France

Nicola Williams

Oliver Berry, Steve Fallon, Emilie Filou, Catherine Le Nevez,

Daniel Robinson, Miles Roddis

NORMANDY (p264)
Discover your inner Impressionist in Monet's garden, time travel with the world's oldest comic strip in Bayeux and ponder the price of peace at the D-Day beaches
PARIS (p108)
Find love (of food, of wine, of the Seine, of someone) in the world's most romantic city
ÉPERNAY (p361)
Discover what all the fuss is about over a glass of bubbly and a cellar tour
NANCY (p402)
Take in gilded wrought ironwork and curvaceous art-nouveau masterpieces
STRASBOURG (p374)
Gaze in awe at the rose-coloured spires and stained glass of the cathedral
BRITTANY (p306)
Cycle around Carnac past fields full of other-worldly megaliths and sip Breton cider on the Crozon Peninsula
CHARTRES (p220)
Wonder at the bluer-than-blue stained glass in the sublime Gothic cathedral
THE LOIRE VALLEY (p416)
Regal châteaux and rich vineyards carpet the banks of France's longest river
WALES
ENGLAND
LONDON
CARDIFF
NORTH SEA
THE NETHERLANDS
BELGIUM
BRUSSELS
GERMANY
LUXEMBOURG
SWITZERLAND
BERN
English Channel (La Manche)
PARIS

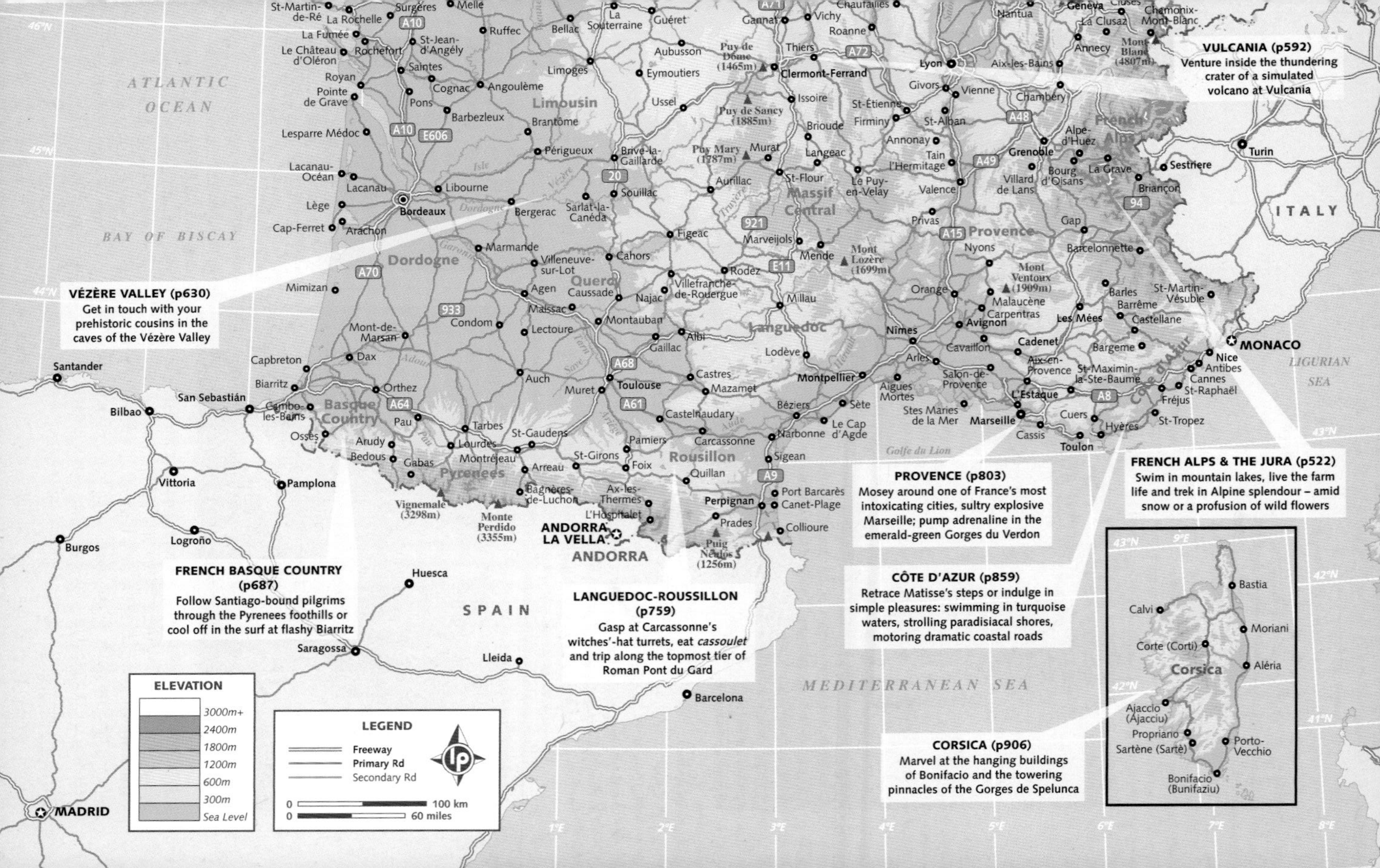
VULCANIA (p592)
Venture inside the thundering crater of a simulated volcano at Vulcania
VÉZÈRE VALLEY (p630)
Get in touch with your prehistoric cousins in the caves of the Vézère Valley
FRENCH ALPS & THE JURA (p522)
Swim in mountain lakes, live the farm life and trek in Alpine splendour – amid snow or a profusion of wild flowers
PROVENCE (p803)
Mosey around one of France's most intoxicating cities, sultry explosive Marseille; pump adrenaline in the emerald-green Gorges du Verdon
CÔTE D'AZUR (p859)
Retrace Matisse's steps or indulge in simple pleasures: swimming in turquoise waters, strolling paradisiacal shores, motoring dramatic coastal roads
FRENCH BASQUE COUNTRY (p687)
Follow Santiago-bound pilgrims through the Pyrenees foothills or cool off in the surf at flashy Biarritz
LANGUEDOC-ROUSSILLON (p759)
Gasp at Carcassonne's witches'-hat turrets, eat *cassoulet* and trip along the topmost tier of Roman Pont du Gard
CORSICA (p906)
Marvel at the hanging buildings of Bonifacio and the towering pinnacles of the Gorges de Spelunca
ATLANTIC OCEAN
BAY OF BISCAY
MEDITERRANEAN SEA
LIGURIAN SEA
Golfe du Lion
ITALY
SPAIN
ANDORRA
MONACO
MADRID
ANDORRA LA VELLA
Limousin
Dordogne
Quercy
Massif Central
Languedoc
Roussillon
Provence
Basque Country
Pyrenees
French Alps
Côte d'Azur
Corsica
Bordeaux
Toulouse
Lyon
Marseille
Montpellier
Nîmes
Avignon
Clermont-Ferrand
Grenoble
Nice
Perpignan
Turin
Santander
Bilbao
San Sebastián
Pamplona
Vittoria
Logroño
Burgos
Huesca
Saragossa
Lleida
Barcelona
Puy de Dôme (1465m)
Puy de Sancy (1885m)
Puy Mary (1787m)
Mont Lozère (1699m)
Mont Ventoux (1909m)
Mont Blanc (4807m)
Vignemale (3298m)
Monte Perdido (3355m)
Puig Neulós (1256m)
Bastia
Calvi
Moriani
Corte (Corti)
Aléria
Ajaccio (Ajacciu)
Propriano
Sartène (Sartè)
Porto-Vecchio
Bonifacio (Bunifaziu)
ELEVATION
3000m+
2400m
1800m
1200m
600m
300m
Sea Level
LEGEND
Freeway
Primary Rd
Secondary Rd
0
100 km
0
60 miles

On the Road

NICOLA WILLIAMS Coordinating Author

Château de Varennes is a biannual date in the diary. Each year in March and again in November, Matthias and I battle it out for the nondriving role, pack the boys in the Twingo and drive two hours from our lakeside village in Haute-Savoie to Marchampt, 'our' village in the Beaujolais (p517), where we wed a decade ago. We lunch like kings in the company of a fruity Beaujolais Villages (March) or a tender young Beaujolais Nouveau (November), and kid around afterwards in the wooded grounds.

OLIVER BERRY Standing at the foot of the gargantuan statue of Notre Dame de France (p603) in Le Puy-en-Velay, deep in the heart of the Massif Central, the view over the city's terracotta rooftops is totally stunning (and worth the climb), but it's even better once you start ascending the clattering cast-iron staircase inside the statue.

STEVE FALLON As far as I'm concerned, any corner café in Paris works for an *apéro* (sundowner). As I'm having dinner with a friend in the 3e, this dive near place de la République proves ever so handy, and they even have a bottle with my name on it: Pastis 51.

EMILIE FILOU Top of Aiguille du Midi (p530), 7am. I'm about to climb Mont Blanc du Tacul (4248m) with my brother and a couple of friends, a couple of summits away from Mont Blanc. Could life be any sweeter?

CATHERINE LE NEVEZ The best part of travelling is the surprises along the way. A combination of a(nother) French transport strike and booked-solid hotels led me fortuitously to this *chambre d'hôte* (B&B) here in Vitré (p353), whose unassuming blank wall unexpectedly conceals an idyllic garden, with hosts who treated me like long-lost family.

DANIEL ROBINSON The Chantier Médiéval de Guédelon (p479), southwest of Auxerre, sounds unbelievable – a 25-year project to build a fortified château using only 13th-century technology. But on the ground, as you watch work progressing at a pace that feels both incredibly slow and remarkably fast, it's fascinating. I'll never look at a Gothic cathedral or a medieval castle in the same way again.

MILES RODDIS Gosh, it was chilly as the Cers (a biting winter wind) swept around the ramparts of Carcassonne's La Cité (p779). But there was one huge compensation: while most visitors shuffle with the throng in high summer, that wintry day a few other hardy souls and I had its streets all to ourselves.

For full author biographies see p989.

France Highlights

France is an extraordinary country boasting an amazing array of attractions and experiences. Here's what our authors, staff and travellers love most about it.

WILL SALTER

1 AV DES CHAMPS-ÉLYSÉES, PARIS

Some say Paris' broadest and most famous boulevard (p153) is now the height of tack, but I've loved it ever since I was a student at the Sorbonne and my kinda-sorta Moroccan boyfriend and I stood beneath the Arc de Triomphe on New Year's Eve and shouted *'C'est pour nous! C'est pour nous! C'est pour nous!'* ('It's for us! It's for us! It's for us!') as the cars raced around, blowing their horns and flashing their headlights. Truth be told, I've done it once or twice again since then.

Steve Fallon, Lonely Planet author, UK

TAKE THE HIGH ROAD

Most travellers who make it over to Corsica (p906) tend to just stick to the coastline (and you can't really blame them), but for me the real Corsica starts once you get up into the high mountains – a wild, untamed landscape of peaks, tarns, chestnuts, forests and mist-filled valleys.

Oliver Berry, Lonely Planet author, UK

2

DAVID TOMLINSON

CHAMPAGNE-TASTING IN ÉPERNAY

We hopped in the car and drove the Route Touristique du Champagne from Reims, stopping in gorgeous villages and drinking in the russet view across the vineyards. At Épernay (p361) we toured Moët & Chandon, and our Champagne thirst was temporarily stilled by a fascinating tour – once you know the full story of how it's made, you realise that Champagne really *is* worth all that money! Back in Reims, our *apéritif* bubbles burst all the sweeter now we knew just how they'd got into that bottle – so much so, we had no choice but to order a second...

Janine Eberle, Lonely Planet staff member, Australia

3

NEIL SETCHFIELD

NEIL SETCHFIELD

4

THROUGH THE HEART OF THE LOIRE VALLEY

The Loire Valley (p416) drive from Blois to Saumur, via Amboise and Tours, is one of the loveliest drives in the world, down rustic lanes past farmhouses, vineyards and châteaux. It feels like nothing has changed here in 100 years.

stoml, traveller

OLIVER STREWE

5 CROIX ROUSSE, LYON

I know Lyon's hilltop quarter of Croix Rousse (p503) inside out: the chic loft apartments where 19th-century silk weavers toiled; the buxom diva of a market with her riot of fruit-and-veg stalls; my favourite cheese man selling impossibly runny St-Marcellin ripened by the legendary Mère Richard; the brass band outside the *mairie* that gets tots and grandmas dancing on Sunday morning; Gérard the charismatic village crier. Sitting on a pavement terrace, sipping white Côtes du Rhône and watching a man with briny hands and a blue plastic apron shuck oysters – the place grabs my soul every time.

Nicola Williams, Lonely Planet author, France

6 LAND'S END, CAMARET-SUR-MER

Brittany has countless enchanting fishing villages scattered around its coastline, but Camaret-sur-Mer (p330) remains my favourite to date. Flung out on the tip of the Presqu'Île de Crozon in Finistère (literally 'land's end'), this former crayfish port–turned–artists' haven is picturesque at any time of year, but never more so than in midsummer, when the rose- and amethyst-hued twilight lingers almost until midnight.

Catherine Le Nevez, Lonely Planet author, Australia

JOHN ELK III

JEAN-BERNARD CARILLET

7 SLURPING OYSTERS

If you are a fan of oysters, be sure to visit Gujan Mestras (p686), the oyster-farming capital about 60km southwest of Bordeaux. Devour them by the dozen on the pier after dousing them with fresh lemon juice, and wash it all down with a glass of chilled white wine.

Lisa Vitaris, traveller, Australia

EXTREME EMBROIDERY

You enter a dimly lit hall, walk up to a long strip of linen behind protective glass and peer at figures embroidered in subdued tones of green, red, yellow and orange – and suddenly, you're back in the year 1066, helping William the Conqueror build and load his ships, crossing the Channel under striped square sails, dining sumptuously on roasted meats and finally watching the spear-wielding Norman horsemen rout the Saxons at Hastings. The Bayeux Tapestry (p279) is more realistic and thrilling than any action-packed video game!

Daniel Robinson, Lonely Planet author, Israel

8

DONALD C & PRISCILLA ALEXANDER EASTMAN

D-DAY BEACHES

The broad stretches of fine sand and the nearby bluffs are quiet now, but early on the morning of 6 June 1944 the beaches of northern Normandy (p283) were a cacophony of gunfire and explosions, the bodies of Allied soldiers lying face-down in the sand as their comrades-in-arms charged inland. Just up the hill from Omaha Beach, the long rows of symmetrical gravestones at the Normandy American Cemetery & Memorial (p285) bear solemn, silent testimony to the horrible price paid for France's liberation from Nazi tyranny.

Daniel Robinson, Lonely Planet author, Israel

9

IZZET KERIBAR

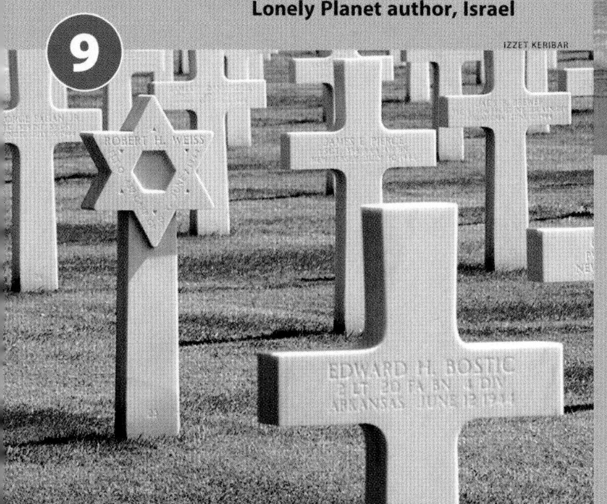

GARETH McCORMACK

10

SURF'S UP

The stylish coastal town of Biarritz (p694) took off as a resort in the mid-19th century. These days, the Atlantic resort is best known for its pipes. Yes, it's a mecca for surfers from around the world, offering some of the best waves on the continent.

anpl, traveller

ADRENALIN KICK

Sure, 007 did it, but so can you: the Vallée Blanche (p532) is a once in a lifetime experience. You won't regret the €70-odd it costs to do it because every minute of the five hours it takes to go down will pump more adrenalin in your body than anything else you've ever done.

Emilie Filou, Lonely Planet author, UK

11

JEFF CANTARUTTI

AMAZING ALPS

After four days of walking in the Parc National de la Vanoise (p555), south of Tignes, we rested at the Refuge du Mont Pourri where we encountered a herd of magnificent ibexes grazing on a pasture below us. Beyond them, a waterfall poured over a cliff and out of sight into a canyon. The setting sun cast deep shadows in the glaciated valley at our feet but the alpenglow tinted the snow-covered peaks and glaciers across the valley a lush orange hue. We sat at this idyllic spot wishing the day would never end.

Glenn van der Knijff, Lonely Planet staff member, Australia

12

GARETH McCORMACK

13

GREG ELMS

EDIBLE BLUE

Roquefort is the most famous of the famous blue cheeses. See how it is made in Roquefort-sur-Soulzon (p793) with a visit to the natural caves where it ages into that pungent bluish mould. And then treat your taste buds to this culinary masterpiece.

Elizabeth Soumya, traveller, India

OUT OF AFRICA

The ancient port of Marseille (p805) has been described as the most North African of European cities. When you're sipping coffee by the water's edge of the Vieux Port, it's easy to be carried away by the illusion that you're in Algiers, Tunis or even Beirut.

anpl, traveller

15

JEAN-BERNARD CARILLET

DELIGHTFUL ANNECY

Annecy (p541) was one of our first destinations on our honeymoon and one of our favourites. Though not on the main tourist trail for foreigners, this wonderful little town has an idyllic setting beside Lac d'Annecy, though perhaps its most captivating feature is the gorgeous Vieille Ville (Old Town). Here, cobblestone lanes, markets, cafés and medieval buildings sit astride the Canal du Thiou, which bisects the historic district. Annecy is a treasure.

Glenn van der Knijff, Lonely Planet staff member, Australia

16

PASCALE BEROUJON

14

BETHUNE CARMICHAEL

TO THE MARKET

For me, a visit to France is all about the markets (p179) – sometimes it's an ancient covered market with stall after stall displaying precious goods, sometimes it's a laid-back alfresco affair in the town square. I love eyeing the piles of pristinely stacked vegetables, pondering the mounds of perfectly ripened cheese and chatting with the fruit-sellers while I assemble my picnic.

Caroline Sieg, Lonely Planet staff member, London

PARIS METRO

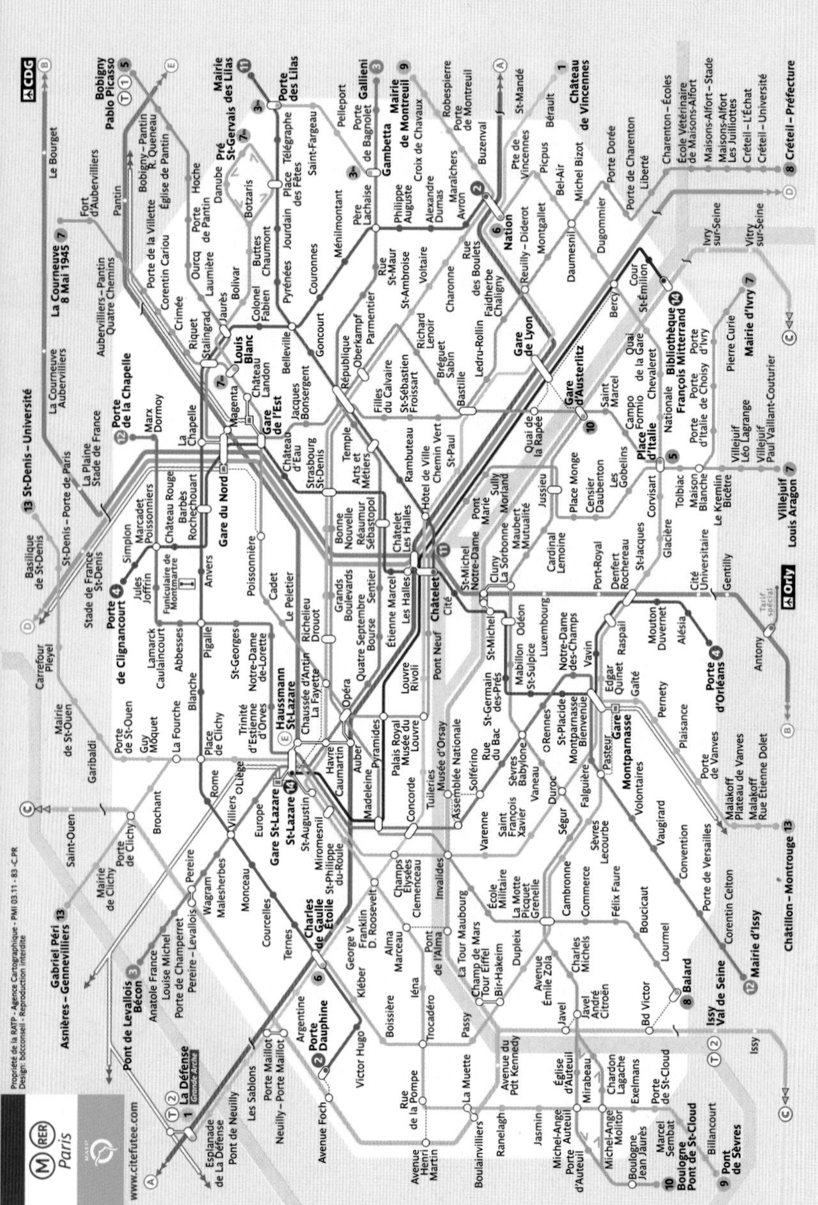

Contents

Regional Map Contents

Destination France

Good, bad or ugly, everyone has an opinion about France and the French: chic, smart, sexy, rude, racist, bureaucratic, or bitchy as hell. Throw the odd urban protest, strike and political scandal into the mix, not to mention a presidential wedding (p47), the funeral of an iconic 20th-century fashion designer (p47) or superstars Angelina Jolie and Brad Pitt plumping for a house in Provence to rear their brood, and the international media is agog too.

This is, after all, Europe's fabled land of good food and wine (p69 and p77), of royal châteaux and restored farmhouses, of iconic landmarks known the world over (p98) and hidden landscapes few know. Savour art and sweet romance in the shining capital on the River Seine. See glorious pasts blaze forth at Versailles. Drink till dawn in a banana-ripening warehouse on the Atlantic Coast (p651). Listen to jazz and blues in Paris (p191). Travel south for Roman civilisation and the sparkling blue Med. Ski the Alps. Sense the subtle infusion of language, music and mythology in Brittany brought by Celtic invaders. Smell ignominy on the beaches of Normandy and battlefields of the Somme. And know that this is the tip of that iceberg the French call culture.

Yes, this is a timeless land whose people exude a natural joie de vivre and savoir faire. Yes, this is the country that entices more travellers into its lovely lair than any other: 82 million visitors in 2007 (4% more than the previous year) ranked it the world's top tourist destination for yet another year.

France's lure in fact, rather like French café society, has never been so strong: vibrant during the days of Jean-Paul Sartre et al who put the world to rights between folkloric clouds of tobacco smoke, since the 1 February 2007 smoking ban, it sparkles like new. Strictly *non fumeur* (nonsmoking) is what this coffee-sipping, Champagne-quaffing, positively seductive society is about these days. Even French wine is slowly becoming in again.

France, moreover, has a new breed of president – personality-driven, American-style – who has hogged the media ever since his arrival at the Élysée Palace in 2007. Not only did Nicolas Sarkozy rewrite the presidential rule book with his divorce and subsequent seduction of an Italian multimillionaire singer during his first few months in office, he also set out a ruthlessly ambitious political agenda for himself, epitomised perhaps by his gargantuan plans for Paris: he wants to develop its surroundings to create a vast metropolitan Greater Paris. Ten of the world's top architects are on the case.

Gargantuan ambition likewise marked the start of France's six-month turn at the presidential helm of the EU in 2008: faced with an economically depressed Europe grappling with soaring fuel prices and living costs, all eyes were on the French president. Sarkozy's goals: to help Europe move forward despite Ireland's rejection of the Lisbon Treaty, broker a European deal on climate change, cut VAT on restaurant bills and oil, and work on immigration which, interestingly, has long been one of the hottest potatoes in his own multicultural country (p55). Unfortunately, his big talk on better defence was belittled in July 2008 when a French soldier accidentally fired a round of live bullets instead of blanks during a military show near Carcassonne, prompting the chief of the country's army to quit in shame and the country to gasp in shock.

Good, bad or physically too short, everyone has an opinion on the sparky Sarkozy. He says the lunch-loving play-hard French, many of whom until recently only worked a 35-hour week (see p50), must change if their country is to move forward economically. Naturally, they don't all agree. *Non fumeur*, yes, but still plenty of sparks ahead.

FAST FACTS

Population: 63.4 million

Area: 551,000 sq km

GDP (end second quarter 2008): €411.93 billion

GDP per capita (2007): US$33,470

GDP growth (2007): 2.1%

Annual inflation (2007): 1.5%

Unemployment (end second quarter 2008): 7.9%

Highest point: Mont Blanc (4807m)

Internet domain: fr

Annual alcohol consumption (per person): wine 78.9L, beer 41L, cider 6.9L, spirits 9.1L

Getting Started

Some parts of France are tried-and-tested, bona fide 'dream destinations' and as such require planning weeks, if not months, in advance in order to snag the best room in the house: be it a castle, a tree house or a golden stone *mas* (farmhouse).

Other areas scarcely score a sentence in newspaper travel sections and as such are perfect for travellers happy to fly by the seat of their pants with no itinerary or advance booking to speak of. Whatever your budget – France allows you to spend a farthing or a fortune – travel is straightforward and generally free of bad surprises.

WHEN TO GO

See Climate Charts (p946) for more information.

Revel in French pleasures any time, although many swear spring is best. In the hot south sun-worshippers bake from June to early September (summer) while winter-sports enthusiasts soar down snow-covered mountains mid-December to late March (winter). Festivals (p950) and gastronomic temptations (p82) around which to plan a trip abound year-round.

School holidays – Christmas and New Year, mid-February to mid-March, Easter, July and August – see millions of French families descend on the coasts, mountains and other touristy areas. Traffic-clogged roads, sky-high accommodation prices and sardine-packed beaches and ski slopes are downside factors of these high-season periods. Many shops take their *congé annuel* (annual closure) in August; Sundays and public holidays (p951) are dead everywhere.

The French climate is temperate, although it gets nippy in mountainous areas and in Alsace and Lorraine. The northwest suffers from high humidity, rain and biting westerly winds, while the Mediterranean south enjoys hot summers and mild winters.

HOW MUCH?

Two-course midrange lunch/dinner *menu* €18/30

Munch-on-the-move baguette sandwich €3.50-6

Half-/full-day bicycle hire €10/15

Cinema ticket in the provinces/Paris €7.50/9.50

Public transport ticket €1.50

COSTS & MONEY

Accommodation is the biggest cost: count on minimum €60 a night for a double room in a midrange hotel and €140 plus for a top-end hotel. Backpackers staying in hostels and living on cheese and *baguette* can survive on €60 a day; those opting for midrange hotels, restaurants and museums will spend upwards of €120. For discount cards, see p948.

TRAVELLING RESPONSIBLY

Since our inception in 1973, Lonely Planet has encouraged our readers to tread lightly, travel responsibly and enjoy the magic independent travel affords. International travel is growing at a jaw-dropping rate, and we still firmly believe in the benefits it can bring – but, as always, we encourage you to consider the impact your visit will have on both the global environment and the local economies, cultures and ecosystems.

Shopping at France's bounty of local food markets (every village and town has at least a weekly one), staying at *chambres d'hôtes* (B&Bs) and *fermes auberges* (farms; p940), entertaining the kids with green activities rather than huge theme parks, spurning domestic flights for the train (p975) and trading in four wheels for two (p969) to get around are ways of minimising your impact and travelling sustainably within France.

Green-themed boxes in most chapters provide destination-specific pointers for travelling responsibly and a top-pick listing of green activities is on opposite.

TOP 10

GREEN PICKS

Go slow, go green and buzz sustainable with our pick of environmentally sweet travel experiences; see destination chapters for more ideas on taking your foot off the accelerator.

1. Try the self-service bike-rental schemes in Paris (p201), Lyon (p516), Marseille (p819), Montpellier (p774), Rouen (p271), Caen (p292), Dijon (p464), Amiens (p259), Toulouse (p746) and Orléans (p422)
2. Build a castle using 13th-century technologies at the Chantier Médiéval de Guédelon (p479)
3. Behave like a Breton: cycle past otherworldly megaliths (p341), hike on the Island of Terror (p327) or bask on Île de Batz (p323)
4. Revel in ravishing gardens: Monet's inspiration in Giverny (p278), subterranean Jardin des Boves in Arras (p250), Menton's Mediterranean paradises (p898), Monaco's Jardin Exotique (p903) and those at Villa Grecque Kérylos in Beaulieu-sur-Mer (p898) and Villa Rothschild in St-Jean Cap-Ferrat (p897)
5. Experience France's first organic village (p894)
6. Paddle along emerald-green waterways at the Maison Flore in France's 'Green Venice' (p660)
7. Follow the footsteps of pilgrims from Le Puy-en-Velay (p602) to St-Jean Pied de Port (p704); or do it by donkey like Robert Louis Stevenson in the Parc National des Cévennes (p786)
8. Bliss out in mud at a Biarritz spa (p696)
9. Celebrate traditional mountain life during the eco-festival, Les Phonies Bergères (p723)
10. Retrace dinosaur steps at the Réserve Géologique (p856) in Digne-les-Bains

A DIFFERENT PERSPECTIVE

Forget the Louvre or the local *musée des beaux arts* (fine-arts museum). Our alternative art spaces are for culture vultures who can't hack another queue or have 'been there, done that'.

1. Cité de l'Architecture et du Patrimoine, Paris – new and esoteric (p152)
2. Musée Rodin, Paris – city soul soother amid sculptures by *The Thinker*'s creator (p151)
3. Château de Vaux-le-Vicomte, near Paris – less visited due to access and size (p217)
4. Maison de l'Outil et de la Pensée Ouvrière, Troyes – tools, tools and more tools, with videos and demos of how they were used (p366)
5. Galerie David d'Angers, Angers – sculptures on display in a converted church (p449)
6. Musée de l'Objet, Blois – playful modern-art museum (p426)
7. Musée d'Art Contemporain, Rochechouart – contemporary art (p614)
8. Fondation Alexandra David-Néel, Digne-les-Bains – inspiration of adventurers (p856)
9. Musée Bartholdi, Colmar – Lady Liberty, eat your heart out! (p395)
10. Musée de l'Impression sur Étoffes and Musée du Papier Peint, Mulhouse – textile printing (p400) and the history of wallpaper (p400)

LIVE DANGEROUSLY

OD on adventure with daredevil France. For more adrenalin-pumping activities, see p943.

1. Scale Europe's highest sand dune (p685)
2. Sail subterranean waters (p647)
3. Drive a Porsche on an ice piste (p566) or fly down the Vallée Blanche off-piste (p532)
4. Learn avalanche survival in the Alps (p525)
5. Embark on a surf safari (p685)
6. Trek Corsica's mythical GR20 (p915)
7. Splash out on white-water sports in the Dordogne (p607), Gorges du Verdon (p97) or Parc National des Pyrénées (p721)
8. Go volcanic (p591)
9. Paraglide the thermals above Puy de Dôme (p592) or hang-glide off Ménez-Hom (p329)
10. Kitesurf, mush, skijor or sledge in a snake gliss (p530)

DON'T LEAVE HOME WITHOUT...

- valid travel insurance (p952).
- ID card or passport and visa if required (p958).
- driving licence, car documents and car insurance (p973).
- sunglasses, hat, mosquito repellent and a few clothes pegs for the hot south.
- a brolly for wet 'n' soggy Brittany, neighbouring northern climes and Paris.
- an adventurous appetite, a pleasure-seeking palate and a thirst for good wine (p77).

TRAVEL LITERATURE

See p59 for 'frog v Rosbif' books, p29 for French history titles and p58 for a cultural focus.

- *Yellow Studio* (Stephen Romer) – Thwarted, unrequited French love is the powerful inspiration behind this dramatic collection of poems by one of Britain's best contemporary poets, at home in France since the 1981.
- *This Night's Cruel Work* (Fred Vargas) – Paris, the Pyrenees and a Normandy village are among the places this award-winning French crime writer takes readers to in her latest spellbinding detective novel.
- *The Man who Married a Mountain* – (Rosemary Bailey) By the author of *Life in a Postcard: Escape to the French Pyrenees,* this elegant piece of travel writing scales the Pyrenees with 19th-century mountaineers.
- *Another Long Day on the Piste* (Will Randall) – Refreshingly different from the 'renovate a farmhouse' norm, this one dissects in hilarious detail a season spent in a ski resort in the French Alps.
- *A Motor-Flight Through France* (Edith Wharton) – A timeless classic, this book follows the Whartons as they embark on a trio of pioneering automobile trips in belle-époque France.

INTERNET RESOURCES

French Government Tourist Office (www.francetourism.com) Official tourist site.
Lonely Planet (www.lonelyplanet.com)
Maison de la France (www.franceguide.com) Main tourist-office website.
Météo France (www.meteo.fr, in French) For details of nationwide weather conditions.
Motorist Information (www.bison-fute.equipement.gouv.fr, in French) Road conditions, closures and school-holiday schedule.
SNCF (www.sncf.com) France's national railways website.

Itineraries

CLASSIC ROUTES

A WHIRLWIND ROMANCE

One Week / Paris to Provence

France's soulful **capital** (p108) seduces: the **Eiffel Tower** (p152) is the peak of romance. Pop the question Gothic-style in **Hôtel St-Merry** (p168). Nip north to chink glasses on **Champagne's wine route** (p360), or west to the **Loire Valley** (p416) and its châteaux: see love blossoming at **Villandry** (p440); a drama of passion and betrayal unfold at **Chenonceau** (p436); or meet your lover on the double-helix staircase at **Château de Chambord** (p429). Don't miss Brittany's haunting **Île d'Ouessant** (p327). Oysters, for which **Cancale** (p316) is famed, are an aphrodisiac. Tempting to lonely hearts and lovers is **Belle Île** (p344), with its caves and beaches steeped in legend. Shouting 'yes' from a huge **sand dune** (p685) or in the **surf** (p685) on the Atlantic Coast is not a bad idea. Or smooching atop **Mont Aigoual** (p785) or paragliding above **Puy de Dôme** (p592). **Provence** (p803) and the **Côte d'Azur** (p859) are love at first sight. Tying the knot aboard a **St-Tropez** (p887) yacht or in a lavender field is old hat. Try in a **Matisse chapel** (p867) or **Van Gogh landscape** (p829); or between **kitesurfs** (p892).

Paris to Provence – 2000km-odd in all – in a whirlwind week is a love affair with old-fashioned romance. But it's not all red roses and fairy-tale castles. Thrills abound for those with a passion for the unconventional.

TIMELESS CLASSICS

Two Weeks / Paris to Nice

There's no better place to kick off a whistle-stop tour of classic French sights than Paris, where the **Eiffel Tower** (p152), the **Arc de Triomphe** (p154), **Notre Dame** (p145) and the **Louvre** (p139) all warrant a postcard home. Stroll the banks of the Seine and the gardens of **Versailles** (p211), then flee the capital for Renaissance royalty at **Châteaux de Chambord** (p429) and **Chenonceau** (p436). Or skip the Loire and spend a couple of days in Normandy marvelling at Rouen's **Cathédrale Notre Dame** (p268), the **Bayeux Tapestry** (p279), **Mont St-Michel** (p302) and the **D-Day landing beaches** (p283).

Venture south through the **Bordeaux wine region** (p669). Surfers can ride waves in **Biarritz** (p694), and the faithful or faithfully curious will like world-famous **Lourdes** (p715). Otherwise, it's straight to **Carcassonne** (p777) and its city walls; Roman **Nîmes** (p760), with a trip to the **Pont du Gard** (p766); and the papal city of **Avignon** (p836), with its **nursery-rhyme bridge** (p837). Finish on the Côte d'Azur, not missing Grace Kelly's **Monaco** (p900), a flutter in **Monte Carlo Casino** (p905), a portside aperitif in **St-Tropez** (p887), a strut in **Cannes** (p877) and a stroll in **Nice** (p861).

Paris to Nice, with a few short detours along the way, is a breathtaking 2000km that can be done in a jam-packed fortnight, but definitely merits as much time as you can give it.

PORT TO PORT

Two Weeks / Calais to Marseille

Step off the boat in **Calais** (p235) and there's 40km of stunning cliffs, sand dunes and windy beaches – not to mention great views of those white cliffs of Dover across the Channel – on the spectacular **Côte d'Opale** (p243). Speed southwest, taking in a fish lunch in **Dieppe** (p271), a cathedral-stop in **Rouen** (p266) or a picturesque cliffside picnic in **Étretat** (p275) on your way to your overnight stop: the pretty Normandy seaside resort of **Honfleur** (p295), **Deauville** (p292) or **Trouville** (p292).

Devote day two to the **D-Day landing beaches** (p283) and abbey-clad **Mont St-Michel** (p302). In Brittany, flop in an old-fashioned beach tent in **Dinard** (p314) then follow fairy-tale forest trails around **Huelgoat** (p325) to art-rich **Camaret-sur-Mer** (p330).

A long drive south along the Atlantic Coast rewards with chic **La Rochelle** (p661) and its lavish seafood and oyster feasts, from where it is simply a matter of wining your way through the **Médoc** (p678) to bustling **Bordeaux** (p669). Next morning, continue south through **Toulouse** (p735) and **Carcassonne** (p777) to the Med. **The Camargue** (p833) – a wonderful wetland of flamingos, horses and incredible bird life – is a unique patch of coast to explore before hitting gritty **Marseille** (p805), immediately east.

The Atlantic to the Mediterranean in two weeks – 2500km in all – rewards with stunning vistas, superb coastal motoring and sensational seafood. Activities abound in, on and out of the sea – and there's always Corsica for the truly coast crazy.

TOUR DE FRANCE

Two Weeks / Strasbourg to Paris

Get set for your race around the country in Strasbourg: stroll canal-clad **Petite France** (p375), marvel at its **cathedral** (p375) and dine in a **winstub** (p383). Moving on to greener climes, pick up the **Route du Vin d'Alsace** (p387) and tipple your way around the **Vosges** (p398) foothills. But keep a clear head for that splendid art-nouveau architecture in **Nancy** (p402), where you should spend at least one night to enjoy romantic **place Stanislas** (p402) illuminated. From Lorraine it is straight to Champagne cellars around **Épernay** (p361), then north to the sobering **Battle of the Somme memorials** (p252) in far northern France.

Then it's the pick of Normandy and Brittany: no time to see everything so choose between **Bayeux** (p279) and its **tapestry** (p279), the **D-Day landing beaches** and **WWII memorials** (p283), **Mont St-Michel** (p302), or mooching megaliths in **Carnac** (p340) in France's Celtic **land of legends** (p306). Then zoom south for more prehistory in the **Vézère Valley** (p630).

The pace hots up in the second week: from the **Dordogne** (p621), wiggle through the **Upper Languedoc** (p782) – through the spectacular **Gorges du Tarn** (p787) – to **Avignon** (p836). Take a break with local café culture then slog like a Tour de France cyclist up **Mont Ventoux** (p848). Speed north next to the majestic city of **Lyon** (p497), from where an **Alpine mountain adventure** (p530) is doable.

The last leg takes in wine-rich Burgundy: **Beaune** (p468), **Dijon** (p457) and **Vézelay** (p485) are the obvious desirable places to stop en route to **Paris** (p108).

This 3000km Tour of France can be done in a fortnight, but warrants mountains more time. As with the world's greatest cycling race, it labours through the Pyrenees and the Alps, and finishes on Paris' Champs-Élysées.

ROADS LESS TRAVELLED

OUTDOOR ACTION

Two Weeks / Chamonix to Cauterets

Kick-start your Alpine adventure in **Chamonix** (p527) at the foot of Europe's highest peak: ride a cable car to the **Aiguille du Midi** (p530) and **Le Brévent** (p531) or a train to the **Mer de Glace** (p531). Skiing the legendary **Vallée Blanche** (p532) and **paragliding** (p534) are daredevil choices. For the truly Alpine-dedicated there are the **Vanoise** (p555) and **Écrins** (p563) national parks to explore.

Hopping across Lake Geneva by boat, the unexplored **Jura** (p570) looms large. This gentle land of cross-country skiing, dog-mushing and cheese dining in **Métabief Mont d'Or** (p578) – not to mention Le Corbusier's **Ronchamp** (p577) chapel – is an oasis of peace.

Or head southwest for week two, breaking the journey in the **Parc Naturel Régional de Chartreuse** (p550), of potent pea-green liqueur fame, or in the cave-riddled **Parc Naturel Régional du Vercors** (p563). Passing through the wild **Cévennes** (p784), walking a stage of Robert Louis Stevenson's **donkey trek** (p786) is doable before hitting the Pyrenees.

In the **Parc National des Pyrénées** (p720), revitalise weary bones with spa waters in **Bagnères de Luchon** (p731) then hit the **Vallée d'Ossau** (p725) and **Vallée d'Aspe** (p721) for a heady cocktail of mountain biking, walking and vulture-spotting. Use **Cauterets** (p727) – from where you can ski in season – as your base.

This highly energetic 1500km tour from the French Alps to the Pyrenees will leave you breathless, especially if you take a few days out to indulge in an adrenaline rush of outdoor activity up, down or on the mountain slopes.

SOMETHING DIFFERENT

One Month / Parisian Sewer to Burgundian Building Site

Forget the Eiffel Tower, St-Tropez and the lavender fields of Provence. This tour ventures out of the ordinary into France's quirkiest sights and sounds – and smells, in the case of the **Paris sewer** (p153) where it starts. Gawp at more skulls than you can imagine in the capital's **catacombs** (p151), then venture north to the spot near **Compiègne** (p260), where WWI officially ended. Top off your day with a subterranean dose of V2 rocket technology in a **bunker** (p241) near St-Omer.

A few drops of Christ's blood in **Fécamp** (p274) on the Normandy coast inspired monks to concoct Benedictine liqueur: visit the **Palais Bénédictine** (p274) and get a free shot – then tell yourself you're not drunk as you tour the 'laboratory of emotions' in Honfleur's wacky **Les Maisons Satie** (p297).

Steering south along the Atlantic Coast, cartwheel down Europe's highest sand dune near **Arcachon** (p685). Afterwards, head east to Quercy and set sail on an underground river in **Gouffre de Padirac** (p647), then nip to Toulouse to tour **Space City** (p740) and see **Airbus planes** (p740) being built.

Learning how silk weavers toiled in the 19th century and walking the tunnels they trod put **Lyon** (p503) in a different light. Returning north, see brickies in costume at the **Chantier Médiéval de Guédelon** (p479) in La Puisaye build a castle using 13th-century tools.

It might well follow a predictable route – enabling it to be mixed-and-matched with other itineraries in this chapter – but that's about it. Covering 2400km in all, one month scarcely does quirky France justice. Take longer if you can.

TAILORED TRIPS

QUICK GETAWAY

Budget airlines (p961) make short breaks easy. For urban souls, sophisticated cities like **Paris** (p108) and **Lyon** (p497) win hands down. Big but not everyone's cup of tea is rough-cut **Marseille** (p805), a heady mix of sea breeze and city grit. Elsewhere along the Med, **Nice** (p861) beckons hard-core punters after sun, sand and sex; **Toulon** (p892) is a slick flit to **St-Tropez** (p887); **Nîmes** (p760) – the stepping-stone alongside student-driven **Montpellier** (p769) to a **Camargue safari** (p833) – combines Roman relics in town with the **Pont du Gard** (p766) out of town; while the **Pyrenees** (p708) tumble into the sea near Spanish-styled **Perpignan** (p794). **Toulouse** (p735), itself a two- or four-day itinerary, is the other Pyrenees launch pad. Fairy-tale castle-clad **Carcassonne** (p777) or the **Loire châteaux** (p431) around **Tours** (p431) vie with the capital for hottest romantic getaway.

In the Alps, **Chamonix' Clubhouse** (p535) – the ultimate in stylish dirty weekends – is a two-hour drive from **Chambéry** (p546) and **Grenoble** (p556), three hours from **Lyon** (p497) and an hour from Geneva (Switzerland). All these cities are first-class stops for **skiing** (p532) and other winter sports.

For an old-fashioned seaside paddle, **Biarritz** (p694), **Dinard** (p314) or **Brest** (p326) are best. **La Rochelle** (p661) is a bridge away from **Île de Ré** (p666); **Poitiers** (p658) neighbours **Green Venice** (p660); **Limoges** (p609) is the place to stockpile crockery; while **Nantes** (p651) and **Bordeaux** (p669) are innovative French cities that surprise and enthral.

ARTISTS' PALETTE

Provence (p803) and the **Côte d'Azur** (p859) are an art paradise: Matisse lapped up the Mediterranean sunlight and vivacity in **Nice** (p867), designing an exceptional chapel in **Vence** (p877). Picasso set up a studio in **Antibes** (p875); Signac and Seurat found inspiration in **St-Tropez** (p887); while Cézanne spent his career in **Aix-en-Provence** (p819). Westward, Van Gogh painted some of his most famous canvases in **Arles** (p826) and **St-Rémy de Provence** (p830).

The Fauvist-favoured port of **Collioure** (p801) on the Côte Vermeille in Roussillon is an essential stop on any art lover's itinerary; as is Henri de Toulouse-Lautrec's hometown of **Albi** (p746), near Toulouse. Artworks of Moulin Rouge cancan girls and prostitutes the bohemian artist painted in Paris hang in the town's **Musée Toulouse-Lautrec** (p748).

A day trip to Monet's garden-clad home and studio in **Giverny** (p277) is irresistible; it is in Paris' **Musée d'Orsay** (p151), incidentally, that Monet's famous painting of **Rouen cathedral** (p268) hangs. Renoir hung out with his impressionist buddies in and around **Le Havre** (p275) on the serene Normandy coast, and is buried in **Essoyes** (p370) in Champagne.

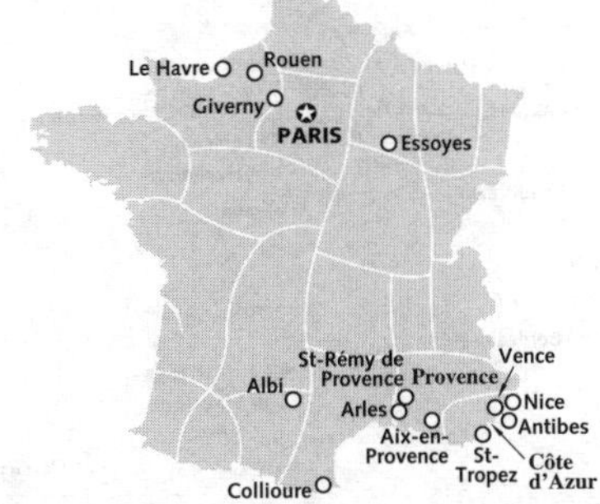

KID TRAVEL

There is no shortage of things to do *en famille:* in **Paris** (p162), kid-friendly capital extraordinaire, scale the **Eiffel Tower** (p152), sail the **Seine** (p201), romp round the **Jardin du Luxembourg** (great playground; p150), meet **Mona Lisa** (kids must see her once; p139), discover wildlife in the **Musée National d'Histoire Naturelle** (p147), explore the **Palais de la Découverte** (p154), and watch horses dance in **Versailles** (p211) or **Chantilly** (p217). Prioritise the **Cité des Sciences et de l'Industrie** (p158) if you want your children to remember (and love) Paris forever.

Elsewhere, the **Loire Valley's** fairy-tale châteaux (p416) are the stuff of little kids' dreams, as is a visit to Saumur's **Cadre Noir** riding school (p446) and a perfume-creation workshop in **Grasse** (p884). For the vehicle-mad, there's Douarnenez' seafaring **Musée du Bateau** (p333), Clermont-Ferrand's **Vulcania** (p592), car museums in **Lyon** (p505), **Monaco** (razz around the F1 Grand Prix track in a Ferrari; p900) and **Mulhouse** (p399), which also sports the **Cité du Train** (p399). Your kid wants to be an astronaut? Build and launch a shuttle at Toulouse's interactive **Cité de l'Espace** (p736).

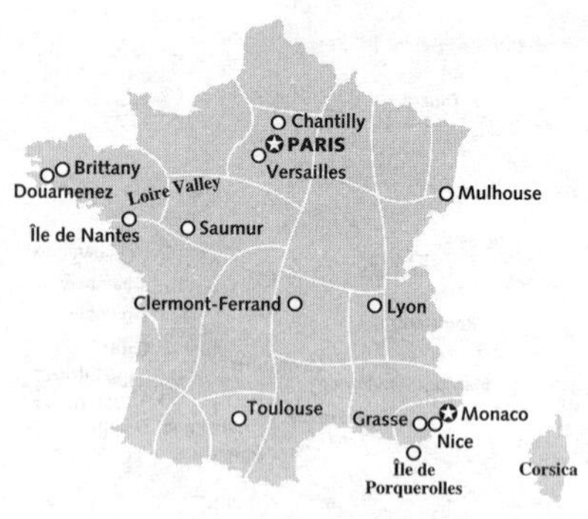

The coastlines drum up bags of old-fashioned fun: Cruise Porto's crystalline caves on **Corsica** (p921), meet sharks in Monaco's **Musée Océanographique** (p903), pedal (or be pedalled) and snorkel on car-free **Île de Porquerolles** (p890), party at the **Nice** Carnival (p869), see how oysters grow at an oyster farm in **Brittany** (p316) and ride a mechanical elephant Jules Verne–style on **Île de Nantes** (p654).

TREASURE TROVE

France flaunts 32 World Heritage Sites (http://whc.unesco.org), including the banks of the Seine in **Paris** (p163) and royal palaces at **Versailles** (p211), **Fontainebleau** (p214) and **Chambord** (p429). The cathedral in **Chartres** (p220) makes a fine foray from the capital, as does the Unesco-hallmarked chunk of the **Loire Valley** (p416) between Sully-sur-Loire and Chalonnes.

Burgundy boasts a medieval Cistercian abbey in **Fontenay** (p472) and Romanesque basilica in fortified **Vézelay** (p485), from where pilgrims head to Santiago de Compostela in Spain. Their paths are World Heritage Sites.

Northern jewels include Strasbourg's **Grande Île** (p375); a trio of public squares in **Nancy** (p402) and buildings in **Reims** (p355); **Le Havre** (p275), bombed in WWII and now an ode to postwar architecture; **Amiens cathedral** (p256); and the hulk of a **citadel in Lille** (p230), one of 13 Vauban citadels (p65) to join Unesco's list in 2008. Sea-splashed **Mont St-Michel** (p302) and its bay are priceless.

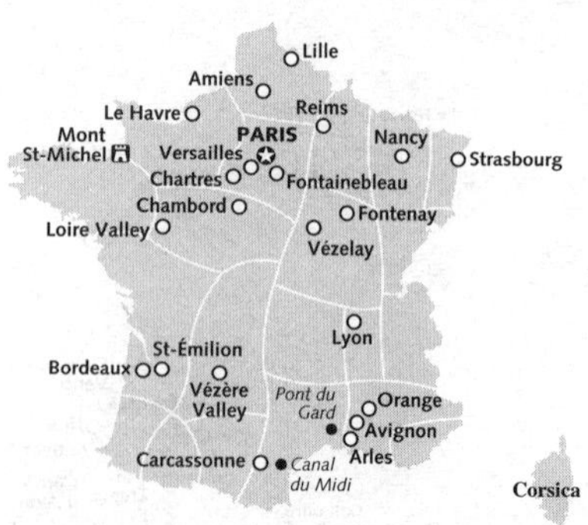

Southbound, stroll the port city of **Bordeaux** (p669), drink Bordeaux reds from listed **St-Émilion vineyards** (p679) and discover prehistory in the **Vézère Valley** (p630). History oozes out of fortified **Carcassonne** (p777); Roman **Pont du Gard** (p766), **Arles** (p826) and **Orange** (p844); papal **Avignon** (p839); and silk-weaving **Lyon** (p497). Sailing a slow boat along the **Canal du Midi** (p776) is a fine way to whittle away time, as is hiking around **Corsica's** capes (p915).

History

PREHISTORIC PEOPLE

Neanderthals were the first people to live in France. Out and about during the Middle Palaeolithic period, these early *Homo sapiens* hunted animals, made crude flake-stone tools and lived in caves. In the late 19th century Neanderthal skeletons were found in caves at Le Bugue in the Vézère Valley (see p630) in Dordogne.

Cro-Magnons, a taller *Homo sapiens* variety who notched up 1.7m on the height chart, followed 35,000 years ago. These people had larger brains than their ancestors, long and narrow skulls, and short, wide faces. Their hands were nimble, and with the aid of improved tools they hunted reindeer, bison, horses and mammoths to eat. They played music, danced and had fairly complex social patterns. You can view archeological treasures from this period in Strasbourg (p379).

Cro-Magnons were also artists. A tour of Grotte de Lascaux II (p635) – a replica of the Lascaux cave where one of the world's best examples of Cro-Magnon drawings was found in 1940 – demonstrates how initial simplistic drawings and engravings of animals gradually became more detailed and realistic. Dubbed 'Périgord's Sistine Chapel', the Lascaux cave is one of 25 known decorated caves in Dordogne's Vézère Valley, the prehistory of which is covered in Les Eyzies de Tayac's Musée National de Préhistoire (p630).

The Neolithic Period produced France's incredible collection of menhirs and dolmens: the Morbihan Coast in Brittany (p341) is an ode to megalithic monuments. During this era, warmer weather caused great changes in flora and fauna, and ushered in farming and stock rearing. Cereals, peas, beans and lentils were grown, and villages were settled. Decorated pottery, woven fabrics and polished stone tools became commonplace household items.

The French invented the first digital calculator, the hot-air balloon, Braille and margarine, not to mention Grand Prix racing and the first public interactive computer network. Find out what else at http://inventors.about.com/od/frenchinventors.

GAULS & ROMANS

The Celtic Gauls moved into the region between 1500 and 500 BC, establishing trading links by about 600 BC with the Greeks, whose colonies included Massilia (Marseille) on the Mediterranean coast.

It was from Wissant in far northern France that Julius Caesar launched his invasion of Britain in 55 BC. Centuries of conflict between the Gauls and the Romans ended in 52 BC when Caesar's legions crushed a revolt by many Gallic tribes led by Celtic Arverni tribe chief Vercingétorix at Gergovia near present-day Clermont-Ferrand. For the next couple of years the Gauls hounded the Romans with guerrilla warfare and stood up to them in several match-drawn pitched battles. But gradually Gallic resistance collapsed and Roman rule in Gaul reigned supreme. Vercingétorix – see him on Clermont-Ferrand's place

TIMELINE

c 30,000 BC

Around 30,000 BC, during the Middle Palaeolithic Period, Cro-Magnons start decorating their homes in the Vézère Valley, Dordogne, with a riot of bestial scenes that remain among the world's best cave paintings.

c 7000–4000 BC

Neolithic man turns his hand to menhirs and dolmen during the New Stone Age, creating a particularly fine collection in Brittany that continues to baffle historians – the tallest stands 20m tall.

1500–500 BC

The Celtic Parisii tribe build a handful of wattle-and-daub huts on what is now the Île de la Cité in Paris; their capital city is christened Lutetia by the Romans.

de Jaude (p585) – meanwhile was captured and carted off to Rome, where he was paraded in chains in Caesar's triumphal procession. As a final insult he was left languishing in prison for six years before being strangled.

Roman France is magnificent, climaxing with the almighty Pont du Gard (p766) aqueduct, built to bring water to the city of Nîmes in southern France. Stand like a plebeian or sit like a Roman patrician in awe-inspiring theatres and amphitheatres at Autun (p489), Lyon (p501), Vienne (p518), Arles (p827) and Orange (p845). Lyon also has an excellent Gallo-Roman civilisation museum (p502). In the Dordogne, Périgueux' 1st-century Roman amphitheatre (p622) was dismantled in the 3rd century and its stones used to build the city walls. The town's stunningly contemporary Musée Gallo-Romain Vesunna (p622) is a feast to behold.

Post-Romans, the Franks adopted important elements of Gallo-Roman civilisation (including Christianity), and their eventual assimilation resulted in a fusion of Germanic culture with that of the Celts and the Romans.

La Reine Margot (Queen Margot) by Alexander Dumas (1802–70) is a compelling tale of murder and intrigue in the Renaissance royal French court. The lead character is based on the queen of King Henri IV.

DYNASTY

The Frankish Merovingian and Carolingian dynasties ruled from the 5th to the 10th centuries, with the Carolingians wielding power from Laon in far northern France. The Frankish tradition, by which the king was succeeded by all of his sons, led to power struggles and the eventual disintegration of the kingdom into a collection of small feudal states.

Charles Martel's grandson, Charlemagne (742–814), extended the boundaries of the kingdom and was crowned Holy Roman Emperor (Emperor of the West) in 800. But during the 9th century Scandinavian Vikings (also called Norsemen, thus Normans) raided France's western coast, settling in the lower Seine Valley and forming the duchy of Normandy a century later. The coronation of Hugh Capet in 987 heralded the birth of the Capetian dynasty, the king's then-modest domain being a humble parcel of land around Paris and Orléans.

The tale of how William the Conqueror and his Norman forces occupied England in 1066 is told on the Bayeux Tapestry, showcased inside Bayeux' Musée de la Tapisserie de Bayeux (p279). In 1152 Eleanor of Aquitaine wed Henry of Anjou (see ornate polychrome effigies of the royal couple in Abbaye Royale de Fontevraud, p447), bringing a further third of France under the control of the English crown. The subsequent rivalry between France and England for control of Aquitaine and the vast English territories in France lasted three centuries.

THE HUNDRED YEARS WAR

During the Hundred Years War (1337–1453) the French suffered particularly nasty defeats at Crécy and Agincourt. Abbey-studded Mont St-Michel (p302) was the only place in northern and western France not to fall into English hands.

1500–500 BC

Celtic Gauls move into the region and establish trading links with the Greeks, whose colonies included Massilia (Marseille) on the Mediterranean coast; the latter bring grapes and olives.

55–52 BC

Julius Caesar launches his invasion of Britain from the Côte d'Opale in far northern France; the Gauls defeat the Romans at Gergovia near present-day Clermont-Ferrand.

c AD 100–300

The Romans revel in their heyday with a riot of splendid public buildings: magnificent baths, temples and aqueducts of almighty proportions such as the Pont du Gard near Nîmes in southern France.

Five years later the dukes of Burgundy (allied with the English) occupied Paris and in 1422 John Plantagenet, duke of Bedford, was made regent of France for England's King Henry VI, then an infant. Less than a decade later he was crowned king of France at Paris' Notre Dame (p145).

Luckily for the French, a 17-year-old virginal warrior called Jeanne d'Arc (Joan of Arc) came along; her tale is told at Orléans' Maison de Jeanne d'Arc (p420). At Château de Chinon (p444) in 1429 she persuaded French legitimist Charles VII that she had a divine mission from God to expel the English from France and bring about Charles' coronation in Reims. Convicted of witchcraft and heresy by a tribunal of French ecclesiastics following her capture by the Burgundians and subsequent sale to the English in 1430, Joan was burned at the stake: the square (p268) where she was burned as a witch remains.

Track France in the news, learn about its history and catch up on stacks more background info with www.discoverfrance.net.

Charles VII returned to Paris in 1437, but it wasn't until 1453 that the English were driven from French territory (with the exception of Calais). At Château de Langeais (p442) in 1491 Charles VIII wed Anne de Bretagne, marking the unification of independent Brittany with France.

RENAISSANCE TO REFORMATION

With the arrival of Italian Renaissance culture during the reign of François I (r 1515–47), the focus shifted to the Loire Valley. Italian artists decorated royal castles in Amboise (p437), Blois (p424), Chambord (p429) and Chaumont (p430), with Leonardo da Vinci making Le Clos Lucé (p439) in Amboise his home from 1516 until his death. Artist and architect disciples of Michelangelo and Raphael were influential, as were writers such as Rabelais, Marot and Ronsard. Renaissance ideas of scientific and geographic scholarship and discovery assumed a new importance, as did the value of secular matters over religious life.

The Reformation swept through Europe in the 1530s. The ideas of Jean (John) Calvin (1509–64), a Frenchman born in Noyon (Picardie) but exiled to Geneva, strengthened it in France. Following the Edict of Jan (1562), which afforded the Protestants certain rights, the Wars of Religion (1562–98) broke out between the Huguenots (French Protestants who received help from the English), the Catholic League (led by the House of Guise) and the Catholic monarchy.

Henri IV (r 1589–1610) kicked off the Bourbon dynasty, issuing the controversial Edict of Nantes (1598) to guarantee the Huguenots many civil and political rights, notably freedom of conscience. Ultra-Catholic Paris refused to allow the new Protestant king entry to the city, and a siege of the capital continued for almost five years. Only when Henri IV embraced Catholicism at the cathedral in St-Denis (p208) did the capital submit to him.

Throughout most of his undistinguished reign, Fontainebleau-born Louis XIII (r 1610–43) remained firmly under the thumb of his ruthless chief minister, Cardinal Richelieu, best known for his untiring efforts to establish an all-powerful monarchy in France and French supremacy in Europe.

c 455–70

France remains under Roman rule until the 5th century, when the Franks (hence the name 'France') and the Alemanii invade and overrun the country from the east.

732

Somewhere near Poitiers, midway along the Atlantic Coast, Charles Martel and his cavalry repel the Muslim Moors and stop them from conquering France and Spain.

800

Charles Martel's grandson, Charlemagne (742–814) extends the boundaries of the kingdom and is crowned Holy Roman Emperor (Emperor of the West).

THE VIRGIN WARRIOR

Never has there been a more legendary *pucelle* (virgin) warrior than Jeanne d'Arc (Joan of Arc), an illiterate peasant girl burnt at the stake by the English in 1431 and France's patron saint since 1920. Scores of stories surround her origins, notably that she was the bastard child of Louis d'Orléans, King Charles VI's brother. The less glamorous but more accurate account pinpoints Domrémy in northeastern France (Domrémy-la-Pucelle today) as the place where she was born in 1412. Her father was Jacques d'Arc, a pious God-fearing farmer who reared his children to clean, sew and tend livestock.

Divine revelations delivered by the Archangel Michael prompted Jeanne d'Arc to flee the fold in 1428. To raise the siege against the city of Orléans (p418) and see Dauphin Charles VII crowned King of France was her mission. In Vaucouleurs, 50km west of Nancy (p402) in Lorraine, the 16-year-old persuaded Robert de Baudricourt to arm her with a sword and two male escorts, with whom she rode to Chinon in February 1429. The fabled scene in which Jeanne d'Arc plucks *le gentil dauphin* (the kind dauphin) out of his court at Château de Chinon (p443) has been immortalised on the silver screen countless times, most notably by Ingrid Bergman in 1948 in Victor Fleming's *Joan of Arc* and again in 1954 in Rossellini's neo-realist *Jeanne au Bûcher.* Ukrainian supermodel Milla Jovovich played Jeanne in Luc Besson's 1999 version starring Dustin Hoffman and Faye Dunaway.

The consequent Poitiers Enquiry, conducted by clergy and university clerks in Poitiers (p658), strived to establish if Jeanne d'Arc was a fraud or a gift, as she claimed, from the King of Heaven to the King of France. Her virginity was likewise certified. Following the six-week interrogation Jeanne was sent by Charles VII to Tours (p431), where she was equipped with intendants, a horse, a sword (found in a church in the Vienne valley) and her own standard featuring God sitting in judgment on a cloud. The armour that was made for her disappeared following her capture in 1430 (to the delight of unscrupulous antique dealers, who sporadically claim to have uncovered the what-would-be priceless suit). In Blois (p424) the divine warrior collected her army, drummed up by Charles VII from his Royal Army Headquarters there. In April 1429 Jeanne d'Arc started her attack on Orléans, besieged by the English since October of the previous year. Defiant to their defences she entered the city, rallying its inhabitants and gaining their support. On 5 and 6 May respectively the French gained control of the Bastille St-Loup and the Bastille des Augustins, followed the next day by the legendary Fort des Tourelles – a fort guarding the only access to the city from the left bank. This last shattering defeat prompted the English to lay down the siege on 8 May and was a decisive turning point in the Hundred Years War.

While in battle Jeanne d'Arc celebrated mass daily. From Orléans she went on to defeat the English at Jargeau, Beaugency and Patay. Charles VII stayed at châteaux in Loches and Sully-sur-Loire at this time and prayed to St Benedict with his protégé at Abbaye de St-Benoît in St-Benoît-sur-Loire. Despite Charles' promised coronation in July 1429, battles between the English and the French waged until 1453, by which time the virginal warrior responsible for turning the war around had long been dead. Jeanne d'Arc was captured by the Burgundians, sold to the English, convicted of witchcraft and heresy by a tribunal of French ecclesiastics in Rouen (p266) in 1431 and burned at the stake.

In 1456 a trail of rehabilitation found the five-month trial of Jeanne d'Arc to be fraudulent and calumnious, and overturned its verdict. The Church beatified her in 1909 and canonised her in 1920.

800–900

Scandinavian Vikings (also called Norsemen, thus Normans) raid France's western coast. They settle in the lower Seine Valley and later form the Duchy of Normandy.

987

Five centuries of Merovingian and Carolingian rule ends with the crowning of Hugh Capet; a dynasty that will rule one of Europe's most powerful countries for the next 800 years is born.

1066

Duke of Normandy William the Conqueror and his Norman forces occupy England, making Normandy and, later, Plantagenet-ruled England formidable rivals of the kingdom of France.

THE SUN KING

At the tender age of five, the Roi Soleil (Sun King) ascended the throne as Louis XIV (r 1643–1715). Bolstered by claims of divine right, he involved France in a rash of wars that gained it territory but terrified its neighbours and nearly bankrupted the Treasury. At home he quashed the ambitious, feuding aristocracy and created the first centralised French state. In Versailles, Louis XIV built an extravagant palace (p211) and made his courtiers compete with each other for royal favour, reducing them to ineffectual sycophants. In 1685 he revoked the Edict of Nantes.

Grandson Louis XV (r 1715–74) was an oafish buffoon whose regent, the duke of Orléans, shifted the royal court back to Paris. As the 18th century progressed, the *ancien régime* (old order) became increasingly at odds with the needs of the country. Enlightened anti-establishment and anticlerical ideas expressed by Voltaire, Rousseau and Montesquieu further threatened the royal regime.

The Seven Years War (1756–63), fought by France and Austria against Britain and Prussia, was one of a series of ruinous wars pursued by Louis XV, leading to the loss of France's flourishing colonies in Canada, the West Indies and India to the British. The war cost a fortune and, even more ruinous for the monarchy, it helped to disseminate in France the radical democratic ideas that had been thrust onto the world stage by the American Revolution.

Winner of the 2008 Ondaatje Prize, Graham Robb's much-lauded *The Discovery of France* is an epic portrait of contemporary France as a re-emerging land of a thousand *pays* (lands); his in-country research saw him cycle some 20,000km around rural France.

REVOLUTION TO REPUBLIC

Social and economic crises marked the 18th century. With the aim of warding off popular discontent, Louis XVI called a meeting of the États Généraux (Estates General) in 1789, made up of representatives of the nobility (First Estate), clergy (Second Estate) and the remaining 90% of the population (Third Estate). When the Third Estate's call for a system of proportional voting failed, it proclaimed itself a National Assembly and demanded a constitution. On the streets, a Parisian mob took the matter into its own hands by raiding the Invalides (p151) for weapons and storming the prison at Bastille (now a very busy roundabout; p144). Said to be something of a clueless idiot, Louis XVI is reckoned to have written *'rien'* (nothing happened) in his diary that day.

France was declared a constitutional monarchy and reforms enacted. But as the new government armed itself against the threat posed by Austria, Prussia and the many exiled French nobles, patriotism and nationalism mixed with revolutionary fervour. Before long the moderate republican Girondins lost power to the radical Jacobins led by Robespierre, Danton and Marat, and in September 1792 France's First Republic was declared. Louis XVI was publicly guillotined in January 1793 on Paris' place de la Concorde (p154) and the head of his queen, the vilified Marie-Antoinette, rolled several months later.

1095

Pope Urban II preaches the First Crusade in Clermont-Ferrand, prompting France to play a leading role in the Crusades and giving rise to some splendid cathedrals – Reims, Strasbourg, Metz and Chartres among them.

1152

Eleanor of Aquitaine weds Henry of Anjou, bringing a further third of France under the control of the English Crown and sparking a French–English rivalry that will last at least three centuries.

1309

French-born Pope Clément V moves the papal headquarters from Rome to the Provençal city of Avignon, where the Holy See remains until 1377; 'home' is the resplendent Palais des Papes built under Benoît XII (1334–42).

REPUBLICAN CALENDAR

During the Revolution, the Convention adopted a calendar from which all 'superstitious' associations (such as saints' days) were removed. Year one began on 22 September 1792, the day the Republic was proclaimed. The 12 months – renamed Vendémiaire, Brumaire, Frimaire, Nivôse, Pluviôse, Ventôse, Germinal, Floréal, Prairial, Messidor, Thermidor and Fructidor – were divided into three 10-day weeks called *décades.*

The poetic names of the months were seasonally inspired: the autumn months, for instance, were Vendémiaire (derived from *vendange,* grape harvest or vintage), Brumaire (from *brume,* mist or fog) and Frimaire (from *frimas,* frost). The last day of each *décade* was a rest day, and the five or six remaining days of the year were used to celebrate Virtue, Genius, Labour, Opinion and Rewards. These festivals were initially called *sans-culottides* in honour of the *sans-culottes,* the extreme revolutionaries who wore pantaloons rather than the short breeches favoured by the upper classes.

While the Republican calendar worked well in theory, it caused no end of confusion and on 1 January 1806 Napoléon switched back to the Gregorian calendar.

The Reign of Terror between September 1793 and July 1794 saw churches closed, cathedrals turned into 'Temples of Reason' and thousands incarcerated in dungeons in Paris' Conciergerie (p146) before being beheaded.

NAPOLÉON BONAPARTE

Beheadings done and dusted, a five-man delegation of moderate republicans set itself up as a Directoire (Directory) to rule the republic...until a dashing young Corsican general named Napoléon Bonaparte (1769–1821) came along. Napoléon Bonaparte's skills and military tactics quickly turned him into an independent political force and in 1799 he overthrew the Directory and assumed power as consul of the First Empire. A referendum in 1802 declared him consul for life, his birthday became a national holiday and in 1804 he was crowned emperor of the French by Pope Pius VII at Paris' Notre Dame (p145). Two years on he commissioned the world's largest triumphal arch (p154) to be built.

To consolidate and legitimise his authority, Napoléon waged several wars in which France gained control of most of Europe. In 1812 his troops captured Moscow, only to be killed off by the brutal Russian winter. Two years later, Allied armies entered Paris, exiled Napoléon to Elba and restored the House of Bourbon to the French throne at the Congress of Vienna (1814–15).

But in 1815 Napoléon escaped from the Mediterranean island-kingdom, landed at Golfe Juan in southern France and marched north, triumphantly entering Paris on 20 May. His glorious 'Hundred Days' back in power ended with the Battle of Waterloo and his return to exile (to the South Atlantic

1337

Incessant struggles between the Capetians and England's King Edward III, a Plantagenet, over the powerful French throne degenerate into the Hundred Years War, which will last until 1453.

1422

John Plantagenet, duke of Bedford, is made regent of France for England's King Henry VI, then an infant. Less than a decade later he is crowned king of France at Paris' Notre Dame.

1431

Jeanne d'Arc (Joan of Arc) is burnt at the stake in Rouen for heresy; the English are not driven out of France until 1453.

island of St Helena, where he died in 1821). In 1840 his remains were moved to Paris' Église du Dôme (p152).

SECOND REPUBLIC TO SECOND EMPIRE

A struggle between extreme monarchists seeking a return to the *ancien régime,* people who saw the changes wrought by the Revolution as irreversible, and the radicals of the poor working-class neighbourhoods of Paris dominated the reign of Louis XVIII (r 1815–24). Charles X (r 1824–30) responded to the conflict with ineptitude and was overthrown in the so-called July Revolution of 1830. Those who were killed in the accompanying Paris street battles are buried in vaults under the Colonne de Juillet in the centre of place de la Bastille (p144).

Louis-Philippe (r 1830–48), a constitutional monarch of bourgeois sympathies, was subsequently chosen as ruler by parliament, only to be ousted by the 1848 Revolution.

The Second Republic was established and elections brought in Napoléon's almost useless nephew, Louis Napoléon Bonaparte, as president. But in 1851 Louis Napoléon led a coup d'état and proclaimed himself Emperor Napoléon III of the Second Empire (1852–70).

France enjoyed significant economic growth at this time. Paris was transformed under urban planner Baron Haussmann (1809–91), who created the 12 huge boulevards radiating from the Arc de Triomphe (p154). Napoléon III threw glittering parties at the royal palace in Compiègne (p260), and breathed in fashionable sea air at Biarritz (p694) and Deauville (p292).

Like his uncle, Napoléon III embroiled France in various catastrophic conflicts, including the Crimean War (1853–56) and the humiliating

OFF WITH HIS HEAD

In a bid to make public executions more humane (hanging and quartering – roping the victim's limbs to four oxen, which then ran in four different directions – was the favoured method of the day for commoners), French physician Joseph Ignace Guillotin (1738–1814) came up with the guillotine.

Several tests on dead bodies down the line, highwayman Nicolas Jacques Pelletie was the first in France to have his head sliced off by the 2m-odd falling blade on 25 April 1792 on place de Grève on Paris' Right Bank. His head rolled into a strategically placed wicker basket. During the Reign of Terror, at least 17,000 met their death by guillotine.

By the time the last person in France to be guillotined (murderer Hamida Djandoubi in Marseille) had been given the chop in 1977 (behind closed doors – the last public execution was in 1939), the lethal contraption had been sufficiently refined to slice off a head in 2/100 of a second. France abolished capital punishment in 1981.

1491

Charles VIII weds Anne de Bretagne at Château de Langeais in the castle-studded Loire Valley. Their marriage marks the unification of independent Brittany with France.

1515

With the reign of François I the royal court moves to the Loire Valley, where a rash of stunning Renaissance châteaux and hunting lodges – enough to last several lifetimes over – are built.

1530s

The Reformation sweeps through France, prompting the core of Catholicism to be questioned, pitting Catholic against Protestant and eventually leading to the Wars of Religion (1562–98).

END TO THE CHURCH–STATE PENAL SYSTEM

Dry Guillotine: 15 Years among the Living Dead by René Belbenoît paints a vivid picture of the hideous island where infamous Jewish army officer Captain Alfred Dreyfus – court-martialled and sentenced to life imprisonment in 1894 for betraying military secrets to Germany – ended up. A notorious penal colony in French Guiana, South America, some 56,000 French prisoners slumbered in misery here between 1864 and 1946. Dreyfus' eventual vindication greatly discredited both the army and Catholic Church, resulting in the legal separation of Church and State in 1905.

Franco-Prussian War (1870–71), which ended with Prussia taking the emperor prisoner. Upon hearing the news, defiant and very hungry Parisian masses took to the streets demanding a republic. The Wall of the Federalists in Paris' Cimetière du Père Lachaise (Père Lachaise Cemetery; p156) serves as a deathly reminder of the subsequent bloodshed.

A BEAUTIFUL AGE

There was nothing beautiful about the start of the Third Republic. Born as a provisional government of national defence in September 1870, it was quickly besieged by the Prussians, who laid siege to Paris and demanded National Assembly elections be held. Unfortunately, the first move made by the resultant monarchist-controlled assembly was to ratify the Treaty of Frankfurt (1871), the harsh terms of which – a 5-billion-franc war indemnity and surrender of the provinces of Alsace and Lorraine – prompted immediate revolt.

During the Semaine Sanglante (Bloody Week), several thousand rebel Communards (supporters of the hard-core insurgent Paris Commune) were killed and a further 20,000 or so executed.

Despite the bloody start, the Third Republic ushered in the glittering belle époque (beautiful age), with art-nouveau architecture, a whole field of artistic 'isms' from Impressionism onwards, and advances in science and engineering, including the construction of the first metro line in Paris. World Exhibitions were held in the capital in 1889 (showcased by the Eiffel Tower, p152) and again in 1901 in the purpose-built Petit Palais (p154).

The horror of trench warfare during WWI sits at the heart of Sebastian Faulks' powerful novel *Birdsong* – essential reading for anyone visiting the Battle of the Somme memorials.

THE GREAT WAR

A trip to the Somme (p252) or Verdun (p414) battlefields goes some way to revealing the unimaginable human cost of WWI. Much of the war took place in northeastern France, with trench warfare using thousands of soldiers as cannon fodder to gain a few metres of territory.

Central to France's entry into war against Austria-Hungary and Germany had been its desire to regain Alsace and Lorraine, lost to Germany in 1871. The Great War officially ended in November 1918 with Germany and the

1588

The Catholic League forces Henri III (r 1574–89), the last of the Valois kings, to flee the royal court at the Louvre, Paris, and the next year he is assassinated by a fanatical Dominican friar.

1598

Bourbon king Henry IV gives French Protestants freedom of conscience with the Edict of Nantes – much to the horror of staunchly Catholic Paris, which refuses to accept the king until he accepts Catholicism.

1643–1715

The Roi Soleil (Sun King), Louis XIV, assumes the French throne and shifts his royal court from Paris 23km west to a fabulous palace in Versailles.

Allies signing an armistice in a clearing (p261) near Compiègne. But the details were not finalised until 1919, when the so-called 'big four' – French Prime Minister Georges Clemenceau, British Prime Minister Lloyd George, Italian Premier Vittorio Orlando and US President Woodrow Wilson – gathered in the Palace of Versailles (p211) to sign the Treaty of Versailles. Its harsh terms included the return of Alsace-Lorraine to France and a reparations bill of US$33 billion for Germany.

Paris sparkled as the centre of the avant-garde in the 1920s and 1930s, with artists pushing into the new fields of cubism and surrealism, Le Corbusier (p65) rewriting the architectural textbook, foreign writers such as Ernest Hemingway and F Scott Fitzgerald drawn to the liberal atmosphere of Paris, and nightlife establishing a cutting-edge reputation for everything from jazz to striptease. In 1922 the luxurious *Train Bleu* (Blue Train) made its first run from Calais, via Paris, to the Côte d'Azur.

WWII

The naming of Adolf Hitler as Germany's chancellor in 1933 signalled the end of a decade of compromise between France and Germany. Initially the French tried to appease Hitler, but two days after Germany invaded Poland in 1939 France joined Britain in declaring war on Germany.

VERDUN: THE STRATEGY BEHIND THE CARNAGE

On the Western Front, the outbreak of WWI in August 1914 was followed by a long period of trench warfare in which neither side made any significant gains. To break the stalemate, the Germans decided to change tactics, attacking a target so vital for both military and symbolic reasons that the French would throw every man they had into its defence. These troops would then be slaughtered, 'bleeding France white' and causing the French people to lose their will to resist. The target selected for this bloody plan by the German general staff was the heavily fortified Lorraine city of Verdun, which had fallen to Prussian forces in 1792 and 1870 and would afford access to the road to Paris.

The Battle of Verdun began on the morning of 21 February 1916. After the heaviest shelling of the war to that date (something like two million shells were fired in 10 hours), German forces went on the attack and advanced with little opposition for four days, capturing, among other unprepared French positions, Fort de Douaumont. Thus began a 300-day battle fought by hundreds of thousands of cold, wet, miserable and ill-fed men, sheltering in their muddy trenches and foxholes amid a moonscape of craters.

French forces were regrouped and rallied by General Philippe Pétain (later the leader of the collaborationist Vichy government during WWII), who slowed the German advance by launching several French counterattacks. The Germans weren't pushed back beyond their positions of February 1916 until American troops and French forces launched a coordinated offensive in September 1918.

1756–63

The Seven Years War, fought by France and Austria against Britain and Prussia, is one of a series of ruinous wars pursued by Louis XV, leading to the loss of France's colonies in Canada, the West Indies and India.

1789–94

Revolutionaries storm the Bastille, leading to the public beheading of Louis XVI and Marie-Antoinette and the Reign of Terror, during which religious freedoms are revoked.

1795–99

A five-man delegation of moderate republicans led by Paul Barras sets itself up as a *Directoire* (Directory) and rules the Republic for five years.

By June 1940 France had capitulated. The British expeditionary force sent to help the French barely managed to avoid capture by retreating to Dunkirk (see the boxed text, below) and crossing the English Channel in small boats. The Maginot Line (see the boxed text, opposite) had proved useless, with German armoured divisions outflanking it by going through Belgium.

The demarcation line between the Nazi-occupied and Vichy zones ran through Château de Chenonceau (p436) in the Loire Valley. Life in the Nazi-occupied north is examined at La Coupole (p241), a WWII museum inside a subterranean Nazi-built rocket-launch site.

The Vichy regime was viciously anti-Semitic, and local police proved very helpful to the Nazis in rounding up French Jews and others for deportation to Auschwitz and other death camps. Museums in Grenoble (p557) and Lyon (p504), among others, examine these deportations. The only Nazi concentration camp on French soil was Natzweiler-Struthof (see the boxed text, p387); it can be visited.

An 80km-long stretch of beach (see the boxed text, p286) and Bayeux' Musée Mémorial 1944 Bataille de Normandie (p281) tell the tale of the D-Day landings on 6 June 1944, when 100,000-plus Allied troops stormed the coastline to liberate most of Normandy and Brittany. Paris was liberated on 25 August by a force spearheaded by Free French units, sent in ahead of the Americans so the French would have the honour of liberating their own capital.

The US general's war room in Reims (see the boxed text, p358), where Nazi Germany officially capitulated in May 1945, is open to the public.

POSTWAR DEVASTATION

France was ruined. Over one-third of industrial production fed the German war machine during WWII, the occupiers requisitioning practically everything that wasn't (and was) nailed down: ferrous and nonferrous

THE EVACUATION OF DUNKIRK

In May and June 1940 Dunkirk earned a place in the history books when the British Expeditionary Force and French and Belgian units in far northern France found themselves almost completely surrounded by Hitler's Blitzkrieg forces. In an effort to salvage what it could, Churchill's government ordered British units to make their way to Dunkirk, where naval vessels and hundreds of fishing boats and pleasure craft – many manned by civilian volunteers – braved intense German artillery and air attacks to ferry 340,000 men to the safety of England. Conducted in the difficult first year of WWII, this unplanned and chaotic evacuation – dubbed Operation Dynamo – failed to save any of the units' heavy equipment but was nevertheless seen as a heroic demonstration of Britain's resourcefulness and determination.

1799–1815

Enter a dashing young Corsican soldier called Napoléon Bonaparte (1769–1821) who, as consul of the First Empire, commissions Paris' most famous triumphal arch to be built.

1851

Louis Napoléon leads a coup d'état and proclaims himself Emperor Napoléon III of the Second Empire (1852–70).

1858

A 14-year-old peasant girl in Lourdes sees the Virgin Mary in a series of 18 visions that come to her in a grotto; the sleepy market town in the Pyrenees later becomes a world pilgrimage site.

THE MAGINOT LINE

The famed Ligne Maginot (www.maginot.org), named after France's minister of war from 1929 to 1932, was one of the most spectacular blunders of WWII. This elaborate, mostly subterranean defence network, built between 1930 and 1940 (and, in the history of military architecture, second only to the Great Wall of China in sheer size), was the pride of prewar France. It included everything France's finest military architects thought would be needed to defend the nation in a 'modern war' of poison gas, tanks and aeroplanes: reinforced concrete bunkers, subterranean lines of supply and communication, minefields, antitank canals, floodable basins and even artillery emplacements that popped out of the ground to fire and then disappeared. The only things visible above ground were firing posts and lookout towers. The line stretched along the Franco-German frontier from the Swiss border all the way to Belgium where, for political and budgetary reasons, it stopped. The Maginot Line even had a slogan: *'Ils ne passeront pas'* (They won't get through).

'They' – the Germans – never did. Rather than attack the Maginot Line straight on, Hitler's armoured divisions simply circled around through Belgium and invaded France across its unprotected northern frontier. They then attacked the Maginot Line from the rear. Most of northern France was already in German hands; some of the fortifications held out for a few weeks.

metals, statues, iron grills, zinc bar tops, coal, leather, textiles and chemicals. Agriculture, strangled by the lack of raw materials, fell by 25%.

In their retreat, the Germans burned bridges (2600 destroyed) and the Allied bombardments tore up railroad tracks (40,000km). The roadways hadn't been maintained since 1939, ports were damaged, and nearly half a million buildings and 60,000 factories were destroyed. The French had to pay for the needs of the occupying soldiers to the tune of 400 million francs a day, prompting an inflation rip tide.

France's humiliation at the hands of the Germans was not lost on its restive colonies. As the war economy tightened its grip the native-born people, poorer to begin with, noticed that they were bearing the brunt of the pain. In North Africa the Algerians coalesced around a movement for greater autonomy, which blossomed into a full-scale independence movement by the end of the war. The Japanese moved into strategically important Indochina in 1940. The Vietnamese resistance movement that developed quickly took on an anti-French, nationalistic tone, setting the stage for Vietnam's eventual independence.

THE FOURTH REPUBLIC & POSTWAR PROSPERITY

After the liberation, General Charles de Gaulle (1890–1970) – France's undersecretary of war who had fled Paris for London in 1940 after France capitulated – faced the tricky task of setting up a viable government. Elections on 21 October 1945 created a national assembly composed largely of

1870

The Third Republic ushers in the bloody-then-beautiful belle époque, a madly creative era that among other things conceives Bohemian Paris, with its raunchy nightclubs and artistic cafés.

1871

The Treaty of Frankfurt is signed, the harsh terms of which – a 5-billion-franc war indemnity and surrender of the provinces of Alsace and Lorraine – prompt immediate revolt.

1903

The world's biggest sporting event after the Olympics and the World Cup sprints around France for the first time; Tour de France riders pedal throughout the night to cover 2500km in 19 days.

THE FRENCH RESISTANCE

Despite the myth of *'la France résistante'* (the French Resistance), the underground movement never actually included more than 5% of the population. The other 95% either collaborated or did nothing. Resistance members engaged in railway sabotage, collected intelligence for the Allies, helped Allied airmen who had been shot down and published anti-German leaflets, among other activities. The impact of their pursuits might have been modest but the Resistance served as an enormous boost to French morale – not to mention fresh fodder for numerous literary and cinematic endeavours.

pro-resistant communists. De Gaulle was appointed head of the government, but quickly sensed that the tide was turning against his idea of a strong presidency and in January 1946 he resigned.

The magnitude of France's postwar economic devastation required a strong central government with broad powers to rebuild the country's industrial and commercial base. Soon after the liberation most banks, insurance companies, car manufacturers and energy-producing companies passed into the hands of the government. Other businesses remained in private hands, the objective being to combine the efficiency of state planning with the dynamism of private initiative. But progress was slow. By 1947 rationing remained and France was forced to turn to the USA for loans as part of the Marshall Plan to rebuild Europe.

One of the aims of the Marshall Plan was to financially and politically stabilise postwar Europe, thus thwarting the expansion of Soviet power. As the Iron Curtain fell over Eastern Europe, the pro-Stalinist bent of the Communist Party put it in a politically untenable position. Seeking at once to exercise power within the government and at the same time oppose its measures as insufficiently Marxist, the communists found themselves on the losing end of disputes involving the colonies, workers' demands and American aid. In 1947 they were booted out of government.

While the Communist Party fulminated against the 'imperialism' of American power, de Gaulle founded a new party, the Rassemblement du Peuple Français (RPF), which argued for the containment of Soviet power.

The economy gathered steam in the 1950s. The French government invested in hydroelectric and nuclear-power plants, oil and gas exploration, petro chemical refineries, steel production, naval construction, auto factories and building construction to accommodate a baby boom and consumer goods.

WAR IN THE COLONIES

The 1950s spelled the end of French colonialism. When Japan surrendered to the Allies in 1945, nationalist Ho Chi Minh launched a push for an autonomous Vietnam that became a drive for independence. Under the brilliant General Giap, the Vietnamese perfected a form of guerrilla warfare that

1904

Colonial rivalry between France and Britain in Africa ends with the Entente Cordiale (literally 'Cordial Understanding'), marking the start of a cooperation that continues, more or less, to this day.

1914–18

The human cost of WWI is enormous: of the eight million French men called to arms, 1.3 million are killed and almost one million crippled.

1918

In the postwar period, industrial production drops by 40% and throws France into financial crisis.

proved highly effective against the French army. After their defeat at Dien Bien Phu in 1954, the French withdrew from Indochina.

The struggle for Algerian independence was nastier. Technically a French *département* (see p953), Algeria was in effect ruled by a million or so French settlers who wished at all costs to protect their privileges. Heads stuck firmly in the Saharan sands (especially in the south, where the oil was), the colonial community and its supporters in the army and the right wing refused all Algerian demands for political and economic equality.

The Algerian War of Independence (1954–62) was brutal. Nationalist rebel attacks were met with summary executions, inquisitions, torture and massacres, which only made Algerians more determined to gain their independence. The government responded with half-hearted reform and reorganisation programs that failed to address the fact that most people didn't want to be part of France.

Keep tabs on the moves and motions of France's National Assembly at www.assemblee-nat.fr.

International pressure on France to pull out of Algeria came from the UN, the USSR and the USA, while *pieds noirs* (literally 'black feet', as Algerian-born French people are known in France), elements of the military and extreme right-wingers became increasingly enraged at what they saw as defeatism in dealing with the problem. A plot to overthrow the French government and replace it with a military-style regime was narrowly avoided when de Gaulle agreed to assume the presidency in 1958.

THE FIFTH REPUBLIC & YESTERDAY'S MAN

While it could claim to have successfully reconstructed the economy and created political stability, the Fourth Republic was hampered by a weak presidential branch and the debilitating situation in Algeria. De Gaulle remedied the first problem by drafting a new constitution (the Fifth Republic), which gave considerable powers to the president at the expense of the National Assembly.

Algeria was a greater problem. De Gaulle's initial attempts at reform – according the Algerians political equality and recognising their right in principle to self-determination – only infuriated right-wingers without quenching the Algerian thirst for independence. Following a failed coup attempt by military officers in 1961, the Organisation de l'Armée Secrète (OAS; a group of French settlers and sympathisers opposed to Algerian independence) resorted to terrorism. It tried to assassinate de Gaulle several times and in 1961 violence broke out on the streets of Paris. Police violently attacked Algerian demonstrators, killing more than 100 people.

By the late 1960s de Gaulle was appearing more and more like yesterday's man. Loss of the colonies, a surge in immigration (p56) and the rise in unemployment had weakened his government. De Gaulle's government by decree was starting to gall the anti-authoritarian baby-boomer generation,

1920s

Paris sparkles as the centre of the avant-garde. The luxurious Train Bleu (Blue Train) makes its first run from Calais, via Paris, to the sparkling blue Mediterranean on the Côte d'Azur.

1939

Nazi Germany occupies France and divides it into a zone under direct German occupation (along the north and western coasts) and a puppet state led by ageing WWI hero General Pétain in the spa town of Vichy.

1944

Normandy and Brittany are the first to be liberated by Allied troops following the D-Day landings in June, followed by Paris on 25 August by a force honourably spearheaded by Free French units.

GAULLISH FACTS

- Charles de Gaulle was a record breaker: he is included in the *Guinness Book of Records* as surviving more assassination attempts – 32 to be precise – than anyone else in the world.
- The present constitution, known as the Fifth Republic and the 11th since 1789, was instituted by good old de Gaulle in 1958.
- Neither he nor his wife could pronounce English *h* – much to the amusement of many (p370).
- 'Of course you can jump up and down on your chair like a little goat, bleating "Europe! Europe! Europe!" but all that leads nowhere and means nothing', said a provocative de Gaulle in 1965.

Find out what else he said and did at www.charles-de-gaulle.org.

now at university and agitating for social change. Students reading Herbert Marcuse and Wilhelm Reich found much to admire in Fidel Castro, Che Guevara and the black struggle for civil rights in America, and vociferously denounced the American war in Vietnam.

Student protests of 1968 climaxed with a brutal overreaction by police to a protest meeting at Paris' most renowned university (p147). Overnight, public opinion turned in favour of the students, while the students themselves occupied the Sorbonne and erected barricades in the Latin Quarter. Within days a general strike by 10 million workers countrywide paralysed France.

But such comradeship between worker and student did not last long. While the former wanted a greater share of the consumer market, the latter wanted to destroy it. After much hesitancy de Gaulle took advantage of this division by appealing to people's fear of anarchy. Just as the country seemed on the brink of revolution and an overthrow of the Fifth Republic, stability returned. The government immediately decentralised the higher-education system and followed through in the 1970s with a wave of other reforms (lowering the voting age to 18, instituting legalised abortion and so on). De Gaulle meanwhile resigned from office in 1969 after losing an important referendum on regionalisation and suffered a fatal heart attack the following year.

POMPIDOU TO LE PEN

Georges Pompidou (1911–74), prime minister under de Gaulle, stepped onto the presidential podium in 1969. Despite embarking on an ambitious modernisation program, investing in aerospace, telecommunications and nuclear power, he failed to stave off inflation and social unrest following the global oil crisis of 1973.

In 1974 Valéry Giscard d'Estaing (b 1926) inherited a deteriorating economic climate and sharp divisions between the left and the right. Hampered by a

1949

France signs the Atlantic Pact uniting North America and Western Europe in a mutual defence alliance (NATO); the council of Europe, of which France is part, is born.

1951

The fear of communism and a resurgent Germany prompts the first steps towards European integration with the European Coal and Steel Community and military accords three years later.

1946–62

French colonialism ends with war in Indochina (1946–54) followed by the Algerian War of Independence (1954–62), brought to a close with the signing of the Accord d'Évian (Evian Accord) in Évian-les-Bains.

lack of media nous and an arrogant demeanour, d'Estaing proved unpopular. His friendship with emperor and accused child-eater Jean-Bédel Bokassa of the Central African Republic did little to win him friends, and in 1981 he was ousted by long-time head of the Parti Socialiste (PS; Socialist Party), François Mitterrand (1916–96). As the only surviving French president to remain in politics, d'Estaing has been nicknamed by the French media *l'Ex* (the Ex).

Despite France's first socialist president instantly alienating the business community (the Paris stock market index fell by 30% on news of his victory) by setting out to nationalise 36 privately owned banks, industrial groups and other parts of the economy, Mitterrand did give France a sparkle. The Minitel – a potent symbol of France's advanced technological savvy – was launched in 1980 and a clutch of *grands projets* (p65) were embarked upon in the French capital. The death penalty was abolished, homosexuality was legalised, a 39-hour work week was instituted, annual holiday time was upped from four to five weeks and the right to retire at 60 was guaranteed.

Yet by 1986 the economy was weakening and in parliamentary elections that year the right-wing opposition, led by Jacques Chirac (Paris mayor since 1977), won a majority in the National Assembly. For the next two years Mitterrand worked with a prime minister and cabinet from the opposition, an unprecedented arrangement known as *cohabitation*. The extreme-right Front National (FN; National Front) meanwhile quietly gained ground by loudly blaming France's economic woes on immigration.

Presidential elections in 1995 ushered Chirac (an ailing Mitterrand did not run) into the Élysée Palace. Whiz-kid foreign minister Alain Juppé was appointed prime minister and several women were placed in top cabinet positions. However, Chirac's attempts to reform France's colossal public sector in order to meet the criteria of European Monetary Union (EMU) were met with the largest protests since 1968, and his decision to resume nuclear testing on the Polynesian island of Mururoa and a nearby atoll was the focus of worldwide outrage. Always the maverick, Chirac called early parliamentary elections in 1997 – only for his party, the Rassemblement pour la République (RPR; Rally for the Republic), to lose out to a coalition of socialists, communists and greens. Another period of *cohabitation* ensued, this time with Chirac on the other side.

Since the end of WWII France has been one of the five permanent members of the UN Security Council. Follow its movements at www.un.org/docs/sc.

The presidential elections in 2002 surprised everybody. Not only did the first round of voting see left-wing PS leader Lionel Jospin eliminated, it also saw the FN's racist demagogue Jean-Marie Le Pen (b 1928) – legendary for his dismissal of the Holocaust as a 'mere detail of history' in the 1980s and his 'inequality of races' jargon in the late 1990s – scoop 17% of the national vote. In the fortnight preceding the subsequent run-off ballot, demonstrators took to the streets with cries of 'Vote for the crook, not the fascist' ('crook' referring to the various party financing scandals floating around Chirac). On the big day itself, left-wing voters – without a candidate of their

1966

France withdraws from NATO's joint military command in 1966; it has maintained an independent arsenal of nuclear weapons since 1960. A year later NATO moves out of its headquarters outside Paris.

1968

Large-scale anti-authoritarian student protests (known since as 'May 1968') at de Gaulle's style of government by decree escalate into a countrywide protest that eventually brings down de Gaulle.

1981

The superspeedy TGV makes its first commercial journey from Paris to Lyon, breaking all speed records to complete the train journey in two hours instead of six.

own – hedged their bets with 'lesser-of-two-evils' Chirac to give him 82% of votes. Chirac's landslide victory was echoed in parliamentary elections a month later when the president-backed coalition UMP (Union pour un Mouvement Populaire) won 354 of the 577 parliamentary seats, ending years of *cohabitation* and leaving Le Pen's FN seatless. Le Pen's subsequent attempt to automatically pass the party leadership to his daughter, Marine, was perceived both within and outside the party as nepotism and only weakened the party further.

HELTER-SKELTER DOWNHILL

France's outright opposition to the US-led war in Iraq in 2003 stirred up anti-French sentiment among Americans: many restaurants in the US changed 'French fries' to 'freedom fries' on their menus, to avoid having to mention the unspeakable, while US defence secretary Donald Rumsfeld publicly dismissed France (along with Germany) as 'old Europe'.

Old Europe indeed – in need of a shake-up: in November 2002 widespread strikes brought France to a standstill as public-sector workers hit out at the government's ambitious privatisation plans aimed at raising cash to reduce an increasingly too-high budget deficit. A few months later, in a bid to appease a discontented electorate, parliament granted greater power to local government (p953) on economic and cultural affairs, transport and further education. The constitutional reform also gave the green light to local referenda – to better hear what the people on the street were saying (though the first referendum subsequently held – in Corsica – threw up a 'No' vote, putting Paris back at square one; for details see p907).

Spring 2003 ushered in yet more national strikes, this time over the government's proposed pension reform, which was pushed through parliament in July. 'We are not going to be intimidated by protestors' was the tough response of centre-right Prime Minister Jean-Pierre Raffarin, in office since May 2002. An extreme heatwave that summer, sending temperatures in the capital soaring above 40° and claiming 11,000 predominantly elderly lives, did little to cool rising temperatures.

SUITE FRANÇAISE

The story behind literary stunner *Suite Française* is as incredible as the novel itself. A twin set of novellas, it evokes the horror of Nazi-occupied Paris from June 1940 until July 1941 through the eyes of Ukrainian-born author Irène Némirovsky, who was arrested as a 'stateless person of Jewish descent' and carted off to Auschwitz, where she died in the gas chamber in August 1942. Months later her husband suffered the same fate, leaving their oldest daughter with a bunch of leather-bound notebooks, which remained unread until the 1990s – when this amazing novel, first published in French in 2004, was discovered.

1994

The 50km-long Channel Tunnel linking mainland France with Britain opens after seven years of hard graft by 10,000 workers; a year later the first land link since the last ice age announces a £925-million loss.

1995

After twice serving as prime minister, Jacques Chirac becomes president of France, winning popular acclaim for his direct words and actions in matters relating to the EU and the war raging in Bosnia.

1998

After resuming nuclear testing in the South Pacific in the early 1990s to the horror of environmentalists, France finally signs the worldwide test-ban treaty, bringing an end to French nuclear testing once and for all.

THE BIRTH OF THE BIKINI

Almost called *atome* (French for atom), rather than bikini, after its pinprick size, the scanty little two-piece bathing suit was the 1946 creation of Cannes fashion designer Jacques Heim and automotive engineer Louis Réard.

Top-and-bottom swimsuits had existed for centuries, but it was the French duo who both made them briefer than brief and plumped for the name 'bikini' – after Bikini, an atoll in the Marshall Islands chosen by the USA in 1946 as the testing ground for atomic bombs.

Once wrapped around the curvaceous buttocks of 1950s sex-bomb Brigitte Bardot on St-Tropez' Plage de Pampelonne, there was no looking back. The bikini was born.

More cracks appeared in France's assured countenance and silky-smooth veneer during 2004. Regional elections saw Chirac's centre-right UMP party sent to the slaughterhouse by the socialists; European elections two months later were equally disastrous. Strikes against various pension, labour and welfare reforms proposed by the government continued and in May 2005 the voice of protest was injected with a new lease of life thanks to French voters' shock rejection of the proposed EU constitution in a referendum. It was no coincidence that the constitution was something Chirac had fervently backed: the overriding message behind the 'No' vote was loud and clear – 'We are fed up with you. Do something!'

What Chirac did was sack his hugely unpopular prime minister, Raffarin, and take his own foot off the reform pedal amid calls in some circles that he should resign. In the face of a five-year high in unemployment (10.2%) and an increasingly sluggish economy (GDP grew by just 1.4% in 2005 compared to 2.1% in 2004), the newly appointed prime minister – the silver-haired and silver-tongued career diplomat Dominique de Villepin (b 1953), who was best known as foreign minister during the Iraq invasion – assumed the gargantuan task of turning around disgruntled public opinion.

The last quarter of 2005 was the final helter-skelter downhill. The catalyst was the death of two teenagers of North African descent in October who, apparently running from police, were electrocuted while hiding in an electricity substation in a northeast Paris suburb. Rioting immediately broke out in the poor, predominantly immigrant neighbourhood and spread like wildfire. Within days the violence was countrywide, as rioters burnt cars, hurled petrol bombs, smashed windows, looted shops and vented months of pent-up anger. Two weeks later the government introduced emergency measures restricting people's movements and imposing curfews in 30 French towns and cities as part of its tough zero-tolerance policy on the urban chaos. Nine thousand burnt cars and buildings later, as peace returned, Chirac assured France there would be no more urban

1999

A lorry carrying flour and margarine catches fire in the 11.6km-long Mont Blanc tunnel in the French Alps, killing 41 people and closing the France–Italy link for three years.

2000

An Air France Concorde bound for New York bursts into flames just after take-off at Roissy Charles de Gaulle airport in Paris and crashes, killing all 109 people on board and four on the ground.

2002

The French franc, first minted in 1360, is dumped on the scrap heap of history as the country adopts the euro as its official currency.

violence. He also swore steps would be made to create equal opportunities for immigrants and better opportunities for their youth.

This did and didn't happen: in what became known as the infamous U-turn, Prime Minister Dominique de Villepin introduced a new youth-employment law in March 2006 giving employers the right to sack under-26s – just like that – during the first two years of their contract. This, the PM argued, removed the risk for employers in hiring young, inexperienced recruits, thus encouraging job creation for youths. The law was slammed by students, however; thousands took to the streets in protest and stayed there for several weeks. Police stormed the Sorbonne in Paris. Finally, squeezed into a corner with street violence increasing by the day, a battered and desperately weak Chirac government finally had no choice but back down.

THE PRESIDENTIAL RACE

Presidential elections, held every five years, threw a woman into the arena in April 2007. Standing tall, dignified and well above any dirty political dog fighting, socialist Ségolène Royal grabbed the country's attention with her glam, squeaky-clean image and tough talk about leading France in a ground-breaking new direction where no man had dared set foot before. Discredited French president *Le Grand Jacques*, now in his 70s and with a twinset of terms under his presidential belt, did not stand again.

Sink your teeth into a meaty discussion on government policy and what France's politicians are saying at government portal www.premier-ministre.gouv.fr.

Then there was 'Sarko', as the French press quickly dubbed the dynamic, high-profile and highly ambitious Nicolas Sarkozy (b 1955) of Chirac's UMP party. Interior minister and ruling party chairman, the centre-right candidate Sarkozy spoke – extremely smoothly and an awful lot – about job creation, lowering taxes, crime crackdown and helping the country's substantial immigrant population, which, given he himself was the son of a Hungarian immigrant, had instant appeal. On polling day, punters even appeared to forgive him for his hardline comments slamming ethnic minorities in the Parisian suburbs as 'scum' during the 2005 riots and for his role (albeit that of innocent victim) in the Clearstream scandal. Falsely implicated in accepting bribes as economic minister in 1991, Sarkozy vowed in 2006 to uncover whoever had framed him after courts ruled the anonymous bribery allegations to be bogus. Chief suspect in the smear campaign according to press reports: floundering prime minister and Chirac favourite in the presidential run, Dominique de Villepin (b 1953).

With none of the 12 presidential candidates winning 50% of the vote, the presidential race went to a second round of voting that pitted Sarkozy against Royal. On 6 May an almost-record 84% of France's 44.7 million eligible voters turned out to cast their ballots, which saw the charismatic, silky tongued, 52-year-old Nicolas Sarkozy bagging the Élysée Palace (with 53% of votes compared to Royal's 47%). A new breed of personality-driven, American-style French president was born.

2003

France opposes the US-led war in Iraq, stirring up anti-French sentiment among Americans and leading US defence secretary Donald Rumsfeld to dismiss France (along with Germany) as 'old Europe'.

2003

A heatwave across Europe brings temperatures of 40°C to Paris in August, killing an estimated 11,000 (mainly elderly) people. In desperation, undertakers had to use refrigerated warehouses outside Paris.

2004

Much to the outrage of French Muslims, the National Assembly says 'yes' to a controversial bill banning overtly religious symbols such as the Islamic headscarf in state schools; riots break out.

SARKOSIS

It's hardly the stuff French people expect of their president. Hardly respectable at all, in fact, say most who have reacted to the Sarkozy soap opera with shock, shame, faint embarrassment and downright dismay. Hanging out your dirty laundry in such an undignified, un-French, bling-bling (brash, vulgar) manner is just not done, at least not in France.

First there was Cécilia, his second wife of 11 years and mother of one of his three children, inconspicuously absent during most of the presidential campaign and certainly not by his side when the president popped his own vote in the ballot box. Disconcertingly vocal about her lack of enthusiasm for the post of *première dame* (First Lady), she braved it for a short while – only for the couple to confirm speculation in October 2007 that they were divorcing. Months later Cécilia tied the knot for a third time – to the lover who had prompted her and Sarkozy to briefly separate in 2005.

Now there's Carla Bruni, a younger Italian version of Cécilia in a nutshell who Sarkozy met at a dinner in Paris a month after the divorce, then whisked off to Egypt for Christmas and wed three months later. A former supermodel, folk singer, songwriter and multimillionaire, the leggy brunette is not coy about her string of past lovers, Mick Jagger and Eric Clapton among them. Nor is she shy about telling the world how she fell madly, passionately, wildly, head-over-heels in love with Sarkozy and his 'five or six brains' at first sight. A month after their marriage, a nude photo of Bruni, taken at the height of her modelling career in the mid-1990s, was auctioned at Christie's in New York for US$91,000. The nude image of France's First Lady was splashed across the tabloids during the couple's official state visit to Britain.

Yet by Sarkozy's side Carla Bruni plays the role of demure First Lady to perfection. Dressed in Dior suits of sombre-coloured fabrics and flat shoes (Sarkozy is short), she is the height of restrained elegance ('First Lady of chic' and '*oh là là* Madame Sarko', screamed headlines in the UK tabloids; 'I can see why you married her', US President Bush was reported as saying). With the release of her latest album, *Comme si de rien n'était* (As if Nothing Happened), in July 2008, her singing career continues as if nothing happened.

Dozens of biographies have been published on the presidential couple, including one in which Bruni, incredibly, spills the beans at length on the intimacies of her relationship with Sarkozy. Indisputably bling-bling, yes, but no one can seem to get enough of the unpopular but charismatic French president, aka 'President Bling-Bling', and his First Lady, who, love it or loathe it, ride high in the public and paparazzi eye.

In May 2008 a psychiatrist in Paris identified people's unhealthy obsession condition with Sarkozy as 'Sarkosis'.

PRESIDENT BLING-BLING

The French nation sat back and waited with bated breathe to see what first step their new president – quickly dubbed President Bling-Bling in the media – would take in his gargantuan task of turning around an economically stagnant, socially discontented France. Legislative elections in June 2007 saw the UMP retain a healthy majority (313 seats) in the 577-seat National Assembly,

2005

Paris loses its bid for the 2012 Olympics to, shock, horror, London.

2005

The French send the fantastic notion of European unity tumbling out the window with its fierce rejection of the European constitution in a referendum.

2006

The government lifts the state emergency it declared in late 2005 in response to street riots and car torching. But the violence continues, this time in protest at the government's Youth Employment Law.

despite losing 44 seats. François Fillon – a motor-sport enthusiast from Le Mans, Anglophile (his wife is Welsh) and political advisor to Sarkozy during the presidential campaign – was appointed prime minister.

Yet far from knuckling down to implementing the rigorous economic reform platform he was elected on, Sarkozy devoted his first months in office to personal affairs – falling out of love, divorcing, falling in love, going on holidays and remarrying (p47), all in a few hasty months. Both his popularity and national morale plummeted.

Peep into the presidential palace and have a good old nosey around at www.elysee.fr.

The honeymoon period was done: local elections in March 2008 confirmed opinion polls as the ruling UMP party lost key seats to the Socialists, including the traditional centre-right strongholds of Toulouse and Strasbourg. Several high-profile members of Sarkozy's cabinet in Paris moreover failed to snag a mayorship, Senegal-born Junior Foreign Minister Rama Yade (suburb of Colombes) and Culture Minister Christine Albanel (4e arrondissement) included. Justice Minister Rachida Dati provided France's disgruntled and substantial ethnic population (p55) with a glimmer of hope by becoming the first mayor of North African origin to head up the 7e.

As national morale moped about at all-time low, French box-office smash-hit film *Bienvenue chez les Ch'tis* (p51) provided a spot of light relief and boosted national pride. A couple of months on, a nation mourned the death of Algerian-born Parisian fashion designer Yves Saint Laurent (1936–2008), the last stalwart of France's Chanel and Dior heyday. Most of the women at his funeral at Paris St-Roch's Church wore a trouser suit in homage to the 20th century's most iconic fashion designer.

2007

France's most significant presidential elections since WWII: son of a Hungarian immigrant Nicolas Sarkozy versus female socialist Ségolène Royal. Sarkozy wins and starts his term by divorcing his wife Cécilia.

2008

President Sarkozy's popularity plummets following his show-biz-style marriage to Italian model and folk singer Carla Bruni.

2008

France's 35-hour work week is effectively scrapped in July as employers are allowed to enforce a longer week on staffers.

The Culture

THE NATIONAL PSYCHE

France is a country whose people have attracted more stubborn myths and stereotypes than any other in Europe. Arrogant, rude, Bolshie, unbelievably bureaucratic, sexist, chauvinistic, superchic and stylish are among the dozens of tags – true or otherwise – pinned on the garlic-eating, beret-wearing, *sacrebleu*-swearing French over the centuries. The French, by the way, don't wear berets or use old chestnuts such as *'sacrebleu'* anymore. Sit in a café some afternoon and you'll soon hear the gentle expressions of surprise favoured by Parisians these days as they slip on dog droppings (a frequent sight on most pavements). *'Merde'* (shit) is quite popular.

Most people are extremely proud to be French and are staunchly nationalistic to boot, a result of the country's republican stance that places nationality – rather than religion, for example – at the top of the self-identity list. This has created an overwhelmingly self-confident nation, both culturally and intellectually, that invariably comes across as a French superiority complex.

Every region in France has its own distinct culture as middle-aged Swedish novelist Bodil Malmsten discovers when he dips into Breton culture in his novel *The Price of Water in Finistère*.

Contrary to popular belief, many French speak a foreign language fairly well, travel and are happy to use their language skills should the need arise. Of course, if monolingual English-speakers don't try to speak French, there's no way proud French linguists will let on they speak fluent English with a great sexy accent! French men, incidentally, deem an English gal's heavily accented French as irresistibly sexy as women deem a Frenchman speaking English. Hard to believe, but true.

On the subject of sex, not all French men ooze romance or light Gitanes all day. Nor are they as civilised about adultery as French cinema would have you believe. Adultery, illegal in France until 1975, was actually grounds for automatic divorce until as late as mid-2004.

Suckers for tradition, the French are slow to embrace new ideas and technologies: it took the country an age to embrace the internet, clinging on for dear life to their own at-the-time innovative Minitel system for eons. Yet the French are also incredibly innovative – a dichotomy reflected in every facet of French life: they drink and smoke more than anyone else, yet live longer. They eat like kings, but are not fat…

DOS & DON'TS

- Say *'Bonjour, monsieur'* when you enter a shop or café and *'Merci, monsieur. Au revoir'* when leaving. Use *'monsieur'* for any male person who isn't a child; *'madame'* for those you'd call 'Mrs' in English; and *'mademoiselle'* for unmarried women (see p57).
- Fondling or picking up fruit, vegetables, flowers or a piece of clothing in shops attracts immediate killer stares from shop assistants. Ask if you want to touch.
- Take a gift – flowers (not chrysanthemums, which are only brought to cemeteries) or wine for more informal gatherings – when invited to someone's home.
- Splitting the restaurant bill is an uncivilised custom. The person who invites generally pays, although close friends often share the cost.
- Never discuss money over dinner.
- Knock what your French textbook at school taught you on the head. These days *'s'il vous plaît'* – never *'garçon'* (meaning 'boy') – is the *only* way to summon a waiter in restaurants.

LIFESTYLE

Be a fly on the wall in the 5th-floor bourgeois apartment of Monsieur et Madame Tout le Monde and you'll see them dunking croissants in bowls of *café au lait* for breakfast, buying a baguette every day from the bakery (Monsieur nibbles the top off on his way home) and recycling nothing bar a few glass bottles. They go to the flicks once a month, work 35 hours a week and view the web-radio production company their 24-year-old son set up and heads in Paris with a mix of pride, amusement and scepticism. Their 20-year-old daughter, who is so BCBG darling (BCBG – *bon chic, bon genre* – a Sloane Ranger in non-Parisian speak), is a student – France's overcrowded state-run universities are free and open to anyone who passes the *baccalauréat,* although Sarkozy had a stab at changing this in 2007 by giving universities the autonomy to select students and seek outside funding.

Sixty Million Frenchmen Can't be Wrong: What Makes the French so French ask Jean-Benoît Nadeau and Julie Barlow in their witty, well-written and at times downright comical musings on one of Europe's most contradictory nationalities.

Madame buys a clutch of hot-gossip weekly mags, Monsieur enjoys boules and August is the *only* month to summer holiday (with the rest of France). Dodging dog poo on pavements is a sport practised from birth and everything goes on the *carte bleue* (credit or debit card) when shopping: this *is* the society, after all, that microchipped credit cards long before anyone else even dreamt of scrapping the swipe-and-sign system. The couple have a landlord: with a tradition of renting rather than buying, home ownership is low (57% of households own their own home; the rest rent).

Slashing the standard working week from 39 to 35 hours in 2000 boosted domestic tourism and redefined peak hours as pleasure-thirsty workers headed out to the country on Thursday night (instead of Friday) and returned to urban life on Monday evening. Given the choice, most French workers would plump for less income and more leisure time – the standard is five weeks holiday and five bank holidays a year – but a sizable chunk of the population still toils 39 hours or more a week (employers can enforce a 39-hour work week for a negotiable extra cost.) In 2008 the minimum gross monthly wage in France was €1309 (€8.63 an hour, compared to €1190 monthly in Britain). On average, women earn 12% less than men.

The family plays a vital role. Nonetheless, fewer couples are marrying (3% less each year), meaning more children born out of wedlock. Those that marry are doing so later (men at the age of 31.3, women at 29.3) and waiting longer to have an average of two children. Divorce adheres to European trends and is rising (42.5% of marriages end in divorce compared to 30.4% in 1985).

Language learners can pick up three news bulletins a day in simple French! Go to Radio France Internationale (www.rfi.fr), select English, and click on 'learn French with RFI'.

Abortion is legal during the first 12 weeks of pregnancy, girls under 16 not needing parental consent provided they are accompanied by an adult of their choice: 30 abortions take place in France for every 100 live births.

Civil unions, called *pactes civils de solidarité* (PACS), between two members of the same (or different) sex have been legal since 1999 and increase year on year by around 25%. But civil partnerships fall short of legal marriages, say gay lobbyists, who want homosexual couples to be granted the same fiscal advantages and adoptive rights in marriage as heterosexuals.

The gay scene thrives in big cities such as Paris, Marseille, Lyon and Grenoble; see p951.

ECONOMY

The economy was the key issue for French voters in the 2007 presidential elections, hence their demand for change in the charismatic shape of Nicolas Sarkozy (p47), who pledged to reduce unemployment and income tax (currently between 5.5% and 40%), create more jobs and boost growth in a sluggish economy that nonetheless ranks as the world's eighth largest.

Unemployment is down (from 8.7% in early 2007 to 7.6% in mid-2008) but the electorate remains unhappy, possibly because of the traditionally high

FRANCE'S NORTH–SOUTH DIVIDE

No film better illustrates what southerners think of those from 'the sticks' in the far north than Dany Boon's *Bienvenue chez les Ch'tis* (Welcome to the Sticks; 2008). With gags a minute, the warm-hearted comedy is a poignant commentary on France's north–south divide – eagerly lapped up by the French, curious to see if Boon's cinematic portrayal of regional prejudices matched up to reality.

For starters, the weather in the cold rainy north is revolting ('1°C in summer and down to -40°C in winter'): the north for a southerner is pretty much anything north of Lyon. So no surprise that post-office chief Philippe, upon setting off north from his native Salon-de-Provence on the sun-drenched Côte d'Azur, dons several jumpers, puffer jacket and scarf as he bids a dramatic farewell to bronzed wife Julie. Bizarrely, the weather doesn't change until he passes the 'Nord-Pas de Calais' sign – at which point it doesn't just rain but slashes down beyond windscreen-wiper control. Even the gendarme on the autoroute, upon stopping him for driving too slowly, lets him off with a sympathetic smile and his deepest condolences when he hears where he's heading: Bergues, a dumpy ex–mining town of 4300 inhabitants, 9km from Dunkirk. (The place exists, is not dumpy, nor as grey and grim as southerners suppose, and is suddenly all the rage as visitors flock to see its post office, its municipal bell tower with lovely melodic carillon, the central square with its chip van and so on.) *Bienvenue chez les Ch'tis* is a kaleidoscope of comic scenes that slowly chip away at the deeply entrenched prejudices surrounding this northern land of redundant coal mines and its unemployed, impoverished, pale, unhealthy and 'uncultured' inhabitants who drink too much beer and speak like this – *Ej t'ermerci inne banes* (that means *Merci beaucoup).* Yes, their thick Ch'timi patois (old Picard peppered with Flemish) is incomprehensible to outsiders. Yes, they dunk stinky Maroilles cheese and bread in *chicorée café* (chicory-flavoured instant coffee) for breakfast. Yes, they skip the traditional French three-course lunch for an alfresco round of *frites fricadelle, sauce picadilly* (chips 'n' meatballs; never ask what's in the balls) from the local *baraque à frites* (chip van) – eaten with their fingers. Yes, their long, sandy and windy beaches are brilliant for *le char à voile* (sand yachting). And yes, their very nickname – *les Ch'tis* – was borne out of prejudice during WWI when French soldiers mocked the thickly accented way their northern comrades spoke – *'ch'est ti, ch'est mi'* (*c'est toi, c'est moi* – it's you it's me), hence 'Ch'ti'.

The north and its regional characteristics are no mystery to director Boon, a born-and-bred northerner who grew up in Armentières, near Lille, on bread-and-butter dishes like *tarte au Maroilles, chicons au gratin* (oven-baked chicory, *chicons* being the Ch'ti word for 'chicories') and *carbonnade flamande* (beef stew). His father was an Algerian-born bus driver, his mother a cleaner and he is one of France's best-known stand-up comics, directors and, since the film, best-paid actors – he plays the buffoonish postal worker, Antoine. Indeed, if anyone is best placed to speak of *les Ch'tis* and their homeland, it's Boon, whose loveable, huge-hearted character in the film says it all: 'An outsider who comes to the north cries twice, once when he arrives, and once when he leaves.'

expectations it has of the economy: this is a country whose people are accustomed to receiving free education (opposite) and health care (employees pay 8% of their salary in social-security contributions, deducted at source), state-subsidised child care for preschoolers, travel concessions for families, ample leisure time and a 35-hour working week – at great cost to state coffers.

Hence Sarkozy, during a speech to civil servants in Nantes, warned of the urgent need to 'change mentalities'. Predictably his first national budget in September 2007, aimed at reducing public spending and rejuvenating the economy, did not go down well: only one in two retiring civil servants would be replaced, income-tax rates for top earners would be reduced, and tax breaks for overtime hours would be introduced to encourage people to work longer hours. Hard-line attempts to reform a pension system which entitles 1.6 million workers in the rail, metro, energy-supply and fishing industries to draw a full state pension after 37.5 working years provoked widespread horror and a series of national strikes and protests – as did his bid to extend the number of working years for a full state pension from 40 to 41.

AN EMOTIONAL AFFAIR

For the French, speaking English is an emotional affair, memorably illustrated a couple of years back when the then French president Jacques Chirac walked out of an EU summit session after one of his fellow countrymen had the audacity to address the meeting in English.

'Don't speak English!' was *Le Monde*'s headline the next day, while the French blogosphere seethed with debate on linguistic patriotism: 'Open your eyes, Mr President, you are on another planet', 'it is a long time since French was the language of the international arena' taunted modern-day French bloggers, many of whom blog in English.

Current French president Sarkozy (p47) is faring marginally better than his monolingual predecessor, the press running endless stories on the English lessons he took in preparation for a trip to Britain in 2008. Yet the bottom line is Sarkozy sticks to what he knows best in public, so much so that the couple of lines he has uttered in English ('we are 'appy for you to invest in France, we will be 'appy to 'elp you make munay in France') were instantly plastered over the internet as a much-viewed video link! Earlier the same year Sarkozy announced controversial plans to kill off the 24-hour multilingual TV channel, France 24 – Chirac's stab at creating a French CNN, launched in 2006 – and replace it with an exclusively French-language station. France 24 broadcasts in French, Arabic and English.

Divine was the title of France's entry in 2008's Eurovision Song Contest that saw, horror of horrors, French electro musician Sébastien Tellier sing in English. Such was the furore raised by the English-language French entry that French MPs got involved, demanding that TV channel France-3, which selected the song, reconsider. While many agreed with politicians that the lyrics were hardly a reflection of the French soul, few could disagree that it was less cringe-worthy than France's entry the previous year – written and performed in Franglais ('I remember *jolie demoiselle,* the last summer, *nous, la Tour Eiffel*/I remember *comme tu étais belle,* so beautiful with your *sac* Chanel).

With English words like 'weekend', 'jogging', 'stop' and 'OK' firmly entrenched in daily French usage, it seems that language purists have lost the battle. One look at the many Anglo-American shop and restaurant signs featured in the online Musée des Horreurs (Museum of Horrors) on the website of the Paris-based Défense de la Langue Française (DLF; Defence of the French Language; www.langue-francaise.org, in French) says it all.

French was the main language of the EU until 1995 when Sweden and Finland came into the EU fold. French broadcasting laws restrict the amount of air time radio and TV stations can devote to non-French music, but little can be done to restrict who airs what on the internet.

Despite ritual denunciations of globalisation by politicians and pundits, the French economy is heavily dependent on the global marketplace. It is the fourth-largest export economy and, within the EU, the largest agricultural producer and exporter, thanks to generous subsidies awarded to the agricultural sector. Its production of wheat, barley, maize (corn) and cheese is particularly significant. The country is, to a great extent, self-sufficient in food except for tropical products such as bananas and coffee.

POPULATION

France is not that densely populated – 107 people inhabit every square kilometre (compared to 235 in Germany, 240 in the UK and 116 in the EU), although 20% of the national population is packed into Paris' greater metropolitan area.

The last 10 years have seen rural and suburban areas gain residents, and Paris and the northeast (except Alsace) lose inhabitants to southern France, an increasingly buoyant part of the country.

In keeping with European trends, France's overall population is ageing: on 1 January 2006 almost 22% of the population was 60 or older (compared to 16% in 1950, 17% in 1980 and 19% in 1990). This demographic phenomenon is less marked in urban areas like Paris and Lyon, and on the Mediterranean coast, where increasing work opportunities ensure a younger, more-active population.

Of France's 4.3 million foreign residents, 13% are Algerian, 13% Portuguese, 12% Moroccan and 9% Italian. Only one-third has French citizenship, which is not conferred at birth but is subject to various administrative requirements; see p55 for more on France's foreign population.

Marseille beat seven French cities, Lyon and Toulouse included, to become France's European capital of culture in 2013 alongside the Slovak city of Košice.

SPORT

Most French wouldn't be seen dead walking down the street in trainers and tracksuit bottoms. But contrary to appearances, they love sport. Shaved-leg cyclists toil up Mont Ventoux, football fans fill stadiums and anyone who can flits off for the weekend to ski.

France has achieved a strikingly high level in international judo, four-time world champion David Douillet being the star. Les 24 Heures du Mans and the F1 Grand Prix in Monte Carlo are the world's raciest dates in motor sports.

With the exception of mogul champion Edgar Grospiron, aka *le boss des bosses,* skiing has produced few stars since the 1968 alpine sweep of Jean-Claude Killy. Alpine downhill skier Antoine Dénériaz (b 1976) scooped gold – just one of three France won – at the 2006 Olympics in Turin, while Chamonix snowboarder Karine Ruby (b 1978), gold medallist in 1998 and holder of more World Cup titles than any other boarder, finished a disappointing 16th.

Losing out to London in its bid to host the 2012 Summer Olympics was a major loss of face for Paris. The French capital last hosted the gargantuan event in 1924.

Football

France's greatest sporting moment came at the 1998 World Cup, which the country hosted and won. But the game has produced no stars since, with France failing to qualify for the 2005 Confederations Cup, losing to Italy in the final of the 2006 World Cup and scraping through the Euro 2008 qualifiers by the skin of its teeth (where it got thrashed by Italy and the Netherlands in the first round).

The land of les Ch'tis, aka the French *région* of Nord-Pas de Calais with over four million inhabitants, is France's most populated region after Île de France: 7% of the French population live there.

Multiculturalism is a dominant feature of French football, with 17 of the 23 players in the last World Cup being of African, West Indian, Algerian or other non-French origin. The country's golden boy of football, Marseille-born midfielder ace Zinedine Zidane (b 1972), now retired, is a classic example. The son of Algerian immigrants, he wooed the nation with a sparkling career of goal-scoring headers and extraordinary footwork that unfortunately ended with him head-butting an Italian player during the 2006 World Cup final. Such was the power of his humble Marseillais grin though (since used to advertise everything from Adidas sports gear to Volvic mineral water and Christian Dior fashion) that the French nation instantly forgave him: *'Merci les Bleus'* became the catch phrase of the moment.

FRENCH BALLS

France's traditional ball games include *pétanque* and the more formal boules which has a 70-page rule book. Both are played by village men in work clothes on a gravel or sand pitch, scratched out wherever a bit of flat and shady ground can be found. World championships are held for both sports. In the Basque Country, the racquet game of *pelota* (p692) is the thing to do with balls.

Current French players include hotshot striker for Barcelona, Thierry Henry, born in a Parisian suburb to parents from Guadeloupe and Martinique; and French-Argentine David Trézéguet who plays for Juventus. Both quietly fly the 'stamp out racism in football' banner on the sidelines, an issue that – despite the pronounced multiethnicity of French football – still rears its ugly head: victorious Parisian club Paris-St-Germain (PSG) was banned from defending the League Cup in 2009 after some of its supporters unfurled a racist banner against les Ch'tis (p51) during the 2008 final (which it won) against northern team Racing Lens. It was the same club whose supporters hurled racial abuse about following its defeat against Israel's Hapoel Tel Aviv in the UEFA Cup in 2006, prompting a plain-clothed Paris policeman to fire on the crowd leaving one PSG fan dead.

Decidedly more upbeat and optimistic than most books on Jewish France, Thomas Nolden looks at the literature Jewish writers in France have produced from the 1960s to the present day in *In Lieu of Memory: Contemporary Jewish Writing in France.*

At club level, Marseille was the first French side to win the European Champions League, thanks to Paris-born football legend Éric Cantona, who transferred to Leeds a year later and subsequently turned the fortunes of Manchester United around. Since the 1995 Bosman decision allowing European clubs to field as many European players as they wish, French football greats have been lured to richer clubs in Italy, Britain, Spain and Germany (Zidane's 2001 transfer from Juventus to Real Madrid for US$64.45 million made him the priciest player in football history).

France's home matches kick off at St-Denis' magnificent 80,000-capacity Stade de France (p196). Other noteworthy stadiums (there are 250-odd in France) include Lyon's Stade de Gerland (p515), home to French national champions Olympique Lyonnais (OL) who have won the title 'Champions de France' seven consecutive times since 2002.

Arsenal's French manager Arsène Wenger was awarded an OBE in 2003 for his contribution to British football.

Rugby

Rugby league (www.francerugby.fr, in French) has a strong following in the south, favourite teams being Toulouse, Montauban and St-Gaudens. Rugby union is more popular still, as the enduring success of the powerful Paris-St-Germain club testifies.

France's home games in the Tournoi des Six Nations (Six Nations Tournament) are held in March and April. The finals of the Championnat de France de Rugby take place in late May and early June.

Cycling

The legendary Tour de France (www.letour.fr), the world's most prestigious bicycle race, brings together 189 of the world's top male cyclists (21 teams of nine) and 15 million spectators in July each year for a spectacular 3000-plus kilometre cycle around the country. The three-week route changes, but always labours through the Alps and Pyrenees and finishes on the Champs-Élysées in Paris. The publicity caravan preceding the cyclists showers roadside spectators with coffee samples, logo-emblazoned balloons, pens and other free junk-advertising gifts – and is almost more fun to watch than the cyclists themselves, who speed through in 10 seconds flat.

In *French Revolutions* 'suburban slouch' Tim Moore cycles around France in a quest to pedal to the bottom of the Tour de France. Great title, great read.

France is the world's top track-cycling nation and has a formidable reputation in mountain biking: Christian Taillefer holds the world speed record on a mountain bike, 212.39km/h, which he hit by flying down a snow-covered ski slope.

Tennis

The French Open (www.fft.fr/rolandgarros) held in Paris' Roland Garros Stadium in late May and early June, is the second of the year's four grand-slam tournaments. Marseille-born Sébastien Grosjean (b 1978), a quarter-

TOUR TRIVIA

- French journalist and cyclist Henri Desgrange came up with the Tour de France in 1903 as a means of promoting his sports newspaper *L'Auto* (now called *L'Équipe*).
- With the exception of two world war–induced intervals, the Tour de France has not missed a year since its inception.
- The 1998 race was the 'tour of shame': fewer than 100 riders crossed the finish line after several teams were disqualified for doping.
- Unfortunately 2004 wasn't much better: even before the race began, the French team had withdrawn and the Spanish were banned on doping grounds.
- *Le Blaireau* (the Badger), alias Brittany-born biking legend Bernard Hinault (b 1954), won the Tour de France five times before retiring in 1986.
- American sports icon Lance Armstrong (b 1971) is the indisputable Tour de France king. He overcame cancer, won seven consecutive times, from 1999 to 2005, then retired, and is set to return to the competitive-cycling circuit in 2009.

finalist in the 2006 Australian Open, has been the highest-ranking French player on the men's circuit for the last few years. On the women's circuit, Amélie Mauresmo – world No 1 for five weeks in 2004 and again in 2006 – is the only real French star. In April, the world's best warm up on clay at the Monte Carlo Masters (http://montecarlo.masters-series.com) in Monaco.

MULTICULTURALISM

The face of France is multicultural (immigrants make up 7.4% of the population), yet its republican code, while inclusive and nondiscriminatory, does little to accommodate a multicultural society. Nothing reflects this dichotomy better than the law, in place since 2004, banning the Islamic headscarf, Jewish skullcap, crucifix and other religious symbols in French schools. Intended to place school children on an equal footing in the classroom, the law is seen by many Muslims in particular as intolerant and evidence that the French State is not prepared to truly integrate them into French society.

During his election campaign, helping ethnic minorities was high on the agenda of the French president (p47), himself the son of a Hungarian immigrant and a mother of Greek Jewish and French descent. And his cabinet is ethnically diverse: his Muslim justice minister Rachida Dati was born to impoverished Algerian and Moroccan parents on a rough housing estate; secretary of state for urban policies Fadela Amara (she blogs in French at http://fadela-amara.net), daughter of Algerian immigrants, grew up with her nine siblings in a Clermont-Ferrand 'shanty town'; and black human-rights minister Rama Yade is from Senegal. Yet not one of the 577 members of the National Assembly represents the immigrant population, first or second generation. French Muslims' strongest national voice remains the French Muslim Council (Conseil Français du Culte Musulman; CFCM), an umbrella organisation of 18 representatives from Muslim associations and mosques in France, established in 2003.

Some 90% of the French Muslim community – Europe's largest – are noncitizens. Most are illegal immigrants living in poverty-stricken *bidonvilles* (tinpot towns) around Paris, Lyon and other metropolitan centres. Many are unemployed (youth unemployment in many suburbs is 40%) and face little prospect of getting a job, let alone a decent one. According to the Washington Post, unlike in Britain, for example, where Muslims account for 11% of inmates, Muslims in French prisons make up between 60% and 70%

THE VOICE OF THE NEW GENERATION

No French writer better delves into the mind, mood and politics of the country's ethnic population than Faïza Guène, sensation of the French literary scene. The young Parisian writer, born and bred on a ghetto housing estate outside Paris, stunned critics with her debut novel, *Kiffe Kiffe Demain* (2004), sold in 27 countries and published in English as *Just Like Tomorrow*. Like the parents of most of her friends and neighbours, Faïza Guène's father moved from a village in western Algeria to northern France in 1952, aged 17, to work in the mines. Only in the 1980s could he return to Algeria where he met his wife, whom he brought back to France – to Les Courtillières housing estate in Seine-St-Denis where 6000-odd immigrants live like sardines in five-storey high-rise blocks stretching for 1.5km. Such is the setting for Guène's first book, as well as her second semi-autobiographical novel, *Dreams from the Endz* (2008).

of inmates – a reflection, Muslim leaders say, of the deep ethnic and social divide in France that discriminates against ethnic minorities.

Years of pent-up anger and resentment exploded in a riot of street violence in Paris following the death of two teenage boys of North African origin in the Parisian suburb of Clichy-sous-Bois in late 2005. The boys were electrocuted to death after hiding in an electrical substation while on the run from the police. Within days, the urban violence was nationwide as youths of all origins, nonimmigrant French included, joined forces to express their burning discontent. The government declared a state of emergency, local authorities imposed curfews in 30 towns and the urban violence receded. The EU pledged €50 million to help France clean up the mess on its streets, but in reality scuffles between youths and police, car burnings and the odd riot have been part of daily life in immigrant-populated Parisian suburbs ever since. An immigration bill passed in late 2007, tightening up restrictions (which could include DNA testing) on immigrant hopefuls wanting to join family already in France, was met with outrage, while government plans unveiled in early 2008 to revitalise impoverished suburbs, invest in better housing and put 4000 more police on suburban streets by 2011 had no price tag attached, leaving critics wondering if it will ever happen. French animal activist and former actress Brigitte Bardot, convicted in June 2008 of racial hatred and discrimination, is by no means alone in her opinions.

French Culture Now (http://frenchculturenow.com) is an informative and comprehensive English-language news service covering anything and everything to do with France and the French.

Multicultural France has always drawn immigrants: 4.3 million from other parts of Europe arrived between 1850 and WWI and another three million came between the world wars. During the post-WWII economic boom years, several million unskilled workers followed from North Africa and French-speaking sub-Saharan Africa. Large-scale immigration peaked in the early 1960s when, as the French colonial empire collapsed, French settlers returned to metropolitan France from Algeria, other parts of Africa and Indochina.

MEDIA

Public licence fees subsidise public broadcaster France Télévisions (www.francetelevisions.fr, in French), which controls 40% of the market with its three TV channels – France 2, 3 and 5 (Arte after 7pm). Yet in the face of increasingly stiff competition from private broadcasters such as TF1 (www.tf1.fr, in French) and M6 (www.m6.fr, in French), its future is uncertain. Equally uncertain is the future of France 24 (www.france24.com), a 24-hour national and international news station broadcast in French, Arabic and English. TF1 and France Télévisions are both shareholders in the channel which is backed by annual public funding of €80 million.

As in Britain, there is a strong distinction between broadcasting and print media. The press, like TV and radio broadcasters, are independent and free of censorship. Unlike Britain, there is no tabloid or gutter press.

On the airwaves, two out of five songs played on French radio must have French lyrics; one in five must be a newcomer.

RELIGION

France maintains a rigid distinction between Church and State. Some 55% of French identify themselves as Catholic, although no more than 10% attend church regularly. Another one million people are Protestant.

Coexisting uneasily with this nominally Christian majority is France's five million–strong Muslim community – 12% of the country's population – most of whom adhere to a moderate Islam. Fears that a more-radical Islam is gaining ground in France have increased calls for the State to help train imams in a French-style Islam and build more mosques.

More than half of France's 600,000-strong Jewish population, Europe's largest, live in and around Paris. Marseille and Strasbourg (p380) likewise have notable Jewish communities. French Jews, who in the late 18th century were the first in Europe to achieve emancipation (abolition of discriminatory laws), have been represented by the Paris-based umbrella organisation, the Consistoire, since 1808.

Despite the huge public outcry following the murder of Jewish telephone salesman Ilan Halimi, tortured for three weeks by a multiracial gang in the Paris suburb of Bagneux in early 2006, anti-Semitic and racist crimes still occur: in 2008, in the same suburb, a 19-year-old Jewish man was kidnapped and kicked, punched and ridiculed for nine hours by a gang of six youths aged between 17 and 28.

France's largest Jewish community – 20,000 mainly second-generation North African Jews – lives in Sarcelles, a predominantly Jewish neighbourhood in Paris.

WOMEN IN FRANCE

Women were granted suffrage in 1945, but until 1964 a woman needed her husband's permission to open a bank account or get a passport. Younger French women, especially, are quite outspoken and emancipated, but self-confidence has yet to translate into equality in the workplace, where women

A MADAME FROM BIRTH *Nicola Williams*

'About time too', a feminist anywhere else on the planet would argue. Indeed, it is only now that French women have decided no more *'mademoiselle'*, meaning 'Miss', 'not married', 'virgin', 'sexually available' and so on, say Paris-based feminist group Les Chiennes de Garde (meaning 'guard dogs', or rather, 'guard bitches'). The group has launched a petition for the term *'mademoiselle'* to be eradicated from the administrative and political arena. It also wants the standard 'maiden name' box struck off official forms and documents.

'Mademoiselle' originates from the medieval word *'damoiselle'*, meaning a young upper-class girl (male equivalents were called *'damoisel'*). Later merged with *'ma'* to denote an unmarried woman, the term was tantamount to 'sad old spinster who can't find a husband' in the 17th and 18th centuries. In the 19th century, novelist Adolphe Belot borrowed the term to depict a frigid wife in *Mademoiselle Giraud, ma Femme*.

So the fight is on to become a *madame* from birth. Already a *madame*, I for one, not to mention practically all my 30-something-with-kids girlfriends, am delighted if someone dares call me *'mademoiselle'*. Despite the kids in tow, dirty washing and first wrinkle, it means I still look young.

are often kept out of senior and management positions. Sexual harassment *(harcèlement sexuel)* in the workplace is addressed with a law imposing financial penalties on the offender. A great achievement in the last decade has been *Parité,* the law requiring political parties to fill 50% of their slates in all elections with female candidates.

Known for their natural chic, style and class, contemporary French women are sassier than ever. Take the Rykiel women: in the 1970s legendary Parisian knitwear designer Sonia Rykiel designed the skin-tight, boob-hugging sweater worn with no bra beneath. In 2006 daughter Nathalie came up with the ultimate stylish sex boutique. The shop – wedged between big-name labels in the chic Parisian quarter of St-Germain-des-Prés – screams design and is aimed squarely at women who know what they want.

ARTS

Literature

COURTLY LOVE TO SYMBOLISM

Lyric poems of courtly love composed by troubadours dominated medieval French literature, while the *roman* (literally 'romance', now meaning 'novel') drew on old Celtic tales such as King Arthur, the search for the Holy Grail and so on. With the *Roman de la Rose,* a 22,000-line poem by Guillaume de Lorris and Jean de Meung, the allegorical figures of Pleasure and Riches, Shame and Fear popped on the scene.

La Pléiade, Rabelais and de Montaigne made French Renaissance literature great: La Pléiade was a group of lyrical poets active in the 1550s and 1560s, of whom the best known is Pierre de Ronsard (1524–85), author of four books of odes. The highly exuberant narrative of Loire Valley–born François Rabelais (1494–1553) blends coarse humour with encyclopaedic erudition in a vast panorama of subjects that includes every kind of person, occupation and jargon existing in mid-16th-century France. Michel de Montaigne (1533–92) wrote essays on everything from cannibals, war horses and drunkenness to the uncanny resemblance of children to their fathers.

Le grand siècle ushered in the great French classical writers with their lofty odes to tragedy. François de Malherbe (1555–1628) brought a new rigour to the treatment of rhythm in poetry; and Marie de La Fayette (1634–93) penned the first major French novel, *La Princesse de Clèves* (1678).

The philosophical work of Voltaire (1694–1778) dominated the 18th century. A century on, the city of Besançon gave birth to Victor Hugo – the key figure of French romanticism. The breadth of interest and technical innovations exhibited in Hugo's poems and novels – *Les Misérables* and

TOP FIVE LITERARY SIGHTS

- The château on the French–Swiss border in the Jura where Voltaire lived from 1759 (p580).
- Colette's Paris: of her many Parisian addresses, the Left Bank cafés of St-Germain-des-Prés and the apartment in the Palais Royal (p141) where she died are the most illustrious. Elsewhere, there's a small museum (p478) in the Burgundian village where she was born.
- The graves of Sartre and Beauvoir in the Cimetière du Montparnasse (p150).
- Musée du Jules Verne in Nantes (p654), home town of the author of *Around the World in 80 Days.*
- Île Ste-Marguerite (p880), the speck of an island off Cannes where the Man in the Iron Mask – immortalised in Alexandre Dumas' novel *Le Vicomte de Bragelonne* (The Viscount of Bragelonne) – was incarcerated in the 17th century.

TOP FIVE FROGS VERSUS ROSBIFS

In the finest of traditions, rivalry between the English *(rosbifs)* and the French (frogs) sells like hotcakes. Our favourites:

- *That Sweet Enemy: the French and the British from the Sun King to the Present,* by Robert and Isabelle Tombs. Cross-Channel rivalry in a historical context, light-hearted nonetheless.
- *Help, the English Are Invading Us!* by José-Alain Fralon. They're everywhere. Slowly but surely the English are invading us…
- *Cross Channel,* by Julian Barnes. A selection of classic short stories zooming in on everything both sides of the English Channel, from sex, art and love to literature, the Channel tunnel and the Eurostar.
- *More France Please! We're British!* by Helen Frith-Powell. France from the perspective of Brits who choose to live there permanently.
- *A Year in the Merde* and *Merde Actually,* by Stephen Clarke. Dog poo everywhere, unnecessary bureaucracy, transport; Clarke spouts on about it all. You'll love it or hate it.

Notre Dame de Paris (The Hunchback of Notre Dame) among them – was phenomenal: after his death, his coffin was laid beneath the Arc de Triomphe for an all-night vigil.

In 1857 literary landmarks *Madame Bovary* by Gustave Flaubert (1821–80), and Charles Baudelaire's (1821–67) collection of poems, *Les Fleurs du Mal* (The Flowers of Evil), were published. Émile Zola (1840–1902) meanwhile strove to convert novel-writing from an art to a science in his powerful series, *Les Rougon-Macquart.*

The expression of mental states rather than the detailing of day-to-day minutiae was the aim of symbolists Paul Verlaine (1844–96) and Stéphane Mallarmé (1842–98). Verlaine's poems – alongside those of Arthur Rimbaud (1854–91), with whom Verlaine shared a tempestuous homosexual relationship – were French literature's first modern poems.

MODERN LITERATURE

The world's longest novel – a seven-volume 9,609,000-character giant by Marcel Proust (1871–1922) – dominated the early 20th century. *À la Recherche du Temps Perdu* (Remembrance of Things Past) explores in evocative detail the true meaning of past experience recovered from the unconscious by 'involuntary memory'.

Surrealism proved a vital force until WWII, André Breton (1896–1966) capturing its spirit – a fascination with dreams, divination and all manifestations of 'the marvellous' – in his autobiographical narratives. In Paris the bohemian Colette (1873–1954) captivated and shocked with her titillating novels detailing the amorous exploits of heroines such as schoolgirl Claudine.

After WWII, existentialism developed around the lively debates of Jean-Paul Sartre (1905–80), Simone de Beauvoir (1908–86) and Albert Camus (1913–60) in Paris' Left Bank cafés of St-Germain-des-Prés. In *L'Étranger* (The Outsider), which scooped the Nobel Prize for Literature in 1957, Camus stresses the importance of the writer's political engagement.

The 1950s' *nouveau roman* saw experimental young writers seek new ways of organising narratives, with Nathalie Sarraute slashing identifiable characters and plot in *Les Fruits d'Or* (The Golden Fruits). *Histoire d'O* (Story of O), an erotic sadomasochistic novel written by Dominique Aury under a pseudonym in 1954, sold more copies outside France than any other contemporary French novel. In the 1960s it was Philippe Sollers' experimental novels that raised eyebrows.

Contemporary authors include Françoise Sagan, Pascal Quignard, Anna Gavalda, Emmanuel Carrère, Stéphane Bourguignon and Martin Page, whose novel *Comment Je Suis Devenu Stupide* (How I Became Stupid) explores a 25-year-old Sorbonne student's methodical attempt to become stupid. Also popular are Frédéric Dard (alias San Antonio), Léo Malet and Daniel Pennac, widely read for his witty crime fiction such as *Au Bonheur des Ogres* (The Scapegoat) and *La Fée Carabine* (The Fairy Gunmother).

Cinema

Watching French classics in the *lyonnaise* factory (p504), where the cinematographic pioneers, the Lumière brothers, shot the world's first motion picture in March 1895, is a must.

French film flourished in the 1920s. Abel Gance (1889–1981) was king of the decade with his antiwar blockbuster *J'Accuse!* (I Accuse!; 1919) – all the more impressive for its location filming on actual WWI battlefields. The switch to sound ushered in René Clair (1898–1981) and his world of fantasy and satirical surrealism.

WWI inspired the 1930s classic *La Grande Illusion* (The Great Illusion; 1937), a devastating portrayal of the folly of war based on the trench warfare experience of director Jean Renoir (1894–1979). Indeed, portraits of ordinary people and their lives dominated film until the 1950s, when realism was eschewed by surrealist Jean Cocteau (1889–1963) in two masterpieces: *La Belle et la Bête* (Beauty and the Beast; 1945) and *Orphée* (Orpheus; 1950) are unravelled in Menton's Musée Jean Cocteau (p899) on the Côte d'Azur.

Sapped of talent and money after WWII, France's film industry found new energy by the 1950s, and so the *nouvelle vague* (new wave) burst forth. With small budgets and no extravagant sets or big-name stars, film-makers produced uniquely personal films using real-life subject matter: Claude Chabrol (b 1930) explored poverty and alcoholism in rural France in *Le Beau Serge* (Bitter Reunion; 1958); Alain Resnais (b 1922) portrayed the problems of time and memory in *Hiroshima, Mon Amour* (1959); and François Truffaut (1932–84) dealt with love.

By the 1970s the new wave had lost its experimental edge, handing over the limelight to lesser-known directors such as Éric Rohmer (b 1920), who made beautiful but uneventful films in which the characters endlessly analyse their feelings. Two 1960s movies ensured France's invincibility as the

OSS 117

OSS 117 is not a cinematic invention. The French secret agent was created by novelist Jean Bruce (1921–63) in 1949 – four years before Ian Fleming's 007. Making his debut in *Tu Parles d'une Ingénue* (You Speak of an Ingénue), Hubert Bonisseur de La Bath, colonel in the Office of Strategic Service (OSS), starred in 87 novels (selling 24 million copies) before his creator died in a car accident in 1963.

But the silky-smooth, dark-haired action man with a penchant for beautiful women, fancy gadgets and dicing with death was not dead. Three years after Bruce's death, wife Josette took over, penning another incredible 143 adventures between 1966 and 1985. Josette died in 1996.

OSS 117 est Mort (OSS 117 is Dead) was the first book written by the couple's children, François and Martine Bruce, who picked up the family tradition in 1987 and churned out 24 more adventures. By the time *OSS 117 Prend le Large* (OSS 117 Takes Off) – the last to be published – hit the streets in 1992, the best-selling French series had been translated into 17 languages and sold 75 million copies. Previous OSS 117s on screen include Ivan Desny in Jean Sacha's 1957 film adaptation of Jean Bruce's 1953 novel *OSS 117 n'est Pas Mort* (OSS 117 is Not Dead): he's clearly not.

KUDOS

For decades all kudos went to *La Grand Vadrouille* (The Great Ramble; 1966), a French comedy, set in 1942, in which five British airmen are shot down over German-occupied France. One is catapulted into Paris' Bois de Vincennes zoo, another in the orchestra pit of its opera house and so the comic tale unfurls.

Watched in France by a record-breaking 17 million cinema spectators, the film ranked as the most watched film of all time until 1997 (when US blockbuster *Titanic* stole the thunder with 20.7 million ticket sales) and the most watched French-made film until 2008 when *Bienvenue Les Ch'tis* (p51) rocketed to top-dog position as the highest grossing film in French cinematic history.

land of romance: Claude Lelouch's *Un Homme et une Femme* (A Man and a Woman; 1966), a love story set in Deauville (p292); and Jacques Demy's *Les Parapluies de Cherbourg* (The Umbrellas of Cherbourg; 1964), a wise and bittersweet love story, likewise filmed in Normandy.

Big-name stars, slick production values and a strong sense of nostalgia were the dominant motifs in the 1980s, as generous state subsidies saw film-makers switch to costume dramas and comedies in the face of growing competition from the USA. Claude Berri's portrait of prewar Provence in *Jean de Florette* (1986), Jean-Paul Rappeneau's *Cyrano de Bergerac* (1990) and *Bon Voyage* (2003), set in 1940s Paris, and *Astérix et Obélix: Mission Cléopâtre* (2002) – all starring France's best-known (and biggest-nosed) actor, Gérard Depardieu – found huge audiences in France and abroad.

French film has enjoyed a massive renaissance in the new millennium thanks to films such as *Le Fabuleux Destin d'Amélie Poulain* (Amélie; 2001), a simple and uncontroversial feel-good story of a Parisian do-gooder directed by Jean-Pierre Jeunet of *Delicatessen* (1991) fame; Jacques Perrin's animal film *Le Peuple Migrateur* (Winged Migration; 2001), about bird migration; the big-name (Omar Sharif and Isabelle Adjani) *Monsieur Ibrahim et les Fleurs du Coran* (Mr Ibrahim and the Flowers of Coran; 2003), about an Arab grocer living on rue Bleue; and the giggle-guaranteed Marseille comedy *Taxi 3* (2003) and *Les Choristes* (The Chorus; 2004), a sentimental tale of a new teacher arriving at a school for troublesome boys in 1949.

Astérix et les Vikings (2005) by Danish director Stefan Fjeldmark wooed French cinema-goers as Europe's most expensive feature-length cartoon – its budget was €22 million – proving once and for all that France's cartoon industry, which currently produces about 15 films a year, means business. Three years later it was another Astérix film, *Astérix aux Jeux Olympiques* (2008), which became the most expensive film to be made in the history of French cinema. Its budget: €78 million.

Charismatic comic actor Jean Dujardin (b 1972) has been the hottest thing since sliced bread since starring in *Brice de Nice* (2005), a piss-take of cult surfing movie *Point Break* in which surfing dude and poseur Brice waits for *sa vague* (his wave) to come in waveless Nice on the French Riviera. The film features great shots of the town. Dujardin went on to play the sexist, racist, macho, uncultured and cringingly outdated 1950s Bond…James Bond, or rather Bonisseur de la Bath…Hubert Bonisseur de la Bath, in *OSS 117: Le Caire, Nid d'Espions* (OSS 117: Cairo Nest of Spies; 2006). The Bond parody (opposite) was an instant hit. His latest comedy, *Lucky Luke* (2008), is a guaranteed classic.

France's leading lady of the moment, meanwhile, the sexy, pouting, dark-haired Marion Cotillard (b 1975), was catapulted to stardom by her role as Édith Piaf in *La Môme* (La Vie en Rose; 2007), a hugely successful film portraying the life of the French singer, from Paris waif to New York superstar. The film landed her an Oscar for best actress in 2008.

FRENCH CINEMATIC HISTORY IN 10 FILMS

- **La Règle du Jeu** (*The Rules of the Game;* 1939) Shunned by the public and censored, Jean Renoir's story of a 1930s bourgeois hunting party in the Loire Valley's soggy Sologne is a dark satirical masterpiece.
- **Les Enfants du Paradis** (*Children of Paradise;* 1945) Made during the Nazi occupation of France, Marcel Carné celebrates the vitality and theatricality of a Paris without Nazis.
- **Et Dieu Créa la Femme** (*And God Created Woman;* 1956) Roger Vadim's tale of the amorality of modern youth, set in St-Tropez, made a star out of Brigitte Bardot.
- **Les Quatre Cents Coups** (*The 400 Blows;* 1959) Partly based on the rebellious adolescence of the best loved of new-wave directors François Truffaut.
- **Les Vacances de M Hulôt** (*Mr Hulôt's Holiday;* 1953) and **Mon Oncle** (*My Uncle;* 1958) Two films starring the charming, bumbling figure of Monsieur Hulôt and his struggles to adapt to the modern age by non-new-wave 1950s director Jacques Tati.
- **Diva** (1981) and **37°2 le Matin** (*Betty Blue;* 1986) Two visually compelling films by Jean-Jacques Beineix. *Diva* stars French icon Richard Bohringer.
- **Shoah** (1985) Claude Lanzmann's 9½-hour-long black-and-white documentary of interviews with Holocaust survivors worldwide is disturbing. It took 11 years to make.
- **Indochine** (*Indochina;* 1993) An epic love story set in 1930s French Indochina with timeless beauty Catherine Deneuve as a French plantation owner.
- **Subway** (1985), **Le Grand Bleu** (*The Big Blue;* 1988), **Nikita** (1990) and **Jeanne d'Arc** (*Joan of Arc;* 1999) Take your pick from these Luc Besson box-office hits.
- **Code Inconnu** (*Code Unknown;* 2001) Intellectual art-house film starring Oscar-winning French actress Juliette Binoche as an actress in Paris.

The runaway hit of the decade was indisputably American film director Ron Howard's *The Da Vinci Code* (2006). Not only did the film bring international acclaim to Audrey Tautou, the waifish French actress of *Amélie* fame who costarred with Tom Hanks in the film, it also brought American tourists in their droves back to Paris. The odds are now on as to whether Dany Boon's hilarious French comedy *Bienvenue chez les Ch'tis* (*Welcome to the Sticks;* 2008; p51) – the film rights of which Warner Brothers bought to make an American equivalent – will do the same for northern France.

The Cannes film festival (www.festival-cannes.fr) in 2008 saw a French film win the Palme d'Or, arguably the world's most coveted film prize, for the first time since 1987. Set in a rough Parisian neighbourhood, Laurent Cantet's *Entre Les Murs* (The Class) used real pupils and teachers and portrayed a year in their school life. The documentary-drama was based on the autobiographical novel of teacher François Bégaudeau (he plays the teacher in the film) and stays firmly in the classroom (hence its French title 'Between the Walls'). The kids are a real mix of cultures and attitudes – an illegal Chinese immigrant, a boy from Mali and another from the Caribbean and so on – rendering the film a brilliant reflection of multiethnic society (p55) in contemporary France.

The French film industry honours its film-makers and actors with the Césars, named after the Marseille-born artist who created the prestigious statue awarded to winners.

Music

There's more to French music than accordions and Édith Piaf. And not just that: from a converted LU biscuit factory (p656) to a cavernous warehouse (p587), venues to catch current sounds outside Paris are industrial chic.

French baroque music influenced European musical output in the 17th and 18th centuries, while French musical luminaries – Charles Gounod (1818–93), César Franck (1822–90) and *Carmen*-creator Georges Bizet (1838–75) among them – were a dime a dozen in the 19th century. Modern orchestration was founded by Hector Berlioz (1803–69), the greatest figure in the French romantic movement. He demanded gargantuan forces: his ideal orchestra included 240 stringed instruments, 30 grand pianos and 30 harps.

Claude Debussy (1862–1918) revolutionised classical music with his *Prélude à l'Après-Midi d'un Faune* (Prelude to the Afternoon of a Fawn), creating a light, almost Asian musical Impressionism; while Impressionist comrade Maurice Ravel (1875–1937) peppered his work, including *Boléro,* with sensuousness and tonal colour. Contemporary composer Olivier Messiaen (1908–92) combined modern, almost mystical music with natural sounds such as birdsong. His student, Pierre Boulez (b 1925), works with computer-generated sound.

Jazz hit 1920s Paris in the banana-clad form of Josephine Baker, a cabaret dancer from the USA (the 15th-century château in the Dordogne where the African-American lived after the war can be visited; p637). Post-WWII ushered in a much-appreciated bunch of musicians – Sidney Bechet, Kenny Clarke, Bud Powell and Dexter Gordon among them. In 1934 a chance meeting between Parisian jazz guitarist Stéphane Grappelli and three-fingered Roma guitarist Django Reinhardt in a Montparnasse nightclub led to the formation of the Hot Club of France quintet. Claude Luter and his Dixieland band were the hot sound of the 1950s.

The *chanson française,* a tradition dating from the troubadours of the Middle Ages, was eclipsed by the music halls and burlesque of the early 20th century, but was revived in the 1930s by Piaf and Charles Trenet. In the 1950s the Left Bank cabarets nurtured *chansonniers* (cabaret singers) such as Léo Ferré, Georges Brassens, Claude Nougaro, Jacques Brel and Serge Gainsbourg. In the 1980s irresistible crooners such as Jean-Pierre Lang and Pierre Bachelet continued the *chanson* tradition with classics like *Les Corons* (1982), a passionate ode to the miners of northern France, which made a comeback in 2008 thanks to the film *Bienvenue chez le Ch'tis* (see boxed text p51).

French pop music has evolved massively since the 1960s *yéyé* (imitative rock) days of Johnny Hallyday. Particularly strong is world music, from

FRENCH KISSING

Kissing is an integral part of French life. (The expression 'French kissing', as in tongues, doesn't exist in French, incidentally.) That said, put a Parisian in Provence and there's no saying they will know when to stop.

Countrywide, people who know each other reasonably well, really well, a tad or barely at all greet each other with a glancing peck on each cheek. Southern France aside (where everyone kisses everyone), two men rarely kiss (unless they are related or artists) but always shake hands. Boys and girls start kissing as soon as they're out of nappies, or so it seems.

Kissing French-style is not completely straightforward, 'how many' and 'which side first' potentially being problematic. In Paris it is definitely two: unless parties are related, *very* close friends or haven't seen each other in an age, anything more is deemed affected. That said, in certain trendy 20-something circles, friends swap three or four cheek-skimming kisses, as do many young teenagers at school *parce qu'ils ont que ça à faire...*

Travel south and the *bisous* (kisses) multiply, three or four being the norm in Provence. The bits of France neighbouring Switzerland around Lake Geneva tend to be three-kiss country (in keeping with Swiss habits); and in the Loire Valley it is four. Corsicans, bizarrely, stick to two but kiss left cheek first – which can lead to locked lips given that everyone else in France starts with the right cheek.

Algerian rai and other North African music (artists include Cheb Khaled, Natacha Atlas, Jamel, Cheb Mami and Rachid Taha) to Senegalese *mbalax* (Youssou N'Dour) and West Indian zouk (Kassav', Zouk Machine). One musician who uses these elements to stunning effect is Manu Chao (www.manuchao.net), the Paris-born son of Spanish parents whose albums are international best sellers. Another hot musical export is Parisian electro-dance duo Daft Punk (www.daftalive.com), whose debut album *Homework* (1997) fused disco, house, funk and techno. Their latest album, *Alive* (2007), adopts a more eclectic approach. Electronica duo Air (an acronym for *'Amour, Imagination, Rêve'* meaning 'Love, Imagination, Dream'), around since the mid-1990s, remains sensational with its fifth album *Pocket Symphony* (2007).

Keep up to the minute with contemporary French literature and what's being translated into English with the French Publishing Agency, online at www.frenchpubagency.com.

For the contemporary younger folk, France is probably best known for its rap, an original 1990s sound spearheaded by Senegal-born, Paris-reared rapper MC Solaar and Suprême NTM (NTM being an acronym for a French expression far too offensive to print), who have since split. Most big-name rappers are French 20-somethings of Arabic or African origin whose prime preoccupation is the frustrations and fury of fed-up immigrants in the French *banlieues* (suburbs). Take Disiz La Peste: hot-shot rapper, 27, Senegalese father, French mother, website http://disizlapeste.artistes.universalmusic.fr, title of third album *Histoires Extra-Ordinaires d'un Jeune de Banlieue* (The Extraordinary Stories of a Youth in the Suburbs; 2005).

Other rappers to listen out for include Monsieur R of Congolese origin, known for his hardcore, antiestablishment 'fuck everything' lyrics (*'La France est une garce, n'oublie pas de la baiser jusqu'à l'épuiser, comme une salope il faut la traiter, mec!'* – 'France is a bad gal, don't forget to fuck her into exhaustion, treat her like a slut, boy!'), which have landed him in court in the past; Parisian heavyweight Booba of Senegalese origin; ghetto kid Rohff (www.roh2f.com, in French) and the trio Malekal Morte. One of France's few female rappers, Cyprus-born Diam's (short for *'diamant'* meaning 'diamond'; www.diams-lesite.com), who arrived in Paris aged seven, was voted MTV's French Artist of the Year in 2007. Rap bands include Marseille's hugely successful home-grown IAM (www.iam.tm.fr, in French), five-piece band KDD from Toulouse and Brittany's Manau (www.manau.com, in French) trio, who fuse hip hop with traditional Celtic sounds.

Architecture et Musique is a fine concept: revel in some fine classical music amid an architectural masterpiece; the concert agenda is at www.architecmusique.com.

Keep on top of who's who and who's hot with Yo La La (www.yolala.org), a podcast about French rap aimed specifically at an anglophone audience. For French speakers, there's www.rap2k.com.

Architecture

PREHISTORIC TO ART NOUVEAU

From the prehistoric megaliths around Carnac (p340) to Vauban's 33 star-shaped citadels (opposite), built to defend France's 17th-century frontiers, French architecture has always been of *grand-projet* proportions.

The south is the place to find France's Gallo-Roman legacy: the Pont du Gard (p766), amphitheatres in Nîmes (p760) and Arles (p827), the theatre at Orange (p845) and Nîmes' Maison Carrée (p760).

Several centuries later, architects adopted elements from Gallo-Roman buildings to create *roman* (Romanesque) masterpieces such as Toulouse's Basilique St-Sernin (p736), Poitiers' Église Notre Dame la Grande (p659) and Caen's two famous Romanesque abbeys (p291).

Northern France's extraordinary wealth in the 12th century lured the finest architects, engineers and artisans, who created impressive Gothic structures with ribbed vaults carved with great precision, pointed arches, slender verticals, chapels along the nave and chancel, refined decoration

VAUBAN'S CITADELS

From the mid-17th century to the mid-19th century, the design of defensive fortifications around the world was dominated by the work of one man: Sébastien le Prestre de Vauban (1633–1707).

Born to a relatively poor family of the petty nobility, Vauban worked as a military engineer during almost the entire reign of Louis XIV, revolutionising both the design of fortresses and siege techniques. To defend France's frontiers, he built 33 immense citadels, many of them shaped like stars and surrounded by moats, and he rebuilt or refined more than 100. Vauban's most famous citadel is situated at Lille, but his work can also be seen at Antibes, Belfort, Belle Île, Besançon, Concarneau, Perpignan, St-Jean-Pied-de-Port, St-Malo and Verdun. In 2008 13 sites (www.sites-vauban.org) made it onto Unesco's World Heritage list under a 'Vauban Fortifications' banner.

and stained-glass windows. Avignon's pontifical palace (p839) is Gothic architecture on a gargantuan scale. With the introduction of flying buttresses around 1230, Gothic masterpieces such as the seminal cathedral at Chartres (p220) and its successors at Reims (p357), Amiens (p256) and Strasbourg (p375) appeared.

By the 15th century architects had shelved size for ornamentation, conceiving the beautifully lacy Flamboyant Gothic. For an example of such decorative overkill, check out the spire of Strasbourg cathedral. To trace the shift from late Gothic to Renaissance, travel along the Loire Valley: Château de Chambord (p429) illustrates the mix of classical components and decorative motifs typical of early Renaissance architecture. In the mid-16th century, François I had Italian architects design Fontainebleau (p214).

In 1635 early baroque architect François Mansart (1598–1666) designed the classical wing of Château de Blois (p424), while his younger rival, Louis Le Vau (1612–70), started work on Louis XIV's palace at Versailles (p211).

A quest for order, reason and serenity through the adoption of the forms and conventions of Greco-Roman antiquity defined neoclassical architecture from 1740 until well into the 19th century. Nancy's place Stanislas (p402) is France's loveliest neoclassical square.

Under Napoléon, many of Paris' best-known sights – the Arc de Triomphe, La Madeleine, the Arc du Carrousel at the Louvre and the Assemblée Nationale building – were designed.

Art nouveau (1850–1910) combined iron, brick, glass and ceramics in ways never before seen. See for yourself in Paris with Hector Guimard's noodlelike metro entrances, the fine art-nouveau interiors in the Musée d'Orsay (p151) and the glass roof over the Grand Palais (p154).

For an alternative guide to contemporary architecture, architects and urban art, look no further than the bilingual www.archi-guide.com.

CONTEMPORARY

Chapelle de Notre-Dame du Haut in the Jura (p577) and Couvent Ste-Marie de la Tourette near Lyon (p520) are architectural icons of the 20th century. Designed in the 1950s by France's most celebrated architect, Le Corbusier (1887–1965), the structures rewrote the architectural style book with their sweeping lines and functionalised forms, adapted to fit the human form.

French political leaders have long sought to immortalise themselves through the erection of huge public edifices, otherwise called *grands projects*. Georges Pompidou commissioned Paris' Centre Pompidou (p141) in 1977; Valéry Giscard d'Estaing transformed a derelict train station into the Musée d'Orsay (p151); while François Mitterrand commissioned the capital's best-known contemporary architectural landmarks, including IM Pei's glass pyramid at the Louvre (p139), the Opéra Bastille (p144), the Grande Arche (p207) in the skyscraper district of La Défense, and the national library

TOP PICKS: URBAN DESIGN

The best of dreamy venues for urban-design buffs:

- Paris' Hôtel Le A (p172), Murano Urban Resort (p175) and Kube Hôtel (p174)
- Lyon's Hotelo (p507) and Collège Hotel (p507)
- Hôtel HI and Hôtel Windsor, Nice (p869)
- Hôtel Le Corbusier, Marseille (p813)
- Les Bains Douches, Toulouse (p742)
- Hôtel 3.14, Cannes (p881)
- Zazpi, St-Jean de Luz (p701)
- L'Hermitage Gantois, Lille (p231)
- Hôtel La Pérouse, Nantes (p655)
- Seeko'o, Bordeaux (p674)

(p156), as well as Jean Nouvel's fabulous riverside architectural icon, the Musée du Quai Branly (p153).

In the provinces, notable buildings include Strasbourg's European Parliament (p379), Dutch architect Rem Koolhaas's Euralille and Jean Nouvel's glass-and-steel Vesunna Musée Gallo-Romain in Périgueux (p622), a 1920s art-deco swimming pool–turned–art museum in Lille (p229) and the fantastic Louvre II (p249) in unknown Lens, 37km south of Lille. Also noteworthy are an 11th-century abbey–turned–monumental sculpture gallery in Angers (p449) and Le Havre's rejuvenated 19th-century docks (p275). Then, of course, there's one of the world's tallest bridges (p792), designed by Sir Norman Foster.

In Lyon a shimmering glass-and-steel cloud (p503) is rising out of the wasteland at the confluence of the Rhône and Saône rivers. Jean Nouvel, meanwhile, clinched the competition in 2008 to design a 300m-tall Millennium tower for Paris' La Défense.

Painting

France's oldest known prehistoric cave paintings (created 31,000 years ago) adorn the Grotte Chauvet-Pont-d'Arc (Ardèche, Rhône Valley) and the underwater Grotte Cosquer (near Marseille); neither can be visited.

According to Voltaire, French painting proper began with Nicolas Poussin (1594–1665), known for his classical mythological and biblical scenes bathed in golden light that the baroque painter created. Wind forward a couple of centuries and modern still life pops onto the scene with Jean-Baptiste Chardin (1699–1779), the first to see still life as an essay in composition rather than a show of skill in reproduction. A century later, neoclassical artist Jacques Louis David (1748–1825) wooed the public with his vast portraits; some are in the Louvre.

While Romantics such as Eugène Delacroix (buried in Paris' Cimetière du Père Lachaise; p156) revamped the subject picture, the Barbizon School effected a parallel transformation of landscape painting. Barbizons included landscape artist Jean-Baptiste Camille Corot (1796–1875) and Jean-François Millet (1814–75). The son of a peasant farmer from Normandy, Millet took many of his subjects from peasant life, and reproductions of his *L'Angélus* (The Angelus; 1857) – the best-known French painting after the *Mona Lisa* – are strung above mantelpieces all over rural France. The original hangs in Paris' Musée d'Orsay (p151).

The Musée d'Orsay is also the place to see the Realists, among them Édouard Manet (1832–83), who zoomed in on Parisian middle-class life, and

Gustave Courbet (1819–77), who depicted the drudgery of manual labour and the difficult lives of the working class.

It was in a flower-filled garden in a Normandy village (p278) that Claude Monet (1840–1926) expounded Impressionism, a term of derision taken from the title of his experimental painting *Impression: Soleil Levant* (Impression: Sunrise; 1874). A trip to the Musée d'Orsay unveils a rash of other members of the school – Boudin, Sisley, Pissarro, Renoir, Degas and so on.

An arthritis-crippled Renoir painted out his last Impressionist days in a villa (p878) on the Côte d'Azur. With a warmth and astonishing intensity of light hard to equal, the French Riviera inspired dozens of artists post-Renoir: Paul Cézanne (1839–1906) is particularly celebrated for his post-Impressionist still lifes and landscapes done in Aix-en-Provence where he was born and worked (visit his studio; p822); Paul Gauguin (1848–1903) worked in Arles; while Dutch artist Vincent van Gogh (1853–90) painted Arles and St-Rémy-de-Provence. In St-Tropez pointillism took off: Georges Seurat (1859–91) was the first to apply paint in small dots or uniform brush strokes of unmixed colour, producing fine mosaics of warm and cool tones, but it was his pupil Paul Signac (1863–1935) who is best known for his pointillist works; see them both in St-Tropez's Musée de l'Annonciade (p888).

Twentieth-century French painting is characterised by a bewildering diversity of styles, including fauvism, named after the slur of a critic who compared the exhibitors at the 1906 autumn Salon in Paris with *fauves* (wild animals) because of their radical use of intensely bright colours, and cubism. Henri Matisse (1869–1954) was the man behind the former (a fauvist trail around Collioure takes you past scenes he captured on canvas in Roussillon; p801) and Spanish prodigy Pablo Picasso (1881–1973), the latter. Both chose southern France to set up studio, Matisse living in Nice (visit the Musée Matisse; p866) and Picasso opting for a 12th-century château (now the Musée Picasso) in Antibes. Cubism, as developed by Picasso and Georges Braque (1882–1963), deconstructed the subject into a system of intersecting planes and presented various aspects of it simultaneously.

Read about buying or selling a home in France, setting up a business and so on with Notaires de France (French Notaries) at www.notaires.fr.

No piece of French art better captures Dada's rebellious spirit than Marcel Duchamp's *Mona Lisa,* complete with moustache and goatee. In 1922 German Dadaist Max Ernst moved to Paris and worked on surrealism, a Dada offshoot that drew on the theories of Freud to reunite the conscious and unconscious realms and permeate daily life with fantasies and dreams.

With the close of WWII, Paris' role as the artistic capital of the world ended, leaving critics ever since wondering where all the artists have gone. The focus shifted back to southern France in the 1960s with new realists such as Arman (1928–2005) and Yves Klein (1928–62), both from Nice. In 1960 Klein famously produced *Anthropométrie de l'Époque Bleue,* a series of imprints made by naked women (covered from head to toe in blue paint) rolling around on a white canvas – in front of an orchestra of violins and an audience in evening dress. A decade on the Supports/Surfaces movement deconstructed the concept of a painting, transforming one of its structural components (such as the frame or canvas) into a work of art instead.

Artists in the 1990s turned to the minutiae of everyday urban life to express social and political angst, using media other than paint to let rip. Conceptual artist Daniel Buren (b 1938) reduced his painting to a signature series of vertical 8.7cm-wide stripes that he applies to every surface imaginable – white marble columns in the courtyard of Paris' Palais Royal (p141) included. The painter (who in 1967, as part of the radical *groupe BMPT,* signed a manifesto declaring he was not a painter) was the *enfant terrible* of French art in the 1980s. Partner-in-crime Michel Parmentier

BLOG ROLL

If there's one country in Europe that deems blogging a national pastime (so *that's* what they do outside their 35-hour work week), it's France. The underbelly of what French people think right now, the French blogosphere is gargantuan, with everyone and everything from streets and metro stops to bars, bands and the president having their own blog.

For an informative overview (did someone say three million bloggers in France and counting?) see **LeMondeduBlog.com** (www.lemondedublog.com) covering just that, the blog world, with loads of links. Parisian *star du blog* **Loïc Le Meur**, probably France's most read and watched blogger, blogs in English and French at www.loiclemeur.com and vid-blogs at www.loic.tv. The self-professed serial entrepreneur recently moved to San Francisco to launch Seesmic, a project aimed at building the first video-conversation community.

French bloggers have serious clout. In the days preceding France's historic vote on the EU constitution (p45), it was the powerful 'No' blog of a humble French law professor that lured an online crowd of 25,000 a day and contributed enormously to France's eventual rejection of the constitution, say political analysts (there was no equivalent 'Yes' blog). The so-called 'workers' revolt' in Paris and elsewhere against the government's proposed new employment law in April 2006 was likewise charted in English by French bloggers who continue to cover events at www.libcom.org/blog.

Hot blogs by the French in English:

- **French Word a Day** (http://french-word-a-day.typepad.com) Fun language learning.
- **Emmanuelle Richard** (www.emmanuelle.net) Wacky musings by a French journalist in Los Angeles with a 'France & Frogs' section and comprehensive links to 'frog blogs', blogs by 'frogs in the US' and blogs by 'Americans in France'.
- **Chocolate & Zucchini** (http://chocolateandzucchini.com) Food-driven blog by Clotilde, a 28-year-old Parisian from Montmartre.
- **La France Profonde** (http://franceprofonde.blogspot.com) Worth noting both for its great title meaning 'the deepest darkest depths of rural France', aka Aveyron in Languedoc-Roussillon, where the American writer has lived for 17-odd years, and its comprehensive list of links to France-related blogs in English.
- **Le Blageur à Paris** (www.parisblagueur.blogspot.com) On-the-ball snapshots of Parisian life from one of the capital's most enigmatic bloggers, a 32-year-old French *fille* called Meg Zimbeck.
- **Libé Labo** (www.libelabo.fr, in French) The audiovisual site of national daily *Libération* is an invaluable resource: podcasts, video, audio and readings.
- **The French Journal** (http://frenchjournal.typepad.com) Well written, informative and cultured site covering most of France in its notes on 'French culture, history, geography, food, wine, travel and more …'

(1938–2000) insisted on monochrome painting for a while – blue in 1966, grey in 1967 and red in 1968.

Paris-born conceptual artist Sophie Calle (b 1953) brazenly exposes her private life in public with her eye-catching installations, which most recently involved 107 women – including Carla Bruni before she became First Lady (p47) – reading and interpreting an email she received from her French lover, dumping her.

Current trends can be tracked at Paris' Palais de Tokyo (www.palaisdetokyo.com), a contemporary art space that opens from noon to midnight six days a week; encourages art visitors to feel, touch, talk and interact; and bends over backwards to turn every expectation of painting and art on its head. La Maison Rouge (www.lamaisonrouge.org) is the other key address.

France's Food Obsession

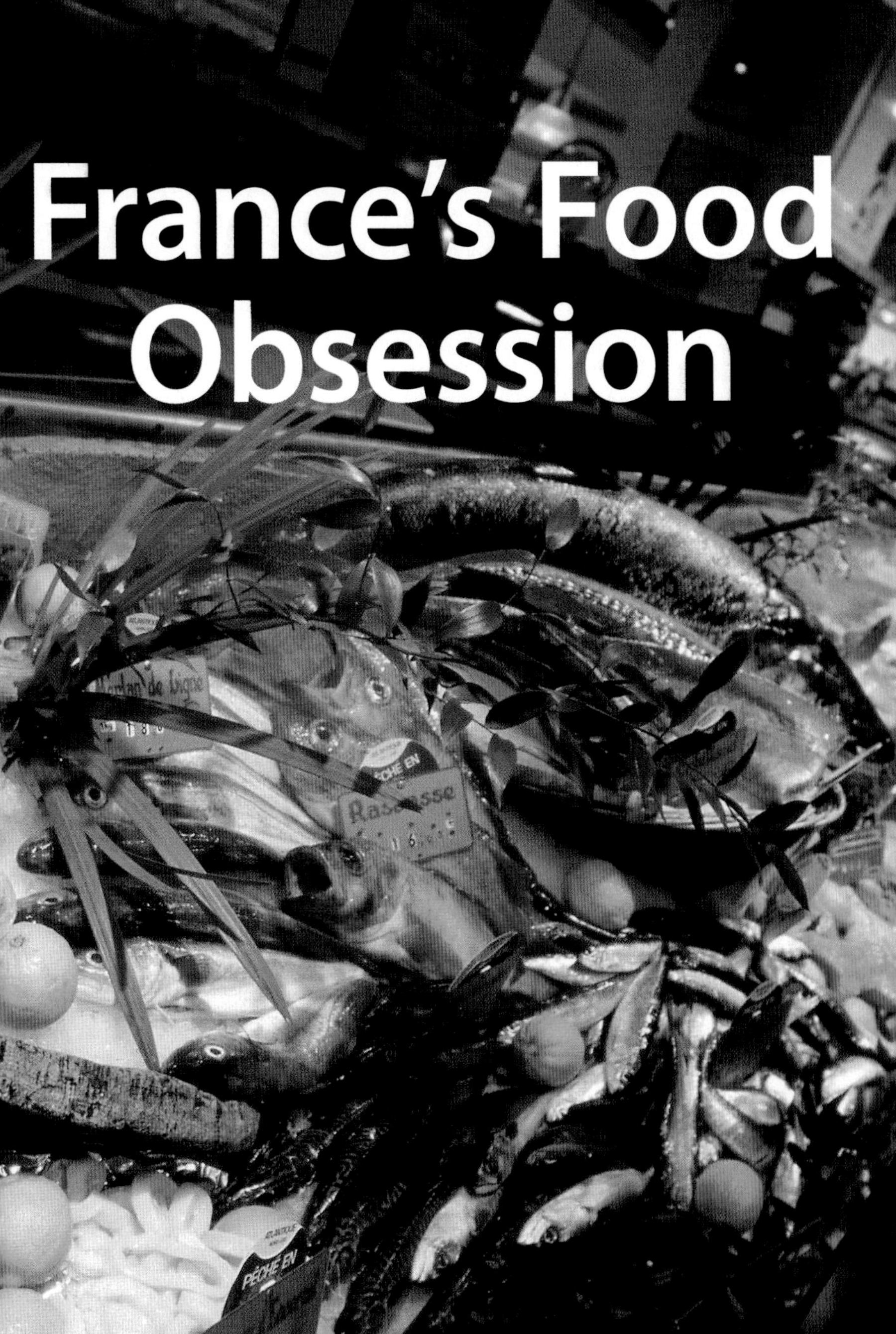

For fresh produce, check out one of France's many local markets and speciality stores JEAN-BERNARD CARILLET

There are many reasons for the amazing variety of regional cuisines in *l'Hexagone* (the Hexagon), as this six-sided nation calls itself. Climatic and geographical factors have been particularly important: the hot south tends to favour olive oil, garlic and tomatoes, while the cooler, pastoral regions to the north emphasise cream and butter. Areas near the coast specialise in mussels, oysters and saltwater fish, while those near lakes and rivers take advantage of the plentiful supply of freshwater fish.

Borders are not firmly drawn, however, and there's much spillover: you'll encounter influences of Gascon cuisine in the Atlantic region and Provence and it is sometimes difficult to distinguish Breton food from the cuisine of the Loire region. And, like everywhere, people do eat dishes from outside their region – an Alsatian-style *choucroute* (sauerkraut with sausage and other prepared meats), say, in a Marseille brasserie, or a *garbure* – a thick soup of cabbage, beans, potatoes, vegetables and herbs and some sort of *confit* (preserved meat) – from the Midi in a restaurant in Dijon. But these dishes will never be as good as they are when they're at home; the ingredients and the preparation just won't be there to give them their authentic tastes.

top five REGIONAL TASTES

Lyon (p508)
Scoff local cuisine in a *bouchon*

Alsace (p383)
Feast on *wädele braisé au pinot noir* (ham knuckles in wine) and *choucroute au canard* (duck sauerkraut) in a cosy old *winstub*

The Jura (p570)
Dip into an authentic fondue

Cancale (p316)
Sink oysters fresh from their *parcs* (beds)

Périgord (p621)
Savour a snail stuffed with foie gras

Regional Specialities

Diverse as it is, French cuisine is typified by certain regions, most notably Normandy, Burgundy, Périgord, Lyon and, to a lesser extent, the Loire region, Alsace and Provence.

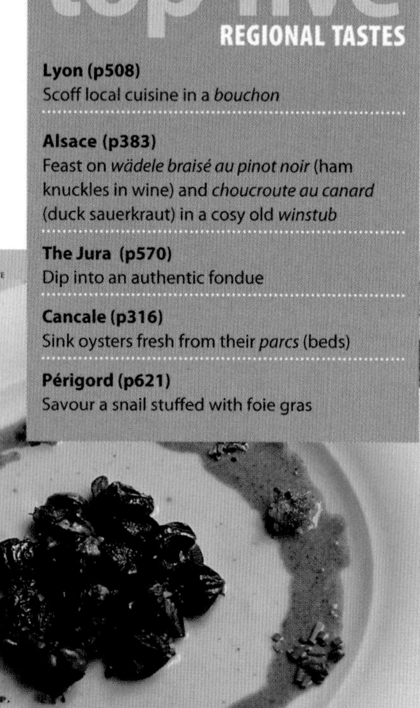

Fricassée d'escargots with Burgundy

OLIVER STREWE

Baguettes, a daily ritual of French life JOHN ELK III

BREAD

Nothing is more French than *pain* (bread). More than 80% of all French people eat it at every meal, and it comes in an infinite variety.

All bakeries have baguettes (and the similar, but fatter, *flûtes*), which are long and thin and weigh 250g, and wider loaves that are simply called *pains*. A *pain*, which weighs 400g, is softer on the inside and has a less crispy crust than a baguette. Both types are at their best if eaten within four hours of baking. You can store them for longer in a plastic bag, but the crust becomes soft and chewy; if you leave them out, they'll soon be hard – which is the way many French people like them at breakfast the next day. If you're not very hungry, ask for a half loaf: a *demi-baguette* or a *demi-pain*. A *ficelle* is a much thinner, crustier 200g version of a baguette – not unlike a very thick breadstick, really.

Most bakeries also carry heavier, more expensive breads made with all sorts of grains and cereals; you will also find loaves studded with nuts, raisins or herbs. These keep much longer than baguettes and standard white-flour breads.

Still others – Brittany, the Auvergne, Languedoc, the Basque Country and Corsica – have made incalculable contributions to what can generically be called French food.

NORMANDY

Cream, apples and seafood are the three essentials of Norman cuisine. Specialities include *moules à la crème normande* (mussels in cream sauce with a dash of cider) and *canard à la rouennaise* ('Rouen-style duck'; duck stuffed with its liver and served with a red-wine sauce), preferably interrupted by a *trou normand* (literally 'Norman hole'; a glass of Calvados) to allow room for more courses.

BURGUNDY

The trinity of the Burgundian kitchen is beef, red wine and mustard. *Bœuf bourguignon* (beef marinated and cooked in young red wine with mushrooms, onions, carrots and bacon) combines the first two; Dijon, the capital of Burgundy, has been synonymous with mustard for centuries.

PÉRIGORD

This southwest region is famous for its truffles and poultry, especially the ducks and geese whose fattened livers are turned into *pâté de foie gras* (duck- or goose-liver pâté), which is sometimes flavoured with cognac and truffles. *Confit de canard* and *confit d'oie* are duck or goose joints cooked very slowly in their own fat. The preserved fowl is then left to stand for some months before being eaten.

ON BOARD WITH CHEESE

Charles de Gaulle, expostulating on the inability of anyone to unite the French on a single issue after WWII, famously grumbled: 'You cannot easily bring together a country that has 265 kinds of cheese.'

The general's comments are well out of date; today France counts upwards of 500 varieties of *fromage* (cheese) made of cow's, goat's or ewe's milk, which can be raw, pasteurised or *petit-lait* ('little-milk', the whey left over after the milk fats and solids have been curdled with rennet). But bear in mind that there are just five basic types (see below).

When cutting cheese at the table, remember that a small circular cheese such as a Camembert is cut into wedges like a pie. If a larger cheese (eg a Brie) has been bought already sliced into a wedge shape, cut from the tip to the rind; cutting off the tip is just not on.

Slice cheeses whose middle is the best part (eg blue or veined cheeses) in such a way as to take your fair share of the rind. A flat piece of semihard cheese like emmental is usually just cut horizontally in hunks.

Wine and cheese are often a match made in heaven. It's a matter of taste, but in general, strong, pungent cheeses require a young, full-bodied red or a sweet wine, while soft cheeses with a refined flavour call for more quality and age in the wine. Some classic pairings include: Alsatian gewürztraminer and Munster; Côtes du Rhone with Roquefort; Côte d'Or (Burgundy) and Brie or Camembert; and mature Bordeaux with emmental or Cantal. Even Champagne can get in on the act; drink it with mushroom-like Chaource.

The number of choices on offer at a *fromagerie* (cheese shop) can be overwhelming, but merchants will always allow you to sample what's on offer before you buy, and are usually very generous with their advice.

The following list divides French cheeses into five main groups as they are usually displayed in a shop and recommends several types to try.

- **Fromage de chèvre** 'Goat's milk cheese' is usually creamy and both sweet and a little salty when fresh, but hardens and gets much saltier as it matures and dries out. Among the best are Ste-Maure de Touraine, a creamy, mild cheese from the Loire region; Crottin de Chavignol, a classic though saltier variety from Burgundy; Cabécou de Rocamadour from Midi-Pyrénées, often served warm with salad or marinated in oil and rosemary; and St-Marcellin, a soft white cheese from Lyon.
- **Fromage à pâté persillée** 'Marbled' or 'blue cheese' is so called because the veins often resemble *persil* (parsley). Roquefort is a ewe's-milk veined cheese from Languedoc that is to many the king of French cheese. Fourme d'Ambert is a very mild cow's-milk cheese from Rhône-Alpes. Bleu du Haut Jura (also called Bleu de Gex) is a mild blue-veined mountain cheese.
- **Fromage à pâté molle** 'Soft cheese' is moulded or rind-washed. Camembert, a classic moulded cheese from Normandy that for many is synonymous with French cheese, and the refined Brie de Meaux are both made from unpasteurised cow's milk. Munster from Alsace and the strong Époisses de Bourgogne are rind-washed, fine-textured cheeses.
- **Fromage à pâté demi-dure** 'Semihard cheese' denotes uncooked, pressed cheese. Among the finest are Tomme de Savoie, made from either pasteurised or unpasteurised cow's milk; Cantal, a cow's-milk cheese from Auvergne that tastes something like English cheddar; St-Nectaire, a strong-smelling pressed cheese that has a complex taste; and Ossau-Iraty, a ewe's-milk cheese made in the Basque Country.
- **Fromage à pâté dure** 'Hard cheese' in France is always cooked and pressed. Among the most popular are Beaufort, a grainy cow's-milk cheese with a slightly fruity taste from Rhône-Alpes; Comté, a cheese made with raw cow's-milk in Franche-Comté; emmental, a cow's-milk cheese made all over France; and Mimolette, an Edam-like bright-orange cheese from Lille that can be aged for as long as 36 months.

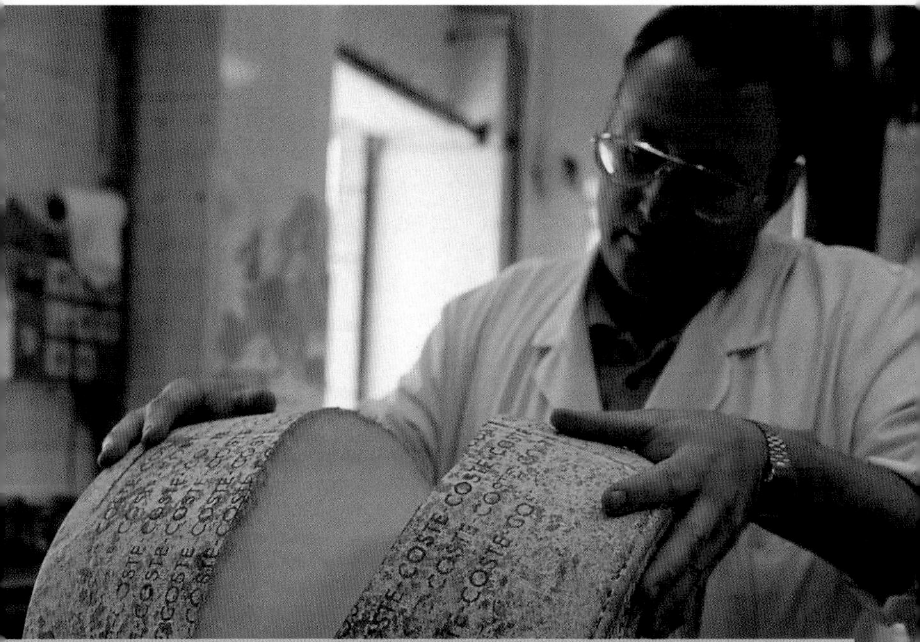

Le fromage français: France is all about cheese, cheese and more cheese, like this tasty Cantal GREG ELMS

LYON

Many people consider France's third-largest city to be its *temple de gastronomie.* A typical type of *charcuterie* is *saucisson de Lyon,* which features in Lyon's trademark dish, *saucisson aux pommes* (sausage with potatoes). Another speciality is the *quenelle,* a poached dumpling made of freshwater fish (usually pike) and served with *sauce Nantua,* made with cream and paste from freshwater crayfish.

Rillettes de Tours is perfect picnic fare GREG ELMS

LOIRE REGION

The cuisine of the Loire, refined in the kitchens of the region's châteaux from the 16th century onwards, ultimately became the cuisine of France as a whole; *rillettes* (potted meat), *coq au vin* (chicken cooked in wine), *beurre blanc* sauce and *tarte Tatin* (a caramelised upside-down apple pie) are specialities from this area, but are now considered generic French cuisine. The Loire region is also known for its *pruneaux de Tours,* prunes dried from luscious damson plums and used in poultry, pork or veal dishes.

Traditional, delicious *charcuterie* PETER WILLIAM THORNTON

CHARCUTERIE

Traditionally *charcuterie* is made only from pork, though a number of other meats (beef, veal, chicken or goose) are used in making sausages, salamis, blood puddings and other cured and salted meats.

Pâtés, terrines and *rillettes* (coarsely shredded potted meat) are also considered types of *charcuterie*.

The difference between a pâté and a terrine is academic: a pâté is removed from its container and sliced before it is served, while a terrine is sliced from the container itself. *Rillettes,* on the other hand, is potted meat or even fish that has not been ground or chopped but shredded with two forks, seasoned, and mixed with fat. It is spread cold over bread or toast.

While every region in France produces standard *charcuterie* favourites as well as its own specialities, Alsace, Lyon and the Auvergne produce the best sausages, and Périgord and the north of France some of the most acclaimed pâtés and terrines.

Some very popular types of *charcuterie* are: *andouillette* (soft raw sausage made from the pig's small intestines that is grilled and eaten with onions and potatoes); *boudin noir* (blood sausage or pudding made with pig's blood, onions and spices, and usually eaten hot with stewed apples and potatoes); *jambon* (ham, either smoked or salt-cured); *saucisse* (usually a small fresh sausage that is boiled or grilled before eating); *saucisson* (usually a large salami eaten cold); and *saucisson sec* (air-dried salami).

ALSACE

A classic dish of this meaty, Teutonic cuisine is *choucroute alsacienne* (also called *choucroute garnie*), sauerkraut flavoured with juniper berries and served hot with sausages, bacon, pork and/or ham knuckle. You should drink chilled riesling or Alsatian pinot noir – not beer – with *choucroute* and follow it with a *tarte alsacienne,* a scrumptious custard tart made with local fruits like *mirabelles* (sweet yellow plums) or *quetsches* (a variety of purple plum).

PROVENCE

The Roman legacy of olives, wheat and wine remain the trinity of *la cuisine provençale,* and many dishes are prepared with olive oil and generous amounts of garlic. Provence's most famous contribution to French cuisine is *bouillabaisse,* a chowder made with at least three kinds of fresh saltwater fish, cooked for about 10 minutes in a broth containing onions, tomatoes, saffron and various herbs, and eaten as a main course with toasted bread and *rouille,* a spicy mayonnaise of olive oil, garlic and chilli peppers.

BRITTANY

Brittany may be a paradise for lovers of seafood, but the crêpe and the galette are the royalty of Breton cuisine. A crêpe is made from wheat flour and is almost always sweet; the flour used in a galette is made from buckwheat, a traditional staple of the region, and the fillings are always savoury. A *galette complète,* for example, comes with ham, egg and cheese.

AUVERGNE

This *rude* ('rugged' or 'harsh') region of the Massif Central specialises in *charcuterie,* and its celebrated *salaisons* (salt-cured meats) are sold throughout the land. Specialities include *lentilles vertes du Puy aux saucisses fumées* (smoked pork sausages with green Puy lentils) and *clafoutis,* a custard and cherry tart baked upside down like a *tarte Tatin.*

HAVE TONGUE, WILL TRAVEL

France has a considerable population of immigrants from its former colonies and protectorates in North and West Africa, Indochina, the Middle East, India, the Caribbean and the South Pacific, as well as refugees from every corner of the globe, so an exceptional variety of reasonably priced ethnic food is available both in big cities and smaller towns.

North African

If curry has become an integral part of Britain's cuisine, the same can be said about *couscous* in France. One of the most delicious and easy-to-find North African dishes, couscous is steamed semolina garnished with vegetables and a spicy, meat-based sauce just before it is served. It is usually eaten with lamb shish kebab, *merguez* (small, spicy sausages), *méchoui* (barbecued lamb on the bone), chicken or some other meat. The Moroccan, Algerian and Tunisian versions all differ slightly. Another Moroccan favourite is *tajine,* a delicious slow-cooked stew of meat, preserved lemons, prunes or other dried fruits, which is usually eaten by dipping small pieces of bread into it.

At the end of a meal, North African restaurants always offer *thé de menthe* (mint tea), which is poured from a great height from brass teapot to tiny cup by the waiter, and an array of luridly coloured, ultra-sweet desserts displayed in the window front, from which you can make your selection. A popular choice is *zlabia,* those tacky (both senses) bright-orange pretzel-shaped things dripping in honey water that you see everywhere in France.

Sub-Saharan African

Sub-Saharan African food is popular in many cities, especially Paris and Marseille. Among Senegalese favourites are *tiéboudienne* (the national dish of rice baked in a thick sauce of fish and vegetables); *yassa* (chicken or fish grilled in onion and lime sauce); *mafé* (beef or chicken stew or curry served with peanut sauce); and *bassissalte* (millet couscous). Specialities from Togo include *lélé* (flat, steamed cakes made from white beans and shrimp and served with tomato sauce); *gbekui* (a sort of goulash made with spinach, onions, beef, fish and shrimp); and *djenkommé* (grilled chicken with special semolina noodles).

Asian

France's many immigrants from Southeast Asia, especially Vietnam and Cambodia, have introduced Asian food to France. Vietnamese restaurants, many of them run by ethnic Chinese who fled Vietnam after the French left, generally offer good value but few authentic dishes. In the big cities, you can also sample the cuisines of Cambodia, Japan, Korea, Tibet and Thailand.

Most dishes will be familiar to you – only the names have been changed: *nem* (small fried Vietnamese spring or egg roll, eaten rolled up in a lettuce leaf with mint and fish sauce); *rouleau de printemps* or *pâté imperial* (Vietnamese soft spring roll with salad, mint and prawns); *pâté aux légumes/au poulet/aux crevettes* (Chinese vegetable/chicken/shrimp spring or egg roll); *bouchée aux crevettes/au porc* (varieties of Chinese dim sum called *siu mai* and *har gau* in Chinese); and *raviolis pékinois* (fried crescent-shaped pork dumplings called *guo tie* in Chinese).

LANGUEDOC

No dish is more evocative of Languedoc than *cassoulet,* a casserole with beans and meat. There are at least three major varieties of *cassoulet* but the favourite is arguably that from Toulouse, which adds *saucisse de Toulouse,* a fat, mild-tasting pork sausage. France's most famous (and expensive) cheese is made at Roquefort, south of Millau.

Classic combo: galette and cider in Brittany OLIVIER CIREN

BASQUE COUNTRY

Among the essential ingredients of Basque cooking are the deep-red chillies that add an extra bite to many of the region's dishes, including the dusting on the signature *jambon de Bayonne,* the locally prepared Bayonne ham. Basques love cakes and pastries; the most popular is *gâteau basque,* a relatively simple layer cake filled with cream or cherry jam.

CORSICA

The hills and mountains of the island of Corsica have always been ideal for raising stock and the dense Corsican underbrush called the *maquis* is made up of shrubs mixed with wild herbs. These raw materials come together to create such trademark Corsican dishes as *stufatu,* a fragrant mutton stew; *premonata,* beef braised with juniper berries; and *lonzo,* a type of Corsican sausage, cooked with white beans, white wine and herbs.

Nip into a local pâtisserie for a slice of heaven on earth, like this *tarte aux poires* (pear tart) GREG E

Food & Drink

'The French think mainly about two things – their two main meals', a well-fed bon-vivant Parisian was once heard to say. 'Everything else is in parentheses.' And it's true. While not every French man, woman and child is a walking *Larousse Gastronomique*, that bible of things culinary, eating and drinking well is still of prime importance to most people of France, and they continue to spend an inordinate amount of time thinking about, discussing and consuming food and wine.

But don't suppose for a moment that this obsession with things culinary means dining out in France has to be a ceremonious occasion or one full of pitfalls for the uninitiated. Approach food and wine here with half the enthusiasm *les français* do, and you will be welcomed, encouraged and very well fed.

For a full culinary tour of France's regional specialities, see p70.

The Food of France by Waverley Root, first published in 1958, remains *the* seminal work in English on *la cuisine française*, with a focus on historical development, by a long-time Paris-based American foreign correspondent.

DRINKS

Alcoholic Drinks

Although alcohol consumption has dropped by 30% in less than two decades – the stereotypical Frenchman no longer starts the day with a shot of red wine in order to *tuer le ver* (kill the worm) followed by a small, black coffee – France still ranks in the top 10 of the world boozing stakes. The average French person consumes 11.4L of pure alcohol a year, compared with 13.7L in Ireland, 11.8L in the UK, 9.7L in New Zealand, 9L in Australia and 8.6L in the USA.

WINE & CHAMPAGNE

Grapes and the art of wine-making were introduced to Gaul by the Romans. In the Middle Ages, important vineyards developed around monasteries as the monks needed wine to celebrate Mass. Large-scale wine production later moved closer to ports (eg Bordeaux), from where it could be exported.

In the mid-19th century, phylloxera aphids were accidentally brought to Europe from the USA. These pests ate through the roots of France's grapevines, destroying some 7000 sq km – 60% of the total – of vineyards. Wine production appeared to be doomed until root stocks resistant to phylloxera were brought from California and original cuttings grafted onto them.

Wine-making is a complicated chemical process, but ultimately the taste and quality of the wine depend on four key factors: the type(s) of grape, the climate, the soil and the art of the vigneron (winemaker).

TROUBLE A-BREWING IN FRANCE'S VINEYARDS

Wine has been the 'totem' drink of France for centuries but, frankly, all is not well in the French wine industry today. At present the nation counts about 8000 sq km of vineyards under cultivation – only 40% of the 2 million hectares under cultivation in 1950. While less *vin de table* (table wine) and *vin de pays* (ordinary wine from a particular village or region) is being produced in favour of more quality wine, overall consumption of wine has dropped by 10% since 1999 and was expected to fall another 7% over the decade to follow as young people continue to reach for multicoloured alcopops and strong lager. At the same time, exports to the US, France's second-biggest wine market after the UK, have fallen steadily for several years due for the most part to the strength of the euro and America's preference for 'bigger', less-complex New World wines, including imports from Australia and New Zealand as well as its own wines.

Some viticulturists have honed their skills and techniques to such a degree that their wine is known as a *grand cru* (literally 'great growth'). If this wine has been produced in a year of optimum climatic conditions it becomes a *millésime* (vintage) wine. *Grands crus* are aged first in small oak barrels and then in bottles, sometimes for 20 years or more, before they develop their full taste and aroma. These are the memorable (and pricey) bottles that wine experts talk about with such passion.

There are dozens of wine-producing regions throughout France, but the seven principal regions are Alsace, Bordeaux, Burgundy, Champagne, Languedoc, the Loire region and the Rhône. With the exception of Alsatian wines, wines in France are generally named after the location of the vineyard rather than the grape varietal.

Appellation d'Origine Contrôlée (AOC; literally, 'label of inspected origin') is bestowed on wines that have met stringent regulations governing where, how and under what conditions they are grown, fermented and bottled. They can cover a wide region, such as Bordeaux, a sub-region such as Haut-Médoc, or a commune or village as in Pomerol. Some wine regions only have a single AOC, such as Alsace, while Burgundy is chopped into scores of individual AOCs. AOC wines are almost always good and usually superb. About a third of all French wine produced carries an AOC guarantee.

La Vie in English (http://lavieinenglish.blogspot.com/) is the enthusiastic food blog of a 'French woman living on the French Riviera and loving America' (go figure); available in French as La Cuisine de Babeth (http://lacuisinedebabeth.blogspot.com).

Alsace

Alsace produces almost exclusively white wines – mostly varieties produced nowhere else in France – that are known for their clean, fresh taste and compatibility with the often heavy local cuisine. Unusually, some of the fruity Alsatian whites also go well with red meat. The vineyards closest to Strasbourg produce light red wines from pinot noir that are similar to rosé and are best served chilled.

Alsace's four most important varietal wines are riesling, known for its subtlety; the more pungent and highly regarded gewürztraminer; the robust pinot gris, which is high in alcohol; and muscat d'Alsace, which is not as sweet as that made with muscat grapes grown further south.

Bordeaux

Britons have had a taste for the full-bodied wines of Bordeaux, known as clarets in the UK, since the mid-12th century when King Henry II, who controlled the region through marriage, tried to gain the favour of the locals by granting them tax-free trade status with England. Thus began a roaring business in wine exporting that continues to this day.

Bordeaux has the perfect climate for producing wine; as a result its 1100 sq km of vineyards produce more fine wine than any other region in the world. Bordeaux reds are often described as well balanced, a quality achieved by blending several grape varieties. The grapes predominantly used are merlot, cabernet sauvignon and cabernet franc. Bordeaux's foremost wine-growing areas are Médoc, Pomerol, Saint Émilion and Graves. The nectar-like sweet whites of the Sauternes area are the world's finest dessert wines.

Burgundy

Burgundy developed its reputation for viticulture during the reign of Charlemagne, when monks first began to make wine here. The vignerons of Burgundy generally only have small vineyards (rarely more than 10 hectares) and produce small quantities of wine. Burgundy reds are produced with pinot noir grapes; the best vintages need 10 to 20 years to age. White wine is made from the chardonnay grape. The five main wine-growing areas are

Chablis, Côte d'Or, Côte Chalonnaise, Mâcon and Beaujolais, which alone produces 13 different types of light gamay-based red wine.

Champagne

Champagne, northeast of Paris, has been the centre for what is arguably France's best-known wine since the 17th century when the innovative monk Dom Pierre Pérignon perfected a technique for making sparkling wine.

Champagne is made from the red pinot noir, the black pinot meunier or the white chardonnay grape. Each vine is vigorously pruned and trained to produce a small quantity of high-quality grapes. Indeed, to maintain exclusivity (and price), the designated areas where grapes used for Champagne can be grown and the amount of wine produced each year is limited. In 2008 the borders that confine the Champagne AOC label were extended to include another 40 villages, increasing the value of their vineyards and its produce by tens of millions of euros (and making party-goers around the world forever grateful). Most Champagne is consumed in France (see the boxed text, p363).

The French Wines website (http://uk.wines-france.com) is as interesting and useful to the cognoscenti as it is to rank novices.

Making Champagne, as carried out by innumerable *maisons* (houses), is a long, complex process. There are two fermentation processes, the first in casks and the second after the wine has been bottled and had sugar and yeast added. The bottles are then aged in cellars for between two and five years (sometimes longer), depending on the *cuvée* (vintage).

During the two months in early spring that the bottles are aged in cellars kept at 12°C, the wine turns effervescent. The sediment that forms in the bottle is removed by *remuage,* a painstakingly slow process in which each bottle – stored horizontally – is rotated slightly every day for weeks until the sludge works its way to the cork. Next comes *dégorgement:* the neck of the bottle is frozen, creating a blob of solidified Champagne and sediment, which is then removed.

If the final product is labelled *brut,* it is extra dry, with only 1.5% sugar content. *Extra-sec* means very dry (but not as dry as *brut*), *sec* is dry and *demi-sec* slightly sweet. The sweetest Champagne is labelled *doux.*

Some of the most famous Champagne houses are Dom Pérignon, Moët & Chandon, Veuve Clicquot, Mercier, Mumm, Krug, Laurent-Perrier, Piper-Heidsieck, Taittinger, De Castellane and Pommery.

Part of the reason the 17th-century monk Dom Pierre Pérignon's technique for making sparkling wine was more successful than earlier efforts was because he put his tipple in strong, English-made glass bottles and capped them with corks brought from Spain.

Languedoc

This is the country's most productive wine-growing region, with up to 40% of France's wine – mainly cheap red table wine – produced here. About 2500 sq km of the region is 'under vine', which represents just over a third of France's total.

About 10% of the wine produced now is AOC standard. In addition to the well-known Fitou label, the area's other quality wines are Coteaux du Languedoc, Faugères, Corbières and Minervois. The region also produces about 70% of France's *vin de pays,* most of which is labelled Vin de Pays d'Oc.

Loire Region

The Loire's 700 sq km of vineyards rank it as the third-largest area in France for the production of quality wines. Although sunny, the climate here is

A GIFT BOX OF BUBBLES

If invited to someone's home or a party in France, you should always bring a gift, but not wine unless it's a bottle of chilled Champagne. The wine your host has chosen will be an expression of his or her tastes and hospitality; Champagne is welcomed and accepted by all.

PHILIPPE FAURE-BRAC: SOMMELIER EXTRAORDINAIRE

The much-decorated Philippe Faure-Brac – he was named Best Sommelier in France in 1988 and Best Sommelier in the World four years later – owns and operates the highly successful **Bistrot du Sommelier** in Paris (p185), produces his own wine label (a Côte du Rhône Villages called Domaine Duseigneur) and has written a half-dozen books on the subject of wine, and wine and food pairing, including *Exquisite Matches* (Éditions EPA, 2005).

Bring me a bottle of... Red from the Rhône – a Châteauneuf-du-Pape, maybe – or a good quality riesling from Alsace.

Is there life beyond French wines? Yes, of course, but understand that my references are French. People are very keen on so-called New World wines and we list bottles from three-dozen different countries on our card, including one from Kent, England (Chapel Down 2006 Bacchus). The best sauvignon outside France is made in New Zealand, shiraz from Australia is especially good and the best malbec is from Argentina.

I'm going to have a glass of red with the chicken and my friend wants white with the lamb. OK with you? The *code de couleur* does not have to be rigid. What you drink is really a matter of taste; at the end of the day a good wine is a good wine. The question you have to ask yourself is: 'What is the dominant characteristic of the food?' Cream sauces can go well with red wine, for example, shellfish with Champagne and certain cheeses (Chaource, Comté) with rosé.

Then what should I have with my Mexican chilli and my (even spicier) Thai tom yam gung? These two cuisines are especially difficult to pair with wines. Try a white or even better a rosé. Avoid reds, particularly complex ones.

About wine whiners... What do you do when someone claims a wine is corked and you know it isn't? We always smell it first, which tells us whether the wine is off. But one can make mistakes, and the customer is always right. Of course we will change it even if we don't believe it is corked.

It's a kind of snobbery, isn't it? It's not easy to stay a wine snob for long. A blind taste test is a great equaliser. Wine snobs don't tend to come here. Instead we get guests who are particularly knowledgeable about wine. If they're not French, they're often Belgian or English.

humid and not all grape varieties thrive. Still, the Loire produces the greatest variety of wines of any region in the country (a particular speciality of the region is rosé). The most common grapes are the muscadet, cabernet franc and chenin blanc varieties. Wines tend to be light and delicate. The most celebrated areas are Pouilly-Fumé, Vouvray, Sancerre, Bourgueil, Chinon and Saumur.

Rhône Region

The Rhône region is divided into northern and southern areas. The different soil, climate, topography and grapes used means there are dramatic differences in the wines produced by each.

Set on steep hills by the river, the northern vineyards produce red wines exclusively from the ruby-red syrah (shiraz) grape; the aromatic viognier grape is the most popular for white wines. The south is better known for quantity rather than quality. The vineyards are also more spread out and interspersed with fields of lavender and orchards of olives, pears and almonds. The grenache grape, which ages well when blended, is used in the reds, while the whites use the ugni blanc grape.

APÉRITIFS & DIGESTIFS

Meals in France are often preceded by an appetite-stirring *apéritif* such as *kir* (white wine sweetened with cassis or blackcurrant syrup), *kir royale* (Champagne with cassis) or *pineau* (cognac and grape juice). Pastis, a 90-proof, anise-flavoured alcoholic drink that turns cloudy when water is added, is especially popular at cafés in the warmer months.

After-dinner drinks are often ordered with coffee. France's most famous brandies are Cognac and Armagnac, both of which are made from grapes in the regions of those names. *Eaux de vie,* literally 'waters of life', can be made with grape skins and the pulp left over after being pressed for wine (Marc de Champagne, Marc de Bourgogne), apples (Calvados) and pears (Poire William), as well as such fruits as plums *(eau de vie de prune)* and even raspberries *(eau de vie de framboise).*

BEER & CIDER

The *bière à la pression* (draught beer) served by the *demi* (about 33cL) in bars and cafés across the land is usually one of the national brands such as Kronenbourg or Heineken-owned Pelforth and totally forgettable. Alsace, with its close cultural ties to Germany, produces some excellent local beers (eg Bière de Scharrach, Schutzenberger Jubilator and Fischer d'Alsace, a hoppy brew from Schiltigheim). Northern France, close to Belgium and the Netherlands, has its own great beers as well, including St-Sylvestre Trois Monts, Terken Brune and the barley-based Grain d'Orge. Castelain brews the Ch'ti beers that played such a prominent role in the hugely successful film *Bienvenue chez les Ch'tis* (Welcome to the Sticks, 2008; see p51).

Cidre (apple cider) is made in many parts of France, including Savoy, Picardy and the Basque Country, but its real home is Normandy and Brittany. You'll also find pear-based *poiré* (perry) here.

General books on the subject of French food are as scarce as hens' teeth in any language, but *Le Grand Atlas des Cuisines de Nos Terroirs* from Éditions Atlas is a beautifully illustrated atlas of regional cooking in France with emphasis on *cuisine campagnarde* (country cooking).

Nonalcoholic Drinks

The most popular nonalcoholic beverages consumed in France are mineral water and coffee.

WATER & MINERAL WATER

All tap water in France is safe to drink, so there is no need to buy pricey bottled water at a restaurant. Just make sure you ask for *une carafe d'eau* (a jug of water). Otherwise you'll most likely get bottled *eau de source* (spring water) or *eau minérale* (mineral water), which comes *plate* (flat or still) like Évian, Vittel and Volvic, or *gazeuse* (fizzy or sparkling) like Badoit and Perrier.

COFFEE

The most ubiquitous form of coffee is espresso, made by a machine that forces steam through ground coffee beans. A small espresso, served without milk, is called *un café noir, un express* or simply *un café.* You can also ask for a *grand* (large) version.

Café crème is espresso with steamed milk or cream. *Café au lait* is lots of hot milk with a little coffee served in a large cup or, sometimes, a bowl. A small *café crème* is a *petit crème.* A *noisette* (literally 'hazelnut') is an espresso with just a dash of milk. Decaffeinated coffee is *café décaféiné.*

TEA & HOT CHOCOLATE

The French have never taken to *thé* (tea) the way the British have, and there's a slightly snobbish, Anglophile association attached to it here. Some people consider it medicinal and drink *thé noir* (black tea) only when they are feeling unwell. Tea is usually served *nature* (plain) or *au citron* (with lemon) and never with milk. *Tisanes* (herbal teas) are widely available.

Chocolat chaud (hot chocolate), available at most cafés, varies greatly and can be excellent or verging on the undrinkable.

SOFT DRINKS & SQUASHES

All the international brands of soft drinks are available in France, as well as many overly sweet, fizzy local ones such as Orangina in its iconic light-bulb-shaped bottle and the lemonade Pschitt.

One popular and inexpensive café drink is *sirop* (fruit syrup or cordial) served *à l'eau* (mixed with water), with soda or with a carbonated mineral water such as Perrier – basically a squash. A *citron pressé* is a glass of iced water (either flat or carbonated) with freshly squeezed lemon juice and sugar.

Chocolate & Zucchini (http://chocolateandzucchini.com) is a food-driven blog with tips, recipes and reviews by a young female foodie named Clotilde from Montmartre in Paris.

CELEBRATIONS

It may sound facile but food itself makes French people celebrate. There are, of course, also birthdays and engagements and weddings and christenings and, like everywhere, special holidays, usually based in religion.

One tradition that is very much alive is *Jour des Rois* (Day of the Kings), which falls on 6 January and marks the feast of the Épiphanie (Epiphany), when the Three Wise Men paid homage to the infant Jesus. Placed in the centre of the table is a *galette des rois* (literally 'kings' cake'; a puff-pastry tart with frangipane cream), which has a little dried bean (or a porcelain figurine) hidden inside and is topped with a gold paper crown. The youngest person in the room goes under the table and calls out which member of the party should get each slice.

The person who gets the bean is named king or queen, dons the crown and chooses his or her consort. This tradition is popular not just among families but also at offices and dinner parties.

At Chandeleur (Candlemas, marking the Feast of the Purification of the Virgin Mary) on 2 February, family and friends gather together in their kitchens to make *crêpes de la Chandeleur* (sweet Candlemas pancakes).

Pâques (Easter) is marked as elsewhere with *œufs au chocolat* (chocolate eggs) – here filled with candy fish and tiny chickens – and there is always an egg hunt for the kids. The traditional meal at Easter lunch is *agneau* (lamb) or *jambon de Pâques* (Easter ham).

After the *dinde aux marrons* (turkey stuffed with chestnuts) eaten at lunch on Noël (Christmas), a *bûche de Noël,* a 'yule log' of chocolate and cream or ice cream, is served.

WHERE TO EAT & DRINK

There's a vast number of eateries in France. Most have defined roles, though some definitions are becoming a bit blurred. On 1 January 2008 France expanded a year-old ban on smoking in public places (schools, hospitals, offices etc) to include *all* bars, night clubs, cafés and restaurants.

Auberge

An *auberge* (inn), which may also appear as an *auberge de campagne* or *auberge du terroir* (country inn), is usually attached to a rural B&B or small hotel and serves traditional country fare. A *ferme-auberge* (literally 'farm-inn') is usually a working farm that serves diners traditional regional dishes made from ingredients produced locally. The food is usually served *table d'hôte* (literally 'host's table'), meaning in set courses with little or no choice.

SEVEN TOP PICKS FOR SEVEN AUTHORS

It wasn't easy and involved a certain amount of gnashing of teeth and rending of garments (not to mention hair-pulling), but the seven authors of *France* have decided on their seven favourite restaurants in France.

- **Bistrot du Sommelier**, Paris (p185) Matchmake food and wine at this delightful Parisian bistro with owner Philippe Faure-Brac, one of the world's foremost sommeliers, on hand to help.
- **La Ribaudière**, Bourg-Charente, near Cognac (p669) Chef Thierry Verrat's gastronomic Michelin-starred palace is set among orchards overlooking the Garonne River.
- **Le Canut et Les Gones**, Lyon (p509) Retro bistro with mustard-yellow facade in Lyon's old silk-weaving quarter of Croix-Rousse. The crowd is hip and the food a creative mix of Lyonnais and French.
- **Le Charlemagne**, Pernand-Vergelesses, near Beaune (p467) With vineyard views, this Japanese-inspired restaurant delightfully melds venerable French traditions with techniques and products from Japan.
- **Mantel**, Cannes (p882) Sensational cuisine and knock-out desserts; eat like a king and spend like a pauper in glamorous Cannes.
- **Le Présidial**, Sarlat-le-Canéda (p628) Wonderful courtyard restaurant in the heart of medieval Sarlat serves up all the classics of Dordogne's cuisine.
- **Tamarillos**, Montpellier (p773) Fruit and flowers play key roles both on and off the plate at this lovely eatery lorded over by chef Philippe Chapon, the 'double champion de France de dessert'.

Bar

A bar or *bar américain* (cocktail bar) is an establishment dedicated to elbow-bending and rarely serves food. A *bar à vins* is a 'wine bar', which often serves full meals at lunch and dinner. A *bar à huîtres* is an 'oyster bar'.

Bistro

A bistro (also spelled *bistrot*) is not clearly defined in France nowadays. It can be simply a pub or bar with snacks and light meals or a fully fledged restaurant.

Brasserie

Unlike the vast majority of restaurants in France, brasseries – which can look very much like cafés – serve full meals, drinks and coffee from morning till 11pm or even later. The dishes served almost always include *choucroute* (sauerkraut) and sausages because the brasserie, which actually means 'brewery' in French, originated in Alsace.

Buffet

A buffet (or *buvette*) is a kiosk, usually found at train stations and airports, selling drinks, filled baguettes and snacks.

Café

The main focus of a café is, of course, *café* (coffee) and only basic food is available at most. Common options include a baguette filled with Camembert or pâté and *cornichons* (gherkins), a *croque-monsieur* (grilled ham and toasted cheese sandwich) or a *croque-madame* (a toasted cheese sandwich topped with a fried egg).

Cafétéria

Many cities in France have *cafétérias* (self-service restaurants), including Flunch, that offer a decent selection of dishes you can see before ordering – a factor that can make life easier if you're travelling with kids.

Crêperie

Crêperies (sometimes known as *galetteries*) specialise in sweet crêpes and savoury galettes.

Relais Routier

A *relais routier* is a transport café or truckstop, usually found on the outskirts of towns and along major roads, which caters to truck drivers and can provide a quick, hearty break from cross-country driving.

The restaurant as we know it today was born in Paris in 1765 when a certain Monsieur A Boulanger opened a small business in rue Bailleuil in the 1er, selling soups, broths and other *restaurants* ('restoratives').

Restaurant

Restaurants come in many guises and price ranges. Generally restaurants specialise in a particular variety of food (eg regional, traditional, North African). There are lots of restaurants where you can get an excellent French meal for under €30; Michelin's *Guide Rouge* is filled with them. Chain restaurants (eg Hippopotamus and Léon de Bruxelles) are a definite step up from fast-food places and usually offer good-value (though formulaic) *menus.*

Almost all restaurants close for at least one and a half days (ie a full day and either one lunch or one dinner) each week, and this schedule will be posted on the front door. Chain restaurants are usually open throughout the day, seven days a week.

Restaurants almost always have a *carte* (menu) posted outside so you can decide before going in whether the selection and prices are to your liking. Most offer at least one fixed-price, multicourse meal known as a *menu, menu à prix fixe* or *menu du jour* (daily menu). A *menu* 'set menu' (not to be confused with a *carte* 'menu') almost always costs much less than ordering à la carte.

When you order a *menu,* you usually get to choose an entrée, such as salad, pâté or soup; a main dish (several meat, poultry or fish dishes, including the *plat du jour* 'daily special', are generally on offer); and a final course (usually cheese or dessert). In some places, you may also be able to order a *formule,* which usually has fewer choices but allows you to pick two of three courses – a starter and a main course or a main course and a dessert.

Boissons (drinks), including wine, cost extra unless the *menu* says *boisson comprise* (drink included), in which case you may get a beer or a glass of mineral water. If the *menu* has *vin compris* (wine included), you'll probably be served a 25cL *pichet* (jug) of wine. The waiter will always ask if you would like coffee to end the meal, but this will almost always cost extra.

Salon de Thé

A *salon de thé* (tearoom) is a trendy and somewhat pricey establishment that usually offers quiches, salads, cakes, tarts, pies and pastries in addition to black and herbal teas.

VEGETARIANS & VEGANS

Vegetarians and vegans make up a small minority in a country where the original meaning of the word *viande* (meat) was 'food'. As a result, vegetarian restaurants are few and far between, even in Paris. On the bright side, more and more restaurants are offering vegetarian choices on their *menus* (set menus), and *produits biologiques* (organic products) are all the rage nowadays, even among carnivores.

Strict vegetarians should be aware that most French cheeses are made with rennet, an enzyme derived from the stomach of a calf or young goat, and that some red wines (especially Bordeaux) are clarified with the albumin of egg whites.

EATING WITH KIDS

Few restaurants in France have high chairs, children's menus or even children's portions, though a few offer a *menu enfant* (children's set menu) to children under 12. This may explain the popularity of American-style fast-food restaurants, *cafétérias* and French chain restaurants, which cater to parents with kids in tow.

HABITS & CUSTOMS

When the French Eat

BREAKFAST

What the French call *petit déjeuner* is not every foreigner's cup of tea. Masters of the kitchen throughout the rest of the day, French chefs don't seem up to it in the morning. Perhaps the idea is not to fill up – *petit déjeuner* means 'little lunch' and the real *déjeuner* (lunch) is just around the corner!

In the Continental style, people traditionally start the day with a bread roll or a bit of baguette left over from the night before, eaten with butter and jam and followed by a *café au lait,* an espresso or even a hot chocolate. Some people now eat cereal, toast, fruit and even yoghurt in the morning – something they never did before.

Contrary to what many foreigners think, the French do not eat croissants every day but usually reserve these for a treat at the weekend when they may also choose brioches (small roll), *pains au chocolat* (chocolate-filled brioche) or other *viennoiserie* (baked goods).

LUNCH & DINNER

Many French people still consider *déjeuner* (lunch) to be the main meal of the day. But as the pace of life is as hectic here as elsewhere in the industrialised world, the two-hour midday meal has become increasingly rare, at least on weekdays. Dinners, however, are still turned into elaborate affairs whenever time and finances permit. A fully fledged, traditional French meal at home is an awesome event, often comprising six distinct *plats* (courses). Each *plat* is served with wine – red, white or rosé – depending on what you're eating. A meal in a restaurant almost never consists of more than three or four courses: the *entrée* (starter or first course), the *plat principal* (main course), *dessert* and perhaps *fromage* (cheese).

TIPS ON TIPPING

French law requires that restaurant and café bills include a service charge, which is usually between 12% and 15%. But a word of warning is in order. *Service compris* (service included, sometimes abbreviated as 'sc' at the bottom of the bill) means that the service charge is built into the price of each dish; *service non-compris* (service not included) or *service en sus* (service in addition) means that the service charge is calculated after the food and/or drink you've consumed has been added up. In either case you pay *only* the total of the bill so a *pourboire* (tip) on top of that is neither necessary nor expected in most cases. However, many French people will leave a few coins on the table in a restaurant, unless the service was particularly bad. They rarely tip in cafés and bars when they've just had coffee or a drink.

EATING ON THE THUMB

Though the French may snack or eat between meals, they do not seem to go in for street food eaten, as they say here, *sur le pouce* (literally 'on the thumb', meaning 'on the run'). Hot-dog stands and noodle carts are nowhere to be seen and eating in public is considered somewhat Anglo-Saxon (English or American) and thus rude. You may encounter a crêpe-maker on a street corner or someone selling roasted *marrons* (chestnuts) in autumn and winter, but generally people will duck into a café for *un truc à grignoter* (something to nibble on) or a pâtisserie for a slice of something sweet.

Self-Catering

Most French people buy a good part of their food from a series of small neighbourhood shops, each with its own speciality (though people are relying more and more on supermarkets and hypermarkets these days). At first, having to go to four shops and stand in four queues to fill the fridge (or assemble a picnic) may seem a waste of time, but the ritual is an important part of French people's daily lives. And as each *commerçant* (shopkeeper) specialises in purveying only one type of food, he or she can almost always provide all sorts of useful tips: which round of Camembert is ripe, which wine will complement a certain food, which type of pot to cook rabbit in and so on. In any case, most products for sale at *charcuteries* (delicatessens), pâtisseries and *traiteurs* 'caterers' or *charcuteries-traiteurs* (delicatessen-caterers) are clearly marked and labelled.

As these stores are geared to people buying small quantities of fresh food each day, it's perfectly acceptable to purchase only meal-size amounts: a few *tranches* (slices) of meat to make a sandwich, perhaps, or a *petit bout* (small hunk) of sausage. You can also request just enough for *une/deux personne(s)* (one/two persons). If you want a bit more, ask for *encore un petit peu,* and if you are being given too much, say *'C'est trop'*.

Fresh bread is baked and sold at *boulangeries;* mouth-watering pastries are available at pâtisseries; a *fromagerie* can supply you with cheese that is *fait* (ripe) to the exact degree that you request; a *charcuterie* offers sliced meat, pâtés and so on; and fresh fruit and vegetables are sold at *épiceries* (greengrocers), supermarkets and open-air markets.

A website that will answer all your questions (and more) about France's 500 different cheeses is All About French Cheeses (www.frencheese.co.uk).

A *boucherie* is a general butcher, but for specialised poultry you have to go to a *marchand de volaille.* A *boucherie chevaline,* easily identifiable by the gilded horse's head above the entrance, sells horse meat, which some people prefer to beef or mutton. Fresh fish and seafood are available from a *poissonnerie.*

Food markets *(marchés alimentaires)* – both open-air street ones *(marchés découverts)* and covered markets *(marchés couverts)* – are a part of life in France.

COOKING COURSES

What better place to discover the secrets of *la cuisine française* than in front of a stove? Cooking courses are available at different levels and lengths of time and the cost of tuition varies widely. In Paris one of the most popular – and affordable – for beginners is the **Cours de Cuisine Olivier Berté** (Map pp120-1; ☎ 01 40 26 14 00; www.coursdecuisineparis.com; 2nd fl, 7 rue Paul Lelong, 2e; Ⓜ Bourse; 3hr course adult/12-14 yr €100/30), which offers three-hour courses at 10.30am from Wednesday to Saturday with an additional class from 6pm to 9pm on Friday. *Carnets* of five/20 courses cost €440/1500.

Much more expensive are the **Paris Cooking Classes with Patricia Wells** (www.patriciawells.com; US$5000) led by the incomparable American food critic and author at her cooking studio in rue Jacob, 6e. The class runs from Monday to Friday, is limited to seven participants and includes market visits, tastings, local transport and daily lunch.

Other cooking schools in Paris include the following:

École Le Cordon Bleu (Map pp124-5; ☎ 01 53 68 22 50; www.cordonbleu.edu; 8 rue Léon Delhomme, 15e; Ⓜ Vaugirard or Convention) Dating back to 1895, the Cordon Bleu school has professional courses as well as one-day themed workshops (€160) on topics like terrines and *viennoiserie* (baked goods), and two- (€299) and four-day courses (€869) on classic and modern sauces and the secrets of bread and pastry making.

École Ritz Escoffier (Map pp118-19; ☎ 01 43 16 30 50; www.ritzescoffier.com; 38 rue Cambon, 1er; Ⓜ Concorde) This prestigious cooking school is based in what is arguably Paris's finest hotel, the Hôtel Ritz Paris (the cooking school's entrance is at the back of the hotel). A four-hour themed workshop (petits fours, truffles, carving fruit and vegetables, pairing food and wine etc) costs €135; a two-day introductory course is €920.

There are a number of regional cooking schools and courses available around France:

Cook In France (☎ 05 53 30 24 05; www.cookinfrance.com; St-Amand de Coly, near Sarlat) Residential cookery courses near Sarlat, run by ex-Masterchef contestant and Rick Stein protégé, Jim Fisher.

Le Bec (p510) Two-hour hands-on cooking sessions (€60) in Lyon with one of France's most creative young chefs, Nicolas Le Bec; advance bookings essential.

Le Marmiton (p842) Learn cooking from famous visiting chefs in a stunning 19th-century château kitchen in Avignon.

Le Viscos (p720) Two- to three-hour cooking classes in English and French (€60) on offer by chef Jean-Pierre St-Martin at a delightful (and remote) hotel-restaurant in Argelès-Gazost, near Lourdes.

Walnut Grove (☎ 02 43 98 50 02; www.walnutgrovecookery.com; Le Hunaudière, Livré-la-Touche, near Rennes) Much-recommended live-in cookery school in the rural Loire Valley, offering a choice of five-day courses.

Our heroine and food guru is Patricia Wells (www.patriciawells.com), France-based writer, teacher (opposite) and author of *The Food Lover's Guide to France*.

EAT YOUR WORDS

For pronunciation guidelines see p981.

Useful Phrases

I'm hungry/thirsty.
J'ai faim/soif. zhay fum/swaf

A table for two, please.
Une table pour deux, s'il vous plaît. ewn ta·bler poor der seel voo play

Do you have a menu in English?
Est-ce que vous avez la carte en anglais? es·ker voo za·vay la kart on ong·glay

What's the speciality of this region?
Quelle est la spécialité de la région? kel ay la spay·sya·lee·tay de la ray·zhon

What is today's special?
Quel est le plat du jour? kel ay ler pla doo zhoor

I'd like the set menu, please.
Je prends le menu, s'il vous plaît. zher pron ler mer·new seel voo play

I'd like some…
Je voudrais du/de la… zher voo·dray doo/de la…

May I have another…please?
Puis-je avoir encore un/une… s'il vous plaît? pwee zher a·vwa ong·kor un/oon… seel voo play

I'm a vegetarian.
Je suis végétarien/végétarienne. (m/f) zher swee vay·zhay·ta·ryun/vay·zhay·ta·ryen

I don't eat (meat).
Je ne mange pas de (viande). zher ne monzh pa de (vyond)

Is service included?
Le service est compris? ler sair·vees ay kom·pree

The bill, please.
L'addition, s'il vous plaît. la·dee·syon seel voo play

Menu Decoder

STARTERS (APPETISERS)

assiette anglaise	a·syet ong·glayz	plate of cold mixed meats and sausages
assiette de crudités	a·syet der krew·dee·tay	plate of raw vegetables with dressings
soufflé	soof·lay	a light, fluffy dish of egg yolks, stiffly beaten egg whites, flour and cheese and other ingredients

SOUP

bouillabaisse	bwee·ya·bes	Mediterranean-style fish soup, originally from Marseille, made with several kinds of fish, including *rascasse* (spiny scorpion fish); often eaten as a main course
bouillon	boo·yon	broth or stock
bourride	boo·reed	fish stew; often eaten as a main course
potage	po·tazh	thick soup made with puréed vegetables
soupe au pistou	soop o pee·stoo	vegetable soup made with a basil and garlic paste
soupe de poisson	soop der pwa·son	fish soup
soupe du jour	soop dew zhoor	soup of the day

MEAT & POULTRY

aiguillette	ay·gwee·yet	thin slice of duck fillet
andouille or **andouillette**	on·doo·yer/ on·doo·yet	sausage made from pork or veal tripe
bifteck	bif·tek	steak
bleu	bler	nearly raw
saignant	sen·yon	very rare (literally 'bleeding')
à point	a pwun	medium rare but still pink
bien cuit	byun kwee	literally 'well cooked', but usually more like medium rare
blanquette de veau	blong·ket der vo	veal stew with white sauce
bœuf bourguignon	berf boor·geen·yon	beef and vegetable stew cooked in red wine
bœuf haché	berf ha·shay	minced beef
boudin noir	boo·dun nwar	blood sausage (black pudding)
brochette	bro·shet	kebab
canard	ka·nar	duck
caneton	ka·ne·ton	duckling
cassoulet	ka·soo·lay	Languedoc stew made with goose, duck, pork or lamb fillets and haricot beans
charcuterie	shar·kew·tree	cooked or prepared meats (usually pork)
chevreuil	sher·vrer·yer	venison
choucroute	shoo·kroot	sauerkraut, usually served with sausage and other prepared meats
civet	see·vay	game stew
confit de canard/ d'oie	kon·fee der ka·nar/ dwa	duck/ goose preserved and cooked in its own fat
coq au vin	kok o vun	chicken cooked in wine
côte	kot	chop of pork, lamb or mutton
côtelette	kot·let	cutlet
cuisses de grenouille	kwees der grer·noo·yer	frogs' legs
entrecôte	on·trer·kot	rib steak
escargot	es·kar·go	snail
faisan	fer·zon	pheasant
faux-filet	fo fee·lay	sirloin steak

filet	fee·lay	tenderloin
foie	fwa	liver
foie gras de canard	fwa gra der ka·nar	duck liver pâté
fricassée	free·ka·say	stew with meat that has first been fried
gibier	zheeb·yay	game
gigot d'agneau	zhee·go da·nyo	leg of lamb
grillade	gree·yad	grilled meats
jambon	zhom·bon	ham
langue	long	tongue
lapin	la·pun	rabbit
lard	lar	bacon
lardons	lar·don	pieces of chopped bacon
lièvre	lye·vrer	hare
mouton	moo·ton	mutton
oie	wa	goose
pieds de cochon/ porc	pyay der ko·shon/ por	pigs' trotters
pintade	pun·tad	guinea fowl
quenelles	ker·nel	dumplings made of a finely sieved mixture of cooked fish or (rarely) meat
rillettes	ree·yet	coarsely shredded potted meat (usually pork)
rognons	ron·yon	kidneys
sanglier	song·glee·yay	wild boar
saucisson	so·see·son	large sausage
saucisson fumé	so·see·son few·may	smoked sausage
steak	stek	steak
steak tartare	stek tar·tar	raw ground meat mixed with onion, raw egg yolk and herbs
tournedos	toor·ner·do	thick slices of beef fillet
volaille	vo·lai	poultry

FISH & SEAFOOD

anchois	on·shwa	anchovy
anguille	ong·gee·yer	eel
brochet	bro·shay	pike
cabillaud	ka·bee·yo	cod
calmar	kal·mar	squid
chaudrée	sho·dray	fish stew
coquille St-Jacques	ko·kee·yer sun·zhak	scallop
crabe	krab	crab
crevette grise	krer·vet greez	shrimp
crevette rose	krer·vet roz	prawn
écrevisse	ay·krer·vees	freshwater crayfish
fruits de mer	frwee der mair	seafood
hareng	a·rung	herring
homard	o·mar	lobster
huître	wee·trer	oyster
langouste	long·goost	crayfish
langoustine	long·goo steen	very small saltwater 'lobster' (Dublin Bay prawn)
maquereau	ma·kro	mackerel
merlan	mair·lan	whiting
morue	mo·rew	cod
moules	mool	mussels
palourde	pa·loord	clam

rouget	roo·zhay	mullet
sardine	sar·deen	sardine
saumon	so·mon	salmon
thon	ton	tuna
truite	trweet	trout

COOKING METHODS, SAUCES & CONDIMENTS

à la provençale	pro·von·sal	with tomato, garlic, herb and olive oil dressing or sauce
à la vapeur	a la va·per	steamed
aïoli	ay·o·lee	garlic mayonnaise
au feu de bois	o fer der bwa	cooked over a wood-burning stove
au four	o foor	baked
béchamel	bay·sha·mel	basic white sauce
en croûte	on kroot	in pastry
farci	far·see	stuffed
fumé	few·may	smoked
gratiné	gra·tee·nay	browned on top with cheese
grillé	gree·yay	grilled
huile d'olive	weel do·leev	olive oil
moutarde	moo·tard	mustard
pané	pa·nay	coated in breadcrumbs
pistou	pee·stoo	pesto (pounded mix of basil, hard cheese, olive oil and garlic)
rôti	ro·tee	roasted
sauté	so·tay	sautéed (shallow fried)
tartare	tar·tar	mayonnaise with herbs
vinaigrette	vee·nay·gret	salad dressing made with oil, vinegar, mustard and garlic

DESSERTS & SWEETS

crêpes suzettes	krep sew·zet	orange-flavoured pancakes flambéed in liqueur
dragées	dra·gay	sugared almonds
éclair	ay·klair	pastry filled with cream
flan	flon	egg-custard dessert
frangipane	fron·zhee·pun	pastry filled with cream and flavoured with almonds
gâteau	ga·to	cake
gaufre	go·frer	waffle
glace	glas	ice cream
île flottante	eel flo·tont	literally 'floating island'; beaten egg white lightly cooked, floating on a creamy sauce
macaron	ma·ka·ron	macaroon (sweet biscuit of ground almonds, sugar and egg whites)
sablé	sa·blay	shortbread biscuit
tarte (aux pommes)	tart (o pom)	(apple) tart or pie
yaourt	ya·oort	yogurt

SNACKS

croque-madame	krok·ma·dam	*croque-monsieur* with a fried egg
croque-monsieur	krok·mer·syer	grilled ham and cheese sandwich
frites	freet	chips (French fries)
quiche	keesh	quiche
tartine	tar·teen	open sandwich

Food Glossary

BASICS

breakfast	per·tee day·zher·nay	*petit déjeuner*
lunch	day·zher·nay	*déjeuner*
dinner	dee·nay	*dîner*
food	noo·ree·tewr	*nourriture*
menu	kart	*carte*
set menu	mer·new/for·mewl	*menu/formule*
starter/appetiser	on·tray	*entrée*
main course	pla prun·see·pal	*plat principal*
wine list	kart day vun	*carte des vins*
waiter/waitress	sair·ver/sair·verz	*serveur/serveuse*
delicatessen	tray·ter	*traiteur*
grocery store	ay·pee·sree	*épicerie*
market	mar·shay	*marché*
fork	foor·shet	*fourchette*
knife	koo·to	*couteau*
spoon	kwee·yair	*cuillère*
bottle	boo·tay	*bouteille*
glass	vair	*verre*
plate/dish	pla/a·syet	*plat/assiette*
hot/cold	sho/frwa	*chaud/froid*
with/without	a·vek/son	*avec/sans*

MEAT & FISH

beef	berf	*bœuf*
chicken	poo·lay	*poulet*
fish	pwa·son	*poisson*
lamb	a·nyo	*agneau*
meat	vyond	*viande*
pork	por	*porc*
turkey	dund	*dinde*
veal	vo	*veau*

FRUIT & VEGETABLES

apple	pom	*pomme*
apricot	ab·ree·ko	*abricot*
artichoke	ar·tee·sho	*artichaut*
asparagus	a·spairzh	*asperge*
banana	ba·nan	*banane*
beans	a·ree·ko	*haricots*
beetroot	be·trav	*betterave*
bilberry (blueberry)	meer·tee·yer	*myrtille*
blackcurrant	ka·sees	*cassis*
cabbage	shoo	*chou*
carrot	ka·rot	*carotte*
celery	sel·ree	*céleri*
porcini (Boletus) mushroom	sep	*cèpe*
cherry	ser·reez	*cerise*
cucumber	kong·kom·brer	*concombre*
French (string) beans	a·ree·ko vair	*haricots verts*
gherkin (pickle)	kor·nee·shon	*cornichon*
grape	ray·zun	*raisin*

grapefruit	pom·pler·moos	*pamplemousse*
leek	pwa·ro	*poireau*
lemon	see·tron	*citron*
lentils	lon·tee·yer	*lentilles*
lettuce	lay·tew	*laitue*
mushroom	shom·pee·nyon	*champignon*
onion	on·yon	*oignon*
peach	pesh	*pêche*
peas	per·tee pwa	*petit pois*
pepper (red/green)	pwa·vron (roozh/vair)	*poivron (rouge/vert)*
pineapple	a·na·nas	*ananas*
plum	prewn	*prune*
potato	pom der tair	*pomme de terre*
prune	prew·no	*pruneau*
pumpkin	see·troo·yer	*citrouille*
raspberry	from·bwaz	*framboise*
rice	ree	*riz*
shallot	eh·sha·lot	*échalote*
spinach	eh·pee·nar	*épinards*
strawberry	frez	*fraise*
sweet corn	ma·ees	*maïs*
tomato	to·mat	*tomate*
turnip	na·vay	*navet*
vegetable	lay·gewm	*légume*

OTHER

bread	pun	*pain*
butter	ber	*beurre*
cheese	fro·mazh	*fromage*
cream	krem	*crème*
egg	erf	*œuf*
honey	myel	*miel*
jam	kon·fee·tewr	*confiture*
oil	weel	*huile*
pepper	pwa·vrer	*poivre*
salt	sel	*sel*
sugar	sew·krer	*sucre*
vinegar	vee·nay·grer	*vinaigre*

DRINKS

beer	bee·yair	*bière*
coffee	ka·fay	*café*
with milk	o lay	*au lait*
with sugar	a·vek sew·krer	*avec sucre*
juice (apple)	zhew (der pom)	*jus (de pomme)*
juice (orange)	zhew (do·ronzh)	*jus (d'orange)*
milk	lay	*lait*
mineral water	o mee·nay·ral	*eau minérale*
tea	tay	*thé*
water	o	*eau*
wine (red)	vun (roozh)	*vin (rouge)*
wine (white)	vun (blong)	*vin (blanc)*

VIVE LA FRANCE!

Be it mooching vineyard to vineyard in a sky-blue Citroën 2CV, pedalling between lavender on an à la mode road racer or taking it all in with traditional walking stick in hand, France is a land of long languid moments spiced with stacks of soul, a zesty spirit, fabulous cuisine and more culture than you could ever hope to absorb in a lifetime. Enjoy.

1

Art & Architecture

With its designer chapels, prehistoric caves and iconic architecture, France is a living art museum. Done and dusted with the capital's extraordinary portfolio of collections, pick a painter to track – Matisse (p867) and Picasso on the Côte d'Azur, Renoir and Monet (p278) in Normandy, the fauvists (p801) in Roussillon…

2

Author tip

For art and architecture lovers who've seen it, done it, the Journées du Patrimoine in September is the time to be around. Countrywide, hundreds of rare and precious treasures, usually closed to visitors, open their doors to voyeurs.

❶ Loire Valley Châteaux

Studded with sky-topping turrets, glittering banquet halls, lavish chapels and crenulated battlements, the hundreds of châteaux, such as Château de Chambord (p429, pictured), littering the Loire Valley paint a compelling history of French high society architecture.

❷ Musée d'Orsay & Musée du Quai Branly

An incomparable collection of Impressionist and post-Impressionist art fills this old Parisian train station, aka the Musée d'Orsay (p151, pictured); stroll afterwards along the waterfront to Jean Nouvel's cutting-edge creation of glass, wood and turf, Musée du Quai Branly (p153), stuffed to the gills with Asian, African and Oceanic art.

❸ Ste-Chapelle

Be stunned and inspired by sublime stained glass which, on sunny days in Paris, bathes this Gothic chapel (p146) – one of Christendom's most beautiful houses of worship – in the most extraordinary of coloured lights.

❹ Abbaye du Mont St-Michel

Rising from flat white sands atop a tiny island, this sea-splashed abbey (p303) and its tidebound bay in northern France are priceless. Illuminated night-time visits to the enchanting sound of music are really quite magical.

❺ Chapelle du Rosaire

Mediterranean sunlight makes stark white walls glow in this bijou 1950s chapel (p867) in Vence, designed inside and out by Matisse. Soak up more 20th-century art next door at the Fondation Maeght (p877) in St-Paul de Vence.

❼ Vézère Valley

Admire a menagerie of mammoths, aurochs etc painted in technicolour red, brown, yellow and black by Cro-Magnon man in the spectacular collection of prehistoric art – Europe's highest concentration of Stone Age art – in the Vézère Valley (p630).

❻ Pont de Millau

Propped up by just seven hollow needlelike pylons, Sir Norman Foster's toll bridge (p792) is a 21st-century icon. Find it slung across the wide Tarn Valley in the wild Grands Causses.

Outdoor Action

Be it kitesurfing on the French Riviera, riding the surf on the Atlantic or rocketing à la surf down slopes in the Alps or Pyrenees, France is one big outdoor playground. It's got mountains, it's got lakes, it's got emerald-green gorges and turquoise-blue coastline – all crying out to be tried and tested.

'So many mythical names, so many expectations, and not a hint of flagging: the Alps' pulling power has never been so strong'

2

❶ Îles Lavezzi

Immerse yourself into one of the most dramatic, diverse and downright gorgeous islands in the Mediterranean with a spot of diving in gin-clear waters off the wild, uninhabited Îles Lavezzi (p934) in Corsica.

❷ Chamonix

The absolute mecca of mountaineering and dream of every hard-core Alpinist, Chamonix (p527) enthrals with its mythical mix of Alpine skiing, off-piste Vallée Blanche and – for armchair action fiends – its heart-stopping Mont Blanc cable car across snow fields into Italy.

❸ Massif Central

This naturally splendid region is paradise for those who like their landscapes rude and raw: tackle Chaîne des Puys hiking trails (p595), ski the slopes of Puy de Sancy (p594) or hurl yourself (aka paraglide) off the icy summit of Puy de Dôme (p592).

❹ Gorges du Verdon

These spectacular gorges with their 800m sheer-drop cliffs and near-fluorescent water set the scene for northern Provence's unspoilt wilderness, a divine mix of Alpine peaks, exceptional sunshine and lingering Provençal flavours – climb, kayak or canyon them (p854).

❺ Anglet

Hit the golden sands of Anglet Beach (p694) in glitzy glam Biarritz for a serious overdose of adrenalin: the waves here are first-class and lure the world's most intrepid surfers.

❻ Vallée d'Ossau

Don your boots in the central Pyrenees and stagger up this pastoral valley (p725) to shimmering lakes and tarns fed by swift mountain streams; watch griffon vultures nest, hatch, feed and soar in the skies.

'The landmark that's more Parisian than Paris itself'

French Icons

Never has there been a country as cancan-fabled, fabulous or sexy as France. Bursting at its baguette-encrusted seams with *oh là là* sights and experiences, this is the land of Eiffel Tower romance, Chanel-chic fashion, architecture of regal proportions and a kitchen table overflowing with world-class food and wine.

1

❶ Eiffel Tower
Do it at least once. For an alternative take on one of the world's most visited monuments, view it below from the saddle of a bicycle (p201), at dark on the hour when it flashes gold or over lunch at the rooftop restaurant of the Musée du Quai Branly (p153).

❷ Boules
Despite its quintessential image of a bunch of old men throwing balls on a dusty patch of gravel beneath plane trees, France's national pastime is a serious sport. Spin with the stars on place des Lices in St-Tropez (p887).

❸ Le Café
Be it over *un café* or sundown *apéro,* whiling away inordinate amounts of time on pavement terraces is a French charm. Café culture is exceptionally vibrant in Lyon (p513) Toulouse (p744), Nantes (p656), Aix-en-Provence (p824) and, of course, Paris (p188).

❹ Champagne
The full-bodied experience: sip bubbly between bites of *biscuits roses* during an Épernay cellar tour (p363), inhale 360-degree views of France's flattest province in Reims from the Cathédrale Notre Dame (p357) and cruise through rolling vineyards by pedal-power.

❺ French Fashion
No one wears berets these days. Catch the *haute couture* trend of the moment with Chanel, Dior, Yves St-Laurent and other iconic designers of the 20th-century in Paris' Triangle d'Or and the hottest in shabby chic at the Marais boutiques (p196).

❻ Markets
Truffles, foie gras, honey, herbs, garlic, olives, dozens of bread types, stinky cheese, organic veg, briny oysters – shop for it all at the market. Every French village, town and city has at least one.

Festivals

France's rich pageant of fun-packed *foires* (fairs) and *fêtes* (festivals) celebrate everything from historic and folkloric tradition to performing arts, a patron saint, seasonal harvest, and one of the country's most impassioned and delicious pastimes, food and wine. Every day is a party somewhere, so go celebrate!

Author tip

No festivals better express the merrymaking spontaneity of the French soul than nationwide dates such as the Fête de la Musique (p950) and Bastille Day (p950) when the entire country explodes in a riot of street parties.

1 Cannes Film Festival

No festival gets camera flashes popping more than this international film festival (p880) in May which sees film stars pose in evening frocks on the red carpet of legendary La Croisette in glitzy glam Cannes.

2 Carnaval de Nice

Nowhere is Mardi Gras celebrated with more gusto and panache than in Nice, the Riviera queen who goes street-mad for two weeks in February with flower battles, floats and phenomenal fireworks (p869).

3 Paris Plages

Don your designer shades and flop on the golden sandbanks of the Seine for a summertime dose of urban beach fun. Sun beds, palm trees, beach umbrellas, atomisers, this is one of Europe's most unique events (p164).

4 Braderie de Lille

Billed as the world's biggest flea market, Lille's September extravaganza is a magnificent riot of street stalls, *moules-frites* (mussels and fries) *menus* to munch and mussel-shell mountains to marvel at (p231)

Environment

THE LAND

Hexagon-shaped France, the largest country in Europe after Russia and the Ukraine, is encircled by water or mountains along every side except in the north-east, where a relatively flat area abuts Germany, Luxembourg and Belgium.

The country's 3200km-long coastline is incredibly diverse, ranging from white chalk cliffs (Normandy) and treacherous promontories (Brittany) to broad expanses of fine sand (Atlantic Coast) and pebbly beaches (Mediterranean Coast).

Europe's highest peak, Mont Blanc (4807m), spectacularly crowns the French Alps, which stagger along France's eastern border. North of Lake Geneva, the gentle limestone Jura Range runs along the Swiss frontier to reach heights of around 1700m, while the rugged Pyrenees define France's 450km-long border with Spain and Andorra, peaking at 3404m.

Stunning as they are, the Alps, the Jura and the Pyrenees are mere babies compared to France's ancient massifs, formed 225 to 345 million years ago. The Massif Central covers one-sixth (91,000 sq km) of the country and is renowned for its chain of extinct volcanoes: Puy de Dôme (1465m) last erupted in 5760 BC, and its geology is the focus of the Vulcania centre near Clermont-Ferrand (p592). Other golden oldies, worn down by time, include the forested upland of the Vosges, between Alsace and Lorraine; the Ardennes, on Champagne's northern edge; and Brittany and Normandy's backbone, the Massif Armoricain.

Five major river systems criss-cross the country: the Garonne (which includes the Tarn, the Lot and the Dordogne) empties into the Atlantic; the Rhône links Lake Geneva and the Alps with the Mediterranean; Paris is licked by the Seine, which slithers through the city en route from Burgundy to the English Channel; and tributaries of the North Sea–bound Rhine drain much of the area north and east of the capital. Then there's France's longest river, the château-studded Loire, which meanders from the Massif Central to the Atlantic.

Some quite miraculous footage of the natural world close-up is screened during the Festival International du Film Nature et Environnement (International Nature & Environment Film Festival; http://frapna.webcastor.fr/isere, in French), held each May in Grenoble.

The Shaping of Environmental Policy in France by Joseph Szarka is a 224-page heavyweight analysis of precisely what its title suggests.

WILDLIFE

France is blessed with a rich variety of flora and fauna, although few habitats have escaped human-induced impacts: intensive agriculture, wetland draining, urbanisation, hunting and the encroachment of industry and tourism infrastructure menace dozens of species.

RESPONSIBLE TRAVEL

Follow common decency in nature reserves and national parks:

- Pack up your litter and carry it out with you.
- Minimise waste by taking minimal packaging and no more food than you need.
- Don't use detergents or toothpaste, even if they are biodegradable, in or near watercourses.
- Stick to designated paths in protected areas, particularly in sensitive alpine areas and on coastal dunes where flora and fauna may be damaged if you stray.
- When camping in the wild (check first with the landowners or a park ranger to see if it's allowed), bury human waste in cat holes at least 15cm deep and at least 100m from any watercourse.
- Obey the 'no dogs, tents and motorised vehicles' rule in national parks.

Animals

France has more mammals (around 110) than any other country in Europe. Couple this with its 363 bird species, 30 types of amphibian, 36 varieties of reptile and 72 kinds of fish, and wildlife-watchers are in paradise. Of France's 39,000 identified insect species, 10,000 creep and crawl in the Parc National du Mercantour (p106) in the Alps.

Follow the progress of France's precious wolf, bear and lynx populations with FERUS, France's conservation group for the wellbeing of these protected predators, online at www.ours-loup-lynx.info, in French.

High-altitude plains in the Alps and the Pyrenees shelter the marmot, which hibernates from October to April and has a shrill and distinctive whistle; the nimble chamois (mountain antelope), with its dark-striped head; and the *bouquetin* (Alpine ibex; see opposite), which can be seen in large numbers in the Parc National de la Vanoise (p555). Mouflons (wild mountain sheep), introduced in the 1950s, clamber over stony sunlit scree slopes in the mountains; red and roe deer and wild boar are common in lower-altitude forested areas. The Alpine hare welcomes winter with its white coat, while 19 of Europe's 29 bat species hang out in the dark in the alpine national parks.

The *loup* (wolf), which disappeared from France in the 1930s, returned to the Parc National du Mercantour in 1992 – much to the horror of the mouflon (on which it preys) and local sheep farmers. Dogs, corrals and sound machines are an effective, nonlethal way of keeping the growing free-roaming wolf population of the Mercantour and other Alpine areas from feasting on domesticated sheep herds.

The brown bear disappeared from the Alps in the mid-1930s. The 150-odd native bears living in the Pyrenees a century ago had dwindled to one orphaned cub following the controversial shooting of its mother – the last female bear of Pyrenean stock – by a hunter in 2004. However another 12 to 18 bears of Slovenian origin also call the French and Spanish Pyrenees home, though the reintroduction program has faced fierce opposition from sheep herders (see p724).

Find out what to spot, where and when with the Ligue de Protection des Oiseaux (LPO; League for the Protection of Birds; www.lpo.fr, in French) and its regional *délégations* (on the website under 'Nos sites web').

A rare but wonderful treat is the sighting of an *aigle royal* (golden eagle): 40 pairs nest in the Parc National du Mercantour, 20 pairs nest in the Vanoise, 30-odd in the Écrins and some 50 in the Pyrenees. Other birds of prey include the peregrine falcon, the kestrel, the buzzard and the bearded vulture, with its bone-breaking habits. The last – Europe's largest bird of prey, with an awe-inspiring wingspan of 2.8m – was extinct in the Alps from the 19th century until the 1980s, when it was reintroduced. More recently, the small, pale-coloured Egyptian vulture (worshipped by the Egyptians, hence its name) has been seen in springtime.

WHERE TO WATCH WILDLIFE

The national parks and their regional siblings offer all sorts of options to visitors who are keen to observe animals in their natural habitat, including nature walks with an expert guide; details are in the regional chapters. The following observation posts are particularly worth a gander:

- Bison in Languedoc at the Réserve de Bisons d'Europe (p784) near Mende.
- Vultures in the Pyrenees at La Falaise aux Vautours (p725) in the Vallée d'Ossau and in Languedoc at the Belvédère des Vautours (p789) in the Parc Naturel Régional des Grands Causses.
- Storks in Alsace at the Centre de Réintroduction des Cigognes in Hunawihr (p392) and the Enclos Cigognes in Munster (p398); on the Atlantic Coast at the Parc Ornithologique in Le Teich (p686) and the Parc Ornithologique du Marquenterre (p248); and at the Parc des Oiseaux outside Villars-les-Dombes near Lyon (p518).
- Wolves in Languedoc at the wolf reserve in the Parc du Gévaudan near Mende (p784).

SURVIVAL OF THE ALPINE IBEX

The nippy *bouquetin des Alpes* (Alpine ibex), with its imposingly large, curly-wurly horns (we're talking 1m long and a good 5kg in weight) and a penchant for sickeningly high crags and ledges, is the animal most synonymous with the French Alps. In the 16th century higher altitudes were loaded with the handsome beast, the males spraying themselves with urine and sporting a strong body odour. Three centuries on, however, its extravagant and unusual horns had become a must-have item in any self-respecting gentleman's trophy cabinet, and within a few years the Alpine ibex had been hunted to the brink of extinction.

In 1963 the Parc National de la Vanoise (p555) was created in the Alps to stop hunters in the Vanoise massif from shooting the few Alpine ibex that remained. The creation of similar nature reserves and the pursuit of rigorous conservation campaigns to protect the animal have seen populations surely and steadily recover – to the point where today the Alpine ibex is thriving. Not that you're likely to encounter one: the canny old ibex has realised that some mammals are best avoided.

Even the eagle-eyed will have difficulty spotting the ptarmigan, a chicken-like species that moults three times a year to ensure a foolproof camouflage for every season (brown in summer, white in winter). It lives on rocky slopes and in alpine meadows above 2000m. The nutcracker, with its loud and buoyant singsong and larch-forest habitat, the black grouse, rock partridge, the eagle owl and the three-toed woodpecker are among the other 120-odd species to keep birdwatchers on their toes in highland realms.

Elsewhere on the French watch-the-birdie front, there are 400 pairs of storks to see in Alsace (p392); 10% of the world's flamingo population hangs out in the Camargue (p834); giant black cormorants – some with a wingspan of 170cm – on an island off the north coast of Brittany (p318); and unique seagull and fishing-eagle populations in the Réserve Naturelle de Scandola on Corsica (p921). The *balbuzard pêcheur* (osprey), a migratory hunter that winters in Africa and returns to France in February or March, today only inhabits two regions of France: Corsica and the Loire Valley-Centre area.

Spotted a bearded vulture? Lucky you! Note down when, where, any distinguishing marks and the bird's behaviour patterns and send the details to the Beared Vulture Reintroduction into the Alps project at www.wild.unizh.ch/bg.

Plants

About 140,000 sq km of forest – beech, oak and pine in the main – covers 20% of France, while 4200 different species of plant and flower are known to grow countrywide (2250 alone grow in the Parc National des Cévennes). In forests near Reims in the Champagne region, mutant beech trees grow in a bizarrely stunted, malformed shape (see p361).

The Alpine and Pyrenean regions nurture fir, spruce and beech forests on north-facing slopes between 800m and 1500m. Larch trees, mountain and arolla pines, rhododendrons and junipers stud shrubby subalpine zones between 1500m and 2000m; and a brilliant riot of spring and summertime wildflowers carpet grassy meadows above the tree line in the alpine zone (up to 3000m).

Alpine blooms include the single golden-yellow flower of the arnica, which has long been used in herbal and homeopathic bruise-relieving remedies; the flame-coloured fire lily, which flowers from December until May; and the hardy Alpine columbine, with its delicate blue petals. The protected 'queen of the Alps' (aka the Alpine eryngo) bears an uncanny resemblance to a purple thistle but is, in fact, a member of the parsley family (to which the carrot also belongs); you will find it on grassy ledges.

The rare twinflower only grows in the Parc National de la Vanoise (p555). Of France's 150 orchids, the black vanilla orchid is one to look out for – its small red-brown flowers exude a sweet vanilla fragrance. At Les Fermes de Marie in Megève (p539), dozens of alpine plants and seeds – gentian, St John's wort, melissa, pulsatilla, pimpernel, cyclamen, hazel seeds and so on – go into beauty products.

The 'Conservatoire du Littoral': Saving the French Coast (€9.91) by Dominique Legrain is a fabulous introduction to France's extraordinarily diverse and nature-rich coastline. Sold online by the Conservatoire du Littoral (www.conservatoire-du-littoral.fr, in French).

Corsica and the Massif des Maures, west of St-Tropez on the Côte d'Azur, are closely related botanically: both have chestnut and cork-oak trees (the bark of which gets stuffed in bottles) and are thickly carpeted with *garrigues* and *maquis* – heavily scented scrubland where dozens of fragrant shrubs and herbs (the secret behind Provençal cooking) find shelter. Particularly enchanting are the rock rose (a shrub bearing white flowers with yellow centres or pinkish-mauve flowers); the white-flowering myrtle, which blossoms in June and is treasured for its blue-black berries (used to make some excellent liqueurs); and the blue-violet-flowering Corsican mint, with its heady summertime aroma.

NATIONAL PARKS

The proportion of protected land in France is surprisingly low, relative to the size of the country. Six small *parcs nationaux* (national parks; www.parcsnationaux-fr.com) fully protect just 0.8% of the country. Another 13% (70,000 sq km) in metropolitan France and its overseas territories, with three million inhabitants, is protected to a substantially lesser degree by 45 *parcs naturels régionaux* (regional nature parks; www.parcs-naturels-regionaux.tm.fr, in French), and a further few percent by 320 smaller *réserves naturelles* (nature reserves; www.reserves-naturelles.org), some of them under the eagle eye of the Conservatoire du Littoral (p107).

Pick up the daily air-pollution and -quality forecast for France at www.prevair.org.

While the central zones of national parks are uninhabited and fully protected by legislation (dogs, vehicles and hunting are banned and camping is restricted), their delicate ecosystems spill over into populated peripheral zones in which economic activities, some of them environmentally unfriendly, are permitted and even encouraged.

Most regional nature parks and reserves were established not only to improve (or at least maintain) local ecosystems, but also to encourage economic development and tourism in areas suffering from economic hardship and diminishing populations (such as the Massif Central and Corsica).

TOP SIX NATURAL CURIOSITIES

Several up-hill-and-down-dales later, here's what especially tickled us in France's incredibly diverse 'natural patrimony':

- Europe's highest **sand dune** (which also happens to move and swallow trees), the Dune du Pilat (p685) near Arcachon on the Atlantic Coast.
- Europe's largest **extinct volcano** (by area), Monts du Cantal (p591), the balding slopes of which can be hiked up in summer and skied down in winter.
- Europe's highest **tides**, with – incredibly – a difference of up to 15m between low and high tides, around Mont St-Michel (p302) in Normandy.
- The lunar landscape of sink holes, caves and streams beneath the **causses** (limestone plateaus) of Languedoc's Parc Naturel Régional des Grands Causses (p788).
- Prehistoric bird footprints and marine-reptile **fossil skeletons** in the Réserve Naturelle Géologique near Digne-les-Bains (p856).
- The navigable **underground river** – over 100m beneath the surface – that flows through the Gouffre de Padirac (p647) in Quercy.

A DEGRADING PROCESS

Make sure that whatever you bring to the mountains leaves with you. Decomposition, always slow, is even more protracted in the high mountains. Typical times:

- paper handkerchief: three months
- plastic bag: 450 years
- apple core: up to six months
- aluminium can: up to 500 years
- cigarette butt: three to five years
- plastic bottle: up to 1000 years
- wad of chewing gum: five years
- glass bottle: up to 4000 years
- cigarette lighter: 100 years

Select pockets of nature – the Pyrenees, Mont St-Michel and its bay, part of the Loire Valley and a clutch of capes on Corsica – have been declared Unesco World Heritage Sites (see p28).

ENVIRONMENTAL ISSUES

The threats to France's environment, its flora and it fauna are many and varied.

As elsewhere in the world, wetlands – incredibly productive ecosystems that are essential for the survival of birds, reptiles, fish and amphibians – are shrinking. More than 20,000 sq km (3% of French territory) are considered important wetlands but only 4% of this land is protected. The vulnerability of these areas was highlighted in early 2003 when lumps of oil landed on beaches in southwestern France following the sinking of the oil tanker *Prestige* off Spain's northwestern coast – to the horror of French environmentalists still seething with fury over the 1999 *Erika* oil-tanker disaster that fouled more than 400km of shoreline in Brittany. Only in 2008 did a French court find the French oil company Total and other parties guilty of causing this *marée noire* (literally, 'black tide').

Environmentalists in Languedoc were none too happy to have one of the world's tallest bridges (p792) slicing across one of their quiet green valleys but the bridge is now widely seen as a triumph of both architecture and engineering. Decide for yourself at www.viaducdemillau.com (in French).

Great tracts of forest land burn each summer, often because of careless day-trippers but occasionally, as is sometimes the case in the Maures and Estérel ranges on the Côte d'Azur, because they're intentionally torched by people hoping to get licences to build on the damaged lands. Since the mid-1970s, between 31 sq km and 615 sq km of land has been reduced to a black stubble each year by an average of 540 fires – although overall, as prevention and fire-fighting improve, the number of fires is falling according to the Office National des Forêts (www.onf.fr, in French), the national forestry commission responsible for public forests in France.

Environmental facts, figures and statistics are available from the Institut Français de l'Environnement (French Institute of the Environment) at www.ifen.fr, in French.

As the globe warms, avalanches have become an ever more severe winter menace in mountainous areas; see p525 for details.

Men with dogs and guns pose a threat to French animal life, brown bears included (p102). While the number of hunters has fallen by more than 20% in the last decade, there are still a lot more hunters in France (1.3 million) than in any other Western European country (Spain is number two with 980,000, followed by the UK with 800,000).

Despite the 1979 Brussels Directive for the protection of wild birds, their eggs, nests and habitats in the EU, the French government has been very slow to make its provisions part of French law, meaning birds that can

NATIONAL PARKS

Park	Features	Activities	Best Time to Visit	Page
Parc National des Cévennes	wild peat bogs, causses, granite peaks, ravines & ridges bordering the Massif Central & Languedoc (910 sq km); red deer, beavers, vultures, wolves, bison	walking, donkey trekking, mountain-biking, horse-riding, cross-country skiing, caving, canoeing, botany (2250 plant species),	spring & winter	p784
Parc National des Écrins	glaciers, glacial lakes & mountain tops soaring up to 4102m in the French Alps (1770 sq km); marmots, lynx, ibex, chamois, bearded vultures	walking, climbing, hang-gliding	spring & summer	p563
Parc National du Mercantour	Provence at its most majestic with 3000m-plus peaks & dead-end valleys along the Italian border; marmots, mouflons, chamois, ibex, wolves, golden & short-toed eagles, bearded vultures	alpine skiing, white-water sports, mountain-biking, walking, donkey trekking	spring, summer & winter	p858
Parc National de Port Cros	Island marine park off the Côte d'Azur forming France's smallest national park & Europe's first marine park (700 hectares & 1288 hectares of water); puffins, shearwaters, migratory birds	snorkelling, birdwatching, swimming, gentle strolling	summer & autumn (for birdwatching)	p891
Parc National des Pyrénées	100km of mountains along the Spanish border (457 sq km); marmots, lizards, brown bears, golden eagles, vultures, buzzards	alpine & cross-country skiing, walking, mountaineering, rock-climbing, white-water rafting, canoeing, kayaking, mountain-biking	spring, summer & winter	p720
Parc National de la Vanoise	postglacial mountain landscape of Alpine peaks, beech-fir forests & 80 sq km of glaciers forming France's 1st national park (530 sq km): chamois, ibex, marmots, golden eagles	alpine & cross-country skiing, walking, mountaineering, mountain-biking	spring, summer & winter	p555

safely fly over other countries can still be shot as they cross France. To put it in statistical bureaucratese: as of 2003, only 22% of France's Important Bird Areas were classified as Special Protection Areas, by far the worst record among the 15 pre-2004 EU member states. A good handful of those not shot – at least 1000 birds of prey a year – are instead electrocuted by high-voltage power lines.

The state-owned electricity company, Electricité de France (http://energies.edf.com), has an enviable record on minimising greenhouse-gas emissions – fossil-fuel-fired power plants account for just 4.6% of its production – but at an environmental price. Clean, renewable hydropower, generated by 220 dams, comprises 8.8% of the company's generating capacity but affects animal habitats. And no less than 78% of France's electricity comes from another controversial carbon-zero source: nuclear power, generated by 58 nuclear reactors at 19 sites.

HIGH-FACTOR PROTECTION BY THE SEA

Over 10% of the coastline of mainland France and Corsica is managed by the **Conservatoire du Littoral** (www.conservatoire-du-littoral.fr), a public coastal-protection body that acquires – sometimes by expropriation – threatened natural areas by the sea in order to restore, rejuvenate and protect them.

Among the *conservatoire*'s rich pageant of *espaces naturels protégés* (protected natural areas) are the rare-orchid-dotted sand dunes east of Dunkirk (p242), a Corsican desert (p917), the Baie de Somme with its ornithological park (p248) and several wet and watery pockets of the horse-studded Camargue (p833).

Books, guides and maps on the 400 natural sites, 1000km of coastline and 1130 sq km of land managed by the Conservatoire du Littoral are sold through its online *boutique*.

For a list of France's 24 **Ramsar Convention wetland sites**, see www.wetlands.org/rsis.

The world's most ambitious nuclear-power program will soon have a new reactor, Flamanville 3 on Normandy's west coast near Cherbourg, due for completion in 2012.

As energy demands increase and global warming looms ever larger in the public energy debate, France's continuing commitment to nuclear power – a position that looked risky and retrograde after Chernobyl, whose fallout raised radiation levels in Alsace, the Lyon and Nice regions and Corsica – now seems possibly prescient.

However, in July 2008 radioactive leaks at two nuclear-power stations brought safety concerns to the fore, and in a sign that the French public's faith in official safety assurances has its limits, winegrowers near the Tricastin nuclear-power plant, north of Avignon, are seeking to have the name of their wine appellation changed to something other than Coteaux de Tricastin, which the recent accident has made about as enticing as Château de Three Mile Island. What is certain is that nuclear energy has helped France meet its Kyoto targets without having to make many inconvenient cuts in its energy use.

Learn the official version of how spent nuclear fuel is reprocessed by visiting France's La Hague Reprocessing plant (www.lahague.areva-nc.com), 25km west of Cherbourg on the Cotentin Peninsula in Normandy.

Europe's largest solar-powered electricity-generating station is being built on a 1000m-high, south-facing slope near the tiny Provence village of Curbans. The 300-hectare array of photovoltaic cells, which will eventually produce 30MW to 50MW, is supposed to generate its first commercial watt in 2009.

Paris

Paris has all but exhausted the superlatives that can reasonably be applied to any city. Notre Dame and the Eiffel Tower have been described countless times, as have the Seine and the differences between the Left and Right Banks. But what writers have been unable to capture is the grandness and the magic of strolling along the city's broad avenues, which lead from impressive public buildings and exceptional museums to parks, gardens and esplanades.

With more famous landmarks than any other city in the world, the French capital evokes all sorts of expectations for first-time visitors: of grand vistas, of intellectuals discussing weighty matters in cafés, of romance along the Seine, of naughty nightclub revues, of rude people who won't speak English. If you look hard enough, you can probably find all of those. But another approach is to set aside the preconceptions of Paris that are so much a part of English-speaking culture, and to explore the city's avenues and backstreets as though the tip of the Eiffel Tower or the spire of Notre Dame weren't about to pop into view at any moment.

You'll soon discover (as so many others before you have) that Paris is enchanting almost everywhere, at any time, even 'in the summer, when it sizzles' and 'in the winter, when it drizzles', as Cole Porter put it. And you'll be back. Trust us.

HIGHLIGHTS

- Introduce yourself to one of Paris' new museums: the architecturally stunning (and content-rich) **Musée du Quai Branly** (p152) or the **Cité de l'Architecture et du Patrimoine** (p152)
- Be stunned (and inspired) by the veritable wall of sublime stained glass in **Ste-Chapelle** (p145), one of the most beautiful houses of worship in Christendom
- Check out the stately *hôtels particuliers* (private mansions) in the **Marais** (p142) by day and the district's throbbing bars and clubs after dark
- Enjoy the collections and the spectacular rooftop views at the **Centre Pompidou** (p138), the world's most successful art and culture centre
- Marvel at the incomparable collection of Impressionist and post-Impressionist art at the waterfront **Musée d'Orsay** (p151)
- Enjoy the views of the timeless **Seine** (p163) from the banks or on an evening cruise
- Go not to the top but the bottom of the **Eiffel Tower** (p152) and look up for a new take on the landmark that's more Parisian than Paris itself
- Relive the *oh-là-là* Paris of cancan and windmills on a walking tour of **Montmartre** (p161)

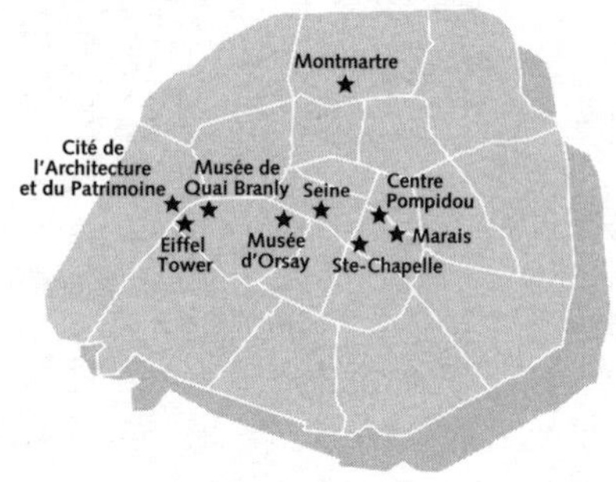

- POPULATION: 2.177 MILLION
- AREA: 105 SQ KM

HISTORY

In the 3rd century BC a tribe of Celtic Gauls known as the Parisii settled on what is now the Île de la Cité. Centuries of conflict between the Gauls and Romans ended in 52 BC, when Julius Caesar's legions crushed a Celtic revolt led by Vercingétorix. Christianity was introduced in the 2nd century AD, but Roman rule ended in the 5th century with the arrival of the Germanic Franks. In 508 Frankish king Clovis I united Gaul as a kingdom and made Paris his seat.

In the 9th century France was beset by Scandinavian Vikings, who raided the western coastal areas; within three centuries these 'Norsemen' (later known as Normans) started pushing towards Paris, which had risen so rapidly in importance that construction had begun on the cathedral of Notre Dame in the 12th century, the Louvre was built as a riverside fortress around 1200, the beautiful Ste-Chapelle was consecrated in 1248 and the Sorbonne opened its doors in 1253.

The incursions heralded the Hundred Years' War between Norman England and the Capetian rulers in Paris, eventually bringing the French defeat at Agincourt in 1415 and English control of the capital in 1420. In 1429 the 17-year-old Jeanne d'Arc (Joan of Arc) rallied the French troops to defeat the English at Orléans. With the exception of Calais, the English were finally driven out of France in 1453.

The Renaissance helped Paris get back on its feet at the end of the 15th century, and many of the city's most famous buildings and monuments were erected at this time. But in less than a century Paris was again in turmoil, as clashes between Huguenot (Protestant) and Catholic groups increased. The worst such incident was the so-called St Bartholomew's Day massacre in 1572, in which 3000 Huguenots who had gathered in Paris to celebrate the wedding of Henri of Navarre (later King Henri IV) were slaughtered.

Louis XIV, also known as the Sun King, ascended the throne in 1643 at the age of five and ruled until 1715, virtually emptying the national coffers with his ambitious building and battling. His greatest legacy is the palace at Versailles, 21km southwest of Paris. The excesses of Louis XVI and his queen, Marie-Antoinette, in part led to an uprising of Parisians on 14 July 1789 and the storming of the Bastille prison – kick-starting the French Revolution.

At first the Revolution was in the hands of moderates, but within a few years the so-called Reign of Terror, during which even the original patriots were guillotined, was in full swing. The unstable post-Revolutionary government was consolidated in 1799 under a young Corsican general named Napoleon Bonaparte, who declared himself First Consul. In 1804 he had the Pope crown him 'Emperor of the French' at Notre Dame and then went forward and conquered most of Europe. Napoleon's ambitions eventually brought about his defeat, first in Russia in 1812 and later at Waterloo in Belgium in 1815. He was exiled to a remote South Atlantic island, where he died in 1821.

France struggled under a string of mostly inept rulers until a coup d'état in 1851 brought Emperor Napoleon III to power. He oversaw the construction of a more modern Paris, with wide boulevards, sculpted parks and – not insignificant – a modern sewer system. Like his pugnacious uncle, however, Napoleon had a taste for blood, which led to his costly and unsuccessful war with Prussia in 1870. When the masses in Paris heard of their emperor's capture by the enemy, they took to the streets, demanding that a republic be declared. Despite its bloody beginnings, the Third Republic ushered in the glittering and very creative period known as the belle époque (beautiful age), celebrated for its graceful art-nouveau architecture and advances in the arts and sciences.

The defeat of Austria-Hungary and Germany in WWI, which regained Alsace and Lorraine for France (lost to Prussia in the previous century), was achieved at an unimaginable human cost; with 20% of all French males aged between 20 and 45 years killed. By the 1930s, however, Paris had become a centre for the artistic avant-garde and had established its reputation among freethinking intellectuals. This was all cut short by the Nazi occupation of 1940; Paris would remain under direct German rule until 25 August 1944.

After the war, Paris regained its position as a creative centre and nurtured a revitalised liberalism that reached a climax in the student-led uprisings of 1968. The Sorbonne was occupied, barricades were set up in the Latin Quarter and some nine million people nationwide were inspired to join in a general

FINDING YOURSELF IN PARIS

In Paris, when a building is put up in a location where they've run out of consecutive street numbers, a new address is formed by fusing the number of an adjacent building with the notation *bis* (twice), *ter* (thrice) or even *quater* (four times). Therefore, the street numbers 17bis and 89ter are the equivalent (more or less) of 17a and 89b in English.

The street doors *(portes cochères)* of most apartment buildings in Paris can be opened only if someone has given you the entry code *(digicode)*, which is usually alphanumeric (eg 26A10) and changed periodically; the days of the concierges, who would vet every caller before allowing them in, are well and truly over. In some buildings the entry-code device is deactivated during the day but to get in (or out) you still have to push a button (usually marked *porte*) to release the electric catch.

The doors of many apartments are unmarked: the occupants' names are nowhere in sight and there isn't even an apartment number. To know which door to knock on, you'll usually be given cryptic instructions, such as *cinquième étage, premier à gauche* (5th floor, first on the left) or *troisième étage, droite, droite* (3rd floor, turn right twice).

strike that paralysed the country, which at one point almost led to civil war.

During the 1980s President François Mitterrand initiated several costly *grands projets*, a series of building projects that garnered widespread approval even when the results were popular failures. In the 1990s the baton passed to right-wing President Jacques Chirac, who won a second five-year term in 2002; in 2007 it was the turn of Chirac's get-tough Interior Minister, current president Nicolas 'Sarko' Sarkozy (see p47).

In May 2001, Bertrand Delanoë, a socialist with support from the Green Party, became Paris' – and a European capital's – first openly gay mayor. He was returned to power in the second round of voting in the elections of March 2008.

ORIENTATION

Central Paris is relatively small, covering an area of just under 87 sq km (or 105 sq km – 9.5km north to south by 11km east to west – if you include the Bois de Boulogne and the Bois de Vincennes). Within the 'oval' of central Paris, which Parisians call *intra-muros* (Latin for 'within the walls'), the Right Bank is north of the Seine, while the Left Bank is south of it.

Paris is quite an easy city to negotiate, but this chapter offers you three ways to find the addresses listed: by district, map reference and metro station.

Arrondissements

Paris is divided into 20 arrondissements (districts), which spiral out clockwise from the centre like a conch shell. City addresses always include the number of the arrondissement, because streets with the same name exist in different districts.

In this chapter, arrondissement numbers are given after a street address using the usual French notation: 1er for *premier* (1st), 2e for *deuxième* (2nd), 3e for *troisième* (3rd) and so on. On some signs or commercial maps, you will see variations such as 2ème, 3ème etc and sometimes IIe, IIIe etc.

Maps

The most ubiquitous (and user-friendly) pocket-sized street atlas available is L'Indispensable's *Paris Practique par Arrondissement* (€4.90), though the similar *Paris Utile* (€4.50) from Blay Foldex has its supporters. If you're looking for a sheet map, Lonely Planet's *Paris City Map* (€7.95) is handy, laminated and has four plans that cover the more popular parts of town, a street index and a metro map. More detailed is Michelin's *Paris Poche Plan* (No 50; €2.20).

The best place to find a full selection of maps is the Espace IGN (p953 and Map pp118–19).

Metro Stations

Paris has 373 metro stations, and there is always a station within 500m of wherever you need to go in Paris (see the Metro map, p12).

Thus all the offices, museums, hotels and restaurants that are mentioned here have the nearest metro stop written immediately after the street address and preceded by the Ⓜ icon.

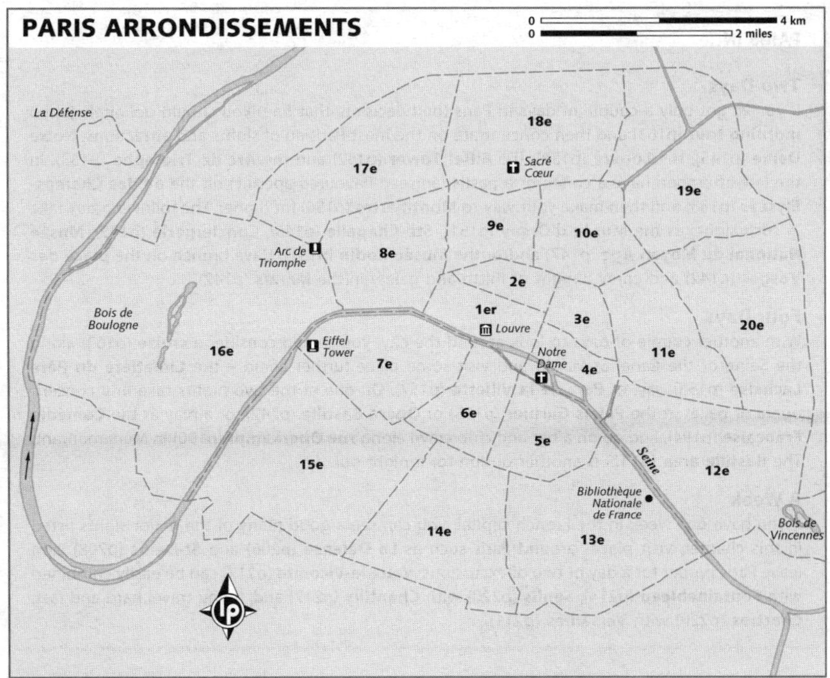

INFORMATION

Bookshops

Abbey Bookshop (Map pp126-7; ☎ 01 46 33 16 24; www.abbeybookshop.net; 29 rue de la Parcheminerie, 5e; Ⓜ Cluny-La Sorbonne; 10am-7pm Mon-Sat) This mellow Canadian-owned bookshop not far from place St-Michel is celebrated for its free tea and coffee (sweetened with maple syrup) and good selection of new and used books.

Les Mots à la Bouche (Map pp126-7; ☎ 01 42 78 88 30; www.motsbouche.com, in French; 6 rue Ste-Croix de la Bretonnerie, 4e; Ⓜ Hôtel de Ville; 11am-11pm Mon-Sat, 1-9pm Sun) 'On the Tip of the Tongue' is Paris' premier gay bookshop and stocks guides as well as some novels in English.

Librairie Ulysse (Map pp126-7; ☎ 01 43 25 17 35; www.ulysse.fr; 26 rue St-Louis en l'Île, 4e; Ⓜ Pont Marie; 2-8pm Tue-Fri) A delightful shop full of travel guides, maps and sage advice from well-travelled staff. The 20,000 back issues of *National Geographic* are not to be sniffed at.

Red Wheelbarrow Bookstore (Map pp126-7; ☎ 01 48 04 75 08; www.theredwheelbarrow.com; 22 rue St-Paul, 4e; Ⓜ St-Paul; 10am-7pm Mon-Sat, 2-6pm Sun) This foreign-owned English-language bookshop has arguably the best selection of literature and 'serious reading' in Paris, and helpful, well-read staff.

Shakespeare & Company (Map pp126-7; ☎ 01 43 26 96 50; 37 rue de la Bûcherie, 5e; Ⓜ St-Michel; 10am-11pm Mon-Sat, 11am-11pm Sun) Paris' most famous English-language bookshop has a varied collection of new and used books in English and is a charm to browse. There's a dusty old library on the 1st floor.

Tea & Tattered Pages (Map pp124-5; ☎ 01 40 65 94 35; 24 rue Mayet, 6e; Ⓜ Duroc; 11am-7pm Mon-Sat, noon-6pm Sun) T&TP is by far the best and most comprehensive second-hand English-language bookshop in Paris, with some 15,000 volumes squeezed into two floors.

Village Voice (Map pp126-7; ☎ 01 46 33 36 47; www.villagevoicebookshop.com; 6 rue Princesse, 6e; Ⓜ Mabillon; 2-8pm Mon, 10am-8pm Tue-Sat, 2-6pm Sun) With an excellent selection of contemporary North American fiction and European literature, lots of readings and helpful staff, Village Voice is a firm favourite.

Emergency

The numbers below are to be dialled in an emergency. See p113 for hospitals with 24-hour accident and emergency departments. For nationwide emergency numbers, see Telephone inside the front cover.

PARIS IN...

Two Days

If you've got only a couple of days in Paris (bad decision, that one) you should definitely join a **morning tour** (p163) and then concentrate on the most Parisian of sights and attractions: **Notre Dame** (p145), the **Louvre** (p138), the **Eiffel Tower** (p152) and the **Arc de Triomphe** (p153). In the late afternoon have a coffee or a pastis (aniseed-flavoured aperitif) on the **av des Champs-Élysées** (p153) and then make your way to **Montmartre** (p156) for dinner. The following day take in such sights as the **Musée d'Orsay** (p151), **Ste-Chapelle** (p145), **Conciergerie** (p145), **Musée National du Moyen Âge** (p147) and/or the **Musée Rodin** (p151). Have brunch on the **place des Vosges** (p142) and enjoy a night of mirth and gaiety in the **Marais** (p142).

Four Days

With another couple of days to look around the city, you should consider a **cruise** (p163) along the Seine or the Canal St-Martin and visit some place further afield – the **Cimetière du Père Lachaise** (p155), say, or **Parc de la Villette** (p157). On one of the two nights take in a concert, opera or ballet at the **Palais Garnier** (p155) or **Opéra Bastille** (p142), or a play at the **Comédie Française** (p194), and go on a bar and club crawl along **rue Oberkampf** (p190) in Ménilmontant. The **Bastille area** (p142) is another option for a night out.

A Week

If you have one week in the French capital, you can see a good many of the major sights listed in this chapter, visit places around Paris such as **La Défense** (p206) and **St-Denis** (p208), and leave Paris proper for a day or two of excursions: **Vaux-le-Vicomte** (p217) can be easily combined with **Fontainebleau** (p214), **Senlis** (p220) with **Chantilly** (p217) and, if you travel hard and fast, **Chartres** (p220) with **Versailles** (p211).

SOS Helpline (☎ 01 47 23 80 80, in English; ⏲ 3-11pm daily)
SOS Médecins (☎ 01 47 07 77 77, 24hr house calls 08 20 33 24 24; www.sosmedecins-france.fr)
Urgences Médicales de Paris (Paris Medical Emergencies; ☎ 01 53 94 94 94; www.ump.fr)

Internet Access

Wi-fi is widely available at midrange and top-end hotels in Paris (sometimes for free but more often for something like €5 per one-off connection) and occasionally in public spaces such as train stations and tourist offices. For a list of almost 100 free-access wi-fi cafés in Paris, visit www.cafes-wifi.com (in French).

If you don't have a laptop or access to wi-fi, Paris is awash in internet cafés with computers, and you'll probably find at least one in your immediate neighbourhood. Some of the biggest, best and/or most central:

Cyber Cube (Map pp124-5; ☎ 01 56 80 08 08; www.cybercube.fr; 9 rue d'Odessa, 14e; Ⓜ Montparnasse Bienvenüe; per 15/30min €1/2, per 5/10hr €30/40; ⏲ 10am-10pm) This branch (there are three) is expensive, but convenient to the Gare Montparnasse.
Milk (☎ 08 20 00 10 00; www.milklub.com; daytime per 1/2/3/5hr €4/7/9/12, night-time per 3/10hr €6/13; ⏲ 24hr) Panthéon (Map pp130-1; 17 rue Soufflot, 5e; Ⓜ Luxembourg); Les Halles (Map pp126-7; 31 bd de Sébastopol, 1er; Ⓜ Les Halles) This chain of seven internet cafés is bright, buzzy and open round the clock.
Phon'net (Map pp132-3; ☎ 01 42 05 10 73; 74 rue de Charonne, 11e; Ⓜ Charonne or Ledru Rollin; per 1/5/15/30hr €5/16/30/45; ⏲ 10am-midnight)
Web 46 (Map pp126-7; ☎ 01 40 27 02 89; 46 rue du Roi de Sicile, 4e; Ⓜ St-Paul; per 15/30/60min €2.50/4/7, per 5hr €29; ⏲ 10am-11pm Mon-Fri, 10am-9pm Sat, noon-11pm Sun) Pleasant, very well-run café in the heart of the Marais.

Internet Resources

Lonely Planet's website (www.lonelyplanet.com) has many useful links. Other recommended English-language websites:
Go Go Paris! Culture! (www.gogoparis.com) Clubs, hang-outs, art gigs, dancing around town, food and drink.
Mairie de Paris (www.paris.fr) Your primary source of information about Paris, with everything from opening times to the latest statistics.
Paris Convention & Visitors Bureau (www.parisinfo.com) The official site of the city's tourist office.
Paris Digest (www.parisdigest.com) Useful for making pre-travel arrangements.
Paris Pages (www.paris.org) Good links to museums and cultural events pages.

Laundry

There's a *laverie libre-service* (self-service launderette) round every corner in Paris; your hotel or hostel can point you to one in the neighbourhood. Machines usually cost €3.50 to €4.50 for a small load (around 6kg) and €5.50 to €8 for a larger one (about 10kg). Drying costs €1 for 10 to 12 minutes.

GARE DU NORD, GARE DE L'EST & RÉPUBLIQUE

Laverie Libre-Service (Map pp120-1; 14 rue de la Corderie, 3e; Ⓜ République or Temple; ⌚ 8am-9pm)
Laverie SBS (Map pp120-1; 6 rue des Petites Écuries, 10e; Ⓜ Château d'Eau; ⌚ 7am-10pm)

LATIN QUARTER & JARDIN DES PLANTES

Laverie Libre-Service (Map pp130-1; 63 rue Monge, 5e; Ⓜ Place Monge; ⌚ 6.30am-10pm) Just south of the Arènes de Lutèce.
Laverie Libre-Service (Map pp130-1; 216 rue St-Jacques, 5e; Ⓜ Luxembourg; ⌚ 7am-10pm) Three blocks southwest of the Panthéon.

LOUVRE & LES HALLES

Laverie Libre-Service (Map pp126-7; 7 rue Jean-Jacques Rousseau, 1er; Ⓜ Louvre-Rivoli; ⌚ 7.30am-10pm) Near the Centre International de Séjour BVJ Paris-Louvre hostel.

MARAIS & BASTILLE

Laverie Libre-Service (Map pp126-7; 35 rue Ste-Croix de la Bretonnerie, 4e; Ⓜ Hôtel de Ville; ⌚ 7am-9pm)
Laverie Miele Libre-Service (Map pp132-3; 4 rue de Lappe, 11e; Ⓜ Bastille; ⌚ 7am-10pm)

MÉNILMONTANT & BELLEVILLE

C'Clean Laverie (Map pp120-1; 18 rue Jean-Pierre Timbaud, 11e; Ⓜ Oberkampf; ⌚ 7am-9pm)

MONTMARTRE & PIGALLE

Salon Lavoir Sidec (Map p136; 28 rue des Trois Frères, 18e; Ⓜ Abbesses; ⌚ 7am-8.50pm)

ST-GERMAIN, ODÉON & LUXEMBOURG

Julice Laverie (Map pp126-7; 56 rue de Seine, 6e; Ⓜ Mabillon; ⌚ 7am-11pm)

Media

There are no local English-language newspapers in Paris, although freebies such as the *Paris Times* (www.theparistimes.com) and *Paris Where* (www.wheremagazine.com) proliferate and are available at English-language bookshops, pubs and so on. *FUSAC* (short for *France USA Contacts*), a freebie issued every fortnight, consists of hundreds of ads placed by companies and individuals. It can be found at the aforementioned places as well as at the **American Church in Paris** (Map pp124-5; ☎ 01 40 62 05 00; www.acparis.org; 65 quai d'Orsay, 7e; Ⓜ Pont de l'Alma or Invalides; ⌚ reception 9am-noon & 1-10pm Mon-Sat, 2-7.30pm Sun), which functions as a community centre for English speakers and is an excellent source of information on au pair work, short-term accommodation etc.

Medical Services

DENTAL SURGERIES

For emergency dental care, contact either of the following:
Hôpital de la Pitié-Salpêtrière (Map pp134-5; ☎ 01 42 16 00 00; rue Bruant, 13e; Ⓜ Chevaleret) This is the only dental hospital with extended hours – from 6.30pm to 10.30am. After 5.30pm use the emergency entrance (Map pp130–1) at 83 bd de l'Hôpital, 13e, Ⓜ St-Marcel.
SOS Dentaire (Map pp130-1; ☎ 01 43 37 51 00; 87 bd de Port Royal, 14e; Ⓜ Port Royal) This is a private dental office that also offers services when most dentists are off duty (8pm to 11pm weekdays, 9.45am to 11pm at the weekend).

HOSPITALS

There are some 50 *assistance publique* (public service) hospitals in Paris. Major hospitals in the city that have 24-hour accident and emergency departments include the following:
American Hospital of Paris (Map pp114-15; ☎ 01 46 41 25 25; www.american-hospital.org; 63 bd Victor Hugo, 92200 Neuilly-sur-Seine; Ⓜ Pont de Levallois Bécon) Offers emergency 24-hour medical and dental care.
Hertford British Hospital (Map pp114-15; ☎ 01 46 39 22 22; www.british-hospital.org; 3 rue Barbès, 92300 Levallois-Perret; Ⓜ Anatole France) A less-expensive private English-speaking option.
Hôpital Hôtel Dieu (Map pp126-7; ☎ 01 42 34 82 34; www.aphp.fr; 1 place du Parvis Notre Dame, 4e; Ⓜ Cité) One of the city's main government-run public hospitals; after 8pm use the emergency entrance on rue de la Cité, 4e.

PHARMACIES

Some pharmacies with extended hours:
Pharmacie Bader (Map pp126-7; ☎ 01 43 26 92 66; 12 bd St-Michel, 5e; Ⓜ St-Michel; ⌚ 9am-9pm)
Pharmacie des Champs (Map pp118-19; ☎ 01 45 62 02 41; Galerie des Champs, 84 av des Champs-Élysées, 8e; Ⓜ George V; ⌚ 24hr)
Pharmacie des Halles (Map pp126-7; ☎ 01 42 72 03 23; 10 bd de Sébastopol, 4e; Ⓜ Châtelet; ⌚ 9am-midnight Mon-Sat, 9am-10pm Sun)

(Continued on page 137)

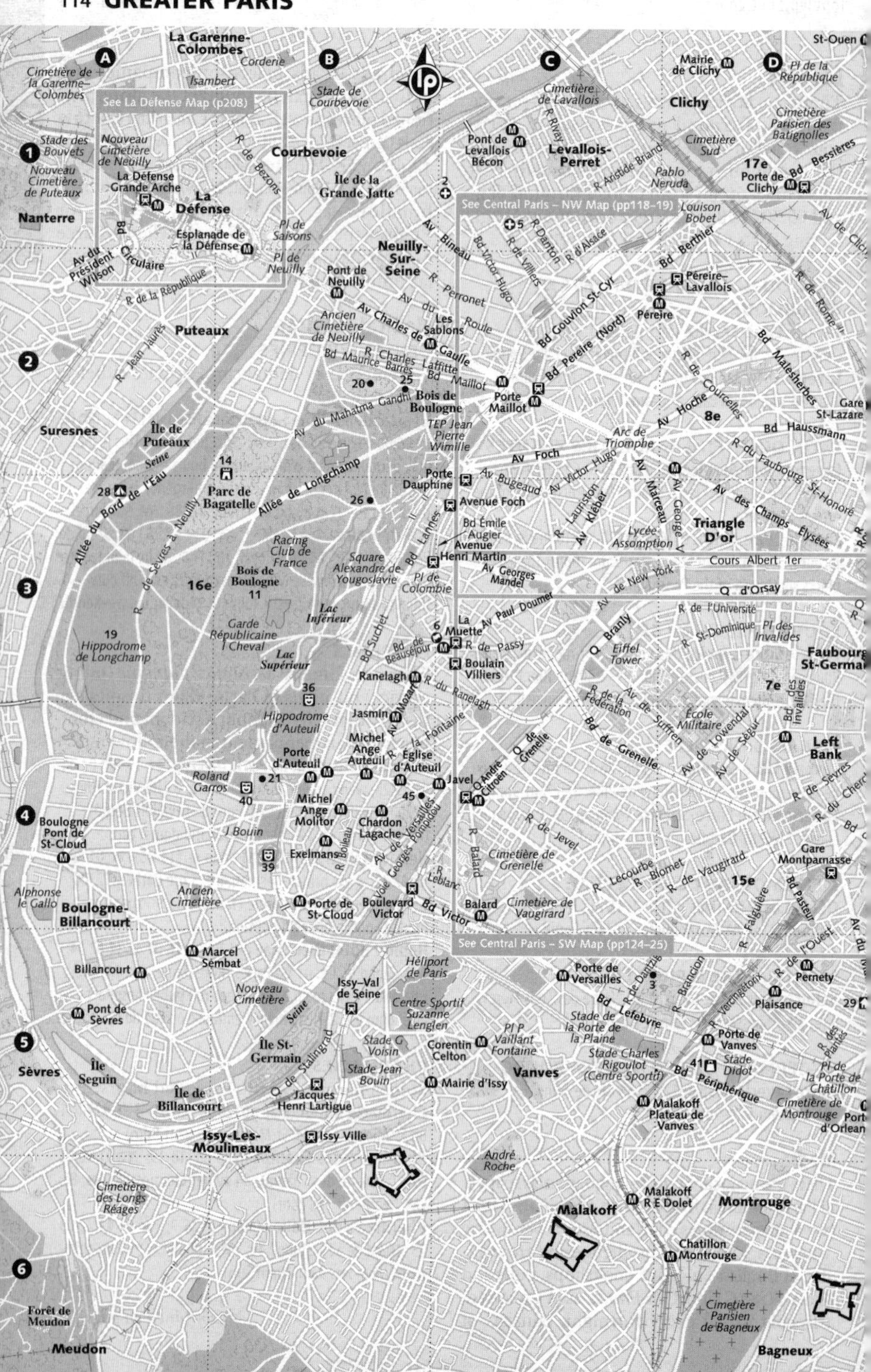

La Garenne-Colombes
Cimetière de la Garenne-Colombes
Stade de Courbevoie
See La Défense Map (p208)
Courbevoie
Cimetière de Lavallois
Levallois-Perret
Mairie de Clichy
Clichy
Pl de la République
Cimetière Parisien des Batignolles
Nanterre
La Défense
Île de la Grande Jatte
Neuilly-Sur-Seine
See Central Paris – NW Map (pp118–19)
Puteaux
Suresnes
Bois de Boulogne
Porte Maillot
Arc de Triomphe
Triangle D'or
Parc de Bagatelle
16e
Hippodrome de Longchamp
Lac Inférieur
Lac Supérieur
Hippodrome d'Auteuil
Eiffel Tower
École Militaire
7e
Faubourg St-Germain
Left Bank
Roland Garros
Boulogne-Billancourt
15e
Gare Montparnasse
See Central Paris – SW Map (pp124–25)
Héliport de Paris
Île St-Germain
Île Seguin
Sèvres
Île de Billancourt
Issy-Les-Moulineaux
Vanves
Malakoff
Montrouge
Cimetière Parisien de Bagneux
Bagneux
Forêt de Meudon
Meudon

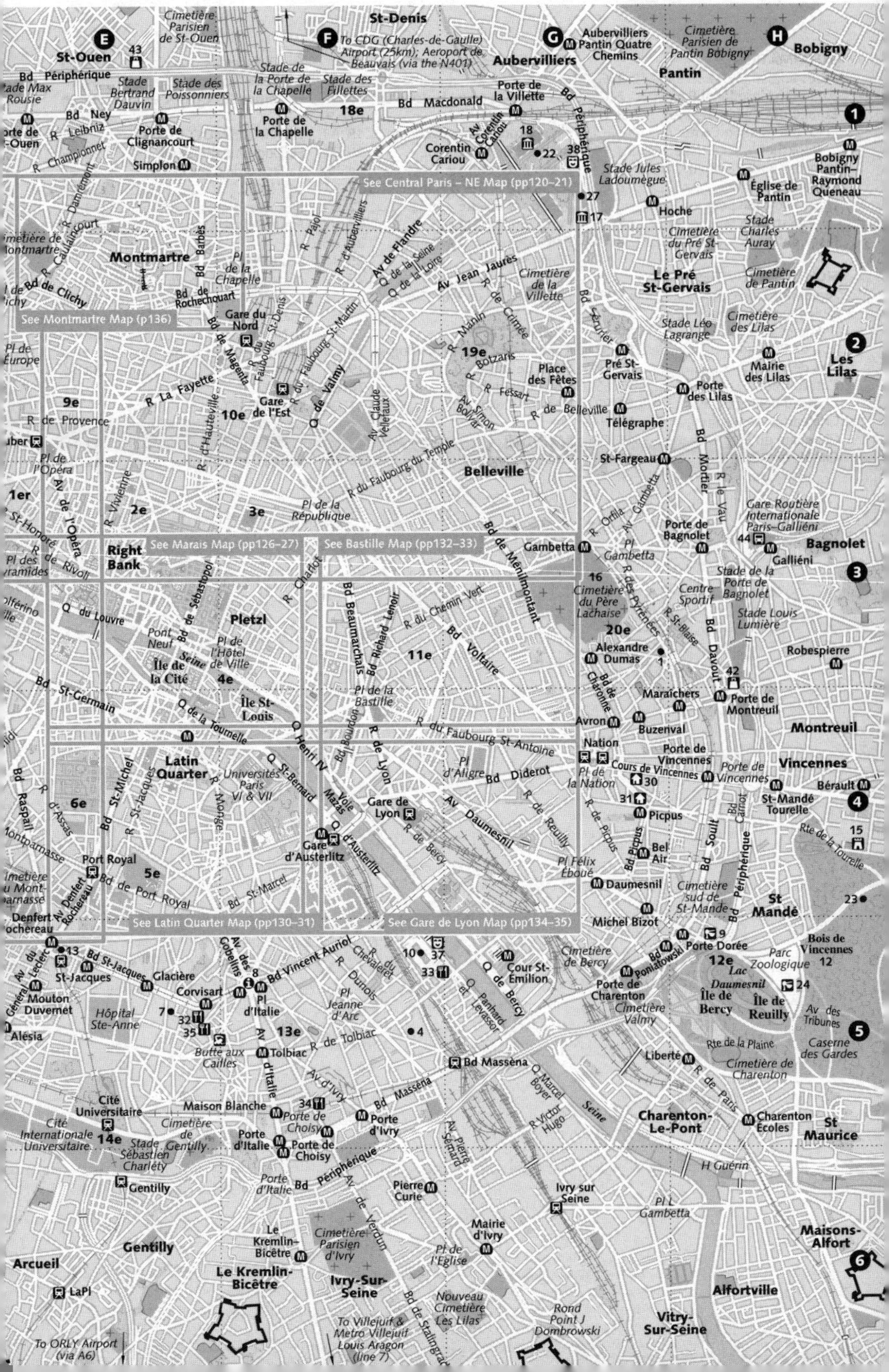

E
F
G
H
St-Ouen
43
Cimetière Parisien de St-Ouen
St-Denis
To CDG (Charles-de-Gaulle) Airport (25km); Aeroport de Beauvais (via the N401)
Aubervilliers
Aubervilliers Pantin Quatre Chemins
Cimetière Parisien de Pantin Bobigny
Bobigny
Pantin
Bd Périphérique
Stade Max Rousie
Stade Bertrand Dauvin
Stade des Poissonniers
Stade de la Porte de la Chapelle
Stade des Fillettes
Porte de la Villette
Bd Macdonald
18e
Porte de la Chapelle
Bd Ney
R Leibniz
Porte de St-Ouen
Porte de Clignancourt
R Championnet
Simplon
Av Corentin Cariou
Corentin Cariou
18
22
38
1
Bobigny Pantin–Raymond Queneau
Stade Jules Ladoumègue
Église de Pantin
Hoche
27
17
See Central Paris – NE Map (pp120–21)
R Damrémont
R Caulaincourt
Cimetière de Montmartre
Montmartre
Barbès
Pl de la Chapelle
R Pajol
R d'Aubervilliers
Av de Flandre
Q de la Seine
Q de la Loire
Av Jean Jaurès
Cimetière de la Villette
Cimetière du Pré St-Gervais
Stade Charles Auray
Le Pré St-Gervais
Cimetière de Pantin
Bd de Clichy
Bd de Rochechouart
See Montmartre Map (p136)
Gare du Nord
R du Faubourg St-Denis
R du Faubourg St-Martin
R de Crimée
R Manin
Bd Sérurier
Stade Léo Lagrange
Cimetière des Lilas
2
Les Lilas
Pl de l'Europe
Bd de Magenta
R La Fayette
19e
R Botzaris
Pré St-Gervais
Mairie des Lilas
Place des Fêtes
Porte des Lilas
9e
Gare de l'Est
Q de Valmy
Av Claude Vellefaux
R Fessart
Av Simon Bolivar
R de Belleville
Télégraphe
R de Provence
R d'Hauteville
10e
Auber
Pl de l'Opéra
R du Faubourg du Temple
Belleville
St-Fargeau
Bd Mortier
R le Vau
Av Gambetta
R Orfila
1er
Av de l'Opéra
R Vivienne
2e
3e
Pl de la République
Bd de Ménilmontant
Porte de Bagnolet
Gare Routière Internationale Paris–Galliéni
44
Galliéni
Bagnolet
R St-Honoré
See Marais Map (pp126–27)
See Bastille Map (pp132–33)
Gambetta
Pl Gambetta
Right Bank
Pl des Pyramides
R de Rivoli
Bd de Sébastopol
R Charlot
Bd Beaumarchais
Bd Richard Lenoir
R du Chemin Vert
16
Cimetière du Père Lachaise
R des Pyrénées
Stade de la Porte de Bagnolet
Centre Sportif
3
Solférino
Q du Louvre
Pletzl
Bd Voltaire
R St-Blaise
Stade Louis Lumière
Pont Neuf
Pl de l'Hôtel de Ville
Seine
11e
20e
Alexandre Dumas
Bd Davout
Robespierre
Île de la Cité
4e
Bd de Charonne
42
Bd St-Germain
Île St-Louis
Pl de la Bastille
Maraîchers
Porte de Montreuil
Q de la Tournelle
Q Henri IV
R de Lyon
Bd Bourdon
R du Faubourg St-Antoine
Avron
Buzenval
Montreuil
Nation
Porte de Vincennes
Vincennes
Bd Raspail
Latin Quarter
R Monge
Universités Paris VI & VII
Q St-Bernard
Pl d'Aligre
Bd Diderot
Pl de la Nation
Cours de Vincennes
30
Porte de Vincennes
Bérault
R d'Assas
6e
Bd St-Michel
R St-Jacques
Voie Mazas
Gare de Lyon
Av Daumesnil
R de Reuilly
R de Picpus
31
Picpus
Bd Carnot
St-Mandé Tourelle
4
Rte de la Tourelle
15
Bd du Montparnasse
Cimetière du Montparnasse
Port Royal
Gare d'Austerlitz
Q d'Austerlitz
R de Bercy
Bd Picpus
Bel Air
Pl Félix Éboué
Bd Soult
Bd Périphérique
5e
Bd de Port Royal
Bd St-Marcel
Av Denfert Rochereau
Daumesnil
Cimetière sud de St-Mandé
St Mandé
23
Denfert Rochereau
See Latin Quarter Map (pp130–31)
See Gare de Lyon Map (pp134–35)
Michel Bizot
9
Bois de Vincennes
13
Bd St-Jacques
Av des Gobelins
8
Bd Vincent Auriol
R Chevaleret
R du Chevaleret
10
37
Cour St-Émilion
Bd Poniatowski
Porte Dorée
12e
Parc Zoologique
12
Av du Général Leclerc
St-Jacques
Glacière
Corvisart
Pl d'Italie
R Dunois
Pl Jeanne d'Arc
33
Q de Bercy
R Panhard et Levassor
Cimetière de Bercy
Porte de Charenton
Lac Daumesnil
24
Île de Bercy
Île de Reuilly
Mouton Duvernet
Hôpital Ste-Anne
7
32
35
Av d'Italie
13e
4
Cimetière Valmy
Av des Tribunes
5
Alésia
Butte aux Cailles
Tolbiac
R de Tolbiac
Bd Masséna
Rte de la Plaine
Caserne des Gardes
Liberté
Cimetière de Charenton
R de Paris
Cité Universitaire
Maison Blanche
34
Av d'Ivry
Bd Masséna
Q Marcel Boyer
Seine
Cité Internationale Universitaire
14e
Cimetière de Gentilly
Stade Sébastien Charléty
Porte de Choisy
Porte d'Ivry
R Victor Hugo
Av Pierre Sémard
Charenton-Le-Pont
Charenton Écoles
St Maurice
Porte d'Italie
Porte de Choisy
Gentilly
Porte d'Italie
Bd Périphérique
Av de Verdun
Pierre Curie
H Guérin
Ivry sur Seine
Pl L Gambetta
Gentilly
Le Kremlin-Bicêtre
Cimetière Parisien d'Ivry
Mairie d'Ivry
Pl de l'Église
Maisons-Alfort
6
Arcueil
Le Kremlin-Bicêtre
Ivry-Sur-Seine
LaPl
Nouveau Cimetière Les Lilas
Rond Point J Dombrowski
Alfortville
Vitry-Sur-Seine
To ORLY Airport (via A6)
To Villejuif & Metro Villejuif Louis Aragon (line 7)
Bd de Stalingrad

GREATER PARIS (pp114–15)

INFORMATION
Aides....................1 G3
American Hospital of Paris..........2 C1
Bureau des Objets Trouvés.........3 C5
FFRP Information Centre & Bookshop....................4 F5
Hertford British Hospital.............5 C1
Italian Consulate.........................6 C3
Ligue Française pour les Auberges de la Jeunesse.........7 E5
Place d'Italie..............................8 F5

SIGHTS & ACTIVITIES
Aquarium Tropical......................9 H5
Bibliothèque Nationale de France..............................10 F5
Bois de Boulogne......................11 B3
Bois de Vincennes.....................12 H5
Catacombes..............................13 E5
Château de Bagatelle................14 B2
Château de Vincennes.............15 H4
Cimetière du Père Lachaise.......16 G3
Cité de la Musique....................17 G1
Cité des Sciences et de l'Industrie.............................18 G1
Cité Nationale de l'Histoire de l'Immigration........................(see 9)
Hippodrome de Longchamp.....19 A3
Jardin d'Acclimatation...............20 B2
Jardin d'Agronomie Tropicale..(see 23)
Jardin des Serres d'Auteuil........21 B4
Parc de la Villette......................22 G1
Parc Floral de Paris...................23 H4
Parc Zoologique de Paris..........24 H5
Paris Cycles..............................25 B2
Paris Cycles..............................26 B3
Philharmonie de Paris Site.........27 G1

SLEEPING
Camping du Bois de Boulogne..28 A3
Hôtel de Blois............................29 D5
Hôtel du Printemps...................30 G4
Hôtel Le Cosy...........................31 G4

EATING
Chez Gladines...........................32 E5
Fil 'O' Fromage.........................33 F5
La Chine Masséna.....................34 F5
Le Temps des Cérises...............35 E5

ENTERTAINMENT
Hippodrome d'Auteuil..............36 B3
La Dame de Canton..................37 F5
Le Zénith..................................38 G1
Parc des Princes........................39 B4
Stade Roland Garros.................40 B4

SHOPPING
Marché aux Puces de la Porte de Vanves.............................41 D5
Marché aux Puces de Montreuil..............................42 H3
Marché aux Puces de St-Ouen................................43 E1

TRANSPORT
Gare Routière Internationale de Paris-Galliéni..........................44 H3
Rent a Car Système...................45 B4

CENTRAL PARIS – NW (pp118–19)

INFORMATION

Art Nouveau Toilets........................ **1** G5
Belgian Embassy........................... **2** C4
Bienvenue à la Ferme...................... **3** D6
Canadian Embassy.......................... **4** D5
Espace IGN................................ **5** E5
France Lodge.............................. **6** D3
German Consulate.......................... **7** A4
German Embassy............................ **8** E6
Irish Embassy & Trade Office.............. **9** C4
Japanese Consulate........................ **10** D3
New Zealand Embassy & Trade Office....... **11** B5
Paris Convention & Visitors Bureau (Main Branch)........... **12** H6
Pharmacie des Champs...................... **13** D5
Ski France................................ **14** F3
Spanish Embassy........................... **15** D6
UK Consulate.............................. **16** F5
UK Embassy & Trade Office................. **17** F5
US Consulate.............................. **18** G5
US Embassy & Trade Office................. **19** F5

SIGHTS & ACTIVITIES

Arc de Triomphe........................... **20** C4
Bateaux Mouches........................... **21** D6
Colonne Vendôme........................... **22** G5
École Ritz Escoffier....................... **23** G5
Église de Ste-Marie Madeleine.............. **24** G5
Flamme de la Liberté...................... **25** D6
Galerie National du Jeu de Paume.......... (see 29)
Galeries Nationales du Grand Palais....... (see 27)
Galeries du Panthéon Bouddhique du Japon et de la Chine........ **26** C6
Grand Palais.............................. **27** E6
Jardin des Tuileries...................... **28** G6
Jeu de Paume.............................. **29** G6
L'Open Tour............................... **30** G4
Musée de l'Opéra.......................... (see 37)
Musée de l'Orangerie...................... (see 32)
Musée des Beaux-Arts de la Ville de Paris........ (see 38)
Musée Guimet des Arts Asiatiques.......... **31** C6
Orangerie................................. **32** F6
Palais de Chaillot........................ **33** B6
Palais de la Découverte................... **34** E6
Palais de l'Élysée........................ **35** F5
Palais de Tokyo........................... **36** C6
Palais Garnier............................ **37** H5
Petit Palais.............................. **38** E6
Place de la Concorde Obelisk.............. **39** F6

SLEEPING

Hôtel Alison.............................. **40** F5
Hôtel Eldorado............................ **41** G2
Hôtel Langlois............................ **42** H4
Hôtel Le A................................ **43** E4
New Orient Hôtel.......................... **44** F3
Style Hôtel............................... **45** G2

EATING

Bistrot du Sommelier...................... **46** F4
Champs-Élysées Bistro Romain.............. **47** D4
Dragons Élysées........................... **48** D4
Franprix Madeleine........................ **49** F5
L'Ardoise................................. **50** G6
Le Roi du Pot au Feu...................... **51** G4
L'Étoile Verte............................ **52** C4
Monoprix Champs-Élysées................... **53** D5
Monoprix Opéra............................ **54** H6

DRINKING

Harry's New York Bar...................... **55** G5

ENTERTAINMENT

Crazy Horse............................... **56** D6
Fnac Champs-Élysées....................... **57** D5
Kiosque Théâtre Madeleine................. **58** G5
Le Lido de Paris.......................... **59** D4
L'Olympia................................. **60** G5
Palais Garnier Box Office................. (see 37)
Salle Pleyel.............................. **61** D4
Virgin Megastore Champs-Élysées........... **62** E5

SHOPPING

Fauchon................................... **63** G5
Fromagerie Alléosse....................... **64** C3
Galeries Lafayette........................ **65** H4
Galeries Lafayette........................ **66** G4
La Maison du Miel......................... **67** G4
Le Printemps de l'Homme................... **68** G4
Le Printemps de la Beauté et Maison....... **69** G4
Le Printemps de la Mode................... **70** G4

TRANSPORT

ADA....................................... **71** F3
Air France Buses.......................... **72** C4
Batobus Stop.............................. **73** E6
Buses from Beauvais Airport............... **74** B3
Parking Pershing (Buses to Beauvais Airport)........ **75** B3
Roissybus................................. **76** G4

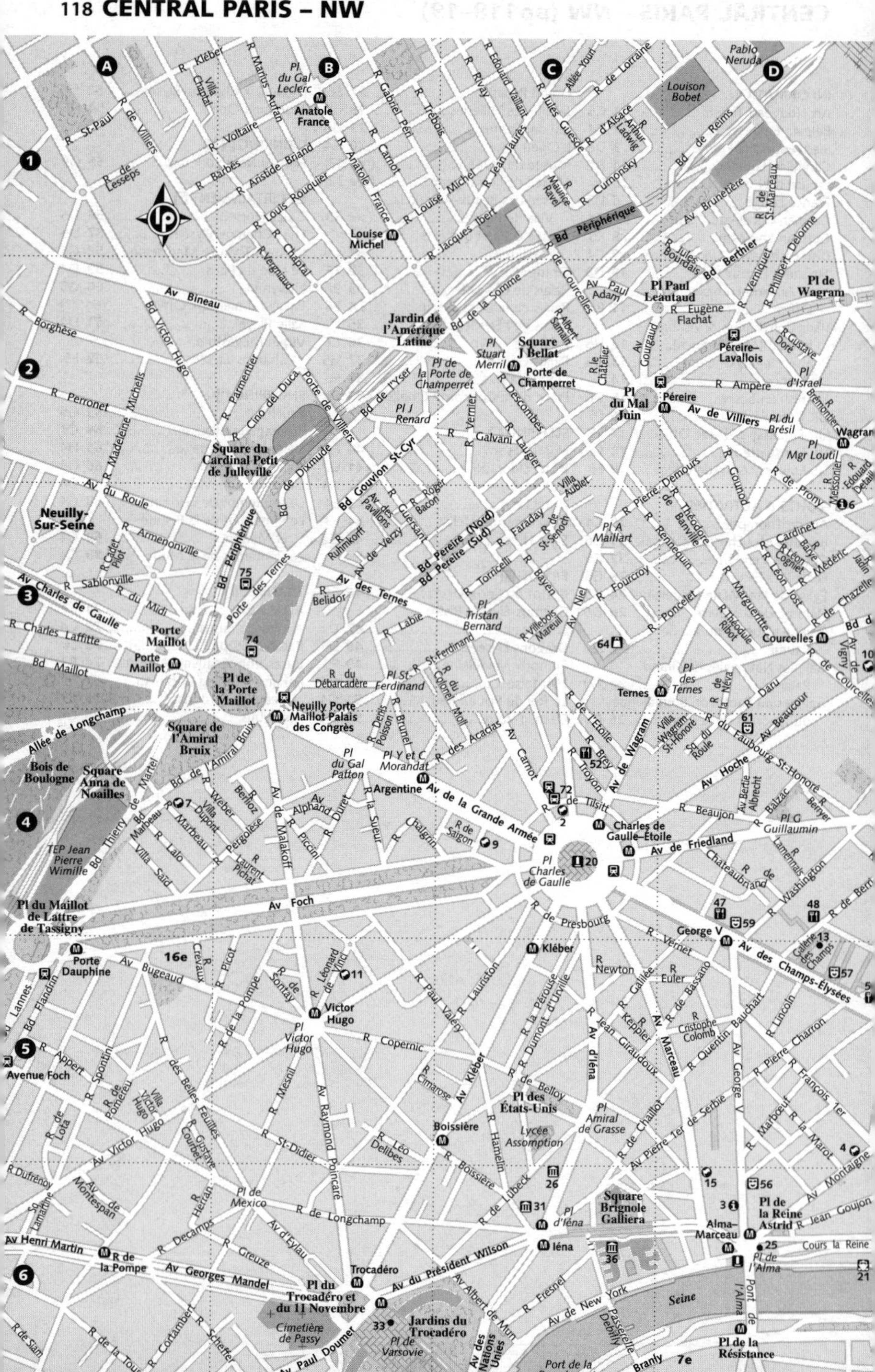
Neuilly-Sur-Seine
Bois de Boulogne
Porte Maillot
Pl de la Porte Maillot
Square de l'Amiral Bruix
Square Anna de Noailles
Pl du Maillot de Lattre de Tassigny
Porte Dauphine
Av Foch
Pl Charles de Gaulle
Charles de Gaulle–Etoile
Av des Champs-Élysées
Av de la Grande Armée
Av des Ternes
Av de Wagram
Bd Périphérique
Jardin de l'Amérique Latine
Square J Bellat
Porte de Champerret
Pl du Mal Juin
Pl de Wagram
Pl Paul Leautaud
Square du Cardinal Petit de Julleville
Louison Bobet
Anatole France
Louise Michel
Pereire
Ternes
Courcelles
Wagram
Argentine
Kléber
George V
Victor Hugo
Pl Victor Hugo
Boissière
Pl des États-Unis
Square Brignole Galliera
Iéna
Alma–Marceau
Pl de la Reine Astrid
Pl de l'Alma
Pl du Trocadéro et du 11 Novembre
Trocadéro
Jardins du Trocadéro
Cimetière de Passy
Pl de Varsovie
Seine
Pl de la Résistance
Port de la Bourdonnais
Av Henri Martin
Av Georges Mandel
Av du Président Wilson
Av Paul Doumer
Av Kléber
Av d'Iéna
Av Marceau
Av George V
Av Montaigne
Av Victor Hugo
Av Raymond Poincaré
Av Hoche
Av de Friedland
Av de Villiers
Av Niel
Av Bineau
Av Charles de Gaulle
Allée de Longchamp
Avenue Foch
16e
7e

0 500 m
0 0.3 miles
E
F
G
H
1
2
3
4
5
6
17e
8e
9e
2e
1er
Guy Môquet
Brochant
La Fourche
Pl de Clichy
Blanche
Pigalle
Rome
Villiers
Monceau
Malesherbes
Liège
Europe
St-Georges
Trinité
St-Lazare
Gare St-Lazare
St-Augustin
Miromesnil
Havre Caumartin
Auber
Chaussée d'Antin
Opéra
Quatre Septembre
Madeleine
Concorde
Tuileries
Pyramides
Palais Royal-Musée du Louvre
St-Philippe du Roule
Franklin D Roosevelt
Champs-Élysées Clemenceau
Invalides
Square des Batignolles
Square Carpeaux
Square S Buisson
Cimetière de Montmartre
Montmartre
Parc de Monceau
Square M Pagnol
Square Louis XVI
Square d'Estienne d'Orves
Pl G Toudouze
Pl Chassaigne-Goyon
Triangle d'Or
Grand Palais
Petit Palais
Jardin des Tuileries
Jardin du Carrousel
Hôtel Ritz Paris
Seine
Right Bank
Bd Pereire (Nord)
Bd Pereire (Sud)
Bd des Batignolles
Bd de Clichy
Bd Malesherbes
Bd Haussmann
Bd des Capucines
Bd de la Madeleine
Bd des Italiens
Av de Clichy
Av des Champs Élysées
Av de l'Opéra
Av Gabriel
Av Matignon
Av de Marigny
Av de Messine
R de Rome
R de Rivoli
R St-Honoré
R du Faubourg St-Honoré
R Royale
R La Fayette
R de Châteaudun
R de Provence
R de Londres
R de Madrid
R de Constantinople
R de Lisbonne
R d'Amsterdam
R de Clichy
R Lamarck
R Caulaincourt
R Lepic
R des Abbesses
Pl de la Concorde
Pl Vendôme
Pl de la Madeleine
Pl de l'Europe
Q des Tuileries
Q d'Orsay
Q de Solférino
Cours Albert 1er
Pont de la Concorde
Pont Alexandre III
Pont des Invalides
See Montmartre Map (p136)
See Central Paris – NE Map (pp120–21)
See Marais Map (pp126–27)

Montmartre
La Goutte d'Or
Gare du Nord
Gare de l'Est
Hôpital Lariboisière
Cimetière de Montmartre
Cimetière St-Vincent
Right Bank
Jardin du Palais Royal
Pletzl
9e
10e
2e
1er
3E
See Marais Map (pp126-27)

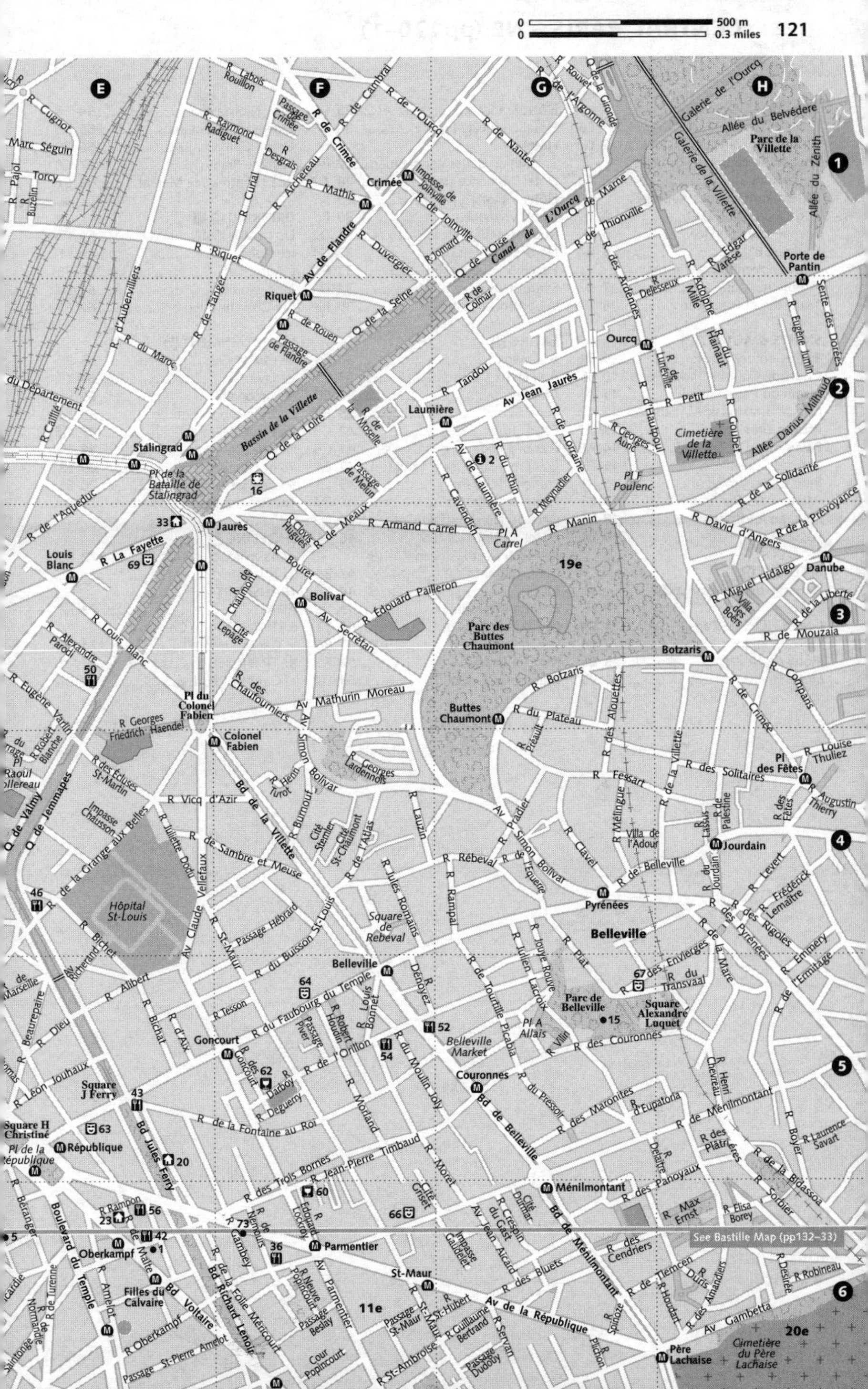
0 500 m
0 0.3 miles
E
F
G
H
1
2
3
4
5
6
Parc de la Villette
Canal de L'Ourcq
Bassin de la Villette
Parc des Buttes Chaumont
19e
11e
20e
Belleville
Hôpital St-Louis
Cimetière de la Villette
Cimetière du Père Lachaise
Crimée
Riquet
Stalingrad
Jaurès
Louis Blanc
Laumière
Bolivar
Colonel Fabien
Buttes Chaumont
Botzaris
Danube
Ourcq
Porte de Pantin
Pl des Fêtes
Jourdain
Pyrénées
Belleville
Goncourt
Couronnes
Ménilmontant
République
Oberkampf
Parmentier
St-Maur
Filles du Calvaire
Père Lachaise
Square J Ferry
Square H Christiné
Parc de Belleville
Square Alexandre Luquet
Belleville Market
Square de Rebeval
Av Jean Jaurès
Av de Flandre
Bd de la Villette
Bd de Belleville
Bd de Ménilmontant
Av de la République
Bd Voltaire
Bd Richard Lenoir
Boulevard du Temple
Q de Valmy
Q de Jemmapes
See Bastille Map (pp132–33)

INFORMATION
C'Clean Laverie......1 E6
Club Alpin Française......2 G2
Fédération Nationale des Gîtes de France......3 A4
Fédération Unie des Auberges de Jeunesse (FUAJ)......4 D2
Laverie Libre Service......5 E6
Laverie SBS......6 C4
Paris Convention & Visitors Bureau......7 D3
Tourisme et Handicaps......8 D2

SIGHTS & ACTIVITIES
13th-Century House......9 D6
Cours de Cuisine Olivier Berté...10 B5
Jardin du Palais Royal......11 B6
Musée des Arts et Métiers......12 C6
Musée Grévin......13 B5
Palais Royal......14 A6
Parc de Belleville......15 G5
Paris Canal Croisières......16 F2
Passage des Panoramas......17 B5
Passage Jouffroy......18 B4
Passage Verdeau......19 B4

SLEEPING
Auberge de Jeunesse Jules Ferry......20 E5
Grand Hôtel de Paris......21 D4
Hôtel Chopin......22 B4
Hôtel de Nevers......23 E6
Hôtel Favart......24 B5
Hôtel Français......25 D4
Hôtel La Vieille France......26 D3
Hôtel Peletier-Haussmann-Opéra...27 B4
Hôtel Résidence des 3 Poussins..28 A3
Hôtel Victoria......29 B5
Hôtel Vivienne......30 B5
Kube Hôtel......31 D2
Nord-Est Hôtel......32 C4
Peace & Love Hostel......33 E3
Sibour Hôtel......34 D4
Woodstock Hostel......35 B3

EATING
Asianwok......36 F6
Aux Deux Canards......37 C5
Chartier......38 B5
Food Shops......39 B3
Food Shops......40 C5
Franprix Faubourg St Denis......41 C5
Franprix Jean-Pierre Timbaud....42 E6
Franprix Jules Ferry......43 E5
Franprix Magenta......44 D4
Gare du Nord Buffalo Grill......45 D2
Hôtel du Nord......46 E4
Jewish & North African Kosher Restaurants......47 B4
Julien......48 C5
Krishna Bhavan......49 D3
Le Chaland......50 E3
Le Grand Colbert......51 B6
Marché Belleville......52 F5
Marché St-Quentin......53 D4
New Nioullaville......54 F5
Opéra Hippopotamus......55 A5
Ossek Garden......56 E6
Passage Brady......57 C5
Rue Montorgueil Market......58 C6

DRINKING
De La Ville Café......59 C5
Ice Kube......(see 31)
L'Autre Café......60 F6
Motown Bar......61 D4
On Cherche Encore......62 F5

ENTERTAINMENT
La Favela Chic......63 E5
La Java......64 F5
Le Limonaire......65 B5
Le Nouveau Casino......66 F6
Le Vieux Belleville......67 G5
New Morning......68 C4
Point Éphémère......69 E3
Social Club......70 B5
Théâtre des Bouffes du Nord....71 D2

SHOPPING
Anna Joliet......72 B6

TRANSPORT
ADA......73 F6
RATP Bus 350 to Charles de Gaulle Airport......74 D3
RATP Bus 350 to Charles de Gaulle Airport......75 D4

INFORMATION
Accueil Familial des Jeunes Etrangers....**1** G3
American Church in Paris....**2** E1
Australian Embassy & Trade Commission....**3** C3
Centre d'Information et de Documentation Jeunesse....**4** B2
Centre des Étudiants Étrangers....**5** D4
Cyber Cube....**6** G5
Fédération Française de Vol à Voile....**7** G3
Italian Embassy....**8** F3
Netherlands Embassy....**9** E4
South African Embassy....**10** E1
Swiss Embassy....**11** F2
Tea & Tattered Pages....**12** F4

SIGHTS & ACTIVITIES
Alliance Française....**13** G4
Cimetière du Montparnasse....**14** G6
Cimetière du Montparnasse Conservation Office....**15** G5
CineAqua....**16** C1
Cité de l'Architecture et du Patrimoine....**17** B1
École Le Cordon Bleu....**18** D6
Église du Dôme....**19** E3
Église St-Louis des Invalides....**20** E2
Fat Tire Bike Tours....**21** C3
Fat Tire Bike Tours Departure Point....**22** C2
Hôtel des Invalides....**23** E2
Hôtel Matignon....**24** F3
Musée d'Orsay....**25** G2
Musée de l'Armée....**26** E2
Musée de l'Homme....**27** B1
Musée de la Marine....(see 27)
Musée des Égouts de Paris....**28** D1
Musée du Quai Branly....**29** C1
Musée Rodin....**30** F3
Palais de Chaillot....**31** B1
Tombeau de Napoléon 1er....(see 19)
Tour Eiffel....**32** C2
Tour Montparnasse....**33** F5

SLEEPING
Celtic Hôtel....**34** G5
Hôtel Aviatic....**35** F4
Hôtel Delambre....**36** G5
Hôtel du Champ-de-Mars....**37** D2
Hôtel du Dragon....**38** G3
Hôtel Lindbergh....**39** G3
Hôtel Muguet....**40** E2
Mayet Hôtel....**41** F4

EATING
Atac....**42** F5
Boulevard Edgar Quinet Food Market....**43** G5
Brasserie Lipp....**44** H3
Crêperies....**45** G5
Inno....**46** F5
La Cagouille....**47** F6
La Coupole....**48** G5
Le Dôme....**49** G5
Marché Grenelle....**50** C3
Rue Cler Market....**51** E2

DRINKING
Cubana Café....**52** G5
Le Rosebud....**53** G5

ENTERTAINMENT
Kiosque Théâtre Montparnasse....**54** F5
Théâtre du Vieux Colombier....**55** G3

SHOPPING
Le Bon Marché....**56** G3

TRANSPORT
Air France Buses....**57** F1
Air France Buses....**58** F5
Aérogare des Invalides....**59** F1
Batobus Stop....(see 62)
Batobus Stop....**60** C2
easyCar....**61** F6
Paris Canal Croisières....**62** G1

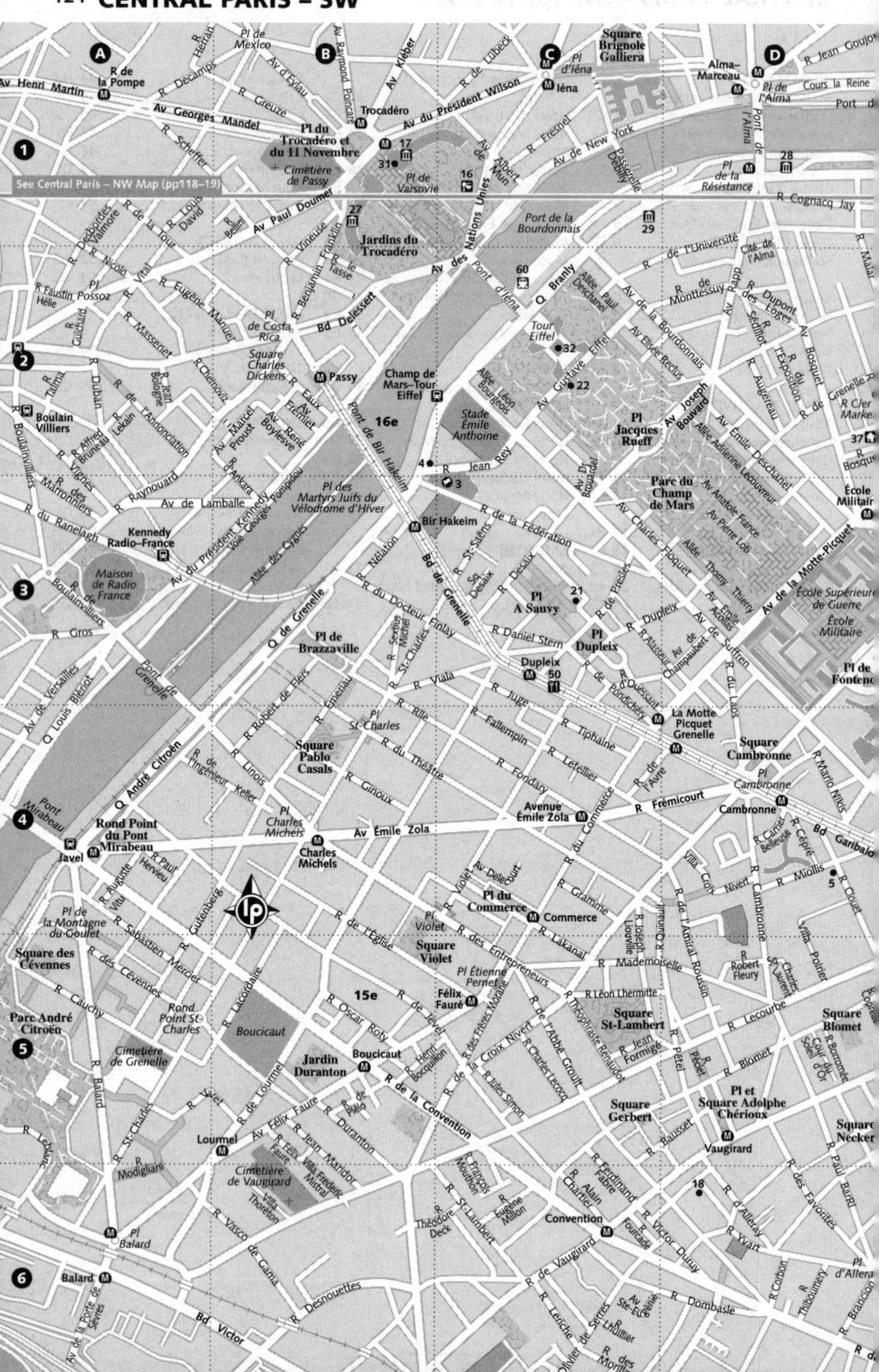
Square Brignole Galliera
Pl du Trocadéro et du 11 Novembre
Cimetière de Passy
See Central Paris – NW Map (pp118–19)
Jardins du Trocadéro
Port de la Bourdonnais
Tour Eiffel
Champ de Mars–Tour Eiffel
Stade Émile Anthoine
Pl Jacques Rueff
Parc du Champ de Mars
Pl des Martyrs Juifs du Vélodrome d'Hiver
Bir Hakeim
Kennedy Radio-France
Maison de Radio France
Pl de Brazzaville
Pl A Sauvy
Pl Dupleix
École Militaire
École Supérieure de Guerre
La Motte Picquet Grenelle
Square Cambronne
Square Pablo Casals
Rond Point du Pont Mirabeau
Avenue Émile Zola
Charles Michels
Pl du Commerce
Square Violet
Square des Cévennes
Parc André Citroën
Boucicaut
Jardin Duranton
Square St-Lambert
Square Blomet
Square Gerbert
Pl et Square Adolphe Chérioux
Square Necker
Cimetière de Grenelle
Cimetière de Vaugirard
Convention
Vaugirard
Balard
15e
16e

0 500 m
0 0.3 miles
Grand Palais
Petit Palais
Av Edward Tuck
Pl de la Concorde
R de Rivoli
R d'Alger
Tuileries
Av de l'Opéra
R de Montpensier
Cours Albert 1er
Conférence
Seine
Pont des Invalides
Pont Alexandre III
Pont de la Concorde
Jardin des Tuileries
1er
Pl des Pyramides
Palais Royal-Musée du Louvre
Palais Royal
Pl de Finlande
Q d'Orsay
Q des Tuileries
See Central Paris – NE Map (pp120–21)
Av Robert Schuman
R Surcouf
Esplanade des Invalides
Invalides
Av du Maréchal Gallieni
R de Constantine
Assemblée Nationale
Pl du Palais Bourbon
Pl du Prést E Harriot
R de Lille
Q Anatole France
Q de Solférino
Musée d'Orsay
Av du Général Lemonnier
Pl du Carrousel
Pl du Palais Royal
Jardin du Carrousel
Cour Napoléon
Right Bank
Jardin de l'Infante
Q du Louvre
R St-Dominique
R Fabert
Passage Jean Nicot
R de la Comète
R Amélie
Pl des Invalides
Square S Rousseau
Solférino
R de Bourgogne
R de Martignac
R Casimir Périer
R Las Cases
R de Villersexel
R de Poitiers
Pont Royal
Q Voltaire
Pont du Carrousel
Seine
Q Malaquais
Pl de l'Institut
Pl Santiago du Chili
La Tour Maubourg
Square Santiago du Chili
Square d'Ajaccio
Varenne
Faubourg St-Germain
R de Verneuil
R de l'Université
R du Bac
École des Beaux-Arts
R Bonaparte
R Mazarine
7e
R Ernest Psichari
R Duvivier
R Chevert
R Louis Codet
Jardin de l'Intendant
R de Bellechasse
Cité Martignac
R de St-Simon
Rue du Bac
Bd St-Germain
R de Luynes
R Jacob
Pl de Furstemberg
See Marais Map (pp126–27)
Cité Vaneau
R de Varenne
Cité de Varenne
R de Grenelle
R St-Guillaume
Pl St-Germain des Prés
Square F Desruelles
St-Germain des Prés
Av de Tourville
Pl Vauban
Bd des Invalides
R Barbet de Jouy
Bd Raspail
R de la Planche
R de la Chaise
Square Chaise Récamier
R des Saints Pères
R du Dragon
R Bernard Palissy
Mabillon
R de Seine
Av de Lowendal
R Bixio
Av Duquesne
Av de Breteuil
Av de Villars
Left Bank
Square des Missions Etrangères
Square des Missions Etragères
R du Four
R des Canettes
R Mabillon
St-François Xavier
R de Babylone
Square Boucicaut
Vieux Colombier
St-Sulpice
R St-Sulpice
Pl St-Sulpice
R d'Estrées
Pl du Prést Mithouard
Square de l'Abbé Esquerré
R Monsieur
Jardin Catherine Labouré
Laennec
R Velpeau
Sèvres Babylone
R du Cherche Midi
R Cassette
R Servandoni
R Férou
R de Condé
Av de Ségur
R Oudinot
R Vaneau
R Pierre Leroux
R Rousselet
R de Rennes
R de Vaugirard
Esplanade du Souvenir Français
R Eblé
R Masseran
Av de Saxe
R du Général Bertrand
R Duroc
Av Constant Coquelin
Vaneau
R de l'Abbé Grégoire
R St-Placide
R du Regard
Rennes
Jardin du Luxembourg
R Guynemer
R Pérignon
R Bellart
Ségur
Pl de Breteuil
R de Sèvres
R St-Romain
Galerie le Sevrien
R Jean Ferrandi
St-Placide
R de Fleurus
R Mayet
Duroc
R Blaise Desgoffe
R Huysmans
Necker
R Littré
Notre Dame des Champs
6e
Sèvres Lecourbe
Pl Henri Queuille
Falguière
Pl P Lafue
R Notre Dame des Champs
R Stanislas
Pl du 18 Juin 1940
Impasse Robiquet
R d'Assas
R Auguste Comte
Jardin R Cavelier-de-la-Salle
R Ernest Renan
R de Staël
Impasse Ronsin
Villa Garnier
Av Maine
Bd du Montparnasse
R Vavin
R Bréa
Université Paris V
Pl et Square Ozanam
Av de l'Observatoire
Bd St-Michel
R Émile Duclaux
R des Volontaires
Pasteur
R Nicholas Chanet
R Dalou
Pl J et T Trefouel
Porte Océane
Montparnasse Bienvenüe
R du Départ
R d'Odessa
Vavin
Jardin du Marco Polo
See Latin Quarter Map (pp130–31)
Volontaires
Bd Pasteur
R Mizon
Bd de Vaugirard
Pl Raoul Dautry
R Delambre
Pl E Denis
Square Gaston Baty
Gare Montparnasse
Edgar Quinet
Bd Edgar Quinet
Pl Camille Julian
R du Dr Roux
Allée du Capitaine Dronne
R de l'Armorique
R de la Gaîté
R Campagne Première
Port Royal
R Mathurin Régnier
R Vigée Lebrun
R Dutot
R Falguière
Jardin de l'Atlantique
Allée du Chef d'Escadron
Raspail
R Boissonade
Passage d'Enfer
R Bargue
R Antoine Payen
R du Cotentin
Pl des Cinq Martyrs du Lycée Buffon
Gaîté
R de la Procession
R Platon
R André Gide
Cimetière du Montparnasse
R Émile Richard
Hôpital St-Vincent de Paul
Av Denfert Rochereau
R Cassini
R Jean Zay
Pl Constantin Brancusi
Pl de Catalogne
R Alain
Av du Maine
R Cels
14e
R Froidevaux
R Schoelcher
Pl Falguière
Square Cardinal Wyszynski
R de l'Ouest
R Fermat
R Daguerre
R Gassendi
R Roger
Observatoire de Paris
R du Faubourg St-Jacques
Square de l'Abbé Lemire
R Guilleminot
R Raymond Losserand
R Édouard Jacques
R Asseline
R Lalande
R Boulard
R Nanteuil
R Labrouste
R Castagnary
R Vercingétorix
R Niepce
R du Château
R de l'Aide Sociale
Passage Tenaille
R Liancourt
Denfert Rochereau
Pl Denfert Rochereau
Bd Arago

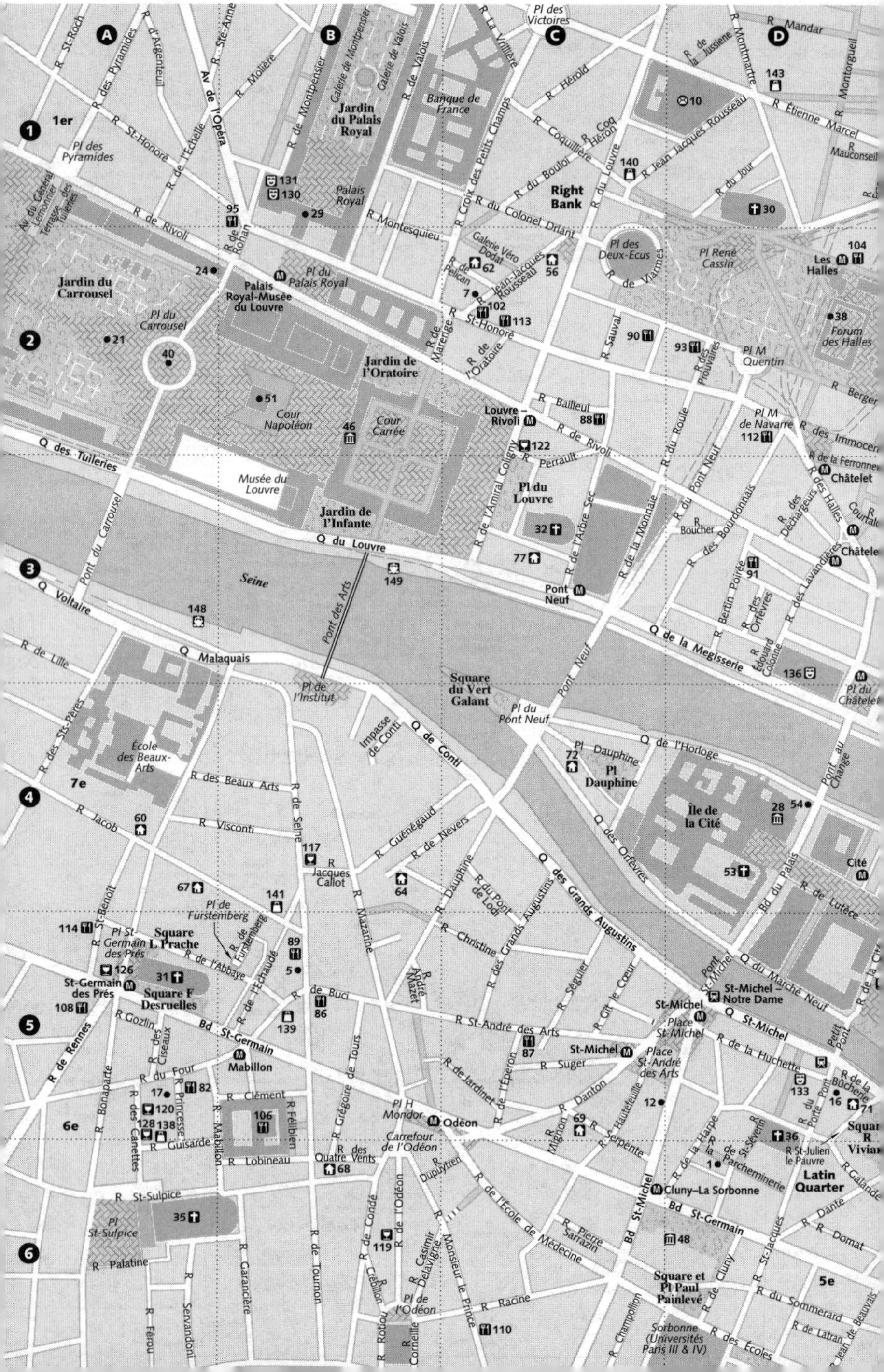

A
B
C
D
1
2
3
4
5
6
1er
7e
6e
5e
Pl des Victoires
Jardin du Palais Royal
Banque de France
Palais Royal
Jardin du Carrousel
Pl du Carrousel
Palais Royal-Musée du Louvre
Jardin de l'Oratoire
Cour Napoléon
Cour Carrée
Musée du Louvre
Jardin de l'Infante
Right Bank
Pl des Deux-Ecus
Pl René Cassin
Les Halles
Forum des Halles
Pl M Quentin
Pl M de Navarre
Louvre – Rivoli
Pl du Louvre
Pont Neuf
Châtelet
Seine
Pont des Arts
Pl de l'Institut
Square du Vert Galant
Pl du Pont Neuf
Pl Dauphine
Île de la Cité
Cité
Pl du Châtelet
École des Beaux-Arts
Square L Prache
Square F Desruelles
St-Germain des Prés
Pl de Furstemberg
Pl St-Germain des Prés
Mabillon
Odéon
Pl H Mondor
Carrefour de l'Odéon
St-Michel
St-Michel – Notre Dame
Place St-Michel
Place St-André des Arts
Cluny–La Sorbonne
Latin Quarter
Square R Viviani
Square et Pl Paul Painlevé
Sorbonne (Universités Paris III & IV)
Pl St-Sulpice
Pl de l'Odéon
R St-Roch
R des Pyramides
R d'Argenteuil
R Ste-Anne
Av de l'Opéra
R Molière
R de Montpensier
Galerie de Montpensier
Galerie de Valois
R de Valois
R La Vrillière
R Hérold
R de la Jussienne
R Montmartre
R Mandar
R Montorgueil
R Étienne Marcel
R Mauconseil
R St-Honoré
R de l'Echelle
Pl des Pyramides
Av du Général Lemonnier
Terrasse des Tuileries
R de Rivoli
R de Rohan
R Montesquieu
R Croix des Petits Champs
R du Bouloi
R Coquillière
R Coq Héron
R du Louvre
R Jean Jacques Rousseau
R du Jour
R du Colonel Driant
Galerie Véro Dodat
R de Pélican
R Jean-Jacques Rousseau
R de Viarmes
R Berger
Pl du Palais Royal
R de Marengo
R de l'Oratoire
R Sauval
R des Prouvaires
R Bailleul
R de Rivoli
R Perrault
R de l'Amiral Coligny
R de l'Arbre Sec
R de la Monnaie
R du Roule
R du Pont Neuf
R des Bourdonnais
R Boucher
R des Déchargeurs
R des Halles
R de la Ferronnerie
R des Innocents
R Courtalon
R des Lavandières
R Bertin Poirée
R des Orfèvres
R Edouard Colonne
Q des Tuileries
Pont du Carrousel
Q du Louvre
Q Voltaire
Q de la Megisserie
R de Lille
Q Malaquais
R des Sts-Pères
Impasse de Conti
Q de Conti
Q de l'Horloge
Pont au Change
R des Beaux Arts
R de Seine
R Jacob
R Visconti
R Guénégaud
R de Nevers
R Jacques Callot
R Dauphine
R du Pont de Lodi
R des Grands Augustins
Q des Grands Augustins
Q des Orfèvres
Bd du Palais
R de Lutèce
R St-Benoît
R de Furstemberg
R de l'Abbaye
R de l'Echaudé
R Mazarine
R Christine
R Séguier
R Git le Cœur
Pont St-Michel
Q du Marché Neuf
Petit Pont
R de la Cité
R de Buci
R André Mazet
R St-André des Arts
Q St-Michel
R de la Huchette
R de Rennes
R Gozlin
R des Ciseaux
Bd St-Germain
R du Four
R Princesse
R des Canettes
R Guisarde
R Mabillon
R Clément
R Félibien
R Lobineau
R Grégoire de Tours
R des Quatre Vents
R Bonaparte
R de Jardinet
R de l'Éperon
R Suger
R Danton
R Mignon
R Serpente
R Hautefeuille
R de la Harpe
R de la Parcheminerie
R de St-Séverin
R St-Julien le Pauvre
R de la Bûcherie
R du Petit Pont
R Galande
R Dupuytren
R de l'École de Médecine
Bd St-Michel
R Pierre Sarrazin
R St-Jacques
R Dante
R Domat
R St-Sulpice
R Palatine
R Garancière
R de Tournon
R de Condé
R de l'Odéon
R Casimir Delavigne
R Monsieur le Prince
R Crébillon
R Rotrou
R Corneille
R Racine
R Servandoni
R Férou
R Champollion
R de Cluny
R du Sommerard
R des Écoles
R de Latran
R Jean de Beauvais
1 7 10 12 16 17 21 24 28 29 30 31 32 35 36 38 40 46 48 51 53 54 56 60 62 64 67 68 69 71 72 77 82 86 87 88 89 90 91 93 95 102 104 106 108 110 112 113 114 117 119 120 122 126 128 130 131 133 136 138 139 140 141 143 148 149

E
F
G
H
1
2
3
4
5
6

R St-Sauveur
R Dussoubs
R Greneta
Passage du Grand Cerf
R Tiquetonne
Étienne Marcel
R de Turbigo
R de Palestro
Bd de Sébastopol
R Cunin Gridaine
Arts et Métiers
R des Fontaines du Temple
R du Temple
R Perrée
R Paul Dubois
R Gabriel Vicaire
R Dupetit Thouars
R Dupuis
R Bailly
R Réaumur
109
R au Maire
R Forez
R Eugène Spuller
Square du Temple
R du Bourg l'Abbé
135
96
81
R des Gravilliers
R des Vertus
R Portefoin
R Caffarelli
R de Picardie
R du Cygne
19
R Chapon
R aux Ours
99
2
R Beaubourg
R de Montmorency
R Grenier St-Lazare
R Pastourelle
3e
R de Beauce
R de Bretagne
142
R St-Martin
R Michel le Comte
R Charlot
R Rambuteau
R Brantôme
R Pierre Lescot
Châtelet les Halles
125
22
Rambuteau
Impasse Berthaud
R des Haudriettes
R des Archives
Rlle Sourdis
R de Saintonge
R Debelleyme
R de Poitou
137
R St-Denis
R Quincampoix
R de Venise
Pl Georges Pompidou
27
45
R Geoffroy Angevin
R de Braque
Passage Ste-Avoie
R des Fils
R du Perche
11
Pl Jean du Bellay
23
134
R de Rambuteau
R du Temple
Jardin de l'Hôtel Salé
R de la Reynie
Pl E Michelet
47
R St-Merri
R Simon le Franc
R Pecquay
R de Thorigny
R Ste-Anastase
127
Pl Igor Stravinsky
43
118
R de la Perle
R des Lombards
75
34
R du Cloître St-Merri
R du Renard
R du Plâtre
R des Francs Bourgeois
13
Square Ch V Langlois
111
R Barbette
R Pernelle
92
R Ste-Croix de la Bretonnerie
6
121
61
R Aubriot
R des Guillemites
R Vieille du Temple
R du Parc Royal
Square Léopold Achille
Square de la Tour St-Jacques
55
R St-Bon
R de Rivoli
R de la Verrerie
15
R de Moussy
R du Bourg Tibourg
8
115
R Elzévir
101
R Payenne
Square G Cain
Av Victoria
Bazar de l'Hôtel de Ville
97
100
R des Rosiers
Pletzl
144
116
R de la Tacherie
52
R des Mauvais Garçons
57
Pl du Bourg Tibourg
R du Trésor
R des Écouffes
R Ferdinand Duval
Q des Gesvres
Pl de l'Hôtel de Ville
Hôtel de Ville
73
65
124
18
129
R Pavée
See Bastille Map (pp132–33)
Pont Notre Dame
39
R Lobau
Place Baudoyer
59
98
145
R de Sévigné
Hôtel de Ville
R François Miron
20
R de Rivoli
R Tiron
R du Roi de Sicile
123
R Malher
Pont d'Arcole
Place St-Gervais
4e
49
58
85
R de Jarente
Q de la Corse
Place Louis Lépin
Seine
R de Brosse
R des Barres
R du Pont Louis Philippe
R Geoffroy l'Asnier
94
76
Pl du Marché Ste-Catherine
R d'Ormesson
St-Paul
4
3
103
80
R de Jouy
41
R de Fourcy
R de l'Hôtel de Ville
44
79
Hôtel Dieu
R de Colombe
R aux Fleurs
R des Ursins
147
Q de l'Hôtel de Ville
Passage St-Paul
R St-Antoine
R d'Arcole
R Chanoinesse
Square A Schweitzer
R des Nonnains d'Hyères
R Charlemagne
107
Pl du Bataillon Français de l'ONU en Corée
78
R Neuve St-Pierre
Pont Louis Philippe
R du Figuier
R du Fauconnier
14
Pl du Parvis Notre Dame
R du Cloître Notre Dame
Pont Marie
Square de l'Ave Maria
R des Jardins St-Paul
R St-Paul
70
50
26
84
R Jean du Bellay
R Charles V
R Beautreillis
25
Q de Bourbon
Q des Célestins
Pont au Double
Square Jean XXIII
Pont St-Louis
74
R St-Louis en l'Île
R Boutarel
63
105
Pont Marie
R des Lions St-Paul
R du Petit Musc
Q de Montebello
R de la Bûcherie
146
Pont de l'Archevêché
Square de l'Île de France
Île St-Louis
Q d'Orléans
R Budé
R des Deux Ponts
9
Q d'Anjou
R Jules Cousin
R Frédéric Sauton
83
33
R Poulletier
Square H Galli
Bd Henri IV
R Lagrange
R Maître Albert
R de Bièvre
Q de la Tournelle
Pont de la Tournelle
Q de Béthune
R de Bretonvilliers
Sully Morland
Q Henri IV
R de Sully
Maubert Mutualité
Pl Maubert
66
R des Bernardins
R de Pontoise
R Cochin
R de Poissy
Seine
Pont de Sully
Square Barye
R Agrippa d'Aubigné
Bd Morland
R des Carmes
Pl Maubert Market
R Monge

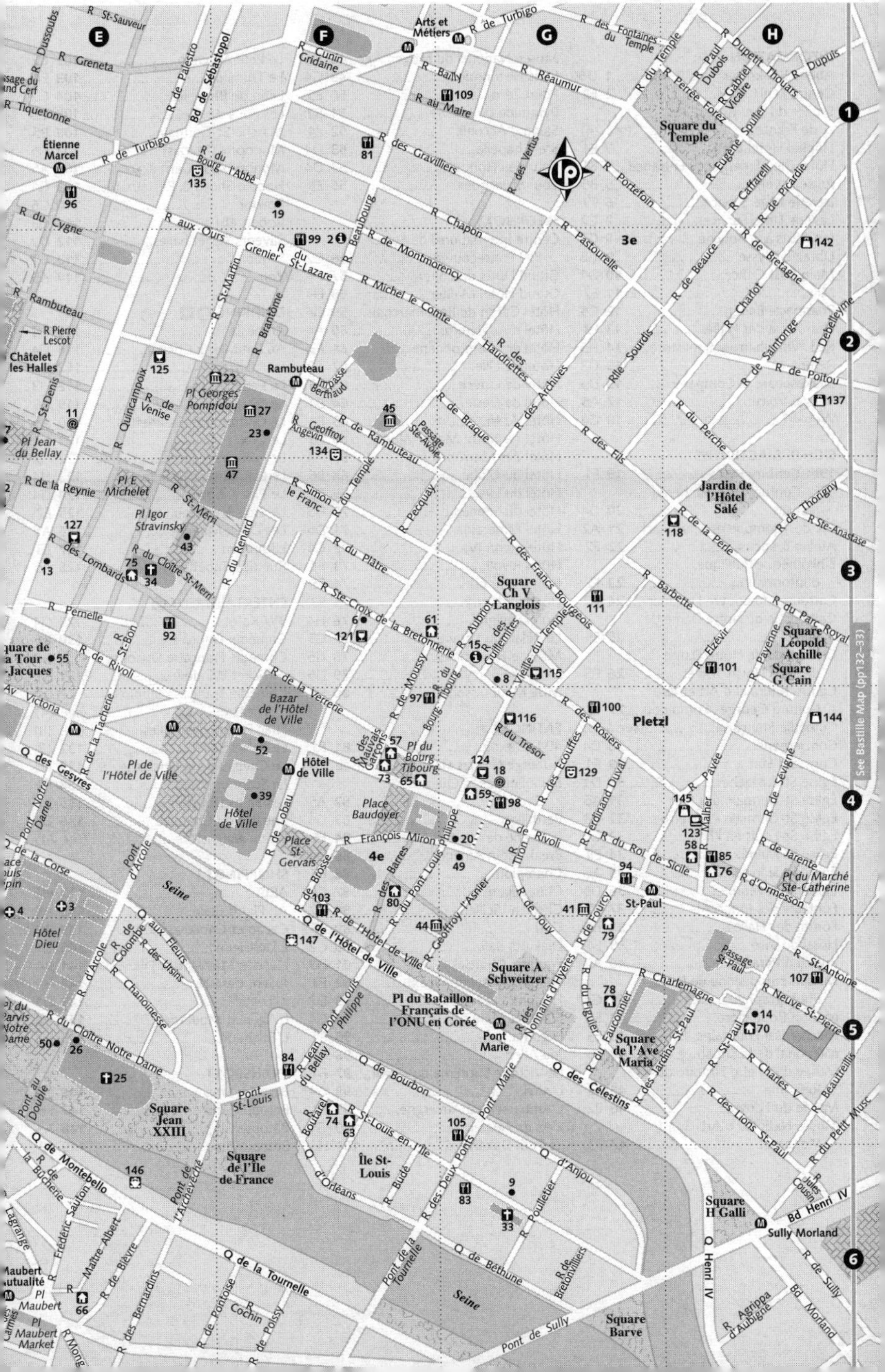

INFORMATION
Abbey Bookshop........................ **1** D6
Centre LGBT Paris........................ **2** F2
Espace du Tourisme d'Île
de France........................ (see 24)
Hôpital Hôtel Dieu........................ **3** E4
Hôtel Dieu Emergency Entrance... **4** E4
Julice Laverie........................ **5** B5
Laverie Libre Service........................ **6** F3
Laverie Libre Service........................ **7** C2
Les Mots à la Bouche........................ **8** G3
Librairie Ulysse........................ **9** G6
Main Post Office........................ **10** D1
Milk........................ **11** E2
Pharmacie Bader........................ **12** C5
Pharmacie des Halles........................ **13** E3
Red Wheelbarrow Bookstore...... **14** H5
Rempart........................ **15** G3
Shakespeare & Company........... **16** D5
Village Voice........................ **17** A5
Web 46........................ **18** G4

SIGHTS & ACTIVITIES
15th-Century House........................ **19** F1
16th-Century Half-Timbered
Houses........................ **20** G4
Arc de Triomphe du Carrousel.... **21** A2
Atelier Brancusi........................ **22** F2
Bibliothèque Publique
d'Information........................ **23** F2
Carrousel du Louvre Entrance..... **24** A2
Cathédrale de Notre Dame de
Paris........................ **25** E5
Cathédrale de Notre Dame
de Paris North Tower............. **26** E5
Centre National d'Art et de
Culture Georges Pompidou.... **27** F2
Comédie Française................ (see 130)
Conciergerie........................ **28** D4
Conseil d'État........................ **29** B1
Église St-Eustache........................ **30** D1
Église St-Germain des Prés.......... **31** A5
Église St-Germain l'Auxerrois...... **32** C3
Église St-Louis en l'Île................ **33** G6
Église St-Merri........................ **34** E3
Église St-Sulpice........................ **35** A6
Église St-Séverin........................ **36** D5
Fontaine des Innocents............... **37** E2
Forum des Halles........................ **38** D2
Hôtel de Ville........................ **39** F4
Inverted Pyramid........................ **40** A2
Maison Européenne de la
Photographie........................ **41** G4
Maison Roue Libre........................ **42** E2
Mechanical Fountains................ **43** E3
Mémorial de la Shoah................ **44** F5
Musée d'Art et d'Histoire du
Judaïsme........................ **45** F2
Musée du Louvre........................ **46** B2
Musée National d'Art
Moderne........................ **47** F3
Musée National du Moyen Âge.. **48** D6
Paris Historique........................ **49** G4
Point Zéro........................ **50** E5
Pyramide du Louvre........................ **51** B2
Salon d'Accueil........................ **52** F4
Ste-Chapelle........................ **53** D4
Tour de l'Horloge........................ **54** D4
Tour St Jacques........................ **55** E3

SLEEPING
Centre International de Séjour
BVJ Paris–Louvre........................ **56** C2
Grand Hôtel du Loiret................ **57** F4
Grand Hôtel Malher................... **58** H4
Hôtel Caron de Beaumarchais.... **59** G4
Hôtel d'Angleterre........................ **60** A4
Hôtel de la Bretonnerie.............. **61** F3
Hôtel de Lille........................ **62** C2
Hôtel de Lutèce........................ **63** F5
Hôtel de Nesle........................ **64** B4
Hôtel de Nice........................ **65** F4
Hôtel de Notre Maître Albert...... **66** E6
Hôtel des Marronniers................ **67** A4
Hôtel du Globe........................ **68** B6
Hôtel du Lys........................ **69** C5
Hôtel du Septième Art................ **70** H5
Hôtel Esmeralda........................ **71** D5
Hôtel Henri IV........................ **72** C4
Hôtel Rivoli........................ **73** F4
Hôtel St-Louis........................ **74** F5
Hôtel St-Merry........................ **75** E3
Hôtel Sévigné........................ **76** H4
Le Relais du Louvre........................ **77** C3
MIJE Le Fauconnier........................ **78** G5
MIJE Le Fourcy........................ **79** G5
MIJE Maubuisson........................ **80** F4

EATING
404........................ **81** F1
Auberge Nicolas Flamel............ (see 19)
Bar à Soupes et Quenelles
Giraudet........................ **82** A5
Berthillon........................ **83** G6
Brasserie de l'Île St-Louis............ **84** F5
Breakfast in America................... **85** H4
Champion........................ **86** B5
Chez Allard........................ **87** C5
Chez La Vieille........................ **88** C2
Cosi........................ **89** B5
Djakarta Bali........................ **90** C2
Franprix Châtelet........................ **91** D3
Franprix Hôtel de Ville................ **92** E3
Franprix Les Halles........................ **93** D2
Franprix Marais........................ **94** G4
Higuma........................ **95** B1
Joe Allen........................ **96** E1
La Victoire Suprême du Cœur.... **97** F4
L'Alivi........................ **98** G4
L'Ambassade d'Auvergne........... **99** F2
L'As de Felafel........................ **100** G4
Le Petit Dakar........................ **101** H3
Le Petit Mâchon........................ **102** C2
Le Trumilou........................ **103** F4
Léon de Bruxelles........................ **104** D2
Les Fous de l'Île........................ **105** G5
Marché St-Germain........................ **106** B5
Monoprix (Marais)........................ **107** H5
Monoprix (St-Germain)............ **108** A5
Noodle Shops & Restaurants..... **109** G1
Polidor........................ **110** C6
Robert et Louise........................ **111** G3
Saveurs Végét'halles................... **112** D2
Scoop........................ **113** C2
Yen........................ **114** A5

DRINKING
Amnésia........................ **115** G3
Au Petit Fer à Cheval............... **116** G4
La Palette........................ **117** B4
La Perle........................ **118** H3
Le 10........................ **119** B6
Le Comptoir des Canettes........ **120** A5
Le Cox........................ **121** F3
Le Fumoir........................ **122** C2
Le Loir dans la Thèière............. **123** H4
Le Pick Clops........................ **124** G4
Le Troisième Lieu........................ **125** E2
Les Deux Magots........................ **126** A5
L'Imprévu........................ **127** E3
Rue des Canettes........................ **128** A5

ENTERTAINMENT
3W Kafé........................ **129** G4
Comédie Française........................ **130** B1
Comédie Française Discount
Ticket Window........................ **131** B1
Comédie Française Studio
Théâtre........................ (see 24)
Fnac Forum des Halles.............. (see 38)
Le Baiser Salé........................ **132** E3
Le Caveau de la Huchette......... **133** D5
Le Scannon........................ **134** F2
Les Bains Douches........................ **135** E1
Théâtre du Châtelet **136** D3
Virgin Megastore..................... (see 24)

SHOPPING
APC........................ **137** H2
Au Plat d'Étain........................ **138** A5
Cacao et Chocolat........................ **139** B5
E Dehillerin........................ **140** C1
Huilerie J Leblanc et Fils............ **141** B4
Julien, Caviste........................ **142** H2
Kiliwatch........................ **143** D1
L'Agende Moderne........................ **144** H4
L'Éclaireur........................ **145** H4

TRANSPORT
Batobus Stop........................ **146** E6
Batobus Stop........................ **147** F5
Batobus Stop........................ **148** A3
Batobus Stop........................ **149** B3

INFORMATION
Hôpital de la Pitié-Salpêtrière Night-Time Entrance....1 H5
Laverie Libre Service....2 C3
Laverie Libre Service....3 F3
Milk....4 C2
SOS Dentaire....5 C5

SIGHTS & ACTIVITIES
École de Botanique....6 G3
Église Royale du Val-de-Grâce....7 C4
Galerie de Minéralogie et de Géologie....8 G4
Gepetto et Vélos....9 E2
Grande Galerie de l'Évolution....10 F4
Institut du Monde Arabe....11 G1
Jardin Alpin....12 G3
Jardin d'Hiver (Serres Tropicales)....13 G3
Jardin des Plantes Entrance....14 F4
Me*énagerie du Jardin des Plantes....15 G3
Mosquée de Paris....16 F4
Musée du Luxembourg....17 A1
Orchards....18 A3
Palais du Luxembourg....19 B2
Panthéon....20 D2
Rucher du Luxembourg....21 A3
Sorbonne....22 D1

SLEEPING
Centre International de Séjour BVJ Paris–Quartier Latin....23 E2
Familia Hôtel....24 E2
Hôtel Cluny Sorbonne....25 C2
Hôtel de l'Espérance....26 E5
Hôtel des 3 Collèges....27 C2
Hôtel des Grandes Écoles....28 E3
Hôtel Gay-Lussac....29 C3
Hôtel La Demeure....30 F5
Hôtel Minerve....31 E2
Hôtel St-Jacques....32 D1
Port Royal Hôtel....33 E6
Select Hôtel....34 C2
Young & Happy Hostel....35 E4

EATING
Bouillon Racine....36 C1
Champion....37 E2
Ed l'Épicier....38 E3
Food Shops....(see 48)
Franprix....39 E4
Indonesia....40 C1
Kootchi....41 E2
La Mosquée de Paris....42 F4
L'AOC....43 F1
Le Baba Bourgeois....44 F1
Le Foyer du Vietnam....45 E4
Le Petit Pontoise....46 F1
Les Cinq Saveurs d'Ananda....47 E3
Marché Maubert....48 E1
Marché Monge....49 E4
Monoprix....50 C1
Perraudin....51 C2
Rue Mouffetard Market....52 E5
Sushi Wasabi....53 D1

DRINKING
Le Piano Vache....54 D2
Le Pub St-Hilaire....55 D2

TRANSPORT
Batobus Stop....56 G2
Eurolines Office....57 D1

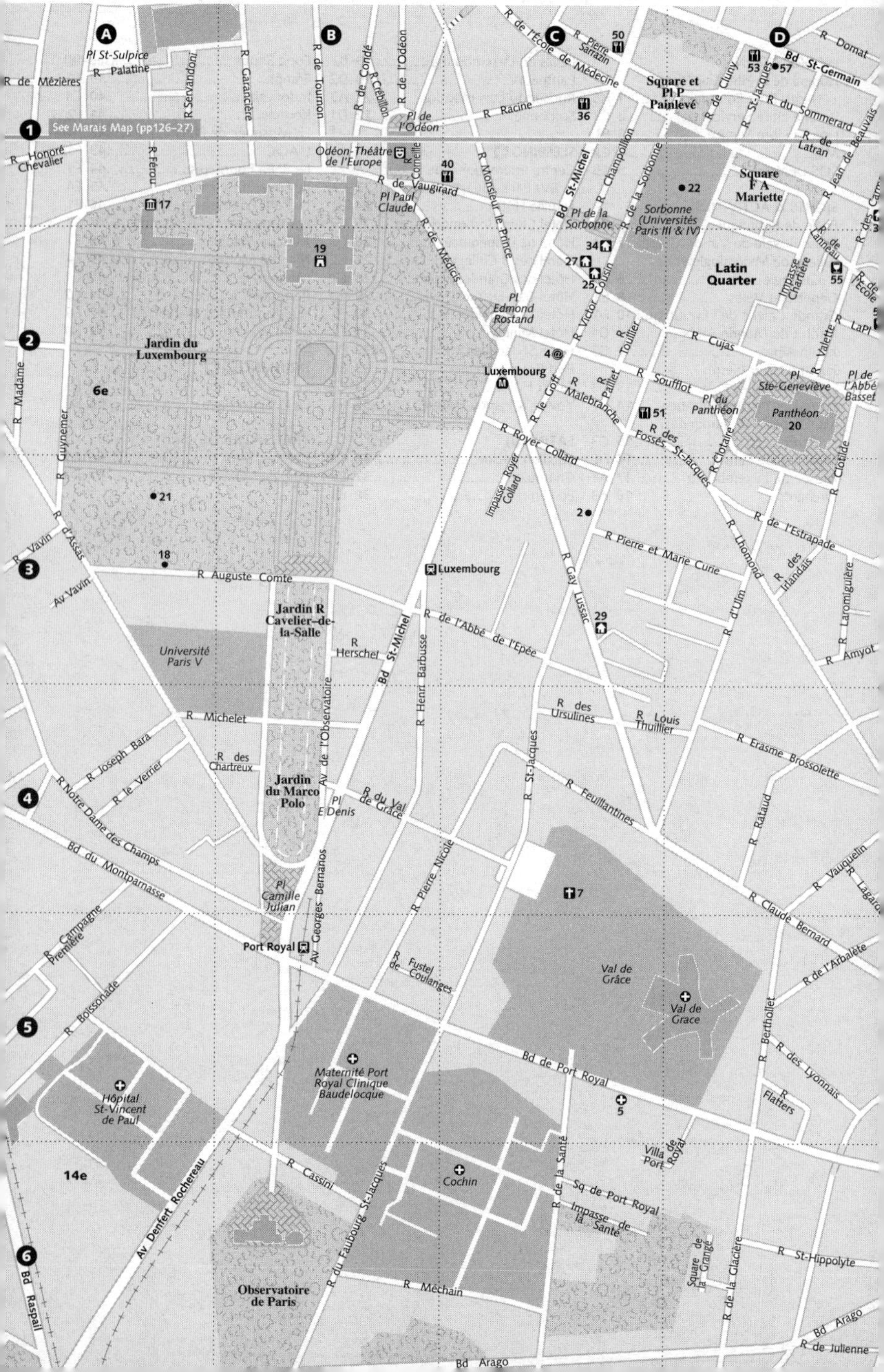
A
B
C
D
1
2
3
4
5
6
See Marais Map (pp126–27)
Pl St-Sulpice
R Palatine
R de Mézières
R Servandoni
R Garancière
R de Tournon
R de Condé
R Crébillon
R de l'Odéon
Pl de l'Odéon
R de l'École de Médecine
R Pierre Sarrazin
50
Square et Pl P Painlevé
R de Cluny
R St-Jacques
53
57
Bd St-Germain
R Domat
R du Sommerard
R de Latran
R Jean de Beauvais
R Racine
36
R Honoré Chevalier
R Férou
Odéon-Théâtre de l'Europe
R Corneille
40
R de Vaugirard
Pl Paul Claudel
R Monsieur le Prince
Bd St-Michel
R Champollion
R de la Sorbonne
22
Square F A Mariette
17
Pl de la Sorbonne
Sorbonne (Universités Paris III & IV)
R de Lanneau
R des Carmes
19
R de Médicis
34
27
25
R Victor Cousin
Latin Quarter
Impasse Chartière
55
R de l'École
Pl Edmond Rostand
R Toullier
R Cujas
R Valette
R Lapl
Jardin du Luxembourg
4
Luxembourg
R Soufflot
Pl Ste-Geneviève
Pl de l'Abbé Basset
6e
R Madame
R Guynemer
R le Goff
R Paillet
R Malebranche
Pl du Panthéon
Panthéon
20
51
R des Fossés St-Jacques
R Royer Collard
Impasse Royer Collard
R Clotaire
R Clotilde
21
2
R de l'Estrapade
R d'Assas
R Vavin
R Pierre et Marie Curie
R Lhomond
R des Irlandais
18
R Auguste Comte
Luxembourg
R Gay Lussac
R Laromiguière
Av Vavin
Jardin R Cavelier-de-la-Salle
R de l'Abbé de l'Epée
29
R d'Ulm
R Amyot
Université Paris V
R Herschel
R Henri Barbusse
R Michelet
Av de l'Observatoire
R des Ursulines
R Louis Thuillier
R Erasme Brossolette
R Joseph Bara
R des Chartreux
R le Verrier
R Notre Dame des Champs
Jardin du Marco Polo
Pl E Denis
R du Val de Grâce
R St-Jacques
R Feuillantines
R Rataud
Bd du Montparnasse
R Pierre Nicole
7
R Vauquelin
R Lagarde
Pl Camille Julian
Av Georges Bernanos
R Claude Bernard
R Campagne Première
Port Royal
R Fustel de Coulanges
Val de Grâce
R de l'Arbalète
R Boissonade
Val de Grace
R Berthollet
Hôpital St-Vincent de Paul
Maternité Port Royal Clinique Baudelocque
Bd de Port Royal
R des Lyonnais
5
R Flatters
14e
Av Denfert Rochereau
R Cassini
Cochin
Villa de Port Royal
R de la Santé
Sq de Port Royal
Impasse de la Santé
R du Faubourg St-Jacques
Square de la Grange
R St-Hippolyte
R de la Glacière
Bd Raspail
Observatoire de Paris
R Méchain
Bd Arago
R de Julienne
Bd Arago

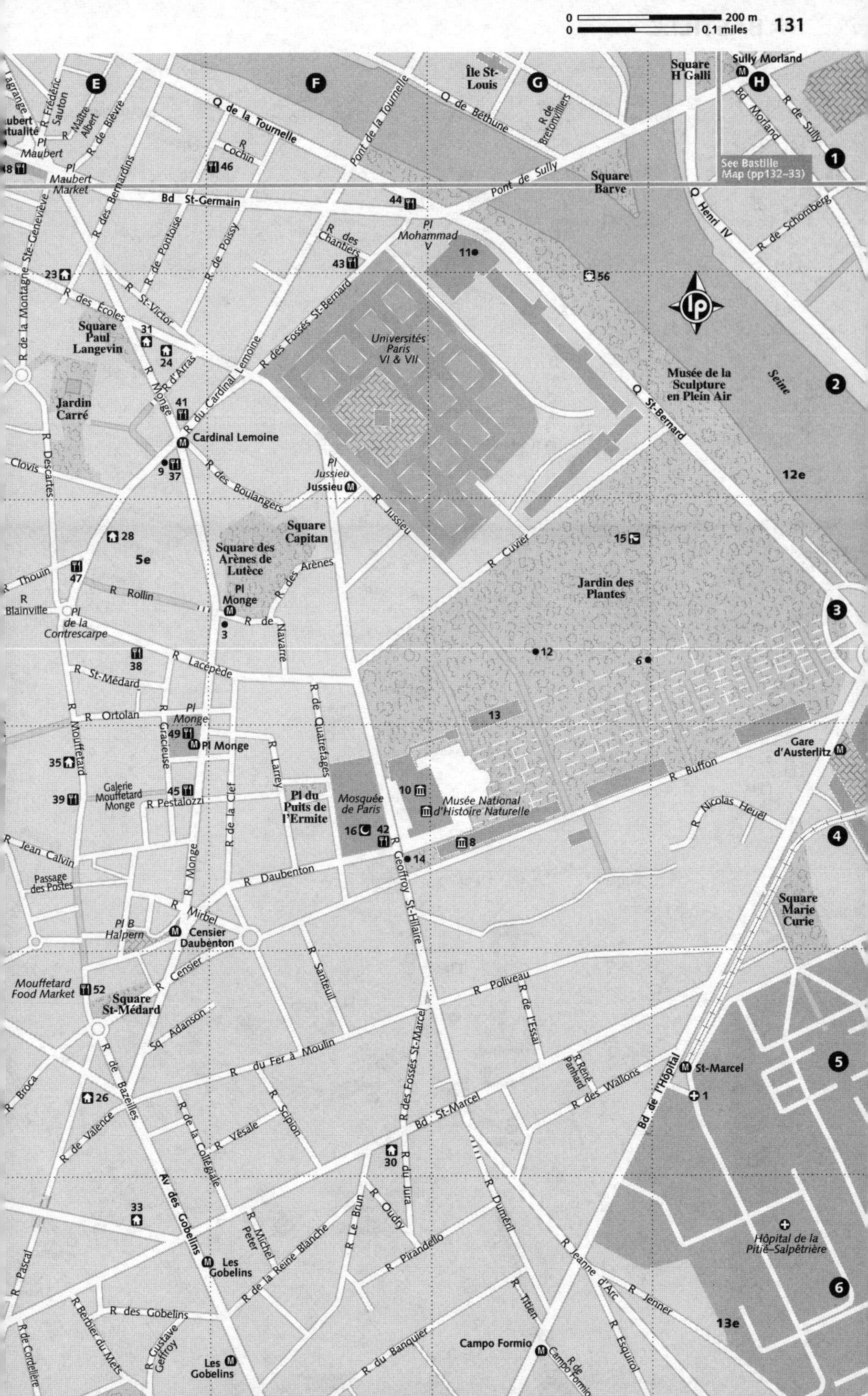

0 200 m
0 0.1 miles
Île St-Louis
Square H Galli
Sully Morland
Q de la Tournelle
Q de Béthune
Pont de la Tournelle
Pont de Sully
See Bastille Map (pp132–33)
Square Barve
Bd St-Germain
Q Henri IV
R de Schomberg
Pl Maubert
Maubert Market
Universités Paris VI & VII
Musée de la Sculpture en Plein Air
Seine
Q St-Bernard
Square Paul Langevin
Jardin Carré
Cardinal Lemoine
Jussieu
Square Capitan
Square des Arènes de Lutèce
Pl Monge
Jardin des Plantes
5e
12e
13e
Pl de la Contrescarpe
R Lacépède
R Mouffetard
R Monge
Pl du Puits de l'Ermite
Mosquée de Paris
Musée National d'Histoire Naturelle
R Buffon
Gare d'Austerlitz
R Daubenton
R Geoffroy St-Hilaire
Square Marie Curie
Censier Daubenton
Mouffetard Food Market
Square St-Médard
R Poliveau
R du Fer à Moulin
Bd St-Marcel
St-Marcel
Bd de l'Hôpital
Hôpital de la Pitié–Salpêtrière
Av des Gobelins
Les Gobelins
Campo Formio
R Jeanne d'Arc
R Jenner
R Dunéril
R du Banquier
R des Gobelins

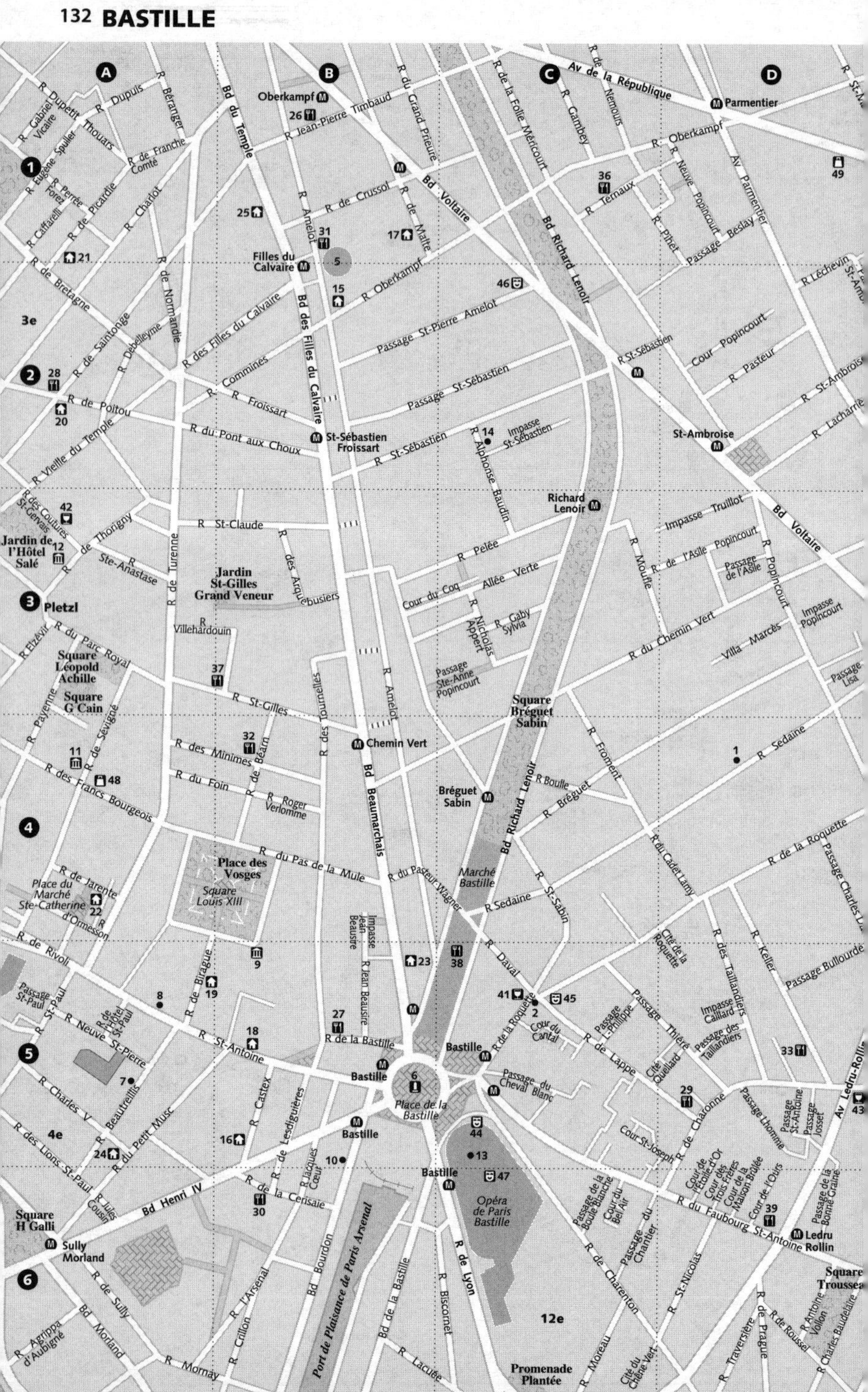

A
B
C
D
1
2
3
4
5
6
Av de la République
Parmentier
Oberkampf
R Jean-Pierre Timbaud
Bd du Temple
R Dupuis
R Béranger
R Gabriel Vicaire
R Eugène Spuller
R de Franche Comté
R Perrée
R Forez
R de Picardie
R Charlot
R Caffarelli
R de Bretagne
R de Normandie
R Amelot
R de Crussol
R de Malte
R du Grand Prieuré
Bd Voltaire
R de la Folie Méricourt
R Gambey
R Nemours
R Oberkampf
R Neuve Popincourt
Av Parmentier
R Ternaux
R Pihet
Passage Beslay
Bd Richard Lenoir
Filles du Calvaire
Bd des Filles du Calvaire
Passage St-Pierre Amelot
R des Filles du Calvaire
R de Saintonge
R Debelleyme
R Commines
R Froissart
R de Poitou
R du Pont aux Choux
St-Sébastien Froissart
Passage St-Sébastien
R St-Sébastien
R Vieille du Temple
R Alphonse Baudin
Impasse St-Sébastien
R Léchevin
Cour Popincourt
R Pasteur
R St-Ambroise
R Lacharrière
St-Ambroise
Richard Lenoir
Impasse Truillot
R de l'Asile Popincourt
Passage de l'Asile
R Popincourt
R Mouffle
R des Coutures St-Gervais
Jardin de l'Hôtel Salé
R de Thorigny
R Ste-Anastase
R St-Claude
R de Turenne
Jardin St-Gilles Grand Veneur
R des Arquebusiers
R Pelée
Allée Verte
Cour du Coq
R Nicholas Appert
R Gaby Sylvia
R du Chemin Vert
Impasse Popincourt
Villa Marcès
Passage Lisa
Pletzl
R Elzévir
R du Parc Royal
R Villehardouin
Square Léopold Achille
Square G Cain
R Payenne
R de Sévigné
R St-Gilles
R des Tournelles
Passage Ste-Anne Popincourt
Square Bréguet Sabin
R Froment
R Sedaine
R des Minimes
R de Béarn
Chemin Vert
R du Foin
R Roger Verlomme
R des Francs Bourgeois
Bd Beaumarchais
Bréguet Sabin
R Boulle
R Bréguet
R de la Roquette
Passage Charles Dallery
R du Cadet Lamy
Place des Vosges
Square Louis XIII
R du Pas de la Mule
R du Pasteur Wagner
Marché Bastille
R Sedaine
R St-Sabin
R de Jarente
Place du Marché Ste-Catherine
R d'Ormesson
Impasse Jean Beausire
R Jean Beausire
R de Rivoli
R Daval
Cité de la Roquette
R des Taillandiers
R Keller
Passage Bullourde
Passage St-Paul
R St-Paul
R de l'Hôtel St-Paul
R Neuve St-Pierre
R de Birague
R St-Antoine
R de la Bastille
Bastille
Passage L-Philippe
Passage Thiéré
Impasse Caillard
Passage des Taillandiers
Cour du Cantal
R de Lappe
Cité Quellard
Passage du Cheval Blanc
Place de la Bastille
R de Charonne
Passage L'homme
Passage St-Antoine
Passage Josset
Av Ledru-Rollin
R Charles V
R Beautreillis
R du Petit Musc
R Castex
R de Lesdiguières
R des Lions St-Paul
R Jacques Cœur
Cour St-Joseph
Cour de l'Étoile d'Or
Cour des Trois Frères
Cour de la Maison Brûlée
Cour de l'Ours
Passage de la Bonne Graine
R Jules Cousin
R de la Cerisaie
Opéra de Paris Bastille
Passage de la Boule Blanche
Cour du Bel Air
Passage du Chantier
R du Faubourg St-Antoine
Ledru Rollin
Square H Galli
Sully Morland
Bd Henri IV
Bd Bourdon
Port de Plaisance de Paris Arsenal
Bd de la Bastille
R de Lyon
R Biscornet
R de Charenton
R St-Nicolas
Square Trousseau
R Antoine Vollon
R de Sully
Bd Morland
R de l'Arsenal
R Crillon
R Agrippa d'Aubigné
R Mornay
R Lacuée
Promenade Plantée
R Moreau
Cité du Chêne Vert
R Traversière
R de Prague
R de Rousset
R Charles Baudelaire
3e
4e
12e
1
2
5
6
7
8
9
10
11
12
13
14
15
16
17
18
19
20
21
22
23
24
25
26
27
28
29
30
31
32
33
36
37
38
39
41
42
43
44
45
46
47
48
49

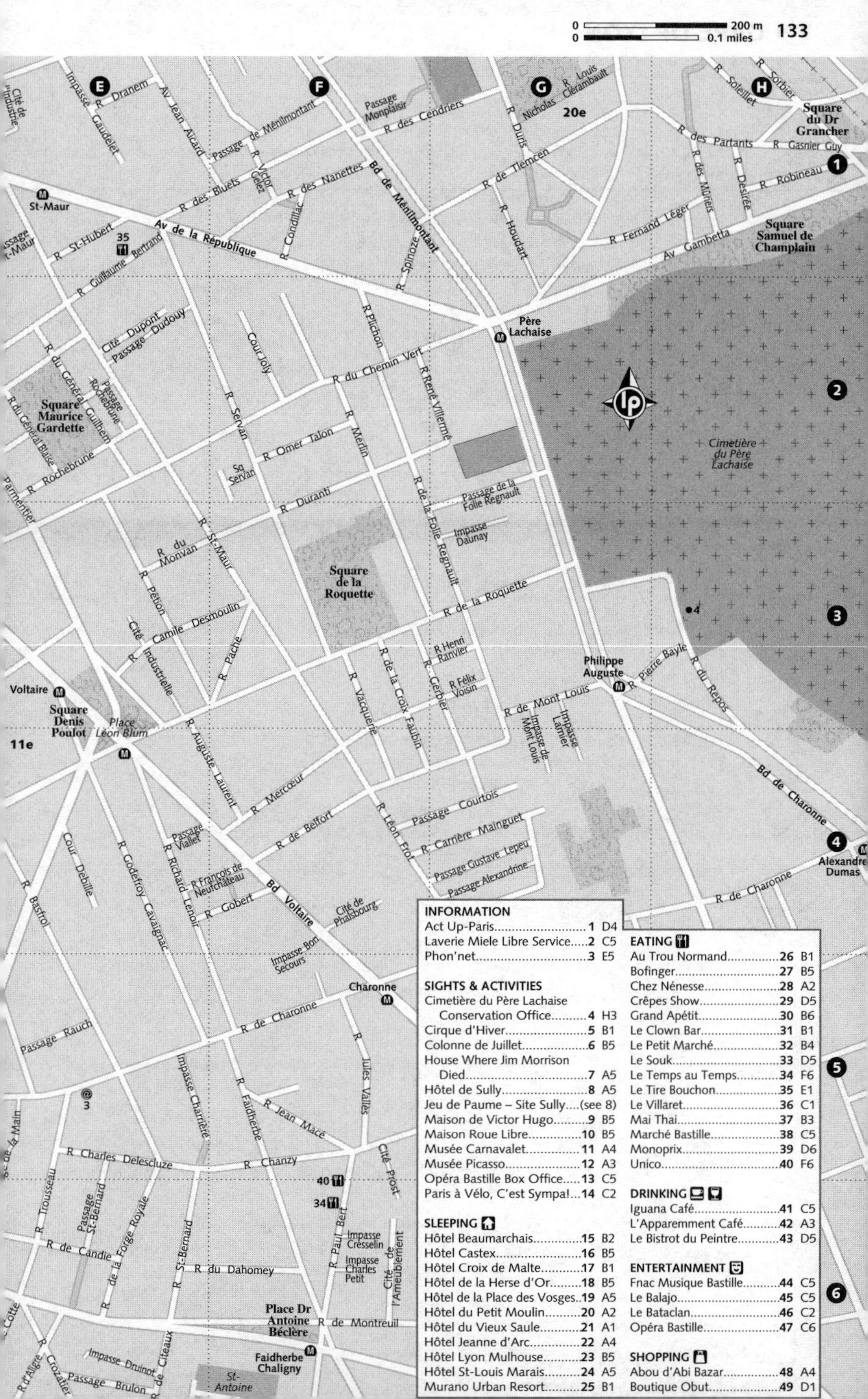
0 200 m
0 0.1 miles
E
F
G
H
1
2
3
4
5
6
20e
11e
Square du Dr Grancher
Square Samuel de Champlain
Square Maurice Gardette
Square de la Roquette
Square Denis Poulot
Place Léon Blum
Place Dr Antoine Béclère
Cimetière du Père Lachaise
St-Maur
Père Lachaise
Philippe Auguste
Voltaire
Alexandre Dumas
Charonne
Faidherbe Chaligny
Av de la République
Bd de Ménilmontant
Av Gambetta
Bd de Charonne
Bd Voltaire
R du Chemin Vert
R de la Roquette
R de Charonne
R de Montreuil
R St-Maur
R de la Folie Regnault
R Léon Frot
R Faidherbe
R Chanzy
R Charles Delescluze
R de Candie
R du Dahomey
R de Mont Louis
R du Repos
R Pierre Bayle
R des Cendriers
R de Tlemcen
R Fernand Léger
R des Partants
R Robineau
R Duranti
R Omer Talon
R Servan
R Merlin
R Pétion
R Camille Desmoulin
R Mercœur
R de Belfort
R Godefroy Cavaignac
R Richard Lenoir
R Basfroi
R Trousseau
R St-Bernard
R Paul Bert
R Jules Vallès
R Jean Macé
INFORMATION
Act Up-Paris....1 D4
Laverie Miele Libre Service....2 C5
Phon'net....3 E5
SIGHTS & ACTIVITIES
Cimetière du Père Lachaise Conservation Office....4 H3
Cirque d'Hiver....5 B1
Colonne de Juillet....6 B5
House Where Jim Morrison Died....7 A5
Hôtel de Sully....8 A5
Jeu de Paume – Site Sully....(see 8)
Maison de Victor Hugo....9 B5
Maison Roue Libre....10 B5
Musée Carnavalet....11 A4
Musée Picasso....12 A3
Opéra Bastille Box Office....13 C5
Paris à Vélo, C'est Sympa!....14 C2
SLEEPING
Hôtel Beaumarchais....15 B2
Hôtel Castex....16 B5
Hôtel Croix de Malte....17 B1
Hôtel de la Herse d'Or....18 B5
Hôtel de la Place des Vosges....19 A5
Hôtel du Petit Moulin....20 A2
Hôtel du Vieux Saule....21 A1
Hôtel Jeanne d'Arc....22 A4
Hôtel Lyon Mulhouse....23 B5
Hôtel St-Louis Marais....24 A5
Murano Urban Resort....25 B1
EATING
Au Trou Normand....26 B1
Bofinger....27 B5
Chez Nénesse....28 A2
Crêpes Show....29 D5
Grand Apétit....30 B6
Le Clown Bar....31 B1
Le Petit Marché....32 B4
Le Souk....33 D5
Le Temps au Temps....34 F6
Le Tire Bouchon....35 E1
Le Villaret....36 C1
Mai Thai....37 B3
Marché Bastille....38 C5
Monoprix....39 D6
Unico....40 F6
DRINKING
Iguana Café....41 C5
L'Apparemment Café....42 A3
Le Bistrot du Peintre....43 D5
ENTERTAINMENT
Fnac Musique Bastille....44 C5
Le Balajo....45 C5
Le Bataclan....46 C2
Opéra Bastille....47 C6
SHOPPING
Abou d'Abi Bazar....48 A4
Boutique Obut....49 D1

A
B
C
D
1
2
3
4
5
6
Sully Morland
Ledru Rollin
Opéra de Paris Bastille
Square Trousseau
R de Sully
R Agrippa d'Aubigné
R l'Arsenal
Bd Bourdon
R Biscornet
R St-Nicolas
Av Ledru Rollin
R Antoine Vollon
See Marais Map (pp126–27)
R Mornay
R Lacuée
R de Lyon
R Moreau
Cité du Chêne Vert
R de Prague
R Charles Baudelaire
R Traversière
Q Henri IV
R de Schomberg
R de Brissac
R Crillon
Bd de la Bastille
R Jules César
Promenade Plantée
R de Charenton
7
Bd Morland
See Latin Quarter Map (pp130–31)
R de Bercy
Av Ledru Rollin
Av Daumesnil
R d'Austerlitz
R Crémieux
R Parrot
R Émile Gilbert
R Michel Chasles
R Abel
R Legraverend
Pont Morland
Sq Georges Lesage
Quai de la Rapée
Pl Mazas
R Traversière
R Abel
R Legraverend
Q St-Bernard
Seine
Voie Mazas
R Audubon
Bd Diderot
Gare de Lyon
R Hector Malot
5
R Jean Bouton
R Guillaumot
Pl H Fresnay
Jardin des Plantes
Pont d'Austerlitz
3
Gare de Lyon
R de Chalon
5e
R Van Gogh
R de Bercy
4
R Buffon
Gare d'Austerlitz
Cour d'Arrivée
Cour Départ
Gare d'Austerlitz
Pont Charles de Gaulle
R Nicolas Houel
Q de la Rapée
Bd de l'Hôpital
R Villiot
Square Marie Curie
Q d'Austerlitz
Av Pierre Mendès-France
Bd de Bercy
13e
R Fulton
1
R Bellièvre
R Giffard
R Edmond Flamand
Pont de Bercy
Quai de la Gare
Q de la Gare
Seine
Q de Bercy
Hôpital de la Pitié-Salpêtrière
R Fernand Braudel
R George Balanchine
R Valery Larbaud
Jardin J Joyce
Pl Jean Vilar
R Abel Gance
Av de France
R Raymond Aron
Passerelle Simone de Beauvoir
R Jenner
R Bruant
Chevaleret
Bd Vincent Auriol

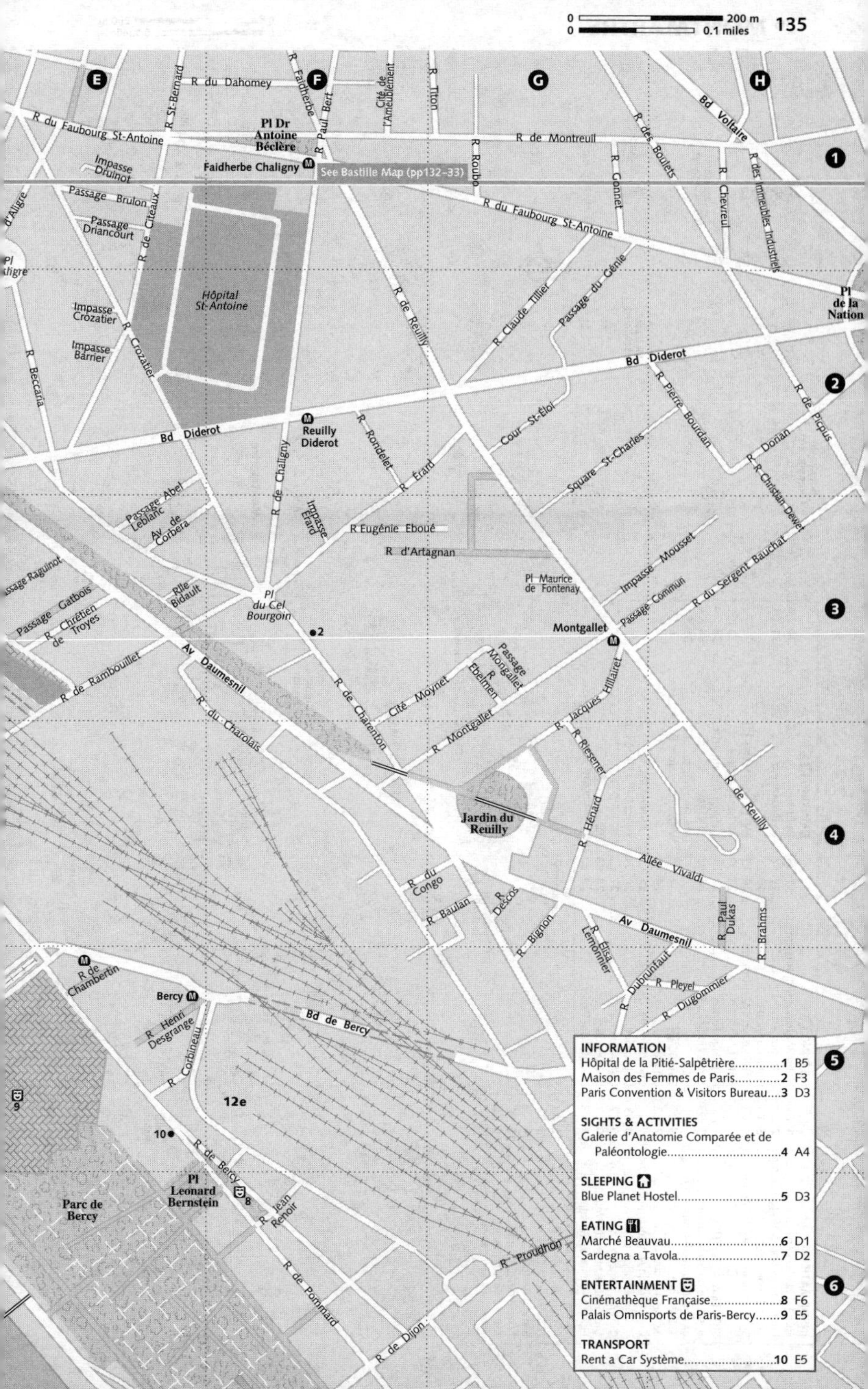
0 200 m
0 0.1 miles
E
F
G
H
1
2
3
4
5
6
See Bastille Map (pp132–33)
R du Dahomey
R St-Bernard
R Faidherbe
R Paul Bert
Cité de l'Ameublement
R Titon
R du Faubourg St-Antoine
Pl Dr Antoine Béclère
Faidherbe Chaligny
R de Montreuil
R des Boulets
Bd Voltaire
R Roubo
R Gonnet
R Chevreul
R des Immeubles Industriels
Impasse Druinot
Passage Brulon
Passage Driancourt
R de Cîteaux
R d'Aligre
Pl d'Aligre
Hôpital St-Antoine
Impasse Crozatier
R Crozatier
Impasse Barrier
R Beccaria
R de Reuilly
R Claude Tillier
Passage du Génie
Pl de la Nation
Bd Diderot
R Pierre Bourdan
R de Picpus
Reuilly Diderot
R Rondelet
Cour St-Éloi
Square St-Charles
R Donan
R Christian Dewet
R Érard
R de Chaligny
Passage Abel Leblanc
Av de Corbera
Impasse Érard
R Eugénie Eboué
R d'Artagnan
Impasse Mousset
R du Sergent Bauchat
Passage Raguinot
Passage Gatbois
R Chrétien de Troyes
Rlle Bidault
Pl du Cel Bourgoin
Pl Maurice de Fontenay
Passage Commun
Montgallet
R de Rambouillet
Av Daumesnil
R du Charolais
R de Charenton
Cité Moynet
Passage Mongallet
R Ebelmen
R Montgallet
R Jacques Hillairet
R Riesener
Jardin du Reuilly
R Hénard
Allée Vivaldi
R du Congo
R Baulan
R Descos
R Bignon
R Elisa Lemonnier
R Paul Dukas
R Brahms
R Dubrunfaut
R Pleyel
R Dugommier
R de Chambertin
Bercy
R Henri Desgrange
Bd de Bercy
R Corbineau
12e
R de Bercy
Pl Leonard Bernstein
Parc de Bercy
R Jean Renoir
R de Pommard
R Proudhon
R de Dijon
INFORMATION
Hôpital de la Pitié-Salpêtrière..........1 B5
Maison des Femmes de Paris..........2 F3
Paris Convention & Visitors Bureau....3 D3
SIGHTS & ACTIVITIES
Galerie d'Anatomie Comparée et de Paléontologie..........4 A4
SLEEPING
Blue Planet Hostel..........5 D3
EATING
Marché Beauvau..........6 D1
Sardegna a Tavola..........7 D2
ENTERTAINMENT
Cinémathèque Française..........8 F6
Palais Omnisports de Paris-Bercy.......9 E5
TRANSPORT
Rent a Car Système..........10 E5

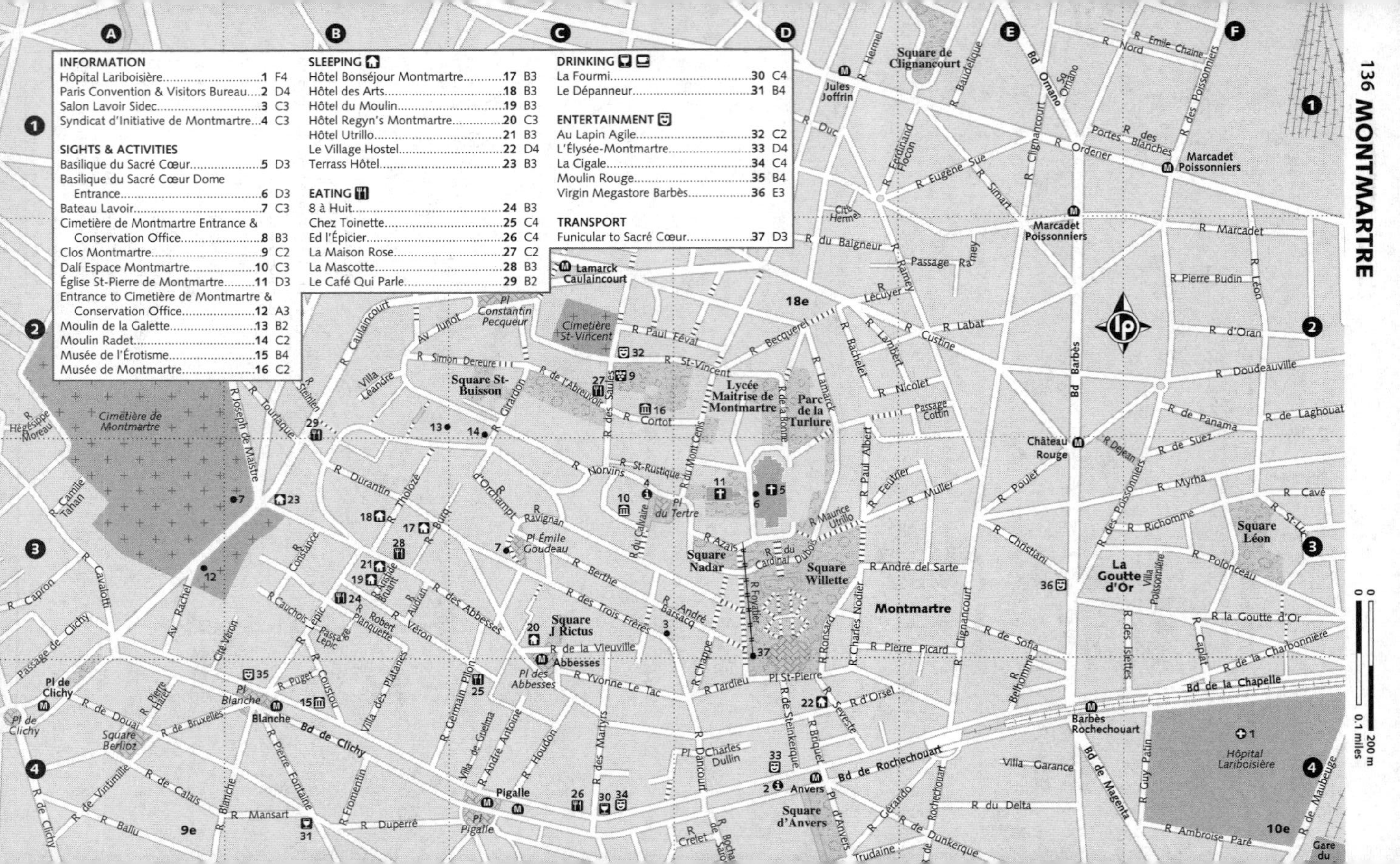
0 200 m
0 0.1 miles
INFORMATION
Hôpital Lariboisière 1 F4
Paris Convention & Visitors Bureau 2 D4
Salon Lavoir Sidec 3 C3
Syndicat d'Initiative de Montmartre 4 C3
SIGHTS & ACTIVITIES
Basilique du Sacré Cœur 5 D3
Basilique du Sacré Cœur Dome Entrance 6 D3
Bateau Lavoir 7 C3
Cimetière de Montmartre Entrance & Conservation Office 8 B3
Clos Montmartre 9 C2
Dalí Espace Montmartre 10 C3
Église St-Pierre de Montmartre 11 D3
Entrance to Cimetière de Montmartre & Conservation Office 12 A3
Moulin de la Galette 13 B2
Moulin Radet 14 C2
Musée de l'Érotisme 15 B4
Musée de Montmartre 16 C2
SLEEPING
Hôtel Bonséjour Montmartre 17 B3
Hôtel des Arts 18 B3
Hôtel du Moulin 19 B3
Hôtel Regyn's Montmartre 20 C3
Hôtel Utrillo 21 B3
Le Village Hostel 22 D4
Terrass Hôtel 23 B3
EATING
8 à Huit 24 B3
Chez Toinette 25 C4
Ed l'Épicier 26 C4
La Maison Rose 27 C2
La Mascotte 28 B3
Le Café Qui Parle 29 B2
DRINKING
La Fourmi 30 C4
Le Dépanneur 31 B4
ENTERTAINMENT
Au Lapin Agile 32 C2
L'Élysée-Montmartre 33 D4
La Cigale 34 C4
Moulin Rouge 35 B4
Virgin Megastore Barbès 36 E3
TRANSPORT
Funicular to Sacré Cœur 37 D3

(Continued from page 113)

Money

Post offices that have a Banque Postale can offer the best exchange rates in Paris, and they accept banknotes (commission €4.50) in various currencies as well as travellers cheques issued by Amex (no commission) or Visa (1.5%, minimum €4.50). *Bureaux de change* are usually faster and easier, open longer hours and give better rates than most banks. For general advice on exchanging money, see p955.

Post

Each arrondissement (p110) in Paris has its own five-digit postcode, formed by prefixing the arrondissement number with '750' or '7500' (eg 75001 for the 1er arrondissement, 75019 for the 19e). The only exception is the 16e, which has two postcodes: 75016 and 75116.

The **main post office** (Map pp126-7; www.laposte.fr; 52 rue du Louvre, 1er; Ⓜ Sentier or Les Halles; 🕑 24hr), five blocks north of the eastern end of the Louvre, is open round the clock for basic services such as sending letters and picking up poste restante (or 'general delivery') mail (window No 11; €0.54 per letter). Other services, including currency exchange, are available only during regular business hours. Be prepared for long queues after 7pm. Poste restante mail not specifically addressed to a particular branch post office in Paris will be delivered here. There is a one-hour closure from 6.20am to 7.20am Monday to Saturday and from 6am to 7am on Sunday.

Toilets

The public toilets in Paris are signposted *toilettes* or *WC*. The tan-coloured, self-cleaning cylindrical toilets you see on Paris' pavements are open 24 hours and are free of charge. Look for the words *libre* ('free'; green-coloured) or *occupé* ('occupied'; red-coloured).

Café owners don't appreciate your using their facilities if you're not a paying customer. If you're desperate, try ducking into a fast-food place, a major department store or even a big hotel with a large lobby. There are free public toilets underground in front of Notre Dame Cathedral (Map pp126–7), near the Arc de Triomphe (Map pp118–19), east down the steps at Basilique du Sacré Cœur (Map p136), at the northwestern entrance to the Jardin des Tuileries (Map pp118–19) and in a few metro stations. Check out the wonderful art-nouveau public toilets below place de la Madeleine, 8e (Map pp118–19), built in 1905.

In older cafés and bars, the amenities may consist of a *toilette à la turque* (Turkish-style toilet), which is what the French call a squat toilet.

Tourist Information

The main branch of the **Paris Convention & Visitors Bureau** (Office de Tourisme et de Congrès de Paris; Map pp118-19; ☎ 08 92 68 30 00; www.parisinfo.com; 25-27 rue des Pyramides, 1er; Ⓜ Pyramides; 🕑 9am-7pm Jun-Oct, 10am-7pm Mon-Sat & 11am-7pm Sun Nov-May, closed 1 May) is about 500m northwest of the Louvre.

The bureau also maintains a handful of centres elsewhere in Paris, which are listed below (telephone numbers and websites are the same as for the main office). For details of the area around Paris, contact **Espace du Tourisme d'Île de France**, p206).

Anvers (Map p136; opp 72 bd de Rochechouart, 18e; Ⓜ Anvers; 🕑 10am-6pm, closed Christmas Day, New Year's Day & 1 May)

Gare de Lyon (Map pp134-5; Hall d'Arrivée, 20 bd Diderot, 12e; Ⓜ Gare de Lyon; 🕑 8am-6pm Mon-Sat, closed Sun & 1 May) In the mainline trains arrivals hall.

Gare du Nord (Map pp120-1; 18 rue de Dunkerque, 10e; Ⓜ Gare du Nord; 🕑 8am-6pm, closed Christmas Day, New Year's Day & 1 May) Beneath the glass roof of the Île de France departures and arrivals area at the eastern end of the train station.

Syndicat d'Initiative de Montmartre (Map p136; ☎ 01 42 62 21 21; 21 place du Tertre, 18e; Ⓜ Abbesses; 🕑 10am-7pm) This locally run tourist office and shop is in Montmartre's most picturesque square and is open year-round.

DANGERS & ANNOYANCES

Crime

In general Paris is a safe city, and random street assaults are rare. The so-called Ville Lumière (City of Light) is generally well lit, and there's no reason not to use the metro before it stops running at some time between 12.30am and just past 1am. As you'll notice, women *do* travel alone on the metro late at night in most areas, though not all who do so report feeling 100% comfortable.

Metro stations that are probably best avoided late at night include: Châtelet-Les Halles and its seemingly endless corridors; Château Rouge in Montmartre; Gare du Nord; Strasbourg St-Denis; Réaumur Sébastopol; and Montparnasse Bienvenüe.

VIEWINGS AT A DISCOUNT

The **Paris Museum Pass** (www.parismuseumpass.fr; 2/4/6 days €30/45/60) is valid for entry to some 38 venues in Paris – including the Louvre, Centre Pompidou, Musée d'Orsay and new Musée du Quai Branly and Cité de l'Architecture et du Patrimoine. Outside the city limits but still within the Île de France region, it will get you into another 22 places, including the basilica at St-Denis (p208) and parts of the châteaux at Versailles (p211) and Fontainebleau (p214). The pass is available online as well as from the participating venues, branches of the Paris Convention & Visitors Bureau (p137), Fnac outlets (p191), RATP (Régie Autonome des Transports Parisians) information desks and major metro stations.

Bornes d'alarme (alarm boxes) are located in the centre of each metro/RER platform and in some station corridors.

Nonviolent crime such as pickpocketing and thefts from handbags and packs is a problem wherever there are crowds, especially crowds of tourists. Places to be particularly careful include Montmartre (especially around Sacré Cœur); Pigalle; the areas around Forum des Halles and Centre Pompidou; the Latin Quarter (especially the rectangle bounded by rue St-Jacques, bd St-Germain, bd St-Michel and quai St-Michel); below the Eiffel Tower; and on the metro during rush hour.

Litter

In theory Parisians can be fined more than €183 for littering (that includes cigarette butts), but we've never heard of anyone having to pay up. Don't be nonplussed if you see locals drop paper wrappings or other detritus along the side of the pavement, however; the gutters in every quarter of Paris are washed and swept out daily, and Parisians are encouraged to use them where litter bins are not available.

A much greater annoyance are all those dog droppings on the pavements. The Paris municipality has made valiant attempts in the past, most notably with the introduction of the *moto-crottes* (motorised pooper-scooters) in 1982. At one stage, the city was spending up to €11 million each year to keep the city's pavements free of *la pollution canine*, but the machines were abandoned in 2004 as both expensive and ineffective. Most recently, plastic-bag dispensers have been placed strategically throughout the city, but the campaign has met less-than-howling success; only 60% of dog owners admit to cleaning up after their pooches, which now number around 150,000 and produce 16 tonnes of dog poo daily.

Lost Property

All objects found anywhere across Paris – except those picked up on the trains or in train stations – are brought to the city's **Bureau des Objets Trouvés** (Lost Property Office; Map pp114-15; ☎ 08 21 00 25 25; www.prefecture-police-paris.interieur.gouv.fr/demarches/article/service_objets_trouves.htm; 36 rue des Morillons, 15e; Ⓜ Convention; 🕐 8.30am-5pm Mon-Thu, 8.30am-4.30pm Fri), which is run by the Préfecture de Police. Since telephone inquiries are impossible, the only way to find out if a lost item has been located is to go there and fill in the forms in person.

Items lost on the **metro** (☎ 32 46; 🕐 7am-9pm Mon-Fri, 9am-5pm Sat & Sun) are held by station agents before being sent to the Bureau des Objets Trouvés.

Anything found on trains or in train stations is taken to the lost-property office (usually attached to the left-luggage office) of the relevant station. Telephone inquiries (in French) are possible:

Gare d'Austerlitz (☎ 01 53 60 71 98)
Gare de l'Est (☎ 01 40 18 88 73)
Gare de Lyon (☎ 01 53 33 67 22)
Gare du Nord (☎ 01 55 31 58 40)
Gare Montparnasse (☎ 01 40 48 14 24)
Gare St-Lazare (☎ 01 53 42 05 57)

SIGHTS

Paris' major sights are distributed more or less equally on the Right and Left Banks of the Seine. We start in the heart of the Right Bank in the area around the Louvre and Les Halles, which largely takes in the 1er and follows, more or less, the order of the arrondissements.

Louvre & Les Halles

The area around the Louvre in the 1er contains some of the most important sights for visitors in Paris. To the northeast, the mostly pedestrian zone between the Centre Pompidou and the Forum des Halles, with rue Étienne Marcel to the north and rue de Rivoli to the south, is filled with people by day and by night, just as it was for the 850-odd years when part of it served as Paris' main marketplace, known as Les Halles.

MUSÉE DU LOUVRE

The vast Palais du Louvre was constructed as a fortress by Philippe-Auguste in the early 13th century and rebuilt in the mid-16th century for use as a royal residence. In 1793 the Revolutionary Convention turned it into the **Musée du Louvre** (Louvre Museum; Map pp126-7; ☎ 01 40 20 53 17; www.louvre.fr; Ⓜ Palais Royal-Musée du Louvre; permanent collections/permanent collections & temporary exhibitions €9/13, after 6pm Wed & Fri €6/11, permanent collections free for under 18yr & after 6pm Fri for under 26yr, admission free 1st Sun of month; 🕑 9am-6pm Mon, Thu, Sat & Sun, 9am-10pm Wed & Fri), the nation's first national museum.

The paintings, sculptures and artefacts on display in the Louvre Museum have been assembled by French governments over the past five centuries. Among them are works of art and artisanship from all over Europe and important collections of Assyrian, Etruscan, Greek, Coptic and Islamic art and antiquities. Traditionally the Louvre's raison d'être is to present Western art from the Middle Ages to about the year 1848 (at which point the Musée d'Orsay takes over), as well as the works of ancient civilisations that informed Western art.

When the museum opened in the late 18th century, it contained 2500 paintings and objets d'art; today some 35,000 are on display. The 'Grand Louvre' project, inaugurated by the late President Mitterrand in 1989, doubled the museum's exhibition space, and new and renovated galleries have opened in recent years devoted to objets d'art such as Sèvres porcelain and the crown jewels of Louis XV (room 66, 1st floor, Apollo Gallery, Denon Wing).

The Louvre may be the most actively avoided museum in the world. Daunted by the richness and sheer size of the place (the side facing the Seine is some 700m long, and it is said that it would take nine months just to glance at every piece of art here), both local people and visitors often find the prospect of an afternoon at a smaller museum far more inviting. Eventually, most people do their duty and come, but many leave overwhelmed, unfulfilled, exhausted and frustrated at having got lost on their way to da Vinci's *La Joconde*, better known as *Mona Lisa* (room 6, 1st floor, Salle de la Joconde, Denon Wing). Your best bet – after checking out a few works you really want to see – is to choose a particular period or section of the Louvre and pretend that the rest is in another museum somewhere across town.

The most famous works from antiquity include the *Seated Scribe* (room 22, 1st floor, Sully Wing), the *Code of Hammurabi* (room 3, ground floor, Richelieu Wing) and that armless duo, the *Venus de Milo* (room 7, ground floor, Denon Wing) and the *Winged Victory of Samothrace* (opposite room 1, 1st floor, Denon Wing). From the Renaissance, don't miss Michelangelo's *The Dying Slave* (ground floor, Michelangelo Gallery, Denon Wing) and works by Raphael, Botticelli and Titian (1st floor, Denon Wing). French masterpieces of the 19th century include Ingres' *The Turkish Bath* (room 60, 2nd floor, Sully Wing), Géricault's *The Raft of the Medusa* (room 77, 1st floor, Denon Wing) and works by Corot, Delacroix and Fragonard (2nd floor, Denon Wing).

The main entrance and ticket windows in the Cour Napoléon are covered by the 21m-high **Pyramide du Louvre**, a glass pyramid designed by the Chinese-born American architect IM Pei. You can avoid the queues outside the pyramid or at the Porte des Lions entrance by entering the complex via the Carrousel du Louvre shopping centre entrance (Map pp126–7), at 99 rue de Rivoli, or by following the 'Musée du Louvre' exit from the Palais Royal-Musée du Louvre metro station. Buy your tickets in advance from the ticket machines in the Carrousel du Louvre or, for an extra €1.10, from the *billetteries* (ticket offices) of Fnac (see p191), online, or by ringing ☎ 08 92 68 36 22 or ☎ 08 25 34 63 46, and walk straight in without queuing. Tickets are valid for the whole day, so you can come and go as you please.

The Louvre is divided into four sections: the Sully, Denon and Richelieu Wings and the Hall Napoléon. **Sully** creates the four sides of the Cour Carrée (literally 'square courtyard') at the eastern end of the complex. **Denon** stretches along the Seine to the south; **Richelieu** is the northern wing along rue de Rivoli.

The split-level public area under the glass pyramid is known as the **Hall Napoléon** (🕑 9am-10pm Wed-Mon). The hall has an exhibition on the history of the Louvre; a bookshop; a restaurant;

AVOIDING MUSEUM FATIGUE

Warm-up exercises, half-hour breathers, a portable seat, bottled water and an energy snack… It might sound as if you're preparing for a trek in the Alps, but these are some of the recommendations for tackling Paris' more than 100 museums. And with almost three dozen major ones free of charge on at least one day of the week, the temptation to see more is huge.

Take the Louvre… Encompassing some 40 sq hectares, the museum has nine enormous departments spread over 60,000 sq metres of gallery space and more than eight million visitors a year, all elbowing each other to see what they want to see in a limited amount of time. It's hardly surprising that many people feel worn out before they've descended into the Cour Napoléon.

To avoid museum fatigue, wear comfortable shoes and make use of the cloakrooms. Be aware that standing still and walking slowly promote tiredness; sit down as often as you can. Reflecting on the material and forming associations with it causes information to move from your short- to long-term memory; your experiences will thus amount to more than a series of visual 'bites'.

Tracking and timing studies suggest that museum-goers spend no more than 10 seconds viewing an exhibit and another 10 seconds reading the label as they try to take in as much as they can before succumbing to exhaustion. To avoid this choose a particular period or section or join a guided tour of the highlights.

a café; auditoriums for concerts, lectures and films; and **CyberLouvre** (10am-5.45pm Wed-Mon), an internet research centre with online access to some 35,000 works of art. The centrepiece of the **Carrousel du Louvre** (Map pp126-7; 01 43 16 47 10; www.carrouseldulouvre.com; 99 rue de Rivoli; 8am-11pm), the shopping centre that runs underground from the pyramid to the **Arc de Triomphe du Carrousel** (Map pp126–7) in the Jardin du Carrousel, is the glass **Pyramide Inversée** *(Inverted Pyramid)*, also created by Pei.

Free English-language maps of the complex entitled *Louvre Plan/Information* are available at the circular information desk in the centre of the Hall Napoléon. Excellent publications to guide you if you are doing the Louvre on your own are *Destination Louvre: A Guided Tour* (€7.50), *Louvre: Guide to the Masterpieces* (€8) and the hefty, 475-page *Guide to the Louvre* (€17). An attractive and useful memento is the DVD entitled *Louvre: The Visit* (€26). All are available from the museum bookshop.

English-language guided tours (01 40 20 52 63) lasting 1½ hours depart from the area under the Grande Pyramide, marked 'Acceuil des Groupes' (Reception for Groups), at 11am, 2pm and (sometimes) 3.45pm Monday to Saturday. Tickets cost €5 in addition to the cost of admission. Groups are limited to 30 people, so it's a good idea to sign up at least 30 minutes before departure time.

Self-paced audioguide tours in six languages with 1½ hours of commentary can be rented for €5 under the pyramid at the entrance to each wing.

JARDIN DES TUILERIES

Beginning just west of the Jardin du Carrousel, the formal, 28-hectare **Jardin des Tuileries** (Tuileries Garden; Map pp118-19; 01 40 20 90 43; M Tuileries or Concorde; 7am-9pm Apr, May & Sep, 7am-11pm Jun-Aug, 7.30am-7.30pm Oct-Mar) was laid out in its present form – more or less – in the mid-17th century by André Le Nôtre, who also created the gardens at Vaux-le-Vicomte (p217) and Versailles (p211). The Tuileries soon became the most fashionable spot in Paris for parading about in one's finery; today it is a favourite of joggers. It forms part of the banks of the Seine World Heritage Site listed in 1991.

The **Voie Triomphale** (Triumphal Way), also called the Axe Historique (Historic Axis), the western continuation of the Tuileries' east–west axis, follows the av des Champs-Élysées to the Arc de Triomphe and, ultimately, to the Grande Arche in the skyscraper district of **La Défense** (p206).

JEU DE PAUME & ORANGERIE

The **Galerie Nationale du Jeu de Paume** (Jeu de Paume National Gallery; Map pp118-19; 01 47 03 12 50; www.jeudepaume.org; 1 place de la Concorde, 1er; M Concorde; adult/senior, student & 13-18yr/under 13yr €6/3/free; noon-9pm Tue, noon-7pm Wed-Fri, 10am-7pm Sat & Sun) is housed in an erstwhile *jeu de paume* (real, or royal, tennis) court built in 1861 during the reign of Napoleon III in the northwestern corner of the Jardin des Tuileries. Once the home of a good part of France's national collection of Impressionist art, now housed across the Seine in the Musée d'Orsay (p151), the two-storey

Jeu de Paume stages innovative exhibitions of contemporary art. A new branch of the gallery, the Jeu de Paume-Site Sully, in the Hôtel de Sully (p143) in the Marais, concentrates on top-notch photography. A joint ticket to both galleries costs €8/4 adult/concession.

The **Musée de l'Orangerie** (Orangery Museum; Map pp118-19; ☎ 01 44 77 80 07; www.musee-orangerie.fr; Jardin des Tuileries, 1er; Ⓜ Concorde; adult/senior, student & 13-18yr €6.50/4.50, admission free 1st Sun of month; ⌚ 12.30-7pm Wed, Thu & Sat-Mon, 12.30-9pm Fri), in the southwestern corner of the Jardin des Tuileries, is, with the Jeu de Paume, all that remains of the once palatial Palais des Tuileries, which was razed during the Paris Commune in 1871. It exhibits important Impressionist works, including a series of Monet's *Decorations des Nymphéas* (Water Lilies) in two huge oval rooms purpose-built in 1927 on the artist's instructions, as well as works by Cézanne, Matisse, Picasso, Renoir, Sisley, Soutine and Utrillo.

PLACE VENDÔME

The octagonal **place Vendôme** (Map pp118-19; Ⓜ Tuileries or Opéra) and the arcaded and colonnaded buildings around it were constructed between 1687 and 1721. In March 1796 Napoleon married Josephine, Viscountess Beauharnais, in the building at No 3. Today, the buildings surrounding the square house the posh **Hôtel Ritz Paris** and some of the city's most fashionable boutiques. The 43.5m-tall **Colonne Vendôme** (Vendôme Column) in the centre of the square consists of a stone core wrapped in a 160m-long bronze spiral made from hundreds of Austrian and Russian cannons captured by Napoleon at the Battle of Austerlitz in 1805. The statue on top depicts Napoleon in classical Roman dress.

PALAIS ROYAL

To the north of place du Palais Royal and the Louvre lies the **Palais Royal** (Royal Palace; Map pp120-1; place du Palais Royal, 1er; Ⓜ Palais Royal-Musée du Louvre), which briefly housed a young Louis XIV in the 1640s. Construction was begun in 1624 by Cardinal Richelieu, though most of the present neoclassical complex dates from the latter part of the 18th century. It now contains the governmental **Conseil d'État** (State Council) and is closed to the public.

The colonnaded building facing place André Malraux is the **Comédie Française** (p194), which was founded in 1680 and is the world's oldest national theatre.

Just north of the palace is the **Jardin du Palais Royal** (Map pp120-1; ☎ 01 47 03 92 16; 6 rue de Montpensier, 1er; ⌚ 7.30am-10pm Apr & May, 7am-11pm Jun-Aug, 7am-9.30pm Sep, 7.30am-8.30pm Oct-Mar), a lovely park surrounded by 19th-century shopping arcades, including **Galerie de Valois** on the eastern side and **Galerie de Montpensier** to the west. Don't miss the zany, crownlike Palais Royal-Musée du Louvre **metro entrance** on the place du Palais Royal.

CENTRE POMPIDOU

Also known as the Centre Beaubourg, the **Centre National d'Art et de Culture Georges Pompidou** (Georges Pompidou National Centre of Art & Culture; Map pp126-7; ☎ 01 44 78 12 33; www.centrepompidou.fr; place Georges Pompidou, 4e; Ⓜ Rambuteau) has amazed and delighted visitors since it was inaugurated in 1977, not just for its outstanding collection of modern art, but also for its radical architectural statement.

The **Forum du Centre Pompidou** (admission free; ⌚ 11am-10pm Wed-Mon), the open space at ground level, has temporary exhibitions and information desks. The 4th and 5th floors of the centre house the **Musée National d'Art Moderne** (MNAM, National Museum of Modern Art; Map pp126-7; adult €10-12, senior & 18-25yr €8-10, admission free under 18yr, 6-9pm Wed for 18-25yr, 1st Sun of month for all; ⌚ 11am-9pm Wed-Mon), France's national collection of art dating from 1905 onwards. About a third of the 50,000-plus works, including the work of the surrealists and cubists, as well as pop art and contemporary works, are on display.

The huge **Bibliothèque Publique d'Information** (BPI; ☎ 01 44 78 12 33; www.bpi.fr, in French; ⌚ noon-10pm Mon & Wed-Fri, 11am-10pm Sat & Sun), which is entered from rue du Renard, takes up part of the 1st as well as the entire 2nd and 3rd floors of the centre. The 6th floor has two galleries for **temporary exhibitions**, the admission to which is usually included in the higher entrance fee. There are **cinemas** (adult/senior & 18-25yr €6/4) and other entertainment venues on the 1st floor and in the basement.

The **Atelier Brancusi** (Map pp126-7; 55 rue Rambuteau, 4e; admission free; ⌚ 2-6pm Wed-Mon), west of the main building, contains some 160 examples of the work of Romanian-born sculptor Constantin Brancusi (1876–1957), as well as some of Brancusi's drawings, paintings and glass photographic plates.

West of the centre, place Georges Pompidou and the nearby pedestrian streets attract buskers, musicians, jugglers and mime artists, and

MUSEUMS: AN OPEN & SHUT CASE

Most museums in Paris close on Monday although more than a dozen (including the Louvre, Centre Pompidou, Musée Picasso and Musée National du Moyen Âge) are shut on Tuesday instead. It's important to remember that *all* museums and monuments in Paris shut their doors between 30 minutes and an hour before their actual closing times, which are the ones listed in this chapter. Therefore if we say a museum or monument closes at 6pm, don't count on getting in much later than 5.30pm, or even 5pm in some cases.

can be a lot of fun. South of the centre on place Igor Stravinsky, the fanciful mechanical fountains (Map pp126–7) of skeletons, hearts, treble clefs and a big pair of ruby-red lips are a delight.

FORUM DES HALLES

Les Halles, the city's main wholesale food market, occupied the area just south of the Église St-Eustache from the early 12th century until 1969, when it was moved to the southern suburb of Rungis. In its place, the unspeakably ugly **Forum des Halles** (Map pp126-7; ☎ 01 44 76 96 56; www.forum-des-halles.com; 1 rue Pierre Lescot, 1er; Ⓜ Les Halles or Châtelet Les Halles; ⏲ shops 10am-7.30pm), a huge underground shopping centre, was constructed in the glass-and-chrome style of the early 1970s. It is now (and finally) undergoing a major makeover, to be completed by 2010.

Atop the Forum des Halles is a popular **rooftop garden**. During the warmer months, street musicians, fire-eaters and other performers display their talents throughout the area, especially at **place du Jean du Bellay**, whose centre is adorned by a multitiered Renaissance fountain, the **Fontaine des Innocents**, erected in 1549. It is named after the Cimetière des Innocents, a cemetery on this site from which two million skeletons were disinterred and transferred to the Catacombes (p151) in the 14e after the Revolution.

ÉGLISE ST-EUSTACHE

One of the most beautiful churches in Paris and consecrated to an early Roman martyr who is the patron saint of hunters, the majestic **Église St-Eustache** (Map pp126-7; ☎ 01 42 36 31 05; www.st-eustache.org, in French; 2 impasse St-Eustache, 1er; Ⓜ Les Halles; ⏲ 9.30am-7pm Mon-Fri, 10am-7pm Sat, 9am-7.15pm Sun) is just north of the gardens above the Forum des Halles. Constructed between 1532 and 1637, St-Eustache is primarily Gothic, though a neoclassical facade was added on the western side in the mid-18th century. Inside, there are some exceptional Flamboyant Gothic arches holding up the ceiling of the chancel, although most of the interior ornamentation is Renaissance and even classical. The gargantuan organ above the west entrance, with 101 stops and 8000 pipes, is used for concerts (long a tradition here) and during High Mass on Sunday (11am and 6.30pm). There's an audioguide (€3 suggested donation) available.

Marais & Bastille

The Marais, the area of the Right Bank north of Île St-Louis in the 3e and 4e, was exactly what its name implies – 'marsh' or 'swamp' – until the 13th century, when it was converted to farmland. In the early 17th century, Henri IV built the place Royale (today's place des Vosges), turning the area into Paris' most fashionable residential district and attracting wealthy aristocrats who then erected their own luxurious *hôtels particuliers*. Today many of them are house museums and government institutions.

When the aristocracy moved from Paris to Versailles and Faubourg St-Germain during the late 17th and 18th centuries, the Marais and its townhouses passed into the hands of ordinary Parisians. The 110-hectare area was given a major facelift in the late 1960s and early 1970s. The Marais has become a much desired address in recent years, while remaining the centre of Paris' gay life and home to a long-established Jewish neighbourhood called the Pletzl.

Today, the Marais is one of the few neighbourhoods of Paris that still has most of its pre-Revolution architecture. Examples include the oldest house in Paris, the 13th-century house (Map pp120–1) at 3 rue Volta in the 3e, parts of which date back to 1292; the 15th-century house (Map pp126–7) at 51 rue de Montmorency in the 3e (dating back to 1407), which is now a restaurant, Auberge Nicolas Flamel (p178); and the 16th-century half-timbered houses (Map pp126–7) at 11 and 13 rue François Miron in the 4e.

After years as a run-down immigrant neighbourhood notorious for its high crime rate, the contiguous Bastille district (11e and 12e) has undergone a fair degree of gentrification, largely due to the opening of the Opéra Bastille (p144) almost two decades ago. Though the area is not the hip nightlife centre it was through most of the 1990s, it still has quite a bit to offer after dark, with numerous pubs, bars and clubs lining rue de Lappe and rue de la Roquette.

HÔTEL DE VILLE

After having been gutted during the Paris Commune of 1871, Paris' **Hôtel de Ville** (City Hall; Map pp126-7; ☎ 39 75; www.paris.fr; place de l'Hôtel de Ville, 4e; Ⓜ Hôtel de Ville) was rebuilt in the neo-Renaissance style (1874–82). The ornate facade is decorated with 108 statues of noteworthy Parisians. There's a **Salon d'Accueil** (Reception Hall; 29 rue de Rivoli, 4e; 🕑 10am-7pm Mon-Sat), which dispenses copious amounts of information and brochures and is used for temporary exhibitions, usually with a Paris theme.

PLACE DES VOSGES

Inaugurated in 1612 as place Royale, **Place des Vosges** (Map pp132-3; Ⓜ St-Paul or Bastille) is an ensemble of three dozen symmetrical houses with ground-floor arcades, steep slate roofs and large dormer windows arranged around a large square. Only the earliest houses were built of brick; to save time and money, the rest were given timber frames and faced with plaster, which was then painted to resemble brick.

The author Victor Hugo lived at the square's Hôtel de Rohan-Guéménée from 1832 to 1848, moving here a year after the publication of *Notre Dame de Paris* (The Hunchback of Notre Dame). The **Maison de Victor Hugo** (Victor Hugo House; Map pp132-3; ☎ 01 42 72 10 16; www.musee-hugo.paris.fr, in French; permanent collections admission free, temporary exhibitions adult/14-26yr/senior & student/under 14yr €7.50/5.50/3.50/free; 🕑 10am-6pm Tue-Sun) is now a municipal museum devoted to the life and times of the celebrated novelist and poet, with an impressive collection of his own drawings and portraits.

HÔTEL DE SULLY

Dating from the early 17th century, the aristocratic mansion called **Hôtel de Sully** (Map pp132-3; 62 rue St-Antoine, 4e; Ⓜ St-Paul) today houses the headquarters of the **Centre des Monuments Nationaux** (☎ 01 44 61 20 00; www.monuments-nationaux.fr; 🕑 9am-12.45pm & 2-6pm Mon-Thu, to 5pm Fri), the body responsible for many of France's historical monuments; there are lots of brochures and information available. Here you'll also find the **Jeu de Paume-Site Sully** (☎ 01 42 74 47 75; www.jeudepaume.org; adult/senior, student & 13-18yr €5/2.50; 🕑 noon-7pm Tue-Fri, 10am-7pm Sat & Sun), a branch of the more famous Galerie Nationale du Jeu de Paume (p140), with excellent rotating photographic exhibitions. Visiting both galleries costs €8/4. The Hôtel de Sully's two Renaissance-style courtyards alone are worth the trip here.

MUSÉE CARNAVALET

Also called the Musée de l'Histoire de Paris (Paris History Museum), the **Musée Carnavalet** (Map pp132-3; ☎ 01 44 59 58 58; www.carnavalet.paris.fr, in French; 23 rue de Sévigné, 3e; Ⓜ St-Paul or Chemin Vert; permanent collections admission free, temporary exhibitions adult/senior & student/14-26yr/under 14yr €7/5.50/3.50/free; 🕑 10am-6pm Tue-Sun) is housed in two *hôtels particuliers*. It charts the history of Paris from the Gallo-Roman period to modern times. Some of the nation's most important documents, paintings and objects from the French Revolution are here (rooms 101 to 113), as is Fouquet's magnificent art-nouveau jewellery shop from the rue Royale (room 142) and Marcel Proust's cork-lined bedroom from his apartment on bd Haussmann (room 147), in which he wrote most of the 7350-page *À la Recherche du Temps Perdu* (In Search of Lost Time).

MUSÉE PICASSO

One of Paris' best-loved art museums, the **Musée Picasso** (Picasso Museum; Map pp132-3; ☎ 01 42 71 25 21; www.musee-picasso.fr, in French; 5 rue de Thorigny, 3e; Ⓜ St-Paul or Chemin Vert; adult/18-25yr/under 18yr €7.70/5.70/free, admission free 1st Sun of month; 🕑 9.30am-6pm Wed-Mon Apr-Sep, 9.30am-5.30pm Wed-Mon Oct-Mar), housed in the mid-17th-century Hôtel Salé, includes more than 3500 of the *grand maître*'s engravings, paintings, ceramic works, drawings and sculptures. You can also see part of Picasso's personal art collection, which includes works by Braque, Cézanne, Matisse, Modigliani, Degas and Rousseau.

MUSÉE DES ARTS ET MÉTIERS

The oldest museum of science and technology in Europe, the **Musée des Arts et Métiers** (Arts & Crafts Museum; Map pp120-1; ☎ 01 53 01 82 00; www.arts-et-metiers.net, in French; 60 rue de Réaumur, 3e; Ⓜ Arts et Métiers; permanent collections admission free, temporary exhibitions adult/student & 6-18yr/under 5yr €5.50/3.50/free;

(10am-6pm Tue, Wed & Fri-Sun, to 9.30pm Thu) is a must for anyone with an interest in how things work. Housed in the 18th-century priory of St-Martin des Champs, some 3000 instruments, machines and working models from the 18th to 20th centuries are displayed on three floors. Taking pride of place is Foucault's original pendulum, which he introduced to the world in 1855.

MUSÉE D'ART ET D'HISTOIRE DU JUDAÏSME

Housed in the sumptuous, 17th-century Hôtel de St-Aignan, the **Musée d'Art et d'Histoire du Judaïsme** (Art & History of Judaism Museum; Map pp126-7; ☎ 01 53 01 86 60; www.mahj.org; 71 rue du Temple, 3e; M Rambuteau; adult/student & 18-26yr/under 18yr €6.80/4.50/free; 11am-6pm Mon-Fri, 10am-6pm Sun) traces the evolution of Jewish communities from the Middle Ages to the present, with particular emphasis on the history of the Jews in France but also communities in other parts of Europe and North Africa. Exhibits include documents relating to the Dreyfus Affair (1894–1900) and works by Paris-based Jewish artists Chagall, Modigliani and Soutine. Temporary exhibitions cost an extra €5.50/4 and a combined ticket is €8.50/6.

MÉMORIAL DE LA SHOAH

Established in 1956, the Memorial to the Unknown Jewish Martyr has metamorphosed into the **Mémorial de la Shoah** (Shoah Memorial; Map pp126-7; ☎ 01 42 77 44 72; www.memorialdelashoah.org; 17 rue Geoffroy l'Asnier, 4e; M St-Paul; admission free; 10am-6pm Sun-Wed & Fri, 10am-10pm Thu) and documentation centre. The permanent collection and temporary exhibitions relate to the Holocaust and the German occupation of parts of France and Paris during WWII; the film clips of contemporary footage and interviews are heart-rending and the displays instructive and easy to follow. The actual memorial to the victims of the Shoah, a Hebrew word meaning 'catastrophe' and synonymous with the Holocaust, stands at the entrance, and there is a wall inscribed with the names of 76,000 men, women and children deported from France to Nazi extermination camps.

MAISON EUROPÉENNE DE LA PHOTOGRAPHIE

Housed in the overly renovated Hôtel Hénault de Cantorbe, dating from the early 18th century, the **Maison Européenne de la Photographie** (European House of Photography; Map pp126-7; ☎ 01 44 78 75 00; www.mep-fr.org, in French; 5-7 rue de Fourcy, 4e; M St-Paul or Pont Marie; adult/senior & 8-25yr/under 8yr €6/3/free, admission free 5-7.45pm Wed; 11am-7.45pm Wed-Sun) has cutting-edge temporary exhibitions (usually retrospectives of single photographers) and a huge permanent collection on the history of photography and its connections with France. There are frequent showings of short films and documentaries on weekend afternoons.

PARIS HISTORIQUE

If you're interested in medieval Paris, **Paris Historique** (Map pp126-7; ☎ 01 48 87 74 31; www.paris-historique.org, in French; 44-46 rue François Miron, 4e; M St-Paul; admission free; 11am-8pm Mon-Sat, 2-7pm Sun), the information centre for the Association for the Conservation and Appreciation of Historic Paris, should be on your tick list. It provides information, has a research library, organises exhibitions and leads guided tours (adult/student and child €9/4) of the area at 2pm or 2.30pm Monday to Saturday.

PLACE DE LA BASTILLE

The Bastille, built during the 14th century as a fortified royal residence, is probably the most famous monument in Paris that no longer exists; the notorious prison – the quintessential symbol of royal despotism – was demolished by a Revolutionary mob on 14 July 1789 and all seven prisoners were freed. **Place de la Bastille** (Map pp132-3; M Bastille) in the 11e and 12e, where the prison once stood, is now a very busy traffic roundabout.

In the centre of the square is the 52m-high **Colonne de Juillet** (July Column), whose shaft of greenish bronze is topped by a gilded and winged figure of Liberty. It was erected in 1833 as a memorial to those killed in the street battles that accompanied the July Revolution of 1830; they are buried in vaults under the column. It was later consecrated as a memorial to the victims of the February Revolution of 1848.

OPÉRA BASTILLE

Paris' giant 'second' opera house, the **Opéra Bastille** (Map pp132-3; ☎ 08 92 89 90 90; www.opera-de-paris.fr, in French; 2-6 place de la Bastille, 12e; M Bastille), designed by the Canadian architect Carlos Ott, was inaugurated on 14 July 1989, the 200th anniversary of the storming of the Bastille. It has three theatres, including the 2700-seat main auditorium. There are 1¼-hour **guided tours** (☎ 01 40 01 19 70; adult/senior, student & 11-25 yr/under 11 yr €11/9/6), which usually depart at

CARA BLACK *interviewed by Steve Fallon*

Cara Black is the author of a best-selling murder-by-arrondissement series set in Paris and featuring the intrepid, half-French, half-American sleuth Aimée Leduc.

A Francophile from California… How does that work? Francophilia goes way back. I had French nuns in school, my uncle studied under Georges Braque on the GI Bill after the war, and in 1971, while travelling through Paris, I went to rue du Bac and knocked on the door of my favourite writer, (two-time Prix Goncourt winner) Romain Gary. He invited me to his café for an espresso and a cigar. We both had both.

Ah, smoke – but fire? All this murder and darkness in the City of Light? That all came about much later, in 1993. I was walking around the place des Vosges and remembered a visit to Paris almost a decade before when I stayed with my friend Sarah. She had taken me on a tour of the pregentrified Marais and shown me the ancient abandoned building where her Jewish mother had hidden during the war and from where the rest of the family had been deported to Auschwitz. The idea for my first book, *Murder in the Marais*, came to me on the plane going home.

Does your research get down and dirty? I crawl under buildings, explore restrooms in old cafés, visit ghost metro stations, go down into the city sewers and even the tunnels under the Palais Royal. I interview police – I'm one of only two American women writers to have spent time in the Préfecture – and private detectives. Some of them have become friends and I take them to dinner.

Now we're cooking! What's on the menu? Murder most fowl? Steak saignant ('bleeding', or rare)? Anything but the *écrévisse* (freshwater crayfish) that come from the Seine. They feed on corpses. I discovered that while researching *Murder on the Île Saint-Louis*. One restaurant was still selling them.

Why are you always Right and not Left? How about murder in the sexy 6e or the louche Latin Quarter? I don't write about the Paris of tourists, where people wear berets and carry baguettes. I'm not really comfortable on the Left Bank. I feel better where my friends live – the Marais, Belleville, Montmartre. I understand these places better.

I wish I could… Tie a scarf the way French women do.

I wish I hadn't… Buried Baudelaire in Père Lachaise cemetery. He's actually in Montparnasse.

I'll always come back to Paris for… Hot chocolate at Ladurée, bicycle rides along the Canal St-Martin, the old stones of the place des Vosges, and the ghosts. Paris is full of ghosts and they communicate. You only need listen.

Cara Black (www.carablack.com) divides her time between Paris and San Francisco. Her latest novel is Murder in the Rue de Paradis.

1.15pm Monday to Saturday. Tickets go on sale 10 minutes before departure at the **box office** (130 rue de Lyon, 12e; 🕒 10.30am-6.30pm Mon-Sat).

The Islands

Paris' twin set of islands could not be more different. Île de la Cité (Map pp126–7) is bigger, full of sights and very touristed (though very few people actually live here). Île St-Louis (Map pp126–7) is residential and much quieter, with just enough boutiques and restaurants – and a legendary ice-cream maker (p181) – to attract visitors.

ÎLE DE LA CITÉ

The site of the first settlement in Paris, around the 3rd century BC, and later the Roman town of Lutèce (Lutetia), the Île de la Cité remained the centre of royal and ecclesiastical power even after the city spread to both banks of the Seine during the Middle Ages. The buildings on the middle part of the island were demolished and rebuilt during Baron Haussmann's great urban renewal scheme of the late 19th century.

Notre Dame Cathedral

The **Cathédrale de Notre Dame de Paris** (Cathedral of Our Lady of Paris; Map pp126–7; ☎ 01 42 34 56 10; www.cathedraledeparis.com; place du Parvis Notre Dame, 4e; Ⓜ Cité; audioguide €5; 🕒 7.45am-6.45pm) is the true heart of Paris; in fact, distances from Paris to all parts of metropolitan France are measured from **place du Parvis Notre Dame**, the square in front of Notre Dame. A bronze star, set in the pavement across from the main entrance, marks the exact location of **point zéro des routes de France** (point zero of French roads).

Notre Dame, the most visited site in Paris, with 10 million people crossing its threshold each year, is not just a masterpiece of French Gothic architecture but has also been the focus of Catholic Paris for seven centuries. Constructed on a site occupied by earlier churches – and, a millennium before that, a Gallo-Roman temple – it was begun in 1163 and largely completed by the mid-14th century. Architect Eugène Emmanuel Viollet-le-Duc carried out extensive renovations in the mid-19th century. The cathedral is on a very grand scale; the interior alone is 130m long, 48m wide and 35m high and can accommodate more than 6000 worshippers.

Notre Dame is known for its sublime balance, although if you look closely you'll see many minor asymmetrical elements introduced to avoid monotony, in accordance with standard Gothic practice. These include the slightly different shapes of each of the three main portals, whose statues were once brightly coloured to make them more effective as a *Biblia pauperum* – a 'Bible of the poor' to help the illiterate understand the Old Testament stories, the Passion of the Christ and the lives of the saints. One of the best views of Notre Dame is from **square Jean XXIII**, the lovely little park behind the cathedral, where you can see the mass of ornate **flying buttresses** that encircle the chancel and support its walls and roof.

Inside, exceptional features include three spectacular **rose windows**, the most renowned of which is the 10m-wide one over the western facade above the 7800-pipe organ, and the window on the northern side of the transept, which has remained virtually unchanged since the 13th century. The central choir, with its carved wooden stalls and statues representing the Passion of the Christ, is also noteworthy. There are free 1½-hour guided tours of the cathedral in English at noon on Wednesday and Thursday and at 2.30pm on Saturday.

The **trésor** (treasury; adult/3-12yr/student €3/1/2; 9.30am-6pm Mon-Sat, 1-6pm Sun), in the south-eastern transept, contains artwork, liturgical objects, church plate and first-class relics – some of them of questionable origin. Among these is the Ste-Couronne, the 'Holy Crown' – purportedly the wreath of thorns placed on Jesus' head before he was crucified – which was brought here in the mid-13th century. It is exhibited between 3pm and 4pm on the first Friday of each month, 3pm to 4pm every Friday during Lent and 10am to 5pm on Good Friday.

The entrance to the **tours de Notre Dame** (Notre Dame towers; ☎ 01 53 10 07 02; www.monuments-nationaux.fr; rue du Cloître Notre Dame; adult/18-25yr/under 18yr €7.50/4.80/free, admission free 1st Sun of the month Oct-Mar; 10am-6.30pm daily Apr-Jun & Sep, 9am-7.30pm Mon-Fri, 9am-11pm Sat & Sun Jul & Aug, 10am-5.30pm daily Oct-Mar), which can be climbed, is from the **North Tower**, to the right and around the corner as you walk out of the cathedral's main doorway. The 422 spiralling steps bring you to the top of the west facade, where you'll find yourself face to face with many of the cathedral's most frightening gargoyles, the 13-tonne bell Emmanuel (all the cathedral's bells are named) in the **South Tower**, and a spectacular view of Paris.

Ste-Chapelle

The most exquisite of Paris' Gothic monuments, **Ste-Chapelle** (Holy Chapel; Map pp126-7; ☎ 01 53 40 60 97; www.monuments-nationaux.fr; 4 bd du Palais, 1er; Ⓜ Cité; adult/18-25yr/under 18yr €6.50/4.50/free, admission free 1st Sun of month Oct-Mar; 9.30am-6pm Mar-Oct, 9am-5pm Nov-Feb) is tucked away within the walls of the **Palais de Justice** (Law Courts). The 'walls' of the **upper chapel** are sheer curtains of richly coloured and finely detailed **stained glass**, which bathe the chapel in extraordinary coloured light on a sunny day. Built in just under three years (compared with nearly 200 years for Notre Dame), Ste-Chapelle was consecrated in 1248. The chapel was conceived by Louis IX to house his personal collection of holy relics (now kept in the treasury of Notre Dame).

A joint ticket with the Conciergerie (below) costs adult/18 to 25 years €11.50/9.

Conciergerie

Built as a royal palace in the 14th century for the concierge of the Palais de la Cité, the **Conciergerie** (Map pp126-7; ☎ 01 53 40 60 97; www.monuments-nationaux.fr; 2 bd du Palais, 1er; Ⓜ Cité; adult/18-25yr/under 18yr €8/6/free, admission free 1st Sun of month Oct-Mar; 9.30am-6pm Mar-Oct, 9am-5pm Nov-Feb) was the main prison during the Reign of Terror (1793–94) and was used to incarcerate alleged enemies of the Revolution before they were brought before the Revolutionary Tribunal in the Palais de Justice next door. Among the 2700 prisoners held in the *cachots* (dungeons) here before being sent in tumbrels to the guillotine were Queen Marie-Antoinette (see a reproduction of her cell) and, as the Revolution began to turn on its own, the radicals Danton, Robespierre and, finally, the judges of the Tribunal themselves.

The Gothic 14th-century **Salle des Gens d'Armes** (Cavalrymen's Hall) is a fine example of the Rayonnant Gothic style. It is the largest surviving medieval hall in Europe. The **Tour de l'Horloge** (clock tower; cnr bd du Palais & quai de l'Horloge) has held a public clock aloft since 1370.

A joint ticket with Ste-Chapelle (p145) costs adult/18 to 25 years €11.50/9.

Pont Neuf

The sparkling-white stone spans of Paris' oldest bridge, **Pont Neuf** (Map pp126-7; Ⓜ Pont Neuf) – literally 'New Bridge' – have linked the western end of the Île de la Cité with both banks of the Seine since 1607, when King Henri IV inaugurated it by crossing the bridge on a white stallion. The seven arches, best seen from the river, are decorated with humorous and grotesque figures of barbers, dentists, pickpockets, loiterers etc.

ÎLE ST-LOUIS

The smaller of the Seine's two islands, Île St-Louis is just downstream from the Île de la Cité. In the early 17th century, when it was actually two uninhabited islets called Île Notre Dame (Our Lady Isle) and Île aux Vaches (Cows Island), a building contractor and two financiers worked out a deal with Louis XIII to create one island out of the two and build two stone bridges to the mainland. In exchange they would receive the right to subdivide and sell the newly created real estate. This they did with great success, and by 1664 the entire island was covered with fine new and airy houses facing the quays and the river.

Today, the island's 17th-century, grey-stone houses and the shops that line the streets and quays impart a village-like, provincial calm. The only sight as such, the French baroque **Église St-Louis en l'Île** (Map pp126-7; 19bis rue St-Louis en l'Île, 4e; Ⓜ Pont Marie; 🕑 9am-noon & 3-7pm Tue-Sun), was built between 1664 and 1726.

Latin Quarter & Jardin des Plantes

The centre of Parisian higher education since the Middle Ages, the Latin Quarter is so called because conversation between students and professors until the Revolution was in Latin. It still has a large population of students and academics affiliated with the Sorbonne (now part of the University of Paris system), the Collège de France, the École Normale Supérieure and other institutions of higher learning, though its near monopoly on Parisian academic life is not what it was. To the southeast, the Jardin des Plantes, with its tropical greenhouses and Musée National d'Histoire Naturelle, offers a bucolic alternative to the chalkboards and cobblestones.

MUSÉE NATIONAL DU MOYEN ÂGE

The **Musée National du Moyen Âge** (National Museum of the Middle Ages; Map pp126-7; ☎ 01 53 73 78 00; www.musee-moyenage.fr; 6 place Paul Painlevé, 5e; Ⓜ Cluny-La Sorbonne or St-Michel; adult/18-25yr/under 18yr €7.50/5.50/free, admission free 1st Sun of month; 🕑 9.15am-5.45pm Wed-Mon) is housed in two structures: the **frigidarium** (cooling room) and other remains of Gallo-Roman baths dating from around AD 200, and the late-15th-century **Hôtel de Cluny**, considered the finest example of medieval civil architecture in Paris.

The spectacular displays at the museum include statuary, illuminated manuscripts, weapons, furnishings, and objets d'art made of gold, ivory and enamel. But nothing compares with *La Dame à la Licorne* (The Lady with the Unicorn), a sublime series of late-15th-century tapestries from the southern Netherlands now hung in circular room 13 on the 1st floor. Five of them are devoted to the senses, while the sixth is the enigmatic *À Mon Seul Désir* (To My Sole Desire), a reflection on vanity.

SORBONNE

Paris' most renowned seat of learning, the **Sorbonne** (Map pp130-1; 12 rue de la Sorbonne, 5e; Ⓜ Luxembourg or Cluny-La Sorbonne) was founded in 1253 by Robert de Sorbon, confessor to Louis IX, as a college for 16 impoverished theology students. Today, the Sorbonne's main complex (bounded by rue de la Sorbonne, rue des Écoles, rue St-Jacques and rue Cujas) and other buildings in the vicinity house most of the 13 autonomous universities that were created when the University of Paris was reorganised after violent student protests in 1968. Parts of the complex are undergoing extensive renovation, scheduled to be completed in 2015.

PANTHÉON

The domed landmark now known simply as the **Panthéon** (Map pp130-1; ☎ 01 44 32 18 00; www.monuments-nationaux.fr; place du Panthéon, 5e; Ⓜ Luxembourg; adult/18-25yr/under 18yr €7.50/4.80/free, admission free 1st

PARIS BREATHES

Now a well-established operation, 'Paris Respire' (Paris Breathes) kicks motorised traffic off certain streets at certain times to let pedestrians, cyclists, in-line skaters and other nonmotorised cruisers take over and, well, breathe. While it drives its usual traffic jams and pollution to other spots in the city instead, it makes Sundays very pedal-pleasurable.

The following tracks are off limits to cars on Sunday and public holidays. For updates on exact routes and detailed maps see www.velo.paris.fr.

- **By the Seine** From quai des Tuileries, 1e, to Pont Charles de Gaulle, 12e, on the Right Bank; and on the Left Bank from the eastern end of quai Branly near Pont d'Alma, 7e, to quai Anatole France, 7e (from 9am to 5pm Sundays).
- **Latin Quarter, 5e** Rue de Cluny and from place Marcelin Berthelot by the Sorbonne to the rue Mouffetard market via rue de Lanneau, rue de l'École Polytechnique and rue des Descartes (from 10am-6pm Sundays).
- **Bastille, 11e** Rue de la Roquette and surrounding streets (from 10am to 6pm Sundays in July and August).
- **Montmartre & Pigalle** All the streets in Montmartre, 18e, encircled by rue Caulaincourt, rue de Clignancourt, bd de Rochechouart and bd de Clichy (from 11am to 7pm April to August, from 11am to 6pm September to March), as well as rue des Martyrs, 9e (from 10am to 1pm Sundays).
- **Canal St-Martin, 10e** The area around quai de Valmy and quai de Jemmapes, 10e (from 10am to 6pm Sundays in winter, to 8pm in summer); in July and August yet more streets running south from quai de Jemmapes become car-free.
- **Bois de Boulogne** (from 9am to 6pm Saturdays and Sundays) and **Bois de Vincennes** (from 9am to 6pm Sundays).
- **Jardin du Luxembourg, 6e** Immediate surrounding streets, including parts of rue Auguste Compte, rue d'Assas, bd St-Michel and rue des Chartreux (from 10am to 6pm Sundays March to November).

Sun of month Oct-Mar; 10am-6.30pm Apr-Sep, to 6.15pm Oct-Mar) was commissioned around 1750 as an abbey church dedicated to Ste Geneviève, but because of financial and structural problems it wasn't completed until 1789 – not a good year for churches to open in France. Two years later, the Constituent Assembly converted it into a secular mausoleum for the *grands hommes de l'époque de la liberté française* (great men of the era of French liberty).

The Panthéon is a superb example of 18th-century neoclassicism, but its ornate marble interior is gloomy in the extreme. The 80-odd permanent residents of the crypt include Voltaire, Jean-Jacques Rousseau, Victor Hugo, Émile Zola, Jean Moulin and Nobel Prize winner Marie Curie, whose remains were moved here in 1995 – the first woman to be interred here.

JARDIN DES PLANTES

Paris' 24-hectare **Jardin des Plantes** (Botanical Garden; Map pp130-1 & Map pp134-5; ☎ 01 40 79 56 01, 01 40 79 54 79; 57 rue Cuvier & 3 quai St-Bernard, 5e; Ⓜ Gare d'Austerlitz, Censier Daubenton or Jussieu; 8am-5.30pm, to 8pm in summer) was founded in 1626 as a medicinal herb garden for Louis XIII. Here you'll find the Eden-like **Jardin d'Hiver** (Winter Garden; Map pp130–1), which is also called the **Serres Tropicales** (Tropical Greenhouses), renovated in 2008; the **Jardin Alpin** (Alpine Garden; Map pp130-1; weekend admission adult/4-15yr/under 4yr €1/0.50/free; 8am-4.30pm Mon-Fri, 1-5pm Sat & Sun Apr-Oct), with 2000 mountain plants; and the gardens of the **École de Botanique** (Map pp130-1; admission free; 8am-5pm Mon-Fri), which is where students of the School of Botany 'practise'.

The **Ménagerie du Jardin des Plantes** (Botanical Garden Zoo; adult/4-15yr/under 4yr €7/5/free; 9am-5pm), a medium-size (5.5-hectare, 1000 animals) zoo in the northern section of the garden, was founded in 1794. During the Prussian siege of Paris in 1870, most of the animals were eaten by starving Parisians.

A two-day combined ticket covering all the Jardin des Plantes sights, including all the sections of the Musée National d'Histoire Naturelle, costs €20/15.

MUSÉE NATIONAL D'HISTOIRE NATURELLE

Created by a decree of the Revolutionary Convention in 1793, the **Musée National d'Histoire Naturelle** (National Museum of Natural History; Map pp130-1; ☎ 01 40 79 30 00; www.mnhn.fr, in French; 57 rue Cuvier, 5e; Ⓜ Censier Daubenton or Gare d'Austerlitz) was the site of important scientific research during the 19th century. It is housed in several different buildings along the southern edge of the Jardin des Plantes.

A highlight for kids, the museum's **Grande Galerie de l'Évolution** (Great Gallery of Evolution; 36 rue Geoffroy St-Hilaire, 5e; adult/4-13yr/under 4yr €8/6/free; 10am-6pm Wed-Mon) has some imaginative exhibits on evolution and humankind's effect on the global ecosystem, spread over four floors and 6000 sq metres of space. Rare specimens of endangered and extinct species dominate the **Salle des Espèces Menacées et des Espèces Disparues** (Hall of Threatened and Extinct Species) on level 2, while the **Salle de Découverte** (Room of Discovery) on level 1 houses interactive exhibits for kids.

To the south, the **Galerie de Minéralogie et de Géologie** (Mineralogy & Geology Gallery; 36 rue Geoffroy St-Hilaire; adult/4-13yr/under 4yr €7/5/free; 10am-5pm Wed-Mon) has an amazing exhibition of giant natural crystals and a basement display of jewellery and other objects made from minerals. Displays on comparative anatomy and palaeontology (the study of fossils) fill the **Galerie d'Anatomie Comparée et de Paléontologie** (Map pp134-5; 2 rue Buffon; adult/4-13yr/under 4yr €6/4/free; 10am-5pm Wed-Mon).

INSTITUT DU MONDE ARABE

Set up by France and 20 Arab countries to promote cultural contacts between the Arab world and the West, the **Institut du Monde Arabe** (Institute of the Arab World; Map pp130-1; ☎ 01 40 51 38 38; www.imarabe.org, in French; 1 place Mohammed V, 5e; Ⓜ Cardinal Lemoine or Jussieu) is housed in a critically praised building (1987) that successfully mixes modern and traditional Arab and Western elements.

The **museum** (adult/18-25yr/under 18yr €5/4/free; 10am-6pm Tue-Sun), spread over three floors and entered via the 7th floor, displays 9th- to 19th-century art and artisanship from all over the Arab world, as well as instruments from astronomy and other fields of scientific endeavour in which Arab technology once led the world. Temporary exhibitions (enter from quai Saint Bernard) charge a separate fee; combined tickets are usually available for around €13/11.

MOSQUÉE DE PARIS

With its striking 26m-high minaret, the central **Mosquée de Paris** (Paris Mosque; Map pp130-1; ☎ 01 45 35 97 33; www.mosquee-de-paris.org; 2bis place du Puits de l'Ermite, 5e; Ⓜ Censier Daubenton or Place Monge; adult/senior & 7-25yr/under 7yr €3/2/free; 9am-noon & 2-6pm Sat-Thu) was built in 1926 in the ornate Moorish style. Visitors must be modestly dressed and remove their shoes at the entrance to the prayer hall. The complex includes a North African–style *salon de thé* (tearoom) and restaurant (p182) and a **hammam** (☎ 01 43 31 38 20; admission €15; men 2-9pm Tue & 10am-9pm Sun, women 10am-9pm Mon, Wed, Thu & Sat, 2-9pm Fri), a traditional Turkish-style bathhouse.

St-Germain, Odéon & Luxembourg

Centuries ago the Église St-Germain des Prés and its affiliated abbey owned most of today's 6e and 7e. The neighbourhood around the church began to develop in the late 17th century, and these days it is celebrated for its heterogeneity. Cafés such as Café de Flore and Les Deux Magots (p189) were favourite hang-outs of postwar Left Bank intellectuals and the birthplaces of existentialism.

ÉGLISE ST-GERMAIN DES PRÉS

Paris' oldest church, the Romanesque **Église St-Germain des Prés** (Church of St Germanus of the Fields; Map pp126-7; ☎ 01 55 42 81 33; 3 place St-Germain des Prés, 6e; Ⓜ St-Germain des Prés; 8am-7pm Mon-Sat, 9am-8pm Sun) was built in the 11th century on the site of a 6th-century abbey and was the dominant church in Paris until the arrival of Notre Dame.

It has since been altered many times, but the **Chapelle de St-Symphorien**, to the right as you enter, was part of the original abbey and is the final resting place of St Germanus (AD 496–576), the first bishop of Paris. The bell tower over the western entrance has changed little since 990, although the spire only dates from the 19th century.

ÉGLISE ST-SULPICE

Lined with 21 side chapels inside, the Italianate **Église St-Sulpice** (Church of St Sulpicius; Map pp126-7; ☎ 01 46 33 21 78; place St-Sulpice, 6e; Ⓜ St-Sulpice; 7.30am-7.30pm) was built between 1646 and

1780. The facade, designed by a Florentine architect, has two rows of superimposed columns and is topped by two towers. The neoclassical decor of the vast interior is influenced by the Counter-Reformation.

The frescos in the **Chapelle des Sts-Anges** (Chapel of the Holy Angels), first to the right as you enter, depict Jacob wrestling with the angel (to the left) and Michael the Archangel doing battle with Satan (to the right) and were painted by Eugène Delacroix between 1855 and 1861.

The monumental 20m-tall organ loft dates from 1781. Listen to it in its full glory during 10.30am Mass on Sunday or the occasional Sunday afternoon organ concert, usually starting at 4pm.

JARDIN DU LUXEMBOURG

When the weather is fine, Parisians of all ages come flocking to the formal terraces and chestnut groves of the 23-hectare **Jardin du Luxembourg** (Luxembourg Garden; Map pp130-1; Ⓜ Luxembourg; 7.30am to 8.15am–5pm to 10pm according to the season) to read, relax and sunbathe. There are a number of activities for children here, and in the southern part of the garden you'll find urban **orchards** as well as the honey-producing **Rucher du Luxembourg** (Luxembourg Apiary).

The **Palais du Luxembourg** (Luxembourg Palace; rue de Vaugirard, 6e), at the northern end of the garden, was built for Marie de Médicis, Henri IV's consort; it has housed the **Sénat** (Senate), the upper house of the French parliament, since 1958. There are **guided tours** (☎ reservations 01 44 54 19 49; www.senat.fr; adult/18-25yr/under 18yr €8/6/free) of the interior, usually at 10.30am one Saturday a month, but you must book by the preceding Tuesday.

The **Musée du Luxembourg** (Luxembourg Museum; ☎ 01 42 34 25 95; www.museeduluxembourg.fr; 19 rue de Vaugirard, 6e; Ⓜ Luxembourg or St-Sulpice; adult/10-25yr/under 10yr €11/9/free; 10.30am-10pm Mon & Fri, 10.30am-7pm Tue-Thu & Sat, 9am-7pm Sun) opened at the end of the 19th century in the orangery of the Palais du Luxembourg as an exhibition space for living artists. It hosts prestigious temporary art exhibitions; admission prices vary depending on the exhibit.

Montparnasse

After WWI, writers, poets and artists of the avant-garde abandoned Montmartre on the Right Bank and crossed the Seine, shifting the centre of artistic ferment to the area around bd du Montparnasse. Chagall, Modigliani, Léger, Soutine, Miró, Kandinsky, Picasso, Stravinsky, Hemingway, Ezra Pound and Cocteau, as well as such political exiles as Lenin and Trotsky, all used to hang out in the cafés and brasseries for which the quarter became famous. Montparnasse remained a creative centre until the mid-1930s. Today, especially since the construction of the Gare Montparnasse complex, there is little to remind visitors of the area's bohemian past except the now very touristed restaurants and cafés.

TOUR MONTPARNASSE

A steel-and-smoked-glass eyesore built in 1974, the 210m-high **Tour Montparnasse** (Montparnasse Tower; Map pp124-5; ☎ 01 45 38 52 56; www.tourmontparnasse56.com; rue de l'Arrivée, 15e; Ⓜ Montparnasse Bienvenüe; adult/student & 16-20yr/7-15yr/under 7yr €9.50/6.80/4/free; 9.30am-11.30pm daily Apr-Sep, 9.30am-10.30pm Sun-Thu, 9.30am-11pm Fri & Sat Oct-Mar) affords spectacular views over the city – a view, we might add, that does not take in this ghastly oversized lipstick tube. A lift takes you up to the 56th-floor enclosed **observatory**, with exhibition centre, video clips, multimedia terminals and Paris' highest café. You can finish your visit with a hike up the stairs to the **open-air terrace** on the 59th floor, but arm yourself with the multilingual guide *Paris Vu d'En Haut* (Paris Seen from the Top; €3), available from the ticket office, to know what you're looking at.

CIMETIÈRE DU MONTPARNASSE

The **Cimetière du Montparnasse** (Montparnasse Cemetery; Map pp124-5; bd Edgar Quinet & rue Froidevaux, 14e; Ⓜ Edgar Quinet or Raspail; 8am-6pm Mon-Fri, 8.30am-6pm Sat, 9am-6pm Sun mid-Mar–early Nov, 8am-5.30pm Mon-Fri, 8.30am-5.30pm Sat, 9am-5.30pm Sun early Nov–mid-Mar) received its first 'lodger' in 1824. It contains the tombs of such illustrious personages as the poet Charles Baudelaire, writer Guy de Maupassant, playwright Samuel Beckett, sculptor Constantin Brancusi, painter Chaim Soutine, photographer Man Ray, industrialist André Citroën, Captain Alfred Dreyfus of the infamous Dreyfus Affair, actor Jean Seberg, philosopher Jean-Paul Sartre, writer Simone de Beauvoir and the crooner Serge Gainsbourg. Maps showing the location of the tombs are available free from the **conservation office** (Map pp124-5; ☎ 01 44 10 86 50; 3 bd Edgar Quinet, 14e).

CATACOMBES

In 1785 it was decided to solve the hygiene and aesthetic problems posed by Paris' overflowing cemeteries by exhuming the bones and storing them in the tunnels of three disused quarries. One ossuary created in 1810 is now known as the **Catacombes** (☎ 01 43 22 47 63; Map pp114-15; www.catacombes.paris.fr, in French; 1 av Colonel Henri Roi-Tanguy, 14e; Ⓜ Denfert Rochereau; adult/14-26yr/under 14yr €7/3.50/free; 🕑 10am-5pm Tue-Sun), which can be visited. After descending 20m (130 steps) from street level, visitors follow 1.7km of underground corridors in which the bones and skulls of millions of former Parisians are neatly stacked along the walls. During WWII these tunnels were used as a headquarters by the Resistance; so-called *cataphiles* looking for cheap thrills are often caught roaming the tunnels at night (there's a fine of €60).

The route through the Catacombes begins at a small, dark-green belle-époque-style building in the centre of a grassy area of av Colonel Henri Roi-Tanguy. The exit is at the top of 83 steps on rue Remy Dumoncel (Ⓜ Mouton Duvernet), 700m to the southwest.

Faubourg St-Germain & Invalides

Paris' most fashionable neighbourhood during the 18th century was Faubourg St-Germain in the 7e, the area between the Seine and rue de Babylone 1km south. Some of the most interesting mansions, many of which now serve as embassies, cultural centres and government ministries, are along three streets running east to west: rue de Lille, rue de Grenelle and rue de Varenne. The **Hôtel Matignon** (Map pp124-5; 57 rue de Varenne, 7e) has been the official residence of the French prime minister since the start of the Fifth Republic in 1958. Here you'll find the richly endowed Musée d'Orsay, home to France's large collection of Impressionist and post-Impressionist art, and the Hôtel des Invalides, containing, among other things, the earthly remains of Napoleon Bonaparte.

MUSÉE D'ORSAY

Facing the Seine from quai Anatole France, the **Musée d'Orsay** (Orsay Museum; Map pp124-5; ☎ 01 40 49 48 14; www.musee-orsay.fr; 62 rue de Lille, 7e; Ⓜ Musée d'Orsay or Solférino; adult/18-30yr/under 18yr €8/5.50/free, admission free 1st Sun of the month; 🕑 9.30am-6pm Tue, Wed & Fri-Sun, 9.30am-9.45pm Thu) is housed in a former train station (1900). It displays France's national collection of paintings, sculptures, objets d'art and other works produced between the 1840s and 1914, including the fruits of the Impressionist, post-Impressionist and art-nouveau movements.

Many visitors to the museum go straight to the upper level (lit by a skylight) to see the famous **Impressionist paintings** by Monet, Pissarro, Renoir, Sisley, Degas and Manet and the **post-Impressionist works** by Cézanne, van Gogh, Seurat and Matisse, but there's also lots to see on the ground floor, including some early works by Manet, Monet, Renoir and Pissarro. The middle level has some superb **art-nouveau rooms**.

English-language tours (☎ information 01 40 49 48 48; admission fee plus €7.50/5.70), lasting 1½ hours, include the 'Masterpieces of the Musée d'Orsay' tour, departing at 11.30am Tuesday to Saturday. The 1½-hour **audioguide tour** (€5), available in six languages, points out around 80 major works. Tickets are valid all day, so you can leave and re-enter the museum as you please. The reduced entrance fee of €5.50 applies to everyone after 4.15pm (6pm on Thursday). Those visiting the Musée Rodin the same day save €2 with a combined ticket (€12).

MUSÉE RODIN

One of our favourite cultural attractions in Paris, the **Musée Rodin** (Rodin Museum; Map pp124-5; ☎ 01 44 18 61 10; www.musee-rodin.fr; 79 rue de Varenne, 7e; Ⓜ Varenne; adult/18-25yr permanent collections or temporary exhibitions plus garden €6/4, both exhibitions plus garden €9/7, garden only €1, admission free under 18yr & 1st Sun of month; 🕑 9.30am-5.45pm Tue-Sun Apr-Sep, 9.30am-4.45pm Tue-Sun Oct-Mar) is both a sublime museum and one of the most relaxing spots in the city, with a lovely **garden**, full of sculptures and shade trees, in which to rest. Rooms on two floors of this 18th-century residence display extraordinarily vital bronze and marble sculptures by Rodin, including casts of some of his most celebrated works: *The Hand of God, The Burghers of Calais (Les Bourgeois de Calais), Cathedral,* that perennial crowd-pleaser *The Thinker (Le Penseur)* and the incomparable *The Kiss (Le Baiser)*. There are also some 15 works by Camille Claudel (1864–1943), sister of the writer Paul Claudel and Rodin's mistress.

HÔTEL DES INVALIDES

The **Hôtel des Invalides** (Map pp124-5; Ⓜ Varenne or La Tour Maubourg) was built in the 1670s by Louis XIV to provide housing for some 4000 *invalides* (disabled war veterans). On 14 July 1789 a mob forced its way into the building and, after some fierce fighting, seized 32,000 rifles before heading on to the prison at Bastille and the start of the French Revolution.

North of the Hôtel des Invalides' main courtyard, in the so-called **Cour d'Honneur**, is the **Musée de l'Armée** (Army Museum; Map pp124-5; ☎ 01 44 42 38 77; www.invalides.org; 129 rue de Grenelle, 7e; adult/18-25yr/under 18yr €8/6/free; 🕒 10am-6pm Apr-Sep, 10am-5pm Oct-Mar, closed 1st Mon of month), which holds the nation's largest collection on the history of the French military.

To the south are the **Église St-Louis des Invalides** (Map pp124–5), once used by soldiers, and the **Église du Dôme** (Map pp124–5), whose sparkling dome (1677–1735) is visible throughout the city. The Église du Dôme received the remains of Napoleon in 1840, and the very extravagant **Tombeau de Napoléon 1er** (Napoleon I's Tomb; 🕒 10am-6pm Apr-Sep, 10am-5pm Oct-Mar, closed 1st Mon of month), in its centre, consists of six coffins that fit into one another rather like a Russian stacking doll.

Eiffel Tower Area & 16e Arrondissement

The very symbol of Paris, the Eiffel Tower, is surrounded by open areas on both banks of the Seine, which take in both the 7e and 16e, the most chichi (and snobby) part of the capital. It's not everyone's *tasse de thé* (cup of tea), but there are several outstanding sights and museums in this part of the Right Bank. The architecturally impressive (and fully loaded) Musée du Quai Branly (p153) is the newly acquired feather in the cap of this area.

TOUR EIFFEL

When it was built for the 1889 Exposition Universelle (World Fair), marking the centenary of the Revolution, the **Tour Eiffel** (Eiffel Tower; Map pp124-5; ☎ 01 44 11 23 23; www.tour-eiffel.fr; Ⓜ Champ de Mars-Tour Eiffel or Bir Hakeim; 🕒 lifts 9am-midnight mid-Jun–Aug, 9.30am-11pm Sep–mid-Jun, stairs 9am-midnight mid-Jun–Aug, 9.30am-6pm Sep–mid-Jun) faced massive opposition from Paris' artistic and literary elite. The 'metal asparagus', as some Parisians snidely called it, was almost torn down in 1909 but was spared because it proved an ideal platform for the transmitting antennas needed for the new science of radiotelegraphy. It welcomed two million visitors the first year it opened and more than three times that number – 6.9 million in 2007 – make their way to the top each year.

The Eiffel Tower, named after its designer, Gustave Eiffel, is 324m high, including the TV antenna at the tip. This figure can vary by as much as 15cm, however, as the tower's 7300 tonnes of iron, held together by 2.5 million rivets, expand in warm weather and contract when it's cold.

Three levels are open to the public. The lifts (in the east, west and north pillars), which follow a curved trajectory, cost €4.80 to the 1st platform (57m above the ground), €7.80 to the 2nd (115m) and €12 to the 3rd (276m). Children aged three to 11 pay €2.50, €4.30 or €6.70, respectively. If you are strong of thigh and lung you can avoid the lift queues by taking the stairs (€4/3.10 over/under 25 years) in the south pillar to the 1st and 2nd platforms.

PALAIS DE CHAILLOT

The **Palais de Chaillot** (Chaillot Palace; Map pp124-5; 17 place du Trocadéro et du 11 Novembre, 16e; Ⓜ Trocadéro) was built for the 1937 World Exhibition held here. Its two curved and colonnaded wings and the terrace in between them afford an exceptional panorama of the Jardins du Trocadéro, the Seine and the Eiffel Tower.

The palace's western wing contains two interesting museums. The **Musée de l'Homme** (Museum of Mankind; ☎ 01 44 05 72 72; www.mnhn.fr; 17 place du Trocadéro et du 11 Novembre, 16e; adult/4-16yr & student/under 4yr €7/5/free; 🕒 10am-5pm Mon & Wed-Fri, to 6pm Sat & Sun), straight ahead as you enter, focuses on human development, ethnology, population and population growth. The **Musée de la Marine** (Maritime Museum; ☎ 01 53 65 69 69; www.musee-marine.fr, in French; 17 place du Trocadéro et du 11 Novembre, 16e; adult/student & 18-25yr/under 18yr €6.50/4.50/free; 🕒 10am-6pm Wed-Mon), to the right of the main entrance, examines France's naval adventures from the 17th century until today.

In the palace's eastern wing is the new **Cité de l'Architecture et du Patrimoine** (☎ 01 58 51 52 00; www.citechaillot.fr, in French; 1 place du Trocadéro et du 11 Novembre, 16e; adult/student & 18-25yr/under 18yr €8/5/free; 🕒 11am-7pm Mon, Wed & Fri-Sun, to 9pm Thu), a mammoth 23,000 sq metres spread over three floors devoted to French architecture and heritage. Exhibits include 350 wood and plaster casts of cathedral portals, columns and altars originally created for the 1878 Exposition Universelle.

JARDINS DU TROCADÉRO

Spreading out below the Palais de Chaillot and fronting the Eiffel Tower are the **Jardins du Trocadéro** (Trocadero Gardens; Map pp124-5; Ⓜ Trocadéro), whose fountains and statue garden are grandly illuminated at night. They are named after a Spanish stronghold near Cádiz that was captured by the French in 1823.

On the eastern side of the Jardins du Trocadéro is **CineAqua** (☎ 01 40 69 23 23; www.cineaqua.com; 2 av des Nations Unies, 16e; adult/13-17yr/3-12yr/under 3yr €19.50/15.50/12.50/free; 10am-8pm), Europe's newest and most ambitious aquarium, with 500 species 'tanked' in more than 3500 sq metres of space.

MUSÉE DU QUAI BRANLY

Housed in architect Jean Nouvel's impressive new structure of glass, wood and turf along the Seine, the long-awaited **Musée du Quai Branly** (Quai Branly Museum; Map pp124-5; ☎ 01 56 61 70 00; www.quaibranly.fr; 37 quai Branly, 7e; M Pont de l'Alma or Alma-Marceau; adult/student & 18-25yr/under 18yr €8.50/6/free, admission free after 6pm Sat for 18-25yr, 1st Sun of month for all; 11am-7pm Tue, Wed & Sun, to 9pm Thu-Sat) introduces the art and cultures of Africa, Oceania, Asia and the Americas through innovative displays, film and musical recordings. The anthropological explanations are kept to a minimum; what is displayed here is meant to be viewed as art. A day pass allowing entry to the temporary exhibits as well as the permanent collection costs adult/concession €13/9.50; an audioguide is €5.

MUSÉE GUIMET DES ARTS ASIATIQUES

France's foremost repository for Asian art, the **Musée Guimet des Arts Asiatiques** (Guimet Museum of Asian Art; Map pp118-19; ☎ 01 56 52 53 00; www.museeguimet.fr; 6 place d'Iéna; M Iéna; permanent collections admission free, temporary exhibitions adult €6.50-8.50, senior, student & 18-25yr €4.50-6; 10am-6pm Wed-Mon) has sculptures, paintings, objets d'art and religious articles from Afghanistan, India, Nepal, Pakistan, Tibet, Cambodia, China, Japan and Korea. Part of the original collection – Buddhist paintings and sculptures brought to Paris in 1876 by collector Émile Guimet – is housed in the **Galeries du Panthéon Bouddhique du Japon et de la Chine** (Buddhist Pantheon Galleries of Japan & China; Map pp118-19; ☎ 01 47 23 61 65; 19 av d'Iéna; M Iéna; admission free; 10am-6pm Wed-Mon) in the sumptuous Hôtel Heidelbach a short distance to the north. Don't miss the wonderful **Japanese garden** (1-5pm Wed-Mon) here.

FLAMME DE LA LIBERTÉ

A replica of the one topping New York's Statue of Liberty, the bronze **Flamme de la Liberté** (Flame of Liberty Memorial; Map pp118-19; place de l'Alma, 8e; M Alma-Marceau) was placed in this square southeast of the Musée Guimet in 1987 on the centenary of the launch of the *International Herald Tribune* newspaper as a symbol of friendship between France and the USA. When, on 31 August 1997 in the place d'Alma underpass below, Diana, Princess of Wales, was killed in a devastating car accident, along with her companion, Dodi Fayed, and their chauffeur, Henri Paul, the Flame of Liberty became something of a memorial to her; for five years it was decorated with flowers, photographs, graffiti and personal notes. It was renovated and cleaned in 2002 and, this being the age of short (or no) memories, apart from a bit of sentimental graffiti on a wall nearby, there are no longer any reminders of the tragedy that happened so close by and that had so much of the Western world in grief.

MUSÉE DES ÉGOUTS DE PARIS

The **Musée des Égouts de Paris** (Paris Sewers Museum; Map pp124-5; ☎ 01 53 68 27 81; place de la Résistance, 7e; M Pont de l'Alma; adult/student & 6-16yr/under 6yr €4.20/3.40/free; 11am-5pm Sat-Wed May-Sep, 11am-4pm Sat-Wed Oct-Dec & Feb-Apr) is a working museum whose entrance – a rectangular maintenance hole topped with a kiosk – is across the street from 93 quai d'Orsay, 7e. Raw sewage flows beneath your feet as you walk through 480m of odoriferous tunnels, passing artefacts illustrating the development of Paris' wastewater disposal system. It'll take your breath away, it will.

Étoile & Champs-Élysées

A dozen avenues radiate out from place de l'Étoile – officially called place Charles de Gaulle – and first among them is the av des Champs-Élysées. This broad boulevard, whose name refers to the 'Elysian Fields' where happy souls dwelt after death, according to the ancient Greeks, links place de la Concorde with the Arc de Triomphe. Symbolising the style and joie de vivre of Paris since the mid-19th century, the avenue is scuzzy in parts but remains a popular tourist destination.

Some 400m north of av des Champs-Élysées is rue du Faubourg St-Honoré (8e), the western extension of rue St-Honoré. It is home to some of Paris' most renowned couture houses, jewellers, antique shops and the 18th-century **Palais de l'Élysée** (Map pp118-19; cnr rue du Faubourg St-Honoré & av de Marigny, 8e; M Champs-Élysées Clemenceau), the official residence of the French president.

ARC DE TRIOMPHE

Located 2km northwest of place de la Concorde in the middle of place Charles de Gaulle (or place de l'Étoile), the **Arc de Triomphe** (Triumphal Arch; Map pp118-19; ☎ 01 55 37 73 77; www.monuments-nationaux.fr; Ⓜ Charles de Gaulle-Étoile; viewing platform adult/18-25yr/under 18yr €9/6.50/free, admission free 1st Sun of month Nov-Mar; 🕑 10am-11pm Apr-Sep, to 10.30pm Oct-Mar) is the world's largest traffic roundabout. It was commissioned by Napoléon in 1806 to commemorate his imperial victories but remained unfinished when he started losing battles and then entire wars. It was not completed until 1836. Since 1920, the body of an **Unknown Soldier** from WWI, taken from Verdun in Lorraine, has lain beneath the arch; his fate and that of countless others is commemorated by a **memorial flame** that is rekindled each evening around 6.30pm.

From the **viewing platform** on top of the arch (50m up via 284 steps and well worth the climb) you can see the dozen broad avenues – many of them named after Napoleonic victories and illustrious generals (including the ultra-exclusive av Foch, which is Paris' widest boulevard) – radiating towards every part of the city. Tickets to the viewing platform of the Arc de Triomphe are sold in the underground passageway that surfaces on the even-numbered side of av des Champs-Élysées. It is the only sane way to get to the base of the arch and is not linked to nearby metro tunnels.

GRAND & PETIT PALAIS

Erected for the 1900 World Exposition, the **Grand Palais** (Great Palace; Map pp118-19; ☎ 01 44 13 17 17, reservations 08 92 68 46 94; www.grandpalais.fr; 3 av du Général Eisenhower, 8e; Ⓜ Champs-Élysées Clemenceau; with/without booking adult €11/10, student & 13-25yr €10/8, under 13yr free; 🕑 10am-10pm Fri-Mon & Wed, to 8pm Thu) now houses the **Galeries Nationales du Grand Palais** beneath its huge art-nouveau glass roof. Special exhibitions, among the biggest the city stages, last three or four months here.

The **Petit Palais** (Little Palace; Map pp118-19; ☎ 01 53 43 40 00; www.petitpalais.paris.fr, in French; av Winston Churchill, 8e; Ⓜ Champs-Élysées Clemenceau; permanent collections admission free, temporary exhibitions adult/senior & student/14-26yr/under 14yr €9/6.50/4.50/free; 🕑 10am-6pm Wed-Sun, 10am-8pm Tue), which was also built for the 1900 fair, is home to the **Musée des Beaux-Arts de la Ville de Paris**, the Paris municipality's Museum of Fine Arts, which contains medieval and Renaissance objets d'art, tapestries, drawings and 19th-century French painting and sculpture.

PALAIS DE LA DÉCOUVERTE

Inaugurated during the 1937 Exposition Universelle and thus the world's first interactive museum, the **Palais de la Découverte** (Palace of Discovery; Map pp118-19; ☎ 01 56 43 20 21; www.palais-decouverte.fr, in French; av Franklin D Roosevelt, 8e; Ⓜ Champs-Élysées Clemenceau; adult/senior, student & 5-18yr/under 5yr €7/4.50/free; 🕑 9.30am-6pm Tue-Sat, 10am-7pm Sun) is a fascinating place to take kids, with hands-on exhibits on astronomy, biology, medicine, chemistry, mathematics, computer science, physics and earth sciences. The **planetarium** (admission €3.50) usually has four shows a day in French at 11.30am, 2pm, 3.15pm and 4.30pm; ring or consult the website for current schedules.

Concorde & Madeleine

The cobblestone expanses of 18th-century place de la Concorde are sandwiched between the Jardin des Tuileries and the parks at the eastern end of av des Champs-Élysées. Delightful place de la Madeleine is to the north. Both are in the 8e arrondissement.

PLACE DE LA CONCORDE

The 3300-year-old pink granite **obelisk** with the gilded top in the middle of **Place de la Concorde** (Map pp118-19; Ⓜ Concorde) once stood in the Temple of Ramses at Thebes (today's Luxor) and was given to France in 1831 by Muhammad Ali, viceroy and pasha of Egypt. The **female statues** adorning the four corners of the square represent France's eight largest cities.

In 1793 Louis XVI's head was lopped off by a guillotine set up in the northwest corner of the square, near the statue representing Brest. During the next two years, a guillotine built near the entrance to the Jardin des Tuileries was used to behead 1343 more people, including Marie-Antoinette and, six months later, the Revolutionary leaders Danton and Robespierre. The square, laid out between 1755 and 1775, was given its present name after the Reign of Terror in the hope that it would be a place of peace and harmony.

PLACE DE LA MADELEINE

Ringed by fine-food shops, the **place de la Madeleine** (Map pp118-19; Ⓜ Madeleine) is 350m north of place de la Concorde at the end of rue Royale. The square is named after the 19th-century neoclassical church in its centre, the **Église de Ste-Marie Madeleine** (Church of St Mary Magdalene; ☎ 01 44 51 69 00; www.eglise-lamadeleine

.com, in French; place de la Madeleine, 8e; ⌚ 9.30am-7pm). Constructed in the style of a Greek temple, what is now simply called 'La Madeleine' was consecrated in 1842 after almost a century of design changes and construction delays. It is surrounded by 52 Corinthian columns standing 20m tall, and the marble and gilt interior is topped by three sky-lit cupolas. You can hear the massive organ being played at Mass at 11am and 7pm on Sunday.

Opéra & Grands Boulevards

Place de l'Opéra (Map pp118–19) is the site of Paris' world-famous (and original) opera house. It abuts the Grands Boulevards, the eight contiguous 'Great Boulevards' – Madeleine, Capucines, Italiens, Montmartre, Poissonnière, Bonne Nouvelle, St-Denis and St-Martin – that stretch from elegant place de la Madeleine in the 8e eastwards to the more plebeian place de la République in the 3e, a distance of just under 3km.

The Grands Boulevards were laid out in the 17th century on the site of obsolete city walls and served as a centre of café and theatre life in the 18th and 19th centuries, reaching the height of fashion during the belle époque. North of the western end of the Grands Boulevards is bd Haussmann (8e and 9e), the heart of the commercial and banking district and known for some of Paris' most famous department stores, including Galeries Lafayette and Le Printemps (p197).

PALAIS GARNIER

One of the most impressive monuments erected in Paris during the 19th century, the **Palais Garnier** (Garnier Palace; Map pp118-19; ☎ 08 92 89 90 90; place de l'Opéra, 9e; Ⓜ Opéra) stages operas, ballets and classical-music concerts. In summer it can be visited on English-language **guided tours** (☎ 08 25 05 44 05; http://visites.operadeparis.fr; adult/senior/10-25yr €12/10/6; Ⓜ 11.30am & 2.30pm daily Jul & Aug, 11.30am & 2.30pm Wed, Sat & Sun Sep-Jun).

Palais Garnier houses the **Musée de l'Opéra** (Map pp118-19; ☎ 08 92 89 90 90, 01 40 01 24 93; adult/senior, student & 10-25yr/under 10yr €8/5/free; ⌚ 10am-5pm Sep-Jun, to 6pm Jul & Aug), which contains three centuries' worth of costumes, backdrops, scores and other memorabilia.

Included in the admission to the museum is a self-paced visit to the opera house itself – as long as there's not a daytime rehearsal or matinee scheduled, in which case it closes at 1pm.

COVERED ARCADES

There are several **passages couverts** (covered shopping arcades) off bd Montmartre (9e), and walking through them is like stepping back into the sepia-toned Paris of the early 19th century. The **passage des Panoramas** (Map pp120-1; 11 bd Montmartre & 10 rue St-Marc, 2e; Ⓜ Grands Boulevards), which was opened in 1800 and received Paris' first gas lighting in 1817, was expanded in 1834 with the addition of four other interconnecting passages: Feydeau, Montmartre, St-Marc and Variétés. The arcades are open till about midnight daily.

On the northern side of bd Montmartre, between Nos 10 and 12, is **passage Jouffroy** (Map pp120-1; Ⓜ Grands Boulevards), which leads across rue de la Grange Batelière to **passage Verdeau** (Map pp120–1).

Both contain shops selling antiques, old postcards, used and antiquarian books, gifts, pet toys, imports from Asia and the like. These arcades are open until 10pm.

MUSÉE GRÉVIN

Inside passage Jouffroy, the **Musée Grévin** (Grévin Museum; Map pp120-1; ☎ 01 47 70 85 05; www.grevin.com; 10 bd Montmartre, 9e; Ⓜ Grands Boulevards; adult/senior & student/6-14yr/under 6yr €18.50/16/11/9.50; ⌚ 10am-6.30pm Mon-Fri, to 7pm Sat & Sun) has some 300 wax figures that look more like caricatures than characters, but where else do you get to see Marilyn Monroe, Charles de Gaulle and Spiderman face to face, or the real death masks of French Revolutionary leaders? The admission charge is positively outrageous and just keeps a-growin' every year.

Ménilmontant & Belleville

A solidly working-class *quartier* (neighbourhood) with little to recommend it until just a few years ago, Ménilmontant in the 11e now boasts a surfeit of restaurants, bars and clubs.

On the other hand, Belleville (20e), home to large numbers of immigrants, especially Muslims and Jews from North Africa and Vietnamese and ethnic Chinese from Indochina, remains for the most part unpretentious and working-class. **Parc de Belleville** (Map pp120-1; Ⓜ Couronnes), which opened in 1992 a few blocks east of bd de Belleville, occupies a hill almost 200m above sea level amid 4.5 hectares of greenery and offers superb views of the city. Paris' most famous necropolis lies just to the south of the park.

CIMETIÈRE DU PÈRE LACHAISE

The world's most visited graveyard, **Cimetière du Père Lachaise** (Père Lachaise Cemetery; Map pp114-15; www.pere-lachaise.com; Ⓜ Philippe Auguste, Gambetta or Père Lachaise; 🕑 8am-6pm Mon-Fri, 8.30am-6pm Sat, 9am-6pm Sun mid-Mar–early Nov, 8am-5.30pm Mon-Fri, 8.30am-5.30pm Sat, 9am-5.30pm Sun early Nov–mid-Mar) opened its one-way doors in 1804. Its 69,000 ornate, even ostentatious, tombs form a verdant, 44-hectare open-air sculpture garden.

Among the 800,000 people buried here are the composer Chopin, the playwright Molière, the poet Apollinaire; the writers Balzac, Proust, Gertrude Stein and Colette; the actors Simone Signoret, Sarah Bernhardt and Yves Montand; the painters Pissarro, Seurat, Modigliani and Delacroix; the chanteuse Édith Piaf; the dancer Isadora Duncan; and even those immortal 12th-century lovers, Abélard and Héloïse, whose remains were disinterred and reburied here together in 1817 beneath a neo-Gothic tombstone.

Particularly frequented graves are those of **Oscar Wilde**, interred in division 89 in 1900, and 1960s rock star **Jim Morrison**, who died in an apartment at 17–19 rue Beautreillis, 4e, in the Marais in 1971 and is buried in division 6.

Père Lachaise has five entrances, two of which are on bd de Ménilmontant. Maps indicating the location of noteworthy graves are available free from the **conservation office** (Map pp132-3; ☎ 01 55 25 82 10; 16 rue du Repos, 20e) in the southwestern corner of the cemetery.

13e Arrondissement & Chinatown

The 13e begins a few blocks south of the Jardin des Plantes in the 5e and has undergone a true renaissance with the advent of the Bibliothèque Nationale de France (BNF), the high-speed Météor metro line (No 14) and the ZAC Paris Rive Gauche project, the massive redevelopment of the old industrial quarter along the Seine. Add to that the stunning new footbridge, Passerelle Simone de Beauvoir, linking the BNF with Parc de Bercy and Docks en Seine, a 20,000-sq-metre riverside warehouse being transformed into a state-of-the-art cultural and design centre, and you've got a district on the upswing. The stylishness of the neighbouring 5e extends to the av des Gobelins, while further south, between av d'Italie and av de Choisy, the succession of Asian restaurants, stalls and shops in the capital's Chinatown gives passers-by the illusion of having imperceptibly changed continents.

BIBLIOTHÈQUE NATIONALE DE FRANCE

Rising up from the banks of the Seine are the four glass towers of the controversial, €2 billion **Bibliothèque Nationale de France** (National Library of France; Map pp114-15; ☎ 01 53 79 53 79, 01 53 79 40 41; www.bnf.fr; 11 quai François Mauriac, 13e; Ⓜ Bibliothèque; temporary exhibitions adult/student 18-26yr from €7/5, under 18yr free; 🕑 10am-7pm Tue-Sat, 1-7pm Sun), which was conceived by the late president François Mitterrand as a 'wonder of the modern world' and opened in 1988.

No expense was spared to carry out a plan that many said defied logic. While many of the books and historical documents were shelved in the sun-drenched, 23-storey, 79m-high towers – shaped like half-open books – readers sat in artificially lit basement halls built around a light well 'courtyard' of 140 50-year-old pines, trucked in from the countryside. The towers have since been fitted with a complex (and expensive) shutter system, but the basement is prone to flooding from the Seine. The national library contains around 12 million tomes stored on some 420km of shelves and can accommodate 2000 readers and 2000 researchers. Temporary exhibitions (use Entrance E) revolve around 'the word', focusing on everything from storytelling to bookbinding. Using the study library costs €3.30/20/35 per day/two weeks/year, while the research library costs €7/53 per three days/year.

Montmartre & Pigalle

During the late 19th and early 20th centuries the bohemian lifestyle of Montmartre in the 18e attracted a number of important writers and artists, including Picasso, who lived at the studio called **Bateau Lavoir** (Map p136; 11bis Émile Goudeau; Ⓜ Abbesses) from 1908 to 1912. Although the activity shifted to Montparnasse after WWI, Montmartre retains an upbeat ambience that all the tourists in the world couldn't spoil.

Only a few blocks southwest of the tranquil residential streets of Montmartre is lively, neon-lit Pigalle (9e and 18e), one of Paris' two main sex districts (the other, which is *much* more low-rent, is along rue St-Denis and its side streets north of Forum des Halles in the 1er). But Pigalle is more than just a sleazy red-light district; there are plenty of trendy nightspots, including clubs and cabarets, here as well. South of Pigalle, the district known as Nouvelle Athènes (New Athens), with its beautiful Greco-Roman architecture and private gardens, has long been favoured by artists.

The easiest way to reach the top of the Butte de Montmartre (Montmartre Hill) is via the RATP's sleek funicular (p203).

BASILIQUE DU SACRÉ CŒUR

Perched at the very top of the Butte de Montmartre, the **Basilique du Sacré Cœur** (Basilica of the Sacred Heart; Map p136; ☎ 01 53 41 89 00; www.sacre-coeur-montmartre.com; place du Parvis du Sacré Cœur, 18e; Ⓜ Anvers; 🕑 6am-10.30pm) was built from contributions pledged by Parisian Catholics as an act of contrition after the humiliating Franco-Prussian War of 1870–71. Construction began in 1873, but the basilica was not consecrated until 1919.

Some 234 spiralling steps lead you to the basilica's **dome** (admission €5; 🕑 9am-7pm Apr-Sep, 9am-6pm Oct-Mar), which affords one of Paris' most spectacular panoramas; they say you can see for 30km on a clear day.

PLACE DU TERTRE

Half a block west of the **Église St-Pierre de Montmartre** (Map p136), which once formed part of a 12th-century Benedictine abbey, is **place du Tertre** (Map p136; Ⓜ Abbesses), once the main square of the village of Montmartre. These days it's filled with cafés, restaurants, tourists and rather obstinate portrait artists and caricaturists who will gladly do your likeness. Whether it looks even remotely like you is another matter.

CIMETIÈRE DE MONTMARTRE

The most famous cemetery in Paris after Père Lachaise, **Cimetière de Montmartre** (Montmartre Cemetery; Map p136; Ⓜ Place de Clichy; 🕑 8am-6pm Mon-Fri, 8.30am-6pm Sat, 9am-6pm Sun mid-Mar–early Nov, 8am-5.30pm Mon-Fri, 8.30am-5.30pm Sat, 9am-5.30pm Sun early Nov–mid-Mar) was established in 1798. It contains the graves of writers Émile Zola, Alexandre Dumas and Stendhal; composer Jacques Offenbach; artist Edgar Degas; film director François Truffaut; and dancer Vaslav Nijinsky – among others. The entrance closest to the Butte de Montmartre is at the end of av Rachel, just off bd de Clichy or down the stairs from 10 rue Caulaincourt. Maps showing the location of the tombs are available free from the **conservation office** (☎ 01 53 42 36 30; 20 av Rachel, 18e) at that entrance.

MUSÉE DE MONTMARTRE

One-time home to painters Renoir, Utrillo and Raoul Dufy, the **Musée de Montmartre** (Montmartre Museum; Map p136; ☎ 01 49 25 89 39; www.museedemontmartre.fr; 12 rue Cortot, 18e; Ⓜ Lamarck Caulaincourt; adult/senior, student & 10-25yr/under 10yr €7/5.50/free; 🕑 11am-6pm Tue-Sun) displays paintings, lithographs and documents, mostly relating to the area's rebellious and bohemian/artistic past, in a 17th-century manor house, the oldest structure in the quarter. It also stages exhibitions of artists still living in the *quartier*. There's an excellent bookshop here that also sells small bottles of the wine produced from grapes grown in the Clos Montmartre (p161).

DALÍ ESPACE MONTMARTRE

More than 300 works by Salvador Dalí (1904–89), the flamboyant Catalan surrealist printmaker, painter, sculptor and self-promoter, are on display at the **Dalí Espace Montmartre** (Dalí Exhibition Space Montmartre; Map p136; ☎ 01 42 64 40 10; www.daliparis.com; 11 rue Poulbot, 18e; Ⓜ Abbesses; adult/senior/student & 8-26 yr/under 8yr €10/7/6/free; 🕑 10am-6.30pm), a surrealist-style basement museum just west of place du Tertre. The collection includes Dalí's strange sculptures (most in reproduction), lithographs, many of his illustrations, and furniture (including the famous 'lips' sofa).

MUSÉE DE L'ÉROTISME

The **Musée de l'Érotisme** (Museum of Erotic Art; Map p136; ☎ 01 42 58 28 73; 72 bd de Clichy, 18e; Ⓜ Blanche; adult/student €8/5; 🕑 10am-2am) tries to put some 2000 titillating statues and stimulating sexual aids and fetishist items from days gone by on a loftier plane, with erotic art – both antique and modern – from four continents spread over seven floors. But most of the punters know why they are here.

La Villette

The Buttes Chaumont, the Canal de l'Ourcq and especially the Parc de la Villette, with its wonderful museums and other attractions, create the winning trifecta of the 19e arrondissement. One new development that will bring in the crowds like never before is the **Philharmonie de Paris** (Map pp114-15; Parc de la Villette; Porte de Pantin), the ambitious new home of the Orchestre de Paris designed by Jean

Nouvel, now under construction and scheduled to open in 2012.

PARC DE LA VILLETTE

The whimsical, 35-hectare **Parc de la Villette** (La Villette Park; Map pp114-15; ☎ 01 04 03 75 75; www.villette.com; Ⓜ Porte de la Villette or Porte de Pantin), which opened in 1993 in the city's far northeastern corner, stretches from the Cité des Sciences et de l'Industrie south to the Cité de la Musique. Split into two sections by the Canal de l'Ourcq, the park is enlivened by shaded walkways, imaginative street furniture, a series of themed gardens for kids and fanciful, bright-red pavilions known as *folies*. It is the largest open green space in central Paris and has been called 'the prototype urban park of the 21st century'.

CITÉ DES SCIENCES ET DE L'INDUSTRIE

At the northern end of Parc de la Villette, the huge **Cité des Sciences et de l'Industrie** (City of Science & Industry; Map pp114-15; ☎ 08 92 69 70 72, reservations 01 40 05 80 00; www.cite-sciences.fr; 30 av Corentin Cariou, 19e; Ⓜ Porte de la Villette; ⏲ 10am-6pm Tue-Sat, to 7pm Sun) has all sorts of high-tech exhibits. Free attractions include the following:

Aquarium (level -2; ⏲ 10am-6pm Tue-Sat, to 7pm Sun)

Carrefour Numérique (level -1; ⏲ noon-7.45pm Tue, to 6.45pm Wed-Sun) Internet centre.

Cité des Métiers (level -1; ⏲ 10am-6pm Tue-Fri, noon-6pm Sat) Information about trades, professions and employment.

Médiathèque (levels 0 & -1; ⏲ noon-7.45pm Tue, to 6.45pm Wed-Sun) Multimedia exhibits dealing with childhood, the history of science, and health.

A free and useful map/brochure in English called *The Keys to the Cité* is available from the information counter at the main entrance to the complex.

The huge, rather confusingly laid-out **Explora** (adult/7-25yr/under 7yr €8/6/free) exhibitions are on levels 1 and 2 and look at everything from space exploration and automobile technology to genetics and sound. Tickets are valid for a full day and allow you to enter and exit at will.

The **Planétarium** (admission €3, 3-7yr free; ⏲ 11am-5pm Tue-Sun) on level 1 has six shows a day on the hour (except at 1pm) on a screen measuring 1000 sq metres.

The highlight of the Cité des Sciences et de l'Industrie is the brilliant **Cité des Enfants** (Children's Village; level 0), whose colourful and imaginative hands-on demonstrations of basic scientific principles are divided into two sections: for two- to seven-year-olds, and for five- to 12-year-olds. In the first, kids can explore, among other things, the conduct of water (waterproof ponchos provided), a building site, and a maze. The second allows children to build toy houses with industrial robots, and stage news broadcasts in a TV studio. A third section has a special exhibition called Ombres et Lumières (Shadows and Light) devoted largely to the five-to-12 age group.

Visits to Cité des Enfants lasting 1½ hours begin four times a day: at 9.45am, 11.30am, 1.30pm and 3.15pm Tuesday to Friday, and at 10.30am, 12.30pm, 2.30pm and 4.30pm on Saturday and Sunday. Each child (€6) must be accompanied by an adult (admission free; maximum two adults per family). During school holidays, book two or three days in advance by phone or via the internet.

CITÉ DE LA MUSIQUE

On the southern edge of Parc de la Villette, the **Cité de la Musique** (City of Music; Map pp114-15; ☎ 01 44 84 44 84; www.cite-musique.fr; 221 av Jean Jaurès, 19e; Ⓜ Porte de Pantin; ⏲ noon-6pm Tue-Sat, 10am-6pm Sun) is a striking triangular-shaped concert hall whose brief is to bring nonelitist music from around the world to Paris' multi-ethnic masses. In the same complex, the **Musée de la Musique** (Music Museum; adult/senior, student & 18-25yr/under 18yr €7/3.40/free) displays some 900 rare musical instruments out of a collection of 4500 warehoused, and you can hear many of them being played through the earphones included in the admission cost.

Outside the Walls: Beyond Central Paris

Two of the city's most important recreational areas lie just 'outside the walls' of central Paris. To the southeast and the southwest are the 'lungs' of Paris, the Bois de Vincennes and the Bois de Boulogne.

BOIS DE VINCENNES

In the southeastern corner of Paris, the **Bois de Vincennes** (Vincennes Wood; Map pp114-15; bd Poniatowski, 12e; Ⓜ Porte de Charenton or Porte Dorée) encompasses some 995 hectares. Most of it, however, is just outside the bd Périphérique.

On the wood's northern edge, **Château de Vincennes** (Map pp114-15; ☎ 01 48 08 31 20; www.chateau

METRO STOPS WORTH STOPPING BY *Jumpbean*

Abbesses (Line 12) Brightly painted murals may ease your journey up the lengthy staircase to the height of Montmartre.

Arts Et Metiers (Line 11) Exposed oversize metal piping turns this station into a Jules Verne submarine.

Bastille (Line 1) Though the ancient prison no longer exists, the tumult of the uprising it sparked lives on in the unfinished mural depicting scenes from the French Revolution.

Concorde (Line 12) Here under the infamous location of the guillotine, lettered tiles on the wall spell out the French translation of the Universal Declaration of Human Rights.

Liège (Line 13) Mosaic tiles evoke the pastoral ambience of the old Flemish city.

Line 14 Paris' newest metro line called the Météor is a journey of its own. Sit in the front car of the fully automated train to watch the eerie depths of the Paris subway system whiz by.

Louvre-Rivoli (Line 1) The museum experience starts from the subway station. Step out of the subway car into the belly of the Louvre. Egyptian artefacts greet you in the yellow gloom of a pyramid's interior.

Palais Royal-Musee Du Louvre (Line 7) The street-level entrance is decorated with bulbous coloured shapes that shine gaudily at the Louvre's northern wall.

Tuilleries (Line 1) Bright murals display the varied history of the city's central park.

Varenne (Line 13) The romance of Rodin's statues graces the platforms at the station closest to his former atelier.

What's your recommendation? www.lonelyplanet.com/france

-vincennes.fr; av de Paris, 12e; Ⓜ Château de Vincennes; 🕑 10am-6pm May-Aug, 10am-5pm Sep-Apr) is a bona fide royal château with massive fortifications and a moat. The château grounds can be strolled for free, but the 52m-high dungeon (1369), a prison during the 17th and 18th centuries, and the Gothic Chapelle Royale (Royal Chapel) can be visited only by guided tour (adult/18 to 25 years/under 18 years €7.50/4.80/free); call ahead for tour times.

South of the château, **Parc Floral de Paris** (Paris Floral Park; Map pp114-15; ☎ 39 75, 08 20 00 75 75; www.parcfloraldeparis.com, in French; rte du Champ de Manoeuvre, 12e; Ⓜ Château de Vincennes; adult/7-18yr €3/1.50; 🕑 9.30am-5pm, to 8pm in summer) is a vast green space with a butterfly garden, nature library, and kids' play areas; it hosts some excellent open-air concerts in summer. At its eastern edge, the **Jardin d'Agronomie Tropicale** (Garden of Tropical Agronomy; ☎ 01 43 94 73 33; 45bis av de la Belle Gabrielle; Ⓜ Nogent-sur-Marne; 🕑 11.30am-5.30pm Sat & Sun) is a vestige of the 1907 Exposition Coloniale, one of two 'world's fairs' held in Paris (the other was in 1931) to introduce metropolitan France to its colonies, their products and peoples.

The well-managed, 15-hectare **Parc Zoologique de Paris** (Paris Zoological Park; Map pp114-15; ☎ 01 44 75 20 10; www.mnhn.fr, in French; 53 av de St-Maurice, 12e; Ⓜ Porte Dorée; admission €5, under 4yr free; 🕑 9am-6pm Mon-Sat, to 6.30pm Sun Apr-Sep, 9am-5pm Mon-Sat, to 5.30pm Sun Oct-Mar), just east of Lac Daumesnil and also known as the Zoo du Bois de Vincennes, is home to some 600 animals.

Fish and other sea creatures from around the globe make their home at the **Aquarium Tropical** (Tropical Aquarium; Map pp114-15; ☎ 01 53 59 58 60; www.palais-portedoree.org, in French; Palais de la Porte Dorée, 293 av Daumesnil, 12e; Ⓜ Porte Dorée; adult/4-25yr/under 4yr €5.70/4.20/free; 🕑 10am-5.15pm Tue-Fri, to 7pm Sat & Sun) on the western edge of Bois de Vincennes.

It was established in 1931 in one of the few buildings left from the Exposition Coloniale of that year.

In the same building is the compelling **Cité Nationale de l'Histoire de l'Immigration** (National City of the History of Immigration; ☎ 01 53 59 58 60; www.histoire-immigration.fr; Palais de la Porte Dorée, 293 av Daumesnil, 12e; Ⓜ Porte Dorée; adult/18-26yr during exhibition periods €5.50/3.50, non-exhibition periods €3/2, under 18yr free; 🕑 10am-5.30pm Tue-Fri, to 7pm Sat & Sun), which documents immigration to France through a series of informative historical displays.

BOIS DE BOULOGNE

On the western edge of Paris just beyond the 16e, the 845-hectare **Bois de Boulogne** (Boulogne Wood; Map pp114-15; bd Maillot, 16e; Ⓜ Porte Maillot) owes its informal layout to Baron Haussmann, who was inspired by Hyde Park in London. Be warned that the Bois de Boulogne becomes a distinctly adult playground after dark, especially along the allée de Longchamp, where male, female and transvestite prostitutes cruise for clients.

The wood's enclosed **Parc de Bagatelle** (☎ 39 75, 08 20 00 75 75; 9.30am-5pm, to 8pm in summer), in the northwestern corner, is renowned for its beautiful gardens surrounding the 1775 **Château de Bagatelle** (Bagatelle Palace; Map pp114-15; ☎ 01 40 67 97 00; route de Sèvres à Neuilly, 16e; adult/student & 7-18yr/under 7yr €3/1.50/free; 9am-6pm Apr-Sep, 9am-5pm Oct-Mar).

The **Jardin des Serres d'Auteuil** (Map pp114-15; ☎ 01 40 71 75 23; av de la Porte d'Auteuil, 16e; M Porte d'Auteuil; admission free; 9.30am-5pm, to 8pm in summer), opened in 1898, is a garden with impressive conservatories at the southeastern end of the Bois de Boulogne.

The 20-hectare **Jardin d'Acclimatation** (Map pp114-15; ☎ 01 40 67 90 82; av du Mahatma Gandhi; M Les Sablons; adult/3-18yr/under 3yr €2.70/1.35/free; 10am-7pm Jun-Sep, 10am-6pm Oct-May), a kids-oriented amusement park whose name is another term for 'zoo' in French, includes the high-tech **Exploradôme** (☎ 01 53 64 90 40; www.exploradome.com, in French; adult/4-18yr/under 4yr €5/3.50/free), a tented structure devoted to science and the media.

The southern part of the wood has two horse-racing tracks, the **Hippodrome de Longchamp** (Map pp114–15) for flat races and the Hippodrome d'Auteuil (p196) for steeplechases. The Stade Roland Garros (p196), home of the French Open tennis tournament, is also here.

Rowing boats (☎ 01 42 88 04 69; per hr €10; 10am-6pm mid-Mar–mid-Oct) can be hired at **Lac Inférieur** (M Av Henri Martin), the largest of the wood's lakes and ponds. They sometimes open at the weekend in winter. **Paris Cycles** (☎ 01 47 47 76 50; per hr €5; 10am-7pm mid-Apr–mid-Oct) hires out bicycles at two locations in the Bois de Boulogne: on **av du Mahatma Gandhi** (M Les Sablons), across from the Porte Sablons entrance to the Jardin d'Acclimatation, and near the **Pavillon Royal** (M Av Foch) at the northern end of Lac Inférieur.

ACTIVITIES

The best single source of information on sports in Paris is the Salon d'Accueil (Reception Hall) of the Mairie de Paris at the **Hôtel de Ville** (Map pp126-7; ☎ 39 75, 08 20 00 75 75; www.sport.paris.fr; 29 rue de Rivoli, 4e; M Hôtel de Ville; 10am-7pm Mon-Sat).

Cycling

A lot more Parisians are pedal-pushing nowadays thanks to **Vélib'** (p201). For imaginative and unusual cycling itineraries suggested by Parisians, subscribe to Vélib's monthly online newsletter (www.velib.paris.fr).

Paris now counts some 370km of bicycle lanes running throughout the city, as well as a dedicated lane running parallel to about two-thirds of the bd Périphérique encircling the capital. On Sundays and holidays, large sections of road are reserved for pedestrians, cyclists and skaters under a scheme called 'Paris Respire' (Paris Breathes; p148).

Before you set out, get hold of a copy of the free booklet *Paris à Vélo* (Paris by Bicycle), published by the Mairie de Paris. More detailed is *Paris de Poche: Cycliste et Piéton* (Pocket Paris: Cyclist and Pedestrian; €3.50), sold in bookshops.

Maison Roue Libre (☎ 08 10 44 15 34; www.rouelibre.fr; 9am-7pm Feb-Oct, 10am-6pm Wed-Sun Nov & Jan; Forum des Halles Map pp126-7; Forum des Halles, 1 passage Mondétour, 1er; M Les Halles; Bastille Map pp132-3; 37 bd Bourdon, 4e; M Bastille), sponsored by RATP, the city's public transport system, is the best place to rent a bicycle in Paris. Bicycles cost €4/10/15/28 per hour/half-day/day/weekend and include insurance, helmet and baby seat. The deposit is €150, and you need some form of ID.

Other outfits that rent bicycles and offer guided bicycle tours:

Fat Tire Bike Tours (Map pp124-5; ☎ 01 56 58 10 54; www.fattirebiketoursparis.com; 24 rue Edgar Faure, 15e; M La Motte Piquet Grenelle; per hr/day/weekend/week €2.50/15/25/50; 9am-6pm)

Gepetto et Vélos (Map pp130-1; ☎ 01 43 54 19 95; www.gepetto-et-velos.com, in French; 59 rue du Cardinal Lemoine, 5e; M Cardinal Lemoine; per half-day/day/weekend/week €7.50/14/23/50; 9am-1pm & 2-7.30pm Tue-Sat, 10am-1pm & 2-7pm Sun)

Paris à Vélo, C'est Sympa! (Map pp132-3; ☎ 01 48 87 60 01; www.parisvelosympa.com, in French; 22 rue Alphonse Baudin, 11e; M St-Sébastien Froissart; per half-day/day/weekend/week €10/13/25/60; 9.30am-1pm & 2-6pm Mon-Fri, 9am-1pm & 2-7pm Sat & Sun Apr-Oct, 9.30am-1pm & 2-5.30pm Mon-Fri, 9am-1pm & 2-6pm Sat & Sun Nov-Mar)

Swimming

Paris has almost 40 swimming pools that are open to the public; check with the **Mairie de Paris** (☎ 39 75, 08 20 00 75 75; www.paris.fr) for the one nearest you. Most are short-length pools, and finding a free lane for lengths can be nigh on impossible. Opening times vary widely; avoid Wednesday afternoon and weekends, when kids off from school take the plunge. The entry cost for most municipal pools is €2.60/21.50 for single ticket/carnet of 10 tickets.

WALKING TOUR

Montmartre, from the French words for hill *(mont)* and martyr, has been a place of legend ever since St Denis was executed here in about AD 250 and began his headless journey on foot to the village north of Paris that still bears his name (p208). In recent times the Montmartre of myth has been resurrected by music, books and especially films like *Le Fabuleux Destin d'Amélie Poulain* (*Amélie*; 2002), which presented the district in various shades of rose, and *Moulin Rouge* (2001), which also made it pretty but gave it a bit more edge.

For centuries Montmartre was a simple country village filled with the *moulins* (mills) that supplied Paris with its flour. When it was incorporated into the capital in 1860, its picturesque charm and low rents attracted painters and writers – especially after the Communard uprising of 1871, which began here. The late 19th and early 20th centuries were Montmartre's heyday, when Toulouse-Lautrec drew his favourite cancan dancers and Picasso, Braque and others introduced cubism to the world.

After WWI such creative activity shifted to Montparnasse, but Montmartre retained an upbeat ambience. The real attractions here, apart from the great views from the Butte de Montmartre (Montmartre Hill), are the area's little parks and steep, winding cobblestone streets, many of whose houses seem about to be engulfed by creeping vines and ivy.

In English-speaking countries, Montmartre's mystique of unconventionality has been magnified by the supposed notoriety of places like the Moulin Rouge, a nightclub on the edge of the Pigalle district that was founded in 1889 and is known for its scantily clad – *oh là là!* – chorus girls. The garish nightlife that Toulouse-Lautrec loved to portray has spread along bd de Clichy, and Pigalle has become decidedly sleazy, though it's pretty tame stuff overall.

WALK FACTS

Start Ⓜ Blanche
Finish Ⓜ Abbesses
Distance 2.5km
Duration 2½ hours
Fuel Stop La Maison Rose

MONTMARTRE WALKING TOUR

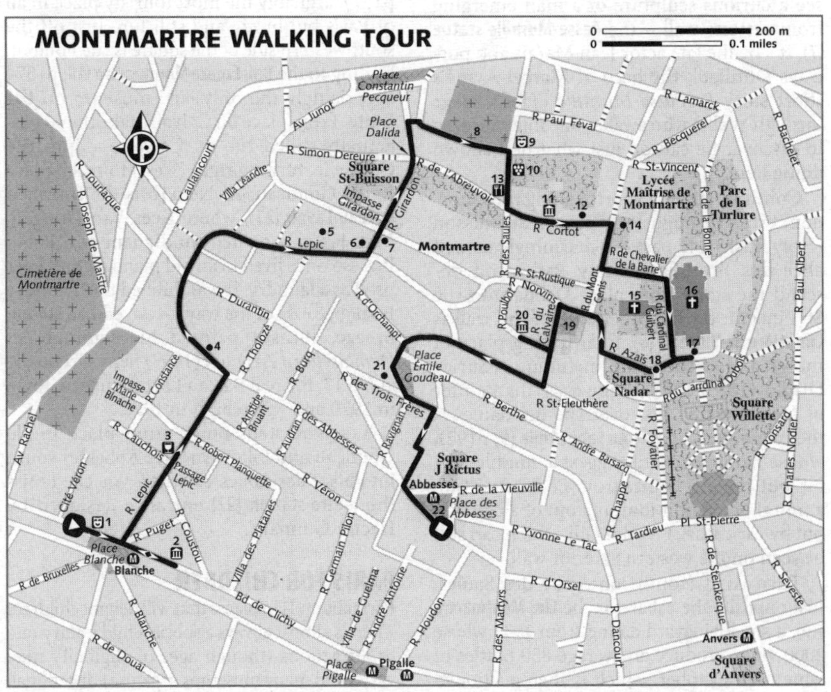

Begin the walk at the Blanche metro station. Diagonally opposite to the left is the legendary **Moulin Rouge** (**1**; p195) beneath its trademark red windmill, while appropriately located to the right is the **Musée de l'Érotisme** (**2**; p157), an institution that likes to portray itself as educational rather than titillating. Walk up rue Lepic and halfway up on the left you'll find the **Café des Deux Moulins** (**3**; ☎ 01 42 54 90 50; 15 rue Lepic, 18e; 🕑 7am-2am), where our heroine Amélie worked in the eponymous film. Follow the curve to the west (left); Théo van Gogh owned the **house at No 54 (4)**, and his brother, the artist Vincent, stayed with him on the 3rd floor from 1886 to 1888.

Further along rue Lepic are Montmartre's famous twinned windmills. The better-known **Moulin de la Galette (5)** was a popular open-air dance hall in the late 19th century and was immortalised by Pierre-Auguste Renoir in his 1876 tableau *Le Bal du Moulin de la Galette* (Dance at the Moulin de la Galette). About 100m to the east, at the corner of rue Girardon is the **Moulin Radet (6)**. Confusingly, it's now a restaurant called Le Moulin de la Galette.

Turn left into place Marcel Aymé and you'll see a curious sculpture of a man emerging from a stone wall – the **Passe-Muraille statue (7)**. It's by the late actor Jean Marais and portrays Dutilleul, the hero of Marcel Aymé's short story *Le Passe-Muraille* (The Walker through Walls) who awakes one fine morning to discover he can do just what he's shown doing here.

Continue straight (north) along rue Girardon, cross through leafy square St-Buisson (Holy Bush) and past the charmingly named allée des Brouillards (Fog Path) and descend the stairs from place Dalida into rue St-Vincent; on the other side of the wall is **Cimetière St-Vincent (8)**, final resting place of the great and the good, including Maurice Utrillo (1883–1955), known as 'the painter of Montmartre'. Just over rue des Saules is the celebrated cabaret **Au Lapin Agile** (**9**; p192), whose name seems to suggest a 'nimble rabbit' but actually comes from *Le Lapin à Gill*, a mural of a rabbit jumping out of a cooking pot by caricaturist André Gill, which can still be seen on the western exterior wall.

Turn right (south) onto rue des Saules. Just opposite the cabaret is the **Clos Montmartre (10)**, a small vineyard dating from 1933 whose 2000 vines produce an average 850 bottles of wine each October, which is then auctioned off for charity in the 18e. You can buy sample bottles of the hooch at the **Musée de Montmartre** (**11**; p157) at 12 rue Cortot, the first street on the left after the vineyard. Further along at No 6 is the **house of Eric Satie (12)**, where the celebrated composer lived from 1892 to 1898. A great place for a bite to eat is **La Maison Rose** (**13**; p187), the quintessential Montmartre bistro and subject of an eponymous lithograph by Utrillo.

Turn right (south) on to rue du Mont Cenis – the attractive **water tower (14)** just opposite dates from the early 20th century – and then left onto rue de Chevalier de la Barre, which will lead you past the back of **Église St-Pierre de Montmartre** (**15**; p157), which was built on the site of a Roman temple to Mercury and did time as a Temple of Reason under the Revolution and as a clothing factory during the Commune. The entrance to the **Basilique du Sacré Cœur** (**16**; p157), and the stunning vista over Paris from **place du Parvis du Sacré Cœur (17)** are just a few steps to the south.

From the basilica follow rue Azaïs west past the upper station of the **funicular** (**18**; p714) and then rue Norvins north into **place du Tertre** (**19**; p157), arguably the most touristy place in all of Paris but buzzy and still fun. Just off the southwestern side of the square is rue Poulbot, leading to the **Dalí Espace Montmartre** (**20**; p157), surprisingly the only 'art' museum on the Butte. From place du Calvaire take the steps – actually called rue du Calvaire – into rue Gabrielle, turning right (west) to reach place Émile Goudeau. At No 11b is the so-called **Bateau Lavoir (21)**, where Kees Van Dongen, Max Jacob, Amedeo Modigliani and Pablo Picasso once lived in an old piano factory later used as a laundry. It was dubbed the 'Laundry Boat' because of the way it swayed in a strong breeze. Picasso painted his seminal *Les Demoiselles d'Avignon* (1907) here. Originally at No 13, the real Bateau Lavoir burned down in 1970 and was rebuilt in 1978.

Take the steps down from place Émile Goudeau and follow rue des Abbesses south into place des Abbesses, where you can't miss the **metro station (22)** entrance designed by Hector Guimard.

PARIS FOR CHILDREN

Paris abounds in places that will delight children. There's almost always a special child's entry rate to attractions (though ages of eligibility may vary), and many museums organise educational, fun-packed *ateliers enfants* (kids workshops) for children aged four or six and upwards. For details about the mother of all kids' destinations, Disneyland Resort Paris, see p210.

The national daily newspaper *Libération* produces an English-language translation of its popular bimonthly supplement *Paris Mômes* (www.parismomes.fr) called *Paris with Kids*. It has listings and other useful information aimed at kids up to age 12; focusing on the 'unusual' is its philosophy.

The weekly entertainment magazine *L'Officiel des Spectacles* (p190) lists *gardes d'enfants* (babysitters) available in Paris. For more ideas of things to see and do with kids, see the 'Kid Travel' itinerary on p28.

TOURS

Bicycle

Fat Tire Bike Tours (Map pp124-5; ☎ 01 56 58 10 54; www.fattirebiketoursparis.com; 24 rue Edgar Faure, 15e; Ⓜ La Motte Picquet Grenelle; ⌚ office 9am-6pm) offers four-hour English-language tours of the city (adult/student €24/22) year-round, except during the second half of January, starting at 11am daily. There is an additional tour at 3pm from April to October. Night bicycle tours (adult/student €28/26) depart at 7pm on Tuesday, Thursday, Saturday and Sunday from mid-February to mid-March and in November, and at the same time daily from mid-March to October. A day-and-night combination tour costs €48/44. Tours depart from opposite the Eiffel Tower's South Pillar at the start of the Champ de Mars; just look for the yellow signs. Costs include the bicycle and, if necessary, rain gear.

Boat

Based on the Right Bank just east of the Pont de l'Alma, **Bateaux Mouches** (Map pp118-19; ☎ 01 42 25 96 10; www.bateauxmouches.com, in French; Port de la Conférence, 8e; Ⓜ Alma Marceau; adult/senior & 4-12yr/under 4yr €9/4/free; ⌚ mid-Mar–mid-Nov), the most famous riverboat company in Paris, runs 1000-seat tour boats, the biggest on the Seine. From April to September, cruises (70 minutes) depart eight times a day between 10.15am and 3.15pm and then every 20 minutes till 11pm. They depart 10 times a day between 10.15am and 9pm the rest of the year. Commentary is in French and English.

If you prefer to see Paris from one of its canals, **Paris Canal Croisières** (Map pp120-1; ☎ 01 42 40 96 97; www.pariscanal.com; Bassin de la Villette, 19-21 quai de la Loire, 19e; Ⓜ Jaurès; adult/senior & 12-25yr/4-11yr/under 4yr €17/14/10/free) has daily 2½-hour cruises departing from quai Anatole France, 7e, just northwest of the Musée d'Orsay (Map pp124–5), for Bassin de la Villette, 19e, via the charming Canal St-Martin and Canal de l'Ourcq. Departures are at 9.30am from quai Anatole France and at 2.30pm from Bassin de la Villette.

Bus

In season, RATP's **Balabus** (☎ 32 46; www.ratp.fr; €1.40 or 1 metro/bus ticket; ⌚ departures 12.30-8pm from La Défense, 1.30pm from Gare de Lyon Sun Apr-Sep) follows a 50-minute route to/from Gare de Lyon (Map pp134–5) and La Défense (Map p206) that passes by many of central Paris' most famous sights. Buses depart about every 20 minutes.

L'Open Tour (Map pp118-19; ☎ 01 42 66 56 56; www.pariscityrama.com; 13 rue Auber, 9e; Ⓜ Havre Caumartin or Opéra; 1 day adult/4-11yr/under 4yr €26/13/free, 2 consecutive days €29/13/free) runs open-deck buses along four circuits (central Paris, 2¼ hours; Montmartre–Grands Boulevards, 1¼ hours; Bastille–Bercy, one hour; and Montparnasse–St-Germain, one hour). You can jump on and off at more than 50 stops. Schedules vary but buses depart roughly every 10 to 15 minutes from 9.30am to 7pm April to October and every 25 to 30 minutes from 9.45am to 6pm November to March.

Walking

Paris Walks (☎ 01 48 09 21 40; www.paris-walks.com; adult/student under 21/under 15yr from €10/8/5) has English-language tours of several different districts, including Montmartre at 10.30am on Sunday and Wednesday (leaving from Ⓜ Abbesses; Map p136) and the Marais at 10.30am on Tuesday and at 2.30pm on Sunday (departing from Ⓜ St-Paul; Map pp126–7). There are other tours focusing on people and themes, such as Hemingway, medieval Paris, the Latin Quarter, fashion, the French Revolution and even chocolate.

FESTIVALS & EVENTS

Innumerable festivals, cultural and sporting events and trade shows take place in Paris throughout the year; weekly details appear in *Pariscope* and *L'Officiel des Spectacles* (p190). You can also find them listed under 'What's On' on the website of the Paris Convention & Visitors Bureau (www.paris info.com).

The following abbreviated list gives you a taste of what to expect throughout the year.

January & February

Festival des Musiques du Nouvel An (www.parisparade.com) The New Year Music Festival, relatively subdued after the previous night's shenanigans (opposite), with marching and carnival bands, dance acts and so on, takes place on the afternoon of New Year's Day at the Palais de Chaillot (Ⓜ Trocadéro).

Fashion Week (www.pretparis.com) Prêt-à-Porter, the ready-to-wear fashion salon that is held twice a year in late January and again in September, is a must for fashion buffs and is held at the Parc des Expositions at Porte de Versailles, 15e (Ⓜ Porte de Versailles).

Chinese New Year (www.paris.fr) Dragon parades and other festivities are held in late January or early February in Paris' two Chinatowns: the smaller in the 3e, taking in rue du Temple, rue au Maire and rue de Turbigo (Ⓜ Temple or Arts et Métiers), and the larger and flashier one in the 13e between porte de Choisy, porte d'Ivry and bd Masséna (Ⓜ Porte de Choisy, Port d'Ivry or Tolbiac).

Salon International de l'Agriculture (www.salon-agriculture.com) A 10-day international agricultural fair with lots to eat and drink, including dishes and wine from all over France. Held at the Parc des Expositions at Porte de Versailles in the 15e (Ⓜ Porte de Versailles) from late February to early March.

March & April

Banlieues Bleues (www.banlieuesbleues.org, in French) 'Suburban Blues' jazz and blues festival is held in March and April in the northern suburbs of Paris, including St-Denis (p208), and attracts big-name talent.

Printemps du Cinéma (www.printempsducinema.com, in French) Cinemas across Paris welcome spring by offering filmgoers a unique entry fee of €3.50 over three days (usually Sunday, Monday and Tuesday) sometime around 21 March.

Foire du Trône (www.foiredutrone.com, in French) Huge funfair with 350 attractions is held on the Pelouse de Reuilly of the Bois de Vincennes (Ⓜ Porte Dorée) for eight weeks from late March to mid-May.

Marathon International de Paris (www.parismarathon.com) The Paris International Marathon, usually held on the first Sunday in April, starts on the av des Champs-Élysées, 8e, and finishes on av Foch, 16e. The Semi-Marathon de Paris is a half-marathon held in early March; see the marathon website for details.

May & June

Nuit des Musées (www.nuitdesmusees.culture.fr, in French) Key museums across Paris throw open their doors at 6pm for one Saturday night in mid-May on 'Museums Night' and don't close till late.

French Tennis Open (www.frenchopen.org) The glitzy Internationaux de France de Tennis – the Grand Slam – takes place from late May to mid-June at Stade Roland Garros (Ⓜ Porte d'Auteuil) at the southern edge of the Bois de Boulogne in the 16e.

Fête de la Musique (www.fetedelamusique.fr, in French) A national music festival welcoming in summer on Midsummer's Night (21 June) that caters to a wide range of tastes with jazz, reggae, classical etc; features both staged and impromptu live performances all over the city.

Gay Pride March (www.gaypride.fr, in French) A colourful, Saturday-afternoon parade held in late June through the Marais to Bastille celebrates Gay Pride Day, with various bars and clubs sponsoring floats, and participants dressing in some eye-catching costumes.

Paris Jazz Festival (www.parcfloraldeparis.com; www.paris.fr) Free jazz concerts every Saturday and Sunday afternoon in June and July in Parc Floral de Paris (Ⓜ Château de Vincennes).

July & August

Bastille Day (www.paris.fr) Paris is *the* place to be on 14 July, France's national day. Late on the night of the 13th, *bals des sapeurs-pompiers* (dances sponsored by Paris' fire brigades, who are considered sex symbols in France) are held at fire stations around the city. At 10am on the 14th, there's a military and fire-brigade parade along av des Champs-Élysées, 8e, accompanied by a fly-past of fighter aircraft and helicopters. In the evening a huge display of *feux d'artifice* (fireworks) is held at around 11pm on the Champ de Mars, 7e (Ⓜ École Militaire).

Paris Plages (www.paris.fr) 'Paris Beaches', one of the most unique and successful city recreational events in the world, sees three waterfront areas transformed into sand-and-pebble 'beaches', complete with sun beds, beach umbrellas, atomisers, lounge chairs and palm trees, for four weeks from mid-July to mid-August.

Tour de France (www.letour.fr) Since 1975 the last stage of the world's most prestigious cycling event has ended with a race up av des Champs-Élysées on the 3rd or 4th Sunday of July.

September & October

Jazz à La Villette (www.villette.com, in French) Super 10-day jazz festival in early September has sessions in Parc de la Villette, at the Cité de la Musique and in surrounding bars (Ⓜ Porte de la Villette or Porte de Pantin).

Festival d'Automne (www.festival-automne.com) The Autumn Festival of arts – including painting, music, dance and theatre – is held in venues throughout the city from mid-September to December.

European Heritage Days (www.journeesdupatrimoine.culture.fr, in French) As done elsewhere in Europe on the third weekend in September, Paris opens doors to buildings (eg embassies, government ministries, corporate offices – even the Palais de l'Élysée) normally off limits to outsiders.

Nuit Blanche (www.paris.fr) 'White Night' is when Paris becomes 'the city that doesn't sleep', with museums across town joining bars and clubs and staying open till the very wee hours on the first Saturday and Sunday of October.

November & December

Africolor (www.africolor.com, in French) African music festival held in venues in the suburbs surrounding Paris from late November to late December.

Jumping International de Paris (www.salon-cheval.com) The annual International Showjumping Competition in the first half of December forms part of the Salon du Cheval at the Parc des Expositions at Porte de Versailles in the 15e (Ⓜ Porte de Versailles), with some of the best showjumpers in the world testing their limits.

Christmas Eve Mass Celebrated at midnight on Christmas Eve at many Paris churches, including Notre Dame (Ⓜ Cité).

New Year's Eve Bd St-Michel (5e), place de la Bastille (11e), the Eiffel Tower (7e) and especially av des Champs-Élysées (8e) are the places to be to welcome in the new year.

SLEEPING

Paris has a very wide choice of accommodation options that cater for all budgets. When calculating accommodation costs in Paris, assume you'll spend from €20 per person per night in a hostel and at least €40 for a washbasin-equipped double in a budget hotel, more if you want your own shower. Communal toilets are standard. Bear in mind that you may be charged extra (up to €3) to use communal showers in budget hotels. If you can't go without your daily ablutions, it can be a false economy staying at such places.

Midrange hotels in Paris offer some of the best value for money of any European capital. Rooms in hotels at this level always have bathroom facilities; all rooms listed in this section have showers or baths unless noted otherwise. These hotels charge between about €70 and €160 for a double and generally offer excellent value, especially at the higher end.

Top-end places run the gamut from tasteful and discreet boutique hotels to palaces with more than 100 rooms. Prices start at €160 a night for two people and can reach the GNP of a medium-sized Latin American republic.

Breakfast – usually a simple continental affair of bread, croissants, butter, jam and coffee or tea, though American-style breakfast buffets are becoming more popular – is served at most hotels with two or more stars and usually costs around €8. A light breakfast is included in the price of a bed or room at most hostels.

Like most cities and towns in France, Paris levies a *taxe de séjour* (tourist tax) of between €0.20 (camping grounds, unclassified hotels) to €1.50 (four-star hotels) per person per night on all forms of accommodation.

Accommodation Services

The Paris Convention & Visitors Bureau (p137), notably the Gare du Nord branch, can find you a place to stay for the night of the day you stop by and will make the booking for free. The only catch is that you have to use a credit card to reserve a room. Be warned: the queues can be very long in the high season.

Two agencies that can arrange bed-and-breakfast accommodation in Paris and get good reviews from readers are **Alcôve & Agapes** (☎ 01 44 85 06 05; www.bed-and-breakfast-in-paris.com) and **Good Morning Paris** (☎ 01 47 07 44 45; www.goodmorningparis.fr). Expect to pay anything from €65 for a double.

If you're interested in renting a furnished flat for anything from a night to a month, consult one of the many agencies listed under the heading 'Furnished Rentals' in the 'Hotels & Accommodation' section of the Paris Convention & Visitors Bureau's website (www.paris info.com).

Louvre & Les Halles

The very central area encompassing the Musée du Louvre and the Forum des Halles, effectively the 1er and a small slice of the 2e, is more disposed to welcoming top-end travellers, but there are some decent midrange places to choose from and the main branch of a popular hostel can also be found here.

Both airports are linked to nearby metro station Châtelet–Les Halles by the RER (Réseau Express Régional regional train service; p203).

BUDGET

Centre International de Séjour BVJ Paris–Louvre (Map pp126-7; ☎ 01 53 00 90 90; www.bvjhotel.com; 20 rue Jean-Jacques Rousseau, 1er; Ⓜ Louvre-Rivoli; dm/d €28/60; 💻 ⊠) This modern 200-bed hostel run by the Bureau des Voyages de la Jeunesse (Youth Travel Bureau) has doubles and bunks in a single-sex room for four to 10 people. Guests must be aged 18 to 35. Rooms are accessible from 2.30pm on the day you arrive. There are no kitchen facilities, and showers are in the hallway. There is usually space in the morning, even in the summer, so stop by as early as you can. Internet access is available for €1 for 10 minutes.

CAMPING IN PARIS

Camping du Bois de Boulogne (Bois de Boulogne Camping Ground; Map pp114-15; ☎ 01 45 24 30 00; www.campingparis.fr; 2 allée du Bord de l'Eau, 16e; sites low/mid-/high season €11/15.20/16.80, with vehicle, tent & 2 people €24/28.60/31.90, first-time booking fee €14) The only camping ground within the Paris city limits, measures 7 hectares and lies along the Seine at the far western edge of the Bois de Boulogne, opposite Île de Puteaux. With upwards of 435 camping pitches and almost two dozen bungalows, it gets very crowded in the summer, but there's usually space for a small tent. More than 50 fully equipped caravans accommodating four to five people are also available for rent; rates – €57 to €102 – depend on the size and the season.

Porte Maillot metro station (Map pp118–19), 4.5km to the northeast through the wood, is linked to the site by RATP bus 244, which runs from 5.40am to 10pm, with slightly different hours at the weekend and in July and August; alight at Les Moulins-Camping stop. From April to October the campground runs a **shuttle bus** (€1.80; 8.45am-12.15pm & 6.30pm-midnight) from the Porte Maillot metro station. In July and August the shuttle departs every half-hour throughout the day.

Hôtel de Lille (Map pp126-7; ☎ 01 42 33 33 42; www.heoteldelille.net; 8 rue du Pélican, 1er; Ⓜ Palais Royal-Musée du Louvre; s €35-38, d €43-50, tr €65-75;) This old-fashioned but spotlessly clean 13-room hotel is down a quiet side street in a 17th-century building. A half-dozen of the rooms have just washbasin and bidet (communal showers cost €3), while the rest have showers as well.

TOP END

Le Relais du Louvre (Map pp126-7; ☎ 01 40 41 96 42; www.relaisdulouvre.com; 19 rue des Prêtres St-Germain l'Auxerrois, 1er; Ⓜ Pont Neuf; s €108, d & tw €165-198, tr €212, ste €237-430;) If you are someone who likes style but in a traditional sense, choose this lovely 21-room hotel just west of the Louvre and south of the Église St-Germain l'Auxerrois. The 10 rooms facing the street and the church are on the petite side; if you are looking for something more spacious, ask for one of the five rooms ending in a '2' and looking on to the garden/patio.

Marais & Bastille

Despite massive gentrification in recent years, there are some fine hostels here and the choice of lower-priced one- and two-star hotels remains excellent. East of Bastille, the relatively untouristed 11e is generally made up of unpretentious, working-class areas and is a good way to see the 'real' Paris up close. Two-star comfort here is less expensive than in the Marais. There are quite a few top-end hotels in the heart of the lively Marais as well as in the vicinity of the elegant place des Vosges.

BUDGET

Auberge de Jeunesse Jules Ferry (Map pp120-1; ☎ 01 43 57 55 60; www.fuaj.fr; 8 bd Jules Ferry, 11e; Ⓜ République or Goncourt; dm/d €21/42;) This 'official' hostel three blocks east of place de la République is somewhat institutional and the rooms could use a refit, but the atmosphere is fairly relaxed. The 99 beds are in two- to six-person rooms, which are locked between 10.30am and 2pm for housekeeping, but there is no curfew. You'll have to pay an extra €2.90 per night if you don't have an HI card or equivalent (€11/17 for those under/over 26).

Maison Internationale de la Jeunesse et des Étudiants (Map pp126-7; ☎ 01 42 74 23 45; www.mije.com; dm/s/d/tr €29/47/68/90;) The MIJE runs three hostels in attractively renovated 17th- and 18th-century *hôtels particuliers* in the heart of the Marais, and it's difficult to think of a better budget deal in Paris. Costs are the same for all three; there are single-sex, shower-equipped dorms with four to eight beds per room, as well as singles, doubles/twins and triples. Rooms are closed from noon to 3pm, and the curfew is 1am to 7am. The maximum stay is seven nights. You can make reservations at any of the three MIJE hostels listed below by calling the central switchboard or emailing; they'll hold you a bed till noon. During the summer and other busy periods, there may not be space after mid-morning. There's an annual membership fee of €2.50.

MIJE Le Fauconnier (11 rue du Fauconnier, 4e; Ⓜ St-Paul or Pont Marie) This 125-bed hostel is two blocks south of MIJE Le Fourcy.

MIJE Le Fourcy (6 rue de Fourcy, 4e; Ⓜ St-Paul) The largest of the three branches, with 180 beds. There's a cheap eatery here called Le Restaurant, with a three-course *menu* (fixed-price meal) including a drink for €10.50.

MIJE Maubuisson (12 rue des Barres, 4e; Ⓜ Hôtel de Ville or Pont Marie) The pick of the three in our opinion, this 99-bed place is half a block south of the *mairie* (town hall) of the 4e.

Hôtel Rivoli (Map pp126-7; ☎ 01 42 72 08 41; 44 rue de Rivoli or 2 rue des Mauvais Garçons, 4e; Ⓜ Hôtel de Ville; s €35-55, d €44-55, tr €70) Long an LP favourite, the Rivoli is forever cheery but not as dirt cheap as it once was, with 20 basic, somewhat noisy rooms. The cheaper singles and doubles have washbasins only but showers are free. The front door is locked from 2am to 7am. Reception is on the 1st floor.

Hôtel de Nevers (Map pp120-1; ☎ 01 47 00 56 18; www.hoteldenevers.com; 53 rue de Malte, 11e; Ⓜ Oberkampf; s €39, d €45-55, tr €75-87; 💻) This 32-room budget hotel around the corner from place de la République, and within easy walking distance of the nightlife of both the Marais and Ménilmontant, is excellent value. Those with allergies may think twice about staying here, though: there are three cats on hand to greet you. Rooms at the low end of the scale share bathing facilities.

Hôtel de la Herse d'Or (Map pp132-3; ☎ 01 48 87 84 09; www.hotel-herse-dor.com; 20 rue St-Antoine, 4e; Ⓜ Bastille; s/d €45/60, d/tr with shower €76/96; 💻) This friendly place just west of place de la Bastille has 35 serviceable rooms off a long stone corridor. It's very basic and very cheap; the lower-priced rooms have washbasins only. Though there's wi-fi, those without laptops can check emails at an internet station in the lobby (€2 for 15 minutes). And, just in case you wondered, *herse* in French is not 'hearse' but 'portcullis'. So let's just call it the 'Golden Gate Hotel'.

Grand Hôtel du Loiret (Map pp126-7; ☎ 01 48 87 77 00; hotelduloiret@hotmail.com; 8 rue des Mauvais Garçons, 4e; Ⓜ Hôtel de Ville or St-Paul; s €50-80, d €50-90, tr/q €100/110; 💻) This 27-room budget hotel in the heart of gay Marais is very popular with young male travellers, not just because it is within easy walking distance of just about everything after dark but because it sits – or does it lie? – on the 'Street of the Bad Boys'. Seven of the rooms have neither shower nor bath or toilet but share facilities off the corridors and are a steal at €50. Internet access costs a whopping €3 for 15 minutes.

MIDRANGE

Hôtel Jeanne d'Arc (Map pp132-3; ☎ 01 48 87 62 11; www.hoteljeannedarc.com; 3 rue de Jarente, 4e; Ⓜ St-Paul; s €60-97, d €84-97, tr/q €116/146; 💻) This cosy, 36-room hotel near lovely place du Marché Ste-Catherine has almost a country feel to it and is a great little base for your peregrinations among the museums, bars and restaurants of the Marais. But everyone knows about it, so book well in advance. Wheelchair access available.

Hôtel Lyon Mulhouse (Map pp132-3; ☎ 01 47 00 91 50; www.1-hotel-paris.com; 8 bd Beaumarchais, 11e; Ⓜ Bastille; s €65-90, d €78-110, tr €110-130; ❄ 💻) A former post house from where carriages would set out for Lyon and Mulhouse in Alsace, this place has 40 quiet and comfortable (though not particularly special) rooms. Place de la Bastille and the delightful market on bd Richard Lenoir (see the boxed text, p179) are just around the corner.

Hôtel du Septième Art (Map pp126-7; ☎ 01 44 54 85 00; www.paris-hotel-7art.com; 20 rue St-Paul, 4e; Ⓜ St-Paul; s €65, d €90-145; 💻) This themed hotel on the south side of rue St-Antoine is a fun place for film buffs (*le septième art*, or 'the seventh art', is what the French call cinema), with a black-and-white-movie theme throughout, right down to the tiled floors and bathrooms. The 23 guestrooms spread over five floors (no lift) are sizeable and quite different from one other. A single with just washbasin is €65.

Hôtel Sévigné (Map pp126-7; ☎ 01 42 72 76 17; www.le-sevigne.com; 2 rue Malher, 4e; Ⓜ St-Paul; s €67, d & tw €80-91, tr €107; ❄ ⊠) This hotel in the heart of the Marais and named after the celebrated 17th-century writer the Marquise de Sévigné is excellent value for its location and price. The hotel's 29 rooms, spread over six floors and accessible by lift, are basically but comfortably furnished.

Hôtel de Nice (Map pp126-7; ☎ 01 42 78 55 29; www.hoteldenice.com; 42bis rue de Rivoli, 4e; Ⓜ Hôtel de Ville; s/d/tr €80/110/135) This is an especially warm, family-run place with 23 comfortable rooms, some of which have balconies high above busy rue de Rivoli. Every square inch of wall space is used to display old prints, and public areas and guestrooms are full of Second Empire–style furniture, Indian carpets and lamps with fringed shades. Reception is on the 1st floor.

Hôtel de la Place des Vosges (Map pp132-3; ☎ 01 42 72 60 46; www.hotelplacedesvosges.com; 12 rue de Birague, 4e; Ⓜ Bastille; r €90-95, ste €150; 💻) This superbly situated 17-room hotel is an oasis of tranquillity due south of sublime place des Vosges. The public areas are quite impressive and the rooms warm and cosy. A tiny lift serves the 1st to 4th floors but it's stairs only from the ground floor and to the 5th floor. A suite on the top floor has choice views and can accommodate up to four people.

Grand Hôtel Malher (Map pp126-7; ☎ 01 42 72 60 92; www.grandhotelmalher.com; 5 rue Malher, 4e; Ⓜ St-Paul; s €95-120, d €115-140, ste €170-185; 💻) This welcoming establishment run by the same family for three generations has a small but pretty courtyard at the back. The 31 guestrooms are of a decent size, and the bathrooms modern and relatively capacious. Room 1 and 2 open on to the courtyard. Wheelchair access available.

Hôtel St-Louis Marais (Map pp132-3; ☎ 01 48 87 87 04; www.saintlouismarais.com; 1 rue Charles V, 4e; Ⓜ Sully Morland; s €99, d & tw €115-140, tr/ste €150/160; 💻) This especially charming hotel in a converted 17th-century convent is more Bastille than Marais but still within easy walking distance of the latter. Wooden beams, terracotta tiles and heavy brocade drapes tend to darken the 19 rooms but certainly add to the atmosphere. Be aware that there are four floors here but no lift.

Hôtel Castex (Map pp132-3; ☎ 01 42 72 31 52; www.castexhotel.com; 5 rue Castex, 4e; Ⓜ Bastille; s/d/ste €120/150/220; ❄ 💻) Equidistant from Bastille and the Marais, the 30-room Castex has modernised but retains some of its 17th-century elements, including a vaulted stone cellar used as a breakfast room, terracotta floor tiles and Toile de Jouy wallpaper. Try to get one of the independent rooms (1 and 2) off the lovely patio; room 3 is a two-room suite or family room.

Hôtel de la Bretonnerie (Map pp126-7; ☎ 01 48 87 77 63; www.bretonnerie.com; 22 rue Ste-Croix de la Bretonnerie, 4e; Ⓜ Hôtel de Ville; r €125-160, ste €185-210; 💻) This is a very charming upper midrange place in the heart of the Marais nightlife area dating from the 17th century. The decor of each of the 22 guestrooms and seven suites is unique, and some rooms have four-poster and canopy beds. Three 'duplex' suites on two levels are huge and can easily accommodate three or four people.

Hôtel Caron de Beaumarchais (Map pp126-7; ☎ 01 42 72 34 12; www.carondebeaumarchais.com; 12 rue Vieille du Temple, 4e; Ⓜ St-Paul; r €125-162; ❄ 💻 ⊠) Decorated like an 18th-century private house – contemporary with Beaumarchais, who wrote *Le Mariage de Figaro* (The Marriage of Figaro) at No 47 of the same street – this themed hotel has to be seen to be believed. The museumlike lobby, with its prized 18th-century pianoforte, gaming tables, gilded mirrors, and candelabras, sets the tone of the place. Downsides: the 19 guestrooms are on the smallish side, and the welcome is never very warm.

TOP END

our pick **Hôtel St-Merry** (Map pp126-7; ☎ 01 42 78 14 15; www.hotelmarais.com; 78 rue de la Verrerie, 4e; Ⓜ Châtelet; d & tw €160-230, tr €205-275, ste €335-407; 💻) The interior of this small hostelry, with beamed ceilings, remade church pews and confessionals, and wrought-iron candelabra, is a goth's wet dream and just the place for the Dracula in you who yearns to breathe free. The 11 rooms and one suite of this hotel, by far our favourite medieval number in the Marais, are in the one-time presbytery of the attached Église St-Merry. So very close are both structures that two flying buttresses straddle the double bed of room 9; the possibilities for in-house gymnastics are endless. Some rooms are on the smallish side – although room 11 is larger than most; room 20 is a suite with eye-popping furnishings and room 12 has a bed board formed of ancient church furnishings and a large table. On the downside: there is no lift connecting the postage-stamp lobby with the four upper floors, no mod cons to speak of (except for recently introduced wi-fi) and no air-conditioning in a hotel that gets quite warm in summer.

Hôtel du Petit Moulin (Map pp132-3; ☎ 01 42 74 10 10; www.hoteldupetitmoulin.com; 29-31 rue de Poitou, 3e; Ⓜ Filles du Calvaire; r €180-280, ste €350; ❄ 💻) This scrumptious boutique hotel in what was once a bakery was designed from top to bottom by Christian Lacroix. It features 17 completely different rooms – from medieval and rococo Marais, sporting exposed beams and dressed in toile de Jouy wallpaper, to a more modern *quartier* with contemporary murals and heart-shaped mirrors just this side of kitsch. 'The Little Mill' is a wonderful new addition to the northern end of the Marais. Wheelchair access available.

The Islands

The smaller of the two islands in the middle of the Seine, Île St-Louis, is by far the more romantic, and it has a string of excellent top-end hotels. It's an easy walk from central Paris. Oddly enough, the only hotel of any sort on the Île de la Cité is a budget one.

BUDGET

Hôtel Henri IV (Map pp126-7; ☎ 01 43 54 44 53; 25 place Dauphine, 1er; Ⓜ Pont Neuf or Cité; s & d €52-76, tr €76) This decrepit place, with 15 worn rooms, is popular for its location, location and – above all else – location on the very tip of the Île de la Cité. It would be impossible to find something this romantic at such a price elsewhere; just don't stay in bed too long. All rooms have showers and are quite large. Book well in advance.

TOP END

Hôtel St-Louis (Map pp126-7; ☎ 01 46 34 04 80; www.hotel-saint-louis.com; 75 rue St-Louis en l'Île, 4e; Ⓜ Pont Marie; r €140-155, ste €220;) One of several hotels lining posh rue St-Louis en l'Île, this place has 19 appealing but unspectacular rooms, though the public areas are lovely. The breakfast room in the basement dates from the early 17th century.

Hôtel de Lutèce (Map pp126-7; ☎ 01 43 26 23 52; www.paris-hotel-lutece.com; 65 rue St-Louis en l'Île, 4e; Ⓜ Pont Marie; s €150, d €170-189, tr €205-225;) An exquisite hotel and more country than city, the Lutèce has an enviable spot on delightful Île St-Louis, and 23 comfortable, tastefully decorated and recently renovated rooms. The lobby/salon, with its ancient fireplace, wood panelling and antique furnishings, sets the welcoming and cosy tone of the whole place.

Latin Quarter & Jardin des Plantes

The northern section of the 5e close to the Seine has been popular with students and young people since the Middle Ages, though there is relatively little budget accommodation left in the area.

There are dozens of attractive two- and three-star hotels in the Latin Quarter, including a cluster near the Sorbonne and another group along the lively rue des Écoles. Midrange hotels in the area are very popular with visiting academics, so rooms are hardest to find when conferences and seminars are scheduled (usually from March to June and in October). In general this part of the city offers better value among top-end hotels than the neighbouring 6e does. The Luxembourg and Port Royal RER stations are linked to both airports by RER and Orlyval.

BUDGET

Young & Happy Hostel (Map pp130-1; ☎ 01 47 07 47 07; www.youngandhappy.fr; 80 rue Mouffetard, 5e; Ⓜ Place Monge; dm/d €23/52;) Although slightly frayed, this is a friendly spot in the centre of the Latin Quarter. It's popular with a slightly older crowd nowadays. The rooms are closed from 11am to 4pm, but the reception remains open; there is no curfew. Beds are in rather cramped rooms for two to eight people, with washbasins. In summer the best way to get a bed is to stop by at about 8am. Internet access costs €2 for half an hour.

Centre International de Séjour BVJ Paris–Quartier Latin (Map pp130-1; ☎ 01 43 29 34 80; www.bvjhotel.com; 44 rue des Bernardins, 5e; Ⓜ Maubert Mutualité; dm/s/d €28/42/64;) This hostel on the Left Bank is a sister branch of the Centre International de Séjour BVJ Paris–Louvre (p165) and has all the same rules. There are 100 beds in singles, doubles and single-sex dorm rooms for four to 10 people. All of the rooms here have showers and telephones.

Hôtel Esmeralda (Map pp126-7; ☎ 01 43 54 19 20; fax 01 40 51 00 68; 4 rue St-Julien le Pauvre, 5e; Ⓜ St-Michel; s €35-95, d €85-95, tr/q €110/120) Tucked away in a quiet street with full views of Notre Dame (choose room No 12!), the Esmeralda has been everyone's secret 'find' for years now, so book well in advance. At these prices and location, the 19 guestrooms – the three cheapest singles have washbasin only – are no great shakes, so expect little beyond the picture postcard through the window. Be advised that there is no lift and some rooms share a toilet.

Port Royal Hôtel (Map pp130-1; ☎ 01 43 31 70 06; www.hotelportroyal.fr; 8 bd de Port Royal, 5e; Ⓜ Les Gobelins; s €41-89, d €52.50-89) It's hard to imagine that this 46-room hotel, owned and managed by the same family for three generations, still only bears one star. The spotless and very quiet rooms overlook a small glassed-in courtyard (eg No 15) or the street (No 14), but we especially like room No 11, with its colourful bed frame and pretty bathroom. Rooms at the lower end of the scale have washbasins only. Wheelchair access available.

Hôtel Gay-Lussac (Map pp130-1; ☎ 01 43 54 23 96; hotel.gay-lussac@club-internet.fr; 29 rue Gay Lussac, 5e; Ⓜ Luxembourg; s/d with washbasin €50/60, s/d with shower €60/70, s/d/tr/q with shower & toilet €65/78/98/110;) The Gay-Lussac, a 35-room threadbare hotel with a certain amount of character in the southern part of the Latin Quarter, has entered the modern age with a website, wi-fi throughout and a lick of paint. Though the single rooms are small, the others are very large indeed and have high ceilings. Furnishings are very basic, but the staff are friendly and helpful.

MIDRANGE

Hôtel Cluny Sorbonne (Map pp130-1; ☎ 01 43 54 66 66; www.hotel-cluny.fr; 8 rue Victor Cousin, 5e; Ⓜ Luxembourg; d €70-95, q €130-150;) This hotel, surrounded by the prestigious buildings of the Sorbonne, is where the poet Arthur Rimbaud dallied in 1872. It has 23 rooms that could do with an upgrade, but the cheery yellow lobby and equally cheery staff make up for that. One of the choicest rooms is No 63, a quad with memorable views of the college and the Panthéon.

Hôtel de l'Espérance (Map pp130-1; ☎ 01 47 07 10 99; www.hoteldelesperance.fr; 15 rue Pascal, 5e; Ⓜ Censier Daubenton; s €71-80, d €80-90;) Just a couple of minutes' walk south of lively rue Mouffetard, the 'Hotel of Hope' is a quiet and immaculately kept 38-room place with faux antique furnishings and a warm welcome from the charming couple who own it. Some of the larger rooms have two double beds. Wheelchair access available.

Hôtel des 3 Collèges (Map pp130-1; ☎ 01 43 54 67 30; www.3colleges.com; 16 rue Cujas, 5e; Ⓜ Luxembourg; s €78-120, d €96-140, tr €130-160;) Under new (and enthusiastic) management, this 44-room hotel is a pleasant and reasonably priced place to stay by the Sorbonne. Furnishings in the smallish rooms are simple – white with splashes of pastel – and some rooms share a toilet. But we love room No 63, with its beamed ceiling and three sun-splashed windows.

Familia Hôtel (Map pp130-1; ☎ 01 43 54 55 27; www.familiahotel.com; 11 rue des Écoles, 5e; Ⓜ Cardinal Lemoine; s incl breakfast €86, d & tw €103-124, tr €161-173, q €184;) This very welcoming and well-situated family-run hotel has attractive sepia murals of Paris' landmarks in 21 of its 30 rooms. Eight rooms have little balconies, from which you can catch a glimpse of Notre Dame. By far the choicest rooms, which carry a premium, are Nos 61, 62 and 65 (the last has a four-poster bed). We love the flower-bedecked windows, lovely parquet floors and complimentary buffet breakfast.

Hôtel Minerve (Map pp130-1; ☎ 01 43 26 26 04; www.parishotelminerve.com; 13 rue des Écoles, 5e; Ⓜ Cardinal Lemoine; s incl breakfast €90-125, d €106-136, tr €156-158;) This 54-room hotel in two buildings is owned by the same family that runs the Familia Hôtel (p169). It has a reception area decked out in oriental carpets and antique books, and we love the frescos of French monuments and reproduction 18th-century wallpapers. Some 10 rooms have small balconies, eight have views of Notre Dame and two have tiny courtyards that are swooningly romantic. The breakfast buffet is complimentary.

Hôtel St-Jacques (Map pp130-1; ☎ 01 44 07 45 45; www.hotel-saintjacques.com; 35 rue des Écoles, 5e; Ⓜ Maubert Mutualité; s €92, d €105-137, tr €168;) This very stylish 38-room hotel has balconies that overlook the Panthéon. Audrey Hepburn and Cary Grant, who filmed some scenes of *Charade* here in the 1960s, would appreciate the mod cons that now complement the original 19th-century details (trompe l'œil ceilings, iron staircase etc). Wheelchair access available.

Hôtel des Grandes Écoles (Map pp130-1; ☎ 01 43 26 79 23; www.hotel-grandes-ecoles.com; 75 rue du Cardinal Lemoine, 5e; Ⓜ Cardinal Lemoine or Place Monge; d €110-135, tr €125-155;) This wonderful and very welcoming hotel just north of place de la Contrescarpe has one of the loveliest situations in the Latin Quarter, tucked away in a courtyard off a medieval street with its own garden. Choose a room in one of three buildings; our favourites are those in the garden annexe, especially the five that are on the ground floor and have direct access to the garden (Nos 29 to 33). Wheelchair access available.

TOP END

Select Hôtel (Map pp130-1; ☎ 01 46 34 14 80; www.selecthotel.fr; 1 place de la Sorbonne, 5e; Ⓜ Cluny-La Sorbonne; d €139-175, tw €155-175, tr €179-189, ste €212;) Smack dab in the heart of the student-filled Sorbonne area, the Select is a very Parisian, art-deco mini-palace, with an atrium and cactus-strewn winter garden, an 18th-century vaulted breakfast room and 67 stylish (though small) rooms.

Hôtel de Notre Maître Albert (Map pp126-7; ☎ 01 43 26 79 00; www.hotel-paris-notredame.com; 19 rue Maître Albert, 5e; Ⓜ Maubert Mutualité; s/d €155/165;) Hidden down a quiet side street of the Latin Quarter but just paces from the Seine, this hotel has some lovely public areas (we adore the tapestry in the lobby, and the oriental carpets), but the 34 rooms, most of which look to rooftops out back and line long narrow corridors, are less impressive.

Hôtel La Demeure (Map pp130-1; ☎ 01 43 37 81 25; www.hotellademeureparis.com; 51 bd St-Marcel, 13e; Ⓜ Gobelins; s/d/ste €165/202/290;) This self-proclaimed *hôtel de caractère*, owned and operated by a charming father-and-son team, is just a bit away from the action at the bottom of the 5e. But the refined elegance of its 43 rooms, the almost 'clubby' public areas and the wraparound balconies of the corner rooms make it worth going that extra distance. Famed for those extra touches, the suite has an iPod, and the modern red fireplace in the lobby actually works.

St-Germain, Odéon & Luxembourg

The well-heeled St-Germain-des-Prés is a delightful area to stay in but has very little in the way of budget places to stay.

What you will find on offer here in that category is competitively priced with other areas, though. On the other hand, there are some excellent midrange hotels in this neighbourhood.

MIDRANGE

Hôtel de Nesle (Map pp126-7; ☎ 01 43 54 62 41; www.hoteldenesleparis.com; 7 rue de Nesle, 6e; Ⓜ Odéon or Mabillon; s €55-85, d €75-100) The Nesle is a relaxed, colourfully decorated hotel with 20 rooms, half of which are painted with murals taken from (mostly French) literature. What is by far its greatest asset, though, is the huge back garden accessible from the 1st floor, with pathways, trellis and even a small fountain. Room 12 looks onto it.

Hôtel du Dragon (Map pp124-5; ☎ 01 45 48 51 05; www.hoteldudragon.com; 36 rue du Dragon, 6e; Ⓜ Sèvres Babylone; s/d €95/115; 💻 ☒) There's no lift at this five-storey hotel, just a rickety-looking old wooden staircase that leads to the 28 brightly coloured rooms. The bedside lamps are on the low-budget side, and we could live without the faux-fur bed coverings. But the bathrooms are large and up to date, and the piano lounge and tiny back patio are just made for relaxing.

Hôtel du Globe (Map pp126-7; ☎ 01 43 26 35 50; www.hotel-du-globe.fr; 15 rue des Quatre Vents, 6e; Ⓜ Odéon; s €95-140, d €115-150, ste €180; 💻) The Globe is an eclectic caravanserai with 14 small but completely renovated rooms just south of the bd St-Germain. Some of the rooms are verging on the minuscule, and there is no lift (you ascend the four floors via a very narrow staircase). Still, we're suckers for armour – there are at least two full sets here – and canopy beds (go for room 43).

Hôtel du Lys (Map pp126-7; ☎ 01 43 26 97 57; www.hoteldulys.com; 23 rue Serpente, 6e; Ⓜ Odéon; s/d/tr €100/120/140) This 22-room hotel situated in what was a *hôtel particulier* in the 17th century has been owned and operated by the same family for six decades. We love the beamed ceiling and the chinoiserie wallpaper in the lobby; rooms to go for include the blue-toned No 13, with its striped ceiling and two windows, or the darker (but more atmospheric) No 14 in terracotta and with rustic old furniture.

TOP END

Hôtel des Marronniers (Map pp126-7; ☎ 01 43 25 30 60; www.hotel-marronniers.com; 21 rue Jacob, 6e; Ⓜ St-Germain des Prés; s €115-181, d & tw €161-181, tr/q €216/256; ❄ 💻) At the end of a small courtyard 30m from the main street, the 'Chestnut Trees' has 37 cosy rooms and a delightful conservatory opening on to a back garden. From the 3rd floor up, rooms ending in 1, 2 or 3 look on to the garden; the rooms on the two uppermost floors – the 5th and the 6th – have pretty views over the courtyard and the roofs of central Paris.

Hôtel d'Angleterre (Map pp126-7; ☎ 01 42 60 34 72; www.hotel-dangleterre.com; 44 rue Jacob, 6e; Ⓜ St-Germain des Prés; s incl breakfast €100-255, d €200-265, ste €285-320; 💻 ☒) The 'England Hotel' is a beautiful 27-room property in a quiet street close to busy bd St-Germain and the Musée d'Orsay. Guests breakfast in the courtyard of this former British Embassy, where the Treaty of Paris ending the American Revolution was signed and where Hemingway once lodged. Duplex suite No 51 at the top has beamed ceiling and No 12 a four-poster bed. Breakfast is included in room rates.

Montparnasse

Just east of Gare Montparnasse, the mammoth train station that also houses the Montparnasse Bienvenüe metro station, there are a number of budget and lower-end midrange places on rue Vandamme and rue de la Gaîté – though the latter street is rife with sex shops and peep shows. Gare Montparnasse is served by Air France buses from both airports. Place Denfert Rochereau is also linked to both airports by Orlybus, Orlyval and RER.

BUDGET

Celtic Hôtel (Map pp124-5; ☎ 01 43 20 93 53; hotel celtic@wanadoo.fr; 15 rue d'Odessa, 14e; Ⓜ Edgar Quinet; s €45-56, d €63-70, tr €80) A cheapie of the old school and still resisting a website, this 29-room hotel is an old-fashioned place with a small modern lift and an up-to-date reception area. The cheaper singles are pretty bare and even the doubles and triples with shower are not exactly *tout confort* (with all the mod cons), but the Gare Montparnasse is only 200m away.

Hôtel de Blois (Map pp114-15; ☎ 01 45 40 99 48; www.hoteldeblois.com; 5 rue des Plantes, 14e; Ⓜ Mouton Duvernet; s €55-75, d €59-80, tw €58-66, tr €70-85; 💻 ☒) This 25-room establishment just off the av du Maine has been completely overhauled and is now a very pleasant, very affordable one-star hotel just south of Gare Montparnasse. Rooms, smallish but fully equipped, have shower or bath, but some share use of the toilet in the hallway.

MIDRANGE

Hôtel Delambre (Map pp124-5; ☎ 01 43 20 66 31; www.hoteldelambre.com; 35 rue Delambre, 14e; Ⓜ Montparnasse; r €80-115, ste €150-160;) This attractive 30-room hotel just east of the Gare Montparnasse takes wrought-iron as a theme and uses it both in functional pieces (bed, lamps, shelving) and decorative items throughout. Room 7 has its own little terrace, while Nos 1 and 2 open on to a small private courtyard. Wheelchair access available.

TOP-END

Hôtel Aviatic (Map pp124-5; ☎ 01 53 63 25 50; www.aviatic.fr; 105 rue de Vaugirard, 6e; Ⓜ Montparnasse Bienvenüe; r €149-270, ste €310-355;) This 42-room hotel with charming, almost Laura Ashley–style decor and a delightful art-deco canopied entrance has been in the business since 1856, so it must be doing something right. The tiny 'winter garden' is a breath of fresh air (literally). Some rooms face the street and some the quieter (and no less light) courtyard.

Faubourg St-Denis & Invalides

The 7e is a lovely arrondissement in which to stay, but apart from the northeastern section – the area east of Invalides and opposite the Louvre – it's fairly quiet and away from all the action.

MIDRANGE

Hôtel du Champ-de-Mars (Map pp124-5; ☎ 01 45 51 52 30; www.hotelduchampdemars.com; 7 rue du Champ de Mars, 7e; Ⓜ École Militaire; s/d/tw/tr €84/90/94/112;) This charming 25-room hotel in the shadow of the Eiffel Tower is on everyone's wish list, so book a good month or two in advance. The attractive shop-front entrance leads to a colourful lobby done up in yellow and charcoal. Rooms on the lower floors can be downright cupboardlike, though; go up higher and you might earn a glimpse of Mademoiselle Eiffel herself.

Mayet Hôtel (Map pp124-5; ☎ 01 47 83 21 35; www.mayet.com; 3 rue Mayet, 6e; Ⓜ Duroc; s incl breakfast €95-120, d €120-140, tr €160;) Light-hearted and loads of fun, this 23-room boutique hotel with drippy murals and a penchant for oversize clocks and primary colours, has good-sized rooms and bathrooms, most with tubs. It offers excellent value and complimentary breakfast too.

Hôtel Lindbergh (Map pp124-5; ☎ 01 45 48 35 53; www.paris-hotel-lindbergh.com; 5 rue Chomel, 7e; Ⓜ Sèvres Babylone; d €98-160, tr €156-180, q €166-190;) We still haven't figured out why this 26-room *hôtel de charme* (charming hotel) is totally kitted out in Charles Lindbergh photos and memorabilia, but it works. We also like the room number plates on the doors with little Paris landmarks, the ample-sized bathrooms and the friendly staff.

Hôtel Muguet (Map pp124-5; ☎ 01 47 05 05 93; www.hotelmuguet.com; 11 rue Chevert, 7e; Ⓜ La Tour Maubourg; s/d/tr €103/135/180;) This hotel strategically placed between Invalides and the Eiffel Tower has 48 generously sized rooms that have been recently renovated. Room 63 is bathed in light and takes in the Église du Dôme (p151), No 62 has a mansard ceiling but wins the lottery with views of the Eiffel Tower. The glassed-in breakfast room opens on to a delightful courtyard garden.

Étoile & Champs-Élysées

This area has some of Paris' finest hotels as well as a couple of real trendsetters.

MIDRANGE

Hôtel Alison (Map pp118-19; ☎ 01 42 65 54 00; www.hotelalison.com; 21 rue de Surène, 8e; Ⓜ Madeleine; s €80-165, d €112-165, tw €135-145, tr €165, ste €204-290;) This excellent-value 34-room midrange hotel, just west of place de la Madeleine, attracts with the bold colours of its carpets and furnishings and modern art in the lobby. Prices depend on whether rooms have bath or shower, as well as the view. Double No 37, for example, looks on to rue Surène, while more-expensive room 31 overlooks a leafy patio.

TOP END

Hôtel Le A (Map pp118-19; ☎ 01 42 56 99 99; www.paris-hotel-a.com; 4 rue d'Artois, 8e; Ⓜ St-Philippe du Roule; r €355-431, ste €485-640;) The 26-room 'A' (think 'list') is an uberstylish minimalist hotel that doesn't have any of the attitude that generally goes with the concept. White, black and grey predominate and help frame the fabulous contemporary art by painter Fabrice Hybert. The airy spaces (the breakfast area and bar are in a glassed-in courtyard), fireplace, and books in the lobby for guests' use are welcome, but rooms are on the petite side.

Clichy & Gare St-Lazare

These areas have some excellent midrange hotels. The better deals are away from Gare St-Lazare, but there are several places along rue d'Amsterdam beside the station worth checking out.

BUDGET

Style Hôtel (Map pp118-19; ☎ 01 45 22 37 59; fax 01 45 22 81 03; 8 rue Ganneron, 18e; Ⓜ La Fourche; s & d €35-50, tr/q €57/67) This 36-room hotel just north of place de Clichy and west of Cimetière de Montmartre is a bit rough around the edges (rough wooden floors, old runner carpets in the hallways) but is loaded with character and the welcome is always charming. There's a lovely double courtyard, but no lift. The cheapest singles and doubles are equipped with washbasin only.

Hôtel Eldorado (Map pp118-19; ☎ 01 45 22 35 21; www.eldoradohotel.fr; 18 rue des Dames, 17e; Ⓜ Place de Clichy; s €35-57, d & tw €68-80, tr €80-90) This bohemian place is one of Paris' greatest finds: a welcoming, somewhat well-run place with 23 colourfully decorated rooms in a main building on a quiet street and in an annexe with a private garden at the back. Cheaper-category singles have washbasin only.

MIDRANGE

New Orient Hôtel (Map pp118-19; ☎ 01 45 22 21 64; www.hotelneworient.com; 16 rue de Constantinople, 8e; Ⓜ Europe; s €89-115, d €106-115, tw €115-140, tr & q €150; ❄ 💻 ⊠) This 30-room nonsmoking hotel is in a neighbourhood of the 8e north of Gare St-Lazare that seems to have only shops that sell musical instruments and/or sheet music. The place has a lot of personality, especially in the common areas. Some rooms (eg twin room No 7 and double No 8) have little balconies.

Hôtel Langlois (Map pp118-19; ☎ 01 48 74 78 24; www.hotel-langlois.com; 63 rue St-Lazare, 9e; Ⓜ Trinité; s €105-120, d & tw €120-140, ste €180; ❄ 💻) Built in 1870, this 27-room hotel has managed to retain its charming belle-époque look and feel. The hotel's rooms and suites (eg Nos 11 and 15) are unusually large for a smallish hotel in Paris. Room 64 has wonderful views of the rooftops of Montmartre.

Opéra & Grands Boulevards

The avenues around blvd Montmartre are popular for their nightlife area and it's a lively area in which to stay. It's very convenient for shopping as this is where you'll find Paris' premium department stores.

MIDRANGE

Hôtel Chopin (Map pp120-1; ☎ 01 47 70 58 10; www.hotelchopin.fr; 46 passage Jouffroy, entrance at 10 blvd Montmartre, 9e; Ⓜ Grands Boulevards; s €50-78, d €81-92, tr €109) Dating back to 1846, the 36-room Chopin is down one of Paris' most delightful 19th-century *passages couverts* (p155). It may be a little faded around the edges, but it's still enormously evocative of the belle époque. The cheapest singles have washbasin only.

Hôtel Vivienne (Map pp120-1; ☎ 01 42 33 13 26; www.hotel-vivienne.com; 40 rue Vivienne, 2e; Ⓜ Grands Boulevards; s €60-114, d & tw €75-114; 💻 ⊠) This stylish 45-room hotel is amazingly good value for Paris. While the rooms are not huge, they have all the mod cons, some have little balconies and the public areas are bright and cheery.

Hôtel Peletier-Haussmann-Opéra (Map pp120-1; ☎ 01 42 46 79 53; www.peletieropera.com; 15 rue Le Peletier, 9e; Ⓜ Richelieu Drouot; s €70-90, d €80-100, tr €86-110; 💻) This is a pleasant, 26-room hotel just off blvd Haussmann and close to the big department stores. There are attractive packages available at weekends, depending on the season. Internet access costs €2 for 15 minutes.

Hôtel Victoria (Map pp120-1; ☎ 01 47 70 20 01; www.hotelvictoria.free.fr; 2bis Cité Bergère, 9e; Ⓜ Grands Boulevards; s/d/tr €71/77/93) This 107-room old-style hotel in a quiet alleyway just off the Grands Boulevards is a good choice if you're looking for central budget accommodation on the Right Bank. The rooms are generally unexceptional but of a good size and the welcome is warm.

Hôtel Favart (Map pp120-1; ☎ 01 42 97 59 83; www.hotel-paris-favart.com; 5 rue Marivaux, 2e; Ⓜ Richelieu Drouot; s €100-130, d €130-160, tr €140-180, q €155-200; ❄ ⊠) With 37 rooms facing the Opéra Comique, the Favart is a stylish art-nouveau hotel that feels like it never let go of the belle époque. We like the prints on the walls in the lobby and the dramatic wrought-iron staircase leading up to the 1st floor. Wheelchair access available.

Gare du Nord, Gare de l'Est & République

The areas east and northeast of the Gare du Nord and Gare de l'Est have always had a more than ample selection of hotels, and there is also a hostel within striking distance. At the same time, there are quite a few two- and three-star places around the train stations in the 10e that are convenient if you are catching an early-morning train to London or want to crash immediately upon arrival. Place de la République is convenient for the nightlife areas of Ménilmontant.

Gare du Nord is linked to Charles de Gaulle airport by RER and RATP bus 350 and to Orly airport by Orlyval. Bus 350 to/from Charles de Gaulle airport also stops right in front of the Gare de l'Est.

BUDGET

Peace & Love Hostel (Map pp120-1; ☎ 01 46 07 65 11; www.paris-hostels.com; 245 rue La Fayette, 10e; Ⓜ Jaurès or Louis Blanc; dm/d €25/60; 💻) This modern-day hippy hang-out is a groovy though chronically crowded hostel with beds in 21 smallish, shower-equipped rooms for two to four people. There's a great kitchen and eating area, but most of the action seems to revolve around the ground floor bar (open till 2am), which has more than two dozen types of beer. Internet access starts at €1 for 15 minutes.

Sibour Hôtel (Map pp120-1; ☎ 01 46 07 20 74; www.hotel-sibour.com; 4 rue Sibour, 10e; Ⓜ Gare de l'Est; s €40-55, d €45-65, tr/q €80/110) This friendly place has 45 well-kept rooms, including some old-fashioned ones – the cheapest singles and doubles – with washbasins only. Hall showers cost €3. Some of the rooms look down on to pretty Église de St-Laurent. Note the trompe l'œil mural in the breakfast room.

Hôtel La Vieille France (Map pp120-1; ☎ 01 45 26 42 37; la.vieille.france@wanadoo.fr; 151 rue La Fayette, 10e; Ⓜ Gare du Nord; s €48, d €75-85, tr €120; 💻) The 'Old France' is an upbeat, 34-room place with relatively spacious and pleasant rooms, though with the Gare du Nord so close it's bound to be somewhat noisy. Singles have washbasins only, but hall showers are free.

MIDRANGE

Nord-Est Hôtel (Map pp120-1; ☎ 01 47 70 07 18; hotel.nord.est@wanadoo.fr; 12 rue des Petits Hôtels, 10e; Ⓜ Poissonnière; s/d/tr/q €65/75/110/145; 💻) This unusual 30-room hotel, charmingly located on the 'Street of Little Hotels', is set away from the street and fronted by a small terrace. It is convenient to both the Gare du Nord and the Gare de l'Est. Internet access costs an outrageous €8/12 for 30/60 minutes.

Grand Hôtel de Paris (Map pp120-1; ☎ 01 46 07 40 56; grand.hotel.de.paris@gofornet.com; 72 bd de Strasbourg, 10e; Ⓜ Gare de l'Est; s/d/tr/q €80/86/105/122) The Grand Hôtel de Paris is a well-run establishment just south of the Gare de l'Est. It has 49 soundproofed rooms and a tiny lift. The quads are especially spacious; try room 53. Room 33 has a small balcony.

Hôtel Français (Map pp120-1; ☎ 01 40 35 94 14; www.hotelfrancais.com; 13 rue du 8 Mai 1945, 10e; Ⓜ Gare de l'Est; s €94-101, d €99-106, tr €134-141; ❄ 💻 ⊠) This two-star hotel facing the Gare de l'Est has 72 attractive, almost luxurious and very quiet rooms, some of which have balconies. The place has recently been freshened up; we love the new mock-café breakfast area.

TOP END

Kube Hôtel (Map pp120-1; ☎ 01 42 05 20 00; www.kubehotel.com; 1-5 passage Ruelle, 18e; Ⓜ La Chapelle; s €250, d €300-400, ste €500-750; ❄ 💻 ⊠) The theme at this ubertrendy boutique hotel is, of course, three-dimensional square – from the glassed-in reception box in the entrance courtyard and the cube-shaped furnishings in the 41 guestrooms to the ice in the cocktails at the celebrated Ice Kube (p190) bar.

Ménilmontant & Belleville

The Ménilmontant nightlife district is an excellent area in which to spend the evening, but the selection of accommodation in all price ranges is somewhat limited, especially in the budget category.

MIDRANGE

Hôtel Croix de Malte (Map pp132-3; ☎ 01 48 05 09 36; www.hotelcroixdemalte-paris.com; 5 rue de Malte, 11e; Ⓜ Oberkampf; s €75-85, d €85-95; 💻 ⊠) With its glassed-in courtyard sporting a giant jungle mural, this cheery hotel will have you thinking you're in the tropics, not Paris. The 40 rooms are in two little buildings, only one of which has a lift.

Hôtel Beaumarchais (Map pp132-3; ☎ 01 53 36 86 86; www.hotelbeaumarchais.com; 3 rue Oberkampf, 11e; Ⓜ Filles du Calvaire; s €75-90, d €110-130, tr €170-190; ❄ 💻) This brighter-than-bright 31-room boutique hotel, with its emphasis on sunbursts and bold primary colours, is just this side of kitsch. But it makes for a different Paris experience and fits in with its surroundings very well indeed. The rooms are of a decent size; the best are Nos 2 and 3, a triple and a double facing the courtyard.

Hôtel du Vieux Saule (Map pp132-3; ☎ 01 42 72 01 14; www.hotelvieuxsaule.com; 6 rue de Picardie, 3e; Ⓜ Filles du Calvaire; s €120, d €140-160, tr €180; ❄ 💻 ⊠) The flower-bedecked 'Old Willow Tree', a 28-room hostelry in the northern Marais bordering Ménilmontant, is something of a find because of its slightly unusual location. The hotel has a small sauna, there is a tranquil little 'garden' on display behind glass off the lobby, and breakfast is served in the 16th-century vaulted cellar.

TOP END

Murano Urban Resort (Map pp132-3; ☎ 01 42 71 20 00; www.muranoresort.com; 13 bd du Temple, 3e; Ⓜ Filles du Calvaire; s €360, d €440-650, ste €750-1200;) This 52-room hotel's subtitle, 'Urban Resort', suggests that you should come, kick off your shoes and sink your toes in the hotel's figurative sand. And with public areas like a new spa with heated pool, a glass-roofed courtyard restaurant, a cool jazz and DJ bar, and guestrooms that allow you to change their colour scheme, that's easily accomplished.

Gare de Lyon, Nation & Bercy

The neighbourhood around the Gare de Lyon has a few budget hotels as well as an independent hostel.

BUDGET

Blue Planet Hostel (Map pp134-5; ☎ 01 43 42 06 18; www.hostelblueplanet.com; 5 rue Hector Malot, 12e; Ⓜ Gare de Lyon; dm €21;) This 43-room hostel is very close to Gare de Lyon – convenient if you're heading south or west at the crack of dawn. Dorm beds are in rooms for two to four people. The hostel closes between 11am and 3pm, but there's no curfew. Internet access costs €3 for 30 minutes.

Hôtel Le Cosy (Map pp114-15; ☎ 01 43 43 10 02; www.hotel-cosy.com; 50 av de St-Mandé, 12e; Ⓜ Picpus; s €40-65, d €50-99;) This family-run budget hotel immediately southeast of place de la Nation positively oozes charm. The 28 rooms, though basic – the cheapest singles and doubles have washbasins only – are all different, decorated in original artwork and with hardwood floors. If feeling flush, choose one of four 'VIP' rooms in the courtyard annexe, especially No 3 or 4 on the 1st floor.

Hôtel du Printemps (Map pp114-15; ☎ 01 43 43 62 31; www.hotel-paris-printemps.com; 80 bd de Picpus, 12e; Ⓜ Picpus; s €50, d €60, tw €65-70, tr €75-80, q €88;) It may not be in the centre of the action, but the 38-room 'Spring Hotel' offers excellent value for its standard and location just steps from place de la Nation. What's more, there's an in-house bar open day and night. Singles have showers but share a toilet; doubles have everything.

Montmartre & Pigalle

Montmartre, encompassing the 18e and the northern part of the 9e, is one of the most charming neighbourhoods in Paris. There is a bunch of top-end hotels in the area, and the attractive midrange places on rue Aristide Bruant are generally less full in July and August than in spring and autumn.

The flat area around the base of the Butte Montmartre has some surprisingly good budget deals. The lively, ethnically mixed area east of Sacré Cœur can be a bit rough; some say it's prudent to avoid Château Rouge metro station at night. Both the 9e and the 18e have a fine hostel.

BUDGET

Woodstock Hostel (Map pp120-1; ☎ 01 48 78 87 76; www.woodstock.fr; 48 rue Rodier, 9e; Ⓜ Anvers; dm/d €19/44 Oct-Mar, €22/50 Apr-Sep;) Woodstock is just down the hill from raucous Pigalle in a quiet, residential quarter. Dorm beds are in rooms for four to six people, and each room has washbasin only; showers and toilets are off the corridor. Rooms are closed from 11am to 3pm, and the (enforced) curfew is at 2am. The eat-in kitchen down the steps from the patio is fully loaded. Internet access is available for €2 for 30 minutes; wi-fi is free.

Le Village Hostel (Map p136; ☎ 01 42 64 22 02; www.villagehostel.fr; 20 rue d'Orsel, 18e; Ⓜ Anvers; dm/d/tr €24/60/81;) A fine 25-room hostel with beamed ceilings and views of Sacré Cœur, this one. Dormitory beds are in rooms for four to six people and all rooms have showers and toilets. Kitchen facilities are available, and there's a popular bar too. Rooms are closed between 11am and 4pm for cleaning, but there is no curfew. Internet access is available for €1/3.50 per 15/60 minutes.

Hôtel Bonséjour Montmartre (Map p136; ☎ 01 42 54 22 53; www.hotel-bonsejour-montmartre.fr; 11 rue Burq, 18e; Ⓜ Abbesses; s €33-40, d €44-55, tr €58-65;) At the top of a quiet street in Montmartre, the 'Good Stay' is a perennial budget favourite. It's a simple place – no lift, linoleum or parquet floors – but welcoming, comfortable, very clean and getting a protracted (and much needed) facelift. Some rooms (Nos 14, 23, 33, 43 and 53) have little balconies attached, and at least one room (No 55) offers a fleeting glimpse of Sacré Cœur. Hall showers cost €2.

MIDRANGE

Hôtel Utrillo (Map p136; ☎ 01 42 58 13 44; www.hotel-paris-utrillo.com; 7 rue Aristide Bruant, 18e; Ⓜ Abbesses or Blanche; s €73, d & tw €83-88, tr €105; 💻) This friendly 30-room hotel, named for the 'painter of Montmartre', Maurice Utrillo (1883–1955), and decorated in primary colours, has a few extras such as a little leafy courtyard in back and a small sauna. Wheelchair access available.

Hôtel des Arts (Map p136; ☎ 01 46 06 30 52; www.arts-hotel-paris.com; 5 rue Tholozé, 18e; Ⓜ Abbesses or Blanche; s €75-95, d & tw €95-105, tr €160; 💻) The 'Arts Hotel' is a friendly and attractive 50-room place convenient to both place Pigalle and Montmartre. Towering over it is the old-style windmill Moulin de la Galette. The resident canine is very friendly.

Hôtel Regyn's Montmartre (Map p136; ☎ 01 42 54 45 21; www.hotel-regyns-paris.com; 18 place des Abbesses, 18e; Ⓜ Abbesses; s €79-89, d & tw €91-111, tr €117-131; 💻 ⊠) This 22-room hotel is a good choice if you want to stay in old Montmartre and not break the bank. It's just opposite the Abbesses metro station, and some of the rooms have views out over Paris.

Hôtel du Moulin (Map p136; ☎ 01 42 64 33 33; www.hotelmoulin.com; 3 rue Aristide Bruant, 18e; Ⓜ Abbesses or Blanche; s/d/tr €83/88/106; 💻) There are 27 good-sized rooms with toilet and bath or shower in both a main building and a garden annexe at this quiet little hotel. The Korean family that owns the place is very kind. Check out their fun website.

Hôtel Résidence des 3 Poussins (Map pp120-1; ☎ 01 53 32 81 81; www.les3poussins.com; 15 rue Clauzel, 9e; Ⓜ St-Georges; s/d €137/152, 1- or 2-person studio €187, 3- or 4-person studio €222; ⁜ 💻) The 'Hotel of the Three Chicks' is a lovely property due south of place Pigalle with 40 rooms, half of which are small studios with their own cooking facilities. This place positively exudes style, and the back patio is a delightful place in the warmer months for breakfast or a drink. Wheelchair access available.

TOP END

Terrass Hôtel (Map p136; ☎ 01 46 06 72 85; www.terrass-hotel.com; 12 rue Joseph de Maistre, 18e; Ⓜ Blanche; r €260-325, ste €355-375; ⁜ 💻 ⊠) This very sedate and stylish hotel at the southeastern corner of Montparnasse Cemetery has 92 spacious and well-designed rooms and suites, an excellent restaurant and bar, and some of the best views in town. For the ultimate Parisian experience, choose double room 608 for stunning views of the Eiffel Tower and Panthéon, or room 802, which has its own private terrace.

EATING

When it comes to food, Paris has everything…and nothing. As the culinary centre of the most aggressively gastronomic country in the world, the city has more 'generic French', regional, and ethnic restaurants than any other place in France. But *la cuisine parisienne* (Parisian cuisine) is a poor relation of that extended family known as *la cuisine des provinces* (provincial cuisine). That's because those greedy country cousins have consumed most of what was once on Paris' own plate, claiming it as their own. Today very few French dishes except maybe vol-au-vent (light pastry shell filled with chicken or fish in a creamy sauce), *potage St-Germain* (thick green pea soup), onion soup, the humble pig's trotters and *gâteau Paris-Brest,* a ring-shaped cake filled with praline and topped with flaked almonds and icing sugar, are associated with the capital.

That said, over the years certain foreign dishes have become as Parisian as pig's trotters (see p75). The *nems* and *pâtés impérials* (spring or egg rolls) and *pho* (soup noodles with beef) of Vietnam, the couscous and *tajines* of North Africa, the *boudin antillais* (West Indian blood pudding) from the Caribbean and the *yassa* (meat or fish grilled in onion and lemon sauce) of Senegal are all eaten with relish throughout the capital. Indian, Chinese and Japanese food are also very popular non-French cuisines in Paris. In fact, foreign food is what Paris does better than any other city in the country.

One of Paris' largest concentrations of foreign restaurants is squeezed into a labyrinth of narrow streets in the 5e arrondissement across the Seine from Notre Dame. The Greek, North African and Middle Eastern restaurants between rue St-Jacques, bd St-Germain and bd St-Michel, including rue de la Huchette, attract mainly foreigners, often under the mistaken impression that this little maze is the whole of the famous 'Latin Quarter'. But you'd be far better off looking elsewhere for ethnic food: bd de Belleville in the 20e for Middle Eastern; nearby rue de Belleville in the 19e for Asian (especially Thai and Vietnamese); rue du Faubourg St-Denis in the 10e for Indian, Pakistani and Bangladeshi; and Chinatown in the 13e for

FAST-FOOD & CHAIN RESTAURANTS

American fast-food chains have busy branches all over Paris, as does the local hamburger chain **Quick** (www.quick.fr, in French). In addition, a number of local chain restaurants have outlets around Paris with standard menus. They are definitely a cut above fast-food outlets and can be good value in areas such as along the av des Champs-Élysées, where restaurants tend to be bad value.

The ever popular Italian-ish bistro-restaurant chain **Bistro Romain** (www.bistroromain.fr, in French; starters €4.90-17.10, pasta €13.30-16.40, mains €14.30-19.40, menus €12.50-33.60; 11am-midnight Sun-Thu, 11am-1am Fri & Sat), with 14 branches in Paris proper, is surprisingly upmarket for its price category. The **Champs-Élysées Bistro Romain** (Map pp118-19; 01 43 59 93 31; 122 av des Champs-Élysées, 8e; M George V), one of a pair along the city's most famous thoroughfare, is a stone's throw from the Arc de Triomphe.

Buffalo Grill (www.buffalo-grill.fr; starters €4.20-10, mains €9.70-20.20, menus from €9.10; 11am-11pm Sun-Thu, 11am-midnight Fri & Sat) counts nine branches in Paris, including the **Gare du Nord Buffalo Grill** (Map pp120-1; 01 40 16 47 81; 9 bd de Denain, 10e; M Gare du Nord). Not surprisingly, the emphasis here is on grills and steak – everything from Canadian buffalo burgers (€10.50) to a huge entrecôte 'cowboy steak' (€17.60).

The ever-expanding **Hippopotamus** (www.hippopotamus.fr, in French; starters €4.80-9.90, mains €11.50-24.50, menus €15.50-29.50; 11.45am-12.30am Sun-Thu, to 1am Fri & Sat) chain, which has 20 branches in Paris proper, specialises in solid, steak-based meals. Three of the outlets stay open to 5am daily, including the **Opéra Hippopotamus** (Map pp120-1; 01 47 42 75 70; 1 bd des Capucines, 2e; M Opéra).

Léon de Bruxelles (www.leon-de-bruxelles.com, in French; starters €5.30-9.90, mains €10.50-16, menus €11.20-15.90; 11.45am-11pm) focuses on one thing and one thing only: *moules* (mussels). Meal-size bowls of the meaty bivalves, served with chips and bread, start at just over €10. There are nine Léons in Paris, including **Les Halles Léon de Bruxelles** (Map pp126-7; 01 42 36 18 50; 120 rue Rambuteau, 1er; M Châtelet-Les Halles).

Chinese, especially av de Choisy, av d'Ivry and rue Baudricourt.

Louvre & Les Halles

The area between Forum des Halles (1er) and the Centre Pompidou (4e) is filled with scores of trendy restaurants, but few of them are particularly good and they mostly cater to tourists, both foreign and French. Streets lined with places to eat include rue des Lombards, the narrow streets north and east of Forum des Halles and pedestrians-only rue Montorgueil, a market street and probably your best bet for something quick.

Those in search of Asian food flock to rue Ste-Anne and other streets of Paris' so-called Japantown, which is just west of the Jardin du Palais Royal. There are also some good-value restaurants serving other Asian cuisine in the area.

FRENCH

Le Petit Mâchon (Map pp126-7; 01 42 60 08 06; 158 rue St-Honoré, 1er; M Palais Royal-Musée du Louvre; starters €7-12.50, mains €14-22; lunch & dinner Tue-Sun) An upbeat bistro with Lyon-inspired specialities convenient to the Louvre. Try the *saucisson de Lyon* (Lyon sausage) studded with pistachios.

Le Grand Colbert (Map pp120-1; 01 42 86 87 88; 2-4 rue Vivienne, 2e; M Pyramides; starters €10-21.50, mains €19.50-30, lunch menus €32-39, dinner menus €39; noon-3am) This former workers' *cafétéria* transformed into a fin-de-siècle showcase is more relaxed than many similarly restored restaurants and a convenient spot for lunch if visiting the *passages couverts* or cruising the streets late at night (last orders: 1am).

Chez la Vieille (Map pp126-7; 01 42 60 15 78; 1 rue Bailleul, 1er; M Louvre-Rivoli; starters €15-21, mains €18-25, lunch menus €23; lunch Mon-Fri, dinner to 9.45pm Mon, Tue, Thu & Fri) Seating 'At the Old Lady's' is on two floors, but don't expect a slot on the more rustic ground floor; that's reserved for regulars. The small menu reflects the size of the place but is universally sublime.

AMERICAN

Joe Allen (Map pp126-7; 01 42 36 70 13; 30 rue Pierre Lescot, 1er; M Étienne Marcel; starters €7.50-10.30, mains €15.50-26, lunch menus €13.90-22.50, dinner menus €18-22.50; noon-1am) An institution in Paris since 1972, Joe Allen is a little bit of New York in Paris. There's an excellent brunch (€19.50 to

€23.50) from noon to 4pm at the weekend. Ribs (€17) are a speciality.

ASIAN

Higuma (Map pp126-7; ☎ 01 58 62 49 22; 163 rue St-Honoré, 1er; Ⓜ Palais Royal-Musée du Louvre; dishes €7-12.50, menus €10-€11.50; ⏰ lunch & dinner) This very authentic, no-nonsense Japanese noodle shop offers incredible value, particularly for its location opposite the Comédie Française. Try the *gyoza* (dumplings) and the fried noodles with pork and vegetables.

Djakarta Bali (Map pp126-7; ☎ 01 45 08 83 11; 9 rue Vauvilliers, 1er; Ⓜ Louvre Rivoli; starters €10.50-14.50, mains €11-22; ⏰ dinner Tue-Sun) Run by the progeny of an Indonesian diplomat exiled when President Sukarno was overthrown in 1967, this place specialises in *rijstafel* (€20 to €45), 'rice table' feasts of between seven and 10 courses that just won't stop coming.

VEGETARIAN

Saveurs Végét'halles (Map pp126-7; ☎ 01 40 41 93 95; 41 rue des Bourdonnais, 1er; Ⓜ Châtelet; starters & salads €4.80-9.80, mains €11.20-17.20, lunch menus €9.80-15.30, dinner menus €15.30; ⏰ lunch & dinner Mon-Sat) This strictly vegan eatery offers quite a few mock-meat dishes such as *poulet végétal aux champignons* ('chicken' with mushrooms) and *escalope de seitan* (wheat gluten 'escalope'). No alcohol is served.

QUICK EATS

Scoop (Map pp126-7; ☎ 01 42 60 31 84; 154 rue St-Honoré, 1er; Ⓜ Palais Royal-Musée du Louvre; dishes €10.90-16.90; ⏰ 11am-7pm) This American-style ice-cream parlour has been making quite a splash for its excellent wraps, burgers, tarts and soups and central, very fashionable location. Sunday brunch (11.30am to 4pm) includes pancakes with maple syrup.

SELF-CATERING

There are several supermarkets around Forum des Halles, including the **Franprix Les Halles** (Map pp126-7; 35 rue Berger, 1er; Ⓜ Châtelet; ⏰ 8.30am-9.50pm Mon-Sat) and the **Franprix Châtelet** (Map pp126-7; 16 rue Bertin Poirée, 1er; Ⓜ Châtelet; ⏰ 8.30am-8pm Mon-Sat).

Marais & Bastille

The Marais, filled with small restaurants of every imaginable type, is one of Paris' premier neighbourhoods for eating out. In the direction of place de la République there's a decent selection of different ethnic cuisines. If you're looking for authentic Chinese food but can't be bothered going all the way to Chinatown in the 13e or Belleville in the 20e, check out any of the small noodle shops and restaurants along rue Au Maire, 3e (Map pp126–7; Ⓜ Arts et Métiers), which is southeast of the Musée des Arts et Métiers. The kosher and kosher-style restaurants along rue des Rosiers, 4e (Map pp126–7; Ⓜ St-Paul), the so-called Pletzl, serve specialities from North Africa, Central Europe and Israel. Many are closed on Friday evening, Saturday and Jewish holidays. Takeaway falafel and *shawarma* (kebabs) are available at several places along the street.

Bastille is another area chock-a-block with restaurants, some of which have added a star or two to their epaulets in recent years. Narrow rue de Lappe and rue de la Roquette, 11e (Map pp132–3), just east of place de la Bastille, may not be as hip as they were a dozen years ago, but they remain popular streets for nightlife and attract a young, alternative crowd.

FRENCH

Le Trumilou (Map pp126-7; ☎ 01 42 77 63 98; 84 quai de l'Hôtel de Ville, 4e; Ⓜ Hôtel de Ville; starters €4.50-13, mains €15-22, menus €16.50 & €19.50; ⏰ lunch & dinner) This no-frills bistro is a Parisian institution in situ for over a century. If you're looking for an authentic menu from the early 20th century and prices (well, almost) to match, you won't do better than this. The *confit aux pruneaux* (duck with prunes) and the *ris de veau grand-mère* (veal sweetbreads in mushroom cream sauce) are particularly good.

Robert et Louise (Map pp126-7; 01 42 78 55 89; 64 rue Vieille du Temple, 3e; Ⓜ St-Sébastien Froissart; starters €6-13, mains €12-18, lunch menus €12; ⏰ lunch & dinner Tue-Sat) This 'country inn', complete with its red gingham curtains, offers delightful, simple and inexpensive French food, including *côte de bœuf* (side of beef, €40 for two), which is cooked on an open fire and prepared by the original owners' daughter and her husband. It's a jolly, truly Rabelaisian evening.

L'Ambassade d'Auvergne (Map pp126-7; ☎ 01 42 72 31 22; 22 rue du Grenier St-Lazare, 3e; Ⓜ Rambuteau; starters €8-16, mains €14-22, lunch menus €20-28, dinner menus €28; ⏰ lunch & dinner) The 100-year-old 'Auvergne Embassy', is the place to go if you're really hungry; the sausages and hams of this region are among the best in France, as are the lentils from Puy and the sublime *clafoutis*, a custard and cherry tart baked upside down like a *tarte Tatin* (caramelised apple pie).

TO MARKET, TO MARKET

Paris counts about 70 *marchés découverts* (open-air markets) that pop up in public squares around the city two or three times a week and another dozen or so *marchés couverts* (covered markets) that keep more regular hours: 8am to 1pm and 3.30pm or 4pm to 7pm or 7.30pm from Tuesday to Saturday (till lunchtime on Sunday). Completing the picture are numerous independent *rues commerçantes,* pedestrian streets where shops set up outdoor stalls. To find out when there's a market near your hotel or hostel, ask the staff or anyone who lives in the neighbourhood.

The following are favourite Paris markets rated according to the variety of their produce, their ethnicity and the neighbourhood. They are the crème de la crème.

Marché Bastille (Map pp132-3; bd Richard Lenoir, 11e; Ⓜ Bastille or Richard Lenoir; 🕐 7am-2.30pm Tue & Sun) Stretching as far north as Richard Lenoir metro station, this is arguably the best open-air market in Paris with many more different national cuisines than ever before.

Marché Beauvau (Map pp134-5; place d'Aligre, 12e; Ⓜ Ledru Rollin; 🕐 8am-1pm & 4-7.30pm Tue-Sat, 8am-1pm Sun) This covered market is a colourful Arab and North African enclave just a stone's throw from the Bastille.

Marché Belleville (Map pp120-1; bd de Belleville btwn rue Jean-Pierre Timbaud & rue du Faubourg du Temple, 11e & 20e; Ⓜ Belleville or Couronne; 🕐 7am-2.30pm Tue & Fri) This market offers a fascinating entry into the large, vibrant communities of the *quartiers de l'est* (eastern neighbourhoods), home to immigrants from Africa, Asia and the Middle East.

Marché Grenelle (Map pp124–5; bd de Grenelle btwn rue de Lourmel & rue du Commerce, 15e; Ⓜ La Motte-Picquet Grenelle; 🕐 7am-2.30pm Wed & Sun) Below an elevated railway and surrounded by stately Haussmann boulevards and art-nouveau apartment blocks, the Grenelle market attracts a well-heeled clientele.

Marché St-Quentin (Map pp120-1; 85 bd de Magenta, 10e; Ⓜ Gare de l'Est; 🕐 8am-1pm & 3.30-7.30pm Tue-Sat, 8.30am-1pm Sun) This iron-and-glass covered market built in 1866 is a maze of corridors lined mostly with gourmet and upmarket food stalls.

Rue Cler (Map pp124-5; rue Cler, 7e; Ⓜ École Militaire; 🕐 8am-7pm Tue-Sat, 8am-noon Sun) This commercial street market is a breath of fresh air in the sometimes stuffy 7e and can almost feel like a party at the weekend, when the whole neighbourhood turns out en masse to squeeze and pinch, pay and cart away.

Rue Montorgueil (Map pp120-1; rue Montorgueil btwn rue de Turbigo & rue Réaumur, 2e; Ⓜ Les Halles or Sentier; 🕐 8am-7.30pm Tue-Sat, 8am-noon Sun) This buzzy market is the closest market to Paris' 700-year-old wholesale market, Les Halles, which was moved from this area to the southern suburb of Rungis in 1969.

Rue Mouffetard (Map pp130-1; rue Mouffetard around rue de l'Arbalète; Ⓜ Censier Daubenton; 🕐 8am-7.30pm Tue-Sat, 8am-noon Sun) Rue Mouffetard is the city's most photogenic market street – the place where Parisians send tourists (travellers go to Marché Bastille).

Le Petit Marché (Map pp132-3; ☎ 01 42 72 06 67; 9 rue de Béarn, 3e; Ⓜ Chemin Vert; starters €8-11, mains €15-25, lunch menus €14; 🕐 lunch & dinner) This great little bistro just up from the place des Vosges attracts a mixed crowd with its hearty cooking and friendly service. The salad starters are popular, as is the *brochette d'agneau aux épices doux* (spicy lamb brochette).

Bofinger (Map pp132-3; ☎ 01 42 72 87 82; 5-7 rue de la Bastille, 4e; Ⓜ Bastille; starters €8-18.50, mains €15.50-31.50, lunch menus €24-31.50, dinner menus €31.50; 🕐 lunch & dinner to 12.30am) Founded in 1864, Bofinger is reputedly the oldest brasserie in Paris and specialities include Alsatian-inspired dishes such as *choucroute* (sauerkraut with assorted meats; €18 to €20) and seafood dishes. Its polished art-nouveau brass, glass and mirrors are all stunning.

L'Alivi (Map pp126-7; ☎ 01 48 87 90 20; 27 rue du Roi de Sicile, 4e; Ⓜ St-Paul or Bastille; starters €9-16, mains €15-23, lunch menus €17-29, dinner menus €25-29; 🕐 lunch & dinner) The ingredients at this rather fashionable Corsican restaurant are always fresh and refined, with Brocciu cheese, *charcuterie* and basil featuring strongly on the menu. Try the Leccia wine with any dish to experience fully the pleasures of what the French call *l'île de beauté* (the beautiful island).

Auberge Nicolas Flamel (Map pp126-7; ☎ 01 42 71 77 78; 51 rue de Montmorency, 3e; Ⓜ Rambuteau or Arts et

Métiers; starters €9.50, mains €16.50, lunch menus €18.50-45, dinner menus €31-45; lunch & dinner Mon-Sat) This charming restaurant with higgledy-piggledy rooms on two floors was once the residence of celebrated alchemist and writer Flamel (1330–1417) and is the oldest building extant in Paris. Expect dishes that are correct but not earth-moving – duck foie gras, lamb cooked in a *tajine* and so on.

Le Temps au Temps (Map pp132-3; 01 43 79 63 40; 3 rue Paul Bert, 11e; M Faidherbe Chaligny; menus €30; lunch & dinner Tue-Sat) This tiny place with about 10 tables has a very exciting three-course menu that changes daily; some of the dishes have been inspired by the *cuisine récréative* (entertaining cuisine) of the great Catalan chef Ferran Adria. You're much more likely to get a seat at lunch.

NORTH AFRICAN & MIDDLE EASTERN

404 (Map pp126-7; 01 42 74 57 81; 69 rue des Gravilliers, 3e; M Arts et Métiers; starters €7-9, couscous & tajines €14-24, lunch menu €17, brunch menu €21; lunch Mon-Fri, dinner daily, brunch 10am-4pm Sat & Sun) As comfortable a Maghreb (North African) caravanserai as you'll find in Paris, the 404 not only has excellent couscous and *tajines* but superb grills (€12 to €22). You'll love the *One Thousand and One Nights* decor, but the tables are set too close to one another.

Le Souk (Map pp132-3; 01 49 29 05 08; 1 rue Keller, 11e; M Ledru Rollin; starters €7.50-13, mains €16-21, menus €20-27; lunch & dinner Tue-Sat) We like coming here almost as much for the decor as for the food – from the clay pots overflowing with spices on the outside to the exuberant but never kitsch Moroccan interior. And the food? As authentic as the decoration, notably the duck *tajine* and vegetarian couscous.

VEGETARIAN

Grand Apétit (Map pp132-3; 01 40 27 04 95; 9 rue de la Cerisaie, 4e; M Bastille or Sully Morland; soups €3-4, dishes €5-11; lunch Mon-Fri, dinner to 9pm Mon-Wed) This simple place near Bastille offers light fare such as miso soup and cereals, as well as strength-building *bols garnis* (bowls of rice and mixed vegetables) and *assiettes* (platters) for those with a, well, 'Big Appetite'.

La Victoire Suprême du Cœur (Map pp126-7; 01 40 41 95 03; 27-31 rue du Bourg Tibourg, 4e; M Châtelet; starters & salads €4-10, mains €14-17, menus €10.50-13.50; lunch & dinner Mon-Sat, brunch 11am-5pm Sun) A welcome addition to the hubbub of the Marais, this Indian-inspired vegan restaurant serves mock-meat dishes as well as *thalis*, a sampling tray of Indian goodies, for €15. For drinks try the mango lassi or spiced tea. Weekend brunch is €21.

OTHER CUISINES

Unico (Map pp132-3; 01 43 67 68 08; 15 rue Paul Bert, 11e; M Faidherbe Chaligny; starters €6.50-11, mains €20-26, lunch menus €19; lunch & dinner Tue-Sat) This very trendy, very orange Argentine *parillada* (steakhouse) has taken over an old butcher and put a modern (well, sort of 1970s, but it works) spin on it. It's all about meat here – especially the barbecued *entrecôte* (rib steak) with chunky *frites* (chips).

Le Petit Dakar (Map pp126-7; 01 44 59 34 74; 6 rue Elzévir, 3e; M St-Paul; starters €7, mains €13-15, lunch menus €15; lunch Tue-Sat, dinner Tue-Sun) Some people think this is the most authentic Senegalese restaurant in Paris, and with the delightful CSAO Boutique & Gallery just up the road, it does feel like a bit of West Africa has fallen onto a quiet Marais street.

Mai Thai (Map pp132-3; 01 42 72 18 77; 24bis rue St-Gilles, 3e; M Chemin Vert; starters €8-11, mains €13-15, lunch menus €13.50; lunch & dinner) This rather stylish place, done up in warm tones of orange, red and yellow and with Buddha figures scattered around, has gained a loyal following that comes for such *classiques de la cuisine du Siam* (classics of the cuisine of Siam) as chicken cooked with sacred basil and the unusual spicy Thai sausages.

Sardegna a Tavola (Map pp134-5; 01 44 75 03 28; 1 rue de Cotte, 12e; M Ledru Rollin; starters & pasta €10-26, mains €16-22; lunch Tue-Sat, dinner Mon-Sat) 'Sardinia at the Table' will introduce you to a little known but delightful Italian cuisine. Try the *poêlon* (pot) of mixed seafood cooked with parsley, tomatoes and garlic and the distinctly Sardinian spaghetti with *bottarga* (cured mullet roe) cooked with oil, garlic, parsley and red pepper flakes.

QUICK EATS

Crêpes Show (Map pp132-3; 01 47 00 36 46; 51 rue de Lappe, 11e; M Ledru Rollin; crêpes & galettes €3-9.80, lunch menus €8.90; lunch Mon-Fri, dinner to 1am Sun-Thu, to 2am Fri & Sat) Head for this unpretentious little restaurant for sweet crêpes and savoury buckwheat *galettes*. There are lots of vegetarian choices, including great salads from around €5.

L'As de Felafel (Map pp126-7; 01 48 87 63 60; 34 rue des Rosiers, 4e; M St-Paul; dishes €5-7; noon-midnight Sun-Thu, noon-5pm Fri) This has always been our favourite place for deep-fried balls of chick-peas and herbs (€6.50). It's always packed, particularly at weekday lunch, so avoid those times if possible.

Breakfast in America (Map pp126-7; ☎ 01 42 72 40 21; 4 rue Malher, 4e; Ⓜ St-Paul; meals €6.50-12; ⏰ 8.30am-11.30pm) This American-style diner, complete with red banquettes and Formica surfaces, is as authentic as you'll find outside the US of A. Breakfast, served all day and with free coffee refills, starts at €6.50, and there are generous burgers, chicken wings and fish and chips.

SELF-CATERING

Markets in the Marais and Bastille area include the incomparable (and open-air) **Marché Bastille** (p179).

In the Marais, there are a number of food shops and Asian delicatessens on the odd-numbered side of rue St-Antoine, 4e (Map pp132–3), as well as several supermarkets. Closer to Bastille there are food shops along rue de la Roquette (Map pp132–3; Ⓜ Voltaire or Bastille) towards place Léon Blum.

Supermarkets include the following:

Franprix Marais (Map pp126-7; 135 rue St- Antoine, 4e; Ⓜ St-Paul; ⏰ 9am-9pm Mon-Sat); Hôtel de Ville (Map pp126-7; 87 rue de la Verrerie, 4e; Ⓜ Hôtel de Ville; ⏰ 9.30am-9pm Mon-Sat)

Monoprix Marais (Map pp126-7; 71 rue St- Antoine, 4e; Ⓜ St-Paul; ⏰ 9am-9pm Mon-Sat); Bastille (Map pp132-3; 97 rue du Faubourg St-Antoine, 11e; Ⓜ Ledru Rollin; ⏰ 9am-9.45pm Mon-Sat).

The Islands

Famed more for its ice cream than dining options, Île St-Louis is a pricey place to eat, although there are a couple of fine places worth a brunch or lunchtime munch. As for Île de la Cité, forget it – eating spots are almost nonexistent and what's there is *touriste* city.

FRENCH

Les Fous de L'Île (Map pp126-7; ☎ 01 43 25 76 67; 33 rue des Deux Ponts, 4e; Ⓜ Pont Marie; starters €6.50-9, mains €14, lunch menus €15-25, dinner menus €19-25; ⏰ noon-11pm Tue-Sat, noon-7pm Sun) Innovative café-style dishes served from an open kitchen into a relaxed but arty setting ensure that this friendly, down-to-earth *salon de thé* and restaurant is always busy. It moonlights as an exhibition space.

Brasserie de l'Île St-Louis (Map pp126-7; ☎ 01 43 54 02 59; 55 quai de Bourbon, 4e; Ⓜ Pont Marie; starters €10-15, mains €17.50; ⏰ 6pm-1am Thu, noon-midnight Fri-Tue) Established in 1870, this brasserie enjoys a spectacular location on the Seine and serves standard brasserie favourites such as *choucroute garnie* (Alsatian dish of sauerkraut with sausage and other prepared meats), *jarret* (veal shank) and *onglet de bœuf* (prime rib of beef).

QUICK EATS

Berthillon (Map pp126-7; ☎ 01 43 54 31 61; 31 rue St-Louis en l'Île, 4e; Ⓜ Pont Marie; ice cream €2-5.40; ⏰ 10am-8pm Wed-Sun) Berthillon is to ice cream what Château Lafite Rothschild is to wine. While the fruit flavours (eg cassis) produced by this celebrated *glacier* (ice-cream maker) are justifiably renowned, the chocolate, coffee, *marrons glacés* (candied chestnuts), *Agenaise* (Armagnac and prunes), *noisette* (hazelnut) and *nougat au miel* (honey nougat) are even richer. Choose from among 70 flavours.

SELF-CATERING

On Île de St-Louis, there are a couple of *fromageries* (cheese shops) along rue St-Louis en l'Île, as well as the small supermarket **Le Prestige d'Alimentation** (67 rue St-Louis en l'Île, 4e; ⏰ 8am-10pm Wed-Mon) and **Boulangerie St-Louis** (80 rue St-Louis en l'Île, 4e).

Latin Quarter & Jardin des Plantes

From cheap-eat student haunts to chandelier-lit palaces loaded with history, the 5e has something to suit every budget and culinary taste. Rue Mouffetard is famed for its food market and food shops; while its side streets, especially pedestrianised rue du Pot au Fer, cook up some fine budget dining.

FRENCH

Le Petit Pontoise (Map pp130-1; ☎ 01 43 29 25 20; 9 rue de Pontoise, 5e; Ⓜ Maubert Mutualité; starters €8-13.50, mains €15-25; ⏰ lunch & dinner) This charming bistro offers a blackboard menu of seasonal delights. Regular dishes to look out for include old-fashioned classics like *rognons de veau à l'ancienne* (calf's kidneys), *boudin campagnard* (black pudding) and sweet apple purée or roast quail with dates.

Perraudin (Map pp130-1; ☎ 01 46 33 15 75; 157 rue St-Jacques, 5e; Ⓜ Luxembourg; starters €10-20, mains €15-30, lunch menus €19-29, dinner menus €29; ⏰ lunch & dinner Mon-Fri) Perraudin is a traditional French restaurant that hasn't changed much since 1910 when it first opened its doors. If you fancy classics such as *bœuf bourguignon* (beef marinated and cooked in young red wine with mushrooms, onions, carrots and bacon), *gigot d'agneau* (leg of lamb), *confit de canard* (preserved duck leg cooked very slowly in its own fat) or *flamiche* (leek pie from northern France), try this reasonably priced and atmospheric (if somewhat frayed) place.

L'AOC (Map pp130-1; ☎ 01 43 54 22 52; 14 rue des Fossés St-Bernard, 5e; Ⓜ Cardinal Lemoine; meals around €35; ⏲ lunch & dinner Tue-Sat) The concept here is AOC (Appellation d'Origine Contrôlée), meaning everything has been reared or made according to strict guidelines designed to protect a product unique to a particular village, town or area. The result? Only the best! Rare is the chance to taste *porc noir de Bigorre*, a type of black piggie bred in the Pyrénées.

NORTH AFRICAN & MIDDLE EASTERN

Kootchi (Map pp130-1; ☎ 01 44 07 20 56; 40 rue du Cardinal Lemoine, 5e; Ⓜ Cardinal Lemoine; mains €12, lunch menus €9.50-15.50, dinner menus €12.50-15.50; ⏲ lunch & dinner Mon-Sat) The welcome at this Afghan caravanserai is warm and the food, warming. Specialities include *qhaboli palawo* (veal 'stew' with nuts and spices); *dogh* (a drink not unlike salted Indian lassi); and traditional halva perfumed with rose and cardamom. Vegetarians keen to spice up their culinary life should plump for *borani palawo* (a spicy vegetable stew) as a main course.

La Mosquée de Paris (Map pp130-1; ☎ 01 43 31 38 20; 39 rue Geoffroy St-Hilaire, 5e; Ⓜ Censier Daubenton or Place Monge; mains €13.50-25; ⏲ lunch & dinner) The central Mosque of Paris (p147) has an authentic restaurant serving 11 types of couscous (€13 to €25) and 10 *tajines* (€15.50 to €17). There's also a North African–style **tearoom** (⏲ 9am-11.30pm) where you can enjoy peppermint tea (€2) and *pâtisseries orientales* (oriental pastries; €2).

VEGETARIAN

Les Cinq Saveurs d'Ananda (Map pp130-1; ☎ 01 43 29 58 54; 72 rue du Cardinal Lemoine, 5e; Ⓜ Cardinal Lemoine; dishes €13.90-14.90, menus €26.90; ⏲ lunch & dinner Tue-Sun) Set back from place de la Contrescarpe, this bright semivegetarian (it serves fish) restaurant is extremely popular among health-food lovers. All ingredients are fresh and guaranteed 100% organic. Decor is simple, refined and stylish.

QUICK EATS

Le Foyer du Vietnam (Map pp130-1; ☎ 01 45 35 32 54; 80 rue Monge, 5e; Ⓜ Place Monge; starters €3-6, mains €6-8.50, menus €8.20-12.20; ⏲ lunch & dinner Mon-Sat) The little 'Vietnam Club' is a favourite meeting spot among the capital's Vietnamese community and serves simple one-dish meals in medium and large portions. Try the 'Saigon' or 'Hanoi' soup (noodles, soy beans and pork flavoured with lemongrass, coriander and chives). Students can fill up for €7.

Sushi Wasabi (Map pp130-1; ☎ 01 44 07 06 88; 86 bd St-Germain, 5e; Ⓜ Maubert Mutualité; sushi €8-9.50, lunch menus €7; ⏲ 11.30am-10.30pm) It's hardly five-star, but at these prices who cares? This cheap and cheerful Japanese *traiteur* (caterer) serves pre-prepared sushi, *maki*, *futo-maki* etc and a good choice of hot meals to a quick-eat crowd.

Le Baba Bourgeois (Map pp130-1; ☎ 01 44 07 46 75; 5 quai de la Tournelle, 5e; Ⓜ Cardinal Lemoine or Pont Marie; mains €15-20; ⏲ lunch & dinner Wed-Sat, 11.30am-5pm Sun) This contemporary eating and drinking space slap bang on the Seine with a pavement terrace facing Notre Dame is a former architect's studio. Its imaginative *tartines* (open-face sandwiches), terrines, *tartes salées* (savoury tarts) and salads make for a simple, stylish bite any time of day. Sunday offers a splendid all-day buffet brunch, *à volonté* (as much as you can eat).

SELF-CATERING

Place Maubert, 5e, becomes the lively food market **Marché Maubert** (Map pp126–7) on Tuesday, Thursday and Saturday mornings. There's a particularly lively food market set out along **rue Mouffetard** (p179). On place Monge is the much smaller market, **Marché Monge** (Map pp130-1; place Monge, 5e; Ⓜ Place Monge; ⏲ 7am-2pm Wed, Fri & Sun).

Supermarkets in the area include the following:

Champion (Map pp130-1; 34 rue Monge, 5e; Ⓜ Place Monge; ⏲ 8.30am-9pm Mon-Sat)

Ed l'Épicier (Map pp130-1; 37 rue Lacépède, 5e; Ⓜ Place Monge; ⏲ 9am-1pm & 3-7.30pm Mon-Fri, 9am-7.30pm Sat)

Franprix (Map pp130-1; 82 rue Mouffetard, 5e; Ⓜ Censier Daubenton or Place Monge; ⏲ 8.30am-8.50pm Mon-Sat)

Monoprix (Map pp130-1; 24 bd St-Michel, 5e; Ⓜ St-Michel; ⏲ 9am-midnight Mon-Sat)

St-Germain, Odéon & Luxembourg

Rue St-André des Arts (Map pp126–7; Ⓜ St-Michel or Odéon) is lined with restaurants, including a few situated down the covered cour du Commerce Saint André. You'll find that there are lots of eateries between Église St-Sulpice and Église St-Germain des Prés as well, especially along rue des Canettes, rue Princesse and rue Guisarde. Carrefour de l'Odéon (Map pp126–7, Ⓜ Odéon) has a cluster of lively bars, cafés and restaurants. Place St- Germain des Prés itself is home to celebrated cafés such as Les Deux Magots and Café de Flore (p189), as well as the equally celebrated Brasserie Lipp.

FRENCH

Polidor (Map pp126-7; ☎ 01 43 26 95 34; 41 rue Monsieur le Prince, 6e; Ⓜ Odéon; starters €4.50-17, mains €11-22, menus €22-32; 🕒 lunch & dinner to 12.30am Mon-Sat, to 11pm Sun) A meal at this quintessentially Parisian *crémerie-restaurant* is like taking a quick trip back to Victor Hugo's Paris – the restaurant and its decor date from 1845 – but everyone knows about it and it's pretty touristy. Specialities include *bœuf bourguignon* (€11), *blanquette de veau* (veal in white sauce; €15) and the most famous *tarte Tatin* (€8) in Paris.

Bouillon Racine (Map pp130-1; ☎ 01 44 32 15 60; 3 rue Racine, 6e; Ⓜ Cluny-La Sorbonne; starters €7.50-14.50, mains €15.50-28, lunch menus €14.90-29, dinner menus €29; 🕒 lunch & dinner) This 'soup kitchen' built in 1906 to feed city workers is an art-nouveau palace. Oh, and the food? Wholly classic, inspired by age-old recipes such as roast snails, *caille confite* (preserved quail) and lamb shank with liquorice. Finish off your foray into gastronomic history with an old-fashioned sherbet.

Chez Allard (Map pp126-7; ☎ 01 43 26 48 23; 41 rue St-André des Arts; Ⓜ St-Michel; starters €8-20, mains €25, menus €25-34; 🕒 lunch & dinner Mon-Sat) One of our favourite places on the Left Bank is this positively charming bistro where the staff couldn't be kinder and more professional – even during its enormously busy lunchtime – and the food is superb. Try 12 snails, some *cuisses de grenouilles* (frogs' legs) or *un poulet de Bresse* (France's most legendary chicken, from Burgundy) for two. Enter from 1 rue de l'Éperon.

Brasserie Lipp (Map pp124-5; ☎ 01 45 48 53 91; 151 bd St-Germain, 6e; Ⓜ St-Germain des Prés; starters €10-15, mains €15.50-25; 🕒 noon-2am) The Lipp is a wood-panelled café-brasserie (1880) where politicians rub shoulders with intellectuals, editors and media moguls, and waiters in black waistcoats, bow ties and long white aprons serve such brasserie favourites as *choucroute garnie* (sauerkraut with sausage and other prepared meats) and *jarret de porc aux lentilles* (pork knuckle with lentils).

ASIAN

Indonesia (Map pp130-1; ☎ 01 43 25 70 22; 12 rue de Vaugirard, 6e; Ⓜ Luxembourg; mains €9-15, lunch menus €11.50-25, dinner menus €18-25; 🕒 lunch Mon-Fri, dinner daily) One of only a couple of Indonesian restaurants in town, this unimaginatively named eatery has all the old favourites – from an elaborate, nine-dish *rijstafel* (rice with side dishes) to *lumpia* (a type of spring roll), *rendang* (beef cooked in peanut and chilli sauce) and gado gado (vegetable salad with peanut sauce). Traditional decor, incense, and the gentle rhythm of the gamelan orchestra create a convincingly Indonesian atmosphere.

Yen (Map pp126-7; ☎ 01 45 44 11 18; 22 rue St-Benoît, 6e; Ⓜ St-Germain des Prés; mains €20-25, lunch menus €30-55, dinner menus €55; 🕒 lunch & dinner Mon-Sat) This Japanese eatery – the last word in minimalism, with its light-wood and charcoal-grey slate floor – is a favourite of resident Japanese and knowledgeable Parisian *gaijin* (non-Japanese). It has a real flair for *soba* (Japanese noodles) and tempura, and you shouldn't leave without trying the aubergine in miso.

QUICK EATS

Bar à Soupes et Quenelles Giraudet (Map pp126-7; ☎ 01 43 25 44 44; 5 rue Princesse, 6e; Ⓜ Mabillon; meals from €7.50; 🕒 10am-5pm Mon, 10am-5pm & 7-11.30pm Tue-Fri, 10am-11.30pm Sat) This soup and dumpling bar serves excellent soups that are packed with unusual combinations – pear and lychee, chestnut or cardoon maybe? – and traditional Lyonnais-style *quenelles* (pike-perch dumplings) topped with a sauce of your choice.

Cosi (Map pp126-7; ☎ 01 46 33 35 36; 54 rue de Seine, 6e; Ⓜ Odéon; sandwich menus €9-11; 🕒 noon-11pm) With sandwich names like Stonker, Tom Dooley and Naked Willi, Cosi (which, incidentally, is of New Zealand origin) could easily run for Paris' most imaginative sandwich maker. Classical music playing in the background and homemade Italian bread, still warm from the oven, only adds to Cosi's natural sex appeal.

SELF-CATERING

With the Jardin du Luxembourg nearby, this is the perfect area for putting together a picnic lunch. There is a large cluster of food shops on **rue de Seine** and **rue de Buci**, 6e (Map pp126–7; Ⓜ Mabillon). The renovated and covered **Marché St-Germain** (Map pp126-7; 4-8 rue Lobineau, 6e; Ⓜ Mabillon; 🕒 8.30am-1pm & 4-7.30pm Tue-Sat,

8.30am-1pm Sun), just north of the eastern end of Église St-Sulpice, has a huge array of produce and prepared food. Nearby supermarkets include the following:

Champion (Map pp126-7; 79 rue de Seine, 6e; Ⓜ Mabillon; 1-9pm Mon, 8.40am-9pm Tue-Sat, 9am-1pm Sun)

Monoprix (Map pp126-7; 50 rue de Rennes, 6e; Ⓜ St-Germain des Prés; 9am-10pm Mon-Sat)

Montparnasse

Since the 1920s the area around bd du Montparnasse has been one of the city's premier avenues for enjoying that most Parisian of pastimes: sitting in a café and checking out the scenery on two legs. Many younger Parisians, however, now consider the area somewhat démodé and touristy, which it is to a certain extent, and avoid it.

Montparnasse offers all types of eateries, especially traditional crêperies, because Gare Montparnasse is where Bretons arriving in Paris to look for work would disembark (and apparently venture no further). There are several at 18 and 20 rue d'Odessa (Map pp124–5) alone and another half-dozen or so around the corner on rue du Montparnasse.

FRENCH

La Coupole (Map pp124-5; ☎ 01 43 20 14 20; 102 bd du Montparnasse, 14e; Ⓜ Vavin; starters €6.50-20, mains €12.50-35, lunch menus €24.50-31.50, dinner menus €31.50; 8am-1am Sun-Thu, to 1.30am Fri & Sat) This 450-seat brasserie, which opened in 1927, has mural-covered columns painted by such artists as Brancusi and Chagall. Its dark-wood panelling and indirect lighting have hardly changed since the days of Sartre, Soutine, Man Ray and Josephine Baker. You can book for lunch, but you'll have to queue for dinner (and then there's always breakfast).

La Cagouille (Map pp124-5; ☎ 01 43 22 09 01; 10 place Constantin Brancusi, 14e; Ⓜ Gaîté; starters €11-15, mains €18-33, menus €26-42; lunch & dinner) Chef Gérard Allemandou, one of the best seafood cooks (and cookbook writers) in Paris, gets rave reviews for his fish and shellfish dishes at this café-restaurant opposite 23 rue de l'Ouest. The *menus* here are exceptionally good value.

Le Dôme (Map pp124-5; ☎ 01 43 35 25 81, 01 43 35 23 95; 108 bd du Montparnasse, 14e; Ⓜ Vavin; starters €12.50-25, mains €29-56; lunch & dinner to 12.30am) An art-deco extravaganza dating from the 1930s, Le Dôme is a monumental place for a meal, with the emphasis on the freshest of oysters, shellfish and fish dishes such as *sole meunière* (sole sautéed in butter and garnished with lemon and parsley).

SELF-CATERING

Opposite the Tour Montparnasse there's the outdoor **Boulevard Edgar Quinet Food Market** (Map pp124-5; bd Edgar Quinet; 7am-2pm Wed & Sat). Supermarkets convenient to the area include the following:

Atac (Map pp124-5; 55 av du Maine, 14e; Ⓜ Gaîté; 9am-10pm Mon-Sat)

Inno (Map pp124-5; 29-31 rue du Départ, 14e; Ⓜ Montparnasse Bienvenüe; 9am-9.50pm Mon-Fri, 9am-8.50pm Sat)

Étoile & Champs-Élysées

With few exceptions, eateries lining the touristy 'Avenue of the Elysian Fields' offer little value for money. However, restaurants in the surrounding areas can be excellent.

FRENCH

L'Étoile Verte (Map pp118-19; ☎ 01 43 80 69 34; 13 rue Brey, 17e; Ⓜ Charles de Gaulle-Étoile; starters €9-13, mains €13-22, lunch menus €14-18, dinner menus €18, menus with wine €25; lunch Mon-Fri, dinner daily) When one of us was a student in Paris (back when the glaziers were still installing the stained glass at Ste-Chapelle), this was the place for both Esperanto speakers (a green star is their symbol) and students in search of old French classics: onion soup, snails, rabbit. That may have changed a bit, but the lunch *menu* is still a great deal for this neighbourhood.

L'Ardoise (Map pp118-19; ☎ 01 42 96 28 18; 28 rue du Mont Thabor, 1er; Ⓜ Concorde or Tuileries; menus €33; lunch Tue-Sat, dinner Tue-Sun) This is a little bistro with no menu as such (*ardoise* means 'blackboard', which is all there is), the food – such as hare in black pepper and beef fillet with morels – is superb, and the three-course set menu offers excellent value. It's touristy, though.

ASIAN

Dragons Élysées (Map pp118-19; ☎ 01 42 89 85 10; 11 rue de Berri, 8e; Ⓜ George V; starters €8-12, mains €15-22; lunch menus €13.50-40, dinner menus €40; lunch & dinner) This mostly Chinese restaurant is a novelty. Below the tables and chairs perched on different levels and scattered about a large dining room is a glass floor below which various types of goldfish cavort. If you enjoy watching your dinner in action, then this is the place for you.

SELF-CATERING

Place de la Madeleine (M Madeleine) is the luxury food centre of one of the world's food capitals. Rue Poncelet and rue Bayen have some excellent food shops, including the incomparable **Fromagerie Alléosse** (p198). Supermarkets include the following:

Franprix Madeleine (Map pp118-19; 12 rue de Surène, 8e; M Madeleine; 8.30am-8pm Mon-Sat)

Monoprix Champs-Élysées (Map pp118-19; 62 av des Champs-Élysées, 8e; M Franklin D Roosevelt; 9am-midnight Mon-Sat)

Opéra & Grands Boulevards

The neon-lit bd Montmartre (M Grands Boulevards or Richelieu Drouot) and nearby sections of rue du Faubourg Montmartre (neither of which are anywhere near the neighbourhood of Montmartre) form one of the Right Bank's most animated café and dining districts. A short distance to the north there's a large selection of kosher Jewish and North African restaurants on rue Richer, rue Cadet and rue Geoffroy Marie, 9e, south of metro Cadet.

FRENCH

Chartier (Map pp120-1; ☎ 01 47 70 86 29; 7 rue du Faubourg Montmartre, 9e; M Grands Boulevards; starters €2.20-12.40, mains €6.50-16, menus with wine €20; lunch & dinner) A real gem for the budget traveller, Chartier is justifiably famous for its 330-seat belle-époque dining room, virtually unaltered since 1896, and its excellent-value menu. Reservations are not accepted and lone diners will have to share a table.

Le Roi du Pot au Feu (Map pp118-19; ☎ 01 47 42 37 10; 34 rue Vignon, 9e; M Havre Caumartin; starters €5-7, mains €17-20, menus €24-29; noon-10.30pm Mon-Sat) The typical Parisian bistro atmosphere adds to the charm of the 'King of Hotpots', but what you really want to come here for is a genuine *pot au feu*, a stockpot of beef, root vegetables and herbs stewed together, with the stock served as an entree and the meat and vegetables as the main course. No bookings.

Aux Deux Canards (Map pp120-1; ☎ 01 47 70 03 23; 8 rue du Faubourg Poissonnière, 10e; M Bonne Nouvelle; starters €5-14.50, mains €16-25, lunch menus €20; lunch Tue-Fri, dinner Mon-Sat) The name of this bistro – 'At the Two Ducks' – reflects much of the menu (there's everything from foie gras to *à l'orange*), but you'll find starters as diverse as mussels with leek and a salad of Jerusalem artichoke and sheep's cheese.

our pick **Bistrot du Sommelier** (Map pp118-19; ☎ 01 42 65 24 85; www.bistrotdusommelier.com; 97 bd Haussmann, 8e; M St-Augustin; starters €14-25, mains €22-32, lunch menus €32 & €39, incl wine €45 & €54, dinner menus incl wine €65, €80 & €110; lunch & dinner Mon-Fri) This is the place in Paris to head for if you are as serious about wine as you are about food. The whole point of this attractive eatery is to match wine with food, and owner Philippe Faure-Brac, one of the world's foremost sommeliers (p145) and a prolific author, is at hand to help. The best way to sample his wine-and-food pairings is on Friday, when a three-course tasting lunch with wine is €45 and a five-course dinner with wine is €70. The food, prepared by chef Jean-André Lallican, is hearty bistro fare, and surprisingly, not all the wines are French.

SELF-CATERING

Both av de l'Opéra and rue de Richelieu have several supermarkets, including a large one in the basement of **Monoprix Opéra** (Map pp118-19; 21 av de l'Opéra, 2e; M Pyramides; 9am-10pm Mon-Fri, 9am-9pm Sat).

Gare du Nord, Gare de l'Est & République

These areas offer all types of food but most notably Indian and Pakistani, which can be elusive elsewhere in Paris. There's a cluster of traditional brasseries and bistros around the Gare du Nord.

FRENCH

Julien (Map pp120-1; ☎ 01 47 70 12 06; 16 rue du Faubourg St-Denis, 10e; M Strasbourg St-Denis; starters €6.90-17, mains €16.70-39, menus €21.50-31.50; lunch & dinner to 1am) In the less-than-salubrious neighbourhood of St-Denis, Julien offers brasserie food that you wouldn't cross town for, but – *sacrebleu* – the decor and the atmosphere: it's an art-nouveau extravaganza perpetually in motion and a real blast to the past. Service is always excellent here, and you'll feel welcome at any time of day.

Le Chaland (Map pp120-1; ☎ 01 40 05 18 68; 163 quai de Valmy, 10e; M Louis Blanc; starters €7, mains €13-14, lunch menus €11.50; lunch & dinner to 11.30pm Mon-Fri, to 2am Sat & Sun) 'The Barge' is a pleasant *café du quartier* serving rock-solid favourites like *blanquette de veau* and *tartes salées* with the occasional leap into the 21st century with gigantic salads. It's one of the more approachable (and affordable) eateries on the Canal St-Martin.

Hôtel du Nord (Map pp120-1; ☎ 01 40 40 78 78; 102 quai de Jemmapes, 10e; Ⓜ Jacques Bonsergent; starters €7-14.50, mains €15-22, lunch menus €13.50; 🕑 lunch & dinner) On the opposite bank of the Canal St-Martin, this wonderful place is the setting for the eponymous 1938 film starring Louis Jouvet and Arletty, and the dining room and bar at the vintage venue feel as if they were stuck in a time warp, with their art-deco posters, zinc counter and old piano. The food is *correct* (adequate) if not mind-blowing; stick with basics like the jumbo hamburger (€16) and its trimmings and you'll be fine.

QUICK EATS

Krishna Bhavan (Map pp120-1; ☎ 01 42 05 78 43; 2 rue Cail, 10e; Ⓜ La Chapelle; dishes €1.50-7.50, menus €10.50; 🕑 lunch & dinner Tue-Sun) This is about as authentic an Indian vegetarian canteen as you'll find in an area that is rapidly overtaking Faubourg St-Denis as Paris' Little India. If in doubt as to what to order, ask for a *thali* (€7.50), a circular steel tray of samosas, dosas and other wrapped goodies.

Passage Brady (Map pp120-1; 46 rue du Faubourg St-Denis & 33 bd de Strasbourg, 10e; Ⓜ Château d'Eau; 🕑 lunch & dinner daily) This derelict covered arcade, which could easily be in Calcutta, has dozens of incredibly cheap Indian, Pakistani and Bangladeshi cafés offering excellent-value lunches (meat curry, rice and a tiny salad €5 to €9.50; chicken or lamb biriani €10.50 to €14.50; *thalis* €7 to €9.50). Dinner menus are from €12.50 to €24, but it must be said that most of the eateries here offer subcontinental food *à la française*.

SELF-CATERING

A covered market in this area is the extravagant **Marché St-Quentin** (p179).

Rue du Faubourg St-Denis (Map pp120-1; 10e, mStrasbourg St-Denis or Château d'Eau), which links bd St-Denis and bd de Magenta, is one of the cheapest places in Paris to buy food, especially fruit and vegetables; the shops at Nos 23, 27–29 and 41–43 are laden with produce. The street has a distinctively Middle Eastern air, and quite a few of the groceries offer Turkish, North African and subcontinental specialities.

There are two Franprix supermarkets convenient to the area:

Franprix Faubourg St-Denis (Map pp120-1; 7-9 rue des Petites Écuries, 10e; Ⓜ Château d'Eau; 🕑 9am-8.20pm Mon-Sat)

Franprix Magenta (Map pp120-1; 57 bd de Magenta, 10e; Ⓜ Gare de l'Est; 🕑 9am-8pm Mon-Sat)

Ménilmontant & Belleville

In the northern section of the 11e and into the 19e and 20e arrondissements, rue Oberkampf and its extension, rue de Ménilmontant (Map pp120–1), are popular with diners and denizens of the night, though rue Jean-Pierre Timbaud, running parallel to the north, is stealing some of their glory these days. Rue de Belleville and the streets running off it are dotted with Chinese, Southeast Asian and a few Middle Eastern places; bd de Belleville has some kosher couscous restaurants, most of which are closed on Saturday.

FRENCH

Chez Nénesse (Map pp132-3; ☎ 01 42 78 46 49; 17 rue Saintonge, 3e; Ⓜ Filles du Calvaire; starters €4-16, mains €10-18; 🕑 lunch & dinner Mon-Fri) The atmosphere at Chez Nénesse, an oasis of simplicity and good taste, is 'old Parisian café' and the dishes are prepared with fresh, high-quality ingredients. Lunchtime starters are €4 and plats du jour (daily specials) are €10 to €12.

Au Trou Normand (Map pp132-3; ☎ 01 48 05 80 23; 9 rue Jean-Pierre Timbaud, 11e; Ⓜ Oberkampf; starters €6-9.50, mains €8.50-14.50, lunch menus €12.50-15; 🕑 lunch & dinner) Even under a younger and more dynamic team 'The Norman Hole' remains the bargain-basement *cafétéria* of the 11e arrondissement. In keeping with the surrounds, the dishes served are simple and portions fairly generous.

Le Tire Bouchon (Map pp132-3; ☎ 01 47 00 43 50; 5 rue Guillaume Bertrand, 11e; Ⓜ St-Maur; starters €7-19, mains €15-18, lunch menus €12-25, dinner menus €17-25; 🕑 lunch Mon-Fri, dinner Mon-Sat) 'The Corkscrew' is a mock old-style bistro close to the flashy rue Oberkampf with a dozen tables arranged around a polished wooden bar. The *cassoulet confit* (casserole or stew with beans and meat) and *millefeuille de dorade* (sea bream in flaky pastry) will tickle your taste buds.

Le Clown Bar (Map pp132-3; ☎ 01 43 55 87 35; 114 rue Amelot, 11e; Ⓜ Filles du Calvaire; starters €7.50-10.50, mains €15-18, weekday/weekend lunch menus €15/18, dinner menus €25; 🕑 lunch & dinner to 1am Mon-Sat) A wonderful wine bar–cum-bistro next to the Cirque d'Hiver, the Clown Bar is like a museum, with its painted ceilings, mosaics on the wall, lovely zinc bar and circus memorabilia that touches on one of our favourite themes: the evil clown. The food is simple and unpretentious traditional French.

Le Villaret (Map pp132-3; ☎ 01 43 57 89 76; 13 rue Ternaux, 11e; Ⓜ Parmentier; starters €8.50-20, mains €18-35, lunch menus €23-28; 🕑 lunch Mon-Fri, dinner Mon-Sat) An excellent neighbourhood bistro serving very rich food, Le Villaret has diners coming from across Paris to sample the house specialities. Tasting menus can range from €50.

ASIAN

New Nioullaville (Map pp120-1; ☎ 01 40 21 96 18; 32 rue de l'Orillon, 11e; Ⓜ Belleville or Goncourt; starters €4.90-7.50, mains €9.80-19.50, menus €7-14; 🕑 lunch & dinner to 1am) This cavernous, 400-seat place tries to please all of the people all of the time. As a result the food is a bit of a mishmash – dim sum sits next to beef satay, as do scallops with black bean alongside Singapore noodles. Order carefully and you should be able to approach some authenticity.

Ossek Garden (Map pp120-1; ☎ 01 48 07 16 35; 14 rue Rampon, 11e; Ⓜ Oberkampf; starters €5-14, barbecues €16-18, lunch menus €9.50-12.50) This Korean place not far from place de la République has excellent barbecues as well as *bibimbap* (€12 to €18) – rice served in a sizzling pot topped with thinly sliced beef (or other meat) and cooked and preserved vegetables, then bound by a raw egg and flavoured with chilli-laced soybean paste.

Asianwok (Map pp120-1; ☎ 01 43 57 63 24; 63 rue Oberkampf, 11e; Ⓜ Parmentier; dishes €13.80-15.20, menus €18.50; 🕑 lunch & dinner Mon-Sat) We can't get enough of the wonderful stir-fries, big salads and ample platters served at this pan-Asian eatery that opened recently in an old vintage bar-café along trendy rue Oberkampf.

SELF-CATERING

Supermarkets in the area include **Franprix Jules Ferry** (Map pp120-1; 28 bd Jules Ferry, 11e; Ⓜ République or Goncourt; 🕑 8.30am-9pm Tue-Sun) and a **Franprix Jean-Pierre Timbaud** (Map pp120-1; 23 rue Jean-Pierre Timbaud, 11e; Ⓜ Oberkampf; 🕑 8.30am-9pm Mon-Sat, 9am-1.30pm Sun).

13e Arrondissement & Chinatown

With the new Simone de Beauvoir footbridge (p156) making Bercy footsteps away from the 13e, foodies are hot-footing it to Paris' Chinatown in search of authentic Asian food: av de Choisy, av d'Ivry and rue Baudricourt are the streets. Another wonderful district for an evening out is the Butte aux Cailles area (Map pp114–15), just southwest of place d'Italie. It's chock-a-block with interesting addresses.

FRENCH

Chez Gladines (Map pp114-15; ☎ 01 45 80 70 10; 30 rue des Cinq Diamants, 13e; Ⓜ Corvisart; starters €5-10, mains €8.50-11.50; 🕑 lunch & dinner to midnight Sun-Tue, to 1am Wed-Sat) This lively Basque bistro in the heart of the Buttes aux Cailles quarter serves enormous 'meal-in-a-bowl' salads (€6.80 to €9), as well as traditional Basque specialities such as *pipérade* (omelette with tomatoes and peppers) and *poulet basque* (chicken cooked with tomatoes, onions, peppers and white wine).

Le Temps des Cérises (Map pp114-15; ☎ 01 45 89 69 48; 18-20 rue de la Butte aux Cailles, 13e; Ⓜ Corvisart or Place d'Italie; starters €8-10, mains €10-21, lunch menus €14.50-22.50, dinner menus €22.50; 🕑 lunch Mon-Fri, dinner Mon-Sat) 'The Time of Cherries' (ie 'days of wine and roses' to English speakers), an easygoing restaurant run by a workers' cooperative for three decades, offers faithfully solid fare in a quintessentially Parisian atmosphere. Buy the *coton-bio* (organic cotton) T-shirt upon departure.

ASIAN

La Chine Masséna (Map pp114-15; ☎ 01 45 83 98 88; 18 av de Choisy, 13e; Ⓜ Porte de Choisy; soups & starters €4.10-11, mains €6.10-14) This enormous restaurant specialises in Cantonese and Chiu Chow cuisine. The dim sum here is especially good, and wait staff still go around with trolleys calling out their wares.

QUICK EATS

Fil'O'Fromage (Map pp114-15; ☎ 01 53 79 13 35; 12 rue Neuve Tolbiac, 13e; Ⓜ Bibliothèque; sandwiches €4.50-7, menus €14.50-15.50; 🕑 10am-7.30pm Mon-Wed, to 10.30pm Thu-Sat) This new *fromagerie* serves lunches and light meals throughout the day six days a week. Everything here involves cheese, including the *assiette froide* (cold plate) of three cheeses, three cold meats and salad and the *poêlons* (pots) of warm cheese.

Montmartre & Pigalle

The 18th arrondissement, where you will find Montmartre and the northern half of place Pigalle, thrives on crowds and little else. When you've got Sacré Cœur, place du Tertre and its portrait artists, and Paris literally at your feet, who needs decent restaurants? But that's not to say everything is a write-off in this well-trodden tourist area. You just have to pick and choose a bit more carefully.

FRENCH

Chez Toinette (Map p136; ☎ 01 42 54 44 36; 20 rue Germain Pilon, 18e; Ⓜ Abbesses; starters €6-9, mains €15-20; 🕑 dinner Tue-Sat) The atmosphere of this convivial restaurant, which has somehow managed to keep alive the tradition of old Montmartre in one of the capital's most touristy neighbourhoods, is rivalled only by its fine cuisine. Game lovers in particular won't be disappointed.

Le Café Qui Parle (Map p136; ☎ 01 46 06 06 88; 24 rue Caulaincourt, 18e; Ⓜ Lamarck Caulaincourt or Blanche; starters €7-14, mains €13.50-20, menus €12.50-17; 🕑 lunch & dinner Thu-Tue) 'The Talking Café' offers inventive, reasonably priced dishes prepared by owner-chef Damian Mœuf amid comfortable surroundings. We love the art on the walls. Brunch (€15) is served from 10am on Saturday and Sunday.

La Maison Rose (Map p136; ☎ 01 42 57 66 75; 2 rue de l'Abreuvoir, 18e; Ⓜ Lamarck Caulaincourt; starters €7.20-13, mains €14.50-16.50, menus €16.50; 🕑 lunch & dinner daily Mar-Oct, lunch & dinner to 9pm Thu-Mon Nov-Feb). Looking for the quintessential Montmartre bistro in a house that was the subject of a lithograph by Maurice Utrillo? Head for the tiny 'Pink House' just north of place du Tertre. It's not so much about food here but rather location, location, location.

La Mascotte (Map p136; ☎ 01 46 06 28 15; 52 rue des Abbesses, 18e; Ⓜ Abbesses; starters €8.50-11.50, mains €19-25, lunch menus €19.50-35, dinner menus €35; 🕑 lunch & dinner) The 'Mascot' is a small, unassuming spot much frequented by regulars who can't get enough of its seafood and regional cuisine. The big terrace is a delight in the warmer months.

SELF-CATERING

Towards place Pigalle there are lots of grocery stores, many of them open until late at night; try the side streets leading off bd de Clichy (eg rue Lepic). Heading south from bd de Clichy, rue des Martyrs, 9e (Map pp120–1), is lined with food shops almost all the way to metro Notre Dame de Lorette. Supermarkets in the area include the following:

8 à Huit (Map p136; 24 rue Lepic, 18e; Ⓜ Abbesses; 🕑 8.30am-10.30pm Mon-Sat)

Ed l'Épicier (Map p136; 6 bd de Clichy, 18e; Ⓜ Pigalle; 🕑 9am-9pm Mon-Sat)

DRINKING

In a country where eating and drinking are as inseparable as cheese and wine, it's inevitable that the line between bars, cafés and bistros is blurred at best. Practically every place serves food of some description, but those featured in this section are favoured, first and foremost, as happening places to drink – be it alcohol, coffee or tea.

Drinking alcohol here has never been cheap, but happy hour – sometimes extending to as late as 9pm – has brought the price of a pint of beer, a glass of wine or a cocktail down to pricey, rather than extortionate, levels. Bear in mind that drinking in Paris essentially means paying the rent for the space you are occupying. So it costs more sitting at tables than it does to stand, more on a fancy square than a backstreet, more in the 8e than in the 18e.

Louvre & Les Halles

Le Fumoir (Map pp126-7; ☎ 01 42 92 00 24; 6 rue de l'Amiral Coligny, 1er; Ⓜ Louvre-Rivoli; 🕑 11am-2am) The 'Smoking Room' is a huge, very stylish colonial-style bar-café just opposite the Louvre. It's a fine place to sip top-notch gin from quality glassware while nibbling on olives; during happy hour (6pm to 8pm) cocktails, usually €8.50 to €11, drop to €6.

L'Imprévu (Map pp126-7; ☎ 01 42 78 23 50; 9 rue Quincampoix, 4e; Ⓜ Rambuteau; 🕑 1pm-2am Sun, noon-2am Tue-Sat) 'The Unexpected', something of an oasis in the busy Les Halles area, is a relatively inexpensive and gay-friendly bar, with mismatched furniture and a relaxed charm. It's popular with students.

Marais & Bastille

Au Petit Fer à Cheval (Map pp126-7; ☎ 01 42 72 47 47; 30 rue Vieille du Temple, 4e; Ⓜ Hôtel de Ville or St-Paul; 🕑 9am-2am) The original horseshoe-shaped zinc counter (1903) leaves little room for much else here, but nobody seems to mind at this tiny and very genial bar overflowing with friendly regulars enjoying a drink or a sandwich (simple meals are served from noon to 1am).

Iguana Café (Map pp132-3; ☎ 01 40 21 39 99; 15 rue de la Roquette, 11e; Ⓜ Bastille; 🕑 3pm-5am) A contemporary, two-level backlit café-pub whose clientele is slipping progressively from 30-somethings to early-20s punters. We love the red, black and silver decor on two levels, and there's a DJ at the weekend, with themed nights twice a month.

La Perle (Map pp126-7; ☎ 01 42 72 69 93; 78 rue Vieille du Temple, 3e; Ⓜ St-Paul or Chemin Vert; 🕑 6am-2am Mon-Fri, 8am-2am Sat & Sun) This is where *bobos* (bohemian bourgeois types) come to slum it over *un rouge* (glass of red wine) until the DJ arrives and things liven up. We like the (for real) distressed look of the place and the locomotive over the bar.

L'Apparemment Café (Map pp132-3; ☎ 01 48 87 12 22; 18 rue des Coutures St-Gervais, 3e; Ⓜ St-Sébastien Froissart; ⏲ noon-2am Mon-Sat, 12.30pm-midnight Sun) Tucked not so 'apparently' behind the Musée Picasso at a merciful distance from the Marais shopping hordes, this tasteful haven looks and feels like a private living room, with wood panelling, leather sofas, scattered parlour games and dog-eared books.

Le Bistrot du Peintre (Map pp132-3; ☎ 01 47 00 34 39; 116 av Ledru-Rollin, 11e; Ⓜ Bastille; ⏲ 8am-2am) This lovely belle-époque bistro and wine bar, with its 1902 art-nouveau bar, elegant terrace and spot-on service, is on our apéritif A-list – and that of local artists, *bobos* and local celebs.

Le Loir dans la Théière (Map pp126-7; ☎ 01 42 72 90 61; 3 rue des Rosiers, 4e; Ⓜ St-Paul; ⏲ 9.30am-7pm) The cutesy-named 'Dormouse in the Teapot' is a wonderful old space filled with retro toys, comfy couches and scenes of *Through the Looking Glass* on the walls. It serves up to a dozen different types of tea, excellent sandwiches and desserts like apple crumble (€8.50 to €12) and brunch at the weekend. Best time to find a table is about 4pm.

Le Pick Clops (Map pp126-7; ☎ 01 40 29 02 18; 16 rue Vieille du Temple, 4e; Ⓜ Hôtel de Ville or St-Paul; ⏲ 7am-2am Mon-Sat, 8am-2am Sun) This retro café-bar – all shades of blue and lit by neon – has Formica tables, ancient bar stools and plenty of mirrors. Attracting a friendly flow of locals and passers-by, it's a great place for morning or afternoon coffee, or that last drink. Try the rum punch.

Latin Quarter & Jardin des Plantes

Le Piano Vache (Map pp130-1; ☎ 01 46 33 75 03; 8 rue Laplace, 5e; Ⓜ Maubert Mutualité; ⏲ noon-2am Mon-Fri, 9pm-2am Sat & Sun) Just down the hill from the Panthéon, the 'Mean Piano' is covered in old posters and couches and drenched in 1970s and '80s rock ambience. Effortlessly underground and a huge favourite with students, it has bands and DJs playing mainly rock, plus some goth, reggae and pop.

Le Pub St-Hilaire (Map pp130-1; www.pubsthilaire.com; 2 rue Valette, 5e; Ⓜ Maubert Mutualité; ⏲ 11am-2am Mon-Thu, 11am-4am Fri, 4pm-4am Sat, 3pm-midnight Sun) 'Buzzing' fails to do justice to the pulsating vibe inside this student-loved pub. Generous happy hours last several hours, and a trio of pool tables, board games, music on two floors and various gimmicks to rev up the party crowd (a metre of cocktails, 'be your own barman', etc) keep the place packed.

St-Germain, Odéon & Luxembourg

La Palette (Map pp126-7; ☎ 01 43 26 68 15; 43 rue de Seine, 6e; Ⓜ Mabillon; ⏲ 8am-2am Mon-Sat) In the heart of 6e gallery land, this fin-de-siècle café and erstwhile stomping ground of Cézanne and Braque attracts a grown-up set of fashion people and local art dealers.

Le 10 (Map pp126-7; ☎ 01 43 26 66 83; 10 rue de l'Odéon, 6e; Ⓜ Odéon; ⏲ 5.30pm-2am) A local institution, this cellar pub groans with students, smoky ambience and cheap sangria. Posters adorn the walls, and an eclectic selection emerges from the jukebox – everything from jazz and the Doors to *chansons françaises* (traditional French songs; p192).

Le Comptoir des Canettes (Map pp126-7; ☎ 01 43 26 79 15; 11 rue des Canettes, 6e; Ⓜ Mabillon; ⏲ noon-2am Tue-Sat) In situ since 1952, a faithful local following pours into this cellar: a stuffy, atmospheric tribute to downtrodden romanticism complete with red tablecloths, melting candles and nostalgic photos of musicians.

Les Deux Magots (Map pp126-7; ☎ 01 45 48 55 25; www.lesdeuxmagots.fr; 170 bd St-Germain, 6e; Ⓜ St-Germain des Prés; ⏲ 7am-1am) This erstwhile literary haunt dates from 1914, although it's best known as the hang-out of Sartre, Hemingway, Picasso and André Breton. Everyone has to sit on the terrace here at least once and have a coffee or the famous hot chocolate served in porcelain jugs.

Montparnasse

The most popular places to while away the hours over a drink or coffee in Montparnasse are large café-restaurants like **La Coupole** (p184) and **Le Dôme** (p184) on bd du Montparnasse.

Cubana Café (Map pp124-5; ☎ 01 40 46 80 81; 47 rue Vavin, 6e; Ⓜ Vavin; ⏲ 11am-3am Sun-Wed, 11am-5am Thu-Sat) The perfect place to have cocktails and tapas (€3.70 to €7.10) before carrying on to the clubs of Montparnasse. A post-work crowd sinks into the comfy leather armchairs beneath oil paintings of everyday life in Cuba.

Le Rosebud (Map pp124-5; ☎ 01 43 35 38 54; 11bis rue Delambre, 14e; Ⓜ Edgar Quinet or Vavin; ⏲ 7pm-2am) Like the sleigh of that name in *Citizen Kane*, Rosebud harkens to the past. Enjoy an expertly mixed champagne cocktail or whisky sour amid the quiet elegance of polished wood and aged leather.

Opéra & Grands Boulevards

De la Ville Café (Map pp120-1; ☎ 01 48 24 48 09; 34 bd de Bonne Nouvelle, 10e; Ⓜ Bonne Nouvelle; ⏰ 11am-2.30am) This one-time brothel has an alluring, slightly confused mix of restored history (original mosaic tiles, distressed walls) and modern design. DJs play most nights, making it a quality 'before' venue for warming up before heading for the clubs.

Harry's New York Bar (Map pp118-19; ☎ 01 42 61 71 14; 5 rue Daunou, 2e; Ⓜ Opéra; ⏰ 10.30am-4am) One of the most popular American-style bars in the interwar years, Harry's manages to evoke a golden past without feeling like a museum piece. Lean upon the bar where F Scott Fitzgerald and Ernest Hemingway once drank and gossiped, and have the expert, white-smocked gentlemen prepare you a killer martini or the house creation: the Bloody Mary. The Cuban mahogany interior was brought over from a Manhattan bar in 1911. There's a basement piano bar with light jazz open in the evening.

Gare du Nord, Gare de l'Est & République

Ice Kube (Map pp120-1; ☎ 01 42 05 20 00; 1-5 passage Ruelle, 18e; Ⓜ La Chapelle; ⏰ 7pm-1.30am Wed-Sat, 2-11pm Sun) Every city worth its, err, salt has got to have an ice bar nowadays, and this *temple de glace* (ice temple) on the first floor of the *très boutique* Kube Hotel (p174) is the French capital's first. The temperature is set at -20°C, there are down jackets on loan and the bar is a shimmering block of carved ice.

our pick **Motown Bar** (Map pp120-1; ☎ 01 46 07 09 79; 81-83 bd de Strasbourg, 10e; Ⓜ Gare de l'Est; ⏰ 24hr except 1am-6pm Tue & Wed) This almost-24-hour place – it's open continuously except for two daytime gaps at the start of the week – is the venue of choice in the wee hours when you have a thirst and a few bob in your pocket but, alas, no friends. You can drink at almost any time of day and eat (mains €7.50 to €11.50) until 11pm; live singers croon on certain nights. There's a warm and festive feel, and the friendly staff and patrons will make Billy-No-Mates feel like he's got a friend or two.

Ménilmontant & Belleville

L'Autre Café (Map pp120-1; ☎ 01 40 21 03 07; 62 rue Jean-Pierre Timbaud, 11e; Ⓜ Parmentier; ⏰ 8am-2am) A young mixed crowd of locals, artists and party-goers remains faithful to this quality café with its long bar, spacious seating areas, relaxed environment, reasonable prices and art-exhibition openings.

On Cherche Encore (Map pp120-1; ☎ 01 49 20 79 56; 2 rue des Goncourt, 11e; Ⓜ Goncourt; ⏰ 11am-4pm Mon, 11am-2am Tue-Fri, noon-2am Sat) This relaxed, modern loft-style bar-café is trying to do it all and succeeding. The DJ spins quality tunes (electro, house and funk) from Thursday to Saturday, which leads to some quality mingling. The corner terrace is positioned for all-afternoon sun and is worth pouncing on.

Montmartre & Pigalle

La Fourmi (Map p136; ☎ 01 42 64 70 35; 74 rue des Martyrs, 18e; Ⓜ Pigalle; ⏰ 8am-2am Mon-Thu, 8am-4am Fri & Sat, 10am-2am Sun) A Pigalle stayer, 'The Ant' hits the mark with its lively yet unpretentious atmosphere. The decor is hip but not overwhelming, the zinc bar is long and inviting, the people laid-back, and the music mostly rock.

Le Dépanneur (Map p136; ☎ 01 44 53 03 78; 27 rue Pierre Fontaine, 9e; Ⓜ Blanche; ⏰ 10am-2am Mon-Thu, 24hr Fri-Sun) An American-style diner-cum-bar with postmodern frills and almost 24-hour service, 'The Repairman' has plenty of tequila and fancy cocktails (€7.50) and DJs after 11pm from Thursday to Saturday.

ENTERTAINMENT

A night on the town in Paris can mean anything from sipping Champagne on the Champs-Élysées or opening unmarked doorways in search of a new club in the *banlieues* (suburbs) to enjoying a Puccini production in the over-the-top surrounds of the Palais Garnier. From jazz cellars to comic theatres; garage beats to go-go dancers; avant-garde artists' squats to world-class symphonies, both home-grown and on tour, this is the place with entertainment choices to suit all budgets and tastes.

Listings

It's virtually impossible to sample the richness of Paris' entertainment scene without first studying *Pariscope* (€0.40) or *Officiel des Spectacles* (€0.35), both of which are in French, come out on Wednesday and are available at newsstands everywhere in the city. Rock, jazz, world and *chansons* (traditional French songs) are among the many genres covered by *Les Inrockuptibles* (www.lesinrocks.com, in French; €3), a national music zine with a strong (inevitably) Paris bias and great soirée and concert listings.

Of the surfeit of various French-language freebies, *À Nous Paris* (www.anous.fr/paris, in French) is among the most informed and posts its contents online; click 'Lieux Branchés' (Trendsetters) to find in-vogue bars, clubs and restaurants of the moment. The pocket-sized booklet *LYLO* (short for Les Yeux, Les Oreilles meaning 'eyes and ears'; www.lylo.fr, in French), freely available at bars and cafés, is a fortnightly low-down on the live music, concert and clubbing scene.

Booking Agencies

Buy tickets for concerts, theatre performances and other cultural events at *billetteries* (ticket offices) in **Fnac** (☎ 08 92 68 36 22; www.fnacspectacles.com, in French) or **Virgin Megastores** (☎ 08 25 12 91 39; www.virginmega.fr, in French). Both accept reservations by phone and the internet, and most credit cards. Tickets generally cannot be returned or exchanged unless a performance is cancelled.

Fnac Champs-Élysées (Map pp118-19; ☎ 01 53 53 64 64; 74 av des Champs-Élysées, 8e; Ⓜ Franklin D Roosevelt; 🕑 10am-midnight Mon-Sat, noon-midnight Sun)

Fnac Forum des Halles (Map pp126-7; ☎ 01 40 41 40 00; Forum des Halles shopping centre, Level 3, 1-7 rue Pierre Lescot, 1er; Ⓜ Châtelet-Les Halles; 🕑 10am-7pm Mon-Sat)

Fnac Musique Bastille (Map pp132-3; ☎ 01 43 42 04 04; 4 place de la Bastille, 12e; Ⓜ Bastille; 🕑 10am-8pm Mon-Sat)

Virgin Megastore Barbès (Map p136; ☎ 01 56 55 53 70; 15 bd Barbès, 18e; Ⓜ Barbès Rochechouart; 🕑 10am-9pm Mon-Sat)

Virgin Megastore Champs-Élysées (Map pp118-19; ☎ 01 49 53 50 00; 52-60 av des Champs-Élysées, 8e; Ⓜ Franklin D Roosevelt; 🕑 10am-midnight Mon-Sat, noon-midnight Sun)

Virgin Megastore Galerie du Carrousel du Louvre (Map pp126-7; ☎ 01 44 50 03 10; 99 rue de Rivoli, 1er; Ⓜ Palais Royal-Musée du Louvre; 🕑 10am-8pm Mon & Tue, to 9pm Wed-Sun)

DISCOUNT TICKETS

On the day of a performance, **Kiosque Théâtre Madeleine** (Map pp118-19; opp 15 place de la Madeleine, 8e; Ⓜ Madeleine; 🕑 12.30-8pm Tue-Sat, 12.30-4pm Sun) sells tickets at half price plus a commission of about €3. Seats available are almost always the most expensive ones in the stalls or 1st balcony. There's also **Kiosque Théâtre Montparnasse** (Map pp124-5; parvis Montparnasse, 15e; Ⓜ Montparnasse Bienvenüe) in Montparnasse between Gare Montparnasse and Tour Montparnasse, open the same hours.

The French-language websites www.billetreduc.com, www.ticketac.com and www.webguichet.com all have online discounts.

Live Music

ROCK, POP & INDIE

There's rock, pop and indie at bars, cafés and clubs around Paris, and a number of venues regularly host acts by international performers. It's often easier to see big-name Anglophone acts in Paris than in their home countries. The most popular stadiums or other big venues for international acts are the **Palais Omnisports de Paris-Bercy** (Map pp134-5; ☎ 08 92 39 01 00; www.bercy.fr, in French; 8 bd de Bercy, 12e; Ⓜ Bercy) in Bercy; the **Stade de France** (Map p209; ☎ 08 92 70 09 00; www.stadedefrance.fr, in French; rue Francis de Pressensé, ZAC du Cornillon Nord, St-Denis La Plaine; Ⓜ St-Denis-Porte de Paris) in St-Denis; and **Le Zénith** (Map pp114-15; ☎ 08 90 71 02 07; www.le-zenith.com, in French; 211 av Jean Jaurès, 19e; Ⓜ Porte de Pantin) at the Cité de la Musique in the Parc de la Villette, 19e. The most central venue (last seen: Material Girl Madge) is **L'Olympia** (Map pp118-19; ☎ 08 92 68 33 68; www.olympiahall.com; 28 bd des Capucines, 9e; Ⓜ Opéra).

La Cigale (Map p136; ☎ 01 49 25 89 99; www.lacigale.fr; 120 bd de Rochechouart, 18e; Ⓜ Anvers or Pigalle; admission €25-60) Now classed as a historical monument, this music hall dates from 1887 but was redecorated 100 years later by Philippe Starck. Having welcomed artists from Jean Cocteau to Sheryl Crow, today it prides itself on its avant-garde program, with rock and jazz concerts.

La Java (Map pp120-1; ☎ 01 42 02 20 52; www.la-java.fr; 105 rue du Faubourg du Temple, 10e; Ⓜ Goncourt; admission €5-24; 🕑 7.30pm-3am Tue-Thu, 11pm-6am Fri & Sat) The dance hall (1922) where Édith Piaf got her first break now reverberates with the sound of live salsa and other Latin music. From 8pm or 9pm until midnight there are concerts, including world music. Afterwards, DJs usually bring in a festive crowd dancing to electro, house, disco and Latin.

L'Élysée-Montmartre (Map p136; ☎ 01 44 92 45 47; www.elyseemontmartre.com; 72 bd de Rochechouart, 18e; Ⓜ Anvers; admission €15-45) A huge old music hall with a great sound system, this is one of the better venues in Paris for one-off rock and indie concerts. It opens for concerts at 6.30pm and hosts club events and big-name DJs at 11.30pm on Friday and Saturday.

Le Bataclan (Map pp132-3; ☎ 01 43 14 00 30; www.bataclan.fr, in French; 50 bd Voltaire, 11e; Ⓜ Oberkampf or St-Ambroise; admission €20-45) Built in 1864, this excellent small concert hall was Maurice Chevalier's debut venue in 1910 and today draws some French and international acts. It also masquerades as a theatre and dance hall.

CLASSICAL

The city hosts dozens of orchestral, organ and chamber-music concerts each week. In addition to the theatres and concert halls listed below, Paris' beautiful churches have much-celebrated organs and can be wonderful places to hear music. Many concerts don't keep to any fixed schedule, but are simply advertised on posters around town. Admission fees vary, but are usually from €20 for adults and half that for students.

Théâtre du Châtelet (Map pp126-7; ☎ 01 40 28 28 40; www.chatelet-theatre.com, in French; 1 place du Châtelet, 1er; Ⓜ Châtelet; concert tickets €10-60, opera €10-90, ballet €10-55; box office 🕑 11am-7pm) This central venue hosts concerts as well as operas, ballets and theatre performances. Tickets go on sale 14 days before the performance date; subject to availability, anyone aged under 26 or over 65 can get reduced-price tickets from 15 minutes before curtain time. The Sunday concerts at 11am (adult/under 26 year €23/12) are a popular fixture. There are no performances in July and August.

Salle Pleyel (Map pp118-19; ☎ 01 42 56 13 13; www.salle pleyel.fr; 252 rue du Faubourg St-Honoré, 8e; Ⓜ Ternes; concert tickets €10-85; 🕑 box office noon-7pm Mon-Sat, to 8pm on day of performance) Dating from the 1920s, this highly regarded hall hosts many of Paris' finest classical music recitals and concerts, including those by the celebrated Orchestre de Paris (www.orchestredeparis.com, in French).

JAZZ & BLUES

After WWII, Paris became Europe's most important jazz centre, and, niche as the style has since become, the city's best clubs and cellars still lure international stars – as does the wonderful Paris Jazz Festival (p164), in the Parc Floral, and Banlieues Bleues (p164), a jazz festival held in March and early April in St-Denis and other Parisian suburbs.

Le Baiser Salé (Map pp126-7; ☎ 01 42 33 37 71; www.le baisersale.com, in French; 58 rue des Lombards, 1er; Ⓜ Châtelet; admission free-€20) 'The Salty Kiss' is one of several jazz clubs on the same street. The *salle de jazz* (jazz hall) on the 1st floor has concerts of traditional jazz, Afro and Latin jazz, and jazz fusion. Combining big names and unknown artists, it is known for its relaxed vibe and its gift for discovering new talents. Music starts at 7pm and again at 10pm.

Le Caveau de la Huchette (Map pp126-7; ☎ 01 43 26 65 05; www.caveaudelahuchette.fr; 5 rue de la Huchette, 5e; Ⓜ St-Michel; admission Sun-Thu/Fri & Sat €11/13; 🕑 9.30pm-2.30am Sun-Wed, to 4am Thu-Sat) Housed in a medieval *caveau* (cellar) that was used as a courtroom and torture chamber during the Revolution, this club is where virtually all the jazz greats have played since the end of WWII. It's touristy, but the atmosphere can often be more electric than at the more serious jazz clubs. Sessions start at 10pm.

New Morning (Map pp120-1; ☎ 01 45 23 51 41; www .newmorning.com in French; 7-9 rue des Petites Écuries, 10e; Ⓜ Château d'Eau; admission €15-21; 🕑 8pm-2am) This is a highly regarded auditorium with excellent acoustics that hosts big-name jazz concerts as well as blues, rock, funk, salsa, Afro-Cuban and Brazilian music. Concerts take place three to seven nights a week at 9pm, with the second set ending at about 1am.

FRENCH CHANSONS

When French music comes to mind, most people hear accordions and *chansonniers* (cabaret singers) such as Édith Piaf, Jacques Brel, Georges Brassens and Léo Ferré. But although you may stumble upon buskers performing *chansons françaises* or playing *musette* (accordion music) in the market, it can sometimes be difficult to catch traditional French music in a more formal setting in Paris. Try these venues to hear it in traditional and modern forms.

Au Lapin Agile (Map p136; ☎ 01 46 06 85 87; www .au-lapin-agile.com; 22 rue des Saules, 18e; Ⓜ Lamarck Caulaincourt; adult €24, students except Sat €17; 🕑 9pm-2am Tue-Sun) This rustic cabaret venue in Montmartre was favoured by artists and intellectuals in the early 20th century, and *chansons* are still performed here and poetry read six nights a week starting at 9.30pm. Admission includes one drink.

Le Limonaire (Map pp120-1; ☎ 01 45 23 33 33; http:// limonaire.free.fr; 18 cité Bergère, 9e; Ⓜ Grands Boulevards; admission free; 🕑 7pm-midnight Mon, 6pm-midnight Tue-Sun) This little wine bar is one of the best places to listen to French *chansons* and other traditional French bistro music. The singers (who change regularly) perform on the small stage every night; the fun begins at 7pm on Sunday, 8.30pm on Monday and at 10pm Tuesday to Saturday. Simple meals (€8.50 to €11) are served.

Le Vieux Belleville (Map pp120-1; ☎ 01 44 62 92 66; www.le-vieux-belleville.com; 12 rue des Envierges, 20e; Ⓜ Pyrénées; admission free; ⏲ performances at 8.30pm Tue, Thu & Fri) This old-fashioned bistro at the top of Parc de Belleville is an atmospheric venue for performances of French *chansons* featuring accordions and an organ grinder three times a week. It serves classic bistro food at lunch Monday to Saturday and at dinner Tuesday to Saturday.

Clubs

Paris does not have a mainstream club scene like that found in London, Berlin or New York; the music, theme and crowd at most clubs changes regularly according to the whims of the moment, and the scene is extremely mobile. As a result, blogs, forums and websites (right) are the best ways to keep apace with what's happening. The best DJs and their followings have short stints in a certain venue before moving on, and the scene's hippest *soirées clubbing* (clubbing events) float between a clutch of venues – including the city's many dance-driven bars (p188).

But the beat is strong. Electronic music is of particularly high quality in Paris' clubs, with some excellent local house and techno. Funk and groove have given the whimsical predominance of dark minimal sounds a good pounding, and the Latin scene is huge; salsa dancing and Latin music nights pack out plenty of clubs. R & B and hip-hop pickings are decent, if less represented than in, say, London.

Club admission costs anything from €5 to €20 and often includes a drink; admission is usually cheaper before 1am and men can't always get in unaccompanied by a woman. Drink prices start at around €6/8 for a beer/mixed drink or cocktail but often cost more.

La Dame de Canton (Map pp114-15; ☎ 01 53 61 08 49, 06 10 41 02 29; www.damedecanton.com, in French; opp 11 quai François Mauriac, 13e; Ⓜ Quai de la Gare or Bibliothèque; admission €10; ⏲ 7pm-2am Tue-Thu, 7pm-dawn Fri & Sat) This floating *boîte* (club) aboard a three-masted Chinese junk hosts concerts (8.30pm) that range from pop and indie to electro, hip-hop, reggae and rock; afterwards DJs keep the young crowd moving.

La Favela Chic (Map pp120-1; ☎ 01 40 21 38 14; www.favelachic.com, in French; 18 rue du Faubourg du Temple, 10e; Ⓜ République; admission free-€10; ⏲ 8pm-2am Tue-Thu, to 4am Fri & Sat) The ambience is more *favela* (shantytown) than chic in this restaurant-bar-cum-dancehall, where Brazilians and French alike get down to the frenetic mix of traditional bossa nova, samba, *baile* (dance) funk and Brazilian pop.

DIGITAL CLUBBING

Track tomorrow's hot 'n' happening *soirée au feeling* with these finger-on-the-pulse Parisian nightlife links (in French).

- www.gogoparis.com (in English)
- www.lemonsound.com
- www.novaplanet.com
- www.parisbouge.com
- www.parissi.com
- www.radiofg.com
- www.tribudenuit.com

Le Balajo (Map pp132-3; ☎ 01 47 00 07 87; www.balajo.fr, in French; 9 rue de Lappe, 11e; Ⓜ Bastille; admission €12-18; ⏲ 10pm-2am Tue & Thu, 9pm-2am Wed, 11pm-5am Fri & Sat, 3-7.30pm Sun) A mainstay of Parisian nightlife since 1936, this ancient ballroom is devoted to salsa classes and Latin music during the week. Weekends see DJs spinning a very mixed bag of rock, disco, funk, R & B and house. While a bit lower-shelf these days, Le Balajo scores a mention for its historical value and its old-fashioned *musette* gigs on Sundays: waltz, tango and cha-cha for aficionados of retro tea-dancing.

Le Nouveau Casino (Map pp120-1; ☎ 01 43 57 57 40; www.nouveaucasino.net, in French; 109 rue Oberkampf, 11e; Ⓜ Parmentier; club admission €5-10, concerts €15-22; ⏲ 7.30pm-midnight or 2am Sun-Thu, to 5am Fri & Sat) 'The New Casino' has an eclectic program – electro, pop, deep house, rock – with both live music concerts and top DJs. Try to get there before everyone pours out of the surrounding bars at 2am.

Les Bains Douches (Map pp126-7; ☎ 01 48 87 01 80; www.lesbainsdouches.net, in French; 7 rue du Bourg l'Abbé, 3e; Ⓜ Étienne Marcel; admission €20; ⏲ 11pm-5am Wed-Sun) Housed in a refitted old *hammam* (Turkish bath), this darling of the 1990s has returned with a new mix of theme nights, Sunday morning 'afters' and gay soirées.

Point Éphémère (Map pp120-1; ☎ 01 40 34 02 48; www.pointephemere.org; 200 quai de Valmy, 10e; Ⓜ Louis Blanc; admission free-€14; ⏲ 10am-2pm) A relatively new arrival by the Canal St-Martin with some of the best electronic music nights in town. Once this self-proclaimed 'centre for dynamic artists' gets in gear, '*on y danse, on danse*' (you'll dance your arse off).

Social Club (Map pp120-1; ☎ 01 40 28 05 55; www.myspace.com/parissocialclub; 142 rue Montmartre, 2e; Ⓜ Grands Boulevards; admission free-€20; ⏰ 11pm-3am Wed & Sun, to 6am Thu-Sat) Once known as Triptyque, this vast and very popular club is set up in three underground rooms and fills something of a gap in inner-city clubbing. Musically they're on to it, with a serious sound system spanning electro, hip-hop and funk, as well as jazz and live acts.

Gay & Lesbian Venues

The Marais, especially those areas around the intersection of rue Ste-Croix de la Bretonnerie and rue des Archives and eastwards to rue Vieille du Temple, has been Paris' main centre of gay and lesbian nightlife for two decades. There are also a few bars and clubs within walking distance of bd de Sébastopol. Other venues are scattered throughout the city. The lesbian scene here is much less public than its gay male counterpart and centres on a few cafés and bars in the Marais.

3W Kafé (Map pp126-7; ☎ 01 48 87 39 26; www.3w-kafe.com, in French; 8 rue des Écouffes, 4e; Ⓜ St-Paul; ⏰ 5.30pm-2am) This glossy lesbian cocktail bar is the flagship venue on a street with several dyke bars. It's relaxed and elegant and there's no ban on men.

Amnésia (Map pp126-7; ☎ 01 42 72 16 94; www.amnesia-café.com; 42 rue Vieille du Temple, 4e; Ⓜ Hôtel de Ville; ⏰ 11am-2am) In the heart of the Marais, cosy Amnésia remains resolutely popular with gay guys but is more mixed than many of its counterparts. There's an attractive lounge area upstairs and a tiny dance floor in the *cave* (wine cellar) downstairs with DJ music from the 1980s and 1990s.

Le Cox (Map pp126-7; ☎ 01 42 72 08 00; www.cox.fr, in French; 15 rue des Archives, 4e; Ⓜ Hôtel de Ville; ⏰ noon-2am Mon-Fri, 1pm-2am Sat & Sun) This small gay bar has become *the* meeting place for an interesting (and maybe interested) and cruisy crowd throughout the evening from 6pm. OK, we don't like the in-your-face name either, but what's a boy to do?

Le Scarron (Map pp126-7; ☎ 01 42 77 44 05; www.lescarron.com; 3 rue Geoffroy l'Angevin, 4e; Ⓜ Rambuteau; ⏰ 10pm-6am Wed-Sat) This rather chic *bar de nuit* hots up as the evening progresses, especially in the vaulted basement. There's a rather subdued piano bar on the ground floor much more suited (key word) to quiet conversation.

Le Troisième Lieu (Map pp126-7; ☎ 01 48 04 85 64; www.letroisiemelieu.com, in French; 62 rue Quincampoix, 4e; Ⓜ Rambuteau; ⏰ 6pm-2am Tue-Sun) This friendly bar is a popular place for chic young lesbians and, at times, for everyone else. There's a large, colourful bar and big wooden tables at street level, with good-value canteen meals. The vaulted cellar below leaves space for dancing to DJs, rock/alternative music concerts and live singers.

Cinemas

Both *Pariscope* and *L'Officiel des Spectacles* (p190) list the full crop of Paris' cinematic pickings. Going to the cinema in Paris is not cheap: expect to pay up to €10 for a first-run film. Students, under 18s, and over 60s get discounted tickets (usually just under €6), except Friday night, all day Saturday and on Sunday matinees. Wednesday yields discounts for everyone.

Cinémathèque Française (Map pp134-5; ☎ 01 71 19 33 33; www.cinemathequefrancaise.com; 51 rue de Bercy, 12e; Ⓜ Bercy; adult/student/under 12yr €6/5/3; ⏰ box office noon-7pm Mon, Wed, Fri & Sat, noon-10pm Thu, 10am-8pm Sun) This national cultural institution is a veritable temple to the 'seventh art' and also sponsors cultural events, workshops and exhibitions. It always leaves its foreign offerings – often rarely screened classics – in their original language.

Theatre

Almost all of Paris' theatre productions, including those written in other languages, are performed in French. There are a few English-speaking troupes around, such as the celebrated Théâtre des Bouffes du Nord. For other English-language productions, look for ads on metro poster boards and in English-language periodicals such as *FUSAC* (p113), *Paris Times* and *Paris Where*, which are free at English-language bookshops, pubs and so on.

Comédie Française (Map pp126-7; ☎ 08 25 10 16 80; www.comedie-francaise.fr, in French; place Colette, 1er; Ⓜ Palais Royal-Musée du Louvre; tickets €5-37; box office ⏰ 11am-6pm) Founded in 1680 during the reign of Louis XIV, 'The French Comedy' theatre bases its repertoire around works of the classic French playwrights such as Molière, Racine and Corneille, though in recent years contemporary and even non-French works have been staged. Tickets for regular seats cost €11 to €37; tickets for the 65 places near the ceiling (€5) go on sale one hour before curtain time (usually 8.30pm) at the discount-ticket window around the corner from the main entrance, facing place André Malraux. This is also when those aged under 27 can purchase any of the better seats remaining for between €10 and €12 at the main box office. There are three venues within the Comédie Française:

Salle Richelieu The main venue on place Colette just west of the Palais Royal.

Studio Théâtre (Map pp126-7; ☎ 01 44 58 98 58; Galerie du Carrousel du Louvre, 99 rue de Rivoli, 1er; Ⓜ Palais Royal-Musée du Louvre; 🕒 box office 2-5pm Wed-Sun)

Théâtre du Vieux Colombier (Map pp124-5; ☎ 01 44 39 87 00; 21 rue du Vieux Colombier, 6e; Ⓜ St-Sulpice; 🕒 box office 11am-6pm)

Théâtre des Bouffes du Nord (Map pp120-1; ☎ 01 46 07 34 50; www.bouffesdunord.com, in French; 37bis bd de la Chapelle, 10e; Ⓜ La Chapelle; adult €12-24, students & under 25yr €10-20; box office 🕒 11am-6pm Mon-Sat) Perhaps best known as the Paris base of Peter Brooks' and Micheline Rozan's experimental troupes, this theatre in the northern reaches of the 10e and just north of the Gare du Nord also hosts works by other directors (eg Declan Donnellan, Stéphane Braunschweig, Krzysztof Warlikowski), as well as classical and jazz concerts.

Opera

Opéra National de Paris (ONP; ☎ 08 92 89 90 90; www.opera-de-paris.fr in French) The ONP splits its performance schedule between the Palais Garnier, its original home built in 1875, and the modern Opéra Bastille, which opened in 1989. Both opera houses also stage ballets and classical-music concerts performed by the ONP's affiliated orchestra and ballet companies. The season runs from September to July.

Opéra Bastille (Map pp132-3; 2-6 place de la Bastille, 12e; Ⓜ Bastille; opera €7-150, ballet €5-80, concert tickets €10-65; box office 🕒 10.30am-6.30pm Mon-Sat) Tickets are available from the box office at 130 rue de Lyon, 11e, some 14 days before the date of the performance. The cheapest opera seats are €7 and are only sold from the box office. Note, on the first day they are released, box office tickets can only be bought from the opera house at which the performance is to be held. At Bastille, standing-only tickets for €5 are available 1½ hours before performances begin. Just 15 minutes before the curtain goes up, last-minute seats at reduced rates (usually €20 for opera and ballet performances) are released to people aged under 28 or over 60.

Palais Garnier (Map pp118-19; ☎ 08 92 89 90 90; place de l'Opéra, 9e; Ⓜ Opéra; box office 🕒 11am-6.30pm Mon-Sat) Ticket prices and conditions (including last-minute discounts) at the city's original opera house are almost exactly the same as those at the Opéra Bastille.

Cabaret

Paris' risqué cabaret revues – those dazzling, pseudo-bohemian productions where the women wear two beads and a feather (or was it two feathers and a bead?) – are another one of those things that everyone sees in Paris except the Parisians themselves. But they continue to draw in the crowds as they did in the days of Toulouse-Lautrec and Aristide Bruant and can be a lot of fun. Times and prices vary with the seasons, but shows usually begin at 7pm or 7.30pm, 8.30 or 9pm, or 11pm, and some venues have matinees and additional evening shows at the weekend. Tickets cost anything from €65 to €120 per person (€140 to €400 with swish dinner and Champagne). All venues sell tickets online.

Crazy Horse (Map pp118-19; ☎ 01 47 23 32 32; www.lecrazyhorseparis.com; 12 av George V, 8e; Ⓜ Alma Marceau) This popular cabaret, whose dressing (or, rather, undressing) rooms were featured in Woody Allen's film *What's New Pussycat?* (1965), now promotes fine art – abstract 1960s patterns as they appear superimposed on the nude female form.

Le Lido de Paris (Map pp118-19; ☎ 01 40 76 56 10; www.lido.fr; 116bis av des Champs-Élysées, 8e; Ⓜ George V) Founded at the close of WWII, the Lido gets top marks for its ambitious sets and the lavish costumes of its 70 *artistes,* including the famed Bluebell Girls and now the Lido Boy Dancers.

Moulin Rouge (Map p136; ☎ 01 53 09 82 82; www.moulinrouge.fr; 82 bd de Clichy, 18e; Ⓜ Blanche) This legendary cabaret founded in 1889, whose dancers appeared in Toulouse-Lautrec's celebrated posters, sits under its trademark red windmill (actually a 1925 copy of the 19th-century original) and attracts viewers and voyeurs by the busload.

Sport

Parisians are mad about watching sport. For details of upcoming sporting events, consult the sports daily *L'Équipe* (www.lequipe.fr, in French) or *Figaroscope* (www.figaroscope.fr, in French), an entertainment and activities supplement published with *Le Figaro* daily newspaper each Wednesday. Branches of Fnac and Virgin Megastore (p191) sell tickets for bigger events.

FOOTBALL

France's home matches (friendlies and qualifiers for major championships) are held at the magnificent **Stade de France** (p208). Tickets cost anything between €20 and €100.

The city's only top-division football team, the red-and-blue-striped **Paris-St-Germain** (☎ 01 47 43 71 71; www.psg.fr), plays its home games at the 48,500-seat **Parc des Princes** (Map pp114-15; ☎ 32 75, 01 47 43 72 56; www.leparcdesprinces.fr; 24 rue du Commandant Guilbaud, 16e; Ⓜ Porte de St-Cloud; tickets €20-80; box office ⏲ 9am-7pm Mon-Fri & 3hr before match), built in 1970.

TENNIS

In late May/early June the tennis world focuses on the clay surface of the 16,500-seat **Stade Roland Garros** (Map pp114-15; ☎ 08 25 16 75 16, 01 47 43 52 52; www.rolandgarros.com, in French; 2 av Gordon Bennett, 16e; Ⓜ Porte d'Auteuil) in the Bois de Boulogne for the French Open, the second of the Grand Slam tournaments. Tickets are expensive and hard to come by; they go on sale in mid-November and bookings must usually be made by March. One week prior to the competition (on the first day of the qualifiers), remaining tickets are sold from the **box office** (☎ 08 25 16 75 16; ⏲ 9.30am-5.30pm Mon-Fri) at the stadium entrance.

The top indoor tournament is the Paris Tennis Open, which usually takes place sometime in late October or early November at the **Palais Omnisports de Paris-Bercy** (Map pp134-5; ☎ 01 40 02 60 60; www.bercy.fr, in French; 8 bd de Bercy, 12e; Ⓜ Bercy). Tickets are available from the **box office** (☎ 08 92 39 01 00, 01 46 91 57 57; ⏲ 11am-6pm Mon-Sat).

CYCLING

Since 1974 the final stage of the **Tour de France** (www.letour.fr), the world's most prestigious cycling event, has ended on the av des Champs-Élysées. The final day varies from year to year, but is usually the 3rd or 4th Sunday in July, with the race finishing sometime in the afternoon. If you want to see this exciting event, find a spot at the barricades before noon.

Track cycling, a sport at which France excels, is held in the velodrome of the Palais Omnisports de Paris-Bercy (above).

HORSE RACING

One of the cheapest ways to spend a relaxing afternoon in the company of Parisians of all ages and backgrounds is to go to the races. The most accessible of the Paris area's half-dozen racecourses is **Hippodrome d'Auteuil** (Map pp114-15; ☎ 01 40 71 47 47; www.france-galop.com; Champ de Courses d'Auteuil, 16e; Ⓜ Porte d'Auteuil), in the southeastern corner of the Bois de Boulogne. It hosts steeplechases six times monthly from February to late June or early July and then early September to early December. Standing on the lawn in the middle of the track is free, but a seat in the stands costs €3 or 4 (under 18 years free). Race schedules are published in almost all national newspapers. If you read French, pick up a copy of *Paris Turf* (€1.20), the horse-racing daily.

SHOPPING

Paris is a wonderful place to shop, whether you're in the market for a diamond-encrusted original Cartier bracelet or you're an impoverished *lèche-vitrine* (literally, 'window-licker') who just enjoys what you see from the outside looking in. From the ultrachic couture houses of av Montaigne and the cubby-hole boutiques of the Marais to the vast underground shopping centre at Les Halles and the flea-market bargains at St-Ouen, Paris is a city that knows how to make it, how to display it and how to charge for it.

Opening Hours

Opening hours for Paris shops are generally 10am to 7pm Monday to Saturday. Smaller shops often shut all day Monday; other days, their proprietors may simply close from noon to around 2pm for a long lunch. Many larger stores hold *nocturnes* (late nights) on Thursdays, remaining open until around 10pm. For Sunday shopping, the Champs-Élysées, Montmartre, the Marais and Bastille areas are the liveliest.

Winter *soldes* (sales) – during which many shops extend their hours – start mid-January; summer ones, in the second week of June.

Clothing & Fashion

HAUTE COUTURE & DESIGNER WEAR

Most of the major French couturiers and ready-to-wear designers have their own boutiques in the capital, but it's also possible to see labelled, ready-to-wear collections at major department stores such as Le Printemps, Galeries Lafayette and Le Bon Marché. The Right Bank, especially the so-called **Triangle d'Or** (Map pp118-19; Ⓜ Franklin D Roosevelt or Alma Marceau, 1er & 8e) formed by av Montaigne and av Georges V, **rue du Faubourg St-Honoré** (Map pp118-19; Ⓜ Madeleine or Concorde, 8e) and its eastern extension, **rue St-Honoré** (Ⓜ Tuileries), **place des Victoires** (Map pp120-1; Ⓜ Bourse or Sentier, 1er & 2e) and the Marais' **rue des Rosiers** (Map pp126-7; Ⓜ St-Paul, 4e), is traditionally the epicentre of Parisian fashion, though **St-Germain** (Map pp126-7; Ⓜ St-Sulpice or St-Germain des Prés) on the Left Bank can also claim a share of boutiques.

FASHION EMPORIA

There are fashion shops offering creations and accessories from a variety of cutting-edge designers.

Abou d'Abi Bazar (Map pp132-3; ☎ 01 42 77 96 98; 10 rue des Francs Bourgeois, 3e; Ⓜ St-Paul; 🕒 2-7pm Sun & Mon, 10.30am-7.15pm Tue-Sat) This fashionable boutique is a treasure trove of smart and affordable ready-to-wear pieces from young designers including Paul & Joe, Isabel Marant, Missoni and Antik Batik.

APC (Map pp126-7; ☎ 01 42 78 18 02; 112 rue Vieille du Temple, 3e; Ⓜ Chemin Vert; 🕒 11.30am-8pm) The focus of the Production and Creation Workshop is on simple lines and straight cuts for guys, though some pieces are more adventurous. It also has women's clothes.

Kiliwatch (Map pp126-7; ☎ 01 42 21 17 37; 64 rue Tiquetonne, 2e; Ⓜ Étienne Marcel; 🕒 11am-7.30pm Tue-Sat) A Parisian institution, Kiliwatch is always packed with hip guys and gals rummaging through rack after rack of new and used street wear and designs. There's a startling range of vintage goods including hats and boots, plus art/photography books, eyewear and the latest trainers.

L'Éclaireur (Map pp126-7; ☎ 01 48 87 10 22; 3ter rue des Rosiers, 4e; Ⓜ St-Paul; 🕒 11am-7pm Mon-Sat) You'll find John Galliano and Dries Van Noten rubbing shoulders with *objets* by Piet Hein Eek and Piero Fornasetti here. Part art space, part lounge and part deconstructionist fashion statement, this collection for women is known for having the next big thing first.

Department Stores

Paris has a number of *grands magasins* (department stores).

Galeries Lafayette (Map pp118-19; ☎ 01 42 82 34 56; 40 bd Haussmann, 9e; Ⓜ Auber or Chaussée d'Antin; 🕒 9.30am-7.30pm Mon-Wed, Fri & Sat, 9.30am-9pm Thu) A vast *grand magasin* in two adjacent buildings, Galeries Lafayette features a wide selection of fashion and accessories and the world's largest lingerie department. A fashion show (☎ 01 42 82 30 25 to book a seat) takes place at 3pm on Friday.

Le Bon Marché (Map pp124-5; ☎ 01 44 39 80 00; 24 rue de Sèvres, 7e; Ⓜ Sèvres Babylone; 🕒 9.30am-7pm Mon-Wed & Fri, 10am-9pm Thu, 9.30am-8pm Sat) Opened by Gustave Eiffel as Paris' first department store in 1852, 'The Good Market' (which also means 'bargain' in French) is less frenetic than its rivals across the Seine, but no less chic. Men's as well as women's fashions are sold.

Le Printemps (Map pp118-19; ☎ 01 42 82 57 87; 64 bd Haussmann, 9e; Ⓜ Havre Caumartin; 🕒 9.35am-7pm Mon-Wed, Fri & Sat, 9.35am-10pm Thu) 'The Spring' (as in the season) is actually three separate stores – one for women's fashion, one for men and one for beauty and household goods – offering a staggering display of perfume, cosmetics and accessories, as well as established and up-and-coming designer wear.

Flea Markets

Paris' *marchés aux puces* (flea markets) can be great fun if you're in the mood to browse for unexpected diamonds in the rough through all the *brocante* (second-hand goods) and bric-a-brac on display. Some new items are also available, and a bit of bargaining is expected.

Marché aux Puces de la Porte de Vanves (Map pp114-15; av Georges Lafenestre & av Marc Sangnier, 14e; Ⓜ Porte de Vanves; 🕒 7am-6pm or later Sat & Sun) The Porte de Vanves flea market is the smallest and, some say, friendliest of the big three. Av Georges Lafenestre has lots of 'curios' that aren't quite old (or curious) enough to qualify as antiques. Av Marc Sangnier is lined with stalls offering new clothes, shoes, handbags and household items.

Marché aux Puces de Montreuil (Map pp114-15; av du Professeur André Lemière, 20e; Ⓜ Porte de Montreuil; 🕒 8am-7.30pm Sat-Mon) Established in the 19th century, this flea market is renowned for its quality second-hand clothing and designer seconds. The 500 stalls also sell engravings, jewellery, linen, crockery, old furniture and appliances.

Marché aux Puces de St-Ouen (Map pp114-15; rue des Rosiers, av Michelet, rue Voltaire, rue Paul Bert & rue Jean-Henri Fabre, 18e; Ⓜ Porte de Clignancourt; 🕒 9am-6pm Sat, 10am-6pm Sun, 11am-5pm Mon) This vast flea market founded in the late 19th century and said to be Europe's largest. It has some 2500 stalls grouped into 10 *marchés* (market areas), each with its own speciality (eg Marché Serpette and Marché Biron for antiques, Marché Malik for second-hand clothing). There are rows and rows of 'freelance' stalls selling anything from used clothing and batteries to rusty tools and stolen mobile phones.

Food & Wine

The food and wine shops of Paris are legendary and well worth seeking out. Many places will vacuum pack or shrink-wrap certain food items to guard against spoilage.

Cacao et Chocolat (Map pp126-7; ☎ 01 46 33 77 63; 29 rue du Buci, 6e; Ⓜ Mabillon; 🕑 10.30am-7.30pm Mon-Sat, 11am-7pm Sun) This place is an exotic and contemporary take on chocolate, showcasing the cocoa bean in all its guises, both solid and liquid. The added citrus flavours, spices and even chilli are guaranteed to tease you back for more.

Fauchon (Map pp118-19; ☎ 01 70 39 38 00; 26 & 30 place de la Madeleine, 8e; Ⓜ Madeleine; 🕑 8.30am-7pm Mon-Sat) Paris' most famous caterer has a half-dozen departments in two buildings selling the most incredibly mouth-watering delicacies from *pâté de foie gras* and truffles to *confitures* (jams).

Fromagerie Alléosse (Map pp118-19; ☎ 01 46 22 50 45; 13 rue Poncelet, 17e; Ⓜ Ternes; 🕑 9.30am-1pm & 4-7pm Tue-Thu, 9am-1pm & 3.30-7pm Fri & Sat, 9am-1pm Sun) To our minds (and taste buds), this is the best cheese shop in Paris and worth a trip across town. Cheeses are sold as they should be: grouped and displayed in five main categories (p72).

Huilerie J Leblanc et Fils (Map pp126-7; ☎ 01 46 34 61 55; 6 rue Jacob, 6e; Ⓜ St-Germain des Prés; 🕑 11am-7pm Tue-Sat) The Leblanc family has made the smoothest of culinary oils from almonds, pistachios, sesame seeds, pine kernels, peanuts etc at its stone mill in Burgundy since 1878. You can taste before you buy.

Julien, Caviste (Map pp126-7; ☎ 01 42 72 00 94; 50 rue Charlot, 3e; Ⓜ Filles du Calvaire; 🕑 9.30am-1.30pm & 3.30-8.30pm Tue-Fri, 9.30am-8pm Sat) This independent wine store on hip rue Charlot focuses on small, independent producers and organic wines. The enthusiastic merchant Julien will locate, explain (and wax lyrical about) the wine for you, whatever your budget.

La Maison du Miel (Map pp118-19; ☎ 01 47 42 26 70; 24 rue Vignon, 9e; Ⓜ Madeleine; 🕑 9.30am-7pm Mon-Sat) In the sticky, very sweet business since 1898, 'The Honey House' stocks over 50 kinds of honey, with such obscure varieties as Corsican chestnut flower, Turkish pine and Tasmanian leatherwood.

Gifts & Souvenirs

Paris has a huge number of speciality shops offering gift items.

Anna Joliet (Map pp120-1; ☎ 01 42 96 55 13; passage du Perron, 9 rue de Beaujolais, 1er; Ⓜ Pyramides; 🕑 10am-7pm Mon-Sat) This wonderful (and minuscule) shop at the Jardin du Palais Royal specialises in music boxes, both old and new. Just open the door and see if you aren't tempted in.

Au Plat d'Étain (Map pp126-7; ☎ 01 43 54 32 06; 16 rue Guisarde, 6e; Ⓜ Mabillon; 🕑 11am-12.30pm & 2-7pm Tue-Sat) People do collect tin and lead soldiers as this fascinating boutique crammed with nail-size, hand-painted military soldiers, drummers, musicians, snipers and cavaliers attests. In business since 1775, the shop itself is practically a collectible.

Boutique Obut (Map pp132-3; ☎ 01 47 00 91 38; 60 av de la République, 11e; Ⓜ Parmentier; 🕑 10am-noon & 12.30-6.30pm Tue-Sat) For the guy who has *everything*, this is the Parisian mecca for fans of *pétanque* (or similar game of *boules*), a form of bowls played with heavy steel balls. They'll kit you out with all the equipment necessary to get a game going.

E Dehillerin (Map pp126-7; ☎ 01 42 36 53 13; 18-20 rue Coquillière, 1er; Ⓜ Les Halles; 🕑 9am-12.30pm & 2-6pm Mon, 9am-6pm Tue-Sat) Spread over two floors and dating back to 1820, E Dehillerin carries an incredible selection of professional-quality *matériel de cuisine* (kitchenware). You're sure to find something even the most well-equipped kitchen is lacking.

L'Agenda Modern (Map pp126-7; ☎ 01 44 54 59 20; 42 rue de Sévigné, 3e; Ⓜ St-Paul; 🕑 9.30am-4.30pm Mon-Fri) Subtitled 'The Shop of Days', this boutique sells handmade diaries beautifully bound in natural or dyed alligator or calf leather. And, fear not, they're bilingual, so the Monday morning blues will not read as *le blues du lundi matin*.

GETTING THERE & AWAY

For information on international air links to Paris, see p961. For information on the transport options between the city and Paris' airports, see opposite.

Air

Paris is served by Aéroport d'Orly and Aéroport Roissy Charles de Gaulle, both well linked by public transport to central Paris. More of a schlep is Aéroport Paris-Beauvais, which handles charter and some budget carriers.

AÉROPORT D'ORLY

Orly (ORY; off Map pp114-15; ☎ 39 50, 01 70 36 39 50; www.aeroportsdeparis.fr), the older and smaller of Paris' two major airports, is 18km south of the city. Its two terminals, Orly Ouest (Orly West) and Orly Sud (Orly South), are linked by a free shuttle-bus service that continues to/from the airport car parks and RER C station Pont de Rungis-Aéroport d'Orly (right); the Orlyval automatic metro links both terminals with the RER B station Antony (right).

AÉROPORT ROISSY CHARLES DE GAULLE

Roissy Charles de Gaulle (CDG; off Map pp114-15; ☎ 39 50, 01 70 36 39 50; www.aeroportsdeparis.fr), 30km northeast of Paris in the suburb of Roissy, consists of three terminal complexes, appropriately named Aérogare 1, 2 and 3, and two train stations served by commuter trains on RER line B3: Aéroport Charles de Gaulle 1 (CDG1), which serves terminals 1 and 3, and the sleek Aéroport Charles de Gaulle 2 (CDG2) for terminal 2. A free shuttle bus connects the terminals with the train stations.

AÉROPORT PARIS-BEAUVAIS

The international airport at **Beauvais** (BVA; off Map pp114-15; ☎ 08 92 68 20 66, 03 44 11 46 86; www.aeroportbeauvais.com), 80km north of Paris, is used by charter companies as well as Ryanair, Central Wings and various other budget airlines

Bus

DOMESTIC

Because French transport is biased in favour of the excellent state-owned rail system, Société Nationale des Chemins de Fer Français (SNCF), the country has extremely limited inter-regional bus services and no internal intercity bus services to or from Paris.

INTERNATIONAL

Eurolines (p963) links Paris with destinations in all parts of Western and Central Europe, Scandinavia and Morocco. The central **Eurolines office** (Map pp130-1; ☎ 01 43 54 11 99; www.eurolines.fr; 55 rue St-Jacques, 5e; Ⓜ Cluny-La Sorbonne; 🕑 9.30am-6.30pm Mon-Fri, 10am-1pm & 2-5pm Sat) takes reservations and sells tickets. The **Gare Routière Internationale de Paris-Galliéni** (Map pp114-15; ☎ 08 92 89 90 91; 28 av du Général de Gaulle; Ⓜ Galliéni), the city's international bus terminal, is in the eastern suburb of Bagnolet.

Train

SNCF (☎ 08 91 36 20 20, for timetables 08 91 67 68 69; www.sncf.fr) mainline train information is available round the clock.

Paris has six major train stations, each of which handles passenger traffic to different parts of France and Europe and also has a metro station bearing its name. For more information on the breakdown of regional responsibility of trains from each station, see the ferries and train map (p966).

Gare d'Austerlitz (Map pp134-5; bd de l'Hôpital, 13e; Ⓜ Gare d'Austerlitz) Spain and Portugal; Loire Valley and non-TGV trains to southwestern France (eg Bordeaux and Basque Country).

Gare de l'Est (Map pp120-1; bd de Strasbourg, 10e; Ⓜ Gare de l'Est) Luxembourg, parts of Switzerland (Basel, Lucerne, Zurich), southern Germany (Frankfurt, Munich) and points further east; regular and TGV Est trains to areas of France east of Paris (Champagne, Alsace and Lorraine).

Gare de Lyon (Map pp134-5; bd Diderot, 12e; Ⓜ Gare de Lyon) Parts of Switzerland (eg Bern, Geneva, Lausanne), Italy and points beyond; regular and TGV Sud-Est and TGV Midi-Méditerranée trains to areas southeast of Paris, including Dijon, Lyon, Provence, the Côte d'Azur and the Alps.

Gare Montparnasse (Map pp124-5; av du Maine & bd de Vaugirard, 15e; Ⓜ Montparnasse Bienvenüe) Brittany and places en route from Paris (eg Chartres, Angers, Nantes); TGV Atlantique Ouest and TGV Atlantique Sud-Ouest trains to Tours, Nantes, Bordeaux and other destinations in southwestern France.

Gare du Nord (Map pp120-1; rue de Dunkerque, 10e; Ⓜ Gare du Nord) UK, Belgium, northern Germany, Scandinavia, Moscow etc (terminus of the high-speed Thalys trains to/from Amsterdam, Brussels, Cologne and Geneva and Eurostar to London); trains to the northern suburbs of Paris and northern France, including TGV Nord trains to Lille and Calais.

Gare St-Lazare (Map pp118-19; rue St-Lazare & rue d'Amsterdam, 8e; Ⓜ St-Lazare) Normandy (eg Dieppe, Le Havre, Cherbourg).

GETTING AROUND

To/From the Airports

AÉROPORT D'ORLY

There is a surfeit of public-transport options to get to and from Orly airport. Apart from RATP bus 183, all services call at both terminals. Tickets for the bus services are sold on board.

Air France bus 1 (☎ 08 92 35 08 20; www.cars-airfrance.com; one-way/return €9/14; 30-45min; every 15min 🕑 6am-11.30pm from Orly, 5.45am-11pm from Invalides) This *navette* (shuttle bus) runs to/from

A MORE PERSONAL APPROACH

Public transport is straightforward and inexpensive to and from the airports. Pricier, door-to-door alternatives include **taxi** (around €40 to €50 between central Paris and Orly, €40 to €60 to/from Roissy Charles de Gaulle; €110 to €150 to/from Beauvais and about €60 between Orly and Roissy Charles de Gaulle; see p204 for taxi telephone numbers) or a private minibus shuttle such as **Allô Shuttle** (☎ 01 34 29 00 80; www.alloshuttle.com), **Paris Airports Service** (☎ 01 55 98 10 80; www.parisairportservice.com) or **PariShuttle** (☎ 01 53 39 18 18; www.parishuttle.com). Count on around €25 per person (€40 between 8pm and 6am) for Orly or Roissy Charles de Gaulle and €150 for one to four people to/from Beauvais. Book in advance and allow ample time for other pickups and drop-offs.

the eastern side of Gare Montparnasse (Map pp124–5; rue du Commandant René Mouchotte, 15e; Ⓜ Montparnasse Bienvenüe) as well as Aérogare des Invalides (Map pp124–5; Ⓜ Invalides) in the 7e. On the way to the city, you can ask to get off at metro stations Porte d'Orléans or Duroc to make other connections.

Jetbus (☎ 01 69 01 00 09; adult/under 5yr €5.70/free; 55min; every 15-25min 6.20am-11.10pm from Orly, 6.15am-10.30pm from Paris) Jetbus runs to/from metro Villejuif Louis Aragon (Map pp114–15), which is a bit south of the 13e on the city's southern fringe. From there a regular metro/bus ticket will get you into the centre of Paris.

Noctilien bus 31 (☎ 08 92 68 77 14, 08 92 68 41 14 in English; adult/4-9yr €6/3; 45min; every 60min 12.30am-5.30pm) Part of the RATP night service, Noctilien bus 31 links Gare de Lyon, Place d'Italie and Gare d'Austerlitz in Paris with Orly-Sud.

Orlybus (☎ 08 92 68 77 14; adult/4-11yr €6.10/3.05; 30min; every 15-20min 6am-11.50pm from Orly, 5.35am-11.25pm from Paris) This RATP bus runs to/from metro Denfert Rochereau (Map pp114–15), in the 14e and makes several stops in the eastern 14e.

Orlyval ☎ 08 92 68 77 14; adult/4-10yr €9.30/4.65; 35-40min; every 4-12min 6am-11pm) This RATP service links Orly with the city centre via a shuttle train and the RER (p203). An automated shuttle train runs between the airport and Antony RER station (eight minutes) on RER line B, from where it's an easy journey into the city; to get to Antony from the city (26 minutes), take line B4 towards St-Rémy-lès-Chevreuse. Orlyval tickets are valid for travel on the RER and for metro travel within the city.

RATP bus 183 (☎ 08 92 68 77 14; adult/4-9yr €1.50/0.75 or 1 metro/bus ticket; 1hr; every 35min 5.35am-8.35pm) This is a cheap but very slow public bus that links Orly-Sud (only) with Ⓜ Porte de Choisy (Map pp114-15), at the southern edge of the 13e.

RER C (☎ 08 90 36 10 10; adult/4-10yr €6/4.25; 50min; every 15-30min 5.30am-11.50pm) An Aéroports de Paris (ADP) shuttle bus links the airport with RER line C at Pont de Rungis-Aéroport d'Orly RER station. From the city, take a C2 train towards Pont de Rungis or Massy-Palaiseau. Tickets are valid for onward travel on the metro.

AÉROPORT ROISSY CHARLES DE GAULLE

Roissy Charles de Gaulle has two train stations: Aéroport Charles de Gaulle 1 (CDG1) and the sleek Aéroport Charles de Gaulle 2 (CDG2). Both are served by commuter trains on RER line B3. A free shuttle bus links all of the terminals with the train stations.

There is public transport between Aéroport Roissy Charles de Gaulle and Paris. Tickets for the bus are sold on board.

Air France bus 2 (☎ 08 92 35 08 20; www.cars-airfrance.com; one-way/return €13/18; 35-50min; every 15min 5.45am-11pm) Air France bus 2 links the airport with two locations on the Right Bank: near the Arc de Triomphe just outside 2 av Carnot, 17e (Map pp118–19; Ⓜ Charles de Gaulle-Étoile) and the Palais des Congrès de Paris (Map pp118–19; bd Gouvion St-Cyr, 17e; Ⓜ Porte Maillot).

Air France bus 4 (☎ 08 92 35 08 20; www.cars-airfrance.com; one-way/return €14/22; 45-55min; every 30min 7am-9pm from Roissy Charles de Gaulle, 6.30am-9.30pm from Paris) Air France bus 4 links the airport with Gare de Lyon (Map pp134–5; 20bis bd Diderot, 12e; Ⓜ Gare de Lyon) and with Gare Montparnasse (Map pp124–5; rue du Commandant René Mouchotte, 15e; Ⓜ Montparnasse Bienvenüe).

Noctilien buses 120, 121 & 140 (☎ 08 92 68 77 14, 08 92 68 41 14 in English; adult/4-9yr €7.50/3.75; every 60min 12.30am-5.30pm) Part of RATP's night service, Noctilien buses 120 and 121 link Montparnasse, Châtelet and Gare du Nord with Roissy Charles de Gaulle, and bus 140 links Gare du Nord and Gare de l'Est with the airport.

RATP bus 350 (☎ 08 92 68 77 14; adult/4-9yr €4.50/2.25 or 3 metro/bus tickets; 1hr; every 30min 5.45am-7pm) This public bus links Aérogares 1 & 2 with Gare de l'Est (Map pp120–1; rue du 8 Mai 1945, 10e; Ⓜ Gare de l'Est) and with Gare du Nord (Map pp120–1; 184 rue du Faubourg St-Denis, 10e; Ⓜ Gare du Nord).

RATP bus 351 (☎ 08 92 68 77 14; adult/4-9yr €4.50/2.25 or 3 metro/bus tickets; 1hr; every 30min 7am-9.30pm from Roissy Charles de Gaulle, 8.30am-8.20pm from Paris) This public bus links the eastern side of place de la Nation (Map pp114–15; av du Trône, 11e; Ⓜ Nation) with the airport.

RER B (☎ 08 90 36 10 10; adult/4-11yr €8.20/5.80; 30min; every 10-15min ⏰ 5am-midnight) RER line B3 links CDG1 and CDG2 with the city. To get to the airport, take any RER line B train whose four-letter destination code begins with E (eg EIRE), and a shuttle bus (every five to eight minutes) will ferry you to the appropriate terminal. Regular metro ticket windows can't always sell RER tickets as far as the airport so you may have to buy one at the RER station where you board.

Roissybus (☎ 08 92 68 77 14; €8.60; 45-60min; every 15min ⏰ 5.45am-11pm) This direct public bus links both terminals with rue Scribe (Map pp118–19; Ⓜ Opéra) behind the Palais Garnier in the 9e.

BETWEEN ORLY & ROISSY

Air France bus 3 (☎ 08 92 35 08 20; www.cars-airfrance.com, in French; adult/2-11yr €16/8; 1hr; every 30min 6am-10.30pm) This bus is free for connecting Air France passengers.

Orlyval (☎ 08 90 36 10 10; adult/4-10yr €9.30/4.65; 1hr, every 10-15min ⏰ 6am-11pm) RER line B connects stations CDG1 and CDG2 at Roissy-Charles de Gaulle and Antony station, from where the Orlyval automatic train links with the two terminals at Orly airport.

AÉROPORT PARIS-BEAUVAIS

The special **Express Bus** (☎ 08 92 68 20 64; €13; 1-1¼hr; ⏰ 8.05am-10.40pm from Beauvais, 5.45am-8.05pm from Paris) leaves **Parking Pershing** (Map pp118-19; 1 bd Pershing, 17e; Ⓜ Porte Maillot), just west of Palais des Congrès de Paris, three hours before Ryanair departures (you can board up to 15 minutes before) and leaves the airport 20 to 30 minutes after each arrival, dropping off just south of Palais des Congrès on Place de la Porte Maillot. Tickets can be purchased up to 24 hours in advance online (http://ticket.aeroportbeauvais.com), at the airport from **Ryanair** (☎ 03 44 11 41 41) or at a kiosk in the car park.

Bicycle

Two-wheeling has never been so good in the city of romance thanks to Vélib' (a crunching of *vélo*, meaning bike, and *liberté*, meaning freedom), a self-service bike scheme whereby you pick up a pearly-grey bike for peanuts from one roadside Vélib' station, pedal wherever you're going, and park it right outside at another.

A runaway success since its launch in 2007, **Vélib'** (☎ 01 30 79 79 30; www.velib.paris.fr; day/week/year subscription €1/5/29, bike hire per 1st/2nd/additional half-hr free/€2/4) has revolutionised how Parisians get around. Its more than 1500 *stations* across the city – one every 300m – sport 20-odd bike stands a head (at the last count there were 20,600 bicycles in all flitting around Paris) and are accessible around-the-clock.

To get a bike, you need a Vélib' account. One- and seven-day subscriptions can be done on the spot at any station with any major credit card, which must have a chip; as deposit you'll need to pre-authorise a direct debit of €150, all of which is debited if your bike is not returned/reported as stolen). If the station you want to return your bike to is full, swipe your card across the multilingual terminal to get 15 minutes for free to find another station. Bikes are geared to cyclists aged 14 and over, and are fitted with gears, antitheft lock with key, reflective strips and front/rear lights. Bring your own helmet!

For more information on cycling in Paris and a list of rental outlets where you can rent wheels for longer periods of time and guided bicycle tours, see p160.

Boat

A river shuttle called **Batobus** (☎ 08 25 05 01 01; www.batobus.com; adult/student/2-16yr 1-day pass €12/8/6, 2-day pass €14/9/7, 3-day pass €17/11/8; every 15-30min ⏰ 10am-9.30pm May-Aug, 10am-7pm Sep–mid-Nov & mid-Mar–Apr, 10.30am-4.30pm mid-Nov–mid-Dec & Feb–mid-Mar, 10.30am-5pm mid-Dec–Jan) docks at the following eight locations. You can jump on and off as you like.

Champs-Élysées (Map pp118-19; port des Champs-Élysées, 8e; Ⓜ Champs-Élysées Clemenceau)

Eiffel Tower (Map pp124-5; port de la Bourdonnais, 7e; Ⓜ Champ de Mars-Tour Eiffel)

Hôtel de Ville (Map pp126-7; quai de l'Hôtel de Ville, 4e; Ⓜ Hôtel de Ville)

Jardin des Plantes (Map pp130-1; quai St-Bernard, 5e; Ⓜ Jussieu)

Musée d'Orsay (Map pp124-5; quai de Solférino, 7e; Ⓜ Musée d'Orsay)

Musée du Louvre (Map pp126-7; quai du Louvre, 1er; Ⓜ Palais Royal-Musée du Louvre)

Notre Dame (Map pp126-7; quai Montebello, 5e; Ⓜ St-Michel)

St-Germain des Prés (Map pp126-7; quai Malaquais, 6e; Ⓜ St-Germain des Prés)

For pleasure cruises on the Seine, Canal St-Martin and Canal de l'Ourcq, see p163.

Car & Motorcycle

The quickest way of turning your stay in Paris into an uninterrupted series of hassles is to drive. If driving the car doesn't destroy your holiday sense of spontaneity, parking the darn thing certainly will. If you must drive, the fastest way to get across the city is usually via the bd Périphérique (Map pp114–15), the ring road that encircles the city.

RENTAL

You can get a small car (eg a Renault Twingo or Opel Corsa) for one day, without insurance and for 250km mileage, from around €80. Most of the larger companies listed below have offices at the airports and main train stations. Several are also represented at **Aérogare des Invalides** (Map pp124-5; Ⓜ Invalides) in the 7e.

Avis (☎ 08 02 05 05 05; www.avis.fr, in French)
Budget (☎ 08 25 00 35 64; www.budget.fr, in French)
Europcar (☎ 08 25 35 83 58; www.europcar.fr, in French)
Hertz (☎ 08 25 88 92 65; www.hertz.fr)
National Citer (☎ 08 25 16 12 12; www.citer.fr)
Sixt (☎ 08 20 00 74 98; www.sixt.fr, in French)

Smaller agencies can offer much more attractive deals. For a wider selection check the *Yellow Pages* (www.pagesjaunes.fr, in French) under 'Location d'Automobiles: Tourisme et Utilitaires'.

ADA (☎ 08 25 16 91 69; www.ada.fr, in French) 8e arrondissement (Map pp118-19; ☎ 01 42 93 65 13; 72 rue de Rome; Ⓜ Rome); 11e arrondissement (Map pp120-1; ☎ 01 48 06 58 13; 34 av de la République; Ⓜ Parmentier)
easyCar (www.easycar.com) Montparnasse (Map pp124-5; Parking Gaîté, 33 rue du Commandant René Mouchotte, 15e; Ⓜ Gaîté) Britain's budget car-rental agency hires cars at train stations and underground car parks and are fully automated systems; you must book in advance. All the forms are online and you must fill them out when you get to the easyCar branch.
Rent a Car Système (☎ 08 91 70 02 00; www.rentacar.fr, in French) 16e arrondissement (Map pp114-15; ☎ 01 42 88 40 04; 84 av de Versailles, 16e); Bercy (Map pp134-5; ☎ 01 43 45 98 99; 79 rue de Bercy, 12e; Ⓜ Bercy)

PARKING

In many parts of Paris you pay €1 to €3 an hour to park your car on the street. Large municipal parking garages usually charge between €1.70 and €2.80 an hour or €20 to €25 per 24 hours. Most are open 24 hours.

Parking fines are €11 to €35, depending on the offence and gravity, and parking attendants dispense them with great abandon. You pay them by purchasing a *timbre amende* (fine stamp) for the amount written on the ticket from any *tabac* (tobacconist), affix a stamp to the pre-addressed coupon and drop it in a postbox.

Public Transport

Paris' public transit system, mostly operated by the **RATP** (Régie Autonome des Transports Parisians; ☎ 32 46, 08 92 69 32 46; www.ratp.fr; 🕑 7am-9pm Mon-Fri, 9am-5pm Sat & Sun) is one of the cheapest and most efficient in the Western world.

Various transport maps are available for free at metro ticket windows. RATP's *Paris 1* provides plans of metro, RER, bus and tram routes in central Paris; *Paris 2* superimposes the same plans over street maps; and *Île-de-France 3* covers the area surrounding Paris. *Grand Plan Touristique* combines all three and adds tourist information. These can also be viewed and downloaded from the highly informative, comprehensive and useful RATP website.

BUS

Paris' bus system, operated by the RATP, runs between 5.45am and 12.30am Monday to Saturday. Services are drastically reduced on Sunday and public holidays (when buses run from 7am to 8.30pm) and from 8.30pm to 12.30am daily when a *service en soirée* (evening service) of 20 buses – distinct from the Noctilien overnight services – runs.

Night Buses

After the 'evening buses' have finished their last runs, some 42 Noctilien (www.noctilien.fr) night buses kick in, departing every hour between 12.30am and 5.30am. The buses serve the main train stations and cross the major arteries of the city before leading out to the suburbs; many go through Châtelet (rue de Rivoli and bd Sébastopol). Look for blue *N* or 'Noctilien' signs at bus stops. There are two circular lines within Paris (the N01 and N02) that link four main train stations, St-Lazare, Gare de l'Est, Gare de Lyon, Montparnasse (but not Châtelet), as well as popular nightspots such as Bastille, the Champs-Élysées, Pigalle and St-Germain.

Noctilien services are free if you have a Navigo pass, Mobilis or Paris Visite pass (opposite) for the zones in which you are travelling. Otherwise you pay a certain number of standard €1.50 metro tickets, depending on the length of your journey. Ask the driver how many you need to get to your destination.

Tickets & Fares

Short bus rides (ie rides in one or two bus zones) cost one metro/bus ticket (€1.50); longer rides require two. Transfer to other buses or the metro is not allowed on the same ticket. Travel to the suburbs costs up to three tickets. Special bus-only tickets can be purchased from the driver.

You must cancel *(oblitérer)* single-journey tickets in the *composteur* (cancelling machine) next to the driver. If you have a Navigo pass, Mobilis or Paris Visite pass (right), flash it as you board. Do not cancel the magnetic coupon that accompanies your pass.

METRO & RER

Paris' underground network, also run by the RATP, consists of two separate but linked systems: the Métropolitain, or *métro,* with 14 lines and 373 stations (one more will open in 2008 and another in 2010); and the RER (Réseau Express Régional), a network of suburban lines, designated A to E and then numbered, that pass through the city centre. When giving the names of stations in this book, the term 'metro' is used to cover both the Métropolitain and the RER system within Paris proper.

Metro

Each metro train is known by the name of its terminus. On maps and plans each line has a different colour and number (from 1 to 14). Nowadays Parisians refer to the line number.

Signs in metro and RER stations indicate the way to the platform for your line. The *direction* signs on each platform indicate the terminus. On lines that split into several branches (such as lines 3, 7 and 13), the terminus served by each train is indicated with backlit panels on the cars, and electronic signs on each platform give the number of minutes until the next train.

Signs marked *correspondance* (transfer) show how to reach connecting trains. At stations with many intersecting lines, such as Châtelet and Montparnasse Bienvenüe, the connection can seem interminable.

Different station exits are indicated by white-on-blue *sortie* (exit) signs. Get your bearings and choose the correct exit by checking the *plan du quartier* (neighbourhood map) posted at each exit.

The last metro train on each line begins its run sometime between 12.35am and 1.04am. The metro starts up again around 5.30am.

RER

The RER is faster than the metro, but the stops are much further apart. Some of Paris' attractions, particularly those on the Left Bank (eg the Musée d'Orsay, Eiffel Tower and Panthéon), can be reached far more conveniently by the RER than by metro.

RER lines have an alphanumeric combination – the letter (A to E) refers to the line, the number to the spur it follows out in the suburbs. Even-numbered lines generally head for Paris' southern or eastern suburbs while odd-numbered ones go north or west. All trains whose four-letter codes (indicated both on the train and on the light board) begin with the same letter share the same terminus. Stations served are usually indicated on electronic destination boards above the platform.

Tickets & Fares

The same RATP tickets are valid on the metro, the RER (for travel within the city limits), buses, the Montmartre funicular and Paris' three tram lines. A single ticket – now white in colour and called *un ticket t+* – costs €1.50; a *carnet* (book) of 10 is €11.10 (€5.55 for children aged four to 11 years). Tickets are sold at all metro stations. Ticket windows and vending machines accept most credit cards.

One metro/bus ticket lets you travel between any two metro stations – no return journeys – for a period of 1½ hours, no matter how many transfers are required. You can also use it on the RER for travel within zone 1. A single ticket can be used to transfer between buses and between buses and trams, but not from the metro to bus or vice versa.

Always keep your ticket until you exit from your station; you may be stopped by a *contrôleur* (ticket inspector) and will have to pay a fine (€25 to €45 on the spot) if you are found to be without a ticket or are holding an invalid one.

Tourist Passes

Mobilis and Paris Visite passes are valid on the metro, the RER, the SNCF's suburban lines (p204), buses, night buses, trams and the Montmartre funicular railway. They do not require a photo but you should write your card number on the ticket. Passes are sold at larger metro and RER stations, SNCF offices in Paris, and the airports.

The Mobilis card coupon allows unlimited travel for one day in two to six zones (€5.60 to €15.90; €4.55 to €13.70 for children aged four to 11 years). Buy it at any metro, RER or SNCF station in the region. Depending how many times you plan to hop on/off the metro in a day, a *carnet* might work out to be cheaper.

The Paris Visite pass allows the holder unlimited travel (including to/from airports) as well as discounted entry to certain museums and activities. They are valid for one, two, three or five consecutive days of travel in three, five or eight zones. The version covering one to three zones costs €8.50/14/19/27.50 for one/two/three/five days. Children aged four to 11 years pay €4.25/7/9.50/13.75.

Travel Passes

The cheapest and easiest way to use public transport in Paris is to get a combined travel pass that allows travel on the metro, RER and buses for a week, a month or a year. You can get passes for travel in two to eight urban and suburban zones but, unless you'll be using the suburban commuter lines extensively, the basic ticket valid for zones 1 and 2 should be sufficient.

The Navigo system (www.navigo.fr, in French), somewhat like London's Oyster cards, provides you with a refillable weekly, monthly or yearly pass that you can recharge at Navigo machines in most metro stations; you simply swipe the card across the electronic panel as you go through the turnstiles. Standard Navigo passes, available to anyone with an address in Paris, are free, but take up to three weeks to be issued; ask at the ticket counter for a form. Otherwise pay €5 for a Nagivo Découverte, issued on the spot but – unlike the Navigo pass – not replaceable if lost or stolen. Both passes require a passport photo and can be recharged for periods of one week or more.

Weekly tickets *(coupon hebdomadaire)* cost €16.30 for zones 1 and 2 and is valid from Monday to Sunday. It can be purchased from the previous Thursday until Wednesday; from Thursday, weekly tickets are available for the following week only. Even if you're in Paris for three or four days, it may work out to be cheaper than buying *carnets* and will certainly cost less than buying a daily Mobilis or Paris Visite pass (see above).

The monthly ticket (*coupon mensuel*; €53.50 for zones 1 and 2) begins on the first day of each calendar month; you can buy one from the 20th of the preceding month. Both are sold in metro and RER stations from 6.30am to 10pm and at some bus terminals.

TRAIN

Suburban Services

The RER and **SNCF commuter lines** (☎ 08 91 36 20 20, 08 91 67 68 69; www.sncf.fr) serve suburban destinations outside the city limits (ie zones 2 to 8). Buy your ticket *before* you board the train or you won't be able to get out of the station when you arrive. You are not allowed to pay the additional fare when you get there.

If you are issued with a full-size SNCF ticket for travel to the suburbs, validate it in a time-stamp pillar *before* you board the train. You may also be given a *contremarque magnétique* (magnetic ticket) to get through any metro/RER-type turnstiles on the way to/from the platform. If you are travelling on a Paris Visite or Mobilis pass, do *not* punch the magnetic coupon in one of SNCF's time-stamp machines. Most – but not all – RER/SNCF tickets purchased in the suburbs for travel to the city allow you to continue your journey by metro. For some destinations, a ticket can be purchased at any metro ticket window; for others you'll have to go to an RER station on the line you need in order to buy a ticket.

Taxi

Prise en charge (flag fall) in a Parisian taxi is €2.10. Within city limits, it costs €0.82 per kilometre between 10am and 5pm Monday to Saturday (*Tarif A*; white light on meter), and €1.10 per kilometre at 'night' (from 5pm to 10am), all day Sunday, and on public holidays (*Tarif B*; orange light on meter). Travel in the suburbs *(Tarif C)* costs €1.33 per kilometre.

There's a surcharge of €2.75 for taking a fourth passenger, but most drivers refuse to accept more than three people anyway for insurance reasons. The first piece of baggage is free; additional pieces over 5kg cost €1 extra, as do pickups from SNCF mainline stations.

To order a taxi, call Paris' **central taxi switchboard** (☎ 01 45 30 30 30; passengers with reduced mobility ☎ 01 47 39 00 91; 24hr). You can also call or book online through the following radio-dispatched taxi companies, on call 24 hours.

Alpha Taxis (☎ 01 45 85 85 85; www.alphataxis.com)
Taxis Bleus (☎ 01 49 36 29 48, 08 91 70 10 10; www.taxis-bleus.com)
Taxis G7 (☎ 01 47 39 47 39; www.taxisg7.fr, in French)

Around Paris

Paris is encircled by the Île de France, the 12,000-sq-km 'Island of France' shaped by five rivers: the Epte in the northwest, the Aisne (northeast), the Eure (southwest), the Yonne (southeast) and the Marne (east). The region was the 'seed' from which the kingdom of France grew, from about AD 1100. Today, excellent rail and road links between the French capital and the sights of this region and neighbouring *départements* make it popular with day trippers.

The Île de France boasts some of the nation's most beautiful and ambitious cathedrals. Closest to Paris is St-Denis, the last resting place for France's kings until the Revolution. Senlis has a magnificent Gothic cathedral said to have inspired the mother of all basilicas, the cathedral at Chartres, with its breathtaking stained glass and intricately carved stone portals.

The region also counts some of the nation's most extravagant châteaux. Foremost is the palace at Versailles, whose opulence was partly what spurred the Revolutionary mob to storm the Bastille in July 1789. The château at Fontainebleau is one of the most important Renaissance palaces in France, while the one at Chantilly is celebrated for its gardens and artwork.

But the Île de France is not stuck in the past. The modern cityscape of La Défense, just west of the city, stands in contrast to the Paris of legend and the imagination. And then there's every kid's favourite, Disneyland Resort Paris, which now has more attractions than ever.

HIGHLIGHTS

- Admire what is Europe's most important collection of funerary sculpture in the crypt of the **Basilique de St-Denis** (p208)
- Get behind the scenes – literally – at **Walt Disney Studios Park** (p210)
- Relive the glory that was the kingdom of France in the 17th and 18th centuries at the **Château de Versailles** (p211)
- Go for a walk, a cycle or even a climb at the Île de France's loveliest wood, the **Forêt de Fontainebleau** (p216)
- Wonder at the colour and richness of the 15th-century *Très Riches Heures du Duc de Berry* illuminated manuscript at the **Château de Chantilly** (p217)
- Get bluer than blue or look at the world through rose-coloured glass under one of the awesome stained-glass windows at the **Cathédrale Notre Dame de Chartres** (p220)

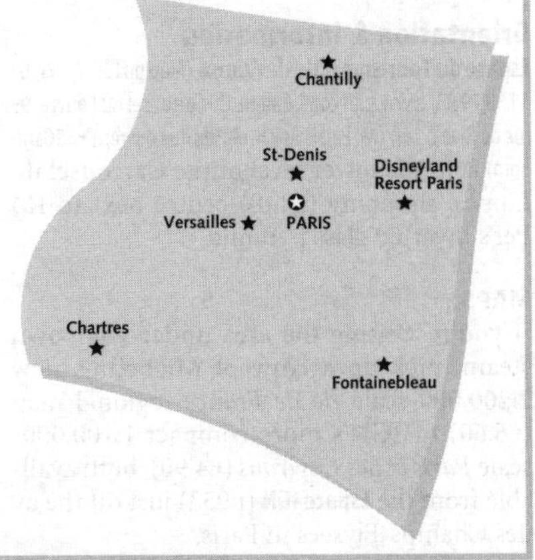

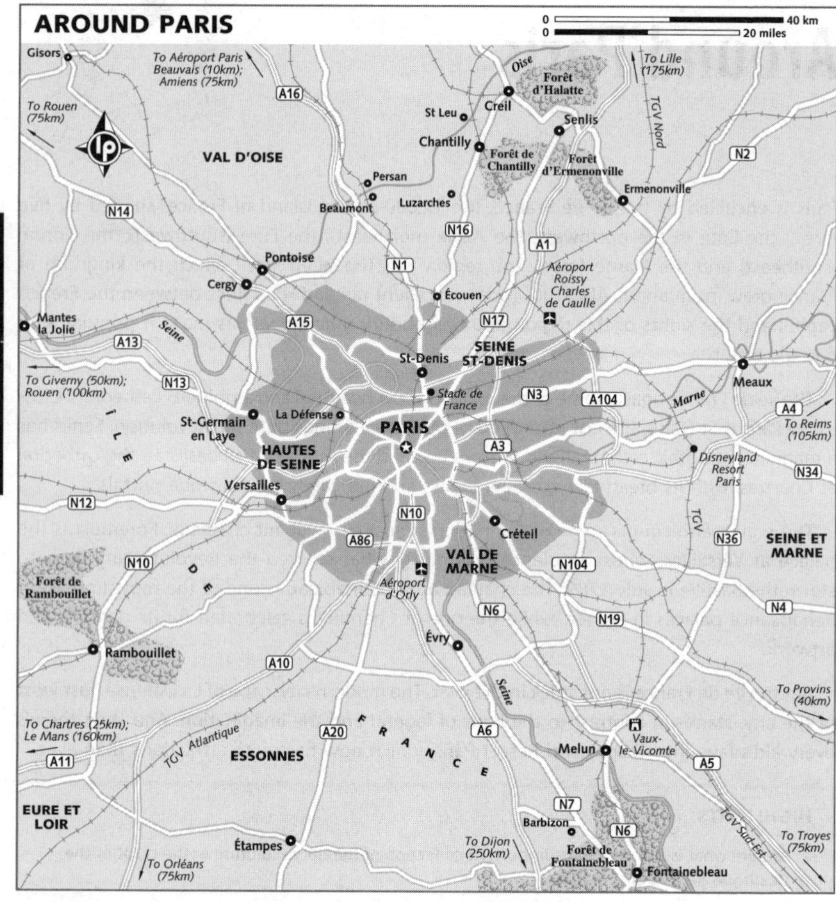

Orientation & Information

Espace du Tourisme d'Île de France (Map pp126-7; ☎ 01 44 50 19 98; www.pidf.com; Galerie du Carrousel du Louvre, 99 rue de Rivoli, 1er; Ⓜ Palais Royal-Musée du Louvre; 🕑 10am-6pm) is in the lower level of the Carrousel du Louvre shopping (p140) centre next to IM Pei's inverted glass pyramid.

MAPS

If you're visiting the area under your own steam, pick up a copy of Michelin's new 1:200,000-scale *Île de France* regional map (€6.60) or IGN's more compact 1:100,000-scale *Paris et Ses Environs* (€4.90), both available from the **Espace IGN** (p953) just off the av des Champs-Élysées in Paris.

LA DÉFENSE

pop 20,000

The ultramodern architecture of La Défense, Paris' skyscraper district on the Seine 3km west of the 17e arrondissement, is so strikingly different from the rest of centuries-old Paris that it's worth a brief visit to put it all in perspective. When development of the 750-hectare site began in the late 1950s, it was one of the world's most ambitious civil-engineering projects. Its first major structure was the vaulted, largely triangular **Centre des Nouvelles Industries et Technologies** (CNIT; Centre for New Industries and Technologies), a giant 'pregnant oyster' inaugurated in 1958, extensively rebuilt 30 years later and revamped as a shopping centre in 2008. Like many of its contemporaries, the centre now feels tired. But later generations still excite: including the **Cœur Défense** (Défense Heart; 2001), the **Tour EDF** (2001) and the **Tour T1** (2005).

Today La Défense counts more than 100 buildings, is home to three-quarters of France's 20 largest corporations and showcases extraordinary monumental art. A total of 1500 companies of all sizes employ some 150,000 people, transforming the oversized, nocturnal ghost town into a hive of high-flying commercial activity.

> **LIGHT BUILDING**
>
> Sky-high future architectural creations at La Défense throw caution to the wind, but outranking them all in size, beauty and sustainability will be **Tour Phare** (Lighthouse Tower), a 299m-tall office and retail tower that torques like a human torso and, through awnings that raise and lower when the sun hits them, uses light as a building material. It is scheduled for completion in 2012.

Information

CIC Courbevoie La Défense bank (11 place de la Défense; M La Défense Grande Arche; 9am-5pm Mon-Fri) Opposite the Espace Info-Défense.

Espace Info-Défense (01 47 74 84 24; www.ladefense.fr; 15 place de la Défense; M La Défense Grande Arche; 9am-5.15pm Mon-Fri) La Défense's tourist office has reams of free information, including the useful *Discover La Défense* brochure, and details on cultural activities.

Post Office (CNIT Bldg, ground fl, 2 place de la Défense; M La Défense Grande Arche)

Sights

GRANDE ARCHE DE LA DÉFENSE

The most important sight is the remarkable cube-shaped **Grande Arche** (Great Arch; 01 49 07 27 27; www.grandearche.com; 1 parvis de la Défense; M La Défense Grande Arche; adult/6-17yr/under 6yr €9/7.50/free, family €19-22; 10am-8pm Apr-Sep, to 7pm Oct-Mar). Housing government and business offices, it is made of white Carrara marble, grey granite and glass, and measures exactly 110m along each side. Inaugurated on 14 July 1989, the arch marks the western end of the 8km-long **Axe Historique** (Historic Axis) stretching from the Louvre's glass pyramid. Lifts enclosed in glass will whisk you up to the 35th floor for views, a film, scale models and a well-received restaurant without (!) a view.

MUSÉE DE LA DÉFENSE

Below the Espace Info-Défense, the **Musée de la Défense** (La Défense Museum; 01 47 74 84 24; www.ladefense.fr; 15 place de la Défense; M La Défense Grande Arche; admission free; 9am-5.15pm Mon-Fri) traces the development of La Défense through the decades with drawings, architectural plans and scale models. Especially interesting are the projects that were never built, including the Tour sans Fin, a 'Never-Ending Tower' that would have been 425m high, but just 39m in diameter.

GARDENS & MONUMENTS

Le Parvis, place de la Défense and Esplanade du Général de Gaulle, which together form a pleasant, 1km-long pedestrian walkway, comprise a **garden of contemporary art**. The more than 60 monumental sculptures and murals along the **Voie des Sculptures** (Sculpture Way) here include colourful and imaginative works by Calder, Miró, César and Torricini, among others.

In the southeastern corner of place de la Défense and opposite the Info-Défense office is a much older monument – **La Défense de Paris**, which commemorates the defence of Paris during the Franco-Prussian War of 1870–71 and from which the district's name is derived. Behind is the **Bassin Agam**, a pool with mosaics and fountains.

Eating

La Défense is mostly fast-food territory. The 3rd floor of the shopping centre **Les Quatre Temps** (01 47 73 54 44; www.les4temps.com, in French; 15 parvis de la Défense; 9am-10pm Mon-Fri, 8.30am-10pm Sat) is loaded with places to eat quick, be it pizza or pancakes, Häagen-Dazs ice cream, Starbucks coffee, soup and juice or stylish Japanese. There's also a convenient branch of the sandwich shop **Lina's** (01 56 37 04 30; www.linascafe.fr; parvis de la Défense; M La Défense Grande Arche; sandwiches €3.90-6.90, soups & salads €4.50-6.10; 9am-4.30pm Mon-Fri).

Globetrotter (01 55 91 96 96; 16 place de la Défense; M La Défense Grande Arche; starters €8-23, mains €15-30; lunch Mon-Fri) This attractive restaurant next to the tourist office has a tropical theme and attempts to take diners on a culinary tour of the world's islands. Tables on the wooden decking terrace face La Grande Arche and those inside woo diners with first-row seats at the Bassin Agam (above).

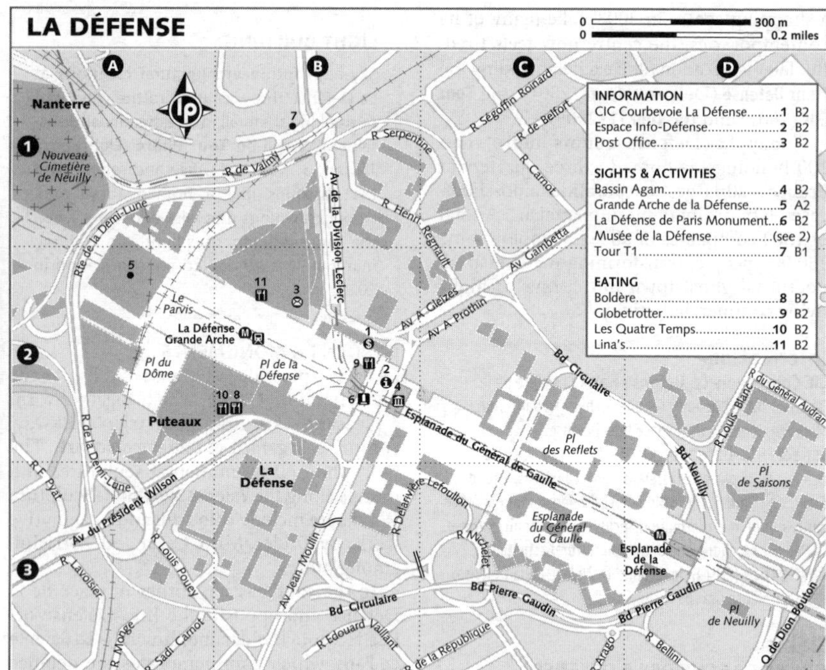

Boldère (☎ 01 47 73 54 44; 15 parvis de la Défense; Ⓜ La Défense Grande Arche; salads €8-15; ⏰ 9am-1am Mon-Fri) The hottest address on the block, this *bar à legumes* (vegetable café) on the 3rd floor of Les Quatre Temps has health-conscious punters building salads from 101 different ingredients or supping one of four different homemade soups. Interior decor is contemporary, the mood chic-casual and the cuisine 100% vegetarian.

Getting There & Away

La Défense Grande Arche metro station is the western terminus of metro line 1; the ride from the Louvre takes about 15 minutes. If you take the faster RER line A, remember that La Défense is in zone 3 and you must pay a supplement (€1.95) if you are carrying a travel pass for zones 1 and 2 only. Beware: the area is patrolled regularly by inspectors.

ST-DENIS

pop 138,600

For 1200 years St-Denis was the burial place of French royalty; today it is a suburb with a very mixed population just north of Paris' 18e arrondissement. The ornate royal tombs, adorned with some truly remarkable statuary, and the Basilique de St-Denis containing them are well worth the trip north, as is the Stade de France, the futuristic stadium just south of Canal de St-Denis.

Information

Office de Tourisme de St-Denis Plaine Commune (☎ 01 55 87 08 70; www.saint-denis-tourisme.com; 1 rue de la République; Ⓜ Basilique de St-Denis; ⏰ 9.30am-1pm & 2-6pm Mon-Sat, 10am-2pm Sun Oct-Mar, 10am-1pm & 2-4pm Sun Apr-Sep)

Post Office (59 rue de la République; Ⓜ Basilique de St-Denis)

Société Générale bank (11 place Jean Jaurès; Ⓜ Basilique de St-Denis; ⏰ 8.45am-1pm & 2-5.15pm Mon-Fri, 8.45am-12.45pm Sat)

Sights

BASILIQUE DE ST-DENIS

Serving as the burial place for all but a handful of France's kings and queens from Dagobert I (r 629–39) to Louis XVIII (r 1814–24), the **Basilique de St-Denis** (St Denis Basilica; ☎ 01 48 09 83 54; www.monuments-nationaux.fr; 1 rue de la Légion d'Honneur;

Ⓜ Basilique de St-Denis; basilica admission free, tombs adult/senior, student & 18-25yr/under 18yr €6.50/4.50/free, admission free 1st Sun of month Nov-Mar; ⏲ 10am-6pm Mon-Sat, noon-6pm Sun Apr-Sep, 10am-5pm Mon-Sat, noon-5pm Sun Oct-Mar) and its tombs and mausoleums constitute one of Europe's most important collections of funerary sculpture.

The single-towered basilica, begun around 1136, was the first major structure to be built in the Gothic style and served as a model for many other 12th-century French cathedrals, including the one at Chartres (p220). Features illustrating the transition from Romanesque to Gothic can be seen in the **choir** and the **ambulatory**, which are adorned with a number of 12th-century **stained-glass windows**.

During the Revolution and the ensuing Reign of Terror the basilica was devastated; skeletal remains from the royal tombs were dumped into two pits outside the church. The mausoleums were put into storage in Paris, however, and survived. They were brought back in 1816, and the royal bones were reburied in the crypt a year later. Restoration of the structure was initially begun under Napoléon Bonaparte, but most of the work was carried out by the Gothic Revivalist architect Eugène Viollet-le-Duc from 1858 until his death in 1879.

The **tombs** are decorated with life-size figures of the deceased. Those built before the Renaissance are adorned with *gisants* (recumbent figures). Those made after 1285 were carved from death masks and are thus fairly, er, lifelike; the 14 figures commissioned under Louis IX (St Louis; r 1214–70) are depictions of how earlier rulers may have looked. The oldest tombs (from around 1230) are those of **Clovis I** (d 511) and his son **Childebert I** (d 558). Don't miss the white-marble catafalque tomb (1597) of **Louis XII** and **Anne of Bretagne**. The graffiti etched on the arms of the seated figures dates from the early 17th century.

Self-paced 1¼-hour audioguide tours of the basilica and the tombs cost €4 (€6.50 for two sharing).

STADE DE FRANCE

Just south of central St-Denis, the 80,000-seat **Stade de France** (Stadium of France; ☎ 08 92 70 09 00; www.stadefrance.com; rue Francis de Pressensé, ZAC du Cornillon Nord, 93216 St-Denis La Plaine; Ⓜ St-Denis-Porte de Paris; adult/student & 6-11yr/under 6yr €10/8/free, family €29; ⏲ tours in French on the hr 10am-5pm Apr-Aug, 4 to 5 daily Sep-Mar, in English 10.30am & 2.30pm Apr-Aug) was

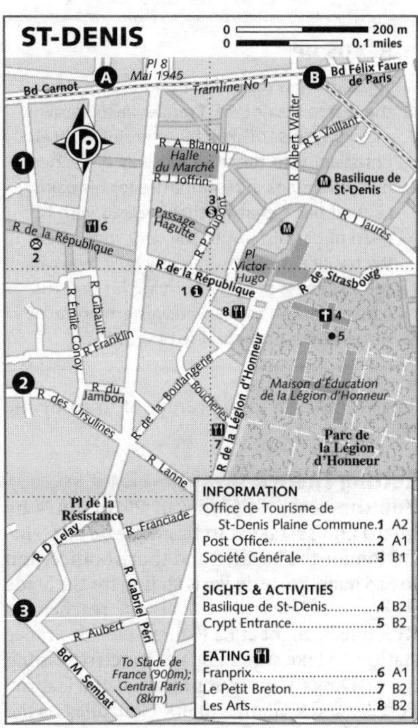

built in time for the 1998 World Cup, which France won by miraculously defeating favourite Brazil 3–0. The futuristic and quite beautiful structure, with a roof the size of place de la Concorde, is now used for football and rugby matches, major gymnastic events and big-ticket music concerts. Visits by guided tour only.

Eating

Les Arts (☎ 01 42 43 22 40; 6 rue de la Boulangerie; Ⓜ Basilique de St-Denis; starters €6-7, mains €11-18, menu €18; ⏲ lunch & dinner to 10.30pm Tue-Sun) This central restaurant has mostly Maghrib cuisine (couscous, *tajines* 'Moroccan stews' etc) though a few traditional French dishes as well, and comes recommended by local people.

Le Petit Breton (☎ 01 48 20 11 58; 18 rue de la Légion d'Honneur; Ⓜ St-Denis-Porte de Paris; menus €11 & €14; ⏲ 10am-3pm Mon-Fri, 11.30am-3.30pm Sat) 'The Little Breton' is a decent spot for a lunch of traditional French fare; don't expect galettes (buckwheat pancakes) or crêpes, despite the name. The plat du jour is a bargain-basement €8.

There is a **Franprix supermarket** (34 rue de la République; ⏲ 9am-8pm Mon, 8.30am-8pm Tue-Sat,

HEADS UP

The basilica is named in honour of St Denis, the patron saint of France (also known as Dionysius of Paris), who introduced Christianity to the city and was beheaded by the Romans in Montmartre for his pains. Legend has it that he then walked with his head under his arm to the very spot where the basilica was subsequently built. You can see a likeness of him – carrying his unfortunate head – on the carved western portal of Notre Dame Cathedral (p145) in Paris.

8.30am-1.30pm Sun) in the centre of town by the post office.

Getting There & Away

You can reach St-Denis in 20 minutes by metro line 13: take it to Basilique de St-Denis station for the basilica and tourist office, and to St-Denis-Porte de Paris station for the Stade de France. (The latter can also be reached via RER line B; alight at La Plaine-Stade de France station.) Make sure to board a metro heading for St-Denis Université and *not* for Gabriel Péri Asnières-Gennevilliers-Courtilles, as the line splits at La Fourche station.

DISNEYLAND RESORT PARIS

Disneyland Resort Paris, 32km east of Paris, consists of three main areas (plus a golf course): **Disney Village**, with its seven hotels, shops, restaurants and clubs; **Disneyland Park**, with its five theme parks; and **Walt Disney Studios Park**, which brings film, animation and TV production to life. The first two are separated by the RER and TGV train stations; the studios neighbour Disneyland Park. Moving walkways whisk visitors to the sights from the far-flung car park.

Disneyland has been on something of a roller coaster financially since it opened in the middle of sugar-beet fields in 1992. Judging from the crowds, however, many visitors – mostly families with young children – can't seem to get enough.

Information

Espace du Tourisme d'Île de France et de Seine et Marne (☎ 01 60 43 33 33; www.pidf.com; place François Truffaut, 77705 Chessy; 🕑 9am-8.45pm) The Île de France tourist office branch northwest of the resort shares space with an office dispensing information on the *département* of Seine et Marne.

Sights

One-day admission fees at **Disneyland Resort Paris** (☎ 01 60 30 60 30; www.disneylandparis.com; adult/3-11yr/under 3yr €46/38/free) include unlimited access to all rides and activities in *either* Walt Disney Studios Park or Disneyland Park. Multiple-day passes are available, including a **Passe-Partout** (adult/3-11yr/under 3yr €56/48/free), which allows entry to both parks for one day, and the two-/three-day **Hopper Ticket** (adult €103/128, 3-11yr €84/105) with which you can enter and leave both parks as often as you like over nonconsecutive days used within one year. Admission fees change from season to season, and a multitude of special offers and accommodation/transport packages are always available.

Disneyland Park (🕑 9am-11pm daily mid-Jul–Aug, 10am-8pm Mon-Fri, 9am-8pm Sat & Sun Sep-Mar, 9am-8pm daily Apr–early May, 10am-8pm Mon-Fri, 9am-8pm Sat & Sun early May–mid-Jun, 9am-8pm daily mid-Jun–early Jul) is divided into five *pays* (lands). **Main Street, USA**, just inside the main entrance, is a spotless avenue reminiscent of Norman Rockwell's idealised small-town America c 1910, complete with Disney characters let loose among the crowds. Adjoining **Frontierland** is a recreation of the 'rugged, untamed American West' with the legendary Big Thunder Mountain ride. **Adventureland**, meant to evoke the Arabian Nights and the wilds of Africa (among other exotic lands portrayed in Disney films), is home to that old favourite, Pirates of the Caribbean, as well as Indiana Jones and the Temple of Peril, a roller coaster that spirals through 360 degrees – in reverse. **Fantasyland** brings fairy-tale characters such as Sleeping Beauty, Pinocchio, Peter Pan and Snow White to life; you'll also find 'It's a Small World' here. **Discoveryland** features a dozen high-tech attractions and rides, including Space Mountain: Mission 2, Star Tours and the Toy Story 2–inspired Buzz Lightyear Laser Blast.

Walt Disney Studios Park (adult/3-11yr/under 3yr €46/38/free; 🕑 9am-6pm daily Jul-Sep, 10am-6pm Mon-Fri, 9am-6pm Sat & Sun Oct-Mar, 10am-6pm daily Apr-Jun) has a sound stage, a production backlot and animation studios, which help illustrate up close how films, TV programs and cartoons are produced.

Eating

You are not allowed to picnic on resort grounds but there's an ample number of themed restaurants to choose from, be it **Buzz Lightyear's Pizza Planet** (Discoveryland); **Planet Hollywood** or the *Happy Days*–inspired **Annette's Diner** (Disney Village); the meaty **Silver Spur Steakhouse** or Mexican **Fuente del Oro** (Frontierland); and the seafaring **Blue Lagoon** restaurant (Adventureland) for future pirates. Most have *menus* (fixed-price menus) for children (around €10) and adults (€20 to €30). Opening hours vary. To avoid another queue, pick your place online and reserve a table in advance (☎ 01 60 30 40 50).

Getting There & Away

Marne-la-Vallée/Chessy, Disneyland's RER station, is served by line A4; trains run every 15 minutes or so from central Paris (€7.50; including park admission adult/ages three to 11 €47/39; 35 to 40 minutes). The last train back to Paris leaves just after midnight.

VERSAILLES

pop 87,100

The prosperous, leafy and very bourgeois suburb of Versailles, 21km southwest of Paris, is the site of the grandest and most famous château in France. It served as the kingdom's political capital and the seat of the royal court for more than a century, from 1682 to 1789 – the year Revolutionary mobs massacred the palace guard and dragged Louis XVI and Marie-Antoinette back to Paris, where they eventually had their heads separated from their shoulders.

Many people consider Versailles a must-see destination. The best way to avoid the queues is to arrive first thing in the morning; if you're interested in just the Grands Appartements, another good time to get here is about 3.30pm or 4pm. The queues are longest on Tuesday, when many of Paris' museums are closed, as well as on Sunday. Most importantly, buy your château ticket in advance: online (www.chateauversailles.fr), from a branch of Fnac or at any SNCF train station or office.

Information

Office de Tourisme de Versailles (☎ 01 39 24 88 88; www.versailles-tourisme.com; 2bis av de Paris; 🕑 10am-6pm Mon, 9am-7pm Tue-Sun Apr-Sep, 9am-6pm Tue-Sat, 9am-6pm Sun Oct-Mar) Sells the Passeport (p213) to Château de Versailles, a detailed visitors guide (€8.50) and a useful IGN walking map of the area (€9.50).

Post Office (av de Paris)

Sights

CHÂTEAU DE VERSAILLES

The splendid and enormous **Château de Versailles** (Versailles Palace; ☎ 08 10 81 16 14; www.chateauversailles.fr; adult/under 18yr €13.50/free, from 3pm €10/free; 🕑 9am-6.30pm Tue-Sun Apr-Oct, to 5.30pm Tue-Sun Nov-Mar) was built in the mid-17th century during the reign of Louis XIV – the Roi Soleil (Sun King) – to project the absolute power of the French monarchy, which was then at the height of its glory. Its scale and decor also reflect Louis XIV's taste for profligate luxury and his boundless appetite for self-glorification. Some 30,000 workers and soldiers toiled on the structure, the bills for which all but emptied the kingdom's coffers. The château has undergone relatively few alterations since its construction, though almost all the interior furnishings disappeared during the Revolution and many of the rooms were rebuilt by Louis-Philippe (r 1830–48). The current €370 million restoration program is the most ambitious yet and until it's completed in 2020 at least a part of the palace is likely to be clad in scaffolding when you visit.

About two decades into his long reign (1643–1715), Louis XIV decided to enlarge the hunting lodge his father had built at Versailles and turn it into a palace big enough for the entire court, which numbered about 6000 people at the time. To accomplish this he hired three supremely talented men: the architect Louis Le Vau (Jules Hardouin-Mansart took over from Le Vau in the mid-1670s); the painter and interior designer Charles Le Brun; and the landscape artist André Le Nôtre, whose workers flattened hills, drained marshes and relocated forests as they laid out the seemingly endless gardens, ponds and fountains.

VERSAILLES IN FIGURES

The château at Versailles counts 700 rooms, 2153 windows, 352 chimneys and 67 staircases under 11 hectares of roof set on 800 hectares of garden, park and woods, including 200,000 trees and 210,000 flowers newly planted each year. There are 50 fountains and 620 fountain nozzles. The walls and rooms are adorned with 6300 paintings, 2100 sculptures and statues, 15,000 engravings and 5000 decorative art objects and furnishings. Oh, and 7.5 million annual visitors, 4.7 million of whom make it inside.

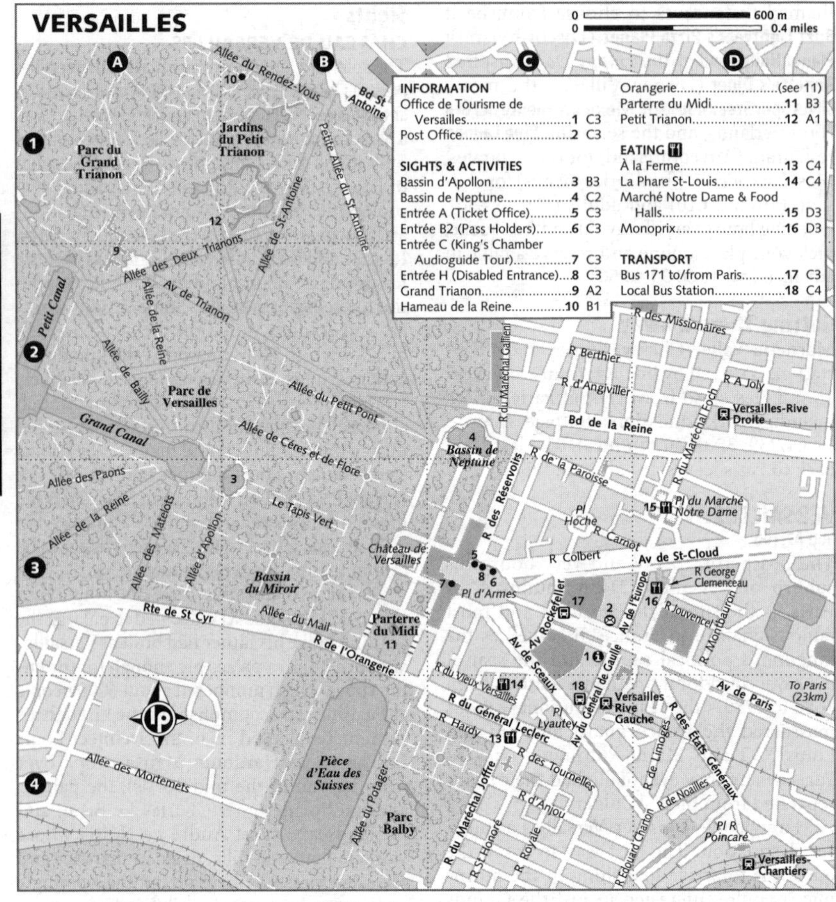

Le Brun and his hundreds of artisans decorated every moulding, cornice, ceiling and door of the interior with the most luxurious and ostentatious of appointments: frescos, marble, gilt and woodcarvings, many with themes and symbols drawn from Greek and Roman mythology. The King's Suite of the **Grands Appartements du Roi et de la Reine** (King's and Queen's State Apartments), for example, includes rooms dedicated to Hercules, Venus, Diana, Mars and Mercury. The opulence reaches its peak in the recently restored **Galerie des Glaces** (Hall of Mirrors), a 75m-long ballroom with 17 huge mirrors on one side and, on the other, an equal number of windows looking out over the gardens and the setting sun.

The château complex comprises four main sections: the palace building, a 580m-long structure with multiple wings, grand halls and sumptuous bedchambers and the Grands Appartements du Roi et de la Reine; the vast gardens, canals and pools to the west of the palace; two much smaller palaces (outbuildings almost!), the **Grand Trianon** and, a few hundred metres to the east, the **Petit Trianon**; and the **Hameau de la Reine** (Queen's Hamlet).

The basic palace ticket includes an English-language audioguide and allows visitors to freely visit the palace's state apartments, the chapel, the **Appartements du Dauphin et de la Dauphine** (Dauphin's and Dauphine's Apartments) and various galleries. The so-called **Passeport** (adult/under 18yr €20/free Tue-Fri, €25/free Sat & Sun Apr-Oct, €16/free Tue-Sun Nov-Mar) includes the same as well as the Grand Trianon and, in high season, the Grandes Eaux Musicales fountain displays (see below). Enter the palace through Entrée A with a palace ticket; Entrée C with a Passeport.

The section of the vast **château gardens** (8.30am-8.30pm Apr-Oct, 8am-6pm Nov-Mar) nearest the palace, laid out between 1661 and 1700 in the formal French style, is famed for its geometrically aligned terraces, flowerbeds, tree-lined paths, ponds and fountains. The 400-odd statues of marble, bronze and lead were made by the most talented sculptors of the era. The English-style **Jardins du Petit Trianon** are more pastoral and have meandering, sheltered paths. Admission to the gardens is free, except on weekends during the Grandes Eaux Musicales (see below), between April and October.

The **Grand Canal**, 1.6km long and 62m wide, is oriented to reflect the setting sun. It is traversed by the 1km-long **Petit Canal**, creating a cross-shaped body of water with a perimeter of more than 5.5km. Louis XIV used to hold boating parties here. In season, you too can paddle around the Grand Canal in four-person **rowing boats**; the dock is at the canal's eastern end. The **Orangerie**, built under the **Parterre du Midi** (Southern Flowerbed) on the southwestern side of the palace, shelters tropical plants in winter.

The gardens' largest fountains are the 17th-century **Bassin de Neptune** (Neptune's Fountain), a dazzling mirage of 99 spouting gushers 300m north of the palace, and the **Bassin d'Apollon** (Apollo's Fountain) at the eastern end of the Grand Canal. The straight side of the Bassin de Neptune abuts a small round pond graced by a winged dragon. Emerging from the water in the centre of the Bassin d'Apollon is Apollo's chariot, pulled by rearing horses.

Try to time your visit for the **Grandes Eaux Musicales** (adult/student & 11-18yr/under 11yr €7/5.50/free, admission free after 4.50pm; 11am-noon & 3.30-5pm Sat & Sun Apr-Sep) or the after-dark **Grandes Eaux Nocturnes** (adult/11-18yr/under 10yr €7/5.50/free; 9.30-11.30pm Sat & Sun Jul & Aug), truly magical 'dancing water' displays set to music composed by baroque- and classical-era composers throughout the grounds in summer.

In the middle of the vast 90-hectare park, about 1.5km northwest of the main palace, is what is now known as **Domaine de Marie-Antoinette** (Marie-Antoinette's Estate; adult/adult after 5pm/under 18yr €9/5/free Apr-Oct, €5/free/free Nov-Mar; noon-6.30pm daily Apr-Oct, noon-5.30pm daily Nov-Mar). The pink-colonnaded **Grand Trianon** was built in 1687 for Louis XIV and his family as a place of escape from the rigid etiquette of the court. Napoléon I had it redone in the Empire style. The much smaller, ochre-coloured **Petit Trianon**, built in the 1760s, was redecorated in 1867 by Empress Eugénie, the consort of Napoléon III, who added Louis XVI–style furnishings similar to the uninspiring pieces that now fill its 1st-floor rooms. Further north is the **Hameau de la Reine**, a mock village of thatched cottages constructed from 1775 to 1784 for the amusement of Marie-Antoinette, who liked to play milkmaid here.

Be advised that high-season tickets cover admission to the Grand Trianon, the Hameau de la Reine, Marie-Antoinette's dairy, the theatre, the English garden and so on; low-season tickets only cover the Grand Trianon and Petit Trianon gardens, which notably are both free on the 1st Sunday of the month between November and March.

Tickets to several different **guided tours** (08 10 81 16 14; adult with/without palace ticket, Passeport or ticket to the Domaine de Marie-Antoinette €7.50/14.50, under 18yr €5.50; 9.45am-3.45pm Tue-Sun) addressing different themes – life at court, classical music, 'Versailles splendours', the private apartments of Louis XV and Louis XI and so on – are sold at the main ticket office. Some are conducted in English.

Eating

Rue Satory is lined with restaurants serving cuisines from all over the world, including Indian, Chinese, Lebanese, Tunisian and Japanese.

our pick **À la Ferme** (01 39 53 10 81; 3 rue du Maréchal Joffre; starters/mains €6/14, menus €17.50 & €21.80; lunch & dinner to 11pm Wed-Sun) Cowhide seats and rustic garlands strung from old wood beams add a country air to 'At the Farm', a temple to grilled meats and cuisine from southwest France.

Le Phare St-Louis (01 39 53 40 12; 33 rue du Vieux Versailles; menus €11-16; lunch & dinner to 11pm) This cosy Breton place heaves. Pick from 15 savoury galettes (€6.70 to €8) and 40-odd different sweet crêpes, including the

Vieux Versailles (€5.60) topped with redcurrant jelly, pear and ice cream then set ablaze with Grand Marnier.

If headed from the tourist office for the outdoor **Marché Notre Dame** (place du Marché Notre Dame; 7.30am-2pm Tue, Fri & Sun) food market, enter via passage Saladin at 33 av de St-Cloud. There are also **food halls** (7am-1pm & 3.30-7pm Tue-Sat) surrounding the marketplace. **Monoprix** (9 rue Georges Clemenceau; 8.30am-8.55pm Mon-Sat) department store, north of av de Paris, has a large supermarket section.

Getting There & Away

RATP bus 171 (€1.50 or one metro/bus ticket, 35 minutes) links Pont de Sèvres (15e) in Paris with the place d'Armes every six to nine minutes from 5am to midnight.

RER line C5 (€2.80) goes from Paris' Left Bank RER stations to Versailles-Rive Gauche station, which is only 700m southeast of the château and close to the tourist office. Trains run every 15 minutes until shortly before midnight.

Less convenient, RER line C8 links Paris' Left Bank with Versailles-Chantiers station, a 1.3km walk from the château.

SNCF operates up to 70 trains a day from Paris' Gare St-Lazare (€2.80) to Versailles-Rive Droite, which is 1.2km from the château. The last train to Paris leaves just after midnight. Versailles-Chantiers is served by half-hourly SNCF trains daily from Gare Montparnasse (€2.80); trains on this line continue to Chartres (€10.90, 45 to 60 minutes). An SNCF package *(forfait loisir)* covering the Paris metro, return train journey to/from Versailles and château admission costs €19.20.

FONTAINEBLEAU

pop 15,900

The town of Fontainebleau, 67km southeast of Paris, is renowned for its elegant Renaissance château, one of France's largest royal residences. It's much less crowded and pressured than Versailles. The town itself has a number of fine restaurants, swish cafés and cultural happenings, and is surrounded by the beautiful Forêt de Fontainebleau, a favourite hunting ground of many French kings and today an important recreational centre in the Île de France. Fontainebleau's lifeblood is INSEAD (www.insead.edu), the international graduate business school that brings some 2000 students here each year.

Information

Office de Tourisme de Pays de Fontainebleau (☎ 01 60 74 99 99; www.fontainebleau-tourisme.com; 4 rue Royale; 10am-6pm Mon-Sat, 10am-1pm & 2-5.30pm Sun May-Oct, 10am-6pm Mon-Sat, 10am-1pm Sun Nov-Mar) The tourist office hires out bicycles (per hour/half-day/full day €5/15/19), as well as self-paced English-language audioguide tours (€4.60, 1½ hours) of both the palace and the Forêt de Fontainebleau.

Post Office (2 rue de la Chancellerie)

Sights

CHÂTEAU DE FONTAINEBLEAU

The enormous, 1900-room **Château de Fontainebleau** (Fontainebleau Palace; ☎ 01 60 71 50 70; www.musee-chateau-fontainebleau.fr, in French, www.chateaudefontainebleau.net; adult/18-25yr/under 18yr €8/6/free, admission free 1st Sun of month; 9.30am-6pm Wed-Mon Jun-Sep, to 5pm Wed-Mon Oct-May), whose list of former tenants or visitors reads like a who's who of French royalty, is one of the most beautifully decorated and furnished châteaux in France. Every centimetre of wall and ceiling space is richly adorned with wood panelling, gilded carvings, frescos, tapestries and paintings. The parquet floors are of the finest woods, the fireplaces are ornamented with exceptional carvings, and many pieces of the furniture date back to the Renaissance era.

The first château on this site was built some time in the early 12th century and enlarged by Louis IX a century later. Only a single medieval tower survived the energetic Renaissance-style reconstruction undertaken by François I (r 1515–47), whose superb artisans, many of them brought from Italy, blended Italian and French styles to create what is known as the First School of Fontainebleau. The *Mona Lisa* once hung here amid other fine works of art in the royal collection.

During the latter half of the 16th century, the château was further expanded by Henri II (r 1547–59), Catherine de Médicis and Henri IV (r 1589–1610), whose Flemish and French artists created the Second School of Fontainebleau. Even Louis XIV got in on the act: it was he who hired Le Nôtre to redesign the gardens.

Fontainebleau, which was not damaged during the Revolution (though its furniture was stolen or destroyed), was beloved by Napoléon, who had a fair bit of restoration work carried out. Napoléon III was another frequent visitor. During WWII the château

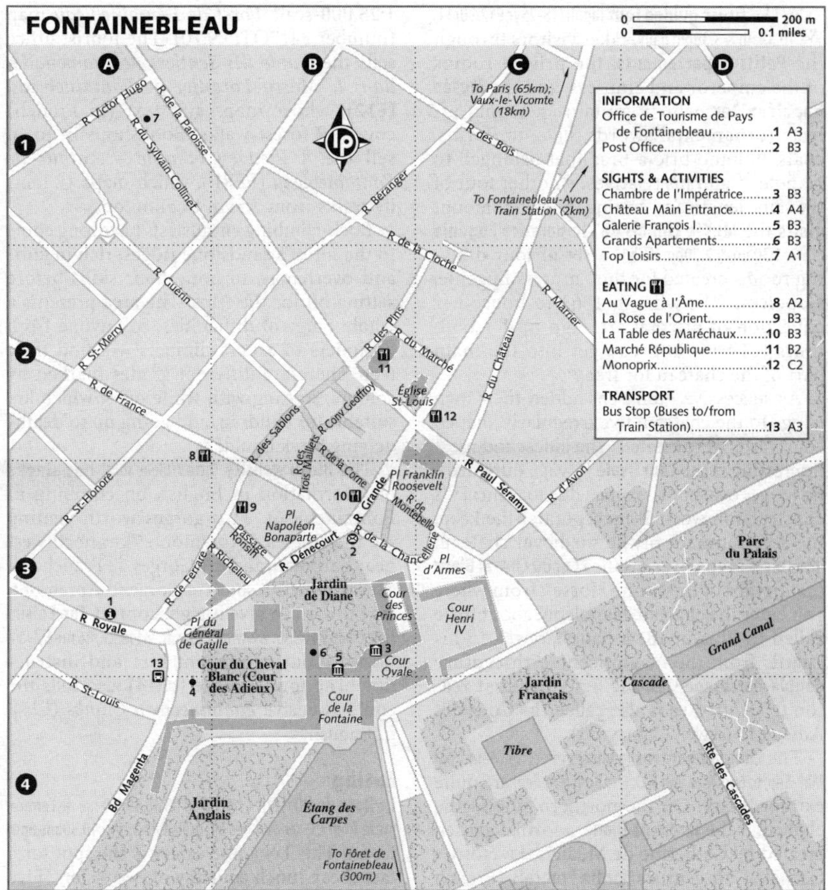

was turned into a German headquarters. After it was liberated by Allied forces under US General George Patton in 1944, part of the complex served as the Allied and then NATO headquarters from 1945 to 1965.

Visits take in the **Grands Appartements** (State Apartments), which contain several outstanding rooms. An informative 1½-hour audioguide (included in the price) leads visitors around the main areas.

The spectacular **Chapelle de la Trinité** (Trinity Chapel), whose ornamentation dates from the first half of the 17th century, is where Louis XV married Marie Leczinska in 1725 and where the future Napoléon III was christened in 1810. **Galerie François 1er**, a jewel of Renaissance architecture, was decorated from 1533 to 1540 by Il Rosso, a Florentine follower of Michelangelo. In the wood panelling, François I's monogram appears repeatedly along with his emblem, a dragon-like salamander.

The **Salle de Bal**, a 30m-long ballroom dating from the mid-16th century that was also used for receptions and banquets, is renowned for its mythological frescos, marquetry floor and coffered ceiling. The large windows afford views of the Cour Ovale (p216) and the gardens. The gilded bed in the 17th- and 18th-century **Chambre de l'Impératrice** (Empress' Bedroom) was never actually used by Marie-Antoinette, for whom it was built in 1787. The gilding in the **Salle du Trône** (Throne Room), the royal bedroom before the Napoléonic period, is in three colours: gold, green and yellow.

A 1¼-hour **guided tour** (adult/18-25yr €12.50/11; 10.30am & 3.30pm daily) takes visitors through the **Petits Appartements**, the private rooms of the emperor and empress, and the **Musée Napoléon 1er**, which contains personal effects (ornamental swords, hats, uniforms, coats etc) and bric-a-brac that belonged to Napoléon and his relatives. Another tour of the same length and costing the same amount visits the **Musée Chinois de l'Imperatice Eugénie** (11.30am & 2.30pm daily), a set of four drawing rooms created for the Empress Eugénie, Napoléon III's wife, in 1863 to house her collection of oriental art. Sign up for both tours (€19/16) and you get into the main part of the château for free.

As successive monarchs added their own wings to the château, five irregularly shaped courtyards were created. The oldest and most interesting is the **Cour Ovale** (Oval Courtyard), no longer oval but U-shaped due to Henri IV's construction work. It incorporates the keep, the sole remnant of the medieval château. The largest courtyard is the **Cour du Cheval Blanc** (Courtyard of the White Horse), from where you enter the château. Napoléon, about to be exiled to Elba in 1814, bade farewell to his guards from the magnificent 17th-century **double-horseshoe staircase** here. For that reason the courtyard is also called the Cour des Adieux (Farewell Courtyard).

The **château gardens** (admission free; 9am-7pm May-Sep, to 6pm Mar, Apr & Oct, to 5pm Nov-Feb) are quite extraordinary. On the northern side of the château is the **Jardin de Diane**, a formal garden created by Catherine de Médicis. Le Nôtre's formal, 17th-century **Jardin Français** (French Garden), also known as the Grand Parterre, is east of the **Cour de la Fontaine** (Fountain Courtyard) and the **Étang des Carpes** (Carp Pond). The **Grand Canal** was excavated in 1609 and pre-dates the canals at Versailles by more than half a century. The informal **Jardin Anglais** (English Garden), laid out in 1812, is west of the pond.

FORÊT DE FONTAINEBLEAU

Beginning 500m south of the château and surrounds the town, the 20,000-hectare **Forêt de Fontainebleau** (Fontainebleau Forest) is one of the prettiest woods in the region. The many trails – including parts of the **GR1** and **GR11** (for further details, see p944) – are excellent for jogging, walking, cycling and horse riding. The area is covered by IGN's 1:25,000-scale *Forêt de Fontainebleau* map (number 2417OT; €9.70). The tourist office sells the *Guide des Sentiers de Promenades dans le Massif Forestier de Fontainebleau* (€12), whose maps and text (in French) cover 19 forest walks. Bookshops in town sell the *À Pied en Famille – Autour de Fontainebleau* (FFRP), which maps 18 family walks from 2.5km to 5km long.

Rock-climbing enthusiasts have long come to the forest's sandstone ridges, rich in cliffs and overhangs, to hone their skills before setting off for the Alps. The area presents a whole range of difficulties, so anyone from beginners to expert climbers will find their feet. There are different grades marked by colours, starting with white ones, which are suitable for children, and going up to death-defying black boulders.

The **Bleau website** (http://bleau.info) has stacks of information in English on climbing in Fontainebleau. Two gorges worth visiting are the Gorges d'Apremont, 7km northwest near Barbizon, and the Gorges de Franchard, a few kilometres south of Gorges d'Apremont. If you want to give it a go, contact **Top Loisirs** (01 60 74 08 50; www.toploisirs.fr, in French; 16 rue Sylvain Collinet) about equipment hire and instruction. The tourist office (p214) also sells the comprehensive *Fontainebleau Climbs* (€25), in English.

Eating

La Rose de l'Orient (06 08 88 36 49; 20 rue de Ferrare; meze from €1, sandwiches €4, grills €7.50; 10.30am-8pm Tue-Sat) This Lebanese eatery is the spot for a fast cheap lunch courtesy of two sisters. Five plastic tables inside or take away a picnic of meze and pitta bread.

our pick **Au Vague à l'Âme** (01 60 72 10 32; 39 rue de France; galettes & crêpes €2.50-9.50, lunch menus €11.50-16, dinner menus €25; lunch Tue-Sun, dinner to 1am Tue-Sat) This cheerful café-restaurant with a vague nautical theme is the place for Breton specialities, including mussels, fresh oysters and an oyster terrine to die for.

La Table des Maréchaux (01 60 39 55 50; 9 rue Grande; starters €15-20, mains €23-30, weekday lunch menus €32, dinner menus €40; lunch & dinner to 11pm) Tucked in fancy Hôtel Napoléon, this romantic restaurant with its flowery interior courtyard garden is a must in summer. Cuisine is inventive: traditional French inspired by foreign flavours and exotic spices.

Options for self-caterers include the following:

Marché République (rue des Pins; ⏰ 8am-1pm Tue, Fri & Sun) Fontainebleau's covered food market, north of the central pedestrian area.

Monoprix (58 rue Grande; ⏰ 8.45am-7.45pm Mon-Sat, 9am-1pm Sun) Supermarket section on the 1st floor.

Getting There & Around

Up to 30 daily SNCF commuter trains link Paris' Gare de Lyon hourly with Fontainebleau-Avon station (€7.60, 40 to 60 minutes); the last train returning to Paris leaves Fontainebleau a bit after 9.45pm weekdays, just after 10pm on Saturday and sometime after 10.30pm on Sunday. An SNCF package (adult/10 to 17 years/4 to 9 years €23/16.70/8.10) includes return transport from Paris, bus transfers and château admission.

Local bus line A links the train station with the château (€1.50), which is 2km southwest, every 10 minutes from 5.30am to 9.30pm. The stop is opposite the main entrance.

VAUX-LE-VICOMTE

Privately owned **Château de Vaux-le-Vicomte** (Vaux-le-Vicomte Palace; ☎ 01 64 14 41 90; www.vaux-le-vicomte.com; adult/6-16yr €12.50/9.90, candlelight visit €15.50/13.70, family €39; ⏰ 10am-1pm & 2-6pm Mon-Fri, 10am-6pm Sat & Sun mid-Mar–early Nov, candlelight visits 8pm-midnight Fri Jul & Aug, Sat May–mid-Oct) and its magnificent **formal gardens** (⏰ 10am-6pm late Mar–mid-Nov), 20km north of Fontainebleau and 60km southeast of Paris, were designed and built by Le Brun, Le Vau and Le Nôtre between 1656 and 1661 as a precursor to their more ambitious work at Versailles. On the second and the last Saturday of every month from April to October, there are elaborate **jeux d'eau** (fountain displays) in the gardens from 3pm to 6pm.

The beauty of Vaux-le-Vicomte turned out to be the undoing of its owner, Nicolas Fouquet, Louis XIV's minister of finance. It seems that Louis, seething with jealousy that he had been upstaged at the château's official opening, had Fouquet thrown into prison, where the unfortunate *ministre* died in 1680.

Today visitors swoon over the château's beautifully furnished interior, including its fabulous dome. In the vaulted cellars an exhibition looks at Le Nôtre's landscaping of the formal **gardens**. A collection of 18th- and 19th-century carriages in the château stables, included in the château admission, forms the **Musée des Équipages** (Carriage Museum).

Getting There & Away

Vaux-le-Vicomte is not an easy place to get to by public transport. The château is 6km northeast of Melun, which is served by RER line D2 from Paris (€7, 45 minutes). A shuttle bus (€3.50 each way) links Melun station with the château shuttle three to five times daily at weekends from April to October; at other times you'll have to take a **taxi** (☎ 01 64 52 51 50), which will cost about €20.

CHANTILLY

pop 11,000

The elegant old town of Chantilly, 48km north of Paris, is small, select and spoiled. Its château sits in a sea of parkland, gardens, lakes and the Forêt de Chantilly, which is packed with walking opportunities; its racetrack is one of the most prestigious hat-and-frock addresses in Europe; and that deliciously sweetened thick *crème* called Chantilly was created here (see the boxed text, p219). Whatever you do, don't come on Tuesday, when the imposing but heavily restored château is closed.

Information

Office de Tourisme de Chantilly (☎ 03 44 67 37 37; www.chantilly-tourisme.com; 60 av du Maréchal Joffre; ⏰ 9.30am-12.30pm & 1.30-5.30pm Mon-Sat, 10am-1.30pm Sun May-Sep, 9.30am-12.30pm & 1.30-5.30pm Mon-Sat Oct-Apr) Ample information on Chantilly, including accommodation lists and a trio of *promenades* leaflets outlining walks through town, along Chantilly's two canals and around the racecourse.

Post Office (26 av du Maréchal Joffre)

Sights

CHÂTEAU DE CHANTILLY

Left in a shambles after the Revolution, the **Château de Chantilly** (Chantilly Palace; ☎ 03 44 27 31 80; www.chateaudechantilly.com; adult/under 18yr €10/free; ⏰ 10am-6pm Wed-Mon Mar-Oct, 10.30am-5pm Wed-Mon Nov-Feb) is of interest mainly because of its gardens and the number of superb paintings it contains. It consists of two attached buildings, which are entered through the same vestibule.

The **Petit Château**, built around 1560 for Anne de Montmorency (1492–1567), who served six French kings as *connétable* (high constable), diplomat and warrior and died doing battle with Protestants in the Counter-

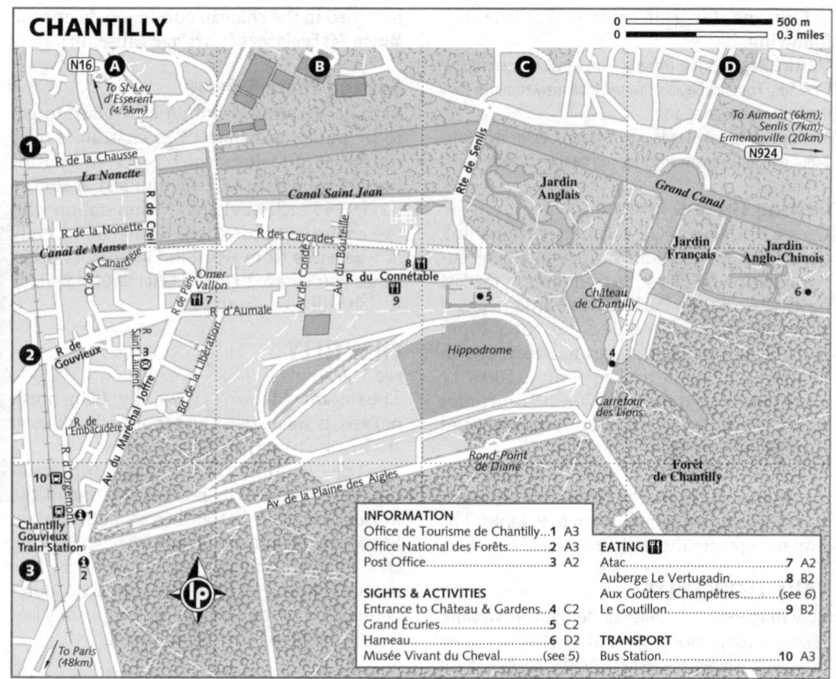

Reformation, contains the **Appartements des Princes** (Princes' Suites). The highlight here is the **Cabinet des Livres**, a repository of 700 manuscripts and more than 30,000 volumes, including a Gutenberg Bible and a facsimile of the *Très Riches Heures du Duc de Berry*, an illuminated manuscript dating from the 15th century that illustrates the calendar year for both the peasantry and the nobility. The **chapel**, to the left as you walk into the vestibule, has woodwork and stained-glass windows dating from the mid-16th century and was assembled by the duke in 1882.

The attached Renaissance-style **Grand Château** was rebuilt 100 years after the Revolution by the Duke of Aumale, son of King Louis-Philippe, and served as a French military headquarters during WWI. It contains the **Musée Condé**, a series of unremarkable 19th-century rooms adorned with paintings and sculptures haphazardly arranged according to the whims of the duke, who donated the château to the Institut de France on the condition that the exhibits not be reorganised and that they remain open to the general public. The most remarkable works are hidden away in a small room called the **Sanctuaire**, including paintings by Raffaelo, Filippino Lippi and Jean Fouquet.

The château's excellent gardens were once among the most spectacular in France. The formal **Jardin Français** (French Garden), with flowerbeds, lakes and a **Grand Canal** laid out by Le Nôtre in the mid-17th century, is northeast of the main building. To the west, the 'wilder' **Jardin Anglais** (English Garden) was begun in 1817. East of the Jardin Français is the rustic **Jardin Anglo-Chinois** (Anglo-Chinese Garden), created in the 1770s. Its foliage and silted-up waterways surround the **hameau**, a mock village dating from 1774 whose mill and half-timbered buildings inspired the Hameau de la Reine at Versailles. *Crème Chantilly* was born here (see the boxed text, opposite).

A normal ticket allows entry to the château, the Musée Condé and the park, though you can visit just the **park** and **gardens** (adult/under 18yr €5/free; 10am-6pm Wed-Mon). Combination tickets, available April to November, include the château, the museum, the park and a boat or minitrain ride through the park (adult/4 to 17 years €14/3) and the château, the museum, the park, a boat or minitrain ride (€19/6). A ticket covering just the park and a ride costs €10/3.

The château's **Grandes Écuries** (Grand Stables), built between 1719 and 1740 to house 240 horses and more than 400 hounds, stand apart from the château to the west and close to Chantilly's famous **hippodrome** (racecourse), inaugurated in 1834. Today the stables house the **Musée Vivant du Cheval** (Living Horse Museum; ☎ 03 44 27 31 80; www.museevivantducheval.fr; adult/12-17yr/4-11yr €9/7/5.50; 🕒 10.30am-6.30pm daily Apr-Oct, 2-6pm Mon & Wed-Fri, 10.30am-6.30pm Sat & Sun Nov-Mar), whose 30 pampered equines live in luxurious **wooden stalls** built by Louis-Henri de Bourbon, the seventh Prince de Condé, who was convinced he would be reincarnated as a horse (hence the extraordinary grandeur!). Displays include everything from riding equipment to rocking horses and portraits, drawings and sculptures of famous nags from the past.

Every visitor, big and small, will be mesmerised by the 30-minute **Présentation Équestre Pédagogique** (Introduction to Dressage; 🕒 11.30am, 3.30pm & 5.15pm Wed-Mon Apr-Oct, 11.30am Mon & Wed-Fri, 11.30am, 3.30pm & 5.15pm Sat & Sun Nov-Mar), which is included in the entry price. Even more magical and highly sought-after are the handful of **equestrian shows** (adult/12-17yr/4-11yr €18.50/14.50/12.50) performed in the stables each year; tickets are like gold dust and can be reserved online.

FORÊT DE CHANTILLY

South of the château is the 6300-hectare **Forêt de Chantilly** (Chantilly Forest), once a royal hunting estate and now criss-crossed by a variety of walking and riding trails. Long-distance trails here include the **GR11**, which links the château with the town of **Senlis** (p220) and its wonderful cathedral; the **GR1**, which goes from **Luzarches** (famed for its cathedral, parts of which date from the 12th century) to **Ermenonville**; and the **GR12**, which goes north-east from four lakes known as the **Étangs de Commelles** to the **Forêt d'Halatte**.

The area is covered by IGN's 1:25,000-scale *Forêts de Chantilly, d'Halatte and d'Ermenonville* map (number 2412OT; €9.80). The 1:100,000-scale *Carte de Découverte des Milieux Naturels et du Patrimoine Bâti* (€6.50), available at the tourist office, indicates sites of interest (eg churches, châteaux, museums and ruins). The **Office National des Forêts** (☎ 03 44 57 03 88; www.onf.fr, in French; 1 av de Sylvie; 🕒 8.30am-noon & 2-5pm Mon-Fri), just southeast of the tourist office, publishes a good walking guide for families called *Promenons-Nous dans les Forêts de Picardie: Chantilly, Halatte & Ermenonville* (€7.50), in French.

AROUND PARIS

Eating

Le Goutillon (☎ 03 44 58 01 00; 61 rue du Connétable; starters €8-10, mains €15-25; 🕒 lunch & dinner to 11pm Mon-Sat) With its red-and-white checked tablecloths, simple wooden tables and classic bistro fare, this wine-bar-cum-restaurant is a cosy French affair much loved by local expats. It's as much wine bar as munch hole.

our pick **Auberge Le Vertugadin** (☎ 03 44 57 03 19; 44 rue du Connétable; starters €14-38, mains €20-32, menu €28; 🕒 lunch daily, dinner to 11pm Mon-Sat) Old-style and elegant, this ode to regional cuisine – think meat, game and terrines accompanied by sweet onion chutney – fills a white-shuttered town house. A warming fire roars in the hearth in winter, and summer welcomes diners to its walled garden.

Aux Goûters Champêtres (☎ 03 44 57 46 21; Château de Chantilly; menus €19.50-41.50; 🕒 11am-7pm Mar-Nov) This fine restaurant in the windmill of the park's *hameau* has local specialities on the menu and is a wonderful place for lunch, particularly

CHÂTEAU DE WHIPPED CREAM

Like every self-respecting French château three centuries ago, the palace at Chantilly had its own *hameau* (hamlet) complete with *laitier* (dairy), where the lady of the household and her guests could play at being milkmaids, as Marie-Antoinette did at Versailles. But the cows at the Chantilly dairy took their job rather more seriously than their fellow bovines at other faux *crémeries* (dairy shops), and the *crème Chantilly* (sweetened whipped cream) served at the hamlet's teas became the talk (and envy) of aristocratic 18th-century Europe. The future Habsburg emperor Joseph II actually visited this *'temple de marbre'* (marble temple), as he called it, clandestinely to try out the white stuff in 1777. Chantilly (or more properly *crème Chantilly*) is whipped unpasteurised cream with a twist. It's beaten with icing and vanilla sugars to the consistency of a mousse and dolloped on berries. Sample it in any café or restaurant in town.

during the summer. Its chief claim to fame: *crème Chantilly* whipped up for the past 20 years by local chef Jean-Michel Duda.

The large **Atac supermarket** (5 place Omer Vallon; 9am-6pm) is midway between the train station and the château. Place Omer Vallon is also the location of the twice-weekly **market** (8.30am-12.30pm Wed & Sat).

Getting There & Away

The château is just over 2km northeast of the train and bus stations; the most direct route from there is to walk along av de la Plaine des Aigles through a section of the Forêt de Chantilly. You will get a better sense of the town, however, by following av du Maréchal Joffre and rue de Paris, so you can connect with rue du Connétable, Chantilly's principal thoroughfare.

Paris' Gare du Nord links with Chantilly-Gouvieux train station (€7, 30 to 45 minutes) by a mixture of RER and SNCF commuter trains (almost 40 a day, 20 on Sunday).

SENLIS

pop 16,500

Senlis, just 10km northeast of Chantilly, is an attractive medieval town of winding cobblestone streets, Gallo-Roman ramparts and towers. It was a royal seat from the time of Clovis to Henri IV and contains four small but fine **museums**, devoted to subjects as diverse as art, archeology, hunting and the French cavalry in North Africa.

The Gothic **Cathédrale de Notre Dame** (place du Parvis Notre Dame; 8am-6pm) was built between 1150 and 1191. The cathedral is unusually bright, but the stained glass, though original, is unexceptional. The magnificent carved-stone **Grand Portal** (1170), on the western side facing place du Parvis Notre Dame, has statues and a central relief relating to the life of the Virgin Mary. It is believed to have been the inspiration for the portal at the cathedral in Chartres.

The **Office de Tourisme de Senlis** (03 44 53 06 40; www.senlis-tourisme.fr; place du Parvis Notre Dame; 10am-12.30pm & 2-6.15pm Mon-Sat, 10.30am-1pm & 2-6.15pm Sun Mar-Oct, 10am-12.30pm & 2-5pm Mon-Sat, 10.30am-12.30pm & 2-5pm Sun Nov-Feb) is just opposite the cathedral.

Getting There & Away

Buses (€3.50, 25 minutes) link Senlis with Chantilly's bus station, just next to its train station, about every half-hour on weekdays and hourly on Saturday, with about a half-dozen departures on Sunday. The last bus returns to Chantilly at 8pm on weekdays (just after 7pm on Saturday and Sunday).

CHARTRES

pop 42,000

The magnificent 13th-century cathedral of Chartres, crowned by two very different spires – one Gothic, the other Romanesque – rises from rich farmland 88km southwest of Paris and dominates the medieval town around its base. The cathedral's varied collection of relics, particularly the Sainte Voile (see the boxed text, p222), attracted many pilgrims during the Middle Ages, who contributed to the building and extensions of the cathedral. With its astonishing blue stained glass and other treasures, the cathedral at Chartres, France's best-preserved medieval basilica, is a must-see for any visitor.

Information

Atlanteam (02 37 36 62 15; 13bis rue Jehan de Beauce; per 15/30/60mins €1/2/3.60; 10.30am-midnight Mon-Sat, 2pm-midnight Sun) Internet café.

Office de Tourisme de Chartres (02 37 18 26 26; www.chartres-tourisme.com; place de la Cathédrale; 9am-7pm Mon-Sat, 9.30am-5.30pm Sun Apr-Sep, 10am-6pm Mon-Sat, 10am-1pm & 2.30-4.30pm Sun Oct-Mar) The tourist office, across the square from the cathedral's main entrance, rents self-paced English-language audioguide tours (for one/two people €5.50/8.50; 1½ hours) of the medieval city and has info on binocular rental, cathedral lectures in English etc.

Post Office (3 blvd Maurice Violette)

Sights

CATHÉDRALE NOTRE DAME DE CHARTRES

The 130m-long **Cathédrale Notre Dame de Chartres** (Cathedral of Our Lady of Chartres; 02 37 21 22 07; www.diocese-chartres.com, in French; place de la Cathédrale; 8.30am-7.30pm), one of the crowning architectural achievements of Western civilisation, was built in the Gothic style during the first quarter of the 13th century to replace a Romanesque cathedral that had been devastated – along with much of the town – by fire on the night of 10 June 1194. Because of effective fund-raising and donated labour, construction took only 30 years, resulting in a high degree of architectural unity.

The cathedral's west, north and south entrances have superbly ornamented triple

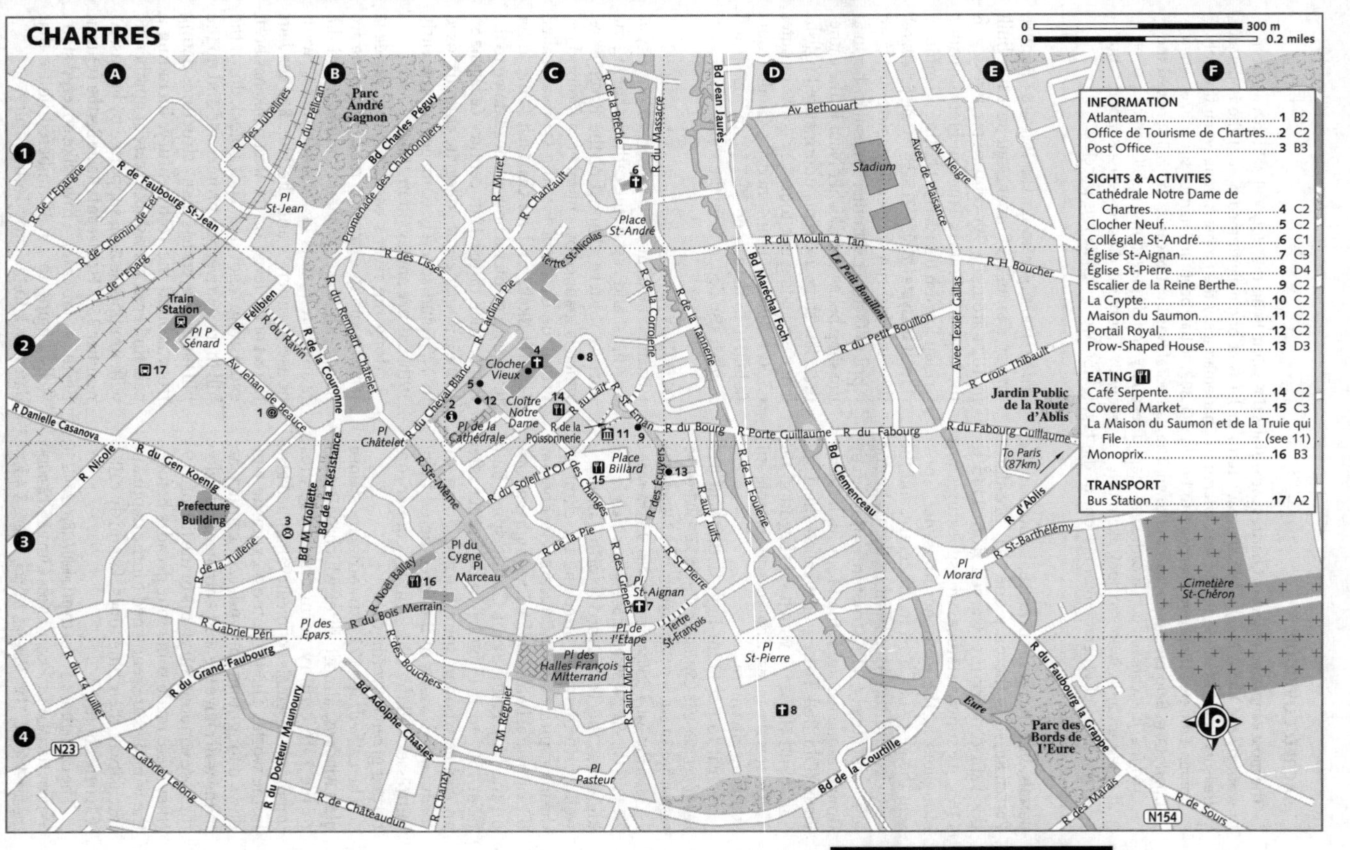
CHARTRES
0 300 m
0 0.2 miles
INFORMATION
Atlanteam 1 B2
Office de Tourisme de Chartres 2 C2
Post Office 3 B3
SIGHTS & ACTIVITIES
Cathédrale Notre Dame de Chartres 4 C2
Clocher Neuf 5 C2
Collégiale St-André 6 C1
Église St-Aignan 7 C3
Église St-Pierre 8 D4
Escalier de la Reine Berthe 9 C2
La Crypte 10 C2
Maison du Saumon 11 C2
Portail Royal 12 C2
Prow-Shaped House 13 D3
EATING
Café Serpente 14 C2
Covered Market 15 C3
La Maison du Saumon et de la Truie qui File (see 11)
Monoprix 16 B3
TRANSPORT
Bus Station 17 A2
Cimetière St-Chéron
Jardin Public de la Route d'Ablis
To Paris (87km)
Parc des Bords de l'Eure
Eure
Le Petit Bouillon
Stadium
Parc André Gagnon
Train Station
Prefecture Building
Pl des Épars
Pl Morard
Pl St-Pierre
Place St-André
Place Billard
Pl de la Cathédrale
Clocher Vieux
Cloître Notre Dame
Pl des Halles François Mitterrand
Pl du Cygne
Pl Marceau
Pl Châtelet
Pl St-Jean
Pl P Sénard
Pl Pasteur
Pl St-Aignan
Pl de l'Étape
Bd Charles Péguy
Bd Jean Jaurès
Bd Maréchal Foch
Bd Clemenceau
Bd de la Courtille
Bd Adolphe Chasles
Bd de la Résistance
Bd M Violette
R de la Couronne
R du Rempart Châtelet
Promenade des Charbonniers
R du Faubourg la Grappe
R d'Ablis
R du Grand Faubourg
R du Docteur Manoury
R du Gen Koenig
R de Faubourg St-Jean
Av Jehan de Beauce
R Félibien
R de la Tannerie
R de la Foulerie
R du Bourg
R Porte Guillaume
R du Fabourg Guillaume
R des Changes
R des Grenets
R de la Pie
R du Soleil d'Or
R Ste-Même
R du Cheval Blanc
R Cardinal Pie
R Noël Ballay
R du Bois Merrain
R des Bouchers
R Gabriel Péri
R du 14 Juillet
R Gabriel Lelong
R Nicole
R Danielle Casanova
N23
N154

SACRED COVER-UP

The most venerated object in Chartres cathedral is the Sainte Voile, the 'Holy Veil' said to have been worn by the Virgin Mary when she gave birth to Jesus. It originally formed part of the imperial treasury of Constantinople but was offered to Charlemagne by the Empress Irene when the Holy Roman Emperor proposed marriage to her in AD 802. It has been in Chartres since 876, when Charles the Bald presented it to the town. The cathedral was built because the veil survived the 1194 fire. It is contained in a cathedral-shaped reliquary and displayed in a small side chapel off the eastern aisle. It doesn't look like much – a yellowish bolt of silk draped over a support – but as the focus of veneration for millions of the faithful for two millennia it is priceless.

portals, but the west entrance, known as the **Portail Royal**, is the only one that pre-dates the 12th-century fire. Carved from 1145 to 1155, its superb statues, whose features are elongated in the Romanesque style, represent the glory of Christ in the centre, and the Nativity and the Ascension to the right and left, respectively. The structure's other main Romanesque feature is the 112m-high **Clocher Vieux** (Old Bell Tower; also called the Tour Sud 'South Tower'), which was begun in the 1140s. It is the tallest Romanesque steeple still standing anywhere.

A visit to the 112m-high **Clocher Neuf** (New Bell Tower; adult/18-25yr/under 18yr €6.50/4.50/free, admission free 1st Sun of certain months; 9.30am-noon & 2-5.30pm Mon-Sat, 2-5.30pm Sun May-Aug, 9.30am-noon & 2-4.30pm Mon-Sat, 2-4.30pm Sun Sep-Apr), which is also known as the Tour Nord (North Tower), is well worth the ticket price and the climb up the long spiral stairway. Access is just behind the cathedral bookshop. A 70m-high platform on the lacy Flamboyant Gothic spire, built from 1507 to 1513 by Jehan de Beauce after an earlier wooden spire burned down, affords superb views of the three-tiered flying buttresses and the 19th-century copper roof, turned green by verdigris.

The cathedral's 172 extraordinary **stained-glass windows**, almost all of which date back to the 13th century, form one of the most important ensembles of medieval stained glass in the world. The three most exquisite windows dating from the mid-12th century are in the wall above the west entrance and below the rose window. Survivors of the fire of 1194 (they were made some four decades before), the windows are renowned for the depth and intensity of their blue tones, famously called 'Chartres blue'.

The cathedral's 110m **crypt** (adult/7-18yr €2.70/2.10; tours 11am Mon-Sat, 2.15pm, 3.30pm, 4.30pm & 5.15pm daily late Jun–late Sep, 11am Mon-Sat, 2.15pm, 3.30pm & 4.30pm daily Apr–late Jun & late Sep–Oct, 11am Mon-Sat & 4.15pm daily Nov-Mar), a tombless Romanesque structure built in 1024 around a 9th-century predecessor, is the largest in France. Tours in French (with a written English translation) lasting 30 minutes start at **La Crypte** (☎ 02 37 21 56 33; 18 Cloître Notre Dame), the cathedral-run shop selling souvenirs, from April to October. At other times they begin at the shop below the Clocher Neuf in the cathedral. The shop also rents informative English-language audioguide tours (25/45/70 minutes €3.20/4.20/6.20) until 4pm daily. Guided tours (adult/10 to 18 years €6.20/4.20) in French and English also depart from the shop.

OLD CITY

Chartres' meticulously preserved old city is northeast and east of the cathedral along the narrow western channel of the River Eure, which is spanned by a number of footbridges. From rue Cardinal Pie, the stairway called **Tertre St-Nicolas** and **rue Chantault** – the latter lined with medieval houses – lead down to the empty shell of the 12th-century **Collégiale St-André**, a Romanesque collegiate church closed in 1791 and severely damaged in the early 19th century and again in 1944.

Along the river's eastern bank, **rue de la Tannerie** and its extension **rue de la Foulerie** are lined with flower gardens, millraces and the restored remnants of riverside trades: wash houses, tanneries and the like. **Rue aux Juifs** (Street of the Jews), on the west bank, has been extensively renovated. Half a block down the hill there's a riverside promenade and up the hill **rue des Écuyers** has many structures dating from around the 16th century, including a half-timbered, **prow-shaped house** at number 26, with its upper section supported by beams. At number 35 is **Escalier de la Reine Berthe** (Queen Bertha's Staircase), a towerlike covered stairwell clinging to a half-timbered house that dates back to the early 16th century.

Rue du Bourg and **rue de la Poissonnerie** also have some old half-timbered houses; on the latter, look for the magnificent **Maison du Saumon** (Salmon House), also known as the Maison de la Truie qui File, at numbers 10 to 12 and now a restaurant (see right), with its carved consoles of the Angel Gabriel and Mary, Michael the Archangel slaying the dragon and, of course, the eponymous salmon.

From **place St-Pierre**, you get a good view of the flying buttresses holding up the 12th- and 13th-century **Église St-Pierre** (place St-Pierre; 9am-noon & 2-6pm). Part of a Benedictine monastery in the 7th century, it was outside the city walls and vulnerable to attack; the fortresslike, pre-Romanesque **bell tower** attached to it was used as a refuge by monks and dates from around 1000. The fine, brightly coloured **clerestory windows** in the nave, the choir and the apse date from the early 14th century.

Église St-Aignan (place St-Aignan; 9am-noon & 2-6pm), first built in the early 16th century, is interesting for its wooden barrel-vault roof (1625), arcaded nave and painted interior of faded blue-and-gold floral motifs (c 1870). The stained glass and the Renaissance **Chapelle de St-Michel** date from the 16th century.

Eating

Café Serpente (02 37 21 68 81; 2 Cloître Notre Dame; starters €6-14.80, mains €15-20; 10am-11pm) Its location bang-slap opposite the cathedral ensures that this atmospheric brasserie and *salon de thé* (tearoom) is always full. Cuisine is traditional, and its chef also constructs well-filled sandwiches (€3.80 to €5.80).

Maison du Saumon et de la Truie qui File (02 37 36 28 00; 10-14 rue de la Poissonnerie; menus €29.80-32.90; lunch Tue-Sun, dinner to 11.30pm Tue-Sat) Inhabiting Chartres' most photographed half-timbered building, this medieval landmark cooks up a bit of everything, ranging from Polish stuffed-cabbage rolls and Hungarian goulash to Alsatian *choucroute* (sauerkraut with sausage and other prepared meats) and Moroccan *tajines* (€18.50 each).

There are a lot of food shops surrounding the **covered market** (place Billard; 7am-1pm Wed & Sat), just off rue des Changes south of the cathedral. The **Monoprix** (cnr 21 rue Noël Ballay & 10 rue du Bois Merrain; 9am-7.30pm Mon-Sat) department store with two entrances has a supermarket on the ground floor.

Getting There & Away

More than 30 SNCF trains a day (20 on Sunday) link Paris' Gare Montparnasse (€12.90, 70 minutes) with Chartres, all of which pass through Versailles-Chantiers (€10.90, 45 minutes to one hour).

The last train to Paris leaves Chartres just after 9pm weekdays, just before 9pm on Saturday and sometime after 10pm on Sunday.

AROUND PARIS

Far Northern France

France's northernmost bits have more to engage the visitor than many realise. True, a tan is easier to come by along the Mediterranean, but when it comes to culture, cuisine, shopping and dramatic views of land and sea – not to mention good old-fashioned friendliness – the Ch'tis (residents of the far north) and their region compete with the best France has to offer. In 2008 the film *Bienvenue chez les Ch'tis* (see the boxed text, p51), which debunks grim stereotypes about the far north with high jinks and hilarity, swept France, becoming the biggest box office hit in the history of French cinema and creating a miniboom in domestic tourism.

Lille is an ideal place to sample Flemish architecture, cuisine and beer. More regional flavour is on offer in Arras, whose Flemish-style squares are unique in France. Amiens, not far from the battlefields of the Somme and a number of moving WWI memorials, boasts a magnificent Gothic cathedral. If you snag a promotional fare on the Eurostar, the region is a superb, reasonably priced weekend getaway from London – with a much smaller carbon footprint than flying.

The most picturesque of the trans-Channel ports is Boulogne-sur-Mer. Dunkirk (Dunkerque), on the other hand, is so uncomely – much of the city was rebuilt after WWII – that you actually feel sorry for the locals, though there are still a few attractions. Although Calais has worthwhile museums and restaurants, not to mention *The Burghers* (see the boxed text, p236), most see it only through the window of an accelerating train, boat or car.

The sublime and spectacular Côte d'Opale stretches southward from Calais along the English Channel (La Manche). Inland, you'll find WWII sites and St-Omer, known for its basilica. Further south, the Somme estuary affords watery pleasures to humans and birds alike.

Just outside Greater Paris, Compiègne serves up the glories of Napoléon III's Second Empire; Beauvais is known for its huge, unfinished cathedral; and romantic Laon offers panoramic views from its hilltop old town.

HIGHLIGHTS

- Ramble along the spectacular, windswept **Côte d'Opale** (p243), facing the white cliffs of Dover
- Visit Lille's superb **museums** (p229) and sample its **restaurants** (p232) and **nightlife** (p233 and p233)
- Contemplate Amiens' breathtaking **Gothic cathedral** (p256) both inside and out
- Stroll around – and under – the Flemish-style centre of **Arras** (p249)
- Ponder the sacrifices and horror of WWI at the evocative **Battle of the Somme memorials** (p252)

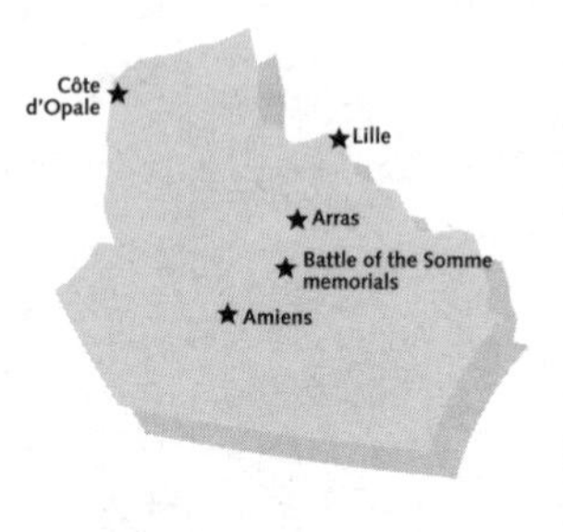

- POPULATION: 5.9 MILLION
- AREA: 31,813 SQ KM

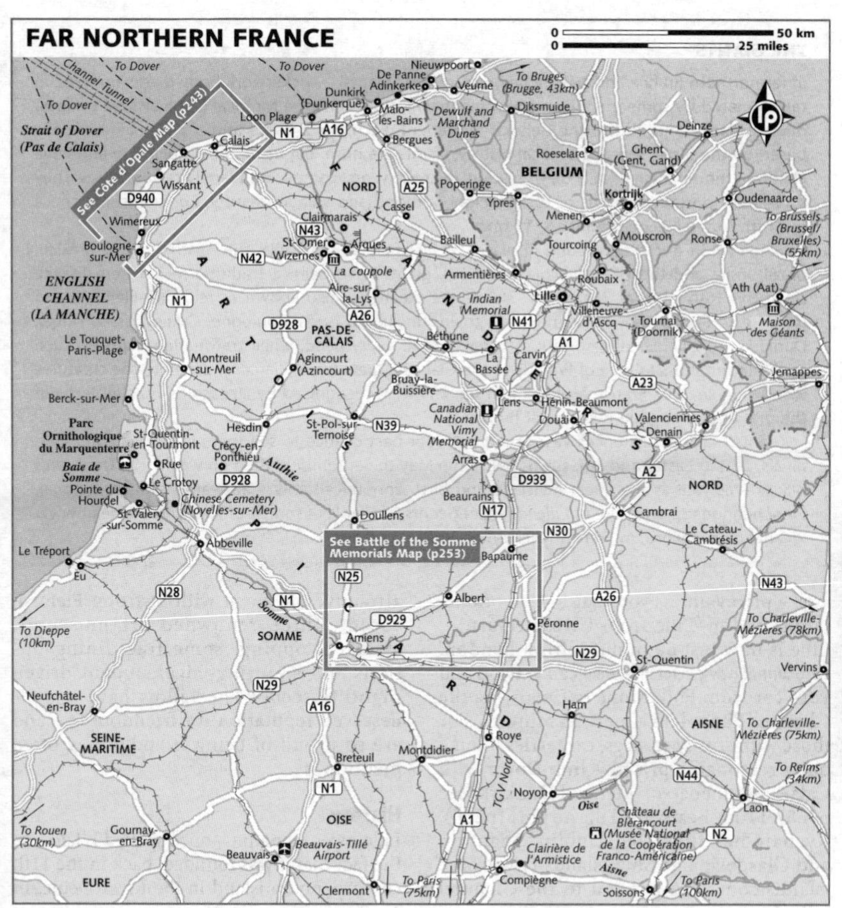

History & Geography

In the Middle Ages, the *département* of Nord (the sliver of France along the Belgian border; www.cdt-nord.fr), together with much of Belgium and part of the Netherlands, belonged to a feudal principality known as Flanders (Flandre or Flandres in French, Vlaanderen in Flemish), which has absolutely nothing to do with Homer Simpson's annoying next-door neighbour Ned and everything to do with John McCrae's famous WWI poem *In Flanders Fields*. Today, many people in the area still speak Flemish – essentially Dutch with some variances in pronunciation and vocabulary – and are very proud of their *flamand* culture and cuisine. Along with the *département* of Pas-de-Calais (www.pas-de-calais.com), the Nord forms the *région* of Nord-Pas de Calais (www.tourisme-nor dpasdecalais.fr).

The area south of the Somme estuary and Albert, towards Paris, forms the *région* of Picardy (Picardie; www.cr-picardie.fr), historically centred on the Somme *département* (www.somme-tourisme.com). The area northeast of Amiens saw some of the bloodiest fighting of WWI. The popular British WWI love song 'Roses of Picardy' (www.firstworldwar.com/audio/rosesofpicardy.htm) was penned here in 1916 by Frederick E Weatherley.

Getting There & Away

Far northern France is a hop, skip and a jump from England. On the **Eurostar** (www.eurostar

THE GIANTS

In far northern France and nearby Belgium, *géants* (giants) – wickerwork body masks up to 8.5m tall animated by someone (or several someones) inside – emerge for local carnivals and on feast days to dance and add to the general merriment. Each has a name and a personality, usually based on the Bible, legends or local history. Giants are born, baptised, grow up, marry and have children (though never really die), creating, over the years, complicated family relationships. They serve as important symbols of town, neighbourhood and village identity. For snapshots check out http://utan.lille.free.fr/geants_1.htm.

Medieval in origin and found in places as far afield as Catalonia, the Austrian Tyrol, Mexico, Brazil, India and the UK (www.giants.org.uk), giants have been a tradition in northern France since the 16th century. More than 300 of the creatures, also known as *reuze* (in Flemish) and *gayants* (in Picard), now 'live' in French towns, including Arras, Boulogne, Calais, Cassel, Douai, Dunkirk and Lille. Local associations cater to their every need, while transnational groups such as the International Circle of Friends of the Giant Puppets (www.ciag.org) promote the creatures worldwide. In 2005 France and Belgium's giants were recognised by Unesco as 'masterpieces of the oral and intangible heritage of humanity'.

Giants make appearances year-round but your best chance to see them is at pre-Lenten carnivals, during Easter and at festivals held from May to September, often on weekends. Dates and places – as well as the latest marriage and birth announcements – appear in the free, annual, French-language brochure *Le Calendrier des Géants*, available at tourist offices; and online at www.geants-carnaval.org, in French (click on 'Agenda, actualités').

.com) – pricey unless you snag a promotional fare (London–Lille from UK£55 return) – Lille is now just 80 minutes from London. **Eurotunnel** (www.eurotunnel.com) can get you and your car from Folkestone to Calais, via the Channel Tunnel, in a mere 35 minutes. For those with sturdy sea legs, car ferries – some quite reasonably priced – link Dover with Calais, Boulogne-sur-Mer and Dunkirk (see p968). From Beauvais-Tillé airport (p260), Ryanair has flights to Dublin, Shannon and Glasgow; and Blue Islands (www.blueislands.com) can get you to the Channel Islands.

On the Continent, superfast Eurostars and TGVs link Lille with Brussels (35 minutes) and TGVs make travel from Lille to Paris' Gare du Nord (one hour) a breeze. Compiègne and Beauvais are close enough to Paris to be visited as day trips.

LILLE

pop 224,900 (1 million in metro area)

Lille (Rijsel in Flemish) may be France's most underrated major city. In recent decades this once-grimy industrial metropolis, its economy based on declining technologies, has transformed itself – with generous government help – into a glittering and self-confident cultural and commercial hub. Highlights for the visitor include an attractive old town with a strong Flemish accent, three renowned art museums, stylish shopping, some fine-dining options and a cutting-edge, student-driven nightlife scene. The Lillois have a well-deserved reputation for friendliness – and are so proud of being friendly they often mention it!

History

Lille owes its name – once spelled L'Isle – to the fact that it was founded, back in the 11th century, on an island in the River Deûle. In 1667 the city was captured by French forces led personally by Louis XIV, who promptly set about fortifying his prize (see p230). Long the centre of France's textile industry, the miserable conditions in which its 'labouring classes' lived were exposed by Victor Hugo in the 1850s.

Lille's textile industry has declined but the city has shown renewed vigour and self-confidence since the TGV came to town in 1993, followed a year later by the Eurostar from London.

Orientation

Place du Général de Gaulle (also called the Grand' Place) separates Lille's main shopping precinct (around pedestrianised rue Neuve), to the south, from the narrow streets of Vieux

Lille (Old Lille), to the north. The Wazemmes neighbourhood is about 1.7km southwest of Place du Général de Gaulle.

Lille's two main train stations, old-fashioned Gare Lille-Flandres and ultramodern Gare Lille-Europe, are 400m apart on the eastern edge of the city centre.

Information

BOOKSHOPS

Le Furet du Nord (☎ 03 20 78 43 43; 15 place du Général de Gaulle; Ⓜ Rihour; ⏲ 9.30am-7.30pm Mon-Sat) One of the largest bookshops in Europe. The 4th floor has plenty of English-language books.

INTERNET ACCESS

4 Players (☎ 03 20 07 43 18; 9 rue Maertens; Ⓜ République Beaux Arts; per 10min/hr prepaid €0.50/3; ⏲ 11am-10.30pm Mon-Fri, 10am-11.30pm Sat, 2-10pm Sun) Yes, it's pronounced 'foreplayers'.

Atlanteam (☎ 03 20 10 05 15; 93 rue Solférino; per hr €3.60; ⏲ 10.30am-midnight Mon-Sat, to 7am on Fri & Sat nights with a reservation, 2-11pm Sun)

Net Arena (☎ 03 28 38 09 20; 10 rue des Bouchers; per hr €3; ⏲ 10am-10pm Mon-Sat, 2-8pm Sun) Has 30 computers.

LAUNDRY

Zombified by too much art and culture? Many experts recommend staring at washing machines going round and round.

Laundrette (4 rue Ovigneur; Ⓜ République Beaux Arts; ⏲ 7am-8pm)

MEDICAL SERVICES

Hôpital Roger Salengro (☎ 03 20 44 61 40/41; rue du Professeur Émile Laine; Ⓜ CHR B Calmette; ⏲ 24hr) The *accueil urgences* (emergency room/casualty ward) of Lille's vast, 15-hospital Cité Hospitalière is 4km southwest of the city centre.

SOS Médecins (☎ 03 20 29 91 91; 3 av Louise Michel; Ⓜ Porte de Douai; consultation at clinic day/weekend €22/48.50, night €64.50-73.50, house calls day/weekend €32/52, night €68-77; ⏲ 24hr) Round-the-clock medical clinic and house calls by doctors.

MONEY

There are commercial banks with ATMs along rue Nationale. The tourist office will usually agree to exchange small sums but the rate is poor.

International Currency Exchange (⏲ 7.30am-8pm Mon-Sat, 10am-8pm Sun) In Gare Lille-Europe next to *accès* (track access) H.

Travelex exchange bureau (⏲ 8am-6.30pm Mon-Fri, 10am-5pm Sat, 10am-4pm Sun & holidays) In Gare Lille-Flandres next to counter N.

POST

Branch Post Office (1 bd Carnot; Ⓜ Rihour) In the Chambre de Commerce building.

Main Post Office (8 place de la République; Ⓜ République Beaux Arts) Changes money.

TOURIST INFORMATION

Tourist Office (☎ from abroad 03 59 57 94 00, in France 08 91 56 20 04; www.lilletourism.com; place Rihour; Ⓜ Rihour; ⏲ 9.30am-6.30pm Mon-Sat, 10am-noon & 2-5pm Sun & holidays) Occupies what's left of the Flamboyant Gothic–style Palais Rihour, built in the mid-1400s for Philip the Good, Duke of Burgundy; a war memorial forms the structure's eastern side. A brochure (€2) outlines five walking tours. City maps cost €0.50.

Sights & Activities

CITY-CENTRE ARCHITECTURE

Vieux Lille (Old Lille), which begins just north of place du Général de Gaulle, is justly proud of its restored 17th- and 18th-century houses. The old brick residences along **rue de la Monnaie** (named after a mint built here in 1685) now house chic boutiques and the Musée de l'Hospice Comtesse (p230). Hard to believe, but in the late 1970s this area was a half-abandoned slum with lots of empty, dilapidated buildings, their windows breeze-blocked-up to keep out vandals and squatters.

The Flemish Renaissance **Vieille Bourse** (Old Stock Exchange; place du Général de Gaulle; Ⓜ Rihour) of 1652, ornately decorated with caryatids and cornucopia, actually consists of 24 separate houses. The courtyard in the middle hosts a **used-book market** (⏲ 1pm or 1.30pm–7pm or 7.30pm Tue-Sun) – old postcards and comic books are also available – and in the warm months locals often gather to play *échecs* (chess).

> **LILLE CITY PASS**
>
> Available in one-/two-/three-day versions (€18/30/45), this pass gets you into almost all the museums in greater Lille (www.destination-lille-metropole.eu) and affords unlimited use of public transport. The three-day version includes eight sites in the Nord-Pas de Calais *région* and the use of regional TER trains. Available at the Lille tourist office.

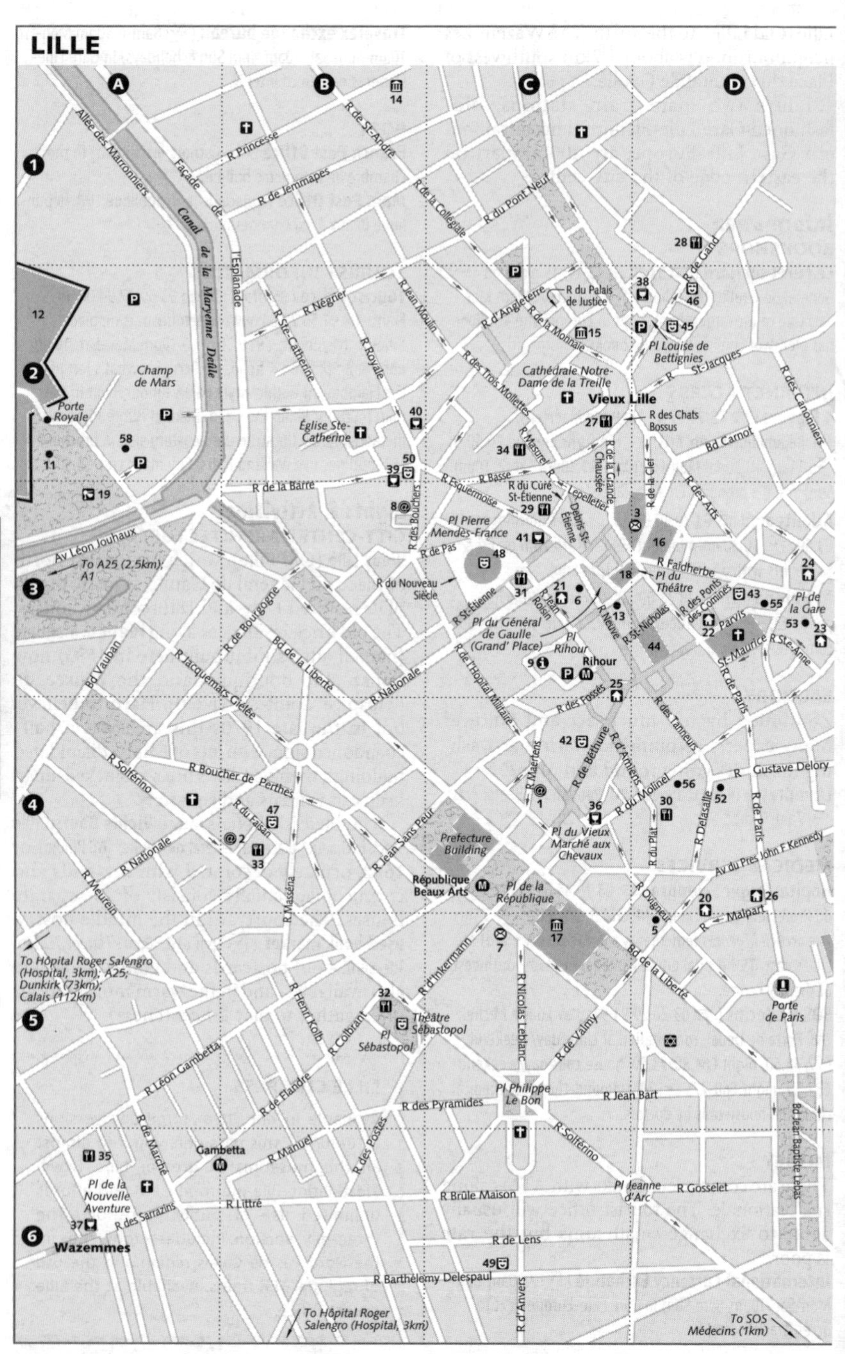
LILLE
Vieux Lille
Champ de Mars
Canal de la Moyenne Deûle
Porte Royale
Cathédrale Notre-Dame de la Treille
Église Ste-Catherine
Pl Pierre Mendès-France
Pl du Général de Gaulle (Grand' Place)
Pl Rihour
Rihour
Pl du Théâtre
Pl Louise de Bettignies
Parvis St-Maurice
Pl de la Gare
Prefecture Building
République Beaux Arts
Pl de la République
Pl du Vieux Marché aux Chevaux
Théâtre Sébastopol
Pl Sébastopol
Pl Philippe Le Bon
Pl Jeanne d'Arc
Porte de Paris
Gambetta
Pl de la Nouvelle Aventure
Wazemmes
To A25 (2.5km); A1
To Hôpital Roger Salengro (Hospital, 3km); A25; Dunkirk (73km); Calais (112km)
To Hôpital Roger Salengro (Hospital, 3km)
To SOS Médecins (1km)
Av Léon Jouhaux
Bd Vauban
Bd de la Liberté
R Nationale
R Solférino
R Esquermoise
R de la Barre
R Royale
R Négrier
R Princesse
R de Jemmapes
R de St-André
R de la Collégiale
R du Pont Neuf
R d'Angleterre
R de la Monnaie
R du Palais de Justice
R des Trois Mollettes
R des Chats Bossus
Bd Carnot
R des Arts
R Faidherbe
R Neuve
R de Béthune
R des Tanneurs
R Gustave Delory
Av du Pres John F Kennedy
R de Paris
R Malpart
R Jean Bart
R des Pyramides
R Gosselet
R Brûle Maison
R de Lens
R Barthélemy Delespaul
R d'Anvers
R Nicolas Leblanc
R de Valmy
R d'Inkermann
R Léon Gambetta
R de Flandre
R des Postes
R Manuel
R Littré
R des Sarrazins
R de Marché
R Meurein
R Masséna
R Jean Sans Peur
R Boucher de Perthes
R Jacquemars Giélée
R de Bourgogne
Bd Jean Baptiste Lebas
Façade de l'Esplanade
Allée des Marronniers
R de Gand
R St-Jacques
R des Canonniers
R du Molinel
R d'Amiens
R des Fossés
R de l'Hôpital Militaire
R St-Étienne
R du Nouveau Siècle
R de Pas
R des Bouchers
R Basse
R du Curé St-Étienne
R Lepelletier
R de la Grande Chaussée
R de la Clef
R St-Nicholas
R des Ponts des Comines
R Ste-Anne
R Maertens
R du Plat
R Delasalle
R Ougneur
R Henri Kolb
R Colbrant
R du Faisan
R Ste-Catherine
R Jean Moulin
R Masurel
Debris St-Étienne
R Jean Roisin
R Esquermoise

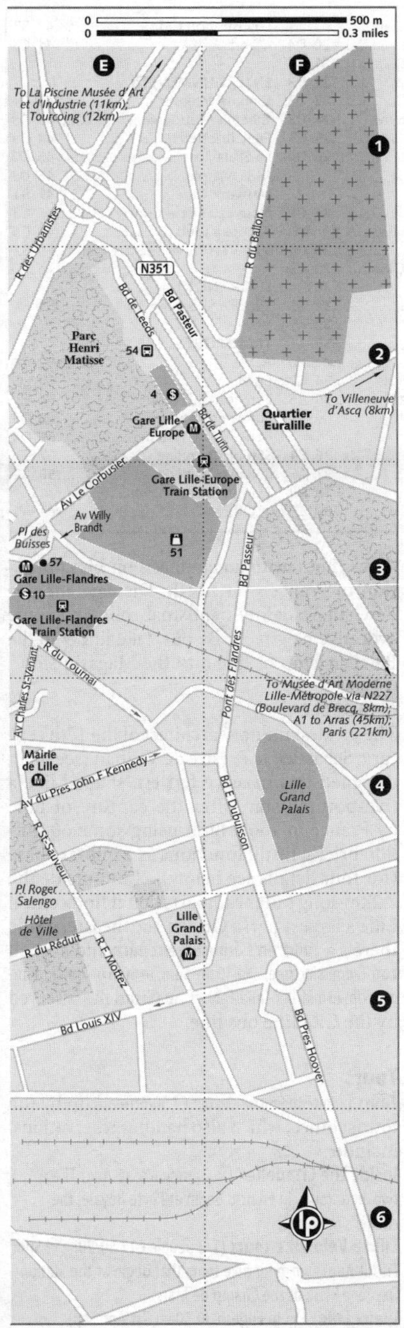

On the southern side of place du Général de Gaulle, the 1932 art-deco home of **La Voix du Nord** (M Rihour), the leading regional daily, has a gilded sculpture of the Three Graces on top. The goddess-topped **column** (1845) in the square's fountain commemorates the city's successful resistance to the Austrian siege of 1792.

Nearby place du Théâtre is dominated by the Louis XVI–style **Opéra** (M Rihour) and the neo-Flemish **Chambre de Commerce** (M Rihour), topped by a 76m-high spire with a gilded clock. Both were built in the early 20th century.

PALAIS DES BEAUX-ARTS

Lille's world-renowned **Palais des Beaux-Arts** (Fine Arts Museum; ☎ 03 20 06 78 00; www.pba-lille.fr; place de la République; M République Beaux Arts; adult/12-25yr/under 12yr €5/3.50/free; 2-6pm Mon, 10am-6pm Wed-Sun), built from 1885 to 1892, has a truly first-rate collection of 15th- to 20th-century paintings, including works by Rubens, Van Dyck and Manet. On the ground floor, there's exquisite porcelain and faïence (pottery), much of it of local provenance, while in the basement you'll find classical archeology, medieval statuary and 18th-century models of the fortified cities of northern France and Belgium. Tickets are valid for the whole day. Information sheets are available in each hall.

MUSÉE D'ART MODERNE LILLE-MÉTROPOLE

The highly regarded **Musée d'Art Moderne Lille-Métropole** (Museum of Modern Art; ☎ 03 20 19 68 68; www.mamlm.fr, in French; 1 allée du Musée, Villeneuve-d'Ascq), in a sculpture park 9km east of Gare Lille-Europe (the route is circuitous, so if you're driving, get a good map), displays colourful, playful and just plain weird works of modern and contemporary art by masters such as Braque, Calder, Léger, Miró, Modigliani and Picasso. It will be closed until sometime in 2009 while a new wing, designed to house France's most important collection of Art Brut, is completed. To get there, take metro line 1 to Pont de Bois and then bus 41 to Parc Urbain-Musée.

LA PISCINE MUSÉE D'ART ET D'INDUSTRIE

If Paris can turn a disused train station into a world-class museum, why not take an art-deco municipal swimming pool (built 1927–32) – an architectural masterpiece inspired by a combination of civic pride and hygienic high-mindedness – and transform it into a temple of the arts? This innovative **museum** (☎ 03 20

INFORMATION
4 Players......1 C4
Atlanteam......2 B4
Branch Post Office......3 D3
International Currenct Exchange......4 E2
Laundrette......5 D5
Le Furet du Nord......6 C3
Main Post Office......7 C5
Net Arena......8 B3
Tourist Office......9 C3
Travelex Exchange Bureau......10 E3

SIGHTS & ACTIVITIES
Chambre de Commerce......(see 3)
Children's Amusement Park......11 A2
Citadelle......12 A2
La Voix du Nord......13 C3
Maison Natale de Charles de Gaulle......14 B1
Musée de l'Hospice Comtesse......15 C2
Opéra......16 D3
Palais des Beaux-Arts......17 C5
Used-Book Market......(see 18)
Vieille Bourse......18 C3
Zoo......19 A3

SLEEPING
Auberge de Jeunesse......20 D4
Grand Hôtel Bellevue......21 C3
Hôtel Brueghel......22 D3
Hôtel Faidherbe......23 D3
Hôtel Flandre-Angleterre......24 D3
Hôtel Kanaï......25 C3
L'Hermitage Gantois......26 D4

EATING
À l'Huîtrière......27 C2
Carrefour Hypermarket......(see 51)
Estaminet 'T Rijsel......28 D1
Fromagerie Philippe Olivier......29 C3
La Source......30 D4
Le Barbu d'Anvers......31 C3
Marché Sébastopol......32 B5
Match Supermarket......33 B4
Outdoor Market......(see 35)
Tous Les Jours Dimanche......34 C2
Wazemmes Food Market......35 A6

DRINKING
Café Citoyen......36 C4
Café Le Relax......37 A6
Café Oz......38 D2
Le Balatum......39 B2
L'Illustration Café......40 B2
Meert......41 C3

ENTERTAINMENT
Cinéma Majestic......42 C4
Cinéma Metropole......43 D3
Fnac Billetterie......44 D3
La Scala......45 D2
Miss Marple......46 D2
Network Café......47 B4
Nouveau Siècle Concert Hall......48 C3
Tchouka Club......49 C6
Vice Versa......50 B2

SHOPPING
Euralille Shopping Mall......51 E3

TRANSPORT
ADA......52 D4
DLM......53 D3
Eurolines Bus Stop......54 E2
Eurolines Office......55 D3
Rent-A-Car Système......56 D4
Station Oxygène......57 E3
Station Oxygène......58 A2
Transpole Information Offices......(see 57)

69 23 60; www.roubaix-lapiscine.com; 23 rue de l'Espérance, Roubaix; Ⓜ Gare Jean Lebas; adult/under 18yr €3.50/free; 11am-6pm Tue-Thu, 11am-8pm Fri, 1-6pm Sat & Sun), 12km northeast of Gare Lille-Europe, showcases fine arts, applied arts and sculpture in a delightfully watery environment. The restaurant and *salon de thé* (tearoom) is run by Meert (p233).

MUSÉE DE L'HOSPICE COMTESSE

Housed in an attractive 15th- and 17th-century poorhouse, the **Musée de l'Hospice Comtesse** (Hospice Comtesse Museum; ☎ 03 28 36 84 00; 32 rue de la Monnaie; adult/student/under 12yr €3/2/free; 10am-12.30pm & 2-6pm, closed Mon morning & Tue) features ceramics, earthenware wall tiles, religious art and 17th- and 18th-century paintings and furniture. A rood screen separates the Salle des Malades (Hospital Hall) from a mid-17th-century chapel with a mid-19th-century painted ceiling.

MAISON NATALE DE CHARLES DE GAULLE

The upper-middle-class house in which Charles André Marie Joseph de Gaulle – WWII Resistance leader, architect of the Fifth Republic and ferocious defender of French interests – was born in 1890 has been turned into a **museum** (☎ 03 28 38 12 05; www.maison-natale-de-gaulle.com; 9 rue Princesse; adult/10-26yr €5/3, English audioguide €1.50; 10am-noon & 2-5pm Wed-Sun) that presents the French leader in the context of his times, with an emphasis on his connection to France's far north. Displays include de Gaulle's dainty baptismal robe and some evocative newsreels. By bus, take line 9 to the Bateliers stop or line 6 to the Magasin stop.

CITADELLE

The greatest military architect of the 17th century, Sébastien le Prestre de Vauban (see p65), designed this massive **fortress**, shaped like a five-pointed star, after the capture of Lille by France in 1667. Built using some 60 million bricks, it still functions as a military base (for tour details see below) – but outside the 2.2km-long outer ramparts you'll find central Lille's largest park. On the southeastern side there's a **children's amusement park** and a small **zoo** (admission free; 10am-5pm, to 6pm or 7pm in summer, closed mid-Dec–mid-Feb). The Citadelle is served by the Citadine bus line.

Tours

Tours (adult/student/under 6yr €7.50/6/free) run by the tourist office, which also handles reservations, include:

Inside the Citadelle (3pm Sun May-Aug) These two-hour tours, in French, begin at Porte Royale, the citadel's main gate.

Lille à Vélo bike tours (1/2 people €12.50/20; 5pm Fri Jul-Aug) Two-hour bike tours that begin at the Station Oxygène kiosk at the Champ de Mars.

Vieux Lille (in English 10.30am Sat Apr-Sep)

Festivals & Events

The **Braderie** (below), a flea market extraordinaire, is held on the first weekend in September. Christmas decorations and edible goodies are sold at the **Marché de Noël** (Christmas market; place Rihour; late Nov–30 Dec). Every two or three years until the year 3000 (so they say), an international cultural event called **Lille 3000** (www.lille3000.com) will link Lille with a different part of the globe – from mid-March to mid-July 2009, 'Les Frontières Invisibles' will focus on Central and Eastern Europe, including Istanbul.

Sleeping

Because of the business market, many of Lille's hotels are at their fullest from Monday to Thursday. Lots of one-, two- and three-star hotels face Gare Lille-Flandres.

BUDGET

Auberge de Jeunesse (03 20 57 08 94; www.hihostels.com; lille@fuaj.org; 12 rue Malpart; M Mairie de Lille; dm incl breakfast €16.85, d €33.70; closed 23 Dec–mid-Jan;) This Spartan former maternity hospital, locked from 11am to 3pm (till 4pm from Friday to Sunday), has 165 beds (two to eight per room). Toilets and showers are down the hall for most rooms; a few doubles have en-suite showers. Kitchen facilities are available.

Hôtel Faidherbe (03 20 06 27 93; hotelfaidherbe@wanadoo.fr; 42 place de la Gare; M Gare Lille-Flandres; d from €47, with washbasin €33) The 40 one-star rooms are compact, cheerful, pastel and very simply furnished. The perfect choice for linoleum fans. Has a lift.

MIDRANGE

Hôtel Kanaï (03 20 57 14 78; www.hotelkanai.com; 10 rue de Béthune; M Rihour; d Mon-Thu €75-95, Fri-Sun €60-65, festival period €105;) You can't get much more central than this two-star place. Completely renovated in 2007, its 31 rooms have clean, minimalist lines; some of the top-floor rooms have great views but there's no lift. By car, take bd de la Liberté, rue Jean Sans Peur and then rue des Fossés.

Hôtel Flandre-Angleterre (03 20 06 04 12; www.hotel-flandre-angleterre.fr; 13 place de la Gare; M Gare Lille-Flandres; s/d Mon-Thu from €60/76, Fri-Sun from €60/69, q €90) This hotel's 44 two-star rooms, though comfortable, clean and quiet, are, shall we say, somewhat lacking in character – but hey, there's plenty of that outside. The best rooms have views of the Lille-Flandres train station.

Hôtel Brueghel (03 20 06 06 69; www.hotel-brueghel.com; 5 parvis St-Maurice; M Gare Lille-Flandres; s/d from €78/84) The 65 two-star rooms here are a mix of modern styling (eg the bathrooms) and antique furnishing, though they don't have nearly as much Flemish charm as the lobby. The tiny wood-and-wrought-iron lift dates from the 1920s.

Grand Hôtel Bellevue (03 20 57 45 64; www.grandhotelbellevue.com; 5 rue Jean Roisin; M Rihour; d €135-165;) This three-star Best Western–affiliated establishment was grandly built in the early 20th century. A charmingly creaky belle-époque lift trundles guests to the 60 spacious rooms, which have high ceilings, antique-style French furnishings and flat-screen TVs. Breakfast is usually free if you stay on a Friday, Saturday or Sunday night.

TOP END

our pick **L'Hermitage Gantois** (03 20 85 30 30; www.hotelhermitagegantois.com; 224 rue de Paris; d €205-275, ste €415;) Occupying a one-time nun-run hospital complex, parts of which were built as far back as the 1460s, this supremely tasteful four-star hotel creates enchanting, harmonious spaces by complimenting its rich architectural heritage – including a

BRADERIE DE LILLE

On the first weekend in September, Lille's entire city centre – 200km of footpaths – is transformed into the Braderie de Lille, billed as the world's largest flea market. The extravaganza – with stands selling antiques, local delicacies, handicrafts and more – dates from the Middle Ages, when Lillois servants were permitted to hawk their employers' old garments for some extra cash.

The city's biggest annual event, the Braderie runs from 3pm on Saturday to midnight on Sunday, when street sweepers emerge to tackle the mounds of mussel shells and old *frites* (French fries) left behind by the merrymakers. Before the festivities, you can make room for all those extra calories by joining in the half marathon held at 9am on Saturday. A free map of the market, *Braderie de Lille – Le Plan,* is available from Lille's tourist office.

Flemish-Gothic facade – with refined ultra-modern elements. The 72 rooms are huge and luxurious, with Starck furnishings next to Louis XV–style chairs and bathrooms sparkling with Carrara marble. One of the four courtyards is home to a 220-year-old wisteria recognised as a historic monument. The chapel, still consecrated, was built in 1637.

Eating

Lille, especially Vieux Lille, has an excellent and varied selection of restaurants and *estaminets* (traditional Flemish eateries, with antique knick-knacks on the walls and plain wooden tables), many of them serving Flemish specialities such as *carbonnade* (braised beef stewed with beer and brown sugar). In Vieux Lille, dining areas include the southern part of rue Royale (an ethnic cuisine hot spot); the eastern end of rue de la Barre; rue de la Monnaie and its side streets; and, a bit to the northeast, rue de Gand. West of the main post office, there are cheap eats on lively, studenty rue d'Inkermann, rue Solférino and rue Masséna. Good-value, *restaurants populaires* can be found around the Wazemmes food market.

Estaminet 'T Rijsel (☎ 03 20 15 01 59; 25 rue de Gand; mains €9.90-19.90; noon-1.30pm & 7.30-9.30pm, to 10pm or 10.30pm Fri & Sat, closed Mon lunch & Sun) Decorated with hops vines and items you'd have found in a Flemish kitchen a century ago, this homey, unpretentious eatery serves up local specialities such as *carbonnade* (€9.90), *pot'je vleesch* (a cold meat terrine; €11.90) and *poulet au Maroilles* (chicken with Maroilles cheese).

Tous Les Jours Dimanche (☎ 03 28 36 05 92; 13 rue Masurel; menus €15.50-16.50; restaurant noon-2.30pm, salon de thé noon-6.30pm, closed Mon, also closed Sun May-Sep) Having tea or a light lunch here, surrounded by a motley mixture of antique furniture and well-chosen objets d'art, is like hanging out in an arty friend's living room. Specialities include salads, sandwiches (€11) and quiche-like tartes (€11). As it is especially popular with women, locals say it has an *ambiance feminine*. On Sundays from October to mid-April, you can have a *brunch anglais* (€19.50) starting at 11.30am.

Le Barbue d'Anvers (☎ 03 20 55 11 68; 1bis rue St-Étienne; M Rihour; menu €38; Mon-Sat, closed Mon Jul & Aug) Named after a race of Belgian chickens, this well-regarded regional restaurant occupies an 18th-century building at the end of a cobblestone courtyard, its three levels decorated with antique Dutch and Flemish furnishings

our pick **À l'Huîtrière** (☎ 03 20 55 43 41; www.huitriere.fr, in French; 3 rue des Chats Bossus; lunch menu €45, other menus €100-140; noon-2pm & 7-9.30pm, closed dinner Sun & late Jul–late Aug) In 1928 the great-grandfather of the present owners turned to the nascent art-deco movement – first exhibited (and named) in Paris just three years earlier – to find suitably elegant decoration for his fish shop, situated on 'Street of the Hunchback Cats'. The sea-themed mosaics and stained glass are worth a look-in even if you're not in the mood to dine on seafood fresh out of the water – accompanied, perhaps, by a wine or two from the over-40,000-bottle cellar. Booking ahead is recommended for Friday dinner and Saturday.

LA SOURCE

Founded way back in 1979 and – thanks to its light and airy restaurant – now a Lille institution, **La Source** (☎ 03 20 57 53 07; 13 rue du Plat; M République Beaux Arts; 2-course menus €8.50-14; meals 11.30am-2.30pm Mon-Sat, 7-9pm Fri, shop 8.30am-7pm Mon-Sat, to 9pm Fri) serves vegetarian, fowl and fish *plats du jour* that are not just for the granola set. Both the decor and the diners exude health, well-being and cheer.

SELF-CATERING

About 1.5km southwest of the tourist office, in Wazemmes, an ethnically mixed, *populaire* (working-class) neighbourhood that's slowly gentrifying, you'll find Lille's beloved **Wazemmes food market** (place de la Nouvelle Aventure; M Gambetta; 8am-2pm Tue-Thu, 8am-8pm Fri & Sat, 8am-3pm Sun & holidays). Right outside, the city's largest **outdoor market** (7am-1.30pm or 2pm Tue, Thu & Sun) is *the* place to be in Lille on Sunday morning – a real carnival scene! There's another outdoor market, **Marché Sébastopol** (place Sébastopol; M République Beaux Arts; 7am-2pm Wed & Sat), a bit nearer the centre.

Other food-shopping options:

Carrefour hypermarket (Euralille shopping mall; M Gare Lille-Europe; 9am-9.30pm Mon-Sat) Vast, with no fewer than 62 checkout counters! Has small, adjacent halal and kosher sections.

Fromagerie Philippe Olivier (☎ 03 20 74 96 99; 3 rue du Curé St-Étienne; M Rihour; 9am or 10am–12.30pm & 3-7.30pm Tue-Fri, 9am-12.30pm & 1-7.30pm Sat) Fine cheeses.

Match supermarket (97 rue Solférino; 8.30am-9pm Mon-Sat) Inside a 19th-century cast-iron covered market.

CAFÉ CITOYEN

Progressive-minded volunteers turned a failing bar into the informal and very friendly **Café Citoyen** (Citizen Café; ☎ 03 20 13 15 73; http://cafecitoyen.org, in French; 7 place du Vieux Marché aux Chevaux; Ⓜ République Beaux Arts; ⏲ noon-midnight Mon-Fri, 2-9pm or later Sat, 2pm or 4pm–7pm or later Sun; 💻) in which social and environmental questions are aired in public debates and discussions. Internet access is free if you order an organic microbrewed beer, a glass of wine (€3.30) or a cup of fair-trade coffee (€1.50) from the friendly fellow wearing round, Trotsky-style glasses. Also serves light meals (salads, soup, hot and cold sandwiches), including vegetarian options; all products are organic and most are sourced locally. A sign in the window welcomes English- and Spanish-speakers.

Drinking

Lille has two main nightlife zones: Vieux Lille (eg rue Royale, rue de la Barre and rue de Gand), where bars tend to be small and oriented towards a fairly chic clientele; and, 750m southwest of the tourist office, rue Masséna and rue Solférino, where inexpensive high-decibel bars draw mainly students. There are a number of edgy cafés around the periphery of the Wazemmes food market.

Meert (☎ 03 20 57 07 44; www.meert.fr; 27 rue Esquermoise; Ⓜ Rihour; ⏲ 9.30am-7.30pm Tue-Fri, 9am-7.30pm Sat, 9am-1pm & 3-7pm Sun) *Gaufres* (waffles; €2.30 each), made with Madagascar vanilla and baked in a hinged iron griddle, are the speciality of Meert, a luxury tearoom-cum-pastry-and-sweets-shop that has served kings, viceroys and generals since 1761. Next door, Meert's chocolate shop has a coffered ceiling, painted wood panels, wrought-iron balcony and mosaic floor almost unchanged since 1839.

L'Illustration Café (☎ 03 20 12 00 90; www.bar-lillustration.com, in French; 18 rue Royale; ⏲ 12.30pm-3am Mon-Sat, 2pm-3am Sun) This mellow bar, adorned with art-nouveau woodwork and rotating exhibits of works by local painters, attracts artists and intellectuals in the mood to read, exchange weighty ideas – or just shoot the breeze. Very French in the best sense of the word.

Le Balatum (☎ 03 20 57 41 81; www.myspace.com/balatum; 13 rue de la Barre; ⏲ 4pm-3am Sun-Fri, 2pm-3am Sat) This funky, dimly lit place, decorated with artwork that changes monthly, is ideal for a tête-à-tête. Attracts a *branché* (cool, in-the-know) crowd, many in their 20s. There's live music (jazz, blues, rock, folk etc) at 8pm on Sunday (and sometimes Saturday) and a DJ from 10.30pm on Thursday, Friday and Saturday nights. Gay friendly.

Café Le Relax (48 place de la Nouvelle Aventure; Ⓜ Gambetta; ⏲ 9am-midnight Tue, Thu & Sun, 10.30am-midnight Mon & Wed, 10.30am-1am Fri, to 2am Sat) A genuine, ungentrified *café de quartier* (neighbourhood café) where locals drop in for an espresso or a strong Belgian beer and to run into friends. A great place to get a feel for this ethnically mixed, working-class part of town. On Sunday morning you can buy edibles at the nearby Wazemmes food market and eat them here with a beer. Local groups perform live music from 9pm to midnight on Friday, Saturday and Sunday; a DJ spins disks – often reggae or ska – on Wednesday night.

Café Oz (☎ 03 20 55 15 15; 33 place Louise de Bettignies; ⏲ 4pm-3am Mon-Fri, 2pm-3am Sat & Sun, opens at noon or 2pm in nice weather, happy hour 6-9pm Mon-Sat) Footy and rugby on a wide screen, Australiana on the walls and cold bottles of Toohey's Extra Dry – what more could you ask for? Popular with English-speakers, including students, this place is packed when DJs do their thing from 9pm to 3am on Thursday, Friday and Saturday nights. The nearest bus stop is Palais de Justice, served by lines 3, 6 and 9.

Entertainment

Lille's free French-language entertainment guide, *Sortir* (www.lille.sortir.eu, in French), comes out each Wednesday and is available at the tourist office, cinemas, event venues and bookshops.

Tickets for Lille's rich cultural offerings can be bought just off rue St-Nicolas at the **Fnac billetterie** (Fnac ticket desk; ☎ 08 92 68 36 22; www.fnacspectacles.com, in French; Ⓜ Rihour; ⏲ 10am-7.30pm Mon-Sat), inside the Fnac store. Events are posted by category on the walls.

CINEMAS

Nondubbed films, some in English, are the speciality of two **cinemas** (☎ 08 36 68 00 73; www.lemetropole.com, in French), the **Cinéma Majestic** (56 rue de Béthune; Ⓜ Rihour), which has six projection spaces, and the **Cinéma Métropole** (26 rue des Ponts des Comines; Ⓜ Gare Lille-Flandres), an art-house cinema.

GAY & LESBIAN

Vice Versa (☎ 03 20 54 93 46; 3 rue de la Barre; ⏰ 1pm-2.30am Tue-Thu, 3pm-2.30am Mon, Fri & Sat, 4pm-2.30am Sun) The rainbow flies proudly at this well-heeled, sophisticated bar, which is as gay as it is popular (and it's very popular). Has retro-themed nights from 10pm every Tuesday and a house-and-electro-oriented DJ from 10.30pm on Friday and Saturday.

Miss Marple (☎ 03 20 39 85 92; www.lemissmarple.com, in French; 18 rue de Gand; ⏰ 4pm-midnight Mon-Thu, 4pm-1am Fri, 4pm-2am Sat) A friendly and unpretentious lesbian and gay bar that welcomes *hétéros* under its crystal chandeliers. The upstairs lounge features 1970s retro styling; the art on the walls changes monthly. There's a DJ from 10pm on some Friday and Saturday nights.

LIVE MUSIC

The **Orchestre National de Lille** (☎ 03 20 12 82 40; www.onlille.com, in French; adult €18-30, under 28yr €10) plays in the circular **Nouveau Siècle concert hall** (place Pierre Mendès-France; Ⓜ Rihour).

NIGHTCLUBS

Although you no longer have to cross the Belgian frontier (eg to Gand) to dance past 4am, some locals still do because, they say, the techno is edgier, the prices lower, substances more available and the closing time even later (1pm!)

Network Café (☎ 03 20 40 04 91; www.network-cafe.net, in French; 15 rue du Faisan; Ⓜ République Beaux Arts; admission free, coat check €1; ⏰ 10.30pm-5.30am Tue & Wed, 9.30pm-5.30am Thu, 10.30pm-7am Fri & Sat, 7.30pm-5.30am Sun) At Lille's hottest late-late discotheque, you can choose between the main room, presided over by two 5m-high statues from faraway lands, and the baroque Venetian room, all crystal chandeliers and velvet settees. A magnet for guest DJs, it's hugely popular with students (especially on Wednesday and Thursday) and the 20-to-40 crowd. Rock sets the tone on Thursday, when there are dance classes (€5) from 9.30pm to 11.30pm, and salsa/R & B dominate on Sunday before/after midnight, but house predominates the rest of the time. The door policy is pretty strict – locals dress up to come here – but tends to be a bit more relaxed for tourists.

La Scala (☎ 03 20 42 10 60; 32 place Louise de Bettignies; admission free; ⏰ 11pm-dawn Mon-Sat) A classic cellar discothèque, with pulsating music and gyrating bodies under ancient brick arches. There are frequent student nights (Wednesday and Thursday) and theme nights (Thursday, Friday and Saturday). Things get going at about 1.30am.

Tchouka Club (☎ 03 20 14 37 50; www.tchoukaclub.com, in French; 80 rue Barthélemy Delespaul; ⏰ 11pm-8am Fri, Sat & holiday eves) This till-dawn, gay and lesbian dance venue has Lille's clubbering classes chattering.

Shopping

Lille's snazziest clothing and housewares boutiques are in the old city in the area bounded by rue de la Monnaie, rue Esquermoise, rue de la Grande Chausée and rue d'Angleterre. The tiny pedestrian streets northwest of Cathédrale Notre Dame de la Treille, including rue Peterinck, reward the inquisitive *flâneur* (aimless stroller).

For more-practical purchases, locals often head either to the pedestrian zone south of place du Général de Gaulle (eg rue Neuve) or to the **Euralille shopping mall** (cnr av Le Corbusier & av Willy Brandt; Ⓜ Gare Lille-Flandres or Gare Lille-Europe).

Getting There & Away

BUS

Eurolines (☎ 03 20 78 18 88; 23 parvis St-Maurice; Ⓜ Gare Lille-Flandres; ⏰ 9.30am-6pm Mon-Fri, 10am-noon & 1-6pm Sat) serves cities such as Brussels (€15, 1½ to two hours), Amsterdam (€30, five hours) and London (€34, 5½ hours). Buses depart from bd de Leeds, to the left as you arrive at Gare Lille-Europe from av Le Corbusier – look for the anonymous white 'Autocars' sign behind the taxi rank, across the street from Lille's 10-storey World Trade Center.

CAR

Driving into Lille is incredibly confusing, even with a good map. To get to the city centre, the best thing to do is to suspend your sense of direction and blindly follow the 'Centre Ville' signs.

Parking at the Champ de Mars (the huge car park just east of the Citadelle) costs €3 a day, including return travel (for up to five people) to central Lille on the Citadine bus line (just show the card issued at the entrance barrier to the driver). If you arrive between 8pm and 7am or on Sunday, parking is free – but you don't get a free bus ticket into the city.

Parking is free along some of the streets southwest of rue Solférino and up around the Maison Natale de Charles de Gaulle.

Avis, Europcar, Hertz and National-Citer have car-hire offices in Gare Lille-Europe. Domestic rental companies include the following:

ADA (☎ 03 20 57 02 25; 2 rue Gustave Delory; Ⓜ Mairie de Lille) Also rents 50cc scooters for €53 per day.

DLM (☎ 03 20 06 18 80; 32 place de la Gare; Ⓜ Gare Lille-Flandres; ⌚ 8am-noon & 2-6pm Mon-Sat)

Rent-A-Car Système (☎ 03 20 40 20 20; 113 rue du Molinel; Ⓜ Rihour or République Beaux Arts)

TRAIN

Lille has been linked to Paris by rail since 1846. The two main train stations are one stop apart on metro line 2 (in the Gare Lille-Europe metro station there's a fabulous mural).

Gare Lille-Flandres is used by almost all regional services and most TGVs to Paris' Gare du Nord (€37.60 to €52.20, one hour, 14 to 18 daily).

Gare Lille-Europe – an ultramodern structure topped by what looks like a 20-storey ski boot – handles pretty much everything else, including Eurostar trains (p965) to London (from the station's far northern end); TGVs/Eurostars to Brussels-Nord (Monday to Friday/weekend €25.20/16.30, 35 minutes, a dozen daily); and TGVs to Nice (€110 to €132.70, 7½ hours, two direct daily) and Strasbourg (€52, 3½ hours, three daily).

For details on getting to/from Amiens, Arras, Boulogne, Calais, Dunkirk and St-Omer, see those sections.

Getting Around

BICYCLE & SEGWAY

Always wanted to try one of those nifty Segway gadgets? Now's your chance! **Station Oxygène**, run by Transpole (right), rents out Segways for €4/15/20 per 30 minutes/half-day/full day (€3.50/12/18 if you have a bus ticket stamped within the hour), not including a mandatory first-time riding lesson (€4) that will get you an official French Segway licence (we're not kidding). Riders must weigh over 40kg and be at least 18 (14 if accompanied by an adult). E-bikes (city bikes with an electric power boost) are available for €1.50/7/10 per 30 minutes/half-day/full day (with a bus ticket €1.30/5.50/8). Both require a credit card deposit of €500.

Station Oxygène has two offices: a shiny glass structure that resembles a hovering flying saucer at the **Champ de Mars** (⌚ 8am-5pm Mon-Fri Apr-Oct); and in the Transpole bus information office on the track level of **Gare Lille-Flandres** (place des Buisses; ⌚ 7.30am-6.30pm Mon-Fri). To reserve, call **Team Segway** (☎ 03 20 81 44 02).

Two car-rental places (opposite) rent bicycles, DLM (city bikes per half-/full day €7/9, for students €5/7) and ADA (mountain bike per day €12).

BUS, TRAM & METRO

Lille's two speedy metro lines (1 and 2), two tramways (R and T) and many urban and suburban bus lines – several of which cross into Belgium – are run by **Transpole** (☎ 08 20 42 40 40; www.transpole.fr, in French), which has **information offices** (⌚ closed Sun) in Gare Lille-Flandres and its metro station. In the city centre, metros run every one to six minutes until about midnight. Useful metro stops include those at the train stations, Rihour (next to the tourist office), République Beaux Arts (near the Palais des Beaux-Arts), Gambetta (near the Wazemmes food market) and Gare Jean Lebas (near La Piscine). Clair de Lune night buses operate from 9.30pm to 12.30am. In this chapter, places with a metro stop within 500m have the name of the stop noted next to the street address.

Tickets (€1.25 for a one-way full fare) are sold on buses but must be purchased (and validated in the orange posts) *before* boarding a metro or tram. A pack of 10 tickets costs €10.30. A Pass Journée (all-day pass) costs €3.50 and needs to be time-stamped just once. A Pass Soirée, good for unlimited travel after 7pm, costs €1.50.

TAXI

Cabs can be ordered 24 hours a day from **Taxi Gare Lille** (☎ 03 20 06 64 00) and **Taxi Rihour** (☎ 03 20 55 20 56).

CALAIS

pop 74,200

As Churchill might have put it, 'never in the field of human tourism have so many travellers passed through a place and so few stopped to visit'. Indeed, there are few compelling reasons for the 15 million people who travel by way of Calais each year to stop and explore – pity the local tourist office, whose job it is to snag a few of the Britons racing south to warmer climes.

That said, the town – a mere 34km from the English town of Dover (Douvres in French) – has enough to offer travellers to make a stop

THE BURGHERS OF CALAIS

Rodin sculpted *Les Bourgeois de Calais* (The Burghers of Calais) in 1895 to honour six local citizens who, in 1347, after eight months of holding off the besieging English forces, surrendered themselves and the keys to the starving city to Edward III. Their hope: that by sacrificing themselves they might save the town and its people. Moved by the entreaties of his consort, Philippa, Edward eventually spared both the Calaisiens and their six brave leaders.

Is it worth a trip to Calais' Flemish Renaissance–style **Hôtel de Ville** (built 1911–25) just to see Rodin's masterpiece? Actually, you don't even have to come to France to see the work. Other casts of the six emaciated but proud figures, with varying degrees of copper-green patination (several were made posthumously), can be seen in London (next to the Houses of Parliament), the USA (New York, Washington, Philadelphia, Omaha, Pasadena, Stanford University) and even Japan (Shizuoka Prefecture).

worthwhile, including three speciality museums, some decent restaurants and, of course, Rodin's *The Burghers of Calais* (above). In addition Calais makes a convenient base for exploring French Flanders and the majestic Channel coast by car or public transport.

Orientation

Gare Calais-Ville (the train station) is 650m south of the main square, place d'Armes, and 700m north of Calais' main commercial district, which stretches south along bd Jacquard from the *Burghers of Calais* statue to place du Théâtre and bd Léon Gambetta. The town centre is ringed by canals and ship docks.

On foot, the car-ferry terminal is 1.5km northeast of place d'Armes (by car the distance is double that). The Channel Tunnel's vehicle-loading area is about 6km southwest of the town centre.

Information

Currency exchange is possible aboard car ferries (at a terrible rate) but *not* at the ferry terminal, which lacks even an ATM.

Change Bureau (☎ 03 21 97 72 66; 5 rue Royale; 🕑 9-11am & 5-7pm Mon-Fri, 10am-noon Sat)

Laundrette (place d'Armes; 🕑 7am-9pm) Be prepared for British border formalities – cross the Channel with clean undies.

Media ServiCenter (☎ 03 21 34 72 85; 1 rue Paul Bert; per hr €3; 🕑 9.45am-4pm & 5.30-8pm Mon, Tue, Thu & Fri, 9.45am-4pm Wed, 2.30-8pm Sat, 3.30-7pm Sun) Internet access.

Médiathèque (☎ 03 21 46 20 40; 16 rue du Pont Lottin; per hr €1; 🕑 10am-noon & 1.30-7pm Tue, Thu & Fri, 10am-7pm Wed, 10am-6pm Sat) Internet access at the public library. Opening an account takes just two minutes.

Post Office (place de Rheims)

Tourist Office (☎ 03 21 96 62 40; www.calais-cotedopale.com; 12 bd Georges Clemenceau; 🕑 10am-1pm & 2-6.30pm Mon-Sat year-round, 10am-1pm Sun Jul & Aug)

Sights & Activities

The 13th-century **tour de guet** (watchtower; place d'Armes), square at the base and octagonal on top, is a rare remnant of pre-20th-century Calais – the rest of the town was virtually demolished during WWII.

The **Musée des Beaux-Arts et de la Dentelle** (Museum of Fine Arts & Lace; ☎ 03 21 46 48 40; 25 rue Richelieu; admission free; 🕑 10am-noon & 2-5.30pm Mon & Wed-Fri, 10am-noon & 2-6.30pm Sat, 2-6.30pm Sun) focuses on just two things: modern sculptures, including pieces by Rodin; and the history of lacemaking both before and after the first lace machines were smuggled over from England – with French government encouragement – in 1816.

In spring 2009, a brand new museum dedicated to Calais' glorious mechanical lacemaking legacy, the **Musée de la Dentelle et de la Mode** (Museum of Lace & Fashion; rue Sambor), is set to open in a 19th-century lace factory whose facade resembles a giant Jacquard punched card.

Willing to exert your thigh muscles for a superb panorama? Try climbing the 271 stairs to the top of the **lighthouse** (☎ 03 21 34 33 34; bd des Alliés; adult/5-15yr €4/2; 🕑 9.30am-12.30pm & 2-6pm 21 Jun–21 Sep, 2-5.30pm Wed & Sat, 10am-noon & 2-5.30pm Sun rest of year, also open 2-5.30pm Mon, Tue, Thu & Fri during school holidays), built in 1848.

Colonne Louis XVIII (Louis XVIII Column; bd des Alliés) commemorates the French king's return from exile in England after the fall of Napoléon (1814). A close inspection will reveal a Hollywood-style imprint of the royal foot.

WWII artefacts (weapons, uniforms, proclamations) fill the display cases of the **Musée**

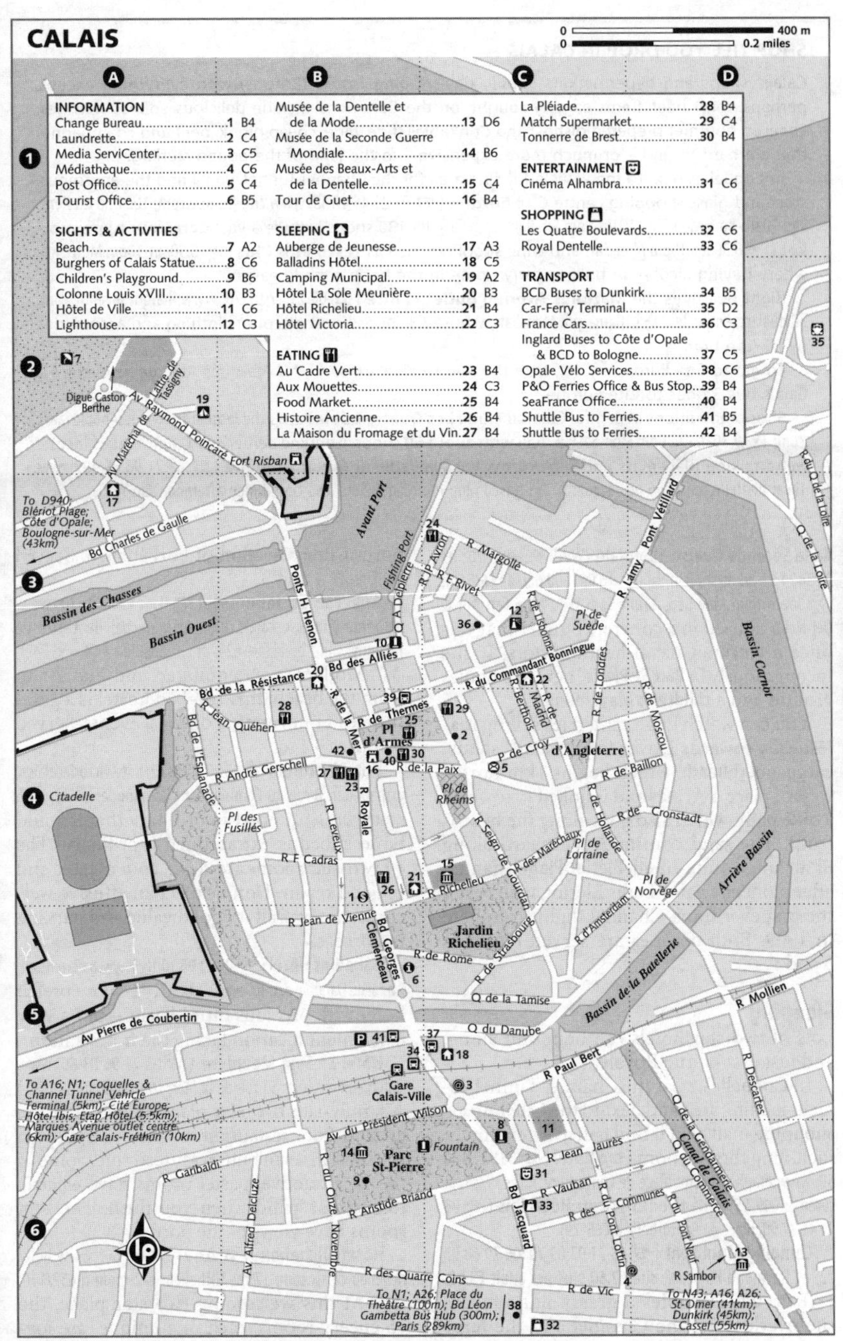

FAR NORTHERN FRANCE

SHOP TILL YOU DROP IN CALAIS

Calais' shops and hypermarkets supply day-tripping *rosbifs* (Britons) with everything except, perhaps, roast beef. Items eagerly sought 'on the Continent' include delicious edibles (terrines, cheeses, gourmet prepared dishes) and drinkables (fine wine, cheap plonk, beer and champagne) that are hard to find – or much more expensive – in the land of the pound sterling.

In Coquelles next to the vehicle-loading area for the Channel Tunnel, you'll find the enormous, steel-and-glass shopping centre **Cité Europe** (☎ 03 21 46 47 48; www.cite-europe.com; 1001 bd du Kent; 🕑 10am-8pm Mon-Thu, 10am-9pm Fri, 9am-8pm Sat). Its 130 shops include a vast **Carrefour hypermarket** (🕑 8.30am-10pm Mon-Sat) and wine suppliers such as **Tesco Vins Plus** (🕑 8.30am-10pm Mon-Sat), where buying alcohol in bulk to carry home in the boot is made easy.

Right nearby is the **Marques Avenue outlet centre** (☎ 03 21 17 07 70; www.marquesavenue.com; bd du Parc, Coquelles; 🕑 10am-7pm Mon-Sat), whose 53 shops boast discount clothing and accessories by 80 'top brands'.

To get to Cité Europe by car, take the A16 to exits 41 or 43; for Marques Avenue, use exit 41. Calais bus 5 goes to Cité Europe.

Shopping options in central Calais include **Les Quatre Boulevards** (bd Jacquard; www.les4boulevards.com; 🕑 9.30am-7.30pm Mon-Sat), a mall with about 50 shops. Genuine *dentelle de Calais* (Calais lace) – we're talking placemats and tablecloths – is available at **Royal Dentelle** (☎ 03 21 96 68 40; www.royal-dentelle.com; 106 bd Jacquard; 🕑 closed Mon morning & Sun, also closed Mon afternoon Jan-Apr).

de la Seconde Guerre Mondiale (WWII Museum; ☎ 03 21 34 21 57; adult/student/family of 5 incl audioguide €6/5/14; 🕑 10am-6pm May-Sep, 11am-5pm Wed-Mon Feb-Apr & Oct-Nov), housed in a concrete bunker that was once a German naval headquarters. It sits incongruously in **Parc St-Pierre**, next to a boules ground and a **children's playground**.

You can watch huge car ferries sailing majestically towards Dover from Calais' sandy, cabin-lined **beach**, which begins 1km northwest of place d'Armes and is linked to town by a bike path, which also goes along the beachfront. The sand continues westward along 8km-long, dune-lined **Blériot Plage**, named after pioneer aviator Louis Blériot, who began the first ever trans-Channel flight from here in 1909. Both beaches are served by buses 3 and 9.

Sleeping

Lots of two-star hotels can be found along, and just east of, rue Royale.

In Coquelles, near the Channel Tunnel vehicle-loading area and next to the Cité Europe shopping mall, you'll find half a dozen hotels, including the 99-room **Etap Hôtel** (☎ 08 92 68 30 59; www.etaphotel.com; place de Cantorbéry; s/tr €39/45, in summer €49/55) and the 86-room **Hôtel Ibis** (☎ 03 21 46 37 00; place de Cantorbéry; d €65-79).

Camping Municipal (☎ 03 21 97 89 79, 06 79 68 93 22; av Raymond Poincaré; site €2.60 plus per adult €3.65; 🕑 Easter-Oct) Occupies a grassy but soulless site overlooking the Channel and the ferry port, inside a section of Fort Risban. Served by buses 3 and 9.

Auberge de Jeunesse (☎ 03 21 34 70 20; www.auberge-jeunesse-calais.com; av Maréchal de Lattre de Tassigny; s incl breakfast €24, dm in double r €18; 🕑 24hr; ☒) Modern, well equipped and just 200m from the beach, this 162-bed hostel is a good source of information on local events. Served by buses 3 and 9.

Hôtel Victoria (☎ 03 21 34 38 32; hotelvictoriacalais@wanadoo.fr; 8 rue du Commandant Bonningue; d €42, with washbasin €30) A hotel so ordinary that it could be described as 'extraordinarily ordinary'. The 14 two-star rooms are clean, comfortable and in good repair. Don't expect an effusive welcome, but overall it's good value and parking is a breeze.

Balladins Hôtel (☎ 03 21 96 10 10; www.balladins.eu; 2 quai du Danube; d/tr from €40/43) A 104-room prefab hotel with precious little charm – but a very convenient location facing the train station.

Hôtel La Sole Meunière (☎ 03 21 96 83 66; www.solemeuniere.com; 53 rue de la Mer; s/d/q €49/59/89; ☒) A family-run two-star place named after the ground-floor restaurant, which – you guessed it – specialises in butter-sautéed sole. Some of the 18 attractive, pastel rooms have electric toilets that grind when you flush. The best rooms have views of the port.

Hôtel Richelieu (☎ 03 21 34 61 60; www.hotelrichelieu-calais.com; 17 rue Richelieu; d/2-room q €57/116; ☒) At this welcoming two-star place, the 15 cheery rooms, each one unique, are lovingly maintained and outfitted with antique furniture redeemed by the owner from local flea markets.

Eating

Calais is a good place for a first or last meal on the Continent. Eateries are plentiful on rue Royale and rue de la Mer and around place d'Armes.

Tonnerre de Brest (☎ 03 21 96 95 35; 16 place d'Armes; weekday lunch menus €10.50-18.50; 🕑 closed Mon except Jul & Aug) At this informal, rustic eatery, run by two sisters, you can wash down with *cidre* (cider) 28 kinds of savoury galettes or 31 sorts of sweet crêpes – or a large salad (€10). Ice cream desserts are a speciality.

Histoire Ancienne (☎ 03 21 34 11 20; www.histoire-ancienne.com; 20 rue Royale; menu du jour from noon-1pm & 6-8pm €11.50, 2-/3-/5-course menus €18/25.50/35.50; 🕑 closed Sun & dinner Mon) Specialising in French and regional meat, fish and vegetarian mains, some grilled over an open wood fire, this 1930s Paris-style bistro also has treats such as *escargots à l'ail* (garlic snails). The toilets take full advantage of the latest self-cleaning technology.

Aux Mouettes (☎ 03 21 34 67 59; 10 rue Jean Pierre Avron; menus €16-34; 🕑 closed dinner Wed, dinner Sun & Mon) Fisherfolk sell their daily catch across the street at the quay – easy to see how this unassuming place manages to serve only the very freshest fish and seafood, including *sole de notre quai* (sole landed at our quay; €22).

Au Cadre Vert (☎ 03 21 34 69 44; 3 rue André Gerschell; menu incl wine €18.50; 🕑 closed Sun, lunch Sat & lunch Wed) A family-run restaurant known for its generous portions and reasonable prices. Specialities include French-style *magret de canard* (duck breast fillet; €14) in raspberry sauce, *pièce de bœuf sauce pleurotte* (beefsteak in mushroom sauce) and large salads (€10 to €12).

La Pléiade (☎ 03 21 34 03 70; 32 rue Jean Quéhen; menus €28-58; 🕑 closed Sun & Mon) At this elegant, family-run restaurant, superfresh North Sea *bar* (sea bass), turbot and sole are prepared differently for each season, using locally grown ingredients. The menu, *gastronomique* but with modern touches, changes every six weeks.

SELF-CATERING

Food market (place d'Armes; 🕑 morning Wed & Sat)

La Maison du Fromage et des Vins (☎ 03 21 34 44 72; 1 rue André Gerschell; 🕑 3-7.30pm Mon, 8.30am-12.30pm & 3-7.30pm Wed-Fri, 8.15am-12.45pm & 2.30-7.30pm Sat, 10am-1pm Sun) Sells cheese and fine wine.

Match supermarket (place d'Armes; 🕑 9am-7.30pm Mon-Sat year-round, 9am-noon Sun Jun-Aug)

Entertainment

Cinéma Alhambra (☎ 03 21 17 73 33; www.cinema-alhambra.org, in French; 2 rue Jean Jaurès) Screens nondubbed films, some in English, in its four halls.

Getting There & Around

For details on options for crossing the Channel by ferry and tunnel, see p968 and p964.

BICYCLE

Opale Vélo Services (☎ 03 21 00 07 41; 39 bd Jacquard; 🕑 9am-noon & 4.30-7pm Mon-Sat, 11am-12.30pm & 5-7pm Sun) rents out city bikes (per half-day/full day/week €4/6/23) and electric-powered bicycles (€5/8/30). A deposit of €200 is required.

BOAT

Every day, 35 to 52 car ferries from Dover dock at Calais' bustling car-ferry terminal, which on foot is about 1.5km northeast of place d'Armes (further by car). Company offices:

P&O Ferries Calais town centre (41 place d'Armes); car-ferry terminal (☎ 03 21 46 10 18; 🕑 6am-10pm); car-ferry parking lot (🕑 24hr)

SeaFrance Calais town centre (2 place d'Armes); car-ferry terminal (☎ 03 21 46 80 05; 🕑 7.30am-7.30pm); car-ferry parking lot (🕑 24hr)

Shuttle buses (€1.50 or UK£1, roughly hourly from about 10am to 7pm or 7.40pm), marked 'Terminal Car Ferry/Centre Ville', link Gare Calais-Ville and place d'Armes (the stop is in front of Café de la Tour) with the car-ferry terminal. Departure times are posted at the bus stop.

Hoverspeed, the company that pioneered the use of hovercraft – the pride of British maritime engineering in the 1960s – ceased operations in 2005.

BUS

Bus 44, run by **Inglard** (☎ 03 21 96 49 54; www.colvert-littoral.com, www.voyages-inglard.com, in French; office in car-ferry terminal), follows the breathtaking Côte d'Opale coastal road (D940), linking Calais' train station with Sangatte, Wissant (€3.10), Audinghen, Ambleteuse and Boulogne-sur-Mer (€5.40, 1¼ hours, three daily except Sunday and holidays). Stops in Boulogne are at Nausicaā and 75 bd Daunou.

Ligne BCD (☎ 08 00 62 00 59) is an express service linking Calais' train station with Dunkirk (€7.70, 45 minutes, 11 daily Monday to Friday, three on Saturday) and Boulogne (€7.20, 40 minutes, five daily Monday to Friday, two on Saturday), where bus stops are at the train station and place Dalton.

CAR & MOTORCYCLE

To reach the Channel Tunnel's vehicle-loading area at Coquelles, follow the road signs on the A16 to 'Tunnel Sous La Manche' (Tunnel under the Channel) and get off at exit 42.

ADA (☎ 03 21 96 49 54), Avis, Budget, Europcar, Hertz and National-Citer have offices at the car-ferry terminal but they're not always staffed. In town, reasonable rates are on offer at **France Cars** (☎ 03 21 96 08 00; 47 bd des Alliés).

TAXI

To order a cab, call **Taxis Radio Calais** (TRC; ☎ 03 21 97 13 14).

TRAIN

Calais has two train stations: Gare Calais-Ville in the city centre; and Gare Calais-Fréthun, a TGV station 10km southwest of town near the Channel Tunnel entrance. They are linked by trains and a *navette* (shuttle bus).

Gare Calais-Ville has services to Amiens (€22.10, 2½ to 3½ hours, six to eight daily), Arras (€18.70, 1¾ hours, 12 daily Monday to Friday, five daily Saturday and Sunday), Boulogne (€7.20, 30 minutes, 15 to 18 daily Monday to Saturday, eight on Sunday), Dunkirk (€7.70, 50 minutes, two to five Monday to Saturday) and Lille-Flandres (€15.30, 1¼ hours, seven to 11 daily).

Gare Calais-Fréthun is served by TGVs to Paris' Gare du Nord (€39.60 to €54.60, 1½ hours, six daily Monday to Saturday, three on Sunday) as well as Eurostars to London (one hour, three daily).

ST-OMER

pop 14,900

St-Omer is said to be the first truly French town you come to after landing at Calais – its river, the Aa, is certainly the first one you'll come across in any alphabetised list of the world's waterways. The town is justly renowned for its richly furnished 13th- to 15th-century **basilica** (entrance via the south transept arm; 🕒 8am-5pm, to 6pm Apr-Oct), downgraded from cathedral status in 1801. The only major Gothic church in the region, it's a real gem; much of the woodwork, including the main altar and breathtaking baroque organ, dates from the 1700s. In the ambulatory, the rough-hewn tomb of the 8th-century Irish monk St Erkembode has on top a neat row of toddlers' shoes, placed there by the parents of children with walking difficulties in the hope of saintly intercession.

The **tourist office** (☎ 03 21 98 08 51; www.tourisme-saintomer.com; 4 rue du Lion d'Or; 🕒 9am-6pm Mon-Sat, 10am-1pm Sun & holidays Easter-Sep, 9am-12.30pm & 2-6pm Mon-Sat except holidays Oct-Easter) is one block north of place Foch, the typically northern-French square in front of the neoclassical **hôtel de ville** (town hall; 1830). The lovely 19th-century **jardin public**, a landscape park, is a block west of place Foch.

Musée de l'Hôtel Sandelin (☎ 03 21 38 00 94; 14 rue Carnot; adult/15-25yr & student €4.50/3; 🕒 10am-noon & 2-6pm, sometimes to 8pm Thu, closed Mon & Tue), with displays that include ceramics, objets d'art and paintings, is housed in a harmonious town house built in 1776. A number of rooms are furnished in the refined style preferred by the Enlightenment elite. To get there from place Foch, walk a block south and then a long block east.

North and northeast of town, the 36-sq-km **Marais Audomarois** (Audomarois Marsh), its market gardens criss-crossed by *watergangs* (canals), is home to all sorts of wildlife, including 250 kinds of bird, 19 species of dragonfly and 11 types of bat. The area can be explored on foot or by boat, including flat-bottomed *bacôves*. In Clairmarais, 5km northeast of St-Omer, **Isnor** (☎ 03 21 39 15 15; www.isnor.fr; 3 rue du Marais; canoe 4hr €25; 🕒 Sat, Sun & holidays Apr, May, Jun & Sep, daily Jul & Aug) rents canoes, row boats, electric boats and bicycles and runs pontoon boat excursions. The tourist office can supply a brochure with walking, cycling and horse-riding options around St-Omer.

About 5km east of St-Omer in Arques, the glassware conglomerate **Arc International** (☎ 03 21 12 74 74; www.arc-international.com; Zone Industrielle, N43; adult/student €6.50/4.20), famous for brands such as Arcoroc, Luminarc and Mikasa, runs 1½-hour guided tours (often in English) of its state-of-the-art production facilities – glowing globules of glass! – at 9.30am, 11am, 2pm and 3.30pm from Monday to Saturday.

The two-star **Hôtel St-Louis** (☎ 03 21 38 35 21; www.hotel-saintlouis.com; 25 rue d'Arras; s/d €59/72), a few blocks southeast of the basilica, has 30 quiet, spacious rooms, rich in yellow and orange tones, and a garden.

There are quite a few good-value restaurants (lunch *menus* from €10) around the perimeter of place Foch (including pedestrianised rue Louis Martel) and adjacent place P Bonhomme. **Le Cygne** (☎ 03 21 98 20 52; www.restaurantlecygne.fr; 8 rue Caventou; menus €15-48; ⏰ closed dinner Sun & Mon), two blocks east of the basilica, is an elegant French restaurant that uses only the freshest seasonal ingredients. For self-catering there's a lively **food market** (place Foch; ⏰ Sat morning).

St-Omer's train station, 1.5km northeast of the *hôtel de ville*, has frequent services to Calais (€7, 30 minutes, nine to 18 daily) and Lille-Flandres (€10.40, 50 minutes, seven to 11 daily).

LA COUPOLE

A top-secret subterranean V2 launch site just five minutes' flying time from London – almost (but not quite) put into operation in 1944 – now houses **La Coupole** (☎ 03 21 12 27 27; www.lacoupole.com; adult/student/5-16yr/family incl audioguide €9/7.50/6/19.50; ⏰ 9am-6pm, to 7pm Jul & Aug, closed 2 weeks from Christmas), an innovative museum that uses lots of moving images to present Nazi Germany's secret programs to build V1 and V2 rockets (which could fly at 650km/h and an astounding 5780km/h respectively); life in northern France during the Nazi occupation; and the postwar conquest of space with the help of V2 rocket technology – and seconded V2 engineers.

La Coupole is 5km south of St-Omer (the circuitous route is signposted, but confusing), just outside the town of Wizernes, near the intersection of the D928 and the D210. From the A26, take exit 3 or 4.

CASSEL

pop 2300

The fortified, very Flemish village of Cassel, 57km southeast of Calais atop French Flanders' highest hill (176m), affords panoramic views of the verdant Flanders plain. A **bagpipe festival** is held here each year on the 3rd weekend in June. Cassel is enormously proud of Reuze Papa and Reuze Maman, its resident giants (see the boxed text, p226).

The main square, fringed by austere brick buildings with steep slate roofs, is where you'll find the **tourist office** (☎ 03 28 40 52 55; www.cassel-horizons.com; 20 Grand' Place; ⏰ 8.30am-noon & 1.30-5.30pm Mon-Fri year-round, 9am-noon Sat Oct-Mar, 8.30am-noon & 1.30-5.45pm Sat, 2-6.30pm Sun Apr-Sep) and

CASSEL AT WAR

Thanks to its elevated position, Cassel served as Maréchal Ferdinand Foch's headquarters at the beginning of WWI. In 1940, it was the site of intensive rearguard resistance by British troops defending Dunkirk during the evacuation.

Cassel Horizons (adult/6-14yr €3/2.50; ⏰ same as tourist office), an interactive museum which presents Cassel's history in an easily digestible form.

Eight or 10 generations ago, wheat flour was milled and linseed oil pressed just as it is today at the wooden **moulin** (windmill; adult/6-14yr €3/2.50; ⏰ 10am-12.30pm & 2-6.30pm Mon-Sat, 10am-1pm & 1.30-7pm Sun Jul & Aug, 2-6.30pm Tue-Fri, 10am-12.30pm & 2-6.30pm Sat & Sun Apr-Jun & Sep, 2-6pm Sat & school holidays, 10am-12.30pm & 2-6.30pm Sun Oct-Mar, closed Dec–early Jan, last tour begins 1hr before closing), perched on the highest point in town to catch the wind. The 45-minute, hands-on tour is noisy but interesting. During the 19th century, the skyline of French Flanders was dotted with 2000 such windmills.

Le Foch (☎ 03 28 42 47 73; www.hotel-foch.net, in French; 41 Grand' Place; d €67; ⊠) has six spacious rooms with antique-style beds, some with views of the square. The elegant **restaurant** (menus €15-25; ⏰ closed dinner Sun & Fri) serves traditional French cuisine, made with fresh local ingredients, amid carved woodwork and sparkling crystal.

Taverne Flamande (☎ 03 28 42 42 59; 34 Grand' Place; menus €12-17, Sunday menu €24.50; ⏰ closed Wed & dinner Tue) occupies a classic 1933 dining room that's as Flemish as the cuisine.

Cassel's train station, 3km up the hill (the tram no longer runs), is on the secondary line linking Dunkirk (€5.50, 25 minutes, 10 daily Monday to Friday, two or three daily weekends) with Arras (€12.30, 1¼ hours, seven daily Monday to Friday, one or two daily weekends).

DUNKIRK

pop 69,400

Dunkirk (Dunkerque), made famous and flattened almost simultaneously in 1940 (see p38), was rebuilt during one of the most uninspired periods in Western architecture. Charming it may not be, but the port city has two worthwhile museums, a mellow beach and several colourful pre-Lent carnivals.

Under Louis XIV, Dunkirk – whose name means 'church of the dunes' in Flemish – served as a base for French privateers, including the daring Jean Bart (1650–1702), whose hugely successful attacks on English and Dutch merchant ships have ensured his infamy in British history and, locally, his status as a national hero: the city centre's main square, suitably adorned with a dashing statue (1845), bears his name, as does a high school.

In the base of a 58m-high **belfry** (adult €2.80) with spectacular views, erected around 1440, is Dunkirk's **tourist office** (☎ 03 28 66 79 21; www.lesdunesdeflandre.fr; rue de l'Amiral Ronarc'h; 9.30am-12.30pm & 1.30-6.30pm Mon-Sat, 10am-noon & 2-4pm Sun & holidays, no midday closure Jul & Aug). Staff can supply you with an **MP3 tour** (€3.50) of the city's WWI and WWII sites and have details on **boat tours** (adult/5-12yr €8.50/6.50; 3pm daily except Wed Jul & Aug, also often possible 3pm Sat, Sun & holidays Apr-May, Sep & Oct) of the port. The **Pass Tourisme** (€12) offers discounts on museums, activities, public transport and shopping.

M+A Informatique (☎ 03 28 64 49 91; 8 rue Thiers; per hr €2.70; 2-10pm or 11pm) offers internet access four blocks southwest of the tourist office.

Sights & Activities

The **Musée Portuaire** (Harbour Museum; ☎ 03 28 63 33 39; www.museeportuaire.com; 9 quai de la Citadelle; adult/student/family €4/3/10; 10am-12.45pm & 1.30-6pm Wed-Mon, also open Tue & no midday closure Jul & Aug), housed in a one-time tobacco warehouse, will delight ship model–lovers of all ages. Guided **tours** (adult/student/family €7.50/6/18, incl museum €9/7.50/22) take visitors aboard a lighthouse ship, a *peniche* (barge) and the *Duchesse Anne*, a three-masted training ship built for the German merchant marine in 1901 and acquired by France as WWII reparations.

The somewhat faded, turn-of-the-20th-century seaside resort of **Malo-les-Bains** is 2km northeast of Dunkirk's city centre (served by buses 3 and 9). Its wide, promenade-lined beach, **Plage des Alliés**, is named in honour of the Allied troops evacuated to England from here in 1940. Just off the coast, vessels sunk during the evacuation can be visited on scuba dives, and some can even be seen at low tide.

The **Musée d'Art Contemporain** (LAAC; ☎ 03 28 29 56 00; av des Bains; 1st/2nd adult €4.50/3, 18-25yr/under 18 €1.50/free; 9am-noon & 2-6.30pm Tue, Wed & Fri, 10am-12.30pm & 2-6.30pm Sat & Sun, to 5.30pm Nov-Mar, 9am-noon & 2-8.30pm Thu year-round), a few hundred metres from the western end of Malo-les-Bains' beach, features often-whimsical, 'evolving' expositions of contemporary art. Outside is a sculpture garden.

The **British Memorial** (rte de Furnes), honouring more than 4500 British and Commonwealth MIAs from 1940, is 1.5km southeast of the tourist office. A military museum dedicated to the evacuation, the **Mémorial du Souvenir** (☎ 03 28 26 27 81; www.dynamo-dunkerque.com; rue des Chantiers de France; adult/under 12yr €3.50/free; 10am-noon & 2-5pm Apr-Sep), is next to the Musée d'Art Contemporain.

Stretching east from Malo-les-Bains to the Belgian border, the *dunes flamandes* (Flemish dunes) represent a unique ecosystem harbouring hundreds of plant species, including rare orchids. The area – including the **Dewulf and Marchand dunes** – is linked to Dunkirk by **DK'BUS** (www.dkbus.com, in French) bus 2B (3B on Sunday and holidays), which continues on to Adinkerke in Belgium (€1.30, an extra €0.90 to cross the border). Tides permitting, you can walk or cycle along the wet sand or the GR from Malo-les-Bains to Bray-Dunes and Westhoek.

Festivals & Events

Dunkirk's **carnivals**, held both before and (mischievously) after the beginning of Lent, originated as a final fling for the town's cod fishermen before they set out for months in the frigid waters off Iceland. The biggest celebration is the *bande* (parade) held on the Sunday right before Mardi Gras, when men traditionally dress up as women, costumed citizens of all genders march around town behind fife-and-drum bands and general merriment reigns. At the climax of the festivities, the mayor and other dignitaries stand on the *hôtel de ville* balcony and pelt the assembled locals with dried salted herrings.

Eating

Dunkirk is not known for its gastronomy but restaurants are scattered around town, including near the tourist office.

Entre Ciel et Mer (☎ 03 28 59 39 00; 16 rue de Flandre, Malo-les-Bains; menus €14.50-23; closed dinner Sun & Mon) Between the beach and place Turenne, this is a good choice for classic French-style fish and meat dishes.

FAR NORTHERN FRANCE

Getting There & Away

For details about getting from Dover to Dunkirk's car-ferry port, about 25km west of the town centre near Loon Plage, see p968.

For details on buses to Calais, see p239.

All but a few express trains from Dunkirk's train station, 1km southwest of the tourist office, to Lille stop at Gare Lille-Flandres (€12.70, 30 to 80 minutes, 30 daily Monday to Friday, 11 to 15 daily weekends).

CÔTE D'OPALE

The 40km of cliffs, sand dunes and beaches between Calais and Boulogne, known as the Côte d'Opale (Opal Coast) because of the ever-changing interplay of greys and blues in the sea and sky, are a dramatic and beautiful introduction to France. The coastal peaks (frequently buffeted by gale-force winds), wide beaches and rolling farmland are dotted with the remains of Nazi Germany's Atlantic Wall, a chain of fortifications and gun emplacements built to prevent the Allied invasion that in the end took place in Normandy. The seashore has been attracting British beach-lovers since the Victorian era.

Part of the **Parc Naturel Régional des Caps et Marais d'Opale** (Opal Coast Headlands & Marshes Regional Park; www.parc-opale.fr), which stretches as far inland as St-Omer, the Côte d'Opale area is criss-crossed by hiking paths, including the GR Littoral (GR120) trail that hugs the coast (except where the cliffs are in danger of collapse). Some routes are also suitable for mountain biking and horse riding. Each village along the Côte d'Opale has at least one campground.

By car, the D940 offers some truly spectacular vistas. For details on Inglard's bus 44, which links all the villages mentioned below with Calais and Boulogne, see p239.

Sights

The Channel Tunnel slips under the Strait of Dover 8km west of Calais at the village of **Sangatte**, known for its wide beach. Southwest of there, the coastal dunes give way to cliffs that culminate in windswept, 134m-high **Cap Blanc-Nez**, which affords breathtaking views of the Bay of Wissant, the port of Calais, the Flemish countryside (pock-marked by Allied bomb craters) and the cliffs of Kent. The grey obelisk, a short walk up the hill from the new parking area, honours the WWI Dover Patrol.

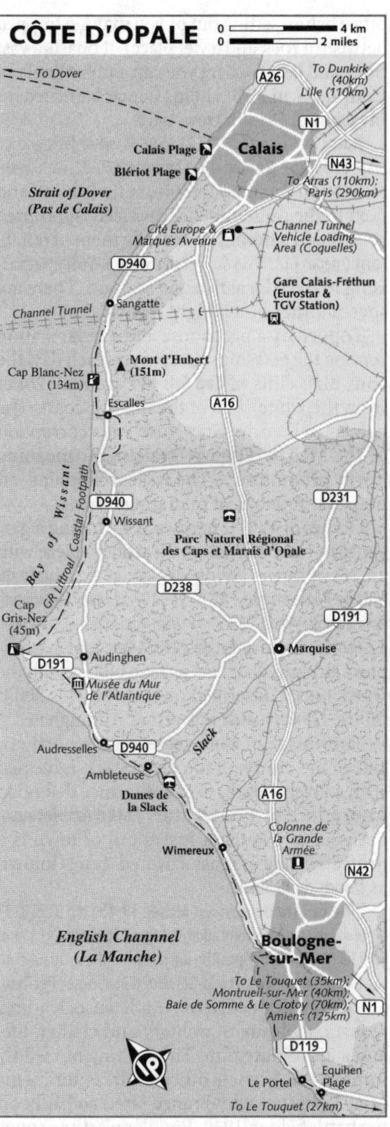

The tidy and very French seaside resort of **Wissant**, home of the Côte d'Opale area's **tourist office** (☎ 08 20 20 76 00; www.tourisme.terredes2caps.fr, in French; 9.30am-noon & 2-6pm Mon-Sat, 10am-1pm & 3-6pm Sun, no midday closure & sometimes to 7pm Jul & Aug), is a good base for walks in the rolling countryside and along the beach from Cap Blanc-Nez to Cap Gris-Nez (check the tides at the tourist

FAR NORTHERN FRANCE

office before setting out or you may get trapped between a rock and a wet place). It boasts a vast fine-sand beach where you can admire England from afar – in 55 BC Julius Caesar launched his invasion of Britain from here.

Hôtel Le Vivier (☎ 03 21 35 93 61; www.levivier.com; place de l'Église, Wissant; d incl breakfast €60-82, with washbasin €44), across the street from the church and next to the millpond, has 39 nicely appointed rooms and a homey, nautically themed **restaurant** (menus €18.50-38.50; closed Tue & Wed) specialising in fresh local fish and seafood. There are several other hotels right nearby.

Topped by a lighthouse and a radar station serving the 600 ships that pass by each day, the 45m-high cliffs of **Cap Gris-Nez** are only 28km from the white cliffs of the English coast. The name – in French, 'Grey Nose' – is a corruption of the archaic English 'craig ness', meaning 'rocky promontory'. The area is a stopping-off point for millions of migrating birds.

Oodles of WWII hardware, including a gargantuan rail-borne German artillery piece with an 86km range, are on display at the **Musée du Mur de l'Atlantique** (☎ 03 21 32 97 33; www.batterietodt.com; adult/8-14yr €5.50/2.50; 9am-7pm Jul & Aug, 9am-noon & 2-6pm Sep-Nov & Feb-Jun, closed Dec & Jan), which occupies a Brobdingnagian German pillbox with the word *'musée'* inscribed on the side. It is 500m off the D940, just southwest of Audinghen.

The village of **Ambleteuse**, on the northern side of the mouth of the River Slack, is blessed with a lovely beach, which was once defended from attack by 17th-century **Fort d'Ambleteuse**, designed by Vauban. Just south of town is a protected area of grass-covered dunes known as **Dunes de la Slack**.

The neatly organised **Musée 39-45** (☎ 03 21 87 33 01; www.musee3945.com; adult/7-14yr €6.50/4.50; 10am-7pm Jul & Aug, 10am-6pm Apr-Jun & Sep–mid-Oct, 10am-6pm Sat, Sun & school holidays mid-Oct–Nov & Mar, closed Dec-Feb), at the northern edge of Ambleteuse, features realistic tableaux of military and civilian life, and a 25-minute film. The dashing but wildly impractical French officers' dress uniforms of 1931 hint at why France fared so badly on the battlefield in 1940. Popular wartime songs accompany your visit.

BOULOGNE-SUR-MER

pop 44,600

Boulogne, the most interesting of France's Channel ports, makes a pretty good first stop in France, especially if combined with a swing north through the Côte d'Opale (p243). Much of the city is an uninspiring mass of postwar reconstruction, but the attractive Ville Haute (Upper City), perched high above the rest of town, is girded by a 13th-century wall. The biggest attraction is Nausicaā, one of Europe's premier aquariums.

Auguste Mariette (1821–81), the archeologist who founded Cairo's Egyptian Museum, was born here, which is why Boulogne has a number of sculptures and artefacts related to the Pharaohs.

Orientation

Central Boulogne consists of the hilltop Ville Haute and, on the flats below, the Basse Ville (Lower City). The main train station, Gare Boulogne-Ville, is 1.2km southeast of the centre.

Information

Several commercial banks can be found on or near rue Victor Hugo. Money can be changed aboard Speed Ferries' trans-Channel catamaran.

Forum Espace Culture (57 rue Adolphe Thiers; per 15 min €1; 2-7pm Mon, 10am-7pm Tue-Sat) Internet access in a bookshop.

Laundrettes 62 rue de Lille (7am to 8pm); 235 rue Nationale (7am to 8pm) Duds meet suds in a gripping contest of wills.

Main Post Office (place Frédéric Sauvage) Exchanges money.

Syrius Connect (☎ 03 21 30 03 47; 23 rue des Religieuses Anglaises; per hr €3; 10am-10pm Mon-Sat) Internet access.

Tourist Office (☎ 03 21 10 88 10; www.tourisme-boulognesurmer.com; parvis de Nauticaā; 10am-7pm Mon-Sat, 10.30am-1pm & 2.30-6pm Sun & holidays Jul & Aug, 10am-12.45pm & 1.45-6.30pm Mon-Sat, 10am-1pm & 3pm–5pm or 6pm Sun & holidays Apr-Jun & Sep–mid-Nov, 10.30am-12.30pm & 2-5.30pm Mon-Sat & sometimes Sun mid-Nov–Mar)

Tourist Office Annexe (forum Jean Noël; 9.30am-12.30pm & 1.45pm or 2pm–6pm or 6.30pm Mon-Sat year-round, 10am-1pm Sun & holidays Apr–mid-Nov, also open 3-6pm Sun Jul & Aug)

Sights

You can walk all the way around the **Ville Haute** – an island of centuries-old buildings and cobblestone streets – atop the rectangular, tree-shaded ramparts, a distance of just under 1.5km. Among the impressive buildings around place Godefroy de Bouillon are the neoclassical **Hôtel Desandrouin**, built in the 1780s

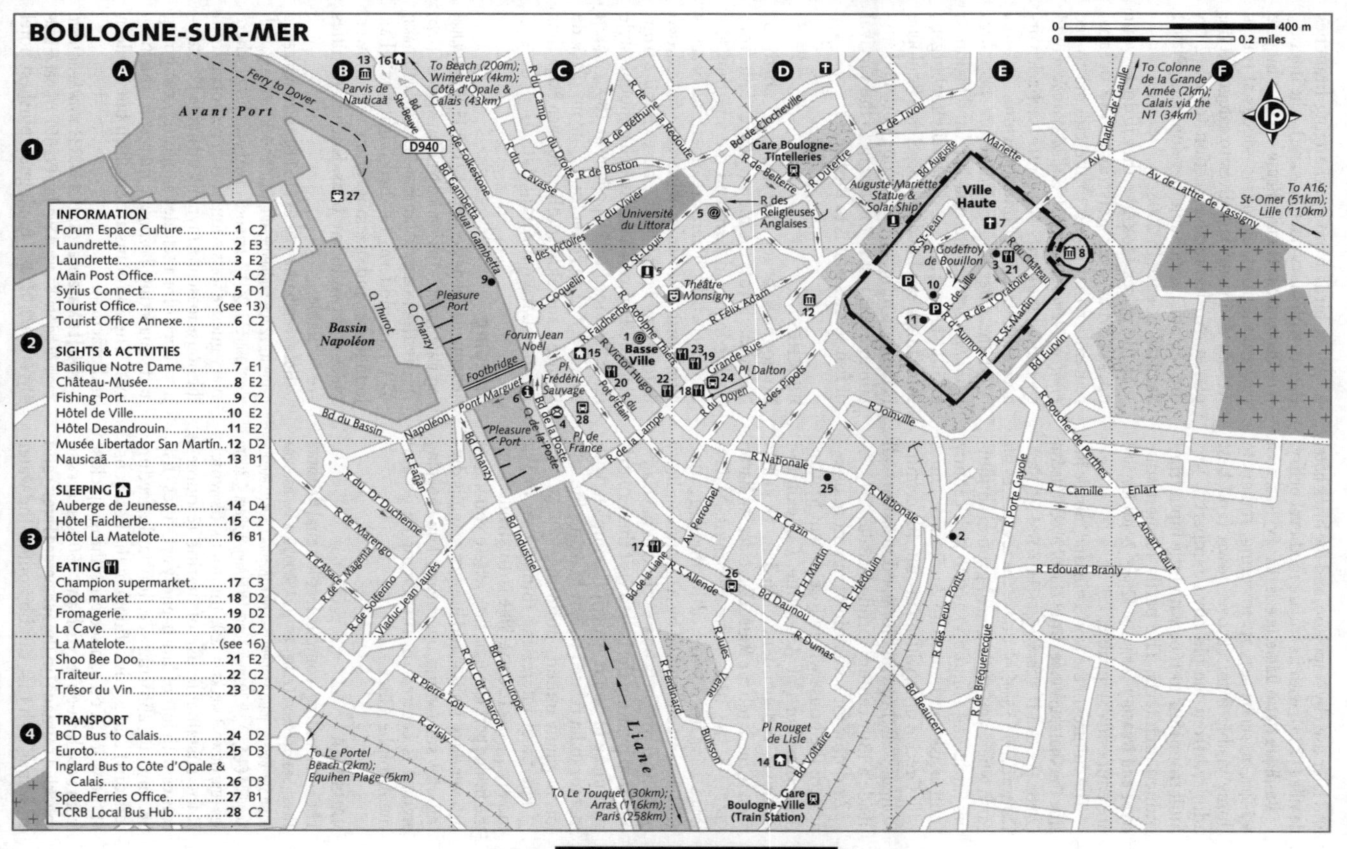

FAR NORTHERN FRANCE

and later used by Napoléon, and the brick **hôtel de ville** (1735), with its square medieval belfry.

Basilique Notre Dame (rue de Lille; 10am-noon & 2-5pm, to 6pm Apr-Aug), its towering, Italianate dome visible from all over town (and best admired from the old city's ramparts), was built from 1827 to 1866 with little input from trained architects. The partly Romanesque **crypt and treasury** (admission €2; 2-5pm Tue-Sun) are eminently skippable.

The cultures of the world mix and mingle inside the **Château-Musée** (03 21 10 02 20; adult/student €2/free; 10am-12.30pm & 2-5pm Mon & Wed-Sat, 10am-12.30pm & 2.30-5.30pm Sun), one of the few places on earth where you can admire Egyptian antiquities (including a mummy) next to 19th-century Inuit masks and compare Andean ceramics with Grecian urns, with an in-situ, 4th-century Roman wall thrown in for good measure – all inside a 13th-century fortified castle.

And now for something even more unexpected: the house where José de San Martín, the exiled hero of Argentine, Chilean and Peruvian independence, died in 1850 has been turned into the **Musée Libertador San Martín** (03 21 31 54 65; 113 Grande Rue; admission free; 10am-noon & 2-6pm Tue-Sat), owned by the Argentine government and staffed by Argentine military personnel who may be surprised to have anyone stop by. Ring the bell to visit this expatriated piece of South America, complete with memorabilia related to San Martín's life and lots of gaudy military uniforms.

The most interesting thing to do in the mostly postwar **Basse Ville** is to stroll along the **fishing port** (quai Gambetta), where you'll find fish vendors' stalls – and hungry seagulls diving and squawking overhead. The **shopping precinct** is centred on rue Victor Hugo and rue Adolphe Thiers.

NAUSICAÃ

The outstanding, completely bilingual **Nausicaã** (French Sea Experience Centre; 03 21 30 99 99; www.nausicaa.fr; bd Ste-Beuve; adult/student/3-12yr €16.50/11.50/10.80, audioguide €4-5; 9.30am-7.30pm Jul & Aug, 9.30am-6.30pm Sep-Jun, closed 3 weeks in Jan), the focus of which is the sustainable use of marine resources, comes with lots of kid-friendly activities (fish petting, a California sea-lion tank, feeding sessions) and is educational in the best sense of the word. You can see everything up close from see-through jellyfish and 250kg sharks to speckled caimans (in the **Submerged Forest**) and arawanas, fish that can hop out of the water to pluck birds from overhanging branches (ladies with fancy hats, beware!). The interactive **Environment-Friendly House** – with a bicycle parked out front, of course – looks at things we can do in our daily lives to safeguard the planet. An interactive section focusing on the sea and sustainable development, **Planet Nausicaã**, opened in 2008.

If the prices look like they'll do to your pocket what drag nets do to the oceans, remember that going to the cinema to see *Finding Nemo* and *A Fish Called Wanda* would cost about the same. The centre is wheelchair-accessible except for one aquarium.

At the cafés you can dine on *specialités boulonnaises* (herring, mackerel and haddock; €5.50) – kind of like a zoo that sells lionburgers, some might say, but don't forget that Boulogne is France's number-one fishing port, and sustainability is just as important to the survival of fish species as it is to the fishers.

BEACHES

Boulogne's beach begins just north of Nausicaã, across the mouth of the Liane from a whirring wind farm and the one-time site of a steelworks. There are other fine beaches 4km north of town at **Wimereux** (served two to four times per hour by buses 1 and 2 from place de France), a partly belle-époque-style resort founded by Napoléon in 1806; 2.5km southwest at **Le Portel** (bus 23 from place de France); and 5km south at **Equihen Plage** (bus Ea and Eb from the train station).

Sleeping

Auberge de Jeunesse (03 21 99 15 30; www.fuaj.org; place Rouget de Lisle; dm incl breakfast & sheets €17.95; closed Jan, reception closed noon-5pm Sat & Sun Oct-Mar;) This modern, 137-bed outfit has a bar, lounge area and spacious rooms with shower, toilet and two to five beds. Kitchen facilities are available.

Hôtel Faidherbe (03 21 31 60 93; www.hotelfaidherbe.fr; 12 rue Faidherbe; d/q €63/96, d Oct-Mar €58, with washbasin €38;) A friendly two-star hotel where every guest elicits some sort of response from the house mascot, a mynah bird named Victor – his repertoire includes laughing, coughing and squawking *'bonjour'*, *'au revoir'* and 'bye-bye'. The 33 rooms are smallish but modern and practical.

Hôtel La Matelote (03 21 30 33 33; www.la-matelote.com; 70 bd Ste-Beuve; d Sun-Thu €95-150, Fri, Sat & holidays €110-170;) Boulogne's plushest hotel has a luxurious Jacuzzi, *hammam* (Turkish baths) and sauna. The 35 spacious four-star rooms, many decorated in rich shades of red and gold, have ultramodern bathrooms and classic wood furnishings, and some come with balconies. Wheelchair access available.

Eating & Drinking

Thanks to its ready supply, Boulogne is an excellent place for fresh fish. In the Ville Haute, rue de Lille is lined with small eateries. In the Ville Basse, the area around place Dalton and rue du Doyen has a good choice of eateries.

Shoo Bee Doo (☎ 03 91 90 55 58; www.shoobeedoo.eu; 2 rue du Château; lunch menus €13.50, dinner menus €17.50-23.50) Yet another of Boulogne's many surprises! Decked out like a Victorian bordello, with dark-red walls, maroon velvet chairs and lots of gilded picture frames, this bar-restaurant puts on *spectacles transformistes* (drag shows; €45) preceded by a meal from 8.30pm to 2am on Friday and Saturday and from 1.30pm to 6pm on many Sundays; reserve ahead. It's also a restaurant (open Tuesday to Thursday and lunch Friday) serving family-style French cuisine; and a gay bar (open 6pm to 1am Tuesday to Sunday) that welcomes *hétéros*.

La Cave (☎ 03 21 32 71 60; 24 rue du Pot d'Étain; menu €25; ⌚ open Tue-Sat & holiday Sun) This restaurant and piano bar, on a desolate side street, serves excellent French cuisine, including *dos de cabillaud* (cod steak). There's often live music in the cellar bar from 8pm to 10pm on Saturday night.

La Matelote (☎ 03 21 30 17 97; 80 bd Ste-Beuve; menus €33-75; ⌚ closed dinner Sun & lunch Thu) A classy establishment with white tablecloths, paper-thin wine glasses, fine porcelain and one Michelin star. Serves French-style *cuisine de saveurs* (cuisine that mixes savours and flavours) with an emphasis on fish, crustaceans and meat.

SELF-CATERING

Food shops are sprinkled around rue de la Lampe and rue Adolphe Thiers.

Champion supermarket (53 bd Daunou; ⌚ 8.30am-8pm Mon-Sat)

Food market (place Dalton; ⌚ morning Wed & Sat) Held the day before if Wednesday or Saturday is a holiday.

Fromagerie (☎ 03 21 87 58 53; 23 Grande Rue; ⌚ 8.30am-12.30pm & 2.30-7.30pm, no midday closure Sat, closed morning Mon & Sun) Fine cheeses.

Traiteur (☎ 03 21 31 53 57; 1 Grande Rue; ⌚ 8.30am-1pm & 3-7.15pm Tue-Fri & morning Sun, 7.30am-7.30pm Sat) Ready-to-eat delicacies.

Trésor du Vin (☎ 03 21 30 39 13; 12 rue Adolphe Thiers; ⌚ 9am-12.30pm & 2-7pm Tue-Sat, sometimes also 10am-12.30pm Sun) A wine shop by and for people who are passionate about wine.

Getting There & Around

For information on car catamarans to Dover, see p968.

For details on buses that service the Côte d'Opale and Calais, see p239.

Euroto (☎ 03 21 30 32 23; 96 rue Nationale) rents cars. There's free parking north of Nausicaä along the beach. To order a cab, call ☎ 03 21 91 25 00.

Gare Boulogne-Ville has rail services to Amiens (€17.60, 1½ hours, six to eight daily), Calais-Ville (€7.20, 30 minutes, 15 to 18 daily Monday to Saturday, eight on Sunday), Étaples-Le Touquet (€5, 20 minutes, 21 Monday to Friday, 13 on weekends), Gare Lille-Flandres or Gare Lille-Europe (€17.60, one to 2¼ hours, 12 daily) and Paris' Gare du Nord (€30.70, 2½ hours, five or six direct daily).

LE TOUQUET

pop 5680

The beach resort of **Le Touquet Paris-Plage**, 30km south of Boulogne, was hugely fashionable during the interwar period, when the English upper crust found it positively smashing (in 1940 a politically oblivious PG Wodehouse was arrested here by the Germans). These days it remains no less posh and no less British. Good spots for a high-profile stroll include the 6km-long **beach**, which features sand sculpture exhibitions, and the leafy area around **place de l'Hermitage**, where you'll find the fabled Hôtel Westminster, the casino and the **tourist office** (☎ 03 21 06 72 00; www.letouquet.com; Palais de l'Europe, place de l'Hermitage; ⌚ 9am-6pm Oct-Mar, to 7pm Apr-Sep, opens 10am Sun & holidays).

Accommodation pricing is highly seasonal. If you're hunting for somewhere central to stay, it's hard to beat the **Hôtel Red Fox** (☎ 03 21 05 27 58; www.hotelredfox.com; 60 rue de Metz; d in winter from €54, in summer €95; ✱ 💻), a two-star hotel just off rue St-Jean, Le Touquet's sparkling, boutique- and eatery-lined main thoroughfare. The 53 functional rooms feature primary colours and brand-new bathrooms.

Just half a block from the beachfront, **Riva Bella** (☎ 03 21 05 08 22; www.rivabella-touquet.com; 12 rue Léon Garat; dm €18-20, d €45; ⌚ mid-Feb–mid-Nov; 💻), Le Touquet's hostel (though it feels more like an old-time hotel), has 50 beds in rooms for two to four people.

There are food shops along rue de Metz, between rue St-Jean and the semicircular **covered market** (morning Thu & Sat, also open Mon mid-Jun–mid-Sep).

Lyddair (www.lyddair.com) links Aéroport Le Touquet Côte d'Opale (www.aeroport-letouquet.com) with Lydd (London Ashford), while Sky South (www.skysouth.co.uk) has flights to Shoreham.

The Étaples-Le Touquet train station, 5km from Le Touquet's centre, is linked with Boulogne (€5, 20 minutes, 21 Monday to Friday, 13 on weekends). Bus 42 links Le Touquet with Boulogne's bd Daunou (€4.60, one hour, four or five Monday to Saturday).

MONTREUIL-SUR-MER

pop 2400

The first thing you should know about Montreuil – so you don't have your hopes cruelly dashed upon arrival – is that this fortified hilltop town is 15km from the sea, the *'sur-mer'* a mere vestige of the time before the River Canche silted up. The second thing you should know – if you like literary trivia – is that Victor Hugo once had lunch here, the result being the great man's decision to set the first scenes of *Les Misérables* in Montreuil.

Montreuil's most interesting bits are inside the walled **Ville Haute** (Upper Town), where you'll find the star-shaped, 16th-century **Citadelle** (adult/student €2.50/1.25, audioguide €1; 10am-noon & 2pm–4pm or 5pm, closed Tue & Dec-Feb); **St-Saulve abbey church** (9am-noon & 2-6pm), whose 12th-century facade is topped by an 18th-century tower; quite a few attractive 18th-century town houses (eg around place Darnétal and along rue de la Chaîne); and some picturesque streets (eg rue du Clape-en-Bas, rue du Clape-en-Haut and cavée St-Firmin). The 3km ramparts walk affords panoramic views of the countryside 40m below but a lack of railings makes it dicey for rambunctious children.

Brochures in English on things to do in and around Montreuil are available from the **tourist office** (03 21 06 04 27; www.tourisme-montreuillois.com; 21 rue Carnot; 10am-12.30pm & 2pm–5pm or 6pm Mon-Sat year-round, 10am-12.30pm Sun Apr-Oct, also open 3-5pm Sun Jul & Aug), just outside the citadel.

Totally renovated in 2006, the **auberge de jeunesse** (/fax 03 21 06 10 83; www.fuaj.org; dm €10.70; check-in 2-6pm except Tue, closed Dec-Feb), with 40 industrial-strength steel single beds, is inside the Citadelle. Kitchen facilities are available. You can usually drop off your bags in the morning.

The three-star **Coq Hôtel** (03 21 81 05 61; www.coqhotel.fr; 2 place de la Poissonnerie; d €115-135), with 19 traditionally styled rooms, occupies a 19th-century building in the heart of the Ville Haute.

The train station, in the Ville Basse, is linked to Boulogne (€6.80, 30 minutes, five to eight daily).

BAIE DE SOMME

The **Somme Estuary** (www.baiedesomme.org, in French, www.baiedesomme.fr), at 5km wide the largest in northern France, affords delightfully watery views as the cycle of the tides alternately hides and reveals vast expanses of sand. **Le Crotoy** is a modest beach resort on the northern bank that makes a good base for exploring the area. From there, across the estuary you can see **Pointe du Hourdel**, famed for its colony of sand-bank-lounging seals and linked to Le Crotoy by a **bike path** (www.baiecyclette.com); lots of duck-hunting huts; and **St-Valery-sur-Somme**, which can be reached on foot (with a bit of knee-deep slogging) at low tide, though only with a guide (the area is notorious for its strong currents and galloping tides) – for details year-round, contact **Promenade en Baie** (03 22 27 47 36; www.promenade-en-baie.com, in French; 5 chemin des Digues).

Le Crotoy's **Tourist Office** (03 22 27 05 25; www.tourisme-crotoy.com; 1 rue Carnot; 9.30am-12.30pm & 2-6pm Mon & Wed-Sat, 10am-12.30pm & 2-5.30pm Sun & holidays, to 7pm Jul & Aug) can supply you with a *horaire des marées* (tide schedule).

Family-run **Les Tourelles** (03 22 27 16 33; www.lestourelles.com; 2-4 rue Pierre Guerlain; s/d €51/74, with washbasin €46/64), a sprawling old two-star hotel overlooking the beach, has an austere, Victorian feel – this is the sort of place where guests take bracing seaside walks before breakfast. One room has 14 bunk beds for kids aged four to 14 (€23, including breakfast), creating a summer-camp atmosphere. The attached **restaurant** (menus €22-32; lunch & dinner) serves French cuisine with Channel Coast touches, including veggie options. From 2.30pm to 6.30pm light meals and oysters are on offer.

The 2-sq-km **Parc Ornithologique du Marquenterre** (Marquenterre Ornithological Park; 03 22 25 68 99; www.parcdumarquenterre.com; adult/6-16yr €9.90/7.90,

MCDONALD'S HAS BRANCHES SO WHY SHOULDN'T THE LOUVRE?

A local branch of the Louvre is coming to a depressed former coal-mining town near you – at least if you live in France's far north. That's right, come 2010, when the Louvre-Lens (www.louvrelens.fr) is set to open in **Lens** (☎ tourist office 03 21 67 66 66; www.tourisme-lenslievin.fr), you'll no longer have to go to Paris to visit the world's most-visited museum.

We may as well be blunt: Lens, 18km northeast of Arras and 37km south of Lille, is known for absolutely nothing, at least as far as tourism is concerned. But thanks to a high-minded effort to 'democratise' the Louvre by bringing its riches to the people – *'la culture est un acteur de la justice sociale'* ('culture is an agent for social justice'), the French prime minister intoned – the town's 37,000 residents are hoping that the Louvre-Lens will do for them what the Guggenheim Museum did for Bilbao. Incidentally, the decision to situate this ultraprestigious project in Lens was apparently helped along by a municipal advert that juxtaposed IM Pei's Louvre pyramid with one of Lens' very own pyramid-like slag heaps!

The new museum, which will occupy the site of long-closed Mineshaft No 9, is being designed by the Japanese architectural firm Sanaa, led by Kazuyo Sejima (said to be the first woman to design a major public monument in France) and Ryue Nishizawa. About two-thirds of the 6000 sq metres of exhibition space will be given over to 600 to 800 major works rotated to Lens from the Louvre (original recipe) for two or three years at a time.

binoculars €4; 🕑 10am-7.30pm Apr-Sep, 10am-6pm mid-Feb–Mar & Oct–mid-Nov, 10am-5pm mid-Nov–mid-Feb, last entry 2hr before closing) in St-Quentin-en-Tourmont, a circuitous 10km northwest of Le Crotoy, is a migratory stopover for more than 200 species of birds on their way from the UK, Iceland, Scandinavia and Siberia to warmer climes in West Africa. While here, our feathered friends – including 12 stork couples (out of 30 in the Somme *département*) – find most of their food in the sandy estuary at low tide. Three marked walking circuits of 2km to 6km take you to marshes, dunes, meadows, freshwater ponds, a brackish lagoon and 14 observation posts.

ARRAS

pop 41,400

Arras (the final *s* is pronounced), former capital of Artois and *préfecture* (capital) of the *département* of Pas-de-Calais, is worth seeing mainly for its harmonious ensemble of Flemish-style arcaded buildings. The city makes a good base for visits to the Battle of the Somme Memorials (p252).

Orientation

The Grand' Place and the almost-adjoining place des Héros (also called the Petite Place), where you'll find the *hôtel de ville*, are Arras' focal point. The train station is 600m to the southeast. Commerce is centred on rue Gambetta, rue Ernestale and the pedestrianised area south of place des Héros, including rue Ronville.

Information

Banks can be found along rue Gambetta and its continuation, rue Ernestale.

The **tourist office** (☎ 03 21 51 26 95; www.ot-arras.fr, in French; place des Héros; 🕑 9am or 10am–noon & 2pm–6pm or 6.30pm Mon-Sat, no midday closure Apr-Sep, 10am–12.30pm or 1pm & 2.30-6.30pm Sun & holidays) is inside the *hôtel de ville*, has an internet terminal, and offers an audioguide tour (adult/student €6/3.20) of the city centre. Le City Pass (adult/student €19/10) gets you into the belfry, the tunnels, Wellington Quarry, the Musée des Beaux-Arts and Cité Nature (a science museum focusing on food, health and nature).

Other handy places:

Copie-Com (☎ 03 21 73 98 02; 121 rue St-Aubert; per hr €1; 🕑 noon-7pm Mon, 10.30am-7pm Tue-Fri, 2-7pm Sat) Internet access.

Laundrette (17 place d'Ipswich; 🕑 7am-8pm) Across the street from an old red British phone box.

Post Office (rue Gambetta) Changes money.

Sights & Activities

Arras' two market squares, **place des Héros** and the **Grand' Place**, are surrounded by 17th- and 18th-century Flemish-baroque houses, especially handsome at night. Although they vary in decorative detail, their 345 sandstone columns form a common arcade unique in France.

The Flemish-Gothic **hôtel de ville** (place des Héros) dates from the 16th century but was completely rebuilt after WWI. Three giants (see the boxed text p226) – Colas, Jacqueline and their son Dédé – make their home in the lobby.

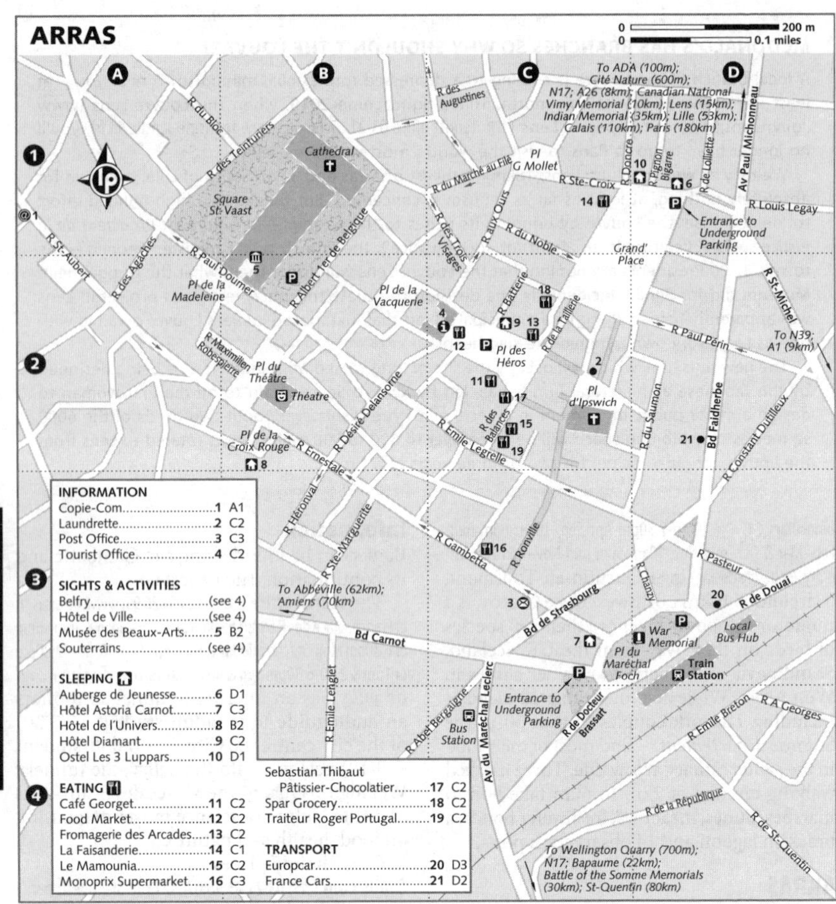

The basement of the *hôtel de ville* is a veritable hub of activity. If you're in the mood for a panoramic view, this is the place to hop on the lift to the top of the 75m **belfry** (adult/student €2.30/1.60; same as tourist office). But for a truly unique perspective on Arras, head into the slimy **souterrains** (tunnels). Also known as *boves* (cellars), they run under place des Héros and were turned into British command posts, hospitals and barracks during WWI. Each spring, in a brilliant juxtaposition of underground gloom and horticultural exuberance, plants and flowers turn the tunnels into the lush, creative, life-affirming **Jardin des Boves** (Cellar Garden; mid- or late Mar–mid- or late Jun). **Tours** (adult/student €4.70/2.70) of the *souterrains* lasting 45 minutes (in English upon request), focusing on the gardens (when they're there), generally begin at about 11am and twice in the afternoon from Monday to Friday, and every 30 minutes or so on Saturday and Sunday.

The staging ground for the spring 1917 offensive in which the poet Siegfried Sassoon was wounded, **Wellington Quarry** (Carrière Wellington; Arras tourist office 03 21 48 58 52; www.carriere-wellington.com; rue Delétoile; adult/student €6.50/2.70; 10am-12.30pm & 1.30-6pm, last tour 1-1½ hr before closing) is a 20m-deep network of old chalk quarries expanded during WWI by tunnellers from New Zealand. Hour-long guided tours in French and English combine imaginative audiovisuals, evocative photos and period items. It's easy to tell who wrote which graffiti when: signs painted in black are British and from WWI, those in red are French and from WWII, when the site was used as a bomb shelter. Opened to the public in 2008, the quarry is about 1km south of the train station; to get there, take av du Maréchal Leclerc or follow the signs around town to the 'Carrière'. It's served by buses 1A and 4.

Highlights at the **Musée des Beaux-Arts** (Fine Arts Museum; ☎ 03 21 71 26 43; 22 rue Paul Doumer; adult/student & over 65yr €4/2; 🕒 9.30am-noon & 2-5.30pm Wed-Mon), housed in a neoclassical former Benedictine abbey with an impressive courtyard, include the original copper lion from the *hôtel de ville* belfry (in the lobby), medieval sculpture (including a 15th-century skeletal figure whose stomach is being devoured by worms) and 17th-century religious paintings.

Sleeping

Auberge de Jeunesse (☎ 03 21 22 70 02; www.fuaj.org; 59 Grand' Place; dm €11.60; 🕒 reception 9am-noon & 5-10pm, closed mid-Nov–Jan) Modern and superbly situated in the town centre, this hostel has cheerful rooms for two to 10; almost all of the 54 beds are bunks. Full kitchen facilities are available.

Hôtel Astoria Carnot (☎ 03 21 71 08 14; www.hotelcarnot.com; 10 place du Maréchal Foch; s/d/q €52/59/80) Above a sleek brasserie, this hotel has 29 spiffy, well-lit rooms with pastel colours, big windows and all-tile bathrooms.

Ostel Les 3 Luppars (☎ 03 21 60 02 03; www.ostel-les-3luppars.com, in French; 47 Grand' Place; s/d/q from €55/70/85) Homey and centred on a courtyard, this lift-equipped 'ho(s)tel' occupies the Grand' Place's only non-Flemish-style building (it's Gothic and dates from 1370). The 42 rooms, some with fine views of the square, are comfortable, if uninspired and a tad small. A half-hour in the sauna costs €5 per person.

Hôtel Diamant (☎ 03 21 71 23 23; www.arras-hotel-diamant.com; 5 place des Héros; s/d from €65/70; 💻 ⊠) The 12 two-star rooms, though smallish, are neat and tasteful, and six have great views of the *place*. Free internet access, coffee and orange juice are available in the lobby.

Hôtel de l'Univers (☎ 03 21 71 34 01; www.hotel-univers-arras.com; 3-5 place de la Croix Rouge; d €95-143; ⊠) Ensconced in a 16th-century former Jesuit monastery, this three-star, Best Western–affiliated hostelry, arrayed in a U around a quiet classical courtyard, is an island of calm – though it's just 50m from No 29 on bustling rue Ernestale. Classic draperies, bedspreads and writing desks give each of the 38 rooms a touch of French class. Civilised comfort at a reasonable price.

Eating

Lots of eateries are hidden away under the arches of the Grand' Place.

Café Georget (☎ 03 21 71 13 07; 42 place des Héros; plat du jour €8; 🕒 lunch Mon-Sat) In her unpretentious café, Madame Delforge has been serving hearty, home-style French dishes to people who work in the neighbourhood since 1985.

Sebastian Thibaut Pâtissier-Chocolatier (☎ 03 21 71 53 20; 50 place des Héros; 🕒 8am-7.30pm Tue-Sun) Sparkling cases of mouth-watering pastries and chocolates greet you at this *salon de thé*, a good place for a light lunch – options include sandwiches (€3 to €4.80), omelettes, quiches and, in the warm months, salads.

Le Mamounia (☎ 03 21 07 99 99; 9 rue des Balances; mains €12-23; 🕒 closed Mon, lunch Sat, dinner Sun) The elegant, multicoloured decor mixes the Maghreb with Provence but the couscous and *tajines* (stews) are 100% Moroccan.

La Faisanderie (☎ 03 21 48 20 76; 45 Grand' Place; menus €24-63; 🕒 closed Mon, dinner Sun & lunch Thu) An especially elegant French restaurant under vaulted brick ceilings. The *menus* change with the seasons to take advantage of fresh seasonal ingredients. Specialities include sole and wild turbot.

SELF-CATERING

Food market (place des Héros, Grand' Place & place de la Vacquerie; 🕒 morning Sat) There's an additional smaller market at place des Héros on Wednesday morning.

Fromagerie des Arcades (37 place des Héros; 🕒 9.30am-12.30pm & 2.30-7.30pm Tue-Sat)

Monoprix supermarket (30 rue Gambetta; 🕒 8.30am-7.50pm Mon-Sat)

PARDON MY FRENCH

Some sensitive matters, it seems, are best mentioned with the discretion implied by foreign vocabulary. Thus, decades ago, a condom was known as a 'French letter' in the UK and a *capote anglaise* (English hood) in France. In Arras' Wellington Quarry (opposite), toilets were treated with similar trans-Channel euphemism: marked *latrines* (a French term) by the British during WWI, they were signposted *WC* (water closet) by the French during WWII.

Spar grocery (9 rue de la Taillerie; 8.30am-1pm & 3.30-8pm Tue-Thu, to 9pm Fri & Sat, 9.30am-1pm & 5.30-8pm Sun)

Traiteur Roger Portugal (03 21 23 44 72; 13 rue des Balances; 9am-1pm & 3-7pm Tue-Sat, 9am-12.30pm Sun & holidays) Delicious ready-to-eat delicacies.

Getting There & Away

BUS

For details on getting to the Canadian National Vimy Memorial, see opposite.

CAR

Car-rental options:

ADA (03 21 55 05 05; 15 av Paul Michonneau)
Europcar (03 21 07 29 54; 5 rue de Douai)
France Cars (03 21 50 22 22; 31 bd Faidherbe)

TAXI

Alliance Arras Taxis-GT (03 21 23 69 69; 24hr) can take you to Somme battlefield sites (eg Vimy).

TRAIN

Arras is on the main line linking Lille-Flandres (€9.40, 24 to 45 minutes, 14 to 25 daily) with Paris' Gare du Nord (€28.70 or €38.90 by TGV, 50 minutes, eight to 12 daily). Other destinations include Amiens (€10.50, 50 minutes, six to 12 daily), Calais-Ville (€18.70, 1¾ hours, 12 daily Monday to Friday, five daily Saturday and Sunday) and Lens (€3.80, 15 minutes, 23 daily Monday to Friday, eight to 11 daily weekends).

BATTLE OF THE SOMME MEMORIALS

The First Battle of the Somme, a WWI Allied offensive waged in the villages and woodlands northeast of Amiens, was designed to relieve pressure on the beleaguered French troops at Verdun. On 1 July 1916, British, Commonwealth and French troops 'went over the top' in a massive assault along a 34km front. But German positions proved virtually unbreachable, and on the first day of the battle an astounding 21,392 British troops were killed and another 35,492 were wounded. Most casualties were infantrymen mown down by German machine guns.

By the time the offensive was called off in mid-November, a total of 1.2 million lives had been lost on both sides. The British had advanced 12km, the French 8km. (Today, 'Ligne de Front' signs mark where the front line stood on specific dates.) The Battle of the Somme has become a symbol of the meaningless slaughter of war and its killing fields have since become a site of pilgrimage (see www.somme-battlefields.co.uk).

GETTING THERE & AWAY

Visiting the Somme memorials is easiest by car but quite a few sites can be reached by train or bus from Amiens and/or Arras; details on public transport options appear after each listing. Cycling is also an option.

The tourist offices in Amiens and Arras can provide details on minibus tours.

COMMONWEALTH CEMETERIES & MEMORIALS

Almost 750,000 soldiers, airmen and sailors from Great Britain, Australia, Canada, the Indian subcontinent, Ireland, New Zealand, South Africa, the West Indies and other parts of the British Empire died during WWI on the Western Front, two-thirds of them in France. According to the Commonwealth tradition, they were buried where they fell, in more than 1000 military cemeteries and 2000 civilian cemeteries now tended by the **Commonwealth War Graves Commission** (www.cwgc.org). French, American and German war dead were reburied in large cemeteries after the war.

Today, hundreds of neatly tended Commonwealth plots – marked by white-on-dark-green road signs – dot the landscape along a wide swathe of territory running roughly from Albert and Cambrai north via Arras and Béthune to Armentières and Ypres (Ieper) in Belgium. Many of the headstones bear inscriptions composed by family members. Twenty-six memorials (20 of them in France) bear the names of more than 300,000 Commonwealth soldiers whose bodies were never recovered or identified.

Except where noted, all the monuments listed in this chapter are always open. Many Commonwealth cemeteries have a bronze plaque with historical information. The bronze cemetery-register boxes contain a booklet with details on the site and brief biographies of each of the identified dead; you can record your impressions in the visitors book.

FAR NORTHERN FRANCE

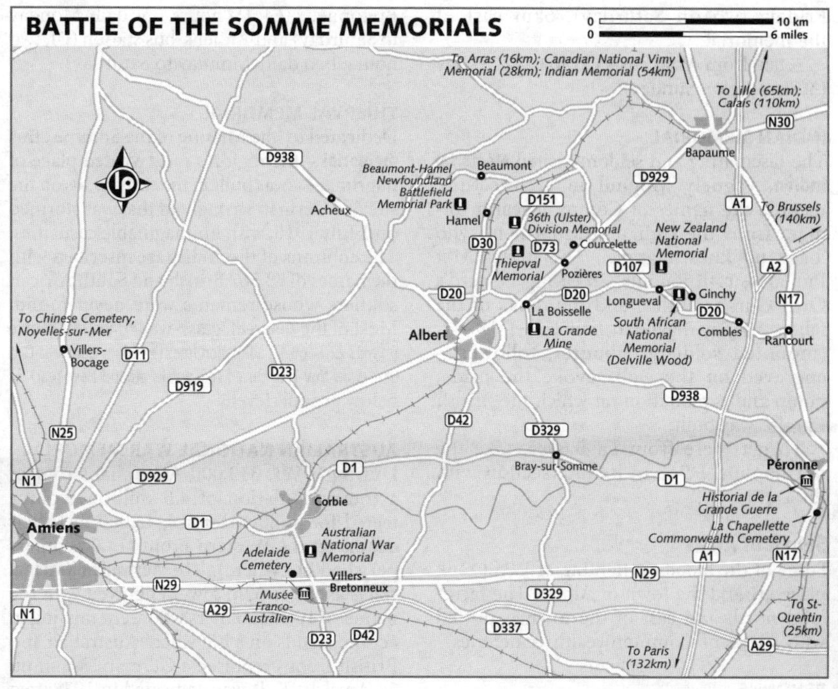

North of Arras

The area towards Lille from Arras has a couple of noteworthy memorials and numerous military cemeteries.

CANADIAN NATIONAL VIMY MEMORIAL & PARK

Whereas the French, right after the war, attempted to erase all signs of battle and return the Somme region to agriculture and normalcy, the Canadians decided that the most evocative way to remember their fallen was to preserve sections of the crater-pocked battlefields. As a result, the best place to get some sense of the unimaginable hell known as the Western Front is at the chilling, eerie moonscape of **Vimy Ridge**. Visitors can also visit **tunnels** (admission free; ⌚ with a guide early May–Nov) and reconstructed **trenches** (⌚ 10am-6pm early May–Oct, 9am-5pm Nov–early May).

Of the 66,655 Canadians who died in WWI, 3589 lost their lives in April 1917 taking this ridge, a German defensive line. Its highest point was later chosen as the site of Canada's **WWI memorial** (built 1925–36, renovated 2007). The allegorical figures, carved from huge blocks of limestone, include a cloaked, downcast female figure representing a young Canada mourning her fallen. The base is inscribed with the names of 11,285 Canadians who 'died in France but have no known graves'. The 1-sq-km park also includes two **Canadian cemeteries** and, at the vehicle entrance to the main memorial, a **monument to the Moroccan Division** (in French and Arabic).

The **Historical Interpretive Centre** (☎ 03 21 50 68 68; www.vac-acc.gc.ca; admission free; ⌚ 10am-6pm early May–Oct, 9am-5pm Nov–early May), in a modest, rust-coloured building at the entrance to the trenches, is staffed by Canadian students, who also serve as tour guides from May to November.

To get to the Canadian memorials from Arras, take bus 191 (€1, 20 minutes, six daily Monday to Saturday) – run by **Tadaõ** (☎ 08 10 00 11 78; www.tadao.fr, in French) – from Arras' bus station, towards Lens, and ask the bus driver to stop a bit before the Thelus–Vert Tilleul turn-off, 3.2km from the memorial.

Trains link Arras with the town of Vimy (€2.70, 12 minutes, six daily Monday to

FAR NORTHERN FRANCE

Friday, two on Saturday), 6km east of the memorial.

A taxi from Arras costs €22 to €24 one-way (30% more on Sunday).

INDIAN MEMORIAL

The fascinating and seldom-visited **Mémorial Indien**, vaguely Moghul in architecture, records the names of Commonwealth soldiers from the Indian subcontinent who 'have no known grave'. The units (31st Punjabis, 11th Rajputs, 2nd King Edward's Own Gurkha Rifles) and the ranks of the fallen – sepoy, havildar, *naik* (chief), *sowar* (mounted soldier), labourer, follower – engraved on the walls evoke the pride, pomp and exploitation on which the British Empire was built.

To get there from La Bassée, take the northbound D947 to its intersection with the D171.

South of Arras

Some of the bloodiest fighting of WWI took place around the town of Albert. The farmland north and east of the town is dotted with scores of Commonwealth cemeteries.

PÉRONNE

Perhaps the best place to start a visit to the Somme battlefields is in the river port of Péronne (population 8400), at the well-designed and informative **Historial de la Grande Guerre** (Museum of the Great War; ☎ 03 22 83 14 18; www.historial.org; Château de Péronne; adult/over 60yr/children 6-18yr incl audioguide €7.50/6/3.80; ⏲ 10am-6pm, closed mid-Dec–mid-Jan). This innovative museum tells the story of the war chronologically, with equal space given to the German, French and British perspectives on what happened, how and why. A great deal of visually engaging material, including period films and the bone-chilling engravings by Otto Dix, capture the aesthetic sensibilities, enthusiasm, naive patriotism and unimaginable violence of the time. The proud uniforms of various units and armies are shown laid out on the ground, as if on freshly – though bloodlessly – dead soldiers. Not much glory here.

On the N17 at the southern edge of town, **La Chapellette Commonwealth Cemetery** has separate British and Indian sections.

Buses 38 and 46 link Péronne with Albert (€4, 35 to 50 minutes, five daily Monday to Saturday); bus 47 goes to both Villers-Bretonneux (€4, 1¼ hours, one daily Monday to Saturday) and Amiens' bus station (€4, two hours, two daily Monday to Saturday).

THIEPVAL MEMORIAL

Dedicated to 'the Missing of the Somme', this **memorial** – the region's most visited place of pilgrimage – was built in the early 1930s on the site of a German stronghold that was stormed on 1 July 1916, with unimaginable casualties. The columns of the arches are inscribed with the names of 73,367 British and South African soldiers whose remains were never found. Most of the discreet, glass-walled **visitors centre** (☎ 03 22 74 60 47; admission free; ⏲ 10am-6pm Mar-Oct, 9am-5pm Nov-Feb, closed two weeks around New Year) is below ground level.

AUSTRALIAN NATIONAL WAR MEMORIAL

During WWI, 313,000 Australians (out of a total population of 4.5 million) volunteered for military service; 46,000 met their deaths on the Western Front (14,000 others perished elsewhere). The **Australian National War Memorial**, a 32m tower engraved with the names of 10,982 soldiers who went missing in action, stands on a hill where Australian and British troops repulsed a German assault on 24 April 1918. It was dedicated in 1938; two years later its stone walls were scarred by the guns of Hitler's invading armies.

The nearest town is **Villers-Bretonneux**, an ugly burg that feels like it hasn't completely recovered from the war. For Aussies, though, it's a heart-warming place that bills itself as *l'Australie en Picardie,* and Anzac Day is religiously commemorated here. In 1993, the unidentified remains of an Australian soldier were transferred from **Adelaide Cemetery**, on the N29 at the western edge of town, to the Tomb of the Unknown Soldier in Canberra.

The town's **Musée Franco-Australien** (☎ 03 22 96 80 79; www.museeaustralien.com, www.villers-bretonneux.com/Australian.htm; École Victoria, 9 rue Victoria; adult/student €4/2.50; ⏲ 10am-12.30pm & 2-6pm Wed-Sat, 2-6pm Tue, 1st & 3rd Sun of month, closed 2 weeks around New Year) has intimate, evocative displays of WWI Australiana, including letters, photographs of life on the Western Front, and a small Anzac (Australian and New Zealand Army Corps) library.

The Villers-Bretonneux train station, 700m south of the museum (along rue de Melbourne) and a walkable 3km south of the Australian National War Memorial, is well served from Amiens (€3.20, 12 minutes, 10 daily Monday to Friday, five or six weekends). Bus 47 links Villers-Bretonneux with Amiens (€1.50, 25 minutes, two or three daily Monday to Saturday) and Péronne (€4, 1¼ hours, one daily Monday to Saturday).

Taking a **taxi** (☎ 03 22 48 49 49) to the memorial from Villers-Bretonneux and getting picked up at a time of your choosing costs €18 to €20 return.

BEAUMONT-HAMEL NEWFOUNDLAND BATTLEFIELD MEMORIAL PARK

Like Vimy (p253), the evocative **Beaumont-Hamel Newfoundland Battlefield Memorial Park** (Mémorial Terre-Neuvien de Beaumont-Hamel) preserves part of the Western Front in the state it was in at fighting's end. The zigzag trench system, which still fills with mud in winter, is clearly visible, as are countless shell craters and the remains of barbed-wire barriers.

On 1 July 1916, the volunteer Royal Newfoundland Regiment stormed entrenched German positions and was nearly wiped out; a plaque notes blandly that 'strategic and tactical miscalculations led to a great slaughter'. You can survey the whole battlefield from the **caribou statue**, surrounded by plants native to Newfoundland. Canadian students based at the **visitors centre** (☎ 03 22 76 70 87; www.vac-acc.gc.ca; admission free; ⌚ 10am-6pm Apr-Oct, to 5pm Nov-Mar, closed 2 weeks around New Year), designed to look like a typical Newfoundland fisher's house, give free guided tours year-round (except perhaps in late December and January).

THIRTY-SIXTH (ULSTER) DIVISION MEMORIAL

Built on a German frontline position assaulted by the overwhelmingly Protestant 36th (Ulster) Division on 1 July 1916, the **Tour d'Ulster** (Ulster Tower; ☎ 03 22 74 87 14; teddy.ulstertower@orange.fr; ⌚ museum 10am-5pm, to 6pm Apr-Sep, closed Dec-Feb), also known as the Mémorial Irlandais, is an exact replica of Helen's Tower at Clanboye, County Down, where the unit did its training. Dedicated in 1921, it has long been a Unionist pilgrimage site. A black obelisk known as the **Orange Memorial to Fallen Brethren** stands in an enclosure behind the tower. In a sign that historic wounds are finally healing, in 2006 the Irish Republic issued a €0.75 postage stamp, showing the 36th Division in action on this site, to commemorate the 90th anniversary of the Battle of the Somme.

Virtually untouched since the war, nearby **Thiepval Wood** can be visited on a guided tour; phone or email the Tour d'Ulster for times.

SOUTH AFRICAN & NEW ZEALAND NATIONAL MEMORIALS

The **South African National Memorial** (Mémorial Sud-Africain) stands in the middle of shell-pocked **Delville Wood**, which was almost captured by a South African brigade in the third week of July in 1916. The avenues through the trees are named after streets in London and Edinburgh. The star-shaped **museum** (☎ 03 22 85 02 17; www.delvillewood.com; admission free; ⌚ 10am-5.30pm, to 4pm outside daylight savings, closed Mon, holidays & Dec–early Feb) was dedicated amid much apartheid-related controversy in 1986.

The **New Zealand National Memorial** is 1.5km due north of Longueval.

LA GRANDE MINE

Just outside the hamlet of La Boisselle, this enormous **crater** looks like the site of a meteor impact. Some 100m across and 30m deep and officially known as the **Lochnagar Crater Memorial**, it was created on the morning of the first day of the First Battle of the Somme by about 25 tonnes of ammonal laid by British sappers in order to create a breach in the German lines – and is a testament to the boundless ingenuity human beings can muster when determined to kill their fellow creatures.

ALBERT

The most noteworthy landmark in this rather unfetching town (population 10,000), virtually flattened during WWI, is neo-Byzantine-style **Basilique Notre Dame de Brebières**, topped by a dazzlingly gilded statue of the Virgin Mary, repaired since famously being left dangling by a German shell.

Right next to the basilica, the underground **Musée Somme 1916** (Somme Trench Museum; ☎ 03 22 75 16 17; www.musee-somme-1916.eu; rue Anicet Godin; adult/6-18yr €5/3; ⌚ 9am-noon & 2-6pm Feb–mid-Dec, no midday closure Jun-Sep) does a good job of evoking the grim, grimy lives of Tommies, *poilus* ('hairy ones', ie French WWI soldiers) and civilians at the front line.

The **tourist office** (☎ 03 22 75 16 42; www.paysducoquelicot.com, in French; 9 rue Léon Gambetta; ⌚ 9am-12.30pm & 1.30-6.30pm Mon-Fri, 9am-noon & 2pm-6.30pm

Sat, 10am-12.30pm Sun & holidays Apr-Sep, to 5pm & closed Sun & holidays Oct-Mar) is 50m towards the train station from the basilica. Year-round, it rents out bicycles (per half-/full day €8/12). A *coquelicot* (as included in the website address) is a poppy.

Trains (14 to 20 Monday to Saturday, seven Sunday) link Albert's train station – the monoplane hanging in the waiting hall is a Potez 36 from 1933 – with Amiens (€5.70, 25 minutes).

CHINESE CEMETERY

Towards the end of WWI, tens of thousands of Chinese labourers were recruited by the British government to perform non-combat jobs in Europe, including the gruesome task of recovering and burying Allied war dead. **Noyelles-sur-Mer**, 65km northwest of Amiens, served as the French base for the Chinese Labour Corps, and it is there (actually, in the neighbouring hamlet of Nolette) that the **Chinese Cemetery**, maintained by the Commonwealth War Graves Commission, bears silent testimony to 849 men from a far-off land who never made it home. To get there, follow the signs along the D111 and the C6 to the 'Cimetière Chinois'.

AMIENS

pop 136,600

One of France's most awe-inspiring Gothic cathedrals is reason enough to spend time in Amiens, the comfy, if reserved, former capital of Picardy, where Jules Verne lived for the last two decades of his life. The clean-lined city centre, rebuilt after the war, has aged remarkably well, thanks in part to recent pedestrianisation and train station renovations. Some 25,000 students give the place a young, lively feel.

Amiens is an excellent base for visits to the Battle of the Somme memorials.

Orientation

The pedestrianised main drag, known as rue de Noyon and rue des Trois Cailloux, stretches from the train station west to place Gambetta, the city's commercial hub, which is three blocks southwest of the cathedral.

Information

Banks can be found around place René Goblet and rue des Trois Cailloux.

Bibliothèque (☎ 03 22 97 10 00; 50 rue de la République; ⏰ 2-7pm Mon, 9.30am-7pm Tue-Fri, 9.30am-6pm Sat) Free internet access in a grand public library, built in the 1820s.

Laundrette 10 rue André (⏰ 8am-6pm); 15 rue des Majots (⏰ 7am-9pm Mon-Sat, 9am-8pm Sun)

Main Post Office (7 rue des Vergeaux) Has currency exchange.

Neurogame Cybercafé (16 rue des Chaudronniers; ☎ 03 22 72 68 79; per hr €3.50; ⏰ 10am-midnight Mon-Sat, 2-8pm Sun) Internet access.

Tourist Office (☎ 03 22 71 60 50; www.amiens.com/tourisme; 40 place Notre Dame; ⏰ 9.30am–6pm or 6.30pm Mon-Sat, 10am-noon & 2-5pm Sun) Can supply details on the Somme memorials and visiting them on minibus tours. Sells the City Pass (€8), which offers all sorts of discounts.

Cathédrale Notre Dame

The largest Gothic cathedral in France (it's 145m long) and a Unesco World Heritage Site, the magnificent **Cathédrale Notre Dame** (place Notre Dame; ⏰ 8.30am-6.15pm Apr-Sep, to 5.15pm Oct-Mar) was begun in 1220 to house the skull of St John the Baptist, now enclosed in gold in the northern outer wall of the ambulatory (on view from about Easter to October). Connoisseurs rave about the soaring Gothic arches (42.3m high over the transept), unity of style and immense interior, but for locals, the 17th-century statue known as the **Ange Pleureur** (Crying Angel), in the ambulatory directly behind the very baroque, 18th-century high altar, remains a favourite.

The black-and-white, octagonal, 234m-long **labyrinth** on the floor of the nave is easy to miss as the soaring vaults draw the eye upward. Plaques in the south transept arm honour Australian, British, Canadian, New Zealand and US troops who died in WWI.

Weather permitting, it's possible to climb the **north tower** (☎ 03 22 80 03 41; adult/18-25yr/under 18yr €6.50/4.50/free; ⏰ visits begin 11am & 2.30-5.15pm Wed-Mon Jul & Aug, 3pm & 4.30pm Mon & Wed-Fri, 2.30-5.15pm Sat & Sun Apr-Jun & Sep, 3.45pm Wed-Mon Oct-Mar except when windy or snowy) with a guide.

Worthwhile, one-hour **audioguides** (1st/2nd person €4/3) of the cathedral's highlights, in six languages, can be rented at the tourist office.

A free 45-minute **light show** bathes the cathedral's facade in vivid medieval colours nightly from mid-June to mid-September and December to 1 January; the photons start flying at 7pm in winter and sometime between 9.45pm (September) and 10.45pm (June) in summer.

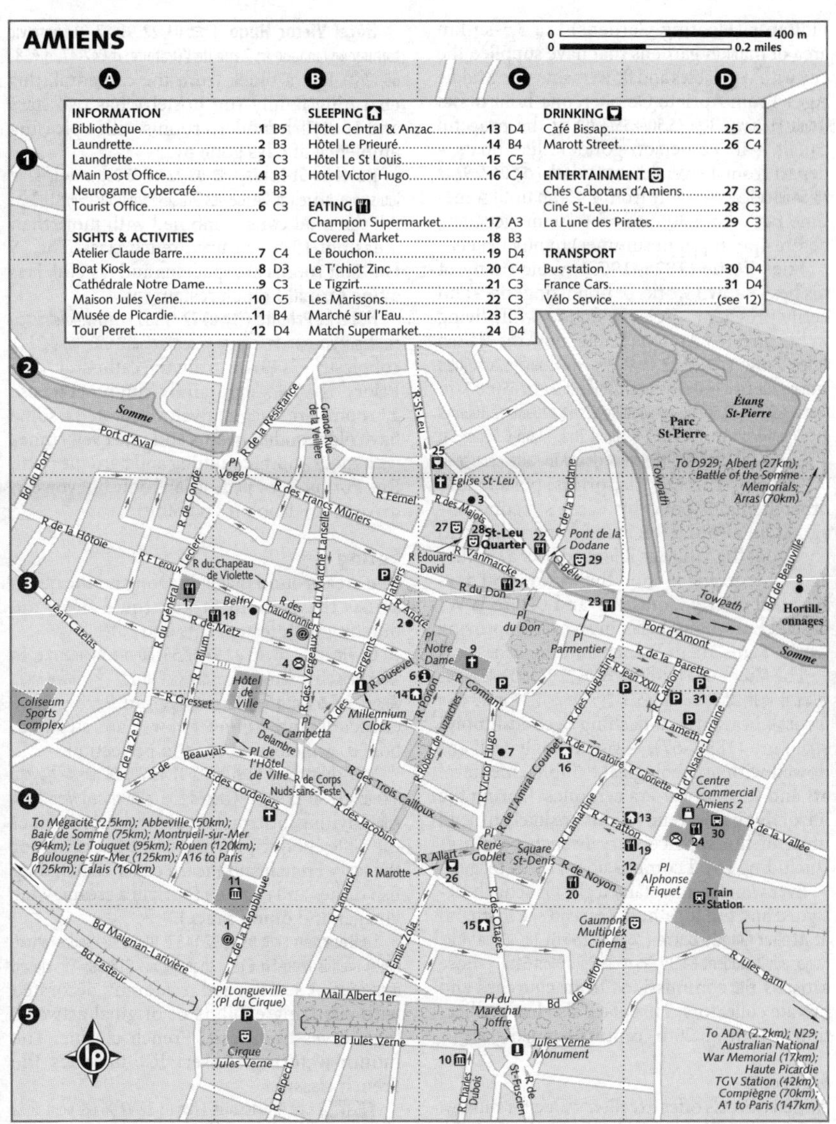

Other Sights & Activities

Postwar renovations have left parts of the medieval **St-Leu Quarter** too cute by half, but the many neon-lit quayside restaurants and pubs make the area especially lively at night.

Another product of postwar exuberance is the concrete **Tour Perret** (built 1948–54), once the tallest building in Europe, across the square from the train station. At night the structure, designed by the Belgian architect Auguste Perret (who also planned postwar Le Havre), is illuminated by ever-changing coloured lights.

The lawns, lakes, waterways and bridges of **Parc St-Pierre** stretch eastward from St-Leu all the way to the **Hortillonnages** – also known as the Jardins

Flottants (Floating Gardens) – a 3.3-sq-km area of market gardens that have supplied the city with vegetables and flowers since the Middle Ages. From April to October, one-hour **cruises** (adult/11-16yr/4-10yr €5.50/4.55/3.70) of the peaceful canals – in 12-person gondola-like boats – depart from a riverside **boat kiosk** (☎ 03 22 92 12 18; 54 bd de Beauvillé) daily from 1.45pm until sometime between 4.30pm and 6.30pm; get there before 4pm (5pm in summer) to buy tickets.

Jules Verne (1828–1905) wrote many of his best-known works of brain-tingling – and eerily prescient – science fiction while living in his turreted Amiens home, now the **Maison Jules Verne** (☎ 03 22 45 45 75; www.amiens.com/julesverne; 2 rue Charles Dubois; adult/student & over 65yr/8-17yr/family €5/3.50/2.50/12, audioguide €2; ⌚ 10am-12.30pm & 2-6.30pm Mon-Wed & Fri, 2-6.30pm Thu, 11am-6.30pm Sat & Sun mid-Apr–mid-Oct, to 6pm & closed Tue afternoon mid-Oct–mid-Apr). The models, prints, posters and other items inspired by Verne's fecund imagination afford a fascinating opportunity to check out the future as it looked over a century ago, when going around the world in 80 days sounded utterly fantastic – and before WWI dashed Europeans' belief in an ever-improving world. Signs are in French and English.

The **Musée de Picardie** (☎ 03 22 97 14 00; 48 rue de la République; adult/student €5/3; ⌚ 10am-12.30pm & 2-6pm Tue-Sun), housed in a dashing Second Empire structure (1855–67), is surprisingly well endowed with archeological exhibits, medieval art and Revolution-era ceramics. During the life of this guide, renovations are likely to send most of the 18th-century French paintings (including royal commissions) into storage.

Ever wonder how stained glass is actually designed and put together? You can see firsthand at **Atelier Claude Barre** (☎ 03 22 91 81 18; 40 rue Victor Hugo; adult/student €4/3; ⌚ tours 3pm Mon-Sat), whose artisans fill commissions from churches and private collectors. This place also has a collection of 11th- to 20th- century stained glass.

FAR NORTHERN FRANCE

Sleeping

Amiens' hotels offer excellent value for money. They often fill up with businesspeople from Monday to Thursday.

Hôtel Central & Anzac (☎ 03 22 91 34 08; www.hotelcentralanzac.com; 17 rue Alexandre Fatton; s/d from €46/54, with washbasin €33/39; ☒) Founded decades ago by an Australian ex-serviceman, this two-star place has 25 clean, well-maintained rooms, many with old-time touches, though some are a bit on the small side.

Hôtel Victor Hugo (☎ 03 22 91 57 91; hotelvictorhugo@wanadoo.fr; 2 rue de l'Oratoire; d €42-47, q €58-66; ☒) Just a block from the cathedral, this charming family-run hostelry has two stars and 10 stylish modern rooms with a pleasing ambience of days gone by.

Hôtel Le St-Louis (☎ 03 22 91 76 03; www.le-saintlouis.com, in French; 24 rue des Otages; d/q from €54/81; ☒) All the mod cons combined with more than a dash of 19th-century French class. The 15 two-star rooms are spacious and tasteful. Has a fine formal French restaurant.

Hôtel Le Prieuré (☎ 03 22 71 16 71; www.hotelrestaurantleprieure.com, in French; 17 rue Porion; d €58-76; ☒) A cobblestone's throw from the cathedral, 'The Priory' is a two-star, family-run hotel whose 23 rooms are imaginatively decorated – some have old wooden beams and one even comes with mock-Gothic vaulting and baroque putti. Rue Porion is for pedestrians only but you can drive up to drop off your stuff.

Eating

The area around place du Don and the quays across the river in St-Leu (quai Bélu) are bursting with restaurants and cafés.

Le Tigzirt (☎ 03 22 91 42 55; 60 rue Vanmarcke, on weekends via 7 place du Don; dishes €10-21; ⌚ closed Mon, dinner Sun & lunch Sat) The Algerian Berber-style couscous and *tajines* (stews) are steamed, boiled, grilled and baked to perfection.

Le T'chiot Zinc (☎ 03 22 91 43 79; 18 rue de Noyon; menus €12.40-25.90; ⌚ closed Sun, also closed Mon Jul & Aug) Inviting, bistro-style decor reminiscent of the belle époque provides a fine backdrop for the tasty French and Picard cuisine, including fish dishes and *caqhuse* (pork in a cream, wine vinegar and onion sauce).

Le Bouchon (☎ 03 22 92 14 32; 10 rue Alexandre Fatton; lunch menus Mon-Fri €13, other menus €18-38; ⌚ closed dinner Sun) A semiformal restaurant, decorated with changing exhibits of original artwork, that serves traditional French cuisine. The mouth-watering dessert list includes the French classics.

our pick **Les Marissons** (☎ 03 22 92 96 66; pont de la Dodane; menus €18.50-46; ⌚ closed Sun, lunch Wed, lunch Sat) Refined *cuisine du marché* (market cuisine), made with fresh local ingredients, is the speciality of this elegant eatery, set under the exposed beams of a 15th-century boatwright's workshop. The chef's personal favourite – it's his own invention – is *lotte rôtie aux abricots* (monkfish roasted with apricots, €25), available whenever monkfish is.

SELF-CATERING

Champion supermarket (22bis rue du Général Leclerc; 8.30am-8pm Mon-Sat)

Covered market (rue de Metz; 9am-1pm & 3-7pm Tue-Thu, 9am-7pm Fri & Sat, 8.30am-12.30pm Sun)

Marché sur l'eau (floating market; place Parmentier; to 12.30pm Sat, to 1pm in summer) Fruit and vegetables grown in the Hortillonnages are sold at this once-floating market, now held on dry land.

Match supermarket (Centre Commercial Amiens 2; 8.30am-8pm Mon-Sat)

Drinking

Café Bissap (03 22 92 36 41; 50 rue St-Leu; 6pm-3am Tue-Sat, 6pm-1am Sun & Mon) A very laid-back, ethnically mixed crowd, including students, sips rum cocktails and West African beers (eg Guinness Foreign Extra, brewed in Cameroon) amid decor from the Senegalese-born proprietor's native land.

Marott Street (03 22 91 14 93; 1 rue Marotte; 11am-1am) Designed by Gustave Eiffel's architectural firm in 1892, this one-time insurance office is now a chic bar where the trendy sip Champagne, suspended – on clear-glass tiles – over the wine cellar.

Entertainment

The tourist office (p256) has details on cultural events.

La Lune des Pirates (03 22 97 88 01; www.lalune.net, in French; 17 quai Bélu) A dynamic venue that hosts cutting-edge concerts one to three times a week.

Chés Cabotans d'Amiens (03 22 22 30 90; www.ches-cabotans-damiens.com, in French; 31 rue Édouard-David) A theatre whose stars are all traditional Picard marionettes. Great fun even if you don't speak Picard or French.

Ciné St-Leu (03 22 91 61 23; www.cine-st-leu.com, in French; 33 rue Vanmarcke) An art-house cinema with nondubbed films, some in English.

Getting There & Away

For details on visiting the Battle of the Somme Memorials (p252) by public transport, see the listing for each memorial site.

The **bus station** (03 22 92 27 03; office 6am-7pm Mon-Fri, 7am-6.35pm Sat), in the basement of the Centre Commercial Amiens 2, is accessible from rue de la Vallée.

Car-rental places include **ADA** (03 22 46 49 49; 387 chaussée Jules Ferry), situated 2.4km southeast of the train station and served by bus 1, and **France Cars** (03 22 72 52 52; 75 bd d'Alsace-Lorraine).

Amiens is an important rail hub. Accessed through a dramatic new entrance, the train station offers direct services to Arras (€10.50, 50 minutes, six to 12 daily), Boulogne (€17.60, 1½ hours, six to eight daily), Calais-Ville (€22.10, 2½ to 3½ hours, six to eight daily), Compiègne (€16.20, 1¼ hours, five to eight daily), Laon (€15.30, 1½ hours, five to seven daily), Lille-Flandres (€17.80, 1½ hours, six to 12 daily), Paris' Gare du Nord (€18.30, one to 1½ hours, 17 to 22 daily) and Rouen (€17.10, four or five daily, 1¼ hours). SNCF buses go to the Haute Picardie TGV station (40 minutes, 16 daily), 42km east of the city.

Getting Around

There's free parking one or two blocks north of the Victor Hugo and Central & Anzac hotels, along rue Lameth, rue Cardon, rue Jean XXIII and rue de la Barette.

Vélam (www.velam.amiens.fr; 1/7 days €1/5), the local version of Paris' Vélib' (p201), has 313 bicycles at 26 automatic rental stations around town. The first half-hour is free.

Vélo Service (Buscyclette; 03 22 72 55 13; per hr/day/weekend €1/6/8, tandems per hr/day €2/8; 9am-12.30pm & 1.30-7pm), a nonprofit organisation that rents bikes, is in the courtyard of Tour Perret, behind the main entrance. Helmets are free.

BEAUVAIS

pop 55,100

Famed for the titanic hubris of its cathedral, doomed to remain forever unfinished, Beauvais became an important tapestry-making centre during the reign of Louis XIV and is often mentioned in the same breath as Gobelins and Aubusson. Today, the city – rebuilt less than enchantingly after WWII – hosts excellent tapestry exhibitions and is a budget airline hub.

Information

Tourist Office (03 44 15 30 30; www.beauvais.fr, in French; 1 rue Beauregard; 9.30am-12.30pm & 1.30-6pm Mon-Sat year-round, 10am-5pm Sun mid-Apr–mid-Oct) About 150m southeast of the cathedral.

Sights

The history of hapless **Cathédrale St-Pierre** (9am-12.15pm & 2-6.30pm May-Oct, 9am-12.15pm & 2-5.30pm Nov-Apr, no midday closure Jul & Aug) has been one of insatiable ambition and colossal failure. When Beauvais' Carolingian cathedral (parts of which, known as the **Basse Œuvre**, can still be seen) was partly destroyed by fire in 1225, the bishop and local nobles decided that its replacement should surpass anything ever built. Unfortunately, their richly adorned creation also surpassed the limits of technology, and in 1284 the 48m-high Gothic vaults – the highest ever built – collapsed. There was further damage in 1573 when the 153m spire, the tallest of its era, came a-tumblin' down. One of the **astronomical clocks** (adult/17-25yr/6-16yr €4/2.50/1) dates from the 14th century; the other, set to solar time and thus 52 minutes behind CET (Central European Time), does its thing at 10.40am, 11.40am, 2.40pm, 3.40pm and 4.40pm. English audioguides of the cathedral (adult/under 26 years €3/2, including astronomical clock €6/4) are available at the tourist office.

Just west of the cathedral, head through the two round bastions – a relic of the early 1300s – to the excellent **Musée Départemental de l'Oise** (☎ 03 44 11 11 30; 1 rue du Musée; admission free; 10am-noon & 2-6pm Wed-Mon, no midday closure Jul-Sep). Highlights in this former bishops' palace include the *Dieu Guerrier Gaulois,* a slender and aristocratic Celtic warrior made of hammered sheet brass in the 1st century AD; the 17th-century funerary monument of a kneeling Charles de Fresnoy, looking more pious than he could possibly have been in real life; and a sinuous art-nouveau dining room.

Themed exhibitions of striking contemporary tapestries make the **Galerie Nationale de la Tapisserie** (☎ 03 44 15 39 10; rue St-Pierre; admission free; 9.30am-12.30pm & 2-6pm Tue-Sun Apr-Sep, 10am-12.30pm & 2-5pm Tue-Sun Oct-Mar, closed btwn exhibitions), France's national tapestry gallery, a place of pilgrimage for fans of this ancient art. Situated next to the cathedral's choir.

Eating

Picnic supplies can be picked up at the **Marché Plus supermarket** (4 rue Pierre Jacoby; 7am-9pm Mon-Sat, 9am-1pm Sun), three short blocks east of the cathedral.

Getting There & Away

Beauvais-Tillé airport (Paris-Beauvais airport; ☎ 08 92 68 20 66; www.aeroportbeauvais.com), a few kilometres northeast of the centre and 80km from Paris, is thriving thanks to Ryanair, whose destinations include Dublin, Glasgow and Shannon. **Blue Islands** (www.blueislands.com) flies to the Channel Islands while **Wizz Air** (http://wizzair.com) goes to Budapest, Warsaw and Cracow. There are buses to/from Paris' Porte Maillot (http://tickets.aeroportbeauvais.com; €13, 1¼ hours).

Local bus 12 (€0.90, six daily except Sunday and holidays) and a *navette* (shuttle bus; €4; eight daily) link the airport with Beauvais' train station and the town centre.

The **train station**, 1.2km southeast of the cathedral, has direct services to Paris' Gare du Nord (€11.70, 1¼ hours, a dozen daily).

COMPIÈGNE

pop 41,700

Compiègne, an easy day trip from Paris, reached its glittering zenith under Napoléon III (r 1852–70), whose legacy is alive and well in the château and adjacent park. The city was the site of the armistice that ended WWI, the French surrender in 1940 and a major Nazi transit camp, now a memorial.

On 23 May 1430, Joan of Arc (Jeanne d'Arc) – honoured by two statues in the city centre – was captured at Compiègne by the Burgundians, who later sold her to their English allies.

Information

Tourist Office (☎ 03 44 40 01 00; www.compiegne-tourisme.fr, in French; place de l'Hôtel de Ville; 9.15am-12.15pm & 1.45-6.15pm Mon-Sat Apr-Sep, to 5.15pm & closed morning Mon Oct-Mar, 10am-12.15pm & 2.15-5pm Sun & holidays Easter-Oct) In a building attached to the ornate, 15th-century Gothic *hôtel de ville,* facing a statue of (who else?) Joan of Arc.

Sights

CHÂTEAU DE COMPIÈGNE

Napoléon III's dazzling hunting parties drew aristocrats and wannabes from all around Europe to his 1337-room **royal palace** (☎ 03 44 38 47 00; www.musee-chateau-compiegne.fr, in French; place du Général de Gaulle; adult/18-25yr/under 18yr €6.50/4.50/free), built around eight courtyards. The sumptuous **Grands Appartements** (Imperial Apartments; 10am-12.30pm & 1.30-5.45pm Wed-Mon, last admission 30min before closing), including the empress's bedroom and a ballroom lit by 15 chandeliers, can be visited with an audioguide in four languages.

Depending on staffing, you may also be able to visit the **Musée du Second Empire**, which illustrates the life of Napoléon III and his family, on a French-language tour; and/or the **Musée de l'Impératrice**, which stars Eugénie and includes

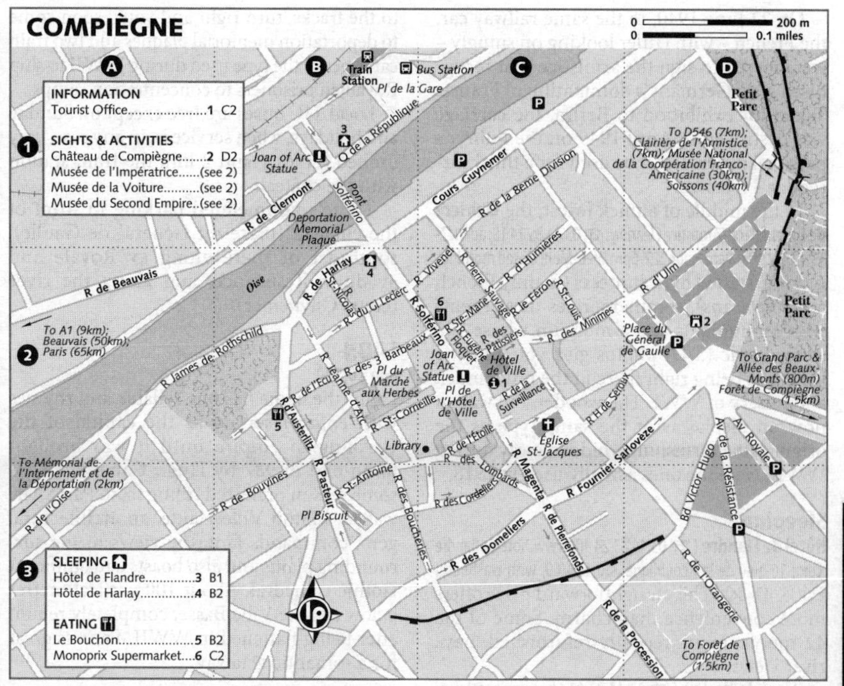

mementos of her dashing, exiled son, 'killed by the Zulus, in Zululand, Africa' in 1879 while serving – with Queen Victoria's express permission – in the British army. Vehicles that predate the internal combustion engine and early motorcars – including the Jamais Contente, a torpedo-shaped motorcar from 1899 – are featured at the **Musée de la Voiture** (Vehicle Museum). Tours (one hour) are in French.

To the east of the château, the 20-hectare, English-style **Petit Parc** (admission free) links up with the **Grand Parc** and the **Forêt de Compiègne**, which surrounds Compiègne on the east and south and is criss-crossed by rectilinear paths. The area is a favourite venue for hiking and cycling (maps available at the tourist office) as well as horse riding. Napoléon I had the 4.5km **allée des Beaux-Monts** laid out so that Empress Marie-Louise wouldn't miss Vienna's Schönbrunn palace quite so much.

MÉMORIAL DE L'INTERNEMENT ET DE LA DÉPORTATION

The new **Mémorial de l'Internement et de la Déportation** (Internment & Deportation Memorial; ☎ 03 44 96 37 00; http://memorial.compiegne.fr, in French; 2bis av des Martyrs de la Liberté; adult/student/under 16yr & WWII veteran €5/2.50/free incl English audioguide; 🕒 10am-6pm Wed-Mon), 2.5km southwest of the city centre, occupies a small part of Camp de Royallieu, a French military base used as a Nazi transit camp from 1941 to 1944. Of the more than 53,000 men, women and children held here – Resistance fighters, political prisoners, POWs, Jews (kept in a special section) and even American civilians arrested after Pearl Harbour – 48,000 were marched through town to the train station for the trip east to concentration and extermination camps, including Auschwitz.

To get to the memorial from pont Solférino, take rue de Harlay southwest along the river, turn left (south) onto bd Gambetta, then right onto rue de Paris; or hop aboard bus 5.

CLAIRIÈRE DE L'ARMISTICE

The armistice that came into force on the 11th hour of the 11th day of the 11th month – the year was 1918 – and finally put an end to WWI was signed 7km northeast of Compiègne (towards Soissons) inside the railway carriage of the Allied supreme commander, Maréchal Ferdinand Foch.

On 22 June 1940, in the same railway car, the French – with Hitler looking on smugly – were forced to sign the armistice that recognised Nazi Germany's domination of France. Taken for exhibition to Berlin, the carriage was destroyed in April 1945 on the Führer's personal orders lest it be used for a third surrender – his own.

In the middle of a thick forest, the **Clairière de l'Armistice** (Armistice Clearing; ☎ 03 44 85 14 18; adult/7-13yr €4/2; 9am-noon & 2-6pm Wed-Mon, closed mornings Jan & Feb), staffed by volunteers (mainly French army veterans), commemorates these events with monuments and a museum whose 700 stereoscopic (3-D) photos give you an eerie feeling of being right there in the mud, muck and misery of WWI. The wooden rail wagon now on display is of the same type as the original; the furnishings, hidden away during WWII, were the ones actually used in 1918.

Sleeping

Hôtel de Flandre (☎ 03 44 83 24 40; www.hoteldeflandre.com; 16 quai de la République; s/d €50/60, with washbasin €30/35;) This straightforward place offers more convenience than charm. Some of the 42 rooms, many recently refurbished, have river views.

Hôtel de Harlay (☎ 03 44 23 01 50; www.hotel-compiegne.net; 3 rue de Harlay; d €72;) A family-run, three-star hotel whose 20 attractive rooms have two-tone walls and rich carpeting.

Eating

Quite a few eateries can be found on the streets southwest of Église St-Jacques, including rue Magenta and narrow, ancient rue des Lombards.

Le Bouchon (☎ 03 44 20 02 03; 4 rue d'Austerlitz; lunch menu €11.50, other menus €19.50-33; closed dinner Sun) In a half-timbered house with out-of-kilter walls, this bistro and wine bar (per glass €2.50 to €4) serves traditional French dishes; specialities include *magret de canard aux figues* (duck's breast with figs; €12).

Monoprix supermarket (37 rue Solférino; 8.30am-8.30pm Mon-Sat, 9am-noon Sun)

Getting There & Around

Compiègne, 65km northeast of Paris, can be visited as a day trip from the capital.

Trains link Compiègne to Paris' Gare du Nord (€12.50, 40 to 80 minutes, 16 to 26 daily) and Amiens (€16.20, 1¼ hours, five to eight daily). As you walk from the station building out to the tracks, turn right and you'll soon come to deportation memorial plaques and two train carriages of the type used during WWII to ship Royallieu prisoners to concentration camps.

Local TIC buses are free except on Sunday and holidays, when service is, in any case, very limited. Lines 1 and 2 link the train station with the château.

There's nonmetered parking in front of the château (place du Général de Gaulle), southeast of there along av Royale and av de la Résistance, and along the river (cours Guynemer).

LAON

pop 26,500

Laon (the name has one syllable and rhymes with *enfant*) served as the capital of the Carolingian empire until it was brought to an end in 987 by Hugh Capet, who for some reason preferred ruling from Paris. The walled, hilltop Ville Haute, an architectural gem, commands fantastic views of the surrounding plains and also boasts a magnificent Gothic cathedral. About 100 vertical metres below sits the Ville Basse, completely rebuilt after being flattened in WWII. Laon is great for a romantic getaway.

Information

Tourist Office (☎ 03 23 20 28 62; www.tourisme-paysdelaon.com, in French; place de la Cathédrale, Ville Haute; 9.30am-1pm & 2-6.30pm early Apr–Sep, 9.30am-12.30pm & 2-5.30pm Mon-Sat, noon-5pm Sun & holidays Oct–early Apr) Next to the cathedral in a 12th-century hospital decorated with 14th-century frescos. Has a 1:600-scale model of Laon in 1854, excellent English brochures, guided tours (in French, although most guides can speak English) and audioguides (€3) for excellent one- to three-hour walking tours of the Ville Haute and the cathedral.

Sights & Activities

A model for a number of its more famous Gothic sisters – Chartres, Reims and Dijon among them – **Cathédrale Notre Dame** (9am–6.30pm or 7pm, to 8pm in summer) was built (1150–1230) in the transitional Gothic style on Romanesque foundations. The 110m-long interior has a gilded wrought-iron choir screen and is remarkably well lit; some of the stained glass dates from the 12th century. A memorial plaque for Commonwealth WWI dead hangs inside the west facade. The structure is best appreciated with an audioguide, available next door at the tourist office. You can climb the **south tower** (adult €3; ⌚ visits begin 11am, 3pm & 4pm Jul & Aug, 3pm & 4pm Fri, Sat, Sun & holidays Apr-Jun & Sep–mid-Nov).

Underneath the cathedral (and indeed most of the old town) are three levels of **souterrains** (subterranean passages); those underneath the citadel can be visited on a **tour** (€3; ⌚ 3pm Wed-Sun & holidays except late Dec, 3pm & 4.30pm daily Jul & Aug), in French – although most guides also speak English. Tickets are available at the tourist office.

The Ville Haute's narrow streets, alleyways and courtyards are rich in historic buildings, making Laon a particularly rewarding place for keen-eyed wandering. The octagonal 12th-century **Chapelle des Templiers** is in the garden of the archeologically oriented **Musée de Laon** (☎ 03 23 22 87 00; 32 rue Georges Ermant; adult/student €3.50/2.60; ⌚ 11am-6pm Tue-Sun Jun-Sep, 2-6pm Tue-Sun Oct-May).

The Ville Haute's 7km-long **ramparts**, with their three fortified gates, are lovely for a stroll; paths known as *grimpettes* take you down the steep forested slopes. For especially panoramic views, head to the 13th-century **Porte d'Ardon**; circular **Batterie Morlot**, a one-time optical telegraph station; and **rue du Rempart St-Rémi**.

Laon-born Jesuit missionary **Jacques Marquette** (1637–75), a pioneer explorer of the Mississippi River and, in 1674, the first European to live in what is now Chicago, is commemorated by an haut-relief statue at square Marquette, at the bottom of rue Franklin Roosevelt (below the Ville Haute Poma station).

Sleeping & Eating

Hôtel Les Chevaliers (☎ 03 23 27 17 50; www.hotel-chevaliers.com, in French; 3-5 rue Sérurier; d incl breakfast €60, s with washbasin €35) Parts of this two-star, family-run, 14-room hostelry, right around the corner from the Haute Ville's *hôtel de ville*, date from the Middle Ages. Rooms are rustic, with ancient stone and brick walls.

Hôtel du Commerce (☎ 03 23 79 57 16; www.hotel-commerce-laon.com, in French; 11 place de la Gare; s/d/t €51/57/63, s/d with toilet €40/46) Facing the train station, this welcoming two-star hotel has 24 modestly furnished but cheery rooms.

Rue Châtelaine, which links the cathedral with place du Général Leclerc, is home to several food shops selling nutritional basics such as chocolate (at No 27).

Getting There & Around

There are direct rail services to Amiens (€15.30, 1½ hours, five to seven daily), Paris' Gare du Nord (€19.70, 1½ to two hours, 14 daily Monday to Friday, eight on Saturday and Sunday) and Reims (€8.50, 45 minutes, eight daily Monday to Friday, four daily weekends).

The Ville Haute is a steep 20-minute walk from the train station – the stairs begin at the upper end of av Carnot – but it's more fun to take the automated, elevated **Poma funicular railway** (return €1; ⌚ every 4min 7am-8pm Mon-Sat except holidays, closed 2 weeks late Jul–early Aug), which links the train station with the upper city in 3½ minutes flat.

Normandy

Known for cows, cider and Camembert, Normandy is bordered to the north and the west by the English Channel (La Manche), Brittany to the southwest, the Paris basin to the east and France's far north to the northeast. It's a place of churned butter and soft cheeses, where gentle fields divided by hedgerows end at chalk-white cliffs and dune-lined beaches.

Ever since the armies of William the Conqueror set sail from its shores in 1066, Normandy has played a pivotal role in European history. It was the front line for Anglo-French hostilities for much of the Hundred Years' War and later became the crucible of Impressionist art, but it was during the D-Day landings of 1944 that Normandy leaped to global importance. Although many towns were shattered during the Battle of Normandy, the landscape is still dotted with sturdy châteaux and stunning cathedrals, as well as the glorious abbey of Mont St-Michel.

These days Normandy is an enticing blend of the maritime, the pastoral and the urban – and of old and new. The D-Day beaches are a short drive from the marvellous Bayeux Tapestry; chic boutiques occupy half-timbered houses near Rouen's famous Gothic cathedral; sheer cliffs meet the sea along the Côte d'Albâtre; fishing boats jostle with designer yachts in the harbours of Honfleur; and postwar concrete exudes 1950s optimism in Le Havre.

Normandy (www.normandie-tourisme.fr) is divided into two French administrative *régions:* Haute Normandie (the Eure and Seine-Maritime *départements*), to the east; and Basse Normandie (the Calvados, Manche and Orne *départements*), to the west.

HIGHLIGHTS

- Admire the architecture and art of the historic city of **Rouen** (p266)
- Discover your inner Impressionist at **Monet's flower-filled garden** (p278) at Giverny
- Travel back a thousand years with the world's oldest comic strip, the **Bayeux Tapestry** (p279)
- Ponder the price of France's liberation at the moving **war cemeteries** (p290 & p285) near the D-Day beaches
- Examine a century of war and peace at Caen's innovative **Mémorial museum** (p288)
- Watch the sun sink into the sands around the abbey of **Mont St-Michel** (p302)
- Savour superfresh seafood at the harbourside restaurants in **Honfleur** (p298) and **Trouville** (p294)

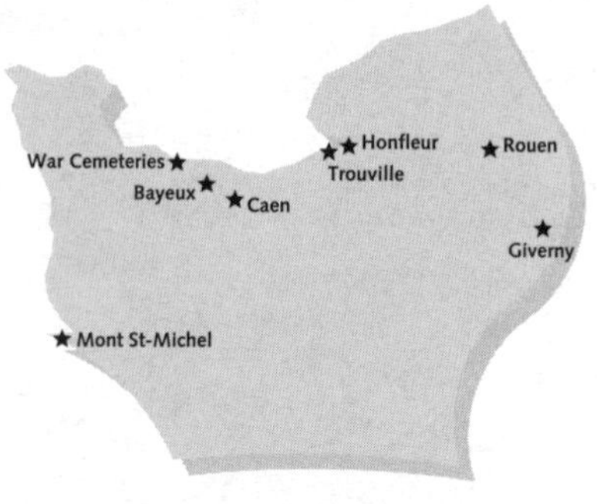

- POPULATION: 3.2 MILLION
- AREA: 29,900 SQ KM

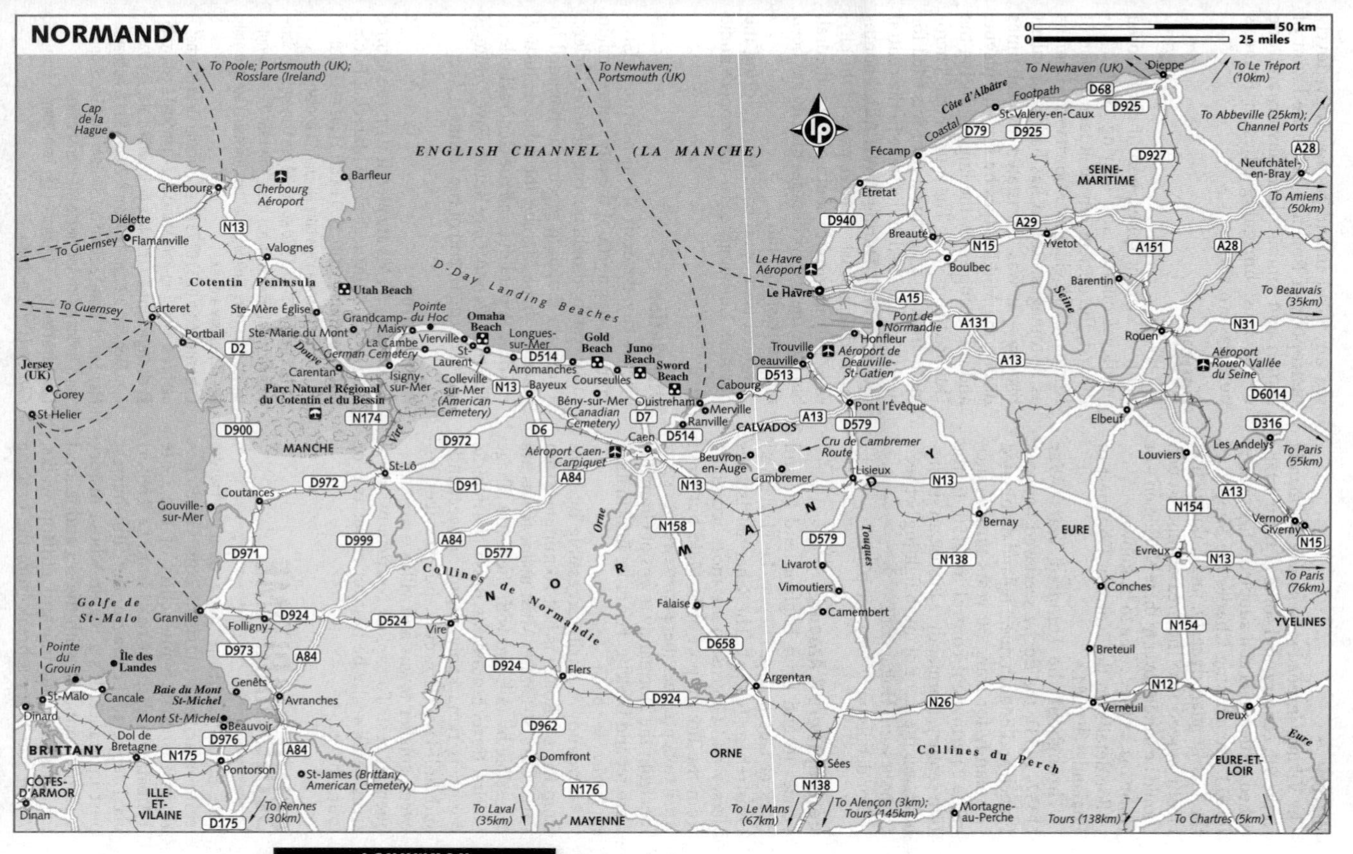
NORMANDY
0 50 km
0 25 miles
ENGLISH CHANNEL (LA MANCHE)
D-Day Landing Beaches
To Poole; Portsmouth (UK); Rosslare (Ireland)
To Newhaven; Portsmouth (UK)
To Newhaven (UK)
To Guernsey
To Guernsey
To Le Tréport (10km)
To Abbeville (25km); Channel Ports
To Amiens (50km)
To Beauvais (35km)
To Paris (55km)
To Paris (76km)
To Chartres (5km)
Tours (138km)
To Alençon (3km); Tours (145km)
To Le Mans (67km)
To Laval (35km)
To Rennes (30km)
Cap de la Hague
Diélette
Flamanville
Cherbourg
Cherbourg Aéroport
Barfleur
Valognes
Cotentin Peninsula
Carteret
Portbail
Ste-Mère Église
Ste-Marie du Mont
Utah Beach
Grandcamp-Maisy
Pointe du Hoc
La Cambe German Cemetery
Vierville
Omaha Beach
St-Laurent
Colleville-sur-Mer (American Cemetery)
Isigny-sur-Mer
Carentan
Douve
Vire
Parc Naturel Régional du Cotentin et du Bessin
MANCHE
Longues-sur-Mer
Arromanches
Gold Beach
Juno Beach
Sword Beach
Bayeux
Courseulles
Bény-sur-Mer (Canadian Cemetery)
Ouistreham
Ranville
Merville
Cabourg
Caen
Aéroport Caen-Carpiquet
CALVADOS
Deauville
Trouville
Honfleur
Aéroport de Deauville-St-Gatien
Pont de Normandie
Le Havre
Le Havre Aéroport
Étretat
Fécamp
Côte d'Albâtre
Coastal Footpath
St-Valery-en-Caux
Dieppe
Neufchâtel-en-Bray
SEINE-MARITIME
Yvetot
Barentin
Rouen
Aéroport Rouen Vallée du Seine
Seine
Boulbec
Breauté
Elbeuf
Louviers
Les Andelys
Vernon
Giverny
YVELINES
Evreux
Conches
Breteuil
Verneuil
Dreux
Eure
EURE-ET-LOIR
EURE
Bernay
Pont l'Évêque
Lisieux
Cru de Cambremer Route
Cambremer
Beuvron-en-Auge
Touques
Camembert
Vimoutiers
Livarot
Falaise
Argentan
Sées
Mortagne-au-Perche
Collines du Perch
ORNE
NORMANDY
Orne
Collines de Normandie
Flers
Domfront
MAYENNE
Vire
St-Lô
Coutances
Gouville-sur-Mer
Granville
Folligny
Avranches
Genêts
Baie du Mont St-Michel
Mont St-Michel
Beauvoir
Pontorson
St-James (Brittany American Cemetery)
Golfe de St-Malo
Île des Landes
Pointe du Grouin
Cancale
St-Malo
Dinard
Dinan
Dol de Bretagne
BRITTANY
CÔTES-D'ARMOR
ILLE-ET-VILAINE
Jersey (UK)
Gorey
St Helier
N13
D2
D900
D971
D973
D924
A84
D976
N175
D175
N174
D972
D999
D524
D91
D6
D577
A84
D962
N176
D514
D7
N158
D658
D924
N13
D513
A13
D579
N138
N26
N12
N154
N13
A13
N15
D316
D6014
N31
A28
A151
D927
D925
D68
D79
A29
N15
A131
A15
D940
NORMANDY

History

The Vikings invaded present-day Normandy in the 9th century, and some of them established settlements and adopted Christianity. In 911 French king Charles the Simple, of the Carolingian dynasty, and Viking chief Hrölfr agreed that the area around Rouen should be handed over to these Norsemen – or Normans, as they came to be known.

For details on the Norman Conquest of England, see p284.

Throughout the Hundred Years' War (1337–1453), the duchy seesawed between French and English rule. England dominated Normandy for some 30 years until France gained permanent control in 1450. In the 16th century, Normandy, a Protestant stronghold, was the scene of much fighting between Catholics and Huguenots.

For details on D-Day, see p286.

Getting There & Around

Ferries to and from England and Ireland dock at Cherbourg, Dieppe, Le Havre and Ouistreham (Caen). The Channel Islands (Jersey and Guernsey) are most accessible from the Breton port of St-Malo but from April to September there are passenger services from the Normandy towns of Granville, Carteret and Diélette. For more information on ferries, see p968.

Normandy is easily accessible by train from Paris – Rouen is just 70 minutes from Paris' Gare St-Lazare. Most major towns are accessible by rail, and with the Carte Sillage Loisirs, travel around the Basse Normandie region is remarkably cheap on weekends and holidays. However, bus services between smaller towns and villages are infrequent at best. To explore Normandy's rural areas you'll really be best on either two or four wheels.

SEINE-MARITIME

The Seine-Maritime *département* (www.seine-maritime-tourisme.com) stretches along the chalk-white cliffs of the Côte d'Albâtre (Alabaster Coast) from Le Tréport via Dieppe to Le Havre, the fifth-busiest port in France. It's a region whose history is firmly bound up with the sea and is ideal for coastal exploring and clifftop walks. When you fancy a break from the bracing sea air, head inland to the lively, lovely metropolis of Rouen, a favourite haunt of Monet and Simone de Beauvoir, and one of the most intriguing cities in France's northeastern corner.

ROUEN

pop 108,300

With its elegant spires, beautifully restored medieval quarter and soaring Gothic cathedral, the ancient city of Rouen is one of Normandy's highlights. Known to the Romans as Rotomagus, Rouen has had a turbulent history – it was devastated several times during the Middle Ages by fire and plague, and was occupied by the English during the Hundred Years' War. The young French heroine Joan of Arc (Jeanne d'Arc) was tried for heresy and burned at the stake in the central square in 1431. During WWII Allied bombing raids laid waste to large parts of the city, especially in the area south of the cathedral, but over the last six decades the city has been meticulously rebuilt.

Rouen is an ideal base for exploring the northern Normandy coast and Monet's home in Giverny.

Orientation

The old city, the heart of which is rue du Gros Horloge, lies north of the city centre's main east–west thoroughfare, rue Général Leclerc. The main shopping precinct is bounded by place du Vieux Marché, the Palais de Justice, rue de la République and rue Général Leclerc. The train station, Gare Rouen-Rive Droite, is at the northern end of rue Jeanne d'Arc.

Information

Banks with ATMs are plentiful on rue Jeanne d'Arc, especially near place Maréchal Foch.

ABC Bookshop (☎ 02 35 71 08 67; 11 rue des Faulx; ⏰ Tue-Sat) Normandy's only all-English bookshop.

Café Chéri (☎ 02 35 70 46 76; 79 rue Ecuyère; ⏰ 9am-8pm Mon-Sat) Free wi-fi has made this café *the* hang-out for road warriors. Online computers (upstairs) are generally free if you buy a drink.

Cybernet (☎ 02 35 07 73 02; 47 place du Vieux Marché; per hr €4; ⏰ 10am-8pm Mon-Sat, 2-7pm Sun) A cybercafé.

Exchange Bureau (25 place de la Cathédrale; ⏰ 9am-7pm Mon-Sat, 9.30am-12.30pm & 2-6pm Sun & holidays May-Sep, 9.30am-12.30pm & 1.30-6pm Mon-Sat, 2-6pm Sun & holidays Oct-Apr) Inside the tourist office.

Laundrettes 56 rue Cauchoise (⏰ 7am-9pm); 55 rue d'Amiens (⏰ 7am- 9pm)

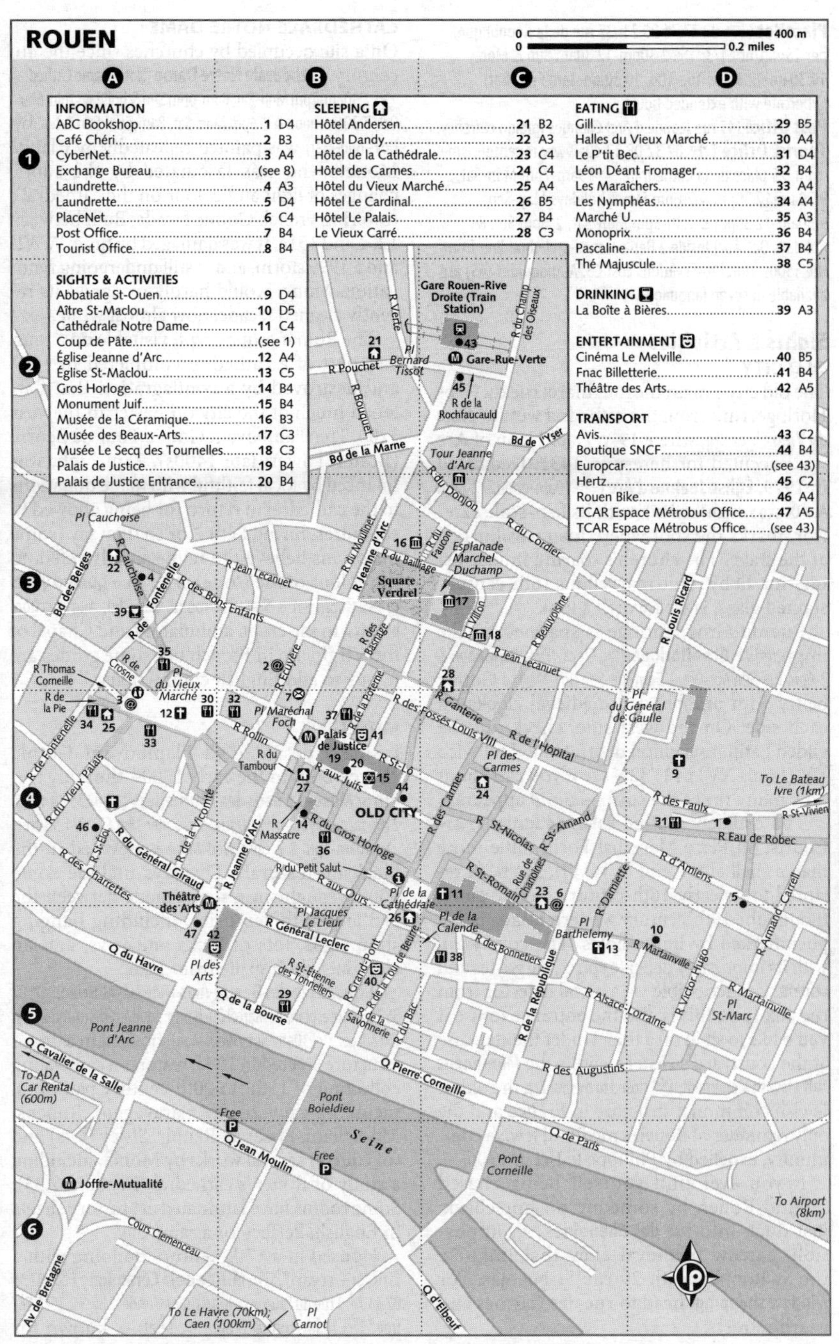

ROUEN
0 400 m
0 0.2 miles
A
B
C
D
1
2
3
4
5
6
INFORMATION
ABC Bookshop....1 D4
Café Chéri....2 B3
CyberNet....3 A4
Exchange Bureau....(see 8)
Laundrette....4 A3
Laundrette....5 D4
PlaceNet....6 C4
Post Office....7 B4
Tourist Office....8 B4
SIGHTS & ACTIVITIES
Abbatiale St-Ouen....9 D4
Aître St-Maclou....10 D5
Cathédrale Notre Dame....11 C4
Coup de Pâte....(see 1)
Église Jeanne d'Arc....12 A4
Église St-Maclou....13 C5
Gros Horloge....14 B4
Monument Juif....15 B4
Musée de la Céramique....16 B3
Musée des Beaux-Arts....17 C3
Musée Le Secq des Tournelles....18 C3
Palais de Justice....19 B4
Palais de Justice Entrance....20 B4
SLEEPING
Hôtel Andersen....21 B2
Hôtel Dandy....22 A3
Hôtel de la Cathédrale....23 C4
Hôtel des Carmes....24 C4
Hôtel du Vieux Marché....25 A4
Hôtel Le Cardinal....26 B5
Hôtel Le Palais....27 B4
Le Vieux Carré....28 C3
EATING
Gill....29 B5
Halles du Vieux Marché....30 A4
Le P'tit Bec....31 D4
Léon Déant Fromager....32 B4
Les Maraîchers....33 A4
Les Nymphéas....34 A4
Marché U....35 A3
Monoprix....36 B4
Pascaline....37 B4
Thé Majuscule....38 C5
DRINKING
La Boîte à Bières....39 A3
ENTERTAINMENT
Cinéma Le Melville....40 B5
Fnac Billetterie....41 B4
Théâtre des Arts....42 A5
TRANSPORT
Avis....43 C2
Boutique SNCF....44 B4
Europcar....(see 43)
Hertz....45 C2
Rouen Bike....46 A4
TCAR Espace Métrobus Office....47 A5
TCAR Espace Métrobus Office....(see 43)
Gare Rouen-Rive Droite (Train Station)
Gare-Rue-Verte
R Verte
R du Champ des Oiseaux
Pl Bernard Tissot
R Pouchet
R Bouquet
R de la Rochfaucauld
Bd de la Marne
Bd de l'Yser
Tour Jeanne d'Arc
R du Donjon
Pl Cauchoise
R Cauchoise
Bd des Belges
R de Fontenelle
R Jean Lecanuet
R des Bons Enfants
R du Moulinet
R Jeanne d'Arc
R du Bailliage
R du Faucon
Esplanade Marchel Duchamp
Square Verdrel
R du Cordier
R J Villon
R des Basnage
R Beauvoisine
R Louis Ricard
R Ecuyère
R Thomas Corneille
R de Crosne
R de la Pie
Pl du Vieux Marché
Pl Maréchal Foch
R de la Poterne
R Ganterie
R des Fossés Louis VIII
R de l'Hôpital
Pl du Général de Gaulle
R Rollin
Palais de Justice
R du Tambour
R aux Juifs
R St-Lô
Pl des Carmes
R du Vieux Palais
R de la Vicomté
R Massacre
OLD CITY
R du Gros Horloge
R des Carmes
R St-Nicolas
R St-Amand
R des Faulx
To Le Bateau Ivre (1km)
R St-Vivien
R Eau de Robec
R St-Eloi
R du Général Giraud
R des Charrettes
R du Petit Salut
R aux Ours
Pl de la Cathédrale
R St-Romain
Rue de Chanoines
R d'Amiens
R Damiette
R Armand Carrel
Théâtre des Arts
Pl Jacques Le Lieur
R Général Leclerc
Pl de la Calende
R des Bonnetiers
Pl Barthelemy
R Martainville
R Grand-Pont
R de la Tour de Beurre
R St-Etienne des Tonneliers
Q du Havre
Pl des Arts
Q de la Bourse
R de la Savonnerie
R du Bac
R de la République
R Alsace-Lorraine
R Victor Hugo
Pl St-Marc
Pont Jeanne d'Arc
Q Cavalier de la Salle
To ADA Car Rental (600m)
Q Pierre Corneille
R des Augustins
Pont Boieldieu
Free
Seine
Q Jean Moulin
Q de Paris
Pont Corneille
Joffre-Mutualité
To Airport (8km)
Cours Clemenceau
Av de Bretagne
To Le Havre (70km); Caen (100km)
Pl Carnot
Q d'Elbeuf

NORMANDY

PlaceNet (☎ 02 77 76 90 21; 37 rue de la République; per 15min/hr €1/3; ⏰ 2.30pm-12.30am Sun & Mon, 10.30am-12.30am Tue-Thu, 10.30am-3am Fri & Sat) Cybercafé with extended hours.

Post Office (45 rue Jeanne d'Arc) Changes foreign currency.

Tourist Office (☎ 02 32 08 32 40; www.rouentourisme.com; 25 place de la Cathédrale; ⏰ 9am-7pm Mon-Sat, 9.30am-12.30pm & 2-6pm Sun & holidays May-Sep, 9.30am-12.30pm & 1.30-6pm Mon-Sat, 2-6pm Sun & holidays Oct-Apr) Inside a Renaissance-style building from the 1500s. Hotel reservations cost €3. Audioguides (€5) are available in seven languages.

Sights & Activities

OLD CITY

The old city's main thoroughfare, rue du Gros Horloge, runs from the cathedral west to **place du Vieux Marché**, where 19-year-old Joan of Arc was executed for heresy in 1431. Dedicated in 1979, **Église Jeanne d'Arc** (⏰ 10am-noon & 2-6pm Apr-Oct, to 5.30pm Nov-Mar), with its fish-scale exterior, marks the spot where Joan was burned at the stake. The church's soaring modernist interior, lit by some marvellous 16th-century stained glass, is well worth a look.

Rue du Gros Horloge is spanned by the impressive **Gros Horloge** (Big Clock; ⏰ 10am-noon & 2-6pm Tue-Sun Apr-Oct, 2-5pm Tue-Sun Nov-Mar), a Gothic belfry with one-handed medieval clocks on each side. On the west side, check out the gilded Latin inscription dedicated to Ludovico XV (Louis XV) in 1732 – see if you can count how many times the suffix *-issimo* appears.

The ornately Gothic **Palais de Justice** (Law Courts; on Place Maréchal Foch), little more than a shell at the end of WWII, has been restored to its early-16th-century Gothic glory, though the 19th-century western facade is still pockmarked by bullet holes. The courtyard, with its impossibly delicate spires, gargoyles and statuary, is accessible via a metal detector from rue aux Juifs; this is also the entrance to use if you'd like to sit in on a trial. Under the staircase at the courtyard's eastern end is the **Monument Juif** (Jewish Monument; ⏰ closed to the public), the oldest Jewish communal structure in France and the only reminder of Rouen's medieval Jewish community, expelled by Philippe le Bel in 1306.

If you ever find yourself being chased around Rouen by someone on horseback, just duck into **rue des Chanoines**, an impossibly narrow medieval alley that links 26 rue St-Romain with 29 rue St-Nicolas. For **window shopping**, head to rue des Carmes and nearby streets.

CATHÉDRALE NOTRE DAME

On a site occupied by churches since the 4th century, **Cathédrale Notre Dame** (Notre Dame Cathedral; ⏰ 7.30am-7pm Mon-Sat, 8am-6pm Sun & holidays mid-Mar–Oct; 7.30am-noon & 2-6pm Mon-Sat, 8am-6pm Sun & holidays Nov–mid-Mar) was painted repeatedly by Claude Monet, who was fascinated by the subtle changes of light and colour on the cathedral's towering French Gothic facade. Built between 1201 and 1514, it was damaged by time, WWII and a 1999 storm, and is still undergoing renovation. Monet would hardly recognise its recently cleaned facade, now almost white.

The Romanesque crypt, visitable on a tour, was part of a cathedral completed in 1062 and destroyed by a conflagration that flattened much of the city on Easter in the year 1200. The Flamboyant Gothic Tour de Beurre (Butter Tower; late 1400s), 75m high, was financed by local faithful who made donations to the cathedral in return for being allowed to eat butter during Lent – or so they say (some historians believe the name simply refers to the colour of the stone). The free **guided visits** (⏰ 2.30pm Sat & Sun year-round, daily Jul, Aug & school holidays) to the crypt, ambulatory and Chapel of the Virgin are in French but some guides are happy to add English commentary.

MUSEUMS

Inside a desanctified Flamboyant Gothic church built in the early 1500s, the truly riveting **Musée Le Secq des Tournelles** (☎ 02 35 88 42 92; 2 rue Jacques Villon; adult/student/under 18yr €2.30/1.55/free; ⏰ 10am-1pm & 2-6pm Wed-Mon) is devoted to the blacksmith's craft. Displays include some 5000 wrought-iron items made between the 3rd and 19th centuries, including hanging shop signs, lots of locks and keys, and an elaborate choir grille from 1202.

The **Musée des Beaux-Arts** (Fine Arts Museum; ☎ 02 35 71 28 40; esplanade Marcel Duchamp; adult/student/under 18yr €3/2/free; ⏰ 10am-6pm Wed-Mon), housed in a grand structure erected in 1870, features a captivating collection of 15th- to 20th-century paintings, including canvases by Caravaggio, Rubens, Modigliani, Pissarro, Renoir, Sisley (lots) and (of course) several works by Monet, including a study of Rouen's cathedral (in room 2.33). Some rooms have laminated art history sheets in English. Perfect for a rainy day.

Housed in a 17th-century building with a fine courtyard, the **Musée de la Céramique** (☎ 02 35 07 31 74; 1 rue du Faucon; adult/student/under 18yr €2.30/1.55/free; ⏰ 10am-1pm & 2-6pm Wed-Sat) is known for its 16th- to 19th-century *faïence* (decorated earthenware) and porcelain. Tickets cost a bit more during temporary expositions.

A one-day ticket valid for all three municipal museums costs €5.35; an annual ticket is €9.15.

CHURCHES

The Flamboyant Gothic **Église St-Maclou** (Place Barthelemy; 10am-noon & 2-6pm Fri-Mon Apr-Oct, to 5.30pm Nov-Mar) was built between 1437 and 1521 but much of the decoration dates from the Renaissance. It is partly surrounded by half-timbered houses inclined at curious angles. The entrance is half-a-block east of 56 rue de la République.

The **Abbatiale St-Ouen** (10am-noon & 2-6pm Tue-Thu, Sat & Sun Apr-Oct, to 5.30pm Nov-Mar), a 14th-century abbey, is a marvellous example of the Rayonnant Gothic style. The entrance is through a lovely garden along rue des Faulx.

AÎTRE ST-MACLOU

For a macabre thrill – perhaps accompanied by a tingly shudder down your spine – check out the courtyard of **Aître St-Maclou** (186 rue Martainville; admission free; 8am-8pm Apr-Oct, to 7pm Nov-Mar), a curious ensemble of half-timbered buildings built between 1526 and 1533. Decorated with lurid woodcarvings of skulls, crossbones, gravediggers' tools and hourglasses, it was used as a burial ground for plague victims as recently as 1781. Aître St-Maclou now houses the regional École des Beaux-Arts (School of Fine Arts).

PASTRY-MAKING CLASSES

Always wanted to learn how to make traditional French pastries or hand-made chocolate? This may be your chance! At **Coup de Pâte** (02 35 71 58 47; www.pastryclasses.blogspot.com; 11 rue des Faulx; 9am-12.30pm Mon-Fri & 1 weekend a month), in the courtyard next to the ABC Bookshop, you can study the art of the *pâtissier* and the *chocolatier* with Arnaud Houley, a congenial chef with decades of experience. A class costs €50 per group (of up to five people), including ingredients and simultaneous English translation. If possible, reserve by phone or email at least 48 hours ahead.

Sleeping

BUDGET

Hôtel Le Palais (02 35 71 41 40; 12 rue du Tambour; s/d €36/42, with hall shower €24/30) The rooms are basic and not all have a private bathrooms, but this old-school cheapie is bang in the middle of the old city – the best of Rouen is literally on your doorstep.

Hôtel Andersen (02 35 71 88 51; www.hotelandersen.com; 4 rue Pouchet; d €53-63, s/d with hall shower €40/45) Ensconced in an early-19th-century mansion, this quiet hotel has an old-world atmosphere, classical music wafting through the lobby and 15 spare but imaginative rooms with Laura Ashley wallpaper. One of half-a-dozen hotels right around the train station.

Hôtel des Carmes (02 35 71 92 31; www.hoteldescarmes.com, in French; 33 place des Carmes; d €49-65, tr €67-77;) This sweet little hotel, trimmed in an imaginative though rather haphazard fashion, has 12 rooms decked out with patchwork quilts and vibrant colours; some even have cerulean-blue cloudscapes painted on the ceilings. You can burn off some Camembert calories by taking one of the less pricey 4th-floor rooms.

MIDRANGE

Hôtel Le Cardinal (02 35 70 24 42; www.cardinal-hotel.fr; 1 place de la Cathédrale; s €47-59, d €58-72, q €96;) In a supercentral spot facing the cathedral, this postwar hotel has 18 simply furnished rooms with lots of natural light and spacious showers. The 4th-floor rooms have fantastic private terraces overlooking the square.

Le Vieux Carré (02 35 71 67 70; www.vieux-carre.fr; 34 rue Ganterie; d €58-62) Set around a cute little garden courtyard, this quiet half-timbered hotel has a delightfully old-fashioned *salon de thé* (tearoom) and 13 smallish rooms eclectically decorated with old postcard blowups and slightly threadbare rugs.

Hôtel de la Cathédrale (02 35 71 57 95; www.hotel-de-la-cathedrale.fr; 12 rue St-Romain; d €66-93, q €115;) Hiding behind a 17th-century half-timbered facade, this atmospheric hotel has 27 unexciting but quiet rooms in shades of white and light blue, decorated with romantic scenes from the 1700s; most overlook a tiny, plant-filled courtyard.

Hôtel Dandy (02 35 07 32 00; www.hotels-rouen.net; 93 rue Cauchoise; d €80-105) Decorated in a contemporary style spiced up with furniture Louis XV would have liked, this welcoming, family-run hotel has 18 rooms with flat-screen TVs and endearingly outdated bathrooms.

Hôtel du Vieux Marché (02 35 71 00 88; www.bestwestern.com; 33 rue du Vieux Palais; d €117-160) Its lobby bedecked with ship models and maritime prints, this modernist hotel has just a smidge of Zen sophistication. The 48 rooms are handsome but uninspiring, with brass lamps, lots of dark wood and ordinary bathrooms. Almost within marshmallow range of place du Vieux Marché.

Eating

Little eateries crowd the north side of rue Martainville, facing Église St-Maclou; for ethnic cuisine head two blocks south to rue des Augustins. More restaurants can be found along rue de Fontenelle (a block west of Église Jeanne d'Arc), and a few blocks east of there along rue Ecuyère.

Thé Majuscule (☎ 02 35 71 15 66; 8 place de la Calende; plat du jour €10.50; restaurant noon-2pm Mon-Sat, salon de thé 2.30-6.30pm Mon-Sat) Downstairs it's a typically chaotic French second-hand bookshop, upstairs a homey tearoom with home-made *tartes* (including one vegetarian pie), salads (in summer), cakes and exotic teas (€3.30). Has a warm-season terrace.

Le P'tit Bec (☎ 02 35 07 63 33; www.leptitbec.com, in French; 182 rue Eau de Robec; lunch menus €13-15.50; lunch Mon-Sat, dinner Fri & Sat, also open dinner Tue-Thu Jun-Aug) The down-to-earth menu is stuffed with pasta, salads, *œufs cocottes* (eggs with grated cheese baked in cream), a few vegetarian options and home-made desserts. Has a warm-season terrace.

Pascaline (☎ 02 35 89 67 44; 5 rue de la Poterne; menus €14.90-26.90; lunch & dinner) A top spot for a great-value *formule midi* (lunchtime fixed-price menu), this bustling bistro serves up traditional French cuisine in typically Parisian surroundings – think net curtains, white tablecloths and chuffing coffee machines. There's live piano nightly, and jazz nights are held two Thursdays a month.

Les Maraîchers (☎ 02 35 71 57 73; www.les-maraichers.fr, in French; 37 place du Vieux Marché; menus €16-25; lunch & dinner) All gleaming mirrors, polished wood and colourful floor tiles, this bistro – established in 1912 and classified a *café historique d'Europe* – has a genuine zinc bar and a warm and very French ambiance. Specialities include Normandy-raised beef.

Les Nymphéas (☎ 02 35 89 26 69; www.lesnympheas-rouen.com, in French; 7-9 rue de la Pie; menus €27-64; 12.15-1.45pm & 7.30-9.30pm Tue-Sat) Its formal table settings arrayed under 16th-century beams, this fine restaurant serves cuisine based on fresh local ingredients (including cider and Calvados), giving a rich Norman twist to dishes such as farm-raised wild duck.

Gill (☎ 02 35 71 16 14; www.gill.fr; 8-9 quai de la Bourse; lunch menu Tue-Fri €35, other menus €65-92; 12.15-1.45pm & 7.30-9.45pm Tue-Sat) *The* place to go in Rouen for *gastronomique* French cuisine of the highest order, served in an ultrachic, ultramodern dining room. Specialities including fresh Breton lobster, scallops with truffles, Rouen-style pigeon and, for dessert, *millefeuille à la vanille*.

SELF-CATERING

Halles du Vieux Marché (place du Vieux Marché; 7am-7pm Tue-Sat, 7am-1pm Sun) A small covered market with an excellent *fromagerie* (cheese shop).

Léon Déant Fromager (18 rue Rollin; 9am-12.45pm & 3-7.30pm Tue-Fri, morning Sat) Normandy cheeses are a speciality.

Marché U (place du Vieux Marché; 8.30am-8.30pm Mon-Sat) Supermarket.

Monoprix (65 rue du Gros Horloge; 8.30am-9pm Mon-Sat) Supermarket.

Drinking

There are several gay nightspots on rue St-Etienne des Tonneliers.

La Boîte à Bières (☎ 02 35 07 76 47; www.laboiteabieres.fr, in French; 35 rue Cauchoise; 5pm-2am Tue-Sat) Affectionately known as BAB, this lively, half-timbered corner bar is a good place to down a few local *bières artisanales* (microbrews) in the company of a loyal student following. Sometimes has karaoke, disco and concert nights.

Le Bateau Ivre (☎ 02 35 70 09 05; http://bateauivre.rouen.free.fr, in French; 17 rue des Sapins; 9pm or 10pm–4am Wed-Sat, sometimes open Tue, closed Wed in summer) A longstanding live venue with a varied program of concerts (French *chansons*, blues, rock reggae etc) except on Thursday, when anyone can join in the jam session.

Entertainment

The tourist office sells tickets to cultural events, as does the **Fnac Billetterie** (☎ 08 92 68 36 22; www.fnacspectacles.com, in French; cnr rue St-Lô & rue de la Poterne; 10am-7pm Mon-Sat).

Cinéma Le Melville (☎ 02 35 07 18 48; 75 rue Général Leclerc) Screens only nondubbed films, many of them in English, in its four halls.

Théâtre des Arts (☎ 02 35 71 41 36; www.operaderouen.com, in French; place des Arts) Home to the Opéra de Rouen, the city's premier concert venue also stages ballets.

Getting There & Away

From **Gare Rouen-Rive Droite** (rue Jeanne d'Arc), an art-nouveau edifice built from 1912 to 1928, trains go direct to Paris' Gare St-Lazare (€19.30, 1¼ hours, 25 daily Monday to Friday, 14 to 19 daily weekends), Amiens (€17.10, four or five daily, 1¼ hours), Caen (€21.80, 1½ hours, eight daily), Dieppe (€9.90, 45 minutes, 10 to 15 daily Monday to Saturday, five Sunday) and Le Havre (€12.90, 50 minutes, 18 daily Monday to Saturday, 10 Sunday).

In the city centre, train tickets are sold at the **Boutique SNCF** (20 rue aux Juifs; 10am-7pm Mon-Sat).

For car rental try **ADA** (02 35 72 25 88; 34 av Jean Rondeaux), **Avis** (02 35 88 60 94); in train station above track 4), **Europcar** (03 32 08 39 09; in train station) or **Hertz** (02 35 70 70 71; 130 rue Jeanne d'Arc).

Getting Around

Free parking is available across the Seine from the city centre, eg along and below quai Jean Moulin.

Rouen's bus lines and partly underground light rail (metro) line are operated by **TCAR** (02 35 52 52 52; www.tcar.fr, in French). The metro runs from 5am (6am on Sunday) to about 11pm and is useful for getting from the train station to the centre of town. One ticket costs €1.40 (10 tickets €10.70, and is valid for an hour; a pass valid for one day is €3.80 (two/three days €5.50/7.20). There are Espace Métrobus ticket offices inside the train station and at 9 rue Jeanne d'Arc.

Radio Taxi (02 35 88 50 50) operates 24 hours a day.

Cy'clic (08 00 08 78 00; http://cyclic.rouen.fr), Rouen's version of Paris' Vélib' (p201), lets you rent a city bike from 14 locations around town. Credit card registration for one/seven days costs €1/5. Use is free for the first 30 minutes; the 2nd/3rd/4th-and-subsequent half-hours cost €1/2/4 each.

Rouen Bike (02 35 71 34 30; 45 rue St-Éloi; 9am-noon & 2-7pm Tue-Sat) rents out mountain bikes for €20/30 per day/weekend.

DIEPPE

pop 33,500

Sandwiched between limestone cliffs, Dieppe – a seaside resort since 1824 – is salty and a bit shabby but authentic, the kind of place where leather-skinned herring fishermen rub shoulders with British day trippers and summertime tourists licking oversized ice creams. It's an excellent spot to try some Norman seafood – the harbour is chock-full of restaurants serving local specialities such as scallops, mussels and sole.

Dieppe is proud of its International Kite Festival (www.dieppe-cerf-volant.org), held in early September in even-numbered years.

History

Privateers from Dieppe pillaged Southampton in 1338 and blockaded Lisbon two centuries later. Explorers based here include Florence-born Giovanni da Verrazano, who in 1524 became the first European to enter New York Harbour. The early European settlers in Canada included many Dieppois and the town was one of France's most important ports during the 16th century, when ships regularly sailed to West Africa and Brazil.

On 19 August 1942 a mainly Canadian force of over 6000 landed on the Dieppe beaches, in part to help the Soviets by drawing Nazi military power away from the Eastern Front. The results were nothing short of catastrophic but lessons learned here proved useful in planning the Normandy landings two years later.

Orientation

Quai Henri IV and almost-perpendicular quai Duquesne line the western side of the port area. Bd de Verdun runs along the lawns bordering the beach. Two blocks inland, most of Grande Rue and rue de la Barre is pedestrianised.

Information

There's no ATM at the ferry terminal.

Banque Populaire (15 place Nationale) One of several banks on place Nationale.
Cybercafé (02 35 83 13 84; 20 rue de l'Épée; 2-7pm Mon, 9am-noon & 2-7pm Tue-Sat; per hr €2)
Laundrettes 44 rue de l'Épée (7am-9pm); 2 rue Notre Dame (7am-9pm) The latter faces the back of Église St-Jacques.
Post Office (2 bd Maréchal Joffre) Changes foreign currency.
Tourist Office (02 32 14 40 60; www.dieppetourisme.com; Pont Jehan Ango; 9am-7pm Mon-Sat, 10am-1pm & 3-6pm Sun Jul & Aug, 9am-1pm & 2-6pm Mon-Sat, 10am-1pm & 3-6pm Sun May, Jun & Sep, 9am-noon & 2-6pm Mon-Sat Oct-Apr) Has useful English brochures on Dieppe and nearby parts of the Côte d'Albâtre.

Sights

The **port**, still used by fishing vessels but dominated by pleasure craft, makes for a bracing sea-air stroll. Two blocks west, the Norman Gothic–style **Église St-Jacques** (place St-Jacques) has

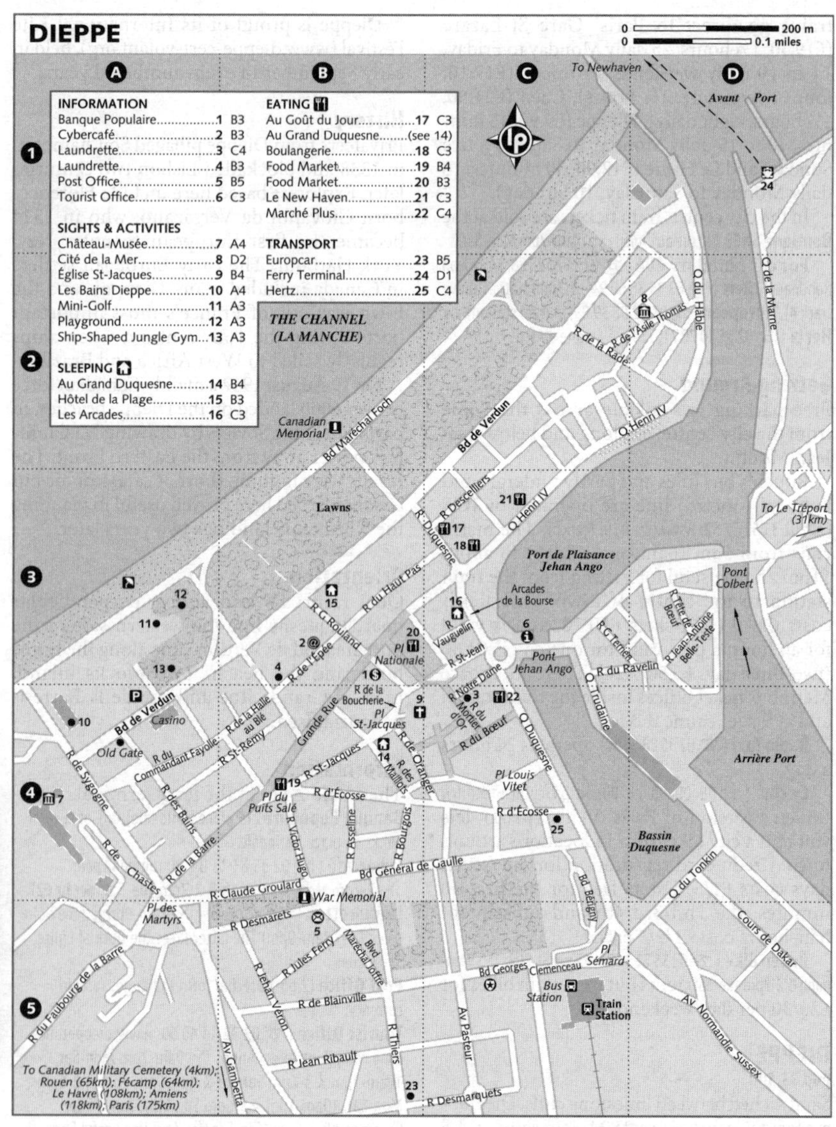

been reconstructed several times since the early 13th century.

Dieppe's often-windy, 1.8km-long **beach** is ideal if you hate sand – or love smooth, round pebbles far too big to make their way into your shoes or undies. The vast **lawns** were laid out in the 1860s by that seashore-loving imperial duo, Napoleon III and his wife, Eugénie. Kids will have a ball at the ship-shaped jungle gym in the **playground** next to the **mini-golf**.

Les Bains Dieppe (☎ 02 35 82 80 90; www.lesbainsdieppe.com, in French; 101 bd de Verdun; adult/3-11yr & over 55yr €5.60/4.60; 🕑 10am–8pm or 9pm Mon-Fri, to 7pm or 8pm Sat & Sun, closed 2-5pm Mon, Tue & Thu when school's in session), established in the 1800s and completely renovated in 2007, has several seawater pools heated to 28°C, including a 50m outdoor pool, and plenty of facilities for kids Also boasts a fitness centre (adult €12) with a *hammam* (Turkish baths)/sauna and a beauty centre.

High above the city on the western cliff, the 15th-century **Château-Musée** (☎ 02 35 06 61 99; rue de Chastes; adult/student/under 12yr €3.50/2/free; 🕑 10am-noon & 2-6pm Jun-Sep, to 5pm Wed-Mon Oct-May) is Dieppe's most imposing landmark. The museum inside is devoted to the city's maritime and artistic history, which often involved separating West African elephants from their tusks and shipping the ivory back to Dieppe. The craft of ivory carving reached extraordinary heights here during the 17th century and the results are on display.

Cité de la Mer (☎ 02 35 06 93 20; 37 rue de l'Asile Thomas; adult/student/4-16yr €5.50/4.50/3.50; 🕑 10am-noon & 2-6pm Sep-May, open longer Jul & Aug) has exhibits on fishing, shipbuilding, the tides, Dieppe's cliffs and the Channel's sea and seaside habitats. Five large aquariums let you admire some especially large specimens of crustaceans and fish most often seen on French plates. An English-language brochure is available at the ticket desk.

There's a **Canadian military cemetery** 4km towards Rouen. Take av des Canadiens (the continuation of av Gambetta) south and follow the signs, or hop on bus 22 (eight to 10 daily Monday to Saturday).

Sleeping

Au Grand Duquesne (☎ 02 32 14 61 10; http://augrandduquesne.free.fr; augrandduquesne@orange.fr; 15 place St-Jacques; d €47-63, with hall shower €42) Central but without harbour views. The 12 blue-themed bedrooms aren't anything special but they're quiet and have floodlit bathrooms.

Hôtel de la Plage (☎ 02 35 84 18 28; www.plagehotel.fr.st; 20 bd de Verdun; d €60-90, q €90-150; 💻) One of several somewhat faded places along the seafront, this hotel has 40 modern, mod-con rooms – three with jacuzzi bathtubs – decorated in pale tones of blue, green and red. Sea-view rooms come at a premium.

Les Arcades (☎ 02 35 84 14 12; www.lesarcades.fr, in French; 1-3 arcades de la Bourse; d €63-79, cheaper Sun-Thu Nov-Mar) Perched above a colonnaded arcade, this 21-room Logis de France hotel has lovely port views, a tiny lift and quiet rooms with yellow walls, blue rugs, efficient bathrooms and flat-screen TVs.

Eating & Drinking

Au Grand Duquesne (☎ 02 32 14 61 10; 15 place St-Jacques; menus €13.90-39.60) A good bet for cuisine that's both *traditionelle* and *créative*, including fish and seafood. Specialities include *crêpiau deippois* (a thick, pear-filled crêpe). The veggie menu costs €18.50.

Le New Haven (☎ 02 35 84 89 72; 53 quai Henri IV; menus €17-29; 🕑 11.45am-2pm & 6.30-9.30pm Thu-Mon, daily Jul & Aug) The harbour front is lined with flashy restaurants but this elegant, though unpretentious fish place is one of the best. Freshly landed specialities include fish, prawns and Norway lobsters with *choucroute* (sauerkraut; €19) and *foie de lotte* (monkfish liver).

Au Goût du Jour (☎ 02 35 84 27 18; 16 rue Duquesne; menus €23-30; 🕑 closed Mon, dinner Sun) At this jazzy restaurant, the reception is as warm and welcoming as the inventive French cuisine is fresh and tasty. Specialities include super-fresh fish, couscous with bass, and home-smoked salmon. Weekday menus ordered before 1.15pm and 9pm are €10.90 to 15.90.

SELF-CATERING

Boulangerie (15 quai Henri IV; 🕑 Wed-Mon)
Food market (place Nationale; 🕑 8.30am-12.30pm Tue & Thu)
Food market (cnr rue St-Jacques & Grande Rue; 🕑 8.30am-12.30pm Sat)
Marché Plus (22 quai Duquesne; 🕑 7am-9pm Mon-Sat, 9am-1pm Sun) Supermarket.

Getting There & Away

Dieppe is 65km north of Rouen, 108km northeast of Le Havre and 118km west of Amiens.

For information on car ferries from the **ferry terminal** to Newhaven, see p968.

Dieppe enjoys direct rail services to Rouen (€9.90, 40 to 60 minutes, 10 to 15 daily Monday to Saturday, six Sunday) but you usually have to change to get to Paris St-Lazare (€25.70, two to three hours, 11 daily Monday to Friday, six to eight weekends) and Le Havre (€20.70, 1½ to two hours, 12 daily Monday to Friday, six daily weekends).

Rental-car companies:
Europcar (☎ 02 35 04 97 10; 33 rue Thiers)
Hertz (☎ 02 32 14 01 70; 5 rue d'Écosse)

CÔTE D'ALBÂTRE

Stretching 130km from Le Tréport southwest to Étretat, the bone-white cliffs of the Côte d'Albâtre (Alabaster Coast) are strikingly reminiscent of the limestone cliffs of Dover, just across the Channel. The dramatic coastline is dotted with small villages and hamlets, lovely gardens, several fine beaches and two nuclear powerplants (Paluel and Penly). The only towns of any note – in addition to Dieppe – are Fécamp, St-Valery-en-Caux and Étretat.

Without a car, the Côte d'Albâtre is pretty inaccessible, though walkers can take the coastal **GR21 hiking trail**, which follows the Côte d'Albâtre all the way from Tréport to Le Havre. If you're driving west from Dieppe, take the coastal roads (D75, D68 and D79) rather than the inland D925.

Fécamp

pop 19,500

Fécamp was an ordinary fishing village until the 6th century, when a few drops of Christ's blood miraculously found their way here and attracted hordes of pilgrims. Benedictine monks soon established a monastery, and the fiery 'medicinal elixir' that a Venetian monk concocted in 1510 (using East Asian herbs) helped keep Fécamp on the map. The recipe, lost during the Revolution, was rediscovered in an old book in the 19th century. Today, Bénédictine is one of the most widely marketed *digestifs* in the world.

INFORMATION

Tourist Office (☎ 02 35 28 51 01; www.fecamptourisme.com, in French; quai Sadi Carnot; 🕑 9am-6.30pm Jul & Aug, 9am-6pm Mon-Fri, 10am-6.30pm Sat, Sun & holidays Apr-Jun, 9am-6pm Mon-Fri, 9.30am-12.30pm & 2-6pm Sat Sep-Mar) Situated at the southern end of the pleasure port, across the parking lot from the train station. Has useful English-language brochures. A beachfront annexe opens in July and August.

SIGHTS

The **port**, still used by fishing craft, is connected to the sea by the narrow *avant port* (outer harbour). North of there rises **Cap Fagnet** (110m), which offers fantastic views of the town and the coastline, while to the south is the **beach**, where you can rent catamarans, kayaks and windsurfers in summer.

All the Bénédictine liqueur in the world is made in the impossibly ornate **Palais Bénédictine** (☎ 02 35 10 26 10; www.benedictine.fr; 110 rue Alexandre Le Grand; adult/12-17yr/under 12yr €6.50/2/free; 🕑 tickets sold 10am-6pm mid-Jul–Aug, 10am-noon & 2-5.30pm Apr–mid-Jul & Sep–mid-Oct, 10-11.45am & 2-5pm mid-Oct–Mar, closed most of Jan), opened in 1900. Tours take you to a surprisingly interesting collection of 13th- to 19th-century religious art and paintings assembled by the company's visionary founder, Alexandre Le Grand, and continue on to the production facilities, where you can admire copper alembics and touch and smell the natural ingredients used to make Bénédictine – the coriander seeds are the most fun to play with. As is only proper, adults end the visit with a shot of liqueur.

Built from 1175 to 1220 by Richard the Lion-Heart, **Abbatiale de la Ste-Trinité** (place des Ducs Richard; 🕑 all day), 1.5km east of the beach (and a few blocks southeast of Fécamp's commercial centre), was the most important pilgrimage site in Normandy until the construction of Mont St-Michel (p302), thanks to the drops of holy blood that miraculously floated to Fécamp in the trunk of a fig tree.

Across from the abbey are the remains of the **fortified château** built by the earliest dukes of Normandy in the 10th and 11th centuries.

SLEEPING & EATING

Quite a few restaurants are situated on the south side of the port, along quai de la Vicomté and nearby parts of quai Bérigny.

Camping de Renéville (☎ 02 35 28 20 97; www.campingdereneville.com; chemin de Nesmond; tent & 2 adults €11-13.50; 🕑 Apr–mid-Nov) Dramatically situated on the western cliffs overlooking the beach. Also rents out chalets (€415 to €595 per week in high season, €240 to €320 per week in low season).

Hôtel Normandy (☎ 02 35 29 55 11; www.normandy-fecamp.com; 4 av Gambetta; s/d €50/62) In a smart fin-de-siècle building just up the hill from the train station, this quiet place has 32 newly refurbished rooms – some quite spacious – with light-yellow walls, baize-green carpets and lots of light. Rooms are often cheaper October to June.

La Ferme de la Chapelle (☎ 02 35 10 12 12; www.fermedelachapelle.fr; Côte de la Vierge; d/q €95/140, apt €145-220, cheaper Oct–mid-Feb; 🏊) High above town near Cap Fagnet, the 17 modern rooms and five kitchenette-equipped apartments overlook a grassy central courtyard, so there's no sea view – for that you'll have to step outside the compound. Guests are often greeted by four vociferous geese.

Le Maupassant (☎ 02 35 29 55 11; 4 av Gambetta; menus €11-24) On the ground floor of the Hôtel Normandy, this very popular brasserie – decorated with glassware suspended from on high – serves French and Norman cuisine, with a few exotic dishes thrown in for good measure.

NORMANDY

Self-Catering

Marché Plus (83 quai Bérigny; 7am-9pm Tue-Sat, 9am-1pm Sun) A supermarket.

GETTING THERE & AWAY

Bus 24, operated by **Cars Perier** (08 00 80 87 03; www.cars-perier.com), goes to Le Havre (€2, 1½ hours, eight daily) via Étretat.

Rail destinations include Le Havre (€7.50, 45 to 75 minutes, seven to 11 daily) and Rouen (€12.30, 1¼ hours, seven to 10 daily).

Étretat

pop 1610

The small village of Étretat, 20km southwest of Fécamp, is known for its twin **cliffs**: the Falaise d'Aval and the Falaise d'Amont, positioned on either side of the pebbly beach.

The **Falaise d'Aval** is renowned for its freestanding arch – compared by French writer Maupassant to an elephant dipping its trunk in the sea – and the adjacent Aiguille, a 70m-high spire of chalk-white rock rising from the surface of the waves. Further along the cliff is a second impressive arch, known as La Manneporte, reached by a steep path up the cliff from the western end of Étretat's beach. On the **Falaise d'Amont**, a memorial marks the spot where two aviators were last seen before their attempt to cross the Atlantic in 1927.

The **tourist office** (02 35 27 05 21; www.etretat.net; place Maurice Guillard; 9am-7pm mid-Jun–mid-Sep, 10am-noon & 2-6pm Mon-Sat rest of year, open Sun during school holidays) has accommodation lists for the area (also available on the website) and a map of the cliff trails.

Bus 24, operated by **Cars Perier** (08 00 80 87 03; www.cars-perier.com), goes to Le Havre (€2, one hour, eight daily) and Fécamp (€2, 30 minutes, eight daily).

LE HAVRE

pop 183,600

All but obliterated in September 1944 by Allied (mainly British) bombing raids that killed 3000 civilians, Le Havre's city centre was totally rebuilt after the war by Belgian architect Auguste Perret, and what emerged from the rubble is something of a love letter to concrete: endless rows of modernist, breeze-block buildings along ruler-straight boulevards that express some of the energy and optimism of 1950s France. Listed by Unesco as a World Heritage Site in 2005, it's a strange and oddly fascinating city, and while it's probably not where you'd want to spend your honeymoon, Le Havre is worth a visit as one of the great examples of idealistic postwar planning.

Orientation

From place de l'Hôtel de Ville, the city's main square, av Foch runs west to the pleasure port; arcaded rue de Paris cuts south past cultural centre Le Volcan; and bd de Strasbourg goes eastward to the train station. Église St-Joseph, whose 107m-high tower makes a good reference point, is three blocks south of the middle of av Foch. Quartier St-François, Le Havre's 'old city', is five blocks southeast of Le Volcan.

Information

There are a number of banks along bd de Strasbourg.

Change Collections (41 chaussée Kennedy; 9am-12.30pm & 2-6.30pm Mon-Fri, to 5pm Sat) An exchange bureau half a block west of the southern end of rue de Paris.

E-Mega (02 35 42 67 55; 119 rue Victor Hugo; per half-hr/1hr/2hr €2.50/4/6; 10am-7pm Wed & Sat, noon-7pm Fri, 2-7pm Tue & Thu) Prepaid internet access a block north of Le Volcan.

Laundrette (5 rue Georges Braque; 7.45am-5pm Mon, Tue, Thu & Fri, 8.30am-5pm Sat) Half a block northwest of the *hôtel de ville* (town hall).

Microminute (02 35 22 10 15; 7 rue Casimir Periér; per hr €3.60; 2-7pm Mon, 10am-7pm Tue-Sat) Internet access a block east of the *hôtel de ville.*

Post Office (place des Halles Centrales)

Tourist Office (02 32 74 04 04; www.lehavretourisme.com; 186 bd Clemenceau; 9am-6.45pm Mon-Sat, 10am-12.30pm & 2.30-5.45pm Sun & holidays Easter-Oct; 9am-12.30pm & 2-6.15pm Mon-Sat, 10am-12.30pm & 2.30-5pm Sun & holidays Nov-Easter) A bit south of the western end of av Foch.

Sights & Activities

ARCHITECTURE

The tourist office can supply you with an English map-brochure for a two-hour self-guided walking tour of the city centre's architectural highlights. As you stroll, your eyes and nose will have trouble missing the city's original, mid-century **pissoirs** (public urinals), once a common sight in French cities.

Le Havre is dominated by Perret's centrepiece, the 107m-high **Église St-Joseph** (bd François 1er), begun in 1951 and inaugurated in 1959, whose 13,000 panels of coloured glass make the interior particularly striking when it's sunny.

The **Appartement Témoin** (Show Apartment; adult/under 18yr €3/free; tours 2pm, 3pm, 4pm & 5pm Wed, Sat & Sun), furnished in impeccable 1950s style, can be visited on a one-hour guided tour that starts at 1 place de l'Hôtel de Ville (in front of the Caron shoe shop). The tourist office has details.

Although it's been compared to a truncated cooling tower or, even worse, a toilet bowl, **Le Volcan** (The Volcano; www.unvolcandanslaville.com, in French; espace Oscar Niemeyer) – one look and you'll know how it got its name – is one of the city's premier cultural venues, with concert halls and an art cinema, L'Eden. It was conceived by Brazilian architect Oscar Niemeyer, who also designed Brasilia.

Le Havre's avant-garde architectural ambitions continue to shape the city, as a rundown docklands area, on the far side of Bassin Vauban from the train station, is redeveloped into **Quartier des Docks**. This cutting-edge magnet for shopping, culture and the arts, designed by Jean Nouvel, is set to open over the next few years.

OTHER SIGHTS

The **Musée Malraux** (02 35 19 62 62; 2 bd Clemenceau; adult/student/under 18yr €5/3/free; 11am-6pm Mon-Fri, 11am-7pm Sat & Sun), at the city centre's southwestern tip, houses a truly fabulous collection of Impressionist works – perhaps the finest in France outside of Paris – by luminaries such as Degas, Monet, Pissarro, Renoir, Sisley and Le Havre native Eugène Boudin. A section is devoted to Fauvist Raoul Dufy, also born in Le Havre.

Le Havre's pebbly **beach** is a few hundred metres northwest of the tourist office.

An old hilltop fortress a bit over 1km north of the tourist office has been transformed into the **Jardins Suspendus** (Hanging Gardens; admission gardens free, hothouses adult/under 12yr €1/free; gardens 10.30am-8pm mid-Jun–Sep, 1-8pm Mon-Fri & 10.30am-8pm Sat, Sun & holidays May–mid-Jun, 1-5pm Mon-Fri & 10.30am-5pm Sat, Sun & holidays Oct-Apr, hothouses 10.30am-5pm daily mid-Jun–Sep, Sat, Sun & holidays Oct–mid-Jun), whose hothouses and outdoor spaces feature rare plants and cacti from five continents.

Sleeping

Hôtel Voltaire (02 35 19 35 35; hotel.voltaire@free.fr; 14 rue Voltaire; d/q €39/66, s with hall shower €34) Le Havre's cheapest hotel has cheery orange hallways and 20 unsurprising rooms with period-appropriate linoleum floors. In a Perret building one block south and around the corner from Église St-Joseph.

Le Petit Vatel (02 35 41 72 07; www.lepetitvatel.com; 86 rue Louis Brindeau; d €58-71, with hall shower €47;) Situated two blocks east of Église St-Joseph, this family-run, two-star hotel, renovated in 2008, has 25 well-kept, space-efficient rooms with straightforward decor.

Hôtel Vent d'Ouest (02 35 42 50 69; www.ventdouest.fr; 4 rue de Caligny; d €98-128, q €194;) The three-star, 38-room West Wind, around the corner from Église St-Joseph, is decorated in shipshape maritime fashion, with nautical memorabilia downstairs and a range of stylish cream-walled rooms upstairs.

Eating

In Quartier St-François, rue du Général Faidherbe and perpendicular rue Jean de la Fontaine are lined with eateries. There are several more restaurants around the periphery of Le Volcan.

Le Bistrot des Halles (02 35 22 50 52; 7 place des Halles; lunch menu €14.70, other menu €31.50; Mon-Sat) Serves classic French food in a traditional bistro atmosphere, with no concrete, steel or glass in sight. Expect brasserie standards (mainly steaks and seafood) and some fine chocolate dessert options.

L'Odyssée (02 35 21 32 42; 41 rue du Général Faidherbe; menus €30-40; closed lunch Sat, dinner Sun & Mon) Elegantly marine in its decor, this French restaurant's specialities include sole, bass, turbot and – in season – scallops.

SELF-CATERING

Halles Centrales (place des Halles Centrales; 8.30am-7.30pm Mon-Sat) A covered market with a dozen food shops and a Marché U supermarket. Situated one block south and two blocks east of Église St-Joseph.

Entertainment

Le Cabaret Electric (02 35 19 91 32; www.cabaretelectric.fr, in French; espace Oscar Niemeyer; bar 6-11pm Tue, Thu & Fri, 2-11pm Wed, 2-8pm Sat, during concerts) Not only do you get to see the inside of Le Havre's most striking building but this funky bar is the city's best venue for live gigs.

Getting There & Away

For details on ferry services to Portsmouth and Newhaven, see p968.

BUS

Bus 20, run by Caen-based **Bus Verts** (☎ 08 10 21 42 14; www.busverts.fr) links the bus station (next to the train station) with Honfleur (€4, 35 minutes), Deauville and Trouville (€6, one hour), and Caen (€10, 2½ hours). There are also express buses to Caen (€14, 1½ hours, four daily Monday to Saturday, two Sunday) via Honfleur.

Bus 24, operated by **Cars Perier** (☎ 08 00 80 87 03; www.cars-perier.com), goes to Fécamp (€2, 1½ hours, eight daily) via Étretat.

CAR

Cars can be hired from **Avis** (☎ 02 35 22 77 73; 87 quai Southampton), **France Cars** (☎ 02 35 19 64 64; 161 bd de Strasbourg) and **National/Citer** (☎ 02 35 21 30 81; 91 quai de Southampton).

TRAIN

Le Havre's **train station** (cours de la République) is 2km east of the *hôtel de ville* at the eastern end of bd de Strasbourg. Destinations include Paris' Gare St-Lazare (€28.10, 2¼ hours, hourly), Rouen (€12.90, 50 minutes, 18 daily Monday to Saturday, 10 Sunday) and Fécamp (€7.50, 45 to 75 minutes, seven to 11 daily).

Getting Around

Year-round, **Vélocéane bicycles** (per 2hr/half-day/full day €2/3/5) can be hired at five sites (seven in summer), including the tourist office (which has bike path maps) and the train station. Tandems and kids' bikes are also on offer.

EURE

Lovely day trips can be made from Rouen, particularly in the landlocked Eure *département* (www.cdt-eure.fr). The beautiful gardens of Claude Monet are at Giverny, while the 12th-century Château Gaillard in Les Andelys affords a breathtaking panorama of the Seine.

LES ANDELYS

pop 9000

Some 40km southeast of Rouen, on a hairpin curve in the Seine, lies Les Andelys (the s is silent), crowned by the ruins of Château Gaillard, the 12th-century hilltop fastness of Richard the Lion-Heart.

Orientation & Information

The town consists of Petit Andely, along the mighty Seine, and long, narrow Grand Andely, whose main square, place Poussin, is 2km east of the river.

Tourist Office (☎ 02 32 54 41 93; http://office-tourisme.ville-andelys.fr, in French; 24 rue Philippe Auguste; 10am-noon & 2-6pm Mon-Sat, 10am-1pm Sun Apr-May, longer hr Jun-Sep, 2-6pm Mon-Fri, 10am-1pm Sat Nov-Feb, longer hr Oct & Mar) In Petit Andely below the château.

Sights

Built from 1196 to 1197, **Château Gaillard** (☎ 02 32 54 41 93; adult/student & senior €3/2.50; 10am-1pm & 2-6pm Wed-Mon mid-Mar–mid-Nov) – whose grounds are always open free-of-charge – secured the western border of English territory along the Seine until Henry IV ordered its destruction in 1603. Fantastic views of the Seine's white cliffs can be enjoyed from the platform a few hundred metres up the one-lane road from the castle. The tourist office has details on tours (€5; in French with English-speaking guides).

From Petit Andely, the château is a 500m climb along a narrow road you can pick up 50m north of the tourist office. By car, take the turn-off opposite Église Notre Dame in Grand Andely and follow the signs.

Sleeping & Eating

our pick **Hôtel & Restaurant de la Chaine d'Or** (☎ 02 32 54 00 31; www.hotel-lachainedor.com; 27 rue Grande, Petit Andely; d €72-120, ste €132; lunch menus €18-29, other menus €45-78; closed Jan, restaurant closed lunch Mon & lunch Tue year-round, dinner Sun & dinner Mon Nov-Mar) Right on the Seine, this little rural hideaway, packed with character, is rustically stylish without being twee. The 12 rooms are spacious, tasteful and romantic, with antique wood furnishings and plush rugs; some are so close to the river you could almost fish out the window. The classy French restaurant is one of the best for miles around – specialities include lobster, escargots and cider sorbet.

GIVERNY

pop 520

The tiny country village of Giverny, 15km south of Les Andelys, is a place of pilgrimage for devotees of Impressionism. Monet lived here from 1883 until his death in 1926, in a rambling house – surrounded by flower-filled gardens – that's now the immensely

CLAUDE MONET

Everyone discusses my art and pretends to understand, as if it were necessary to understand, when it is simply necessary to love.

Claude Monet

The undisputed leader of the Impressionists, Claude Monet was born in Paris in 1840 and grew up in Le Havre, where he found an early affinity with the outdoors. Monet disliked school and spent much of his time sketching his professors in the margins of his exercise books. By 15 his skills as a caricaturist were known throughout Le Havre, but Eugène Boudin, his first mentor, convinced him to turn his attention away from portraiture towards the study of colour, light and landscape.

In 1860 military service interrupted Monet's studies at the Académie Suisse in Paris and took him to Algiers, where the intense light and colours further fuelled his imagination. The young painter became fascinated with capturing a specific moment in time, the immediate impression of the scene before him, rather than the precise detail.

From 1867 Monet's distinctive style began to emerge, focusing on the effects of light and colour and using the quick, undisguised broken brushstrokes that would characterise the Impressionist period. His contemporaries were Pissarro, Renoir, Sisley, Cézanne and Degas. The young painters left the studio to work outdoors, experimenting with the shades and hues of nature, arguing and sharing ideas. Their work was far from welcomed by critics; one of them condemned it as 'impressionism', in reference to Monet's *Impression: Sunrise* (1874). Much to the critic's chagrin, the name stuck.

From the late 1870s Monet concentrated on painting in series, seeking to re-create a landscape by showing its transformation under different conditions of light and atmosphere. *Haystacks* (1890–91) and *Rouen Cathedral* (1891–95) are some of the best-known works of this period. In 1883 he moved to Giverny, planting his property with a variety of flowers around an artificial pond, the Jardin d'Eau, (below), in order to paint the subtle effects of sunlight on natural forms. It was here that he painted the *Nymphéas* (Water Lilies) series. The huge dimensions of some of these works, together with the fact that the pond's surface takes up the entire canvas, meant the abandonment of composition in the traditional sense and the virtual disintegration of form. A *Nymphéas* canvas from 1919, likely to be the last ever to come up for auction, sold in June 2008 for an astounding US$80 million.

For more info on Monet and his work, visit www.giverny.org.

popular Maison et Jardins de Claude Monet. The nearby Musée d'Art Américain is also worth a visit.

Sights

Monet's home for the last 43 years of his life is now the delightful **Maison et Jardins de Claude Monet** (☎ 02 32 51 28 21; www.fondation-monet.com; adult/student/7-12yr €5.50/4/3, gardens only €4; ⏰ 9.30am-6pm Tue-Sun Apr-Oct). His pastel-pink house and Water Lily studio stand on the periphery of the **Clos Normand**, with its symmetrically laid-out gardens bursting with flowers. Monet bought the **Jardin d'Eau** (Water Garden) in 1895 and set about creating his trademark lily pond, as well as the famous Japanese bridge (since rebuilt).

Draped with purple wisteria, the bridge blends into the asymmetrical foreground and background, creating the intimate atmosphere for which the 'painter of light' was renowned.

Seasons have an enormous effect on Giverny. From early to late spring, daffodils, tulips, rhododendrons, wisteria and irises appear, followed by poppies and lilies. By June, nasturtiums, roses and sweet peas are in flower.

Around September, there are dahlias, sunflowers and hollyhocks.

The **Musée d'Art Américain** (☎ 02 32 51 94 65; www.maag.org; 99 rue Claude Monet; adult/student & senior/12-18yr €5.50/4/3; ⏰ 10am-6pm Tue-Sun Apr-Oct), also surrounded by gardens, displays works by American Impressionist painters who flocked to France in the late 19th and early 20th centuries.

It's 100m down the road from the Maison de Claude Monet.

Getting There & Away

Giverny is 76km northwest of Paris and 66km southeast of Rouen.

From Paris' Gare St-Lazare two early morning trains run to Vernon (€11.90, 50 minutes), 7km to the west of Giverny. For the return trip there's one direct train every hour or two from 3pm till at least 8.40pm (10pm on Sunday). From Rouen (€9.60, 40 minutes) several trains leave before noon; to get back, there's about one train every hour between 5pm and 10pm (till 9pm on Saturday).

Shuttle buses (€2; seven daily Tuesday to Sunday April to October), run by **Veolia** (☎ 08 25 07 60 27; www.mobiregion.net, in French), meet most trains to and from Paris.

Facing the train station, you can rent a bike at the **Café de Chemin de Fer** (L'Arrivée de Giverny; ☎ 02 32 21 16 01; 7am-1am) for €12 a day.

CALVADOS

The *département* of Calvados (www.calvados-tourisme.com) stretches from Honfleur in the east to Isigny-sur-Mer in the west and includes Caen, Bayeux – world-renowned for its tapestry – and the D-Day beaches. The area is famed for its rich pastures and farm products, including butter, cheese, cider and the distinctive apple brandy that bears the name of the *département*.

BAYEUX

pop 14,600

Bayeux has become famous throughout the English-speaking world thanks to a 68m-long piece of painstakingly embroidered cloth: the 11th-century Bayeux Tapestry, whose 58 scenes vividly tell the story of the Norman invasion of England in 1066. But there's more to Bayeux than this unparalleled piece of needlework – the first town to be liberated after D-Day (on the morning of 7 June), it is one of the few in Calvados to have survived WWII practically unscathed. A great place to soak up the Norman atmosphere, Bayeux' delightful city centre is crammed with 13th- to 18th-century buildings, including lots of wood-framed Norman-style houses, and a fine Gothic cathedral.

Bayeux makes an ideal launch pad for exploring the D-Day beaches just to the north.

Orientation

Central Bayeux is surrounded by France's very first ring road (bd de Eindhoven, bd Maréchal Leclerc etc), built by British military engineers right after D-Day. The cathedral, 1km northwest of the train station, is the most visible landmark in the city centre. The main commercial streets are east–west rue St-Martin and rue St-Jean.

Information

La Paillote (☎ 02 31 10 08 73; 25 rue Montfiquet; 5pm-2am, to 3am Fri & Sat, closed Sun & Mon in winter) A laid-back pub with a tropical vibe and internet access.

Laundrettes 67 rue des Bouchers (7am-9pm); 13 rue Maréchal Foch (7am-9pm)

Post Office (14 rue Larcher) Changes foreign currency.

Pub Fiction (☎ 02 31 10 17 41; 14 rue du Petit Rouen; per 15min €1; 8.30pm-2am, to 3am Fri & Sat, from 6pm Jul & Aug) A popular, saloon-style pub with three internet computers.

Société Générale (26 rue St-Malo) A bank.

Tourist Office (☎ 02 31 51 28 28; www.bayeux-bessin-tourism.com; pont St-Jean; 9am-7pm Mon-Sat, 9am-1pm & 2-6pm Sun & holidays Jul & Aug, 9.30am-12.30pm & 2-6pm Apr-Jun, Sep & Oct, 9.30am-12.30pm & 2-5.30pm Nov-Mar) Covers both Bayeux and the surrounding Bessin region, including the D-Day beaches. Has a walking tour map of town, English books on D-Day and the tapestry, and bus and train schedules. Charges €2 to book hotels and B&Bs.

Sights

BAYEUX TAPESTRY

Undoubtedly the world's most celebrated embroidery, the **Bayeux Tapestry** (wool thread embroidered onto linen cloth) vividly recounts the story of the Norman conquest of England in 1066. Divided into 58 scenes briefly captioned in almost-readable Latin, the main narrative – told from an unashamedly Norman perspective – fills up the centre of the canvas, while religious allegories and depictions of daily life in the 11th century unfold along the borders. The final showdown at the Battle of Hastings is depicted in truly graphic fashion, complete with severed limbs and decapitated heads (along the bottom of scene 52). Halley's comet, which blazed across the sky in 1066, makes an appearance at the top of scene 32, while at the bottom of scene 15 there's – no, it can't be! – an 11th-century 'full Monty'.

Scholars believe that the 68.3m-long tapestry was commissioned by Bishop Odo

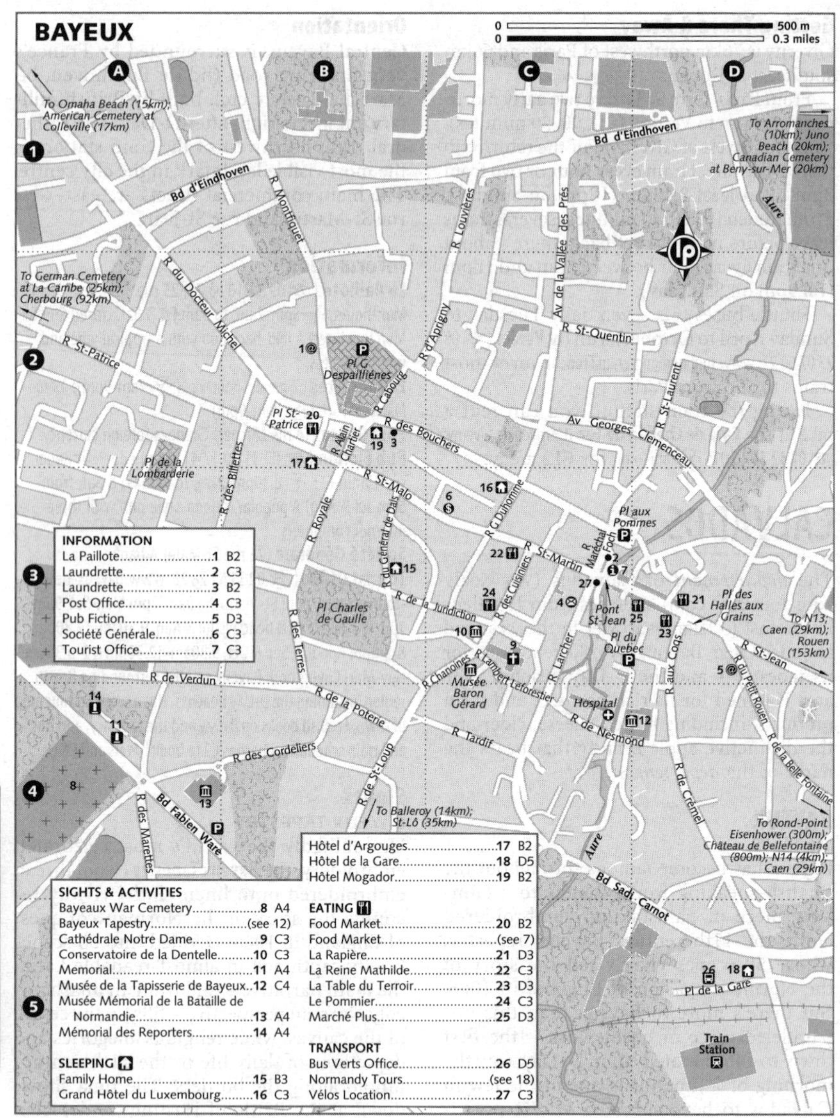

of Bayeux, William the Conquerer's half-brother, in southern England (probably Canterbury) for the opening of Bayeux cathedral in 1077.

The tapestry is housed in the **Musée de la Tapisserie de Bayeux** (☎ 02 31 51 25 50; www.tapisserie-bayeux.fr; rue de Nesmond; adult/student incl audioguide €7.80/3.80; ⌚ 9am-6.30pm mid-Mar–mid-Nov, to 7pm May-Aug, 9.30am-12.30pm & 2-6pm mid-Nov–mid-Mar). Upstairs is an excellent new exhibition on the tapestry's creation, its remarkable history and its conservation; a new 15-minute film is screened alternately in English and French.

For an animated version of the Bayeux Tapestry, check out David Newton's very creative short film on YouTube.

CATHÉDRALE NOTRE DAME

Most of Bayeux' spectacular Norman Gothic **Cathédrale Notre Dame** (rue du Bienvenu; 8.30am-7pm Jul-Sep, 8.30am-6pm Apr-Jun & Oct, 9am-5pm Nov-Mar) dates from the 13th century, though the crypt (accessible from the north side of the choir), the arches of the nave and the lower portions of the entrance towers are 11th-century Romanesque. The central tower was added in the 15th century; the copper dome dates from the 1860s. First prize for tackiness has got to go to 'Litanies de la Sainte Vierge', a 17th-century retable in the first chapel on the left as you enter the cathedral.

CONSERVATOIRE DE LA DENTELLE

At the **Conservatoire de la Dentelle** (Lace Conservatory; 02 31 92 73 80; http://dentelledebayeux.free.fr; 6 rue du Bienvenu; admission free; 10am-12.30pm & 2.30-6pm Mon-Sat), dedicated to the preservation of traditional Norman lacemaking, you can watch some of France's most celebrated lacemakers create intricate designs using dozens of bobbins and hundreds of pins. At its height, the local lace industry employed 5000 lacemakers.

MUSÉE MÉMORIAL DE LA BATAILLE DE NORMANDIE

Using well-chosen photos (some in original colour), personal accounts, dioramas and wartime objects, this **museum** (02 31 51 46 90; bd Fabien Ware; adult/student €6.50/3.80; 9.30am-6.30pm May-Sep, 10am-12.30pm & 2-6pm Oct-Apr) offers a first-rate introduction to WWII in Normandy. Signs are in French and English. A new 25-minute film on the Battle of Normandy is screened in English three to five times a day.

BAYEUX WAR CEMETERY

This peaceful **cemetery** (bd Fabien Ware), a few hundred metres west of the Musée Mémorial, is the largest of the 18 Commonwealth military cemeteries in Normandy. It contains 4848 graves of soldiers from the UK and 10 other countries, including Germany. Across the road is a memorial for 1807 Commonwealth soldiers whose remains were never found; the Latin inscription across the top reads 'We, whom William once conquered, have now set free the conqueror's native land'. See p290 for details on other war cemeteries.

MÉMORIAL DES REPORTERS

Just west of the Musée Mémorial, this landscaped promenade lists the names of nearly 2000 journalists killed in the line of duty since 1944. A project of Reporters Without Borders (www.rsf.org) and the City of Bayeux, it was inaugurated in 2006.

Sleeping

The tourist office has a list of *chambres d'hôtes* (B&Bs; €40 to €80) around Bayeux.

Family Home (02 31 92 15 22; www.fuaj.org; 39 rue Général de Dais; dm/s €19/30) One of France's most charming youth hostels, this place – in a mainly 18th-century neighbourhood – sports a 17th-century dining room, a delightful 16th-century courtyard and 80 beds in rooms for one to four people. Check-in is possible all day – if reception isn't staffed, phone and someone will pop by.

Hôtel de la Gare (02 31 92 10 70; www.normandy-tours-hotel.com; 26 place de la Gare; d with hall bathroom €28, d/q with shower €38/55) Across the parking lot from the train station, this place has 15 tired but serviceable rooms. Pay when you check in.

Hôtel Mogador (02 31 92 24 58; hotel.mogador@wanadoo.fr; 20 rue Alain Chartier; d €44-54;) Situated on the main market square, this friendly, family-run, two-star hotel has 14 rooms with pastel curtains and lots of old wood beams. The small patio is a lovely spot for a morning croissant. An excellent bet.

Grand Hôtel du Luxembourg (02 31 92 00 04; www.hotels-bayeux-14.com; 25 rue des Bouchers; r €80-145) With its grand 17th-century facade, this Best Western–affiliated hotel has 27 comfortable rooms with old-time touches. There are 34 less-expensive rooms, smallish and nondescript, in the adjacent Hôtel de Brunville.

Hôtel d'Argouges (02 31 92 88 86; www.hotel-dargouges.com; 21 rue St-Patrice; d €90-120, q €280) This graceful three-star hotel, in a stately 18th-century residence, has an elegant breakfast room overlooking a private garden, squeaky parquet floors and 28 rooms, some with period features such as marble chimneys.

our pick **Château de Bellefontaine** (02 31 22 00 10; www.hotel-bellefontaine.com; 49 rue de Bellefontaine; d €125-140, ste €160;) Swans and a bubbling brook welcome you to this majestic 18th-century château, which is surrounded by a 2ha private park and has 20 enormous rooms, some with marble chimneys and period mouldings. The decor is an intelligent mix of tradition and modernity, and the rural location couldn't be more pastoral. Situated 1.5km southeast of the tourist office (500m south of rond-point Eisenhower).

PASSIONATE ABOUT THE BAYEUX TAPESTRY

Looking back on her life, Isabelle Robert-Attard can hardly believe how lucky she is to be the director of the Musée de la Tapisserie de Bayeux (p279), a job that 'brings together everything I love – archeology, history, tourism and the Vikings, or at least Scandinavia'.

Robert-Attard grew up with the tapestry – or, more precisely, with a 1:10-scale poster of it hung on the wall of her family's living room in Orléans. She visited the real tapestry for the first time at age two and returned as a teenager, shocked to discover how 3-D the scenes appeared.

While attending a sports high school in the Pyrenees, Robert-Attard specialised in orienteering – precisely the skill that Harold lacked when he got lost on the Norman coast; in 1986 she was France's national junior orienteering champion. However, she admits that the first time she walked around the museum as director, 'I got lost', adding, 'I do better in the woods'. She has since had the route visitors follow redesigned.

For family reasons Robert-Attard ended up living for five years in Sweden – in fact, in Lappland, where she studied Nordic archeology and set up a tourism consulting company. But life that far north 'was quite extreme. You have nine months of winter and snow and two months of summer and mosquitoes'. Like the Viking Normans over a millennium earlier, she decided that France was a more convivial place to live. In 2007 Robert-Attard found herself transformed into a character named Pénélope Breuil in an erudite, *Da Vinci Code*–like best-seller, *Intrigue à l'Anglaise* by Adrien Goetz, which purports to solve a thousand-year-old mystery: the circuitous fate of 3m of scenes missing from the end of the Bayeux Tapestry. Some people, it seems, want to get their hands on them badly enough to commit murder!

More usually, the Bayeux Tapestry is the subject of scholarly rather than novelistic interest, and every year a new PhD is written about it. Though more reputable research is the norm, Robert-Attard says that 'in 1941 the Nazis studied the tapestry, looking for their Aryan and Germanic ancestors' among the supposedly Aryan Normans.

Despite the publication of innumerable academic works, Robert-Attard says, 'there are many things that we can't explain because we have lost the clues to read them properly. Why do a fox and a crow appear on the tapestry three times? Is the fox William and the crow Harold?'

She adds: 'I am also passionate about the object itself, which survived so many things – there were fires in the cathedral, and during the Revolution they tried to cut it into small pieces to cover horse-drawn carriages. I won't say the fact of its survival is a miracle – I don't like that word – but it certainly involved an amazing quantity of luck.' One factor that seems to have worked in its favour is the fact that 'the tapestry was made of common materials. It's wool and linen, not silk and silver and gold so there was no value in the materials and therefore no reason to steal it'.

As for the question of the Bayeux Tapestry's name, Robert-Attard acknowledges that there's no simple solution. The object is not, in fact, a *tapisserie* (tapestry) at all but rather a *broderie* (embroidery), 'but it's too late to change the name to "Broderie de Bayeux" – people won't recognise it. And a small *toile* (piece of cloth) is a *toilette*. I'm afraid "Toilette de Bayeux" won't do either'.

Eating

Local specialities to keep an eye out for include *cochon de Bayeux* (Bayeux-style pork). Rue St-Jean and rue St-Martin are home to a variety of eateries and food shops. Appropriately, rue des Cuisiniers (north of the cathedral) also has some restaurants.

La Reine Mathilde (☎ 02 31 92 00 59; 47 rue St-Martin; cakes €2.30; 🕑 8.30am-7.30pm Tue-Sun) A sumptuous, c 1900–style *pâtisserie* and *salon de thé* that's ideal if you've got a hankering for something soft and sweet.

La Table du Terroir (☎ 02 31 92 05 53; 42 rue St-Jean; lunch menus €12.50-14, dinner menus €21-28; 🕑 closed dinner Sun) At this country-style restaurant, crimson chairs and white tablecloths provide an enjoyable backdrop for specialities such as grilled salmon, pork fillet and *tripes à la Caen*.

Le Pommier (☎ 02 31 21 52 10; www.restaurantlepommier.com; 38-40 rue des Cuisiniers; lunch menu €14, other menus €23-36.25; 🕑 closed Tue & Wed Nov–mid-Mar) Specialities at this smart restaurant include filet of roast duck, *filet mignon de porc* and a varied selection of imaginative French dishes made with fresh Norman products, including rare legacy vegetables.

La Rapière (☎ 02 31 21 05 45; 53 rue St-Jean; lunch menu €15, dinner menus €27-33; 🕑 closed Wed & Thu)

Housed in a late-1400s mansion held together by its original oak beams, this restaurant specialises in hearty home cooking – the *timbale de pêcheur* (fisherman's stew) is served up piping hot in a cast-iron pan. For dessert, an excellent option is *trou normand* (apple sorbet with a dash of Calvados).

SELF-CATERING

Food markets rue St-Jean (Wed morning); place St-Patrice (Sat morning)

Marché Plus (16 rue St-Jean; 7am-9pm Mon-Sat, 8.30am-12.30pm Sun) Supermarket.

Getting There & Away

Bus Verts (08 10 21 42 14; www.busverts.fr), whose **office** (9.30am-1.15pm & 2.30-4.45pm Mon-Sat early Jun–Aug; 8.30am-12.05pm & 2.30-6pm Mon-Fri Sep, 10am-noon Mon & 3-5pm Wed & Fri Oct–early Jun) faces the train station, links the train station and place St-Patrice with Caen (bus 30; €4, one hour, three or four daily Monday to Friday except holidays). Travellers under 25 get a 15% discount.

Bus Verts also runs regular buses to the D-Day beaches (see p284).

Train destinations from Bayeux include Caen (€5.50, 20 minutes, 13 to 19 daily Monday to Saturday, eight Sunday), whence there are connections to Paris' Gare St-Lazare (€32) and Rouen (€24.60); Cherbourg (€14.60, one hour, 11 daily Monday to Friday, three to five on weekends); Coutances (€11.40, 50 minutes, eight daily Monday to Saturday, four Sunday); and Pontorson (Mont St-Michel; €19.60, 1¾ hours, two or three direct daily). To get to Deauville change at Lisieux.

Getting Around

A **taxi** (02 31 92 92 40) can take you around Bayeux or out to the D-Day sites.

Vélos Location (Le Verger de l'Aure; 02 31 92 89 16; 5 rue Larcher; per half-/full day €10/15; 8am-8pm) Offers year-round bike rental in a grocery store near the tourist office.

D-DAY BEACHES

Code-named 'Operation Overlord', the D-Day landings (p286) were the largest military operation in history. On the morning of 6 June 1944, swarms of landing craft – part of an armada of over 6000 ships and boats – hit the northern Normandy beaches and tens of thousands of soldiers from the USA, the UK, Canada and elsewhere began pouring onto French soil.

The majority of the 135,000 Allied troops stormed ashore along 80km of beaches north of Bayeux code-named (from west to east) Utah, Omaha, Gold, Juno and Sword. The landings on D-Day – known as 'Jour J' in French – were followed by the 76-day Battle of Normandy, during which the Allies suffered 210,000 casualties, including 37,000 troops killed. German casualties are believed to be around 200,000; another 200,000 German soldiers were taken prisoner. About 14,000 French civilians also died.

Caen's Mémorial (p288) and Bayeux' Musée Mémorial (p281) provide a comprehensive overview of the events of D-Day, and many of the villages near the landing beaches (eg Arromanches) have local museums with insightful exhibits.

If you've got wheels, you can follow the D514 along the D-Day coast or several signposted circuits around the battle sites – look for signs for 'D-Day-Le Choc' in the American sectors and 'Overlord-L'Assaut' in the British and Canadian sectors. A free booklet called *The D-Day Landings and the Battle of Normandy*, available from tourist offices, has details on the eight major visitors' routes

For details on D-Day and its context, see www.normandiememoire.com and www.6juin 1944.com.

INFORMATION

Maps of the D-Day beaches are available at *tabacs* (tobacconists), newsagents and bookshops in Bayeux and elsewhere. The area is also sometimes called the Côte de Nacre (Mother-of-Pearl Coast). Towns along the coast, including Arromanches, have lots of small hotels.

TOURS

An organised minibus tour is an excellent way to get a sense of the D-Day beaches and their place in history. The Bayeux tourist office can handle reservations.

Normandy Sightseeing Tours (02 31 51 70 52; www.normandywebguide.com) From May to October (and on request the rest of the year), this experienced outfit offers morning (adult/student/under 10 years €40/35/25) and afternoon tours (€45/40/30) of various beaches and cemeteries. These can be combined into an all-day excursion (€75/65/45).

WILLIAM CONQUERS ENGLAND

Born out of wedlock to Robert the Magnificent, future Duke of Normandy, and Arlette, daughter of a furrier, William the Bastard (1027–87) – better known to posterity as William the Conqueror – became Duke of Normandy at the tender age of eight when his father died while on the way back from Jerusalem. Having survived several assassination attempts by rivals, including members of his own family, William assumed full control of the province at age 15 and set about regaining his lost territory and quashing rebellious vassals.

William had twice been promised the throne of England: once by the king himself, Edward the Confessor (his cousin), and once by the most powerful Saxon lord in England, Harold Godwinson of Wessex, who had the misfortune of being shipwrecked on the Norman coast. But in January 1066 Edward died without an heir and Harold was immediately crowned king with the support of the great nobles of England.

One of several pretenders to the throne, William was preparing to send an invasion fleet across the Channel when a rival army (consisting of an alliance between Harold's estranged brother Tostig and Harold Hardrada of Norway) landed in the north of England. After a September battle at Stamford Bridge, near York, Hardrada was hard done by and Tostig was toast – in short, Harold defeated and killed them both.

Meanwhile, William had crossed the Channel unopposed with an army of about 6000 men, including a large cavalry force. They landed at Pevensey before marching to Hastings, where, on 13 October, Harold faced off against William with about 7000 men from a strong defensive position. The battle began the next day.

Although William's archers scored many hits, the Saxon army's ferocious defence ended a charge by the Norman cavalry and drove them back in disarray. William faced the real possibility of losing the battle. Summoning the experience and tactical ability he had gained in numerous campaigns against rivals back in Normandy, he used the cavalry's rout to draw the Saxon infantry out of their defensive positions, whereupon the Norman infantry turned and caused heavy casualties among the undisciplined Saxon troops. Late in the afternoon the battle started to turn against Harold, who was slain – by an arrow through the eye, according to the Bayeux Tapestry. The embattled Saxons fought on until sunset and then fled. William immediately marched to London, ruthlessly quelled the opposition, and was crowned king of England on Christmas Day.

William thus became the ruler of two kingdoms, bringing England's feudal system of government under the control of Norman nobles. Ongoing unrest among the Saxon peasantry soured William's opinion of the country and, after 1072, he spent the rest of his life in Normandy, only going to England when compelled to do so. William left most of the governance of the country to the bishops.

In Normandy William continued to expand his influence through military campaigns, strategic marriages and the ruthless elimination of all opposition. In 1087 he was injured during an attack on Mantes. He died at Rouen a few weeks later and was buried in Caen (see p291).

Normandy Tours (☎ 02 31 92 10 70; www.normandy-tours-hotel.com; 26 place de la Gare; adult/student €41/36; ⌚ year-round) This local operator offers four- or five-hour tours of the main sites at 8.15am and 1.15pm, as well as personally tailored trips. Based at Bayeux' Hotel de la Gare (p281).

Mémorial (☎ 02 31 06 06 45; www.memorial-caen.fr; adult/under 18yr €69/55; ⌚ 1pm Oct-Mar, 9am & 2pm Apr-Sep) Conducts excellent four- to five-hour minibus tours around the landing beaches. The price includes entry to the Mémorial (p288). You can book online (under Day Pass) or by telephone.

GETTING THERE & AWAY

Run by **Bus Verts** (☎ 08 10 21 42 14; www.busverts.fr, in French), bus 70 (two or three daily Monday to Saturday, more frequently and on Sunday and holidays in summer) goes northwest from Bayeux to Colleville-sur-Mer (Omaha Beach and the American Cemetery; €2, 35 minutes), Pointe du Hoc (€4) and Grandcamp-Maisy. Bus 74 (bus 75 in summer; three or four daily Monday to Saturday, more frequently and on Sunday and holidays in summer) links Bayeux with Arromanches (€2, 30 minutes),

Gold and Juno Beaches, and Courseulles (€3, one hour).

The D-Day sites can also be visited by bicycle, eg from Bayeux.

Arromanches

To make it possible to unload the vast quantities of cargo needed by the invasion forces without having to capture – intact! – one of the heavily defended Channel ports (a lesson of the 1942 Dieppe Raid; see p271), the Allies set up prefabricated marinas, code-named **Mulberry Harbours**, off two of the landing beaches. These consisted of 146 massive cement caissons towed over from England and sunk to form a semicircular breakwater in which floating bridge spans were moored. In the three months after D-Day, the Mulberries facilitated the unloading of a mind-boggling 2.5 million men, four million tonnes of equipment and 500,000 vehicles.

The harbour established at Omaha was completely destroyed by a ferocious gale just two weeks after D-Day, but the remains of the second, **Port Winston** (named after Winston Churchill), can still be seen near **Arromanches**, 10km northeast of Bayeux. At low tide you can walk out to one of the caissons from the beach. The best view of Port Winston and nearby **Gold Beach** is from the hill east of town, marked with a statue of the Virgin Mary.

Right on the beach, the **Musée du Débarquement** (Landing Museum; ☎ 02 31 22 34 31; www.normandy1944.com; place du 6 Juin; adult/student €6.50/4.50; ⌚ 9am-7pm May-Aug, 9am-6pm Sep, 9.30am-12.30pm & 1.30-5.30pm Mar, Apr & Oct, 10am-12.30pm & 1.30-5pm Feb, Nov & Dec, closed Jan), redesigned in 2004 for the 60th anniversary of D-Day, makes an informative stop before visiting the beaches. Dioramas, models and two films explain the logistics and importance of Port Winston. Written material is available in 18 languages.

Juno Beach

Dune-lined **Juno Beach**, 12km east of Arromanches, was stormed by Canadian troops on D-Day. A Cross of Lorraine marks the spot where General Charles de Gaulle came ashore shortly after the landings. He was followed by Winston Churchill on 12 June and King George VI on 16 June.

The area's only Canadian museum, **Centre Juno Beach** (☎ 02 31 37 32 17; www.junobeach.org; adult/concession €6.50/5, WWII veterans & widows free; ⌚ 9.30am-7pm Apr-Sep, 10am-6pm Mar & Oct, 10am-1pm & 2-5pm Feb, Nov & Dec, closed Jan), has multimedia exhibits on Canada's role in the war effort and the landings. Guided tours of Juno Beach (€4.50) are available from April to October.

Longues-sur-Mer

Part of the Nazis' Atlantic Wall, the massive casemates and 150mm German guns near Longues-sur-Mer, 6km west of Arromanches, were designed to hit targets some 20km away, including both Gold Beach (to the east) and Omaha Beach (to the west). Over six decades later, the mammoth artillery pieces are still in their colossal concrete emplacements – the only in situ large-calibre weapons in Normandy. For details on tours (€4), available from April to October, contact the **Longues tourist office** (☎ 02 31 21 46 87).

Parts of the classic D-Day film, *The Longest Day* (1962), were filmed both here and at Pointe du Hoc. On clear days, Bayeux' cathedral, 8km away, is visible to the south.

Omaha Beach

The most brutal fighting on D-Day took place on the 7km stretch of coastline around Vierville-sur-Mer, St-Laurent-sur-Mer and Colleville-sur-Mer, 15km northwest of Bayeux, known as 'Bloody Omaha' to US veterans. Sixty years on, little evidence of the carnage unleashed here on 6 June 1944 remains except for concrete German bunkers, though at very low tide you can see a few remnants of the Mulberry Harbour (left).

These days Omaha is a peaceful place, a glorious stretch of fine golden sand partly lined with sand dunes and summer homes. Near the car park in St-Laurent, a memorial marks the site of the first US military cemetery on French soil. There's also a sculpture on the beach called *Les Braves*, by the French sculptor Anilore Banon, commissioned to commemorate the 60th anniversary of the landings in 2004. **Circuit de la Plage d'Omaha**, trail-marked with a yellow stripe, is a self-guided tour all along Omaha Beach.

On a bluff above the beach, the huge **Normandy American Cemetery & Memorial** (Cimetière Militaire Américain; ☎ 02 31 51 62 00; www.abmc.gov; Colleville-sur-Mer; ⌚ 9am-6pm mid-Apr–mid-Sep, 9am-5pm mid-Sep–mid-Apr), 17km northwest of Bayeux at Colleville-sur-Mer, is the largest American cemetery in Europe. Featured in the opening scenes of Steven Spielberg's

THE BATTLE OF NORMANDY

In early 1944 an Allied invasion of Continental Europe seemed inevitable. Hitler's disastrous campaign on the Russian front and the Luftwaffe's inability to control the skies over Europe had left Germany vulnerable. Both sides knew a landing was coming – the only questions were where and, of course, when.

Several sites were considered. After long deliberations, it was decided that the beaches along Normandy's northern coast – rather than the even more heavily fortified coastline further north around Calais, where Hitler was expecting an attack – would serve as a surprise spearhead into Europe.

Code-named 'Operation Overlord', the invasion began on the night between 5 and 6 June 1944 when three paratroop divisions were dropped behind enemy lines. At about 6.30 on the morning of 6 June, six amphibious divisions stormed ashore at five beaches, backed up by an unimaginable 6000 sea craft and 13,000 aeroplanes. The initial landing force involved some 45,000 troops; 15 more divisions were to follow once successful beachheads had been established.

The narrow Straits of Dover had seemed the most likely invasion spot to the Germans, who set about heavily reinforcing the area around Calais and the other Channel ports. Allied intelligence went to extraordinary lengths to encourage the German belief that the invasion would be launched north of Normandy: double agents, leaked documents and fake radio traffic, buttressed by phoney airfields and an entirely fictitious American army group, supposedly stationed in the southeast of England, all suggested the invasion would centre on the Pas de Calais.

Because of the tides and unpredictable weather patterns, Allied planners had only a few dates available each month in which to launch the invasion. On 5 June, the date chosen, the worst storm in 20 years set in, delaying the operation. The weather had only marginally improved the next day, but General Dwight D Eisenhower, Allied commander-in-chief, gave the go-ahead: 6 June would be D-Day.

In the hours leading up to D-Day, teams of the French Resistance set about disrupting German communications. Just after midnight on 6 June, the first Allied troops were on French soil. British commandos and glider units captured key bridges and destroyed German gun emplacements, and the American 82nd and 101st Airborne Divisions landed west of the invasion site. Although the paratroops' tactical victories were few, they caused confusion in German ranks and, because of their relatively small numbers, the German high command was convinced that the real invasion had not yet begun.

Omaha & Utah Beaches

The assault by the US 1st and 29th Infantry Divisions on Omaha Beach (Vierville, St-Laurent and Colleville) was by far the bloodiest of the day. From the outset the Allies' best-laid plans were thrown into chaos. The beach was heavily defended by three battalions of heavily armed, highly trained Germans supported by mines, underwater obstacles and an extensive trench system. Strong winds blew many of the landing craft far from their carefully planned landing sectors. Many troops, overloaded with equipment, disembarked in deep water and simply drowned; others were cut to pieces by machine-gun and mortar fire from the cliffs. Only two of the 29 Sherman tanks expected to support the troops made it to shore and it proved almost impossible to advance up the beach as planned.

By noon the situation was so serious that General Omar Bradley, in charge of the Omaha Beach forces, considered abandoning the attack; but eventually, metre by metre, the GIs gained a precarious toehold on the beach. Assisted by naval bombardment, the US troops blew through a key German strongpoint and at last began to move off the beach. But of 2500 American casualties sustained there on D-Day, over 1000 were fatalities, most of them killed within the first hour of the landings.

The soldiers of the US 4th and 8th Infantry Divisions who landed at Utah fared much better than their comrades at Omaha. Most of the landing craft came ashore in a relatively lightly protected sector, and by noon the beach had been cleared and soldiers of the 4th Infantry had linked with paratroopers from the 101st Airborne. By nightfall, some 20,000 men and 1700 vehicles had arrived on French soil via Utah Beach. However, during the three weeks it took to get from this sector to Cherbourg, US forces suffered one casualty for every 10m they advanced.

Sword, Juno & Gold Beaches

These beaches, stretching for about 35km from Ouistreham to Arromanches, were attacked by the British 2nd Army, which included significant Canadian units and smaller groups of Commonwealth, Free French and Polish forces.

At Sword Beach, initial German resistance was quickly overcome and the beach was secured within hours. Infantry pushed inland from Ouistreham to link up with paratroops around Ranville, but they suffered heavy casualties as their supporting armour fell behind, trapped in a massive traffic jam on the narrow coastal roads. Nevertheless, they were within 5km of Caen by 4pm, but a heavy German counterattack forced them to dig in and Caen was not taken on the first day as planned.

At Juno Beach, Canadian battalions landed quickly but had to clear the Germans trench by trench before moving inland. Mines took a heavy toll on the infantry, but by noon they were south and east of Creuilly.

At Gold Beach, the attack by the British forces was at first chaotic, as unexpectedly high waters obscured German underwater obstacles. By 9am, though, Allied armoured divisions were on the beach and several brigades pushed inland. By afternoon they'd linked up with the Juno forces and were only 3km from Bayeux.

The Beginning of the End

By the fourth day after D-Day, the Allies held a coastal strip about 100km long and 10km deep. British Field Marshal Montgomery's plan successfully drew the German armour towards Caen, where fierce fighting continued for more than a month and reduced the city to rubble. The US Army, stationed further west, pushed northwards through the fields and *bocage* (hedgerows) of the Cotentin Peninsula.

The prized port of Cherbourg fell to the Allies on 27 June after a series of fierce battles. However, its valuable facilities were sabotaged by the retreating Germans and it remained out of service until autumn. Having foreseen such logistical problems, the Allies had devised the remarkable Mulberry Harbours (p285), two huge temporary ports set up off the Norman coast.

By the end of July, US army units had smashed through to the border of Brittany. By mid-August, two German armies had been surrounded and destroyed near Argentan and Falaise (the so-called 'Falaise Pocket'), and on 20 August US forces crossed the Seine at several points about 40km north and south of Paris. Lead by General Charles de Gaulle, France's leader-in-exile, Allied and Free French troops arrived on the streets of Paris on 25 August and by that afternoon the city had been liberated.

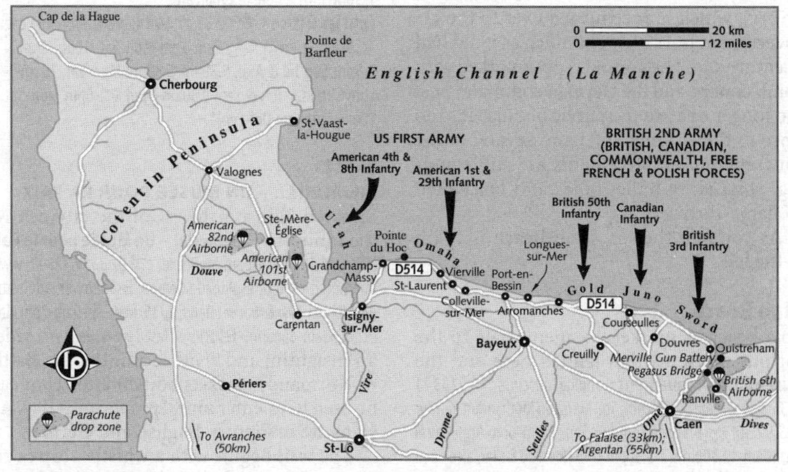

Saving Private Ryan, it contains the graves of 9387 American soldiers, including 41 pairs of brothers, and a memorial to 1557 others whose remains were never found. White marble crosses and Stars of David stretch off in seemingly endless rows, surrounded by an immaculately tended expanse of lawn. The cemetery is overlooked by a large colonnaded memorial, centred on a statue dedicated to the spirit of American youth. Nearby is a reflective pond and a small chapel.

Opened in 2007, the **Visitor Center** (admission free), mostly underground so as not to detract from the site, has an excellent multimedia presentation on the D-Day landings, told in part through the stories of individuals. Be prepared for airport-type security. **Tours** of the cemetery (one in the afternoon year-round, a second in the morning in summer) focus on personal stories.

Pointe du Hoc Ranger Memorial

At 7.10am on 6 June 1944, 225 US Army Rangers commanded by Lt Col James Earl Rudder scaled the 30m cliffs at Pointe du Hoc, where the Germans had a battery of huge artillery guns perfectly placed to rain shells onto the beaches of Utah and Omaha. Unbeknown to Rudder and his team, the guns had already been transferred inland, and they spent the next two days repelling fierce German counterattacks. By the time they were finally relieved on 8 June, 81 of the rangers had been killed and 58 more had been wounded.

Today the **site** (☎ 02 31 51 90 70; admission free; 24hr), which France turned over to the US government in 1979, looks much as it did half a century ago. The ground is pockmarked with bomb craters, and the German command post (no longer open to the public because it's too close to the eroding cliff) and several of the concrete gun emplacements are still standing, scarred by bullet holes and blackened by flame-throwers.

As you face the sea, Utah Beach is 14km to the left.

Utah Beach

This beach is marked by memorials to the various divisions that landed here and the **Musée du Débarquement** (Landing Museum; ☎ 02 33 71 53 35; www.utah-beach.com; Ste-Marie du Mont; adult/6-14yr €5.50/2.50; 9.30am-7pm Jun-Sep, 10am-6pm Apr, May & Oct, 10am-12.30pm & 2-5.30pm 1-15 Nov, Feb & Mar, also open Sat, Sun & school holidays mid-Nov–Dec).

CAEN

pop 108,900

Founded in the 11th century by William the Conqueror, Caen – capital of the Basse Normandie region – was 80% destroyed during the 1944 Battle of Normandy. Rebuilt in the 1950s and '60s in a typically utilitarian style, modern-day Caen offers visitors a walled medieval château, two ancient abbeys and a clutch of excellent museums, including a groundbreaking museum of war and peace.

The city can be used as a base for exploring the D-Day beaches but Bayeux is more atmospheric.

Orientation

Just south of the château lies Caen's modern commercial heart, centred around pedestrianised, east–west-oriented rue St-Pierre. From there, av du 6 Juin – and its tram line – heads southeast, crossing the river Orne on the way to the train station. What remains of Caen's old city can be found around rue du Vaugueux, just east of the château.

Information

There are several ATMs along rue St-Pierre.

Hemisphères (☎ 02 31 86 67 26; 15 rue des Croisières; Mon afternoon & Tue-Sat) Carries Lonely Planet titles, including some in English.

Laundrette (3 rue de Geôle; 7am-9pm)

L'Espace (☎ 02 31 93 37 14; 1 rue Basse; per hr €3.80; 10am-10pm Mon-Fri, 10am-11pm Sat, 10am-2pm & 3-9pm Sun) A deluxe cybercafé.

Tourist Office (☎ 02 31 27 14 14; www.tourisme.caen.fr; place St-Pierre; 9am-7pm Mon-Sat, 10am-1pm & 2-5pm Sun Jul & Aug, 9.30am-6.30pm Mon-Sat, 10am-1pm Sun Mar-Jun & Sep, 9.30am-1pm & 2-6pm Mon-Sat, 10am-1pm Sun Oct-Feb)

Sights

MÉMORIAL – UN MUSÉE POUR LA PAIX

Situated 3km northwest of the city centre, the innovative **Mémorial – Un Musée pour la Paix** (Memorial – A Museum for Peace; ☎ 02 31 06 06 45; www.memorial-caen.fr; esplanade Général Eisenhower; adult/student/under 10yr & war veteran €16/15/free; 9am-7pm Mar-Oct, 9.30am-6pm Nov-Feb, closed last 3 weeks Jan) provides an insightful and vivid account of the Battle of Normandy. Tickets bought after 1pm can be used to re-enter until 1pm the next day. All signs are in French, English and German.

The visit begins with a whistle-stop overview of Europe's descent into total war,

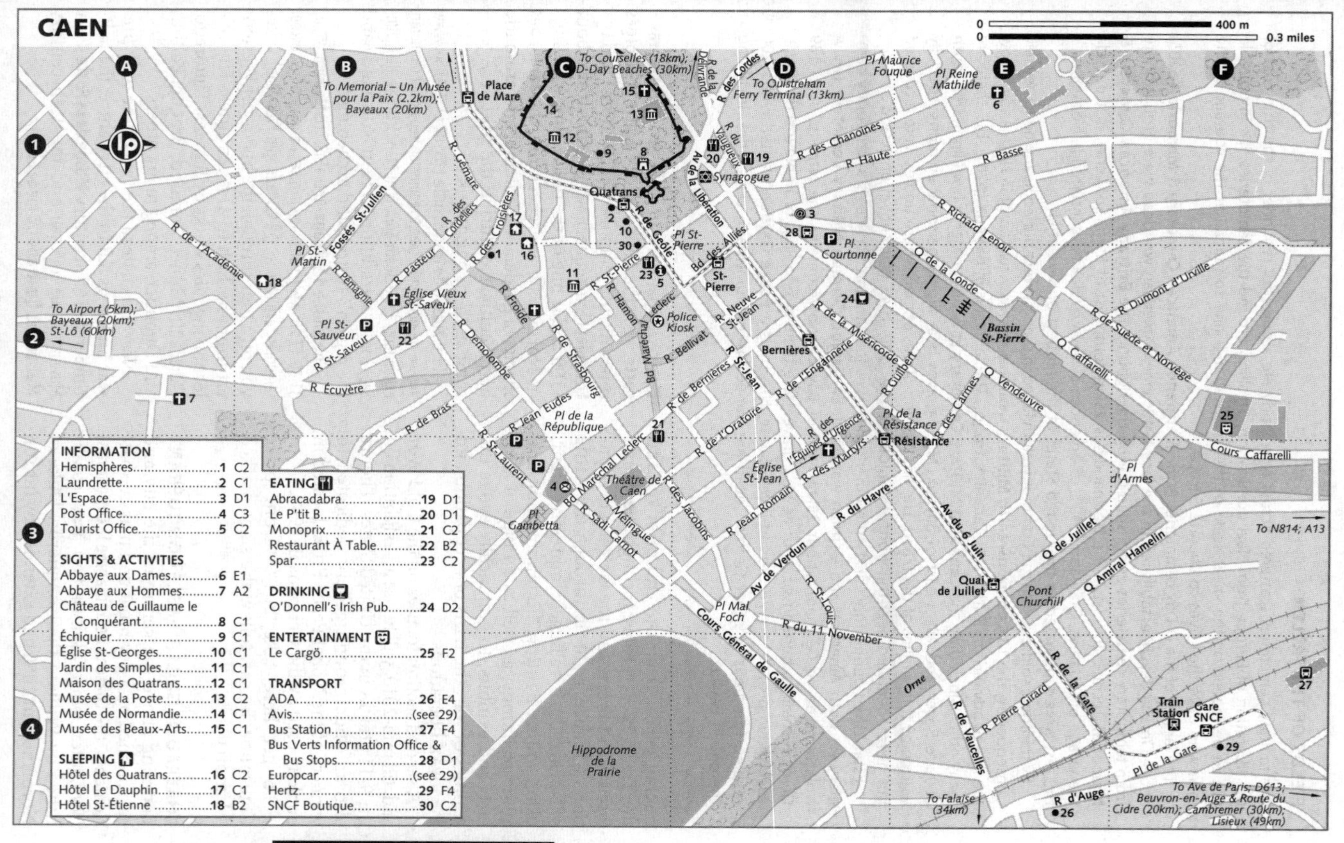
CAEN
0 400 m
0 0.3 miles
To Airport (5km); Bayeux (20km); St-Lô (60km)
To Memorial – Un Musée pour la Paix (2.2km); Bayeux (20km)
To Courseulles (18km); D-Day Beaches (30km)
To Ouistreham Ferry Terminal (13km)
To N814; A13
To Ave de Paris; D613; Beuvron-en-Auge & Route du Cidre (20km); Cambremer (30km); Lisieux (49km)
To Falaise (34km)
Place de Mare
Quatrans
Synagogue
St-Pierre
Bernières
Résistance
Quai de Juillet
Train Station
Gare SNCF
Église St-Jean
Église Vieux St-Sauveur
Police Kiosk
Théâtre de Caen
Hippodrome de la Prairie
Bassin St-Pierre
Pont Churchill
Orne
Pl Maurice Fouque
Pl Reine Mathilde
Pl Courtonne
Pl St-Pierre
Pl d'Armes
Pl de la Résistance
Pl Mal Foch
Pl de la République
Pl Gambetta
Pl St-Sauveur
Pl St-Martin
Pl de la Gare
Av de la Libération
Av du 6 Juin
Av de Verdun
Cours Général de Gaulle
Cours Caffarelli
Fossés St-Julien
Q de la Londe
Q Vendeuvre
Q Caffarelli
Q de Juillet
Q Amiral Hamelin
R de la Gare
R de Vaucelles
R d'Auge
R Pierre Girard
R St-Jean
R de Geôle
R des Cordes
R de la Délivrande
R du Vaugueux
R des Chanoines
R Haute
R Basse
R Richard Lenoir
R de Suède et Norvège
R Dumont d'Urville
R de la Miséricorde
R Guilbert
R des Carmes
R de l'Engannerie
R des Martyrs
R des l'Équipes d'Urgence
R du Havre
R St-Louis
R du 11 November
R Jean Romain
R des Jacobins
R de l'Oratoire
R de Bernières
R Neuve St-Jean
R Bellivat
R Hamon
R St-Pierre
Bd Maréchal Leclerc
Bd des Alliés
R Froide
R Demolombe
R de Strasbourg
R Jean Eudes
R St-Laurent
R Sadi Carnot
R Mélingue
R des Croisières
R Gémare
R des Cordeliers
R Pasteur
R Pémagnie
R St-Saveur
R Écuyère
R de Bras
R de l'Académie
INFORMATION
Hemisphères 1 C2
Laundrette 2 C1
L'Espace 3 D1
Post Office 4 C3
Tourist Office 5 C2
SIGHTS & ACTIVITIES
Abbaye aux Dames 6 E1
Abbaye aux Hommes 7 A2
Château de Guillaume le Conquérant 8 C1
Échiquier 9 C1
Église St-Georges 10 C1
Jardin des Simples 11 C1
Maison des Quatrans 12 C1
Musée de la Poste 13 C2
Musée de Normandie 14 C1
Musée des Beaux-Arts 15 C1
SLEEPING
Hôtel des Quatrans 16 C2
Hôtel Le Dauphin 17 C1
Hôtel St-Étienne 18 B2
EATING
Abracadabra 19 D1
Le P'tit B 20 D1
Monoprix 21 C2
Restaurant À Table 22 B2
Spar 23 C2
DRINKING
O'Donnell's Irish Pub 24 D2
ENTERTAINMENT
Le Cargö 25 F2
TRANSPORT
ADA 26 E4
Avis (see 29)
Bus Station 27 F4
Bus Verts Information Office & Bus Stops 28 D1
Europcar (see 29)
Hertz 29 F4
SNCF Boutique 30 C2

FIELDS OF THE FALLEN

The military cemeteries scattered across Normandy are a powerful reminder of the true cost of the liberation of Europe from Nazi domination. Strolling around the cemeteries, it's impossible not to be moved by the sheer scale of the devastation – and to marvel at the courage of the men who gave their lives to liberate Europe.

The largest of the D-Day cemeteries is the **Normandy American Cemetery & Memorial** (p285) above Omaha Beach, established in the late 1940s when American war dead were brought here from temporary cemeteries established during the fighting. The **Brittany American Cemetery & Memorial**, technically just inside Normandy, is 25km southeast of Mont St-Michel, just outside the village of St-James. Only about 40% of American D-Day war dead are interred in Normandy – the rest were repatriated to the United States at the request of next-of-kin.

By tradition, soldiers from the Commonwealth killed in the war were buried near where they fell. Consequently, the 18 **Commonwealth Military Cemeteries** (www.cwgc.org) in Normandy follow the line of advance of British and Canadian troops. The largest is in **Bayeux** (p281), but there are many others, including the **Canadian Military Cemetery** at Bény-sur-Mer, a few kilometres south of Juno Beach and 18km east of Bayeux. Many graves bear highly personal epitaphs, specially written by the families of the fallen. The final resting places of men whose bodies were recovered but never identified bear the words 'A Soldier of the 1939–1945 War Known unto God'.

Established during the war by the American Graves Registration Service as a temporary cemetery for both American and German war dead, **La Cambe German Military Cemetery** (www.volksbund.de, in German), about 25km west of Bayeux, now contains the remains of 21,139 German soldiers, buried two or three to a grave. Here there are no flags or noble inscriptions – each grave bears a simple ground-level plaque. Nearby is a **Peace Garden** planted with 1200 maples. Hundreds of other German dead are buried in Commonwealth cemeteries, including the one in Bayeux.

tracing events from the end of WWI and the Treaty of Versailles, through the rise of fascism in Europe and the German occupation of France, right up through the Battle of Normandy. It's a hugely impressive affair, using sound, lighting, film, animation and audio testimony, as well as a range of artefacts and exhibits, to graphically evoke the realities of war, the trials of occupation and the joy of liberation.

A second section focuses on the Cold War and, till mid-2010, will house an exhibition on the 9/11 attacks in the United States. There's also an underground gallery dedicated to winners of the Nobel Peace Prize, located in bunkers used by the Germans in 1944.

To get here take bus 2 from place Courtonne. By car, follow the signs marked 'Mémorial'.

NORMANDY

CHÂTEAU DE GUILLAUME LE CONQUÉRANT

Looming above the centre of the city and surrounded by a dry moat and massive battlements, the **Château de Guillaume le Conquérant** (www.chateau.caen.fr; admission free) was established by William the Conqueror, Duke of Normandy, in 1060 and extended by his son Henry I. Visitors can walk around the **ramparts**; visit the 12th-century **Église St-Georges** (open during temporary exhibitions) and the **Échiquier** (Exchequer), which dates from about 1100 and is one of the oldest civic buildings in Normandy; and check out the **Jardin des Simples**, a garden of medicinal and aromatic herbs cultivated during the Middle Ages – some of them poisonous.

The **Musée de Normandie** (☎ 02 31 30 47 60; www.musee-de-normandie.caen.fr; admission free except temporary exhibitions; 9.30am-6pm Wed-Mon Oct-May, daily Jun-Sep) looks at traditional life in Normandy and the region's history and archeology.

The **Musée des Beaux-Arts** (Fine Arts Museum; ☎ 02 31 30 47 70; www.ville-caen.fr/mba; admission free except temporary exhibitions; 9.30am-6pm Wed-Mon) takes you on a tour through the history of Western art from the 15th to 21st centuries. The collection includes works by Rubens, Tintoretto, Géricault, Monet, Bonnard, Braque, Balthus and Dubuffet, among many others.

Near the château are two of the only prewar buildings left in the city centre: the half-timbered, 16th-century **Musée de la Poste** (Postal Museum; 52 rue St-Pierre); and the 15th-century **Maison des Quatrans** (25 rue de Geôle).

ABBEYS

Caen's two Romanesque abbeys were founded in the mid-11th century by William the Conqueror and his wife, Matilda of Flanders, as part of a deal in which the Church pardoned these 5th cousins for having semi-incestuously married each other.

The **Abbaye aux Hommes** (Men's Abbey; ☎ 02 31 30 42 81; adult/student/under 18yr €2.20/1.10/free, admission free Sun; 🕑 8.15am-noon & 2-7.30pm except during services, tours 9.30am, 11am, 2.30pm & 4pm), with its multiturreted Église St-Étienne, is near the western end of rue Écuyère. This was William's final resting place, though the original tomb was ruined by a 16th-century Calvinist mob and, in 1793, by fevered Revolutionaries – a solitary thighbone is all that's left of Will's mortal remains. Today, the 18th-century convent buildings house the town hall.

The **Abbaye aux Dames** (Women's Abbey; ☎ 02 31 06 98 98; 🕑 tours 2.30pm & 4pm), at the eastern end of rue des Chanoines, includes the Église de la Trinité. Access to the abbey, which houses regional government offices, is by guided tour (free). Look for Matilda's tomb behind the main altar.

Sleeping

There are several hotels around the northwestern end of Bassin St-Pierre.

Hôtel St-Étienne (☎ 02 31 86 35 82; www.hotel-saint-etienne.com; 2 rue de l'Académie; s €27-38, d €42-46; ⊠) Friendly and upbeat, this classic budget hotel – in a charming late-18th-century building with creaky wooden stairs – has just 11 rooms, some with old-fashioned features such as wooden wardrobes and stone fireplaces.

Hôtel des Quatrans (☎ 02 31 86 25 57; www.hotel-des-quatrans.com; 17 rue Gémare; s/d/q €56/65/75) Named after a historically prominent local family, this tidy, two-star hotel, built mid-century in a modern style, has 47 comfy, unfussy rooms, some with balconies and all with subdued furnishings in pleasing colours.

Hôtel Le Dauphin (☎ 02 31 86 22 26; www.le-dauphin-normandie.com; 29 rue Gémare; d €85-190; ⊠) Although this Best Western–affiliated hotel is partly housed in a former priory, the facilities – including a sauna and a fitness room – are thoroughly modern. Some of the 35 rooms have antique furniture and ancient exposed beams. The pricier rooms are cheerier.

Eating

A variety of eateries line rue du Vaugueux and the streets running off it, home to some of Caen's few surviving medieval buildings. More restaurants can be found three blocks to the southeast along quai Vandeuvre.

Abracadabra (☎ 02 31 43 71 38; 4 rue du Vaugueux; pizzas €7-15; 🕑 closed lunch Sun & Wed) A local favourite since 1995, this superconvivial pizzeria serves up 40 kinds of pizzas, each with its own often-surprising name, as well as pasta and salads. Even some of the desserts are served in pizza crust.

Restaurant À Table (☎ 02 31 86 57 75; 43 rue St-Sauveur; menus €14.90-20; 🕑 closed Sun & Mon) An excellent option for traditional French cuisine – including four fish and four meat mains – at reasonable prices. Specialities include home-smoked salmon and some scrumptious desserts.

Le P'tit B (☎ 02 31 93 50 76; 15 rue du Vaugueux; menu €25; 🕑 lunch & dinner) This classy little stone-walled eatery gives traditional flavours a contemporary twist – the *wok de trois poissons* (three-fish stew) and beef filet are a treat for the tastebuds. The menu changes four times a year.

SELF-CATERING

There are several food shops along rue St-Pierre.

Monoprix (45 bd Maréchal Leclerc; 🕑 8.30am-8.50pm Mon-Sat) Supermarket.

Spar (23 rue St-Pierre; 🕑 8.30am-8pm Mon-Sat) Supermarket.

Drinking & Entertainment

O'Donnell's Irish Pub (☎ 02 31 85 51 50; 20 quai Vendeuvre; 🕑 4.30pm-2.30am Mon, Tue & Thu, to 3.30pm Wed, Fri & Sat, to midnight Sun) This Irish-style bar, with posters on the ceiling and upside-down barrel-tables on the terrace, serves over 30 whiskies as well as Guinness and Beamish Red on tap. Popular with Anglophone students, it screens football and rugby matches and has live music from 10pm on Friday.

Le Cargö (☎ 02 31 86 79 31; www.lecargo.fr, in French; 9 cours Caffarelli; admission free–€20) At the far end of the pleasure port, this *scène de musique actuelle* (venue for contemporary music) presents cutting-edge local bands with names like Sickbag, Psykoside and Pain Society, as well as more-established groups.

Getting There & Away

AIR

Skysouth (www.skysouth.co.uk) has three flights a week from Brighton to **Caen-Carpiquet airport** (☎ 02 31 71 20 10; www.caen.aeroport.fr), 5km west of town.

BUS

Run by Caen-based **Bus Verts** (☎ 08 10 21 42 14; www.busverts.fr, in French; place Courtonne; 🕑 7.30am-7pm Mon-Fri, 9am-7pm Sat), bus 20 goes to Le Havre (€10, 2½ hours) via Deauville, Trouville and Honfleur. The Caen–Le Havre route is also served by an express bus (€14, 1½ hours, four daily Monday to Saturday, two Sunday) via Honfleur.

Bus 30 goes to Bayeux (€4, on the hour, three or four daily Monday to Friday except holidays); bus 1 serves the ferry port at Ouistreham; and bus 3 will get you to Courseulles-sur-Mer.

See p284 for details on buses serving the D-Day beaches.

In Caen, most buses stop at the bus station and place Courtonne. When arriving or departing, your Bus Verts ticket is valid for an hour on Caen's buses and trams.

CAR

Rental places include **ADA** (☎ 02 31 34 88 89; 34 rue d'Auge), **Avis** (☎ 08 20 61 16 81; 44 place de la Gare), **Europcar** (☎ 08 25 89 54 70; 36 place de la Gare) and **Hertz** (☎ 02 31 84 64 50; 34 place de la Gare).

FERRY

For details on ferries from Portsmouth to Ouistreham, 14km northeast of Caen, see p968.

TRAIN

Caen, on the Paris–Cherbourg line, has regular connections to Paris' Gare St-Lazare (€29.10, two hours, 12 daily), Bayeux (€5.50, 20 minutes, 13 to 19 daily Monday to Saturday, eight Sunday), Cherbourg (€18.40, 1¼ hours, seven to 13 daily), Deauville (€11.70, one hour, eight to 10 daily), Dieppe (€9.90, 45 minutes, 10 to 15 daily Monday to Saturday, five Sunday), Pontorson (Mont St-Michel; €22.80, two hours, three or four daily) and Rouen (€21.80, 1½ hours, eight daily).

In the city centre, tickets are sold at the **SNCF Boutique** (8 rue St-Pierre; 🕑 9.15am-7pm Mon-Fri, 10am-7pm Sat).

Getting Around

Twisto (☎ 02 31 15 55 55; www.twisto.fr, in French) runs the city's buses and the two tram lines, A and B, which link the train station with the city centre. A single/24-hour ticket costs €1.25/3.30.

For a taxi call **Abbeilles Taxi** (☎ 02 31 52 17 89).

V'eol (☎ 08 00 20 03 06; www.veol.caen.fr, in French; 1st 30min free), Caen's answer to Paris' Velib' (p201), has 350 bicycles available at 40 automatic stations. The only problem: you need to sign up (one week/year €1/15).

TROUVILLE & DEAUVILLE

The twin seaside towns of Trouville (population 5400) and Deauville (population 4400), 15km southwest of Honfleur, are hugely popular with Parisians, who flock here year-round on weekends and all week long from April to September.

Chic Deauville – once a swamp, as Trouvillians are quick to point out – has been a playground of the wealthy ever since it was founded by Napoleon III's half-brother, the Duke of Morny, in 1861. Exclusive, expensive and brash, it's packed with designer boutiques, deluxe hotels and public gardens of impossible neatness, and is home to two racetracks and a high-profile American film festival.

Trouville, also a veteran beach resort, is in addition a working fishing port and, in many ways, a much more attractive place to visit. The town was frequented by painters and writers during the 19th century, including Mozin and Flaubert, and many French celebrities have holiday homes here, lured by the sandy, 2km-long beach and the laid-back seaside ambience.

To see what's on many visitors' minds, check out the windows of the many real-estate agencies in both towns.

Orientation

From the mouth of the River Touques, Deauville is to the west, while Trouville is to the east; both have long beaches along their northern sides. In Trouville, bd Fernand Moureaux runs along the river.

The towns are linked by pont des Belges, just east of Deauville's train and bus stations, and by a low-tide footpath near the river's mouth (replaced at high tide by a boat that runs from mid-March to September and on weekends and during school holidays the rest of the year).

NORMANDY

CIDER HOUSE RULES

Normandy's signposted 40km **Route du Cidre** (Cider Route) circuit, about 20km east of Caen, wends its way through the **Pays d'Auge**, a rural area of orchards, pastures, hedgerows, half-timbered farmhouses and stud farms, through picturesque villages such as **Cambremer** (www.cambremer.com) and **Beuvron-en-Auge**. Along the way, signs reading **Cru de Cambremer** indicate the way to about 20 small-scale, traditional producers who are happy to show you their facilities and sell you their home-grown cider (€3 a bottle) and Calvados. The area's AOC cider, made with a blend of apple varieties, is known for being fruity, tangy and slightly bitter – nothing like the mass-produced, pasteurised '*cidre*' sold in French supermarkets.

Traditional Normandy **cider** takes about six months to make. The apples are shaken off the trees – traditionally planted only 100 per hectare to ensure maximum sunlight – or gathered from the ground sometime between early October and early December. After being stored for two or three weeks to let them mature, they are pressed. The next step is *défécation* (purification), a process that separates the *chapeau brun* ('brown hat'), ie the floating solid matter, from the clear juice, which is then slow-fermented at 10°C or less for three months. Finally, the partly fermented juice is bottled – using a bottling machine towed from farm to farm by a tractor – with just the right amount of yeast so that over the course of two months, the cider becomes naturally carbonated (but not explosively so) inside the bottle, just like Champagne (p79). Alcohol levels range from about 3% for *doux* (sweet) to 4% or 5% for *brut* (dry), with *demi-sec* (semi-dry) coming in at 3% or 4%.

Making **Calvados** (apple brandy) – 'the finest destiny of the apple' – takes even longer. First the raw apple juice – including the solid matter left by the pressing – is fermented for six months, with a fast fermentation followed by a slow one. When all the sugar has turned to alcohol, the juice is distilled, usually twice. The resulting liquid is clear but takes on a delicate golden colour from the oak casks in which it's aged for anything from two years to many decades. As with Cognac (p668), ageing ends the moment Calvados is bottled.

Another Normandy favourite is **pommeau**, an amber-coloured aperitif made by mixing unfermented apple juice with Calvados.

Information

Deauville Post Office (rue Robert Fossorier) Exchanges currency.

Deauville Tourist Office (☎ 02 31 14 40 00; www.deauville.org; place de la Mairie; 🕑 9am-7pm Mon-Sat, 10am-6pm Sun & holidays Jul–mid-Sep, 10am-6pm Mon-Sat, 10am-1pm & 2-5pm Sun & holidays mid-Sep–Jun) Situated about 400m west of the train station. Can supply you with an English-language walking tour brochure and a Deauville map from which Trouville is completely missing.

Internet (per 15min €1) At the Trouville tourist office.

Laundrette (91 rue des Bains, Trouville; 🕑 7am-8pm)

Société Générale (9 place Morny, Deauville & 6 rue Victor Hugo, Trouville) Bank.

Trouville Tourist Office (☎ 02 31 14 60 70; www.trouvillesurmer.org; 32 bd Fernand Moureaux; 🕑 9.30am-7pm Mon-Sat, 10am-4pm Sun Jul & Aug, 9.30am-6.30pm Mon-Sat & 10am-1pm Sun Apr-Jun, Sep & Oct, 9.30am-6pm Mon-Sat & 10am-1pm Sun Nov-Mar) Situated about 200m north of pont des Belges. Has a free, Deauville-less map of Trouville and sells maps for a self-guided architectural tour and two rural walks (7km and 11km).

Sights & Activities

In Deauville, the rich and beautiful strut their stuff along the beachside **Promenade des Planches**, a 643m-long boardwalk lined with cabins named after famous Americans (mainly film stars), before swimming in the nearby 50m covered **Piscine Olympique** (Olympic swimming pool; 🕑 closed 3 wks in Jan & 2 wks in Jun) or losing a wad at the **casino** 200m inland. Trouville, too, has a **casino**, and a 583m **boardwalk** where you can swim in freshwater swimming pools, rent sailboats, windsurf and even surf. Nearby are lots of imposing **19th-century villas**.

The **Musée de Trouville** (☎ 02 31 88 16 26; 64 rue du Général Leclerc; adult/student €2/1.50; 🕑 11am-1pm & 2pm–5.30pm or 6pm Wed-Mon Easter–mid-Nov), in the fine Villa Montebello, is 1km to the northeast of the Trouville tourist office. With a panoramic view over the beach, the museum recounts Trouville's history and features works by Charles Mozin and Eugène Boudin.

Trouville's beach is home to the **Natur' Aquarium** (☎ 02 31 88 46 04; www.natur-aquarium.com, in French; 17 rue de Paris; adult/3-14yr €7/5; 🕑 10am-noon

& 2-6.30pm daily Easter-Jun, Sep & Oct, 10am-7pm Jul & Aug, 2-6pm Nov-Easter), an aquarium packed with multicoloured fish, fearsome reptiles and weird insects.

Festivals & Events

Deauville's 10-day **American Film Festival** (www.festival-deauville.com) is an altogether more welcoming affair than its better-known cousin at Cannes. Tickets for most screenings are on sale to the public, and you're bound to catch glimpses of a few Hollywood stars when the festival's in full swing in early September. There's also an **Asian Film Festival** (www.deauvilleasia.com) for five days in mid-March.

Deauville is renowned for its equestrian tradition. **Horse racing** takes place in July, August and October – with a few winter races – at two *hippodromes* (racetracks; www.hippodromesdedeauville.com, in French): La Touques for flat races; and Clairefontaine (www.hippodrome-deauville-clairefontaine.com) for flat, trotting and jumping races (steeplechases and hurdles).

Sleeping

Trouville offers much better accommodation value than Deauville. Prices are highest in July and August and on weekends, and lowest from October to Easter except during Paris' school holidays.

Le Trouville (☎ 02 31 98 45 48; www.hotelletrouville.com, in French; 1-5 rue Thiers, Trouville; s/d €40/58) This two-star, family-run hotel may be small and simple but the rates are great, especially considering its proximity to the beach. The colourful bedcovers and wallpaper add a hint of much-needed character to the 15 smallish rooms.

La Maison Normande (☎ 02 31 88 12 25; www.maisonnormande.com, in French; 4 place de Lattre de Tassigny, Trouville; d €46-66; ⊠) Stay in this late-17th-century Norman house and you'll feel like you're visiting your new Norman grandma. The 17 rooms are decorated in warm colours and some have views of the church. Situated right across from the church on rue Victor Hugo.

Le Fer à Cheval (☎ 02 31 98 30 20; www.hotel-trouville.com; 11 rue Victor Hugo, Trouville; d €85-97 Jul, Aug, Sat & holidays, €73-85 rest of year) Occupying three beautiful turn-of-the-20th-century buildings, this modern hotel has 34 comfortable rooms with big windows, horse-themed decor and bright bathrooms. Owned by a retired *boulanger* (baker) who loves to bake fresh croissants.

FRESH OYSTER PICNIC

The **Poissonnerie** (fish market; cnr bd Fernand Moureaux & rue des Bains, Trouville; 🕑 9am-7pm) is *the* place in Trouville to head for a waterfront picnic of fresh oysters with lemon (just €6.50 to €8.50 a dozen) – or for locally caught raw fish. Everything is fresh so no energy is wasted on freezing, and since there are almost no middlemen you pay reasonable prices and the fishermen get a fair share of the proceeds. It's housed in temporary stalls while the market building – which burned down in 2006 – is being rebuilt.

Eating

In Trouville, there are lots of restaurants along bd Fernand Moureaux and perpendicular rue des Bains.

Brasserie Le Central (☎ 02 31 88 13 68; 158 bd Fernand Moureaux, Trouville; menus €18.40-27.50; 🕑 7.30am-midnight or later) This buzzy brasserie adds a touch of Parisian class to the Trouville waterfront. The menu offers few surprises – fresh fish (all of it wild except for the salmon), mussels and seafood are the mainstays – but the atmosphere is fantastic on a summer evening.

SELF-CATERING

Champion (49 av de la République, Deauville; 🕑 9am-8pm Tue-Sat, 9am-1pm Sun) Supermarket.

Food market (🕑 Wed morning) In Trouville along bd Fernand Moureaux between pont des Belges and the Poissonnerie.

Monoprix (166 bd Fernand Moureaux, Trouville; 🕑 9am-7.30pm Mon-Sat) Supermarket.

Entertainment

Nightlife is centred in Deauville.

Bar Le Zoo (☎ 02 31 81 02 61; www.lezoo.fr, in French; 53 rue Désiré-le-Hoc, Deauville; 🕑 6pm-3am) A sleek and sophisticated urban-style hang-out, tailor-made for cocktails (€8.50) and checking out the beautiful people. Has a DJ from 10pm on Friday and Saturday, when you can dance in the cellar. The website has details on theme nights.

Shopping

Shopping in Deauville (for instance right around the casino and along rue Eugène Colas) tends towards well-known Parisian brand names, while Trouville features less-glitzy wares along its main commercial street, rue des Bains.

Getting There & Around

Nine-seat Pipers operated by **Skysouth** (☎ in UK 01273-446 400; www.skysouth.co.uk) link **Aéroport de Deauville-St-Gatien** (☎ 02 31 65 65 65; www.deauville.aeroport.fr), 10km northeast of Deauville and Trouville, with Brighton Shorham.

From next to Deauville's train station, **Bus Verts** (☎ 08 10 21 42 14; www.busverts.fr, in French) has hourly services to Caen (€5, 1¼ hours), Honfleur (€2, 40 minutes) and Le Havre (direct or via Honfleur; €6, 1¼ hour).

Except for a handful of direct trains to Paris' Gare St-Lazare (€27.40, 2¼ hours, six to nine daily), rail travel to and from Deauville and Trouville requires a change at Lisieux (€5.50, 20 minutes, eight to 12 daily). Destinations include Caen (€11.70, one hour, eight to 10 daily) and Rouen (€19.80, 1½ to two hours, four daily).

For a cab, call **Central Taxis** (☎ 02 31 87 11 11).

HONFLEUR

pop 8200

Long a favourite with painters but now more popular with the Parisian jet set, Honfleur is arguably Normandy's most charming seaside town.

Its heart is the Vieux Bassin (Old Harbour), from where explorers once set sail for the New World. Now filled with pleasure vessels, this part of the port is surrounded by a jumble of brightly coloured buildings that evoke maritime Normandy of centuries past.

History

Honfleur's seafaring tradition dates back over a millennium. After the Norman invasion of England in 1066, goods bound for the conquered isle were shipped across the Channel from here.

In 1608 Samuel de Champlain set sail from Honfleur on his way to founding Quebec City, and in 1681 Cavelier de La Salle set out from here to explore the New World, reaching the mouth of the Mississippi and naming the area Louisiana in honour of Louis XIV.

During the 17th and 18th centuries Honfleur achieved a degree of prosperity through maritime trade – including slave trade – with the west coast of Africa, the West Indies and the Azores.

Orientation

Honfleur's focal point is the rectangular Vieux Bassin. Along its northwest side is café-lined quai Ste-Catherine; on its northeast edge are the ancient stone Lieutenance building, the Avant Port (Outer Harbour) and a drawbridge; from its southwestern side, rue de la République, the town's main commercial thoroughfare, heads southwest; and on its southeast side lies an old quarter known as the Enclos.

The tourist office is south across the street from the Enclos' southern edge. From the Lieutenance, quai des Passagers leads 100m north to bd Charles V.

Information

CIC-Banque (7 quai Lepaulmier) Currency exchange across the little park from the tourist office.

Jardin des Peintres (11 bd Charles V; per hr €4; 🕑 9am-9pm, closed Wed) A café with internet computers and free wi-fi.

Laundrette (4 rue Notre Dame; 🕑 7am-8pm) Around the corner from the tourist office.

Médiathèque (quai Lepaulmier; per 30min €2.50; 🕑 2.30-6pm Tue-Fri, 2.30-5.30pm Sat, also open 9.30am or 10am–12.30pm Wed & Sat) This public library has several internet computers.

Post Office (7 cours Albert Manuel) On the southwestern continuation of rue de la République. Changes foreign currency.

Tourist Office (☎ 02 31 89 23 30; www.ot-honfleur.fr; quai Lepaulmier; 🕑 9.30am-7pm Mon-Sat, 10am-5pm Sun Jul & Aug, 9.30am-12.30pm & 2pm–6pm or 6.30pm Mon-Sat, 10am-12.30pm & 2-5pm Sep-Jun, closed Sun afternoon Oct–mid-Mar) Situated inside the Médiathèque (library) building. Has a free map detailing a 2km walking circuit. Internet access costs €5 for 30 minutes.

Sights

HARBOURS & WALKS

On the west side of the Vieux Bassin, with its many pleasure boats, **quai Ste-Catherine** is lined with tall, taper-thin houses – many protected from the elements by slate tiles – dating from the 16th to 18th centuries. The **Lieutenance**, at the mouth of the old harbour, was once the residence of the town's royal governor. The **Avant Port**, just northeast of the Lieutenance, is home to Honfleur's 30 or so fishing vessels, which moor in the area northeast of quai de la Quarantaine.

There are quite a few **art galleries** around Église Ste-Catherine (for instance on the

CAMEMBERT COUNTRY

Some of the most enduring names in the pungent world of French *fromage* come from Normandy, including **Pont L'Évêque, Livarot** and, most famous of all, **Camembert**, all of which are named after towns south of Honfleur, on or near the D579.

It's thought that monks first began experimenting with cheese-making in the Pays d'Auge sometime in the 11th century, but the present-day varieties didn't emerge until around the 17th century. The invention of Camembert is generally credited to Marie Herel, who was supposedly given the secret of soft cheese–making by an abbot from Brie on the run from Revolutionary mobs in 1790. Whatever the truth of the legend, the cheese was a huge success at the local market in Vimoutiers, and production of Camembert quickly grew from a cottage industry into an international operation – it even received the imperial seal of approval from Napoleon III at the World Fair in 1855.

Since 1983 the Camembert name has been protected by an official AOC (Appellation d'Origine Contrôlée) designation, just like fine French wines. Between 10,000 and 15,000 tonnes of Camembert are produced in Normandy every year and it remains one of the country's most popular cheeses – two-thirds of French cheese buyers consider it an essential element of any self-respecting cheeseboard.

Camembert is traditionally made from unpasteurised cow's milk and requires two special moulds – *Penicillium candida* and *Penicillium camemberti* – to mature, a process that usually takes around three weeks. The distinctive round wooden boxes in which Camembert is wrapped have been around since 1890; they were designed by a local engineer by the name of Monsieur Ridel to protect the soft disk during long-distance travel.

If you're interested in seeing how the cheese is made, you can take a guided tour of the **Président Farm** (☎ 02 33 36 06 60; www.fermepresident.com; adult/child €5/2; 🕑 10am-noon & 2-6pm Jun-Aug, by reservation Mar-May, Sep & Oct), an early 19th-century farm restored by Président, one of the region's largest Camembert producers. It's in the centre of the town of Camembert, which is about 60km south of Honfleur.

And in case you're new to the world of Camembert, here are a couple of tips from those in the know. Most French people squeeze their cheese before buying it to test its ripeness – the texture should be soft, but not runny. A good Camembert should have a white rind with a sprinkling of reddish spots, and the taste should be strong and quite fruity. Remove it from the fridge a couple of hours before eating and let it rest at room temperature. Serve on crusty French bread.

narrow cobblestone streets northwest of place Hamelin) and in the Enclos quarter.

Honfleur is superb for aimless ambling. One option is to head north from the Lieutenance along quai des Passagers to **Jetée de l'Ouest** (Western Jetty), which forms the west side of the Avant Port, out to the broad mouth of the Seine. Possible stops include the **Jardin des Personalités**, a park featuring figures from Honfleur history; **Naturospace** (☎ 02 31 81 77 00; www.naturospace.com, in French; bd Charles V; adult/under 15yr €7.70/5.90; 🕑 10am-1pm & 2-7pm Apr-Sep, to 5.30pm Feb, Mar, Oct & Nov, 10am-7pm Jul & Aug), a tropical greenhouse filled with 60 different species of free-flying butterflies; and the **beach**.

Built between 1600 and 1613, **Chapelle Notre Dame de Grâce** is at the top of the Plateau de Grâce, a wooded, 100m-high hill about 2km west of the Vieux Bassin. There's a great view of the town and port.

ÉGLISE STE-CATHERINE

Initially intended as a temporary structure, this extraordinary **church** (place Ste-Catherine; 🕑 9am-6pm Easter-Sep, to 5.15pm Oct-Easter) has been standing in the square for over 500 years. Built by the people of Honfleur during the late 15th and early 16th centuries after its stone predecessor had been destroyed during the Hundred Years' War, wood was used in an effort to save funds for strengthening the fortifications around the Enclos. The structure is particularly notable for its double-vaulted roof and its twin naves, which from the inside resemble a couple of overturned ships' hulls.

Across the square is the church's free-standing wooden bell tower, **Clocher Ste-Catherine** (☎ 02 31 89 54 00; admission €2; 🕑 10am-noon & 2-6pm Wed-Mon mid-Mar–Sep, 2.30-5pm Mon & Wed-Fri, 10am-noon & 2.30-5pm Sat & Sun Oct–mid-Nov, closed mid-Nov–mid-Mar), supposedly built away from the church in order to avoid lightning strikes and damage from the clock's clanging bells.

MUSÉE EUGÈNE BOUDIN

Named in honour of Eugène Boudin, an early Impressionist painter born here in 1824, this **museum** (☎ 02 31 89 54 00; opposite 50 rue de l'Homme de Bois; adult/student & senior €4.70/3, Jul-Sep €5.40/3.90; 🕑 10am-noon & 2-6pm Wed-Mon mid-Mar–Sep, 2.30-5pm Mon & Wed-Fri, 10am-noon & 2.30-5pm Sat & Sun Oct–mid-Mar) is three blocks northwest of the Lieutenance. It features a collection of Impressionist paintings from Normandy, including works by Dubourg, Dufy and Monet. One room is devoted to Boudin, whom Baudelaire called the 'king of skies' for his luscious skyscapes.

LES MAISONS SATIE

The quirky **Les Maisons Satie** (☎ 02 31 89 11 11; 67 bd Charles V; adult/student & senior/under 10yr €5.40/3.90/free; 🕑 10am-7pm Wed-Mon May-Sep, 11am-6pm Wed-Mon Oct-Apr, closed Jan) captures the spirit of the eccentric, avant-garde composer Erik Satie (1866–1925), who lived and worked in Honfleur and was born in the half-timbered house that now contains the museum. 'Esoteric' Satie was known for his surrealistic wit as much as for his starkly beautiful piano compositions. Visitors wander through the museum with a headset playing Satie's music and excerpts from his writings (in French or English). Each room is a surreal surprise – winged pears and self-pedalling carousels are just the start.

MUSÉE DE LA MARINE

Located in the Enclos quarter, the **Musée de la Marine** (☎ 02 31 89 14 12; quai St-Etienne; adult/student & senior €3.30/2.10; 🕑 10am-noon & 2-6.30pm Tue-Sun Apr-Sep, 2.30-5.30pm Tue-Fri, 10am-noon & 2.30-5.30pm Sat & Sun Oct–mid-Nov & mid-Feb–Mar, closed mid-Nov–mid-Feb) has nautically themed displays of model ships, carpenters' tools and engravings. It is inside the deconsecrated 13th- and 14th-century Église St-Étienne.

MUSÉE D'ETHNOGRAPHIE ET D'ART POPULAIRE NORMAND

Next to the Musée de la Marine, the **Musée d'Ethnographie et d'Art Populaire Normand** (rue de la Prison; adult/student & senior €3.30/2.10; 🕑 10am-noon & 2-6.30pm Tue-Sun Apr-Sep, 2.30-5.30pm Tue-Fri, 10am-noon & 2.30-5.30pm Sat & Sun Oct–mid-Nov & mid-Feb–Mar, closed mid-Nov–mid-Feb) occupies a couple of period houses and a former prison. Its nine rooms re-create the world of Honfleur during the 16th to 19th centuries using a mix of costumes, furniture and artefacts. A combined ticket with the Musée de la Marine costs €4.50 for adults, or €2.90 for students and seniors.

> **PONT DE NORMANDIE**
>
> Opened in 1995, this futuristic bridge (€5 each way) stretches in a soaring 2km arch over the Seine between Le Havre to Honfleur. It's a typically French affair, as much sophisticated architecture as engineering, with two huge V-shaped columns – somewhat reminiscent of giant toast tongs – holding aloft a delicate net of cables. Crossing is quite a thrill – and the views of the Seine are magnificent. In each direction there's a narrow footpath and a bike lane.

Tours

Some of the tourist office's 1½- to two-hour **walking tours** (€7) of Honfleur are in English, including one that leaves at 3pm every Wednesday in May and June and from September to mid-October. Atmospheric night-time tours begin at 9pm on Friday and Saturday in May and June and from September to mid-October, and on Saturday in July and August.

From about March to mid-October, you can take a **boat tour** from the Avant Port (across the street from the Lieutenance) out to the Seine Estuary and the Pont de Normandie (above) – look for the *Cap Christian*, *L'Évasion III* or the larger *Jolie France*.

Sleeping

Etap Hôtel (☎ 08 92 68 07 81; rue des Vases; www.etaphotel.com; d €38.60-46.60) Has 63 cheap, charmless, chain-hotel rooms.

Hôtel Belvédère (☎ 02 31 89 08 13; www.hotel-belvedere-honfleur.com; 36 rue Emile Renouf; d €66) Offering the best value in town, this cosy, welcoming hotel has nine well-kept rooms, some with views of the Pont de Normandie, others of the delightful, grassy back garden. Situated 1km southeast of the tourist office.

Hôtel du Dauphin (☎ 02 31 89 15 53; www.hoteldudauphin.com; 10 place Pierre-Berthelot; d €69-98, q €139) Behind a 17th-century, slate and half-timbered facade, this welcoming hotel has 34 modern, smallish rooms with brass lamps and marine prints. The pricier rooms even have spa bathtubs with water jets. Situated one block south of Église Ste-Catherine.

Hôtel L'Écrin (☎ 02 31 14 43 45; www.honfleur.com/default-ecrin.htm; 19 rue Eugène Boudin; d €100-190, ste €220-250;) The parlour and public spaces of this lavish Norman manor house are stuffed with porcelain, oil paintings and antique furniture, re-creating the opulence of times long past. The 30 three-star rooms, which come with thoroughly modern bathrooms, retain touches of the 1800s – alongside thin-screen TVs hung on the walls like oil paintings. To get here from Église Ste-Catherine, go southwest along rue Brûlée and turn right.

our pick **La Maison de Lucie** (☎ 02 31 14 40 40; www.lamaisondelucie.com; 44 rue des Capucins; d €150-220, ste €315) Former home of the novelist Lucie Delarue Mardrus (1874–1945), this marvellous little hideaway has just 10 rooms and two suites, the latter decorated with a mixture of antiques and contemporary objects d'art from far-off lands. Some of the bedrooms, panelled in oak, have Moroccan-tile bathrooms and boast fantastic views across the harbour to the Pont de Normandie. The shady terrace is a glorious place for a summer breakfast. There's a chic jacuzzi in the old brick-vaulted cellar. Situated five short blocks west of the Lieutenance.

Eating

Quai Ste-Catherine is lined with brasseries and restaurants with warm-season terraces, chock-a-block with sharply dressed Parisians on summer weekends. More eateries can be found around place Hamelin and adjacent rue de l'Homme de Bois, one block northwest of the Lieutenance, and on the cobblestone streets just north of the tourist office.

La Cidrerie (☎ 02 31 89 59 85; 26 place Hamelin; menu incl drink €10.90; closed Tue & Wed except Jul, Aug & school holidays) This tidy little crêperie – down a short alleyway – is a good find if you fancy washing your meal down with *cidre Normand*.

La Tortue (☎ 02 31 81 24 60; www.restaurantlatortue.fr, in French; 36 rue de l'Homme de Bois; lunch menu €13, other menus €19-34; closed Tue & dinner Mon Oct-Mar) This traditionally styled eatery serves up French cuisine with Norman touches, offering four meat and six fish mains. Starters include oysters in aniseed sauce (€9). Situated two blocks northwest of the Lieutenance.

L'Ascot (☎ 02 31 98 87 91; 76 quai Ste-Catherine; menus €24.50-30.50; closed Tue) A great spot for fresh seafood on a summer evening, with tightly packed tables on the outside terrace and an intimate candle-lit ambience inside. Also serves eight kinds of fish and several steak options.

L'Absinthe (☎ 02 31 89 39 00; 10 quai de la Quarantaine; menus €33-68; lunch & dinner) Facing the Vieux Port, this well-regarded restaurant serves up sumptuous, sophisticated French cuisine – made with seasonally fresh products – in the finest *gastronomique* tradition. Specialities include fillet of bass, roasted pigeon and blue Breton lobster. It's a good idea to reserve ahead for Saturday dinner and Sunday lunch.

SELF-CATERING

There are several food shops along rue de la République.

Champion (opp 55 rue de la République; 8.30am-12.30pm & 2.30-7.30pm Mon-Sat, no midday closure Sat) Supermarket.

Food market (place Ste-Catherine; 8am-1pm Sat)

Organic food market (place Ste-Catherine; 8am-1pm Wed)

Petit Casino (16 quai Lepaulmier; 8am-1pm & 3-8pm Tue-Fri, no midday closure Sat, to 7pm Sun) A supermarket a block east of the tourist office.

Drinking

Café L'Albatros (☎ 02 31 89 25 30; 32 quai Ste-Catherine; 8am-1am Oct-Apr, to 2am May-Sep) Sailors, students, philosophers and layabouts are all at home at this café-bar, from breakfast through sandwiches and beer and on to nightcaps. Serves light meals till 10pm.

Le Perroquet Vert (☎ 02 31 89 14 19; 52 quai Ste-Catherine; 8am-1am Oct-Mar, to 2am Apr-Sep) The brick-vaulted 'green parrot' has an excellent selection of beers and a fine terrace for people-watching. Serves breakfast, afternoon sandwiches (noon to 3pm) and tapas (7pm to closing).

Getting There & Around

The **bus station** (☎ 02 31 89 28 41) is two blocks east of the tourist office. Bus 20, operated by **Bus Verts** (☎ 08 10 21 42 14; www.busverts.fr, in French), goes via Deauville and Trouville (€2, 30 minutes) to Caen (€7, two hours, 12 daily Monday to Saturday, six Sunday) and, in the other direction, to Le Havre (€4, 30 minutes, eight daily Monday to Saturday, four Sunday) via the Pont de Normandie. There's also an express bus to Caen (€9.80, one hour).

To catch the train (eg to Paris), take the bus to Deauville, Le Havre or Lisieux (€4, 50 minutes, four or five daily).

Free parking is available next to Naturospace, which is 600m from the Avant Port on bd Charles V. East of the Avant Port at Parking du Mole, you can park all day for €2.

MANCHE

The Manche *département* (www.manchetourisme.com) encompasses the entire Cotentin Peninsula, stretching from Utah Beach northwest to Cherbourg and southwest to the magnificent Mont St-Michel. The peninsula's northwest corner is especially captivating, with unspoiled stretches of rocky coastline sheltering tranquil bays and villages. The fertile inland areas, criss-crossed with hedgerows, produce an abundance of cattle, dairy products and apples. The British crown dependencies of Jersey and Guernsey lie 22km and 48km offshore, respectively.

Manche is also known for its nuclear facilities, including an electricity-generating complex at Flamanville, a reprocessing facility at Cap de la Hague and a shipyard for building nuclear submarines at Cherbourg.

For details on Utah Beach, see p288.

CHERBOURG

pop 40,500

At the top of the Cotentin Peninsula sits Cherbourg, the largest – but hardly the most appealing – town in this part of Normandy. Transatlantic cargo ships, passenger ferries from Britain and Ireland, yachts and warships pass in and out of Cherbourg's monumental port. During WWII, most of the petrol used by the Allied armies during the Normandy campaign was supplied by an underwater pipeline laid from England to Cherbourg shortly after D-Day.

Modern-day Cherbourg – now united with adjacent Octeville – is a far cry from the romantic city portrayed in Jacques Demy's 1964 film *Les Parapluies de Cherbourg* (The Umbrellas of Cherbourg) but it's a useful base if you're crossing the Channel by ferry.

Orientation

The city centre is west of the Bassin du Commerce, with lots of shopping around rue Maréchal Foch and the pedestrian streets north of there. The attractive Avant Port (Outer Harbour) is north of pont Tournant; further north, east across the harbour entrance from the pleasure port, is Cité de la Mer, with the ferry terminal further east.

Information

Archesys (☎ 02 33 53 04 93; 16 rue de l'Union; per 6min/hr €0.50/5; 🕑 11.30am-10pm Tue-Fri, 11.30am-midnight Sat, 2-10pm Sun) Internet access.

Change Bourse Monnaies (☎ 02 33 20 08 27; 53 rue Maréchal Foch; 🕑 8.30am-12.15pm & 1.45-6.15pm Mon-Fri & 8.30am-12.15pm Sat) Currency exchange.

Forum Espace Culture (☎ 02 33 78 19 30; place Centrale; per 10/30min €1.50/2.35; 🕑 2-7pm Mon, 10am-7pm Tue-Sat) This bookshop has an internet café on the upper floor.

Laundrette (62 rue au Blé; 🕑 7am-8pm)

Post Office (1 rue de l'Ancien Quai) Exchanges currency.

Tourist Office (☎ 02 33 93 52 02; www.ot-cherbourg-cotentin.fr; 2 quai Alexandre III; 🕑 9am-noon & 2-6pm Mon-Sat Sep-Jun, to 6.30pm Jul & Aug) Has useful information on visiting the city, the Cotentin Peninsula and D-Day sites.

Tourist Office Annexe (☎ 02 33 44 39 92; ferry terminal) Open for ferry arrivals.

Sights & Activities

Housed in Cherbourg's art-deco transatlantic ferry terminal, built in the 1930s, **Cité de la Mer** (☎ 02 33 20 26 26; www.citedelamer.com; Gare Maritime Transatlantique; adult/child €14/10; 🕑 9.30am-7pm Jul & Aug, 9.30am-6.30pm May, Jun, Sep & school holidays, 10am-6pm Feb-Apr & Oct-Dec, closed Jan) is both an aquarium – the deepest in Europe – and a showcase for French submarine prowess. This may be your only chance to go inside a French nuclear submarine, *Le Redoubtable*, in service from 1967 to 1991.

Musée Thomas Henry (☎ 02 33 23 39 30; 4 rue Vastel; admission free; 🕑 10am-noon & 2-6pm Tue-Sat, 2-6pm Sun & Mon May-Sep, 2-6pm Wed-Sun Oct-Apr) has 300 works by French and European artists, including Fra Angelico, David, Camille Claudel and Cotentin-born Jean-François Millet.

Sleeping

Auberge de Jeunesse (☎ 02 33 78 15 15; www.fuaj.org; 55 rue de l'Abbaye; dm €16.80; 🕑 check-in 9am-1pm & 6pm-11pm; 💻) Situated 1km northwest of the tourist office, this 99-bed hostel, opened in 1998 in the French navy's old archives buildings, has a small kitchen for self-caterers. Rooms have two to five beds. Take bus 3 or 5 to the Hôtel de Ville stop.

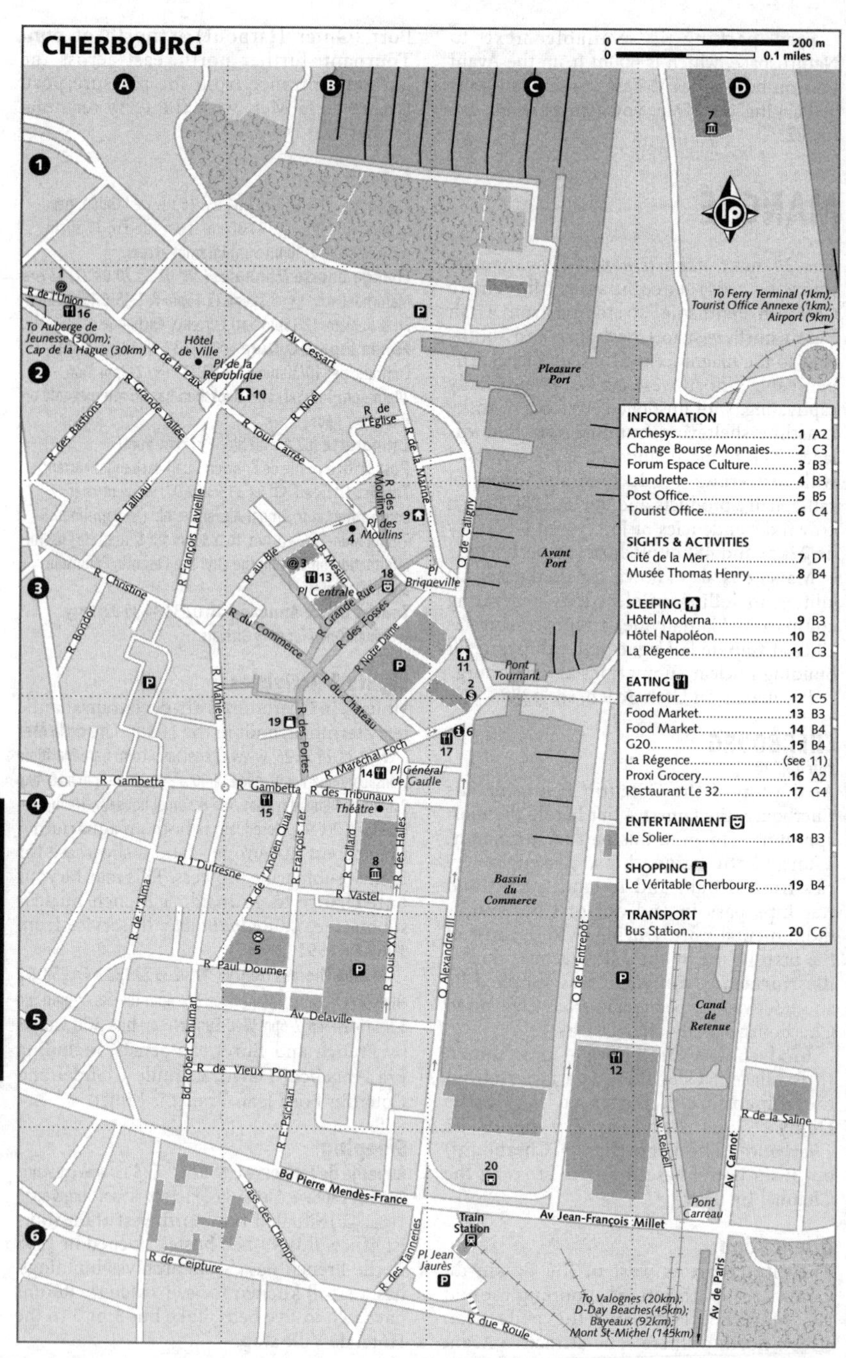
CHERBOURG
0 200 m
0 0.1 miles
A
B
C
D
1
2
3
4
5
6
To Ferry Terminal (1km); Tourist Office Annexe (1km); Airport (9km)
To Auberge de Jeunesse (300m); Cap de la Hague (30km)
R de l'Union
Hôtel de Ville
Pl de la République
Av Cessart
R de la Paix
R Grande Vallée
R des Bastions
R Noël
R Tour Carrée
R de l'Église
R de la Marine
R des Moulins
Pl des Moulins
Pleasure Port
Avant Port
Q de Caligny
R Talluau
R François Lavieille
R au Blé
R B Meslin
Pl Centrale
R Grande Rue
R des Fossés
Pl Briqueville
R Christine
R Bondor
R du Commerce
R Notre Dame
R Mahieu
R du Château
Pont Tournant
R des Portes
R Maréchal Foch
Pl Général de Gaulle
R Gambetta
R des Tribunaux
Théâtre
R J Dufresne
R de l'Ancien Quai
R François 1er
R Collard
R des Halles
R Vastel
R de l'Alma
Bassin du Commerce
R Paul Doumer
R Louis XVI
Q Alexandre III
Q de l'Entrepôt
Av Delaville
Canal de Retenue
Bd Robert Schuman
R de Vieux Pont
R E Psichari
Av Reibell
R de la Saline
Av Carnot
Bd Pierre Mendès-France
Pass des Champs
Av Jean-François Millet
Pont Carreau
Train Station
R des Tanneries
Pl Jean Jaurès
R de Ceinture
Av de Paris
R due Roule
To Valognes (20km); D-Day Beaches (45km); Bayeux (92km); Mont St-Michel (145km)
INFORMATION
Archesys 1 A2
Change Bourse Monnaies 2 C3
Forum Espace Culture 3 B3
Laundrette 4 B3
Post Office 5 B5
Tourist Office 6 C4
SIGHTS & ACTIVITIES
Cité de la Mer 7 D1
Musée Thomas Henry 8 B4
SLEEPING
Hôtel Moderna 9 B3
Hôtel Napoléon 10 B2
La Régence 11 C3
EATING
Carrefour 12 C5
Food Market 13 B3
Food Market 14 B4
G20 15 B4
La Régence (see 11)
Proxi Grocery 16 A2
Restaurant Le 32 17 C4
ENTERTAINMENT
Le Solier 18 B3
SHOPPING
Le Véritable Cherbourg 19 B4
TRANSPORT
Bus Station 20 C6

NORMANDY

Hôtel Napoléon (☎ 02 33 93 32 32; www.hotel-napoleon.fr; 14 place de la République; s €24-40, d €35-52) In one of the area's few surviving 19th-century buildings, the Napoléon offers 14 upbeat, pastel bedrooms, some with a limited view across the port.

Hôtel Moderna (☎ 02 33 43 05 30; www.moderna-hotel.com; 28 rue de la Marine; s €36-42, d €41-51, q €67; ☒) In a classic 1950s building, this friendly hotel has 25 rooms whose rich colours add a warm, homey feeling. Has a patio for breakfast. Excellent value.

La Régence (☎ 02 33 43 05 16; www.laregence.com; 42-44 quai de Caligny; d €51-99) This three-star Logis de France establishment offers 21 tasteful, well-kept rooms (most of modest size) with brass light fittings. The pricier rooms have great harbour views.

Eating & Entertainment

Restaurants can be found north of the tourist office on quai de Caligny and northwest along rue Tour Carrée and rue de la Paix.

Restaurant Le 32 (☎ 02 33 94 30 39; 32 rue Maréchal Foch; 2-/3-course menus €10.50/20; closed Sun, Mon & holidays) Good-value, home-made French cuisine is the order of the day at this unpretentious, family-run *resto*. Specialities include beef carpaccio and scallops on skewers.

La Régence (☎ 02 33 43 05 16; 42-44 quai de Caligny; mains €19-34; lunch & dinner) An old-time French restaurant with traditional fish, seafood and meat mains. Specialities include mussels, fish soup and *tartiflette au Camembert*.

Le Solier (☎ 02 33 94 76 63; 52 rue Grande Rue; 6pm-1am Tue-Sat Oct-May, to 2am Jun-Sep) Opened in 1982, this convivial place is a cross between an English pub and a French bar. Hosts live traditional Irish music on the 2nd Thursday of the month and jazz the last Thursday.

SELF-CATERING

Carrefour (quai de l'Entrepôt; 8.30am-9pm Mon-Sat, to 9.30pm Fri) Supermarket.

Food markets place Centrale & around (to 4pm Thu & morning Sat); place Général de Gaulle (Tue morning)

G20 (57 rue Gambetta; 8.30am-7.30pm Mon-Sat) Supermarket.

Proxi grocery (15 rue de l'Union; 8.30am-8.30pm Mon-Sat, 9am-12.45pm & 5-8pm Sun & holidays)

Shopping

For a fine selection of top-quality *parapluies* (umbrellas), check out **Le Véritable Cherbourg** (☎ 02 33 93 23 77; www.parapluie-cherbourg.com; 30 rue des Portes; closed Mon morning & Sun). Prices range from €85 to €150.

Getting There & Away

Cherbourg is 92km northwest of Bayeux and 145km north of Mont St-Michel.

For details on car ferry services from Cherbourg's **ferry terminal** (www.port-cherbourg.com) to Poole, Portsmouth and Rosslare (Ireland), see p968 and p967.

Direct trains go to Paris' Gare St-Lazare (€41.20, 3½ hours, two to four direct daily), Bayeux (€14.60, one hour, 11 daily Monday to Friday, three to five daily weekends) and Caen (€18.40, 1¼ hours, seven to 13 daily). With a change at Lison, there are services to Coutances (€17.30, 1½ hours, five to 10 daily) and Pontorson (Mont St-Michel; €24.50, 2¼ hours, two daily).

Getting Around

In the warm months, a shuttle-bus service links the ferry terminal with the town centre and the train station.

For a taxi, call ☎ 02 33 53 36 38. A daytime trip between the train station and ferry terminal costs about €9.

COUTANCES

pop 9500

A fine Norman Gothic cathedral and a lovely landscape garden make Coutances, a medieval hilltop town 77km south of Cherbourg, worth a stop, perhaps on the way to or from Mont St-Michel.

Orientation & Information

The main north–south street is known as rue Geoffroy de Montbray south of the cathedral and place du Parvis (home of the town hall), and as rue Tancrède north of there. The train and bus stations are 1km southeast of the cathedral.

Post Office (10 rue St-Dominique) Exchanges money.

Tourist Office (☎ 02 33 19 08 10; tourismecoutances@wanadoo.fr; place Georges Leclerc; 9.30am-6.30pm Mon-Sat, 10am-1pm Sun Jul & Aug, 9.30am-12.30pm & 2-6pm Mon-Fri, no midday closure Thu, 10am-noon & 2-5pm Sat Sep-Jun) Around the side of the battle-scarred town hall, which is on the square in front of the cathedral. Has several excellent brochures on Coutances. Internet costs €2 per hour.

Sights & Activities

Built on elements left over from its 11th-century Romanesque predecessor, the

PARC NATUREL RÉGIONAL DU COTENTIN ET DU BESSIN

Inland from Utah Beach, to the south and southwest, is the 1450-sq-km **Parc Naturel Régional du Cotentin et du Bessin** (www.parc-cotentin-bessin.fr), with its waterways, marshes, moors and hedgerows. For details on hiking and cycling in the park and elsewhere in the Manche *département*, see www.mancherandonnee.com (in French).

13th-century **Cathédrale de Coutances** (admission free; 9am-7pm) has an airy, if sober, Norman Gothic design enhanced by the use of light-hued limestone.

Interior highlights include several 13th-century windows, a 14th-century fresco of St Michel skewering the dragon, and an organ and high altar from the mid-1700s. You can climb the lantern tower on a **tour** (adult/student €6.50/5.50; in French 11am & 3pm Mon-Fri, 3pm Sun Jul & Aug, in English 11.45am Tue Jul & Aug). The tourist office has an excellent trilingual brochure on the cathedral.

About 100m west of the tourist office, across the square, is the splendid **Jardin des Plantes** (9am-11.30pm Jul & Aug, 9am-8pm Apr-Jun & Sep, 9am-5pm Oct-Mar), a grand landscape garden laid out in the 1850s that mixes French-, Italian- and English-style elements in its terraces, flower beds, fountains, statues and maze. On summer evenings (July and August), classical music wafts through the gardens

Both the cathedral and gardens light up with a son-et-lumière (sound-and-light) show on summer nights.

Sleeping

Hôtel La Pocatière (☎ 02 33 45 13 77; www.hotelapocatiere.com; 25 bd Alsace-Lorraine, D971; d €29-49, q €63) Situated at the northern tip of the old city (750m north of the cathedral), this welcoming two-star hotel has 18 spotless, newly renovated rooms with red or blue drapes, cheery wallpaper and bright little bathrooms.

Hotel La Taverne du Parvis (☎ 02 33 45 13 55; latavernedu parvis@wanadoo.fr; place du Parvis; s/d/q €34/43/57) Facing the cathedral's west facade, this brasserie-cum-hotel has 12 good-value rooms without frills, some with great cathedral views.

Eating

Several restaurants are clustered around the tourist office. Food shops can be found on rue Tancrède.

La Taverne du Parvis (☎ 02 33 45 13 55; place du Parvis; 2-course lunch menu €12.50, other menus €21.50) A popular café-brasserie facing the cathedral.

SELF-CATERING

Food market (place du Général de Gaulle; 7am-1pm Thu) Below the retaining wall at the back of the cathedral garden. Look for the delicious local Coutances cheese.

Marché Plus (23 rue Tancrède; 7am-9pm Mon-Sat, 9am-1pm Sun) Supermarket about 100m north of the cathedral.

Getting There & Around

The SNCF runs buses to the seaside town of Granville (€7.20, 30 minutes, three or four daily, more in summer). Bus 110, operated by **Manéo** (☎ 08 00 15 00 50; www.mobi50.com, in French), goes to several beaches south of Gouville-sur-Mer.

Train destinations include Bayeux (€11.40, 50 minutes, eight daily Monday to Saturday, four Sunday), Cherbourg (€17.30, 1½ hours, five to 10 daily) and Pontorson (Mont St-Michel; €10.50, 40 minutes, two or three daily).

City centre parking is free if your car is not registered in the Manche *département*.

MONT ST-MICHEL

pop 46

It's one of France's most iconic images: the slender towers and sky-scraping turrets of the abbey of Mont St-Michel rising from stout ramparts and battlements, the whole ensemble connected to the mainland by a narrow causeway. Fortunately, although it's visited by huge numbers of tourists, both French and foreign, the Mont still manages to whisk you back to the Middle Ages, its fantastic architecture set against the backdrop of the area's extraordinary tides.

The bay around Mont St-Michel is famed for having Europe's highest tidal variations. Depending on the gravitational pull of the moon and the sun (greatest 36 to 48 hours after the full and new moon, when both bodies are lined up with the earth), the difference between low and high tides can reach an astonishing 15m, although the Mont is only completely surrounded by the sea every month or two, when the tidal coefficient is above 100 and high tide above 14m. Regardless of the time of year, the waters sweep in at an astonishing clip, said to be as fast as a galloping horse. At low tide the Mont is surrounded by bare sand for kilometres around, but at high tide, barely six hours later, the whole bay – including some of the Mont's car parks – can be submerged.

Be prepared for lots of steps, some of them spiral – alas, the Mont is one of the least wheelchair-accessible sites in France.

Mont St-Michel's 1300th anniversary is being celebrated in 2008 and 2009 – the tourist office website has details on events.

History

According to Celtic mythology, Mont St-Michel was one of the sea tombs to which the souls of the dead were sent. Bishop Aubert of Avranches is said to have built a devotional chapel at the summit of the island in 708, following his vision of the Archangel Michael, whose gilded figure, perched on the vanquished dragon, crowns the tip of the abbey's spire. In 966 Richard I, duke of Normandy, gave Mont St-Michel to the Benedictines, who turned it into a centre of learning and, in the 11th century, into something of an ecclesiastical fortress, with a military garrison at the disposal of the abbot and the king.

In the 15th century, during the Hundred Years' War, the English blockaded and besieged Mont St-Michel three times. The fortified abbey withstood these assaults and was the only place in western and northern France not to fall into English hands. After the Revolution, Mont St-Michel was turned into a prison. In 1966 the abbey was symbolically returned to the Benedictines as part of the celebrations marking its millennium. Mont St-Michel and the bay became a Unesco World Heritage Site in 1979.

Orientation

The only opening in the ramparts, Porte de l'Avancée, is to the left at the end of the causeway. The Mont's single street – an alley deceptively called Grande Rue – is lined with restaurants, a few hotels and an exuberant array of tacky souvenir shops.

There are several large car parks (€4 per day) along the causeway. Unless you're trying to get rid of your car in an insurance scam, it's a good idea to pay attention to the signs that warn visitors which areas will soon be under water due to the incoming tide. Tides above 13.10m submerge the two lots closest to the Mont.

Pontorson (population 4200), the nearest real town to Mont St-Michel, is 9km to the south and is the base for many travellers. The north–south-oriented D976 links Mont St-Michel with Pontorson's main thoroughfare, east–west-oriented rue du Couesnon.

Information

Internet – Mont St-Michel (Hôtel de la Croix Blanche, Grande Rue; per hr €4) If you're so addicted to email that not even one of the glories of the Middle Ages can tear you away, this hotel, halfway up the Grande Rue, has a terminal.

Internet – Pontorson (per 30min/1hr €4.50/8) In the tourist office.

Post Office – Mont St-Michel (Grande Rue) Changes currency and has an ATM.

Post Office – Pontorson (place de l'Hôtel de Ville) Changes currency.

Tourist Office – Mont St-Michel (☎ 02 33 60 14 30; www.ot-montsaintmichel.com; 🕑 9am-7pm Jul & Aug, 9am-12.30pm & 2-6.30pm Mon-Sat, 9am-noon & 2-6pm Sun Apr-Jun & Sep, 9am-noon & 2-6pm Mon-Sat, 10am-noon & 2-5pm Sun Oct-Mar) Just inside Porte de l'Avancée, up the stairs to the left. An *horaire des marées* (tide table) is posted just inside the door. A detailed map of the Mont costs €3.

Tourist Office – Pontorson (☎ 02 33 60 20 65; www.mont-saint-michel-baie.com, in French; place de l'Hôtel de Ville; 🕑 9am-12.30pm & 2-6.30pm Mon-Fri, 10am-12.30pm & 3-6.30pm Sat, 10am-noon Sun Jul & Aug, 9am-noon & 2-6pm Mon-Fri, 10am-noon & 3-6pm Sat Sep-Jun) Has details on traversing the Bay of Mont St-Michel on foot and on local events. Situated on rue St-Michel half a block south of rue Couesnon.

Société Générale (Mont St-Michel) ATM just inside Porte de l'Avancée.

Sights

ABBAYE DU MONT ST-MICHEL

The Mont's major attraction is the stunning **abbey** (☎ 02 33 89 80 00; www.monuments-nationaux.fr; adult/18-25yr/under 18yr incl guided tour €8.50/5/free; 🕑 9am-7pm May-Aug, 9.30am-6pm Sep-Apr, last entry 1hr before closing), at the top of the Grande Rue and up a steep stairway. From Monday to Saturday in July and August, there are illuminated *nocturnes* (night-time visits) with music from 7pm to 10pm.

Most rooms can be visited without a guide but it's worth taking the one-hour tour, included in the ticket price. The frequency of English tours ranges from twice a day (11am and 3pm) in the dead of winter to hourly in summer; the last leaves at least 1½ hours before closing time. Audioguides (one for €4, two for €6) are available in six languages. Don't forget to pick up the excellent brochure-guide, available in 10 languages.

The **Église Abbatiale** (Abbey Church) was built at the rocky tip of the mountain cone. The transept rests on solid rock, while the nave, choir and transept arms are supported by the rooms below. The church is famous for its mix of architectural styles: the nave and south transept (11th and 12th centuries) are solid Norman Romanesque, while the choir (late 15th century) is Flamboyant Gothic. Mass is held at 12.15pm from Tuesday to Sunday and at 11.30am on Sunday.

The buildings on the northern side of the Mont are known as **La Merveille** (The Marvel). The famous **cloître** (cloister) is surrounded by a double row of delicately carved arches resting on granite pillars. The early-13th-century, barrel-roofed **réfectoire** (dining hall) is illuminated by a wall of recessed windows – remarkable, given that the sheer drop precluded the use of flying buttresses. The Gothic **Salle des Hôtes** (Guest Hall), dating from 1213, has two enormous fireplaces. Look out for the **promenoire** (ambulatory), with one of the oldest ribbed vaulted ceilings in Europe, and the **Chapelle de Notre Dame sous Terre** (Underground Chapel of Our Lady), one of the abbey's oldest rooms, rediscovered in 1903.

The masonry used to build the abbey was brought to the Mont by boat and pulled up the hillside using ropes. The contraption that looks like a treadmill for gargantuan gerbils was in fact powered in the 19th century by half-a-dozen prisoners who, by turning the wheel, hoisted the supply sledge up the side of the abbey. Experts doubt that they sang the Oompah-Loompah song while trudging round and round.

NORMANDY

GRANDE RUE

None of the four private **museums** (adult/child €8/4.50, for all 4 museums €16/9) along Grande Rue is up to much, although a couple might intrigue the kids. The **Archéoscope** (☎ 02 33 89 01 85) is a smart 20-minute multimedia history of the Mont with lights, video and even a few spurts of dry ice, while the **Musée de la Mer et de l'Écologie** explains Mont St-Michel's complex tidal patterns.

Tours

When the tide is out, you can walk all the way around Mont St-Michel, a distance of about 1km. Straying too far from the Mont can be very risky: you might get stuck in wet sand – from which Norman soldiers are depicted being rescued in one scene of the Bayeux Tapestry (p279) – or be overtaken by the incoming tide, providing your next-of-kin with a great cocktail party story.

Experienced outfits offering **guided walks** (€6.50) out into – or even across – the bay include **Découverte de la Baie du Mont-Saint-Michel** (☎ 02 33 70 83 33; www.decouvertebaie.com, in French) and **Chemins de la Baie** (☎ 02 33 89 80 88; www.cheminsdelabaie.com, in French), both based across the bay from Mont St-Michel in Genêts. Local tourist offices have details.

Sleeping

There are eight rather pricey hotels on the Mont itself but most people choose to stay in one of the chain-style hotels in Beauvoir, on the mainland, or in the rather ordinary town of Pontorson, 9km due south of the Mont. The places mentioned below are in Pontorson.

Auberge de Jeunesse (Centre Duguesclin; ☎ 02 33 60 18 65; aj.pontorson@wanadoo.fr; 21 bd du Général Patton, Pontorson; dm €11.30; 🕑 mid-Apr–Sep) Situated 1km west of the train station near the new Gendarmerie building, this modern, 62-bed hostel has four- to six-bed rooms and kitchen facilities. Reception closes from noon to 5pm (except from mid-July to late August) but there's no curfew.

Hôtel La Tour Brette (☎ 02 33 60 10 69; www.latourbrette.com; 8 rue du Couesnon, Pontorson; d €36-42) A family-run place with 10 unsurprising, good-value rooms.

Hôtel de Bretagne (☎ 02 33 60 10 55; www.lebretagnepontorson.com; 59 rue du Couesnon, Pontorson; d/q €59/79; 🕑 closed mid-Jan–Feb) This half-timbered, two-star place looks a bit shabby from the outside but the flowery bedspreads and curtains add a touch of brightness to the 12 spacious but otherwise average rooms.

Hôtel Montgomery (☎ 02 33 60 00 09; www.hotel-montgomery.com; 13 rue du Couesnon, Pontorson; d €93-117, ste €180-250) In a 16th-century mansion, this three-star, Best Western–affiliated hotel has a vine-covered Renaissance facade and, inside, creaky wood-panelled corridors and 32 rooms. One room comes with hefty Renaissance furniture and a four-poster bed just 135cm wide!

Eating

MONT ST-MICHEL

The Grande Rue is jammed with sandwich shops and crêperies.

Crêperie La Sirène (☎ 02 33 60 03 60; crêpes €2.10-8.60; 9am-8pm, to 10.30pm or 11.30pm summer) Not a bad budget option, with a good selection of sweet crêpes and savoury galettes and salads. Up an ancient spiral staircase from a souvenir shop.

La Mère Poulard (☎ 02 33 89 68 68; lunch menu €39, dinner menus €65-85; 11.45am-4.30pm & 6.45-9.30pm, no afternoon closure in summer) Established in 1888, this tourist institution churns out its famous soufflé omelettes, cooked in a wood-fired oven, and charges astronomical prices for them.

PONTORSON

Rue du Couesnon has a few cheap eateries but the best restaurants belong to the hotels.

Hôtel La Tour Brette (☎ 02 33 60 10 69; 8 rue du Couesnon; menus €11.30-33; closed Wed) Home-style French and Normandy cuisine, including oysters, mussels and fish soup.

Hôtel Montgomery (☎ 02 33 60 00 09; 13 rue du Couesnon; mains €12.60-19.60; 7.15-9.15pm) One of Pontorson's best restaurants for French, Normandy and Brittany cuisine.

Hôtel de Bretagne (☎ 02 33 60 10 55; 59 rue du Couesnon; lunch menu €12.90, dinner menus €15.90-26.90; closed lunch Mon & Sun) A formal restaurant that serves up local specialities such as oysters with Camembert, and scallops cooked in cider.

SELF-CATERING

Pontorson has five full-size supermarkets, all well signposted.

Proxi (5 rue du Couesnon, Pontorson; 8am-12.45pm & 2.30-7.30pm Tue-Sat, 9am-12.30pm Sun year-round, also 9am-12.30pm & 3.30-7.30pm Mon Jun-Aug) Supermarket.

Super Marché (Beauvoir) Supermarket about 2km from the Mont near the end of the causeway.

Getting There & Around

Mont St-Michel is linked to Beauvoir (eight minutes) and Pontorson (€2; 13 minutes) by bus 6, operated by **Manéo** (☎ 08 00 15 00 50; www.mobi50.com, in French), six to eight times daily (more frequently in July and August). Times are coordinated with the arrival in Pontorson of some trains from Caen and Rennes. **Les Couriers Bretons** (☎ 02 99 19 70 80) links Pontorson with St-Malo (1¼ hours, one round trip daily); times are coordinated with bus 6.

Train destinations from Pontorson include Bayeux (€19.60, 1¾ hours, two or three direct daily), Cherbourg (€24.50, 2¼ hours, two daily), Coutances (€10.50, 40 minutes, two or three daily) and Rennes (€11.90, 1¾ hours, two or three daily).

Brittany

Thrust out into the Atlantic, France's westernmost promontory might be called Finistère, meaning 'land's end', but its Breton name, Penn ar Bed, translates as 'head of the world', highlighting how Bretons have long viewed it and, by extension, the rest of this spirited, independent region.

Historically cut off from the rest of the mainland by dense, impenetrable forest, in an era when sea travel was all, Brittany (Bretagne in French) was for all intents and purposes an island. Patchwork farming fields now take the forest's place, though pockets still remain. But Brittany still stands with its back to the rest of the country, looking oceanward.

The sea crashing against the granite coast and scattered islands provides numerous nautical pursuits as well as prized mussels, sea bass, oysters and lobster – ideally accompanied by cider, Breton beer, and Muscadet wine from its former capital, Nantes (covered in the Atlantic Coast chapter, p651). Within its deep, mysterious interior, Brittany's woodlands and wending rivers and canals are ideal for hiking, cycling, or punting lazily by boat.

Brittany's language is undergoing a revival that is seeing it forge beyond its former frontiers, buoyed by enduring customs and celebrations. Dancing needle-and-thread style, interlinked by little fingers, to music played with *biniou* (something like a bagpipe) and *bombarde* (a double-reeded oboe) at *festoù-noz* (night festivals) is a fantastic way to experience Breton culture – which is as interwoven with French culture today as the intricate lace of women's traditional headdresses and the churches' filigreed stone steeples.

HIGHLIGHTS

- Sip Breton cider and learn about its production at the **Musée du Cidre** (p329) on the Crozon Peninsula at Argol
- See where artists such as Gaugin set up their easels at **Pont-Aven** (p338), which has inspired some 60 galleries today
- Stroll along the walled city's **ramparts** (p309) at sunset for kaleidoscopic views over St-Malo

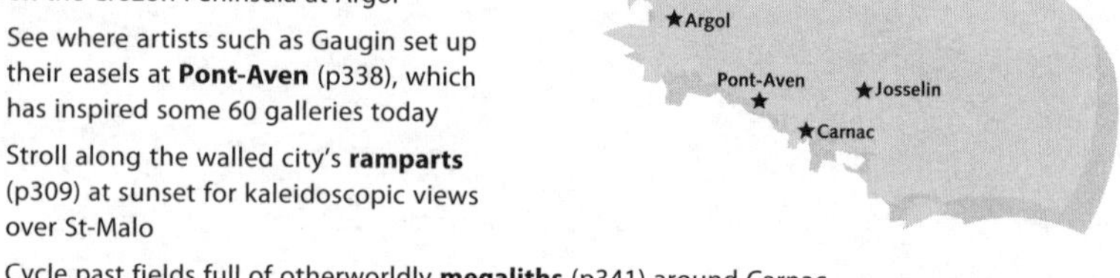

- Cycle past fields full of otherworldly **megaliths** (p341) around Carnac
- Tour the turreted medieval castle looming over the fairy-tale forest village of **Josselin** (p347)

POPULATION: 2.9 MILLION	AREA: 27,210 SQ KM

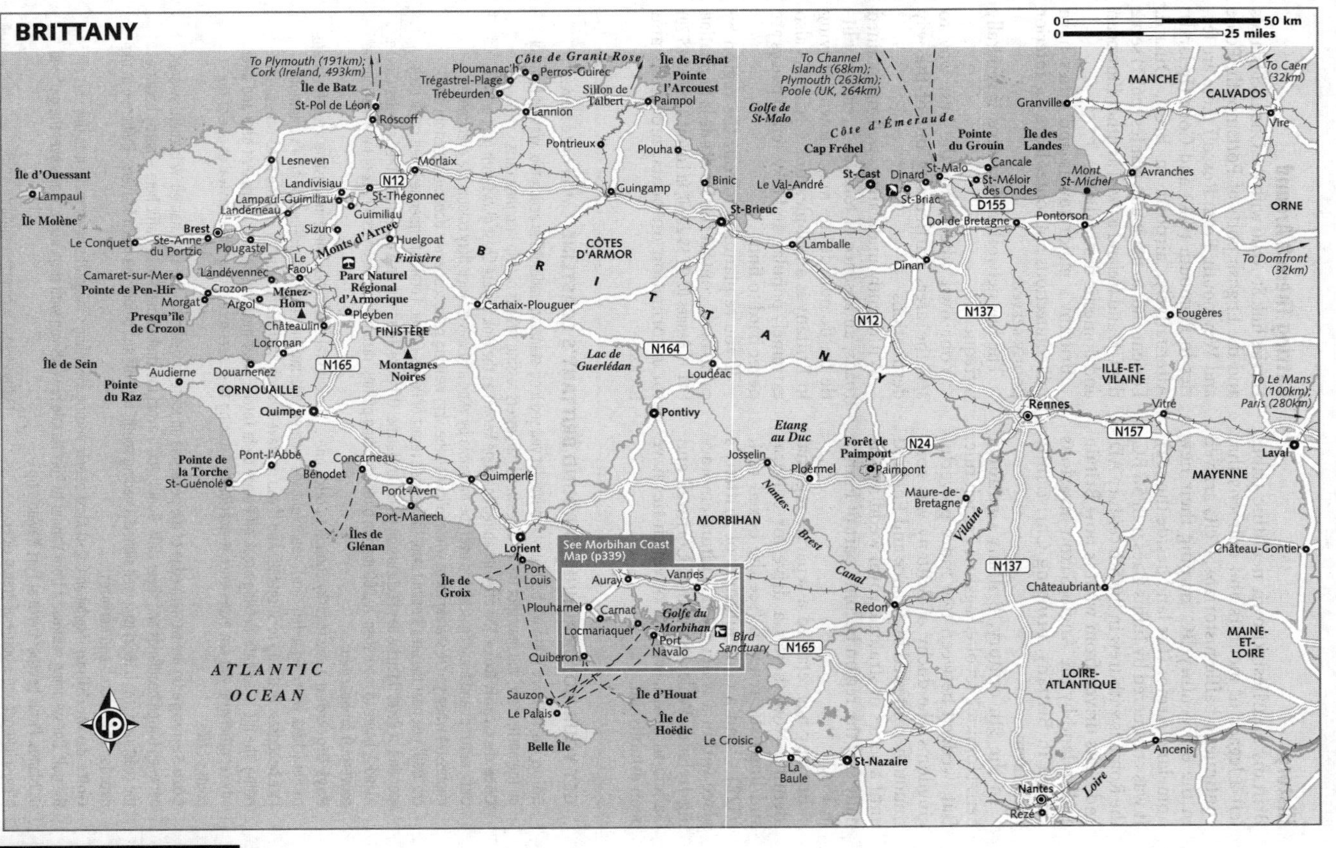
BRITTANY
0 50 km
0 25 miles
To Plymouth (191km); Cork (Ireland, 493km)
Île de Batz
St-Pol de Léon
Roscoff
Côte de Granit Rose
Ploumanac'h
Perros-Guirec
Trégastrel-Plage
Trébeurden
Lannion
Sillon de Talbert
Île de Bréhat
Pointe l'Arcouest
Paimpol
To Channel Islands (68km); Plymouth (263km); Poole (UK, 264km)
Golfe de St-Malo
Côte d'Émeraude
Cap Fréhel
Pointe du Grouin
Île des Landes
MANCHE
CALVADOS
To Caen (32km)
Granville
Vire
Lesneven
Morlaix
N12
Landivisiau
St-Thégonnec
Lampaul-Guimiliau
Guimiliau
Landerneau
Pontrieux
Plouha
Binic
Guingamp
Le Val-André
St-Cast
Dinard
St-Malo
Cancale
St-Méloir des Ondes
St-Briac
D155
Mont St-Michel
Avranches
ORNE
Île d'Ouessant
Lampaul
Île Molène
Brest
Ste-Anne du Portzic
Le Conquet
Plougastel
Sizun
Monts d'Arrée
Huelgoat
Finistère
Le Faou
Landévennec
Camaret-sur-Mer
Pointe de Pen-Hir
Crozon
Morgat
Argol
Ménez-Hom
Presqu'île de Crozon
Parc Naturel Régional d'Armorique
Pleyben
Châteaulin
FINISTÈRE
Carhaix-Plouguer
B R I T T A N Y
CÔTES D'ARMOR
St-Brieuc
Lamballe
Dinan
Dol de Bretagne
Pontorson
To Domfront (32km)
N137
N12
Fougères
Locronan
Île de Sein
Audierne
Douarnenez
N165
Montagnes Noires
Lac de Guerlédan
N164
Loudéac
Pointe du Raz
CORNOUAILLE
Quimper
Pontivy
ILLE-ET-VILAINE
Rennes
Vitré
To Le Mans (100km); Paris (280km)
N157
Laval
Etang au Duc
Forêt de Paimpont
N24
Josselin
Ploërmel
Paimpont
Pointe de la Torche
St-Guénolé
Pont-l'Abbé
Bénodet
Concarneau
Pont-Aven
Port-Manech
Quimperlé
Maure-de-Bretagne
MAYENNE
Îles de Glénan
Lorient
MORBIHAN
Nantes-Brest Canal
Vilaine
Château-Gontier
See Morbihan Coast Map (p339)
Île de Groix
Port Louis
Auray
Vannes
N137
Châteaubriant
Plouharnel
Carnac
Golfe du Morbihan
Redon
Locmariaquer
Port Navalo
Bird Sanctuary
N165
MAINE-ET-LOIRE
Quiberon
ATLANTIC OCEAN
LOIRE-ATLANTIQUE
Sauzon
Le Palais
Île d'Houat
Île de Hoëdic
Belle Île
Le Croisic
La Baule
St-Nazaire
Ancenis
Nantes
Loire
Rezé

History

Brittany's earliest known neolithic tribes left a legacy of menhirs and dolmens that continue to baffle historians. Celts arrived in the 6th century BC, naming their new homeland Armor (the land beside the sea). It was conquered by Julius Caesar in 56 BC; the Romans withdrew in the 5th century AD; and Celts driven from what is now Britain and Ireland by the Anglo-Saxon invasions settled in Brittany, bringing Christianity with them.

In the 9th century, Brittany's national hero Nominoë revolted against French rule. But, wedged between two more powerful kingdoms, the duchy of Brittany was continuously contested by France and England until a series of strategic royal weddings finally saw the region become part of France in 1532.

Brittany has retained a separate regional identity. Now there's a drive for cultural and linguistic renewal (see the boxed text, p322) – and a consciousness of Brittany's place within a wider Celtic culture embracing Ireland, Wales, Scotland, Cornwall and Galicia in Spain, with all of which ties have been established.

Getting There & Around

Ferries link St-Malo with the Channel Islands and the English ports of Portsmouth, Poole and Weymouth. From Roscoff there are ferries to Plymouth (UK) and Cork (Ireland). Alternatively, airports in Brest, Dinard, Lorient and, to the south, Nantes (p657) serve the UK and Ireland as well as other European and domestic destinations.

Brittany's major towns and cities have rail connections but routes leave the interior poorly served.

The bus network is extensive, if generally infrequent.

Your own wheels are the best way to see the area, particularly out-of-the-way destinations.

With gently undulating, well-maintained roads, an absence of tolls, and relatively little traffic outside the major towns, driving in Brittany is a real pleasure. Cycling is also extremely popular, and bike-rental places are never hard to find.

If you're planning to tour the region by canal boat, contact the **Service de la Navigation** (☎ in Rennes 02 99 59 20 60, in Lorient 02 97 64 85 20) for information on boats, moorings and locks.

GET YOUR MOTOR RUNNING AROUND BRITTANY'S COASTLINE *Catherine Le Nevez*

Sillon de Talbert Brittany's best coastal drives let you see long-standing traditions in action too. West of Paimpol on the north coast, you may spot the local seaweed harvesters tossing strands of kelp into their carts.

Côte de Granit Rose The otter-inhabited coastline known as the Pink Granite Coast glows with pink granite cliffs, outcrops and boulders sculpted over the millennia by wind and waves. Their fiery colours are even more impressive when you're scaling them while following the 5km walking path, *sentier des douaniers* (custom officers' trail) just near the area's main town, the seaside resort of Perros-Guirec. Local fishermen sell their catch each morning at Peros' Marché des Pêcheurs on place du Marché. Offshore, head out on a boat trip to the Sept-Îles (Seven Islands), home to more than 20,000 marine birds including puffins, razorbills and fulmars. Check out www.armor-decouverte.fr for boat info.

Pays Bigouden If you're lucky enough to catch one of the cultural celebrations here in Finistère's southwestern corner (check www.bigouden.com), you might see women wearing the *coiffe bigoudène,* the area's traditional lace headdress that's up to 30cm tall. And if you're brave enough, you might want to join the hard-core surfers riding 'the lift' – a death-defying break off Pointe de la Torche. Near the car park, surf shops rent gear and offer advice; otherwise you can experience it vicariously listening to surfers recounting their survival at one of the point's cafés.

Côte Sauvage On the western edge of the peninsula en route to Quiberon, the aptly named 'wild coast' swoops between barren headlands and sheer cliffs. Bonus: you'll avoid the choked main-road traffic here – partly because the coast road (the D186a) isn't well signed. Heading south, turn off just before you reach St-Pierre-Quiberon, in the direction of Kemiscob and Kervozès.

Golfe du Morbihan (Morbihan Coast) Most people visiting Morbihan's megaliths never make it to this part of the gulf. But swinging southwest from Vannes to Port Navalo rewards you with stupendous views over the gulf and its islands. Picnic benches perch at Port Navalo's tip – bring a hamper and a bottle of Breton cider.

What's your recommendation?
www.lonelyplanet.com/france

NORTH COAST

Enveloped by belle-époque beach resorts, fishing villages and curled headlands, Brittany's central north coast spans the *départements* of Ille-et-Vilaine and Côtes d'Armor. Green shallows give rise to the name Côte d'Émeraude (Emerald Coast) to the east; westwards, boulders blush along the Côte de Granit Rose (Pink Granite Coast; opposite).

ST-MALO

pop 49,600

The mast-filled port of St-Malo has a cinematically changing landscape. With one of the world's highest tidal ranges, brewing storms under blackened skies see waves lash over the top of the ramparts ringing its walled city. Hours later, the blue sky merges with the deep marine-blue sea, exposing beaches as wide and flat as the clear skies above and creating land bridges to the granite outcrop islands.

Construction of the walled city's fortifications began in the 12th century. The town became a key port during the 17th and 18th centuries as a base for both merchant ships and government-sanctioned privateers (pirates, basically) against the constant threat of the English. These days English arrivals are tourists, for whom St-Malo, a short ferry hop from the Channel Islands, is a summer haven.

Orientation

The St-Malo conurbation consists of the harbour towns of St-Malo and St-Servan plus the modern suburbs of Paramé and Rothéneuf to the east. The old walled city of St-Malo is known as Intra-Muros ('within the walls') or Ville Close. From the train station, it's a 15-minute walk westwards along av Louis Martin.

Information

INTERNET ACCESS

Cyberm@lo (☎ 02 99 56 07 78; 68 chaussée du Sillon; per 15min/hr €1.50/4; 🕑 10am-1am Mon-Sat, 11am-11pm Sun mid-Jun–mid-Sep, 11am-9pm Tue-Thu, 11am-11pm Fri & Sat, 3-8pm Sun mid-Sep–mid-Jun) Your best bet year-round; situated east along the seafront.

Mokamalo (☎ 02 99 56 60 17; 5 rue de l'Orme; 🕑 9am-8pm daily in summer, reduced hours in winter) Internet access inside the walls.

LAUNDRY

Laundrette (rue de la Herse; 🕑 7.30am-9pm)

POST

Main Post Office (1 bd de la République) Outside the walls.

Post Office (place des Frères Lamennais) Intra-Muros.

TOURIST INFORMATION

Tourist Office (☎ 08 25 13 52 00, 02 99 56 64 43; www.saint-malo-tourisme.com; esplanade St-Vincent; 🕑 9am-7.30pm Mon-Sat, 10am-6pm Sun Jul & Aug, 9am-12.30pm & 1.30pm–6pm or 6.30pm Mon-Sat Sep-Jun, 10am-12.30pm & 2.30-6pm Sun Easter-Jun & Sep)

Sights & Activities

WALLED CITY

St-Malo's first inhabitants originally lived in St-Servan but later moved to this former island, which became linked to the mainland by the sandy isthmus of Le Sillon in the 13th century.

For the best views of the walled city, stroll along the top of the **ramparts**, constructed at the end of the 17th century under military architect Vauban, and measuring 1.8km. Free access includes all of the main city *portes* (gates).

Though you'd never guess it from the cobblestone streets and reconstructed monuments in 17th- and 18th-century style, during August 1944 the battle to drive German forces out of St-Malo destroyed around 80% of the old city. Damage to the town's centrepiece, **Cathédrale St-Vincent** (place Jean de Châtillon; 🕑 9.30am-6pm except during Mass), constructed between the 12th and 18th centuries, was severe. A mosaic **plaque** on the floor of the nave marks the spot where Jacques Cartier received the blessing of the bishop of St-Malo before his 'voyage of discovery' to Canada in 1535. Cartier's tomb – all that remains of it post-1944 is his entombed head – is in a chapel on the north side of the choir.

MONUMENT COMBO

A **combined ticket** (adult/child €12.30/6.15) gives you access to St-Malo's three major monuments: the Musée du Château de St-Malo, Musée International du Long Cours Cap-Hornier and Mémorial 39-45. It can be purchased at any of the three participating museums and is valid for the duration of your stay in St-Malo.

BRITTANY

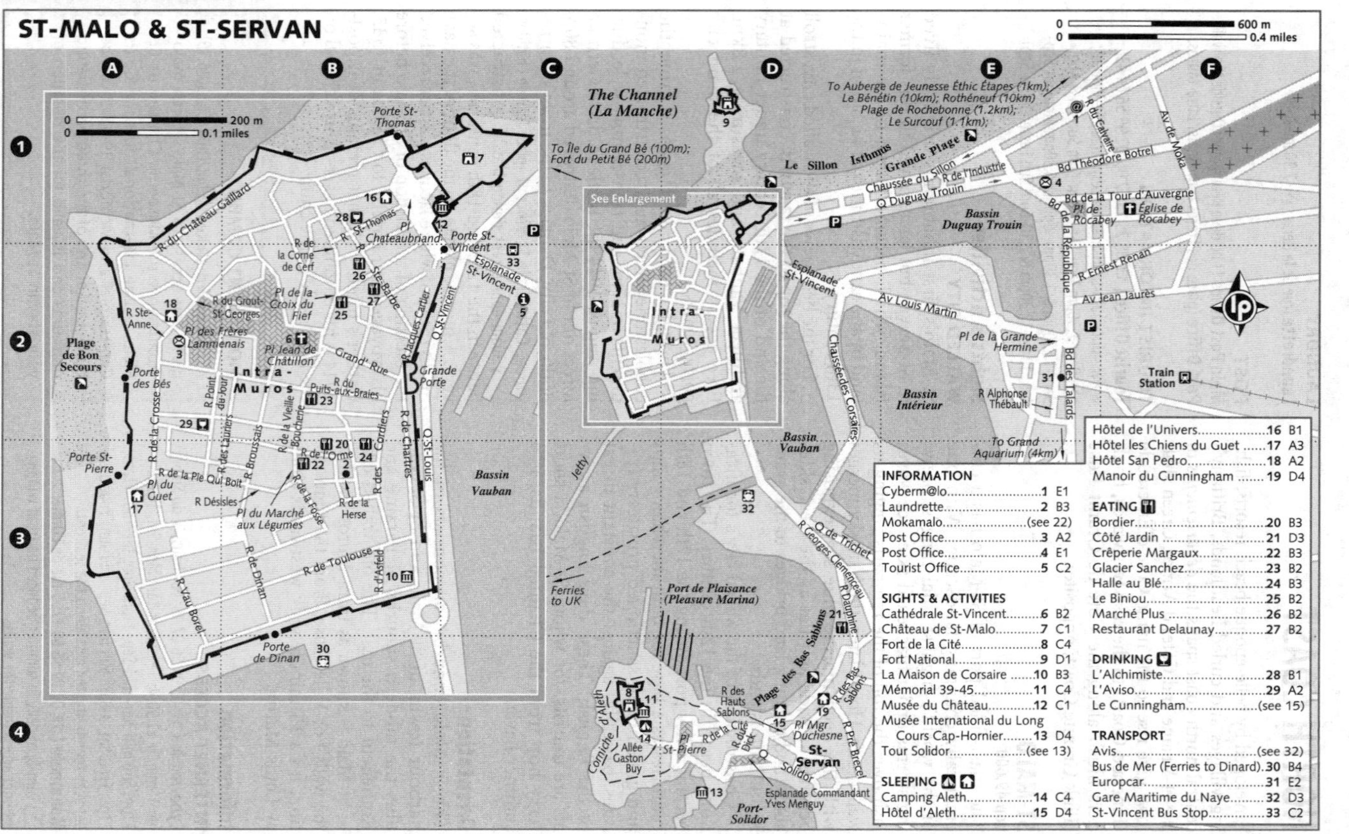
ST-MALO & ST-SERVAN
0 600 m
0 0.4 miles
0 200 m
0 0.1 miles
INFORMATION
Cyberm@lo 1 E1
Laundrette 2 B3
Mokamalo (see 22)
Post Office 3 A2
Post Office 4 E1
Tourist Office 5 C2
SIGHTS & ACTIVITIES
Cathédrale St-Vincent 6 B2
Château de St-Malo 7 C1
Fort de la Cité 8 C4
Fort National 9 D1
La Maison de Corsaire 10 B3
Mémorial 39-45 11 C4
Musée du Château 12 C1
Musée International du Long Cours Cap-Hornier 13 D4
Tour Solidor (see 13)
SLEEPING
Camping Aleth 14 C4
Hôtel d'Aleth 15 D4
Hôtel de l'Univers 16 B1
Hôtel les Chiens du Guet 17 A3
Hôtel San Pedro 18 A2
Manoir du Cunningham 19 D4
EATING
Bordier 20 B3
Côté Jardin 21 D3
Crêperie Margaux 22 B3
Glacier Sanchez 23 B2
Halle au Blé 24 B3
Le Biniou 25 B2
Marché Plus 26 B2
Restaurant Delaunay 27 B2
DRINKING
L'Alchimiste 28 B1
L'Aviso 29 A2
Le Cunningham (see 15)
TRANSPORT
Avis (see 32)
Bus de Mer (Ferries to Dinard) 30 B4
Europcar 31 E2
Gare Maritime du Naye 32 D3
St-Vincent Bus Stop 33 C2
The Channel (La Manche)
To Île du Grand Bé (100m); Fort du Petit Bé (200m)
To Auberge de Jeunesse Éthic Étapes (1km); Le Bénétin (10km); Rothéneuf (10km) Plage de Rochebonne (1.2km); Le Surcouf (1.1km);
Le Sillon Isthmus
Grande Plage
Chaussée du Sillon
R de l'Industrie
Q Duguay Trouin
Bd Théodore Botrel
R du Calvaire
Av de Moka
Bd de la Tour d'Auvergne
Pl de Rocabey
Église de Rocabey
Bd de la République
R Ernest Renan
Av Jean Jaurès
Bassin Duguay Trouin
Esplanade St-Vincent
Av Louis Martin
Pl de la Grande Hermine
Bd des Talards
Train Station
R Alphonse Thébault
Bassin Intérieur
To Grand Aquarium (4km)
Chausséedes Corsaires
Bassin Vauban
See Enlargement
Intra-Muros
Jetty
Ferries to UK
Port de Plaisance (Pleasure Marina)
Q de Trichet
R Georges Clemenceau
R Dauphine
Plage des Bas Sablons
R des Bas Sablons
R des Hauts Sablons
Pl Mgr Duchesne
R Pré Brecel
St-Servan
Solidor
R de la Cité
R du Dick
Pl St-Pierre
Corniche d'Aleth
Allée Gaston Buy
Esplanade Commandant Yves Menguy
Port-Solidor
Porte St-Thomas
Porte St-Vincent
Pl Chateaubriand
R St-Thomas
R du Château Gaillard
R de la Corne de Cerf
Ste-Barbe
Pl de la Croix du Fief
R du Grout-St-Georges
R Ste-Anne
Pl des Frères Lamennais
Pl Jean de Châtillon
Grand' Rue
R Jacques Cartier
Q St-Vincent
Grande Porte
Plage de Bon Secours
Porte des Bés
R du Puits-aux-Braies
R Point du Jour
R de la Crosse
R des Lauriers
R Broussais
R de la Vieille Boucherie
R de l'Orme
R des Cordiers
R de Chartres
Q St-Louis
Porte St-Pierre
R de la Pie Qui Boit
Pl du Guet
R Désilles
Pl du Marché aux Légumes
R de la Fosse
R de la Herse
R de Dinan
R de Toulouse
R d'Asfeld
R Vau Borel
Porte de Dinan

The ramparts' northern stretch looks out across to the remains of the former prison, **Fort National** (adult/child €4/2; Jun-Sep), accessible only at low tide. Within **Château de St-Malo**, built by the dukes of Brittany in the 15th and 16th centuries, is the **Musée du Château** (02 99 40 71 57; adult/child €5.20/2.60; 10am-noon & 2-6pm daily Apr-Sep, Tue-Sun Oct-Mar), also known as the Musée d'Histoire de la Ville (city history museum). The museum's most interesting exhibits – the history of cod fishing on the Grand Banks and photos of St-Malo after WWII – are in the Tour Générale.

You can visit the 18th-century mansion and historic monument **La Maison de Corsaire** (02 99 56 09 40; www.demeure-de-corsaire.com, in French; 5 rue d'Asfeld; adult/child €5.50/4; 10am-noon & 2-6pm daily in summer, Tue-Sun in winter), once owned by corsair (privateer) François Auguste Magon. Guided tours are in French; descriptions are available in English.

ÎLE DU GRAND BÉ

At low tide, cross the beach to walk out via the Porte des Bés to the rocky islet of **Île du Grand Bé**, where the great St-Malo–born 18th-century writer Chateaubriand is buried. Once the tide rushes in, the causeway remains impassable for about six hours – check tide times with the tourist office. Depths can be deceptive; if you get caught out, stay on the islet until the tide subsides.

About 100m beyond the Île du Grand Bé is the Vauban-built 17th-century **Fort du Petit Bé** (06 08 27 51 20), also accessible at low tide.

ST-SERVAN

The pretty fishing port of St-Servan sits south of the walled city. Constructed in the mid-18th century, **Fort de la Cité** was used as a German base during WWII. One of the bunkers now houses **Mémorial 39-45** (02 99 82 41 74; adult/child €5.20/2.60; guided visits 2pm, 3.15pm & 4.30pm Tue-Sun Apr-Jun & Sep-Mar, 6 times daily Jul & Aug), which depicts St-Malo's violent WWII history and liberation and includes a 45-minute film in French. Some guided visits are conducted in English; call ahead to confirm times.

Musée International du Long Cours Cap-Hornier (Museum of the Cape Horn Route; 02 99 40 71 58; adult/child €5.20/2.60; 10am-noon & 2-6pm daily Apr-Sep, Tue-Sun Oct-Mar) is in the 14th-century Tour Solidor. Presenting the life of the hardy sailors who followed the Cape Horn route, it offers superb views from the top of the tower.

GRAND AQUARIUM

Allow around two hours to see the excellent **Grand Aquarium** (02 99 21 19 00; av Général Patton; adult/child €15.50/10.50; 10am-6pm Feb-Oct & Dec, to 8pm Jul & Aug, closed Nov). About 4km south of the city centre, it's a great wet-weather alternative for kids, with a minisubmarine descent and a *bassin tactile* (touch pool), where you can fondle rays, turbot – even a baby shark. Bus C1 from the train station passes by every half-hour.

BEACHES

You can splash in the protected tidal pool west of the city walls at **Plage de Bon Secours** or climb its ladder to jump off into the sea.

St-Servan's **Plage des Bas Sablons** has a cement wall to keep the sea from receding completely at low tide.

The much larger **Grande Plage** stretches northeast along the isthmus of Le Sillon. Spectacular sunsets can be seen along the stretch from Grande Plage to Plage des Bas Sablons. Less crowded **Plage de Rochebonne** is another 1km to the northeast.

To learn how to windsurf (lessons from €35 for one hour) or sail a catamaran (lessons from €50 for one hour), contact **Surf School** (02 99 40 07 47; www.surfschool.org, in French).

BOAT TRIPS

Compagnie Corsaire (08 25 13 80 35; www.compagnie corsaire.com) runs ferries from just outside Porte de Dinan to Îles Chausey (adult/child return €28.50/17; daily July and August, Sunday April, May, June and September), Île Cézembre (adult/child return €13.50/8; daily July and August, Sunday April, May, June and September) and along the river to Dinan (adult/child one-way €22.50/13.50, return €28.50/13.50, April to September). Other boat trips (with commentary in French) from April to September include the Bay of St-Malo (adult/child €18.50/11, 1½ hours) and, during July and August, Cancale's bay and Pointe du Grouin (adult/child €27/16, 2½ hours).

The company can also take you *pêche en mer* (deep-sea fishing) for about four hours (€38, Monday, Wednesday and Friday July and August).

Vedettes de St-Malo (02 23 18 41 08; www.vedettes-saint-malo.com) also runs boat excursions.

For ferries to Dinard see p313.

Sleeping

St-Malo has plenty of hotels, but accommodation books up quickly in summer – the tourist office website has continuous updates of availability. For *chambres d'hôtes* (B&Bs), try the nearby towns of Cancale, Dinan and their surrounds.

BEYOND THE WALLS

Camping Aleth (☎ 02 99 81 60 91; camping@ville-saint-malo.fr; allée Gaston Buy, St-Servan; camping €12; ⏰ May-Sep) Perched on top of a peninsula next to Fort de la Cité, Camping Aleth (also spelt Alet) has panoramic 360-degree views and is close to beaches, and close but not *too* close to some lively bars.

Auberge de Jeunesse Éthic Étapes (☎ 02 99 40 29 80; www.centrevarangot.com; 37 av du Père Umbricht; dm incl breakfast €15.50-18.70; 💻 ⊠) This efficient place has a self-catering kitchen (and supermarket two minutes' walk away) as well as free sports facilities. Take bus C1 from the train station.

Hôtel d'Aleth (☎ 02 99 81 48 08; www.st-malo-hotel-cunningham.com; 2 rue des Hauts Sablons; r €38-60, q €100) Just a short stumble upstairs from the nautical pub, Le Cunningham (opposite), it's well worth a few extra euros for a sea view. Light sleepers beware: it's noisy to say the least. Frills are few: no lift, no in-room phones and no reception desk (check in at Manoir du Cunningham, below).

Le Surcouf (☎ 02 99 56 30 19; www.surcoufhotel.com; s €45-70, d €75; ⊠) In a peaceful residential quarter 1km from the walled town and five minutes' walk from the beach, this welcoming hotel is ideal if you're driving, with free street parking out front. Rooms are spacious, immaculate and contemporary, if sparingly decorated (no pictures on the walls). Wi-fi's free.

Manoir du Cunningham (☎ 02 99 21 33 33; 9 place Mgr Duchesne; r €90-190) If you're averse to noise and/or have more cash to splash, the Hôtel d'Aleth's owners operate this 13-room, mahogany-rich guesthouse in a 17th-century half-timbered house a stroll from the ferry, with views out to sea.

INTRA-MUROS

Hôtel les Chiens du Guet (☎ 02 99 40 87 29; www.leschiensduguet.com, in French; 4 place du Guet; r €41-57) A narrow stone staircase next to this welcoming no-star place pops you directly up on top of the ramparts; adjacent Porte St-Pierre opens directly to the beach. The 12 simple, sunlit rooms are homey if somewhat snug. There's a convivial on-site restaurant; *menus* start at €9.50.

Hôtel San Pedro (☎ 02 99 40 88 57; www.sanpedro-hotel.com; 1 rue Ste-Anne; s €46-48, d €53-70; ⏰ Feb-Nov; ⊠) Tucked at the back of the old city, the San Pedro has cool, crisp, neutral-toned decor with subtle splashes of colour, friendly service and superb sea views, as well as free wi-fi. Breakfast is an €8 feast.

Hôtel de l'Univers (☎ 02 99 40 89 52; www.hotel-univers-saintmalo.com, in French; place Chateaubriand; s €48-78, d €63-95) Right by the most frequently used gateway to the old city (Porte St-Vincent), and handy for the tourist office, this cream-coloured two-star place with 63 rooms is perfectly poised for all of St-Malo's attractions – not the least of which is its own all-wood, in-house maritime bar.

Eating

Browse the menus of the plethora of restaurants between Porte St-Vincent, the cathedral and the Grande Porte.

Le Biniou (☎ 02 99 56 47 57; 3 place de la Croix du Fief; crêpes €2-8, menus around €10; ⏰ 10am-1am in summer, closed Thu in winter) St-Malo has no shortage of crêperies but this one – with cute little illustrations of traditional Breton *biniou* (bagpipes) is a time-honoured favourite. Take a seat on the tiny terrace or the mezzanine with velour settees to choose from well over 100 different artisan galettes (savoury buckwheat crêpes), sweet crêpes (including the house speciality of caramelised apples flambéed in Calvados), or a heaping kettle of mussels.

Crêperie Margaux (☎ 02 99 20 26 02; 3 place du Marché aux Légumes; crêpes €7.50-13; ⏰ closed Tue & Wed, daily during school holidays) Watch the owner of this wonderful little crêperie on violet-filled Marché aux Légumes making traditional crêpes by hand (her motto: 'if you're in a hurry, don't come here'). The aromas wafting through the timber-lined dining room, and the scads of happy diners, prove it's well worth the wait.

Côté Jardin (☎ 02 99 81 63 11; 36 rue Dauphine, St-Servan; menus €25; ⏰ lunch Tue-Sun, dinner Tue & Thu-Sun) The charming, friendly Côté Jardin presents regional and traditional French cuisine, with a scenic terrace overlooking the marina and St-Malo's walled city. Doodlers can draw on the table with coloured pencils provided.

Restaurant Delaunay (☎ 02 99 40 92 46; 6 rue Ste-Barbe; menus €33-49; ⏰ closed Sun year-round & Mon in winter) Chef Didier Delaunay creates

COUNTING THE BEAT

Celtic culture is synonymous with music, and Brittany is no exception. Its wealth of indoor and outdoor festivals and concerts feature traditional instruments through to electronica (and everything in between), including big-name international acts. Keep your finger on the pulse by picking up the free monthly zine **Ty Zicos** (www.tyzicos.com, in French) in cafés and bars.

In addition to the festivals and events listed throughout this chapter, tune in to the region's top trio each year:

Les Vieilles Charrues de Carhaix (www.vieillescharrues.asso.fr; Carhaix; mid-Jul) Old-school crooners, electronic beats and much more attract crowds of 300,000-plus.

Astropolis (www.astropolis.org; Brest; early Aug) Electronic music fest with the main event atmospherically set in a castle.

Les Transmusicales de Rennes (www.lestrans.com; Rennes; early Dec) Groundbreaking indie bands.

standout gastronomic cuisine at his aubergine-painted restaurant inside the walls. The menu features succulent dishes both from the surf (Breton lobster's a speciality) and turf (tender lamb).

SELF-CATERING

Cheeses and butters handmade by Jean-Yves **Bordier** (9 rue de l'Orme; Tue-Sat) are shipped to famous restaurants all over the world. Just down the street is the covered market, **Halle au Blé** (rue de la Herse; 8am-noon Tue & Fri).

Glacier Sanchez (02 99 56 67 17; 9 rue de la Vieille Boucherie; Apr-Sep) serves up great ice cream.

Pick up beach-picnic supplies inside the walls at **Marché Plus** (cnr rue St-Vincent & rue St-Barbe; 7am-9pm Mon-Sat, to noon Sun).

Drinking

L'Alchimiste (02 23 18 10 06; 7 rue St-Thomas; 5pm-1am Tue-Sun Oct-Apr, to 2am daily May-Sep) Ben Harper–type music creates a mellow backdrop at this magical place filled with old books and a toy flying fox. Take a seat at the bar draped with a red, tasselled theatre curtain, on the carved timber mezzanine (including a pulpit), or in the wood-heated basement.

L'Aviso (02 99 40 99 08; 12 rue Point du Jour; 5pm-2am) Regular live music features at this cosy place, which has more than 300 beers on offer (and over 10 – including Breton beer – on tap). If you can't decide, ask the friendly owner/connoisseur.

Le Cunningham (2 rue des Hauts Sablons; 6pm-2am Mon-Fri, 4pm-3am Sat & Sun) Sail away at this curved wood bar with a wall of timber-framed windows looking out over water. Year-round live entertainment includes jazz, soul and Brazilian beats.

Entertainment

In summer, classical music concerts are held in Cathédrale St-Vincent and elsewhere in the city, and the pubs, bars and cafés have lots of live music – check the 'what's on' section of the tourist office's website (www.saint-malo-tourisme.com).

Getting There & Away

AIR

See p316 for flight details.

BOAT

Brittany Ferries (reservations in France 08 25 82 88 28, in UK 0870 556 1600; www.brittany-ferries.com) sails between St-Malo and Portsmouth, and **Condor Ferries** (in France 08 25 13 51 35, in UK 0870 243 5140; www.condorferries.co.uk) runs to/from Poole and Weymouth via Jersey or Guernsey. Car ferries leave from the Gare Maritime du Naye.

From April to September, **Compagnie Corsaire** (08 25 13 80 35) and **Vedettes de St-Malo** (02 23 18 41 08; www.vedettes-saint-malo.com) run a **Bus de Mer** (Sea Bus; adult/child return €6/4; hourly) shuttle service (10 minutes) between St-Malo and Dinard.

BUS

All intercity buses stop by the train station.

Courriers Bretons (02 99 19 70 80) has services including Cancale (€1, 30 minutes) and Mont St-Michel (€4.50, 1½ hours, three to four daily). It also offers all-day tours to Mont St-Michel (€9) – check for seasonal schedules.

TIV (02 99 82 26 26) has buses to Dinard (€1.50, 30 minutes, hourly) and Rennes (€3, one to 1½ hours, three to six daily).

Tibus (08 10 22 22 22) goes to Dinan (€2, 50 minutes, three to eight daily).

CAR & MOTORCYCLE

Avis (☎ 02 99 40 18 54) and **ADA** (☎ 02 99 56 06 15) have offices at the train station. Avis also has a desk at the Gare Maritime du Naye. **Europcar** (☎ 02 99 56 75 17; 16 bd des Talards) is about 300m north towards the walled city.

TRAIN

TGV trains run between St-Malo and Rennes (€12.10, one hour, frequent), Dinan (€8.30, one hour, requiring a change), and a direct service to Paris' Gare Montparnasse (€58, three hours, three daily).

Getting Around

St-Malo city buses (single journey €1.05, 24-hour pass €3) operate until about 8pm, with some lines extending until around midnight in summer. Between esplanade St-Vincent and the train station, take buses C1 or C2.

Call ☎ 02 99 81 30 30 for a taxi.

DINARD

pop 10,700

Visiting Dinard 'in season' is a little like stepping into one of the canvases Picasso painted here in the 1920s. Belle-époque mansions built into the cliffs form a timeless backdrop to the beach dotted with blue-and-white striped bathing tents and the beachside carnival. Out of season, when holidaymakers have packed up their buckets and spades, the town is decidedly dormant, but wintry walks along the coastal paths are spectacular.

Orientation

Dinard's focal point is the gently curved beach Plage de l'Écluse (also called Grande Plage), flanked by Pointe du Moulinet and Pointe de la Malouine. To get to the beach from the Embarcadère (where boats from St-Malo dock), climb the stairs and walk 200m northwest along rue Georges Clemenceau.

Information

Cyberspot (☎ 02 99 46 28 30; 6 rue Winston Churchill; per hr €6; 🕑 11am-midnight Wed-Mon in winter, daily in summer)

Lavomatic de la Poste (10 rue des Saules; 🕑 8am-7pm Jun-Sep, Mon-Sat Oct-May) Laundrette.

Post Office (place Rochaid)

Tourist Office (☎ 02 99 46 94 12; www.ot-dinard.com, in French; 2 bd Féart; 🕑 9.30am-7pm Jul & Aug, 9.30am-12.15pm & 2-6pm Mon-Sat Sep-Jun) Staff book accommodation for free.

Sights & Activities

The romantically named **promenade du Clair de Lune** (moonlight promenade) has views across the Rance River estuary to St-Malo's walled city, and nightly sound-and-light spectacles in summer.

Two-hour **guided walks** (🕑 2.30pm, days vary) explaining the town's history, art and architecture in English and French depart from the tourist office.

Beautiful **seaside trails** extend along the coast in both directions. Walkers can follow the shoreline from Plage du Prieuré to Plage de St-Énogat via Pointe du Moulinet, while cyclists can shadow the coastline on the road. Pack the Institut National Géographique (IGN) 1:50,000 map *Ille-et-Vilaine: Randonnées en Haute Bretagne*, which highlights walking trails throughout the *département*.

BARRAGE DE LA RANCE

This 750m bridge over the Rance estuary carries the D168 between St-Malo and Dinard, lopping a good 30km off the journey. A feat of hydroelectrics, the **Usine Marémotrice de la Rance** (below the bridge) generates electricity by harnessing the lower estuary's extraordinarily high tidal range – a difference of 13.5m between high and low tide.

If you're mechanically minded, visit **Espace Découverte** (admission free; 🕑 10am-6pm May-Sep) on the Dinard bank, illustrating the power station's construction and environmental impact, with a film in English.

BEACHES & SWIMMING

Framed by fashionable hotels, a casino and neo-Gothic villas, **Plage de l'Écluse** is the perfect place to shade yourself in style by renting one of Dinard's trademark blue-and-white striped **bathing tents** (☎ 02 99 46 18 12; per half-day €6.80-10.80, per day €7.45-14.15); you can also hire parasols and deckchairs. Reproductions of Picasso's paintings are often planted in the sand here in high summer.

Filled with heated seawater, the Olympic-sized indoor pool **Piscine Olympique** (☎ 02 99 46 22 77; promenade des Alliés; adult/student €4.10/3.25; 🕑 hr vary) is beside the beach.

Less chic (and less crowded) than the Plage de l'Écluse is **Plage du Prieuré**, 1km to the south. **Plage de St-Énogat** is 1km west of Plage de l'Écluse, on the far side of Pointe de la Malouine.

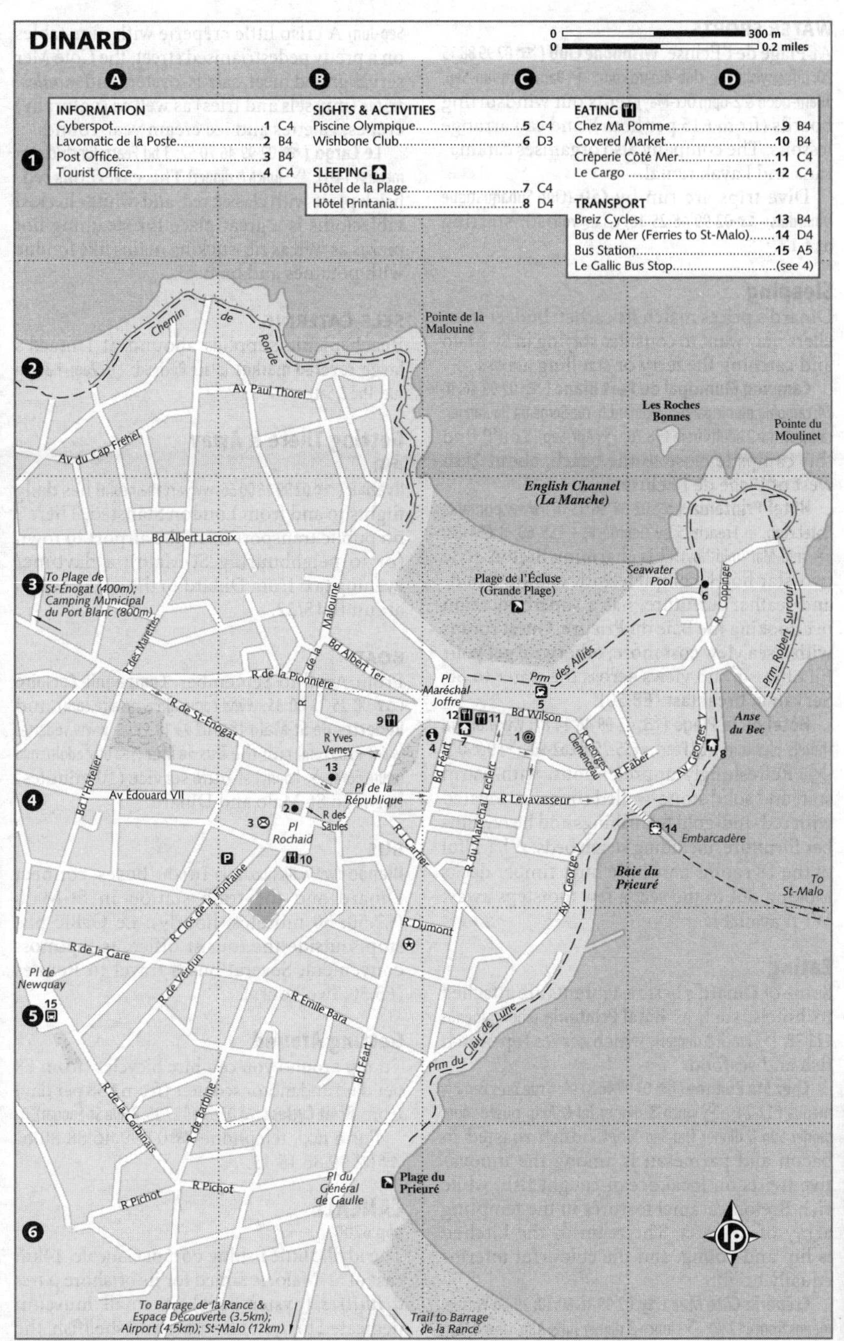
DINARD
0 300 m
0 0.2 miles
A
B
C
D
1
2
3
4
5
6
INFORMATION
Cyberspot....1 C4
Lavomatic de la Poste....2 B4
Post Office....3 B4
Tourist Office....4 C4
SIGHTS & ACTIVITIES
Piscine Olympique....5 C4
Wishbone Club....6 D3
SLEEPING
Hôtel de la Plage....7 C4
Hôtel Printania....8 D4
EATING
Chez Ma Pomme....9 B4
Covered Market....10 B4
Crêperie Côté Mer....11 C4
Le Cargo....12 C4
TRANSPORT
Breiz Cycles....13 B4
Bus de Mer (Ferries to St-Malo)....14 D4
Bus Station....15 A5
Le Gallic Bus Stop....(see 4)
Chemin de Ronde
Pointe de la Malouine
Av Paul Thorel
Les Roches Bonnes
Pointe du Moulinet
Av du Cap Fréhel
English Channel (La Manche)
Bd Albert Lacroix
To Plage de St-Énogat (400m); Camping Municipal du Port Blanc (800m)
Seawater Pool
Plage de l'Écluse (Grande Plage)
R Coppinger
Prm Robert Surcouf
R de la Malouine
Bd Albert 1er
R des Marettes
R de la Pionnière
Prm des Alliés
Pl Maréchal Joffre
Bd Wilson
R de St-Énogat
R Yves Verney
R Georges Clemenceau
Anse du Bec
Av Georges V
R Faber
Bd l'Hôtelier
Av Édouard VII
Pl de la République
Bd Féart
R du Maréchal Leclerc
R Levavasseur
R des Saules
Pl Rochaid
R J Cartier
Embarcadère
R Clos de la Fontaine
Baie du Prieuré
Av George V
To St-Malo
R Dumont
R de la Gare
Pl de Newquay
R de Verdun
R Émile Bara
Prm du Clair de Lune
R de la Corbinais
R de Barbine
Bd Féart
Pl du Général de Gaulle
Plage du Prieuré
R Pichot
R Pichot
To Barrage de la Rance & Espace Découverte (3.5km); Airport (4.5km); St-Malo (12km)
Trail to Barrage de la Rance
BRITTANY

WATER SPORTS

At Plage de l'Écluse, **Wishbone Club** (☎ 02 99 88 15 20; info@wishbone-club-dinard.com; 9am-9pm Jun-Sep, 10am-noon & 2-6pm Oct-May) rents out windsurfing boards (from €15 per hour), and can arrange lessons. The company also organises catamarans and kayak rental.

Dive trips are run by **CSD** (Club Subaquatique Dinardais; ☎ 02 99 46 25 18; c.s.d@voila.fr), starting at €17.

Sleeping

Dinard's prices match its cachet: budget travellers may want to consider staying in St-Malo and catching the ferry or strolling across.

Camping Municipal du Port Blanc (☎ 02 99 46 10 74; camping.municipal@ville-dinard.fr; rue Sergeant Boulanger; campsite for 2 adults from €18.70; Apr-Sep) You'll find this campsite close to the beach, about 2km west of Plage de l'Écluse.

Hôtel Printania (☎ 02 99 46 13 07; www.printaniahotel.com, in French; 5 av George V; s €55-60, d €54-88; mid-Mar–mid-Nov) This charming Breton-style two-star hotel, complete with mature wood-and-leather furniture, has a superb location overlooking the Baie du Prieuré. Guest rooms with a sea view cost more; otherwise get your fill of the grand views across the water to St-Servan at breakfast (€8.50).

Hôtel de la Plage (☎ 02 99 46 14 87; www.dinard-hotels-plus.com; 3 bd Féart; s €55-75, d €62-90; Dec-Oct; ⊠) Refreshingly unpretentious, with warm staff and solid stone-walled rooms renovated with red-and-gold furnishings and heavy timber furniture, including sleigh beds. A handful of the 18 rooms here have huge timber decks looking out to the sea, a few footsteps away. Wi-fi available.

Eating

Some of Dinard's best restaurants are attached to hotels, such as **Hôtel Printania** (above; menus €25-38; lunch & dinner), which serves top-notch fish and seafood.

Chez Ma Pomme (☎ 02 99 46 81 90; 6 rue Yves Verney; menus €12-24; lunch & dinner Jul & Aug, closed Mon, dinner Sun & dinner Thu Sep-Jun) Codfish roasted in bacon and parmesan is among the innovative twists on local ocean-caught fish, while rich Breton caramel features in the tempting array of desserts. The team in the kitchen is hip and young, and the colourful interior equally bright.

Crêperie Côté Mer (☎ 02 99 16 80 30; 29 bd Wilson; menus from €12.90; lunch & dinner Jul & Aug, closed Mon Sep-Jun) A crisp little crêperie with pine tables on a pretty pedestrianised street, the Côté Mer serves grilled meat, salads, oysters and *moules-frites* (mussels and fries) as well as (naturally) crêpes, galettes and ice cream year-round.

Le Cargo (☎ 02 99 46 70 52; 3 bd Féart; lunch/dinner menus €14-17; lunch & dinner) This cavernous red-brick place with classic red-and-white checked tablecloths is a great place for steaming hot pizzas as well as rib-sticking mains like fondue with potatoes and ham.

SELF-CATERING

Beach-picnic supplies abound at Dinard's large **covered market** (place Rochaid; 7am-1.30pm Tue, Thu & Sat).

Getting There & Away

AIR

Ryanair (☎ 02 99 16 00 66; www.ryanair.com) has daily flights to and from London Stansted. There's no public transport from the airport to town (or to neighbouring St-Malo); a daytime/evening taxi from Dinard to the airport costs around €15/22.

BOAT

From April to September, **Compagnie Corsaire** (☎ 08 25 13 80 35; www.compagniecorsaire.com) and **Vedettes de St-Malo** (☎ 02 23 18 41 08; www.vedettes-saint-malo.com) run the **Bus de Mer** (Sea Bus; adult/child return €6/4; hourly) shuttle service (10 minutes) between St-Malo and Dinard.

BUS

Illenoo (www.illenoo.fr, in French) buses connect Dinard and the train station in St-Malo (€2.50, 30 minutes, hourly). Le Gallic bus stop, outside the tourist office, is the most convenient. Several buses travel to Rennes (€3.50, two hours).

Getting Around

To nip around you can hire bicycles (from €8 per day) and motor scooters (from €38 per day) from **Breiz Cycles** (☎ 02 99 46 27 25; 8 Rue St-Énogat).

For a taxi, telephone ☎ 02 99 46 88 80 or ☎ 02 99 88 15 15.

CANCALE

pop 6200

The idyllic little fishing port of Cancale, 14km east of St-Malo, is famed for its offshore *parcs à huîtres* (oyster beds). A small museum dedicated to oyster farming and shellfish, the

Ferme Marine (Marine Farm; ☎ 02 99 89 69 99; corniche de l'Aurore; adult/child €6.70/3.50; ⏲ mid-Feb–Oct) runs guided tours in English at 2pm from mid-June to mid-September.

The **tourist office** (☎ 02 99 89 63 72; www.cancale-tourisme.fr; ⏲ 9am-12.30pm & 2-6pm Mon-Sat Sep-Jun, 9am-12.30pm & 2-7pm Mon-Sat, 9am-12.30pm Sun Jul & Aug) is at the top of rue du Port. In July and August only, there's a tourist office **annexe** (quai Gambetta; ⏲ hr vary) in the wooden house where the fish auction takes place.

Sleeping

It's an easy day trip to Cancale from St-Malo or Dinard, but there are some appealing places if you want to spend the night.

Auberge de Jeunesse (☎ 02 99 89 62 62; cancale@fuaj.org; Port Pican; dm €12.10-13.10; ⏲ Feb-Nov; ⊠) Right by the seaside, Cancale's HI-affiliated youth hostel at Port Pican is 3km northeast of the town – take the bus (July and August only) to the Cancale Église or Port Pican stop and walk 500m towards the seafront. Breakfast's an extra €3.60; campers can pitch up here for €6 per night.

Camping Municipal Le Grouin (☎ 02 99 89 63 79; marie@ville-cancale.fr; Pointe du Grouin; campsite €13.50; ⏲ Mar-Oct) Overlooking a fine-sand beach 6km north of Cancale near Pointe du Grouin, this place has 200 well-spaced sites, and facilities for wheelchairs.

La Pastourelle (☎ 02 99 89 10 09; pastourelle@baie-saintmichel.com; Les Nielles, St-Méloir des Ondes; s incl breakfast €48-54, d €54-72; ⊠) The countryside around Cancale shelters some really lovely *chambres d'hôtes* (ask the tourist office for a complete list). One of the most delightful is this vine-covered traditional Breton *longère* (long house) looking out to sea. Rooms are crisp and countrified, and convivial *tables d'hôtes* (€26 per person) are available by reservation. It's on the D155.

Hôtel La Mère Champlain (☎ 02 99 89 60 04; www.lamerechamplain.com; 1 quai Thomas; d €65-145) Reached by a newly installed lift (making it wheelchair accessible), the 15 delightfully renovated rooms at this quayside hotel have a relaxed port ambience and pretty-as-a-picture port views. The nautical-style restaurant (*menus* €16 to €40), complete with crisp linen, specialises in grilled lobster and has amazing desserts.

Le Continental (☎ 02 99 89 60 16; www.hotel-cancale.com, in French; 4 quai Thomas; d €88-148; ⏲ mid-Feb–early Jan) Above its portside, red-awning-shaded restaurant (*menus* €19 to €42), this *hôtel de charme* with good wheelchair access has beautiful timber-rich rooms. Sea-facing rooms are at a premium but the views, especially on the higher floors, are worth it.

Les Maisons de Bricourt (www.maisons-de-bricourt.com) Chef Olivier Roellinger (below) rents out several seasonally opening guest rooms (double from €170) and cottages including old seamen's cabins (double from €290) under the umbrella Les Maisons de Bricourt.

Eating

Around 25 specialist seafood restaurants are strung along the seafront – strolling along the port where the catches unload is the best way to whet your appetite. See also listings under Sleeping.

L'Huitière (☎ 02 99 89 75 05; 5 quai Gambetta; mains from €7.50, seafood platters for 1/2 people €21.50/42; ⏲ 10am-10pm Easter-Sep, 10am-7pm Oct-Easter) This low-key blue-and-yellow-painted joint on the waterfront has a chilly dining room but a warm welcome and absolutely delicious oysters, plus magnificent bowls of *moules* cooked with crème fraîche and *frites* crisped to perfection, as well as Breton *far* cake (like a solidified custard, filled with prunes) for dessert.

our pick **O Roellinger** (☎ 02 99 89 64 76; 1 rue Duguesclin; menus €100-172; ⏲ closed mid-Dec–mid-Mar) Up the hill from the port, one of the region's (and indeed France's) most acclaimed chefs, Olivier Roellinger, has his triple-Michelin-starred restaurant. Olivier was born in this 1760-built former East India Company house, where he has been creating extraordinary cuisine for the past two-and-a-half decades. Signature dishes include the 'route of the south seas' – a knock-out combination of oysters, *iraches* (local baby squid caught only 'while the lilacs are in bloom'), and poached Easter cabbage laced with spiced curry. Opening hours and days vary, but booking ahead's essential in any case.

Clustered by the Pointe des Crolles lighthouse, stalls at the **marché aux huîtres** (oyster market; ⏲ 9am-6pm) sell oysters from €3.50 per dozen for small *huîtres creuses* to upwards of €20 for saucer-sized *plates de Cancale*.

Getting There & Around

Buses stop behind the church on place Lucidas and at Port de la Houle, next to the pungent fish market. **Courriers Bretons** (☎ 02 99 19 70 80) has year-round services to and from St-Malo (€2,

30 minutes). In summer, at least three daily Courriers Bretons buses continue to Port Pican and Port Mer, near Pointe du Grouin.

It's a stunning 35km walk along the coast from Cancale to St-Malo.

A variety of bikes can be hired at **Les 2 Roues de Cancale** (☎ 02 99 89 80 16; 7 rue de L'Industrie; per day from €13).

POINTE DU GROUIN

At the northern tip of the wild coast between Cancale and St-Malo, this **nature reserve** juts out on a windblown headland. Just east offshore, **Île des Landes** is home to a colony of giant black cormorants whose wingspans can reach 170cm.

Via the GR34 coastal hiking trail, Pointe du Grouin is a stunning 7km hike from Cancale and 28km from St-Malo. By the D201 road, it's 4km from Cancale. Cancale tourist office's free map covers the local coastline.

DINAN

pop 11,200

Set high above the fast-flowing River Rance, the narrow cobblestone streets and squares lined with crooked half-timbered houses making up Dinan's old town is straight out of the Middle Ages – something that's not lost on the deluge of summer tourists. No less than 100,000 visitors turn up to join Dinannais townsfolk dressed in medieval garb for the two-day Fête des Remparts, held every even-numbered year in late July.

Orientation

Situated 22km south of Dinard, Dinan's most interesting sights are tucked within the tight confines of the old city. Dinan's picturesque riverside port is about 400m downhill to the northeast.

Information

Post Office (7 place Duclos)

Tourist Office (☎ 02 96 87 69 76; www.dinan-tourisme.com; 9 rue du Château; 🕑 9am-7pm Mon-Sat, 10am-12.30pm & 2.30-6pm Sun Jul & Aug, 9am-12.30pm & 2-6pm Mon-Sat Sep-Jun)

Zonzon (☎ 02 96 87 95 86; 9 rue des Rouairiesaux; per hr €4; 🕑 10am-10pm Mon-Thu, to 1am Fri & Sat, 3-10pm Sun) Internet access, west of the walled city.

Sights

The half-timbered houses overhanging place des Cordeliers and place des Merciers mark the heart of the old town. A few paces south, climb up to the little balcony of the **Tour de l'Horloge** (☎ 02 96 87 02 26; rue de l'Horloge; adult/under 18yr €2.90/1.85; 🕑 10am-6.30pm Jun-Sep, 2-6.30pm Easter-May), a 15th-century clock tower whose chimes ding every quarter-hour.

Basilique St-Sauveur (place St-Sauveur; 🕑 9am-6pm), with a soaring Gothic chancel, has in the north transept a 14th-century grave slab reputed to contain the heart of Bertrand du Guesclin, a 14th-century knight noted for his hatred of the English and his fierce battles to expel them from France. (Ironically, Dinan today has one of the largest English expat communities in Brittany.)

Just east of the church, beyond the tiny **Jardin Anglais** (English Garden), a former cemetery and nowadays a pleasant little park, is the 13th-century **Tour Ste-Cathérine**, with great views down over the viaduct and port.

Rue du Jerzual and its continuation, the steep (and slippery when wet) stone **rue du Petit Fort**, both lined with art galleries, antiques shops and restaurants, lead down to the **Vieux Pont** (Old Bridge). From here the little **port** extends northwards, while the 19th-century **Viaduc de Dinan** soars high above to the south.

Atmospherically housed in the keep of the ruined 14th-century **Château de Dinan**, the town's **museum** (☎ 02 96 39 45 20; rue du Château; adult/child €5.35/1.70; 🕑 10am-6.30pm Jun-Sep, 1.30-5.30pm Oct-Dec & Feb-May) showcases the town's textile industry, with a fine collection of *coiffes* (traditional Breton lace headdresses).

Activities

Between May and September, **Compagnie Corsaire** (☎ 08 25 13 81 00; www.compagniecorsaire.com) runs boats along the River Rance to Dinard and St-Malo (one-way/return €22.50/28.50, 2½ hours). Sailing schedules vary according to the tides. From Dinard or St-Malo you can easily return to Dinan by bus (and, from St-Malo, by train too).

Ask at the tourist office for its free leaflet *Discovery Tours*, available in several languages including English, which plots three **walking itineraries** around town.

Sleeping

In summer, advance reservations are recommended. Ask the tourist office for a list of *chambres d'hôtes* in the surrounding area.

Camping Municipal Châteaubriand (☎ in summer 02 96 39 11 96, rest of yr 02 96 39 22 43; 103 rue Chateaubriand; adult €2.40-2.60, tent € €2.70-2.90, car €2-2.10; 🕑 late May-

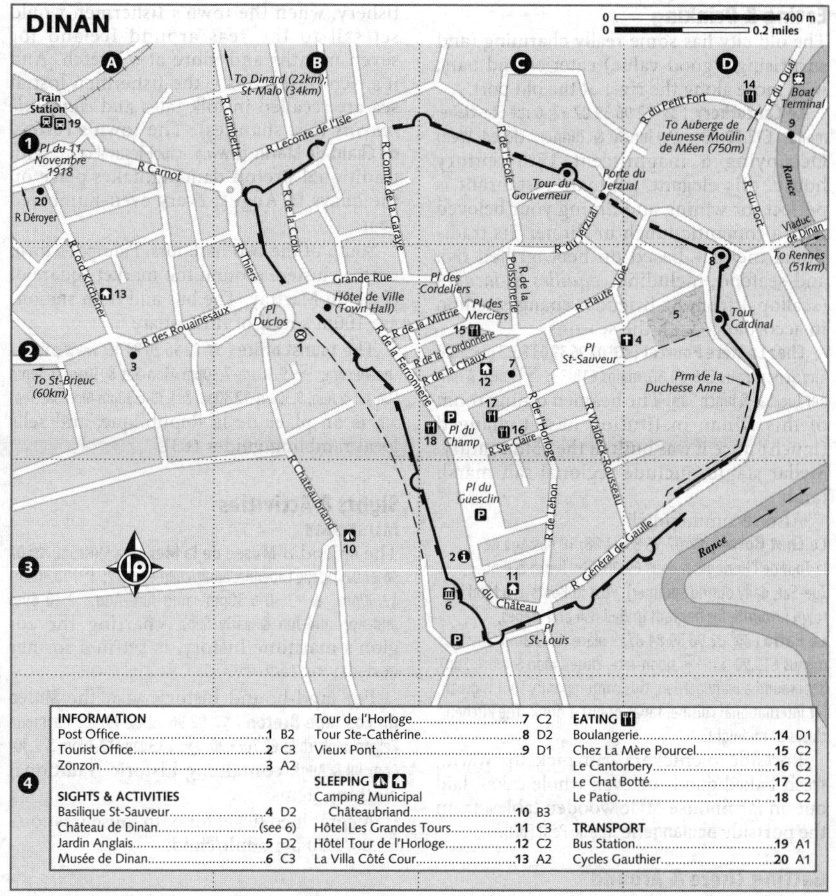

late Sep) This two-star campsite at the foot of the ramparts is the closest to the old town.

Auberge de Jeunesse Moulin de Méen (☎ 02 96 39 10 83; dinan@fuaj.org; Vallée de la Fontaine des Eaux; camping €6, dm incl breakfast €15.70; reception 9am-noon & 5-9pm, closed late Dec–early Feb;) Dinan's HI-affiliated youth hostel is in a lovely vine-covered old water mill about 750m north of the port.

Hôtel Tour de l'Horloge (☎ 02 96 39 96 92; hiliotel@wanadoo.fr; 5 rue de la Chaux; s €42-57, d €47-62) In the centre of the old town, the 12-room Horloge occupies a charming 18th-century house on a cobbled, car-free lane, which contrasts with its brand-new renovations in colourful North African style. Head to the top floor, where rooms have exposed wooden beams and a lofty view of the hotel's namesake clock tower.

Hôtel Les Grandes Tours (☎ 02 96 85 16 20; www.hotel-dinan-grandes-tours.com; 6 rue du Château; s €48-52, d €51-55; Feb–mid-Dec) In its former life as the Hôtel des Messageries, this hotel was fabled as the place Victor Hugo stayed with his very good friend Juliette Drouet in 1836. Blue-shaded rooms (especially those on the sloped-ceilinged top floor) are snug but conducive to snuggling up, and there's lock-up parking (€5 from mid-March to mid-November, free during winter).

La Villa Côté Cour (☎ 02 96 39 30 07; www.villa-cote-cour-dinan.com; 10 rue Lord Kitchener; s €77.50-87.50, d €85-160, q €190-210;) Live the dream…opening onto a delightful garden, this exquisite *chambre d'hôte* has just four countrified rooms with checked fabrics, scrubbed floorboards and a decadent sauna (€9.50).

Eating & Drinking

The old city has some really charming (and surprisingly good-value) eateries and bars; with more along the river at the old port.

Le Cantorbery (☎ 02 96 39 02 52; 6 rue Ste-Claire; menus €12.50-38; ⏰ lunch & dinner, closed Wed) Occupying a magnificent 17th-century house, this elegant, intimate restaurant is perfect for wining and dining your beloved over a romantic lunch or dinner. Its traditional menu – based on beef, grilled fish and seafood, including *coquilles St-Jacques* (scallops) from St-Brieuc – changes tempo in accordance with the seasons.

Chez La Mère Pourcel (☎ 02 96 39 03 80; 3 place des Merciers; menus €28-62.50, mains €18-33; ⏰ lunch & dinner Tue-Sat & lunch Sun) The beamed dining room of this Dinan institution hasn't changed (much) since it was built in the 15th century. Stellar staples include regional salt-marsh lamb.

Also recommended:

Le Chat Botté (☎ 02 96 85 31 58; 18 passage de la Tour de l'Horloge; menus €9-15; ⏰ lunch & dinner Tue-Sat, daily during summer) 'Puss in Boots' is a local old-town favourite for fragrant grilled fish and crêpes.

Le Patio (☎ 02 96 39 84 87; 9 place du Champ Clos; menus €10.90-13; ⏰ noon-late, closed Mon & lunch Sun) Set around a leafy garden, this contemporary spot is great for international cuisine, tapas or just a drink. The kitchen closes at midnight.

Portside picnickers can pick up warm, fresh-baked goods or even whole cakes, laid out on farmhouse-style wooden tables, from the portside **boulangerie** (rue du Petit Fort).

Getting There & Around

Buses leave from place Duclos and the bus station. **Illenoo** (☎ 02 99 26 16 00) runs five daily services to Dinard (€2, 30 minutes) and Rennes (€3, 1¼ hours).

There are trains to St-Malo (€7.90, one hour, five daily) and Rennes (€12.20, one hour), both with a change.

Cycles Gauthier (☎ 02 96 85 07 60; 15 rue Déroyer; ⏰ 9am-noon & 2-7pm Tue-Sat) rents out bikes for €15 per day.

For taxi services call ☎ 02 96 39 67 20.

PAIMPOL

pop 7900

Set around a working fishing harbour and ringed by half-timbered buildings, Paimpol (Pempoull in Breton) is rich in history, as the one-time home port of the Icelandic fishery, when the town's fishermen would set sail to the seas around Iceland for seven months and more at a stretch. And it's rich in legends – the fishermen lost at sea are recalled in folk tales and *chants de marins* (sea shanties). The town's **Festival de Chant de Marin** (www.paimpol-festival.com), with traditional Breton dancing, takes place on the quays in August every even-numbered year.

South of the two harbours, Paimpol's town centre clusters around the market square of place du Martray. The bus and train stations are 100m south of this square.

The **tourist office** (☎ 02 96 20 83 16; www.paimpol-goelo.com; ⏰ 9.30am-7.30pm Mon-Sat & 10am-1.30pm Sun Jul & Aug, 9.30am-12.30pm & 1.30-6.30pm Mon-Sat Sep-Jun) is on place de la République, and sells local rambling guides (€3).

Sights & Activities

MUSEUMS

The splendid **Musée de la Mer** (Sea Museum; ☎ 02 96 22 02 19; rue Labenne; adult/child €4.60/2; ⏰ 10.30am-12.30pm & 2.30-6.30pm mid-Jun–Aug, 2.30-6pm mid-Apr–mid-Jun & early Sep), charting the region's maritime history, is set in a former cod-drying factory.

For land-bound history, visit the **Musée du Costume Breton** (☎ 02 96 22 02 19; rue Raymond Pellier; adult/child €2.70/1.20; ⏰ 10.30am-12.30pm & 2.30-6pm Jul & Aug), containing historic traditional clothing items.

A combined ticket for both museums costs €5.80/2.70 per adult/child.

STEAM TRAIN

Between May and September, the 1922 steam train **La Vapeur du Trieux** (☎ 08 92 39 14 27; adult/child return €22/11) chuffs along the river bank from Paimpol's station to the artists' town of Pontrieux. Reserve ahead.

ABBAYE DE BEAUPORT

If you have wheels (or you're up for a glorious 1½-hour walk along the seashore from the town harbour), head 3.5km east to the romantic maritime **Abbaye de Beauport** (☎ 02 96 55 18 58; www.abbaye-beauport.com, in French; adult/child €5/3; ⏰ 10am-7pm mid-Jun–mid-Sep, 10am-noon & 2-5pm mid-Sep–mid-Jun). En route, stop at the Pointe de Guilben for beautiful bay views. The tourist office has a free map.

ÎLE DE BRÉHAT

Paimpol is the closest port to **Île de Bréhat** (Enez Vriad in Breton), a tiny, car-free island 8km offshore to the north. With a population of 350, it stretches just 5km from north to south. The most idyllic time to visit is in spring, when Mediterranean wildflowers bloom in its gentle microclimate. In the citadel on the southwestern edge you can visit the **glass-making factory** (☎ 02 96 20 09 09; www.verreriesdebrehat.com; admission €1; ⏰ hr vary). It's possible to rent bikes, but the best way to protect the fragile environment is to walk. There is a seasonal municipal campsite; contact Paimpol's tourist office for information.

Vedettes de Bréhat (☎ 02 96 55 79 50; www.vedettesdebrehat.com) operates ferries (adult/child return €8.50/7, 15 minutes, at least eight sailings daily) to Île de Bréhat from Pointe L'Arcouest, 6km north of Paimpol. Tickets are also available at Paimpol's tourist office. Bikes cost an extra €15 return to transport, which is only possible on certain in- and out-bound journeys. It's cheaper to rent a bike on the island; shops line the right-hand side of the road when you get off the boat.

Sleeping & Eating

Camping Municipal de Cruckin (☎ 02 96 20 78 47; rue de Cruckin; camping for 1/2 adults €7.50/12.90; ⏰ Easter-Sep) Near the Abbaye de Beauport, this eco-campsite runs an environmentally conscious program of energy, water and waste management. It's beautifully sited on the Baie de Kérity, 3.5km southeast of town off the road to Plouha.

L'Artimon (☎ 08 71 11 73 71, 06 24 17 73 12; La Madeleine, Plouezec; dm incl breakfast €15) Backpackers have the informal option of staying at L'Artimon, 8km southeast of town, with a pick-up service in Paimpol if required – call directly or check with Paimpol's tourist office for more info.

Hôtel Le Terre-Neuvas (☎ 02 96 55 14 14; fax 02 96 20 47 66; 16 quai Duguay Trouin; d from €32; ⏰ mid-Jan–mid-Dec) Perched right beside the harbour and a few steps from the historic town centre as well as the seafront, the two-star Terre-Neuvas has comfortable, incredibly inexpensive rooms, some with views out to sea. Its restaurant (*menus* €19 to €31) is a popular port of call for guests and nonguests.

K' Loys (☎ 02 96 20 40 01; www.k-loys.com; 21 quai Morand; d €65-95) Each of the 15 rooms at the cosy three-star 'Chez Louise', a former ship owner's mansion with good wheelchair access, is individually decorated with striped walls and paisley-pattern prints. There are lovely private lounges with richly upholstered booths to relax over a drink.

Crêperie-Restaurant Morel (☎ 02 96 20 86 34; 11 place du Martray; crêpes & galettes €2-9.20; ⏰ lunch & dinner) Over two timber-balustraded levels *packed* with Paimpolaises (who wait outside for the doors to open), this cornerstone of the community on Paimpol's pretty main square prepares perfectly buttered Breton crêpes, as well as scrumptious fillings such as chocolate-laced chestnut cream. In summer more laden tables spill onto a pavement terrace. Order a pitcher of cider and settle back for an authentic slice of Breton life.

L'Islandais (☎ 02 96 20 93 00; 19 quai Morand; menus €18-35; ⏰ lunch & dinner) You'll find a clutch of laid-back, quality seafood restaurants along the western side of the harbour, including this popular spot where the seafood platters are large enough to share between two.

Paimpol's Tuesday-morning **market** spreads over place Gambetta and place du Martray. On weekends, vendors sell freshly shucked oysters at quai Duguay Trouin.

Getting There & Around

TS Loisirs (☎ 02 96 20 51 02; 23 av Chateaubriand), behind the train station, and **Intersport Paimpol** (☎ 02 96 20 59 46; zone de Kerpuns), near the massive Carrefour supermarket complex, both rent a wide variety of bikes and kayaks.

Tibus (☎ 08 10 22 22 22) runs buses to and from St-Brieuc (€2, 1½ hours). In summer most continue to Pointe L'Arcouest.

There are several trains or SNCF buses daily between Paimpol and Guingamp (€6.40, 45 minutes), where you can pick up connections to Brest, St-Brieuc and Rennes.

FINISTÈRE

France's westernmost *département*, Finistère, has a wind-whipped coastline scattered with lighthouses and beacons lashed by waves. Finistère's southern prow, Cornouaille, takes its name from early Celts who sailed from Cornwall and other parts of Britain to settle here, and today it harbours the Breton language, customs and culture.

BRETON LANGUAGE REDUX

Should you happen past a Brittany outlet of fast-food giant McDonald's, you'll receive a *trugarez* (thank you) for using the rubbish bins, and be wished *kenavo* (goodbye) in the car park.

Presumably, this bilingual French and Breton (Breizh) signage isn't included for now-elderly, first-language (non-French-speaking) Bretons. And it's not for bilingual French/Breton speakers, since, of course, they already speak and read French. Rather, it's a symbolic way of localising the multinational in the region.

This trend isn't confined to burger chains. Throughout Brittany you'll see bilingual Breton street and transport signs, and many other occurrences of the language popping up.

Historically speaking, Breton is a Celtic language related to Cornish and Welsh, and more distantly, to Irish and Scottish Gaelic. Following on from the French Revolution, the government banned the teaching of Breton in schools, punishing children who spoke their mother tongue. As happened with other marginalised Celtic cultures, speakers of all ages were stigmatised. For the next century and a half it remained a language spoken in the sanctum of private homes. Education, post-WWII economics, mass media, and, most of all, fluid transportation between Brittany and the rest of the country also saw French rapidly gain ground. Between 1950 and 1990 there was an 80% reduction in Breton usage.

But what constitutes 'Breton' these days is trickier to pin down. The seeds of the language's revival were planted in the 1960s, particularly after France's May 1968 protests, driven by the younger generation rebelling against their oppressed cultural heritage. Bringing about the rebirth of the language, no longer passed on generationally, wasn't straightforward. More often spoken than written (and both spoken and written with regional differences), settling on a standardised Breton for teaching in schools is still complex.

There's also a distinct difference between the Breton of first-generation speakers and 'neo-Breton', particularly as the new incarnation often replaces French words long intermingled with Breton with completely Breton ones. Case in point: *Aotrou* and *Itron* are now used for the French *Monsieur* and *Madame*. Traditionally, though, they denote someone of exceedingly high rank (*Itron* is the respectful term of address for the Virgin Mary) – creating another generational language gap. (Imagine some stranger you encounter in the street saying, without irony, 'Hello, Exalted One', or the like. Bizarre.) Some older Breton speakers also find it hard to shake the ostracism inflicted on them for their language, and aren't comfortable conversing in it openly.

Breton now also extends beyond its historic boundaries. Originally, Basse Bretagne (Lower Brittany, in the west) spoke variants of the Breton language, while Haute Bretagne (Upper Brittany, in the east, including areas such as St-Malo) spoke Gallo, a language similar to French. But today you'll find Breton signage in Rennes' metro stations and in many other parts of the east, emblemising Brittany's culture across the entire region.

When today's students integrate their school-taught Breton into society, Breton will evolve yet again, as France's mosaic of cultures also continues to evolve. For now as the language regenerates, so does the sense of Breton identity. Bolstered, ironically, by usage by such companies as McDonald's. (And just in case you were wondering, the term in Brittany for a Big Mac is, yep, a Big Mac.)

ROSCOFF

pop 3700

Arriving across the Channel into Roscoff (Rosko in Breton) provides a captivating first glimpse of Brittany. Granite houses dating from the 16th century wreathe this pretty port, which is surrounded by emerald-green fields producing cauliflower, onions, tomatoes, new potatoes and artichokes. Roscoff farmers in distinctive horizontally striped tops, known as 'Johnnies', loaded-up boats with plaited strings of locally grown, small, pink onions, crossed the Channel to the UK, then peddled – and pedalled – with their onions hanging from their bikes' handlebars. Today, Johnnies have a near mythical status in the area, with a number still continuing the trade and a new wave of younger-generation Johnnies ensuring the survival of this iconic tradition.

Roscoff's waters conceal beds of *goémon* (algae), harvested for foodstuffs as well as *thalassothérapie* health and beauty treatments.

Orientation

Roscoff ranges around a north-facing bay, with its fishing port and pleasure harbour on the western side. Quai d'Auxerre leads northwest – becoming quai Charles de Gaulle, then rue Amiral Réveillère – to the main place Lacaze-Duthiers.

The car-ferry terminal is at Port de Bloscon, 2km east of the town centre.

Information

The ferry terminal has an ATM, but change currency on board as there's no exchange service in town.

Ferry Laverie (23 rue Jules Ferry; 7.30am-9pm)
Post Office (19 rue Gambetta)
Tourist Office (02 98 61 12 13; www.roscoff-tourisme.com; quai d'Auxerre; 9am-12.30pm & 1.30-7pm Mon-Sat, 10am-12.30pm Sun Jul & Aug, 9am-noon & 2-6pm Mon-Sat Sep-Jun) By the time you're reading this, the tourist office will have moved to its new home next to the lighthouse. There's a computer for visitors to check their email.

Sights & Activities

With its Renaissance belfry rising above the flat landscape, the 16th-century Flamboyant Gothic **Église Notre Dame de Kroaz-Batz** (place Lacaze-Duthiers; 9am-noon & 2-6pm excl religious services) is one of Brittany's most impressive churches.

Wander through 3000 species of exotic plants, many from the southern hemisphere, at **Le Jardin Exotique de Roscoff** (02 98 61 29 19; www.jardinexotiqueroscoff.com; adult/child €5/2; 10am-7pm Jun-Sep, 10.30am-12.30pm & 2-6pm Apr, May & Oct, 2-5pm Nov & Mar).

Photographs trace Roscoff's roaming onion farmers from the early 19th century at the **Maison des Johnnies** (02 98 61 25 48; 48 rue Brizeux; adult/child €4/2.50; tours in English & French 10.30am Tue & 3pm Thu outside school holidays, 3pm Mon, Tue, Thu & Fri school holidays, additional tours 11am & 5pm Mon, Tue, Thu & Fri & 3pm & 5pm Sun mid-Jun–mid-Sep). Tours at 5pm on Tuesdays between mid-June and mid-September include a free hour-long meeting with Johnnies from 6pm to 7pm. Check ahead, as it's anticipated that the number of tours will increase.

You can learn about local seaweed harvesting at the **Centre de Découverte des Algues** (02 98 69 77 05; 5 rue Victor Hugo; admission free, walks per adult/child €5/3.50; 9am-noon & 2-7pm Mon-Sat), which also organises guided walks, and gives regular free lectures (often in English and German). Then immerse yourself in the stuff at **Thalasso Roscoff** (08 25 00 20 99; www.thalasso.com, in French; rue Victor Hugo; closed Dec), which offers health-inducing activities including a heated seawater pool, a *hammam* (Turkish baths) and a jacuzzi (€11 for all three).

ÎLE DE BATZ

Bordering what is basically a 4-sq-km vegetable garden fertilised by seaweed, the beaches on the **Île de Batz** (pronounced ba; Enez Vaz in Breton) are a peaceful place to bask. The mild island climate tends the luxuriant **Jardins Georges Delaselle** (02 98 61 75 65; adult/child €4.50/2; 1-6.30pm daily Jul & Aug, 2-6pm Wed-Mon Apr-Jun & Sep-Oct), founded in the 19th century, with over 1500 plants from all five continents.

Ferries (adult/child €7.50/4 return, bike €7 return, 20 minutes each way) between Roscoff and Île de Batz run every 30 minutes between 8am and 8pm from late June to mid-September; there are about eight sailings daily during the rest of the year.

On the island, **Le Saout** (02 98 61 77 65) and **Roulez Jeunesse** (02 98 61 76 91) rent bicycles for around €10 per day.

Sleeping & Eating

Roscoff's hotels are home to some first-rate restaurants.

Camping de Perharidy (02 98 69 70 86; www.camping-aux4saisons.fr, in French; Le Ruguel; campsites €8.70-11; Easter-Sep) Close to a sandy beach in the grounds of a lovely 19th-century mansion, this campsite is approximately 3km southwest of Roscoff.

Hôtel Les Arcades (02 98 69 70 45; www.hotel-les-arcades-roscoff.com, in French; 15 rue Amiral Réveillère; d €46-70; Easter–early Nov;) Perched right above the rocks on the waterfront in the town's heart, this cosy two-star hotel, run by the same family for nearly a century, has 24 light-filled, light-coloured rooms and a glass-paned restaurant (mains around €15) serving up seafood and spectacular views.

Hôtel Les Chardons Bleus (02 98 69 72 03; www.chardonsbleus.fr.st, in French; 4 rue Amiral Réveillère; d €55-80; mid-Mar–Jan) Set back just 100m from the port, in the town centre, the 'Thistles', a Logis de France, has 10 comfortable rooms, and an old-fashioned formal restaurant (*menus* €10 to €40) specialising in seafood.

Hôtel du Centre (02 98 61 24 25; www.chezjanie.com; r €59-108; mid-Feb–mid-Nov) Contemporary, artistic rooms at this boutique hotel look like they've been lifted out of a magazine, and indeed they've featured in many. Sea-view rooms looking out over the postcard-pretty old port cost around 20% more. But it's perhaps best known for its restaurant, Chez Janie (*menu* €24), serving Breton classics like *kig ha farz* – a farmers' family meal based around the Breton cake *far*, cooked in a linen bag within a boiling bacon and vegetable stew.

Also recommended:

La P'tite Fabrik (☎ 02 98 69 92 69; 18 rue Jules Ferry) Watch artisan crêpes being handmade in the open kitchen of this crêpe shop in the old town, and perhaps pick some up for a beach picnic.

Le Surcouf (☎ 02 98 69 71 89; 14 rue Amiral Réveillère; menus €10-25; lunch & dinner) A reliable year-round opener, this brasserie-restaurant is unsurprisingly popular with locals. Specific opening hours and days can vary slightly.

Brasserie Restaurant Les Alizés (☎ 02 98 69 75 90; quai d'Auxerre; menus €12.50-31; lunch & dinner Jun–mid-Sep, closed 1 day per week mid-Sep–May) This sophisticated 1st-floor restaurant has a lift for wheelchair access, a nautical area in its sea-view dining room, and top-quality seafood.

Getting There & Away

Brittany Ferries (☎ reservations 08 25 82 88 28; www.brittany-ferries.com) links Roscoff to Plymouth in England (five to nine hours, one to three daily year-round) and Cork in Ireland (14 hours, once-weekly June to September). Boats leave from Port de Bloscon, about 2km east of the town centre.

The combined bus and train station is on rue Ropartz Morvan.

Cars Bihan (☎ 02 98 83 45 80) operates buses from Roscoff to Brest (€2, 1½ to two hours, up to four daily), departing from the ferry terminal (Port de Bloscon) and passing by the town centre.

There are regular trains and SNCF buses to Morlaix (€5.20, 45 minutes), where you can make connections to Brest, Quimper and St-Brieuc.

MORLAIX

pop 17,000

At the bottom of a deep valley sluicing through northeastern Finistère, Morlaix is an engaging and easily accessed city that's also a good gateway to the coast and the *enclos paroissiaux* (enclosed parishes), the rich sculptures surrounding many of the parish churches fanning out to the south (such as the 16th-century masterpiece in the village of Pleyben).

Towering above the town, the arched 58m-high railway viaduct was built in 1863. Below, a few steps southwest, is the **tourist office** (☎ 02 98 62 14 94; officetourisme.morlaix@wanadoo.fr; place des Otages; 10am-2.30pm & 2-7pm Mon-Sat, 10am-12.30pm Sun Jul & Aug, 9am-12.30pm & 2-6pm Tue-Sat Sep-Jun). From the train station, take rue de Léon south, then turn left and descend the stairs of rue Courte.

Café de l'Aurore (☎ 02 98 88 03 05; 17 rue Traverse; Mon-Sat) has a free internet terminal for bar customers, and regular live music. Or log on at **Cyberarena** (☎ 02 38 88 15 83; 16 rue Basse; per hr €4.50, 11am-1am Mon-Sat, 1pm-1am Sun).

Sights & Activities

The late-15th-century Flamboyant Gothic **Église St-Melaine** (9am-noon & 2-6pm) bears a star-studded barrel-vault roof and polychrome wooden statues, including St Peter and the eponymous St Melaine.

The area's history, archeology and art are showcased at **Le Musée de Morlaix** (☎ 02 98 88 68 88; place des Jacobins; 10am-12.30pm & 2-6.30pm daily Jul & Aug, 10am-noon & 2-6pm Mon & Wed-Fri, 2-6pm Sat Easter-May & Sep, 10am-noon & 2-5pm Mon & Wed-Fri, 2-5pm Sat Oct-Easter & Jun). The museum also incorporates the beautifully preserved half-timbered house nearby, **La Maison à Pondalez** (☎ 02 98 62 14 94; 9 Grand' Rue; 10.30am-12.30pm & 3-6pm Tue-Sat Jul & Aug, 10.30am-12.30pm & 2-6pm Wed-Sat Sep-Jun). Tickets per adult/child cost €4.10/2.20 for both the museum and the house.

A great way to see the area by land and sea combines a boat trip through the islands of the Baie de Morlaix and a picturesque train trip between Roscoff and Morlaix with **Le Léon à Fer et à Flots** (☎ 02 98 62 07 52; www.aferaflots.org, in French; adult/child €23/12; Apr-Sep, hours depend on tides).

Sleeping & Eating

Rue Ange de Guernisac has several enticing restaurants.

Ty Pierre (☎ 02 98 63 25 75, pierreyvesjacquet@hotmail.com; 1bis place de Viarmes; s/d/tr with shared bathroom incl breakfast €31/47/62) Artworks and artefacts Pierre-Yves Jacquet's picked up on his Asian travels now decorate his *chambre d'hôte*'s 10 spacious rooms. No, at this price there's no lift (count on climbing three or four floors). And most rooms don't have their own bathroom (they're just along the wide corridors). But bikes are available for rent from €15 per day. Bonus: the B&B's just across from the cosy Breton bar, La Chope (closed Monday), with French football on the telly and cider on tap.

Hôtel de l'Europe (☎ 02 98 62 11 99; www.hotel-europe-com.fr; 1 rue d'Aiguillon; r €85-150) Regal, refined, yet still relaxed, the Hôtel de l'Europe occupies an elegant 19th-century building. Moulded ceilings, carved panelling and sculpted woodwork fill the sweeping public areas (with wi-fi); the romantic guest rooms have rich apricot and rose tones and mod cons including free broadband.

Grand Café de la Terrasse (☎ 02 98 88 20 25; 31 place des Otages; mains €12.50-19.80; 🕑 7am-midnight Mon-Sat) In the heart of town, Morlaix's showpiece is this stunning 1872-established brasserie with an original central spiral staircase. Sip tea, coffee or something stronger, or sup on classical brasserie fare like rabbit and leek crumble.

Getting There & Away

Morlaix has frequent train services including to Brest (€9.40, 45 minutes), Roscoff (€5.20, 30 minutes) and Paris (Gare Montparnasse; from €65.40, four hours).

HUELGOAT

pop 1709

Visitors to Brittany often stick to the coast, but the mystical wooded interior, steeped in Breton mythology and legend, reveals a completely different side to the region. One of the most enchanting inland villages is Huelgoat (An Uhelgoat in Breton), 30km south of Morlaix. The village borders the unspoiled Forêt d'Huelgoat, a forest with otherworldly rock formations, caves, menhirs and abandoned silver and lead mines. To the east and northeast are the Forêt de St-Ambroise and the Forêt de Fréau.

Orientation & Information

Huelgoat hugs a small Y-shaped lake. Its **tourist office** (☎ /fax 02 98 99 72 32; 🕑 10am-12.30pm & 2-5.30pm Mon-Sat Jul & Aug, 10am-noon & 2.30-4.30pm Mon-Fri Sep-Jun) is in the Moulin du Chaos, an old mill beside the bridge at the eastern end of the lake.

Activities

The forest's **walking tracks** are a haven of calm in spring and autumn, but get busy in summer and muddy in the wet winter months. An undemanding walking trail (45 minutes round trip) leads walkers downstream from the bridge, on the opposite bank to the tourist office. From here, the trickling River Argent disappears into a picturesque, wooded valley that is punctuated by giant, moss-covered granite boulders.

Longer hikes (1½ to two hours) lead along the Promenade du Canal to some old silver mines and to the unremarkable Grotte d'Artus (Arthur's Cave).

Sleeping & Eating

Camping Municipal du Lac (☎ 02 98 99 78 80; rue Général de Gaulle; per person/site from €3/3.50; 🕑 mid-Jun–mid-Sep) This 80-place lakeside campsite sits 1km west of the town centre.

Hôtel-Restaurant du Lac (☎ 02 98 99 71 14; fax 02 98 99 70 91; 9 rue Général de Gaulle; r €49-85; 🕑 closed Jan) Huelgoat's only hotel, a lime-green Logis de France with forest-green trimmings, fronts the lake in the centre of town. Below its 15 soundproofed rooms it has a good on-site restaurant (*menus* €28 to €34) serving French fare from around the country, such as chicken breast with walnut and cheese sauce, as well as pizzas (€6.80 to €10.80) and warming Irish coffees. Wi-fi's free.

Crêperie des Myrtilles (☎ 02 98 99 72 66; 26 place Aristide-Briand; crêpes €1.90-6.20, menus €9.20-14.50; 🕑 lunch & dinner Jan-Oct, closed Mon except Jul & Aug) Inside this slate-floored place with low wooden ceilings, located on the town's main square, you can tuck into the signature *crêpe aux myrtilles* (crêpes with locally picked blueberries) or an egg-and-cheese-concocted *crêpe forestière*. There's a lovely outdoor summer terrace. Afterwards, peek in at the art gallery **Les Stéles** (☎ 02 98 99 79 20; www.les.steles.fr, in French; 24 place Aristide Briand) next door.

Huelgoat has a trio of charming *chambres d'hôtes* right in the village:

Finistère B&B (☎ 02 98 99 83 72; 18 rue des Cieux; s/d incl breakfast €41/57) Two of these four light, airy rooms are self-catering; the rate drops by €6 if you forgo breakfast. No credit cards.

O'Brien's (☎ 02 98 99 82 73; www.chateaubrien.com; 4 rte de Berrien; r incl breakfast from €50) Kids are warmly welcomed at this countrified spot, which has a convivial guest lounge with club sofas and a beamed ceiling.

Laura's (☎ 02 98 99 91 62; 2 impasse de Cendres; r incl breakfast from €55) This pretty blue-shuttered place opens to a sunny garden. Wi-fi's free.

Getting There & Away

At least two services daily travel to/from Morlaix (€2, one hour). Buses stop in front of the church in place Aristide-Briand.

BREST

pop 145,100

Today much of Brest's mid-20th-century architecture is maturing as the city settles into its new skin after it – as one of France's most important naval and commercial ports – was virtually reduced to rubble by Allied air attacks during WWII. The city was rapidly rebuilt after the war to provide housing for its residents, many of whom lived in temporary accommodation for an entire generation.

The town is still a major port and military base; you'll see French sailors' blue uniforms with gold epaulettes throughout the town, as well as plenty of students from Brest's university.

Brest's built-up city centre provides a dramatic contrast to the seaswept Île d'Ouessant (opposite), accessible by boat or plane from Brest.

Orientation

Brest sprawls along the northern shore of the deep natural harbour known as the Rade de Brest. Its 13th-century castle (one of the few buildings to survive the bombing), the naval base (Arsenal Maritime) and Port de Commerce are on the waterfront. From the castle, rue de Siam runs northeast to place de la Liberté, the city's main square, then it intersects with av Georges Clemenceau, the main northwest–southeast traffic artery.

Information

Point Bleu (7 rue de Siam; 7am-8.30pm) Launderette.

Post Office (place Général Leclerc)

Tourist Office (02 98 44 24 96; www.brest-metropole-tourisme.fr; place de la Liberté; 9.30am-7pm Mon-Sat & 10am-noon Sun late Jun–Aug, 9.30am-6pm Mon-Sat Sep-Jun)

Sights & Activities

With 50 tanks in three thematic pavilions – polar, tropical and temperate – the gleaming modern aquarium **Océanopolis** (02 98 34 40 40; www.oceanopolis.com; port de Plaisance; adult/child €15.80/11; 9am-6pm daily May-Jun & early–mid-Sep, to 7pm daily Jul & Aug, 10am-5pm Tue-Fri, 10am-6pm Sat & Sun Oct-Mar) is great, especially on (not uncommon) rainy days. Tip: buying your ticket from the tourist office for the same price allows you to skip the queues and head straight in to view the kelp forests, seals, crabs, anemones, penguins, sharks and more. It's about 3km east of the city centre; take bus 15 from place de la Liberté.

Learn about Brest's maritime military history at the **Musée de la Marine** (Naval Museum; 02 98 22 12 39; adult/child €5/free; 10am-6.30pm Apr–mid-Sep, 10am-noon & 2-6pm Wed-Mon mid-Sep–Mar). The museum is housed within the fortified 13th-century **Château de Brest**, built to defend the harbour on the River Penfeld. Following the 1532 union of Brittany and France, both the castle and its harbour became a royal fortress. From its ramparts there are striking views of the harbour and the naval base. Museum tickets cost €3 from Brest's tourist office.

A sobering reminder of how Brest was on the eve of WWII can be seen at the 14th-century tower, **Tour Tanguy** (02 98 00 88 60; place Pierre Péron; admission free; 10am-noon & 2-7pm daily Jun-Sep, 2-5pm Wed-Thu & 2-6pm Sat & Sun Oct-May). Other exhibits on the town's history include the documented visit of three Siamese ambassadors in 1686 who presented gifts to the court of Louis XIV; rue de Siam was renamed in their honour.

La Société Maritime Azenor (02 98 41 46 23; adult/child €15/10; Apr-Sep) offers 1½-hour cruises around the harbour and the naval base two or three times daily from both the Port de Commerce (which is near the castle) and the Port de Plaisance (which is opposite Océanopolis).

Festivals & Events

Les Jeudis du Port (Harbour Thursdays; admission free; 7.30pm-midnight Thu mid-Jul–late Aug) Try to plan to be in Brest on a Thursday night during summer when Les Jeudis du Port fill the port with live rock, reggae and world music, as well as street performances and children's events.

Sleeping

Camping du Goulet (02 98 45 86 84; www.campingdugoulet.com, in French; Ste-Anne du Portzic; campsite €13-23;) This huge, hilly, three-star campsite is in Ste-Anne du Portzic, 6km southwest of Brest and 400m from the sea. Take bus 28 from rue Georges Clemenceau (near the tourist office) to the Le Cosquer stop.

Auberge de Jeunesse Éthic Étapes (02 98 41 90 41; brest.aj.cis@wanadoo.fr; rue de Kerbriant; dm incl sheets & breakfast €16;) Near Océanopolis and a stone's throw from the artificial beach at Moulin Blanc, this bright, modern, 118-bed hostel has bike storage and good wheelchair access. Take bus 15 from the train station to the terminus (Port de Plaisance).

Hôtel Bellevue (02 98 80 51 78; www.hotelbellevue.fr, in French; 53 rue Victor Hugo; d €42-82) With shades of blue and yellow throughout the 26 rooms and the welcoming bar area (open 2pm to 11pm), this cheerful, clean, two-star hotel has the convenience of on-site parking (€5) and a lift, as well as Brest's shopping streets, train station and port a short stroll away.

Hôtel Continental (☎ 02 98 80 50 40; continental-brest@hotel-sofibra.com; rue Émile Zola; s €101-133, d €165-170;) With sleek, streamlined rooms and crisp white bathrooms finished off with tiled friezes, the classy three-star Continental has a much more lavish, art-deco-styled interior than its plain exterior lets on. All 73 soundproofed rooms are equipped with mod cons including satellite TV. Considerable reductions on room rates on weekends.

Eating

Amour de Pomme de Terre (☎ 02 98 43 48 51; 23 rue Halles St-Louis; menus €15-30; lunch & dinner, closed Sun & lunch Sat) 'Potato Love' serves up all manner of potato-oriented dishes such as gratins, along with fresh fruit and vegetable salads from the covered market opposite, and a dip into a basket of rich dried sausages, from which you hack off a hunk.

Ma Petite Folie (☎ 02 98 42 44 42; Port de Plaisance; menus €20-40; lunch & dinner Mon-Sat) Aboard an old green-and-white lobster-fishing boat strung with buoys and forever beached at Moulin Blanc, this character-filled restaurant has exceptional crab, prawns and fresh fish in butter sauce, ideally finished off with pear tart for dessert and washed down with crisp white wine.

Fleur de Sel (☎ 02 98 44 38 65; 15bis rue de Lyon; mains €22-41; lunch & dinner, closed Sun, lunch Sat & Mon) Its style is minimalist art deco but the atmosphere is warm and welcoming at this creative place, run by the same owners as Amour de Pomme de Terre, but serving up a wider variety of creative French cuisine such as veal kidneys sizzled in truffle vinegar.

Head to **Les Halles St-Louis** (9am-1pm & 4-7pm Mon-Sat, 9am-1pm Sun), Brest's covered market, for self-catering supplies. An **open-air market** takes place out front on Sunday mornings.

Getting There & Away

AIR

Brest's newly expanded **airport** (www.brest.aeroport.fr) has regular Ryanair flights to/from London (Luton), and Flybe flights to/from Birmingham, Exeter, Southampton and Edinburgh, with services to additional destinations on the cards.

BOAT

Ferries to Île d'Ouessant (see p328) leave from the Port de Commerce. In summer, **Azénor** (☎ 02 98 41 46 23; www.azenor.com, in French) connects Brest with Camaret-sur-Mer on the Crozon Peninsula (one-way adult/child €9/7, one hour, twice daily except Saturday during July and August).

BUS

Brest's **bus station** (☎ 02 98 44 46 73) is beside the train station. Routes include Le Conquet (€2, 45 minutes, six daily) and Roscoff (€2, 1½ hours, four daily).

CAR & MOTORCYCLE

Hire companies include **ADA** (☎ 02 98 44 44 88; 9 av Georges Clemenceau), which also rents bikes, and **Europcar** (☎ 02 98 44 66 88; rue Voltaire).

TRAIN

There are frequent trains or SNCF buses to Quimper (€14.60, 1¼ hours) and Morlaix (€9.40, 45 minutes), which has connections to Roscoff. There are also around 15 TGV trains daily to Rennes (€30, two hours) and Paris (Gare Montparnasse; from €86.80, 4½ hours).

Getting Around

Shuttle buses (one-way €4.60) connect the bus station and the airport approximately hourly; a taxi for the 10km trip costs around €15.

The local bus network **Bibus** (☎ 02 98 80 30 30) sells tickets good for two hours for €1.20 and day passes for €3. There's an information kiosk on place de la Liberté.

From June to September, the tourist office rents bikes for €8 per day (€4 with a bus day pass).

To order a taxi call ☎ 02 98 80 18 01 or ☎ 02 98 80 68 06.

ÎLE D'OUESSANT

pop 950

Although it's frequented by summer visitors by the ferryload, free-roaming little black sheep and traditional houses give the windswept Île d'Ouessant (Enez Eusa in Breton, meaning 'Island of Terror'; Ushant in English) an ends-of-the-earth feel – best experienced by hiking its 45km craggy coastal path.

Orientation & Information

Ferries land at Port du Stiff on the east coast. The island's only village is Lampaul, 4km west on the sheltered Baie de Lampaul. A handful of hotels, restaurants and shops are sprinkled along the west coast.

Île d'Ouessant's **tourist office** (☎ 02 98 48 85 83; www.ot-ouessant.fr, in French; place de l'Église, Lampaul; ⏰ 10am-noon & 1.30-5pm Mon-Sat, 10am-noon Sun Jun-Sep, closed Oct-May) sells walking brochures and can hook you up with operators offering horse riding, sailing and other activities.

Sights & Activities

MUSEUMS

The black-and-white-striped **Phare de Créac'h** is the world's most powerful lighthouse. Beaming two white flashes every 10 seconds, visible for over 50km, it serves as a beacon for over 50,000 ships entering the Channel each year. Beneath is the island's main museum, the **Musée des Phares et des Balises** (Lighthouse & Beacon Museum; ☎ 02 98 48 80 70; adult/child €4.10/2.60; ⏰ 10.30am-6.30pm Apr-Sep, 1.30-5pm Oct-Mar), which tells the story of these vital navigation aids; more interesting is the section on shipwrecks and underwater archeology.

Two typical local houses make up the small **Écomusée d'Ouessant** (☎ 02 98 48 86 37; Maison du Niou; adult/child €3.30/2.10; ⏰ 10.30am-6.30pm Apr-Sep, 1.30-5pm Oct-Mar). One recreates a traditional homestead, furnished like a ship's cabin, with furniture fashioned from driftwood and painted in bright colours to mask its imperfections; the other explores the island's history and customs.

A combined ticket giving entry to both museums costs €6.50/4.10 for an adult/child. Check ahead as schedules are liable to change.

BEACHES

Plage de Corz, 600m south of Lampaul, is the island's best beach. Other good spots to stretch out are **Plage du Prat**, **Plage de Yuzin** and **Plage Ar Lan**. All are easily accessible by bike from Lampaul or Port du Stiff.

Sleeping & Eating

Camping Municipal (☎ 02 98 48 84 65; fax 02 98 48 83 99; Stang Ar Glan, Lampaul; per person from €2.80; ⏰ Apr-Sep) About 500m east of Lampaul, this sprawling 100-pitch place looks more like a football field than a campsite.

Auberge de Jeunesse (☎ 02 98 48 84 53; fax 02 98 48 87 42; La Croix-Rouge, Lampaul; dm incl breakfast €15; ⏰ closed last 3 weeks Jan) This friendly hostel, on the hill above Lampaul, has two- to six-person rooms. It's popular with school and walking groups; reservations are essential.

Hôtel Roc'h Ar Mor (☎ 02 98 48 80 19; roch.armor@wanadoo.fr; Lampaul; d €55-87, tr €66.50-87; ⏰ mid-Feb–Dec) It's worth paying a tad extra for a panoramic sea view and a balcony at this appealing 15-room hotel with sunlit blue-and-white rooms and good wheelchair access. In a superb location next to the Baie de Lampaul, there's also a good restaurant (mains from €7), with a terrace overlooking the ocean.

Crêperie Ti A Dreuz (☎ 02 98 48 83 01; Lampaul; crêpes around €3-8; ⏰ Easter–mid-Sep) You could be forgiven for thinking you'd been at sea too long, or knocked back too much Breton cider, but 'the slanting house' is so-named for its wonky walls. This quaint island crêperie serves delicious galettes: try the *ouessantine*, with creamy potato, cheese and sausage.

Ty Korn (☎ 02 98 48 87 33; Lampaul; lunch/dinner menus €15/30) The ground floor of this hyperfriendly place is a bar, serving Breton black-wheat beers (made from the same *blé noire* as Breton galettes); upstairs there's an agreeable restaurant. Opening hours can vary.

If you forgot the sandwich filling, you'll find minimarkets in Lampaul.

Getting There & Away

AIR

Finist'air (☎ 02 98 84 64 87; www.finistair.fr) flies from Brest's airport to Ouessant in a mere 15 minutes. There are two flights daily (one-way adult/child €63/36); transporting a bicycle costs €15 one-way.

BOAT

Ferries depart from Brest and the tiny town (and Brittany's most westerly point) of Le Conquet (Konk Leon in Breton). Buses operated by **Les Cars St-Mathieu** (☎ 02 98 89 12 02) link Brest with Le Conquet (€2, 45 minutes, six daily).

In high summer it's a good idea to reserve at least one day in advance and to check in 30 minutes before departure. Transporting a bicycle costs €11.40. Ferry fares quoted are all return.

Penn Ar Bed (☎ 02 98 80 80 80; www.pennarbed.fr) sails from the Port de Commerce in Brest (adult/child €33.40/19.10, 2½ hours) and from Le Conquet (€29.20/16.60, 1½ hours). Boats run between each port and the island two to five times daily from May to September and once daily between October and April.

Getting Around

BICYCLE

Bike-hire operators have kiosks at the Port du Stiff ferry terminal and compounds just up the hill as well as outlets in Lampaul. The going rate for town/mountain bikes is €10/14. You can save by booking and prepaying for a mountain bike (€10) at the Brest tourist office.

Cycling on the coastal footpath is forbidden – the fragile turf is strictly reserved for walkers.

MINIBUS

Islander-run minibus services such as **Ouessant Voyage** (☎ 06 07 90 07 43) meet the ferry at Port du Stiff and will shuttle you to Lampaul or your accommodation for a flat fare of €2 (to guarantee a seat in July and August, book ahead at the island tourist office, or at the tourist office in Brest). For the return journey, the pick-up point is the car park beside Lampaul's church.

Minibus owners also offer two-hour guided tours (€15 per person) of the island, in French.

PRESQU'ÎLE DE CROZON

The anchor-shaped Crozon Peninsula is part of the Parc Naturel Régional d'Armorique, and one of the most scenic spots in Brittany. The partly forested peninsula is criss-crossed by some 145km of signed walking trails, with crêperies in traditional stone buildings tucked in and around the hinterland.

Ménez-Hom

To feel Brittany's wind beneath your wings, the **Club Celtic de Vol Libre** (☎ 02 98 81 50 27; www.vol-libre-menez-hom.com, in French; hang-gliding & paragliding from €75) offers three-hour hang-gliding and paragliding sessions off the rounded, 330m-high, heather- and grass-clad hump of Ménez-Hom. Situated at the peninsula's eastern end, a surfaced road leads to the top of the summit, which has sublime views over the Baie de Douarnenez.

Landévennec

pop 371

To the north of Ménez-Hom, the River Aulne flows into the Rade de Brest beside the pretty village of Landévennec, home to the ruined Benedictine **Abbaye St-Guenolé**. The abbey **museum** (☎ 02 98 27 35 90; adult/child €4/3; 🕓 10am-7pm daily Jul–mid-Sep, 2-6pm Sun-Fri May-Jun & late Sep) records the history of the settlement, founded by St Guenolé in AD 485 and the oldest Christian site in Brittany. Nearby, a new abbey is home to a contemporary community of monks, which runs a little shop selling homemade fruit jellies.

Argol

pop 746

Argol is a quaint village in its own right, but its main draw is the **Musée du Cidre du Bretagne** (Breton Cider Museum; ☎ 02 98 27 35 85; adult/child €5/free; 🕓 10am-noon & 2-7pm Apr-Sep & school holidays, 10am-1pm & 2-7pm Jul & Aug). This former dairy's old stone buildings have been transformed into a working *cidrerie* producing over 300,000 bottles annually. A visit (allow around an hour, including a French-language but very visual film) takes you through the history of cider in Brittany and present-day production. And, of course, you get to taste it too. In July and August only, one of the barns is used as a crêperie (crêpes €4.50 to €7.50; open noon to 10pm nonstop).

Crozon & Morgat

pop 8000

The area's largest town, Crozon, is the engine room for the peninsula. On the water 2km south, Morgat was built in the 1930s by the Peugeot brothers (of motor-vehicle fame) as a summer resort.

Every Tuesday during July and August free concerts take place on place d'Ys, and each year in mid-August the area hosts the **Festival du Bout du Monde** (Festival of the End of the World; www.festivalduboutdumonde.com, in French), featuring world music.

INFORMATION

Housed in the former railway station, the **Crozon tourist office** (☎ 02 98 27 07 92; www.crozon.com, in French; bd Pralognan; 🕓 9.15am-12.30pm & 2-7pm Mon-Sat, 10am-noon Sun Jul & Aug, 9.15am-noon & 2pm–5.30pm or 6pm Mon-Sat Sep-Jun) is on the main road to Camaret.

The **Morgat tourist office** (☎ 02 98 27 29 49; 🕓 9am-noon Mon-Fri) overlooks the promenade at the corner of bd de la Plage and doubles as the town's **post office**.

ECOBUZZ

Tucked away on the road to Crozon 8km west of Le Faou, **Ferme Apicole de Terenez** (☎ 02 98 81 06 90; Rosnoën; www.ferme-apicole-de-terenez.com; s incl breakfast €30-33, d €37-43; ☒) is abuzz with live bees that you can view in its **honey museum** (admission free; ⏲ 9am–at least 7pm daily). Depending on the season, you might also see *apiculteurs* (beekeepers) Irène and Stéphane Brindeau using environmentally friendly cold-extraction methods to extract all-natural honey, produced with the pollen of flowers and trees, from giant combs in the workshop here. You can buy honey, nougat and other homemade honey products like *hydromel* (*chouchen* in Breton; a fermented, alcoholic drink made from honey and water).

But this little haven is more than just a hive of honey-making. The grounds extend to a private forest and even a private island (accessible by foot at low tide; you can walk around it in about 30 minutes), which guests can explore while staying in one of the farm's six timber-lined *chambre d'hôte* rooms. Rates include the sweetest of breakfasts, with the farm's honey baked into cakes, biscuits and more. The Brindeau family (who describe their work here as 'not a job, a passion') can also help organise kayak rental to paddle around the property and beyond. You can cook up a feast on the barbecue, or head just 200m down the road to the postcard-perfect waterfront restaurant, **L'Ermitage** (☎ 02 98 81 93 61; menus €16.50-33.50; ⏲ lunch & dinner Tue-Sun, daily Aug, closed Mar), serving fish caught right outside the door.

ACTIVITIES

Beyond the marina at the southern end of Morgat's fine sandy **beach**, the coastal path offers an excellent 13km hike (part of the GR34) along the sea cliffs to **Cap de la Chèvre**.

Morgat-based companies **Vedettes Rosmeur** (☎ 02 98 27 10 71) and **Vedettes Sirènes** (☎ 02 98 26 20 10) operate 45-minute boat trips to the colourful **sea caves** along the coast. Tours (adult/child €10/7) depart from Morgat harbour several times daily from April to September.

SLEEPING & EATING

Morgat's seafront and place d'Ys are good spots to trawl for seafood restaurants.

Camping Les Pieds Dans l'Eau (☎ 02 98 27 62 43; http://lespiedsdansleau.free.fr, in French; St-Fiacre; per person/tent/car from €4/4/2.30; ⏲ mid-Jun–mid-Sep) 'Camping feet in the water' (almost literally, at high tide) is one of 16 campsites along the peninsula.

Mana Mana Backpacker (☎ 02 98 26 20 97; www.mana-mana.net; rte de Penfrat, Le Pouldu; dm €15-16, sheets €3; ⏲ closed mid-Jan–Mar) In the best free-spirited travellers' tradition, this 30-bed independent hostel has a cosy lounge/party room, a self-catering kitchen, good wheelchair access and a garden, as well as free wi-fi. You can rent surfboards and bikes for €5 each per day; breakfast costs €5.50. There are discounts for longer stays. From the bus stop, head north along the beach and turn left on rue de Trelez for 900m.

Hôtel de la Baie (☎ 02 98 27 07 51; hotel.delabaie@presquile-crozon.com; 46 bd de la Plage, Morgat; d €40-65) One of the *very* few places to remain open year-round, this simple, friendly, family-run spot on Morgat's promenade has views over the ocean and is one of the best deals around – even better if you take a room with shower only (from €33). Parking's free; breakfast costs €6.50.

Saveurs et Marées (☎ 02 98 26 23 18; 52 bd Plage, Morgat; menus €17-45; ⏲ lunch & dinner, closed Feb) Our pick of Morgat's clutch of restaurants is this lemon-yellow cottage overlooking the sea for its breezy dining room, sunny terrace and consistently good, locally caught seafood (including succulent lobster).

Camaret-sur-Mer

pop 2600

At the western extremity of the Crozon Peninsula, Camaret is a classic little fishing village – or at least, it was until early last century, as France's then biggest crayfish port. Abandoned fishing-boat carcasses now decay in its harbour, but it remains an enchanting place that lures artists, with an ever-increasing number of **art galleries** (15 to date) dotted around town, particularly along rue de la Marne and around place St-Thomas, one block north of the waterfront.

Camaret's **tourist office** (☎ 02 98 27 93 60; www.camaret-sur-mer.com, in French; 15 quai Kléber; ⏲ 9am-7pm Mon-Sat & 10am-1pm Sun Jul & Aug, 9am-noon & 2-6pm Mon-Sat Sep-Jun) is on the waterfront.

The **Chapelle Notre-Dame-de-Rocamadour** (⏲ school holidays only), its timber roof like an inverted ship's hull, is dedicated to the sailors of Camaret, who have adorned it with votive offerings of oars, life buoys and model ships.

Pointe de Pen-Hir, 3km south of Camaret, is a spectacular headland bounded by steep, sheer sea cliffs, with two WWII memorials.

SLEEPING & EATING

Hôtel Vauban (☎ 02 98 27 91 36; fax 02 98 27 96 34; 4 quai du Styvel; d €37-45; ⌚ Feb-Nov) Its airy rooms are contemporary, but the Vauban's old-fashioned hospitality extends to its large rear garden with a barbecue to grill your own fish; and a piano to play. Its bar remains a favourite with Camaret's old-timers too.

Crêperie Rocamadour (☎ 02 98 27 93 17; quai Kléber; mains €10-14; ⌚ lunch & dinner Wed-Sun Sep-Jun, daily Jul & Aug) Close to the tourist office, this beamed-ceilinged place turns out carefully prepared galettes as well as mains like citrus-infused salmon. Finish off with a flaming flambéed crêpe or one smothered in melted chocolate.

Del Mare (☎ 02 98 27 97 22; 16 quai Gustave Toudouze; menus €13.50-26.50; ⌚ lunch & dinner daily Jul & Aug, closed Tue & Wed early Apr–Jun & Sep–mid-Nov) Seafood is the order of the day at this marine-styled place on the main stretch of waterfront, with a clutch of tables on its little timber terrace. Service is prompt and friendly.

There are supermarkets on quai du Styvel and rue de Loc'h.

Getting There & Around

Azénor (p327) runs seasonal ferries between Brest and the Presqu'Île de Crozon.

From mid-April to mid-September, **Penn Ar Bed** (☎ 02 98 80 80 80; www.pennarbed.fr) sails between Camaret and Île d'Ouessant (adult/child return from €30.10/17.10, slightly higher in peak season)

Five buses daily run from Quimper to Crozon (€2, 1¼ hours), continuing to Camaret (€2), and up to four from Camaret and Crozon to Brest (€2, 1¼ hours, daily). Buses also run between Morgat, Crozon and Camaret several times daily (€2, 10 minutes).

To rent a bike, contact **Point Bleu** (☎ 02 98 27 09 04; quai Kador, Morgat) or, in summer, the open-air stall in front of Morgat's tourist office. The going rate is about €10 per day.

QUIMPER

pop 64,900

Small enough to feel like a village with its slanted half-timbered houses and narrow cobbled streets, and large enough to buzz as the troubadour of Breton culture and arts, Quimper (pronounced kam·pair) is Finistère's thriving capital. Derived from the Breton word *kemper*, meaning 'confluence', Quimper sits at the juncture of the small Rivers Odet and Steïr, criss-crossed by footbridges with cascading flowers.

Orientation

The magnolia-shaded, mainly pedestrianised old city clusters around the cathedral on the north bank of the Odet, overlooked by Mont Frugy on the south bank. Most of Quimper's historic architecture concentrates in the tight triangle formed by place Médard, rue Kéréon, rue des Gentilhommes and its continuation, rue du Sallé, to place au Beurre.

Information

Eixxos (☎ 02 98 64 40 56; 12 bd Dupleix; per hr €3.50; ⌚ 11am-10pm Mon-Thu, 11am-1am Fri & Sat, 2-10pm Sun) Internet access.

Laverie de la Gare (4 av de la Gare; ⌚ 8am-8pm) Launderette.

Main Post Office (bd Amiral de Kerguélen)

Tourist Office (☎ 02 98 53 04 05; www.quimper-tourisme.com, in French; place de la Résistance; ⌚ 9am-7pm Mon-Sat, 10am-12.45pm & 3-5.45pm Sun Jul & Aug, 9.30am-12.30pm & 1.30–6pm or 6.30pm Mon-Sat Sep-Jun, 10am-12.45pm Sun Jun & 1-15 Sep) Runs weekly 1½-hour guided city tours in English (€5.20) in July and August, and sells the Pass' Quimper (€13) whereby two people can access four attractions/tours of your choice (from a list of participating organisations).

Sights & Activities

Quimper's **cathedral** (⌚ 9.30am-noon & 1.30-6.30pm Mon-Sat, 1.30-6.30pm Sun May-Oct, 9am-noon & 1.30-6.30pm Mon-Sat, 1.30-6.30pm Sun Nov-Apr) has a distinctive kink built into its soaring light-filled interior – said by some to symbolise Christ's head inclined on one shoulder as he was dying on the cross. Begun in 1239, the cathedral wasn't completed until the 1850s, with the seamless addition of its dramatic twin spires. Between them, high on the west facade, is an equestrian statue of King Gradlon, the city's mythical 5th-century founder.

The ground-floor halls are home to some fairly morbid 16th- to 20th-century European paintings, but things lighten up on the upper levels of the **Musée des Beaux-Arts** (☎ 02 98 95 45 20; 40 place St-Corentin; adult/child €4.50/2.50; ⌚ 10am-7pm daily Jul & Aug, 10am-noon & 2-6pm Wed-Mon Apr-Jun, Sep-Oct, 10am-noon & 2-6pm Wed-Sat & Mon, 2-6pm Sun Nov-Mar). A room dedicated to Quimper-born poet Max Jacob includes sketches by Picasso.

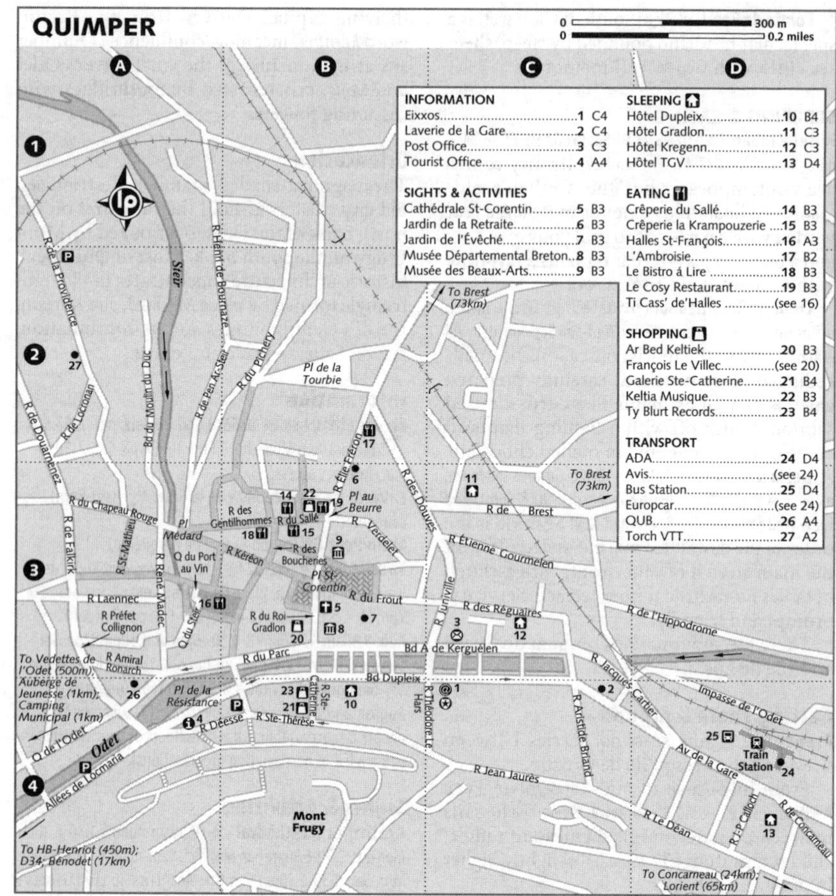

Recessed behind a magnificent stone courtyard beside the cathedral, the **Musée Départemental Breton** (☎ 02 98 95 21 60; 1 rue du Roi Gradlon; adult/child €4/2.50; 🕒 9am-6pm daily Jun-Sep, 9am-noon & 2-5pm Tue-Sat, 2-5pm Sun Oct-May) is housed in the former bishop's palace. Superb exhibits showcase Breton history, furniture, costumes, crafts and archeology. Adjoining the museum is the **Jardin de l'Évêché** (Bishop's Palace Garden; admission free; 🕒 9am–5pm or 6pm).

For even more serenity, pop into the hidden, flower-filled **Jardin de la Retraite** (🕒 9am-7.15pm daily mid-Apr–mid-Oct), secluded behind high walls.

You will be able to watch Quimper's traditional *faïence* pottery being made during 40-minute workshop tours (in French or English) of *faïencier* **HB-Henriot** (☎ 08 00 62 65 10; adult/child €4/2.50; 🕒 Mon-Fri). There are at least two tours daily year-round (up to eight daily in summer). Ask about creative workshops to try your hand at this delicate art too.

Following the switchback path just east of the tourist office up the 72m-high **Mont Frugy** rewards with captivating city views.

Tours

From May to September, **Vedettes de l'Odet** (☎ 08 25 80 08 01, 02 98 57 00 58) runs boat trips (adult/child €24/15, 1¼ hours) from Quimper along the serene Odet estuary to Bénodet, departing from quai Neuf.

Festivals & Events

The **Festival de Cornouaille** (www.festival-cornouaille.com, in French), a celebration of traditional Celtic music, costumes and culture, takes place between the third Saturday and the fourth Sunday of July. After the traditional festival, classical-music concerts are held at different venues around town.

Sleeping

Quimper unfortunately has a chronic shortage of inexpensive accommodation, and none in the old city.

Auberge de Jeunesse (☎ 02 98 64 97 97; quimper@fuaj.org; 6 av des Oiseaux; camping €6, dm incl breakfast €15.20, sheets €2.80; Apr-Sep) Quimper's seasonal youth hostel has self-catering facilities.

Camping Municipal (☎/fax 02 98 55 61 09; av des Oiseaux; campsites from €9; tents Apr-Sep, campervans year-round) This wooded park is 1km west of the old city (3km from the train station). From quai de l'Odet follow rue Pont l'Abbé northwestwards and continue straight ahead where it veers left. Alternatively, take bus 1 from the train station to the Chaptal stop.

Hôtel TGV (☎ 02 98 90 54 00; www.hoteltgv.com; 4 rue de Concarneau; s/d €36/38) The cheapest and best value of several hotels around the train station, 800m from the old city, the TGV has 22 small but bright en-suite rooms. Light sleepers will find the top-floor rooms quieter. Wi-fi's free.

Hôtel Dupleix (☎ 02 98 90 53 35; www.hotel-dupleix.com, in French; 34 bd Dupleix; s €65-68, d €79-83; closed Christmas period) Part of a business complex overlooking the River Odet (with good winter weekend deals), this efficient, modern hotel is fronted by a concrete forecourt with a fountain. Some rooms have a balcony overlooking the cathedral, and it's a handy option if you're driving, with a lock-up garage on site.

Hôtel Gradlon (☎ 02 98 95 04 39; www.hotel-gradlon.com; 30 rue de Brest; r €82-160; closed mid-Dec–mid-Jan) Quimper's most charming hotel is this former 19th-century coach house. Recently renovated with floral and checked fabrics (and wheelchair access), its 22 rooms include three elegant junior suites set around a rose-garden courtyard. There's a cosy bar with a toasty open fire, as well as free wi-fi. Parking costs €8.

Hôtel Kregenn (☎ 02 98 95 08 70; www.hotel-kregenn.fr; 11-15 rue des Réguaires; r €100-180, ste €210;) A Zen timber-decked courtyard and a guest lounge with outsized mirrors and white leather sofas give you the initial impression that Quimper's newest hotel is contemporary in style, but the plush rooms (in pistachio green, ocean blue or chocolate) evoke a traditional feel, as does the warm-hearted welcome. Higher-priced rooms have air-con; two rooms are equipped for wheelchairs. Broadband internet's free; parking costs €6.

Eating & Drinking

As a bastion of Breton culture, Quimper has some exceptional crêperies. Rue du Frout near the cathedral has a couple of small pubs that attract a Breton-speaking clientele.

our pick **Crêperie la Krampouzerie** (☎ 02 98 95 13 08; 9 rue du Sallé; galettes €3.50-7.70; lunch & dinner Tue-Sat) In an atmospheric space with blue-and-white tiled wooden tables, crêpes and galettes are made from organic flours and regional ingredients like *algues d'Ouessant* (seaweed from the Île d'Ouessant), Roscoff onions and homemade ginger caramel. Tables fill the square out front in fine weather, giving it a street-party atmosphere.

Crêperie du Sallé (☎ 02 98 95 95 80; 6 rue du Sallé; galettes €3.90-8.80; lunch & dinner Tue-Sat) For a quarter of a century, locals have crowded into this crêperie decorated with lace curtains,

WORTH THE TRIP – DOUARNENEZ

Explore Brittany's maritime heritage in depth at Douarnenez' **Port-Musée** and **Musée du Bateau** (☎ 02 98 92 65 20; quai du Port Rhu; combined ticket adult/child €6.20/3.80; 10am-7pm mid-Jun–mid-Sep, 10am-12.30pm & 2-6pm Tue-Sun early Apr–mid-Jun & mid-Sep–early Nov, closed early Nov–early Apr). Moored at the open-air Port-Musée, traditional vessels range from a Breton *langoustier* (cray-fishing boat) to a Norwegian masted sailing ship. Within the vast Musée du Bateau, occupying a former sardine cannery (Douarnenez locals are affectionately nicknamed *penn sardin* – sardine head), are smaller traditional boats such as an Inuit kayak and a Welsh coracle, as well as local craft.

Buses run between Douarnenez and Quimper (€2, 35 minutes, six to 10 daily). You'll find appealing cafés scattered around Douarnenez's port.

wooden dressers and painted plates on the walls. Breton specialities include *saucisse fumée* (smoked sausage) and the house speciality, *forestière* made with mushrooms, smoked lard (fatty bacon) and cheese.

Le Bistro á Lire (☎ 02 98 95 30 86; 18 rue des Boucheries; snacks around €4.50, mains €7.80; ⏰ lunch Tue-Sat, salon de thé 9am-7pm Tue-Sat, plus Mon afternoon Jul & Aug) Amid the shelves at this bookshop–*salon de thé*, hungry bookworms can enjoy lunch mains like lasagne or a hot drink and a slice of the *gâteau du jour* (cake of the day) for €5.50. The sunny rear courtyard is reserved for diners during lunch hours.

Le Cosy Restaurant (☎ 02 98 95 23 65; 2 rue du Sallé; mains €11.50-15; ⏰ lunch & dinner Tue-Sat Jul & Aug, lunch Tue-Sat, dinner Fri & Sat Sep-Jun) *Pas de crêpes!* (No crêpes!) the blackboard menu on the street proclaims. Inside, make your way through the *épicerie* (specialist grocer) crammed with locally canned sardines, ciders and other Breton specialities and up the narrow staircase to the eclectic, artistic dining room, where you can tuck in to specialities like gratins and *tartines* (open sandwiches), made from market ingredients.

L'Ambroisie (☎ 02 98 95 00 02; www.ambroisie-quimper.com; 49 rue Elie Fréron; menus €23-48, mains €29; ⏰ lunch & dinner Tue-Sat, lunch Sat, closed mid-Jun–mid-Jul) Quimper's most celebrated gastronomic restaurant is sumptuously decorated with contemporary art and elegant china on snow-white tablecloths. Regional produce provided by chef Gilbert Guyon's friends is used in the creation of house specials like sole with new potatoes and caramelised onions. Cooking classes are available by request.

SELF-CATERING

The covered market **Halles St-François** in the old town has a slew of salad and sandwich options. One of the best, with a clutch of outdoor terrace tables, is **Ti Cass' de'Halles** (☎ 09 98 95 87 56; 3 Halles St-François; dishes from €3.30; ⏰ 10am-3pm Mon-Thu, 10am-7pm Fri & Sat).

Entertainment

From mid-June to mid-September traditional Breton music and dance takes place every Thursday evening at 9pm in the Jardin de l'Évêché (admission €5).

Check posters and leaflets pasted up around town or ask the tourist office for times and venues of a local **fest-noz** (night festival). On average there's one in or near Quimper every couple of weeks.

Shopping

Several shops located in the old town sell Quimper's traditional *faïence* pottery, including **Ar Bed Keltiek** (Celtic World; ☎ 02 98 95 42 82; 2 rue du Roi Gradlon) and **François Le Villec** (☎ 02 98 95 31 54; 4 rue du Roi Gradlon). Breton and Celtic music and art are available at **Keltia Musique** (☎ 02 98 95 45 82; 1 place au Beurre), which carries an excellent range of books and CDs.

For a total change of tune, flip through '70s pop, French punk and rock vinyl at **Ty Blurt Records** (☎ 06 63 52 80 02; 7 rue Ste-Catherine; ⏰ 2-7pm Mon-Sat). A few doors up you can check out traditional and contemporary art on sale at **Galerie Ste-Catherine** (☎ 02 98 90 18 22; 13 rue Ste-Catherine; ⏰ 11am-12.30pm & 2.30-7pm Tue-Sat).

Getting There & Away

BUS

CAT/Connex Tourisme (☎ 02 98 90 68 40) bus destinations include Brest (€6, 1¼ hours) and Douarnenez (€2, 35 minutes, six to 10 daily).

Le Coeur (☎ 02 98 54 40 15) runs buses to Concarneau (€2, 45 minutes, seven to 10 daily); three daily continue to Quimperlé (€2, 1½ hours).

CAR

ADA (☎ 02 98 52 25 25), **Europcar** (☎ 02 98 65 10 05) and **Avis** (☎ 02 98 90 31 34) all have offices right outside the train station.

TRAIN

There are frequent trains to Brest (€14, 1¼ hours, up to 10 daily), Lorient (€10, 40 minutes, six to eight daily), Vannes (€16.30, 1½ hours, seven daily), Rennes (€30.10, 2½ hours, five daily) and Paris (Gare Montparnasse; €68.20, 4¾ hours, eight daily).

Getting Around

Torch VTT (☎ 02 98 53 84 41; 58 rue de la Providence; ⏰ Tue-Sat) rents out mountain bikes for €18 per day. The friendly owner is a fount of information about local cycle routes.

QUB (☎ 02 98 95 26 27; 2 quai de l'Odet), the Quimper bus network, has an information office opposite the tourist office; a single/day ticket costs €1/3.

For a taxi, call ☎ 02 98 90 21 21.

NAME GAME

Brittany's toponymy (the study of place names) gives an insight into words you'll often see on road signs and maps (sometimes with local spelling variations). And you will see them often – over 40,000 Breton place names alone incorporate the word *'ker'*, combined with a family name, place name or a description.

aven, avon – river
bihan – little
braz – big
conk – shelter
ker – town, village, home
loc (6th century), lan (8th and 9th century) – religious settlement
men, mein – stone(s)
menez – mount
mor – sea
nevet – forest
nevez – new
plou – parish (usually followed directly by a saint's name)
trev, tre, treo – parish division
ti, ty – house

CONCARNEAU

pop 20,000

The sheltered harbour of Concarneau (Konk-Kerne in Breton), 24km southeast of Quimper, radiates out from its trawler port, which brings in close to 200,000 tonnes of *thon* (tuna) from the Indian Ocean and off the African coast (the adjacent Atlantic's too cold). Jutting out into the port, the old town, Ville Close, is circled by medieval walls.

Orientation

Concarneau concentrates around the western side of the harbour at the mouth of the River Moros. Ville Close and its fortifications separate the Port de Plaisance, to the south, from the busy fisheries area of the Port de Pêche. Quai d'Aiguillon, becoming quai Peneroff, runs from north to south beside the harbour.

Information

Espace Informatique (☎ 02 98 60 76 37; 23 rue des Écoles; per 15min €1.20; 9am-noon & 2-7pm Mon-Fri, 9am-noon & 2-5pm Sat) Internet access.

Post Office (14 quai Carnot)

Tourist Office (☎ 02 98 97 01 44; www.tourismeconcarneau.fr; quai d'Aiguillon; 9am-7pm Jul & Aug, 9am-12.30pm & 1.30-6.30pm Mon-Sat, 10am-1pm Sun Apr-Jun & 1-15 Sep, 9am-noon & 2-6pm Mon-Sat mid-Sep–March)

Sights & Activities

MUSEUMS & TOURS

The **walled town**, fortified in the 14th century and modified by Vauban two centuries later, huddles on a small island linked to place Jean Jaurès by a footbridge.

Between 15 June and 15 September the walled town can also be accessed through the **Maison du Patrimoine** (☎ 02 98 60 76 06; admission €0.80 mid-Jun–mid-Sep, free mid-Sep–mid-Jun), which has exhibits on the town's history – ask for an English-language brochure. Within the walls, rue Vauban and place St-Guénolé are enchanting for their old stone houses converted into shops, restaurants and galleries.

Return to the mainland via the **fortifications** on the southern side of the island for magical views over the town, the port and the bay.

Concarneau's seafaring traditions, offshore fishing trawlers, model ships and fishing exhibits feature at the **Musée de la Pêche** (Fisheries Museum; ☎ 02 98 97 10 20; 3 rue Vauban; adult/child €6/4; 9.30am-8pm Jul & Aug, 10am-noon & 2-6pm Sep-Jun, closed 3 weeks in Jan).

Founded in 1859, the **Marinarium** (☎ 02 98 50 81 64; place de la Croix; adult/child €5/3; 10am-7pm Jul & Aug, 10am-noon & 2-6pm Apr-Jun & Sep, 2-6pm Oct-Dec, Feb & Mar) is the world's oldest institute of marine biology. Alongside its 10 aquariums are exhibits on oceanography and marine flora and fauna.

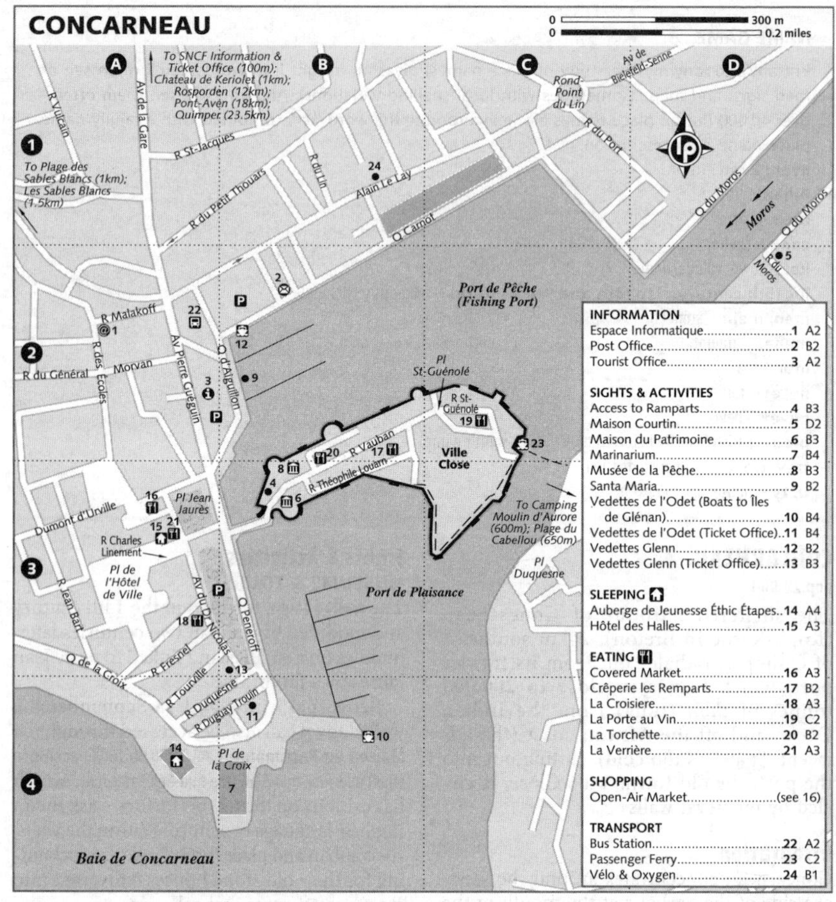

One of Concarneau's last functioning canneries, **Maison Courtin** (Conserverie Courtin; ☎ 02 98 97 01 80; 3 quai du Moros; admission free), conducts tours including a film of the cannery in peak production, and free sampling. Contact the cannery or the tourist office for tour times. If fish are your thing, you can also tour the **fishing port** (☎ 02 98 50 55 18; www.alassautdesremparts.fr, in French; tours €2-6 depending on program; 🕓 9.30-10am & 5-9pm by reservation), 100m from the tourist office, to discover all facets of this age-old Breton industry.

Château de Keriolet (☎ 02 98 97 36 50; adult/child €5/3; 🕓 10.30am-1pm & 2-6pm Sun-Fri, 10.30am-1pm Sat Jun-Sat, by reservation Easter-May) is an exquisite example of 19th-century architecture. Its intriguing Russian connections are revealed during a guided tour. The castle is a well-signed five-minute drive from town (turn right just before the large Leclerc supermarket).

BEACHES

Plage des Sables Blancs is on Baie de la Forêt, 1.5km northwest of the town centre; take bus 2, northbound, from the tourist office. For Plage du Cabellou, 5km south of town, take bus 2, southbound.

WALKING & CYCLING

The tourist office sells two excellent guides: *Balades au Pays des Portes de Cornouaille* (€2.50; in French), describing 18 walks around Concarneau, and *VTT de Cornouaille* (€3.50), outlining 39 cycling circuits.

SEA ANGLING

To reel in some fish of your own, the **Santa Maria** (☎ 06 62 88 00 87; adult/child incl equipment hire €36/21; ⏲ sailing 8am & 1.30pm or 2pm Mon-Fri Jul & Aug) sets out on four-hour sea-angling trips from quai d'Aiguillon near the tourist office. All-day deep-sea fishing expeditions (8am to 6pm on Saturdays in July and August) cost €80.

BOAT TRIPS

In July and August **Vedettes Glenn** (☎ 02 98 97 10 31; 17 av du Dr Nicolas) does four-hour river trips (adult/child €27/15, sailing 2.15pm Tuesday to Friday and Sunday) from Concarneau along the gorgeously scenic estuary of the River Odet. Boat trips also operate to the Îles de Glénan – a cluster of nine little islands about 20km south of Concarneau – starting at €26/14.

Vedettes de l'Odet (☎ 08 25 80 08 01; www.vedettes-odet.com, in French; 1 rue Duguay Trouin) also runs boat trips to both destinations – check with the tourist office or the company directly for seasonal sailing schedules and departure points.

Sleeping

Camping Moulin d'Aurore (☎ 02 98 50 53 08; www.moulinaurore.com, in French; 49 rue de Trégunc; per person/site/car €5.50/5/1.50; ⏲ Apr-Sep) Facilities at this campsite 600m southeast of the harbour and a mere 50m from the sea include a bar/TV room and a laundry. Take bus 1 or 2 to Le Rouz stop from the tourist office or the ferry from Ville Close, then walk southeast along rue Mauduit Duplessis.

Auberge de Jeunesse Éthic Étapes (☎ 02 98 97 03 47; www.ajconcarneau.com; quai de la Croix; dm incl breakfast €14.50; ☒) Fall asleep listening to the waves at this welcoming waterfront hostel next to the Marinarium. Extras include a wraparound barbecue terrace, a self-catering kitchen and pastries for breakfast.

Hôtel des Halles (☎ 02 98 97 11 41; www.hoteldeshalles.com; place de l'Hôtel de Ville; d €52-80; ☒) A few steps from Ville Close, this 22-room hotel looks plain on the outside, but its renovated rooms come in a rainbow of colour combinations like pistachio green and hot pink, with lavender trimmings throughout the public areas (even the lift doors). Breakfast (€8) includes homemade marmalade and bread straight from the oven. Broadband internet's free and the family owners are ultrahelpful.

Les Sables Blancs (☎ 02 98 50 10 12; www.hotel-les-sables-blancs.com; d €105-370; ⊠) Right on the 'white sands' of the beach from which it takes its name, this ultrachic new pad has spacious rooms (with wi-fi) and an excellent restaurant, with good deals on half-board (from €115 per person).

Eating

Cafés, pizzerias and crêperies line the waterfront, and there are more inside the walls of Ville Close.

La Verrière (☎ 02 98 60 55 78; 3 rue des Halles; menus €8.50-27; ⏲ daily in summer, closed Mon) Barbecued fish is the speciality of Concarneau's hippest new hang-out, set around a covered courtyard garden. You can also drop by for tapas or just a drink and take advantage of the free wi-fi.

Crêperie les Remparts (☎ 02 98 50 65 66; 31 rue Théophile Louarn; menu €12; ⏲ Easter-Oct) Enjoy a very Breton lunchtime *menu* of fish soup, *moules-frites* (mussels and fries) and *far* (Breton cake). There's also has an inventive range of savoury crêpes with fillings such as mushrooms in cream sauce.

La Croisiere (☎ 02 98 97 01 87; 11 av du Dr Nicolas; menus €16.50-27; ⏲ lunch Tue-Fri & Sun, dinner Tue-Sat, daily in summer) Just back from the boat-filled marina, the lively La Croisiere is a local fave for its seafood straight off the boat.

La Porte au Vin (☎ 02 98 97 38 11; 9 place St-Guénolé; menus €18-25; ⏲ lunch & dinner Apr-Oct) Highly recommended, this place in the centre of the walled city is a lovely spot in fine weather, with a pretty patio terrace shaded by a red awning. It's consistently strong on traditional cooking (which in Concarneau means fish).

SELF-CATERING

There's a **covered market** (⏲ 9am-noon Tue-Sun) on place Jean Jaurès and a busy **open-air market** in the same square on Monday and Friday mornings.

Enticing *biscuiteries* within Ville Close include **La Torchette** (☎ 02 98 60 46 87; 9 rue Vauban; ⏲ 10.30am-6.30pm, to 11pm Jul & Aug), with chocolate sculptures and Breton biscuits by the bucketful.

Getting There & Away

L'Été Évasion (☎ 02 98 56 82 82) runs up to 10 buses daily between Quimper and Quimperlé, calling by Concarneau (€2 to or from Quimper).

Vélo & Oxygen (☎ 02 98 97 09 77; 65 av Alain Le Lay; ⏲ Tue-Sat) rents out bikes for €10 per day.

WORTH THE TRIP – PONT-AVEN

Once the railway was pushed through in the 19th century, the tiny Breton village of Pont-Aven (population 3000), nestled in the 'valley of willows', was discovered by artists. American painters were among the first to uncover it, but things really took off when France's Paul Gaugin and Emile Bernard set up a colony here in the 1850s. Their work, and that of their disciples, morphed into a movement known today as the Pont-Aven School.

There is some debate in artistic and sociological circles as to whether these works folklorised the local Breton people, but they certainly capture the beauty of the little village and the surrounding countryside. For an insight into the town's place in art history, stop by the **Musée des Beaux-Arts de Pont-Aven** (☎ 02 98 06 14 43; place de l'Hôtel de Ville; adult/child €4.50/2.50; ⏰ 10am-7pm Jul & Aug, 10.30am-12.30pm & 2pm–6pm or 6.30pm Sep-Dec & Feb-Jun, closed Jan). And to see the spots where the masters set up their easels, pick up a free walking-trail map from the **tourist office** (☎ 02 98 06 04 70; place de l'Hôtel de Ville; ⏰ 9.30am-7.30pm Jul & Aug, 9.30am-12.30pm & 2-6.30pm Apr, May & Sep, 10am-12.30pm & 2-6pm Oct-Mar, closed Sun Nov-Easter), which can also help with accommodation if you want to spend the night.

Charming spots for a drink or a meal include the bar-restaurant **Auberge de la Fleur d'Ajonc** (☎ 02 98 06 10 65; place de l'Hôtel de Ville; menus €16-23, mains €8.50-12; ⏰ lunch Tue-Sun, dinner Tue-Sat), in an atmospheric medieval building of sloping stone floors and low ceilings held up by hefty beams; and **Le Moulin de Rosmadec** (☎ 02 98 06 00 22; www.moulinderosmadec.com; menus €35-50, mains €21-28; ⏰ lunch Tue-Wed & Fri-Sun, dinner Mon-Wed, Fri & Sat, closed Feb & Oct), serving gastronomic fare overlooking the town's namesake *pont* (bridge) and *aven* (river in Breton). Le Moulin de Rosmadec also has four delightful guest rooms upstairs (doubles €85 to €90).

Since the 1960s, Pont-Aven has again become a magnet for artists, with no fewer than 60 galleries here in summer. Even in winter, you'll still find around 20 galleries open on weekends.

Pont-Aven is an easy 18km drive southeast of Concarneau. **Buses** (☎ 02 98 44 46 73; €2) – five Monday to Saturday and two on Sunday – connect Pont-Aven with Quimperlé in the east (30 minutes), Concarneau (30 minutes) and Quimper (one hour).

A stubby **passenger ferry** (fare €0.80; ⏰ 8am-11pm daily Jul-Aug, 8am–6.30pm or 8.30pm Mon-Sat, 9am-12.30pm & 2-6.30pm Sun Sep-Jun) links Ville Close with place Duquesne on the eastern side of the harbour.

Call ☎ 02 98 97 10 93 or ☎ 02 98 50 70 50 for a taxi.

MORBIHAN COAST

In the crook of Brittany's southern coastline, the Golfe du Morbihan (Morbihan Coast) is a haven of islands, oyster beds and birdlife. But the area is perhaps best known for its proliferation of mystifying Celtic megaliths, which are strewn throughout most of the *département*.

LORIENT

pop 61,844

Like Brest, the port city of Lorient (An Oriant in Breton) was largely wiped out during WWII. Rapidly reconstructed in the following decades, today it sprawls along the western side of the Rade de Lorient, a natural harbour at the mouth of the River Scorff. Lorient's name is an abbreviation of Port de l'Orient, dating from the 17th century, when Compagnie des Indes (the French East India Company) ships docked here. It doesn't have a concentrated dining and entertainment hub, but the boat-filled port has its charms.

Orientation

The centre of town is near the canal-like Port de Plaisance, about 1km south of the train and bus stations – take cours de Chazelles and its continuation, rue Maréchal Foch, or catch bus D (direction Carnel).

Information

There are two laundrettes on bd Cosmao Dumanoir beside the bus station.

No Work Tech (☎ 02 97 84 72 09; 5 place de la Libération; per hr €4; ⏰ 2pm-1am Mon, 10am-1am Tue-Sat, 3-11pm Sun) Internet access.

Post Office (9 quai des Indes)

Tourist Office (☎ 02 97 21 07 84; www.lorient-tourisme.fr, in French; quai de Rohan; ⏰ 9am-7pm daily Jul

& Aug, 10am-noon & 2-6pm Mon-Fri, 2-5pm Sat Sep & Apr-Jun, 10am-noon & 2-5pm Mon-Fri, 10am-noon Sat Oct-Mar) Lorient's tourist office has some seven different sets of opening hours, all of which change annually, but those listed here are a general rule of thumb.

Sights

Permanently moored at the Port de Plaisance, the research vessel **Thalassa** (☎ 02 97 35 13 00; quai de Rohan; adult/child €6.90/5.30; ⏰ 10am-7pm daily Jul & Aug, 9.30am-12.30pm & 2-6pm Mon-Fri, 2-6pm Sat & Sun May, Jun, Sep & other school holidays, closed rest of yr) makes a fascinating setting for this hands-on, wheelchair-accessible oceanography museum.

In **Port Louis**, 5km south of Lorient, the magnificent 16th-century **citadel** (adult/concession/child €5.50/4/free; ⏰ 10am-6.30pm Wed-Mon Apr–mid-Sep, 2-6pm Wed-Mon mid-Sep–mid-Dec & Feb-Mar) has two museums (again, it's worth checking ahead to confirm annual opening hours). **Musée de la Compagnie des Indes** (☎ 02 97 82 19 13) traces the history of the French East India Company and its lucrative trade with India, China, Africa and the New World from 1660 to the end of the 18th century through its fascinating display of documents, maps and artefacts. Safety at sea and underwater archeology are addressed at the **Musée National de la Marine** (☎ 02 97 82 56 72), with a treasure trove from the world's oceans.

To reach Port Louis and the museum, take the **Batobus** (☎ 02 97 21 28 29; one-way €1.25) ferry, which runs between Lorient and Port Louis, leaving every half-hour between 6.30am and 8pm. It departs Lorient's Port de Pêche from Monday to Saturday and the Embarcadère de la Rade on Sunday.

Île de Groix, 8km long by 3km wide and about 14km offshore, was once a major tuna-fishing port. With its excellent beaches and a 25km coastal footpath, it makes a great day trip (for ferries, see p340).

Festivals & Events

Celtic communities from Ireland, Scotland, Wales, Cornwall, the Isle of Man and Galicia in northwest Spain congregate with Bretons at the **Festival Interceltique** (☎ 02 97 21 24 29; www.festival-interceltique.com) over 10 days in early August. Book way ahead if you're planning to stay here at this time, when upwards of 600,000 people descend on the city.

Sleeping

Auberge de Jeunesse (☎ 02 97 37 11 65; lorient@fuaj.org; 41 rue Victor Schoelcher; dm incl sheets & breakfast €15.70; ⏰ closed mid-Dec–Jan; ⊠) On the banks of the River Ter, 4km from town, Lorient's hostel has a lively bar and table tennis. From the bus stop on cours de Chazelles, outside the bus station, take bus B2.

Hôtel Victor Hugo (☎ 02 97 21 16 24; www.hotelvictorhugo-lorient.com; 36 rue Lazare Carnot; d €47-72) A handy 200m from the Gare Maritime's ferries to Île de Groix, this brightly lit, soundproofed hotel has 28 warm, welcoming rooms with cheerful striped fabrics, satellite TVs and telephones, and free wi-fi in many rooms. If you don't mind taking a shower outside the room, rates drop as low as €35. Parking costs €7.

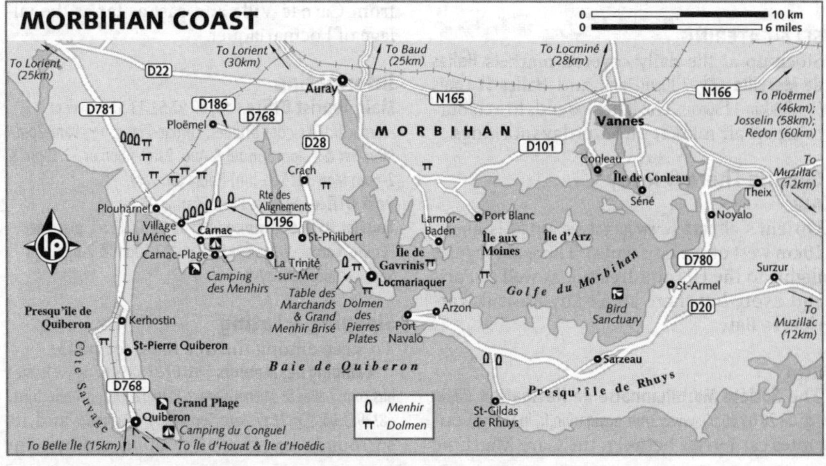

Rex Hôtel (☎ 02 97 64 25 60; www.rex-hotel-lorient.com; 28 cours de Chazelles; s/d €56/58; closed Christmas period) Rooms positively gleam at this tautly run ship – which it is almost literally: the reception desk has the shape of a boat's prow, polished woodwork lines the public areas and a tape of waves breaking and seagulls mewing plays in the small lounge. Each of the 23 rooms has a shining bathroom and broadband internet. Secure parking costs €4 (or €8 for garaged). The hotel is gay-friendly.

Eating

Tout Sucre Tout Miel (☎ 02 97 21 47 67; bd Franchet d'Esperey; crêpes €1.70-6.80; lunch Mon-Sat, dinner Tue-Sat) Everything at this cosy, convivial crêperie is homemade from fresh produce. If you're heading off for a picnic, you can order your meal to take away.

Tavarn Ar Roue Morvan (☎ 02 97 21 61 57; 1 place Polig-Montjarret; mains €7-11.90; lunch & dinner Mon-Sat) Attracting an artistic, cultural crowd, and *the* place to hang out during the Festival Interceltique (at which time, like most places in Lorient, it's open daily), this traditional Breton tavern turns out hearty Breton cuisine, and often has live music throughout the year.

Le Jardin Gourmand (☎ 02 97 64 17 24; 46 rue Jules-Simon; menus €26-38; lunch Wed-Sun, dinner Wed-Sat) Chef Natalie Beauvais has recently garnered a string of awards at this garden-set spot a couple of blocks north of the train station. The minimalist decor contrasts with Natalie's hearty regional cuisine, which is inspired by what's best in the market each morning.

SELF-CATERING

Stock up at the daily covered markets **Halles de Merville** (7.30am-1pm) and **Halles St-Louis** (7.30am-12.30pm). The latter extends to a colourful open-air market on Saturday mornings.

Getting There & Away

AIR

Lorient's **airport** (www.lorient.aeroport.fr) is about 10km west of the city centre. There are regular flights to the UK and Ireland, as well as Paris and Lyon, but there aren't any no-frills carriers to date.

BOAT

The **Société Morbihannaise de Navigation** (SMN; ☎ 08 20 05 60 00; www.smn-navigation.fr, in French) operates car ferries between the Gare Maritime and Île de Groix (adult/child return €25/20, 45 minutes, seven to eight daily). From mid-July to the end of August, SMN runs a passenger-only ferry to Sauzon on Belle Île (adult/child return €25/20 one hour, once daily).

BUS

The **bus station** (☎ 02 97 21 28 29) is linked to the train station by a footbridge. Destinations include Josselin (€12.50, one to 1½hours).

TRAIN

Several trains a day connect Lorient with Quimper (€10.40, 40 minutes), Vannes (€8.60, 40 minutes), Rennes (€23.50) and Paris (Gare Montparnasse; from €78.90, 3¾ hours).

Getting Around

City **buses** (☎ 02 97 21 28 29; single/day ticket €1.20/3.50) run until around 8pm.

For a taxi, call ☎ 02 97 21 29 29.

CARNAC

pop 4600

Pre-dating Stonehenge by around 100 years, Carnac (Garnag in Breton) tops it too with sheer numbers, making this the world's greatest concentration of megalithic sites. There are no fewer than 3000 of these upright stones, most around thigh-high, erected between 5000 and 3500 BC.

Carnac, some 32km west of Vannes, comprises the old stone village Carnac-Ville and the seaside resort of Carnac-Plage, 1.5km south, bordered by the 2km-long sandy beach. Its megaliths stretch 13km north from Carnac-Ville and east as far as the village of Locmariaquer.

Information

Main Tourist Office (☎ 02 97 52 13 52; www.ot-carnac.fr; 74 av des Druides, Carnac-Plage; 9am-7pm Mon-Sat & 3-7pm Sun Jul & Aug, 9am–noon or 12.30pm & 2-6pm Mon-Sat Sep-Jun) Hours can vary.

Post Office (av de la Poste, Carnac-Ville)

Tourist Office Annexe (☎ 02 97 52 13 52; place de l'Église, Carnac-Ville; 9.30am-12.30pm & 2-6pm Apr-Sep & school holidays)

Sleeping & Eating

To sleep among the tree tops, see p343.

Camping des Menhirs (☎ 02 97 52 94 67; www.lesmenhirs.com; 7 allée St-Michel, Carnac-Plage; adult/pitch/electricity €8/29/3.65; May–late Sep) Carnac and its surrounds have over 15 camping grounds, in-

MORBIHAN'S MIGHTY MEGALITHS

Two perplexing questions arise from the Morbihan region's neolithic menhirs, dolmens, cromlechs, tumuli and cairns.

Just *how* did the original constructors hew, then haul, these blocks (the heaviest weighs 300 tonnes), millennia before the wheel and the mechanical engine reached Brittany?

And why? Theories and hypotheses abound. A phallic fertility cult? Sun worship? Representation of a long-forgotten divinity? For the moment, the vague yet common consensus is that they served some kind of sacred, religious purpose – the same spiritual impulse behind so many monuments built by humankind.

The best way to appreciate the stones' sheer numbers is to walk or bike between the Le Ménec and Kerlescan groups, with menhirs almost continuously in view. Between June and September seven buses a day run between the two sites and both Carnac-Ville and Carnac-Plage.

Because of severe erosion the sites are fenced off to allow the vegetation to regenerate. However, between 10am and 5pm from October to May you can wander freely through parts (check site billboards or ask at the Maison des Mégalithes for updates). You can see them on a one-hour **guided visit** (€4), regularly in French year-round and usually in English at 3pm Wednesday, Thursday and Friday from early July to late August. Sign up for guided visits at the **Maison des Mégalithes** (☎ 02 97 52 89 99; rte des Alignements; admission free; 🕑 9am-8pm Jul & Aug, to 5.15pm Sep-Apr, to 7pm May & Jun), which also has a rolling video, topographic models and views of the menhirs from its rooftop terrace. Opposite the Maison des Mégalithes, the largest menhir field – with no less than 1099 stones – is the **Alignements du Ménec**, 1km north of Carnac-Ville; the eastern section is accessible in winter. From here, the D196 heads northeast for about 1.5km to the equally impressive **Alignements de Kermario**. Climb the stone observation tower midway along the site to see the alignment from above. Another 500m further on are the **Alignements de Kerlescan**, a smaller grouping also accessible in winter.

Tumulus St-Michel, at the end of rue du Tumulus and 400m northeast of the Carnac-Ville tourist office, dates back to at least 5000 BC and offers sweeping views.

Between Kermario and Kerlescan, 500m to the south of the D196, deposit your fee in an honour box at **Tumulus de Kercado** (admission €1; 🕑 year-round). Dating from 3800 BC and the burial site of a neolithic chieftain, during the French Revolution it was used as a hiding place for Breton royalists. From the parking area 300m further along the D196, a 15-minute walk brings you to the **Géant du Manio**, the highest menhir in the complex, and the **Quadrilatère**, a group of minimenhirs, close-set in a rectangle.

Near Locmariaquer, 13km southeast of Carnac-Ville, the major monuments are the **Table des Marchands**, a 30m-long dolmen, and the **Grand Menhir Brisé** (adult/student/child €5/3.50/free; 🕑 10am-7pm Jul & Aug, to 6pm Apr-Jun, to 5pm Sep-Mar), the region's largest menhir, which once stood 20m high but now lies broken on its side. Both are off the D781, just before the village.

Just south of Locmariaquer by the sea is the **Dolmen des Pierres Plates**, a 24m-long chamber with still-visible engravings.

For some background, the **Musée de Préhistoire** (☎ 02 97 52 22 04; 10 place de la Chapelle, Carnac-Ville; adult/child €5/2.50; 🕑 10am-6pm Jul & Aug, 10am-12.30pm & 2-6pm Wed-Mon Apr, May, Jun & Sep, 10am-12.30pm & 2-5pm Wed-Mon Oct-Mar) chronicles life in and around Carnac from the Palaeolithic and neolithic eras to the Middle Ages.

cluding this luxury complex of 100-sq-metre pitches. It's just 300m north of the beach; amenities range from a sauna to a cocktail bar and wi-fi. You'll score a better deal outside peak summer.

Auberge Le Ratelier (☎ 02 97 52 05 04; www.le-ratelier.com; 4 Chemin du Douet, Carnac-Ville; d €46-60; 🕑 Feb-Dec) This vine-clambered former farmhouse, now an eight-room inn with low ceilings and traditional timber furnishings – is in a quiet street one block southwest of place de l'Église. Rooms with showers only start from €38. *Menus* (from €19) at its whitewashed, wood-beamed restaurant (lunch and dinner May to September, closed Wednesday October to December and from February to April) revolve around fresh seafood, particularly lobster.

Crêperie au Pressoir (☎ 02 97 52 01 86; village du Ménec; galettes €3-8; ⌚ lunch & dinner Easter-Aug) Opening hours fluctuate, so we recommend checking ahead, but this artisan crêperie in a traditional long Breton house is a rare opportunity to dine right in the middle of a 70-strong cromlech (circle of menhirs). From Carnac-Ville, take rue St-Cornély northwest and turn right on rue du Ménec and follow it north for about 1km.

Crêperie St-George (☎ 02 97 52 18 34; 8 allée du Parc, Carnac-Plage; menus from €9; ⌚ lunch & dinner Apr-Sep) For consistently great-value crêpes close to the beach, try the contemporary Crêperie St-George in the Galeries St-George centre.

Getting There & Away

The main bus stops are in Carnac-Ville, outside the police station on rue St-Cornély, and in Carnac-Plage, beside the tourist office. **Cariane Atlantique** (☎ 02 97 47 29 64) buses go to Auray (€4), Vannes (€7) and Quiberon (€3).

The nearest year-round train station is in Auray, 12km to the northeast. SNCF has an office in the Carnac-Plage tourist office.

Hire bikes for around €9/17 per half-/full day from **Lorcy** (☎ 02 97 52 09 73; 6 rue de Courdiec, Carnac-Ville) and **Le Randonneur** (☎ 02 97 52 02 55; 20 av des Druides, Carnac-Plage).

For a taxi, call ☎ 02 97 52 75 75.

QUIBERON

pop 5200

Quiberon (Kiberen in Breton) sits at the southern tip of a sliver-thin, 14km-long peninsula flanked on the western side by the rocky, wave-lashed Côte Sauvage (Wild Coast). The town fans out around the port where ferries depart for Belle Île, and is wildly popular in summer.

Orientation & Information

The D768 leads along the peninsula and into Quiberon, ending at the seasonally operating train station. From here rue de Verdun winds down to the sheltered bay of Port-Maria, pincered by the town's main beach, La Grande Plage, to its east and the ferry harbour to the west.

The **tourist office** (☎ 08 25 13 56 00; www.quiberon.com; 14 rue de Verdun; ⌚ 9am-1.30pm & 2-7pm Mon-Fri, to 5pm Sat, 10am-1pm & 2-5pm Sun Jul & Aug, 9am-12.30pm & 2-6pm Mon-Sat Sep-Jun) is between the train station and La Grande Plage.

Sights & Activities

Conserverie La Belle-Iloise (☎ 02 97 50 08 77; rue de Kerné; ⌚ visits 10am, 11am, 3pm & 4pm daily Jul & Aug, 10-11am & 3-4pm Mon-Fri Sep-Jun), north of the train station, offers guided visits around its former sardine cannery, with bargain-priced sardines available from the adjacent shop.

La Grande Plage attracts families; bathing spots towards the peninsula's tip are larger and less crowded. The **Côte Sauvage** is great for a windy walk, but you'll need a permit for any nautically based activity (such as a diving certificate) to swim in the rough seas, or risk a fine – and your safety. Alternatively you can splash in the brand-new indoor aquatic centre **Neptilude** (☎ 02 97 50 39 07; 1 rue Neptune; adult/child €5.50/4.50; ⌚ at least 2-6.30pm school holidays & weekends year-round).

Sleeping

Camping du Conguel (☎ 02 97 50 19 11; www.campingduconguel.com; bd de la Teignouse; campsites €12.40-43.25, electricity €3.65; ⌚ Apr-Oct; 🏊) This splashy four-star option, with an aqua park including water slides, is one of the peninsula's 15 campsites. Just 2km east of the town centre, it's beside Plage du Conguel, with four- to six-berth cabins also available, starting at €94 for two nights.

Auberge de Jeunesse – Les Filets Bleus (☎ 02 97 50 15 54; 45 rue du Roch Priol; dm €10; ⌚ Apr-Sep) Quiberon's HI-affiliated hostel is in a peaceful part of town 800m east of the train station and 500m from the beach. There's limited camping (€5.90) in the grounds; breakfast costs €3.50.

Hôtel L'Océan (☎ 02 97 50 07 58; http://hotel-de-locean.com, in French; 7 quai de l'Océan; d €53.50-71; ⌚ Easter-Sep) Overlooking the harbour, you can't miss this huge white house with multicoloured shutters. The cheapest of its 37 rooms don't have TVs, but rooms at the other end of the price scale get you a fabulous harbour view. Parking (very welcome in summer) costs €5.50.

Eating & Drinking

La Closerie de St-Clément (☎ 02 97 50 40 00; 36 rue de St-Clément; crêpes €4-9; ⌚ lunch & dinner daily Jul & Aug, closed Mon & dinner Sun Sep-Jun) This rustic place with gnarled timber beams and chunky wooden furniture has a peaceful, tree-shaded garden terrace to keep diners cool in summer, and a cosy fireplace to warm your cockles in winter.

TREETOP SLEEPING

For the ultimate eco-escape, the only way you can go past **Dihan** (☎ 02 97 56 88 27; www.dihan-evasion.org, in French; Kerganiet, Ploëmel; d guestroom/yurt incl breakfast €50/70, d tree house €110-120, table d'hôte from €20;) is in the literal sense, as secluded as it is in a leafy dell just outside Ploëmel (follow the black signs from the village).

Run by a fun-loving young couple, Myriam and Arno Le Masle, in its former life the property was Myriam's grandparents' working farm. The farmhouse and barns now house guest rooms, while the grounds shelter two yurts imported from Mongolia, and five tree houses, reached by climbing ladders (the highest – at 12m – requires you to strap on a harness to reach it). Should nature call, there are biodegradable dry toilets up here as well as conserved water (you'll find brightly tiled bathrooms and a sauna in the reception building). Rates include breakfast, which is a combination of organic, fair-trade and local artisan produce, such as a finger-licking *caramel au beurre salé* (Breton caramel spread). Eco-initiatives also include rare-for-France recycling. Fabulous *tables d'hôtes* (a combination of Myriam's Breton, Mauritian and Indian heritage; by reservation) take place in the converted *cidrerie*, where pianist Arno hits the keys and bands sometimes drop by. Otherwise, guests can fire up the barbecue and dine beneath a bamboo-sheltered pergola.

All of which would be enough to recommend it heartily, but you can also rent bikes (€8 per day), book a massage (from €60) or even an on-site beauty treatment with biological cosmetics.

And both guests and nonguests can saddle up, with **horse riding** starting at €18 per hour (there are also ponies for kids).

L'Embarcadère (☎ 02 97 50 17 84; 2 quai de l'Océan; mussels from €8, mains €14.90-18.90; 7am-9pm Mon-Sat, 10am-9pm Sun) Of the bar-restaurants lined up along the quayfront, L'Embarcadère offers value that's hard to beat. It also serves whopping bowls of *moules-frites*, and mixes a great kir.

our pick **Villa Margot** (☎ 02 97 50 33 89; 7 rue de Port Maria; lunch menus €17.50-21.50, dinner menus €21.50-36, mains €19.50-27; lunch & dinner Thu-Mon) The interior of this stunning stone restaurant looks like it'd be at home in a chic Parisian *quartier*, with original art on the walls (painted on adjacent Belle Île), flower-shaped opaque glass light fittings, hot-pink and brown colour schemes and lobsters clawing in the live tank (caught the night before, along with the fish). That is until you head out onto the timber deck, which has direct access to the beach for a post-repast stroll.

La Criée (☎ 02 97 30 53 09; 11 quai de l'Océan; mains €25-45; lunch & dinner Tue-Sun Feb-Dec) Within the former fish auction house (hence the name), and an easy walk from the ferry terminal, this long-established seaside restaurant keeps with its traditions by laying out its seafood on a table for you to take your pick.

Getting There & Away

BOAT

For ferries between Quiberon and Belle-Île, see p344.

BUS

Quiberon is connected by **Cariane Atlantique** (☎ 02 97 47 29 64) buses with Carnac (€3, 45 minutes), Auray (€7, 1¼ hours) and Vannes (€9.10, 1¾ hours). Buses stop at the train station and at place Hoche near the tourist office and the beach.

CAR & MOTORCYCLE

High-summer traffic is hellish – consider leaving your vehicle at the 1200-place Sémaphore car park (€3.60 for up to four hours, €12.50 for 24 hours), 1.5km north of the beach, and walking or taking the free shuttle bus into town.

TRAIN

In July and August only, a shuttle train called the *Tire-Bouchon* (corkscrew) runs several times a day between Auray and Quiberon (€3, 40 minutes). Tickets cost €2.80 if purchased at the tourist office. From September to June an SNCF bus service links Quiberon and Auray train stations (€6.30, 50 minutes) at least seven times a day.

Getting Around

Cycles Loisirs (☎ 02 97 50 31 73; 3 rue Victor Golvan), 200m north of the tourist office, rents touring/mountain bikes from €8/14 a day. **Cyclomar** (☎ 02 97 50 26 00; 47 place Hoche), around 200m south of the tourist office, rents out bikes for similar prices as well as scooters including helmet from €38 per day plus insurance. It also runs an operation from the train station during July and August.

To order a **taxi** ring ☎ 02 97 50 19 09.

BELLE ÎLE

pop 5200

Accessed by ferries from Quiberon, the population of Belle Île (in full, Belle-Île-en-Mer) swells tenfold in summer thanks to its namesake beauty. But as it's Brittany's largest island (at 20km by 9km), there's room to escape the crowds.

Information

Turn left as you leave the ferry in Le Palais to reach the main **tourist office** (☎ 02 97 31 81 93; www.belle-ile.com; quai Bonnelle; 8.45am-7.30pm Mon-Sat & to 1pm Sun Jul & Aug, 9am-12.30pm & 2-6pm Mon-Sat, 10am-12.30pm Sun Sep-Jun).

There's a summer-only **information kiosk** (☎ 02 97 31 69 49; Easter-Sep) on the quay in Sauzon.

Sights & Activities

The dramatic **citadel**, strengthened by Vauban in 1682, dominates the little Le Palais port. Inside, the **Musée Historique** (☎ 02 97 31 84 17; adult/child €6.10/3.05; 9.30am-6pm May-Oct, 9.30am-noon & 2-5pm Nov-Apr) interprets the history of both the defensive system and the island.

Belle Île's fretted southwestern coast has spectacular rock formations and caves including **Grotte de l'Apothicairerie** (Cave of the Apothecary's Shop), where waves roll in from two sides.

Plage de Donnant has awesome surf, though swimming here is dangerous. Sheltered **Port Kérel**, to the southwest, is better for children, as is the 2km-long **Plage des Grands Sables**, the biggest and busiest strand, spanning the calm waters of the island's eastern side.

The tourist office sells walking and cycling guides. The ultimate hike is the 95km **coastal footpath** that follows the island's coastline.

Sleeping & Eating

About 10 campsites are pitched around Belle Île; most open from April or May to September or October.

Auberge de Jeunesse Haute Boulogne (☎ 02 97 31 81 33; www.fuaj.org; Le Palais; dm incl sheets & breakfast €15.30; closed Oct & Christmas; ☒) This modern 96-bed HI-affiliated hostel with a self-catering kitchen is to the north of the citadel.

Hôtel Vauban (☎ 02 97 31 45 42; www.hotelvauban.com, in French; 1 rue des Remparts, Le Palais; d €61-74; Mar–early Nov) This comfy place is perched high on the coastal path, with views of the ferry landing below from many of its 16 spacious rooms.

The hotel rents out mountain bikes, and there's good wheelchair access and a guest-only restaurant (*menus* €20) serving seafood from April to September.

Crêperies and pizzerias are scattered across the island; many of the higher-end hotels have good restaurants.

For all-out luxury, the **citadel** (www.citadellevauban.com) also incorporates a lavish hotel with doubles for €151 to €271 (plus suites from €451) and a gastronomic restaurant, La Table du Gouverneur (*menus* from €30 to €65).

Getting There & Away

Travelling to Belle Île can involve a bit of planning, as taking a car on the ferry is prohibitively expensive for a short trip, and needs to be booked well ahead even outside peak season. On the upside, bikes can be carried free on board ferries.

FROM QUIBERON

The shortest crossing to Belle Île is from Quiberon. **Compagnie Océane** (☎ 02 97 35 02 00; www.compagnie-oceane.fr) operates car/passenger ferries (45 minutes, year-round) and fast passenger ferries to Le Palais and to Sauzon in July and August. An adult return passenger fare is €26.50; transporting a small car costs a hefty €149 return *plus* passenger fares. There are five crossings a day (up to 13 in July and August).

FROM VANNES

Navix (☎ 02 97 46 60 29; www.navix.fr, in French with English sections) operates ferries (return €31 to €44) between May and mid-September.

FROM LORIENT

From mid-July to the end of August, Compagnie Océane runs a fast passenger-only ferry (one-way from €16.46, one hour, once daily) to Sauzon.

Getting Around

Lots of places in Le Palais rent out bicycles/motor scooters for around €12/35 a day.

Seasonal buses run by **Taol Mor** (☎ 02 97 31 32 32) criss-cross the island.

Car-rental rates on the island start at about €65 for 24 hours; you'll find outlets at the harbour as you disembark.

VANNES

pop 58,000

Street art, sculptures and intriguing galleries pop up unexpectedly through the half-timbered, cobbled city of Vannes (Gwened in Breton), which has a quirky, creative bent.

The city's integral role in Brittany's history stretches back to pre-Roman times, when it was the capital of the Veneti, a Gaulish tribe of sailors who fortified the town. Conquered by Julius Caesar in the 1st century BC, it became the centre of Breton unity in the 9th century under Breton hero Nominoë, and in 1532 the union of the duchy of Brittany with France was proclaimed here. These days it's a vibrant hub for students attending the city's Université de Bretagne-Sud.

Orientation

Vannes' lively little marina sits at the end of a canal-like waterway about 1.5km from the gulf's entrance. Roughly 3.5km south of town, Île de Conleau, also known as Presqu'Île de Conleau (Conleau Peninsula) is linked to the mainland by a causeway.

Information

Cyber Athalie (☎ 02 97 47 59 02; 4 rue Porte Poterne; per hr €3.50; 🕑 9.30am-12.30pm & 2-8pm Mon-Sat) Internet access.

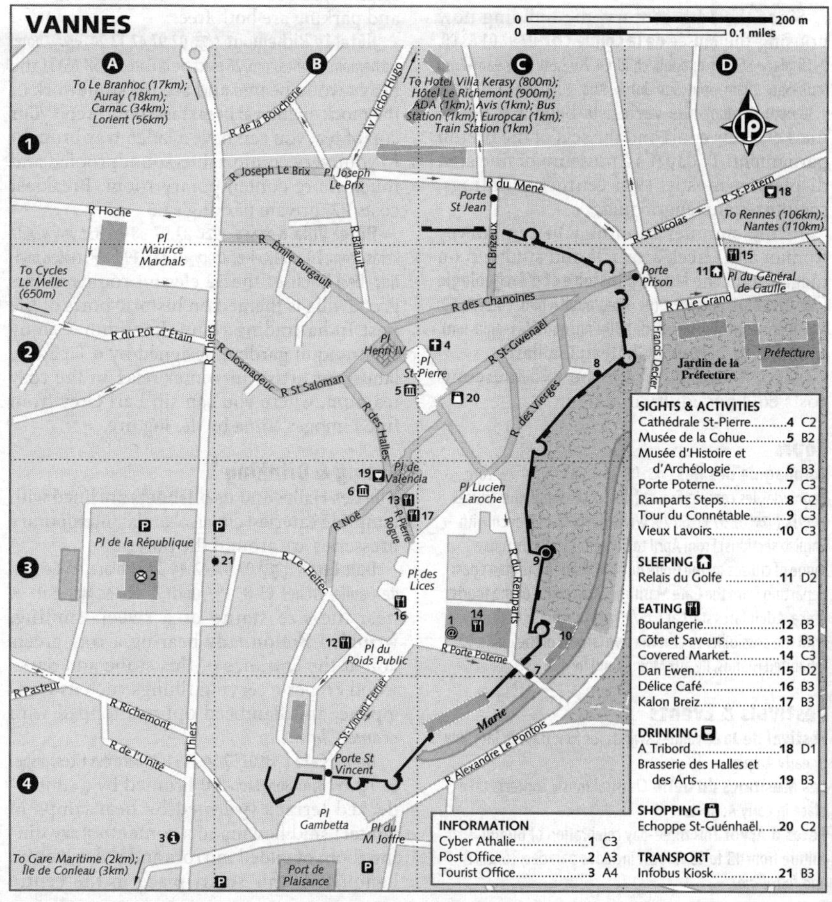

Post Office (2 place de la République)
Tourist Office (☎ 02 97 47 24 34; www.tourisme-vannes.com, in French; 1 rue Thiers; 🕑 9am-7pm daily Jul & Aug, 9.30am-12.30pm & 2-6pm Mon-Sat Sep-Jun) Occupies a distinctive 17th-century half-timbered house.

Sights

Surrounding Vannes' walled **old town** is a flower-filled moat. Inside, you can weave through the web of narrow alleys ranged around the 13th-century Gothic **Cathédrale St-Pierre**. Tucked away behind rue des Vierges, stairs lead to the accessible section of the **ramparts**. From here, you can see the black-roofed **Vieux Lavoirs** (Old Laundry Houses), though you'll get a better view from the **Tour du Connétable** or from the **Porte Poterne** to the south.

Since the 14th century, the building now housing the **Musée de la Cohue** (☎ 02 97 01 63 00; 9-15 place St-Pierre; adult/child €4.20/2.60; 🕑 9am-7pm Mon-Sat, 10am-6pm Sun Jul & Aug, 9.30am-12.30pm & 1.30-6pm Sep-Jun) has variously been a produce market, a law court and the seat of the Breton parliament. Today it's a museum of fine arts, displaying mostly 19th-century paintings, sculptures and engravings.

In the summer months you can survey Roman and Greek artefacts and study up on megaliths at the **Musée d'Histoire et d'Archéologie** (☎ 02 97 01 63 00; 2 rue Noë; adult/child €4.20/2.60; 🕑 10am-6pm mid-Jun–Sep, 1.30-6pm mid-May–mid-Jun), in the 15th-century Château Gaillard.

A combined ticket for the two museums costs €6/4 per adult/child.

Tours

Compagnie des Îles (☎ 08 25 13 41 00; www.compagniedesiles.com, in French) Offers seasonal gulf cruises.
Navix (☎ 02 97 46 60 29; www.navix.fr, in French with English sections) From April to September, Navix runs a range of cruises on the Golfe du Morbihan (Morbihan Coast), departing from the Gare Maritime, 2km south of the tourist office. Adult fares start at €15/29 per two hours/half-day, with the possibility to visit the two largest of the gulf's 40 inhabited islands, Île aux Moines and Île d'Arz.

Festivals & Events

Festival de Jazz Vannes swings for four days in late July or early August.
Les Musicales du Golfe Classical music concerts take place in early August.
Fêtes d'Arvor This three-day celebration of Breton culture from 13 to 15 August includes parades, concerts and *festoù-noz*.

Sleeping

The tourist office can book accommodation for a €1 fee.

Relais du Golfe (☎ 02 97 47 14 74; fax 02 97 42 52 48; 10 place du Général de Gaulle; d with bathroom €52-60, d with shared bathroom €37-47; ☒) Its name suggests something more flash than these rooms (wedged above a café-bar) actually are. But it's the most central budget option, and staff are welcoming.

Le Branhoc (☎ 02 97 56 41 55; www.auditel-hotel.fr; 5 rte du Bono, Auray; s €47-57, d €49-59) Situated 17km west of Vannes just outside the pretty riverside town of Auray (itself well worth a wander), this peacefully situated, family-run hotel is a handy base for exploring both Vannes and Morbihan's megalithic sites. Rooms are bright, spacious and spotlessly clean, and wi-fi and parking are both free.

Hôtel Le Richemont (☎ 02 97 47 17 24; www.hotel-richemont-vannes.com; 26 place de la Gare; d €58-65) If the heavy wood beams and arched stonework of the mock-medieval breakfast room aren't your cup of tea, you can have a laden tray brought to your very comfortable, soundproofed and much more contemporary room. Breakfast costs €7; private parking's €6.

Hôtel Villa Kerasy (☎ 02 97 68 36 83; www.villakerasy.com; 20 av Favrel-et-Lincy; d €125-190; 🕑 closed mid-Nov–Dec) Each of the 12 elegant rooms in this grand villa is themed on historic ports of the East India trading route. In summer enjoy the tranquil garden, designed by a Japanese landscape artist. In winter relax in the cosy tearoom, where you can sip Earl Grey from fine Limoges china by the log fire.

Eating & Drinking

Rue des Halles and its offshoots are lined with tempting eateries; classical and contemporary brasseries arc around the port.

Dan Ewen (☎ 02 97 42 44 34; 3 place du Général de Gaulle; crêpes €3-8; 🕑 lunch & dinner Mon-Sat) A near-life-size statue of a sweet, smiling, wrinkled Breton lady bearing a tray greets you at the entrance of this stone and dark-wood crêperie serving fillings such as frangipane, and flambéed options topped with *crème Chantilly*.

Délice Café (☎ 02 97 54 23 31; 7 place des Lices; dishes €6-11; 🕑 8am-8pm Mon-Sat) Fronted by a timber-decked terrace (warmed by heat lamps in winter), and flowing to a contemporary dining room of gilded mirrors and red velveteen banquettes, this smart place in the centre of the old town has healthy salads and hot dishes like *croques-monsieur* (grilled ham-and-cheese sandwiches). Terrace dining costs roughly 10% more.

Kalon Breiz (☎ 02 97 54 27 20; 6 rue Pierre-René Rogues; menus €11-13.50; ⏰ lunch & dinner) Tasty sweet and savoury crêpes keep this cosy place packed to the rafters day and night. Even at its busiest, staff remain friendly and efficient.

Côte et Saveurs (☎ 02 97 47 21 94; 8 rue Pierre-René Rogues; menus €19-29, mains €13-18.50; ⏰ lunch & dinner) A spiral staircase winds through the centre of the ground-floor dining room to the upper level of this airy, contemporary restaurant serving fresh fish such as red tuna with lemon and thyme.

A Tribord (☎ 02 97 42 76 94; www.atribord-vannes.com; 28 rue St-Patern; ⏰ 6pm-2am daily) Everything from folk music to club nights with DJs hitting the decks takes place at this eclectic venue. You'll find a couple of other bars in the same street.

Brasserie des Halles et des Arts (☎ 02 97 54 08 34; 9 rue des Halles; ⏰ noon-midnight) You can eat at this buzzing brasserie (mains €9.50 to €18), but it's an equally good spot for a drink while browsing the art – such as the Breton images made from tiles that adorn its colourful walls.

SELF-CATERING

On Wednesday and Saturday mornings, a produce market takes over place du Poids Public and the surrounding area. Vannes' **covered market** (Les Halles; ⏰ 8.30am-1.30pm) is adjacent.

Three-tiered displays of cakes, tarts and Breton pastries spin at the place du Poids Public's **boulangerie** (☎ 02 97 47 33 55; 11 place du Poids Public; ⏰ 7am-8pm Mon-Sat).

Shopping

In keeping with Vannes' artistic spirit, galleries such as **Echoppe St-Guénhaël** (☎ 02 97 47 92 37; 29 rue St-Guénhaël) sell innovative (and often amusing) contemporary Breton art. Look out for rainbow-hued shell-and-watercolour collages by Vannes artist 'Fred'.

Getting There & Away

BUS

The small bus station is opposite the train station. Services include **Cariane Atlantique** (☎ 02 97 47 29 64), which runs to Carnac (€7, 1¼ hours) and on to Quiberon (€9.10, 45 minutes).

CAR & MOTORCYCLE

Europcar (☎ 02 97 42 43 43), **Avis** (☎ 02 97 01 29 13), and **ADA** (☎ 02 97 42 59 10) are at the train station.

TRAIN

There are frequent trains westwards to Auray (€3.60, 11 minutes), Lorient (€8.60, 40 minutes) and Quimper (€17, 1½ hours). Eastbound trains serve Rennes (€17.80, 1½ hours) and Nantes (€18.60, 1½ hours).

Getting Around

TPV (☎ 02 97 01 22 23; tickets €1.20) runs eight city bus lines until 8.15pm. Its Infobus kiosk is on place de la République. Buses 3 and 4 link the train station with place de la République.

You can hire bikes from **Cycles Le Mellec** (☎ 02 97 63 00 24; 51ter rue Jean Gougaud) from €12 a day. Contact **Vélo & Co** (☎ 02 97 54 24 59; www.veloandco.fr) to rent bikes (from €8.50/11 per half-/full day) and scooters (from €8/30 per hour/half-day) at various points around town.

To order a taxi, ring ☎ 02 97 54 34 34.

EASTERN & CENTRAL BRITTANY

The one-time frontier between Brittany and France, fertile eastern Brittany fans out around the region's lively capital, Rennes. Central Brittany conceals the enchanting Forêt de Paimpont, sprinkled with villages and ancient Breton legends.

JOSSELIN

pop 2400

In the shadow of an enormous, witch's-hat-turreted 14th-century castle that was the long-time seat of the counts of Rohan, the storybook village of Josselin lies on the banks of the River Oust 43km northeast of Vannes. Today, visitors in their thousands continue to fall under its spell.

Orientation & Information

A beautiful square of 16th-century half-timbered houses, place Notre Dame, is the little village's heart. The castle and the tourist office are south, below rue des Trente, the main through street.

The small but friendly **tourist office** (☎ 02 97 22 36 43; www.paysdejosselin-tourisme.com; place de la Congrégation; 🕑 10am-6pm daily Jul & Aug, 10am-noon & 2-6pm Mon-Fri, 10am-noon Sat Sep-Jun) is beside the castle entrance. You can check your emails (up to 15 minutes) for free. Directly opposite, the **English Bookshop** (☎ 02 97 75 62 55; rue des Trente; 🕑 10am-6pm Mon-Sat May-Sep, 11am-4pm Tue-Thu & Sat Oct-Apr) stocks second-hand novels and nonfiction titles.

Sights & Activities

Guarded by its three round towers, the **Château de Josselin** (☎ 02 97 22 36 45; adult/child €7.50/5; 🕑 10am-6pm daily mid-Jul–Aug, 2-6pm Jun–mid-Jul & Sep, 2-6pm Sat & Sun Apr-May & Oct, closed Nov-Mar) can only be visited by guided tour. One English-language tour departs daily from June to September; the rest of the year you can ask for a leaflet in English. Within the château is the **Musée de Poupées** (Doll Museum; adult/child €6.40/4.60). A combination ticket for both costs €11.90/8.20 per adult/child.

The hulking château makes an evocative backdrop for the village's two-day **Medieval Festival**, featuring feasting and fireworks, held in mid-July in even-numbered years.

Older still, parts of the **Basilique Notre Dame du Roncier** in place Notre Dame date from the 12th century; superb 15th- and 16th-century stained glass illuminates the south aisle.

Sleeping & Eating

Camping du Bas de la Lande (☎ 02 97 22 22 20; camping basdelalande@wanadoo.fr; Guégon; campsite €8.70-11; 🕑 Apr-Oct) This peaceful spot is 2km west of Josselin, on the south bank of the Oust.

Chez Janny (☎ 02 97 73 94 72; 61 rue Glatinier; broce liande.chambres@orange.fr; d €55; ⊠) There's a casual, homey feel to this *chambre d'hôte* located 50m from the château, particularly in its brightly coloured toy- and book-strewn lounge/breakfast room in an old shopfront.

Hôtel-Restaurant du Château (☎ 02 97 22 20 11; www.hotel-chateau.com, in French; 1 rue Général de Gaulle; d €61-70; 🕑 closed 3 weeks Feb, 1 week Nov, 1 week Dec) It's worth the few extra euros for a magnificent view of the château looming above this cosy hotel. Cheaper rooms, which don't have in-room showers or toilets, start at €35.50. Its restaurant *menus* range from €15 to €55 and regional specialities include a moist caramel cake.

Restaurant Café France (☎ 02 97 70 61 93; 6 place Notre Dame; menus €8.90-18.90; 🕑 lunch & dinner Apr-Sep) does good omelettes, while just down the hill **Crêperie-Grill Sarrazine** (☎ 02 97 22 37 80; 51 rue Glatinier; menus €8.80-13.90, galettes & salads from €6; 🕑 lunch & dinner) packs in the locals.

Getting There & Away

CTM (☎ 02 97 01 22 01) bus destinations include Rennes (€12.50, 1¼ hours).

FORÊT DE PAIMPONT

Also known as Brocéliande, the Paimpont Forest is about 40km southwest of Rennes, and legendary as the place where King Arthur received the Excalibur sword (forget that these stories are thought to have been brought to Brittany by Celtic settlers and hence probably took place offshore – it's a magical setting all the same).

The best base for exploring the forest is the lakeside village of **Paimpont**. Some 95% of the forest is private land, but the **tourist office** (Syndicat d'Initiative; ☎ 02 99 07 84 23; syndicat-dinitiative paimpont@wanadoo.fr; 🕑 10am-noon & 2-6pm daily Apr-Sep, 10am-noon & 2-6pm Tue-Sun Oct-Mar), beside the 12th-century **Église Abbatiale** (Abbey Church), has a free brochure outlining a 62km-long driving circuit with numerous short walks along the way that are accessible to the public. It also sells more-detailed walking and cycling guides.

In July and August the tourist office leads **guided tours** (morning/afternoon/full day €6/10/12) of the forest (the availability of English-speaking guides varies).

Campers can set up their tents at the lakeside **Camping Municipal de Paimpont** (☎ 02 99 07 89 16; rue du Chevalier Lancelot du Lac; camping €11.90; 🕑 May-Sep), while backpackers will want to head to the **Auberge de Jeunesse** (☎ 02 97 22 76 75; www.fuaj.org; dm €10.50; 🕑 Jun-Sep; ⊠), in a lovely old stone farmhouse at Choucan-en-Brocéliande, 5km north of Paimpont.

For more creature comforts, try the **Hôtel Le Relais de Brocéliande** (☎ 02 99 07 84 94; www.le-relais-de-broceliande.fr; 5 rue du Forges, Paimpont; r with/without bathroom €55/34), with rustic rooms and canopied beds. Its on-site restaurant (*menus* €17 to €36) specialises in local river-caught fish. **Illenoo** (www.illenoo.fr, in French) runs buses to/from Rennes (€2.50, one hour) from Monday to Saturday (none on Sunday).

You can rent mountain bikes (per half-/full day €9/12) from **Pays de Merlin** (☎ 02 99 07 80 23; rue Général de Gaulle).

RENNES

pop 210,500

A crossroads since Roman times, Brittany's vibrant capital sits at the junction of highways linking northwestern France's major cities. Its contemporary and medieval quarters are woven with waterways, which are best explored by renting a boat. At night, this student city has no end of lively places to pop in for a pint.

Orientation

The centre is divided by La Vilaine, a river channelled into a cement-lined canal that disappears underground just before the central square, place de la République. The northern area includes the pedestrianised old city; the south is garishly modern. The metro runs north through the city from the main train station.

Information

Comédie des Langues (☎ 02 99 36 72 95; 25 rue St-Malo; 🕑 9am-7pm Mon-Sat) Stocks English-language books.

Laundrette (23 rue de Penhoët; 🕑 7am- 8pm)

NeuroGame (☎ 02 99 65 53 85; www.neurogame.com; 2 rue Dinan; per 20min €1; 🕑 10am-1am Mon-Thu, to 3am Fri, noon-3am Sat, 2-10pm Sun) Internet access.

Post Office (place de la République)

Tourist Office (☎ 02 99 67 11 11; www.tourisme-rennes.com; 11 rue St-Yves; 🕑 1-6pm Mon, 9am-7pm Tue-Sat, 11am-1pm & 2-6pm Sun Jul & Aug, 1-6pm Mon, 9am-6pm Tue-Sat, 11am-1pm & 2-6pm Sun Sep-Jun) Staff can book accommodation for free.

Sights & Activities

OLD CITY

Much of Rennes was gutted by the great fire of 1720, started by a drunken carpenter who accidentally set alight a pile of shavings. Half-timbered houses that survived line the old city's cobbled streets such as **rue St-Michel** and **rue St-Georges**. The latter runs alongside the place de la Mairie and the site of the 17th-century **Palais du Parlement de Bretagne**, the former seat of the rebellious Breton parliament and, more recently, the Palais de Justice. In 1994 this building too was destroyed by fire, started by demonstrating fishermen. Now restored, it houses the Court of Appeal. In July and August, guided tours in English (adult/child €6.80/4; book at the tourist office) take you through the ostentatiously gilded rooms.

Crowning the old city is the 17th-century **Cathédrale St-Pierre** (🕑 9.30am-noon & 3-6pm), which has a stunning neoclassical interior.

MUSEUMS

Rooms devoted to the Pont-Aven school (p338) are the highlight of the **Musée des Beaux-Arts** (☎ 02 99 28 55 85; 20 quai Émile Zola; adult/student/child €4.30/2.20/free; 🕑 10am-noon & 2-6pm Tue-Sun), which also has a 'curiosity gallery' of antiques and illustrations amassed in the 18th century. It also hosts temporary exhibitions, which attract an additional charge.

Rennes' futuristic cultural centre, **Champs Libres** (☎ 02 23 40 66 00; 10 cours des Alliés), is home to the **Musée de Bretagne** (☎ 02 23 40 66 70; www.musee-bretagne.fr), with displays on Breton history and culture. Under the same roof is **Espace des Sciences** (☎ 02 23 40 66 40; www.espace-sciences.org), an interactive science museum, along with a planetarium, a temporary exhibition space and a library. A combined ticket for all sections costs €10/7 per adult/child.

Tours

urbaVag (☎ 02 99 33 16 88, 06 82 37 67 72; www.urbavag.fr, in French; rue Canal St-Martin; per hr €26-31) Cruise Rennes' waterways on a whisper-quiet electric boat rented from urbaVag. Boats take up to seven passengers; the price drops significantly with each extra hour of rental.

Festivals & Events

Les Mercredis du Thabor Traditional Breton dancing and music take place in Rennes' beautiful Parc du Thabor on Wednesdays during June and July (usually from 4pm).

Tombées de la Nuit Rennes' old city comes alive during this music and theatre festival in the first week of July.

Yaouank (☎ 02 99 30 06 87) A huge *fest-noz*, held on the third Saturday in November.

Sleeping

Camping des Gayeulles (☎ 02 99 36 91 22; www.camping-rennes.com; rue Professeur Audin; per adult/campervan/tent €3.50/7.60/5.70; 🕑 Apr-Oct) Rennes' only campsite is in Parc des Bois, 4.5km northeast of the train station. It's open for campervans year-round. Take bus 3 from place de la République to the Gayeulles stop.

Auberge de Jeunesse (☎ 02 99 33 22 33; rennes@fuaj.org; 10-12 Canal St-Martin; dm incl breakfast €16.90, sheets €2.80; 🕑 7am-1am) Rennes' well-equipped youth hostel has a self-catering kitchen and a canalside setting 2km north from the centre. Take bus 18 from place de la Mairie.

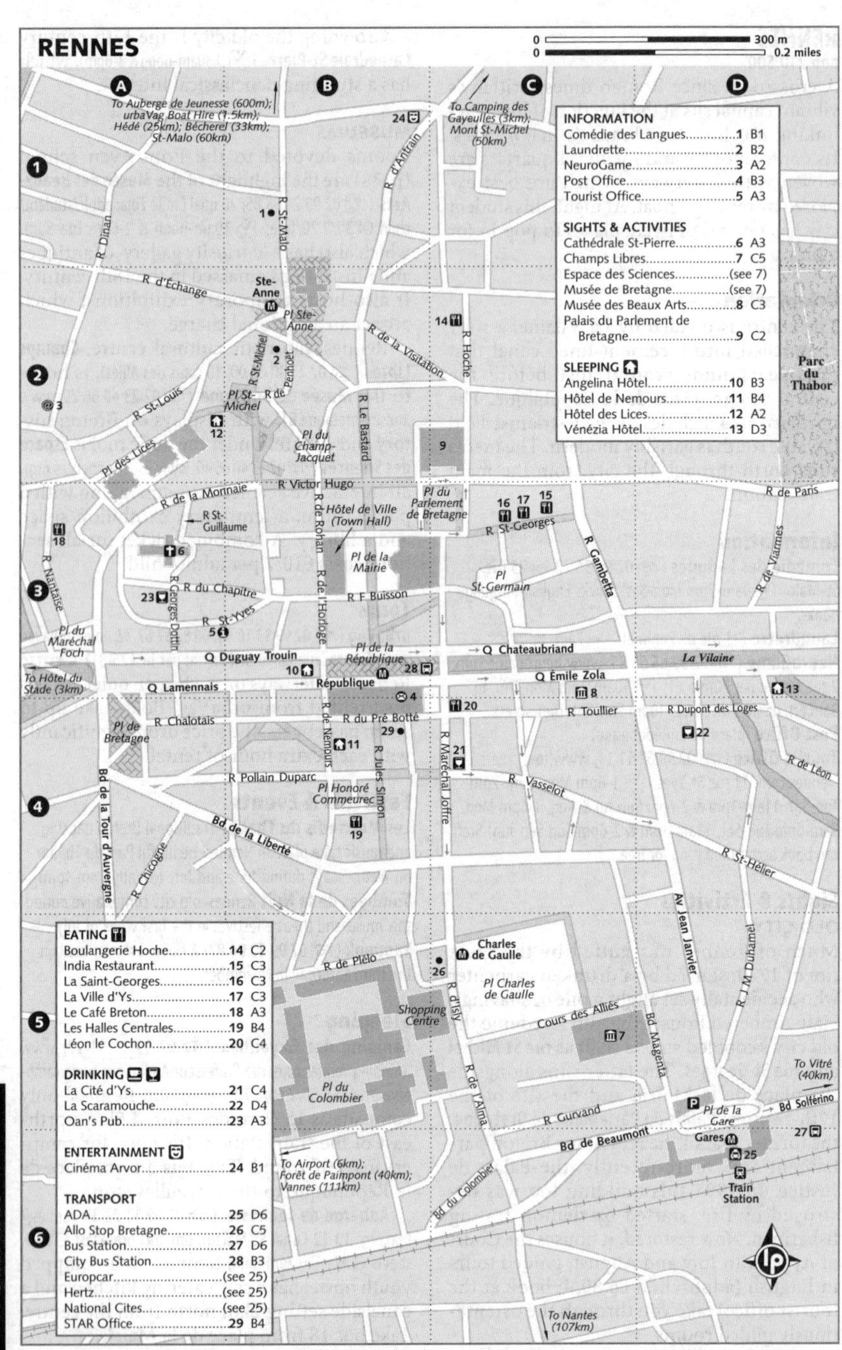
RENNES
0 300 m
0 0.2 miles
INFORMATION
Comédie des Langues....1 B1
Laundrette....2 B2
NeuroGame....3 A2
Post Office....4 B3
Tourist Office....5 A3
SIGHTS & ACTIVITIES
Cathédrale St-Pierre....6 A3
Champs Libres....7 C5
Espace des Sciences....(see 7)
Musée de Bretagne....(see 7)
Musée des Beaux Arts....8 C3
Palais du Parlement de Bretagne....9 C2
SLEEPING
Angelina Hôtel....10 B3
Hôtel de Nemours....11 B4
Hôtel des Lices....12 A2
Vénézia Hôtel....13 D3
EATING
Boulangerie Hoche....14 C2
India Restaurant....15 C3
La Saint-Georges....16 C3
La Ville d'Ys....17 C3
Le Café Breton....18 A3
Les Halles Centrales....19 B4
Léon le Cochon....20 C4
DRINKING
La Cité d'Ys....21 C4
La Scaramouche....22 D4
Oan's Pub....23 A3
ENTERTAINMENT
Cinéma Arvor....24 B1
TRANSPORT
ADA....25 D6
Allo Stop Bretagne....26 C5
Bus Station....27 D6
City Bus Station....28 B3
Europcar....(see 25)
Hertz....(see 25)
National Cites....(see 25)
STAR Office....29 B4
To Auberge de Jeunesse (600m); urbaVag Boat Hire (1.5km); Hédé (25km); Bécherel (33km); St-Malo (60km)
To Camping des Gayeulles (3km); Mont St-Michel (50km)
To Hôtel du Stade (3km)
To Airport (6km); Forêt de Paimpont (40km); Vannes (111km)
To Nantes (107km)
To Vitré (40km)
Parc du Thabor
R Dinan
R St-Malo
R d'Antrain
R d'Échange
Ste-Anne
Pl Ste-Anne
R de la Visitation
R Hoche
R St-Michel
R de Penhoët
Pl St-Michel
R St-Louis
Pl des Lices
Pl du Champ-Jacquet
R Le Bastard
R Victor Hugo
Pl du Parlement de Bretagne
R de la Monnaie
R St-Guillaume
R de Rohan
Hôtel de Ville (Town Hall)
R St-Georges
R Gambetta
R de Paris
R de Viarmes
R Nantaise
Pl de la Mairie
R du Chapitre
R Georges Dottin
R F Buisson
R de l'Horloge
Pl St-Germain
R St-Yves
Pl du Maréchal Foch
Q Duguay Trouin
Pl de la République
Q Chateaubriand
La Vilaine
République
Q Lamennais
Q Émile Zola
R Toullier
R Dupont des Loges
R du Pré Botté
R de Nemours
R Chalotais
Pl de Bretagne
R Jules Simon
R Maréchal Joffre
R de Léon
R Pollain Duparc
R Vasselot
Pl Honoré Commeurec
Bd de la Tour d'Auvergne
Bd de la Liberté
R St-Hélier
R Chicogne
Av Jean Janvier
R J M Duhamel
Charles de Gaulle
R de Plélo
Pl Charles de Gaulle
R d'Isly
Shopping Centre
Cours des Alliés
Bd Magenta
R de l'Alma
Pl du Colombier
R Gurvand
Pl de la Gare
Bd Solférino
Bd de Beaumont
Gares
Train Station
Bd du Colombier

Vénézia Hôtel (☎ 02 99 30 36 56; hotel.venezia@wanadoo.fr; 27 rue Dupont des Loges; s €28-38, d €38-48) Named for the Venice-like canals surrounding this small 'island' in the city centre; half of this charming hotel's 16 rose-toned rooms have pretty views over the canalside garden. The cheapest have a toilet, but share showers. The kind owner can recommend any number of crêperies nearby.

Angelina Hôtel (☎ 02 99 79 29 66; angelina-hotel@voila.fr; 1 quai Lamennais; d €45-62) It doesn't get more central than this cavernous hotel right next to République, with the old city and shopping district on the doorstep. Reception's on the 3rd floor of this creaking old building (there's a lift), but the wicker-furnished rooms are surprisingly well kept and come with bright modern bathrooms, as well as free wi-fi.

Hôtel des Lices (☎ 02 99 79 14 81; www.hotel-des-lices.com; 7 place des Lices; r €48-78; ❄ ⊠) You can peer down from the steel balconies or through the floor-to-ceiling glass doors to see the Saturday-morning market, which snakes right past the front door of this modern six-storey hotel. Inside, rooms are small but sleek with pared-down contemporary furnishings and textured walls. Breakfast (€8) is served in a sunlit ground-floor salon with limed floorboards, white tables and fresh flowers. Wi-fi's free.

Hôtel du Stade (☎ 02 99 59 19 19; www.hoteldustade.fr; 167 rte de Lorient; r €45-68; ❄ ⊠) Parking is limited in Rennes' city centre, so what this shiny new hotel lacks in centrality, it more than makes up for with its free secured parking and spacious and uncluttered rooms (three of which are wheelchair-accessible). Wi-fi's free.

Hôtel de Nemours (☎ 02 99 78 26 26; www.hotelnemours.com, in French; 5 rue de Nemours; r €54-90; ❄ ⊠) Lined with historic black-and-white photographs of Rennes, boutique Hôtel de Nemours is an understatement in elegance, with cream, chocolate- and caramel-coloured furnishings, high-thread-count white linens, flat-screen TVs and free wi-fi. Slide into a corduroy-upholstered banquette for a breakfast buffet feast (€7.50).

Eating

Rennes has a wide choice of restaurants. Rues St-Malo and St-Georges are the city's two main 'eat streets'; the latter particularly specialises in crêperies. See also p352.

La Saint-Georges (☎ 02 99 38 87 04; 31 rue St-Georges; crêpes €2.50-15; ⏰ lunch & dinner Tue-Sat) Innovative crêpes at this smart spot are named after famous people called George: Georges Pompidou, George Michael and so on, through to the most lavish concoction, the Giorgio Armani, with warm foie gras.

Léon le Cochon (☎ 02 99 79 37 54; 1 rue Maréchal Joffre; menu €25, mains €11-24; ⏰ lunch & dinner, closed Sun Jul & Aug) Basking in the plaudits of almost every French gastronomic guidebook, but still fun and informal, 'Leon the Pig' specialises not just in pork but porcine products in all their many and varied manifestations.

Le Café Breton (☎ 02 99 30 74 95; 14 rue Nantaise; menus €13-30; ⏰ lunch & dinner Mon-Sat) Diminutive rue Nantaise has a handful of top restaurants, including this local fave for its tarts, salads and gratins. Definitely book ahead.

India Restaurant (☎ 02 99 87 09 01; 41 rue St-Georges; veg/nonveg menus €14/18; ⏰ lunch & dinner) For a change from crêpes, head to this richly decorated red-and-gold eatery serving up impeccably presented, high-quality Indian cuisine with an extensive choice of vegetarian dishes.

SELF-CATERING

Fresh produce and Breton specialities are available daily at Rennes' covered markets, **Les Halles Centrales** (place Honoré Commeurec; ⏰ 7am-7pm Mon-Sat, 9.30am-12.30pm Sun); on Saturdays, a fabulous **open-air market** fills the surrounding streets and squares.

Pick up exquisite pastries and still-warm bread at **Boulangerie Hoche** (☎ 02 99 63 61 01; 17 rue Hoche, ⏰ 7am-7.30pm Mon-Sat).

Drinking & Entertainment

Rue St-Michel – nicknamed rue de la Soif (Street of Thirst) for its bars, pubs and cafés – is the best-known drinking strip, but it can get rowdy (and sometimes aggressive) late at night.

our pick **Oan's Pub** (☎ 02 99 31 07 51; 1 rue Georges Dottin; ⏰ 2pm-1am Mon-Sat) Locals habitually turn up with instruments for impromptu Celtic jam sessions at this cosy, cavelike, stone-walled pub with Brittany-brewed Coreff beer on tap.

La Cité d'Ys (☎ 02 99 78 24 84; 31 rue Vasselot; ⏰ noon-1am Mon-Sat) If you want to practise your Breton with Breton-speaking locals and bar staff (lubricated by Breton beer), this wooden mezzanine pub is prime. *Yec'hed mat* (Cheers)!

BRETON CRÊPES

Crêpes are Brittany's traditional staple, and ubiquitous throughout the region. Unlike the rolled-up crêpes sold at stalls on Paris' street corners, Breton crêpes are folded envelope-style at the edges, served flat on a plate and eaten using cutlery.

Rennes, as Brittany's capital, has dozens of enticing crêperies, including **La Ville d'Ys** (☎ 02 99 36 70 28; 5 rue St-Georges; crêpes €2.20-5.50; lunch & dinner), named for the fabled Atlantis-style submerged city of Breton legend, and tucked inside a two-storey, 15th-century house with a slanted wooden staircase and colourful crockery displayed on the walls. We spoke to the crêperie's owner-chef, 60-year-old Claudine Thomas as she cooked in her open kitchen, to find out the secrets behind making Breton crêpes:

What are the essential ingredients in a basic galette?

Blé noir – sarrasin in Breton (buckwheat flour); and salted Breton butter. It's important to keep the Breton tradition; locals take crêpes very seriously. Well, crêpes are crêpes!

Favourite traditional toppings?

Andouille (local sausage), and for sweet crêpes, *caramel au beurre salé – salidou* in Breton (salty caramel sauce), which I make here with ingredients from the market.

What's the ideal cooking temperature?

A *galettier – bilig* in Breton (the hotplate) – has no temperature dial, only numbers from one to eight. It can't be too hot – the crêpe needs to be brown at the edges; crispy but not burnt.

Do you use a particular recipe?

I use a recipe from Finistère – the crêpes are a finer texture and crispier than other recipes. People always come in because of this recipe; they don't want any other kind.

If you want to learn how to create your own crêpes, the **Écoles de Treblec** (☎ 02 99 34 86 76; www.ecole-maitre-crepier.com, in French with English sections; 66 rue de Guer, Maure-de-Bretagne), 38km southwest of Rennes, runs a variety of courses; a day-long course costs €79.80.

Le Scaramouche (☎ 02 99 31 55 53; 3bis rue Duhamel; 8am-1am Mon-Sat) This huge space with art and film projected onto the walls attracts lots of local actors, artists and philosophic types.

Nondubbed films screen at **Cinéma Arvor** (☎ 02 99 38 72 40; 29 rue d'Antrain).

To find out about upcoming football matches and obtain tickets, check www.staderennais.com (in French).

Getting There & Away

BUS

Among Rennes' many bus services, **Illenoo** (www.illenoo.fr, in French) runs five times daily to Dinard (€3.50, two hours) via Dinan (€3, 1½ hours), as well Paimpont (€2.50, one hour, none on Sunday).

CAR & MOTORCYCLE

ADA (☎ 02 99 67 43 79), **Europcar** (☎ 02 23 44 02 72), **National Citer** (☎ 02 23 44 02 78) and **Hertz** (☎ 02 23 42 17 01) all have offices at the train station.

HITCHING

Allo Stop Bretagne (☎ 02 99 35 04 40; www.allostoprennes.com, in French; 20 rue d'Isly; 9.30am-12.30pm & 2-6pm Mon-Fri, 9am-1pm & 1.30-3pm Sat), in the Trois Soleils shopping centre, matches up hitchers with drivers for a fee (from €6 for a one-off, one-way journey).

TRAIN

Destinations with frequent services include St-Malo (€12.10, one hour), Dinan (€12.70, one hour including a change), Vannes (€17.80, 1½ hours), Nantes (€20.10, 1¼ hours), Brest (€30, two hours), Quimper (€30.10, 2½ hours) and Paris' Gare Montparnasse (€52.20, 2¼ hours).

Getting Around

Rennes has an efficient local bus network and (incredibly, for a city its size) its own single-line metro, both run by **STAR** (☎ 08 11 55 55 35; www.star.fr, in French; 12 rue Pré Botté). Bus and metro tickets (single journey €1, 10-trip carnet €9.70, 24-hour pass €3) are interchangeable.

The metro line runs northwest to southeast. Main stations include République (place de la République) in the centre, and Ste-Anne (old town).

Ring ☎ 02 99 30 79 79 for a taxi.

VITRÉ

pop 17,000

With its narrow cobbled streets, half-timbered houses and colossal castle topped by witch's-hat turrets, Vitré rivals Dinan as one of Brittany's best-preserved medieval towns – with far fewer tourists and a more laissez-faire village air.

Orientation & Information

Situated 40km east of Rennes, Vitré's compact old town sits immediately north of the train station, between place de la République and the castle.

The **tourist office** (☎ 02 99 75 04 46; www.ot-vitre.fr; place Général de Gaulle; 9.30am-12.30pm & 2-6.30pm Mon-Sat, 10am-12.30pm & 3-6pm Sun Jul & Aug, 2.30-6pm Mon, 9.30am-12.30pm & 2.30-6pm Tue-Fri, 10am-12.30pm & 3-5pm Sat Sep-Jun) is right outside the train station.

Check your email at **Gamer's** (☎ 02 23 55 10 37; 1bis bd Pierre Landais; per 15min/hr €1/4; 2-7pm Mon, 10am-12.30pm & 2-7pm Tue-Sat).

Sights & Activities

You can visit Vitré's **museums** over any number of days for a single entry fee of €4/2.50 per adult/child. The highlight is the **Musée du Château** at the southern corner of the majestic **medieval castle** (☎ 02 99 75 04 54; place du Château; 10am-6pm Jul-Sep, 10am-noon & 2-5.30pm Apr-Jun, 10am-noon & 2-5.30pm Wed-Fri, 2-5.30pm Sat-Mon Oct-Mar). Rising on a rocky outcrop overlooking the River Vilaine, it was built in 1060, and was expanded in the 14th and 15th centuries. A twin-turreted gateway leads you from the cobbled square of place du Château into the triangular inner courtyard.

Sleeping

Vitré has a shortage of accommodation, so it's worth booking ahead any time of year.

Hôtel du Château (☎ 02 99 74 58 59; hotel-du-chateau2@wanadoo.fr; 5 rue Rallon; s €37-53, d €47-59) Wake up to the aroma of freshly baked bread and, on upper floors, fantastic vistas of the castle, at this family-run hotel at the base of the ramparts. The friendly owners are a fount of local information. Free wi-fi, good wheelchair access, a brimming €6.50 breakfast and €3 garaged parking make this one of Brittany's gems.

Mme Faucher (☎ 02 99 75 08 69; http://bnb.faucher.info; 2 chemin des Tertres Noirs; s/d incl breakfast €40/46; ☒) In a rambling 18th-century stone house looking out over a large leafy garden, this *chambre d'hôte* run by Mme and M Faucher is the kind of familial, down-to-earth place you hoped still existed in France. Their home is filled with family memorabilia, bathrooms are shared, and travellers are welcomed with open arms. Breakfast is a hearty basketful of brioches and baguettes, along with strong coffee. It's just a short downhill stroll to the town centre, but driving is a bit complicated due to the one-way road system. Check directions online or ask the tourist office for a route map.

Eating & Drinking

Quaint crêperies and gastronomic restaurants are tucked throughout the old town.

Le Green'Otoire (☎ 02 23 55 08 41; Les Rochers-Sévigné; menus from €8; lunch Thu-Tue, dinner Fri-Sun) Well worth the 4km drive southeast of town along the D88, this 'semi-gastronomic' with exposed stone walls faces an ancient castle and is a favourite with locals for its daily-changing chef's suggestions as well as its feather-light pastries for dessert.

Le Pichet (☎ 02 99 75 24 09; 17 bd de Laval; menus €18-50, mains €12-27; lunch Mon-Sat, dinner Mon-Tue, Fri & Sat) Classical French cuisine incorporating local fish and regional produce fresh from the market is served on a charming terrace overlooking the garden when the sun's shining, and in front of the crackling open fire in winter.

Bressan (☎ 02 99 75 23 64; 3 rue de la Trémouille; 3pm-3am Mon-Sat) Vitré's funky, laid-back microbrewery creates artisan beers in its gleaming copper boilers, which it serves on tap. In summer try the *blanche*, brewed with citrus zest; in winter, go for the robust *noire* (stout).

Getting There & Away

Frequent trains travel between Vitré and Rennes (€6.60, 35 minutes).

Champagne

Known in Roman times as Campania, meaning 'plain', Champagne is a largely agricultural region and is celebrated around the world for the sparkling wines that have been produced here for more than three centuries. According to French law, only bubbly originating from this region – grown in designated areas (now being expanded to meet growing demand), then aged and bottled according to the strictest of rules – can be labelled as Champagne.

The production of this prestigious sparkling wine takes place mainly in two *départements:* Marne, whose metropolis is the 'Coronation City' of Reims, and the less prestigious (though increasingly respected) Aube, whose *préfecture* (departmental capital) is the ancient and picturesque city of Troyes, home to several exceptional museums and entire streets lined with half-timbered houses.

The town of Épernay, 30km to the south of Reims, is the de facto capital of Champagne (the drink, that is) and is the best place to head for *dégustation* (tasting session). The Champagne Route wends its way through the region's diverse vineyards, taking visitors from one picturesque – and prosperous – wine-growing village to the next. A number of name-brand *maisons* (literally 'houses', meaning Champagne producers) have achieved international renown, but much of the region's liquid gold is made by almost 5000 small-scale vignerons (wine makers) in 320-odd villages, many of whose family-run facilities welcome visitors.

HIGHLIGHTS

- Climb to the top of the tower at Cathédrale Notre Dame in **Reims** (p357) for 360-degree views across France's flattest province
- Sip bubbly and nibble *biscuits roses* (pink bicuits) at the end of a cellar tour in **Épernay** (p363), the 'capital of Champagne'
- Explore the rolling vineyards along the various sections of Champagne's scenic **Champagne Route** (p360) by car or even by bicycle
- Wander through the back streets and alleys of the old city in **Troyes** (p366), one of the best-preserved in Europe

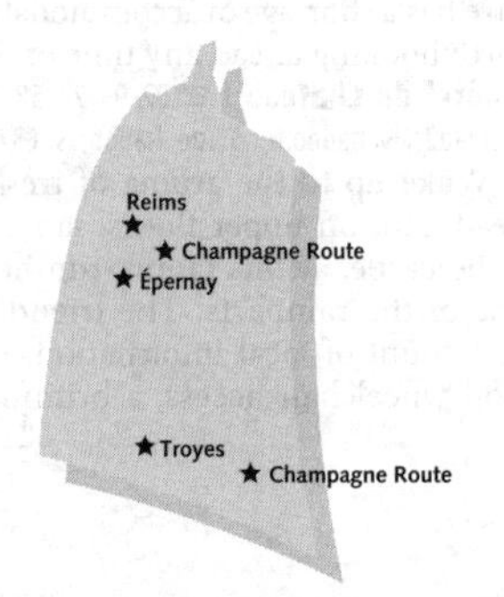

- POPULATION: 1.3 MILLION
- AREA: 25,606 SQ KM

History

Champagne's most famous convert to Christianity was the Merovingian warrior-king Clovis I, who founded the Frankish kingdom in the late 5th century and began the tradition of holding royal coronations in Reims. In the Middle Ages, the region – especially Troyes – grew rich from commercial fairs at which merchants from around Europe bought and sold products from as far afield as the Mediterranean.

The region's name has been associated with bubbly since the late 17th century, when a Benedictine monk named Dom Pierre Pérignon perfected the process of using a second fermentation to make ho-hum still wine sparkle. But while the province may appear to be living the good life now, that hasn't always been the case. Champagne is dominated by an infertile chalk plain 'branded for its poverty and sterility with the unseemly name La Champagne Pouilleuse (literally 'flea-bitten Champagne')', to quote Sir Walter Scott in his *The Life of Napoleon Buonaparte, Emperor of the French* (1827).

Getting There & Around

Champagne (www.tourisme-champagne-ardenne.com), just north of Burgundy, makes a refreshing stopover if you're driving from far northern France or Paris eastward to Lorraine or Alsace. With the TGV Est Européen line (p975) now up and running, both Reims and Épernay can be visited on a one-day excursion from Paris.

France's rail lines radiate out from Paris like the spokes of a wheel and, as it so happens, Reims, Épernay and Troyes are each on a different spoke (more or less). Although there are pretty good rail connections between Reims and Épernay, the best way to get from Reims to Troyes is by bus.

REIMS

pop 202,600

Over the course of a millennium (816 to 1825), some 34 sovereigns – among them two dozen kings – began their reigns as rulers in Reims' famed cathedral. Meticulously reconstructed after WWI and again following WWII, the city – whose name is pronounced something like 'rance' and is often anglicised as Rheims – is neat and orderly, with wide avenues and well-tended parks. Along with Épernay, it is the most important centre of Champagne production.

Orientation

In the commercial centre (north and northwest of the cathedral), the main streets are rue Carnot, rue de Vesle, rue Condorcet and, for shopping, rue de Talleyrand. The train station is almost exactly 1km northwest of the

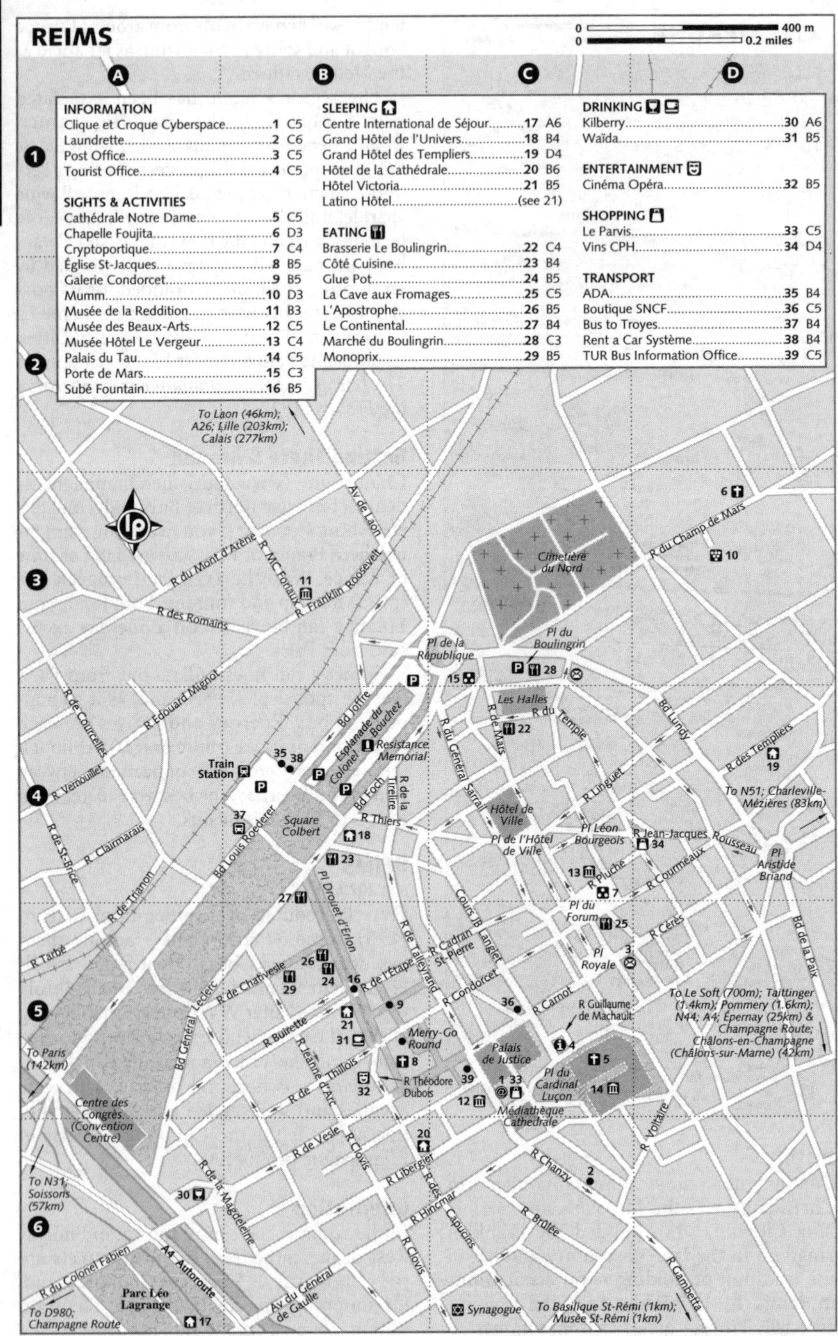
REIMS
0 400 m
0 0.2 miles
A
B
C
D
1
2
3
4
5
6
INFORMATION
Clique et Croque Cyberspace 1 C5
Laundrette 2 C6
Post Office 3 C5
Tourist Office 4 C5
SIGHTS & ACTIVITIES
Cathédrale Notre Dame 5 C5
Chapelle Foujita 6 D3
Cryptoportique 7 C4
Église St-Jacques 8 B5
Galerie Condorcet 9 B5
Mumm 10 D3
Musée de la Reddition 11 B3
Musée des Beaux-Arts 12 C5
Musée Hôtel Le Vergeur 13 C4
Palais du Tau 14 C5
Porte de Mars 15 C3
Subé Fountain 16 B5
SLEEPING
Centre International de Séjour 17 A6
Grand Hôtel de l'Univers 18 B4
Grand Hôtel des Templiers 19 D4
Hôtel de la Cathédrale 20 B6
Hôtel Victoria 21 B5
Latino Hôtel (see 21)
EATING
Brasserie Le Boulingrin 22 C4
Côté Cuisine 23 B4
Glue Pot 24 B5
La Cave aux Fromages 25 C5
L'Apostrophe 26 B5
Le Continental 27 B4
Marché du Boulingrin 28 C3
Monoprix 29 B5
DRINKING
Kilberry 30 A6
Waïda 31 B5
ENTERTAINMENT
Cinéma Opéra 32 B5
SHOPPING
Le Parvis 33 C5
Vins CPH 34 D4
TRANSPORT
ADA 35 B4
Boutique SNCF 36 C5
Bus to Troyes 37 B4
Rent a Car Système 38 B4
TUR Bus Information Office 39 C5
To Laon (46km); A26; Lille (203km); Calais (277km)
Av de Laon
R du Mont d'Arène
R MC Foriaux
R Franklin Roosevelt
R des Romains
Cimetière du Nord
R du Champ de Mars
Pl de la République
Pl du Boulingrin
Les Halles
R du Temple
R de Mars
Bd Lundy
R des Templiers
To N51; Charleville-Mézières (83km)
R de Courcelles
R Edouard Mignot
Bd Joffre
Esplanade du Colonel Bouchez
Resistance Memorial
R du Général Sarrail
R Vernouillet
Train Station
R de St-Brice
R Clairmarais
Bd Louis Roederer
Square Colbert
Bd Foch
R de la Tirelire
R Thiers
Hôtel de Ville
Pl de l'Hôtel de Ville
Pl Léon Bourgeois
R Linguet
R Jean-Jacques Rousseau
Pl Aristide Briand
R Pluche
R Courmeaux
Pl du Forum
R de Trianon
Pl Drouet d'Erlon
Cours JB Langlet
R Cérès
Bd de la Paix
R Tarbé
R de Talleyrand
R Cadran St-Pierre
Pl Royale
R de Chativesle
R de l'Etape
R Condorcet
R Carnot
R Guillaume de Machault
To Le Soft (700m); Taittinger (1.4km); Pommery (1.6km); N44; A4; Épernay (25km) & Champagne Route; Châlons-en-Champagne (Châlons-sur-Marne) (42km)
Bd Général Leclerc
R Buirette
Merry-Go Round
To Paris (142km)
R Jeanne d'Arc
R de Thillois
R Théodore Dubois
Palais de Justice
Pl du Cardinal Luçon
Médiathèque Cathédrale
Centre des Congrès (Convention Centre)
R de Vesle
R Clovis
R Voltaire
To N31; Soissons (57km)
R de la Magdeleine
R Libergier
R Chanzy
R des Capucins
R Hincmar
R Brûlée
R du Colonel Fabien
A4 Autoroute
R Clovis
R Gambetta
Parc Léo Lagrange
Av du Général de Gaulle
Synagogue
To Basilique St-Rémi (1km); Musée St-Rémi (1km)
To D980; Champagne Route

cathedral, across square Colbert from place Drouet d'Erlon, the city's major nightlife strip. Virtually every street in the city centre is one-way.

Information

Commercial banks can be found on rue Carnot and at the southern end of place Drouet d'Erlon. The tourist office can change money every day, including Sundays and holidays.

Clique et Croque Cyberspace (☎ 03 26 86 93 92; www.cliqueetcroque.com; 19 rue Chanzy; per min/hr/5hr/10hr €0.07/4/18/30; 🕑 10am-midnight Mon-Sat, 2-8pm Sun) Internet access opposite the Musée des Beaux-Arts.

Laundrette (59 rue Chanzy; 🕑 7am-9.30pm)

Post Office (2 rue Cérès; 🕑 8.30am-6pm Mon-Fri, to noon Sat) Through the arches on the eastern corner of place Royale.

Tourist Office (☎ 03 26 77 45 00, 08 92 70 13 51; www.reims-tourisme.com; 2 rue Guillaume de Machault; 🕑 9am-7pm Mon-Sat, 10am-6pm Sun & holidays mid-Apr–mid-Oct, 10am-6pm Mon-Sat, 11am-4pm Sun & holidays mid-Oct–mid-Apr) The Reims City Card (€14) gets you a Champagne-house tour, an all-day bus ticket, entry to all four municipal museums and a guided tour of the cathedral.

Sights

All four museums run by the municipality – St-Rémi, Beaux-Arts, Reddition (see the boxed text, p358) and the Ancienne Collège des Jésuites (under renovation at the time of research) – along with the 1966 **Chapelle Foujita** (☎ 03 26 40 06 96; 33 rue du Champ de Mars; 🕑 2-6pm Thu-Tue May-Oct or by appointment), are covered by the **Pass Découverte** (adult/student €3/free), which is valid for one month. All city museums are free on the first Sunday of the month.

CHURCHES & MUSEUMS

Imagine the extravagance, the over-the-top costumes and the egos writ large of a French royal coronation… The focal point of such pompous occasions was **Cathédrale Notre Dame** (www.cathedrale-reims.com, in French; place du Cardinal Luçon; 🕑 7.30am-7.30pm, closed Sun morning), a Gothic edifice begun in 1211 on a site occupied by churches since the 5th century and mostly completed 100 years later. The most famous event to take place here was the coronation of Charles VII, with Joan of Arc (Jeanne d'Arc) at his side, on 17 July 1429.

Very badly damaged by artillery and fire during WWI, the 138m-long cathedral, now a Unesco World Heritage Site, is more interesting for its dramatic history than its heavily restored architectural features. The finest stained-glass windows are the western facade's 12-petalled **great rose window**, its almost cobalt-blue neighbour below, and the rose window in the north transept (to the left), above the Flamboyant Gothic organ case (15th and 18th centuries) topped with a figure. Nearby is a 15th-century wooden **astronomical clock**. There are windows by Chagall (constructed in 1974) in the central axial chapel behind the high altar, one of which portrays Christ and Abraham, and, two chapels to the left, there is a statue of Joan of Arc. The tourist office rents audioguides (€5/9 for one/two people) with self-paced tours of the cathedral.

Those strong-of-thigh might want to climb the 250 steps of the **cathedral tower** (adult/12-25yr €6.50/4.50; 🕑 Tue-Sat & Sun afternoon early May–early Sep, Sat & Sun afternoon mid-Mar–early May & early Sep–Oct) on a one-hour tour. Times and frequencies vary. Book at the Palais du Tau.

Next door, the **Palais du Tau** (☎ 03 26 47 81 79; www.palais-du-tau.fr, in French; 2 place du Cardinal Luçon; adult/student/under 18yr €6.50/4.50/free; 🕑 9.30am-6.30pm Tue-Sun early May–early Sep, 9.30am-12.30pm & 2-5.30pm Tue-Sun early Sep–early May), a former archbishop's residence constructed in 1690, was where French princes stayed before their coronations and where they hosted sumptuous banquets afterwards. Now a museum, it displays truly exceptional statuary, liturgical objects and tapestries from the cathedral, some in the impressive Gothic Salle de Tau (Great Hall).

The rich collections of the **Musée des Beaux-Arts** (☎ 03 26 47 28 44; 8 rue Chanzy; 🕑 10am-noon & 2-6pm Wed-Sun), housed in an 18th-century building a short distance to the west, include one of only four versions of Jacques-Louis David's world-famous *The Death of Marat* (yes, the bloody corpse in the bathtub), 27 works by Camille Corot (only the Louvre has more) and 13 portraits by German Renaissance painters Cranach the Elder and the Younger, lots of Barbizon School landscapes, art-nouveau creations by Émile Gallé and two works each by Monet, Gauguin and Pissarro.

At **Musée Hôtel Le Vergeur** (☎ 03 26 47 20 75; 36 place du Forum; adult/student/under 18yr €4/3/free; 🕑 2-6pm Tue-Sun), in a 13th- to 16th-century town house, highlights include a series of furnished period rooms (kitchen, smoking room, Napoleon III's bedroom), engravings by Albrecht Dürer and a stunning Renaissance facade facing the interior garden.

V-E DAY IN REIMS

Nazi Germany, represented by General Alfred Jodl, surrendered unconditionally at 2.41am on 7 May 1945 at US General Dwight D Eisenhower's headquarters in Reims, now a museum known as the **Musée de la Reddition** (Surrender Museum; ☎ 03 26 47 84 19; 12 rue Franklin Roosevelt; 🕑 10am-noon & 2-6pm Wed-Mon). On display are military uniforms, contemporary photographs and original Allied battle maps affixed to the walls behind glass. There's a 12-minute film in French, German and English.

The 121m-long **Basilique St-Rémi** (place du Chanoine Ladame; 🕑 8am-7pm) is named in honour of Bishop Remigius, who baptised Clovis and 3000 Frankish warriors in 498. Once a Benedictine abbey church and now a Unesco World Heritage Site, its Romanesque nave and transept – worn but stunning – date mainly from the mid-11th century. The choir (constructed between 1162 and 1190) is in the early Gothic style, with a large triforium and, way up top, tiny clerestory windows. The 12th-century-style chandelier has 96 candles, one for each year of the life of St Rémi, whose tomb (in the choir) is marked by a mausoleum from the mid-1600s. The basilica is about 1.5km south-southeast of the tourist office; take the Citadine 1 or 2 or bus A or F to the St-Rémi stop.

Next door, **Musée St-Rémi** (☎ 03 26 85 23 36; 53 rue Simon; 🕑 2-6.30pm Mon-Fri, 2-7pm Sat & Sun), in a 17th- and 18th-century abbey, features local Gallo-Roman archeology, tapestries and 16th- to 19th-century military history in more than a dozen rooms and halls.

CHAMPAGNE HOUSES

The musty *caves* (cellars) and dusty bottles of eight Reims Champagne houses can be visited on guided tours. The following places all have fancy websites, cellar temperatures of 8°C to 10°C and frequent English-language tours that end, *naturellement*, with a tasting session. For details on how Champagne is made, see p77.

Mumm (☎ 03 26 49 59 70; www.mumm.com; 34 rue du Champ de Mars; tours adult/under 12yr €8/free; 🕑 tours 9am-11am & 2-5pm Mar-Oct, Sat Nov-Feb) Mumm (pronounced 'moom'), the only *maison* in the centre of Reims, was founded in 1827 and is now the world's third-largest producer (eight million bottles a year), offering edifying one-hour cellar tours in cellars containing 25 million bottles. Phone ahead for weekday tours from November to February. A tasting session with oenological commentary is available for €14/19.50 for two/three Champagnes.

Pommery (☎ 03 26 61 62 55; www.pommery.fr; 5 place du Général Gouraud; tours adult/student & 12-17yr/under 12yr €10/7/free; 🕑 tours 9.30am-7pm Apr–mid-Nov, 10am-6pm Sat & Sun mid-Nov–Mar) Pommery occupies an Elizabethan-style hilltop campus (built 1868–78) 1.8km southeast of the cathedral. The year-round cellar tours take you 30m underground to Gallo-Roman quarries and 25 million bottles of bubbly. Phoning ahead for reservations is recommended. The complex often hosts contemporary art exhibitions. Take the E or V bus to the Gouraud stop.

Taittinger (☎ 03 26 85 84 33; www.taittinger.com; 9 place St-Niçaise; tours adult/under 12yr €10/free; 🕑 tours 9.30am-noon & 2pm-4.30pm, closed Sat & Sun mid-Nov–mid-Mar) The headquarters of Taittinger, 1.5km southeast of the cathedral, is an excellent place to come for a clear, straightforward presentation on how Champagne is actually made; there's no claptrap about 'the Champagne mystique' here. On the one-hour tours visitors are shown everything from *remuage* (bottle turning) to *dégorgement* (sediment removal at -25°C) to the corking machines. Parts of the cellars occupy 4th-century Roman stone quarries; other bits were made by 13th-century Benedictine monks. Take the Citadine 1 or 2 bus to the St-Niçaise stop.

OTHER SIGHTS

Pedestrianised **place Drouet d'Erlon** has almost as much neon as Las Vegas. Southeast of the **Subé Fountain** (built in 1907) – crowned by a gilded statue of Winged Victory – is a delightful covered shopping arcade called **Galerie Condorcet**. In rue Marx Dormoy, 12th- to 14th-century **Église St-Jacques**, the only medieval parish church extant in Reims, has some pretty awful postwar stained glass.

The handsome, mid-18th-century **place Royale**, surrounded by neoclassical arcades, reflects the magnificence of Louis XV's France (that's him as a Roman emperor up on the pedestal).

Roman relics from the 3rd century include the **Porte de Mars** (place de la République), a triumphal arch located just north of the centre, and the **Cryptoportique** (place du Forum; admission free; 🕑 2-6pm Tue-Sun Jun–mid-Oct), one of three galleries below street level thought to have been used for grain storage.

Sleeping

BUDGET

Centre International de Séjour (CIS; ☎ 03 26 40 52 60; www.cis-reims.com; chaussée Bocquaine; bed in s/d/q per person €40.60/24.90/18.90, with shared toilet €26.90/18.20/16.40; 24hr;) The 85 brightly painted rooms are institutional and utterly devoid of charm but the price is right and it's just across the canal in Parc Léo Lagrange. To get there, take bus B, K, M or N to the Comédie stop or bus H to the Pont de Gaulle stop.

Hôtel Victoria (☎ 03 26 47 21 79; hotel-victoria-reims@wanadoo.fr; 35 place Drouet d'Erlon; s & d €30-69, tr & q €59-99;) It sure ain't the Ritz but this 29-room hostelry on six floors above a friendly little café is central and cheap and there's a lift. Not all rooms have their own WC or air-con; room 52 looks straight onto the Subé Fountain.

Latino Hôtel (☎ 03 26 47 48 89; www.latinocafe.fr, in French; 33 place Drouet d'Erlon; s & d €54-74, apt €130;) This almost boutique hotel above a buzzy musical café has a dozen gaily (think fruity) painted guestrooms (think cherry, pumpkin and aubergine) over five floors but no lift. The furnishings are fun, the welcome exceptionally warm and we love the quotes from the great and the good (Gandhi, Boris Vian) sgraffitoed on the hall walls. The apartment on the top floor looking straight onto the Cathédrale Notre Dame can accommodate up to five people.

Hôtel de la Cathédrale (☎ 03 26 47 28 46; www.hotel-cathedrale-reims.fr; 20 rue Libergier; s/d/q €54/62/78;) Charm, graciousness and a resident Yorkshire terrier greet guests at this hostelry run by a music-loving couple. The 17 tasteful rooms are smallish but pleasingly chintzy and some have recently been renovated. There are four floors but no lift. Go for room 14 with two windows or room 43 with views of Basilique St-Rémi and the hills to the south.

MIDRANGE

Grand Hôtel de l'Univers (☎ 03 26 88 68 08; www.hotel-univers-reims.com, in French; 41 bd Foch; s/d from €77/85, Nov-Apr from €70/79;) This venerable three-star place has 42 large rooms, tastefully appointed, with high ceilings and bathrooms big enough to do jumping jacks in. We love the mix of artwork and vintage posters in the hallways and the attached art-deco Au Congrès restaurant. Corner room 222 is filled with light and catches fleeting glimpses of the cathedral.

TOP END

our pick **Grand Hôtel des Templiers** (☎ 03 26 88 55 08; http://pagesperso-orange.fr/hotel.templiers; 22 rue des Templiers; r €190-280, ste €350;) Built in the 1800s as the home of a rich Champagne merchant, this luxurious four-star neo-Gothic extravaganza retains its original ceilings, stained glass and furnishings. The sweeping wooden staircase imparts a certain retro theatricality but the 17 rooms and suites come with luscious fabrics and modern marble bathrooms. A bonus is the basement swimming pool. Wheelchair access available.

Eating

Côté Cuisine (☎ 03 26 83 93 68; 43 bd Foch; starters €6-21, mains €11.80-22.50, weekday lunch menus €13.50-16.90, dinner menus €32.50; lunch & dinner Mon-Sat) A spacious, modern place with well-regarded traditional French cuisine. Try to get a table giving on to square Colbert.

Brasserie Le Boulingrin (☎ 03 26 40 96 22; www.boulingrin.fr; 48 rue de Mars; starters €6.50-14, mains €13-24, menus €18-25; Mon-Sat) This place, whose name is derived from the English 'bowling green' (as in lawn bowling), offers a minitrip back in time with original decor and fittings, including an old-time zinc bar, dating to 1925. The culinary focus is on *fruits de mer* (seafood).

L'Apostrophe (☎ 03 26 79 19 89; 59 place Drouet d'Erlon; starters €6.50-15.10, mains €14.50-25, weekday lunch menu €14; lunch & dinner) This stylish (and sprawling) café-brasserie dispenses some mean *piscines* (enormous cocktails for several people) along with its French and international cuisine. It's a perennial favourite thanks to its chic atmosphere, summertime terrace and good value. Open as a café straight through from 9am to 1am.

Glue Pot (☎ 03 26 47 36 46; 49 place Drouet d'Erlon; meals €7.50-17; 10am-3am, meals noon-2.30pm & 7-11pm, to 1.30am Fri & Sat) This eclectic pub doubles as a decent Tex-Mex eatery (fajitas are €17) that also serves burgers (the €15 Big Boy has an egg on top) and pizzas (€9.30 to €11.90) to patrons seated on bright red banquettes under ersatz Tiffany lamps.

Le Continental (☎ 03 26 47 01 47; 95 place Drouet d'Erlon; starters €15.90-27, mains €16.90-39, menus, some incl wine, €18.90-55; lunch daily, dinner Mon-Sat) Built in the early 20th century, this classy, marble-floored place with an extravagant golden 'tree' holding up the ceiling serves up panoramic views and classic French dishes such as *magret de canard au miel d'acacia* (duck breast fillet with acacia honey; €15.90). It's open for drinks all afternoon and is a great spot for a teatime glass/bottle of Champagne (€8/44).

SELF-CATERING

The **Marché du Boulingrin** (place du Boulingrin; 5am-3pm Sat), a sprawling food market under a tent, may someday move back into the *halles* (covered market) due south, which has been shut tight since telephone numbers had six digits. Along the south side of place du Forum you'll find several food shops, including a *fromagerie* (cheese shop) called **La Cave aux Fromages** (12 place du Forum; Tue-Sat). There's also a **Monoprix supermarket** (21 rue de Chativesle; 9am-9pm Mon-Sat).

Drinking & Entertainment

Brasseries and cafés line brightly lit place Drouet d'Erlon, the focal point of Reims' nightlife. *Le Monocle*, a free guide available at the tourist office, lists pubs and bars, clubs and cultural venues.

Cinéma Opéra (☎ 03 26 47 13 54; 3 rue Théodore Dubois; adult/concession €7.60/6) shows nondubbed films.

Kilberry (☎ 03 26 88 46 47; 182 rue de Vesle; 10am-12.15am Mon-Thu, to 1.15am Fri, 4pm-1.15am Sat) Almost at the canal, the Kilberry is festooned with 'olde Oirish' farm implements and has Beamish on tap. Happy hour is 5.30pm to 7.30pm.

our pick **Waïda** (☎ 03 26 47 44 49; 5 place Drouet d'Erlon; 7.30am-7.30pm Wed-Sun) An old-fashioned *salon de thé* (tearoom) and confectioner with mirrors, mosaics and marble, Waïda is the place to buy a box of *biscuits roses* (€3.30), traditionally nibbled with Champagne.

Le Soft (☎ 03 26 35 78 19; www.softclub.fr; 2bis av Georges Clemenceau; bar from 5.30pm, club from 10.30pm-late Thu-Sat) Sprawling and *dynamique*, this bar-disco, about 1km southeast of the cathedral, has more flashing blue light than a cop shop. It's House Electro on Thursday, Lady's Night on Friday and free before 1am on Saturday.

Shopping

Vins CPH (☎ 03 26 40 12 12; www.vinscph.com; 3 place Léon Bourgeois; 9am-12.30pm & 2-7.30pm Mon-Fri, 9am-7.30pm Sat) In the cellar at the end of a courtyard is where locals buy good-value wines.

Le Parvis (☎ 03 26 47 44 44; place du Cardinal Luçon; 9am-8pm Apr-Oct, to 7pm Nov-Mar) This excellent bet faces the cathedral and has an enormous range of Champagnes and regularly scheduled tastings (€7 to €10).

Getting There & Away

BUS

The best way to get to Troyes (€21.80, 1¾ to 2¼ hours, three or four daily on weekdays, two at the weekend and holidays) is to take a bus operated by **TransChampagneArdenne** (☎ 03 26 65 17 07; www.stdmarne.fr, in French). The stop is in front of the train station to the southwest; hours are posted in the bus shelter.

CAR

Rental companies with offices facing the train station car park include **ADA** (☎ 03 26 82 57 81) and **Rent a Car Système** (☎ 03 26 77 87 77).

TRAIN

Direct services link Reims with Épernay (€5.70, 22 to 38 minutes, 23 daily weekdays, 14 daily weekends), Laon (€8.50, 35 to 55 minutes, eight daily Monday to Friday, six on Saturday, two on Sunday) and Paris' Gare de l'Est (€22.70, 1¾ hours, 10 to 15 daily), half of which are TGVs (€28, 45 minutes).

In the city centre, seek information and buy tickets at the **Boutique SNCF** (1 cours Jean-Baptiste Langlet; 9am-7pm Mon-Fri, 10am-6pm Sat).

Getting Around

An outfit called **Arthemys Véloservices** (☎ 06 25 49 52 57; www.arthemys-services.com) will deliver a bike 'ready to roll' wherever you're staying in Reims for €6/10/15 per half-day/full day/weekend.

Two circular bus lines, the clockwise Citadine 1 and the anticlockwise Citadine 2 (single ticket €1, all-day *ticket journée* €3, 10-ticket *carnet* €8.60), operated by **TUR** (☎ 03 26 88 25 38; www.tur.fr, in French; 6 rue Chanzy; 7.30am-7.30pm Mon-Fri, 10am-7pm Sat), serve most of the major sights of Reims. Most TUR lines begin their last runs at about 8.50pm; the five night lines operate until 12.15am.

Pay-and-display **car parking** (per hr €0.70, maximum 5hr) is in effect from 9am to noon and 2pm to 7pm Monday to Saturday. Construction of a new tram line, scheduled to start running in 2010, was creating traffic congestion at the time of writing, especially in the centre near the Palais de Justice.

For a taxi, ring ☎ 03 26 47 05 05.

AROUND REIMS

The **Champagne Route** (Route du Champagne) weaves its way among neatly tended vines covering the slopes between small villages, some with notable churches or speciality museums, some quite ordinary. All along the route, beautiful panoramas abound and small-scale *producteurs* (Champagne producers) welcome travellers in search of bubbly, though you should phone ahead before stopping by: many are closed around the *vendange* (grape harvest, ie September and into October). Tourist offices, including the one at Reims, can supply you with an excellent (and free) colour-coded, 210-page booklet, *The Discovery Guide*.

The signposted tertiary roads that make up the Champagne Route meander through the Marne's four most important wine-growing areas. The first two start in Reims, the last two in Épernay.

Massif de St-Thierry (70km; mainly pinot noir and meunier vines) – northwest of Reims, through such villages as Cormicy (WWI national cemetery), St-Thierry (Benedictine monastery with 12th-century chapel), Trigny (where French kings-to-be began their journey to Reims and coronation), flower-bedecked Vandeuil and Savigny-sur-Ardre (where Charles de Gaulle first broadcast his appeal for French resistance).

Montagne de Reims (70km; mainly pinot noir vines) – between Reims and Épernay, through Sacy (the church has an elegant spire), Verzenay (identifiable from afar by the lighthouse), Bouzy (famed for its nonsparkling reds) and Mutigny (has a 2km *sentier de vignoble* 'vineyard walking path').

Vallée de la Marne (90km; mainly pinot meunier vines) – west of Épernay towards Dormans, through Champillon (panoramic views), Hautvillers (see right), Damery (medieval church), Châtillon-sur-Marne (huge statue of Pope Urban II, initiator of the First Crusade) and Dormans (château and park).

Côte des Blancs (100km; chardonnay vines) – south of Épernay towards Sézanne, through Cuis (Romanesque church), Oger (flowers galore), Vertus (fountains and a medieval church), Étoges (church and 17th-century château) and medieval Sézanne.

> **ON THE FACE OF IT**
>
> Louis XVI's attempt to escape from Paris in 1791 ended at **Ste-Ménehould**, 79km east of Reims, when the monarch, by then known by the commoner name of Louis Capet (all kings since the 10th-century Hugh Capet were declared to have ruled illegally) and his consort Marie-Antoinette were recognised by the postmaster thanks to the king's portrait having been printed on a banknote.

Parc Natural Régional de la Montagne de Reims

The Montagne de Reims (see left) section of the Champagne Route skirts the Parc Natural Régional de la Montagne de Reims, endowed with extensive forests and a botanical curiosity, the mutant beech trees known as **faux de Verzy** (see http://verzy.verzenay.free.fr for photos). To get to the *faux* from the village of Verzy in the northeastern corner of the park, follow the signs up the D34; the first trees can be seen about 1km from 'Les Faux' car park.

Across the D34, a short trail leads through the forest to a *point de vue* (panoramic viewpoint) atop 288m-high **Mont Sinaï**.

Hautvillers

pop 865

It was in this tidy village, 7km north of Épernay, that, more than three centuries ago, Dom Pérignon (1639–1715) created Champagne as we know it. It thus lays claim to being *le berceau du champagne* (the cradle, or birthplace, of Champagne). The good Dom's tomb is in front of the altar of the hilltop **Église Abbatiale** (abbey church), which has lots of 17th-century woodwork (eg choir stalls); the bones in the box to the right are those of St Nivard, 7th-century archbishop of Reims and the abbey's founder. Astonishing vineyard views await a few hundred metres north of the centre along route de Fismes (D386) and south along route de Cumières (a road leading to the D1). Hautvillers is twinned with the Alsatian town of Eguisheim, which may help explain why two **storks** – Petrus and Leontine, if you must know – live in a *voilière* (aviary) 800m towards Épernay along the D386. They had five *cigogneaux* (storklings) in May 2007, boosting France's stork population of 700 by almost three-quarters of a percentage point. (See the boxed text, p392.)

Details on the village and region are available at the **tourist office** (☎ 03 26 57 06 35; www.tourisme-hautvillers.com, in French; place de la République; ⏲ 9.30am-1pm & 1.30-6pm Mon-Sat, 10am-5pm Sun Apr–mid-Oct, 10am-noon & 2-5pm Mon-Sat mid-Oct–Mar).

ÉPERNAY

pop 24,500

Prosperous Épernay, the self-proclaimed *capitale du champagne* and home to many of the world's most celebrated Champagne houses, is the best place in Champagne for touring cellars and sampling bubbly. The

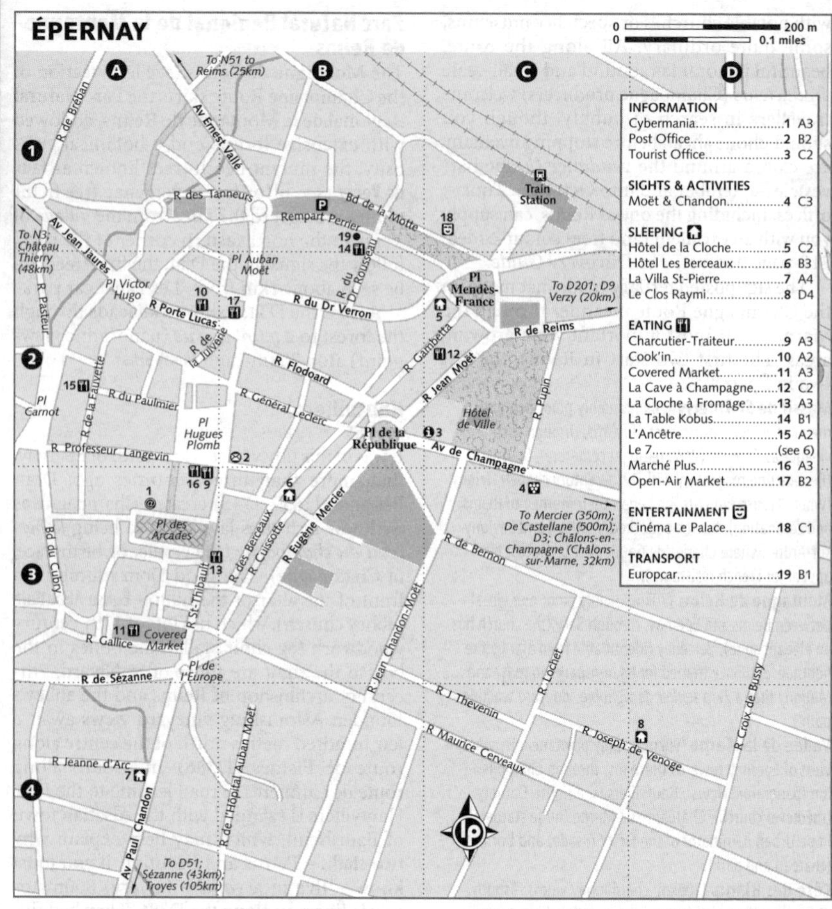

town also makes a good base for exploring the Champagne Route. By rail, Épernay, which is 25km south of Reims, can be visited as a day trip from Reims – or even Paris on the new TGV Est Européen line.

Beneath the streets in 110km of subterranean cellars, more than 200 million bottles of Champagne, just waiting to be popped open for some sparkling occasion, are being aged. In 1950, one such cellar – owned by the irrepressible Mercier (see opposite) – hosted a car rally without the loss of a single bottle!

Orientation

Av de Champagne, where many of Épernay's Champagne houses are based, stretches east from the town's commercial heart, whose liveliest streets are rue Général Leclerc and rue St-Thibault. South of place de la République are car parks.

Information

Cybermania (☎ 03 26 52 26 26; www.cybermania51.com, in French; 11 place des Arcades; per 30min/hr €2/3; 🕑 2pm-midnight Mon, from 11am Tue-Sat, 2-8pm Sun)

Post Office (place Hugues Plomb; 🕑 8.30am-6.30pm Mon-Fri, to noon Sat) Has currency exchange.

Tourist Office (☎ 03 26 53 33 00; www.ot-epernay.fr; 7 av de Champagne; 🕑 9.30am-12.30pm & 1.30-7pm Mon-Sat, 11am-4pm Sun & holidays mid-Apr–mid-Oct, 9.30am-12.30pm & 1.30-5.30pm Mon-Sat mid-Oct–mid-Apr) Has details on cellar visits, car touring, and walking and cycling options.

Tours

CHAMPAGNE HOUSES

Many of the *maisons* on or near av de Champagne offer interesting, informative cellar tours, followed by tasting and a visit to the factory-outlet bubbly shop. For details on the Champagne production process, see p77.

Moët & Chandon (☎ 03 26 51 20 20; www.moet.com; 1/2 glasses adult €11/18, 10-18yr €6.70, under 10yr free; 20 av de Champagne; 🕑 tours 9.30-11.30am & 2-4.30pm, closed Sat & Sun mid-Nov–Mar) This prestigious *maison* offers frequent one-hour tours that are among the region's most impressive. If you sell your car you might be able to buy a 6L methuselah of superpremium Dom Pérignon *millésime* (vintage Champagne) of 1995, a bargain at €6000 plus.

De Castellane (☎ 03 26 51 19 11; www.castellane.com, in French; 64 av de Champagne; 1/2/3 glasses adult €7/12/18, under 10yr free; 🕑 tours 10.30-11.15am & 2.30-5.15pm mid-Mar–Dec, Sat & Sun Jan–mid-Mar) The 45-minute tours take in the *maison*'s informative bubbly museum, dedicated to elucidating the *méthode champenoise* and its diverse technologies. The reward for climbing the 237 steps up the 66m-high tower is a panoramic view.

Mercier (☎ 03 26 51 22 22; www.champagnemercier.com; 68-70 av de Champagne; adult/12-17yr €7/3; 🕑 tours 9.30-11.30am & 2-4.30pm mid-Mar–late Nov, closed Tue & Wed late Nov–mid-Mar) The most popular brand in France (and No 2 in overall production) has thrived on unabashed self-promotion since it was founded in 1847 by Eugène Mercier, a trailblazer in the field of eye-catching publicity stunts and the virtual creator of the cellar tour. Everything here is flashy, including the 160,000L barrel that took two decades to build (for the Universal Exposition of 1889), the lift that transports you 30m underground and the laser-guided touring train. No gimmick: the *chef de cave* (cellar manager) is a woman.

VINEYARDS

Champagne Domi Moreau (☎ 06 30 35 51 07, after 7pm 03 26 59 45 85; www.champagne-domimoreau.com; tours €20; 🕑 tours 9.30am & 2.30pm except Wed, no tours 2nd half of Aug, Christmas period & Feb school holidays) Runs three-hour minibus tours (in French and English) to nearby vineyards. Pick-up is across the street from the tourist office on av de Champagne. It also organises two-hour bicycle tours of the vineyards for €10. Call ahead for reservations.

Sleeping

Épernay's hotels are often full on weekends from Easter to September and on weekdays in May, June and September.

La Villa St-Pierre (☎ 03 26 54 40 80; www.villasaintpierre.fr, in French; 1 rue Jeanne d'Arc; d €33-50, with washbasin €23; 💻 ⊠) In an early-20th-century mansion that has hardly changed in half a century, this homey and very friendly one-star place has 15 simple rooms that retain the charm and atmosphere of yesteryear.

Hôtel de la Cloche (☎ 03 26 55 15 15; hotel-de-la-cloche.c.prin@wanadoo.fr; 5 place Mendès France; d from €48; 💻) This rather snooty place has two stars and 19 cheerful rooms with bright, compact bathrooms. Some rooms have park views. The attached restaurant gets rave reviews.

Hôtel Les Berceaux (☎ 03 26 55 28 84; www.lesberceaux.com; 13 rue des Berceaux; d €95-115, ste €130; 💻) This three-star institution, founded in 1889, has 28 comfortable rooms, each different and all with a modern *champenois* ambience. Businesspeople usually stay here.

Le Clos Raymi (☎ 03 26 51 00 58; www.closraymi-hotel.com; 3 rue Joseph de Venoge; d from €100, ste €160; 💻 ⊠) Staying at this delightful three-star place away from the centre is like being a

STAY-AT-HOME TIPPLE

Unlike Cognac, 95% of which is consumed outside France, about 46% of the 330 million-plus bottles of Champagne produced each year are popped open, sipped and savoured in France itself. That doesn't leave much for the rest of us, especially when you consider how many bottles are wasted christening ships or showering victorious football players! But help is at hand. The body that regulates the Champagne AOC (Appellation d'Origine Contrôlée; trademark body for food and wine) label has agreed to expand the wine-growing area for the first time since 1927. An additional 40 very lucky villages will henceforth be able to label their sparkling wine 'Champagne'.

Large *maisons* with global brand recognition, many of them owned by international luxury-goods conglomerates, send a high percentage of their production to other countries (Moët & Chandon, for example, exports 80% of its bubbly), in part because profit margins are higher, but the many small *producteurs* continue to serve an almost exclusively domestic clientele. Just under 151 million bottles left France in 2007, destined for the following countries (among others): UK (38.9 million bottles), US (21.7 million), Japan (9.1 million), Russia (1.03 million) and China (656,000).

personal guest of Monsieur Chandon of Champagne fame, who occupied this luxurious home over a century ago. The seven romantic rooms have giant beds, 3.7m-high ceilings, ornate mouldings and parquet floors. In winter there's often a fire in the cosy modernist living room.

Eating

Rue Gambetta is home to five pizzerias and two kebab joints.

L'Ancêtre (☎ 03 26 55 57 56; 20 rue de la Fauvette; starters €8.30-12, mains €13-22, menus €15.50-29; ⌚ closed Mon & lunch Wed) A rustic eatery with a grape-patterned stained-glass door, traditional French cuisine and a mere half-dozen tables. Book ahead.

Le 7 (☎ 03 26 55 28 84; Hôtel Les Berceaux, 13 rue des Berceaux; starters €9-15, mains €19-27, menus €17.50 & €24; ⌚ closed Mon & Tue) This bistro at the Hôtel Les Berceaux (it also has a more formal restaurant) has traditional French fare and a relaxed vibe.

La Cave à Champagne (☎ 03 26 55 50 70; 16 rue Gambetta; starters €9-15, mains €12-16, menus €16.50 & €32; ⌚ closed Tue & Wed) 'The Champagne Cellar' is well regarded by locals for its Champenois cuisine, including *potée à la champenoise* (poultry and pork oven-baked with cabbage; €14).

Cook'in (☎ 03 26 32 04 23; 20 rue Porte Lucas; starters €10.85-16.85, mains €13.50-18, menus €17.50-27.50; ⌚ closed Sun, lunch Mon & dinner Wed) This very stylish bistro with black, white and red leather banquettes near the open-air market serves excellent 'enlightened' French provincial cuisine.

La Table Kobus (☎ 03 26 51 53 53; 3 rue du Docteur Rousseau; menus €20-47; ⌚ closed Mon, dinner Sun & Thu) French cuisine in versions traditional and creative, all served amid fin-de-siècle decor.

SELF-CATERING

Covered market (Halle St-Thibault; rue Gallice; ⌚ 8am-noon Wed & Sat)
Open-air market (place Auban Moët; ⌚ Sun morning)
Charcutier-Traiteur (9 place Hugues Plomb; ⌚ 8am-12.45pm & 3-7.30pm, closed Sun & Wed) Sells scrumptious prepared dishes.
La Cloche à Fromage (19 rue St-Thibault; ⌚ 9am-12.15pm & 3.15-7pm Tue-Sat) Has wonderful cheeses and other food products.
Marché Plus (13 place Hugues Plomb; ⌚ 7am-9pm Mon-Sat, 9am-1pm Sun) Grocery store.

Entertainment

Cinéma Le Palace (☎ 08 92 68 07 51; www.le-palace.fr; 33 bd de la Motte; adult/concession €7.50/6.50) Shows nondubbed films just southwest of the train station.

Getting There & Around

From the **train station** (place Mendès France) there are direct services to Nancy (€26.40, two hours, five or six daily), Reims (€5.70, 23 to 32 minutes, 23 daily weekdays, 14 daily weekends) and Paris' Gare de l'Est (€19.40, 1¼ hours, eight to 13 daily).

Cars can be hired from **Europcar** (☎ 03 26 54 90 61; 20 rempart Perrier; 8am-noon & 2-6.30pm Mon-Fri, 9am-noon & 2-5pm Sat).

Parking in the lots south of place de la République is free for the first hour and costs €1.10 for the 2nd and subsequent hours.

TROYES

pop 60,500

Troyes – like Reims, one of the historic capitals of Champagne – has a lively old centre that's graced with one of France's finest ensembles of Gothic churches and medieval and Renaissance half-timbered civic buildings. It is one of the best places in France to get a sense of what Europe looked like back when Molière was penning his finest plays and the Three Musketeers were swashbuckling. Several unique and very worthwhile museums are another lure.

Troyes does not have any Champagne cellars. However, you can shop till you drop in its scores of outlet stores that carry brand-name clothing and accessories, a legacy of the city's long-time role as France's knitwear capital.

Orientation

Although the Aube was almost strong-armed out of the Champagne trade (see Côte des Bar, p369), Troyes' medieval city centre – bounded by bd Gambetta, bd Victor Hugo, bd du 14 Juillet and the Seine – is, cruelly, shaped like a Champagne cork *(bouchon)*. The main commercial street is rue Émile Zola.

Information

The tourist office annexe changes money when the banks are closed but the rate is poor.

Cyber Café Viardin Micro (8 rue Viardin; per 1/10/20hr €2/6/14; ⌚ 2-7pm Mon, 9.30am-noon & 2-7pm Tue, to midnight Wed-Sat)

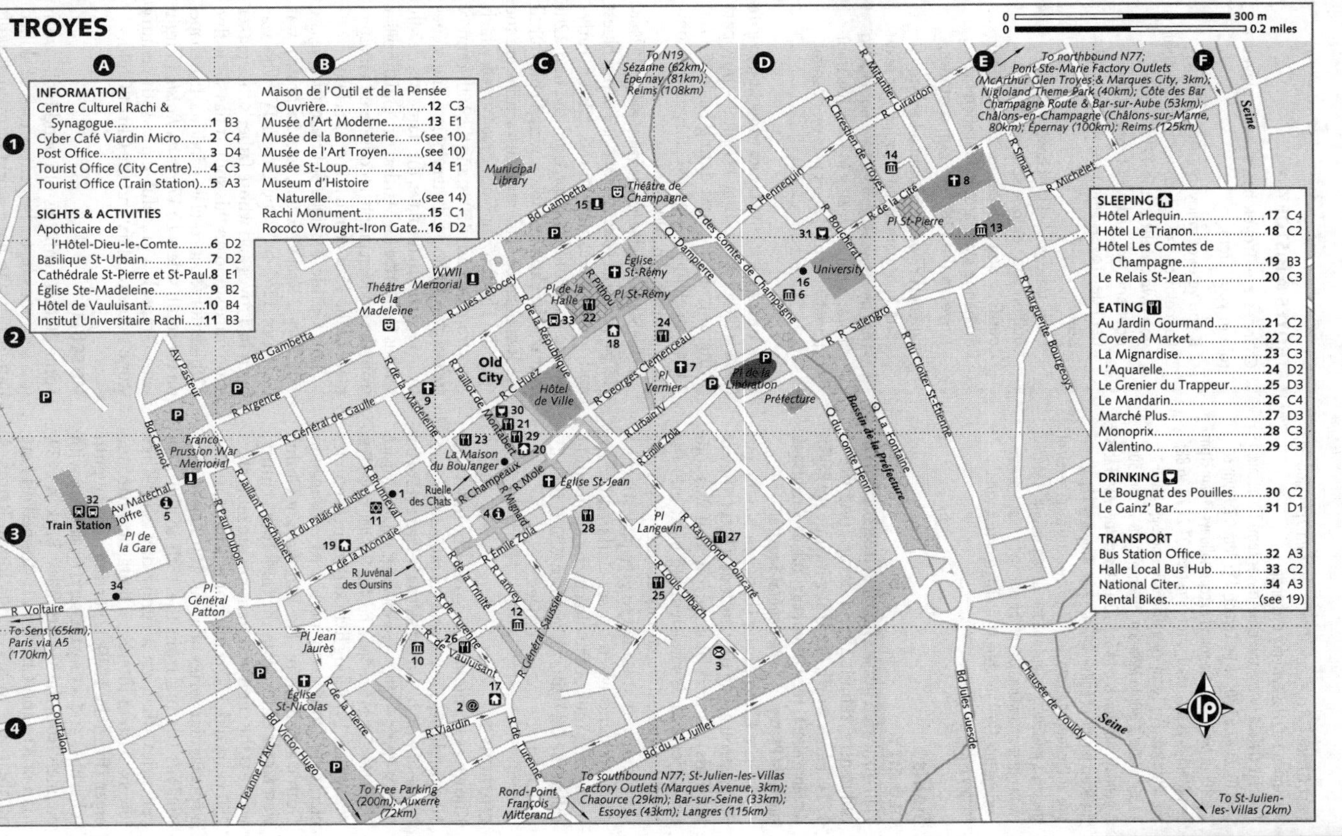
TROYES
INFORMATION
Centre Culturel Rachi & Synagogue....1 B3
Cyber Café Viardin Micro....2 C4
Post Office....3 D4
Tourist Office (City Centre)....4 C3
Tourist Office (Train Station)....5 A3
SIGHTS & ACTIVITIES
Apothicaire de l'Hôtel-Dieu-le-Comte....6 D2
Basilique St-Urbain....7 D2
Cathédrale St-Pierre et St-Paul....8 E1
Église Ste-Madeleine....9 B2
Hôtel de Vauluisant....10 B4
Institut Universitaire Rachi....11 B3
Maison de l'Outil et de la Pensée Ouvrière....12 C3
Musée d'Art Moderne....13 E1
Musée de la Bonneterie....(see 10)
Musée de l'Art Troyen....(see 10)
Musée St-Loup....14 E1
Museum d'Histoire Naturelle....(see 14)
Rachi Monument....15 C1
Rococo Wrought-Iron Gate....16 D2
SLEEPING
Hôtel Arlequin....17 C4
Hôtel Le Trianon....18 C2
Hôtel Les Comtes de Champagne....19 B3
Le Relais St-Jean....20 C3
EATING
Au Jardin Gourmand....21 C2
Covered Market....22 C2
La Mignardise....23 C3
L'Aquarelle....24 D2
Le Grenier du Trappeur....25 D3
Le Mandarin....26 C4
Marché Plus....27 D3
Monoprix....28 C3
Valentino....29 C3
DRINKING
Le Bougnat des Pouilles....30 C2
Le Gainz' Bar....31 D1
TRANSPORT
Bus Station Office....32 A3
Halle Local Bus Hub....33 C2
National Citer....34 A3
Rental Bikes....(see 19)
0 300 m
0 0.2 miles
To northbound N77; Pont Ste-Marie Factory Outlets (McArthur Glen Troyes & Marques City, 3km); Nigloland Theme Park (40km); Côte des Bar Champagne Route & Bar-sur-Aube (53km); Châlons-en-Champagne (Châlons-sur-Marne, 80km); Épernay (100km); Reims (125km)
To N19; Sézanne (62km); Épernay (81km); Reims (108km)
To southbound N77; St-Julien-les-Villas Factory Outlets (Marques Avenue, 3km); Chaource (29km); Bar-sur-Seine (33km); Essoyes (43km); Langres (115km)
To St-Julien-les-Villas (2km)
To Free Parking (200m); Auxerre (72km)
To Sens (65km); Paris via A5 (170km)
Seine
Bassin de la Préfecture
Old City
Train Station
Pl de la Gare
Pl Général Patton
Pl Jean Jaurès
Pl de la Halle
Pl St-Rémy
Pl Vernier
Pl de la Libération
Pl Langevin
Pl St-Pierre
Rond-Point François Mitterand
Municipal Library
Théâtre de Champagne
Théâtre de la Madeleine
WWII Memorial
Franco-Prussian War Memorial
Hôtel de Ville
Église St-Rémy
Église St-Jean
Église St-Nicolas
Préfecture
University
La Maison du Boulanger
Ruelle des Chats
Bd Gambetta
Bd Carnot
Bd Victor Hugo
Bd du 14 Juillet
Bd Jules Guesde
Av Pasteur
Av Maréchal Joffre
Q des Comtes de Champagne
Q Dampierre
Q La Fontaine
Q du Comte Henri
R de la République
R de la Madeleine
R Général de Gaulle
R Paillot de Montabert
R Champeaux
R Émile Zola
R Urbain IV
R Georges Clemenceau
R Raymond Poincaré
R Louis Ulbach
R Général Saussier
R de Turenne
R de Vauluisant
R Viardin
R de la Trinité
R Larivey
R Mignard
R Mole
R C Huez
R Brunneval
R du Palais de Justice
R de la Monnaie
R Juvénal des Oursins
R de la Pierre
R Jaillant Deschainets
R Paul Dubois
R Argence
R Jules Lebocey
R Pithou
R Boucherat
R de la Cité
R Chrestien de Troyes
R Mitantier
R Girardon
R Hennequin
R Salengro
R du Cloître St-Étienne
R Simart
R Michelet
R Marguerite Bourgeoys
Chaussée de Vouldy
R Jeanne d'Arc
R Courtalon
R Voltaire

Post Office (38 rue Louis Ulbach; 8am-7pm Mon-Fri, 9am-noon Sat) Has currency exchange.

Tourist Office (www.tourisme-troyes.com) Train Station (03 25 82 62 70; 16 bd Carnot; 9am-12.30pm & 2-6.30pm Mon-Sat year-round except holidays, 10am-1pm Sun & holidays Nov-Mar); City Centre (03 25 73 36 88; rue Mignard; 10am-7pm daily Jul–mid-Sep, 9am-12.30pm & 2-6.30pm Mon-Sat, 10am-noon & 2-5pm Sun & holidays Apr-Jun & mid-Sep–Oct, closed Nov-Mar) Faces the west facade of Église St-Jean. Pass' Troyes (€12), on sale at the tourist offices, includes free entry to all seven of the city's museums, a Champagne tasting session, a tour (with guide or audioguide) of the old city, a horse-drawn carriage ride (July and August) and discounts at various factory outlet shops.

Sights

OLD CITY

Half-timbered houses line the streets of Troyes' old centre, rebuilt after a devastating fire in 1524. Lanes worth exploring include **rue Paillot de Montabert**, **rue Champeaux**, **rue de Vauluisant**, **rue de la Pierre** and **rue Général Saussier**.

Off rue Champeaux (between No 30 and 32), a stroll along tiny **ruelle des Chats** (Alley of the Cats), as dark and narrow as it was four centuries ago, is like stepping back into the Middle Ages. The stones at intervals along the sides were installed to give pedestrians a place to stand when horses clattered by. An hour-long tour of the old city by audioguide, called the **Cat Trail** (adult/concession €5.50/3), is available from the tourist offices.

CHURCHES

Known as *la ville aux 10 églises* (the town with 10 churches), Troyes sees its most important house of worship in **Cathédrale St-Pierre et St-Paul** (place St-Pierre; 10am-7pm daily Jul & Aug, 10am-1pm & 2-6pm Mon-Sat, to 5pm Sun & holidays Sep-Jun, closed Mon Nov-Mar), a 114m-long hybrid that incorporates elements from every period of *champenois* Gothic architecture. The Flamboyant Gothic **west facade** dates from the mid-16th century, whereas the choir and transepts are more than 250 years older. The interior is illuminated by a spectacular series of about 180 **stained-glass windows** (dating from the 13th to the 17th centuries) that, on a sunny day, shine like jewels. Also of interest: a fantastical baroque **organ** (from the 1730s) sporting musical putti (cherubs) and a tiny **treasury** (Jul & Aug) with enamels from the Meuse Valley. Back in 1429, Joan of Arc and Charles VII stopped off here on their way to his coronation in Reims. A block to the west, the **rococo wrought-iron gate** (rue de la Cité) of a one-time hospital – now part of the university – and dating back to 1760 glitters in glamorous gilded glory after a complete overhaul in 2000.

Église Ste-Madeleine (rue Général de Gaulle; 9.30am-12.30pm & 2-5.30pm, closed Sun morning), Troyes' oldest and most interesting church, has an early-Gothic nave and transept from the mid-12th century; the choir and tower weren't built until the Renaissance. The main attractions are the splendid Flamboyant Gothic **rood screen**, which dates from the early 1500s, and the 16th-century **stained glass** in the presbytery portraying scenes from Genesis. In the nave, the statue of a deadly serious **Ste-Marthe** (St Martha), around the pillar from the wooden pulpit, is considered a masterpiece of the 15th-century Troyes School.

The Gothic **Basilique St-Urbain** (place Vernier; 9.30am-12.30pm & 2-5.30pm, closed Sun morning) was begun in 1262 by Pope Urban IV, who was born in Troyes and whose father's shoemaker shop once stood on this spot. It has some fine 13th-century stained-glass windows. In a chapel on the south side is *La Vierge au Raisin* (Virgin with Grapes), a graceful, early-15th-century stone statue of Mary and the Christ Child.

MUSEUMS

Some 10,000 centuries-old hand tools, worn to a sensuous lustre by generations of skilled hands, bring to life a world of manual skills

TROYES & HISTORY

Chances are Troyes has already played a role in your life:

- If you've ever enjoyed a story about Lancelot or the search for the Holy Grail you owe a debt to the 12th-century poet and troubadour Chrétien (Chrestien) de Troyes, who was, well, a local boy.
- Every time you've purchased gold bullion you've done so using the troy ounce, a unit of measure derived from exchange standards established in Troyes in the 12th and 13th centuries.
- Whenever you've bought a Lacoste shirt, Petit Bateau kids clothing or sexy Dim underwear, you've paid homage to a brand name created in what has traditionally been France's knitwear capital.

made obsolete by the Industrial Revolution at **Maison de l'Outil et de la Pensée Ouvrière** (Museum of Tools & Crafts; ☎ 03 25 73 28 26; www.maison-de-l-outil.com; 7 rue de la Trinité; adult/student & 12-18yr/under 18yr €6.50/3/free, admission free 1st Sun of month; 🕐 10am-6pm). Run by a national crafts guild, this unique and – if you'll excuse the expression – riveting museum is in the magnificent Renaissance-style Hôtel de Mauroy (built in 1556). Videos show how the tools were used and what they produced. Definitely worth a visit, even if you're not a 'boy'.

Musée d'Art Moderne (☎ 03 25 76 26 80; place St-Pierre; adult/student under 25yr, under 18yr €5/free, admission free 1st Sun of month; 🕐 10am-1pm & 2-6pm Tue-Sun) owes its existence to all those alligator shirts, whose global success allowed the museum's benefactors, Lacoste entrepreneurs Pierre and Denise Lévy, to amass this outstanding collection. Housed in an erstwhile bishop's palace (from the 16th to 18th centuries), the museum focuses on glass (especially the work of local glassmaker Maurice Marinot), ceramics and French painting (including lots of fauvist works) created between 1850 and 1950. Featured artists include Derain, Dufy, Matisse, Modigliani, Picasso and Soutine

Musée St-Loup (☎ 03 25 76 21 68; 1 rue Chrestien de Troyes; adult/student under 25yr, under 18yr €4/free, admission free 1st Sun of month; 🕐 9am-noon & 1-5pm Tue-Sun), across the street from the cathedral, has a wide-ranging and sometimes surprising collection of medieval sculpture, enamel, archeology and natural history. In the same building is the **Museum d'Histoire Naturelle** (Museum of Natural History), which is included in the Musée St-Loup entry fee and keeps the same hours.

If you come down with an old-fashioned malady – scurvy, perhaps, or unbalanced humours – the place to go is the **Apothicaire de l'Hôtel-Dieu-le-Comte** (☎ 03 25 80 98 97; quai des Comtes de Champagne; adult/student under 25yr, under 18yr €2/free, admission free 1st Sun of month; 🕐 9am-noon & 1-5pm Tue-Sun), a fully outfitted, wood-panelled pharmacy from 1721. The empty ground storey of the building across the little courtyard, now a herb garden, once served as a morgue.

Hôtel de Vauluisant (☎ 03 25 73 05 85; 4 rue de Vauluisant; adult/student under 25yr, under 18yr €3/free, admission free 1st Sun of month; 🕐 9am-noon & 1-5pm Tue-Sun), a haunted-looking Renaissance-style mansion-turned-museum, has two sections. **Musée de l'Art Troyen** (Museum of Troyes Art) features the evocative paintings, stained glass and statuary (stone and wood) of the Troyes School, which flourished here during the economic prosperity and artistic ferment of the early 16th century. **Musée de la Bonneterie** (Hosiery Museum) showcases the sock-strewn story of Troyes' 19th-century knitting industry. Some of the machines on display look not unlike enormous Swiss watches.

Sleeping

A number of two- and three-star hotels face the train station.

Hôtel Le Trianon (☎ 03 25 73 18 52; 2 rue Pithou; d with washbasin/shower €25/34, tr/q €72/82; 🕐 reception 11am-8pm Mon, 6.30am-8pm Tue-Sat, 9am-1pm Sun) At this gay-owned very convivial place, the rainbow flag flies proudly from the balcony. The eight

RASHI

During the 11th and 12th centuries, a small Jewish community was established in Troyes under the protection of the counts of Champagne. Its most illustrious member was Rabbi Shlomo Yitzhaki (1040–1105), better known as Rashi (Rachi in French).

Rashi's commentaries on the Bible and the Talmud, which combine literal and nonliteral methods of interpretation and make extensive use of allegories and parables as well as symbolic meanings, are still vastly important to Jews and have also had an impact on interpretations of the Christian Bible. Rashi's habit of explaining difficult words and passages in the local French vernacular – transliterated into Hebrew characters – has made his writings an important resource for scholars of Old French. In 1475 (a mere three decades after Gutenberg), Rashi's Bible commentary became the first book to be printed in Hebrew.

The striking **Rachi monument** (next to the Théâtre de Champagne), a white and black globe with Hebrew letters, stands very near the site of a medieval Jewish cemetery where Rashi is believed to have been buried. A local institute of Jewish studies, the **Institut Universitaire Rachi** (2 rue Brunneval) and the new **Centre Culturel Rachi** (☎ 03 25 73 53 01; 5 rue Brunneval) just opposite are named in his honour.

rooms, above a jaunty yellow bar, are spacious but ordinary, though most have fireplaces.

Hôtel Les Comtes de Champagne (☎ 03 25 73 11 70; www.comtesdechampagne.com; 56 rue de la Monnaie; d/q from €50/70, d with washbasin €33;) For centuries, the same massive wooden ceiling beams have kept this superwelcoming place from collapsing into a pile of toothpicks. We love the bright courtyard lobby and the flower boxes; a huge and very romantic double goes for €83. Bicycles (see opposite) are available for rent.

our pick **Hôtel Arlequin** (☎ 03 25 83 12 70; www.hotelarlequin.com; 50 rue de Turenne; d with shower/shower & WC from €41/58; reception 8am-12.30pm & 2-10pm Mon-Sat, 7am-12.30pm & 6.30-10pm Sun & holidays;) The 22 cheerful rooms at this charming and very yellow two-star hostelry come with antique furnishings, high ceilings and commedia dell'arte playfulness. The whole place, lovingly kept and efficiently run, is furnished in exceptionally good taste, from the smart custard facade to the lemony breakfast room. Rooms on the top floor (numbers 304, 305 and 307) are the cheapest and there is no lift.

Le Relais St-Jean (☎ 03 25 73 89 90; www.relais-st-jean.com; 51 rue Paillot de Montabert; s €85-130, d €95-135;) On a narrow medieval street in the heart of the old city, this four-star hotel has 25 rooms that were the last word in ultramodern back in the 1980s – gotta love the marble, black leather and glass-covered surfaces! The hotel has its own little conservatory with tropical plants and good wheelchair access.

Eating

The people of Troyes are enormously proud of the local speciality, *andouillette de Troyes* (pork or veal tripe sausage). As far as most non-French are concerned, it's an acquired taste.

Rue Champeaux (just north of Église St-Jean) is lined with restaurants. Student-oriented eateries can be found just west of the cathedral along rue de la Cité and rue Georges Clemenceau.

L'Aquarelle (☎ 03 25 73 87 82; 24 rue Georges Clemenceau; lunch menu €12.50; noon-late, closed dinner Mon & Sun Nov-Mar) Delicious savoury galettes (€3.30 to €7.80), sweet crêpes (€2.80 to €6.50), salads (€6.50 to €8.50) and local Pays de l'Othe *cidre* served by a softly spoken chap from Belfast.

Le Mandarin (☎ 03 25 73 01 54; 14 rue Turenne; starters €4-11, mains €5.60-10.80, menus €8.90-13.50; closed Mon & Tue lunch) If like us you can't go for too long without a fix of rice and noodles even in provincial France, the Mandarin can oblige. Dim sum is a snip at €4.10 per serving.

Le Grenier du Trappeur (☎ 03 25 73 21 86; 24 rue Louis Ulbach; starters €4.50-12, mains €9.50-18, menus €11-16; lunch & dinner to 9.30-10pm Mon-Sat) Pancake-flat Champagne is a long way from the mountains but this Savoyard restaurant with its chalet decor will whisk you back to the Alps with its all-you-can-eat *raclette* (€18) and *gratins*.

Au Jardin Gourmand (☎ 03 25 73 36 13; 31 rue Paillot de Montabert; starters €9-14, mains €17-25, weekday lunch menu €17; closed Sun & lunch Mon) Elegant without being overly formal, this intimate restaurant uses only the freshest ingredients for its French and *champenois* dishes, including no fewer than 13 kinds of *andouillette*. The estimable wine list offers more than two dozen vintages by the glass. There's a terrace in summer.

Valentino (☎ 03 25 73 14 14; 35 rue Paillot de Montabert; starters €15-22, mains €24-34, menus €22-50; Tue-Sat) This is a modern restaurant whose chef takes the *fusionista* approach, combining classic French ingredients and savoir faire with East Asian spices and textures. It's in a quiet medieval courtyard.

our pick **La Mignardise** (☎ 03 25 73 15 30; 1 ruelle des Chats; starters €18-28.50, mains €27.50-32, menus €26-53; closed dinner Sun & Mon) An elegant restaurant whose traditional French cuisine is served beneath ancient wooden beams, 19th-century mouldings and ultramodern halogen lamps. The menu changes every six to eight weeks. The chef is a particular fan of fish, with more than half of the 15 mains on offer from the briny deep.

SELF-CATERING

Covered market (place de la Halle; 8am-12.45pm & 3.30-7pm Mon-Thu, 7am-7pm Fri & Sat, 9am-12.30pm Sun)

Monoprix (1st fl, 71 rue Émile Zola; 8.30am-8pm Mon-Sat) Supermarket upstairs in this half-timbered house.

Marché Plus (37 rue Raymond Poincaré; 7am-9pm Mon-Sat, 9am-1pm Sun) Grocery store.

Drinking

Le Bougnat des Pouilles (☎ 03 25 73 59 85; www.bougnatdespouilles.com, in French; 29 rue Paillot de Montabert; noon-3am Mon-Sat) A funky wine bar that doubles as an art gallery. Attacks of the munchies can be overcome with plates of cold cuts and cheese (€7.50) or *tartines* (open sandwiches; €3.80 to €4.20). There's live music two or three times a month, often on Thursdays from 8.30pm or so.

WAY TO GO

A 42km-long bike path called **Vélovoie** (☎ 03 25 42 50 00; www.aube-champagne.com) links the southeastern Troyes suburb of St-Julien-les-Villas with Lac d'Orient and two adjacent lakes (Lac du Temple and Lac Amance) further north. The lakes are known for their birdlife (cranes, kingfishers), and there's a hide on a narrow isthmus between Lac d'Orient and Lac du Temple for budding birders. At least 15 daily trains a day from Paris' Gare de l'Est (up to a dozen at the weekend) allow passengers to transport their bicycles. Ask the tourist office in Troyes for the brochure-map *Vélovoie Troyes > Les Lacs* or download it from the Aube-Champagne website.

Le Gainz' Bar (☎ 03 25 80 60 76; 37-39 rue de la Cité; ⏰ 10am-3am Mon-Sat) Named in honour of the legendary balladeer Serge Gainsbourg (that's him in the shades on the wall), this friendly, rambling place is Troyes' most popular student hang-out. There's a student night on Thursday, a DJ on Friday and a theme night on Saturday.

Shopping

Troyes is famous across France for its **magasins d'usine** (factory outlets; ⏰ generally 10am-7pm Mon-Fri, from 9.30am Sat, closed Sun), a legacy of the local knitwear industry. Brand-name sportswear, underwear, baby clothes, shoes and so on – discontinued styles, unsold stock, returns, prototypes – attract bargain-hunters by the coachload.

Most stores are situated in two main zones. The first is **St-Julien-les-Villas**, about 3km south of the city centre on bd de Dijon (the N71 to Dijon), where you'll find **Marques Avenue** (☎ 03 25 82 80 80; www.marquesavenue.com; av de la Maille), which boasts 230 name brands. The second is **Pont Ste-Marie**, about 3km northeast of Troyes' city centre along rue Marc Verdier, which links av Jean Jaurès (the N77 to Châlons-en-Champagne) with av Jules Guesde (the D960 to Nancy). There you'll find **McArthur Glen Troyes** (☎ 03 25 70 47 10; www.mcarthurglen.fr), a huge strip mall with more than 100 shops, and **Marques City** (☎ 03 25 46 37 48; www.marquescity.com), which brings together another 50 or so stores.

Getting There & Away

The **bus station office** (☎ 03 25 71 28 42; ⏰ 8.30am-12.30pm & 2-6.30pm Mon-Fri), run by Courriers de l'Aube, is in the train station building. Schedules are posted next to each bus berth. For details on getting to Reims see p360.

Cars can be rented from **National Citer** (☎ 03 25 73 27 37; 18 rue Voltaire; ⏰ 8am-noon & 2-6.30pm Mon-Fri, 8.30am-noon & 2-6pm Sat) south of the station.

Troyes is on the rather isolated train line linking Basel (Bâle; €40.20, four hours) in Switzerland and Mulhouse (€37.50, three hours) in Alsace with Paris' Gare de l'Est (€22.20, 1½ hours, 12 to 15 daily). A change of trains gets you to Dijon (€27.10, 2½ to four hours, three to five daily) via Chaumont.

Getting Around

The Hôtel Les Comtes de Champagne (see opposite) arranges **rental bikes** for €8/12/20/60 per half-day/full day/two days/week. The local bus company, **TCAT** (☎ 03 25 70 49 00; www.tcat.fr, in French; place de la Halle; ⏰ 8am-12.45pm & 1.35-7pm Mon-Fri, to 6.30pm Sat) has its main bus hub, known as Halle, next to the covered market.

To order a taxi, call ☎ 03 25 78 30 30 or ☎ 03 25 76 06 60.

CÔTE DES BAR

Although the Aube *département*, of which Troyes is the capital, is a major producer of Champagne (it has 6813 sq km of vineyards, 85% of them pinot noir and 15% chardonnay), it gets little of the recognition accorded the Marne *département*. Much of the acrimony dates back to 1909, when winemakers of the Aube were excluded from the growing area for Champagne's AOC. Two years later, they were also forbidden to sell their grapes to producers up north, provoking a revolt by local *vignerons*, months of strikes and a situation so chaotic that the army was called in. It was another 16 years before the Aube growers were fully certified as producers of genuine Champagne but by then the Marne had established market domination.

Today, Champagne production in the southeastern corner of the Aube (about 35km southeast of Troyes) – just north of Burgundy's Châtillonnais vineyards (see p473) – is relatively modest in scale, though the reputation of the area's wines, especially rosés, has been on an upward trajectory in recent years.

The Côte des Bar section of the **Champagne Route** (p360) 30km east of Troyes passes through **Bar-sur-Aube** (☎ tourist office 03 25 27

THE TROUBLE WITH DROPPING YOUR 'H'

Like him or leave him, Charles de Gaulle was a patriot, a man of valour and knew something about his compatriots. Who can ever forget his famous lament: *'On ne peut pas rassembler à froid un pays qui compte 265 spécialités de fromages'* (You cannot easily bring together a country that has 265 kinds of cheese)? Ah, but what about his wife Yvonne, known as 'Tante Yvonne' (Aunt Yvonne) for her reserve and conservatism? Didn't she once say something, well, unforgettable too?

It's an apocryphal story and has many variations, and even the time frame is unclear, but it goes something like this. The de Gaulles are lunching with the British prime minister (Harold Wilson?) and his wife on the eve of the general's retirement from political life (in 1969?). Mrs Wilson apparently turns to Mme de Gaulle and asks her – in English – what she is most looking forward to in the coming months of new-found freedom. To the shock, horror and, no doubt, amusement of everyone within earshot, *la tante* replies: 'A penis'.

After what is the most pregnant of pauses, de Gaulle turns to his wife and says *'Chérie*, in English it eez pronounced "APpiness".'

24 25; www.barsuraube.net, in French; place de l'Hôtel de Ville), graced by a medieval quarter and two churches, notably the 13th-century **Église St-Pierre** (rue St-Pierre). The town is on the rail line linking Troyes (€8.80, 30 minutes, five to 10 a day) with Langres (€11.40, 31 to 54 minutes, five or six daily). Nearby **Bayel** (tourist office ☎ 03 25 92 42 68; www.bayel-cristal.com; 2 rue Belle Verrière) is known for crystal; tours of the **Cristallerie Royale de Champagne** (Royal Champagne Glassworks; ☎ 03 25 92 37 60; place de l'Église) next to the tourist office begin at 9.30am and 11am weekdays.

The Champagne Route also takes you to **Colombey-les-Deux-Églises**, where Charles de Gaulle is buried in the village-centre churchyard. **La Boisserie** (☎ 03 25 01 50 50; adult/12-18yr/under 12yr €4/4/free, incl memorial €7/6/free; 🕑 10am-12.30pm & 2-6.15pm daily mid-Apr–mid-Oct, to 5.15pm Wed-Mon mid-Oct–Nov & Feb–mid-Apr), the general's home from 1934 to 1970, is now a museum. Nearby, the ugly 43.5m-high **Croix de Lorraine** (Lorraine Cross; built in 1972), symbol of the Resistance, was paid for by public subscription.

Also along the route is **Essoyes** (☎ tourist office 03 25 29 64 64; place de la Mairie), where Renoir spent his last 25 summers and is buried; the **Atelier Renoir** (☎ 03 25 38 56 28; adult/under 12yr €2/free; 🕑 2.30-6.30 daily Easter-Oct) in the centre is where the great Impressionist worked. **Les Riceys** (☎ tourist office 03 25 29 15 38; place des Héros de la Résistance) is a *commune* noted for its three churches, three different AOCs and exceptional rosé wines.

Langres

pop 9500

Langres, 75km southeast of Bar-sur-Aube and about the same distance north of Dijon (it's 125km to Troyes), is both an elongated hilltop bastion, with six towers and seven fortified gates, and a pungent cheese with a concave orangey-yellow crust. The town's most famous son is Denis Diderot (1713–84), the great encyclopedist; his statue graces place Diderot, the main square in the centuries-old town centre.

The **tourist office** (☎ 03 25 87 67 67; www.tourisme-langres.com; square Olivier Lahalle; 🕑 9am-noon & 1.30-7pm daily May-Sep, to 5.30pm Mon-Sat Oct-Apr) is next to one of the **Porte des Moulins**, the town gates dating from 1647.

Two blocks northeast of place Diderot is **Cathédrale St-Mammès**, whose classical facade (built in 1758) and two monolithic towers hide a late-Romanesque and early-Gothic interior. The modern **Musée d'Art et d'Histoire** (☎ 03 25 87 08 05; place du Centenaire; admission free; 🕑 10am-noon & 2pm–5pm or 6pm Wed-Mon), two short blocks west of the cathedral, has a collection that ranges from Gallo-Roman archeology to 17th- and 18th-century painting and sculpture. Circumambulating the **ramparts** is a 3.5km affair.

The two-star, Logis de France–affiliated **Grand Hôtel de l'Europe** (☎ 03 25 87 10 88; www.relais-sud-champagne.com; 23 rue Diderot; s/d/tr/q from €55/67/86/96; 🕑 reception to 11pm daily), in a one-time post house two blocks north of place Diderot, has 26 rooms that boast 'bourgeois comfort'. The rustic French **restaurant** (starters €8-20, mains €18-28.50, menus €17.50-47) specialises in game (in season) and dishes made with local cheese.

Langres' train station, on the flats about 3km west of the old town centre, has services to Dijon (€12.90, one hour, three or four daily) and Troyes (€18.80, 1¼ hours, five or six daily), Chaumont (€22.70, 20 minutes, up to 12 daily) and Paris' Gare de l'Est (€34.60, 2½ to three hours, up to eight daily).

Alsace & Lorraine

Though often spoken of as if they were one, Alsace and Lorraine, neighbouring *régions* in France's northeastern corner, are linked by little more than the Massif des Vosges (Vosges Mountains) and the imperialism of 19th-century Germany. In 1871, after the Franco-Prussian War, the German Reich annexed Alsace and the northern part of Lorraine (the Moselle *département*), making the *régions'* return to rule from Paris a rallying cry of French nationalism.

Charming and beautiful Alsace, long a meeting place of Europe's Latin and Germanic cultures, is nestled between the Vosges and the River Rhine – along which the long-disputed Franco-German border has at last found a final resting place. Popularly known as a land of storks' nests and colourful half-timbered houses sprouting geraniums, Alsace also offers a wide variety of outdoor activities – including hiking, cycling and skiing – in and around its vineyards and gentle, forested mountains. Strasbourg, the region's main city, is the seat of the European Parliament. Throughout France, the people of Alsace have a reputation for being well organised, hard-working and tax-paying.

Lorraine, a land of prairies and forests popularly associated with quiche and de Gaulle's double-barred cross *(croix de Lorraine),* has little of the picturesque quaintness of Alsace. However, it is home to two particularly handsome cities, both former capitals. Nancy, one of France's most refined and attractive urban centres, is famed for its neoclassical architecture and art-nouveau museums, while Metz, 54km to the north, is known for its Germanic neighbourhoods, the stunning stained glass of its marvellous cathedral, and the new Centre Pompidou–Metz, set to open in late 2009. Verdun bears silent testimony to the destruction and insanity of WWI.

HIGHLIGHTS

- Crane (or should that be stork) your neck to see the rose-coloured spires and stained glass of Strasbourg's splendiferous **cathedral** (p375)
- Watch storks glide majestically above their rooftop nests in **Hunawihr** (p392) and around the other towns of the Route du Vin d'Alsace
- Marvel at Colmar's medieval **Issenheim Altarpiece** (p395)
- Take in Nancy's refined **place Stanislas** (p402) and **art nouveau museums** (p403)
- Be dazzled by the curtains of stained glass in Metz' **Gothic cathedral** (p407)

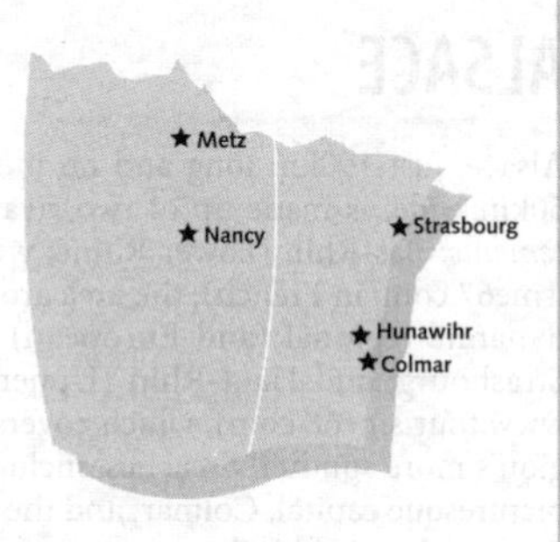

- ALSACE POPULATION: 1.7 MILLION
- LORRAINE POPULATION: 2.3 MILLION
- ALSACE AREA: 8280 SQ KM
- LORRAINE AREA: 23,547 SQ KM

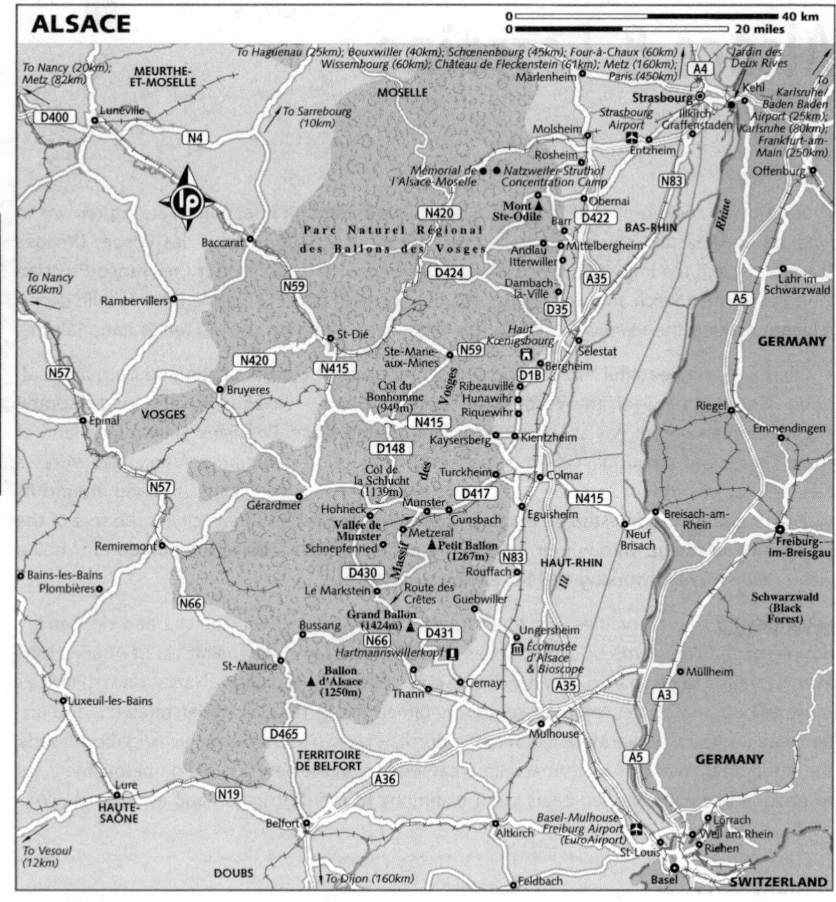

ALSACE

Alsace, just 190km long and no more than 50km wide, is made up of two rival *départements*: Bas-Rhin (Lower Rhine; www.tourisme67.com, in French), the area around the dynamic regional (and European) capital, Strasbourg; and Haut-Rhin (Upper Rhine; www.tourisme68.com), which covers the region's more southerly reaches, including the picturesque capital, Colmar, and the historic industrial city of Mulhouse.

Germany is just across the busy Rhine, whose left bank is Alsatian as far south as the Swiss city of Basel.

History

French influence in Alsace began during the Wars of Religion (1562–98) and increased during the Thirty Years War (1618–48) when Alsatian cities, caught between opposing Catholic and Protestant factions, turned to France. Most of the region was attached to France in 1648 under the Treaty of Westphalia. Today one-fifth of Alsatians are Protestants.

By the time of the French Revolution, Alsatians felt far more connected to France than to Germany, but the passage of time did little to dampen Germany's appetite for the region known in German as Elsass. The Franco-Prussian War of 1870–71, a supremely humiliating episode in French history, ended with the Treaty of Frankfurt (1871), by which an embittered France was forced to cede Alsace to the Kaiser. Following Germany's defeat in WWI, the region was returned to France but it was reannexed by Nazi Germany in 1940.

After WWII, Alsace was once again returned to France. Intra-Alsatian tensions ran high, however, as those who had fled came back and confronted neighbours whom they suspected of having collaborated with the Germans: 140,000 Alsatians, as annexed citizens of the Third Reich, had been conscripted into Hitler's armies. These conscripts were known as the 'Malgré-Nous' (literally 'despite ourselves') because the vast majority had gone off to war against their will; over half never returned from the Russian front and postwar Soviet prison camps. To make Alsace a symbol of hope for future Franco-German (and pan-European) coexistence and cooperation, Strasbourg was chosen as the seat of the Council of Europe (in 1949) and, later, of the European Parliament.

Opened in 2005, the impressive **Mémorial de l'Alsace-Moselle** (☎ 03 88 47 45 50; www.memorial-alsace-moselle.org, in French & German; adult/under 21yr, student & over 65yr/family incl audioguide €10/7/20; 🕒 10am-6pm or 7pm Tue-Sun, closed early Jan–early Feb, last entry 1hr before closing), 53km southwest of Strasbourg in Schirmeck (not far from the Natzweiler-Struthof Concentration Camp, p387), takes an unblinking but reconciliatory look at the region's traumatic modern history, which saw residents change nationality four times in 75 years.

Getting There & Around

Alsace is *almost* in central Europe. Situated 456km east of Paris, it's midway between Calais and Prague (about 630km from each) and is slightly closer to Berlin (801km) than to Marseille (814km).

From Strasbourg, the A4 heads northwest towards Metz and Paris, while from Mulhouse the A36 goes southwest towards the Jura and Dijon. The Massif des Vosges gets very snowy in winter so winter tyres and/or chains may be required, eg to cross Col de la Schlucht or Col du Bonhomme.

Thanks to the new TGV Est Européen, inaugurated in June 2007, the train ride from Paris to Strasbourg now takes just two hours and 20 minutes.

Special discount rail fares are available for travel within Alsace. The Pass Evasion, available on Saturday, Sunday and holidays, costs €8.50 for unlimited all-day travel within either the Bas-Rhin or Haut-Rhin *département*, or €13.50

THE LOCAL LINGO

The roots of Alsatian (Elsässisch; www.heimetsproch.org, in French and German), the language of Alsace, go back to the 4th century, when the Alemanni, a group of Germanic tribes, arrived here and assimilated the local Celts (Gauls) and Romans. Similar to the dialects spoken in nearby parts of Germany and Switzerland, it has no official written form (spelling – including on menus – is something of a free-for-all), and pronunciation varies considerably from one area to another (especially between the north and south).

Despite a series of heavy-handed attempts by both the French and the Germans to impose their language on the region, in part by restricting (or even banning) the use of Alsatian, it is still used in everyday life by people of all ages, especially in rural areas (particularly in the north). You're likely to hear its singsongy cadences whenever you happen upon locals who are just being themselves – for instance, in a *bäkerlààda* (*boulangerie;* bakery) and at Strasbourg's La Choucrouterie (p385).

Three other minority languages are still in use in Alsace. Francique, the language of the Franks, is spoken in areas north of Haguenau. Welsche, a Latin-based dialect that dates from the Gallo-Roman period, can still be heard in the Vosges valleys. And the local version of Yiddish, similar to Alsatian but with its own peculiarities, is central to Alsatian Jewish identity.

In mid-2008 France's National Assembly voted to add a line to the French constitution recognising regional languages such as Alsatian as 'part of France's heritage', but after a scathing broadside from the Académie Française, which declared the amendment no less than 'an attack on French national unity', the Senate scuttled the bill.

for travel anywhere in Alsace. A 'Mini-Groupe' version valid for two/five people travelling together costs €16.50/26 – perfect for day trips to the wine towns! You can get 25% off on all regional rail travel if you're aged 12 to 25, over 60 or – with an 'Escapade en TER Alsace' ticket – travelling in a group of three to nine people.

Alsace has *lots* of bike trails (see p388). Bicycles can be brought along on virtually all regional TER trains and autorails (but not SNCF buses).

STRASBOURG

pop 427,000

Prosperous, cosmopolitan Strasbourg (City of the Roads) is France's great northeastern metropolis and the intellectual and cultural capital of Alsace. Situated only a few kilometres west of the Rhine, the city is aptly named, for it is on the vital transport arteries that have linked northern Europe with the Mediterranean since Celtic times.

Strasbourg continues to serve as an important European crossroads thanks to the presence of the European Parliament, the Council of Europe, the European Court of Human Rights, the Eurocorps (www.eurocorps.org), the Franco-German TV network Arte (www.arte-tv.com, in French and German) and a student population of some 53,000 (more than any other French city except Paris), 22% from outside France. Strasbourg is one of Europe's most cycle-friendly cities.

Towering above the restaurants, *winstubs* (traditional Alsatian eateries) and pubs of the lively old city – a wonderful area to explore on foot – is the cathedral, a medieval marvel in pink sandstone. Nearby you'll find one of the finest ensembles of museums anywhere in France.

History

Before it was attached to France in 1681, Strasbourg was effectively ruled for several centuries by a guild of citizens whose tenure accorded the city a certain democratic character.

Johannes Gutenberg worked in Strasbourg from about 1434 to 1444, perfecting his printing press and the movable metal type that made it so revolutionary. A university was founded in 1566 and several leaders of the Reformation took up residence here.

Orientation

The train station is 400m west of the Grande Île (Big Island), the core of ancient and modern Strasbourg, whose main squares are place Kléber, place Broglie (*broag*·lee), place Gutenberg and place du Château. The quaint Petite France area, on the Grande Île's southwestern corner, is subdivided by canals. The Krutenau District is southeast across the river from the cathedral.

The European Parliament building and Palais de l'Europe are about 2.5km northeast of the cathedral.

Information

BOOKSHOPS

Bookworm (☎ 03 88 32 26 99; www.bookworm.fr; 3 rue de Pâques; Ancienne Synagogue; 9.30am-6.30pm Tue-Fri, 10am-6pm Sat) A well-stocked English bookshop where you can find Lonely Planet guides and *Images of Alsace*, the only English-language coffee-table book on Alsace, written by the owners. A good source of information on goings-on in Strasbourg.

Géorama (☎ 03 88 75 01 95; 20-22 rue du Fossé des Tanneurs; Homme de Fer; 2-7pm Mon, 9.30am-7pm Tue-Sat) Has a huge selection of hiking maps and topoguides.

INTERNET ACCESS

A number of phonecard shops near the train station offer internet access, eg at Nos 2 and 8 on rue du Maire Kuss.

Bibliothèque (public library; ☎ 03 88 43 64 77; 3 rue Kuhn; Ancienne Synagogue; 10am-6pm Tue, Wed

VISITING THE MAGINOT LINE

Parts of the Maginot Line (p39) are open to visitors thanks to local volunteer organisations (the French government considers the Maginot Line an embarrassing failure that's best forgotten and so provides no funding or publicity). In Lorraine, visitors can tour more than a dozen sites, including Fort du Hackenberg (p412). Maginot sites in Alsace include **Schœnenbourg** (☎ Hunspach tourist office 03 88 80 59 39; www.lignemaginot.com; adult/6-18yr €6/4; self-guided tours begin 2-4pm Sat & 9.30-11am & 2-4pm Sun Apr–early Nov, 2-4pm Mon-Fri mid-Apr–early Oct), a concrete behemoth about 45km north of Strasbourg. The self-guided tour follows a 3km route that takes two hours; signs are in English.

& Fri, 1-7pm Thu, 10am-5pm Sat) Access is free but you may have to reserve a bit ahead.

L'Utopie (☎ 03 88 23 89 21; 21-23 rue du Fossé des Tanneurs; Homme de Fer; per 1/20hr €3/20; 7am-11.30pm) A proper café with free wi-fi; the computers are downstairs.

Milk (☎ 03 88 32 06 02; 32-34 rue du Vieux Marché aux Vins; Homme de Fer; per hr €4, discounts available; 24hr) Has about 100 computers.

NeT SuR CouR (☎ 03 88 35 66 76; 18 quai des Pêcheurs; Gallia; per hr €2; 9.30am-8.30pm Mon-Sat, 1.30-7.30pm Sun & holidays) Hidden at the end of a narrow courtyard.

Tele SM (☎ 03 90 23 53 70; 3 quai St-Jean; Faubourg National; per hr €2; 8am or 9am–midnight)

LAUNDRY

Laundrettes 29 Grand' Rue (Alt Winmärik; 7.30am-8pm); 8 rue de la Nuée Bleue (Broglie; 7am-9pm); 15 rue des Veaux (7am-9pm)

Laverie Net (☎ 03 88 75 11 78; 4 rue Déserte; Faubourg National; per 7kg €9, incl drying & folding; 9am-12.30pm & 1.30-7pm Mon-Sat, 9am-7pm Fri & Sat) Full-service laundry.

MEDICAL SERVICES

Nouvel Hôpital Civil (☎ 03 88 11 67 68; www.chru-strasbourg.fr, in French; rue Koeberlé; 24hrs) The *urgences* (casualty ward/emergency room), opened in 2008, is served by bus 15 (get off at Lycée Pasteur) and the Navette Hôpital Civil shuttle, which links the Porte de l'Hôpital and Musée d'Art Moderne tram stops.

MONEY

Société Générale (☎ 03 88 23 46 50; 8 place de la Gare; Gare Centrale; 2-6pm Mon, 8.30am-noon & 1.45-6pm Tue-Fri)

POST

Branch Post Office (place de la Cathédrale; Langstross Grand' Rue; 8am-6.30pm Mon-Fri, 8am-5pm Sat) Has extended Saturday hours and currency exchange.

Main Post Office (5 av de la Marseillaise; République) In a neo-Gothic structure built by the Germans in 1899. Has exchange services.

TOURIST INFORMATION

Agence de Développement Touristique en Bas-Rhin (ADT; ☎ 03 88 15 45 88; www.tourisme67.com, in French; 9 rue du Dôme; Broglie; 9.30am or 10am–6pm Mon-Fri Jun-Aug, 9am-noon & 1-5pm Sat Jul & Aug, 9.30am or 10am–6pm Mon-Sat late Nov–Dec, 10am-noon & 2-5pm Mon-Fri rest of year) The *départementa*l tourist board has excellent English-language brochures – some downloadable (on the website go to *'Obtenez nos brochures'*) – on hiking, cycling, skiing, Jewish sites and activities for families with young children.

Main Tourist Office (☎ 03 88 52 28 28; www.otstrasbourg.fr; 17 place de la Cathédrale; Langstross Grand' Rue; 9am-7pm) Next door to the ornately carved, 16th-century Maison Kammerzell. A city-centre walking map with English text costs €1; bus/tram and cycling maps are free. *Strolling in Strasbourg* (€4.50) details six architectural walking tours. The Strasbourg Pass (adult/child €11.40/5.70), a coupon book valid for three consecutive days, may save you some cash.

Tourist Office Annexe (☎ 03 88 32 51 49; Gare Centrale; 9am-7pm) In the train station's southern wing.

Sights

GRANDE ÎLE

With its bustling public squares, busy pedestrianised precincts and upmarket shopping streets, the Grande Île – a Unesco World Heritage Site since 1988 – is a paradise for the aimless ambler. The narrow streets of the **old city** are especially enchanting at night, particularly right around the cathedral (eg rue du Sanglier). Also worth a look is **place Gutenberg**, with its Renaissance-style **Chambre de Commerce et d'Industrie** (Chamber of Commerce) building. There are watery views from the paths along the **River Ill** and its canalised branch, the **Fossé du Faux Rempart**; the grassy quays, frequented by swans, are great venues for a picnic or a romantic stroll.

Criss-crossed by narrow lanes, canals and locks, **Petite France** is the stuff of fairy tales. The half-timbered houses, meticulously maintained and sprouting veritable thickets of geraniums, and the riverside parks attract multitudes of tourists. However, the area still manages to retain its Alsatian atmosphere and charm, especially in the early morning and late evening.

The romantic **Terrasse Panoramique** (admission free; 9am-7.30pm) on top of **Barrage Vauban** (7.30am-7.30pm), a dam built to prevent riverborne attacks on the city (and now used to store bits and pieces of stone statuary), affords panoramas of the River Ill.

CATHÉDRALE NOTRE DAME

Strasbourg's lacy, almost fragile-looking Gothic **cathedral** (Langstross Grand' Rue; 7am-7pm) is one of the marvels of European architecture. The west facade, most impressive if approached from rue Mercière, was completed in 1284, but the 142m spire – the tallest

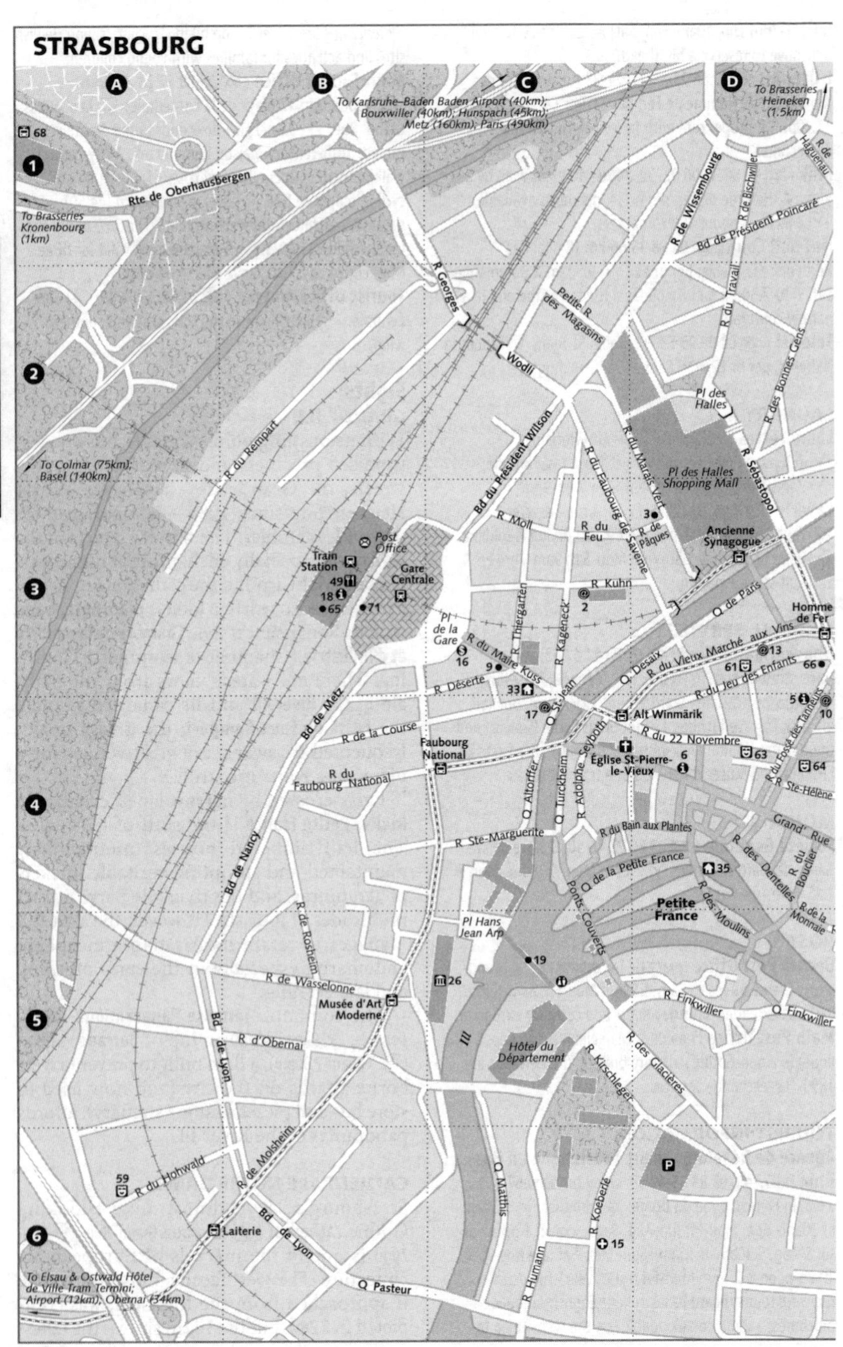
STRASBOURG
To Karlsruhe–Baden Baden Airport (40km); Bouxwiller (40km); Hunspach (45km); Metz (160km); Paris (490km)
To Brasseries Heineken (1.5km)
To Brasseries Kronenbourg (1km)
To Colmar (75km); Basel (140km)
To Elsau & Ostwald Hôtel de Ville Tram Termini; Airport (12km); Obernai (34km)
Rte de Oberhausbergen
R Georges
Wodli
R de Wissembourg
Bd de Président Poincaré
R du Travail
Petite R des Magasins
R du Rempart
Bd du Président Wilson
R du Marais Vert
R du Faubourg de Saverne
Pl des Halles
Pl des Halles Shopping Mall
R Sébastopol
R des Bonnes Gens
R Moll
R du Feu
R de Pâques
Ancienne Synagogue
Post Office
Train Station
Gare Centrale
Pl de la Gare
R Kuhn
Q de Paris
Homme de Fer
R du Maire Kuss
R Thiergarten
R Kageneck
Q Desaix
R du Vieux Marché aux Vins
R du Jeu des Enfants
R Déserte
Q St-Jean
Alt Winmärik
R de la Course
Faubourg National
R du Faubourg National
Bd de Metz
R du 22 Novembre
Église St-Pierre-le-Vieux
R du Fossé des Tanneurs
R Ste-Hélène
Grand' Rue
Q Altorffer
Q Turckheim
R Adolphe Seyboth
R du Bain aux Plantes
R Ste-Marguerite
Q de la Petite France
R des Dentelles
R du Boucher
Bd de Nancy
R de Rosheim
Ponts Couverts
R des Moulins
Petite France
R de la Monnaie
Pl Hans Jean Arp
R de Wasselonne
Musée d'Art Moderne
R Finkwiller
Q Finkwiller
Ill
Bd de Lyon
R d'Obernai
Hôtel du Département
R des Glacières
R Kirschleger
R du Hohwald
R de Molsheim
Q Matthis
R Koeberlé
Laiterie
Q Pasteur
R Humann
R de Haguenau
R de Bischwiller
A
B
C
D
1
2
3
4
5
6

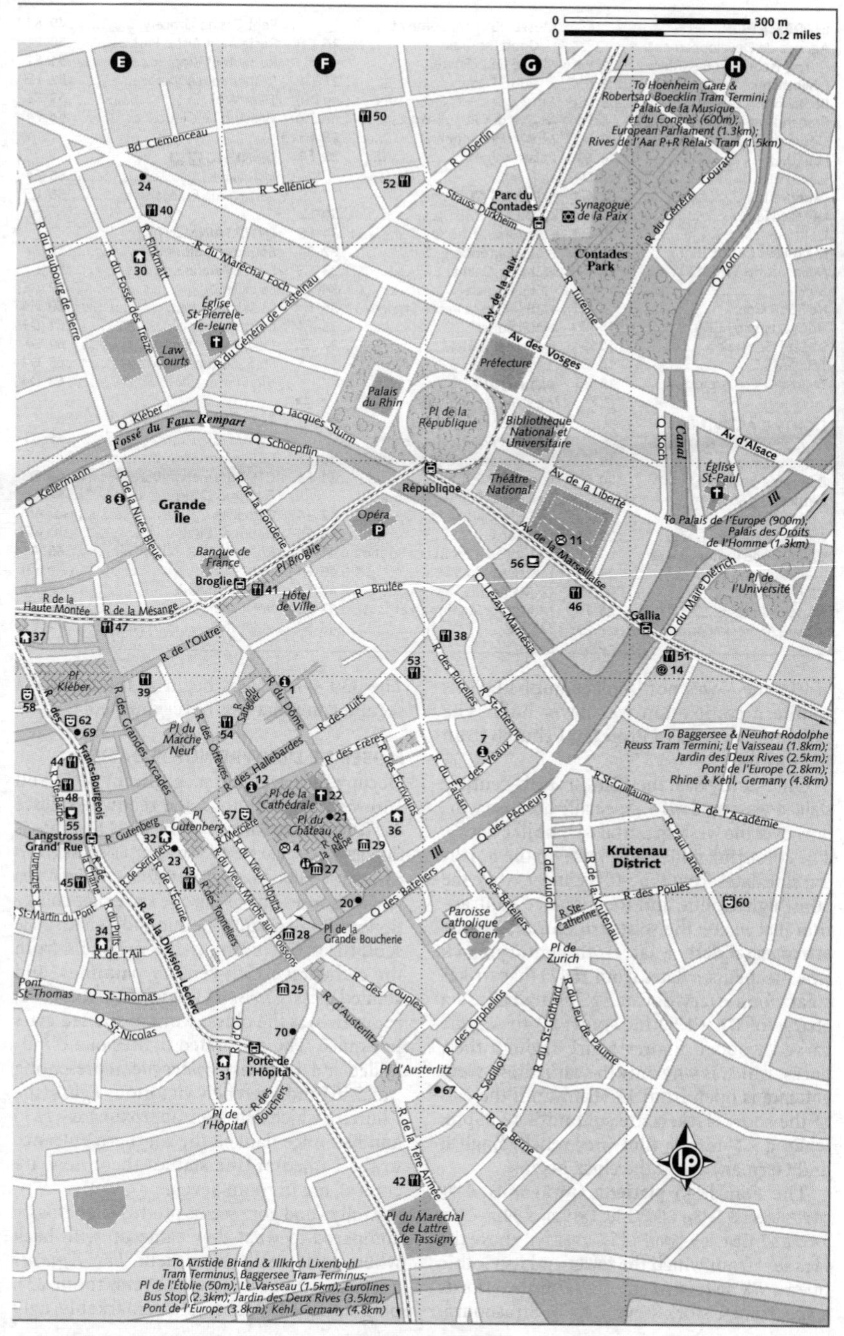

0 300 m
0 0.2 miles
E
F
G
H
To Hoenheim Gare & Robertsau Boecklin Tram Termini; Palais de la Musique et du Congrès (600m); European Parliament (1.3km); Rives de l'Aar P+R Relais Tram (1.5km)
Bd Clemenceau
R Sellénick
R Oberlin
R Strauss Durkheim
Parc du Contades
Synagogue de la Paix
Contades Park
R du Général Gourard
Q Zorn
R du Faubourg de Pierre
R du Fossé des Treize
R Finkmatt
R du Maréchal Foch
R du Général de Castelnau
Église St-Pierre-le-Jeune
Law Courts
Av de la Paix
R Turenne
Av des Vosges
Préfecture
Palais du Rhin
Pl de la République
Bibliothèque National et Universitaire
Q Koch
Canal
Av d'Alsace
Q Kléber
Fossé du Faux Rempart
Q Jacques Sturm
Q Schoepflin
Q Kellermann
R de la Nuée Bleue
Grande Île
R de la Fonderie
République
Théâtre National
Av de la Liberté
Église St-Paul
Ill
To Palais de l'Europe (900m); Palais des Droits de l'Homme (1.3km)
Opéra
Banque de France
Pl Broglie
Av de la Marseillaise
Broglie
Hôtel de Ville
R Brulée
Q Lezay-Marnésia
Q du Maire Dietrich
Pl de l'Université
R de la Haute Montée
R de la Mésange
Gallia
R de l'Outre
R des Pucelles
Pl Kléber
R du Sanglier
R du Dôme
R des Juifs
R des Grandes Arcades
R des Orfèvres
Pl du Marché Neuf
R des Francs-Bourgeois
R St-Étienne
To Baggersee & Neuhof Rodolphe Reuss Tram Termini; Le Vaisseau (1.8km); Jardin des Deux Rives (2.5km); Pont de l'Europe (2.8km); Rhine & Kehl, Germany (4.8km)
R des Frères
R des Hallebardes
R des Écrivains
R du Faisan
R des Veaux
R St-Guillaume
R Ste-Barbe
Pl de la Cathédrale
Pl du Château
R de l'Académie
R Paul Janet
R Gutenberg
Pl Gutenberg
R Mercière
R de la Râpe
Langstross Grand' Rue
Q des Pêcheurs
Krutenau District
R du Vieux Hôpital
R de Serruriers
R de l'Écurie
R des Tonneliers
R du Vieux Marché aux Poissons
Q des Bateliers
R des Bateliers
R de Zurich
R de la Krutenau
R Salzmann
R de la Chaîne
R des Poules
R Ste-Catherine
St-Martin du Pont
R du Puits
Pl de la Grande Boucherie
Paroisse Catholique de Cronen
R de l'Ail
R de la Division Leclerc
Pl de Zurich
Pont St-Thomas
Q St-Thomas
R des Couples
R d'Austerlitz
R des Orphelins
R du St-Gothard
R du Jeu de Paume
Q St-Nicolas
R d'Or
Porte de l'Hôpital
Pl d'Austerlitz
R Sédillot
Pl de l'Hôpital
R des Bouchers
R de la 1ère Armée
R de Berne
Pl du Maréchal de Lattre de Tassigny
To Aristide Briand & Illkirch Lixenbuhl Tram Terminus, Baggersee Tram Terminus; Pl de l'Étoile (50m); Le Vaisseau (1.5km); Eurolines Bus Stop (2.3km); Jardin des Deux Rives (3.5km); Pont de l'Europe (3.8km); Kehl, Germany (4.8km)
ALSACE & LORRAINE

INFORMATION
Agence de Développement Touristique en Bas-Rhin....1 F4
Bibliothèque....2 C3
Bookworm....3 D3
Branch Post Office....4 F4
Géorama....5 D4
Laundrette....6 E3
Laundrette....7 D4
Laundrette....8 G4
Laverie Net....9 C3
L'Utopie....10 D4
Main Post Office....11 G3
Main Tourist Office....12 F4
Milk....13 D3
NeT SuR CouR....14 H3
Nouvel Hôpital Civil....15 C6
Société Générale....16 C3
Tele SM....17 C4
Tourist Office Annexe....18 B3

SIGHTS & ACTIVITIES
Barrage Vauban & Terrasse Panoramique....19 C5
Batorama Boat Excursions....20 F5
Cathedral's South Entrance....21 F4
Cathédrale Notre Dame....22 F4
Chambre de Commerce et d'Industrie....23 E4
Club Vosgien....24 E1
Musée Alsacien....25 F5
Musée Archéologique....(see 29)
Musée d'Art Moderne et Contemporain....26 C5
Musée de l'Œuvre Notre Dame....27 F4
Musée des Arts Décoratifs....(see 29)
Musée des Beaux-Arts....(see 29)
Musée Historique....28 F5
Palais Rohan....29 F4

SLEEPING
CIARUS....30 E2
Hôtel Au Cerf d'Or....31 F5
Hôtel Gutenberg....32 E4
Hôtel Le Colmar....33 C3
Hôtel Patricia....34 E5
Hôtel Régent Petite France....35 D4
Hôtel Suisse....36 F4
Le Kléber Hôtel....37 E3

EATING
Au Coin des Pucelles....38 G3
Au Crocodile....39 E4
Casher Price Naouri Kosher Supermarket....40 E1
Food Market....41 F3
Galeries Lafayette Gourmet Supermarket....42 E4
La Bourse....43 F6
La Cloche à Fromage Boutique....44 E4
L'Assiette du Vin....45 E4
Le Michel....46 G3
Monoprix Supermarket....47 E3
Moozé....48 E4
Petit Casino Grocery....49 B3
Restaurant Autre Part....50 F1
Restaurant King....51 F1
Restaurant La Victoire....52 H3
Tiger Wok....53 F3
Winstub Le Clou....54 F4

DRINKING
Irish Times....55 E4
La Taverne Française....56 G3

ENTERTAINMENT
Boutique Culture....57 F4
Fnac Billeterie....58 E4
La Laiterie....59 A6
La Salamandre....60 H5
Le Star Cinema....61 D3
Odyssée Cinema....62 E4
Star St-Exupéry Cinema....63 D4
Virgin Megastore....64 D4

TRANSPORT
Avis....65 B3
CTS Information Bureau....(see 71)
CTS Information Bureau....66 D3
Eurolines Office....67 G5
Europcar....(see 65)
National-Citer....(see 65)
Rotonde P+R Relais Tram....68 A1
Sixt....(see 65)
SNCF Boutique....69 E4
Vélocation....70 F5
Vélocation....71 B3

of its time – was not in place until 1439; its southern companion was never built. The cathedral served as a Protestant church from 1521 to 1681.

On a sunny day, the 12th- to 14th-century **stained-glass windows** – especially the rose window over the western portal – shine like jewels. The colourful, gilded **organ case** on the northern side dates from the 14th century, while the 30m-high Gothic and Renaissance contraption just inside the southern entrance is the **astronomical clock**, a late-16th-century clock (the mechanism dates from 1842) that strikes solar noon every day at 12.30pm. There's a charge of €2 (€1.50 for students) to see the carved wooden figures whirl through their paces, which is why only the cathedral's **south entrance** is open from 11.30am until the end of the show. Tickets are sold until 12.05pm, when a 22-minute film (in French, English and German) about the clock begins.

The 66m-high **platform** (☎ 03 88 43 60 40; adult/student & 5-18yr €4.60/2.30; 9am or 10am–btwn 5.45pm & 7.15pm, to 9.45pm Fri & Sat in summer) above the facade – from which the **tower** and its Gothic openwork **spire** soar another 76m – affords a spectacular stork's-eye view of Strasbourg. The 330 spiral steps begin at the base of a second spire that was never finished.

MUSÉE DE L'ŒUVRE NOTRE DAME

Occupying a group of magnificent 14th- and 16th-century buildings, the renowned **Musée de l'Œuvre Notre Dame** (☎ 03 88 32 88 17; 3 place du Château; Langstross Grand' Rue; adult/student under 25yr & senior/under 18yr incl audioguide €4/2/free; noon-6pm Tue-Sun) houses one of Europe's premier collections of Romanesque, Gothic and Renaissance sculptures (including many originals from the cathedral), 15th-century paintings, and stained glass. *Christ de Wissembourg* (c 1060; room two) is the oldest work of stained glass in France. The celebrated figures of a blindfolded and downcast *Synagogue* (representing Judaism) and a serenely victorious *Église* (the Church), which date from approximately 1230 and had once flanked the southern entrance to the cathedral (the statues there now are copies), are in room Seven.

Hollywood gore seems pretty Milquetoasty compared to what they came up with back when Hell really was hell. *Les Amants Trépassés* (the Deceased Lovers; room 23), painted in 1470, shows a remarkably ugly couple being punished for their illicit lust: both of their entrails are being devoured by dragon-headed snakes while a toad feasts on her pudenda. If this work isn't enough to scare you into a life of chastity, nothing will!

MUSÉE D'ART MODERNE ET CONTEMPORAIN

The outstanding **Musée d'Art Moderne et Contemporain** (MAMC, Museum of Modern & Contemporary Art; 03 88 23 31 31; place Hans Jean Arp; Musée d'Art Moderne; adult/student under 25yr & senior/under 18yr €5/2.50/free; noon-7pm Tue, Wed & Fri, noon-9pm Thu, 10am-6pm Sat & Sun) displays a permanent collection of 'modern' (pre-WWII) art representing all the major movements (including Impressionism, symbolism, fauvism, cubism, Dadaism and surrealism) and hosts temporary exhibits of contemporary works as well as contemporary exhibits of temporary works.

PALAIS ROHAN

The majestic **Palais Rohan** (03 88 52 50 00; 2 place du Château; for whole complex adult/student under 25yr & senior/under 18yr €6/3/free, for each museum €4/2/free; noon-6pm Mon & Wed-Fri, 10am-6pm Sat & Sun) was built between 1732 and 1742 as a residence for the city's princely bishops. In the basement, the **Musée Archéologique** (audioguide included in ticket price) takes you from the Palaeolithic period to AD 800. On the ground floor is the **Musée des Arts Décoratifs**, which has a series of lavish rooms featuring the lifestyle of the rich and powerful during the 18th century. Louis XV and Marie-Antoinette once slept here – in 1744 and 1770, respectively. On the 1st floor the **Musée des Beaux-Arts** has a rather staid collection of French, Spanish, Italian, Dutch and Flemish masters from the 14th to the 19th centuries.

MUSÉE HISTORIQUE

The excellent, trilingual (French, German and English) **Musée Historique** (Historical Museum; 03 88 52 50 00; 3 place de la Grande Boucherie; Porte de l'Hôpital; adult/student under 25yr & senior/under 18yr incl audioguide €4/2/free; noon-6pm Tue-Fri, 10am-6pm Sat & Sun), reopened in 2007 after a complete redesign, traces the city's history from its beginnings as a 1st-century AD Roman military camp called Argentoratum. Highlights include a famous painting of the first-ever performance of *La Marseillaise*, France's stirring national anthem, which – despite its name – was written in Strasbourg in 1792; a 1:600-scale model of the city, created in the 1720s to help Louis XV visualise the city's fortifications; and a Gutenberg Bible from 1485. There's lots for kids to do – they can try on medieval-style knights' helmets, and many objects, including ancient pots and tiles and 18th-century cannons, can be touched.

MUSÉE ALSACIEN

Tucked away in three typical houses from the 1500s and 1600s, the **Musée Alsacien** (03 88 52 50 01; 23 quai St-Nicolas; Porte de l'Hôpital; adult/student under 25yr & senior/under 18yr €4/2/free; noon-6pm Mon & Wed-Fri, 10am-6pm Sat & Sun), affords a fascinating glimpse into Alsatian life over the centuries. Displays in the museum's two dozen rooms include kitchen equipment (stoves, ceramics, biscuit cutters), children's toys, colourful furniture and even a tiny 18th-century synagogue.

EUROPEAN INSTITUTIONS

The home of the rather toothless, 730-member **European Parliament** (Parlement Européen; 03 88 17 20 07; www.europarl.eu.int; rue Lucien Fèbvre; Parlement Européen), used just 12 times a year for four-day 'part-sessions' (plenary sessions), is 2.5km northeast of the cathedral. When it's in session (dates are available from the tourist office or on the website – click 'Activities', then 'Parliament's Calendar'), you can sit in on **debates** (5-6pm Mon, 9am-noon & 3-6pm Tue & Wed, 10am-noon & 3-5pm Thu) for up to one hour. Reservations are possible only for groups,

STRASBOURG'S MUSEUMS

The **Pass Musées** (1-day/3-day/annual €6/8/20, 1-day version for students under 26yr & seniors €3) gets you into all of Strasbourg's museums (where it's sold), including temporary exhibitions.

Admission to all of Strasbourg's **museums** (www.musees-strasbourg.org, in French) and the cathedral's platform is free on the first Sunday of the month. On other days tickets are valid all day long, so you can enter and re-enter as you please.

The following are closed on Monday: Musée de l'Œuvre Notre Dame, Musée d'Art Moderne et Contemporain, Musée Historique, Le Vaisseau.

Closed on Tuesday: Palais Rohan museums, Musée Alsacien.

JEWISH ALSACE

Interest in Alsace's rich Jewish heritage (http://judaisme.sdv.fr/histoire/historiq/anglais/history.htm, in English, http://judaisme.sdv.fr, in French), spanning 1000 years, has grown tremendously in recent years. Indeed, the **European Day of Jewish Culture** (www.jewisheritage.org), marked on the first Sunday of September in 30 countries, grew out of a local initiative in northern Alsace. Famous people of Alsatian-Jewish origin include Captain Alfred Dreyfus (of the Dreyfus Affair), Léon Blum (thrice prime minister of France in the 1930s and 1940s), the Marx Brothers (of *Duck Soup*), Marcel Marceau (the mime artist) and Julia Louis-Dreyfus (Elaine Benes on *Seinfeld*).

Today most Alsatian Jews live in Strasbourg, whose vibrant Jewish community – proud of its unique liturgical and musical traditions – numbers about 15,000. Alsace is the only region in France in which the majority of the Jews are Ashkenazim, ie spoke Yiddish in centuries past (nationwide, some 70% of French Jews immigrated from North Africa in the mid-20th century).

Towns all over the region, including many along the Route du Vin d'Alsace (p387), have historic **synagogues**. Museums with exhibits related to Alsatian Judaism include Strasbourg's Musée de l'Œuvre Notre Dame (p378) and Musée Alsacien (p379); Colmar's Musée Bartholdi (p395); and the **Musée Judéo-Alsacien** (☎ 03 88 70 97 17; http://judaisme.sdv.fr/today/musee, in French; 62 Grand' Rue; adult/child €6/3; 🕑 2-5pm Tue-Fri, 2-6pm Sun, closed Sat Easter–mid-Sep) in Bouxwiller, 40km northeast of Strasbourg. In Lorraine, displays related to that region's Jewish history can be found at Nancy's Musée Lorrain (p403) and Metz' Musée La Cour d'Or (p407).

The Agence de Développement Touristique en Bas-Rhin (p375) publishes an excellent brochure, *Discovering Alsatian Judaism,* downloadable from its website (click on *'Obtenez nos brochures'*).

Theso for individuals it's first-come first-served (bring ID). The rest of the time the building is inaccessible (except to groups) because of strict post–9/11 security measures.

Across the Ill, the Council of Europe's **Palais de l'Europe** (Palace of Europe; ☎ 03 88 41 20 29; www.coe.int; 🚊 Droits de l'Homme), once used by the European Parliament, can be visited on free one-hour weekday tours; phone ahead for times and reservations. During the four annual Monday-to-midday-Friday sessions of the council's 47-country *assemblée parlementaire*, you can sit in on debates (no reservations required; dates are on the website).

Just across Canal de la Marne, the striking **Palais des Droits de l'Homme** (Human Rights Law Courts; ☎ 03 90 21 52 17; www.echr.coe.int; 🚊 Droits de l'Homme), home of the European Court of Human Rights, completes the city's ensemble of major European institutions. If there's space it's possible to sit in on one of the two to five monthly court sessions (in French and/or English with simultaneous translation), which generally begin at 9am on Tuesday, Wednesday or Thursday and last 90 minutes – check the website under 'Pending Cases' for dates and get there with ID a half-hour ahead. Three or more people should reserve by email.

OTHER SIGHTS

Many of Strasbourg's most impressive public buildings, built when the city was ruled by the German Reich, are just northeast of the Grande Île around **place de la République** (🚊 République). The neighbourhood that stretches from there eastwards to Parc de l'Orangerie is dominated by solid, stone buildings inspired by late-19th-century Prussian tastes. Most are some sort of 'neo' – romantic, Gothic or Renaissance – and you can see that some had the initials RF (for 'République Française') hastily added after 1918 to replace the original German insignia.

Across av de l'Europe from Palais de l'Europe, the flowerbeds, playgrounds, shaded paths and swan-dotted lake of **Parc de l'Orangerie** (🚊 Droits de l'Homme) are hugely popular with local families, especially on sunny Sundays. In the warm months you can rent **row boats** on Lac de l'Orangerie.

Le Vaisseau (☎ 03 88 44 44 00; www.levaisseau.com; 1bis rue Philippe Dollinger; 🚊 Winston Churchill; adult/3-17yr €8/7; 🕑 10am-6pm Tue-Sun, last entry 5pm, closed 1st 3 weeks of Sep), 2.5km southeast of the cathedral, is an interactive, hands-on science and technology museum aimed at kids aged three to 15. Everything is trilingual (English, French and German).

As a concrete (but very green) expression of Franco-German friendship, Strasbourg and its German neighbour Kehl have turned areas once used by customs posts and military installations into the 60-hectare **Jardin des Deux Rives** (Two-Shores Garden), whose play areas, promenades and parkland stretch along both banks of the Rhine just south of Pont de l'Europe. The centrepiece is a sleek (and hugely expensive) **suspension bridge**, designed by Marc Mimram, that's proved a big hit with pedestrians and cyclists; one of the walkways is 275m long, the other 387m long. To get to the park, take tram D to Aristide Briand, and from there walk east or take bus 21 for three stops.

Tours

CITY TOURS

The main tourist office has 1½-hour **audioguides** (adult/student/under 12yr €5.50/3.50/free) of the cathedral and the old city in five languages.

Scenic boat excursions (70 minutes) in nine languages that take in Petite France and the European institutions are run by **Batorama** (☎ 03 88 84 13 13; www.batorama.fr, in French; 9 rue de Nantes; Porte de l'Hôpital; adult/student 25yr & under €7.60/3.80; excursions begin at 10.30am, 1pm, 2.30pm & 4pm Nov & Jan-Mar, more frequently rest of year, to 9pm or 10pm Apr-Oct).

BREWERIES

Brasseries Heineken (☎ 03 88 19 57 55; annabelle.ferry@exirys.com; 4 rue St-Charles; admission free; tours Mon-Fri) is 2.5km north of the Grande Île in Schiltigheim, near the intersection of rue St-Charles and rte de Bischwiller. Tours last two hours and are sometimes in English; phone or email for reservations. Take bus 4 (northbound) to the Schiltigheim Mairie stop.

Brasseries Kronenbourg (☎ 03 88 27 41 59; siege.visites@kronenbourg-fr.com; 68 rte d'Oberhausbergen; Ducs d'Alsace; adult/12-18yr/family €5/3/14; tours approx hourly Mon-Sat, closed Jan) sells 800 million litres of beer in France every year – enough beer to fill about 250 Olympic swimming pools! The two-hour tours (some in English) of its brewing facilities, 2.5km northwest of the Grande Île in the suburb of Cronenbourg, are both interesting and thirst-quenching. Call or email for reservations.

Festivals & Events

Strasbourg's beloved **Marché de Noël** (Christmas Market; place Broglie, place Gutenberg, place d'Austerlitz, place de la Cathédrale, place Kléber, Petite France), known as Christkindelsmärik in Alsatian and a tradition since at least 1570, runs from the last Saturday in November until 5pm on 24 December (till 31 December at place de la Cathédrale and place d'Austerlitz).

Sleeping

It is *extremely* difficult to find last-minute accommodation from Monday to Thursday when the European Parliament is in plenary session (generally for one week each month; see www.europarl.eu.int and click 'Activities', then 'Parliament's Calendar' for dates). Because of the Christmas Market, weekends in December are also tight so reserve ahead if at all possible.

The tourist office and its website (www.otstrasbourg.fr; click 'Your Stay', then 'Accommodation' to opt for a French-language search engine) can provide details about same-night room availability; if you drop by, staff are happy to help reserve a room. Reservations can also be made via www.lonelyplanet.com/hotels.

Many hotels apply high-season rates during European Parliament sessions and in May, June, September, October and December. Since Strasbourg is far from any sea coast, July and August are low season.

BUDGET

CIARUS (☎ 03 88 15 27 88; www.ciarus.com; 7 rue Finkmatt; dm in 8-/4-/2-bed room incl breakfast €21.50/25.50/28, s €44.50;) Hostels don't get much more

ALSACE & LORRAINE

> **HIKING, CYCLING & SNOWSHOEING**
>
> The Strasbourg section of the **Club Vosgien** (☎ 03 88 35 30 76; www.club-vosgien-strasbourg.net, in French; 71 av des Vosges; staffed 4-6.30pm Mon-Fri, 10am-noon Sat), a regional walking organisation founded in 1872, offers walks, cycling excursions and snowshoe trips for its members (guests welcome) in the Vosges and other parts of Alsace; there are trips bright and early each Sunday and often on other days too – the website has details (in French). No reservations are needed for trips by private car (passengers pay a small sum per kilometre) or train; reserve a few days ahead for bus trips (about €12, depending on the distance). Insurance costs €4.

stylish than this welcoming, 295-bed hostel, nominally Protestant-affiliated. Dorm rooms have industrial-strength furniture, toilets and showers. Parking is also available. Often accommodates rambunctious school groups. By bus, take bus 2, 4 or 10 to the place de Pierre stop.

Hôtel Le Colmar (☎ 03 88 32 16 89; hotel.le.colmar@wanadoo.fr; 1 rue du Maire Kuss; Alt Winmärik; s/d €42/45, with washbasin €27/34, hall shower €1.50) This one-star cheapie offers a unique mix of light and linoleum – stylish it ain't but it's convenient and good value. Some rooms have great river views. Payment is in cash only.

Hôtel Patricia (☎ 03 88 32 14 60; www.hotelpatricia.fr; 1a rue du Puits; Langstross Grand' Rue; d €43-45, s with washbasin €28; reception 8-11am & 2-8pm Mon-Sat, 8-11am Sun) The dark, rustic interior and Vosges sandstone floors – the 16th-century structure was once a convent – fit in well with the local ambience. The 22 rooms are simply furnished but immaculate and spacious; some (eg rooms 3 and 6) have great views. The best budget bet on the island.

MIDRANGE

Two- and three-star hotels, many of them chain-affiliated, line place de la Gare.

Hôtel Suisse (☎ 03 88 35 22 11; www.hotel-suisse.com; 2-4 rue de la Râpe; s/q €59/99, d €75-85, €10 less on weekends in Jan, Feb, Jul & Aug;) Just two short blocks from the cathedral, this charming hostelry has two stars, 26 comfortable rooms and the cosy ambience of a half-timbered Alsatian cottage. Often full.

Hôtel Au Cerf d'Or (☎ 03 88 36 20 05; www.cerf-dor.com, in French; 6 place de l'Hôpital; Porte de l'Hôpital; r €61-110;) A jacuzzi, 5m swimming pool and sauna (half-hour €8) are the cherry on the icing of this 43-room, Logis de France hotel, which has a golden *cerf* (stag) hanging proudly out front. On the ground floor there's a traditional French restaurant and a homey sitting area.

Le Kléber Hôtel (☎ 03 88 32 09 53; www.hotel-kleber.com; 29 place Kléber; Homme de Fer; d €65-78;) The 30 rooms (see website for photos) are named after fruits, spices, pastries and other high-calorie treats and are decorated accordingly – Meringue is all white, of course, while Noisette is light brown and, being smallish, makes you feel like you're inside a giant hazelnut. Dieters might want to avoid staying in Pavlova or Kougelopf. Very central.

Hôtel Gutenberg (☎ 03 88 32 17 15; www.hotel-gutenberg.com; 31 rue des Serruriers; Langstross Grand' Rue; d €74-98;) Built in 1745, this is one of the city's best-value two-star hotels – and it's just two blocks from the cathedral. The 42 tasteful rooms have antique touches and sparkling, all-tile bathrooms.

TOP END

Hôtel Régent Petite France (☎ 03 88 76 43 43; www.regent-hotels.com; 5 rue des Moulins; Alt Winmärik; d from €276, ste €401-526;) Guests of this opulent four-star hotel enjoy sleekly modern public spaces, romantic watery views and marble bathrooms worthy of a Roman emperor. The 1970s-style breakfast room is decorated with brazen shades of orange not seen since mood rings went out of style. Bringing along Fido or Mitzi will set you back €20. parking is available.

Eating

Strasbourg is a gastronomer's dream. Just south of place Gutenberg, pedestrianised rue des Tonneliers and nearby streets (eg rue de l'Écurie) are lined with midrange restaurants of all sorts. Petite France has quite a few Alsatian places, while several more modest places are situated a bit south along quai Finkwiller. Inexpensive eateries catering to students can be found northeast of the cathedral along rue des Frères, especially towards place St-Étienne.

WINSTUBS & FRENCH

Restaurant La Victoire (☎ 03 88 35 39 35; 24 quai des Pêcheurs; Gallia; menu €8.70; 11.30am-2pm & 6.30pm-1am, closed Sat & Sun) A great place for a hearty French or Alsatian meal, especially late at night. Vegetarians can order *bibeleskaes* (€8.50). Excellent value.

Le Michel (☎ 03 88 35 45 40; 20 av de la Marseillaise; Gallia; menus €9.50-15; 6am-9pm Mon-Fri, 6am-7pm Sat) Hugely popular with locals, this Paris-style café-brasserie – known by Strasbourgeois cognoscenti as Snack Michel – serves solid French mains, pastries made fresh all day, and breakfast any time you want it. Founded just before the strikes of May 1968, it's now run by the sons of the founders.

Winstub Le Clou (☎ 03 88 32 11 67; 3 rue du Chaudron; Broglie; lunch menu €15; 11.45am-2.15pm & 5.30pm-midnight except Sun, holidays & lunch Wed) Diners sit together at long tables so come here for an evening in the company of fellow diners, not an intimate tête-à-tête. Specialities include *wädele braisé au pinot noir* (€16.40) and

WINSTUBS

A *winstub* (literally 'wine room') is a traditional Alsatian restaurant renowned for its warm, homey atmosphere. Most dishes are based on pork and veal; specialities include *baeckeoffe* (meat stew; also spelled *'bæckeoffe'*), *jambonneau* (knuckle of ham), *wädele braisé au pinot noir* (ham knuckles in wine) and *jambon en croûte* (ham wrapped in a crust). Vegetarians can usually order *bibeleskas* (*fromage blanc;* soft white cheese mixed with fresh cream; also spelled *'bibeleskäs'* and *'bibelskaes'*) and *pommes sautées* (sautéed potatoes). Few *winstubs* offer *menus* (fixed-price multicourse meals); many have nonstandard opening hours.

bibeleskäs (€12.20). A dozen Alsatian wines are available by the glass.

L'Assiette du Vin (☎ 03 88 32 00 92; 5 rue de la Chaîne; Langstross Grand' Rue; lunch menus incl wine €15-25, other menus €25-30; closed lunch Mon, Sat & Sun) Inspired by what's available fresh in the marketplace, this chic-rustic French restaurant changes its menu monthly. The summer flowers come from the chef's mother's garden. The award-winning wine list encompasses 400 vintages (with 10,000 more cellared), 19 of which can be sampled by the glass (€3 to €9).

Au Coin des Pucelles (☎ 03 88 35 35 14; 12 rue des Pucelles; Broglie; 6.30pm-1am, closed Sun, Mon & holidays) A *winstub* with just six tables, a red-checked tablecloth on each, and solid Alsatian fare such as *choucroute au canard* (sauerkraut with six kinds of duck meat; €22.10). Perfect for a late dinner.

La Bourse (☎ 03 88 36 40 53; 1 place du Maréchal de Lattre de Tassigny; Étoile; menus €24-32; 11.45am-2.30pm & 6.30-11pm, to 11.30pm Fri, Sat & Sun) Under a trompe l'œil sky and grouchy putti, this art-deco brasserie serves excellent *tartes flambées* (Alsatian pizzas made with crème fraîche, €8 to €10; vegetarian options available) and *bæckeoffe* (€18) as well as meat specialities such as *fleischschnäcke* (minced meat rolls) and *lewerknepfle* (ground liver balls with cream sauce). Sam tickles the ivories nightly from 7.30pm to 11.30pm.

our pick Au Crocodile (☎ 03 88 32 13 02; www.au-crocodile.com; 10 rue de l'Outre; Broglie; 2-/3-course lunch menus €58/80, incl wine €87/114, other menus €88-127; lunch & dinner Tue-Sat) Named after a stuffed toothy critter (now suspended over the foyer) brought back from Egypt by an Alsatian aide-de-camp of one of Napoléon's generals, this hushed temple of French gastronomy serves up all-out *gastronomique* indulgence in impeccable surroundings. Specialities include *foie de canard cuit en croûte de sel* (duck liver cooked in a crust of salt crystals; €56). Reservations are a good idea in the evening, especially on Friday and Saturday.

ASIAN

Moozé (☎ 03 88 22 68 46; cnr 1 rue de la Demi-Lune & rue Ste-Barbe; Langstross Grand' Rue; dishes €2.50-6; lunch & dinner Mon-Sat) A hip and hugely popular Japanese fusion place where colour-coded plates go round on a dual-carriageway conveyor belt. The bathrooms are integrated into a Zen rock garden, so those who come seeking physical relief will find spiritual repose as well.

Tiger Wok (☎ 03 88 36 44 87; 8 rue du Faisan; Broglie; lunch menus €13.60-16.60, dinner menus €14.60-24.90, all-you-can-eat lunch/dinner €20.95/22.92; noon-2.15pm & 7-10.30pm Sun-Tue, to 11pm Wed & Thu, to 11.30pm Fri & Sat) At this popular wokkery you choose your ingredients (veggies, fish, meat) and then tell your personal *wokeur* (wok guy) – muscular and short-sleeved – how to prepare them and with which sauces. The result: a quick, crunchy meal you can down with Thai Singha beer.

VEGETARIAN & KOSHER

Restaurant Autre Part (☎ 03 88 37 10 02; 60 bd Clemenceau; Sun-Thu) Informal, lively and a wee bit brusque, this kosher-dairy restaurant has plenty of tasty 100% vegetarian options, including pizzas (€6.50 to €9.50), *tartes flambées* (€7 to €9.70) and pasta, as well as fish (€13 to €17).

Restaurant King (☎ 03 88 52 17 71; 28 rue Sellénick; Parc du Contades; meat mains €8-17; closed Sat & dinner Fri) In the heart of Strasbourg's Jewish neighbourhood, this strictly kosher place specialises in steaks, grilled meats and chicken.

SELF-CATERING

For picnic supplies:

Casher Price Naouri (22 rue Finkmatt; 8.30am-7.30pm Sun-Thu, to btwn 2.30pm & 4pm Fri) An all-*cacher* (kosher) supermarket serving Strasbourg's large Jewish community.

Food market (place Broglie; Broglie; 7am–5pm or 5.30pm, to 6pm Wed & Fri, closes earlier in winter)

Galeries Lafayette Gourmet supermarket (4 rue Ste-Barbe; Langstross Grand' Rue; 9am-8pm Mon-Sat) On the ground floor of the department store.

La Cloche à Fromage boutique (☎ 03 88 52 04 03; 32 rue des Tonneliers; Langstross Grand' Rue; 9.15am or 10am–12.15pm & 2.30-7pm Mon-Fri, 8.15am-6.30pm Sat) First-rate cheeses.
Monoprix supermarket (5 rue des Grandes Arcades; Homme de Fer; 8.30am-8.30pm Mon-Sat)
Petit Casino grocery (inside the train station; Gare Centrale; 7am-8pm, 365 days a year)

Drinking

Strasbourg's legions of pubs and bars include a number of student-oriented places on the small streets east of the cathedral.

Irish Times (☎ 03 88 32 04 02; 19 rue St-Barbe; Langstross Grand' Rue; 4pm-1am daily, opens at 2pm Fri, Sat & Sun year-round & Mon-Thu May-Sep) A congenial and genuinely Irish pub that attracts a very international crowd, including English-speaking students. Sunday features a general knowledge quiz with prizes (9pm). Major sports events are shown on two wide screens.

La Taverne Française (☎ 03 88 24 57 89; 12 av de la Marseillaise; République or Gallia; 8.30am-2am Mon-Thu, 8.30am-3am Fri, 2pm-3am Sat) A mellow café favoured by actors from the national theatre, musicians from the opera house, and students. A mixture of the old-fashioned and the endearingly tacky creates the ideal atmosphere for stimulating conversation.

Entertainment

The Strasbourgeois may head to bed earlier than their urban counterparts elsewhere in France but the city's entertainment options are legion. Details on cultural events appear in the free monthly *Spectacles* (www.spectacles-publications.com, in French), available at the tourist office.

Ticket outlets:
Boutique Culture (☎ 03 88 23 84 65; place de la Cathédrale cnr rue Mercière; Langstross Grand' Rue; noon-7pm Tue-Sat)
Fnac billetterie (☎ 08 92 68 36 22; www.fnacspectacles.com, in French; 2nd fl, 22 place Kléber; Homme de Fer; 10am-7pm Mon-Fri, 9.30am-7.30pm Sat)
Virgin Megastore (☎ 08 92 39 28 00; www.ticketnet.fr; 30 rue du 22 Novembre; Homme de Fer; 9am or 9.30am–7pm Mon-Sat)

CINEMAS

Cinemas with nondubbed films, some in English:
Le Star (☎ 03 88 32 44 97/67 77, 08 92 68 72 12; www.cinema-star.com, in French; 27 rue du Jeu des Enfants; Homme de Fer)
Odyssée (☎ 03 88 75 10 47; www.cinemaodyssee.com, in French; 3 rue des Francs-Bourgeois; Langstross Grand' Rue) An art-house cinema.
Star St-Exupéry (☎ 03 88 22 28 79/32 67 77, 08 92 68 72 12; www.cinema-star.com, in French; 18 rue du 22 Novembre; Alt Winmärik)

LIVE MUSIC

La Laiterie (☎ 03 88 23 72 37; www.artefact.org, in French; 11-13 rue du Hohwald; Laiterie; closed Jul–mid-Sep & last week of Dec) Strasbourg's most vibrant venue for live music puts on about 200 concerts a year. Tickets (€10 to €28) are available at the door (but cannot be reserved by phone), via the website, at the Boutique Culture or, for a surcharge, at Virgin Megastore and Fnac. On Friday nights from midnight to 5am, La Laiterie turns into a laid-back disco featuring *musique électronique* (€5). Situated about 1km southwest of the train station.

NIGHTCLUBS

La Salamandre (☎ 03 88 25 79 42; www.lasalamandre-strasbourg.fr, in French; 3 rue Paul Janet; admission Fri & Sat €5, other nights €3-5, major concerts up to €25; 10pm-4am Thu-Sat & night before holidays Sep-Jul, 10pm-4am Fri & Sat Aug, sometimes also open Mon-Wed) Billed as a *bar-club-spectacles*, this discotheque – warmly lit, friendly and with a marble fountain in the middle – has a theme night each Friday (salsa, 1980s etc). Events on Thursday (and sometimes other nights – see website) are often sponsored by student groups (open to all). Another attraction is the **bal musette** (adult/student €10/5; 5-10pm 1 or 2 Sun a month mid-Sep–May), where you can dance to live French accordion music, salsa, tango and 1950s rock and roll. At the **apéritif linguistique** (admission free; 7–10pm or later 1st Tue of each month except Jul & Aug) language fans gather at about 20 tables – one for each language – to converse and meet people from around the world.

Shopping

The city's fanciest shopping can be found on and around rue des Hallebardes, a block north of the cathedral, whose superelegant window displays are real eye candy (Baccarat is at No 44). Somewhat less exclusive shops line rue des Grandes Arcades and, to the west, the Grand' Rue.

Getting There & Away

AIR

Strasbourg's international **airport** (☎ 03 88 64 67 67; www.strasbourg.aeroport.fr) is 12km southwest of

ON-STAGE & OFF, ALSATIAN IS ALIVE & LAUGHING

Alsace's language, Alsatian (p373), has a tireless and appropriately irreverent advocate in **Roger Siffer** (http://rogersiffer.choucrouterie.com, in French), director of Strasbourg's **La Choucrouterie** ('The Sauerkraut Factory'; www.choucrouterie.com, in French and German), a trilingual (Alsatian, French and German) theatre he founded in 1984. Siffer is also a singer, comedian, actor and producer known for his biting satire. His office at 'La Chouc' is – as you'd expect – a well-lived-in mess, with overloaded bookshelves, posters from his old cabaret revues, wooden guitars piled on top of each other, an accordion, superannuated costumes and a vest and hat worn by 'Professor Knatschke', a satirical character created by the Alsatian illustrator Hansi (p391).

Siffer's career in music and cabaret – and as a hirsute poster boy for Alsatian – began almost by accident. 'I was going to become a philosophy teacher', he explains. 'During my university studies – this was in 1968, when I was 20 – I used to sing Buddy Holly, Little Richard, that sort of stuff, but when I'd drink too much I'd sing in Alsatian – and everybody loved it! So I started performing Alsatian children's songs, which are filled with scatology to shock the bourgeoisie. It reminded people of their childhood' – not so surprising, then, that Siffer achieved success almost overnight.

'When I arrived in Strasbourg at the age of 16 to attend high school, I told everyone that I didn't know Alsatian, that I was born in Blida in North Africa, that I was a *pied-noir* – the *pied-noirs* were the toughest kids in the neighbourhood. Like lots of people of my generation, I was ashamed of speaking Alsatian, considered a language for peasants, and of having an Alsatian accent. French was the language of success. "If you want to be something you had better master French" – that's what parents told children of my generation', Siffer remembers.

'I started learning French at age four, when I began school. Before that, with my family, I spoke only Alsatian. In elementary school, when I was eight or nine years old, I was punished for speaking Alsatian. At school there was a rule – French only. But during breaks, when we'd play football, Alsatian would come back spontaneously. A teacher heard me and made me copy out the school regulations by hand. The thing is, that teacher was himself Alsatian and' – Siffer shakes his head – 'when he left the school grounds, he too spoke Alsatian.'

the city centre (towards Molsheim), near the village of Entzheim.

Ryanair, forced to halt flights to Strasbourg because of legal action by Air France, now links Dublin and London Stansted with **Karlsruhe/Baden Baden airport** (www.badenairpark.de), across the Rhine in Germany, 40km northeast of Strasbourg.

BUS

The **Eurolines office** (☎ 03 90 22 14 60; 6D place d'Austerlitz; Porte de l'Hôpital; 9.30am-12.30pm & 2-6pm Mon-Fri, 10am-12.30pm Sat) is just a few blocks southeast of the Grande Île, but because of governmental strictures intended to hinder private-sector competition with the state-owned SNCF, their buses must use a **bus stop** (Lycée Couffignal) 2.5km south of there on rue du Maréchal Lefèbvre, at Parking Couffignal (facing the Citroën garage).

Strasbourg city bus 21 (€1.30) links the Aristide Briand tram terminus with Kehl, the German town just across the Rhine.

CAR

Rental companies with offices in the south wing of the **train station** (Gare Centrale) include **Avis** (☎ 03 88 32 30 44), **Europcar** (☎ 03 88 22 96 48), **National-Citer** (☎ 03 88 23 60 76) and **Sixt** (☎ 03 88 23 09 31).

TRAIN

The train station, built in 1883, was given a 120m-long, 23m-high glass facade and underground galleries in order to welcome the new TGV Est Européen in grand style.

Domestic destinations include Paris' Gare de l'Est (€63.70 to €19.80, two hours and 20 minutes, 13 to 17 daily), Lille (Gare Lille-Europe; €52, 3½ hours, three daily), Lyon (€48.30, five hours, five daily), Marseille (€80.50 to €100, 6½ hours, one TGV daily), Metz (€21.50, 1¼ to 1¾ hours, seven to 11 daily) and Nancy (€20.70, 1½ hours, seven to 12 daily).

Internationally, destinations with direct services include Basel SNCF (Bâle; €19.30, 1¼ hours, 16 to 25 daily), Brussels-Nord (€61.70, five hours, two or three daily), Karlsruhe (€22, 40 minutes, four daily) and Stuttgart (€39, 1¼ hours, four TGVs daily). If you take the Eurostar via Lille, London is just five hours away, city centre to city centre.

Route du Vin destinations include Colmar (€10.20, 31 to 65 minutes, 20 to 30 daily), Dambach-la-Ville (€7.40, one hour, 12 daily on weekdays, four to six daily on weekends), Obernai (€5.20, 30 minutes, 20 daily weekdays, five to nine daily on weekends) and Sélestat (€7.30, 20 minutes, 24 to 46 daily).

On the Grande Île, tickets are available at the **SNCF Boutique** (5 rue des Francs-Bourgeois; Langstross Grand' Rue; 10am-7pm Mon-Fri, to 5pm Sat).

Getting Around

TO/FROM THE AIRPORT

The Navette Aéroport (airport shuttle), run by CTS (right), links the Baggersee tram stop, southwest of the city, with Strasbourg's airport (€5.20 including tram ticket from Baggersee to anywhere in the city, 15 minutes, three times an hour until at least 10.20pm). Tickets are sold at all tram stops.

Flight Liner buses (www.flightliner.de) link Strasbourg with Karlsruhe/Baden Baden airport (€17, one hour), across the Rhine. Bus times are coordinated with Ryanair's London services.

BICYCLE

Strasbourg, a world leader in bicycle-friendly planning, has an extensive and ever-expanding *réseau cyclable* (network of cycling paths and lanes; www.strasbourg.fr/deplacement, in French). Free maps are available at the tourist office.

The city government's **Vélocation** (www.velocation.net) system can supply you with a well-maintained one-speed bike (per half-/full day €5/8, Monday to Friday €12), kid's bike (per day €5) or child seat (€2). Helmets are not available. A €100 to €200 deposit is required. Outlets:

City Centre (03 88 24 05 61; 10 rue des Bouchers; Porte de l'Hôpital; 9.30am-12.30pm & 1.30-7pm Easter–mid-Oct, 9.30am-12.30pm & 1-5pm mid-Oct–Easter)

Train Station (03 88 23 56 75; Gare Centrale; 7am-8pm Mon-Fri, 9.30am-12.30pm & 1.30-7pm Sat, Sun & holidays Easter–mid-Oct, 7am-8pm Mon-Fri, 9.30am-12.30pm & 1.30-5.30pm Sat mid-Oct–Easter) Situated on Level -1, at the southern end of the glass-topped underground gallery. Adjacent is an 820-place bicycle parking lot (€2 for 24 hours) that's open from 6am to 10pm Monday to Friday and from 8am to 6pm Saturday.

BUS & TRAM

Five highly civilised tram lines, known as A through E, form the centrepiece of Strasbourg's outstanding public transport network, run by **CTS** (03 88 77 70 70; www.cts-strasbourg.fr; information bureaus in train station, Gare Centrale, & 56 rue du Jeu des Enfants, Homme de Fer; Mon-Sat). The main tram hub is Homme de Fer. Trams generally operate until midnight or 12.30am; buses – few of which pass through the Grande Île – run until about 11pm, though just once an hour after 9pm. This being earnest, hard-working Strasbourg, there are no night buses.

Tickets, valid on both buses and trams, are sold by bus drivers and ticket machines at tram stops (English instructions available) and cost €1.30 (€2.50 return). The Ticket 24H00 (for one/three people €3.50/4.80), valid for 24 hours from the moment you time-stamp it, is sold at tourist offices and tram stop ticket machines. The weekly Hebdopass, good for seven days from when it's time-stamped, costs €17, plus €3 for a magnetic Carte Badgeo (photo required), issued at CTS offices.

In this section, tram stops less than 400m from sights, hotels, restaurants etc are mentioned right after the street address and indicated with a tram icon.

PARKING

Virtually the whole city centre is either pedestrianised or a hopeless maze of one-ways, so don't even think of getting around the Grande Île by car – or parking there for more than a couple of hours. For details on city centre parking garages see www.par cus.com.

At Strasbourg's nine P+R (park-and-ride) car parks, all on tram routes, the €2.70 all-day fee, payable from 7am to 8pm, gets the driver and each passenger a free return tram ride into the city centre. If you'd like to visit the city without parking hassles, this is the way to do it. From the autoroute, follow the signs marked 'P+R Relais Tram'. Locals figure that your vehicle is least likely to be burnt to a crisp by bored youths if you park north of the city centre at **Rives de l'Aar** (Rives de l'Aar), northwest of the centre at **Rotonde** (Rotonde) or south of the centre at **Baggersee** (Baggersee). Elsau is said to be potentially dicey.

NATZWEILER-STRUTHOF CONCENTRATION CAMP

About 60km southwest of Strasbourg stands Natzweiler-Struthof, the only Nazi concentration camp on French territory. (There were also a number of transit camps, such as the notorious Camp de Drancy, 22km northeast of Paris.) The site was chosen by Himmler because of the nearby deposits of valuable pink granite, in whose extraction – in the **Grande Carrière** (Large Quarry) – many inmates were worked to death. In all, some 22,000 (40% of the total) of the prisoners interned here and at nearby annexe camps died; many were shot or hanged. In early September 1944, as US Army forces approached, the 5517 surviving inmates were sent to Dachau.

The camp provided the Reichsuniversität (Reich University) in Strasbourg with inmates for use in often lethal pseudomedical experiments involving chemical warfare agents (mustard gas, phosgene) and infectious diseases (hepatitis, typhus). In April 1943, 86 Jews – 56 men and 30 women – specially brought from Auschwitz were gassed here to supply the university's Anatomy Institute (on the grounds of the Strasbourg's Hôpital Civil) with skulls and bones for its anthropological and racial skeleton collection. After liberation, their bodies, preserved in alcohol, were found by Allied troops.

Today, the remains of the **camp** (☎ 03 88 47 44 57; www.struthof.fr; adult/student & under 18yr €5/2.50; ⌚ 10am-6pm May–mid-Sep, 10am-5pm Mar, Apr & mid-Sep–24 Dec, last entry 1hr before closing, closed Christmas-Feb) are still surrounded by guard towers and concentric, once electrified barbed-wire fences. The **four crématoire** (crematorium oven), the **salle d'autopsie** (autopsy room) and the **chambre à gaz** (gas chamber), an ordinary-looking building 1.7km down the D130 from the camp gate, bear grim witness to the atrocities committed here. The nearby **Centre Européen du Résistant Déporté** (⌚ same as camp), opened in 2005, pays homage to Europe's Resistance fighters.

To get to Natzweiler-Struthof from Obernai, take the D426, D214 and D130; follow the signs to 'Le Struthof' or 'Camp du Struthof'.

TAXI

Round-the-clock companies:

Alsace France Taxi (☎ 03 88 22 19 19)
Taxi Treize (☎ 03 88 36 13 13)

ROUTE DU VIN D'ALSACE

Meandering for some 120km along the eastern foothills of the Vosges, the **Route du Vin d'Alsace** (Alsace Wine Route) passes through villages guarded by ruined hilltop castles, surrounded by vine-clad slopes and joyously coloured by half-timbered houses in lurid pastels. Combine such charms with numerous roadside *caves* (wine cellars), where you can sample Alsace's crisp white varietal wines (in particular riesling, pinot blanc and gewürztraminer), and you have one of France's busiest tourist tracks.

The Route du Vin, at places twee and commercial, stretches from Marlenheim, about 20km west of Strasbourg, southwards to Thann, about 35km southwest of Colmar. En route are some of Alsace's most picturesque villages (and some very ordinary ones, too), many extensively rebuilt after being flattened in WWII. Ramblers can take advantage of the area's *sentiers viticoles* (signposted vineyard trails) and the paths leading up the eastern slopes of the Vosges to the remains of medieval bastions.

Local tourist offices can supply you with an English-language map/brochure, *The Alsace Wine Route* (free), and *Alsace Grand Cru Wines,* which details Alsace's 50 most prestigious AOC (Appellation d'Origine Contrôlée; system of French wine classification) wine-growing micro-regions. Lots more information is available online from the Alsace Wine Committee (www.vinsal sace.com).

The villages mentioned in the following section – listed from north to south – all have plenty of hotels and restaurants and some have campsites. *Chambres d'hôtes* (B&Bs) generally cost €35 to €55 for a double – tourist offices can provide details on local options.

TOURS

For minibus tours of the Route du Vin (reservations can be made via Colmar's tourist office) try these agencies:

LCA Top Tour (☎ 03 89 41 90 88, 06 72 37 17 11; www.alsace-travel.com; 3rd fl, 8 place de la Gare, Colmar; half-day €53)

Regioscope (☎ 03 89 44 38 21, 06 88 21 27 15; www.regioscope.com; morning/afternoon tour €44/52)

PEDALLING THROUGH THE VINES

Perhaps the most rewarding way to experience the Route du Vin is by bicycle, taking back roads and field access tracks to avoid the heavily trafficked main roads, which tend to have narrow shoulders. An excellent network of bike paths also runs along both the French and the German banks of the Rhine (www.2rives3ponts.eu, in French and German). Bicycles can be rented in towns such as Colmar, Sélestat and Munster.

Maps and guides you may want to pick up (eg at the Colmar tourist office):

- **Escapades à Bicyclettes** (€2.50) – a map indicating the bike paths that run along both banks of the Rhine, and the bike paths and cyclable tertiary roads that link Colmar with the German university town of Freiburg.
- **L'Alsace à Vélo** (€5.95) – a pocket guide in French that's not all that detailed but does show quite a few cycling circuits around Alsace.
- **Le Haut-Rhin à Vélo** (€5.50) – a trilingual (French, German and English) 1:105,000-scale IGN Découvertes Régionales map detailing bike paths (in blue) and low-traffic tertiary roads and agricultural tracks (in red) between Sélestat and Basel, including many that take you right through the vineyards. Also shows cycling options in the Munster Valley and on the French bank of the Rhine.

GETTING THERE & AROUND

The Route du Vin is not just one road but a composite of several roads (D422, D35, D1B and so on). It is signposted but you might want to pick up a copy of Blay's colour-coded map, *Alsace Touristique* (€5.30). Cyclists have a wide variety of on- and off-road options (see the boxed text, above).

Parking can be a nightmare in the high season, especially in Ribeauvillé and Riquewihr, so your best bet is to park a bit out of the town centre and walk for a few minutes. As elsewhere in France, *never* leave valuables in a parked car.

It's entirely possible, if a bit cumbersome, to get around the Route du Vin by public transport, since almost all the towns and villages mentioned here are served by train from Strasbourg (p385) or by train and/or bus from Colmar (p397). Bicycles can be brought along on virtually all trains.

Obernai

pop 10,800

The walled town of Obernai ('nai' rhymes with 'day'), 31km south of Strasbourg, is centred on the picturesque **place du Marché**, an ancient market square that's still put to use each Thursday morning. Around the square you'll find the mainly 16th-century **hôtel de ville** (town hall), decorated with baroque trompe l'œil; the Renaissance **Puits aux Six Seaux** (Well of the Six Buckets), just across rue du Général Gouraud (the main street); and the bell-topped **Halle aux Blés** (Corn Exchange; 1554), from whose flanks pedestrianised rue du Marché and tiny parallel ruelle du Canal de l'Ehn – just a hand's breadth wide – lead to the Vosges-sandstone **synagogue** (1876). The cool, flower-bedecked courtyards and alleyways (such as little ruelle des Juifs, next to the tourist office) are fun to explore, as are the 1.75km-long, 13th-century **ramparts**, accessible from the lot in front of double-spired **Église St-Pierre et St-Paul** (19th century).

A number of wine growers have cellars a short walk from town (the tourist office has a map). The 1.5km **Sentier Viticole du Schenkenberg**, which wends its way through vineyards, begins at the hilltop cross north of town – to get there, follow the yellow signs from the cemetery behind Église St-Pierre et St-Paul.

The **tourist office** (☎ 03 88 95 64 13; www.obernai.fr; place du Beffroi; 🕑 9.30am-12.30pm & 2-7pm daily Jul & Aug, 9am-noon & 2-6pm daily Easter-Jun, Sep & Oct, 9am-noon & 2-5pm except Sun & holidays Nov-Easter, 9am-noon & 2-6pm Sun Dec) is behind the *hôtel de ville*, across the car park from the 59m **Kapellturm** (Belfry; 1280).

La Cloche (☎ 03 88 95 52 89; www.la-cloche.com; 90 rue du Général Gouraud; d/q €55/75; ⊠), a two-star Logis de France–affiliated hotel facing the *hôtel de ville*, has 20 spacious, wood-furnished rooms, some with classic views of the ancient town centre. The rustic ground-floor **restaurant** (menus €15.50-28.50; 🕑 closed dinner Sun Jan-Mar) serves delicious Alsatian cuisine, including *spaetzle* (an egg-based noodle dish).

The train station is about 300m east of the old town.

Mittelbergheim

pop 620

A solid hillside village with no real centre, Mittelbergheim sits amid a sea of sylvaner grapevines and seasonal wild tulips, its tiny streets lined with ancient houses in subdued tones of tan, mauve and terracotta. From **Parking du Zotzenberg** (on the D362 at the upper edge of the village next to the cemetery), named after the local *grand cru* (Alsace's top AOC wine designation), a paved *sentier viticole* (vineyard trail) heads across the slopes towards the two towers of the **Château du Haut Andlau** and the Vosges. A stroll along rue Principale (the main street, perpendicular to the D362) takes you past the red-sandstone, Catholic **Église St-Martin** (next to No 17), built in 1893, and a block down is the Protestant **Église St-Étienne** (next to No 30), dating from the 12th to 17th centuries. Each of Mittelbergheim's *caves* has an old-fashioned, wrought-iron sign hanging out front.

Private accommodation is easy to come by – you'll see *Chambres/Zimmer* signs in windows all over town. For information, see www.pays-de-barr.com.

our pick **Hôtel Gilg** (☎ 03 88 08 91 37; www.hotel-gilg.com; 1 rte du Vin, D362; d €57-87; reception closed Tue & Wed, hotel closed Jan & late Jun–mid-Jul), built in 1614 (the trompe l'œil dates from 2001), is a two-star establishment with wood-panelled rooms (reached via a spiral stone staircase) that are almost as romantic as the village. Reserve well in advance for May, September and October. If you'll be arriving on Tuesday or Wednesday call ahead. The rustically elegant **restaurant** (menus €28-66; closed Tue & Wed) serves classic French and Alsatian cuisine.

Dambach-la-Ville

pop 2000

Surrounded by vines, this village has plenty of *caves* but manages to avoid touristic overload. The 14th-century, pink-granite **ramparts** are pierced by four **portes** (gates), three holding aloft ancient watchtowers and bearing quintessentially Alsatian names: Ebersheim, Blienschwiller and Dieffenthal. Some of the superb half-timbered houses date from before 1500.

Neo-Romanesque **Église St-Étienne** (place de l'Église) and the **synagogue** (rue de la Paix) – the latter unused since WWII – both date from the 1860s.

The **tourist office** (☎ 03 88 92 61 00; www.pays-de-barr.com; place du Marché; 9am-noon & 1.30-6pm Mon-Sat, 10am-noon Sun & holidays Jul & Aug, 10am-noon & 2pm–5pm or 6pm Mon-Fri, 10am-noon Sat Sep-Jun), in the mid-16th-century Renaissance-style **hôtel de ville**, can supply you with a brochure for a walking tour of Dambach and has details on cycling to Itterwiller.

The renowned Frankstein *grand cru* vineyards cover the southern and southeastern slopes of four granitic hills west and southwest of Dambach. The 1½-hour **Sentier Viticole du Frankstein**, which begins 70m up the hill from the tourist office on rue du Général de Gaulle, meanders among the hallowed vines, passing by hillside **Chapelle St-Sébastien** (9am-7pm May-Oct, also open Sat, Sun & holidays Nov-Apr), known for its Romanesque tower, Gothic choir, Renaissance windows and baroque high altar.

The train station is about 1km east of the old town.

Sélestat

pop 19,200

Sélestat is the largest town between Strasbourg, 50km to the north, and Colmar, 23km to the south. Its claim to cultural fame is the 15th- and 16th-century **Bibliothèque Humaniste** (Humanist Library; ☎ 03 88 58 07 20; 1 rue de la Bibliothèque; adult/student & senior €3.80/2.30, audioguide €1.80; 9am-noon & 2-6pm Mon & Wed-Fri year-round, 9am-noon Sat year-round, also open 2-5pm Sat & Sun Jul & Aug), whose displays include a 7th-century book of Merovingian liturgy, a 10th-century treatise on Roman architecture and a copy of *Cosmographiae Introductio* (printed in 1507 in the Vosges town of St-Dié), in which the New World was referred to as 'America' for the very first time. Explanatory sheets are available in six languages.

The 13th- to 15th-century **Église St-Georges**, one of Alsace's loveliest Gothic churches, has curtains of stained glass – some from the 1300s and 1400s – in the choir. Nearby, 12th-century Romanesque **Église St-Foy** was heavily restored in the 19th century.

Vieux Sélestat, the old town area south and southwest of the churches, is a mainly postwar commercial precinct dotted with half-timbered and trompe-l'œil shop buildings. A huge **outdoor market**, held since 1435, takes over the streets all around Église St-Foy from 8am to noon every Tuesday. Locally grown fruits and vegies are sold at the *marché du terroir* (local-produce market), held on Saturday morning at place Vanolles, on the southern edge of the old town.

The turn-off to the **Cimetière Israélite** (Jewish Cemetery; 8am-6pm Apr-Sep, to 4pm Oct-Mar, closed Sat & Jewish holidays), one of many around Alsace, is 1.8km north of Sélestat's yellow-brick water tower on the west side of N83; look for the black-on-white sign. The half-hidden key is attached to the upper hinge of the cemetery's right-hand door.

The **tourist office** (☎ 03 88 58 87 20; www.selestat-tourisme.com; bd du Général Leclerc; 9am-noon & 2-5.45pm Mon-Sat, closed Sun & holidays Sep-Jun, 9.30am-12.30pm & 1.30-6.30pm Mon-Sat, 10.30am-3pm Sun & holidays Jul & Aug) is on the edge of the town centre, two short blocks from the Bibliothèque Humaniste. Well signposted, it rents out bicycles (two hours/half-day/full day €5.50/8/12.50) in summer.

The train station is 1km west of the Bibliothèque Humaniste.

Bergheim

pop 1830

The delightful walled town of Bergheim – overflowing with geraniums, dotted with flowerbeds and enlivened by half-timbered houses in shocking pastels – is more spacious than its neighbours. But things have not always been so cheerful: over the centuries the town has passed from one overlord to another, having been sold, ceded or captured some 20 times; and between 1582 and 1630, 35 women and one man were burnt at the stake here for witchcraft.

The centre, spared from the ravages of WWII, is dominated by an early Gothic **church** (14th century), significantly modified in the early 1700s. The wall-mounted **sundial** at 44 Grand' Rue has its origins in 1711. The 14th-century, Gothic **Porte Haute**, square and imposingly medieval, is the only one of the village's original three main gates that's still extant. Outside across the grassy park, the **Herrengarten linden tree**, planted around 1300, is hanging in there – a sort of steel bra is providing support – but looks like it could use a hug. A map of the town stands nearby. A 2km path, marked 'Remparts XIVème Siècle', circumnavigates the town's ramparts. Bergheim's *grands crus* labels are Kanzlerberg and Altenberg de Bergheim.

The tiny **tourist office** (point info; ☎ 03 89 73 31 98; www.ribeauville-riquewihr.com; 10am-noon & 2-5pm Mon-Sat, closed Sun & holidays early Oct–Easter, 9.30-noon & 2-6pm Mon-Sat, 10am-1pm Sunday & holidays Easter–early Oct) is between the well-proportioned **hôtel de ville** (1767), which can supply you with a brochure on the town (€1), and the deconsecrated **Ancienne Synagogue** (rue des Juifs/Judagass), built in 1863 on the site of an early-14th-century synagogue and now a cultural centre.

Just inside the Porte Haute, **La Cour du Bailli** (☎ 03 89 73 73 46; www.cour-bailli.com; 57 Grand' Rue; r €78-145 mid-Jul–Oct & Dec, r €62-132 rest of year; reception 9am-7pm;), a three-star hotel and apartment hotel centred on a flowery 16th-century courtyard, has 38 spacious, rustic rooms and kitchenette-equipped studios and, in the cellar, an **Alsatian restaurant** (menus €19.50-27; lunch & dinner daily Easter-Oct, lunch Sat & Sun, dinner Fri-Sun in winter). There are several more **restaurants** between here and the *hôtel de ville.*

NAH-NAH!

At eye-level on the exterior of Bergheim's 14th-century Porte Haute (left), a bas-relief sandstone figure exposes his posterior and thumbs his nose at his pursuers, recalling the time, from the 14th to 17th centuries, when Bergheim granted asylum to people guilty of unpremeditated crimes.

Haut Kœnigsbourg

Perched on a lushly forested promontory offering superb vistas, the imposing red-sandstone **Château du Haut Kœnigsbourg** (☎ 03 88 82 50 60; www.haut-koenigsbourg.fr; adult/student/under 18yr €7.50/5.70/free; 9.30am-6.30pm Jun-Aug, 9.30am-5.30pm Apr, May & Sep, 9.45am-5pm Mar & Oct, 9.45am-noon & 1-5pm Nov-Feb, last entry 30min before closure) makes a very medieval impression despite having been reconstructed in 1908 – with German imperial pomposity – by Kaiser Wilhelm II (r 1888–1918). Audioguides are available.

Ribeauvillé

pop 4900

Ribeauvillé, some 19km northwest of Colmar, is arguably the most heavily touristed of all the villages on the Route du Vin. It's easy to see why: this little village, nestled in a valley and brimming with 18th-century overhanging houses and narrow alleys, is picture-perfect. The local *grands crus* are Kirchberg de Ribeauvillé, Osterberg and Geisberg.

Along the main street, don't miss the 17th-century **Pfifferhüs** (Fifers' House; 14 Grand' Rue), which once housed the town's fife-playing minstrels and is now home to a friendly *wistub (winstub);* the **hôtel de ville** (across from 64 Grand' Rue) and its Renaissance fountain; or the nearby clock-equipped **Tour des Bouchers** (Butchers' Bell Tower; 13th and 16th centuries).

Just across two traffic roundabouts from the tourist office, the lemon-coloured **Cave de Ribeauvillé** (☎ 03 89 73 61 80; www.cave-ribeauville.com; 2 rte de Colmar; admission & tasting free; 🕑 8am-noon & 2-6pm Mon-Fri, longer hours Jul & Aug, 10am-12.30pm & 2.30-7pm Sat & Sun, slightly shorter hours Jan-Easter), France's oldest wine growers' cooperative (founded in 1895), has a small viniculture museum, informative brochures and excellent wines (including 10 *grands crus*) made with all seven of the grape varieties grown in Alsace. On weekends it's staffed by local wine growers.

West and northwest of Ribeauvillé, the ruins of three 12th- and 13th-century hilltop castles – **St-Ulrich** (530m), **Giersberg** (530m) and **Haut Ribeaupierre** (642m) – can be reached on a hike (three hours return) beginning at place de la République (at the northern tip of the Grand' Rue).

The **tourist office** (☎ 03 89 73 23 23; www.ribeauville-riquewihr.com; 1 Grand' Rue; 🕑 9.30am or 10am–noon & 2-6pm Mon-Sat, 10am-1pm Sun & holidays Easter–early Oct & Dec, 10am-noon & 2-5pm Mon-Fri & 2nd & 4th Sat of month rest of year), the area's best equipped, is at the southern end of the main street, the one-way (south-to-north) Grand' Rue.

Hunawihr

pop 500

You're absolutely guaranteed to see storks in the quiet hamlet of Hunawihr, about 1km south of Ribeauvillé, which is surrounded by a 14th-century wall and feels more solid and serious than its neighbours. On a hillside just outside the centre, the 16th-century fortified **church**, surrounded by a hexagonal wall, has been a *simultaneum* – that is, it has served both the Catholic and Protestant communities – since 1687.

About 500m east of Hunawihr, the delightful **Centre de Réintroduction des Cigognes** (Stork Reintroduction Centre; ☎ 03 89 73 28 48; www.cigogne-loutre.com, in French; adult/5-12yr €8/5.50; 🕑 10am-12.30pm & 2pm–btwn 5.30pm & 7pm Apr-Oct, no midday closure weekends & Jun-Aug, 10am-noon & 2-4.30pm Wed, Sat, Sun & holidays late Mar & 1-11 Nov) is home base for 200 free-flying storks (p392). Cormorants, penguins, otters and a sea lion show off their fishing prowess several times each afternoon.

At the nearby **Jardins des Papillons** (Butterfly Gardens; ☎ 03 89 73 33 33; www.jardinsdespapillons.fr; adult/5-14yr €7/4.50; 🕑 10am–5pm or 6pm Easter–1 Nov) you can stroll among exotic free-flying butterflies.

Riquewihr

pop 1200

About 5km south of Ribeauvillé, heavily touristed Riquewihr is the most medieval stop along the Route du Vin, with 13th- and 16th-century **ramparts** and a maze of alleyways and courtyards that are great for exploring. Several shops sell *macarons* (macaroons), a tradition since coconuts were first brought up the Rhine in the 1700s.

The **Sentier Viticole des Grands Crus** (2km; yellow signage) takes you away from the souvenir shops and out to the most prestigious local vineyards, Schœnenbourg (north of town) and Sporen (southeast of town), while a 15km trail with red trail markers takes you to five nearby villages. Both can be picked up next to Auberge du Schœnenbourg, 100m to the right of the *hôtel de ville* (through which the road passes) as you approach the old town from the Route du Vin.

The late-13th-century **Dolder** (admission €2.50, incl Tour des Voleurs €4; 🕑 1.45-6.30pm daily Jul & Aug, 1.45-6.30pm Sat, Sun & holidays Easter-Jun & Sep–1 Nov) is a stone and half-timbered gate – topped by a 25m bell tower – with panoramic views and a small local-history museum. From there, rue des Juifs (site of the medieval Jewish quarter) leads down the hill to the **Tour des Voleurs** (Thieves' Tower; admission €2.50; 🕑 10am-12.30pm & 2-6.30pm Easter–1 Nov). Tucked inside the town's medieval stone fortifications, this fascinating place features a gruesome torture chamber with English commentary and an old-style wine grower's kitchen.

The **Maison de Hansi** (☎ 03 89 47 97 00; 16 rue du Général de Gaulle; adult/under 16yr €2/free; 🕑 10am-6pm Tue-Sun Apr-Dec) presents delightful posters, children's books, engravings and even wine labels created by the celebrated Colmar-born illustrator Jean-Jacques Waltz (1873–1951), aka Hansi, whose idealised images of Alsace are known around the world.

The Château des Princes de Wurtemberg-Montbéliard (1540) now houses the **Musée de la Communication** (☎ 03 89 47 93 80; adult/student & senior €4/3.50; 🕑 10am-5.30pm Tue-Sun Easter–1 Nov & 2 weeks in

STORKS

White storks *(cigognes)*, long a feature of Alsatian folklore, are one of the region's most beloved symbols. Believed to bring luck (as well as babies), they winter in Africa and then spend the warmer months in Europe, feeding in the marshes (their favourite delicacies include worms, insects, small rodents and frogs) and building their nests of twigs and sticks on church steeples and rooftops.

When mid-August arrives, instinct tells young storks – at the age of just a few months – to fly south for a two- or three-year, 12,000km trek to sub-Saharan Africa (Alsatian storks are particularly fond of Mali and Mauritania), from where they return to Alsace ready to breed – if they return at all. Research has shown that something like 90% die en route because of electrocution, pesticides (eg those used to combat locusts), hunting, exhaustion and dehydration. In subsequent years, the adult storks – 1m long, with a 2m wingspan and weighing 3.5kg – make only a short trek south for the winter, returning to Alsace to breed after a few months in Africa.

In the mid-20th century, environmental changes, including the draining of the marshes along the Rhine, and high-tension lines reduced stork numbers catastrophically. By the early 1980s there were only two pairs left in the wild in all of Alsace.

Research and breeding centres were set up with the goal of establishing a permanent, year-round Alsatian stork population. The young birds spend the first three years of their lives confined to large cages, which causes them to lose their migratory instinct and thus avoid the rigours and dangers of migration. The program has been a huge success, and today Alsace is home to more than 400 pairs.

See p391 and p398 for details on stork-breeding centres.

Dec), whose exhibits trace the history of written and voice communications in Alsace.

The **tourist office** (☎ 03 89 73 23 23; www.ribeauville-riquewihr.com; 2 rue de la Première Armée; ⏰ 9.30am or 10am–noon & 2-6pm Mon-Sat, 10am-1pm Sun & holidays Easter–early Oct & Dec, 10am-noon & 2-5pm Mon-Fri & 1st & 3rd Sat of month rest of year) is smack in the centre of the old town.

Kaysersberg

pop 2700

In the postcard-perfect centre of Kaysersberg, 10km northwest of Colmar, stand the ornate Renaissance **hôtel de ville** (1605) and, next door, the red-sandstone **Église Ste Croix** (⏰ 9am-4pm), a 12th- to 15th-century Catholic church whose **altar** (1518) has 18 painted haut-relief panels of the Passion and the Resurrection. Out front, a Renaissance **fountain**, in red sandstone, holds aloft a statue of Emperor Constantine. Up the main street, av du Général de Gaulle (one-way going west to east, ie downhill), you'll find lots of colourful old houses, many half-timbered, others showing baroque influences; further along is a squat, **fortified bridge** (next to No 84) built to span the River Weiss in 1514.

You can see master glass-blowers practising their magic at **Verrerie d'Art** (☎ 03 89 47 14 97; 30 rue du Général de Gaulle; ⏰ 10am-12.15pm & 2-5.45pm, closed Sun, Mon, holidays & sometimes Thu afternoon).

The house where the musicologist, medical doctor and 1952 Nobel Peace Prize winner Albert Schweitzer (1875–1965) was born is now the **Musée Albert Schweitzer** (☎ 03 89 47 36 55; 126 rue du Général de Gaulle; adult/student €2/1; ⏰ 9am-noon & 2-6pm daily Apr–11 Nov, Fri afternoon, Sat & Sun late Nov–late Dec), with exhibits on the good doctor's life in Alsace and Gabon.

Footpaths lead in all directions through glen and vineyard. A 10-minute walk above town, the remains of the massive, crenulated **Château de Kaysersberg** stand surrounded by vines; other destinations include Riquewihr (two hours one-way via the château and over the hill, 1½ hours via the vineyards). These paths begin through the arch to the right as you face the entrance to the *hôtel de ville*.

The **tourist office** (☎ 03 89 78 22 78; www.kaysersberg.com; 37 rue du Général de Gaulle; ⏰ 9.30am-noon & 2-5.30pm Mon-Sat mid-Sep–mid-Jun, 9am-12.30pm & 2-6pm Mon-Sat, 10am-12.30pm Sun & holidays mid-Jun–mid-Sep), inside the *hôtel de ville*, can supply you with a walking-tour brochure as well as hiking and cycling maps, and helps with *chambres d'hôtes* reservations. Internet and wi-fi are free. Audioguides of town (1½ to two hours) cost €5.

Hôtel Constantin (⏰ 03 89 47 19 90; www.hotel-constantin.com; 10 rue du Père Kohlmann; d €56-72), a three-star place in the heart of the old town (half a block from 38 rue du Général de Gaulle), has

20 modern rooms whose wood furnishings fit in well with the local vibe.

COLMAR

pop 65,300

Capital of the Haut-Rhin *département*, harmonious – and very conservative – Colmar is a maze of cobbled pedestrian malls and centuries-old Alsatian-style buildings, many painted in surprising tones of blue, orange, red or green. The Musée d'Unterlinden is renowned worldwide for the profoundly moving *Issenheim Altarpiece*.

Colmar is an excellent base for exploring the Route du Vin by car, bike, train or bus. And for something a bit different, it's easy to take day trips to the German university city of Freiburg (by bus) and the Swiss city of Basel (by train), each about an hour away (see www.tourismtrirhena.com).

Orientation

Av de la République links the train station and the adjacent bus terminal with the Musée d'Unterlinden and the nearby tourist office, a distance of about 1km. The old city, much of it pedestrianised, is southeast of the Musée d'Unterlinden. The Petite Venise (Little Venice) quarter runs along the River Lauch, at the southern edge of the old city.

Information

Cyber Didim (☎ 03 89 23 20 44; 9 rue du Rempart; per hr €2.50; ⏲ 10am–10pm or later Mon-Sat, 2-10pm Sun) Upstairs at the doner kebab place.

Hôpital Pasteur (☎ 03 89 12 40 94; 39 av de la Liberté; ⏲ 24hr) Situated 700m west of the train station and served by bus lines 1, 3, 10, A, C and S. The casualty ward is in Building 39.

Laundrette (1bis rue Ruest; ⏲ 7am-9pm)

Main Post Office (36 av de la République) Has exchange services.

Tourist Office (☎ 03 89 20 68 92; www.ot-colmar.fr; 4 rue d'Unterlinden; ⏲ 9am-noon & 2-6pm Mon-Sat, to 7pm Jul & Aug, no midday closure Apr-Sep & Dec, 10am-1pm Sun & holidays) Can help find accommodation and supply you with information on hiking, cycling and bus travel (including schedules) along the Route du Vin and in the Massif des Vosges. Exchanges US dollars, pounds sterling and Swiss francs.

Sights

OLD CITY

The medieval streets of the old city, including **rue des Clefs**, the **Grand' Rue** and **rue des Marchands**, are lined with dozens of restored, half-timbered houses – and lots of attractive shops – and are great for an aimless stroll. **Maison Pfister** (1537), opposite 36 rue des Marchands, is remarkable for its exterior decoration, including delicately painted panels, an elaborate oriel window and a carved wooden balcony.

The house next door at 9 rue des Marchands, which dates from 1419, has a wooden sculpture of an uptight-looking *marchand* (merchant) – has his tulip portfolio just tanked? – on the corner. **Maison des Têtes** (Kopfhüs in Alsatian; House of the Heads; 19 rue des Têtes), built in 1609, has a fantastic facade crowded with 106 grimacing stone faces and animal heads.

Colmar has a number of small *quartiers* (quarters) – often not much more than a single street – which preserve the ambience that reigned back when each was home to a specific guild. **Rue des Tanneurs**, with its tall houses and rooftop verandahs for drying hides, intersects **quai de la Poissonnerie**, the former fishers' quarter, which runs along the Lauch. The river provides the delightful **Petite Venise** area – also known as Quartier de la Krutenau – with its rather fanciful appellation. It is best appreciated from the **rue de Turenne bridge**.

At the southeastern end of rue des Marchands is the **Ancienne Douane** (Koïfhus in Alsatian; Old Customs House), built in 1480 and topped with a variegated tile roof. Now used for temporary exhibitions and concerts,

> **LADY LIBERTY IN COLMAR**
>
> Colmar celebrated the centenary of the death of Frédéric Auguste Bartholdi (1834–1904) by erecting a 12m-high replica of his most famous work, the Statue of Liberty. Made of stratified resin supported by an Eiffelesque internal metal frame, Lady Liberty – given a convincing copper-green patina – bears her torch aloft 3km north of the old city on route de Strasbourg (N83), in the middle of a traffic roundabout near Colmar-Houssen airfield. Around her base congregate the huddled masses, yearning to shop at the nearby American-style strip malls... By the way, the copper-skinned New York original (www.nps.gov/stli), dedicated in 1886, is four times as tall (eight times as tall including the pedestal).

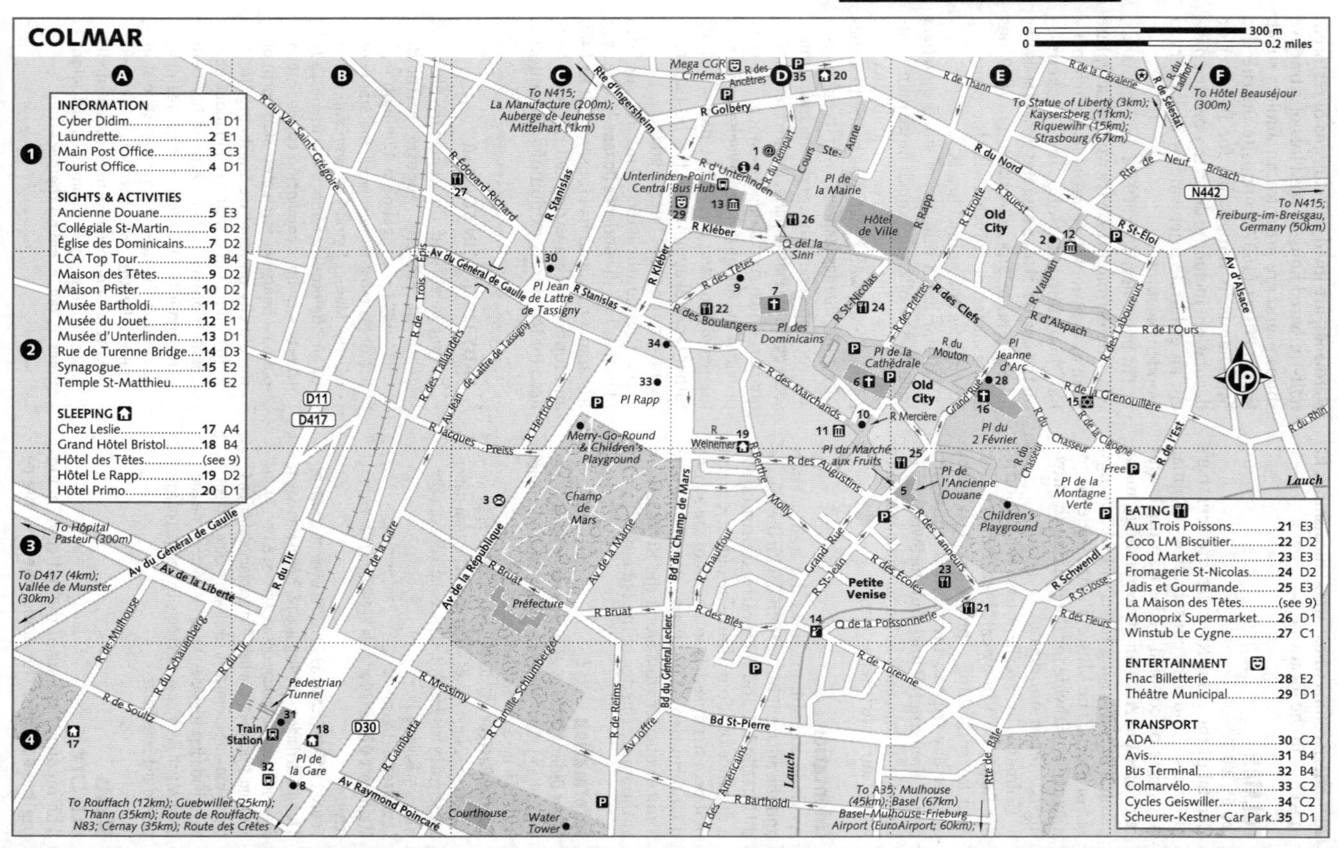
COLMAR
INFORMATION
Cyber Didim 1 D1
Laundrette 2 E1
Main Post Office 3 C3
Tourist Office 4 D1
SIGHTS & ACTIVITIES
Ancienne Douane 5 E3
Collégiale St-Martin 6 D2
Église des Dominicains 7 D2
LCA Top Tour 8 B4
Maison des Têtes 9 D2
Maison Pfister 10 D2
Musée Bartholdi 11 D2
Musée du Jouet 12 E1
Musée d'Unterlinden 13 D1
Rue de Turenne Bridge 14 D3
Synagogue 15 E2
Temple St-Matthieu 16 E2
SLEEPING
Chez Leslie 17 A4
Grand Hôtel Bristol 18 B4
Hôtel des Têtes (see 9)
Hôtel Le Rapp 19 D2
Hôtel Primo 20 D1
EATING
Aux Trois Poissons 21 E3
Coco LM Biscuitier 22 D2
Food Market 23 E3
Fromagerie St-Nicolas 24 D2
Jadis et Gourmande 25 E3
La Maison des Têtes (see 9)
Monoprix Supermarket 26 D1
Winstub Le Cygne 27 C1
ENTERTAINMENT
Fnac Billetterie 28 E2
Théâtre Municipal 29 D1
TRANSPORT
ADA 30 C2
Avis 31 B4
Bus Terminal 32 B4
Colmarvélo 33 C2
Cycles Geiswiller 34 C2
Scheurer-Kestner Car Park 35 D1
0 300 m
0 0.2 miles
To Hôtel Beauséjour (300m)
To N415; Freiburg-im-Breisgau, Germany (50km)
To Statue of Liberty (3km); Kaysersberg (11km); Riquewihr (15km); Strasbourg (67km)
To N415; La Manufacture (200m); Auberge de Jeunesse Mittelhart (1km)
To Hôpital Pasteur (300m)
To D417 (4km); Vallée de Munster (30km)
To Rouffach (12km); Guebwiller (25km); Thann (35km); Route de Rouffach; N83; Cernay (35km); Route des Crêtes
To A35; Mulhouse (45km); Basel (67km); Basel-Mulhouse-Frieburg Airport (EuroAirport; 60km)
Old City
Petite Venise
Hôtel de Ville
Pl de la Mairie
Pl de la Cathédrale
Pl des Dominicains
Pl du Marché aux Fruits
Pl de l'Ancienne Douane
Pl du 2 Février
Pl Jeanne d'Arc
Pl de la Montagne Verte
Children's Playground
Pl Rapp
Merry-Go-Round & Children's Playground
Champ de Mars
Préfecture
Courthouse
Water Tower
Train Station
Pedestrian Tunnel
Pl de la Gare
Pl Jean de Lattre de Tassigny
Unterlinden-Point Central Bus Hub
Mega CGR Cinémas
Lauch
Free

it is the town's best example of late-medieval civil architecture.

MUSEUMS

The outstanding **Musée d'Unterlinden** (☎ 03 89 20 15 50; www.musee-unterlinden.com; 1 rue d'Unterlinden; adult/student under 30yr/over 65yr/under 12yr €7/5/6/free; ⌚ 9am-6pm daily May-Oct, 9am-noon & 2-5pm Wed-Mon Nov-Apr), whose pride and joy is the Issenheim Altarpiece (see below), is set around a Gothic-style Dominican cloister in which several dwarf-mutant hazelnut trees grow. Medieval stone statues, prints by Martin Shongauer (late 1400s) and an exceptional ensemble of 15th-century Upper Rhine Primitives let visitors peer into the medieval European mind. The entry price includes an excellent audioguide, available in six languages.

Dedicated to the Colmar native who created New York's Statue of Liberty (see the boxed text, p393), the **Musée Bartholdi** (☎ 03 89 41 90 60; 30 rue des Marchands; adult/student/under 12yr €4.50/2.90/free; ⌚ 10am-noon & 2-6pm Wed-Mon Mar-Dec) displays the works (including models) and memorabilia of Frédéric Auguste Bartholdi in the house where he was born. Highlights include a full-size plaster model of the Lady Liberty's left ear (the lobe is watermelon-sized!) and the Bartholdi family's sparklingly bourgeois apartment. A ground-floor room is dedicated to 18th- and 19th-century Jewish ritual objects.

At the **Musée du Jouet** (Toy Museum; ☎ 03 89 41 93 10; www.museejouet.com; 40 rue Vauban; adult/8-17yr €4.50/3.50, groups of 4 or more adult/8-17yr €3.50/1.70; ⌚ 10am-noon & 2-6pm, to 7pm Jul & Aug, no midday closure Jul, Aug & Dec, closed Tue Oct, Nov & Jan-Jun), kids of every age will delight at the sight of toys, dolls and trains from generations past, including a whole miniature French village complete with working trams and trains.

HOUSES OF WORSHIP

The 13th- and 14th-century Gothic **Collégiale St-Martin** (place de la Cathédrale; ⌚ 8am–6.30pm or 7pm except Sun morning) has a sombre ambulatory and a peculiar, Mongol-style copper spire (1572).

The celebrated triptych *La Vierge au Buisson de Roses* (The Virgin in the Rose Bush), painted by Martin Schongauer in 1473, can be seen inside the desanctified Gothic **Église des Dominicains** (place des Dominicains; adult/student €1.50/1; ⌚ 10am-1pm & 3-6pm mid-Mar–Dec). In 1972 the work made world headlines when it was stolen, not to be recovered for 18 months. The stained glass dates from the 14th and 15th centuries.

Temple St-Matthieu (Grand' Rue; ⌚ 10am-noon & 3-5pm late Apr–mid-Jun & late Jul–mid-Oct), quintessentially Protestant in its austerity, has something of a split personality. From 1715 to 1987, a wall cut off the soaring 14th-century Gothic choir – a Catholic hospital chapel until 1937 – from the nave, long a Protestant church. This arrangement allowed the 14th-century *jubé* (rood screen) to survive the counter-Reformation. The elaborate Silbermann organ is used for concerts.

God only knows why Colmar's classical **synagogue** (☎ 03 89 41 38 29; office at 3 rue de la Cigogne), built from 1839 to 1842, has its very own tiny belfry (Jews have no tradition of ringing bells), but if 19th-century neo-Moorish synagogues (eg the Great Synagogue of Budapest) can have faux-minarets, why not? Call ahead to visit the interior.

Festivals & Events

From mid-May to mid-September, **Soirées Folkloriques** (free performances of Alsatian music and dancing) are held at 8.30pm (or a bit later) on Tuesday at place de l'Ancienne Douane.

THE ISSENHEIM ALTARPIECE

The late-Gothic **Rétable d'Issenheim** (c1500), acclaimed as one of the most dramatic and moving works of art ever created, illustrates with unrelenting realism scenes from the New Testament, including the Nativity, the Crucifixion, the Entombment and the Resurrection. Ascribed to the painter Mathias Grünewald and the sculptor Nicolas of Haguenau, it is a work of profound faith whose emotion, imagination and layers of symbolism have engaged and captivated spectators for five centuries. The work originally opened up on hinges to form three different configurations.

The gruesome *Temptation of St Anthony* shows the unfortunate saint being set upon by a mob of hideous monsters far more grotesque than anything in the bar scene of *Star Wars*. In the *Concert of Angels*, a figure lurks at the back – Lucifer! – but why is he covered in feathers? *The Issenheim Altar* (€4), an excellent booklet on sale at Colmar's Musée d'Unterlinden (above), where the altarpiece is the star attraction, helps decipher many of its mysteries.

During summer, villages all over Alsace hold **Fêtes du Vin** (Wine Festivals) featuring wine and song; the tourist office has details.

Colmar's magical **Marché de Noël** (Christmas Market; www.noel-colmar.com) runs from the last Saturday in November to 31 December.

Sleeping

In December (during the Christmas Market), around Easter and from mid-July to mid-August hotels are booked up well in advance.

BUDGET

Auberge de Jeunesse Mittelhart (☎ 03 89 80 57 39; fax 03 89 80 76 16; 2 rue Pasteur; dm/s/d incl breakfast €13/18/35, sheets €4; ⏲ reception 7-10am & 5-11pm, to midnight during daylight-saving time, closed late Dec–mid-Jan) This one-time orphanage isn't cheery (it's not hard to imagine lonely children crying themselves to sleep) but the management does its best. An old-style place with 110 beds, hall showers and kitchen facilities, it's situated 1.2km northwest of the tourist office, around the corner from 76 rte d'Ingersheim. By bus, take bus 4, 5 or 15 to the Pont Rouge stop.

Hôtel Primo (☎ 03 89 24 22 24; www.villes-et-vignoble.com/hotel-primo.html; 5 rue des Ancêtres; d €39-55, with washbasin €29) Best described as 'cheap and horrible', this centrally located 84-room prefab place is most notable for the cigarette burns on its linoleum tile floors, is the only bottom-end hotel left in Colmar.

MIDRANGE & TOP END

Chez Leslie (☎ 03 89 79 98 99; www.chezleslie.com; 31 rue de Mulhouse; d incl breakfast €68, 4-person apt per week €400; ☒) Run by an expat from San Francisco, this superfriendly, four-room *chambre d'hôte* (B&B) occupies a private home of the sort that made bourgeois Germans of a century ago pat their paunches with satisfaction. Each spacious room is unique.

Hôtel Le Rapp (☎ 03 89 41 62 10; www.rapp-hotel.com; 1-5 rue Weinemer; d €88-138; ❄ 💻 🏊) Right at the edge of the old city, this three-star, Logis de France hotel has 38 comfortable rooms with classic decor as well as a pool, sauna, hammam and fitness room.

Hôtel Beauséjour (☎ 03 89 20 66 66; www.beausejour.fr; 25 rue du Ladhof; d high season €90-140, low season €70-110; 💻) This venerable three-star hostelry, run by the Keller family for five generations, has 40 rooms, some with Provençal or Louis XV decor, others merely modern and comfortable, with garden-view balconies. Has an elegant restaurant. Situated 600m northeast of the Musée du Jouet.

Grand Hôtel Bristol (☎ 03 89 23 59 59; www.grand-hotel-bristol.fr; 7 place de la Gare; d €93-149; 💻) At this Best Western–affiliated, three-star place, built in 1925, a marble stairway leads from the Persian-carpeted lobby to grand hallways and 91 comfortable rooms. Has a sauna, fitness room and good wheelchair access.

Hôtel des Têtes (☎ 03 89 24 43 43; www.maisondestetes.com; 19 rue des Têtes; d €115-239, low season from €98; ❄ ☒) This impeccable four-star hostelry, luxurious but never flashy, occupies the magnificent Maison des Têtes (p393). Each of its 21 rooms offers rich wood panelling, an elegant sitting area, a mostly marble bathroom and romantic views – definitely honeymoon material.

Eating

Restaurants are sprinkled around Colmar's old city, especially around place de l'Ancienne Douane (eg Grand' Rue, rue St-Jean).

ALSATIAN & FRENCH

Jadis et Gourmande (☎ 03 89 41 73 76; 8 place du Marché aux Fruits; plats du jour €8.50-10.50; ⏲ 8am-6pm Mon-Sat) A wood-panelled *salon de thé* (tearoom) that serves breakfast (€5.20 to €6.90), light lunches (eg quiche, salad; from noon to 3pm), Alsatian wines by the glass (€2.20 to €3.30) and luscious homemade desserts, including apple strudel with vanilla ice cream (€5.50).

Winstub Le Cygne (☎ 03 89 23 76 26; 17 rue Édouard Richard; ⏲ noon-2pm & 7pm-midnight, closed Sun, lunch Sat & dinner Mon) Hidden in an untouristed side street, this is where locals come when they want to 'eat Alsatian' – and eat well – but are tired of sauerkraut, mild though the Alsatian version may be. Authentic specialities include *fleischschnacka* (literally 'meat snails'; dough filled with chopped beef and baked with beef broth; €13.50) and *lawerknaepfa* (grilled heifer liver dumplings; €13.50).

Aux Trois Poissons (☎ 03 89 41 25 21; 15 quai de la Poissonnerie; menus €21-45; ⏲ closed Wed, dinner Sun & dinner Tue) Oil paintings on the walls and Persian carpets on the floor give this mainly fish restaurant a hushed atmosphere of civilised elegance. The chef's speciality is *sandre dur lit de choucroute* (pike-perch on a bed of sauerkraut; €18). Provençal frogs' legs will hop onto your plate for €15.

La Maison des Têtes (☎ 03 89 24 43 43; 19 rue des Têtes; menus €29.90-60; ⏲ closed Mon, lunch Tue & dinner

Sun) Behind the leaded windows of the spectacular Maison des Têtes awaits a truly grand dining room, built in 1898 and decorated with grape bunches in wood, wrought iron and stained glass. The chef's *cuisine française actuelle* (contemporary French cuisine) includes *caille farcie à la choucroute et foie d'oie* (quail stuffed with sauerkraut and goose liver) and, in season, fish and game. Known for its superb wine list.

SELF-CATERING

Coco LM Biscuitier (☎ 03 89 41 79 02; www.coco-lm.com; 16 rue des Boulangers; 🕑 9am-7pm) Bakes scrumptious Alsatian cookies *(lekerli, brünsli)*, cakes *(kougelhopf)*, sweet and salty *bretzels* and a type of startlingly spicy ginger biscuit dubbed a *gingerli*. The website has recipes.

Fromagerie St-Nicolas (☎ 03 89 24 90 45; 18 rue St-Nicolas; 🕑 9am-12.30pm & 2-7pm Tue-Fri, 2-7pm Mon, 9am-6.30pm Sat) Prepare yourself to be overcome by the heady odours of unrepentantly unpasteurised cheese. BYOB (bring your own baguette) and they'll make you a sandwich.

Other places to buy edibles:

Food market (rue des Écoles; 🕑 8am-1pm Thu) Market gardeners once unloaded their produce directly from boats at this handsome sandstone 1865 *marché couvert* (covered market).

Monoprix supermarket (across the square from the Musée d'Unterlinden; 🕑 8am-8pm Mon-Sat)

Entertainment

Colmar's main performance venues, hosting concerts, ballet, theatre and even the occasional opera, are **La Manufacture** (☎ 03 89 24 31 78; www.atelierdurhin.com, in French; 6 rte d'Ingersheim), housed in a former factory 400m northwest of the tourist office, and the **Théâtre Municipal** (☎ 03 89 20 29 02), next to the Musée d'Unterlinden.

Tickets are available at the **Fnac billetterie** (☎ 08 92 68 36 22; www.fnacspectacles.com, in French; 1 Grand' Rue; 🕑 2-7pm Mon, 10am-7pm Tue-Fri, 9am-7pm Sat).

Getting There & Away

AIR

The trinational **Basel-Mulhouse-Freiburg airport** (EuroAirport; www.euroairport.com) is 60km south of Colmar.

BUS

Public buses are not the quickest way to explore Alsace's Route du Vin but they *are* a viable option; destinations served include Riquewihr, Hunawihr, Ribeauvillé, Kaysersberg and Eguisheim. In the Vosges you can bus it to Munster, Col de la Schlucht and Col du Bonhomme.

The open-air bus terminal is to the right as you exit the train station. Timetables are posted and are also available at the tourist office or online (www.l-k.fr, in French). Services are very limited on Sunday and holidays.

Line 1076 goes to the German city of Freiburg (€7.40, 1¼ hours, seven daily Monday to Friday, four daily weekends and holidays), sometimes with a change to a train at Breisach.

CAR

Cars can be hired from **ADA** (☎ 03 89 23 90 30; 22bis rue Stanislas). Avis has an agency in the train station.

TRAIN

Colmar has train connections to Basel SNCF (Bâle; €11.40, 44 minutes, 16 to 25 direct daily), Mulhouse (€7, 20 minutes, 28 to 38 daily), Paris' Gare de l'Est (€65.70 to €86.80, 2¾ hours by direct TGV, two daily) and Strasbourg (€10.20, 31 to 65 minutes, 20 to 30 daily).

Route du Vin destinations from Colmar include Dambach-la-Ville (€5.30) and Obernai (€7.50), both of which require a change of trains at Sélestat (€4.10, 13 minutes, 23 to 30 daily). About 20 daily autorails or SNCF buses (seven to 10 daily on weekends) link Colmar with the Vallée de Munster towns of Munster (€3.40, 35 minutes) and Metzeral (€4.30, 50 minutes); the last run back, by bus, begins a bit after 9pm (7pm on Saturday, Sunday and holidays).

Getting Around

TO/FROM THE AIRPORT

To get to the Basel-Mulhouse-Freiburg airport (EuroAirport), take one of the frequent trains to St-Louis and catch an airport shuttle bus (€1, eight minutes, every 20 or 30 minutes).

BICYCLE

Colmarvélo (☎ 03 89 41 37 90; place Rapp; per half-/full day €5/6; 🕑 8.30am-12.15pm & 1.15-7.15pm Apr-Oct), run by the municipality, rents city bikes (deposit €50).

Hybrid bikes for Route du Vin touring can be rented from **Cycles Geiswiller** (☎ 03 89 41 30 59; 4-6 bd du Champ de Mars; per half-/full day €6/11;

THE CONTINENTAL DIVIDE

The Massif des Vosges serves as a *ligne de partage des eaux* (continental divide): a raindrop that falls on the range's eastern slopes will flow to the Rhine and eventually make its way to the icy waters of the North Sea, while a drop of rain that lands on the southern slopes of the Ballon d'Alsace – perhaps only a few metres from its Rhine-bound counterpart – will eventually end up in the Rhône before merging with the warm waters of the Mediterranean. The Vosges' western slopes feed the Moselle, which joins the Rhine at Koblenz.

The Danube, which meanders through Vienna and Budapest on its way to the Black Sea, rises just 100km east of the Vosges in the mountains of the Black Forest, visible on clear days from the area's *ballons* (peaks).

9am-noon & 2-6pm Tue-Sat), which has free helmets and cycling maps.

PARKING

Free parking can be found in the Scheurer-Kestner car park just north of the Hôtel Primo; a few blocks east of the train station around the German-era, brick-built water tower; and in *part* of the car park at place de la Montagne Verte.

TAXI

For a taxi call **Radios Taxis** (☎ 03 89 80 71 71) or **Taxi Gare** (☎ 03 89 41 40 19).

MASSIF DES VOSGES

The sublime **Parc Naturel Régional des Ballons des Vosges** covers about 3000 sq km in the southern part of the Vosges range. In the warm months, the gentle, rounded mountains, deep forests, glacial lakes and rolling pastureland are a walker's paradise, with an astounding 10,000km of marked trails, including GRs (*grandes randonnées;* long-distance hiking trails) and their variants. Cyclists have hundreds of kilometres of idyllic trails and hang-gliding enthusiasts have plenty of places for launching. In winter three dozen inexpensive skiing areas offer modest downhill pistes and cross-country options.

For details on outings sponsored by the Strasbourg section of the Club Vosgien, see p381.

For information on bus and train connections to the Vosges area, see p397.

Vallée de Munster

This lush river valley – its pastureland dotted with 16 villages, its upper slopes thickly forested – is one of the loveliest in the Vosges. From the town of Metzeral, hiking destinations include Schnepfenried, Hohneck, the Petit Ballon and Vallée de la Wormsa, which has a section of the GR5 and three small lakes.

MUNSTER

pop 4900

This streamside town (the name means 'monastery'), famed for its notoriously smelly eponymous cheese, is a good base for exploring the valley (the GR531 passes by here). At **place du Marché** (food market on Tuesday and Saturday mornings), it's easy to spot several storks' nests. About eight young storks live in the **Enclos Cigogne** (Stork Enclosure) – and more hang out on top of it – 250m behind the Renaissance **hôtel de ville**; on foot, cross the creek and turn left.

Information

Maison du Parc Naturel Régional des Ballons des Vosges (☎ 03 89 77 90 34; www.parc-ballons-vosges.fr, in French; 1 cour de l'Abbaye; 10am-noon & 2-6pm Tue-Sun mid-Jun–Sep, 2-6pm Mon-Fri Oct–mid-Jun, also 2-6pm Sat & Sun Dec) The regional park's visitors centre has ample printed information in English, including a translation of the exhibits. To get there walk through the arch from place du Marché.

Tourist Office (☎ 03 89 77 31 80; www.la-vallee-de-munster.com; 1 rue du Couvent; 9.30am-12.30pm & 1.30–6pm or 6.30pm Mon-Sat, 10am-12.30pm Sun Jul & Aug, 9.30am-12.30pm & 2-6pm Mon-Fri, 10am-noon & 2-4pm Sat Sep-Jun) Has information, some in English, on the Munster Valley, including visits to cheesemakers. Sells hiking maps and topoguides in French. In the same building as the Maison du Parc but downstairs (or around the other side).

Activities

Cimes et Sentiers (☎ 06 74 32 12 59; www.sentiersrando.com, in French) is one of several outfits offering guided walking and cycling tours of the Vosges year-round and, in winter, snowshoe hikes. The Munster tourist office can provide details.

Cycle Hop Evasion (☎ 06 07 16 56 35; stephane.aylies@cegetel.net; 5 rue de la République; per day €16; ⏲ 8.30am-noon & 1.30pm or 2-7pm mid-Apr–Oct, by reservation rest of year), based 200m east of Munster's tourist office, rents mountain bikes, arranges professional cycling guides and can supply you with details on cycling routes.

Sleeping & Eating

Hôtel des Vosges (☎ 03 89 77 31 41; www.hotelbardesvosges.fr; 58 Grand' Rue; d/q €48/66; ⏲ reception closes at 1pm Sun except Jun-Sep) This family-run, two-star hotel, on the main commercial street, has 15 simply outfitted but well-tended rooms with spacious bathrooms.

Near the Hôtel des Vosges are several restaurants and the delightful **Salon de Thé Gilg** (☎ 03 89 77 37 56; 11 Grand' Rue; ⏲ closed Sun afternoon except Dec, closed Mon year-round).

The **Super U supermarket** (⏲ 8am-7pm Mon-Thu, to 8pm Fri, to 6.30pm Sat) is 1.7km south of the tourist office on the D417 (towards Colmar).

Getting Around

Cycle Hop Evasion (opposite) rents out mountain bikes.

ROUTE DES CRÊTES

Partly built during WWI to supply French frontline troops, the **Route des Crêtes** (Route of the Crests) takes you to (or near) the Vosges' highest *ballons* (bald, rounded mountain peaks) as well as to several WWI sites. Mountaintop lookouts afford spectacular views of the Alsace plain, the Schwartzwald (Black Forest) across the Rhine in Germany, and – on clear days – the Swiss Alps and Mont Blanc.

The route links **Col du Bonhomme** (949m), about 20km west of Kaysersberg, with Cernay, 15km west of Mulhouse, along the D148, D61, D430 and D431. To minimise disruption to the lives of local fauna, sections north and south of Col de la Schlucht are left unploughed and thus closed from the first big snow (usually around November) until about April.

At the dramatic, windblown summit of the **Grand Ballon** (1424m; accessible year-round), the highest point in the Vosges, a short trail takes you to an aircraft-radar ball and a weather station. If the unsurpassed panorama doesn't blow you away, the howling wind just might.

From **Col de la Schlucht** (1139m), home to a small ski station, trails lead in various directions; walking north along the GR5 will take you to three lakes, **Lac Vert**, **Lac Noir** and **Lac Blanc** (Green, Black and White Lakes).

Ballon d'Alsace

This 1250m-high *ballon*, 20km southwest of the Grand Ballon as the crow flies (by road, take the D465 from St-Maurice), is the meeting point of four *départements* (Haut-Rhin, Territoire de Belfort, Haute-Saône and Vosges) and three *régions* (Alsace, Franche-Comté and Lorraine). Between 1871 and WWI, the frontier between France and Germany passed by here, attracting French tourists eager to catch a glimpse of France's 'lost province' of Alsace from the heroic **equestrian statue of Joan of Arc** (1909) and the cast-iron **orientation table** (1888). During WWI the mountaintop was heavily fortified, but the trenches, whose shallow remains can still be seen, were never used in battle.

The Ballon d'Alsace is a good base for day walks. The GR5 passes by here, as do other trails; possible destinations include **Lac des Perches** (four hours).

MULHOUSE

pop 110,900

The multi-ethnic industrial city of Mulhouse (moo·*looze*), 43km south of Colmar, was allied with the cantons of nearby Switzerland before voting to join Revolutionary France in 1798. Largely rebuilt after the ravages of WWII, it has little of the quaint Alsatian charm that you

A ROOM AT THE TOP OF ALSACE

Built all in wood in 1922 and run by the Club Vosgien, the region's veteran hiking organisation, the **Chalet Hôtel du Grand Ballon** (☎ 03 89 48 77 99; www.chalethotel-grandballon.com, in French; s/d €31/56, with washbasin from €24/43) sits atop the Grand Ballon in splendid isolation – amid a web of hiking and cycling trails. The rooms are spartan but with views this breathtaking you won't be spending much time inside. The Alsatian restaurant (veggie *menu* €16, other *menus* €15 to €26.50) is perfect for hearty après-hike dining. By car, it's 17km up the hill from Willer-sur-Thur (the road is kept open year-round), northwest of Mulhouse.

find further north – but the city's world-class industrial museums are well worth a stop.

About 700m northwest of the train station, the **tourist office** (☎ 03 89 66 93 13; www.tourism-mulhouse.com; place de la Réunion; République; 10am-6pm Mon-Sat, to 7pm Jul, Aug & Dec, 10am-noon & 2-6pm Sun & holidays Apr-Dec, 10am-1pm Sun & holidays Jan-Mar) is in the heart of the old city in the 16th-century, trompe-l'œil-covered former **hôtel de ville**, also home to the municipal **Musée Historique** (Historical Museum; ☎ 03 89 33 78 17; closed Tue).

The wonderful **Musée National de l'Automobile** (☎ 03 89 33 23 23; www.collection-schlumpf.com; 192 av de Colmar; Musée de l'Auto; adult/student incl audioguide in 6 languages €10.50/8.10; 10am-6pm, to 5pm early Nov–early Apr, from 1pm Mon-Fri early Jan–early Feb) displays 400 rare and beautiful European motorcars produced since 1878 by more than 100 different companies, including Bugatti, whose factory was in nearby Molsheim. By car, get off the A36 at the Mulhouse Centre exit.

A railway enthusiast's dream, the **Cité du Train** (French Railway Museum; ☎ 03 89 42 83 33; www.citedutrain.com; 2 rue Alfred de Glehn; adult/7-17yr & student incl audioguide €10/7.60, incl Musée National de l'Automobile €17.50/12.60, family discounts available), the largest rail museum in Europe, displays the SNCF's marvellous collection of locomotives and carriages. Situated about 4km northwest of the centre, it's served by bus 20 (bus 62 on Sunday and holidays) from the train station. By car, get off the A35 at Mulhouse Dornach.

Mulhouse was once known as the 'French Manchester', which is why it's home to the **Musée de l'Impression sur Étoffes** (Museum of Textile Printing; ☎ 03 89 46 83 00; www.musee-impression.com; 14 rue Jean-Jacques Henner; Gare Centrale; adult/student €6/3; 10am-noon & 2-6pm Tue-Sun), whose unique and very colourful collection of more than six million printed fabric samples, assembled since 1833, make it a mecca for fabric designers. It's situated one long block northeast of the train station.

Has wallpaper always been something of a wallflower in your life? The delightful **Musée du Papier Peint** (Wallpaper Museum; ☎ 03 89 64 24 56; www.museepapierpeint.org; 28 rue Zuber, Rixheim; adult/student/under 12yr €6/4.50/free; 10am-noon & 2-6pm, closed Tue Oct-May), home to an unparalleled collection of the stuff and the machines used to make wallpaper since the 18th century, will change all that. Situated a couple of kilometres southeast of central Mulhouse on the D66, it's easy to get to: by car take the A36 and get off at Rixheim; by bus take line 18 from the train station to the Temple stop.

Getting There & Around

France's second train line, linking Mulhouse with Thann, opened in 1839. Today, the **train station** (10 av du Général Leclerc; Gare Centrale), just south of the city centre, has frequent direct services to Colmar (€7, 20 minutes, 28 to 38 daily), St-Louis (on the Swiss border near EuroAirport), Basel and Strasbourg (€15.10).

ÉCOMUSÉE D'ALSACE

In Ungersheim about 17km northwest of Mulhouse (off the A35 to Colmar), **Écomusée d'Alsace** (☎ 03 89 62 43 00; www.ecomusee-alsace.com, in French; adult/4-14yr/student €12/8.50/11, Jul & Aug €16/11/11, family discounts available; 10am-7pm Jul & Aug, 10am–5pm or 6pm Apr-Jun & Sep-11 Nov, closed Mon & Tue except during school holidays, also open 2-8pm Wed, Sat, Sun & holidays Dec–early Jan, last entry 1hr before closing, restaurant & park open till later) is a 'living museum' in which smiths, cartwrights and coopers do their thing in and among 70 centuries-old Alsatian buildings – a veritable village – brought here for preservation (and so storks can build nests on them). Sounds cheesy but many Alsatians really like the place. That towering industrial relic is the **Rodolphe Potassium Mine**, shut in 1976.

BIOSCOPE

The new **Bioscope** (☎ 03 89 62 43 00; www.lebioscope.com, in French & German; same prices as Écomusée, discounts if you visit both; 10am-7pm Jul & Aug, to 6pm May, Jun & Sep, to 5pm Apr & Oct–11 Nov) is an innovative, family-oriented theme park that's supposed to make it fun for kids aged from five to the early teens to learn about the relationship between human beings and the environment through *vulgarisation scientifique* – no, not scientifically turning your children into vulgarians (TV is probably taking care of that already) but rather the 'popularisation of science'. Signs are in French, English and German. Situated 5km by road from the Écomusée.

LORRAINE

Lorraine, between the plains and vines of Champagne and the Massif des Vosges, is fed by the Meurthe, Moselle and Meuse Rivers – hence the names of three of its four *départements* (the fourth is Vosges).

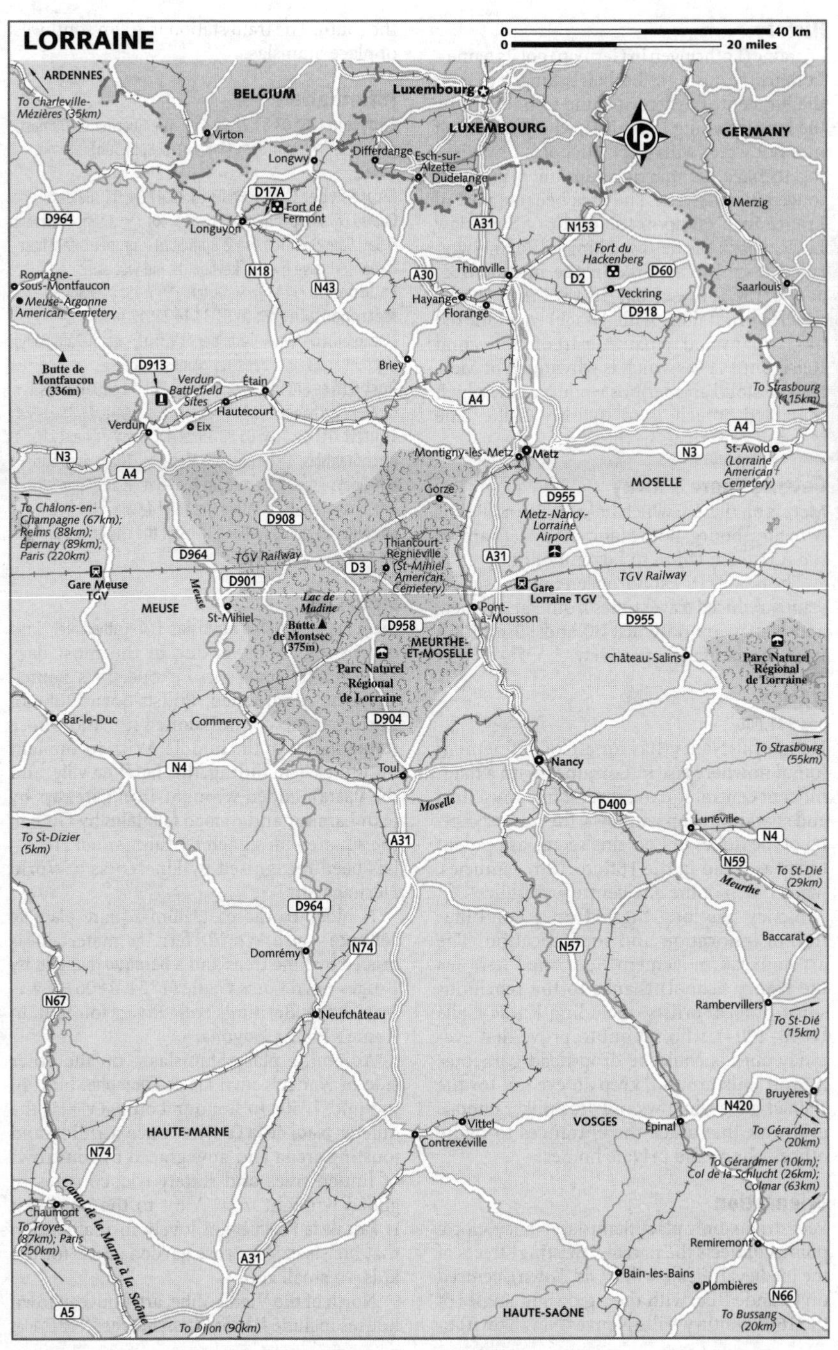

ALSACE & LORRAINE

History

Lorraine (Lothringen in German) got its name – Lotharii regnum, ie Lothair's kingdom – in the 9th century when it came to be ruled by the Frankish king Lothair II, who got himself into hot water with Pope Nicholas I by seeking to have his marriage annulled in order to wed his mistress. The area became part of France in 1766 upon the death of Stanisław Leszczyński, the deposed king of Poland who ruled Lorraine as duke in the middle decades of the 18th century. In 1871 the Moselle *département* (along with Alsace) was annexed by Germany and remained part of the Second Reich until 1918, which is why much of Metz feels so stolid and serious while Nancy, which remained French, is so stylishly Gallic. The two cities are rivals to this day.

Getting There & Away

Metz is on the A4, which links Paris and Reims with Strasbourg. Both Nancy and Metz are on the A31 from Dijon to Luxembourg.

The new TGV Est Européen line has significantly reduced travel times from Paris – Metz and Nancy are now just 80 and 90 minutes from the capital, respectively.

NANCY

pop 331,000

Delightful Nancy has an air of refinement found nowhere else in Lorraine. With a magnificent central square, several fine museums and sparkling shop windows, the former capital of the dukes of Lorraine seems as opulent today as it did in the 16th to 18th centuries, when much of the city centre was built.

Nancy has long thrived on a combination of innovation and sophistication. The art-nouveau movement flourished here (as the Nancy School) thanks to the rebellious spirit of local artists, including Émile Gallé (1846–1904), who set out to prove that everyday objects could be drop-dead gorgeous. As you walk around, keep an eye out for the stained-glass windows and dreamlike, sinuous grillwork that grace the entrances to many offices, shops and private homes.

Orientation

Pedestrians-only place Stanislas, Nancy's focal point, connects the narrow, twisting streets of the medieval Vieille Ville (Old Town), centred on Grande Rue, with the rigid right angles of the 16th-century Ville Neuve (New Town) to the south. The train station is 800m southwest of place Stanislas.

Information

Copycom (☎ 03 83 22 90 41; 3 rue Guerrier de Dumast; per hr €2; 9am-8pm Mon-Sat, 3-8pm Sun) Internet access.

E-café Cyber Café (☎ 03 83 35 47 34; 11 rue des Quatre Églises; per min/hr €0.09/5.40; 11am-9pm Mon & Sat, 9am-9pm Tue-Fri, 2-8pm Sun) A proper café whose computers have qwerty keyboards and webcams.

Laundrette (124 rue St-Dizier; 7.45am-9.30pm)

Métropolitain (☎ 03 83 33 14 71; 12 rue Mazagran; Nancy Gare; per hr €3; noon-2am daily) Internet access in a bar-cum-games arcade.

Post Office (10 rue St-Dizier; Point Central) Does currency exchange.

Tourist Office (☎ 03 83 35 22 41; www.ot-nancy.fr; place Stanislas; 9am-7pm Mon-Sat, 10am-5pm Sun & holidays Apr-Oct, 9am-6pm Mon-Sat, 10am-1pm Sun & holidays Nov-Mar) Inside the *hôtel de ville*. Has free brochures detailing walking tours of the city centre and art-nouveau architecture.

Sights

Neoclassical **place Stanislas** (Cathédrale), laid out in the 1750s, is one of the most dazzling public spaces in Europe. It is named after the enlightened, Polish-born Duke of Lorraine who commissioned it – and whose **statue** stands in the middle. With its opulent buildings (including the **hôtel de ville** and the **Opéra**), gilded wrought-iron **gateways** by Jean Lamour and rococo **fountains** by Guibal, the square – designed by Emmanuel Héré – has been recognised by Unesco as a World Heritage Site.

A block to the east, 90m-square **place de l'Alliance** – also World Heritage material – is graced by lime trees and a **baroque fountain** by Bruges-born Louis Cyfflé (1724–1806); it was inspired by Bernini's *Four Rivers* fountain in Rome's Piazza Navona.

Adjoining place Stanislas – on the other side of Nancy's own **Arc de Triomphe**, built in the mid-1750s to honour Louis XV – is the quieter **place de la Carrière**, once a riding and jousting arena and now graced by four rows of linden trees and stately rococo gates in gilded wrought iron. A bit to the northeast is **Parc de la Pépinière**, a lovely formal garden that boasts cafés, a rose garden and – for the kids – a small zoo.

North of the Vieille Ville, art-nouveau town houses include **Maison Weissenburger** (1 bd Charles

V), built in 1904, and **Maison Huot** (92 quai Claude de Lorrain), constructed a year earlier.

The interior of the domed, 18th-century **cathédrale** (pl Monseigneur Ruch; Cathédrale) is a sombre mixture of neoclassical and baroque. The organ loft and the ironwork, by Jean Lamour and his students, are from the end of the 1750s.

Just south of the train station is a bizarre **bronze sculpture** (av Foch; Nancy Gare), a square column with a pile of – no, it can't be! – on top. Clues about its meaning can be found on the nearby brass plaques.

MUSEUMS

A highlight of any visit to Nancy, the brilliant **Musée de l'École de Nancy** (School of Nancy Museum; ☎ 03 83 40 14 86; 36-38 rue du Sergent Blandan; adult/student & senior €6/4 incl audioguide, students free Wed; 10am-6pm Wed-Sun) brings together a heady collection of furnished rooms and curvaceous glass produced by the turn-of-the-20th-century art-nouveau (Jugendstil) movement. It's housed in a 19th-century villa about 2km southwest of the city centre – to get there take bus 123 to the Nancy Thermal stop or buses 122, 126, 134 or 135 to the Painlevé stop.

Star attractions at the excellent **Musée des Beaux-Arts** (Fine Arts Museum; ☎ 03 83 85 30 72; 3 place Stanislas; adult/student & senior incl audioguide €6/4; 10am-6pm Wed-Mon) include a superb collection of Daum-made art-nouveau glass and a rich and varied selection of paintings from the 14th to 18th centuries. Laminated information sheets are available in each room in French, English and German.

The mostly 16th-century Palais Ducal, the splendid former residence of the dukes of Lorraine, now houses the **Musée Lorrain** (Lorraine Museum; ☎ 03 83 32 18 74; 64 & 66 Grande Rue; adult/student & senior for both sections €5.50/3.50, student admission free Wed; 10am-12.30pm & 2-6pm Wed-Mon). The part dedicated to **fine arts & history** (64 Grande Rue; €4/2.50) possesses rich collections of medieval statuary, engravings and *faïence* (pottery), as well as Judaica from before and after the Revolution; the section dedicated to **regional art & folklore** (66 Grande Rue; €3.50/2) is housed in the 15th-century **Couvent des Cordeliers**, a former Franciscan monastery. Inside, the late-15th-century Gothic **Église des Cordeliers** and the adjacent **Chapelle Ducale** (Ducal Chapel; 1607), modelled on the Medici Chapel in Florence, served as the burial place of the dukes of Lorraine.

MUSEUM PASSES

The discount **Pass Nancy Trois Musées** (€8), valid for three months, gets you into the Musée de l'École de Nancy, the Musée Lorrain and the Musée des Beaux-Arts and is sold at each museum.

The **City Pass Nancy Culture** (€9), available year-round at the tourist office, gets you reduced-price entry to six museums, a guided or MP3 tour of the city, bike rental, a bus and/or tram return trip and a cinema ticket. From May to October, the **City Pass Nancy Loisirs** (€13) bestows a few additional benefits.

Tours

The tourist office offers MP3 tours (€6) of the historic centre (two hours) and the art-nouveau quarters (up to three or four hours).

Sleeping

Hôtel de l'Académie (☎ 03 83 35 52 31; fax 03 83 32 55 78; http://academie-hotel.com; 7bis rue des Michottes; d €32-36, q €49, s/d with shower €25/30) This offbeat, 29-room, one-star place has a tacky fountain that tinkles like a broken urinal, and very simply furnished rooms with acoustic tile ceilings and plastic shower pods. Gallé would have been appalled but it's clean and you can't beat the price.

Hôtel des Portes d'Or (☎ 03 83 35 42 34; www.hotel-lesportesdor.com; 21 rue Stanislas; d €55-65) This two-star hostelry, superbly situated just metres from place Stanislas, has 20 comfortable but uninspiring rooms with upholstered doors. It's often full so call ahead. Breakfast (€6) is mandatory except from December to February. By car, take rue St-Dizier, turn right onto pedestrians-only rue Stanislas and press the intercom button.

Hôtel de Guise (☎ 03 83 32 24 68; www.hoteldeguise.com; 18 rue de Guise; d €64-100;) A grand stone staircase leads to extra-wide hallways and 48 bright, spacious, two-star rooms. The bathrooms are as modern as the 18th-century hardwood floors are charmingly creaky. The building, in the heart of the old city, dates from 1680.

Hôtel des Prélats (☎ 03 83 30 20 20; www.hoteldesprelats.com; 56 place Monseigneur Ruch; Cathédrale; d €104;) In a grand building that's been a hotel since 1906, this three-star place with good wheelchair access, completely renovated in 2005, has 41 rooms with parquet floors, antique-style furnishings and creative tile bathrooms.

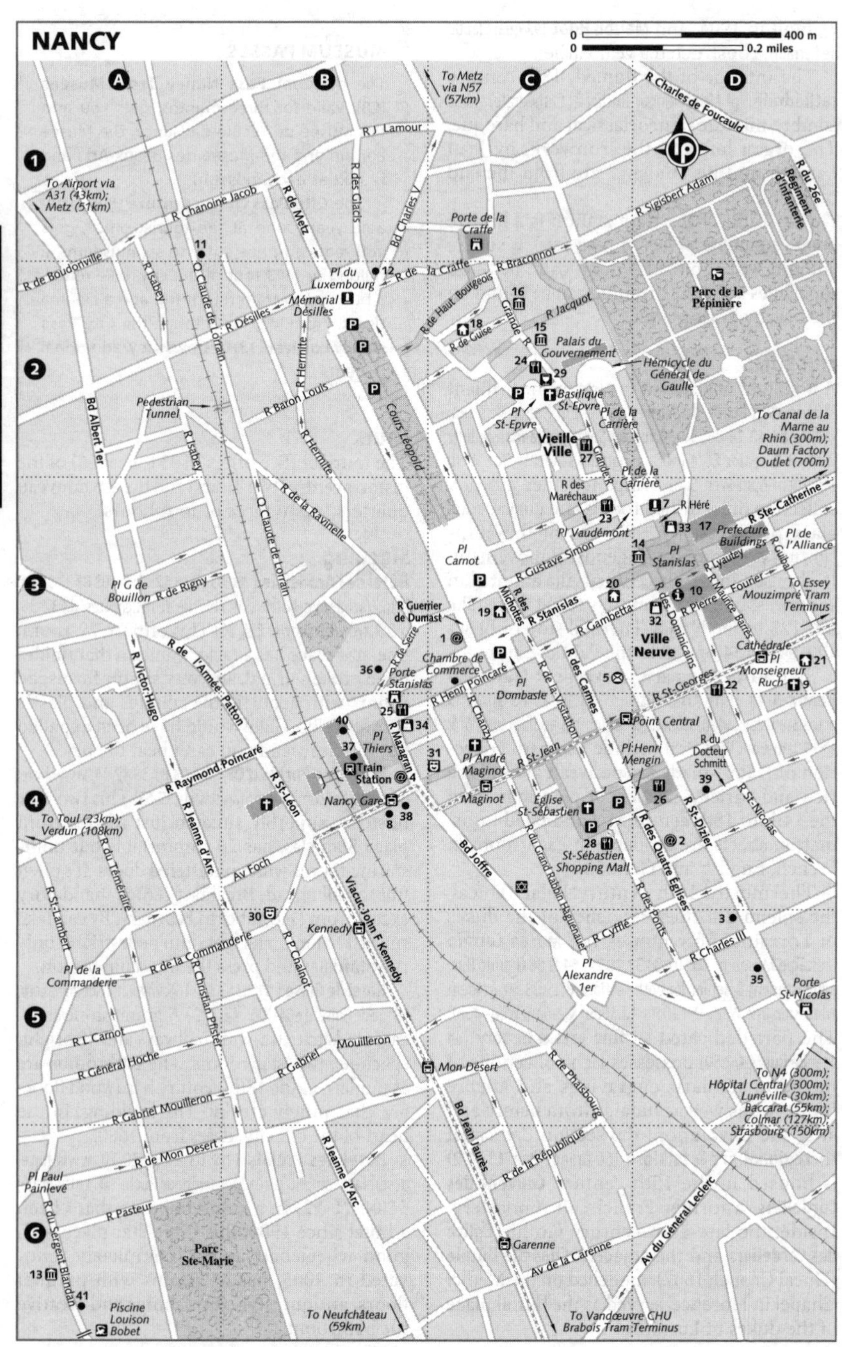
NANCY
0 400 m
0 0.2 miles
To Metz via N57 (57km)
To Airport via A31 (43km); Metz (51km)
R Charles de Foucauld
R J Lamour
R des Glacis
Bd Charles V
R de Metz
R Chanoine Jacob
R Sigisbert Adam
R du 26e Régiment d'Infanterie
Porte de la Craffe
R Braconnot
Parc de la Pépinière
Pl du Luxembourg
R de la Craffe
R de Boudonville
R Isabey
Q Claude de Lorrain
Mémorial Désilles
R Désilles
R de Haut Bourgeois
Grande R
R Jacquot
R de Guise
Palais du Gouvernement
Hémicycle du Général de Gaulle
R Hermite
R Baron Louis
Cours Léopold
Basilique St-Epvre
Pl St-Epvre
Pl de la Carrière
Pedestrian Tunnel
Bd Albert 1er
Vieille Ville
To Canal de la Marne au Rhin (300m); Daum Factory Outlet (700m)
R de la Ravinelle
R des Maréchaux
R Héré
R Ste-Catherine
Pl Vaudémont
Prefecture Buildings
Pl de l'Alliance
Pl Carnot
R Gustave Simon
Pl Stanislas
R Lyautey
R Guibal
Pl G de Bouillon
R de Rigny
R des Michottes
R Stanislas
R Guerrier de Dumast
R Gambetta
R des Dominicains
R Pierre Fourier
R Maurice Barrès
To Essey Mouzimpré Tram Terminus
Ville Neuve
Cathédrale
Pl Monseigneur Ruch
R de Serre
Chambre de Commerce
R de l'Armée Patton
Porte Stanislas
R Henri Poincaré
Pl Dombasle
R des Carmes
R de la Visitation
R St-Georges
R Victor Hugo
R Chanzy
Point Central
R Mazagran
Pl Thiers
R du Docteur Schmitt
R Raymond Poincaré
Pl André Maginot
R St-Jean
Pl Henri Mengin
R St-Léon
Train Station
Maginot
Nancy Gare
Église St-Sébastien
R St-Dizier
R St-Nicolas
To Toul (23km); Verdun (108km)
R Jeanne d'Arc
R du Téméraire
R des Quatre Églises
St-Sébastien Shopping Mall
Av Foch
Bd Joffre
R du Grand Rabbin Haguenauer
R St-Lambert
Viaduc John F Kennedy
R des Ponts
R Cyffle
Kennedy
R P Chalnot
R Charles III
Pl de la Commanderie
R de la Commanderie
R Christian Pfister
Pl Alexandre 1er
Porte St-Nicolas
R L Carnot
Mouilleron
R Général Hoche
R Gabriel
Mon Désert
R de Phalsbourg
To N4 (300m); Hôpital Central (300m); Lunéville (30km); Baccarat (55km); Colmar (127km); Strasbourg (150km)
R Gabriel Mouilleron
R Jeanne d'Arc
Bd Jean Jaurès
R de la République
R de Mon Desert
Pl Paul Painlevé
R Pasteur
R du Sergent Blandan
Av du Général Leclerc
Garenne
Parc Ste-Marie
Av de la Garenne
Piscine Louison Bobet
To Neufchâteau (59km)
To Vandœuvre CHU Brabois Tram Terminus

INFORMATION		
Copycom	1	C3
E-café Cyber Café	2	D4
Laundrette	3	D5
Métropolitain	4	B4
Post Office	5	C3
Tourist Office	6	D3
SIGHTS & ACTIVITIES		
Arc de Triomphe	7	D3
Bronze Sculpture	8	B4
Cathédrale	9	D3
Hôtel de Ville	10	D3
Maison Huot	11	A1
Maison Weissenburger	12	B2
Musée de l'École de Nancy	13	A6
Musée des Beaux-Arts	14	D3
Musée Lorrain (Fine Arts & History Section)	15	C2
Musée Lorrain (Regional Art & Folklore Section)	16	C2
Opéra	17	D3
SLEEPING		
Hôtel de Guise	18	C2
Hôtel de l'Académie	19	C3
Hôtel des Portes d'Or	20	C3
Hôtel des Prélats	21	D3
EATING		
Au Vieux Gourmet	22	D3
Aux Croustillants	23	C3
Aux Délices du Palais	24	C2
Brasserie Excelsior	25	B4
Covered Market	26	D4
Le Gastrolâtre	27	C2
Monoprix Supermarket	28	C4
DRINKING		
Le Ch'timi	29	C2
Le Varadero	(see 27)	
ENTERTAINMENT		
Blue Note Why Not Club	(see 19)	
Caméo Commanderie Cinema	30	B5
Fnac Billetterie	31	C4
SHOPPING		
Baccarat Shops	32	D3
Daum	33	D3
Lefèvre-Lemoine	34	B4
TRANSPORT		
ADA	35	D5
Europcar	36	B3
National-Citer	37	B4
SNCF Office	(see 29)	
STAN Office	38	B4
STAN Office	39	D4
Vélostan	40	B4
Vélostan (Espace Thermal)	41	A6

Eating

No fewer than 20 moderately priced eateries of all sorts – including French, Italian, tapas, fish and seafood, South American, sushi and Indian (including vegetarian) – line rue des Maréchaux, just west of the Arc de Triomphe; lunch *menus* start at €10. North of there, intimate, midrange eateries can be found all along Grande Rue. There are lots of cheapies in the vicinity of the covered market along rue St-Dizier and rue des Quatre Églises.

Aux Délices du Palais (☎ 03 83 30 44 19; 69 Grande Rue; starters €5, mains €9, desserts €4; ⏰ Mon-Fri & dinner Sat) Billing itself as *bistronomique* (whatever that means), this informal place serves whatever the jovial chef's muse inspires him to make – everything from chicken *tajine* (North African–style stew) to beef fajitas to endive tartes. Great value, so it's no surprise it's got an enthusiastic local following.

Brasserie Excelsior (☎ 03 83 35 24 57; 50 rue Henri Poincaré; 🚊 Nancy Gare; after-10pm menu €18.90, other menus €30.50; ⏰ 8am-12.30am Mon-Sat, 8am-11pm Sun, meals served noon-3pm & 7pm–closing time) Built in 1910, this sparkling brasserie's art-nouveau decor makes every glance at the ceiling memorable – and the food's excellent too. The sauerkraut options include *choucroute à trois poissons* (sauerkraut with salmon, haddock and monkfish).

Le Gastrolâtre (Chez Tanésy; ☎ 03 83 35 51 94; 23 Grande Rue; lunch menu €25, other menus €42; ⏰ Tue-Sat) A 16th- and 17th-century town house has been transformed into a homey, intimate bistro specialising in mouth-watering Lorraine- and Provence-inspired cuisine, including fowl.

SELF-CATERING

Aux Croustillants (10 rue des Maréchaux; ⏰ 24hr except from 8pm Sun–5.30am Tue) An almost–24/7 *boulangerie-pâtisserie*.

Au Vieux Gourmet (26 rue St-Georges; 🚊 Cathédrale; ⏰ 9am-8pm Mon-Fri, 9am-7.30pm Sat, 9.30am-12.30pm Sun) A grocery since 1889, this place carries luxury products (Fauchon, Hédiard) as well as staples.

Covered market (place Henri Mengin; 🚊 Point Central; ⏰ 7am-6pm Tue-Thu, 7am-6.30pm Fri & Sat)

Monoprix supermarket (rue des Ponts; ⏰ 8.30am-8.30pm Mon-Sat) Deep inside the St-Sébastien shopping mall.

Drinking

There are several bars along Grande Rue.

Le Ch'timi (☎ 03 83 32 82 76; 17 place St-Epvre; ⏰ 9.30am-2am Mon-Sat, 9.30am-9pm Sun) On three brick-and-stone levels, Le Ch'timi is *the* place to go for beer. Popular with students, this unpretentious bar has 150 brewskies, 16 of them (including Guinness and Kilkenny) on tap.

Le Varadero (☎ 03 83 36 61 98; 27 Grande Rue; ⏰ 6pm-2am Tue-Sat May-Oct, 9pm-2am Tue-Sat Nov-Apr) Named after a beach in Cuba, this trendy but laid-back bar, popular with the 25-to-35 demographic, has live Latin and jazz on the terrace from 7pm to 10pm on Friday and Saturday in the warm season. Year-round there's a DJ from 10pm to 2am on Thursday, Friday and Saturday.

Entertainment

Details on cultural events appear in the free monthly *Spectacles* (www.spectacles-publications.com, in French). Tickets are available at the tourist office and the **Fnac billetterie** (☎ 08 92 68 36 22; www.fnacspectacles.com, in French; 2nd fl, 2 av Foch; 🚊 Nancy Gare; ⏰ 10am-7pm Mon-Sat).

CINEMAS

Caméo Commanderie (☎ 08 92 68 00 29; www.cine-cameo.com, in French; 16 rue de la Commanderie; 🚊 Kennedy) Screens nondubbed films, including some in English.

LIVE MUSIC

Blue Note Why Not Club (☎ 03 83 30 31 18; www.bluenotenancy.com; 3 rue des Michottes; admission free except €10 Fri, Sat & theme nights; 🕒 11pm-4am Wed & Sun, 9pm-4am Thu, 11pm-5am Fri & Sat) This vaulted subterranean discotheque, at the far end of the courtyard, has jazz and blues concerts (€8 to €10) each Thursday (except during school holidays) from 9pm to 11pm or midnight; karaoke on Sunday from 11.30pm to 2am; and, from about 11pm (2am on Sunday), two dance floors, one Latin, the other disco.

Shopping

Nancy's main – and most sparkling – commercial thoroughfares are rue St-Dizier, rue St-Jean and rue St-Georges.

Baccarat shops (☎ 03 83 30 55 11; www.baccarat.fr; cnr rue des Dominicains & rue Gambetta; 🕒 closed Mon morning & Sun) Exquisite crystal of the sort enjoyed by royalty the world over, and jewellery, are on display at these shops, where the simplest wine glass – impossibly delicate – goes for €63.

Daum (☎ 03 83 32 21 65; 14 place Stanislas; 🕒 closed Sun & Mon morning) At this flagship shop, you can admire limited-edition crystal knick-knacks and watch a video showing crystal artisans at work.

Daum factory outlet (☎ 03 83 32 14 55; www.daum.fr; 17 rue des Cristalleries; 🚊 Cristalleries; 🕒 9.30am-12.30pm & 2-6pm Mon-Sat, closed Mon Jul & Aug) About 1km northeast of place Stanislas, this place sells discontinued Daum designs and unsigned seconds.

Bergamotes de Nancy, the local confectionery speciality, are hard candies made with bergamot, a citrus fruit (used to flavour Earl Grey tea) that grows on Mt Etna. Selling Bergamottes (with two *t*'s) is **Lefèvre-Lemoine** (Au Duché de Lorraine; ☎ 03 83 30 13 83; 47 rue Henri Poincaré; 🚊 Nancy Gare; 🕒 8.30am-7pm Mon-Sat, 9.30am-12.30pm Sun), founded in 1840 and last redecorated – with Gilded Age panache – back in 1928. One of its old-fashioned red sweets tins made a cameo appearance in the film *Amélie*.

Getting There & Away

CAR

Rental options:

ADA (☎ 03 83 36 53 09; 138 rue St-Dizier)

Europcar (☎ 03 83 37 57 24; 18 rue de Serre)

National-Citer (☎ 03 83 37 38 59; train station departure hall; 🚊 Nancy Gare)

TRAIN

The **train station** (place Thiers; 🚊 Nancy Gare), spiffed up for the arrival of the TGV Est Européen in 2007, is on the line linking Paris' Gare de l'Est (€50.50 by TGV, 1½ hours, eight to 10 direct daily) with Strasbourg (€20.70, 1½ hours, seven to 12 daily). Other destinations include Baccarat (€5, 45 minutes, eight to 15 daily) and Metz (€5, 37 to 53 minutes, 22 to 48 daily).

Tickets can be purchased at the **SNCF office** (18 place St-Epvre; 🕒 12.30-6pm Mon, 9.30am-1pm & 2-6pm Tue-Fri).

Getting Around

There's free parking along the north and east sides of Parc de la Pépinière (rue Sigisbert Adam and rue du 26e RI) and on some side streets in the working-class neighbourhoods west of the train tracks.

The local public transport company, **STAN** (☎ 03 83 30 08 08; www.reseau-stan.com, in French; office 3 rue du Docteur Schmitt; 🕒 7am-7.30pm Mon-Sat), with offices next to the Nacy Gare tram stop, has its main transfer points at Nancy République and Point Central. One/10 tickets cost €1.20/8.70.

In this section, tram stops 200m or less from sights, hotels etc are mentioned right after the street address and indicated with a tram icon 🚊.

Vélostan (www.velostan.com, in French; per half-day/day/week €3/5/10) is not in Central Asia – it's STAN's bike-rental scheme, with rental sites inside the **train station** (☎ 03 83 32 50 85; 🕒 7.30am-7.30pm Mon-Fri, 9am-6pm weekends & holidays) and, near the Musée de l'École de Nancy, in **Espace Thermal** (☎ 03 83 90 20 96; 43bis rue du Sergent Blandan; 🕒 10am-1pm & 3-6pm Mon-Fri, 9am-6pm Sat).

A **taxi** (☎ 03 83 37 65 37) is just a telephone call away.

BACCARAT

pop 4750

The famous Baccarat *cristallerie* (crystal glassworks), founded in 1764, is 55km southeast of Nancy. The **Musée du Cristal** (Crystal Museum; ☎ 03 83 76 61 37; www.baccarat.fr; 2 rue des Cristalleries; adult/under 10yr €2.50/free; 🕒 9am-noon & 2-6pm), on the grounds of the factory, has 1100 exquisite pieces of lead crystal made by hand over the last two centuries. At the time of writing, the museum was expected to be closed for part of 2009. The **Baccarat boutique** out front is almost as captivating as the museum; nearby **crystal shops** sell lesser, though more affordable brands.

On the other bank of the park-lined River Meurthe, the dark sanctuary of **Église St-Rémy** (⌚ 8am-5pm), built in the mid-1950s to replace a church destroyed by Allied bombing in 1944, is lit by 20,000 Baccarat crystal panels set in brutalist-style concrete walls.

The **tourist office** (☎ 03 83 75 13 37; www.ot-baccarat.fr; 11 rue de la Division Leclerc; ⌚ 9am-noon & 1.30-5.30pm Mon-Fri year-round, 9am-noon & 2-5pm Sat, 10am-noon Sun mid-Jun–mid-Sep), a bit north of the Musée du Cristal, has hiking maps.

Baccarat's train station, a few hundred metres north of the Musée du Cristal, has trains to Nancy (€5, 45 minutes, eight to 15 daily). By car, Baccarat makes an easy stop on the way from Nancy to Colmar via the Vosges' Col du Bonhomme.

METZ

pop 323,000

Present-day capital of the Lorraine *région*, Metz (pronounced 'mess') is a dignified city with stately public squares, shaded riverside parks, and a lively, pedestrians-only commercial centre. Quite a few of the city's most impressive buildings date from the 48-year period when Metz was part of the German Reich.

The Gothic cathedral, with its stunning stained glass, is the most outstanding attraction. The city also has a first-rate museum of antiquities and art and, at the time of writing, it was expected to be home to a branch of Paris' Centre Pompidou from late 2009.

Orientation

The cathedral, on a hill above the River Moselle, is a bit over 1km north of the train station. The city centre's main public squares are place d'Armes, next to the cathedral; place St-Jacques, in the heart of the pedestrianised commercial precinct; place St-Louis; and, 400m to the west of the latter, place de la République.

Information

The tourist office charges a 5.5% commission to change money.

Bar St-Jacques (☎ 03 87 75 08 20; 10 place St-Jacques; per hr €2; ⌚ 7am–midnight or later, from 9am Sun) This road warriors' watering hole has free wi-fi and two internet computers.

Diacom Internet Café (☎ 03 87 63 08 85; 20 rue Gambetta; per hr €3; ⌚ 9am-8pm Mon-Sat, to 8.30pm Jun-Aug, 11.30am-8pm Sun)

Hospital (Notre Dame de Bonsecours CHR; ☎ 03 87 55 34 91/2; 1 place Philippe de Vigneulles; ⌚ 24hr) The emergency room/casualty ward is in Building F.

Laundrettes 11 rue de la Fontaine (⌚ 7am-8pm); 23 rue Taison (⌚ 7am-8pm)

Main Post Office (9 rue Gambetta) Has currency exchange.

Office du Commerce et des Services (☎ 03 87 75 97 13; 9 rue des Clercs; per hr €3; ⌚ 10am-12.30pm & 1.30-7.30pm Tue-Sat) Internet access.

Police (Hôtel de Police; ☎ 03 87 16 17 17; 10 rue Belle Isle; ⌚ 24hr)

Tourist Office (☎ 03 87 55 53 76; http://tourisme.mairie-metz.fr; 2 place d'Armes; ⌚ 9am-7pm Mon-Sat, 10am-3pm Sun, to 5pm Sun Apr-Sep) In a one-time guardroom built in the mid-1700s. Has free walking-tour and cycling maps, free wi-fi and an internet terminal that works with a phonecard.

Tourist Office Annexe (Metz Métropole Découverte; ⌚ 10am-1pm & 2-6pm Mon-Sat except holidays) Inside the train station at the far eastern end. Has free wi-fi.

Sights

CATHÉDRALE ST-ÉTIENNE

Metz' stupendous Gothic **Cathédrale St-Étienne** (place St-Étienne; ⌚ 8am-7pm mid-Apr–Sep, to 6pm Oct–mid-Apr), built between 1220 and 1522, is famed for its veritable curtains of 13th- to 20th-century stained glass, among the finest in France. The superb **Flamboyant Gothic windows** (1504), on the main wall of the north transept arm, provide a remarkable stylistic contrast with the glorious **Renaissance windows** on the main wall of the south transept arm, created a mere two decades later. There are windows by **Chagall** on the western wall of the north transept arm (yellow predominates) and in the nearby section of the ambulatory (over the entrance to the Grande Sacristie; reds and blues set the tone), where you'll also find the **treasury** (adult/student €2/1; ⌚ approx 10am-12.30pm & 2pm–5pm or 6pm, closed Jan). In the 15th-century **crypt** (below the altar; adult/student €2/1; ⌚ approx 10am-12.30pm & 2pm–5pm or 6pm, closed Jan) you can see a 15th-century sculpture of the **Graoully** ('*grau*·lee' or '*grau*·yee'), a dragon that is said to have terrified pre-Christian Metz. Try to visit on a bright day. Beautifully illuminated at night.

MUSÉE LA COUR D'OR

The superb **Musée La Cour d'Or** (☎ 03 87 68 25 00; 2 rue du Haut Poirier; adult/over 65yr/student under 26yr/under 18yr €4.60/3.30/2.30/free; ⌚ 9am-5pm Mon & Wed-Fri, 10am-5pm Sat & Sun) has a first-rate collection

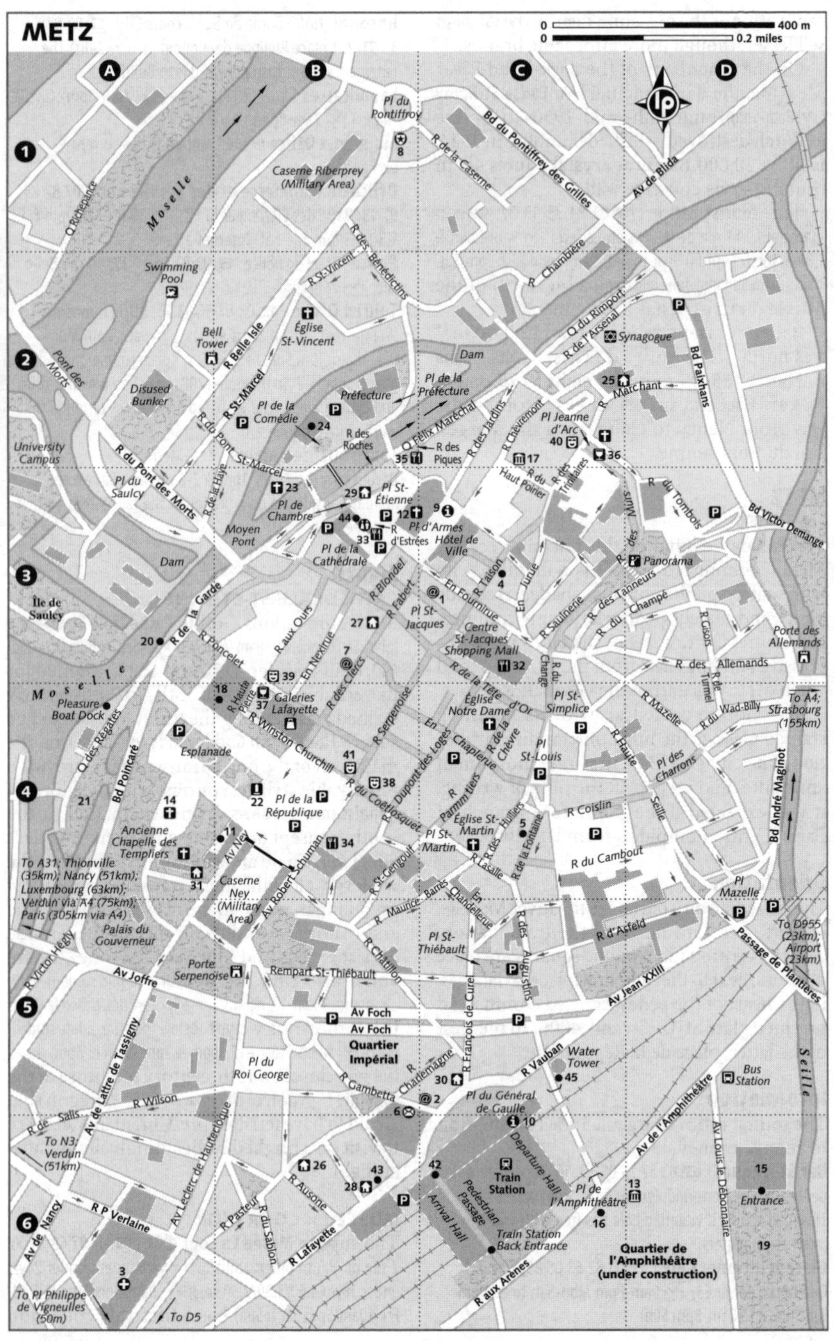
METZ
0 400 m
0 0.2 miles
Pl du Pontiffroy
Caserne Riberprey (Military Area)
Bd du Pontiffrey des Grilles
R de la Caserne
Av de Blida
Moselle
Q Richepance
Swimming Pool
R des Bénédictins
R St-Vincent
Église St-Vincent
R Chambière
Q du Rimport
R de l'Arsenal
Synagogue
Bd Paixhans
Bell Tower
R Belle Isle
Pont des Morts
Disused Bunker
R St-Marcel
Pl de la Comédie
Préfecture
Pl de la Préfecture
Dam
R Marchant
Pl Jeanne d'Arc
R du Pont St-Marcel
R des Roches
Q Félix Maréchal
R des Piques
R des Jardins
R Chèvremont
University Campus
R du Pont des Morts
Pl du Saulcy
R de la Haye
Pl de Chambre
Pl St-Étienne
Pl d'Armes
Hôtel de Ville
R du Haut Poirier
R des Trinitaires
R des Murs
R du Tombois
Bd Victor Demange
Moyen Pont
R d'Estrées
Pl de la Cathédrale
Panorama
Île de Saulcy
R Blondel
R Taison
En Jurue
R des Tanneurs
R du Champé
R Fabert
En Fournirue
Pl St-Jacques
Centre St-Jacques Shopping Mall
R Saulnerie
R de la Garde
R Poncelet
R aux Ours
En Nexirue
R des Clercs
R du Change
R Gisors
Porte des Allemands
R des Allemands
R de Turmel
R de la Tête d'Or
Moselle
Pleasure Boat Dock
R Haute Pierre
Galeries Lafayette
R Winston Churchill
R Serpenoise
Église Notre Dame
Pl St-Simplice
R Mazelle
R du Wad-Billy
To A4; Strasbourg (155km)
Q des Régates
Esplanade
En Chaplerue
R de la Chèvre
Pl St-Louis
R Haute Seille
Pl des Charrons
Bd Poincaré
R du Coëtlosquet
R Dupont des Loges
R Parmentiers
Pl de la République
Bd André Maginot
R Coislin
Ancienne Chapelle des Templiers
Av Ney
Av Robert Schuman
Pl St-Martin
Église St-Martin
R des Huiliers
R de la Fontaine
R Lasalle
R du Cambout
To A31; Thionville (35km); Nancy (51km); Luxembourg (63km); Verdun via A4 (75km); Paris (305km via A4)
Caserne Ney (Military Area)
R St-Gengoult
R Maurice Barrès
En Chandellerue
R des Augustins
R d'Asfeld
Pl Mazelle
Palais du Gouverneur
R Victor-Hegly
R Chatillon
Pl St-Thiébault
To D955 (23km); Airport (23km)
Passage de Plantières
Porte Serpenoise
Rempart St-Thiébault
Av Joffre
Av Jean XXIII
Av Foch
Av Foch
Quartier Impérial
R François de Curel
R Vauban
Water Tower
Seille
Av de Lattre de Tassigny
Pl du Roi George
R Charlemagne
R Gambetta
Bus Station
R Wilson
R de Salis
Pl du Général de Gaulle
Departure Hall
Av de l'Amphithéâtre
Av Louis le Débonnaire
To N3; Verdun (51km)
Av Leclerc de Hauteclocque
Train Station
Pedestrian Passage
Arrival Hall
Pl de l'Amphithéâtre
Entrance
R Ausone
R Pasteur
R du Sablon
R P Verlaine
Av de Nancy
R Lafayette
Train Station Back Entrance
Quartier de l'Amphithéâtre (under construction)
R aux Arènes
To Pl Philippe de Vigneulles (50m)
To D5

INFORMATION
Bar St-Jacques....1 C3
Diacom Internet Café....2 C5
Hospital (Notre Dame de Bonsecours CHR)....3 A6
Laundrette....4 C3
Laundrette....5 C4
Main Post Office....6 B5
Office du Commerce et des Services....7 B3
Police....8 B1
Tourist Office....9 C3
Tourist Office Annexe....10 C6

SIGHTS & ACTIVITIES
Arsenal Cultural Centre....11 B4
Cathédrale St-Étienne....12 B3
Centre Pompidou–Metz (2009)....13 D6
Église St Pierre-aux-Nonains....14 A4
Les Arènes....15 D6
Maison du Project....16 C6
Musée La Cour d'Or....17 C2
Palais de Justice....18 B4
Parc de la Seille....19 D6
Pedal Boat & Rowboat Hire....20 A3
Riverside Park....21 A4
Statue of Marshall Ney....22 B4
Temple Neuf....23 B3
Théâtre....24 B2

SLEEPING
Auberge de Jeunesse Carrefour..25 C2
Cécil Hôtel....26 B6
Grand Hôtel de Metz....27 B3
Hôtel Bristol....28 B6
Hôtel de la Cathédrale....29 B3
Hôtel Métropole....30 C5
La Citadelle....31 A4

EATING
Atac Supermarket....32 C3
Covered Market....33 B3
La Baraka....(see 29)
L'Étude....34 B4
Restaurant Thierry....35 B2

DRINKING
Café Jehanne d'Arc....36 C2
L'Appart....37 B4

ENTERTAINMENT
Arsenal Cultural Centre....(see 11)
Fnac Billetterie....(see 32)
Les Arènes....(see 15)
Le Tiffany....38 B4
L'Endroit....39 B3
Salle des Trinitaires....40 C2
Virgin Megastore....41 B4

TRANSPORT
Avis....42 C6
Budget....43 B6
Europcar....(see 42)
Hertz....(see 42)
Mob Emploi....44 B3
Mob Emploi (Train Station Bureau)....45 C5
National-Citer....(see 42)

of Gallo-Roman antiquities, among them a statue of the Egyptian goddess Isis unearthed right here in Metz; art from the Middle Ages, including objects from around the year 1000 and several rare painted ceilings; paintings from the 15th century onwards, among them some fine works by lesser-known local artists; and objects that trace the history of Metz' ancient Jewish community. A room-by-room brochure in English is available.

CITY CENTRE

On the eastern edge of the city centre, triangular **place St-Louis** – renovated in 2008 – is surrounded by medieval arcades and merchants' houses dating from the 14th to 16th centuries.

Neoclassical **place de la Comédie**, bounded by one of the channels of the Moselle, is home to the city's **Théâtre** (1738–53), the oldest theatre building in France that's still in use. During the Revolution, place de l'Égalité (as it was then known) was the site of a guillotine that lopped the heads off 63 'enemies of the people'. The neo-Romanesque **Temple Neuf** (Protestant Church; only during services), sombre and looming, was constructed under the Germans in 1904.

The formal flowerbeds of the **Esplanade** – and its **statue** of a gallant-looking Marshall Ney, sword dangling at his side (1859) – are flanked by imposing public buildings, including the **Arsenal cultural centre** (1863; see p411) and the sober, neoclassical **Palais de Justice** (late 18th century). **Église St-Pierre-aux-Nonains** (admission free; 1-6pm Tue-Sat & 2-6pm Sun Jul-Sep, 1-6pm Sat & 2-6pm Sun Oct-Jun, closed holidays) was originally built around 380 as part of a Gallo-Roman spa complex (the wall sections with horizontal red-brick stripes are Roman originals). For almost a thousand years – from the 7th to the 16th centuries – the structure served as the abbey church of a Benedictine women's monastery.

West and northwest of the Esplanade, on both sides of bd Poincaré, is a lovely **riverside park** graced with statues, ponds, swans and a fountain. In the warm months, **pedal boats** and **row boats** can be rented on quai des Régates.

QUARTIER IMPÉRIAL

The solid, bourgeois buildings and broad avenues of the **German Imperial Quarter**, including rue Gambetta and av Foch, were constructed in the decades before WWI. Built with the intention of Germanising the city by emphasising Metz' post-1871 status as an integral part of the Second Reich, the area's neo-Romanesque and neo-Renaissance buildings are made of dark-hued sandstone, granite and basalt, rather than the yellow-tan Jaumont limestone characteristic of French-built, neoclassical structures. Because of the area's unique ensemble of Wilhelmian architecture, it is a candidate for Unesco World Heritage status.

The massive, grey-sandstone **train station**, completed in 1908, was designed to detrain 100,000 of the Kaiser's troops and their equipment in just 24 hours, should great power rivalries make this necessary. Built in a style known as Rhenish neo-Romanesque, it is decorated with Teutonic sculptures – some of them quite amusing – whose common theme is German imperial might.

The massive **main post office**, built in 1911 of red Vosges sandstone, is as solid and heavy as the cathedral is light and lacy.

QUARTIER DE L'AMPHITHÉÂTRE

Until recently a wasteland of abandoned hangars and depots, 'the wrong side of the tracks' is undergoing a transformation thanks to Metz' seemingly boundless cultural ambitions (and development budget). The Amphitheatre Quarter – named after a Gallo-Roman amphitheatre – boasts **Les Arènes** (Palais Omnisports), a vast steel-and-glass venue for sports events and concerts (see opposite), and the green riverside lawns of **Parc de la Seille**.

But you ain't seen nothin' yet: at the time of writing, the **Centre Pompidou–Metz** (www.centrepompidou-metz.fr) – a branch of the inside-out original in Paris – was supposed to open its doors to aficionados of modern and contemporary art from the fall of 2009. The design, by Shigeru Ban (Tokyo) and Jean de Gastines (Paris), is like nothing else ever conceived by the human mind. Locals hope the museum, covered by an undulating, translucent membrane of teflon-coated fibreglass designed to trap rainwater for irrigation, will do for Metz what the Guggenheim did for Bilbao. Until the grand opening, you can learn about the project at the **Maison du Projet** (1-8pm May-Sep, 11am-5pm Oct-Apr), next to the construction site.

Tours

The tourist office's audioguides (€7), available in three languages (English, French and German), cover the city centre (1½ hours) and the Quartier Impérial (45 minutes).

Sleeping

Metz' hotels are great value. Except in summer, they're fullest Monday to Thursday.

BUDGET

Auberge de Jeunesse Carrefour (☎ 03 87 75 07 26; ascarrefour@wanadoo.fr; 6 rue Marchant; dm €15.70, s/d incl breakfast €19.15/38.30; 24hr;) A hostel for young working women that also functions as a youth hostel. The rooms, accessible all day long, are spartan; some have a shower and toilet. From the train station, take bus 3 or 11 to the St-Georges stop.

Hôtel Bristol (☎ 03 87 66 74 22; www.hotel-bristol-57.com; 7 rue Lafayette; s/d from €30/35, larger d €44-49) Bring your bell-bottoms – at the Bristol it's still the 1970s, the period authenticity enhanced by fusty furnishings virtually undisturbed since Elvis didn't die. The cheaper rooms can charitably be termed 'compact' but cash-strapped backpackers should do just fine at this family-run, 53-room place.

MIDRANGE

A number of two-star hotels can be found facing the train station and along nearby rue Lafayette.

Hôtel Métropole (☎ 03 87 66 26 22; www.hotelmetropole-metz.com; 5 place du Général de Gaulle; d €52-63;) Built at the tail end of the German period (1912), this two-star place, facing the train station, has 72 spotless, orange-yellow rooms that are so bright and cheery they're almost uplifting. Excellent value.

our pick Hôtel de la Cathédrale (☎ 03 87 75 00 02; www.hotelcathedrale-metz.fr; 25 place de Chambre; d €58-105, ste €110) Ensconced in a gorgeous 17th-century town house, this three-star place positively oozes romance! The 30 large rooms – 10 with spectacular views of the cathedral – are tastefully furnished with antiques and rugs that complement perfectly the ancient wooden beams overhead. The wrought iron is by Jean Lamour (1698–1771), creator of the gilded masterpieces that adorn Nancy's place Stanislas.

Grand Hôtel de Metz (☎ 03 87 36 16 33; www.hotel-metz.com; 3 rue des Clercs; d from €61-95;) At this supercentral, 62-room place you can luxuriate in a giant bathtub looking out on a minisuite (€95) big enough for ballroom dancing (our advice to management: lose the plastic plants), and make your own poached eggs at the buffet breakfast (€7). Standard rooms are comfortable but not luxurious. By car, take rue Fabert from the cathedral, push the button on the intercom and explain you're going to the hotel.

Cécil Hôtel (☎ 03 87 66 66 13; www.cecilhotel-metz.com; 14 rue Pasteur; d/tr €64/69;) Built right after Metz was returned to France (1920), this family-run, two-star hotel, mercifully devoid of pastels, is popular with value-minded business people. The 39 modern rooms have spacious tile bathrooms. If you stay Friday and Saturday, or Saturday and Sunday, the buffet breakfast (€7) is free. Parking available.

TOP END

La Citadelle (☎ 03 87 17 17 17; www.citadelle-metz.com; d €205-265; 5 av Ney;) Opened in 2005 in a one-time military supplies depot built 4½ centuries ago, Metz' only four-star hotel has good wheelchair access, parking and 79 huge, ultramodern rooms – in stark red, white and black – with more than a hint of Japanese sleekness and harmony.

Eating

Place St-Jacques is taken over by cafés in the warmer months. The arcades of place St-Louis are home to a number of moderately priced restaurants. Quite a few small eateries can be found along the streets down the hill from the cathedral, along and near the river.

La Baraka (☎ 03 87 36 33 92; 25 pl de Chambre; 🕑 closed Wed & mid-Jul–mid-Aug) Serves Metz' finest Algerian Berber couscous (€11.50 to €16.50), *tajines* (€12) and *brick* (a fried pastry filled with egg, capers and either chopped meat or tuna; €4).

our pick L'Étude (☎ 03 87 36 35 32; www.l-etude.com, in French; 11 av Robert Schuman; 2-/3-course lunch menus €13/15, other menus €22/27, during concerts €29/35; 🕑 Mon-Sat) Hugely popular with local cognoscenti, this eatery is a quintessentially French mixture of the intellectual (the walls are lined with weighty tomes) and the gastronomic (French, of course) – a coming together of the mind and the stomach, if you will. There's live music (jazz, *chansons*, Cuban, Roma – the website has the schedule) from about 8.30pm on Friday and Saturday, except in July and August; reservations are recommended.

Restaurant Thierry (☎ 03 87 74 01 23; www.restaurant-thierry.fr; 5 rue des Piques; weekday menu €21.50, Fri night & Sat €33.50; 🕑 closed Wed & Sun) Brings culinary insights from the Caribbean Basin, Louisiana and Vietnam together with French gastronomic traditions to create avant-garde cuisine 'without taboos'. The bistro ambience is both chic and relaxed. Often full, so call ahead if possible.

SELF-CATERING

For picnic supplies:

Atac supermarket (near place St-Jacques; 🕑 8.30am-7.30pm Mon-Sat) On the lowest level of the Centre St-Jacques shopping mall.

Covered market (place de la Cathédrale; 🕑 approx 7am-6pm Tue-Sat)

Drinking

Café Jeanne d'Arc (☎ 03 87 37 39 94; place Jeanne d'Arc; 🕑 11.30am-midnight Mon-Wed, 11.30am-2am Thu & Fri, 3pm-3am Sat) This bar bears its long history – the roof beams are from the 1500s, the faint frescos two or three centuries older – with good humour and mellowness. The soundtrack ranges from Dizzie Gillespie to Brel and Gainsbourg to Western classical. There's a refreshing terrace when it's warm.

L'Appart (☎ 03 87 18 59 26; www.l-endroit.com, in French; 2 rue Haute Pierre; 🕑 8pm-2.30am Sun & Tue-Thu, 8pm-3.30am Fri & Sat) The house in which the poet Paul Verlaine – Arthur Rimbaud's lover and, almost, his assassin – was born in 1844 is now a lively, mixed (gay and hetero) bar with a retro 1950s ceiling, backlit bottles and a centuries-old carved wood panelling that's protected by law. There's a DJ on Friday, Saturday and Sunday nights, karaoke on Thursday and a drag show at midnight on Sunday.

Entertainment

Details on cultural events appear in *Spectacles* (www.spectacles-publications.com, in French) and *Ce Mois-Ci à Metz*, both in French, free, monthly and available at the tourist office.

Le Tiffany (☎ 03 87 75 23 32; www.letiffany.net, in French; 24 rue du Coëtlosquet; admission free except Thu/Fri & Sat €5/15; 🕑 11pm-5am Mon & Wed-Sat) The gyrating bodies here – most belonging to people aged 20 to 30 – would have knocked the socks off the medieval people who built the vaulted cellar this classic discotheque has occupied since 1972. The DJs tend towards house. Thursday is student night; Friday is often theme night.

L'Endroit (☎ 03 87 18 59 26; www.l-endroit.com, in French; 20 rue aux Ours; admission €10; 🕑 12.30am-5.30am Fri, Sat & Sun night & holiday eve) A gay disco open to all with industrial style interior design, including a stainless-steel dance floor, and house music on the turntable. Every other Friday or Saturday there's a theme night.

Events tickets are available at the **Fnac billetterie** (☎ 08 92 68 36 22; www.fnacspectacles.com, in French; near place St-Jacques; 🕑 10am-7.30pm Mon-Fri, 9am-7.30pm Sat), on the ground level of the Centre St-Jacques shopping mall; and at **Virgin Megastore** (☎ 08 92 39 28 00; www.ticketnet.fr; 61-63 rue Serpenoise; 🕑 9am-8pm Mon-Sat).

The city's main concert venues are the **Arsenal cultural centre** (☎ 03 87 39 92 00; www.mairie-metz.fr/arsenal; 3 av Ney), **Les Arènes** (www.arenes-de-metz.com, in French; Quartier de L'Ampithéâtre) and the **Salle des Trinitaires** (☎ 03 87 20 03 03; www.lestrinitaires.com, in French; place Jeanne d'Arc).

Getting There & Away

CAR

Avis (☎ 03 87 50 60 30), **Europcar** (☎ 03 87 62 26 12), **Hertz** (☎ 03 87 66 63 33) and **National-Citer** (☎ 03 87

38 09 99) have rental offices in the train station's arrival hall. You can also try **Budget** (☎ 03 87 66 36 31; 5 rue Lafayette).

TRAIN

Metz' **train station** (pl du Général de Gaulle), fixed up to greet the TGV Est Européen in style, is on the line linking Paris' Gare de l'Est (€50.50 to €62.70 by TGV, 80 minutes, four to six daily) with Luxembourg (€12.80, 50 minutes, at least 15 daily). Direct trains also go to Nancy (€5, 37 to 53 minutes, 22 to 48 daily), Strasbourg (€21.50, 1¼ to 1¾ hours, seven to 11 daily) and Verdun (€6, 1½ hours, five daily each weekday, one daily weekends).

Getting Around

BICYCLE

Six-speed city bikes and mountain bikes can be rented from **Mob Emploi** (☎ 03 87 74 50 43; per half-/full day/week €5.50/8/18), a nonprofit place that's *not* affiliated with the mafia ('mob' is short for *mobilité*). Helmets and locks are free; rental options include kids' bikes, child carriers and even a tandem. The deposit is €100 per bike. There are two bureaus:

Rue d'Estrées (🕒 8am-6pm Mon-Fri, 9am-6pm Sat & Sun Apr-Sep or mid-Oct)

Train station (rue Vauban; 🕒 5.45am-8pm Mon-Fri) At the base of the water tower just east of the train station.

PARKING

Free parking can be found near the train station under the trees on av Foch; northeast of the train station along bd André Maginot; and east of Auberge de Jeunesse Carrefour along bd Paixhans.

TAXI

Radio Taxis de Metz (☎ 03 87 56 91 92) is on duty day or night.

FORT DU HACKENBERG

The largest single Maginot Line bastion (see p374) in the Metz area was the 1000-man **Fort du Hackenberg** (☎ 03 82 82 30 08; www.maginot-hackenberg.com; adult/under 16yr €8/4; 🕒 tours begin every 15min 2-3.30pm Sat, Sun & holidays & 3pm Wed Apr–11 Nov, additional tours at 3pm Mon, Tue, Thu & Fri mid-Jun–mid-Sep, 2pm Sat in winter), 30km northeast of Metz near the village of Veckring, whose 10km of galleries were designed to be self-sufficient for three months and, in battle, to fire four tonnes of shells a minute. An electric trolley takes visitors along 4km of underground tunnels – always at 12°C – past a variety of subterranean installations (kitchen, hospital, electric plant etc). Tours last two hours.

Readers have been enthusiastic about the **tours** (www.maginot-line.com) of Fort du Hackenberg, other Maginot Line sites and Verdun led by Jean-Pascal Speck, an avid amateur historian and owner of the charming, three-star, 14-room **Hôtel L'Horizon** (☎ 03 82 88 53 65; www.lhorizon.fr; 5 rte du Crève Coeur; d €98-150; 🕒 closed 2 or 3 weeks around New Year) in Thionville. If he's unavailable, he can put you in touch with other English-speaking guides.

VERDUN

pop 19,300

The horrific events that took place in and around Verdun between February 1916 and August 1917 – *l'enfer de Verdun* (the hell of Verdun; see p37) – have turned the town's name into a byword for wartime slaughter. These days, Verdun is an economically depressed and profoundly provincial backwater – some would say it's a throwback to the more insular France of 50 years ago – though the dispatch of French troops based nearby to missions abroad has made world politics a very local and, for some, personal affair.

History

After the annexation of Lorraine's Moselle *département* and Alsace by Germany in 1871, Verdun became a frontline outpost. Over the next four decades, it was turned into the most important – and most heavily fortified – element in France's eastern defence line.

During WWI Verdun itself was never taken by the Germans, but the evacuated town was almost totally destroyed by artillery bombardments. In the hills to the north and east of Verdun, the brutal combat – carried out with artillery, flame-throwers and poison gas – completely wiped out nine villages. During the last two years of WWI, more than 800,000 soldiers (some 400,000 French and almost as many Germans, along with thousands of the Americans who arrived in 1918) lost their lives in this area.

Orientation

The main commercial street, known as rue St-Paul and rue Mazel, and the Ville Haute (Upper Town) are on the west bank of the River Meuse. The train station is 700m northwest of the cathedral.

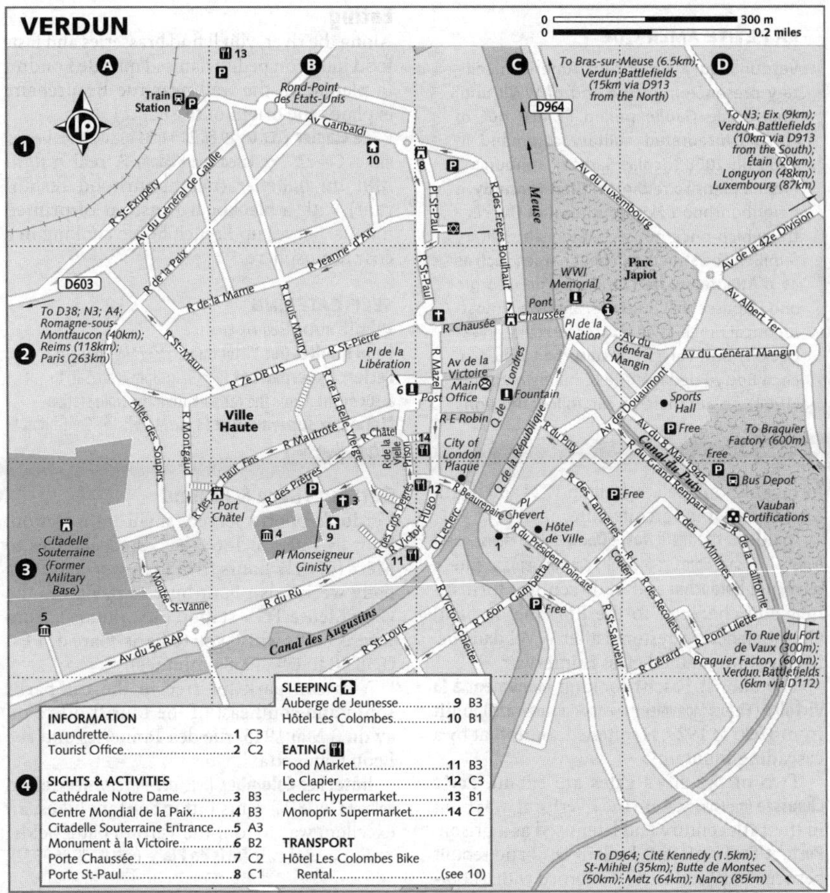

Information

Laundrette (2 place Chevert; 6.30am-9pm)

Tourist Office (☎ 03 29 84 55 55; Pavillon Japiot, av du Général Mangin; 9am-7pm Mon-Sat, 9am-noon & 2-6pm Sun Jul & Aug, 9.30am-12.30pm & 1.30-6pm Mon-Sat, 10am-noon & 2-5pm Sun Sep-Jun) A brand-new tourist office run by the city.

Sights

Verdun's huge **Citadelle Souterraine** (☎ 03 29 86 62 02; tourist entrance on av du 5e RAP; adult/5-15yr €6/2.50; 9am or 10am–noon or 12.30pm & 2pm–btwn 5pm & 7pm, no midday closure Apr-Sep, closed Jan, last tour begins 45min before closing), with its 7km of underground galleries, was designed by Vauban (p65) in the 17th century and completed in 1838. In 1916 it was turned into an impregnable command centre in which 10,000 *poilus* (French WWI soldiers) lived, many waiting to be dispatched to the front. About 10% of the galleries have been converted into an imaginative audiovisual re-enactment of the war, making this an excellent introduction to the WWI history of Verdun. Half-hour tours in battery-powered cars are available in six languages.

The **Centre Mondial de la Paix** (World Centre for Peace; ☎ 03 29 86 55 00; www.cmpaix.fr, in French; place Monseigneur Ginisty; admission free; 9.30am-7pm Jul & Aug, 9.30am-noon & 2-6pm Sep-Jun, closed Christmas-Jan) has a new permanent exhibit that looks at wars, their causes and solutions; human rights; and the fragility of peace. It is housed in Verdun's handsomely classical (and classically handsome)

LA PETITE AMERIQUE

Verdun had a significant American military presence from the end of WWII until Charles de Gaulle pulled France out of NATO's integrated military command in 1966 (in 2008 Nicolas Sarkozy announced French plans to rejoin). In **Cité Kennedy**, a neighbourhood 2km southeast of the centre, which once housed American military families, the streets still bear names such as av d'Atlanta, av de Floride, av de Géorgie and impasse de Louisiane, and the almost-identical ranch-style houses look like an especially dull version of suburban America, circa Betty Friedan's *The Feminine Mystique* (1963). To get there by car, follow the signs to Lycée Freyssinet.

former bishop's palace, built in 1724 and worth a look just for the architecture.

Inside **Cathédrale Notre Dame** (place Monseigneur Ginisty; 8am-6pm Oct-Mar, till 7pm Apr-Sep), a gilded baroque **baldachin** and 18th-century furnishings add character to the Romanesque and Gothic structure, restored after WWI damage. Much of the stained glass is interwar.

The almost Fascist-looking **Monument à la Victoire** (Victory Monument; overlooking rue Mazel), built from 1920 to 1929, is softened somewhat by a cascading fountain.

Two of the city's gates are extant. **Porte Chaussée** (rue Chaussée), on the riverfront, was built in the 14th century and later used as a prison. **Porte St-Paul** (rue St-Paul), built in 1877 and rebuilt between 1919 and 1929, is adorned with a bombastic marble plaque that goes on about the 'victorious peace' that inspired a 'cry of joy'.

Sleeping

Auberge de Jeunesse (03 29 86 28 28; www.fuaj.org; place Monseigneur Ginisty; dm €12.10; reception 8am-12.30pm & 5-11pm Mon-Fri, 8-10am & 5-9pm Sat, Sun & holidays, hostel closed Christmas-Jan;) This modern hostel, situated behind the cathedral, has 77 bunks of generous proportions in rooms for five to 12 people. Rooms are accessible all day long; a kitchenette is available.

Hôtel Les Colombes (03 29 86 05 46; www.hotel-a-verdun.com, in French; 9 av Garibaldi; d/q €35/45; closed Dec) Named to honour the dove of peace, this friendly, family-run hostelry, modest like Verdun itself, has 31 practical, well-lit rooms. Near the train station.

Eating

Along the river, you'll find brasseries and fast-food joints on pedestrianised quai de Londres (a plaque on the wall near rue Beaurepaire explains the origin of the name).

Le Clapier (03 29 86 20 14; 34 rue des Gros Degrés; menus €14-22; closed Sun & Mon) A real *restaurant du quartier* (neighbourhood restaurant) with a blackboard instead of printed menus. Serves up French home cooking in a cosy atmosphere.

SELF-CATERING

Picnic supplies options:

Food market (rue Victor Hugo; 7am-1pm Fri)

Leclerc hypermarket (9am-8pm Mon-Sat, to 8.30pm Fri) Across the car park from the train station.

Monoprix supermarket (3 rue Mazel; 9am-noon & 2-7pm Mon-Sat)

Getting There & Around

Verdun's poorly served, small train station, built by Eiffel in 1868, has direct services to Metz (€7, 1½ hours, five each weekday, one daily weekends). Four buses a day go to the Gare Meuse TGV station (30 minutes), from where TGVs whisk you to Paris' Gare de l'Est (€38.40 to €40.40, 80 minutes).

You can park for free in the car parks south and southeast of the tourist office on av du 8 Mai 1945, rue des Tanneries and rue Léon Gambetta.

Hôtel Les Colombes (left; per 4hr/day/weekend incl helmet €10/18/30) rents out mountain bikes, an excellent way to tour the Verdun battlefields.

For a taxi call **Taxis de Place** (03 29 86 05 22).

VERDUN BATTLEFIELDS

Much of the Battle of Verdun (p37) was fought 5km to 8km (as the crow flies) northeast of Verdun. Today, the area – still a jumble of trenches and artillery craters, now forested – are on and along the D913 and D112; by car follow the signs to 'Douamont', 'Vaux' or the 'Champ de Bataille 14–18'. Signposted paths lead to dozens of minor remnants of the war. Site interiors are closed in January.

Mémorial de Verdun

The village of Fleury, wiped off the face of the earth in the course of being captured and recaptured 16 times, is now the site of the **Mémorial de Verdun** (03 29 84 35 34; adult/11-16yr €7/3.50; 9am-6pm daily, closed noon-2pm 12 Nov-19 Jan & Feb–mid-Mar, totally closed 20 Dec-Jan), a museum –

renovated in 2008 – that tells the story of '300 days, 300,000 dead, 400,000 wounded' with insightful displays, including both war matériel and personal items, in French, English and German. Downstairs is a recreation of the battlefield as it looked on the day the guns finally fell silent. Admission includes a 20-minute film, shown twice an hour.

In the grassy crater-pocked centre of what was once **Fleury**, a few hundred metres down the road from the memorial, signs among the low ruins indicate the village's former layout.

Ossuaire de Douaumont

The sombre, 137m-long **Douaumont Ossuary** (☎ 03 29 84 54 81; www.verdun-douaumont.com; 🕒 closed 24 Dec–mid-Feb), inaugurated in 1932, is one of France's most important WWI memorials. It contains the remains of about 130,000 unidentified French and German soldiers collected from the Verdun battlefields and buried together in 52 mass graves according to where they fell. A ticket to the excellent, 20-minute **audiovisual presentation** (adult/8-12yr €4/3; 🕒 no morning screenings in Dec or 2nd half of Feb) on the battle and its participants, in four languages, also lets you climb the 46m-high **bell tower**, which houses a museum re-outfitted in 2008.

Out front, the **French military cemetery** is flanked by **memorials to Muslim and Jewish soldiers** (to the east and west, respectively) who died fighting for France in WWI. The former, its architecture evocative of a North African mosque, was inaugurated in 2006.

Fort de Douaumont

About 2km northeast of the Douaumont Ossuary, on the highest of the area's hills stands **Fort de Douaumont** (☎ 03 29 84 41 91; adult/8-15yr €3/1.50; 🕒 10am–6pm or 6.30pm Apr-Sep, 10am-5pm Oct-Dec, 10am-1pm & 2-5pm Feb & Mar, last entry 30min before closing), the strongest of the 38 fortresses and bastions built along a 45km front to protect Verdun. When the Battle of Verdun began, 400m-long Douaumont – whose 3km network of cold, dripping galleries was built between 1885 and 1913 – had only a skeleton crew. By the fourth day it had been captured easily, a serious blow to French morale; four months later it was retaken by colonial troops from Morocco. Panoramic views can be had from atop the fort's crater-pocked roof. Signs are in French, English, Dutch and German; information sheets are available in 13 languages.

Charles de Gaulle, then a young captain, was wounded and taken prisoner near here in 1916.

Tranchée des Baïonnettes

On 12 June 1916 two companies of the 137th Infantry Regiment of the French army were sheltered in their *tranchées* (trenches), *baïonnettes* (bayonets) fixed, waiting for a ferocious artillery bombardment to end. It never did – the incoming shells covered their positions with mud and debris, burying them alive. They weren't found until three years later, when someone spotted several hundred bayonet tips sticking out of the ground. The victims were left where they died, their bayonets still poking through the soil. The site is always open. The tree-filled valley across the D913 is known as the **Ravin de la Mort** (Ravine of Death).

AMERICAN MEMORIALS

More than one million American troops participated in the Meuse-Argonne Offensive of late 1918 (http://us.offensives1918-meuse.com), the last Western Front battle of WWI. The bitter fighting northwest of Verdun, in which more than 26,000 Americans died, convinced the Kaiser's government to cable US President Woodrow Wilson with a request for an armistice. The film *Sergeant York* (1941) starring Gary Cooper is based on events that took place here. The website of the Meuse *département*'s tourism board is at www.tourism e-meuse.com.

The largest US military cemetery in Europe, the WWI **Meuse-Argonne American Cemetery**, is at Romagne-sous-Montfaucon, 41km northwest of Verdun along the D38 and D123. Just east of Montfaucon d'Argonne (about 10km southeast of the cemetery), a 58m-high Doric column atop the 336m-high **Butte de Montfaucon** commemorates the Meuse-Argonne Offensive.

About 40km southeast of Verdun, the WWI **St-Mihiel American Cemetery** is on the outskirts of Thiaucourt-Regniéville. From there, a 15km drive to the southwest takes you to the 375m-high **Butte de Montsec**, site of a US monument with a bronze relief map surrounded by a round, neoclassical colonnade.

The WWII **Lorraine American Cemetery** is about 45km east of Metz, just outside of St-Avold.

All these sites are managed by the **American Battle Monuments Commission** (www.abm c.gov).

The Loire Valley

Flowing for over 1000km from its trickling source in the Massif Central west towards the Atlantic Ocean, the regal Loire is often dubbed one of the last *fleuves sauvages* (wild rivers) in France. It's a fickle and unruly body of water that frequently breaks its banks and floods the flat pastureland on either side of the river. For centuries before the Industrial Revolution, this huge waterway was one of France's great commercial highways, but these days most of the river traffic has long since sailed into the sunset, and the freight barges and steamers that once plied the waters have been replaced by occasional canoes and flat-bottomed *futreaux* (barges).

In centuries past, the Loire River was a key strategic area, one step removed from the French capital and poised on the crucial frontier between northern and southern France. Throughout the centuries kings, queens, dukes and nobles established their feudal strongholds and country seats along the Loire, and the valley is littered with some of the most extravagant architecture this side of Versailles. From sky-topping turrets and glittering banquet halls to slate-crowned cupolas, lavish chapels and crenellated towers, the hundreds of châteaux dotted around the Loire Valley provide a comprehensive cross-section of the changing architectural tastes over 1000 years of French high society. The result is an astonishingly rich collection of architectural treasures, ranging from the medieval fortresses of Chinon, Angers and Loches through to the extravagant pleasure palaces of Azay-le-Rideau, Chenonceau and Chambord. If it's aristocratic pomp and architectural splendour you're looking for, the Loire Valley is a place to linger.

HIGHLIGHTS

- Join the Joan of Arc trail in the historic city of **Orléans** (p418)
- Explore the cloisters and chapels of the Loire Valley's greatest ecclesiastical complex, **Abbaye Royale de Fontevraud** (p447)
- Climb up the fabulous double-helix staircase to the turret-covered rooftop of **Chambord** (p429), the Loire Valley's most over-the-top château
- Visit the retirement home of the original Renaissance Man, Leonardo da Vinci, at **Clos Lucé** (p439)
- Admire the fabulous kitchen gardens and floral displays of **Villandry** (p440)
- Wander around the hobbit houses and mushroom museums of the **Troglodyte Valley** (p448)

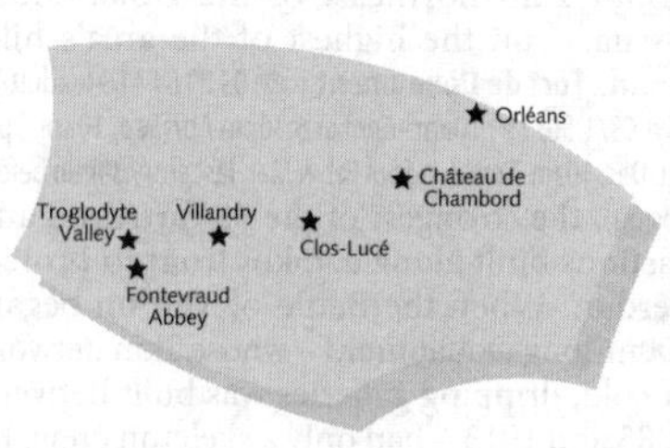

- POPULATION: 2,589,000
- AREA: 33,646 SQ KM

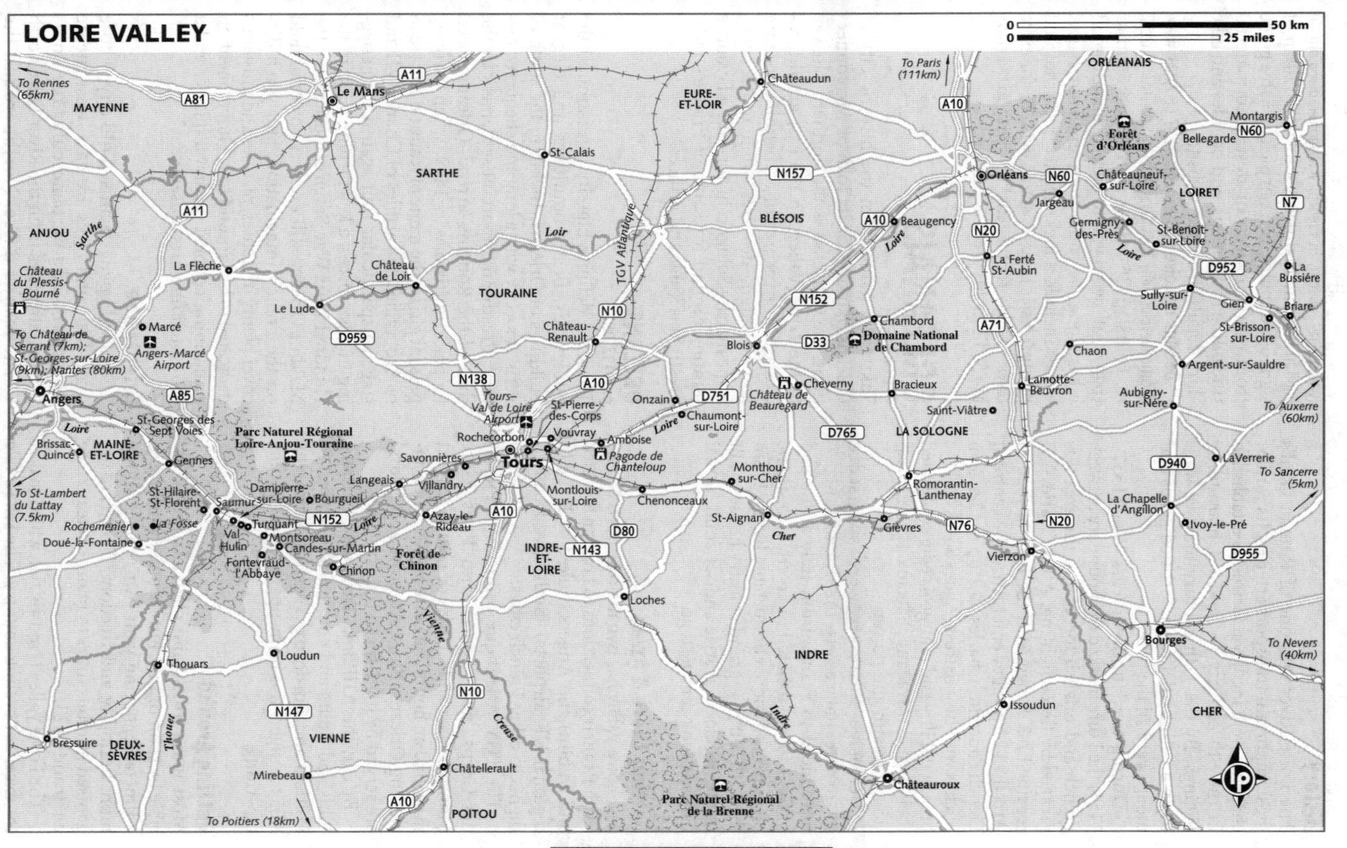

THE LOIRE VALLEY

History

The Loire River was one of Roman Gaul's most important transport arteries. Its earliest châteaux were medieval fortresses established in the 9th century to fend off marauding Vikings. By the 11th century massive walls topped with battlements, fortified keeps and moats were all the rage.

During the Hundred Years War (1337–1453) the Loire marked the boundary between French and English forces and the area was ravaged by fierce fighting. After Charles VII regained his crown with the help of Joan of Arc, the Loire Valley emerged as the centre of French court life. Charles took up residence in Loches with his mistress, Agnes Sorèl, and the French nobility and bourgeois elite established their own extravagant châteaux as an expression of wealth and power.

Defensive fortresses were superseded by ornate palaces as the Renaissance – introduced to France from Italy at the end of the 1400s – ushered in an era of aesthetic pleasure and more comfortable living. From the 17th century, grand country houses built in the neoclassical style and set amid formal gardens took centre stage.

Getting There & Away

The Loire Valley has two main airports: Tours (with Ryanair connections to London Stansted and Dublin) and Angers (linked by Flybe to regional UK airports). Both have frequent flights to other French cities.

The TGV Atlantique connects St-Pierre-des-Corps, near Tours, with Paris' Gare Montparnasse and Charles de Gaulle Airport in around an hour. The Loire's other cities (including Orléans, Blois, Amboise and Tours) are served by high-speed trains to Paris.

By car, the A10 links Paris with Orléans, Blois and Tours and continues southwest to Poitiers and Bordeaux. West of Tours, the A85 to Angers was being upgraded at the time of writing.

Getting Around

Most main towns and châteaux are accessible by train or bus, but if you're working to a timetable, having your own wheels allows more flexibility and freedom. There are organised minibus tours to many châteaux, see p430 and p423.

The Loire Valley is mostly flat, which makes for excellent cycling country. The **Loire à Vélo** (www.loire-a-velo.fr, in French, www.loireradweg.org, in English) scheme maintains a total of 120km of signposted routes: you can pick up a free guide from tourist offices, or download material (including route maps, audioguides and bike-hire details) from the website.

Détours de Loire (☎ in Tours 02 47 66 22 23; www.locationdevelos.com) has three bike-rental shops, in Tours (p436), Blois (p429) and Saumur (p447), allowing you to pick up and drop off bikes along the route for a small surcharge. Prices include a lock, helmet, repair kit and pump; classic bikes cost €14, with €7 for extra days; weekly rentals cost €57 with extra days at €5. Tandems are €38 per day.

ORLÉANAIS

Taking its name from the historic city of Orléans, famous for its Joan of Arc connections, the Orléanais is the northern gateway to the Loire Valley. In the east are the ecclesiastical treasures of St-Benoît-sur-Loire and Germigny-des-Prés, while to the south is the marshy Sologne, historically a favourite hunting ground for some of France's most prestigious kings and princes.

ORLÉANS

pop 113,000

There's a definite big-city buzz around the boulevards, flashy boutiques and elegant buildings of Orléans, 100km to the south of Paris. It's a city with a long and chequered history: already an important settlement by the time of the Romans' arrival, Orléans sealed its place in history in 1429, when a young peasant girl by the name of Jeanne d'Arc (Joan of Arc) rallied the armies of Charles VII and staged a spectacular rout against the besieging English forces, a key turning point in the Hundred Years War. Seven centuries later, the Maid of Orléans still exerts a powerful hold on the French imagination, and you'll discover plenty of statues, plaques and museums dedicated to her around town, not to mention a charming cobbled medieval quarter and a top-notch fine-arts museum.

Orientation

The mostly pedestrianised old city, whose main thoroughfares are east–west rue de Bourgogne and perpendicular rue Louis Rouget, stretches from the River Loire north to rue Jeanne d'Arc. North, around the

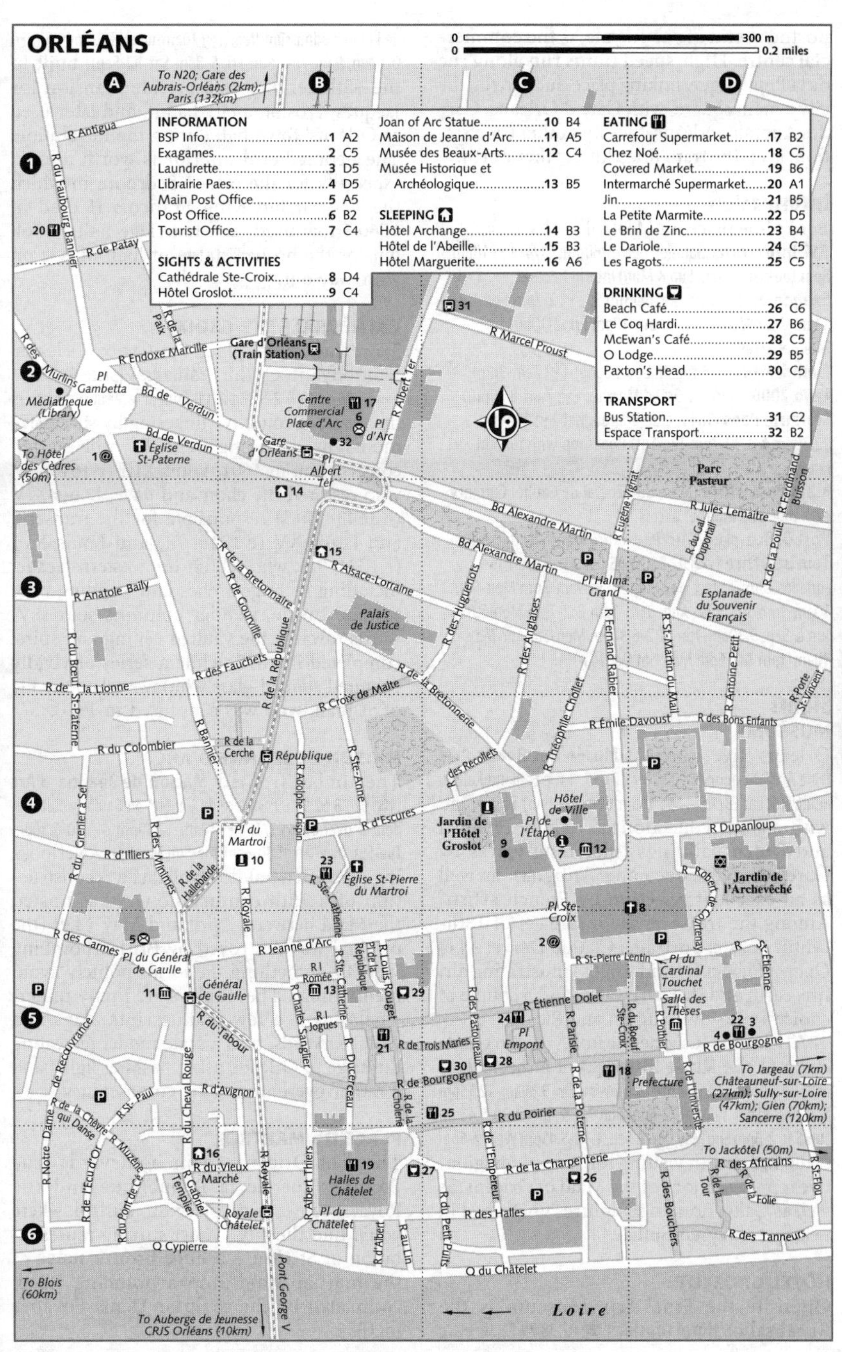
ORLÉANS
0 300 m
0 0.2 miles
A
B
C
D
1
2
3
4
5
6
To N20; Gare des Aubrais-Orléans (2km); Paris (132km)
INFORMATION
BSP Info 1 A2
Exagames 2 C5
Laundrette 3 D5
Librairie Paes 4 D5
Main Post Office 5 A5
Post Office 6 B2
Tourist Office 7 C4
SIGHTS & ACTIVITIES
Cathédrale Ste-Croix 8 D4
Hôtel Groslot 9 C4
Joan of Arc Statue 10 B4
Maison de Jeanne d'Arc 11 A5
Musée des Beaux-Arts 12 C4
Musée Historique et Archéologique 13 B5
SLEEPING
Hôtel Archange 14 B3
Hôtel de l'Abeille 15 B3
Hôtel Marguerite 16 A6
EATING
Carrefour Supermarket 17 B2
Chez Noé 18 C5
Covered Market 19 B6
Intermarché Supermarket 20 A1
Jin 21 B5
La Petite Marmite 22 D5
Le Brin de Zinc 23 B4
Le Dariole 24 C5
Les Fagots 25 C5
DRINKING
Beach Café 26 C6
Le Coq Hardi 27 B6
McEwan's Café 28 C5
O Lodge 29 B5
Paxton's Head 30 C5
TRANSPORT
Bus Station 31 C2
Espace Transport 32 B2
R Antigua
R du Faubourg Bannier
R de Patay
R de la Paix
R des Murlins
Pl Gambetta
Médiathèque (Library)
To Hôtel des Cèdres (50m)
R Endoxe Marcille
Bd de Verdun
Église St-Paterne
Gare d'Orléans (Train Station)
Centre Commercial Place d'Arc
Pl d'Arc
Gare d'Orléans
Pl Albert Ier
R Albert Ier
R Marcel Proust
Parc Pasteur
Bd Alexandre Martin
R Jules Lemaitre
R Ferdinand Buisson
R Eugène Vignat
R du Gal Duportail
R de la Poule
Pl Halmagrand
Esplanade du Souvenir Français
R Anatole Baily
R de la Bretonnaire
R de Gourville
R Alsace-Lorraine
Palais de Justice
R des Huguenots
R des Anglaises
R Fernand Rabier
R St-Martin du Mail
R Antoine Petit
R Porte St-Vincent
R du Boeuf St-Paterne
R des Fauchets
R de la République
R de la Lionne
R Croix de Malte
R de la Bretonnerie
R Théophile Chollet
R Émile Davoust
R des Bons Enfants
R du Colombier
R Bannier
R de la Cerche
République
R Adolphe Crispin
R Ste-Anne
R des Recollets
R d'Escures
Jardin de l'Hôtel Groslot
Hôtel de Ville
Pl de l'Étape
R Dupanloup
R du Grenier à Sel
R des Minimes
Pl du Martroi
R d'Illiers
R de la Hallebarde
R Royale
Église St-Pierre du Martroi
R Ste-Catherine
R Robert de Courtenay
Jardin de l'Archevêché
Pl Ste-Croix
R des Carmes
Pl du Général de Gaulle
R Jeanne d'Arc
R Louis Rouget
R St-Pierre Lentin
Pl du Cardinal Touchet
R St-Étienne
Général de Gaulle
R l Romée
R Charles Sanglier
R l Jogues
R Étienne Dolet
Salle des Thèses
R du Tabour
R Pothier
R du Boeuf Ste-Croix
R de Notre Dame de Recouvrance
R de Trois Maries
Pl Empont
R des Pastoureaux
R de Bourgogne
R Parisie
Prefecture
R de l'Université
To Jargeau (7km) Châteauneuf-sur-Loire (27km); Sully-sur-Loire (47km); Gien (70km); Sancerre (120km)
R d'Avignon
R St-Paul
R de la Chèvre qui Danse
R du Cheval Rouge
R Ducerceau
R de la Cholerie
R du Poirier
R de la Poterne
R Muzène
R de l'Écu d'Or
R du Vieux Marché
R Gabriel Templier
Halles de Châtelet
R Albert Thiers
R de l'Empereur
R de la Charpenterie
To Jackôtel (50m)
R des Africains
R de la Tour
R de la Folie
R St-Flou
R du Pont de Cé
Royale Châtelet
Pl du Châtelet
R d'Albert
R au Lin
R du Petit Puits
R des Halles
R des Bouchers
R des Tanneurs
Q Cypierre
Q du Châtelet
To Blois (60km)
Pont George V
Loire
To Auberge de Jeunesse CRJS Orléans (10km)

northern end of rue Royale, is the commercial centre. High-speed trams run along rue de la République, linking place du Martroi, the city's main square, with Gare d'Orléans. Gare des Aubrais-Orléans, the city's other train station, is on the tram line 2km further north.

Information

Banks line place du Martroi.

BSP Info (125 rue Bannier; per 15/60min €1/4; 10am-8pm Tue-Sat, 2-8pm Sun & Mon) Internet access.

Exagames (5 rue Parisie; per hr €5; 2-7pm Sun-Tue, 11am-7pm Wed & Thu, 11am-10pm Fri, 2-10pm Sat) Internet access.

Laundrettes (176 rue de Bourgogne; 7am-9pm)

Lavo 2000 (place du Grand Marché; 7am-8.30pm)

Librairie Paes (184 rue de Bourgogne; 10am-12.30pm & 1.30-7pm Tue-Sat) Bookshop with foreign-language titles.

Main Post Office (place du Général de Gaulle) Currency exchange and internet access.

Post Office (place d'Arc) Post-office branch by the station.

Tourist Office (02 38 24 05 05; www.tourisme-orleans.com; 2 place de l'Étape; 9am-7pm Mon-Sat, 10am-1pm Sun Jul & Aug, 9am-1pm & 2-7pm Mon-Sat Jun & Sep, 9.30am-1pm & 2-6.30pm Mon-Sat Apr-May, 10am-1pm & 2-6pm Mon-Sat Oct-Mar)

Sights

MUSEUMS

Orléans' five-storeyed **Musée des Beaux-Arts** (Fine Arts Museum; 02 38 79 21 55; 1 rue Fernand Rabier; adult/student €3/1.50; 10am-6pm Tue-Sun) is a treat, with a huge collection of Italian, Flemish and Dutch paintings (including works by Coreggio, Velázquez and Antigna), as well as an excellent selection by French artists. Among the treasures are a rare set of 18th-century pastel portraits, Claude Dervet's *Les Quatre Éléments* (mid-1600s) illustrating air, fire, earth and (frozen) water, and a couple of choice works by Gauguin and Picasso.

A ticket to Musée des Beaux-Arts also grants entry to the **Musée Historique et Archéologique** (02 38 79 25 60; sq Abbé Desnoyers; 9.30am-12.15pm & 1.30-5.45pm Tue-Sat, 2-6pm Sun Jul & Aug, 1.30-5.45pm Tue-Sat, 2-6pm Sun May, Jun & Sep, 1.30-5.45pm Wed, 2-6pm Sun Oct-Apr), worth visiting for several imaginative representations of the Maid of Orléans, as well as Gallo-Roman sculptures unearthed in nearby Neuvy-en-Sullias.

HÔTEL GROSLOT

Opposite the Fine Arts Museum is the Renaissance **Hôtel Groslot** (02 38 79 22 30; place de l'Étape; admission free; 10am-noon & 2-6pm Sun-Fri Oct-Jun, 9am-7pm Sun-Fri, 5-8pm Sat Jul-Sep), built in the 15th century as a private mansion for Jacques Groslot, a city bailiff, and later used as Orléans' town hall during the Revolution. The neomedieval interior is worth a look, especially for the ornate bedroom in which the 17-year-old King François II died in 1560 (now used as a marriage hall). Look out for the bronze statue of Joan of Arc on your way out.

CATHÉDRALE STE-CROIX

Towering above place Ste-Croix, Orléans' Flamboyant Gothic **cathedral** (place Ste-Croix; 10am-noon & 2-5.30pm, till 6pm or later in summer) is the result of collective tinkering by successive monarchs, including Henri IV, who started construction in 1601, Louis XIII (r 1610–43) who restored the choir and nave, Louis XIV (r 1643–1715) responsible for the transept, and Louis XV (r 1715–74) and Louis XVI (r 1774–92), who rebuilt the western facade, including its huge arches and wedding-cake towers. Inside, slender columns soar skywards towards the vaulted ceiling and spire, completed in 1895, while a series of vividly coloured stained-glass windows relate the life of St Joan, who was canonised in 1920.

MAISON DE JEANNE D'ARC

The timber-fronted **Maison de Jeanne d'Arc** (02 38 52 99 89; 3 place du Général de Gaulle; adult/student & over 65yr €2/1; 10am-12.30pm & 1.30-6.30pm Tue-Sun May-Oct, 1.30-6pm Tue-Sun Nov-Apr), overlooking place Général de Gaulle, is a reconstruction of a 15th-century house that hosted the Maid between April and May 1429 (the original was destroyed by British bombing in 1940, something the locals politely avoid mentioning). The displays are pretty underwhelming – a few manuscripts, flags and vintage swords, plus a scale model recreating the siege of Orléans using flashing lights and a rather overenthusiastic commentary.

PLACE DU MARTROI

Three of Orleáns' main boulevards (rue Bannier, rue de la République and rue Royale) converge on place du Martroi, where you'll find the city's most stirring representation of St Joan – a huge bronze **statue** of the martial Maid atop a prancing steed, completed by the sculptor Denis Foyatier in 1855.

Activities

WALKING TOURS

In July and August the tourist office runs guided tours (generally in French, but sometimes with an English commentary) of the old city and Orléans' monuments, buildings and historical sites. There are occasional tours during the rest of the year, as well as walking tours combined with a riverboat cruise and picnic lunch (€19 to €52) – contact the office to see what's on offer.

Festivals & Events

Since 1430 the Orléanais have celebrated the annual **Fêtes de Jeanne d'Arc** in early May, commemorating the liberation of the city from the occupying English. A week of street parties, medieval costume parades and concerts ends with a solemn morning Mass at the cathedral on 8 May.

Sleeping

Auberge de Jeunesse CRJS Orléans (☎ 02 38 53 60 06; auberge.crjs45@wanadoo.fr; 7 av de Beaumarchais; dm with member's card under 26yr €10.70, over 26yr €15.25; ⏲ reception 8am-7pm) A bare-bones municipal hostel at the Stade Omnisports (sports stadium) 10km south of Orleans. Sixty beds spread out over 16 spartan modern rooms (expect cardboard mattresses, standard-issue furnishings and one bathroom between two rooms). Perks include a restaurant and DVD room with video projector. Reception is often closed on weekends, so phone ahead. Jump off the tram or Bus 20 at Université L'Indien.

Jackôtel (☎ 02 38 54 48 48; www.jackotel.com; 18 Cloître St-Aignan; d €40-70) Cute little two-star place tucked in a former cloister shaded with chestnut trees. Beams, bricks and slate are dotted around the old house, with floral patterns and catalogue furniture in the rooms; a few are jazzed up with skylights and original fireplaces, and it's whisper-quiet.

Hôtel Archange (☎ 02 38 54 42 42; www.hotelarchange.com; 1 bd de Verdun; s €39-43, d €47-53.50) Gilded mirrors, cherub murals and sofas shaped like giant hands greet you at this peculiar station hotel. Indian-style wallpapers and citrus colour schemes spice up some rooms, but most err towards standard beiges and off-whites, with en-suite bathrooms and shuttered windows throughout. Tram noise might be a problem for late sleepers.

Hôtel Marguerite (☎ 02 38 53 74 32; www.hotel-orleans.fr; 14 place du Vieux Marché, s €52-63, d €61-72, tr €66-77) Solid, basic and worth recommending for its central spot and wallet-friendly prices. Expect floral-print bedrooms and neutral colours in a town house atmosphere – opt for a superior room if you like your bathroom sparkling and your shower powerful.

Hôtel de l'Abeille (☎ 02 38 53 54 87; www.hoteldelabeille.com; 64 rue Alsace-Lorraine; s €42-51, d €45-89) Bees buzz, floorboards creak and vintage Orléans posters adorn the walls at this gorgeous turn-of-the-century pile off rue de la République. It's deliciously old-fashioned, from the scuffed pine floors and wildly floral wallpapers to the hefty dressers and bee-print curtains, and for breakfast there's a choice of coffees, teas, pâtisseries and exotic jams.

Hotel des Cèdres (☎ 02 38 62 22 92; www.hoteldescedres.com; 17 rue du Maréchal Foch; s €59, d €66-78; ⊠) Modern, efficient and cosy, in a red-brick building in downtown Orléans. The rooms are short on character, decked out in peach-and-creams, pine desks and generic bathrooms, but travellers *en famille* will appreciate the interconnecting rooms. Free wi-fi and eco-friendly bath goodies are a bonus.

Eating

Le Brin de Zinc (☎ 02 38 53 38 77; 62 Rue St-Catherine; mains €9-18) Battered signs, old telephones and even a vintage scooter decorate this old-world bistro, serving up lashings of mussels and oysters at lunchtime and platters of rich bistro food till late. The daily blackboard *plat du jour* at €7.60 is about the best value in the city.

Chez Noé (☎ 02 38 53 44 09; 195 rue de Bourgogne; lunch menus €11, €13.50 & €50, dinner menus €15.80, €21 & €32; ⏲ closed Sat lunch, Sun & Mon) Characterful, cheery and crammed at lunchtime, this lively brasserie is about uncomplicated food at a decent price, from garlic snails to chilli con carne and salmon steak.

Les Fagots (☎ 02 38 62 22 79; 32 rue du Poirier; mains €11.50-16.50) Covered with ancient pots and antique bric-a-brac, this charming place feels like a cross between a junk shop and a country kitchen, specialising in granny's traditional recipes – *brochette de lotte* (monkfish kebabs), *andouillette artisanale* (tripe sausage), and even *pavé d'ane* (donkey steak) for the seriously heartless.

Jin (☎ 02 38 53 80 95; 13 rue Louis Roguet; mains €12.50-18) Zingy Japanese restaurant serving authentic sushi, *yakitori* and *maki* in a metro setting, all puce-and-mauve bucket seats, scarlet lanterns and shiny chrome.

Le Dariole (☎ 02 38 77 26 67; 25 rue Étienne Dolet; menus €16.50-21; ⌚ lunch Mon-Fri, dinner Fri, salon de thé 2.30-7pm Mon-Sat) This rustic *salon de thé* (tea house) is a fine place for afternoon tea, with loads of types from rare Jasmine to Georgian and Chinese Dragon, as well as home-made cakes, pâtisseries and *fine tarte aux pommes* (apple tart). After nightfall it transforms into a smart restaurant specialising in regional food.

La Petite Marmite (☎ 02 38 54 23 83; 178 rue de Bourgogne; menus €20-34; ⌚ closed Tue & Wed) Sheltering behind awnings and clipped conifers, this hugger-mugger restaurant is a riot of wonky beams, terracotta tiles and low ceilings: the perfect place to tuck into portions of provincial French food, from rabbit stew to wild Sologne mushrooms and stonking pork steaks.

SELF-CATERING

Places for picnic supplies:

Carrefour supermarket (Centre Commercial Place d'Arc; ⌚ 8.30am-9pm Mon-Sat)

Covered market (place du Châtelet; ⌚ 7.30am-7.30pm Tue-Sat, 8am-1pm Sun) Inside the Halles de Châtelet shopping centre.

Intermarché supermarket (49 rue du Faubourg Bannier; ⌚ 8.45am-7.30pm Mon-Sat, 9am-12.30pm Sun)

THE LOIRE VALLEY

Drinking & Entertainment

The free **Orléans Poche** (www.orleanspoche.com, in French) details cultural hot spots and happenings in Orléans. Rue de Bourgogne and rue du Poirier are chock-a-block with drinking holes.

O Lodge (☎ 02 38 77 70 15; place de la République; ⌚ lunch & dinner daily) Bar, diner and gig spot at the same time; local bands and DJs provide the tunes while you tuck into steak sandwiches, burgers, cocktails and cold beers.

Le Coq Hardi (☎ 02 38 53 04 35; 12 place du Chatelet; ⌚ all day till midnight daily) This old neighbourhood bar has been pulling *demi-bières* (half-beers) for donkey's years, and it's a gorgeously Gallic place to sink a few brews, surrounded by old signs and scruffy seats.

McEwan's Café (☎ 02 38 54 65 70; 254 rue de Bourgogne; ⌚ 4pm-3am Mon-Sat) A Scottish-themed bar favoured by beer and whisky drinkers, as well as barflies watching sports on the big screen.

Paxton's Head (☎ 02 38 81 23 29; 264-266 rue de Bourgogne; ⌚ 3pm-3am Tue-Sat) Traditional Brit-style boozer with a murky cellar-bar that hosts jazz combos and bands on weekends.

Beach Café (☎ 02 38 81 04 55; 45 rue de la Charpenterie; ⌚ 5pm-3am) A lively student hang-out with cocktails and beers on the blackboard and a surfy vibe, just the ticket on warm summer nights.

Getting There & Away

BUS

The catch-all municipal transport service **Ulys** (www.ulys-loiret.com) brings together information for local bus companies serving the Orléanais area. There's a flat-rate €2 tariff for journeys. Bus 7, run by **Les Rapides du Val de Loire** (www.rvl-info.com), travels to Jargeau (40 minutes) and Sully-sur-Loire (1¾ hours, three daily Monday to Friday). Bus 3 travels to Châteauneuf-sur-Loire (40 minutes, four to six daily, two on Sunday). Tickets can be bought on board or from Orléans' **bus station** (☎ 02 38 53 94 75; 2 rue Marcel Proust).

TRAIN

The city's two stations, Gare d'Orléans and Gare des Aubrais-Orléans (the latter is 2km to the north), are linked by tram and frequent shuttle trains. Most Loire Valley destinations stop at both stations, but trains to/from Paris' Gare d'Austerlitz (€17.10, one hour 10 minutes, hourly) use Gare des Aubrais-Orléans. Orléans has frequent services to Blois (€9.40, 40 minutes) and Tours (€16.80, one to 1½ hours).

Getting Around

BUS & TRAM

Orléans buses and trams are run by Semtao. Information and tickets are available from **Espace Transport** (☎ 08 00 01 20 00; www.semtao.fr; Gare d'Orléans; ⌚ 6.45am-7.15pm Mon-Fri, 8am-6.30pm Sat). Fares are €1.30/11.90 for a single ticket/10-ticket *carnet*; trams run until around 12.30am, buses till 8pm or 9pm.

BICYCLE

Orléans operates an on-street bike-hire system, **Vélo+** (☎ 0 80 00 83 56; www.agglo-veloplus.fr; deposit €3, first 30min free, next 30min €0.50, per subsequent hr €2) with drop-off stations all over town (including the train station, place du Martroi, place du Général de Gaulle and outside the cathedral).

ORLÉANS TO SULLY-SUR-LOIRE

North of Orléans stretches the 350-sq-km Forêt d'Orléans (one of the few remaining places in France where you can spot wild ospreys), while east of Orléans towards the

Burgundy border are intriguing churches and little-known châteaux.

Châteauneuf-sur-Loire's **château** explores the history of river shipping on the Loire, with a collection of model boats and riverine artefacts displayed in the castle's former stables, now the **Musée de la Marine** (☎ 02 38 46 84 46; 1 place Aristide Briand; adult/7-18yr €3.50/2; 🕒 10am-6pm Wed-Mon Apr-Oct, 2-6pm Wed-Mon Nov-Mar).

Another 6km southeast is the **Église de Germigny-des-Prés**, one of France's few Carolingian churches, renowned for its unusual Maltese-cross layout and gilt-and-silver 9th-century mosaic. Twelve kilometres upstream is St-Benoît-sur-Loire and the Romanesque **Abbaye de Fleury** (☎ 02 38 35 72 43; www.abbaye-fleury.com; 🕒 6.30am-10pm), still home to a practising Benedictine brotherhood, who conduct summertime abbey tours. Look out for the famous decorated portal and the relics of St Benedict (480–547) in the abbey basilica.

Nine kilometres southeast of St-Benoît, the **Château de Sully-sur-Loire** (☎ 02 38 36 36 86) is a grand example of a fairy-tale castle, with machicolated ramparts and turrets rising from a glassy moat. Built from 1395 to defend one of the Loire's crucial crossings, the castle underwent major refurbishment in 2007–08; contact the Sully **tourist office** (☎ 02 38 36 23 70; http://ot.sully.sur.loire@wanadoo.fr; 21 bd Jeanne d'Arc; 🕒 9.45am-12.15pm & 2.30-6.30pm Mon-Sat, 10.30am-1pm Sun May-Sep, 10am-noon & 2-6pm Wed-Sat, 10am-noon Mon, 2-6pm Tue Oct-Apr) for the latest news. The château also hosts an annual outdoor **music festival** (www.festival-sully.com) every June.

For buses see opposite.

LA SOLOGNE

For centuries, the boggy wetland and murky woods of La Sologne have formed one of France's great hunting grounds, with deer, boars, pheasants and stags roaming the woodland, and eels, carp and pike filling its deep ponds and rivers. François I (r 1515–47) established it as a royal playground, but years of war, disease and floods turned it into malaria-infested swamp; only in the mid-19th century, after it was drained under Napoléon III, did La Sologne regain its hunting prestige.

In winter it can be a desolate place, with drizzle and thick fog blanketing the landscape, but in summer it's a riot of wildflowers and blooming foliage, and makes for great country to explore on foot, bike or horseback. Paths and trails criss-cross the area, including the GR31 and the GR3C, but stick to the signposted routes if you're visiting during hunting season, unless you fancy getting some buckshot up your backside. **La Malle aux Raboliots** (☎ 02 54 88 43 75; 8 rue de la Paix, St-Viâtre; adult/child €25/18) offers a guided bike trip around the Sologne area, including a home-made picnic, or you can hire bikes for €7.50/15 per half-/full day.

For further info on hikes and walks in the Sologne, contact the **tourist office** (☎ 02 54 76 43 89; www.tourisme-romorantin.com; 🕒 10am-noon & 2-6.30pm Mon-Fri, 9am-noon & 1.30-6pm Sat) in **Romorantin-Lanthenay**, 41km southeast of Blois.

The best time to visit is the last weekend in October, when the annual **Journées Gastronomiques de Sologne** fills the streets of Romorantin with local delicacies such as stuffed trout, wild-boar pâté and Sauvignon cheese, as well as freshly baked *tarte Tatin*, the upside-down apple tart accidentally created in 1888 by two sisters in the village of Lamotte-Beuvron.

You can catch trains from Romorantin-Lanthenay to Tours (via Gièvres; €13.30, 1¼ to 1½ hours, four to eight daily).

BLÉSOIS

The countryside around the former royal seat of Blois is surrounded by some of the country's finest châteaux, including graceful Cheverny, little-visited Beauregard, and the turret-topped supertanker château to end them all, Chambord.

Château Tours

The *départemental* bus company **TLC** (☎ 02 54 58 55 44; www.tlcinfo.net; adult/child excl admission fees €11.20/8.96; 🕒 departures at 9.10am & 1.45pm mid-May–early Sep) runs châteaux tours from Blois to Chambord and Cheverny; tickets can be bought on the bus, or preferably in advance at the Blois tourist office.

Transport Touristique de Voyageurs (☎ 06 08 14 71 41; deveaux.pierre@wanadoo.fr; Chissay-en-Touraine; per bus for up to 6 people per day €230) offers tailored trips to local châteaux in air-conditioned minibuses.

BLOIS

pop 49,200

Looming on a rocky escarpment, Blois' historic château (formerly the feudal seat of the powerful counts of Blois) has been repeatedly redeveloped over the last seven centuries, and its grand halls, spiral staircases and sweeping courtyards provide a whistle-stop tour through the key periods of French architecture. Blois suffered heavy bombardment during WWII, and the modern-day town is mostly the result of speedy postwar reconstruction. Inland from the river the twisting streets of the old town give you some idea of how Blois might have looked to its medieval inhabitants; and if you're suffering from château fatigue, there are some intriguing diversions to explore, including a museum of magic and a mischievous gallery of modern art. Sadly for chocoholics, Blois' historic chocolate factory, Poulain, is strictly off-limits to visitors.

Orientation

Blois, on the northern bank of the Loire, is fairly compact. The train station is at the top of the hill along av Jean Laigret, which travels east downhill towards the château and the river. The old city is to the east of the château, while the commercial district centres on pedestrianised rue du Commerce, rue Porte Chartraine, and rue Denis Papin connected to rue du Palais by the 19th-century Escalier Denis Papin.

Information

Laundrettes 1 rue Jeanne d'Arc (⌚ 7am-9pm); 4 rue St-Lubin (⌚ 7am-9pm)

Post Office (rue Gallois) Changes money.

Tourist Office (☎ 02 54 90 41 41; www.bloispaysdechambord.com; 23 place du Château; ⌚ 9am-7pm Mon-Sat, 10am-7pm Sun Apr-Sep, 9.30am-12.30pm & 2-6pm Mon-Sat, 10am-4pm Sun Oct-Mar)

Sights & Activities

CHÂTEAU ROYAL DE BLOIS

Blois' **château** (☎ 02 54 90 33 32; place du Château; adult/student/6-17yr €7.50/5/3; ⌚ 9am-7pm Jul & Aug, 9am-6.30pm Apr-Jun & Sep, 9am-12.30pm & 1.30-5.30pm Oct-Mar) was intended more as an architectural showpiece than a military stronghold, and successive French kings have left their creative mark over the centuries. From the château's huge **central courtyard** you can view four distinct periods of French architecture: the Gothic Salle des États and original medieval castle; François I's Renaissance north wing (1515–24) with its spiral loggia staircase; the classical west wing (1635–38), constructed by the architect François Mansart under Gaston d'Orléans, brother to Louis XIII; and the Flamboyant Gothic east wing (1498–1503), constructed in the Italianate style by Louis XII using red brick and creamy stone (a horseback statue of Louis can be seen above the ticket office).

First stop is the cavernous **Salle des États Généraux** (Estates General Hall), with its soaring double barrel–vaulted roof decorated in royal blues and golden *fleurs-de-lys*. Blois' medieval lords meted out justice here in the Middle Ages, and Luc Besson used the hall for the dramatic trial scene in his 1999 biopic *Jeanne d'Arc* (1999).

The **Renaissance wing** was remodelled in the early 16th century as royal apartments for François I and his wife Queen Claude. Its most famous feature is the loggia staircase, decorated with salamanders and curly 'F's (heraldic symbols of François I). The wing suffered heavily during the Revolution and served as a military barracks from 1788 to 1861, before being painstakingly restored by the architect Felix Duban in the 19th century. Highlights include the guards' hall and the bedchamber in which Catherine de Médicis (Henri II's machiavellian wife) died on 5 January 1589 aged 69. According to Alexandre Dumas, the queen supposedly stashed her poisons in secret cupboards behind the elaborately panelled walls of the *studiolo* (domestic chamber).

On the 2nd floor are the king's apartments, housing a council room, private study, and the king's gallery and bedchamber – the setting for one of the bloodiest episodes in the château's history, when Henri III had his arch-rival, the Duke de Guise, murdered by royal bodyguards (the king himself courageously hid behind a tapestry). Period paintings and portraits recreate the gruesome event in the **Halles des Guises**. Ironically, Henri III was himself murdered just eight months later by a vengeful monk.

The Renaissance kitchens have been converted into a **sculpture gallery** of columns, statues and friezes torn down during the Revolution. Look out for lots of salamanders, mythological scenes and plenty of leering gargoyles.

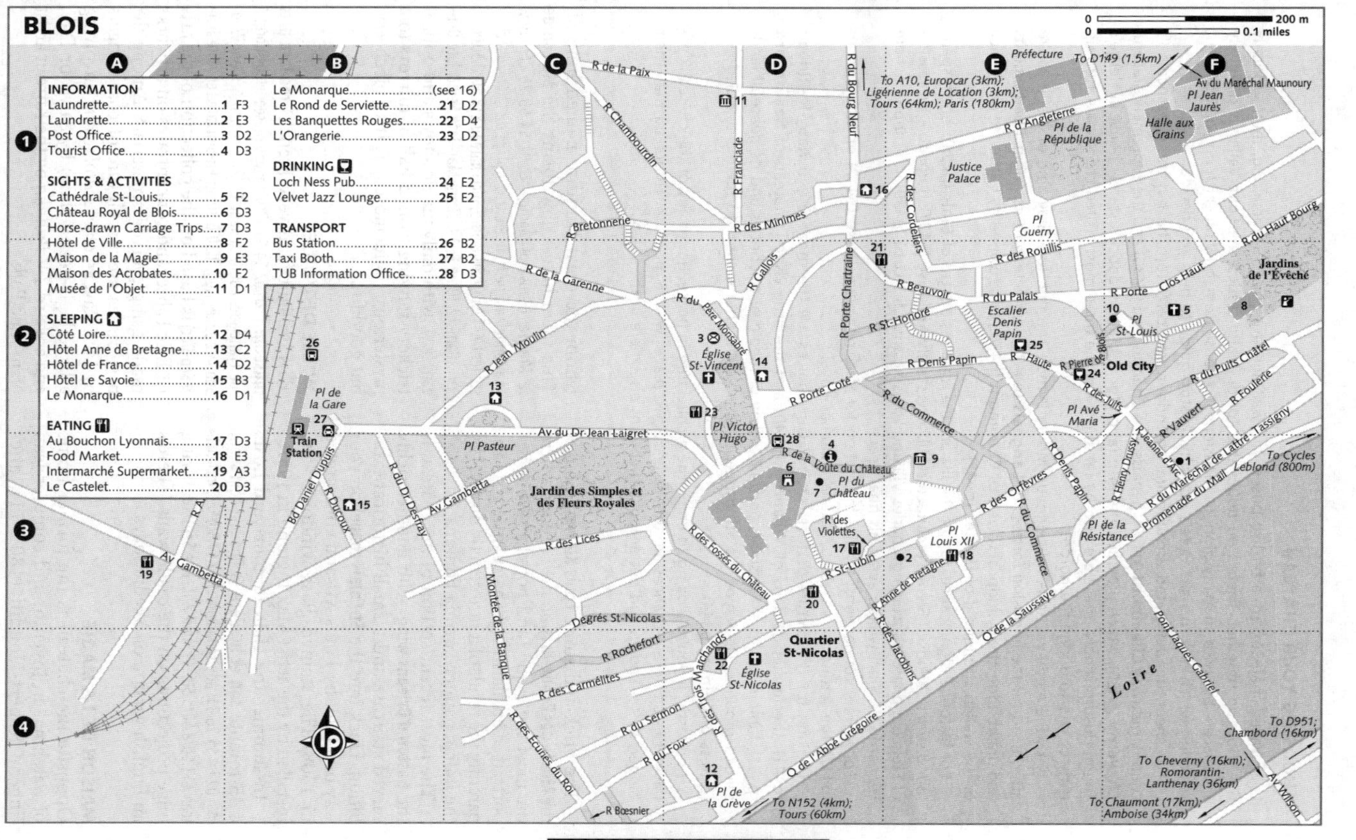
BLOIS
INFORMATION
Laundrette 1 F3
Laundrette 2 E3
Post Office 3 D2
Tourist Office 4 D3
SIGHTS & ACTIVITIES
Cathédrale St-Louis 5 F2
Château Royal de Blois 6 D3
Horse-drawn Carriage Trips 7 D3
Hôtel de Ville 8 F2
Maison de la Magie 9 E3
Maison des Acrobates 10 F2
Musée de l'Objet 11 D1
SLEEPING
Côté Loire 12 D4
Hôtel Anne de Bretagne 13 C2
Hôtel de France 14 D2
Hôtel Le Savoie 15 B3
Le Monarque 16 D1
EATING
Au Bouchon Lyonnais 17 D3
Food Market 18 E3
Intermarché Supermarket 19 A3
Le Castelet 20 D3
Le Monarque (see 16)
Le Rond de Serviette 21 D2
Les Banquettes Rouges 22 D4
L'Orangerie 23 D2
DRINKING
Loch Ness Pub 24 E2
Velvet Jazz Lounge 25 E2
TRANSPORT
Bus Station 26 B2
Taxi Booth 27 B2
TUB Information Office 28 D3
0 200 m
0 0.1 miles
To A10, Europcar (3km); Ligérienne de Location (3km); Tours (64km); Paris (180km)
To D149 (1.5km)
Préfecture
Pl de la République
Halle aux Grains
Pl Jean Jaurès
Av du Maréchal Maunoury
Justice Palace
Pl Guerry
Jardins de l'Évêché
Old City
Pl St-Louis
Pl Avé Maria
Escalier Denis Papin
Pl Louis XII
Pl du Château
Pl Victor Hugo
Église St-Vincent
Quartier St-Nicolas
Église St-Nicolas
Pl de la Grève
Pl de la Résistance
Jardin des Simples et des Fleurs Royales
Pl Pasteur
Pl de la Gare
Train Station
Loire
Pont Jacques Gabriel
To Cycles Leblond (800m)
To D951; Chambord (16km)
To Cheverny (16km); Romorantin-Lanthenay (36km)
To Chaumont (17km); Amboise (34km)
To N152 (4km); Tours (60km)
R du Bourg Neuf
R des Cordeliers
R d'Angleterre
R Porte Chartraine
R des Minimes
R Franciade
R Chambourdin
R de la Paix
R de la Garenne
R Jean Moulin
Av du Dr Jean Laigret
Av Gambetta
R du Dr Desfray
R Ducoux
Bd Daniel Dupuis
R Denis Papin
R du Commerce
R Porte Côté
R St-Lubin
R des Jacobins
Q de la Saussaye
Q de l'Abbé Grégoire
R des Fossés du Château
R des Lices
Montée de la Banque
R des Écuries du Roi
R des Carmélites
R Rochefort
Degrés St-Nicolas
R du Sermon
R du Foix
R des Trois Marchands
Promenade du Mail
R du Maréchal de Lattre Tassigny
Av Wilson
R Henry Drussy
R Jeanne d'Arc
R Vauvert
R Foulerie
R du Puits Châtel
R Porte Clos Haut
R du Haut Bourg
R du Palais
R des Rouillis
R Beauvoir
R St-Honoré
R Haute
R Pierre de Blois
R des Juifs
R des Orfèvres
R Anne de Bretagne
R des Violettes
R de la Voûte du Château
R Gallois
R du Père Monsabré
R Bretonnerie
R Bœsnier

CHOOSING YOUR CHÂTEAU

Loire Valley châteaux are a bit like buses: you wait ages for one to come along, then suddenly five show up together. There's no doubt that for dramatic castles, the Loire Valley is definitely the place – but with so many glorious mansions to choose from, how on earth do you go about selecting which one to visit? Here's our whistle-stop guide to help you decide…

For sheer, unadulterated architectural splendour, you can't top the big three: François I's country getaway **Chambord** (p429), Renaissance **Chenonceau** (p436) and the supremely graceful **Cheverny** (p430), which provided the inspiration for Captain Haddock's stately home in Hergé's Tintin. Unsurprisingly, these are also by far and away the three most visited châteaux – turn up early or late to dodge the hordes.

If it's the medieval, serf-and-seigneur, Monty Python and the Holy Grail kind of castle you're after, head for the imposing fortress of **Langeais** (p442), complete with its original battlements and drawbridge; the cylindrical towers of **Chaumont** (p430), once owned by Catherine de Medici; or the walled stronghold of **Loches** (p442).

For historical significance, top of the list are the royal residences of **Blois** (p424), which spans four distinct periods of French architectural history; stately **Amboise** (p437), home to a succession of French monarchs including Charles VIII and Louis XI; and **Clos Lucé** (p439) in Amboise, where Leonardo da Vinci whiled away his final years.

For literary connections, try the inspiration for *Sleeping Beauty*, **Ussé** (p442) or **Montsoreau** (p447), the setting for a classic Alexandre Dumas novel.

Looking for the picture-perfect setting? Our choices are the moat-ringed **Azay-le-Rideau** (p441), the formal gardens of **Villandry** (p440) and the little-visited château of **Beauregard** (p431), famous for its astonishing portrait gallery of medieval celebrities and its peaceful landscaped grounds. Or maybe it's atmospheric ruins you're after – then go for the tumbledown fortress of **Chinon** (p444).

And lastly, if you're looking to enjoy the architecture in peace, go for any of the châteaux we haven't listed here – chances are the lesser-known places will be much, much quieter than their bigger, better-known and better-looking cousins elsewhere in the valley.

The brick-and-stone **Louis XII wing** houses the **Musée des Beaux-Arts** on the 1st floor, where the most grotesque (and popular) work is a portrait of an alarmingly hairy little girl (apparently the result of a rare genetic disease) by the Italian painter Lavinia Fontana.

The most recent section of the château is the **Gaston d'Orléans wing**, with another richly carved staircase and a small historical exhibition. Duck into the **St-Calais chapel** on your way out, built by Louis XII and consecrated in 1508. The stained-glass windows were installed by the artist Max Ingrand in 1957.

In summer the château courtyard hosts a 45-minute **son et lumière** (sound-and-light show; ☎ 02 54 55 26 31; adult/student/child €7.50/5/3, incl château €11.50/8.50/5.50; ⌚ mid-Apr–late Sep) featuring huge projections on the castle walls. There's an English version on Wednesdays.

MAISON DE LA MAGIE

Opposite the château is the former home of watchmaker, inventor and conjurer Jean Eugène Robert-Houdin (1805–71), after whom the great Houdini named himself. This town house now forms the **Maison de la Magie** (House of Magic; ☎ 02 54 55 26 26; www.maisondelamagie.fr, in French; 1 place du Château; adult/student/6-17yr €7.50/6.50/5, incl château €12.50/8.50/5.50; ⌚ 10am-12.30pm & 2-6.30pm Mar–late Sep & late Oct–early Nov), with daily magic shows and optical trickery ranging from a hall of mirrors to a mysterious 'Hallucinoscope'. It's a bit cheesy, but good fun.

MUSÉE DE L'OBJET

This brilliant (and very French) **modern arts museum** (☎ 02 54 55 37 45; www.museedelobjet.org; 6 rue Franciade; adult/student €4/2; ⌚ 1.30-6.30pm Wed-Sun late June–Aug, 1.30-6.30pm Fri-Sun late Feb–late June & Sep-Dec) is based on the collection of the artist Eric Fabre, and concentrates on artworks made using everyday materials. Among the best pieces are a sculpture of coat-hangers by Man Ray, an *objet scatologique* (involving a large high-heeled shoe) by Salvador Dalí, and a weird *TV Buddha* by the Korean artist Nam June Paik.

OLD CITY

Despite serious damage by German attacks in 1940, Blois' old city is worth exploring, especially around the 17th-century **Cathédrale St-Louis** (place St-Louis; 9am-6pm), with its lovely multi-storeyed bell tower, dramatically floodlit after dark. Most of the stained glass inside was installed by Dutch artist Jan Dibberts in 2000.

Across is the **Maison des Acrobates** (3bis rue Pierre de Blois), decorated with wooden sculptures taken from medieval farces, and one of the few 15th-century houses to survive the WWII bombardment. There's another example at No 13 known as the **Hôtel de Villebrême**.

Lovely panoramas unfold across town from the peaceful **Jardins de l'Évêché** and the top of the **Escalier Denis Papin.**

CARRIAGE RIDES

Horse-drawn carriage trips (adult/child €6/4; 9am-7pm Jul & Aug, 2-6pm Apr-Jun & Sep) clop around town from the château's main gate. Book at the tourist office, or just wait outside the château for the next carriage.

Sleeping

Le Monarque (02 54 78 02 35; lemonarque@free.fr; 61 rue Porte Chartraine; s €38, d €55-57) The Anne de Bretagne's sister hotel sits at the edge of the old city, and offers similar levels of colour and comfort, with the added bonus of a downstairs restaurant (*menus* €18 to €28).

Hôtel Le Savoie (02 54 74 32 21; hotel.le.savoie@wanadoo.fr; 6 rue Ducoux; s/d €45/54, with shower only €41/48) Straightforward station hotel, decorated with multinational flags and a whitewashed facade. The modern chain-style rooms are hardly award-winning: expect prefab furniture and easy-to-clean fabrics. It's handy for train travellers and there's a useful bike shed for cyclists.

Hôtel de France (02 54 78 00 53; www.franceetguise.com; 3 rue Gallois; s €45, d 49-53) Chandeliers, glass and brass left from this hotel's belle-époque heyday still decorate the lobby, but some of the musty rooms are looking pretty tired: ask for one of the balcony rooms overlooking the Église St-Vincent.

Côté Loire (02 54 78 07 86; www.coteloire.com; 2 place de la Grève; d early Nov–Mar €48-67, Apr–early Nov €53-72) If it's charm and colours you want, head for the homely Loire Coast, with haphazard rooms decked out in cheery checks, bright pastels and the odd bit of exposed brick. There's free wi-fi and a wooden-decked breakfast patio.

Hôtel Anne de Bretagne (02 54 78 05 38; http://annedebretagne.free.fr; 31 av du Dr Jean Laigret; d €54-58) At the top of town overlooking a crescent, this creeper-covered hotel is a more traditional option, with a bar full of polished wood, soft lighting and vintage pictures, and modern rooms finished in flowery wallpaper and stripy bedspreads. Parking is available.

Eating

Au Bouchon Lyonnais (02 54 74 12 87; 25 rue des Violettes; mains €12-14) Classic neighbourhood bistro with a flavour of bygone days, where ancient net curtains sit alongside battered tables and rustic rafters, and the food is straight out of the Lyonnaise cookbook: snails, duck steaks and *la veritable andouillette* (true tripe sausage). Peasant food done to perfection.

Le Castelet (02 54 74 66 09; 40 rue St-Lubin; menus €17-28.20; closed Wed & Sun) Rusticana and rural frescoes cover the walls of this country restaurant, while piped medieval music fills the air: the perfect setting for more filling Touraine food, with a heavy emphasis on seasonal ingredients.

Les Banquettes Rouges (02 54 78 74 92; 16 rue des Trois Marchands; menus €22.50 & €28.50; lunch & dinner Tue-Sat) Handwritten slate menus and homely food distinguish the Red Benches: rabbit with marmalade, duck with lentils and pike with red cabbage, all done with a spicy twist and a smile.

LE PASS'-CHÂTEAUX

Many of the châteaux in the Blésois are covered by the **Pass'-Châteaux**, which offers savings of between €1.20 and €5.30 depending on which châteaux you visit; contact the tourist offices in Blois, Cheverny and Chambord. There are also additional formulas which include the smaller châteaux at Villesavin, Troussay and Talcy.

Chambord–Cheverny–Blois: €19
Chambord–Cheverny–Beauregard: €19
Chambord–Blois–Chaumont: €18.70
Blois–Chambord–Cheverny–Beauregard: €24.80
Blois–Cheverny–Chaumont–Chambord: €25.20

RIVER CRUISING

Unlike many of France's other rivers, the Loire offers relatively few opportunities to get out on the water: it's often too unstable and unpredictable to navigate safely, so you won't see too many holiday barges or canal boats cruising around. But the river's not completely off-limits…

Croisières de Loire (☎ 02 47 23 98 64; www.labelandre.com) offers cruises on the Loire and Cher, departing from Amboise (€8.50/5.50 per adult/child, running May to September) and Chenonceaux (€9.25/6 per adult/child, from April to October), with great views of both châteaux; hop aboard the flat-bottomed *gabarre* (barge; adult/child €8.50/5.50) in Chenonceaux for the authentic boatman's experience.

Ligérienne de Navigation (☎ 02 47 52 68 88; www.naviloire.com; adult/under 12yr €9/6; Apr-Nov) runs one of the few river cruises on the Loire proper, in a 66-seat boat departing from Rochecorbon to some of the Loire's wild islets and nature reserves.

Promenades en Futreau (Blois Tourist Office ☎ 02 54 90 41 41; adult/under 12yr €8.50/6.50; Mon-Sat Jul & Aug, Tue-Sat May, Jun & Sep) sets out from the Blois quayside aboard a traditional *futreau* (flat-bottomed barge).

La Margaretifera et la Candaise (☎ 02 47 95 93 15; Candes-sur-Martin; adult/under 12yr €7.50/5.50) provides atmospheric boat trips in traditional high-cabined Loire vessels known as *toues*, departing from Candes-sur-Martin.

THE LOIRE VALLEY

our pick L'Orangerie (☎ 02 54 78 05 36; 1 av du Dr Jean Laigret; menus €32-74) Polish up those pumps and dust off that evening dress – the Orangery is Blois' most respected table. Tucked behind wrought-iron gates in a timber-storeyed building opposite the château, it's cloud nine for connoisseurs of *haute cuisine* – plates are artfully stacked with ingredients, from duck liver to langoustine and foie gras (fattened liver), and the sparkling *salon* would make Louis XIV green with envy. On summer nights, opt for a courtyard table and prepare to be pampered.

SELF-CATERING

Food market (rue Anne de Bretagne; 7.30am or 8am-1pm Tue, Thu & Sat)
Intermarché supermarket (16 av Gambetta)

Drinking

The best bars are in the old town, particularly in the small alleys off rue Foulerie.

Velvet Jazz Lounge (☎ 02 54 78 36 32; www.velvetjazz.fr; 15bis rue Haute; 6pm-2am Mon, 3pm-2am Tue-Sat; ⊠) Lodged under artful lights, 13th-century vaults and contemplative Buddhas, Blois' funkiest bar hosts regular jazz acts after dark, and offers a selection of 32 (count 'em) hot chocolates in its alternative guise as an afternoon *salon de thé*.

Loch Ness Pub (☎ 02 54 56 08 67; cnr rue des Juifs & rue Pierre de Blois; 3pm-3am) The Scottish theme isn't convincing, but the boozing students and late-night drinkers at this ever-popular drinking hole don't seem to mind. Big-screen sports, karaoke and occasional gigs pack in the punters.

Getting There & Away

BUS

TLC (☎ 02 54 58 55 44; www.tlcinfo.net) handles buses to and from Blois, with destinations including Chambord (line 2, €3.99; 40 minutes, four Monday to Saturday, one on Sunday), Beaugency (line 1, €10.55; 55 minutes, four Monday to Friday, two on Saturday) and Cheverny (line 4, €1.10; 45 minutes, six to eight Monday to Friday, three on Saturday, two on Sunday). TLC also runs château tours in summer (see p423).

CAR

To rent a vehicle:
Avis (☎ 02 54 45 10 61; train station; 8am-noon & 2-6pm Mon-Fri)
Europcar (☎ 02 54 43 22 20; 4 rue Gutenberg; 8am-noon & 2-6.30pm Mon-Fri, 8am-noon & 2-5pm Sat)
Ligérienne de Location (☎ 02 54 78 25 45; 96-100 av de Vendôme; 8am-noon & 2-6.30pm Mon-Fri, 8am-noon & 3-6pm Sat)

TRAIN

There are regular trains to Amboise (€6, 20 minutes, at least 10 daily), Orléans (€9.30, 45 minutes, at least hourly) and Tours (€9.10, 40 minutes, hourly), plus Paris' Gare d'Austerlitz (€23.30, two hours, eight to 13 daily).

Getting Around

BICYCLE

The **Châteaux à Vélo** (www.chateauxavelo.com) network offers 11 waymarked cycling routes in the Blois area. You can download a free route map from the website or pick up a copy from the tourist office; there are also 40 downloadable guides for your MP3 player. For bike hire:

Cycles Leblond (☎ 02 54 74 30 13; 44 Levée des Tuileries; per half-/full day €9/12; ⏲ 9am-9pm)

Randovélo (☎ 02 54 78 62 52; www.randovelo.fr; 29 rue du Puits Neuf; per day €14; ⏲ 9am-6pm Mon-Fri Apr-Oct)

BUS

TUB (☎ 02 54 78 15 66; www.tub-blois.fr; 2 place Victor Hugo; ⏲ 1.30-6pm Mon, 8am-noon & 1.30-6pm Tue-Fri, 9am-noon & 1.30-4.30pm Sat) operates local buses in Blois. A one-way ticket costs €1.10; buses run until about 8pm Monday to Saturday, with hardly any on Sunday.

TAXI

Taxi Radio (☎ 02 54 78 07 65; place de la Gare; ⏲ 24hr) Can be found at the train station.

CHÂTEAU DE CHAMBORD

For full-blown château splendour, you can't top **Chambord** (☎ 02 54 50 50 20; www.chambord.org; adult/18-25yr/under 18yr €9.50/7.50/free, €1 reduction Jan-Mar & Oct-Dec; ⏲ 9am-7.30pm mid-Jul–mid-Aug, 9am-6.15pm mid-Mar–mid-Jul & mid-Aug–Sep, 9am-5.15pm, Jan–mid-Mar & Oct-Dec), one of the crowning examples of French Renaissance architecture, and by far the largest, grandest and most visited château in the Loire Valley.

Begun in 1519 as a weekend hunting lodge by François I, it quickly snowballed into one of the most ambitious (and expensive) architectural projects ever attempted by any French monarch. Though construction was repeatedly halted by financial problems, design setbacks and military commitments (not to mention the kidnapping of the king's two sons in Spain), by the time Chambord was finally finished 30-odd years later, the castle boasted some 440 rooms, 365 fireplaces, and 84 staircases, not to mention a cityscape of turrets, chimneys and lanterns crowning its rooftop, and a famous **double-helix staircase**, supposedly designed by the king's chum, Leonardo da Vinci. Ironically, François ultimately found his elaborate palace too draughty, preferring the royal apartments in Amboise and Blois – he only stayed here for 42 days during his entire reign from 1515 to 1547.

Despite its apparent complexity, Chambord is laid out according to simple mathematical rules. Each section is arranged on a system of symmetrical grid squares around a Maltese cross. At the centre stands the rectangular keep, crossed by four great hallways, and at each corner stands one of the castle's four circular bastions. Through the centre of the keep winds the great staircase, with two intertwining flights of stairs leading up to the great **lantern tower** and the castle's **rooftop**, from where you can gaze out across the landscaped grounds and marvel at the Tolkienesque jumble of cupolas, domes, chimneys and lightning rods.

It's worth picking up the multilingual audioguide (€4) to explore the rest of the château, if only to avoid getting lost around the endless rooms and corridors. The most interesting rooms are on the 1st floor, including the king's and queen's chambers (complete with interconnecting passages to enable late-night nooky) and a wing devoted to the thwarted attempts of the Comte de Chambord to be crowned Henri V after the fall of the Second Empire. On the 2nd floor is the eerie **Museum of Hunting**, with an endless display of weapons and macabre hunting trophies, and there's an interesting multilanguage film on the history of the castle's construction, screened on the ground floor. In a place of such ostentatious grandeur, it's often the smallest things that are most interesting – look out for a fascinating display of hundreds of cast-iron keys (one for each door in the château) and an equally fascinating display case containing broken pottery, tableware and goblets found in the castle's latrine.

Several times daily there are 1½-hour **guided tours** (€4) in English, and during school holidays there are **costumed tours** to entertain the kids. Free son et lumière shows, known as **Les Clairs de Lune**, are projected onto the château's facade nightly from July to mid-September, and there are outdoor concerts held throughout summer, including a daily **spectacle équestre** (dressage show; adult/child €8.50/6.50; ⏲ Tue-Sun May, Jun & Sep).

Domaine National de Chambord

This huge hunting reserve (the largest in Europe) stretches for 54 sq km around the château, and is reserved solely for the use of

CHÂTEAU TOURS

Hard-core indie travellers might baulk at the idea of a minibus tour, but don't dismiss it out of hand. Most companies offer a choice of well-organised itineraries, taking in various combinations of Azay-le-Rideau, Villandry, Cheverny, Chambord and Chenonceau (plus wine-tasting tours): entry to the châteaux isn't included, although you'll get a discount on the standard price. Half-day trips cost between €18 and €33; full-day trips range from €40 to €50 including lunch. You can reserve places via the Tours tourist office.

Acco-Dispo (☎ 06 82 00 64 51; www.accodispo-tours.com)
Alienor (☎ 02 47 61 22 23, 06 10 85 35 39; www.locationdevelos.com)
Quart de Tours (☎ 06 85 72 16 22; www.quartdetours.com)
St-Eloi Excursions (☎ 02 47 37 08 04; www.saint-eloi.com)

high-ranking French government personalities (though somehow it's difficult to imagine Sarkozy astride a galloping stallion). About 10 sq km of the park is publicly accessible, with trails open to walkers, mountain bikers and horse riders.

It's great for wildlife-spotting, especially in September and October during the stag mating season. There are **aires de vision** (observation towers) around the park; set out at dawn or dusk to spot stags, boars and red deer.

Bikes can be hired from a **rental kiosk** (☎ 02 54 33 37 54; per half-/full day €10/13; ⌚ Apr–early Nov) near the *embarcadère* (jetty) on the River Cosson, where you can also rent boats. There are guided **evasions à vélo** (bike trips; adult/child €10/6 plus bike hire) from mid-August to September, and half-day horse rides (€70) in July and August.

To see the rest of the reserve, jump aboard a **Land Rover Safari** (☎ 02 54 50 50 06; adult €18; ⌚ Apr-Sep), conducted by French-speaking guides with an intimate knowledge of where and when to see the best wildlife.

Getting There & Away

Chambord is 16km east of Blois, 45km southwest of Orléans and 17km northeast of Cheverny. For details on public transport options see p428.

CHÂTEAU DE CHEVERNY

Thought by many to be the most perfectly proportioned château of all, **Cheverny** (☎ 02 54 79 96 29; www.chateau-cheverny.fr; adult/7-14yr €7/3.40; ⌚ 9.15am-6.45pm Jul & Aug, 9.15am-6.15pm Apr-Jun & Sep, 9.45am-5.30pm Oct, 9.45am-5pm Nov-Mar) represents the zenith of French classical architecture, the perfect blend of symmetry, geometry and aesthetic order.

Built from gleaming stone from the nearby Bourré quarries and surrounded by lush parkland, Cheverny is one of the few châteaux whose original architectural vision has survived the centuries practically unscathed. Since its construction between 1625 and 1634 by Jacques Hurault, an intendant to Louis XII, the castle has hardly been altered, and its interior decoration includes some of the most sumptuous furnishings, tapestries and objets d'art anywhere in the Loire Valley. Owned by the Hurault family for the last six centuries, the apartments include a formal dining room, bridal chamber and children's playroom (complete with Napoléon III–era toys), as well as a guards' room full of pikestaffs, claymores and suits of armour. Behind the main château is the 18th-century **Orangerie**, where many priceless artworks (including the *Mona Lisa*) were stashed during WWII.

Tintin fans might find the château's facade oddly familiar: Hérgé used it as a model (minus the two end towers) for Moulinsart (Marlinspike) Hall, the ancestral home of Tintin's irascible sidekick, Captain Haddock. A small exhibition, **Les Secrets de Moulinsart** (combined ticket with château adult/7-14yr €11.80/6.80), explores the Tintin connections.

Near the château's gateway are the **kennels**, home to the pedigree hunting dogs still used by the owners of Cheverny: feeding time, known as the **Soupe des Chiens**, takes place daily at 5pm from April to September.

Cheverny is 16km southeast of Blois and 17km southwest of Chambord. For information on the bus from Blois see p428.

CHÂTEAU DE CHAUMONT

Set on a defensible bluff behind the Loire, **Chaumont-sur-Loire** (☎ 02 54 51 26 26; adult/12-18yr/6-12yr €7.50/5/free; ⌚ 10am-6pm mid-May–mid-Sep, 10.30am-5.30pm Apr–mid-May & mid-Sep–end Sep, 10am-5pm Oct-Mar) presents a resolutely medieval face,

THE LOIRE VALLEY

with its cylindrical corner turrets and sturdy drawbridge, but the interior mostly dates from the 19th century. At least two earlier fortresses occupied the site (whose name derives from Chauve Mont 'Bald Hill'), but the main phase of construction for the present château began sometime around 1465 under Pierre d'Amboise. Originally a strictly defensive fortress, the castle became a short-lived residence for Catherine de Médicis following the death of Henry II in 1560, and later passed into the hands of Diane de Poitiers (Henry II's mistress), who was forced to swap the altogether grander surroundings of Chenonceau for Chaumont by the ruthless Catherine.

The château was thoroughly renovated by Princess de Broglie, heiress to the Say sugar fortune, who bought it in 1875 (and knocked down one entire wing to provide a better view of the river). The most impressive room is the Council Chamber, with its original maiolica-tiled floor, plundered from a palace in Palermo, but the château's finest architecture is arguably reserved for the **Écuries** (stables), built in 1877 to house the Broglie's horses in truly sumptuous style (the thoroughbreds all had their own personal padded stalls). A collection of vintage horse-drawn carriages is now displayed inside the stables; buzz on the gate to be let in.

Chaumont's English-style park hosts the annual **Festival International des Jardins** (International Garden Festival; ☎ 02 54 20 99 22; www.chaumont-jardins.com; adult/12-18yr/6-12yr €9/6.50/3; ⌚ 9.30am-nightfall) between April and October.

Getting There & Away

Chaumont-sur-Loire is 17km southwest of Blois and 20km northeast of Amboise. Onzain, an easyish walk from Chaumont across the Loire, has trains to Blois (€3, 10 minutes, 10 to 14 daily) and Tours (€7.20, 35 minutes).

CHÂTEAU DE BEAUREGARD

Less visited than its sister châteaux, **Beauregard** (☎ 02 54 70 40 05; adult/8-18yr €6.50/4.50; ⌚ 9.30am-6.30pm Jul & Aug, 9.30am-noon & 2-6.30pm Apr-Jun, Sep & Oct, 9.30am-noon & 2-5pm Nov, Feb & Mar, closed Dec & Jan & Wed Oct-Mar) has some special charms all of its own. Built as yet another hunting lodge by François I, the castle's highlight is an amazing portrait gallery depicting 327 notables of European aristocratic society. Spot famous faces including Christopher Columbus, Cardinal Richelieu, Catherine de Médicis, Anne de Bretagne, Henry VIII of England and his doomed wife Anne Boleyn, and every French king since Philippe VI: underfoot, the porcelain floor is decorated with handmade Delft tiles.

TOURAINE

Often dubbed the 'Garden of France', the Touraine region is famous for its rich food, tasty cheeses and notoriously pure French accent, as well as a smattering of glorious châteaux: some Renaissance (Azay-le-Rideau, Villandry and Chenonceau), others medieval (Chinon and Loches). The historical capital, Tours, makes a good base, with regular bus and train links.

Getting Around

Châteaux accessible by train or SNCF bus from Tours include Chenonceau, Villandry, Azay-le-Rideau, Langeais, Amboise, Chaumont, Chinon and Loches – see each château listing for details.

TOURS

pop 298,000

Though not quite as cosmopolitan as its sister city of Orléans, Tours has long been considered one of the principal cities of the Loire Valley. It's a smart, solidly bourgeois kind of place, filled with wide 18th-century boulevards, parks and imposing public buildings, as well as a busy university of some 25,000 students. Hovering somewhere between the style of Paris and the conservative sturdiness of central France, Tours makes a useful staging post for exploring the Touraine, with Azay-le-Rideau, Villandry and Langeais all a short drive away.

Orientation

Tours' 18th-century planners laid out the city in efficient fashion, with the central hub of place Jean-Jaurès connecting the main thoroughfares – west–east bd Béranger and bd Heurteloup, and north–south rue Nationale and av de Grammont. About 300m east of place Jean-Jaurès is the train station, while the city centre and commercial district stretches northwards towards the Loire River. The old city encircles place Plumereau (locally known as Place Plum), about 400m west of rue Nationale.

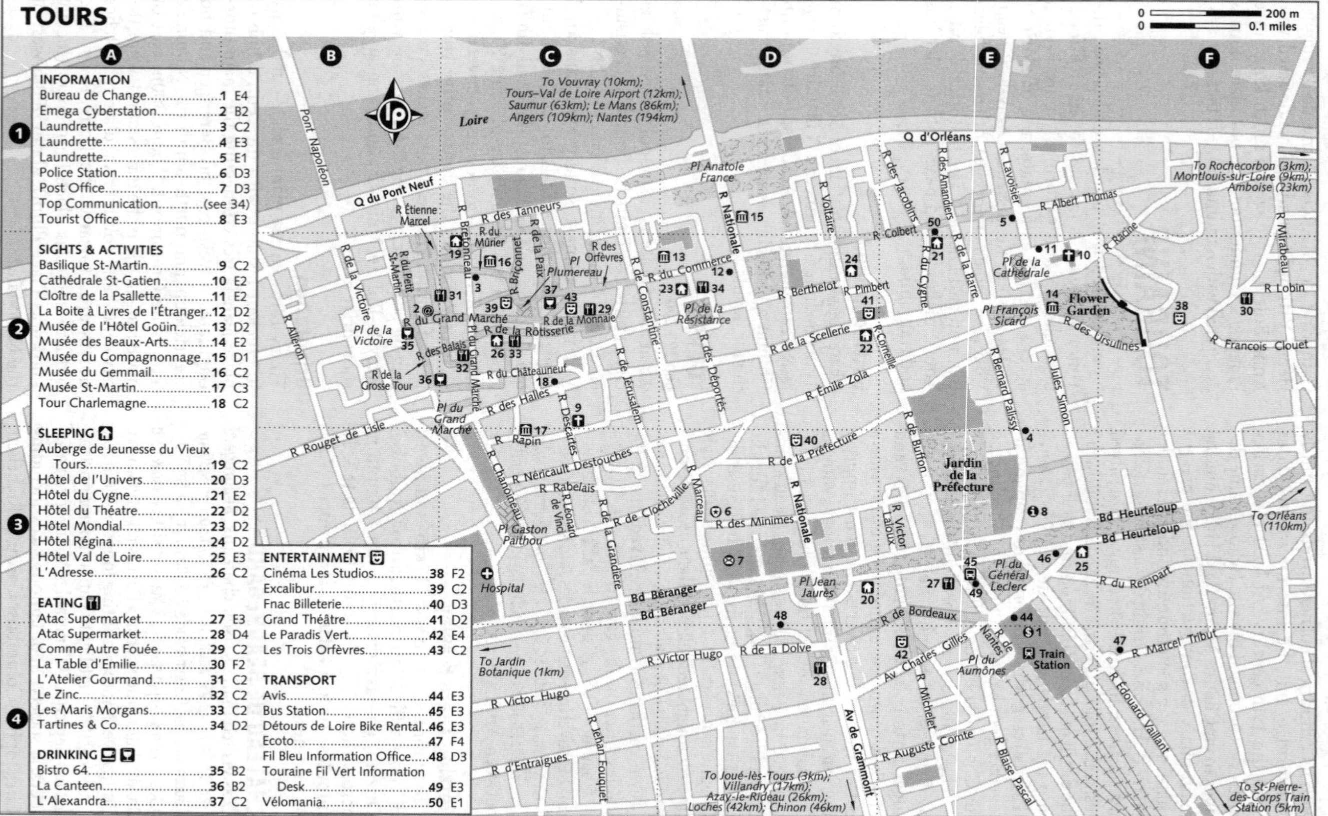
TOURS
0 200 m
0 0.1 miles
INFORMATION
Bureau de Change....1 E4
Emega Cyberstation....2 B2
Laundrette....3 C2
Laundrette....4 E3
Laundrette....5 E1
Police Station....6 D3
Post Office....7 D3
Top Communication....(see 34)
Tourist Office....8 E3
SIGHTS & ACTIVITIES
Basilique St-Martin....9 C2
Cathédrale St-Gatien....10 E2
Cloître de la Psallette....11 E2
La Boite à Livres de l'Étranger..12 D2
Musée de l'Hôtel Goüin....13 D2
Musée des Beaux-Arts....14 E2
Musée du Compagnonnage....15 D1
Musée du Gemmail....16 C2
Musée St-Martin....17 C3
Tour Charlemagne....18 C2
SLEEPING
Auberge de Jeunesse du Vieux Tours....19 C2
Hôtel de l'Univers....20 D3
Hôtel du Cygne....21 E2
Hôtel du Théatre....22 D2
Hôtel Mondial....23 D2
Hôtel Régina....24 D2
Hôtel Val de Loire....25 E3
L'Adresse....26 C2
EATING
Atac Supermarket....27 E3
Atac Supermarket....28 D4
Comme Autre Fouée....29 C2
La Table d'Emilie....30 F2
L'Atelier Gourmand....31 C2
Le Zinc....32 C2
Les Maris Morgans....33 C2
Tartines & Co....34 D2
DRINKING
Bistro 64....35 B2
La Canteen....36 B2
L'Alexandra....37 C2
ENTERTAINMENT
Cinéma Les Studios....38 F2
Excalibur....39 C2
Fnac Billeterie....40 D3
Grand Théâtre....41 D2
Le Paradis Vert....42 E4
Les Trois Orfèvres....43 C2
TRANSPORT
Avis....44 E3
Bus Station....45 E3
Détours de Loire Bike Rental..46 E3
Ecoto....47 F4
Fil Bleu Information Office....48 D3
Touraine Fil Vert Information Desk....49 E3
Vélomania....50 E1
To Vouvray (10km); Tours–Val de Loire Airport (12km); Saumur (63km); Le Mans (86km); Angers (109km); Nantes (194km)
Loire
To Rochecorbon (3km); Montlouis-sur-Loire (9km); Amboise (23km)
To Orléans (110km)
To Joué-lès-Tours (3km); Villandry (17km); Azay-le-Rideau (26km); Loches (42km); Chinon (46km)
To St-Pierre-des-Corps Train Station (5km)
To Jardin Botanique (1km)
Pont Napoléon
Q du Pont Neuf
Q d'Orléans
R Nationale
Av de Grammont
Bd Heurteloup
Bd Béranger
Pl Anatole France
Pl Plumereau
Pl du Grand Marché
Pl de la Victoire
Pl de la Résistance
Pl de la Cathédrale
Pl François Sicard
Pl Jean Jaurès
Pl du Général Leclerc
Pl Gaston Pailhou
Pl du Aumônes
Jardin de la Préfecture
Flower Garden
Train Station
Hospital

Information

There are commercial banks around place Jean Jaurès.

Bureau de Change (8.45am-6pm Mon-Sat Feb-May & Oct-Dec, to 6.30pm Jun-Sep, closed Jan) Inside the train station. The commission is €4.50.

Emega Cyberstation (43 rue du Grand Marché; per hr €2; noon-midnight Mon-Sat, 2-11pm Sun) Internet access.

La Boîte à Livres de l'Étranger (02 47 05 67 29; 2 rue du Commerce; Mon-Sat) Multilingual bookshop with English titles.

Laundrettes 22 rue Bernard Palissy (7am-8pm); 149 rue Colbert (7am-7.45pm); cnr rue Bretonneau & rue du Mûrier (7am-8.30pm)

Police Station (02 47 33 80 69; 70-72 rue Marceau; 24hr)

Post Office (1 bd Béranger) Currency exchange.

Top Communication (68-70 rue Colbert; per hr €2; 10am-midnight Mon-Sat, 3-10pm Sun) Internet access.

Tourist Office (02 47 70 37 37; www.ligeris.com; 78-82 rue Bernard Palissy; 8.30am-7pm Mon-Sat, 10am-12.30pm & 2.30-5pm Sun mid-Apr–mid-Oct; 9am-12.30pm & 1.30-6pm Mon-Sat, 10am-1pm Sun mid-Oct–mid-Apr)

Sights

MUSÉE DES BEAUX-ARTS

Arranged around the courtyard of the former archbishop's palace, the **Musée des Beaux-Arts** (02 47 05 68 73; 18 place François Sicard; adult/student/under 13yr €4/2/free; 9am-12.45pm & 2-6pm Wed-Mon) is a fine example of a French provincial arts museum, with palatial rooms decorated to reflect the period of the artworks on display – look out for works by Delacroix, Degas and Monet, as well as a rare Rembrandt miniature and a Rubens portrait of the Virgin Mary. The massive 1804 Lebanese cedar in front of the museum measures a whopping 7.5m around the base. Wheelchair access is available.

CATHÉDRALE ST-GATIEN

In a country of jaw-dropping churches, the **Cathédrale St-Gatien** (place de la Cathédrale; 9am-7pm) still raises a gasp. With its twin west towers, stretching skyward through a latticework of Gothic decorations, arches, flying buttresses and gargoyles, it's a show-stopper. The cathedral is especially known for its intricate stained glass, particularly the rose windows above the organ; the interior dates from the 13th to 16th centuries, and the domed tops of the two 70m-high **towers** date from the Renaissance. On the north side is the **Cloître de la Psallette** (02 47 47 05 19; adult/under 18yr €2.50/free; 9.30am-12.30pm & 2-6pm Mon-Sat, 2-6pm Sun Apr-Sep, 9.30am-12.30pm & 2-5pm Wed-Sat & 2-5pm Sun Oct-Mar), a cloister built from 1442 to 1524.

MUSÉE DU GEMMAIL

The fashion for *gemmail* (pronounced zheh·mai) – pieces of backlit stained glass embedded in enamel – flourished briefly during the 1950s, but it never quite caught on in the way its inventors had hoped. You can see examples of this odd art form at the **Musée du Gemmail** (02 47 61 01 19; rue du Mûrier; adult/student €5.40/3.90; 2-6.30pm Tue-Sun Easter–mid-Oct).

MUSÉE DU COMPAGNONNAGE

France has long prided itself on the work of its 20,000-odd *compagnons* (craftsmen), whose skills have been in demand since the first showpiece cathedrals started appearing in the early Middle Ages (when the Statue of Liberty was restored in the mid-1980s, French *compagnons* were responsible for the intricate metalwork). In addition to traditional professions such as stonemasonry, carpentry and ironmongery, the *compagnonnages* (guild organisations) welcome in many skilled labourers, including pastry chefs, coopers and locksmiths. You can view their work at the **Musée du Compagnonnage** (02 47 61 07 93; 8 rue Nationale; adult/student/under 12yr €5/3/free; 9am-12.30pm & 2-6pm daily mid-Jun–mid-Sep, 9am-noon & 2-6pm Wed-Mon mid-Sep–mid-Jun), where displays range from handmade clogs to booby-trapped locks, vintage barrels and enormous cakes.

MUSÉE DE L'HÔTEL GOÜIN

The city's **archeological museum** (02 47 66 22 32; 25 rue du Commerce) had been closed since January 2008 for restoration works at the time of writing, but you can still admire the Italianate exterior of the building, originally a Renaissance residence built for a wealthy merchant around 1510.

BASILIQUE ST-MARTIN

Tours was once an important pilgrimage city thanks to the soldier-turned-evangelist St Martin (c 317–97), bishop of Tours in the 4th century. After his death a Romanesque basilica was constructed above his tomb, but today only the north tower, the **Tour Charlemagne**, remains (the rest was torn down during the Wars of Religion and the French Revolution). A replacement basilica was built in 1862 on a new site a short distance south along rue Descartes to house his relics, while the small **Musée St-Martin** (☎ 02 47 64 48 87; 3 rue Rapin; adult/concession €2/1; ⏰ 9.30am-12.30pm & 2-5.30pm Wed-Sun mid-Mar–mid-Nov) displays various artefacts relating to the lost church.

JARDIN BOTANIQUE

Tours has several public parks, including the 19th-century **botanic garden** (bd Tonnelle; admission free; ⏰ 7.45am-sunset) a 5-hectare landscaped park with a tropical greenhouse, medicinal herb garden and petting zoo. The park is 1.6km west of place Jean Jaurès; bus 4 along bd Béranger stops nearby.

WINE TOURS

The tourist office organises two wine tours around local vineyards: a half-day White Tour (€35) through the Vouvray area, or a full-day Red Tour (€58) through Chinon and Bourgueil, both including lunch.

Sleeping

Auberge de Jeunesse du Vieux Tours (☎ 02 47 37 81 58; www.ajtours.org; 5 rue Bretonneau; dm €17.40; ⏰ reception 8am-noon & 6-11pm; 💻) Friendly, bustling hostel with a large foreign-student and young-worker contingent; there are lots of kitchens (mostly small) and lounges to hang out in, but no en-suite bathrooms. Bike hire is available on-site.

Hôtel Régina (☎ 02 47 05 25 36; fax 02 47 66 08 72; 2 rue Pimbert; d with shower €26.60-44, d with shower & toilet €31.60-50) Budget cheapie with a bedsit vibe, offering simple rooms with mix-and-match furniture and second-hand wall prints in a choice of pinks, blues and pale whites. Curfew is 1am, and the matronly *madame* stands for no nonsense.

Hôtel Val de Loire (☎ 02 47 05 37 86; hotel.val.de.loire@club-Internet.fr; 33 bd Heurteloup; s €30-40, d €40-50) Higgledy-piggledy rooms spread around an 1870 town house, with period features including parquet floors, faded rugs and scruffy furniture, as well as wi-fi and double glazing to shut out the road noise. The top-floor rooms are jammed into the rafters; ask for one lower down for more space (and be prepared for weird push-button showers).

our pick **L'Adresse** (☎ 02 47 20 85 76; www.hotel-ladresse.com; 12 rue de la Rôtisserie; s €50, d €70-90) Looking for Parisian style in provincial Tours? Then you're in luck – 'The Address' is a boutique bonanza, with rooms finished in sleek slates, creams and ochres, topped off with wi-fi, flat-screen TVs, designer sinks, wicker bathchairs and reclaimed rafters: best are the ones with sexy shuttered balconies over the bustling alley. Drop-dead cool.

Hôtel du Théâtre (☎ 02 47 05 31 29; www.hotel-du-theatre37.com; 57 rue de la Scellerie; s €51-56, d €56-62) As its name suggests, this characterful hotel is down the street from the city theatre. Inside a spiral staircase reaches up a tiny timber-framed courtyard to the 1st-floor lobby; the rooms are comfortably old-fashioned, with wi-fi and a beamed dining room for breakfast.

Hôtel Mondial (☎ 02 47 05 62 68; www.hotelmondialtours.com; 3 place de la Résistance; s €52-62, d €56-72) Overlooking place de la Résistance, this hotel boasts a fantastic city-centre position: the modernised, metropolitan attic rooms in funky greys, browns and scarlets are the nicest, but even the older-style ones are decent. Breakfast is served in-room or in the 1st-floor lounge diner. Wi-fi available.

Hôtel du Cygne (☎ 02 47 66 66 41; www.hotel-cygne-tours.com; 6 rue du Cygne; d €53-96) One of Tours' oldest hotels, and showing its age in places, but still a charming place if you like your rooms old world. Slatted shutters on the exterior, chandeliers, terracotta pots and a bustling *madame* in the lobby: rooms range from small and poky to large and grand with gilded mirrors and floor-to-ceiling drapes.

Hôtel de l'Univers (☎ 02 47 05 37 12; www.hotel-univers.fr; 5 bd Heurteloup; d €137-272; ❄ 💻 ⊠) Everyone from Ernest Hemingway to Édith Piaf has kipped at the Universe over its 150-year history, and it's still a prestigious address. Previous guests gaze down from the frescoed balcony above the lobby (look out for Churchill and Edward VII), and the rooms are appropriately glitzy, if corporate: beds are huge, bathrooms are gleaming, and some have odd interconnecting windows between bedroom and bathroom. Wheelchair access is available.

Eating

Place Plum is crammed with cheap eats, but the quality can be variable.

Tartines & Co (☎ 02 47 20 50 60; 6 rue des Fusillés; mains from €8.50, lunch menu €13.20; ⏰ 10am-5pm) Snazzy little bistro that reinvents the traditional *croque* (toasted sandwich). Choose your topping – gourmet chicken, roasted veg, carpaccio beef – and it's served up quick as a flash on toasted artisan bread. Our tip is the Paysan, featuring roasted goat's cheese, walnuts and ham.

Comme Autre Fouée (☎ 02 47 05 94 78; 11 rue de la Monnaie; lunch menu €10, other menus €16-19.50; ⏰ lunch Sat & Sun, dinner Tue-Sat, also lunch Tue-Thu mid-May–mid-Sep) For local flavour, you can't top this place, which churns out the house speciality of *fouées*, a pitta-like disc of dough stuffed with pork rillettes, *haricots blancs* (white beans) or goat's cheese.

La Table d'Emilie (☎ 02 47 05 05 30; 1 rue Lobin; mains €10.50-13.30; ⏰ closed Sat & Aug) Giant poppies and crimson tablecloths brighten up the *salon* of this much-recommended local's restaurant, run by a friendly team passionate about honest, straightforward cooking – go for the St-Jacques scallops or the market-fresh *poisson du jour* (fish of the day).

Les Maris Morgans (☎ 02 47 64 95 34; 6 rue de la Rôtisserie; menus €16-35; ⏰ dinner Wed-Mon) *Avast, me hearties* – this ship-shape place (named after naughty water fairies) is all about the fruits of the sea, from just-cooked crab to sea bass and fresh oysters. The chef's special is *bisquines* (a seafood platter of mussels, langoustines, fish and prawns), and the dining room is draped in nautical knick-knacks and fishing tackle.

L'Atelier Gourmand (☎ 02 47 38 59 87; 37 rue Étienne Marcel; menu €20; ⏰ closed Mon) Another one for the foodies, but you'll need your dark glasses – the puce-and-silver colour scheme is straight out of a Brett Easton Ellis novel. You might not love the interior decor, but there's no quibbling with the food – hunks of roast lamb, green-pepper duck and authentic bouillabaisse, delivered with a modern spin.

Le Zinc (☎ 02 47 20 29 00; 27 place du Grand Marché; menus €20.50-25.50; ⏰ closed Wed & lunch Sun) One of the new breed of French bistros, more concerned with simple, classic staples and market-fresh ingredients (sourced direct from the local Halles) than Michelin stars and *haute cuisine* cachet. Country dishes – duck breast, beef fillet, river fish – served up in a buzzy terracotta-floored dining room. Attractive and authentic.

SELF-CATERING

For all your picnicking needs:

Atac supermarket 5 place du Général Leclerc (⏰ 7.30am-8pm Mon-Sat); 19 place Jean Jaurès (⏰ 9am-7.30pm Mon-Sat) The place Jean Jaurès branch is inside the shopping centre.

Les Halles (covered market; place Gaston Pailhou; ⏰ 7am-7pm)

Drinking

Place Plum and the surrounding streets are plastered in grungy bars and drinking dens, all of which get stuffed to bursting on hot summer nights.

Bistro 64 (64 rue du Grand Marché; ⏰ 11am-2am Mon-Sat) Cosy neighbourhood that's one step removed from the place Plum hustle. Scuffed-up decor, jazz combos and plenty of house beers keep the local crowd happy.

L'Alexandra (☎ 02 47 61 48 30; 106 rue du Commerce; ⏰ noon-2am Mon-Fri, 3pm-2am Sat & Sun) Popular Anglo-Saxon bar crammed with students and late-night boozers, with attractions including house-special cocktails and internet access (€2).

La Canteen (☎ 02 34 74 10 30; 10 rue de la Grosse Tour; ⏰ noon-2.30pm & 7.30-11pm Mon-Sat) For something smoother and sexier, swing by this designer wine bar, where rough stone walls sit alongside leather sofas, chrome artworks, razor-sharp tables and a neon-lit bar. Loads of wines by the glass, including Loire vintages.

Entertainment

Get the low-down from the free monthly *Tours.infos* (www.tours.fr, in French), available all over town. Tickets are sold at **Fnac billeterie** (☎ 08 92 68 36 22; 72 rue Nationale).

Cinémas Les Studios (☎ for recorded information 08 92 68 37 01; www.studiocine.com, in French; 2 rue des Ursulines) Screens nondubbed films.

Excalibur (☎ 02 47 64 76 78; 35 rue Briçonnet; admission from €8; ⏰ 11pm-6am Tue-Sat) Hot-and-heavy club lodged in a converted ecclesiastical building not far from the Basilique St-Martin. Varied music – from pop tunes to house and drum-and-bass – pack in plenty of Tourangeaux clubbers.

Grand Théâtre (☎ 02 47 60 20 20; 34 rue de la Scellerie; ⏰ box office 9.30am-12.30pm & 1.30-5.45pm Mon-Sat & 30min before performances) Hosts opera and symphonic music.

Le Paradis Vert (☎ 02 47 66 00 94; 9 rue Michelet; adult/student billiard table per hr €10/8; ⏰ 10am-2am) Fast Eddie eat your heart out – France's biggest pool hall is right here in Tours, with 36 tables and a weekly pool contest open to all comers. If you get knocked out, you can always surf the net instead.

Les Trois Orfèvres (☎ 02 47 64 02 73; 6 rue des Orfèvres; admission €3-10; ⏰ 11pm-5am Wed-Sat) Grungy nightspot and gig venue in the heart of the medieval quarter, where the DJs lean towards rock classics, alternative and indie, and the students hang out in force in the vaulted-roof bar.

Getting There & Away

AIR

Tours–Val de Loire Airport (☎ 02 47 49 37 00; www.tours-aeroport.com), about 5km northeast of central Tours, is linked to London's Stansted and Dublin by Ryanair.

BUS

Touraine Fil Vert (☎ 02 47 47 17 18; www.touraine-filvert.com, in French) serves destinations in the Indre-et-Loire *département*, including Line C to Amboise (35 minutes, 12 daily Monday to Saturday) and onward to Chenonceaux (1¼ hours, two daily). Single-journey tickets in the surrounding area cost a flat-rate €1.50. There is an **information desk** at the bus station (☎ 02 47 05 30 49; place du Général Leclerc; 🕑 7am-7pm Mon-Sat).

CAR

Tours' one-way system and hectic traffic make driving a real headache, so you'll be glad not to bring a car. If you need to hire, there are rental agencies around the station, including **Avis** (☎ 02 47 20 53 27; in the train station; 🕑 8am-12.30pm & 1.30-6pm Mon-Fri, 9am-noon & 2-6pm Sat) and **Ecoto** (☎ 02 47 66 75 00; www.ecoto.fr; 8 rue Marcel Tribut; 🕑 8am-noon & 2-6pm Mon-Fri).

TRAIN

Tours is the Loire Valley's main rail hub. The train station is linked to St-Pierre-des-Corps, Tours' TGV train station, by frequent shuttle trains.

Trains run at least hourly between Tours and Orléans (€16.60, one to 1½ hours, some change at Vierzon or St-Pierre-des-Corps), stopping at Amboise (€4.60, 20 minutes) and Blois (€9.10, 40 minutes).

SNCF lines go west to Saumur (€10, 35 minutes, eight to 12 daily) and Angers (€15.30, one hour, eight to 12 direct daily); southwest to Chinon (€8.10, 45 minutes, 10 daily on weekdays, five daily on weekends); southeast to Loches (€7.80, 50 minutes, 10 to 15 daily) by train or coach; and east to Chenonceaux (€5.70, 30 minutes, six daily).

High-speed TGVs rocket to Paris-Gare Montparnasse (€39.10 to €55.10, 1¼ hours, around 15 daily); slow-coach Corails run to Gare d'Austerlitz (€28.70, two to 2¾ hours, nine to 15 daily).

TGVs also serve Bordeaux (€45, 2¾ hours), La Rochelle (€31 to €36.40, 2½ to 3¼ hours), Poitiers (€18.50 to €20.40, one hour) and Nantes (€25 to €26.90, 1½ hours).

Getting Around

TO/FROM THE AIRPORT

A shuttle bus (€5) leaves the bus station two hours before and half an hour after each Ryanair flight.

BICYCLE

Détours de Loire (☎ 02 47 61 22 22; www.locationdevelos.com; 31 bd Heurteloup; 1 day €14, subsequent days per day €7, 1 week €57; 🕑 9am-1pm & 2-7pm Mon-Sat, 9.30am-12.30pm & 6-7pm Sun Easter–early Oct, 9am-1pm & 2-6pm Mon-Sat early Oct–Easter) is part of the Loire à Vélo network (p418).

Vélomania (☎ 02 47 05 10 11; 109 rue Colbert; 🕑 10.30am-1.30pm & 3.30-7.30pm Mon-Sat) also rents bikes (per day/week €14.50/50.50).

BUS

Local buses are operated by **Fil Bleu** (☎ 02 47 66 70 70; www.filbleu.fr, in French; information office 5bis rue de la Dolve; 🕑 closed Sat afternoon & Sun). Most lines stop near place Jean-Jaurès. Tickets cost €1.20 and remain valid for an hour. Most lines run until about 8.30pm; hourly Bleu de Nuit night buses run until about 1am.

AROUND TOURS

Vineyards carpet the area around Vouvray (population 3100) and Montlouis-sur-Loire (population 8000), 10km east of Tours, and there are many *caves* (wine cellars) dotted around the area where you can taste and buy wine. Contact the **Vouvray tourist office** (☎ 02 47 52 68 73; 12 rue Rabelais; 🕑 9.30am-1pm & 2-6.30pm daily May-Oct, 9.30am-1pm & 2-5.30pm Tue-Sat Nov-Apr) for a list of local wine sellers, or book into the organised wine trip offered by the Tours tourist office.

Fil Bleu bus 61 links Tours' train station with Vouvray (€1.20, 20 minutes) while Fil Vert Line C (€1.50, 10 minutes, hourly) travels to Montlouis-sur-Loire.

CHÂTEAU DE CHENONCEAU

Spanning the languid Cher River via a series of supremely graceful arches, and encircled by formal gardens and landscaped parkland, **Chenonceau** (☎ 02 47 23 90 07; www.chenonceau.com; adult/student & 7-18yr €10/7.50, with audioguide €14/11.50; 🕑 9am-8pm Jul & Aug, 9am-7.30pm Jun & Sep, 9am-7pm Apr

& May, 9.30am-5pm or 6pm rest of year), not to be confused with the village spelled Chenonceaux, is one of the most elegant and unusual of the Loire Valley châteaux. In stark contrast to the ostentatious drama of Chambord and Blois, or the martial posturing of Chaumont and Loches, Chenonceau feels curiously serene and superior, delighting purely in the aesthetic quality of its architecture and its glorious surroundings.

So it's perhaps unsurprising to find that this architectural fantasy land is largely the work of several remarkable women (hence its alternative name, Le Château des Dames 'Ladies' Chateau'). The initial phase of construction started in 1515 on the orders of Thomas Bohier, a court minister of King Charles VIII, although much of the work and design was actually overseen by his wife, Katherine Briçonnet. The château's distinctive arches and one of the formal gardens were added by Diane de Poitiers, mistress of King Henri II. Following Henri's death, Diane was forced to exchange Chenonceau for the rather less grand château of Chaumont by the king's scheming widow, Catherine de Médicis, who completed the construction and added the huge yew-tree *labyrinthe* (maze) and the western rose garden. But Chenonceau's heyday was under the aristocratic Madame Dupin, who made the château a centre of fashionable 18th-century society and attracted guests including Voltaire and Rousseau (the latter tutored the Madame's son). Legend also has it that it was she who single-handedly saved the château from destruction during the Revolution, thanks to her popularity with the local populace.

The château's interior is crammed with wonderful furniture, tapestries and paintings, as well as several stunning original tiled floors; the *pièce de la resistance* is the black-and-white chessboard floor of the 60m-long **Grande Gallerie** spanning the Cher, scene of many a wild party under the auspices of Catherine de Médicis and Madame Dupin. During WWII, the Cher apparently marked the boundary between free and occupied France; local legend has it that the Grand Gallery was used as the escape route for many refugees fleeing the Nazi occupation.

Getting There & Away

The château is 34km east of Tours, 10km southeast of Amboise and 40km southwest of Blois. There are trains and buses from all three towns, and you can take boat trips from the château in summer (see p428).

AMBOISE

pop 11,500

The childhood home of Charles VIII and the final resting place of the great Leonardo da Vinci, upmarket Amboise is an elegant provincial town, pleasantly perched along the southern bank of the Loire and overlooked by its fortified 15th-century château. With some seriously posh hotels and a wonderful weekend market, Amboise makes a less hectic base for exploring the nearby châteaux than Blois or Tours, except in summer, when the coach tours arrive *en masse* to visit da Vinci's mansion home at Clos Lucé, where the great man whiled away his last three years under the patronage of François I.

Orientation

The train station, across the river from the town centre, is about 800m north of the Château Royal d'Amboise. Le Clos Lucé is 500m southeast of the château along rue Victor Hugo. The island in the middle of the Loire is called Île d'Or.

Place Michel Debré, sometimes called place du Château, stretches west from rue de la Tour to pedestrianised rue Nationale, Amboise's main commercial street.

Information

Several banks dot rue Nationale.

Laundrette (7 allée du Sergent Turpin; 7am-8pm)

Playconnect (119 rue Nationale; per hr €3; 3-10pm Sun & Mon, 10am-10pm Tue-Sat) Internet access.

Post Office (20 quai du Général de Gaulle)

Tourist Office (☎ 02 47 57 09 28; www.amboise-valdeloire.com; 9am-8pm Mon-Sat & 10am-6pm Sun Jul & Aug, 10am-1pm & 2-6pm Mon-Sat, 10am-1pm Sun Apr-Jun & Sep, 10am-1pm & 2-6pm Mon-Sat Oct-Mar) In a detached riverside building opposite 7 quai du Général de Gaulle. Sells walking and cycling maps and a discount ticket for the château, Clos Lucé and the Pagode de Chanteloup.

Sights & Activities

CHÂTEAU ROYAL D'AMBOISE

Like many of the older Loire Valley castles, the **Château Royal d'Amboise** (☎ 02 47 57 00 98; place Michel Debré; adult/15-25yr/7-14yr €9/7.50/5.30; 9am-7pm Jul & Aug, 9am-6.30pm Apr-Jun, 9am-6pm Sep & Oct, 9am-5.30pm Mar & early Nov, 9am-12.30pm Jan, Feb & mid-Nov–Dec) uses

THE LOIRE VALLEY

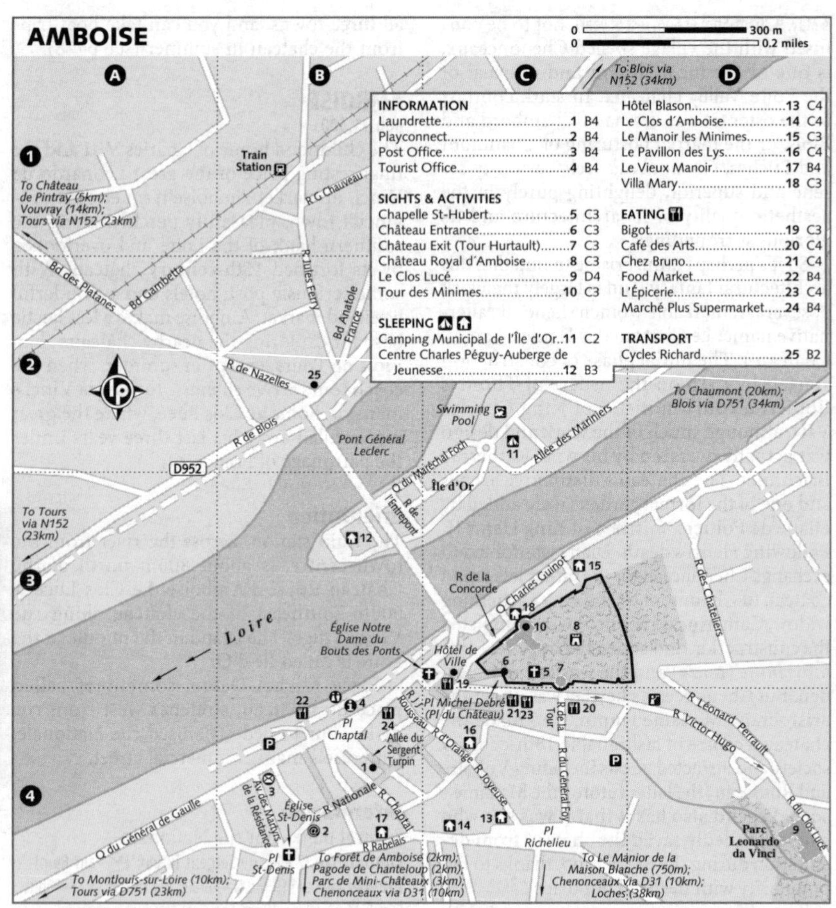

the natural terrain to maximise its defensive potential. Sprawling across a rocky escarpment with panoramic views of the river and surrounding countryside, it presented a formidable prospect to would-be attackers, but in fact saw little military action; it was more often used as a weekend getaway from the official royal seat at nearby Blois. Charles VIII (r 1483–98), was born and brought up here, and was responsible for the château's Italianate remodelling in 1492. François I (r 1515–47), who constructed Chambord (p429), also grew up here alongside his sister Margaret of Angoulême, and later invited da Vinci to work at nearby Clos-Lucé under his patronage.

The château entrance is at the top of the ramp at place Michel Debré. Today, just a few of the original 15th- and 16th-century structures survive, notably the **Flamboyant Gothic wing** and the **Chapelle St-Hubert**, a small chapel dedicated to the patron saint of hunting (note the carved stag horns and hunting friezes outside) and believed to be the final resting place of da Vinci. The interior highlights include a **guards' room**, a lovely **belvedere** overlooking the river, and a vaulted **Council Chamber** decorated with the initials of Charles VIII and his wife, Anne de Bretagne. Charles died suddenly in 1498 after hitting his head on a lintel while playing *jeu de paume* (an early form of tennis); the widowed Anne was later forced to remarry the new king, Louis XII.

From 1848 to 1852, Abd el-Kader, the leader of the Algerian resistance against

French colonialism, was imprisoned here with his family and entourage; a monument in the château's landscaped grounds commemorates the event.

The exit from the château is through the circular **Tour Hurtault**, with an ingenious sloping spiral ramp designed to allow carriages and horses to easily ascend to the château from the town below.

LE CLOS LUCÉ

Leonardo da Vinci (pronounced van·see in French) installed himself in the grand manor house at **Le Clos Lucé** (☎ 02 47 57 00 73; www.vinci-closluce.com; 2 rue du Clos Lucé; adult/student/6-15yr Mar–mid-Nov €12.50/9.50/7, mid-Nov–Mar €9.50/7/6; 9am-8pm Jul & Aug, 9am-7pm Feb-Jun, Sep & Oct, 9am-6pm Nov-Jan) in 1516 on the invitation of François I, who was greatly enamoured with the Italian Renaissance. Already 64 by the time he arrived, da Vinci seems to have spent his time at Clos Lucé sketching, tinkering and dreaming up new contraptions: the house and landscaped grounds house scale models of many of his inventions, including a protoautomobile, tank, parachute, hydraulic turbine and even a primitive helicopter.

PAGODE DE CHANTELOUP

Two kilometres south of Amboise is the curious **Pagode de Chanteloup** (☎ 02 47 57 20 97; www.pagode-chanteloup.com; adult/7-15yr/student €7/6/5; 9.30am-7.30pm Jul & Aug, 10am-7pm Jun, 10am-6.30pm May & Sep, 10am-6pm Mar & Apr, 2-4.30pm Mon-Fri Feb, plus 10am-noon & 2-5pm Sat & Sun Feb, Oct & Nov bank holidays & school holidays), the only remains of a demolished château. Built between 1775 and 1778, the pagoda is an odd blend of classical French architecture and Chinese motifs, which were all the rage at the time of the pagoda's construction; clamber to the top and you'll be rewarded with glorious views of the surrounding park and the forested Loire Valley. Gourmet picnic hampers (€11 to €25) are on sale in summer, and you can while away the afternoon larking about in a rowboat or playing free outdoor games.

Nearby, the **Parc de Mini-Châteaux** (☎ 08 25 08 25 22; www.mini-chateaux.com; adult/child €12.75/8.75; 10am-8pm mid-Jul–mid-Aug, 10am-7pm Jun–mid-Jul & late August, 10.30am-6pm Sep–mid-Nov, 10.30am-7pm Apr & May, closed mid-Nov–Mar) collects intricate scale models of 44 of the Loire Valley's most famous châteaux – squint a bit and it's just as good as a hot-air balloon trip over the Loire for a fraction of the price. Well, almost.

Sleeping

Amboise has some of the smartest places to stay in the Loire Valley, but you'll need deep pockets unless you're camping.

BUDGET

Camping Municipal de l'Île d'Or (☎ 02 47 57 23 37; Île d'Or; adult €2.45-2.50, tent €3.25-3.30; mid-Mar–early Oct;) Pleasant campsite on a peaceful river island, with facilities including tennis courts, ping pong and canoe hire.

Centre Charles Péguy-Auberge de Jeunesse (☎ 02 47 30 60 90; www.mjcamboise.fr; Île d'Or; dm €12; reception 2-8pm Mon-Fri, 5-8pm Sat & Sun;) Efficient boarding school–style hostel on the Île d'Or, with 72 beds mostly in three- or four-bed dorms, and treats including ping pong, table football and bike hire.

Hotel Blason (☎ 02 47 23 22 41; www.leblason.fr; 11 place Richelieu; d €44-58, tr €66-68;) Quirky, creaky budget hotel, on a quiet square in a wood-fronted building that previously served as a convent school, laundry and blacksmith's. The 25 higgledy-piggledy rooms are wedged in around the corridors: most are titchy, flowery and timber-beamed. Parking available.

MIDRANGE

Villa Mary (☎ 02 47 23 03 31; www.villa-mary.fr; 14 rue de la Concorde; d €60-120;) Four tip-top rooms in an impeccably furnished 18th-century town house, crammed with beeswaxed antiques, glittering chandeliers and antique rugs. Choose from Red, Violet, Pink and Blue, all with period pieces and patterned wallpaper – a couple have separate bathrooms across the corridor. Parking is also available.

Le Clos d'Amboise (☎ 02 47 30 10 20; www.leclosamboise.com; 27 rue Rabelais; r €75-170;) Another posh pad finished with oodles of style and lashings of luxurious fabrics. Features range from wood-panelling to timber joints and antique beds; some rooms have separate sitting areas, others original fireplaces and toile de Jouy–style fabrics, and the best give views over the lovingly manicured grounds and pool. There's even a sauna and gym in the old stables, and parking is available.

La Pavillon des Lys (☎ 02 47 30 01 01; www.pavillondeslys.com; 9 rue d'Orange; d €90-140, ste €180-210;) Beautiful hotel drenched with the kind of chichi style more suited to the Côte d'Azur. Take a cappuccino-coloured 18th-century town house and fill it with designer lamps, just-so furniture, roll-top baths, hi-fis and deep sofas, and you're halfway there; chuck in a locally renowned restaurant, an elegant patio garden and boutiquey treats and you're getting there. Parking is also available.

Le Vieux Manoir (☎ 02 47 30 41 27; 13 rue Rabelais; r €140-190, ste €275-305; ⊠) Run by expat Americans who cut their teeth at an award-winning Boston B&B, this shuttered mansion (with parking available) is stuffed floor to ceiling with period charm – vintage dressers, reclaimed sinks, old portraits, chintzy rugs. Rooms are named after French notables (from Colette to George Sand) – our choice is Madame de Lafayette with its burnished 19th-century dresser and cupboard bathroom. Cosy, inviting, but a little pricey.

Other options:

Le Manoir de la Maison Blanche (☎ 02 47 23 16 14; www.lamaisonblanche-fr.com; 18 rue de l'Épinetterie; d €80-90) Another sweet mansion B&B, with four rooms in a converted outbuilding, a lovely garden setting, and parking.

Le Manoir Les Minimes (☎ 02 47 30 40 40; www.manoirlesminimes.com; 34 quai Charles Guinot; d €115-170, ste €270-460) Check into the prestige suites at this pricey pamper-palace, set around a private courtyard that would put most châteaux to shame. Parking available.

Eating & Drinking

Café des Arts (☎ /fax 02 47 57 25 04; 32 rue Victor Hugo; meals €4-12) Spit-and-sawdust local's bar, dishing up beer and bar snacks steps from the château's old gate. Local *chanteurs* occasionally croon away while you sip your aperitif.

Bigot (☎ 02 47 57 59 32; 2 rue Nationale; 🕑 9am-7.30pm Tue-Fri, 8.30am-7.30pm Sat & Sun) Since 1913 this award-winning chocolatier and pâtisserie has been whipping up some of the Loire's creamiest cakes and gooiest treats: multicoloured *macarrons*, buttery biscuits and handmade chocolates, éclairs and *petits fours*, best appreciated at the fabulously frilly *salon de thé*.

Chez Bruno (☎ 02 47 57 73 49; place Michel Debré; 2-/3-course menu €11/15; 🕑 lunch Wed-Sun, dinner Fri & Sat) Amboise's new boy uncorks a host of local vintages in a coolly contemporary setting (white tablecloths, big gleaming glasses, snazzy artwork), accompanied by honest, inexpensive regional cooking. If you're after Loire Valley wine tips or oenological instruction, this is the place.

L'Épicerie (☎ 02 47 57 08 94; 46 place Michel Debré; menus €20.90, €25.60 & €30.90; 🕑 Wed-Sun) For a more time-honoured atmosphere head along the street from Chez Bruno to the Grocery, where rich wood and neo-Renaissance decor is matched by filling fare such as *cuisse de lapin* (rabbit leg) and *tournedos de canard* (duck fillet).

SELF-CATERING

For self-catering supplies, Amboise's excellent outdoor **food market** (🕑 8am-1pm Fri & Sun) fills the river-bank car parks west of the tourist office. For general supplies there's a **Marché Plus supermarket** (5 quai du Général de Gaulle; 🕑 7am-9pm Mon-Sat, 10am-2pm Sun).

Getting There & Around

Amboise is 34km downstream from Blois and 23km upstream from Tours.

BICYCLE

Hire mountain bikes at **Cycles Richard** (☎ 02 47 57 01 79; 2 rue de Nazelles; per day €15; 🕑 9am-noon & 2.30-7pm Tue-Sat).

BUS

Touraine Fil Vert's (p436) line C1 links Amboise's post office with Tours' bus terminal (€1.50, 45 minutes, nine daily Monday to Saturday). One bus daily continues on to Chenonceaux (15 minutes) from Monday to Saturday, with an extra afternoon bus in the summer.

TRAIN

The **train station** (bd Gambetta), across the river from the centre of town, is served by trains from Paris' Gare d'Austerlitz (€24.20, 2¼ to three hours, 11 daily), Blois (€5.60, 20 minutes, 10 to 20 daily) and Tours (€4.50, 15 minutes, 10 to 20 daily).

CHÂTEAU DE VILLANDRY

Completed in 1756, one of the last major Renaissance châteaux to be built in the Loire Valley, **Villandry** (☎ 02 47 50 02 09; www.chateauvillandry.com; château & gardens adult/8-18yr & student €9/5, gardens only €6/3.50; 🕑 château 9am-6.30pm Jul & Aug, 9am-6pm Apr-Jun, Sep & Oct, 9am-5.30pm Mar, 9am-5pm Feb & early Nov, gardens 9am-btwn 5pm & 7.30pm year-round) is more famous for what lies outside the château's walls than what lies within. Sheltered with enclosing walls, the château's glorious landscaped gardens are some of the finest in France, occupying over 6 hectares filled with impeccably manicured lime trees, tinkling fountains, ornamental vines and razor-sharp box hedges.

The original gardens and château were built by Jean le Breton, who served François I as finance minister and Italian ambassador (as well as supervisor for the construction of Chambord). During his time as ambassador, le Breton became enamoured by the art of Italian Renaissance gardening, and determined to create his own ornamental masterpiece at his newly constructed château at Villandry.

Some sections are purely aesthetic, others profoundly practical: wandering around the pebbled walkways you'll see formal **water gardens**, a **maze**, **vineyards** and the **Jardin d'Ornement** (Ornamental Garden), which depicts various aspects of love (fickle, passionate, tender and tragic) using geometrically pruned hedges and coloured flowerbeds. But the highlight is the 16th-century **potager** (kitchen garden), where even the vegetables are laid out in regimental colour-coordinated fashion. Sadly, the original gardens were destroyed in the 19th century to make way for a more fashionable English-style park, but over recent years they have been painstakingly restored to resemble the original Renaissance layout. Once inside the gardens you can stay as long as you like; the after-hours exit is next to the village church.

Make sure you time your visit when the gardens are in bloom between April and October – midsummer is the most spectacular season.

While the gardens steal the show, it's worth visiting the château's interior, mostly finished in luxurious 18th-century style by the Marquis de Castellane, who owned the château after le Breton. Highlights include a stunning gallery of Spanish art and an over-the-top Oriental Room, complete with a gilded ceiling plundered from a 15th-century Moorish palace in Toledo. From the corner **tower** (the only remnant from the original medieval château) and the **belvedere**, there are bird's-eye views across the gardens and the nearby Loire and Cher rivers.

Getting There & Away

Villandry is 17km southwest of Tours, 31km northeast of Chinon and 11km northeast of Azay-le-Rideau. Bikes are a great way to get around between the nearby châteaux; the D88 and D288 are more roundabout but much less trafficky than the main D7.

Touraine Fil Vert's (p436) Bus V travels between Tours and Azay-le-Rideau (€1.50, 50 minutes), stopping at Villandry (30 minutes from Tours), twice daily in July and August, and on Wednesdays and Saturdays in June, September and October. There's space at the back to carry a few bikes.

The nearest trains stop in Savonnières, 4km northeast of Villandry. Destinations include Tours (€2.90, 10 minutes, three Monday to Saturday, one on Sunday) and Saumur (€8.20, 35 minutes).

CHÂTEAU D'AZAY-LE-RIDEAU

Conjure up a classic French château and chances are it will be close to **Azay-le-Rideau** (☎ 02 47 45 42 04; adult/18-25yr €7.50/4.80; ⏰ 9.30am-7pm Jul & Aug, 9.30am-6pm Apr-Jun & Sep, 10am-12.30pm & 2-5.30pm Oct-Mar), a wonderful moat-ringed mansion decorated with geometric windows, ordered turrets and decorative stonework, wrapped up within a shady landscaped park. Built in the 1500s on a natural island in the River Indre, the château is one of the Loire's loveliest – Honoré de Balzac called it a 'multi -faceted diamond set in the River Indre'. The most famous feature is its open loggia staircase, overlooking the central courtyard and decorated with the salamanders and ermines of François I and Queen Claude; the interior is mostly 19th century, remodelled by the Marquis de Biencourt from the original 16th-century château built by Gilles Berthelot, a tax collector and chief treasurer for François I. The elegant billiard room and enormous castle kitchens are impressive, but the château's most photogenic side is its elegant exterior, especially when it's reflected in the still waters of the moat encircling the castle's walls. In summer, a son et lumière (one of the Loire's oldest and best) is projected onto the castle walls every evening. Audioguides (€4) are available in several languages.

Getting There & Away

Château d'Azay-le-Rideau is 26km southwest of Tours. The D84 and D17, on either side of the Indre, are a delight to cycle along.

Touraine Fil Vert's (p436) Bus V travels from Tours to Azay-le-Rideau (€1.50, 50 minutes) twice daily from July to August, and on Wednesdays and Saturdays in June, September and October. The train station is 2.5km from the château: connections include Tours (€4.80, 20 to 50 minutes, six to eight daily) and Chinon (€4.30, 20 minutes).

CHÂTEAU D'USSÉ

This main claim to fame of this grand **château** (☎ 02 47 95 54 05; www.chateaudusse.fr; adult/8-16yr/under 8yr €12/4/free; 9.30am-7pm daily Jul & Aug, 10am-7pm daily Apr-Jun, 10am-6pm daily Sep–mid-Nov & mid-Feb–mid-Mar) is as the inspiration for Charles Perrault's classic fairy tale, *La Belle au Bois Dormant* (better-known to English-speakers as *Sleeping Beauty*).

Ussé's creamy white towers and slate roofs jut out from the edge of the glowering forest of Chinon, offering sweeping views across the flat Loire countryside and the flood-prone River Indre. The castle mainly dates from the 15th and 16th centuries, built on top of a much earlier 11th-century fortress; its most notable features are the wonderful formal gardens designed by Le Nôtre, architect of Versailles, and a warren of twisting corridors, crackling hearths and refurbished rooms (some of which are starting to show their age).

You can even climb up inside one of the castle towers, where a series of dodgy wax models recount the tale of *Sleeping Beauty*, or descend into the cellar for a glimpse at the massive boiler that once piped heat around the castle's chilly hallways. Rather fittingly, there's also a popular local rumour that Ussé was one of the main inspirations Walt Disney had in mind when he was dreaming up his magic kingdom (check out the Disney logo and you might be inclined to agree).

Ussé is on the edge of the small riverside village of Rigny-Ussé, about 14km north of Chinon.

CHÂTEAU DE LANGEAIS

In contrast to the showy splendour of many châteaux, **Langeais** (☎ 02 47 96 72 60; adult/10-17yr €8/5; 9am-7pm Jul & Aug, 9.30am-6.30pm Apr-Jun & Sep–mid-Nov, 10am-5pm mid-Nov–Jan, 9.30am-5.30pm Feb & Mar) was constructed first and foremost as a fortress, built in the 1460s to cut off the likely invasion route from Brittany. It's every inch the medieval stronghold: crenellated ramparts and defensive towers jut out from the jumbled rooftops of the surrounding village, presenting a forbidding proposition to any would-be attacker and reminding any disgruntled local serfs of the enduring power of the castle's seigneur.

Langeais is one of the few châteaux to have preserved much of its medieval interior. Inside the castle (reached via a creaky drawbridge), you'll find original 15th-century furniture (including chairs, four-poster beds and a famous gilded chest) dotted around the castle's flag-stoned rooms, as well as many fine Flemish and Aubusson tapestries: look out for a famous one depicting nine 'worthy' knights, representing the epitome of medieval courtly honour. In one room, a waxwork display illustrates the marriage of Charles VIII and Anne of Brittany, which was held here on 6 December 1491 and brought about the historic union of France and Brittany. Up top you can stroll around the castle's ramparts for a soldier's-eye view of the town: gaps underfoot enabled boiling oil, rocks and ordure to be dumped on attackers. Across the château's interior courtyard is a ruined **keep**, constructed by the 10th-century warlord, Count Foulques Nerra: built in 944, it's the oldest such structure in France.

Getting There & Away

Langeais is 14km west of Villandry and about 31km southwest of Tours. Its train station, 400m from the château, is on the line linking Tours (€5.20, 15 minutes, six to 10 daily) and Saumur (€6.80, 25 minutes).

LOCHES

pop 6300

Billed as the capital of southern Touraine, the historic town of Loches spirals around the base of its medieval citadel, another forbidding stronghold begun by Foulques Nerra in the 10th century, and later enlarged by Charles VII. Loches earned a lasting footnote in the history books in 1429, when Joan of Arc persuaded Charles VII to march north from here to belatedly claim the French crown, but these days the town is a sleepy kind of place, best known for its lively Saturday morning market.

Orientation & Information

The Ville Haute (Citadelle or Cité Médiévale) is above the Ville Basse (lower town or Vieille Ville), still accessible via two medieval gates (Porte Picois and Porte des Cordeliers). The main commercial street, rue de la République, is just outside the citadel walls.

Éspace Public Numerique (☎ 02 47 59 49 85; 24 av des Bas-Clos; per hr €2.15; 2-8pm Tue, Thu & Fri, 10am-1pm & 2-7pm Wed, 1-5.30pm Sat May-Sep) Internet access.

Tourist Office (☎ 02 47 91 82 82; www.loches-tourainecotesud.com; place de la Marne; 9am-7pm Mon-Sat, 9.45am-12.30pm & 2.15-6pm Sun Jul & Aug, 9am-12.30pm & 2-6.30pm Mon-Sat, 10am-12.30pm &

2.30-6pm Sun May, Jun & Sep, 9am-12.30pm & 2-6pm Mon-Sat Mar & Apr, 10am-12.30pm & 2.30-6pm Mon, Tue, Thu & Fri, 9.30-12.30pm & 2.30-6pm Wed & Sat Oct-Feb) Beside the river near the end of rue de la République.

Sights

From rue de la République, the old gateway of Porte Picois leads through the cobbled Vieille Ville towards the **Porte Royale** (Royal Gate), the citadel's sole entrance, flanked by two forbidding 13th-century towers. As you climb uphill you'll pass the **Maison Lansyer** (adult/child €3/2; 🕐 10am-noon & 2-6pm Wed-Mon Jun-Sep, 2-5pm Wed-Fri, 10am-noon & 2-5pm Sat & Sun Apr, May & Oct), the former home of the landscape painter Emmanuel Lansyer (1838–93), featuring his original canvases alongside works by Canaletto, Millet, Piranese and Delacroix.

Inside the church, the **Collegiale St-Ours**, lies the tomb of Agnés Sorel, Charles VII's mistress, who lived in the château during her illicit affair with the king. Notoriously beautiful and fiercely intelligent, Agnés earned many courtly enemies due to her powerful influence over Charles' decisions; having borne three daughters, she died in mysterious circumstances while pregnant with their fourth child. The official cause was dysentery, although some scientists have speculated that elevated levels of mercury in her body indicate she may have been poisoned by persons unknown.

At the northern end of the Citadelle is the **Logis Royal** (☎ 02 47 59 01 32; www.chateau-loches.fr; adult/12-18yr €7/4.50; 🕐 9am-7pm mid-Mar–Sep, 9.30am-5pm Oct–mid-Mar), built as a royal residence for Charles VII and his successors, and later used as a prison until the 1920s. In the basement is a circular chamber where the unfortunate Cardinal Balue was supposedly kept suspended from the ceiling in a wooden cage for betraying Louis XI. In fact, it was more likely used as a grain store, although you can see a replica of the cardinal's actual cage elsewhere in the castle, as well as a chilling Salle des Questions (otherwise known as a torture chamber). Louis XI also constructed the notorious **Tour Ronde** (Round Tower) and **Tour Martelet**, both of which incarcerated prisoners during the Revolution (you can still read some of their graffiti etched on the walls).

At the southern end of the promontory is the 36m-high **Donjon** (keep) built in the 11th century by Foulques Nerra. Though the interior floors have fallen away, dizzying catwalks allow you to climb right to the top for fantastic (and rather unsteadying) views across town.

Sleeping & Eating

Hôtel de France (☎ 02 47 59 00 32; www.hoteldefranceloches.com; 6 rue Picois & 11 rue de la République; d €40-80) An arched gateway leads into the paved courtyard of this old *relais de poste* (post house), now a trim if rather tired Logis de France. The best rooms are above the traditionally themed restaurant (*menus* €18 to €50) in the main building: rather frilly and dated, they're a darn sight more attractive than the battered duplex rooms in the courtyard annexe.

Le Moulin L'Étang (☎ 02 47 59 15 10; d €70-80, meals from €30; 🅿) A better option is this lovingly converted mill 3.2km from Loches along the N143, with thick-beamed rooms peeking out through titchy blue shutters onto a private millpond and 2.8-hectare garden, and home-cooked food dripping with local ingredients. Parking is available.

SELF-CATERING

If you fancy your own feast, head for Loches' **market** (🕐 7am-3pm Wed, 7am-1pm Sat), which takes over rue de la République and the surrounding streets every Wednesday and Saturday and attracts punters from far and wide.

Getting There & Around

Loches is 67km southwest of Blois and 41km southeast of Tours. Trains and SNCF buses link the train station, across the River Indre from the tourist office, with Tours (€7.80, 55 minutes, 12 daily, six on weekends).

CHINON

pop 8700

Peacefully placed along the northern bank of the Vienne and dominated by its hulking hillside château, Chinon is best known as one of the Loire's main wine-producing areas. Vineyards stretch along both sides of the river; within the muddle of white tufa houses and black slate rooftops of the town centre you'll discover an interesting medieval quarter, although the château itself is largely ruined and is currently the focus of a major restoration project.

Orientation & Information

Rue Haute St-Maurice, the main street of the hillside medieval quarter, becomes rue Voltaire as you move east. The train station

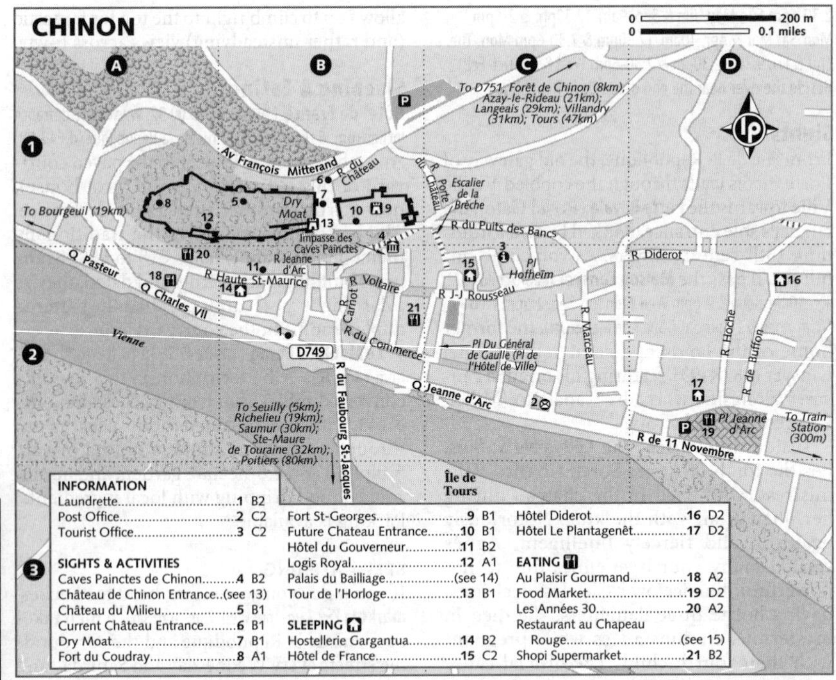

is 1km east of the commercial hub, place du Général de Gaulle (also called place de l'Hôtel de Ville).

Laundrette (40 quai Jeanne d'Arc; 7am-9pm)

Post Office (80 quai Jeanne d'Arc)

Tourist Office (☎ 02 47 93 17 85; www.chinon.com; place Hofheïm; 10am-7pm May-Sep, 10am-noon & 2-6pm Mon-Sat Oct-Apr)

Sights

CHÂTEAU DE CHINON

Since 2005 – no doubt spurred along by the sudden and disastrous collapse of the ramparts at Saumur (p446) – Chinon's **Forteresse Royale** (☎ 02 47 93 13 45; during restoration works adult/under 12yr €3/free; 9am-7pm Apr-Sep, 9.30am-5pm Oct-Mar) is engaged in one of the region's largest restoration projects, costing €14.5 million and originally scheduled to finish in 2008, but still well under way at the time of writing. The château is split into three sections separated by dry moats. The 12th-century **Fort St-Georges** and the **Logis Royal** (Royal Lodgings) are bearing the brunt of the restoration work and are currently off-limits to the public, but the rest of the castle is still open. The most interesting sights are the 14th-century **Tour de l'Horloge** (Clock Tower), which houses a collection of Joan of Arc memorabilia, and the wonderful valley panorama from the top of the 13th-century **Fort du Coudray**; there's also a small historical exhibition in the **Château du Milieu** (the Middle Castle).

Entry to the castle is currently via a tunnel behind the castle, accessed from av François Mitterand; look out for the replica trebuchet beside the main road.

OLD TOWN

The author François Rabelais (1483–1553), whose works include *Gargantua and Pantagruel* grew up in Chinon; you'll see Rabelais-related names dotted all around Chinon's old town, which offers a fine cross-section of medieval architecture, best seen along **rue Haute St-Maurice** and **rue Voltaire**. Look out for the remarkable **Hôtel du Gouverneur** (rue Haute St-Maurice), an impressive town house with a double-flighted staircase ensconced behind a carved gateway, and the nearby Gothic **Palais du Bailliage**, the former residence of Chinon's bailiwick (now occupied by the Hostellerie

Gargantua). The tourist office has a free walking-tour leaflet and offers **guided tours** (adult/under 18yr €4.50/2.50).

Hidden at the end of a cobbled alleyway off rue Voltaire are the **Caves Painctes de Chinon** (☎ 02 47 93 30 44; impasse des Caves Painctes; admission €3; 🕑 guided tours 11am-3pm & 4.30-6pm, Tue-Sun Jul–mid-Sep), former quarries converted into wine cellars during the 15th century. Tours of the *caves* are run by the Confrérie des Bons Entonneurs Rabelaisiens (www.entonneursrabelaisiens.com), a brotherhood of local wine growers.

Sleeping

Hôtel Le Plantagenêt (☎ 02 47 93 36 92; www.hotel-plantagenet.com; 12 place Jeanne d'Arc; s €40-60, d €48-75, tr €54-85; ❄ ⊠) Basic, dated but perfectly serviceable hotel halfway between centre and station, with rooms spread over three buildings – a 19th-century house, a garden annexe, and a separate *maison bourgeoise*.

Hôtel Diderot (☎ 02 47 93 18 87; www.hoteldiderot.com; 4 rue de Buffon; s €43-53, d €53-75) Can this really be a two-starrer? A gorgeous shady town house on the edge of Chinon (parking available), crammed with polished antiques and rose-filled gardens, run with the kind of tip-top charm you'd expect of a hotel twice the price. It's creaky and squeaky in places, but full of charm: rooms are all individually styled, from over-the-top Napoleonic to stripped-back art deco.

Hostellerie Gargantua (☎ 02 47 93 04 71; www.hotel-gargantua.com; 73 rue Voltaire; r €49-77) Harry Potter would feel right at home at this turret-topped, soaring medieval mansion, once occupied by the town bailiwick, and now a simple, endearingly offbeat period hotel. Spiral staircases, pitch-dark wood and solid stone conjure the Middle Ages atmosphere: all the rooms are named after Rabelais characters, but the Superior rooms are worth the cash, including Grangousier with its fireplace and four-poster, and Badebec with its oak beams and château views. Rather incongruously, there are also mod-cons including flat-screen TVs and wi-fi. Verily good fun.

Hôtel de France (☎ 02 47 93 33 91, www.bestwestern.com/fr/hoteldefrancechinon; 47 place du Général de Gaulle; d from €84, tr from €120) Yes, it's a Best Western, but there's nary a corporate connotation in sight at this lovely place overlooking the town's prettiest square. It's full of Gallic allure – old carpets, mismatched furniture, rich wall-papers – and the rooms are quaint and cosy (try and bag one of the front-facing balconies).

Eating & Drinking

Restaurant au Chapeau Rouge (☎ 02 47 98 08 08; place du Général de Gaulle; menus €21, €37 & €56, mains €21-24) There's an air of a Left Bank brasserie hanging around the Red Hat, sheltered behind red and gold awnings and net curtains; hare fondant, smoked fish and other countrified dishes fill the chalkboards.

our pick **Au Plaisir Gourmand** (☎ 02 47 93 20 48; 2 rue Parmentier; menu €39, mains €26-38; 🕑 closed dinner Sun & Mon) Some of the Loire's finest cuisine is served in a delightful 17th-century Chinon town house under the Michelin-starred eye of owner-chef Jean-Claude Rigollet. Rich and sophisticated recipes revolve around top-quality produce – perch, beef fillet, pike, langoustine, scallops – and the setting is heart-meltingly lovely, especially if you can secure one of the highly sought-after courtyard tables on a sultry summer's evening. If you're going to splash out anywhere in the Loire, this is definitely the place to do it.

Les Années 30 (☎ 02 47 93 37 18; 78 rue Voltaire; menus €27, €34 & €40; 🕑 closed Tue & Wed) Diners eat elbow-to-elbow in this diminutive bistro in the medieval quarter, regardless of whether you choose to dine in the bric-a-brac *salle* or the streetside pergola-topped patio. The menu ranges from traditional coq au vin and sea bream to unusual choices such as wild boar.

SELF-CATERING

Food market (place Jeanne d'Arc; 🕑 Thu morning)

Shopi supermarket (22 place du Général de Gaulle; 🕑 7.30am-1pm & 2.30-7.30pm Mon-Sat, 8.30am-12.30pm Sun)

Getting There & Around

Chinon is 47km southwest of Tours, 21km southwest of Azay-le-Rideau and 80km north of Poitiers.

Trains or SNCF buses (12 daily, six on weekends) go to Tours (€8.50, 45 to 70 minutes) and Azay-le-Rideau (€4.30, 25 minutes).

ANJOU

In Anjou, Renaissance châteaux give way to chalky white tufa cliffs concealing an astonishing underworld of wine cellars, mushroom farms and monumental art sculptures. Above ground, black slate roofs pepper the vine-rich land.

Angers, the historic capital of Anjou, is famous for its fortified hilltop château and a stunning medieval tapestry. Architectural gems in Anjou's crown include the city's cathedral and, to the southeast, the Romanesque Abbaye de Fontevraud. Europe's highest concentration of troglodyte dwellings dot the banks of the Loire around Saumur.

The area along the Rivers Loire, Authion and Vienne from Angers southeast to Azay-le-Rideau form the **Parc Naturel Régional Loire-Anjou-Touraine** (www.parc-loire-anjou-touraine.fr, in French), a 2530-sq-km regional park whose mission is to protect both the landscape and the area's extraordinary architectural *patrimoine* (patrimony).

SAUMUR & TROGLODYTE VALLEY

pop 30,000

Like many of the Loire's riverside towns, there's an air of Parisian sophistication around Saumur: stately, solidly bourgeois, and just a touch snooty, the town is renowned for its École Nationale d'Équitation, a national cavalry school that's been home to the crack horsemen of the Cadre Noir since 1828. Soft white tufa cliffs stretch along the riverbanks east and west of Saumur, pock-marked by the unusual man-made caves known as *habitations troglodytes*.

Orientation & Information

Saumur's main commercial streets are rue Franklin Roosevelt and its southeastern continuation, rue d'Orléans, which lead inland from Pont Cessart; and perpendicular rue St-Jean, which is pedestrianised.

The **Saumur Tourist Office** (☎ 02 41 40 20 60; www.saumur-tourisme.com; ⏰ 9.15am-12.30pm & 2-6pm Mon-Sat, 10am-noon Sun) is in the theatre building, facing the river.

Sights & Activities

Lording above the town's rooftops, Saumur's fairy-tale **château** (☎ 02 41 40 24 40; adult/under 11yr €3/free; ⏰ gardens 10am-1pm & 2-5.30pm Wed-Mon Apr-Sep) was largely built during the 13th century by Louis XI, and has variously served as a dungeon, fortress and country residence, but its defensive heritage took a hefty knock in 2001 when a large chunk of the western ramparts collapsed without warning, triggering an enormous restoration project that has already lasted seven years and still shows no sign of being completed. While the interior remains closed, you can still wander around the outside grounds and take a guided tour exploring the castle's history (ask at the tourist office).

Three kilometres west of the town in St-Hilaire-St-Florent, the **École Nationale d'Équitation** (National Equestrian School; ☎ 02 41 53 50 60; www.cadrenoir.fr; rte de Marson; adult/3-12yr €7.50/4.50; ⏰ 9am-6pm Tue-Fri, 9am-12.30pm Sat, 2-6pm Mon Apr–mid-Oct) is one of France's foremost riding academies, responsible for training the country's Olympic teams and members of the elite Cadre Noir display team. Famous for their acrobatic manoeuvres and astonishing discipline, Cadre Noir horses take around 5½ years to train to display standard; their riders are distinguished by a special black jacket, cap, gold spurs and three golden wings on their whips.

There are guided tours every half-hour during opening hours until 4pm; morning tours usually include a Cadre Noir training session. Advance reservations are essential, and enquire about the availability of English-language tours.

Saumur's many mushroom farms provide a useful outlet for the 10 tonnes of droppings dumped daily by the school's 400-odd horses: you can get acquainted with the fabulous fungus at the **Musée du Champignon** (Mushroom Museum; ☎ 02 41 50 31 55; www.musee-du-champignon.com; rte de Gennes; adult/student/child €7/5.50/4.50; ⏰ 10am-7pm Feb–mid-Nov), tucked into a cave at the western edge of St-Hilaire-St-Florent. Further on 300m is **Pierre et Lumiere** (☎ 02 41 50 70 04; ⏰ 10am-7pm Feb–mid-Nov), an underground miniature park featuring many local landmarks crafted from tufa stone.

Sleeping

Camping l'Île d'Offard (☎ 02 41 40 30 00; www.cvtloisirs.com; rue de Verden; sites for 2 people €16-25.50; ⏰ Mar-Oct) Well-equipped and very pretty campsite on a natural river island, about 1.5km from town.

Hôtel de Londres (☎ 02 41 51 23 98; www.lelondres.com; 48 rue d'Orléans; s €40, d €45-65;) Small-town hotel run with big-city efficiency: refurbished rooms in jolly checks, crisp blues and sunshine yellows, all with gleaming bathrooms and thoughtful spoils including wi-fi, afternoon tea and a well-stocked comic library for kids (big and little). Parking available.

Hôtel Saint-Pierre (☎ 02 41 50 33 00; www.saintpierresaumur.com; 8 rue Haute St-Pierre; r €70-155) Squeezed down a miniscule alleyway op-

STÉPHANE MICHON, CURATOR AT THE MUSHROOM MUSEUM

'I never really planned on venturing into the weird and wonderful world of the mushroom… it was just one of those things that happened really! I originally studied History of Art and Archeology, and became involved with various tourism projects around Saumur after completing my studies – including managing the Musée du Champignon (see opposite).

'There are more than 1500km of subterranean caves around Saumur which provide the perfect environment for cultivating mushrooms: a constant year-round temperature (of 13°C to 14°C) and very high humidity (more than 90%). Thanks to Saumur's equestrian connections, we also have ready access to plenty of top-quality fertiliser for our mushroom crops! The caves keep us sheltered from the rain, but they can be quite chilly and damp to work in – I've also nearly lost myself on several occasions, hardly surprising really since there are dozens of kilometres of caves around Saumur, and no maps!

'In addition to the *champignon de Paris* (button mushroom), some of our other famous fungi include the *pied bleu* (blue foot), the shiitake and the *pleurote* (oyster mushroom). For me, the best way to eat them is simply either fried with parsley and oil, or in the local speciality, *Galipette*: a large *champignon de Paris,* grilled and then stuffed with goat's cheese, parsley butter or *rillettes* (potted meat). I try to eat mushrooms at least once a week – they're really healthy, and naturally I'm lucky enough to be able to pick a fresh crop every day!'

posite the cathedral, this effortlessly smart hideaway mixes up heritage architecture with modern-day comforts: pale stone, thick rugs and vintage lamps sit happily alongside wi-fi, minibars and satellite TV (smallish rooms range from Tradition to Prestige). It's one of those places where every nook and cranny seems to hide a secret: tiled mosaics in the bathrooms; black-and-white dressage photos in the lobby; flagstones, character-packed furniture and twisted beams throughout.

our pick **Château de Verrières** (☎ 02 41 38 05 15; http://chateau-verrieres.com; 53 rue d'Alsace; r €120-290;) Despite its stonking size, there are actually only 10 rooms at this wonderful 1890 château, ensconced within the woods and ponds of a 1.6-hectare English park (parking is available). As you might expect, the feel's classic and kingly: luxurious rooms feature free-standing roll-top baths, floor-to-ceiling curtains, antique writing desks, wood panelling and heritage wallpaper (not to mention views over the Cadre Noir training ground); the top-of-the-line Rising Sun suite even boasts a dash of modish Japanese minimalism. Regal with a capital R.

Getting There & Around

See p453 for details on bus options from Angers.

Trains from Saumur travel to Tours (€10 to €13.10, 35 to 55 minutes, 10 to 16 daily) and Angers (€7.40, 20 minutes, 12 daily, six on Sunday).

Détours de Loire (☎ 02 41 53 01 01; 1 rue David d'Angers; 9am-12.30pm & 4.30-6.30pm) rents out bikes (see p418).

EAST OF SAUMUR

The tufa bluffs east of Saumur are home to some of the area's main wine producers: you'll see notable *vignobles* (vineyards) and *viticulteurs* (wine growers) dotted all along the riverside D947, most offering free *dégustation* (tasting) sessions from around 10am to 6pm between spring and autumn (the French-language website www.producteurs-de-saumur-champigny.fr has useful background information).

The smart château of **Montsoreau** (☎ 02 41 67 12 60; adult/student 15-17yr/5-14yr €8.30/6.60/5.20; 10am-7pm May-Sep, 2-6pm Apr & Oct–mid-Nov, 2-6pm weekend Mar) houses an interesting museum exploring the river trade that once sustained the Loire Valley. The castle itself was built in 1455 by one of Charles VII's advisers, and later became famous thanks to an Alexandre Dumas novel, *La Dame de Monsoreau*. The nearby village of **Candes-sur-Martin** occupies an idyllic spot at the confluence of the Vienne and the Loire.

The most interesting attraction east of Saumur is the **Abbaye Royale de Fontevraud** (☎ 02 41 51 71 41; www.abbaye-fontevraud.com; adult/18-25yr/under 18yr €7.90/5.90/free, €1.40 discount Nov-Apr; 9am-6.30pm Jun-Sep, 10am-6pm Oct, Apr & May, 10am-5.30pm Nov-Mar), 4km south of Montsoreau in Fontevraud l'Abbaye.

VALLEY OF THE TROGLODYTES

For centuries, the creamy white tufa cliffs around Saumur have provided a key source of local building materials; in fact, many of the Loire's grandest châteaux were constructed from the distinctive stone quarried around Saumur and the surrounding area. But the cliffs weren't only used for their stone; as in the Vézère Valley in the Dordogne (p630), the rocky bluffs also provided shelter and storage for the local inhabitants, leading to the development of a unique *culture troglodyte* (cave culture). Originally used as human dwellings, the cool, dank caves now provide the perfect natural cellars for everyone from wine growers to mushroom farmers. Eat your heart out, Bilbo Baggins.

You'll see *habitations troglodytes* dotted all around the valley east and west of Saumur, but a good base is the small village of Doué-la-Fontaine. About 6km north of Doué is one of the best examples of troglodytic culture, the abandoned village of **Rochemenier** (☎ 02 41 59 18 15; www.troglodyte.info; adult/7-18yr €4.90/2.50; 9.30am-7pm Apr-Oct, 2-6pm Sat, Sun and bank holidays Nov, Feb & Mar), inhabited right up until the 1930s. You can wander around the remains of two farmsteads (complete with houses, stables, outbuildings and even an underground chapel). More hobbit-style houses can be seen at **Les Maison Troglodytes** (☎ 02 41 59 00 32; adult/10-18yr €5.50/3; 9.30am-7pm Jun-Sep, 9.30am-12.30pm & 2-6.30pm Mar-May & Oct) in La Fosse, where the only trace of the underground dwellings are the chimneys poking up from the ground. Other sites include the former stone quarries of **Les Perrières** (☎ 02 41 59 71 29; Doué-la-Fontaine; adult/child €5/3; 10.30am-7pm daily mid-Jun–mid-Sep, 2.30-7pm, Tue-Sun mid-Sep–Oct & mid-Apr–mid-Jun), sometimes called the 'cathedral caves' due to their lofty caverns, and the **Troglodytes et Sarcophages** (☎ 02 41 59 24 95; www.troglo-sarcophages.fr; Doué-la-Fontaine; adult/6-11yr €4.50/3; 2.30-7pm daily Jun-Aug, Sat & Sun May), a Merovingian mine where sarcophagi were produced from the 6th to the 9th centuries. Atmospheric lantern-lit tours of the caves take place on Tuesdays and Fridays at 8.30pm (by reservation only) in July and August (adult/child costs €7/5).

You'll also find some strange pieces of artwork dotted around the valley, including the **Hélice Terrestre de l'Orbière** (☎ 02 41 57 95 92; adult/child €4/2; 11am-8pm May-Sep, 2-6pm Wed-Sun Oct-Apr), in St-Georges des Sept Voies, 23km northwest of Saumur – a startling piece of symbolic rock art sculpted by local artist Jacques Warminski (1946–96). Even weirder is the grotesque sculpture gallery at **La Cave aux Sculptures** (☎ 02 41 59 15 40; Dénezé-sous-Doué; adult/6-13yr €4/2.50; 10.30am-1pm & 2-6.30pm Tue-Sun Apr-Oct), full of leering faces, contorted figures and bestial gargoyles carved sometime between the 16th and 17th century. No one's quite sure whether the sculptures are the work of early cartoonists, political protestors, or just local artists with a penchant for the peculiar.

But perhaps oddest of all is the **Troglo des Pommes Tapées** (☎ 02 41 51 48 30; adult/8-16yr €5.50/3.50; 10am-6.30pm Wed-Sun, 2-6.30pm Tue mid-Mar–Oct) near Turquant, one of the last places in France to produce the traditional dried apples known as *pommes tapées*. Once dried and cored, each apple is skilfully 'tapped' to ensure its readiness, and the powerfully flavoured fruits can be used in all kinds of recipes, from apple sauce to *tarte aux pommes*.

Until its closure in 1793, this huge complex was one of the largest ecclesiastical centres in Europe; unusually, both nuns and monks were governed by an abbess (generally a lady of noble birth retiring from public life). Around the enormous complex you can visit the former dormitories, workrooms and prayer halls, as well as the spooky underground sewer system and a wonderful barrel-vaulted refectory, where the monks and nuns would eat in silence while being read to from the scriptures.

Look out too for the space rocket–shaped kitchens, built entirely from stone to make them fireproof.

The highlight is undoubtedly the massive, movingly simple **abbey church**, notable for its soaring pillars, Romanesque domes, and the polychrome tombs of four illustrious Plantagenets: Henry II, king of England from 1154 to 1189; his wife Eleanor of Aquitaine (who retired to Fontevraud following Henry's death); their son Richard the Lion-Heart; and his wife Isabelle of Angoulème.

THE LOIRE VALLEY

Sleeping & Eating

Chez Teresa (☎ 02 41 51 21 24; 6 av Rochechouart; d €49-55, mains €6.50-8.50) Keeping up Fontevraud's English connections, this frilly little teashop is run by an expat Englishwoman with a passion for traditional teatime fare: tea for two with sandwiches, scones and cakes is just €8.50, and there are cute upstairs rooms if you fancy staying overnight.

Hôtel Abbaye Royale de Fontevraud (☎ 02 41 51 73 16; www.hotelfp-fontevraud.com;, menus €23, €32, €38, & €47; dinner Mar-Nov) For something altogether more upmarket, try this gastronomic godsend at the base of the valley below the abbey, serving seriously *haute cuisine* (pigeon, duck, lobster, foie gras) under the arches of the old priory cloisters. The rooms (€55 to €115 for a double) are a bit corporate in comparison to the stellar food, but comfy nonetheless.

ANGERS

pop 151,000

Often dubbed 'Black Angers' due to the murky stone and dark slate used in its buildings, the riverside city is the eastern gateway to the Loire Valley. It's best known for its public parks and famous tapestries: the 14th-century *Tenture de l'Apocalypse* is housed in the city's old château, while its modern-day counterpart, the *Chant du Monde,* is housed at the intriguing Jean Lurcat museum.

Orientation

Angers is split into two halves by the River Maine: the largely modern district of La Doutre occupies the western bank, while the historic old quarter occupies the eastern bank, bordered by bd Ayrault, bd du Maréchal Foch and bd du Roi René. The commercial centre is southeast of the cathedral, with the train station about 800m south of central place du Président Kennedy.

Information

There are commercial banks on bd du Maréchal Foch.

Ambiances Multimedia (10 rue Bodinier; per hr €3; 10.30am-8pm Mon-Sat, 3-8pm Sun) Internet access.

Cyber Espace (25 rue de la Roë; per hr €3; 10am-10pm Mon-Thu, 10am-midnight Fri & Sat, 2-8pm Sun) Internet access.

Laundrettes rue St-Laud (2 rue St-Laud; 7am-9pm); rue Talot (rue Talot; 7am-10pm); rue Val de Maine (rue Val de Maine; 7am-10pm)

Post Office (1 rue Franklin Roosevelt) Exchanges currency.

Tourist Office (☎ 02 41 23 50 00; www.angersloiretourisme.com; 7 place du Président Kennedy; 10am-7pm Mon, 9am-7pm Tue-Sat, 10am-6pm Sun May-Sep, 2-6pm Mon, 9am-6pm Tue-Sat, 10am-1pm Sun Oct-Apr) Currency exchange for €4, also sells a joint ticket to the city's château and museums for €15.

Sights & Activities

CHÂTEAU D'ANGERS

Angers' brooding black-stone **château** (☎ 02 41 86 48 77; 2 promenade du Bout du Monde; adult/under 18yr €7.50/free; 9.30am-6.30pm May-Aug, 10am-5.30pm Sep-Apr) looms behind quai de Ligny, ringed by battlements and 17 watchtowers. Formerly the seat of power for the counts of Anjou, the principal reason to visit these days is the **Tenture de l'Apocalypse** (Apocalypse tapestry), a 101m-long series of tapestries commissioned by Louis I, duke of Anjou around 1375 to illustrate the Book of Revelation. It recounts the story of the Day of Judgment from start to finish, complete with the Four Horsemen of the Apocalypse, the Battle of Armageddon and the coming of the Beast: look out for graphic depictions of St Michael battling a satanic seven-headed dragon and the fall of Babylon. Free multilingual audioguides provide useful context, and there are guided tours in French, English, German and Italian in July and August.

CATHÉDRALE ST-MAURICE

In the heart of the Quartier de la Cité is **Cathédrale St-Maurice** (8.30am-7pm Apr-Nov, 8.30am-5.30pm Dec-Mar), one of the earliest examples of Plantagenet or Angevin architecture in France, distinguished by its rounded ribbed vaulting, 15th-century stained glass and a 12th-century portal depicting the Day of Judgment.

Across the square from the cathedral on place Ste-Croix is the **Maison d'Adam** (c 1500), one of the city's best-preserved medieval houses, decorated with a riot of carved (and often rather bawdy) figurines. From the square in front of the cathedral a monumental staircase, the **Montée St-Maurice**, leads down to the river.

GALERIE DAVID D'ANGERS

Angers' most famous son is the sculptor Pierre-Jean David (1788–1856), often just known as David d'Angers. Renowned for lifelike busts and sculptures, his work adorns public monuments all over France, notably at the Panthéon, the Louvre and Père Lachaise cemetery (where he carved many tombstones, including Honoré de Balzac's). His work forms the cornerstone of the **Galerie David d'Angers** (☎ 02 41 05 38 90; 33bis rue Toussaint;

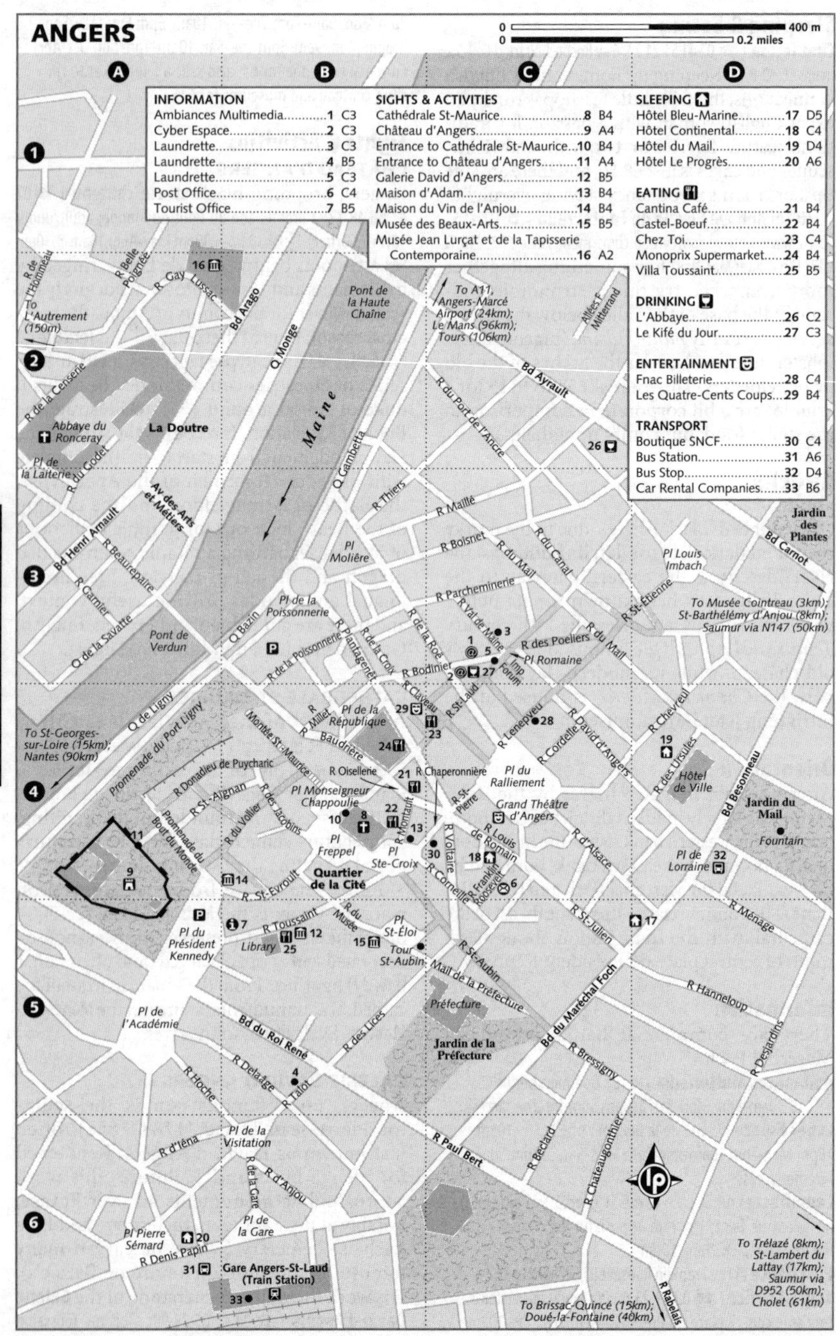

THE LOIRE VALLEY

adult/student/under 18yr €4/3/free; ⌚ 10am-7pm daily mid-Jun–mid-Sep, 10am-noon & 2-6pm Tue-Sun mid-Sep–mid-Jun), housed in the converted 12th-century Toussaint Abbey, flooded with light through a striking glass-and-girder roof.

MUSÉE JEAN LURÇAT ET DE LA TAPISSERIE CONTEMPORAINE

Providing an interesting counterpoint to Angers' other famous piece of needlework, the **Musée Jean Lurçat et de la Tapisserie Contemporaine** (☎ 02 41 24 18 45; 6 bd Arago; adult/under 18yr €4/free; ⌚ 10am-7pm daily Jun-Sep, 10am-noon & 2-6pm Tue-Sun Oct-May) collects major 20th-century tapestries by Jean Lurçat, Thomas Gleb and others inside the Hôpital St-Jean, a 12th-century hospital founded by Henry Plantagenet. The centrepiece is the *Chant du Monde* (Song of the World), an amazing tapestry sequence depicting the trials and triumphs of modern humanity, from nuclear holocaust and space exploration to the delights of drinking champagne. Odd and unmissable.

MUSÉE DES BEAUX-ARTS

Angers' heavily restored **Musée des Beaux-Arts** (Fine Arts Museum; ☎ 02 41 05 38 00; 14 rue du Musée; adult/student/under 18yr €4/3/free, during special exhibitions €6/5/free; ⌚ 10am-7pm daily Jun-Sep, noon or 1-6pm Tue-Sun Oct-May) sits on the lovely paved place St-Éloi, surrounded by polished-up, pale stone buildings. Mixing plate glass and steel with the fine lines of the typical Angevin *maison particulier* (aristocratic house), the Logis Barrault, the museum has a collection of 18th- to 20th-century works, as well as a section on the history of Angers.

WINE TASTING

Still thirsty? Head for the **Maison du Vin de l'Anjou** (☎ 02 41 88 81 13; mdesvins-angers@vinsvaldeloire.fr; 5bis place du Président Kennedy; ⌚ 9am-1pm & 3-6.30pm Tue-Sun Apr-Sep, 9.30am-1pm & 3-6.30pm Tue-Sat Oct-Mar) for the lowdown on local vintages and tips on where to buy Anjou and Loire wines.

Sleeping

Hôtel du Mail (☎ 02 41 25 05 25; www.hotel-du-mail.com; 8-10 rue des Ursules; s €39-65, d €55-75, tr €85) Converted convent with an old-world atmosphere. The funky lobby, with its parquet flooring, arty lights and curvy desk, is more exciting than the rather dated rooms, reached via a creaky spiral staircase; but the quiet courtyard location, huge buffet breakfast and thoughtful touches (daily newspapers, free umbrellas, wi-fi) make this a peaceful Angers base. Parking is also available.

Hôtel Le Progrès (☎ 02 41 88 10 14; www.hotelleprogres.com; 26 rue Denis Papin; s/tr €42/66, d €54-64; ❄) It's nothing fancy, but this reliable station hotel is solid, friendly and squeaky clean, decked out in plain style with free extras including air-con and wi-fi.

Hôtel Continental (☎ 02 41 86 94 94; www.hotellecontinental.com; 12-14 rue Louis de Romain; s €57-66, d €68; ❄ ☒) Wedged into a weird wafer-shaped building in the city centre, this is a great metro-style hotel, with 25 rooms decked out in cosy checks and sunny colours, plus plenty of mod-cons (wi-fi, satellite TV, and a good downstairs café, Le Green). Street noise is a drawback.

Hôtel Bleu-Marine (☎ 02 41 87 37 20; www.marinehotel-angers.com; bd du Maréchal Foch; ❄) The choice for the design-conscious. Clean lines, minimalist decor, businessy styling and wall-mounted LCD TVs conjure up Angers' sharpest rooms, though the look occasionally borders on the spartan. It has free wi-fi, and parking is also available.

Eating

Castel-Boeuf (☎ 02 41 87 11 44; 14 rue Montault; menus €12.50 & €18.50; ⌚ closed Sun, dinner Mon & Tue) Homely little restaurant near the cathedral specialising in unpretentious country food – it's especially popular for its *carpaccio* beef (with Roquefort, shallots or Italian dressing).

Cantina Café (☎ 02 41 87 36 34; 9 rue Oisellerie; mains €15-25; ⌚ closed Mon & lunch Sun) Southern flavours with Spanish accents are the mainstays at this pleasant diner, recommended for its mussels, salads and steaks.

Villa Toussaint (☎ 02 41 88 15 64; 43 rue Toussaint; mains €16.80-26.80) With its sliding doors, plate-glass and decked patio (complete with an overarching tree), you know you're in for a treat at this fusion place, combining pan-Asian flavours with classic French ingredients. The *combinaisons* bring together several dishes onto one plate, from sushi to Thai chicken and tapas.

Chez Toi (☎ 02 41 87 85 58; 44 rue St-Laud; mains €12.90-20.90; ⌚ 9am-1.30am Mon-Sat) Minimalist furniture and technicolour trappings meet head-to-head in this zippy little lounge-bar, much favoured by the trendy young Angevin set. All the *menus* are named after *amis* (friends) to emphasise the chummy vibe, and you're positively encouraged to share.

ORANGE PEEL & ANISEED

Some of France's most distinctive **liqueurs** are distilled in the Loire Valley, including bitter orange Cointreau and the aniseedy (and allegedly hallucinogenic) brew known as absinthe, the tipple of choice for every self-respecting artist during the Belle Époque.

Cointreau has its origins in the experiments of two enterprising brothers: Adolphe Cointreau, a sweet-maker, and his brother Édouard-Jean Cointreau, who founded a factory in Angers in 1849 to produce fruit-flavoured liqueurs. Having toyed around with various flavours, in 1875 Édouard-Jean's son (also called Édouard) hit upon the winning concoction of sweet and bitter oranges, flavoured with intensely orangey peel, which formed the basis for their new world-beating brew. The liqueur was a massive success; by the early 1900s over 800,000 bottles of Cointreau were being produced to the brothers' top-secret recipe, and a century later every single one of the 13 million bottles is still distilled to the same formula at the original factory site in Angers. You can visit **Le Musée Cointreau** (☎ 02 41 31 50 50; www.cointreau.fr; bd des Bretonnières; adult/concession €6/5.40; ⏲ tours 11am-6pm Mon-Sat May-Oct, 11am-6pm Tue-Sat Nov-Apr) on a guided tour, which includes a visit to the distillery and entry to the Cointreau archive: look out for some fascinating early advertising posters featuring the company's trademark clown, Pierrot, and a cinema advert produced by none other than the Lumière brothers. The museum is off the ring road east of Angers. By bus, take No 7 from the train station. By contrast, **absinthe** has had a more chequered history. Brewed from a heady concoction of natural herbs, true absinthe includes three crucial components: green anise, fennel and the foliage of *Artemisia absinthium* (wormwood), which has been used as a traditional remedy since the time of the ancient Egyptians. Legend has it that modern-day absinthe was concocted by a French doctor (rather wonderfully called Dr Pierre Ordinaire) in the late 1790s, before being acquired by a father-and-son team who established the first major absinthe factory, Maison Pernod-Fils, in 1805.

The popularity of the drink exploded in the 19th century, when it became the tipple of choice for bohemian poets and painters (as well as French troops, who were given the drink as an antimalarial drug). Seriously potent (usually between 45% and 90% proof), absinthe's traditional green colour and supposedly psychoactive effects led to its popular nickname of 'the green fairy'; everyone from Rimbaud to Vincent van Gogh sang its praises (Ernest Hemingway even invented his own absinthe cocktail, ominously dubbed *Death in the Afternoon*). Some scholars even believe that by the late 19th century there was more absinthe being drunk in France than wine.

But the drink's fearsome reputation was ultimately its own downfall: fearing widespread psychic degeneration, governments around the globe banned it in the early 20th century (including France in 1915), leading directly to the growth of other aperitifs such as pastis and ouzo. Faced with dwindling sales, the last absinthe factory closed down in the 1960s, but in the 1990s a group of dedicated *absintheurs* reverse-engineered the vivid green liqueur, chemically analysing century-old bottles that had escaped the ban. One of the modern distilleries to resurrect this famous firewater is the **Distillerie Combier** (☎ 02 41 40 23 00; www.combier.fr; 48 rue Beaurepaire; adult €3; ⏲ 10am-noon & 2-6pm Jul & Aug, closed Tue Sep, closed Tue-Thu May & Oct) near Saumur, where you can taste authentic absinthe alongside other liqueurs including Royal Combier, Triple Sec and Pastis d'Antan.

SELF-CATERING

The **Monoprix supermarket** (across from 59 rue Plantagenêt; ⏲ 8.30am-9pm Mon-Sat) has a food hall.

Drinking & Entertainment

The free *Angers Poche* details local listings, and tickets are sold at **Fnac billeterie** (☎ 08 92 68 36 22; 25-29 rue Lenepveu; ⏲ 10am-7pm Mon-Sat).

Le Kifé du Jour (☎ 02 41 86 80 70; 10am-2.30pm Mon-Sat, 5.30pm-2.30am Wed-Sat) A laid-back little wine bar with lots of local wines (pink, red and white) by the glass or the *pichet* (€2.70 to €3.80).

L'Autrement (☎ 02 41 87 61 95; www.lautrementcafe.com; 90 rue Lionnaise; ⏲ 6.30pm-2am Wed-Sat) Jazz troupes, roots bands and local acts grace the stage at Angers' smoothest cabaret bar, about 100m west of Abbaye du Ronceray.

L'Abbaye (☎ 02 41 88 47 92; www.abbayecafe.fr; 40 bd Ayrault; ⏲ 3pm-2am Mon-Sat, 5pm-1am Sun) This old abbey, now a popular cocktail and beer bar, is crammed with students in term-time.

Les Quatre-Cents Coups (☎ 02 41 88 70 95; www.les400coups.org; 12 rue Claveau) Good little multi-screen arts cinema showing art-house films from home and abroad (some nondubbed).

Getting There & Away

Angers is 107km west of Tours and 90km east of Nantes.

AIR

Angers-Marcé Airport (☎ 02 41 33 50 00; www.angers.aeroport.fr), 24km northeast of the centre in Marcé (off the A11), has flights to Southampton, Belfast, Dublin, Edinburgh, Glasgow, Leeds, Manchester and Newcastle with **Flybe** (www.flybe.com).

BUS

Anjou Bus (☎ 08 20 16 00 49; www.cg49.fr/themes/transports/anjoubus/default_v3.asp; 6.15am-7pm Mon-Sat) handles local buses from its base next to the new train station.

Buses 5 and 11 travel to Saumur (€7.30, 1½ hours, two daily Monday to Saturday). Bus 9 travels to Brissac-Quincé (€1.50, 25 minutes, three or four Monday to Saturday) and Doué-La-Fontaine (€5.60, one hour).

TRAIN

Angers' train station, Gare Angers-St-Laud, has connections to Saumur (€7.40, 20 minutes, 12 daily, six on Sunday) and Tours (€16, eight to 14 daily). TGVs travel to Paris' Gare Montparnasse (€46.10 to €61.60, 1½ hours, hourly).

Buy tickets at the city-centre **Boutique SNCF** (5 rue Chaperonnière; 1.30-7pm Mon, 9.30am-7pm Tue-Fri, to 6.30pm Sat).

Getting Around

At the time of writing, work was still continuing on Angers' much-vaunted (and hugely expensive) tram system – look out for updates.

BICYCLE

The tourist office rents bikes as part of the Détours de Loire network.

BUS

Local buses are run by **Keolis Angers** (☎ 02 41 33 64 64; www.cotra.fr). Tickets cost €1.20/10 for a single/10-ticket carnet.

CAR

All the major car-rental companies (including Avis, Hertz, Europcar and National) have **kiosks** (6.30am-7.30pm Mon-Sat) inside the train station.

AROUND ANGERS

South of Angers, the River Maine joins the Loire for the final leg of its journey to the Atlantic. The river banks immediately west of this confluence remain the source of some of the valley's most notable wines, including Savennières and Coteaux du Layon.

Château de Serrant

Built from cream-and-fawn tufa stone and topped by bell-shaped, slate-topped towers, the grand **Château de Serrant** (☎ 02 41 39 13 01; www.chateau-serrant.net; adult/child €9.50/6; 9.45am-5.45pm mid-May–mid-Sep, 9.45am-noon & 2-5.15pm mid-Mar–mid-May & mid-Sep–mid-Nov) is a wonderful slice of Renaissance style, reminiscent of Cheverny but on a more modest scale. Begun by the aristocrat Charles de Brie in the 16th century and later completed by a wealthy bureaucrat Guillaume de Bautru, the château is notable for its 12,000-tome library, huge kitchens and an extravagant domed bedroom known as the **Chambre Empire**, designed to host an overnight stay by the Emperor Napoléon (who actually only hung around for about two hours).

The château is near St-Georges-sur-Loire, 15km southwest of Angers on the N23. Anjou bus 18 travels from Angers (€1.50, 40 minutes, four to six Monday to Saturday).

Château de Brissac

The tallest castle in France, the **Château de Brissac** (☎ 02 41 91 22 21; www.chateau-brissac.fr; adult/15-18yr/7-14yr incl tour €8.50/7.50/4.50, grounds only €3.50; 10am-6.30pm daily Jul & Aug, 10.15am-12.15pm & 2-6pm Wed-Mon Apr-Jun, Sep & Oct) is 15km south of Angers in Brissac-Quincé. Spread over seven storeys and 204 rooms, this chocolate-box mansion was built by the duke of Brissac in 1502, and is one of the most luxuriously furnished in the valley, with a riot of posh furniture, ornate tapestries, twinkling chandeliers and luxurious bedrooms – even a private theatre. Around the house are 8 sq km of grounds filled with cedar trees, 19th-century stables and a vineyard, boasting no less than three AOC (Appellation d'Origine Contrôlée) vintages.

Four of the château's bedrooms are offered as ridiculously extravagant **chambres d'hôtes** (d €390, dinner €90;), perfect if you've always dreamt of sleeping on an antique four-poster under priceless tapestries and ancestral portraits.

Anjou Bus 9 links Angers with Brissac-Quincé (€1.50, 25 minutes, six daily).

Burgundy

With the vineyards and plains of Champagne to the north and the Rhône Valley, gateway to the Midi-Pyrénées, to the south, Burgundy (Bourgogne in French) can make a strong case for being the real heartland of France. Amid some of the country's most gorgeous countryside, two great French passions, wine and food, come together here in a particularly enticing and hearty form.

Burgundy's towns and its dashingly handsome capital, Dijon, are heirs to a glorious architectural heritage that goes back to the Renaissance, the Middle Ages and beyond, into the mists of Gallo-Roman and Celtic antiquity. Many civil and religious buildings, including Beaune's stunning Hôtel-Dieu, are topped with colourful tile roofs. Dijon, Beaune, Châtillon-sur-Seine and other towns have truly outstanding museums (www.musees-bourgogne.org, in French).

Burgundy is a paradise for lovers of the great outdoors. You can hike and cycle through the highly civilised vineyards of the Côte d'Or, on a network of cycling trails (such as the Voie Verte in Saône-et-Loire) that are also great for in-line skating, and in the wild reaches of the Parc Naturel Régional du Morvan (Morvan Regional Park); glide along the waterways of the Yonne in a canal boat; or float above the vineyards in a hot-air balloon.

The majority of Burgundy's most interesting historical sights are found in three *départements:* Côte-d'Or (capital: Dijon) in the northeast; Yonne (capital: Auxerre) in the northwest, almost at the gates of Paris; and Saône-et-Loire (capital: Mâcon) in the south. Most of the lightly populated Parc Naturel Régional du Morvan is in the region's fourth *département,* Nièvre.

HIGHLIGHTS

- Marvel at the glories of the late Middle Ages at **Dijon's Musée des Beaux-Arts** (p461) and **Beaune's Hôtel-Dieu** (p468)
- Sample Burgundy's most renowned vintages in **Beaune** (p468) and along the vine-carpeted slopes of the **Côte d'Or** (p465)
- Explore the hilltop village of **Vézelay** (p485) and stroll into the surrounding countryside
- Conjure up monastic life in the Middle Ages at the abbeys of **Cluny** (p492), **Fontenay** (p472), **Pontigny** (p480) and **Vézelay** (p485)
- Watch a 13th century–style château being built with 13th-century technology at the **Chantier Médiéval de Guédelon** (p479)

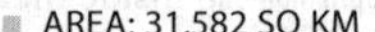

- POPULATION: 1.6 MILLION
- AREA: 31,582 SQ KM

History

At its height during the 14th and 15th centuries, the duchy of Burgundy was one of the richest and most powerful states in Europe, a vast swathe of territory stretching from modern-day Burgundy to Alsace and from there northwest to Lorraine, Luxembourg, Flanders and Holland. This was a time of bitter rivalry between Burgundy and France – indeed, it was the Burgundians who sold Jeanne d'Arc (Joan of Arc) to the English – and for a while it seemed quite possible that the kingdom of France would be taken over by Burgundy. In the end, though, it worked out the other way around, and in 1477 Burgundy became French.

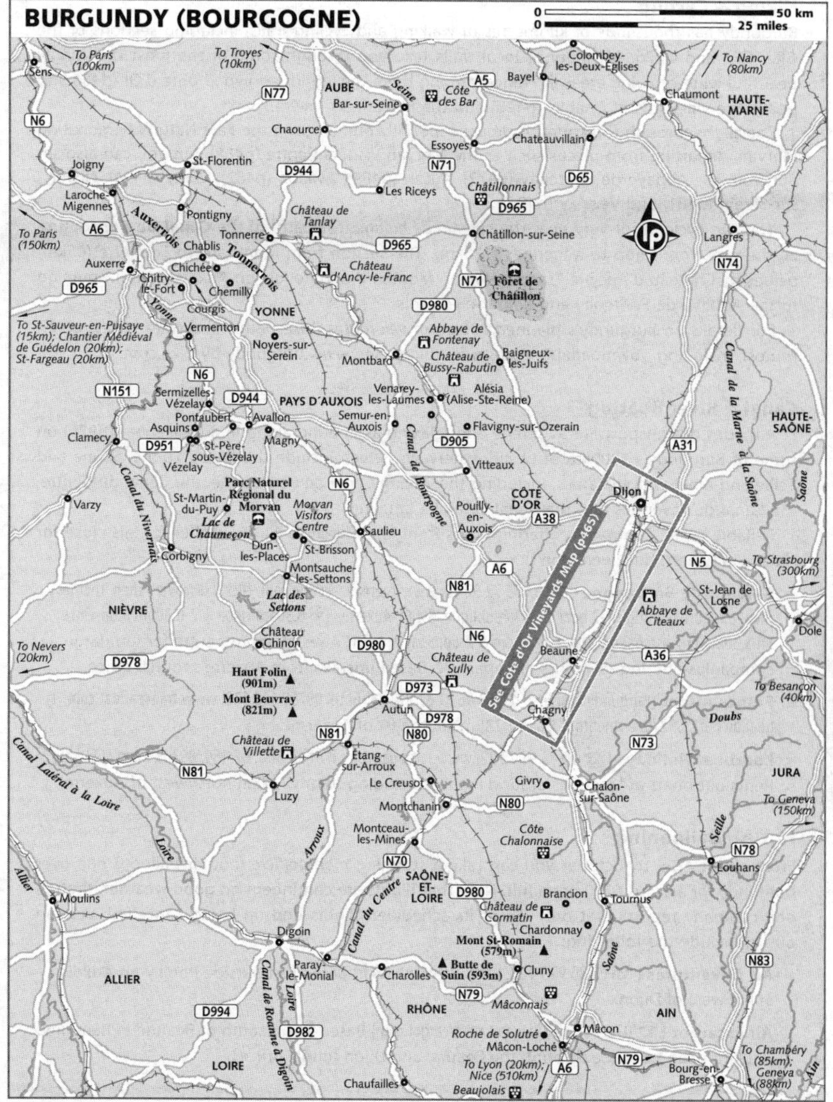

ON THE GROUND, UPON THE WATER & IN THE AIR

Tasting fine wines often involves hanging out in dimly lit cellars – but Burgundy is also a paradise for lovers of the great outdoors.

The **Comité Régional de Tourisme de Bourgogne** (Burgundy Regional Tourist Board; www.burgundy-tourism.com) publishes excellent brochures on Burgundy's outdoors options, including *Burgundy by Bike* and *Boating Holidays in Burgundy*, available at tourist offices.

Hiking & Cycling

Burgundy has thousands of kilometres of walking and cycling trails, including sections of the GR2, GR7 and GR76. A variety of local trails take you through some of the most ravishingly beautiful wine-growing areas in France, among them the world-renowned Côte d'Or (p466 and p470), the vineyards of Chablis (p478) and the Mâconnais (p494).

Footpaths through the countryside are especially numerous in the Parc Naturel Régional du Morvan, departing from places such as the Morvan Visitors Centre (p488), but you can also set out from the Abbaye de Fontenay (p472), Autun (p489), Avallon (p482), Cluny (p494), Noyers-sur-Serein (p481) and Vézelay (p486).

You can cycle on or very near the *chemin de halage* (towpath) of the **Canal de Bourgogne** all the way from Dijon to Migennes (225km). The section from Montbard to Tonnerre (65km) passes by Château d'Ancy-le-Franc; between Montbard and Pouilly-en-Auxois (58km), spurs go to the Abbaye de Fontenay and Semur-en-Auxois.

For details on Burgundy's planned 800km of *véloroutes* (bike paths) and *voies vertes* (green routes), including downloadable maps and guides, see www.burgundy-by-bike.com.

Canal & River Boating

Few modes of transport are as serene and relaxing as floating along in a houseboat (p970) on some of Burgundy's 1200km of placid waterways, which include the Rivers Yonne, Saône and Seille and a network of canals, including the 242km Canal de Bourgogne, the Canal du Centre, the Canal du Nivernais and the Canal Latéral à la Loire.

Reliable rental companies offering boats from late March to 11 November (canals close for repairs in winter, but rivers don't):

- **Bateaux de Bourgogne** (☎ 03 86 72 92 10; www.tourisme-yonne.com, click 'I discover', then 'themes', then 'pleasure boating'; 1-2 quai de la République, 89000 Auxerre; 🕓 8.30am-noon & 2-6.30pm Mon-Thu, till 5.30pm Fri, also open 9.30am-12.30pm & 2-6pm Sat Apr-Oct) A reservations centre for four large companies offering 15 points of departure. Based upstairs from Auxerre's tourist office.
- **France Afloat** (Burgundy Cruisers; ☎ 03 86 81 67 87, ☎ in UK 08700 110 538; www.franceafloat.com; 1 quai du Port, 89270 Vermenton) Based 23km southeast of Auxerre.
- **Locaboat Holidays** (☎ 03 86 91 72 72; www.locaboat.com; Port au Bois, BP 150, 89303 Joigny CEDEX) Rents out boats at locations around France, including Joigny (27km northwest of Auxerre).

Hot-Air Ballooning

From about April to October you can take a stunning *montgolfière* (hot-air balloon) ride over Burgundy for around €220 per adult. Note that flights are contingent on good weather, though one company reports that only 7% of its scheduled flights end up being cancelled. Veteran outfits include the following:

- **Air Adventures** (☎ 03 80 90 74 23; www.airadventures.fr) Based just outside Pouilly-en-Auxois, 50km west of Dijon.
- **Air Escargot** (☎ 03 85 87 12 30; www.air-escargot.com) Based 16km south of Beaune in Remigny. Bookings can be made through the Beaune and Dijon tourist offices.

During the Middle Ages, two Burgundy-based monastic orders exerted significant influence across much of Christendom. The ascetic Cistercians were headquartered at Cîteaux (see the boxed text, p464), while their bitter rivals, the powerful and worldly Benedictines, were based at Cluny (p492).

Getting There & Around

By car or rail (including the TGV Sud-Est), Burgundy makes an easy stopover on the way from the English Channel or Paris to the Alps, Lyon, Provence or the Côte d'Azur. From Dijon, autoroutes stretch northeast to Alsace (A36), north to Lorraine (A31), north and then west to Champagne (A31, A5 and A26) and south to the Rhône Valley (A6). There's no quick way to go west to the Loire Valley.

All the cities and towns and some of the villages mentioned in this chapter are served by trains and public buses, though patience and planning are a must as services in many areas are infrequent (especially on Sunday and during school holidays) or have to be booked the day before. For details on touring the Côte d'Or wine villages by public transport, see p471 and p464. Details on train and bus options around Burgundy are available from **Mobigo** (☎ 08 00 10 20 04; www.mobigo-bourgogne.com, in French).

Tourist offices can supply brochures and maps with details on dedicated bike paths and cycling circuits.

CÔTE-D'OR

The Côte-d'Or *département* is named after one of the world's foremost wine-growing regions, which stretches from Dijon – bursting with cultural riches – south to the wine town of Beaune and beyond. In the far northwest, on the border with Champagne, Châtillon-sur-Seine displays spectacular Celtic treasures, while in the west you can explore the walled, hilltop town of Semur-en-Auxois.

DIJON

pop 237,000

Dijon is one of France's most appealing provincial cities. Filled with elegant medieval and Renaissance buildings, the lively centre is wonderful for strolling, especially if you like to leaven your cultural enrichment with excellent food, fine wine and shopping.

Dijon wears its long and glorious history with grace, and with a self-confidence that's never smug or off-putting because it's so obviously and richly deserved. The city's 25,000 students get much of the credit for keeping the nightlife scene snappy, though people of all ages participate in the city's thriving cultural life.

History

Dijon served as the capital of the duchy of Burgundy from the 11th to 15th centuries, enjoying a golden age during the 14th and 15th centuries under Philippe-le-Hardi (Philip the Bold), Jean-sans-Peur (John the Fearless) and Philippe-le-Bon (Philip the Good). During their reigns, some of the finest painters, sculptors and architects from around the Burgundian lands were brought to Dijon, turning the city into one of the great centres of European art.

Orientation

Dijon's main thoroughfare, known for much of its length as rue de la Liberté, stretches from the train station eastwards past the tourist office annexe and the Palais des Ducs to Église St-Michel. The main shopping precinct is around rue de la Liberté and perpendicular rue du Bourg. The focal point of the old town is place François Rude. The main university campus is 2km east of the centre.

Information

Centre Hospitalier Universitaire (☎ 03 80 29 30 31; 3 rue du Faubourg Raines; 🕑 24hr) Huge hospital complex with a 24-hour *urgences* (emergency room/casualty ward).

Cyberbisey (☎ 03 80 30 95 41; 53 rue Berbisey; per hr €3; 🕑 10am-8pm Mon-Fri, noon-8pm Sat) Internet access.

Cyberspace 21 (☎ 03 80 30 57 43; 46 rue Monge; per hr €4; 🕑 11am-midnight Mon-Sat, 2pm-midnight Sun & holidays) Internet access.

Institut Géographique National (IGN; ☎ 03 80 49 98 58; 2 rue Michelet; 🕑 9am or 10am-noon & 1-6pm Mon-Sat) Has an unsurpassed selection of driving, walking, cycling and other maps published by the IGN.

Laundrettes 41 rue Auguste Comte (🕑 6am-9pm); 28 rue Berbisey (🕑 6am-9pm); 55 rue Berbisey (🕑 7am-8.30pm); 8 place de la Banque (🕑 7am-8.30pm)

Main Post Office (place Grangier) Exchanges foreign currency, including US$100 bills.

Multi-Rezo UnderCity (☎ 03 80 42 13 89; 55 rue Guillaume Tell; per 15min/1hr €1/4; 🕑 9am-2am Mon-Fri, 11am-2am Sat, 2pm-midnight Sun) Prepaid internet access.

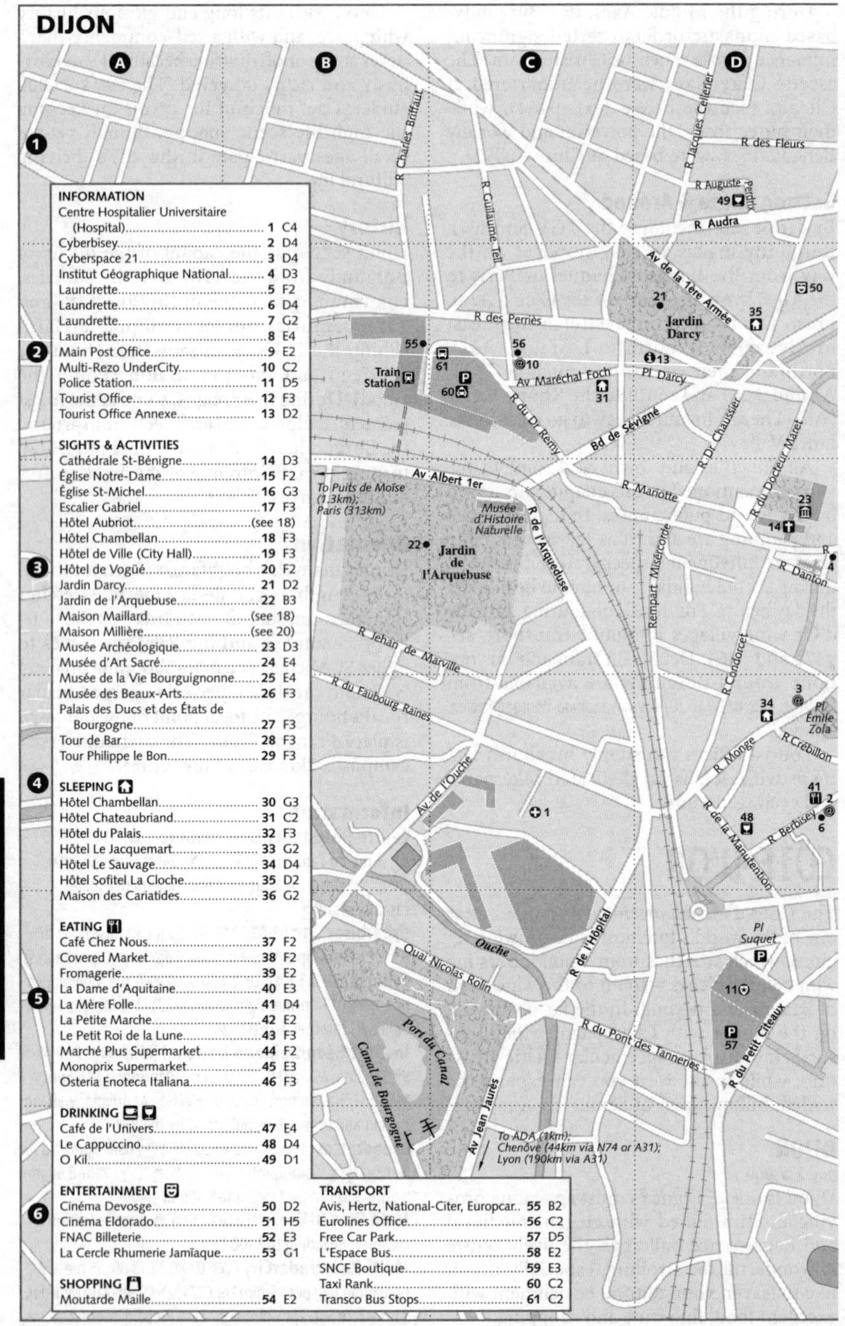
DIJON
INFORMATION
Centre Hospitalier Universitaire (Hospital) 1 C4
Cyberbisey 2 D4
Cyberspace 21 3 D4
Institut Géographique National 4 D3
Laundrette 5 F2
Laundrette 6 D4
Laundrette 7 G2
Laundrette 8 E4
Main Post Office 9 E2
Multi-Rezo UnderCity 10 C2
Police Station 11 D5
Tourist Office 12 F3
Tourist Office Annexe 13 D2
SIGHTS & ACTIVITIES
Cathédrale St-Bénigne 14 D3
Église Notre-Dame 15 F2
Église St-Michel 16 G3
Escalier Gabriel 17 F3
Hôtel Aubriot (see 18)
Hôtel Chambellan 18 F3
Hôtel de Ville (City Hall) 19 F3
Hôtel de Vogüé 20 F2
Jardin Darcy 21 D2
Jardin de l'Arquebuse 22 B3
Maison Maillard (see 18)
Maison Millière (see 20)
Musée Archéologique 23 D3
Musée d'Art Sacré 24 E4
Musée de la Vie Bourguignonne 25 E4
Musée des Beaux-Arts 26 F3
Palais des Ducs et des États de Bourgogne 27 F3
Tour de Bar 28 F3
Tour Philippe le Bon 29 F3
SLEEPING
Hôtel Chambellan 30 G3
Hôtel Chateaubriand 31 C2
Hôtel du Palais 32 F3
Hôtel Le Jacquemart 33 G2
Hôtel Le Sauvage 34 D4
Hôtel Sofitel La Cloche 35 D2
Maison des Cariatides 36 G2
EATING
Café Chez Nous 37 F2
Covered Market 38 F2
Fromagerie 39 E2
La Dame d'Aquitaine 40 E3
La Mère Folle 41 D4
La Petite Marche 42 E2
Le Petit Roi de la Lune 43 F3
Marché Plus Supermarket 44 F2
Monoprix Supermarket 45 E3
Osteria Enoteca Italiana 46 F3
DRINKING
Café de l'Univers 47 E4
Le Cappuccino 48 D4
O Kil 49 D1
ENTERTAINMENT
Cinéma Devosge 50 D2
Cinéma Eldorado 51 H5
FNAC Billeterie 52 E3
La Cercle Rhumerie Jamïaque 53 G1
SHOPPING
Moutarde Maille 54 E2
TRANSPORT
Avis, Hertz, National-Citer, Europcar 55 B2
Eurolines Office 56 C2
Free Car Park 57 D5
L'Espace Bus 58 E2
SNCF Boutique 59 E3
Taxi Rank 60 C2
Transco Bus Stops 61 C2
R Charles Briffaut
R Guillaume Tell
R Jacques Cellerier
R des Fleurs
R Auguste Perdrix
R Audra
Av de la 1ère Armée
Jardin Darcy
R des Perrièes
Train Station
Av Maréchal Foch
Pl Darcy
R du Dr Remy
Bd de Sévigné
R Dr Chaussier
R du Docteur Maret
Av Albert 1er
To Puits de Moïse (1.3km); Paris (313km)
Musée d'Histoire Naturelle
R Mariotte
Jardin de l'Arquebuse
R de l'Arquebuse
Rempart Miséricorde
R Danton
R Jehan de Marville
R du Faubourg Raines
R Condorcet
Pl Émile Zola
R Crébillon
R Monge
Av de l'Ouche
R de la Manutention
R Berbisey
Ouche
R de l'Hôpital
Pl Suquet
Quai Nicolas Rolin
Port du Canal
Canal de Bourgogne
R du Pont des Tanneries
R du Petit Citeaux
Av Jean Jaurès
To ADA (1km); Chenôve (44km via N74 or A31); Lyon (190km via A31)

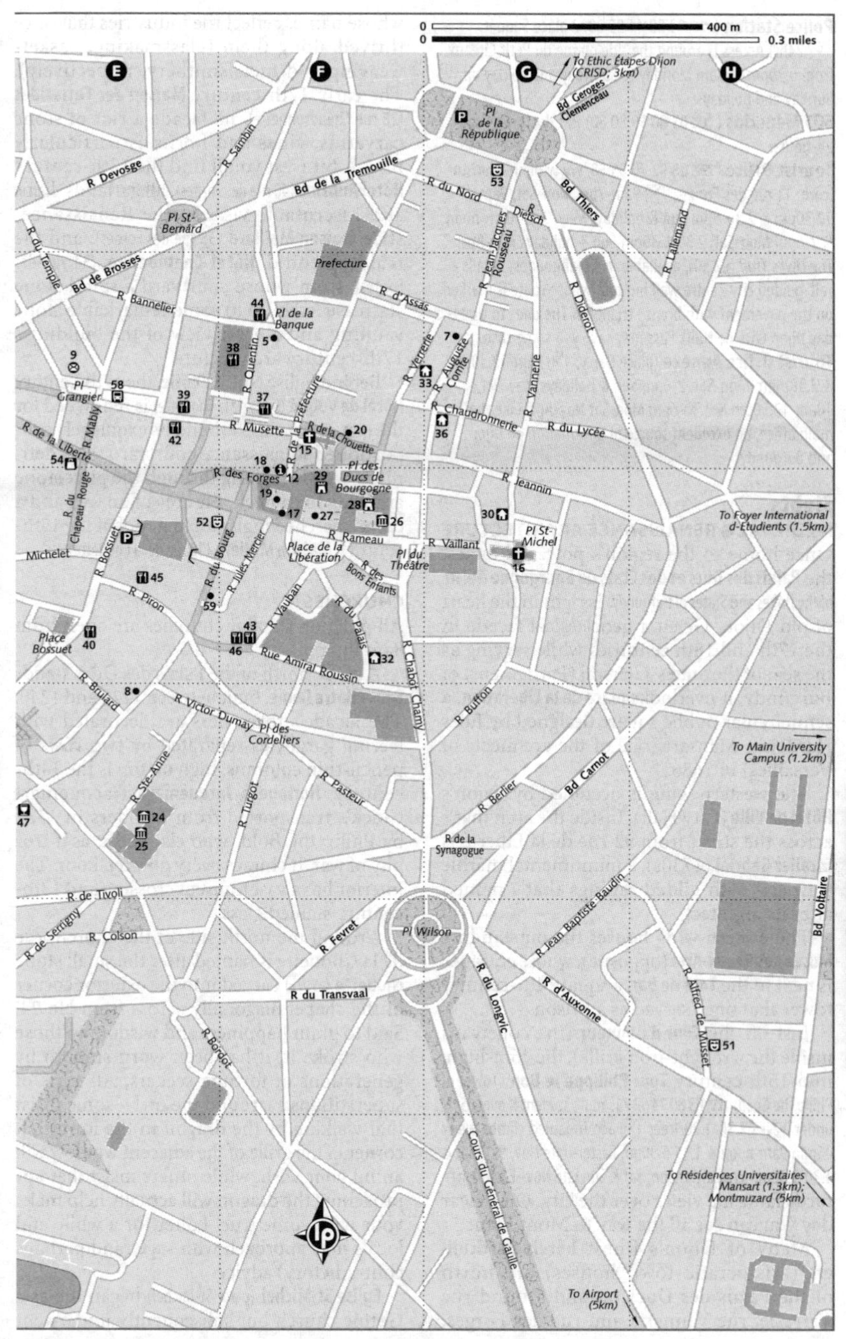
0 400 m
0 0.3 miles
E
F
G
H
To Ethic Étapes Dijon (CRISD; 3km)
Bd Geroges Clemenceau
Pl de la République
53
R Devosge
R Sambin
Bd de la Tremouille
R du Nord
Bd Thiers
R Dietsch
Pl St-Bernard
R du Temple
Bd de Brosses
Prefecture
R Jean-Jacques Rousseau
R Lallemand
R Diderot
R d'Assas
R Bannelier
44
Pl de la Banque
5
7
38
R Quentin
R Verrerie
R Auguste Comte
R Vannerie
9
Pl Grangier
58
39
37
R de la Préfecture
33
R Chaudronnerie
R du Lycée
42
R Musette
R de la Chouette
20
R de la Liberté
R Mably
15
36
54
18
R des Forges
12
29
Pl des Ducs de Bourgogne
R Jeannin
R du Chapeau Rouge
19
28
17
27
26
30
To Foyer International d'Etudients (1.5km)
52
Pl St-Michel
R Rameau
R Vaillant
Michelet
R Bossuet
Place de la Libération
Pl du Théâtre
16
45
R du Bourg
R Jules Mercier
R des Bons Enfants
R Piron
59
R Vauban
R du Palais
Place Bossuet
40
43
46
32
Rue Amiral Roussin
R Chabot Charny
R Brulard
8
R Victor Dumay
Pl des Cordeliers
R Buffon
To Main University Campus (1.2km)
Bd Carnot
R Ste-Anne
R Pasteur
R Berlier
47
24
R Turgot
25
R de la Synagogue
R de Tivoli
R Jean Baptiste Baudin
Bd Voltaire
R de Serrigny
R Colson
Pl Wilson
R Fevret
R du Longvic
R d'Auxonne
R du Transvaal
R Alfred de Musset
R Bordot
51
Cours du Général de Gaulle
To Résidences Universitaires Mansart (1.3km); Montmuzard (5km)
To Airport (5km)

BURGUNDY

Police Station (☎ 03 80 44 55 00; 2 place Suquet; ⌚ 24hr) Access is around the side on rue du Petit Cîteaux from 6.30pm to 8am Monday to Saturday and all day on Sunday and holidays.
SOS Médecins (☎ 03 80 59 80 80) Has doctors on call 24-hours.
Tourist Office (☎ 08 92 70 05 58; www.dijon-tourism.com; 11 rue des Forges; ⌚ 9am-7pm Mon-Sat, 9am-12.30pm & 2.30-5pm Sun & holidays May-Oct, 10am-noon & 2-6pm Mon-Sat, 2.30-5.30pm Sun & holidays Nov-Apr). *The Owl's Trail* (€2.50), available in 11 languages, details a self-guided city-centre walking tour whose route is marked on the pavement with bronze triangles. The one- to three-day Dijon Côte de Nuits Pass may save you some cash.
Tourist Office Annexe (place Darcy; ⌚ 9am-12.30pm & 2.30-6pm Mon-Sat, 2-6pm Sun & holidays May-Oct, 10am-12.30pm & 2.30-6pm Mon-Sat Nov-Apr) Like the main office, an excellent source of information on Dijon and Burgundy.

Sights

MEDIEVAL & RENAISSANCE ARCHITECTURE

Once home to the region's powerful dukes, the **Palais des Ducs et des États de Bourgogne** (Palace of the Dukes and States of Burgundy) is right in the heart of old Dijon. Given a neoclassical facade in the 17th and 18th centuries while serving as the seat of the States-General (Parliament) of Burgundy, it overlooks **place de la Libération**, a semicircular public square designed by Jules Hardouin-Mansart (one of the architects of Versailles) in 1686.

The western wing is occupied by Dijon's **Hôtel de Ville** (City Hall). Inside the arch that's across the street from 92 rue de la Liberté is **Escalier Gabriel** (1730s), a monumental marble stairway with gilded railings that's named after its architect.

The eastern wing houses the outstanding **Musée des Beaux-Arts** (opposite), whose entrance is next to the **Tour de Bar**, a squat 14th-century tower that once served as a prison.

Just off the **Cour d'Honneur** (the courtyard inside the wrought-iron grille), the 46m-high, mid-15th-century **Tour Philippe le Bon** (Tower of Philip the Good; ☎ 03 80 74 52 71; adult/student & over 65yr/under 12yr €2.30/1.20/free; ⌚ accompanied climbs every 45min 9am-noon & 1.45-5.30pm Easter–late Nov, 9-11am & 1.30-3.30pm Wed afternoon, Sat & Sun late Nov–Easter) affords fantastic views over the city. On a clear day you can see all the way to Mont Blanc.

Many of Dijon's finest **hôtels particuliers** (aristocratic town houses) are north of the Palais des Ducs on and around rue Verrerie, rue Vannerie and rue des Forges, whose names reflect the industries that once thrived along them (glassmaking, basket-weaving and metalsmithery, respectively). The early-17th-century **Maison des Cariatides** (28 rue Chaudronnerie), its facade a riot of stone caryatids, vines and horns, is particularly fine. A bit west you'll find the 13th-century **Hôtel Aubriot** (40 rue des Forges), all garlands, lions and inscrutable visages; the Renaissance-style **Maison Maillard** (38 rue des Forges); and the truly splendid **Hôtel Chambellan** (34 rue des Forges), from whose courtyard a spiral stone staircase leads up to some remarkable stone vaulting and a great view of the building's 17th-century architecture.

Behind Église Notre Dame, the 17th-century **Hôtel de Vogüé** (8 rue de la Chouette) is renowned for the ornate carvings around its exquisitely proportioned Renaissance courtyard – it's definitely worth walking through the pink stone archway for a peek. Figures of an owl and a cat are perched high atop the roof of the 15th-century **Maison Millière** (10 rue de la Chouette).

CHURCHES

All of Dijon's major churches are open from 8am to 7pm.

A block north of the Palais des Ducs stands **Église Notre Dame**, built between 1220 and 1240. The facade's three tiers are decorated with leering gargoyles separated by two rows of pencil-thin columns; high on top is the 14th-century **Horloge à Jacquemart** (Jacquemart Clock), transported from Flanders in 1382 by Philip the Bold, who claimed it as a trophy of war. It chimes every quarter-hour. The interior has a vast transept crossing and 13th-century stained glass.

Around the north side of the church, rue de la Chouette is named after the small stone **chouette** (owl) carved into the exterior corner of the chapel diagonally across from No 24. Said to grant happiness and wisdom to those who stroke it, it has been worn smooth by generations of fortune-seekers. All sorts of superstitions surround the owl – some insist that walking by the dragon in the lower left corner of the grille of the adjacent window will annul your wish, while others insist that approaching the dragon will actually help make your wish come true. Loiter for a while and locals may approach with sage (and perhaps contradictory) advice.

Église St-Michel (place St-Michel) began life as a Gothic church but subsequently underwent a facade-lift operation in which it was given a richly ornamented Renaissance west front considered among the most beautiful in France, perhaps because it looks like it should be in Italy. The two 17th-century towers are topped with cupolas and, higher still, glittering gold spheres.

Situated above the tomb of St Benignus (who is believed to have brought Christianity to Burgundy in the 2nd century), Dijon's Burgundian Gothic–style **Cathédrale St-Bénigne** (place St-Philibert; 9am-6.30pm Sat, till 7pm Wed & Fri, to 7.30pm Mon, Tue & Thu, to 9pm Sun) was built around 1300 as an abbey church. Some of Burgundy's great figures are buried inside. The **crypt** (admission €2; 10am-6pm Mon, 9am-6pm Tue-Fri, 9am-4pm Sat, 1-6pm Sun) is all that's left of an 11th-century Romanesque basilica.

MUSEUMS

All of Dijon's municipal museums are free except, occasionally, for special exhibitions.

Housed in the eastern wing of the Palais des Ducs, the **Musée des Beaux-Arts** (03 80 74 52 09; audioguide €3.90; 9.30am-6pm Wed-Mon May-Oct, 10am-5pm Wed-Mon Nov-Apr) is one of the most outstanding museums in France. From 2009 to 2017 it is supposed to undergo a section-by-section renovation intended to double exhibition space.

The wood-panelled **Salle des Gardes** (Guards' Room), once warmed by a gargantuan fireplace that's as Gothic as Gothic can be, houses three impossibly intricate, gilded Gothic retables from the 1300s, and the late-medieval sepulchres of two Valois dukes. Other highlights include a fine collection of **primitives** that give you a good sense of how artistic and aesthetic sensibilities varied between Italy, Switzerland and the Rhineland in the 13th and 14th centuries; the painting *Galerie d'Objets d'Art* (mid-17th century) by Cornelis de Baellieur, which shows a room rendered with such precision that you can actually enjoy the minuscule artwork hanging on its walls (photography made this sort of painterly tour de force obsolete; hung at eye level in room 1.19); and quite a few **Rude sculptures** – nude though never lewd, they're by the Dijon-born artist François Rude (1784–1855), so don't be a prude or become unglued, dude! The modern and contemporary art section, with works by Manet and Monet, is closed from 11.30am to 1.45pm. In the courtyard, the **ducal kitchens** (1433) often host exhibitions of works by local artists.

The **Musée Archéologique** (03 80 30 88 54; 5 rue du Docteur Maret; 9am-12.30pm & 1.30-6pm Wed-Sun, plus Mon mid-May–Sep) displays some truly surprising Celtic, Roman and Merovingian artefacts, including a particularly fine 1st-century AD bronze of the Celtic goddess Sequana standing on a dual-prowed boat. Upstairs, the early Gothic hall (12th and 13th centuries), with its ogival arches held aloft by two rows of columns, once served as the dormitory of a Benedictine abbey.

The **Musée de la Vie Bourguignonne** (03 80 48 80 90; 17 rue Ste-Anne; 9am-noon & 2-6pm Wed-Mon), in a 17th-century Cistercian convent, explores village and town life in Burgundy in centuries past with evocative tableaux illustrating dress, headgear, cooking and traditional crafts. A detailed, case-by-case guide in English and German is available at the ticket desk. Down the alley to the right as you exit the cloister, the **Musée d'Art Sacré** (03 80 48 80 90; 15 rue Ste-Anne; same hr) displays gleaming Catholic ritual objects from the 12th to 19th centuries inside the convent's green copper–domed chapel (1709).

PARKS

Dijon has plenty of green spaces that are perfect for picnics, including **Jardin Darcy**, next to the tourist office annexe; and **Jardin de l'Arquebuse**, the botanic gardens, whose stream, pond and formal gardens are south across the tracks from the train station.

Tours

The tourist office offers a two-hour **MP3 tour** (€6, incl a PDA with images €12) of the city centre and runs various English-language **walking tours** (adult/student/under 18yr/couple €6/3/1/9; 3pm daily, additional tours 5pm May-Oct, 11am daily & 10pm Mon-Sat Jul & Aug) with departures from the main tourist office.

Taking a tour (in French with a printed text in English) is the only way to see the famous **Puits de Moïse** (Well of Moses; 1395–1405), a grouping of six Old Testament figures by Claus Sluter that's 1.2km west of the train station on the grounds of a psychiatric hospital.

Segway tour (adult/12-16yr €15/7; 3pm & 4.30pm daily Jul & Aug, 3pm & 4.30pm Sat, Sun & holidays Apr & May, Fri-Sun & holidays Jun, Sep & Oct) Run by the tourist office, this 1½-hour tour zips around the city centre.

Wine & Voyages (03 80 61 15 15; www.wineandvoyages.com; 2/3hr tours €55/65; Mon-Sat Mar–mid-Dec) Runs minibus tours in English of the Côte de Nuits vineyards. Reserve by phone or internet or via the tourist office.

Sleeping

Accommodation can be booked via the tourist office website (www.dijon-tourism.com) or on www.lonelyplanet.com.

Ethic Étapes Dijon (CRISD; ☎ 03 80 72 95 20; www.auberge-cri-dijon.com; 1 bd Champollion; dm/s/d incl breakfast €19.50/36.50/49, €1.50 less per person after 1st night; 💻) This institutional (though friendly) 216-bed hostel, 2.5km northeast of the centre, was completely renovated in 2006. Most beds are in modern, airy rooms for two. By bus, take Liane 4 to the Epirey CRI stop.

Hôtel Chambellan (☎ 03 80 67 12 67; www.hotel-chambellan.com; 92 rue Vannerie; s/d from €43/48, with washbasin only €29/32) Built in 1730, this two-star place has a vaguely medieval feel. Most of the rooms, decorated in cheerful tones of red, orange, pink and white, have views of a quiet courtyard.

Hôtel Le Jacquemart (☎ 03 80 60 09 60; www.hotel-lejacquemart.fr; 32 rue Verrerie; d €52-62, s/d with washbasin only €29/32; 💻) Right in the heart of old Dijon, this two-star hotel has 31 tidy, comfortable rooms; the pricier ones are quite spacious and some come with marble fireplaces. The window boxes make the 18th-century building especially pretty in summer.

Hôtel Chateaubriand (☎ 03 80 41 42 18; www.hotelchateaubriand.fr, in French; 3 av Maréchal Foch; d €40.60-45.60, with washbasin only €35.60) An old-fashioned cheapie like the ones your parents stayed in when they backpacked around Europe. This 23-room place has the air of a well-worn dive but, thanks to the Victorian breakfast room, far more character than the sterile chain hotels down the block. Alas, not as romantic as the writer and nowhere near as self-indulgent as the legendarily thick steak named after him.

Hôtel du Palais (☎ 03 80 67 16 26; www.hoteldupalais-dijon.com; 23 rue du Palais; d €44-68, q €83) A great little two-star place in a 17th-century *hôtel particulier*. The 13 rooms are spacious and welcoming and the public spaces exude old-fashioned charm. The breakfast room has an 18th-century painted coffered ceiling.

Hôtel Le Sauvage (Hostellerie du Sauvage; ☎ 03 80 41 31 21; www.hotellesauvage.com; 64 rue Monge; d €48-58, tr €58-80) In a 15th-century *relais de poste* (relay post house) set around a cobbled, vine-shaded courtyard, this good-value two-star hotel is just off lively rue Monge. The 22 rooms are sparse and practical.

Hôtel Sofitel La Cloche (☎ 03 80 30 12 32; www.hotel-lacloche.com; 14 place Darcy; d €190-220, €20 less in Jul & Aug, ste €300-500; ❄ 💻) This venerable four-star hostelry, built in 1884, boasts a huge lobby chandelier, an immaculate back garden, a sauna and a small fitness room. The 68 rooms are hushed and very comfortable, some mixing shiny brass with burgundy carpets, others sleek wood furnishings with grey carpeting.

Eating

Loads of restaurants can be found on buzzy rue Berbisey, around place Émile Zola and around the perimeter of the covered market (eg along rue Bannelier and rue Quentin). Rue Amiral Roussin is lined with intimate eateries. In the warm months, outdoor cafés sprout at semicircular place de la Libération.

RESTAURANTS

Le Petit Roi de la Lune (☎ 03 80 49 89 93; 28 rue Amiral Roussin; lunch menu €13.80; 🕐 closed Sun & lunch Mon) 'The Little King of the Moon' serves French cuisine that – explains the chef – has been *revisitée, rearrangée et decalée* (revisited, rearranged and shifted), resulting in dishes such as the hugely popular *Camembert frit avec gelée de mûre* (Camembert wrapped in breadcrumbs, fried, baked and then served with blackberry jelly; €9.80) and the heretical *aiguillettes de canard au Coca Cola* (strips of duck filet in a Coca-Cola sauce; €14.90).

La Mère Folle (☎ 03 80 50 19 76; 102 rue Berbisey; lunch menu €10, other menus €15-23; 🕐 closed Tue, lunch Sat & lunch Wed) A 23-seat Burgundian restaurant with specialities such as *magret de canard au miel, thym et mirabelles* (fillet of duck with honey, thyme and cherry plums; €13). Crammed with character, from the baroque putti and gilded wall mirrors to the pineapple-shaped table lamps and retro chandelier.

AS FRENCH AS THEY COME

Café Chez Nous (☎ 03 80 50 12 98; impasse Quentin; 🕐 lunch noon-2pm, bar 10am-2am, closed Mon till 2pm & Sun) A quintessentially French *bar du coin* (neighbourhood bar), often crowded, down a tiny alleyway from the covered market. Serves lunches (details are on the chalkboard) generally made with organic ingredients – the *plat du jour* (meat or fish) costs €8, salads are about €7 and wine by the glass is a bargain at €1.20 to €2.40. On Monday evenings a customer who's in the mood sometimes cooks dinner (€3 to €4) for everyone – sign up on the chalkboard.

La Petite Marche (☎ 03 80 30 15 10; 27-29 rue Musette; menus €10.50-14; ⏰ lunch Mon-Sat) An organic restaurant with seven types of salad and quite a few vegetarian options (as well as meat and fish) – a good choice if you're tired of heavy Burgundian classics. Upstairs from an organic food shop.

Osteria Enoteca Italiana (☎ 03 80 50 07 36; 32 rue Amiral Roussin; lunch/dinner menu €15/39; ⏰ closed Mon & dinner Sun) An intimate *ristorante* that's proud of its authentic, traditional Italian pasta (including vegetarian fettucine), meat and fish dishes, some made with white Italian truffles (in season), and its scrumptious home-made desserts (think tiramisu). The decor hints at Venice, the chef's hometown.

La Dame d'Aquitaine (☎ 03 80 30 45 65; 23 place Bossuet; lunch menu €22, other menus €29-45; ⏰ closed Sun & lunch Mon) Excellent Burgundian and southwestern French cuisine served – to the accompaniment of Western classical music – under the sumptuously lit bays of a 13th-century cellar. Options include *coq au vin rouge* and *magret de canard aux baies de cassis* (duck's breast with blackcurrant sauce). The Middle Ages at their most civilised.

SELF-CATERING

For picnic treats:

Covered Market (Halles du Marché; rue Quentin; ⏰ 7am-1pm, Tue & Thu-Sat) A huge market on Fridays and Saturdays, with a smaller version on Tuesdays and Thursdays.

Fromagerie (28 rue Musette; ⏰ 6am or 7am-12.30pm or 1pm & 2.30-7pm, no midday closure Fri & Sat, closed Mon morning & Sun) A friendly, top-quality cheese shop.

Marché Plus supermarket (2 rue Bannelier; ⏰ 7am-9pm Mon-Sat, 9am-1pm Sun)

Monoprix supermarket (11-13 rue Piron; ⏰ 9am-8.45pm Mon-Sat)

Drinking

There are quite a number of bars along rue Berbisey.

Le Cappuccino (☎ 03 80 41 06 35; 132 rue Berbisey; ⏰ 5pm-2am Mon-Sat) Coffee isn't even served at this convivial and often packed bar (the name is left over from an earlier Starbucksian incarnation), but wine by the glass and a varied selection of 80 beers are, including Mandubienne, the only beer brewed in Dijon. Occasionally hosts live music.

O Kil (☎ 03 80 30 02 48; www.lekil.com, in French; 1 rue Auguste Perdrix; ⏰ 5pm-2am Tue-Sat) Under stone cellar vaulting, this cosy pub hosts live music once a month. Fans of English and other languages gather here to converse at the 'Café Polyglotte', which begins at 7.30pm each Tuesday.

Café de l'Univers (☎ 03 80 30 98 29; 47 rue Berbisey; ⏰ 5pm-2am) This ground-floor bar, the walls covered with mirrors and beer ads, has its menu on a chalkboard. In the cellar there's live music from 9pm to 1am on Friday and Saturday. Popular with students but ages are varied.

Entertainment

For the latest on Dijon's cultural scene, pick up the monthly *Spectacles* (www.spectacles-publications.com, in French), available free from the tourist office. Events tickets are sold at the **Fnac billeterie** (☎ 08 92 68 36 22; www.fnacspectacles.com, in French; 24 rue du Bourg; ⏰ 1-7pm Mon, 10am-7pm Tue-Sat).

A number of nightclubs can be found near the northwest corner of place de la République (eg rue Marceau). Places listed under Drinking (left) host live music.

Le Cercle Rhumerie Jamaïque (☎ 03 80 73 52 19; www.lecerclejamaique.com, in French; 14 place de la République; admission free; ⏰ 3pm-5am Tue-Sat) Decked out like a bordello, with bold-red walls and gilded mirrors, this nightclub has live music (Cuban, flamenco, jazz, rock and roll) nightly from 11pm to 3am. Rum-based cocktails are the speciality. Le Night Club (admission free; open 11pm to 5am Thursday to Saturday), the downstairs disco, has a blue galactic ceiling and music that's as mixed as the clients' ages (mostly 20 to 40).

Nondubbed films flicker nightly:

Cinéma Eldorado (☎ 03 80 66 51 89, recorded information 08 92 68 01 74; www.cinema-eldorado.fr, in French; 21 rue Alfred de Musset) A three-screen art cinema.

Cinéma Devosge (☎ 03 80 30 74 79, recorded information 08 92 68 73 33; http://cinealpes.allocine.net, in French; 6 rue Devosge) Five screens.

Shopping

Moutarde Maille (☎ 03 80 30 41 02; 32 rue de la Liberté; ⏰ 9am-7pm Mon-Sat) The factory boutique of the company that makes Grey Poupon. When you walk in, tangy odours assault the nostrils, as they well should in a place with 36 different kinds of mustard, including three on tap that you can sample (from €76 per kilogram).

Shops near the covered market sell samplers with up to 10 different kinds of Edmond Fallot mustard in tiny jars (€9.50).

Getting There & Away

AIR

At the time of research, no scheduled international flights used **Dijon-Bourgogne Airport** (☎ 03 80 67 67 67; www.dijon.aeroport.fr), 5km southeast of the city centre, but budget airlines may resume flights during the life of this guide.

BUS

A single train station **information and ticket counter** (⏲ 5.45am-9pm Sun-Thu, to 9.30pm Fri, to 8pm Sat) deals with TER trains, Divia local buses and the *départemental* bus company, **Transco** (☎ 08 00 10 20 04). Bus stops are in front of the train station; schedules appear in the free *Guide Horaire* booklet (available at the information and ticket counter); tickets are sold on board.

Transco bus 60 (18 to 21 daily Monday to Friday, 10 Saturday, two Sunday) links Dijon with the northern Côte de Nuits wine villages of Marsannay-la-Côte, Couchey, Fixin and Gevrey-Chambertin (30 minutes). Dijon's local Divia Ligne 15 (right) goes to Marsannay-la-Côte.

Information on bus services to/from Dijon appears under Avallon, Beaune, Châtillon-sur-Seine and Semur-en-Auxois in this chapter.

International bus travel is handled by **Eurolines** (☎ 03 80 68 20 44; 53 rue Guillaume Tell; ⏲ Mon-Fri & Sat morning).

CAR

Avis, Hertz, National-Citer and Europcar have bureaux in the train-station complex. **ADA** (☎ 03 80 51 90 90; 109 av Jean Jaurès) is 2km south of the train station (take the Liane 4 bus line to Bourroches Jaurès).

TRAIN

The newly refurbished **train station** (rue du Dr Remy) is linked with Paris' Gare de Lyon (€43.40 to €54.10 by TGV, 1¾ hours, 10 to 14 daily, most frequent in the early morning and evening), Lyon–Part Dieu (€25.10, two hours, 11 to 19 daily), Nice (€79.10 to €91.30 by TGV, 6¼ hours, two direct daily) and Strasbourg (€38.90, 3½ hours, three or four nondirect daily).

For details on travelling by rail to destinations within Burgundy, see the city and town listings in this chapter.

In the city centre, tickets can be purchased at the **SNCF Boutique** (55 rue du Bourg; ⏲ 12.30-7pm Mon, 10am-7pm Tue-Sat).

Getting Around

BICYCLE

The main tourist office rents mountain bikes year-round for €12/18 per half-/full day, €50 for three days. Helmets are free.

Velodi (☎ 08 00 20 03 05; www.velodi.net, in French), with 400 heavy city bikes available at 33 sites around town, is Dijon's version of Paris' Vélib' automatic rental system (see p201).

BUS

Details on Dijon's bus network, operated by Divia, are available at **L'Espace Bus** (☎ 08 00 10 20 04; www.divia.fr, in French; place Grangier; ⏲ 7.30am-6.45pm Mon-Fri, 8.30am-6.30pm Sat). Single tickets, sold by drivers, cost €0.95 and are valid for any number of trips made within a single hour; a Forfait Journée ticket (€3.20), good for unlimited trips all day long, is available from the tourist office or L'Espace Bus. A seven-day pass costs just €9.20.

ABBAYE DE CÎTEAUX

In contrast to the showy Benedictines of Cluny (p492), the medieval Cistercian order was known for its austerity, discipline and humility – and for the productive manual labour of its monks. Named after **Cîteaux Abbey** (Cistercium in Latin; ☎ 03 80 61 32 58; www.citeaux-abbaye.com, in French), south of Dijon, where it was founded in 1098, the order enjoyed phenomenal growth in the 12th century under St Bernard (1090–1153), and some 600 Cistercian abbeys soon stretched from Scandinavia to the Near East.

Cîteaux was pretty much destroyed during the Revolution and the monks didn't return until 1898 but today it is home to about 35 modern-day monks. You can visit the monastery on a two-hour **guided tour** (adult/student & monk €7.50/4; ⏲ tours begin 10.30am, 11.30am & several times 2-4.45pm or 5pm Wed-Sat & Sun afternoon May–early October, plus Tue Jul & Aug) described as 'more spiritual than architectural' (in French with printed English commentary; includes an audiovisual presentation on monastic life). Phone ahead or email for reservations. Visitors are invited to attend daily prayers and Sunday Mass (10.30am). The boutique sells edibles made at monasteries around France.

BURGUNDY

Dijon has two kinds of bus lines: 'Liane' lines, which are numbered from 1 to 7 and run every 10 minutes or less from about 5.30am (on Sunday from 9am) to midnight or 12.30am; and less frequent 'Ligne' lines, which are numbered from 10 to 46. Bus lines are known by their number and end-of-the-line station.

The free Diviaciti minibus shuttle does a city-centre circuit every six minutes from 7am to 8pm Monday to Saturday. Liane 1, 3, 5 and 6 run along rue de la Liberté.

CAR & MOTORCYCLE

All city-centre parking is metered. Free spots are available (clockwise from the train station): northwest of rue Devosge, northeast of bd Thiers, southeast of bd Carnot, south of rue du Transvaal and on the other side of the train tracks from the city centre. There's a big free car park at place Suquet, just south of the police station.

TAXI

A taxi is just a phone call away on ☎ 03 80 41 41 12 (24 hours a day).

CÔTE D'OR VINEYARDS

Burgundy's most renowned vintages come from the vine-covered Côte d'Or (Golden Hillside), the narrow, eastern slopes of a range of hills made of limestone, flint and clay that runs south from Dijon for about 60km. The northern section, the **Côte de Nuits**, stretches from Marsannay-la-Côte south to Corgoloin and produces reds known for their robust, full-bodied character. The southern section, the **Côte de Beaune**, lies between Ladoix-Serrigny and Santenay and produces great reds and great whites.

Tourist offices en route can provide local brochures; *The Burgundy Wine Road*, an excellent free booklet published by the Burgundy Tourist Board (www.bourgogne-tourisme.com); and a useful map, *Roadmap to the Wines of Burgundy* (€0.50).

Activities

WINE TASTING

The villages of the Côte d'Or offer innumerable places to sample and purchase world-class wines – a short walk from where they were made! Look for signs reading *dégustation* (tasting), *domaine* (wine-making

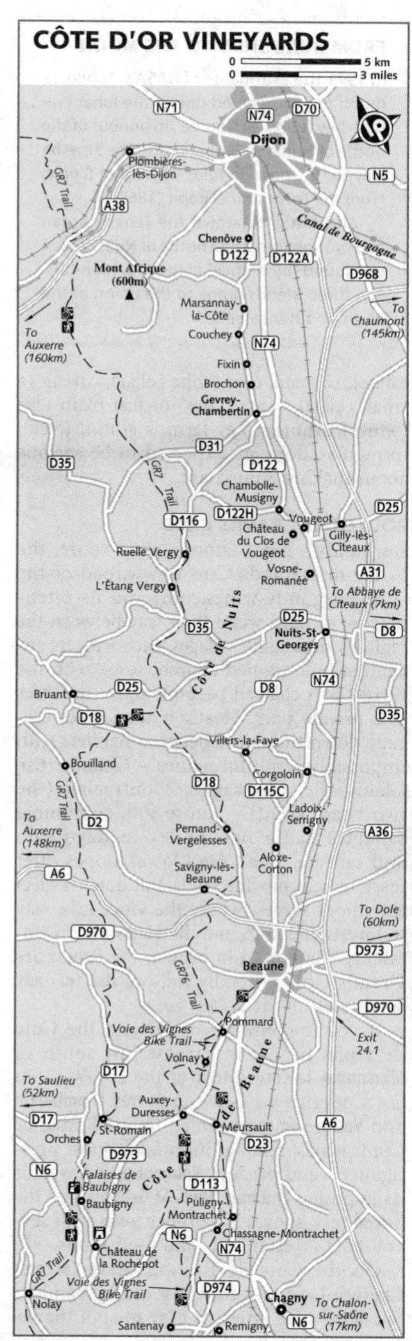

FROM BURGUNDY TO THE MOON

In 1971 the astronauts of NASA's Apollo 15 moon mission named one of the lunar craters they found 'St George', in honour of the bottle of Nuits-St-Georges consumed on the way to the moon in Jules Verne's sci-fi epic, *From the Earth to the Moon* (1865):

'And lastly, to crown the repast, Ardan had brought out a fine bottle of Nuits, which was found "by chance" in the provision-box. The three friends drank to the union of the earth and her satellite.'

estate), *château, cave* (wine cellar), *caveau* (a small cellar), *vente* (sales) or just plain *vins* (wines). Another key term is *gratuit* (free), though visitors are expected to be serious about making a purchase.

ROUTE DES GRANDS CRUS

Burgundy's most famous wine route, the Route des Grands Crus (www.road-of-the-fine-burgundy-wines.com) and its often-narrow variants wend their way between the region's stone-built villages, each with its ancient steeple-topped church, some with the turrets of a château peeping above the trees of a private park. Neatly tended vines cascade down the slopes between hamlets with impossibly beautiful names – Chambertin, Chambolle, Chassagne, Montrachet (the two *ts* are silent) – whose soft, subliminal syllables cause oenophiles to daydream and salivate. The Côte's lower slopes offer luscious seas of wine fields, but don't neglect the upper slopes, where the vines give way to forests and cliffs and the views are breathtaking. Signposted in brown, the Route des Grands Crus generally follows the tertiary roads west of the N74.

If you're coming from Dijon, the Côte de Nuits begins in earnest just south of **Marsannay-la-Côte**. Most of the area's *grand cru* vineyards are between **Gevrey-Chambertin** and **Vosne-Romanée**, famed for its Romanée Conti wines, among Burgundy's most prestigious – and priciest. **Vougeot** is known for its imposing château. **Nuits-St-Georges** (see the boxed text, above) is a proper town with several hotels, restaurants and food shops.

On the Côte de Beaune, **Aloxe-Corton's** Château Corton-André, just off the hamlet's one-lane main street, is easy to spot thanks to its impossibly steep coloured-tile roof. **Pernand-Vergelesses** (see Eating, opposite) is nestled in a little valley that's completely hidden from the N74.

South of Beaune, the **Château de Pommard** (www.chateau-de-pommard.tm.fr), surrounded by a stone wall, is on the D973 on the northeast edge of town. **Volnay** is notable for its hillside church. A bit off the main track, **St-Romain** is a bucolic village situated right where vineyardland meets pastureland, forests and cliffs. Hiking trails from here include the spectacular **Sentier des Roches**, a circuit that follows part of the GR7 and the D17I along the top of the **Falaises de Baubigny** (Baubigny cliffs), 300m above the Saône. This trail takes you via the hillside hamlet of **Orches** to the 15th-century **Château de La Rochepot** (☎ 03 80 21 71 37; www.larochepot.com; adult/6-14yr €7.50/4; closed Tue, tours 10am-6pm Jul & Aug, 10am-5.30pm Jun & Sep, 10-11.45am & 2-5.30pm Apr & May, 10-11.45am & 2-4.30pm Oct), whose conical towers rise from thick woods above the ancient village of Rochepot. Tours are in French but most guides speak English and an English text is provided.

WALKING

The GR7 and its variant, the GR76, run along the Côte d'Or from a bit west of Dijon to the hills west of Beaune, from where they continue southwards. The Beaune tourist office sells an excellent guide, *Walks in the Beaune Countryside* (€3), which details 30 marked routes.

CYCLING

To get from Dijon to Beaune by bike, follow the quiet (but almost vergeless/shoulderless) D122, which gradually becomes pretty south of Couchey, to Nuits-St-Georges. From there, take either the challenging D8 and the D115C, or the flatter D20, just east of the N74, which offers fine views of the wine slopes. The ride takes three or four hours and covers about 50km. To avoid cycling both ways (or through Dijon's ugly and heavily trafficked urban sprawl, which stretches as far south as Marsannay-la-Côte), you can take your bike along on most Dijon–Beaune trains – look for the bicycle symbol on train schedules.

The 20km **Voie des Vignes** (Vineyard Way), a bike route marked by rectangular green-on-white signs, goes from Beaune's Parc de la Bouzaize via Pommard, Volnay, Meursault, Puligny-Montrachet and Chassagne-

Montrachet to Santenay, where you can pick up the **Voie Verte** (see p494) to Cluny. The Beaune tourist office sells a detailed map, *The Beaune-Santenay Cycle Track* (€2).

Sleeping

Along the Route des Grands Crus, signs reading *chambres* announce the presence of a B&B. Tourist offices have lists of the area's plentiful accommodation options.

Gilly-lès-Cîteaux may be on the flat (ie eastern) side of the N74 but it's home to one of the Côte d'Or's most luxurious hotels, the four-star **Château de Gilly** (☎ 03 80 62 89 98; www.chateau-gilly.com; d €160-312, 10% more on Fri & Sat, ste €422-723; 💻 🏊), which occupies the 14th- and 17th-century residence of the abbots of Cîteaux. The 48 spacious rooms are luxuriously appointed and all have lovely views. Bicycle use is free.

Nearby **La Closerie de Gilly** (☎ 03 80 62 87 74; www.closerie-gilly.com; d €75-85, per week €300-400; ☒ 🏊) is a homey, five-room B&B inside a delightful 18th-century *maison bourgeoise* with a huge, flowery garden. Has bicycles for rent and offers wine-tasting with commentary.

In Ladoix-Serrigny, 10 unsurprising two-star rooms are available at **Les Terrasses de Corton** (☎ 03 80 26 42 37; www.terrasses-de-corton.com; d/q from €55/79), on the N74 near the southern edge of town.

Eating

Lots of excellent restaurants are tucked away in the villages of the Côte d'Or.

Les Terrasses de Corton (☎ 03 80 26 42 37; menus €17.50-40; 🕑 noon-1.45pm & 7.30-9pm, closed Wed & lunch Thu, also closed dinner Sun late Oct–early Mar) In Ladoix-Serrigny, on the N74 near the southern edge of town, this place looks a bit like a motel but in fact serves good-value French and Burgundian cuisine, including home-style bœuf bourguignon (€13.50).

La Cabotte (☎ 03 80 61 20 77; 24 Grand' Rue, Nuits-St-Georges; menus €27-49; 🕑 closed lunch Sat, Mon & Sun) In Nuits-St-Georges, this 22-seat restaurant serves up refined, 'inventive' versions of French dishes. No artifice or posing here, just excellent, if sometimes surprising, food. To get there walk half a block south from Beffroi de Nuits, the town's 17th-century chiming clock tower.

Le Chambolle (☎ 03 80 62 86 26; 28 rue Basse, Chambolle-Musigny; menus €26-42; 🕑 12.15-1.30pm or 2pm & 7.15-8.30pm Fri-Tue) In Chambolle-Musigny on the D122, a bit east of Vougeot, traditional Burgundian cuisine made with the freshest ingredients is the order of the day at this rustic restaurant.

our pick **Le Charlemagne** (☎ 03 80 21 51 45; www.lecharlemagne.fr, in French; Pernand-Vergelesses; lunch menus Mon-Fri €27-33, other menus €43-82; 🕑 12.15-1.30pm & 7.15-9.30pm, closed Tue & lunch Wed, also closed dinner Wed Sep-May) With vineyard views as mouth-watering as the imaginatively prepared *escargots de Bourgogne,* the serene, Japanese-inspired dining room is the perfect spot to experience delicious dishes melding venerable French traditions with techniques and products from Japan – surprises involving *gari* (pickled ginger root), *nori* (dried seaweed) and *yazu* (a tiny Japanese lemon) await. Several tables are almost inside the ultramodern kitchen. Situated on the D18 at the town's southern entrance.

Getting Around

For information on visiting the Côte d'Or by train and bus from Beaune and Dijon, see p471 and p464.

REPENT, O SINNERS, BEFORE IT'S TOO LATE!

On the left side of the *Polyptych of the Last Judgement* (1443) by the Flemish painter Roger van der Weyden, on display in Beaune's Hôtel-Dieu (p468), naked dead people climb out of their graves and are welcomed into Heaven (a golden cathedral) by a winged angel, while on the right the terror-stricken damned are dragged shrieking into the fiery depths of Hell, their faces frozen in agony.

The message to the illiterate medieval masses was clear: Judgement Day means payback time, with the trumpets a-blarin', the scales a-swingin' and your fate for all Eternity lying in the balance. God is loving and beneficent but that angel – the one holding the scales – isn't going to cut anyone any slack, so if you think that supplications, implorations and entreaties will help at this late stage – well, you are sadly mistaken! Repent, repent, O Sinners, for if you do not this is what awaits you! Rated PG13 – parental discretion advised, depicts nudity and harsh divine justice.

BEAUNE

pop 21,300

Beaune (pronounced similarly to 'bone'), 44km south of Dijon, is the unofficial capital of the Côte d'Or. This thriving town's raison d'être and the source of its joie de vivre is wine – making it, tasting it, selling it, but most of all, drinking it. Consequently Beaune is one of the best places in all of France for wine tasting.

The jewel of Beaune's old city is the magnificent Hôtel-Dieu, France's most splendiferous medieval charity hospital.

Orientation

The amoeba-shaped old city, enclosed by ramparts and a stream, is encircled by a one-way boulevard with seven names. The tourist office and the old town's commercial centre are about 1km west of the train station.

Information

Athenaeum de la Vigne et du Vin (☎ 03 80 25 08 30; www.athenaeumfr.com; 7 rue de l'Hôtel-Dieu; 🕑 10am-7pm, till 7.30pm Jul & Aug) Stocks thousands of titles on oenology (the art and science of wine making), including quite a few in English, as well as recipe books and wine-related gifts.

Laundrettes 19 rue du Faubourg St-Jean (🕑 6am-9pm); 63 rue de Lorraine (🕑 7am-9pm)

Le Clos Carnot (☎ 03 80 22 73 43; 34 place Carnot; per hr €3; 🕑 8am-midnight) A café-brasserie with two internet computers.

Post Office (7 bd St-Jacques) Does currency exchange.

Tourist Office (☎ 03 80 26 21 30; www.beaune-burgundy.com; 6 bd Perpreuil; 🕑 9am-7pm Mon-Sat, 9am-6pm Sun Easter–mid-Nov, 9am-12.30pm & 1.30-6pm Mon-Sat, 10am-12.30pm & 1.30-5pm Sun mid-Nov–Easter) Has an internet computer (€1.50 per 15 minutes) and sells Pass Beaune ticket combos that save 5% to 15%.

Sights

Founded in 1443 and used as a hospital until 1971, the celebrated Gothic **Hôtel-Dieu des Hospices de Beaune** (☎ 03 80 24 45 00; rue de l'Hôtel-Dieu; adult/student/under 18yr €6/4.80/2.80; 🕑 tickets sold 9am-6.30pm Easter–mid-Nov, 9am-11.30am & 2-5.30pm mid-Nov–Easter, interior closes 1hr later), open 365 days a year, is topped by ornate turrets and pitched rooftops covered in multicoloured tiles. Interior highlights include the barrel-vaulted **Grande Salle** (look for the dragons up on the roof beams); an 18th-century **pharmacy** lined with flasks once filled with volatile oils, unguents, elixirs and powders such as *beurre d'antimoine* (antimony butter) and *poudre de cloportes* (woodlouse powder); the huge **kitchens**, with their open hearths and industrious nuns; and the brilliant **Polyptych of the Last Judgement** (see the boxed text, p467).

Notable for its extra-large porch, **Basilique Collégiale Notre Dame** (place Général Leclerc; 🕑 8.30am-7pm, till 6pm in winter), built in the Romanesque and Gothic styles from the 11th to 15th centuries, was once affiliated with the monastery of Cluny. Medieval tapestries are displayed inside from Easter till the third weekend in November.

Beaune's thick stone **ramparts**, which shelter wine cellars and are surrounded by overgrown gardens, are ringed by a pathway that makes for a lovely stroll.

Activities

WINE TASTING

Underneath Beaune's buildings, streets and ramparts, millions of dusty bottles of wine are being aged to perfection in cool, dark, cobweb-lined cellars. At a number of places you can sample and compare fine local wines.

Cellier de la Vieille Grange (☎ 03 80 22 40 06; 27 bd Georges Clemenceau; 🕑 9am-noon & 2-7pm Tue-Sat, by appointment Sun & Mon) This is where locals come to buy Burgundy wines *en vrac* (in bulk) for as little as €1.25 per litre (from €3.40 per litre for AOC). Tasting is done direct from 114L and 228L barrels using a pipette. Bring your own jerrycan or buy a *cubitainer* (5/20L for €2.75/7.60) or something memorably – and horribly – called a *Vinibag*.

Lycée Viticole (☎ 03 80 26 35 81; www.lavitibeaune.com, in French; 16 av Charles Jaffelin; 🕑 8am-noon & 2-5.30pm Mon-Thu, to 5pm Fri, 8am-noon Sat, closed 2 weeks mid-Aug) One of about 20 French secondary schools – at least one in each wine-growing region – that train young people in every aspect of wine growing, from tending the vines to fermentation, bottling and ageing. You can visit the cellars and taste the prize-winning wines made by the students, something they're officially not allowed to do till they're 18. (Decades ago wine used to be served with lunch in the school cafeteria!)

Marché aux Vins (☎ 03 80 25 08 20; www.marcheauxvins.com, in French; 2 rue Nicolas Rolin; admission €10; 🕑 9.30-11.30am & 2-5.30pm, no midday closure mid-Jun–Aug) Using a *tastevin* (flat silvery cup whose shiny surfaces help you admire the wine's colour) you can sample an impressive 15 wines (including three whites) in the candle-lit former Église des Cordeliers and its cellars. Wandering among the vintages takes about an hour. The finest wines are at the end – look for the *premiers crus* and the *grand cru*.

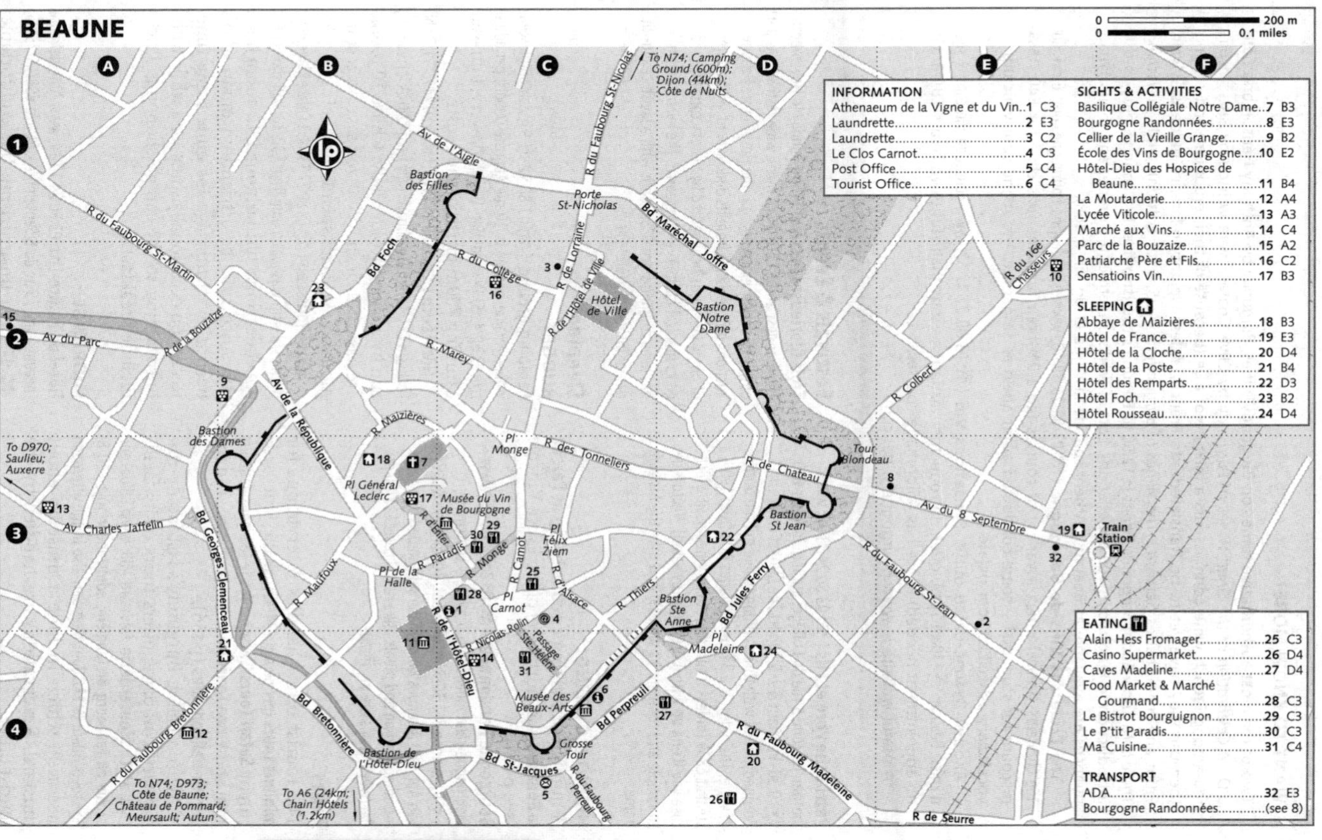
BEAUNE
0 200 m
0 0.1 miles
INFORMATION
Athenaeum de la Vigne et du Vin..1 C3
Laundrette..2 E3
Laundrette..3 C2
Le Clos Carnot..4 C3
Post Office..5 C4
Tourist Office..6 C4
SIGHTS & ACTIVITIES
Basilique Collégiale Notre Dame..7 B3
Bourgogne Randonnées..8 E3
Cellier de la Vieille Grange..9 B2
École des Vins de Bourgogne..10 E2
Hôtel-Dieu des Hospices de Beaune..11 B4
La Moutarderie..12 A4
Lycée Viticole..13 A3
Marché aux Vins..14 C4
Parc de la Bouzaize..15 A2
Patriarche Père et Fils..16 C2
Sensatioins Vin..17 B3
SLEEPING
Abbaye de Maizières..18 B3
Hôtel de France..19 E3
Hôtel de la Cloche..20 D4
Hôtel de la Poste..21 B4
Hôtel des Remparts..22 D3
Hôtel Foch..23 B2
Hôtel Rousseau..24 D4
EATING
Alain Hess Fromager..25 C3
Casino Supermarket..26 D4
Caves Madeline..27 D4
Food Market & Marché Gourmand..28 C3
Le Bistrot Bourguignon..29 C3
Le P'tit Paradis..30 C3
Ma Cuisine..31 C4
TRANSPORT
ADA..32 E3
Bourgogne Randonnées..(see 8)
To N74; Camping Ground (600m); Dijon (44km); Côte de Nuits
To D970; Saulieu; Auxerre
To N74; D973; Côte de Baune; Château de Pommard; Meursault; Autun
To A6 (24km; Chain Hôtels (1.2km)
Train Station
Tour Blondeau
Grosse Tour
Bastion des Filles
Bastion Notre Dame
Bastion St Jean
Bastion Ste Anne
Bastion de l'Hôtel-Dieu
Bastion des Dames
Porte St-Nicholas
Hôtel de Ville
Musée du Vin de Bourgogne
Musée des Beaux-Arts
Pl Monge
Pl Général Leclerc
Pl Félix Ziem
Pl Carnot
Pl de la Halle
Pl Madeleine
Passage Ste-Hélène
Av de l'Aigle
Bd Foch
Bd Maréchal Joffre
Av de la République
Bd Georges Clemenceau
Bd Bretonnière
Bd St-Jacques
Bd Perpreuil
Bd Jules Ferry
Av du 8 Septembre
Av du Parc
Av Charles Jaffelin
R du Faubourg St-Martin
R du Faubourg St-Nicolas
R du Faubourg St-Jean
R du Faubourg Madeleine
R du Faubourg Bretonnière
R du Faubourg Perreuil
R de la Bouzaize
R du Collège
R de Lorraine
R de l'Hôtel de Ville
R Marey
R Maizières
R des Tonneliers
R de Chateau
R Colbert
R du 16e Chasseurs
R d'Enfer
R Paradis
R Monge
R Carnot
R d'Alsace
R Thiers
R Maufoux
R Nicolas Rolin
R de l'Hôtel-Dieu
R de Seurre
BURGUNDY

WANT TO KNOW MORE?

Two of the most authoritative tomes on Burgundy wines, *Burgundy* by Anthony Hanson and *Côte d'Or: A Celebration of the Great Wines of Burgundy* by Clive Coates, were written by Brits, inspiring among French wine connoisseurs a mixture of awe (because of their erudition) and chagrin (because they have yet to be translated into French). A less weighty reference guide is Sylvain Pitiot and Jean-Charles Servant's *The Wines of Burgundy* (€14.25, 11th edition), while *Everything There Is To Know About Burgundy Wines* (€12.50 at Beaune's tourist office) is a concise, easy-to-use introduction to Burgundy's 100 appellations. Lots of works on fermented grapes and their myriad nuances are available at Beaune's Athenaeum de la Vigne et du Vin (p468).

The **École des Vins de Bourgogne** (☎ 03 80 26 35 10; www.ecoledesvins-bourgogne.com; 6 rue du 16e Chasseurs, Beaune) offers a variety of courses (eg a 2¾-hour fundamentals class for €40; 15% discount for students) – some conducted as far afield as Singapore – to refine your vinicultural vocabulary as well as your palate.

Another Beaune-based outfit, **Sensations Vin** (☎ 03 80 22 17 57; www.sensation-vin.com; 1 rue d'Enfer, Beaune; 10am-7pm), offers introductory tasting sessions (half-/full-/two hours €8/18/33; no appointment needed) as well as tailor-made courses.

A useful website is www.bourgogne-wines.com.

Patriarche Père et Fils (☎ 03 80 24 53 78; www.patriarche.com; 5 rue du Collège; audioguide tour €10; 9.30-11.30am & 2-5.30pm) The largest cellars in Burgundy, lined with three million to five million bottles of wine. The oldest is a Beaune Villages AOC from 1904, a steal at €839 (unless it turns out to be vinegar, in which case you'll end up with a pretty pricey salad). Visitors get to sample and compare 13 wines – and take the *tastevin* home.

HIKING & CYCLING

A number of walking circuits begin at **Parc de la Bouzaize**, just northwest of the Lycée Viticole (see p466).

Bourgogne Randonnées (☎ 03 80 22 06 03; www.bourgogne-randonnees.com; 7 av du 8 Septembre; 9am-noon & 1.30-7pm Mon-Sat, 10am-noon & 2-7pm Sun Apr-Oct) Arranges tailor-made self-guided bike tours, including lodging and meals. Bike rental costs €17/90 per day/week; maps are provided.

Tours

The tourist office handles reservations for **minibus tours** (per person €34-43) of the vineyards run by **Safari Tours** (www.burgundy-tourism-safaritours.com) and **Vinea Tours** (www.vineatours.com), and for **hot-air-balloon rides** (p456).

Maison Fallot, Burgundy's last family-run mustard company, offers tours of its facilities at **La Moutarderie** (Mustard Mill; www.fallot.com; 31 rue du Faubourg Bretonnière; adult/under 10yr €10/8; tours 10am & 11.30am Mon-Sat, also in the afternoon in summer), which include a museum about mustard. Reservations are handled by the tourist office.

Festivals & Events

Trois Glorieuses Festival (Third Sunday in November) The grandest of the Côte d'Or's many wine festivals. As part of this three-day extravaganza, the Hospices de Beaune auctions off the wines from its endowment, 61 hectares of prime vineyards bequeathed by benefactors; proceeds go to medical facilities and research. The event, which has been running since 1859, ends with a lavish candle-lit dinner inside the Hôtel-Dieu.

Sleeping

BUDGET

Camping ground (☎ 03 80 22 03 91; campinglescentvignes@mairie-beaune.fr; 10 rue Auguste Dubois; per adult/tent €3.60/4.35; mid-Mar–Oct) A flowery, four-star camping 700m north of the centre.

Hôtel Foch (☎ 03 80 24 05 65, fax 03 80 24 75 59; 24 bd Foch; s/d €33/38, with washbasin only from €28) A cheapie, run by a friendly older lady, whose 10 rooms are basic but clean. What you save on accommodation you can spend on wine!

Hôtel Rousseau (☎ 03 80 22 13 59; 11 place Madeleine; d €55, s/d with washbasin only from €30/38, hall shower €3) An endearingly old-fashioned, 12-room hotel run since 1959 by a friendly woman who's been *d'un certain âge* for quite some time. Reception occasionally shuts for a while without warning so she can go shopping. Prices include breakfast.

MIDRANGE

Hôtel de France (☎ 03 80 24 10 34; www.hoteldefrance-beaune.com; 35 av du 8 Septembre; s/d/tr/q €56/65/75/85;) An unsurprising but comfortable, sound-proofed two-star place with 21 decent rooms. Ideal if you're arriving by train.

Hôtel de la Cloche (☎ 03 80 24 66 33; www.hotel-cloche-beaune.com; 40-42 rue du Faubourg Madeleine; d €57-98;) The 32 rooms at this veteran three-star establishment mix classic decor with contemporary comfort.

Abbaye de Maizières (☎ 03 80 24 74 64; www.beaune-abbaye-maizieres.com; 19 rue Maizières; d €77-107, ste €133-149;) An idiosyncratic hotel inside a 12th-century abbey whose 13 tastefully converted rooms, with modern bathrooms, make creative use of the old brickwork and ancient wooden beams.

Hôtel des Remparts (☎ 03 80 24 94 94; www.hotel-remparts-beaune.com; 48 rue Thiers; d €92-108, low season €79-95, ste €116-150;) Set around two delightful courtyards, this three-star place – in a 17th-century town house – has 22 rooms with red tile floors, antique furniture and luxurious bathrooms. An excellent bet.

TOP END

Hôtel de la Poste (☎ 03 80 22 08 11; www.hoteldelapostebeaune.com; 1 bd Georges Clemenceau; d €130-220;) A four-star establishment on a site that's been home to a hostelry since 1660. Has an old-time wooden lift and 36 spacious, soothing rooms – no bling here, just understated elegance. Good wheelchair access.

Eating

Local restaurants are renowned for helping diners select just the right wine to go with each dish. You'll find quite a few cafés and restaurants around place Carnot, place Félix Ziem and place Madeleine.

Caves Madeleine (☎ 03 80 22 93 30; 8 rue du Faubourg Madeleine; menus €12-22; closed Thu, Sun & lunch Fri) A convivial Burgundian restaurant, much appreciated by locals who prize good value, with regional classics such as bœuf bourguignon, *cassolette d'escargots* and *jambon persillé* (jellied moulded ham). Most guests sit at long communal tables.

Le Bistrot Bourguignon (☎ 03 80 22 23 24; www.restaurant-lebistrotbourguignon.com; 8 rue Monge; lunch menu €12.90; Tue-Sat) A cosy bistro-style restaurant and wine bar that serves good-value cuisine billed as *régionale et originale* and 17 Burgundy wines by the glass (€2.60 to €7). Hosts live jazz at least once a month.

Le P'tit Paradis (☎ 03 80 24 91 00; 25 rue Paradis; lunch menu €18, other menus €27-35; Tue-Sat) An intimate restaurant on a narrow medieval street – an excellent place for *cuisine elaborée* (creatively transformed versions of traditional dishes) made with fresh local products. Has a terrace in summer.

Ma Cuisine (☎ 03 80 22 30 22; passage Ste-Hélène; menu €22; 12.15-1.30pm & 7.30-9pm Mon, Tue, Thu & Fri, closed Aug) A low-key, 13-table place hidden down an alley. The traditional French and Burgundian dishes, all excellent, include *pigeon de Bresse entier rôti au jus* (whole Bresse pigeon roasted in its juices; €32). The award-winning wine list includes 850 vintages listed by colour, region and ascending price (€18 to €830).

SELF-CATERING

The covered market hall at place de la Halle hosts a **food market** (until 12.30pm Sat) and a much smaller **marché gourmand** (gourmet market; Wed morning).

Alain Hess Fromager (7 place Carnot; 9am-12.15pm & 2.30-7.15pm Mon-Sat, plus 10am-1pm Sun Easter-Dec) Fine cheeses.

Casino supermarket (28 rue du Faubourg Madeleine; 8.30am-7.30pm Mon-Sat, 9am-noon Sun) Through an archway on rue du Faubourg Madeleine.

Getting There & Away

BUS

Bus 44, run by **Transco** (☎ 08 00 10 20 04), links Beaune with Dijon (€6.30, one hour, seven daily Monday to Friday, six Saturday, two Sunday and holidays), stopping at Côte d'Or wine-growing villages such as Vougeot, Nuits-St-Georges and Aloxe-Corton. Some line 44 buses also serve villages south of Beaune, including Pommard, Volnay, Meursault and La Rochepot. Services are somewhat reduced in July and August.

In Beaune, buses stop along the boulevards around the old city. Timetables can be consulted at the tourist office.

CAR

Cars, scooters (50cc per day €26, 125cc per day €58) and mountain bikes (€13 per day) can be rented from **ADA** (☎ 03 80 22 72 90; 26 av du 8 Septembre).

TRAIN

Beaune has frequent rail connections to Dijon (€6.50, 25 minutes, 25 to 40 daily) via the Côte d'Or village of Nuits-St-Georges (€3, 10 minutes). The last train from Beaune to Dijon departs a bit after 11pm.

Other destinations include Paris' Gare de Lyon (€50.50 to €62.40, two direct TGVs daily), Lyon–Part Dieu (€21.60, 1¾ hours, 11 to 17 daily) and Mâcon (€12.90, 50 minutes, 11 to 18 daily).

Getting Around

Parking is free outside the town walls.

If your legs feel wobbly from walking or wine, you can take a **taxi** (☎ 06 09 42 36 80, 06 09 43 12 08).

Near the train station, **Bourgogne Randonnées** (p470) and **ADA** (p471) rent bicycles.

PAYS D'AUXOIS

The area northwest of Dijon along and around the Canal de Bourgogne is verdant and rural, with broad fields, wooded hills and escarpments dotted with fortified hilltop towns, including Semur-en-Auxois.

Semur-en-Auxois

pop 4450

Surrounded by a hairpin curve in the River Armançon, this beguiling town is guarded by four massive, 13th- and 14th-century pink-granite bastions. Fear not, the 44m-high **Tour de la Orle d'Or** is not likely to collapse any time soon – those menacing cracks have been there since 1589!

Next to two concentric medieval gates, **Porte Sauvigne** (1417) and fortified **Porte Guillier** (13th century), the **tourist office** (☎ 03 80 97 05 96; www.ville-semur-en-auxois.fr, in French; 2 place Gaveau; 9am-1pm & 2-7pm Mon-Sat, 10am-12.30pm & 3-6pm Sun & holidays Jul & Aug, 9am-noon & 2-5pm or 6pm Mon-Sat Sep-Jun, closed Mon Oct-Apr) has a free walking-tour brochure in English and an SNCF train ticket machine.

Carpe Diem (right) offers free internet and wi-fi access with a drink or meal.

Most of the **old city**, easily explorable on foot, was built when Semur was an important religious centre boasting no less than six monasteries. Pedestrianised **rue Buffon**, through the gates from the tourist office, is lined with 17th-century houses; the **confectionary shop** (14 rue Buffon; Tue-Sun) produces **Semurettes**, delicious dark-chocolate candies invented here a century ago. The **Promenade du Rempart** affords panoramic views from atop the western part of Semur's medieval battlements.

Inside the twin-towered, Gothic **Collégiale Notre Dame** (9am-noon & 2-6.30pm, till 5pm or 6pm Nov-Easter), a collegiate church restored in the mid-19th century, are a stained-glass window (1927) and a plaque commemorating American soldiers who fell in France in WWI.

The **Musée Municipal** (☎ 03 80 97 24 25; rue Jean-Jacques Collenot; admission free; 2-5pm Mon & Wed-Fri Oct-Mar, 2-6pm Wed-Mon & holidays Apr-Sep) is fun because its eclectic exhibits – from fossils and stuffed fauna to archeology, sculptures and oil paintings – are still arranged just as they were back in the 19th century.

SLEEPING & EATING

Hôtel des Cymaises (☎ 03 80 97 21 44; www.hotelcymaises.com; 7 rue du Renaudot; d/q €64/93) Set around a quiet courtyard in an 18th-century *maison bourgeoise*, this two-star hotel has 18 comfortable, modern rooms, four apartments and a bright verandah for breakfast. It's just 100m from the tourist office – to get there go through the ancient gates and turn right.

Hôtel de la Côte d'Or (☎ 03 80 97 24 54; www.auxois.fr; 1 rue de la Liberté; d €95;) Across from the tourist office, this three-star place – totally renovated in 2008 – has 18 rooms whose contemporary furnishings blend nicely with the old beams and (in some rooms) stone fireplaces.

Carpe Diem (☎ 03 80 97 00 35; 4 rue du Vieux Marché; menus €11.50-21; 10.30am-2am Tue-Sun Jun-Sep, 10.30am-10pm Tue & Wed, till 2am Thu-Sat, 10.30am-4.30pm Sun Oct-May) This friendly neighbourhood bar serves bistro-style meals and wine by the glass (€2 to €2.50). Often hosts live music (jazz, blues) on Friday or Saturday from 6.30pm to 7.30pm and after 9.30pm.

There's a **Petit Casino grocery** (32 place Notre Dame; 8am-1pm & 3-8pm, closed Sun afternoon & Mon) near the church.

GETTING THERE & AWAY

Transco (☎ 08 00 10 20 04) bus 49 (two or three daily) goes to Dijon (€10.80, 1¼ hours) and Avallon (40 minutes), while bus 70 goes to Montbard (on the Paris–Dijon rail line; 20 to 60 minutes, seven to nine daily Monday to Saturday, three Sunday).

Abbaye de Fontenay

Founded in 1118 and restored to its stone-built medieval glory a century ago, **Abbaye de Fontenay** (Fontenay Abbey; ☎ 03 80 92 15 00; www.abbayedefontenay.com; adult/student under 26yr €8.90/4.20; 10am-6pm Apr–11 Nov, 10am-noon & 2-5pm 12 Nov–Mar) offers a fascinating glimpse of the austere, serene surroundings in which Cistercian monks lived lives of contemplation, prayer and manual

ESCARGOTS

One of France's trademark culinary habits, the consumption of gastropod molluscs – preferably with butter, garlic, parsley and fresh bread – is inextricably linked in the public mind with Burgundy because *Helix pomatia,* though endemic in much of Europe, is best known as *escargot de Bourgogne* (the Burgundy snail). Once a regular – and unwelcome – visitor to the fine-wine vines of Burgundy and a staple on Catholic plates during Lent, the humble hermaphroditic crawler has been decimated by overharvesting and the use of agricultural chemicals, and is now a protected species. As a result, the vast majority of the critters impaled on French snail forks (the ones with two tongs) are now imported from Turkey, Greece and Eastern Europe.

For *lots* more information – and perhaps a new career – see the article 'Start Your Own Snail Farm', issued by the **United States Department of Agriculture** (www.totse.com/en/technology/science_technology/snails.html).

labour. Set in a bucolic wooded valley along a stream called Ru de Fontenay, the abbey – a Unesco World Heritage Site – includes an exquisitely unadorned Romanesque church, a barrel-vaulted monks' dormitory, landscaped gardens and the 'first metallurgical factory in Europe'. Guided **tours** (departures hourly 10am-5pm except 1pm Apr–11 Nov) are in French (printed information is available in six languages).

From the parking lot, the **GR213 trail** forms part of two verdant walking circuits, one to Montbard (13km return), the other (11.5km) through Touillon and Le Petit Jailly. Maps are available at the ticket counter.

The abbey is 25km north of Semur-en-Auxois. A **taxi** (☎ 03 80 92 31 49, 03 80 92 04 79) from the Montbard train station – served from Dijon (€11, 40 minutes) and Paris' Gare de Lyon (one hour by TGV) – costs €11 (€15 on Sunday and holidays).

CHÂTILLON-SUR-SEINE

pop 6300

Châtillon's main claim to fame is the **Trésor de Vix**, a treasure trove of Celtic, Etruscan and Greek objects from the 6th century BC on display at the **Musée du Pays Châtillonnais** (☎ 03 80 91 24 67; rue de la Libération; adult/student under 26yr €4.50/2.50; 10am-6pm Jul & Aug, 9.30am-noon & 2-5pm Wed-Mon Sep-Jun). The outstanding collection includes a jaw-droppingly massive bronze Greek *krater* – 1.64m high and weighing 208kg! – that could hold 1100L of wine. In mid-2009 the museum will move to **Abbaye Notre Dame**, founded in 1132, situated a few hundred metres north of place Marmont. Signs are in French, English and German.

Châtillon's **tourist office** (☎ 03 80 91 13 19; www.pays-chatillonnais.fr; place Marmont; 9am-noon & 2-6pm Mon-Sat year-round, plus 10am-noon Sun & holidays May-Sep) is at the fountain roundabout though there are plans to move it to larger quarters. Internet access is available at **Au Stand** (☎ 03 80 91 22 53; 41 rue Maréchal de Lattre; per hr €4; 8am-9pm Tue-Sat, 8am-1pm Sun).

The town's commercial centre, rebuilt after the war, is bordered by two branches of the Seine, here hardly more than a stream. A short walk east is the idyllic **Source de la Douix** (pronounced dwee; 24hr), a 600L-a-second artesian spring that flows from the bottom of a 30m cliff. Perfect for a picnic, it is one of the oldest Celtic religious sites in Europe. Nearby you can climb up to the round, crenellated **Tour de Gissey** (1500s), which affords fine views; access is via the cemetery. Also overlooking the town, next to the cemetery, is the pre-Romanesque **Église St-Vorles**, built in the 10th century and partly rebuilt in the 13th century.

Among the wines produced in the **Châtillonnais vineyards**, north of town, is Burgundy's own bubbly, *Crémant de Bourgogne* (www.cremantdebourgogne.fr, in French). Vineyards can be visited by following the new **Route du Crémant**, marked by white-on-brown signs. The Champagne region's **Côte des Bar vineyards** (p369) are just a few kilometres further north.

The three-star **Hôtel de la Côte d'Or** (☎ 03 80 91 13 29; cotedor.chatillon@club-internet.fr; 2 rue Charles Ronot; d €60-70), a block off the main street, is a pleasant Logis de France place whose 10 rooms come with antique furnishings and surprising carpets. The rustic **restaurant** (*menus* €18 to €40) serves traditional French and regional cuisine, including Charolais beef and Bresse chicken.

Châtillon is an easy stopover if you're travelling between Burgundy and Champagne. Bus 50, run by **Transco** (☎ 08 00 10 20 04), goes to Dijon (€14.40, 1¾ hours, two or three daily).

SNCF buses go to the main-line train station in Montbard (40 minutes, three to five daily Monday to Friday, two daily weekends).

YONNE

The Yonne *département* (www.tourisme-yonne.com), roughly midway between Dijon and Paris, has long been Burgundy's northern gateway. For visitors, attractions include the verdant countryside, the magical hilltop village of Vézelay, the white-wine powerhouse of Chablis and canal-boat cruising from ancient river ports such as Auxerre.

Getting Around

Bus services in the Yonne are cheap but extremely limited. Most lines operated by **Les Rapides de Bourgogne** (☎ in Auxerre 03 86 94 95 00, in Avallon 03 86 34 00 00; www.rapidesdebourgogne.com, in French; office at 39 rue de Paris, Avallon; ⌚ 9.30-11.15am Mon-Sat, often open other times) run only once or twice a day on school days, with two more daily services available on demand – that is, you must make a reservation the day before, prior to 5pm, by internet or phone (☎ 08 00 30 33 09). Line 1 links Auxerre with Pontigny, Line 4 goes from Auxerre to Chablis and Tonnerre, and Line 5 links Avallon's Café de l'Europe taxi stand with Noyers-sur-Serein and Tonnerre. Tourist offices have timetables.

AUXERRE

pop 37,100

The alluring riverside town of Auxerre (pronounced oh-sair) has been a port since Roman times. Wandering through the maze of cobbled streets in the old city, you come upon Roman remains, Gothic churches and timber-framed medieval houses – and have views across a jumble of belfries, spires and steep tiled rooftops leading down to the boats bobbing on the River Yonne.

Auxerre makes a good base for exploring northern Burgundy, including Chablis (p478), and the city's port is an excellent place to rent a canal boat (see the boxed text, p456).

Orientation

The old city clambers up the hillside on the west (left) bank of the River Yonne, while

CAPTIVATED BY THE CELTS

Jean-Louis Coudrot, an archeologist and protohistorian who has been director of the **Musée du Pays Châtillonnais** (p473) since 1995, is fascinated by all things Celtic. Not surprisingly, given that his museum's pride and joy is the breathtaking **Trésor de Vix** (Vix Treasure), discovered in 1953 in the tomb of the **Dame de Vix**, a Celtic princess who controlled the trade in Cornish tin in the 6th century BC – OTEC (the Organisation of Tin-Exporting Celts), if you will. Mined in Cornwall, it was brought by boat up the Seine as far as Vix and then carried overland to the Saône and the Rhône, whence river vessels conveyed it south to Marseilles and its most eager consumers, the Greeks, who alloyed it with copper to make bronze.

Coudrot has been fascinated by archeology since the age of 10. 'My father sentenced me to do some work in the garden of our house and I found a polished stone axe. I immediately started researching what it was and got in touch with a local archeologist, with whom I started working on excavations, on weekends, starting at age 13.' The excavation site, near Troyes, had belonged to the Celts, known as the Celtoi to the Greeks and the Galli to the Romans.

'For me it was miraculous! We found torques, belts made of interlocking rings and fibulas (clothing clasps), all in bronze.' Bronze, of course, cannot be made without tin, which is why trade with the Dame de Vix was so important to the Greeks – and why, eager to maintain their supply of the strategic metal, 'they sent the Dame de Vix all manner of gifts, including ornate *kraters*, Greek ceramics and also, certainly, amphorae of wine, which was not grown in this region at that time'.

The trade created 'a commercial network, just like today. Globalisation had already begun', Coudrot says. 'For the past 2500 years we've had the same axis of transportation and trade between northwest Europe and the southeast. Basically, the Dame de Vix controlled a Greco-Celtic version of the Calais-Provence autoroute and the TGV from London to Marseilles.'

THE CELTS IN BURGUNDY *Daniel Robinson*

Bibracte The Celts take centre stage at the Museum of Celtic Civilisation, which is in the Parc Naturel Régional du Morvan at Bibracte, the site of Vercingétorix' selection as chief of the Gaulish coalition in 52 BC.

The goddess Sequana The 1st-century AD bronze statue of the Celtic goddess Sequana, standing on a boat, is one of the highlights of a visit to Dijon's Musée Archéologique.

Trésor de Vix A truly stunning collection of Celtic, Greek and Etruscan objects, found in the tomb of the Dame de Vix, a Celtic princess who lived 2500 years ago, is the centrepiece of the Musée du Pays Châtillonnais in Châtillon-sur-Seine.

the train station is 700m east of the river. The commercial centre stretches from the cathedral to the post office, with shops lining rue de Paris and, further south, rue du Temple. The liveliest areas are around pedestrianised rue de l'Horloge and place Charles Surugue.

Information

The tourist office will change small amounts of money on Sunday and holidays.

Laundrette (138 rue de Paris; 6.30am-10pm)
Post Office (place Charles Surugue) Changes currency.
Speed Informatique 89 (32 rue du Pont; per 10min/1hr €1/5; 2-9pm Mon-Sat) Internet access.
Tourist Office (03 86 52 06 19; www.ot-auxerre.fr; 1-2 quai de la République; 9am-1pm & 2-7pm Mon-Sat, 9.30am-1pm & 3-6.30pm Sun & holidays mid-Jun–mid-Sep, 9.30am-12.30pm & 2-6pm Mon-Fri, 9.30am-12.30pm & 2-6.30pm Sat, 10am-1pm Sun mid-Sep–mid-Jun) Runs English tours of the city from July to mid-September. The brochure *In the Steps of Cadet Roussel* takes you on a self-guided architectural walking tour.
Tourist Office Annexe (7 place de l'Hôtel de Ville; 10am-noon or 12.30pm & 1.30-6pm Tue-Sat, till 7pm mid-Jun–mid-Sep) Next to Tour de l'Horloge.

Sights & Activities

Wonderful views of the city, perched on the hillside, can be had from **Pont Paul Bert** (1857) and the arched footbridge opposite the main tourist office.

From Easter to September from Wednesday to Sunday and on holidays, the main tourist office rents **electric boats** (one hour/two hours/half-day/full day costs €20/32/48/85). It takes at least 1½ hours to get to one or more of the locks on the Canal du Nivernais.

Cycling options include the **towpath** along the Canal du Nivernais to Clamecy (about 60km). Bicycles can be rented at the tourist office.

ABBAYE ST-GERMAIN

The ancient **Abbaye St-Germain** (St-Germain Abbey; 03 86 18 05 50; place St-Germain; adult/student under 26yr Oct-May €4.50/free, Jun-Sep €6.30/free; 10am-12.30pm & 2-6.30pm Wed-Mon Jun-Sep, 10am-noon & 2-6pm Wed-Mon Oct-May) began as a basilica above the tomb of St Germain, the 5th-century bishop who made Auxerre an important Christian centre. Over the centuries, as the site's importance grew, so did the abbey, and by the Middle Ages it was attracting pilgrims from all over Europe.

The **crypt**, visitable only on a tour (in French with printed information in English; departures on the hour until 5pm in winter, on the half-hour till 5.30pm in summer), contains some of Europe's finest examples of Carolingian architecture. Supported by 1000-year-old oak beams, the walls and vaulted ceiling are decorated with 9th-century frescoes; the far end houses the tomb of St Germain himself. Excavations under the nave have uncovered sarcophagi – left in situ – from as early as the 6th century.

Housed around the abbey's cloister, the **Musée d'Art et d'Histoire** displays prehistoric artefacts, Gallo-Roman sculpture and pottery discovered in and around Auxerre. The medieval section includes a mock-up of a scriptorium (where monks copied over manuscripts); nearby rooms have medals and coinage.

The same ticket gets you into the **Musée Leblanc-Duvernoy** (03 86 52 44 63; 9bis rue d'Égleny; separate admission €2.20; 2-6pm Wed-Mon), which has a pretty good collection of *faïence* (pottery) and 18th-century Beauvais tapestries.

CATHÉDRALE ST-ÉTIENNE

The vast Gothic **Cathédrale St-Étienne** (place St-Étienne; 7.30am-6pm Easter-Oct, 7.30am-5pm Nov-Easter) and its stately 68m-high bell tower dominate Auxerre's skyline. The choir, ambulatory and some of the vivid **stained-glass windows** (eg in

BURGUNDY

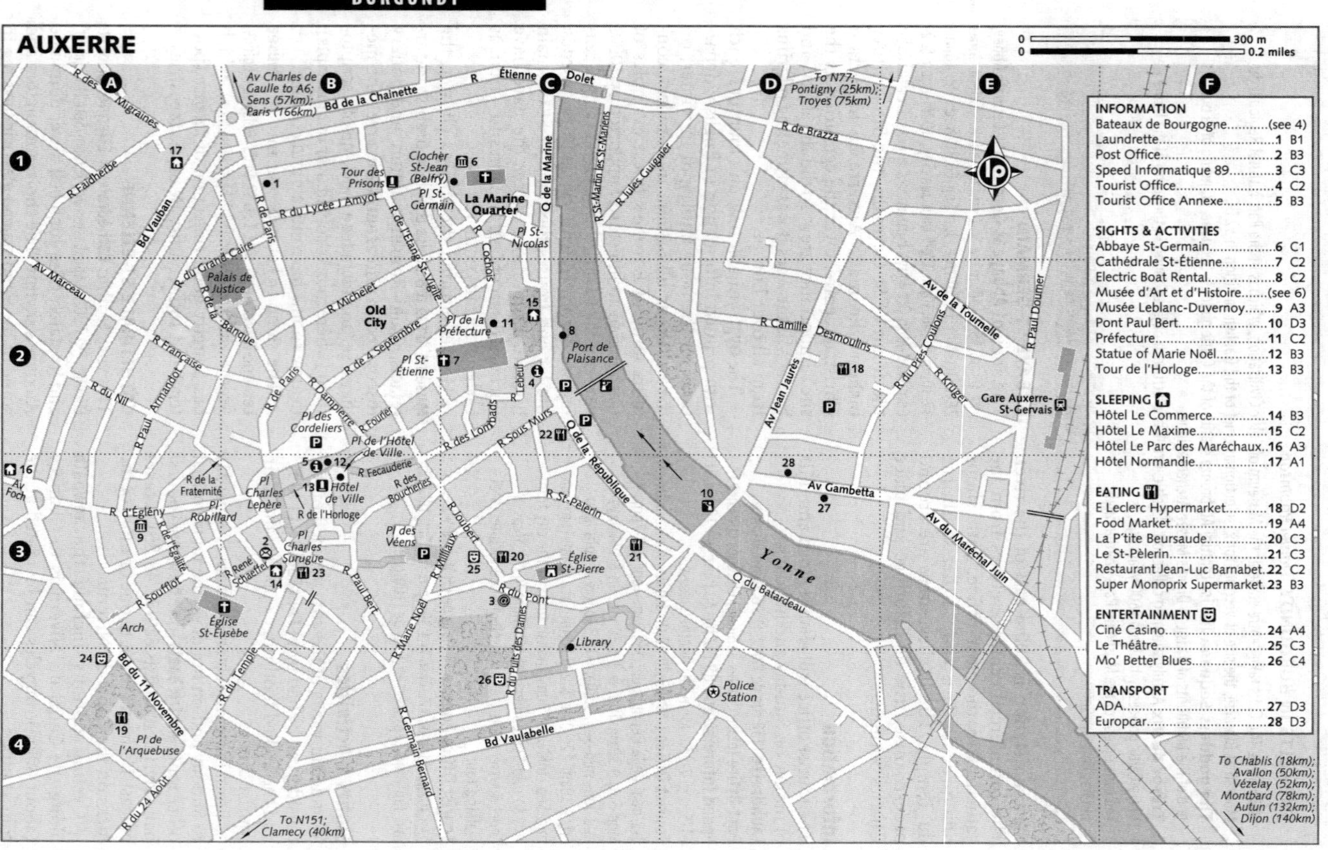
AUXERRE
0 300 m
0 0.2 miles
INFORMATION
Bateaux de Bourgogne (see 4)
Laundrette 1 B1
Post Office 2 B3
Speed Informatique 89 3 C3
Tourist Office 4 C2
Tourist Office Annexe 5 B3
SIGHTS & ACTIVITIES
Abbaye St-Germain 6 C1
Cathédrale St-Étienne 7 C2
Electric Boat Rental 8 C2
Musée d'Art et d'Histoire (see 6)
Musée Leblanc-Duvernoy 9 A3
Pont Paul Bert 10 D3
Préfecture 11 C2
Statue of Marie Noël 12 B3
Tour de l'Horloge 13 B3
SLEEPING
Hôtel Le Commerce 14 B3
Hôtel Le Maxime 15 C2
Hôtel Le Parc des Maréchaux 16 A3
Hôtel Normandie 17 A1
EATING
E Leclerc Hypermarket 18 D2
Food Market 19 A4
La P'tite Beursaude 20 C3
Le St-Pèlerin 21 C3
Restaurant Jean-Luc Barnabet 22 C2
Super Monoprix Supermarket 23 B3
ENTERTAINMENT
Ciné Casino 24 A4
Le Théâtre 25 C3
Mo' Better Blues 26 C4
TRANSPORT
ADA 27 D3
Europcar 28 D3
Av Charles de Gaulle to A6; Sens (57km); Paris (166km)
To N77; Pontigny (25km); Troyes (75km)
To Chablis (18km); Avallon (50km); Vézelay (52km); Montbard (78km); Autun (132km); Dijon (140km)
To N151; Clamecy (40km)
Yonne
Old City
La Marine Quarter
Gare Auxerre-St-Gervais
Port de Plaisance
Police Station
Library
Palais de Justice
Église St-Eusèbe
Église St-Pierre
Clocher St-Jean (Belfry)
Tour des Prisons
Hôtel de Ville
Arch
R des Migraines
R Faidherbe
Bd Vauban
Av Marceau
Bd de la Chainette
R Étienne Dolet
R de Paris
R du Lycée J Amyot
R du Grand Caire
R de la Banque
R Michelet
R de l'Étang St-Vigile
R Cochois
Pl St-Germain
Pl St-Nicolas
Q de la Marine
R St-Martin les St-Mariens
R Jules Guignier
R de Brazza
R Française
R du Nil
R Paul Armandot
R de 4 Septembre
Pl de la Préfecture
Pl St-Étienne
R Dampierre
R Fourier
Pl des Cordeliers
Pl de l'Hôtel de Ville
R Fecauderie
R des Lombards
R Sous Murs
R Lebeuf
Q de la République
R Camille Desmoulins
Av Jean Jaurès
R du Prés Coulons
Av de la Tourmelle
R Krüger
R Paul Doumer
Av Gambetta
Av du Maréchal Juin
Av Foch
R de la Fraternité
Pl Robillard
Pl Charles Lepère
R de l'Horloge
R d'Églény
R de l'Égalité
Pl Charles Surugue
R René Schaeffer
R Soufflot
R des Boucheries
Pl des Véens
R Joubert
R Milliaux
R St-Pèlerin
R du Pont
R Paul Bert
R Marie Noël
R du Puits des Dames
Q du Batardeau
Bd du 11 Novembre
R du Temple
Pl de l'Arquebuse
R du 24 Août
R Germain Bernard
Bd Vaulabelle

the axial chapel and the ambulatory) date from the 1200s. The Gothic western front was badly damaged by the hammer-happy Huguenots, who decapitated most of the statues during the Wars of Religion.

The 11th-century Romanesque **crypt** (adult/under 12yr €3/free; 9am-6pm Mon-Sat, 2-6pm Sun Easter-Oct, 10am-5pm Mon-Sat Nov-Easter) is ornamented with remarkable frescoes, including a scene of **Christ à Cheval** (Christ on Horseback; late 11th century) unlike any other known in Western art. Upstairs, the **treasury** (adult/under 12yr €1.90/free; same as crypt) has an Entombment painting by Luca Penni (16th century), illuminated manuscripts, Limoges enamels and the usual chalices. Tickets are sold in the gift shop off the choir.

From June to September at 9.30pm or 10pm, a 70-minute **sound-and-light show** (€5) is held nightly inside the cathedral. In July and August **organ concerts** (€5) take place every Sunday at 5pm.

TOUR DE L'HORLOGE

In the heart of Auxerre's partly medieval commercial precinct, the spire-topped **Tour de l'Horloge** (Clock Tower; btwn place de l'Hôtel de Ville & rue de l'Horloge) was built in 1483 as part of the city's fortifications. On the 17th-century clock faces (there's one on each side), the sun-hand indicates the time of day; the moon-hand shows what day of the lunar month it is, making a complete rotation every 29½ days. A full-colour **statue of Marie Noël** (15 place de l'Hôtel de Ville), Auxerre's best-known poet, stands nearby.

Sleeping

Hôtel Le Commerce (☎ 03 86 52 03 16; hotelducommerceauxerre@wanadoo.fr; 5 rue René Schaeffer; s/d €45/49; reception 5.30-9pm Mon, 7.30am-3pm & 5.30-9pm Tue-Sat, closed Sun) A welcoming two-star place smack in the centre of town. The 16 rooms, in deep pastels and the colours of the sea, have either shower pods or bath-tubs. The old building's cheerful, creative decor was inspired by distant sunny lands.

Hôtel Normandie (☎ 03 86 52 57 80; www.hotelnormandie.fr; 41 bd Vauban; d €67-95; closed Christmas–early Jan;) In a 19th-century building on tree-lined bd Vauban, this two-star hotel has ivy-covered frontage and 47 rooms with views that make it feel like a country inn. Amenities include a billiard table, a workout room and a sauna (€6 per person).

Hôtel Le Maxime (☎ 03 86 52 14 19; www.lemaxime.com; 2 quai de la Marine; d €87-113, Oct-Feb €5-10 less, ste for 2/4 people €140/200;) In a wonderful spot overlooking the River Yonne, this three-star place offers 26 spacious rooms – some with river views, others with views of the old city – and first-class service.

Hôtel Le Parc des Maréchaux (☎ 03 86 51 43 77; www.hotel-parcmarechaux.com; 6 av Foch; d €92-123, in winter €5 less;) Once a mansion of château-like proportions, this three-star place has 25 rooms decorated with impeccable taste, all named after French marshals. The two best rooms – great for a romantic getaway – have balconies overlooking the private park.

Eating

Restaurant Jean-Luc Barnabet (☎ 03 86 51 68 88; 14 quai de la République; weekday only menus €21-29, other menus €46-73, children's menu €17.50; closed dinner Sun & Mon & lunch Tue) A truly refined place to dine. The chef's innovative versions of traditional French fish and meat dishes have earned many accolades, including a Michelin star.

La P'tite Beursaude (☎ 03 86 51 10 21; 55 rue Joubert; menus €18-27; Thu-Mon) An intimate, rustic place with half a dozen fish and meat dishes prepared according to the traditions of Burgundy and France. Specialities include *entrecôte poêlée à la crème d'Époisses* (fried rib steak with Époisses cheese). The waitresses wear traditional Morvan dress.

Le St-Pèlerin (☎ 03 86 52 77 05; 56 rue St-Pèlerin; menus €21-28; Tue-Sat) Diners come back satiated from this rustic restaurant, where French and Burgundian dishes are prepared over a wood fire. Specialities include escargots, *œufs meurette* (eggs poached in Burgundy wine sauce) and *jambon à la Chablisienne* (ham in Chablisienne sauce).

SELF-CATERING

Places for picnic supplies:

E Leclerc hypermarket (14 av Jean Jaurès; 9am-8pm Mon-Thu & Sat, till 8.30pm Fri)

Food market (place de l'Arquebuse; 7am-1pm Tue & Fri, small market also Sat morning)

Super Monoprix supermarket (place Charles Surugue; 8.30am-8pm Mon-Sat)

Entertainment

Mo' Better Blues (☎ 03 86 51 36 64; www.addim89.org, www.citedesmusiques.org, both in French; 36-38 rue du Puits des Dames; admission free; 9pm-1am Wed & Thu,

7pm-2am Fri, 9pm-2am Sat) A dynamic jazz bar with live concerts. Also has jam sessions at 9.30pm on Thursday and salsa courses from 7pm to 9pm on Wednesday.

Ciné Casino (☎ 03 86 52 36 80, 08 92 68 81 08; www.cinefil.com, in French; 1 bd du 11 Novembre) generally screens a nondubbed film or two.

Le Théâtre (☎ 03 86 72 24 24; www.auxerre-le-theatre.com, in French; 54 rue Joubert; Sep-Jun), housed in a sleek art-deco building, puts on music and dance performances and hosts **top jazz talent** (www.jazzclubdauxerre.com, in French; 2 or 3 times a month Oct-May).

Getting There & Away

CAR

Car-rental companies:
ADA (☎ 03 86 46 01 02; 6bis av Gambetta)
Europcar (☎ 03 86 46 99 08; 9 av Gambetta)

TRAIN

Trains run from **Gare Auxerre-St-Gervais** (rue Paul Doumer) to the main-line Laroche-Migennes station (€3.60, 15 minutes, 15 daily), where you may have to change for Dijon (€23.30, two hours, five to seven daily) and Paris' Gare de Lyon or Gare de Bercy (€23, 1½ to 2½ hours, 11 to 14 daily). Trains also go to Avallon (€8.80, 1¼ hours, four or five daily), Autun (€19.50, 70 minutes, two or three daily) and Sermizelles-Vézelay (€7, 50 minutes, four or five daily).

Getting Around

Free parking is available along the river on quai de la Marine and quai de la République, and on the boulevards that circle the old city: bd de la Chainette, bd Vauban, bd du 11 Novembre and bd Vaulabelle.

Phone for a **taxi** (☎ 03 86 94 02 02, 03 86 52 30 51).

The main tourist office rents out bicycles (three/seven hours costs €10/18).

AROUND AUXERRE

Between the River Yonne and the Canal de Bourgogne lie the Auxerrois and the Tonnerrois, rural areas covered with forests, fields, pastures and vineyards. The quiet back roads (eg the D124) and many of the walking trails make for excellent cycling.

La Puisaye

The countryside west of Auxerre, known as **La Puisaye**, is a lightly populated landscape of woods, winding creeks and dark hills. The area is best known as the birthplace of Colette (1873–1954), author of *La Maison de Claudine* and *Gigi* (and 50 other novels), who lived till age 18 in the tiny town of St-Sauveur-en-Puisaye, 40km southwest of Auxerre, and of particular interest because much of her work explores her rural Burgundian childhood.

The **Musée Colette** (☎ 03 86 45 61 95; adult/10-25yr €5/2; 10am-6pm Wed-Mon Apr-Oct, 2-6pm Sat & Sun, public holidays & school holidays Nov-Mar), in the château of St-Sauveur-en-Puisaye, features letters, manuscripts, two furnished rooms from her apartment in Paris' Palais Royal and photos featuring her iconic hairdo. An explanatory sheet in (charmingly mangled) English is available.

Chablis

pop 2600

The well-to-do but sleepy town of Chablis, 19km east of Auxerre, has made its fortune growing, ageing and marketing the dry white wines that have carried its name to the four corners of the earth.

Chablis is made exclusively from chardonnay grapes and is divided into four Appellations d'Origine Contrôlées (AOC): Petit Chablis, Chablis, Chablis Premier Cru and, most prestigious of all, Chablis Grand Cru. The seven *grands crus*, lovingly grown on just 1 sq km of land on the hillsides northeast of town, are Blanchot, Bougros, Les Clos, Grenouilles, Preuses, Valmur and Vaudésir.

ORIENTATION & INFORMATION

Chablis' main street is known as rue Auxerroise (west of the main square, place Charles de Gaulle) and rue du Maréchal de Lattre de Tassigny (east of place Charles de Gaulle). Most of Chablis' shops are closed on Monday and noon to 3pm on other days.

Tourist Office (☎ 03 86 42 80 80; www.chablis.net; 1 rue du Maréchal de Lattre de Tassigny; 10am-12.30pm & 1.30-6pm, till 7pm Jun-Aug, closed Sun Nov-Mar) Just east of place Charles de Gaulle. Can supply you with a free English walking-tour booklet and maps of Chablis' vineyards.

SIGHTS & ACTIVITIES

The 12th- and 13th-century Gothic **Église St-Martin** (Jul & Aug), first founded in the 9th century by monks fleeing the Norman attacks on Tours, is two short blocks northwest of place Charles de Gaulle. Southeast along rue Porte Noël are the twin bastions of **Porte**

BURGUNDY

THEY DON'T BUILD 'EM LIKE THEY USED TO

In the year 1228 (better known to most of us as 1997), an imaginary nobleman of modest rank but great ambition began constructing a fortified château. A team of skilled artisans, using the latest 13th-century technologies, has been hard at work ever since and is right on schedule to finish the project, as planned, in 25 years. Stone is quarried on-site using iron hand tools forged by a team of blacksmiths, who also produce vital items such as door hinges. Clay for tiles – fired for three days using locally cut wood – is quarried nearby, and the mortar, made on-site with lime, is transported in freshly woven wicker baskets. An impressive château fort is now rising in the woods where there was none before.

Welcome to the fantastic **Chantier Médiéval de Guédelon** (☎ 03 86 45 66 66; www.guedelon.fr; adult/5-17yr €9/7; ⏲ 10am-7pm daily Jul & Aug, 10am-5.30pm or 6pm Thu-Tue mid-Mar–Jun & Sep–2 Nov, to 7pm Sun & holidays Apr-Jun, closed 3 Nov–mid-Mar), 45km southwest of Auxerre and 7km southwest of St-Sauveur-en-Puisaye, run by craftspeople who are passionate about what they're creating, something you can sense when you talk with them (some speak English). Archeologists, too, are enthusiastic – the period processes, which often require years of trial and error before they're reperfected, provide invaluable insights for their research.

Excellent English material on Guédelon is available. A very worthwhile guided tour, sometimes in English, costs €2 per person. Your visit is not likely to be 'nasty, brutish and short' but rather engaging, friendly and leisurely, though it may be messy unless you wear closed shoes, as the site, ever true to life, is often a sea of muck. Kids-oriented activities include stone carving (using especially soft stone). After a visit you'll never look at a medieval cathedral or château in quite the same way again.

Noël (1778), which hosts art exhibitions from June to August. Nearby, the enigmatic 16th-century building known as the **synagogue** (☎ 03 86 18 96 08; 10-14 rue des Juifs) was recently restored. The 12th-century cellar of **Petit Pontigny** (rue de Chichée) was once used by Pontigny's Cistercian monks to ferment wine.

Vineyard walks from Chablis include the **Sentier des Grands Crus** (8km) and the **Sentier des Clos** (13km to 24km, depending on your route). The tourist office sells French-language topoguides (€3).

Cycling is a great way to tour the Chablis countryside. One flat, verdant option is the 45km **Chemin de Serein** (www.chemin-serein.com), which follows the old Tacot rail line southeast to Noyers-sur-Serein (p481) and L'Isle-sur-Serein. The tourist office helpfully hires **bikes** (per two hours/half-day/full day €4/7.50/12) from Easter to October.

Nearby villages worth exploring include **Courgis**, which offers great views; **Chichée** and **Chemilly**, both on the River Serein; and **Chitry-le-Fort**, famous for its fortified church.

Wine can be tasted and purchased at dozens of places (eg along rue des Moulins) – the tourist office has a comprehensive list. A variety of vintages, including five of Chablis' seven *grands crus,* can be sampled at **La Chablisienne** (☎ 03 86 42 89 98; 8 bd Pasteur; ⏲ 9am-12.30pm & 2-7pm, to 6pm Jan-Mar, no midday closure Jul & Aug), a large cooperative cellar founded in 1923. It's situated 700m south of place Charles de Gaulle – follow rue Auxerroise and then av de la République (D62).

SLEEPING

Hôtel Le Bergerand's (☎ 03 86 18 96 08; www.chablis-france.fr; 4 rue des Moulins; d incl breakfast €78-128; ❄ 💻 ⊠) A rustic two-star hotel whose 22 B&B-style rooms, with antique wood furniture and cheerful spring colours, occupy a one-time coaching inn. The French-born *patronne,* who lived in Los Angeles for 35 years, likes stirring local affairs up a bit.

Hôtel du Vieux Moulin (☎ 03 86 42 47 30; www.larochehotel.fr; 18 rue des Moulins; d €125-175, low season €100-135, ste €190-270; ❄ 💻 ⊠) In a one-time mill, the five rooms and two suites – understated and very contemporary – afford luscious views of a branch of the Serein. The breakfast room, as homey as a living room, has *grand cru* views.

EATING

Le Bistrot des Grands Crus (☎ 03 86 42 19 41; 8-10 rue Jules Rathier; main with wine €9.50, menu €20; ⏲ closed mid-Jan–mid-Feb) A block southeast of Porte Noël, this sleek place serves *cuisine du terroir* (cooking that's deeply connected to the land) made with the freshest local ingredients, including Chablis.

Restaurant de la Poste (☎ 03 86 42 11 94; 24 rue Auxerroise; weekday lunch menu €11, other menus €15-28.50) Unpretentious and popular with locals, this place serves pasta as well as French fish and meat dishes.

Le Wine Bar (☎ 03 86 42 47 30; 18 rue des Moulins; mains €15-25; lunch Tue-Sat, dinner Fri & Sat, also open dinner Tue-Thu Jun-Sep) Attached to the Hôtel du Vieux Moulin, this establishment serves traditional Burgundian dishes as well as fusion cuisine.

Chablis has an **outdoor food market** (place Charles de Gaulle; until 1pm Sun). Except for the **Petit Casino grocery** (rue du Maréchal Leclerc; 7.30am-1pm & 3-7.30pm Mon-Sat), 50m down the hill from place Charles de Gaulle, all the food shops along rue Auxerroise are closed on Sunday afternoon and Monday.

Pontigny

pop 800

Rising from the flat fields 25km north of Auxerre, Pontigny's **Abbatiale** (abbey church; ☎ 03 86 47 54 99; www.abbayedepontigny.eu, in French; admission free; 9am or 10am-5pm in winter, till 7pm in summer), founded in 1114, is one of the last surviving examples of Cistercian architecture in Burgundy. The simplicity and purity of its construction reflect the austerity of the Cistercian order (see p464). On summer days sunshine filtering through the high windows creates an amazing sense of peace and tranquillity. *Discovering Pontigny* (€2.50), on sale in the little gift shop, points out fascinating architectural details.

The Gothic sanctuary, 108m long and lined with 23 chapels, was built in the mid-12th century; the wooden choir screen, stalls and organ loft were added in the 17th and 18th centuries. Monks from here were the first to perfect the production of Chablis wine.

The **tourist office** (☎ 03 86 47 47 03; http://pontignytourisme.free.fr; 22 rue Paul Desjardins; 10am-12.30pm & 2-6pm Apr-Oct, 10am-12.30pm & 2-4.30pm Nov-Mar, closed Sun & sometimes Mon), across the road from the Abbatiale (next to the post office), has information on accommodation (including B&Bs) and sells hiking maps and topoguides of the area.

There are a couple of restaurants on the N77, north across the stream from the tourist office. Edibles are available at the **Panier Sympa grocery** (43 rue Paul Desjardins; 7am-1pm & 3-8pm Mon-Sat, 8am-1pm & 4-8pm Sun).

THE ENGLISH CONNECTION

Three archbishops of Canterbury played a role in the history of Pontigny's abbey: Thomas Becket spent the first three years of his exile here (1164–66); Stephen Langton, a refugee from political turmoil in England, lived here for six years (from 1207 to 1213); and Edmund Rich, who fell ill and died at Soissy in 1240 while on his way to the Vatican, was brought here for burial.

Tonnerre

pop 6000

The less-than-prosperous town of Tonnerre, on the Canal de Bourgogne, is best known for the **Hôtel-Dieu** (Vieil Hôpital; rue de l'Hôpital; adult/student €4.50/3.50; 9.30am-noon & 1.30-6pm Mon-Sat, 10am-12.30pm & 2-6pm Sun & holidays Apr-Sep, 9am-noon & 2-6pm except Wed, Sun & holidays Oct-Mar), a charity hospital founded in 1293 by Marguerite de Bourgogne, sister-in-law of St Louis. At the eastern end of the barrel-vaulted patients' hall, near the chapel and Marguerite's tomb, is an extraordinary 15th-century *Entombment of Christ*, carved from a single block of stone.

The **tourist office** (☎ 03 86 55 14 48; www.tonnerre.fr, in French; rue de l'Hôpital; same as Hôtel-Dieu), at the entrance to the Hôtel-Dieu, has a walking-tour brochure, *Tonnerre and Its Heritage*, and rents bicycles (half-day/full day for €10/18).

About 400m west of the tourist office, some 200L of water per second gush from **Fosse Dionne**, a natural spring that was sacred to the Celts and whose weird, almost nuclear blue-green tint hints at its great depth. Legend has it that a serpent lurks at the bottom. The pool is surrounded by a mid-18th-century washing house, a semicircle of ancient houses and forested slopes. To get there, follow the signs on rue François Mitterrand (across the street from the Hôtel-Dieu) past the **covered market** (Sat morning), built in 1903.

A steep staircase heads up the slope from Fosse Dionne to the hilltop **Église St-Pierre**.

About the only reason to overnight in Tonnerre is **La Ferme de Fosse Dionne** (☎ 03 86 54 82 62; www.fermefossedionne.com; 11 rue de la Fosse Dionne; d with breakfast €65). In a late-18th-century farmhouse overlooking Fosse Dionne, this delightful hostelry has six lovingly kept rooms of varying shapes and colours. Downstairs, the friendly owner runs a café and antique shop that stocks hard-to-find edibles from northern Burgundy, including Tonnerre's almost unknown wines. Ask nicely and he might provide some hiking tips, or even play one of his old gramophones.

By rail, Tonnerre – 16km northeast of Chablis – is linked to Dijon (€16.80, one hour, eight to 10 daily) and, via Laroche-Migennes, to Auxerre (€9.70, one hour, eight daily).

Château de Tanlay

The French Renaissance–style **Château de Tanlay** (☎ 03 86 75 70 61; adult/child €8/3.50; ⏲ tours 10am, 11.30am, 2.15pm, 3.15pm, 4.15pm & 5.15pm Wed-Mon & holiday Tue Apr–mid-Nov), an elegant product of the 17th century, is surrounded by a wide moat and elaborately carved outbuildings. Interior highlights include the **Grande Galerie**, whose walls and ceiling are completely covered with trompe l'œil. The château is 10km east of Tonnerre in the village of Tanlay.

Château d'Ancy-le-Franc

The Italian Renaissance makes a cameo appearance at **Château d'Ancy-le-Franc** (☎ 03 86 75 14 63; www.chateau-ancy.com; adult/student/6-15yr €8/7/5; ⏲ tours 10.30am, 11.30am, 2pm, 3pm & 4pm Tue-Sun & holiday Mon late Mar or Apr–mid-Nov, also 5pm Apr-Sep), built in the 1540s by the celebrated Italian architect Serlio. The richly painted interior is mainly the work of Italian artists brought to Fontainebleau by François I.

Overlooking huge stables, a large park and the Canal de Bourgogne, the château is 19km southeast of Tonnerre.

Noyers-sur-Serein

pop 880

The medieval village of Noyers (pronounced nwa·yair), 30km southeast of Auxerre, is surrounded by rolling pastureland, wooded hills and a hairpin curve in the River Serein. Stone ramparts and fortified battlements enclose much of the village, and between the two imposing stone gateways, cobbled streets lead past 15th- and 16th-century gabled houses, wood and stone archways and a number of art galleries. Many of the streets still bear their medieval names – look out for place du Grenier à Sel (Salt Store Square) and place du Marché au Blé (Flour Market Square). Noyers lives by its own rules so don't be surprised if places are closed when they're supposed to be open and vice versa.

Lines carved into the facade of the 18th-century **mairie** (town hall), next to the library, mark the level of historic floods. Diagonally across the street is the **tourist office** (☎ 03 86 82 66 06; www.noyers-sur-serein.com; 22 place de l'Hôtel de Ville; ⏲ 10am-1pm & 2-6pm Mon-Sat Oct-May, daily Jun-Sep).

Musée de Noyers (☎ 03 86 82 89 09; 25 rue de l'Église; adult/senior/student €4/3/2; ⏲ 11am-6.30pm Wed-Mon Jun-Sep, 2.30-6.30pm Sat, Sun & school holidays Oct-Dec & Feb-May), near the 15th-century church, is proud of its colourful collection of naive art, figurines and boxes.

Noyers is a superb base for walking. Just outside the clock-topped southern gate, Chemin des Fossés leads eastwards to the River Serein and a **streamside walk** around the village's 13th-century **fortifications**, 19 of whose original 23 towers are extant. The 9km **Balade du Château**, trail-marked in red, follows the Serein's right bank past the utterly ruined château just north of Noyers. For details on the walkable and cyclable **Chemin de Serein**, see p479.

La Vieille Tour (☎ 03 86 82 87 69; fax 03 86 82 66 04; place du Grenier à Sel; d incl breakfast €55-70, with washbasin only €45; ⏲ Apr-Sep), in a rambling 17th-century house, has five simply furnished *chambres d'hôte*, loads of local colour and a lovely back garden. It is run by a Dutch art historian who promises a warm welcome but adds, 'I cannot guarantee I have no spiderwebs'. Bicycle parking available.

One or the other of Noyers' two **grocery shops**, situated on either side of an ATM and the *mairie*, is open daily till 7pm or 8pm except from 12.30pm or 1pm to 3pm weekdays, Sunday afternoon and every other Sunday morning.

A KNIGHT IN SHINING PETTICOATS

Speculation about the cross-dressing habits of the French secret agent Charles Geneviève d'Éon de Beaumont (1728–1810), born in Tonnerre, has been rife for centuries, especially in sex-obsessed England, where he spent part of his life wearing the latest women's fashions and spying for Louis XV. The locals, at least, have no doubt about the brave chevalier's suitability as a role model for today's youth – they've named the local high school after him – though a local tourist brochure, hedging its bets, refers to him as a *chevalier(e) tonnerrois(e)* (male/female knight from Tonnerre).

AVALLON

pop 8200

The once-strategic walled town of Avallon, on a picturesque hilltop overlooking the green terraced slopes of two River Cousin tributaries, was in centuries past a stop on the coach road from Paris to Lyon. At its most animated during the Saturday morning market, the city makes a good base for exploring Vézelay, the Vallée du Cousin (River Cousin Valley) and the rolling countryside of the Parc Naturel Régional du Morvan.

A promotional brochure cheerfully and succinctly sums up the city's history: 'Avallon was often burned, pillaged, and its inhabitants slaughtered or decimated by outbreaks of the plague. The Tourism Office wishes you a pleasant stay.'

Orientation

The old city, built on a triangular granite hilltop with ravines to the east and west, is about 1km southwest of the train station. The main commercial thoroughfares are the old city's Grande Rue Aristide Briand and, outside the walls, rue de Paris and rue de Lyon.

Information

Internet access (per 30min €2) In the tourist office.

Post Office (9 place des Odebert)

Tourist Office (☎ 03 86 34 14 19; www.avallonnais-tourisme.com; 6 rue Bocquillot; 9.30am-1pm & 2.30-6.30pm daily mid-Jun–mid-Sep, 9.30am-12.30pm & 2-6pm Mon-Sat rest of year, open Sun morning school holidays) In a 15th-century house.

BURGUNDY

Sights

Tour de l'Horloge, a solid, 15th-century clock tower, spans Grande Rue Aristide Briand. The nearby **Musée de l'Avallonnais** (☎ 03 86 34 03 19; place de la Collégiale; admission free; 2-6pm Wed-Mon Jul-Sep & school holidays, also open Sat, Sun & bank holidays Oct-Jun), founded in 1862, displays religious art, fossils and expressionist sketches by Georges Rouault (1871–1958).

Eight centuries ago, the early-12th-century **Collégiale St-Lazare** (rue Bocquillot; until 6pm in summer, may close earlier in winter) drew huge numbers of pilgrims thanks to a piece of the skull of St Lazarus, believed to provide protection from leprosy. The church once had three **portals** but one was crushed when the northern belfry came a-tumblin' down in 1633; the two remaining portals are grandly decorated in the Burgundian Romanesque style, though much of the carving has been damaged. Summertime art exhibitions are held next door in **Église St-Pierre** and across the street in the 18th-century **Grenier à Sel** (Salt Store).

South of the church is one of the city's ancient gateways, the **Petite Porte**, from where a pathway descends, affording fine views over the Vallée du Cousin. Walking around the walls, with their 15th- to 18th-century towers, ramparts and bastions, is a good way to get a sense of the local geography.

About 100 costumes from the 18th century to 1970, changed each year, are on display at the **Musée du Costume** (☎ 03 86 34 19 95; 6 rue Belgrand; adult/student €4/2.50; 10.30am-12.30pm & 1.30-5.30pm mid-Apr–1 Nov), housed in a 17th-century hunting manor. It is run by a friendly older woman who describes herself as a monarchist – though her grandfather was a socialist and her daughter is a '68er. Napoléon, she says, was something of a *parvenu* (upstart).

Activities

For a bucolic walk or bike ride in the **Vallée du Cousin**, take the shaded, one-lane D427, which follows the gentle rapids of the River Cousin through dense forests and lush meadows. From Avallon's Hôtel du Rocher, you can head either west towards Pontaubert (under the viaduct; 3km) and Vézelay, or east towards Magny.

The tourist office sells hiking maps (eg IGN 2722 ET) and has information in French on the Parc Naturel Régional du Morvan.

Sleeping

Avallon and its riverside surrounds have some excellent accommodation options.

AVALLON

Hôtel Les Capucins (☎ 03 86 34 06 52; www.avallonlescapucins.com; 6 av Paul Doumer; d €55, 7-person ste €110;) This two-star, Logis de France place, decorated with all manner of *papillons* (butterflies), has 18 comfortable rooms. The newer ones are on the practical side.

Hôtel d'Avallon Vauban (☎ 03 86 34 36 99; www.avallonvaubanhotel.com; 53 rue de Paris; s/d €54/60, studio apt €75-90;) The trompe l'œil trees make the facade look a bit like a camouflaged battleship, but there really are trees – lots of them – in the parklike private garden. The 26 two-star rooms and four ski chalet–like studio apartments are tidy and spacious, though functional as far as furnishings go. Bicycle parking available.

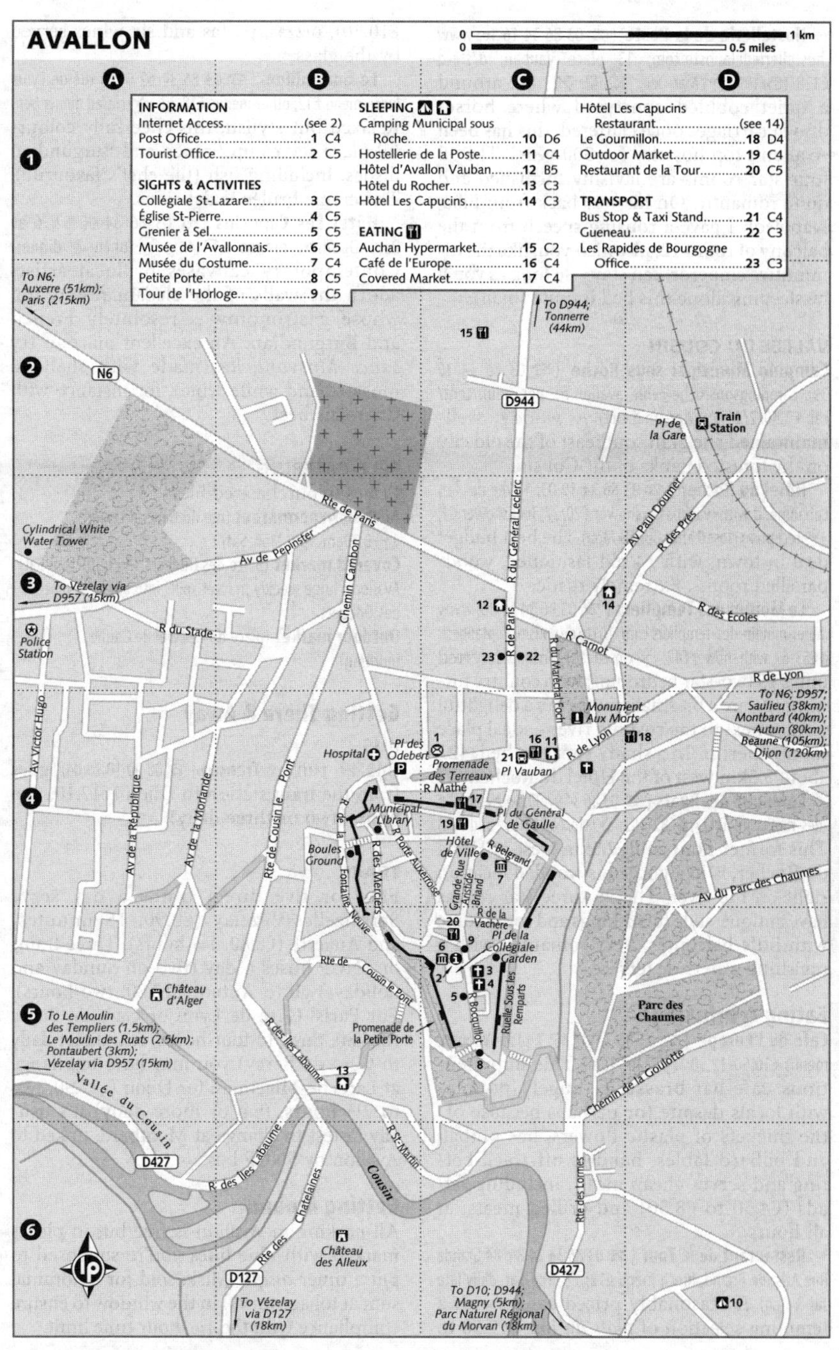
AVALLON
0 1 km
0 0.5 miles
INFORMATION
Internet Access (see 2)
Post Office 1 C4
Tourist Office 2 C5
SIGHTS & ACTIVITIES
Collégiale St-Lazare 3 C5
Église St-Pierre 4 C5
Grenier à Sel 5 C5
Musée de l'Avallonnais 6 C5
Musée du Costume 7 C4
Petite Porte 8 C5
Tour de l'Horloge 9 C5
SLEEPING
Camping Municipal sous Roche 10 D6
Hostellerie de la Poste 11 C4
Hôtel d'Avallon Vauban 12 B5
Hôtel du Rocher 13 C3
Hôtel Les Capucins 14 C3
EATING
Auchan Hypermarket 15 C2
Café de l'Europe 16 C4
Covered Market 17 C4
Hôtel Les Capucins Restaurant (see 14)
Le Gourmillon 18 D4
Outdoor Market 19 C4
Restaurant de la Tour 20 C5
TRANSPORT
Bus Stop & Taxi Stand 21 C4
Gueneau 22 C3
Les Rapides de Bourgogne Office 23 C3
To N6; Auxerre (51km); Paris (215km)
To D944; Tonnerre (44km)
N6
D944
Pl de la Gare
Train Station
Rte de Paris
Av de Pepinster
Chemin Cambon
R du Général Leclerc
Av Paul Doumer
R des Prés
Cylindrical White Water Tower
To Vézelay via D957 (15km)
Police Station
R du Stade
R de Paris
R Carnot
R des Écoles
R du Maréchal Foch
R de Lyon
To N6; D957; Saulieu (38km); Montbard (40km); Autun (80km); Beaune (105km); Dijon (120km)
Monument Aux Morts
Av Victor Hugo
Av de la République
Av de la Morlande
Rte de Cousin le Pont
Hospital
Pl des Odebert
Promenade des Terreaux
Pl Vauban
R Mathé
Municipal Library
Pl du Général de Gaulle
R de la Fontaine Neuve
R des Merciers
R Porte Auxerroise
Boules Ground
Hôtel de Ville
R Belgrand
Grande Rue Aristide Briand
R de la Vachère
Pl de la Collégiale
Garden
Av du Parc des Chaumes
Rte de Cousin le Pont
R Bocquillot
Ruelle Sous les Remparts
Promenade de la Petite Porte
Parc des Chaumes
Château d'Alger
To Le Moulin des Templiers (1.5km); Le Moulin des Ruats (2.5km); Pontaubert (3km); Vézelay via D957 (15km)
R des Îles Labaume
Vallée du Cousin
Chemin de la Goulotte
R St-Martin
D427
Cousin
Rte des Chatelaines
Château des Alleux
Rte des Lormes
D127
To Vézelay via D127 (18km)
To D10; D944; Magny (5km); Parc Naturel Régional du Morvan (18km)

Hostellerie de la Poste (☎ 03 86 34 16 16; www.hostelleriedelaposte.com; 13 place Vauban; d/ste/q €128/185/199; Mar-Dec) Set around a quiet cobbled courtyard where horse-drawn carriages once clattered, this has been Avallon's top hostelry for 300 years. The 30 four-star rooms are lavishly furnished and quite romantic. On his way back from Elba, Napoléon I gave a rousing speech from the balcony of room 12, in which you, like the diminutive emperor, can stay – so long as you'll be sleeping alone (his bed is quite small).

VALLÉE DU COUSIN

Camping Municipal sous Roche (☎ 03 86 34 10 39; campingsousroche@ville-avallon.fr; per adult/tent/car €3.40/2/2; Apr–mid-Oct) A woody, well-maintained site 2km southeast of the old city on the forested banks of the Cousin.

Hôtel du Rocher (☎ 03 86 34 19 03; 11 rue des Îles Labaume; d with washbasin/shower €20/27, hall shower €1; reception closed after 8pm & Mon) The best budget deal in town, with 14 old-fashioned, wood-panelled rooms. Extremely rustic.

Le Moulin des Templiers (☎ 03 86 34 10 80; www.hotel-moulin-des-templiers.com; 10 rte de Cousin, Pontaubert; d €53-62, with shower €42; closed Jan) This converted mill's 15 two-star bedrooms, with country furnishings, are a bit small but there's a delightful terrace next to the rushing river – ideal place for an aperitif. In a shady spot on the D427 about 3.5km west of the Hôtel du Rocher.

Le Moulin des Ruats (☎ 03 86 34 97 00; www.moulin-des-ruats.com; D427; d €82-152; closed 11 Nov–mid-Feb) This former flour mill, 2.5km west of Hôtel du Rocher, is in a gorgeous wooded location right on the river. The 25 three-star rooms have antique-style furnishings and some come with little balconies. Very romantic, with a ravishing waterside terrace.

BURGUNDY

Eating & Drinking

Café de l'Europe (☎ 03 86 34 04 45; 7 place Vauban; menus €10.50-12.50; 7am-1am) This unpretentious café-bar-brasserie, hugely popular with locals despite (or perhaps because of) the thickets of plastic flowers, has pinball and billiard tables, handles off-track betting and serves cheap meals, including salads (€4.50 to €8.50) and grilled meats, at all hours.

Restaurant de la Tour (☎ 03 86 34 24 84; 84 Grande Rue Aristide Briand; lunch menu €12; Tue-Sat, daily late Jul & Aug) A reasonably priced eatery with a tempting selection of *plats du jour* (€7.50 to €10.50), pizzas, pastas and six wines served by the glass.

Le Gourmillon (☎ 03 86 31 62 01; 8 rue de Lyon; lunch menu €12, other menus €18-32; closed dinner Sun) Relaxed but stylish, this cheerfully colourful place serves up French and Burgundian dishes, including fish (the chef's favourite). The crème brûlée is delicious.

Hôtel Les Capucins (☎ 03 86 34 06 52; 6 av Paul Doumer; menus €14-44; lunch & dinner) Contemporary canvases by local artists adorn the walls of the elegant restaurant, whose gastronomy is resolutely French and Burgundian. An excellent place to try *sauce Morvandelle* (made with shallots, mustard and white wine), for instance with Charolais beef.

SELF-CATERING

Places to purchase edibles:

Auchan hypermarket (rue du Général Leclerc; 8.30am-9pm Mon-Sat)

Covered market (place des Odebert until 1pm Sat) Avallon's huge weekly market spills into adjacent place des Odebert.

Outdoor market (place du Général de Gaulle; Thu morning)

Getting There & Away

BUS

Bus 49, run by **Transco** (☎ 08 00 10 20 04), goes from the train station to Dijon (€17.10, two hours, two or three daily).

TRAIN

Four or five direct trains a day serve Sermizelles-Vézelay (€2.90, 15 minutes) and Auxerre (€8.80, 1¼ hours). Three trains or SNCF buses a day (two on Sunday and holidays) go to Autun (€12.80, two hours). For Paris' Gare de Lyon or Gare de Bercy (€26.80, three to four hours, two direct daily to Gare de Bercy) you may have to change at Laroche-Migennes; for Dijon (€17.90, two to 2½ hours, two or more daily) it's usually fastest to change at Montbard, linked to Avallon by SNCF bus.

Getting Around

All parking in Avallon is free but in places marked with blue lines you're supposed to put a timer *disque* (disk; sold for a nominal sum at tobacconists) in the window to ensure compliance with the 1½-hour time limit.

Gueneau (☎ 03 86 34 28 11; 26 rue de Paris; half day/full day/2 days €8/16/28; 🕒 8am-noon & 2-6pm or 6.30pm Tue-Sat) rents out hybrid and mountain bikes but does not have helmets.

VÉZELAY

pop 490

Despite the hordes of tourists who descend on Vézelay in summer, this tiny hilltop village – part of the Parc Naturel Régional du Morvan (p487) and a Unesco World Heritage Site – is one of France's architectural gems. Perched on a rocky spur crowned by a medieval basilica and surrounded by a sublime patchwork of vineyards, sunflower fields and sheep, Vézelay seems to have been lifted from another age.

One of the main pilgrimage routes to Santiago de Compostela in Spain starts here (www.amis-saint-jacques-de-compostelle.asso.fr, in French).

History

Thanks to the relics of St Mary Magdalene, Vézelay's Benedictine monastery became an important pilgrimage site in the 11th and 12th centuries. St Bernard, leader of the Cistercian order (see boxed text, p464), preached the Second Crusade here in 1146. King Philip Augustus of France and King Richard the Lion-Heart of England met up here in 1190 before setting out on the Third Crusade.

Vézelay's vineyards, founded in Gallo-Roman times, were wiped out in the late 1800s by phylloxera and were only re-established in 1973.

Information

Internet (per 10min €2) At the tourist office.

Post Office (17 rue St-Étienne) Has an ATM.

Tourist Office (☎ 03 86 33 23 69; www.vezelaytourisme.com; 12 rue St-Étienne; 🕒 10am-1pm & 2-6pm, closed Thu Oct-May & Sun Nov-Easter) Sells IGN hiking maps and cards (€0.80) with details on four walking circuits (1½ to three hours; trail markings in yellow), each of which heads out of Vézelay in a different direction.

Sights

BASILIQUE STE-MADELEINE

Founded in the 880s, **Basilique Ste-Madeleine** (🕒 all day) has had a turbulent history. Rebuilt

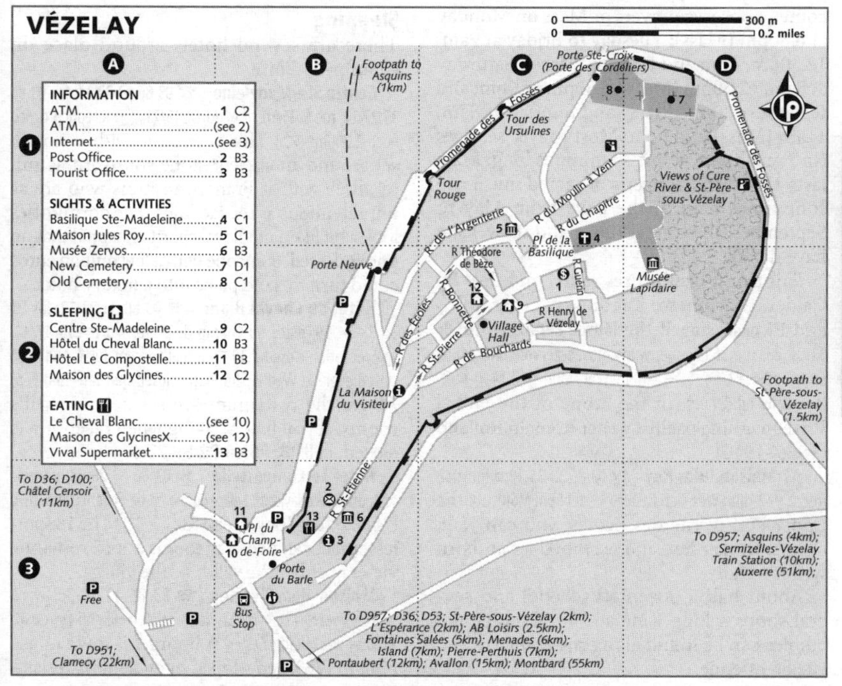

between the 11th and 13th centuries, it was trashed by the Huguenots in 1569, desecrated during the Revolution and, to top off the human ravages, repeatedly struck by lightning. By the mid-1800s it was on the point of collapse. In 1840 the architect Viollet-le-Duc undertook the daunting task of rescuing the structure. His work, which included reconstructing the western facade and its doorways, helped Vézelay – previously a ghost town – spring back to life.

On the 12th-century **tympanum**, visible from the narthex (enclosed porch), Romanesque carvings show Jesus seated on a throne, radiating his holy spirit to the Apostles. The **nave**, rebuilt following the great fire of 1120, has round arches and tiny windows, typical features of the Romanesque style; the transept and choir (1185) have ogival arches and larger windows, hallmarks of Gothic architecture. Under the transept is a mid-12th-century **crypt** with a reliquary containing what is believed to be one of Mary Magdalene's bones.

Prayers, sometimes held in the cloister chapel, are sung in haunting four-voice harmony by the monks and nuns of the Fraternité Monastique de Jérusalem. Visitors are welcome to observe prayers or Mass on Monday at 6.30pm (Mass); Tuesday to Friday at 7am, 12.30pm, 6pm and 6.30pm (Mass); Saturday at 8am, 12.30pm (Mass), 5.30pm or 6pm, and 6.30pm or 7pm (Mass) and Sunday at 8am, 11am (Mass) and 6pm. Most prayer services (in French) are about 30 minutes long; Mass lasts 1¼ hours. Concerts of sacred music are sometimes held in the nave from May to September; the tourist office and its website have details.

Paintings, sculptures and mobiles by Calder, Giacometti, Kandinsky, Léger, Mirò and Picasso star at the **Musée Zervos** (☎ 03 86 32 39 26; rue St-Étienne; www.musee-zervos.com; adult/under 18yr €3/free; 2-6pm Wed-Mon mid-Mar–mid-Nov, daily Jul & Aug), in the home of the Nobel Prize–winning pacifist writer Romain Rolland (1866–1944).

At **Maison Jules Roy** (☎ 03 86 33 35 10; admission free; 2-6pm Wed-Sun Easter-Oct, till 5pm Mon), at the upper end of rue des Écoles, you can walk around the gardens and see the Algerian-born writer's study.

About half a dozen **art galleries** and several shops selling wine and local crafts and edibles can be found along rue St-Pierre and rue St-Étienne.

Activities

WALKING

Squirrels frolic in the **park** behind the basilica, which affords wonderful views of the Vallée de Cure and nearby villages, including St-Père-sous-Vézelay. A dirt road leads north to the **old** and **new cemeteries**. **Promenade des Fossés** circumnavigates Vézelay's medieval ramparts. A footpath with fine views of the basilica links Porte Neuve, on the northern side of the ramparts, with the village of **Asquins** (pronounced ah·kah) and the River Cure. The GR13 trail passes by Vézelay.

CYCLING & CANOEING

Mountain bikes are rented out (year-round; €25 per day) and outdoor activities – kayak trips (8/18km from €15/27), rafting (€42), cave exploration (half-day €37) and horse riding – arranged by **AB Loisirs** (☎ 03 86 33 38 38; www.abloisirs.com, in French; rte du Camping, St-Père-sous-Vézelay; 9.30am-6pm daily Jul & Aug, weekends in spring & most days rest of year except mid-Dec–mid-Jan), whose base is a few kilometres southeast of Vézelay (400m southeast of the D957 along the D36). It's best to phone ahead. Bikes can be brought to your hotel.

Sleeping

There are several hotels around place du Champ-de-Foire.

Centre Ste-Madeleine (☎ 03 86 33 22 14; fax 03 86 33 22 14; rue St-Pierre; dm/s/d €8/15/21; reception closed noon-1.30pm; ☒) This very basic 38-bed hostel, set around an ancient stone courtyard, is run by three with-it Franciscan nuns who are as unpretentious as the facilities. The dormitories look a bit like a medieval charity hospital that no one endowed. Someone with a few million euros could turn this old place into a luxury hotel.

Hôtel du Cheval Blanc (☎ 03 86 33 22 12; fax 03 86 33 34 29; place du Champ-de-Foire; s/d/tr €38/42/46; reception closed 3.30-6pm daily except Jul & Aug, also closed evening Wed & Thu, hotel closed mid-Jan–mid-Feb) Above the restaurant are six neat, no-frills rooms. If you'll be arriving when reception is closed, call ☎ 06 60 72 89 77.

Hôtel Le Compostelle (☎ 03 86 33 28 63; www.lecompostellevezelay.com; 1 place du Champ-de-Foire; d €49-61, tr/q €74/84; closed early Jan–mid-Feb; ☒) The 18 spotless, practical, two-star rooms afford romantic views of either the valley or the village.

Maison des Glycines (☎ 03 86 32 35 30; www.glycines-vezelay.com; rue St-Pierre; s €35, d €65-82; closed 11 Nov–week before Easter) A bourgeois town house built in 1763 – enveloped by ancient wisterias –

has been turned into a three-star hotel that's positively overflowing with old-fashioned character. The hexagonal floor tiles, doors and wooden beams haven't changed in several generations. The 11 rooms are all named after famous artists – 'Paul Claudet' is the one to get. No TV or telephones.

Eating

Eateries can be found along rue St-Pierre and rue St-Étienne and around place du Champ-de-Foire.

Maison des Glycines (☎ 03 86 32 35 30; rue St-Pierre; menus €18-23; 🕑 12.30-4pm Fri-Wed, closed 11 Nov–week before Easter) Serves *gastronomique* cuisine, made with fresh regional products, and wine by the glass (€5 to €8) in a mid-18th-century dining room. Functions as a *salon de thé* (tearoom) from 3.30pm to 7pm.

Le Cheval Blanc (☎ 03 86 33 22 12; place du Champ-de-Foire; lunch menus €20-26, other menus €25-34; 🕑 closed dinner Wed & Thu except on holidays, Jul & Aug) Serves French cuisine, made with fresh seasonal products, mixing traditional recipes with *nouvelle* ideas. Rustic but classic.

Vival supermarket (🕑 9am-8pm mid-May–mid-Sep, 9am-12.30pm & 3.30-7.30pm Mon-Sat, 9.30am-1pm Sun mid-Sep–mid-May, closed afternoon Mon & afternoon Wed Nov-Jan) For groceries; near the bottom of rue St-Étienne.

Getting There & Away

Vézelay is 15km from Avallon (19km if you take the gorgeous D427 via Pontaubert). There's a free car park 250m from place du Champ-de-Foire (towards Clamecy).

Four or five trains a day link the Sermizelles-Vézelay train station, about 10km north of Vézelay, with Avallon (€2.90, 15 minutes) and Auxerre (€7, 50 minutes). **Allô Taxi** (☎ 03 86 32 31 88) and **Taxi TLS** (☎ 03 86 33 19 06) can get you from Sermizelles-Vézelay to Vézelay for about €17 (€23 after 7pm and on Sunday).

If all goes as planned, it should be possible to make an all-day trip to Vézelay from Avallon and Montbard (on the Paris–Dijon rail line) by SNCF bus (daily in July and August, weekends in May, June, September and October).

AROUND VÉZELAY

Southeast of Vézelay at the base of the hill, **St-Père-sous-Vézelay** has a Flamboyant Gothic church but is best known for **L'Espérance** (☎ 03 86 33 39 10; www.marc-meneau.com; r €150-470; menus €65-210; 🕑 restaurant closed Tue, lunch Mon & lunch Wed, also closed mid-Jan–early Mar), a legendary French restaurant (and 30-room hotel) with two Michelin stars.

Three kilometres south along the D958 are the **Fontaines Salées** (☎ 03 86 33 26 62; adult/6-12yr €4/1.60; 🕑 Apr–11 Nov), saltwater hot springs where excavations have uncovered a Celtic sanctuary (2nd century BC) and Roman baths (1st century AD). About 2km south is the village of **Pierre-Perthuis** (literally 'pierced stone'), named after a natural stone arch; nearby, a graceful stone bridge (1770) spans the River Cure underneath a modern highway bridge.

PARC NATUREL RÉGIONAL DU MORVAN

The 2990-sq-km Morvan Regional Park, bounded more or less by Vézelay, Avallon, Saulieu and Autun and situated mainly in the Nièvre *département,* encompasses 700 sq km of dense woodland, 13 sq km of lakes and vast expanses of rolling farmland broken by hedgerows, stone walls and stands of beech, hornbeam and oak. The sharp-eyed can observe some of France's largest and most majestic birds of prey perched on trees as they scan for field rodents – or wait lazily for road kill.

The majority of the thinly populated area's 73,000 residents earn their living from farming, ranching, logging and – it's a tough job but someone has to do it – growing Christmas trees. The time when the impoverished Morvan (a Celtic name meaning 'Black Mountain') supplied wet nurses to rich Parisians passed long ago.

Activities

The Morvan offers an abundance of options to fans of outdoor activities. On dry land you can choose from rambling (the park has over 2500km of marked trails; see Morvan Visitors Centre, p488), mountain biking, horse riding, rock climbing, orienteering and fishing, while waterborne activities such as rafting, canoeing and kayaking are possible on several lakes and the Rivers Chalaux, Cousin, Cure and Yonne.

In addition to **AB Loisirs** (opposite), the following outfits rent out mountain bikes and

MAQUIS BERNARD RÉSISTANCE CEMETERY

Seven RAF men – the crew of a bomber shot down near here in 1944 – and 21 *résistants* are buried in the neatly tended **Maquis Bernard Résistance Cemetery** (www.ouroux-en-morvan.com – select English, 'Map of Site', then 'The Maquis Bernard'), surrounded by the dense forests in which British paratroops operated with Free French forces. The nearby **drop zone** is marked with signs.

The cemetery is about 8km southwest of Montsauche-les-Settons (along the D977) and 5.6km east of Oroux-en-Morvan (along the D12), near the tiny hamlet of Savelot. From the D977, go 2.8km along the narrow dirt road to Savelot.

can also arrange water sports such as canoeing and rafting:

Activital (www.activital.net, in French) Lac de Chaumeçon (☎ 03 86 22 61 35) Based in St-Martin-du-Puy; Lac des Settons (☎ 03 86 84 51 98) Based in Montsauche-les-Settons.

Okheanos (☎ 03 86 84 60 61; www.okheanos.com, in French) Based in Dun-les-Places.

MORVAN VISITORS CENTRE

Surrounded by hills, forests and lakes, the Morvan Regional Park's visitors centre, known as Espace St-Brisson, is 14km west of Saulieu in St-Brisson. To get there by car, follow the signs to the 'Maison du Parc'.

All sorts of information, including hiking and cycling maps and guides, is available at the helpful **tourist office** (☎ 03 86 78 79 57; www.parcdumorvan.org, in French; 🕓 9.30am or 10am-12.30pm & 2-5.30pm Mon-Sat, 10am-1pm & 3-5.30pm Sun Easter–mid-Nov, 9.30am-12.30pm & 2-5pm Mon-Fri mid-Nov–Easter). Guided walks of the park (€4 to €10), some at night (eg to observe owls), set out from April to October, and there are activities for children in July and August. The website has details (in French) on local festivals, cultural events, outdoor activities and lodging. Other useful (though not necessarily up-to-date) websites include www.morvan-tourisme.org and www.patrimoinedumorvan.org, both in French.

The **Écomusée du Morvan** (☎ 03 86 78 79 10), which explores traditional Morvan life and customs, has six sites around the park, including one at Espace St-Brisson, **Maison des Hommes et des Paysages** (adult/student €3/1.50; 🕓 10am-1pm & 2-6pm May-Sep, to 5pm Apr & Oct–mid-Nov, closed Tue except Jul & Aug), whose theme is the interplay between humans and landscapes. Everything is in French.

The Morvan was a major stronghold for the Resistance during WWII; the **Musée de la Résistance en Morvan** (☎ 03 86 78 79 10/06; adult/student €4/2.50, incl Écomusée €6/3.50; 🕓 same as Maison des Hommes) chronicles key events and characters. An English audioguide costs €1.

The **Verger Conservatoire** (Conservation Orchard) preserves some 200 varieties of legacy fruit trees that are no longer commercially grown; the **Herbularium** features 170 species of Morvan plants.

Trails that can be picked up in St-Brisson include three 5km circuits (Coteaux de St-Brisson, Autour de la Maison du Parc and Autour du Vignan), a 12km circuit to Dolmen Chevresse and a 20km circuit to the village of Gouloux.

BIBRACTE

The Celtic town on **Mont Beuvray** where Vercingétorix was proclaimed chief of the Gaulish coalition in 52 BC – shortly before his defeat by Julius Caesar at Alésia – is now the site of archeological excavations and the **Museum of Celtic Civilisation** (☎ 03 85 86 52 35; www.bibracte.fr; St-Léger-sous-Beuvray; adult/concession/under 11yr €5.75/4.25/free; 🕓 10am-6pm mid-Mar–mid-Nov, till 7pm Jul & Aug). It is 25km west of Autun.

SAÔNE-ET-LOIRE

In the southern Saône-et-Loire *département* (www.bourgogne-du-sud.com), midway between Dijon and Lyon, highlights include the Gallo-Roman ruins in Autun, Cluny's glorious Romanesque heritage, the fascinating industrial history of Le Creusot and, around Mâcon, vineyards galore. Several rivers and the Canal du Centre meander among its forests and pastureland.

AUTUN

pop 15,100

Autun, 85km southwest of Dijon, is now a quiet subprefecture, but almost two millennia ago – known as Augustodunum – it was one of the most important cities in Roman Gaul, boasting 6km of ramparts, four monumental gates, two theatres, an amphitheatre and a system of aqueducts. Beginning in AD 269, the city was repeatedly sacked by barbarian tribes and its fortunes declined, but things improved considerably in the Middle Ages, making it possible to construct an impressive cathedral.

If you have a car, Autun is an excellent base for exploring the southern parts of the Parc Naturel Régional du Morvan (p487).

Orientation

The train station is linked to the common-turned–car park, Champ de Mars, by the town's main thoroughfare, av Charles de Gaulle. The hilly area around Cathédrale St-Lazare, reached via narrow cobblestone streets, is known as the old city. The main shopping area is just south of Champ de Mars around rue St-Saulge and rue des Cordeliers.

Information

Elge Interactive (☎ 03 85 86 13 07; 6 Grande Rue Chauchien; per hr €4.50; ⏰ generally 9am-noon & 2-6.30pm Mon-Fri, sometimes Sat Jun–mid-Sep) Internet and wi-fi access.
Laundrette (1 rue Guérin; ⏰ 7am-9pm)
Post Office (8 rue Pernette)
Tourist Office (☎ 03 85 86 80 38; www.autun-tourisme.com; 13 rue du Général Demetz; ⏰ 9.30am-12.30pm & 2-6pm year-round except Mon morning & Sun Oct–mid-May, longer hr daily mid-May–Sep) Sells a self-guided walking-tour brochure (€2) and local IGN hiking map 2825E (€7.70); also has free pamphlets in French on the Parc Naturel Régional du Morvan.

Sights & Activities

GALLO-ROMAN SITES

Built during the reign of Constantine, **Porte d'Arroux** was once one of Augustodunum's four gates. Constructed wholly without mortar, it supports four semicircular arches of the sort that put the 'Roman' in Romanesque: two for vehicles and two for pedestrians. **Porte St-André** is similar in general design and here, too, it's not difficult to imagine a Roman chariot clattering through, a helmeted legionnaire at the reins.

You can also let your imagination run wild at the **Théâtre Romain** (Roman Theatre; ⏰ 24hr), designed to hold 16,000 people – try picturing the place filled with cheering (or jeering), toga-clad spectators. From the top look southwest and you'll see the **Pierre de Couhard** (Rock of Couhard), the 27m-high remains of a Gallo-Roman pyramid that was probably a tomb.

Long associated (wrongly) with the Roman god Janus, the 24m-high **Temple de Janus** (www.temple-de-janus.net, in French for a 3-D visit) – in the middle of farmland 800m north of the train station – is thought to have been a site for Celtic worship. Only two of its massive walls are still standing.

OLD CITY

Many of Autun's buildings date from the 17th and 18th centuries.

Napoléon Bonaparte and his brothers Joseph and Lucien studied in Autun as teenagers. Their old Jesuit college, now a high school known as **Lycée Joseph Bonaparte**, on the west side of Champ de Mars, has a wrought-iron gate (1772) decorated with the municipal coat of arms. Next door is classical **Église Notre Dame** (1757).

The Gothic **Cathédrale St-Lazare** (place du Terreau; ⏰ 8am-7pm Sep-Jun, plus 9-11pm Jul & Aug) was built in the 12th century to house the sacred relics of St Lazarus. Later additions include the 15th-to 16th-century bell tower over the transept and the 19th-century towers over the entrance. Over the main doorway, the Romanesque **tympanum** showing the Last Judgement was carved in the 1130s by Gislebertus, whose name is written below Jesus' right foot. Across the bottom, the saved are on the left while the damned – including a woman whose breasts are being bitten by snakes (symbolising lust) – are on the right. The Renaissance-style fountain next to the cathedral, **Fontaine St-Lazare**, dates from the 16th century.

The **Musée Rolin** (☎ 03 85 52 09 76; 5 rue des Bancs; adult/student €3.40/free; ⏰ 9.30am-noon & 1.30-6pm Wed-Mon Apr-Sep, 10am-noon & 2pm or 2.30-5pm Wed-Mon Oct-Mar) has a worthwhile collection of Gallo-Roman artefacts; 12th-century Romanesque art, including the *Temptation of Eve* by Gislebertus; and 15th-century paintings such as the *Autun Virgin* by the Maître de Moulins. A recently built hall features 20th- and 21st-century art.

The adjacent **prison** (2bis place St-Louis; admission €1; ⏰ 2-6pm Wed-Sun approximately Jul-Sep), a forbidding circular structure built in 1854, was used to house baddies until 1955.

WALKING & CYCLING

For a **stroll** along the city walls (part-Roman but mostly medieval), walk from av du Morvan south to the 12th-century **Tour des Ursulines** and follow the walls to the northeast.

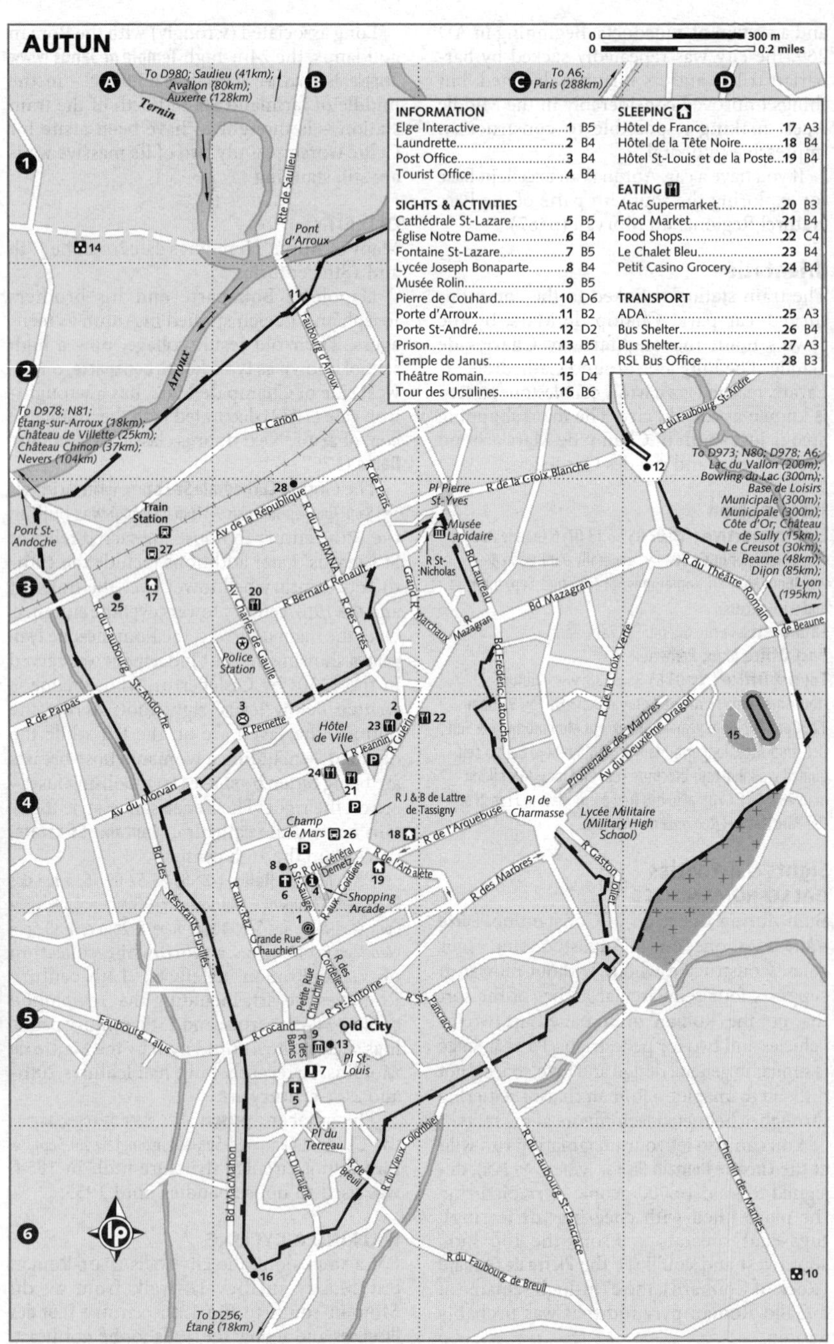
AUTUN
0 300 m
0 0.2 miles
INFORMATION
Elge Interactive 1 B5
Laundrette 2 B4
Post Office 3 B4
Tourist Office 4 B4
SIGHTS & ACTIVITIES
Cathédrale St-Lazare 5 B5
Église Notre Dame 6 B4
Fontaine St-Lazare 7 B5
Lycée Joseph Bonaparte 8 B4
Musée Rolin 9 B5
Pierre de Couhard 10 D6
Porte d'Arroux 11 B2
Porte St-André 12 D2
Prison 13 B5
Temple de Janus 14 A1
Théâtre Romain 15 D4
Tour des Ursulines 16 B6
SLEEPING
Hôtel de France 17 A3
Hôtel de la Tête Noire 18 B4
Hôtel St-Louis et de la Poste 19 B4
EATING
Atac Supermarket 20 B3
Food Market 21 B4
Food Shops 22 C4
Le Chalet Bleu 23 B4
Petit Casino Grocery 24 B4
TRANSPORT
ADA 25 A3
Bus Shelter 26 B4
Bus Shelter 27 A3
RSL Bus Office 28 B3
To D980; Saulieu (41km); Avallon (80km); Auxerre (128km)
To A6; Paris (288km)
Ternin
Arroux
Rte de Saulieu
Pont d'Arroux
Faubourg d'Arroux
To D978; N81; Étang-sur-Arroux (18km); Château de Villette (25km); Château Chinon (37km); Nevers (104km)
R Carion
R du Faubourg St-André
To D973; N80; D978; A6; Lac du Vallon (200m); Bowling du Lac (300m); Base de Loisirs Municipale (300m); Municipale (300m); Côte d'Or; Château de Sully (15km); Le Creusot (30km); Beaune (48km); Dijon (85km); Lyon (195km)
R de la Croix Blanche
Pl Pierre St-Yves
Musée Lapidaire
R St-Nicholas
Train Station
Pont St-Andoche
Av de la République
R du 22 BMNA
R de Paris
Bd Laureau
R du Théâtre Romain
R de Beaune
R Bernard Renault
Av Charles de Gaulle
R des Cités
Grand R Marchaux
R Mazagran
Bd Mazagran
R du Faubourg St-Andoche
Police Station
Bd Frédéric Latouche
R de la Croix Verte
R de Parpas
R Pernette
Hôtel de Ville
R Jeannin
R Guérin
Promenade des Marbres
Av du Deuxième Dragon
Av du Morvan
R J & B de Lattre de Tassigny
Pl de Charmasse
Lycée Militaire (Military High School)
Champ de Mars
R de l'Arquebuse
R du Général Demetz
R St-Saulge
R aux Cordiers
R de l'Arbalete
R Gaston Joliet
R des Marbres
Shopping Arcade
Bd des Résistants Fusillés
R aux Raz
Grande Rue Chauchien
Petite Rue Chauchien
R des Cordeliers
R St-Antoine
R St-Pancrace
Faubourg Talus
R Cocand
R des Bancs
Old City
Pl St-Louis
Pl du Terreau
R Dufraigne
R de Breuil
R du Vieux Colombier
R du Faubourg St-Pancrace
Chemin des Manies
Bd MacMahon
R du Faubourg de Breuil
To D256; Étang (18km)

BURGUNDY

The Chemin des Manies leads out to the Pierre de Couhard, where you can pick up the **Circuit des Gorges**, three marked forest trails ranging from 4.7km to 11.5km. The map to take along is IGN 2925 O (€7.70).

Sleeping

AUTUN

Hôtel de France (☎ 03 85 52 14 00; www.hotel-de-france-autun.fr; 18 av de la République; d €41, with washbasin only €26; reception closed after 3pm Sun, closed 1st 3 weeks in Feb) A one-star, family-run hostelry with 26 basic, clean rooms.

Hôtel St-Louis et de la Poste (☎ 03 85 52 01 01, 08 20 87 68 76; www.hotelsaintlouis.net; 6 rue de l'Arbalète; d €69-89, Napoleonic ste €250; reception open 9am-noon & 5-8pm;) In a grand 17th-century building that hosted Napoléon no less than four times, this two-star, 39-room establishment has a lavish 1920s lobby. Stay two nights and the breakfast and buffet dinner are free.

Hôtel de la Tête Noire (☎ 03 85 86 59 99; www.hoteltetenoire.fr; 3 rue de l'Arquebuse; d/tr €72/85; closed approximately 20 Dec–late Jan;) A two-star, Logis de France place with 31 easy-to-like rooms, some quite large, accessible by lift. Has a good restaurant.

WEST OF AUTUN

our pick **Château de Villette** (☎ 03 86 30 09 13; www.stork-chateau.com; d €135-225, ste €265-365; whole château per week €8750-12,000;) Set in a 5-sq-km private estate, this delightful 16th- and 18th-century château lets you sample the luxurious life of Burgundy's landed aristocracy. After waking up in a ravishingly furnished period room, you can ramble, cycle or hunt escargots (from mid-July to mid-August) in the rolling, partly forested countryside before sitting down to a superb, multicourse French meal (available two nights a week). Worthy of a honeymoon! Situated 20km southwest of Autun – take the N81, then the D192 for 3km to Poil, then the C1 for 2km.

Eating

There are a number of restaurants located along the north side of Champ de Mars and several more up towards the cathedral, along Grande Rue Chauchien and Petite Rue Chauchien and around place du Terreau.

Le Chalet Bleu (☎ 03 85 86 27 30; 3 rue Jeannin; www.lechaletbleu.com; menus €18-58; closed Tue, dinner Sun & dinner Mon) Serves creative French gastronomic cuisine in a light, leafy dining room. Specialities include *meurette d'œufs pochés et escargots* (poached eggs with red-wine sauce and escargots), coq au vin and thick Charolais steaks.

Stock up for a picnic at the following:

Atac supermarket (opposite 35 av Charles de Gaulle; 8.30am-7pm Mon-Sat)

Food market (under & outside the Hôtel de Ville; until noon or 12.30pm Wed & Fri)

Food shops There are several on rue Guérin, northeast of Champ de Mars.

Petit Casino grocery (6 av Charles de Gaulle; 7.30am-12.30pm & 3-8pm Tue-Sat, 8.30am-12.30pm & 4-7pm Sun)

Entertainment

Autun is pretty sleepy but its nightlife scene has one unpretentious bright spot: **Bowling du Lac** (☎ 03 85 52 06 06; www.bowling-autun.com; rte de Chalon-sur-Saône; 11am-2am Tue-Thu, 11am-4am Fri, 3pm-4am Sat, 3pm-2am Sun), a few hundred metres east of the old city next to the McDonald's. Hugely popular with locals of all ages, it has eight bowling lanes, billiard tables, a bar and a restaurant and hosts live music about once a month.

Getting There & Away

From the bus shelters next to the train station and at Champ de Mars, buses go to Le Creusot (Line 3; €5.17, one hour, three daily Monday to Friday, two Saturday except school holidays) and the Le Creusot TGV station (Line 90; €6, 45 minutes, five daily Monday to Friday, two daily weekends); timetables are posted. The **RSL bus office** (☎ 03 85 86 92 55; www.r-s-l.fr, in French; 13 av de la République; 8.15am-noon & 2-6pm Mon-Thu, to 5pm Fri) has details.

You can rent cars from **ADA** (☎ 03 85 86 37 36; 8 av de la République).

Autun's **train station** (av de la République) is on a slow tertiary line that requires a change of train (or bus) to get almost anywhere except Auxerre (€19.50, 70 minutes, two or three daily) and Avallon (€12.80, two hours, two or three daily).

CHÂTEAU DE SULLY

This Renaissance-style **château** (☎ 03 85 82 09 86; www.chateaudesully.com, in French; adult/under 18yr €7.30/5.90, gardens only €3.50/2.80; Apr–11 Nov), on the outskirts of the village of Sully (15km northeast of Autun along the D973), has a beautifully furnished interior and a lovely English-style garden. It was the birthplace of Marshall MacMahon, duke of Magenta and president of France from 1873 to 1879, whose ancestors fled Ireland several centuries ago and whose descendents still occupy the property. Tours of the interior begin hourly on the half-hour from 10.30am to 4.30pm except at 12.30pm (also at 5.30pm July and August).

LE CREUSOT

pop 23,600

Let's be frank: Le Creusot – 30km southeast of Autun along the gorgeous N80 – is an ugly industrial town, but the story of how it got that way is fascinating (at least if you like industrial history). After all, this is where the power hammer was invented in 1841 – the towering gadget (which looks like a Jules Verne spaceship) at the southern entrance to town was the mightiest (and loudest) steam hammer in the world when it was built in 1876. (For the record, it's 21m high, weighs 545 tonnes and could apply 500 tonnes of force.)

Thanks to nearby coal deposits and cheap transport via the **Canal du Centre** (1793), which links the Saône with the Loire and thus the Mediterranean with the Atlantic, Le Creusot became a major steel-making centre during the 19th century. The story of the smoke-belching Schneider steelworks, which at one time employed 15,000 workers, is told at **Château de la Verrerie** (☎ 03 85 73 92 00; adult/11-18yr/family €6/3.80/15.25), a late 18th-century glassworks turned into a private mansion by the paternalistic Schneiders, undisputed masters of their company town.

The château houses two museums that may soon be merged. The **Musée de l'Homme et de l'Industrie** (🕒 10am-noon & 2-6pm Mon-Fri, 2-6pm Sat & Sun, till 7pm May-Sep) has exhibits on the Schneider dynasty and some marvellous 1:14–scale steam locomotives. Across the courtyard, the **Académie François Bourdon** (www.afbourdon.com, in French; 🕒 11am-1pm & 2-6.30pm Mon-Fri, 2-6pm Sat, Sun & holidays Jul & Aug, 11am-12.30pm & 3-6pm Mon & Wed-Fri, 3-6pm Sat, Sun & holidays Feb-Jun, Sep & Oct, 3-6pm Wed-Mon Feb-Easter & Nov, closed Dec & Jan) has models of flagship Schneider products, including railway locomotives, bridges, naval vessels and nuclear powerplants. The 18-hectare forested **park** behind the château is always open.

The **tourist office** (☎ 03 85 55 02 46; www.le-creusot.fr, www.creusot.net, in French; 🕒 10am-noon or 12.30pm & 2-5.30pm or 6pm Mon-Fri, 2-6pm Sat, also open afternoons Sun & holidays approximately May–mid-Sep) is inside the château's gatehouse. A two-hour MP3 walking guide to the town costs €3.

Le Creusot's train station, a 10-minute walk northeast of the château, and place Schneider (next to the château) are linked to Autun (p491) and, by the Navette TGV run by **CTC** (☎ 03 85 73 01 10; www.bus-ctc.fr, in French), to Le Creusot TGV station (€2.50, 20 minutes, four or five daily Monday to Saturday).

CLUNY

pop 4400

The remains of Cluny's great abbey – Christendom's largest church until the construction of St Peter's Basilica in the Vatican – are fragmentary and scattered, barely discernible among the houses and green spaces of the modern-day town. But with a bit of imagination, it's possible to picture how things looked in the 12th century, when Cluny's Benedictine abbey, renowned for its wealth and power and answerable only to the Pope, held sway over 1100 priories and monasteries stretching from Poland to Portugal.

Orientation & Information

Cluny's main street is known (from southeast to northwest) as place du Commerce, rue Filaterie, rue Lamartine and rue Mercière.

Cyber Espace (☎ 03 85 59 25 36; Portes d'Honneur; per hr €3; 🕒 10am-noon & 2-7pm Tue, Wed, Fri & Sat, 2-7pm Thu) Public internet access.

Post Office (chemin du Prado) Changes foreign currency.

Tourist Office (☎ 03 85 59 05 34; www.cluny-tourisme.com; 6 rue Mercière; 🕒 10am-12.30pm & 2.30-6.45pm Apr-Sep, no midday closure Jul & Aug, closed Sun Apr & Sep, 10am-12.30pm & 2.30-6pm Tue-Sat Oct-Mar) Has excellent English-language brochures.

Sights

Cluny's vast **Église Abbatiale** (Abbey Church; ☎ 03 85 59 12 79; adult/18-25yr/under 18yr €6.50/4.50/free), built between 1088 and 1130, once stretched from the rectangular **map table** in front of the **Musée d'Art et d'Archéologie** (🕒 tickets sold 9.30am-6.10pm May-Aug, 9.30-11.40am & 1.30-4.40pm Sep-Apr) all the way to the trees near the octagonal **Clocher de l'Eau Bénite** (Tower of the Holy Water) and its neighbour, the square **Tour de l'Horloge** – a distance of 187m!

A visit to the abbey begins at the Musée d'Art et d'Archéologie, where tickets are sold and an English brochure is available. Displays include a model of the Cluny

BURGUNDY

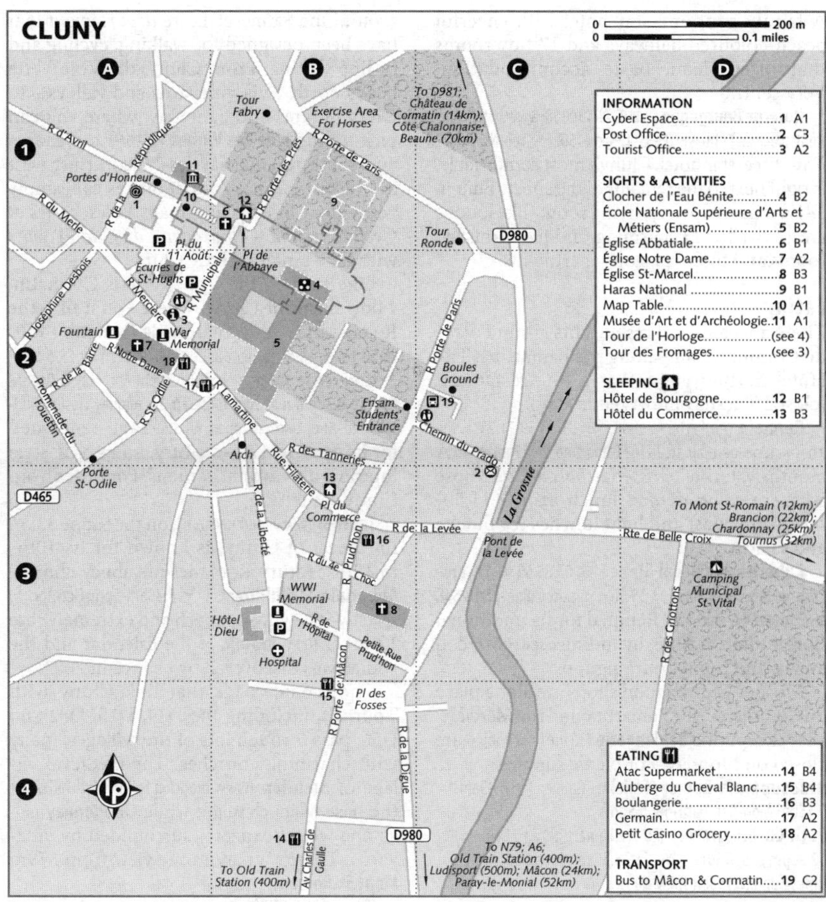

complex and some superb Romanesque carvings. It continues on the grounds of the **École Nationale Supérieure d'Arts et Métiers** (Ensam; place du 11 Août), an institute for training mechanical and industrial engineers that's centred on an 18th-century cloister. The visit includes a 10-minute computer-generated 'virtual tour' of the abbey as it looked in the Middle Ages. You can wander around the grounds at midday and for an hour after the museum closes. Free guided tours in English are held in July and August.

The best place to appreciate the abbey's vastness is from the top of the **Tour des Fromages** (adult/student €1.25/0.80; same as tourist office), once used to ripen cheeses. Access to the tower's 120 steps is through the tourist office.

Cluny has two other churches: **Église St-Marcel** (rue Prud'hon; closed to public), topped by an octagonal, three-storey belfry; and 13th-century **Église Notre Dame** (generally 9am-7pm), across from the tourist office.

The **Haras National** (National Stud Farm; 2 rue Porte des Prés), founded by Napoléon in 1806, houses some of France's finest thoroughbreds, ponies and draught horses. It can be visited on a **guided tour** (06 22 94 52 69; adult/12-17yr/4-11yr €5/3/2; 2pm, 3.30pm & 5pm Tue-Sun early Apr–Sep, 2pm Tue-Fri mid-Mar–early Apr & Wed, Fri & Sat Oct).

Sleeping

Hôtel du Commerce (03 85 59 03 09; www.hoteldu commerce-cluny.com, in French; 8 place du Commerce; d €42, with washbasin only €26; reception closed noon-4.30pm)

A family-run, one-star hotel with cheerful peach-coloured hallways and 17 tidy rooms that offer clean, basic accommodation. Very central.

Hôtel de Bourgogne (☎ 03 85 59 00 58; www.hotel-cluny.com; place de l'Abbaye; d €85-125, q €150; Feb-Nov;) This three-star hotel, Cluny's most comfortable, is right next to the remains of the abbey. Built in 1817, it has a flowery, living room–like lounge area, as well as 13 charming, antique-furnished rooms and three spacious apartments.

Eating

There are cafés and restaurants around place du Commerce and along rue Lamartine. The Hôtel de Bourgogne has a fine restaurant (closed Tuesday and Wednesday).

Germain (Au Péché Mignon; ☎ 03 85 59 11 21; www.chocolaterie-germain.fr; 25 rue Lamartine; 7am-8pm) A mouth-watering *pâtisserie-chocolaterie* whose adjacent *salon de thé* (lunch *menu* €11.50) serves breakfast and light lunches (eg quiche and salad).

Auberge du Cheval Blanc (☎ 03 85 59 01 13; 1 rue Porte de Mâcon; menus €17-39.50; closed dinner Fri & Sat, also closed Dec–mid-Mar) Reputed for its traditional Burgundian cuisine, including escargots, coq au vin and bœuf bourguignon.

Most of Cluny's food shops are along place du Commerce, rue Lamartine and rue Mercière; all – except one **boulangerie** (36 rue Prud'hon) – are closed on Monday. For picnic supplies:

Atac supermarket (av Charles de Gaulle; 8.45am-7.15pm Mon-Sat, 9am-noon Sun)

Petit Casino grocery (29 rue Lamartine; 8am-12.30pm & 3-7.30pm Tue-Sat, 8.30am-noon Sun, sometimes Sun afternoon Jul & Aug)

BURGUNDY

Getting There & Around

The bus stop on rue Porte de Paris is served by **Buscéphale** (☎ 03 85 39 93 40; www.cg71.fr, in French) Line 7 (six or seven daily), which goes to Mâcon (45 minutes), the Mâcon-Loché TGV station (30 minutes) and Cormatin (20 minutes). Schedules are posted at the bus stop and available at the tourist office.

Ludisport (☎ 06 62 36 09 58; www.ludisport.com; at old train station; per half-/full day €10/18; 9am-noon & 2-5pm Jul & Aug, 10am-noon & 2-4pm Feb-Jun & Sep-Nov), about 1km south of the centre, rents out bicycles.

NORTH OF CLUNY

An old railway line and parts of a former canal towpath have been turned into the **Voie Verte** (Green Road), a series of paved paths around the Saône-et-Loire *département* that have been designed for walking, cycling and in-line skating. From Cluny, the Voie Verte heads north – via vineyards and valleys – to Givry (42km) and Santenay, where you can pick up the **Voie des Vignes** (p466) to Beaune, and south to Charnay-les-Mâcon (just west of Mâcon; 19km). Tourist offices can supply you with a free cycling map, *Voies Vertes et Cyclotourisme – Bourgogne du Sud*. Towns with bike rental include Cluny.

One stop on the Voie Verte is Cormatin, 14km north of Cluny, where you'll find the Renaissance-style **Château de Cormatin** (☎ 03 85 50 16 55; adult/student under 25yr/under 17yr €9/5.50/4; tours begin 10am-noon & 2-5.30pm Apr, May & Oct–12 Nov, to 6.30pm mid-Jun–mid-Sep, no midday closure mid-Jul–mid-Aug, gardens open till sundown), renowned for its opulent 17th-century, Louis XIII-style interiors and formal gardens. For buses from Cluny see left.

Tournus (www.tournugeois.fr), on the Saône 33km northeast of Cluny, is known for its 10th- to 12th-century Romanesque abbey church, **Abbatiale St-Philibert** (8.30am-6pm Oct-Apr, to 7pm May-Sep), whose superb and extremely rare 12th-century **mosaic** of the calendar and the zodiac was discovered by chance in 2002.

The scenic roads that link Cluny with Tournus, including the D14, D15, D82 and D56, pass through lots of tiny villages, many with charming churches. The medieval village of **Brancion** (www.brancion.fr, in French) sits at the base of its château, while **Chardonnay** is – as one would expect – surrounded by vineyards. There's a panoramic view from 579m **Mont St-Romain**.

The **Côte Chalonnaise** wine-growing area runs from St-Gengoux-le-National north to **Chagny** and is just south of the Côte de Beaune (p465).

MÂCON

pop 34,100

The town of Mâcon, 70km north of Lyon on the right (west) bank of the Saône, is a good base for exploring the **Mâconnais**, Burgundy's southernmost wine-growing area, which produces mainly dry whites.

The **tourist office** (☎ 03 85 21 07 07; www.macon-tourism.com; 1 place St-Pierre; 9.30am-12.30pm & 2-6.30pm Mon-Sat mid-Jun–Sep, 10am-noon or 12.30pm & 2-6pm Mon-Sat Oct–mid-Jun, closed Mon Nov-Apr), across the street from the 18th-century **town hall**, and its riverfront **annexe** (esplanade Lamartine; 10am-

1.30pm & 3-7pm daily Jul-Sep) have information on visiting the vineyards of the Mâconnais (including hiking maps) and, a wee bit further south, the **Beaujolais** (p517).

Mâcon's main commercial streets are rue Carnot and rue Dombey, a block west of the river, and perpendicular rue Sigorgne. The all-wood **Maison de Bois**, facing 95 rue Dombey and built around 1500, is decorated with carved wooden figures, some of them very cheeky indeed.

The **Musée Lamartine** (☎ 03 85 38 96 19; 41 rue Sigorgne; adult/student €2.50/free; 🕑 10am-noon & 2-6pm Tue-Sat, 2-6pm Sun) explores the life and times of the Mâcon-born Romantic poet and left-wing politician Alphonse de Lamartine (1790–1869).

The **Musée des Ursulines** (☎ 03 85 39 90 38; adult/student €2.50/free, incl entry to Musée Lamartine €3.40/free; 🕑 10am-noon & 2-6pm Tue-Sat, 2-6pm Sun), housed in a 17th-century Ursuline convent, features Gallo-Roman archeology, 16th- to 20th-century paintings and displays about 19th-century Mâconnais life.

About 10km west of town in the wine country, the **Musée de Préhistoire de Solutré** (☎ 03 85 35 85 24; adult/student/under 18yr €3.50/2/free 🕑 10am-6pm Apr-Sep, 10am-noon & 2-5pm Jan-Mar, Oct & Nov) displays finds from one of Europe's richest prehistoric sites, occupied from 35,000 to 10,000 BC. A lovely 20-minute walk will get you to the top of the rocky outcrop known as the **Roche de Solutré**, from where Mont Blanc can sometimes be seen, especially at sunset.

The fin de siècle grandeur of the two-star **Hôtel d'Europe et d'Angleterre** (☎ 03 85 38 27 94; www.hotel-europeangleterre-macon.com; 92-109 quai Jean Jaurès; d €50-70; 🕑 reception closed noon-2pm, till 4pm Sun Dec-Mar), facing the river five short blocks north of Pont St-Laurent, has faded somewhat since Queen Victoria is said to have stayed here, but some of the old-time atmosphere remains, eg in the breakfast room (c 1900). The first giraffe ever to set foot on French soil – a gift of Muhammad Ali, Viceroy of Egypt – stayed here for two days in 1826 while on its way from Marseille to Paris. Many of the 29 spacious rooms have marble fireplaces and river views.

L'Ethym' Sel (☎ 03 85 39 48 84; 10 rue Gambetta; menus €14.50-32; 🕑 closed Wed & dinner Tue Sep-Jun, Sun & Mon Jul & Aug), two blocks south of the tourist office, is a modern bistro whose French and Burgundian specialities include locally raised Charolais steak (€15).

For buses from Cluny see opposite. The Mâcon-Ville train station is on the main line (11 to 18 daily) linking Dijon (€17.60, 1¼ hours), Beaune (€12.90, 50 minutes) and Lyon–Part Dieu (€11.30, 50 minutes). The Mâcon-Loché TGV station is 5km southwest of town.

Lyon & the Rhône Valley

Gourmets, eat your heart out: Lyon *is* the gastronomic capital of France, with lavish piggy-driven dishes, delicacies to savour, and a bounty of eating spaces. Be it an old-fashioned bistro with checked tablecloths and slipper-shuffling grandma or smart, minimalist space with state-of-the-art furnishings and chic city-slicker crowd, this French cuisine king thrills. Throw two mighty rivers, majestic Roman amphitheatres and elegant Renaissance architecture into the pot and the city will have you captivated. Most travellers turn up here unexpectedly (for business or en route south from Paris), are pleasantly surprised and instantly yearn to return.

Plumb at the crossroads to central Europe and the Atlantic, the Rhineland and the Mediterranean, the Rhône Valley has been the envy of many a soul for centuries. Ensnaring the Rhône River on its 813km-long journey from Lake Geneva to the Mediterranean, the valley forges downstream from Lyon past Gallo-Roman ruins at Vienne (of jazz festival fame), nougat-making workshops in Montélimar and an extraordinary wealth of centuries-old Côtes du Rhône vineyards from which some of France's most respected reds are born.

Design-driven St-Étienne with its no-frills airport is a handy gateway to this region. For action-seeking souls, the green 'n' wild Gorges de l'Ardèche, which bring the River Ardèche tumbling to the gates of Provence and Languedoc, promise adventure by the kayakload.

HIGHLIGHTS

- Breakfast on oysters and a glass of crisp white Côtes du Rhône on a pavement terrace in village-like **Croix Rousse** (p503)
- Stroll the city: gorge on medieval and Renaissance architecture under the beady eyes of gargoyles and other cheeky stone characters in **Vieux Lyon** (p501) and cool down afterwards in Daniel Buren's polka-dot fountains on the **presqu'île** (p502)
- Enjoy twinkling views of **Fourvière** (p502) lit at night; next day hike (or ride the funicular) up the 'hill of prayer' for a stunning panorama of the city and its two rivers
- Feast on trotters, ears and other piggy parts in a traditional Lyonnais **bouchon** (p508)
- Learn the secret of French cuisine with France's only female three-starred Michelin chef at Anne-Sophie Pic's state-of-the-art cookery school in **Valence** (p519)
- Revel in the romance of a bygone era: pedal from A to B, eat frogs' legs and sleep in a 1920s *roulotte* (traditional caravan) in wine-rich **Beaujolais** (p517);
- Overdose on outdoor action in the racy white waters of the **Gorges de l'Ardèche** (p520)

POPULATION: 5,646,000	AREA: 43,698 SQ KM

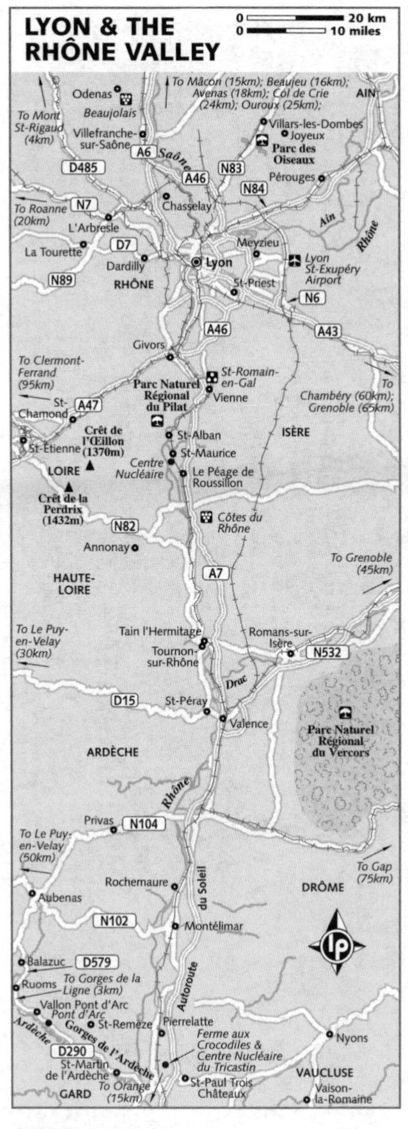

LYON

pop 467,400

Commercial, industrial and banking powerhouse for the past 500 years, grand old Lyon (Lyons in English) is the focal point of a prosperous urban area of almost two million people, France's second-largest conurbation where international police agency Interpol has been headquartered since 1989. Outstanding art museums, a dynamic cultural life, a busy clubbing and drinking scene, not to mention a thriving university and fantastic shopping, lend the city a distinctly sophisticated air.

Green parks, riverside paths, a wonderfully successful city bicycle scheme and a historical old town sufficiently precious to be protected as a Unesco World Heritage Site ensure a bounty of discoveries – on foot or bicycle – for the first-time visitor, while adventurous gourmets (particularly those with a penchant for piggie parts) can indulge their wildest gastronomic fantasies in a dining scene that is chic, sharp and savvy.

History

In 43 BC the Roman military colony of Lugdunum (Lyon) was founded. It served as the capital of the Roman territories known as the Three Gauls under Augustus, but had to wait until the 15th century for fame and fortune to strike: with the arrival of moveable type in 1473, Lyon became one of Europe's foremost publishing centres, with several hundred resident printers contributing to the city's extraordinary prosperity. By the mid-18th century, the city's influential silk weavers – 40% of Lyon's total workforce – transformed what had already been a textiles centre since the 15th century into the silk-weaving capital of Europe.

A century on, Lyon had tripled in size, boasting a population of 340,000 people and 100,000 weaving looms (40,000 of which were in the hilltop neighbourhood of Croix Rousse). A weaver spent 14 to 20 hours a day hunched over his loom breathing in silk dust, two-thirds were illiterate and everyone was paid a pittance. Strikes in 1830–31 and 1834 only resulted in the death of several hundred weavers.

In 1870 the Lumière family moved to Lyon, and sons Louis and Auguste shot the first moving picture – of workers exiting their father's photographic factory – in 1895. Cinema's birth was an instant winner.

During WWII some 4000 people (including Resistance leader Jean Moulin) were killed and 7500 others deported to Nazi death camps under Gestapo chief Klaus Barbie (1913–91), the 'butcher of Lyon'. Nazi rule ended in September 1944, when the retreating Germans blew up all but two of Lyon's 28 bridges. A Lyon court sentenced Barbie to death in absentia in 1952

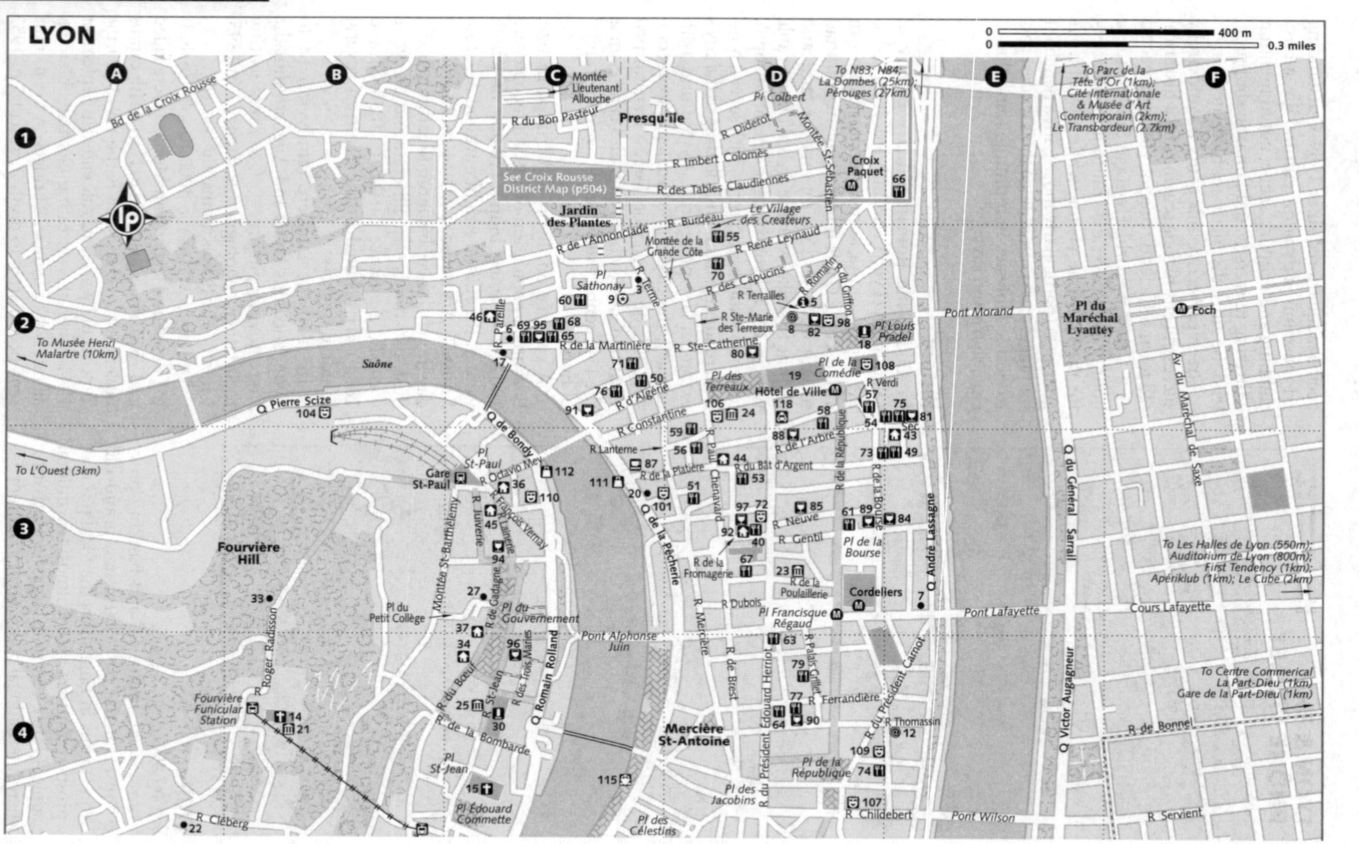
LYON
0 400 m
0 0.3 miles
A B C D E F
1 2 3 4
Bd de la Croix Rousse
To Musée Henri Malartre (10km)
To L'Ouest (3km)
To Parc de la Tête d'Or (1km); Cité Internationale & Musée d'Art Contemporain (2km); Le Transbordeur (2.7km)
To N83; N84; La Dombes (25km); Pérouges (27km)
To Les Halles de Lyon (550m); Auditorium de Lyon (800m); First Tendency (1km); Apériklub (1km); Le Cube (2km)
To Centre Commerical La Part-Dieu (1km); Gare de la Part-Dieu (1km)
See Croix Rousse District Map (p504)
Montée Lieutenant Allouche
R du Bon Pasteur
Presqu'île
Pl Colbert
R Diderot
Montée St-Sébastien
R Imbert Colomès
R des Tables Claudiennes
Croix Paquet
Jardin des Plantes
R de l'Annonciade
R Burdeau
Le Village des Createurs
Montée de la Grande Côte
R René Leynaud
Pl Sathonay
R Terme
R des Capucins
R Terraillès
R Romarin
R du Griffon
R Ste-Marie des Terreaux
R Pareille
R de la Martinière
R Ste-Catherine
Pl Louis Pradel
Pont Morand
Pl du Maréchal Lyautey
Foch
Saône
Pl de la Comédie
Pl des Terreaux
Hôtel de Ville
R Verdi
R d'Algérie
Q Pierre Scize
Q de Bondy
R Constantine
R de l'Arbre Sec
R Lanterne
R de la Platière
R Paul Chenavard
R du Bât d'Argent
R de la République
R de la Bourse
Av du Maréchal de Saxe
Q du Général Sarrail
Pl St-Paul
Gare St-Paul
R Octavio Mey
R François Vernay
R Juiverie
R Lainerie
Montée St-Barthélemy
Q de la Pêcherie
R Neuve
R Gentil
Pl de la Bourse
Fourvière Hill
R de la Fromagerie
R de la Poulaillerie
Q André Lassagne
Cordeliers
R Dubois
Pl du Petit Collège
R de Gadagne
Pl du Gouvernement
Pl Francisque Régaud
Pont Lafayette
Cours Lafayette
R Mercière
Pont Alphonse Juin
R Roger Radisson
R des Trois Maries
R Palais Grillet
R de Brest
Q Romain Rolland
R du Bœuf
R St-Jean
R du Président Carnot
R Ferrandière
Q Victor Augagneur
Fourvière Funicular Station
R de la Bombarde
R Thomassin
Mercière St-Antoine
R de Bonnel
R du Président Edouard Herriot
Pl St-Jean
Pl de la République
Pl Édouard Commette
Pl des Jacobins
R Childebert
Pont Wilson
R Servient
R Cléberg
Pl des Célestins
3 5 6 7 8 9 12 14 15 17 18 19 20 21 22 23 24 25 27 30 33 34 36 37 40 43 44 45 46 49 50 51 53 54 55 56 57 58 59 60 61 63 64 65 66 67 68 69 70 71 72 73 74 75 76 77 79 80 81 82 84 85 87 88 89 90 91 92 94 95 96 97 98 101 104 106 107 108 109 110 111 112 115 118

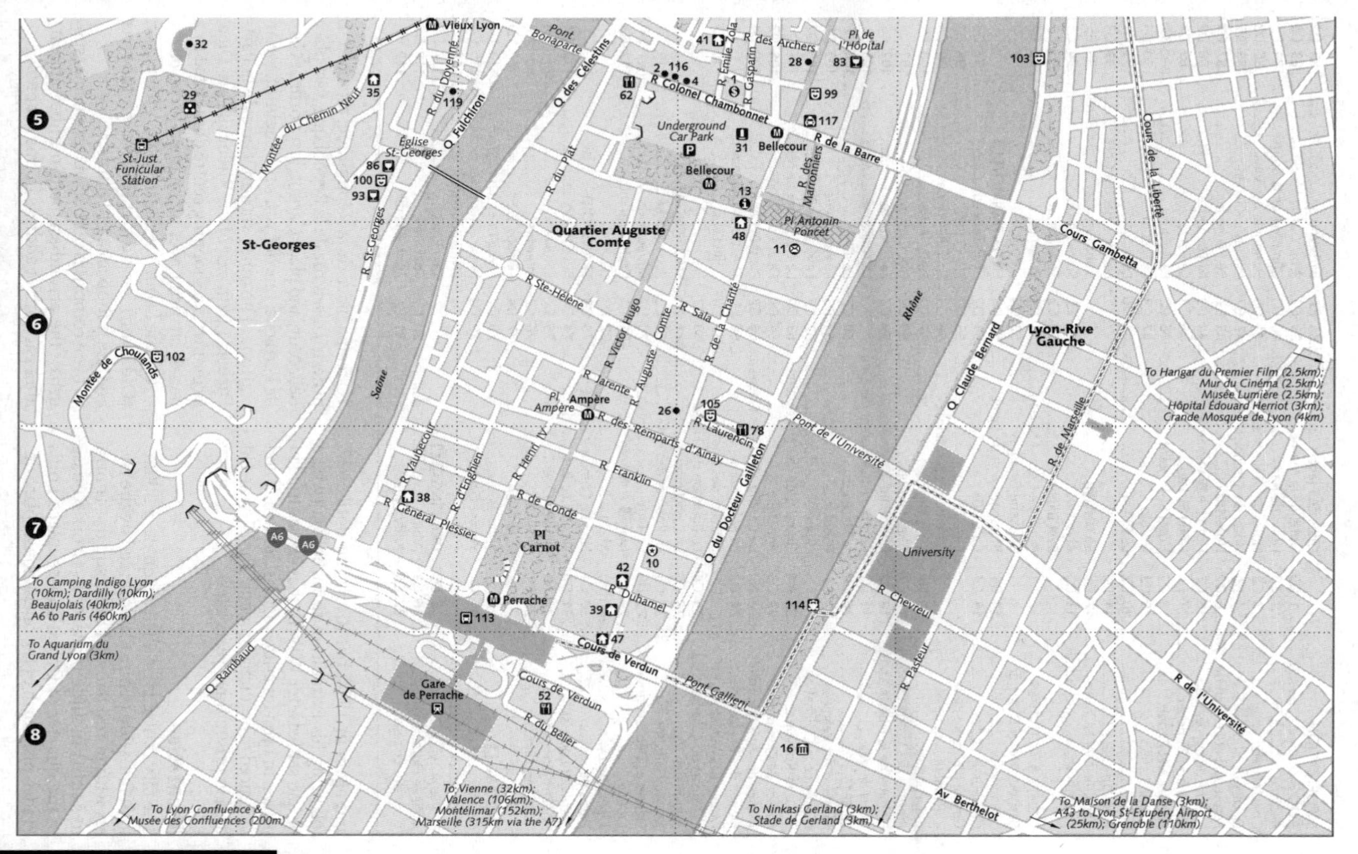
Vieux Lyon
Pont Bonaparte
Q des Célestins
R des Archers
R Émile Zola
R Gasparin
Pl de l'Hôpital
R Colonel Chambonnet
R du Doyenné
Montée du Chemin Neuf
St-Just Funicular Station
Q Fulchiron
Église St-Georges
Underground Car Park
Bellecour
R de la Barre
R des Marronniers
R du Plat
Pl Antonin Poncet
Cours de la Liberté
Cours Gambetta
St-Georges
R St-Georges
Quartier Auguste Comte
R Ste-Hélène
R Sala
R de la Charité
R Victor Hugo
R Auguste Comte
Rhône
Lyon-Rive Gauche
Q Claude Bernard
Montée de Choulands
Saône
R Jarente
Pl Ampère
Ampère
R des Remparts d'Ainay
R Laurencin
Pont de l'Université
R de Marseille
To Hangar du Premier Film (2.5km); Mur du Cinéma (2.5km); Musée Lumière (2.5km); Hôpital Édouard Herriot (3km); Grande Mosquée de Lyon (4km)
R Vaubecour
R d'Enghien
R Henri IV
R Franklin
Q du Docteur Gailleton
R Général Plessier
R de Condé
Pl Carnot
University
A6
To Camping Indigo Lyon (10km); Dardilly (10km); Beaujolais (40km); A6 to Paris (460km)
R Duhamel
Perrache
R Chevreul
To Aquarium du Grand Lyon (3km)
Cours de Verdun
Q Rambaud
Gare de Perrache
Pont Galliéni
R Pasteur
R de l'Université
R du Bélier
To Lyon Confluence & Musée des Confluences (200m)
To Vienne (32km); Valence (106km); Montélimar (152km); Marseille (315km via the A7)
To Ninkasi Gerland (3km); Stade de Gerland (3km)
Av Berthelot
To Maison de la Danse (3km); A43 to Lyon St-Exupéry Airport (25km); Grenoble (110km)

INFORMATION
- AOC Exchange 1 D5
- Badiane 2 C5
- Cool Waters 3 C2
- Decitre 4 D5
- Forum Gai et Lesbien de Lyon 5 D2
- Laverie de la Fresque 6 C2
- Pharmacie Blanchet 7 E3
- Planète Net Phone 8 D2
- Police Station 9 C2
- Police Station 10 C7
- Post Office 11 D6
- Raconte-Moi La Terre 12 E4
- Tourist Office 13 D5

SIGHTS & ACTIVITIES
- Basilique Notre Dame de Fourvière 14 B4
- Cathédrale St-Jean 15 C4
- Centre d'Histoire de la Résistance et de la Déportation 16 D8
- Fresque des Lyonnais 17 C2
- Homme de la Liberté Statue 18 D2
- Hôtel de Ville 19 D2
- La BF15 20 C3
- Musée d'Art Religieux 21 B4
- Musée de la Civillisation Gallo-Romaine 22 A4
- Musée de l'Imprimerie 23 D3
- Musée des Arts Décoratifs (see 26)
- Musée des Beaux-Arts 24 D2
- Musée des Miniatures et Décors du Cinéma 25 C4
- Musée des Tissus 26 C6
- Musée Gadagne 27 C3
- Nature et Découvertes 28 D5
- Odéon 29 A5
- Opéra de Lyon (see 108)
- Palais de Justice 30 C4
- Statue of Louis XIV 31 D5
- Théâtre Romain 32 A5
- Tour Métallique 33 B3

SLEEPING
- Artelit 34 C4
- Auberge de Jeunesse du Vieux Lyon 35 B5
- Collège Hotel 36 C3
- Cour des Loges 37 C3
- Gîtes de France 38 B7
- Hôtel de la Marne 39 C7
- Hôtel de Paris 40 D3
- Hôtel des Célestins 41 D5
- Hôtel du Simplon 42 C7
- Hôtel Iris 43 E3
- Hôtel Le Boulevardier 44 D3
- Hôtel St-Paul 45 C3
- Hôtel St-Vincent 46 C2
- Hôtelo 47 C8
- Le Royal 48 D6

EATING
- Alyssaar 49 E3
- Best Bagels 50 C2
- Bistro Le Casse Museau 51 D3
- Brasserie Georges 52 C8
- Brasserie Léon de Lyon 53 D3
- Café 203 54 D2
- Café Cousu 55 D2
- Café des Fédérations 56 D3
- Chez Georges 57 D2
- Chez Hugon 58 D2
- Chez Paul 59 D3
- Comptoir-Restaurant des Deux Places 60 C2
- Fubuki 61 D3
- Giraudet 62 C5
- Grand Café des Négociants 63 D4
- Jim-Deli 64 D4
- La Cantine des Sales Gosses 65 C2
- La Mère Brazier 66 E1
- L'Atelier des Chefs 67 D3
- Le Bouchon des Filles 68 C2
- Le Café Epicerie (see 37)
- Le Potager des Halles 69 C2
- Le Tiafé 70 D2
- Magali et Martin 71 C2
- Matsuri 72 D3
- Neo Le Comptoir 73 D3
- Nicolas Le Bec 74 D4
- Ninkasi Opéra 75 E2
- Oblik 76 C2
- Pain & Cie 77 D4
- Thomas 78 D7
- Yinitial G&G 79 D4

DRINKING
- Albion 80 D2
- Andy Walha 81 E2
- Barberousse 82 D2
- Broc' Café 83 D5
- Comptoir de la Bourse 84 E3
- Harmonie des Vins 85 D3
- Johnny's Kitchen 86 B5
- Ké Pêcherie 87 C3
- La Fée Verte 88 D3
- Le Bar 89 D3
- La Ruche (see 89)
- Le Forum 90 D4
- Le Voxx 91 C2
- Le Wine Bar d'à Côté 92 D3
- Saint Just: Caviste pas Pareil 93 B5
- Smoking Dog 94 C3
- Soda Bar 95 C2
- St-James 96 C4

ENTERTAINMENT
- CNP-Terreaux Cinema 97 D3
- F & G Bar 98 D2
- Fnac Billetterie 99 D5
- Furib' Arts 100 B5
- Hot Club de Lyon 101 C3
- La Chapelle 102 A6
- La Marquise 103 E5
- Le 42 104 B2
- Le Bastringue 105 D6
- Le Kiosque Théâtre 106 D2
- Le New York Le Medley 107 D4
- Opéra de Lyon 108 D2
- Planète OL 109 D4
- Théâtre Le Guignol de Lyon 110 C3

SHOPPING
- Book Market 111 C3
- Boutique du Musée (see 24)
- Crafts Market 112 C3

TRANSPORT
- Bus Station 113 C7
- Eurolines (see 113)
- Intercars (see 113)
- Linebús (see 113)
- Navig'Inter (cruises) 114 D7
- Navig'Inter (river excursions) 115 C4
- SNCF Boutique 116 C5
- Taxi Rank 117 D5
- Taxi Rank 118 D2
- Zone Cycable 119 B5

and again in 1954, but it was not until 1987, following his extradition from Bolivia (where he had settled after WWII), that he was tried in person in Lyon for crimes against humanity and sentenced to life imprisonment. The 72-year-old died in prison three years later.

Orientation

The city centre is on the Presqu'île, a 500m-to 800m-wide peninsula bounded by the rivers Rhône and Saône. Public squares (north to south) include place de la Croix Rousse in the quarter of Croix Rousse; place Louis Pradel, just north of the opera house; place des Terreaux; place de la République, attached to pedestrianised rue de la République; vast place Bellecour; and place Carnot, just north of Gare de Perrache, one of Lyon's two main-line train stations. The other station, Gare de la Part-Dieu, is 1.5km east of the Rhône in Part-Dieu, a commercial shopping centre dominated by a pencil-shaped tower nicknamed *le crayon*.

On the Saône's western bank, Vieux Lyon (Old Lyon) is sandwiched between the river and the hilltop area of Fourvière.

Lyon comprises nine arrondissements (suburbs); the arrondissement number appears after each street address in this chapter.

Information

BOOKSHOPS

Badiane (Map pp498-9; ☎ 04 72 41 18 00; www.badiane.fr; 1 place Bellecour, 2e; Ⓜ Bellecour; 🕑 2-7pm Mon, 10am-7pm Tue-Sat) Culinary and gastronomic bookshop with astonishing selection of titles on food, wine etc; cooking courses, demonstrations and food and wine tastings.

Decitre (Map pp498-9; ☎ 04 26 68 00 30; 6 place Bellecour, 2e; Ⓜ Bellecour) English-language fiction, travel guides and maps.

Raconte-Moi La Terre (Map pp498-9; ☎ 04 78 92 60 22; www.raconte-moi.com; 38 rue Thomassin, 2e; Ⓜ Cordeliers; 🕑 10am-7.30pm Mon-Sat) Travel bookshop.

EMERGENCY

Police Station (Commissariat de Police) 5 place Sathonay, 1er (Map pp498-9; ☎ 04 78 28 11 87; Ⓜ Hôtel de Ville); 47 rue de la Charité, 2e (Map pp498-9; ☎ 04 78 42 26 56; Ⓜ Perrache or Ampère)

SOS Médecins (☎ 04 78 83 51 51) Medical emergencies.

INTERNET ACCESS

Planète Net Phone (Map pp498-9; ☎ 04 78 39 72 41; 21 rue Romarin, 1er; Ⓜ Hôtel de Ville; per hr €2; 🕑 10am-7pm Mon-Fri, 2-7pm Sat) Cheap access in a cheap phone centre.

Raconte-Moi La Terre (Map pp498-9; ☎ 04 78 92 60 22; www.raconte-moi.com; 38 rue Thomassin, 2e; Ⓜ Cordeliers; per hr €4; 🕑 10am-7.30pm Mon-Sat) Stylish surfing on several terminals in the 1st-floor café of this travel bookshop; free wi-fi for laptop users.

INTERNET RESOURCES

www.bullesdegones.com (in French) Exhaustive guide for families: what to do with the kids (up to 12 years) in and around Lyon.

www.lyon.fr Official city website.

www.lyonblog.fr One-stop shop (in French) for 300 blogs about Lyon.

www.lyonresto.com Restaurant listings (in French) with reviews, videos, menu prices and ratings for food, atmosphere, service, quality and quantity.

www.petitpaume.com City guide (in French) written by local university students.

www.rhonealpes-tourisme.com Regional tourist information site.

LAUNDRY

Cool Waters (Map pp498-9; rue Terme, 1er; Ⓜ Hôtel de Ville; 🕑 6am-9pm)

Laverie de la Fresque (Map pp498-9; 1 rue de la Martinière, 1er; Ⓜ Hôtel de Ville; 🕑 6am-10pm)

MEDICAL SERVICES

Hôpital Édouard Herriot (off Map pp498-9; ☎ 08 20 08 20 69, 04 72 10 73 11; www.chu-lyon.fr, in French; 5 place d'Arsonval, 3e; Ⓜ Grange Blanche) Emergency room open 24-7.

Maisons Médicales de Garde (☎ 04 72 33 00 33; www.gardemedicale.com, in French; 🕑 8am-midnight Mon-Fri, noon-midnight Sat, 8am-midnight Sun)

Pharmacie Blanchet (☎ 04 78 42 12 42; 5 place des Cordeliers, 2e; Ⓜ Cordeliers; 🕑 24hr)

MONEY

AOC Exchange (Map pp498-9; 20 rue Gasparin, 2e; Ⓜ Bellecour; 🕑 9.30am-6.30pm Mon-Sat) Currency exchange.

POST

Post Office (Map pp498-9; 10 place Antonin Poncet, 2e; Ⓜ Bellecour)

TOURIST INFORMATION

Tourist Office (Map pp498-9; ☎ 04 72 77 69 69; www.lyon-france.com; place Bellecour, 2e; Ⓜ Bellecour; 🕑 9am-6pm)

Sights

VIEUX LYON

Old Lyon, with its cobblestone streets and **medieval and Renaissance houses** below Fourvière hill, is divided into three quarters: St-Paul (north), St-Jean (middle) and St-Georges (south). Facing the river is the grandiose **Palais de Justice** (Law Courts; Map pp498-9; quai Romain Rolland; Ⓜ Vieux Lyon).

Lovely old buildings languish on **rue du Bœuf**, **rue St-Jean** and **rue des Trois Maries**. Crane your neck upwards to see gargoyles and other cheeky stone characters carved on window ledges along **rue Juiverie**, home to Lyon's Jewish community in the Middle Ages.

On tourist-busy rue St-Jean, the **Musée des Miniatures et Décors du Cinéma** (☎ 04 72 00 24 77; www.mimlyon.com, in French; 60 rue St-Jean, 5e; Ⓜ Vieux Lyon; adult/4-15yr €7/5.50; 🕑 10am-6.30pm Tue-Fri, 10am-7pm Sat & Sun) provides an unusual insight into the making of movie sets and special effects achieved with the use of miniatures. Fans of *Star Trek*, *Terminator*, *Titanic* or *Perfume* (based on Patrick Süskind's novel) will particularly enjoy it. A couple of ghoulish exhibits (parents, watch out for the black curtain) are not suitable for young children.

Partly Romanesque **Cathédrale St-Jean** (Map pp498-9; place St-Jean, 5e; Ⓜ Vieux Lyon; 🕑 8am-noon &

CITY SLICKER

The **Lyon City Card** (1/2/3 days adult €19/29/39, 4-18yr €5/15/20) covers admission to every Lyon museum and the roof of Basilique Notre Dame de Fourvière. It also includes a guided or audioguided city tour organised by the tourist office, a river excursion (April to October) and 10% off Cyclopolitan cycling tours and Le Grand Tour (p506).

The card, sold by the tourist office and some hotels, allows unlimited travel on buses, trams, the funicular and the metro; it also yields 10% discount in selected shops.

2-7.30pm Mon-Fri, 8am-noon & 2-7pm Sat & Sun), seat of Lyon's 133rd bishop, was built between the late 11th and early 16th centuries. The portals of its Flamboyant Gothic facade completed in 1480 are decorated with 280 square stone medallions. Don't miss the enchanting chimes of the **astronomical clock** in the north transept at noon, 2pm, 3pm and 4pm daily.

The **Musée Gadagne** (Map pp498-9; ☎ 04 78 42 03 61; www.museegadagne.com, in French; place du Petit Collège, 5e; Ⓜ Vieux Lyon; ⏲ 11am-6pm Wed-Sun), in a 16th-century mansion built for two rich Florentine bankers, was at the time of writing set to reopen and house a local-history and puppet museum.

FOURVIÈRE

Over two millennia ago, the Romans built the city of Lugdunum on the slopes of Fourvière. Today, Lyon's 'hill of prayer' – topped by a basilica and the **Tour Métallique** (Map pp498–9), an Eiffel Tower–like structure built in 1893 and used as a TV transmitter – affords spectacular views of the city and its two rivers. Footpaths wind uphill but the funicular departing from place Édouard Commette is the least taxing way up; a return ticket costs €2.20.

Crowning the hill – and proffering a stunning city view from its terrace – is the 66m-long, 19m-wide and 27m-high **Basilique Notre Dame de Fourvière** (Map pp498-9; ☎ 04 78 25 86 19; www.fourviere.org; ⏲ 7am-7pm), a superb example of the exaggerated enthusiasm for embellishment that dominated French ecclesiastical architecture in the late 19th century. Free organ **concerts** (⏲ 6pm 2nd & 4th Sun of the month Sep-Jun) are fabulous for lapping up its magnificence. Otherwise, one-hour **discovery visits** (€2; ⏲ several times daily Mon-Sat Apr-Jan) take in the main features of the basilica, crypt and so on; **rooftop tours** (adult/under 12yr €5/3; ⏲ 2.30pm & 4pm daily Jun-Sep, 2.30pm & 4pm Wed & Sun Apr, May & Oct, 2.30pm & 3.30pm Wed & Sun Nov) climax on the wonderfully stone-sculpted roof. An unparalleled city panorama unfolds from the **Tour de l'Observatoire** (Observatory Tower), should it ever reopen again following much-needed restoration. Between 2008 and 2011, €5 million in all will be ploughed into preserving and restoring the basilica.

Fourvière treasures, including works of sacred art, are showcased in the **Musée d'Art Religieux** (☎ 04 78 25 13 01; 8 place de Fourvière, 5e; Ⓜ Fourvière funicular station; adult/under 26yr €6/4; ⏲ 10am-12.30pm & 2-5.30pm daily), host to some worth-the-trip temporary exhibitions alongside its permanent collection.

Artefacts found in the Rhône Valley are displayed in the **Musée de la Civilisation Gallo-Romaine** (Museum of Gallo-Roman Civilisation; Map pp498-9; ☎ 04 72 38 39 30; www.musees-gallo-romains.com, in French; 17 rue Cléberg, 5e; Ⓜ Fourvière funicular station; adult/18-25yr/under 18yr €3.80/2.30/free, Thu free; ⏲ 10am-6pm Tue-Sun). Next door the **Théâtre Romain**, built around 15 BC and enlarged in AD 120, sat an audience of 10,000. Romans held poetry readings and musical recitals in the smaller **odéon** next door.

PRESQU'ÎLE

The centrepiece of Presqu'île's beautiful **place des Terreaux** (Ⓜ Hôtel de Ville), 1er, is a 19th-century fountain made of 21 tonnes of lead and sculpted by Frédéric-Auguste Bartholdi (of Statue of Liberty fame). The four horses pulling the chariot symbolise rivers galloping seawards. The **Hôtel de Ville** (Town Hall; Map pp498–9) fronting the square was built in 1655 but given its present ornate facade in 1702. Best of all is Daniel Buren's polka-dot 'forest' of 69 granite fountains embedded in the ground across much of the square. When the fountains are on, join the kids in a mad dash as the water dances up, down, disappears for a second and gushes back again – fabulous fun on hot summer days.

Nearby, the **Musée des Beaux-Arts** (Museum of Fine Arts; Map pp498-9; ☎ 04 72 10 17 40; www.mba-lyon.fr; 20 place des Terreaux, 1er; Ⓜ Hôtel de Ville; adult/under 18yr €6/free; ⏲ 10am-6pm Wed, Thu & Sat-Mon, 10.30am-6pm Fri) showcases France's finest collection of sculptures and paintings, outside Paris, from every period of European art. Its **cloister garden** is a great picnic venue. Pick up stylish, art-driven jewellery pieces and other souvenirs in its upmarket **Boutique du Musée** (21 rue Paul Chenavard, 1er; Ⓜ Hôtel de Ville ; 10am-6pm Tue-Fri, 10am-7pm Sat).

Lyon's neoclassical **opera house** (Map pp498-9; 1 place de la Comédie, 1er; Ⓜ Hôtel de Ville), built in 1832, is topped with a striking glass-domed roof by top French architect Jean Nouvel. Boarders and bladers buzz around the fountains of **place Louis Pradel**, surveyed by the **Homme de la Liberté** (Man of Freedom) on roller skates, sculpted from scrap metal by Marseille-born César (1921–98).

West of place des Terreaux, well-known Lyonnais peer out from the seven-storey **Fresque des Lyonnais** (Map pp498-9; cnr rue de la Martinière & quai de la Pêcherie, 1er; Ⓜ Hôtel de Ville), a mural featuring loom inventor Joseph-Marie Jacquard (1752–1834), Renaissance poet Maurice Scève (c 1499–c 1560), superstar chef Paul Bocuse and the yellow-haired Little Prince, created by Lyon-born author Antoine de St-Exupéry (1900–44).

South along the quay, inspired contemporary art installations fill the white space of **La BF15** (☎ 04 78 28 66 63; www.labf15.org; 11 quai de la Pêcherie, 1er; Ⓜ Bellecour; admission free; 2-7pm Wed-Sat), a cutting-edge riverside art gallery.

The **Musée de l'Imprimerie** (Printing Museum; Map pp498-9; ☎ 04 78 37 65 98; www.imprimerie.lyon.fr, in French; 37 rue de la Poulaillerie, 2e; Ⓜ Cordeliers; adult/concession/under 18yr €3.80/2/free; 9.30am-noon & 2-6pm Wed-Sun) focuses on a technology established in Lyon by the 1480s.

Extraordinary Lyonnais silks are showcased at the **Musée des Tissus** (Textile Museum; Map pp498-9; ☎ 04 78 38 42 00; www.musee-des-tissus.com, in French; 34 rue de la Charité, 2e; Ⓜ Ampère; adult/16-25yr/under 16yr €6/3.50/free; 10am-5.30pm Tue-Sun). Next door, the **Musée des Arts Décoratifs** (Decorative Arts Museum; Map pp498-9; with Musée des Tissus ticket free; 10am-noon & 2-5.30pm Tue-Sun) displays 18th-century furniture, tapestries, wallpaper, ceramics and silver.

Laid out in the 17th century, **place Bellecour** (Ⓜ Bellecour) – one of Europe's largest public squares – is pierced by an equestrian **statue of Louis XIV**. From here, pedestrianised **rue Victor Hugo** runs south to place Carnot and Gare de Perrache.

South of Perrache, across Pont de la Mulatière next to the confluence of the Rhône and the Saône (see the boxed text, below), is the well-thought-out **Aquarium du Grand Lyon** (off Map pp498-9; ☎ 04 72 66 65 66; www.aquariumlyon.fr; 7 rue Stéphane Déchant, La Mulatière; adult/under 12yr/under 1m tall €13/9/free; 11am-7pm Wed-Sun, 11am-7pm daily during school holidays). Bus 15 links it with place Bellecour.

CROIX ROUSSE

Soulful **Croix Rousse** (Map p504; Ⓜ Croix Rousse), a hilltop quarter with its own village crier (p506), quietly buzzes north up the steep *pentes* (slopes). Famed for its bohemian inhabitants and lush outdoor food market, it is historically known for its silk-weaving tradition, illustrated by the **Mur des Canuts** (off Map p504; cnr bd des Canuts & rue Denfert Rochereau, 4e; Ⓜ Hénon), a fresco painted on the side of an apartment block. Following the introduction of the mechanical Jacquard loom in 1805, Lyonnais *canuts* (silk-weavers) built workshops in this quarter with large windows to let in light and hefty wood-beamed ceilings

LYON'S MOST EXCITING URBAN SPACE

... is the **Lyon Confluence** (www.lyon-confluence.fr), the spot where the Rhône and the Saône meet south of Gare de Perrache. An industrial wasteland for decades, the riverside site – suddenly prime real estate – is the focus of a €780-million rejuvenation project.

Watch this space for the incredible **Musée des Confluences** (off Map pp498-9; Confluence Museum; www.museedesconfluences.fr), a spacey science-and-humanities museum housed in a futuristic steel-and-glass transparent crystal topped by a floating 'cloud'. Inside, three of the 10 vast exhibition areas will grapple with eternal questions like 'Where do we come from?', 'Where are we going?' and 'Who are we and what are we doing?'. Remaining spaces will hone in on hot issues of the future – cloning, genetically modified organisms, global warming, biotechnology and so on.

Prior to the museum's grand opening in 2010, sneak previews of its future collection can be enjoyed in situ at the **Local d'Information du Musée des Confluences** (☎ 04 78 37 30 00; 86 quai Perrache, 2e; tram line 1, Montrochet stop; admission free; 1-6pm Wed-Sat, 10am-noon & 1-6pm Sun).

Two auditoriums, café, restaurant, shop and riverside garden will complete the ambitious cultural ensemble, the creation of world-famous Austria-based architecture agency Coop Himmelb(l)au.

more than 4m high to accommodate the huge new machines. These workshops are chic loft apartments today.

During the bitter 1830–31 *canut* uprisings, triggered by low pay and dire working conditions, hundreds of weavers were killed. Learn about their labour-intensive life and the evolution of Lyon's silk industry at the **Maison des Canuts** (Map p504; ☎ 04 78 28 62 04; www.maisondescanuts.com; 10-12 rue d'Ivry, 4e; Ⓜ Croix Rousse; adult/student/under 12yr €6/3/free; ⏰ 10am-6.30pm Tue-Sat, guided tours 11am & 3.30pm), a museum with a boutique selling silk; and the riveting **Atelier de Passementerie** (off Map p504; ☎ 04 78 27 17 13; www.soierie-vivante.asso.fr; 21 rue Richan, 4e; adult/student €4/3; ⏰ 2-6.30pm Tue, 9am-noon & 2-6.30pm Wed-Sat, guided visits & loom demonstration 2pm & 4pm Tue-Sat), a workshop, run by the Soierie Vivante association, that functioned until 1979.

Silk, stained glass and other visual arts are the soul of the galleries and workshops that come and go the length of **Montée de la Grande Côte** (Map p504; Ⓜ Croix Rousse), a walkway linking Croix Rousse with place des Terreaux, 1er. Several more tiny galleries stud the eastern end of rue Burdeau, 1er (Map pp498-9; Ⓜ Croix Paquet).

CROIX ROUSSE DISTRICT

0 — 200 m
0 — 0.1 miles

See Lyon Map (p498)

SIGHTS & ACTIVITIES

Cours des Voraces	1	B2
Maison des Canuts	2	B1
Montée de la Grande Côte	3	A2

SLEEPING

Lyon Guest House	4	A2

EATING

Azur Afghan	5	A1
Gd Kfé de la Soierie	6	A2
Outdoor Food Market	7	A2
Toutes les Couleurs	8	B2

DRINKING

La Bistro Fait Sa Broc'	9	B1

Hidden Croix Rousse gems include **place Bertone**, a leafy square that doubles as an open-air stage for music, theatre and other ad-hoc street entertainment in summer; and the **Jardin Rosa Mir** (off Map p504; 83 Grande Rue, 4e; Ⓜ Croix Rousse; ⏰ 3-6pm Sat Apr-Nov), a walled garden decorated with thousands upon thousands of seashells.

RIVE GAUCHE

Lyon's graceful 117-hectare **Parc de la Tête d'Or** (off Map pp498-9; ☎ 04 72 69 47 60; bd des Belges, 6e; Ⓜ Masséna; ⏰ 6am-11pm mid-Apr–mid-Oct, to 9pm mid-Oct–mid-Apr), landscaped in the 1860s, is graced by a lake, botanic garden with greenhouses, rose garden and zoo. In summer rent boats, ride ponies, take a twirl on a fairground ride or watch a puppet show. Buses 41 and 47 link it with metro Part-Dieu.

The park's northern realms sit snug against the brick-and-glass **Cité Internationale**, designed by Italian architect Renzo Piano to host the G7 summit in 1996 and developed a decade later with the Roman-inspired **Salle 3000**, an amphitheatre and congress centre baptised in 2006. Equally cutting edge are the temporary exhibitions and permanent collection of post-1960 art in the **Musée d'Art Contemporain** (Museum of Contemporary Art; off Map pp498-9; ☎ 04 72 69 17 17; www.moca-lyon.org; 81 quai Charles de Gaulle, 6e; adult/18-25yr/under 18yr/family €8/6/free/10; ⏰ noon-7pm Wed-Fri, 10am-7pm Sat & Sun).

The WWII headquarters of Gestapo commander Klaus Barbie (p497) from 1942 to 1944 houses the evocative **Centre d'Histoire de la Résistance et de la Déportation** (CHRD; Map pp498-9; ☎ 04 78 72 23 11; 14 av Berthelot, 7e; Ⓜ Perrache or Jean Macé; adult/student/under 18yr €4/2/free; ⏰ 9am-noon & 2-5.30pm Wed-Fri, 9am-6pm Sat & Sun). Multimedia exhibits present the history of Nazi atrocities and the heroism of French Resistance fighters.

Cinema's glorious beginnings are showcased at the **Musée Lumière** (off Map pp498-9; ☎ 04 78 78 18 95; www.institut-lumiere.org; 25 rue du Premier Film, 8e; Ⓜ Monplaisir-Lumière; adult/under 18yr €6/5, audiogude €3; ⏰ 11am-6.30pm Tue-Sun), 3km southeast of place Bellecour along cours Gambetta. This film-buff must is inside the art-nouveau home of Antoine Lumière who moved to Lyon with sons Auguste and Louis in 1870 and shot the first reels of the world's first motion picture, *La Sortie des Usines Lumières* (Exit of the Lumières Factories) in one of their factories here on 19 March 1895. Today classic films are screened in the **Hangar du Premier Film** (see p514) – the film

TRABOULES

There's more to parts of Lyon than meets the eye. Beneath the city in Vieux Lyon and Croix Rousse, dark dingy *traboules* (secret passages) wind their way through apartment blocks, under streets and into courtyards. In all, 315 passages link 230 streets and have a combined length of 50km.

A couple of Vieux Lyon's *traboules* date from Roman times, but most were constructed by *canuts* (silk-weavers) in the 19th century to facilitate the transport of silk in inclement weather. Resistance fighters found them equally handy during WWII.

Genuine *traboules* (derived from the Latin *trans ambulare*, meaning 'to pass through') cut from one street to another, often wending their way up fabulous spiral staircases en route. Passages that fan out into a courtyard or cul-de-sac are not *traboules* but *miraboules*.

Vieux Lyon's most celebrated *traboules* include those linking 27 rue St-Jean with 6 rue des Trois Maries; 54 rue St-Jean with 27 rue du Bœuf (push the intercom button to buzz open the door); 10 quai Romain Rolland with 2 place du Gouvernement; 17 quai Romain Rolland with 9 rue des Trois Maries; and 31 rue du Bœuf with 14 rue de la Bombarde.

Step into Croix Rousse's underworld at 9 place Colbert, crossing cours des Voraces – renowned for its monumental staircase that zigzags up seven floors – and emerging at 29 rue Imbert Colomès. Other *traboules* in this fashionable quarter include those linking 1 place Colbert with 10 montée St-Sébastien and 9 place Colbert with 14bis montée St-Sébastien; and the plethora of passages on rue des Capucins: at Nos 3, 6, 13, 22 and 23.

The tourist office distributes a free map of Croix-Rousse and Vieux Lyon marked up with all the *traboules* alongside interesting courtyards, building facades and staircases.

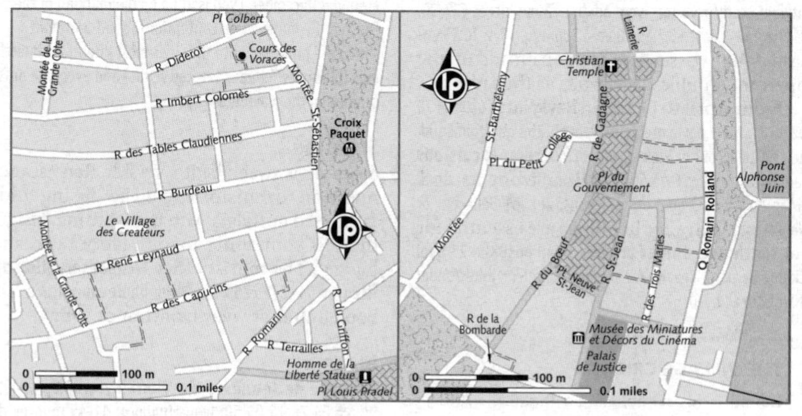

set for *La Sortie des Usines Lumières* – that somehow escaped demolition when the rest of the Lumière factories were bulldozed in the 1970s.

Nearby, the **Mur du Cinéma** (Cinema Wall; off Map pp498-9; cnr cours Gambetta & Grande Rue de la Guillotière, 7e; Ⓜ Guillotière), a painted wall, recaps Lyon's marvellous cinematic story in still-image form.

The **Grande Mosquée de Lyon** (off Map pp498-9; ☎ 04 78 76 00 23; www.mosquee-lyon.org; 146 bd Pinel, 8e; Ⓜ Laënnec; 9am-noon Sat-Thu), 5km east of Presqu'île, fuses traditional North African architecture and calligraphy with contemporary Western styles.

NORTHERN SUBURBS

Vintage cars are showcased inside a 15th-century château 11km north of Lyon along the D433. Motoring enthusiasts can drool over Hitler's Mercedes, Jean-Paul II's Renault Espace, 50-odd motorbikes, bicycles and other historical modes of Lyonnais public transport at the **Musée Henri Malartre** (off Map pp498-9; ☎ 04 78 22 18 80; www.musee-malartre.com, in French; 645 rue du Musée, Rochetaillée-sur-Saône;

adult/under 18yr €5.30/free; 9am-6pm Tue-Sun Sep-Jun, 10am-7pm Jul & Aug). Take bus 40 or 70 to the Rochetaillée stop.

Activities

Rollerbladers (www.generationsroller.asso.fr, in French) hook up on place Bellecour for a mass scoot around town every Friday at 9pm for beginners (12km, 1¼ hours) and 10.30pm for speed fiends (25km, 1½ hours).

Silky smooth **cycling paths** run beside both rivers; see p516 for bike hire.

Tours

The tourist office has audioguides and runs English-language **walking tours** (adult/8-18yr €10/5) of Vieux Lyon and Croix Rousse. Tiny and/or tired feet might prefer the pedal-powered Presqu'île tours run by **Cyclopolitain** (☎ 04 78 30 35 90; www.cyclopolitain.com, in French; 30-/60-min tour 2 people €18/25; 10.30am-7pm Mar-Jul & Sep, 3-7pm last 2 weeks Aug, 10.30am-5.30pm Oct-Dec).

With **Le Grand Tour** (☎ 04 78 56 32 39; www.pariscityrama.com/fr/visiter_lyon; adult 1-/2-day ticket €17/20, 4-11yr 1 or 2 days €8; 10am-6.30pm Apr-Oct, 10.45am-5pm Nov-Mar), passengers can hop on and off the open-top double-decker bus as they please.

From April to October, **Navig'inter** (☎ 04 78 42 96 81; www.naviginter.fr, in French; 13bis quai Rambaud, 2e; Ⓜ Bellecour or Vieux Lyon) runs **river excursions** (adult/under 10yr €9/5.50; 1 or 1¼ hr) from its **dock** (Map pp498-9; 3 quai des Célestins, 2e; Ⓜ Bellecour or Vieux Lyon). Advance bookings are essential for its **lunch and dinner cruises** (Map pp498-9; 23 quai Claude Bernard, 7e; Ⓜ Ampère or Guillotière; adult/under 10yr from €44/25).

THE VILLAGE CRIER

Gérald is his name, Gérald Rigaud… And he's an institution in Croix Rousse where he stands up and shouts all about it at the bohemian quarter's very own Speakers' Corner on place de la Croix Rousse each Sunday at 11am. In between political rants about Sarkozy et al, the highly entertaining village crier, an actor by trade, reads out love letters, poems, riddles and other community messages left for him in shop letterboxes or his own electronic mailbox (ministeredesrapportshumains@yahoo.fr9). Spot him pedalling around Croix Rousse on his bike, megaphone in hand, flat black hat on head.

DIP INTO NATURE

Observe the night sky, birdwatch, build a wooden cabin or discover virgin forest with a nature-discovery *sortie* (outing) organised by **Nature et Découvertes** (Map pp498-9; ☎ 04 78 38 38 74; 58 rue de la République, 3e; Ⓜ Bellecour) – the pick of the crop when it comes to green activities in and around the city.

Festivals & Events

Les Nuits de Fourvière (Fourvière Nights; www.nuitsdefourviere.fr, in French) Open-air concerts in Fourvière's Roman amphitheatre from early June to early August.

Biennale d'Art Contemporain (Contemporary Art Biennial; www.biennale-de-lyon.org) Art Biennial, from July to September in odd-numbered years.

Biennale de la Danse (Dance Biennial; www.biennale-de-lyon.org) Month-long Dance Biennial, held in September in even-numbered years.

Fête des Lumières (Festival of Lights) For several days around 8 December, Lyon is lit up by the marking of the Feast of the Immaculate Conception. Sound-and-light shows are projected onto the city's most important buildings (place des Terreaux is a key venue) and everyone puts candles on the window sills.

Sleeping

Sleeping is sweet: be it riverside Renaissance mansion or historic college fusing old-fashioned nostalgia with hard-hitting design, there is something to suit every taste and budget. The tourist office–run **reservation office** (☎ 04 72 77 72 50; resa@lyon-france.com) has a list; book online at www.lyon-france.com.

BUDGET

Auberge de Jeunesse du Vieux Lyon (Map pp498-9; ☎ 04 78 15 05 50; lyon@fuaj.org; 41-45 montée du Chemin Neuf, 5e; Ⓜ Vieux Lyon; dm incl breakfast €16.60; reception 7am-1pm, 2-8pm & 9pm-1am) The main draw of this superbly located hostel above Vieux Lyon is the sweeping city views from its garden and terrace. Dorms sleep two to seven people.

Hôtel Le Boulevardier (Map pp498-9; ☎ 04 78 28 48 22; 5 rue de la Fromagerie, 1er; Ⓜ Hôtel de Ville; s/d/tr €49/51/62, s/d with shared shower €40/42) A jazzy number, Le Boulevardier is an excellent-value hotel above a bistro and jazz club of the same name. Decor is as colourful and eclectic as Cédric, the charismatic Lyonnais behind this alluring act.

Hôtel Iris (Map pp498-9; ☎ 04 78 39 93 80; hoteliris@freesurf.fr; 36 rue de l'Arbre Sec, 1er; Ⓜ Hôtel de Ville; s/d/tr €50/60/72, s/d with shared bathroom €40/42) The location of this colourful dame in a centuries-old convent couldn't be better: its street brims with hip places to eat and drink. For a taste of authentic Lyonnais architecture, ask for a room reached via the open-air staircase.

our pick **Hôtel de Paris** (Map pp498-9; ☎ 04 78 28 00 95; www.hoteldeparis-lyon.com; 16 rue de la Platière, 1er; Ⓜ Hôtel de Ville; s/d from €48/62;) This fantastic-value hotel resides in a 19th-century bourgeois building in central Lyon's shop-packed heart. The funkiest rooms sport a retro 1970s decor with chocolate-and-turquoise or candyfloss-pink colour scheme. Check the latest best places to dine with charismatic owner and energy bomb Claude Chevanne.

Hôtel de la Marne (Map pp498-9; ☎ 04 78 37 07 46; www.hoteldelamarne.fr; 78 rue de la Charité, 2e; Ⓜ Gare de Perrache; s/d/tr/q €51/57/73/81) A real charmer, this Perrache hotel has 23 rooms, some of which open onto a sky-topped courtyard. Blue carpets, slate-grey paintwork and three white walls are uniform features. But throw in a fuchsia wall and a sweet collection of individual pictures and knick-knacks and you have a delightful place to stay. Yes, the reception desk is a vintage hot-air-balloon basket. Wheelchair access is available.

Hôtel St-Vincent (Map pp498-9; ☎ 04 78 27 22 56; www.hotel-saintvincent.com, in French; 9 rue Pareille, 1er; Ⓜ Hôtel de Ville; s/d/tr €55/65/75; Sep-Jul) High-beamed ceilings, giant-sized windows, a couple of old stone walls and original wooden floors make this three-floor, 32-room hotel a fine place for lapping up authentic Lyonnais atmosphere. Free wi-fi.

MIDRANGE

Hôtel des Célestins (Map pp498-9; ☎ 04 72 56 08 98; www.hotelcelestins.com; 4 rue des Archers, 2e; Ⓜ Bellecour; s/d from €62/68; reception 7am-10pm;) A stone's throw from 18th-century Théâtre des Célestins, this cosy hotel is surrounded by designer boutiques. The priciest rooms face the theatre, the cheaper ones a quiet courtyard.

Hôtel St-Paul (Map pp498-9; ☎ 04 78 28 13 29; 6 rue Lainerie, 5e; Ⓜ Vieux Lyon; d €66-74, tr €83;) With its classic oyster-grey facade and line-up of large symmetrical windows, this bijou hotel in the old town has enjoyed a renaissance in recent years. Its 20 rooms might be too *bijou* for some tastes, but its value for money is a dead cert. Free wi-fi.

Hôtel du Simplon (Map pp498-9; ☎ 04 78 37 41 00; www.hoteldusimplon.com; 11 rue Duhamel, 2e; Ⓜ Perrache; s/d €71/100) With its heart-warming measure of old-fashioned charm and chivalry, the well-run house of Madame Alix Reverchon is enchanting. A loyal clientele seeks out its 37 individual rooms year after year, but why the cherries everywhere? *Reverchon* is a type of cherry.

Hotelo (Map pp498-9; ☎ 04 78 37 39 03; www.hotelo-lyon.com; 37 cours de Verdun, 2e; Ⓜ Perrache; s/d/tr from €79/90/97) Our hot choice around Gare de Perrache, this striking newbie with a refreshingly contemporary design is simple, stylish and well thought out. Studios have a kitchenette and one room is perfectly fitted out for disabled travellers. Wheelchair access is available and there's free wi-fi too.

our pick **Collège Hotel** (Map pp498-9; ☎ 04 72 10 05 05; www.college-hotel.com; 5 place St-Paul, 5e; Ⓜ Vieux Lyon; d €110-140;) What style this college hotel has, although those with a dislike of white might not appreciate it. With reception decked out in warm, cosy ochre tones, the white minimalism of the bedrooms is quite dazzling. Enjoy breakfast on your balcony or in the *salle de classe petit dejeuner* (breakfast classroom), bedecked like a classroom of a yesteryear. A roof-terrace garden tops off this refreshingly different hotel.

TOP END

our pick **Le Royal** (Map pp498-9; ☎ 04 78 37 57 31; www.lyonhotelleroyal.com; 20 place Bellecour, 2e; Ⓜ Bellecour; d around €150-250;) 'Home away from home' is the philosophy of this timeless visiting card, in business since 1895. Recently

CAMPING INDIGO LYON

Fancy a bijou wooden chalet between trees or a green plot of shade to pitch up on? Then head out of town to **Camping Indigo Lyon** (☎ 04 78 35 64 55; www.camping-indigo.com; Porte de Lyon, Dardilly; tent/adult/2-7yr €9.90/4.40/3, 5-person chalet per night/week from €50/210;), a campsite founded on mountains of strict environmental respect. Open year-round, it rents five-person chalets and mobile homes that sleep two to six, and sports loads of family fun in the shape of an outdoor pool, kids' paddling pool, playground and so on.

redesigned from top to toe, it envelopes guests in an elegant family-residence environment with stylish *salons* (lounges), an unusual open-plan kitchen and only the best in fabrics and furnishings. Rates vary wildly depending on date and availability.

Cour des Loges (Map pp498-9; ☎ 04 72 77 44 44; www.courdesloges.com; 2-8 rue du Bœuf, 5e; Ⓜ Vieux Lyon; d/ste from €240/510;) Four 14th- to 17th-century houses wrapped around a Vieux Lyon *traboule* (secret passage) make this an exquisite place to stay. Individually designed rooms woo guests with Philippe Stark bathroom fittings and a bounty of antiques and carefully preserved historical features. Italianate loggias and spiral staircases add a twist to public areas.

Eating

Memorable dining is guaranteed. This is the French gastronomic capital after all, with a flurry of big-name chefs behind a sparkling restaurant line-up that embraces all genres: be it French, fusion or fast you want, Lyon has it.

Cobbled **rue Mercière, rue des Marronniers** and the northern side of **place Antonin Poncet** – all in the 2nd arrondissement (metro Bellecour) – are chock-a-block with eating options, pavement terraces overflowing in summer. Near the opera house, **rue Verdi**, 1er, is likewise table-filled.

BOUCHONS

Watch out for **La Mère Brazier** (Map pp498-9; rue Royale, 1er; Ⓜ Croix Paquet) to reopen near the opera house – at the time of writing, chef Mathieu Vianney was reinventing the mythical 1930s restaurant that earned Lyon its first trio of Michelin stars in 1933.

Comptoir-Restaurant des Deux Places (Map pp498-9; ☎ 04 78 28 95 10; 5 place Fernand Rey, 1er; Ⓜ Hôtel de Ville; lunch/dinner menu €15/28; lunch & dinner Tue-Sat) Red-and-white checked curtains, an

GO LOCAL

A *bouchon* might be a 'bottle stopper' or 'traffic jam' elsewhere in France, but in Lyon it's a small, friendly bistro that cooks up traditional city cuisine.

Kick-start what will surely be a memorable gastronomic experience with a *communard,* an aperitif of red Beaujolais wine and *crème de cassis* (blackcurrant liqueur), named after the supporters of the Paris Commune killed in 1871. Blood-red in colour, the mix is considered criminal elsewhere in France. When ordering wine, don't ask for a wine list. Simply order a *pot* – a 46cL glass bottle adorned with an elastic band to prevent wine drips – of local Brouilly, Beaujolais, Côtes du Rhône or Mâcon. Price: €9 to €12.50.

Next comes the entrée of *tablier de sapeur* (literally 'fireman's apron', but actually meaning breaded, fried tripe) or *salade de cervelas* (salad of boiled pork sausage sometimes studded with pistachio nuts or black truffle specks) perhaps. Hearty main dishes to sink meat-mad fangs into include *boudin blanc* (veal sausage), *boudin noir aux pommes* (blood sausage with apples), *quenelles* (a lighter-than-light flour, egg and cream dumpling), *quenelles de brochet* (pike dumplings served in a creamy crayfish sauce), *andouillette* (sausage made from pigs' intestines) and *gras double* (a type of tripe). If none appeal, bite into some *pieds de mouton/veau/couchon* (sheep/calf/piggie trotters) instead.

The cheese course usually comprises a choice of three things: a bowl of *fromage blanc* (a cross between cream cheese and natural yoghurt) with or without thick whipped cream; *cervelle de canut* (literally 'brains of the silk-weaver'), which is *fromage blanc* mixed with chives and garlic that originated in Croix Rousse and accompanied every meal for 19th-century weavers; or a round of local St Marcellin ripened to gooey perfection by the legendary Mère Richard for three generations. Desserts are grandma-style. Think *tarte aux pommes* (apple tart) or *fromage blanc* (again) with a fruit coulis dribbled on top.

Little etiquette is required in *bouchons.* Seldom do you get clean cutlery for each course, and mopping your plate with a chunk of bread is fine. If the tablecloth is paper, that's where the bill will be totted up.

In keeping with tradition, most *bouchons* don't accept diners after 9.30pm and are closed weekends (although this is slowly changing) and the entire month of August. Advance reservations are essential.

B&BS

Slowly but stylishly, *chambres d'hôtes* are making headway in Lyon. A trio of umbrella organisations have B&Bs in and around Lyon on their books, easy to view and bookable via the internet: **B&B Lyon** (☎ 04 72 32 02 74; www.bb-lyon.com); **Chambres Lyon** (☎ 04 72 13 99 35; www.chambreslyon.com) and **Gîtes de France** (Map pp498-9; ☎ 04 72 77 17 50; www.gites-de-france-rhone.com; 1 rue Général Plessier, 2e; Ⓜ Perrache).

The belles of Lyon's B&B ball:

- **Artelit** (Map pp498-9; ☎ 04 78 42 84 83; www.dormiralyon.com; 16 rue du Bœuf, 5e; Ⓜ Vieux Lyon; d incl breakfast €150-250) A reflection of the artist who runs this three-room *chambre d'hôte,* Artelit is a soulful place to sleep with centuries of history behind every last nook and cranny. 'Reception' is the workshop-cum-shop of Lyonnais photographer Frédéric Jean.
- **Lyon Guesthouse** (☎ 04 78 29 62 05, 06 07 37 45 32; www.lyonguesthouse.com; 6 montée Lieutenant Allouche, 1er; Ⓜ Croix Rousse; s €60-75, d/tr/q €85/105/120) Perched on the *pentes* (slopes) of Croix Rousse, this B&B with prime views of Fourvière is the creation of art collector and gallery owner Françoise Besson (www.francoisebesson.com). Its three rooms are modern and minimalist, breakfast is a wholly organic affair, and the art gallery's collection hangs on the crisp white walls.

old-world interior crammed with antiques and a menu scribed in black ink contribute to the overwhelmingly traditional feel here. Its pavement terrace beneath trees on a quiet village-like square off place Sathonay is particularly idyllic.

Chez Georges (Map pp498-9; ☎ 04 78 28 30 46; 8 rue du Garet, 1er; Ⓜ Hôtel de Ville; lunch menus €18 & €25; ⏰ lunch & dinner Mon-Fri, dinner Sat) One of the most respected *bouchons* with a flurry of guidebook entries to prove it, Chez Georges got its name in 1951. Service is endearingly familiar, despite the vaguely upmarket feel this one has.

Chez Paul (Map pp498-9; ☎ 04 78 28 35 83; www.chezpaul.fr; 11 rue Major Martin, 1er; Ⓜ Hôtel de Ville; menus €19 & €23.50; ⏰ lunch & dinner Mon-Fri May-Jul, lunch & dinner Mon-Fri, dinner Sat Sep-Apr) Another red-and-white-checked-tablecloth place with modern-day Lyonnais *mère* (mother) – 62-year-old Josiane – in the kitchen, Paul's Place is memorable: the sugar cubes spiked in a fiery pea-green alcohol served as a digestive after coffee are tongue-numbing.

Café des Fédérations (Map pp498-9; ☎ 04 78 28 26 00; www.lesfedeslyon.com, in French; 8 rue Major Martin, 1er; Ⓜ Hôtel de Ville; lunch/dinner menu €19.50/24; ⏰ lunch & dinner Mon-Fri) B&W photos of old Lyon speckle the wood-panelled walls of the city's best-known *bouchon* where nothing has changed for decades. Feast on *caviar de la Croix Rousse* (lentils dressed in a creamy sauce), followed perhaps by an *andouillette* (sausage made from pigs' intestines) doused in a mustard sauce.

Chez Hugon (Map pp498-9; ☎ 04 78 28 10 94; 12 rue Pizay, 1er; Ⓜ Hôtel de Ville; menu €22; ⏰ lunch & dinner Mon-Fri) The original 1937 interior is a real blast from the past at Madame Hugon's place.

Two new kids on the *bouchon* block already praised for their traditional but less stomach-heavy, more creative *bouchon* cuisine:

Magali et Martin (☎ 04 72 00 88 01; 11 rue Augustins, 1er; Ⓜ Hôtel de Ville; 2-/3-course menu €17/19; ⏰ lunch & dinner Mon-Fri) No secrets here: peep into the third of the trio of large glass windows fronting this fantastic eating space to watch the chefs in action.

Le Bouchon des Filles (☎ 04 78 30 40 44; www.lebouchondesfilles.com; 20 rue Sergent Blandan, 1er; Ⓜ Hôtel de Ville; menu €25; ⏰ dinner Thu-Sat, lunch Sun) Ode to the legendary culinary *mères* of 1930s Lyon, run by two *filles* (daughters) no less.

FRENCH

Brasserie Léon de Lyon (Map pp498-9; ☎ 04 72 10 11 12; www.leondelyon.com; 1 rue Pléney, 1er; Ⓜ Hôtel de Ville; 2-/3-course menu du jour €22.80/26, entrée/plat/dessert du jour €7/14.80/5.80; ⏰ lunch & dinner Mon-Sun) In keeping with dining trends, legendary Lyonnais chef Jean-Paul Lacombe has turned his Michelin-starred gastronomic restaurant into a soulful brasserie – same 1904 decor, similar culinary products, more affordable prices.

Le Canut et Les Gones (off Map p504; ☎ 04 78 29 17 23; 29 rue de Belfort, 4e; Ⓜ Croix Rousse; plat du jour €9, lunch/dinner menu €15/35; ⏰ lunch & dinner Tue-Sat) The culinary experience at this retro bistro is as promising as its mustard-yellow facade with mint-green window frames suggests. The crowd is hip and local, and the food a creative mix of local and French.

Le Potager des Halles (Map pp498-9; ☎ 04 72 00 24 84; www.lepotagerdeshalles.com, in French; 3 rue de la Martinière, 1er; Ⓜ Hôtel de Ville; plat du jour €9, 2-/3-course lunch menu Tue-Fri €13/15, dinner menus €32 & €35; lunch & dinner Tue-Sat) The decor is nothing to write home about but the cuisine at the Market Hall's Vegetable Garden is an impassioned ode to seasonal produce. Franck Delhoum is the magician in the kitchen.

Brasserie Georges (Map pp498-9; ☎ 04 72 56 54 54; www.brasseriegeorges.com; 30 cours de Verdun, 2e; Ⓜ Perrache; breakfast €11.50-14, menus €20-25, seafood platters €36.50-66; 8am-11.15pm Sun-Thu, 8am-12.15am Fri & Sat) In fashion since 1836, the sheer size of this brasserie with 1920s art-deco interior takes your breath away – it can feed 2000 a day! Food is a mix of onion soup, mussels, sauerkraut, seafood and local specialities.

Thomas (Map pp498-9; ☎ 04 72 56 04 76; www.restaurant-thomas.com; 3 & 6 rue Laurencin, 2e; Ⓜ Ampère; starters/mains €13/19, lunch/dinner menu €17/39; lunch & dinner Mon-Fri) Only the best products is a prerequisite for dishes served at this twinset ode to good food: ingenious chef Thomas Ponson gives taste buds the choice between formal dining or more casual fare in his tapas-inspired wine bar, Comptoir Thomas, opposite.

Le Bec (☎ 04 78 42 15 00; www.nicolaslebec.com; 14 rue Grolée; menus €68 (lunch only), €118 & €158; lunch & dinner Tue-Sat, closed three weeks in August) Best to experience the extraordinary cuisine of Lyon's hottest chef (opposite) in the company of friends who share the same tastes as you – *menus* are only served to an entire table. Given the price tag, clientele is predominantly business.

Also recommended:

La Cantine des Sales Gosses (Map pp498-9; ☎ 04 78 27 65 81; www.la-cantine-des-sales-gosses.com; 5 rue de la Martinière, 1er; Ⓜ Hôtel de Ville; starters/mains/desserts €9/15/7; lunch & dinner Mon-Sun) Near the Martinière indoor food market.

Bistro Le Casse Museau (Map pp498-9; ☎ 04 72 00 20 52; 2 rue Chavanne, 1er; Ⓜ Hôtel de Ville; lunch Tue-Sat, dinner Thu-Sat) Slurp Côtes du Rhone in the company of a retro-clock collection and weathered floor tiles.

OTHER

Toutes les Couleurs (Map p504; ☎ 04 72 00 03 95; 26 rue Imbert Colomès, 1er; Ⓜ Croix-Paquet; plat du jour €9.50, 2-course menus €13 & €16.50, 3-course menus €18, €21 & €25; lunch Tue-Fri, lunch & dinner Fri & Sat) Vegetarians in France for a while will be in seventh heaven at this 100% authentic *restaurant bio*. Its exclusively vegetarian, season-driven menu includes *végétalien* (no eggs or dairy products) and gluten-free dishes. No cow's milk here – only soya, almond or rice milk.

Oblik (Map pp498-9; ☎ 04 72 30 14 97; 26 rue Hippolyte Flandrin, 1er; Ⓜ Hôtel de Ville; plat du jour €9.50, menus €12, €15 & €23; 10am-3pm & 5pm-1am Tue-Fri, 5pm-1am Sat) Red banquette seating, six-odd tables, free wi-fi and an eclectic choice of music make this small space one of Lyon's most atmospheric. Food is unstartling but the vibe is contagious; come 11pm the place morphs into a jam-packed bar.

Fubuki (Map pp498-9; ☎ 04 78 30 41 48; 17 rue Gentil, 2e; Ⓜ Cordeliers; lunch menus €10.50-15.50, dinner menus €19-46; lunch & dinner Mon-Sat) Tables are *chauf-*

COOK YOUR OWN LUNCH *Nicola Williams*

It might sound like a raw deal, but the cooking workshops over lunch at **L'Atelier des Chefs** (Map pp498-9; ☎ 04 78 92 46 30; www.atelierdeschefs.com; 8 rue St-Nizier, 2e; Ⓜ Cordeliers; 11am-7pm Mon-Sat) are inspired – and a snip at €17.

The day I turned up at 1pm, stomach rumbling, eager beaver to don the white apron, I spent no more than 15 minutes chopping and slicing, another 15 stirring over a trendy stainless-steel stove, and a delightful half-hour or so around a shared table with new-found friends and a welcome glass of red, tucking into the result of my endeavours – a chorizo-spiced chicken filet served on a bed of baby spinach and *poivronnade* (red peppers, leeks and tomato fried with garlic, thyme and bay leaf).

Not only that, chef Stéphane Ranieri had already made dessert for us, the coffee came with a startlingly green kiwi-and-lime macaroon and I left, head reeling with the dozens of tips and tricks cleverly peppered throughout the one-hour session: adding salt to the leeks at the start of frying prevents them burning; peeled peppers cook quicker and are easier to digest; to ensure a moist chicken, pan-fry it skin-down fast until it sticks then flip it over, pour in boiling water and let it gently simmer… Food for thought indeed.

CHALK & CHEESE: JOSIANE CHANAUX & NICOLAS LE BEC

From slurping oysters at the market to salivating for hours over a 12-course feast too pretty to eat, dining in Lyon satisfies. So is this, the city with a riot of piggy-driven dishes in its soul and a backbone of offal and other ghoulish parts, France's gastronomic capital?

In the kitchen at Chez Paul (p509) Josiane Chanaux, a 62-year-old buxomly figure with red nail varnish and large jewellery, cracks the whip with the same formidable ease as Mère Brazier, Mère Filloux and other 'mothers' (who made Lyon's culinary reputation) did in the 1930s. Formal training? No way! This is a woman who has spent a lifetime behind a gas stove and knows a thing or two about making tongues wag with her staunchly traditional Lyonnais cooking.

'I've been in the restaurant business for almost 45 years, starting as a waitress and gradually moving into the kitchen. My favourite time of day – 7am, before anyone else arrives, when it's just me and my saucepans', says Josiane, whose typical morning might entail boiling up *tête de veau* (calf's head to you and me), preparing a wintertime *blanquette de veau* (mushroom, cream and white-wine veal stew) or a summertime tomato-and-olive equivalent.

'The spirit here is *familiale*. People come to eat as if at home or at their parents' house', she adds. 'Chez Paul's *tablier de sapeur* is particularly popular. Most *bouchons* serve it with a thick sauce similar to tartare sauce; I make it with a creamier sauce.'

Then there's Nicolas Le Bec (see Le Bec opposite), a high-flying, travel-mad 30-something who wouldn't be seen dead with an *andouillette* (sausage made from pigs' intestines) in his oven or wearing whites (this highly stylised chef wears black). His self-named Lyon restaurant with magic mirror in one room (allowing privileged diners to peep in his kitchen) scooped a Michelin star within months of it opening, and the much-vaunted dynamo is now all out to democratise fine dining with his lounge bar and laid-back eating space Espace Le Bec at St-Exupéry airport that opened in mid-2008, and a ground-breaking drinking and dining venue planned for the Confluence (p503) in 2009.

'My cuisine is a product-driven cuisine. It changes every month and is seasonal – it is what nature proposes' – says Nicolas Le Bec, charmingly boy-next-door, astonishingly humble and nowhere near as suave as most photos of him in the media suggest. Friends lucky enough to spend a couple of hours with him in a **cookery workshop** (www.espace-lebec.com; €60) rave about his infectious passion, energy and muck-in attitude in the kitchen.

'Travel is my biggest inspiration. Discovering the market, the market cuisine, the street cuisine of a place – that's the interesting part', says Le Bec, who isn't known for one signature dish. Rather, he constantly plays with different combinations, playing around with green asparagus in spring, tomatoes in summer, mushrooms and anything else autumn cooks up in October and so on.

Josiane Chanaux, aka Chez Paul, and Nicolas Le Bec, the chalk and cheese of Lyon's culinary scene: lunch at both to understand the full force of this city's extra-special gastronomy.

fantes (heated) – literally – at this highly rated Japanese restaurant where traditionally dressed chefs armed with very big knives chop and cook a sizzling fiesta of grilled and raw fish before your eyes. Book ahead to snag a hot seat.

Yinitial G&G (Map pp498-9; ☎ 04 78 42 14 14; 14 rue Palais Grillet, 2e; Ⓜ Cordeliers; menus €19.50, €27 & €32; ⏲ lunch & dinner Tue-Sat Sep-Jul) Taste buds are kept on the move at this ode to design – a minimalist space with low-hanging table lights, an open kitchen and a world cuisine that throws a pinch of European in the wok alongside Asian. Good vegetarian choice.

L'Ouest (off Map pp498-9; ☎ 04 37 64 64 64; www.bocuse.com; 1 quai du Commerce, 9e; Ⓜ Gare de Vaise; starters/mains around €15/20; ⏲ lunch & dinner) With the emphasis at The West being island (any island) cuisine, chefs trained by legendary Lyon chef Paul Bocuse cook up everything from king-prawn spring rolls with fresh mint and saffron-spiced crab soup to wok-fried Asian cod and straightforward roast fish in a state-of-the-art open kitchen. Decor is minimalist, avant-garde and includes a vast wood decking space outside overlooking the Saône.

Also recommended:

Azur Afghan (Map p504; ☎ 04 72 39 66 19; 6 rue Villeneuve, 4e; Ⓜ Croix Rousse; meat/veg menu €18/15; ⏲ 8-11pm Tue-Sat) Afghan hidey-hole with floor cushions, low tables and authentic Afghan food.

WANT TO DO LUNCH OR BRUNCH?

Head to the indoor market, Les Halles de Lyon (opposite), for a sit-down lunch of local produce at one of the many stalls, lip-smacking *coquillages* (shellfish) included, or try one of our top picks:

- **Pain & Cie** (Map pp498-9; ☎ 04 78 38 29 84; 13-15 rue des Quatre Chapeaux, 2e; Ⓜ Bellecour; salads €3.50-14.50; 🕑 7am-10.30pm Mon-Sat, 7am-7pm Sun) Join the crowds for a well-topped *tartine* (thick toast with topping), meal-sized salad or weekend brunch (€9 to €21).
- **Jim-Deli** (Map pp498-9; ☎ 04 78 38 31 67; 14 rue des Quatre Chapeaux, 2e; Ⓜ Bellecour; starters/pasta €8/15; 🕑 lunch & dinner Mon-Sat) Half of this Italian duo serves panini to take away; the other half carpaccio, pasta, salads and other Italian dishes emblazoned with an Italian Mama stamp of approval.
- **Neo Le Comptoir** (Map pp498-9; ☎ 04 78 30 51 01; www.neolecomptoir.com, in French; 21 rue du Bât d'Argent, 1er; Ⓜ Hôtel de Ville; salads €8-15; 🕑 11am-3pm or 3.30pm daily Sep-Jun, Mon-Sat Jul & Aug) Pick and mix your own salad and while it's being tossed, decide which room you fancy eating in at this refreshingly different eating space with lime-green-and-pink walls in a bourgeois town house. Weekend brunch.
- **Café 203** (Map pp498-9; ☎ 04 78 28 66 65; 9 rue du Garet, 1er; Ⓜ Hôtel de Ville; lunch menu €13, plat du jour €9.20; 🕑 7am-2am) One of the city's busiest addresses, Parisian-styled 203 is great for breakfast, lunch, dinner or a drink. It became a national celebrity in 2008 when it flounced France's blanket smoking ban, only to eventually give in several hefty fines and the threat of closure later. Its tables – plastered in images of stubbed-out fags – shout defiance.
- **Giraudet** (Map pp498-9; ☎ 04 72 77 98 58; www.giraudet.fr, in French; 2 rue Colonel Chambonnet, 2e; Ⓜ Bellecour; 🕑 11am-7pm Mon, 9am-7pm Tue-Sat) This sleek *quenelle* (flour, egg and cream dumplings) boutique off place Bellecour has a bar where you can taste both the Lyonnais speciality and unusual homemade soups (eg watercress, curry, broad bean and cumin). It runs another lunch bar at Les Halles de Lyon (opposite).
- **Le Café Épicerie** (Map pp498-9; ☎ 04 72 77 44 40; 6 rue du Bœuf, 5e; Ⓜ Vieux Lyon; 🕑 lunch & dinner Thu-Mon) Ignore the fact that this trendy eating space with pavement seating in Vieux Lyon is attached to one of the city's most romantic hotels; it's one of old Lyon's most stylish lunch spots.
- **Gd Kfé de la Soierie** (Map p504; ☎ 04 78 28 11 26; place des Tapis, 4e; Ⓜ Croix Rousse; 🕑 7am-1am daily) Plop down on a Fermob chair outside this timeless café on a Sunday morning when the Croix Rousse market is in full swing and you'll love this hilltop quarter forever. Zinc bar is one of many original features at this retro café, perfect for lapping up local atmosphere.

Le Tiafé (Map pp498-9; ☎ 04 78 27 85 88; 14 rue René Leynaud, 1er; Ⓜ Croix Paquet; lunch menu €17; 🕑 6pm-1am Tue-Sat) Cameroon cuisine opposite Le Village des Createurs (p515).

Alyssaar (Map pp498-9; ☎ 04 78 29 57 66; 29 rue du Bât d'Argent, 1er; Ⓜ Hôtel de Ville; menus €17-26; 🕑 dinner Tue-Sat) Cheap cheerful Syrian.

CAFÉS

Cafés spill across place des Terreaux and the lower flanks of Vieux Lyon in summer. December to April, Croix Rousse café life revolves around oyster and white-wine breakfasts shucked outdoors on crisp sunny mornings.

Café Cousu (Map pp498-9; ☎ 04 72 98 83 38; www.café-cousu.com; Passage Thiaffait, 19 rue René Leynaud, 1er; Ⓜ Croix Paquet; lunch menu €7; 🕑 8am-8pm Tue-Fri, 10am-9pm Sat, 11am-6.30pm Sun) This *bijou* concept café wedged between fashion designers in Le Village des Createurs (p515) entices a hip lunchtime crowd with its wholly home-made soups, tarts and cakes. Weekend brunch €10.

Grand Café des Négociants (Map pp498-9; ☎ 04 78 42 50 05; 2 place Francisque Regaud, 2e; Ⓜ Cordeliers; 🕑 7am-1am) Affectionately called Les Négos locally, this café-cum-brasserie with mirror-lined walls, impeccable service and a pavement terrace beneath trees has been a favourite meeting point with Lyonnais since

1864. Look for the gargantuan shocking-pink flower pot out front.

QUICK EATS

Rue Ste-Marie des Terreaux and rue Ste-Catherine, 1er (metro Hôtel de Ville) are lined with cheap-eat Chinese, Turkish and Indian joints.

Best Bagels (Map pp498-9; ☎ 04 78 27 65 61; 1 place Tobie Robatel, 1er; Ⓜ Hôtel de Ville; bagel menus €2.90-4.90; 🕑 11.30am-10pm Mon & Tue, 11.30am-11pm Wed-Fri, 9.30am-11pm Sat, 11am-2.30pm Sun) Filled or frosted bagels, coffee to go and other American delights are doled out at this bagel bar and grocery store.

Matsuri (Map pp498-9; ☎ 04 78 27 83 06; www.matsuri.fr, in French; 7 rue de la Fromagerie, 1er; Ⓜ Hôtel de Ville; 🕑 lunch & dinner Mon-Sat) For a stylish instant-eat, duck down on a bar stool at this bright sushi bar and pick from the colour-coded plates of raw fish (€3 to €6) that glide past on a conveyor belt.

Ninkasi Opéra (Map pp498-9; ☎ 04 78 28 37 74; www.ninkasi.fr, in French; 27 rue de l'Arbre Sec, 1er; Ⓜ Hôtel de Ville; salads €6-9, burgers €5.20; 🕑 10am-1am Mon-Thu, 10am-3am Fri & Sat, 6pm-midnight Sun) If meaty burgers or fish and chips is your cup of tea, this microbrewery grub stop is for you. DJs spin tunes on Saturdays, and film screenings, live bands etc fulfil its Sunday-evening entertainment pledge.

SELF-CATERING

Les Halles de Lyon (off Map pp498-9; 102 cours Lafayette, 3e; Ⓜ Part-Dieu; 🕑 8am-7pm Tue-Sat, 8am-2pm Sun) The city's legendary indoor food market. Buy a round of impossibly runny St Marcellin (€2.60) from legendary cheesemonger Mère Richard or a fat knobbly Jésus de Lyon from pork butcher Collette Sibilia.

Lyon has two **outdoor food markets**: Croix Rousse (Map p504; bd de la Croix Rousse, 4e; Ⓜ Croix Rousse; 🕑 Tue-Sun morning); Presqu'île (Map pp498-9; quai St-Antoine, 2e; Ⓜ Bellecour or Cordeliers; 🕑 Tue-Sun morning).

Drinking

The bounty of café terraces on place des Terreaux, 1er (metro Hôtel de Ville) buzz with drinkers all hours. English-style pubs serving €5 pints are clustered on rue Ste-Catherine, 1er, and in Vieux Lyon: firm favourites open daily until 1am include the **Albion** (Map pp498-9; ☎ 04 78 28 33 00; 12 rue Ste-Catherine, 1er), **Smoking Dog** (Map pp498-9; ☎ 04 78 28 38 27; 16 rue Lainerie, 5e) and Irish **St-James** (Map pp498-9; ☎ 04 78 37 36 70; 19 rue St-Jean, 5e).

Barberousse (Map pp498-9; ☎ 04 72 00 80 53; 18 rue Terrailles, 1er; Ⓜ Hôtel de Ville; 🕑 7pm-3am Tue-Sat) The busiest time of day at this student-loved shooter bar, one of a handful of nightlife venues on back-alley rue Terrailles, is between 8pm and 10pm when its flavoured rums are downed *sur le pouce* (on the cheap). Cinnamon, chestnut, violet or rhubarb and caramel…the choice is exotic.

Ké Pêcherie (Map pp498-9; ☎ 04 78 28 26 25; quai de la Pêcherie, 1er; Ⓜ Hôtel de Ville; 🕑 7am-1.30am) Trendy with an older set, this Saône-side space spans the whole spectrum of drinking: daytime café, late-afternoon lounge bar, post-work aperitif and heaving music venue.

Andy Walha (Map pp498-9; ☎ 04 78 30 54 48; 29 rue de l'Arbre Sec, 1er; Ⓜ Hôtel de Ville; 🕑 11am-3am) Warhol inspires the pop-art decor at this cocktail bar where a beautiful set quaffs champagne, cocktails and elderflower cordial well past midnight. Food too: smoked salmon, foie gras (fattened liver) and gourmet half- or full-sized mixed platters (€14/26).

Soda Bar (Map pp498-9; ☎ 06 50 25 55 44; www.soda-bar.fr, in French; 7 rue de la Martinière, 1er; Ⓜ Hôtel de Ville; 🕑 6pm-1am Mon-Wed, 6pm-3am Thu & Fri, 8pm-3am Sat) Spirited bar staff juggle bottles between drinks (called 'flair bartending' apparently) at this contemporary cocktail bar with an exotic drinks menu. Step behind the bar Monday night and learn how to shake your own.

Le Bar (Map pp498-9; ☎ 04 78 31 51 08; 10bis rue de la Bourse, 1er; Ⓜ Cordeliers; 🕑 6pm-midnight) Its name is a pallid reflection of the minimalist steely interior and chic cocktails for which it's known.

Le Voxx (Map pp498-9; ☎ 04 78 28 33 87; 1 rue d'Algérie, 1er; Ⓜ Hôtel de Ville; 🕑 8am-2am Mon-Sat, 10am-2am Sun) Less fashion-conscious than its cocktail-fuelled contemporaries, the Voxx gets packed with a real mix of people, from student to city slicker.

Johnny's Kitchen (Map pp498-9; ☎ 04 78 37 94 13; www.myspace.com/johnnyskitchen; 48 rue St-Georges, 5e; Ⓜ Vieux Lyon; 🕑 noon-1am daily) A young carefree crowd spills onto the street at this busy pub in St-Georges where Johnny dishes up Irish and burger-shaped world cuisine, art by local artists, televised sport and great music – bands jam for free in its *cave* (cellar).

Broc' Café (Map pp498-9; ☎ 04 72 40 46 01; 2 place de l'Hôpital, 2e; Ⓜ Bellecour; 🕑 8am-1am Mon-Sat) This laid-back café-bar with a pavement terrace oozes a certain *je ne sais quoi*. It serves reasonably priced food, its retro interior is decked out à la second-hand (*'broc'* is short for *'brocante'*, meaning second-hand or jumble) and its student crowd oozes street cred – a great drinking choice any time.

La Bistro fait sa Broc' (Map p504; ☎ 04 72 07 93 97; 1-3 rue Dumenge, 4e; Ⓜ Croix Rousse; 🕑 5pm-1am Mon-Sat) A hip lime-green and candyfloss-pink facade greets punters at this retro wine bar where no two chairs match and the furniture is constantly rearranged. Bands occasionally play here.

La Fée Verte (Map pp498-9; ☎ 04 78 28 32 35; www.lafeeverte.fr, in French; 4 rue Pizay, 1er; Ⓜ Hôtel de Ville; 🕑 9am-2am Mon-Wed, 9am-3am Thu & Fri, 10am-1am Sat & Sun) Hit the Green Fairy (as in the bar, not devilish old absinthe) for a drink in a steely setting, set alive with live bands come dusk. Steel aside, furnishings are a predictable green.

modernartcafé (off Map p504; ☎ 04 72 87 06 82; www.modernartcafe.net; 65 bd de la Croix Rousse, 4e; Ⓜ Croix Rousse; 🕑 11.50am-1.50am Mon-Fri, 3.30pm-2am Sat, 11am-2am Sun, shorter hours in winter & rain) Retro furnishings, changing art on the walls, a pocket-sized beach with deckchairs, free wi-fi, weekend brunch and a clutch of music- and video-driven happenings make Croix Rousse's art bar one cool place to be.

Also worth a visit:

Comptoir de la Bourse (Map pp498-9; ☎ 04 72 41 71 52; 33 rue de la Bourse, 1er; Ⓜ Cordeliers; 🕑 7.30am-3.30am Mon-Sat)

Karma (☎ 04 78 92 86 20; 37 rue de la Bourse, 1er; Ⓜ Cordeliers; 🕑 10am-1am Fri, 3pm-1am Sat).

Entertainment

The scene is dynamic. Listings guides include weekly publication **Lyon Poche** (www.lyonpoche.com, in French; at newsagents €1); free weekly **Le Petit Bulletin** (www.petit-bulletin.fr, in French), available on street corners; and quarterly **Scope** (www.progrescope.com, in French), distributed with local daily **Le Progrès** (www.leprogres.fr, in French).

Tickets are sold at **Fnac Billetterie** (Map pp498-9; ☎ 08 92 68 36 22; www.fnac.com/spectacles; 85 rue de la République, 2e; Ⓜ Bellecour; 🕑 10am-7pm Mon-Sat). For half-price same-day theatre tickets, try **Le Kiosque Théâtre** (16 place des Terreaux, 1er; Ⓜ Hôtel de Ville; 🕑 12.30-7.30pm Tue-Sat; commission €3).

CINEMAS

Nondubbed films are the staple diet of **CNP-Terreaux** (Map pp498-9; ☎ 08 92 68 69 33; 40 rue du Président Édouard Herriot, 1er; Ⓜ Hôtel de Ville; tickets €7.50).

Hangar du Premier Film (off Map pp498-9; ☎ 04 78 78 18 95; www.institut-lumiere.org; 25 rue du Premier Film, 8e; Ⓜ Monplaisir Lumière; tickets regular/special screenings €6.80 & €8.30) shows films of all genres and eras. From June to September, the big screen moves outside.

LIVE MUSIC

Furib' Arts (Map pp498-9; ☎ 04 72 00 26 41; www.myspace.com/lefuribart; 60 rue St-Georges, 5e; Ⓜ Vieux Lyon; admission free-€4; 🕑 3pm-1am Tue-Sat) Tune into a local band at this grungy cellar bar loved by a loyal set. The size of the crowd will tell you where the band is from.

Le Bastringue (Map pp498-9; ☎ 06 70 15 81 39; http://lebastringue.free.fr, in French; 14 rue Laurencin, 2e; Ⓜ Ampère; 🕑 8pm-1am Tue-Sat) In a similar vein, this *bar à vin associatif* hosts an eclectic choice of sounds and events – Afro blues, acoustic rock, games evenings etc.

Hot Club de Lyon (Map pp498-9; ☎ 04 78 39 54 74; www.hotclubjazz.com, in French; 26 rue Lanterne, 1er; Ⓜ Hôtel de Ville; admission €9-12; 🕑 9pm-1am Tue-Thu, 9.30pm-1am Fri, 4-7pm & 9.30pm-1am Sat Sep-Jun) A nonprofit musical landmark since 1948, Lyon's premier jazz club stages live jazz concerts and a weekly jam session (4pm to 7pm Saturday).

Ninkasi Gerland (off Map pp498-9; ☎ 04 72 76 89 00; www.ninkasi.fr, in French; 267 rue Marcel Mérieux, 7e; Ⓜ Stade de Gerland; 🕑 10am-1am Mon-Wed, 10am-2am Thu, 10am-3am Fri, 10am-4am Sat, 4pm-midnight Sun) Drink beer, listen to DJ beats and jive to bands with a frenetic crowd at this microbrewery near the stadium.

Le Transbordeur (off Map pp498-9; ☎ 04 78 93 08 33; www.transbordeur.fr, in French; 3 bd de Stalingrad, Villeurbanne) Take bus 59 from metro Part-Dieu to Cité Inter Transbordeur stop, to get to Lyon's prime concert venue. Located in an old industrial building, it is on the European concert-tour circuit and draws international stars.

NIGHTCLUBS

Track new offerings at www.lyonclubbing.com, www.lyon2night.com and www.night4lyon.com (all in French).

Le 42 (Map pp498-9; ☎ 04 78 28 35 05; www.le42.com, in French; 42 quai Pierre Scize, 9e; Ⓜ Hôtel de Ville; 🕑 midnight-4am Wed-Sat) Of the clutch of riverside bars and clubs on quai Pierre Scize, the 42 stands out for its atmospheric setting – an old beamed family home.

F & G Bar (Map pp498-9; ☎ 04 72 00 99 13; 20 rue Terraille, 1er; Ⓜ Hôtel de Ville; admission free-€10; 🕑 4pm-

GREEN PICK: VEG PATCH ON WHEELS

Take two food-mad students, a bicycle and the pick of the morning's fresh seasonal market produce and what do you get? **Potager City** (www.potagercity.fr, in French; 4-5kg fresh fruit or veg €14.90; 9am-9pm Mon-Fri), a fruit-and-veg-on-wheels service that shops at markets and delivers by bicycle to your home or hotel in central Lyon. *Potager* means 'vegetable patch' or 'garden'.

3am Tue-Sat) F & G – Filles et Garçons (girls and boys) – is a hot bet with Lyon's 20-something crowd that piles in from the surrounding bars on this dead-central party street.

La Chapelle (Map pp498-9; ☎ 04 78 37 23 95; 60 montée de Choulans, 5e; Ⓜ Perrache; admission Mon-Thu free, Fri & Sat €10-20; 6pm-2am Mon-Wed, 6pm-5am Thu-Sat, closed Tue winter) 'Open-minded' and 'a garden of Eden' are labels the Chapel wears. Set in the chapel of a 16th-century château surrounded by a vast green park (to which the drinking 'n' dancing spills), the setting is unique. Decor: art deco and age-old. Music: house and techno.

La Marquise (Map pp498-9; ☎ 04 72 61 92 92; www.marquise.net, in French; 20 quai Victor Augagneur, 3e; Ⓜ Guillotière; admission free-€15; 7pm or 8pm-11pm Thu, to 5am Fri & Sat) Step aboard this 'good vibes generator', aka a concert club moored on a barge where DJs belt out an ear-popping barrage of electronic, hip hop, breakbeat, boogie, soul and rap.

Le Cube (off Map pp498-9; ☎ 04 78 17 29 84; 115 bd Stalingrad, Villeurbanne; admission free; 7pm-5am Thu-Sat) The Cube is just that – a glass box where the Lyonnais jet set flock to eat, drink and jive the night away. House reigns at this trend temple.

In the hip Gare de Brotteaux quarter, start at **ApériKlub** (☎ 04 37 24 19 46; 13-14 place Jules Ferry; Ⓜ Brotteaux; 6.30pm-3am Wed-Fri, 8.30pm-4am Sat) and end at **First Tendency** (☎ 04 37 24 19 46; 13-14 place Jules Ferry; Ⓜ Brotteaux; admission free; 11pm-5am Thu-Sat). Dress sharp for both.

SPORT

When at home, national football champs Olympique Lyonnais (http://olweb.fr) kick off at the **Stade de Gerland** (off Map pp498-9; Gerland Stadium; ☎ 04 72 76 01 70; 353 av Jean Jaurès, 7e; Ⓜ Stade de Gerland), a 40,000-seater stadium built in the 1920s. Match tickets are sold online and at club boutique **Planète OL** (Map pp498-9; ☎ 04 78 37 49 49; cnr rue de Jussieu & rue Grolée, 2e; Ⓜ Cordeliers; 10am-1.30pm & 2-6pm Tue-Sat).

THEATRE, DANCE & CLASSICAL MUSIC

Opéra de Lyon (Map pp498-9; ☎ 08 26 30 53 25; www.opera-lyon.com, in French; place de la Comédie, 1er; Ⓜ Hôtel de Ville; mid-Sep–early Jul) Opera, ballet and classical concerts.

Maison de la Danse (off Map pp498-9; ☎ 04 72 78 18 18; www.maisondeladanse.com; 8 av Jean Mermoz, 8e) Contemporary dance. Take bus 23, 24 or 25.

Auditorium de Lyon (off Map pp498-9; ☎ 04 78 95 95 95; www.auditorium-lyon.com, in French; 82 rue de Bonnel, 3e; Ⓜ Part-Dieu; Sep-Jun) Home to the National Orchestra of Lyon; workshops, jazz and world-music concerts.

Théâtre Le Guignol de Lyon (Map pp498-9; ☎ 04 78 28 92 57; www.guignol-lyon.com, in French; 2 rue Louis Carrand, 5e; Ⓜ Vieux Lyon) Traditional puppet theatre.

Shopping

On the Presqu'île, mainstream shops line rue de la République and rue Victor Hugo. Upmarket boutiques and big-name design houses stud parallel rue du Président Édouard Herriot, rue de Brest and the trio of streets fanning from place des Jacobins to place Bellecour.

More big-name fashion designers are clustered between art galleries and antique shops in **Quartier Auguste Comte**, an exclusive quarter south of place Bellecour around rue Auguste Comte, 2e.

For cutting-edge work by local, just-known or yet-to-make-their-name designers, browse the fashion boutiques in **Le Village des Createurs** (☎ 04 78 27 37 21; www.villagedescreateurs.com; Passage Thiaffait, 19 rue René Leynaud, 1er; Ⓜ Croix Paquet; 2-7pm Wed-Sat).

Centre Commercial La Part-Dieu (off Map pp498-9; Ⓜ Part-Dieu; 9.30am-7.30pm Mon-Sat) is Lyon's vast indoor shopping centre.

For fans of markets there's a riverside **Book Market** (Map pp498-9; quai de la Pêcherie, 1er; Ⓜ Hôtel de Ville; 7am-6pm Sat & Sun) and **Crafts Market** (Map pp498-9; quai de Bondy, 5e; Ⓜ Vieux Lyon; 9am-noon Sun).

Getting There & Away

AIR

Flights to/from European cities land at **Lyon-St-Exupéry Airport** (off Map pp498-9; ☎ 08 26 80 08 26; www.lyon.aeroport.fr), 25km east of the city.

BUS

In the Perrache complex, **Eurolines** (Map pp498-9; ☎ 04 72 56 95 30), **Intercars** (Map pp498-9; ☎ 04 78 37 20 80) and Spain-oriented **Linebús** (Map pp498-9; ☎ 04 72 41 72 27) have offices on the bus-station level of the Centre d'Échange (follow the 'Lignes Internationales' signs).

CAR & MOTORCYCLE

Car-rental companies have offices at Gare de la Part-Dieu and Gare de Perrache.

TRAIN

Lyon has two main-line train stations: **Gare de la Part-Dieu** (off Map pp498-9; Ⓜ Part-Dieu), 1.5km east of the Rhône, and **Gare de Perrache** (Map pp498-9; Ⓜ Perrache). A handful of local trains stop at **Gare St-Paul** (Map pp498-9; Ⓜ Vieux Lyon) in Vieux Lyon. Buy tickets at all three stations or at the **SNCF Boutique** (Map pp498-9; 2 place Bellecour, 2e; Ⓜ Bellecour; 🕑 9am-6.45pm Mon-Fri, 10am-6.30pm Sat).

Destinations by direct TGV include Paris' Gare de Lyon (€61, two hours, every 30 to 60 minutes), Lille-Europe (€80.20, 3¼ hours, nine daily), Nantes (€89.20, 4½ hours, five daily), Beaune (€21.60, 2¼ hours, up to nine daily), Dijon (€28.50, 2¾ hours, at least 12 daily) and Strasbourg (€52.80, 5¼ hours, five daily).

Getting Around

TO/FROM THE AIRPORT

Satobus (☎ 04 72 68 72 17; www.satobus.com) links the airport with the centre every 20 minutes between 5am or 6am and midnight. Journey time is 35/45 minutes to Gare de la Part-Dieu/Gare de Perrache and the single/return fare (€8.60/15.20) includes one hour's travel on public transport; kids aged four to 12 years pay half-fare.

By taxi, the 30-minute trip between the airport and the city centre costs around €40/55 during the day/between 7pm and 7am.

BICYCLE

Pick up a pair of red-and-silver wheels at one of 200-odd bike stations dotted around the city and drop them off at another with Lyon's hugely successful **vélo'v** (☎ 08 00 08 35 68; www.velov.grandlyon.com, in French) bike-rental scheme. The first 30 minutes are free and the first/subsequent hours cost €1/2 with a *carte courte durée* (a short-duration card, costing €1 and valid for seven days) and €0.50/1 if you buy a *carte longue durée* (long-duration card, costing €5 and valid for one year). Buy either card with a credit card from machines installed at bike stations: central stations are located in front of the town hall on bd de la Croix Rousse, 4e (Map p504; metro Croix Rousse); beside the opera house (1er; Map pp498–9; metro Hôtel de Ville); and opposite Cathédrale St-Jean on place St-Jean (5e; Map pp498–9; metro Vieux Lyon). A city map showing every station and cycling path is posted at each station.

Less leg work is required with the chauffeur-driven tricycles with soft roofs operated by **Cyclopolitain** (☎ 04 78 30 35 90; www.cyclopolitain.com, in French; 🕑 10.30am-7pm Mar-Jul & Sep, 3-7pm last 2 weeks Aug, 10.30am-5.30pm Oct-Dec). Pick up a *cyclo* at several points around the city, including place Bellecour, or order one by telephone; they cost €2 per person per kilometre.

WINE TASTING

Our trio of addresses guarantee to swirl, sniff and sip:

- **Harmonie des Vins** (Map pp498-9; ☎ 04 72 98 85 59; 9 rue Neuve, 1er; Ⓜ Hôtel de Ville; 🕑 10am-2am Tue-Sat) Find out all about French wine at this stylish wine bar with old stone walls and contemporary furnishings. Tasty food fills the place at lunchtime.
- **Le Wine Bar d'à Côté** (Map pp498-9; ☎ 04 78 28 31 46; www.cave-vin-lyon.com, in French; 7 rue Pleney, 1er; Ⓜ Cordeliers) Furnished like an English gentlemen's club with leather sofa seating, and a library of reference books including every Michelin *Guide Rouge* from 1965 to 1980, this cultured wine bar is a treat. Thematic evenings must be reserved in advance. Look for the Harley parked on the street, in front of its wine shop, La Cave.
- **Saint Just: Caviste pas Pareil** (Map pp498-9; ☎ 06 80 47 21 09; www.myspace.com/lesaintjus; 76 rue St-Georges, 5e; Ⓜ Vieux Lyon; 🕑 5-9pm Thu-Sat) The alternative space for *dégustation* (tasting), this far-from-mainstream hideout runs fun and relaxed wine-tasting workshops (€18) or otherwise invites punters to sit back and indulge in an oenological *grand tour* (€7).

GAY & LESBIAN LYON

The city has its fair share of venues; free monthly newspaper *Hétéoculte* is a one-stop shop for finding out what's on where, as are the **Forum Gai et Lesbien de Lyon** (Map pp498-9; ☎ 04 78 39 97 72; www.fgllyon.org, in French; 17 rue Romarin, 1er; Ⓜ Croix Paquet; 🕑 6-8pm Tue-Fri) and **ARIS** (Accueil Rencontres Informations Service; ☎ 04 78 27 10 10; www.aris-lyon.org, in French; 19 rue des Capucins, 1er; Ⓜ Croix Paquet). Lyon's **Lesbian and Gay Pride** (www.fierte.net, in French) hits the streets each year in June.

Gay bars include **Le Forum** (Map pp498-9; ☎ 04 78 37 19 74; 15 rue des Quatre Chapeaux, 2e; Ⓜ Cordeliers; 🕑 5pm-1am Sun-Thu, 5pm-3am Fri & Sat) and **La Ruche** (Map pp498-9; ☎ 04 78 37 42 26; 22 rue Gentil, 2e; Ⓜ Cordeliers; 🕑 5pm-3am). After hours, don your dancing shoes at gay nightclub **Le New York Le Medley** (Map pp498-9; ☎ 04 78 38 23 96; 19 rue Childebert, 2e; Ⓜ Cordeliers; admission free; 🕑 10pm-5am Wed, 11pm-5am Thu-Sat).

The website www.lyongay.net is an online gay guide to Lyon.

If you want to pedal yourself but need a spurt of electric power, rent a three- or seven-gear Swiss-made electric bicycle with 2kg battery (good for 30km) from **Zone Cycable** (Map pp498-9; ☎ 04 72 77 83 40; www.zonecyclable.com; 3 rue du Vieil Renversé, 5e; Ⓜ Vieux Lyon; 🕑 9.30am-noon & 2-7pm, closed Sun Dec–mid-Apr). Book bikes (€6/20/40 per hour/day/weekend) and guided bike tours (3½ hours, €39) in advance.

PUBLIC TRANSPORT

Buses, trams, a four-line metro and two funiculars linking Vieux Lyon to Fourvière and St-Just is run by **TCL** (☎ 08 20 42 70 00; www.tcl.fr, in French; 5 rue de la République, 1er; Ⓜ Bellecour; 🕑 7.30am-6.30pm Mon-Fri, 9am-noon & 1.30-5pm Sat). Public transport runs from around 5am to midnight.

Tickets valid for all forms of public transport cost €1.50/12.50 for one/carnet of 10 and are available from bus and tram drivers and machines at metro entrances. Tickets allowing unlimited travel for two hours/one day cost €2.20/4.40 and a Ticket Liberté Soirée allowing unlimited travel after 7pm is €2.20. Time-stamp tickets on all forms of public transport or risk a €40 fine.

In this chapter, the nearest metro stops for sights, hotels etc are mentioned right after the street address and indicated with a metro icon, Ⓜ.

TAXI

Taxis hover in front of both train stations, on the place Bellecour end of rue de la Barre (2e), and at the northern end of rue du Président Édouard Herriot (1er).

Allo Taxi (☎ 04 78 28 23 23; www.allotaxi.fr, in French)
Taxis Lyonnais (☎ 04 78 26 81 81; www.taxilyonnais.com, in French)

NORTH & WEST OF LYON

Cosmopolitan Lyon is ensnared by green hills, lakes and vineyards.

Beaujolais

Hilly Beaujolais, 50km northwest of Lyon is a land of streams, granite peaks (the highest is 1012m Mont St-Rigaud), pastures and forests.

The region is famed for its fruity red wines, especially its 10 premium *crus*, and the Beaujolais *nouveau*, drunk at the tender age of just six weeks. Vineyards stretch south from Mâcon along the right bank of the Saône for some 50km.

At the stroke of midnight on the third Thursday (ie Wednesday night) in November – as soon as French law permits – the *libération* (release) or *mise en perce* (tapping; opening) of the first bottles of cherry-bright Beaujolais *nouveau* is celebrated with much hype and circumstance around France and the world.

In **Beaujeu** (population 1904), 64km northwest of Lyon, there's free Beaujolais *nouveau* for all during the **Sarmentelles de Beaujeu** – one big street party.

For details on wine cellars where you can taste and buy wine, contact Beaujeu's **tourist office** (☎ 04 74 69 22 88; www.aucoeurdubeaujolais.fr; place de l'Église; 🕑 10am-noon & 2.30-6pm Wed-Sun). Ask for its list of the many *chambres d'hôtes* mushrooming in this nature-rich area.

Exploring Beaujolais by **mountain bike** is uplifting, its gentle hills being suitable for the least experienced (or even the laziest) of cyclists. Fifteen routes (230km) are detailed in the topoguide *Le Beaujolais à VTT*. **Walking** the area's many footpaths is equally delightful.

Pérouges & La Dombes

Film star **Pérouges** (population 850), a yellow-stone medieval village too perfectly restored, lures day trippers like crazy in spring and summer.

They flock there to stroll its cobbled alleys, admire its half-timbered stone houses, ogle at the weary old **liberty tree** planted in 1792 on place de la Halle and wolf down *galettes de Pérouges* (sweet tarts, served warm and crusted with sugar) and cider. Buses link the village, 27km northeast of Lyon on a hill, with Lyon's Gare de Perrache.

Northwest is **La Dombes**, a marshy area whose hundreds of *étangs* (shallow lakes), created from malarial swamps over the past six centuries by farmers, are used as fish ponds and then drained so crops can be grown on the fertile lake bed. The area, famed for its production of frogs' legs, attracts lots of wildlife, particularly waterfowl. Observe local and exotic birds, including dozens of pairs of storks, at the **Parc des Oiseaux** (☎ 04 74 98 05 54; www.parcdesoiseaux.com, in French; adult/6-14yr/under 6yr €13/10/free; 🕑 9am-7pm), a landscaped bird park outside Villars-les-Dombes on the N83.

Lunch local at **La Bicyclette Bleue** (☎ 04 74 98 21 48; www.labicyclettebleue.fr, in French; menus €11-35; 🕑 lunch & dinner Thu-Mon, lunch Tue), a family affair 7.5km southeast of Villars-les-Dombes in Joyeux, renowned for its *grenouilles fraîches en persillade* (fresh frogs' legs in butter and parsley). It also rents out bicycles (bikes/tandems per hour €4.50/8, per half-day €12.50/20) to explore the lakeland. Cyclists can pick from 11 mapped circuits, 12km (one hour) to 59km (four hours) long.

ST-ÉTIENNE

pop 175,500

No doubt about it: down-to-business St-Étienne, an industrial hub 62km southwest of Lyon, is dreary. But it does have one redeeming feature.

Enter St-Étienne's **Musée d'Art Moderne** (MAM; Modern Art Museum; ☎ 04 77 79 52 52; www.mam-st-etienne.fr, in French; rue Fernard Léger, St-Priest-en-Jarez; adult/12-18yr/under 18yr €4.50/3.70/free, 1st Sun of month free; 🕑 10am-6pm Wed-Mon), with its internationally renowned collection of 20th-century and contemporary paintings, sculptures and photographs. Tram 4 (direction Hôpital Nord) links it with the centre. The cutting-edge **Biennale Internationale Design** (www.citedudesign.com), a design fair hosted every two years in November, is the city's other big drawcard. The next is in 2010.

The **tourist office** (☎ 04 77 49 39 00; www.tourisme-st-etienne.com; 16 av de la Libération; 🕑 9am-1pm & 2-7pm Mon-Sat, 9am-noon Sun Apr-Sep, 9am-1pm & 2-6pm Mon-Sat, 9am-noon Sun Oct-Mar), 1km southwest of the train station, has accommodation details.

St-Étienne International Airport (☎ 04 77 55 71 71; www.saint-etienne.aeroport.fr) is 12km northwest of the city. Hourly trains link St-Étienne Châteaucreux with Lyon (€9.40, 50 minutes).

DOWNSTREAM ALONG THE RHÔNE

South of Lyon, vineyards meet nuclear powerplants – not the most auspicious juxtaposition, but worth a stop for Lyon-based day trippers or the southbound.

Vienne

pop 30,600

This one-time Gallo-Roman city, now a disappointingly average town 30km south of Lyon, appeals most to aficionados of the Romans

GREEN BEAUJOLAIS

Tap into green Beaujolais with **Billebaudez en Beaujolais Vert** (☎ 04 74 04 77 07; www.billebaudez.com, in French), a group formed by local farmers, cheese-makers, oil producers, artists and so on to promote the nature-rich region in which they live and work. Through the organisation tourists can, among other things, visit local farms, fish, horse-ride, paint, participate in a fruit harvest, learn about bee-keeping – or sleep in one of a trio of romantically furnished *roulottes* (traditional gypsy caravans) from the 1920s and 1950s at **Les Roulottes de la Serve** (☎ 04 74 04 76 40; www.lesroulottes.com; La Serve, Ouroux; d incl breakfast €47-60, heating per night €3-5; 🕑 Apr-Nov). Run by traditional caravan-maker Pascal and his hippie wife, Pascaline, the B&B is amid fields, while showers, toilets and breakfast (and optional evening meal) are provided in the main farmhouse. Follow the road from Avenas to the Col de Crie for 5km, and at the La Serve crossroads, head to Ouroux; after 100m turn right down the track signposted *chambres d'hôtes en roulottes*.

NUCLEAR TOURISM

Nuclear tourism enjoys a twist at the **Ferme aux Crocodiles** (☎ 04 75 04 33 73; www.lafermeauxcrocodiles.com, in French; adult/3-12yr €11/7; 9.30am-7pm Mar-Sep, 9.30am-5pm Oct-Feb), a crocodile farm, 20km south of Montélimar near Pierrelatte, where 350-odd grouchy Nile crocodiles slumber in tropical pools heated by a neighbouring nuclear powerplant.

The **Centre Nucléaire du Tricastin** plant has four 915-megawatt reactors, sufficiently productive to heat 42 hectares of greenhouses and 2400 local homes. Nearby, the **Centre Nucléaire de St-Alban–St-Maurice**, 20km south of Vienne on the Rhône's left bank, has two pressurised water reactors rated at a mighty 1300 megawatts, enough to supply the needs of Lyon 10 times over.

or jazz fans: its two-week **jazz festival** (☎ 08 92 70 20 07; www.jazzavienne.com, in French) in June is famous.

The Corinthian columns of the **Temple d'Auguste et de Livie** (place Charles de Gaulle) in the old town, built around 10 BC to honour Emperor Augustus and his lovely wife Livia, are superb. Across the river in St-Romain-en-Gal, the excavated remains of the Gallo-Roman city form the **Musée Gallo-Romain** (☎ 04 74 53 74 01; www.musees-gallo-romains.com, in French; 2 chemin de la Plaine Gal; adult/18-25yr/under 18yr €3.80/2.30/free, 1st Sun of month free; 10am-6pm Tue-Sun).

Savour great town views from the **Belvédère de Pipet**, a balcony with a 6m-tall statue of the Virgin Mary, immediately above Vienne's fabulous **Théâtre Romain** (☎ 04 74 85 39 23; rue du Cirque; adult/under 18yr €2.30/free, 1st Sun of month free; 9.30am-1pm & 2-6pm Apr-Aug, 9.30am-1pm & 2-6pm Tue-Sun Sep & Oct, 9.30am-12.30pm & 2-5pm Tue-Sat, 1.30-5.30pm Sun Nov-Mar). The vast Roman amphitheatre, built around AD 40–50, stands majestically on the hillside and is a key jazz-festival venue.

Gen up on guided walks, festivals, markets and other activities at the **tourist office** (☎ 04 74 53 80 30; www.vienne-tourisme.com, in French; 3 cours Brillier; 9am-noon & 1.30-6pm Mon-Sat, 10am-noon & 2-5pm Sun Sep-Jun, 9am-6pm Mon-Sat, 10am-5pm Sun Jul & Aug).

SLEEPING & EATING

Auberge de Jeunesse (☎ 04 74 53 21 97; mjcvienne.auberge@laposte.net; 11 quai Riondet; dm €9.30, sheets/breakfast €2.80/3.50; reception 5-8pm Mon-Thu mid-Sep–mid-Jun, 5-9pm daily mid-Jun–mid-Sep) Vienne's 54-room riverside hostel is a two-minute strut south of the tourist office. Call ahead to make sure someone is in when you arrive.

Hôtel de la Pyramide (☎ 04 74 53 01 96; www.lapyramide.com, in French; 14 bd Fernand-Point; s/d from €190/200; lunch menus €61, dinner menus €106-161; restaurant Thu-Mon;) Overlooking La Pyramide de la Cirque (a 15.5m-tall obelisk that in Roman times pierced the centre of a hippodrome), this apricot-coloured villa with powder-blue shutters is a four-star haven of peace. French chef Patrick Henriroux creates in the kitchen with lobsters, foie gras, black truffles, scallops and other seasonal gourmet treats.

Run-of-the-mill eating options abound along cours Romestang and cours Brillier.

GETTING THERE & AWAY

Trains link Vienne with Lyon (€5.90, 20 to 32 minutes, at least hourly), Valence (€15.30, one hour, at least hourly) and Valence TGV station (€11.40, 40 minutes, at least hourly).

Towards Valence

The **Parc Naturel Régional du Pilat** spills across 650 sq km southwest of Vienne and offers breathtaking panoramas of the Rhône Valley from its highest peaks, Crêt de l'Œillon (1370m) and Crêt de la Perdrix (1432m). The Montgolfier brothers, inventors of the hot-air balloon in 1783, were born and held their first public *montgolfière* (hot-air balloon) demonstration in **Annonay**, on the park's southeastern boundary.

The north section of the Côtes du Rhône wine-growing area stretches from Vienne south to Valence. Two of its most respected appellations, St Joseph and Hermitage, grow around **Tain l'Hermitage** on the Rhône's left bank.

One or two trains an hour link Tain l'Hermitage with Valence (€3.60, 10 minutes) and Lyon (€12.60, 50 minutes).

Valence

pop 64,900

Several Rhône Valley towns claim to be the gateway to Provence, including Valence, complete with quaint old town and a crunchy, orange rind–flavoured shortbread shaped like a Vatican Swiss guard to commemorate Pope Pius VI's imprisonment and death in Valence in 1799. Fancy a bite? Ask for *un suisse* in any pâtisserie.

Vieux Valence is crowned by the **Cathédrale St-Apollinaire**, a late-11th-century pilgrimage church (thus the ambulatory), largely destroyed in the Wars of Religion and rebuilt in the 17th century. Allegorical sculpted heads adorn **Maison des Têtes** (57 Grande Rue), a blend of Flamboyant Gothic and Renaissance from 1530. The main commercial streets are rue Émile Augier and Grande Rue. Get the full lowdown from the **tourist office** (☎ 04 75 44 90 40; www.tourisme-valence.com; 1 bd Bancel; 9.30am-12.30pm & 1.30-6pm Mon-Fri, until 5pm Sat Sep-May, 9.30am-6.30pm Mon-Fri Jun-Aug) at the train station.

Anne-Sophie Pic (b 1969), the only female chef in France with three Michelin stars, reigns over Valence gastronomy. Her culinary creations form the backbone of upmarket **Hôtel des Senteurs** (☎ 04 75 44 15 32; www.pic-valence.com; 285 av Victor Hugo; d €280-310, ste €400-880, menus €30-150; Feb-Dec), a century-old inn run by her family for four generations and oozing style, alongside a couple of stunning restaurants – the bourgeois **Restaurant Pic** (menus €110 & €195) and more affordable **Le 7** (menus €17 & €28). Real fun for lunch are the 1½ hour hands-on cookery sessions held Tuesday to Friday at Anne-Sophie's latest creation, **Scook** (☎ 04 75 44 14 14; www.scook.fr; 243 av Victor Hugo; half-/full-day course €95/230), a cutting-edge cooking school where food-lovers can learn a couple of tricks of the trade. Lunch sessions (€45) involve cooking two courses, then tucking into them *sur place* (in situ).

From the central train station, Valence-Ville, there are trains to/from Montélimar (€7.70, 23 minutes, five daily), Lyon (€15.30, 1¼ hours, 12 daily), Avignon (€21.40, 1¼ hours, four to six direct daily) and Grenoble (€14.40, 1¼ hours, nine daily). Many stop at Valence TGV Rhône-Alpes Sud station, 10km east.

Gorges de l'Ardèche

The serpentine River Ardèche slithers past towering cliffs of mauve, yellow and grey limestone, dotted with vegetation typical of the Midi-Pyrénées, as it makes its way from near **Vallon Pont d'Arc** to **St-Martin de l'Ardèche**, a few kilometres west of the Rhône. Eagles nest in the cliffs and there are numerous caves to explore. One of the area's most famous features is the **Pont d'Arc**, a natural stone bridge created by the river's torrents.

About 300m above the waters (which can be canoed) of the gorge is the **Haute Corniche** (D290), which affords a magnificent series of *belvédères* (panoramic viewpoints). It turns into a huge and chaotic traffic jam in summer. On the plateaux above the gorges, typical Midi villages (eg St-Remèze) are surrounded by garrigue, lavender fields and vineyards.

From Vallon Pont d'Arc, the scenic D579 takes cyclists and motorists northwest to **Ruoms**; across the river, the D4 snakes wildly along the **Défilé de Ruoms** (a narrow tunnel of rock) and the **Gorges de la Ligne** for 8km. From Bellevue, head north for 2km on the D104 to Uzer, then east on the D294 to pretty village **Balazuc**.

From Balazuc the D579 leads northwards to **Aubenas**, from where a multitude of scenic roads fan into the surrounding countryside. This is chestnut land, where the dark-brown

AN ARCHITECTURAL PILGRIMAGE

It is only for hardened fans of architecture, 'it' being a far-from-pretty futuristic concrete priory. But with the signature of modern-architecture icon Le Corbusier (for more, see p65) behind it, stark **Couvent Ste-Marie de la Tourette** (☎ 04 74 26 79 70; www.couventlatourette.com; adult/12-18yr/under 12yr €8/6/free; guided tours 10.30am, 3pm & 5pm Mon-Sat, 3pm & 5pm Sun Jul & Aug, 2.30pm Mon-Fri, 10.30am, 2.30pm & 4pm Sat, 2.30pm & 4pm Sun Sep & Oct, 3.30pm daily Nov-Mar), 30km west of Lyon in La Tourette, lures a prestigious set into its lair. Inhabited by white-robed Dominican monks, the working monastery can be visited by one-hour guided tour.

From Lyon's Gare de Perrache (10 daily) and Gare St-Paul (20 daily) in Vieux Lyon, trains go to L'Arbresle (€6.80, 45 minutes), 2km north of La Tourette, from where you can call ☎ 04 74 26 90 19 for a taxi or walk (around 25 minutes). By car, follow the westbound N7 or more scenic D7 from Lyon.

AS NUTTY AS NOUGAT

There is just one sweet reason to stop in Montélimar – nougat.

Produced in the otherwise ordinary town, 46km south of Valence, since the 17th century, *nougat de Montélimar* took off after WWII when holidaying motorists on their way to the French Riviera stopped off in the Rhône-side town to buy the sweeter-than-sweet treat to munch en route.

Traditional Montélimar nougat consists of at least 28% almonds, 25% lavender honey, 2% pistachio nuts, sugar, egg white and vanilla. Nougat varies in texture (more or less tender), honey taste (more or less strong) and crispness of the nuts. Some nougats are coated in chocolate and others have fruit (try the one with figs), but traditional Montélimar nougat is quite simply off-white.

A dozen nougat producers offer free tours of their factories; pick a small (rather than an industrial) confectioner, such as Le Gavial or Le Chaudron d'Or. The **tourist office** (☎ 04 75 01 00 20; www.montelimar-tourisme.com; allées Provençales; 🕑 9am-12.15pm & 2-5.30pm Mon-Sat) has details.

Montélimar is on the train line linking Valence-Ville (€7.70, 20 minutes, five daily) with Avignon-Centre (€12.30, 50 minutes, hourly).

fruit is turned into everything from *crème de châtaigne* (a sweet purée served with ice cream, crêpes or cake) to *bière aux marrons* (chestnut beer) and *liqueur de châtaigne*, a 21% alcohol-by-volume liqueur which makes a sweet aperitif when mixed with white wine. Buy a bottle at the **Palais du Marron** (☎ 04 75 64 35 16; 10 cours de l'Esplanade) in **Privas**.

WHITE-WATER SPORTS

Bomb down the Ardèche in a canoe or kayak at the **Base Nautique du Pont d'Arc** (☎ 04 75 37 17 79; www.canoe-ardeche.com; rte des Gorges de l'Ardèche; 🕑 Apr-Nov) in Vallon Pont d'Arc. A half-day descent (8km) costs €13/9 per adult/seven- to 12-year-old; longer one-day trips up the river are also possible.

French Alps & the Jura

Mont Blanc, Grandes Jorasses and Barre des Écrins for mountaineers. Val d'Isère, Chamonix and Les Trois Vallées for adrenalin junkies. Vanoise, Vercors and Jura for great-outdoors fans. So many mythical names, so many expectations, and not a hint of flagging: the Alps' pulling power has never been so strong.

Their magnetic beauty has played no small part in their soaring popularity: people will take four-hour bus trips from the airport, pay an arm and a leg for a lift pass and give up creature comforts for a piece of Alpine wonder. The summit bug is incurable and terribly infectious.

What is so enticing about the Alps and the Jura is their almost beguiling range of qualities: under Mont Blanc's 4810m of raw wilderness lies the most spectacular outdoor playground for activities ranging from skiing to canyoning, but also a vast historical and architectural heritage, a unique place in French cuisine (cheese, more cheese!), and some very happening cities boasting world-class art. So much for the old cliché that you can't have it all.

Celebrity chefs and DJs ride the popularity wave and compete for the best spots, resorts outbid each other in outlandish activities, and spa-chalet hotels rival in obscene luxuries. Get away from the mad, trendy circus deep inside the national parks or the Jura forests.

Summer too provides some respite, a wild-flower infusion of walking, wildlife-spotting and lake swimming. Life on a farm slows the clock and that's where you realise what this is all about: life that little bit closer to nature.

HIGHLIGHTS

- Go mountaineering or head down the mythical Vallée Blanche in **Chamonix** (p532) before a drink or three at the town's **bars** (p537)
- Swim in beautiful Lac d'Annecy before strolling in its chic lakeside namesake, **Annecy** (p541)
- Experience life (not to mention a feast of a dinner) on a **Jurassien farm** (p574)
- **Trek** in one of the Alps' two national parks and four regional parks (p524)
- Go green and learn the ropes of eco-living and eating at **La Juliane** (p569)
- Make sure you enjoy one of the Alps' supreme cheese **raclettes** or **fondues** (p551)

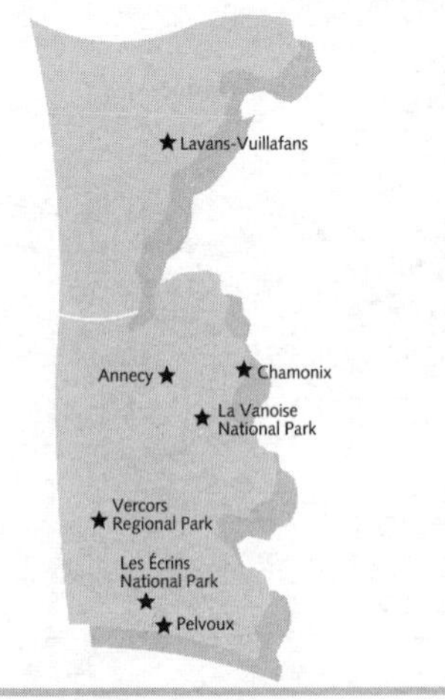

- POPULATION: 3,313,000
- AREA: 210,000 SQ KM

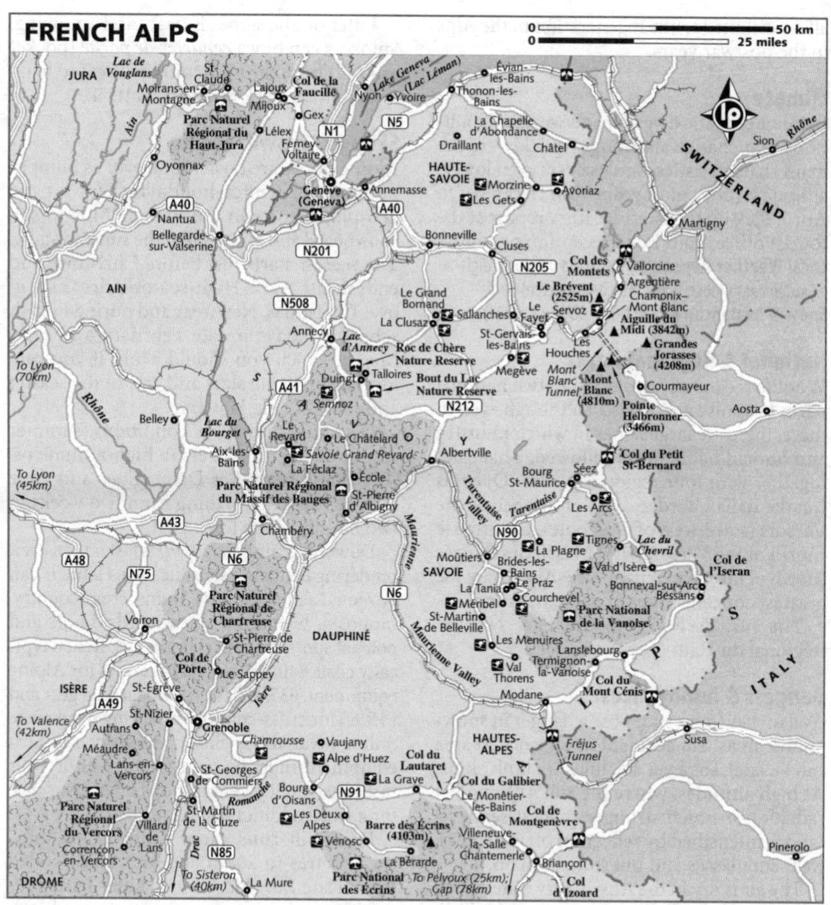

History

Migrant tribes of Celtic, Gaulish and Teutonic origin arrived in the Alps first, and by the time of Christ, permanent communities were well established, especially around the lakes of Geneva, Bourget and Annecy, and the Tarentaise and Maurienne Valleys.

During the Roman conquest the Alps were a strategic stronghold, falling under Roman control during Augustus' reign. The Frankish kings of the Merovingian and Carolingian empires laid the foundations for the modern Alps with their distinctive dialects, traditions and cultures.

The 13th and 14th centuries saw the feudal houses of Savoy, the Dauphiné and Provence fiercely contesting the Alps. The ensuing centuries were marked by successive wars and occupations, with each side swapping and reoccupying territories. This cycle ended with the union of Savoy with France in 1860. Savoy was split into two *départements,* Savoie (73) and Haute-Savoie (74).

The Industrial Revolution bombarded the region with heavy industry. The first holidaymakers made their way to the area around Chamonix and Mont Blanc in the late 19th century.

German and Italian forces occupied the Alps during WWII, while the mountains became one of the main strongholds for the French resistance. Modern industry, the development of hydroelectric energy, huge urban development and large-scale tourism all contributed to the regeneration of the Alps in the postwar years.

Climate

Extreme climatic diversity and weather conditions that change alarmingly quickly are the main characteristics. Snow covers even lower-altitude stations most years from December to April. Pick up the latest weather report at the tourist office, your hotel reception or call:

Local Weather Report (☎ 08 36 68 02 plus 2-digit *département* number; www.meteofrance.com)
Snow & Avalanche Report (☎ 08 36 68 10 20)

National & Regional Parks

Wildlife is carefully protected in two national parks (Vanoise and Écrins), although even in these, there are large zones in which industry and human habitation is allowed. That said, together with four regional parks – Queyras (on the Italian border south of Briançon), the Vercors (southwest of Grenoble), Chartreuse (north of the Vercors) and Massif des Bauges (north of the Chartreuse) – the Alps enjoy the greatest concentration of parks in France.

The Jura is home to the Parc Naturel Régional du Haut-Jura.

Dangers & Annoyances

Avalanches (opposite) pose a danger in snowbound areas. An accident in an isolated area can be fatal, so never ski, hike or climb alone. At high altitudes, where the sun's ultraviolet radiation is much stronger than at sea level (and is intensified by reflection off the snow), wear sunglasses and put sunscreen on.

The air is dry in the Alps. Carry water when hiking, and drink more than you would at lower altitudes. Always bring extra layers too: the weather can turn very suddenly, and be aware of the possibility of hypothermia after a long climb or a sudden storm, as you'll cool off quickly while enjoying the cold, windy panorama.

Litter on the slopes is nasty and annoying. Smokers can buy a *cendrier de poche* (pocket ashtray) from the local tourist offices to hang around their neck and stick butts in.

Skiing & Snowboarding

Alpine slopes are busier than ever as bumper numbers of winter holidaymakers hit the 200-plus resorts in the French Alps to ski, snowboard and après-ski in the sun and snow. The season starts just before Christmas and ends in late April. High-season prices kick in over Christmas, New Year and during French school holidays in late February and early March, which you should avoid if you can; low season is the start and end of the season and most of cold January.

Dependent on snow conditions, summer Alpine skiing on glaciers in high-altitude resorts Val d'Isère, Les Deux Alpes and Alpe d'Huez runs for anything from two weeks to two months, June to August.

Downhill skiing *(ski alpin)* is faster then ever, rendering helmets a sensible idea. Helmets can be rented alongside skis (Alpine, cross-country, monoski, telemark), snowboards, boots and poles at sport shops in every resort. Rental typically costs €40/170 per day/six days for Alpine equipment, €35/150 for snowboarding gear and €15/65 for cross-country; reserving in advance online invariably yields a 15% discount. Lost equipment must be paid for by you or your insurance policy; rental shops offer insurance for a small additional charge.

Downhill runs range from a few hundred metres to 20km and are colour-coded to indicate how kid-easy or killer-hard they are: green (beginners), blue (intermediate), red (advanced) and black (very advanced). Summer glacial skiing is on short greens or blues. Snowboarders are brilliantly catered for in larger resorts with a riot of snowparks kitted out with half-pipes, quarter-pipes, shape kickers, gaps and ramps. Long, rambling

TOP SURFS

ANENA (www.anena.org, in French) Get to the bottom of what makes an avalanche with the in-depth studies of the National French Association for the Study of Snow & Avalanches.

Natives (www.natives.co.uk) Perfect to find that dream season job in Méribel or Les Deux Alpes.

pistehors.com (http://pistehors.com) Essential surfing for anyone heading off-piste.

Planet Subzero (www.planetsubzero.com) Book seasonal and long-term accommodation online.

Ski France International (http://ski-resort-france.co.uk) Excellent website to prepare your holiday in the Alps, winter or summer, with detailed resort guides, maps, snow reports and more.

AVALANCHE AWARENESS

People die from avalanches every year. We can't repeat it enough. Casualties peaked at an all-time high in 2005–06, with 55 deaths. Figures have since levelled, with 20 deaths and fewer avalanche incidents in 2007–08. Whether it is due to increased awareness or better climatic conditions for the last couple of seasons (or a combination of both) is hard to say.

Ski resorts announce the daily avalanche risk through signs and coloured flags outside ticket kiosks, at the base of ski lifts and dotted around the resort and slopes. Yellow means 'low risk', black-and-yellow checks stand for 'heightened risk' and black is 'severe risk'. Ignoring an avalanche warning can be the death of you. Once buried beneath snow, you have no more than 15 minutes to get out.

Off-piste *(hors piste)* skiers should never leave home without an avalanche pole, ARVA transceiver, a shovel – and, most importantly, a professional local mountain guide. Staying firmly *on* piste is safer still.

Essential surfing for snow adventurers is **pistehors.com** (http://pistehors.com), an excellent English-language website devoted to French off-piste and snowboarding news. **Henry's Avalanche Talk** (☎ 04 79 06 16 58; www.henrysavalanchetalk.com), among other things, translates the daily avalanche forecast issued by Méteo France into English during the ski season and runs links to other useful avalanche-related sites. Val d'Isère–based Henry also runs mountain-safety and avalanche-awareness clinics – something more and more resorts are doing in a bid to, bluntly put, save lives. Most are free.

The French courts have adopted a zero-tolerance policy towards irresponsible skiers and boarders who trigger avalanches.

cross-country *(ski de fond)* trails are at their most scenic in the Jura.

France's leading ski school, the **École de Ski Français** (ESF; www.esf.net) – its instructors wear red – teaches snowboarding and skiing. It has a branch in every resort and touts competitive rates against the crop of smaller private schools it competes against; lessons typically cost €40/50 per hour for two/four people and €30 per person for a two-hour group lesson. Kids can start learning from the age of four; from the age of three, nappyless tots can lark about in the *jardin de neige* (snow garden).

LIFT PASSES

You must buy a lift pass *(forfait)* to ride the various *remontées mécaniques* – drag lifts or buttons *(téléskis)*, chairlifts for two to eight people *(télésièges)*, gondolas *(télécabines)*, cable cars *(téléphériques)* and funicular railways *(funiculaires)*.

Passes – a big chunk out of your budget, €200 or thereabouts for a week in big resorts – give access to one or more ski sectors. They can be valid for a half or full day or as many days as you want, and rarely require a passport photo. Any self-respecting lift pass is 'hands-free' – like a credit card with a built-in chip that barriers detect automatically – and can be bought and recharged online. One-way and return tickets are available on chairlifts and cable cars for walkers.

Children aged under five ski for free but still need a pass; bring along a passport as proof of age. Many places offer the same deal to veterans aged 75 or more.

Cheaper passes – usually around €6 a day – are also needed for cross-country ski trails, although passes are rarely checked.

INSURANCE

When buying your lift pass, think about insurance – a vital necessity. If you're hurt on the slopes, all the services that come to your aid – the helicopter, the guy who skis you and your stretcher down the mountain, the doctor who treats you – charge *a lot* of money (we're talking up to €2000 here).

Most packages include insurance or you might have the **Carte Neige** (www.ffs.fr/site/carteneige, in French), an annual policy that covers mountain-rescue costs and medical treatment. It costs €35 to €42 per year (€30 for cross-country skiing only), depending on the level of cover you choose and where you buy it. Resorts sell it (usually through the ESF, left) and it's sold online.

If you are not insured, buy **Carré Neige** (www.carreneige.com) with your lift pass. Every resort offers the daily insurance scheme – effectively

RESORT RECCE

Resort	Profile	Elevation	Alpine Runs
Chamonix-Mont-Blanc	Good off-piste but too much transport; trendy & full of fun	1037m	182km
St-Gervais & Megève	Pricey & a bit snobby	810m & 1113m	445km
Les Portes du Soleil	12 connected resorts luring families	1000-1800m	650km
Morzine-Les Gets	Busiest & biggest resort in Portes du Soleil	1000m	110km
Avoriaz	Chic 1960s Portes du Soleil village-resort	1800m	80km
La Clusaz	Cheaper spot; ski for the day from Annecy	1100m	128km
Le Grand Bornand	Day trip from Annecy, hot locally	1000m	90km
Savoie Grand Révard	Day trip from Chambéry; cheap, local & big on cross-country	1100m	50km
Les Trois Vallées	Hot, trendy, vast & fast ski area	2000m	600km
Méribel	Heavy traffic & Brit-packed bars in Les Trois Vallées	1450m	150km
Courchevel	Superchic 'Three Valleys' skiing	1550, 1650m & 1850m	150km
Val Thorens	Europe's highest; third of the 'Three Valleys' trio	2300m	140km
St-Martin de Belleville	Authentic, picture-postcard Savoyard village linked to Les Trois Vallées	1450m	160km
Val d'Isère	Unrivalled winter/summer skiing & boarding; buzzy nightlife	1850m	300km
Tignes	Ruthlessly modern (ugly); summer skiing & glacial snowpark for boarders	2100m	300km
Chamrousse	Weekend skiing from Grenoble	1700m	92km
Les Deux Alpes	Snowboarders' delight; summer ski & board	1660m	225km
Alpe d'Huez	Snowboarding park; Europe's longest black run; summer skiing	1860m	245km
Serre-Chevalier	Door-to-door skiing from 13 resorts; best sunshine	1200m	250km
Métabief Mont d'Or	Predominantly cross-country in the Jura	1000m	40km
Les Rousses	Predominantly cross-country; ideal for French & Swiss day trippers	1100m	50km

a daily version of *Carte Neige* – that covers mountain rescue, transport and medical costs and costs €2.50 a day.

Getting There & Away

On a clear day the view through the plane window is the best introduction to the Alps you could dream of: chances are you're landing at **Lyon St-Exupéry airport** (p515; www.lyon.aeroport.fr), 25km east of Lyon; or **Geneva Airport** (Aéroport International de Genève; www.gva.ch) in neighbouring Switzerland.

From both airports there are buses to numerous ski resorts with Geneva's **Aeroski-Bus** (☎ +41 22 798 20 00; www.alpski-bus.com) and Lyon's **Satobus-Alpes** (☎ from abroad 04 79 68 32 96, ☎ within France 08 20 32 03 68; www.satobus-alps.com); fares and frequencies are listed in this chapter under Getting There & Away in resort sections.

Traffic on steeply climbing, winding mountain roads leading to resorts can be hellish, especially on Friday and Saturday. After heavy snowfalls, you may need snow chains. Winter tyres (automatically provided with most hire cars picked up at Lyon and Geneva airports) are a good idea. The Fréjus and Mont Blanc road tunnels connect the French Alps with Italy, as do several mountain passes. Road signs indicate if passes are blocked.

Eurostar ski trains (see p965) provide a more environment-friendly alternative between London and Moûtiers or Bourg St-Maurice. Within France, train services to the Alps are excellent.

SAVOY

'The Alps par excellence' could be the strap line of this northern half of the French Alps. Glaciers and lakes, mineral deserts and dense Alpine forests, magnificent land-

Cross-Country Trails	Difficulty	Lifts	One-/Six-Day Lift Pass
36km	Intermediate, advanced, serious off-piste	47	€47/225
75km	Beginners, intermediate	108	€34.50/166
214km	All abilities	209	€39/200
69km	All abilities	48	€28.20/141.50
45km	All abilities, super kid-friendly	36	€32/na
86km	Beginners, intermediate	45	€28.50/149.50
60km	Beginners, intermediate	31	€26.50/121.80
140km	Beginner, intermediate	16	€15.20/na
130km	All levels, advanced	200	€44/220
33km	All abilities, kid-friendly	57	€37/178
66km	All abilities, advanced	62	€37/178
0km	All abilities	26	€36.50/172
28km	All abilities	36	€35.50/172
44km	Intermediate, advanced, off-piste	89	€42/202.50
44km	Intermediate, advanced, off-piste	89	€42/202.50
44km	Beginner, intermediate	23	€26.50/139
15km	Intermediate, advanced	51	€36.40/172
50km	All abilities	87	€38.20/198.50
35km	All abilities, off-piste	66	€38/181
200km		20	€19/100.50
220km		40	€19.80/103.40

scapes and everlasting snow, this is what would qualify as proper mountains in most people's books.

Flanked by Switzerland and Italy, Savoy (Savoie, pronounced sav·wa) rises from the southern shores of Lake Geneva, Europe's largest Alpine lake, and culminates at the roof of Europe, Mont Blanc's mighty 4810m. In between is a collection of adrenalin-pumped ski resorts such as Chamonix and party-central Val d'Isère, as well as some lesser-known nonskiing gems starting with the historical château towns Annecy and Chambéry to the southwest.

As well as skiing, Savoy is big for…sailing. Glacial lakes from Lake Geneva in the north to Lac d'Annecy and France's biggest natural lake Lac du Bourget in the south make for great nautical playgrounds.

Rural life, unchanged for centuries, strikes in the region's most remote realms like the Bauges massif (so little known it is often mistaken for the northeastern Vosges region), and the wild Parc National de la Vanoise.

CHAMONIX

pop 9086 / elevation 1037m

Cliché as it sounds, Chamonix is the mecca of mountaineering, its birthplace, its flag-bearer, its heart and soul. Its surrounding landscapes have enthralled and inspired countless adventurers and other thrill-seekers. Even James Bond thought it worthy of one of his adrenalin shots: that spectacular stunt-riddled ski chase by 007 in *The World Is Not Enough* (1999) was filmed in Chamonix.

Chamonix retains a hard-core mountain image for most French people, but over the last decade, young Brits have brushed off any preconceived ideas and gradually adopted Chamonix as their favourite winter party place (even stag dos have started coming). It does mean there is growing discontent among some locals that bar staff don't speak French, but the upshot is that if you want good après-ski, you're in for a treat.

More diplomatic Chamoniards say that it's only fair: Chamonix after all was 'discovered' by Brits William Windham and Richard Pococke in 1741, and much of the early tourism in Chamonix was British. The town's popularity grew and reached consecration in 1924 with the organisation of the first Winter Olympics.

To this day, fun is indeed on an Olympic scale in Chamonix: there are more winter and summer activities than you'll be able to fit in your holiday and, French–English rivalry aside, 250 years on, the wow factor is still there.

Orientation

Chamonix town runs along the banks of the River Arve for about 2km, wedged in a valley between the Mont Blanc massif (east) and the Aiguilles Rouges massif (west) with 2525m-high Le Brévent as its peak.

Sports and souvenir shops, restaurants, cafés and bars line the main street, pedestrianised rue du Docteur Paccard and its continuation, rue Joseph Vallot. Cross the river to reach the bus and train stations and the happening Chamonix Sud quarter where hip bars and clubs cluster around the foot of the Aiguille du Midi cable car (p530).

Chamonix' most exceptional downhill skiing is in Les Grands Montets (1235m to 3300m), a ski area accessible from Argentière, 9km north of Chamonix; shuttle buses (p538) link the two.

Information

BOOKSHOPS

Maison de la Presse (☎ 04 50 53 29 76; 93 rue du Docteur Paccard; ⏲ 9am-7pm Mon-Sat, 9am-12.30pm & 3-7pm Sun) Huge selection of books, maps, topoguides and the press in six languages.

Photo Alpine Tairraz (☎ 04 50 53 14 23; 162 av Michel Croz) Skiing and walking guides, maps, mountaineering books and local guidebooks.

EMERGENCY

PGHM (Peloton de Gendarmerie de Haute-Montagne; ☎ 04 50 53 16 89; 69 rue de la Mollard) Mountain-rescue service for the entire Mont Blanc area.

Police Station (☎ 04 50 53 00 55; 111 rue de la Mollard)

> **SOS**
>
> If you need help getting off the mountain, the Gendarmerie de Montagne is the emergency service to SOS. Comprising 15 Pelotons de Gendarmerie de Haute-Montagne (PGHM) and five Pelotons de Gendarmerie de Montagne (PGM) countrywide, these highly skilled mountain-rescue specialists are based in key towns and stations in the French Alps:
>
> **Annecy** (☎ 04 50 09 47 47; 33 av Plaine)
> **Bourg St-Maurice** (☎ 04 79 07 01 10; 945 av Maréchal Leclerc)
> **Briançon** (☎ 04 92 22 22 22; 37 rue Pasteur)
> **Chamonix** (☎ 04 50 53 16 89; 69 rue de la Mollard)
>
> When an emergency strikes, if you don't know which number to call, don't waste time looking for it; simply call ☎ 17.

INTERNET ACCESS

Surf for free on your own laptop in the wi-fi-savvy tourist office (p530). Mojo's (p536) also has six computers for use (per minute/two hours €0.10/10) as does Camp de Base (p537).

Shop 74 (☎ 04 50 90 73 17; impasse du Bartavel; per hr €6; ⏲ 10am-8pm)

INTERNET RESOURCES

www.chamonix.com Tourist office website.

www.chamonix.net Independent companion site; advice on accommodation, entertainment and nightlife.

www.compagniedumontblanc.com Buy ski passes online, get weather forecasts and snow conditions, download piste maps and ski-area opening hours.

LAUNDRY

Laverie Automatique (174 av de l'Aiguille du Midi; 7/16kg wash €5.50/10; ⏲ 8am-10pm)

MEDICAL SERVICES

The tourist office (p530) has a list of doctors, dentists, pharmacists, physiotherapists etc.

Duty Dentist (☎ 04 50 66 17 19)

Duty Doctor (☎ 15)

Hospital (Centre Hospitalier; ☎ 04 50 53 84 00; 509 rte des Pélerins) In Les Favrands, 2km south of Chamonix centre.

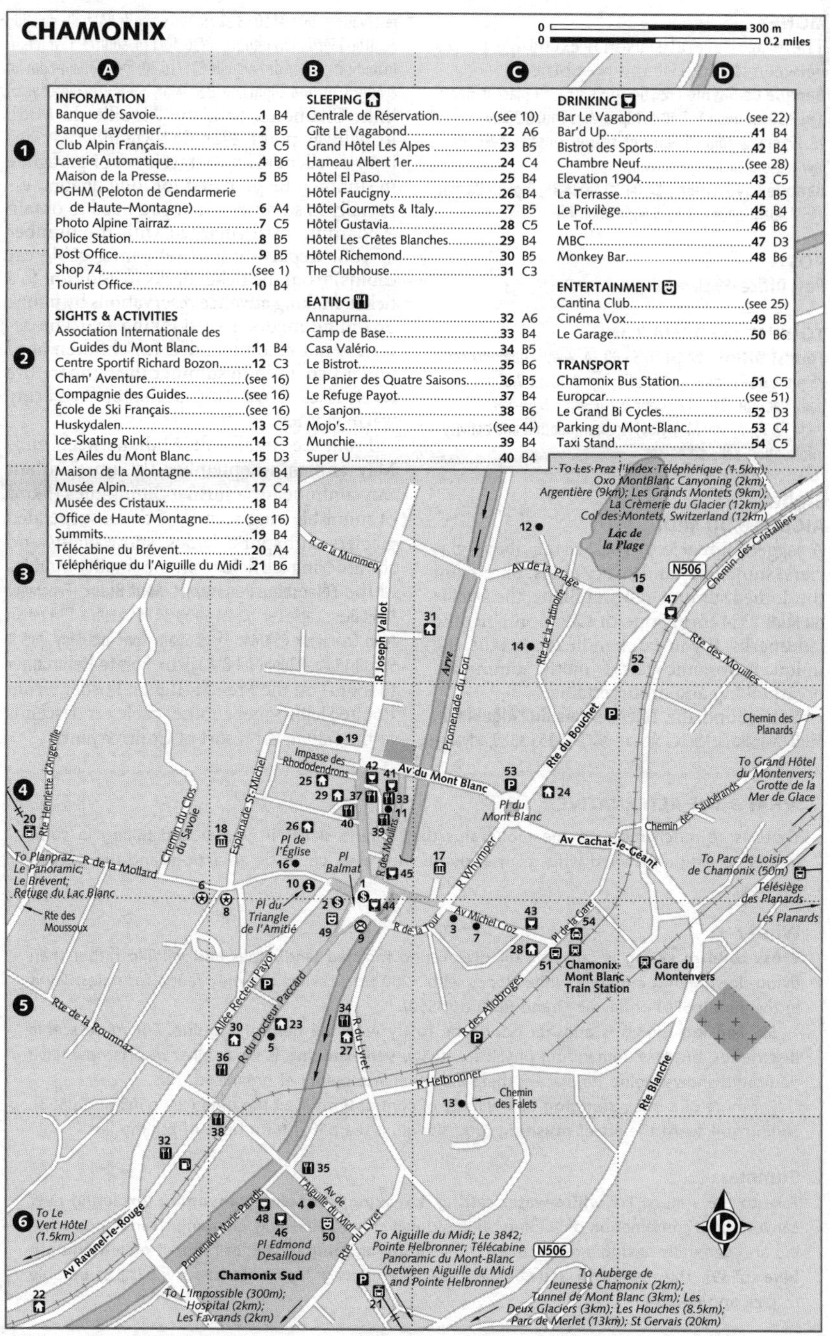
CHAMONIX
0 300 m
0 0.2 miles
A
B
C
D
1
2
3
4
5
6
INFORMATION
Banque de Savoie....1 B4
Banque Laydernier....2 B5
Club Alpin Français....3 C5
Laverie Automatique....4 B6
Maison de la Presse....5 B5
PGHM (Peloton de Gendarmerie de Haute–Montagne)....6 A4
Photo Alpine Tairraz....7 C5
Police Station....8 B5
Post Office....9 B5
Shop 74....(see 1)
Tourist Office....10 B4
SIGHTS & ACTIVITIES
Association Internationale des Guides du Mont Blanc....11 B4
Centre Sportif Richard Bozon....12 C3
Cham' Aventure....(see 16)
Compagnie des Guides....(see 16)
École de Ski Français....(see 16)
Huskydalen....13 C5
Ice-Skating Rink....14 C3
Les Ailes du Mont Blanc....15 D3
Maison de la Montagne....16 B4
Musée Alpin....17 C4
Musée des Cristaux....18 B4
Office de Haute Montagne....(see 16)
Summits....19 B4
Télécabine du Brévent....20 A4
Téléphérique du l'Aiguille du Midi....21 B6
SLEEPING
Centrale de Réservation....(see 10)
Gîte Le Vagabond....22 A6
Grand Hôtel Les Alpes....23 B5
Hameau Albert 1er....24 C4
Hôtel El Paso....25 B4
Hôtel Faucigny....26 B4
Hôtel Gourmets & Italy....27 B5
Hôtel Gustavia....28 C5
Hôtel Les Crêtes Blanches....29 B4
Hôtel Richemond....30 B5
The Clubhouse....31 C3
EATING
Annapurna....32 A6
Camp de Base....33 B4
Casa Valério....34 B5
Le Bistrot....35 B6
Le Panier des Quatre Saisons....36 B5
Le Refuge Payot....37 B4
Le Sanjon....38 B6
Mojo's....(see 44)
Munchie....39 B4
Super U....40 B4
DRINKING
Bar Le Vagabond....(see 22)
Bar'd Up....41 B4
Bistrot des Sports....42 B4
Chambre Neuf....(see 28)
Elevation 1904....43 C5
La Terrasse....44 B5
Le Privilège....45 B4
Le Tof....46 B6
MBC....47 D3
Monkey Bar....48 B6
ENTERTAINMENT
Cantina Club....(see 25)
Cinéma Vox....49 B5
Le Garage....50 B6
TRANSPORT
Chamonix Bus Station....51 C5
Europcar....(see 51)
Le Grand Bi Cycles....52 D3
Parking du Mont-Blanc....53 C4
Taxi Stand....54 C5
To Les Praz l'Index Téléphérique (1.5km); Oxo MontBlanc Canyoning (2km); Argentière (9km); Les Grands Montets (9km); La Crèmerie du Glacier (12km); Col des Montets, Switzerland (12km)
Lac de la Plage
N506
Chemin des Cristalliers
Av de la Plage
R de la Mummery
R Joseph Vallot
Arve
Promenade du Fori
Rte de la Patinoire
Rte des Mouilles
Rte du Bouchet
Chemin des Planards
To Grand Hôtel du Montenvers; Grotte de la Mer de Glace
Impasse des Rhododendrons
Av du Mont Blanc
Pl du Mont Blanc
Chemin des Saubérands
Av Cachat-le-Géant
To Parc de Loisirs de Chamonix (50m)
Télésiège des Planards
Les Planards
Rte Henriette d'Angeville
Chemin du Clos du Savoie
Esplanade St-Michel
Pl de l'Église
Pl Balmat
R des Moulins
R Whymper
To Planpraz; Le Panoramic; Le Brévent; Refuge du Lac Blanc
R de la Mollard
Rte des Moussoux
Pl du Triangle de l'Amitié
R de la Tour
Av Michel Croz
Pl de la Gare
Chamonix-Mont Blanc Train Station
Gare du Montenvers
Allée Recteur Payot
R du Docteur Paccard
Rte de la Roumnaz
R des Allobroges
R du Lyret
R Helbronner
Chemin des Falets
Rte Blanche
To Le Vert Hôtel (1.5km)
Av Ravanel-le-Rouge
Promenade Marie Paradis
Av de l'Aiguille du Midi
Pl Edmond Desailloud
Rte du Lyret
Chamonix Sud
To Aiguille du Midi; Le 3842; Pointe Helbronner; Télécabine Panoramic du Mont-Blanc (between Aiguille du Midi and Pointe Helbronner)
To Auberge de Jeunesse Chamonix (2km); Tunnel de Mont Blanc (3km); Les Deux Glaciers (3km); Les Houches (8.5km); Parc de Merlet (13km); St Gervais (20km)
To L'Impossible (300m); Hospital (2km); Les Favrands (2km)

MONEY

There are several seasonal exchange places between the tourist and post offices.

Banque de Savoie (☎ 04 50 53 30 25; 1 place Balmat; 🕑 8.30am-noon & 1.40-5.30pm Mon-Thu, 8.30am-12.30pm & 2-7pm Fri-Sun high season, closed weekends low season) Exchange bureau.

Banque Laydernier (☎ 04 50 53 26 39; 2 place Balmat, 🕑 8.40am-noon & 1.45-5.50pm Mon-Fri)

POST

Post Office (89 place Balmat)

TOURIST INFORMATION

Tourist Office (☎ 04 50 53 00 24; www.chamonix.com; 85 place du Triangle de l'Amitié; 🕑 8.30am-7.30pm daily Dec-Apr, 9am-12.30pm & 2-6.30pm Mon-Sat, 9am-12.30pm Sun May-Nov) Accommodation and activity information, sells ski passes.

Sights

AIGUILLE DU MIDI

A jagged pinnacle of rock rising above glaciers, snowfields and rocky crags, 8km from the domed summit of Mont Blanc, the **Aiguille du Midi** (3842m) is one of Chamonix' iconic landmarks. If you can handle the height, the unique panoramic views from the summit are breathtaking and unforgettable.

Year-round the **Téléphérique du l'Aiguille du Midi** (Aiguille du Midi Cable Car; ☎ 04 50 53 30 80, advance reservations 24hr 04 50 53 22 75; 100 place de l'Aiguille du Midi; adult/4-15yr/family return €38/30.40/114, adult/4-15yr return to midstation Plan de l'Aiguille €21/16.80; 🕑 6.30am-6pm Jul & Aug, 8.30am-4.30pm late-Dec–Mar, hours vary rest of year) links Chamonix with the Aiguille du Midi; its halfway point, Plan de l'Aiguille (2317m) is an excellent place to start hikes or paraglide in summer. Be prepared for long queues, especially in summer when you need to obtain a boarding card (marked with the number of your departing *and* returning cable-car cabins) from the ticket desks in addition to a ticket. Making advance reservations by phone or online incurs a €2 booking fee. The ascent is not recommended for children aged under two. Even in summer the temperature rarely rises above -10°C at the top – so bring warm clothes!

From the Aiguille du Midi, between mid-May and mid-September the unrepentant can continue for a further 30 minutes (5km) of mind-blowing scenery – think suspended glaciers and spurs, seracs, snow plains and shimmering ice fields – in the smaller bubbles of the **Télécabine Panoramic Mont Blanc** (Panoramic Mont Blanc Cable Car ☎ 04 50 53 30 80; adult/4-15yr return from Chamonix €54/44; 🕑 8.50am-4pm mid-May–Jun & Sep, 8.15am-4.30pm Jul & Aug) to **Pointe Helbronner** (3466m) on the French–Italian border. From Pointe Helbronner another cable car descends to the Italian ski resort of Courmayeur.

WHAT'S THE ALTERNATIVE?

There is so much more to the mountains than Alpine skiing in winter and hiking in summer. So we thought we'd whet your appetite with what could be an action- and fun-packed holiday.

Winter

Cross-country skiing is fantastic for discovering forested landscapes and wildlife rather than flying downhill on infinitely white slopes with 5000 other skiers the only fauna for miles. Try it in the Jura (p579) or Savoie Grand Révard (p550).

Ski touring (p533) is another good one to try with the help of a guide. For more scenic discoveries, but less demanding physical activity, **snowshoeing** is ideal. Most resorts now have dedicated snowshoeing itineraries; there are otherwise plenty of organised trips.

For more of a buzz, **sledging** on a variety of contraptions is all the rage (see p563 and p553). Sliding still, learn the art of **mushing** (dog sledging, see p552) for a taste of Eskimo life.

Summer

Take to the waters! Try **white-water rafting**, **kayaking**, **canoeing**, **canyoning** (exploring river canyons by a combination of wading, sliding down chutes, abseiling, climbing, swimming, jumping and generally having a great time). Or fly: go **paragliding** (p534); or bomb it on a **mountain bike** (p539). These summer activities are available in *every* Alpine resort so you'll just be able to pick and choose.

ADVENTURE KNOW-HOW

These guides have it. So go, create your own adventure:

Association International des Guides du Mont Blanc (☎ 04 50 53 27 05; www.guides-du-montblanc.com; 98 rue des Moulins) Chamonix-based international guides; extreme skiing, mountaineering, glacier trekking, ice and rock climbing, and paragliding.

Aventure en Tête (☎ 04 50 54 05 11; www.aventureentete.com; 620 rte du Plagnolet, Argentière) Ski touring and ski-alpinism expeditions, heli-skiing/boarding, free ride and off-piste security courses; mountaineering and climbing in summer.

Chamonix Experience (☎ 04 50 54 09 36; www.chamex.com; 141 rue Charlet Straton, Argentière) Courses in off-piste skiing, avalanche awareness, heli-skiing, ice climbing and ski touring; in summer, rock and alpine climbing.

Compagnie des Guides (☎ 04 50 53 00 88; www.chamonix-guides.com; 190 place de l'Église) Crème de la crème of mountain guides, founded in 1821 and the oldest organisation of its kind in the world. Guides for skiing, mountaineering, snowshoeing, ice climbing, hiking, mountain biking and every other Alpine pastime.

LE BRÉVENT

The highest peak on the western side of the valley, **Le Brévent** (2525m) has fabulous views of the Mont Blanc massif and a multitude of hiking trails, ledges to paraglide from and a summit restaurant (p536).

Reach it with the **Télécabine du Brévent** (☎ 04 50 53 13 18; 29 rte Henriette d'Angeville; Chamonix-Brévent adult/4-15yr/family return €22/17.40/66, Chamonix-Planpraz adult/4-15yr return €12/9.60; 8am-5.45pm Jun-Aug, 8.45am-4.45pm mid-Dec–Apr), from the end of rue de la Mollard to midstation **Planpraz** (2000m), then continuing on another cable car to the top.

MER DE GLACE

The **Mer de Glace** (Sea of Ice), the second-largest glacier in the Alps, is 14km long, 1800m wide and up to 400m deep. During a visit to Chamonix in 1741, Englishman William Windham was the first foreigner to set eyes on the glacier, which he described as 'a sort of agitated sea that seemed suddenly to have become frozen' (hence the name). The glacier moves 45m a year at the edges, and up to 90m a year in the centre, and has become a popular tourist attraction thanks to the rack-and-pinion railway line built between 1897 and 1908.

Since 1946, the **Grotte de la Mer de Glace** (late Dec–Apr & mid–Jun-Sep) – an ice cave – has been carved every spring. The interior temperature is between -2°C and -5°C. Look down the slope for last year's cave to see how far the glacier has moved. Be prepared to climb 100 or so steps to access the cave.

A quaint red mountain train links **Gare du Montenvers** (☎ 04 50 53 12 54; 35 place de la Mer de Glace; adult/4-15yr/family €21/16.80/63; 9am-4.30pm mid-Dec–Apr, 8am-6.30pm Jul & Aug, hours vary rest of year) in Chamonix with Montenvers (1913m), from where a cable car transports tourists in summer down to the glacier and cave. The journey takes 20 minutes and admission includes entry to the caves and the cable car. Before catching the train back to Chamonix, nip into the **Grand Hôtel de Montenvers** (1880; p536) for a gander at its nine-room local-history museum and a drink on its dramatically placed terrace.

The Mer de Glace can be reached on foot via the Grand Balcon Nord trail from Plan de l'Aiguille. The two-hour uphill trail from Chamonix starts near the summer luge track. Traversing the glacier and its crevasses requires proper equipment and an experienced guide.

MUSEUMS

Pay for one Chamonix museum and visit the other for free. Discounts also apply for *carte d'hôte* (p538) pass-holders.

The town's illustrious Alpine history (the cliffhanging tale of local crystal-hunter Jacques Balmat and doctor Michel Gabriel Paccard summiting Mont Blanc for the first time in 1786, the creation of the winter season etc) zooms into focus at the **Musée Alpin** (Alpine Museum; ☎ 04 50 53 25 93; 89 av Michel Croz; adult/carte d'hôte/12-18yr €5.20/4/1.50; 2-7pm, also 10am-noon school holidays).

Rocks, minerals and geology are examined in the **Musée des Cristaux** (Crystal Museum; ☎ 04 50 55 53 93; Esplanade St-Michel; adult/carte d'hôte/12-18yr €5.20/4/1.50; 2-7pm, also 10am-1pm school holidays), in addition to fantastic temporary exhibitions such as the history of mountaineering or the impact of climate change on mountains.

Activities

WINTER ACTIVITIES

Make the **Maison de la Montagne** (190 place de l'Église; 8.30am-noon & 3-7pm), across the square from the tourist office, your first port of call for finding out everything about the Mont Blanc area.

Inside is the highly regarded **Compagnie des Guides** (p531); the **École de Ski Français** (ESF); Argentière (☎ 04 50 54 00 12; www.esf-argentiere.com; 329 rue Charlet Straton); Chamonix (☎ 04 50 53 22 57; www.esf-chamonix.com); and the **Office de Haute Montagne** (OHM; ☎ 04 50 53 22 08; www.ohm-chamonix.com), which has information on trails, hiking conditions, weather forecasts and *refuges* (mountain huts), and runs a huge library of topoguides and maps that are free to consult.

Skiing & Snowboarding

The biggest problem with skiing in Chamonix is that there is so much transport involved since many of its areas are very spread out and not connected. Of Chamonix' nine main skiing and snowboarding areas, the best for beginners are Le Tour, Les Planards and Les Chosalets. Brévent-Flégère, above Chamonix (connected by *téléphérique*), and Les Grands Montets, accessible from Argentière, 9km north of Chamonix, offer accomplished skiers the greatest challenges. For boarders, there is a snowpark with half-pipe, kicker ramps and other thrill-filled obstacles in Les Grands Montets, and a natural half-pipe in Le Tour.

The region has several marked but ungroomed trails suitable for skiers looking for off-piste thrills. The famous 20km **Vallée Blanche descent** – a lifelong dream for most serious skiers – is one of the world's most celebrated runs. The route leads from the Aiguille du Midi over the Mer de Glace and through the forests back to Chamonix, covering a drop in altitude of up to 2800m. It must *only* be tackled with a guide; the route crosses the crevasse-riddled glacier and passes through avalanche-prone areas. It takes four to five hours and a guide costs €270 per group

VINCENT LAMEYRE

Age: 43
Guide since: 1993
Mont Blanc ascents: about 70 (rough average; the record is 400, by a guide from St-Gervais)
Vallée Blanche descents: too many to remember
Likes: skiing and touring in winter; rock climbing in summer
Dislikes: people who think mountaineering is a walk in the park – there are plenty

How does one become a member of the Compagnie? Obviously you have to be a qualified guide (state diploma). Then you have to be born here. If there are no native applicants one year, 'foreigners' are accepted. That's my case; I'm from Paris. The first foreigner to be accepted was Roger Frison-Roche (legendary mountaineer, explorer, journalist and author) in 1930, 109 years after the creation of the organisation! Applicants become lifelong members after a two-year introduction; they are consecrated at the annual Fête des Guides on 15 August. That was one of the most beautiful days of my life.

What is it like within the organisation? The organisation is unlike anything I've ever seen: we're all pretty strong-minded. You have to be; on the mountain you're the sole judge, there's no room for meekness. But when you put 180 strong tempers together, you get a lot of sparks! It's never serious though: we'll argue and then make up over a beer. It's very sociable and there is a lot of solidarity.

What's changed over the years? Twenty years ago, we hardly worked in winter. But the Compagnie has marketed itself well for the past 10 years, and now we do a huge amount of off-piste skiing, the Vallée Blanche in particular. There's nothing else like it in the world. The downside of all this commercialisation is that many people think mountaineering is fun. It's not. It's a different sensation and it's a lot of effort. You also need good technique.

Any highlights or a favourite ascent? For me it's about having the right people at the right place at the right time. And there's something exciting about taking beginners: you know they have a whole mountaineering career ahead of them.

Have you ever been scared? Of course, we're always scared. That's what keeps you on your toes. That's also what makes you stop: you become very weary after 30 years of guiding. We are, statistically, very exposed. Every year we lose colleagues: it's sinister when it happens, but we're a little fatalistic about it. The show must go on.

Vincent Lameyre is a guide at the Compagnie des Guides de Chamonix

CHAMONIX CLIFFHANGERS

Cliffhanging is an understatement for many of the 18 *refuges* (mountain huts) that the **Club Alpin Français** (CAF; ☎ 04 50 53 16 03; www.clubalpin-chamonix.com; 136 av Michel Croz; ⌚ 3.30-7pm Mon, Tue, Thu & Fri, 9.30am-noon Sat Sep-Jun, 9.30am-noon daily Jul & Aug) runs in the Mont Blanc massif, poised perilously on the mountain edge or teetering precariously over a stomach-churning drop.

Most *refuges* are staffed by a warden from around mid-June to mid-September and must be reserved in advance by telephone. Snow permitting, many are open – albeit without a warden – for several more months of the year. Expect to pay anything from €8 to €15 for a dorm bed (with or without a warden) plus around €6/15 for breakfast/dinner prepared by the hut-keeper.

(for up to four people; €16 per person for additional people up to eight people max) through the Compagnie des Guides, ESF or any of the Chamonix guides (opposite). Snowboarders require an even better level than skiers and mixed skier/boarder groups are not possible.

Lift Passes

The tourist office, some hotels and kiosks next to ski lifts sell hands-free ski passes for the Chamonix area. The **Chamonix Le Pass** (1/6 days €37/185) gives access to all Chamonix' ski domains but does not include the Aiguille du Midi (for the Vallée Blanche), nor the Montenvers train nor the higher reaches of Les Grands Montets. Cheaper passes covering single ski areas are available, as is the more expensive **Ski Pass Mont Blanc**, which covers basically everything (including the Courmayeur ski area in Italy; one/six days €47/225). View all options and buy passes online at www.compagnied umontblanc.com.

Ski Touring & Heli-Skiing

Ski de randonnée (ski touring, generally between March and May) is big in Chamonix, the range of tours being seemingly endless. The king of ski tours is the classic six-day **Haute Route** (from €825 per person including guide and full board in *refuges*) from Chamonix to Zermatt in Switzerland, opened by guides in 1927. Skiers need to be experienced in off-piste skiing and extremely fit. Shorter two-day trips (about €310 per person) are suitable for experienced skiers but *ski de randonnée* novices.

Heli-skiing (€300 to €540 per person) is reserved strictly for top-level skiers, as proficient off as on killer-black pistes: contact the Compagnie des Guides (opposite), ESF (opposite) or **Chamonix Mont-Blanc Hélicoptères** (CMBH; ☎ 04 50 54 13 82; www.cmbh.net, in French).

Mushing

Huskydalen (☎ 04 50 47 77 24; www.huskydalen.com, in French; chemin des Falets) runs introductory courses in **mushing** (dog sledging, €65 for 1½ hours) from December to April, as well as various summer activities including an original version of dog-walking: it's the dog that walks you (or rather pulls you from a harness).

SUMMER ACTIVITIES

Walking

From late spring until October, 310km of spectacular walking trails open up to hikers. The most rewarding are the high-altitude trails reached by cable car; lifts shut down in the late afternoon but in June and July it is light enough to walk until at least 9pm.

From the top of Les Praz l'Index cable car (€16) or La Flégère (€10), the line's midway point, easy 1¼- to two-hour trails lead to **Lac Blanc** (literally 'White Lake'), a turquoise-coloured lake ensnared by mountains at 2352m. Star-lovers can overnight in the **Refuge du Lac Blanc** (☎ 04 50 53 49 14; dm with half board €47; ⌚ Jun-Sep), a wooden chalet with romantic Mont Blanc views.

The **Grand Balcon Sud** trail along the western side of the valley stays at around 2000m and also affords fabulous Mont Blanc views. Reach it on foot from behind Le Brévent's *télécabine* station.

Several routes start from Plan de l'Aiguille, including the **Grand Balcon Nord**, which takes you to the Mer de Glace, from where you can walk or take the Montenvers train down to Chamonix.

For the less ambitious, **Parc de Merlet** (☎ 04 50 53 47 89; www.parcdemerlet.com, in French; adult/4-12yr €5.50/3.50; ⌚ 10am-6pm May, Jun & Sep, 9.30am-7.30pm Jul & Aug) in Les Houches offers a unique opportunity to see marmots, chamois and other typical Alpine animals close up. Some marked footpaths through the animal park are wheelchair- and pushchair-friendly.

White-Water Sports

Cham' Aventure (☎ 04 50 53 55 70; www.cham-aventure.com; 190 place de l'Église), with an office inside the Maison de la Montagne, organises canyoning (half-/full day €64/98 per person), rafting (€36/130 for two hours/day) and hydrospeed (€47 for two hours) on Chamonix' River Arve and the Dora Baltea in neighbouring Italy (an hour's drive). Most of these activities are unsuitable for children under 10, sometimes even 13.

Chamonix guide companies (p531) arrange canyoning, as does **Oxo MontBlanc Canyoning** (☎ 06 77 88 24 50; www.canyoning-chamonix.com; 44 chemin de l'Ordon), a smaller set-up that offers some excellent expeditions.

Summer Luge

The highlight of the **Parc de Loisirs de Chamonix** (☎ 04 50 53 08 97; www.planards.com, in French; 🕑 2-6pm Sat & Sun Apr, May & Oct, 2-6pm daily Jun & Sep, 10am-7.30pm daily Jul & Aug), the **summer luge track** (luge d'été; 1/6 descents €5/25, 1/1½hr €12.50/15), winds through trees at an electrifying speed near the chairlift in Les Planards. Kids under six ride for free with an adult. Other activities for kidding around include trampolines, electric cars, a forest-adventure obstacle course and funfair rides.

Cycling

Lower-altitude trails like the Petit Balcon Sud (250m) from Argentière to Servoz are perfect for biking; for bike rental see p538. Most outdoor-activity specialists arrange guided mountain-biking expeditions.

Paragliding

The sky above Chamonix is often dotted with paragliders wheeling down from the snowy heights. Tandem flights from Planpraz (elevation 2000m) cost €90 per person (€220 from the Aiguille du Midi). Paragliding schools include **Summits** (☎ 04 50 53 50 14, 06 84 01 26 00; www.summits.fr; 27 allée du Savoy) and **Les Ailes du Mont Blanc** (☎ 04 50 53 96 72, 06 20 46 55 57; www.lesailesdumontblanc.com; 24 av de la Plage).

Ice Skating, Swimming et al

The **ice-skating rink** (☎ 04 50 53 12 36; carte d'hôte adult/child €4.80/2.85, skate rental €3.40; 🕑 2-5pm Thu-Tue, 2-5pm & 9-11pm Wed, high season only) provides skiing alternatives when the weather packs up, as do activities offered at the **Centre Sportif Richard Bozon** (☎ 04 50 53 23 70; http://sports.chamonix.com; 214 av de la Plage), a sports complex with indoor and outdoor **swimming pools** (carte d'hôte adult/child €4.80/2.85; 🕑 noon-7.30pm Mon-Fri, 2-7.30pm Sat & Sun), **sauna and hammam** (incl pool & gym €14.50), **climbing wall** (€4.20), **squash** (€8) and **tennis courts** (per hr €14.50). Gentlemen, the French have a penchant for tiny speedos – you can buy one there if all you have is trunks.

Festivals & Events

The two-day **Fête des Guides** in mid-August sees Chamonix' illustrious Compagnie des Guides welcome new members (see boxed text, p532) and honour lost ones with a dramatic son et lumière, fireworks, concerts and mountaineering displays.

Sleeping

Most establishments close in May and November. The tourist office–based **Centrale de Réservation** (Central Booking Office; ☎ 04 50 53 23 33; www.chamonix.com) accepts reservations by telephone or online. In high season many hotels, hostels and *refuges* only take weekly bookings or half-board deals.

BUDGET

Chamonix sports a dozen campsites, open May or June to September or October. In summer, the **Grand Hôtel du Montenvers** (see boxed text, p536), dramatically perched at the foot of a glacier, has an atmospheric *refuge*-style dormitory.

Les Deux Glaciers (☎ 04 50 53 15 84; les2glaciers.com; 80 rte des Tissières; 2-adults tent pitch €14.30; 🕑 mid-Dec–mid-Nov) The only campsite to stay open almost all year (it has heated bungalows for rent), the Two Glaciers sits at the foot of its namesakes in Les Bossons, 3km south of Chamonix. Ride the train to Les Bossons, or the Chamonix bus to the Tremplin-le-Mont stop.

Gîte Le Vagabond (☎ 04 50 53 15 43; www.gitevagabond.com; 365 av Ravanel-le-Rouge; dm €16.80, with breakfast/half-board €19.40/38.60; 🕑 reception 8-10am & 4.30-10pm; 💻 ⊠) This legendary bunkhouse, where cool dudes free-ride by day and eat, drink and party by night, is run and populated almost exclusively with Brits. Find Chamonix' hippest hostelry in a 150-year-old stagecoach inn on the edge of town. Beds are in four- or six-person dorms.

Auberge de Jeunesse Chamonix (☎ 04 50 53 14 52; www.fuaj.org; 127 montée Jacques Balmat; dm incl sheets &

breakfast €18, half-board €27.80; reception 8am-noon, 5-7.30pm & 8.30-10pm Dec-May & Jun-Sep) A very FUAJ (Fédération Unie des Auberges de Jeunesse) establishment: bright, spacious, well run, with impeccable two- to six-bed dorms. The only downside is that it is 2km south of Chamonix in Les Pélerins. Take the Chamonix–Les Houches bus line and get off in Les Pélerins d'en Haut (in front of the hostel). There's no kitchen but bargain half-board deals.

Hôtel El Paso (04 50 53 64 20; www.cantina.fr; 37 impasse des Rhododendrons; s/d/tr/q from €25/35/50/60, with shower & toilet from €35/45/55/65) The accommodation leg of nightclub Cantina Club (p537), rooms at El Paso are basic but clean and superconvenient for Tex-Mex food and party downstairs. The upshot is that if you'd like to sleep, you'll have to invest in ear plugs.

Le Vert Hôtel (04 50 53 13 58; www.verthotel.com; 964 route des Gaillands; low season s/d/tr/q from €25/40/60/75, high season €62/78/108/122) Self-proclaimed 'Chamonix' house of fun, sports and creativity', this hotel 2km out of town takes itself almost too seriously. Rooms are unremarkable (some with bathroom cabins the size of an aeroplane toilet), but what people really come for is the all-happening bar: polished, ultrahip, and a regular venue for DJs and live music.

Hôtel Les Crêtes Blanches (04 50 53 05 62; www.cretes-blanches.com; 16 impasse du Génépy; s/d/tr/chalet summer from €50/56/78/105, winter from €62/76/96/119) The good news? This tip-top establishment in the centre of Chamonix with crisp, modern bedrooms is excellent value for money. The bad news? Student tour operator STA has been quick to spot the bargain and books much of the hotel in advance. There is also a funky five-person chalet in the courtyard with a self-catering kitchen.

Hôtel Gustavia (04 50 53 00 31; www.hotel-gustavia.com; 272 av Michel Croz; s/d/tr from €50/80/111) Going strong since 1890, this charming manor-house hotel with bottle-green wooden shutters and wrought-iron balconies oozes soul. Rooms are elegant with their denim-coloured duvets and amber wood furnishings, and the clientele is young and fun, thanks partly to Chambre Neuf (p537) – its stylish après-ski bar.

Hôtel Richemond (04 50 53 08 85; www.richemond.fr; 228 rue du Docteur Paccard; s incl breakfast €58-66, d €91-106, tr €110-133, q €123-148) Run by the same family since 1914, Hôtel Richemond has had a tumultuous history: WWII saw the hotel taken over by the Gestapo (who painted a huge red cross on the roof to avoid it getting bombed). English and American prisoners were kept on the 5th floor. Nowadays it's still the same grand building, with imposing volumes and thick carpets (and very flowery wallpaper), but the bathrooms and corridors look like they've seen better days.

MIDRANGE

Hôtel Faucigny (04 50 53 01 17; www.hotelfaucigny-chamonix.com; 118 place de l'Église; d/tr/q low season €68/82/98, high season €79/93/112; mid-May–mid-Nov & mid-Dec–mid-Apr;) This tidy hotel has been carefully and cleverly renovated by owners Jacqueline and Guy Écochard to optimise space and comfort (made-to-measure furniture, heating mirrors etc) in a charming old building. There is a lovely flower-decked terrace at the front with vertigo-inducing views of Mont Blanc.

Hôtel Gourmets & Italy (04 50 53 01 38; www.hotelgourmets-chamonix.com; 96 rue du Lyret; d €78-99, tr €104-150;) One of Chamonix' most understated addresses: rooms are fairly neutral in beige but comfortable, with great designer bathrooms. The cosy downstairs lounge is perfect to read the paper or use the wi-fi to catch up on emails. You can also wind down in the sauna or swim in the pool in summer, with unrivalled Mont Blanc views to gawp at.

Hameau Albert 1er (04 50 53 05 09; www.hameaualbert.fr; 38 rte du Bouchet; d summer/winter from €125/160;) Five generations of Carriers have run this exquisite hotel – a hamlet of traditional Savoyard farms and wooden chalets turned exclusive resort thanks to an unusual mix of ultramodern and period furniture and no end of luxurious comforts (on-site spa, huge plasma-screen TV etc).

TOP END

Grand Hôtel Les Alpes (04 50 55 37 80; www.grandhoteldesalpes.com; 89 rue du Docteur Paccard; d low/high season from €140/330; mid-Dec–mid-Apr, mid-Jun–Sep;) Dating from 1840, this grand old dame goes down in the chronicles of Chamonix history as one of the resort's first and finest. What distinguishes this hotel from other high-end places, however, is its friendliness: in winter, a scrumptious cake buffet greets skiers back from the slopes, and evenings start off with a similar spread of nibbles, the perfect opportunity for people to mingle.

Clubhouse (04 50 90 96 56; www.clubhouse.fr; 74 promenade des Sonnailles; d 3-nights full-board from €865; Dec-Sep;) Provocatively decadent, the Clubhouse lures a moneyed set into its luxurious lair – Chamonix' only remaining

A LOFTY LUNCH

Feast on fine fodder and even finer mountain views at these high-altitude favourites:

Grand Hôtel du Montenvers (☎ 04 50 53 87 70; 35 place de la Mer de Glace; half-board per person dm/d €38.50/54.40, dm/d per person with breakfast €23.60/38.50, menus €8-10; ⌚ hotel Jul & Aug, restaurant late Dec–mid-Oct) Ride the red mountain train up to Montenvers and dine in Alpine splendour at the foot of the Alps' second-largest glacier. The place dates back to 1880 and has kept many of its original features (parquet floors, enormous fireplace).

Le 3842 (☎ 04 50 55 82 23; Aiguille du Midi; menu €38, mains €8-10; ⌚ restaurant mid-Jun–mid-Sep, snack bar all year) Stylish summit dining and drinking at the top of the Aiguille du Midi in what claims to be Europe's highest café. Make sure you don't gawp at the view with your mouth full.

La Crémerie du Glacier (☎ 04 50 54 07 52; 766 chemin de la Glacière; mains €6-15) Crazy as it sounds for a piste restaurant, you might have to book to get a chance to bite into La Crémerie's world-famous *croûtes au fromage* (chunky slices of toasted bread topped with melted cheese). Ski to it with the red Pierre à Ric piste in Les Grands Montets.

Le Panoramic (☎ 04 50 53 44 11; Le Brévent; menus from €15; ⌚ mid-Dec–Apr & Jun-Sep) Views of Mont Blanc are included in the menu of cheeses, cured meats and BBQ fare. For something a little more frugal, a *vin chaud* (hot mulled wine) at the terrace will do just fine.

art-deco mansion, dating from 1927, a cross between a James Bond movie set and a retro Alpine chalet. The seven quirky rooms scream design (from the dirty-weekend suite to the big kids' – 30-something boys – bunk rooms). Members only (membership €150 for a year), and stays are restricted to three, four or six nights. All rates are full-board.

Eating

Most restaurants are open seven days a week in season but have reduced hours out of season. Call ahead to check.

Mojo's (21 place Balmat; sandwich €5-6; ⌚ 9am-8pm) The latest arrival on the tasty sandwich scene, Mojo has also bagged the best location in town: smack bang on the main square, with views of Le Brévent to the right, a Mont Blanc full-frontal straight ahead and l'Aiguille du Midi to your left. *Bon appétit.*

Annapurna (☎ 04 50 55 81 39; 62 av Ravanel-le-Rouge; mains €10-15; ⌚ lunch & dinner Wed-Sun, dinner Tue) Named after the 8000m-plus Himalayan mountain first summited by French Alpine climbers in 1950, this mountain restaurant doesn't disappoint. The menu contains all the regulars (tandoori, biriani, korma etc), which you can also order as takeaway.

Casa Valério (☎ 04 50 55 93 40; 88 rue du Lyret; mains €10-20; ⌚ lunch & dinner, closes at 2am) One of Chamonix' most popular eateries, this restaurant doubles up as a happening hang-out in the evenings when young 'seasonaires' crowd the front of the restaurant to devour pasta or pizza by the bar counter.

Le Sanjon (☎ 04 50 53 56 44; 5 av Ravanel-le-Rouge; menus €12-35; ⌚ lunch & dinner) The usual cheese overload on the menu, with the slightly more unusual additions of *Potée Savoyarde* (*diot* sausage, potatoes, onions and, yes, cheese) and *Moëlleux Savoyard* (cheese cooked in pine-tree bark with a dash of Génépi for good measure and served with potatoes and smoked ham).

Le Bistrot (☎ 04 50 53 57 64; www.lebistrotchamonix.com; 151 av de l'Aiguille du Midi; lunch menu €17, dinner menus €42 & €65; ⌚ lunch & dinner) Chamonix' very own gastronomic wonder, this is a real foodie's place where chef Mickey's prowess will bowl over even the most discerning crowd. The warm chocolate macaroon with a raspberry and red pepper coulis is out of this world.

Munchie (☎ 04 50 53 45 41; 87 rue des Moulins; mains €17-25; ⌚ dinner Mon-Sun) Think fusion at this trendy hang-out with great pan-Asian food. Mains include sashimi, sushi, laksa, fish cakes and spare ribs, all delicious and beautifully presented. It is, predictably, very popular so book if you can.

Le Panier des Quatre Saisons (☎ 04 50 53 98 77; 24 Galerie Blanc Neige, rue du Dr Paccard; mains €20-25; ⌚ dinner Thu, lunch & dinner Fri-Sun & Tue Dec-May & mid-Jun–Oct) Incredibly (for France), this little place offers veggie options that are actually worth having. The menu changes every season and always delivers. Don't let its location at the back of a somewhat drab shopping mall put you off.

L'Impossible (☎ 04 50 53 20 36; 9 chemin du Cry; mains €20-30; ⌚ lunch & dinner daily Dec-Apr, Jul & Aug) In a barn dating back to 1754 near the Aiguille du Midi cable car, this stunning rustic-chic eating space – lots of wood, warm lighting, gilded gold frames and period paintings – serves quintessential French cuisine with a modern twist.

SELF-CATERING

A food market fills place du Mont Blanc on Saturday morning.

Camp de Base (☎ 04 50 18 47 76; 107 rue des Moulins; 🕒 3-8pm) For those in need of a PG Tips cup of tea or chocolate digestive biscuits, an English grocery shop, combined with internet café (per hour €5).

Le Refuge Payot (☎ 04 50 53 18 71; www.refugepayot.com; 166 rue Joseph Vallot) Local produce: cheese, smoked and air-dried meats, sausages, wine, honey etc.

Super U (117 rue Joseph Vallot) A supermarket.

Drinking

Chamonix nightlife rocks. In the centre, quaint old riverside rue des Moulins touts a line-up of drinking holes. **Bar'd Up** (☎ 04 50 53 91 33; 123 rue des Moulins; 🕒 4.30pm-2am) and **Le Privilège** (☎ 06 33 76 86 00; 26 rue des Moulins; 🕒 4pm-2am) are still going strong. Elsewhere, young 'n' fun **Bar Le Vagabond**, at Gîte Le Vagabond (p534), and Le Vert Hôtel's **bar** (p535) are worth checking out. Online, go to www.lepetitcanardchx.com.

Many of these après-ski joints serve grub alongside grog:

Bistrot des Sports (☎ 04 50 33 00 46; 182 rue Joseph Vallot; 🕒 11am-midnight) This inconspicuous brasserie is steeped in history: an old meeting place for muleteers and guides on their way up or down the mountain, it was bought by legendary mountaineer and explorer Roger Frison-Roche in 1934. It's changed hands since but the place has kept an undeniable charm and a certain authenticity. The street terrace is perfect for a mellow drink.

Chambre Neuf (☎ 04 50 55 89 81; 272 av Michel Croz; 🕒 8pm-1am) Particularly popular with Scandinavians, this is one of the liveliest party places in Chamonix, with raucous après-ski drinking and conversations about monster jumps, epic off-pistes and, like, totally mental, man, at every table.

Elevation 1904 (☎ 04 50 53 00 52; 259 av Michel Croz; 🕒 7pm-2am) Alpine paraphernalia lines the walls of this merry bet by the train station. The snack shack outside dishes out panini and salads more or less all day. Inside, words flow as much as the drinks late into the night.

our pick MBC (☎ 04 50 53 61 59; www.mbchx.com; 350 rte du Bouchet; 🕒 4pm-2am) This trendy microbrewery run by four Canadians is fab. Be it with their burger, cheesecake of the week, live music or amazing locally brewed and named beers (Blonde de Chamonix, Stout des Drus, Blanche des Guides etc), MBC really delivers.

Monkey Bar (☎ 04 50 96 64 34; 81 place Edmond Desailloud; 🕒 1pm-2am) Popular with locals (foreign staff have actually made an effort to speak French) and visitors alike, Monkey has a slight retro feel with its Brooklyn-style brick wall and fairy lights. It's an easygoing place for a fun but mellow evening.

La Terrasse (☎ 04 50 53 09 95; www.laterrassechamonix.com; 43 place Balmat; 🕒 4pm-2am) Race the clock for cheap drinks (5pm €5, 6pm €6 etc) and take position on the strategically placed balcony and terrace on Chamonix' main square. There's live music (of varying quality) every night of the week.

Le Tof (☎ 04 50 53 45 28; 158 place Edmond Desailloud; 🕒 10pm-4am) Chamonix' gay scene struts its stuff in the town's only gay bar and disco. Sip aperitifs, munch tapas and dance to house, new wave and retro in a trendy lounge atmosphere.

Office (☎ 04 50 54 15 46; www.the-office-bar.eu; 274 rue Charlet Stratton, Argentière; 🕒 3pm-2am) Sunday roast, English footie and a load of Brits, this is Argentière's party headquarters. Wi-fi throughout.

Entertainment

NIGHTCLUBS

Le Garage (☎ 04 50 53 64 49; 200 av de l'Aiguille du Midi; 🕒 1am-4am) An electro-house club that opens for a short and sweet three hours of pumping beats every night.

Cantina Club (☎ 04 50 53 83 80; www.cantina.fr; 37 impasse des Rhododendrons; 🕒 7pm-3am) Deep house, Afrobeat, drum and bass, breakbeat and hip hop are the varied DJ sounds pumped out at this happening underground club. The street-level restaurant cooks up Tex-Mex food from 7pm.

CINEMA

Films are shown in English at **Cinéma Vox** (☎ 04 50 53 03 39; cour Bartavel; adult/student €7.50/6.50). Check out the program at www.chamonix.com.

Getting There & Away

BUS

From **Chamonix bus station** (☎ 04 50 53 01 15; www.altibus.com; 🕒 6.45-10.30am & 1.25-4.45pm Mon-Fri, 6.45-11am Sat & Sun), located next to the train station,

THE GREEN CARD

Chamonix has long battled with air-pollution problems: the valley is a major road axis between France and Italy, and with 2000m-plus summits on either side, exhaust fumes just stagnate above Chamonix. In a bid to encourage locals and visitors to leave the car at home, the Chamonix valley now offers free public transport. All you have to do is get a **carte d'hôte** from your hotel or campsite and on you go for freeeeee!

The card also offers reductions for a number of activities. Details are listed on the card leaflet.

there are buses to/from Geneva airport and bus station (one way/return €35/55, 1½ to two hours, three daily) and Courmayeur (one way/return €11/18, 45 minutes, two to three daily). Advanced booking is required for both.

CAR

Approaching Chamonix from Italy, you arrive via the 11.6km-long **Tunnel de Mont Blanc** (www.atmb.net; toll one-way/return €32.30/40.30), which enters town in the southern suburb of Les Pélerins. From France, the A40 motorway – the Autoroute Blanche – hooks up with the Chamonix-bound N205, dual carriageway for the last leg.

Parking in town can be tricky although **Parking du Mont-Blanc** (☎ 04 50 53 65 71; place du Mont Blanc; 1st hr free, then per hr/24hr/week €2/9.50/35) is a reliable car park. Other car parks are scattered along rte du Bouchet, around rue des Allobroges and in Chamonix Sud.

Car-rental companies include **Europcar** (☎ 04 50 53 63 40; 36 place de la Gare).

TRAIN

From Chamonix–Mont Blanc **train station** (☎ 04 50 53 12 98; place de la Gare) the Mont Blanc Express narrow-gauge train trundles from the St-Gervais–Le Fayet station, 23km west of Chamonix, to Martigny, 42km northeast of Chamonix in Switzerland, stopping en route in Les Houches, Chamonix and Argentière. There are nine to 12 return trips between Chamonix and St-Gervais (€9.10, 40 minutes). Travelling between Servoz and Vallorcine is free with the *carte d'hôte* (see boxed text, above).

From St-Gervais–Le Fayet, there are trains to most major French cities (see opposite).

Getting Around

BICYCLE

Le Grand Bi Cycles (☎ 04 50 53 14 16; 240 rte du Bouchet; 9am-7pm Jul & Aug, 9am-7pm Tue-Sun Sep-Jun, closed Nov) rents out bikes for €25 a day and can advise you on where to go.

BUS

Local bus transport is handled by **Chamonix Bus** (☎ 04 50 53 05 55; www.chamonix-bus.com; 591 promenade Marie-Paradis; 7am-7pm winter, 8am-noon & 2-7pm Jun-Aug).

From mid-December to the end of April lines to the ski lifts and central car parks depart every 10 minutes or so between 7am and 7pm (town-centre shuttles 8.30am to 6.30pm). All buses are free with the *carte d'hôte* scheme (see the boxed text, left), except the Chamo-Nuit night buses linking Chamonix with Argentière and Les Houches (last departures from Chamonix 11.30pm or midnight; €2).

TAXI

There's a **taxi stand** (☎ 04 50 53 13 94) outside the train station. Minibuses for two to eight people are available from **Chamonix Transfer** (☎ 06 07 67 88 85, 06 62 05 57 38; www.chamonix-transfer.com, in French).

MEGÈVE & ST-GERVAIS

A chic ski village developed in the 1920s for a French baroness disappointed with Switzerland's crowded St-Moritz, **Megève** (population 3878, elevation 1113m) looks almost too perfect to be true: horse-drawn sledges, exquisitely arranged boutique windows and carefully grown pot plants spill into medieval-style streets. In winter it attracts a rather snobby, moneyed crowd, but the attitude is more laid-back in summer.

Sitting snug below Mont Blanc, 36km southwest of Chamonix, Megève's neighbour is **St-Gervais-les-Bains** (better known as simply St-Gervais, population 5400, elevation 850m), another picture-postcard winter and summer resort linked to Chamonix by the legendary Mont Blanc Express.

Information

Megève Tourist Office (☎ 04 50 21 27 28; www.megeve.com; 70 rue de Monseigneur Conseil; 9am-7pm daily mid-Dec–mid-Apr, Jul & Aug, 9am-12.30pm & 2-6.30pm Mon-Sat Sep–mid-Dec & mid-Apr–Jun)

St-Gervais Tourist Office (☎ 04 50 47 76 08; www.st-gervais.net; 115 av Mont Paccard; 9am-noon &

2-7pm daily mid-Dec–mid-Apr, Jul & Aug, 9am-noon & 2-6pm Mon-Fri Sep–mid-Dec & mid-Apr–Jun)

Activities

Skiing is the winter biggie, with Megève downhill split into three separate areas: Mont d'Arbois-Princesse (linked to St-Gervais), Jaillet-Combloux and Rochebrune-Côte 2000. Ski passes for the 445km of piste served by 108 lifts are sold online at **SAEM** (www.skiamegeve.com, in French); a one-/six-day pass covering the entire area costs €34.50/166 but cheaper passes valid for one area are available.

Megève's **ESF** (☎ 04 50 21 00 97; www.megeve-ski.com) and **Compagnie des Guides et Accompagnateurs** (☎ 04 50 21 55 11; www.guides-megeve.com) are inside the **Maison de la Montagne** (176 rue de la Poste). The latter organises off-piste skiing, heli-skiing, ice climbing, rock climbing and paragliding.

Summer hiking trails in the Bettex, Mont d'Arbois and Mont Joly areas are accessible from both villages. Mountain biking is also popular; some of the best terrain is found along marked trails between Val d'Arly, Mont Blanc and Beaufortain. **Accro'bike** (☎ 04 50 47 76 77; 78 impasse Bédière) in St-Gervais runs guided biking expeditions (from €35).

For staggering mountain views with no legwork, hop aboard France's highest train. The **Tramway du Mont Blanc** (☎ 04 50 47 51 83; rue de la Gare; adult/4-15yr/family return €18/14/54; 🕑 mid-Dec–mid-Apr, Jul & Aug) has laboured up to Bellevue (1800m) from St-Gervais–Le Fayet in winter and further up to the Nid d'Aigle (Eagle's Nest) at 2380m in summer since 1913.

Sleeping & Eating

Both tourist offices run an **accommodation service** Megève (☎ 04 50 21 29 52); St-Gervais (☎ 04 50 47 76 08).

Alp Hôtel (☎ 04 50 21 07 58; www.alp-hotel.fr; 434 rte de Rochebrune; d €55-100) This two-star chalet with 20 tidy if a little old-fashioned rooms near the Rochebrune cable car is the cheapest you'll get in pricey Megève. Count another €8 for a wholesome *petit déjeuner* (breakfast) each morning.

Au Coeur de Megève (☎ 04 50 21 25 30; www.hotel-megeve.com; 44 rue Charles Feige; d mid-/high season from €148/164, Jul & Aug from €100) For a little Alpine fantasy at just about affordable prices, this is a very nice option. Bang-slap in pedestrian Megève, this three-generation family affair has delightful rooms fragrant with candles and woodwax, lined with flowered balconies.

Les Fermes de Marie (☎ 04 50 93 03 10; www.fermesdemarie.com; chemin de Riante Colline; d low/mid-/high season from €177/250/396; 🕑 mid-Dec–mid-Apr, Jul & Aug; 💻 🅟) One of the most renowned Alpine spa resorts, this gorgeous nine-chalet hamlet oozes opulence. Rooms look like they're permanently arranged for a glossy-magazine photo shoot, and the trio of restaurants within the hotel – formal dining room, rotisserie specialising in roast meats, and fondue-driven bistro – pleases the most demanding of palates.

L'Igloo (☎ 04 50 93 05 84; www.ligloo.com; 3120 rte du Crêt; mains €5-15; 🕑 lunch & dinner mid-Jun–mid-Sep & mid-Dec–mid-Apr) Feast on a fiesta of incredible Mont Blanc mountain views at this high-altitude eating joint plump on the top of Mont d'Arbois (1833m). Ski here or ride the Télécabine du Mont d'Arbois. In summer the Igloo has an open-air swimming pool.

Getting There & Away

From **Megève bus station** (☎ 04 50 21 25 18), there are seven daily services to/from St-Gervais–Le Fayet and Sallanches train stations. In winter, airport shuttles run three times daily to/from Geneva airport (one way/return €40/70, 1½ hours) from both villages.

The closest train station to Megève is in Sallanches, 12km north; for train information in Megève go to the SNCF information desk inside the bus station.

St-Gervais is the main train station for Chamonix and is linked to the latter by the Mont Blanc Express (opposite). Services to/from St-Gervais include several day trains and one night train to/from Paris' Gare d'Austerlitz (€83.10, five hours; overnight train €92.20, 9½ hours), Lyon (€29, 3½ hours), Annecy (€12.70, 1½ hours) and Geneva (€11.40, 1½ hours).

LES PORTES DU SOLEIL

Poetically dubbed 'the Gates of the Sun' (elevation 1000–2466m; www.portesdusoleil.com), this gargantuan ski area – the world's largest – is formed from a chain of villages strung along the French-Swiss border. Some 650km of downhill slopes and cross-country trails criss-cross it, served by 209 ski lifts covered by a single ski pass (one/six days €39/200), or a cheaper, more restricted pass valid for one pocket. In spring and summer mountain-bike enthusiasts revel in 380km of invigorating biking trails, including the 100km-long circular Portes du Soleil tour.

Morzine (population 3000, elevation 1000m) – the best known of the 12 interconnected ski resorts – retains a smidgen of traditional Alpine village atmosphere. It's frantically busy in winter but summer sees the pace slow down as enchanting visits to Alpine cheese dairies and traditional slate workshops kick in. For local know-how on summer activities – hiking, biking, climbing, canyoning and paragliding – contact the **Bureau des Guides** (☎ 04 50 75 96 65; www.bureaudesguides.net), which can advise on mountain-bike hire and Morzine's heart-stopping 3300m-long **bike descent** (free; 🕐 Jun-Sep) from the top of the Plénéy cable car (one/10 ascents €4.50/35). Accommodation can be booked through **Morzine Réservation** (☎ 04 50 79 11 57; www.resa-morzine.com) inside the **tourist office** (☎ 04 50 74 72 72; www.morzine-avoriaz.com; place de la Crusaz).

our pick **Farmhouse** (☎ 04 50 79 08 26; www.thefarmhouse.fr; Morzine; d with breakfast €94-370, dinner €40) is Morzine's oldest and loveliest building, a 1771 farmhouse run for the past 17 years by the charming Dorrien Ricardo. The Farmhouse is your quintessential wood-beamed manor house. Five rooms (some with Victorian-style bathrooms to die for, and one room called the Cell which was indeed, once upon a time, Morzine's only prison cell) are in the main house, and a trio of cottages (including the old *mazot*, or miniature mountain chalet, where the family Bible and deeds of the house would have been stored) sit in the lovely grounds. Dining – open to nonguests too and strictly around one huge long table – is a lavish affair and very much an experience in itself.

Chic but small **Avoriaz** (elevation 1800m), purpose-built a few kilometres up the valley atop a rock, appeals for its no-cars policy. Horse-drawn sleighs piled high with luggage romantically ferry new arrivals – wealthy families in the main – to and from the snowy village centre where wacky 1960s mimetic architecture gets away with an 'avant-garde' tag. The place is so hip that French chef Christophe Leroy has opened a restaurant at **Hôtel des Dromonts** (☎ 04 94 97 91 91; www.christophe-leroy.com, in French; place des Dromonts; d from €199, full board extra €29; 🕐 mid-Dec–mid-Apr; 💻). The hotel looks a little outdated with its 1970s rendering and thinning carpets, but definitely edgy with its weird volumes and minimalist decor.

With just three other hotels, accommodation in Avoriaz is limited to self-catering studios and apartments, which can be booked through the **tourist office** (☎ 04 50 74 02 11; www.avoriaz.com; place Centrale). Motorists unload in bays close to the resort but must park in car parks (€7/43 per day/week) a short walk away.

Arriving by road via Cluses you hit **Les Gets** (population 1300, elevation 1172m) – smaller, less pretentious than Morzine and Avoriaz, and a good deal for families and those looking to save a bob. Its **tourist office** (☎ 04 50 75 80 80; www.lesgets.com; place de la Mairie) and **accommodation service** (☎ 04 50 75 80 51; reservations@lesgets.com) can point you in the right direction. For ski-pass information see www.sagets.fr.

Should scrimping not be your priority, check into spa-clad **Ferme de Montagne** (☎ 04 50 75 36 79; www.fermedemontagne.com; full board per person per week €1450-2100; 🕐 Jun-Sep & Nov-Apr), an exclusive five-star Savoyard farmhouse labelled one of Europe's top boutique ski hotels by glossy-mag critics.

Getting There & Away

Free shuttle buses serve the lifts of Télécabine Super Morzine, Télécabine du Pléney and Téléphérique Avoriaz.

During the ski season, Morzine (one way/return €33.50/55.50), Avoriaz (€37/63) and Les Gets (€30.50/51) are linked by bus to Geneva airport, 50km-odd west. From Morzine there are regular **SAT buses** (☎ 04 50 79 17 73) to Les Gets and Avoriaz. There are also buses from Morzine to its closest train stations: Thonon-les-Bains (34km north) and Cluses (31km south).

THONON-LES-BAINS

pop 30,700 / elevation 430m

Just across the water from the Swiss city of Lausanne on the French side of Lake Geneva (Lac Léman), Thonon-les-Bains – a fashionable spa town during the belle époque – sits on a bluff above the lake. Winter is deathly dull, but its summer lake cruises and lakeside strolls appeal.

A 230m-long **funicular railway** (☎ 04 50 71 21 54; one way/return €1/1.80; 🕐 8am-11pm Jul & Aug, 8am-9pm mid-Apr–Jun & Sep, 8am-12.30pm & 1.30pm-6.30pm Mon-Sat & 2-6pm Sun Oct-Mar) links the upper town and **tourist office** (☎ 04 50 71 55 55; www.thononlesbains.com; place du Marché; 🕐 9am-12.15pm & 1.45-6.30pm Mon-Fri, 10am-12.15pm & 1.45-6.30pm Sat Sep-Jun, 9am-7pm Mon-Fri, 10am-7pm Sat Jul & Aug) with the marina. Buy boat tickets (www.cgn.ch) at the lakeside **tourist office chalet** (☎ 04 50 26 19 94; 🕐 10am-12.30pm & 2-6.30pm Jul & Aug).

You can fill your water bottle with Thonon mineral water for free at the mosaic-lined

TAKING THE WATERS

Trot 9km east from Thonon along Europe's largest Alpine lake and you hit **Évian-les-Bains** (population 7800), the spa town from which that world-famous mineral water originates. Dubbed the 'Pearl of Lake Geneva', lakeside Évian was a favourite country retreat of the dukes of Savoy, razed during the Wars of Religion and reinvented as a luxury spa resort in the 18th century when wallowing in tubs of mineral water was all the rage. Wallowing in a tub of Évian can still be done at **Les Thermes Évian** (☎ 04 50 75 02 30; www.lesthermesevian.com; place de la Libération; ⏰ 8.30am-6.30pm Mon-Fri, to 6pm Sat), although it is the bottled mineral water that accounts for the biggest chunk of the town's economy. The water takes 15 years to trickle down through the Chablais Mountains, gathering minerals en route, before emerging at a constant temperature of 11.4°C. It was 'discovered' in 1790 and has been bottled since 1826.

Tours (☎ 04 50 26 80 29; visits-usine-evian@danone.com; admission free, transport €2; ⏰ Jun-Sep) of the Évian bottling plant, on an industrial estate 5km out of town, can be arranged through the factory. The **tourist office** (☎ 04 50 75 04 26; www.eviantourism.com; place d'Allinges) can also help.

Fontaine de la Versoie in the Parc Thermal de Thonon. Locals do it too by the jerrycan.

Château de Ripaille (☎ 04 50 26 64 44; www.ripaille.fr, in French; 1hr guided tour €6; ⏰ 1-5 tours daily Feb-Nov, grounds 10am-7pm Tue-Sun May-Sep, 10am-4.30pm Tue-Sun Oct-Apr), 1km east along quai de Ripaille, is a turreted castle rebuilt in the 19th century on the site of its 15th-century ancestor. It has vineyards, a garden for summer dining (mid-June to mid-September) and forested grounds to explore.

The beautiful fortified medieval village of **Yvoire**, 16km west of Thonon on the shores of Lake Geneva, makes for a great day trip. A riot of cob houses and geranium-lined streets, you can get familiar with its 700-year history on a 1½-hour **guided tour** (€5.50; ⏰ Jul & Aug) organised by the **tourist office** (☎ 04 50 72 80 21; www.yvoiretourism.com).

The garden-clad **Hôtel à l'Ombre des Marronniers** (☎ 04 50 71 26 18; www.hotellesmarronniers.com, in French; 17 place de Crête; d from €50) is an in-town sleeping option, but out-of-town **La Ferme du Château** (☎ 04 50 26 46 68; www.lafermeduchateau.com; Hameau de Maugny; d €85; ⊠ 🅿), 10km inland in Draillant, is way more charming. Sophie and Didier run the *chambre d'hôte* in a renovated 18th-century stone Savoyard farm and cook up excellent evening meals (€25 with wine).

From **Thonon bus station** (place des Arts), **SAT** (☎ 04 50 71 00 88) runs regular buses to/from Évian-les-Bains (€1.50, 30 minutes) and into the Chablais Mountains, including to Morzine (€11, one hour). The **train station** (place de la Gare) is southwest of place des Arts, the main square. Trains run to/from Geneva (€6.90, one hour) direct or via Annemasse (€5.50, 30 minutes).

ANNECY

pop 51,000 / elevation 448m

As you stroll along the shores of shimmering Lac d'Annecy, it seems impossible to think that Annecy's biggest asset very nearly became its downfall in the 1950s: a reeking, insalubrious mess, the lake was an open-air sewer for every town and village in the vicinity. Public health issues aside, the city quickly realised that unless it cleaned up its act, its burgeoning tourism would disappear.

Forward 60 years and Lac d'Annecy is now one of the purest in the world, receiving only rainwater, spring water and mountain streams thanks to an extensive decontamination plan. Swimming in the lake surrounded by snowy mountains really is an Alpine highlight, as is strolling in the warren of geranium-lined medieval streets of Vieil Annecy. So much so in fact that Annecy gets a whopping two million visitors a year, the bulk of it in summer. Luckily there is plenty to do away from the crowds, with walking and cycling galore in the surrounding mountains.

Orientation

The train and bus stations are about 500m northwest of Vieil Annecy, also called the Vieille Ville (Old Town), which is huddled around the River Thiou (split into Canal du Thiou to the south and Canal du Vassé to the north). The town centre is between the post office and the purpose-built shopping mall, Centre Bonlieu, near the shores of Lac d'Annecy.

Annecy-le-Vieux, a primarily residential quarter not to be confused with Vieil Annecy, straddles the lake's north.

Information

EMERGENCY

Hospital (☎ 04 50 88 33 33; 1 av de Trésum)
Police Station (☎ 04 50 52 32 00; 15 rue des Marquisats)

INTERNET ACCESS

Larache Télécom (☎ 04 50 33 08 95; 3 rue de l'Industrie; per 15min/1hr €1/3; 9am-11pm)
Planète Telecom (☎ 04 50 33 92 60; 4 rue Jean Jaurès; per hr €3; 9.30am-8.30pm)

LAUNDRY

Lav'Confort Express (6 rue de la Gare; 7am-9pm)

MONEY

Crédit Lyonnais (1 rue Jean Jaurès, Centre Bonlieu)

POST

Post Office (4bis rue des Glières)

TOURIST INFORMATION

Tourist Office (☎ 04 50 45 00 33; www.lac-annecy.com; 1 rue Jean Jaurès, Centre Bonlieu; 9am-12.30pm & 1.45-6pm Mon-Sat mid-Sep–mid-May, 9am-6.30pm Mon-Sat mid-May–mid-Sep, 10am-1pm Sun Mar-May)

Sights & Activities

Wandering around the Vieille Ville and the lakefront is the essence of Annecy. Just east, behind the Hôtel de Ville, are the **Jardins de l'Europe**, linked to popular park **Champ de Mars** by the poetic iron arch of **Pont des Amours** (Lovers' Bridge).

VIEILLE VILLE

With labyrinthine narrow streets and colonnaded passageways, the old town retains much of its 17th-century appearance. On the central island, imposing **Palais de l'Isle** (☎ 04 50 33 87 30; 3 passage de l'Île; adult/concession €3.40/1, 1st Sun of month Oct-May free; 10.30am-6pm daily Jun-Sep, 10am-noon & 2-5pm Wed-Mon Oct-May) was a prison, but now hosts local-history displays. A combined ticket covering the palace and the Musée Château costs €6.20.

CHÂTEAU D'ANNECY

In the 13th- to 16th-century castle above town, the eclectic **Musée Château** (☎ 04 50 33 87 30; adult/concession €4.80/2; 10.30am-6pm Jun-Sep, 10am-noon & 2-5pm Wed-Mon Oct-May) explores traditional Savoyard art, crafts and Alpine natural history.

SUNBATHING & SWIMMING

Parks and grassy areas in which to picnic and sunbathe line the lakefront. Public beach **Plage d'Annecy-le-Vieux** (admission free; Jul & Aug) is 1km east of Champ de Mars. Closer to town, privately run **Plage Impérial** (admission €3.50; Jul & Aug) slumbers in the shade of the elegant pre-WWI **Impérial Palace**.

Plage des Marquisats (admission free; Jul & Aug) is 1km south of the Vieille Ville along rue des Marquisats. Located next door is a water-sports centre, the **Piscine des Marquisats** (☎ 04 50 33 65 40; 29 rue des Marquisats; May-Aug), with three outdoor swimming pools (€3.95).

WALKING

A fine stroll goes from the Jardins de l'Europe along quai Bayreuth and quai de la Tournette to the Stade Nautique des Marquisats and beyond. Another excellent walk begins at Champ de Mars and meanders eastwards around the lake towards Annecy-le-Vieux.

Forêt du Crêt du Maure, south of Annecy, has many walking trails, as do **Bout du Lac** (20km from Annecy on the southern tip of the lake) and **Roc de Chère** (10km from town on the eastern shore of the lake); Voyages Crolard buses (see Billetterie Crolard, p546) serve both.

Walking guides and maps, including IGN's excellent *Lac d'Annecy* (No 3431OT; 1:25,000) or *Walks and Treks Lake of Annecy* which details 15 itineraries in the area (€6.50), are sold at the tourist office and neighbouring sports shop, **Go Sport** (Centre Bonlieu).

CYCLING & BLADING

Biking and blading are big, thanks to 46km of cycling tracks – equally popular with rollerbladers – around the lake. The tourist office and rental outlets (p546) have free maps.

The Friday-evening jaunts around town organised by local rollerblading club **Roll 'n Cy** (☎ 06 76 73 47 12; www.roll-n-cy.org, in French; 8pm Fri Mar–mid-Dec) are fun, free and open to anyone on rollerblades. The club meets on place de la Mairie.

WATER SPORTS

From late March to late October, pedal boats and small motorboats can be hired at several points along the quays of the Canal du Thiou and Canal du Vassé.

From June to September the **Stade Nautique des Marquisats** (31 rue des Marquisats) is an aquatic-activity hub: the **Canoë-Kayak Club d'Annecy**

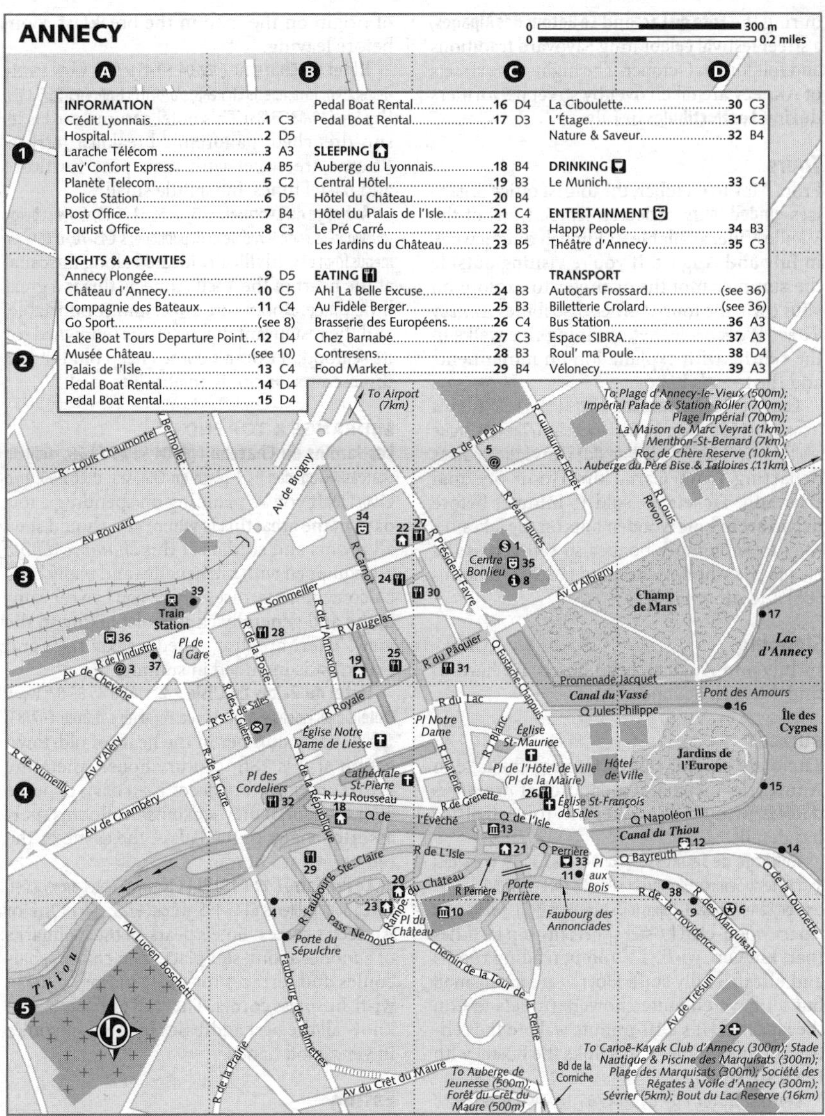

(☎ 04 50 45 03 98) rents kayaks and canoes, and the **Société des Régates à Voile d'Annecy** (SRVA; ☎ 04 50 45 48 39; 31 rue des Marquisats) rents sailing boats from €30 for two hours. Nearby, **Annecy Plongée** (☎ 04 50 45 40 97; www.annecyplongee.com; 6 rue des Marquisats) rents and sells diving gear and arranges baptism dives.

On the other side of the lake, Station Roller (p546) also rents kayaks (per hour/day €7/20).

Festivals & Events

Highlights include a **Venetian carnival** in February, fireworks over the lake in August during the **Fête du Lac**, and **Le Retour des Alpages**, a street festival celebrating Savoyard traditions and folklore in October. The night-time streets of Annecy are taken over by street performers during **Les Noctibules** in July.

Tours

From May to October, the tourist office organises **guided tours** (adult/under 12yr €5.70/free) of the Vieille Ville, available in English once a week in July and August. If you're visiting outside the summer months or prefer to explore on your own, the tourist office distributes *Annecy Town Walks,* a leaflet outlining five walks in the centre, with explanation on monuments and the town's history.

Compagnie des Bateaux (☎ 04 50 51 08 40; www.annecy-croisieres.com; 2 place aux Bois; 1/2hr lake cruise adult €11.40/14.60; ⌚ mid-Mar–Oct) runs lake cruises departing from Canal du Thiou on quai Bayreuth. Tickets are sold 15 minutes before departure at blue wooden huts on the lakeside. May to September boats also sail across the lake to Menthon-St-Bernard (€4.90), Talloires (€6) and other villages.

Sleeping

In July and August cheap hotels are hard to find; book in advance.

BUDGET

There are several campsites near the lake in Annecy-le-Vieux and a handful of *chambres d'hôtes* around the lake; the tourist office has details.

Auberge de Jeunesse (☎ 04 50 45 33 19; www.fuaj.org; 4 rte du Semnoz; dm incl breakfast & sheets €17.60; ⌚ reception 8am-noon & 3-10pm mid-Jan–Nov; ⊠) Annecy's smart wood-clad hostel sports tip-top facilities (bar, kitchen, wi-fi, TV room, reading room) and ultrafriendly staff. Dorms are a tad small but all have en-suite showers (toilets are on the landing). It's a 10-minute walk to the centre, and in summer a bus links the hostel with the train station.

Central Hôtel (☎ 04 50 45 05 37; www.hotelcentralannecy.com, in French; 6bis rue Royale; d/tr €33/42, with shower €40/47, with shower & toilet €45/52) Spread across three floors in a rambling building, the rooms at this establishment are simple but cosy. The owner has been gradually improving the place and the eight rooms (out of 16) with balconies overlooking the canal are big hits with visitors. Stick a pin in your country of origin on the map in the breakfast room before leaving.

Hôtel du Château (☎ 04 50 45 27 66; www.annecy-hotel.com; 16 rampe du Château; s/d/tr/q Oct-Apr €43/55/73/83, May-Sep €49/68/73/83) This hotel's trump card is its sun-drenched, panoramic breakfast terrace. Rooms are sweet with their pine furniture and pastel tones, but a little small.

Auberge du Lyonnais (☎ 04 50 51 26 10; www.auberge-du-lyonnais.com; 9 rue de la République; s €45-70, d €50-75, menus from €23) Idyllically located along the canal at the heart of the Vieil Annecy, this is a great little place. Rooms are sweet and comfortable, and the restaurant downstairs is renowned for its seafood; it doesn't come cheap but the €23 three-course *menu* is an absolute steal.

MIDRANGE & TOP END

Les Jardins du Château (☎ 04 50 45 72 28; jardinduchateau@wanadoo.fr; 1 place du Château; d €65-90, tr/q €100/130) If you're planning on spending a few days in the area, this is where you should stay: all rooms and studios at this *chambre d'hôte* are equipped with kitchenettes and many have balconies and terraces where you can eat, sunbathe and generally chill whilst taking in the view. There are discounted weekly rates and breakfast is included in summer.

Hôtel du Palais de L'Isle (☎ 04 50 45 86 87; www.hoteldupalaisdelisle.com; 13 rue Perrière; s/d from €67/83; 💻) Guests slumber in the heart of old-town action at this 18th-century house where the crisp contemporary decor is an oasis of peace after the tourist mayhem outside. Rooms sport assorted views of the Palais, the castle or the old town's sea of roofs.

Le Pré Carré (☎ 04 50 52 14 14; www.hotel-annecy.net; 27 rue Sommeiller; s €145-195, d from €225; 💻) One of Annecy's chicest hotels bears all the hallmarks of a modern four-star place: Zen colours, balconies and terraces for most rooms, jacuzzi, wi-fi, business corner. The staff also happen to know all the best addresses in town so you're in very good hands.

Eating

The quays along both sides of Canal du Thiou in the Vieille Ville are jam-packed with touristy cafés and restaurants.

Chez Barnabé (☎ 04 50 45 90 62; 29 rue Sommeiller; mains from €3.60; ⌚ 10am-7pm Mon-Sat) The concept of hot or cold buffet from which you can fill different-sized boxes is nothing new (imported from the US) but when it's done as well

LAKESIDE LEGENDS

Dining à la lakeside legend requires a certain amount of nous and loads of dosh.

La Maison de Marc Veyrat (☎ 04 50 60 24 00; www.marcveyrat.fr; 13 vieille rte des Pensières, Veyrier; d €300-670, menu €368; ⏰ Thu-Sun late May–Sep) Small fortune needed aside, snagging a table is tough at Marc Veyrat's lakeside 'Maison Bleue', a baby-blue house with a handful of extraordinary hotel rooms, 1km east of the centre. Cuisine is highly creative and flamboyant, reflecting Veyrat's signature use of herbs.

Auberge du Père Bise (☎ 04 50 60 72 01; www.perebise.com; rte du Port, Talloires; d €240-580, menus €82, €130 & €175; ⏰ lunch & dinner Thu-Mon) The other big name on Lake Annecy's chic shores, this one is substantially more affordable in the form of a fab brunch worth-every-last-cent feast (€32, served at weekends in June and September and every day in July and August). You'll still need to book about a week in advance though. Père Bise has been run by four generations of Bise since 1901; female chef Sophie Bise currently heads up the kitchen.

as it is here (everything is fresh and prepared on the premises), it's a winning formula. The brownies and cookies are just the ticket to undo the goodness of the salad bar.

Au Fidèle Berger (☎ 04 50 45 00 32; 2 rue Royale; ⏰ 9.15am-7pm Tue-Sat) This old-England style tearoom serves decadent cakes, mountains of macaroons and home-made ice creams for the sweet-toothed among you. Breakfast is a treat, with delicious pastries and a cup of *thé*.

Ah! La Belle Excuse (☎ 04 50 51 20 05; cour du Pré Carré, 10 rue Vaugelas; mains €10-15; ⏰ lunch & dinner Mon-Sat) In a funky, red-and-green wood-clad house with an unbeatable summer deck, the Beautiful Excuse serves up unpretentious grub of grilled meats, salads and *parmentiers* (mashed potato baked with different toppings).

Contresens (☎ 04 50 51 22 10; 10 rue de la Poste; mains €15; ⏰ lunch & dinner Tue-Sat) The menu looks a little bit like a mathematic formula but it all becomes clear in the end: starters are annotated A, mains B, sides C and desserts D, and you can order any combination of the above for set prices. The food is as creative as the menu (sun-dried tomato, Beaufort cheese and rocket salad burger, mussel ravioli, Nutella mousse with Rice Krispies squares etc) and totally divine.

L'Étage (☎ 04 50 51 03 28; 13 rue du Pâquier; mains €15; ⏰ lunch & dinner) Glorious, glorious cheese! At L'Étage *le fromage* is given pride of place, even if you're not having a Savoyard speciality (think steak with cheese sauce, yum). The decor is a little passé but the cheerful staff more than make up for it (a word of warning though, they do not take kindly to people not finishing their plate).

Brasserie des Européens (☎ 04 50 45 00 81; place de l'Hôtel de Ville; mains €15-25; ⏰ lunch & dinner) Hang in there for the mother of all seafood platters (a cool €185 for four people) and seven different types of steak tartare (raw beef, plain, with toast, parmesan, peppercorns, Mexican spices etc), this is the real McCoy of French brasseries.

Nature & Saveur (☎ 04 50 45 82 29; www.nature-saveur.com; place des Cordeliers; lunch €18-22, dinner with/without wine €36-42/52; ⏰ lunch Tue-Sat, dinner Fri & Sat) The new kid on the 'alternative' block, Nature & Saveur only uses organic and wholesome ingredients from local farms, from obscure legumes to freshly ground flours, extra fresh farm eggs or locally raised meat and almond milk. But don't be fooled: this is no tree-hugger's hut. Chef Laurence Salomon's restaurant is sophisticated and attracts a discerning boho-chic clientele.

La Ciboulette (☎ 04 50 45 74 57; cour du Pré Carré, 10 rue Vaugelas; mains €30-35; ⏰ lunch & dinner Tue-Sat) In a sophisticated amber-coloured dining room, this is Annecy's affordable gastronomic gem. The works of locally born chef Georges Paccard, it specialises in fish and wonderful seasonal food. This being Savoy, the cheese platter is phenomenal.

SELF-CATERING

In the Vieille Ville, there is a **food market** (rue Faubourg Ste-Claire; ⏰ 8am-noon Sun, Tue & Fri).

Entertainment

Théâtre d'Annecy (☎ 04 50 33 44 00; www.bonlieu-annecy.com, in French; Centre Bonlieu) is the main stage in Annecy for theatre.

For a chilled evening beer, **Le Munich** (☎ 04 50 45 02 11; quai Perrière; ⏰ 8am-2am daily Jun-Sep, 10am-2am

Tue-Sun Apr, May & Oct, 10am-2am Wed-Sun Nov-Mar) is a great place to watch the world go by on the edge of the canal. Choose from 13 draught beers. Disco-bar **Happy People** (☎ 04 50 51 08 66; 48 rue Carnot; admission €11; 🕐 11pm-5am), Annecy's main gay venue, is also worth checking out for a few late ones.

Getting There & Away

BUS

From the **bus station** (Gare Routière Sud; rue de l'Industrie), adjoining the train station, the **Billetterie Crolard** (☎ 04 50 45 08 12; www.voyages-crolard.com; 🕐 7.15am-12.30pm & 1.30-7.15pm Mon-Sat, plus Sun high season) sells tickets for hourly buses to other lakeside destinations including Menthon-St-Bernard (€2.30, 20 minutes) and Talloires (€2.70, 30 minutes), and for local ski resorts La Clusaz and Le Grand Bornand (single/return/return with lift pass €8/13.50/27, 50 and 60 minutes respectively). It also runs up to five buses daily to/from Lyon St-Exupéry airport (one way/return €30/45, two hours).

Next door, **Autocars Frossard** (☎ 04 50 45 73 90; 🕐 7.45-11am & 2-7.15pm Mon-Fri, 7.45am-1pm Sat) sells tickets for Geneva (€10.50, 1¾ hours, up to 12 daily), Thonon-les-Bains (€16.50, two hours, twice daily), Évian-les-Bains (€18.50, 2½ hours, twice daily) and Chambéry (€6, one hour).

TRAIN

From Annecy's **train station** (place de la Gare), there are frequent trains to/from Aix-les-Bains (€6.80, 30 minutes), Chambéry (€8.60, 45 minutes), St-Gervais (€12.70, 1¾ hours), Lyon (€21.60, 2¼ hours) and Paris' Gare de Lyon (€69.80, four hours).

Getting Around

BICYCLES & ROLLERBLADES

Bikes can be hired from **Vélonecy** (☎ 04 50 51 38 90; place de la Gare; 🕐 9.30am-noon & 1.30-6.30pm Wed-Sat, 1.30-6.30pm Tue), situated at the train station, for adult/student €15/3 per day. People with a valid bus or train ticket qualify for a €5 per day tariff.

Roul' ma Poule (☎ 04 50 27 86 83; www.annecy-location-velo.com; 4 rue des Marquisats; 🕐 9.30am-12.30pm & 2-6pm Wed-Mon Apr-Jun, Sep & Oct, 9am-8pm Jul & Aug) rents rollerblades (€9/14 per half-/full day), bikes (€10/15), tandems (€18/28) and trailers (€7/11). They can recommend excellent day trips in the area.

Near the Impérial Palace at the start of the lakeside cycling path, **Station Roller** (☎ 04 50 66 04 99; www.roller-golf-annecy.com, in French; 2 av du Petit Port; 🕐 9am-10pm) is another bike and blade outlet.

BUS

Get info on local buses at **Espace SIBRA** (☎ 04 50 10 04 04; www.sibra.fr; 21 rue de la Gare; 🕐 7.30am-7pm Mon-Fri, 9am-noon & 2-5pm Sat), opposite the bus station. Buses run from 6am to 8pm and a single ticket/day pass/carnet of 10 costs €1.10/2.70/9.

TAXI

Taxis hover outside the bus and train stations. Otherwise call ☎ 04 50 45 05 67.

AROUND ANNECY

When the sun shines, the villages of **Sévrier**, 5km south on Lake Annecy's western shore, and **Menthon-St-Bernard**, 7km south on the lake's eastern shore, make good day trips (p544). South of Menthon, **Talloires** is the most exclusive lakeside spot. All have wonderful beaches.

In winter, ski-keen Annéciens make a beeline for the cross-country resort of **Semnoz** (elevation 1700m; www.semnoz.fr, in French), 18km south; or downhill stations **La Clusaz** (elevation 1100m; www.laclusaz.com), 32km east, and **Le Grand Bornand** (elevation 1000m; www.legrandbornand.com), 34km northeast.

CHAMBÉRY

pop 57,800 / elevation 270m

On paper, Chambéry has everything going for it: strategic Alpine location at the crossroads of the main Alpine valleys, scenic setting near Lac du Bourget and two regional parks and a rich heritage of alternately French, Italian and Savoy rules. But in practice, the city doesn't quite meet these expectations: the centre is quiet, a little neglected even, the sights few and not easily accessible and the hotel scene in the centre drab (thankfully much better on the outskirts). There is plenty to see and do in the surrounding area, however, so Chambéry makes a logical base. And on the plus side, there are some very nice little restaurants in town.

The city was Savoy's capital from the 13th century until 1563 when the dukes of Savoy shifted their capital to Turin in Italy. The castle – which once served as the seat of power for the House of Savoy, founded by Humbert

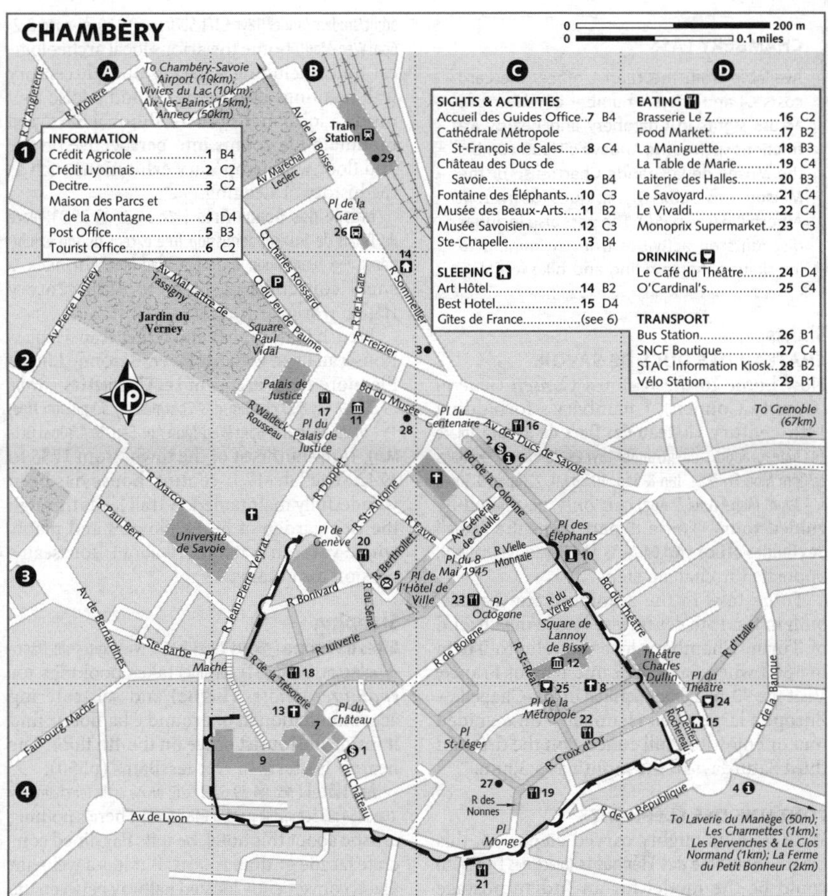

I (the Whitehanded) in the mid-11th century – now houses the administration for the Savoie *département*.

Information

BOOKSHOPS

Decitre (☎ 04 79 62 80 80; 75 rue Sommeiller) English-language novels, travel guides and maps.

LAUNDRY

Laverie du Manège (393 rue de la République; per 8kg €4.50; 🕑 7am-9pm)

MONEY

Crédit Agricole (place du Château)
Crédit Lyonnais (26 bd de la Colonne)

POST

Post Office (11 place de l'Hôtel de Ville)

TOURIST INFORMATION

Tourist Office (☎ 04 79 33 42 47; www.chambery-tourisme.com; 24 bd de la Colonne; 🕑 9am-noon & 1.30-6pm Mon-Sat Sep-Jun, 9am-6pm Mon-Sat, 9.30am-12.30pm Sun Jul & Aug) Guided old-town tours, including night visits, as well as information on the local cheese and wine routes.

Maison des Parcs et de la Montagne (☎ 04 79 60 04 46; www.maisondesparcsetdelamontagne.fr, in French; 256 rue de la République; 🕑 10am-noon & 2-7pm Tue-Sat) Stocks information and exhibitions on the three local parks: national park La Vanoise, and regional parks Les Bauges and La Chartreuse.

CHAMBÉRY PASS

Available from the tourist office, the card costs €4 and offers a number of reductions across sights in Chambéry and nearby attractions such as the Abbaye d'Hautecombe, the Musée de la Grande Chartreuse or the Maison des Jeux Olympiques d'Hiver in Albertville (see p550). The pass also includes discounts on activities from swimming to ice skating, horse riding and bike rentals.

Sights

CHÂTEAU DES DUCS DE SAVOIE

Now home to the region's *Conseil Général* (County Council), Chambéry's forbidding 14th-century **Château des Ducs de Savoie** (place du Château; adult/student/under 18yr €4/2.50/free; tours 2.30pm Mon-Fri May, Jun & Sep, 10.30am, 2.30pm, 3.30pm & 4.30pm Mon-Fri Jul & Aug) can only be visited by guided tours. Tours depart from the **Accueil des Guides office** (04 79 33 42 47; place du Château), opposite the château steps.

Tours take in the adjoining **Ste-Chapelle**, built in the 15th century to house the Shroud of Turin. Chambéry lost the relic to Turin in 1860 when Savoy became part of France. Visit the 70-bell **Grand Carillon** in Ste-Chapelle – Europe's largest bell chamber – on a guided tour or enjoy it in full concert on the first and third Saturdays of the month at 5.30pm.

FONTAINE DES ÉLÉPHANTS

With its four mighty carved elephants, this bizarre **Fontaine des Éléphants** (place des Éléphants) could be the model for an Indian postage stamp. It was sculpted in 1838 in honour of Général de Boigne (1751–1830), a local who made his fortune in the East Indies. When he returned home, he bestowed some of his wealth on the town and was honoured posthumously with this monument. Among his various local projects was the construction of the arcaded street that leads from the fountain to Château des Ducs de Savoie.

MUSEUMS

Admission is free on the first Sunday of the month.

South of the fountain in an old Franciscan monastery, near the 15th- and 16th-century **Cathédrale Métropole St-François de Sales** (place de la Métropole; 8am-noon & 2-6.30pm), is the fantastic **Musée Savoisien** (04 79 33 44 48; sq de Lannoy de Bissy; adult/student/under 18yr €3/1.50/free; 10am-noon & 2-6pm Wed-Mon), home to various local archeological finds including a gallery of 13th-century wall paintings discovered behind a false roof inside a local mansion. Traditional Savoyard mountain life zooms into perspective on the 2nd floor with temporary exhibitions such as the history of sledging.

Musée des Beaux-Arts (04 79 33 75 03; place du Palais de Justice; admission free except during exhibitions; 10am-noon & 2-6pm Wed-Mon) houses a small collection of 14th- to 18th-century Italian works.

French philosopher and writer Jean-Jacques Rousseau lived with his lover, Baronne Louise Éléonore de Warens, at **Les Charmettes** (04 79 33 39 44; 890 chemin des Charmettes; admission free; 10am-noon & 2-6pm Wed-Mon Apr-Sep, to 4.30pm Oct-Mar), 1km southeast of the town, from 1736 to 1742. The late-17th-century house has been wonderfully maintained. A trail leads through the rich garden of herbs, flowers and plants where you can learn more about Rousseau's passion for botany.

Sleeping

Gîtes de France (04 79 33 22 56; www.gites-de-france-savoie.com; 24 bd de la Colonne) takes bookings for *chambres d'hôtes* (B&Bs) and self-catering accommodation in or around Chambéry; find it inside the tourist office on the 4th floor. The nearest hostel is in Aix-les-Bains (p550).

Art Hôtel (04 79 62 37 26; www.arthotel-chambery.com; 154 rue Sommeiller; s/d/tr €48/56/66) There's nothing artistic about this hotel, be it its flag-lined concrete facade or drab rooms. But it is a well-run place, conveniently located halfway between the town centre and the train station, which is why so many business people and visiting academics to the Université de Savoie stay here.

Best Hotel (04 79 85 76 79; www.besthotel.fr/chambery; 9 rue Denfert Rochereau; s/d/tr €55/63/79) The decor at this hotel won't rock the design world but rooms are comfortable, clean and the best ones overlook place du Théâtre. It's also supercentral. The buffet breakfast is €9 – watch out for the egg-cooking machine, it practically takes an engineer to get it going.

Les Pervenches (04 79 33 34 26; 600 chemin des Charmettes; r €60-80) In a quiet hamlet just 1km from the centre and 200m from Rousseau's former house Les Charmettes, Les Pervenches offers nine cosy rooms with bucolic views of the surrounding hills. The on-site restaurant, Le Clos Normand (mains €15), serves plenty of cheesy goodies but from a different part of France this time (the owners' native Normandy).

La Ferme du Petit Bonheur (☎ 04 79 85 26 17; www.fermedupetitbonheur.fr; 538 chemin Jean-Jacques; s/d/tr €75/85/105) It really will be 'little happiness' if you choose to stay with Eric and Chantal at their wonderful *chambre d'hôte* in the hills. Eric is a musician, Chantal a painter, and their exquisite tastes show throughout their five beautifully appointed rooms and the amazing home-made croissants for breakfast. In summer, Toscane the Labrador will beg children to throw the ball one more time, and for those long winter nights, what better than reading a book by the wood-burning stone in the cosy living room?

Eating

Le Vivaldi (☎ 04 79 33 58 42; 32 rue Croix d'Or; mains from €8; ⏰ lunch & dinner) Decorated as if this were someone's living room, Le Vivaldi serves excellent pizzas and pasta for trivial prices. The streetside terrace fills up the minute the sun starts shining, but if you can't get a seat, you can always opt for takeaway.

Le Savoyard (☎ 04 79 33 36 55; 35 place Monge; mains €10-20; ⏰ lunch & dinner Mon-Sat) The decor is resolutely non-Alpine (think urban design den rather than Savoyard chalet), but the menu sure is with a wondrous selection of cheesy specialities. Those on a diet or in search of alternative flavours will be pleased to know that there is plenty to cater for them too, such as scallop risotto or steak with home-made *frites*.

Brasserie Le Z (☎ 04 79 85 96 87; www.zorelle.com, in French; 12 av des Ducs de Savoie; mains €10-25; ⏰ lunch & dinner) In rather quiet Chambéry, this is a very pleasant surprise indeed: tall tables, bizarrely shaped plates, chandeliers and psychedelic colours play host to some very fine and beautifully presented food (grilled fish, tasty meats, creamy risottos). Even more surprising (and welcome!), Le Z is open seven days a week, rescuing you from picnic leftover gloom on Sunday night.

La Table de Marie (☎ 04 79 85 99 76; 193 rue Croix d'Or; mains €12; ⏰ lunch Wed-Sun, dinner Sat only) This pocket-sized restaurant is an odd combination of prim, flowery decor which seems suitable for the tea-house part of the business (scrumptious cakes washed down with organic tea and hot chocolate), but less so perhaps for the lunchtime steaks and Savoyard specialities!

La Maniguette (103 rue Juiverie; mains €16, 3-course menu €29; ⏰ lunch Tue, lunch & dinner Wed-Sat) The strapline of this restaurant is *Chercheurs de Goût* (Taste Explorers), and everything here does go the extra mile to add a touch of originality: the bread is home-baked, the menu changes every month and always adds a faraway twist to local flavours.

SELF-CATERING

Chambéry's Saturday morning **food market** (on place du Palais de Justice until 2010 while the covered market on place de Genève gets some much-needed renovation) is a gastronome's rendezvous. Pedestrian rue du Sénat otherwise boasts butcher, baker and chocolate-maker shops.

Laiterie des Halles (☎ 04 79 33 77 17; 2 place de Genève; ⏰ 7.30am-12.15pm & 3-7.15pm Tue-Sat) Cheese fiends will go gaga at this dairy shop.

Monoprix supermarket (place du 8 Mai 1945; ⏰ 8.30am-8pm Mon-Sat)

Drinking

The huge open square of place St-Léger is the summertime heart of Chambéry's drinking scene.

O'Cardinal's (☎ 04 79 85 53 40; 5 place de la Métropole; ⏰ 5pm-1.30am Sun & Mon, 10am-1.30am Tue-Sat) Leather banquet seating, superfriendly staff and great pub grub (noon to 2pm Tuesday to Saturday) have turned this into Chambéry students' favourite pub. In warmer – and since the smoking ban even cold – weather the cheer spills out onto cathedral-shaded place de la Métropole.

Le Café du Théâtre (☎ 04 79 33 16 53; place du Théâtre; ⏰ 7am-1.30am) This tiny café seems like a concentrate of Chambéry's local life. Business people stop for a coffee on the way to work, retired people come for a prelunch drink with their mates, schoolchildren order a crêpe on their way home and students come here to kick-start or even spend the evening. Join them all, whatever the time of day.

Getting There & Away

AIR

Chambéry-Savoie Airport (☎ 04 79 54 49 54; www.chambery-airport.com), 10km north in Viviers du Lac, is serviced by no-frills flights to/from Oslo, Stockholm and a bunch of regional British airports; see p961 for details.

BUS

From the **bus station** (☎ 04 79 69 11 88; place de la Gare; ⏰ ticket office hours vary) there are buses to/from local ski resort La Féclaz (€7.10, 50 minutes, up to seven daily), Aix-les-Bains (€3, 25 minutes, two daily), Annecy (€9.20, one hour, seven daily) and Grenoble (€5.10, two hours, 10 daily). There are three daily buses to/from Geneva airport (€30, 1½ hours) and up to five a day to/from Lyon St-Exupéry airport (€20, one hour).

TRAIN

From Chambéry **train station** (place de la Gare; ticket office 5.45am-9pm Mon-Thu & Sat, 5.25am-11pm Fri, 5.45am-10pm Sun) there are major rail connections running to/from Paris' Gare de Lyon (€68.20, three hours, 11 daily), Lyon (€15.20, 1½ hours, 12 daily), Annecy (€8.60, 45 minutes, 25 daily), Geneva (€14.60, 1½ hours, five daily) and Grenoble (€9.90, one hour, 10 to 13 daily). Trains also run through the Maurienne Valley to Modane (€14.30, 1¼ hours, nine daily) and onwards into Italy.

In town, buy tickets at the **SNCF Boutique** (21 place St-Léger; 9am-12.45pm & 1.30-6pm Mon-Fri, 9.30am-12.30pm & 2-5.30pm Sat).

Getting Around

TO/FROM THE AIRPORT

Frustratingly, there are no bus services from Chambéry centre to the airport. The 15-minute journey by taxi costs around €17 – call **Allo Taxi Chambéry** (04 79 69 11 12).

BICYCLE

Pick up wheels for €1/5/10 per hour/day/week and advice on marked trails and itineraries from **Vélo Station** (04 79 96 34 13; 6.30am-7pm Mon-Fri, 9am-7pm Sat & Sun Apr-Oct, closed Sun Nov-Mar) at the train station. The greater Chambéry area boasts 66km of cycling lanes.

BUS

City buses run from 6am to around 8pm Monday to Saturday and are operated by **STAC** (04 79 68 67 00). A single ticket/carnet of 10 cost €1.10/6.78. They are sold at tobacconists and the **STAC information kiosk** (23 bd du Musée; 7.30am-12.30pm & 1-6.30pm Mon-Fri, 8.30am-12.30pm & 2.30-5.30pm Sat).

Buses 3, 5, 6, 7 and 9 link the train station with Fontaine des Éléphants.

AROUND CHAMBÉRY

Chambéry is sandwiched by two green-rich regional nature parks. Southwest, the **Parc Naturel Régional de Chartreuse** (www.parc-chartreuse.net, in French) safeguards the wild forested slopes of the Chartreuse massif, dubbed the 'desert' by the Chartreux monks who settled here more than 1000 years ago, and best known for the bright-green herbal liquor made here by the monks since 1737. The **park headquarters** (04 76 88 75 20; www.chartreuse-tourisme.com) in St-Pierre de Chartreuse, 40km south of Chambéry, has information on visiting the Voiron **distillery** where the liquor is produced, as well as the **Musée de la Grande Chartreuse** (04 76 88 60 45; www.musee-grande-chartreuse.fr; La Correrie, St-Pierre de Chartreuse; adult/student €4/2; Feb-Oct), which explores the monastery's millennium-long history and the monks' reclusive lifestyle.

Northeast, outdoor enthusiasts can delve into 800 sq km of royal hiking and biking opportunities in the little-known **Parc Naturel Régional du Massif des Bauges** (www.parcdesbauges.com) with its endless pastures and plateaux. Several marked trails kick off from the **Maison Faune-Flore** (04 79 52 22 56; adult/7-18yr €2.50/1.50; 10.30am-1pm & 1.30-6.30pm Tue-Sun Jul & Aug, 2-6pm Wed & Sun May, Jun, Sep & Oct) in École, where you can learn how to spot some of the 600-odd chamois and plethora of mouflons inhabiting the park.

Snow fiends could do worse than **Savoie Grand Révard** (www.savoiegrandrevard.com), the nearest ski resort to Chambéry, where Baujus (people from the Massif des Bauges) ski at weekends. Downhill skiing is limited to 50km of pistes (€15.20 per day), but cross-country skiing (€8) is big with 140km of trails (the biggest domain in France), as is snowshoeing with 60km of marked itineraries. Tourist offices in **Le Revard** (04 79 54 01 60), **La Féclaz** (04 79 25 80 49) and **Le Châtelard** (04 79 54 84 28; www.lesbauges.com) – the main office in the park – have more information.

Self-pamperers can seek solace in **Aix-les-Bains** (population 27,500), a small thermal spa 11km northwest of Chambéry from where you can sail, swim, pedal-boat, stroll or skate around France's largest natural lake, **Lac du Bourget**. Contact **Compagnie des Bateaux** (04 79 63 45 00; www.gwel.com) at the waterfront Grand Port or the **tourist office** (04 79 88 68 00; www.aixlesbains.com; place Maurice Mollard) in town about lake cruises. A two-hour cruise costs €15.50 and a return trip to the 12th-century **Abbaye d'Hautecombe** on the other side of the lake is €12.20.

The highs and lows of the 1992 Winter Olympics are colourfully retold at **Maison des Jeux Olympiques d'Hiver** (04 79 37 75 71; 11 rue Pargoud; adult/family €3/8; 9am-7pm Mon-Sat, 2-7pm

SAY CHEESE!

Every restaurant in the Alps worth its regional reputation offers **raclette, tartiflette** or **fondue**. To save on pennies but maximise the cheese, opt for the DIY option. Most dairy or grocery shops will lend you the required apparatus provided you buy the ingredients from them. So here's a quick 'how to' guide for your own cheesy fest.

- **Fondue Savoyarde**: The age-old favourite is made with three types of cheeses in equal proportions (Emmental, Beaufort and Comté) and dry white wine (proportions should be about 0.4L of wine for 1kg of cheese). The mix should be melted in a cast-iron dish on a hob, which can then be kept warm with a small burner on the table (that'll be the fondue set for you). As for eating, dunk chunks of dry bread or baguette in the cheesy goo. **Our tip:** Rub or add garlic to the dish – you'll have cheesy breath anyway, so what the hell.
- **Raclette:** Named after the Swiss cheese of the same name (with just a quick gender change in the process: *Le* Raclette is the cheese, *La* Raclette the dish), a raclette is a combination of melting cheese, boiled potatoes, charcuterie (deli meats) and baby gherkins. Traditionally, half a Raclette cheese is placed under a grill and the top layer regularly scraped in all its melting glory. Less spectacular but far more practical, is the home raclette kit: an oval hot plate with a grill underneath and individual dishes to melt slices of cheese. **Our tip:** Try to squeeze cheese, potato, charcuterie and gherkins in every mouthful (not a whole potato obviously).
- **Tartiflette**: Easy-peasy. You don't even need special equipment with that one, just an ovenproof dish and the oven to put it in. Buy one whole Reblochon cheese. Slice it in half lengthwise (ie you should end up with two thinner rounds, not two semicircles). In the dish, mix together slices of parboiled potatoes, crème fraîche, onions and lardons (diced bacon). Whack the two cheese halves on top, bake for about 40 minutes at 180°C, and ta-da! **Our tip:** More crème fraîche and more lardons (a sprinkle of nutmeg is also really good)!

Sun Jul & Aug, 9.30am-12.30pm & 2-6pm Mon-Sat Sep-Jun) in Albertville, a disappointingly uninspiring town 39km east of Chambéry.

Sleeping

our pick **Château des Allues** (☎ 06 75 38 61 56; www.chateaudesallues.com; Les Allues, St-Pierre d'Albigny; d €100-140, q €170, dinner adult/child €40/18) Be prepared to be wowed by this beautiful 19th-century bourgeois mansion perched at the top of a hill and proffering sweeping views of the Belledonne range. Painstakingly restored by Stéphane and Didier, it's taken three years of gutting, scrubbing, painting and trawling antique markets up and down the region to get it in that shape, but what a result. The whole place oozes charm, elegance and originality: the wood panelling in the dining room was salvaged from a 17th-century pharmacy, the floor tiles are the château's original – as is the re-enamelled bath-tub with legs in one of the five spacious, lavishly furnished rooms – and Didier's old childhood toy cars crowd the lobby's glass shelves. Stéphane's cooking is as stylish as the rest of the house, with many of the fresh products coming from the vegetable garden.

LES TROIS VALLÉES

Named after its valley trio, this sought-after ski area is vast, fast and the largest in the world – 600km of pistes and 200 lifts across three ritzy resorts: **Val Thorens**, Europe's highest at a heady 2300m; wealthy old **Méribel** (elevation 1450m) created by Scotsman Colonel Peter Lindsay in 1938; and trendsetting **Courchevel** (a fave of Victoria Beckham), a series of purpose-built resorts at altitudes of 1550m, 1650m and 1850m, where fashion is as hot on as off the slopes. In between is a sprinkling of lesser-known villages – **Le Praz** (elevation 1300m), **St-Martin de Belleville** (elevation 1450m) and **La Tania** (elevation 1400m), linked by lifts to their big-sister resorts.

Information

Courchevel 1850 Tourist Office (☎ 04 79 08 00 29; www.courchevel.com; 🕒 9am-7pm Jul-Aug & Dec-Apr, 9am-noon & 2-6pm Mon-Fri Sep-Nov, May & Jun) Sister offices at 1650m, 1550m and 1300m.

Méribel Tourist Office (☎ 04 79 08 60 01; www.meribel.net; Maison du Tourisme; ⌚ 9am-7pm Dec-Apr, 9am-noon & 2-5pm Mon, Tue, Thu & Fri, 9am-noon Wed & Sat Sep-Nov, May & Jun, 9am-noon & 3-7pm Jul & Aug)
Val Thorens Tourist Office (☎ 04 79 00 08 08; www.valthorens.com; Maison de Val Thorens; ⌚ 8.30am-7pm)

Activities

The three valleys will appease the feistiest of outdoor-action appetites, Méribel Valley alone boasting 57 downhill ski runs (150km), 57 ski lifts, two snowboarding parks, a slalom stadium and two Olympic downhill runs. In Courchevel there's another 150km of downhill piste to explore and a superb 2km-long floodlit toboggan run (a great adrenalin-pumping après-ski alternative); while Val Thorens, though smaller, proffers summer skiing on the Glacier de Péclet. A Trois Vallées pass costing €44/220 for one/six days covers the entire area, but cheaper single-valley passes are also available.

Courchevel is big on alternative snow action, the key info point being **La Croisette** (place du Forum; ⌚ 7am-8pm) in Courchevel 1850, where the **ESF** (☎ 04 79 08 07 72; www.esfcourchevel.com) resides in winter and the superfriendly **Maison de la Montagne** year-round. The latter takes bookings for guided off-piste adventures, heli-skiing, snowshoeing and ski mountaineering as well as go-karting or driving on ice, snowmobile treks and snow-rafting, and is home to the **Bureau des Guides** (☎ 04 79 01 03 66; www.guides-courchevel-meribel.com). You can also try your hands at mushing with **Traineau Évasion** (☎ 04 79 08 81 55; Le Plantain, La Tania; per hr €55); this is surprisingly hard work and not suitable for children under 12.

In summer, rock climbing, mountain biking, hiking and paragliding are rife in all three valleys. In July and August **Chardon Loisirs** (☎ 04 79 08 39 60; www.chardonloisirs.com; La Croisette) organises canyoning and rafting on the Doron de Belleville and Isère Rivers.

Sleeping & Eating

All three resorts have a **central accommodation service** (Courchevel ☎ 04 79 08 14 44; www.courchevel-reservation.com; Méribel ☎ 04 79 00 50 00; infos@meribel-reservations.com; Val Thorens ☎ 04 79 00 01 06; www.valthorens.com/resa).

Hôtel Olympic (☎ 04 79 08 08 24; rue des Tovets, Courchevel 1850; d €42-99, per week €279-659) This is Courchevel's cheapest hotel and a nice place to boot. Rooms are unpretentious, with white walls, crisp colourful duvet covers and balconies. In the evenings, chill out by the fireplace in the bar-lounge; and fill up for a day of fun at the gargantuan buffet breakfast in the morning.

Le Doron (☎ 04 79 08 60 02; hotel_doron@wanadoo.fr; rte de la Chaudanne, Méribel; low/high season d €96/146, tr €117/177) Among the cheapest options – not cheap – is this place, above a rowdy Brit-styled pub opposite Méribel tourist office.

Les Peupliers (☎ 04 79 08 41 47; www.lespeupliers.com; Le Praz; summer only d €110, half-board per person d low/high season €130/190) This hotel has managed the rare feat of combining authentic village feel with plush, stylish creature comforts such as hammam and jacuzzi. The downstairs bar fills up every night with a jolly après-ski crowd, many of whom then move to La Table de Mon Grand-Père, the hotel's restaurant.

La Bouitte (☎ 04 79 08 96 77; www.la-bouitte.com; St-Marcel; summer d/tr from €200/250, winter €248/417; 2-/3-course menu €69/86, mains €50-100; ⌚ Jul, Aug & mid-Dec–Apr) This is a fairy-tale chalet, with everything just the way you'd imagine it to be in a perfect Alpine world. The eight exquisite rooms are an ode to centenary-old wood, and the food at the two-Michelin-starred restaurant is out of this world. Find it in the hamlet of St-Marcel, 1km south of St-Martin de Belleville.

There are plenty of very expensive hangouts in Courchevel, but normal human beings can hang out at **Prends Ta Luge et Tire-Toi** (Take Your Sledge And Piss Off; ☎ 04 79 08 78 68; www.laluge.com; Le Forum, Courchevel 1850; ⌚ 9am-2am daily), an odd combination of surf shop, Caribbean-themed bar and internet café (€8 per hour). Extra points awarded for the most random name ever.

Getting There & Away

The four-lane A43 links Chambéry (88km northwest) with the nearest town, Moûtiers, 18km north of Méribel. All ski resorts are signposted as you approach Moûtiers.

Shuttle buses link all three resorts with Geneva (€70, 3½ hours) and Lyon St-Exupéry (€64, three to four hours) airports. There are also regular weekend buses between Chambéry airport and Moûtiers (€40, one hour), from where you can catch the shuttles to the resorts.

Moûtiers is the nearest train station, with trains to/from Chambéry (€11.70, 1¼ hours) and TGVs galore to Paris between late

A BOWL OF FARM AIR

Unlike many purpose-built ski resorts, Val d'Isère is a genuine village with year-round inhabitants. Claudine is one of them and she runs one of the town's most delectable shops, **La Fermette de Claudine** (☎ 04 79 06 13 89; www.lafermettedeclaudine.com; Val Village). All dairy products – fresh unpasteurised milk, the wonderful cheeses, the yoghurts – come from her dairy farm, **La Ferme de l'Adroit**, just 1km down the road in the direction of Col de l'Iseran. The farm is open to the public and you can watch cheese production (Tomme, Avalin, Beaufort) in the morning or milking in the afternoon. As well as fab cheeses, the town shop sells wondrous *saucissons* (sausages) and can lend you raclette and fondue kits.

December and March (€76.80, 4¾ hours). **Eurostar** (www.eurostar.com) also operates direct trains to/from London during the winter season (return from €220, eight hours, overnight or day service, weekends only).

Transdev Savoie (☎ 08 20 22 74 13; www.altibus.com) operates up to 12 regional buses daily between Moûtiers and Méribel (€12.50, 45 minutes), Courchevel (€9.70 to €12.50, 40 to 60 minutes) and Val Thorens (€16, one hour).

VAL D'ISÈRE

pop 1660 / elevation 1850m

It's hard to say what people come to Val d'Isère for, whether it's for the awesome skiing or the never-ending party. The fact that you can actually dance on the slopes has somehow blurred the distinction. If you're seeking traditional Alpine atmosphere, you may have to reconsider your choice of destination, which is ironic since Val d'Isère is one of the few ski resorts to have a year-round village life. The resort is located in the upper Tarentaise Valley, 31km southeast of Bourg St-Maurice, and attracts a mostly young, foreign crowd.

Lac du Chevril looms up large on the approach to Val d'Isère. The dark reservoir lake and its dam slumber on the grave of Tignes-le-Lac, the village flooded by the 1950s electricity-generating project. Out of its ashes rose **Tignes** (elevation 2100m), a purpose-built lakeside village that – together with Val d'Isère – forms the **Espace Killy** skiing area (named after home-grown triple Olympic gold medallist Jean-Claude Killy). In February 2009 it staged the World Alpine Skiing Championships.

Information

Tourist Office (☎ 04 79 06 06 60; www.valdisere.com; place Jacques Mouflier; 🕑 8.30am-7.30pm Dec-Apr, Jul & Aug, 9am-noon & 2-6pm Mon-Fri rest of the year) Internet access here costs €9 per hour or €5 for wi-fi.

Activities

WINTER ACTIVITIES

Espace Killy offers fabulous skiing on 300km of marked pistes between 1550m and 3450m. Ski touring is also excellent, especially in the Parc National de la Vanoise. The snowboarders' Snowspace Park in La Daille has a half-pipe, tables, gaps, quarter-pipes and kicker ramps, while the runs around Tignes are popular with both snowboarders and skiers. In July and August you can ski on the glacier.

Ski schools teaching boarding, cross-country and off-piste skiing are a dime a dozen. The **ESF** (☎ 04 79 06 02 34; carrefour des Dolomites; www.esfvaldisere.com) is in Val Village, a hub of shops and services backing onto the slopes. Nearby, **STVI** (🕑 8.30am-7pm Mon-Fri & Sun, 8am-8pm Sat Dec-Apr) sells lift passes covering Espace Killy (one/six days €42/202.50) and – for five-day or longer passes – one day's skiing in La Plagne, Les Arcs, Les Trois Vallées or Valmorel. Unusually, beginner lifts opposite Val Village are free. Glacial summer skiing starts in late June and lasts for anything from two weeks to two months.

Heli-skiing in Italy (it is illegal in France), ice climbing, snowshoeing, snowmobiling, mushing and paragliding with skis (to land!) are other snow-driven activities. Fun-driven are the floodlit airboarding and snake-gliss sledging sessions held four times a week on the Savonette nursery slope opposite Val Village.

SUMMER ACTIVITIES

The valleys and trails from Val d'Isère into the nearby Parc National de la Vanoise (p555) proffer an orgy of outdoor action. Be it walking, mountain biking, trekking or rock climbing, the **Bureau des Guides** (☎ 06 14 62 90 24; www.guide-montagne-tarentaise.com) in the Killy Sport shop next to the tourist office can arrange it.

ALPINE PARADISE

Valérie Graziano, owner of **La Ferme d'Angèle** (☎ 04 79 41 05 71; www.ferme-angele.com; Le Noveray, Séez; half-board per person dm/d €70/75), has turned this beautiful 1830 stone mountain farm into the Alpine equivalent of a '1001 night' palace. Beds disappear under enormous feather duvets, bathroom sinks are made of old brass tubs, thick Afghan rugs cover original stone floors, the reading room looks out to scenic Alpine skyline, and whole legs or shoulders of meat roast in the roaring fireplace while home-made soups bubble up in a Harry Potter–sized cauldron. Rooms vary from double to six-people duplex and all have access to the sauna and outdoor hot tub. La Ferme d'Angèle is only a couple of minutes away from La Rosière ski area (cross-border with Italy) or half an hour by car to Les Arcs or 45 minutes to Val d'Isère.

Find La Ferme d'Angèle 4km from Bourg St-Maurice, in the direction of Italy and La Rosière in the hamlet of Le Noveray above Séez.

Sleeping

Find out about availability and make hotel reservations (essential in high season) through the **Centre de Réservation Hôtellerie** (☎ 04 79 06 18 90; valhotel@valdisere.com). For self-catering accommodation, contact **Val Location** (☎ 04 79 06 06 60; vallocation@valdisere.com). Prices vary widely, pricey being the common factor.

Hôtel Bellevue (☎ 04 79 06 00 03; d with half-board per person €80, with bathroom & half-board per person €105) This central, family-run hotel on the main street screams 1960s. Rooms in the hotel, annexe and chalet are basic but good value for skiers who are in town to ski rather than self-pamper. Half-board is a no-frills home-cooking kind of deal.

Relais du Ski & La Bailletta (☎ 04 79 06 02 06; http://lerelaisduski.valdisere.com; rte Fornet; s/d/tr/q incl breakfast Relais from 70/88/102/124, Bailletta from 117/136/171/196; ⌚ Dec-Apr, Jul & Aug) A 500m stroll from the centre, this is effectively two hotels rolled into one. La Bailletta does comfortable midrange rooms while Relais du Ski has nine basic rooms with shared bathrooms reminiscent of student accommodation. Both hotels share the buffet breakfast, which is a feast. Half- and full-board deals available.

Eating

Many restaurants cater to a largely English clientele, making quality varied and unpredictable. Better deals can be had opting for full-board in your hotel. Goodies, lots of them, are sold at main-street **Maison Chevallot** (⌚ 7am-8pm).

Quicksilver & Billabong Coffee Shops (☎ 04 79 06 09 54; burgers & wraps €8-15; ⌚ 9am-10pm) What do you get when you mix two of the trendiest surf brands in a French Alpine resort? An American diner! With massive burgers, huge portions of *frites* and gooey brownies.

Bananas (☎ 04 79 06 04 23; mains €15; ⌚ 11.30am-2am) A bizarre, but somehow very popular, mix of Tex-Mex and Indian is dished up at this party shack at the bottom of La Face, behind the Bellevarde Express. It starts filling as skiers pack up for the day and doesn't empty till close.

La Fruitière (☎ 04 79 06 07 17; mains €20; ⌚ lunch Dec-Apr) At the top of the La Daille bubble at 2400m, this piste-side oasis of fine dining is legendary. Snuggle under a rug to keep warm on the terrace and savour traditional but creative cuisine in a hip dairy setting.

Sur la Montagne (☎ 04 79 40 06 12; mains €20; ⌚ lunch & dinner) Pizza à la Val d'Isère: Italy may only be on the other side of the mountain but at La Montagne, mozzarella has been trumped by local cheeses St-Marcellin and Reblochon. There are some creative pasta, fish and meat dishes too.

Le Blizzard (☎ 04 79 06 02 07; mains €20-30; ⌚ lunch & dinner) Fine dining in a refined chalet atmosphere is what one of Val d'Isère's chicest hotel-restaurants offers. Views from the dining room's bay windows are stupendous. It's just a shame diners are not allowed to use the tantalisingly close pool.

Casino (⌚ 7.30am-1.30pm & 3-9pm) Supermarket on the main street opposite the Boutique Autocars Martin.

Drinking & Entertainment

Get hold of a copy of the free weekly *Mountain Echo* (a tongue-in-cheek resort mag put together by the resort's anglophone seasonal workers) or *Valscope* (which lists events, film screenings and other organised fun) to find out what's happening. Here's our pick of the hottest bars:

Dick's Tea Bar (☎ 04 79 06 14 87; www.dicksteabar.com; admission before/after midnight free/€13.50; ⏲ 8am-4am) Val d'Isère's party HQ. Live music starts from 4.30pm; DJs follow later on in the night, all night.

La Folie Douce (☎ 04 79 06 01 47; ⏲ 11am-5.30pm) If you can't wait to party until you're back in the village, DJs and live bands big it up every day on this outdoor terrace at the top of La Daille's cable car from 3pm. Ibiza in the Alps.

Le Lodge (☎ 04 79 06 02 01; ⏲ 11.30am-2am) Attracting a slightly more discerning (dare we say it, older) crowd, Le Lodge is definitely more of a bar than a pub.

Le Petit Danois (☎ 04 79 06 27 97; ⏲ 8am-1.30am) Cheap beer and lairy crowd; thank God they serve full English breakfast the next morning to mop up the mess.

Warm Up (☎ 04 79 08 27 00; ⏲ 11.30am-2am) Oh the cosy retro leather sofas, the beers, the free wi-fi, the pool table, the fun; it's the perfect après-ski spot.

Getting There & Away

Six daily buses in season link Val d'Isère with Tignes (€7.20) and Bourg St-Maurice train station (€13.10, 45 minutes). Tickets must be reserved 48 hours in advance at the **Boutique Autocars Martin** (☎ 04 79 06 00 42; ⏲ 8.30-11am & 12.30-7pm Mon-Fri, 6.30am-7pm Sat, 6.30-11am & 12.30-7pm Sun) on the main street in the resort centre. The **SNCF desk** (⏲ 10am-12.30pm & 3-6.30pm Tue-Sat) here sells train tickets.

> **SNOWMAN'S LARDER**
>
> Whenever you think every good business idea under the sun has been taken up, something else comes up and you think, genius! **Snowman's Larder** (☎ 06 24 09 20 09; www.snowmans-larder.com) is one of those: online shopping for self-catering skiers.
>
> It's cheaper than resort supermarkets and you can either pick and choose from their list or go for their ready-made packs of groceries, some of which include ingredients for staple meals such as spaghetti bolognese or chicken curry. Party animals will like the booze-packed kit while families will thank the mother in Snowmans' Larder who remembered the fruit and veg and the mini Baby Bells in the Kids' pack.
>
> Snowman's Larder delivers in Val d'Isère and Tignes in winter.

In Bourg, you can connect to buses for Chambéry airport (one way/return €40/70, 1½ hours weekend only). Other seasonal bus services include three or four daily to/from Geneva airport (one way/return €70/118, four hours) and two to five daily to/from Lyon St-Exupéry airport (one way/return €62/94, four hours). Again, advance reservations are obligatory. **Eurostar** (www.eurostar.com) operates direct winter weekend services between Bourg St-Maurice and London (return from €220, nine hours, overnight or day service).

PARC NATIONAL DE LA VANOISE

A wild mix of high mountains, steep valleys and vast glaciers, the **Parc National de la Vanoise** (www.vanoise.com) sports 530 sq km of spectacular scenery between the Tarentaise (north) and Maurienne (south) Valleys: snowcapped peaks mirrored in icy lakes is just the start! It was the country's first national park in 1963 and is very much a green haven. Five designated nature reserves and an inhabited peripheral zone embracing 28 villages border the highly protected core of the park where marmots, chamois and France's largest colony of Alpine ibexes graze freely and undisturbed beneath the larch trees. Overhead, 20 pairs of golden eagle and the odd bearded vulture fly in solitary wonder.

A hiker's heaven, yes, although **walking trails** are limited and accessible for a fraction of the year – June to late September usually. The **Grand Tour de Haute Maurienne**, a hike of five days or more around the upper reaches of the valley, takes in the very best of the national park. The **GR5** and **GR55** cross it, and other trails snake south to the Park National des Écrins (p563) and east into Italy's Grand Paradiso National Park.

Lanslebourg and **Bonneval-sur-Arc**, two pretty villages along the southern edge of the park, are the main accommodation bases from which to explore. The **Maison du Val Cénis** (☎ 04 79 05 23 66; www.valcenis.com; ⏲ 9am-noon & 2-7pm mid-Dec–Apr, Jul & Aug, shorter hr rest of year) in Lanslebourg, and Bonneval-sur-Arc's **tourist office** (☎ 04 79 05 95 95; www.bonneval-sur-arc.com; ⏲ 9am-noon & 2-6.30pm Mon-Sat high season, to 5.30pm rest of year) stock practical information on the limited skiing (cross-country and downhill), walking and other activities in the park. In Termignon-la-Vanoise, 6km southwest of Lanslebourg, the tiny national park–run

Maison de la Vanoise (☎ 04 79 20 51 67; admission free; ⌚ hr vary) portrays the park through ethnographical eyes.

Getting There & Away

All three mountain passes linking the national park with Italy – the Col du Petit St-Bernard, Col de l'Iseran and Col du Mont Cénis – are shut in winter.

Trains serving the valley leave from Chambéry and run as far as Modane, 23km southwest of Lanslebourg, from where **Transdev Savoie** (☎ 08 20 22 74 13; www.transavoie.com) runs three to four daily buses to/from Termignon-la-Vanoise (€7.90, 40 minutes), Lanslebourg (€10.60, 50 minutes) and Bonneval-sur-Arc (€15.90, 1¼ hours).

DAUPHINÉ

Apart from its celebrated gratin *(gratin dauphinois)*, the Dauphiné's other big legacy to the French lexicon is historical. In 1339 Dauphiné ruler Humbert II established a university in Grenoble. A decade later, lacking money and a successor, he sold Dauphiné to the French king, Charles V, who started the tradition whereby the eldest son of the king of France (the crown prince) ruled Dauphiné and bore the title 'dauphin'.

Now a defunct administrative entity, the Dauphiné refers to territories south and southwest of Savoy, stretching from the River Rhône in the west to the Italian border in the east. It includes the city of Grenoble and, a little further east, the mountainous Parc National des Écrins. The gentler terrain of the western part of Dauphiné is typified by the Parc Naturel Régional du Vercors, much loved by cross-country skiers. In the east, the town of Briançon stands guard on the Italian frontier.

GRENOBLE

pop 155,100

One of the great things about Grenoble is that every corner you turn and every street you take yields spectacular views of the surrounding Alps. It's intoxicating to think this is only the tip of the iceberg and that there are 10 times more mountain marvels just on your doorstep…

But Grenoble isn't just an Alpine base: since the 1960s the city has grown into a leading technology hub, with cutting-edge work in nuclear physics and nanotechnology. Culturally too, Grenoble has some outstanding museums showcasing world-class modern art and a busy performing-arts scene, which the city's 60,000 students lap up. So whatever you go to Grenoble for, you'll certainly get a lot more than you bargained for.

Orientation

Grenoble is tricky to negotiate from behind the wheel thanks to the bewildering one-way system and disorientating tram network. The old city is centred on place Grenette and place Notre Dame, both 1km east of the train and bus stations. The main university campus is a couple of kilometres east of the old centre, on the southern side of the River Isère.

Information

BOOKSHOPS

Decitre (☎ 04 76 03 36 36; 9-11 Grande Rue) Mainstream bookshop with English titles.

EMERGENCY

Duty Pharmacy (☎ 04 76 63 42 55)

Grenoble University Hospital (☎ 04 76 76 75 75) Hôpital Nord La Tronche (av de Marquis du Grésivaudan; tram stop 'La Tronche' on tramway line B); Hôpital Sud (av de Kimberley, Echirolles; bus 11 & 13)

INTERNET ACCESS

Log in to the tourist office's two computers (below) for €2 per 15 minutes or €5 an hour.

Celsius Café (☎ 04 76 00 13 60; 15 rue Jean-Jacques Rousseau; per 30/60min €1.50/2.50; ⌚ 9am-11pm Mon-Sat, 1-8pm Sun) Top location and facilities.

Neptune Internet (☎ 04 76 63 94 18; 2 rue de la Paix; per 30/60min €2.50/3.50; ⌚ 1-7pm Mon-Sat, 2-6pm Sun) A funky, tidy place with lots of QWERTY keyboards.

Pl@net Internet (☎ 04 76 47 44 74; 1 place Vaucanson; per hr €3.50; ⌚ 8.30am-10pm Mon-Sat)

LAUNDRY

Pay about €3.50 to wash a 7kg load:

Au 43 Viallet (43 av Félix Viallet; ⌚ 7am-8pm)

Laverie Berriat (88 cours Berriat; ⌚ 7am-8pm)

POST

Post Office (rue de la République) Next to the tourist office.

TOURIST INFORMATION

Tourist Office (☎ 04 76 42 41 41; www.grenoble-isere-tourisme.com; 14 rue de la République; ⌚ 9am-

6.30pm Mon-Sat, 10am-1pm Sun Oct-Apr, 10am-1pm & 2-5pm May-Sep) Inside the Maison du Tourisme. Sells maps and guides, arranges city tours.

Sights

FORT DE LA BASTILLE

Looming above the old city on the northern side of the River Isère, this grand 16th-century fort is Grenoble's best-known landmark. Built to control the approaches to the city, the stronghold has long been a focus of military and political action.

These days, the strategic importance of **Fort de la Bastille** (498m; www.bastille-grenoble.com) is of the touristy variety thanks to its spectacular mountain views. Three viewpoint indicators explain the surrounding vistas, and panels map out hiking trails, some of which lead down the hillside.

To get to the fort, hop aboard the riverside **Téléphérique Grenoble Bastille** (☎ 04 76 44 33 65; quai Stéphane Jay; adult/student/under 5yr one-way €4.15/3.35/free, return €6.10/4.85/free; ⌚ Feb-Nov). The ascent in egg-shaped pods, which climb 264m from the quay over the swift waters of the River Isère, is almost more fun than the fort itself. Unsurprisingly, it gets crowded in summer – leave early to avoid the worst queues. Or better, walk: it's a pleasant one hour uphill and just over half an hour down.

MUSEUMS

The city has a wealth of great museums, many free.

Musée de Grenoble

The sleek glass and steel exterior of Grenoble's boldest museum spans an entire block between the river Isère and av Maréchal Randon. Also called Musée des Beaux-Arts, **Musée de Grenoble** (☎ 04 76 63 44 44; www.museedegrenoble.fr, in French; 5 place de Lavalette; adult/student €5/2, 1st Sun of month free; ⌚ 10am-6.30pm Wed-Mon) is renowned for its distinguished modern collection, including various works by famous artists Chagall, Matisse, Modigliani, Monet and Picasso, among others. Its classic collection is equally impressive, spanning works from the 13th to 19th century.

Centre National d'Art Contemporain (CNAC)

Housed in the city's other architectural biggie, Grenoble's **Centre National d'Art Contemporain** (CNAC; National Centre of Contemporary Art) is a must-see. Considered one of Europe's leading centres of contemporary art, it is dramatically placed in **Le Magasin** (☎ 04 76 21 95 84; www.magasin-cnac.org; 155 cours Berriat; adult/student/under 10yr €3.50/2/free; ⌚ 2-7pm Tue-Sun), a vast and hugely impressive glass and steel warehouse built by Gustave Eiffel. There are two exhibition areas: the 1000-sq-metre space with a huge glass roof called 'La Rue', in which artists create works designed specifically for this space, and a flexible 900-sq-metre space known as 'The Galleries' which is adapted to the artist's work. Take tram A to Berriat–Le Magasin stop.

Musée Dauphinois

The **Musée Dauphinois** (☎ 04 57 58 89 01; www.musee-dauphinois.fr, in French; 30 rue Maurice Gignoux; admission free; ⌚ 10am-7pm Wed-Mon Jun-Sep, until 6pm Oct-May) beautifully documents the cultures, crafts and traditions of Alpine life, including a fantastic exhibition devoted to the region's skiing history. The museum occupies a beautiful 17th-century convent, nestled at the foot of the hill below Fort de la Bastille. From the city centre, it is most easily reached by the Pont St-Laurent footbridge.

Musée de l'Ancien Évêché

On place Notre Dame, the imposing **Cathédrale Notre Dame** and adjoining 14th-century **Bishops' Palace** – home to Grenoble's bishops until 1908 – form the **Musée de l'Ancien Évêché** (☎ 04 76 03 15 25; www.ancien-eveche-isere.com; 2 rue Très Cloîtres; admission free; ⌚ 9am-6pm Wed-Sat & Mon, 10am-7pm Sun, 1.30-6pm Tue). The palace museum traces local history from prehistory to the 21st century, and takes visitors beneath the cathedral square to a crypt safeguarding old Roman walls and a baptistery dating from the 4th to 10th centuries.

Musée de la Résistance et de la Déportation de l'Isère

The moving **Musée de la Résistance et de la Déportation de l'Isère** (Museum of Resistance and Deportation of Isère; ☎ 04 76 42 38 53; www.resistance-en-isere.com, in French; 14 rue Hébert; admission free; ⌚ 9am-6pm Mon & Wed-Fri, 1.30-6pm Tue, 10am-6pm Sat & Sun Sep-Jun, 10am-7pm Mon & Wed-Sun, 1.30-7pm Tue Jul & Aug) examines the deportation of Jews and other 'undesirables' from Grenoble to Nazi camps during WWII in a cool-headed way. It also documents the role of the Vercors region in the French Resistance. Captions are in French, English and German.

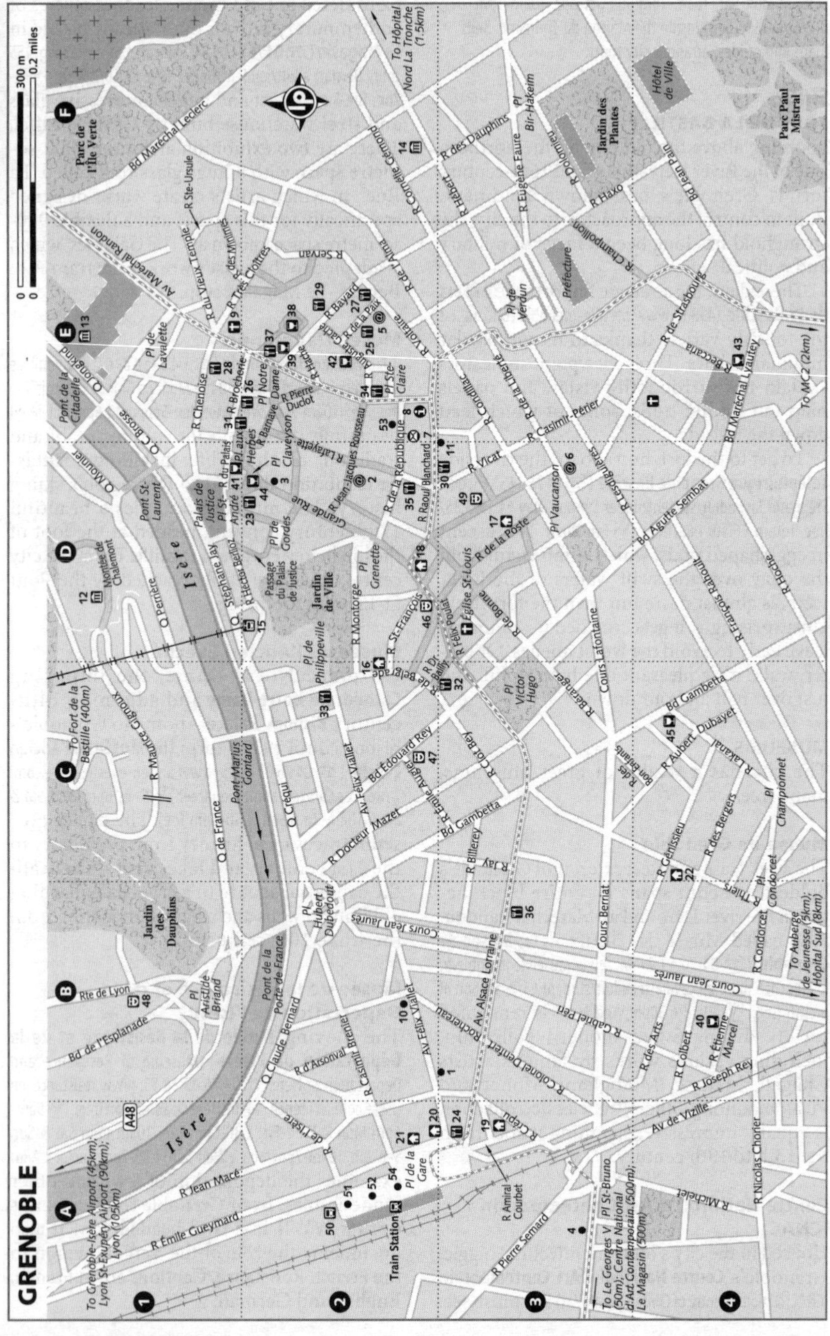
GRENOBLE
0 300 m
0 0.2 miles
To Grenoble-Isère Airport (45km); Lyon St-Exupéry Airport (90km); Lyon (105km)
To Fort de la Bastille (400m)
To Hôpital Nord La Tronche (1.5km)
To MC2 (2km)
To Auberge de Jeunesse (5km); Hôpital Sud (8km)
To Le Georges V (50m); Centre National d'Art Contemporain (500m); Le Magasin (500m)
Parc de l'Ile Verte
Jardin des Dauphins
Jardin de Ville
Jardin des Plantes
Parc Paul Mistral
Hôtel de Ville
Préfecture
Palais de Justice
Train Station
Pl de la Gare
Pl Victor Hugo
Pl Grenette
Pl de Gordes
Pl Claveyson
Pl aux Herbes
Pl St-André
Pl Notre Dame
Pl Ste-Claire
Pl de Verdun
Pl Hubert Dubedout
Pl Aristide Briand
Pl de Philippeville
Pl de Lavalette
Pl St-Bruno
Pl Condorcet
Pl Championnet
Pl Bir-Hakeim
Église St-Louis
Isère
Pont de la Citadelle
Pont St-Laurent
Pont Marius Gontard
Pont de la Porte de France
Passage du Palais de Justice
Montée de Chalemont
Bd Maréchal Leclerc
Av Maréchal Randon
Q Jongkind
Q Mounier
Q C Brosse
Q Perrière
Q de France
Q Créqui
Q Claude Bernard
Q Stéphane Jay
Rte de Lyon
Bd de l'Esplanade
R Maurice Gignoux
R Jean Macé
R Émile Gueymard
R Amiral Courbet
R Pierre Semard
R Casimir Brenier
R d'Arsonval
Av Félix Viallet
R Docteur Mazet
Bd Édouard Rey
Bd Gambetta
Cours Jean Jaurès
Av Alsace Lorraine
Cours Berriat
Cours Lafontaine
Bd Agutte Sembat
Bd Maréchal Lyautey
Bd Jean Pain
R Haxo
R de Strasbourg
R Casimir-Périer
R Lafayette
R de la République
R Raoul Blanchard
R Jean-Jacques Rousseau
Grande Rue
R Montorge
R St-François
R Félix Poulat
R de Bonne
R de la Poste
R Vicat
R Hector Berlioz
R Brocherie
R Chenoise
R Très Cloîtres
R du Vieux Temple
R des Minimes
R Ste-Ursule
R Servan
R Bayard
R Hache
R Barnave
R Pierre Duclot
R Voltaire
R de la Paix
R Cornélie Gémond
R de l'Alma
R Hébert
R des Dauphins
R Eugène Faure
R Dolomieu
R Champollion
R Lesdiguières
R Beccaria
R Hoche
R François Raoult
R Aubert Dubayet
R des Bons Enfants
R Lakanal
R des Bergers
R Génissieu
R Thiers
R Condorcet
R Nicolas Chorier
R Michelet
R Joseph Rey
Av de Vizille
R Colbert
R Étienne Marcel
R des Arts
R Gabriel Péri
R Colonel Denfert Rochereau
R Crépu
R Billerey
R Jay
R Lt Rey
R Émile Augier
R Béranger
Pl Vaucanson
R de Belgrade
R Dr Bailly
R Condillac
R de la Liberté
R Auguste Gache
R du Palais
R Clot Bey

INFORMATION
- Au 43 Viallet....1 B3
- Celsius Café....2 D2
- Decitre....3 D2
- Laverie Berriat....4 A3
- Neptune Internet....5 E2
- Pl@net Internet....6 D3
- Post Office....7 E2
- Tourist Office....8 E2

SIGHTS & ACTIVITIES
- Bishop's Palace....(see 9)
- Bureau des Guides de Grenoble et Accompagnateurs....(see 11)
- Cathédrale Notre Dame....9 E1
- Club Alpin Français de l'Isère....10 B2
- Maison de la Montagne....11 D3
- Musée Dauphinois....12 D1
- Musée de Grenoble....13 E1
- Musée de la Résistance et de la Déportation de l'Isère....14 F2
- Musée de l'Ancien Évêché....(see 9)
- SIPAVAG....(see 11)
- Téléphérique Grenoble Bastille....15 D2

SLEEPING
- Hôtel Acacia....16 C2
- Hôtel de la Poste....17 D3
- Hôtel de l'Europe....18 D2
- Hôtel Lux....19 A3
- Hôtel Suisse et Bordeaux....20 A2
- Hôtel Terminus....21 A2
- Splendid Hôtel....22 C4

EATING
- Café de la Table Ronde....23 D2
- China Moon....24 A3
- Ciao a Te....25 E2
- La Fondue....26 E2
- La Panse....27 E2
- L'Amphitryon....28 E1
- Le Mal Assis....29 E2
- Le Mandala....30 D3
- L'Épicurien....31 E1
- Les Archers....32 C3
- Les Dix Vins....33 C2
- Les Halles Ste-Claire....34 E2
- Monoprix Supermarket....35 D2
- Pivano....36 B3
- Shaman Café....37 E2

DRINKING
- Barberousse....38 E2
- Le 365....39 E2
- Le Code Bar....40 B4
- Le Couche Tard....41 D1
- Le Tord Boyaux....42 E2
- Momento....43 E4
- Styx....44 D2
- Subway....45 C4

ENTERTAINMENT
- Fnac....46 D2
- La Nef....47 C2
- La Soupe aux Choux....48 B1
- Les 6 Rex....49 D3

TRANSPORT
- Bus Station....50 A2
- Car Rental Companies....51 A2
- Eurolines....(see 50)
- Métrovélo....52 A2
- SNCF Boutique....53 E2
- TAG Office....54 A2
- TAG Office....(see 8)

Activities

The authorities on mountain activities around Grenoble – skiing, snowboarding, ski mountaineering, ice climbing, walking, mountain biking, rock climbing etc – reside in the **Maison de la Montagne** (☎ 04 76 44 67 03; 3 rue Raoul Blanchard; 9.30am-12.30pm & 1-6pm Mon-Fri, 10am-1pm & 2-5pm Sat). Staff are a mine of information and can help you plan day trips and treks with *refuge* stays, or book activities. They also sell a number of maps and walking books, including the excellent *TopoGuides* series, and run a library of more than 700 maps and walking references that are free to consult. For walks around Grenoble, ask for the free **SIPAVAG** (☎ 04 76 24 48 59; www.sipavag.fr, in French) maps and itineraries (*La Carte des Sentiers des Franges Vertes* or *Guide Balades*, in French).

If it's a guide you're after, the **Bureau des Guides de Grenoble et Accompagnateurs** (☎ 04 76 44 67 03; www.guide-grenoble.com, in French; Maison de la Montagne) runs the whole gamut of summer and winter activities.

You can also try the **Club Alpin Français de l'Isère** (☎ 04 76 87 03 73; 32 av Félix Viallet; www.clubalpin-grenoble.com, in French; 2-6pm Tue & Wed, 2-8pm Thu & Fri). They run most of the *refuges* in the area. Their program of activities is posted in the window.

To jump lift-pass queues in Grenoble's surrounding ski resorts (p563), buy your pass in advance from the tourist office or the *billetterie* inside Fnac (p562).

Tours

The tourist office organises imaginative thematic **walking tours** (adult €6-12.50, student €4-12.50, in French only), including a two-hour stroll in the footsteps of Grenoble-born novelist Stendhal, museums and various industry-focused tours. Those who'd rather go it alone can rent an MP3 audioguide (English available; €7 plus €80 deposit; two-hour tour with 13 stops) at the tourist office.

Festivals & Events

Jazz greats have hit Grenoble for a fiesta of concerts during the annual **Grenoble Jazz Festival** (☎ 04 76 51 65 32; www.jazzgrenoble.com, in French; tickets free-€30, 3-/6-evening pass €42/65) in March since 1973; the venue for many concerts is MC2 (p562).

Sleeping

Sleeping in Grenoble is a bit of a let-down. Hotels tend to be soulless and the reluctant preserve of passing business people. Parking can also be expensive (few street spaces, expensive public car parks).

Auberge de Jeunesse (☎ 04 76 09 33 52; grenoble@fuaj.org; 10 av du Grésivaudan; B&B €16.70; reception 7.30am-11pm) This excellent hostel has everything you could possibly want: a lively bar, a self-catering kitchen (and a huge supermarket two minutes away to fill up the fridge), a wicked sun deck, private car park and impeccable two- to four-bed dorms, many with en suite. The only downside: it's 5km south of the train station in the Echirolles district. From cours Jean Jaurès, take bus 1 to the Quinzaine stop (just outside the Casino supermarket) or tram A to La Rampe stop and walk 15 minutes.

Hôtel de l'Europe (☎ 04 76 46 16 94; www.hoteleurope.fr; 22 place Grenette; s with washbasin/shower €31/42, d €40-80) This is a good bet for cheap accommodation in the centre as there are a few non–en suite rooms. The catch: the shared bathroom is on the 2nd floor, which is a bit of a bummer if your room is two floors up. You'll have a choice of grand spiral staircase or lift to get around.

Hôtel de la Poste (☎ 04 76 46 67 25; 25 rue de la Poste; s/d/tr €34/41/50) Beautifully renovated and oozing old-school charm, the rooms in the rambling flats that make up Hôtel de la Poste are Grenoble's best-kept secret. Some have shared bathroom and toilets but these facilities are so clean you won't have a second thought about using them. And best of all, you even get the use of the kitchen. Rooms B3 and B5 are top picks.

Hôtel Lux (☎ 04 76 46 41 89; www.hotel-lux.com; 6 rue Crépu; s €37-50, d €51-55) Despite its name, Hôtel Lux is not a luxurious affair: rooms are pretty basic and the decor neutral, but its charming owners keep the place spotless. It's close to the station and has wi-fi throughout.

Hôtel Acacia (☎ 04 76 87 29 90; 13 rue de Belgrade; s €40, d €44-62) As boxy and boring as it is, this dead-central hotel could not be closer to the action. Rooms with shared toilets (but their own shower) are cheaper. Definitely go for a nonsmoking room though to avoid the smell.

Hôtel Suisse et Bordeaux (☎ 04 76 47 55 87; www.hotel-sb-grenoble.com; 6 place de la Gare; s/d/t €48/57/69) They've gone a little overboard with the old flowery bedspread and matching curtains, but it's otherwise spacious and clean. Rooms overlooking the backyard are much quieter than those at the front, but then you'll miss out on the balconies.

Splendid Hôtel (☎ 04 76 46 33 12; www.splendid-hotel.com; 22 rue Thiers; s €57, d €71-89) Colourful, fresh and with funky paintings on the walls, this is a welcome break from the dreary two-star scene in Grenoble. Rooms are simple but cosy, some with air-con and all with wi-fi. There is a lovely garden at the back, a great breakfast buffet and last but not least, a car park. A great choice all round.

Hôtel Terminus (☎ 04 76 87 24 33; www.terminus-hotel-grenoble.fr; 10 place de la Gare; d €68-149; ❄ 💻) The rooms are comfortable and rather spacious, the staff helpful and the buffet breakfast copious, but there is no escaping the fact that it is a chain (Best Western), attracting a mostly 'passing-by' clientele.

Eating

Unlike its sleeping options, Grenoble boasts some excellent restaurants, thanks partly to its vibrant student crowd. As Dauphiné capital, Grenoble is *the* place to sample that quintessential French dish *gratin dauphinois* (finely sliced potatoes oven-baked in cream and a pinch of nutmeg).

RESTAURANTS

L'Amphitryon (☎ 04 76 51 38 07; 9 rue Chenoise; mains €10; ⏲ dinner Mon-Sat) The decor is an odd, slightly tacky mix of cardboard cut-out dunes, steel door, blue lights and 16th-century building. Thankfully, no such identity crisis on the menu: a resolutely modern oriental cuisine, the house speciality being *brik*, a thin pastry stuffed with mouth-watering fillings.

Shaman Café (☎ 04 38 37 23 56; 1 place Notre Dame; menu from €12.50; ⏲ 8am-midnight) With its oriental decor and big chill music, this place smacks of Buddha Bar wannabe. It's not quite there yet but it is still a decent option, particularly for lunch with a three-course meal for €12.50. The cuisine is in turn Japanese, Lebanese, Chinese or Thai.

Ciao a Te (☎ 04 76 42 54 41; 2 rue de la Paix; mains €15; ⏲ lunch & dinner Tue-Sat, closed Aug) A genuinely Italian address, so don't come here for pizza but for the real, rich and generous Italian cuisine: lots of veal, seafood and superfresh pasta. Unsurprisingly, Ciao has become one of Grenoble's most popular restaurants, so book.

Le Mandala (☎ 04 76 44 49 80; 7 rue Raoul Blanchard; mains €15; ⏲ lunch & dinner Mon-Sat, lunch Sun) The outside looks a little stern but the mood inside Le Mandala is anything but: behind his glass kitchen wall, Joël cooks up a storm (do try his *tarte au citron:* you've never had anything like it) while Cyril hands out menus, dishes and jokes in the small but perfectly formed dining room.

Les Archers (☎ 04 76 46 27 76; 2 rue Docteur Bailly; mains €15; ⏲ 11am-2am Tue-Sat, 11am-1am Sun & Mon) This green-fronted, old-school French brasserie is the perfect place for a seafood platter, a load of snails or a winter-warming sauerkraut, and late-night eating generally speaking. In summer, tables spill into the square.

La Fondue (☎ 04 76 15 20 72; 5 rue Brocherie; fondue per person €17; ⌚ dinner Mon, lunch & dinner Tue-Sat) No surprise here, La Fondue does what it says on the tin: 16 different types of fondue (with Génépi, chartreuse, kirsch, different types of cheeses etc), including the dessert variety (chocolate). There is also an assortment of raclettes and *tartiflettes* to complete the mountain cheese trilogy (see boxed text, p551).

Les Dix Vins (☎ 04 76 17 14 72; 4 rue Belgrade; menus €17-38; ⌚ lunch & dinner Mon-Sat) The seriously funky decor (pink chairs, purple walls and oddly shaped lampshades) is matched by a fun (and very affordable) cuisine, a formula that attracts a young crowd keen for a bit of the action. There's also a very well-supplied bar if you'd just like to take in the atmosphere.

La Panse (☎ 04 76 54 09 54; 7 rue de la Paix; menus €18, €22 & €34; ⌚ lunch & dinner Mon-Sat) The food, the decor, the crowd, the atmosphere, it's all very sophisticated here, except for the bill: surprisingly small for a place of that calibre. Which means you'll be able to tuck into your *croustillant de Reblochon* (little parcels of Reblochon cheese and apple) and your *entrecôte aux morilles* (a tender piece of beef with a creamy morel sauce) even more merrily.

Le Mal Assis (☎ 04 76 54 75 93; 7 rue Bayard; mains €20; ⌚ dinner Tue-Sat) 'The Badly Seated' is an intimate little place where traditional French dishes turn up as the usual tasty mains (*andouillette,* an aniseed-flavoured fish stew, and *bourride,* a type of sausage) or the less conventional platters (crostini, foie gras, terrines) for a more tapas-style meal. And really, the seats are not that bad; there are just not that many of them, so book ahead.

L'Épicurien (☎ 04 76 51 96 06; 1 place aux Herbes; mains €20; ⌚ lunch & dinner Mon-Sat, closed Aug) In a rustic setting with sloped beamed ceiling and a mezzanine, L'Épicurien serves solid French cuisine: the rabbit with apricot and foie gras is a-okay and the *gratin dauphinois* a mound of creamy goodness. And let's have one last squeeze for the regional dessert of choice, the *tarte aux noix*. No mercy for the stomach.

CAFÉS & QUICK EATS

Pivano (☎ 04 76 50 62 13; 33 av Alsace Lorraine; mains €5; ⌚ 7.30am-7pm Mon-Sat) 'Gastronomic snacks' are the hallmark of this chic boutique café. Their breakfast formula beats any of the neighbouring hotels' morning offerings: €3.80 for supertasty bread with lovely spreads and a hot drink. They even have wi-fi.

China Moon (☎ 04 76 43 14 15; 52 av Alsace Lorraine; mains from €4; ⌚ 9am-11pm daily) Fried rice, sweet and sour pork, spring rolls and dumplings, this is perfect to grab a quick bite that is not a sandwich on your way to or from the station. Takeaway is also available.

Café de la Table Ronde (☎ 04 76 44 51 41; 7 place St-André; dishes €10-22; ⌚ 7am-midnight Mon-Sat) All hail the *ardoise du jour* at this historic 1739 café opposite the Palais de Justice, and Stendhal and Rousseau's favourite haunt: there's something for every purse from €9 cheapies such as hot goat's cheese salad to carnivorous treats like *Tournedos Rossini* (€20), a succulent piece of beef served with a pan-fried slice of foie gras and a Madeira wine sauce – sinful!

SELF-CATERING

Les Halles Ste-Claire (place Ste-Claire; ⌚ 7am-1pm Tue-Thu & Sun, 7am-1pm & 3-7pm Fri & Sat) Grenoble's lovely old covered market since 1874.

Monoprix (22 rue Lafayette; ⌚ 8.30am-8pm Mon-Sat) Supermarket with street-level *boulangerie* (bakery; rue Raoul Blanchard entrance).

Drinking

Like every good student city, Grenoble does a mean party. Here are just a few places to get you started.

Le 365 (☎ 04 76 51 73 18; 3 rue Bayard; ⌚ 3pm-1am or 2am Tue-Sat) If Dionysos (god of wine) had a house, we reckon that's what it would look like: an irresistible clutter of bottles, frames, candles and ultrarelaxed atmosphere, the ideal setting for sipping one of the many wines on offer or a decadent *chocolat chartreuse* (hot chocolate with herbal liquor chartreuse, quite the winter-warmer!)

Le Tord Boyaux (☎ 04 76 44 18 90; 4 rue Auguste Gaché; ⌚ 6pm-2am) More than 30 flavoured wines, some of them quite extravagant (violet, chestnut, Génépi, fig etc), and a blind test every Tuesday night to see how many your taste buds can recognise: how's that for a good night out?

Barberousse (☎ 04 76 57 14 53; 8 rue Hache; ⌚ 6pm-2am Tue-Sat) If you're after cheap drinks and a boogie, this is the place to come: shots and loud music are regular fixtures, as is the lairy crowd of students who down aromatic rum and sing on top of their head as if there was no tomorrow.

momento (☎ 04 76 26 21 59; 2 rue Beccaria; ⌚ noon-1am Sun-Wed, to 2am Thu-Sat) A feast of fluoro lights, this establishment is a bit like an American

GAY GRENOBLE

Student-studded Grenoble enjoys a rich gay life, kicking off with a wealth of gay organisations (think everything from rugby to mountain sports, singing and a support network for gay and lesbian parents) spearheaded by **CIGALE** (Collectif Inter-Associations Gays et Lesbiennes; www.cigalegrenoble.free.fr, in French; 8 rue Sergent Bobillot). The fabulously cutting-edge **Festival Vues d'en Face** (www.vuesdenface.com), an international gay and lesbian film festival, is held each year in April.

Le Georges V (☎ 04 76 84 16 20; 124 cours Berriat; admission €12; ⌚ 11pm-5.30am Wed-Sun) is a happening gay nightclub and **Le Code Bar** (☎ 04 76 43 58 91; 9 rue Étienne Marcel; ⌚ 6pm-1am Tue-Sun) a hip and friendly gay bar.

diner à la 21st century: big burgers, big cocktails (pitchers), big music. Its location is a bit odd: next to a multistorey car park and fairly out-centred.

Subway (☎ 04 76 87 31 67; 2 rue Lakanal; ⌚ 8.30am-1am Mon-Wed, 8.30am-2am Thu & Fri, 2pm-2am Sat, 4pm-1am Sun) The favourite local drinking hole of an unpretentious young crowd. It's happy hour all night on Thursday, wahey!

Styx (☎ 04 76 44 09 99; 6 place Claveyson; ⌚ 1pm-2am Mon-Sat) If you're too cool for school, this is the place for you: designer cocktails, DJs, soft red light and attitude by the shaker-load. The terrace is the place to hang out on sunny afternoons or warmer evenings.

Le Couche Tard (☎ 04 76 44 18 79; 1 rue du Palais; ⌚ 7pm-2am Mon-Sat) The 'go to bed late' grungy pub must be the only place on earth that will encourage you to graffiti its walls, so make the best of it! Happy hour is until 10pm every day, even better.

Entertainment

Pick up the weekly *Grenews* and *Le Petit Bulletin* (both free) at the tourist office to discover what's happening when and where.

La Nef (☎ 08 92 68 00 31; 18 bd Édouard Rey; tickets €7.50) shows a great selection of art-house and independent films. For new releases try **Les 6 Rex** (☎ 08 92 68 00 31; 1 rue Émile Augier; tickets €7.80-8). Find programs (in French) at www.cine-loisirs.com.

The most exciting all-rounder for theatre, dance, opera, jazz (p559) and other music is **MC2** (Maison de la Culture; ☎ 04 76 00 79 00; www.mc2grenoble.fr, in French; 4 rue Paul Claudel; ⌚ box office 12.30-7pm Tue-Fri, 2-7pm Sat), 2km south of the centre on tram line A (tram stop MC2).

La Soupe aux Choux (☎ 04 76 87 05 67; http://jazzalasoupe.free.fr, in French; 7 rte de Lyon; show only/dinner & show €10/28; ⌚ 8pm-1am Tue-Sat), going strong for 25 years, is the tip-top address for getting down to live jazz. Get into the groove of dozens more venues with flyers at the *billetterie* (ticket office) inside **Fnac** (☎ 08 25 02 00 20; 4 rue Félix Poulat; ⌚ 10am-7pm Mon-Sat).

Getting There & Away

AIR

A clutch of budget airlines, including Ryanair and easyJet, fly to/from **Grenoble-Isère Airport** (☎ 04 76 65 48 48; www.grenoble-airport.com), 45km northwest of Grenoble, from London, Glasgow, Stockholm and Warsaw; see p961 for details.

BUS

The **bus station** (☎ 04 76 87 90 31; rue Émile Gueymard), next to the train station, is the main terminus for several bus companies, including **VFD** (☎ 08 20 83 38 33; www.vfd.fr, in French) and **Transisère** (☎ 08 20 08 38 38; www.transisere.fr, in French). Destinations include Chambéry (€5.10, two hours), Geneva airport (€43, 2½ hours), Lyon St-Exupéry airport (€20, one hour), Chamrousse (€4, 1¼ hours), Bourg d'Oisans (€5.10, 50 minutes), Les Deux Alpes (€5.10, 1¾ hours) and the Vercors ski stations (opposite).

Eurolines (☎ 04 76 46 19 77; www.eurolines.fr; ⌚ 10am-noon & 2-7pm Tue-Sat) handles international destinations (p964).

TRAIN

From the **train station** (rue Émile Gueymard), next to the Gare Europole tram stop, trains run to/from Paris' Gare de Lyon (from €74.70, 3½ hours), Chambéry (€9.90, one hour, 10 to 13 daily) and Lyon (€18, 1½ hours, five daily). Train tickets are sold at the station and in town at the **SNCF boutique** (15 rue de la République; ⌚ 9am-12.30pm & 2-6.30pm Mon-Fri, 9.30am-12.30pm & 2-6pm Sat).

Getting Around

TO/FROM THE AIRPORT

Shuttle buses run by **Transisère** (☎ 08 20 08 38 38) to/from Grenoble-Isère Airport use the bus station (one-way/return €4/8, 45 minutes, four to eight daily).

BICYCLE

Métrovélo (☎ 08 20 22 38 38; 🕑 7am-8pm Mon-Fri, 9am-noon & 2-7pm Sat & Sun Apr-Oct, 9am-noon Sat & 2-7pm Sun Nov-Mar), underneath the train station, rents out bikes for €3/5 per half-/full day. Helmets, child's seat and locks are free. You'll need an ID and a €50 deposit per bike.

BUS & TRAM

Grenoble's three pollution-free tram lines – called A, B and C – run through the heart of town. A single-trip bus and tram ticket costs €1.30 from ticket machines at tram and bus stops or drivers. Time-stamp tickets in the blue machines at stops before boarding. Carnets of 10 tickets (€10.90) and day passes (€3.60) can only be bought at the **TAG office** (☎ 08 20 48 60 00; www.semitag.com; 🕑 8.30am-6.30pm Mon-Fri, 9am-6pm Sat) inside the tourist office or next to the train station. Trams run from around 5am to 1am; buses stop between 6pm and 9pm.

CAR

Find the major car-rental agencies in the Europole complex underneath the train station.

TAXI

Call the **central reservation line** (☎ 04 76 54 42 54) to order a taxi.

AROUND GRENOBLE

Grenoble's low-altitude surrounds lure city dwellers seeking a weekend fix of snow action. The Vercors is sweet for cross-country, while family-driven **Chamrousse** (elevation 1700m), built for the 1968 Winter Olympics 35km southeast from Grenoble, is OK for beginner-level downhill – its **tourist office** (☎ 04 76 89 92 65; www.chamrousse.com, in French; 42 place de Belledonne) has the full lowdown. Serious skiers must head east to Les Deux Alpes, Alpe d'Huez and La Grave for serious action.

Several daily VFD buses link Grenoble with all the surrounding resorts (details listed in respective sections), including Chamrousse (€4, 1¼ hours). For day trippers, the Skiligne operated by VFD to 13 different ski resorts in the region are a good deal; rates (from €13 in Chamrousse and Villard de Lans to €35 for Les Deux Alpes and Alpe d'Huez) include a one-day ski pass as well as return bus fare.

Parc Naturel Régional du Vercors

Immediately southwest of Grenoble, this gently rolling nature park (1750 sq km) is a slow-paced oasis of calm and an ideal family destination, cheaper, easier and smaller than big Alpine resorts. If you're not an adrenalin junkie, you'll love it here. Known for its cross-country skiing, snowshoeing, caving and hiking, it was also a Resistance stronghold during WWII, nicknamed *Forteresse de la Résistance*.

From humble **Lans-en-Vercors** (population 2300, elevation 1020m), 25km southwest of Grenoble, buses shuttle downhill skiers 4km east to its 14-piste Montagnes de Lans ski area. **Villard de Lans** (population 4000, elevation 1050m), 9km up the valley, is linked by ski lifts to **Corrençon-en-Vercors** (population 358, elevation 1111m) for 125km of winter-wonderland downhill pistes at melting prices (€28 for a day). For alternative fun, the **Colline des Bains** (half-/full day €6/8), in Villars-de-Lans, offers six sledging tracks: pick your vehicle (sledge train for extra chaos, solo sledge, rubber ring or bobsleigh), pick your track and whiz down.

Villard de Lans' dynamic **tourist office** (☎ 04 76 95 10 38; www.villarddelans.com; place Mure Ravaud) should be your first port of call for activities in the Vercors (which run the gamut of mountain fun, from paragliding to canyoning). Their booking service **Vercors Réservations** (☎ 04 76 95 96 96; www.vercors-reservations.com) can help with accommodation throughout the park, including farmstays. **Les Accompagnateurs Nature et Patrimoine** (☎ 04 76 95 08 38; www.accompagnateur-vercors.com, in French) organises great guided walking or snowshoeing trips to learn about the park's flora and fauna.

GETTING THERE & AWAY

Up to seven **VFD** (☎ 08 20 08 38 38; www.vfd.fr, in French) buses daily link Lans-en-Vercors with Grenoble (€4, 45 minutes), Villard de Lans (€1.80, 15 minutes) and Corrençon-en-Vercors (€1.80, 35 minutes).

Parc National des Écrins

The spectacular **Parc National des Écrins** (www.les-ecrins-parc-national.fr), France's second-largest

INSIDE TASTE

The Vercors has some amazing chalets and farmhouses to stay in. Here is a selection of this author's favourites.

Les Allières (☎ 04 76 94 32 32; www.aubergedesallieres.com, in French; Lans-en-Vercors; half-board per person €51, mains €20) It takes about half an hour from the nearest car park to walk to Les Allières, a forest chalet 1500m up in the mountain that offers basic accommodation (bunk beds and shared toilets) and wondrous mountain food. The wood-fire raclette and *tarte aux myrtilles* (blueberry tart, a regional speciality) are legendary. Take the direction of Montagnes de Lans from Lans-en-Vercors. Park in the first car park on your left (about 1.5km up the road); the path to Les Allières is signposted across the road.

À la Crécia (☎ 04 76 95 46 98; www.gite-en-vercors.com, in French; Lans-en-Vercors; s/d/tr/q €52/57/72/87; dinner €17) Goats, pigs, poultry and lambs rule the roost at this authentic 16th-century farm, renovated with zeal by Véronique and Pascal who run this charming *chambre d'hôte*. Stylish rooms are rustic but modern with wooden beams, delicate natural tones and stunning mosaic bathrooms. Hot water and heating in winter come courtesy of the roof's solar panels.

Gîte La Verne (☎ 04 76 95 21 18; http://gite.laverne.free.fr; La Verne, Méaudre; d with half board €124, apt for 4/8 people per week €500/780) Not your average *gîte* (cottage for rent) at all, La Verne is a beautiful Alpine chalet split into six exquisite flats that can be rented out on a *gîte* (self-catering) or *chambre d'hôte* (half-board) basis. Flats are fitted with fully equipped kitchens. But whatever the formula, you'll be able to enjoy the hammam and outdoor Norwegian bath as well as owner Edwige's brilliant aperitifs and her wonderful hospitality.

national park (918 sq km), was created in 1973. Stretching between the towns of Bourg d'Oisans, Briançon and Gap, the area is enclosed by steep, narrow valleys, and sculpted by the Romanche, Durance and Drac rivers and their erstwhile glaciers. It peaks at 4102m with the legendary summit Barre des Écrins (a mountaineer's dream).

Bourg d'Oisans (population 3352, elevation 720m), 55km southeast of Grenoble, and **Briançon** (p566), another 67km in the same direction, are good bases for exploring the park. In Bourg d'Oisans, the **Maison du Parc** (☎ 04 76 80 00 51; rue Gambetta; ⏲ 10.30am-12.30pm & 3-7pm Jul & Aug, 9-11am & 2-5pm Mon-Fri Sep-Jun) sells maps and guides. The town's **tourist office** (☎ 04 76 80 03 25; www.bourgdoisans.com; quai Girard; ⏲ 9am-7pm Jul & Aug, 9am-noon & 2-6pm Jun, 9am-noon & 2-6pm Mon-Sat Sep–mid-Dec & mid-Apr–May, 9am-noon & 2-6pm Mon-Sat, 9-11am Sun mid-Dec–mid-Apr) is also useful. The **Oisans website** (www.tourisme-oisans.com) is an excellent source of information on the area, with accommodation and activities listings.

SIGHTS & ACTIVITIES

In Bourg d'Oisans the **Musée des Minéraux et de la Faune des Alpes** (☎ 04 76 80 27 54; place de l'Église; adult/6-18yr €4.60/2; ⏲ 2-6pm Wed-Mon Sep-Jun, 10am-6pm Jul & Aug) paints park geology, flora and fauna, including ibexes, chamois and stoats.

In summer you can mammal-spot amid spectacular scenery from the window of **Chemin de Fer de la Mure** (☎ 08 92 39 14 26; www.trainlamure.com; adult/student/4-16yr return €19/12.50/9.50; ⏲ 2-4 departures daily Apr-Oct), a small red 1920s mountain train that chugs 30km (1¾ hours) between St-Georges de Commiers and La Mure.

Age-old footpaths used by shepherds and smugglers centuries before – 700km in all – ensnare the national park, making it prime **hiking** territory. **Kayaking** along the Drac's turquoise waters, rock climbing, *via ferrata*, **paragliding** and **mountain biking** are other activities; tourist and park offices have details.

SLEEPING & EATING

The tourist office in Bourg d'Oisans knows about **gîtes d'étape** (walkers' guesthouses; dm €13-21) open year-round.

There are campsites galore in and around Bourg d'Oisans, open June to September, including the pretty **La Cascade** (☎ 04 76 80 02 42; www.premiumwanadoo.com/lacascadesarenne; rte de l'Alpe d'Huez; 2-adult tent pitch €17.50-25; ⏲ mid-Dec–Sep; 🏊), 1.5km from the centre; and well-equipped **Le Colporteur** (☎ 04 76 79 11 44; www.camping-colporteur.com; Le Mas de Plan; 2-adult tent pitch €19-24; ⏲ mid-May–mid-Sep, 💻 🏊), with a restaurant-bar, a two-second hop from town.

Bourg has a clutch of uninspiring hotels. Instead try **Au Fil des Saisons** (☎ 04 76 30 07 01; www.chambresdhotes-afs.com, in French; Ferme du Cros, Les Côtes de Corps; d with B&B €50, dinner €17; ⌚ Feb–mid-Dec). It is a beautiful 1731 mountain farm with beamed and vaulted ceilings where Dany (Danielle) and Domi (Dominique) welcome you with incredible warmth. Dinner is a regal but wholesome spread of home-made everything: the bread is home-baked as are all the cakes, the vegetables are home-grown, the honey is Domi's very own (he's a bee-keeper in his spare time) and the lamb and cheeses come from their son's sheep farm next door. Find the Ferme du Cros 2km from Corps in Les Côtes de Corps; follow the southbound N85 from Grenoble. Advance reservations essential.

GETTING THERE & AWAY

From Bourg d'Oisans **bus station** (av de la Gare), on the main road into town, there are two or three buses daily to/from Briançon (€13.90, two hours), Les Deux Alpes (€1.80, 40 minutes) and Alpe d'Huez (€1.80, 40 minutes), and up to eight daily to/from Grenoble (€5.10, 50 minutes).

Les Deux Alpes

elevation 1600m

It's Glacier du Mont de Lans – an enormous 3200m- to 3425m-high glacier – and its year-round skiing that creates the buzz in Les Deux Alpes, a busy ski resort 28km southeast of Bourg d'Oisans. The village's lowly beginnings as mountain pasture for sheep flocks are belied by the never-ending stream of traffic that clogs up the main street, av de la Muzelle.

Free-riders come from far and wide to tackle the mythical **Vallons de la Meije** descent in **La Grave** (www.la-grave.com), 21km east. The stuff of legend, the off-piste run plummets 2150m and is strictly for the crème de la crème of off-piste riders.

INFORMATION

Slope-side **Maison des Deux Alpes** (place des Deux Alpes) is the key source: inside you'll find the **tourist office** (☎ 04 76 79 22 00; www.les2alpes.com; ⌚ 8am-7pm mid-Dec–mid-Apr, Jul & Aug, 9am-noon & 2-6pm Mon-Fri rest of year), **accommodation service** (☎ 04 76 79 24 38; reservation@les2alpes.com), **ESF** (☎ 04 76 79 21 21; www.esf2alpes.com) and the **Bureau des Guides** (☎ 04 76 11 36 29; www.guides2alpes.com, in French).

SIGHTS

Metre-tall animals, Alpine flowers and shepherds are among the monumental ice sculptures filling the **Grotte de Glace** (Ice Cave; admission €4; ⌚ 10am-3pm), a cave carved into the Glacier du Mont de Lans at Dôme de Puy Salié (3425m). To reach it, ride the Jandri Express *télécabine* to 3200m (change of *télécabine* at 2600m) and then a lift down the underground Funiculaire Dôme Express to 3400m. Allow an hour to get there. A ticket covering cable cars and the cave costs €20.90/16.70 per adult/under 13 years.

Go for a scenic ride aboard a caterpillar-track minibus on **La Croisière Blanche** (The White Cruise; ☎ 04 76 79 75 03; per ride €6; ⌚ 10.30am-3pm Sun-Fri mid-Dec–mid-Apr, 10am-3pm Jul & Aug). It is very gimmicky but it does allow nonskiers to tickle the summit at 3600m and enjoy breathtaking 360° views. Wrap up as you would when skiing: the temperature is in the minus and the ride takes about 50 minutes. Cruise plus cable cars plus ice cave costs €26.90/22.70 for adult/child. You *must* book before you head off.

ACTIVITIES

Les Deux Alpes sports 225km of marked downhill pistes and a snowpark (2600m) with an 800m-long axe pipe, 120m-long half-pipe, and numerous jumps as well as technical courses along cornice drops, canyons and corridors in the 'slide' zone. The main skiing domain at Les Deux Alpes lies below La Meije (3983m), one of the highest peaks in the Parc National des Écrins. A one-/six-day pass covering the entire area costs €36.40/172; access to La Grave and La Meije off-piste is free for six-day (or more) Les Deux Alpes lift-pass holders and costs €12 a day for one- to five-day pass holders. Riders wanting to access La Grave from Les Deux Alpes are pulled by a snowcat from the top of the Dôme de la Lauze lift.

Skiing and snowboarding aside, snow fiends can bomb downhill on a mountain bike at the Bike Park des Lutins, nip around the rink in an ice-glider (dodgems on ice) or go on a snowmobile *(motoneige)* expedition. Contact the **Bureau des Guides** (left) for organised ice climbing, snowshoeing, off-piste skiing and mountaineering. In summer guides run rock climbing, walking, canyoning and biking expeditions.

The summer skiing season on the glacier – Europe's largest summer skiing area against a panoramic backdrop of Mont Blanc, Massif Central and Mont Ventoux – runs from mid-June to the end of August. Otherwise there are 26 nail-biting descents and five cross-country trails for mountain bikers, numerous hiking trails and plenty of paragliding. Phew!

SLEEPING

The fun, action-packed **Auberge de Jeunesse** (☎ 04 76 79 22 80; www.fuaj.org; dm €17.60, full board only in winter 1 night €35-42, 6 nights incl 6-day lift pass €335-455; ⏲ Dec-Apr & mid-Jun–Aug) offers very good-value full-board deals in winter, where you can nip down for lunch to fill up on hot food or order a pack lunch to eat on the slopes.

The tourist office can help you find anything from a self-catering flat to a hotel room.

GETTING THERE & AWAY

VFD buses link Grenoble and Les Deux Alpes (€5.10, 1¾ hours, up to 10 daily) via Bourg d'Oisans; return journeys to Grenoble must be booked 72 hours in advance in Les Deux Alpes at **Agence VFD** (☎ 04 76 80 51 22; 112 av de la Muzelle) or the tourist office. There are also services to/from Lyon St-Exupéry airport (one-way/return €29/44, 3½ hours).

Alpe d'Huez

elevation 1860m

Number of hairpin bends: 21. Length: 14km. Average slope gradient: 7.9%. Record time: 37 minutes 35 seconds. Portrait of a mythical *étape* of the Tour de France between Bourg d'Oisans and Alpe d'Huez, a purpose-built resort in the Massif des Grandes Rousses. Apart from legendary cycling, Alpe d'Huez has 245km of motorway pistes that range from dead-easy to deadly; at 16km La Sarenne, accessible from the Pic Blanc cable car, is the French Alps' longest black run. Experienced skiers can also ski in July and August on glaciers ranging from 2530m to 3330m. Off the slopes, speed fiends can ice-drive…in a Porsche.

Views from Pic du Lac Blanc (3330m), the highest point accessible year-round by the Tronçons and Pic Blanc cable cars, take in about a fifth of the French territory as well as neighbouring Italy and Switzerland. Summer unveils mountains threaded through with marked hiking and biking trails.

Information hub **Maison de l'Alpe** (place Paganon) sells ski passes (one/six days €38.20/198.50) and houses the tip-top **tourist office** (☎ 04 76 11 44 44; www.alpedhuez.com; ⏲ 9am-7pm high season, 9am-12.30pm & 2.30-6pm Mon-Fri low season), **accommodation reservation centre** (☎ 04 76 80 90 00; www.alpe-vacances.com) and **ESF** (☎ 04 76 80 94 23; www.esf-alpedhuez.com).

GETTING THERE & AWAY

VFD buses (left) link Alpe d'Huez and Grenoble (€5.10, 1¾ hours, up to 10 daily) via Bourg d'Oisans. Buses shuttle skiers from Alpe d'Huez to Les Deux Alpes (return €6, 45 minutes, twice daily).

BRIANÇON

pop 12,100 / elevation 1320m

Strolling along the old town's ramparts, it's obvious why Briançon got its fortifications: five valleys tumble down into a plateau crowned by the rocky outcrop that is Briançon Vieille Ville. Italy is a mere 20km away, the town therefore played a major border-control role for centuries.

Invasions and wars over, Briançon still manages to play the location card: at 1320m and boasting 300 days of sunshine a year, air quality is excellent, with little pollution and humidity, making it an ideal destination for athletes and asthmatics in need of fresh air.

Military engineering and acclimatisation aside, cheap skiing (with no après-ski scene

MOUNTAIN TECHNOLOGY

Ever wondered where all that snow comes from? Take a tour of Alpe d'Huez's hi-tech **Usine à Neige du Plat des Marmottes** (Plat des Marmottes Snow Factory; admission & cable car €15; ⏲ 2pm Thu) at 2300m, where artificial snow is made for up to 200 of the resort's 785 snow-making machines. Access Plat des Marmottes with the Marmottes cable car.

Roughly ten per cent of France's electricity comes from hydroelectric plants, many of them in the Alps. The excellent **Musée Hydrelec** (☎ 04 76 80 78 00; www.musee-hydrelec.fr; Le Verney, Vaujany; admission free; ⏲ 10am-6pm mid-Jun–mid-Sep, 2-6pm weekends & school holidays mid-Sep–mid-Jun) explores the ins and outs of this form of energy. There is plenty of info in English and loads of interactive displays. Find Hydrelec halfway between Allemont and Vaujany on Lac du Verney, off the D526.

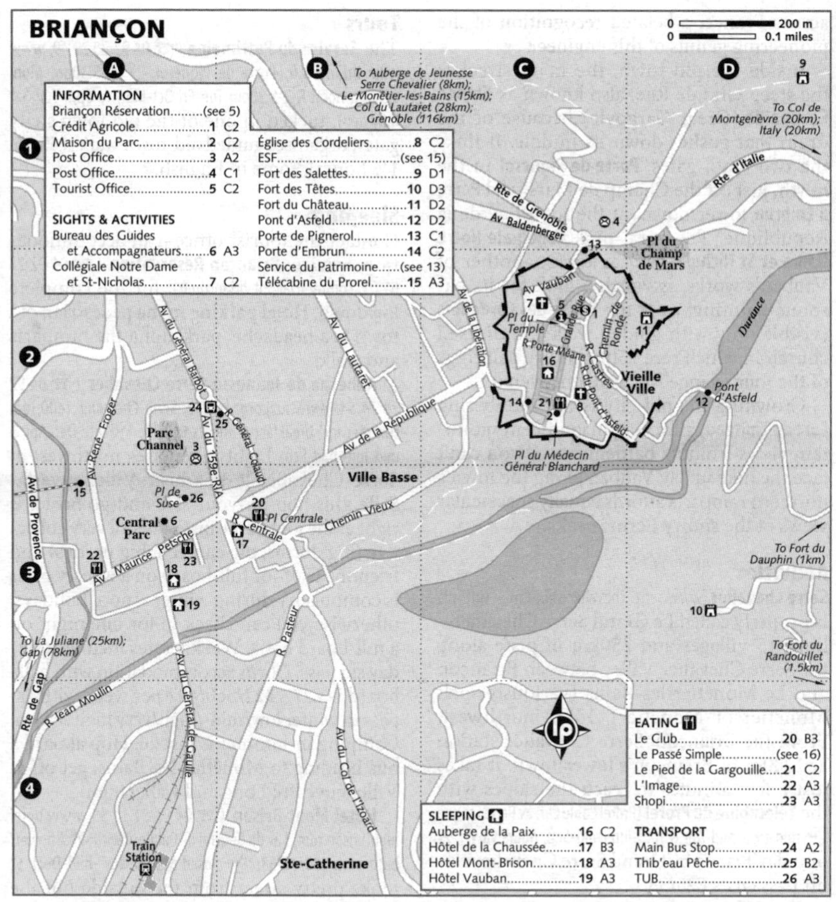

or nightlife to speak of) and walking are the best reasons to bed down in Briançon. Serre Chevalier (p568) offers 250km of fine pistes with sunshine on a plate, while the nearby Parc National des Écrins (p563) and Parc Naturel Régional du Queyras are criss-crossed by miles of scenic trails.

Information

Crédit Agricole (10 Grande Rue; 8.15am-noon & 1.30-4.45pm Mon-Fri, until 3.45pm Sat) Bank with currency exchange.

Maison du Parc (04 92 21 42 15; ecrins.brianconnais@espaces-naturels.fr; place du Médecin Général Blanchard; 10am-noon & 3-7pm Jul & Aug, 2-6pm Mon-Fri Sep-Jun) Comprehensive information on the Parc National des Écrins (p563).

Post Offices (place du Champ de Mars; av du 159e RIA)

Tourist Office (04 92 21 08 50; www.ot-briancon.fr, in French; Maison des Templiers, 1 place du Temple; 9am-noon & 2-6pm Mon-Sat, 10am-12.30pm & 3-5pm Sun Sep-Jun, 9am-7pm Jul & Aug) In Vieille Ville.

Sights

Briançon's star attraction is its extensive 17th- and early-18th-century Vauban heritage, including the Vieille Ville (Old Town) signature star-shaped fortications, surrounding forts (**Fort des Têtes**, **Fort des Salettes**, **Fort du Dauphin** and **Fort du Randouillet**) and bridge (**Pont d'Asfeld**). This architectural ensemble was in fact listed as a Unesco World Heritage Site in 2008 along with 11 other Vauban sites across France, a belated recognition of the pioneering genius of this engineer.

Inside the old town, the main street is the steep Grande Rue, also known as **Grande Gargouille** (Great Gargoyle) because of the drain that gushes down its middle. It links the two main gates, **Porte de Pignerol** in the north, just off the Champ de Mars, and **Porte d'Embrun** lower down, at the top of av de la République. The coral-pink **Collégiale Notre Dame et St Nicholas** (place du Temple), another of Vauban's works, is worth a look for its baroque painting, as is the **Église des Cordeliers** (visible only with guided walks), a disused church in which rare 15th-century paintings of the four evangelists were uncovered.

Crowning the old city is the slumbering **Fort du Château**, affording magnificent mountain views from its battlements. If you can't face the hike up, av Vauban along the town's northern ramparts affords equally spectacular views of the snowy Écrins peaks.

Activities

Serre Chevalier (www.serre-chevalier-ski.com) – which is properly called Le Grand Serre Chevalier – links 13 villages and 250km of piste along the Serre Chevalier Valley between Briançon and Le Monêtier-les-Bains (variously spelt Mônetier or Monétier), 15km northwest. From the Briançon–Serre Chevalier station at 1200m in Briançon's lower town, it takes just a few minutes to reach the slopes with the **Télécabine du Prorel** (Prorel Cable Car; av René Froger; mid-Dec–mid-Apr & mid-Jun–mid-Sep, hours vary). A one-day Briançon/Grand Serre Chevalier ski-lift pass costs €25/38.

The **ESF** (04 92 20 30 57; www.esf-serrechevalier.com; 7 av René Froger; 8.45am-6pm Dec-Apr) runs a seasonal office inside the Prorel cable-car station. The **Bureau des Guides et Accompagnateurs** (04 92 20 15 73; www.guides-briancon.fr, in French; Central Parc) organises the usual off-piste outings as well as treks, paragliding, rafting, cycling, canyoning and via ferrata in summer. For information on walking in the nearby Écrins national park, the Maison du Parc (p567) has plenty of info and maps.

The tourist office also hands out the excellent booklet *Guide des Itinéraires dans la Vallée de Serre Chevalier* (sadly in French only) detailing cultural walks and snowshoeing itineraries for those not so keen on skiing.

Tours

The **Service du Patrimoine** (04 92 20 29 49; www.ville-briancon.fr; Porte de Pignerol; 2-5.30pm Mon, 9.30am-noon & 2-5.30pm Tue-Fri Oct-Mar, to 6pm Tue-Sat May-Sep), tucked in one of the old town's city gates, organises guided old-town walks (€5.35, 1½ hours), some in English.

Sleeping

Contact the tourist office–run accommodation service, **Briançon Réservation** (04 92 21 01 01; commercial@ot-briancon.fr), for the complete lowdown. Hotel parking in the pedestrian old town is a headache; park along the ramparts and walk.

Auberge de Jeunesse Serre Chevalier (04 92 24 74 54; www.fuaj.org; Le Bez, Serre Chevalier 1400; dm summer incl breakfast & sheets €12.10; late Dec-Apr & mid-Jun–mid-Sep) Eight kilometres northwest at Serre Chevalier-le-Bez near Villeneuve-la-Salle, this hop-on-your-skis-and-go hostel is right at the foot of the pistes. It's all very collective (big dorms, big canteen, big parties) and friendly. Half- or full-board on a weekly basis is compulsory during winter school holidays; otherwise you can check in for one night on a full-board basis. Weekly rates include a six-day ski pass. Dorm accommodation with half-board is €277/322/360/407 per week with ski pass in winter low/mid-/high/very high season. Camping in summer is just €6. Hop aboard a bus heading to Monêtier-les-Bains, get off at Villeneuve Pré Long and walk 600m.

Hôtel Mont-Brison (04 92 21 14 55; www.hotelmontbrison.com; 3 av du Général de Gaulle; d with sink/shower/bathroom €30/40/53; closed May & Nov–mid-Dec) It looks pretty sweet from the outside but the rooms inside are very uninspiring, not to say shabby, with paper-thin mattresses. On the plus side, there is free wi-fi and most rooms have balconies with good views.

Auberge de la Paix (04 92 21 37 43; www.auberge-de-la-paix.com; 3 rue Porte Méane; d/tr €43/53, with bathroom €49/64) Three floors, no lift, creaky wooden floors, minuscule windows and plenty of 1960s flower power are the trademarks of Briançon's oldest hotel, an old-town inn dating from 1845. The attached restaurant Le Passé Simple (open for lunch and dinner Tuesday to Saturday and lunch Sunday) is part of the Vauban menu club (*menu* €22); it also serves a vast range of regional specialities (€20).

Hôtel de la Chaussée (04 92 21 10 37; www.hotel-de-la-chaussee.com; 4 rue Centrale; d/tr/q €65/75/90) The

UNLEASH YOUR GREEN SELF

Perched on a hill surrounded by the majestic peaks of the Écrins national park, this story-book chalet is also a textbook example of responsible tourism. At **La Juliane** (☎ 04 92 23 47 49; www.lajuliane.com; Le Martouret, Pelvoux; dm/d €17/44, incl half-board per person €37/41.50) electricity comes from solar panels (which also provide heating and hot water), a wind mill and a micro-hydroelectric turbine. The chalet is built out of logs of *mélèze* (a local tree) and dry stone and the insulation is a mix of sheep wool and hemp. So no hairdryers or leaving the lights on, and no letting the water run while you brush your teeth.

Despite this rustic-sounding set up, La Juliane is wonderfully cosy with pretty rooms and delicious (mostly organic) food prepared by owner Jean-Claude. The setting helps too: many are the guests who have forsaken a day on the slopes for the simple pleasure of enjoying one of the area's 300 days of sunshine on the terrace.

For the energetic types, snowshoeing, skiing, hiking, climbing and mountain biking are available locally. As for curious minds, Jean-Claude runs wild plant–picking and cooking courses in the spring, where you can learn to prepare anything from jams to gratins mountain-style.

La Juliane is 25km southwest of Briançon in the Vallée de la Vallouise: from Pelvoux-le-Saret turn right on route de l'Eychauda. Drive 500m up the hill until you get to a large car park. From there, La Juliane is signposted up a small path (muddy and/or snowy in winter): it takes about 15 minutes to walk and Jean-Claude can come and pick up luggage and young children by 4WD.

renovated rooms on the 2nd and 3rd floors should fulfil every Alpine chalet fantasy: wooden-clad, beautifully furnished, subtly scented and oh so cosy. The restaurant downstairs follows suit with tasty comfort food and a touch of originality thanks to its Vauban menu. Definitely the best hotel in town.

Hôtel Vauban (☎ 04 92 21 12 11; www.hotel-vauban.fr; 13 av du Général de Gaulle; d €70-95; 💻) The corridors are depressing and there is a bit of a nostalgic atmosphere at Hôtel Vauban, but the rooms are comfortable, there is a sauna and the place is well run and friendly.

Eating

Briançon is milking the Vauban heritage in every possible way, and that includes eating. Five restaurants across town have agreed on a cartel of Vauban menus: no one is allowed to copy the others' recipes of 17th-century fare (think pigeon, rabbit stews and never-heard-of vegetables). The tourist office has a list of participating venues.

Le Club (☎ 04 92 21 99 06; 3 place Centrale; mains €8; 🕑 lunch & dinner Mon-Sat) Think local café gone hip at this 'kitchen and bar' establishment. The decor is definitely trendy and the food international (burgers, big desserts), but the atmosphere has retained that of a local hang-out with its permanently propped counter and popular sunny terrace.

L'Image (☎ 04 92 20 66 66; 7 av Maurice Petsche; lunch menu €11, mains €10.50-16.60; 🕑 lunch & dinner Mon-Sun) The idea of a restaurant in a casino might normally make you want to steer clear but on this particular occasion, the contemporary decor, glass fireplace and excellent food (sublime mushroom and white-truffle ravioli and sinful chocolate fondue) mean that Casino Barrière's restaurant is a top choice.

Le Pied de la Gargouille (☎ 04 92 20 12 95; 64 Grande Rue; menus €17.50 & €19.50; 🕑 dinner Mon-Sun) The Gargoyle's Foot – an old-town homage to fondue, raclette and tartiflette (see boxed text, p551) – is a Briançon staple. Call ahead to reserve the house speciality, *gigot d'agneau à la ficelle* (whole leg of lamb strung over an open fire), and bring three friends to finish it.

SELF-CATERING

Shopi (av Maurice Petsche; ☎ 8.30am-12.30pm & 2.30-7.30pm Mon-Sat, 8.45am-12.30pm Sun) A supermarket.

Getting There & Away

BUS

Grenoble-based **VFD** (☎ 08 20 28 38 38; www.vfd.fr) runs buses to/from Grenoble (€27.50, 2¾ hours, two or three daily) via Bourg d'Oisans. Tickets must be booked at least 72 hours in advance either online or at the fishing shop **Thib'eau Pêche** (☎ 04 92 21 36 09; 16 av du 159e RIA; 🕑 9am-noon & 2-7pm Tue-Sat) which acts as a bus-ticket office (very odd indeed).

Other services operated by **SCAL** (☎ 04 92 51 06 05) and leaving from the bus stop on the corner of av du 159e RIA and rue Général Colaud include seven daily buses (except Sunday) to/from Gap (€9.50, two hours), Marseille (€29.80, five to six hours) and Aix-en-Provence (€26.70, five hours). Buses shuttle skiers and boarders to/from Villeneuve-la-Salle every 20 minutes (€40 for a six-day pass, 20 minutes). In winter **Altibus** (☎ 08 20 32 03 68) also runs two daily services to/from Lyon St-Exupéry airport (one-way/return €52/90, four hours).

CAR & MOTORCYCLE

The Col de Montgenèvre (1850m) is the main road link between Briançon and neighbouring Italy. It stays open year-round, as does the nearby Col du Lautaret (2058m) that links Briançon and Grenoble. Both do occasionally get snow-bogged; to check road conditions call ☎ 04 92 24 44 44.

TRAIN

From the **train station** (av du Général de Gaulle), about 1.5km from the Vieille Ville, there is an overnight train to Paris' Gare d'Austerlitz (€93.20, 10½ hours). There are speedier daytime services between Paris and Oulx (€95, five hours) in Italy, about 30km from Briançon, with regular shuttle buses between Oulx and Briançon (€10.50, one hour). Other destinations include Gap (€12.20, 1½ hours, seven daily) and Marseille (€36.60, five hours, two daily).

Getting Around

Local buses run by **TUB** (☎ 04 92 20 47 10; tub@wanadoo.fr; place de Suse; 9am-noon & 1.30-4.30pm Mon-Fri) connect the train station with place du Champ de Mars and the Prorel cable-car station. A single ticket/carnet of 10 costs €1.10/8.

THE JURA

From its fragrant yellow wine to liquid cheese, *Jésus* sausage and authentic farmstays, Jurassien travel really is a memorable feast. Moreover, the dark wooded hills and granite plateaux of the Jura Mountains that stretch in an arc for 360km along the Franco-Swiss border from the Rhine to the Rhône are one of the least explored pockets in France. If it is peace, tranquillity and a true taste of humble mountain life you're seeking, the Jura is an instant winner.

The Jura – from a Gaulish word meaning 'forest' – is France's premier cross-country skiing area. The range is dotted with ski stations and every year the region hosts the Transjurassienne, one of the world's toughest cross-country skiing events.

The region is not short of culture or history either. From heavy metallurgy to precious gem-cutting, its contribution hasn't gone unnoticed in the country's economy, neither has its historical role as the hotbed of the French Resistance during WWII.

BESANÇON

pop 116,100

Old town, young heart: that's Besançon, capital of the Franche-Comté region. The city boasts one of the country's largest foreign-student populations and an innovative spirit, most obvious in its hip buzzing bars and historic quarters such as the Battant (originally the winemakers' district).

First settled in Gallo-Roman times, Besançon became an important stop on the early trade routes between Italy, the Alps and the Rhine. This historical transport role is about to come full circle with the opening of a new TGV station outside Besançon (in the village of Auxon, 10km north) in December 2011 on the new Rhine-to-Rhône TGV line (allowing connections from Germany all the way to the south of France without going through Paris). Once again, Besançon will be at the centre of Europe.

Orientation

The old city is encased by the curve of the River Doubs (Boucle du Doubs). The tourist office and train station sit just outside this loop. The Battant quarter straddles the north-west bank of the river around rue Battant. Grande Rue, the pedestrianised main street, slices through the old city from the bank of the river to the gates of the citadel.

Information

ID PC (28 rue de la République; per hr €3; 9.30am-noon & 2-7pm Tue-Sat) Computer shop with internet terminals.
Le Lavoir (14 rue de la Madeleine; per 5kg €3.50; 8am-8pm) Laundrette.
Post Office (23 rue Proudhon; 8am-7pm Mon-Fri, 8.30am-noon Sat) In the old city.
Tourist Office (☎ 03 81 80 92 55; www.besancon-tourisme.com; 2 place de la 1ère Armée Française;

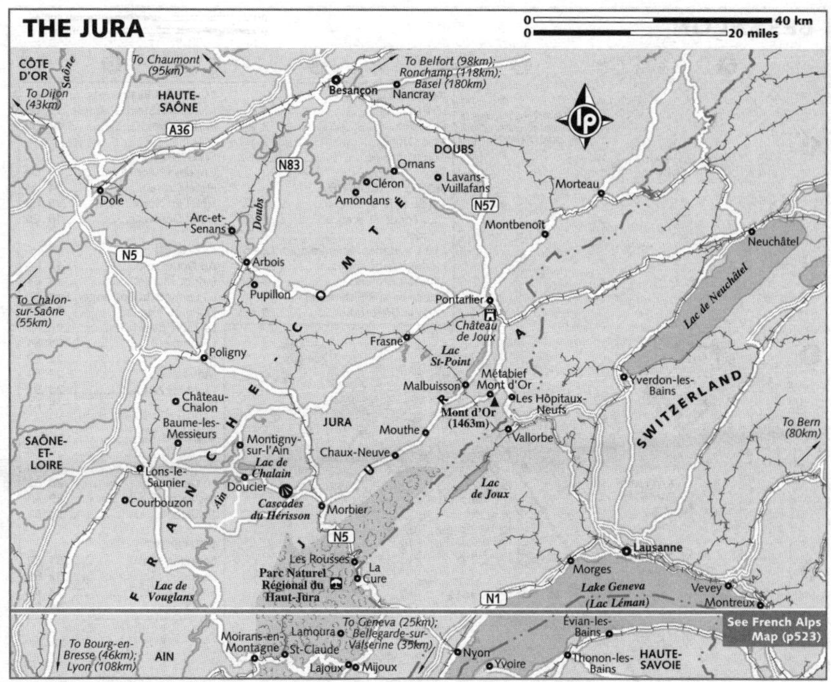

9.30am-7pm Tue-Sat, 10am-6pm Mon, 11am-1pm Sun) Sells city maps and guides; organises thematic city tours (in French only).

Sights

MUSEUMS

Built by Vauban for Louis XIV between 1688 and 1711, Besançon's **citadel** (☎ 03 81 87 83 33; www.citadelle.com; rue des Fusillés de la Résistance; adult/4-14yr €7.80/4.50; 9am-7pm Jul & Aug, 9am-6pm Apr-Jun, Sep & Oct, 10am-5pm Nov-Mar) is a steep 15-minute walk from **Porte Noire** (Black Gate; rue de la Convention), a triumphal arch left over from the city's Roman days, dating from the 2nd century AD. Inside the citadel walls there are three museums to visit: the **Musée Comtois** zooms in on local traditions, the **Musée d'Histoire Naturelle** covers natural history, and the harrowing **Musée de la Résistance et de la Déportation** examines the rise of Nazism and fascism, and the French Resistance movement.

Less sobering are the insects, fish and other animals inhabiting the **insectarium** (including some meaty tarantulas), **aquarium**, **noctarium** and **parc zoologique**. Citadel admission covers entry to all the museums.

Thought to be France's oldest museum, the **Musée des Beaux-Arts** (☎ 03 81 87 80 49; www.musee-arts-besancon.org; 1 place de la Révolution; adult/student €5/2.50; 9.30am-noon & 2-6pm Wed-Mon) houses an impressive collection of paintings, including archeological, medieval and Renaissance works in a very modern building.

HORLOGE ASTRONOMIQUE

Housed in the 18th-century **Cathédrale St-Jean** (rue de la Convention; adult/under 18yr €3/free; 7 guided tours Wed-Mon Apr-Sep, Thu-Mon Oct-Mar), this incredible astronomical clock has 30,000 moving parts, 57 faces, 62 dials and, among other things, tells the time in 16 places around the world, the tides in eight different ports of France, and the time of the local sunrise and sunset. It really has to be seen to be believed.

Tours

In summer vessels dock beneath Pont de la République to take passengers on 1¼-hour

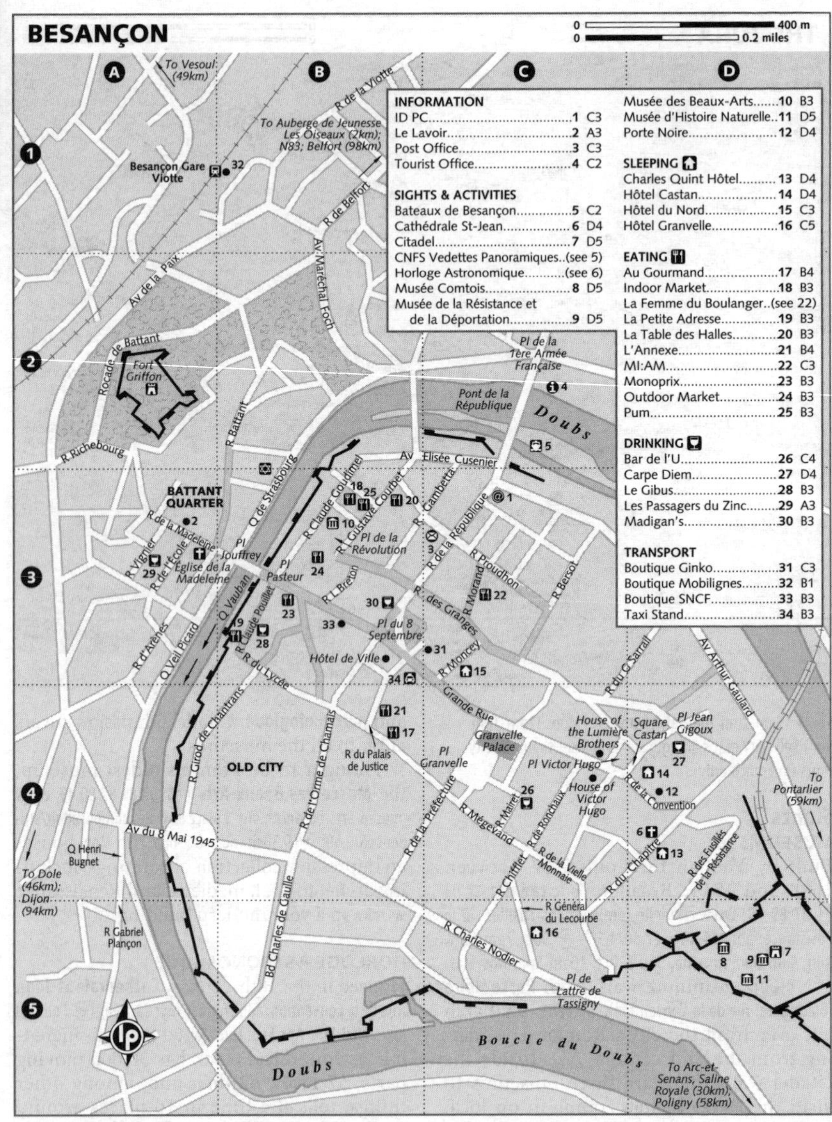

river cruises along the Boucle du Doubs, organised by **Bateaux de Besançon** (☎ 03 81 68 13 25; www.sautdudoubs.fr, in French; adult/child €10.50/8; ⏲ Apr-Oct) and **CNFS Vedettes Panoramiques** (☎ 03 81 68 05 34; www.vedettes-panoramiques.com, in French; adult/child €10.50/8; ⏲ Jul & Aug). In summer there are usually three trips a day. Both companies sail along a 375m-long tunnel underneath the citadel.

Sleeping

Les Oiseaux (☎ 03 81 40 32 00; www.fjtlesoiseaux.fr, in French; 48 rue des Cras; dm incl breakfast €23; ⏲ reception 8am-8pm) This hostel is about 2km east of the train station. The tower block which houses the rooms is quite a bit of an eyesore but the rooms themselves are clean and good value. Take bus number 7 from the tourist office in the direction of Orchamps and get off at Les Oiseaux.

Hôtel du Nord (☎ 03 81 81 34 56; www.hotel-du-nord-besancon.com; 8 rue Moncey; d €39-61, q €61-77) Right in the centre of town, this is a good-value hotel: rooms are fairly old-fashioned but clean, there is free wi-fi, a private garage just 200m from the hotel and lovely staff at hand. Ask for a nonsmoking room if you don't like the smell of cold tobacco.

Hôtel Granvelle (☎ 03 81 81 33 92; www.hotel-granvelle.fr; 13 rue Général du Lecourbe; d €50-60, tr €62-71) You'll find 30 clean, functional rooms in this lovely stone building at the back of a courtyard below the citadel. 'Interactive' rooms are equipped with internet-linked computers; otherwise there's free wi-fi in the rest of the hotel. Good wheelchair access.

Charles Quint Hôtel (☎ 03 81 82 05 49; www.hotel-charlesquint.com; 3 rue du Chapitre; d €87-138;) Besançon's stunning boutique hotel in an 18th-century town house oozes charm, with waxed parquet floors, period furniture, sumptuous fabrics, a heavenly garden with a tiny green swimming pool and splendid wood-panelled dining room. Find this nine-room oasis of old-style elegance slumbering in the shade of the citadel, behind the cathedral.

Hôtel Castan (☎ 03 81 65 02 00; www.hotelcastan.fr; 6 square Castan; d €110-170; closed 2 or 3 weeks Aug;) Original monumental fireplaces, canopy beds, hunted stag heads, terracotta floors and ornate grandfather clocks add authenticity to this lovely ivy-covered 18th-century town house, exquisitely furnished by a retired dentist with a passion for collecting antiques. Find Besançon's grandest hotel on a peaceful old-town square.

Eating

Au Gourmand (☎ 03 81 81 40 56; 5 rue Mégevand; mains from €7; lunch & dinner Tue-Fri, lunch Sat) With its vinyl-coated tablecloths, salt straight out of the supermarket pot and profusion of knick-knacks on the walls, this is a no-frills but charming place. Food is simple, with the humble potato being king, particularly in the form of *les parmentières* (a mound of mashed potato with various toppings).

Pum (☎ 03 81 81 18 47; cnr rue Jean Petit & rue Gustave Courbet; mains from €7.50; lunch & dinner, until 1am Sun-Thu, to 2am Fri & Sat) Bright-orange Pum is a great place for tight budgets: the restaurant downstairs follows the popular 'hot-seating' formula, where you take a seat wherever there's space on one of the long wooden tables. Thai staples such as stir-fries and green curries feature prominently. Upstairs, the bar serves cocktails and beers with an exotic Thai twist.

La Petite Adresse (☎ 03 81 82 35 09; 28 rue Claude Pouillet; mains €15; lunch & dinner Mon-Sat) Enjoy some solid regional cooking in the gregarious atmosphere of this tiny hole-in-the-wall establishment on Besançon's most happening street. The owner sometimes organises competitions whereby if you recognise the song he plays, you win…a sausage. Need we say more?

MI:AM (☎ 03 81 82 09 56; 8 rue Morand; mains €15; 11.30am-midnight Tue-Sun) *Apéro dînatoire* (a light casual dinner) is what trendy MI:AM (as in YUM!) is best at. Waltz through the heavy velvet curtain to enter or snag a seat on the buzzing street terrace. The lunchtime *tartines* (thick slice of toasted bread topped with various ingredients) are not bad either.

La Femme du Boulanger (☎ 03 81 82 86 93; 6 rue Morand; 8am-7pm Mon-Sat), run by the same set as MI:AM next-door, is paradise for cake and tart lovers.

La Table des Halles (☎ 03 81 50 62 74; 22 rue Gustave Courbet; lunch/dinner menus €16/20; lunch & dinner Tue-Sat) The urban loft decor wouldn't look out of place in New York's trendy meat-packing district: industrial rigging for the lights, starch-white walls and massive bay windows instead of walls. But in the plate, the cuisine is resolutely French and regional: Morteau sausages with Mont d'Or mash, poultry in savagnin (a local white wine) sauce or banana gratin with praline mousse. Fabulous.

L'Annexe (☎ 03 81 53 17 12; 11 rue du Palais de Justice; mains €20; lunch & dinner Mon-Fri, dinner Sat) Small, swanky and supertrendy, L'Annexe attracts a chic crowd seeking a fun but sophisticated evening. The menu is as small as the restaurant but as refined too, emphasising fresh market products and premium ingredients (beef, scallops etc).

Self-caterers can shop for food at the **indoor market** (cnr rue Paris & rue Claude Goudimel), the **outdoor market** (place de la Révolution; Tue, Fri & Sat morning) or the supermarket, **Monoprix** (10 Grande Rue; 8.30am-8pm Mon-Sat).

Drinking

Nightlife is concentrated in the old Battant quarter and around the river along rue Claude Pouillet and parallel quai Vauban.

Madigan's (☎ 03 81 81 17 44; 19 place du 8 Septembre; 7.30am-1am) French pop music and a young crowd for Irish-style shenanigans on one of town's main squares.

Le Gibus (☎ 03 81 81 09 99; 11 rue Claude Pouillet; 5pm-1am) A rocking crowd gathers in the 1950s pin-up decor most evenings for live or recorded music and always plenty of good times.

Carpe Diem (☎ 03 81 83 11 18; 2 place Jean Gigoux; 9am-1am Mon-Thu, 9am-2am Fri & Sat, 9am-8pm Sun) The archetypal local French café with a crowd of regulars, on the respectable side of 60 during the day and the carefree side of 30 at night. Regular gigs feature, when a drink surcharge of €0.40 kicks in.

Les Passagers du Zinc (☎ 03 81 81 54 70; 5 rue Vignier; 5pm-1am Tue-Fri, 5pm-2am Sat & Sun) A grungy bar and club with battered leather sofas and multicoloured lights, the regular live bands and music nights keep this place high on the list of best venues in town. Step through the bonnet of an old Citroën DS to reach the cellar.

Bar de l'U (☎ 03 81 81 55 95; 5 rue Mairet; 8am-1am Mon-Thu, to 2am Fri, 11am-2am Sat, 5pm-midnight Sun) Live music most nights and slamming competitions every second Monday of the month, this is student mainstay. Many events require a student card to attend.

Getting There & Away

BUS

There is no bus station in Besançon. Daily services to Ornans (€3.30, 45 minutes) and Pontarlier (€7.50, 1¼ hours) stop at the train-station bus stop. You can buy tickets at the **Boutique Mobilignes** (☎ 08 25 00 22 44; www.mobilignes.com, in French; 8.30am-noon & 2.30-6.30pm Mon-Fri, 8.30am-noon Sat), at the far end of the Besançon Gare Viotte train station.

TRAIN

From Besançon Gare Viotte, 800m uphill from the city centre, there are trains to/from Paris' Gare de Lyon (€63.60, 2¾ hours, three daily), Dijon (train/TGV €13.30/17.60, 50/70 minutes, 20 daily), Lyon (€31, 2¼ hours, seven daily), Belfort (€14, 1¼ hours, 15 daily), Arbois (€8.10, 45 minutes, eight to 10 daily) and Arc-et-Senans (€6.10, 30 minutes, up to 10 daily). Buy tickets at the train station or

THE STUFF OF DREAMS

Get away from it all at these two more-idyllic-than-idyllic Jurassien hideouts.

Amondans (☎ 03 81 86 53 53; www.amondans.com; place du Village, Amondans; half-board s/d/tr €71/102/141; May-Oct) This funky find of a village inn – a stunning 18th-century farm 30km south of Besançon in sleepy Amondans (population 87) – fuses retro 1930s to 1960s furnishings (picked up in second-hand shops and jumble sales) with century-old features to create a contemporary eating and sleeping space. Rooms overlook open fields and are vast and minimal. Guests – groups and couples rather than families – are very much hip, happy, outdoor types who mountain-bike, hike, canoe, cave or horse-ride by day and hang out after dinner in the inn's magnificent *coin salon* – an entire converted barn with the most enormous fireplace you're ever likely to see. Swiss couple George and Geneviève, who run the place, can organise most outdoor activities, rent out mountain bikes (€15 per day), supply picnics (€10) and occasionally serve a barbecued dinner in the hills.

Ferme Auberge du Rondeau (☎ 03 81 59 25 84; http://ferme-rondeau.fr.cc; Lavans-Vuillafans; s/d €42/53, menus €23-33; mid-Jan–Nov; ☒) Coo over 200 goats, 50 boar and a handful of dairy cows at this idyllic organic farm, 2km from the village of Lavans-Vuillafans. Run by the friendly Bourdier family for three generations, this farm really is the stuff childhood dreams are made of: cosy rooms are wood-panelled and breakfast is a veritable feast of farm produce – home-made yoghurt and jam, fresh farm-baked bread and brioche. And 90% of what you'll eat for dinner or lunch comes from the farm: *sanglier* (boar) saucisson, seven different types of *chèvres* (goat's cheese) and a main course of goat, kid or boar depending on the season. You can also buy a range of unbelievably warm hand-knitted mohair plaids and jumpers made with the wool of the farm's angora goats. Advance reservations for eating, sleeping or both are essential.

LIQUID GOLD

Jura's signature wine, *vin jaune* (yellow wine), is made following a unique vinification. Savagnin grapes are harvested late, their sugar-saturated juices left to ferment for a minimum of six years and three months in oak barrels. A thin layer of yeast forms over the wine to prevent it from oxidising, and evaporation (called *la part des anges*, 'the angels' share') is not compensated by additional top-ups. It is this long and undisrupted fermentation process that gives the wine its unique flavour. In the end, 100L of grape juice ferment down to 62L of *vin jaune* (lucky bloody angels), which is then bottled in special 0.62L bottles called *clavelin*. *Vin jaune* is actually renowned for it ageing qualities, with prime vintages easily keeping for more than a century. The oldest bottle enjoyed was a 1774 vintage, a cool 220 years old when sipped by an awestruck committee of experts in 1994.

Legend has it that *vin jaune* was invented when a winemaker rediscovered a forgotten barrel, six years and three months after he'd initially filled it, its content miraculously transformed into a gold-coloured wine (hence the name).

Myth or reality, the tradition lives on. **La Percée du Vin Jaune** festival takes place every year in early February to celebrate the first tasting of the vintage produced six years and three months earlier. Villages in the Jura wine area take it in turn to hold the two-day celebrations when the new vintage is blessed and rated, and street tastings, cooking competitions, cellar visits and vintage auctions keep a crowd of *vin jaune* aficionados fulfilled. Check www.jura-vins.com or www.percee-du-vin-jaune.com (both in French) for more info.

from the **Boutique SNCF** (44 Grande Rue; 9am-7pm Mon-Fri, 9am-6pm Sat) in town.

Getting Around

Borrow a bicycle, pushchair or shopping caddie on wheels to cruise around town – free with a valid bus ticket – from the local bus company office, **Boutique Ginko** (☎ 08 25 00 22 44; www.ginkobus.com; 4 place du 8 Septembre; 10am-7pm Mon-Sat). The boutique sells bus tickets costing €1.15/3.50/9.80 for a single ticket/day ticket/carnet of 10.

Call a **taxi** (☎ 03 81 88 80 80) or pick one up next to the town hall.

AROUND BESANÇON

Saline Royale

Envisaged by its designer, Claude-Nicolas Ledoux, as the 'ideal city', the 18th-century **Saline Royale** (Royal Saltworks; ☎ 03 81 54 45 45; www.salineroyale.com, in French; adult/16-25yr/6-15yr €7.50/5/3.50; 9am-7pm Jul & Aug, 9am-noon & 2-6pm Apr-Jun, Sep & Oct, 10am-noon & 2-5pm Nov-Mar, closed Jan) in **Arc-et-Senans** (population 1400), 30km southwest of Besançon, is a showpiece of early Industrial Age town planning. Although his urban dream was never realised, Ledoux's semicircular saltworks is now listed as a Unesco World Heritage Site.

Regular trains link Besançon and Arc-et-Senans (€6.10, 30 minutes, up to 10 daily).

Route Pasteur

Almost every single town in France has at least one street, square or garden named after Louis Pasteur, the great 19th-century chemist who invented pasteurisation and developed the first rabies vaccine. In the Jura, it is even more the case since the illustrious man was a local lad, born and raised in the region, and a regular visitor for holidays (he worked mostly in Paris).

Pasteur was born in **Dole**, 20km west of Arc-et-Senans along the D472. His childhood home, **La Maison Natale de Pasteur** (☎ 03 84 72 20 61; www.musee-pasteur.com; 43 rue Pasteur; adult/student/under 12yr €5/3/free; 10am-6pm Mon-Sat, 2-6pm Sun Jul & Aug, 10am-noon & 2-6pm Mon-Sat, 2-6pm Sun Apr-Jun, Sep & Oct, 10am-noon & 2-6pm Sat & Sun Nov-Mar), overlooking the Canal des Tanneurs in the old town, is now an atmospheric museum housing letters, artefacts and exhibits including his university cap and gown.

In 1827 the Pasteur family settled in the rural community of **Arbois** (population 3509), 35km east of Dole. His laboratory and workshops in Arbois are on display at **La Maison de Louis Pasteur** (☎ 03 84 66 11 72; 83 rue de Courcelles; adult/7-15yr €5.80/2.90; guided tours hourly 9.45-11.45am & 2-6pm Jun-Sep, 2.15-5.15pm Apr, May & 1-15 Oct). The house is still decorated with its original 19th-century fixtures and fittings.

Route du Vin

No visit to Arbois, the Jura wine capital, would be complete without a glass of *vin jaune*. The history of this nutty 'yellow wine' (see boxed text, p575), is told in the **Musée de la Vigne et du Vin** (☎ 03 84 66 40 45; museevignevin@wanadoo.fr; adult/child €3.50/2.70; 10am-12.30pm & 2-6pm Wed-Mon Mar-Jun, Sep & Oct, 10am-12.30pm & 2-6pm Jul & Aug, 2-6pm Wed-Mon Nov-Feb). Don't miss out on doing the **Chemin des Vignes**, a 2.5km-long walking trail that wends its way in a loop through vineyards from the museum. Cyclists might prefer the 8km-long **Circuit des Vignes**, a mountain-bike trail likewise through vineyards.

Complete the wine trip with lunch at Arbois' **La Balance Mets et Vins** (☎ 03 84 37 45 00; 47 rue de Courcelles; menus €24/32; lunch & dinner Thu-Mon, lunch Tue), a fantastic restaurant making the very best of local specialities. Its signature rooster casserole, *coq au vin jaune et aux morilles*, and crème brûlée doused in local *vin jaune* are must-tastes, as are the wine menus with five different glasses of either Jurassienne wine (€16) or *vin jaune* (€27, including one from 1976). La Balance also dabbles in that most non-French of practices: the doggy bag!

High above Arbois is **Pupillon** (population 220), a cute yellow-brick village famous for its wine production. Some 10 different *caves* (wine cellars) are open to visitors. Mountain bikers can follow the **Circuit de Pupillon** (13km) marked trail from Arbois.

Arbois **tourist office** (☎ 03 84 66 55 50; www.arbois.com; rue de l'Hôtel de Ville; 9am-noon & 2-6pm Mon-Sat) has cycling itinerary information, a list of *caves* where you can taste and buy the local vintage and a treasure-hunt itinerary (in French) for kids.

Trains link Arbois and Besançon (€8.10, 45 minutes, eight to 10 daily).

POLIGNY TO BAUME-LES-MESSIEURS

Comté is indisputable king of the Jura, small-town **Poligny** (population 4518) serving as the capital of the industry that produces 40 million tonnes of the venerable cheese a year. Learn how 450L is transformed into a 40kg wheel of cheese and smell some of its 83 different aromas at the **Maison du Comté** (☎ 03 84 37 78 40; www.comte.com; av de la Résistance; adult/student/6-16yr €4/3/2.50; 10am-noon & 2-6pm Jul & Aug, 2-6pm May, June & Sep, 2-5pm Tue-Sun Apr & Oct). There are dozens of *fruitières* (dairy cooperatives where farmers combine their milk productions to make cheese) open to the public. Poligny **tourist office** (☎ 03 84 37 24 21; tourisme.poligny@wanadoo.fr; place des Déportés; 9am-noon & 2-6pm Tue-Sat, 2-6pm Mon) stocks an abundance of cheesy info.

Heading south, wiggle along the pretty D68 to Plasne, then continue south to **Château-Chalon** (population 167), the pretty hilltop village of medieval yellow stone ensnared by vineyards known for their legendary *vin jaune* (see boxed text, p575). There is an excellent **tourist office** in the nearby village of Voiteur (☎ 04 84 44 62 47; www.hauteseille.com; 3 place de la Mairie; 9.30am-12.30pm & 2-6pm Mon-Sat Jul & Aug, 9.30am-12.30pm Mon-Fri Sep-Jun, 9.30am-12.30pm & 2-6pm Mon-Fri school holidays) with plenty of info on surrounding villages, wine and walking in the area (the €3 *Walking and Mountain-Biking Tours in the Coteaux of Haute Seille* is worth its weight in gold).

Enchanting **Baume-les-Messieurs** (population 196) is another extraordinarily pretty village of cob houses and red-tiled rooftops, wedged between three glacial valleys, 20km south of Poligny. Its abandoned Benedictine **Abbaye Impériale** (Imperial Abbey; ☎ 03 84 44 99 28; admission €3.60; 10am-noon & 2-6pm mid-May–Sep) can only be visited by guided tour. Nearby, the 30-million-year-old **Grottes de Baume** (Baume Caves; ☎ 03 84 48 23 02; adult/children €5/2.50; 10am-5pm mid-Apr–mid-Jun, 10am-6pm mid-Jun–mid-Sep, guided tours only) feature some impressive stalagmites and stalactites.

Immediately east lies the Jura's **Région des Lacs** (Lakes District), the highlight being the majestic waterfalls of the **Cascades du Hérisson**.

Sleeping & Eating

From November to April, it can be difficult if not impossible to find somewhere open for dinner in rural areas on week nights.

Le Comptois (☎ 03 84 25 71 21; www.lecomptoisdoucier.com; Doucier; d €35-45, half-board per person €50, mains €12-18) This simple village restaurant opposite the post office with eight rooms up top (four dead-basic for hikers) really has no airs and graces, but it serves excellent food with a wonderful wine list to match.

Le Grand Jardin (☎ 03 84 44 68 37; www.legrandjardin.fr; rue des Grands Jardins, Baume-les-Messieurs; s/d/tr/q incl breakfast €39/47/57/74; Feb–mid-Dec) Book well ahead in summer to snag one of the three rooms at this delightful *chambre d'hôte*, enviably placed opposite the abbey in Baume-les-Messieurs. Rooms, one of which sleeps seven, are quainter than picture-postcard quaint.

Au Douillet Gourmet (☎ 03 84 51 27 24; www.au-douillet-gourmet.com; rue du Château, Montigny-sur-l'Ain; s/d/tr incl breakfast €40/50/63, incl dinner €55/80/108) If you decide to stay at Pascal and Christelle's gregarious and slightly chaotic dairy farm, this is your chance to learn and even help with milking the cows, bottle-feeding the calves or collecting eggs from the hen hutch. Christelle also does wonderful home-made food and pretty much everything you'll eat comes from the farm.

our pick **Escargot Comtois** (☎ 03 84 24 15 29; www.escargot-comtois.com, in French; 215 rue de Montorient, Courbouzon; s/d incl breakfast €41/49, tr incl breakfast €59-69, dinner with/without snails €23/20; 💻) Spending a night at this highly original *chambre d'hôte* makes a great story to tell the folks back home. This is one of France's 400 snail farms so, between May and September, you'll witness a hive of snail activity, from the 200,000 gastropods binging on grass in their 'pen' to harvesting. The result lines the shelves and fills the freezers of the snail lab on the ground floor of Muriel and David Blanchard's lovingly restored 1747 stone village house. Rooms are cosy and sport a computer with internet access. Evening meals are around a shared table, the optional entrée being snails. Find Courbouzon 22km south of Baume-les-Messieurs.

Le Relais des Abbesses (☎ 03 84 44 98 56; www.chambres-hotes-jura.com; rue de la Roche, Château-Chalon; d incl breakfast €65-68, dinner €24) An unusual B&B in the heart of beautiful Château-Chalon: Agnès and Gérard have decorated their rooms with Asian antiques acquired over many years. They are both fine cooks, and their *table d'hôte* is a treat, be it in the view-studded dining room or the garden.

Café Restaurant de l'Abbaye (☎ 03 84 44 63 44; Baumes-les-Messieurs; menu €20; 🕑 lunch & dinner Mon-Sat May-Sep, shorter hr rest of year) Tucked in one of the abbey's old buildings, this old-fashioned eating and drinking venue hits the spot as far as tasty lunches go. Try the *cassolette franc-comtoise* (a casserole of potatoes, onions, cheese and local sausage) for a real taste of the country.

BELFORT

pop 50,700

Squeezed between north and east, France and Germany, art and industry, Belfort has grown into its own distinctive identity (it calls itself a *territoire*, not a *département*). Historically part of Alsace, it only became part of the Franche-Comté region in 1921 and is best known today as the manufacturer of the speedy TGV train and host to three-day open-air rock festival **Les Eurockéennes** (www.eurockeennes.fr) in early July and international film festival **Entre Vues** (www.festival-entrevues.com) in late November.

The city centrepiece is a **Vauban citadel** (p65), host to open-air concerts in summer and the **Musée d'Histoire** (☎ 03 84 54 25 51; 🕑 10am-6pm, Wed-Mon Jun-Sep, 10am-noon & 2-6pm Wed-Mon Oct-May). On duty at its foot is an 11m-tall lion sculpted in sandstone by Frédéric-Auguste Bartholdi (of Statue of Liberty fame) to commemorate Belfort's resistance to the Prussians in 1870–71. While the rest of Alsace was annexed as part of the greater German Empire, Belfort stubbornly remained part of France.

Belfort **tourist office** (☎ 03 84 55 90 90; www.ot-belfort.fr; 2bis rue Clémenceau; 🕑 9am-noon & 1.45-6.30pm Mon-Fri, to 6pm Sat mid-Jun–mid-Sep, 9am-noon & 1.45-6pm Mon-Fri, to 5.30pm Sat mid-Sep–mid-Jun) distributes free city maps and has plenty of information on accommodation and things to see and do around Belfort. Car enthusiasts can visit the **Musée de l'Aventure Peugeot** (☎ 03 81 99 42 03; www.musee-peugeot.com; Carrefour de l'Europe; adult/10-18yr/under 10yr €7/3.50/free; 🕑 10am-6pm), 12km south in Sochaux; the modernist **Église du Sacré Cœur**, 4km southeast in Audincourt, is an architecture-buff must; and outdoor adventures are bountiful in the **Massif du Ballon d'Alsace** (1247m), 20km north of Belfort in the southern Vosges Mountains.

Ronchamp

The only reason to rendezvous in Ronchamp, 20km west of Belfort, is to visit Le Corbusier's striking modernist chapel on a hill overlooking the old mining town. Built between 1950 and 1955, the surreal **Chapelle de Notre Dame du Haut** (Chapel of Our Lady of the Height; ☎ 03 84 20 65 13; www.chapellederonchamp.fr, in French; adult/student €3/2; 🕑 9.30am-7pm Apr-Sep, 10am-5pm Oct & Mar, 10am-4pm Nov-Feb) with a sweeping concrete roof, coloured-glass windows and plastic features is one of the 20th century's architectural masterpieces. It's a pilgrimage site for thousands of architects every year, and 3000-odd religious pilgrims each year on 8 September (the Virgin Mary's birth day).

A 15-minute walking trail leads uphill to the chapel from the centre of Ronchamp village; the **tourist office** (☎ 03 84 63 50 82; 14 place du 14 Juillet; ☎ 9am-12.30pm & 1.30-6pm Tue-Fri, 9am-12.30pm Sat, 1.30-6pm Mon) can guide you.

Sleeping & Eating

Don't leave Belfort without biting into a *Belflore*, a scrumptious almond-flavoured pastry filled with raspberries and topped with hazelnuts.

Relais d'Alsace (☎ 03 84 22 15 55; www.arahotel.com; 5 av de la Laurencie; s/d/tr/q from €38/50/60/70) Just like Belfort's signature festival, this place rocks! Run by the legendary Kim, this is the coolest place to hang out within a 200km radius: partysome but chilled, laid-back but impeccably held, Kim has effortlessly managed to combine professionalism and fun. Rooms are simple but bright with funky animal cartoons sketched on the doors. At the time of research Kim had just bought the next-door restaurant and hoped to soon be able to serve solid regional snacks.

Getting There & Away

Connections from Belfort **train station** (av Wilson) include Paris' Gare de Lyon via Besançon (from €72.30, four hours, seven daily), Montbéliard (€3.40, 20 minutes, 20 daily), Besançon (€14, 1¼ hours, 14 daily) and Ronchamp (€4.10, 20 minutes, four daily).

MÉTABIEF MONT D'OR

pop 907 / elevation 1000m

Métabief Mont d'Or, 18km south of Pontarlier on the main road to Lausanne, is the region's leading cross-country ski resort. All year, lifts take you almost to the top of Mont d'Or (1463m), the area's highest peak, from where a fantastic 180° panorama stretches over the foggy Swiss plain to Lake Geneva (Lac Léman) and all the way from the Matterhorn to Mont Blanc.

Métabief is famed for its unique *Vacherin Mont d'Or*. It has been produced alongside Comté and Morbier by the Sancey-Richard family at the **Fromagerie du Mont d'Or** (☎ 03 81 49 02 36; 2 rue Moulin; 🕒 cheese shop 9am-12.15pm & 3-7pm Mon-Sat, 9am-noon Sun) since 1953. To see cheese being made, arrive with the milk lorry around 9am.

The closest **tourist office** (☎ 03 81 49 13 81; www.tourisme-metabief.com, in French; 1 place de la Mairie, Les Hôpitaux-Neufs; 🕒 9am-12.30pm & 1.30-6pm Mon-Sat, 9am-noon Sun) open year-round is in Les Hôpitaux-Neufs. The annexe in Métabief is closed out of season, much like everything else in the village. Family-run **Hôtel Étoile des Neiges** (☎ 03 81 49 11 21; www.hoteletoiledesneiges.fr, in French; 4 rue du Village; s/d/tr/q €54/66/80/94, half-board €65/96/132/160; ♿) stays open more or less year-round. The restaurant looks a little like a hospital canteen but the rooms are spotless, with great mezzanine family rooms. Good wheelchair access.

Getting there and away: use your own wheels!

AROUND MÉTABIEF MONT D'OR

Skiers can break from the slopes at **Parc Polaire** (Polar Park; ☎ 03 81 69 20 20; www.parcpolaire.com, in French; adult/4-11yr €7/5.40; 🕒 10am-6pm Jul & Aug, 2-6pm Tue-Sun Mar, April & Jun, 2-6pm Mon-Fri & Sun Sep & Oct, 10am-5pm Tue-Sun Jan & Feb), a husky-and-reindeer park in Chaux-Neuve where Claude and Gilles Malloire will introduce you to their 40 huskies and their life as a pack.

The dramatic **Château de Joux** (☎ 03 81 69 47 95; www.chateaudejoux.com, in French; adult/student/6-14yr €5.80/4.70/3; 🕒 9am-6pm Jul & Aug, 10-11.30am & 2-4.30pm Apr-Jun & Sep–mid-Nov, guided tours only), 10km north of Métabief, used to guard the

HOT BOX, CHRISTMAS ICE & JESUS

It's hot, it's soft and it's packed in a box. *Vacherin Mont d'Or* is the only French cheese to be eaten with a spoon – hot (or cold for that matter). Made between 15 August and 15 March with *lait cru* (unpasteurised milk), it derives its unique nutty taste from the spruce bark in which it's wrapped. Connoisseurs top the soft-crusted cheese with chopped onions, garlic and white wine, wrap it in aluminium foil and bake it for 45 minutes to create a *boîte chaude* (hot box). Only 11 factories in the Jura are licensed to produce *Vacherin Mont d'Or*.

Mouthe, 15km south of Métabief Mont d'Or, is the mother of *liqueur de sapin* (fir-tree liqueur). *Glace de sapin* (fir-tree ice cream) also comes from Mont d'Or, known as the North Pole of France due to its seasonal subzero temperatures (record low -38°C). Sampling either is rather like ingesting a Christmas tree. Then there's *Jésus* – a small, fat version of *saucisse de Morteau* (Morteau sausage), easily identified by the wooden peg on its end, attached after the sausage is smoked with pinewood sawdust in a traditional *tuyé* (mountain hut).

GRANDE TRAVERSÉE DU JURA

Cross-country skiing, mountain biking, walking or even snowshoeing, the Grande Traversée du Jura (GTJ) – the Grand Jura Crossing – is a cross-country track running some 200km from Villers-le-Lac (north of Pontarlier) to Hauteville-Lompnes (southwest of Bellegarde). The exact itinerary varies between disciplines but the track peaks at 1500m near the town of Mouthe (south of Métabief) and follows one of the coldest valleys in France. After the first 20km the route briefly crosses into Switzerland, but mostly runs along the border on the French side. Well maintained and very popular, the track takes 10 full days of skiing to cover – a feat even for the ultrafit.

Part of the GTJ, the 76km from Lamoura to Mouthe is covered each year by 4000 skiers during the world's second-largest cross-country skiing competition, the **Transjurassienne** (www.transjurassienne.com) held in early February, and several hundred rollerbladers and rollerskiers during the **Trans' Roller** (www.transroller.com) in September.

For complete information on the GTJ, including maps and accommodation along the route, contact **Les Grandes Traversées du Jura** (☎ 03 84 51 51 51; www.gtj.asso.fr; 15 & 17 Grande Rue, Les Planches-en-Montagne).

route between Switzerland and France. Today it houses France's most impressive arms museum, and a 100m-deep well (watch your guide pour water into it and hold your breath until you hear it hit the bottom, several long seconds later). Guided tours are gripping, full of anecdotes and stories, and available in English (ring ahead). In summer, torch-lit night-time tours are organised for extra spookiness.

PARC NATUREL RÉGIONAL DU HAUT-JURA

Experience the Jura at its rawest in the Haut-Jura Regional Park, an area of 757 sq km stretching from Chapelle-des-Bois in the north almost to the western tip of Lake Geneva. Each year in February its abundant lakes, mountains and low-lying valleys host the Transjurassienne, the world's second-longest cross-country skiing race (above). Forget about exploring the region without a car.

A great place to start is the **Maison du Parc** (☎ 03 84 34 12 30; www.parc-haut-jura.fr; Lajoux; adult/child €5/3; ⌚ 10am-noon & 2-7pm Tue-Fri, 10am-7pm Sat & Sun Jul, Aug & school holidays, 9am-noon & 2-6pm Tue-Fri rest of year), an interactive sensorial museum that will help you discover the region and its history through sounds, films, touching, feeling and smelling.

There's not much to **St-Claude** (population 12,296) – the largest town in the park – bar its illustrious diamond-cutting industry which, unfortunately, is off-limits to visitors. Further west, however, is a gem of another kind very much within your reach: **our pick** **Les Louvières** (☎ 03 84 42 09 24; www.leslouvieres.com, in French; Pratz; 2-/3-course menu €28/34; ⌚ lunch & dinner Wed-Sat, lunch Sun), a solar-powered farmhouse restaurant to rave about in the middle of nowhere. Philippe's creations in the kitchen (foie gras maki-zushi with maple syrup, fish in wasabi sauce etc) are strictly fusion, and Canadian waiter Sol's welcome in the very hip dining room is warm enough to make Jura winter snow melt.

The so-called French capital of wooden toys, **Moirans-en-Montagne**, 14km west, hosts the **Musée du Jouet** (Toy Museum; ☎ 03 84 42 38 64; www.musee-du-jouet.fr, in French; 5 rue du Murgin; adult/6-15yr/3-5yr €5/2.50/2; ⌚ 10am-6.30pm Jul & Aug, 10am-12.30pm & 2-6pm Mon-Fri, 2-6pm Sat & Sun Sep & Apr-Jun, 2-6pm Tue-Sun Oct-Mar) – a far-from-playful 'look but don't touch' (rather than interactive) museum.

Fall asleep to absolute silence at the nearby **Le Clos d'Estelle** (☎ 03 84 42 01 29; www.leclosdestelle.com; Hameau La Marcantine, Charchilla; d/tr incl breakfast €70/82, dinner incl wine €25), four *chambres d'hôtes* run by the lovely Christine and Jean-Pierre Thévenet, Jura locals through and through, who'll enthusiastically share their knowledge of the area with you.

Les Rousses (population 3018, elevation 1100m), on the northeastern edge of the park, is the park's prime sports hub, winter (skiing) and summer (walking and mountain biking) alike. Dubbed *la station aux quatre villages* (the four-village resort), it comprises four small ski areas – predominantly cross-country with a dash of downhill thrown in for good measure: Prémanon, Lamoura, Bois d'Amont and the village Les Rousses. Find out more at the **Maison du Tourisme** (square du 19 Mars 1962;

CROSS-BORDER

'I think you're going to sleep very well, with your head in Switzerland and your feet in France,' the owner said. He was right. **Hôtel Franco-Suisse** (☎ 03 84 60 02 20, +41 22 360 13 96; www.arbezie-hotel.com; La Cure; s/d/tr/q €49/59/69/79, for half-board per person add €29; ⌚ bistro lunch & dinner Wed-Mon) is a unique bistro inn with both French and Swiss telephone numbers (!) that sits smack on the French-Swiss border, 2.5km from Les Rousses. Run by the Arbez family since 1920, the decor is best described as Parisian bistro meets Alpine chalet. Rooms are simple but comfortable (those in the annexe have been done up in real chalet style) and the next-door neighbour is the Douane La Cure (La Cure customs and border crossing). Find Hôtel Franco-Suisse in the hamlet of La Cure, wedged between the Col de la Faucille (France) and Col de la Givrine (Switzerland).

⌚ 9am-noon & 2-6pm Mon-Sat, 9.30am-12.30pm Sun, longer hr in high season), home to the **tourist office** (☎ 03 84 60 02 55; www.lesrousses.com, in French), **ESF** (☎ 03 84 60 01 61; www.esf-lesrousses.com) and **Espace Loisirs Les Rousses** (☎ 03 84 60 02 55) where ski passes for both Les Rousses and the neighbouring ski resorts of La Dôle and St-Cergue in Switzerland are sold. Lunch, dinner and/or kip the night on the Swiss border (above).

The Jura's most staggering view is from the **Col de la Faucille**, 20km south of Les Rousses. Savour incredible views (extra incredible at sunset) from the restaurant terrace (or the pool in summer) of **La Mainaz** (☎ 04 50 41 31 10; www.la-mainaz.com; 5 rte du Col de la Faucille; d from €77; ⌚ mid-Dec–mid-Oct; 🅿), a hotel-restaurant midway along the mountain pass.

As the N5 twists and turns its way down the Jura Mountains past the small ski resort of **Mijoux**, the panoramic view of Lake Geneva embraced by the French Alps and Mont Blanc beyond is equally startling. For the best vantage point, ride the **Telesiège Val Mijoux** (chairlift; return €6; ⌚ 9am-1pm & 2.15-5.30pm Fri-Sun mid-Jul–mid-Aug) from Mijoux to the foot of the **Télécabine du Mont Rond** and continue up to Mont Rond (elevation 1533m).

Continuing a further 25km southeast you arrive at the French-Swiss border, passing through **Ferney-Voltaire** (☎ tourist office 04 50 28 09 16; www.ferney-voltaire.net), 5km north of Geneva en route. Following his banishment from Switzerland in 1759, Voltaire lived in Ferney until his return to Paris and death in 1778. Guided tours (55 minutes) of his humble home, **Château de Voltaire** (☎ 04 50 40 53 21; allée du Château; admission free; ⌚ tours 10.30am, 11.30am, 2.30pm, 3.30pm & 4.30pm Tue-Sun mid-May–mid-Sep), take in the château, chapel and surrounding 7-hectare park. Past visitors include Auden, Blake and Flaubert, all of whom wrote about the philosopher's home in exile.

Massif Central

Between the knife-edge Alps and the green fields of the Limousin sprawls the Massif Central, one of the wildest, emptiest and least-known corners of France. Cloaked with a mantle of grassy cones, snow-flecked peaks and high plateaus left behind by long-extinct volcanoes, the Massif Central is a place where you can feel nature's heavy machinery at work. Deep underground, hot volcanic springs bubble into the spa baths and mineral-water factories of Vichy and Volvic, while high in the mountain massifs, trickling streams join forces to form three of France's greatest rivers: the Dordogne, the Allier and the Loire.

Deeply traditional and still dominated by the old industries of agriculture and cattle farming, the Massif Central and the surrounding Auvergne region is home to the largest area of protected landscape in all of France, formed by two huge regional parks: the Parc Naturel Régional des Volcans d'Auvergne and its neighbour, the Parc Naturel Régional du Livradois-Forez. With so much natural splendour on offer, the Massif Central is, unsurprisingly, a paradise for those who like their landscapes really rude and raw – whether that means hikers tackling the trails around the Chaîne des Puys, skiers plunging down the slopes of the Puy de Sancy, or paragliders launching themselves from the icy summit of Puy de Dôme.

But the Auvergne isn't just about the great outdoors. History buffs can delve into the belle-époque streets of Vichy or wander the backstreets of Le Puy-en-Velay, once one of the busiest pilgrimage cities in Europe, while gastronomes can stuff themselves silly with five varieties of trademarked cheese and some of the halest, heartiest food anywhere in France.

HIGHLIGHTS

- Staring out across the rooftops of **Le Puy-en-Velay** from inside the statue of Notre Dame de France (p602)
- Puffing your way to the summit of the **Puy de Dôme** (p592) for the finest views in central France
- Venturing inside the booming volcano at **Vulcania** (p592)
- Hiking the high-altitude trails around **Puy de Sancy** (p595) and **Le Mont-Dore** (p595)
- Soothe those bones and sample the waters at the spa town of **Vichy** (p588)

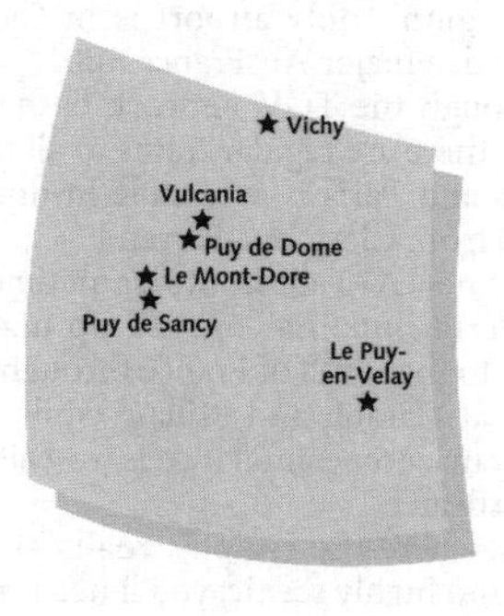

- POPULATION: 1,310,000
- AREA: 26,015 SQ KM

History

The historical province of the Auvergne derives its name from a Gallic tribe, the Arverni, who ruled the area until the all-conquering Romans arrived under the command of Julius Caesar. An Arverni chieftain called Vercingétorix put up the only real resistance to Caesar's legions. Despite several spirited victories, his armies were finally crushed near Alésia in Burgundy, and the Auvergne fell under Roman rule (Vercingétorix is commemorated with a statue in Clermont-Ferrand).

The Romans founded a number of settlements, notably the city of Augustonemetum (later Clermont-Ferrand). Following the fall of the Empire, the Auvergne entered a period of infighting between rival factions of Franks, Aquitanians and Carolingians, before being split into feudal domains during the Middle Ages under the powerful dukes of Auvergne, whose governmental seat was established in Riom.

After the French Revolution, the capital switched to Clermont-Ferrand, and the city became a focus of industrial and educational expansion, especially following the arrival of the industrious Michelin brothers and their rubber factories in the late 19th century.

Meanwhile well-to-do aristocrats flocked to the region's fashionable spas and built countless belle-époque mansions, notably in Vichy (p588) and La Bourboule (p596). During WWII Vichy became the capital of the collaborationist regime under Maréchal Pétain.

Getting There & Around

The region's only airport is in Clermont-Ferrand, a major Air France hub.

Though the TGV network hasn't yet arrived, there are regular trains to all the main towns and Paris is accessible in under four hours from Clermont-Ferrand.

The new A75 autoroute (sometimes called *La Méridienne*) has opened up high-speed travel to the south of France through the viaducts at Garabit and Millau, while the A89 (La Transeuropéenne) travels west all the way to Bordeaux.

Elsewhere the region's roads are twisty, slow and highly scenic: you'll need your own car to reach the more remote spots, as the bus network is almost nonexistent.

CLERMONT-FERRAND & AROUND

CLERMONT-FERRAND

pop 141,000 / elevation 400m

Sprawling around a long-extinct volcano, slap bang in the middle of the Massif Central, Clermont-Ferrand is the capital of the Auvergne and the region's only metropolis. The spiritual home of the roly-poly Michelin Man (known to the French as Bibendum) and the Michelin tyre empire, Clermont-Ferrand has been a thumping industrial powerhouse for over a century. Beyond the smokestack factories and suburban warehouses, you'll discover a soaring twin-spired cathedral, some interesting museums and one of the most atmospheric old cities in the Auvergne.

Orientation

The old town is bounded by av des États-Unis to the west, rue André Moinier to the north and bd Trudaine to the east. The commercial centre stretches westward from the cathedral to av des États-Unis and place de Jaude, then along rue Blatin.

Information

Laundrette (6 place Hippolyte Renoux; ⌚ 7am-8pm)
Laundrette (rue du Port)
Lepton (22 av des Paulines; per hr €2.50; ⌚ 10am-midnight Mon-Fri, 2pm-midnight Sat & Sun) Online games and internet access.
Main Post Office (rue Maurice Busset)
Tourist Office (☎ 04 73 98 65 00; www.clermont-fd.com; place de la Victoire; ⌚ 9am-7pm Mon-Fri, 10am-7pm Sat & Sun May-Sep, 9am-6pm Mon-Fri, 10am-1pm & 2-6pm Sat, 9.30am-12.30pm & 2-6pm Sun Oct-Apr) Opposite the cathedral on place de la Victoire. There's a multimedia exhibition on the Auvergne's churches downstairs.
Visio2 (11 av Carnot; per hr €2.50; ⌚ 10am-midnight Mon-Sat) Internet access.

Sights

OLD CITY

Perched at the top of the rue des Gras, the jet-black **Cathédrale Notre Dame** (⌚ 8am-noon & 2-6pm Mon-Sat, 9.30am-noon & 3-7.30pm Sun) looks like it's fallen from the pages of *The Lord of the Rings*. Carved from the inky volcanic rock

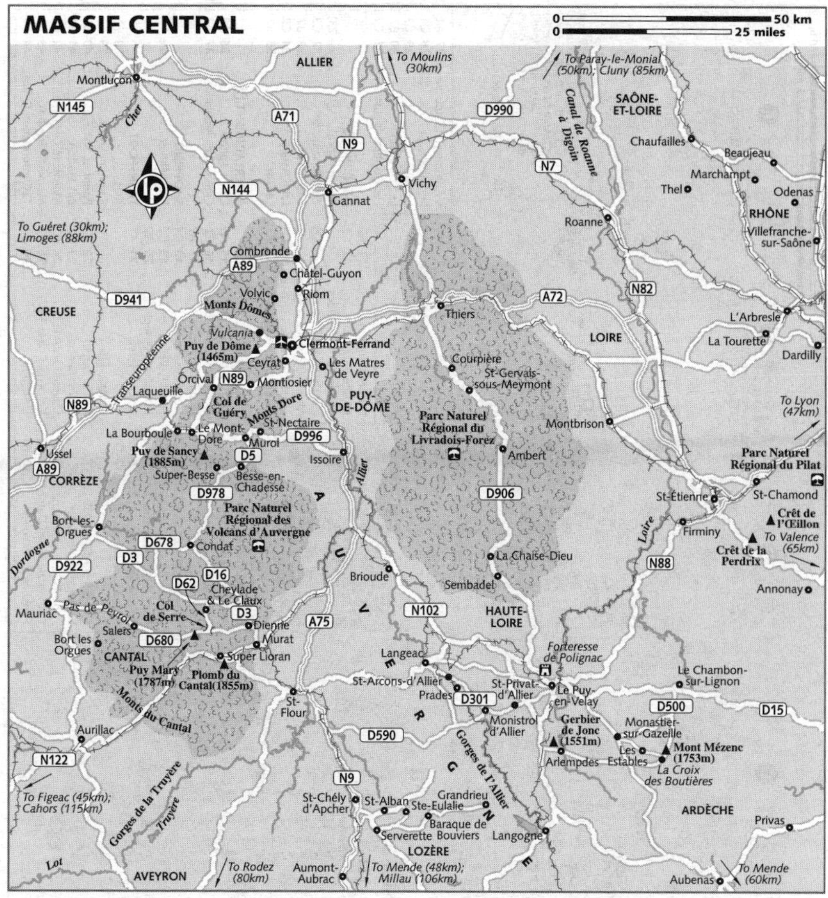

from the quarries of Volvic, it's one of the weirdest sights in the Auvergne, with its twin soaring towers and massive Gothic facade, partly designed by the architect Viollet-le-Duc. Constructed between the 13th and 19th centuries, the interior is a striking contrast of light and shade: murky chapels lurk along each side of the nave, lit up brilliantly by afternoon sunshine through the technicolour transept windows.

North of the cathedral is the early-16th-century **Fontaine d'Amboise**, with a panoramic view of the Puy de Dôme and nearby peaks. South is the café-filled place de la Victoire, and the city's **Michelin Boutique** (☎ 04 73 90 20 50; 2 place de la Victoire; ⏰ 2-7pm Mon, 10am-1pm & 2-7pm Tue-Sat), where you can pick up souvenirs ranging from roadmaps and restaurant guides to bouncy Bibendum key rings.

The twisting lanes of Clermont-Ferrand's **old city** circle outwards from the cathedral, dotted with mansions dating from the 17th and 18th centuries. The old street of rue Blaise Pascal is a jumble of antique-sellers, craft-shops and cafés. Nearby is the 12th-century **Basilique Notre Dame du Port**, a historic Romanesque chapel listed as a Unesco World Heritage Site. It's currently closed for refurbishment, but a neighbouring shop has been converted into an exhibition space, the **Basilique Renovation Exhibition**, where you can see how the work's coming along.

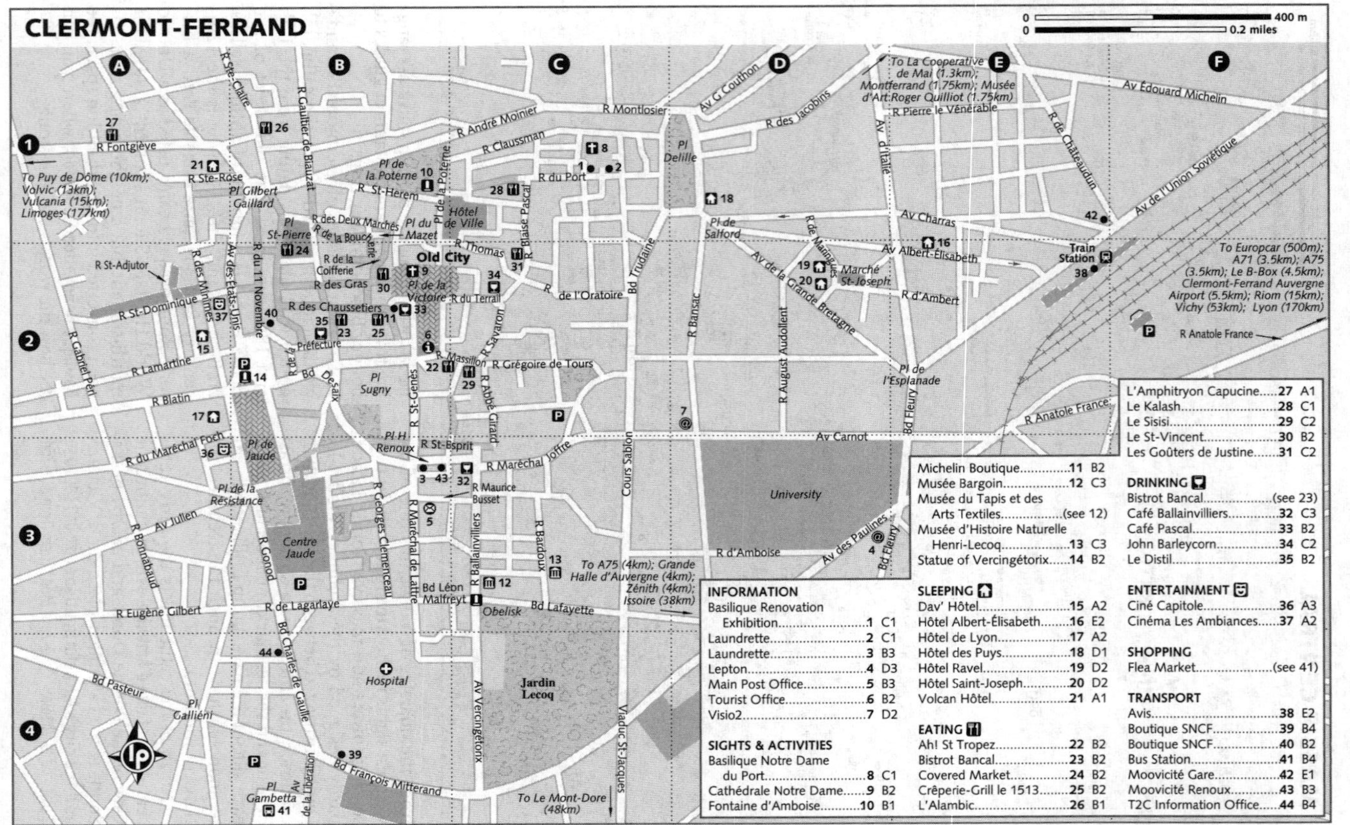
CLERMONT-FERRAND
0 400 m
0 0.2 miles
A
B
C
D
E
F
1
2
3
4
To Puy de Dôme (10km); Volvic (13km); Vulcania (15km); Limoges (177km)
To La Cooperative de Mai (1.3km); Montferrand (1.75km); Musée d'Art Roger Quilliot (1.75km)
To Europcar (500m); A71 (3.5km); A75 (3.5km); Le B-Box (4.5km); Clermont-Ferrand Auvergne Airport (5.5km); Riom (15km); Vichy (53km); Lyon (170km)
To A75 (4km); Grande Halle d'Auvergne (4km); Zénith (4km); Issoire (38km)
To Le Mont-Dore (48km)
Old City
Train Station
University
Hospital
Jardin Lecoq
Centre Jaude
Hôtel de Ville
Obelisk
Pl Delille
Pl de Salford
Pl de l'Esplanade
Pl de la Poterne
Pl Gilbert Gaillard
Pl St-Pierre
Pl du Mazet
Pl de la Victoire
Pl Sugny
Pl H Renoux
Pl de Jaude
Pl de la Résistance
Pl Galliéni
Pl Gambetta
Av Édouard Michelin
Av de l'Union Soviétique
Av d'Italie
Av Charras
Av Albert-Élisabeth
Av de la Grande Bretagne
Av Carnot
Av des Paulines
Av G Couthon
Av des États-Unis
Av Julien
Av Vercingétorix
Av de la Libération
Bd Fleury
Bd Trudaine
Bd Désaix
Bd Léon Malfreyt
Bd Lafayette
Bd Charles de Gaulle
Bd François Mitterand
Bd Pasteur
Cours Sablon
Viaduc St-Jacques
R de Châteaudun
R Pierre le Vénérable
R des Jacobins
R Montlosier
R André Moinier
R Claussman
R du Port
R Blaise Pascal
R Thomas
R de l'Oratoire
R du Terrail
R Savaron
R Massillon
R Grégoire de Tours
R Abbé Girard
R St-Genès
R St-Esprit
R Maréchal Joffre
R Maurice Busset
R Maréchal de Lattre
R Georges Clemenceau
R Ballainvilliers
R Bardoux
R Bansac
R August Audollent
R de Maringues
Marché St-Joseph
R d'Ambert
R Anatole France
R d'Amboise
R St-Herem
R des Deux Marchés
R de la Boucherie
R de la Coifferie
R des Gras
R des Chaussetiers
Préfecture
R du 11 Novembre
R des Minimes
R St-Dominique
R St-Adjutor
R Ste-Claire
R Ste-Rose
R Fontgiève
R Gaultier de Biauzat
R Gabriel Péri
R Lamartine
R Blatin
R du Maréchal Foch
R Bonnabaud
R Gonod
R de Lagarlaye
R Eugène Gilbert
INFORMATION
Basilique Renovation Exhibition 1 C1
Laundrette 2 C1
Laundrette 3 B3
Lepton 4 D3
Main Post Office 5 B3
Tourist Office 6 B2
Visio2 7 D2
SIGHTS & ACTIVITIES
Basilique Notre Dame du Port 8 C1
Cathédrale Notre Dame 9 B2
Fontaine d'Amboise 10 B1
Michelin Boutique 11 B2
Musée Bargoin 12 C3
Musée du Tapis et des Arts Textiles (see 12)
Musée d'Histoire Naturelle Henri-Lecoq 13 C3
Statue of Vercingétorix 14 B2
SLEEPING
Dav' Hôtel 15 A2
Hôtel Albert-Élisabeth 16 E2
Hôtel de Lyon 17 A2
Hôtel des Puys 18 D1
Hôtel Ravel 19 D2
Hôtel Saint-Joseph 20 D2
Volcan Hôtel 21 A1
EATING
Ah! St Tropez 22 B2
Bistrot Bancal 23 B2
Covered Market 24 B2
Crêperie-Grill le 1513 25 B2
L'Alambic 26 B1
L'Amphitryon Capucine 27 A1
Le Kalash 28 C1
Le Sisisi 29 C2
Le St-Vincent 30 B2
Les Goûters de Justine 31 C2
DRINKING
Bistrot Bancal (see 23)
Café Ballainvilliers 32 C3
Café Pascal 33 B2
John Barleycorn 34 C2
Le Distil 35 B2
ENTERTAINMENT
Ciné Capitole 36 A3
Cinéma Les Ambiances 37 A2
SHOPPING
Flea Market (see 41)
TRANSPORT
Avis 38 E2
Boutique SNCF 39 B4
Boutique SNCF 40 B2
Bus Station 41 B4
Moovicité Gare 42 E1
Moovicité Renoux 43 B3
T2C Information Office 44 B4

MUSEUMS & SIGHTS

Historic exhibits, from excavated Roman coins to neolithic wood carvings, are displayed at the **Musée Bargoin** (☎ 04 73 91 37 31; 45 rue Ballainvilliers; adult/under 18yr €4.30/free; 10am-noon & 1-5pm Tue-Sat, 2-7pm Sun), the city's main archeological museum. Upstairs, the **Musée du Tapis et des Arts Textiles** has a collection of Oriental and Middle Eastern carpets, including examples from Tibet, Iran, Syria and China.

Just down the street, the **Musée d'Histoire Naturelle Henri-Lecoq** (☎ 04 73 91 93 78; 15 rue Bardoux; adult/under 18yr €4.30/free; 10am-noon & 2-5pm or 6pm Mon-Sat, 2-6pm Sun) is named after the celebrated pharmacist and natural scientist who lived in Clermont-Ferrand in the 19th century. A passionate student and compulsive collector of the flora and fauna of the Auvergne, Lecoq amassed a huge collection of rocks, fossils, plants and stuffed animals – look out for a stunning gallery of Auvergnat butterflies and a collection of over 50 native orchids.

Place de Jaude, the city's monumental square, has recently been pedestrianised. Crisscrossed by clanking trams and pottering pedestrians, the square is overlooked by a **statue of Vercingétorix**, the Celtic chief who nearly thwarted Caesar's conquest of Gaul.

A couple of kilometres northeast is the suburb of **Montferrand**, which joined forces with nearby Clermont in 1630 under the orders of Louis XIII, laying the foundations for the modern-day city. Montferrand is dotted with Gothic and Renaissance houses, especially around rue de la Rodade and rue des Cordeliers, but today it feels rather rundown and unloved beside its bigger, buzzier neighbour.

The main attraction in Montferrand is the **Musée d'Art Roger Quilliot** (☎ 04 73 16 11 30; place Louis Deteix; adult/under 18yr €4.20/free; 10am-6pm Tue-Sun), an ambitious fine-arts museum in a converted Ursuline convent. Exhibits range from the late Middle Ages to the 20th century: look out for significant works by Delacroix, the Ryckaert family and François Boucher, as well as work by local artists Maurice and Simone Combe. Jump aboard Tram A from place de Jaude or Bus 31 from the train station.

If you're visiting several museums, there's a three-museum pass for €8 available from the tourist office.

Sleeping

Hôtel Saint-Joseph (☎ 04 73 92 69 71; 10 rue de Maringues; s €38-45, d €43-50) Bargain-basement hotel above a corner bar near Marché St-Joseph, and the best value for shoestringers in Clermont. Considering the knock-down prices, the rooms are decent: all have private bathroom or shower, satellite TV and sunny or stripy colour schemes, and there's even free wi-fi.

Hôtel Ravel (☎ 04 73 91 51 33; hotelravel63@wanadoo.fr; 8 rue de Maringues; s/d €40/48) With its mosaic facade and musty corridors, this budget family hotel has more character than most. It feels faded, with clunky plumbing and patchy wallpaper, but the rooms are well kept, clean, and have en-suite bathrooms, and the nicest overlook the busy St-Joseph morning market.

Hôtel Albert-Élisabeth (☎ 04 73 92 47 41; www.hotel-albertelisabeth.com; 37 av Albert-Élisabeth; r €49-57) Halfway between the centre and the station, this hotel is bland but makes a useful midrange base. Expect no surprises – functional rooms and chain-hotel fixtures are the watchword – but it's efficient and easily recognised at night thanks to its blinking neon sign. There's street parking opposite and wi-fi (both for a fee).

Dav' Hôtel (☎ 04 73 93 31 49; www.davhotel.fr; 10 rue des Minimes; d €50-58) The main draw at this alley hotel is the central location, steps from place de Jaude and a short uphill stroll to the Vieille Ville. The decor's sparse bordering on spartan, with plain soundproofed rooms equipped with the usual mod cons (hairdryer, satellite TV).

Volcan Hôtel (☎ 04 73 19 66 66; www.volcanhotel.fr; 6 rue Sainte-Rose; s €58-72, d €63-77) If it's midprice modernism you're after, then the Volcan is a good choice, plonked along a quiet street near the Vieille Ville. Charming it ain't: the style is flat-pack functional, with beige carpets, red-check bedspreads and cookie-cutter furniture, plus wi-fi and Canal+. Some have a mezzanine with old-city views.

Hôtel de Lyon (☎ 04 73 17 60 80; hotel.de.lyon@wanadoo.fr; 16 place de Jaude; r €69-95; P) You'll glimpse Vercingétorix from your window at this old-city crash pad, perched above a brasserie on place de Jaude. Despite its classic exterior, the rooms are motel-modern: expect check curtains, pine furniture and country prints, plus the best city views in town, with wi-fi and double-glazing to keep the late-night noise to a minimum.

Hôtel des Puys (☎ 04 73 91 92 06; www.hoteldespuys.fr; 16 place Delille; s €72-109, d €107-161;) The exterior has all the charm of a municipal car park, but inside you'll find plush three-star rooms, most with a balcony over trafficky place Delille. More cash buys extra space, separate sitting areas and big bathrooms, but the highlight is the panoramic breakfast room with views over Clermont's rooftops. Parking (€9) and breakfast (€13) are chronically overpriced.

Eating

BUDGET

The area north of place de Jaude and around rue St-Dominique is full of cheap eateries, including lots of ethnic restaurants and inexpensive French bistros.

Les Goûters de Justine (☎ 04 73 92 26 53; 11bis rue Blaise Pascal; cakes €2-5; ⌚ noon-7pm Tue-Fri, 2.30-7pm Sat) For afternoon tea and home-made cakes, seek out this snug little tearoom with its jumble of mismatched furniture and granny's-kitchen atmosphere.

Crêperie-Grill le 1513 (☎ 04 73 92 37 46; 3 rue des Chaussetiers; crepes €3-8; ⌚ daily) Ever-popular crêperie lodged inside the stone-vaulted cellars of a medieval mansion built in 1513 (hence the name). The usual selection of galettes and crêpes are on offer – for local flavours try the Galette Auvergnate, with local ham and St-Nectaire cheese, washed down with a bowl of cider.

Le Kalash (☎ 04 73 90 19 22; 10 rue du Port; mains €12-16; ⌚ lunch & dinner Mon-Sat) Things are hot and spicy at Le Kalash, one of several decent Indian eateries around town, serving authentic tandooris and tikkas in an Eastern-themed setting. Turn up on the right night and you might catch a Bollywood epic projected onto the back wall.

MIDRANGE

Ah! St Tropez (☎ 04 73 90 44 64; mains €15-17; 10 rue Massillon; ⌚ lunch & dinner Tue-Sat) A little corner of Provence in Clermont-Ferrand, decorated with painted murals and sunbaked colours, and stuffed with filling southern dishes such as grilled peppers, fish soup and crunchy figs with lavender. There aren't many tables, so booking's essential.

Bistrot Bancal (☎ 04 73 14 23 92; 15 rue des Chaussetiers; mains €15-17 ⌚ dinner Tue-Sun) Half buzzy wine bar, half gastro-brasserie, this fine restaurant is one of Clermont's secret places to try hand-picked local wines accompanied by authentic *saveurs de terroir* (country dishes), charcuterie and cheese.

Le St-Vincent (☎ 04 73 90 63 45; 10, rue de la Coifferie; menus €24/29/37; ⌚ Mon-Sat) Cosy, rustic and reassuringly old-fashioned, this small restaurant feels like an antique shop, with a hotchpotch of haphazard beams, country trinkets and solid wood furniture. The three *menus* are dominated by Auvergnat dishes, with more choices as you clamber up the price scale.

Le Sisisi (☎ 04 73 14 04 28; rue Massillon; mains €25-35; ⌚ Tue-Sat) Funky little café-bar-cum-bistro in an old-town location: the ambiance is scruffy-chic, but the food is top-notch, with a menu of fish, meats and salads, served either in the lively bar or the back-room bistro, dotted with contemporary artwork.

L'Amphitryon Capucine (☎ 04 73 31 38 39; 50 rue Fontgiève; menus €25-70; ⌚ Tue-Sat) Gastronomic with a capital G, this much-vaunted restaurant is one of the best addresses in Clermont, but you'll need to dig out your glad rags – jeans and trainers certainly won't cut the mustard in the swag-draped dining room. Dress appropriately and you'll be rewarded with the city's finest cooking spread over several courses (including a belt-busting eight-course *menu gourmand*).

L'Alambic (☎ 04 73 36 17 45; 6 rue Ste-Claire; menus €26/36; ⌚ lunch Tue & Thu-Sat, dinner Mon-Sat) 'The Still' has a formidable reputation for its traditional Auvergnat dishes, especially its charcuterie and gut-busting *aligot,* a local concoction of potato, garlic, cream and Cantal cheese.

SELF-CATERING

Looking like a modern-art experiment gone wrong, the Lego-brick facade of Clermont's **covered market** (⌚ 6am-7pm Mon-Sat) is on place Saint-Pierre.

Drinking

Café Ballainvilliers (☎ 04 73 91 57 88; 18 rue Ballainvilliers; ⌚ till 1am Tue-Sat) A lively bistro-bar that's popular for summertime alfresco drinking thanks to the outside terrace.

Bistrot Bancal (see left) One of the city's best-stocked wine bars, especially good for organic and locally grown Auverganat wines.

Café Pascal (4 place de la Victoire) A good all-round street café, whether you're after big-screen sports or a quick aperitif. There are patio tables outside with views of the floodlit cathedral at night.

Le Distil (☎ 04 73 37 64 15; 8 rue de la Préfecture; ⌚ 7.30pm-1.30am) Another good hang-out for oenophiles, this brick-and-wood wine bar has vintages by the glass, including both New World and French.

John Barleycorn (9 rue du Terrail; 🕑 2pm-2am Mon-Sat May-Aug, 5pm-2am Mon-Sat Sep-Apr) Traditional Celtic-themed boozer serving up beers, whiskies and wines in a laid-back, spit-and-sawdust atmosphere.

Entertainment

The pocket-sized *Le P'tit Bougnat* is the most useful guide to Clermont's after-dark scene (there's a digital version at www.cyber bougnat.net).

La Cooperative de Mai (☎ 04 73 14 48 08; www.lacoope.org; rue Serge Gainsbourg) One of Clermont's main gig and concert venues, a cavernous warehouse space that plays host to visiting bands (mostly French, but sometimes from further afield). Catch Tram A and get off at place du 1er Mai.

Le B-Box (☎ 04 73 28 59 74; www.bboxclub.com; av Ernest Cristal, La Pardieu; entry from €12; 🕑 11pm-5am Thu-Sat) Massive (in every sense), this city-sized warehouse contains one of the largest clubs in France, split into several levels: DJs spin everything from cheesy chart choons to house, jungle and hardcore.

Fans of *le septième art* can swing by the historic **Cinéma Les Ambiances** (☎ 08 75 56 09 46; www.cinema-lesambiances.fr; 7 rue Saint-Dominique; tickets €8.50), a wonderful art-house cinema dedicated to showing the latest flicks in *version originale* (nondubbed), with recent nondubbed releases also at the multiplex **Ciné Capitole** (☎ 08 92 68 73 33; 32 place de Jaude).

Stadium bands and large-scale touring shows are hosted at Clermont's main arena, **Zénith** (☎ 04 73 77 24 24; www.zenith-auvergne.com), for up to 8500 spectators. Part of the Grande Halle d'Auvergne complex, it's southeast of the city centre.

> **SHORT FILM CENTRAL**
>
> Clermont's answer to Cannes is the annual **Festival International du Court Métrage** (www.clermont-filmfest.com), one of the world's foremost festivals of short film. Held every February since 1979, the festival celebrates the best and brightest shorts from across the world, with three competitions for international and domestic shorts, as well as a touring 'Coup de Cœurs' program that visits cinemas across the Auvergne.

Getting There & Away

AIR

Clermont-Ferrand Auvergne airport (☎ 04 73 62 71 00; www.clermont-aeroport.com; airport code CFE) is 7km east of the city centre. It's a major hub for domestic and European flights, especially for Air France; destinations include Nice, Marseille, Strasbourg, Paris Orly and Paris Charles de Gaulle. An airport shuttle (€4) runs around eight times daily (two on Sunday) from the centre via the bus and train stations. Bus No 20 travels to/from the airport four times daily Monday to Friday.

BUS

The **bus station** (☎ 04 73 93 13 61; place Gambetta) has an efficient information office. Bus 73 travels to Riom (35 minutes) six to nine times Monday to Saturday, and bus 1 serves Thiers (1¼ hours, eight to 12 Monday to Saturday). For other destinations, trains are faster and more frequent. The bus station also hosts Clermont's weekly **flea market** (🕑 7am-1pm Sun).

CAR

Car-rental agencies:

Avis airport (☎ 04 73 91 18 08); town (☎ 04 73 91 72 94)
Europcar airport (☎ 04 73 91 18 07); town (☎ 04 73 92 70 26)
Hertz (☎ 04 73 62 71 93) Located at the airport.

TRAIN

Clermont is the region's main rail hub. You can buy tickets at the two **boutiques SNCF** (SNCF ticketing offices; ☎ 08 92 35 35 35; 43 rue du 11 Novembre, 80 bd François Mitterand) in the city centre.

Long-haul destinations include Paris' Gare de Lyon (€45.10 to €51, 3½ hours direct, six to 10 daily) and Lyon (€23.30 to €28.20, three hours via St-Étienne, more than 10 daily). The cross-Cévennes railway to Nîmes (€35.70, five hours, three daily), known as Le Cévenol, is one of the most scenic in France (and one of the oldest, built in 1870 at a cost of 520 million francs).

Short hauls run to/from Vichy (€8.80 to €12.40, half-hour, hourly), Le Mont-Dore (€11.70, 1¼ hours, four or five daily), Thiers (€7.70, 45 minutes, 10 daily) and Le Puy-en-Velay (€20.10, 2¼ hours, three or four direct daily).

Getting Around

Clermont's public-transport system is handled by **T2C** (☎ 04 73 28 00 00; www.t2c.fr; 24 bd Charles de Gaulle; 8.30am-6pm Mon-Fri, 8.30am-12.15pm & 2-5pm Sat). A single ticket costs €1.30 and remains valid for three onward connections within an hour on either tram or bus; a day ticket costs €4.20. Tram B is the quickest way into the city from the station, while tram A connects place de Jaude with Montferrand; both lines run between 5am and 11pm.

Moovicité (☎ 08 10 63 00 63; www.moovicite.com) rents bikes for a knock-down €2/3 per half/full day, plus a deposit of €150/225 for traditional/electric bikes. Rentals of up to one hour are free. There are two offices, **Moovicité Gare** (43 av de l'Union Soviétique; 7am-7pm Mon-Fri, 8am-7pm Sat) and **Moovicité Renoux** (20 place H Renoux; 7am-7pm Mon-Fri, 8am-7pm Sat). You can drop bikes off at either one.

NORTH OF CLERMONT-FERRAND

Riom

pop 19,300

During the Middle Ages, Riom was the capital of the Auvergne region. Mansions and *hôtels particuliers*, mostly built from dark volcanic stone, line the boulevards of the old quarter, and the town has a brace of museums and a landmark clock tower to explore.

The town's main thoroughfares are the east–west rue de l'Hôtel de Ville and rue St-Amable, and the north–south rue de l'Horloge and rue du Commerce. The **tourist office** (☎ 04 73 38 59 45; www.tourisme-riomlimagne.fr; 16 rue du Commerce; 9.30am-1pm & 2-6.30pm Mon-Sat, 10am-1pm Sun Jul & Aug, 9.30am-noon & 2-5.30pm Tue, Wed, Fri & Sat, 2-5.30pm Mon & Thu Sep-Jun) is on the west side of town, very near the pretty Romanesque church of **Église St-Amable** (rue St-Amable; 9am-5pm Oct-May, 9am-7pm Jun-Sep).

Riom's 15th-century **Tour de l'Horloge** (Clock Tower; rue de l'Horloge; admission €0.50; 10am-noon & 2-6pm Jul & Aug; 10am-noon & 2-5pm Tue-Sun Sep-Jun) has a wonderful view of both town and mountains from the upper stories.

To the east are the town's museums, **Musée Régional d'Auvergne** (☎ 04 73 38 17 31; 10bis rue Delille; admission €4.20; 10am-noon & 2.30-6pm Tue-Sun mid-May–Oct), which explores the customs and traditions of life in the Auvergne, and the **Musée Francisque Mandet** (☎ 04 73 38 18 53; 14 rue de l'Hôtel de Ville; admission €4.20; 10am-noon & 2.30-6pm Tue-Sun Jun-Sep, 10am-noon & 2-5.30pm Tue-Sun Oct-May), displaying classical finds and 15th- to 19th-century paintings.

South along rue du Commerce is the 15th-century **Église Notre Dame du Marthuret** (rue du Commerce; 9am-6pm), which hold's Riom's treasured relics: a typically severe Vierge Noire (Black Madonna) and the tender Vierge à l'Oiseau, depicting the Virgin and Child accompanied by a fluttering bird.

Riom is 15km north of Clermont on the N9; to get there by bus, see p587.

Vichy

pop 26,900

Pootling pensioners, pocket-sized dogs and curative springs sum up the well-to-do town of Vichy, 70km northeast of Clermont-Ferrand. Famous for its volcanic mineral waters since Napoléon III and his entourage sojourned here during the 19th century, and later infamous as the seat of Marshal Pétain's collaborationist regime during WWII, these days Vichy is a curious mix of spa resort, provincial shopping centre and old-age retirement home. Its belle-époque heyday has long since passed, but there's still an air of understated grandeur about its stately streets and landscaped parks; and if you've got a dicky elbow or a dodgy knee, you can join the queues of *curistes* who flock to Vichy to try its therapeutic waters for themselves.

ORIENTATION

The heart of Vichy is the Parc des Sources, 800m west of the train station. Rue Georges Clemenceau, the main shopping thoroughfare, crosses the city centre. The busy ringroads of bd du Président Kennedy and bd des États-Unis run along the Allier River south of the centre.

INFORMATION

Échap (☎ 04 70 32 28 57; 12 rue Source de l'Hôpital; €0.07 per min; noon-midnight Tue-Sat, 2pm-midnight Sun) Internet access.

Le Chantier (☎ 04 70 32 10 04; 23 av E Gilbert; per hr €2; 9.30am-11pm Tue-Fri, noon-1am Sat, 10am-3pm Sun) Internet access in a funky art space, gallery and bar.

Main Post Office (place Charles de Gaulle)

Tourist Office (☎ 04 70 98 71 94; www.vichytourisme.com; 19 rue du Parc; 9am-7pm Mon-Sat, 9.30am-12.30pm & 3-7pm Sun Jul & Aug, 9am-12.30pm & 1.30-7pm Mon-Sat, 9.30am-12.30pm & 3-7pm Sun Apr-Jun & Sep, 10am-noon & 2-6pm Mon-Sat & 3-6pm Sun Oct-Mar)

SIGHTS & ACTIVITIES

First stop in Vichy is the huge **Parc des Sources**, laid out by Napoléon III in 1812. Filled by chestnut and plane trees and encircled by a

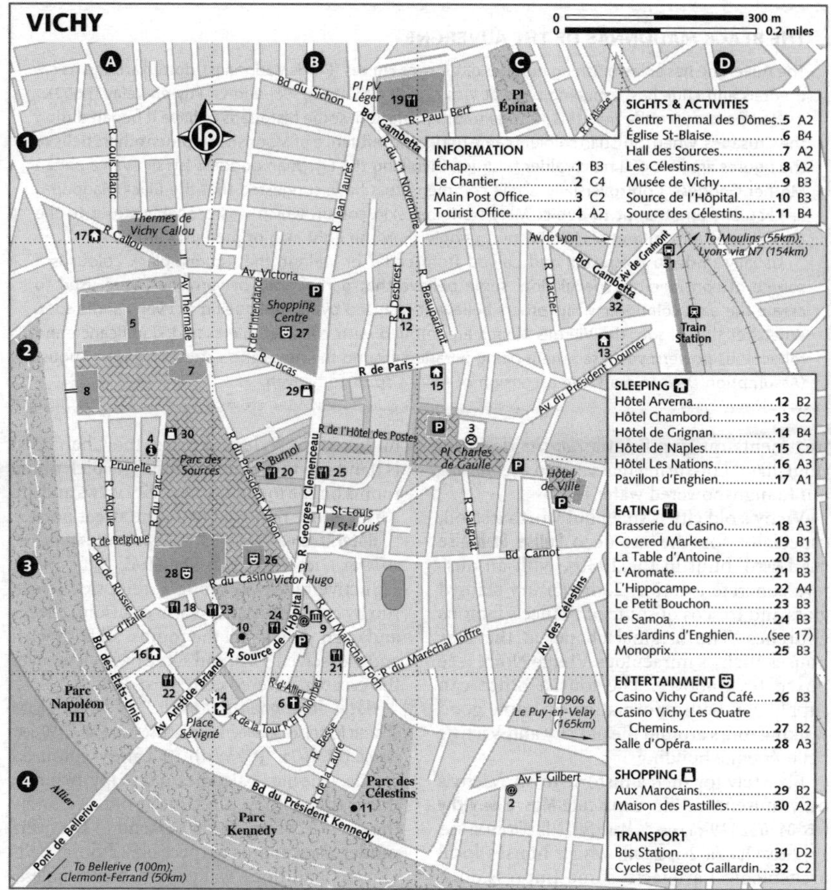

wrought-iron colonnade (which allows *curistes* to perambulate the park without getting wet), the park's main feature is the **Hall des Sources** (6am-7.30pm Mon-Sat, 7.45am-7.30pm Sun, later in summer), an elegant glass hall that houses three of the city's natural springs. In the centre is an enclosed area where you can sample Vichy's waters, from the mild and bubbly Célestins to the hot and salty Chômel, which emerges at a natural temperature of 43.5°C. You can buy a plastic cup (€0.20) or fill your bottle for free with Célestins water, but for the more adventurous concoctions you'll need a pass (and a prescription!) from the nearby Centre Thermal.

The **Source de l'Hôpital** is across the park, while the **Source des Célestins** (bd du Président Kennedy; 8am-8.30pm Apr-Sep, 8am-6pm Oct-Mar) is further south near the river. Over 60 million bottles of Célestins water are sold annually, but you can join the locals and fill up for nothing here from the brass taps, which are shut in winter to prevent frozen pipes.

North of the Hall des Sources is the **Centre Thermal des Dômes** (08 00 30 00 63; 132 bd des États-Unis; 8am-7.45pm Mon-Fri, 8am-7.15pm Sat, 8.30am-12.30pm Sun), with its Byzantine dome, Moorish arches and tiled towers. In Vichy's heyday, this complex housed the city's thermal baths, and the area was a lavish playground of upmarket boutiques, shops and cafés, but these days it's looking decidedly dowdy. The most luxurious of Vichy's three spas is **Les Célestins** (04 70 30 82 82; 111 bd des États-Unis), which offers pricey

THE BLACK MADONNAS OF THE AUVERGNE

The Auvergne has an astonishing number of **Vierges Noires** (Black Madonnas), dotted around its cathedrals and churches, including ones at Vichy (p588), Murat (p598) and Le Puy-en-Velay (p602).

No one knows quite how this strange tradition started: some historians believe it began during the Crusades, when Christian soldiers came under the influence of Moorish sculptors; others believe the figures are part of a much older tradition involving the Egyptian goddess Isis or even a pagan Mother Goddess. Controversially, some commentators have suggested that the Black Madonnas are actually an attempt to depict Mary's original skin colour, which was probably closer to the dark skin of African and Middle Eastern people than the light skin of modern Europeans.

Usually under a metre tall and carved from cedar or walnut, the figures' black colour is a source of considerable speculation: some believe that dark woods or varnishes were used to create the dark colouring, while others believe it's caused by natural ageing or even candle soot. Whatever the reason, the Vierges Noires are imbued with considerable sacred significance and miraculous powers: you'll see them being paraded around the Auvergne's streets on 15th August (Assumption Day) to mark the ascension of Mary's spirit to heaven.

treatments ranging from a *douche de Vichy* (four-hand hot-spring massage) to a *jet tonifiant* (a high-powered water jet).

Vichy's old city is small but worth a stroll, especially for the art-deco **Église St-Blaise** (rue d'Allier), built in the 1930s, with an austere concrete exterior, 20th-century stained glass and frescos of some of France's famous churches. The original chapel at the rear houses Vichy's miraculous Vierge Noire (see boxed text, above). The tourist office can supply you with information on some good walking tours around the old city and Vichy's belle-époque buildings.

Bizarrely for such a historic town, Vichy's only museum is the miniscule **Musée de Vichy** (☎ 04 70 32 12 97; 15 rue du Maréchal Foch; admission free; 🕑 2-6pm Tue-Fri, 2-5pm Sat), which houses local archeological artefacts, some Impressionist paintings and a set of letters and coins from the Pétain régime.

Vichy has some lovely parks, including the riverside **Parc Kennedy** and **Parc Napoléon III**. Look out for the Swiss-style 19th-century chalet houses along the parks' edge, which once lodged the city's visiting *curistes*.

SLEEPING

Hotel de Naples (☎ 04 70 97 91 33; www.hoteldenaples.fr; 22 rue de Paris; r €33-41; Ⓟ) Luxury it ain't, but the Naples is fab for budget travellers, with about the cheapest sleeps in Vichy. The clean, spartan rooms are split between the main building and a quiet rear annexe overlooking the hotel's garden and car park. Wi-fi's available.

Hôtel Chambord (☎ 04 70 30 16 30; le.chambord@wanadoo.fr; 82-84 rue de Paris; s €42-50, d €48-60) Solidly midrange in style and price, the Chambord is handy to town and station. The pick of the rooms on the top floors have city views and are a little more removed from the street noise.

Hôtel Arverna (☎ 04 70 31 31 19; www.hotels-vichy.com, in French; 12 rue Desbrest; s €45-50, d €50-65; ⊠ Ⓟ) A seductive hideaway along a quiet side street, run by expat Parisians. Warm crimsons, checks and corn yellows fill the rooms, all with wi-fi and flat-screen TVs, and some have views over the creeper-covered courtyard garden.

Hôtel de Grignan (☎ 04 70 32 08 11; www.hotelgrignan.fr; 7 place Sévigné; s/d/q high season €50/77/90, low season €46/61/75; Ⓟ) With its candy-coloured facade, pale blue balconies and stripy awnings, this is the prettiest place in the old city. Sadly the period charm doesn't extend to the over-modernised rooms (expect bland floral bedspreads and flock wallpaper). Nevertheless, the views over the old town's rooftops are sublime, and there's wi-fi and parking.

Pavillon d'Enghien (☎ 04 70 98 33 30; www.pavillondenghien.com; 32 rue Callou; r €48-78;) A converted mansion with bedrooms in soothing whites and creams, livened up with the odd splash of colour, funky lampshade or original fireplace. Ask for one overlooking the interior courtyard and cute pool.

Hôtel Les Nations (☎ 04 70 98 21 63; www.lesnations.com; 13 bd de Russie; s €49-101, d €55-101 depending on season) Smart hotel with touches of art-deco style, overlooking tree-filled place Général Leclerc. Green-wicker lobby chairs and wrought-iron gates set the swish tone, and the rooms don't disappoint: the more expensive 'Confort Plus' rooms are worth the cash, with their own sitting areas and power showers.

EATING

Le Samoa (☎ 04 70 59 94 46; 13 rue Source de l'Hôpital; mains €3-8) For a quick *croque* or an ice-cream sundae, the Samoa's the place, shaded by trees with a terrace by the bandstand and the Parc des Sources.

Le Petit Bouchon (☎ 04 70 31 21 04; 1 rue de Banville; mains €11-20; Tue-Sat) Forget haute cuisine – this ramshackle bistro dishes out totally authentic lyonnaise staples cooked in the time-honoured fashion. Checked tablecloths and wooden tables fill the dining room, and the menu's crammed with gems like *pavé de boeuf* (thick-cut beef steak) and *grenouilles de poulet*; afterwards you can even do as other diners have done and write your review on the wall. The €12 lunch menu is the best bang for your buck in Vichy.

Brasserie du Casino (☎ 04 70 98 23 06; 4 rue du Casino; mains €16-22; Thu-Mon Mar–mid-Oct & mid-Nov–mid-Feb) Prewar style haunts this ultra-Gallic brasserie, all shiny brass, faded wood and squeaky leather, with a wall of photos featuring the actors and *chanteurs* who've stopped by from the opera house. The food's substantial (duck *confit*, rabbit stew) and the feel unmistakably French.

Les Jardins d'Enghien (☎ 04 70 98 33 30; www.pavillondenghien.com; 32 rue Callou; menus €19-32; lunch daily, dinner Tue-Sat) The poolside garden at Pavillon d'Enghien (see opposite) makes a sweet spot for supper alfresco, with market-fresh ingredients and plenty of Auvergnat recipes.

La Table d'Antoine (☎ 04 70 98 99 11; 8 rue Burnol; menus €21-59.90; lunch Tue-Sun, dinner Tue-Sat) This high-class temple to French fine dining is a fave of the gourmet guidebooks. Abstract portraits and high-backed chairs create a boutique feel, and the food is seriously fancy, from coconut-poached chicken to langoustines and smoked fish.

L'Aromate (☎ 04 70 32 13 22; 9 rue Besse; menus €19.50-36, mains €18-20; lunch Thu-Tue, dinner Mon & Thu-Sat) The atmosphere's starchier than a nun's wimple, but you can't beat the Aromate for upmarket dining. Classical music tinkles and the cavernous dining room is filled with gilt mirrors and stone columns, creating a fittingly ritzy setting for the rich, classic food.

L'Hippocampe (☎ 04 70 97 68 37; 3 bd de Russie; menus €16-50; Tue-Sun) Appropriately enough for a restaurant called the Sea Horse, this place specialises in seafood – scallops, sole and oak-smoked sardines, not to mention a truly monumental *assiette de fruits de mer* (seafood platter).

Self-Catering

The **covered market** is on place PV Léger. There's also a **Monoprix** (rue Georges Clemenceau; 8.30am-7pm Mon-Sat, 9.30am-12.30pm & 2.30-7pm Sun).

ENTERTAINMENT

Vichy's turn-of-the-century **Salle d'Opéra** (☎ 04 70 30 50 50; rue du Casino), still hosts regular productions. The town's casino was one of the first to be opened in France, and Vichy is still a popular gambling getaway: one-armed-bandit fans should check out the **Casino Vichy Grand Café** (7 rue du Casino; 10am-3am) or **Casino Vichy Les Quatre Chemins** (☎ 04 70 97 93 37; 10am-4am).

Vichy Mensuel, a free monthly what's-on guide, can be picked up all over town.

SHOPPING

Vichy's had a sweet tooth since the 1820s, when the first *pastilles de Vichy* were created using mineral water mixed with sugar and flavoured with mint, aniseed or lemon. Octagonal in shape and stamped with the Vichy logo, you can pick some up at the **Maison des Pastilles** (10am-noon & 3-7pm Tue-Sat, 3-7pm Sun Apr-Oct) in the Parc des Sources.

Vichy's also well-known for its *confiseries* and *chocolateries*, including **Aux Marocains** (☎ 04 70 98 30 33; 33 rue Georges Clemenceau), chock-a-block with handmade sweets, petits fours and caramels.

GETTING THERE & AROUND

Train destinations include Paris' Gare de Lyon (€40.70 to €47.10, three hours, six to eight daily), as well as Clermont-Ferrand (€8.80 to €12.40, half-hour, hourly) and Riom (€7, 25 minutes, frequent).

Cycles Peugeot Gaillardin (☎ 04 70 31 52 86; 48 bd Gambetta; Mon morning & Tue-Sat) hire bikes (half/full day €5/8) plus €80 deposit.

PARC NATUREL RÉGIONAL DES VOLCANS D'AUVERGNE

A vast tract of cloud-shrouded peaks, snowy uplands and jade-green valleys, the huge **Parc Naturel Régional des Volcans d'Auvergne** (☎ 04 73 65 64 00; www.parc-volcans-auvergne.com) occupies most of the western Massif Central, stretching for around 3950 sq km and 120km from base to

FIERY FURNACES

With its peaceful pastures and verdant hills, it's hard to believe that the Massif Central was once one of the most active volcanic areas in Western Europe. The area consists of three geological bands. The **Chaîne des Puys** and **Monts Dômes**, a chain of extinct volcanoes and cinder cones stretching in a 40km north–south line across the northern Massif Central, thrust up around 100,000 years ago. The central **Monts Dores** are much older, created between 100,000 and three million years ago, while the real grandaddies are the **Monts du Cantal**, formed by a nine-million-year-old volcano which collapsed inwards, leaving only its caldera (fragmented rim).

Though the volcanoes have been silent for several thousand years (the last serious eruption occurred around 5000 BC), reminders of the region's turbulent volcanic past are dotted across the region. Deep beneath the earth, fiery forces are still at work: volcanic activity is responsible for the mineral waters of **Volvic**, north of Clermont, and the geothermal springs of **Vichy** (p588), **Le Mont-Dore** (opposite) and the spa town of **Châtel-Guyon** (www.ot-chatel-guyon.com). It also explains the distinctive black rock often used as a building material across the region, notably at Clermont-Ferrand's cathedral (p582) and the town houses of Riom (p588).

The multimedia theme park of Vulcania (below) is a fantastic place to get acquainted with the region's volcanic history.

tip. Its northerly area extends from the chain of extinct volcanoes known as the Chaîne des Puys and Monts Dômes, centring on the high point of Puy de Dôme (below). Further south are the Monts Dore and the snowy Puy de Sancy, a popular ski station and the Massif Central's highest point. The park's southern edge is marked by the wild, rugged Monts du Cantal, formed by an ancient supervolcano worn down over the millennia, and dominated by the lofty summit of the Plomb du Cantal (1855m).

Unsurprisingly, this is fantastic terrain for outdoor enthusiasts, including skiers, hikers and mountain bikers, as well as hang-gliders and paragliders who can often be seen drifting around the region's peaks.

PUY DE DÔME & AROUND

The ice-flecked summit of Puy de Dôme (1465m) looms 15km to the west of Clermont-Ferrand. Crested by snow between September and May, the mountain was formed by a volcanic eruption some 10,000 years ago, and was later used as a Celtic shrine and Roman temple, but these days it's more popular with *parapenteurs* (paragliders) and hikers. You can still visit the remains of the Roman temple, dedicated to Mercury, and the views from the summit stretch to the Alps in clear weather – the only drawback is the blinking TV mast and the 2000-odd other visitors you'll share the views with on a fine summer's day.

You can reach the summit either by the 'mule track' – a steep hour's climb from the Col de Ceyssat, 4km off the D941A – or by the 4km **toll road** (cars/motorbikes €6/4; 8am-dusk Mar-Nov). The road is closed to cars from 10am to 6pm in July and August and from 12.30pm to 6pm weekends in May, June and September, replaced by regular shuttle buses (adult costs €4). There are also daily **shuttles** (adult/child €5/2.50; July & Aug) from the station and place de Jaude in Clermont-Ferrand in summer; ask at the tourist office for times.

Vulcania

Surrounded by the plugs and domes of the Chaîne des Puys, 15km to the west of Clermont on the D941B, the volcanic theme park of **Vulcania** (08 20 82 78 28; www.vulcania.com; adult/child €21/13.50, 1 child free with 2 adults; 9.30am-7pm Jul & Aug, 10am-6pm mid-Mar–mid-Nov) brings the Auvergne's long-extinct volcanoes back to life in spectacular style.

Opened in 1992, the museum was dreamt up by French geologists Katia and Maurice Krafft, who were tragically killed in a volcanic eruption on Mt Unzen in Japan a year before the museum's opening. Controversially built inside the protected Parc des Volcans, Vulcania is designed to resemble a giant cinder cone: entry is via a glittering gold volcanic dome and a simulated crater, complete with billowing steam and booming eruptions. Spread out over three levels, the park is a combination of educational museum and thrills-and-spills theme park: alongside state-of-the-art multimedia displays exploring the role of volcanoes in earth's history, attractions include the '4D' film *Awakening of the Auvergne Giants,* which depicts volcanic eruptions complete with air blasts and water spray; the 20m-high 'Grand Geyser'; a section about the Mount St Helens eruption in 1982, complete with rock samples and vulcanised artefacts; and a highly dubious new '4D' Dragon Ride – not very scientific, but good fun all the same.

ORCIVAL

pop 250 / elevation 860m

Halfway between Puy de Dôme and Le Mont-Dore is Orcival, a huddle of slate rooftops and tumbledown barns gathered around the banks of the Sioulet River. The birthplace of ex–French president Giscard d'Estaing, it's a traditional typically Auvergnat village, centred around the beautiful **Basilique Notre-Dame**. The church is renowned for its sober Romanesque architecture and elegant crypt, as well as the 12th-century **Virgin of Orcival**, which (as always in the Auvergne) takes its annual walkabout on Assumption Day. Look out for the rare decorative ironwork depicting apocalyptic scenes on the main door.

Orcival's tiny **tourist office** (☎ 04 73 65 89 77; www.terresdomes-sancy.com; ⌚ 10am-noon & 2-6pm Tue-Sat) is opposite the church, and can supply you with suggestions for local hikes including trips to nearby Lac de Servières and Lac de Guéry.

North of the village is the15th-century **Château de Cordès** (☎ 04 73 65 81 34; adult/student/child €4/3/2.30; ⌚ 10am-noon & 2-6pm Easter-Oct), with rich 18th-century furnishings and formal grounds laid out by Le Nôtre, designer of the gardens of Versailles.

Sleeping & Eating

Camping de la Haute Sioule (☎ 04 73 65 83 32; www.camping-auvergne.info; St-Bonnet-près-Orcival; 2-person sites €12; ⌚ Easter-Oct) Spacious hillside campsite with a choice of fixed chalets and tent sites in a shady park with views of the Chaîne des Puys. It's about 5km northwest of Orcival on the D27.

Hôtel Notre Dame (☎ 04 73 65 82 02; d €36-45; ⌚ Feb-Dec) This simple hotel is right next door to the Basilique, so you can expect to be woken up by church bells on a Sunday. The seven refurbished rooms are snug, and No 26 even has its own miniature terrace. Hearty portions of *chou farci* (pork-stuffed cabbage) and *aligot* (see p600) are served up at the rustic restaurant.

Hôtel du Mont-Dore (☎ 04 73 65 82 06; fax 04 73 65 80 61; d from €40) More homely rooms (all with private bathrooms and simple furnishings) inside a converted town house, complete with its own turret.

COL DE GUÉRY

South of Orcival, the snaking D27 climbs up to the lofty pass of **Col de Guéry**, which offers fantastic mountain views on every side.

There's a car park from where you can admire the scenery near the **Maison des Fleurs d'Auvergne** (☎ 04 73 65 20 09; http://maisondesfleurs.free.fr; ⌚ 10am-7pm mid-Jun–mid-Sep, 10am-7pm Sat & Sun May–mid-Jun), which presents colourful displays of the Auvergne's flowers and other plants in summer. In winter, as soon as the first snow falls, the surrounding area is a centre for cross-country skiing, organised by the **Foyer Ski de Fond Guéry-Orcival** (☎ 04 73 65 20 09; www.leguery.fr).

Beyond the pass is the chilly **Lac de Guéry**, the highest lake in the Massif Central and a haven for trout and perch fishing (even in winter – this is the only lake in France that permits ice-fishing!)

The **Auberge du Lac de Guéry** (☎ 04 73 65 02 76; www.auberge-lac-guery.fr; d €57; ⌚ mid-Jan–mid-Oct) has an unbeatable position right on the lake shore and a fine country restaurant that serves up fresh fish straight from the lake.

LE MONT-DORE

pop 1700 / elevation 1050m

Winter skiers, summer walkers and spa bathers all make a beeline for Le Mont-Dore, nestled in a narrow wooded valley beneath the Puy de Sancy, 44km southwest of Clermont-Ferrand. The Massif Central's main winter-sports base is a good deal quieter than the adrenalin-junky resorts of the Alps to the east, which makes Le Mont-Dore a haven for hikers and skiers who prefer to explore the mountains in (relative) peace and quiet.

Information

Laundrette (place de la République; ⌚ 9am-7pm)
Post Office (place Charles de Gaulle)
s@ncyber (☎ 04 73 65 28 84; sancyber@orange.fr; allée Georges Lagaye; per hr €4.50; ⌚ 2-11pm Fri & Sat, 2-7pm Sun) Le Mont-Dore's cybercafé opens extra days during holidays and the ski season.
Tourist Office (☎ 04 73 65 20 21; www.sancy.com; av de la Libération; ⌚ 9am-12.30pm & 1.30-6pm Mon-Sat, 9am-12.30pm & 1.30-5pm Sun) There's a daily weather forecast and ski bulletin posted outside.

Sights & Activities

Long before anyone thought of hurtling down the hillsides strapped to a pair of wooden planks, Le Mont-Dore was visited for its hot springs, which bubble out at a temperature between 37°C and 40°C. The first bathers were (of course) the cleanliness-obsessed Romans, and you can still see traces of their original baths at the **Thermes du Mont-Dore** (☎ 04 73 65 05 10; 1 place du Panthéon; 9am-noon & 2-5.30pm Mon-Fri, 9am-noon Sat), where the pricey treatments range from hot-stone therapy to reiki massage. In low season, you can visit the 19th-century neo-Byzantine building on a guided tour (adult/child €3.20/2.20; phone for times).

Four kilometres to the south of Le Mont-Dore is **Puy de Sancy** (1886m), the highest peak in central France. The mountain's snowcapped summit can be reached by the **Téléphérique du Sancy** (adult single/return €5.60/7.30; 9am-7pm Jul & Aug, 9am-12.10pm & 1.30-5pm mid-Apr–Jun & Sep, 9am-12.15pm & 1.30-5pm weekends Oct & Easter holidays), originally built in 1936, followed by a short walk along the maintained trail and staircase to the top. With fabulous views of the northern *puys* (volcanic hills) and the Monts du Cantal, it's a popular tourist attraction, and can be uncomfortably crowded in summer. Set out early or late to dodge the worst crowds.

Built in 1898, France's oldest funicular railway (now a historic monument), the **Funiculaire du Capucin** (av René Cassin; single/return €3.30/4.20; 9.30am-6.40pm Jul–mid-Aug, 10am-12.10pm & 2-5.40pm Wed-Sun mid-May–Jun & mid-Aug–Sep), crawls at 1m per second up to the plateau of Les Capucins, 1270m above town. Various trails lead off the plateau, including the GR30, which wends southward towards the Puy de Sancy, continuing to the Pic du Capucin (1450m; about 45 minutes one way) or dropping steeply back to town.

If the weather's bad, escape to Le Mont-Dore's **ice-skating rink** (☎ 04 73 65 06 55; allée Georges Lagaye; Dec-Aug) for a spot of skating (adult/child costs €6.35/5.05) or bowling (after 8pm €5.75, before 8pm €4.70).

SKIING

There are two ski fields near Le Mont-Dore: **Puy de Sancy** and **Super-Besse**, on the mountain's southeastern slopes, encompassing 85km of downhill runs, plus a further 40km of cross-country trails. A joint lift pass costs €24/63 for one/three days (€16.80/44 for children under 12, or €19.40/51 for children 12 to 18 years

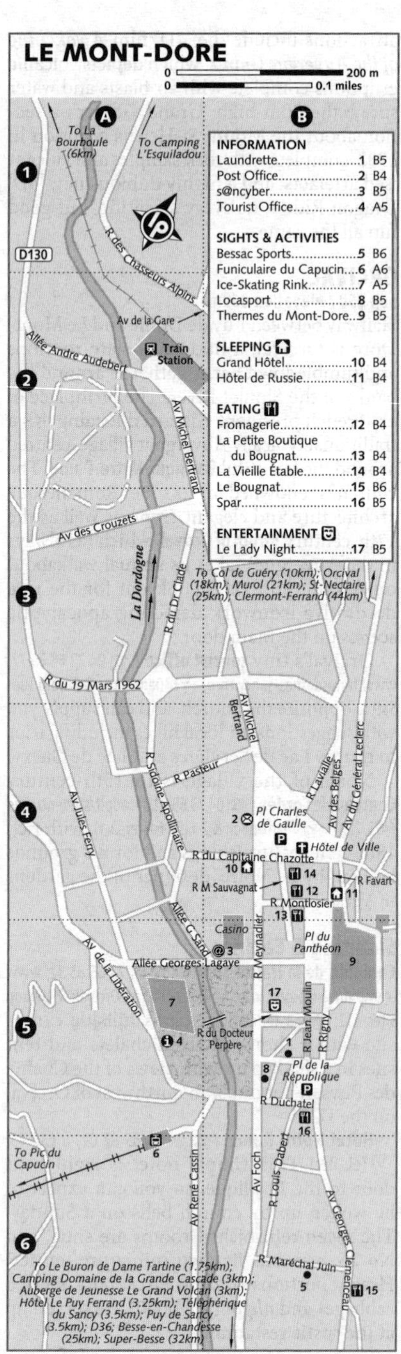

TRAIL CENTRAL

The Massif Central is prime walking country, with a network of well-signed trails and as many as 13 GR tracks (including the north–south **GR4**) criss-crossing the region, supplemented by hundreds of smaller footpaths. Key areas include the Parc des Volcans d'Auvergne and the Monts du Cantal around Murat (p598), roughly circled by the **GR400**, and the mountainous area around Le Mont-Dore (p593), Puy de Sancy, and the Col de Guéry.

Routes range from day hikes to multiweek epics: hard-core hikers tackle the 290km **Traverse of the High Auvergne** through the Chaîne des Puys, via Volvic and the GR4; the **Robert Louis Stevenson Trail** from Monastier-sur-Gazeille via the GR70, tracing the author's famous routes through the Cévennes; and the **Via Podensis** (p602) pilgrimage route from Le Puy-en-Velay.

Good walking guidebooks include Lonely Planet's own *Walking in France*, and the French-language Chamina guidebooks (www.chamina.com), *Week-end dans le Massif Central* and *Week-end en Auvergne*.

There are also some excellent online resources: www.rando-massifcentral.com has a database of more than 400 Massif Central walks (described in French).

old). There are plenty of places to hire kit: try **Bessac Sports** (☎ 04 73 65 02 25; 3 rue Maréchal Juin) or **Locasport** (☎ 04 73 65 29 13; 67 rue Meynadier), which both also hire out mountain bikes and hiking equipment in summer.

WALKING

There are lots of walks around Le Mont-Dore, all superbly signposted and clearly marked on good trail maps such as Chamina's 1:30,000-scale map *Massif du Sancy* (€5.35) or the more extensive Massif du Sancy guidebook (€6.70), which outlines 30 hikes in the area.

CYCLING

You can't avoid the ups and downs (even though the Funiculaire du Capucin does allow bikes on board) but this is still great cycling terrain. The tourist office has a free mountain bike–trail map, *Circuit VTT: Le Mont-Dore Sancy*.

Sleeping

CAMPING

Camping Domaine de la Grande Cascade (☎ 04 73 65 06 23; colon.daniel@orange.fr; rte de Besse; sites for 2 people €10; 🕒 Jun–early Sep) At a kilometre up, this campsite is always on the chilly side, but it's a grand spot to pitch a tent, peacefully sited near a 30m waterfall with wondrous views of the surrounding mountains. It's 3km from town on the D36.

Camping L'Esquiladou (☎ 04 73 65 23 74; camping .esquiladou@wanadoo.fr; rte des Cascades; sites for 2 people from €9; 🕒 May–mid-Oct) This woody municipal site is less dramatic, but it's handy to town and the train station, with Le Mont-Dore about 1.5km away along the D996.

HOSTELS & HOTELS

Auberge de Jeunesse Le Grand Volcan (☎ 04 73 65 03 53; le-mont-dore@fuaj.org; rte du Sancy; B&B €15.70; 🕒 Dec–mid-Nov; 💻) Always jammed with skiers and hikers, this HI-linked hostel hunkers in the shadow of Puy de Sancy, 3.5km south of town. Two- to six-bed rooms all have their own bathrooms, and fun facilities include ping pong, table football and an in-house bar.

Grand Hôtel (☎ 04 73 65 02 64; www.hotel-mont-dore .com; 2 rue Meynadier; s €42-49, d €52-79, tr €62-69; 🕒 mid-Dec–mid-Mar & mid-Apr–mid-Nov; P) Come sunshine or snow, this slate-roofed pile hotel is Le Mont-Dore's funkiest sleep. Built in 1850, the hotel has been refurbished with imagination and lashings of style: deep-red leather sofas, Chagall-style wall murals and designer lighting in the lobby, plus boutiquey bedrooms with thick duvets, patchwork throws and deep tubs, including a few with balconies. Handmade jams, freshly squeezed juice and minipatisseries for brekkie complete the plush package.

Hôtel de Russie (☎ 04 73 65 05 97; www.lerussie.com; 3 rue Favart; d €49.90-69.90, q €69.90-135; P) Carefully modernised with dashes of designer style, this town hotel is a treat, from the scrubbed-up parquet floor and colour-washed walls to reclaimed wood and lobby lanterns. The rooms are lovely, finished in cappuccino browns and ice whites, with luxury touches including rattan furniture, wi-fi and flat-screen TVs: the duplex rooms are brilliant for families.

THIERRY DUPONT: PARAGLIDER

The Massif Central is a paradise for people who love nature and the great outdoors. I've always been into adrenalin sports – I started off skateboarding and BMXing when I was younger, and graduated onto mountain biking and rock climbing later on. But I always wanted to get higher, and I got into paragliding when I was about 17.

I try to get up to the mountains to fly at least twice a month in summer, but I can't always manage that because of work. It's the most amazing feeling, stepping out into the air and catching the currents on the mountain – it's the closest I'll ever come to real flying, unless I manage to grow my own wings! It gives you a whole new way of looking at the world, seeing the land beneath you and the sky above – it makes you feel tiny and massive all at the same time.

Hôtel Le Puy Ferrand (☎ 04 73 65 18 99; www.hotel-puy-ferrand.com; d €62-72, studio flats €72-82; 🕒 late Dec-Oct;) A traditional chalet-style ski hotel, a quick stomp from the Puy de Sancy cable car. Wood-clad walls create the alpine atmosphere, and for skiers travelling *en famille* there are self-contained flats with kitchens, as well as a sauna, ski-drying room and a homely Savoyard restaurant.

Le Buron de Dame Tartine (☎ 04 73 65 28 40; www.auberge-dame-tartine.com; rte du Sancy; d €65-80, menus €18-32) This renovated *buron* (shepherd's hut) serves mountain recipes, including *truffade* (see p600) and *tartiflette* (a potato, cheese and meat gratin), in a suitably countrified setting. Stout stone, rough brick and hefty rafters fill the dining room, and the same rustic feel runs into the four rooms, with stripped pine furniture, polished floors and to-die-for mountain views.

Eating

Lots of Le Mont-Dore's hotels offer half board, often compulsory during ski season.

La Vieille Étable (☎ 04 73 65 20 49; rue Maurice Sauvagnat; mains €13-18) Rich mountain food and Auvergnat recipes rule the roost at this country crêperie, perennially popular for its fondues and *aligot* (see p600), as well as its house-special galettes – try the Montdorienne (with Auvergnat ham and *bleu d'Auvergne* cheese).

Le Bougnat (☎ 04 73 65 28 19; av Georges Clemenceau; mains €13.50-19) Hearty mountain dishes are the order of the day at this Savoyard-style restaurant, with stews and fondues served up at solid wooden tables.

SELF-CATERING

La Petite Boutique du Bougnat (1 rue Montlosier) sells a smorgasbord of local goodies, including sausages, hams and Auvergnat wine, with cheeses available at the **fromagerie** (rue Montlosier; 🕒 9.30am-12.30pm & 3-7pm Mon-Sat) across the street. There's also a **Spar** (rue Duchatel; 🕒 7.30am-12.30pm & 3-7.15pm Mon-Sat).

Drinking & Entertainment

Le Lady Night (☎ 04 73 65 06 43; rue du Docteur Perpère; 🕒 11pm-5am Fri-Sun, 10pm-5am daily in high season) This dubiously named nightclub is the town's main *aprés-ski* joint, but it's supercheesy – expect chunky chart tunes and cheap booze aplenty.

Getting There & Around

From the sleepy train station, you can reach Clermont-Ferrand (€11.70, 1¼ hours, around six daily including some that change at Laqueuille) with connections to Paris' Gare de Lyon (€54.80, 5½ hours).

In winter, a free skiers' *navette* (shuttle bus) plies regularly between Le Mont-Dore and the Sancy cable car.

AROUND LE MONT-DORE

La Bourboule

Seven kilometres downriver from Le Mont-Dore, **La Bourboule** is another well-heeled spa resort known for its hot-water **thermes** (☎ 04 73 81 21 00; www.grandsthermes-bourboule.com), rinky-dink casino and faded belle-époque buildings. Sometimes known as *'la station oxygène'*, it's a lovely place to stroll the boulevards and drink in the clear mountain air. From the landscaped **Parc Fenestre**, filled with giant sequoias, pine trees and open-air games, you can catch a *téléferique* up the **Plateau de Charlannes** (1300m) to lots of summer hiking trails.

The **tourist office** (☎ 04 73 65 57 71; www.sancy.com; place de la République; 🕒 9am-7pm Mon-Sat Jul & Aug, 9am-noon & 1.30-6pm Mon-Sat Sep-Jun) is in the Hôtel de Ville.

If you're staying, the **Hôtel Le Parc des Fées** (☎ 04 73 81 01 77; www.parcdesfees.com; 107 quai

Maréchal-Fayolle; s €49-56, d €61-67; ⊠ P) is a superior choice, mixing metro furnishings with belle-époque architecture: leather armchairs and potted plants in the lobby, a dedicated playroom for the kids, and cool shades in the rooms (insist on one with Puy de Sancy views). Wheelchair accessible.

Le Pavillon (☎ 04 73 65 50 18; www.hotellepavillon.fr; 209 av de l'Angleterre; d €47-62; P) Art-deco architecture meets boutique tweaks at this smooth hotel, offering recently redone rooms tweaked with caramel colours, soft lighting and plush throws, as well as a zingy **restaurant** (dinner Fri, Sat & Mon, lunch Sat & Mon) and a book-filled lounge where you can curl up with coffee and magazines.

The train to Le Mont-Dore (€1.50, 10 daily) takes just eight minutes, with connections onto Clermont-Ferrand.

Murol & Lac Chambon

About 10km east of Le Mont-Dore, the 12th-century **Château de Murol** (☎ 04 73 88 67 11; adult/4-15yr €7.50/6; Sun-Tue, Thu & Fri Jun-Aug, Mon, Tue, Thu & Fri May, Tue & Thu Mar, Apr, Sep & Oct) squats on a knoll above the surrounding village. Once owned by both the Murol and d'Estaing families, it's worth visiting for the intriguing keep and chapels, as well as the medieval guided tours, when costumed guides, scullery maids and jesters recreate daily life in the castle, and knights knock lumps out of each other beneath the keep. You'll need to book your places: there are usually five daily tours in summer, dropping to two or three in the low season.

About 1.5km west of Murol is the popular water-sports playground of **Lac Chambon**, where you can rent out canoes and windsurf boards from several operators along the lakeshore.

Besse-en-Chandesse & Around

Lava-brick cottages and cobbled lanes make up the mountain village of **Besse-en-Chandesse**, 25km southeast of Le Mont-Dore, where life still ticks along at a laid-back country pace. Apart from its basalt architecture, best seen along the rue de la Boucherie, Besse is known for its *fromage* – a hefty proportion of the region's St-Nectaire cheese is produced on the surrounding mountain slopes. The town is also home to a small **ski museum** (☎ 04 73 79 57 30; admission €2.50; 9am-noon & 2-7pm school holidays), where you can browse vintage skis and Old World alpine kit.

The most interesting time to visit is during the **Transhumance de la Vierge Noire**, which marks the move of the local cow herds to and from the rich upland pastures on 21 July and the first Sunday after 21 September. To mark the occasion, the local Black Madonna is paraded from the Église St-André in Besse to La Vassivière chapel, near **Lac Pavin**, about 4km west of Besse, accompanied by street fairs and fireworks.

The popular ski resort of **Super-Besse** is about 7km west of the village, accessible by the D978 or via the GR30 trail in summer, with an optional detour to the summit of **Puy de Montchal** (1407m). A further 13.5km south along the D978 is **Égliseneuve-d'Entraigues**, where you can wander around displays and demonstrations of traditional cheesemaking at the quirky **Maison du Fromage** (☎ 04 73 71 93 69; place du Foirail; admission €3.50; 10am-12.30pm & 2.30-7pm Wed-Mon Jul & Aug, 2-6pm Wed-Sun end Jun & early Sep).

MASSIF CENTRAL

St-Nectaire

Six kilometres to the east of Murol is **St-Nectaire**, stretched out along the river beside the D996 road. The village is split into two sections: modern **St-Nectaire-Le-Bas**, with a smattering of belle-époque buildings left from the town's former incarnation as a spa resort; and the much older **St-Nectaire-Le-Haut**, reached via a steep switchback lane from the main road. Despite its well-known name, St-Nectaire's cheesemaking heyday has long since passed, and these days most of the famous *fromage* is produced by large dairy operations elsewhere in the Auvergne.

St-Nectaire's main architectural sight is the Romanesque **church** (9am-7pm Apr-Oct, 10am-12.30pm & 2-6pm Nov-Mar) in the upper village, famed for its multicoloured capitals and a fine 12th-century statue of the Virgin. You can also visit the remains of the town's Roman baths at the **Grottes du Cornadore** (☎ 04 73 88 57 97; adult/6-12yr €6.20/4.70; mid-Feb–Oct), and the interconnecting caves and medieval frescoes of the **Site Troglodyte de Jonas** (☎ 04 73 88 57 98; adult/6-12yr €6.20/4.70; daily mid-Jun–mid-Sep, Feb & Easter holidays, weekends in May, early Jun & Oct), 6km south of town.

St-Nectaire's hotels include an improbably huge Mercure, but a much better option is **Villa St-Hubert** (☎ 04 73 88 41 30; www.villasthubert.com; St-Nectaire-Le-Haut; d €40-72; P), a deluxe *chambre d'hôte* in a lavish mansion built by a Parisian émigré in the 17th century. It's an

LE CHASTEL MONTAIGU

Ever fancied staying in a fairy-tale castle? Then try this fabulously over-the-top **château** (☎ 04 73 96 28 49; www.lechastelmontaigu.com; Montaigut-le-Blanc; r €125; ⊠ P) with its very own private hilltop. Rebuilt from ruins using authentic medieval materials, it's a regal residence through and through. Heavy stone, rich fabrics and antique wall hangings fill the four bewitching rooms, which range from the smallish Chambre Guerin (with rustic-tiled bathroom and reclaimed font sinks) to the palatial Chambre des Templiers, complete with its own private turret terrace. Needless to say, every room has blindingly good views across the valley, and you'll feel like a true *seigneur* wandering around the spiral staircases and medieval terraces. Montaigut-le-Blanc is 11km east of St-Nectaire on the D996.

utter spoil – patterned wallpaper, delicate lighting and deep, soft beds in the rooms, a gorgeous chestnut-shaded garden out back, and a seriously opulent dining room lit by chandeliers and a roaring hearth where you can tuck into local dishes courtesy of your hosts. *Oh là là.*

MURAT

pop 2300 / elevation 930m

Tumbling down a steep basalt crag topped by a statue of the Virgin Mary, Murat is an excellent base for exploring the Monts du Cantal. With a cluster of dark stone houses huddled beneath the Rocher Bonnevie, it's one of the prettiest towns in the Cantal and a popular hiking centre. To the west are the three lofty peaks of **Puy Mary** (1787m), **Plomb du Cantal** (1855m) and **Puy de Perse-Arse** (1686m), the last remnants of an exploded supervolcano that once covered the Cantal Massif.

Information

The **tourist office** (☎ 04 71 20 09 47; www.officedetourismepaysdemurat.com; 2 rue du Faubourg Notre-Dame; ⏲ 9am-12.30pm & 1.30-7pm Mon-Sat, 9.30am-12.30pm & 2.30-6.30pm Sun Jul & Aug, 9am-noon & 2-6pm Mon-Sat & 10am-noon Sun Sep-Jun) is near the town hall, and has lots of info on walks and activities in the Cantal area.

Sights & Activities

Murat's fine old town, with its twisting streets and wonky stone cottages, makes a lovely afternoon stroll. The tourist office has an audioguide and pamphlet describing a good walking route, but for the best views you'll need to brave the lung-busting climb up to the top of the **Rocher Bonnevie**. Local fitness freaks often hold races up to the top, but ordinary mortals reach the summit after about 45 minutes. Follow the red-and-white GR flashes northwestwards out of town, followed by signs for the Rocher.

Down in the town itself, the **Église Notre-Dame-des-Oliviers** is worth a look for its 15th-century bell tower and *Vierge Noire*, typical of many in the Auvergne. Budding entomologists will make a beeline for the **Maison de la Faune** (☎ 04 71 20 00 52; just above place de l'Hôtel de Ville; adult/child €4/2.50; ⏲ 10am-noon & 3-5pm Mon-Sat, 2-6pm Sun), which houses over 10,000 insects, butterflies and stuffed beasties from the Auvergne to the Amazon.

Sleeping & Eating

Camping Municipal Stalapos (☎ 04 71 20 01 83; rue du Stade; sites from €6; ⏲ May-Sep) Beside the Alagnon River, this attractive campsite is 750m south of the train station. Look out for food and folklore nights in high summer.

Aux Globe-Trotters (☎ 04 71 20 07 22; www.murathotelglobetrotters.com; r €35-41; 💻) The best budget choice by miles, this cosy place has a choice of brightly shaded rooms, some jammed up into the top-floor rafters, some overlooking the hotel garden, and some facing the lively street. All are cute and colourful, with plain pine and a choice of tub or shower.

Auberge de Maître Paul (☎ 04 71 20 14 66; www.auberge-paul.fr; 14 place du Planol; s €40, d €50-55, tr €65-70; ⏲ closed last week Jun & 1st week Nov; ⊠) In the middle of Murat, this jovial *gîte* is an old favourite for hikers and family travellers, with plain, peach-and-yellow rooms spread around the creaky corridors of a 16th-century house. It's warm, welcoming and child-friendly, with a reliable Auvergnat restaurant and planet-sized pizzas for the nippers. If you're hiking, ask nicely and the owner might even ferry your bags to the next stop.

Hostellerie Les Breuils (☎ 04 71 20 01 25; www.hostellerie-les-breuils.com; 34 av du Docteur Mallet; r €65-76.50; ⏲ Feb & mid-May–Oct; 🏊) Covered with slate tiles and gabled windows, this 19th-century *maison bourgeoise* is crammed from top to bottom with Old World rooms, resplendent with polished floors, sleigh beds and original fireplaces (as well as original family furniture). Some have interconnecting doorways (perfect for travellers *en famille*). There's even a heated pool and a sauna.

Near the tourist office, **Caldera** (3 rue Justin Vigier) sells local cheese, cold cuts, honey, jam and liqueur.

Getting There & Around

Murat has northerly train connections to Clermont-Ferrand (€17, 1¾ hours, six daily), and in the opposite direction to Aurillac (€7.90, 45 minutes).

The countryside makes for splendid, if taxing, cycling. Both **Loisirs et Deux Roues** (☎ 04 71 20 06 54; rue Bon Secours) and **Ô P'tit Montagnard** (☎ 04 71 20 28 40; rue Faubourg Notre Dame) rent reliable machines.

PARC NATUREL RÉGIONAL LIVRADOIS-FOREZ

Blanketed in pine forest and hilly uplands, the nature park of Livradois-Forez is one of the largest protected areas in France, stretching from the plains of Limagne in the west to the Monts du Forez in the east. Formerly a centre for logging and agriculture, it's now a haven for nature-lovers and weekend walkers, but you'll need your own wheels to get around.

The **park information office** (☎ 04 73 95 57 57; www.parc-livradois-forez.org, in French; 🕒 9am-12.30pm & 1.30-7pm Mon-Fri, 3-7pm Sat & Sun May-Sep, 9am-12.30pm & 1.30-5.30pm Mon-Fri Oct-Apr) is off the D906 in St-Gervais-sous-Meymont. It's stocked with leaflets, including the *Route des Métiers* (The Cottage-Industry Trail), detailing local honey shops, lace-makers and perfumers, and the *Guide de la Randonnée et des Loisirs de Plein Air*, indicating walking trails and mountain-bike routes linked in with IGN (Institut Géographique National) topoguides.

Getting Around

A lovely **train touristique** (☎ 04 73 82 43 88; http://pagesperso-orange.fr/..agrivap/; 🕒 Jul & Aug) runs through the park between Courpière (15km south of Thiers) via Ambert to La Chaise-Dieu. There are a couple of routes, either aboard a double-decker *train panoramique* or a vintage steam train; contact the park office or the Ambert tourist office for details.

THIERS

pop 14,000 / elevation 420m

Hovering on the hillside above the Gorges de la Durolle, the industrial town of Thiers is the undisputed capital of French cutlery. For centuries this sober town has been churning out pocket knives and tableware, and though the industry has fallen on hard times, the town still produces some 70% of the nation's knives.

For an overview head for the **Musée de la Coutellerie** (Cutlery Museum; ☎ 04 73 80 58 86; 23 & 58 rue de la Coutellerie; adult/child Jun-Sep €6.30/2.70, Oct-May €5/2.50; 🕒 10am-12.30pm & 1.30-7pm Jul & Aug, 10am-noon & 2-6pm Jun & Sep, 10am-noon & 2-6pm Tue-Sun Oct-May), which is split over two buildings along rue de la Coutellerie. No 23 explores the historical side of cutlery-making, while No 58 houses the museum's unparalleled collection of knives past and present.

About 4km upstream from Thiers is the **Vallée des Rouets** (Valley of the Waterwheels; 🕒 noon-7pm Jul & Aug, noon-6pm Tue-Sun Jun & Sep), an open-air museum dedicated to the knife-makers who once toiled here in front of water-driven grindstones. The admission price includes a ticket for the shuttle-bus trip from the town museum.

If you fancy picking up your own shiny souvenir, there are lots of knife-sellers dotted round the town's medieval streets – ask at the friendly **tourist office** (☎ 04 73 80 65 65; www.tourisme-thiers.fr, in French; 1 place du Pirou; 🕒 9am-1pm & 1.30-7pm Mon-Sat, 10am-noon & 2-6pm Sun mid-Jun–mid-Sep, 9.30am-noon & 2-6pm Mon-Sat mid-Sep–mid-Jun) for recommended shops.

Thiers isn't worth staying in overnight – it's easily reached by train from Clermont-Ferrand (€7.70, 45 minutes, every two hours).

AMBERT

pop 7700

In the 16th century, Ambert, 30km north of La Chaise-Dieu, boasted more than 300 water-powered mills supplying the demands of the French paper industry, but the town is better-known today as an agricultural centre and the spiritual home of one of the Auvergne's classic cheeses, Fourme d'Ambert.

The **tourist office** (☎ 04 73 82 61 90; www.tourisme.fr/office-de-tourisme/ambert.htm; 4 place de l'Hôtel de

COUNTRY COOKERY

Unsurprisingly for a region covered by so much lush green grass, the Auvergne has a long tradition of producing some of France's finest cheeses. The region has five AOC (Appellation d'Origine Contrôlée) cheeses: the semihard, cheddarlike **Cantal** and premium-quality **Salers**, both made from the milk of high-pasture cows; **St-Nectaire**, rich, flat and semi-soft; **Fourme d'Ambert**, a mild, smooth blue cheese; and **Bleu d'Auvergne**, a powerful, creamy blue cheese with a Roquefort-like flavour. For more info check out www.fromages-aoc-auvergne.com.

The Auvergne's traditional dishes include **aligot** (puréed potato with garlic and Tomme cheese), **truffade** (sliced potatoes with Cantal cheese), **chou farci** (cabbage stuffed with pork or beef) and **potée Auvergnate**, a rich bean, pork and vegetable soup-stew. There's also another AOC label to look out for, the **lentille verte de Puy** (green Puy lentil), often used in local sauces and stews.

Ville; 9.30am-12.30pm & 1.30-6pm Mon-Sat, 10am-noon Sun Jun-Sep, 10am-12.30pm & 2-5pm Tue-Sat Oct-May) is opposite the Hôtel de Ville.

You can explore the town's paper-making past at the **Moulin Richard de Bas** (☎ 04 73 82 03 11; adult/child €5.50/3.60; 9am-8pm Jul & Aug, 9am-noon & 2-6pm Sep-Jun), a restored 14th-century mill where paper is still made using strictly traditional techniques. It's 4km out of town on the D57.

Cheese connoisseurs will prefer the small **Maison de la Fourme d'Ambert** (☎ 04 73 82 49 23; 29 rue des Chazeaux; adult/child €4.60/3.70; 9am-7pm Jul & Aug, 9am-noon & 2-7pm Sep, 9am-noon & 2-7pm Tue & Thu-Sat Oct-Dec, Feb & Mar, 9am-noon & 2-7pm Tue-Sat Apr-Jun), with displays on the history and manufacture of the town's trademark *fromage*.

The Thursday morning **market** is popular with local organic farmers, and it's also a great place to pick up Auvergnat cheeses.

LA CHAISE-DIEU

The sleepy village of La Chaise-Dieu, 42km north of Le Puy-en-Velay, is famed for its monumental church, the **Église Abbatiale de St-Robert** (9am-noon & 2-7pm Jun-Sep, 10am-noon & 2-5pm Oct-May), built in the 14th century atop an earlier abbey chapel by Pope Clement VI, who served here as a novice monk.

Most of the sights are in the **Chœur de l'Église** (adult/under 7yr €3.70/1); the ticket office is through the right-hand door as you enter the cathedral, and left along the old cloister. Highlights include the massive 18th-century organ, Clement VI's marble tomb and some fine 16th-century Flemish tapestries, but the most celebrated relic is the chilling **Danse Macabre**, a weird fresco in which Death dances a mocking jig around members of 15th-century society. The church is also the centre for La Chaise-Dieu's renowned **festival of sacred music**, held in late August.

Behind the cathedral is the **Salle de l'Echo** – an architectural oddity that allows people on opposite sides of the room to hear each other talking, rather like the Whispering Gallery in St Paul's; legend has it that the gallery was built to enable monks to hear lepers' confessions without contracting the dread disease.

Hotel de l'Echo (☎ 04 71 00 00 45; fax 04 71 00 00 22; place de l'Echo; menus €17, €29 & €46, d €49-70; P), peacefully positioned behind the cathedral in a refurbished stone town house, with prim rooms overlooking the square and the church, has a hearty restaurant lodged inside the old abbey kitchens.

Alternatively, **La Jacquerolle** (☎ 04 71 00 07 52; www.lajacquerolle.com; rue Marchédial; s €52, d €57-60) is a cute-as-a-button B&B run by a mother-and-daughter team, full of frilly rooms (all named after flowers) characterised by plush quilts, antique furniture and wood-panelled walls.

LE PUY-EN-VELAY

pop 22,000 / elevation 630m

Cradled at the base of a broad mountain valley, the lively town of Le Puy-en-Velay is one of the most striking sights in central France. Three volcanic pillars thrust skywards from the town's terracotta rooftops, crowned with Le Puy's trio of ecclesiastical landmarks: a 10th-century church, a soaring Romanesque cathedral and a massive cast-iron statue of the Virgin Mary and Child, which has stood watch above the town since 1860. Down in Le Puy itself, you'll discover a beautifully preserved old city and plenty of shops selling the town's trademark exports: lace and lentils.

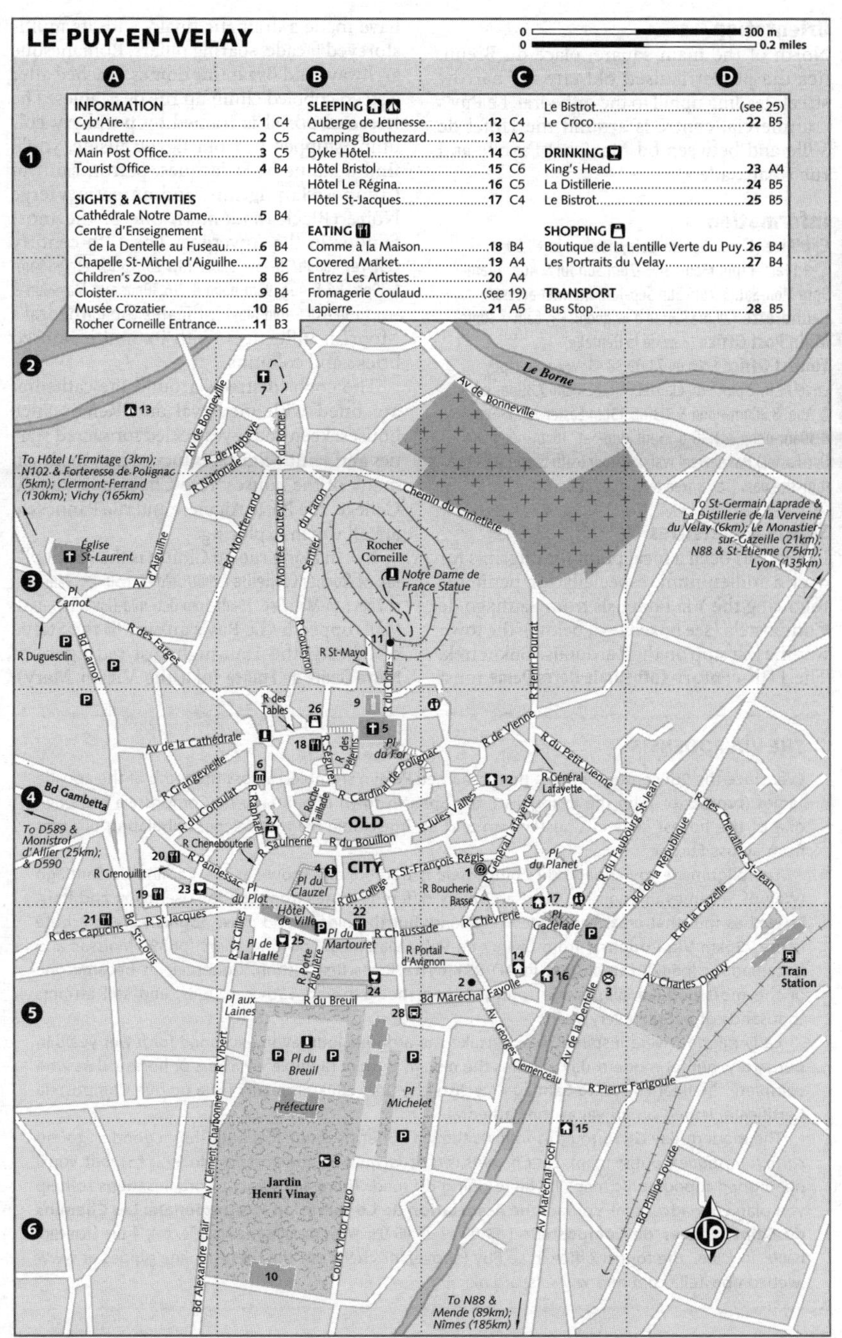
LE PUY-EN-VELAY
0 300 m
0 0.2 miles
INFORMATION
Cyb'Aire 1 C4
Laundrette 2 C5
Main Post Office 3 C5
Tourist Office 4 B4
SIGHTS & ACTIVITIES
Cathédrale Notre Dame 5 B4
Centre d'Enseignement de la Dentelle au Fuseau 6 B4
Chapelle St-Michel d'Aiguilhe 7 B2
Children's Zoo 8 B6
Cloister 9 B4
Musée Crozatier 10 B6
Rocher Corneille Entrance 11 B3
SLEEPING
Auberge de Jeunesse 12 C4
Camping Bouthezard 13 A2
Dyke Hôtel 14 C5
Hôtel Bristol 15 C6
Hôtel Le Régina 16 C5
Hôtel St-Jacques 17 C4
EATING
Comme à la Maison 18 B4
Covered Market 19 A4
Entrez Les Artistes 20 A4
Fromagerie Coulaud (see 19)
Lapierre 21 A5
Le Bistrot (see 25)
Le Croco 22 B5
DRINKING
King's Head 23 A4
La Distillerie 24 B5
Le Bistrot 25 B5
SHOPPING
Boutique de la Lentille Verte du Puy 26 B4
Les Portraits du Velay 27 B4
TRANSPORT
Bus Stop 28 B5
Le Borne
Av de Bonneville
To Hôtel L'Ermitage (3km); N102 & Forteresse de Polignac (5km); Clermont-Ferrand (130km); Vichy (165km)
To St-Germain Laprade & La Distillerie de la Verveine du Velay (6km); Le Monastier-sur-Gazeille (21km); N88 & St-Étienne (75km); Lyon (135km)
Rocher Corneille
Notre Dame de France Statue
Chemin du Cimetière
Église St-Laurent
Pl Carnot
R Duguesclin
Bd Carnot
R des Farges
Av d'Aiguilhe
Bd Montferrand
Montée Gouteyron
Sentier du Faron
R du Rocher
R de l'Abbaye
R Nationale
R Gouteyron
R St-Mayol
R du Cloître
R des Tables
Pl du For
R des Pèlerins
R Séguret
Av de la Cathédrale
R Grangevieille
R Cardinal de Polignac
R de Vienne
R Henri Pourrat
R du Petit Vienne
R Général Lafayette
Bd Gambetta
To D589 & Monistrol d'Allier (25km); & D590
R du Consulat
R Raphaël
R Roche Taillade
OLD CITY
R Jules Vallès
R du Bouillon
R Chenebouterie
R Saulnerie
R Pannessac
R Grenouillit
Pl du Plot
Pl du Clauzel
R du Collège
R St-François Régis
R Boucherie Basse
Pl du Planet
R du Faubourg St-Jean
Bd de la République
R des Chevaliers St-Jean
R de la Gazelle
Hôtel de Ville
R des Capucins
R St Jacques
Bd St-Louis
R St Gilles
Pl de la Halle
Pl du Martouret
R Chaussade
R Chèvrerie
Pl Cadelade
R Portail d'Avignon
R Porte Aiguière
Av Charles Dupuy
Train Station
Pl aux Laines
R du Breuil
Bd Maréchal Fayolle
Av Georges Clemenceau
Av de la Dentelle
R Pierre Farigoule
Pl du Breuil
R Vibert
Préfecture
Pl Michelet
Av Clément Charbonnier
Jardin Henri Vinay
Bd Alexandre Clair
Cours Victor Hugo
Av Maréchal Foch
Bd Philippe Jourde
To N88 & Mende (89km); Nîmes (185km)
MASSIF CENTRAL

Orientation

North of the main square, place du Breuil, lies the pedestrianised old city, its narrow streets leading uphill to the cathedral. Le Puy's commercial centre is around the Hôtel de Ville and between bd Maréchal Fayolle and rue Chaussade.

Information

Cyb'Aire (17 rue Général Lafayette; per hr €3.50; 11am-11pm Mon-Sat, 3-7pm Sun Jul & Aug, 11am-9pm Mon-Sat, 3-7pm Sun Sep-Jun) Internet access.
Laundrette (24 rue Portail d'Avignon; 8am-7.30pm)
Main Post Office (8 av de la Dentelle)
Tourist Office (04 71 09 38 41; www.ot-lepuy envelay.fr; 2 place du Clauzel; 8.30am-7.30pm Jul & Aug, 8.30am-noon & 1.30-6.15pm Easter-Jun & Sep, 8.30am-noon & 1.30-6.15pm Mon-Sat, 10am-noon Sun Oct-Easter) Has several walking-tour leaflets and sells the four-site pass (see boxed text, opposite).

Sights & Activities

Le Puy has been a focal point for pilgrims for over a millennium, especially for penitents following the Via Podensis from Santiago de Compostela (see boxed text, below): the town was the last stop on their arduous 736km trek. The 11th-century **Cathédrale Notre Dame** must have made a dramatic finale, with its multi-storeyed facade, soaring pillars, Romanesque archways and Byzantine domes, reached after a steep cobbled climb up rue des Tables. The frescoed portal is framed by porphyry columns shipped in from Egypt: inside, you'll find a statue of St Jacques, patron saint of Compostela pilgrims, and an eerie Vierge Noire (Black Madonna), one of the most famous in the Auvergne. The 12th-century **cloister** (adult/18-25yr/under 18yr €5/3.50/free; 9am-6.30pm Jul & Aug, 9am-noon & 2-6.30pm mid-May–Jun & Sep, to 5pm Oct–mid-May) indicates the cathedral's Moorish influences, with its multicoloured bricks and columns.

The cobbled streets around the cathedral are lined with medieval and Renaissance houses: keep your eyes peeled for sacred statues and saintly figurines tucked into niches in many of the houses. Rue Chaussade, rue du Collège, rue Porte Aiguière and rue Pannessac are all worth exploring.

North along rue du Cloître is the 757m pillar of **Rocher Corneille** (adult/child €3/1.50; 9am-6pm or 7pm mid-Mar–Sep, 10am-5pm Oct–mid-Nov & Feb–mid-Mar), topped by Le Puy's answer to the Statue of Liberty: the 16m-high rust-red figure of **Notre Dame de France** (aka the Virgin Mary),

THE VIA PODENSIS

Ever since the 9th century, when a hermit named Pelayo stumbled across the tomb of the apostle James (brother of John the Evangelist), the Spanish town of Santiago de Compostela has been one of the holiest sites in Christendom and an irresistible magnet for perambulating pilgrims from across Europe.

The pilgrimage to Santiago de Compostela is traditionally known as the Camiño de Santiago (Way of St James in English). There are many different routes from London, Germany and Italy, as well as four that cross the French mainland. But the oldest (and most popular) French route is the 736km **Via Podensis** from Le Puy-en-Velay via Figeac (p645), Cahors (p639), Moissac and Rocamadour (p647). Established in AD 951 by Le Puy's first bishop, Godescalc, it became one of the most popular pilgrimage routes during the 12th and 13th centuries, and still attracts thousands of people every year.

Early pilgrims were inspired to undertake the arduous journey in exchange for fewer years in purgatory, but for modern-day pilgrims the reward is more tangible – walkers or horse-riders who complete the final 100km to Santiago (cyclists the final 200km) qualify for a unique Compostela Certificate, issued on arrival at the cathedral.

The modern-day **GR36** roughly follows the Via Podensis route, IGN publishes a good all-round *carte touristique* (tourist map), *Les Chemins vers St-Jacques de Compostelle* (No 922; €5), but you'll need good topographic maps if you're going off road. There are plenty of organisations to help you plan your adventure: contact the **Association de Coopération Interrégionale: Les Chemins de Saint-Jacques de Compostelle** (05 62 27 00 05; www.chemins-compostelle.com; 4 rue Clémence Isaure, Toulouse), the tourist office in Le Puy (above), or check out the useful online guides at www.webcompostella.com and www.csj.org.uk.

fashioned from cannons captured during the Crimean War. Inside the statue, a creaky spiral staircase winds its way to the top, with tiny portholes affording vertiginous views over the town's rooftops.

Further north is the **Chapelle St-Michel d'Aiguilhe** (adult/child €2.75/2.25; 9am-6.45pm Jul & Aug, 9am-6.30pm May, Jun & Sep, 9.30am-noon & 2-5.30pm mid-Mar–Apr & Oct–mid-Nov, 2-5pm Feb–mid-Mar & Christmas holidays), Le Puy's oldest chapel, perched atop another 85m-high volcanic plug reached via a 268-step staircase. Stepping inside feels like a lost scene from *Indiana Jones* – the chapel follows the natural contours of the rock, and the simple architecture, strange carvings and 12th-century frescos create an otherworldly atmosphere. Established by Bishop Godescalc in the 10th century, the chapel was rebuilt in the 12th, 14th and 19th centuries.

At the southern end of the Jardin Henri Vinay is **Musée Crozatier** (04 71 06 62 40; adult/child €3.20/free; 10am-noon & 2-6pm Wed-Mon Feb-Nov), founded by Puy-born sculptor Charles Crozatier (1795–1855). Its hotchpotch of artefacts range from dinosaur bones and Dutch paintings to Le Puy lace and the first 'praxinoscope', an image-projecting machine that predated modern-day cinema.

Le Puy's great lace industry has fallen on hard times: in its heyday, there were over 5000 lace workshops in the Haute-Loire, but only a handful now remain. You can learn more (and even take a crash course) at the **Centre d'Enseignement de la Dentelle au Fuseau** (04 71 02 01 68; www.ladentelledupuy.com; 38-40 rue Raphaël; adult/under 10yr €3.50/free; 8.30-11.30am & 1.30-5pm Mon-Fri, 9.30am-4.30pm Sat).

Along with its lentils and lace, Le Puy is famous for its very own fiery-green liqueur, Verveine, invented in 1859. **La Distillerie de la Verveine du Velay** (04 71 03 04 11; www.verveine.com; 45min tour adult/student/child €5.80/4.20/2; 10am-12.30pm & 1.30-6.30pm Jul & Aug, 10am-noon & 1.30-6.30pm Tue-Sat Mar-Jun & Sep-Dec, 1.30-4.30pm Tue-Sat Jan & Feb) is 6km east along the N88 in St-Germain Laprade.

Festivals & Events

Le Puy's annual four-day street party, the **Fête du Roi de l'Oiseau** (www.roideloiseau.com) takes place in mid-September. The tradition dates back to 1524, when the title of King *(Roi)* was bestowed on the first archer to shoot down a straw *oiseau* (bird) in return for a year's exemption from taxes, but these days it's just an excuse for an annual bash full of music, cinema, street theatre and outlandish costumes.

> **PILGRIM'S PASS**
>
> Le Puy's four major sites (the cathedral, the Rocher Corneille, the Chapelle St-Michel d'Aiguilhe and the Musée Crozatier) can be visited on a joint **museum pass** (€8). You can buy it at any of the sites or from the tourist office.

Altogether less raucous are Le Puy's **Latin Music Festival**, held in mid-July, and the weeklong folk festival, **Interfolk**, at the end of July.

Sleeping

Auberge de Jeunesse (04 71 05 52 40; auberge.jeunesse@mairie-le-puy-en-velay.fr; 9 rue Jules Vallès; dm €10.50; daily Easter-Nov, Mon-Fri Nov-Easter) Inside a former convent, this HI hostel is typically well run, with a choice of four-bed rooms or boarding-school 20-bed dorms, but the titchy kitchen feels cramped when it's busy with summer hikers.

Camping Bouthezard (Camping Le Puy-en-Velay; 04 71 09 55 09; chemin de Bouthezard; sites €12; Easter-Sep) Le Puy's campsite enjoys an attractive berth beside the River Borne. Bus 6 delivers you outside.

Dyke Hôtel (04 71 09 05 30; dykehotel@wanadoo.fr; 37 bd Maréchal Fayolle; s €36, d €40-48) Despite the curious choice of name (which refers to a volcanic pillar, in case you're wondering), this small hotel is efficient if unexciting. Downstairs there's a café-bar; upstairs there are clean, modernish rooms of varying dimensions, all with bathrooms and some with balconies onto the (very) busy road.

Hôtel St-Jacques (04 71 07 20 40; www.hotel-saint-jacques.com; 7 place Cadelade; s €40-50, d €55-65; Feb-Dec; ⊠) It's showing its age, but this intimate little hotel is a good budget base. Spread over four floors, the pick of the rooms have wood floors, dinky bathrooms and views of the square, with a patio café for summer brekkie. Wi-fi's free.

Hôtel Bristol (04 71 09 13 38; www.hotelbristol-lepuy.com; 7-9 av Maréchal Foch; s €48-58, d €58-70; P) Typically solid Logis de France, with 40 businessy rooms around a small garden-cum-car-park, plus a smart restaurant filled with brass fixtures and leather armchairs. The ones in the rear annexe are roomier and smarter; ask for the top floor for rooftop views. Wi-fi and parking on site.

Hôtel L'Ermitage (☎ 04 71 07 05 05; http://hotelermitage.perso.cegetel.net; 75 av de l'Ermitage; d €50-75; ⊠ P) Modern, corporate-style hotel 3km from the centre, with a selection of boxy rooms that are on the bland side (laminate floors, generic furnishings, small TVs), but with the bonus of views of the hotel garden or across the valley and town.

Hôtel Le Régina (☎ 04 71 09 14 71; www.hotelrestregina.com; 34 bd Maréchal Fayolle; s €53, d €60-110; ⊠) Topped by a neon-lit art-deco turret, the Régina's rooms range from old and shabby to modern and swish, with a considerable difference in quality depending on price. The off-street rooms are much quieter, but the *appartements* are the plushest, with stripped wood, contemporary furnishings and separate office suites. There's wi-fi (free), parking (€6.50) and a refined restaurant complete with grand piano (mains €17 to €24).

Eating

Le Bistrot (☎ 04 71 02 27 08; 7 place de la Halle; mains €9.50-15; Tue-Sat) Brasserie staples are served with a Gallic shrug at this occasionally shambolic bistro-bar. Steaks, casseroles and lentil stews are chalked up daily, and you can choose from lots of world beers while you tuck in at the patio tables.

Entrez les Artistes (☎ 04 71 09 71 78; 29 rue Pannessac; mains €10-20; lunch Tue-Sat, dinner Thu-Sun) Frilly and irresistibly feminine, this cosy place is decorated with quirky style and lashings of local lace. Good, solid local dishes served up in simple style – nothing too fancy, but dead filling.

Le Croco (☎ 04 71 02 40 13; 5 rue Chaussade; mains €12.50-14.10; Tue-Sat) The cute Croco specialises in huge salads and veggie platters featuring Auvergnat ingredients (including Bleu d'Auvergne, Cantal and *chèvre chaud*).

Lapierre (☎ 04 71 09 08 44; 6 rue des Capucins; menus €18-28, mains around €15; Mon-Sat) A much-recommended Auvergnat restaurant run by a talented female chef, Estelle Lapierre. The atmosphere's posh and prissy, with lacy lampshades, fresh plants and razor-sharp napkins dotted around and top-notch traditional food – expect hearty meat, fish and cheese dishes, and handmade desserts featuring a *soupçon* of Verveine.

our pick **Comme à la Maison** (☎ 04 71 02 94 73; rue Séguret; menus €22-39; lunch Tue-Fri & Sun, dinner Tue-Sat) This little restaurant is easy to miss, but if you manage to find it, you'll be rewarded with Le Puy's most adventurous food, created by up-and-coming chef Guillaume Fourcade. Inventive dishes such as fennel-and-mackerel tart or foie gras with dried fruit are served in a funky dining room blending old architecture with bold colours. Excellent and bang up to date.

SELF-CATERING

Le Puy's weekly market takes over place du Plot and nearby streets every Saturday morning, or there's a **covered market** just off rue Grenouillit. **Fromagerie Coulaud** (24 rue Grenouillit; Tue-Sat) sells a good selection of local cheeses.

Drinking

Le Puy has plenty of places for a quiet café or a late-night Kronenbourg. One of the best is **La Distillerie** (29 place du Breuil; till 1am or 2am Mon-Sat), a traditional boozer filled with upturned beer barrels and a decommissioned still.

Le Bistrot (place de la Halle; Tue-Sat) packs in a loyal local crowd for its extensive beer selection, as does the **King's Head** (place du Marché Couvert; till 1am Tue-Sat), an English-style pub run by a friendly Anglo-Saxon owner.

Shopping

The two souvenirs to pick up in Le Puy are (obviously) lace and lentils. Several shops sell handmade lace, including **Les Portraits du Velay** (☎ 04 71 06 00 94; www.dentelledupuy.com, in French; 10 rue Raphaël), while you can pick up authentic AOC lentils at the local market or the **Boutique de la Lentille Verte du Puy** (☎ 04 71 02 60 44; 23 rue des Tables; Jul & Aug).

Getting There & Away

Le Puy's bus connections are pretty limited and practically nonexistent during school holidays, so you're far better off catching the train. Connections to the **train station** (av Charles Dupuy) include Lyon (€19.90, 2½ hours, three to five daily) via St-Étienne and Clermont-Ferrand (€20.10, two hours, four to six direct).

Getting Around

All five lines of the local TUDIP buses (single ticket/10-trip carnet €1.10/7.50) stop at place Michelet.

For a taxi call ☎ 04 71 05 42 43.

AROUND LE PUY-EN-VELAY

Fortresse de Polignac

Five kilometres northwest from Le Puy is the château of **Polignac** (☎ 04 71 04 06 04; adult/6-18yr €5/3; 🕒 9am-7pm Jun–mid-Sep, 10am-12.30pm & 1.30-6.30pm Tue-Sun Apr, May & mid-Sep–mid-Nov), built in the 11th century by the powerful Polignac family, who once controlled access to the city from the north. Perched atop another volcanic dome, the castle is ringed by a practically continuous wall dotted with lookout towers and a 32m-high rectangular keep at the castle's highest point.

Gorges de l'Allier

About 30km west of Le Puy, the salmon-filled Allier River – paralleled by the scenic Clermont-Ferrand–Nîmes rail line – weaves between rocky, scrub-covered hills and steep cliffs. Above the river's east bank, the narrow D301 gives fine views as it passes through wild countryside and remote, mud-puddle hamlets.

The wide-open landscape is the main attraction, but there are interesting detours, including a Romanesque church in **Prades**, and the 15th-century **Collégiale St-Gal** (☎ 04 71 77 05 41; 🕒 8.30am-7pm) and **Jacquemard folk museum** (☎ 04 71 77 05 51; 🕒 2-7pm Jul & Aug, 3-7pm early Sep), both in Langeac.

The gorges are hugely popular with outdoor enthusiasts. Walking trails criss-cross the valley walls, and if you're after more thrills and spills, several companies offer canyoning, adventure sports and white-water rafting – try **Tonic Rafting** (☎ 04 71 57 23 90; www.raft-canyon.fr, in French; €55-110; 🕒 Apr-Sep) or **Rivière Nature** (☎ 04 71 57 22 54; St-Privat-d'Allier; per day €75; 🕒 Apr-Sep).

For a lazier way of exploring the valley, hop aboard the scenic **Train des Gorges de l'Allier** (☎ 04 71 77 70 17; www.trainstouristiques-ter.com; tickets €13-28; 🕒 Mon-Fri Jul & Aug), which trundles between Langeac and Langogne via Prades and Monistrol d'Allier.

There are plenty of campsites in the valley, including the riverside **Camping les Gorges de l'Allier** (☎ 04 71 77 05 01; www.campinglangeac.com; sites €12.50) in Langeac and **Camping Le Vivier** (☎ 04 71 57 24 14; mairie.monistroldallier@wanadoo.fr; sites from €10; 🕒 Apr-Sep) in Monistrol d'Allier.

If you're after something more comfortable, the rustic **Auberge de l'Île d'Amour** (☎ 04 71 77 00 11; 17 av de Gévaudan, Langeac; menus €20-35, d €50-60) in Langeac makes a homely base, with small, snug rooms and free-standing chalets as well as a solid *table de terroir* (country table) restaurant.

Alternatively, you can sleep in charmingly renovated stone cottages at **Le Moulin Ferme-Auberge** (☎ 04 71 74 03 09; www.gite-aubergedumoulin.com; St-Arcons-d'Allier; d €55, with half board €95; P), with dinner served at a big communal table in the 15th-century windmill.

La Montagne Protestante

Around 40km east of Le Puy is the highland area known as La Montagne Protestante, so called because of the stout Protestant principles (and occasionally odd customs) of the local population. It's a sparsely populated area, carpeted in rich pastureland and thick fir forest; the area's most distinctive landmarks are the peaks of Mont Meygal (1436m) and Mont Mézenc (1753m), whose summit is accessible via the GR73 and GR7 hiking trails. On a clear day, you can take in panoramic views across southeastern France, from Mont Blanc, 200km to the northeast, to Mont Ventoux, 140km to the southeast.

Villages are few and far between, but one particular place is worth a visit – the trim village of **Le Chambon-sur-Lignon**, 45km east of Le Puy-en-Velay, which played a courageous role in WWII. Chambon and the surrounding hamlets sheltered over 3000 refugees, including hundreds of Jewish children, from deportation by the Nazis, and every July and August there's an exhibition on the town's WWII history. The **tourist office** (☎ 04 71 59 71 56; http://ot-lechambonsurlignon.fr; rue des Quatre Saisons; 🕒 9am-noon & 2-6.30pm Mon-Sat, 10am-noon Sun Jun-Sep, 9am-noon & 3-6pm Mon-Sat Oct-May) has details.

Limousin, the Dordogne & Quercy

If it's the heart and soul of France you're searching for, then look no longer. Tucked away in the country's southwestern corner, the neighbouring regions of the Limousin, Dordogne and Quercy sum up all that's best about *la belle France*. The is a land of dense oak forests, rolling green fields and rich country cooking, where historic châteaux and cobblestone villages line the river banks and wooden-hulled *gabarres* (barges) still meander along the waterways. While the rest of France seems desperate to catch up to its European neighbours, this is one corner of the country that seems perfectly content to keep things just the way they are.

Of the three areas, Limousin is the most traditional, dominated by country farms and sleepy backcountry hamlets. Known for its emerald-green countryside and famously rich food, Limousin is home to the bustling city of Limoges, the undisputed capital of French fine china.

Slightly to the south, the Dordogne is best known for its history and heritage. With a bevy of dramatic monuments, from sturdy *bastides* (fortified towns) to clifftop châteaux and medieval towns, the Dordogne is also celebrated for its astonishing prehistoric sites, including some of the most spectacular cave paintings in Europe.

Still further south is the old region of Quercy, closer in many ways to the nearby Mediterranean regions of Toulouse and Languedoc than its northern neighbours. Sliced through by the snaking River Lot, and pock-marked by limestone valleys and subterranean caverns, Quercy is home to the fairy-tale *fortresse royale* of Najac and the holy city of Rocamadour, as well as the vintage vineyards around the capital city of Cahors.

HIGHLIGHTS

- Marvel at the prehistoric cave paintings of the **Vézère Valley** (p630)
- Venture into the underworld at the **Gouffre de Padirac** (p647)
- Stroll around an excavated Roman villa at the **Musée Gallo-Romain Vesunna** (p622) in Périgueux
- Shop till you drop at the hectic street markets of **Sarlat-la-Canéda** (p626) and **Périgueux** (p621)
- Drink in the panoramas from the hilltop fortresses of **Monpazier** (p637) and **Domme** (p637)
- Take to the waterways aboard a traditional river **gabarre** (p636)

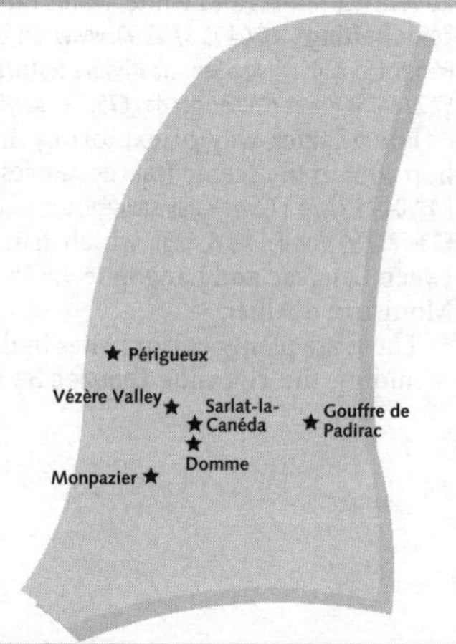

- POPULATION: 1,134,959
- AREA: 25,654 SQ KM

Activities

KAYAKING & CANOEING

Cruising the waterways in a self-powered canoe is one of the most memorable ways to explore the region. There are lots of operators along the Dordogne and Vézère Rivers; hire fees include compulsory life jackets *(gilets)* and an introduction to basic safety procedures (such as how to survive capsizing). Prices vary according to your chosen route – most places charge around €20 to €25 per day, including minibus transport.

Dordogne

Canoë Vacances (☎ 05 53 28 17 07; www.canoevacances.com; La Roque Gageac) Canoe and kayak trips between Carsac and Les Milandes via Vitrac, Domme, Marqueyssac and Castelnaud (trips €10 to €17).

Canoës-Loisirs (☎ 05 53 28 23 43; www.canoes-loisirs.com; Pont de Vitrac, Domme) Trips include Carsac–Vitrac (9km, €10), Carsac–Beynac (25km, €19), Vitrac–Castelnaud (12km, €12) and Vitrac–Beynac (16km, €15).

Safaraïd (☎ 05 65 37 44 87; www.canoe-kayak-dordogne.com; Vayrac canoe/kayak per day €19/22) Based in Vayrac, this operator has various stations between Argentat and Beynac, with lots of possible routes in between, as well as a seven-day canoe safari (€197 to €312 for two people, including campsites).

Vézère

Canoës Vallée Vézère (☎ 05 53 05 10 11; www.canoesvalleevezere.com; Les Eyzies) Trips from Les Trois Chateaux (26km, €22 to €24), Saint-Léon-sur-Vézère (19km, €16 to €18), La Saint-Christophe (13km, €14 to €16) and La Marzac (10km, €10 to €14). A 5km initiation course costs €8.

Canoëric (☎ 05 53 03 51 99; www.canoe-perigord.com; Le Bugue) Runs day trips of between 9 and 21km to Le Bugue (€9 to €23).

WALKING, CYCLING & HORSE RIDING

This corner of France is renowned for its natural beauty and has three *parcs naturels régionaux:* **Périgord-Limousin** (Map p608; ☎ 05 53 60 34 65; www.parc-naturel-perigord-limousin.fr) in the northwest, **Millevaches en Limousin** (☎ 05 55 67 97 90; www.pnr-millevaches.fr) in the east and **Causses de Quercy** (☎ 05 65 24 20 50; www.parc-causses-du-quercy.org) in the south.

There's fantastic walking and mountain biking in all three parks; you can pick up *balades à la journée* (day walk) leaflets and *VTT* (*vélo tout terrain;* mountain bike) guides from tourist offices. Serious walkers will prefer the dedicated park topoguides, which detail major walking routes, including the GR (Grands Randonées) trails. Many of the trails and bridleways can also be explored on horseback.

Major areas for walking include the Monts de Blond, le Massif des Monédières and Monts de Chalus in northwest Limousin, the area around Cahors (on the GR36 and the GR65) and the Lot Valley, and the classic Santiago de Compostela trail which runs through many of the region's southerly towns.

Getting There & Around

The major transport hub is Limoges (see p613), which has regular flights to many French and UK cities. Bergerac (p639) also has budget flights to the UK. The A20 motorway heads north from Limoges to Paris and continues south to Toulouse.

As always in rural France, having your own wheels is really handy. The bus network is patchy and frustratingly geared around school timetables; most towns and small villages can be reached faster and more easily by train. A useful rail link meanders down to Toulouse from Limoges via Brive, Souillac and Cahors, and Limoges and Périgueux are both on the southwest main line from Paris.

LIMOUSIN

The rich green fields and hummocky hills of Limousin are less well known than the

MONKEY BUSINESS

For adrenalin junkies looking for their next fix, head for one of the **Parcours Aventures dans les Arbres** (Tree Adventure Parks). With a network of walkways, swings and bridges running between towering trees and linked with cross-country trails and obstacle courses, these woodland playgrounds are suitable for everyone from six-year-olds to septuagenarians. Eat your heart out, Tarzan…

La Foret des Ecureuils (☎ 06 89 30 92 99; www.laforetdesecureuils.com; St-Vincent-le-Paluel)

L'Appel de la Forêt (☎ 05 53 46 35 06; www.appel-de-la-foret.com; Thenon)

Indian Forest Périgord (☎ 05 53 31 22 22; www.indianforestperigord.com; Carsac-Aillac)

Parcours Aventure des Jaumâtres (☎ 05 55 65 43 11; www.lespierresjaumatres.fr; near Guéret)

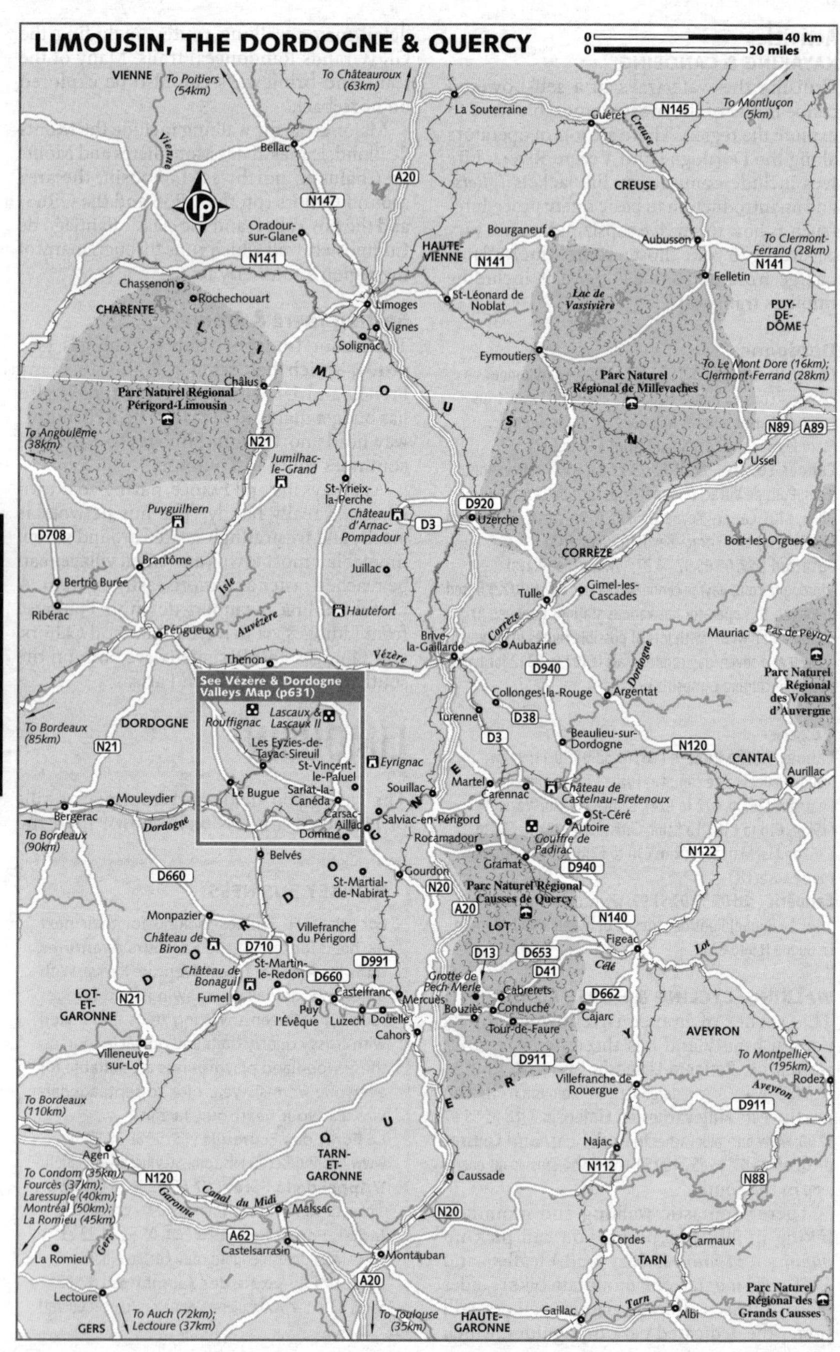
LIMOUSIN, THE DORDOGNE & QUERCY
0 40 km
0 20 miles
VIENNE
To Poitiers (54km)
To Châteauroux (63km)
La Souterraine
Guéret
N145
To Montluçon (5km)
Creuse
Bellac
Vienne
A20
CREUSE
N147
Oradour-sur-Glane
Bourganeuf
HAUTE-VIENNE
Aubusson
To Clermont-Ferrand (28km)
N141
N141
N141
Felletin
Chassenon
Rochechouart
St-Léonard de Noblat
Lac de Vassivière
CHARENTE
Limoges
Vignes
PUY-DE-DÔME
Solignac
Eymoutiers
To Le Mont Dore (16km); Clermont-Ferrand (28km)
Châlus
Parc Naturel Régional de Millevaches
Parc Naturel Régional Périgord-Limousin
LIMOUSIN
To Angoulême (38km)
N21
N89
A89
Ussel
Jumilhac-le-Grand
St-Yrieix-la-Perche
D920
Puyguilhern
Château d'Arnac-Pompadour
D3
Uzerche
D708
Bort-les-Orgues
Brantôme
CORRÈZE
Juillac
Bertric Burée
Isle
Gimel-les-Cascades
Tulle
Ribérac
Hautefort
Auvézère
Périgueux
Corrèze
Mauriac
Pas de Peyrol
Brive-la-Gaillarde
Aubazine
Thenon
Vézère
D940
Parc Naturel Régional des Volcans d'Auvergne
See Vézère & Dordogne Valleys Map (p631)
Dordogne
Collonges-la-Rouge
Argentat
Rouffignac
Lascaux & Lascaux II
Turenne
D38
To Bordeaux (85km)
DORDOGNE
D3
Beaulieu-sur-Dordogne
N21
Les Eyzies-de-Tayac-Sireuil
N120
St-Vincent-le-Paluel
Eyrignac
CANTAL
Aurillac
Le Bugue
Sarlat-la-Canéda
Souillac
Martel
Carennac
Château de Castelnau-Bretenoux
Mouleydier
Carsac-Aillac
Bergerac
Salviac-en-Périgord
St-Céré
Autoire
To Bordeaux (90km)
Dordogne
Domme
Rocamadour
Gouffre de Padirac
N122
Belvès
Gramat
D940
D660
St-Martial-de-Nabirat
Gourdon
N20
Parc Naturel Régional Causses de Quercy
A20
Monpazier
LOT
N140
Château de Biron
Villefranche du Périgord
D710
Figeac
Lot
D13
D653
St-Martin-le-Redon
D991
Célé
Château de Bonaguil
D660
D41
Grotte de Pech Merle
Castelfranc
Mercuès
Cabrerets
D662
LOT-ET-GARONNE
N21
Fumel
Puy l'Évêque
Luzech
Douelle
Bouziès
Conduché
Cajarc
Cahors
Tour-de-Faure
AVEYRON
Villeneuve-sur-Lot
D911
To Montpellier (195km)
Villefranche de Rouergue
Rodez
To Bordeaux (110km)
Aveyron
D911
QUERCY
DORDOGNE
Agen
Najac
TARN-ET-GARONNE
N112
To Condom (35km); Fourcès (37km); Laressuple (40km); Montréal (50km); La Romieu (45km)
N120
Caussade
N88
Garonne
Canal du Midi
Moissac
N20
A62
Cordes
Carmaux
Gers
Castelsarrasin
La Romieu
Montauban
TARN
A20
Lectoure
Parc Naturel Régional des Grands Causses
To Auch (72km); Lectoure (37km)
To Toulouse (35km)
HAUTE-GARONNE
Gaillac
Tarn
Albi
GERS

ALL ABOARD!

For a unique view of the gloriously green Limousin, clamber aboard the carriages of the **Chemin Touristique Limousin-Périgord** (☎ 05 55 69 57 62; www.trainvapeur.com), a 1932 steam engine which that its way across fields and forests between Limoges and Ussel.

The railway runs between mid-July and mid-August; reservations are essential and can be made through the Limoges tourist office (below). There are six circuits in all. The following lines run three times a season.

Limoges–Eymoutiers (adult/6-12yr/under 6yr €24/10/free; 8hr) Follows the old upland railway via St-Leonard-de-Noblat.

Limoges–Pompadour (adult/6-12 yr/under 6yr €12/5/free; 1½hr) Includes a visit to the gardens and stables of Pompadour.

Eymoutiers–Châteauneuf–Bujaleuf (adult/6-12yr/under 6yr €12/5/free; 1½hr) Via the plunging Gorges de la Vienne.

Dordogne and Lot Valleys to the south, but that doesn't mean that the region is without its charms. With its quiet lanes, flower-filled villages and country markets, it's tailor-made for walkers and cyclists. It's also the perfect place to escape the summertime crowds further south, and a destination *par excellence* for fans of homely, hearty French cuisine.

Limousin is made up of three *départements*: Haute-Vienne, in the west, whose *préfecture* is the city of Limoges; the rural Creuse, in the northeast; and, in the southeast, the Corrèze, home to many of the region's most beautiful sights.

LIMOGES

pop 135,100

If you're a china connoisseur, you'll already be familiar with the legendary name of Limoges. For over 200 years, this elegant city has been the preferred place for the French upper crust to pick up their tableware, and though the heyday of porcelain production has long since passed, Limoges is still an excellent place to get acquainted with French china. If you fancy stocking up on some crockery, you'll find several factories still dotted around the city, as well as a clutch of medieval buildings and museums in the neighbourhood known as La Cité and in the city centre.

Orientation

Limoges is compact. The commercial centre radiates out from the partly pedestrianised Château quarter, bordered by the thoroughfares of av de la Liberation and bd Gambetta. The medieval quarter La Cité and the cathedral are 500m east of the centre, while the train station is 750m northeast, past place Jourdan.

Information

INTERNET ACCESS

The tourist office has a free wi-fi zone.

Point Cyber (☎ 05 55 79 03 28; 7 av Charles de Gaulle; 🕑 9.30am-midnight Mon-Sat, 2pm-midnight Sun; per hr €2.80)

TendanceWeb (☎ 05 55 10 93 61; 5 bd Victor Hugo; 🕑 8am-4am Mon-Fri, 9am-6am Sat, 2pm-4am Sun; per hr €3)

LAUNDRY

Laundrette (28 rue Delescluze; 🕑 7am or 8am-9pm)

Laundrette (9 rue Monte à Regret; 🕑 7am or 8am-9pm)

MONEY

There are banks on place Jourdan and place Wilson, and the post office changes cash and has an ATM.

POST

Main Post Office (29 av de la Libération) Offers currency-exchange services and has an ATM.

Post Office (6 bd de Fleurus) Has an ATM.

TOURIST INFORMATION

Tourist Office (☎ 05 55 34 46 87; www.tourismelimoges.com; 12 bd de Fleurus; 🕑 9am-7pm Mon-Sat, 10am-6pm Sun Jun-Sep, 9am-6pm Mon-Sat Jan-Apr, Nov & Dec) Has a free wi-fi zone and offers several guided walks around the city.

Sights

PORCELAIN & ENAMEL

For over three hundred years, the name of Limoges has been synonymous with *les arts du feu*: *émail* (enamel) and *porcelaine*

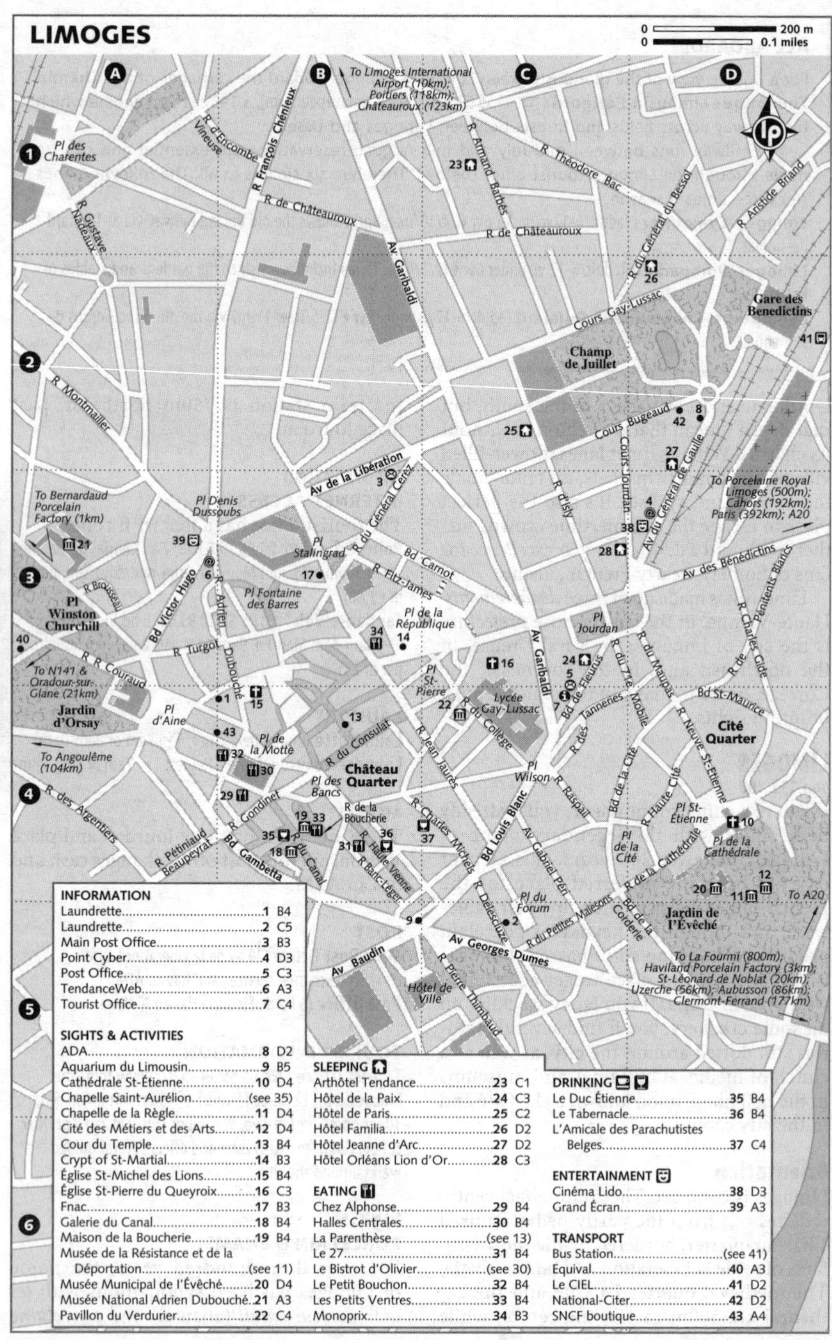
LIMOGES
0 200 m
0 0.1 miles
To Limoges International Airport (10km); Poitiers (118km); Châteauroux (123km)
Pl des Charentes
R d'Encombe Vineuse
R François Chénieux
R Armand Barbès
R Théodore Bac
R Aristide Briand
R de Châteauroux
R Gustave Nadeaux
Av Garibaldi
R du Général du Bessol
Cours Gay-Lussac
Gare des Benedictins
Champ de Juillet
R Montmailler
Cours Bugeaud
Av de la Libération
R du Général Cerez
Cours Jourdan
R d'Isly
Av du Général de Gaulle
To Porcelaine Royal Limoges (500m); Cahors (192km); Paris (392km); A20
To Bernardaud Porcelain Factory (1km)
Pl Denis Dussoubs
Pl Stalingrad
Bd Carnot
R Fitz-James
Av des Bénédictins
R Brousseau
Bd Victor Hugo
R Adrien Dubouché
Pl Fontaine des Barres
Pl de la République
Pl Jourdan
R des Pénitents Blancs
R Charles Gide
Pl Winston Churchill
R Turgot
R Couraud
To N141 & Oradour-sur-Glane (21km)
Jardin d'Orsay
Pl d'Aine
Pl St-Pierre
Lycée Gay-Lussac
R du Collège
Bd de Fleurus
R du 71e Mobile
R du Maupas
Bd St-Maurice
R Neuve St-Étienne
Cité Quarter
R des Tanneries
To Angoulême (104km)
Pl de la Motte
R du Consulat
Château Quarter
Pl des Bancs
R Jean Jaurès
Pl Wilson
R Raspail
Bd de la Cité
R Haute Cité
Pl St-Étienne
Pl de la Cathédrale
R des Argentiers
R Gondinet
R de la Boucherie
R Charles Michels
Bd Louis Blanc
Av Gabriel Péri
Pl de la Cité
R de la Cathédrale
R Pétiniaud Beaupeyrat
Bd Gambetta
R du Canal
R Haute Vienne
R Banc-Léger
R Delescluze
Pl du Forum
R du Petites Maisons
Bd de la Corderie
Jardin de l'Évêché
To A20
Av Georges Dumes
Av Baudin
R Pierre Thimbaud
Hôtel de Ville
To La Fourmi (800m); Haviland Porcelain Factory (3km); St-Léonard de Noblat (20km); Uzerche (56km); Aubusson (86km); Clermont-Ferrand (177km)
INFORMATION
Laundrette 1 B4
Laundrette 2 C5
Main Post Office 3 B3
Point Cyber 4 D3
Post Office 5 C3
TendanceWeb 6 A3
Tourist Office 7 C4
SIGHTS & ACTIVITIES
ADA 8 D2
Aquarium du Limousin 9 B5
Cathédrale St-Étienne 10 D4
Chapelle Saint-Aurélion (see 35)
Chapelle de la Règle 11 D4
Cité des Métiers et des Arts 12 D4
Cour du Temple 13 B4
Crypt of St-Martial 14 B3
Église St-Michel des Lions 15 B4
Église St-Pierre du Queyroix 16 C3
Fnac 17 B3
Galerie du Canal 18 B4
Maison de la Boucherie 19 B4
Musée de la Résistance et de la Déportation (see 11)
Musée Municipal de l'Évêché 20 D4
Musée National Adrien Dubouché 21 A3
Pavillon du Verdurier 22 C4
SLEEPING
Arthôtel Tendance 23 C1
Hôtel de la Paix 24 C3
Hôtel de Paris 25 C2
Hôtel Familia 26 D2
Hôtel Jeanne d'Arc 27 D2
Hôtel Orléans Lion d'Or 28 C3
EATING
Chez Alphonse 29 B4
Halles Centrales 30 B4
La Parenthèse (see 13)
Le 27 31 B4
Le Bistrot d'Olivier (see 30)
Le Petit Bouchon 32 B4
Les Petits Ventres 33 B4
Monoprix 34 B3
DRINKING
Le Duc Étienne 35 B4
Le Tabernacle 36 B4
L'Amicale des Parachutistes Belges 37 C4
ENTERTAINMENT
Cinéma Lido 38 D3
Grand Écran 39 A3
TRANSPORT
Bus Station (see 41)
Equival 40 A3
Le CIEL 41 D2
National-Citer 42 D2
SNCF boutique 43 A4

(porcelain). Limoges had been producing decorative enamel since at least the 12th century, but its fortunes were transformed by the discovery of kaolin near St-Yrieix-La-Perche in 1768. This china clay, a vital ingredient in porcelain manufacture, had previously been imported at huge expense from the Far East; the discovery of kaolin on home soil led to an explosion of porcelain production in Limoges in the late 18th and 19th centuries.

The **Musée National Adrien Dubouché** (☎ 05 55 33 08 50; 8bis place Winston Churchill; adult/18-25yr/under 18yr €4/2.60/free; ⌚ 10am-12.25pm & 2-5.40pm Wed-Mon Sep-Jun, 10am-5.40pm Wed-Mon Jul & Aug, 1st Sun of month free), founded by a wealthy cognac merchant with a penchant for porcelain, houses one of the two great china collections in France (the other is in Sèvres, near Paris). Spread over two floors, the museum concentrates on the golden age of Limoges porcelain, but you'll also find examples from rival factories such as Meissen, Royal Doulton and Worcester amongst the 12,000 pieces, which range from dinner services and hand-painted vases to porcelain clocks and delicate figurines. Foreign-language brochures and audioguides are available at the ticket desk.

Despite suffering a long decline during the early 20th century, many of the city's famous factories are still in business. The celebrated *marques* (brands) of **Haviland** (☎ 05 55 30 21 86; av du Président Kennedy; ⌚ factory shop 10am-1pm & 2-6pm Mon-Sat Sep-Jun, 10am-6.30pm Jul & Aug) and **Bernardaud** (☎ 05 55 10 55 91; 27 av Albert Thomas; ⌚ factory shop 9am-6.30pm Mon-Sat Oct-May, 9am-7pm Jun-Sep) both have small museums and factory shops, and offer guided tours (phone ahead for times or ask at the tourist office).

One of the oldest factories, **Porcelaine Royal Limoges** (☎ 05 55 33 27 30; 28 rue Donzalot; ⌚ shop 10am-6.30pm Mon-Sat, plus 10am-6.30pm Sun Jul & Aug, oven 11am-6pm Mon-Sat), houses the **Four des Casseaux**, the only surviving example of the mighty brick kilns originally used to fire porcelain; standing at 19.5m high and capable of reaching temperatures of 900°C to 1400°C, it certainly puts your microwave into perspective.

Keep your eyes peeled while you wander around the city: many of Limoges' buildings and public spaces are decorated with porcelain and *émail* tiles, and a number of galleries have *émail* work on display. The **Halles Centrales** (p612) has a porcelain fresco depicting the goodies on sale in the market, while on place St-Pierre is the **Pavillon du Verdurier**, an octagonal, porcelain-faced structure dating from 1900, now used as an art gallery. For more contemporary work, the **Galerie du Canal** (☎ 05 55 33 14 11; 15 rue du Canal; ⌚ 10am-noon & 2-7pm Tue-Sat Jan-Jun & Sep-Nov, 10am-noon & 2-7pm Mon-Sat Jul, Aug & Dec) is a cooperative gallery run by local enamellers.

CHÂTEAU QUARTER

This bustling corner of Limoges is the heart of the old city. Just off place St-Aurélien, the **rue de la Boucherie** – named after the butcher's shops that lined the street in the Middle Ages – contains many of the city's loveliest timbered houses. The **Maison de la Boucherie** (36 rue de la Boucherie; admission free; ⌚ 10am-1pm & 2-7pm Jul-Sep) houses a small history museum, and nearby is the tiny **Chapelle Saint-Aurélien**, dedicated to the patron saint of butchers.

A little way north is place de la Motte, home to the Halles Centrales (Covered Market) and the **Église St-Michel des Lions** (rue Adrien Dubouché), named for the two granite lions flanking the door. Built between the 14th and 16th centuries, it contains St-Martial's **relics** (including his head) and some beautiful 15th-century stained glass, but its most notable feature is the huge copper ball perched atop its 65m-high spire.

Nearby is the **Cour du Temple**, a tiny enclosed courtyard reached via an alleyway from rue du Temple. The courtyard was formerly a private garden belonging to the nearby *hôtels particuliers* (private mansions): look out for various coats-of-arms and the 16th-century stone staircase around the edge of the courtyard.

All that remains of the great pilgrimage abbey of St-Martial, founded in AD 848, is an outline on place de la République. The **Crypt of St-Martial** (⌚ mid-Jun–mid-Sep) contains the tomb of Limoges' first bishop, who converted the population to Christianity. Just to the east is the moody **Église St-Pierre du Queyroix** (place St-Pierre), notable for its characteristic Limousin belfry and stained glass.

Once you've done your cultural duty, chill out at the **Aquarium du Limousin** (☎ 05 55 33 42 11; 2 bd Gambetta; adult/12-18yr/3-12yr €6.50/5/4; ⌚ 10.30am-6.30pm), which houses 2500 fish in the subterranean surroundings of Limoges' old water reservoirs.

LA CITÉ

More fine medieval buildings can be found east of the city centre in the Cité quarter, dominated by the sombre **Cathédrale St-Étienne**, one of the few Gothic churches south of the Loire. Built between 1273 and 1888, the cathedral's famous features include the richly decorated **Portail St-Jean**, as well as a glorious rose window and a Renaissance rood screen.

Around the cathedral is the **Jardin de l'Évêché**, Limoges' botanical garden, where you'll find both medicinal and toxic herbs. At the base of the gardens is the **Musée de la Résistance et de la Déportation** (☎ 05 55 45 98 10; admission free; ⏰ 2-5pm Wed-Mon mid-Sep–May, 10am-noon & 2-6pm Wed-Mon Jun, 10am-noon & 2-6pm daily Jul–mid-Sep), temporarily housed in the **Chapelle de la Règle** during work on the municipal museum. The Limousin was a stronghold of the Resistance during WWII, and the museum has lots of intriguing material ranging from radios to weapons, diaries, letters and even a Free French aeroplane. The museum is dedicated to Georges Guingouin, a Resistance commander who subsequently became mayor of Limoges.

Near the cathedral is the **Cité des Métiers et des Arts** (☎ 05 55 32 57 84; 5 rue de la Règle; adult/child €5/2.50; ⏰ 2-6pm Wed, Sat & Sun Apr-May, 2-6pm daily Jun, Sep & Oct, 10.30am-1pm & 2.30-7pm daily Jul & Aug), which showcases work by top members of France's craft guilds.

The **Musée Municipal de l'Évêché** (☎ 05 55 45 98 10; place de la Cathédrale) was undergoing a massive refurbishment program at the time of research. Temporary exhibits from the museum's huge decorative-arts collection will be still be on display during the refurbishment – ask at the tourist office.

Sleeping

BUDGET

Hôtel de Paris (☎ 05 55 77 56 96; hoteldeparis4@wanadoo.fr; 5 cours Vergniaud; d from €35) In a typical Limoges town house on Champ-de-Juillet, this solid one-starrer is quiet, clean and convenient, but it's run on a budget. The rooms are mixed, furnished with simple bathrooms, creaky old beds and well-worn furniture; the lightest rooms overlook the square in front.

Hôtel Familia (☎ 05 55 77 51 40; www.hotelfamilia.fr; 18 rue du Général du Bessol; s €41-53, d €47-58) This small family-run hotel is the pick of the budget places near the station. Forget decorative frills – '70s bathroom suites, easy-clean fabrics and pastel colours are the order of the day – but it's good value, especially if you get a room over the flowery back garden.

MIDRANGE

Hôtel de la Paix (☎ 05 55 34 36 00; 25 place Jourdan; d €45-69, with shower & shared toilet from €41) This creaky classic is a bit faded, but it's still our favourite spot in Limoges. The ground floor is occupied by the owner's Mechanical Music Museum, stuffed with gramophones, rinky-dink record players, barrel organs and other musical oddities, while the upper corridors hide small, serviceable rooms livened up by the odd theatrical knick-knack. Chic it ain't, but it's full of charm.

Hôtel Orléans Lion d'Or (☎ 05 55 77 49 71; www.orleansliondor.com; 9 & 11 cours Jourdan; s €47-51, d €55-60, tr €63-68; **P**) Another solid, slightly drab hotel geared toward the business crowd, with the focus on convenience rather than character. Pastels and florals predominate, but it's convenient for both station and centre.

Arthôtel Tendance (☎ 05 55 77 31 72; www.arthoteltendance.com; 37 rue Armand Barbès; s/d €59/65) Quirky hotel that plunders decorative touches from across the globe. Its *chambres de thème* include a maple-clad Canadian cabin, a Balinese room with Lombok furniture, and a Grecian room decked out in whites and sea-blues. Other choices include Africa, Egypt, Provence and Morocco, all with wi-fi and LCD TVs.

Hôtel Jeanne d'Arc (☎ 05 55 77 67 77; www.hoteljeannedarc-limoges.fr; 17 av du Général de Gaulle; s €62-79, d €74-92, tr 85-95; **P**) This smart hotel (originally a *relais de poste* 'post house') makes a fine base as long as you're not after anything avant-garde. The decor's classic (checks, stripes and rich colours for the fabrics; heavy drapes and hefty furniture for the rooms), while the amenities include private parking (€5) and wi-fi (€5 per hour).

Eating

La Parenthèse (☎ 05 55 33 18 25; Cour du Temple, 22 rue du Consulat; teas €3-6, mains €6.60-9.80; ⏰ 10am-2.30pm Mon, to 6.30pm Tue-Fri, to 7pm Sat) Forty teas and 14 coffees (presented, of course, in Limoges porcelain) are served at this tearoom. For something more filling, there are home-made cakes, pastries and sweets, as well as savoury pies and gratins.

Le Bistrot d'Olivier (☎ 05 55 33 73 85; Halles Centrales; menus €10-15; ⏰ lunch Mon-Sat) Restaurants don't get more Gallic than this tiny diner inside the Halles Centrales. It's rough-and-ready – everyone from local office workers to market traders cram themselves into the benches for the lunchtime *menus* – but the cooking's as authentic as it gets. If it's full, try Chez François opposite.

Chez Alphonse (☎ 05 55 34 34 14; 5 place de la Motte; mains €11-21; ⌚ lunch & dinner Mon-Sat) Hearty ingredients, rich sauces and hard-core French cooking define Alphonse' Place. Here it's all about the food, not the frills; the menu's stuffed with regional dishes (including horse steak and veal head), so if you want to try traditional Limousine cuisine, this is definitely the place.

Le Petit Bouchon (☎ 05 55 33 35 60; 17 place de la Motte; mains from €11; ⌚ lunch Tue-Sat) This scruffy little bistro opposite the market dishes up lunchtime staples in a cosy dining room decked with old posters and straw hats above the bar.

our pick **Le 27** (☎ 05 55 32 27 27; 27 rue Haute-Vienne; mains €17-21; ⌚ lunch & dinner Mon-Sat) Limoges' freshest, funkiest place to eat, blending contemporary decor with culinary invention. Teardrop lanterns twinkle, neon lights buzz and waistcoated waiters bustle, while the menu takes in everything from gingered guinea-fowl to 'mysterious meringue'. One whole wall is taken up by the wine selection, so you won't be short of a tipple.

Les Petits Ventres (☎ 05 55 34 22 90; 20 rue de la Boucherie; menus €23.50-34; ⌚ dinner) In the old butchers' district, this atmospheric, wood-beamed restaurant specialises in meat-heavy classics, from *andouillettes* (tripe sausages) to *fricassée de rognons* (fried kidneys). Veggies should probably look elsewhere.

SELF-CATERING

Limoges' covered market, the **Halles Centrales** (place de la Motte; ⌚ to 1pm), is full of local-produce stalls that run the gourmet gamut from local cheese to Limousin beef. For the basics, try **Monoprix** (42 rue Jean Jaurès; ⌚ 8.30am-8.30pm Mon-Sat).

Drinking

The large student crowd keeps Limoges' nightspots ticking; you'll find most of the drinking holes around rue Charles Michels.

L'Amicale des Parachutistes Belges (☎ 05 55 10 12 39; 17 rue Charles Michels; ⌚ 7pm-2am) Belgian beers and a buzzy gig scene are the draws at this scruffy boozer on rue Charles Michels. Soul, funk, ragga and rock acts regularly grace the stage.

La Fourmi (☎ 05 55 34 54 13; 3 rue de la Font Pinot; ⌚ 9pm-5am Wed-Sat) The best place in town for musos, with breaking acts, alternative bands and theatrical spectacles in a twin-floored warehouse-style space. It's a bit out of town, but worth the trek.

Le Duc Étienne (place St-Aurélien; ⌚ 2pm-1am Mon-Wed, to 2am Thu-Sat) A long-standing hangout in the medieval quarter, with a snug little bar dishing out European beers and late-night coffee to a pre-club crowd. In summer things spill onto the terrace in front of Église St-Aurélien.

Le Tabernacle (☎ 05 55 34 69 80; 19 rue de la Loi; ⌚ 11pm-4am Wed-Thu, to 5am Fri & Sat) Part pub, part club, part grungy gig venue, this is another good place to check out Limoges' late-night music scene. Bare brick and industrial styling conjure up a lived-in vibe.

Entertainment

Event tickets are sold at **Fnac** (☎ 08 25 02 00 20; 8 rue des Combes; ⌚ 2-7pm Mon, 10am-7pm Tue-Sat).

Limoges has two cinemas – the multiplex **Grand Écran** (☎ 0 892 682 015; 9-11 place Denis Dussoubs) and the artier **Cinéma Lido** (☎ 05 36 68 20 15; 3 av du Général de Gaulle).

Getting There & Away

AIR

Just off the A20, **Limoges International Airport** (☎ 05 55 43 30 30; www.aeroportlimoges.com, in French) is 10km west of Limoges, with domestic connections including Paris Orly, Toulouse, Nice and Strasbourg. It's also served by British budget carriers Ryanair (London Stansted, Nottingham and Liverpool) and Flybe (Southampton), while Air France flies to Edinburgh and Manchester. There's no shuttle bus into town; a taxi takes 15 minutes and costs around €20.

BUS & TRAIN

Limoges is the main bus hub for the Haute-Vienne *département*, administered by **Equival** (☎ 05 55 10 10 03; www.equival.fr; 14 rue de l'Amphithéâtre; ⌚ 9am-6pm Mon-Fri). The bus station is across the tracks from the train station.

The area is split into five zones, with tariffs based on how many zones you cross. Bus 12 goes to Oradour-sur-Glane (€3, 45 minutes, five daily Monday to Saturday), buses 14 and 21 service Rochechouart (€4, one hour, four to six daily Monday to Saturday), and SNCF line 9 coaches travel to St-Léonard de Noblat (€4, 30 minutes, five to eight daily).

CAR

Hire cars from **ADA** (☎ 05 55 79 61 12; 27 av du Général de Gaulle) or **National-Citer** (☎ 05 55 77 10 10; 3 cours Bugeaud).

TRAIN

Completed in 1929, the stunning art-deco **Gare des Bénédictins** (☎ 08 36 35 35 35) is one of France's finest, graced by a copper dome, carved frescoes and an elegant clock tower, restored following a 1997 fire.

Destinations include Paris' Gare d'Austerlitz (€49, three hours, hourly), Périgueux (€14.30, one hour, daily), Cahors (€28.70, 2¼ hours, four daily), Brive-la-Gaillarde (€16.90, one hour, 15 to 18 daily), Tulle (€13.50, 1¼ hours, five to seven daily) and Aubusson (€13.40, 1¾ hours, three daily Monday to Saturday, one on Sunday). Tickets can be bought at the station and at the town-centre **SNCF boutique** (4 rue Othon Péconnet; 9am-7pm Mon-Sat).

WEST OF LIMOGES

Rochechouart & Chassenon

pop 3815

There are two reasons to visit the walled town of **Rochechouart**, 45km west of Limoges: meteorites and modern art. Rochechouart witnessed one of the most devastating impacts in Earth's history 200 million years ago when a massive 1.5km-radius lump of intergalactic rock slammed into the Earth at 72,000km/h with the force of 14 million Hiroshima bombs. The impact site, 4km west of town, created a crater 20km wide and 6km deep, but the only visible traces are the unusual rocks, frequently used as local building material, left behind by the massive explosion. The **Éspace Météorite Paul Pellas** (☎ 05 55 03 02 70; 16 rue Jean-Parvy; adult/under 15yr €4/free; 10am-noon & 1.30-6pm Mon-Fri Jul & Aug, 2-6pm Sat & Sun Sep-Jun) explores this cosmic cataclysm through minerals, models and video displays.

A typically French blend of architectural adventure and artistic invention, the **Musée Départemental d'Art Contemporain** (☎ 05 55 03 77 91; place du Château; adult/12-16yr/under 12yr €4.60/3/free; 10am-12.30pm & 1.30-6pm Mar-Sep, 10am-12.30pm & 1.30-5pm Oct-Feb), is housed in the town's refurbished château. Highlights include a collection of works by the Dadaist Raoul Haussman and sculptures by the 'German School', as well as an installation of white stones by the British artist Richard Long in a room decorated by 16th-century frescoes.

LA VILLAGE MARTYR

On the afternoon of 10 June, 1944, the little town of **Oradour-sur-Glane**, 21km northwest of Limoges, witnessed one of the worst Nazi war crimes committed on French soil. German lorries belonging to the SS 'Das Reich' Division surrounded the town and ordered the population on to the market square. The men were divided into groups and forced into *granges* (barns), where they were machine-gunned before the structures were set alight. Several hundred women and children were herded into the church, and the building was set on fire, along with the rest of the town. Only one woman and five men survived the massacre; 642 people, including 193 children, were killed. Chillingly, the same SS Division committed a similarly brutal act in Tulle two days earlier, in which 99 Resistance sympathisers were strung up from the town's balconies as a macabre warning to others.

Since these events, the entire **village** (admission free; 9am-7pm mid-May–mid-Sep, 9am-6pm mid-Sep–Oct & Mar–mid-May, 9am-5pm Nov-Feb) has been left untouched, complete with tram tracks, pre-war electricity lines, the blackened shells of buildings and the rusting hulks of 1930s automobiles – an evocative memorial to a once-peaceful village caught up in the brutal tide of war. At the centre of the village is an underground memorial inscribed with the victims' names; poignantly, there are also display cases collecting their recovered belongings, including watches, wallets, hairpins and a couple of children's bikes.

Entry is via the **Centre de la Mémoire** (adult/7-18yr, student & veteran €7.50/5.20), which contextualises the massacre using historical exhibitions, video displays and survivors' testimonies. Various theories have been put forward to try to explain the event – perhaps German panic following the Allied landings four days earlier, or reprisal for sabotage raids committed by the Resistance following the invasion – but it may one of those terrible events that simply defies any rational explanation.

After the war, Oradour was rebuilt a few hundred metres west of the ruins. Several buses travel from the bus station in Limoges to Oradour-sur-Glane (€3, 30 minutes, daily except Sundays in winter). By car, take the D9 and follow signs to the *village martyr* (martyred village).

THE LION OF THE LIMOUSIN

The spectre of Richard, Coeur de Lion (Richard the Lion-Heart), looms over the Haute-Vienne *région*. The crusading king waged several bloody campaigns here in the 12th century before meeting his end at the now-ruined keep of **Château de Chalûs-Chabrol,** 40km west of Limoges, where he was mortally wounded by a crossbowman in 1199. Legend has it that once the keep was captured, Richard pardoned the crossbowman (actually a young boy), before expiring on 6 April 1199 in the arms of his mother, Eleanor of Aquitaine. Richard's heart was buried in Rouen (p266), his brain in the abbey of Charroux in Poitiers and his body in the Abbaye de Fontevraud (p447) beside his father, Henry II; rather unsportingly, the crossbowman was later skinned alive by Richard's captain, Mercadier.

There are several other medieval châteaux and monuments nearby that share a Lionheart connection: pick up the leaflet *Route de Richard Coeur de Lion* from local tourist offices.

About 5km from Rochechouart are the Gallo-Roman baths of **Chassenon** (☎ 05 45 89 32 21; adult/child €5/2.50; ⏰ 10am-7pm Jul–mid-Sep, 2-5.30pm mid-Sep–mid-Nov & Mar-May, 10am-noon & 2-7pm Jun). Discovered in 1844 and excavated in 1958, this luxurious former way station known to the Romans as *Cassinomagnus* was an important crossroads on the Via Agrippa, the road that crossed France via Saintes, Périgueux, Limoges, Clermont-Ferrand and Lyon. Much of the complex (including a temple and amphitheatre) were plundered for stone, but you can still make out the baths, plunge pools and hypocausts, the Roman equivalent of underfloor heating.

Sleeping and Eating

OUR PICK Domaine des Chapelles (☎ 05 55 78 29 91; www.domainedeschapelles.com; Oradour-sur-Vayres; d €55-90, villas per week €390-540; ♿ P) This former shepherd's barn, in open countryside near Oradour-sur-Vayres, has been transformed into a swish, sexy hideaway. In five impeccably finished rooms, walk-in showers, hi-fis and cappuccino-and-cream colour schemes sit alongside exposed stone, rustic tiles and private terraces. For utter privacy, try the self-contained villas, which have designer kitchens, wood-burning stoves, heated pool and even a rental quad bike. The country restaurant (mains €15 to €25) is also superb (check out the funky sheep murals!). Wheelchair access available.

La Météorite (☎ 05 55 02 86 80; www.hotel-lameteorite.fr; 1 place Marquet; d €55-85) A sweet little hotel in Rochechouart with a touch of quirky flair. The seven rooms are all cosy and different, from apple-green doubles to more spacious suites with pine headboards, rustic brick and original beams.

Getting There & Away

There are buses to Rochechouart from Limoges (see p613).

EAST OF LIMOGES

Guéret & Bourganeuf

pop (Guéret) 15,000 / pop (Bourganeuf) 3500

The busy town of **Guéret** grew up around a 12th-century monastery and the 15th-century Château de Moneyroux, now the administrative HQ for the *conseil general* of the Creuse *département*, of which Guéret is capital. Guéret itself isn't that exciting, but it's a handy base for exploring nearby attractions, including the fascinating wolf sanctuary at **Le Parc Animalier des Monts de Guéret** (☎ 05 55 81 23 23; www.loups-chabrieres.com; adult/4-12yr €7.50/6; ⏰ 10am-8pm May–mid-Sep, 1.30-6pm Feb-Apr & mid-Sep–Nov), where black and grey wolves roam free across a 12-hectare park, and the **Labyrinthe Géant** (Giant Maze; ☎ 05 55 41 01 97; ⏰ 10am-8pm Fri-Wed, plus 10am-10pm Thu Jul & Aug, 2-7pm weekends only Easter-Jun & Sep-Nov), where you can get well and truly lost in the middle of one of France's largest mazes, 3km from Guéret.

The bourgeois town of **Bourganeuf** is also worth a stroll, especially for its atmospheric old town; its main claim to fame came in 1886, when it became one of the first places in France to be connected to mains electricity. The **Musée de l'Électrification, de l'Eau et de la Lumière** (☎ 05 55 64 26 26; rte de la Cascade; 10am-noon & 2-6pm Mon-Sat Jul & Aug; €4) explores this electrifying event .

South of Bourganeuf, the Limousin is at its lushest and loveliest, especially around **Plateau de Millevaches** and the glassy **Lac de Vassivière** (www.vassiviere.com), a popular spot for water sports and afternoon picnics.

Sleeping & Eating

La Ferme de la Gorce (☎ 05 55 41 11 55; fermedelagorce@wanadoo.fr; 86 av du Limousin, Guéret; d from €60; P) A mile from Guéret, this charming farm-stay is a reassuringly rustic base, with plenty of wood and solid stone in the low-ceilinged bedrooms, and friendly hosts who are full of info on the surrounding area.

our pick **Abbaye du Palais** (☎ 05 55 64 02 64; www.abbayedupalais.com; d from €65, ste €85-150, cottages per week €550-1450; P) Between Bourganeuf and Guéret, this bewitching B&B is one of the loveliest places in the Creuse: a former Cistercian abbey turned cosy family home, run by a Dutch couple. Cats, dogs, rabbits and kids charge around the grounds, where you'll find the ruins of a chapel, a monks' dorm and a pet farm. Inside the grand house are three doubles and four suites filled with antiques, tapestries and fireplaces, and outside there are self-contained *gîtes* (cottages for rent) in refurbished outbuildings. There's even a 'cookery clinic' if you fancy polishing up your knife skills.

Le Moulin Noyé (☎ 05 55 52 81 44; www.moulin-noyé.com; Glénic; mains around €25) This backcountry restaurant a mile northwest of Guéret is a fave of local gourmets and restaurant guides, so you can be assured of a slap-up feed. The restaurant's focus is on local produce, from lake fish to hearty slabs of Limousin beef, and the dining room overlooks wooded countryside above the Creuse river. The enticing upstairs rooms are all named after composers.

Aubusson

pop 4250

Along with pottery and porcelain, the northern Limousin is famous for its **tapestries**, which once adorned the walls of aristocratic houses from London to the Loire Valley. The small town of **Aubusson**, 90km east of Limoges, was once the clacking centre of French carpet production, rivalled only by the Gobelins factories in Paris. Characterised by their vivid colours, fine detail and exquisite craftsmanship, Aubusson's tapestries were true works of art and took pride of place in many of the country's grandest châteaux. Following the French Revolution, the industry suffered a steady decline before being revived after WWII by inventive new designers such as Jean Lurçat and Sylvaine Dubuisson.

Today, there are around 20 tapestry workshops in Aubusson and nearby Felletin (10km south). The **tourist office** (☎ 05 55 66 32 12; rue Vieille; tourisme.aubusson@wanadoo.fr; 10am-7pm Mon-Sat, 10am-noon & 2.30-5.30pm Sun Jul & Aug, 9.30am-12.30pm & 2-6pm Mon-Sat Jun & Sep), in Aubusson, arranges visits to local tapestry *ateliers* (workshops), and can supply you with a list of local galleries and showrooms.

Recent work is displayed at the **Exposition Tapisseries d'Aubusson–Felletin** (☎ 05 55 66 32 12; Grande Rue; admission €3; 9am-12.30pm & 2-6pm Jun & Sep, 9am-6pm daily Jul & Aug), inside Aubusson's town hall.

For a historical overview, head to the **Musée Départemental de la Tapisserie** (☎ 05 55 83 08 30; av des Lissiers; adult/child €4/2.50; 9.30am-noon & 2-6pm Wed-Mon Jun & Sep, 9.30am-6pm Jul & Aug), which houses wonderful examples of both antique and modern tapestries produced in Aubusson. The **Maison de Tapissier** (☎ 05 55 66 32 12; rue Vieille; adult/12-18yr/under 12yr €5/3/free; 9.30am-12.30pm & 2-6pm Mon-Sat, plus 10am-noon & 2.30-5.30pm Sun Easter-Sep), in a 16th-century mansion in the middle of Aubusson, is also worth a visit: various exhibits recreate the atmosphere of a 17th-century weaver's workshop, with tools, original furniture and (of course) plenty of vintage tapestries.

SLEEPING & EATING

Villa Adonis (☎ 05 55 66 46 00; www.villa-adonis.com; 14 av de la République; d €52; P) From the funky watch-battery keys to the flat-screen TVs, power showers and stripped-back colour schemes, this excellent hotel on Aubusson's outskirts has an edge of big-city style. All rooms overlook a lovely garden, and the buffet breakfast includes fresh fruit jams and proper espresso.

L'Hôtel de France (☎ 05 55 66 10 22; www.aubussonlefrance.com; 6 rue des Déportés; d €59-95) Former post house turned upmarket Logis de France with 23 plush rooms – some modern, some old-fashioned and frilly, some tucked into the attic with sloping ceilings and roof beams. The restaurant's the best in town, with a smorgasbord of Limousine dishes served to the tune of a tinkling lounge piano.

SOUTH OF LIMOGES

Solignac

pop 1350

In the thickly wooded Briance valley, 10km south of Limoges, the tiny medieval village of Solignac was a major stop on the pilgrimage route to Santiago de Compostela. Its

LIVE LIKE A KING

For the aristocratic high life, how about a night or three in a fairy-tale château?

Château de Castel-Novel (☎ 05 55 85 09 03; www.castelnovel.com; Varetz; d €108-340; P) Immortalised by the French author Colette, who based herself here while writing *Le Blé en Herbe* and *Chéri,* this château 10km north of Brive-la-Gaillarde is a beauty. Topped by turrets, gables and slate tiles, filled with idiosyncratic rooms (including a turret room and Colette's Louis XVI apartment), and surrounded by sweeping lawns and an 18th-century orangery, it's no wonder Madame Colette found it inspiring.

our pick **Château les Merles** (☎ 05 53 63 13 42; www.lesmerles.com; Tuilières; d €120-180, ste €220-290; P) Despite its 19th-century neoclassical facade, this eye-popping hotel is a study in modish minimalism: black-and-white sofas, slate-grey throws and monochrome colour schemes run throughout the rooms, most of which would look more at home in downtown Paris than the deep Dordogne. It's got wit, style and sexiness in spades: tripod floor lamps, gilt-framed mirrors, just-so objets d'art and an utterly ravishing fusion restaurant to boot. 'Boutique' just doesn't do it justice.

Château Ribagnac (☎ 05 55 39 77 91; www.chateauribagnac.com; St Martin-Terressus; r €220-265; P) This aristocratic estate 25 minutes west of Limoges is owned by two British ex-lawyers, whose struggles to renovate the château were documented in the fly-on-the-wall UK TV series *No Going Back*. Despite the ups and downs, it's a real palace, with rooms ranging from a chandelier-lit grand suite to a super romantic honeymoon suite complete with its own balcony.

11th-century church is a Romanesque wonder, renowned for its 14m-wide domed roof. The stalls in the nave are decorated with carved wooden sculptures of human heads, fantastical animals and a monk mooning the world, and the columns depict human figures being devoured by dragons.

Five kilometres southeast are the ruins of the **Château de Chalucet,** a 12th-century keep occupied by the English during the Hundred Years War. The ruins make a fine picnic spot, with valley views from the tumbledown keep. Nearby in Le Vigen, the **Parc Zoologique du Reynou** (☎ 05 55 00 40 00; www.parczooreynou.com; adult/3-12yr €10.50/7.50; 10am-8pm Apr-Sep, 10am-7pm Wed, Sat & Sun Oct-Mar, last entry 2 hr before closing) is a 35-hectare safari park established on land once owned by the Haviland dynasty. Its exotic denizens include wolves, giraffes, wildebeest, snowy owls and a pair of breeding tigers.

Hôtel Le St-Eloi (☎ 05 55 00 44 52; www.promenades-gourmandes.com; 66 av St-Eloi; d €55-85) is about the only place to stay nearby, with 15 sunny rooms inside a shuttered building opposite the church. The ones with jacuzzis and terraces are fantastic value, and half board is available at the **restaurant** (mains €16-22; lunch & dinner, closed Sun evening).

Three or four buses daily (except Sunday) link Limoges with Solignac (€3, 25 minutes) and Le Vigen (€3, 35 minutes). The Solignac–Le Vigen train station is linked to Limoges (€3, 10 minutes) and Uzerche (€9.60, 40 minutes) by several trains daily.

Arnac-Pompadour

pop 1280

The village of Arnac-Pompadour revolves around its **château**, notorious for its association with the mistress of Louis XV, Madame de Pompadour (born Jeanne-Antoinette Poisson). Having been presented the château in 1745, the *madame* actually stayed here, but she also helped develop Arnac into one of France's foremost *haras* (stud farms) – hence the village's local moniker, *Cité de Cheval* (*cheval* is French for 'horse'). Renowned for its Anglo-Arab pedigrees, Arnac-Pompadour became an Haras National in 1872. You can arrange visits to the château, the *écuries des étalons* (stallions' stables) and the *jumenterie de la rivière* (mares' stable) by contacting **Les Trois Tours** (☎ 05 55 98 51 10; www.les3tours-pompadour.com) at the château, or asking at the **tourist office** (☎ 05 55 98 55 47; www.pompadour.net; 9.30am-6pm daily Jul & Aug, 9.30am-noon & 1.30-6pm daily May & Jun & Sep, 10am-noon & 1.30-4.30pm Mon-Sat Oct-Apr). There are regular race meetings, as well as a grand horse show on 15 August and a whole day dedicated to the humble *âne* (donkey) on 14 July.

Arnac-Pompadour is about 60km south of Limoges, from where there are daily trains

(€10.30, 1¼ hours, six to eight daily Monday to Saturday).

Uzerche

pop 3500

The walled town of Uzerche, teetering on a promontory above the rushing Vézère River, is one of the Limousin's most appealing hilltop hamlets. The village's main attraction is its medieval architecture, including the **Porte Bécharie**, one of the nine original gates that granted access to the village in the 14th century, and the 15th- and 16th-century **maisons à tourelles** (turret houses), whose spiky turrets jut out from the walls like witches' hats. From the main gate Uzerche's single street leads uphill to the **Église St-Pierre**, a fortified church with one of the oldest crypts in the Limousin, dating from the 11th century. In front of the church there's a fine panorama over the river valley from place de la Lunade, which takes its name from a pagan summer solstice (now rejigged as a Christian procession).

The **tourist office** (☎ 05 55 73 15 71; www.pays-uzerche.com; place de la Libération; ⌚ 10am-7pm Mon-Fri, 10am-12.30pm & 2.30-6.30pm Sat & Sun Jul & Aug, 10am-noon & 2-6pm daily late Jun & early Sep, 10am-noon Mon-Fri mid-Sep–mid-Jun) is near the church, and sells work by local artists (including patchwork teddy bears and handmade pottery).

SLEEPING & EATING

There are only a couple of hotels in Uzerche, the best of which is **Hôtel Jean Teyssier** (☎ 05 55 73 10 05; www.hotel-teyssier.com; rue du Pont-Turgot; d €54-78; P), pleasantly placed below the village beside the river. Despite its well-worn exterior, inside you'll find a comfortable modern hotel: the 14 rooms are fresh and well furnished (expect magnolia walls and country-style fabrics), and downstairs there's a restaurant serving Limousin staples (mains €16 to €25), with a panoramic dining room overlooking the river.

The other choice is **Hôtel Ambroise** (☎ 05 55 73 28 60; hotelambroise@orange.fr; av Charles de Gaulle; d €35-65; ⌚ closed Nov) with snug, old-fashioned rooms (some with river views) and a pleasant **restaurant** (menus €15-31) beside the hotel gardens.

GETTING THERE & AWAY

Uzerche is linked to Limoges, 56km to the north, by train (€9.60, 40 minutes, six to eight daily). The train station is 2km north of the old city along the N20.

BRIVE-LA-GAILLARDE

pop 49,900

The main commercial and administrative centre for the Corrèze *département* is Brive-la-Gaillarde, best known for its rugby team (currently coached by former national player Olivier Magne) and hectic weekly markets, which burst into life every Tuesday, Thursday and Saturday on the central place du 14 Juillet. Apart from the market, the town's short on sights, but it's a good base for exploring the Corrèze.

The **tourist office** (☎ 05 55 24 08 80; www.brive-tourisme.com; place du 14 Juillet; ⌚ 9am-7pm Mon-Sat, 3-7pm Sun Jul & Aug, 9am-12.30pm & 1.30-6pm Mon-Sat Apr-Jun & Sep, 9am-noon & 2-6pm Mon-Sat Oct-Mar) is housed in a former water tower, locally known as the *phare* (lighthouse), overlooking the market square.

Sights & Activities

The town's main museum is the **Musée Labenche** (☎ 50 55 18 17 70; www.musee-labenche.com; 26bis, bd Jules-Ferry; adult/child €4.70/2.50; ⌚ 10am-6.30pm Wed-Mon Apr-Oct, 1.30-6pm Wed-Mon Nov-Mar) with exhibits exploring local history and archeology, as well as a unique collection of 17th-century English tapestries and a piano that once belonged to Debussy.

The **Maison Denoix** (☎ 05 55 74 34 27; 9 bd du Maréchal-Lyautey; admission free; ⌚ 9am-noon & 2.30-7pm Tue-Sat Sep-Jun, Mon-Sat Jul & Aug) is a traditional distillery that since 1839 has been producing the favourite local tipple of the Corrèze, *l'eau de noix* (walnut liqueur), alongside more adventurous concoctions such as chocolate liqueur, quince liqueur and curaçao. You can wander around the old copper cauldrons and stills, or take a guided tour at 2.30pm on Tuesdays and Thursdays in July and August. There's also a well-stocked shop where you can sample the wares.

The Romanesque **Collegiale St-Martin**, in the heart of town, dates from the 11th century, but it's taken a battering over the centuries: the only original parts are the transept and a few decorated columns depicting fabulous beasties and Biblical scenes.

Sleeping and Eating

Hôtel Andrea (☎ 05 67 73 29 93; www.landrea.fr; 39 av Jean-Jaurès; d €35-55) A decent budget choice near the station, offering cheap and cheery rooms above a café-bar. The budget price buys dated bathrooms, tiny TVs and a bit of street noise, but the cheerful interior keeps things bright and welcoming.

Hôtel du Chapon Fin (☎ 05 55 74 23 40; www.chaponfin-brive.com; 1 place de Lattre-de-Tassigny; s/d/tr from

TULLE ACCORDIONS

Whether its Édith Piaf, Johnny Hallyday or Parisian hiphop, France has always been fiercely proud of its musical heritage, and there's nothing more Gallic than the sound of an **accordion** pumping out a few traditional tunes from a street corner. Ask any accordion aficionado where the world's finest instruments are made, and chances are they'll all give you the same answer: the industrial town of **Tulle**, 28km northeast of Brive. A single accordion consists of between 3500 and 6800 parts and requires up to 200 hours' labour, so mass production has never been an option. The very best instruments can fetch a staggering €9000.

Tulle's celebrated **Maugein factory** (☎ 05 55 20 08 89; rte de Brive; 🕑 8am-noon & 2-5.30pm Mon-Thu) is one of the town's oldest accordion makers, and guided visits are free by reservation. You can see the craftspeople at work, browse the accordion museum, and maybe even pick up an instrument for yourself.

If you're in town in mid-September, check out the **Nuits de Nacre**, an annual four-day street music festival in which the accordion, of course, takes centre stage.

€53/63/78; 💻) The rooms in this smart white-shuttered hotel are all spick-and-span and contemporary, although the colour schemes are occasionally eye-searing – ask for one overlooking the park. Free wi-fi.

La Truffe Noire (☎ 05 55 92 45 00; www.la-truffe-noire.com; 22 bd Anatole-France; d €110-130) By far the town's top spot, this grand old girl has 30 rooms decked out in stylish fashion: beige and cream fabrics, flat-screen TVs, big beds and the odd beam or two. The rooms are swish, but the restaurant's even better: expect rich Limousin food with a price tag to match (mains €15 to €30).

Getting There and Away

Brive is a major rail and bus junction – there are regular trains to all the main regional towns, including Limoges (€16.90, one hour, 15 to 18 daily), Périgueux (€11.50, 50 minutes, six to eight daily) and Cahors (€14.90, one hour, eight to 10 daily). For trains to Sarlat (€8.70, 1¼ to 1½ hours, three to five daily), you'll need to change at Souillac. The **bus station** (☎ 05 55 17 91 19; place du 14 Juillet; 🕑 8.15am-noon & 2-6.15pm Mon-Sat) is next to the tourist office.

The **train station** (av Jean Jaurès) is 1.3km from the town centre and the tourist office, and can be reached via most buses heading south out of town.

EAST OF BRIVE

Gimel-les-Cascades

This tiny, typically Corrèzien village is one of the region's prettiest, with a huddle of slate roofs, flower-filled balconies and higgledy-piggledy cottages gathered along the banks of a rushing brook. In summer it can feel far from peaceful, though, especially once the day trippers and coach tours roll in. But visit out of season and you might well have it all to yourself. It's a place to wander the lanes, drink in the atmosphere, and stroll along the banks of the river. The three crashing **Cascades**, after which the village is named, are reached via a riverside path at the foot of the village. The local church also contains a beautiful enamelled reliquary known as the **Châsse de St-Étienne**, made in the 12th century by Limoges craftsmen.

Other nearby sights include the remains of the Cistercian **Abbaye d'Aubazine** (☎ 05 55 84 61 12; 🕑 guided visits 10.30am, 3pm & 4pm Jul & Aug, rest of year by appointment) and the **Étang de Ruffaud**, a glassy pond that offers a refreshing dip and a shady place for a picnic.

Gimel's seasonal **tourist office** (☎ 05 55 21 44 32; www.gimellescascades.fr; 🕑 10am-6pm Jul & Aug) is 50m up the hill from the church.

The **Hostellerie de la Vallée** (☎ 05 55 21 40 60; hostellerie_de_la_vallee@hotmail.com; d €53-56.50; 🕑 Mar-Dec) makes for a sweet stopover, with nine small, pleasant rooms tucked around the corridors of an old stone cottage in the heart of the village. The restaurant is a down-home treat, too, with an old-fashioned dining room and plenty of hearty dishes including rabbit and beef stew.

SOUTH OF BRIVE

Rolling countryside and green pastures unfold south of Brive to the banks of the Dordogne and the border with northern Quercy (p647).

Turenne

pop 770

Rising up from a solitary spur of rock, the hilltop village of Turenne is an arresting sight:

honey-coloured stone cottages and wonky houses are stacked up like dominoes beneath the towering **château** (☎ 05 55 85 90 66; www.chateau-turenne.com; adult/10-18yr/under 10yr €3.80/2.60/free; 10am-7pm Jul & Aug, 10am-noon & 2-6pm Apr-Jun, 2-5pm Sun or by reservation Sep-Mar), built to protect the feudal seat of the Vicomtes de Turenne. The castle's most upstanding feature is the Tour de César, an arrow-straight tower which provides heart-melting views of the surrounding countryside. Apart from a few ramparts and a 14th-century guard room, the rest of the castle and lordly lodgings have crumbled away, and are now occupied by an ornamental garden.

The **tourist office** (☎ 05 55 85 94 38; 9am-12.30pm & 2.30-6.30pm Jul & Aug, 10am-12.30pm & 3-6pm Apr-Jun & Sep) is at the base of the village, and runs guided visits (adult/child under 12 years costs €4/free) as well as night-time costumed promenades in summer.

From Brive, there are usually three daily buses from Monday to Saturday (35 minutes); if you're catching a train (€3, 15 minutes), you'll arrive at **Turenne Gare**, 3km southeast of the village, and will have to make your way on foot.

Collonges-la-Rouge

pop 50

Red by name, red by nature, Collonges-la-Rouge is one of the classic postcard villages of the Corrèze, with its skyline of conical turrets, rickety rooftops and rust-coloured houses. The part-Romanesque **church**, constructed from the 11th to the 15th centuries on an 8th-century Benedictine priory, was an important resting place on the pilgrimage to Santiago de Compostela. In a stirring show of ecclesiastical unity, during the late 16th century local Protestants held prayers in the southern nave and their Catholic neighbours prayed in the northern nave. Nearby, the slate roof of the ancient **covered market** shelters an ancient baker's oven.

The **tourist office** (☎ 05 55 25 47 57; www.ot-pays-de-collonges-la-rouge.fr; 10am-7pm Jul & Aug, 10am-12.30pm & 2-6pm Apr-Jun & Sep, 10am-noon & 2-5pm Mon-Sat Oct-Mar) is next to the town hall on the village's 'main' road, off the D38.

Jeanne Maison d'Hôtes (☎ 05 55 25 42 31; www.jeannemaisondhotes.com; r incl breakfast €90) is a grandiose B&B in a towering 15th-century *maison bourgeoise* on the village's edge that is a real home away from home. The five rooms all have quirky fixtures and antique furniture, from writing desks and decorative screens to chaises longues and latticed windows (our favourite is the chimney room, with its own enormous inglenook fireplace). The home-cooked dinners are a delight too – and a steal at €32 with wine.

Relais du Quercy (☎ 05 55 25 40 31; www.relaisduquercy.com.fr; Meyssac; d €52-65; P) is a mile or so down the road in the village of Meyssac. It is a jaunty little hotel, complete with slate roof, brick facade and backyard swimming pool. The rooms are comfy and cosy, if unremarkable. The nicest look out over the rear terrace, but all have TVs with Canal+, spick-and-span bathrooms and soft beds.

Collonges is linked by bus with Brive, 18km to the northwest along the D38 (€4, 30 minutes, four to six daily on weekdays and one on Saturday).

Beaulieu-sur-Dordogne

pop 1300

Peacefully perched on a curve of the Dordogne near northern Quercy, and hemmed in by lush woods and fields, Beaulieu (literally, beautiful place) fully deserves its name. Like Collonges, the town was once an important stop for Compostela pilgrims, and the beautifully preserved medieval quarter is one of the region's finest: a network of curving lanes lined with timber-framed houses and smart mansions, many dating from the 14th and 15th centuries.

The **tourist office** (☎ 05 55 91 09 94; www.beaulieu-sur-dordogne.fr; place Marbot; 9.30am-1pm & 2.30-7pm Jul & Aug, 9.30am-12.30pm & 2.30-6pm Mon-Sat, 9.30am-12.30pm Sun Apr-Jun & Sep, 10am-12.30pm & 2.30-5pm Oct-Mar) is on the main square.

Beaulieu's most celebrated feature is the **Abbatiale St-Pierre**, a 12th-century Romanesque abbey church with a wonderful **tympanum** (c 1130) depicting scenes from the Last Judgment including dancing apostles and resurrected sinners. Nearby is the **Faubourg de la Chapelle**, a neighbourhood of 17th- and 18th-century houses, and the **Chapelle des Pénitents**, built to accommodate pious parishioners – access to the abbey church was strictly reserved for monks and paying pilgrims.

Beaulieu's biggest event is the **Fête de la Fraise** (Strawberry Festival) held to mark the harvest in mid-May. Strawberry-focussed events fill the town's streets, including strawberry auctions, strawberry parades and the eating of a gargantuan strawberry tart to close the festival in style.

SLEEPING & EATING

Auberge de Jeunesse (☎ 05 55 91 13 82; www.fuaj.org/aj/beaulieu; place du Monturu; dm €11.60-15.20; ⏰ Apr-Oct) Parts of this quirky little hostel date from the 15th century, and it certainly looks vintage: latticed windows and a miniature turret decorate the exterior, while inside you'll find a cosy chimney-side lounge, well-stocked kitchen and dinky four-bed rooms, all with private bathrooms.

Camping des Îles (☎ 05 55 91 02 65; www.camping-des-iles.net; per person €11.90-18.90; ⏰ Apr-Oct) This shady campsite is on an island sandwiched between two branches of the Dordogne. Its three-star facilities include tennis courts and a children's play area.

Auberge Les Charmilles (☎ 05 55 91 29 29; www.auberge-charmilles.com; 20 bd Rodolphe de Turenne; d from €60) Beaulieu's strawberry fetish continues at the Charmilles, where the rooms of the *maison bourgeoise* are named after different types of the summer berry. The decor's fresh and fruity, with puffy bedspreads, summery bathrooms, wooden floors and wi-fi. The best rooms overlook garden and river. The restaurant specialises in traditional duck and meat dishes (menus €19 to €45), and there's a waterside terrace for summer suppers.

Le Château de Doux (☎ 05 55 91 94 00; www.chateaududoux.com; Altillac; s €63-66, d €69-71; 🅟) Just across the river from Beaulieu is this age-old beauty, a hilltop château turned country hotel surrounded by 3 hectares of private park. All the château trappings are present and correct – sweeping staircase, vaulted lobby, wooden rafters, creaky corridors – and the 21 rooms are fittingly Olde Worlde.

Manoir de Beaulieu (☎ 05 55 91 01 34; www.manoirdebeaulieu.com; 4 place du Champ-de-Mars; s €65-85, d €75-155; 🅟) Half old-fashioned auberge, half modern pamper-pad, this smart village-centre hotel is a find. The rooms mix the best of old and new – stripped wood floors, glass sinks and digital TVs meet solid furniture, velvet armchairs, and the odd cartwheel or reclaimed desk. It's pricey and posh, but a super place to splash, and the courtyard restaurant is superb (mains €17 to €42).

Beaulieu's market is on Wednesday and Saturday mornings, and there are grocery stores on place Marbot, near the tourist office.

GETTING THERE & AWAY

Beaulieu is 70km east of Sarlat-la-Canéda and 47km northeast of Gouffre de Padirac (p647).

From Monday to Saturday, there are buses linking Beaulieu with Brive (€6.50, one hour, one to three daily).

THE DORDOGNE

Rich food, heady history and rolling countryside sum up the delightful Dordogne. Long a favourite place of escape for second-homing Brits and French families on *les grandes vacances*, it remains one of the most popular parts of France. During the Hundred Years War the Dordogne marked the frontier between French and English forces, and the area is sometimes known as the 'Land of 1001 Châteaux' thanks to its abundance of historic castles. But the castle-builders weren't the first to settle on the riverbanks; Cro-Magnon man was here long before, and the Vézère Valley has the most spectacular series of prehistoric cave paintings anywhere in Europe, including the astonishing Grotte de Lascaux (p634) near Montignac.

Strictly speaking, the Dordogne is a *département*, not a region: this area is better known to the French as the Périgord. It's been divided into four colour-coded areas for easy navigation: Périgord Blanc (white) after the limestone hills around the capital city, Périgueux; Périgord Pourpre (purple) for the wine-growing regions around Bergerac; Périgord Vert (green) for the forested regions of the northwest; and Périgord Noir (black) for the dark oak forests around the Vézère Valley and Sarlat-la-Canéda.

PÉRIGUEUX

pop 29,600

There's been a settlement on the site of present-day Périgueux for over 2000 years. Initially occupied by Gallic tribes, and later developed by the Romans into the city of Vesunna, Périgueux is still the biggest (and busiest) city of the Dordogne *département*, with a bustling commercial centre and a bevy of bars, restaurants and shops. But despite its big-city facade, history still seeps through the cracks: Roman remains, including a ruined temple and a luxurious provincial villa discovered in 1959, can be found in the suburb of La Cité, while medieval buildings and Renaissance mansions are dotted around the rabbit-warren city centre.

Orientation

The medieval and Renaissance old city, known as Puy St-Front, is on the hillside between the

River Isle (to the east), bd Michel Montaigne and place Francheville (to the west). West of place Francheville is La Cité, where you'll find most of the city's Roman remains. The train station is 1km northwest of the old city.

Information

EMERGENCY

Hôtel de Police (police station; ☎ 05 53 06 44 44; place du Président Roosevelt; 24hr) Across from 20 rue du 4 Septembre.

LAUNDRY

Laundrette (place Hoche; 8am-8pm)
Laundrette (18 rue des Mobiles de Coulmiers; 8am-9pm)
Laundrette (61 rue Gambetta; 8am-9pm, to 8pm Sat)

MONEY

There are several banks on place Bugeaud.

POST

Post Office (1 rue du 4 Septembre) Offers money exchange.

TOURIST INFORMATION

Espace Tourisme Périgord (☎ 05 53 35 50 24; 25 rue du Président Wilson; 8.30am-5.30pm Mon-Fri) Provides information on the Dordogne *département*.
Tourist Office (☎ 05 53 53 10 63; www.tourisme-perigueux.fr; 26 place Francheville; 9am-6pm Mon-Sat, 10am-1pm & 2-6pm Sun Jun-Sep, 9am-1pm & 2-6pm Mon-Sat mid-Sep–mid-Jun)

Sights

PUY ST-FRONT

Périgueux' most distinctive landmark is the **Cathédrale St-Front** (place de la Clautre; admission free; 8am-12.30pm & 2.30-7.30pm), notable for its five Byzantine bump-studded domes (inspired by either St Mark's Basilica in Venice or the church of the Holy Apostles of Constantinople, depending on whom you ask). Built in the 12th century, and heavily restored by Abadie (the architect of Sacré Cœur, p157), the interior is laid out in a Greek cross, with the soaring domes supported by svelte arches. The carillon sounds the same on the hour chime as Big Ben. The best views of the cathedral are from **Pont des Barris**, which crosses the River Isle to the east.

Périgueux' medieval quarter is north of the cathedral, where the city's broad boulevards give way to a tangle of cobblestone streets lined with haphazard houses: the best examples are along **rue du Plantier**, **rue de la Sagesse** and **rue de la Miséricorde. Rue Limogeanne** has graceful Renaissance buildings at Nos 3 and 12, and the elaborately carved **Maison du Pâtissier** is at the end of rue Éguillerie. Most impressive of all is the **Hôtel d'Abzac de Ladouze** (16 rue Aubergerie), which was a fortified merchant's house in the 15th century.

Of the 28 towers that formed Puy St-Front's medieval fortifications, only the 15th-century **Tour Mataguerre**, a stout, round bastion next to the tourist office, now remains. The tourist office supplies a street map detailing the city's other architectural sites.

The **Musée du Périgord** (☎ 05 53 06 40 70; 22 cours Tourny; adult/student/under 18yr €4/2/free; 10.30am-5.30pm Mon & Wed-Fri, 1-6pm Sat) houses archeological finds, including some fine Roman mosaics and unique examples of prehistoric scrimshaw.

The **Musée Militaire** (☎ 05 53 53 47 36; 32 rue des Farges; adult/child €4/free; 1-6pm Mon-Sat Apr-Sep, 2-6pm Mon-Sat Oct-Dec, 2-6pm Wed & Sat Jan-Mar) has an eclectic collection of swords, firearms, uniforms and insignia dating from the Middle Ages until WWII, with sections devoted to WWI and the French Resistance.

LA CITÉ

Périgueux (or Vesunna, to give it its Roman name) was among the most important cities in Roman Gaul, but the only remains of this once-thriving outpost are in **La Cité**, west of the city centre. The **Tour de Vésone**, the last remaining section of a massive Gallo-Roman temple dedicated to the Gaulish goddess Vesunna, is just south of the **Église St-Étienne de la Cité** (place de la Cité), which served as Périgueux' cathedral until 1669.

To the north are the ruins of the city's **Roman amphitheatre**, designed to hold over 30,000 baying spectators and one of the largest such structures in Gaul: today only a few creeper-covered arches remain, and its gladiatorial arena is occupied by a peaceful park, the **Jardins des Arènes**.

Just west of the Tour de Vésone is the **Musée Gallo-Romain Vesunna** (☎ 05 53 53 00 92; www.semitour.com; rue Claude Bernard; adult/6-12yr €5.70/3.70; 10am-7pm Jul & Aug, 10am-12.30pm & 2-6pm Tue-Sun Apr-Jun & Sep-Nov, 10am-12.30pm & 2-5.30pm Tue-Sun Dec-Mar), constructed by renowned French architect Jean Nouvel above a 1st-century Roman villa uncovered in 1959. Light floods in through the glass-and-steel structure, and walkways circumnavigate the excavated villa; it's still

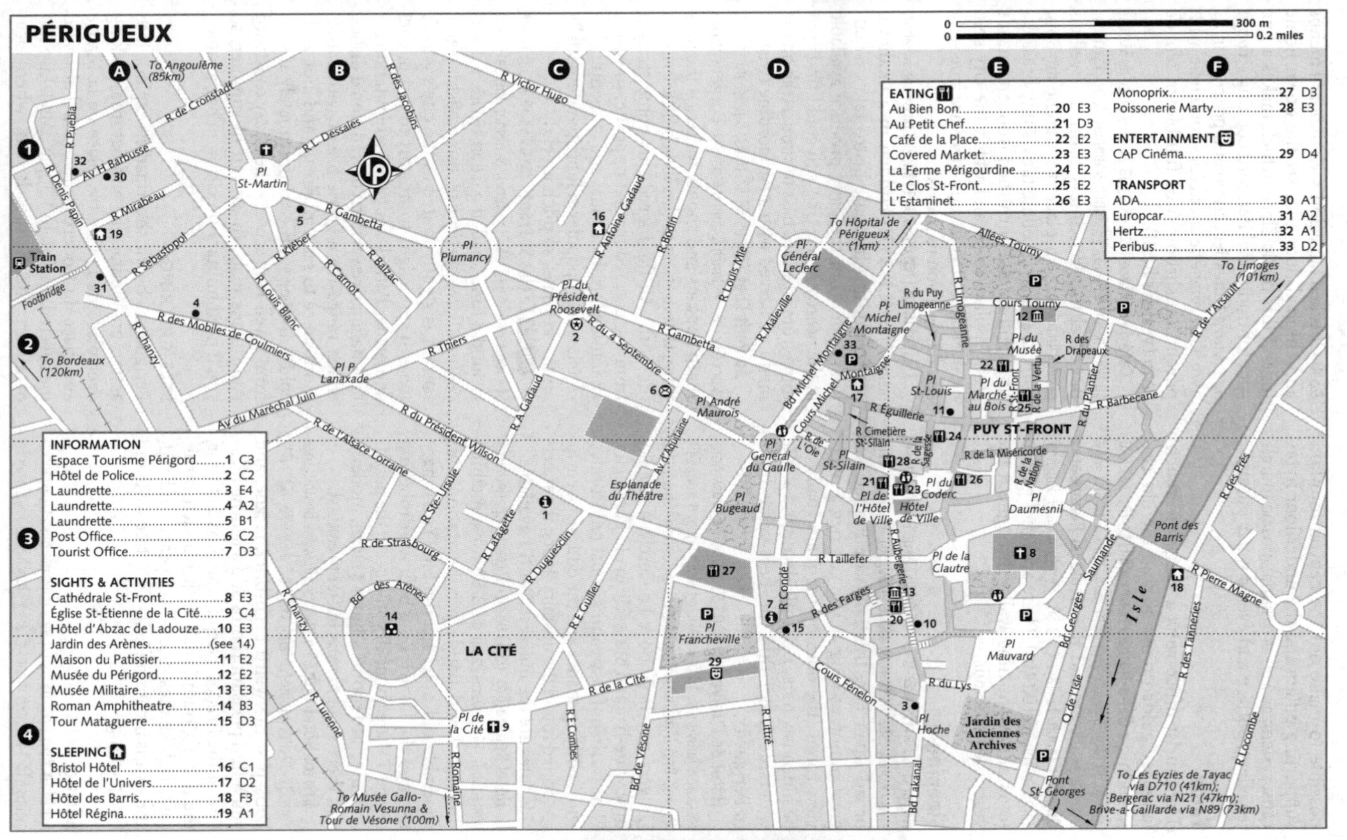
PÉRIGUEUX
0 300 m
0 0.2 miles
EATING
Au Bien Bon 20 E3
Au Petit Chef 21 D3
Café de la Place 22 E2
Covered Market 23 E3
La Ferme Périgourdine 24 E2
Le Clos St-Front 25 E2
L'Estaminet 26 E3
Monoprix 27 D3
Poissonerie Marty 28 E3
ENTERTAINMENT
CAP Cinéma 29 D4
TRANSPORT
ADA 30 A1
Europcar 31 A2
Hertz 32 A1
Peribus 33 D2
INFORMATION
Espace Tourisme Périgord 1 C3
Hôtel de Police 2 C2
Laundrette 3 E4
Laundrette 4 A2
Laundrette 5 B1
Post Office 6 C2
Tourist Office 7 D3
SIGHTS & ACTIVITIES
Cathédrale St-Front 8 E3
Église St-Étienne de la Cité 9 C4
Hôtel d'Abzac de Ladouze 10 E3
Jardin des Arènes (see 14)
Maison du Patissier 11 E2
Musée du Périgord 12 E2
Musée Militaire 13 E3
Roman Amphitheatre 14 B3
Tour Mataguerre 15 D3
SLEEPING
Bristol Hôtel 16 C1
Hôtel de l'Univers 17 D2
Hôtel des Barris 18 F3
Hôtel Régina 19 A1
To Angoulême (85km)
To Bordeaux (120km)
To Hôpital de Périgueux (1km)
To Limoges (101km)
To Musée Gallo-Romain Vesunna & Tour de Vésone (100m)
To Les Eyzies de Tayac via D710 (41km); Bergerac via N21 (47km); Brive-a-Gaillarde via N89 (73km)
Train Station
Footbridge
PUY ST-FRONT
LA CITÉ
Isle
Pont des Barris
Pont St-Georges
Jardin des Anciennes Archives
Pl St-Martin
Pl Plumancy
Pl du Président Roosevelt
Pl P Lanaxade
Pl Général Leclerc
Pl André Maurois
Pl General du Gaulle
Pl Bugeaud
Pl Francheville
Pl Michel Montaigne
Pl St-Louis
Pl du Marché au Bois
Pl du Musée
Pl Daumesnil
Pl de la Clautre
Pl Mauvard
Pl Hoche
Pl de la Cité
Pl St-Silain
Pl du Coderc
Pl de l'Hôtel de Ville
Hôtel de Ville
Esplanade du Théâtre
R Denis Papin
R Puebla
Av H Barbusse
R Mirabeau
R de Cronstadt
R Sebastopol
R Chanzy
R des Mobiles de Coulmiers
R L Dessales
R Gambetta
R Kléber
R Louis Blanc
R Carnot
R Balzac
R des Jacobins
R Victor Hugo
R Thiers
Av du Maréchal Juin
R de l'Alsace Lorraine
R du Président Wilson
R A Gadaud
R Antoine Gadaud
R Bodin
R Louis Mie
R Maleville
R du 4 Septembre
Av d'Aquitaine
Bd Michel Montaigne
Cours Michel Montaigne
R Ste-Ursule
R Lafayette
R Duguesclin
R E Guiller
R E Combes
R Romaine
R de Strasbourg
Bd des Arènes
R Turenne
R de la Cité
Bd de Vésone
R Littré
R Condé
R des Farges
R Taillefer
Cours Fénelon
R Aubergerie
Bd Lakanal
R du Lys
R Limogeanne
R du Puy Limogeanne
R Éguillerie
R de l'Ole
R Cimetière St-Silain
R de la Sagesse
R de la Miséricorde
R de la Nation
R St-Front
R de la Vertu
R des Drapeaux
R du Plantier
R Barbecane
Cours Tourny
Allées Tourny
R de l'Arsault
R des Prés
R Pierre Magne
R des Tanneries
R Locombe
Bd Georges Saumande
Q de l'Isle

possible to make out the central fountain, supporting pillars and the underfloor hypocaust system, as well as original mosaic murals, jewellery, pottery and even a water pump.

Tours

The tourist office runs a range of French-language guided tours around the old city, including a **Gallo-Roman tour** (adult/12-18yr €5/3.80; 10.30 Mon-Sat Jun-Sep, 3pm Mon, Wed & Fri Oct-May) and a walk around the **Medieval-Renaissance Quarter** (adult/12-18yr €5/3.80; 3pm daily Jun-Sep, 3pm Tue, Thu & Sat Oct-May). There are other guided tours and night-time walks throughout the year: ask for details.

Sleeping

Hôtel des Barris (05 53 53 04 05; 2 rue Pierre-Magne; www.hoteldesbarris.com; s/d/tr €44/50/56) Beside the broad River Isle, this Logis de France is a great option as long as you can bag a river-view room (the ones by the main road can be hideously noisy). Simple decor and a cute waterside make this the best-value hotel in Périgueux.

Hôtel de l'Univers (05 53 53 34 79; www.hotelrestaurantlunivers.fr; 18 cours Michel Montaigne; d from €49; Feb-Dec) You won't get more central than the Univers, perched above Le Cercle, a swanky little wine-bar and brasserie in old Périgueux. Nine fresh, unfussy rooms, most redecorated with soothing shades and the odd rustic curio, are dotted round the upstairs floors; the street-side ones are the quietest. Wi-fi's available.

Hôtel Régina (05 53 08 40 44; comfort.perigueux@wanadoo.fr; 14 rue Denis Papin; d €53-60) For something functional and handy for the station, this venerable old hotel fits the bill. You'll have to forgo the luxuries – a bed, wardrobe and digital TV are about all you'll get in the peach-and-mustard rooms – but it's clean, modern, and there's a generous buffet breakfast.

Bristol Hôtel (05 53 08 75 90; www.bristolfrance.com; 37-39 rue Antoine Gadaud; s €58-67, d €64-76; P) Look past the weird Lego-brick facade, and you'll find pleasant rooms and a central location at the Bristol. Despite the boxy exterior, the decor's traditional, with wooden furniture, rich shades of orange, peach and red, and extras including LCD TVs, free wi-fi and free parking.

Eating

Au Bien Bon (05 53 09 69 91; 15 rue des Places; lunch menus €10-14, dinner menus €22; lunch Mon-Fri, dinner Fri & Sat) Checked tablecloths, chalkboard menus and chipped floor tiles set the down-home tone at this rustic place, which makes a fine spot for traditional Périgord cooking – *confit de canard* (duck leg, cured and poached in its own fat), *omelette aux cèpes* (omelette with porcini mushrooms) or full-blown *tête de veau* (vealer's head).

Café de la Place (05 53 08 21 11; 7 place du Marché au Bois; mains €11-15; lunch & dinner) You can almost feel the Frenchness at this marvellous streetside café on place du Marché au Bois, with its spinning ceiling fans, shiny brass fittings and smoke-burnished wooden bar. It's really a place to sit and watch the city spin by over a *petit café*, but there are brasserie standards if you're peckish.

L'Estaminet (05 53 06 11 38; 2 Impasse Limogeanne; menus €15, €18.50 & €25) Hidden in a medieval courtyard, this intimate bistro takes its culinary cue from the daily produce available at the nearby market, so you could find anything from fresh sea bass to rump steak on the menu, all served with a Périgordine twist.

Au Petit Chef (05 53 53 16 03; 5 place du Coderc; mains €12-18; lunch & dinner Mon-Sat) Forget razor-sharp napkins and snooty waiters – the only thing that matters at this kitsch little bistro is the nosh. All the ingredients come straight from the covered market opposite, so you're guaranteed fresh flavours and authentic *plats régionaux*. It's popular at lunchtime, especially on market days, so pitch up early.

our pick **Le Clos St-Front** (05 53 46 78 58; 12 rue St-Front; mains €15-25; lunch & dinner Tue-Sat) Set around a lime-shaded garden beside a 16th-century *hôtel particulier*, this ravishing restaurant is rightly touted as the city's *grande table*. It's a delight from start to finish: chef and owner Patrick Feuga has a reputation for his imaginative versions of traditional dishes, which range from goose breast with cardamom sauce to sashimi Bream and 'hot-and-cold' caramel soufflé. Unfortunately it's far from a well-kept secret – the buzzy courtyard patio is *the* place to eat out in summer, so you'll need military precision to bag a table.

SELF-CATERING

Périgueux' chaotic **street markets** explode into action on Wednesday and Saturday, taking over place de la Clautre, place de la Mairie and place du Coderc (where you'll also find the covered market, to 1.30pm daily). Liveliest of all are the **Marchés de Gras**, when local delicacies such as truffles, wild mushrooms and foie gras are sold on place St-Louis from mid-November to mid-March.

There are lots of *charcuteries* (butcher shops) and *fromageries* (cheese shops) in the old city; try **La Ferme Périgourdine** (☎ 05 53 08 41 22; 9 rue Limogeanne; 🕑 8am-12.30pm & 3-7pm Tue-Sat) for cheese or **Poissonerie Marty** (☎ 05 53 03 45 62; 11 rue des Chaines; 🕑 8am-6pm Mon-Sat) for fish. There's also a city-centre **Monoprix** (🕑 8.30am-8pm Mon-Sat; place Bugeaud).

Entertainment

The 10-screen **CAP Cinéma** (☎ 08 92 68 01 21; place Francheville) screens mainly new-release films, some in *version originale* (nondubbed).

Getting There & Away

BUS

The main local operator is **Peribus** (☎ 05 53 53 30 37; place Michel Montaigne; 🕑 9.45am-12.30pm & 1.30-5.45pm Mon-Fri). Single fares around town cost €1.25.

For buses further afield, contact **Trans Périgord** (☎ 05 53 02 20 85; 33 rue St-Front). There are 10 regular lines, with a flat fee of €2/1 per adult/child. Destinations include Sarlat (Line 7A; 1½ hours, two daily Monday to Friday), Montignac (Line 7B; one hour 40 minutes, one daily Monday to Friday) and Bergerac (70 minutes, six daily Monday to Friday).

CAR

All the rental agencies are around the station, including **Europcar** (☎ 05 53 08 15 72; 7 rue Denis Papin), **ADA** (☎ 05 53 05 40 28; 4 av H Barbusse) and **Hertz** (☎ 05 53 54 61 80; cnr rue Puebla & av H Barbusse 1).

TRAIN

The **train station** (rue Denis Papin) is served by buses 1, 4 and 5. Direct services run to Bordeaux (€18, one hour 20 minutes, hourly), Limoges (€14.30, one hour, hourly) and Brive-la-Gaillarde (€11.30, one hour, hourly). Fewer trains run on Sunday.

From Limoges there are connections to Paris Austerlitz (€55.90 to €70.50, four to five hours). To get to Sarlat-la-Canéda (€13.20, around three daily) you have to change at Le Buisson.

BRANTÔME

pop 2122

Often dubbed the 'Venice of the Périgord' thanks to its five medieval bridges and elegant riverfront architecture, **Brantôme** hugs a comely curve in the River Dronne 27km north of Périgueux. Surrounded by grassy parks and willow-filled woodland, it's a glorious spot to while away an afternoon or embark on a pleasure cruise.

Brantôme's most illustrious landmark is the former **Benedictine Abbey**, built and rebuilt from the 11th to 18th centuries and now occupied by the Hôtel de Ville. Next door is the Gothic **abbey church** and Brantôme's **tourist office** (☎ 05 53 05 80 63; ot.brantome@wanadoo.fr; 🕑 10am-7pm mid-Jun–mid-Sep, 10am-12.30pm & 2-6pm Wed-Mon mid-Sep–mid-Jun), which runs daily guided tours around Brantôme's main sights for €6/3 per adult/child.

Behind the modern-day abbey and the tourist office are the remains of Brantôme's original abbey, known as the **Parcours Troglodytique** (🕑 10am-7pm mid-Jun–mid-Sep, 10am-12.30pm & 2-6pm Wed-Mon mid-Sep–mid-Jun), cut from the rock face by industrious monks in the 8th century. Its most famous feature is a 15th-century rock frieze supposedly depicting the Last Judgement. Of more interest is the abbey's 11th-century Romanesque **clocher** (belltower), allegedly the oldest (and arguably most beautiful) in France.

Cruise boats run from the banks of the river in front of the abbey, including **Promenade en Bateau** (☎ 05 53 04 74 71; adult/child €7/5) and **L'Arche de Noë** (☎ 06 10 81 20 05; adult/child €7/5). Cruises last about 50 minutes and depart hourly in season.

Sleeping & Eating

Maison Fleurie (☎ 05 53 53 17 04; www.maison-fleurie.net; 54 rue Gambetta; d €45-85) Behind the wrought-iron doors of this smart stone house are five spick-and-span B&B rooms, furnished in impeccably good taste by the expat British owners, and a sunny interior courtyard filled with geraniums and petunias.

Hostellerie du Périgord (☎ 05 53 05 70 58; www.hotel-hpv.fr; 7 av André Maurois; d €48-55, tr €72; 🅿) Creepers cover the outside of this old roadside inn, arranged around a private courtyard set back from the main road and riverfront. The rooms are pleasant in an everyday kind of way, all with wi-fi, stout beds, plain bathrooms and a choice of courtyard or pool views. Southwest wines and *cuisine de terroir* (country cuisine) make the restaurant popular for Sunday lunch (*menus* €17 to €39, mains €11 to €27.

our pick Hostellerie les Griffons (☎ 05 53 45 45 35; www.griffons.fr; Bourdeilles; d €85-135; ; P) Fantastically atmospheric hotel–cum–*chambre d'hôte* (B&B) in a converted mill with views of the river through its blue-shuttered windows. The rooms are an enticing jumble of medieval fireplaces, head-scraping beams and porthole windows – ask for No 6, with its ceiling of muddled crossbeams, or No 2, with stone hearth and town views. The hotel is in the nearby town of Bourdeilles, about 9km southwest of Brantôme along the D78.

Getting There & Away

Brantôme is 27km north of Périgueux along the D939. There is a very early morning bus to Périgueux (line 1AB; 50 minutes) which returns in the evening around 6pm except on Wednesday, when it returns at around 1pm. There's no bus station – buses leave from various streetside stops around town.

SARLAT-LA-CANÉDA

pop 10,000

A picturesque tangle of honey-coloured buildings, alleyways and secret squares make up Sarlat-la-Canéda, one of the unmissable villages of the Dordogne. Ringed by forested hilltops and boasting some of the best-preserved medieval architecture in France, Sarlat makes a charming launch pad for exploring the Périgord Noir and the Vézère Valley. But be warned – it's also one of region's most popular tourist spots, and you may find it almost impossible to appreciate the town's charms among the summer throngs.

Orientation

The heart-shaped Cité Médiévale (Medieval Town) is bisected by the rue de la République (La Traverse). The train station is around 2km from the Cité Médiévale, which is centred on place de la Liberté, rue de la Liberté and place du Peyrou.

Information

There are several banks along rue de la République, all with ATMs.

Easy Planet (Map p626; ☎ 05 53 31 22 37; av Gambetta; 10am-8pm Mon-Sat, & 2-7pm Sun) Internet access is €3 per hour.

Post Office (Map p626; place du 14 Juillet) Currency exchange.

Tourist Office (Map p628; ☎ 05 53 31 45 45; www.ot-sarlat-perigord.fr; rue Tourny; 9am-7pm Mon-Sat,

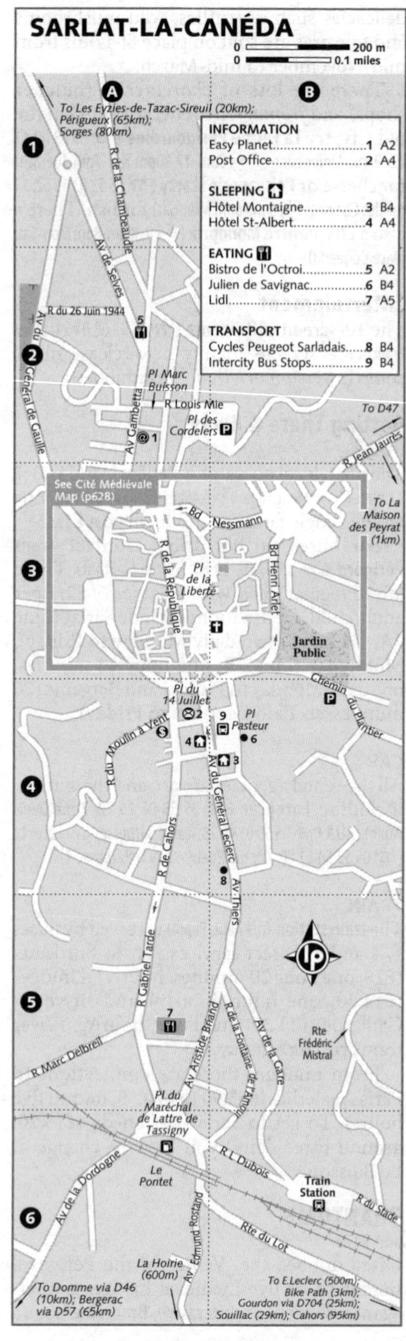

10am-noon Sun Apr-Oct, 9am-noon & 2-7pm Mon-Sat Nov-Mar) Fantastically efficient; ask for the free walking tour around the medieval town.

Sights & Activities

Part of the fun of wandering around Sarlat is getting well and truly lost in the network of twisting alleyways and back streets. **Rue Jean-Jacques Rousseau** (Map p628) or the area around **Le Présidial** (p628) both make good starting points, but for the grandest buildings and *hôtels particuliers* you'll want to explore **rue des Consuls**. Look out for the medieval fountain, tucked away down steps at the rear of a mossy grotto.

Whichever street you take, sooner or later you'll end up at the **Cathédrale St-Sacerdos** (Map p628) on place du Peyrou, once part of Sarlat's Cluniac abbey. The original abbey church was built in the 1100s, redeveloped in the early 1500s and remodelled again in the 1700s, so it's a real mix of styles. The belfry and western facade are the oldest parts of the building, while the nave, organ and interior chapels are later additions.

Opposite the cathedral is the 16th-century timber-framed **Maison de la Boétie** (Map p628), birthplace of the writer Étienne de la Boétie (1530–63), a close friend of the French essayist Michel de Montaigne (1533–92).

Two medieval courtyards, the **Cour des Fontaines** and the **Cour des Chanoines** (Map p628), can be reached via an alleyway off rue Tourny. Duck down the passage from Cour des Chanoines to the **Chapelle des Pénitents Bleus** (Map p628), a Romanesque chapel that provided the architectural inspiration for the cathedral.

Nearby is the **Jardin des Enfeus** (Map p628), Sarlat's first cemetery, and the rocket-shaped **Lanterne des Morts** (Lantern of the Dead; Map p628), built to honour a visit by St Bernard, one of the founders of the Cistercian order, in 1147.

Sleeping

Hotel rooms in Sarlat in summer are like gold dust, and budget rooms are thin on the ground at any time. Shoestringers should ask at the tourist office about *chambres d'hôtes*.

Hôtel Les Récollets (Map p628; ☎ 05 53 31 36 00; www.hotel-recollets-sarlat.com; 4 rue Jean-Jacques Rousseau; d €43-69) Lost in the medieval maze of the old town, the Récollets is a budget beauty. Nineteen topsy-turvy rooms and a charming vaulted breakfast room are rammed in around the medieval *maison*. Our favourites are 305 and 308, with exposed brick and king-size beds.

Hôtel La Couleuvrine (Map p628; ☎ 05 53 59 27 80; www.la-couleuvrine.com; 1 place de la Bouquerie; d €52-80) Gables, chimneys and red-tile rooftops adorn this rambling hotel, which originally formed part of Sarlat's city wall. It's old, odd and endearingly musty. Strange-shaped rooms are sandwiched between solid stone and wooden rafters, and for maximum quirk factor there are a couple of rooms in the hotel's turret.

La Maison des Peyrat (off Map p626; ☎ 05 53 59 00 32; www.maisondespeyrat.com; le Lac de la Plane; r €53-95; 🅿) Variously used as a plague hospital, nuns' rest-home and hunting retreat, this sweet 10-room hotel is a total sanctuary, peacefully positioned on a hilltop 1.5km from Sarlat. The 11 shuttered rooms are cool and uncluttered, with touches of country-tinged charisma; the best overlook the courtyard gardens and the countryside beyond.

Hôtel Montaigne (Map p626; ☎ 05 53 31 93 88; www.hotelmontaigne.fr; 2 place Pasteur; d €54-64; 🅿) Popular with the coach-tour crowd, this imposing stone-front hotel lacks the intimacy of some of Sarlat's hotels, but it's cheaper than most. The modern rooms, all with private bathrooms and cosy decor, aren't massively exciting, but the buffet brekkie is great. There's also a handy car park in front of the hotel, and wi-fi, too.

Hôtel St-Albert (Map p626; ☎ 05 53 31 55 55; www.hotel-saintalbert.eu; place Pasteur; r from €60) Pared back, stylish hotel with the barest of boutique touches: minimal clutter, chocolate-and-cream tones and posh bath goodies make it feel closer to a metropolitan crash pad than an old-town *auberge*. Free wi-fi.

La Hoirie (Map p626; ☎ 05 53 59 05 62; www.lahoirie.com; La Giragne; d €89-138; 🅿) This turreted 18th-century lodge, surrounded by a huge private garden, makes a delightful escape from the hectic hum of downtown Sarlat. The rooms (named after local sights) have a trace of Cistercian simplicity, finished in soothing tones and local stone.

Villa des Consuls (Map p628; ☎ 05 53 31 90 05; www.villaconsuls.com; 3 rue Jean-Jacques Rousseau; d €69-89, apt €110-162;) Despite its Renaissance exterior, the four huge rooms and three self-catering apartments here are modern through and through. Some have wood floors, tall windows, sofas and original beams; others are tucked into the attic with split-level staircases, nook-and-cranny windows and lofty ceilings. At this price, it's a steal.

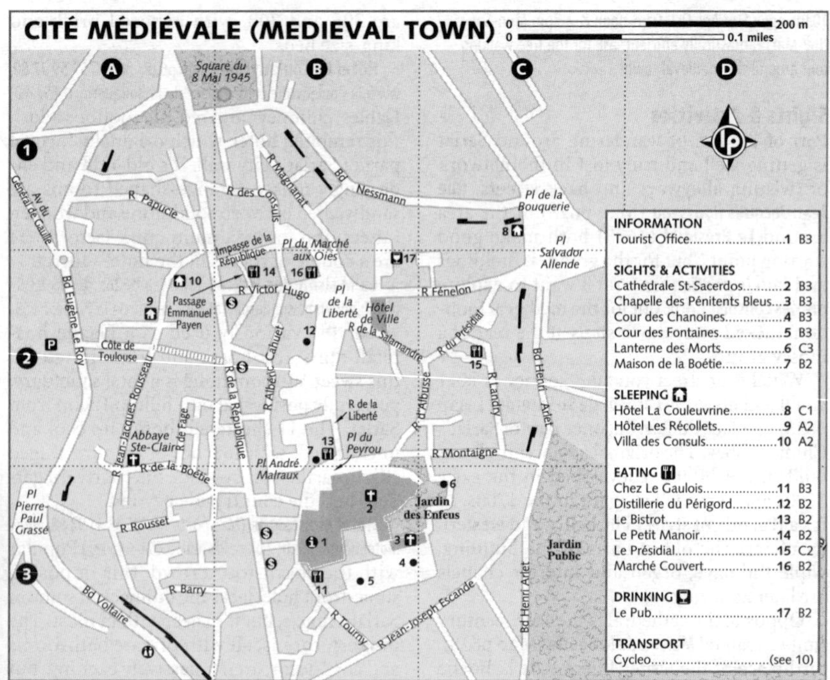

Eating

Sarlat isn't short on restaurants, but many of them are more concerned with packing in the punters than titillating the tastebuds. Choose wisely.

Chez Le Gaulois (Map p628; ☎ 05 53 59 50 64; 3 rue Tourny; mains €9-13; lunch & dinner Tue-Sat) If you've worked up an appetite, this Alpine *auberge* is a fine place to refuel. Stonking plates of smoked sausage, cold meats and cheese are served up Savoyard-style on wooden platters, as well as authentic *tartiflettes* (cheese, potato and bacon bake) and fondues laced with mountains of Reblochon cheese.

Le Bistrot (Map p628; ☎ 05 53 28 28 40; place du Peyrou; menus €15-24; lunch & dinner Mon-Sat) This diminutive bistro is the best of the bunch on café-heavy place du Peyrou. Red-check tablecloths and twinkling fairy lights create an intimate atmosphere, and the menu's heavy on Sarlat classics – especially walnuts, *magret de canard* (duck breast) and *pommes sarlardaises* (potatoes cooked in duck fat).

Le Petit Manoir (Map p628; ☎ 05 53 29 82 14; 13 rue de la République; menus €24-29; lunch Thu-Sun, dinner Wed-Sat) Global flavours, local ingredients and fusion-style cooking come together in sophisticated fashion at the 'Little Manor', lodged inside an elegant Sarlat mansion. Choose a table inside the Renaissance-style dining room or the front courtyard and prepare for culinary adventures.

Bistro de l'Octroi (Map p626; ☎ 05 53 30 83 40; 111 av de Selves; menus €18 & €26; lunch & dinner) This local's tip is a little way out of town, but worth the walk. Sarladais punters pack into the dining room for the comforting cooking and cosy town-house setting. Top choices are the generous slabs of Limousin beef, good seafood and a fantastic mint-chocolate *panna cotta* (Italian dessert made from cream, milk and sugar).

our pick Le Présidial (Map p628; ☎ 05 53 28 92 47; 6 rue Landry; menus from €29; lunch Tue-Sat, dinner Mon-Sat) Housed in one of Sarlat's most historic buildings (originally a 17th-century courthouse), the superswish Présidial is one of the Dordogne's top tables. Stout gates swing back to reveal the city's loveliest terrace, filled with summer flowers and climbing ivy – the perfect place to sit back and enjoy authentic *saveurs de terroir* (country flavours). Goose, duck and foie gras dominate the menu, and the wine list is super (especially for Sarlat and Cahors vintages). But it's the romantic courtyard setting that steals the show. A complete *coup de cœur*.

SELF-CATERING

Practically every other shop in Sarlat is stocked with local goodies, from duck *confit* to walnut cake, but the best place for supplies is the **Marché Couvert** (Map p628; 🕒 8.30am-2pm Sat-Thu, 8.30am-8pm Fri mid-Apr–mid-Nov, 8.30am-1pm Tue, Wed, Fri & Sat mid-Nov–mid-Apr) inside the converted Église Ste-Marie, with lots of stalls supplied by local producers. Other good shops include **Distillerie du Périgord** (Map p628; ☎ 05 53 59 20 57; place de la Liberté) for local liqueurs, and **Julien de Savignac** (Map p626; ☎ 05 53 31 29 20; place du Pasteur) for wine.

For the full-blown French market experience, you absolutely mustn't miss Sarlat's chaotic **Saturday market** (place de la Liberté & rue de la République), which takes over the streets around the cathedral from 8am. Depending on the season, delicacies on offer include foie gras, mushrooms, duck- and goose-based products, and even the holy *truffe noir* (black truffle). A smaller **fruit and vegetable market** (🕒 8.30am-1pm) is held on Wednesday mornings on place de la Liberté.

Out-of-town supermarkets include **E.Leclerc** (off Map p626; ☎ 05 53 31 35 35; rte de Souillac; 🕒 Mon-Sat 9am-8pm) and **Lidl** (Map p626; av Aristide Briand; 🕒 9am-12.30pm & 2.30-7.30pm Mon-Fri, 9am-7pm Sat).

Drinking

Sarlat's drinking scene is pretty limited – about the only option apart from the cafés is **Le Pub** (Map p628; ☎ 05 53 59 57 98; 1 passage de Gérard du Barry; 🕒 from 7pm), which is especially popular in summer, when the enclosed courtyard springs to life with alfresco drinkers. Closing times vary widely according to the season.

Getting There & Away

Useful bus destinations are Périgueux (bus 7A; 1½ hours, two daily) via Montignac (30 minutes), which leaves from place Pasteur, and Souillac (bus 6; 40 minutes, four or five Monday to Saturday, two on Sunday), which travels to and from the train station. Tickets cost a flat rate of €2.

Rather inconveniently, Sarlat's **train station** (Map p626; ☎ 05 53 59 00 21) is 1.3km south of the old city along av de la Gare. Destinations include Périgueux (via Le Buisson; €13.20, 1¾ hours, three daily), Les Eyzies (change at Le Buisson; €8.20, 50 minutes to 2½ hours depending on connections, three daily) and Bergerac (€10.70, 2½ hours, six daily).

Getting Around

Bikes can be rented for around €10 per day from **Cycles Peugeot Sarladais** (Map p626; ☎ 05 53

LES DIAMANTS NOIRS

From walnuts to strawberries, *cèpe* (porcini) mushrooms, foie gras and *chanterelles*, the Dordogne is famous for its gourmet goodies. But for true culinary connoisseurs there's only one ingredient that matters, and that's the *diamant noir* – otherwise known as the black truffle.

A subterranean fungi that grows naturally in chalky soils (often around the roots of oak and hazelnut trees), this mysterious little mushroom is notoriously capricious; a good truffle spot one year can be inexplicably bare the next, which has made farming them on any kind of serious scale practically impossible. The art of truffle-hunting is a closely guarded secret; it's a matter of luck, judgment and hard-earned experience, and serious truffle hunters often employ specially trained dogs (and sometimes even pigs) to help them in the search. But it's not simply a matter of culinary perfection – truffles are seriously big business, with a vintage crop fetching as much as €850 a kilogram.

The height of truffle season is between December and March, when special truffle markets are held around the Dordogne, including Périgueux (p621), Sarlat (p626) and most notably Sorges (locally championed as France's truffle capital). For more background on this flavoursome fungi, the **Ecomusée de la Truffe** (☎ 05 53 05 90 11; www.truffe-sorges.org; Le Bourg, Sorges; 🕒 9.30am-12.30pm & 2.30-6.30pm Jul & Aug, 10am-noon & 2-5pm Tue-Sun Sep-Jun) in Sorges has lots of truffle-themed exhibits and might even be able to help you hook up with a truffle hunt in season…

As for the best way to eat them – well, those in the know say that the best way to savour the taste is in a plain omelette or simply on a slice of fresh crusty bread. Whether the truffle deserves its culinary reputation is something only your tastebuds can tell you…

28 51 87; 36 av Thiers) and **Cycleo** (Map p628; ☎ 05-53-31-90-05; 3 rue Jean-Jacques Rousseau).

Parking is free along bd Nessmann, bd Voltaire and bd Henri Arlet. Cars are banned in Cité Médiévale from June to September, and rue de la République is pedestrianised in July and August.

PREHISTORIC SITES & THE VÉZÈRE VALLEY

Flanked by limestone cliffs, subterranean caverns and ancient woodland, the Vézère Valley is world famous for its incredible collection of prehistoric paintings – the highest concentration of Stone Age art found in Europe. The many underground caves around the Vézère provided shelter for Cro-Magnon man, and the area is littered with prehistoric monuments such as the Lascaux caves near Montignac (p634), the Abri du Cap Blanc (p632) and the Grotte de Rouffignac (p632).

Most of the key sites are between Le Bugue and Montignac, 25km to the northeast. If you're driving, the best bases are Les Eyzies (below), and Sarlat-la-Canéda (p626). Most of the valley's sites are closed in winter, and the otherworldly atmosphere is pretty much shattered by the summer crowds, so spring and autumn are definitely the best times to visit.

Getting Around

Public transport is limited, with few trains and even fewer buses. You can get to most towns fairly easily, but there's usually no way of getting to the caves themselves. Cycling is an option, and hire bikes are often available from campsites, tourist offices or rental outlets, but as always in rural France, having your own car makes things easier.

Les Eyzies-de-Tayac-Sireuil

pop 850

At the heart of the Vézère Valley, Les Eyzies makes a fairly uninspiring introduction to the wonders of the Vézère. Touristy and a little tatty, the town caters for the massive influx of tourists who descend on the valley every summer, and judging by the endless postcard sellers, cafés and souvenir shops lining the street, business must be brisk. Despite the town's commercial gloss, it's a useful base with some pleasant hotels and campsites, and an excellent museum of prehistory.

INFORMATION

Librairie de la Préhistoire (🕑 8.30am-12.30pm & 3-7pm Mar-Nov, 8.30am-7pm Jun-Aug, 8.30am-noon Dec-Feb) Sells IGN maps and topoguides.

Tourist Office (☎ 05 53 06 97 05; www.leseyzies.com; 🕑 9am-7pm Mon-Sat, 10am-noon & 2-6pm Sun Jul & Aug, 9am-noon & 2-6pm Mon-Sat, 10am-noon & 2-5pm Sun Sep-Jun, closed Sun Oct-Apr) Has a small internet kiosk where you can check email for €1.50 for 15 minutes.

SIGHTS

The **Musée National de Préhistoire** (National Museum of Prehistory; ☎ 05 53 06 45 45; adult/18-25yr/under 18yr €5/3.50/free, 1st Sun of month free; 🕑 9.30am-6.30pm Jul & Aug, 9.30am-6pm Wed-Mon Jun & Sep, 9.30am-noon & 2-5.30pm Wed-Mon Oct-May) provides a fine prehistory primer (providing your French is good). Inside a marvellous modern building underneath the cliffs, it houses the most comprehensive collection of prehistoric finds in France. Highlights include a huge gallery of Stone Age tools, weapons and jewellery, and skeletons from some of the animals that once roamed the Vézère (including bison, woolly rhinoceros, giant deer and cave bears), as well as a collection of carved reliefs on the 1st floor – look out for an amazing frieze of horses and a bison licking its flank. Much of the jewellery is fashioned from bone, antlers and seashells, and intricately marked with chevrons, dots, dashes and other designs.

About 250m north of the museum is the **Abri Pataud** (☎ 05 53 06 92 46; www.semitour.com; adult/6-12yr/under 6yr €5.80/3.80/free; 🕑 10am-7pm Jul-Sep, 10am-12.30pm & 2-6pm Mon-Sat Sep-Jun), a Cro-Magnon *abri* (shelter) inhabited over a period of 15,000 years starting some 37,000 years ago; bones and other excavated artefacts are on display. The ibex carved into the ceiling dates from about 19,000 BC. The admission price includes a one-hour guided tour in French (and some English if you're lucky).

SLEEPING & EATING

Les Eyzies has lots of campsites, but they get heavily oversubscribed so reserve well ahead.

Camping La Rivière (☎ 05 53 06 97 14; www.larivierel eseyzies.com; per person €8.40-12.85; 💻 🏊) The nearest campsite to Les Eyzies is a stroll west of town and pleasantly plonked beside the river. Great facilities – including a restaurant, bar, laundry and on-site grocery – ensure it's packed in high season.

Camping Le Vézère Périgord (☎ 05 53 06 96 31; www.levezereperigord.com; route de Montignac, Tursac; per person €9-13; 🏊) This tranquil, forested site 6km north

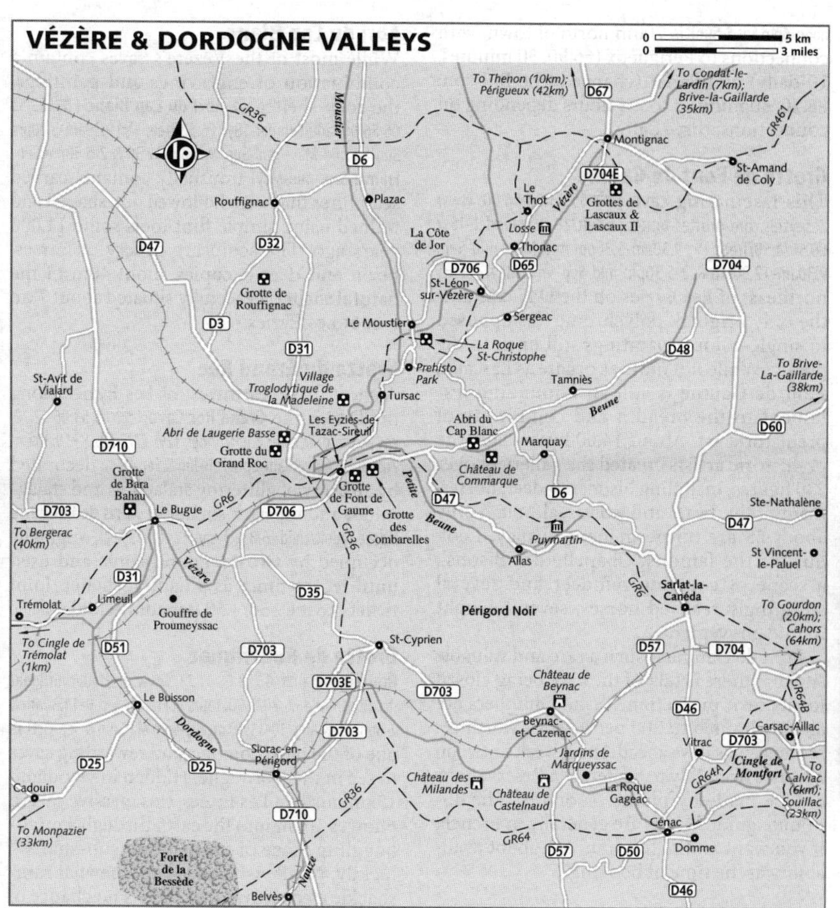

of Les Eyzies is popular with holidaying families. There's a swimming pool, tennis courts, ping pong, trampolines and even a pizzeria, as well as mountain-bike and kayak hire.

Hôtel des Roches (☎ 05 53 06 96 59; www.roches-les-eyzies.com; s €71-75, d €84.80-101.60; ⏲ Apr-Nov;) For a modern feel, try this smart hotel, chunkily constructed from the area's pale stone and decorated in simple pastoral style. The rear rooms overlook the garden and swimming pool, but you'll have to pay for the privilege.

Hostellerie du Passeur (☎ 05 53 06 97 13; www.hostellerie-du-passeur.com; place de la Mairie; d €87.50-108; ⏲ Feb-Oct) This ivy-clad hotel is in the middle of Les Eyzies, overlooking the meandering Vézère. It's traditional in style, with rooms divided into 'Charme', 'Elegance' and 'Prestige' – the better rooms are worth the cash, with valley views, flash TVs and deep, luxurious beds.

Hôtel des Glycines (☎ 05 53 06 97 07; www.les-glycines-dordogne.com; Les Eyzies; d €86-232; P) Les Eyzies' old post house has been converted into this pricey pamper-pad, with four categories of plush rooms ranging from cream-and-check 'Classics' to full-blown private suites, complete with private terrace and garden outlook. (Avoid the 'courtyard rooms' if you can, which overlook the main road out of Les Eyzies). Prince Charles once stayed here, so it can't be too shabby.

GETTING THERE & AWAY

Les Eyzies is on the D47, 21km west of Sarlat. The **train station** (☎ 05 53 06 97 22; ⏲ 7am-6pm Mon-Fri, noon-6pm Sat & Sun) is 700m north of town, with connections to Périgueux (€6.90, 30 minutes, 10 daily) and Sarlat (change at Le Buisson; €8.20, 50 minutes to 2½ hours depending on connections, three daily) .

Grotte de Font de Gaume

This fascinating **cave** (☎ 05 53 06 86 00; www.leseyzies.com/grottes-ornees; adult/18-25yr/under 18yr €6.50/4.50/free; 9.30am-5.30pm mid-May–mid-Sep, 9.30am-12.30pm & 2-5.30pm mid-Sep–mid-May) 1km northeast of Les Eyzies on the D47 contains the only original 'polychrome' (as opposed to single-colour) paintings still open to the public. While not quite as ornate as Lascaux, Font de Gaume is still an astounding testament to the breadth and complexity of prehistoric art. About 14,000 years ago, the prehistoric artists created the gallery of over 230 figures, including bison, reindeer, horses, mammoths, bears and wolves, although only about 25 are on permanent display. Look out for the famous 'Chapelle des Bisons', a scene of courting reindeer and several stunningly realised horses, several caught in mid-movement.

Font de Gaume is such a rare and valuable site that there is talk of the cave being closed for its own protection. Visitor numbers are already limited to 200 per day: it's worth reserving a few days ahead, and a week or two in advance from July to September. Reservations can be made by phone or online. The 45-minute guided tours are generally in French; if you want an English tour, ask about availability at the time of booking.

Grotte des Combarelles

The narrow cave of **Combarelles**, discovered in 1901 about 1.5km east of Font de Gaume, is renowned for its animal engravings, many of which cleverly use the natural contours of the rock to sculpt the animals' forms: the most impressive examples are delicately drawn mammoths, horses and reindeer, as well as a fantastic mountain lion that seems to leap from the rock face. One wall seems to have been used as a kind of prehistoric sketchpad, with many animals and geometric symbols superimposed on one another.

The six- to eight-person group tours last about an hour, and can be reserved through the Font de Gaume ticket office. Opening hours and admission costs are the same for both sites.

Abri du Cap Blanc

While most of the Vézère's caves contain a combination of engravings and paintings, the rock shelter of **Abri du Cap Blanc** (☎ 05 53 06 86 00; adult/under 18yr €6.50/free; 9.30am-5.30pm Sun-Fri mid-May–mid-Sep, 9.30am-12.30 & 2-5.30pm Sun-Fri mid-Sep–mid-May) unusually contains carved sculptures that were hollowed out, shaped and refined using simple flint tools some 14,000 years ago. The sculpture gallery of horses, bison and deer occupies about 40m of the natural shelter, peacefully situated about 7km east of Les Eyzies.

Grotte du Grand Roc

A short drive northwest of Les Eyzies along the D47 is the **Grand Roc Cave** (☎ 05 53 06 92 70; www.grandroc.com; adult/under 12yr €7/3.50; 9.30am-7pm Jul & Aug, 10am-6pm Feb-Jun & Sep-Dec), decorated by an array of glittering stalactites and stalagmites, and the rock shelter of **Abris de Laugerie Basse** (adult/child €6/3; same as Grand Roc), originally occupied by Cro-Magnon people and used until recent times as a natural shelter. Joint tickets cost €9.50/4.50 per adult/child.

Grotte de Rouffignac

Rouffignac (☎ 05 53 05 41 71; www.grottederouffignac.fr; adult/child €6.20/3.90; tours in French 9-11.30am & 2-6pm Jul & Aug, 10-11.30am & 2-5pm Mar-Jun & Sep-Oct) is one of the most complex and rewarding caves to see in the Dordogne. Hidden in woodland 15km north of Les Eyzies, this massive cavern plunges 10km into the earth through a mind-boggling maze of tunnels and sub-shafts – luckily, you'll visit aboard a somewhat ramshackle electric train, so there's no chance of getting lost.

Rouffignac is sometimes known as the 'Cave of 100 Mammoths' and with good reason: you'll see many painted pachyderms on your trip into the underworld, including a frieze of 10 mammoths in procession, one of the largest cave paintings ever discovered. At the end of the tour the train grinds to a halt and you stumble out into a hidden gallery where the entire ceiling is covered in mammoths, ibex, enormous horses, and even a few rhinoceros – some intricately painted, others reduced to simple strokes and lines. Keep your eyes peeled for scratches and hollows on the cave floor, left behind by the long-extinct cave bears who once shared this cave with our prehistoric ancestors. Certainly beats a cat…

PREHISTORY 101

If you're visiting the cave paintings around the Vézère and Lot, it helps to know a little about the prehistoric artists who created them. Most of the valley's cave paintings date from the end of the last ice age, between 20,000 BC and 10,000 BC, and were painted by Cro-Magnon people – descendants of the first *homo erectus* settlers who arrived in Europe from North Africa between 700,000 BC and 100,000 BC. These early humans were an entirely separate species from the shorter, burlier Neanderthals who lived in Europe around the same time, and died out suddenly around 35,000 BC.

Until around 20,000 BC much of Northern Europe was still covered by vast glaciers and ice sheets: Cro-Magnon people lived a loose hunter-gatherer lifestyle, using natural caves as temporary hunting shelters while they followed the migration routes of their prey (including woolly mammoths, woolly rhinoceros, reindeer and aurochs, an ancestor of the modern cow).

The first cave art appears in the so-called Gravettian period, consisting of abstract engravings or paintings of female genitalia or 'Venus' figures and developing into complex animal figures and friezes such as those at **Lascaux** (p634), **Rouffignac** (opposite) and **Font de Gaume** (opposite), which date from around 15,000 BC to 10,000 BC. Curiously, the artwork in more recent caves is often less sophisticated than the ones at Lascaux, suggesting that different tribes had differing traditions and levels of artistry, but also indicating that Lascaux seems to have held an unusual significance for its painters.

Using flint tools for engraving, natural fibre brushes, pads or sponges for painting, and paints derived from minerals such as magnesium and charcoal (black), ochre (red/yellow) and iron (red), the prehistoric painters worked by the light of primitive oil torches. Usually they painted the animals they hunted, but occasionally they also left hand tracings, or depicted abstract figures and scenes (such as the celebrated picture of an injured hunter and bull in Lascaux). As well as the paintings, Cro-Magnon artists also created jewellery from shells, bones and antlers, and scrimshaw decorated with animal scenes and geometric patterns, examples of which can be seen at the **Museum of Prehistory** p630, in Les Eyzies.

It's interesting to note the things they chose not to draw – there are no landscapes, trees, rivers, skies or rocks in any of the Vézère's caves, only animals – suggesting that the cave paintings had some kind of ritual or shamanic significance, possibly as shrines or magical sanctuaries. Most mysterious of all are the strange geometric shapes common to all the caves. Although many theories have been put forward to explain them, ranging from primitive writing to magic markers, in truth no one has the faintest idea what these weird signs signified to our Cro-Magnon cousins.

The paintings seem to have come to an abrupt halt around 10,000 BC, around the same time the last ice sheets disappeared and humans settled down to a more fixed lifestyle of farming and agriculture.

Village de la Madeleine

Cro-Magnons weren't the only ones to use the Vézère's caves for shelter. As in the Loire, many of the area's caves were used for storage, defence or protection as recently as the Middle Ages. **Le Village Troglodytique de la Madeleine** (Cave Village; ☎ 05 53 46 36 88; adult/child €5.50/3.50; ⏲ 10am-7.30pm Jul & Aug, 10am-7pm May-June & Sep, 10am-6pm Mar, Apr, Oct & Nov) is a good example: carved out from the cliff face above the winding Vézère River, the lower level was occupied by prehistoric people 10,000 to 14,000 years ago, while the upper level was used as a fortified village by medieval settlers. Though largely ruined, you can still visit the Ste-Madeleine chapel (after which the Magdalenian era is named), but most of the archeological artefacts are at the Musée National de Préhistoire in Les Eyzies (p630).

La Roque St-Christophe

This 900m-long series of terraces and **caves** (☎ 05 53 50 70 45; www.roque-st-christophe.com; adult/12-16yr/5-11yr €7/4/3; ⏲ 10am-8pm Jul & Aug, 10am-6.30pm Apr-Jun & Sep, 10am-6pm Feb, Mar & Oct–mid-Nov, 2-5pm mid-Nov–Jan) sits on a sheer cliff face 80m above the Vézère. Thanks to its commanding position high above the valley, the cave complex makes a practically unassailable stronghold, and it's been employed as a natural fortress for almost 50 millennia – initially by Mousterian (Neanderthal) people 50,000 years ago, followed by successive generations until the 16th century. The sweeping views are stunning, though the caverns themselves are largely empty and some of the plastic reconstructions are decidedly lame.

La Roque St-Christophe is on the D706, 9km northeast of Les Eyzies.

Le Thot

In an effort to bring the prehistoric age to life, the museum and animal park at **Le Thot** (☎ 05 53 50 70 44; www.semitour.com; adult/6-12yr €5.80/3.80, joint ticket with Lascaux €11.50/7.80; 9am-7pm Jul & Aug, 10am-noon & 2-5.30pm Tue-Sun Sep-Jun, closed Jan) places displays about Cro-Magnon life alongside real-life beasties depicted by our prehistoric forebears, including reindeer, stags, horses, ibex and European bison. The kids even get to try their hand at a spot of cave painting.

Montignac

pop 3101

The riverside town of Montignac, 25km northeast of Les Eyzies, is most famous for its proximity to the Grottes de Lascaux, which are hidden away on the thickly wooded hilltops a couple of miles from town. Huddled along both banks of the Vézère, Montignac is a peaceful, attractive place and makes a less hectic base than Les Eyzies or Sarlat. The old city and commercial centre is on the river's right bank, but you'll find most of the hotels on the left bank around place Tourny.

LIMOUSIN, THE DORDOGNE & QUERCY

INFORMATION

There are three banks near the tourist office.

Post Office (place Tourny) Offers currency exchange.

Tourist Office (☎ 05 53 51 82 60; www.bienvenue-montignac.com; place Bertrand de Born; 9am-7pm Jul–mid-Sep, 9am-noon & 2-6pm Mon-Sat Apr-Jun & mid-Sep–Oct, 10am-noon & 2-5pm Mon-Sat Nov-Mar) Around 200m west of place Tourny, next to the 14th-century Église St-Georges le Prieuré.

SLEEPING & EATING

Hôtel de la Grotte (☎ 05 53 51 80 48; www.hoteldelagrotte.fr; place Tourny; d €30-75; P) Small, sweet and chichi, this unpretentious country *auberge* makes a charming stop as long as you don't mind frilly bedspreads and floral wallpaper. The gingerbread rooms themselves are a little poky (especially the attic ones, huddled in around the roof beams), but they're reasonably priced and quite comfortable.

Hotel le Lascaux (☎ 05 53 51 82 81; www.hotel-le-lascaux.fr; 109 av Jean-Jaurès; d €45-64; P) Candy-cane awnings and climbing ivy decorate the front of this family-owned place on the main road to Lascaux from Montignac. It's relaxed and unfussy, with snug, simple rooms, some with striped wallpaper and wooden beds, others more on the drab side. Bag one with a view on to the tree-shaded back garden and you'll be a very happy camper.

La Roseraie (☎ 05 53 50 53 92; www.laroseraie-hotel.com; 11 place des Armes; r €80-170;) The name gives the game away: the highlight of this lovely mansion-cum-hotel is the gorgeous rose garden behind the house, set around box-edged grounds and a palm-tinged pool. Inside the house are rococo rooms in various shades of damask pink and sunflower yellow, all with solid furniture, sparkling bathrooms and those essential garden views. Truffles, chestnuts, pork and guineafowl find their way on to the seasonal menu (*menus* from €21), and on warm summer nights the canopy-shaded terrace is the only place to be.

GETTING THERE & AWAY

Montignac is on the 7A and 7B bus routes between Périgueux (€2, 1½ hours, one or two daily) and Sarlat (€2, 35 minutes, one or two daily). Buses stop on place Tourny.

Grotte de Lascaux

France's most famous prehistoric cave paintings are to be found at the **Grotte de Lascaux**, 2km southeast of Montignac. Discovered in 1940 by four teenage boys who were out searching for their lost dog, Lascaux contains a vast network of chambers and galleries adorned with some of the most extraordinary and complex prehistoric paintings ever found.

Far from the comparatively crude etchings of some of the Vézère's other caves, Lascaux' paintings are renowned for their astonishing artistry: the 600-strong menagerie of animal figures are depicted in Technicolor shades of red, black, yellow and brown, and range from reindeer, aurochs, mammoths and horses to a monumental 5.5m-long bull, the largest cave drawing ever found. Lascaux is sometimes referred to as the prehistoric equivalent of the Sistine Chapel, and it's a fitting comparison: after a visit in 1940, Picasso allegedly muttered, 'We have invented nothing'.

LOCAL VOICES: PHILIPPE CAMBA, CAVE GUIDE AT LASCAUX

Officially I'm a teacher by profession but I've always been fascinated by prehistory. I originally studied eco-biology and palaeontology, and for the last three years I've been combining teaching in the winter with my work as a cave guide in the summer.

In the summer season we can have up to 2000 visitors a day at Lascaux, and take up to six tours each. I do tours in English and French. The most amusing ones are the tours for Japanese and Chinese visitors, who usually bring along their own tour guide to do the translation but don't always know all the right words – so over the last few years I've learned all the names of the colours, animals and the different body parts in Japanese. It helps a lot!

Lascaux is a unique place, with over 2000 of the finest polychrome paintings ever discovered, as well as the largest cave painting ever found. It's amazing to think that these paintings were all done in one go – they never used sketches or drafts because they couldn't rub out their mistakes. They were real artists, who understood perspective, colour and form. In their own way, Lascaux' paintings are just as complex as those of Picasso or van Gogh. For me, the best scenes are the ones that show the animals in mid-movement. They're like prehistoric movies.

Sadly, I've never been able to see the original paintings, which were closed for good in 2000. It's a real shame, but I hope one day I might get the chance. You never know!

Carbon dating has shown that the paintings are between 15,000 and 17,000 years old. But despite endless discussion and academic study, no one really knows why the prehistoric painters devoted so much time and effort to their creation, or why this particular site seems to have been so important to them.

The original cave was opened to visitors in 1948, and public interest was unsurprisingly massive. But within a few years it became apparent that human breath and body heat was causing irreparable damage to the paintings, and they were closed just 15 years later in 1963. (More recently a mysterious white fungus has caused new concerns about the paintings' safety).

In response to public demand, a replica of the most famous sections of the original cave was meticulously recreated a few hundred metres away – a massive undertaking that required the skills of some 20 artists and took over 11 years. **Lascaux II** (☎ 05 53 51 95 03; www.semitour.com; adult/6-12yr €8.30/5.30, joint ticket with Le Thot €11.50/7.80; 🕑 9am-8pm Jul & Aug, 9.30am-6.30pm Sep & Apr-Jun, 10am-12.30pm & 2-6pm Oct–mid-Nov, 10am-12.30pm & 2-5.30pm mid-Nov–Mar) was opened in 1983, and although the idea sounds rather contrived, the reproductions are enormously moving – especially when the lights are turned off and the paintings seem to spring to life in the light of a flickering torch.

As one of France's most famous sites, the caves can get extremely busy in the height of summer, so it's definitely worth visiting outside July and August if you can. There are several guided tours every hour. Ask at the ticket office about the availability of tours in English, Spanish, German and Japanese.

Reservations aren't strictly necessary, but it's worth booking ahead just in case. From April to October, tickets are sold *only* in Montignac (next to the tourist office).

Domme

pop 1030

Commanding an unparalleled view across the surrounding countryside from a dizzying outcrop above the Dordogne, the fortified village of **Domme** is one of the area's best preserved *bastides* and still retains most of its 13th-century ramparts and three original gateways. Approached via a tortuous switchback road from the valley below, it's the perfect defensive stronghold – a fact certainly not lost on Philippe III of France, who founded the town in 1281 as a stronghold against the English. The town's imposing clifftop position is best appreciated from the **esplanade du Belvédère** and the adjacent **promenade de la Barre**, which both offer panoramic views across the valley.

Honeycombing the stone underneath the village is a series of large caves, known as the **grottes naturelles à concrétions** (adult/student/5-14yr incl museum €6.50/5.50/4; 🕑 10am-7pm Jul & Aug, 10am-noon & 2-6pm Sep-Dec & Feb-Jun), decorated with some of the most ornate stalactites and stalagmites in the Dordogne. A lift whisks you back up at the end of the 30-minute tour. Tickets are available from the **tourist office** (☎ 05 53 31 71 00; place de la Halle; 10am-7pm Jul & Aug, 10am-noon & 2-6pm Feb-Jun & Sep–mid-Nov, 2-5pm Mon-Fri mid-Nov–Dec, closed Jan), opposite the entrance to the caves.

Across the square from the tourist office, the **Musée d'Arts et Traditions Populaires** (adult/student/child €3/2.50/2, free with cave ticket; Apr-Sep) has nine rooms of artefacts, including clothing, toys and tools, mainly from the 19th century. Domme is about 18km south of Sarlat along the D46.

SLEEPING & EATING

Le Nouvel Hôtel (☎ 05 53 28 38 67; domme-nouvel-hotel@wanadoo.fr; 1 Grand Rue; d from €50) Up to date it certainly ain't, but this pocket-size *auberge* on the corner of the main square still has plenty of old-fashioned appeal. The 17 rooms are small and country-cosy: think scuffed wooden furniture, rough stone walls and well-worn rugs, and you won't be far wrong.

La Guérinière (☎ 05 53 29 91 97; www.la-gueriniere-dordogne.com; Cénac et St-Julien; d €54-79, q €94-129; P) Surrounded by its own 15-acre grounds, this wonderful *chambre d'hôte* offers five rooms and two self-contained cottages just along the D46 near Domme. The rooms are all named after flowers and finished with impeccably good taste: our faves are Mimosa, with its sloping roof and chinoiserie wardrobe, and the super-size Blue room.

L'Esplanade (☎ 05 53 28 31 41; rue du Pont-Carral; www.esplanade-perigord.com; d low season €77-128, high season €85-150) This place is an absolute spoil from start to finish. Teetering on the edge of the village ramparts, it's a traditional family-owned hotel with a twist of designer chic: four-poster beds, antique desks and upholstered armchairs fill the elegant rooms, some of which have balconies with mind-boggling valley views. Downstairs there's a top-notch restaurant (*menus* €42 to €78) with a to-die-for terrace overlooking the esplanade du Belvédère.

Château de Castelnaud

The **Château de Castelnaud** (☎ 05 53 31 30 00; www.castelnaud.com; adult/10-17yr €7.60/3.80; 9am-8pm Jul & Aug, 10am-7pm Apr-Jun & Sep, 10am-6pm Feb, Mar & Oct–mid-Nov, 2-5pm mid-Nov–Jan) certainly fits the blueprint for the quintessential castle. Its massive ramparts and metre-thick walls are topped by crenellations and sturdy towers from where you can see right across the Dordogne Valley to Castelnaud's arch-rival, the Château de Beynac (opposite). Inside the castle is a **museum of medieval warfare**, displaying daggers, spiked halberds and huge trebuchets. If you fancy seeing them in action, mock battles are staged throughout July and August, and there's a nightly guided tour (€9.60/5 for an adult/child) conducted by Jeanette, the castle's costumed cook. Castelnaud is 11km west of Domme along the D50 and D57.

La Roque Gageac

The jumble of amber buildings of La Roque Gageac, crammed into the cliff above a hairpin curve in the River Dordogne, has earned it official recognition as one of France's *beaux villages* (beautiful villages). It's certainly an entrancing spot, with a warren of meandering lanes leading up to the **Jardin Exotique** (Exotic Garden), the **church**, and the dramatic **Fort Troglodyte** (☎ 05 53 31 61 94; adult/child €4/2; 10am-7pm Mon-Sat Jul & Aug, Mon-Fri Apr–mid-Nov), where a series of defensive positions constructed by medieval engineers have been carved out from the overhanging cliffs.

MESSING ABOUT ON THE RIVER

One of the most atmospheric ways to explore the region's scenery is aboard a **gabarre**, a flat-bottomed, wooden boat used to transport freight up and down the rivers of the Périgord and Lot Valley. *Gabarres* were once a common sight in this part of France, but they had practically died out by the early 20th century, eclipsed by the rise of the railway and the all-conquering automobile. But these days they've been reinvented as river-going pleasure-vessels, and you can hop aboard for a tranquil cruise in several places, including the small village of La Roque Gageac.

Gabarres Caminade (☎ 05 53 29 40 95; vecchio@tiscali.fr; La Roque Gageac)

Gabarres de Bergerac (☎ 05 53 24 58 80; perigord.gabarres@worldonline.fr; Bergerac)

Gabarres de Beynac (☎ 05 53 28 51 15; www.gabarre-beynac.com; St-Martial de Nabirat) Ten kilometres south of Domme on the D46.

Gabarres Norbert (☎ 05 53 29 40 44; www.norbert.fr; La Roque Gageac)

Several canoe companies are based in the town, including **Canoë Dordogne** (☎ 05 53 29 58 50; contact@canoe-dordogne.fr; Le Bourg; 🕑 9am-7pm) next to the car park, which offers self-guided canoe trips of between one and five hours from various points upriver of La Roque Gageac, as well as guided trips in an eight to 10 person canoe.

Just out of town, **Canoë Vacances** (☎ 05 53 28 17 07; www.canoevacances.com; La Peyssière; 🕑 9am-7pm) offers three itineraries from La Roque Gageac to Les Milandes (€10, 9km), from Carsac to La Roque Gageac (€12, 16km) and Carsac to Les Milandes (€17, 25km). There's a choice of two- to four-person canoes or single kayaks, and minibus trips are included in the price. Adventurous types can even try out a spot of canyoning (from €4 to €7).

Down below, the quay also serves as a launch point for short **river cruises** aboard a traditional *gabarre* (see boxed text, opposite).

La Roque Gageac sits on a curve in the Dordogne 15km south of Sarlat, via the D46 and D703.

Château de Beynac

Looming ominously from atop a limestone bluff, the 12th-century **Beynac Château** (☎ 05 53 29 50 40; adult/5-11yr €7/3; 🕑 10am-6pm Mar-Sep, 10am-dusk Oct-Feb) commands a panoramic position above the Dordogne, making it a key defensive position during the Hundred Years War. Apart from a brief interlude under Richard the Lionheart, Beynac remained fiercely loyal to the French monarchy, often placing it at odds with the English-controlled stronghold of nearby Castelnaud. Protected by 200m cliffs, a double wall and double moat, it presented a formidable proposition for any would-be attackers, but in fact Beynac saw little direct action; frontal assaults were far too costly in terms of money and manpower, and the châteaux of the Dordogne were defeated more often through machiavellian intrigue than brute force.

The château's main points of interest are the Romanesque keep, a grand Salle des États (State Room) and frescoed chapel, and the 16th- and 17th-century apartments built to lodge the castle barons. From the battlements, there's a dizzying view along the Dordogne to the château of Marqueyssac. Below the castle, a steep trail leads to the village of **Beynac-et-Cazenac**, 150m below on the river bank (and the D703).

From mid-March to mid-November, one-hour guided tours (in French) take place every half-hour.

Château des Milandes

This 15th-century **château** (☎ 05 53 59 31 21; www.milandes.com; adult/4-15yr €8/5.50; 🕑 9.30am-7.30pm Jul & Aug, 10am-6.30pm May, Jun, Sep & Oct) is less famous for its architecture than its former owner: the African-American dancer, singer and music-hall star Josephine Baker (1906–75), who took the Parisian cultural scene by storm in the 1920s with her raunchy performances at the Folies Bergères and La Revue Nègre. Baker was notorious for her outrageous fashion sense and eccentric habits – her most famous stage outfit consisted of nothing but a string of pearls and a skirt of bananas, and she often liked to walk her pet cheetah, Chiquita, on a lead around Paris, terrifying her fellow pedestrians.

Having made a fortune on the stage in the 1920s and early 1930s, Baker purchased the castle in 1936 and lived here until 1958. She was awarded the Croix de Guerre and the Legion of Honour for her work with the French Resistance during WWII, and was later active in the US civil-rights movement, but she is best remembered for her 'Rainbow Tribe' – 12 children from around the world adopted as 'an experiment in brotherhood' (Brangelina, take note).

The château houses a museum of artefacts relating to the great Ms Baker, and her famous tunes tinkle out from the speaker system as you stroll around the rooms. Oddly, there are also daily displays by the château's birds of prey between May and October. There are bilingual guided tours every hour or so – ask ahead if you're after one in English.

MONPAZIER

pop 560

Picturesquely poised on a hilltop 45km from Sarlat, Monpazier is the best-preserved *bastide* town in southwest France. Founded in 1284 by a representative of Edward I (king of England and duke of Aquitaine), Monpazier had a turbulent time during the Wars of Religion and the Peasant Revolts of the 16th century, but despite numerous assaults and campaigns, the town has survived remarkably intact. From the town's three gateways, Monpazier's grid-straight streets lead to the arcaded market square, **place des Cornières** (place Centrale), surrounded by a motley collection of stone houses that reflect centuries of building and rebuilding. In one corner is an old *lavoir* (washing place), once used for washing clothes. Thursday is market day, as it has been since the Middle Ages.

The **tourist office** (☎ 05 53 22 68 59; www.pays-des-bastides.com, in French; place des Cornières; 🕑 10am-7pm Jul & Aug, 10am-12.30pm & 2.30-6.30pm Tue-Sat, 2.30-6.30pm Sun Sep-Jun) is in the southeastern corner of the square.

There are several excellent campsites around Monpazier, including the four-star **Moulin de David** (☎ 05 53 22 65 25; www.moulin-de-david.com; campsite €16-25; 🕑 May-Aug), halfway between Monpazier and Biron in a quiet valley with 160 shady sites.

Hotel de France (☎ 05 53 22 60 06; www.hoteldefrancemonpazier.fr; 21 rue Saint Jacques; d €40-70; 🕑 Apr-Oct) Parts of this yellow-brick *auberge* date back centuries (the central staircase was built in the 1400s), so it certainly feels historic. There are wooden furnishings, old rugs and flowery wallpaper in the rooms, a solid country restaurant, and small shuttered windows overlooking the town's rooftops.

Hotel Edward 1er (☎ 05 53 22 44 00; www.hoteledward1er.com; 5 rue St-Pierre; d €64-116, ste €102-178; 🅿) This tower-topped château-cum-mansion is perfect for wannabe lords of the manor. Rooms get more luxuriant the more you pay: top-of-the-line suites have a choice of jacuzzi or Turkish bath, and views of surrounding hills. It feels slightly dated considering the price tag, but on the upside there's wi-fi and satellite TV throughout and the Dutch owners are full of beans.

Bistrot 2 (☎ 05 53 22 60 64; Monpazier; mains €13; 🕑 lunch Sun-Fri, dinner Tue-Thu & Sat) Modern bistro in a square stone-front inn, opposite one of the medieval gateways. Minimalist dishes, contemporary flavours and metropolitan style reinvent traditional Périgord staples, and the fine outside terrace is perfect for Sunday lunch or twilight suppers.

BERGERAC

pop 27,000

Rich vineyards and flat fields surround the solidly bourgeois town of Bergerac, capital of the Périgord Pourpre, one of the largest wine-growing areas of the Aquitaine. The town's main claim to fame is the dramatist and satirist Savinien Cyrano de Bergerac (1619–55), whose romantic exploits (and oversize nose) have inspired everyone from Molière to Steve Martin. Despite the legend (largely invented by the 19th-century playwright Edmond Rostand), Cyrano's connection with the town is pretty tenuous – he's thought to have only stayed here a few nights at most. Bergerac's cobbled old town and medieval harbour are worth exploring, though, and it's a handy stopover between Périgueux (47km to the northeast) and Bordeaux (93km to the west).

The **tourist office** (☎ 05 53 57 03 11; www.bergerac-tourisme.com; 97 rue Neuve d'Argenson; 🕑 9.30am-7.30pm Mon-Sat, 10.30am-1pm & 2-7pm Sun Jul & Aug, 9.30am-1pm & 2-7pm Mon-Sat Sep-Jun) has lots of information on local wine-tasting.

The prettiest parts of Bergerac's old town are the **place de la Mirpe**, with its tree-shaded square and timber houses, and **place Pelissière**, where a jaunty statue of Cyrano de Bergerac looks up at the nearby church.

The town's museums are dedicated to Bergerac's twin vices: wine and tobacco. The musty **Musée du Vin et de la Batellerie** (Wine and Shipping Museum; ☎ 05 53 57 80 92; place de la Mirpe; adult/child €2.50/1.50; 🕑 10am-noon & 2-5.30pm Tue-Fri, 10am-noon Sat) has displays of vintage wine-making equipment and scale models of local river boats, while the **Musée du Tabac** (☎ 05 53 63 04 13; 10 rue de l'Ancien Port; adult/child €3/1.50; 🕑 10am-noon & 2-6pm Tue-Fri year-round, 2-6pm Sat & Sun Mar-Nov, 2-6pm Mon Jul & Aug) collects lots of ornate pipes and tobacco-centred artefacts inside the 17th-century Maison Peyrarède.

Bergerac's vintages can be sampled at the **Maison des Vins** (☎ 05 53 63 57 55; admission free; 🕑 10am-12.30pm & 2-6pm Mon-Sat May-Sep, Tue-Sat Oct-Apr), which offers tasting sessions and sells wines produced by local châteaux.

Sleeping & Eating

Hotel du Commerce (☎ 05 53 27 30 50; 36 place Gambetta; d €39-55) This modern, lemon-coloured hotel is in a relaxed spot on place Gambetta, with functional if rather characterless rooms, all with free wi-fi, contemporary furnishings and up-to-date bathrooms.

La Bourbonnière (☎ 05 23 56 23 99; 15 place de la Mirpe; d €60) There are several sweet *chambres d'hôtes* around place de la Mirpe; this former riverboatman's cottage is one of the prettiest, with a couple of pocket-size rooms tucked around its wonky corridors, and chocolate-box windows peeking on to the shady square.

Le Logis Plantaganet (☎ 05 53 57 15 99; 5 rue du Grand Moulin; www.lelogisplantagenet.com; d €90) A more

CASTLE COUNTRY

While not quite in the same league as the Loire Valley, the châteaux of the Dordogne and Quercy are still well worth exploring. Here are some of our favourites:

Biron (Map p608; ☎ 05 53 63 13 39; adult/child €5.70/3.70; ⏰ Feb-Dec) This much-filmed château, 8km south of Monpazier, is a glorious mishmash of styles, having been fiddled with by eight centuries of successive heirs. Finally the castle was flogged in the early 1900s to pay for the extravagant lifestyle of a particularly irresponsible son.

Hautefort (Map p608; ☎ 05 53 50 51 23; www.chateau-hautefort.com; adult/child €8.50/4; ⏰ 9.30am-7pm daily Jun-Sep, 10am-12.30pm & 2-6pm Apr & May, 2-6pm weekends & holidays Mar & Oct–mid-Nov, closed mid-Nov–Feb) An imposing neoclassical château 40km east of Périgueux set around a central square and surrounded by formal gardens and flower terraces.

Jumilhac-le-Grand (Map p608; ☎ 05 53 52 42 97; château adult/child €6/4, château and gardens €7.50/5.50; ⏰ 10am-7pm daily Jun-Sep, 2-6pm Oct-Easter, 2-5pm Sun or by reservation Easter-May) This spiky-turreted, slate-topped château, 50km northeast of Périgueux, is renowned for its formal gardens and lavish rooms. Guides dressed in period costume conduct night-time tours in summer.

Losse (Map p631; ☎ 05 53 50 80 08; www.chateaudelosse.com; adult/child €7.50/3; ⏰ noon-7pm Jun-Aug, noon-6pm May & Sep) This château 5km southwest of Montignac features an original 15th-century moat and battlements, plus grandly furnished rooms filled with antique tapestries and furniture.

Puymartin (Map p631; ☎ 05 53 59 29 97; adult/child €7/3.50; ⏰ 10am-6.30pm daily Aug, 10am-noon & 2-6.30pm July, 10am-noon & 2-6pm Apr-Jun & Sep, 2-5.30pm Oct–mid-Nov, mornings by reservation) A partly furnished château 8km northwest of Sarlat, it's best known for its elegant interior and the mysterious Dame Blanche, whose restless spirit is said to haunt the château corridors.

upmarket B&B, with soft-coloured decor, polished floors and swanky fabrics in a timber-fronted building in the old city, and a communal kitchen or flowery back garden for breakfast.

Château Les Farcies du Pech' (☎ 05 53 82 48 31; www.chambre-hote-bergerac.com; Hameau de Pécharmant; 🅿) If you don't mind staying a little out of Bergerac, this château-winery-B&B (complete with its own brace of vintages) is a delight, with five rooms all finished in the same scrubbed-up style: patterned rugs, colour-washed walls, hardwood floors and the odd patch of original stonework. The French brekkie, served in the wood-beamed kitchen, is a treat.

L'Enfance de Lard (☎ 05 53 57 52 88; place Pélissière; menus from €30; ⏰ dinner Wed-Mon) Reached via a rickety staircase, this tiny 1st-floor restaurant only has six tables, but if you secure a seat you'll be treated to Bergerac's most comforting cooking. The carefully crafted menu only features a few dishes, hand-picked according to the season – grilled pigeon, perhaps, or rabbit with mustard – but here it's all about quality, not quantity.

Getting There & Away

Bergerac is on the regional train line between Bordeaux (€14.30, 1½ hours, hourly) and Sarlat (€10.70, 1½ hours, every two hours); for other destinations change at Le Buisson. The airport, 4km southeast of town, is served by budget flights from Paris (Air France). There are also seasonal flights to Bristol, Stansted, East Midlands and Liverpool (Ryanair), and to Birmingham, Exeter, Leeds, Southampton and Gatwick (Flybe).

QUERCY

Southeast of the Dordogne *département* lies the warm, unmistakably southern region of Quercy, many of whose residents still speak Occitan (Provençal), as well as French with a heavy southern accent. The dry limestone plateau in the northeast is covered with oak trees and riddled with canyons carved by the serpentine River Lot. The main city of Cahors is surrounded by some of the region's finest vineyards.

CAHORS

pop 21,432

Sheltered in a U-shape *boucle* (curve) in the River Lot, the bustling city of Cahors has the feel of a sunbaked Mediterranean town, a reminder that the southern region of Languedoc lies just to the south. Pastel-coloured buildings line the shady squares of the old medieval quarter, criss-crossed by a labyrinth of alleyways and cul-de-sacs, while around the edge of the old town run the hectic

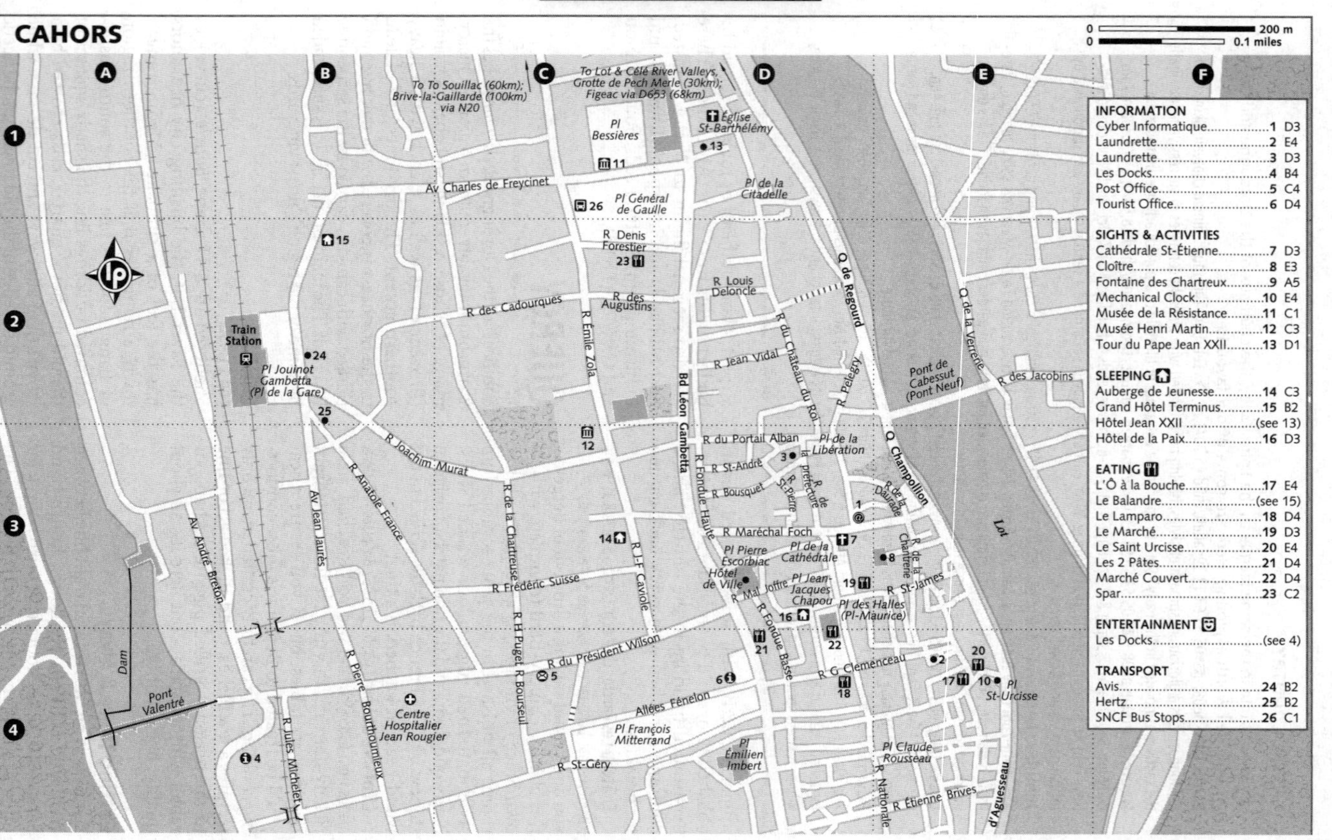
CAHORS
0 200 m
0 0.1 miles
INFORMATION
Cyber Informatique 1 D3
Laundrette 2 E4
Laundrette 3 D3
Les Docks 4 B4
Post Office 5 C4
Tourist Office 6 D4
SIGHTS & ACTIVITIES
Cathédrale St-Étienne 7 D3
Cloître 8 E3
Fontaine des Chartreux 9 A5
Mechanical Clock 10 E4
Musée de la Résistance 11 C1
Musée Henri Martin 12 C3
Tour du Pape Jean XXII 13 D1
SLEEPING
Auberge de Jeunesse 14 C3
Grand Hôtel Terminus 15 B2
Hôtel Jean XXII (see 13)
Hôtel de la Paix 16 D3
EATING
L'Ô à la Bouche 17 E4
Le Balandre (see 15)
Le Lamparo 18 D4
Le Marché 19 D3
Le Saint Urcisse 20 E4
Les 2 Pâtes 21 D4
Marché Couvert 22 D4
Spar 23 C2
ENTERTAINMENT
Les Docks (see 4)
TRANSPORT
Avis 24 B2
Hertz 25 B2
SNCF Bus Stops 26 C1
To To Souillac (60km); Brive-la-Gaillarde (100km) via N20
To Lot & Célé River Valleys; Grotte de Pech Merle (30km); Figeac via D653 (68km)
Église St-Barthélémy
Pl Bessières
Av Charles de Freycinet
Pl Général de Gaulle
Pl de la Citadelle
R Denis Forestier
R Louis Deloncle
Q de Regourd
Q de la Verrerie
R des Jacobins
Pont de Cabessut (Pont Neuf)
R des Cadourques
R des Augustins
R Émile Zola
R du Château du Roi
R Jean Vidal
R Pelegry
Train Station
Pl Jouinot Gambetta (Pl de la Gare)
Bd Léon Gambetta
R du Portail Alban
Pl de la Libération
Q Champollion
R Joachim Murat
R St-André
R Bousquet
R St-Pierre
R de la préfecture
R de la Daurade
R Anatole France
Av Jean Jaurès
R de la Chartreuse
R Fondue Haute
R Maréchal Foch
Lot
Av André Breton
R J-F Caviole
Pl Pierre Escorbiac
Pl de la Cathédrale
R de la Chantrerie
Hôtel de Ville
R Mal Joffre
Pl Jean-Jacques Chapou
R St-James
R Frédéric Suisse
Pl des Halles (Pl-Maurice)
R Fondue Basse
R du Président Wilson
R H Puget
R Bourseul
R G Clemenceau
R Pierre Bourthoumieux
Dam
Pont Valentré
Centre Hospitalier Jean Rougier
Allées Fénelon
Pl St-Urcisse
Pl François Mitterrand
Pl Émilien Imbert
Pl Claude Rousseau
R Jules Michelet
R St-Géry
R Nationale
R Étienne Brives
d'Aguesseau

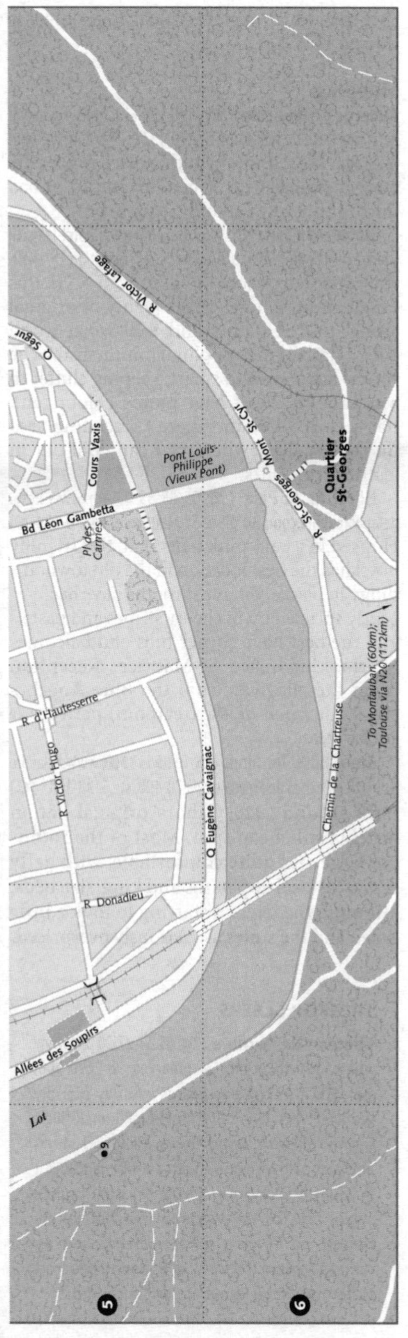

boulevards of the modern city and the medieval quays. Known for its delicious wines and a famous three-towered bridge, the Pont du Valentré, Cahors is an ideal base for exploring the Lot.

Orientation

Slicing through the centre of Cahors, and neatly dividing the old and new city, is bd Léon Gambetta (named after the French statesman who was born in Cahors in 1838). The modern city lies to the west, while Vieux Cahors (Old Cahors) is to the east. At Gambetta's northern end is place Général de Gaulle, essentially a giant car park; about 500m to the south is place François Mitterrand and the tourist office, currently the focus of a major municipal redevelopment project.

Information

INTERNET ACCESS

Cyber Informatique (☎ 05 65 53 66 98; place Clement Marot; per hr €2; ⏰ 10am-8pm Mon-Sat, 2-8pm Sun)
Les Docks (430 allées des Soupirs; per hr €3; ⏰ 2-6pm & 8-10pm Tue, 2-6pm Wed, Fri & Sat) Free wi-fi or fixed computers in Cahors' buzzy arts centre.

LAUNDRY

Laundrette (place de la Libération; ⏰ 7am-9pm)
Laundrette (208 rue Georges Clémenceau; ⏰ 7am-9pm)

MONEY

There are several high-street banks along bd Léon Gambetta, open either Tuesday to Saturday or Monday to Friday.

POST

Post Office (257 rue Président Wilson)

TOURIST INFORMATION

Tourist Office (☎ 05 65 53 20 65; officetourisme@mairie-cahors.fr; place François Mitterrand; ⏰ 9am-6.30pm Mon-Sat, 10am-1pm Sun Jul & Aug, 9am-12.30pm & 1.30-6pm Mon-Sat Sep-Jun)
Comité Départemental du Tourisme (☎ 05 65 35 07 09; www.tourisme-lot.com; 1st fl, 107 quai Eugène Cavaignac; ⏰ 8am-12.30pm & 1.30-6pm Mon-Thu, to 5.30pm Fri) Provides information on the Lot *département*.

Sights & Activities

Cahors is ringed on three sides by the **quays**, which once harboured the city's river-going traffic, but are now mostly used by cyclists, rollerbladers and afternoon strollers. On the west side of Cahors is the **Pont Valentré**, one

LIMOUSIN, THE DORDOGNE & QUERCY

of France's finest medieval bridges, consisting of six arches and three tall towers, two of which have projecting parapets designed to allow defenders to drop missiles on attackers below. The main body of the bridge was built in the 14th century and the towers were added later. The bridge was built as part of the town's defences, not to carry traffic.

On the bank opposite the bridge, the natural spring known as the **Fontaine des Chartreux**, dedicated to the city's Gallo-Roman goddess Divona, still supplies the city's drinking water. Many Roman coins have been found here, and the subterranean cavern has been explored to 137m.

In the Middle Ages, Cahors was a prosperous commercial centre, and the old city is densely packed with timber-fronted houses and galleried mansions (many of which are marked on the *Itinéraires à Travers la Ville* leaflet from the tourist office) built by the city's medieval merchants.

The Romanesque **Cathédrale St-Étienne** (admission free), consecrated in 1119, is similar in style to the Cathédrale St-Front in Périgueux (p622), with an airy nave topped by two cupolas (at 18m wide, the largest in France). Some of the frescoes are 14th century, but the side chapels and carvings in the **cloître** (cloister; Jun-Sep) mainly date from the Flamboyant Gothic period in the 16th century. On the cathedral's north facade is a carved tympanum depicting Christ surrounded by fluttering angels and pious saints; while not quite as ambitious as the one in Beaulieu (p620), it's still impressive.

Near the cathedral at place St-Urcisse, there's a weird **mechanical clock** (1997) that looks like something out of Tim Burton's sketchbook.

At the top of the old city is the **Tour du Pape Jean XXII** (1-3 bd Léon Gambetta), the town's tallest building at 34m high, and originally part of a 14th-century mansion belonging to Jacques Duèse (later Pope John XXII), who constructed the Pont Valentré and founded Cahors' university. The building is not open to the public.

Cahors' only museums are the **Musée Henri Martin** (Musée Municipal; 05 65 30 15 13; 792 rue Émile Zola; adult/6-18yr/under 6yr €3/1.50/free; 11am-6pm Mon & Wed-Sat, 2-6pm Sun), with works by the Cahors-born pointillist painter Henri Martin (1893–1972), and the little **Musée de la Résistance** (05 65 22 14 25; place Général de Gaulle; admission free; 2-6pm), which explores the city's experiences during WWII.

Sleeping

Auberge de Jeunesse (05 65 35 64 71; fjt46@wanadoo.fr; 20 rue Frédéric Suisse; dm €12.10-15.70; 9am-12.30pm & 2-7pm;) Cahors' youth hostel is friendly and functional, with 50 beds in four- to 10-bed dorms housed in an old city convent.

Hôtel Jean XXII (05 65 35 07 66; www.hotel-jeanxxii.com; 2 rue Edmond-Albé; s/d/tr €44/53/57; reception 4.40-8pm) Huddled next to the Tour Jean XXII, this excellent little hotel mixes plenty of original stone, potted plants and well-worn wood with a flash of metropolitan minimalism. The rooms are plain and smart, keeping clutter to a minimum. Most have muted colours and flat-screen TVs, and there's a reading area on the 1st floor where you can chill out in leather armchairs.

Hôtel de la Paix (05 65 35 03 40; www.hoteldelapaixcahors.com; 30 place St-Maurice; s €48, d €54-70) Housed in a pale-pink tenement, this friendly hotel has the best location in the old town. It's dingy in places, but most rooms have been recently spruced up in cheery stripes and pastels and the best have corner tubs and balconies overlooking place St-Maurice. Reception is up the alleyway from the Blue Angel, a streetside *salon de thé* (tearoom) perfect for sticky treats.

Grand Hôtel Terminus (05 65 53 32 00; www.balandre.com; 5 av Charles de Freycinet; d €70-100, ste €130-160;) Built around 1920, Cahors' original station hotel is still a top spot. Most of the rooms are large and quite comfortable, with hefty radiators, roll-top baths and king-size beds, although the decor's starting to look a little dated and the suites are seriously overpriced.

TREETOP SLEEPS

Château de Gauthie (05 53 27 30 33; www.chateaugauthie.com; Monmarves; d €90-100; P) This château B&B is a family-friendly wonder, with five delightful knick-knack-filled rooms, all with wood floors, parkland views and a choice of wooden or cast-iron beds. But if you're looking for a truly unusual night's sleep, ask for the wooden tree house, accessed via its own spiral staircase and arranged around the trunk of a soaring oak tree. Note that credit cards are not accepted.

THE GOOD LIFE

If you're looking to get back to the land, take some tips from the owners of **Tondes** (☎ 05 63 94 52 13; Castelsagrat; d €47; P), a pair of expat Brits who upped sticks for rural France to set up an eco-friendly, sustainable, 100% organic farm. All the eggs, milk, yoghurt and organic vegetables are produced on the farm, and even the bread's home-baked, so you couldn't really ask for a greener place to stay. The simple B&B rooms are decked out with country fabrics, walk-in showers and rustic decor, and if you fancy trying your hand at a spot of milking or vegetable tending, the owners will be only too happy to oblige. It's about 56km southwest of Cahors.

Eating

Les 2 Pâtes (bd Leon Gambetta; pastas €5-8) For a quick lunchtime fix, this Italianate takeaway is a great bet. Pick a panini, a sandwich or a pasta-and-sauce combo and it's served up pronto (the ice-cream sundaes are good, too). You can either eat on the move or sit in on the streetside terrace.

Le Lamparo (☎ 05 65 35 25 93; 76 rue Georges Clémenceau; menus €15.60-21.80; lunch & dinner) Uncomplicated Italian cuisine packs in the punters at the Lamparo, where you'll find the usual wood-fired pizzas, pastas and meat-based staples served in a Med-style dining room. The waiters might come across as Mafia rejects, but the food's decent enough.

Le Saint Urcisse (☎ 05 65 35 06 06; place St-Urcisse; mains €19.50-25.50; lunch & dinner Tue-Sat) Homespun cooking *à la grand-mère*, served in a cosy kitchen-style dining room or a walled courtyard filled with fairy lights and birdsong. It's popular for its *picadors brochettes* (kebabs), which come with duck, chicken, prawns or lamb.

L'O à la Bouche (☎ 05 65 35 65 69; 134 rue St-Urcisse; menus €19.50-26.50; lunch & dinner Tue-Sat) Things are more sophisticated across the street at the Michelin-rated O, where '*cuisine creative*' is the watchword and classic ingredients are given a fresh spin by the Belgian-born chef, such as cod in a peanut crust and a gorgeous '*tout coco*' chocolate pudding.

Le Marché (☎ 05 65 35 27 27; place Jean-Jacques Chapon; menus €25-35; lunch & dinner Tue-Sat) Fusion food in funky surroundings is the order of the day at the Market. Puce-and-cream armchairs, razor-edge wood and slate walls set the designer tone, and the menu's just as swish, swinging from roast tarragon beef to lemon-scented sea bass.

Le Balandre (☎ 05 65 53 32 00; www.balandre.com; 5 av Charles de Freycinet; menus €42-60; lunch & dinner) If it's posh and pricey you want, then Le Balandre is the place. The long-standing gourmet restaurant at the Grand Hotel Terminus commands a devoted following, especially for timeless slices of foie gras and *confit de canard*. Expect chandeliers, sparkling glasses and napkins you could cut your finger on.

SELF-CATERING

Top place for supplies is the **Marché Couvert** (place des Halles; 8am-12.30pm & 3-7pm Tue-Sat, 9am-noon Sun), usually referred to as Les Halles. The twice-weekly open-air market takes place on nearby place Chapon on Wednesdays and Saturdays. For emergencies there's a **Spar** (place Général de Gaulle; 8.30am-12.30pm & 3-7.30pm Mon-Sat).

Entertainment

Les Docks (☎ 05 65 22 36 38; 430 allées des Soupirs) is a former warehouse turned cultural centre, with regular gigs, theatre, films and a multimedia café.

Getting There & Away

BUS

The tourist office has a booklet of bus timetables, *Les Bus du Lot*, but most routes are geared around school-term times, making buses a frustrating way of getting around. Destinations from Cahors include Figeac (line 16; 80 minutes, four to six daily), via Bouziès (30 minutes), and Villefranche-de-Rouergue (line 1 or 2; one daily) .

CAR

Car-hire firms include **Avis** (☎ 05 65 30 13 10; place de la Gare) and **Hertz** (☎ 05 65 35 34 69; 385 rue Anatole France), opposite the train station.

Parking is free along the river and at place Charles de Gaulle.

TRAIN

Cahors' **train station** (place Jouinot Gambetta, aka place de la Gare) is on the main line to Paris' Gare d'Austerlitz (€63.80, five hours, eight to 10 daily) via Brive-la-Gaillarde (€16.90, one hour), Limoges (€28.70, two hours), and Souillac (€12.30, 40 minutes), from where there are coaches to Sarlat (€15, three hours, two daily).

EAST OF CAHORS

The narrow, winding and wonderfully scenic D662 (signposted 'Vallée du Lot') tracks the banks of the River Lot eastwards from Cahors towards Figeac, passing through the peaceful towns of Bouziès and Conduché and the gravity-defying hillside village of St-Cirq Lapopie.

Grotte de Pech Merle

Discovered in 1922, the 1200m-long **Pech Merle Cave** (☎ 05 65 31 27 05; www.pechmerle.com; adult/5-18yr mid-Jun–mid-Sep €7.50/4.50, mid-Sep–mid-Jun €6/3.80; 9.30-noon & 1.30-5pm Easter-Nov) is perched high on the hills above the riverside town of Les Cabrerets, 30km northeast of Cahors. One of the few decorated caves to be discovered around the Lot Valley, Pech Merle makes an intriguing comparison to those in the Vézère, with several wonderful galleries of mammoths, cows, bison and dappled horses, as well as some unique hand tracings, fingerprints and human figures. But the most memorable part of the cave is saved till last – a beautifully preserved adolescent footprint, clearly imprinted into the muddy clay floor.

Entry is by guided tour (usually in French, but some have an English translation); the time of your visit will be imprinted on your ticket. Reserve well ahead in July and August, as visitor numbers are limited to 700 per day.

St-Cirq Lapopie

pop 50

Teetering at the crest of a sheer cliff high above the River Lot, the miniscule village of St-Cirq Lapopie is one of the most popular places in the Lot, and with good reason. With a muddle of terracotta-roof villages and ramshackle streets tumbling down the steep hillside, it's a gorgeous place to stroll and admire the panoramic valley views, but be warned – if it's peace and tranquillity you're looking for, you won't find it in high summer.

The **tourist office** (☎ 05 65 31 29 06; saint-cirq .lapopie@wanadoo.fr; 10am-1pm & 2-7.30pm daily Jun-Sep, closed Sun Apr, May & Oct, closed Sun & Mon Nov-Mar) is in the village hall. Nearby is the early-16th-century **Gothic church** and the steep path up to the ruined **château** at the summit of the village, where you'll be rewarded with a jaw-dropping panorama across the Lot Valley.

Many of the village's houses have been converted into artists studios producing pottery, craftwork and jewellery. There's a small town museum, the **Maison de la Fourdonne** (☎ 05 65 31 21 51; adult/under 10yr €1.50/1, free with car-park ticket; 2.30-7pm Tue-Sun Apr-Nov), housing a collection of old postcards, pots and archeological artefacts, while the **Musée Rignault** (admission €2; 10am-12.30pm & 2.30-6pm Apr-Oct, to 7pm Jul & Aug) has a delightful garden and an eclectic collection of French furniture and African and Chinese art.

There are some good campsites near St-Cirq, including the riverside **La Plage** (☎ 05 65 30 29 51; www.campingplage.com; sites per person €5.50-8, plus €5.10; Apr-Nov) on the left bank of the Lot, and **La Truffière** (☎ 05 65 30 20 22; http://camping-truffiere .com; Le Causse; sites €5.50-8, plus per person €5.10), 3km from St-Cirq along the D42.

St-Cirq's hotels are seriously oversubscribed (and mostly overpriced), but if you want to stay, the **Auberge de Sombral** (☎ 05 65 31 26 08; www.lesombral.com; d €50-78) is a gorgeous option, with seven cosy doubles and a titchy attic room peppered around the red-roofed house, opposite the tourist office.

Even better is the homely **Hôtel de La Pelissaria** (☎ 05 65 31 25 14; http://perso.wanadoo.fr /hoteldelapelissaria; r €79-156; Apr-Oct;), at the bottom of the steep main street in a lovingly restored 16th-century house filled to the rafters with curios, antiques and objets d'art. All the rooms are endearingly different: some have cast-iron beds and hefty roof beams, others stained glass and exposed brickwork, and there are a few dotted around the garden in converted outbuildings.

Le Gourmet Quercynois (☎ 05 65 31 21 20; menus €19.90-36.80; lunch & dinner) is the village's top table, a charmingly chaotic place with a menu of biblical proportions ranging from *nougat de porc* to country *cassoulet* (stew). The tables are packed in tight, but you can always escape to the little patio to catch the evening rays. The in-house deli sells local spoils, including *cèpe* (porcini) mushrooms, gingerbread and chestnut cake.

St-Cirq is 25km east of Cahors and 44km southwest of Figeac. The main car park (€3) is at the top of the village. There's also a free one further down from where a path leads up to St-Cirq's main street. The No 16 bus between Cahors and Figeac (see p643) stops at Tour-de-Faure; from here, it's a lung-busting 3km uphill walk to the village.

Figeac

pop 9500

The riverside town of Figeac, 70km northeast of Cahors, has a rough-and-ready charm that comes as a refreshing change after many of the primped and prettified towns of the Dordogne and Lot. Traffic buzzes along the river boulevards and the old town has an appealingly lived-in feel, with shady streets lined with ramshackle medieval and Renaissance houses, many with open-air galleries on the top floor (once used for drying leather). History fills the streets of Figeac: founded by Benedictine monks, and later an important medieval trading post and pilgrim's stopover, the town's most recent claim to fame is as the birthplace, in 1790, of Jean-François Champollion, the brilliant linguist who deciphered the Rosetta Stone.

INFORMATION

Allô Laverie (6am-10pm) This laundrette is next to the tourist office.

Post Office (8 av Fernand Pezet) Offers currency exchange.

Tourist Office (05 65 34 06 25; www.tourisme-figeac.com; place Vival; 10am-7.30pm Jul & Aug, 10am-12.30pm & 2.30-6pm Mon-Sat, 10am-12.30pm Sun Sep-Jun)

SIGHTS

The historic centre of Figeac is place Vival, where the tourist office occupies the ground floor of an arcaded 13th-century building, part of Figeac's lost abbey. Upstairs the **Musée du Vieux Figeac** (adult/child €2/1; 10am-7.30pm Jul & Aug, 10am-12.30pm & 2.30-6pm Mon-Sat, 10am-12.30pm Sun May, Jun & Sep, 10am-noon & 2.30-6pm Mon-Sat Oct-Apr) has a collection of antique clocks, coins, minerals and a propeller blade made by a local aerospace firm.

For a guide to the town's medieval and Renaissance architecture, pick up the leaflet *Les Clefs de la Ville* from the tourist office. **Rue de Balène** and **rue Caviale** have the best examples of 14th- and 15th-century houses, many with wooden galleries, timber frames and original stone carvings, while **rue de Colomb** has several fine *hôtels particuliers* dating from the Renaissance.

The lively Saturday morning market still takes place under the 19th-century cast-iron arcade on place Carnot, while on place Champollion you'll find the lavishly restored **Musée Champollion** (05 65 50 31 08; rue des Frères Champollion; adult/child €4/2; 10.30am-6pm Jul & Aug, 10.30am-12.30 & 2-6pm Tue-Sun Apr-Jun & Sep, 2-5.30pm Tue-Sun Oct-Mar), named after the Figeac-born Egyptologist and linguist Jean-François Champollion (1790–1832), whose efforts in deciphering the Rosetta Stone provided the key for cracking Egyptian hieroglyphics. The museum is now devoted to the history of writing, with exhibits ranging from illustrated medieval manuscripts to Chinese writing tools.

Behind the museum on **place des Écritures** is a huge replica of the Rosetta tablets, created by the artist Joseph Kosuth in 1990.

SLEEPING & EATING

Hôtel des Bains (05 65 34 10 89; www.hoteldesbains.fr; 1 rue Griffoul; d €45-68) Sailing along by the riverside like a salmon-pink pleasure vessel, this dainty family-owned hotel makes a cheap, cheery stopover in Figeac. Formerly a public bathhouse (hence the name), the hotel's 19 rooms are small and low-key, decked out in crisp whites and sunny pastels; the choicest ones have balconies overlooking the river.

Hostellerie de l'Europe (05 65 34 10 16; www.hostelleriedeleurope.com; 51 allée Victor Hugo; r €45-65;) An efficient Inter Hotel just behind the river on one of the town's main exit roads. Behind the crimson-shuttered facade you'll find up-to-date rooms with spacious bathrooms, functional fixtures and wi-fi throughout, although most are short on character. The frilly hotel restaurant, La Table de Marinette (mains €15 to €20), is a good bet for old-fashioned Quercy dishes; Marinette takes the orders herself before bustling off to the kitchen to supervise the cooking.

Hôtel-Café Champollion (05 65 34 04 37; fax 05 65 34 61 69; 3 place Champollion; mains from €10-16; lunch & dinner) This cool and contemporary café-bar, decked out in zingy colours and modern art is as popular for a morning café as a late-night *bière à la pression* (draught beer). The lunchtime salads are also really good. Rooms (from €50 to €70) are available upstairs, but the late-night noise can be taxing.

Brasserie 5 (05 65 50 10 81; place Champollion; menus €17-24; dinner Wed-Mon) This ritzy new restaurant is dripping with designer style, with plenty of dark wood, plate-glass windows and rich colour schemes for that boutique feel. Thankfully it's not a case of style over substance: the food's the best in Figeac, with inventive variations on classic dishes such as roasted sea bream and *carpaccio de boeuf*.

For self-caterers there's an **E Leclerc Express** (🕑 8.30am-12.30pm & 3-7.30pm Mon-Fri, 8.30am-1pm & 2.30-7.30pm Sat) on the corner of rue 11 Novembre, but the choicest ingredients can be found at the Saturday morning market on place Carnot.

GETTING THERE & AWAY

The most useful trains from Figeac are west to Cahors (€11.40, one hour 40 minutes, four to six daily Monday to Saturday) via Tour-de-Faure; south to Villefranche de Rouergue (€6.40, 35 minutes, six to eight daily) and Najac (€8.70, 50 minutes, six to eight daily); and north to Brive-la-Gaillarde (€12.90, 80 minutes, six daily).

Villefranche de Rouergue

pop 12,300

Villefranche's origins as a *bastide* town are barely recognisable beneath the main roads, refurbished buildings and busy shopping streets, but at the centre of the timber-framed old town is the arcaded **place Notre Dame** – a typical example of a *bastide* square – which still hosts the lively Thursday-morning market. Nearby is the square-pillared 15th-century **Collégiale Notre Dame**, with its never-completed bell tower and choir stalls, ornamented with a menagerie of comical and cheeky figures.

A few blocks to the southwest, the **Musée Urbain Cabrol** (☎ 05 65 45 44 37; rue de la Fontaine; 🕑 10am-noon & 2-6.30pm Tue-Sat Jul & Aug, 2-6pm Tue-Sat Apr-Jun & Sep) has an eclectic collection of religious art, local folk art and 19th-century medical equipment. The **fountain** out front, decorated with 14th-century carvings, gushes from a natural spring.

The **tourist office** (☎ 05 65 45 13 18; www.villefranche.com; promenade du Guiraudet; 🕑 9am-noon & 2-6pm Mon-Sat May-Oct, 9am-noon & 2-6pm Mon-Sat, 10am-noon Sun Jul & Aug, 9am-noon & 2-6pm Mon-Fri Nov-Apr) is next to the town hall.

Villefranche's hotels are patchy. The best value and most central is **L'Univers** (☎ 05 65 45 15 63; 2 place de la République; d €55-58), a decent Logis de France with passable rooms – all furnished in similar style with '80s furniture and dated bathrooms. Get one with a river balcony if you can.

A more luxurious option is **Le Relais de Farrou** (☎ 05 65 45 18 11; www.relaisdefarrou.com; rte de Figeac; s €52-69.50, d €63.50-86.50, ste €95-115;), a ruthlessly modernised *relais de poste* 4km from town with a smorgasbord of upmarket facilities: tennis courts, minigolf, secluded gardens and even a helipad (just in case you brought your chopper).

Buses from Villefranche are erratic due to the school-centred timetable, but there are regular trains to Figeac (€6.30, 40 minutes, every two hours) and Najac (€3.20, 15 minutes, every two hours).

Najac

pop 250

If you were searching for a film set for Camelot, Najac would unquestionably be it. Jutting out from a hilltop above a hairpin curve in the River Aveyron, the town's medieval castle, the **Fortresse Royal** (☎ 05 65 29 71 65; admission €3.75; 🕑 10am-1pm & 3-7pm Jul & Aug, 10am-12.30pm & 3-6.30pm Jun, 10am-12.30pm & 3-5.30pm Apr, May & Sep), looks like it's fallen from the pages of a fairy tale: slender towers and fluttering flags rise from the crenellated ramparts, surrounded on every side by dizzying *falaises* (cliffs) dropping to the valley floor below. A masterpiece of medieval military planning, and practically unassailable thanks to its hilltop position, Najac was a key stronghold during the Middle Ages, and was hotly contested by everyone from English warlords to the powerful Counts of Toulouse. The castle's medieval architecture is beautifully preserved, and the view from the central keep is unsurprisingly superb.

The castle is reached via a steep 1.2km cobbled street from **place du Faubourg**, a beguiling central square surrounded by a hotchpotch of timber-framed houses, some from the 13th century. Beyond the castle is the austere Gothic **Église St-Jean**, constructed and financed by local villagers on the orders of the Inquisition as punishment for their heretical tendencies. The **tourist office** (☎ 05 65 29 72 05; otsi.najac@wanadoo.fr; place du Faubourg; 🕑 9am-12.30pm & 2-6.30pm Mon-Sat, longer in Jul & Aug) is on the southern side of the square.

The town's best place to stay is **Oustal del Barry** (☎ 05 65 29 74 32; www.oustaldelbarry.com; place du Faubourg; d €53.50-75; 🕑 late Mar–mid-Nov), a wonderfully worn and rustic *auberge*, with haphazard rooms filled with trinkets and solid furniture to match its venerable timber-framed facade. Its country **restaurant** (menus €23.50-43; 🕑 lunch &

dinner daily, closed lunch Mon & Tue Oct-Jun) is renowned for miles around for its traditional dishes and southwest cuisine.

Simple little **La Salamandre** (☎ 05 65 29 74 09; rue du Barriou; mains around €15; 🕑 lunch & dinner, closed dinner Wed Dec & Jan) is worth a visit for its local dishes and a wonderful panoramic terrace overlooking the castle.

Trains run regularly to Figeac (€8.50, 50 minutes, two to four daily).

WEST OF CAHORS

Downstream from Cahors, the lower River Lot twists its way through the rich **vineyards** of the Cahors Appellation d'Origine Contrôlée (AOC) region, passing the dams at **Luzech**, whose medieval section sits at the base of a donjon, and **Castelfranc**, with a dramatic suspension bridge. Sights in this region are few and far between – this is working land first and foremost, and the landscape becomes increasingly industrial the further west you travel from Puy l'Évêque. Along the river's right bank, the D9 affords superb views of the vines and the river's many hairpin curves.

Château de Bonaguil

This imposing feudal **fortress** (☎ 05 53 71 90 33; www.bonaguil.org; Fumel; adult/7-16yr/under 7yr €6/3.50/free; 🕑 10am-7pm Jul & Aug, 10am-12.30pm & 2-6pm Jun & Sep, 10.30am-12.30pm & 2-5.30pm Apr-May & Oct, 10.30am-12.30pm & 2-5pm Feb-Mar, 10.30am-12.30pm & 2-5pm weekends & school holidays Nov, 2-5pm weekends & school holidays Dec & Jan) is a fine example of late-15th-century military architecture, featuring the artful integration of cliffs, outcrops, towers, bastions, loopholes, machicolations and crenellations. It's about 15km west of Puy l'Évêque (and on the GR36 footpath). Optional guided tours (1½ hours) are given in English three times daily in July and August, with the last one about an hour before closing time.

About 5km to the southeast is the attractive village of **St-Martin-le-Redon**, in a quiet little valley along the River Thèze (and just off the D673).

Rocamadour

pop 630

A favourite image for many a postcard and tourist brochure, the cliffside silhouette of Rocamadour is one of the Lot's most dramatic sights. This celebrated pilgrimage spot, 59km north of Cahors and 51km east of Sarlat, looks like something out of *The Da Vinci Code*, with a cluster of chapel steeples and pale stone houses clamped to a vertical cliffside beneath the ramparts of a 14th-century château. Famed for the miraculous powers of its Vierge Noire (Black Madonna), Rocamadour drew a steady stream of pilgrims and worshippers from across Europe in the Middle Ages, and the tourist traffic is still going strong several centuries on.

Rocamadour is split into two parts: the **Cité** (old city) and the largely modern and touristy suburb of L'Hospitalet, perched on the plateau above the cliff. Unless you're parking your car or visiting the tourist office, L'Hospitalet is of limited interest, although kids might enjoy the stalactites and stalagmites of the **Grotte des Merveilles** (☎ 05 65 33 67 92; admission adult/5-11yr €6/4, 🕑 9.30am-7pm Jul & Aug, 10am-noon & 2-6pm Sep-Nov & Apr-Jun).

Access to the Cité itself is from the ramparts of Rocamadour's **château** (€2.50), 1.5km from L'Hospitalet. You can either follow the switchback staircase down to the old town (which the pious once climbed on their knees) or take the lazy option and ride on a cable car for €4/2.50 one way/return. Halfway down the cliff are the **Sanctuaires**, a series of 12th- to 14th-century chapels containing the city's most prized relics, including the spooky Vierge Noire in the **Chapelle Notre Dame**. More steps lead from the Sanctuaires down to Rocamadour's main commercial thoroughfare, the **Grande Rue**, crammed (just as in the pilgrims' day) with souvenir shops and touristy restaurants. One of the city's original medieval gateways can be seen at the street's far end.

You'd be better off giving the overpriced hotels and restaurants around Rocamadour a wide berth – prices for even the dingiest room skyrocket in summer, and most hotels are booked out well in advance by coach parties.

Gouffre de Padirac

The sparkling subterranean caverns of the **Gouffre de Padirac** (☎ 05 65 33 64 56; www.gouffre-de-padirac.com; adult/4-12yr €8.70/5.50; 🕑 9.30am-6pm Jul, 8.30am-6.30pm Aug, 10am-5pm Sep–mid-Nov, 9.30am-5.30pm mid-Mar–Jun) are among the most breathtaking in France. Discovered in 1889, the cave's navigable river, 103m below ground level, is reached through a 75m-deep, 33m-wide chasm. Boat pilots ferry visitors along 1km of the subterranean waterway, visiting a series of glorious floodlit caverns en route, including the soaring **Salle de Grand Dôme** and the **Lac des Grands Gours**, a glittering 27m-wide subterranean lake. The cave is 15km northeast of Rocamadour.

Château de Castelnau-Bretenoux

Not to be confused with the Château de Castelnaud (p636), Castelnau-Bretenoux (☎ 05 65 10 98 00; adult/18-25yr/under 18yr €6.50/4.50/free; 10am-7pm Jul & Aug, 10am-12.30pm & 2-6.30pm May & Jun, 10am-12.30pm & 2-5.30pm Sep-Apr) was originally constructed in the 12th century and saw heavy action during the Hundred Years War, before being redeveloped in the Middle Ages following the advent of new forms of artillery. The castle is laid out around a roughly triangular courtyard, with stout towers linked by ramparts and bulwarks. Most of the rooms open to visitors date from the 17th and 18th centuries, when the castle was mainly used as a residential home rather than a defensive fortress. Having fallen into disrepair in the 19th century, the castle was refurbished by a Parisian opera singer, Jean Mouliérat, before being gifted to the state in 1932. The castle is about 5km south of Beaulieu-sur-Dordogne along the D940.

Carennac

pop 370

A jumble of amber houses and brick cottages make up tiny Carennac, beautifully nestled on the left bank of the Dordogne. The village's main landmark is the 16th-century **Château du Doyen**, which now houses a heritage centre, **L'Espace Patrimoine** (☎ 05 65 33 81 36; patrimoine-vallee-dordogne@wanadoo.fr; admission free; 10am-noon & 2-6pm Tue-Fri Apr-Jun, Tue-Sun Jul-Sep), showcasing the art and history of the region. Above is the square **Tour de Télémaque**, named after the hero of Fénelon's *Les Aventures de Télémaque*, written here in 1699.

Just inside the castle gateway is the **priory** and the Romanesque **Église St-Pierre**, with another remarkable Romanesque tympanum of Christ in majesty, similar in style to those in Cahors (p641) and Beaulieu (p620). Just off the **cloître** (adult/child €2.50/0.80), which was heavily damaged in the Revolution, is a remarkable, late-15th-century **Mise au Tombeau** (Statue of the Entombment), once vividly painted. The church's opening hours are the same as those of the **tourist office** (☎ 05 65 10 97 01; ot.intercom.carennac@wanadoo.fr; 10am-7pm mid-Jun–Sep, 10am-noon & 2-6pm Mon-Sat, 2-6pm Sun Oct–mid-Jun) next door.

La Petite Vigne (☎ 05 65 50 23 84; www.lapetitevigne-carennac.com; d €65), a boutique B&B on the edge of the village, is a real find. Crisp cotton sheets, pine furniture, designer wallpaper and carefully chosen colour accents distinguish the gleaming rooms, all lodged inside a solid shuttered house. There's a back garden for breakfast or home-cooked summer suppers (mains €12 to €20), served Friday to Sunday.

Hôtel Fenelon (☎ 05 65 10 96 46; www.hotel-fenelon.com; s €48-56, d €52-66;) has flower-filled hanging baskets and stripy awnings that evoke the feel of an Alsatian summer house. The rooms are fairly unremarkable (think pink-tiled bathrooms, flowery bedspreads and sunflower-coloured walls), but the pricier ones have top-notch views over the river and the tree-covered Île Calypso. Half-board at the downstairs restaurant is particularly good value (*menus* €22.50, €31 and €41).

Atlantic Coast

Sandwiched by Brittany to the north and the Basque country to the south, the area in this chapter slices through three distinct regions: Pays de la Loire, around the dynamic city of Nantes; Poitou-Charentes, spanning the history-rich university city of Poitiers to the arcaded port of La Rochelle (and its offshore islands); and Aquitaine, spreading from its neoclassical capital, Bordeaux.

These key cities will give you a taste of each region, but quiet country roads winding through vine-striped hills lead to countless other treats. Among them are the charming town of Cognac, tantamount with its double-distilled spirit; the country's largest wine-growing area, encompassing the Médoc's magnificent châteaux and the golden-hued, medieval, hilltop hamlet, St-Émilion; and the tranquil Bay of Arcachon, home to a dazzling variety of birdlife and weathered wooden oyster shacks.

Fresh-from-the-ocean seafood proliferates on menus, of course, but the regions have their own equally distinct traditional cuisines – from crêpes (in the north) to snails (through the centre) and foie gras (further south), just for starters.

The regions' exceptional wining and dining is offset by a smorgasbord of outdoor activities, thanks to more sunshine than anywhere in France apart from the Mediterranean. Much more laid-back than the Med, all along this stretch of coastline you'll find reasonably priced beach havens with pine-forested dunes and some world-class surf breaks, as well as myriad cycling trails.

With more packed into these regions than could possibly fit in these pages, allow yourself time to savour spur-of-the-moment detours and new discoveries, too.

HIGHLIGHTS

- Glide through the emerald-green waterways of the **Marais Poitevin** (p660)
- Cycle the smooth, flat bike paths criss-crossing the sunbaked **Île de Ré** (p666)
- Hang onto your seat for a wild, cinematically simulated ride at the futuristic theme park, **Futuroscope** (p660)
- Tour the dramatically floodlit buildings and monuments making up the world's largest Unesco-listed urban area in central **Bordeaux** (p672)
- Ride a three-storey-high, 60-ton, 50-passenger mechanical elephant in **Nantes** (p654)

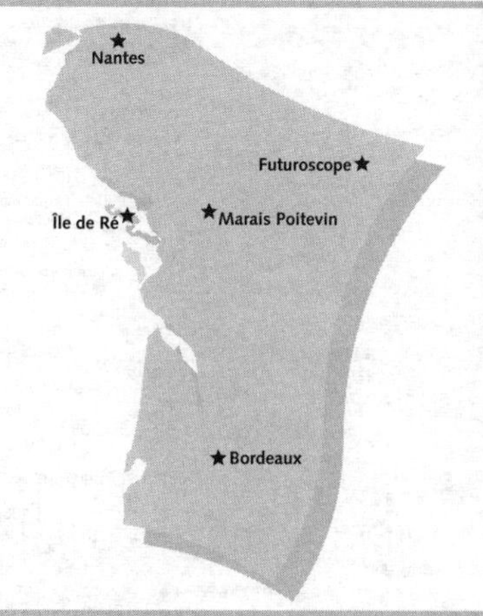

- POPULATION: 4,529,642
- AREA: 51,597 SQ KM

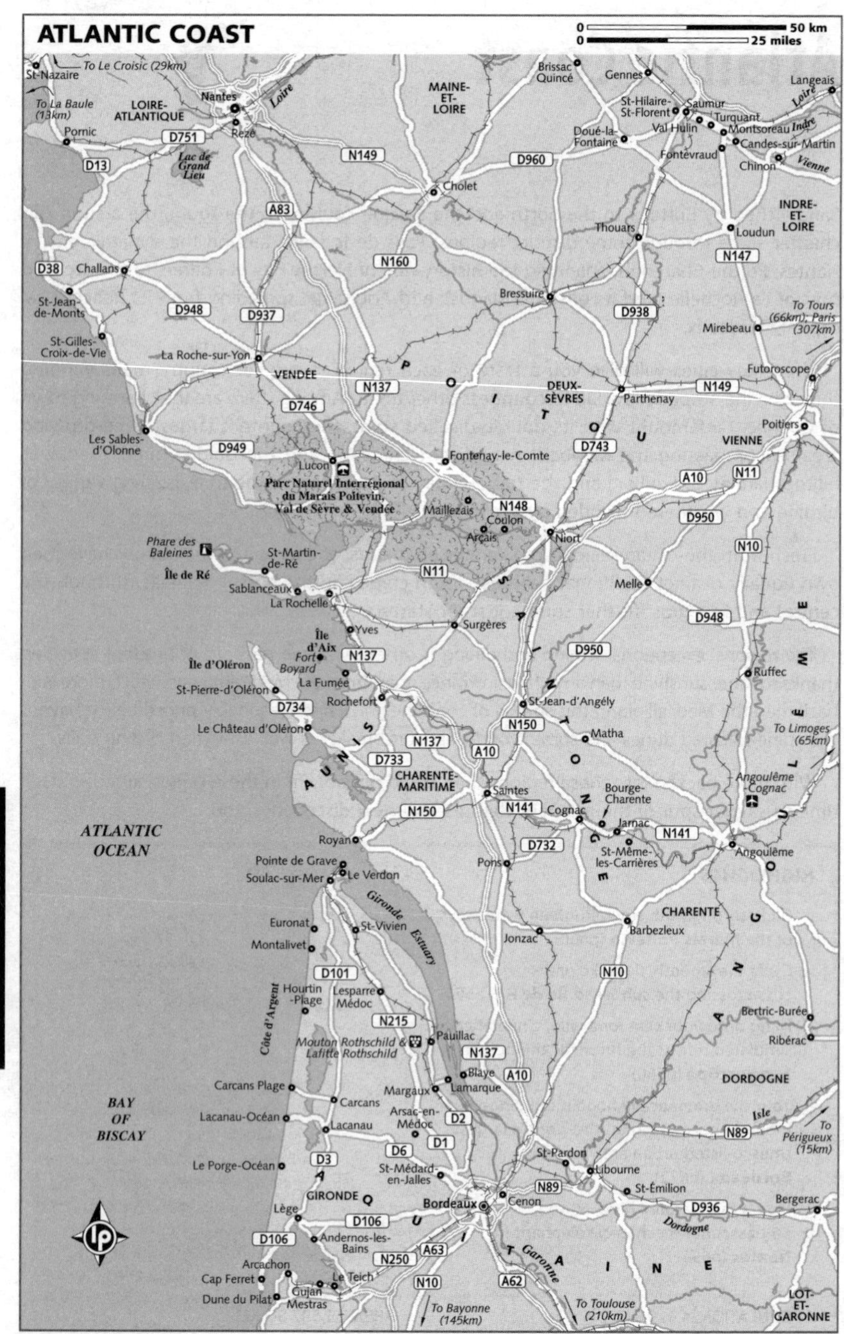

ATLANTIC COAST

History

Nantes was, until 1941, the capital of Brittany, and still retains strong Breton roots. Most of the other areas in this chapter were historically part of Aquitaine. The Aquitaine came under English control when the marriage of Eleanor of Aquitaine (c 1122–1204) to the French king Louis VII was dissolved in 1152 and she married Henry Plantagenet, the future King Henry II of England. In 1361, during the Hundred Years' War, Edward III of England established the principality of Aquitaine. Less than a century later, in 1453, it was recaptured by the French and has since remained part of France.

The Atlantic Coast's ports and harbours were integral to trade with France's colonies, notably in salt and wine – and slaves, something that is increasingly addressed in historical exhibits.

Voyagers inspired by the coast included many of the early French settlers in Canada, among them the founders of Montreal, who set sail from La Rochelle in the 17th century. The loss of French Canada (and the right to trade with North America) to the English in 1763 dealt an economic blow, which was softened by the arrival of rail the following century.

Rapid rail links with the rest of the country have today made the Atlantic Coast popular with seachangers, as well as with students attending the area's many major universities.

Getting There & Away

Bordeaux is the main transport hub for the region, reached in three hours by TGV from Paris. From here, trains can take you pretty much anywhere in France. Nantes, Poitiers and La Rochelle are also well served by TGV, and a good rail service links most of the main attractions within the region. A car gives added freedom for the wine-tasting trail.

The region also has good air services, particularly from the UK, with airports at Nantes, Poitiers, La Rochelle and Angoulême-Cognac (all served by low-cost operator Ryanair among others) and Bordeaux (including easyJet flights).

UPPER ATLANTIC COAST

This bite of the Loire-Atlantique *département*, where the Loire empties into the ocean, might as easily be termed 'lower Brittany'. Breton in every sense – cultural, architectural and historical – its centrepiece is Brittany's former capital, Nantes.

NANTES

pop 280,600

You can take Nantes out of Brittany (as happened when regional boundaries were redrawn during WWII), but you can't take Brittany out of its long-time capital, Nantes (Naoned in Breton).

Spirited and innovative, this city on the banks of the Loire, 55km east of the Atlantic, has a long history of reinventing itself. Founded by Celts around 70 BC, in AD 937 Alain Barbe-Torte, the grandson of the last king of Brittany, established the duchy of Brittany here following a series of invasions. A landmark royal charter guaranteeing civil rights to France's Huguenots (Protestants), the Edict of Nantes, was signed in the city by Henri IV in 1598. Its revocation in 1685 led to a Huguenot exodus from the region.

By the 18th century Nantes was France's foremost port, and in the 19th century – following the abolition of slavery – it became a cutting-edge industrial centre; the world's first public transport service, the omnibus, began here in 1826. Shipbuilding anchored the city's economy until the late 20th century. When the shipyards relocated to St-Nazaire to the west, Nantes transformed itself into a thriving student and cultural hub. The city centre has now nudged past Bordeaux's as the country's sixth-largest metropolis, and it's growing, with one in two Nantais today aged under 40.

Its renaissance extends from the extensive redevelopment of the former shipyards, to its brand new museum in the former Dukes of Brittany's magnificent castle.

Orientation

On the Loire's northern bank, central Nantes' two main arteries, both served by tram lines, are the north–south, partly pedestrianised cours des 50 Otages and a broad east–west boulevard (successively called bd de Stalingrad, alleé Commandant Charcot, cours John Kennedy and cours Franklin Roosevelt), which connects the train station with quai de la Fosse. They intersect near the Gare Centrale bus/tram hub.

The old city is to the east, between cours des 50 Otages and the Château des Ducs de Bretagne.

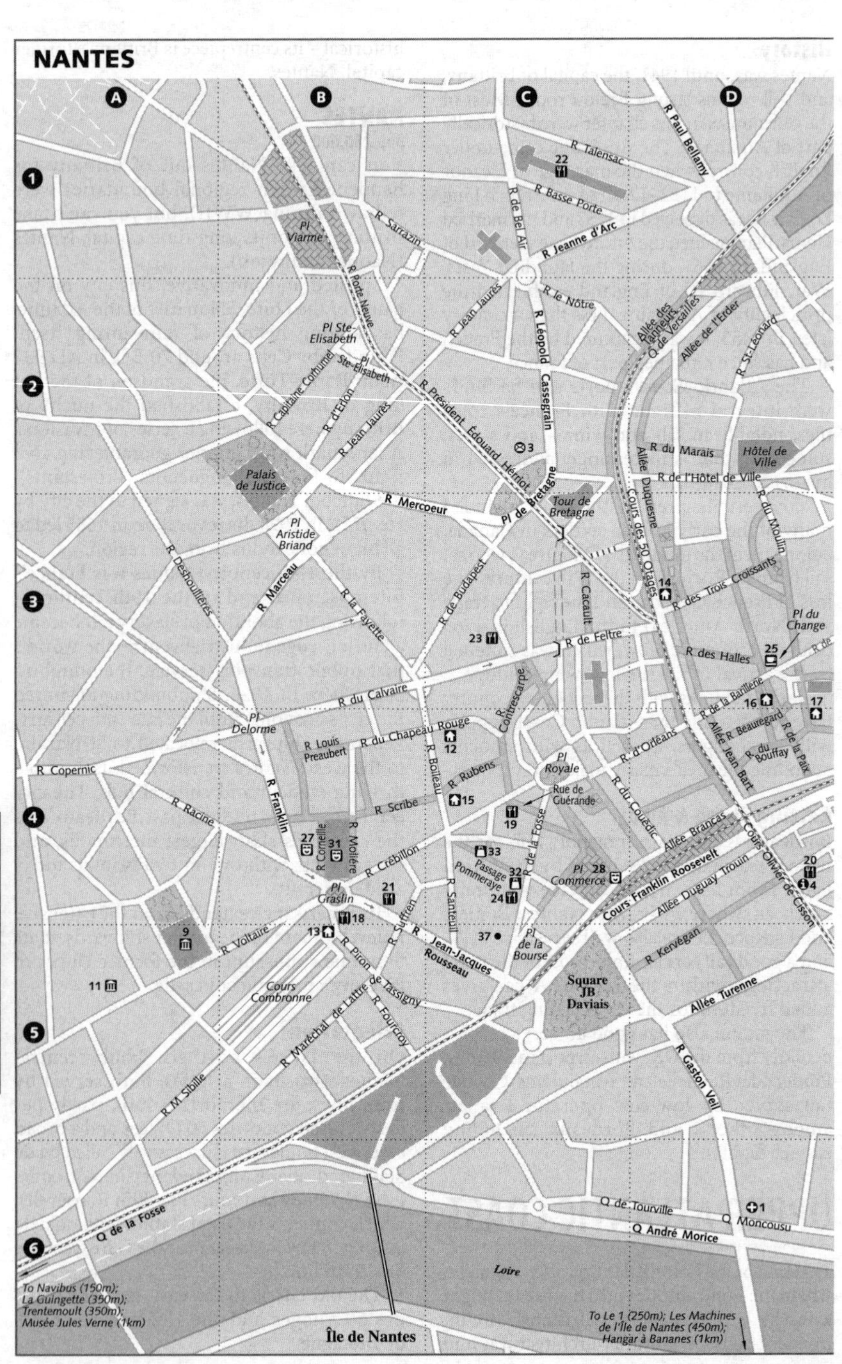
NANTES
R Talensac
R Paul Bellamy
R Basse Porte
Pl Viarme
R Sarrazin
R de Bel Air
R Jeanne d'Arc
R Porte Neuve
R Jean Jaurès
R le Nôtre
R Léopold Cassegrain
Allée des Tanneurs
Q de Versailles
Allée de l'Erder
R St-Léonard
Pl Ste-Elisabeth
Pl Ste-Elisabeth
R Capitaine Corhumel
R d'Erlon
R Jean Jaurès
R Président Édouard Herriot
R du Marais
Hôtel de Ville
R de l'Hôtel de Ville
Palais de Justice
R Mercoeur
Pl de Bretagne
Tour de Bretagne
Allée Duquesne
Cours des 50 Otages
R du Moulin
Pl Aristide Briand
R Deshoulières
R Marceau
R la Fayette
R de Budapest
R Cacault
R des Trois Croissants
Pl du Change
R de Feltre
R des Halles
R du Calvaire
R Contrescarpe
R de la Barillerie
Pl Delorme
R Louis Preaubert
R du Chapeau Rouge
R Beauregard
R du Bouffay
R de la Paix
Allée Jean Bart
R Copernic
R Franklin
R Boileau
R Rubens
Pl Royale
R d'Orléans
Rue de Guérande
R Racine
R Scribe
R du Couëdic
R Corneille
R Molière
R Crébillon
R de la Fosse
Passage Pommeraye
Allée Brancas
Cours Olivier de Clisson
Pl Commerce
Cours Franklin Roosevelt
Allée Duguay Trouin
Pl Graslin
R Voltaire
R Suffren
R Santeuil
R Jean-Jacques Rousseau
Pl de la Bourse
R Kervégan
R Piron
Cours Combronne
Square JB Daviais
R Maréchal de Lattre de Tassigny
R Fourcroy
Allée Turenne
R Gaston Veil
R M Sibille
Q de Tourville
Q Moncousu
Q André Morice
Q de la Fosse
Loire
To Navibus (150m); La Guingette (350m); Trentemoult (350m); Musée Jules Verne (1km)
Île de Nantes
To Le 1 (250m); Les Machines de l'Île de Nantes (450m); Hangar à Bananes (1km)
ATLANTIC COAST

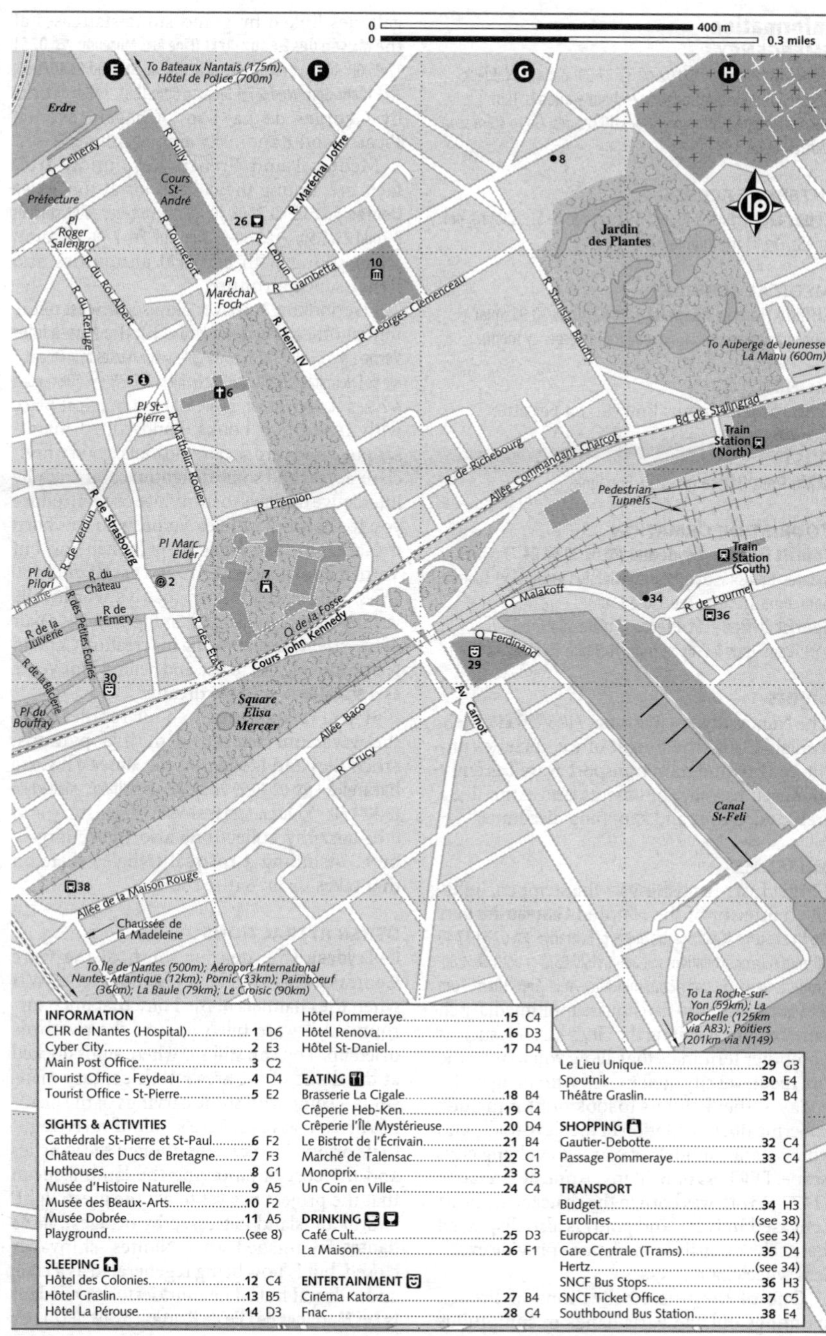

INFORMATION
CHR de Nantes (Hospital)....1 D6
Cyber City....2 E3
Main Post Office....3 C2
Tourist Office - Feydeau....4 D4
Tourist Office - St-Pierre....5 E2

SIGHTS & ACTIVITIES
Cathédrale St-Pierre et St-Paul....6 F2
Château des Ducs de Bretagne....7 F3
Hothouses....8 G1
Musée d'Histoire Naturelle....9 A5
Musée des Beaux-Arts....10 F2
Musée Dobrée....11 A5
Playground....(see 8)

SLEEPING
Hôtel des Colonies....12 C4
Hôtel Graslin....13 B5
Hôtel La Pérouse....14 D3
Hôtel Pommeraye....15 C4
Hôtel Renova....16 D3
Hôtel St-Daniel....17 D4

EATING
Brasserie La Cigale....18 B4
Crêperie Heb-Ken....19 C4
Crêperie l'Île Mystérieuse....20 D4
Le Bistrot de l'Écrivain....21 B4
Marché de Talensac....22 C1
Monoprix....23 C3
Un Coin en Ville....24 C4

DRINKING
Café Cult....25 D3
La Maison....26 F1

ENTERTAINMENT
Cinéma Katorza....27 B4
Fnac....28 C4
Le Lieu Unique....29 G3
Spoutnik....30 E4
Théâtre Graslin....31 B4

SHOPPING
Gautier-Debotte....32 C4
Passage Pommeraye....33 C4

TRANSPORT
Budget....34 H3
Eurolines....(see 38)
Europcar....(see 34)
Gare Centrale (Trams)....35 D4
Hertz....(see 34)
SNCF Bus Stops....36 H3
SNCF Ticket Office....37 C5
Southbound Bus Station....38 E4

Information

EMERGENCY

Hôtel de Police (☎ 02 40 37 21 21; 6 place Waldeck Rousseau) Police Nationale's 24-hour station is 1km northeast of the Monument des 50 Otages. Go to tram stop Motte Rouge.

INTERNET ACCESS

Cyber City (☎ 02 40 89 57 92; 14 rue de Strasbourg; per hr €3; 11am-midnight)

MEDICAL SERVICES

CHR de Nantes hospital (☎ 02 40 08 38 95; quai Moncousu) Has a *service d'urgence* (emergency room).

MONEY

Commercial banks line rue La Fayette.

POST

Main Post Office (place de Bretagne)

TOURIST INFORMATION

Tourist Office – Feydeau (☎ 02 72 64 04 79; www.nantes-tourisme.com; cours Olivier de Clisson; 10am-6pm, from 10.30am Thu, closed Sun)

Tourist Office – St-Pierre (2 place St-Pierre; 10am-1pm & 2-6pm, from 10.30am Thu, closed Mon)

Sights

The Nantes **city pass** (Pass Nantes; 24/48/72hr €16/27/32), available from the tourist office, includes unlimited bus and tram transport as well as entry to museums and monuments, and extras like a free guided tour and shopping discounts.

MUSEUMS

Forget fusty furnishings – the stripped, light-filled interior of the restored **Château des Ducs de Bretagne** (Castle of the Dukes of Brittany; ☎ 02 51 17 49 00; museum or exhibitions per adult/child €5/3 or both €8/4.80, grounds free; 9am-8pm mid-May–mid-Sep, 10am-7pm Wed-Mon mid-Sep–mid-May) houses multimedia-rich new exhibits detailing the city's history, such as computer terminals that allow you to tour the old medieval city, juxtaposed with images of it today. Other exhibits to look out for include sobering documentation of the slave trade, and vintage scale models of Nantes' evolving cityscape. Duchess of Brittany, Anne de Bretagne (1477–1514), was born in the château; her heart (encased in ivory and gold) is also displayed here. The extensive renovations provide excellent wheelchair access.

One of the finest collections of French paintings outside Paris hangs in sumptuous galleries linked by grand stone staircases at the **Musée des Beaux-Arts** (Fine Arts Museum; ☎ 02 51 17 45 00; 10 rue Georges Clemenceau; adult/child €3.10/1.60; 10am-6pm Wed & Fri-Mon, to 8pm Thu), with works by Georges de La Tour, Chagall, Monet, Picasso and Kandinsky among others.

Medieval and French Revolution artefacts are among the collections at the **Musée Dobrée** (☎ 02 40 71 03 50; 18 rue Voltaire; adult/student & child €3/1.50; 1.30-5.30pm Tue-Fri, 2.30-5.30pm Sat & Sun), along with classical antiquities and Renaissance furniture.

Overlooking the river 2km southwest of the tourist office (Feydeau branch), the **Musée Jules Verne** (☎ 02 40 69 72 52; www.julesverne.nantes.fr, in French; 3 rue de l'Hermitage; adult/student & child €3/1.50; 10am-noon & 2-6pm Mon & Wed-Sat, 2-6pm Sun) is a magical place with 1st-edition books, hand-edited manuscripts, cardboard theatre cut-outs, good wheelchair access and some delightful child-friendly interactive displays to introduce or reintroduce you to the work of Jules Verne, who was born in Nantes in 1828. Signs are in French only but Verne's books, such as *Around the World in 80 Days*, are so well known that it's worthwhile visiting regardless. The adjoining park has a pair of life-size **statues**, showing his creation Captain Nemo looking out to sea, and behind him Verne as a small boy with big dreams.

If you're squeamish about reptiles, skip the vivarium packed with live pythons, crocodiles and iguanas at the **Musée d'Histoire Naturelle** (☎ 02 40 99 26 20; 12 rue Voltaire; adult/child €3.10/1.60; 10am-6pm Wed-Mon). Prehistory and ethnography collections also figure largely here, including a rorqual (whale) skeleton that takes up an entire room.

OTHER ATTRACTIONS

Île Feydeau (the quarter south of the Gare Centrale) ceased to be an island after WWII when the channels of the Loire that once surrounded it were filled in after the riverbeds dried up. You can still see where ships docked at the doors of the area's 18th-century mansions – some with stone carvings of the heads of African slaves. There's talk of reverting it to its original river status, though the logistics and the cost of emptying the landfill mean that the project has yet to get the green light.

Still an island (accessed by bridges), **Île de Nantes** languished after Nantes' shipyards closed, but is now being regenerated as a civic and cultural hub. The quirkiest new resident is **Les Machines de l'Île de Nantes** (☎ 08 10 12 12 25;

www.lesmachines-nantes.fr), which creates amazing mechanisms such as a 12m-high mechanical elephant (40-minute rides per adult/child cost €6/4.50) which plods along at 26cm per second, carrying up to 50 passengers. You can also visit the adjacent gallery (adult/child costs €6/4.50), which displays and demonstrates prototypes and projects on the drawing board, including a triple-decker, 25m-high, 80-person carousel with Jules Verne–inspired mechanical sea creatures, due for completion in 2010. Gallery tickets are also good for the workshop, where you can watch these fantastical contraptions being built. Opening hours and elephant departures vary – check ahead.

Back in town, inside the Flamboyant Gothic **Cathédrale St-Pierre et St-Paul** (place St-Pierre), the **tomb of François II** (r 1458–88), duke of Brittany, and his second wife, Marguerite de Foix, is a masterpiece of Renaissance art.

Founded in the early 19th century, the **Jardin des Plantes** is one of the most exquisite botanical gardens in France, filled with flowerbeds, duck ponds, fountains and towering redwoods (sequoias). There are **hothouses** and a **children's playground** at the northern end.

Sleeping

Nantes makes a good weekend break, when hotel rates often drop. Bookings (including weekend packages with freebies thrown in) can be made through www.resanantes.com.

BUDGET

Auberge de Jeunesse La Manu (☎ 02 40 29 29 20; nanteslamanu@fuaj.org; 2 place de la Manu; dm incl breakfast €17; ⏰ reception closed noon-5pm, hostel closed Christmas period; 💻) Housed in an old converted factory with good wheelchair access, this well-equipped 123-bed hostel is a 15-minute walk from the centre. Alas, there's a lock-out from 10am to 5pm. Take tram 1 to the Manufacture stop.

Hôtel Renova (☎ 02 40 47 57 03; www.hotel-renova.com, in French; 11 rue Beauregard; s €35-45, d €45-50, tr €70; ⊠) Over six steep mosaic-tiled flights of stairs, this narrow hotel of 24 rooms with original polished floorboards is a simple little one-star place with an absolutely superstar location in the old city.

Hôtel St-Daniel (☎ 02 40 47 41 25; www.hotel-saintdaniel.com, in French; 4 rue du Bouffay; r €35-51; ⊠) Peacefully situated overlooking the St-Croix church courtyard in the heart of the old town, this clean, cheery place has a variety of room sizes including some whoppers, as well free wi-fi.

MIDRANGE & TOP END

Hôtel Pommeraye (☎ 02 40 48 78 79; www.hotel-pommeraye.com; 2 rue Boileau; s €54-114, d €59-114, ste €118-188; 💻) Sleek and chic with shimmering short-pile carpet and textured walls in shades of pale grey, gold, chocolate and violet blue, rooms at this boutique place on the corner of Nantes' smartest shopping street are sized like clothes (M, L, XL, XXL), with prices to match.

Hôtel des Colonies (☎ 02 40 48 79 76; www.hoteldescolonies.fr; 5 rue du Chapeau Rouge; s €54-72.50, d €61-72.50; 💻) Local art exhibitions rotate monthly in the lobby of this central spot featuring cherry-red public areas and rooms fitted out with purple, green and orange feature walls and boxy resin light fittings. Hotel-wide wi-fi's free.

Hôtel Graslin (☎ 02 40 69 72 91; www.hotel-graslin.com; 1 rue Piron; r €82-94; ⊠) An unlikely (but very Nantes) marriage of the art deco and '70s eras at this refurbished hotel includes details like velour, eggplant-and-orange wing chairs in the lounge (where wi-fi's free), and the spiffy rooms (wi-fi at additional charge) that feature faux timber and edgy colour combinations like peppermint and bone, plus shag-carpeted rooms in the attic.

Hôtel La Pérouse (☎ 02 40 89 75 00; www.hotel-laperouse.fr; 3 allée Duquesne; r €86-179; ❄ 💻 ⊠) Styled to reflect the city's shipbuilding traditions, a wooden gangway entrance leads to this design hotel's stone-and-wood lobby and 46 rooms with zigzag chairs, canvas sail-like curtains, and glass bathroom basins and wardrobes. Breakfast (€12) includes 17 flavours of jam and freshly squeezed OJ.

Eating

For cosmopolitan dining, head to the medieval Bouffay quarter, a couple of blocks west of the château around rue de la Juiverie, rue des Petites Écuries and rue de la Bâclerie. Breton crêperies abound throughout town. West of cours des 50 Otages, rues Jean-Jacques Rousseau and Santeuil are lined with eateries.

See also the listings under Drinking and Entertainment.

Crêperie Heb-Ken (☎ 02 40 48 79 03; 5 rue de Guérande; crêpes €4.80-17.90; ⏰ lunch & dinner Mon-Sat) Dozens of varieties of crêpe (such as a delicious trout-and-leek combo, or honey, lemon and almond for dessert) are made with love at this cosy spot. A sure sign of its authenticity: you can order *lait ribot* (thickened milk) by the *bolée* (drinking bowl) or pitcher.

Crêperie l'Île Mystérieuse (☎ 02 40 47 42 83; 13 rue Kervégan; menus €8-14; ⌚ lunch & dinner Tue-Sat) Jules Verne's legacy lives on at this lovely little place serving crêpes with local cheeses and cured hams amid decor such as a hot-air balloon, old-fashioned maps and books lining uneven stone walls glittering with coins.

Brasserie La Cigale (☎ 02 51 84 94 94; 4 place Graslin; breakfast €11, brunch €20, mains €12.20-24.50; ⌚ 7.30am-12.30am) No visit to Nantes is complete without a café and cake or an all-out feast at 1890s Brasserie La Cigale – several salons of original gilded tilework and frescoed ceilings, attended by white-aproned waiters. Its name comes from the cautionary fable of the *cigale* (cicada) and the ant, in which the cicada is too busy enjoying himself to plan for the winter ahead (hence the all-work, no-play ant doesn't get billing here).

Le Bistrot de l'Écrivain (☎ 02 51 84 15 15; 15 rue Jean-Jacques Rousseau; menus €14.50-18.50; ⌚ lunch & dinner Mon-Sat) Splashed in shades of red, with wine bottles lining the walls and checked tablecloths, Le Bistrot de l'Écrivain serves authentic Nantaise cuisine like *sandre* (pike-perch) in *beurre blanc* (white sauce), and local Muscadet wines. (For more on Muscadet, visit www.vinsdenantes.fr.)

Un Coin en Ville (☎ 02 40 20 05 97; 2 place de la Bourse; mains €15-19.50; ⌚ lunch Tue-Fri, dinner Tue-Sat) Flickering tea-light candles, soulful jazz and blues, and cooking that combines local produce with exotic styles, such as Moroccan *tajines* with local leeks and turnips, and a banana crumble made with Lu biscuits set the scene for a romantic meal.

Le 1 (☎ 02 40 08 28 00; 1 rue Olympe de Gouges; lunch menu €17, dinner menu €23; ⌚ lunch & dinner) Legal eagles from Nantes' gleaming 21st-century law court next door lounge in the ultracontemporary bar and dine on fabulous fusion dishes at this spanking-new spot overlooking the Loire. Book ahead for the chef's table, in a small glassed-in room looking into the Paul Valet–designed kitchen (no extra cost). The wine cellar is also a see-through affair, with over 2000 bottles on stainless-steel racks in a glass cool room.

SELF-CATERING

Sardines are sold at street stalls throughout town between March and November.

Stock up on picnic supplies at this huge marketplace, **Marché de Talensac** (rue Talensac; ⌚ 7.30am-1pm Tue-Sun). Central supermarkets include **Monoprix** (2 rue du Calvaire; ⌚ 9am-9pm Mon-Sat).

MOVEABLE FEAST

Glide along the River Erdre with an ever-changing view of châteaux as you dine aboard **Bateaux Nantais** (☎ 02 40 14 51 14; www.bateaux-nantais.fr; quai de la Motte Rouge, Nantes; lunch €53-86, dinner €58-86; ⌚ by reservation), accompanied by ambient music, local Muscadet wines and chef-prepared regional specialities. There are regular departures in summer; in winter boats operate only when there are sufficient numbers.

Drinking

Nantes has no shortage of lively spots for a drink. Two prime areas are the medieval Bouffay quarter, and the hot new **Hangar à Bananes** (www.hangarabananes.com, in French; 21 quai des Antilles; ⌚ daily until late), a former banana-ripening warehouse on the Île de Nantes. Here you'll find over a dozen restaurants, bars and clubs (and combinations thereof), each hipper than the next, including the stark monochrome **Téo** (☎ 02 40 08 90 28; www.teo-time.com; ⌚ restaurant lunch Mon-Fri, dinner Mon-Sat, bar daily noon-2am), and **Altercafé** (☎ 02 28 20 01 06; www.altercafe.fr; ⌚ noon-midnight Mon, noon-2am Tue, noon-4am Wed-Fri, 3pm-5am Sat, 3pm-midnight Sun, nonstop food service until 10pm daily), where even the beer is organic. Their front terraces face onto the Anneaux de Buren, a permanent art installation of metal rings, that light up at night.

La Maison (☎ 02 40 37 04 12; 4 rue Lebrun; ⌚ 3pm-2am) You have to see to believe this trip of a place, decorated room by room like a home furnished in *bad* 1970s taste, playing (what else?) house music – but not so loud that you can't chat with the local students who make it their home from home.

Café Cult (☎ 02 40 47 18 49; www.lecult.com, in French; place du Change; ⌚ 2pm-2am Mon & Sat, from noon Tue-Fri) Squeezed inside a darkened half-timbered house and hung with local art, this bohemian place draws a student crowd and sometimes hosts concerts.

Entertainment

Good what's-on websites include www.leboost.com (in French). Tickets for most events are available at **Fnac** (☎ 08 25 02 00 20; place Commerce; ⌚ 10am-8pm Mon-Sat).

Le Lieu Unique (☎ 02 40 12 14 34; www.lelieuunique.com, in French; 2 rue de la Biscuiterie), within the one-time Lu biscuit factory (crowned by a replica of its original tower, which you can ascend for

€2), this industrial-chic space is the venue for dance and theatre performances, eclectic and electronic music, philosophical sessions and contemporary-art exhibitions. Also here is an always-buzzing restaurant, a polished concrete bar, and a decadent hammam (Turkish bath) complex in the basement.

Beautifully refurbished, the 1788-built **Théâtre Graslin** (☎ 02 40 69 77 18; place Graslin) is the home of the Nantes Opera.

In a small turquoise-coloured space with an eclectic collection of stainless-steel and brass clocks (none of which show the same time), **Spoutnik** (☎ 02 40 47 65 37; 6 allée du port Maillard; 5pm-2am Mon-Sat) has regular live independent rock as well as 40 different flavours of vodka and good tap beer.

The six-screen **Cinéma Katorza** (☎ 02 51 84 90 60; 3 rue Corneille) shows nondubbed films.

Shopping

Gautier-Debotte (☎ 02 40 48 18 16; 9 rue de la Fosse; 9am-7.15pm Tue-Sat) When Jules Verne was a young boy he too was awed by this beautiful chocolate shop's chandeliers, marble floors and circular velvet banquette where Nantais have waited while their orders were filled since 1823. Handmade specialities include *mascarons* (finely ground chocolates in a dark-chocolate shell) and a rainbow of hard-boiled sweets.

Pedestal statues symbolise traditional Nantais industries inside the ornate three-tiered shopping arcade **Passage Pommeraye**, built in 1843.

Getting There & Away

AIR

Aéroport International Nantes-Atlantique (☎ 02 40 84 80 00; www.nantes.aeroport.fr) is 12km southeast of town.

BICYCLE

Detours de Loire (☎ 02 40 48 75 37; www.locationdevelos.com; per day/week €14/57) lets you pick up and drop off bikes along the Loire Valley, including Nantes. Check the website for the current pick-up and drop-off points.

BUS

The southbound **bus station** (☎ 08 25 08 71 56), across from 13 allée de la Maison Rouge, is used by CTA buses serving areas of the Loire-Atlantique *département* south of the Loire River, while the **Lila** (☎ 08 25 08 71 56) bus web covers the entire Loire-Atlantique *département*. Tickets cost €2/16 per single/10 rides.

Eurolines (☎ 02 51 72 02 03; allée de la Maison Rouge; 9.30am-12.30pm & 1.30-6pm Mon-Sat) has an office in town.

CAR

Budget, Europcar and Hertz are right outside the train station's southern entrance.

TRAIN

The **train station** (☎ 36 35; 27 bd de Stalingrad) is well connected to most of the country. Destinations include Paris' Gare Montparnasse (€49.10 to €61.40, 2¼ hours, 15 to 20 daily), Bordeaux (€37, four hours, three or four daily) and La Rochelle (€21, 1¾ hours, three or four daily).

Tickets and information are also available at the **SNCF ticket office** (La Bourse, 12 place de la Bourse; 10am-7pm Mon, 9am-7pm Tue-Sat) in the city centre.

Getting Around

TO/FROM THE AIRPORT

The public bus TAN-Air links the airport with the Gare Centrale bus-and-tram hub and the train station's southern entrance (€6, 20 minutes) from about 5.30am until 9pm. For information call **Allotan** (☎ 08 10 44 44 44).

BICYCLE

Nantes' new pick-up, drop-off bicycle system, **Bicloo** (☎ 08 10 44 44 50; www.bicloo.nantesmetropole.fr, in French), has stations all over town, open from 4am to 1am (but you can keep bikes overnight). Rates are just €1/5 per 24 hours/week.

BUS & TRAM

The **TAN network** (☎ 08 10 44 44 44; www.tan.fr, in French) includes three modern tram lines that intersect at the Gare Centrale (Commerce), the main bus/tram transfer point, and a first-for-France 'Busway'. Buses run from 7.15am to 9pm. Night services continue until 12.30am.

Bus/tram tickets can be individually purchased (€1.20) from bus (but not tram) drivers and at tram-stop ticket machines. They're valid for one hour after being time-stamped. A *ticket journalier*, good for 24 hours, costs €3.30; time-stamp it only the first time you use it.

CAR & MOTORCYCLE

For a full list of free and pay parking areas in Nantes – including access maps – click on

ACROSS THE RIVER

For the cost of a tram ticket, the little **Navibus** (shuttle boat; ☎ 08 10 44 44 44) ferries you across the river from the Gare Maritime tram stop to the villagelike quarter of **Trentemoult**. Lined with fishermen's cottages and ship's captains' houses, this artsy community has an island feel, despite being on the Loire's southern banks. On weekends especially, drop by **La Guingette** (☎ 02 40 75 88 96; 20 quai Marcel Broissard; mains €8.50-11.50; 🕑 lunch & dinner), where locals congregate for board-game tournaments, French tapas and a drink at the boat-shaped timber bar.

www.nantesmetropole.fr/67868597/0/fiche_pagelibre (in French).

TAXI

To order a taxi, call ☎ 02 40 69 22 22.

AROUND NANTES

The classic seaside town of **Le Croisic** (population 4300) centres on a pretty, half-timbered fishing harbour adjoining its old town, where shrimp, lobster, crab, scallop and sea bass are unloaded. From Nantes, an all-day *MétrOcéane* (www.metroceane.fr, in French) train ticket to Le Croisic costs €14.80 and includes public transport throughout Nantes. En route to Le Croisic, the same ticket allows you to stop at **St-Nazaire** (population 68,600), where cruise ships – including the *Queen Mary II* – are built and where Airbus has a factory, which can be toured. Also along this stretch of coast is the glamorous belle-époque resort of **La Baule** (population 16,400), boasting what's purportedly Europe's largest beach.

TGVs also run directly from Paris' Gare Montparnasse to Le Croisic (€57.70, 3¼ hours).

CENTRAL ATLANTIC COAST

The Poitou-Charentes region, midway along the Atlantic Coast, scoops up a pot-pourri of attractions – from the history-rich capital, Poitiers, to the portside panache of La Rochelle, the languid beaches of Île de Ré, and the eponymous home of Cognac.

POITIERS

pop 87,000

Inland from the coast, history-steeped Poitiers was founded by the Pictones, a Gaulish tribe, and rose to prominence as the former capital of Poitou, the region governed by the Counts of Poitiers in the Middle Ages. A pivotal turning point came in AD 732, when somewhere near Poitiers (the exact site is not known) the cavalry of Charles Martel defeated the Muslim forces of Abd ar-Rahman, governor of Córdoba, thus ending Muslim attempts to conquer France. The Romans built up the city, and there are numerous reminders still evident, such as extensive ruins uncovered when the large Cordeliers shopping centre was built in the town centre about a decade ago. The city's remarkable Romanesque churches are in part a legacy of Eleanor of Aquitaine's financial support.

Poitiers has one of the oldest universities in the country, first established in 1432 and today a linchpin of this lively city.

Orientation

The train station is about 600m downhill (west) from the old city, which begins just north of Poitiers' main square, place du Maréchal Leclerc, and stretches northeast to Église Notre Dame la Grande. Rue Carnot heads south from place du Maréchal Leclerc.

Information

Banks can be found around place du Maréchal Leclerc.

Post Office (21 rue des Écossais) Changes money.

Tourist Office (☎ 05 49 41 21 24; www.ot-poitiers.fr; 45 place Charles de Gaulle; 🕑 10am-11pm Mon-Sat, 10am-6pm & 7-11pm Sun 21 Jun-Aug, 10am-10pm Mon-Sat, 10am-6pm & 7-10pm Sun 1-17 Sep, 10am-6pm Mon-Sat 18 Sep-20 Jun) Near Église Notre Dame.

Virtual 86 (☎ 05 49 53 63 42; 13 rue Magenta; per 15min/1hr €0.50/2; 🕑 10am-2am) Internet access.

Sights

Strolling Poitiers' history-trodden streets is the best way to get a feel for the city's past. Along the pavements, red, yellow and blue lines correspond with three **self-guided walking tours** of the city detailed on a free city map handed out by the tourist office.

Every evening from 21 June to the third weekend in September, spectacular colours are cinematically projected onto the west facade of the Romanesque **Église Notre Dame la Grande** (place Charles de Gaulle; 8.30am-7pm Mon-Sat, 2-7pm Sun). The earliest parts of the church date from the 11th century; three of the five choir chapels were added in the 15th century, with the six chapels along the northern wall of the nave added in the 16th century. The only original frescoes are the faint 12th- or 13th-century works that adorn the U-shaped dome above the choir.

Within today's Palais de Justice (law courts), at the northeastern end of rue Gambetta, the vast, partly 13th-century great hall, **Salle des Pas-Perdus** (8.45am-6pm Mon-Fri), flanked by three huge fireplaces, is a not-so-subtle reminder of the building's history as the former palace of the counts of Poitou and the dukes of Aquitaine.

The 13th-century stained-glass window illustrating the Crucifixion and the Ascension at the far end of the choir of the Gothic-style **Cathédrale St-Pierre** (rue de la Cathédrale; 8am-6pm) is one of the oldest in France.

Constructed in the 4th and 6th centuries on Roman foundations, **Baptistère St-Jean** (rue Jean Jaurès; adult/child €1.50/0.75; 10.30am-12.30pm & 3-6pm Wed-Mon Apr-Oct, 2.30-4.30pm Wed-Mon Nov-Mar), 100m south of the cathedral, was redecorated in the 10th century and used as a parish church. The octagonal hole under the frescoes was used for total-immersion baptisms, practised until the 7th century.

Seven signed statues by Camille Claudel are the highlight of the **Musée Ste-Croix** (05 49 41 07 53; www.musees-poitiers.org, in French; 3 rue Jean Jaurès; adult/child €3.70/free; 1.15-6pm Mon, 10am-noon & 1.15-6pm Tue-Fri, 10am-noon & 2-6pm Sat & Sun Jun-Sep, to 5pm Mon-Fri & afternoons Sat & Sun Oct-May). Admission here is also good for the **Musée Rupert de Chièvre** (05 49 41 07 53; 9 rue Victor Hugo), which displays 19th-century furniture, paintings and art.; it has the same opening hours as the Musée Ste-Croix

Sleeping

In addition to chains such as Ibis, Poitiers has a handful of atmospheric, well-located hotels.

Hôtel Griotte Central (05 49 01 79 79; www.centralhotel86.com, in French; 35 place du Maréchal Leclerc; d €36-53) At the southern edge of this charming pedestrian district of half-timbered houses, this two-star place is a terrific little bargain. It has snug but sunlit rooms with showers or bath-tubs, and a lift to save you and your suitcases from scaling its three storeys.

Hôtel de l'Europe (05 49 88 12 00; www.hotel-europe-poitiers.com; 39 rue Carnot; d €52-83) Behind a dramatically recessed entrance, the main building of this elegant, very un-two-star-like hotel with good wheelchair access dates from 1710, with a sweeping staircase, oversized rooms and refined furnishings. The annexe has modern rooms for the same price.

Le Grand Hôtel (05 49 60 90 60; www.grandhotelpoitiers.fr; 28 rue Carnot; s €67-70, d €77-85;) Poitiers' premier hotel lives up to its name. Faux-art-deco furnishings and fittings fill the public areas with character, and rooms are spacious and well equipped. Service comes with all the trimmings including a porter and a lock-up garage (€6).

Eating & Drinking

Prime dining spots tend to be south of place du Maréchal Leclerc.

our pick **La Serrurerie** (05 49 41 05 14; 28 rue des Grandes Écoles; mains €12-17.50, weekend brunch €15; 8am-2am) Showcasing local art, sculpture and a fantastic collection of retro toys, this mosaic-and-steel bistro-bar is Poitiers' communal lounge-dining room. Its social scene peaks during the weekend brunches, where you have the option of a vegetarian-friendly version or the full posthangover bacon-and-eggs works. A chalked blackboard menu lists specialities like *tournedos* (thick slices) of salmon, sensational pastas, and a *crème brûlée* you'll be dreaming about until your next visit.

Other good dining bets are the atrium-style bistro **La Gazette** (05 49 61 49 21; 1 rue Gambetta; menus €11-12; lunch & dinner Mon-Sat), and little **La Table du Jardin** (05 49 41 68 46; 42 rue du Moulin à Vent; menu €9.90, mains €13-18; closed Sun, Mon & last 2 weeks Jun), serving exclusively seasonal market-fresh produce.

The covered market **Marché Notre Dame** (7am-1pm Tue-Sat) is right next to Église Notre Dame la Grande; the area out front hosts an open-air market from 7am to 1pm on Saturdays. About 200m to the south, the **Monoprix supermarket** is across from 29 rue du Marché Notre Dame (in the Cordeliers shopping centre).

You'll find the best bars and pubs one block north of place du Maréchal Leclerc along rue du Chaudron d'Or; and around place Notre Dame.

For live music, including jam sessions on Thursdays, swing by **Le Pince Oreille** (☎ 05 49 60 25 99; www.lepince-oreille.com, in French), and for electronica head to the very *hype* **Le Confort Moderne** (☎ 05 49 46 08 08; www.confort-moderne.fr, in French). Programs and cover charges are posted on the websites.

Shopping

Unique shops in Poitiers include **Fabrique de Parapluies** (137 Grand Rue), which has been making umbrellas by hand for centuries, and **Macarons Rannou-Metivier** (30 & 13bis rue des Cordeliers), which makes the local almond-based biscuits with seasonal flavours such as citrus. Behind-the-scenes peeks are possible at candle-maker **Ciergerie Guedon** (☎ 05 49 41 07 43; 113 Grand Rue), and violin-maker **Luthier L Gayraud** (☎ 05 49 60 97 96; 7 place de la Liberté; admission €5; by reservation).

Getting There & Away

The **train station** (☎ 08 36 35 35 35; bd du Grand Cerf) has direct links to Bordeaux (from €29.70, 1¾ hours), La Rochelle (€20.10, one hour and 20 minutes), Nantes (€25.70, 3¼ hours) and many other cities including Paris' Gare Montparnasse (from €48.20, 1½ hours, 12 daily).

AROUND POITIERS

Futuroscope

Futuristic theme park **Futuroscope** (☎ 05 49 49 30 80; www.futuroscope.com; Jaunay-Clan; adult €33, child under 16yr €25; from 10am, seasonal closing times vary, closed Jan–early Feb) is refreshingly uncommercial, focused instead on the cinematic technological wizardry of its attractions, as well as lakeside laser and firework shows. To keep things cutting edge, one-third of the attractions change annually. Many are motion-seat setups (some, such as the five-minute roller-coaster-effect **The Best of Dynamic Cinema**, give you a pretty vigorous shake), requiring a minimum height of 120cm. However, there's a new play area for littlies (miniature cars and so on).

Other standouts are **The Future is Wild**, where you can 'catch' various creatures in your hands, thanks to virtual-reality goggles and a sensor strapped to your wrist; and a 3-D journey through the solar system at **Destination Cosmos**. Free infrared headsets provide soundtracks in English, German and Spanish.

Allow at least five hours to see the major attractions; two days to see everything. Futuroscope's numerous hotels are bookable through the website, or directly at the lodging desk. Restaurants in the park span all price ranges up to the gastronomic **Le Cristal** (menus €23-39), serving gourmet fare (succulent fish with beetroot and a seafood-rich sauce) with 'futuristic' twists like strawberries and fairy floss accompanied by bubbling test-tubes of syrup for dessert, plus table centrepieces of frothing dry ice. There are also picnic areas if you want to self-cater.

Futuroscope is 10km north of Poitiers in Jaunay-Clan (take exit No 28 off the A10). TGV trains link the park's TGV station with cities including Paris and Bordeaux; times and prices are similar to those to/from Poitiers.

Local **Vitalis** (☎ 05 49 44 66 88) bus 9 links Futuroscope (Parc de Loisirs stop) with Poitiers' train station (the stop in front of Avis car rental; €1.30, 30 minutes); there are one to two buses an hour from 6.15am until 7.30pm or 9pm.

Marais Poitevin

Within the protected Parc Naturel Interrégional du Marais Poitevin, these tranquil bird-filled wetlands are dubbed Venise Verte (Green Venice) due to the duckweed that turns its maze of waterways emerald green each spring and summer. Covering some 800 sq km of wet and drained marsh, the marshlands are interspersed with villages and woods threaded by bike paths.

Boating and **cycling** are ideal for exploring the area. Try **Venise Verte Loisirs** (☎ 05 49 35 43

SLEEPING GREEN IN FRANCE'S 'GREEN VENICE'

To get even closer to nature in the Marais Poitevin, choose from one of 10 rooms at the waterside **Maison Flore** (☎ 05 49 76 27 11; www.maisonflore.com; rue du Grand Port, Arçais; s/d/tr/q €48/63/76/85; ⊠), which are themed after local marsh plants such as pale-green Angelica and purple-hued Iris. But the environmental connection runs much deeper, with solar hot water, geothermal heating and cooling, and an organic breakfast (€9) of freshly squeezed OJ, Fair Trade coffee and home-made cakes and yoghurt. There's a cosy guest lounge with books and board games, and you can rent boats on the premises.

34; www.veniseverteloisirs.fr, in French; 10 chemin du Charret, Arçais; guided/unguided 'plate' boats per 35 mins from €15/9, canoes per hr from €12, kayaks per hr from €10; Mar-Nov by appointment) and **La Bicyclette Verte** (www.bicyclette-verte.com, in French; 36 rte de St-Hilaire, Arçais; per half-day/full day from €9/13; 9am-7pm Apr-Sep, by reservation Oct-Mar).

Dining is sublime at **Hôtel-Restaurant Le Central** (05 49 35 90 20; www.hotel-lecentral-coulon.com; 4 rue d'Autremont, Coulon; s €49-76, d €56-123, menus €18.50-41, mains €19-22; lunch Tue-Sun, dinner Tue-Sat, hotel & restaurant closed 3 weeks Feb, restaurant only closed 2 weeks early Oct;). Specialties include crispy eel, sorbet made from angelica, a local herbal plant, and a mouth-watering cheeseboard. Its 13 rooms have artistic touches like pressed-metal bedheads made by a local blacksmith, and free wi-fi.

Sympathetic to this protected area is the environmentally friendly Maison Flore (opposite).

LA ROCHELLE

pop 77,300

Known as La Ville Blanche (The White City), La Rochelle's luminous limestone facades glow in the bright coastal sunlight. Arcaded walkways, half-timbered houses (protected from the salt air by slate tiles) and ghoulish gargoyles are rich reminders of the city's seafaring past. One of France's foremost seaports from the 14th to 17th centuries, early French settlers of Canada, including the founders of Montreal, set sail from here in the 17th century.

This 'white city' is also commendably green, with innovative public transport and open spaces. It's kid-friendly too, with lots of activities for little visitors.

La Rochelle's late-20th-century district of Les Minimes was built on reclaimed land, and now has one of the largest marinas in the country. Unlike the Med with its motor cruisers, the 3500 moorings here are mostly used by yachts, which fill the harbour with billowing spinnakers.

Orientation

La Rochelle is centred on its lively Vieux Port (Old Port). The old city unfolds to its north. The train station is linked to the Vieux Port by the 500m-long av du Général de Gaulle, with the tourist office about halfway between, at the edge of a quarter of brightly painted wooden buildings known as Le Gabut. Les Minimes is 3km southwest of the old city.

Information

There are a number of banks on rue du Palais in the old city.

Akromicro (05 46 34 07 94; rue de l'Aimable Nanette; per hr €2; 10am-midnight) Internet access.

Hospital (05 46 45 50 50; rue du Dr Schweitzer) Has an emergency room.

Hôtel de Police (Police Station; 05 46 51 36 36; 2 place de Verdun; 24hr)

Post Office (6 rue de l'Hôtel de Ville) Changes money.

Tourist Office (05 46 41 14 68; larochelle-tourisme.com, www.ville-larochelle.fr; Le Gabut, 2 quai Georges Simenon; 9am-8pm Mon-Sat, 11am-5.30pm Sun Jul & Aug, 9am-7pm Mon-Sat, 11am-5pm Sun Jun & Sep, 10am-12.30pm & 1.30-6pm Mon-Sat, 10am-1pm Sun Oct-May) Sells the *Pass Rochelais,* offering various discounts for public transport, sights and activities.

Sights & Activities

TOWERS

The most economical way to visit the three **defensive towers** (05 46 34 11 81; 10am-6.30pm Apr-Sep, 10am-1pm & 2.15-5.30pm Oct-Mar) is on a combined ticket (adult/18 to 25 years/child costs €10.50/7/free), but there are also combinations if you only want to visit two of the three. Opening hours may vary; check with the tourist office.

To protect the harbour at night in times of war, an enormous chain was raised between the two 14th-century stone towers at the harbour entrance, giving rise to the name of **Tour de la Chaîne** (Chain Tower). There are superb views from the top and a whizz-bang new permanent exhibit about the Canadian voyagers.

Across the harbour it's also possible to climb the 36m-high, pentagonal **Tour St-Nicolas**.

So named because of its role as the harbour's lighthouse (lit by an enormous candle), and one of the oldest of its kind in the world, the conical 15th-century **Tour de la Lanterne** is also referred to as Tour des Quatre Sergents in memory of four local sergeants, two of whom were held here for plotting to overthrow the newly reinstated monarchy before their execution in Paris in 1822. The English-language graffiti on the walls was carved by English privateers held here during the 18th century.

The gateway to the old city, **Tour de la Grosse Horloge** (quai Duperré) is a steadfast Gothic-style clock tower, with a 12th-century base and an 18th-century top. For safety reasons, it's not possible to enter. The tower's grand arch leads to the arcaded **rue du Palais**, La Rochelle's main

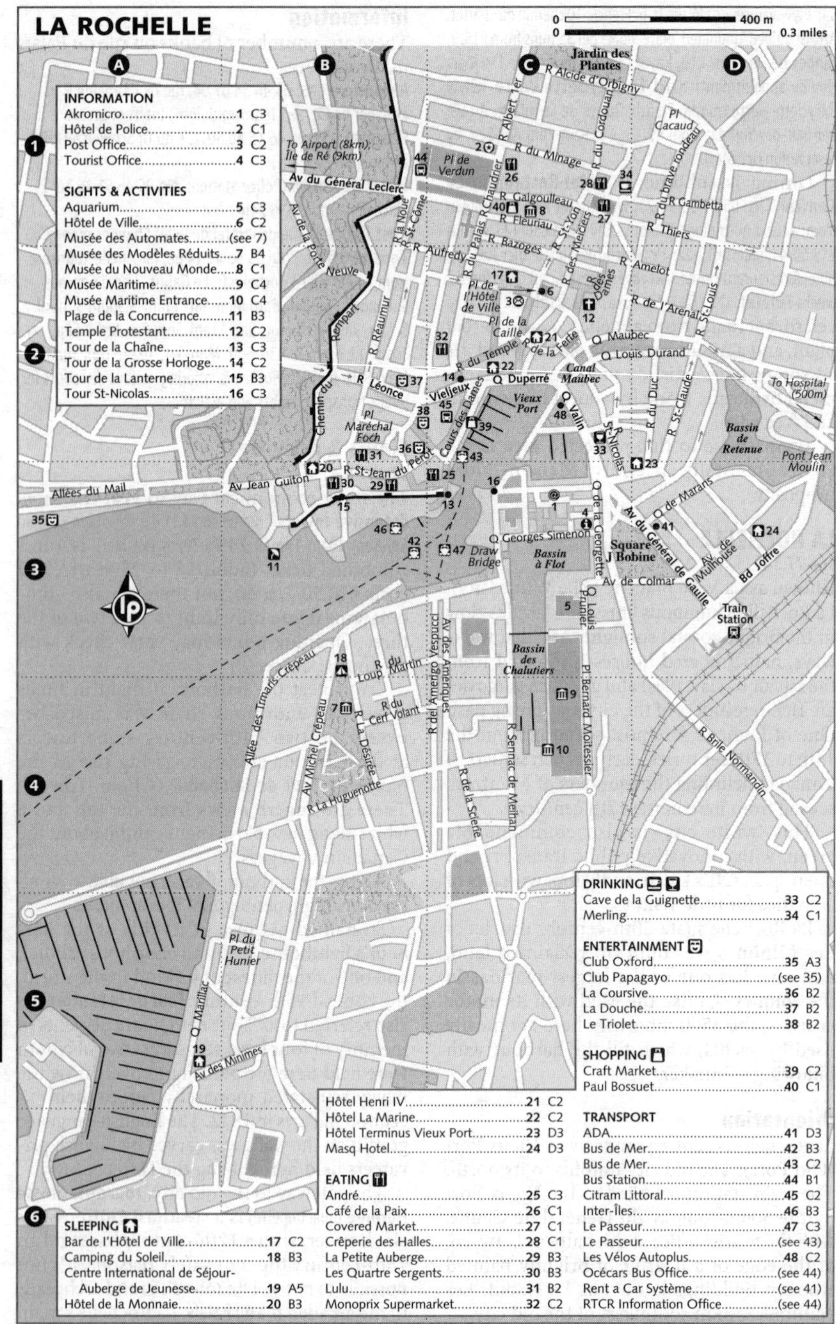

ATLANTIC COAST

shopping street, lined with 17th- and 18th-century shipowners' homes. Two blocks to the east, **rue des Merciers** is also lined with arcades.

AQUARIUM

Colourful tropical fish, sea flora and ominous 2.7m-long bull sharks swim in some 3 million litres of seawater at La Rochelle's 21st-century, state-of-the-art **aquarium** (☎ 05 46 34 00 00; quai Louis Prunier; adult/student & child €13/10, audioguide €3.50; 🕑 9am-11pm Jul & Aug, to 8pm Apr-Jun & Sep, 10am-8pm Oct-Mar), alongside local Atlantic fish and sea creatures. Even non-aquarium visitors can still head to its rooftop café for a meal or a drink while taking in the panoramic city and harbour views.

MUSEUMS

Moored at Bassin des Chalutiers are the two ships comprising the **Musée Maritime** (Maritime Museum; ☎ 05 46 28 03 00; adult/student & child €8/5.50; 🕑 10am-7.30pm Jul & Aug, until 6.30pm Apr-Jun & Sep): the meteorological research vessel *France 1*, and *Angoumois*, a *chalutier* (fishing boat).

Two treats for kids (and kids-at-heart), both wheelchair accessible, can be visited on a combined ticket (adult/child under 10 costs €11/6.50). **Musée des Automates** (Automation Museum; ☎ 05 46 41 68 08; 14 rue La Désirée; adult/3-10yr €7.50/5; 🕑 9.30am-7pm Jul & Aug, 10am-noon & 2-6pm Sep-Jun) is a small theme-park-style display showing 300 automated dolls from the last two centuries, including a near-life-size recreation of bygone Montmartre in Paris, right down to the Moulin Rouge and the funicular railway. Trainspotters will love the **Musée des Modèles Réduits** (Scale Model Museum; ☎ 05 46 41 64 51; rue La Désirée; adult/under 10yr €7.50/5; 🕑 9.30am-7pm Jul & Aug, 10am-noon & 2-6pm Jan-Jun & Sep-Dec), with miniature cars, computer-automated naval battles, and a tootling model railway. In July and August (weather permitting) children under 10 can ride aboard a little train (€2 train only or €1 plus entrance fee).

La Rochelle's role as a departure point for North America is interpreted at the 18th-century mansion housing the **Musée du Nouveau Monde** (New World Museum; ☎ 05 46 41 46 50; 10 rue Fleuriau; adult/under 18yr €4/free; 🕑 10am-12.30pm & 2-6pm Mon & Wed-Sat, 2.30-6pm Sun Apr-Sep, 9.30am-12.30pm & 1.30-5pm Mon & Wed-Fri, 2.30-6pm Sat & Sun Oct-Mar).

ISLAND EXCURSIONS

Several islands are scattered around La Rochelle, including the nearby Île de Ré (p666), as well as a trio further south.

Accessible only by boat, the tiny crescent-shaped **Île d'Aix** (pronounced eel dex), 16km due south of La Rochelle, has some blissful beaches. Between the Île d'Aix and the larger **Île d'Oléron** (linked to the mainland by a free bridge) is the fortress-island **Fort Boyard**, built during the first half of the 19th century.

Inter-Îles (☎ 08 25 13 55 00; cours des Dames) has sailings from Easter to early November to Fort Boyard (adult/child costs €18/11) and Île d'Aix and Île d'Oléron (each €26/17), plus sailings to Île de Ré (€17/10.50) from Easter to September.

La Rochelle's tourist office also has information about reaching the islands by public and private transport.

OTHER SIGHTS & ACTIVITIES

The austere **Temple Protestant** (2 rue St-Michel) was built in the late 17th century, though it became a Protestant church only after the Revolution. After the St Bartholomew's Day Massacre of 1572, many surviving Huguenots took refuge in La Rochelle before the city was besieged in 1627 by Louis XIII's forces under the command of Cardinal Richelieu.

Small artificial **beaches** near town include Plage de la Concurrence, and Plage des Minimes.

Tours

Flanked by a 15th-century Flamboyant Gothic wall and a resplendent 17th-century Renaissance-style courtyard, the **Hôtel de Ville** (Town Hall; ☎ 05 46 41 14 68; place de l'Hôtel de Ville) has guided tours in French (€4/1.50 for adult/child) at 3pm on weekends and school holidays; at 3pm daily in June and September; and 3pm and 4pm daily in July and August. Tours in English are available during July and August (schedules vary).

Summer's wealth of French-language **city tours** (☎ 05 46 41 14 68) includes horse-drawn-carriage tours (adult/child costs €9/6) and night tours (€10.50/7) led by characters in costume, as well as gastronomic tours and bike tours (each €6/4); reservations are essential.

Festivals & Events

Festival International du Film (☎ 01 48 06 16 66, 05 46 51 54 00) Silent classics, as well as new nondubbed films, are screened during the 10-day film festival in early July.

Francofolies (☎ 05 46 28 28 28; www.francofolies.fr, in French) A cutting-edge, contemporary music and performing arts festival held over six days in mid-July.

Jazz Festival (☎ 05 46 27 11 19) October sees jazz fans jive to La Rochelle's jazz festival, which is themed each year according to an artist or genre.

Sleeping

BUDGET

During the warmer months, dozens of campsites open up (and fill up just as quickly) around La Rochelle and Île de Ré. The tourist office has a list of camping grounds outside the town. The closest to the city is **Camping du Soleil** (☎ 05 46 44 42 53; av Michel Crépeau; adult & tent €8.50; late Jun-late Sep). Take bus 10.

Cut-price chain hotels proliferate in and around La Rochelle, the best being **B&B** (www.hotelbb.com).

Centre International de Séjour-Auberge de Jeunesse (☎ 05 46 44 43 11; www.fuaj.net/homepage/larochelle; av des Minimes; dm incl breakfast €16.60-17.50, d incl breakfast €37; reception 9am-noon, 2-7pm & 9-10pm, closed Christmas period) This popular HI hostel is 2km southwest of the train station in Les Minimes. Nonmembers incur an extra €2.90 per night.

Bar de l'Hôtel de Ville (☎ 05 46 41 30 25; 5 rue St-Yon; d €45-60) This bustling bar with an attached hotel has just nine rooms. Don't expect luxury – rooms are supersimple, but they offer great value for money given the price and proximity to the Vieux Port and the old town.

MIDRANGE

Hôtel Henri IV (☎ 05 46 41 25 79; henriIV@wanadoo.fr; 31 rue des Gentilshommes; d €58-95) Housed in a classified late-16th-century building, this hotel is smack-bang in the middle of the pedestrianised old city, a block back from the Vieux Port. Even the cheapies among the Hôtel Henri IV's 24 rooms have satellite TVs.

Hôtel Terminus Vieux Port (☎ 05 46 50 69 69; http://hotelterminus.17-flash.com, in French; 7 rue de la Fabrique; d €60-69) Bedecked with navy-blue awnings, this welcoming hotel has 32 comfortable, freshly renovated rooms whimsically named after the islands offshore from La Rochelle. The pick are the bright, sun-filled rooms at the front. There's also a cheery in-house bar. Free wi-fi; parking's €6.50.

Hôtel La Marine (☎ 05 46 50 51 63; www.hotel-marine.com, in French; 30 quai Duperré; d €60-150;) For captivating views of La Rochelle's iconic towers, try for rooms 1, 6, 9 or 13 in this boutique hotel by the Vieux Port. Each of the 13 rooms is individually decorated with cool, neutral-toned decor and smart designer furniture. Wi-fi's free; nearby parking costs €6.

Hôtel de la Monnaie (☎ 05 46 50 65 65; www.hotel-monnaie.com; 3 rue de la Monnaie; d €105-120;) Rooms at this epicentral spot are more up-to-the-minute than the vine-draped 17th-century floodlit facade and statue-studded courtyard suggest, with mod cons and good wheelchair access. Parking's €12.

TOP END

our pick **Masq Hotel** (☎ 05 46 41 83 83; www.masqhotel.com; 17 rue de l'Ouvrage à Cornes; r €115-168, ste €170-250;) La Rochelle's first-ever, new-from-the-ground-up design hotel takes its cue from a chance meeting between owner-creator Michel Dufour and two Balinese brothers, Hindu artists Mantra and Geredeg, whom he commissioned to paint the abstract canvases that hang in all 76 rooms as well as the artistically lit neo-retro foyer. Other conversation pieces include Philippe Starck Carrara marble tables, and Pierluigi Cerri–designed apple-green leather chairs in the breakfast room. A couple of the ultraspacious suites have terraces. Wi-fi's free; parking's €8.

Eating

The port has a plethora of restaurants and cafés, especially on the northern side. In summer, the quays in front of the Vieux Port are closed to traffic from 8pm to midnight Monday to Saturday and 2pm to midnight on Sunday, giving it the ambience of a giant street party.

Away from the tourist crowds, locals' favoured dining areas are rue St-Jean du Pérot and the streets surrounding place du Marché such as rue des Cloutiers.

Most restaurants offer a kids' menu for around €8.50.

Crêperie des Halles (☎ 05 46 27 93 97; 1 rue des Cloutiers; dishes €5-8.50; lunch & dinner Mon-Sat) Crowds spill out the doors of this cosy, convivial crêperie tucked behind the covered market. Sweet crêpes and savoury galettes are topped with market-fresh ingredients, and prices are equally convivial.

Café de la Paix (☎ 05 46 41 39 79; 54 rue Chaudrier; menu €19.50, mains €11-18.50; 7am-10pm Mon-Sat) A visual feast as much as a dining one, this belle-époque brasserie-bar serves up traditional cuisine like beef, duck, foie gras and fish, as well as breakfasts and afternoon teas amid the splendour of soaring frescoed ceilings and gold-edged arched mirrors.

La Petite Auberge (☎ 05 46 41 28 43; 25 rue St-Jean du Pérot; menu €28, mains €15-17; lunch Tue & Thu-Sat, dinner Mon-Sat) Roasted monkfish with bacon and orange, saddle of lamb with apricots and rosemary, and king prawns in coconut curry sauce with saffron risotto are among the aromatic dishes served at this crisp newcomer. The smart, neutral-toned dining room is tiny, so booking ahead's a good idea during busy periods.

our pick **Lulu** (☎ 05 46 50 69 03; 19ter place de la Préfecture; menus €19-35, mains €16; lunch & dinner) Decorated in striking shades of fuchsia, Lulu is La Rochelle's grooviest new kid on the block, with a hip young team in the kitchen turning out gourmet fare and a loungey vibe that comes into its own during regular piano soirées.

André (☎ 05 46 41 28 24; www.bar-andre.com; 8 place de la Chaîne; menus €32-39, mains €17-30; noon-4pm & 7pm-midnight) First opened in the 1950s as a small seafood café, André's popularity saw it begin buying adjacent shops. There's now a maze of interconnecting rooms, each with its own individual ambience (like a port-holed cabin) but all serving fish caught the night before.

Les Quartre Sergents (☎ 05 46 41 35 80; 49 rue St-Jean du Pérot; menus €17-42; lunch & dinner) Set inside a beautifully tiled, historic former greenhouse and still filled with plants today, this is the city's premier address for white-tableclothed elegance and gastronomic French fare such as frogs' legs in creamy Pineau (sweet white wine with a Cognac base) sauce.

SELF-CATERING

The lively, 19th-century **covered market** (place du Marché; 7am-1pm) seethes with stallholders selling fresh fruit and vegetables, fish splayed on beds of ice, and just-killed meat. On Friday afternoons an **open-air market** sprawls across Place Verdun.

In the old city you can pick up staples at **Monoprix supermarket** (30-36 rue du Palais).

Drinking

There's no shortage of places to drink along the main dining strips, but some of the city's best bars (most open to 2am) are sprinkled along the bohemian-feel rue St-Nicolas. On a hot summer's afternoon here, try a glass of Guignette (white wine with tiny bubbles, flavoured with natural fresh fruit) at **Cave de la Guignette** (☎ 05 46 41 05 75; 8 rue St-Nicolas; 4-8pm Mon, 10am-1pm & 4-8pm Tue & Wed, 10am-1pm & 3-8pm Thu-Sat).

For fresh-roasted coffee, head to the 1st-floor tearoom of **Merling** (25 rue Gambetta; closed Mon morning & Sun), which supplies most cafés in town with their brews.

Entertainment

Entry to clubs generally costs around €10 depending on the night. The dual discos **Club Oxford** and **Club Papagayo** (☎ 05 46 41 51 81 for both; complexe de la Pergola; 11pm-5am Wed-Mon, plus Tue Jul-Sep) are on the waterfront about 500m west of Tour de la Lanterne. Oxford spins techno and house; Papagayo goes for '70s and '80s, with karaoke on Sundays. Further east, **La Douche** (☎ 05 46 41 24 79; 14 rue Léonce; 11pm-5am Thu-Sun) draws a trendy gay and straight crowd.

Le Triolet (☎ 05 46 41 03 58; 8 rue des Carmes; 11pm-3am) has been *le* cool club for an older crowd since 1970.

The two auditoriums at **La Coursive** (☎ 05 46 51 54 00; 4 rue St-Jean du Pérot; late Aug–mid-Jul) host regular concerts and nondubbed art films.

Shopping

Authentic, handmade leather crafts, jewellery, sand sculptures and more are sold by the artists themselves at the waterfront **craft market** (cours des Dames; daily Jul–mid-Sep, Sat & Sun Easter-Jun). Cognac and Pineau produced by local vintner **Paul Bossuet** (21 rue Gargoulleau) make great souvenirs, not least for their decorative bottles.

BIRDWATCHING IN THE MARAIS D'YVES

An easy 15km drive south of La Rochelle, the **Réserve Naturelle Marais d'Yves** (☎ 05 46 56 41 76; www.marais.yves.reserves-naturelles.org, in French; N137, Yves; 2-6pm Sun & school holidays plus additional openings during the year) has a free Centre Nature, where you can pop in and peer through telescopes to watch some of the 192-hectare reserve's 250 bird species amid the wetlands (depending on the season, you might see flocks of over 20,000 fill the sky on their migratory path). The website lists various guided walks and cycle rides through the wetlands (available in English), where you'll also learn about the area's 750 species of frogs, flowers and insects.

Getting There & Away

AIR

La Rochelle Airport (☎ 05 46 42 30 26; www.larochelle.aeroport.fr, in French), north of the city centre off the N237, has domestic flights as well as services to London Stansted and Dublin (with Ryanair), Southampton, Manchester, Glasgow and Birmingham (with Flybe), London Gatwick and Bristol (with easyJet) and Leeds and Edinburgh (with Jet2).

At the time of research there was no ATM here (though one is planned), so bring euros for transport.

BUS

From the **bus station** (place de Verdun), **Océcars** (☎ 05 46 00 95 15) runs services to regional destinations. See opposite for details on bus services to Île de Ré.

Eurolines ticketing is handled by **Citram Littoral** (☎ 05 46 50 53 57; 30 cours des Dames; closed Sat afternoon, Mon morning & Sun).

CAR

Inexpensive car-rental companies close to the train station include **ADA** (☎ 05 46 41 02 17; 19 av du Général de Gaulle) and **Rent A Car Système** (☎ 05 46 27 27 27; 27 av du Général de Gaulle).

TRAIN

The **train station** (☎ 08 36 35 35 35) is linked by TGV to Paris' Gare Montparnasse (€57.60, three hours, five or six direct daily). Other destinations served by regular direct trains include Nantes (€22.30, two hours), Poitiers (€19.30, 1½ hours) and Bordeaux (€23.80, two hours).

Getting Around

TO/FROM THE AIRPORT

Bus 7 runs from the airport to the town centre (€1.20); schedules are available at www.rtcr.fr (in French). A taxi costs about €10.

BICYCLE

The city's distinctive yellow bikes can be rented at **Les Vélos Autoplus** (☎ 05 46 34 02 22; quai Valin; 9am-7pm Jul & Aug, 9am-12.30pm & 1.30-7pm May, Jun & Sep, 9.15am-12.15pm & 1.50-6pm Mon-Sat Oct-Apr). The first two hours are free; after that bikes cost €1 per hour. Child seats, but not bike helmets, are available. From May to September bikes can also be picked up at the Vieux Port (across the street from 11 quai Valin).

BOAT

Le Passeur (tickets €0.60; 7.45am-8pm, to 10pm Apr & May, to midnight Jul & Aug) is a three-minute ferry service linking Tour de la Chaîne with the Avant Port. It runs when there are passengers – press the red button on the board at the top of the gangplank.

The ferry Bus de Mer links Tour de la Chaîne with Les Minimes (€1.50, €1.70 July and August, 20 minutes). It runs daily April to September; at weekends and holidays only from October to March. Boats from the Vieux Port depart every hour on the hour (except at 1pm) from 10am to 7pm (every half-hour and until 11.30pm in July and August).

BUS

Electric buses buzz around town. Local transport system **RTCR** (☎ 05 46 34 02 22) has a main bus hub and **information office** (place de Verdun; 7.30am-6.30pm Mon-Fri, 8am-6.30pm Sat). Most lines run until some time between 7.15pm and 8pm. Tickets cost €1.20.

Bus 1 runs from place de Verdun to the train station, returning via the Vieux Port. Bus 10 links place de Verdun with the youth hostel and Les Minimes.

CAR & MOTORCYCLE

A free shuttle bus connects the low-cost Park and Ride (P+R) car park off av Jean Moulin.

TAXI

Call ☎ 05 46 41 55 55 for a taxi.

ÎLE DE RÉ

pop 16,000

Spanning 30km from its most easterly and westerly points, and just 5km at its widest section, Île de Ré is scattered with 10 villages of traditional green-shuttered, whitewashed buildings with red Spanish-tile roofs. Even with the advent of the bridge linking it to La Rochelle, Île de Ré retains an isolated feel. Its name is thought to originate from the Egyptian sun god, Ra, as a combination of the offshore gulf stream and the westerly winds bathe the island in sunshine, particularly in summer (when hotels and campsites fill *completely*).

Sights & Activities

On the northern coast about 12km from the toll bridge, the quaint fishing port of **St-Martin-de-Ré** (population 2500) is the

ATLANTIC COAST

island's main town. Surrounded by 17th-century fortifications, you can stroll along most of the ramparts, but the **citadel** (1681), which has been a prison for over two centuries, is closed to the law-abiding public. St-Martin's **tourist office** (☎ 05 46 09 20 06; www.iledere.com; av Victor Bouthillier; ⏰ 10am-6pm Mon-Sat, to noon Sun May-Sep, 10am-noon & 2-6pm Mon-Sat Oct-Apr) is about 100m on your right, across the port, from the Rébus stop.

The island's best **beaches** are along the southern edge – including unofficial **naturist beaches** at Rivedoux Plage and La Couarde-sur-Mer – and around the western tip (northeast and southeast of Phare-des-Baleines). Many beaches are bordered by dunes that have been fenced off to protect the vegetation.

Criss-crossed by an extensive network of well-maintained bicycle paths, the pancake-flat island is ideal for **cycling**. A biking map is available at tourist offices; in summer practically every hamlet has somewhere to hire bikes. Year-round try **Cycland** (☎ 05 46 09 65 27), which can deliver bikes to the bridge.

Sleeping & Eating

Île de Ré is an easy day trip from La Rochelle; however, if you want to spend longer on the island, each village has a tourist information office with lists of local accommodation options, including campsites. (Pitching your tent anywhere but designated camping areas is forbidden.)

Restaurants throughout the island's villages include elegant seafood places overlooking St-Martin harbour's flotilla of boats. Pick up beach picnic supplies at St-Martin's **covered market** (rue Jean Jaurès; ⏰ 8.30am-1pm Tue-Sun) or from a cluster of nearby food shops. You'll also find minimarts in the island's villages.

Getting There & Away

The one-way automobile toll (paid on your way to the island) is €9 (a whopping €16.50 from mid-June to mid-September).

Year-round excruciatingly slow buses run by **Rébus** (☎ 05 46 09 20 15) link La Rochelle (the train station car park, Tour de la Grosse Horloge and place de Verdun) with all the major towns on the island; the one-hour trip to St-Martin costs €5.40. The company also covers intra-island routes.

COGNAC

pop 19,400

On the banks of the River Charente amid vine-covered countryside, Cognac is known worldwide for the double-distilled spirit that bears its name, and on which the local economy thrives. Most visitors head here to visit the famous cognac houses, but it's a picturesque stop even if you're not a fan of the local firewater.

Orientation & Information

Cognac's central, café-ringed roundabout place François 1er, is 200m northeast of the **tourist office** (☎ 05 45 82 10 71; www.tourism-cognac.com; 16 rue du 14 Juillet; ⏰ 9am-7pm Mon-Sat, 10am-4pm Sun Jul & Aug, 9.30am-5.30pm Mon-Sat May, Jun & Sep, 10am-5pm Mon-Sat Oct-Apr), which has free wi-fi. It's linked to the river by bd Denfert Rochereau.

There are banks in the town centre, but nowhere to change money.

Sights & Activities

Half-timbered 15th- to 17th-century houses line the narrow streets of the **Vieille Ville** (old city), which sits snugly between the partly Romanesque **Église St-Léger** (rue Aristide Briand) and the river.

At the southern corner of the leafy **Jardin Public** (Public Park) is the **Musée de Cognac** (☎ 05 45 32 07 25; 48 bd Denfert Rochereau; adult/child €4.50/free; ⏰ 10am-6pm Apr-Oct, 2-5.30pm Wed-Mon Nov-Mar), showcasing the town's history. Admission here also covers **Le Musée des Arts du Cognac** (☎ 05 45 32 07 25; 48 bd Denfert Rochereau; ⏰ 10am-6pm Apr-Oct, 2-5.30pm Tue-Sun Nov-Mar), taking you step by step through the production of cognac – from vine to bottle. Next door, the free **Espace Découverte** (☎ 05 45 36 03 65; ⏰ 10am-6.30pm Jul & Aug, to 6.30pm Tue-Sun Jun-Sep, 10.30am-6pm Tue-Sun Apr, May & Oct, 2-6pm Tue-Sun Mar & Nov, by appointment Dec-Feb), an interpretive centre covering the history of the Cognac region through to the present day, has some engaging interactive exhibits as well as models and paintings.

See the boxed text, p668, for information on tours and tastings.

Sleeping & Eating

Hôtel Le Cheval Blanc (☎ 05 45 82 09 55; www.hotel-chevalblanc.fr; 6 place Bayard; s/d €46/52; ✿) Miniature bottles of Cognac in the vending machine satiate midnight cravings at this two-star

ATLANTIC COAST

THE HOME OF COGNAC

According to local lore, divine intervention plays a role in the production of Cognac. Made of grape *eaux-de-vie* (brandies) of various vintages, Cognac is aged in oak barrels and blended by an experienced *maître de chai* (cellar master). Each year some 2% of the casks' volume – *la part des anges* (the angels' share) – evaporates through the pores in the wood, nourishing the tiny black mushrooms that thrive on the walls of cognac warehouses.

The best-known **Cognac houses** are open to the public, and also run tours of their cellars and production facilities, ending with a tasting session. Opening times vary annually; it's a good idea to reserve in advance.

Camus (☎ 05 45 32 28 28; www.camus.fr; 29 rue Marguerite de Navarre; adult from €7, under 18yr free) Located 250m northeast of the Jardin Public.

Hennessey (☎ 05 45 35 72 68; www.hennessey-cognac.com; 8 rue Richonne; adult from €9, 12-18yr €7, under 12yr free; closed Jan & Feb) Situated 100m uphill from quai des Flamands. Tours include a film (in English) and a boat trip across the Charente to visit the cellars.

Martell (☎ 05 45 36 33 33; www.martell.com; place Édouard Martell; adult/12-18yr/under 12yr €7/3/free) Found 250m northwest of the tourist office; last entry is one hour prior to closing.

Otard (☎ 05 45 36 88 86; www.otard.com; 127 bd Denfert Rochereau; adult/12-18yr/under 12yr €7/3.50/free) Housed in the 1494 birthplace of King François I, the Château de Cognac, 650m north of place François 1er.

Rémy Martin (☎ 05 45 35 76 66; www.remymartin.com) Two locations: the **estate** (adult/12-18yr/under 12yr €14/7/free; closed Oct-Apr), 4km southwest of town towards Pons; and, in town, the **house** (adult/12-18yr/under 12yr €25/14/7; year-round by appointment), for intimate tastings in groups of eight.

The tourist office has a list of smaller cognac houses near town; most close between October and mid-March.

place (with good wheelchair access) 100m west of the tourist office in the town centre. Although the rooms here aren't vast, they're immaculate, well equipped and have wi-fi. Parking costs €6.

Hôtel Héritage (☎ 05 45 82 01 26; www.hheritage.com; 25 rue d'Angoulême; d €68-74) Renovated in striking shades of lime green, fuchsia and cherry red, this wi-fi'd 17th-century mansion in the heart of town proves period elegance and contemporary style don't have to be mutually exclusive. Adjacent to the beautifully restored belle-époque bar, the hotel's restaurant, La Belle Époque specialises in reintroducing long-lost regional classics (*menus* €18 to €29).

La Courtine (☎ 05 45 82 34 78; Parc François 1er; menus €19.50-26.50, mains €14; lunch & dinner) Set about 2km west of the town centre in lush parklands, you can sit in the dining room or out on the terrace and watch the ducks at this riverside restaurant while dining on them too – with dishes such as roasted duck filet in raspberry sauce. The house speciality is *oeufs meurette* (poached eggs in red wine with foie gras).

You'll find an **Ecofrais supermarket** (32 place Bayard) opposite the post office. About 300m to the north of place François 1er, the **covered market** (57 bd Denfert Rochereau; until 1pm) is just across from the Musée de Cognac.

Getting There & Away

Angoulême-Cognac airport (www.aeroport-angouleme-cognac.com) is about 30km northwest of town and is connected to London (Stansted) by three Ryanair flights per week. A shuttle to/from Cognac costs €5 one-way (bring euros with you); there's also a Hertz car-rental office here.

Cognac's **train station** (1km south of the town centre, on av du Maréchal Leclerc) has regular trains to/from La Rochelle (€14.30, 1¼ hours).

By car, take the A10 exit EO5 for Pons (from the south) or St-Jean d'Angely (from the north).

Call ☎ 05 45 82 14 31 for a taxi.

AROUND COGNAC

Within a short drive of Cognac are some fascinating towns and villages worth seeking out. Just a couple of highlights include the former Gallo-Roman capital of Aquitaine, **Saintes** (population 26,300), on the River Charente. Dating from the 1st century AD, its Roman legacies include a double arch that served as the town gate, an amazing overgrown amphitheatre built during the reign of Claudius, and an archeology museum with unearthed statues and even a chariot and harness. Its pedestrianised old town spills over with lively places to shop, eat and drink.

Also straddling the Charente is **Jarnac** (population 5000), the 1916 birthplace of former president François Mitterrand. The house where he was born has been transformed into a museum; he's now buried in the town's cemetery. The waters around Jarnac are prime for fishing.

Situated 7km outside Jarnac, in the hamlet of **St-Même-Les-Carrières**, the cosy restaurant **L'Auberge** (☎ 05 45 81 93 03; place de l'Église; menus €23-33, mains €10.50-19.50; lunch Tue-Fri & Sun, dinner Mon-Sat plus Sun Jul & Aug) turns out solid regional classics like snails in garlic butter.

our pick **La Ribaudière** (☎ 05 45 81 30 54; Bourg-Charente; menus €40-76; lunch Wed-Sun, dinner Mon-Sat) This gastronomic haven is set among orchards overlooking the Charente river, in the tiny village Bourg-Charente (midway between Cognac and Jarnac). Chef Thierry Verrat grows his own vegetables to accompany his seasonally changing, Michelin-starred creations. Despite the bucolic setting, the dramatically modernised, violet-and-peppermint-painted restaurant is anything but rustic, with a geometric '70s-style chill-out lounge, bold contemporary art and TV screens above the outsized, arctic-white tables, where you can watch your meal being prepared in the kitchen via webcam.

Cognac's tourist office has details of these and other areas in its surrounds.

LOWER ATLANTIC COAST

At the lower edge of the Atlantic Coast, the expansive Aquitaine region extends to the Dordogne in the east, and the Basque Country in the south. The gateway to the region's wealth of attractions, set amid glorious vine-ribboned countryside, is its capital, Bordeaux.

BORDEAUX

pop 229,500

The new millennium was a major turning point for the city long known as La Belle Au Bois Dormant (Sleeping Beauty), when the mayor, ex–Prime Minister Alain Juppé, roused Bordeaux, pedestrianising its boulevards, restoring its neoclassical architecture, and implementing a high-tech public transport system.

Although Juppé was convicted for abusing public funds in Paris in 2004, it was soon water under the bridge for the Bordelaise, and he was re-elected to the mayorship in 2006 and again in 2008. His efforts paid off: in mid-2007 half of the entire city (1810 hectares, from the outer boulevards to the banks of the Garonne) was Unesco listed, making it the largest urban World Heritage Site.

Bolstered by its high-spirited university-student population (not to mention 2.5 million tourists annually), La Belle Bordeaux now scarcely seems to sleep at all.

History

Rome colonised the Aquitaine region in 56 BC; the area 100km east of the Atlantic at the lowest bridging point on the River Garonne he named Burdigala. From 1154 to 1453, after Eleanor of Aquitaine married would-be King Henry II of England, the city prospered under the English. Their fondness for the region's red wine (known across the Channel as claret) provided the impetus for Bordeaux's enduring international reputation for quality wines.

Orientation

The city centre lies between flower-filled place Gambetta and the wide River Garonne, which flows both ways depending on the tides. From place Gambetta, place de Tourny is 500m northeast of here; the tourist office is 200m to the southeast.

Bordeaux's train station, Gare St-Jean, is about 3km southeast of the city centre. Cours de la Marne stretches from the train station to place de la Victoire, which is linked to place de la Comédie by the pedestrianised shopping street, rue Ste-Catherine.

Information

BOOKSHOPS

Bradley's Bookshop (☎ 05 56 52 10 57; 8 cours d'Albret; 9.30am-7pm Tue-Sat, 2-7pm Mon) Stocks English-language books.

Librairie Mollat (☎ 05 56 56 40 40; 15 rue Vital Carles; 9.30am-7.30pm Mon-Sat) Great range of travel guides and maps.

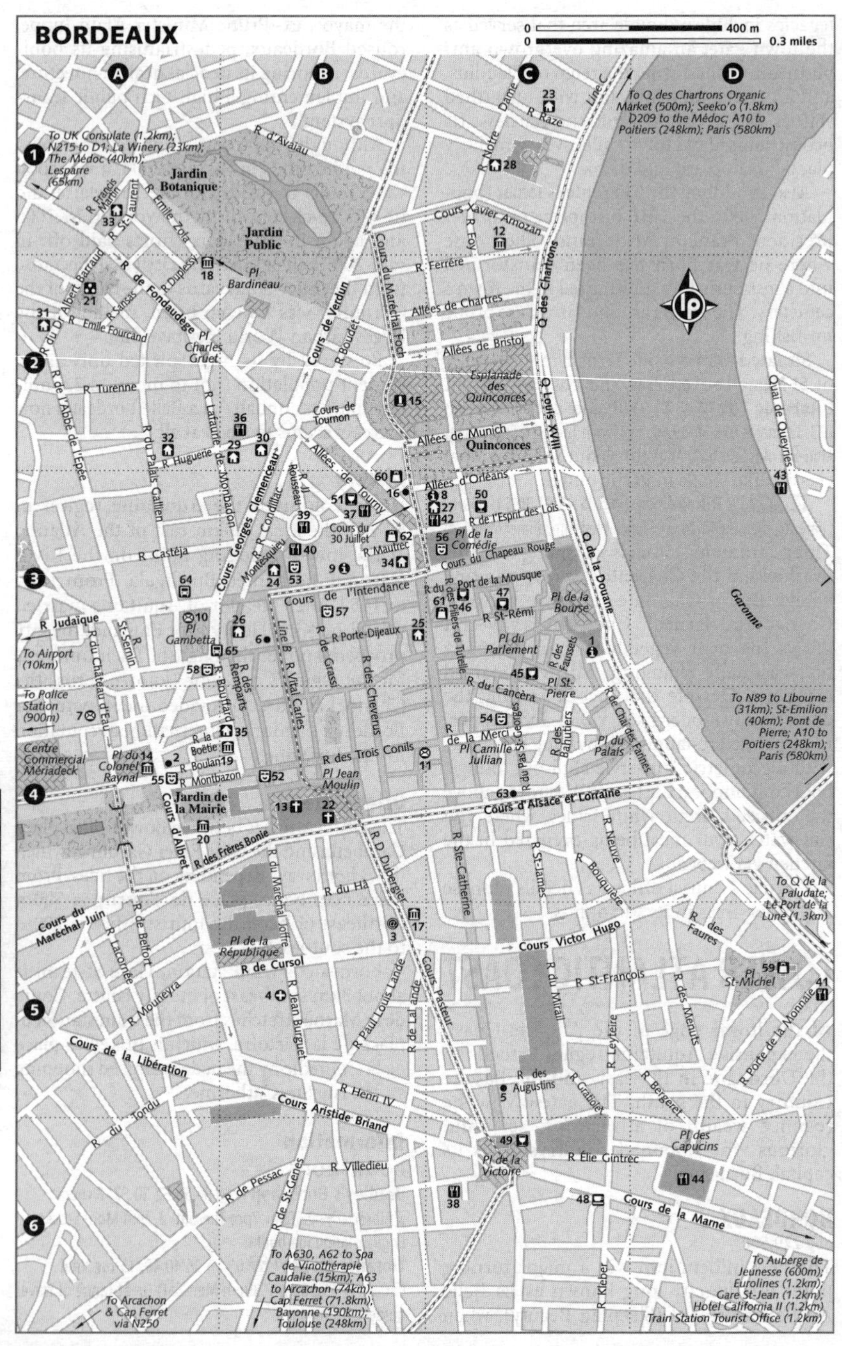
BORDEAUX
0 400 m
0 0.3 miles
To UK Consulate (1.2km); N215 to D1; La Winery (23km); The Médoc (40km); Lesparre (65km)
To Q des Chartrons Organic Market (500m); Seeko'o (1.8km) D209 to the Médoc; A10 to Poitiers (248km); Paris (580km)
Jardin Botanique
Jardin Public
Pl Bardineau
Pl Charles Gruet
Cours de Verdun
Cours du Maréchal Foch
Q des Chartrons
Esplanade des Quinconces
Quinconces
Allées de Tourny
Pl de la Comédie
Cours de l'Intendance
Pl Gambetta
Pl du Parlement
Pl de la Bourse
Garonne
Pl St-Pierre
Q de la Douane
Q Louis XVIII
Quai de Queyries
To Airport (10km)
To Police Station (900m)
Centre Commercial Mériadeck
Pl du Colonel Raynal
Jardin de la Mairie
Pl Jean Moulin
Cours d'Alsace et Lorraine
To N89 to Libourne (31km); St-Emilion (40km); Pont de Pierre; A10 to Poitiers (248km); Paris (580km)
Pl de la République
Cours Victor Hugo
Cours Pasteur
To Q de la Paludate; Le Port de la Lune (1.3km)
Pl St-Michel
Cours de la Libération
Cours Aristide Briand
Pl de la Victoire
Pl des Capucins
Cours de la Marne
To A630, A62 to Spa de Vinothérapie Caudalie (15km); A63 to Arcachon (74km); Cap Ferret (71.8km); Bayonne (190km); Toulouse (248km)
To Arcachon & Cap Ferret via N250
To Auberge de Jeunesse (600m); Eurolines (1.2km); Gare St-Jean (1.2km); Hotel California II (1.2km) Train Station Tourist Office (1.2km)
ATLANTIC COAST

INFORMATION
Bordeaux Monumental....1 C3
Bradley's Bookshop....2 A4
Cyberstation....3 B5
Hôpital St-André....4 B5
Laundrette....5 C5
Librarie Mollat....6 B3
Main Post Office....7 A4
Main Tourist Office....8 C3
Maison du Tourisme de la Gironde....9 B3
Post Office - Place Gambetta....10 A3
Post Office - Place St-Projet....11 B4

SIGHTS & ACTIVITIES
CAPC Musée d'Art Contemporain....12 C1
Cathédrale St-André....13 B4
École du Vin....(see 16)
Galerie des Beaux-Arts....14 A4
Girondins Fountain Monumenent....15 B2
Maison du Vin de Bordeaux....16 B3
Musée d'Aquitaine....17 B5
Musée d'Histoire Naturelle....18 A2
Musée des Arts Décoratifs....19 B4
Musée des Beaux-Arts....20 A4
Palais Gallien....21 A2
Tour Pey-Berland....22 B4

SLEEPING
Ecolodge des Chartrons....23 C1
Hotel de France....24 B3
Hôtel de la Presse....25 B3
Hôtel de la Tour Intendance....26 B3
Hôtel des 4 Soeurs....27 C3
Hôtel Notre Dame....28 C1
Hôtel Studio....29 B2
Hôtel Touring....30 B2
La Maison Bordeaux....31 A2
La Maison du Lierre....32 A2
Petit Hôtel Labottiere....33 A1
Regent Grand Hotel Bordeaux....34 B3
Une Chambre en Ville....35 B4

EATING
Baillardran....(see 39)
Baud et Millet....36 B2
Brasserie Le Noailles....37 B3
Cassolette Café....38 C6
Champion Supermarket....39 B3
Fromagerie....40 B3
La Tupina....41 D5
L'Entrecôte....42 C3
L'Estaquade....43 D3
Marché des Capucins....44 D6

DRINKING
Absolut Lounge....45 C3
Bodega Bodega....46 C3
Café Brun....47 C3
Café Pop....48 C6
Chez Auguste....49 C6
Chez Greg Le Grand Théâtre....50 C3
Villa Tourny....51 B3

ENTERTAINMENT
Bar de l'Hôtel de Ville....52 B4
Centre Jean Vigo....53 B3
Cinéma Utopia....54 C4
Connemara Bar....55 A4
Grand Théâtre....56 C3
Théâtre Femina....57 B3
Virgin Megastore Billeterie....58 A3

SHOPPING
Antique Market....59 D5
Bordeaux Magnum....60 B3
Galerie Bordelaise....61 C3
L'Intendant....62 B3

TRANSPORT
Bordeaux Scooter....63 C4
Jet'Bus....64 A3
TBC Bus Information Office....65 A3

INTERNET ACCESS

Cyberstation (☎ 05 56 01 15 15; 23 cours Pasteur; per hr €2; ⏰ 9.30am-2am Mon-Sat, 2pm-2am Sun)

LAUNDRY

Laundrette (32 rue des Augustins; ⏰ 7.30am-9pm)

MEDICAL SERVICES & EMERGENCY

Hôpital St-André (☎ 05 56 79 56 79; 1 rue Jean Burguet) Has a 24-hour casualty ward.

Police Station (☎ 05 57 85 77 77; 23 rue François de Sourdis; ⏰ 24hr)

MONEY

Banks offering currency exchange can be found near the tourist office on cours de l'Intendance, rue de l'Esprit des Lois and cours du Chapeau Rouge.

POST

The post offices at 43 place Gambetta and place St-Projet are open from 9am to 12.30pm and 1.30pm to 5pm on Saturday in addition to weekdays.

Main Post Office (37 rue du Château d'Eau)

TOURIST INFORMATION

Bordeaux Monumental (☎ 05 56 48 04 24; 28 rue des Argentiers; ⏰ 9.30am-1pm & 2-7pm Mon-Sat, 10am-1pm & 2-6pm Sun Jul & Aug, 9.30am-1pm & 2-6pm Mon-Sat, 10am-1pm & 2-6pm Sun May, Jun, Sep & Oct, 10am-1pm & 2-6pm Mon-Sat, 2-6pm Sun Nov-Apr) Specialist tourist office dedicated to the city's history. Free multimedia presentations plus temporary exhibitions with a historical theme (admission prices varies).

Main Tourist Office (☎ 05 56 00 66 00; www.bordeaux-tourisme.com; 12 cours du 30 Juillet; ⏰ 9am-7.30pm Mon-Sat, 9.30am-6.30pm Sun Jul & Aug, 9am-6.30pm Mon-Sat, 9.30am-6.30pm Sun May, Jun, Sep & Oct, 9am-6.30pm Mon-Sat, 9.45am-4.30pm Sun Nov-Apr) Runs an excellent range of city and regional tours; see p672 and the boxed text, p675.

Maison du Tourisme de la Gironde (☎ 05 56 52 61 40; www.tourisme-gironde.cg33.fr; 21 cours de l'Intendance; ⏰ 9am-6pm Mon-Fri, to 7pm Apr-Oct, 10am-1pm & 2-6.30pm Sat) Information on the Gironde *département*.

Train Station Tourist Office (⏰ 9am-noon & 1-6pm Mon-Sat, 10am-noon & 1-3pm Sun May-Oct, 9.30am-12.30pm & 2-6pm Mon-Fri Nov-Apr) Small but helpful branch of Bordeaux's main tourist office outside the train station building.

Dangers & Annoyances

Bordeaux is generally a safe city, but the train station and its surrounding streets can be dicey, especially at night. Place de la Victoire can become aggressive late at night.

Sights & Activities

On the first Sunday of every month, Bordeaux's city centre is closed to cars, and attractions often have extended hours. Added events on the day include a **contemporary art bus** (tickets €5; 2.30-6.30pm), which visits galleries showcasing emerging artists (commentary in French). Reserve through the main tourist office.

CATHÉDRALE ST-ANDRÉ

Lording over the city is **Cathédrale St-André**. A Unesco World Heritage Site even prior to the city's classification, the cathedral's oldest section dates from 1096; most of what you see today was built in the 13th and 14th centuries. Exceptional masonry carvings can be seen in the north portal. Even more imposing than the cathedral itself is the gargoyled, 50m-high Gothic belfry, **Tour Pey-Berland** (adult/student/child €5/3.50/free; 10am-1.15pm & 2-6pm Jun-Sep, 10am-12.30pm & 2-5.30pm Tue-Sun Oct-May). Erected between 1440 and 1466, its spire was added in the 19th century, and in 1863 it was topped off with the statue of Notre Dame de l'Aquitaine (Our Lady of Aquitaine). Scaling the tower's 232 narrow steps rewards you with a spectacular panorama of the city.

MUSEUMS

Bordeaux's museums have free entry for permanent collections; temporary exhibits cost €5 for adults, €2.50 for children.

Gallo-Roman statues and relics dating back 25,000 years are among the highlights at the impressive **Musée d'Aquitaine** (Museum of Aquitaine; 05 56 01 51 00; 20 cours Pasteur; 11am-6pm Tue-Sun). Ask to borrow an English-language catalogue.

Built in 1824 as a warehouse for French colonial produce like coffee, cocoa, peanuts and vanilla, the cavernous Entrepôts Lainé creates a dramatic backdrop for more than 700 post-1960s works by over 140 European and American artists at the **CAPC Musée d'Art Contemporain** (Museum of Contemporary Art; 05 56 00 81 50; Entrepôt 7, rue Ferrére; 11am-6pm Tue, Thu-Sun, to 8pm Wed, closed Mon). The rooftop **café** (brunch €25, menus €20-32, mains €13-21; 11am-6pm Tue-Sun) does a fantastic Sunday brunch.

The evolution of Occidental art from the Renaissance to the mid-20th century is on view at Bordeaux's **Musée des Beaux-Arts** (Museum of Fine Arts; 05 56 10 20 56; 20 cours d'Albret; 11am-6pm Wed-Mon). Occupying two wings of the 1770s-built Hôtel de Ville, either side of the **Jardin de la Mairie** (an elegant public park), the museum was established in 1801; highlights include 17th-century Flemish, Dutch and Italian paintings. Temporary exhibitions are regularly hosted at its nearby annexe, **Galerie des Beaux-Arts** (place du Colonel Raynal).

Faïence pottery, porcelain, gold, iron, glasswork and furniture are displayed at the **Musée des Arts Décoratifs** (Museum of Decorative Arts; 05 56 00 72 50; 39 rue Bouffard; museum 2-6pm Wed-Mon, temporary exhibits from 11am Mon-Fri); for your own decorative treasures browse rue Bouffard's antique and homewares shops.

The **Musée d'Histoire Naturelle** (Natural History Museum; 05 56 48 29 86; 5 place Bardineau; 11am-6pm Mon & Wed-Fri, 2-6pm Sat & Sun) has lots of stuffed animals and birds (many of them local), but is really only worthwhile if you're a natural-history nut.

PALAIS GALLIEN

The only remains of Burdigala today are the crumbling ruins of the 3rd-century amphitheatre, **Palais Gallien** (rue du Docteur Albert Barraud; adult/child €3/2.50; 2-7pm Jun-Sep).

PARKS

Landscaping is artistic as well as informative at the **Jardin Public** (cours de Verdun). Established in 1755 and laid out in the English style a century later, the grounds incorporate the meticulously catalogued **Jardin Botanique** (05 56 52 18 77; admission free; 8.30am-6pm), founded in 1629 and at this site since 1855.

At the vast square **esplanade des Quinconces**, laid out in 1820, you'll see the fountain **monument to the Girondins**, a group of moderate, bourgeois National Assembly deputies during the French Revolution, 22 of whom were executed in 1793 after being convicted of counter-revolutionary activities.

The facelift of the 4km-long **riverfront esplanade** incorporates playgrounds and bicycle paths.

Pretty **place Gambetta**, a central open area ringed by shaded benches, also has its share of history – during the Reign of Terror that followed the Revolution, a guillotine placed here severed the heads of 300 alleged counter-revolutionaries.

Courses & Tours

The tourist office runs a packed program of bilingual tours, including a wheelchair-accessible two-hour **morning walking tour** (adult/concession/child €7/6.50/5 plus optional wine tasting €3.50; 10am daily plus extra tour 3pm mid-Jul–mid-Aug) of the city; a **night-time walking tour** (ticket €15; varies) taking in the floodlit buildings and monuments; and a **gourmet trail tour** (ticket €22; 9.45am 1st & 3rd Sat of each month), where you can learn about the region's cuisine the best way there is – by sampling it (four tastings are included in the price). Contact the tourist office for details of dozens of other tour options, including **river cruises** in the warmer months.

See the boxed text, p675, for highlights of wine-related tours including day trips further afield, as well as wine courses. Short **cooking courses** also run periodically and are bookable through the tourist office.

All tours take a limited number of participants; reserve ahead.

Sleeping

Accommodation options are plentiful across all categories. The *Découverte* ('Discover Bordeaux') package is a neat little offering from the tourist office that bundles up two nights at your choice of participating hotels along with free public transportation, a guided city tour, a vineyard tour including wine tasting (both tours in English and French), and a bottle of wine. Prices start at €190 for a two-night package for two people in a two-star hotel; kids under 12 stay for free in their parents' room. Book 10 or more days in advance.

BUDGET

Auberge de Jeunesse (05 56 33 00 70; www.auberge-jeunesse-bordeaux.com; 22 cours Barbey; dm incl sheets & breakfast €21; reception 7.30am-1.30pm & 3.30-9.30pm;) Bordeaux's only hostel is housed in an ultramodern building with a self-catering kitchen, good wheelchair access and foosball, to boot. From the train station, follow cours de la Marne northwest for 300m and turn left opposite the park; the hostel's about 250m ahead on your left.

Hôtel Studio (05 56 48 00 14; www.hotel-bordeaux.com; 26 rue Huguerie; s/d €29/35;) Hôtel Studio's private en-suite rooms work out cheaper for two people than a couple of dorm beds at Bordeaux's hostel (though breakfast here is an extra €5 per person). Sure, there are no lifts, and the blue-and-white rooms are pretty plain (with incredibly thin walls – bring ear plugs). But they're comfortable, and some have small balconies and/or TVs.

Hôtel Touring (05 56 81 56 73; www.hoteltouring.fr; 16 rue Huguerie; s €42-45, d €49-53, s/d with shared bathroom €35/40) Run with pride by a warm-hearted local family, the Touring's rooms are furnished with original 1940s and '50s furniture, like flip-up school-style desks and club chairs, and most have fridges, TVs and telephones.

Also recommended:

Hôtel Notre Dame (05 56 52 88 24; www.hotelnotredame33.com; 36-38 rue Notre Dame; s €43-48, d €50-55, Suite Notre Dame s/d €55/62;) Spick-and-span 22-room hotel a stone's throw from the riverfront with a lift, wheelchair access and almost-free wi-fi (there's a one-off €1.50 set-up fee).

Hôtel de France (05 56 48 24 11; www.hotel-france-bordeaux.fr; 7 rue Franklin; d €55-59) Simple but charming hotel in the heart of the city, with welcoming multilingual staff and freshly renovated rooms decorated with Monet prints.

MIDRANGE

Hôtel de la Presse (05 56 48 53 88; www.hoteldelapresse.com; 6-8 rue Porte-Dijeaux; d €50-113;) Just off the pedestrianised rue Ste-Catherine. Elegant touches at Hôtel de la Presse include

SWEET ECODREAMS IN BORDEAUX

Hidden away in a little side street off the quays in Bordeaux's Chartrons wine merchants district, the brand-new *chambre d'hôte* **Ecolodge des Chartrons** (05 56 81 49 13; www.ecolodgedeschartrons.com; 23 rue Raze; s incl breakfast €90-100, d €110-140;) is blazing a trail for ecofriendly sleeping in the city.

Owners-hosts Veronique and Yann have added a solar-powered hot-water system, energy-efficient gas heating, insulation of compacted wood and cellulose, and hemp-based soundproofing, while preserving the 'soul' of this old wine merchant's house. They've stripped back and limewashed the stone walls, scrubbed the wide floorboards, and recycled antique furniture (including a wooden baby cot). Each of the five guest rooms has a bathroom built from natural materials such as basalt. You can curl up with a book in the lounge, access the island kitchen, and start the day with an organic breakfast, served at a long timber table. Wi-fi's hit-and-miss in parts of the historic building, but it's free.

silk and dried flowers, and guest baskets of fruit and nuts in the rooms. Service is polished and professional.

Hotel California II (☎ 05 56 91 17 25; www.hotelcalifornia33.com, in French; 22 rue Charles Domercq; s/d €52/58) Situated directly opposite the train station. Windows are all double-glazed, and rose motifs and natural light lend a countrified ambience to the rooms, which have BBC and kettles for a late-night cuppa.

Hôtel de la Tour Intendance (☎ 05 56 44 56 56; www.hotel-tour-intendance.com; 14-16 rue de la Vieille Tour; d €58-129;) Wake up to soaring exposed-sandstone walls, stone-laid floors and wood-beamed ceilings at this stylised boutique hotel tucked into a quiet corner of the city. Light-filled rooms have neutral-toned natural fabrics and fibres, limewashed timber panelling and geometric-embossed vinyl, with pebbled bathrooms screened by milky opaque glass.

Hôtel des 4 Soeurs (☎ 05 57 81 19 20; 4soeurs.free.fr; 6 cours du 30 Juillet; s/d from €65/75;) A romantic relic from the reign of Louis-Philippe, Hôtel des 4 Soeurs' sophisticated rooms recall the private home it once was, with stencilled wood panelling, snow-white damask drapes, and old-fashioned chrome bathroom fittings. Try for one of the front rooms overlooking place de la Comédie, such as room 22, where Richard Wagner stayed in 1850.

La Maison du Lierre (☎ 05 56 51 92 71; www.maisondulierre.com; 57 rue Huguerie; d €78-99;) The delightfully restored 'House of Ivy' has a welcoming *chambre d'hôte* feel. A beautiful Bordelaise stone staircase (no lift, unfortunately) leads to sunlit rooms with polished floorboards, rose-printed fabrics and sparkling bathrooms. The vine-draped garden is a perfect spot to sip fresh orange juice at breakfast (from €7.90).

Une Chambre en Ville (☎ 05 56 81 34 53; www.bandb-bx.com; 35 rue Bouffard; d €89, junior ste €99, 6-person apt per week €1300) Within the walls of a former gallery and an adjoining Bordelaise town house, each of these five *chambres en ville* (rooms in the city) is an individual work of art. Burnished chrome kettles let you brew up your own tea and coffee. Une Chambre en Ville is gay-friendly (and all-welcoming).

TOP END

La Maison Bordeaux (☎ 05 56 44 00 45; www.lamaisonbordeaux.com; 113 rue du Docteur Albert Barraud; s €145-195, d €180-230) You'd expect to find a sumptuous 18th-century château with a conifer-flanked courtyard and stable house in the countryside, but this stunning *maison d'hôte* is right in the middle of the city. Public areas include a library with shelves of books and CDs. A *table d'hôte* is available by arrangement (*menus* €30 to €150 including wine). Breakfast is included in the price.

Petit Hôtel Labottiere (☎ 05 56 48 44 10; www.chateauxcountry.com; 14 rue Francis Martin; d €180;) Staying in one of just two antique-filled guest rooms in this private heritage-listed 18th-century mansion is like sleeping in a museum (which, essentially, you are). A banquet-sized breakfast/brunch is served in a triple-chandeliered gallery space or the hedged central courtyard. Nonguests can tour the property by appointment (tour prices vary depending on duration); guests receive a free private tour.

our pick **Seeko'o** (☎ 05 56 39 07 07; www.seekoo-hotel.com; 54 quai de Bacalan; d €180-220, ste €360;) The monochrome lobby of Bordeaux's iceberg-shaped, first-ever design hotel leads to 45 retro-futuristic vinyl-and-leather-decorated rooms (some with circular beds), fitted out by Bordeaux designers. Unwind in the free Turkish hammam, or the 1st-floor Champagne bar (open 6pm to 2am Tuesday to Saturday including nonguests); or rent a bike (€10/15 per half-day/full day).

Regent Grand Hotel Bordeaux (☎ 05 57 30 44 44; www.theregentbordeaux.com; 2-5 place de la Comédie; d €390-460;) Bordeaux finally gained a hotel on par with its prestigious wines with the 2008 opening of this palatial 'urban resort'. Behind its 1779 facade are 150 plush guest rooms conceived by French designer Jacques Garcia – as well as two brasseries, a mini 'fashion avenue' lined with boutiques (Versace et al), plus a gastronomic restaurant and an enormous day spa (all also open to nonguests).

Eating

All that wine needs fine cuisine to accompany it, and Bordeaux has some excellent restaurants. Place du Parlement, rue du Pas St-Georges and rue des Faussets have a plethora. There are also scads of inexpensive cafés and restaurants around place de la Victoire.

Sandwich joints become pricier but offer better quality around the top end of rue Ste-Catherine; you'll also find good ones scattered along rue du Palais Gallien.

See also listings under Drinking, p676.

Cassolette Café (☎ 05 56 92 94 96; 20 place de la Victoire; menu €11.90, dishes €2.60-7.60; noon-midnight)

ATLANTIC COAST

ON THE WINE TRAIL

Thirsty? The 1000-sq-km wine-growing area around the city of Bordeaux is, along with Burgundy, France's most important producer of top-quality wines.

The Bordeaux region is divided into 57 appellations (production areas whose soil and microclimate impart distinctive characteristics on the wine produced there) that are grouped into seven *familles* (families), and then subdivided into a hierarchy of designations (eg *premier grand cru classé,* the most prestigious) that often vary from appellation to appellation. The majority of the Bordeaux region's reds, rosés, sweet and dry whites and sparkling wines have earned the right to include the abbreviation AOC (Appellation d'Origine Contrôlée) on their labels, indicating that the contents have been grown, fermented and aged according to strict regulations that govern such viticultural matters as the number of vines permitted per hectare and acceptable pruning methods.

Bordeaux has over 5000 châteaux (also known as *domaines, crus* or *clos*), referring not to palatial residences but rather to the properties where grapes are raised, picked, fermented and then matured as wine. The smaller châteaux sometimes accept walk-in visitors, but at many places, especially the better-known ones, you have to make advance reservations. Many close during the *vendange* (grape harvest) in October.

Whet your palate with the tourist office's informal introduction to wine and cheese courses (adult/concession €23/20), every Thursday at 4.30pm year-round, where you sip two to three different wines, and sup on cheese straight out of the cellar.

Serious students of the grape can enrol at the **École du Vin** (Wine School; ☎ 05 56 00 22 66; ecole .vins-bordeaux.fr), within the **Maison du Vin de Bordeaux** (Bordeaux House of Wine; 3 cours du 30 Juillet; %8.30am-4.30pm Mon-Fri), located across the street from the tourist office. Introductory two-hour courses are held Friday to Wednesday from 3pm to 5pm between June and September (€25). To really develop your nose (and your dinner-party skills), sign up for one of three progressively more complex two- to three-day courses (from €335/218 per adult/student) scheduled between May and October, including châteaux visits.

Châteaux visits are also included in many tours run by Bordeaux's tourist office. The program changes annually, with most tours operating between May and October. Day trips generally start at €72 per adult for those closest to town, and around €83 for areas such as the **Médoc** (p678) or **St-Émilion** (p679), including wine tastings and lunch. Some also incorporate a tour of the city's Chartrons wine merchants district. Separate three-hour tours of the Chatrons district at 9.30am on Saturday and Sunday from April to mid-November cost €10/9.50/7 per adult/concession/child.

For DIY wine trailing, the Maison du Vin de Bordeaux supplies free, colour-coded maps of production areas, details on châteaux, and the addresses of local *maisons du vin* (tourist offices that mainly deal with winery visits). A good starting point is Philippe Raoux's **La Winery** (☎ 05 56 39 04 90; www.lawinery.fr, in French; Rond-point des Vendangeurs, D1, Arsac-en-Médoc; 🕑 11am-7pm Tue-Sun Sep-Jun, to 8pm Tue-Sun Jul & Aug), 23km from Bordeaux. A first for France, this vast glass-and-steel wine centre mounts concerts and contemporary-art exhibits alongside various fee-based tastings, including innovative tastings that determine your *signe œnologique* ('wine sign'; booking required) costing €16 (€29 for rare *grands crus*), and stocks over 1000 different wines. See p679 for a peek behind the scenes, and p677 for wine shops in Bordeaux's city centre.

If you'd rather imbibe than drive, **Bordeaux Excursions** (www.bordeaux-excursions.com) customises private wine-country tours, starting from €190 for one to four people (excluding châteaux fees) for a half-day trip.

And to immerse yourself, literally, in the local liquid, at the **Spa de Vinothérapie Caudalie** (☎ 05 57 83 83 83; www.sources-caudalie.com; chemin de Smith Haut Lafitte, Martillac; treatments from €58) you can try a red-wine bath, a merlot wrap or a cabernet body scrub, said to promote blood-strengthening and anti-ageing. The spa is 20 minutes south of Bordeaux next to Château Smith Haut Lafitte, with overnight packages available at the attached hotel. It's best reached by your own wheels; exit the A62 at junction 1.

But even if the wine trail only leads you as far as the supermarket, it's possible to pick up exceptional wines off the shelves from just a few euros – the same wines that command a small fortune at some very flash restaurants around the world.

Fun, friendly and fantastic value, this lively place at the southwestern edge of place de la Victoire serves up *cassoulets* (casserole dishes) cooked on terracotta plates, created from ingredients you tick off on a checklist. There's a good kids' menu (€6) and it's wi-fi'd.

Brasserie Le Noailles (☎ 05 56 81 94 45; 12 allées de Tourny; mains €14.50-29.50; ⏰ lunch & dinner) Fronted by a winter garden, this classical French brasserie of dark timber-panelled interior with red-velour booths serves elegant fare, including its signature king prawn salad.

L'Entrecôte (☎ 05 56 81 76 10; 4 cours du 30 Juillet; menu €16.50; ⏰ lunch & dinner) Opened in 1966, this unpretentious place doesn't take reservations, and it only has one menu option. But Bordeaux locals continue to queue for its succulent thin-sliced meat (heated underneath by tea-light candles and topped with a 'secret recipe' sauce made from shallots and bone marrow), salad and unlimited home-made *frites*. The only choices are among the desserts (all €5.50), and the house red or rosé.

Baud et Millet (☎ 05 56 79 05 77; 19 rue Huguerie; menus €19-24; ⏰ 10am-11pm Mon-Sat) Over 250 different cheeses are offered at this cosy, mostly vegetarian (albeit far from vegan) place, with almost as many international wines lining the walls. Serious *fromage* fans should go for the all-you-can-eat cheese buffet.

La Tupina (☎ 05 56 91 56 37; 6 rue Porte de la Monnaie; menus €32-48, mains €19-44; ⏰ lunch & dinner) Filled with the aroma of soup simmering inside an old *tupina* ('kettle' in Basque) over an open fire, this white-tableclothed place is feted far and wide for its seasonal southwestern French specialities such as a minicasserole of foie gras and eggs, milk-fed lamb or goose wings with potatoes and parsley. A €16 lunch *menu* is available on weekdays.

L'Estaquade (☎ 05 57 54 02 50; quai de Queyries; mains €22-26; ⏰ lunch & dinner) Set on stilts, jutting out off the river's eastern bank, the seafood (bass, cod, scampi, scallops etc) and meat dishes (like braised pork knuckle) here can't help but be eclipsed by the magical views of Bordeaux's neoclassical architecture, particularly when the floodlights reflect in the water by night. On weekdays there's a €16 lunch *menu*.

SELF-CATERING

For a taste of Bordeaux (that for once doesn't involve wine!), head to **Baillardran** (☎ 05 56 79 05 89; www.baillardran.com; place des Grands Hommes), which has several branches in town, including this one in the Galerie des Grands Hommes shopping centre, where you can watch them make *canelés*, a local vanilla-infused fluted cake. In the shopping centre's basement is a **Champion supermarket**. Nearby, you'll find Jean D'Alos' fine **fromagerie** (4 rue Montesquieu; ⏰ closed Mon morning & Sun), with over 150 raw-milk and farm cheeses.

On Sunday mornings head to the quai des Chartrons' open-air bio (organic) market; otherwise, stock up at the covered market, **Marché des Capucins** (place des Capuchins; ⏰ 6am-1pm Tue-Sun).

Drinking

Considering its synonymity with wine, Bordeaux has surprisingly few bars, meaning restaurants and bistros tend to fill the gap.

Villa Tourny (☎ 05 56 44 60 48; 20 allées de Tourny; 8am-2am Mon-Sat) The hottest address in Bordeaux, thanks to its ruby-coloured velveteen banquettes, stylish food (mains €15 to €24.50) and local football stars who hang out here.

Chez Greg Le Grand Théâtre (☎ 05 56 31 30 30; 29 rue de l'Esprit des Lois; ⏰ lunch & dinner Mon-Sat, bar to 2am Mon-Sat) Glitzy retro decor with unusual twists like white-vinyl wall hangings held together with spoons make this a prime dining spot (lunch *menus* €20 to 35, dinner *menu* €35), but it comes into its own after the dinner plates are cleared away.

Bodega Bodega (☎ 05 56 01 24 24; 4 rue des Piliers de Tutelle; ⏰ lunch Mon-Sat, dinner daily, bar to 2am) Bordeaux's beloved Spanish bar has two floors of tapas, tunes and trendy types.

Café Brun (☎ 05 56 52 20 49; 45 rue St-Rémi; ⏰ 10am-2am) A warm atmosphere and cool jazz makes this bar-bistro great for an evening apéritif.

Absolut Lounge (☎ 05 56 48 80 00; 14 rue de la Devise; ⏰ 6pm-2am Mon-Sat) Chill to electro-jazz amid turquoise decor and red lamps while sipping a classic mojito.

Student hang-outs ring place de la Victoire, such as perennial favourite **Chez Auguste** (☎ 05 56 91 77 32; 3 place de La Victoire; ⏰ 7am-2am). For a postmodern vibe and cool French tunes, pop into nearby **Café Pop** (Café Populaire; ☎ 05 56 94 39 06; 1 rue Kleber; ⏰ 8pm-2am Tue-Sat).

Entertainment

Details of events appear in *Clubs & Concerts* (www.clubsetconcerts.com, in French), available for free at the tourist office.

Concert and event tickets can be purchased from the **Virgin Megastore billeterie** (☎ 05 56 56

05 56; 15-19 place Gambetta; 9.30am-7.30pm Mon-Thu, to 8pm Fri & Sat, noon-7pm Sun).

NIGHTCLUBS & LIVE MUSIC

Trendy pedestrianised streets like rue St-Rémi are good bets to get the evening started. For zoning reasons, many of the city's late-night dance venues are a few blocks northeast of Gare St-Jean along the river, on quai de la Paludate, such as the dark, atmospheric jazz club **Le Port de la Lune** (05 56 49 15 55; www.leportdelalune.com; 58 quai de la Paludate; admission varies; 7pm-2am), which also has a restaurant (*menu* €22; lunch and dinner daily); gigs are posted on the website. Clubs also cluster along the river north of the city centre. Bouncers can be selective but there's normally no cover charge.

Catch regular live bands as well as football on the big screen at the lively **Connemara Bar** (05 56 52 82 57; 18 cours d'Albret; noon-2am), which also has free wi-fi, darts, pool and good pub grub.

A mainly gay crowd kicks up its heels at **Bar de l'Hôtel de Ville** (05 56 44 05 08; 4 rue de l'Hôtel de Ville; 6pm-2am), which often has shows on Sundays.

THEATRE & CLASSICAL MUSIC

Designed by Victor Louis (of Chartres Cathedral fame), the 18th-century **Grand Théâtre** (05 56 00 85 95; place de la Comédie; ticket office 11am-6pm Tue-Sat Oct-Jul) stages operas, ballets and concerts of orchestral and chamber music. The tourist office also organises bilingual one-hour guided behind-the-scenes tours of the building (adult/child costs €6/5); tour times depend on performances and rehearsals.

Plays, dance performances, variety shows and concerts (such as French singer-songwriter Renan Luce) take place at **Théâtre Femina** (10 rue de Grassi).

CINEMAS

Nondubbed art-house films are screened at **Centre Jean Vigo** (05 56 44 35 17; www.jeanvigo.com, in French; 6 rue Franklin), and **Cinéma Utopia** (05 56 52 00 03; www.cinemas-utopia.org/bordeaux, in French; 3 place Camille Jullian).

Shopping

Europe's longest pedestrian shopping street, rue Ste-Catherine, is paved with raised, polished Bordelaise stone, becoming increasingly upmarket as it stretches 1.2km north from place de la Victoire to place de la Comédie.

Galerie Bordelaise (rue de la Porte Dijeaux & rue Ste-Catherine) is a 19th-century shopping arcade. Luxury-label boutiques concentrate within *le triangle*, formed by the allées de Tourny, cours Georges Clemenceau and cours de l'Intendance. An **antique market** (place St-Michel) fills the square on Sunday mornings.

Speciality wine shops include **Bordeaux Magnum** (05 56 48 00 06; 3 rue Gobineau) and **l'Intendant** (05 56 48 01 29; 2 allées de Tourny). The latter has a central spiral staircase climbing four floors, surrounded by cylindrical shelves holding 15,000 bottles of regional wine.

Getting There & Away

AIR

Bordeaux airport (05 56 34 50 50; www.bordeaux.aeroport.fr) is in Mérignac, 10km west of the city centre, with domestic and some international services. A taxi from the airport into town costs about €20 (around €25 at night, on Sundays and on public holidays).

BUS

Citram Aquitaine (05 56 43 68 43; www.citram.fr, in French) runs most buses to destinations in the Gironde.

International bus operator **Eurolines** (05 56 92 50 42; 32 rue Charles Domercq; 9am-12.30pm & 1.30-7pm Mon-Fri, 9am-noon & 2-6pm Sat) faces the train station.

CAR

Rental companies have offices in the train-station building.

TRAIN

Bordeaux is one of France's major rail-transit points. The station, Gare St-Jean, is about 3km from the city centre at the southern terminus of cours de la Marne.

Destinations include Paris' Gare Montparnasse (€66.20, three hours, at least 16 daily), Bayonne (€28.80, 1¾ hours), Nantes (€41.60, four hours), Poitiers (€33.90, 1¾ hours), La Rochelle (€25, two hours) and Toulouse (€33.30, 2¼ hours).

Getting Around

TO/FROM THE AIRPORT

The train station, place Gambetta and the main tourist office are connected to the airport (one-way €7) by **Jet'Bus** (05 56 34 50 50). The first bus leaves the airport at 7.45am Monday to Friday, and at 8.30am Saturday and Sunday from outside Terminal B (last at 10.45pm daily); the first departure to the airport from the train station is at 6.45am Monday to Friday, and 7.30am Saturday and Sunday (last at 9.45pm daily), with buses at 45-minute intervals throughout the day. The trip takes approximately 45 minutes.

BICYCLE

Bordeaux Scooter (☎ 05 57 59 10 18; bordeauxscooters@wanadoo.fr; 63 cours d'Alsace et Lorraine; ⏰ varies by arrangement) rents out bicycles (€11 for 24 hours) and scooters (from €29 per 24 hours).

BUS & TRAM

Urban buses and trams are run by **TBC** (☎ 05 57 57 88 88; www.infotbc.com, in French). The company has Espace Bus information/ticket offices at the train station and place Gambetta (4 rue Georges Bonnac) and at esplanade des Quinconces. Tram line C links the train station with the city centre via the riverside.

Single tickets (€1.30) are sold on board buses, and from machines at tram stops (stamp your ticket on board). Tickets aren't valid for transfers.

Night buses operate until 1.30am on Thursday, Friday and Saturday nights; line S11 links place de la Victoire with the nightclub zone on quai de la Paludate.

CAR

City parking is pricey and hard to find. Look for free spaces in the side streets north of the Musée d'Art Contemporain and west of the Jardin Public.

TAXI

To order a taxi try ☎ 05 569 148 11 or ☎ 05 568 199 15.

THE MÉDOC

Northwest of Bordeaux, along the western shore of the Gironde Estuary – formed by the confluence of the Garonne and Dordogne Rivers – lie some of Bordeaux' most celebrated vineyards. To their west, fine-sand beaches, bordered by dunes and *étangs* (lagoons), stretch from Pointe de Grave south along the Côte d'Argent (Silver Coast) to the Bassin d'Arcachon and beyond, with some great surf – see the boxed text, p685. The coastal dunes are enveloped by a pine forest, planted to stabilise the drifting sands and prevent them from encroaching on areas further inland.

Orientation & Information

On the banks of the muddy Gironde, the port town of **Pauillac** (population 1300) is at the heart of the wine country, surrounded by the distinguished Haut-Médoc, Margaux and St-Julien appellations. The Pauillac wine appellation encompasses 18 *crus classés* (see p675) including the world-renowned Mouton Rothschild, Latour and Lafite Rothschild.

Pauillac's tourist office houses the **Maison du Tourisme et du Vin** (☎ 05 56 59 03 08; www.pauillac-medoc.com, in French; La Verrerie; ⏰ seasonal hours vary annually), which has information on châteaux and how to visit them.

Sleeping & Eating

From Bordeaux, the Médoc makes an easy and enjoyable day trip. To stay and/or dine under the vines, the tourist offices in Bordeaux and in the Médoc have information, including *chambres d'hôtes* in the area.

Le Pavillon de Margaux (☎ 05 57 88 77 54; www.pavillonmargaux.com; 3 rue Georges Mandel, Margaux; d €70-120) In an old schoolhouse, this welcoming, family-run place has 14 rooms styled according to famous local châteaux. You can taste the family's wines at the on-site restaurant (mains €16 to €20; call to check closing days during mid-November to March), which serves a small but stellar selection of dishes, such as veal escalope with sage and ham, under a canopy of fairy lights.

Le Wy (☎ 05 56 39 04 91; La Winery; 3-course menus €23, discovery menu €63, mains €19-26; ⏰ lunch Tue-Sun, dinner Tue-Sat) Gastronomic fare like truffle-infused risotto and foie gras with green apples blends with a relaxed atmosphere (not a white tablecloth in sight) and over 400 different wines by the glass. At La Winery, p675; gourmet picnic baskets are available for €15.

Getting There & Away

The region is best explored by car. The Médoc's northern tip, Pointe de Grave, is linked to Royan by **car ferries** (☎ 05 46 38 35 15; www.ot-royan.fr; per person/bicycle/motorcycle/car one way €3.10/1.60/10/21.90) that operate approximately six times daily in winter and every 45 minutes in summer. The service runs around 6.30am to 8.30pm (7.15am and 9.30pm from Royan, 25 minutes one-way), depending on the season.

Another **car ferry** (☎ 05 57 42 04 49; www.tourisme-blaye.com, in French; per person/bicycle/car/motorcycle one way €3.10/1.60/7.40/13) links Lamarque (between Pauillac and Margaux on the D2) with Blaye, running five to 10 times daily (every 1½

PHILIPPE RAOUX: OWNER, LA WINERY

What inspired you to open La Winery? My family have been wine merchants since 1923; my father operated a wine mail-order business and I previously worked with customers only by mail, phone and internet. So I wanted to create a place where people can experience the wines. We opened in 2007.

Do you make wine yourself? We have four properties in the Médoc, so we have a foot in the production. But it's a tiny part of what we sell here, only 5%, which is different to the way châteaux work in France. It's a new concept. At first our neighbours (the châteaux owners) didn't understand – they're not wine merchants, they're winemakers, it's two different professions. But now they understand and are happy, because we introduce people to their wine too.

How did you come up with the idea of the 'signe œnologique' ('wine sign')? We wanted to invent a tasting process where people could be sure what wines they will like by knowing what qualities they like. It's a blind tasting; people are asked 10 questions and answer with a keypad. Then they can choose wines according to their 'sign', such as 'sensual', which reflects fruity wines.

Are all of the wines here from the Bordeaux region? About 60% are from Bordeaux; 35% are from other regions in France and 5% are foreign.

What's the reaction to foreign wines here? Connoisseurs are open to tasting them, comparing them. But they represent only 2% of wine consumption in France. French consumers are very traditional. Everyone in France knows someone working in the wine industry. Speaking about wine is speaking about family – you do not make infidelity to your family!

What gives Bordeaux wines their reputation? The harmony, the balance…other wines can depend on the season and be too alcoholic, too much colour, unbalanced. But every component of Bordeaux wines is on the same level, whether it's a good year or not. Even if it's not a 'good year', nothing is so bad that you don't like the wine.

Your favourite Bordeaux wine (your properties' wines aside)? St-Émilion Cheval Blanc *grand cru*. It's always fresh – as if it was harvested the day before.

hours June to September). The service starts around 7.30am and ends between 6.30pm and 8pm (until 9pm Saturday and Sunday June to September).

Citram Aquitaine buses (☎ 05 56 43 68 43) link Bordeaux with Margaux (€6.50, 50 minutes), Pauillac (€9.80, 1½ hours) and Lesparre Médoc (€13.10, 1½ hours). In Lesparre, buses depart for Soulac-sur-Mer (€7.60, two hours) and Point de Grave (€8.70, 2¼ hours).

To reach the Médoc by car from Bordeaux, take *sortie* (exit) 7 to get off the Bordeaux Rocade (ring road).

Trains run from Bordeaux's Gare St-Jean station to Margaux (€6.80, 50 minutes) and Pauillac (€9.60, one hour 10 minutes) several times a day.

ST-ÉMILION

pop 2345

The medieval village of St-Émilion perches above vineyards renowned for producing full-bodied, deeply coloured red wines. Named after Émilion, a miracle-working Benedictine monk who lived in a cave here between 750 and 767, it soon became a stop on pilgrimage routes, and the village and its vineyards are now Unesco-listed. Today, although it's definitely a stop on the tourist route, too, it's well worth venturing 40km east from Bordeaux to experience St-Émilion's magic, particularly when the sun sets over the valley and the limestone buildings glow with halolike golden hues.

Orientation & Information

Wear flat, comfortable shoes: the village's steep, uneven streets are hard going. The rocky terrain also make it difficult for travellers with disabilities to get around, but three new trails that allow mobility-impaired visitors to see at least some of the sites are plotted on free maps available from the tourist office.

The pharmacy and most banks are along rue Guadet.

Chai Pascal (☎ 05 57 24 52 45; 37 rue Gaudet; 🕒 11am-11pm, closed Sun in low season) New wine bar with online computers due to have opened by the time you're reading this.

Post Office (rue Guadet) Can exchange currency.

Tourist Kiosk (place de l'Église Monolithe) Summertime kiosk with varying hours (usually 10am to noon and 2pm to 6pm Monday to Friday and some weekends).

Tourist Office (☎ 05 57 55 28 28; www.saint-emilion-tourisme.com; place des Créneaux; 🕑 9.30am-8pm Jul-Aug, to 7pm mid-late Jun & early-late Sep, 9.30am-12.30pm & 1.45-6.30pm Apr–mid-Jun & late Sep-Oct, 9.30am-12.30pm & 1.45-6pm Nov-Mar) Stacks of brochures in English and details on visiting over 100 nearby châteaux.

Sights

The only (but highly worthwhile) way to visit the town's most interesting historical sites – many of them concealed beneath the village streets in a labyrinth of catacombs – is with one of the tourist office's 45-minute **guided tours** (adult/student/child incl site entry €6.50/4.10/3.20). Highlights are the hermit saint's famous cave, **Grotte de l'Ermitage**, and the 11th-century church **Église Monolithe**, carved out of limestone between the 9th and the 12th centuries. Tours in French depart regularly throughout the day – call ahead to check English tour times (usually 2pm). It's chilly below ground; bring a jumper.

For captivating views of the hilltop hamlet, collect the key from the tourist office to climb the **clocher** (bell tower; ☎ 05 57 55 28 28; admission €1) above the church. The entrance is on place des Créneaux; it has the same opening hours as the tourist office.

A domed Romanesque 12th-century nave dominates the former **Collégiale** (Collegiate Church), which also boasts an almost-square vaulted choir built between the 14th and 16th centuries. **Cloître de l'Église Collégiale**, the church's tranquil 12th- to 14th-

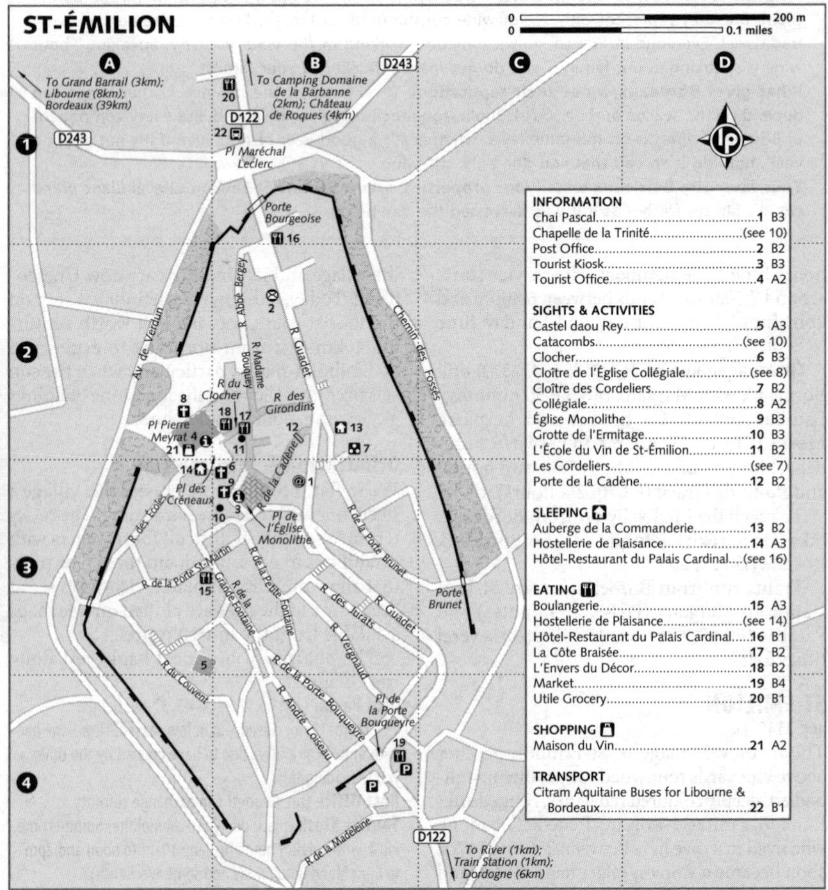

century cloister, is the venue for special events – see below.

Surviving sections of the town's medieval walls and gates include **Porte de la Cadène** (Gate of the Chain), off rue Guadet.

Within the ruined monastery, **Cloître des Cordeliers** (rue Porte Brunet; admission free; year-round), the winery **Les Cordeliers** (05 57 24 58 32; guided cellar tours €4; tour hrs vary daily) has made sparkling wine for over a century.

The 13th-century donjon known as the **Castel daou Rey** (Tour du Roi, King's Tower; admission €1; 11am-7.15pm Jul & Aug, variable hrs out of season) has exceptional views of the town and the Dordogne Valley.

Activities

Blind tastings and games (available in English) are a fun and informative introduction to wine tasting at **L'École du Vin de St-Émilion** (05 57 24 61 01; www.vignobleschateaux.fr; 4 rue du Clocher; tasting courses €29; 3pm daily Apr-Oct, by reservation Nov-Mar). The adjacent **Maison du Vin** (05 57 55 50 55; place Pierre Meyrat; classes €17; mid-Jul–mid-Sep) also offers bilingual, 1½-hour classes starting at 11am.

Eight **hiking circuits** loop, from 4km to 14km, through the greater World Heritage jurisdiction; the tourist office has maps.

Tours

The tourist office organises two-hour afternoon **château visits** (adult/child €9.60/6; Mon-Sat May-Sep) in French and English. It also runs various events throughout the year, such as **Les Vendredis Vignerons** (Winemakers' Friday; tickets €68; 11am-5pm Fri Jun-Sep) that combines a day in the vineyards and lunch with a local winemaker.

Festivals & Events

Between March and December, classical concerts are held at various châteaux as part of **Les Grandes Heures de St-Émilion**. Tickets (€28) must be booked in advance; the program is posted on the tourist-office website.

Each year from 10 to 15 October, the **Marché du Gout**, a market selling regional products, sets up in the village cloister. The cloister is also the venue for **free concerts** from May to November; the tourist office has the program.

Sleeping & Eating

The village and its surrounds have some charming boutique hotels. Ask the tourist office for a list of nearby *chambres d'hôtes*, as well as details of its two-day packages for two (€880) at *chambre d'hôte* accommodation including meals, tours and château visits. Many of St-Émilion's best restaurants are attached to hotels.

VILLAGE CENTRE

Auberge de la Commanderie (05 57 24 70 19; www.aubergedelacommanderie.com; 2 rue Porte Brunet; d €70-100, apt €135-207; mid-Feb–mid-Jan;) Inside this hotel's 13th-century walls, rooms are modernised with massive murals depicting a Technicolorised pop-art version of an old black-and-white postcard of the village. Wi-fi's available, and there's free parking in the private lock-up car park.

Hôtel-Restaurant du Palais Cardinal (05 57 24 72 39; www.palais-cardinal.com; place du 11 Novembre 1918; s €67-208, d €70-266;) Run by the same family for five generations. The hotel's heated pool is set in rambling flower-filled gardens and framed by sections of the original medieval town-wall fortifications, dating from the 13th century. Gastronomic fare at its restaurant (*menus* €19 to €40, closed lunch Wednesday and Thursday, and closed from December to March) includes the likes of cognac-glazed shrimp and spiced St-Émilion wine plums accompanied by blackcurrant sorbet.

our pick **Hostellerie de Plaisance** (05 57 55 07 55; www.hostellerie-plaisance.com; place du Clocher; d €310-520, ste €620; closed Jan;) With a spice-coloured bar opening to a wraparound terrace, this intimate gem in the shadow of the bell tower recently expanded to house 17 whimsical rooms. (A glass lift concealed in a gazebo whisks you through the rock face down to the new wing.) Its twin-Michelin-starred restaurant (*menus* €55 to €120; closed Wednesday lunch and all day Sunday and Monday) is now housed in a dining room of eggshell blue and white gold. Start your meal with local caviar and move on to line-caught bass with black-pork belly; or go for chef Philippe Etchebest's 'discovery menu'.

La Côte Braisée (05 57 24 79 65; www.la-cote-braisee.com; 3 rue du Tertre de la Tente; menus €14.50-37; closed lunch Wed in high season, closed dinner Tue & all day Wed in low season) On a slanting, rocky laneway, this rustic, cavelike restaurant is renowned for its foie gras, either stuffed inside roast duck with local grapes, or pan-fried with caramelised apples. At separate premises, the proprietors rent out five charming guest rooms (doubles €50 to €75); the restaurant acts as the reception point.

L'Envers du Decor (☎ 05 57 74 48 31; 11 rue du Clocher; lunch menus €18-28, dinner menu €28; 🕑 lunch & dinner) Warmed by a wood fire in the cooler months, this local favourite serves market-fresh *menus* and opens to a quiet rear courtyard garden.

AROUND ST-ÉMILION

Camping Domaine de la Barbanne (☎ 05 57 24 75 80; www.camping-saint-emilion.com; rte de Montagne; camping €18-28, cabins €54; 🕑 Apr-Sep;) This family-friendly, three-star place is about 2km north of St-Émilion on the D122. There's a five-night minimum for camping in July and August. Cabins, sleeping up to five people, are spacious and well equipped.

Château de Roques (☎ 05 57 74 55 69; www.chateau-de-roques.com; Puisseguin; d €68-108;) If you've dreamed of staying in a romantic countryside château but your budget – or lack thereof – was a rude awakening, you'll be delighted by this affordable 16th-century place in the vineyards, 5km outside St-Émilion. Its restaurant (*menus* €26 to €33, open lunch and dinner, closed late December to early February) serves foie gras with cognac and jelly made from locally produced Sauternes white wine. Wi-fi's free and there's good wheelchair access. The best road is the D122 (north from St-Émilion) – the château is just near the junction of the D21.

Grand Barrail (☎ 05 57 55 37 00; www.grand-barrail.com; rte de Libourne/D243; d €185-320, ste €510-620;) Grand doesn't even begin to describe this immense 1850-built château 3km from the village, with its decadent on-site spa, stone-flagged heated swimming pool, free state-of-the-art fitness room, wheelchair access and, if you happen to be arriving by helicopter, its own helipad on the front lawns. Undoubtedly the best seat in its restaurant (*menus* €40 to €61) is the corner table framed by 19th-century stained glass.

ATLANTIC COAST

SELF-CATERING

Boulangeries (bakeries), such as the one on rue de la Grande Fontaine, open to around 6pm. A **market** fills place de la Porte Bouqueyre every Sunday. **Utile Grocery** (🕑 8am-7pm Mon-Sat, to 1pm Sun May–mid-Sep, 8am-12.30pm & 3.15-7pm Mon-Fri, 8am-1pm Sun mid-Sep–Apr) is a supermarket on the D122, 150m north of town.

Shopping

St-Émilion's sloping streets and squares are lined with about 50 wine shops – one for every eight of the old city's residents. The best value is the **Maison du Vin** (☎ 05 57 55 50 55; place Pierre Meyrat; 🕑 9.30am-12.30pm & 2-6pm Sep-Jul, 9.30am-7pm Aug), which is owned by the 250 châteaux whose wines it sells at cellar-door prices. It also has a free aromatic exhibit and sells specialist publications.

Ursuline nuns brought the recipe for *macarons* (macaroons – almond biscuits) to St-Émilion in the 17th century. Specialist shops around town charge €6 per two dozen.

Getting There & Away

Citram Aquitaine (☎ 05 56 43 68 43) buses to/from Bordeaux's train station run at least once daily (except on Sunday and holidays from October to April) to Libourne (€5.50, 45 minutes); from there you take a **Marchesseau** (☎ 05 57 40 60 79) bus to St-Émilion (€2.10, 10 minutes). On Friday, Saturday and Sunday, there are two direct buses each way between Bordeaux and St-Émilion (€7.60, one hour, 15 minutes).

Trains run three times daily (two on Sunday and holidays) from Bordeaux (€7.70, 40 minutes); the train station is 1km south of the base of the village. (Stations aren't announced on these small trains, so it's easy to miss your stop.) A shuttle service between the train station and the village is expected to start operating in the summer months.

By car from Bordeaux, follow the signs for Libourne and take the D243. Year-round the tourist office rents out bicycles for €10/14.70 per half-day/full day. Call for a **taxi** (☎ 05 57 25 17 59; www.taxi-st-emilion.com).

ARCACHON

pop 11,800

A long-time oyster-harvesting area on the southern side of the tranquil, triangular Bassin d'Arcachon (Arcachon Bay), this seaside town lured bourgeois Bordelaise at the end of the 19th century. Its four little quarters are romantically named for each of the seasons, with villas that evoke the town's golden past amid a scattering of 1950s architecture.

Arcachon seethes with sun-seekers in summer, but you'll find practically deserted beaches a short bike ride away.

Orientation

Arcachon's main commercial streets run parallel to the beach: bd de la Plage, cours Lamarque de Plaisance and cours Héricart de Thury. Perpendicular to the beach, busy streets include av Gambetta and rue du Maréchal de Lattre de Tassigny.

Information

Crédit Agricole (252 bd de la Plage) Only bank with currency exchange.
Le Bistrot du Boulevard (☎ 05 56 83 45 67; 230 bd de la Plage; per 15min €1.50; 🕑 10am-2am) Internet access.
Post Office (place Président Roosevelt)
Tourist Office (☎ 05 57 52 97 97; www.arcachon.com; Esplanade Georges Pompidou; 🕑 9am-7pm Jul & Aug, 9am-6.30pm Mon-Fri, to 5pm Sat, 10am-noon & 1-5pm Sun Apr-Jun & Sep, 9am-6pm Mon-Fri, 9am-5pm Sat Oct-Mar)

Sights

In the **Ville d'Été** (Summer Quarter) Arcachon's sandy beach, **Plage d'Arcachon**, is flanked by two piers. Lively **Jetée Thiers** is at the western end. In front of the eastern pier, **Jetée D'Eyrac**, stands the town's turreted **Casino de la Plage** – built by Adalbert Deganne in 1953 as an exact replica of Château de Boursault in the Marne. Inside, it's a less-grand blinking and bell-ringing riot of poker machines and gaming tables.

The old-fashioned **Aquarium et Musée** (☎ 05 56 54 89 28; 2 rue du Professeur Jolyet; adult/student/under 10yr €4.80/3.20/3; 🕑 9.45am-12.15pm & 1.45-7pm Jul & Aug, 9.45am-12.15pm & 1.45-6.30pm late Mar–Oct, closed Nov–late Mar), in a wooden shack opposite the casino, has a small collection of fish in floodlit tanks.

On the tree-covered hillside south of the Ville d'Été, the century-old **Ville d'Hiver** (Winter Quarter) has over 300 villas, many decorated with delicate wood tracery, ranging in style from neo-Gothic through to colonial. It's an easy stroll or a short ride up the **art-deco public lift** (admission free; 🕑 9am-12.45pm & 2.30-7pm) in Parc Mauresque.

A tree-lined **pedestrian promenade** runs west from the Plage d'Arcachon to **Plage Péreire**, **Plage des Abatilles** and the **Dune du Pilat** (p685).

Activities

Cycle paths link Arcachon with the Dune du Pilat and Biscarosse (30km to the south), and around the Bassin d'Arcachon to Cap Ferret. From here, a cyclable path parallels the beaches north to Pointe de Grave.

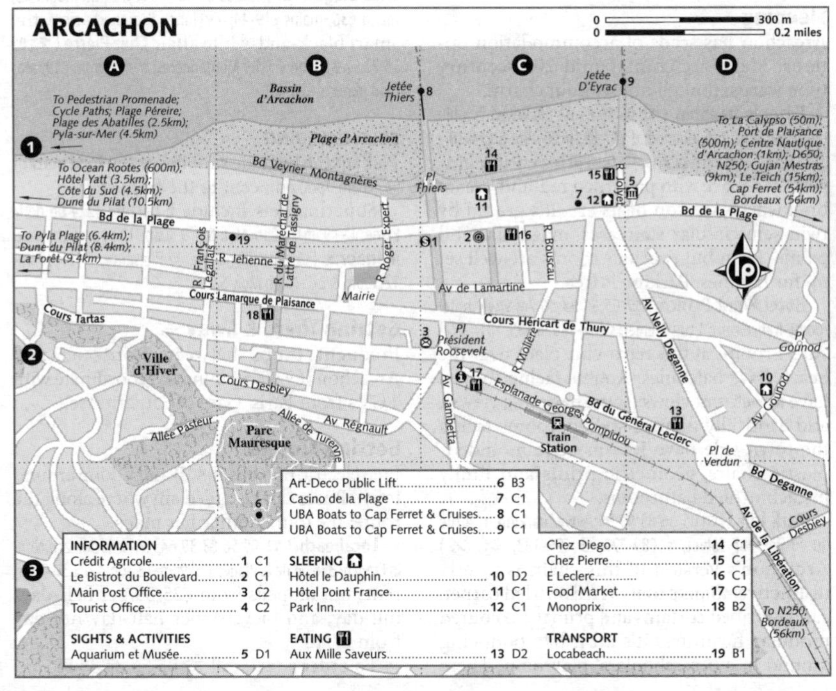

The exposed ocean beaches to the south of town generally offer good conditions for surfing. **Ocean Roots** (☎ 06 62 26 04 11; oceanrootsclub@aol.com; 27 av St-Francois Xavier; ⏲ varies) offers lessons and rents out equipment. For more surf spots, see the boxed text, opposite.

Centre Nautique d'Arcachon (☎ 05 56 83 77 42; quai Goslar; ⏲ Apr-Sep), 1.5km east of the Jetée d'Eyrac at the Port de Plaisance (Pleasure Boat Port), rents out sea kayaks, and windsurfing and diving equipment, and offers courses.

The tourist office has details of stacks of other activities including **tandem parachuting**, **seaplane flights**, **wakeboarding** and more.

Tours

Les Bateliers Arcachonnais (UBA; ☎ 05 57 72 28 28; www.bateliers-arcachon.asso.fr, in French) runs daily, year-round cruises around the **Île aux Oiseaux** (adult/child €13.50/9.50), the uninhabited 'bird island' in the middle of the bay. It's a haven for tern, curlew and redshank, so bring your binoculars. In summer there are regular all-day excursions (11am to 5.30pm) to the **Banc d'Arguin**, the sand bank off the Dune du Pilat (€16/11 per adult/child).

Sleeping

Arcachon has scads of accommodation options. Many are chintzy mid-20th-century time warps, though not without charm.

Hôtel le Dauphin (☎ 05 56 83 02 89; www.dauphin-arcachon.com; 7 av Gounod; d €57-88, tr €64-95, q €71-107; ❄ 🅿) Don' miss this late-19th-century gingerbread place with patterned red-and-cream brickwork. An icon of its era, it's graced by twin semicircular staircases, magnolias and palms. Plain but spacious rooms are well set up for families. Parking is free.

Hôtel Point France (☎ 05 56 83 46 74; www.hotel-point-france.com; 1 rue Grenier; s €82-140, d €85-181; ❄) All 34 rooms at this retro-chic place near the beach have balconies. Rooms facing the sea have knock-out views (some have side views), and exotically themed styling; rooms facing the town side have Jetsons-style moulded-plastic chairs, geometric prints and funky pistachio-tiled bathrooms.

Park Inn (☎ 05 56 83 99 91; www.parkinn.fr; 4 rue du Professeur Jolyet; s €89-172, d €99-183; ❄ ⊠) Arcachon's version of this chain is utterly distinctive, thanks to its vivid swirled carpet, candy-striped curtains and primary-coloured modular furniture. It's a bit like bouncing around in a pre-schoolers' playroom. There are three wheelchair-equipped rooms, wi-fi, and the staff are a pleasure to deal with.

Eating

The bay's oysters (served raw and accompanied by the local small, flat sausages, *crepinettes*) appear on *menus* everywhere.

Aux Mille Saveurs (☎ 05 56 83 40 28; 25 bd du Général Leclerc; menus €18-35, tasting menu €45; ⏲ closed dinner Tue & Wed low season) In a light-filled space of flowing white tablecloths, this genteel restaurant is renowned for traditional French fare artistically presented on fine china. Seafood aside, specialities include rabbit with thyme and coriander.

La Calypso (☎ 05 56 83 65 08; 84 bd de la Plage; menu €25; ⏲ closed Wed & Thu Sep-Jun) Beneath beamed ceilings, with a cosy open fire flickering in the chillier months, this is an amiable place to tuck in to specialities like sole stuffed with crab, honey-glazed duck, and a delicious *bouillabaisse arcachonnaise* (fish soup) made from local sea critters.

The beachfront promenade between Jetée Thiers and Jetée d'Eyrac is lined with restaurants and places offering pizza and crêpes, plus a couple of standout places serving seafood: **Chez Diego** (☎ 05 56 83 84 46; bd Veyrier-Montagnères; menu €36, mains €19-44; ⏲ lunch & dinner), and the smart black-and-white affair **Chez Pierre** (☎ 05 56 22 52 94; 1 bd Veyrier Montagnères; menus from €19, seafood platters €20-48).

SELF-CATERING

Pick up fresh picnic supplies at the **food market** (⏲ 8am-1pm) adjacent to the train station.

Supermarkets include **E Leclerc** (224 bd de la Plage; ⏲ 9am-7.30pm Mon-Sat, 9.30am-12.30pm Sun) and **Monoprix** (46 cours Lamarque de Plaisance; ⏲ 8.30am-12.30pm & 2-7.30pm Mon-Sat).

Getting There & Away

Frequent trains between Bordeaux and Arcachon (€9.90, 50 minutes) coordinate with TGVs from Paris' Gare Montparnasse.

Getting Around

Free electric Ého buses A, B and C loop around town. Buses can be hailed anywhere along the route; the tourist office has maps.

Locabeach (☎ 05 56 83 39 64; www.locabeach.com, in French; 326 bd de la Plage; ⏲ 9am-12.30pm & 2.30-7pm) rents out mopeds from €25/39 per half-day/full day, and bicycles per half-day/full day from €7/10.

To order a taxi, call ☎ 05 56 83 88 88.

SURF'S UP: TOP SURF SPOTS ON THE ATLANTIC COAST

France's Atlantic Coast has some of Europe's best surf. Autumn is prime time for riding the waves, with warm(ish) water temperatures, consistent(ish) conditions and few(er) crowds. The biggest swells tend to roll in around Biarritz (p694), but the waves along this stretch of coast are mighty *malade* (sick)!

- Hit the beaches south of Arcachon around the **Dune du Pilat** (below).
- Take a lesson in the mellow waves at **Soulac-sur-Mer**. Reserve through Soulac's **tourist office** (☎ 05 56 09 86 61; www.soulac.com; 68 rue de la Plage; 9am-12.30pm & 2-5.15pm Mon-Sat year-round plus Sun Apr-Oct), or check out www.soulac-surf.com (in French). Beginners lessons start at €32.
- Watch the pros contest August's **ASP** (Association of Surfing Professionals; www.aspeurope.com) event at **Lacanau-Océan**.
- Paddle out from the tip of pine-forested **Cap Ferret peninsula** (below).
- Other hot spots (but don't let on we told you!) are **Le Porge-Océan**, **Montalivet** and **Hourtin-Plage**.

And for the best wave *away* from the coast, longboarders can attempt the **mascaret** (bore; mascaretgironde.free.fr), a tidal wave travelling inland from the Gironde Estuary. The best place to pick it up is St-Pardon (you'll need boots to get in).

AROUND ARCACHON

Dune du Pilat

This colossal sand dune (sometimes referred to as the Dune de Pyla because of its location in the resort town of Pyla-sur-Mer), 8km south of Arcachon, stretches from the mouth of the Bassin d'Arcachon southwards for almost 3km. Already the largest in Europe, it's spreading eastwards at 4.5m a year – it has swallowed trees, a road junction and even a hotel.

The view from the top – approximately 114m above sea level – is magnificent. To the west you can see the sandy shoals at the mouth of the Bassin d'Arcachon, including the **Banc d'Arguin bird reserve** and **Cap Ferret**. Dense dark-green pine forests stretch from the base of the dune eastwards almost as far as the eye can see.

Take care swimming in this area: powerful currents swirl out to sea from the deceptively tranquil *baïnes* (little bays).

SLEEPING & EATING

The area's swag of seasonal campsites are listed at www.campings-bassinarcachon.com.

La Forêt (☎ 05 56 22 73 28; rte de Biscarosse; campsites €16-34; Apr–early Nov;) A well-run, three-star campsite, 'the forest' has shady pine trees and spotless amenities.

Hôtel Yatt (☎ 05 57 72 03 72; www.yatt-hotel.com, in French; 253 bd Côte D'Argent, Moulleau village; d €45-105, tr €60-105, q €70-115, mini-ste €80-135; closed mid-Nov–week before Easter;) Built in 1950 and renovated with a designer's eye (backlit floor-to-ceiling woodcut panels, floating blond-timber floors, funky yellow bath towels), this hip hotel in the café-clad Moulleau fishing village, 400m north of Pyla-sur-Mer, is footsteps from the jetty and the beach. Wi-fi's free.

Côte du Sud (☎ 05 56 83 25 00; www.cote-du-sud.fr; 4 av du Figuier; d €59-130; closed Dec–early Feb;) This chic little beachside boutique hotel has eight exotic rooms inspired by a spectrum of continents, with details such as rattan ceilings, seashells, cacti and stainless-steel basins. This airy restaurant (*menus* €23 to €30) specialises in – what else? – seafood.

GETTING THERE & AWAY

Cycling is the most popular way to reach the dune from Arcachon (see opposite).

Local bus company **Baia** (☎ 08 10 20 17 14; www.baia-cobas.fr, in French) has daily buses from Arcachon's train station to the Pyla Plage (Haïtza), 1km north of the dune (adult/child one-way €1/0.50). From mid-June to mid-September, buses continue south to the dune's car park at the northern end.

Cap Ferret

pop 6392 (peninsula)

Hidden within a canopy of pine trees at the tip of the Cap Ferret peninsula, the tiny village of Cap Ferret spans a mere 2km between the tranquil bay and the crashing Atlantic surf. It's

ATLANTIC COAST

> **OYSTER TASTE TEST**
>
> Oysters from each of the Bassin d'Arcachon's four oyster-breeding zones hint at subtly different flavours. See if you can detect these:
>
> **Banc d'Arguin** – milk and sugar
> **Île aux Oiseaux** – minerals
> **Cap Ferret** – citrus
> **Grand Banc** – roasted hazelnuts

crowned by its 53m-high, red-and-white **lighthouse** (☎ 05 57 70 33 30; adult/child €4.50/3; 🕑 10am-7.30pm Jul & Aug, 10am-12.30pm & 2-6.30pm Apr-Jun & Sep, 2-5pm Wed-Sun Oct-Mar), with interactive exhibits and stunning views from the top.

Federation Française de Surf member **Surf Center** (☎ 05 56 60 61 05; 22 allées des Goëlands; 🕑 approximately Jun-Sep) rents out boards and offers lessons for all levels; information is also available from the **tourist office** (☎ 05 56 60 63 26; www.lege-capferret.com, in French; 12 av de l'Océan; 🕑 10am-6.30pm Mon-Sat, 10am-1pm & 3-6.30pm Sun Jul & Aug, 10am-1pm & 3-6pm daily Jun & Sep). The outlying office can be reached on the same telephone number and the website during the rest of the year.

SLEEPING & EATING

Auberge de Jeunesse (☎ 05 56 60 64 62; www.fuaj.org; 87 av de Bordeaux; dm incl sheets & breakfast €13.80, camping €6; 🕑 Jul & Aug, reception 8am-1pm & 6-9pm) This ultrabasic summertime youth hostel is a 500m stroll from the beach.

Hôtel L'Océane (☎ 05 56 60 68 13; www.hotel-oceane.com, in French; 62 av de l'Océane; d €49-94, tr €117, 5-person ste €158) Some of Hôtel L'Océane's coir-carpeted, marine-coloured rooms open to private breezy decks or a communal timber-decked patio. There's a clutch of cafés and pizzerias mere footsteps from the hotel.

La Maison du Bassin (☎ 05 56 60 60 63; www.lamaisondubassin.com; 5 rue des Pionniers; s €100-200, d €120-230, apt €300; 🕑 closed Jan–early Feb) Four dreamy rooms the size of suites are situated in a separate annexe of this quixotic hideaway, while cosy rooms in the main house have details like a muslin-canopied sleigh bed, or a curtained bath-tub in the centre of the room. Its chocolate-toned contemporary restaurant, Le Bistrot du Bassin (*menus* €25 to €39, mains €17 to €34), has a wi-fi'd bar area.

GETTING THERE & AWAY

Les Bateliers Arcachonnais (UBA; ☎ 05 57 72 28 28; www.bateliers-arcachon.asso.fr, in French) runs ferries from Arcachon to Cap Ferret (adult/child return €11.50/8), year-round (check Arcachon departure jetties beforehand). In the warmer months seasonally operating lines include ferries linking Cap Ferret and the Dune du Pilat, and Cap Ferret and Moulleau. Schedules are posted on the website and available from tourist offices.

Cap Ferret is a scenic drive around Bassin d'Arcachon or, to drive here directly from Bordeaux (71.8km) take the D106.

Gujan Mestras

pop 15,367

Picturesque oyster ports are dotted around the town of Gujan Mestras, which sprawls along 9km of coastline.

You'll find the **tourist office** (☎ 05 56 66 12 65; www.ville-gujanmestras.fr, in French; 19 av de Lattre de Tassigny; 🕑 9.30am-12.30pm & 2-6pm Mon-Sat, 9.30am-12.30pm Sun mid-Jun–mid-Sep, 9.30am-12.30pm & 2-5.30pm Mon-Sat mid-Sep–mid-Jun) at the western edge of town in La Hume.

Flat-bottomed oyster boats moored to weathered wooden shacks line the largest port, **Port de Larros**, about 4km to the east. The small **Maison de l'Huître** (☎ 05 56 66 23 71; adult/child €4.50/2.50; 🕑 10am-12.30pm & 2.30-6pm Mon-Sat year-round plus 10am-12.30pm & 2.30-6pm Sun Jun-Aug) has a display on oyster farming, including a short film in English. Locally harvested oysters are sold nearby and served at seafood restaurants with waterside terraces.

Gujan Mestras' train station is on the train line linking Bordeaux with Arcachon.

Le Teich Parc Ornithologique

Just 29% of the shallow 155-sq-km Bassin d'Arcachon is under water at low tide, attracting 260 species of migratory and nonmigratory birds each year. Committed to their preservation is the idyllic **Parc Ornithologique** (Bird Reserve; ☎ 05 56 22 80 93; www.parc-ornithologique-du-teich.com; adult/child €6.80/4.80; 🕑 10am-8pm Jul & Aug, to 7pm mid-Apr–Jun & early Sep–mid-Sep, to 6pm mid-Sep–mid-Apr) situated in Le Teich, 15km east of Arcachon. Le Teich's train station, 1.2km south of the park, is linked with Bordeaux and Arcachon.

French Basque Country

Gently sloping from the western foothills of the Pyrenees into the deep sapphire-blue Bay of Biscay, the Basque Country (Euskal Herria in the Basque language; Le Pays Basque in French) straddles modern-day France and Spain. Yet this feisty, independent land remains profoundly different from either of the nation states that have adopted it.

The French side (or as it's diplomatically referred to here, the 'northern side'; 'Iparralde' in Basque) accounts for roughly 20% of the Basque country, and is famed for its glitzy beach resort, Biarritz. Bronzed surfers zoom around Biarritz's hilly coastline on mopeds, and oiled sun-seekers pack its beaches like glistening sardines.

Together with sprawling Anglet and Bayonne, 8km to the east, Biarritz forms an urban area often called BAB, with a population around 110,000. Biarritz, however, is the least Basque of the trio. Easily the most Basque is the French Basque Country's cultural and economic capital, Bayonne, whose authentically preserved old town is bisected by bridges arcing over its confluence of rivers. Traditional Basque music, sports and festivals are an integral part of Bayonne's local culture, and its good transport links make it an ideal base for discovering the region.

To the southwest of this conurbation is St-Jean de Luz, a delightful seaside township and working fishing port.

Up in the French Basque Country's lush hills, little one-street villages and green valleys traversed by hiking trails are easily explored from the walled town of St-Jean Pied de Port, an age-old pit stop for pilgrims heading over the border to Santiago de Compostela.

HIGHLIGHTS

- Discover just what makes the local chocolate so scrumptious during a behind-the-scenes factory tour in **Bayonne** (p691)
- Chug up the scenic mountainside railway, **Le Petit Train de la Rhune** (p704)
- Watch world-class surfers from fashionable café terraces or ride the waves yourself in and around **Biarritz** (p694)
- Taste traditional Basque dishes incorporating freshly caught seafood at **St-Jean de Luz** (p702)
- Browse local produce and handmade products at the farmers market in the age-old pilgrims' outpost, **St-Jean Pied de Port** (p704)

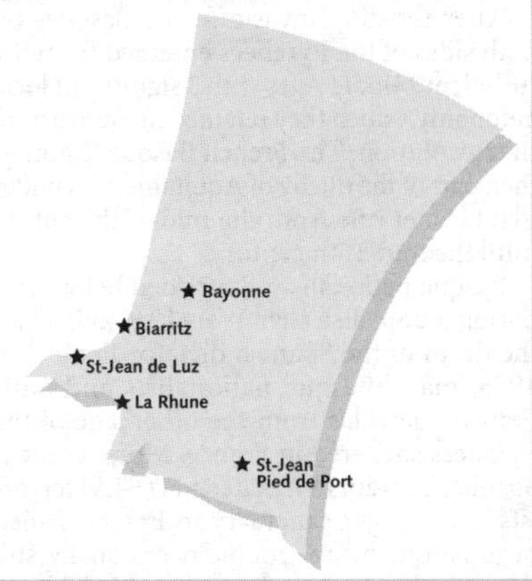

- POPULATION: 600,000
- AREA: 13,400 SQ KM

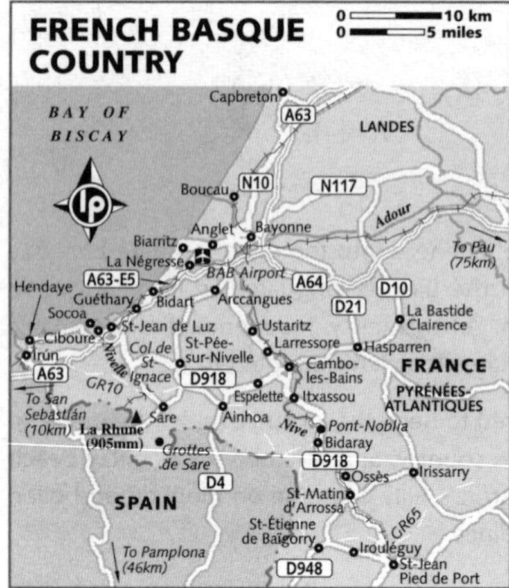

History

Recent DNA testing shows that the Basque people have inhabited the region for at least 30,000 years – the only people in Europe to have remained in their region for so long. This was made possible by the fact that the area was still inhabitable during the last ice age. Roman sources mention a tribe called the Vascones living in the area and it's attested that the Basques took over what is now southwestern France in the 6th century. The Romans never managed to conquer the area, however, as the Basques were able to shelter in the mountains and continue to live off fishing in the ocean. Converting to Christianity in the 10th century, they are still known for their strong Catholicism.

After resisting invasions, the Basques on both sides of the Pyrenees emerged from the turbulent Middle Ages with a significant local autonomy, which they retained in France until the Revolution. The French Basque Country, then part of the duchy of Aquitaine, was under Plantagenet rule from the mid-12th century until the mid-15th century.

Basque nationalism flourished before and during the Spanish Civil War (1936–39). Until the death of the Spanish dictator Franco, in 1975, many Basque nationalists and anti-Franco guerrillas from the other side of the Pyrenees sheltered in France. More recently, Spanish Euskadi ta Azkatasuna (ETA) terrorists have sought sanctuary in France. Failed negotiations mean trouble occasionally still flares up (such as the attack on Madrid airport in 2007 that killed two people), but it's a small, extremist minority that doesn't reflect the peaceful nationalism that predominates in the region.

Getting There & Away

All roads and train lines lead to Bayonne, which is easily accessible from the rest of France.

Rail travel to Spain involves switching trains at the frontier since the Spanish track gauge is narrower. Take an SNCF train to Hendaye, where you can pick up the EuskoTren, familiarly known as 'El Topo' (The Mole), a shuttle train that runs regularly via Irún to San Sebastián.

Buses travel between Bayonne and Bilbao, Spain, via Biarritz, St-Jean de Luz and San Sebastián twice daily – see p693.

The airport (p693) serving Bayonne and Biarritz has domestic flights as well as services to the UK, Ireland and other European destinations.

BAYONNE

pop 44,200

Bayonne (Baiona in Basque) is defined by the so-name 'river junction' of the River Adour and the smaller River Nive, as well as by its compactness. Until 1907, it was forbidden to build outside the town's fortifications, resulting in the narrow, curved streets of Petit Bayonne, with riverside buildings clad in red and green shutters and shoals of waterside restaurants. Although you can cross the architecturally preserved town centre on foot in about 15 minutes, you can easily spend hours discovering its hidden laneways and staircases, and remnants of its medieval past.

In addition to its chocolates, Bayonne is famous for its prime cured ham, and for the *baïonnette* (bayonet), developed here in 1640 on rue des Faures ('Blacksmiths' Street').

History

Bayonne prospered from the 13th to 15th centuries under the protection of the Plantagenet kings who ruled Aquitaine. The town's subsequent 18th-century commercial prosperity was fuelled by Basque privateers, who landed cargoes much more valuable and sweeter scented than the tonnes of cod caught off the coast of Newfoundland by the substantial Basque fishing fleet. This already-lively town now buzzes even more with the recent opening of the city's new university.

LOCAL LINGO

According to linguists, Euskara, the Basque language, is unrelated to any other tongue on earth, and is the only tongue in southwest Europe to have withstood the onslaught of Latin and its derivatives.

Basque is spoken by about a million people in Spain and France, nearly all of whom are bilingual. In the French Basque Country, the language is widely spoken in Bayonne and the hilly hinterland. However, while it is an official language in Spain, it isn't recognised as such in France (although some younger children are educated in Basque at primary-school level). The language also has a higher survival rate on the Spanish (aka 'southern') side, which is more industrialised, hence its employment opportunities allow native speakers to stay in the area.

But you'll still encounter the language here on Basque-language TV stations, and the occasional sign reading *'Hemen Euskara emaiten dugu'* (Basque spoken here) on shop doors. You'll also see the Basque flag (similar to the UK's but with a red field, a white vertical cross and a green diagonal one) flying throughout the region, as well as another common Basque symbol, the *lauburu* (like a curly four-leaf clover), signifying good luck or protection.

Orientation

The Rivers Adour and Nive split central Bayonne into three: St-Esprit, the area north of the Adour; Grand Bayonne, the oldest part of the city, on the western bank of the Nive; and the very Basque Petit Bayonne quarter to its east.

To the west, Bayonne meets the suburban sprawl of Anglet (famed for its beaches, p694) and the glamorous seaside resort of Biarritz (p694).

Information

BOOKSHOPS

Elkar (☎ 05 59 59 35 14; place de l'Arsenal) A wealth of texts on Basque history and culture, walking in the Basque Country, maps and CDs of Basque music.

INTERNET ACCESS

Multimedia Services (☎ 05 59 59 00 32; 6 rue des Faures; per hr €4; 🕑 2-7pm Mon, 10am-7pm Tue-Fri, 10am-noon Sat)

LAUNDRY

Hallwash (6 rue d'Espagne; 🕑 8am-8pm) Machines shut down and doors lock on the dot of closing time.

POST

Post Office (11 rue Jules Labat)
Post Office (21 bd Alsace-Lorraine)

TOURIST INFORMATION

Tourist Office (☎ 08 20 42 64 64; www.bayonne-tourisme.com; place des Basques; 🕑 9am-7pm Mon-Sat, 10am-1pm Sun Jul & Aug, 9am-6.30pm Mon-Fri, 10am-6pm Sat Sep-Jun) Efficient, friendly office providing stacks of informative brochures and free bike rental (p694), plus French-language guided city tours (€5; 10.30am Monday to Saturday mid-July to mid-September).

Sights & Activities

RAMPARTS

Vauban's 17th-century fortifications (see the boxed text, p65) are now covered with grass and dotted with trees, enveloping the city centre in a green belt. You can walk the stretches of the old ramparts that rise above bd Rempart Lachepaillet and rue Tour de Sault.

CATHÉDRALE STE-MARIE

The twin towers of Bayonne's Gothic **cathedral** (🕑 8am-noon & 3-7pm Mon-Sat) soar above the city. Construction began in the 13th century, and was completed in 1451; the mismatched materials in some ways resemble Lego blocks. Above the north aisle are three lovely stained-glass windows, the oldest, in the Chapelle Saint Jérôme, dating from 1531. The entrance to the stately 13th-century **cloister** (🕑 9am-12.30pm & 2-6pm Jun-Sep, to 5pm Oct-May) is on place Louis Pasteur.

MUSEUMS

The seafaring history, traditions and cultural identity of the unique Basque people are all explored at the **Musée Basque et de l'Histoire de Bayonne** (☎ 05 59 59 08 98; www.musee-basque.com, in French; 37 quai des Corsaires; adult/student/under 18yr €5.50/3/free; 🕑 10am-6.30pm daily Jul & Aug, closed Mon Sep-Jun) through exhibits including a reconstructed farm and the interior of a typical *etxe* (home).

Treasures crammed in the **Musée Bonnat** (☎ 05 59 59 08 52; 5 rue Jacques Lafitte; adult/student/child

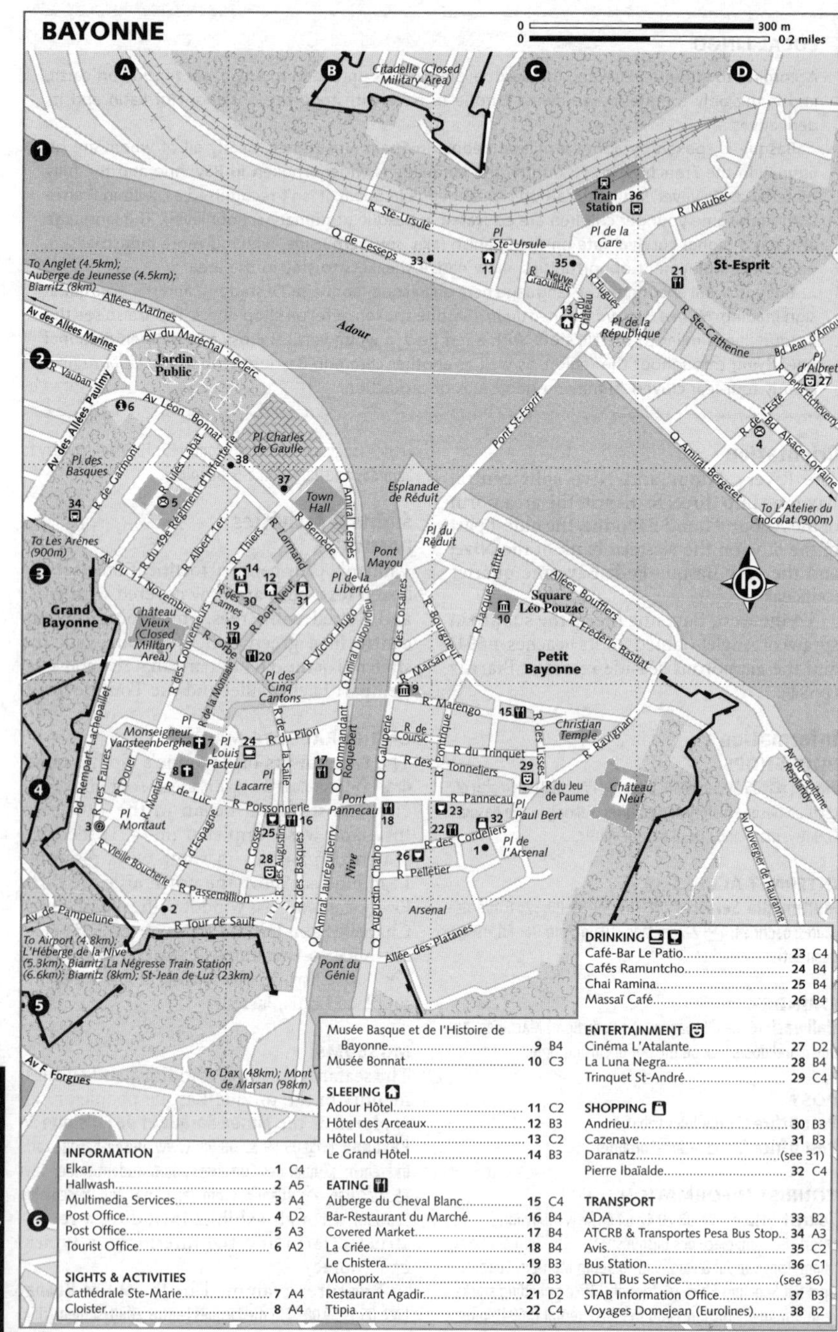
BAYONNE
0 300 m
0 0.2 miles
Citadelle (Closed Military Area)
Train Station 36
R Ste-Ursule
Q de Lesseps
Pl Ste-Ursule
Pl de la Gare
R Maubec
St-Esprit
R Neuve Graouillats
R Hugues
R du Château
Pl de la République
R Ste-Catherine
Bd Jean d'Amou
Pl d'Albret
R Denis Etcheverry
R de l'Esté
Bd Alsace-Lorraine
Q Amiral Bergeret
To L'Atelier du Chocolat (900m)
To Anglet (4.5km); Auberge de Jeunesse (4.5km); Biarritz (8km)
Allées Marines
Av des Allées Marines
Adour
Av du Maréchal Leclerc
Jardin Public
R Vauban
Av des Allées Paulmy
Av Léon Bonnat
Pl Charles de Gaulle
Pl des Basques
R de Garmont
R Jules Labat
R du 49e Régiment d'Infanterie
Town Hall
R Bernède
Q Amiral Lespès
Pont St-Esprit
Esplanade de Réduit
Pl du Réduit
To Les Arènes (900m)
Av du 11 Novembre
R Albert 1er
R Thiers
R Lormand
R des Carmes
R Port Neuf
Pont Mayou
Pl de la Liberté
R Jacques Laffitte
Allées Boufflers
Square Léo Pouzac
R Frédéric Bastiat
Grand Bayonne
Château Vieux (Closed Military Area)
R des Gouverneurs
R Orbe
R Victor Hugo
Q Amiral Dubourdieu
Q des Corsaires
R Bourgneuf
R Marsan
Petit Bayonne
Pl des Cinq Cantons
R de la Monnaie
R Marengo
R des Lisses
Christian Temple
Pl Monseigneur Vansteenberghe
Pl Louis Pasteur
R du Pilori
R de la Salie
Q Commandant Roquebert
Q Galuperie
R de Coursic
R du Trinquet
R Pontrique
R des Tonneliers
R Ravignan
Av du Capitaine Resplandy
Château Neuf
Bd Rempart Lachepaillet
R des Faures
R Douer
R Montaut
R de Luc
Pl Lacarre
R Poissonnerie
Pont Pannecau
R Pannecau
R du Jeu de Paume
Pl Paul Bert
Pl Montaut
R d'Espagne
R Gosse
R des Augustins
R des Basques
R des Cordeliers
Pl de l'Arsenal
Av Duvergier de Hauranne
R Vieille Boucherie
R Passemillion
Q Amiral Jauréguiberry
Nive
Q Augustin Chaho
R Pelletier
Arsenal
Av de Pampelune
R Tour de Sault
Allée des Platanes
To Airport (4.8km); L'Héberge de la Nive (5.3km); Biarritz La Négresse Train Station (6.6km); Biarritz (8km); St-Jean de Luz (23km)
Pont du Génie
Av F Forgues
To Dax (48km); Mont de Marsan (98km)
INFORMATION
Elkar 1 C4
Hallwash 2 A5
Multimedia Services 3 A4
Post Office 4 D2
Post Office 5 A3
Tourist Office 6 A2
SIGHTS & ACTIVITIES
Cathédrale Ste-Marie 7 A4
Cloister 8 A4
Musée Basque et de l'Histoire de Bayonne 9 B4
Musée Bonnat 10 C3
SLEEPING
Adour Hôtel 11 C2
Hôtel des Arceaux 12 B3
Hôtel Loustau 13 C2
Le Grand Hôtel 14 B3
EATING
Auberge du Cheval Blanc 15 C4
Bar-Restaurant du Marché 16 B4
Covered Market 17 B4
La Criée 18 B4
Le Chistera 19 B3
Monoprix 20 B3
Restaurant Agadir 21 D2
Ttipia 22 C4
DRINKING
Café-Bar Le Patio 23 C4
Cafés Ramuntcho 24 B4
Chai Ramina 25 B4
Massaï Café 26 B4
ENTERTAINMENT
Cinéma L'Atalante 27 D2
La Luna Negra 28 B4
Trinquet St-André 29 C4
SHOPPING
Andrieu 30 B3
Cazenave 31 B3
Daranatz (see 31)
Pierre Ibaïalde 32 C4
TRANSPORT
ADA 33 B2
ATCRB & Transportes Pesa Bus Stop 34 A3
Avis 35 C2
Bus Station 36 C1
RDTL Bus Service (see 36)
STAB Information Office 37 B3
Voyages Domejean (Eurolines) 38 B2

BAYONNE CHOCOLATE

Bayonne's long association with chocolate stems from the Spanish Inquisition, when Jews who fled Spain set up their trade in St-Esprit. By 1870, Bayonne boasted 130 *chocolatiers* (specialist makers of chocolate), more than in all of Switzerland. Today, 11 are still in business, including **Daranatz** (☎ 05 59 59 03 05; 15 rue Port Neuf); the 19th-century **Cazenave** (☎ 05 59 59 03 16; 19 rue Port Neuf), which does a sublime *chocolat mousseaux* (rich hot chocolate; €5.20); and **Andrieu** (☎ 05 59 25 72 95; rue des Carmes), which organises visits of its workshop, **L'Atelier du Chocolat** (☎ 05 59 55 70 23; www.atelierduchocolat.fr; 1 allée de Gibéléou; adult/child €5.60/2.80; 9.30am-6.30pm Mon-Sat Jul & Aug, 9.30am-12.30pm & 3-6pm Mon-Sat Sep-Jun) including a historical overview of chocolate in Bayonne and, of course, tastings.

Tastings are also the highlight of the weekend-long **Journées du Chocolat** each May, when master chocolatiers set up the tools of their craft in front of their shops.

€5.50/3/free; 10am-6.30pm Wed-Mon May-Oct, 10am-12.30pm & 2-6pm Wed-Mon Nov-Apr) include canvases by El Greco, Goya, Ingres and Degas, and a roomful of works by Rubens.

A combined ticket (adult/student for €9/4.50) covers both museums.

Festivals & Events

Ham Fair During Easter week, the town hosts a Ham Fair, honouring *jambon de Bayonne*, the acclaimed local ham.

Journées du Chocolat May (see boxed text, above).

La Ruée au Jazz Four days of stompin' in mid-July, attracting jazz lovers from all over France.

Fêtes de Bayonne The town's premier fiesta is the five-day Fêtes de Bayonne, beginning on the first Wednesday in August. They do a 'running of the bulls', as in Pamplona, Spain, only here it's more benign; they use cows not bulls and most of the time participants are chasing the frisky heifers rather than vice versa. The festival also includes Basque music, bullfights, fireworks, a parade of floats, and rugby.

Sleeping

It's tough to find a bed from mid-July to mid-August and near impossible during the Fêtes de Bayonne.

Auberge de Jeunesse (☎ 05 59 58 70 00; www.hibiarritz.org; 19 rte des Vignes, Anglet; dm incl breakfast €16.30-17.30, camping incl breakfast €9.90-10.90; reception 8.30-11.30am & 6-9pm, to noon & 10pm Apr-Sep, closed early Nov–Mar;) Anglet's party-hard hostel comes complete with a basement Scottish pub screening surf films. From the Mairie de Bayonne (Town Hall) bus stop, take bus 7 (C on Sunday and public holidays) to the Les Sables stop, from where it's a 500m uphill walk. Alternatively, from Biarritz train station, take bus 9 (C on Sundays and public holidays) to the Auberge de Jeunesse stop.

L'Héberge de la Nive (☎ 05 59 42 39 22; www.nivaugalop.com; chemin de Halage, Bassussarry; d €34, q €60, 6-person r €90) On the riverbank 5km from central Bayonne, this basic but delightful two-storey farmhouse has an on-site restaurant (mains €7 to €11.90; open for lunch Wednesday to Monday) and a stable of horses (hour-long rides from €20) for guests and nonguests to saddle up.

Adour Hôtel (☎ 05 59 55 11 31; www.adourhotel.net; 13 place Ste-Ursule; r from €65) Just north of the River Adour and conveniently near the station, this friendly family establishment has bright, airy rooms decorated according to a Basque theme – bullfighting, rugby, chocolate, cuisine and more. Wi-fi is free.

Le Grand Hôtel (☎ 05 59 59 62 00; www.legrandhotelbayonne.com, in French; 21 rue Thiers; s €66-144, d €72-155;) This old building was once a convent, though you'd never guess from the spacious cream-toned rooms and cosy on-site bar. Wi-fi and wheelchair-accessible rooms are available; parking's €13.

Hôtel des Arceaux (☎ 05 59 59 15 53; www.hotel-arceaux.com, in French; 26 rue Port Neuf; r from €79) These 17 spick-and-span rooms are decorated in a fresh palette of colours reflecting the Basque sky, green hills, warm earth and golden sands, and some can accommodate families.

Hôtel Loustau (☎ 05 59 55 08 08; www.hotel-loustau.com; 1 place de la République; s €80-115, d €90-130, tr €94-140;) This tall 18th-century building in St-Esprit has spacious, comfortable and impeccably clean rooms with wi-fi. On the southern side of the building, twin sets of full-length French windows open out onto views of the lamp-lit bridge crossing the swirling River Adour. It also runs an excellent restaurant (*menus* cost €17 to €26).

Eating

Restaurants proliferate around the covered market and along quai Amiral Jauréguiberry as well as quai Galuperie and quai des Corsaires across the River Nive.

our pick **La Criée** (☎ 05 59 59 56 60; 14 quai Chaho; mains €8-13.50; lunch Mon-Sat, dinner Tue-Sat) Decked out in marine colours, this unassuming little find does delicious Basque seafood specialities (such as *les chipirons à l'espagnole* – squid with sweet peppers served with finely ground rice), but you can also get fresh oysters, mussels and even fish and chips. For dessert, don't miss the *ardi gasna* (local cheese with cherry jam).

Restaurant Agadir (☎ 05 59 55 66 56; 3 rue Ste-Catherine; menu €16, mains €9-13; lunch & dinner, closed lunch Mon) Shimmering with red and gold, this St-Esprit restaurant serves up mountains of southern Moroccan–style couscous.

Le Chistera (☎ 05 59 59 25 93; 42 rue Port Neuf; mains €10-16; lunch Tue-Sun, dinner Thu-Sun) A local gathering spot, this aromatic, traditional Basque place is named for the *chistera* (basket) that *pelota* players strap to their wrists, and is decorated with motifs from the sport, thanks to two generations of owners who are ex-professional players (see below).

Bar-Restaurant du Marché (☎ 05 59 59 22 66; 39 rue des Basques; menu €12.50; lunch Mon-Sat) Run by a welcoming, Basque-speaking family, this unpretentious place dishes up ample home cooking using produce from the nearby market.

Ttipia (☎ 05 59 46 13 31; 27 rue des Cordeliers; menu €28; lunch Tue-Sun, dinner Mon-Sat) Help yourself to unlimited cider direct from the huge barrels and take a seat at long communal tables to tuck into Ttipia's only offering, a set menu comprising an omelette with *morue* (salt cod) and *merlu* (hake) wrapped in paper, and salted pork with salad, followed by local cheese and nuts.

Auberge du Cheval Blanc (☎ 05 59 59 01 33; 68 rue Bourgneuf; menus €30-75; lunch & dinner Tue-Fri,

PELOTA

Even in the tiniest of Basque villages, you'll find a church, a cemetery, a town hall and at least one *pelota* court.

The term *pelota* (*pelote basque* in French) is actually the generic name for a group of 16 different native Basque games. The courts differ, but all are played using a hard ball with a rubber core (the *pelote*), which is struck with bare hands *(mains nues),* a wooden paddle *(pala* or *paleta),* or a scooplike racquet made of wicker, leather or wood and strapped to the wrist *(chistera).* The latter is used in *cesta punta,* also known as *jaï alaï,* which, with its three-walled court, is the world's fastest ball game (up to 250km/h) and electrifying to watch.

The sport's evolution is equally intriguing, as Bayonne champion player Jean-Pierre Marmouyet explained:

My father played professionally, and sent me to the *jaï alaï* school. When I was 18, a talent scout from Spain came to see me play and gave me a contract, and I played professionally for over 20 years, including 14 years in the US. Now I'm in charge of a big school in Biarritz where I teach players aged 14 to 18. I want to give them the opportunities I was given.

Cesta punta is very big in America, especially Miami, but not many Americans play it. The reason is that it was mostly played in [the Basque province of] Biscaye and then in Cuba. Many of the 'high society' colonials came to Cuba from Biscaye; it was introduced as a form of gambling. Hemingway used to gamble a lot on *pelota* in Cuba. When Fidel came to Cuba, he closed the gambling, and it was brought to Miami by the people who could leave, the upper class. That's why it's mostly played by imported immigrant workers… It's like horse racing [the players being like jockeys]. When I played there I helped organise the players, like a union, for better conditions. But here [in the Basque Country] it's all about the sport.

The technique is very important. The legend is that the *chistera* was invented in the 1870s when a small boy, whose hand was too fragile to hit the ball, used a basket from the markets to catch and throw the ball instead. I like this legend and this object because it's like in every sport: little by little you find ways to play it more efficiently. In addition to teaching, I still play socially every week.

Throughout the French Basque Country matches are open to the public, with tickets generally costing around €10; see the Entertainment sections of this chapter for details.

dinner Sat, lunch Sun) This refined eatery with pastel tones and original artwork fully deserves its Michelin star for its mouth-watering and creative French cuisine.

SELF-CATERING

The turquoise-coloured **covered market** (quai Commandant Roquebert) sits on the riverfront. There are a number of tempting food shops and delicatessens along rue Port Neuf and rue d'Espagne. Pick up staples at **Monoprix** (8 rue Orbe).

Drinking

Petit Bayonne is awash with pubs and bars (all generally open from noon to 2am, Monday to Saturday), especially along rue Pannecau, rue des Cordeliers and quai Galuperie. In fine weather, rue Poissonnerie is completely blocked by the huge crowds spilling out of **Chai Ramina** (11 rue Poissonnerie). Other lively night-time spots include **Café-Bar Le Patio** (38 rue Pannecau) and **Massaï Café** (14 rue des Cordeliers).

To sip (or buy to take home) no fewer than 380 different teas (reputedly the most in France), take a seat amid the metal canisters of the **Cafés Ramuntcho** (☎ 05 59 59 12 37; 9 rue du Pilori; cakes €1, menu €7; 9am-7pm Wed-Sat, noon-7pm Tue), established in 1920.

Entertainment

Upcoming cultural events are listed in *À l'Affiche* and the trimestrial *Les Saisons de la Culture*, both available free at the tourist office.

Every Thursday in July and August, there's traditional **Basque music** (admission free; 9.30pm) in place Charles de Gaulle.

Between October and June **Trinquet St-André** (☎ 05 59 59 18 69; rue du Jeu de Paume; tickets around €9) stages *main nue pelota* matches (see boxed text, opposite) every Thursday at 4.30pm.

In summer, bullfights are held at **Les Arènes** (☎ 05 59 25 65 30; 19 av du Maréchal Foch), 1km west of the city centre. The tourist office has details of upcoming corridas and also sells tickets.

Cinéma l'Atalante (☎ 05 59 55 76 63; www.cinema-atalante.org, in French; 7 rue Denis Etcheverry) screens art-house, nondubbed films.

Catch live jazz, salsa and tango evenings and concerts of world music at the alternative cabaret/theatre venue, **La Luna Negra** (☎ 05 59 25 78 05; rue des Augustins; 7pm-2am Wed-Sat).

There are no clubs in central Bayonne; booty-shakers should head for nearby Biarritz.

Shopping

To buy Bayonne's famous ham at the lowest prices, visit the covered market (left). For the best quality, visit a specialist shop, such as **Pierre Ibaïalde** (☎ 05 59 25 65 30; 41 rue des Cordeliers), where you can taste before you buy. See the boxed text, p691 for shops selling the town's other gastronomic claim to fame, chocolate.

Getting There & Away

AIR

Biarritz-Anglet-Bayonne airport (☎ 05 59 43 83 83; www.biarritz.aeroport.fr) is 5km southwest of central Bayonne and 3km southeast of the centre of Biarritz. It's served by low-cost carriers including easyJet and Ryanair, as well as Air France, with daily domestic flights and flights to the UK, and regular flights to Ireland and other European destinations.

Bus 6 links both Bayonne and Biarritz with the airport (buses depart roughly hourly). A taxi from the town centre costs around €15 to €20.

BUS

From place des Basques, **ATCRB buses** (☎ 05 59 26 06 99) follow the coast to the Spanish border. There are nine services daily to St-Jean de Luz (€3, 40 minutes) with connections for Hendaye (€3, one hour). Summer beach traffic can double journey times. **Transportes Pesa** (☎ in Spain 902 10 12 10; www.pesa.net) buses leave twice a day Monday to Saturday for Bilbao in Spain, calling by Biarritz, St-Jean de Luz, Irún and San Sebastián.

From the train station, **RDTL** (☎ 05 59 55 17 59; www.rdtl.fr, in French) runs services northwards into Les Landes. For beaches north of Bayonne, such as Mimizan Plage and Moliets Plage, get off at Vieux Boucau (1¼ hours, six or seven daily).

Eurolines is represented by **Voyages Domejean** (☎ 05 59 59 19 33; 3 place Charles de Gaulle). Buses stop in the square, opposite this travel agent's office.

CAR & MOTORCYCLE

Among several rental agencies near the train station are **ADA** (☎ 05 59 50 37 10; 10bis quai de Lesseps) and **Avis** (☎ 05 59 55 06 56; 1 rue Ste-Ursule).

TRAIN

TGVs run between Bayonne and Paris' Gare Montparnasse (€75.60, five hours, eight daily).

There are five trains daily to St-Jean Pied de Port (€8.20, 1¼ hours) and fairly frequent services to St-Jean de Luz (€4.30, 25 minutes) via Biarritz (€2.30, nine minutes), plus the Franco-Spanish border towns of Hendaye (€6.40, 40 minutes) and Irún (€6.60, 45 minutes). For travel between Bayonne and Biarritz, however, buses (p699) are cheaper and more frequent.

There are also train services to Bordeaux (€28.80, 2¼ hours, at least 10 daily), Pau (€15, 1¼ hours, nine daily) and Toulouse (€37.30, 3¾ hours, five daily).

Getting Around

BICYCLE

Bayonne's tourist office lends out bikes for free (not overnight); you simply need to leave some ID as a deposit. For longer rental try Adour Hôtel (p691), which charges €16/23 per 24 hours/three days and also has weekly rates.

BUS

STAB buses link Bayonne, Biarritz and Anglet. A single ticket costs €1.20, while *carnets* of five/10 are €4.75/9.50. Timetables are available from STAB's **information office** (☎ 05 59 52 59 52; www.bus-stab.com, in French; rue Thiers; 🕑 8.15am-noon & 1.30-6pm Mon-Sat). Buses 1 and 2 run between Bayonne and Biarritz about 50 times daily, stopping at the *hôtels de ville* (town halls) and stations of both towns. No 1, which runs every 15 minutes until 8.30pm, is the fastest and most frequent.

A free bright-orange *navette* (shuttle bus) loops around the heart of town.

For buses to/from the airport, see p693.

CAR & MOTORCYCLE

There's free parking along the southern end of av des Allées Paulmy, within easy walking distance of the tourist office.

TAXI

Call **Taxi Bayonne** (☎ 05 59 59 48 48).

BIARRITZ

pop 30,700

As ritzy as its name suggests, this stylish coastal town, 8km west of Bayonne, took off as a resort in the mid-19th century when Napoléon III and his Spanish-born wife, Eugénie, visited regularly. Along its rocky coastline are architectural hallmarks of this golden age, and the belle-époque and art-deco eras that followed. Although it retains a high glamour quotient (and high prices to match), it's also a magnet for vanloads of surfers, with some of Europe's best waves.

Orientation

Place Clemenceau, the heart of town, is just south of the main beach (La Grande Plage). Pointe St-Martin, topped with a lighthouse, rounds off Plage Miramar, the northern continuation of La Grande Plage, which is bounded on its southern side by Pointe Atalaye.

Both the train station and airport are about 3km southeast of the centre.

Information

Form@tic (☎ 05 59 22 12 79; 15 av de la Marne; per hr €4; 🕑 9am-8pm Mon-Sat) Bright, stylish internet café with full facilities.

Post Office (rue de la Poste)

Tourist Office (☎ 05 59 22 37 00; www.biarritz.fr; square d'Ixelles; 🕑 9am-7pm daily Jul & Aug, 9am-6pm Mon-Sat, 10am-5pm Sun Sep-Jun) Has internet access (€3 for every 15 minutes) and publishes *Biarritz Scope et Shops,* a free monthly what's-on guide. In July and August there are tourist office annexes at the train station, and at the roundabout just off the Biarritz *sortie* (exit) No 4 from the A63; annex opening hours vary.

There are central **laundrettes** (🕑 7am-9pm) at 11 av de la Marne and 4 av Jaulerry.

Sights & Activities

BEACHES

Biarritz' fashionable beaches, particularly the **Grande Plage** and **Plage Miramar**, are end-to-end bodies on hot summer days. North of Pointe St-Martin, the adrenaline-pumping surfing beaches of **Anglet** (the final *t* is pronounced) continue northwards for more than 4km. Take eastbound bus 9 (Line C on Sunday and public holidays) from the bottom of av Verdun (just near av Édouard VII).

Beyond long, exposed **Plage de la Côte des Basques**, some 500m south of Port Vieux, are **Plage de Marbella** and **Plage de la Milady**. Take westbound bus 9 (Line C on Sunday and public holidays) from rue Gambetta where it crosses rue Broquedis.

MUSÉE DE LA MER

Undergoing a rolling series of renovations over the next couple of years, Biarritz' **Musée de la Mer** (Sea Museum; ☎ 05 59 22 33 34; www.musee

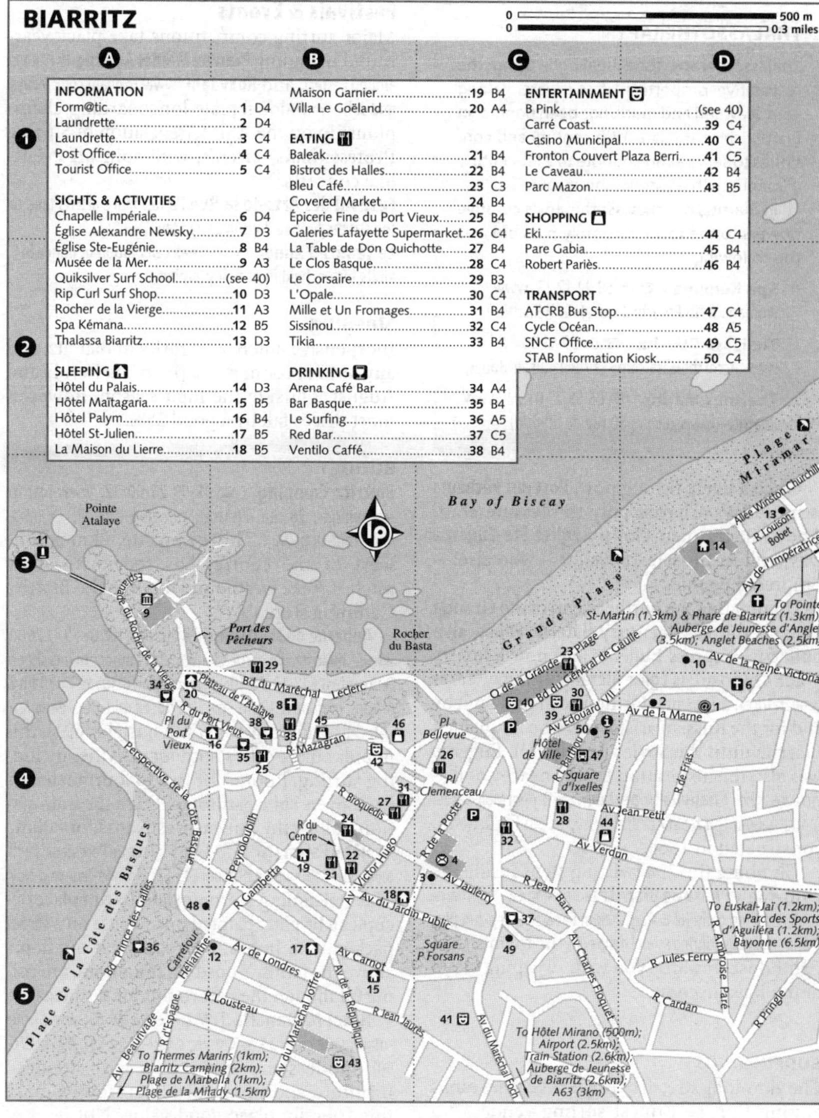

delamer.com; Esplanade du Rocher de la Vierge; adult/child €7.80/5; 9.30am-12.30pm & 2-6pm, closed Mon Nov-Mar) has brand-new tanks seething with underwater life from the Bay of Biscay (Golfe de Gascogne), as well as exhibits on fishing and whaling, recalling Biarritz' whaling past. Tickets are €0.80 cheaper if you buy them at the tourist office.

OTHER ATTRACTIONS

If the swell's big, you might get a drenching as you cross the footbridge at the end of Pointe Atalaye to **Rocher de la Vierge** (Rock of the Virgin). Named after its white statue of the Virgin and child, views from this impressive outcrop extend to the mountains of the Spanish Basque Country.

THALASSOTHERAPY

Thalassotherapy ('sea healing'), using the restorative properties of sea water (along with seaweed and mud), has been popular in Biarritz since the late 18th century and continues to serve as an antidote to 21st-century ailments such as stress and insomnia.

In Biarritz, put thalassotherapy's curative powers to the test – or simply bliss out – at the following:

- **Spa Kémana** (☎ 05 59 22 12 13; www.kemana.fr, in French; 3 carrefour Hélianthe)
- **Thalassa Biarritz** (☎ 05 59 41 30 01; www.accorthalassa.com; 11 rue Louison-Bobet)
- **Thermes Marins** (☎ 05 59 23 01 22; www.biarritz-thalasso.com; 80 rue de Madrid)

Once a lively fishing port, **Port des Pêcheurs** is nowadays a haven only to pleasure craft. Above it, the neo-Gothic **Église Ste-Eugénie** was built in the late 1800s for – who else? – Empress Eugénie.

Dominating the northern end of the Grande Plage is the 19th-century **Hôtel du Palais**, also built for Empress Eugénie and now a luxury hotel. Opposite is **Église Alexandre Newsky** (8 av de l'Impératrice), a Russian Orthodox church built by and for the Russian aristocrats who frequented Biarritz until the Soviet Revolution. Eugénie was also the inspiration for the nearby doll's-house-size **Chapelle Impériale** (🕑 3-6pm Mon-Sat Jul & Aug, 3-6pm Thu & Sat Apr-Jun & Sep, 3-5pm Thu Oct-Mar), constructed in 1864.

Climbing the 258 twisting steps inside the 73m-high **Phare de Biarritz** (admission €2; 🕑 10am-noon & 3-7pm daily Jul & Aug, 2-6pm Sat & Sun Sep-Jun plus 2-5pm weekdays during school holidays), the town's 1834 lighthouse, rewards you with sweeping views of the Basque coast.

SURFING

The 4km-long stretch of Anglet's beaches ranks among Europe's finest surfing venues. No fewer than a dozen places around town offer gear and lessons; try **Rip Curl Surf Shop** (☎ 05 59 24 38 40; 2 av de la Reine Victoria) or the **Quiksilver Surf School** (☎ 05 59 22 03 12; www.biarritz-boardriders.com, in French) under the Casino Municipal.

For surf conditions, ring the French-language **Swell Line** (☎ 08 92 68 40 64) or check out www.swell-line.com (in French).

Festivals & Events

Major surfing competitions take place year-round including **Biarritz Maider Arosteguy** (3 days, around Easter), and **Roxy Jam** (www.roxyjam.com; 5 days, mid-Jul), a major female longboarding championship on the ASP (Association of Surfing Professionals) circuit, with spin-off events like concerts.

Festival des Arts de la Rue Performance artists take to the streets for five days in early May.

Le Temps d'Aimer A two-week celebration of dance in all its forms, held in mid-September.

Sleeping

Inexpensive hotels are a rarity in Biarritz, and any kind of room is at a premium in July and August. Outside the high season, however, most prices fall by a good 25%.

BUDGET

Biarritz Camping (☎ 05 59 23 00 12; www.biarritz-camping.fr; 28 rue d'Harcet; camping €15-23; 🕑 mid-May–mid-Oct; 🚌) This camp site, 2km southwest of the centre, has spacious, shady pitches. Take westbound bus 9 to the Biarritz Camping stop.

Auberge de Jeunesse de Biarritz (☎ 05 59 41 76 00; www.hibiarritz.org; 8 rue Chiquito de Cambo; dm incl sheets & breakfast €17.10-18.10; 🕑 reception 8.30am-11.30am & 6-9pm, to noon & 10pm Apr-Sep, closed mid-Dec–early Jan; 💻 ⊠) Like Anglet's youth hostel (p691), this popular place offers outdoor activities including surfing. Rooms for two to four hostellers have an en-suite bathroom. From the train station, follow the railway westwards for 800m.

Hôtel Palym (☎ 05 59 24 16 56; 7 rue du Port Vieux; r with toilet only €40, r with bathroom €45-58; 🕑 mid-Jan–mid-Nov) This welcoming 20-room, family-run place occupies a brightly painted town house on a street packed with hotels. Bedrooms, on the floors above the family's bustling restaurant, are colourful though the bathrooms are a squeeze.

Hôtel Maïtagaria (☎ 05 59 24 26 65; www.hotel-maitagaria.com; 34 av Carnot; s €49-54, d €57-69, tr €76-90) Spotless modern rooms with art-deco furniture and immaculate bathrooms make this friendly place good value. Not least of its charms is its summer terrace opening off the comfy guest lounge, which is warmed in winter by a toasty open fire.

La Maison du Lierre (☎ 05 59 24 06 00; www.maisondulierre.com; 3 av du Jardin Public; r €56-139; ⊠) This brand-new sister establishment of the *chambre d'hôte*–style La Maison du Lierre in Bordeaux (p674) has 23 exquisitely decorated rooms named for local plants in the adjacent Jardin Public, and many of the rooms have garden views. Rooms have polished floors and beautiful printed fabrics; breakfast (€7.90 to €9.90) includes freshly squeezed juice.

MIDRANGE & TOP END

Hôtel St-Julien (☎ 05 59 24 20 39; www.saint-julien-biarritz.com, in French; 20 av Carnot; r €65-114, q €103-148) A bright shuttered facade graces this attractive late-19th-century villa, with original parquet flooring inside. Third-floor rooms have views of both mountains and sea. Wi-fi is available for €5 per day; parking is free.

Hôtel Mirano (☎ 05 59 23 11 63; www.hotelmirano.fr, in French; 11 av Pasteur; r €70-110) Squiggly purple, orange and black wallpaper and oversize orange perspex light fittings are some of the rad '70s touches at this boutique retro hotel, a 10-minute stroll from the town centre, with the 21st-century bonus of free wi-fi.

Maison Garnier (☎ 05 59 01 60 70; www.hotel-biarritz.com; 29 rue Gambetta; r €90-140) The seven boutique rooms of this elegant mansion are tastefully decorated and furnished in cool, neutral tones; those up at attic level are especially romantic.

Villa Le Goëland (☎ 05 59 24 25 76; www.villagoeland.com; 12 plateau de l'Atalaye; r €130-280; 💻 ⊠) This stunning family home with its château-like spires perches high on a plateau above Pointe Atalaye. Rooms, tastefully furnished with antiques, family photos and mementos, have panoramic views of town, the sea and across to Spain. There are only four rooms (opt for *chambre Goëland* with its huge 35-sq-metre private terrace), so advance booking is essential. Wi-fi is available.

Eating

See-and-be-seen cafés and restaurants line Biarritz' beachfront. Anglet's beaches are also becoming increasingly trendy, with cafés strung along the waterfront.

Bleu Café (☎ 05 59 22 34 53; Grand Plage; breakfast €9, dishes €7-9; 🕑 9am-midnight Jul & Aug, 9am-5pm Sep-Jun) Snag a seat on the terrace to sip Lavazza coffee or dine on Poilâne bread with fresh vegies while watching surfers battle the rollers.

Le Corsaire (☎ 05 59 24 63 72; Port des Pêcheurs; mains €11-23.50; 🕑 lunch & dinner Tue-Sat) Down by the water's edge, sit out on the terrace to savour dishes like grilled cod with chorizo. On either side, the neighbouring seafood restaurants in this little harbourside setting offer similar quality and prices, and are equally appealing.

Tikia (☎ 05 59 24 46 09; 1 place Ste-Eugénie; menus €12.80-20; 🕑 lunch & dinner) The premises may be *tikia* ('small' in Basque) but the same can't be said of this rustic restaurant's giant *brochettes* (skewers) of duck, steak or seafood, accompanied by local wines and friendly service.

Bistrot des Halles (☎ 05 59 24 21 22; 1 rue du Centre; mains €14.50-17; 🕑 lunch & dinner) One of a cluster of decent restaurants along rue du Centre that get their produce directly from the nearby covered market, this bustling place serves excellent fish and other fresh fare from the blackboard menu in an interior adorned with old metallic advertising posters.

Baleak (☎ 05 59 24 58 57; 8 rue du Centre; lunch/dinner menus €16/28, mains €16; 🕑 lunch & dinner daily Jul-Sep, Tue-Sun Oct-Jun) Fish-lovers will be hooked by the fresh catches served in this trendy new place amid exposed stone walls. Great wine list, too.

Le Clos Basque (☎ 05 59 24 24 96; 12 rue Louis Barthou; menus €27; 🕑 lunch Tue-Sun, dinner Tue-Sat) With its tiles and exposed stonework hung with abstract art, this tiny place could have strayed in from Spain. The cuisine, however, is emphatically Basque, traditional with a contemporary twist or two, such as sirloin with green mustard, or stuffed eggplant with saffron. Reserve ahead to secure a terrace table.

Also recommended:

L'Opale (☎ 05 59 24 30 30; 17 av Édouard VII; mains €18-28; 🕑 lunch & dinner, closed Sun low season) Adjacent to designer boutiques and opening onto the seafront, serves seafood in ultrastylish surrounds.

Sissinou (☎ 05 59 22 51 50; 5 av du Maréchal Foch; mains €25; 🕑 lunch & dinner) Gastronomic Basque cuisine in a sleek, streamlined space. One to watch.

SELF-CATERING

Just downhill from Biarritz' **covered market**, **La Table de Don Quichotte** (12 av Victor Hugo) sells all sorts of Spanish hams, sausages, pickles and wines. You'll find a tempting array of cheeses, wines and pâtés at nearby **Mille et Un Fromages** (8 av Victor Hugo). At sea level, **Épicerie Fine du Port Vieux** (41bis rue Mazagran) is another excellent delicatessen.

There's a good-size supermarket in the basement of the **Galeries Lafayette** (17 place Clemenceau) department store.

Drinking

There are some great bars on and around rue du Port Vieux, place Clemenceau and the central food-market area. Places generally open from 11am to 2am unless noted otherwise.

Bar Basque (☎ 05 59 24 60 92; 1 rue du Port Vieux) This rustic-chic newcomer serves bite-size Basque tapas (€1.20 to €7) washed down with a fantastic selection of wines.

Le Surfing (☎ 05 59 24 78 72; 9 bd Prince des Galles) After a hard day's surfing, drop in to this memorabilia-filled surf bar to compare waves and wipe-outs.

Arena Café Bar (☎ 05 59 24 88 98; Plage du Port Vieux; 🕑 9am-2am daily Apr-Sep, 10am-2am Wed-Sun Oct-Mar) Tucked into a tiny cove, this beachfront hangout combines a style-conscious restaurant (mains €15 to €22) with a fuchsia- and violet-tinged bar with DJs on the turntables.

Red Bar (9 av du Maréchal Foch; 🕑 Tue-Sun) You mightn't think a rugby bar would attract trendsetters, but this temple to Biarritz Olympique (their colours are red and white – hence the name), with reggae and '70s rock in the background, will make you think again.

Ventilo Caffé (rue du Port Vieux; 🕑 Wed-Sun Sep-Jun, daily Jul & Aug) This revamped café continues to lure a young crowd and gets packed to the gills on summer nights.

Entertainment

Free classical music concerts take place in high summer at various atmospheric outdoor venues around town; the tourist office has the program.

Constructed in 1928, Biarritz' landmark **Casino Municipal** (1 av Édouard VII) has 200-plus fruit machines that whirr and chink until the wee hours.

Central clubs include **Le Caveau** (☎ 05 59 24 16 17; 4 rue Gambetta; 🕑 11pm-5am); **B Pink** (☎ 05 59 22 77 59; 🕑 11pm-5am Tue-Sat), within the Casino Municipal; and the sizzling new **Carré Coast** (☎ 05 59 24 64 64; Grand Plage; 🕑 11pm-5am), with a cool sea-facing lounge bar and some of the coast's hottest DJs spinning funk, house and disco – see who's hitting the decks at www.myspace.co m/lecarrecoast.

SPORT

At the **Fronton Couvert Plaza Berri** (☎ 05 59 22 15 72; 42 av du Maréchal Foch), there's *pelota* (p692) virtually year-round; ask the tourist office for schedules. From July to mid-September, the open-air *fronton* (*pelota* court) at **Parc Mazon** has regular *chistera* matches at 9pm on Thursdays. Admission to each venue is around €8.

Between mid-June and mid-September, **Euskal-Jaï** (☎ 05 59 23 91 09; av Henri Haget) in the Parc des Sports d'Aguiléra complex, 2km east of central Biarritz, has regular professional *cesta punta* matches (admission €10 to €20) at 9pm. Bus 1 stops nearby.

Shopping

At **Pare Gabia** (☎ 05 59 24 22 51; 18 rue Mazagran), Vincent Corbun continues his grandfather's business, established in 1935, making and selling espadrilles in a rainbow of colours and styles (customised with ribbons and laces while you wait). A pair starts from €10. For Basque music, crafts and guidebooks, visit **Eki** (☎ 05 59 24 79 64; 21 av de Verdun). **Robert Pariès** (1 place Bellevue) will test your willpower with scrumptious chocolates and Basque sweets.

Getting There & Away

AIR

To reach Biarritz-Anglet-Bayonne airport (p693), take STAB bus No 6 or, on Sunday, line C to/from Biarritz' *hôtel de ville*. Each runs once or twice hourly, from 7am to about 7pm.

BUS

Nine daily **ATCRB buses** (☎ 05 59 26 06 99) and buses to Spain (p693) stop just near the tourist office beside square d'Ixelles.

TRAIN

Biarritz–La Négresse train station is about 3km south of the town centre, although walking to the centre isn't advised due to busy roads without footpaths; buses 2 and 9 (B and C on Sundays) connect the two. **SNCF** (13 av du Maréchal Foch; 🕑 Mon-Fri) has a town-centre office. Times, fares and destinations are much the same as Bayonne's (p693), a nine-minute train journey away. Between Bayonne and Biarritz, however, buses run far more frequently (opposite) and work out much cheaper, as you'll pay the same to get from Biarritz' train station to its town centre as you will to get from Bayonne to Biarritz directly on the bus.

Getting Around

BICYCLE

Cycle Océan (☎ 05 59 24 94 47; www.cycleocean.com; 24 rue Peyroloubilh) rents out mountain bikes (€12 per day) and scooters (from €31).

BUS

Most services stop beside the Hôtel de Ville, from where route Nos 1 and 2 (€1.20, about 50 daily) go to Bayonne's Hôtel de Ville and station. **STAB** (☎ 05 59 24 26 53) has an information kiosk adjacent to the tourist office.

For buses to Biarritz-Anglet-Bayonne airport, see p693.

TAXI

Call **Taxis Biarritz** (☎ 05 59 03 18 18).

ST-JEAN DE LUZ & CIBOURE

pop 13,600

If you're searching for the quintessential Basque seaside town – with atmospheric narrow streets, a sheltered bay, good surf nearby and a lively fishing port pulling in large catches of sardines, tuna and anchovies that are cooked up at authentic restaurants – you've found it.

St-Jean de Luz, 24km southwest of Bayonne, sits at the mouth of the River Nivelle. The town and its long beach are on the eastern side of Baie de St-Jean de Luz.

Its sleepy, smaller alter ego, Ciboure, is on the western curve of the bay, separated from St-Jean de Luz by the fishing harbour. Several timber-framed whitewashed Basque houses, with shutters in green or ox-blood red, survive here just south of rue Agorette.

Information

Internet World (☎ 05 59 26 86 92; 7 rue Tourasse; per hr €6; 🕑 9am-9pm daily Jun-Aug, 10am-6pm Mon-Sat Sep-May) Friendly internet café.

Laverie du Port (place Maréchal Foch; 🕑 7am-9pm) Laundrette.

Post Office Ciboure (quai Maurice Ravel); St-Jean de Luz (cnr bd Victor Hugo & rue Sallagoity)

Tourist Office (☎ 05 59 26 03 16; www.saint-jean-de-luz.com; 20 bd Victor Hugo; 🕑 9am-7.30pm Mon-Sat, 10am-1pm & 3-7pm Sun Jul & Aug, 9am-12.30pm & 2.30-6.30pm Mon-Sat, 10am-1pm Sun Sep-Jun) Runs an extensive program of French-language tours around the town and across the Spanish border; ask about English-language tours in summer.

Sights

A superb panorama of the town unfolds from the promontory of **Pointe Ste-Barbe**, at the northern end of the Baie de St-Jean de Luz and about 1km beyond the town beach. Go to the end of bd Thiers and keep walking.

BEACHES

St-Jean de Luz' family-friendly sandy beach sprouts bathing tents (€6.25 per day) from June to September. Ciboure has its own modest beach, Plage de Socoa.

Plage de Socoa, 2km west of Socoa on the corniche (the D912), is served by ATCRB buses (p703) en route to Hendaye and, in the high season, by boats (p703). See p701 for surf beaches.

CHURCHES

The plain facade of France's largest and finest Basque church, **Église St-Jean Baptiste** (rue Gambetta; 🕑 8.30am-noon & 2-7pm), conceals a splendid interior with a magnificent baroque altarpiece. It was in front of this very altarpiece that Louis XIV and María Teresa, daughter of King Philip IV of Spain, were married in 1660. After exchanging rings, the couple walked down the aisle and out of the south door, which was then sealed to commemorate peace between the two nations after 24 years of hostilities. You can still see its outline, opposite No 20 rue Gambetta.

In Ciboure, the 17th-century **Église St-Vincent** (rue Pocalette) has an octagonal bell tower topped by an unusual three-tiered wooden roof. Inside, the lavish use of wood and tiered galleries are typically Basque.

ÉCOMUSÉE BASQUE

Basque traditions are brought to life on one-hour audioguide tours of this illuminating multimedia **museum** (☎ 05 59 51 06 06; adult/student/child €5.50/5/2.30; 🕑 10am-6.30pm daily Jul & Aug, 10-11.15am & 2.45-4.45pm Mon-Sat Apr-Jun, Sep & Oct), 2km north of St-Jean de Luz beside the N10. Three entire rooms are devoted to Izarra (Basque for 'star'), a liquor made from 20 different local plants, and the museum is one of 10 stops along the Route Gourmande de Basque (see boxed text, p701).

PLACE LOUIS XIV

This pretty, pedestrianised square is home to **Maison Louis XIV** (☎ 05 59 26 01 56; 🕑 10.30am-noon & 2.30-5.30pm Jun & Sep–mid-Oct, 10.30am-12.30pm & 2.30-6.30pm Jul & Aug), built in 1643 by a wealthy shipowner and furnished in period style. Here, Louis XIV lived out his last days of bachelorhood before marrying María Teresa. Half-hour guided tours (with English text) cost €4.80/3 per adult/child.

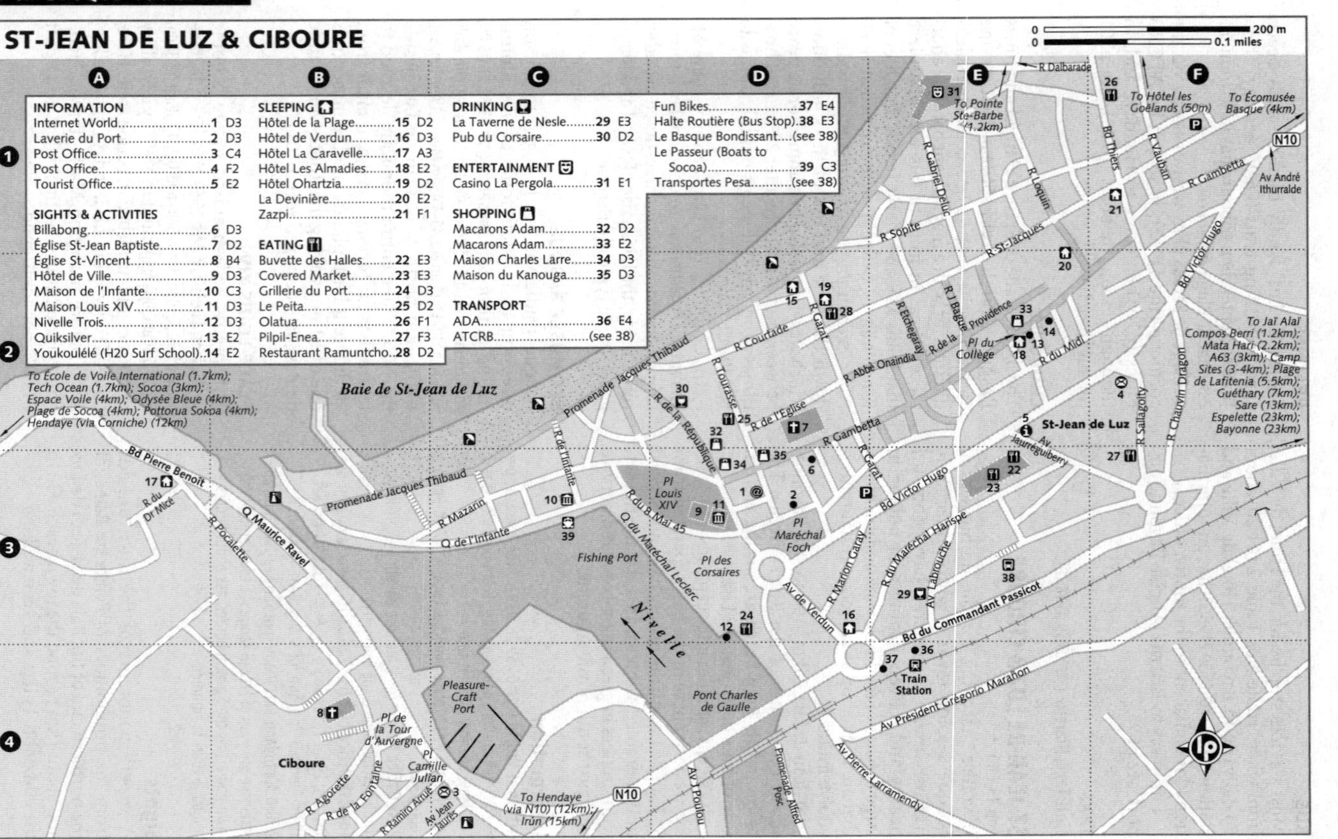
ST-JEAN DE LUZ & CIBOURE
0 200 m
0 0.1 miles
INFORMATION
Internet World....1 D3
Laverie du Port....2 D3
Post Office....3 C4
Post Office....4 F2
Tourist Office....5 E2
SIGHTS & ACTIVITIES
Billabong....6 D3
Église St-Jean Baptiste....7 D2
Église St-Vincent....8 B4
Hôtel de Ville....9 D3
Maison de l'Infante....10 C3
Maison Louis XIV....11 D3
Nivelle Trois....12 D3
Quiksilver....13 E2
Youkoulélé (H20 Surf School)....14 E2
SLEEPING
Hôtel de la Plage....15 D2
Hôtel de Verdun....16 D3
Hôtel La Caravelle....17 A3
Hôtel Les Almadies....18 E2
Hôtel Ohartzia....19 D2
La Devinière....20 E2
Zazpi....21 F1
EATING
Buvette des Halles....22 E3
Covered Market....23 E3
Grillerie du Port....24 D3
Le Peita....25 D2
Olatua....26 F1
Pilpil-Enea....27 F3
Restaurant Ramuntcho....28 D2
DRINKING
La Taverne de Nesle....29 E3
Pub du Corsaire....30 D2
ENTERTAINMENT
Casino La Pergola....31 E1
SHOPPING
Macarons Adam....32 D2
Macarons Adam....33 E2
Maison Charles Larre....34 D3
Maison du Kanouga....35 D3
TRANSPORT
ADA....36 E4
ATCRB....(see 38)
Fun Bikes....37 E4
Halte Routière (Bus Stop)....38 E3
Le Basque Bondissant....(see 38)
Le Passeur (Boats to Socoa)....39 C3
Transportes Pesa....(see 38)
To École de Voile International (1.7km); Tech Ocean (1.7km); Socoa (3km); Espace Voile (4km); Odysée Bleue (4km); Plage de Socoa (4km); Pottorua Sokoa (4km); Hendaye (via Corniche) (12km)
To Pointe Ste-Barbe (1.2km)
To Hôtel les Goëlands (50m)
To Écomusée Basque (4km)
To Jaï Alaï Compos Berri (1.2km); Mata Hari (2.2km); A63 (3km); Camp Sites (3-4km); Plage de Lafitenia (5.5km); Guéthary (7km); Sare (13km); Espelette (23km); Bayonne (23km)
To Hendaye (via N10) (12km); Irún (15km)
Baie de St-Jean de Luz
St-Jean de Luz
Ciboure
Nivelle
Fishing Port
Pleasure-Craft Port
Pont Charles de Gaulle
Train Station
Pl Louis XIV
Pl Maréchal Foch
Pl des Corsaires
Pl du Collège
Pl de la Tour d'Auvergne
Pl Camille Julian
Promenade Jacques Thibaud
Promenade Alfred Posc
Bd Pierre Benoit
Q Maurice Ravel
R Pocalette
R du Dr Micé
R Mazarin
Q de l'Infante
R de l'Infante
R du 8 Mai 45
Q du Maréchal Leclerc
R de la République
R Tourasse
R Courtade
R Garat
R de l'Église
R Gambetta
R Abbé Onaindia
R Etchegaray
R J Bague
R de la Providence
R du Midi
R St-Jacques
R Sopite
R Gabriel Deluc
R Loquin
R Dalbarade
Bd Thiers
R Vauban
Av André Ithurralde
Bd Victor Hugo
R Chauvin Dragon
R Sallagoity
Av Jaurréguiberry
R du Maréchal Harispe
Av Labrouche
R Marion Garay
Av de Verdun
Bd du Commandant Passicot
Av Président Grégorio Marañon
Av Pierre Larramendy
Av J Poulou
R Agorette
R de la Fontaine
R Ramiro Arrué
Av Jean Jaurès
N10

ECO EATING & DRINKING

Artisan produce abounds along the **Route Gourmande de Basque** (Basque Gourmand Route; ☎ 05 59 54 56 70; www.routegourmandebasque.com). The route links 10 producers over 126km, but if you're short on time you can cherry-pick among them. Along the way, you can learn about and taste Basque specialities including ham, trout, wine, cheese, chilli peppers, Basque cake, cider, Izarra liquor (see p699), chocolate and honey, all utilising traditional methods for minimal environmental impact and deliciously rich, natural flavours.

Alongside, and rather dwarfed by its more imposing neighbour, is St-Jean de Luz' **Hôtel de Ville**, built in 1657.

In the days before her marriage, María Teresa stayed in another shipowner's mansion, the brick-and-stone Maison Joanoenia, off place Louis XIV, nowadays called **Maison de l'Infante** (☎ 05 59 26 36 82; quai de l'Infante; adult/child €2.50/free; 11am-12.30pm & 2.30-6.30pm Tue-Sat, 2.30-6.30pm Mon mid-Jun–mid-Oct), which has fine architectural detail.

SOCOA

The heart of **Socoa** is about 2.5km west of Ciboure along the continuation of quai Maurice Ravel (named for the *Boléro* composer, who was born in Ciboure in 1875). Its prominent fort was built in 1627 and later improved by Vauban. You can walk out to the Digue de Socoa breakwater or climb to the lighthouse via rue du Phare, then out along rue du Sémaphore for fabulous coastal views.

Activities

Opportunities to get out on, in and under the water abound.

SURFING

For prime waves, head 5.5km northeast of St-Jean de Luz to **Plage de Lafitenia**; ATCRB's Biarritz and Bayonne buses pass within 1km (Martienia or Bubonnet stop).

Surf schools based in the **Youkoulélé** (H20 Surf School; ☎ 05 59 26 81 95; 72 rue Gambetta), **Quiksilver** (☎ 06 86 94 95 27; 64 rue Gambetta) and **Billabong** (☎ 05 59 26 07 93; 16 rue Gambetta) surf shops will transport you to the waves. Two-hour lessons start at €40.

OTHER ACTIVITIES

École de Voile International (☎ 05 59 47 06 32) and **Espace Voile** (☎ 05 59 47 21 21) in Socoa offer windsurfing lessons and yachting courses. The former also rents out dinghies and motor boats and the latter, sea kayaks.

Diving schools in Socoa:

Odysée Bleue (☎ 06 63 54 13 63; hangar 4, chemin des Blocs)

Pottorua Sokoa (☎ 05 59 47 1 7; 53 av Commandant Passicot)

Tech Ocean (☎ 05 59 47 96 75; 45 av Commandant Passicot)

From May to mid-September, the **Nivelle Trois** (☎ 05 59 47 06 24) leaves quai du Maréchal Leclerc for morning deep-sea fishing trips and afternoon cruises.

Festivals & Events

Festival de Film de Surf (International Surf Film Festival; www.surf-film.com) Four days of surf movies in mid-May.

Fêtes de la St-Jean Bonfires, music and dancing take place on the weekend nearest 24 June.

Régates de Traînières A weekend of boat races on the first weekend in July.

La Fête du Thon The Tuna Festival, on another July weekend, fills the streets with brass bands, Basque music and dancing, while stalls sell sizzling tuna steaks.

Danses des Sept Provinces Basques Folk dancers from all across the Spanish and French Basque Country meet in early summer.

La Nuit de la Sardine The Night of the Sardine – a night of music, folklore and dancing – is held twice each summer on a Saturday in early July and the Saturday nearest 15 August.

Sleeping

July to mid-September are packed; low-season prices can drop significantly.

Between St-Jean de Luz and Guéthary, 7km northeast up the coast, are no fewer than 16 camp sites. ATCRB's Biarritz and Bayonne buses stop within 1km of them all.

Hôtel de Verdun (☎ 05 59 26 02 55; 13 av de Verdun; r without bathroom €28, r with shower only €33-36, r with shower & toilet €45) Opposite the train station in St-Jean de Luz, this simple place is a popular staging post for Chemin de St-Jacques pilgrims. Rooms are relatively spacious, if plain. Good meals (*menu* €12) are available

CONSERVATION-CONSCIOUS VILLAS

Accommodation devoted to ecological principles is still a rarity in the French Basque Country (in part because it's pretty green to begin with). But St-Jean de Luz's **Hôtel les Goëlands** (☎ 05 59 26 10 05; www.hotel-lesgoelands.com; 4 & 6 av d'Etcheverry; s €50-64, s with shared bathroom €40, d €74-104, q €94-158; ☒) goes all out. In a pair of traditional Basque villas, this family-run, very family-friendly place not only scrupulously recycles, limits waste and conserves energy (including solar hot water) but also rents electric bikes to guests and cooks meals made from fresh local produce (half board is obligatory in July and August, starting from €72 per person). Driving might not be the most eco-friendly way to get here, but if you do come by car, parking is free.

onsite; half board is obligatory from July to September.

Hôtel La Caravelle (☎ 05 59 47 18 05; www.hotellacaravelle.com; bd Pierre Benoît; r €50-140, tr €70-140, q €70-150) In Ciboure, this nautical-themed place was originally two fishermen's cottages. Seven of its 19 light-filled, modernised rooms have beautiful bay views. Parking costs €10.

Hôtel Ohartzia (☎ 05 59 26 00 06; www.hotel-ohartzia.com, in French; 28 rue Garat; r low season €68-72, high season €79-89) Framed by cobalt-blue shutters, this flower-bedecked Basque house is just a few steps from the beach. Immaculate rooms are well furnished and equipped, and the welcome's friendly. The highlight is its oasislike garden courtyard. Wi-fi is available in the bar area, but alas, not in the rooms.

Hôtel Les Almadies (☎ 05 59 85 34 48; www.hotel-les-almadies.com, in French; 58 rue Gambetta; r €75-130; 🖳) Four of the seven rooms at this family-run gem open to balconies overlooking St-Jean de Luz' pedestrianised shopping street, and all blend restrained countrified fabrics with contemporary furnishings (which are immaculate, thanks in part to the no-pets rule). The timber-decked breakfast room has a plumbed-in espresso machine and opens to a sunny terrace. Parking is €9, and wi-fi is free. It's closed for three weeks in November.

Hôtel de la Plage (☎ 05 59 51 03 44; www.hoteldelaplage.com; 33 rue Garat; r incl breakfast low season €88-138, high season €108-158; ⏲ mid-Feb–mid-Nov & school holidays; ❄) This red-shuttered building overlooks the beach, with sea views from most rooms (many of which have small balconies). There's a great on-site bar-restaurant (also open to nonguests). Wi-fi is available. Valet parking costs €12.

La Devinière (☎ 05 59 26 05 51; www.hotel-la-deviniere.com; 5 rue Loquin; r €120-180) You have to love a place that forsakes TVs for antiquarian books (room 11 even has its own mini-library). Beyond the living room, with its piano and comfy armchairs, there's a delightful small patio equipped with lounges. It's charming.

Zazpi (☎ 05 59 26 07 77; www.zazpihotel.com; 21 bd Thiers; r €160-280, ste €300-450; ❄ 🖳) Seriously hip. In Basque, *zazpi* means 'seven', reflecting the number of rooms (including two suites) in this mansion-turned-designer-hotel, each named after one of the Basque provinces. It's fronted by a snazzy bar with lime and olive modular sofas and a tearoom (open 11am to 8pm) serving soups, salads and pastas (€12 to €17). Breakfast is a pricey €15; parking costs €10. It's wheelchair accessible and has wi-fi.

Eating

Tempting restaurants line rue de la République, rue Tourasse and place Louis XIV.

Grillerie du Port (☎ 05 59 51 18 29; quai du Maréchal Leclerc; ⏲ mid-Jun–mid-Sep) In this old shack by the port, join the crowds gorging on fresh sardines, salads and slabs of tuna steak fresh off the boat. It's informal and economical (prices depend on the day's catch but are always reasonable).

Buvette des Halles (☎ 05 59 26 73 59; bd Victor Hugo; dishes €7-14; ⏲ 6am-2pm Tue-Sat Oct-May, 6am-2pm & dinner daily Jun-Sep) Tucked into a corner of the covered market, this minuscule restaurant serves goat's cheese, Bayonne ham, grilled sardines, fish soup, mussels and much more outside beneath the plane trees on the small square between June and September. The rest of the year, stop by for fresh, tasty sandwiches, but go early for the best pickings.

Pilpil-Enea (☎ 05 59 51 20 80; 3 rue Sallagoity; lunch mains €10-14, menus from €28, dinner mains €16-30; ⏲ lunch & dinner Thu-Mon) Strung with fishing nets, this small, simple dark-timber and blue-and-white-checked restaurant is set apart from the tourist throng, and is a firm local favourite for its quality cooking.

Restaurant Ramuntcho (☎ 05 59 26 03 89; 24 rue Garat; menus €18-30, mains €11-15; ⏲ closed Mon low season) You can scarcely see the walls for the photos and posters of vintage vehicles and motorbikes at this lively place, which successfully blends the cuisine of southwest France with the owner's native Normandy. Duck and fish dishes feature prominently.

Le Peita (☎ 05 59 26 86 66; 21 rue Tourasse; mains €14.50-20, combination plates €12.50-14.50; 🕑 lunch & dinner Wed-Sun) Dried Espelette chilli peppers and hams hang from the ceiling at this authentic place with crushed-silk tablecloths and friendly owners. For a taste of the local produce on display, order one of the combination plates accompanied by fresh local cheese.

Olatua (☎ 05 59 51 05 22; 30 bd Thiers; 2-course menus €33, 3-course menus €35, mains €25; 🕑 lunch & dinner) This bright brasserie-style restaurant serves market-fresh fare like St-Jacques scallops with risotto and a cloudlike chocolate soufflé with pistachio ice cream for dessert.

SELF-CATERING

There's a food market every Tuesday and Friday morning inside the **covered market** (bd Victor Hugo).

Drinking & Entertainment

La Taverne de Nesle (☎ 05 59 26 60 93; 5 av Labrouche; 🕑 5pm-2am Wed-Mon Oct-Jun, daily Jul-Sep) This cheery neighbourhood pub has a DJ every Friday year-round (twice a week in July and August).

Pub du Corsaire (☎ 05 59 26 10 74; 16 rue de la République; 🕑 5pm-2am) Ten of nearly 100 different beers are on draft at this place, which also mixes some mean cocktails.

Mata Hari (☎ 05 59 26 04 28; 48 av André Ithurralde; admission €10; 🕑 varies) Although swarming with people in the high season, St-Jean de Luz has only three clubs, all outside town. This sophisticated spot, 2km east of the train station and open year-round (generally Thursday to Saturday; daily in July and August), is far and away the most popular.

Casino La Pergola (☎ 05 59 51 58 58; rue Dalbarade; 🕑 slot machines 11am-3am daily, gaming 9pm-3am Tue-Sun) Bang on the beach.

SPORT

In July and August catch *cesta punta* at the **Jaï Alaï Compos Berri** (☎ 05 59 51 65 30; rte de Bayonne, N10), 1km northeast of the train station. Matches start at 9pm every Tuesday and Friday, and half-time is spiced up with music or dancing. Tickets are available at the tourist office and cost €8 to €18, depending on the crowd-pulling capacity of the players.

Shopping

Basque sweets at **Maison du Kanouga** (9 rue Gambetta) include *kanouga* – chewy chocolate cubes invented by the owner's grandfather – and more varieties of marzipan than you've imagined in your sweetest dreams. Equally tempting are the two branches of **Macarons Adam** (49 rue Gambetta & 6 rue de la République).

St-Jean de Luz is also a good place to purchase Basque linen – for example, at **Maison Charles Larre** (4 rue de la République).

Getting There & Away

BUS

Buses run by **ATCRB** (☎ 05 59 26 06 99) pass the **Halte Routière** bus stop near the train station on their way northeast to Biarritz (€3, 30 minutes, nine daily) and Bayonne (€3, 40 minutes, nine daily). Southwestward, there are around 10 services daily to Hendaye (€1, 35 minutes).

Also passing the Halte Routière is **Transportes Pesa** (p693), serving San Sebastián and Bilbao.

From April to October **Le Basque Bondissant** (The Leaping Basque; ☎ 05 59 26 25 87; www.basquebondissant.com, in French) runs buses to La Rhune (p704; including Le Petit Train adult/child costs €17/12) and the Grottes de Sare (p704; adult/child including admission costs €10.50/7.50). Buses leave from the Halte Routière.

TRAIN

There are frequent trains to Bayonne (€4.30, 25 minutes) via Biarritz (€2.70, 15 minutes) and to Hendaye (€2.70, 15 minutes), with connections to Spain.

Getting Around

BICYCLE

Based at the train station, **Fun Bikes** (☎ 06 27 26 83 01) rents out cycles (from €7 per half day) and scooters (from €21 per half day).

BOAT

The good ship **Le Passeur** (☎ 06 81 20 84 98) plies between quai de l'Infante and Socoa (€2 one way) every half-hour between June and September.

BUS

Between June and September, the Navette Intercommunale, run by ATCRB, provides a local daily bus service, with a skeleton service during the rest of the year. From the Halte Routière, take Line A for Erromardie and the camp sites north of town, Line D for Socoa via Ciboure.

CAR

Car-rental companies at the train station include **ADA** (☎ 05 59 26 26 22).

TAXI

Call ☎ 05 59 26 10 11.

AROUND ST-JEAN DE LUZ

La Rhune

Symbolically, half of the 905m-high, antenna-topped mountain La Rhune ('Larrun' in Basque), 10km south of St-Jean de Luz, is in the French Basque Country, while the other half lies on the Spanish side. Views are spectacular from its peak, best approached from **Col de St-Ignace**, 3km northwest of Sare on the D4 (the St-Jean de Luz road). From here, you can take a fairly strenuous walk or hop on **Le Petit Train de la Rhune** (☎ 05 59 54 20 26; www.rhune.com; single/return adult €12/14, child €7/8). This charming little wooden train takes 35 minutes to haul itself up the 4km from col to summit. It runs from Easter to September with departures roughly every 35 minutes, and on Monday and Thursday during October at 10am and 3pm. Be prepared for a wait of up to an hour in high summer.

Grottes de Sare

Who knows what the first inhabitants of the **Grottes de Sare** (☎ 05 59 54 21 88; www.sare.fr/grottes_sare.html; adult/child €6.50/3.50; 10am-7pm Jul & Aug, 10am-6pm Apr-Jun & Sep, 10am-5pm Oct & school holidays, 2-5pm Nov-Mar), some 20,000 years ago, would make of today's whiz-bang technology including lasers and holograms during sound-and-light shows at these caves. Multilingual 45-minute tours take you through a gaping entrance via narrow passages to a huge central cavern. Follow the D306 6km south of the village of Sare.

Ainhoa

pop 599

'Un des plus jolis villages de la France', says the sign as you enter this, indeed, very pretty village. Only this being the Basque country, someone has painted over *'la France'*...

Ainhoa's elongated main street is flanked by imposing 17th-century houses, half-timbered and brightly painted. Look for the rectangular stones set above many of the doors, engraved with the date of construction and the name of the family to whom the house belonged. The fortified church has the Basque trademarks of an internal gallery and an embellished altarpiece.

For a memorable Basque meal, stop at the Michelin-starred **Ithurria** (☎ 05 59 29 92 11; www.ithurria.com; Ainhoa; s €89-100, d €120-150, menus €35-58;), established by the Isabal family in an old pilgrims' hostel and now run by Maurice Isabal's two sons (one the sommelier, the other the chef). To make a night of it, its rainbow-hued rooms are equipped with mod cons, and to compensate for gastronomic overload, there's an on-site sauna and fitness room.

Espelette

pop 1879

The whitewashed Basque town of Espelette is famous for its dark-red chilli peppers, an integral ingredient in traditional Basque cuisine. So prized is *le piment d'Espelette* that it's been accorded Appellation d'Origine Contrôlée (AOC) status, like fine wine. In autumn you can scarcely see the walls of the houses, strung with rows of chilli peppers drying in the sun. The last weekend in October marks Espelette's **Fête du Piment**, with processions, a formal blessing of the chilli peppers and the ennoblement of a *chevalier du piment* (a knight of the pimiento).

If you prefer sugar to spice, stop by for free tastings from specialist chocolate-maker **Chocolats Anton** (☎ 05 59 93 80 58; place du Marché).

The **tourist office** (☎ 05 59 93 95 02; www.espelette.fr, in French), within a small stone château, shares its premises with the Hôtel de Ville.

Chilli peppers star on the menu at the renowned **Hôtel Restaurant Euzkadi** (☎ 05 59 93 91 88; www.hotel-restaurant-euzkadi.com; r €51-68, menus €17-32;) in dishes such as *axoa* (tender minced veal simmered with onions and fresh chilli peppers). Its comfortable rooms are a true bargain.

ST-JEAN PIED DE PORT

pop 1700

At the foot of the Pyrenees, the walled town of St-Jean Pied de Port, 53km southeast of Bayonne, was for centuries the last stop in France for pilgrims heading south over the Spanish border, a mere 8km away, and on to Santiago de Compostela in western Spain.

Today it remains a popular departure point for hikers attempting the pilgrim trail, but there are plenty of shorter hikes and opportunities for mountain biking in the area.

St-Jean Pied de Port makes an ideal day trip from Bayonne, particularly on Monday when the market is in full swing. Half the reason for coming here is the scenic journey south of Cambo-les-Bains, as both railway and road (the D918) pass through rocky hills, forests and lush meadows dotted with white farmhouses selling *ardi* ('cheese' in Basque).

Information

Bar Paris (☎ 05 59 37 01 47; 33 av Renaud; per hr €3; 🕒 7.15am-12.30pm & 3-8.30pm) Internet access; a few steps from the station.

Maison de la Presse (place Charles de Gaulle) Carries a good selection of walking maps.

Tourist Office (☎ 05 59 37 03 57; www.pyrenees-basque.com; place Charles de Gaulle; 🕒 9am-7pm Mon-Sat, 10am-4pm Sun Jul & Aug, 9am-noon & 2-6pm Mon-Sat Sep-Jun)

Sights & Activities

OLD TOWN

The **Église Notre Dame du Bout du Pont**, with foundations as old as the town itself, was thoroughly rebuilt in the 17th century. Beyond **Porte de Notre Dame** is the photogenic **Vieux Pont** (Old Bridge), from where there's a fine view of whitewashed houses with balconies leaning out above the water. Fishing is forbidden where the River Nive passes through town,

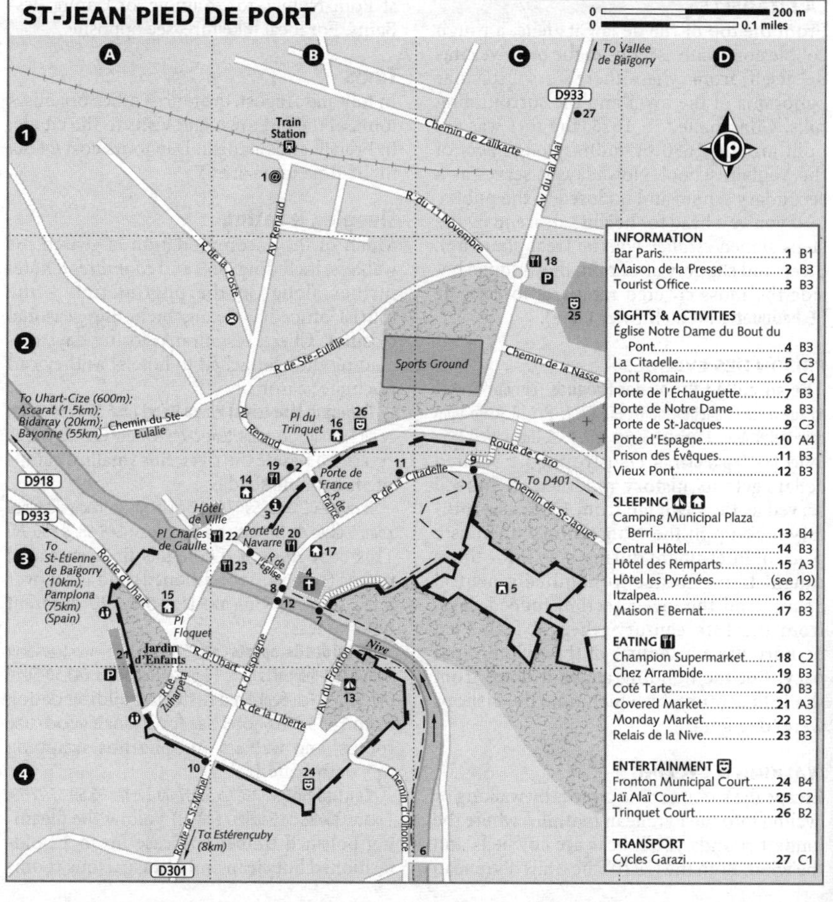

and the fat, gulping trout seem to know it. A pleasant 500m riverbank stroll upstream leads to the steeply arched **Pont Romain** (meaning Roman Bridge, but in fact dating from the 17th century).

Rue de la Citadelle is edged by substantial, pink-granite, 16th- to 18th-century houses. Look for the construction date on door lintels (the oldest we found was 1510). A common motif is the scallop shell, symbol of St Jacques (St James or Santiago) and of the Santiago de Compostela pilgrims. Pilgrims would enter the town through the **Porte de St-Jacques** on the northern side of town, then, refreshed and probably a little poorer, head for Spain through the **Porte d'Espagne**, south of the river.

LA CITADELLE

From the top of rue de la Citadelle, a rough cobblestone path ascends to the massive citadel itself, from where there's a spectacular panorama of the town and the surrounding hills. Constructed in 1628, the fort was rebuilt around 1680 by military engineers of the Vauban school. Nowadays it serves as a secondary school and is closed to the public.

If you've a head for heights, descend by the steps signed *escalier poterne* (rear stairway). Steep and slippery after rain, they plunge beside the moss-covered ramparts to **Porte de l'Échauguette** (Watchtower Gate).

PRISON DES ÉVÊQUES

The so-called **Prison des Évêques** (Bishops' Prison; 41 rue de la Citadelle; adult/child €3/2; 10.30am-9pm daily Jul & Aug, 11am-12.30pm & 2.30-6.30pm Wed-Mon Easter-Jun, Sep & Oct), a claustrophobic vaulted cellar, gets its history muddled. It indeed served as the town jail from 1795, as a military lock-up in the 19th century, then as a place of internment during WWII for those caught trying to flee to nominally neutral Spain. And the lower section indeed dates from the 13th century when St-Jean Pied de Port was a bishopric of the Avignon papacy. But the building above it dates from the 16th century, by which time the bishops were long gone.

WALKING & CYCLING

Escape the summertime crowds by walking or cycling into the Pyrenean foothills, where the loudest sounds you'll hear are cowbells and the wind. Both the GR10 (the trans-Pyrenean long-distance trail running from the Atlantic to the Mediterranean) and the GR65 (the Chemin de St-Jacques pilgrim route) pass through town. Outside the summer season, check with the tourist office or hostels for snow reports and possible rerouting, and plan your accommodation ahead as many places on the Spanish side close.

Pick up a copy of *55 Balades et Randonnées en Pays Basque* (in French; €8) from the tourist office, which maps walking and mountain-bike excursions.

To cycle the easy way while enjoying the best of Nive Valley views, load your bicycle onto the train in Bayonne – they're carried free – and roll back down the valley from St-Jean Pied de Port. If you find the ride all the way back to the coast daunting, rejoin the train at Pont-Noblia, for example, or Cambo-les-Bains. For local bike hire, see opposite.

Tours

In July and August, the tourist office organises tours of the old town and visits to the citadel in French and Spanish. Day tours cost €4.50; night-time tours are €7.

Sleeping & Eating

Much of the accommodation is geared for walkers, including *gîtes* and *chambres d'hôtes* further along on the pilgrim trail – the tourist office has details including seasonal closures. Check restaurant closing days (including those attached to hotels) as they can fluctuate seasonally.

Camping Municipal Plaza Berri (05 59 37 11 19; av du Fronton; per adult/tent/car/electricity €2.50/2/2/2.50; Apr-Oct) Beside the river, this smallish campsite has ample shade.

Itzalpea (05 59 37 03 66; www.maisondhotes-itzalpea.com; 5 place du Trinquet; s incl breakfast €48-58, d €56-76) This cosy *maison d'hôte* has five renovated rooms (some air-conditioned) and is set over a tea shop serving no less than 20 different types of teas.

Hôtel des Remparts (05 59 37 13 79; www.touradour.com/hotel-remparts.htm; 16 place Floquet; s €43.50-50, d €49-54; Feb-Sep) In a historic building dating from 1643, this hotel has functional, good-size rooms, and walkers and pilgrims swapping tips in the café-bar.

Central Hôtel (05 59 37 00 22; fax 05 59 37 27 79; 1 place Charles de Gaulle; r €60-71) Follow the gleaming polished timber staircase up to 12 old-fashioned but clean and ultraspacious rooms at this eponymously situated hotel. The owners are welcoming and there's an on-site restaurant (*menus* €19.50 to €45) opening to a riverside terrace.

our pick **Maison E Bernat** (☎ 05 59 37 23 10; www.ebernat.com; 20 rue de la Citadelle; d incl breakfast €66-86, extra person €24; 💻) There are only four bedrooms in this welcoming 17th-century place with thick stone walls, but they're airy, well furnished and meticulously kept, and each has a double bed and a single bed. There's a great little restaurant on-site, spilling onto a tiny terrace (*menus* from €11), and the hosts run a program of gourmet-themed weekends.

Hôtel les Pyrénées (☎ 05 59 37 01 01; www.hotel-les-pyrenees.com; 19 place Charles de Gaulle; r €100-160, apt €185-250; 🕑 mid-Jan–mid-Nov; ❄ 💻 ⊠ 🏊) Some of the large, well-furnished rooms at this one-time coaching inn take in stunning mountain views from balconies.

Chez Arrambide (menus €40-85, mains €20-49) This twin Michelin-starred restaurant, the real reason to stop by Hôtel les Pyrénées, is where chef Firmin Arrambide does wonders with market produce, such as pan-fried duck breast with ginger and cinnamon or foie gras–stuffed hare. Wi-fi is available; parking costs €10.

Other dining recommendations:

Côté Tarte (☎ 05 59 49 16 78; 5 rue de la Citadelle; menus €14-16; 🕑 9am-6pm Mon & Wed-Sat) Fresh, contemporary little place – all limed tables and coir carpets – specialising in delicious sweet and savoury tarts.

Relais de la Nive (☎ 05 59 37 04 22; place Charles de Gaulle; menus €20-23; 🕑 lunch & dinner Fri-Sun Mar-Nov) Bar-restaurant with views of the Vieux Pont, perfectly reflected in the adjacent Nive river by day and floodlit at night.

SELF-CATERING

Farmers from the surrounding hills bring fresh produce – chilli peppers and local cheeses and much more – to the town's **Monday market** (place Charles de Gaulle). In high summer a weekly handicraft and food fair is held most Thursdays in the covered market.

Walkers can stock up at the **Champion supermarket** (av du Jaï Alaï) near the train station.

Entertainment

Year-round, variants of *pelota* (admission €7 to €10) are played at the *trinquet*, *fronton* municipal and *jaï alaï* courts, including a barehanded *pelota* tournament at the *trinquet* court at 5pm every Monday. Check schedules at the tourist office.

In high summer, catch Basque music and dancing in the *jaï alaï* court at 9.30pm on Thursdays.

Getting There & Away

Train is the best option to/from Bayonne (€8.20, 1¼ hours, up to five daily) since the irregular bus service makes a huge detour (and drops you at the station, rather than the centre of town, despite passing right through it – go figure).

Getting Around

Cycles Garazi (☎ 05 59 37 21 79; 32 av du Jaï Alaï) rents mountain bikes (per half day/day €10/15).

Parking is a real pain in summer. The car parks beside the covered market and by the *jaï alaï* court, both free, are the largest.

To order a taxi, call ☎ 05 59 37 05 00 or ☎ 05 59 37 13 37.

AROUND ST-JEAN PIED DE PORT

The village of **St-Étienne de Baïgorry** and its outlying hamlets straddle the Vallée de Baïgorry. Tranquillity itself after busy St-Jean Pied de Port and stretched thinly along a branch of the Nive, the village has, like so many Basque settlements, two focal points: the church and the *fronton* (*pelota* court).

Irouléguy (white, rosé and red) is the French Basque Country's only AOC wine – and most of it comes from the Vallée de Baïgorry. Just north of town, the **wine-growers' cooperative** (☎ 05 59 37 41 33; www.cave-irouleguy.com; 🕑 closed Sun Oct-Apr) organises vineyard visits (€3) in July and August by reservation. It's open year-round for sales and tastings.

The Pyrenees

Snow-capped for much of the year, the jagged peaks of the Pyrenees (les Pyrénées) form a natural, 430km-long boundary between France and Spain.

With sufficient time and energy, you could follow the GR10 walking trail that bucks and twists from Hendaye beside the Bay of Biscay on France's Atlantic Coast all the way to Banyuls beside the Mediterranean Sea – but you'll probably have to select from its three distinct zones.

Rising steadily from the Atlantic through mist and cloud, the Pyrénées-Atlantiques cradle the mountains' largest and most stylish town, Pau.

The Hautes Pyrénées, the focus of this chapter, are wilder and higher. Their rugged ridges and precarious cols fall within the narrow strip of the Parc National des Pyrénées that shadows the frontier for about 100km. You can disappear into these protected mountains for days and spot only other walkers, marmots, izards (cousin to the chamois) and, perhaps, one of the Pyrenees' few brown bears. Pastoral valleys, such as the Vallée d'Aspe and the Vallée d'Ossau, cut laterally into the central Pyrenees, steepening and narrowing as they climb to shimmering lakes and tarns fed by swift mountain streams. Small-scale winter ski resorts and summer walking bases such as Cauterets and Bagnères de Luchon defer to the sheer grandeur of the mountains. To the north sits Lourdes, one of Christianity's most revered pilgrimage sites.

Eastwards, in the Pyrénées Orientales, the climate becomes warmer and drier, and the vegetation pricklier, squatter and more abundant as the mountains taper down into Roussillon, then finally dip into the Mediterranean.

HIGHLIGHTS

- Ride the century-old, timber-seated funicular to the panoramic **bd des Pyrénées** (opposite) in Pau
- Swoosh down the slopes from the ski station of Cirque du Lys, linked by *télécabine* (cable car) to **Cauterets** (p727)
- Immerse yourself in an icy **bath** (p715) at the spiritual sanctuary in Lourdes
- Learn to make traditional Pyrenean dishes at a **cooking class** (p720) in the storybook-pretty village of St-Savin
- Watch griffon vultures nest, hatch, feed and glide in the skies above **La Falaise aux Vautours** (p725) in Aste-Béon

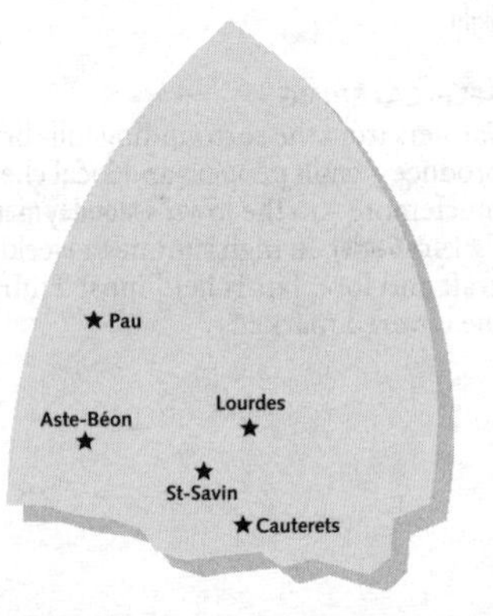

- POPULATION: 3,050,000
- AREA: 8400 SQ KM

Getting There & Away

The two main towns, Pau and Lourdes, are well served by rail. Both also have airports. Pau is served by Ryanair flights to and from the UK and Belgium, while Air France has domestic services, and Transavia connects Pau with Amsterdam. Lourdes' airport primarily handles charter flights, but also has scheduled services to Paris.

Outside of the towns there are limited bus services but to really explore you'll need your own wheels. Drivers needn't worry – the roads are well maintained and nowhere near as hair-raising as other precipitous regions such as the Alps. Alternatively, you can get around with good hiking boots and a healthy amount of lung power.

THE TOWNS

PAU

pop 80,600

Palm trees might seem out of place in this mountainous region, but its chief city, Pau (rhymes with 'so'), has long been famed for its mild climate. In the 19th century it was a favourite wintering spot for wealthy English and Americans, who left behind grand villas, English-style flower-filled public parks and promenades with dizzying vistas of the snow-dusted peaks.

In recent years the city has owed its prosperity to a high-tech industrial base and a huge natural-gas field, plus spin-off chemical plants, at nearby Lacq. It's also at the cutting edge of communications technology. Yet it retains the elegance and style of its past, bolstered by an energetic student population.

Orientation

The town centre sits on a small hill with the Gave de Pau (River Pau) at its base. Along its crest stretches bd des Pyrénées, a wide promenade offering panoramic views of the mountains. The town's east–west axis is the thoroughfare of cours Bosquet, rue Maréchal Foch and rue Maréchal Joffre. Separating the latter two is the main square, place Clemenceau.

Information

C Cyber Café (☎ 05 59 82 89 40; 20 rue Lamothe; per hr €4.50; ⌚ 10am-2am Mon-Fri, 2pm-2am Sat & Sun) One of over a dozen internet cafés around town.

Laundrette (☎ 05 59 83 90 51; 81 rue Castetnau)

Librairie des Pyrénées (☎ 05 59 27 78 75; 14 rue St-Louis) Sells an excellent selection of walking maps.

Main Post Office (21 cours Bosquet)

Tourist Office (☎ 05 59 27 27 08; www.tourismepau.com; place Royale; ⌚ 9am-6pm Mon-Sat, 9.30am-noon & 2-6pm Sun, closed Sun afternoon Sep-Jun) Stacks of information on the city and surrounds, including a pair of free booklets in English: *History & Heritage* and *Parks & Gardens* for DIY walking tours around town.

Dangers & Annoyances

Pau itself poses no problems, but avoid Parc Lawrence, which can be dodgy both day and night.

Sights

CHÂTEAU

Originally the residence of the monarchs of Navarre, Pau's **château** (☎ 05 59 82 38 02; www.musee-chateau-pau.fr, in French; adult/18-25yr/under 18yr €5/3.50/free; ⌚ 9.30am-12.15pm & 1.30-5.45pm mid-Jun–mid-Sep, 9.30-11.45am & 2-5pm mid-Sep–mid-Jun) was transformed into a Renaissance château amid lavish gardens by Marguerite d'Angoulême in the 16th century. Marguerite's grandson, the future Henri IV, was born here – cradled, so the story goes, in an upturned tortoise shell.

The painstakingly restored château holds one of Europe's richest collections of 16th- to 18th-century Gobelins tapestries and some fine Sèvres porcelain. These items apart, most of the ornamentation and furniture, including an oak dining table that can seat 100, dates from Louis-Philippe's intervention. In the room where Henri IV was born is the tortoise-shell cradle.

Within the brick-and-stone **Tour de la Monnaie** below the main château, a modern lift (free) hauls you from place de la Monnaie up to the ramparts.

Admission includes an obligatory one-hour guided tour in rapid-fire French (departing every 15 minutes), but you can pick up an English-language guide sheet at the reception desk.

PYRENEES PANORAMA

A mesmerising panorama of the Pyrenean summits unfolds from the majestic bd des Pyrénées. An **orientation table** details the names of the peaks. For information on the funicular, see p714.

THE PYRENEES (LES PYRÉNÉES)

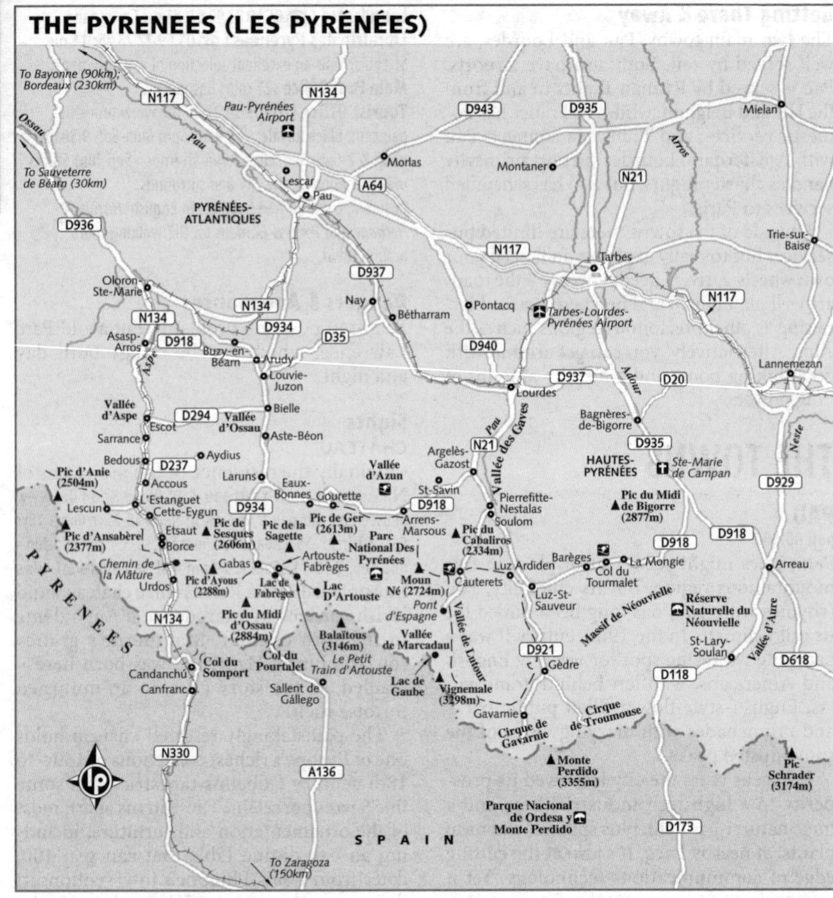

VIEILLE VILLE

Of Pau's old centre, only an area of around 300m in diameter abutting the château remains, yet it is rich in restored medieval and Renaissance buildings.

MUSÉE BERNADOTTE

The **Musée Bernadotte** (☎ 05 59 27 48 42; 8 rue Tran; adult/student/child €3/1.50/free; 🕑 10am-noon & 2-6pm Tue-Sun) has exhibits illustrating the improbable yet true story of how a French general, Jean-Baptiste Bernadotte, born in this very building, became king of Sweden and Norway in 1810, when the Swedish Riksdag (parliament) reckoned that the only way out of the country's dynastic and political crisis was to stick a foreigner on the throne. The present king of Sweden, Carl Gustaf, is the seventh ruler in the Bernadotte dynasty. You'll spot it by the blue-and-yellow Swedish flag fluttering outside.

MUSÉE DES BEAUX-ARTS

Works by Rubens, El Greco and Degas are among the rich collection of 15th- to 20th-century European paintings at Pau's **Musée des Beaux-Arts** (Fine Arts Museum; ☎ 05 59 27 33 02; rue Mathieu Lalanne; adult/student/child €3/1.50/free; 🕑 10am-noon & 2-6pm Wed-Mon).

Activities

The tourist office has reams of information about aerial activities like **hot-air ballooning**, **gliding** and **parachuting** in the clear mountain

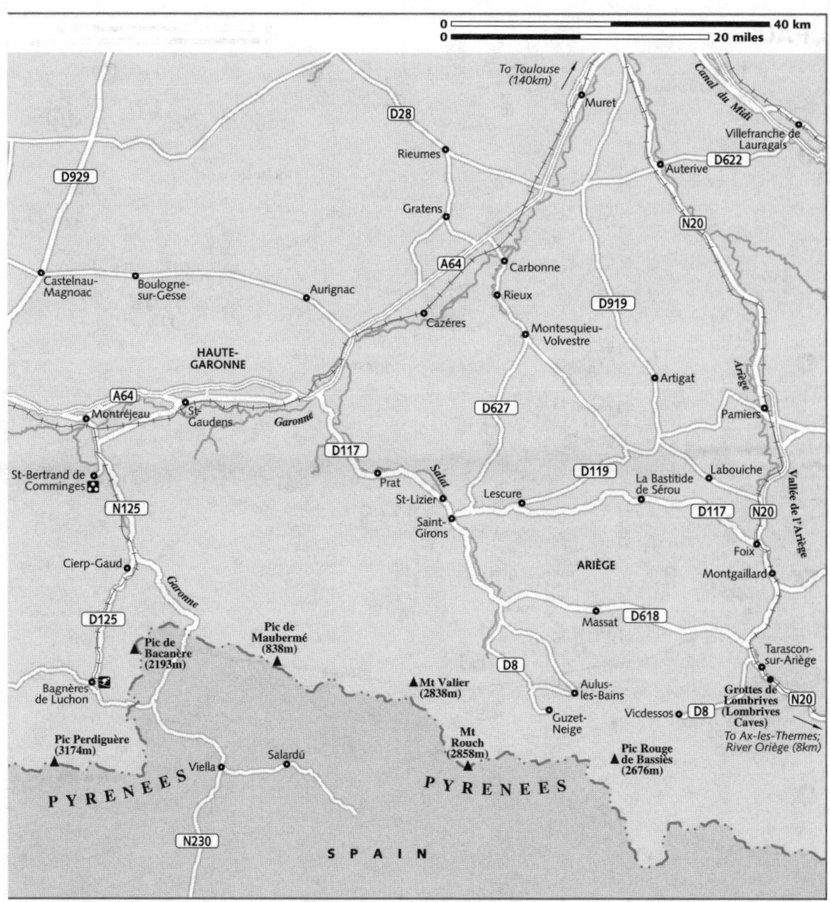

skies, as well as down-to-earth pursuits such as **walking** and **horse riding**.

Festivals & Events

Carnival Week The prelude to Lent brings winter gaiety to the town around late February.

Festival de Dance March brings a month-long celebration of contemporary dance.

Grand Prix Historique In the week before Whitsuntide: vintage vehicles parade through town on the first weekend, while Formula 3 WTCC Grand Prix motor race through the city's streets on the second weekend.

L'Été à Pau (Summer in Pau) Free, often high-quality music concerts at venues throughout the town.

Concours Complet International Some of the world's best horse riders compete in dressage, cross-country and jumping during October.

Sleeping

Pau is a popular venue for congresses so it's a good idea to book ahead at any time of year. Rates can spike during festivals and special events.

Hôtel Adour (☎ 05 59 27 47 41; www.hotel-adour-pau.com; 10 rue Valérie Meunier; s €44-46, d €44-60; ☒) Even though the street isn't particularly noisy, rooms overlooking this central hotel are *triple* glazed. High-ceilinged rooms are colourful and comfy, and secure parking from €4 is a bargain.

Hôtel Central (☎ 05 59 27 72 75; www.hotelcentralpau.com, in French; 15 rue Léon Daran; s €50-57, d €53-72; 💻 ☒) Eye-catching rooms are individually decorated at this appealing and friendly spot that, true to its name, is in a prime spot 50m

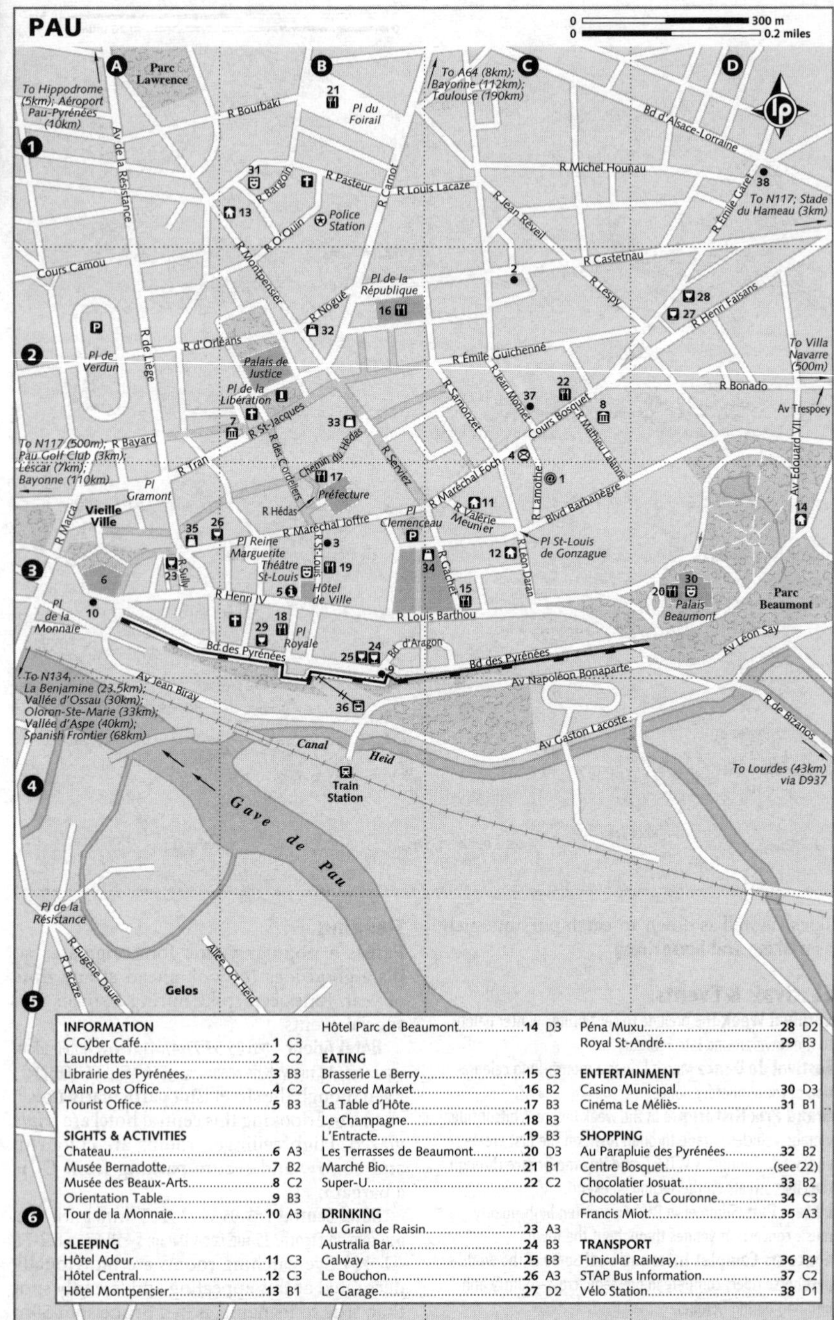
PAU
0 300 m
0 0.2 miles
A
B
C
D
1
2
3
4
5
6
To Hippodrome (5km); Aéroport Pau-Pyrénées (10km)
Parc Lawrence
Pl du Foirail
To A64 (8km); Bayonne (112km); Toulouse (190km)
R Bourbaki
Bd d'Alsace-Lorraine
Av de la Résistance
R Pasteur
R Bargoin
R Carnot
R Louis Lacaze
R Michel Hounau
Police Station
R O'Quin
R Jean Réveil
R Émile Garet
To N117; Stade du Hameau (3km)
R Montpensier
Cours Camou
R Castetnau
Pl de la République
R Lespy
R Nogué
R Henri Faisans
R d'Orléans
Pl de Verdun
R de Liège
Palais de Justice
R Émile Guichenné
To Villa Navarre (500m)
R Bonado
Pl de la Libération
R Samonzet
R Jean Monnet
Cours Bosquet
R Mathieu Lalanne
Av Trespoey
R St-Jacques
R des Cordeliers
Chemin du Hédas
R Serviez
To N117 (500m); Pau Golf Club (3km); Lescar (7km); Bayonne (110km)
R Bayard
R Tran
Pl Gramont
Préfecture
R Hédas
R Maréchal Foch
R Lamothe
Blvd Barbanègre
Av Édouard VII
R Marca
Vieille Ville
R Maréchal Joffre
Pl Clemenceau
R Valérie Meunier
Pl Reine Marguerite
R St-Louis
Théâtre St-Louis
Pl St-Louis de Gonzague
R Léon Daran
R Sully
R Gachet
Hôtel de Ville
R Henri IV
Palais Beaumont
Parc Beaumont
Pl de la Monnaie
Pl Royale
R Louis Barthou
Bd d'Aragon
Bd des Pyrénées
Av Léon Say
Av Napoléon Bonaparte
To N134, La Benjamine (23.5km); Vallée d'Ossau (30km); Oloron-Ste-Marie (33km); Vallée d'Aspe (40km); Spanish Frontier (68km)
Av Jean Biray
R de Bizanos
Canal Heid
Av Gaston Lacoste
To Lourdes (43km) via D937
Train Station
Gave de Pau
Pl de la Résistance
R Eugène Daure
R Lacaze
Allée Oct Heid
Gelos
INFORMATION
C Cyber Café 1 C3
Laundrette 2 C2
Librairie des Pyrénées 3 B3
Main Post Office 4 C2
Tourist Office 5 B3
SIGHTS & ACTIVITIES
Chateau 6 A3
Musée Bernadotte 7 B2
Musée des Beaux-Arts 8 C2
Orientation Table 9 B3
Tour de la Monnaie 10 A3
SLEEPING
Hôtel Adour 11 C3
Hôtel Central 12 C3
Hôtel Montpensier 13 B1
Hôtel Parc de Beaumont 14 D3
EATING
Brasserie Le Berry 15 C3
Covered Market 16 B2
La Table d'Hôte 17 B3
Le Champagne 18 B3
L'Entracte 19 B3
Les Terrasses de Beaumont 20 D3
Marché Bio 21 B1
Super-U 22 C2
DRINKING
Au Grain de Raisin 23 A3
Australia Bar 24 B3
Galway 25 B3
Le Bouchon 26 A3
Le Garage 27 D2
Péna Muxu 28 D2
Royal St-André 29 B3
ENTERTAINMENT
Casino Municipal 30 D3
Cinéma Le Méliès 31 B1
SHOPPING
Au Parapluie des Pyrénées 32 B2
Centre Bosquet (see 22)
Chocolatier Josuat 33 B2
Chocolatier La Couronne 34 C3
Francis Miot 35 A3
TRANSPORT
Funicular Railway 36 B4
STAP Bus Information 37 C2
Vélo Station 38 D1

from the pedestrian zone and not far from the leafy sprawl of Parc Beaumont. Wi-fi's free; parking costs €5.

Hôtel Montpensier (☎ 05 59 27 42 72; www.hotel-montpensier-pau.com; 36 rue Montpensier; s €75-95, d €85-95;) Sunlit, coir-carpeted rooms spill over with shimmering taffeta and silk cushions, and metallic and timber furniture at this boutique gem. In fine weather you can take breakfast (€9) on the garden terrace; wi-fi and parking are both free.

La Benjamine (☎ 05 59 21 48 27; www.labenjamine.net; Quartier Candeloup, Monein; r incl breakfast €85-110;) Expansive timber floors and crisp neutral fabrics fill the four guest rooms at this dreamy *chambre d'hôte* (B&B) 23.5km southwest of Pau. Occupying a renovated farmhouse, the rooms take their cue from aromatic plants growing in the rambling garden. Breakfast is an outdoor feast including flaky pastries and homemade jam. *Tables d'hôtes* are available by reservation for €42 with wine (€35 without).

Hôtel Parc de Beaumont (☎ 05 59 11 84 00; www.hotel-parc-beaumont.com; 1 av Edouard VII; r from €195;) Built from striking materials including steel, wood and glass, public areas at this ultracontemporary hotel are hung with original works of art. Rooms – most with balconies overlooking the park – are particularly spacious. So are the 2m-by-2m beds (they can even hitch on an extension for visiting basketball teams). There's an inviting indoor pool, a sauna, a hammam (Turkish bath) and a Jacuzzi, all free to guests. Wi-fi's available; parking costs €12.

Eating

our pick **Pau Golf Club** (☎ 05 59 13 18 56; www.paugolfclub.com; rue du Golf; menus €10-20, mains €7-15; lunch daily) A veritable museum, this 1856-built, still-operating golf course was the first ever on the European continent. Dining at its brass-and-timber restaurant allows you to survey its antique golf clubs, artworks painted at various stages of its history, and cabinets full of old trophies. The food is hearty and regional, and diners often break spontaneously into song (it's a Pyrenean thing…). There's a wonderful bar here too.

L'Entracte (☎ 05 59 27 68 31; 2bis rue St-Louis; mains €12-20; lunch & dinner Tue-Sat) For something light and/or late, L'Entracte (The Interval – it's right opposite Pau's main theatre) is a winner, serving crunchy salads and quality pizzas until midnight.

Brasserie Le Berry (☎ 05 59 27 42 95; 4 rue Gachet; mains €13-18; lunch & dinner) Adored by locals for its top value, original 1950s ambience and classical brasserie fare including scrumptious homemade desserts, Le Berry's tables are hotly contested (they don't take reservations). Be sure to arrive early, especially at lunchtime, when there's a €7.80 *plat du jour*.

Villa Navarre (☎ 05 59 14 65 65; www.villanavarre.fr; 59 av Trespoey; menus €16-55, mains €39-50; closed dinner Sun) In a turreted 19th-century villa, this sumptuous spot is strong on fish (baked sea bass encrusted in lime juice and salt, citrus-marinated bream and the like) as well as tender meats (rack of lamb with dried fruit and lemon balm, say). The villa also shelters an ultraluxe hotel (rooms from €192).

La Table d'Hôte (☎ 05 59 27 56 06; 1 rue Hédas; menus €18-31; lunch & dinner Wed-Sun) On a little country-like lane, this 17th-century tannery is all beams, mellow exposed brickwork and rough plaster. Service is cheerful, and dishes – such as *cochon noir Gascon,* locally reared pork stuffed with frilly mushrooms and soaked in its juices – are creative and delightfully presented.

Le Champagne (☎ 05 59 27 72 12; 5 place Royale; menus €19-23; lunch & dinner Mon-Sat) Traditional Béarnaise cuisine using local produce is dished up at this laid-back linchpin of Pau's social scene. Tables spill out onto place Royale when the weather's warm; you can also just drop by for a drink.

SELF-CATERING

Stock up on picnic goodies at the big **covered market** (place de la République). The smaller **Marché Bio** sells exclusively organic food on place du Foirail every Wednesday and Saturday morning.

There's a large **Super-U** supermarket in the basement of the **Centre Bosquet** (cours Bosquet) shopping mall in the heart of town.

Drinking

Pau has several distinct drinking zones; bars open from 10am to 2am unless noted otherwise.

'Le Triangle', bounded by rue Henri Faisans, rue Émile Garet and rue Castetnau, is the centre of student nightlife. Good bets are **Le Garage** (☎ 05 59 83 75 17; 49 rue Émile Garet) – look for the giant stucco mechanic sitting on the roof – and **Péna Muxu** (☎ 05 59 83 92 37; 35 rue Émile Garet; 7pm-2am Wed-Sat), which sometimes has live music.

A short string of international bars (**Galway** and **Australia** among them) extends along bd des Pyrénées and around the corner into bd d'Aragon. Also on bd des Pyrénées, you can flop in a deck chair and gaze at the mountains at the chic *salon de thé,* **Royal St-André** (☎ 05 59 98 44 02; 26 bd des Pyrénées; ⏰ 10am-2am May-Oct, 2-7pm Nov-Apr).

Congenial wine bars near the château include **Au Grain de Raisin** (11 rue Sully), which also has a good range of draft beers, and **Le Bouchon** (46 rue Maréchal Joffre). Look out for the local **Jurançon wines** (www.cavedejurancon.com), whose vineyards ribbon the surrounding countryside.

Entertainment

For theatre, music, dance and upcoming exhibitions, get hold of *La Culture à Pau,* published every three months and available free from the tourist office.

Exclusively nondubbed films screen at **Cinéma Le Méliès** (☎ 05 59 27 60 52; 6 rue Bargoin), Pau's only cinema.

Casino Municipal (☎ 05 59 27 06 92; ⏰ 10am-3am Mon-Fri, to 4am Sat & Sun) occupies a sumptuous building, the Palais Beaumont, within Parc Beaumont. In the same building is a free, permanent exhibition commemorating the Wright brothers, who established the world's first-ever flying school in Pau in 1912. There's also a snazzy on-site restaurant, Les Terrasses de Beaumont (mains €19.50 to €24, open lunch and dinner daily).

The renowned **Hippodrome du Pont Long** (☎ 05 59 13 07 07; 462 bd du Cami-Salié), 5km north of the town centre, has steeplechases from December to April. Rugby fans will want to take in a home game of **Section Paloise** (www.section-paloise.com/accueil.php, in French), one of France's leading club sides at **Stade du Hameau** (☎ 05 59 02 50 91; bd de l'Aviation); schedules are posted on the team's website.

Shopping

Pau's renowned chocolatiers include **La Couronne** (place Clemenceau) and **Josuat** (23 rue Serviez). Champion jam-maker **Francis Miot** (48 rue Maréchal Joffre) also makes wonderfully quirky sweets and handmade chocolates.

If you've ever despaired of finding a windproof, soak-proof umbrella, stop by **Au Parapluie des Pyrénées** (12 rue Montpensier), whose traditional beech-handled, rattan-ribbed umbrellas are used by Pyrenean shepherds.

Getting There & Away

AIR

The **Aéroport Pau-Pyrénées** (☎ 05 59 33 33 00; www.pau.aeroport.fr) is about 10km northwest of town. There are regular Ryanair flights to/from London (Stansted), Bristol and Brussels (Charleroi). Transavia flies direct to/from Amsterdam, while Air France has frequent flights to Paris (both Orly and Roissy) and Lyon.

BUS

Citram Pyrénées (☎ 05 59 27 22 22) buses roll up the Vallée d'Ossau to Laruns (€4, one hour, two to four daily).

TRAIN

Up to 10 daily trains or SNCF buses link Pau and Oloron-Ste-Marie (€6.10, 40 minutes) via Buzy-en-Béarn (€3.80, 25 minutes). There are three onward SNCF bus connections from Buzy into the Vallée d'Ossau and three to four from Oloron-Ste-Marie into the Vallée d'Aspe. Most of the latter continue to the Spanish railhead of Canfranc, from where trains run to Zaragoza (Saragossa). Regular trains link Pau with Lourdes (€6.80, 30 minutes).

Around 10 direct trains run to Bayonne (€15, 1¼ hours) and Toulouse (€27.10, 2¾ hours). There are five daily TGVs to Paris' Gare Montparnasse (from €79.70, 5½ hours).

Getting Around

TO/FROM THE AIRPORT

Shuttle-bus services from the train station to the airport had been suspended at the time of research, but are expected to resume – check with the tourist office for updates. A taxi costs around €25.

BICYCLE

Vélo Station (☎ 05 59 02 27 54; 9 bd Alsace Lorraine) rents out all manner of bikes.

CAR & MOTORCYCLE

There's extensive free parking on place de Verdun. Major rental-car companies such as **Avis** (☎ 05 59 12 80 01) have branches at both the airport and the train station.

FUNICULAR RAILWAY

The train station is linked to bd des Pyrénées by a free **funicular railway** (⏰ 6am-10pm, approximately every 3 min), a wonderful creaky little contraption dating from 1908. (The short walk, even uphill, takes much the same time.)

PUBLIC TRANSPORT

The local bus company, **STAP** (☎ 05 59 14 15 16; www.bus-stap.com, in French), has a sales and information office on rue Jean Monnet. Single tickets/daily passes/eight-ride *carnets* (books of tickets) cost €1.10/2.50/5.60.

TAXI

For a taxi, call ☎ 05 59 02 22 22 or reserve online at http://pau-taxi.com (in French).

LOURDES

pop 15,700 / elevation 400m

Descending the steep streets of Lourdes towards its Santuaires Notre Dame de Lourdes initially feels like entering a religious theme park.

Lourdes, 43km southeast of Pau, has become one of the world's most important pilgrimage sites since 1858, when 14-year-old Bernadette Soubirous (1844–79) saw the Virgin Mary in a series of 18 visions that came to her in a grotto. The Vatican confirmed them as bona-fide apparitions and the little country girl turned nun was beatified in 1933.

Catering to some six million visitors annually, the town is now awash with neon-signed hotels and over 220 souvenir shops selling cut-price statues, rosaries and crucifixes and Virgin Mary–shaped plastic bottles (just add holy water at the shrine).

But beyond the tacky commercialism are humbling reminders that some people spend their life savings to come here. Each year sees some 70,000 invalids in wheelchairs and on stretchers cared for by over 100,000 self-funded volunteers, in addition to numerous elderly visitors. And the commercialism doesn't extend to the sanctuaries, which are free of charge, and mercifully without a souvenir shop in sight.

Orientation

Lourdes' two main east–west streets are rue de la Grotte and bd de la Grotte, both leading to the Sanctuaires Notre Dame de Lourdes, which lies west of the River Pau. The principal north–south thoroughfare, called av du Général Baron Maransin where it passes above bd de la Grotte, connects the train station with place Peyramale, where you'll find the tourist office.

Information

Forum Information office (☎ 05 62 42 78 78; www.lourdes-france.com; Esplanade des Processions; 🕑 8.30am-6.30pm Apr-Oct, 9am-noon & 2-6pm Nov-Mar) For information on the Sanctuaires Notre Dame de Lourdes.

Laundrette (10 av du Général Baron Maransin; ☎ 8am-7pm)

Micro Point Com (8 place du Champ Commun; per hr €4; 🕑 2-7pm Mon, 9.30am-noon & 2-7pm Tue-Sat) Internet.

Tourist Office (☎ 05 62 42 77 40; www.lourdes-info tourisme.com; place Peyramale; 🕑 9am-7pm Mon-Sat, 10am-6pm Sun Jul & Aug, 9am-6.30pm Mon-Sat, 10am-12.30pm Sun Apr-Jun & Sep, 9am-noon & 2-6pm Mon-Sat Jan-Mar & Oct-Dec) Has details of various discount passes to the town's sites.

Sights

SANCTUAIRES NOTRE DAME DE LOURDES

The development of the Sanctuaries of Our Lady of Lourdes began within a decade of Ste Bernadette's apparitions in 1858. The most revered site is known variously as the **Grotte de Massabielle** (Massabielle Cave or Grotto), the Grotte Miraculeuse (Miraculous Cave) and the Grotte des Apparitions (Cave of the Apparitions). Open 24 hours, its walls are worn smooth by the touch of millions of hands over the years. Hundreds of candles, donated by pilgrims, flicker. Adjacent are 19 individual **baths** (🕑 generally 9-11am & 2.30-4pm Mon-Sat, 2-4pm Sun & holy days), separated into men's and women's areas. Volunteers in the change rooms shield you with blue cloaks as you strip off your clothes (yep, all of them), swaddle you in a wet, white, cotton sheet, then – after you step into the bath, walk to the end and kiss the Virgin Mary statue – they take you by the arms and lower you backwards, dipping you into the bath's seriously icy stream water for a few seconds. The baths are often used by invalids seeking cures (see p718) but are open to all-comers (of any or no religious affiliation).

The main 19th-century section of the sanctuaries has three parts. On the western side of Esplanade du Rosaire, between the two ramps, is the neo-Byzantine **Basilique du Rosaire** (Basilica of the Rosary). One level up is the **crypt**, reserved for silent worship. Above is the spire-topped, neo-Gothic **Basilique Supérieure** (Upper Basilica).

From Palm Sunday to at least mid-October, solemn **torchlight processions** nightly start from the Massabielle Grotto at 9pm, while at 5pm there's the **Procession Eucharistique** (Blessed

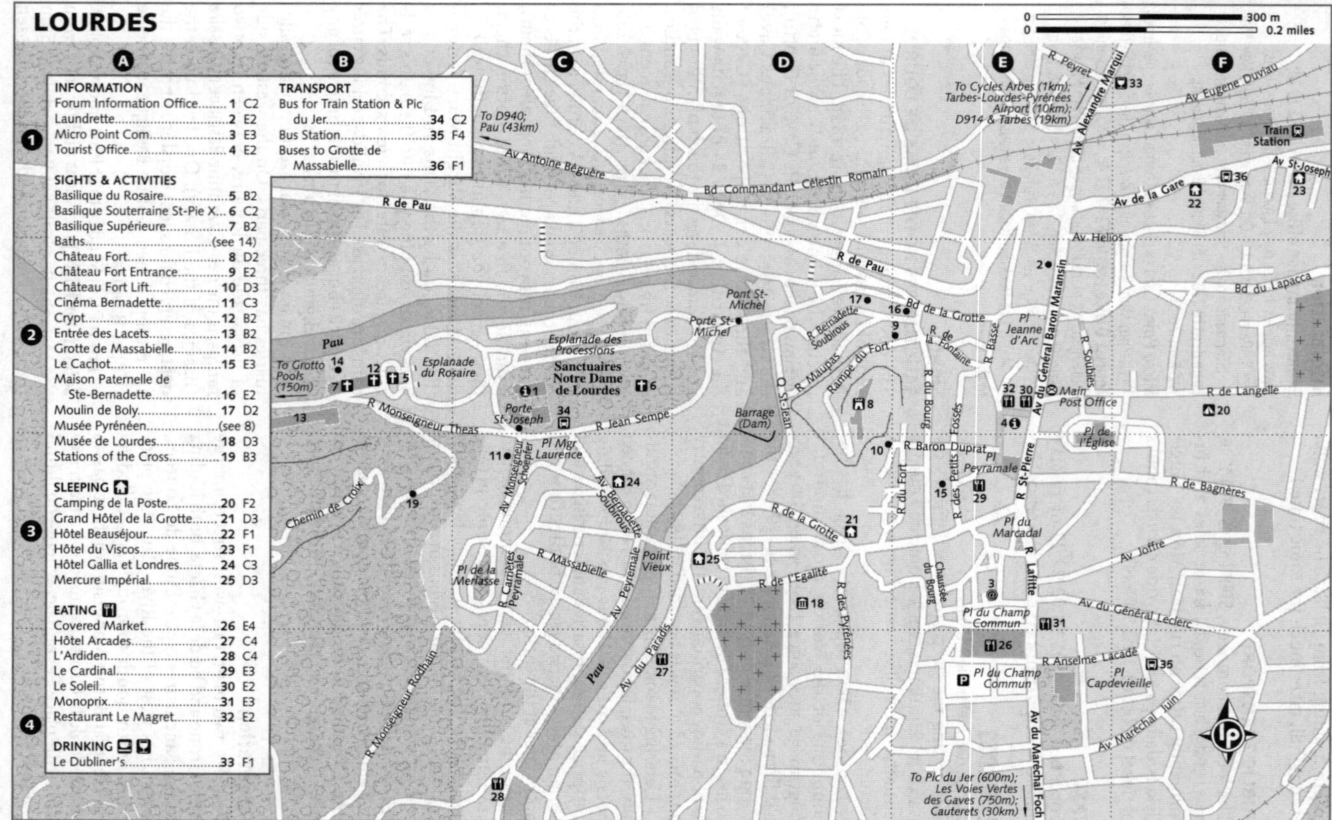
LOURDES
INFORMATION
Forum Information Office 1 C2
Laundrette 2 E2
Micro Point Com 3 E3
Tourist Office 4 E2
SIGHTS & ACTIVITIES
Basilique du Rosaire 5 B2
Basilique Souterraine St-Pie X 6 C2
Basilique Supérieure 7 B2
Baths (see 14)
Château Fort 8 D2
Château Fort Entrance 9 E2
Château Fort Lift 10 D3
Cinéma Bernadette 11 C3
Crypt 12 B2
Entrée des Lacets 13 B2
Grotte de Massabielle 14 B2
Le Cachot 15 E3
Maison Paternelle de Ste-Bernadette 16 E2
Moulin de Boly 17 D2
Musée Pyrénéen (see 8)
Musée de Lourdes 18 D3
Stations of the Cross 19 B3
SLEEPING
Camping de la Poste 20 F2
Grand Hôtel de la Grotte 21 D3
Hôtel Beauséjour 22 F1
Hôtel du Viscos 23 F1
Hôtel Gallia et Londres 24 C3
Mercure Impérial 25 D3
EATING
Covered Market 26 E4
Hôtel Arcades 27 C4
L'Ardiden 28 C4
Le Cardinal 29 E3
Le Soleil 30 E2
Monoprix 31 E3
Restaurant Le Magret 32 E2
DRINKING
Le Dubliner's 33 F1
TRANSPORT
Bus for Train Station & Pic du Jer 34 C2
Bus Station 35 F4
Buses to Grotte de Massabielle 36 F1
0 300 m
0 0.2 miles
To D940; Pau (43km)
To Cycles Arbes (1km); Tarbes-Lourdes-Pyrénées Airport (10km); D914 & Tarbes (19km)
To Grotto Pools (150m)
To Pic du Jer (600m); Les Voies Vertes des Gaves (750m); Cauterets (30km)
Sanctuaires Notre Dame de Lourdes
Esplanade des Processions
Esplanade du Rosaire
Train Station
Main Post Office
Barrage (Dam)
Pont St-Michel
Porte St-Michel
Porte St-Joseph
Point Vieux
Pau
Bd Commandant Célestin Romain
R de Pau
Av Alexandre Marqui
Av du Général Baron Maransin
R St-Pierre
Av du Maréchal Foch
Av de la Gare
R de la Grotte
Bd de la Grotte
R de Bagnères
Av Bernadette Soubirous
R Monseigneur Rodhain
Chemin de Croix
R Monseigneur Theas
Av Monseigneur Schoepfer
Av Peyramale
Av du Paradis
Av du Général Leclerc
Av Joffre
R Lafitte
R du Bourg
Chaussée du Bourg
R des Pyrénées
R de l'Egalité
Q St-Jean
R Baron Duprat
R des Petits Fossés
R Basse
Pl Jeanne d'Arc
Pl de l'Église
Pl du Marcadal
Pl Peyramale
Pl du Champ Commun
Pl Capdevieille
R Anselme Lacadé
Av Maréchal Juin
R Soubies
Av Helios
Bd du Lapacca
R de Langelle
Av St-Joseph
Av Eugene Duviau
R Peyret
Av Antoine Béguère
R Massabielle
R Carrières Peyramale
Pl de la Merlasse
Pl Mgr Laurence
R Jean Sempe
R Bernadette Soubirous
R Maupas
Rampe du Fort
R du Fort
R de la Fontaine

Sacrament Procession) along the Esplanade des Processions. When it's wet, the latter ceremony is held inside the vast, bunkerlike **Basilique Souterraine St-Pie X** (Underground Basilica of St Pius X), with a capacity for 25,000 worshippers and vibrant backlit works of *gemmail* (superimposed pieces of coloured glass embedded in enamel).

All four places of worship open 6am to 10pm in summer and 7am to 7pm in winter. You can enter the grounds around the clock via the **Entrée des Lacets** (rue Monseigneur Theas). The **Porte St-Michel** and **Porte St-Joseph** entrances are open 5am to midnight year-round.

STATIONS OF THE CROSS

Also called Chemin du Calvaire (Way of Calvary), the 1.5km Chemin de Croix (Way of the Cross), leading up the forested hillside from near the Basilique Supérieure, is punctuated by the 14 **Stations of the Cross**. Especially devout pilgrims mount to the first station on their knees.

OTHER BERNADETTE SITES

On rue Bernadette Soubirous are the **Moulin de Boly** (Boly Mill; No 12; admission free), Bernadette's birthplace; and the **Maison Paternelle de Ste-Bernadette** (No 2; admission €1), the house that the town of Lourdes bought for the Soubirous family after Bernadette saw the apparitions. **Le Cachot** (15 rue des Petits Fossés; admission free), a former prison, is where Bernadette lived during the period when she saw the apparitions.

MUSÉE DE LOURDES

The **Musée de Lourdes** (☎ 05 62 94 28 00; adult/child €5.50/2.70; ⌚ 9am-noon & 1.30-6.30pm Apr-Oct), in the Parking de l'Égalité, portrays the life of Ste Bernadette as well as the general history of Lourdes.

CINÉMA BERNADETTE

To learn yet more about Ste Bernadette (or to simply rest your feet), **Cinéma Bernadette** (☎ 05 62 42 79 19; 6 av Monseigneur Schoepfer; adult/disabled/child €6.50/5/4.50) shows the two-hour feature film *Bernadette* (with optional English dialogue) at 2pm, 4.30pm and 8.30pm daily from Easter to mid-October.

CHÂTEAU FORT

On a rocky pinnacle, the **Château Fort** (Fortified Castle; adult/child/disabled €5/2.30/2; ⌚ 9am-noon & 1.30-6.30pm Easter-Sep, 9am-noon & 2-6pm Oct-Easter) is home to the **Musée Pyrénéen**, with displays on folk art and local traditions.

Take the free lift (elevator) from rue Baron Duprat or walk up the ramp at the northern end of rue du Bourg.

PIC DU JER

Panoramic views of Lourdes and the central chain of the Pyrenees unfurl from the summit of Pic du Jer (948m). It's a six-minute ride from valley level by the **funicular railway** (☎ 05 62 94 00 41; bd d'Espagne; adult/child one-way €6.50/5, return €9/6.50; ⌚ 10am-6pm Mar-Nov).

The signed trail to the summit from the lower station is a more strenuous route (allow 2½ to three hours for the return journey) or simply ride up and walk down. The ticket booth has a free map.

While here, you can take a 45-minute **guided cave tour** (adult/child €3.50/2; ⌚ by reservation); English tours can be arranged.

Take bus 2 from place Monseigneur Laurence.

Activities

To get away from Bernadette Soubirous for a day, cycle along all or part of **Les Voies Vertes des Gaves** (Mountain Streams Green Routes). The route follows the old, long-abandoned Lourdes–Cauterets train line up the lovely Vallée des Gaves to Cauterets, where you can catch a bus back to Lourdes.

Festivals & Events

Lourdes' renowned **Festival International de Musique Sacrée** is a week of sacred music held around Easter.

Sleeping

Lourdes has over 270 hotels – more than anywhere in France outside Paris. Even so, you may have to scout around during religious holidays and from August to the first week of October. Conversely, the town is so quiet in winter that most hotels shut down. Virtually all hotels have facilities for travellers with disabilities. The tourist office has details of self-catering apartments.

Camping de la Poste (☎ 05 62 94 40 35; 26 rue de Langelle; camping for 2 people €10; ⌚ Easter–mid-Oct) There are a dozen or so campsites ringing town, but this tiny, friendly place is right in the heart of town – and consequently often full.

Hôtel du Viscos (☎ 05 62 94 08 06; fax 05 62 94 26 74; 6 av St-Joseph; d €36-60, with shared bathroom €32; Feb–mid-Dec) A true bargain, this friendly, family-run place has a bustling bar (guests only), has free parking and couldn't be handier for the station.

Hôtel Beauséjour (☎ 05 62 94 38 18; www.hotel-beausejour.com; 16 av de la Gare; d €66-185;) The Beauséjour, with its scrubbed white and ox-blood facade, offers free parking, and runs a good restaurant (*menu* €15). Rooms at the rear have impressive views of town and the Pyrenees beyond.

MIRACLE CURES

There's only around one certifiable miracle cure in Lourdes every decade, but there are thousands at various stages of consideration, and more every week. The most recent 'official miracle', the 67th overall, confirmed in 2005, was that of Italian Anna Santaniello, crippled by and cured of chronic rheumatism.

To find out what makes a cure miraculous, we spoke to Dr Patrick Theillier, Director of the Lourdes Medical Bureau.

How did you come to work in this field?
In 1998, the Bishop of Tarbes-Lourdes, Jacques Perrier, asked me to come here as a permanent doctor to receive people who've been cured, to see whether there's a medical explanation or not.

Do you have a clerical background?
I'm married with six children and 16 grandchildren, so I'm not a priest! I'm a traditional doctor but I've done many works and studies about the spiritual dimension of medicine.

What's the difference between a cure and a miracle?
The church has seven criteria: the illness must have a fatal prognosis; the diagnosis must be precise; the illness must be organic; the cure can't have been caused by medical treatment; the healing must be sudden, unexpected and instantaneous; the cure must be complete; and it mustn't be remission but lasting healing. The process of determining takes many years. The first thing is to check for medical explanations, then (if there aren't any) analyse the patient's case against the church's criteria.

How many 'miracle' candidates do you see?
Every year about 40 unexplained cases, but there are others that we don't know about (inexplicably cured people who don't contact the medical bureau).

What have the patients done to be cured in Lourdes?
Sometimes it's because they prayed, sometimes it's the water…you find all cases. There's a 'prayer climate' here…not just for Catholics, but Muslims and all other religions. Cures can happen the first time people come in the sanctuary or the 15th time…there's no rule, everything's possible. It's always a surprise. An 81-year-old man came to see me this week; he had been diagnosed with liver cancer at Christmas and was sent home to die within three weeks. His children came to say goodbye and one brought him some water from Lourdes and got him to drink it. He started getting better in January, and by 1 February he was going so well he swam 1km.

Does his cure qualify as a 'miracle'?
I need to see his test results but I don't feel it strongly; it's an intuitive thing. A Spanish woman came this week who has recovered from muscular disease – I think it's a miracle but it will never be recognised as one because her prognosis was serious but not fatal. Another woman, with MS, came to receive the sacrament for sick people last year and went to the bath; from that point she started to get better and was later able to stand, walk, and now drives a car again. It's not clear if it's a miracle, because it's a gradual improvement, not a sudden halt of the disease.

Worst thing about your job?
Sometimes people believe they're getting better but they're not. It's difficult, but it's part of the job of any doctor… you have to tell them.

Best thing about your job?
Seeing people who've suffered for years find life again…it shows that life is stronger than death.

Mercure Impérial (☎ 05 62 94 06 30; www.mercure.com; 3 av du Paradis; r €69-145; Feb–mid-Dec) Don't be dissuaded because it's part of a chain: this 1930s hotel preserves its original ambience, and its roof terrace is a sublime place to sip an aperitif, overlooking the river and Pont Vieux. The lounge opens out onto a rear garden, and the restaurant (mains cost €11 to €15) is splendid. It's wi-fi'd; parking costs €11 to €13.

our pick **Grand Hôtel de la Grotte** (☎ 05 62 94 58 87; www.hotel-grotte.com; 66 rue de la Grotte; s/d/tr from €71/80/94; mid-Feb–mid-Oct) Established in 1871, Lourdes' first-ever hotel has belonged to the same family for four generations. With richly coloured rooms and suites, a gorgeous garden, a bar and a couple of restaurants (mains cost €18 to €22), it embodies old-world courtesy. Rates rise by 10% in peak season.

Hôtel Gallia et Londres (☎ 05 62 94 35 44; www.hotelgallialondres.com; 26 av Bernadette Soubirous; d €120-240; Apr-Oct) The spacious bedrooms (some with sanctuary views) are individually and attractively decorated à la Louis XVI. You'll gasp at the chandeliers and the wooden panelling of the dining room with its side alcoves for intimate eating. Equally seductive is the lovely little garden.

Eating

Alas, your options aren't great in this town of pack-'em-in, fill-'em-up hotels with accompanying restaurants. Most offer half or full board; many even require guests to stay on those terms, especially in the high season. On the upside, prices are reasonable.

Se also listings under Sleeping.

Le Cardinal (☎ 05 62 42 05 87; 11 place Peyramale; dishes from €5, daily menu €8.50; Mon-Sat) Popular with locals, this unpretentious bar-brasserie is great for a drink or for tucking in to huge, healthy salads and filling daily *menus*.

Hôtel Arcades (☎ 05 62 94 20 59; 13 av du Paradis; menus €16-21.50, mains €10.50-13) The restaurant of Hôtel Arcades, open daily year-round, could save you from starvation. Entry is directly from the street, the service is swift and smiling and the food more than acceptable (if not perhaps 'gastronomic').

Le Soleil (☎ 05 62 94 53 22; 8 rue des Quatre Frères Soulas; mains €12-15; Tue-Sun) A bold Muslim presence in such a fervently Catholic town (that nevertheless welcomes visitors of all persuasions), this North African restaurant dishes up delicious couscous.

Restaurant le Magret (☎ 05 62 94 20 55; 10 rue des Quatre Frères Soulas; weekday lunch menu €13, dinner menus €26-33, mains €17-23; Tue-Sun Feb-Dec) Rustic decor embellished with early photos of Lourdes makes an evocative backdrop for dining on innovative regional cuisine including a crayfish 'cappuccino' with wild nettles, served in a glass; raw Pyrenean black-pork ham; and Vallée d'Ossau cheese.

L'Ardiden (☎ 05 62 42 24 35; 48 av Peyramale; mains from €13; Wed-Sun) It's well worth the short walk upstream to L'Ardiden, pleasantly situated beside Pont Peyramale and the river. It's strong on pizza and pasta, along with fresh seafood and southwestern French specialities. It's a good bet if you're travelling with littlies, with a kid's *menu* for €6.50.

SELF-CATERING

Lourdes' **covered market** (place du Champ Commun) occupies most of the square. Opposite you'll find a **Monoprix supermarket** (9 place Champs Commun).

Drinking

Unsurprisingly, nightlife is not Lourdes' forte – the town has only one Madonna and she's far from a Material Girl (despite the merchandising around town). Your best year-round bet is the pub–piano bar **Le Dubliner's** (☎ 05 62 42 16 38; 7 av Alexandre Marqui), which usually has music from 8pm.

Getting There & Away

AIR

Tarbes-Lourdes-Pyrénées airport (www.tarbes-lourdes.aeroport.fr) is 10km north of Lourdes on the N21. It mainly handles charter flights, but has up to three scheduled daily Air France flights to/from Paris (Orly). The airport is not served by public transport.

BUS

The small **bus station** (place Capdevieille) has services northwards to Pau (though trains are much faster) and is a stop for buses running between Tarbes and Argelès-Gazost (at least eight daily), the gateway to the Pyrenean communities of Cauterets, Luz-St-Sauveur and Gavarnie. SNCF buses to Cauterets (€7, one hour, at least five daily) leave from the train station.

TRAIN

Lourdes is well connected by train to French cities including Bayonne (€17.70, 1¾ hours, up to four daily), Pau (€6.80, 30 minutes, 10-plus daily) and Toulouse (€23.40, two hours, six daily). There are four daily TGVs to Paris' Gare Montparnasse (from €88.80, six hours).

Getting Around

BICYCLE

Opposite Leclerc supermarket, **Cycles Arbes** (☎ 05 62 94 05 51; 10 av François Abadie) hires out a variety of bikes.

BUS

Citybus (☎ 08 00 10 02 39) bus 1 links the train station with place Monseigneur Laurence and the Sanctuaries (€1.20).

CAR & MOTORCYCLE

To keep things fair for the souvenir traders, the one-way traffic routing through the town is reversed every 15 days (the only town in France to do so). This, combined with the caterpillar of tour coaches, swarms of pedestrians and fuming summer traffic jams, means that you're better off leaving your vehicle near the train or bus stations, where there's free parking, and walk.

Major car-rental companies have desks at the airport and the train station.

TAXI

For a taxi, call ☎ 05 62 94 31 30.

AROUND LOURDES

The **Grottes de Bétharram** (☎ 05 62 41 80 04; www.betharram.com; adult/child €11/7; 🕒 2.30-4pm Mon-Fri Jan-Mar, 9am-noon & 1.30-5.30pm daily Apr-Oct, closed Nov & Dec), 14km west of Lourdes along the D937, are among France's most spectacular limestone caves. Guided visits, by minitrain and barge, last 1½ hours.

To see fauna that you would be extremely lucky to stumble across in the Parc National des Pyrénées, visit **Parc Animalier des Pyrénées** (☎ 05 62 97 91 07; www.parc-animalier-pyrenees.com, in French; adult/child €10/6; 🕒 9am-7pm Jun-Aug, 9am-noon & 2-6pm Apr, May & Sep, 1-6pm Oct), at the northern side of the village **Argelès-Gazost**. Animals in this small park include marmots, wolves, lynx, otters and a couple of brown bears.

Just 4km south of Argelès-Gazost (16km south of Lourdes) is one of the Pyrenees' jewels, St-Savin. Not only is it officially 'one of France's prettiest villages', but it's home to the wonderful hotel-restaurant **Le Viscos** (☎ 05 62 97 02 28; www.hotel-leviscos.com; d €85-126; 🕒 closed 2 weeks Jan). Run by the seventh generation of the St-Martin family, its clutch of countrified rooms have hand-sewn bedspreads, cushion covers and canopies. But the real draw is the gastronomic restaurant (*menus* €27 to €78; closed dinner Sunday and all day Monday for nonguests), where you can savour chef Jean-Pierre St-Martin's regional fare, including *pomme farçie au boudin et foie gras* (blood-sausage-stuffed apple topped with pan-fried foie gras and caramel), in its elegant dining room, the winter garden or the summer courtyard. Jean-Pierre also offers two- to three-hour **cooking classes** (in English and French) for €60 per person, including the fruits of your labour plus two glasses of wine (reservations essential). The tiny village has long been a haven for artists and writers; check out the photo of guest Paulo Coelho at Le Viscos' reception (oh yeah, and Michael and Kirk Douglas and President Sarkozy, among other celebs seeking time out of the spotlight).

HATS OFF?

The archetypal beret-wearing, baguette-carrying Frenchman may be a caricature, but berets are still sported by plenty of folk in these parts (often carrying baguettes, too).

This quintessential headgear is honoured at the **Musée du Béret** (Beret Museum; ☎ 05 59 61 91 70; place St-Roch; adult/child under 10yr €4/free; 🕒 10am-noon & 2-6pm Tue-Sun Apr-Oct, 2-6pm Tue-Sat Nov-Mar), in the bustling little market town of Nay (a well-signed 24km west of Lourdes along the D937 towards Pau), and have been made here since 1812. Cap off a visit by browsing its boutique's rainbow of colours.

PARC NATIONAL DES PYRÉNÉES

Rich in plant life and teeming with fauna, the Pyrenees National Park extends for about 100km along the Franco-Spanish border – from the Vallée d'Aspe in the west to the Vallée d'Aure in the east. Its boundaries are marked by a red izard head on a white background, painted on rocks and trees. Within are 230 lakes and Vignemale (3298m), the French Pyrenees' highest summit. It interlinks and collaborates closely with Spain's 156-sq-km Parque Nacional de Ordesa y Monte Perdido, to its south.

Glance up to spot birds of prey like golden eagles, griffon vultures, bearded vultures, booted eagles, buzzards and falcons. Some 42 of France's 110 species of mammal are also here; some reintroduced including marmots, the izard (close relative of the chamois, all but blasted out of existence half a century ago), and brown bears (see the boxed text, p724).

MAPS & BOOKS

Each of the six park valleys (Vallée d'Aure, Vallée de Luz, Vallée de Cauterets, Val d'Azun, Vallée d'Ossau and Vallée d'Aspe) has a national park folder or booklet in French, *Randonnées dans le Parc National des Pyrénées,* describing 10 to 15 walks. Worthwhile for the route maps alone, they're on sale at local parks and tourist offices.

The park is covered by IGN's 1:25,000 Top 25 maps 1547OT *Ossau,* 1647OT *Vignemale,* 1748OT *Gavarnie* and 1748ET *Néouvielle.*

Information

There are **national park offices** (www.parc-pyrenees.com) with visitor centres at (from west to east) Etsaut, Laruns, Arrens-Marsous, Cauterets, Luz-St-Sauveur, Gavarnie and St-Lary-Soulan. All are open year-round; call ahead to check closing days in May and November.

Activities

WALKING

Some 350km of waymarked trails (including the Mediterranean-to-Atlantic GR10) criss-cross the park; some link up with trails in Spain.

Within the park are about 20 *refuges* (mountain huts), primarily run by the Club Alpin Français (CAF). Most are staffed only from July to September but maintain a small wing year-round.

WHITE-WATER SPORTS

Rivers racing from the Pyrenean heights offer some of France's finest white water, since spring snow melt is supplemented by modest (sometimes not-so-modest) year-round rain, bringing a fairly steady annual flow. Organisations offering rafting and canoeing within or downstream from the national park include **A Boste Sport Loisir** (☎ 05 59 38 57 58; www.aboste.com; rue Léon Bérard, 64390 Sauveterre de Béarn) and **Centre Nautique de Soeix** (☎ 05 59 39 61 00; http://soeix.free.fr; quartier Soeix, 64400 Oloron-Ste-Marie).

THE VALLEYS

VALLÉE D'ASPE

The Vallée d'Aspe has been a transfrontier passage ever since Julius Caesar's Roman legionnaires marched through. South of Pau, the Gave d'Aspe (River Aspe) flows for some

SKIING IN THE FRENCH PYRENEES

Let's be frank: the best Pyrenees skiing lies across the watershed, in Spain's Baqueira-Beret and Andorra's Gran Valira. But the more modest resorts on the French side offer reasonable downhill skiing and snowboarding for beginners and intermediates.

The Pyrenees receive less snow than the much higher Alps and the falls are generally moister and heavier. In addition to downhill skiing, the potential for cross-country skiing, ski touring and, increasingly, snowshoeing, is also good.

The French side has over 20 downhill ski stations, and more than 10 cross-country areas. See also www.bearn-basquecountry.com.

Ax Trois Domaines Above Ax-les-Thermes (p733) are 75km of gentle runs, tracing their way through pine forest and, higher up, the open spaces of Campels.

Barèges-La Mongie This combined resort, on either side of Col du Tourmalet and at the foot of the Pic du Midi de Bigorre (p730), has 69 runs, making it the French Pyrenees' most extensive skiing area.

Cauterets Snow lingers late at this long-established spa town-ski resort (p727); you can still whiz downhill here when other resorts have closed down for the season.

Superbagnères A cabin lift hurtles up from the spa town of Bagnères de Luchon (p731) for skiing above the tree line at 1800m.

Val d'Azun The best cross-country skiing in the Pyrenees, about 30km southwest of Lourdes, where you can plough along 110km of trails between 1350m and 1600m. There's a tourist office in Arrens-Marsous.

50km from the Col du Somport, which marks the frontier with Spain, down to Oloron-Ste-Marie. Fewer than 3000 people live in the valley's 13 villages. Its upper reaches are still among the most remote corners of the French Pyrenees and one of the final refuges of their more timid wildlife. But such seclusion may soon be lost due to the much-protested Tunnel de Somport, the Pyrenees' newest, 8km-long road tunnel.

MAPS

The 1:50,000-scale *Béarn: Pyrénées Carte No 3*, published by Rando Éditions, is a practical general trekking map of the area. A more detailed option is IGN's 1:25,000-scale Top 25 map No 1547OT, *Ossau*.

The national park's *Randonnées dans le Parc National des Pyrénées: Aspe* is a pack of information sheets on 11 walks, varying from 1½ hours to eight hours, in and around the valley.

Information

The valley's **tourist office** (☎ 05 59 34 57 57; www.aspecanfranc.com, in French & Spanish; place Sarraillé; 9am-12.30pm & 2-5.30pm or 6.30pm Mon-Sat) is in the main square of Bedous. It carries a reasonable selection of walking maps.

The **Maison du Parc National des Pyrénées** (Park Information Centre; ☎ 05 59 34 88 30; 10.30am-12.30pm & 2-6.30pm May-Oct) occupies the old train station in Etsaut (trains have long since stopped serving the valley) and houses a good display (in French) about the fauna of the Pyrenees.

Getting There & Away

SNCF (☎ 08 92 35 35 35) buses and trains connect Pau and Oloron-Ste-Marie up to 10 times daily. From Oloron there are three to four onward bus connections into the valley via Bedous to Etsaut, the majority continuing to Somport and the Spanish railhead of Canfranc.

Bedous & Around

Bedous, the valley's largest village (albeit with a population of just 578) is 25km south of Oloron-Ste-Marie. Despite its diminutive size, it's still surprisingly easy to get lost in its little maze of narrow stone streets.

Breathtaking scenery notwithstanding, there's little in the way of sights, although the village's 18th-century working watermill, **Moulin d'Orcun** (☎ 05 59 34 51 70; adult/child €4/3; visits 11am, 3pm & 6pm Jul, Aug & school holidays), 500m out of Bedous on the Aydius road, opens for visits during holiday periods.

A further 7km up the N134, towards Pau, the storybook-pretty village of Sarrance is an age-old stop on the pilgrim's route to Santiago, with a historic cloister and church, and the **Écomusée de la Vallée d'Aspe** (☎ 05 59 34 57 65; adult/child €4/2.50; 10am-noon & 2-7pm Jul-Sep, 2-6pm Sat, Sun & school holidays Oct-Christmas & Feb-Jun, closed Christmas-Jan), which evokes the myths, legends and origins of the village.

ACTIVITIES

The tourist office in Bedous (left) and other outlets in the valley sell the excellent locally produced guide *45 Randonnées en Béarn: la Vallée d'Aspe* (€9). It can also put you in touch with organisers of a whole host of outdoor activities: mountain biking, canyon clambering, rafting, climbing, skiing, snowshoeing and winter mountaineering trips.

SLEEPING & EATING

Camping Municipal de Carole (☎ 05 59 34 59 19; per person/tent/car €2.50/2/2; Mar–mid-Nov) Small and quiet (it's a good 300m west of the N134), it's well signposted from the main highway.

Le Mandragot (☎ 05 59 34 59 33; place Sarraillé; dm €10) This welcoming *gîte d'étape* (walkers' guest house) is a frequent staging post for walkers undertaking the Chemin de St Jacques. Accommodation is in rooms for two

VALLEY HOPPING

If you're hopping from one valley to the next, you can cut kilometres by skipping the main thoroughfares in favour of scenic back roads rolling over the valleys' lower flanks.

The narrow D294 between Escot and Bielle corkscrews for 21km over the Col de Marie-Blanque (1035m) between the Aspe and Ossau valleys. A gentler alternative is the road linking Asasp-Arros and Arudy, which primarily traverses forest.

The drive along the D918 between Laruns (Vallée d'Ossau) and Argelès-Gazost (Vallée des Gaves) is a true summer spectacular, but closes due to snow from approximately October to May. Year-round, the D35 between Louvie-Juzon and Nay is easier going, lined with farms selling cheese.

to eight. There's a cosy common room and self-catering facilities.

Chez Michel (☎ 05 59 34 52 47; michel.abrioux@wanadoo.fr; rue Gambetta; r with breakfast €45, menus €10-20) Overnight guests can unwind here after a hard day's walking, either in the sauna or in the neat little restaurant, which dishes up regional treats like *garbure* (a pork-based gruel, thick with vegetables and pulses), trout with wild mushrooms, and bilberry pie. The restaurant is closed Saturday lunch July and August, as well as lunch Friday and Saturday and dinner Sunday September to June.

Restaurant des Cols (☎ 05 59 34 70 25; Aydius; d €33; closed dinner Sun & Mon except school holidays, plus 1-15 Oct) A 6.5km (uphill) drive east of Bedous in the hamlet of Aydius. It also has three delightful double guest rooms with self-catering facilities.

A heady variety of local cheeses fill the *fromagerie* **Ferme Miramon** (☎ 05 59 34 53 76; N134), situated just near the post office.

Accous

At the yawning mouth of the Vallée Berthe, 2.5km south of Bedous and 800m east of the highway, this little village has a splendid backdrop of 2000m-plus peaks. For the ultimate panorama, sign up with one of its two *parapente* (paragliding) schools. **Ascendance** (☎ 05 59 34 52 07; www.ascendance.fr, in French) offers accompanied 15-minute introductory flights (€65) and five-day induction courses (€400). **Air Attitude** (☎ 05 59 34 50 06; www.air-attitude.com, in French) has similar prices.

The **Fermiers Basco-Béarnais cheese centre** (☎ 05 59 34 76 06; 8.30am-noon & 2-6pm Mon-Fri, 10am-noon & 2.30-6pm Sat, Sun & school holidays), a farmers cooperative and thriving *fromagerie* (cheese shop), is beside the N134. It has free sampling and offers a 20-minute audiovisual presentation in French, plus the opportunity to buy the best of local ewe's-, goat's- and cow's-milk cheeses.

SLEEPING & EATING

Camping Despourrins (☎ 05 59 34 71 16; per person/site €2.80/3.10; Mar-Oct) This tiny campsite is just off the N134, tucked behind the Fermiers Basco-Béarnais cheese centre.

Maison Despourrins (☎ 05 59 34 53 50; http://maison-despourrins.vallee-aspe.com, in French; dm €14, cold/hot meals €7/14) Colourfully decorated and ecominded, this *gîte d'étape* has 23 beds in two- to four-share rooms. Meals made using local produce will revitalise the weariest walkers, or you can use the kitchen facilities to self-cater.

Auberge Cavalière (☎ 05 59 34 72 30; www.auberge-cavaliere.com; s half board €56.60, d half board €119; year-round by reservation) The low-beamed restaurant with sheep and goat pelts around the walls at this well-established place is like eating in a cosy barn. The hotel also arranges horse treks of four to seven days (from €595 and €1010 respectively, including full board). It's about 3km south of Accous and just off the main road.

Lescun

It's worth risking vertigo along the steeply hairpinned, 5.5km detour south of Bedous to the mountain village of Lescun (900m) for jaw-dropping westerly views of the Cirque de Lescun, an amphitheatre of jagged limestone mountains, backed by the 2504m Pic d'Anie.

WALKING

Several great walks start from Lescun. For a day walk with spectacular views back over the Vallée de Lescun and the distinctive Pic du Midi d'Ossau (2884m), follow the GR10 northwest via the Refuge de Labérouat and along the base of Les Orgues de Camplong (Camplong Organ Pipes) up to the Cabane

ECOFESTIVAL

Some 30% of the Pyrenees is agricultural, compared to just 3% on average of the nation as a whole. Animals graze naturally, production is still small-scale and artisan, and products are made directly on the farms and sold locally. These generations-old traditions mean that sustainability and 'green' practices are already entrenched in the Pyrenean way of life, hence measures like renewable energy and solar power, which are gaining ground in more populated areas, are slow to catch on here. But the natural environment is celebrated in the Vallée d'Aspe during **Les Phonies Bergères** (www.phoniesbergeres.fr, in French; May of even-numbered years). This three-day festival features unique art exhibits set in nature, such as giant impressions created by mown mountainside grass, various sculptures and paintings, as well as ecothemed concerts and performance art.

BEARS, OH MY!

In 2004 in the Vallée d'Aspe, a boar hunter shot the one animal that might (with a great deal of luck) have ensured the genetic survival of the Pyrenean bear. 'In self-defence', he claimed, maintaining that the bear charged him. France was in uproar; even then-President Chirac weighed in, declaring it 'a great loss for French and European biodiversity'.

So the Pyrenean brown bear is emphatically dead. But over the past decade-and-a-half, bears have been imported from Slovenia, released, and have now bred successfully. Today, between 15 and 20 brown bears roam the Pyrenees. (Tragically, in 2007 one of them was killed by a car on the road between Argelèse-Gazost and Lourdes.)

The reintroduction of bears is not universally welcomed, though, particularly in the western Pyrenees, where free-roaming sheep are bred for meat (as opposed to fenced sheep producing cheese as in the east). Some 124 sheep were killed and around 15 beehives destroyed by bears in 2007. Effective protection requires nightly vigils or the construction of kilometres of fencing to protect flocks. As one valley resident told us, 'It's easy for people to sit in their offices in Paris and care about the bears, but they're not out here trying to protect their sheep.'

As bear numbers increase, so too does the controversy. You'll see slogans daubed on rocks, such as '*Non aux ours*' (No to the bears) or '*Pas d'ours*' (No bears), which proliferate throughout the valleys. But the bears still have fans, as evidenced by occasional signs of support such as '*Bonne année et longue vie aux ours!*' (Happy New Year and long life to the bears!).

du Cap de la Baigt, a *fromagerie* (open only in summer) where you can buy cheese directly from the shepherd.

SLEEPING & EATING

Gîte & Camping du Lauzart (☎ 05 59 34 51 77; campinglauzart@wanadoo.fr; camping for 2 people €10.40; ⏰ May–mid-Sep) Spacious, friendly and beautifully situated, 1.5km southwest of the village, the on-site *gîte* has dorm beds for €11 to €12.

Maison de la Montagne (☎ 05 59 34 79 14; t.croquefer@tiscali.fr; per person €15, half board €30) An old barn has been atmospherically converted into this cosy, rustic *gîte*, where rooms sleep four or five. The owner, a qualified guide, leads mountain walks.

Chambre d'Hôte Pic d'Anie (☎ 05 59 34 71 54; www.vallee-aspe.com/hebergement/pic-anie, in French; r €53; ⏰ mid-Jun–mid-Sep) In the village itself, this summertime-only *chambre d'hôte* has five simple, well-maintained rooms.

Au Château d'Arance (☎ 05 59 34 75 50; www.auchateaudarance.com, in French; r €58-63) From the hamlet of Cette-Eygun, 12km from Lescun, climb eastwards up a narrow, winding lane for 2.25km to reach this intimate 13th-century castle. There are eight rooms, one of which is wheelchair accessible. Its restaurant (*menus* €16 and €26) is equally captivating, and the sweeping view of the valley below from the terrace makes a sundowner taste all the sweeter.

Etsaut & Borce

The twin villages of Etsaut and Borce are set back on either side of the N134, 11km south of Bedous. Both are popular bases for higher-elevation walks. The **Maison du Parc National des Pyrénées** (Park Information Centre; ☎ 05 59 34 88 30; ⏰ 10.30am-12.30pm & 2-6.30pm May-Oct) is in the old train station in Etsaut (hours can vary). For more information on the area, visit www.haute-aspe.net (in French).

Up the hill, the trim little hamlet of Borce has been restored and documented with care yet it's still a living community, just the right side of twee.

One route for medieval pilgrims heading for Santiago de Compostela (nowadays the GR653 long-distance trail) was via the Vallée d'Aspe, through Borce and over the Col du Somport. **Hospitalet de St-Jacques de Compostelle** (☎ 05 59 34 88 99; admission free; ⏰ 10am-6.30pm) in Borce is a tiny museum, housed in a former pilgrims' lodging and 15th-century chapel. Pop €2 in the slot for 20 minutes of haunting plainsong.

Espace Animalier (☎ 05 59 34 89 33; adult/child €8/4.60; ⏰ 9.30am-7pm Jun-Sep, 1.30-6pm Apr, May, Oct & Nov) is a large open area above the village where three brown bears together with izards, roe deer, marmots and mouflons (wild mountain sheep) live in semicaptivity – though authorities, under pressure from local herders, did veto plans to introduce a small pack of wolves.

WALKING

For a challenging half-day walk, join the GR10 in Borce or Etsaut and follow it south to **Fort du Portalet**, a 19th-century fortress used as a prison in WWII by the Germans and the Vichy government. In summer, two- to three-hour tours (€3; English tours possible) are organised through the tourist office in Bedous. From the fort, head east to negotiate the Chemin de la Mâture, a vertiginous path originally hacked into the vertical cliff face to allow bullock trains to transport timber for ships' masts from the upper slopes.

To lighten the load, Rand'en Âne, run by **La Garbure** (☎ 05 59 34 88 98; www.garbure.net, in French), can line you up with a donkey (per hour/half-/full-day €11/23/35).

SLEEPING & EATING

La Garbure (☎ 05 59 34 88 98; www.garbure.net, in French; per person €11.50, half board €23.50) This popular *gîte d'étape*, down the alleyway beside Etsaut's parish church, has donkeys to rent and can arrange a host of other outdoor activities. The owners have mountains of info about local walks. There's a kitchen for self-caterers and even free wi-fi. Rooms accommodate between two and eight people.

The same family also runs **La Maison de l'Ours** (which has the same rates and hours as La Garbure) in the village square. In July and August you can sit on its terrace and savour its lip-smacking homemade ice cream.

VALLÉE D'OSSAU

The River Ossau makes a 60km journey from the watershed at Col du Pourtalet (1794m) to its confluence with the Aspe at Oloron-Ste-Marie. The Vallée d'Ossau, through which the river cuts a swath, is one of contrasts. The lower northern reaches, as far as Laruns, are broad, green and pastoral. As it cuts more deeply and more steeply into the Pyrenees, it becomes narrow, confined, wooded and looming before broadening out again near the hamlet of Gabas.

MAPS & BOOKS

The most practical general walking map of the area is the 1:50,000-scale *Béarn: Pyrénées Carte No 3,* published by Rando Éditions. For more detail, consult three IGN 1:25,000-scale Top 25 maps – numbers 1547OT *Ossau,* 1647OT *Vignemale* and 1546ET *Laruns.*

The tourist office produces *Randonnées en Vallée d'Ossau* (€7), describing 30 signed walks between 5km and 16km long, plus five mountain-bike routes. The national-park visitor centre stocks *Randonnées dans le Parc National des Pyrénées: Vallée d'Ossau* (€6.40), describing 14 more challenging walks in the area, supported by 1:50,000-scale maps.

Information

La Maison de la Vallée d'Ossau Office de Tourisme (☎ 05 59 05 31 41; ossau.tourisme@wanadoo.fr; place de La Mairie, Laruns; 🕑 9am-noon & 2-6pm Mon-Sat, 9am-noon Sun & public holidays, plus 2-6pm Sun Jul & Aug) On Laruns' main square, dispensing valley-wide information.

National Park Visitor Centre (☎ 05 59 05 41 59; pnpossau@espaces-naturels.fr; 🕑 9am-noon & 2-5.30pm Jun-Sep, Tue-Sat only Oct-May) Beside the tourist office.

Activities

The valley's tourist office, La Maison de la Vallée d'Ossau Office de Tourisme, can reserve a host of activities including summertime caving, climbing, kayaking and rafting, and winter snowshoe treks and guided cross-country ski outings.

Getting There & Around

Citram Pyrénées (☎ 05 59 27 22 22) runs buses from Pau to Laruns (€4, one hour, two to four daily).

SNCF trains from Pau stop at Buzy-en-Béarn from where there are three onward bus connections daily as far as Laruns (40 minutes).

During school holidays, **Transports Canonge** (☎ 05 59 05 30 31) runs a morning and an evening bus between Laruns and Artouste-Fabrèges (€2 return, 40 minutes, daily). The summer service continues as far as Col du Pourtalet.

For scenic routes between the Ossau and Aspe valleys, see the boxed text, p722.

Falaise aux Vautours

The gliding flight of the griffon vulture *(Gyps folvus)* is once more a familiar sight over the Pyrenees. It feeds exclusively on carrion, fulfilling the role of alpine dustman.

The 82-hectare protected area of the Falaise aux Vautours was originally a haven for 10 griffon-vulture pairs nesting in the limestone cliffs above the villages. Now there are more than 120 couples, plus various other raptors – notably a couple of Egyptian vultures which come back each spring; miniature cameras beam images from the heart of their nest.

La Falaise aux Vautours (Cliff of the Vultures; ☎ 05 59 82 65 49; www.falaise-aux-vautours.com, in French;

adult/child €7/5; ⌚ 10.30am-12.30pm & 2-6.30pm Jun-Aug, 2-5pm Apr & other school holidays, 2-6pm May & Sep) in Aste-Béon shows live, big-screen, round-the-clock images from nests on the cliffs 500m higher up; you can peek in on nesting, hatching and feeding in real time. There's also a good display about vultures, with captions in English.

Laruns

pop 1500 / elevation 536m

Laruns, 6km south of Aste-Béon and 37km from Pau, is the valley's principal village.

SLEEPING & EATING

Campsites sprawl nearby, though you're often hemmed in by caravans and mobile homes.

Camping du Valentin (☎ 05 59 05 39 33; per person/site €3.35/7.05; ⌚ May-Oct) By contrast, this highly recommended campsite, 2.4km south of the village beside the D918, has separate zones for mobile homes, caravans and family tents. Overlooking all, and enjoying the best of the impressive views northwards, is a grassy area for lightweight campers.

Refuge-Auberge L'Embaradère (☎ 05 59 05 41 88; 13 av de la Gare; dm €15, half board €29; ⌚ closed 1-21 May) This long-standing walkers' budget option is a reasonable bet but you'll need to plan ahead as there are no meals or self-catering facilities.

Hôtel de France (☎ 05 59 05 33 71; www.vallee-ossau.com/hotel/france, in French; av de la Gare; r €50, with shared bathroom €29) Although no longer young (and all the more characterful for that), this place is spotless and spruce. It serves real jam for breakfast, unlike the usual sealed plastic goo. The friendly family owners readily dispense information about hiking opportunities.

L'Arrégalet (☎ 05 59 05 35 47; 37 rue du Bourguet; menus €15-30; ⌚ lunch Tue-Sun) Sit out on the terrace of this highly recommended place about 200m northeast of Laruns' main square, which smokes its own trout, bakes all its bread and marinates its own duck foie gras in Armagnac. The tempting desserts (many of them cream-based) are all homemade, too.

Eaux-Bonnes

If you've a penchant for faded glamour (with an emphasis on faded), take the briefest of detours to this sad spa that got left behind. Frequented by no less than the Empress Eugénie herself in its 19th-century heyday, it's now all but a ghost resort. The once magnificent Hôtel des Princes stares unseeing, all shutters closed, across the oval square at Hôtel du Parc, once its keenest rival, and now closed over 40 years. More recently, some slick, quick-buck cartel took over the casino – and promptly dropped the place when it failed to squeeze out the profit it had banked on. The **tourist office** (☎ 05 59 05 33 08; ⌚ 9am-12.30pm & 1.30-6pm Mon-Fri year-round plus 9am-12.30pm & 1.30-6pm Sat May-Oct, 10am-noon & 3-6pm Sun Jul & Aug), God bless it, squats lonely in what was once the town's bandstand.

The valley's largest ski resort of Gourette is a mere 10-minute drive away. Even higher, the col beyond is a favourite torture point of the Tour de France.

Gabas

Tiny Gabas, with fewer than 50 souls, is now mainly a trekking base, 13km south of Laruns. Its equally small-scale 12th-century **chapel** is the only vestige of what was once a monastery, the very last Chemin de St-Jacques pilgrim hostel before the Spanish frontier. Pick up a hunk of tangy *fromage d'Ossau*, made here in the high mountains from ewe's milk and matured in this very hamlet.

The CAF **refuge** (☎ 05 59 05 33 14; half board per person €26-31; ⌚ Jun-Sep & school holidays, Sat & Sun only other times, closed Nov & Dec), 500m south of Gabas, offers cheery accommodation in rooms for four to 12, and a culinary reputation that extends way beyond the valley; Marie-France's homemade desserts are to die for.

Hôtel-Restaurant le Biscaü (☎ 05 59 05 31 37; fax 05 59 05 43 23; d €36-46; menus around €15; ⌚ mid-Dec–Oct) Le Biscaü is the most comfortable option in Gabas, offering hearty cuisine (save room for the cheese course; the owner himself matures cheeses brought in by the local shepherds).

From the CAF *refuge*, a 3.5km forest track brings you to Lac de Bious-Artigues (1420m) and a superb view southeast to Pic du Midi d'Ossau and southwest to Pic d'Ayous.

Le Petit Train d'Artouste

Winter skiers and summer holidaymakers converge upon charmless lakeside Artouste-Fabrèges (1250m), 6km by road east of Gabas, to squeeze into the **cable car** (return fare €7; ⌚ 9.30am-6pm), which soars up the flanks of the 2032m Pic de la Sagette. Between June and September, an open-topped **train** (☎ reservations 05 59 05 36 99; www.trainartouste.com, in French; adult/child €21/17; ⌚ half-hourly 9am-5pm Jul & Aug, hourly 9am-3pm Jun & Sep), built for dam workers in the 1920s, runs for 10km at 2000m from the upper cable-car station to Lac d'Artouste

(1991m). Views are heart-stopping and the 'little train' tucks away over 100,000 passengers in its four months of operation. Allow a good four hours.

There's a seasonal **tourist office** (☎ 05 59 05 34 00; 9am-noon & 2-7pm Mon-Sat, 9am-noon Sun Jun-Sep & Christmas-Mar) beside the cable car.

CAUTERETS

pop 1300 / elevation 930m

Crowded in by slopes towering to 2800m, the thermal spa and ski resort of Cauterets, less than 30km south of Lourdes, is a superb summertime base for exploring the forests, meadows, lakes and streams of the Parc National des Pyrénées. In winter Cauterets is doused with snow; it's usually the first of France's Pyrenean ski stations to open and the last to close.

Information

Laundrette (19 rue Richelieu; 8am-8pm)

Maison de la Presse (8 place Maréchal Foch) Stocks walking maps.

Maison du Parc National des Pyrénées (☎ 05 62 92 52 56; place de la Gare; 9.30am-noon & 3-7pm Jun–mid-Sep, 9.30am-noon & 3-6pm Mon-Fri mid-Sep–Apr) Sells walking maps, has an impressive free exhibition on Pyrenean flora and fauna, and shows park-related films. Organises guided walks (€9.15/15.25 per half-/full day in July and August; free for children under 16).

Pont d'Espagne Information Office (☎ 05 62 92 52 19; Dec-Sep, hours vary)

Tourist Office (☎ 05 62 92 50 50; www.cauterets.com, in French; place Maréchal Foch; 9am-12.30pm & 2-7pm Mon-Sat, 9am-noon & 3-6pm Sun school holidays, otherwise 9am-noon & 2-6pm Mon-Sat, 9am-noon Sun, closed Sun Nov & May)

Sights & Activities

WALKING

Dozens of walks start right from town or from Pont d'Espagne at the end of the spectacular D920 road, 8km south, 600m higher and accessible in season by shuttle bus (p730).

The area west of Cauterets is covered by IGN's 1:25,000-scale Top 25 map No 1647OT *Vignemale;* land east of town features on No 1748OT *Gavarnie*. Rando Éditions' *Bigorre Carte No 4* covers the region at 1:50,000.

The national park produces *Randonnées dans le Parc National des Pyrénées: Vallée de Cauterets* (in French; €6.40), which maps 15 walks. The tourist office carries *Sentiers du Lavaudon* (in French; €5), outlining seven easy walks in the area.

For a pleasant day walk from Cauterets (allow around six hours), follow the Vallée de Lutour southwards as far as Lac d'Estom, where the lakeside *refuge* offers refreshments.

From the giant car park at **Pont d'Espagne** (where you can rent a multimedia guide to the valley's flora and fauna in summer for €6), Chemin des Cascades passes by a series of spectacular waterfalls as it drops northwards towards Cauterets.

Heading south from Pont d'Espagne, you've a choice of two valleys, each different in character. Following the Gave de Gaube upstream through a pine wood brings you to the popular **Lac de Gaube** and, nearby, Hôtellerie de Gaube, where you can sip a drink or recharge with a snack or midday *menus* (around €15) on the terrace, overlooking a waterfall. Three hours, not counting breaks, is generous for this out-and-back walk.

A longer trek up the gentler, more open **Vallée de Marcadau** leads to **Refuge Wallon** (☎ 05 62 92 64 28; dm €15, half board €36.90; Feb–mid-Apr & Jun-Sep) at 1866m. Allow about five hours for the round trip.

SKIING

The shining new Télécabine du Lys cabins shoot up to 2000 skiers per hour from Cauterets to the 21-run **Cirque du Lys**. The 36km of runs here, ranging from 2415m to 1850m, are best for beginner and intermediate **downhill skiers**. Lift passes cost €27 per day or €140 for six days. In summer it morphs into a mountain-biking area, including a kids' bike park with a 1500m drop in altitude.

Pont d'Espagne (1450m) is primarily a **cross-country skiing** area. From it, 37km of maintained trails, paralleled in their lower reaches by a 6km circuit for walkers and snowshoers, lead up the Vallée du Marcadau. A one-day trail pass with/without cable-car transport costs €7.30/8.30.

Several shops in Cauterets hire out ski equipment. Typical prices per day are downhill €12 to €20, snowboards €19 to €25 and cross-country gear €8 to €10.

SNOWSHOE TREKS

Several mountain guides organise day and half-day treks into spectacular scenery. Typical prices are around €21 to €26 for a three-hour outing and €29 to €32 for a full day including transport and hire of snowshoes and poles. Ask at the tourist office or try **Bureau des Guides** (☎ 06 12 94 81 88).

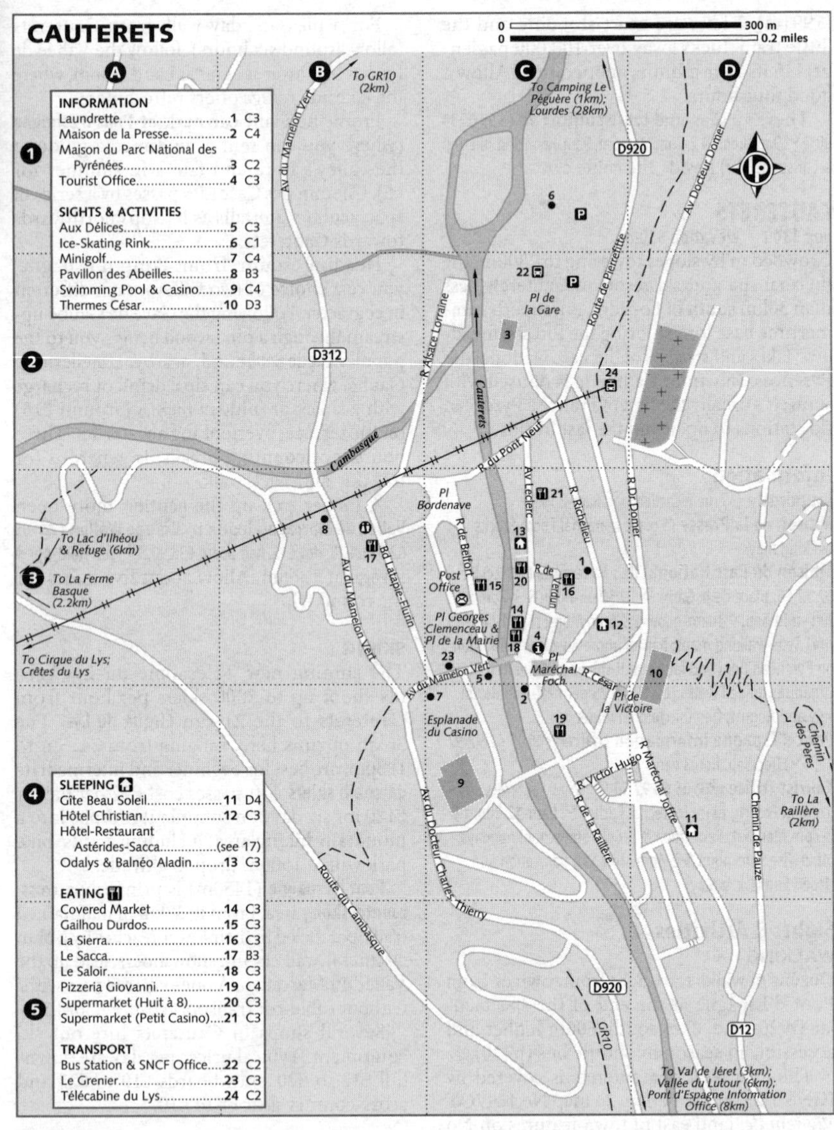

THERMAL SPAS

Cauterets' hot springs, bubbling from the earth at 36°C to 53°C, have attracted visitors keen to soak up the springs' health-giving properties since the 19th century. Some use artificially heated water, but for the real deal try the variety of water-based facilities (starting from €8) at **Thermes César** (☎ 05 62 92 14 20; www.thermesdecauterets.com, in French; rue Docteur Domer; ⏲ Feb-Nov).

OTHER ACTIVITIES

Esplanade du Casino and Esplanade des Œufs (Egg Esplanade, named in an age before public-relations officers and spin doctors, for the stench the sulphurous waters gave off) are

A LITTLE SWEETENER

When the 19th-century *curistes* (those seeking a cure) in Cauterets had swallowed their daily dose of sulphurous spa water, they – and their nearest and dearest – were inflicted instead with halitosis. But an enterprising villager set about making a boiled sweet that would mask it.

Brightly coloured, these pillow-shaped, striped *berlingots* are made by a quartet of small producers in Cautrets including **Aux Délices** (☎ 05 62 92 07 08; www.berlingots.com, in French; place Clemenceau). They'll always give you a sample and if you call by in the late afternoon you can usually see a batch being made.

home to cafés, a swimming pool, **minigolf** and the town's large **casino** (☎ 05 62 92 52 14; www.casino-cauterets.fr, in French; esplanade des Œufs). It would be an even more lovely little open space for promenading if they'd banish the parked cars.

Pavillon des Abeilles (☎ 05 62 92 50 66; 23bis av du Mamelon Vert; admission free; 🕒 10.30am-12.30pm & 2.30-7pm Mon-Sat school holidays, otherwise 3-7pm Wed-Sat) is all about bees, with a glass-sided hive, video and honey of every possible flavour.

Cauterets also has an **ice-skating rink** (place de la Gare; adult/child €8/5.50).

Sleeping

Cauterets has a wide-ranging choice of accommodation in all categories. The tourist office can also provide details of apartments to rent by the week.

Camping Le Péguère (☎ 05 62 92 52 91; www.les-campings.com/peguere; per site €10.32-13, cabins per person with/without bathrooms from €25/35; 🕒 May-Sep) This grassy, shady campsite, 1.5km north of town on the D920, has some choice pitches right beside the Gave de Cauterets, and a variety of bright, clean chalets and cabins available on a weekend or weekly basis.

Gîte Beau Soleil (☎ 05 62 92 53 52; gite.beau.soleil@wanadoo.fr; 25 rue Maréchal Joffre; per person incl breakfast €22-23, half board €36-37; 🕒 closed Nov–first snow) The Beau Soleil has the comfort of a hotel as well as the friendly informality of a *refuge*. Beds are in spick-and-span en-suite doubles or quad-shares, and there's a green rear garden, a large lounge, and a kitchen for self-caterers.

Hôtel-Restaurant Astérides-Sacca (☎ 05 62 92 50 02; www.asterides-sacca.com; 11 bd Latapie-Flurin; r €38-85; 🕒 closed 10 Oct–20 Dec) On one of the Pyrenees' prettiest streets, lined with 19th-century buildings and often used as a film set, is this venerable, family-run establishment. The checked-fabric rooms have a more contemporary feel than the pastel, floral ones but all are spacious and appealing. Half- and full-board options let you take full advantage of its renowned restaurant (below).

Odalys & Balnéo Aladin (☎ 05 62 92 60 00; www.hotelbalneoaladin.com, in French; 11 av Général Leclerc; d incl breakfast €106-150, half board per person €65-114; 🕒 Christmas–mid-May & Jun-Sep) The Aladin also doubles as a spa (though with artificially heated water; also open to nonguests) and offers every luxury, including a fitness centre and a sauna. The minimum four-night stay is negotiable outside peak periods, but half board is obligatory during the ski season.

Hôtel Christian (☎ 05 62 92 50 04; www.hotel-christian.fr, in French; 10 rue Richelieu; r incl breakfast €66-80; 🕒 Dec-Sep) Rooms are large and comfortable at this friendly hotel, in the hands of the same Cauterets family for three generations. There's a charming rear garden, and wi-fi.

Eating & Drinking

Dining prices are competitive around town.

Pizzeria Giovanni (☎ 05 62 92 57 80; 5 rue de la Raillère; pizza around €9, menus around €15; 🕒 lunch & dinner daily school holidays, otherwise dinner only, closed Wed & mid-May–mid-Jun & Nov–mid-Dec; 💻) Pizzas (eat in or take away) are superior, steaks are hearty and generous and the home-baked desserts are a dream. Bonus: diners can log on to the internet for free (nondiners pay €3 per hour).

La Sierra (☎ 05 62 42 68 97; 8 rue Verdun; menus around €15; 🕒 Thu-Tue) Tucked away down a side street, this intimate little place consistently offers a variety of good-value deals such as a bottomless *garbure*.

En So de Bedau (☎ 05 62 92 60 21; 11 rue de la Raillère; menus €15-20; 🕒 seasonal hours vary) This very regional place is a valley favourite for tapas accompanied by good beers and wines, or a hearty mountain meal.

Le Sacca (☎ 05 62 92 50 02; www.asterides-sacca.com; 11 bd Latapie-Flurin; menus €16.50-42; 🕒 lunch & dinner, closed 10 Oct–20 Dec) By common consent the finest place to dine in Cauterets (read: book ahead). Chef Jean-Marc Canton's cuisine blends classical French fare and artistic presentation with subtle mountain flavours. Kids are welcomed warmly with a well-priced *menu* (€10) too. For accommodation here, see left.

La Ferme Basque (☎ 05 62 92 54 32; rte de Cambasque; ⌚ seasonal hours vary) With a plunging view of Cauterets from its terrace, this place 4km west of town by road makes a great spot for a daylight drink.

SELF-CATERING

Follow your nose to Cauterets' **covered market** (av Leclerc; ⌚ daily during school holidays, individual traders' hours vary), where a couple of stalls do tasty takeaway dishes while another sells wonderful mountain cheeses. Regional cheeses and jams are also sold at **Le Saloir** (av Leclerc).

Still on av Leclerc, you'll spot two small supermarkets, **Huite à 8** and **Petit Casino**.

Gailhou Durdos (rue de Belfort), opposite the post office, has a rich selection of local wines and specialities.

Getting There & Away

The last train steamed out of Cauterets' magnificent, all-wood station in 1947. Like something left over from a cowboy film set, it now serves as the **bus station** (☎ 05 62 92 53 70; place de la Gare).

SNCF buses run between Cauterets and Lourdes train station (€7, one hour, at least five daily).

Getting Around

BICYCLE

Le Grenier (4 av du Mamelon Vert; ⌚ closed Nov & May) rents out winter ski equipment and mountain bikes (per half-/full day from €16/25) in summer.

BUS

Navette d'Espagne is a shuttle service (single/return €4/6.50) between the bus station and Pont d'Espagne during the ski season (twice daily) and in summer (six times daily).

CABLE CAR

The fast new **Télécabine du Lys** operates mid-June to mid-September and from December to the end of April. It rises over 900m to the Cirque du Lys, where in summer you can catch the Grand Barbat chairlift up to Crêtes du Lys (2400m). A return trip costs €8/6 per adult/child to Cirque du Lys or €10/7.50 including the chairlift.

TAXI

Ring **Bordenave Frères** (☎ 05 62 92 53 68) for a taxi. The trip between Cauterets and Pont d'Espagne costs €16 one-way.

VALLÉE DES GAVES & AROUND

Gentle and pastoral, the Vallée des Gaves (Valley of the Mountain Streams) extends south from Lourdes to Pierrefitte-Nestalas. Here the valley forks: the narrow, rugged eastern tine twists via Gavarnie while the western prong corkscrews up to Cauterets.

Pic du Midi de Bigorre

Once the preserve of astronomers and scientists, the Pic du Midi (2877m) is now accessible to all by **cable car** (☎ 08 25 00 28 77; adult/student/child €25/22/15; ⌚ daily Feb & Jun–late Sep, closed last 3 weeks Nov, call for closing days rest of yr). Leaving from the ski resort of La Mongie (1800m), it gives access to one of the Pyrenees' most soul-stirring panoramas.

Gavarnie

pop 165 / elevation 1360m

In winter, Gavarnie, 52km south of Lourdes at the end of the D921, offers limited downhill and decent cross-country skiing plus snowshoe treks. In summer it's a popular take-off point for walkers – consult the IGN Top 25 map No 1748OT *Gavarnie* or the National Park pack *Randonnées dans le Parc National des Pyrénées: Vallée de Luz* (€10) for the rich menu of routes.

The most frequented trail, accessible to all (in winter too, with skis or snowshoes), leads to the **Cirque de Gavarnie**, a breathtaking rock amphitheatre, 1500m high, fringed by ice-capped peaks. The round-trip walk to its base takes two hours. Between Easter and October you can clip-clop along on a horse or donkey (€24 round trip). In late July, Gavarnie hosts an **arts festival** in the dramatic setting of the Cirque.

The helpful **tourist office** (☎ 05 62 92 49 10; www.gavarnie.com; ⌚ 8.30am-12.30pm & 2-6.30pm daily school holidays, otherwise 9am-12.30pm & 2-6.30pm Mon-Sat) is at the northern entrance to the village. You'll find the **national park office** (☎ 05 62 92 42 48; ⌚ 9.30am-noon & 1.30-5.30pm Mon-Fri, 9am-noon & 1.30-6.30pm daily school holidays) 200m beyond.

Camping Le Pain de Sucre (☎ 05 62 92 47 55; www.camping-gavarnie.com; per person/site €3.60/3.80; ⌚ mid-Dec–mid-Apr & Jun-Sep) enjoys a lovely riverside spot a little north of town.

Hôtel Le Marboré (☎ 05 62 92 40 40; www.lemarbore.com; half board per person €62; ⌚ mid-Dec–mid-Nov; ☒) stands out among Gavarnie's few overnight options as much for its acclaimed restaurant as for the comfort of its rooms. In a characterful, thoroughly modernised, 19th-century

NO PASARÁN!

'No pasarán', say the banners and posters around Lourdes and the Vallée des Gaves: 'They shall not pass', echoing the famous Republican slogan of the Spanish Civil War. The long environmental campaign to save the Vallée d'Aspe was lost and the tunnel de Somport now allows easy truck access to the valley. The battlefield has now moved two valleys eastward, to Vallée des Gaves, as residents and environmentalists resist plans for the Traversée Centrale des Pyrénées (TCP), or Central Pyrenees Crossing.

The TCP is still being actively pursued by the governments of the Midi-Pyrenees region and of Aragón, over the Spanish frontier, despite the opposition of local councils in the valley. What's proposed is a 42km tunnel burrowed under Vignemale, France's highest Pyrenean peak. Should it go ahead, it will facilitate land crossings into Spain, with more than 250 trains set to use this twin-track rail-freight link per day. But not if its opponents get their way.

building, it's family-run and friendly. Kick back in Le Swan, its pub, or work out in its fitness centre. Half board is compulsory in the ski season and high summer.

During school holidays only, two SNCF buses run daily between Gavarnie and Luz-St-Sauveur (€7), from where there are connections to Lourdes (€7).

Cirque de Troumouse

From Gèdre, 6.5km north of Gavarnie, a toll road (€4 per vehicle) winds southeast up a desolate valley into the Pyrenees to the base of the wild and little-explored Cirque de Troumouse. Snows permitting, the road is open between May and October.

UPPER GARONNE VALLEY

St-Bertrand de Comminges

On an isolated hillock, St-Bertrand and its **Cathédrale Ste-Marie** (adult/child incl audioguide in English €4/1.50; 9am-7pm Mon-Sat, 2-7pm Sun May-Sep, 10am-noon & 2-5pm Mon-Sat, 2-5pm Sun Oct-Apr) loom over the Vallée de Garonne and the much pillaged remains of the Gallo-Roman town of Lugdunum Convenarum, where you can wander at will for free.

The splendid Renaissance oak choir stalls, carved in 1535 by local artisans, sit below the soaring Gothic east end of the cathedral.

Bagnères de Luchon

pop 3032 / elevation 630m

Bagnères de Luchon (or simply Luchon) is a trim little town of gracious 19th-century buildings, expanded to accommodate the *curistes* who came to take the waters at its splendid spa.

Tourist Office (☎ 05 61 79 21 21; www.luchon.com; 18 allées d'Étigny; 9am-7pm daily Jul & Aug, 9am-7pm Mon-Sat, 9am-12.30pm & 2.30-6pm Sun Dec-Mar, 9am-12.30pm & 1.30-7pm Sep-Nov & Apr-Jun)

SIGHTS & ACTIVITIES

Once only for the ailing, the **Thermes** (Health Spa; ☎ 05 61 79 22 97; Apr–mid-Oct), at the southern end of allées d'Étigny, now also offers relaxation and fitness sessions for weary skiers and walkers, the mainstay of the town's tourism-based economy. It's €14 to loll in the scented steam of the 160m-long underground *vaporarium*, then dunk yourself in the caressing 32°C waters of its pool. (Specific seasonal opening hours are exceptionally complex, even for France, so call ahead or check with the tourist office.) Follow this with a flutter in the elegant surroundings of the casino and you'll have had a good night out.

The stylish allées d'Étigny, flanked by cafés and restaurants, link place Joffre with the Thermes. Just to the west of this boulevard is the base of the **cabin lift** (single/return €5.90/7.90) that hauls you up to **Superbagnères** (1860m), the starting point for winter skiing and summer walking and mountain biking. It operates daily in the ski season and during July and August (weekends only during most other months).

Cycling

Although you'll huff and puff, the area is rich in opportunities for mountain biking. The tourist office has copies of the free *Guide des Circuits VTT*, prepared by the local mountain-bike club, and also a miniguide to four runs starting from the top of the cabin lift. To rent a bike, see p732.

Walking

Pull on your boots and head for the hills: an amazing 250km of marked trails, ranging from gentle valley-bottom strolls to more demanding high-mountain treks, thread their way from Luchon and Superbagnères. The tourist office carries a useful free pamphlet, *Sentiers Balisés du Pays de Luchon,* and also sells the detailed *Randonnées autour de Luchon* (€10.95). Alternatively, pick up IGN 1:25,000 map No 1848OT *Bagnères de Luchon.*

Other Activities

For the full range of outdoor possibilities, ask the tourist office for a copy of its free *La Montagne Active* brochure. The skies above Superbagnères are magnificent for **parapenting**. Contact **École Soaring** (☎ 05 61 79 29 23; www.soaring.fr, in French; 31 rue Sylvie). More down-to-earth, **Pyrénées Aventure** (☎ 05 61 79 20 59; www.pyreneesaventure.com, in French; 9 rue Docteur Germès) arranges canyon clambering and guided walks.

SLEEPING & EATING

Camping Beauregard (☎ 05 61 79 30 74; camp.beauregard@wanadoo.fr; 37 av de Vénasque; adult €3.50-4, site €4-5; Apr-Oct) This is the larger and more welcoming of Luchon's two campsites. A mere 300m from Les Thermes, it's popular with *curistes.*

Hôtel des Deux Nations (☎ 05 61 79 01 71; www.hotel-des2nations.com; 5 rue Victor Hugo; r €52-58, with shared bathroom €30-35) Nearly into its second century, this hotel has been run by the same family for five generations. Rooms are comfortable and good value, but the major attraction is its restaurant (*menus* €15 to €35, closed Sunday dinner and Monday November to January), fronted by a striped awning, which serves hearty local cuisine like flaming locally reared lamb chops in gargantuan quantities.

The allées d'Étigny are packed with bars and restaurants, some fine delicatessens and the usual pizza-and-pasta joints.

Caprices d'Étigny (☎ 05 61 94 31 05; 30bis allées d'Étigny; menus €10.50-23.50; closed dinner Thu) Staffed by a young, friendly crew, this central spot does great grilled meats on its open fire.

L'Arbesquens (☎ 05 61 79 33 69; 47 allées d'Étigny; menus €11-23; closed Wed & dinner Sun) Beneath its hefty timber beams (or the steel-frame winter garden), dip into the house speciality, fondue (minimum two people), in some 17 varieties.

Self-caterers should pass by Luchon's 1897-established **market** (rue Docteur Germès; daily Apr-Oct, Wed & Sat only rest of yr).

GETTING THERE & AROUND

SNCF trains and buses run between Luchon and Montréjeau (€6.30, 50 minutes, seven daily), which has frequent connections to Toulouse (€14.90) and Pau (€16.30).

For bicycle hire, contact **Luchon Location Loisirs** (2 allées d'Étigny; from €8/12 per half-/full day).

VALLÉE DE L'ARIÈGE

The Vallée de l'Ariège offers some great pre-Pyrenean walking, caving and canoeing. Ask at any tourist office for the *Carte Touristiques: Guide Pratique,* which lists in French a host of local entrepreneurs.

Foix

pop 9700

In the crook of the confluence of the Rivers Ariège and Arget, Foix merits a small detour from the N20 to visit its castle, an 11th-century church and streets lined with medieval, half-timbered houses on the west bank of the Ariège.

The **tourist office** (☎ 05 61 65 12 12; www.ot-foix.fr, in French; 9am-7pm Mon-Sat, 9.30am-12.30pm & 2-6pm Sun Jul & Aug, 9am-noon & 2-6pm Mon-Sat Sep-Jun) is near the covered market on cours Gabriel Fauré, the wide main thoroughfare.

SIGHTS

The triple-towered **Château des Comtes de Foix** (☎ 05 34 09 83 83; www.sesta.fr, in French; adult/student/child €4.30/3.20/2.20; 9.45am-6.30pm Jul & Aug, 9.45am-noon & 2-6pm Jun & Sep, 10.30am-noon & 2-5.30pm Wed-Sun Oct-Dec & Feb-May, Sat & Sun Jan, daily in school holidays) stands guard above the town. Constructed in the 10th century as a stronghold for the counts of Foix, it served as a prison from the 16th century onwards; look for the graffiti scratched into the stones by some hapless inmate. Today it houses a small **archaeological museum**. Guided tours in English depart at 1.30pm in July and August.

ACTIVITIES

Canyon clambering, canoeing, mountain biking and hiking can all be arranged through **Pyrénévasion** (☎ 05 61 65 01 10; www.pyrenevasion.com). The tourist office sells *Le Pays de Foix à Pied* (€7.80), an excellent guide to short and more challenging walks in the area.

SLEEPING & EATING

Camping du Lac (☎ 05 61 65 11 58; www.campingdulac.com, in French; per person €3-8, car free-€3; year-round;)

Beside the RN20 2.5km north of Foix, this attractive campsite has a good restaurant serving hearty mountain fare as well as tasty pizzas.

Hôtel Restaurant Lons (☎ 05 34 09 28 00; www.hotel-lons-foix.com; 6 place Dutilh; d from €52.50) Several of the colourful, good-value rooms at this former coaching inn overlook the river, and bike rental can be arranged for forays into the mountains. The attached restaurant (lunch/dinner *menus* from €11/14; closed from late December to late January) offers similar river views through its picture windows.

GETTING THERE & AWAY

Regular trains connect Toulouse and Foix (€12.30, 1¼ hours, 10-plus daily).

Around Foix

Beneath **Labouiche**, 6km northwest of Foix, flows Europe's longest navigable underground river, Rivière Souterraine de Labouiche. You can take a spectacular 1500m, 75-minute **boat trip** (☎ 05 61 65 04 11; adult/child €8.50/6.50; 9.30am-5.15pm Jul & Aug, 10-11.15am & 2-5.15pm Apr-Jun & Sep, 10-11.15am & 2-4.30pm Sat & Sun Oct–mid-Nov) along part of its length.

Les Forges de Pyrène (☎ 05 34 09 30 60; adult/child €7.50/4; 10am-7pm Jul & Aug, 1.30-6pm Apr–mid-Nov, plus 10am-noon Jun & Sep), in Montgaillard, 4.5km south of Foix, is a living museum of Ariège folk tradition with its own blacksmith, a baker, a cobbler and a basket weaver. Spread over 5 hectares, it illustrates a host of lost or dying trades such as glass-blowing, tanning, thatching and nail-making.

Ax-les-Thermes

pop 1500 / elevation 720m

Ax-les-Thermes flourishes as a small skiing and walking base and, with over 60 hot-water springs, as a spa town. Like Foix, 43km northwest, it lies at the confluence of two rivers: the Ariège and – here's scope for confusion – the Oriège.

Several detailed walking guides (€5) are sold at the **tourist office** (☎ 05 61 64 60 60; www.vallees-ax.com, in French; av Delcassé; 9am-1pm & 2-7pm Mon-Sat, 2-6pm Sun ski season, 9am-noon & 2-6pm non–ski season, closed Sun during Nov), which also has information on the area's spas, including **Thermes du Teich** (☎ 05 61 65 86 60; treatments from €7; Easter–mid-Nov), with a pool, a sauna, a hammam and an aqua gym.

The heart of town is place du Breilh. On one side of the square is the faded elegance of the casino. On the other is the **Bassin de Ladres**, a shallow pool originally built to soothe the wounds of Knights Templar injured in the Crusades; pull off your socks and steep your feet in its waters. A couple of interesting narrow streets with overhanging buildings are tucked between place du Breilh and place Roussel.

La Petite Fringale (☎ 06 87 74 03 21; 6 rue Rigal; menus €15-30) is a popular, friendly place, down a pedestrianised alley near the Bassin de Ladres, with a small summertime terrace. It does lots of tempting cheese-based dishes, including steaming fondues.

Most trains serving Foix (see left) continue as far as Ax.

Around Ax-les-Thermes

At **Lombrives** (☎ 05 61 05 98 40; May-Sep & school holidays), 22km north of Ax on the N20 near the village of Ussat-les-Bains, is Europe's largest underground cave. Routes range from 1½ hours underground (€7.50/4.50 per adult/child) to a five-hour 'journey to the centre of the earth' (€34.70/25) by prior reservation.

Toulouse Area

Once Languedoc's traditional centre, Toulouse, not quite the Pyrenees, was hived off when regional boundaries were redrawn almost half a century ago. Geographical limbo aside, this is a land rich in historical sights, and fascinating to explore.

Toulouse itself is one of France's liveliest and fastest-growing cities. Bolstered by its booming hi-tech industries (notably aerospace; this is the epicentre of the huge Europe-wide EADS aircraft manufacturing consortium), this city is dynamic, confident and bags of fun. Party with students until dawn in its packed bars, cafés and clubs, and know that Spain is just around the corner.

In the south the Pyrenees stride out, spiky and snowcapped on the horizon in five small, historic and stunningly scenic towns: Toulouse-Lautrec's red-brick Albi, 75km northeast; the 16th-century Huguenot stronghold of Montauban, 53km north; Condom, 110km to the northwest, with its elegant 18th-century mansions and cheeky museum; Roman Auch, 77km west; and Moissac, 70km to the north, with its magnificent Abbaye St-Pierre and cloister where Chemin de St-Jacques hikers en route to Spain and Santiago de Compostela continue to picnic pilgrim-style. Delve into the quiet lanes and narrow alleys of this town and spot the odd rucksack strung from a 1st-floor window – a sure sign of a warm welcome for walkers seeking a bed for the night.

West of Toulouse city, the region of Gascony (Gascogne) rolls all the way to the Atlantic. Famous for its lush countryside, fine Gaillac wine, foie gras (fattened liver), ducks, and Armagnac liqueur, slow-paced Gascony is ideal for experiencing some of France's finest examples of medieval and Renaissance architecture – not to mention one of France's richest regional cuisines. Devote at least a day, luxuriously lazy lunch obligatory, to exploring the cluster of sleepy *bastides* (fortified medieval villages) northwest of Toulouse.

HIGHLIGHTS

- Sip an *apéro* on **place St-Pierre** (p744), catch a local band and party until dawn with Toulouse's student-busy **nightlife** (p744)
- Play astronauts at Toulouse's interactive **Cité de l'Espace** (p740)
- Grab a **bike** (p746) and go for a spin along the pea-green **Canal du Midi**, taking time out afloat at the **Buddha Boat Spa** (p740)
- Delve into the life, work and mind of an artistic master at Albi's **Musée Toulouse-Lautrec** (p748)
- Invade Condom's army of surrounding **bastides** (fortified medieval villages; p756)
- Fatten up on fattened goose and duck liver in the gastronomic village of **Gimont** (p753), not missing its seasonal Fat Market

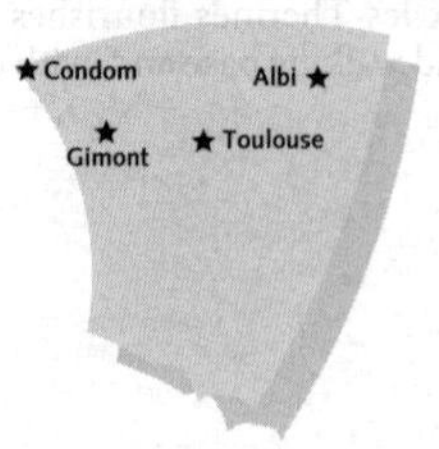

- POPULATION: 2,560,000
- AREA: 45,350 SQ KM

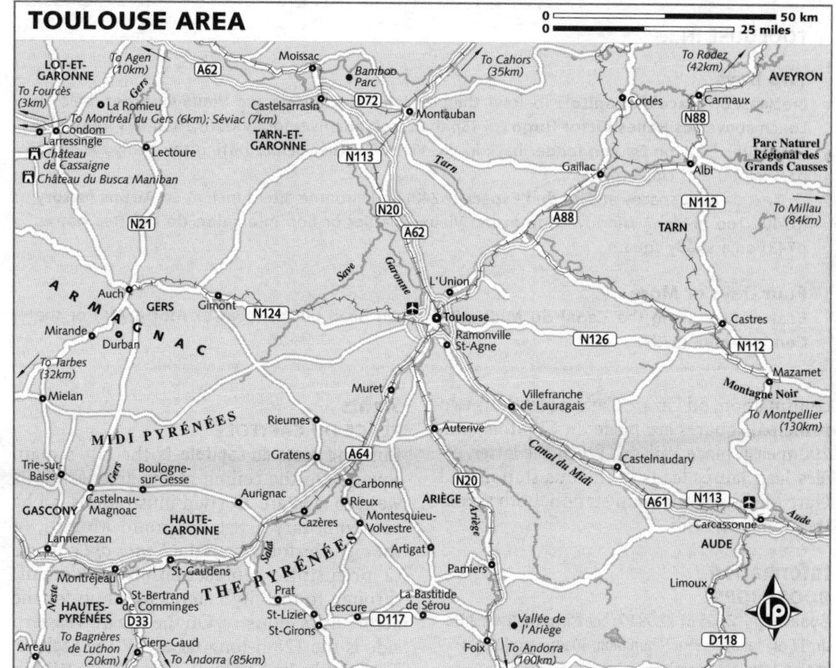

TOULOUSE

pop 437,100

From the fun 'n' funky works of contemporary art in its sleek two-line metro (take a tour; see p741) to its dynamic dining and café scene, this friendly city – pink by day, bright by night, thanks to its mirage of rose-red brick buildings – is dazzling: no surprise really given *la ville rose* (the pink city) is France's fourth-largest city.

From its narrow medieval streets and alleys to the many churches and cathedrals, Toulouse oozes a rich and tumultuous history. Its sizeable student population of 115,000 gives the place a youthful kick and injects an infectious energy into its riverside bars, live-music venues and late-night clubbing alternatives.

Two waterways slice through the city: the pea-green Canal du Midi and the mucky brown River Garonne, both peaceful and romantic any time of day.

History

Toulouse, Tolosa to the Romans, was the Visigoth capital from AD 419–507. In the 12th and 13th centuries the counts of Toulouse supported the Cathars (see p799). Three centuries later, during the Wars of Religion, the city sided with the Catholic League. Toulouse merchants grew rich in the 16th and 17th centuries from the woad (blue dye) trade, until the Portuguese began importing indigo from India. The Toulouse parliament ruled Languedoc from 1420 until the 1789 Revolution.

During WWI, Toulouse became an arms and aircraft manufacturing centre. In the 1920s, Antoine de St-Exupéry, author of *Le Petit Prince (The Little Prince)*, and other daring pilots pioneered mail flights to northwest Africa and South America, often staying in the city between sorties. After WWII, Toulouse became the nucleus of the country's aerospace industry. Passenger planes built here have included the Caravelle and Concorde as well as the 555-seat Airbus A380, and local factories also produce the Ariane space rocket.

French crooner Claude Nougaro (1929–2004), born and bred here, sang about Toulouse in the bittersweet tribute *Oh! Toulouse*.

Orientation

The heart of Toulouse is bounded by the River Garonne (west) and bd de Strasbourg and its

TOULOUSE IN...

Two Days

Breakfast on **place du Capitole** (below), then explore the **Capitole** and **Vieux Quartier** (below). Lunch above **Les Halles Victor Hugo** (p743), then cross the river for modern art at **Les Abattoirs** (opposite). Dine on Gascon fodder back in the Vieux Quartier before hitting the many excellent bars (p744) and clubs (p745).

Next day get spacey at **Cité de l'Espace** (p740) and airborne after lunch at an **Airbus factory** (p740). Too hi-tech? Window-shop in the Vieux Quartier or flop in a **salon de thé** (tea house; p743) on a shady square.

Four Days or More

Boat or bike along the **Canal du Midi** (p740), then head out of town to **Albi** (p746) or the **Condom area** (p754).

continuation, bd Lazare Carnot (east). Its two principal squares are place du Capitole and, 200m east, place Wilson. From the latter, allées Jean Jaurès leads to the bus station and Gare Matabiau, the train station, both across the Canal du Midi.

Information

BOOKSHOPS

Bookshop (☎ 05 61 22 99 92; bookshop.tlse@wanadoo.fr; 17 rue Lakanal; 🕑 2-7pm Mon, 10am-7pm Tue-Sat) English-language bookshop.

Ombres Blanches (☎ 05 34 45 53 33; www.ombres-blanches.fr; 48-50 rue Gambetta; 🕑 10am-7pm Mon-Sat) Maps and travel guides.

INTERNET ACCESS

Laverie des Lois (☎ 05 61 23 71 45; 19 rue des Lois; http://laveriedeslois.spaces.live.com; per hr €4; 🕑 cybercafé 11am-9pm Tue-Sat, laundrette 8am-9pm daily) Surf the net while your smocks wash.

Le Ch@t de la Voisine (☎ 05 61 57 36 18; 25 rue des Sept Troubadours; per hr €2; 🕑 10am-midnight daily)

LAUNDRY

Toulouse's abundance of laundrettes includes one with a cybercafé (see above).

Bulle de Savon (56 rue Blancheurs; 🕑 8am-10pm)

POST

Post Office (9 rue la Fayette)

TOURIST INFORMATION

Tourist Office (☎ 05 61 11 02 22; www.toulouse-tourisme.com; square Charles de Gaulle; 🕑 9am-7pm Mon-Sat, 10am-1pm & 2-6.15pm Sun Jun-Sep, 9am-6pm Mon-Fri, 9am-12.30pm & 2-6pm Sat, 10am-12.30pm & 2-5pm Sun Oct-May) Inside a 16th-century tower.

Sights

PLACE DU CAPITOLE

Bustling **place du Capitole** is the city's main square. On the ceiling of the arcades on its western side are 29 vivid illustrations, all by contemporary artist Raymond Moretti, of the city's history, from the *Venus of Lespugue* (a prehistoric representation of woman) through to the city's status as a hub for the aeronautics industry. On the square's eastern side is the 128m-long facade of the **Capitole**, Toulouse's city hall built in the 1750s. Within is the **Théâtre du Capitole**, one of France's most prestigious opera venues, and the over-the-top, late 19th-century **Salle des Illustres** (Hall of the Illustrious).

VIEUX QUARTIER

The predominantly 18th-century **Vieux Quartier** is a tiny web of narrow lanes and squares.

BASILIQUE ST-SERNIN

Once an important stop on the Chemin de St-Jacques pilgrimage route, the **Basilique St-Sernin** (☎ 05 61 21 80 45; place St-Sernin; 🕑 8.30am-6.15pm Mon-Sat, 8.30am-7.30pm Sun Jul-Sep, 8.30-11.45am & 2-5.45pm Mon-Sat, 8.30am-12.30pm & 2-7.30pm Sun Oct-Jun) still lures plenty of walkers. It is France's largest and most complete Romanesque structure and is topped by a magnificent eight-sided 13th-century tower and 15th-century spire.

Above the double-level crypt is the 18th-century tomb of St-Sernin beneath a sumptuous canopy. In the north transept is a 12th-century fresco of Christ's Resurrection. Note the shorter visiting hours for the ambulatory chapels and **crypt** (admission €2; 🕑 10-11.30am & 2.30-5pm Mon-Sat, 2.30-5pm Sun).

MUSÉE ST-RAYMOND

Inside an 11th-century hospital, this **museum** (☎ 05 61 22 31 44; place St-Sernin; adult/child €3/1.50, temporary exhibitions €2/1.50, 1st Sun of month free; 10am-7pm Jun-Aug, to 6pm Sep-May) has displayed its collection of exceptional Roman sculptures, early Christian sarcophagi and treasure trove of gold Gaulish torques since 1891.

MUSÉE DES AUGUSTINS

The beautiful **Musée des Augustins** (☎ 05 61 22 21 82; 21 rue de Metz; adult/under 18yr €3/free, temporary exhibitions €6/free, 1st Sun of month free; 10am-6pm Thu-Tue, 10am-9pm Wed) houses a superb fine-art collection ranging from Roman stone artefacts to paintings by Rubens, Delacroix and Toulouse-Lautrec. It's in a former Augustinian monastery, and its two 14th-century cloister gardens are postcard-pretty.

ENSEMBLE CONVENTUEL DES JACOBINS

The church is the centrepiece of this magnificent ensemble. Indeed the extraordinary Gothic structure of **Église des Jacobins** (Parvis des Jacobins; 9am-7pm), flooded by day in multicoloured natural light from the huge stained-glass windows, practically defies gravity. A single row of seven 22m-high columns, running smack down the middle of the nave, appear like palm trees as they spread their fanned vaulting.

Artillery barracks in the 19th century, this is the mother church of the order of Dominican friars. Construction began soon after St Dominic founded the order in 1215 to preach church doctrine to the heretical Cathars and it took 170 years to complete, 45m-tall octagonal belfry included. Interred below the modern, marble altar are the remains of St Thomas Aquinas (1225–74), early head of the Dominican order.

Equally arresting is a stroll around the **Cloître des Jacobins** (admission €3, 1st Sun of month free), a meditative cloister with boxed-hedge garden and stage for piano recitals (p741) in September. Art exhibitions fill the 14th-century refectory, **Les Jacobins** (☎ 05 61 22 23 82; 69 rue Pargaminières; admission free; 9am-7pm).

> **CENT SAVERS**
>
> With the plastic **Toulouse en Liberté** card, enjoy discounts on sights, accommodation, shopping, guided tours and so on. The annual card costs €10/5 for adults/kids and is sold at the tourist office and participating hotels.
>
> To blitz museums buy a **Passeport 3 Musées** (€6) or **Passeport 6 Musées** (€9) covering admission to three and six city museums respectively. Admission to several museums is free on the first Sunday of the month.

CATHÉDRALE ST-ÉTIENNE

The **Cathédrale St-Étienne** (Cathedral of St Stephen; place St-Étienne; 8am-7pm Mon-Sat, 9am-7pm Sun) is in a hotchpotch of styles: the vast 12th-century nave being out of kilter with the equally monumental late-13th-century choir designed to realign the cathedral along a different axis. Improvised Gothic vaulting links the two sections. The glorious western rose window dates from 1230.

HÔTEL D'ASSÉZAT

Toulouse boasts 50-odd *hôtels particuliers* – private mansions mostly dating from the 16th century. One of the finest is **Hôtel d'Assézat**, built for a woad merchant in 1555 and home to the **Fondation Bemberg** (☎ 05 61 12 06 89; www.fondation-bemberg.fr; place d'Assézat; adult/8-18yr €4.60/2.75, guided tour €7.35/5.50; 10am-12.30pm & 1.30-6pm Tue-Sun, to 9pm Thu), with its lovely collection of paintings, bronzes and objets d'art from the Renaissance to the 20th century. Guided tours depart daily at 3.30pm and the foundation hosts history-of-art workshops (€8/5.50 for adults/eight to 18 year olds).

ÉGLISE NOTRE DAME DU TAUR

The 14th-century **Église Notre Dame du Taur** (12 rue du Taur; 2-7pm Mon-Fri, 9am-1pm Sat & Sun) was constructed to honour St-Sernin, patron of the basilica that bears his name, who was reputedly martyred on this very spot. The middle of three chapels at the end of the nave has a 16th-century Black Madonna known as Notre Dame du Rempart.

LES ABATTOIRS

This former municipal red-brick abattoir built in 1831 on the *rive gauche* (left bank) has been transformed into a vast public space. The main building has been recycled as Toulouse's cutting-edge **Musée d'Art Moderne et Contemporain** (☎ 05 62 48 58 00; www.lesabattoirs.org, in French; 76 allées Charles de Fitte;

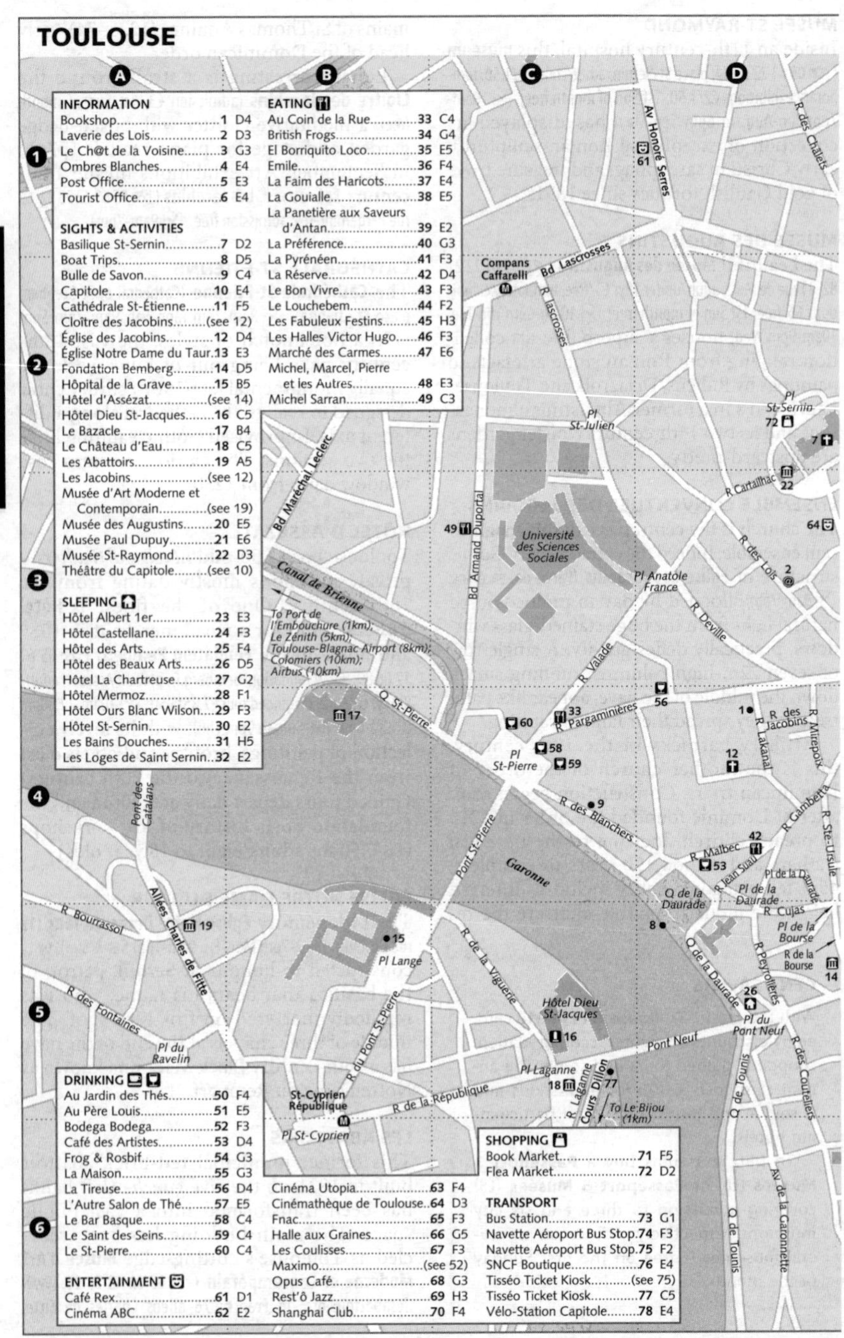
TOULOUSE
INFORMATION
Bookshop....1 D4
Laverie des Lois....2 D3
Le Ch@t de la Voisine....3 G3
Ombres Blanches....4 E4
Post Office....5 E3
Tourist Office....6 E4
SIGHTS & ACTIVITIES
Basilique St-Sernin....7 D2
Boat Trips....8 D5
Bulle de Savon....9 C4
Capitole....10 E4
Cathédrale St-Étienne....11 F5
Cloître des Jacobins....(see 12)
Église des Jacobins....12 D4
Église Notre Dame du Taur....13 E3
Fondation Bemberg....14 D5
Hôpital de la Grave....15 B5
Hôtel d'Assézat....(see 14)
Hôtel Dieu St-Jacques....16 C5
Le Bazacle....17 B4
Le Château d'Eau....18 C5
Les Abattoirs....19 A5
Les Jacobins....(see 12)
Musée d'Art Moderne et Contemporain....(see 19)
Musée des Augustins....20 E5
Musée Paul Dupuy....21 E6
Musée St-Raymond....22 D3
Théâtre du Capitole....(see 10)
SLEEPING
Hôtel Albert 1er....23 E3
Hôtel Castellane....24 F3
Hôtel des Arts....25 F4
Hôtel des Beaux Arts....26 D5
Hôtel La Chartreuse....27 G2
Hôtel Mermoz....28 F1
Hôtel Ours Blanc Wilson....29 F3
Hôtel St-Sernin....30 E2
Les Bains Douches....31 H5
Les Loges de Saint Sernin....32 E2
EATING
Au Coin de la Rue....33 C4
British Frogs....34 G4
El Borriquito Loco....35 E5
Emile....36 F4
La Faim des Haricots....37 E4
La Gouialle....38 E5
La Panetière aux Saveurs d'Antan....39 E2
La Préférence....40 G3
La Pyrénéen....41 F3
La Réserve....42 D4
Le Bon Vivre....43 F3
Le Louchebem....44 F2
Les Fabuleux Festins....45 H3
Les Halles Victor Hugo....46 F3
Marché des Carmes....47 E6
Michel, Marcel, Pierre et les Autres....48 E3
Michel Sarran....49 C3
DRINKING
Au Jardin des Thés....50 F4
Au Père Louis....51 E5
Bodega Bodega....52 F3
Café des Artistes....53 D4
Frog & Rosbif....54 G3
La Maison....55 G3
La Tireuse....56 D4
L'Autre Salon de Thé....57 E5
Le Bar Basque....58 C4
Le Saint des Seins....59 C4
Le St-Pierre....60 C4
ENTERTAINMENT
Café Rex....61 D1
Cinéma ABC....62 E2
Cinéma Utopia....63 F4
Cinémathèque de Toulouse....64 D3
Fnac....65 F3
Halle aux Graines....66 G5
Les Coulisses....67 F3
Maximo....(see 52)
Opus Café....68 G3
Rest'ô Jazz....69 H3
Shanghai Club....70 F4
SHOPPING
Book Market....71 F5
Flea Market....72 D2
TRANSPORT
Bus Station....73 G1
Navette Aéroport Bus Stop....74 F3
Navette Aéroport Bus Stop....75 F2
SNCF Boutique....76 E4
Tisséo Ticket Kiosk....(see 75)
Tisséo Ticket Kiosk....77 C5
Vélo-Station Capitole....78 E4
Av Honoré Serres
R des Chalets
Bd Lascrosses
Compans Caffarelli
R Lascrosses
Pl St-Sernin
Pl St-Julien
R Cartailhac
Bd Maréchal Leclerc
Bd Armand Duportal
Université des Sciences Sociales
Pl Anatole France
R des Lois
Canal de Brienne
To Port de l'Embouchure (1km); Le Zénith (5km); Toulouse-Blagnac Airport (8km); Colomiers (10km); Airbus (10km)
R Deville
R Valade
R Pargaminières
R des Jacobins
R Lakanal
R Mirepoix
Q St-Pierre
Pl St-Pierre
R des Blanchers
R Gambetta
R Ste-Ursule
R Malbec
R Jean Suau
Pl de la Daurade
Q de la Daurade
R Cujas
Pl de la Bourse
R de la Bourse
Pont des Catalans
Pont St-Pierre
Garonne
R Bourrassol
Allées Charles de Fitte
Pl Lange
R de la Viguerie
R Peyrolières
Hôtel Dieu St-Jacques
Pl du Pont Neuf
Pont Neuf
R des Fontaines
Pl du Ravelin
R du Pont St-Pierre
Pl Laganne
R Laganne
Cours Dillon
To Le Bijou (1km)
St-Cyprien République
R de la République
Pl St-Cyprien
Q de Tounis
R des Couteliers
Av de la Garonnette

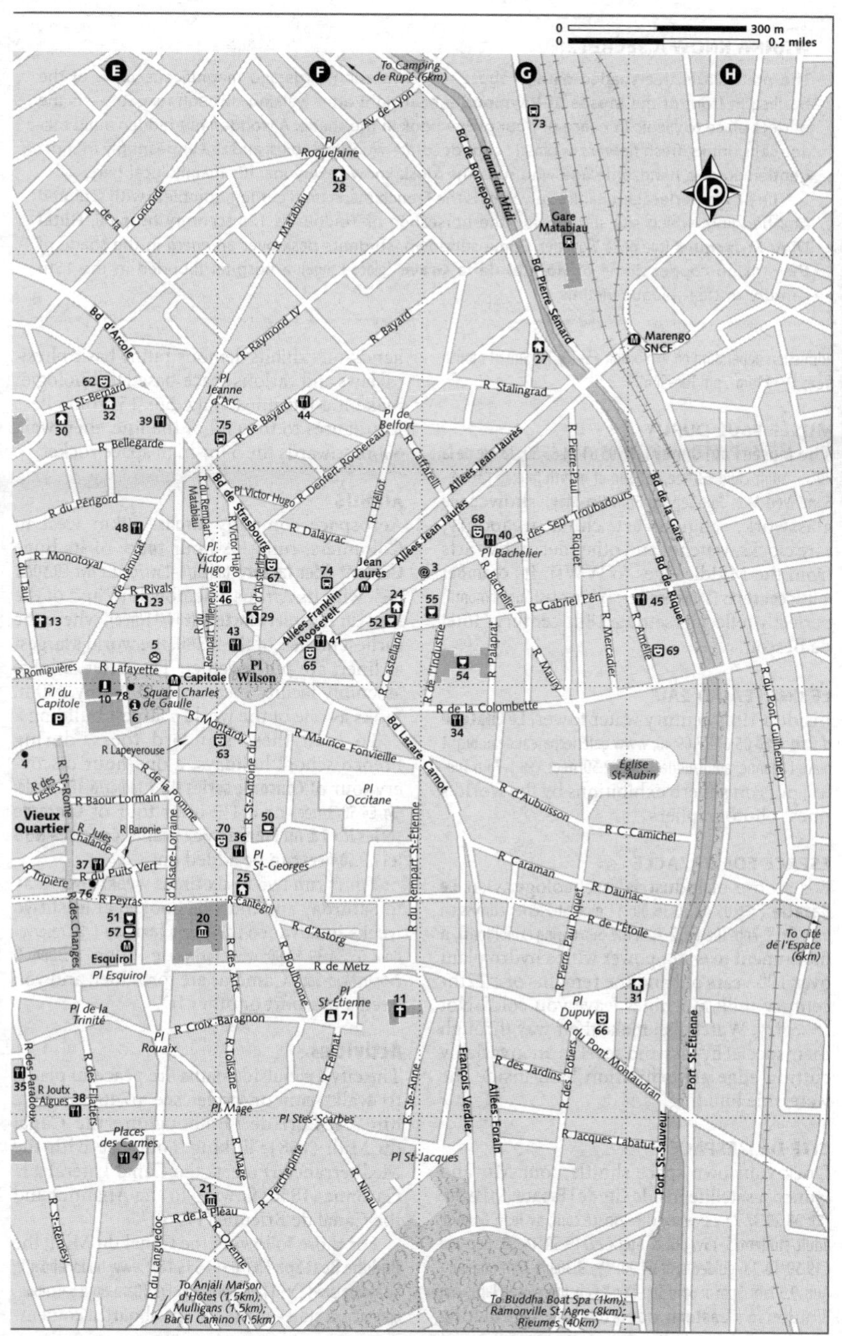
0 300 m
0 0.2 miles
E
F
G
H
To Camping de Rupé (6km)
Av de Lyon
Pl Roquelaine
Bd de Bonrepos
Canal du Midi
R de la Concorde
R Matabiau
Gare Matabiau
Bd Pierre Sémard
Bd d'Arcole
R Raymond IV
R Bayard
Marengo SNCF
R Stalingrad
Pl Jeanne d'Arc
R St-Bernard
R de Bayard
Pl de Belfort
R Bellegarde
R Caffarelli
Allées Jean Jaurès
R Pierre-Paul Riquet
Bd de la Gare
Bd de Strasbourg
Pl Victor Hugo
R Denfert Rochereau
R du Périgord
R Héliot
R des Sept Troubadours
R du Rempart Matabiau
R Victor Hugo
R Dalayrac
Pl Bachelier
R Monotoyal
R de Rémusat
Pl Victor Hugo
R d'Austerlitz
Jean Jaurès
Bd de Riquet
R du Taur
R Rivals
Allées Franklin Roosevelt
R Bachelier
R Gabriel Péri
R Mercadier
R Amélie
R du Rempart Villeneuve
R de l'Industrie
R Castellane
R Palaprat
R Maury
R Romiguières
R Lafayette
Capitole
Pl Wilson
R du Pont Guilhemery
Pl du Capitole
Square Charles de Gaulle
R Montardy
R de la Colombette
R Lapeyrouse
R St-Antoine du T
R Maurice Fonvieille
Bd Lazare Carnot
Église St-Aubin
R des Gestes
R St-Rome
R de la Pomme
Pl Occitane
R d'Aubuisson
R Baour Lormain
Vieux Quartier
R Baronie
R d'Alsace-Lorraine
R C Camichel
R Jules Chalande
Pl St-Georges
R Caraman
R Tripière
R du Puits Vert
R du Rempart St-Étienne
R Dauriac
R Peyras
R Cantegril
R des Changes
R de l'Étoile
R d'Astorg
R Pierre Paul Riquet
To Cité de l'Espace (6km)
Esquirol
R des Arts
R Boulbonne
R de Metz
Pl Esquirol
Pl de la Trinité
Pl St-Étienne
Pl Dupuy
R Croix Baragnon
Pl Rouaix
R du Pont Montaudran
R des Paradoux
R Tolisane
R Fermat
R Ste-Anne
François Verdier
Allées Forain
Port St-Étienne
R des Jardins
R Joutx Aigues
R des Filatiers
R des Potiers
Pl Mage
Pl Stes-Scarbes
Places des Carmes
R Mage
R Jacques Labatut
Port St-Sauveur
Pl St-Jacques
R Ninau
R Perchepinte
R de la Pleau
R Ozenne
R St-Rémésy
R du Languedoc
To Anjali Maison d'Hôtes (1.5km); Mulligans (1.5km); Bar El Camino (1.5km)
To Buddha Boat Spa (1km); Ramonville St-Agne (8km); Rieumes (40km)
3 4 5 6 10 11 13 20 21 23 24 25 27 28 29 30 31 32 34 35 36 37 38 39 40 41 43 44 45 46 47 48 50 51 52 54 55 57 62 63 65 66 67 68 69 70 71 73 74 75 76 78

WANNA KNOW A SECRET...

The pretty little tree-shaded garden abuzz with twittering birds and magnificent views of the basilica in front of the **Musée St-Raymond** – bear right after walking through its gates – is the perfect place to picnic in peace or pour over a book in the shade. A wooden hut hidden amid foliage sells drinks, fresh flowers in plastic cups decorate wooden tables, and the endearingly friendly gentleman of a handsome age who runs the kiosk knows everyone; it's mainly local here.

The picnic-perfect Left Bank equivalent is the French manicured garden, complete with sculpted box hedging, which sits snug inside the horseshoe of Toulouse's 12th-century hospital, **Hôtel Dieu St-Jacques** (rue de la Viguerie). Come sundown, students bask over an *apéro* in the shade of the striking copper dome of **Hôpital de la Grave** (place Lange), a hospital founded in the 15th century to treat plague victims.

admission depending on exhibition €5-10, 1st Sun of month free; 11am-7pm Tue-Sun).

MUSÉE PAUL DUPUY

The **Musée Paul Dupuy** (05 61 14 65 50; 13 rue de la Pléau; adult/child €3/free, 1st Sun of month free; 10am-6pm Wed-Mon Jun-Sep, to 5pm Oct-May) showcases glasswork, religious art, china, weaponry, rare clocks, watches and other decorative arts from the Middle Ages to WWII. Its **chamber music concerts** (admission free; 3pm last Sun of month) perfectly reflect its setting: 18th-century Hôtel de Besson.

LE CHÂTEAU D'EAU

Inside a 19th-century water tower, **Le Château d'Eau** (05 61 77 09 40; www.galeriechateaudeau.org; 1 place Laganne; adult/under 18yr €2.50/free; 1-7pm Tue-Sun) puts on superb exhibitions by the world's finest photographers.

ESPACE EDF BAZACLE

For a dose of industrial archeology, visit **Le Bazacle** (05 62 30 16 00; 11 quai St-Pierre; admission free; 2-7pm Tue-Fri, 2-7pm Tue-Sun during exhibitions), a monument to water power with a hydro plant over 100 years old and the remains of a 12th-century mill. Machines leave you cold? Not to worry. Watch fish make their way through their special bypass and revel in an invariably cutting-edge art exhibition held inside the waterside building.

CITÉ DE L'ESPACE

Dock your own space shuttle, tour Mir and launch a satellite inside **Cité de l'Espace** (Space City; 08 20 37 72 23; www.cite-espace.com; av Jean Gonord; adult/student/5-15yr Jul & Aug €22/19.50/14.50, Sep-Jun €19.50/16/13, guided visit €4.90; 9.30am-7pm mid-Jul–Aug, 9.30am-5pm or 6pm Sep-Dec & Feb-Jun, closed Jan), on Toulouse's eastern outskirts. Its stimulating hands-on exhibits demonstrating basic physical laws and various space-based technologies make it a kid-must. Take bus 15 from allées Jean Jaurès to the end of the line, then walk 600m towards the 53m-high space rocket.

AIRBUS

Aerospace company **Airbus**, 10km west in Colomiers, runs 1½-hour **tours**: of its huge **Clément Ader factory** (adult/6-18yr/under 6yr €9.50/8/free), with its Airbus assembly line, and of the **Jean Luc Lagardère factory** (€14/11/free), where the earliest models of the A380, the world's largest airliner, are put together. The latter, a huge assembly facility measuring 490m by 250m, ranks as one of the world's largest buildings.

To both these standard tours, during French school holidays, a one-hour discovery tour of **Concorde series No 1** (adult/6-18yr/under 6yr €4.50/3/free) or a 1½-hour tour of **Concorde series No 1 & Air France's 'Fox Charlie' Concorde No 9** (€11/9.50/free) can be added on.

Tours run two to six times weekly Monday to Saturday and must be booked at least two weeks in advance through **Taxiway** (reservations 05 34 39 42 00; www.taxiway.fr; 9am-12.30pm & 2-6pm Mon-Sat). Cameras are forbidden and you need a passport or other ID.

Activities

The city's canalside paths are peaceful places to walk, run or cycle; see p746 for bike hire. At Port de l'Embouchure the Canal du Midi (1681; linking Toulouse with the Mediterranean) meets the Canal Latéral à la Garonne (1856; flowing to the Atlantic) and the Canal de Brienne (1776).

For those following the Canal du Midi, the **Buddha Boat Spa** (05 61 55 54 87; www.buddhaboat.fr; bd Montplaisir; 11am-8pm Mon-Fri, 10am-8pm Sat, noon-6pm Sun), a state-of-the-art spa aboard a contemporary wooden barge, is a dreamy pit-stop. The €35 fee for two hours includes use of Turkish bath, sauna, CD library, sun deck etc.

Tours

The tourist office runs **walking tours** (2hr; adult/10-16yr €9/6) of historic Toulouse, metro art and Toulouse illuminated at night on foot (€10/7 for adults/10 to 16 year olds) or by coach (€14/10). To really get under the skin of the city, stride out on an urban stroll with **La Gargouille** (☎ 05 34 60 12 75; www.la-gargouille.org; adult/student €6/3); two-hour city hikes depart twice monthly from a designated metro station.

Boat trips along the Canal du Midi and River Garonne run by **Toulouse Croisières** (☎ 05 61 25 72 57; www.toulouse-croisieres.com, in French) and **Les Bateaux Toulousains** (☎ 05 61 80 22 26; www.bateaux-toulousains.com) leave from quai de la Daurade.

Festivals & Events

Festival de la Violette Celebration of Toulouse's favourite flower in early February.

Le Marathon des Mots (www.lemarathondesmots.com, in French) 'Word Marathon' revelling in language and literature for four days in June.

Toulouse d'Été Jazz, classical and other music around town in July and August.

Piano aux Jacobins (www.pianojacobins.com) Piano recitals in Église des Jacobins in September.

Jazz sur Son 31 International jazz festival in October.

Sleeping

Toulouse hotels cater to a business clientele, meaning cheaper rates at weekends and in July and August.

BUDGET

Camping de Rupé (☎ 05 61 70 07 35; 21 chemin du Pont de Rupé; 2 adults with tent & car €14.50; reception 9am-12.30pm & 5-8pm daily) Find this jam-packed campsite 6km northwest of the train station; take bus 59 from place Jeanne d'Arc. Pitch tents in summer; caravans year-round.

our pick **Hôtel La Chartreuse** (☎ 05 61 62 93 39; www.chartreusehotel.com; 4bis bd de Bonrepos; d/tr €37/48) *Bon repos* (good rest) is what this extraordinary good-value and clean hotel amid several scruffy offerings across from the train station provides. Canalside cyclists are catered for with free, safe bike parking.

Hôtel des Arts (☎ 05 61 23 36 21; couleurs.suds@club-internet.fr; 1bis rue Cantegril; d with shared/private shower €42/54) Price is the trump card for this modest place where every room shares a toilet. Those with shower can get steamy since only a plastic curtain separates the cubicle from the room itself.

our pick **Hôtel St-Sernin** (☎ 05 61 21 73 08; www.hotelstsernin.com; 2 rue St-Bernard; s/d/tr from €58/68/83) Exciting change is afoot at this boutique hotel with prime views of Basilique St-Sernin – rooms four, nine, 15 and 20 are to die for: Parisian couple Julien and Aurore bought it as the hotel of their dreams in 2008 and are renovating floor by floor. Free wi-fi.

Hôtel Ours Blanc Wilson (☎ 05 61 21 62 40; www.hotel-oursblanc.com; 2 rue Victor Hugo; s/d/tr €59/69/91;) One of a trio of Ours Blanc (Polar Bear; no, nobody could tell us why) hotels, the Wilson is a solid choice sporting an original 1930s vintage lift. Risk it to the 5th floor for great pigeon's-eye views over the rooftops.

SOMETHING DIFFERENT

First up is a canal boat moored 8km south in Ramonville St-Agne, the last stop on the metro line. Comprising three rooms and two teeny-weeny cabins to bunk up in, **Péniche Soléïado** (☎ 05 62 19 07 71, 06 86 27 83 19; www.peniche-soleiado.com; Pont Mange Pommes, rue Riquet, Ramonville St-Agne; s/d incl breakfast €60/80, dinner adult/under 12yr €30/15) is paradise for kid-clad families (assuming the kids can swim – if not, a stay could be stressful). Handsome sage-green in colour with plenty of colourful potted flowers and a sundeck for dining, it is moored beneath a poetically named bridge whose very name conjures up the carefree, *mange pommes* (apple-eating) lifestyle the boat embodies. Bicycles are aboard allowing guests to explore the bijou port nearby or pedal the easy 30 minutes along a shaded canalside towpath to Toulouse. Dinner on deck is a must, as well as a day cruise with lunch (adult/under 12 years costs €115/80) that Marie and Pascal, the creative couple behind the nautical venture, run twice a month.

And what about a tree house or tepee between trees at **Tepacap Rieumes** (☎ 05 62 14 71 61; www.tepacap.fr; rte de l'Isle en Dodon, Rieumes; tepee per person €20, breakfast €5, tree house d incl breakfast €135; Mar-Nov), an *accrobranche* (tree-climbing) park 40km southwest of Toulouse along the D632 and D7.

A TWINSET OF MAISONS D'HÔTES

Enjoy the intimacy of a Toulousien home at these superb *maisons d'hôtes:*

- **Anjali Maison d'Hôtes** (☎ 09 54 22 42 93, 06 84 29 78 09; www.anjali.fr; 86 Grande Rue St-Michel; s/d/tr/q incl breakfast from €75/85/125/150; 💻) Taking a 19th-century house with wooden shutters and a secret walled garden as her canvas, Delphine has created four delightful rooms, each with its own art-inspired quirk. Hampi is as serene as the journeys to southern India that inspired it; Brédoury is family-friendly with a kids' room kitted out with boatlike bunk beds and a tiny window to play 'I Spy' from; Tolosa is for wheelchair guests; and black-and-white Cinema Paradiso has its own bedside projector to screen films on the wall opposite.
- **Les Loges de Saint Sernin** (☎ 05 61 24 44 44; www.logessaintsernin.fr; 12 rue St-Bernard; d incl breakfast Mon-Fri/weekend €120/105) Sylviane Tatin, busy mother of four, is the creative soul behind this designer B&B on the 2nd floor of an 18th-century town house. Its four rooms mix old with new and reflect their natural surroundings – Saint Sernin is a romantic red-brick colour, Capitole is orange, Garonne is soft beige and Canal du Midi is vibrant green. Breakfast in summer is on a balcony overlooking Sylviane's husband's courtyard golf course!

MIDRANGE

Hôtel Albert 1er (☎ 05 61 21 17 91; www.hotel-albert1.com; 8 rue Rivals; d Sat & Sun from €69, Mon-Fri from €84; ❄ 💻) Centuries-old Albert Premier ('the first') was adopted in 1956 by the parents of Anne-Marie Hilaire, who runs this perfectly mannered hotel with her two grown-up sons. Don't miss the shopping, dining and drinking guide the hotel compiles for guests.

Hôtel Castellane (☎ 05 61 62 18 82; www.castellanehotel.com, in French; 17 rue Castellane; d/tr/q €72/84/88; ❄) Unbeatable value, brilliantly placed and ranking sky-high in the friendliness stakes, this unpretentious two-star hotel with a generous quota of family rooms and – *quelle surprise!* – sunlit interior patio is hard to fault. Children under 12 years breakfast for free.

Hôtel Mermoz (☎ 05 61 63 04 04; www.hotel-mermoz.com; 50 rue Matabiau; d/tr €125/140; ❄) Walk into this pretty little art-deco nook with its peaceful garden and bright rooms and you leave the city behind. The theme of its decor recalls aviation's pioneering days from Antoine de Saint-Exupéry's *Vol de Nuit* (Night Flight). Free wi-fi; garage parking €10.

Hôtel des Beaux Arts (☎ 05 34 45 42 42; www.hoteldesbeauxarts.com; 1 place du Pont Neuf; d without river view €108, with river view €128-220; ❄) The romantic 18th-century facade of the Beaux Arts (Fine Arts) – soft, mellow caramel-coloured bricks framing nine windows adorned with green awnings and wrought-iron balconies – promises great things. And its interior, arranged as country-style home rather than hotel, doesn't disappoint. Free wi-fi.

TOP END

our pick Les Bains Douches (☎ 05 62 72 52 52; www.hotel-bainsdouches.com; 4 & 4bis rue du Pont Guilhemery; s/d from €140/160; ❄) The urban creation of Monsieur and Madame Henriette, motorbike designer and interior designer respectively, this design hotel stuns. Hidden in the old city baths, the Henriettes took the historic two-storey facade with original 1950s mosaics and added two more floors on top – in glass. Inside, waxed concrete floors, stainless-steel surfaces and subtle neon lighting pave the way to 19 rooms and three suites, each individually designed and oozing New Yorker panache.

Eating

Bd de Strasbourg, place St-Georges and the western side of place du Capitole are one big café-terrace line-up, perfect for lunch and hot in summer when everything spills outside. Cheap student places stud rue Blanchers while nearby rue Pargaminières is the street for kebabs, burgers and other late-night fast food.

Michel, Marcel, Pierre et les Autres (☎ 05 61 22 47 05; www.michelmarcelpierre.com; 35 rue de Rémusat; starter/main/dessert €7/13/7, 2-/3-course menu €17/23; 🕑 lunch & dinner Tue-Sat) This classic bistro with a quirk is *the* place for delicious bistro fare (mackerel fillets, pastry-baked cheese, *rillettes de canard* etc). Its marketing spin – 'not a restaurant but a place of life and good humour' – is spot on.

our pick Les Halles Victor Hugo (place Victor Hugo; menus €10-20; 🕑 lunch Tue-Sun) Many of Toulouse's best-value places are the small, spartan, lunchtime-only restaurants above the appetite-sharpening food stalls of Toulouse's busy covered market. Fast, packed and no-nonsense, catering for market vendors and shoppers alike, they serve up generous, delicious *menus* of hearty fare.

El Borriquito Loco (☎ 05 61 25 34 54; www.restaurant-borriquito.com; 25 rue des Paradoux; plat du jour €10, lunch menus €10-26; ⏲ lunch & dinner Mon-Sat) This Spanish tapas bar is a bit mad with its jumble of masks, vintage clothing, red wedge shoes et al strung in its wrought-iron balconies. But it's as cheap as chips (€12.50 for a three-course lunch including wine and coffee) and morphs into a DJ club with a dance floor in the evening.

La Réserve (☎ 05 61 21 84 00; 8 rue Jean Suau; lunch menu €12.50, mains €10-15; ⏲ lunch & dinner Mon-Fri, all day Sat & Sun) When you need a break from duck, hit this stylish restaurant with an industrial interior and plenty of pavement seating. Its menu has everything – salads, pizza and pasta alongside the city's signature *confit*. Weekends, the kitchen's open all day.

our pick Chez Navarre (☎ 05 62 26 43 06; 49 Grande Rue Nazareth; lunch/dinner menu €12.50/20; ⏲ lunch & dinner Tue-Fri, dinner Sat) Fed up with restaurant dining? This fabulous 16th-century *table d'hôtes* with red-brick walls, old wooden bar, beamed ceiling and shared candlelit tables is perfect. The rustic French cuisine of simple terrines, soups and one fixed meal ooze the same charming 'at home' feel.

Au Coin de la Rue (☎ 05 61 21 99 45; 2 rue Pargaminières; 2-/3-course menu €19/22, salads €14; ⏲ lunch & dinner daily) A quintessential French bistro with wooden shutters and a well-aged bottle of Armagnac planted firmly on the bar, this contemporary spot has a handful of tables in the sun and several in the shade. A glass chandelier adds a touch of funk inside. Wi-fi hot spot and student hangout.

Le Bon Vivre (☎ 05 61 23 07 17; www.lebonvivre.com; 15bis place Wilson; menus €25-36; ⏲ lunch & dinner daily) Old-style regional cuisine doesn't get meatier at this local favourite: *ris de veau à l'ancienne* (calf sweetbreads old-style), *cassoulette de lentils* spiced with *museaux* (muzzles) and pig's ears or a humble plate of cured ham *(noir de Bigorre)* courtesy of the region's precious Bigorre Gascony black pig.

Michel Sarran (☎ 05 61 12 32 32; 21 bd Armand Duportal; lunch/dinner menu €48/98; ⏲ lunch & dinner Mon-Fri) As with many Michelin twin-starred gastronomic restaurants, lunch is good value at Michel Sarran's delightful town house on a tree-lined avenue; the *menu* includes wine and coffee.

Also recommended:

Le Louchebem (☎ 05 61 99 21 26; www.lelouchebem.com; 24 rue de Bayard; starters/mains €9/14, menu €20-23; ⏲ 8pm-4am Tue-Thu, 8pm-6am Fri & Sat) Meaty choice – *cassoulet* and choice of grills – for night owls out 'til dawn; by day find it in the Halles Victor Hugo (opposite).

Les Fabuleux Festins (☎ 05 61 62 08 31; www.lesfabuleuxfestins.com; 32 rue Gabriel Péri; starters/mains €11/13, menu €28; ⏲ lunch & dinner Tue-Sat) Fabulous sums up this exotic space which lures a distinctly jet-setting, trendy crowd.

Emile (☎ 05 61 21 05 56; www.restaurant-emile.com; place St-Georges; lunch menus €20 & €30, dinner menus €36 & €41; ⏲ lunch & dinner Tue-Sat) Top address, around since the 1940s, for the reputedly perfect *cassoulet*.

SELF-CATERING

Buy fresh produce (and/or wine for €1.20 a litre!) at covered food markets **Les Halles Victor Hugo** (place Victor Hugo; ⏲ 7am-1pm Tue-Sun) or **Marché des Carmes** (place des Carmes; ⏲ 7am-1pm Tue-Sun).

Imaginative bread (chestnut, nut, chorizo, onion, and fig among others) and *baguette* sandwiches (Camembert and walnut) make bakery **La Panetière aux Saveurs d'Antan** (39 bd de Strasbourg; ⏲ 7am-8.30pm Wed-Mon) a very satisfying picnic stop.

TEA FOR TWO

Check out these two addresses:

- **Au Jardin des Thés** (☎ 05 61 23 46 67; 16 place St-Georges; lunch menu €13.80, breakfast/brunch €8/16; ⏲ 11am-7pm daily) This equally civilised tea house has a buzzing terrace on perhaps the city's loveliest green squares (playground in the middle for the kid-clad) and pours a good range of Darjeelings and greens. Its good-value savoury tarts and salads pack it out at lunchtime.
- **L'Autre Salon de Thé** (☎ 05 61 22 11 63; 45 rue des Tourneurs; lunch menu €12-14, Sun brunch €17; ⏲ noon-7pm) An old-world tea room wedged onto Toulouse's oldest bar (p744), this atmospheric spot is perfect for a tart-and-salad lunch or a simple cuppa poured from a flowery old-fashioned china teapot. Its cakes, laid on a table in the centre of the small salon, are divine.

Ginger cake, jammy dodgers, baked beans and other British products are what grocer **British Frogs** (☎ 05 61 62 69 78; 13 rue de la Colombette; ⏰ 10am-7pm Tue-Sat, 10am-1pm Sun) sells.

Drinking

Almost every square in the Vieux Quartier has at least one café, busy day and night. Other busy after-dark streets include rue Castellane, rue Gabriel Péri and near the river around place St-Pierre.

Au Père Louis (☎ 05 61 21 33 45; 45 rue des Tourneurs; ⏰ 8.30am-3pm & 5-10.30pm Mon-Sat) Top of our list for irresistible old-fashioned charm, At Father Louis' is Toulouse's oldest bar franked 1889. A hybrid retro bar-cum-café and lunch spot, it deserves at least one drink.

La Maison (☎ 05 61 62 87 22; 9 rue Gabriel Péri; ⏰ 5pm-2am Sun-Fri, 5pm-5am Sat) 'At home' atmosphere is what this crumbling old house with a retro collection of second-hand chairs, wine list chalked above the (decorative) fireplace and the odd visiting pigeon is all about. Overtly hip, students flop on the sofa sipping tea early on, cocktails late.

Bodega Bodega (☎ 05 61 63 03 63; 1 rue Gabriel Péri; menu €19.50, tapas €4.50-9; ⏰ 7pm-2am Mon-Fri, 7pm-6am Sat, 8pm-2am Sun) Find all the fun of the *feria* at this vast party space in a historic building where the tax authority once lived. It heaves at weekends with live music and a frenetic tapas-quaffing crowd.

La Tireuse (☎ 05 61 12 28 29; 24 rue Pargaminières; ⏰ 5pm-2am Mon-Sat, 6pm-2am Sun) Much loved by students, this friendly beer bar has 20 beers *en pression* (on tap) and is a fine place to drink away the night. Should the munchies strike, the street it sits on is studded with kebab and burger joints.

Frog & Rosbif (14 rue de l'Industrie; ⏰ 5.30pm-2am Mon-Fri, 1.30pm-3.30am Sat, 1.30pm-2am Sun) Lively British pub with dartboard, TV screen and its own microbrewery churning out very palatable real ales and stouts. A pint during 'happy hour' from 5.30pm to 8pm weekdays costs €4.50.

Near the river, place St-Pierre is Toulouse's terrace hot spot with its row of student-busy bars, including psychedelic **Le Saint des Seins** (☎ 06 07 81 90 52; www.myspace.com/lesaintdesseins; 5 place St-Pierre; ⏰ 5pm-2am Wed-Fri, 5pm-4am Sat) with its hip clientele, jam sessions and rock concerts; mainstream pub **Le St-Pierre** (☎ 05 61 21 74 13; 10 place St-Pierre; ⏰ 9am-2am Mon-Fri, noon-5am Sat, noon-2am Sun); and sports bar **Le Bar Basque** (☎ 05 61 21 55 64; 7 place St-Pierre; ⏰ 11am-2am Mon-Fri, 1pm-5am Sat, 1pm-2am Sun) with bench seating in a massive courtyard with dramatic rugby-pitch backdrop.

A skip away on place de la Daurade is another trio of café-bars with packed terraces, including the very romantic at sunset **Café des Artistes** (☎ 05 61 12 06 00; 13 place de la Daurade; ⏰ 11am-2am daily) with river view and soft apricot-coloured, timber-framed facade.

Entertainment

The scene buzzes. Pick up free listings guides at the *billetterie spectacles* (box office) in **Fnac** (☎ 08 92 68 36 22; 16 allées Franklin Roosevelt). Online see http://toulouse.sortir.eu.

CINEMAS

Watch nondubbed foreign films at **Cinéma Utopia** (☎ 05 61 23 66 20; 24 rue Montardy), **Cinéma ABC** (☎ 05 61 29 81 00; 13 rue St-Bernard) and art-house **Cinémathèque de Toulouse** (☎ 05 62 30 30 10; www.lacinemathequedetoulouse.com, in French; 69 rue du Taur).

LIVE MUSIC

Venues abound. For classical music and theatre, head for the city's elegant 1860s market hall **Halle aux Graines** (☎ 05 61 63 13 13; www.onct.mairie-toulouse.fr; place Dupuy), now a concert hall

EAT GREEN

Hard to believe in this land of foie gras and duck, but wholly vegetarian restaurants do exist. For a complete listing, nip to the St-Sernin Sunday morning market and visit the stall of Toulouse's **Association Végétarienne et Végétalienne** (http://avis.free.fr; ⏰ 11am-1pm Sun), on the corner of rue St-Bernard and place St-Sernin.

Not only does **La Faim des Haricots** (☎ 05 61 22 49 25; www.lafaimdesharicots.fr, in French; 3 rue du Puits Vert; menus €10-13; ⏰ lunch Mon-Wed, lunch & dinner Thu-Sat) cook up a different *plat du jour* (daily special) every day alongside a handsome choice of homemade salads, savoury tarts and soups which you can play pick 'n' mix with, but the deal is *à volonté* meaning eat as much as you want. Desserts, also *à volonté,* include homely favourites like bread pudding, carrot cake, chocolate tart and vanilla flan. Vegetarian options available.

THOMAS SALACROUP

This native of Villefranche de Rouergue, a village few know in the Massif Central, is a political-science student in Toulouse.

Hot spots to drink: The city's Irish soul **Mulligans** (☎ 05 61 14 04 21; www.mulligans.fr; 39 Grande Rue St-Michel); beer bar **La Tireuse** (opposite); and **Bar El Camino** (☎ 05 62 26 60 51; 138 Grande Rue St-Michel) where the owner César serves cheap drinks with excellent tapas.

And for dinner: For students and people who like the concept of *bonne franquette* (cheap well-cooked food), it's **La Gouaille** (☎ 05 61 25 65 66; 6 rue Joutx Aigues) – the *menu* is cheap, about €13. I like **La Préférence** (☎ 05 61 13 62 74; www.lapreference.fr; 41 place Bachelier) because it's cheap, you can bring you own wine and the chef takes time to explain his dishes which combine traditional French with French island (like La Martinique in the Caribbean). Another is **La Pyrénéen** (☎ 05 61 23 38 88; 14 allées Franklin Roosevelt) – very French, very *bistro à la française,* very much like a living museum – try the *magret* (duck breast) with honey.

Where do you club? I don't so much, though **Maximo** (☎ 05 61 62 08 07; www.maximo-café.com; 3 rue Gabriel Péri) is a beautiful place in the centre for a couple of drinks. I prefer to listen to bands and Toulouse has some good venues. **Le Filochard** (☎ 05 61 52 66 80; 8 place du Pont Neuf) has eclectic gigs, is often full of people and must be tried if only to test *le chouchen*, a Breton drink, very sweet!

Hot tip: For any true jazz fan – I am – the best place is unfortunately a restaurant: **Rest'ô Jazz** (☎ 05 61 57 96 95; www.restojazz.com; 8 rue Amélie) is dark, atmospheric, uniquely friendly, soulful, with eclectic jazz-band concerts every week, closed Sunday.

and home to Toulouse's Orchestre National du Capitole.

Le Bijou (☎ 05 61 42 95 07; www.le-bijou.net; 123 av de Muret; admission free-€15) World music and upcoming artists predominate at this experimental venue tucked behind a neighbourhood bistro 1km south of the town centre (République metro stop); concerts start at 9.30pm.

Havana Café (☎ 05 62 88 34 94; www.havana-café.fr; 2 av des Crêtes, Ramonville St-Agne; admission free-€20) All sounds, reggae, rock, blues, heavy metal and gospel included, make this popular venue at the end of metro line B, 8km south of the city (Ramonville metro stop), Toulouse's biggest and best.

Le Bikini (☎ 05 62 24 09 50; www.lebikini.com; rue Hermès, Ramonville St-Agne; admission €5-20) The stuff of Toulousien legend around for 25 years or so, also at the end of metro line B (Ramonville metro stop).

Le Zénith (☎ 05 62 74 49 49; 11 av Raymond Badiou) Premier concert venue on the international circuit. Near Arènes and Patte d'Oie metro stops.

NIGHTCLUBS

Several bars double up as clubs, as do concert venues **Havana Café** and **Le Bikini** (see above).

Opus Café (24 rue Bachelier; admission free; midnight-5am Mon-Wed, 11pm-6am Thu-Sat) Dance until dawn at this much-loved venue for seasoned clubbers who flock here late for that quintessential French *l'after.*

Café Rex (☎ 05 61 12 16 39; 15 av Honoré Serres; admission €10; 8pm-2am Tue-Fri, 8pm-5am Sat) A bar-cum-club with a young crowd, lots of happenings and an Australian soul, near Campons Cottarelli metro stop.

Shopping

Mainstream shopping embraces rue du Taur, rue d' Alsace-Lorraine, rue de la Pomme, rue des Arts and nearby streets. The place St-Georges area is boutique-fashionable.

GAY & LESBIAN TOULOUSE

It's not called *la ville rose* (the pink city) for nothing; for a complete low-down on the gay scene see www.gaytoulouse.net. Gay venues include **Shanghai Club** (12 rue de la Pomme; www.shanghai-leclub.com; 12.30am-10am, to 11am Sun), a gay club and disco around since 1970; and **Les Coulisses** (5 bd de Strasbourg; tapas €8-12; 6pm-2am Mon-Fri, to 5am Sat), a mixed, gay-friendly champagne bar with shimmering-silver floor-length curtains, boxed-hedge terrace painted black, and resident DJ Luke Skywalker spinning tunes on Friday.

Markets include a bit-of-everything **market** (Place du Capitole; ⌚ Wed), a **flea market** (place St-Sernin; ⌚ Sat & Sun) and an antiquarian **book market** (place St-Étienne; ⌚ Sat).

Getting There & Away

AIR

From **Toulouse-Blagnac Airport** (☎ 08 25 38 00 00; www.toulouse.aeroport.fr), 8km northwest of the centre, there are daily flights to/from Paris (Air France and easyJet) and other European cities.

BUS

Regional services to/from Toulouse **bus station** (☎ 05 61 61 67 67; bd Pierre Sémard) include the following:

Destination	One-way Fare (€)	Duration (hr)	Daily Frequency
Albi	12.90	1½	3
Auch	10.90	1¼	2
Castres	10.90	1½	6
Millau	26.50	4	1
Montauban	7.50	1¼	4

TRAIN

Buy tickets at the **SNCF boutique** (5 rue Peyras) in town or at train station **Gare Matabiau** (bd Pierre Sémard), 1km northeast of the centre. Destinations include the following:

Destination	One-way Fare (€)	Duration (hr)
Albi	11.40	1¼
Auch	12.90	1½
Bayonne	37.30	3¾
Bordeaux	34.80	2-3
Carcassonne	13.30	1
Castres	12.70	1¼
Lourdes	23.40	1¾
Montauban	10.50	½
Pau	29.50	2¾

Getting Around

TO/FROM THE AIRPORT

The **Navette Aéroport** (airport shuttle; ☎ 05 34 60 64 00; www.navette-tisseo-aeroport.com) links the airport with town (one-way/return €4/6.30m, 20 minutes, every 20 minutes from 5am to 8.20pm from town and 7.25am to midnight from the airport). Catch the bus in front of the bus station, outside the Jean Jaurès metro station or at place Jeanne d'Arc.

A **taxi** (☎ 05 61 30 02 54, 06 07 41 29 33) to/from town costs €25.

BICYCLE

Take to the streets with the city's bike-rental scheme, **Vélô Toulouse** (www.velo.toulouse.fr, in French; ⌚ pick-up 5.30am-2am, drop-off 24hr), with 135 bike stations dotted every 300m around the city. A one-/seven-day ticket (including a bonus 20/30 minutes' free rental) costs €1/5, plus a €150 credit-card deposit; pay €0.50/1.50/2 for first/second/subsequent hours. Short-term subscribers need a credit card with a chip and PIN.

Otherwise, **Vélo-Station Capitole** (☎ 05 34 30 03 00; square Charles de Gaulle; per half-/full day €1/2, credit-card deposit €260; ⌚ 8am-7pm Mon-Fri, 10am-7pm Sat & Sun) rents out bikes.

BUS & METRO

Local buses and the two-line metro are run by **Tisséo** (☎ 05 61 41 70 70; www.tisseo.fr, in French), which has ticket kiosks located on place Jeanne d'Arc and cours Dillon. A one-way/return ticket for either costs €1.40/2.50, a 10-ticket carnet is €11.70 and a one-/two-day pass is €4.20/7.

Most bus lines run daily until at least 8pm (night bus lines 10pm to midnight).

ALBI

pop 48,600

The fortress-like Gothic cathedral dwarfing Albi is a dramatic reminder of its violent religious past. The town was at the heart of the Albigensian heresy of the 12th and 13th centuries and the bloody crusade that crushed it. Almost all of central Albi, including the cathedral, is built from bricks of reddish clay, dug from the River Tarn that casually meanders through town.

Two things merit the trip: that extraordinary cathedral and the excellent museum dedicated to artist Henri de Toulouse-Lautrec, who hailed from Albi.

Information

Lavotop (10 rue Émile Grand; ⌚ 7am-9pm) Laundrette.

Ludi.com (64 rue Séré de Rivières; per hr €4; ⌚ 11am-midnight Mon-Sat) Internet access.

Post Office (place du Vigan)

Tourist Office (☎ 05 63 49 48 80; www.albi-tourisme.fr; place Ste-Cécile; ⌚ 9am-7pm Mon-Sat, 10am-12.30pm & 2.30-6.30pm Sun Jul & Aug, 9am-12.30pm & 2-6pm Mon-Sat, 10am-12.30pm & 2.30-5pm Sun Oct-Jun) The leaflet *To Discover* maps six thematic walks around town, including an enchanting 'secret gardens' tour. Staff make hotel reservations (free by phone or email, €2 in situ).

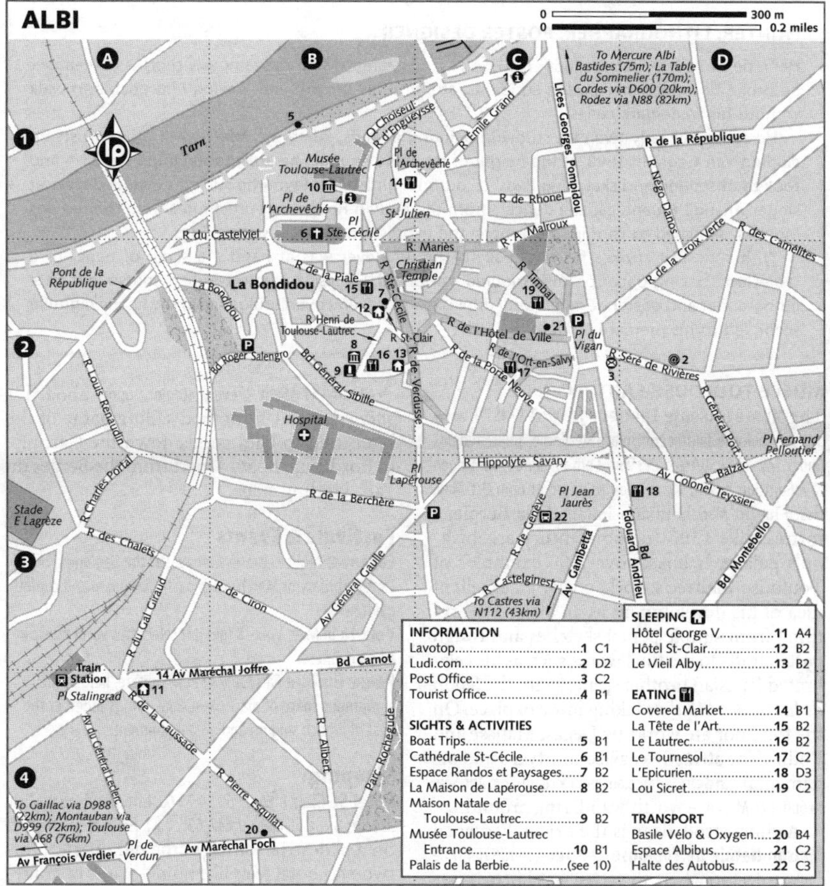

Sights & Activities

CATHÉDRALE STE-CÉCILE

As much fortress as church, the mighty **Cathédrale Ste-Cécile** (place Ste-Cécile; 9am-6.30pm Jun-Sep, 9am-noon & 2-6.30pm Oct-May) was begun in 1282. Built to impress and subdue, it took over a hundred years to complete. Attractive isn't the word – what strikes you most is its sheer mass rising over town like some Tolkienesque dark lord's tower rather than a place of Christian worship.

Step inside and the contrast with that brutal exterior is total. No surface was left untouched by the Italian artists who, in the early 16th century, painted their way, chapel by chapel, the length of its vast nave. An intricately carved, lacy rood screen, many of its statues smashed in the Revolution, spans the sanctuary. The stained-glass windows in the apse and choir date from the 14th to 16th centuries.

On no account miss the **grand chœur** (great choir; adult/under 12yr €2/free, adult Jul & Aug €1.50) with its frescos, chapels and 30 biblical polychrome figures, finely carved in stone.

At the western end, behind today's main altar, is *Le Jugement Dernier* (The Last Judgement; 1490), a vivid doomsday horror show of the damned being boiled in oil, beheaded or tortured by demons and monsters.

Look out for organ concerts in July and August (5pm Wednesday, 4pm Sunday).

PAINTER, LITHOGRAPHER, POSTER DESIGNER

Henri de Toulouse-Lautrec (1864–1901), Albi's most famous son, was famously short. As a teenager he broke both legs in separate accidents, stunting his growth and leaving him unable to walk without his trademark canes.

He spent his early twenties studying painting in Paris, where he mixed with other artists including Van Gogh. In 1890, at the height of the belle époque, he abandoned Impressionism and took to observing and sketching Paris' colourful nightlife. His favourite subjects included cabaret singer Aristide Bruant, cancan dancers from the Moulin Rouge and prostitutes from the rue des Moulins, sketched to capture movement and expression in a few simple lines.

With sure, fast strokes he would sketch on whatever was at hand – a scrap of paper or a tablecloth, tracing paper or buff-coloured cardboard. He also became a skilled and sought-after lithographer and poster designer until drinking and general overindulgence in the heady nightlife scene led to his premature death in 1901.

MUSÉE TOULOUSE-LAUTREC

The **Musée Toulouse-Lautrec** (☎ 05 63 49 48 70; www.musee-toulouse-lautrec.com; place Ste-Cécile; adult/student/under 14yr €5/2.50/free; 🕑 9am-6pm Jul & Aug, 9am-noon & 2-6pm Jun & Sep, 10am-noon & 2-5pm or 6pm Oct-May, closed Tue Oct-Mar) is inside Palais de la Berbie, a fortress-like 13th- to 15th-century archbishop's palace. It boasts over 500 examples of Toulouse-Lautrec's work, giving an excellent idea of his development as an artist – everything from simple pencil sketches and rough pastel drafts to the final works such as his celebrated Parisian brothel scenes, with the *Salon de la rue des Moulins* taking pride of place. On the top floor are works by Degas, Matisse and Rodin. The attractive palace courtyard and ornamental **gardens** (admission free; 🕑 8am-7pm Apr-Sep, to 6pm Oct-Mar) are worth wandering around.

A short stroll away is the privately owned **Maison Natale de Toulouse-Lautrec** (14 rue Henri de Toulouse-Lautrec) where the artist was born. Next-door neighbour is **La Maison de Lapérouse** (14 rue Henri de Toulouse-Lautrec) where the Albi-born explorer lived before sailing around the Pacific in 1785. Both are shut to the public.

BOAT TRIPS

From mid-June to mid-September, **Albi Croisières** (☎ 05 63 43 59 63; www.albi-croisieres.com) runs half-hour **boat trips** (adult/3-12yr €6/4; 🕑 11am, 11.45am & every 40min 2-6pm) aboard a *gabarre*, a flat-bottomed sailing barge of the kind used to haul goods down the Garonne to Bordeaux. Boats depart from the Berges du Tarn landing stage.

ALBI PASS

This card (€6.50), sold at the tourist office, gives free admission to the Musée Toulouse-Lautrec and cathedral choir and offers other reductions and concessions around town.

Festivals & Events

Carnaval Albi celebrates Carnaval at the beginning of Lent (February or March) with particular gusto and confetti galore.

Voix-là In May, Voix-là (get it?) celebrates vocal music in all its richness.

Pause Guitare Early July's Pause Guitare, held in the sumptuous space of place Ste-Cécile, brings together the best of French singing and accompaniment.

Sleeping

Hôtel St-Clair (☎ 05 63 54 25 66; http://andrieu.michele.free.fr; 8 rue St-Clair; d €42-65;) Sweetly placed on a pedestrian street in the old quarter, this two-star hotel feels like home. Wafts of home-cooking drift across the small flower-filled courtyard and an old-fashioned bar gives reception a cosy air. Free wi-fi.

Le Vieil Alby (☎ 05 63 54 14 69; http://pagesperso-orange.fr/le-vieil-alby; 25 rue Henri de Toulouse-Lautrec; s/d €44/53; 🕑 closed Jan) This tiny old-town hotel falls under the Logis de France umbrella group and is located above a restaurant cooking up local fare.

Hôtel George V (☎ 05 63 54 24 16; www.hotelgeorgev.com; 29 av Maréchal Joffre; s/d/tr €45/50/55) Friendly, welcoming and family-run, this nine-room hotel with red bricks and blue shutters is excellent value. Rooms are spacious and breakfast is served on a small terrace. Free wi-fi.

Mercure Albi Bastides (☎ 05 63 47 66 66; www.accorhotels.com; 41 rue Porta; d €82-97;) Occupying an 18th-century brick building that served as a mill and later pasta factory, this hotel on the other side of the water enjoys an idyllic riverside spot. Its 58 rooms are handsomely furnished, and prime views of red-brick Albi grace its restaurant terrace. Free wi-fi and parking.

Eating

Old Albi is bespeckled with places to eat, including a tasty line-up along the western leg of V-shaped rue Henri de Toulouse Lautrec.

Lou Sicret (☎ 05 63 38 26 40; 1 rue Timbal; mains €15, entrée/plat du jour €4/7.90; ⏲ lunch & dinner Tue-Sat) Hidden at the end of a shop-clad alley, this very Occitan, arty restaurant serves regional *cuisine d'oc* on a tree-shaded patio.

La Table du Sommelier (☎ 05 63 46 20 10; 20 rue Porta; lunch menus €13-16, dinner menus €25; ⏲ lunch & dinner Tue-Sat) Cross the 11th-century red-brick Pont Vieux to find this delightful bistro where the best of wines (the owner's a qualified sommelier) are married with fine food. The menus (€32) built around white, rosé or Gaillac wines are a particular delight.

Le Lautrec (☎ 05 63 54 86 55; 13-15 rue Henri de Toulouse-Lautrec; 2-/3-course menu €15/17, dinner menu €30; ⏲ lunch & dinner Tue-Sat, lunch Sun) Dine on the terrace or in the former stables of the Lautrec family – the house where Toulouse-Lautrec was born is opposite. Cuisine is market-driven and a *promenade gourmande* (€18/26/32/38 for one/two/three/four courses) takes diners on a tasty regional tour.

L'Epicurien (☎ 05 63 53 10 70; www.restaurantlepicurien.com; 42 place Jean Jaurès; starters/mains €15/25, menus €28 & €37; ⏲ lunch & dinner Tue-Sat) The steely grey and glass facade says it all: this dedicated gastronomy space by Swedish chef Rikard and Belgian front-of-house Patricia is hip, smart and trend savvy. Cuisine is Mediterranean with a creative hint of fusion.

Also recommended:

Le Tournesol (☎ 05 63 38 38 14; 11 rue de l'Ort-en-Salvy; starters/mains €6.90/9.50; ⏲ lunch Tue-Sat & dinner Fri) The 100% vegetarian choice.

La Tête de l'Art (☎ 05 63 38 44 75; 7 rue de la Piale; menus €15-30; ⏲ lunch & dinner May-Jul & Sep, Thu-Mon Aug & Oct-Apr) Tripe and boned pig's trotter mix with a more traditional local fare.

SELF-CATERING

Buy fresh fare and fill your water bottle with wine (€1.10 a litre) at the striking, red-brick and glass **covered market** (place St-Julien; ⏲ 8am-2pm Tue-Thu, 8am-2pm & 5-8pm Fri, 7am-2pm & 5-8pm Sat, 8am-2pm Sun).

Getting There & Away

From the **Halte des Autobus** (☎ 05 63 54 58 61; place Jean Jaurès), buses serve Castres (€2, 50 minutes, up to 10 daily).

From the **train station** (place Stalingrad) there are trains to/from Rodez (€12.60, 1½ hours, seven daily), Millau (€20.80, 2¾ hours, two daily) and Toulouse (€11.40, 1¼ hours, at least hourly).

Getting Around

Rent town bikes from **Basile Vélo & Oxygen** (☎ 05 63 38 43 09; http://chrisbas.ifrance.com, in French; 28 av Maréchal Foch; per day/week €15/75; ⏲ 1.30-6.30pm Mon, 9am-noon & 1.30-7pm Tue-Sat).

Pick up information on local bus services at the **Espace Albibus** (☎ 05 63 38 43 43; 14 rue de l'Hôtel de Ville; ⏲ 2-5pm Mon, 10am-5pm Tue-Fri).

Call ☎ 05 63 54 85 03 for a taxi.

CASTRES

pop 42,900

Founded by the Romans as a *castrum* (settlement), this town with place Jean Jaurès at its heart is something of an ode to its most famous son, the founding father of French socialism.

Downstream from the **tourist office** (☎ 05 63 62 63 62; www.tourisme-castres.fr; 2 place de la République; ⏲ 9.30am-12.30pm & 1-6pm Mon-Sat, 10.30am-noon & 2-4pm Sun Jul & Aug, 9.30am-12.30pm & 2-6pm Mon-Sat, 2.30-4.30pm Sun Sep-Jun), on the eastern bank of the River Agoût, are the one-time workshops of tanners, weavers and dyers who made the city's wealth.

The lovely formal gardens of the **Musée Goya** (☎ 05 63 71 59 30; Hôtel de Ville, rue de l'Hôtel de Ville; adult/under 18yr €2.30/free; ⏲ 10am-6pm Jul & Aug, 9am-noon & 2-5pm or 6pm Tue-Sat, 10am-noon & 2-5pm or 6pm Sun Sep-Jun) were designed by Le Nôtre, architect

À PIED

Dump the car and opt for exploration *à pied* (on foot): Albi's **Espace Randos et Paysages** (☎ 05 63 47 33 70; www.ffrandonnee-tarn.org; 6 rue St-Clair; ⏲ 10am-noon & 3-6pm Tue-Fri, to 7pm Sat), run by the Comité Régional de la Randonnée Pédestre, sells walking maps and topoguides – many outlining short family-orientated walks – and stocks a mountain of leaflets outlining walks around Albi. *L'Echappe Verte d'Albi* details three 1km-long 'green' strolls in the city itself.

of Versailles' parkland. The museum's collection of Spanish art includes several works by Goya himself and canvases by Murillo, Ribera and Picasso.

Parc de Gourjade (av de Roquecourbe, D89), north of town, has campsites, golf course, 15km of jogging trails, riding centre, swimming pool and ice-skating rink. Take bus 6 or 7 from the Arcades stop on place Jean Jaurès or hop aboard **Le Miredames** (☎ 05 63 62 41 76; return adult/6-13yr/under 5yr/family €4/1.60/free/10; ⌚ up to 5 daily May-Oct), a wooden river barge that links the park with the quay in front of the tourist office.

MONTAUBAN

pop 53,200

Montauban, southern France's second-oldest *bastide* on the right bank of the River Tarn, was founded in 1144 by Count Alphonse Jourdain of Toulouse who, legend says, was so charmed by its trailing willow trees (*alba* in Occitan) that he named the place Mont Alba. It was badly battered during the Albigensian crusade and later became a Huguenot stronghold, only to again suffer persecution when the Edict of Nantes (1598) was repealed by Louis XIV a century later.

Montauban's attractive arcaded 17th-century brick buildings around place Nationale date from the prosperous decades following the Catholic reconquest.

Information

Tourist Office (☎ 05 63 63 60 60; www.montauban-tourisme.com; 4 rue du Collège; ⌚ 9.30am-6.30pm Mon-Sat, 9.30am-12.30pm Sun Jul & Aug, 9.30am-12.30pm & 2-6.30pm Sep-Jun)

Sights

Jean Auguste Dominique Ingres, the sensual neoclassical painter and accomplished violinist, was a native of Montauban. Many of his works, plus canvases by Tintoretto, Van Dyck, Courbet and others, are in the **Musée Ingres** (☎ 05 63 22 12 91; 13 rue de l'Hôtel de Ville; adult/under 18yr €4/free; ⌚ 10am-6pm daily Jul & Aug, 10am-noon & 2-6pm Tue-Sat Sep-Jun, 10am-noon & 2-6pm Sun Easter-Jun & Sep–mid-Oct), a riverside bishop's palace. The entry ticket also admits you to the nearby Histoire Naturelle (natural history), Terroir (local costumes and traditions) and Résistance et Déportation (with mementos of WWII) museums.

An Ingres masterpiece, *Le Vœu de Louis XIII*, depicting the king pledging France to the Virgin, hangs in the 18th-century **Cathédrale Notre Dame de l'Assomption** (place Franklin Roosevelt; ⌚ 10am-noon & 2-6pm Mon-Sat). The fine 13th-century **Église St-Jacques**, in mellow pink brick, still bears cannonball marks from Louis XIII's 1621 siege of the town.

Festivals & Events

Alors Chante A festival of traditional French song in May.

Jazz à Montauban A week-long jam in July.

Légende des Quatre-Cent Coups (400 Blows) This weekend street festival at the end of August commemorates the moment when, says local lore, a fortune-teller told Louis XIII, besieging Montauban, to blast off 400 cannons simultaneously against the town, which still failed to fall.

Sleeping

Hôtel du Commerce (☎ 05 63 66 31 32; www.hotel-commerce-montauban.com; 9 place Franklin Roosevelt; s/d/q €52.50/64/81; ⌘) Overlooking the cathedral, this is a charming family affair run by the Passedats for generations. A highlight is the breakfast salon with original 1930s Villeroy & Boch floor tiles, Calais lace curtains and Botticelli reproductions on the walls. Free wi-fi.

Hôtel d'Orsay (☎ 05 63 66 06 66; www.hotel-restaurant-orsay.com, in French; 29 av Roger Salengro; d €55-65; ⌘) A stone's throw from the station, this hotel has comfortable if dated rooms within a solid building of mellow red. In summer, lounge on its floral terrace. Its upmarket restaurant, La Cuisine d'Alain, is open for lunch Tuesday to Friday and dinner Monday to Saturday (lunch/dinner *menu* costs €23/60).

Eating

Place Nationale is ringed with several cheapish if unstartling brasseries.

La Mangeoire (☎ 05 63 20 70 64; 12 rue d'Auriol; starters €10-12, mains €15-17; ⌚ lunch & dinner) Young, fun and bursting with creativity, La Mangeoire is a tapas bar and drinking haunt where a cultured set enjoys Mediterranean cuisine and an energising dose of contagious atmosphere. Everything spills outside in summer. Dessert? *Si tu es sage* (if you're good)!

Le Couvert des Brasseurs (☎ 05 63 91 30 61; 27 place Nationale; meat/cheese platter €22/16; ⌚ lunch & dinner) Seafood is what this contemporary space with exposed stone walls and pillar-box red chairs cooks up. Feast on a *plateau royal* (€40/75 for one/two people) or a dozen oysters (€15).

Au Fil de l'Eau (☎ 05 63 66 11 85; aufildeleau@wanadoo.fr; 14 quai du Dr Lafforgue; lunch menu Tue-Fri €18, menus €35-55; ⌚ lunch & dinner Tue-Sat, lunch Sun) An interior decorated with modern art for sale offsets a tempting menu crammed with local products at this riverside restaurant. *Crème brulée de foie gras* drizzled with balsamic vinegar, followed by a pig-trotter mousse on a bed of Le Puy lentils, formed part of our memorable feast.

Morning **farmers markets** are on Saturday (place Prax-Paris) and Wednesday (place Lalaque), in addition to a smaller daily one (place Nationale).

Getting There & Away

From the **train station** (av Mayenne), about 1km from place Nationale across the Tarn, trains serve Toulouse (€10, 30 minutes, frequent), Bordeaux (€26.70, two hours, frequent) and Moissac (€5.20, 20 minutes, five daily).

MOISSAC

pop 12,300

Pretty riverside Moissac, an easy trip from Montauban or Toulouse, remains a well-trodden halt for walkers following in the footsteps of Santiago de Compostela pilgrims on the Spain-bound GR65 route.

Abbaye St-Pierre (place Durand de Bredon), resplendent with France's finest Romanesque sculpture, became a model for more modest ecclesiastical buildings throughout southern France. Above the **south portal**, completed around 1130, is a superb tympanum depicting St John's vision of the Apocalypse, with Christ in majesty flanked by the apostles, angels and 24 awestruck elders. In the **cloister** (adult/12-18yr €5/3.50; 9am-7pm Jul & Aug, 9am-noon & 2-6pm Mon-Fri, 10am-noon & 2-6pm Sat & Sun Apr-Jun, Sep & Oct, 10am-noon & 2-5pm Mon-Fri, 2-5pm Sat & Sun Nov-Mar) 116 delicate marble columns support wedge-shaped, deeply carved capitals, each a little masterpiece of foliage, earthy figures or biblical scenes. The Revolution's toll is sickening – nearly every face is smashed.

Enter through the **tourist office** (☎ 05 63 04 01 85; www.moissac.fr; 6 place Durand de Bredon; as cloister). Cloister admission includes a museum of folk art and furnishings, and a library containing replicas of the monastery's beautiful illuminated manuscripts.

Le Pont Napoléon (☎ 05 63 04 01 55; www.le-pont-napoleon.com; 2 allée Montebello; s/d from €35/40) stands guard over the bridge that Napoleon built after his stay here in 1808. This historic 12-room hotel is a delight. Its retro rooms are stylish and its gastronomic restaurant, **Le Table de Nos Fils** (menus €25-38; lunch & dinner Fri-Tue, dinner Thu), creates a real buzz. Chef Patrick Delaroux runs weekend cooking courses.

Le Moulin de Moissac (☎ 05 63 32 88 88; www.lemoulindemoissac.com, in French; esplanade du Moulin; d €68-85) is a grain mill built on the banks of the Tarn in 1474. It exported flour to the young USA in the 18th century, was shelled during WWI and sheltered Jewish children and clandestine Resistance activity in WWII. Revel in unparalleled river views from its hotel rooms and waterside **restaurant** (lunch/dinner menu €22/34).

Five trains daily run to/from Montauban (€5.20, 20 minutes), most serving Toulouse (€12.10).

AUCH

pop 23,500

Auch (it rhymes with Gosh!) has been an important trade crossroads ever since the Romans conquered a Celtic tribe called the Auscii and established Augusta Auscorum on the flats east of the River Gers. The town's heyday was in the Middle Ages when the counts of Armagnac and their archbishops together ran the city and built its cathedral. Its second flowering was in the late 18th century, as new roads were pushed southwards to Toulouse and into the Pyrenees. A slide into rural obscurity followed the Revolution in 1789.

BAMBOO BONANZA

You don't get any greener that the attractively landscaped, well thought-out forest of the **Bamboo Parc** (☎ 06 70 64 55 28; www.bamboo-parc.com; Château de Lériet, Gandalou; adult/2-12yr €6/3; 2-6pm Wed, Sat & Sun Mar-May & Sep-Nov, 2-6pm Wed, Fri & Sat, 10am-6pm Sun Jun, 2-6pm Mon-Sat, 10am-6pm Sun Jul & Aug), an 9-hectare park arranged around the ruins of a château where 100-year-old banana trees rub leaves with bonsais and 80 types of Chinese bamboo. Log cabins, water-spouting dragons, witches and *lutins* (elves) keep kids enchanted, and the monthly *bien être* (well-being) shiatsu sessions (two hours, €25) create a Zen Sunday moment. Music concerts complete the open-air repertoire. Find it 8km east of Moissac, signposted off the D72 (direction Gandalou).

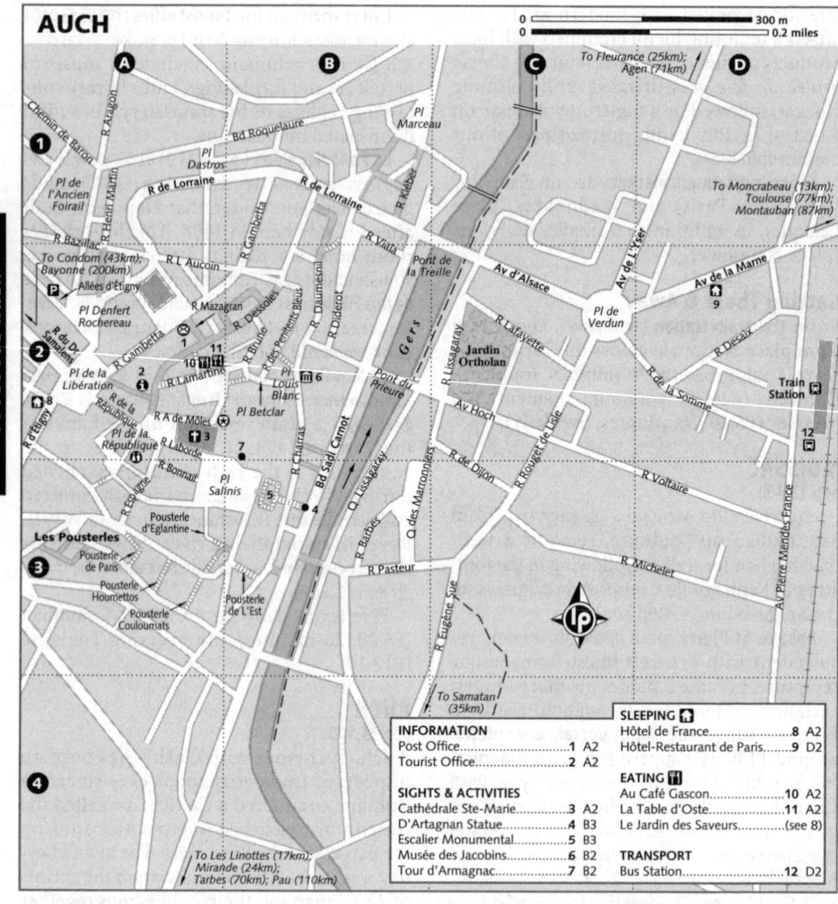

INFORMATION	
Post Office	1 A2
Tourist Office	2 A2
SIGHTS & ACTIVITIES	
Cathédrale Ste-Marie	3 A2
D'Artagnan Statue	4 B3
Escalier Monumental	5 B3
Musée des Jacobins	6 B2
Tour d'Armagnac	7 B2
SLEEPING	
Hôtel de France	8 A2
Hôtel-Restaurant de Paris	9 D2
EATING	
Au Café Gascon	10 A2
La Table d'Oste	11 A2
Le Jardin des Saveurs	(see 8)
TRANSPORT	
Bus Station	12 D2

Orientation

Hilltop Auch, with place de la Libération, place de la République and the cathedral at its heart, has most of the sights, restaurants, shops and hotels. Pedestrianised rue Dessoles is the principal shopping street. The old town, tumbling away to the south, is a web of lanes, steps and little courtyards. Across the River Gers is the 'new' Auch and adjacent train and bus stations.

Information

Post Office (rue Gambetta)

Tourist Office (☎ 05 62 05 22 89; www.auch-tourisme.com; 1 rue Dessoles; ⌚ 9.30am-6.30pm Mon-Sat, 10am-12.15pm & 3-6pm Sun mid-Jul–mid-Aug, 9.15am-noon & 2-6pm Mon-Sat mid-Aug–mid-Jul, 10am-12.15pm Sun May–mid-Jul & mid-Aug–Sep) Inside 15th-century Maison Fedel.

Sights

CATHÉDRALE STE-MARIE

This magnificent building, a Unesco World Heritage Site, moved Napoléon II to exclaim 'A cathedral like this should be put in a museum!' Constructed over two centuries, **Cathédrale Ste-Marie** (⌚ 8.30am-noon & 2-5pm) ranges in style from pure Gothic to Italian Renaissance. To appreciate the contrast, take a look at the doorway in the external north wall; the lower part is lacy Gothic while the upper, unadorned arch is purest Florentine.

The heavy western facade impresses with its sheer bulk – and looks imposingly grand when illuminated at night – but the real splendour lies within: 18 vivid 16th-century Renaissance stained-glass windows and an astonishing **choir** (admission incl audioguide €2), featuring over 1500 individual carvings of biblical scenes and mythological creatures in the 113 oak choir stalls.

For a multisensory experience, enjoy a free **recital** (6pm Sun Jul & Aug) on the cathedral's grand booming organ or look out for occasional chamber-music concerts (tickets €10).

Behind the cathedral, the 14th-century, 40m-high **Tour d'Armagnac** (closed to the public) served Auch's archbishops as their archive, then briefly became a lock-up during the Revolution and later times of trouble.

MUSÉE DES JACOBINS

An old boy around since 1793, the **Musée des Jacobins** (05 62 05 74 79; 4 place Louis Blanc; adult/under 18yr €3/free; 10am-noon & 2-6pm Apr-Oct, 2-5pm Mon-Fri, 10am-noon & 2-5pm Sat & Sun Nov, Dec, Feb & Mar) fills an elegant 14th-century Dominican monastery. Its eclectic collection came from property seized during the Revolution and includes early Gallo-Roman villa frescos, pre-Columbian artefacts from the Americas and a rich collection of 19th-century Gascon costumes. Show your ticket to the cathedral's choir to get half-price admission to the museum, and vice versa.

ESCALIER MONUMENTAL

Auch's 234-step **Escalier Monumental** (Monumental Stairway) drops to the river from place Salinis. Near the bottom postures a **statue of d'Artagnan**, the fictional swashbuckling Gascon hero immortalised by Alexandre Dumas in *Les Trois Mousquetaires (The Three Musketeers)*. Nearby, a series of narrow, stepped alleyways, collectively called Les Pousterles, also plunge to the plain.

Sleeping

Hôtel Restaurant de Paris (05 62 63 26 22; 38 av de la Marne; s/d €40/43, with shower €32/37, with shared bathroom €27/30; Dec-Oct) Cheap as chips and old-fashioned, the Paris has been run by one family for over 70 years. With few concessions to the passing years, it nevertheless has cosily furnished rooms, a well-stocked bar and restaurant serving copious quantities.

Hôtel de France (05 62 61 71 71; www.hoteldefrance-auch.com; 1 place de la Libération; s/d from €70/86;) Shabby from the outside, this age-old hotel is sweetness and light inside. Its *chambres prestiges* (€140) and jacuzzi-clad suites (€230 to €330) are grand in size and decor, as is Le Jardin des Saveurs (lunch *menu* €20.50, dinner *menu* €27 to €55), its splendid restaurant in a glorious Second Empire salon.

Eating & Drinking

A stroll along rue Dessoles uncovers several informal, friendly bars-cum-bistros.

La Table d'Oste (05 62 05 55 62; www.table-oste-restaurant.com; 7 rue Lamartine; lunch/dinner menu €16/37; lunch & dinner Tue-Fri, lunch Sat, dinner Mon mid-Jun–Oct, lunch & dinner Tue-Sat Nov–mid-Jun) Strung with copper

GIMONT: A GOURMET GALLIVANT

Foodies with a fetish for *foie* (liver) should gallivant to **Gimont**, a village in the Gers (www.foie-gras-gers.com), 28km east of Auch on the Toulouse-bound N124, where two fine-food houses conserve the corn-fattened livers of ducks *(canards)* and geese *(oies)* to make France's best foie gras (fattened liver).

Comtesse du Barry (05 62 67 85 44; www.comtessedubarry.com; 9am-12.30pm & 2-7pm Mon-Sat, 10am-12.30pm & 2.30-7.30pm Sun Sep–mid-Jul), with upmarket *épiceries* (specialists grocers) from all over France, has been in business in Gimont since 1908 and offers free guided visits of its factory at 9am Thursday; advance bookings only. Drool over foie gras in all its guises – *frais* (fresh) and *entier* (whole), *mi-cuit* (semicooked) or preserved in the form of a *bloc de foie gras* – in its boutique.

Direct competitor **Ducs de Gascogne** (05 62 67 84 75; www.ducsdegascogne.com; 3 av de Cahuzac; starters €7-16.50, mains €10-15; lunch Tue-Sun) arrived in Gimont in 1953 and runs a restaurant with a museum above its shop. Liver predictably hogs the menu, the highlight being an inspired tasting platter of three foie-gras types – oven-baked to golden, spiced with black pepper and salt crystals or laced with black truffles. No time to stop? Grab a foie-gras sandwich (€6) to eat in the car.

Unforgettable is a trip around Gimont's weekly **Marché du Foie** (Liver Market; 8am-2pm Wed) and seasonal **Marché du Gras** (Fat Market; 8am-2pm Wed & Sun Nov-Mar) which ushers in a line-up of hundreds of ducks and geese – dead, but with head, beak and fattened liver very much intact.

LES LINOTTES

Lazily set amid gently rolling fields of yellow canola with a soul-stirring view of the spiky snow-capped Pyrenees as a backdrop, **Les Linottes** (☎ 05 62 61 04 79; www.leslinottes.com; Porteteny, Durban; d incl breakfast €60; dinner from €20), 17km south of Auch, is country living at its best. Everything at this three-bedroom *chambre d'hôte* – a converted hay barn – is ecological: the interior walls are built from bales of hay 'plastered' in a mix of earth and straw, stones cobble the floors of the spacious bathrooms with fabulous walk-in showers, and a waxed mud floor in the book-busy kitchen-cum-dining room lends it a distinctly modern air. Each room has its own terrace with table and chairs overlooking a lovely garden, and breakfast is a 100% homemade feast. Psychologist Laurence and TV producer Patrice, the creative couple behind the project, are planning an ecological swimming pool next, filtered naturally by frogs, aquatic plants and other wildlife.

pans from its beamed ceiling and bedecked with a wooden terrace, this local favourite cooks up a cosy dining experience, with ample beef, pork and duck to fill you to bursting.

Au Café Gascon (☎ 05 62 61 88 08; café.gascon@wanadoo.fr; 5 rue Lamartine; menus €35 & €48; lunch & dinner) Next-door neighbour Georges Nosella envelopes diners in an all-embracing Gascon experience with his regional fare, cultural happenings and so on. *Menus* must be booked at least two hours in advance; otherwise the only choice is the fixed €22 meal.

Getting There & Away

From the **bus station** (☎ 05 62 05 76 37; av Pierre Mendès-France) buses serve Condom (€6.50, 50 minutes, three daily) and Agen (€11, 1½ hours, five to seven daily). Trains or SNCF buses link Auch with Toulouse (€13.30, 1½ hours) from the neighbouring **train station** (av Pierre Mendès France).

CONDOM

pop 7250

Poor Condom, whose name has made it the butt of so many nudge-snigger, English-language jokes (the French don't even use the word, preferring *préservatif* or, more familiarly, *capote anglaise*, meaning 'English hood' – touché!).

Condom, whose name is actually a derivation of the old Gallo-Roman name Condatomagus, is a self-confident town on the River Baïse, worth a visit for its cathedral, locally produced Armagnac appreciated by Santiago de Compostela pilgrims for aeons, sober neoclassical mansions…and seasonal condom museum.

Information

Tourist Office (☎ 05 62 28 00 80; www.tourisme-tenareze.com; 1 place Bossuet; 9am-7pm Mon-Sat, 10.30am-12.30pm Sun Jul & Aug, 9am-noon & 2-6pm Mon-Sat Sep-Jun) Within the 13th-century Tour Auger d'Andiran.

Sights & Activities

Condom's 16th-century **Cathédrale St-Pierre** (place St-Pierre), with its lofty nave and elaborately carved chancel, is a rich example of southern Flamboyant Gothic architecture. Its most richly sculpted entrance – much defaced during the Revolution – gives onto the square. Abutting the cathedral on its northern side is the vast but delicately arched 16th-century **cloister**, topped with a tent-like structure to provide shelter to picnicking walkers heading south along the Chemin de St-Jacques.

Musée de l'Armagnac (☎ 05 62 28 47 17; 2 rue Jules Ferry; adult/child €2.20/1.10; 10am-noon & 3-6pm Apr-Oct, 2-5pm Wed-Sun Nov, Dec, Feb & Mar, closed Jan) portrays the traditional production of Armagnac, Gascony's fiery rival to cognac, distilled to the north in the Bordeaux vineyards.

For the real stuff, head to **Armagnac Ryst-Dupeyron** (☎ 05 62 28 08 08; 36 rue Jean Jaurès; admission free; 10am-noon & 2-6.30pm Mon-Fri year-round, plus 3.30-6.30pm Sat & Sun Jul & Aug), one of several Armagnac producers offering free sampling. Or try the **Cave Cooperative** (☎ 05 62 28 12 16) on the D931.

If you can't beat 'em, join 'em, must be the rationale behind Condom's seasonal **Musée du Preservatif** (Condom Museum; ☎ 05 62 68 25 69; 2 rue Jules Ferry; adult/under 18yr €3/1.50; 10am-noon & 3-7pm early-Jul–mid-Sep), a space relating the contraceptive's history from its birth in 1665.

Down by the Baïse on quai Bouquerie, **Gascogne Navigation** (☎ 05 62 28 46 46; www.gascogne-navigation.com; La Capitainerie, 3 av d'Aquitaine; 9am-noon & 2.30pm or 3pm–7pm) runs 1½-hour river cruises (adult/child costs €7.80/5.80) and 2½-hour bring-your-own-picnic (€12/8) or lunch cruises (€33/19). From April to October, it rents small boats (hour/half-day/full day costs €29/59/99) for up to six people to frolic in the sun afloat.

Festivals & Events

Bandas à Condom (www.festival-de-bandas.com) Marching and brass bands from all over Europe for 48 hours of nonstop oompah on the second weekend in May.

Les Nuits Musicales Operetta in the cloister in July and August.

Sleeping

Camping Caravaning Municipal de l'Argenté (☎ 05 62 28 17 32; campingmunicipal@condom.org; chemin de l'Argenté; tent/adult/under 7yr €3.42/3.19/1.37; 🕒 Apr-Sep, reception 1.30-8pm) This well-equipped campsite is beside the River Baïse where, come July and August, you can paddle in a canoe or kayak. Find it 2.3km southwest of town along the D931.

Le Relais de la Ténarèze (☎ 05 62 28 02 54; 22 av d'Aquitaine; d/tr €51/74) This welcoming *étape pélerin* (pilgrim stop) run by pinny-clad Madame for the past 15 years gets packed with groups of Spain-bound cyclists and walkers of Chemin de St-Jacques. For hearty home cooking, invest in the evening *menu du terroir* (local-produce set menu; €19) of gigantic dimensions. From April to October reservations are essential.

Le Logis des Cordeliers (☎ 05 62 28 03 68; www.logisdescordeliers.com; rue de la Paix; d €52-65, tr €68; 🕒 Feb-Dec) A modern building, this family-run, family-friendly abode is peaceful and proffers lovely pool views from most of its 21 rooms with small balconies strung with flowers.

Côté Remparts (☎ 05 62 28 38 97; bolac.ph@orange.fr; 7 rue Jules Ferry; s/d/tr/q incl breakfast €70/85/100/115) Near the cathedral, Philippe and Catherine Bolac's mellow-hued *chambre d'hôte* with oyster-grey painted shutters hosts seven guests. One room faces the street; the other the garden.

Les Trois Lys (☎ 05 62 28 33 33; www.lestroislys.com; 38 rue Gambetta; d €130-170) Ten individually and tastefully furnished rooms languish within this 18th-century mansion on Condom's main street. A pool, cosy bar and superb restaurant make it an ideal self-contained retreat.

Eating

For feisty appetites, Le Relais de la Ténarèze (see left) is a sound choice.

Librairie Gourmande (☎ 05 62 28 17 35; 3 place Bossuet; plat du jour €7; 🕒 10am-12.30pm & 3.30-7pm Tue-Fri,

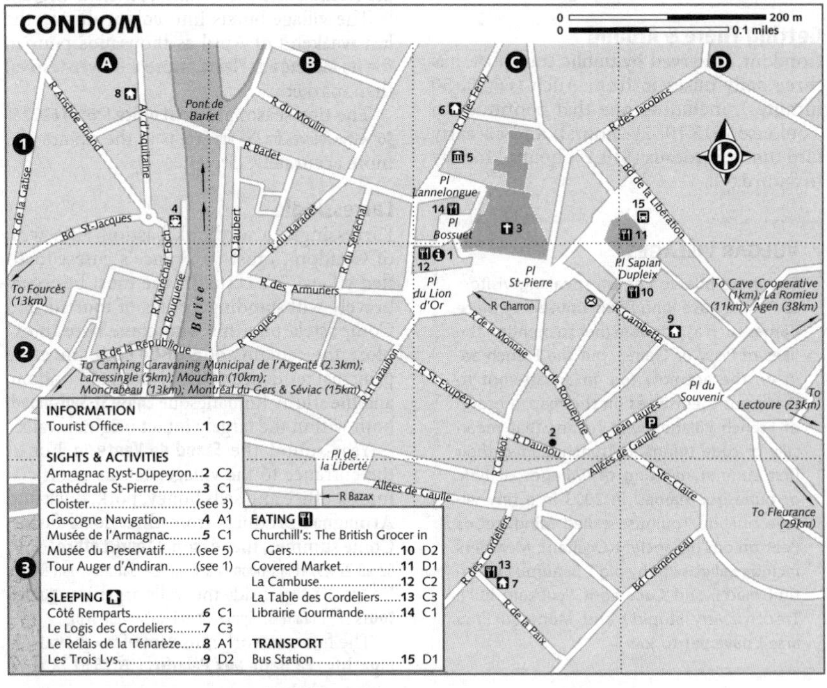

10am-12.30pm Sat) Grab a couple of titles from the bookshop and plop yourself down at a table in the café to browse in leisure over a light lunch or a slice of Armagnac-laced fruit cake.

La Cambuse (☎ 05 62 68 48 95; place Bossuet; 2-/3-course menu €10/12, salads & bruschettas €10-13; ⏰ lunch Mon-Sat, dinner Fri & Sat) This quick-fix place next to the tourist office cooks up snacks and more substantial fare to eat around a gay violet-pink bar, on place Bossuet in summer, or for takeaway.

La Table des Cordeliers (☎ 05 62 68 43 82; www.latabledescordeliers.fr; 1 rue des Cordeliers; weekday lunch menu €22, dinner menus €39 & €58, with wine €90; ⏰ lunch & dinner Thu-Sat, lunch Sun, dinner Tue & Wed) There aren't many places you can dine beneath the sweeping stone arches of a 13th-century chapel: A Michelin-starred, Gascon-inspired cuisine befits the stylish setting.

SELF-CATERING

The weekly Marché au Gras held Wednesday and Saturday morning in the **covered market** (place Sapian Dupleix) is more experience than shopping trip. **Churchill's: The British Grocer in Gers** (☎ 05 62 68 43 89; place Sapian Dupleix; ⏰ 10am-12.30pm & 2-5.30pm Tue-Sat) sells British groceries.

Getting There & Around

Condom, ill-served by public transport, has three daily buses to/from Auch (€6.50, 50 minutes), including one that continues to Toulouse (€15.10, 2½ hours), and an early bird run to Bordeaux (€19, 2¾ hours, Monday to Saturday).

VULGAR VILLAGES

The more puerile English-speaking visitors to France have long been amused by place names such as Condom (not to mention the likes of Pissy or Stains), but the French are in on the act now too. In an attempt to really put themselves on the map, a group of French villages with names that mean silly or rude things in French staged their first summit meeting of 'Villages of lyric or burlesque names' in 2003 in a tiny village outside Toulouse called Mingocebos ('eat onions' in ancient Occitan). Members include Saligos ('filthy pig'), Beaufou ('beautiful mad'), and Cocumont ('cuckold hill'). Trecon ('very stupid') and Montcuq ('my arse') have yet to join.

AROUND CONDOM

This swath of the ancient province of Gascon was in its time wild frontier country, caught between the French, entrenched in Toulouse, and the English with their power base in Bordeaux. The better-endowed of the hapless villages caught in the crossfire fortified themselves against all comers, creating what are known as *bastides*. You can drive from one to another in a long morning. But better to take them at a more gentle pace; these mild undulating lands are ideal for cycling. Or view them from the basket of a hot-air balloon (see p758).

The area's claim to contemporary fame is as a producer of Armagnac, a feisty liqueur that invariably finds its way into the local Gascon cuisine, be it as a lacing for prune soufflé, with foie gras or duck.

Fourcès

Fourcès (pronounce that *s*), 13km northwest of Condom, is a picturesque *bastide* on the River Auzoue. Uniquely circular, it was founded by the English invaders. Nowadays, its shady expanse is ringed by well-restored medieval houses. In one corner is the tiny, dusty **Musée des Vieux Métiers** (Museum of Ancient Crafts).

The village bursts into colour during the last weekend of April as thousands pour in for its **Marché aux Fleurs**, more a flower festival than market.

The tiny seasonal **tourist office** (☎ 05 62 29 50 96; www.fources.fr; ⏰ Jun-Sep) is in the square (or, more accurately, circle).

Larressingle

Larressingle, a textbook bastion 5km west of Condom, must be France's cutest fortified village. It's certainly the most besieged, bravely withstanding armies of tourists and Compostela pilgrims who come here to explore the remains of a **castle keep**, once the principal residence of the bishops of Condom, and the sturdy Romanesque **Église St-Sigismond**, both within the largely intact original walls.

Year-round the **Stand de Vente**, a hut at the entrance to the village, acts as unofficial tourist office and sells honey, pork, duck and Armagnac products from three local farms. Come summer, the seasonal **tourist office** (☎ 05 62 68 22 49; 10am-noon & 3-7pm Tue-Sat May, Jun & Sep, Tue-Sun Jul & Aug) inside the walls organises **guided tours** (⏰ 11am, 3.30pm & 5pm Tue-Sat Jun-Sep).

The fun waxwork museum of medieval village life, **La Halte aux Pèlerins** (☎ 05 62 28 11 58;

ARMAGNAC

Ask any Gascon: Armagnac slips down just as smoothly as the more heavily produced and marketed Cognac to the north. Produced from white grapes that ripen in the sandy soils hereabouts and aged in barrels of local black oak, it was originally taken for medicinal reasons but is drunk with gusto today, often as a digestive. In local restaurants, Floc de Gascogne – a liqueur wine made from Armagnac and red or white grape juice – is the traditional aperitif.

A couple of major distillers are headquartered in Condom (p754), and driving or cycling among the vineyards, you'll stumble upon one siren-call notice after another, signalling you to taste and buy direct from a small-scale farmer-distiller in his *chais* (traditional wine cellar).

Two dreamy addresses oozing history are 13th-century **Château de Cassaigne** (☎ 05 62 28 04 02; www.chateaudecassaigne.com; Cassaigne; 🕑 10am-7pm daily Jul & Aug, 9am-noon & 2-6pm Tue-Sun Sep-Jun), 6.5km southwest of Condom, just off the D931 to Eauze, where you can visit the cellars and sample the Armagnac from its 18th-century distillery; and 17th-century **Château du Busca Maniban** (☎ 05 62 28 40 38; www.buscamaniban.com; Mansencome; 🕑 2-6pm Mon-Sat Apr-Nov), the stuff of dreams 5.5km further south along the scenic D229 in Mansencome.

adult/12-18yr €7.50/5; 🕑 10.30am-12.30pm & 2-7pm Jul-Sep, 2.30-6pm Tue-Sun Apr-Jun & Oct, 2.30-5.30pm Sun Nov-Mar), has optional English commentary. Outside the fortifications, **Cité des Machines du Moyen Âge** (☎ 05 62 68 33 90; adult/child €5/3; 🕑 10am-7pm Jul & Aug, 2-6pm school holidays, Sat & Sun Mar-Jun & Sep–mid-Nov) particularly excites the male species with its feisty displays of catapults, canons and other medieval war machines, arranged as if about to assault the city.

With the Chemin St-Jacques passing footsteps away, **Auberge de Larressingle** (☎ 05 62 28 29 67; http://auberge.larressingle.free.fr; d €55, half-board per person €49.50), with six rooms and prime village views, is a busy pit stop for hikers. Decor is countryside rustic and fare is local – foie gras, *magret de canard* (duck breast) or *confit de canard* (preserved duck) and lots of Gers poultry.

Montréal du Gers & Séviac

Montréal du Gers, dating to 1255, was one of Gascony's first *bastides*. Its chunky Gothic church squats beside place Hôtel de Ville, the arcaded main square.

At Séviac, 1.5km southwest, are the excavated remains – a work in progress – of a luxurious 4th-century **Villa Gallo-Romaine** (☎ 05 62 29 48 57; adult/under 12yr €4/free; 🕑 10am-7pm Jul & Aug, 10am-noon & 2-6pm Mar-Jun & Sep-Nov), part of the agricultural estate of a Roman aristocrat. Archeologists so far have revealed the villa's baths, outbuildings and large areas of spectacular mosaic floors.

Admission includes entry to the small museum within Montréal's **tourist office** (☎ 05 62 29 42 85; place Hôtel de Ville; 🕑 9.30am-12.30pm & 2-6pm Tue-Sat) displaying artefacts from Séviac.

Abbaye de Flaran

Founded in 1151 by Pyrenees monks from Escaladieu, this delightful Cistercian **abbey** (☎ 05 62 28 50 19; Valence sur Baïse; adult/student/under 18yr €4/2/free, 1st Sun of month Nov-Mar free; 🕑 9.30am-7pm Jul & Aug, 9.30am-noon & 2-6pm Feb-Jun & Sep–mid-Jan), guarded by a 14th-century fortress door turned pigeon loft, is southwest France's loveliest. Built in a remote green spot, it was occupied until the French Revolution, by which point no more than a handful of monks remained. Its vaulted chapter hall propped up by coloured marble columns, refectory with 15th-century triple arch window and decorative moulding (spot the phoenix and pelican), and recently renovated monks' cells are particularly fine. Watch for art exhibitions and classical-music concerts in its grounds.

La Romieu

This tiny village, 11km northeast of Condom, takes its name from the Occitan *roumieu*, meaning 'pilgrim'. It's dominated by the magnificent 14th-century **Collégiale St-Pierre** (adult/under 12yr €4.80/free; 🕑 9.30am-7pm Mon-Sat, 2-7pm Sun Jul & Aug, 9.30am-6.30pm Mon-Sat, 2-6.30pm May, Jun & Sep, 10am-12.30pm & 1.30-6.30pm Mon-Sat, 2-6pm Sun Apr, 10am-noon & 2-6pm Mon-Sat, 2-6pm Sun Oct-Mar). Embracing the church are two 33m-tall towers and a fine Gothic cloister with pretty garden. Left of the altar is the sacristy where original medieval frescos include arcane biblical characters, black angels and esoteric symbols. Climb the 136 steps of the double-helix stairway to the top of the octagonal tower for a countryside panorama. Buy tickets and access the ensemble via the helpful **tourist office** (☎ 05 62 28 86 33; www.la-romieu.com; ⌚ same hours as church).

About 800m west of the village, **Les Jardins de Coursiana** (☎ 05 62 68 22 80; www.jardinsdecoursiana.com, in French; adult/7-16yr €6/4; ⌚ 10am-8pm Mon-Sat mid-Apr–Oct) is the landscaped handiwork of a local agricultural engineer. Over 700 trees and rare plants, each clearly labelled, flourish in the arboretum English garden, aromatic herb garden and *potager familial* (family vegetable patch).

A ticket covering the church and gardens costs €8.50.

Lectoure

Juicy melons aside, Lectoure's lure is its **Musée Archéologique** (☎ 05 62 68 70 22; place du Général de Gaulle; adult/child €4/free; ⌚ 10am-noon & 2-6pm Mar-Sep, 10am-noon & 2-6pm Wed-Mon Oct-Feb) in the former episcopal palace, now the town hall. View finds from local Gallo-Roman sites (including 20 bull- or ram-head pagan altars, used for sacrifice), Roman jewellery and mosaics.

Rearing up above the museum is the bulk of the 15th-century **Cathédrale St-Gervais et St-Protais** (place du Général de Gaulle) with its curious, ornate tower. The **tourist office** (☎ 05 62 68 76 98; www.lectoure.fr, in French; place du Général de Gaulle; ⌚ 9am-12.30pm & 2.30-7pm Jul & Aug, 9am-noon & 2-6pm Mon-Sat, 2-5pm Sun Sep-Jun) is next door.

Nearby, 18th-century mansion **Hôtel de Bastard** (☎ 05 62 68 82 44; www.hotel-de-bastard.com; rue Lagrange; d €50-65, menus €28, €50 & €62; ⌚ lunch & dinner Wed-Sat, lunch Sun, dinner Tue early Feb–mid-Dec) is best known for its Gascon cuisine served on a terrace overlooking the hotel's cypress-framed pool and the valley beyond.

West out of town on the road to Condom at **Bleu de Lectoure** (☎ 05 62 68 78 30; www.bleu-de-lectoure.com; ⌚ 10am-12.30pm & 2-6.30pm Mon-Sat, 2-6pm Sun, closed Mon Jan & Feb), a dedicated Franco-American couple have revived the extraction of blue dye from the fermented leaves of the woad plant. You can visit the workshop in a former tannery and buy a whole host of products dyed in woad.

The best view of Lectoure and its surrounding *bastides* has to be aboard a hot-air balloon courtesy of **Montgolfières de Gascogne** (☎ 05 62 64 69 92, 06 82 76 46 01; www.montgolfieres-gascogne.fr, in French). A ride for one/two/three people costs €220/210/190 per person, and romantics can indulge in a two-hour flight at sunrise for €320 per person, Champagne included.

Languedoc-Roussillon

Languedoc-Roussillon is a three-eyed hybrid, cobbled together in the 1980s by the merging of two historic regions. Bas-Languedoc (Lower Languedoc), land of bullfighting, rugby and robust red wines, looks towards the more sedate Provence. On the plain are the major towns: Montpellier, the vibrant capital; sun-baked Nîmes with its fine Roman amphitheatre; and fairy-tale Carcassonne, with its witches'-hat turrets. On the coast, old Agde lies somnolent beside the Hérault River, and Sète, a thriving port, adds commercial vigour.

Deeper inland, Haut-Languedoc (Upper Languedoc) is quite distinct from the sunny lowlands. A continuation of the Massif Central, this sparsely populated mountainous terrain shares trekking, mountain pasture, forests and hearty cuisine with Auvergne, to its north. Within the greater wilderness, the small towns of Mende, Florac, Alès and Millau are oases. The Parc National des Cévennes has long been the refuge of exiles and is criss-crossed by ancient trails. Trekking country too are the bare limestone plateaux of the Grands Causses, sliced through by deep canyons such as the Gorges du Tarn, perfect for a day's canoeing.

Roussillon, abutting the Pyrenees, gives more than a glance over the frontier to Spanish Catalonia, with which it shares a common language and culture. Alongside the rocky coastline lies pretty Collioure, which drew the likes of Matisse and Picasso, while the gentle Têt and Tech Valleys stretch away inland. To their south, the Mont Canigou, the highest summit in the eastern Pyrenees and symbol of Catalan identity, pokes its nose to the clouds while, further east, the foothills are capped by stark, lonely Cathar fortresses.

HIGHLIGHTS

- Gasp at your first glimpse of La Cité's witches'-hat turrets above **Carcassonne** (p779)
- Spend a morning and more exploring the delights of Montpellier's freshly renovated **Musée Fabre** (p771)
- Spot vultures looping and swooping high above **Gorges de la Jonte** (p789)
- Swim under the bridge for an original perspective of the **Pont du Gard** (p766)
- Drift lazily down the **Gorges du Tarn** (p788) in a canoe
- Walk a stage or two of Robert Louis Stevenson's **donkey trek** (p786) in Parc National des Cévennes
- Enjoy spectacular Pyrenean scenery from the trundling **Train Jaune** (Yellow Train; p800), near Villefranche de Conflent
- Take a slow boat along the **Canal du Midi** from Agde (p779)

Gorges du Tarn
Gorges de la Jonte
Parc National des Cévennes
Pont du Gard
Montpellier
Carcassonne
Agde
Villefranche de Conflent

- POPULATION: 2,295,000
- AREA: 27,375 SQ KM

BAS-LANGUEDOC

Languedoc takes its name from *langue d'oc*, a language closely related to Catalan and quite distinct from *langue d'oïl*, the forerunner of modern French, spoken to the north (the words *oc* and *oïl* meant 'yes'). The plains of Bas-Languedoc boast all Languedoc's towns of consequence, its beaches, rich Roman heritage and France's largest wine-producing area.

History

Phoenicians, Greeks, Romans, Visigoths and Moors all passed through Languedoc before it came under Frankish control in the 8th century. The Franks were generally happy to leave affairs in the hands of local rulers and around the 12th century Occitania (today's Languedoc) reached its zenith. At the time, Occitan was the language of the troubadours and the cultured speech of southern France. However, the Albigensian Crusade, launched in 1208 to suppress the 'heresy' of Catharism, led to Languedoc's annexation by the French kingdom. The treaty of Villers-Cotterêts (1539), which made *langue d'oïl* the realm's official language, downgraded Occitan. Continuing to be spoken in the south, it enjoyed a literary revival in the 19th century, spearheaded by the poet Frédéric Mistral, and is nowadays more often called Provençal.

NÎMES

pop 145,000

Plough your way through the bleak, traffic-clogged outskirts of Nîmes to reach its true heart, still beating where the Romans established their town more than two millennia ago. Here, you'll find some of France's best-preserved classical buildings, together with some stunning modern constructions as the city continues its centuries-old rivalry with Montpellier, just down the autoroute.

The city's other, less obvious claim to fame is sartorial. During the 1849 Californian gold rush, one Levi Strauss was making trousers for miners. Looking for a tough, hard-wearing fabric, he began importing the traditionally blue *serge de Nîmes,* nowadays known as denim.

Orientation

Almost everything, including traffic, revolves around Les Arènes, the Roman amphitheatre. North of here, the fan-shaped, largely pedestrianised old city is bounded by bd Victor Hugo, bd Amiral Courbet and bd Gambetta. The main squares are place de la Maison Carrée, place du Marché and place aux Herbes.

Information

Avenue PC Gamer (2 rue Nationale; per hr €2; 🕒 10.30am-11.30pm) Internet access.

Laundrette (14 rue Nationale; 🕒 7am-9pm)

Main Post Office (bd de Bruxelles)

Net@Games (place de la Maison Carrée; per hr €2.50, wi-fi per hr €2; 🕒 9am-1am Mon-Sat, noon-1am Sun) Internet access.

Tourist Office (☎ 04 66 58 38 00; www.ot-nimes.fr; 6 rue Auguste; 🕒 8.30am-8pm Mon-Fri, 9am-7pm Sat, 10am-6pm Sun Jul & Aug; core hr 8.30am-6.30pm Mon-Fri, 9am-6.30pm Sat, 10am-5pm Sun Sep-Jun) Rents out audioguides to central Nîmes (one/two terminals €8/10).

Sights

Nîmes has recently added a high-tech, 21st-century dimension to its two major classical sights.

LES ARÈNES

Nîmes' magnificent **Roman Amphitheatre** (adult/7-17yr/under 7yr incl audioguide €7.70/5.90/free; 🕒 9am-7pm Jun-Aug, 9am-6pm or 6.30pm Mar-May, Sep & Oct, 9.30am-5pm Nov-Feb), the best preserved in the whole of the Roman Empire, was built around AD 100 to seat 24,000 spectators. It's easy to forget, as one marvels at the architectural accomplishments of the Romans, what a nasty streak they had too. The amphitheatre hosted animal fights to the death, stag hunts, man against lion or bear confrontations and, of course, gladiatorial combats. In the contemporary arena, it's only the bulls that get killed. An advance of a kind, you might say.

There's a mock-up of the gladiators' quarters and, if you time it right, you'll see a couple of actors in full combat gear slugging it out in the arena.

Buy your ticket at the reception point, tucked into the northern walls.

MAISON CARRÉE & CARRÉ D'ART

The **Maison Carrée** (Square House; place de la Maison Carrée; adult/7-17yr/under 7yr €4.50/3.70/free; 🕒 10am-7pm or 7.30pm Apr-Sep, 10am-6.30pm Mar & Oct, 10am-1pm & 2-5pm Nov-Feb) is a remarkably preserved rectangular Roman temple, constructed around AD 5 to honour Emperor Augustus' two adopted sons. Within, a 22-minute 3D film, **Héros de Nîmes**, is screened every

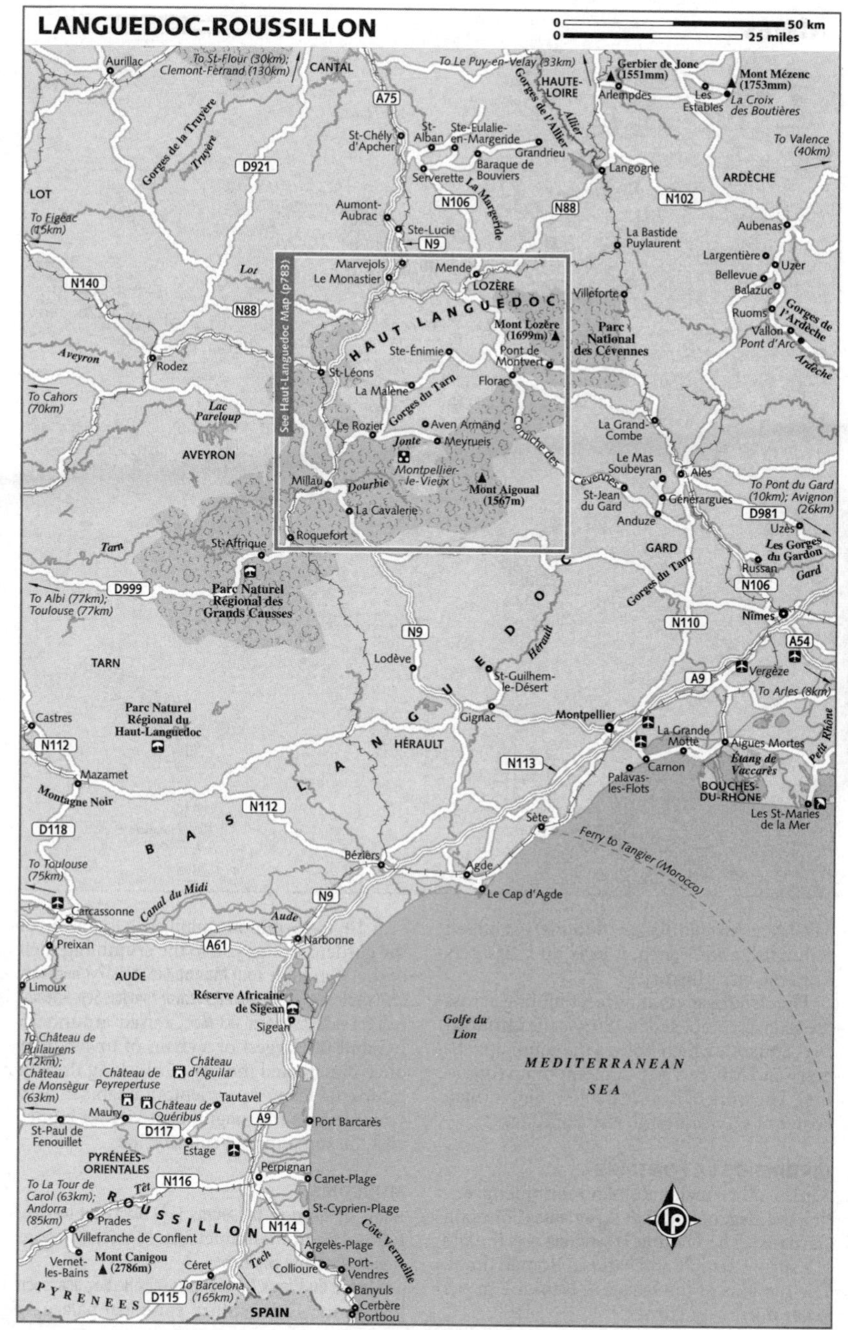

LANGUEDOC-ROUSSILLON

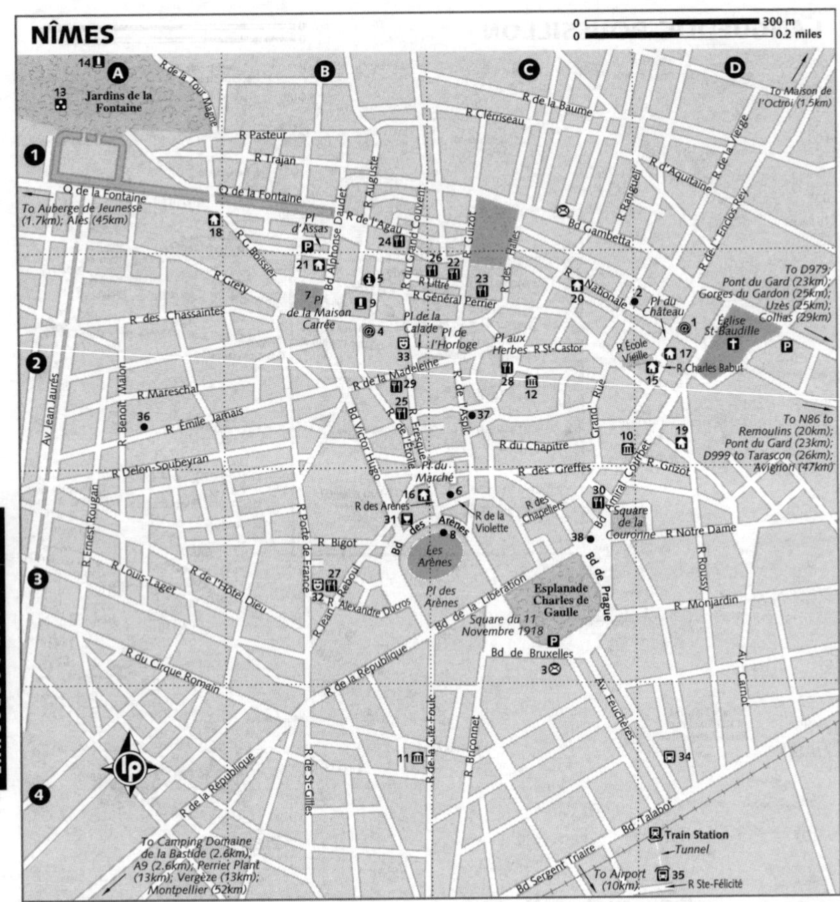

half-hour. An epic piece of flummery subtitled in English and French, it calls up characters from the city's history.

The striking glass and steel building across the square, completed in 1993, is the **Carré d'Art** (Art Square), which houses the municipal library and Musée d'Art Contemporain (opposite). The work of British architect Sir Norman Foster, it's a wonderful, airy building.

JARDINS DE LA FONTAINE

Nîmes' other major Roman monuments enrich the elegant **Jardins de la Fontaine** (Fountain Gardens). The **Source de la Fontaine** was the site of a spring, temple and baths in Roman times. The remains of the **Temple de Diane** are in the lower northwest corner.

A 10- to 15-minute uphill walk to the top of the gardens brings you to the crumbling shell of the 30m high **Tour Magne** (adult/7-17yr/under 7yr €2.70/2.30/free; 9.30am-6.30pm or 7pm Jun-Sep, 9.30am-1pm & 2-4.30pm or 6pm Oct-Mar), raised around 15 BC and the largest of a chain of towers that once punctuated the city's 7km-long Roman ramparts. There's an orientation table to help you interpret the magnificent view of Nîmes and the surrounding countryside.

MUSEUMS

Each of Nîmes' **museums** (10am-6pm Tue-Sun) follows a common timetable. Most are in sore need of a new broom.

Musée du Vieux Nîmes (place aux Herbes; admission free), in the 17th-century episcopal palace, is

INFORMATION
Avenue PC Gamer....................1 D2
Laundrette....................2 D2
Main Post Office....................3 C3
Net@Games....................4 B2
Tourist Office....................5 B2

SIGHTS & ACTIVITIES
Billeterie des Arènes....................6 C3
Carré d'Art....................7 B2
Les Arènes Entrance....................8 C3
Maison Carrée....................9 B2
Musée d'Archéologie....................10 C2
Musée d'Art Contemporain....................(see 7)
Musée des Beaux Arts....................11 B4
Musée d'Histoire Naturelle....................(see 10)
Musée du Vieux Nîmes....................12 C2
Temple de Diane....................13 A1
Tour Magne....................14 A1

SLEEPING
Hôtel Acanthe du Temple....................15 D2
Hôtel Amphithéâtre....................16 B3
Hôtel Central....................17 D2
Hôtel Imperator Concorde....................18 A1
Kyriad....................19 D2
New Hôtel La Baume....................20 C2
Royal Hôtel....................21 B2

EATING
Au Plaisir des Halles....................22 C2
Covered Food Market....................23 C2
Haddock Café....................24 B1
Le 9....................25 B2
Le Marché sur la Table....................26 C2
Les Olivades....................27 B3
L'Oustaù Nadal....................28 C2
Maison Villaret....................29 B2
Monoprix Supermarket....................30 C3

DRINKING
Grand Café de la Bourse....................31 B3
La Bodeguita....................(see 21)
Le Ciel de Nîmes....................(see 7)

ENTERTAINMENT
Ciné Sémaphore....................32 B3
Théâtre de Nîmes....................33 B2

TRANSPORT
Airport Bus Stop....................34 D4
Bus Station....................35 D4
Commavélo....................36 A2
SNCF Sales Office....................37 C2
TANGO Bus Information Kiosk....................38 C3

a small museum that, in addition to the usual period costumes and furniture, has a whole room showcasing denim, with smiling pin-ups of Elvis, James Dean and Marilyn Monroe.

Musée d'Archéologie (Archeological Museum; 13 bd Amiral Courbet; admission free) brings together Roman and pre-Roman tombs, mosaics, inscriptions and artefacts unearthed in and around Nîmes. It also houses a hotchpotch of artefacts from Africa, piled high and tagged with yellowing captions such as 'Abyssinia' and 'Dahomey'. In the same building, **Musée d'Histoire Naturelle** (Natural History Museum; admission free) has a musty collection of stuffed animals gazing bleakly out. Only the custodians, protected from visitors inside their own glass case, have life.

Musée des Beaux-Arts (Fine Arts Museum; rue de la Cité Foulc; adult/7-17yr/under 7yr €5.10/3.70/free) has a wonderfully preserved Roman mosaic (look down upon it from the 1st floor). This apart, it houses a fairly pedestrian collection of Flemish, Italian and French works.

The refreshing **Musée d'Art Contemporain** (Contemporary Art Museum; place de la Maison Carrée; adult/7-17yr/under 7yr €5.10/3.70/free) in the Carré d'Art makes a welcome contrast. Housing both permanent and rotating exhibitions of modern art, it merits a visit, if only to prowl the innards of this striking building.

THE CROCODILE OF NÎMES

Around town and in tourist literature, you'll see the city's shield: a crocodile chained to a palm tree. It recalls the city's foundation, when retiring Roman legionnaires who had sweated with Caesar during his River Nile campaign, were granted land to cultivate hereabouts.

Tours

The tourist office runs 1½- to two-hour French-language city tours (€5.50), both general and themed, year-round. Its pamphlet *Laissez-Vous Conter Nîmes* has full details.

Taxis TRAN (☎ 04 66 29 40 11) offer a 30- to 40-minute tour of the city (around €30 for up to six people) with a cassette commentary in English. Reserve by phone or in person at the tourist office.

Festivals & Events

In July and August there's an abundance of dance, theatre, rock, pop and jazz events. Year-round, the tourist office regularly updates its list of events, *Les Rendez-Vous de Nîmes*.

FÉRIAS & BULLFIGHTS

Nîmes becomes more Spanish than French during its two *férias* (bullfighting festivals): the five-day **Féria de Pentecôte** (Whitsuntide Festival) in June, and the three-day **Féria des Vendanges** celebrating the grape harvest on the third weekend in September. Each is marked by daily *corridas* (bullfights). The **Billeterie des Arènes** (☎ 04 66 02 80 90; www.arenesdenimes.com, in French; 2 rue de la Violette) sells tickets both to callers-in and via its website.

JEUDIS DE NÎMES

Between 6pm and 10.30pm every Thursday in July and August, artists, artisans and vendors of local food specialities take over the main squares of central Nîmes, where

BILLET NÎMES ROMAINE

You can make something of a saving by purchasing a **combination ticket** (adult/child €9.80/7.50). This admits you to Les Arènes, Maison Carrée and Tour Magne and is valid for three days. Pick one up at the first site you visit.

there are also free concerts of music in all its many genres.

Sleeping

During Nîmes' *férias*, many hotels raise their prices significantly and accommodation is hard to find.

BUDGET

Auberge de Jeunesse (☎ 04 66 68 03 20; www.hinimes.com; 257 chemin de l'Auberge de Jeunesse, la Cigale; dm/d/q €12.75/32/51; Feb-Dec) This sterling, well-equipped youth hostel with self-catering facilities has everything from dorms to cute houses for two to six in its extensive grounds, 3.5km northwest of the train station. It rents out bikes (per day €14) and there's limited camping (per person €6.35). Take bus I, direction Alès or Villeverte, and get off at the Stade stop.

Camping Domaine de la Bastide (☎ 04 66 62 05 82; www.camping-nimes.com; route de Générac; site & 2 persons €13.90; year-round) This campsite is 4km south of town on the D13. Take bus D and get off at La Bastide, the terminus.

Hôtel Central (☎ 04 66 67 27 75; www.hotel-central.org; 2 place du Château; s/d/tr/q €43/48/58/68, s/d with shared bathroom €35/40) With its creaky floorboards and bunches of wild flowers painted on each bedroom door, this friendly hotel is full of character. Room 20, on the 5th floor, has great rooftop views. Free wi-fi.

Hôtel Amphithéâtre (☎ 04 66 67 28 51; http://pagesperso-orange.fr/hotel-amphitheatre; rue des Arènes; s €41-45, d €53-70; Feb-Dec;) The welcoming, family-run Amphithéâtre is just up the road from its namesake. Once a pair of 18th-century mansions, it has 15 rooms decorated in warm, woody colours, each named after a writer or painter. We suggest dipping into Montesquieu or Arrabal, both large and with a balcony overlooking pedestrian place du Marché. Rooms on the 3rd floor enjoy air-conditioning.

Hôtel Acanthe du Temple (☎ 04 66 67 54 61; www.hotel-temple.com; 1 rue Charles Babut; s €42-50, d €52-60, tr/q €70/80;) Just opposite the Central, this jolly place has spick-and-span rooms with wallpaper that differs in each one. Five rooms have air-con, the rest come with fans, some have separate toilets and around 40% are nonsmoking.

MIDRANGE

Royal Hôtel (☎ 04 66 58 28 27; www.royalhotel-nimes.com, in French; 3 bd Alphonse Daudet; s €60-65, d €75-85) You can't squeeze this hotel, popular with visiting artists and raffishly bohemian, into a standard mould. Rooms, all with ceiling fans and nearly all with bathtubs, are furnished with flair. Some overlook pedestrian place d'Assas, a work of modern art in its own right – fine for the view, though the noise might be intrusive on summer nights. Free wi-fi.

Maison de l'Octroi (☎ 04 66 27 15 95; www.bed-breakfast-nimes.com; 209 chemin de Russan; r incl breakfast €65-75;) Host Nicole Crès keeps her two *chambre d'hôte* rooms spick and span and serves delicious breakfasts. Rooms overlook a 5000-sq-metre garden shaded by oak and lime trees. Her house is 1.5km north of the city centre; parking is free.

Kyriad (☎ 04 66 76 16 20; www.hotel-kyriad-nimes.com; 10 rue Roussy; r €69-75;) On a quiet street, the Kyriad's decor follows a bullfighting theme. Its 28 rooms are smallish but satisfyingly furnished and have complimentary tea and coffee. Head up high to the top floor for the two best rooms (€80), each with a terrace and views over the city. Free wi-fi.

New Hôtel La Baume (☎ 04 66 76 28 42; www.new-hotel.com; 21 rue Nationale; s/d €110/140;) In an unfashionable part of town and in fact far from new, this 34-room hotel occupies an attractive 17th-century town mansion with a glorious interior courtyard and twisting stairway. The bedrooms, decorated in sensuous ochre, beige and cream, blend the traditional and strictly contemporary. Wi-fi available.

TOP END

Hôtel Imperator Concorde (☎ 04 66 21 90 30; www.hotel-imperator.com; quai de la Fontaine; r incl breakfast Apr-Oct €190-255, Nov-Mar €165-225;) This *grande dame* of Nîmes hotels is a favourite of visiting matadors. Its bar, the 'Hemingway', commemorates the swaggering author's brief presence here in room 310. The 62 rooms are richly draped and furnished and there's a large garden with a playing fountain. Its highly regarded restaurant, L'Enclos de la Fontaine, is equally grand and distinguished. Free wi-fi.

Eating

Nîmes' gastronomy owes as much to Provence as to Languedoc. Spicy southern delights, such as aïoli and *rouille* (spicy mayonnaise of olive oil, garlic and chilli peppers), are as abundant as cassoulet. Sample the Costières de Nîmes wines from the pebbly vineyards to the south.

Haddock Café (☎ 04 66 67 86 57; www.haddock-café.fr, in French; 13 rue de l'Agau; daily special €8, menus €15-20, mains €10-14.50; ⏰ lunch & dinner Mon-Fri, 7pm-2am Sat) This cheerful, welcoming place to eat, drink and, at least twice weekly, enjoy live music began life as a convent. Its great selection of local wines, by the glass and bottle, rotates regularly and meals are especially good value.

Au Plaisir des Halles (☎ 04 66 36 01 02; 4 rue Littré; menus €21.50-44, mains €10; ⏰ Tue-Sat) Just around the corner from the covered market, ingredients here are the freshest and the lunchtime three-course *menu* is excellent value. The photo portraits around the walls are of the winegrowers whose products feature on its impressive list of Languedoc vintages.

Les Olivades (☎ 04 66 21 71 78; 18 rue Jean Reboul; 3-course lunch menu €12, dinner menu €22, mains around €12; ⏰ Tue-Fri & dinner Sat) To the rear of this excellent wine shop, which merits a visit in its own right, there's an intimate dining area, where Madame in the kitchen and her husband as maître will treat you royally. Their tempting dinner *menu* offers plenty of choice within each of its three courses.

Le Marché sur la Table (☎ 04 66 67 22 50; 10 rue Littré; mains €15-18; ⏰ Tue-Sun) You *could* just pop in for a glass of wine at this friendly spot, run by up-and-coming young chef Éric Vidal (see his impressive culinary credentials on the toilet wall, no less) and his partner, Caroline. But you'd be missing a lot. Éric buys everything fresh from the food market just down the road and his fish is never farmed. Eat in the attractively furnished interior or quiet, green rear courtyard.

Le 9 (☎ 04 66 21 80 77; 9 rue de l'Étoile; lunch menu €15, mains €15-18; ⏰ Mon-Sat & lunch Sun May-Sep, dinner Fri & Sat only Oct-Apr) Have a meal or simply drop in for a drink at this mildly eccentric place, tucked away behind high green doors with just a sign swinging outside. Eat in the vast, arched former stables or in the leafy, vine-clad courtyard. Everything except the lunch *menu* is à la carte.

SELF-CATERING

There are colourful Thursday markets in the old city in July and August.

Maison Villaret (☎ 04 66 67 41 79; 13 rue de la Madeleine) This family bakery makes 25 different kinds of bread, cakes, biscuits and local specialities such as *caladons* (honey and almond-studded biscuits).

L'Oustaù Nadal (place aux Herbes) is packed with goodies such as brandade, tapenade, honey from the hills and olive oil, including a couple of kinds on draught.

Other options:

Covered food market (rue Général Perrier) Large and particularly rich.

Monoprix (3 bd Amiral Courbet) Supermarket.

Drinking

Place aux Herbes is one communal outside café in summer. Place du Marché beneath the huge palm tree that flops its fronds over the centre, is equally bustling.

Le Ciel de Nîmes (place de la Maison Carrée; ⏰ 10am-6pm Tue-Sun year-round, to 10.30pm Fri & Sat May-Sep) On the rooftop terrace of the Carré d'Art, this is the perfect place for a relaxing drink, lording it over the hubbub in the square below.

Grand Café de la Bourse (bd des Arènes) This vast, flamboyant café right opposite Les Arènes, is a great spot for breakfast, a quick coffee or a sundowner, either on the terrace or inside.

La Bodeguita (place d'Assas; ⏰ 6pm-late Mon-Sat) With a Spanish click of the heels and attached to the Royal Hôtel, this is a popular venue for the local intelligentsia. On summer evenings, there's often live music.

Entertainment

Les Arènes is a major venue for theatre performances and concerts.

Ciné Sémaphore (☎ 04 66 67 83 11; www.semaphore.free.fr; 25 rue Porte de France) has five screens and shows nondubbed films.

Théâtre de Nîmes (☎ 04 66 36 02 04; place de la Calade) is the major venue for drama and music performances.

Getting There & Away

AIR

Nîmes' **airport** (☎ 04 66 70 49 49), 10km southeast of the city on the A54, is served only by Ryanair, which flies to/from London (Luton), Liverpool and Nottingham East Midlands in the UK.

BUS

The **bus station** (☎ 04 66 38 59 43; rue Ste-Félicité) connects with the train station. International operators **Eurolines** (☎ 04 66 29 49 02) and **Line Bus** (☎ 04 66 29 50 62) both have kiosks there.

Regional destinations include Pont du Gard (€6.50, 30 minutes, five daily), Uzès (€5.30, 45 minutes, at least five daily) and Alès (€8, 1¼ hours, five daily).

CAR & MOTORCYCLE

Europcar has kiosks at the airport (☎ 04 66 70 49 22) and train station (☎ 04 66 29 07 94).

TRAIN

In town, there's a convenient **SNCF sales office** (11 rue de l'Aspic).

More than 12 TGVs daily run to/from Paris' Gare de Lyon (€68.50 to €96, three hours). There are frequent services to/from Alès (€8.10, 40 minutes), Arles (€7.20, 30 minutes), Avignon (€8.10, 30 minutes), Marseille (€17.90, 1¼ hours), Sète (€11.60, one hour) and Montpellier (€8.20, 30 minutes).

Getting Around

TO/FROM THE AIRPORT

An airport bus (€5, 30 minutes) meets and greets Ryanair flights, leaving from the train station. To confirm times, ring ☎ 04 66 29 27 29.

BICYCLE

Commavélo (☎ 04 66 29 19 68; www.commavelo.com; 28 rue Émile Jamais; 9.30am-1pm & 2-7pm) rents out town bikes (per half-day/full day/three days €7/12/30) and mountain bikes (per half-day/full day/three days €9/15/37.50).

Drivers who leave their vehicles in the car parks of Les Arènes, Porte Auguste or place d'Assas can borrow a town bike for free. Present your parking ticket at the pay desk.

PUBLIC TRANSPORT

Local buses are run by **TANGO** (☎ 08 20 22 30 30), which has an information kiosk in the northeast corner of esplanade Charles de Gaulle. A single ticket/five-ticket carnet costs €1/4.

TAXI

Ring ☎ 04 66 29 40 11 for a taxi.

AROUND NÎMES

Perrier Plant

Ever wondered how they get the bubbles into a bottle of Perrier water? Or why it's that stubby shape? Take the one-hour tour in French of **Perrier's bottling plant** (☎ 04 66 87 61 01; adult/child €5/2; tours approx hourly 10am or 10.30am-4pm). It's in Vergèze, on the RN113, 13km southwest of Nîmes. We trust their tongue is firmly in their cheek when they advertise *dégustation gratuité* (free tasting)! Ring to reserve – recommended in high summer and required for the rest of the year.

Pont du Gard

The **Pont du Gard**, a Unesco World Heritage Site, is an exceptionally well-preserved, three-tiered Roman aqueduct, once part of a 50km-long system of canals built around 19 BC to bring water from nearby Uzès to Nîmes. The scale is huge: the 35 arches of its 275m-long upper tier, running 50m above the River Gard, contain a watercourse designed to carry 20,000 cu metres of water per day. Its largest construction blocks weigh more than five tonnes.

It's about a 400m walk with excellent wheelchair access from car parks on both left and right banks of the River Gard to the bridge itself. The road bridge, built in 1743, runs parallel with the aqueduct's lower tier. The best view is from upstream, where you can swim on hot days.

At the **visitors centre** (☎ 08 20 90 33 30; www.pontdugard.fr; 9.30am-7pm Tue-Sun, 1-7pm Mon May-Sep; to 5pm or 6pm Oct-Apr) on the left, northern bank, there's an impressive, high-tech **museum** (admission €7), a 25-minute large-screen **film** (admission €4) showing the bridge from land and air and **Ludo** (per hr €5), a children's activity play area. A **combination ticket** (adult/6-17yr/under 6yr €12/9/free) gives access to all three activities. A **family ticket** (€24) gives the same access to two adults and up to four children. The Richesses du Gard information office rents audioguides (€6) to the site.

You can walk, for free, **Mémoires de Garrigue**, a 1.4km trail with interpretive signs that winds through this typical Mediterranean bush and scrubland – though you'll need the explanatory booklet in English (€4) to get the most out of it.

In July and August, for an extra €2 on top of your museum entry or combination ticket, it's possible to walk the bridge's topmost tier. A guide leads groups every half-hour between 10am and 11.30am and from 2pm to 5.30pm.

If you simply want to enjoy the bridge, just head on down. You can walk about for free around the clock, though the car parks close between 1am and 6am.

GETTING THERE & AWAY

The Pont du Gard is 21km northeast of Nîmes and 26km west of Avignon. Buses normally stop on the D981, 500m north of the visitors centre. In summer, some make a diversion to the Pont du Gard car park.

Lignes du Gard (☎ 04 66 29 27 29; www.stdgard.fr) bus 168 runs five times daily to/from Nîmes, while bus 205 leaves Avignon three times daily, at 7.40am, 12.15pm and 6.08pm.

The extensive car parks on each bank of the river cost €5.

River Gard

The wild, unpredictable River Gard descends from the Cévennes mountains. Torrential rains can raise the water level by as much as 5m in a flash. During long dry spells, by contrast, sections may disappear completely, as the water continues to trickle through an underground channel.

The river has sliced itself a meandering 22km gorge (Les Gorges du Gardon) through the hills from **Russan** to the village of **Collias**, about 6km upstream from the Pont du Gard. The GR6 hiking trail runs beside it most of the way.

In Collias, 4km west of the D981, **Le Tourbillon** (☎ 04 66 22 85 54; www.canoe-le-tourbillon), **Kayak Vert** (☎ 04 66 22 80 76; www.canoefrance.com/gardon) and **Canoë Collias** (☎ 04 66 22 87 20; www.canoe-collias.com, in French) rent out kayaks and canoes. Kayak Vert also offers mountain-bike hire.

You can paddle 8km down to the Pont du Gard (€19.50 per person, two hours), or arrange to be dropped upstream at Russan, from where a great descent leads back to Collias through Gorges du Gardon (€33, full day), usually possible only between March and mid-June, when the river is high enough.

Uzès

pop 7860

Uzès, 25km northeast of Nîmes, once derived wealth from silk, linen and, bizarrely, liquorice. When all three industries collapsed it went through hard times, but it's again on the upsurge thanks to tourism, as visitors come to enjoy its faithfully restored Renaissance facades, impressive Duché (Ducal Palace) and splendid place aux Herbes, the shady, arcaded central square, all odd angles and off kilter.

Farmers from all around sell their produce at the market, held each Wednesday and Saturday on place aux Herbes.

The **tourist office** (☎ 04 66 22 68 88; www.uzes-tourisme.com; ⏲ 9am-6pm or 7pm Mon-Fri, 10am-1pm & 2-5pm Sat & Sun Jun-Sep, 9am-12.30pm & 2-6pm Mon-Fri, 10am-1pm Sat Oct-May) is on place Albert I, just outside the old quarter. It rents out audioguides (€5) for a self-guided walking tour.

SIGHTS & ACTIVITIES

The tourist office's free multilingual pamphlet, *Uzès: Premier Duché de France,* presents a walking tour of the historic centre's highlights.

The **Duché** (☎ 04 66 22 18 96; ⏲ 10am-1pm & 2-6.30pm Jul–mid-Sep, 10am-noon & 2-6pm mid-Sep–Jun) is a fortified château that belonged to the Dukes of Uzès for more than 1000 years. Altered almost continuously from the 11th to 18th century, it has fine period furniture, tapestries and paintings. You can take the French-language one-hour **guided tour** (adult/12-16yr/7-11 yr/under 7yr €13/8/4/free) or wander at will around the **keep** (admission €8).

The **Jardin Médiéval** (Medieval Garden; admission €4; ⏲ 10.30am-12.30pm & 2-6pm Jul & Aug, 2-6pm Mon-Fri, 10.30am-12.30pm & 2-6pm Sat & Sun Apr-Jun & Sep, 2-5pm daily Oct), in the shadow of the Duché's keep and set back from rue Port Royal, is a delightful garden of medieval plants and flowers, impressively researched and documented (with English translation too).

Musée du Bonbon (☎ 04 66 22 74 39; Pont des Charrettes; adult/child €4.50/2.50; ⏲ 10am-7pm Jul-Sep, 10am-1pm & 2-6pm Tue-Sun Oct-Dec & Feb-Jun) is the place for a little indulgence. A plaque at the entrance declares 'This museum is dedicated to all who have devoted their lives to a slightly guilty passion – greed'. All signs at this candy museum belonging to manufacturers Haribo are multilingual, and parents will be pestered to go away with kilos of goodies at wholesale prices.

FESTIVALS & EVENTS

Uzès positively reeks on 24 June, the date of the **Foire à l'Ail** (Garlic Fair), while the third Sunday in January sees a full-blown **Foire aux Truffes** (Truffle Fair). The town is also renowned for its **Nuits Musicales d'Uzès**, an international festival of baroque music held in the second half of July.

SLEEPING & EATING

Hôtel La Taverne (☎ 04 66 22 13 10; www.lataverne-uzes.com, in French; 4 rue Xavier Sigalon; d/tr €64/76) Up a pedestrianised side street beside the tourist office, this Logis de France hotel has nine simply furnished rooms, all with air-con and tiled floors. Its restaurant (*menus* €24 to €28), just along the street, has a pretty internal patio and serves classic French cuisine. Free wi-fi.

our pick **Terroirs** (☎ 04 66 03 41 90; www.enviedeterroirs.com; 5 place aux Herbes; tapas around €4.50, mixed platters €10-13; ⏰ 9am-10.30pm Apr-Sep, 9.30am-6pm Wed-Sun Oct-Mar) Snack copiously under the deep arcades or on the cobbled square at this restaurant and delicatessen where Tom and Corinne Graisse source nearly all their goods locally. Their mixed platters and toasted open sandwiches are filled with delights, described explicitly in the English version of the menu.

SHOPPING

At the splendid **Maison de la Truffe** (27 place aux Herbes), it's truffles with everything – adding aroma to chocolate, steeped in oil, bagged with rice and much more.

GETTING THERE & AWAY

The bus station – grandly named and in fact merely a bus stop – is on av de la Libération, beside Banque Populaire. Buses running between Avignon (€8.70, one hour) and Alès (€7.30, 40 minutes) call by two to five times daily. There are also at least five daily services to/from Nîmes (€5.30, 45 minutes).

ALÈS & AROUND

pop 39,300

Alès, 45km from Nîmes and 70km from Montpellier, snuggles against the River Gard. Gateway to the Cévennes, it's the Gard *département*'s second-largest town. Coal was mined here from the 13th century, when monks first dug into the surrounding hills, until the last pit closed in 1986.

The pedestrianised heart of town, having long ago shed its sooty past, is pleasant, if unexciting. Fountains play in public places and it's bright with flowers in summer.

The **tourist office** (☎ 04 66 52 32 15; www.ville-ales.fr, in French; place Hôtel de Ville; ⏰ 9am-7pm Mon-Sat, 9am-noon Sun Jul & Aug, 9am-noon & 1.30-5.30pm Mon-Sat Sep-Jun) occupies a modern building set into the shell of a baroque chapel.

Sights & Activities

From April to October the **Train à Vapeur des Cévennes** (Cévennes Steam Train; ☎ 04 66 60 59 00; adult/child one-way €9/6, return €12/7; ⏰ Apr–mid-Sep, Tue-Sun mid-Sep–Oct) takes 40 minutes to chug the 13km between St-Jean du Gard and Anduze via the Bambouseraie (below), making three to four return trips each day.

MINE TÉMOIN

At **Mine Témoin** (☎ 04 66 30 45 15; chemin de la Cité Ste-Marie; adult/child €6/4; ⏰ 10am-7pm Jul & Aug, 9am-5pm Jun, 9.30am-12.30pm & 2-6pm Mar-May & Sep–mid-Nov) in Alès, don a safety helmet, arm yourself with the guide booklet in English and take the cage down to explore an actual mine that was used to train apprentice colliers. Preceded by a 20-minute video (in French), the one-hour **guided tour** (also in French) leads you along 700m of underground galleries.

BAMBOUSERAIE DE PRAFRANCE

It's over 150 years since the first shoots of this huge, mature **bamboo grove** (☎ 04 66 61 70 47; adult/child €7.50/4.50; ⏰ 9.30am-dusk Mar–mid-Nov) were planted by a spice merchant returning from the tropics. Here in Générargues, 12km southwest of Alès, 150 bamboo species sprout amid aquatic gardens, a Laotian village and a Japanese garden. The Cévennes steam train (left) stops right beside the reception.

MUSÉE DU DÉSERT

The **Musée du Désert** (Museum of the Wilderness; ☎ 04 66 85 02 72; www.museedudesert.com; adult/10-18yr/under 10yr €4.50/3.50/free; ⏰ 9.30am-7pm Jul & Aug, 9.30am-noon & 2-6pm Mar-Jun & Sep-Nov) portrays the way of life of the Huguenots (see boxed text, opposite), their persecution, clandestine resistance for more than a century and emigration of up to half a million to more tolerant lands. It's in the charming hamlet of Le Mas Soubeyran, 5.5km north of the Bambouseraie.

LA CARACOLE

Here's one to make the kids squirm. **La Caracole** (☎ 04 66 25 65 70; www.lacaracole.fr; St-Florent sur Auzonnet; adult/child €5/3.50; ⏰ tours 10.30am, 3pm, 4.30pm & 6pm Jul & Aug, 3pm & 4.30pm Wed & Sun Apr-Jun & Sep), with a cast of over 250,000, presents 'the astonishing, exciting world of the snail'. In this snail farm's appropriately small museum, there's information on – oh yes – the snail in religion, the snail in art and the snail through the centuries. After the 1½ hour tour (in English and French), there's free sampling and the chance to buy a tin of two of former farm members embalmed in a variety of tempting sauces. It's 12km from Alés. Take the D904 northwards (towards Aubenas), then turn left onto the D59.

THE CAMISARD REVOLT

Early in the 18th century, a guerrilla war raged through the Cévennes as Protestants took on Louis XIV's army. The revocation of the Edict of Nantes in 1685 removed rights that the Protestant Huguenots had enjoyed since 1598. Many emigrated, while others fled deep into the wild Cévennes, from where a local leader, Roland Laporte, only 22 at the time, led the resistance against the French army sent to crush them.

Poorly equipped, the outlaws resisted for two years. They fought in their shirts (*camiso* in *langue d'oc*); hence their popular name, Camisards. Once the royal army gained the upper hand, the local population was either massacred or forced to flee. Their leader was killed and most villages were destroyed.

On the first Sunday of September, thousands of French Protestants meet at Roland's birthplace in Le Mas Soubeyran. It's now the Musée du Désert (opposite), which details the persecution of Protestants in the Cévennes between 1685 and the 1787 Edict of Tolerance, which marked the reintroduction of religious freedom.

Sleeping & Eating

Camping la Croix Clémentine (☎ 04 66 86 52 69; www.clementine.fr, in French; site & 2 people according to season €13-24; Apr-Sep;) This four-star campsite is in Cendras, 5km northwest of Alès. Sites, within or on the fringes of an oak wood, are shady and there are plenty of activities to keep the children occupied.

Hôtel Durand (☎ 04 66 86 28 94; www.hotel-durand.fr, in French; 3 bd Anatole France; s/d/tr €32/38/46;) This modest choice, down a side street 100m east of Hôtel Le Riche, is spruce and well maintained. Bathrooms have recently been overhauled, each of its 17 rooms has air-con, and there's a small rear garden.

Hôtel Le Riche (☎ 04 66 86 00 33; www.leriche.fr, in French; 42 place Pierre Sémard; s/d/tr €48/59/70; Sep-Jul;) Opposite the train station, this great-value hotel is highly recommended as much for its 19 pleasant, modern rooms as for the fine cuisine of the restaurant (*menus* €18 to €48) with its wonderful stucco mouldings.

Mas de Rochebelle (☎ 04 66 30 57 03; www.masderochebelle.fr; 44 chemin Ste Marie; r €60-80;) Near the Mine Témoin, this welcoming *chambre d'hôte* was once the mine director's residence. It has five attractive rooms and a vast garden, where you can wander, swim or simply relax under its magnificent yew tree.

Getting There & Away

BUS

From the **Gare Routière** (place Pierre Sémard), immediately south of the train station, one bus heads into the Cévennes to Florac (€13.50, 1¼ hours, daily except Sunday), and two to five serve Uzès (€7.30, 40 minutes), two continuing to Avignon (€14.60, 1¾ hours). Five buses daily link Alès and Nîmes (€8.30, 1¼ hours).

TRAIN

There are up to 10 trains daily to/from Montpellier (€14.30, 1½ hours), some requiring a change in Nîmes (€8.10, 40 minutes). Three trains daily run between Alès and Mende (€16.20, 2½ hours).

MONTPELLIER

pop 244,300

The 17th-century philosopher John Locke may have had one glass of Minervois wine too many when he wrote: 'I find it much better to go twise (sic) to Montpellier than once to the other world'. Paradise it ain't, but Montpellier, where students make up around a third of the population, is innovative, fast-growing, self-confident and a worthy rival to Toulouse for the title of southern France's most vital city. Two high-speed tram routes cut across this most pedestrian-friendly of cities, where more than 12,000 parking spaces, over 1000 bikes for borrowing and around 150km of cycling paths encourage motorists to leave their cars behind.

History

Montpellier, one of the few cities in southern France without a Roman heritage, started lateish. Founded by the Counts of Toulouse, it's first mentioned in a written document in 985. By medieval times, it had become a prosperous city with trading links all over the Mediterranean. Its scholastic tradition is a long one: Europe's first medical school was founded here in the 12th century. The

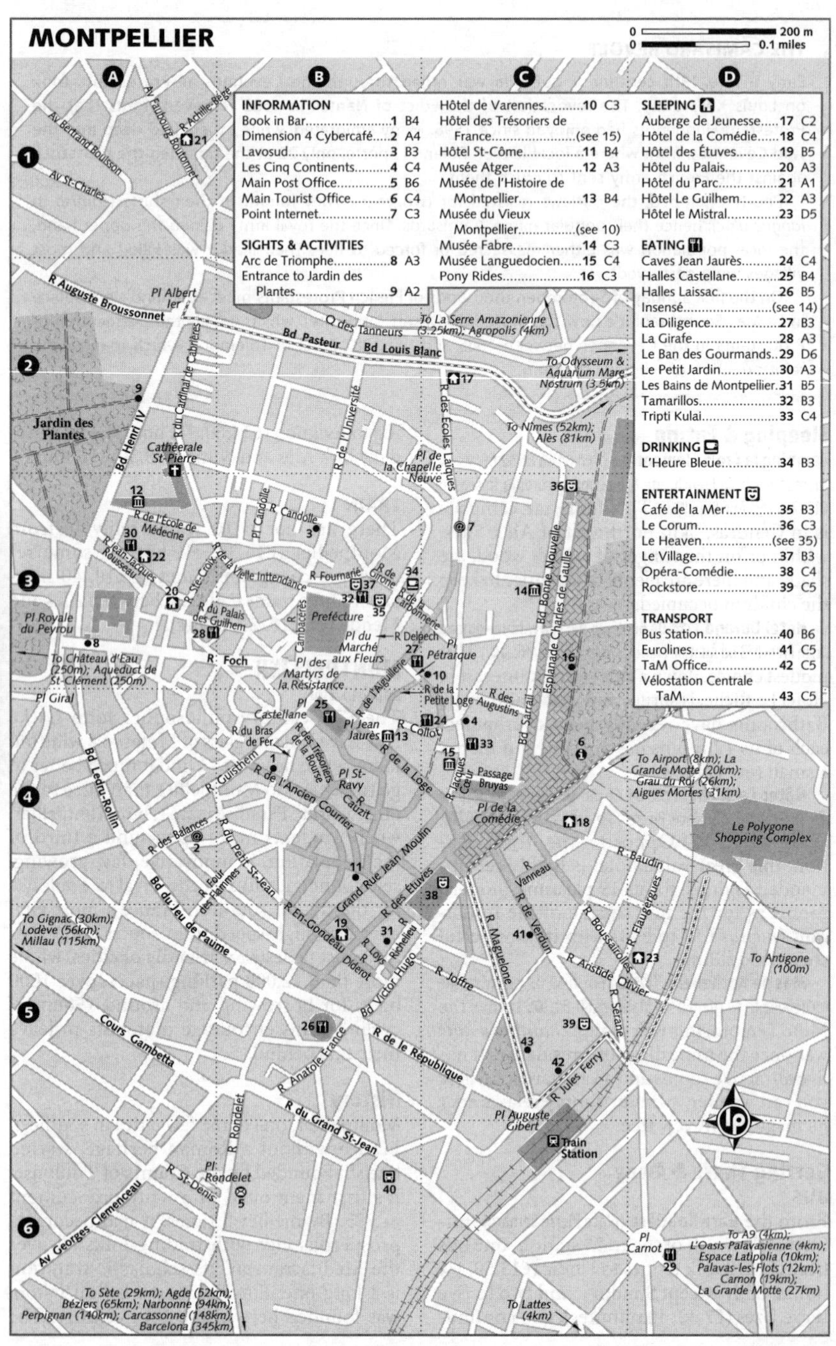
MONTPELLIER
0 200 m
0 0.1 miles
INFORMATION
Book in Bar....1 B4
Dimension 4 Cybercafé....2 A4
Lavosud....3 B3
Les Cinq Continents....4 C4
Main Post Office....5 B6
Main Tourist Office....6 C4
Point Internet....7 C3
SIGHTS & ACTIVITIES
Arc de Triomphe....8 A3
Entrance to Jardin des Plantes....9 A2
Hôtel de Varennes....10 C3
Hôtel des Trésoriers de France....(see 15)
Hôtel St-Côme....11 B4
Musée Atger....12 A3
Musée de l'Histoire de Montpellier....13 B4
Musée du Vieux Montpellier....(see 10)
Musée Fabre....14 C3
Musée Languedocien....15 C4
Pony Rides....16 C3
SLEEPING
Auberge de Jeunesse....17 C2
Hôtel de la Comédie....18 C4
Hôtel des Étuves....19 B5
Hôtel du Palais....20 A3
Hôtel du Parc....21 A1
Hôtel Le Guilhem....22 A3
Hôtel le Mistral....23 D5
EATING
Caves Jean Jaurès....24 C4
Halles Castellane....25 B4
Halles Laissac....26 B5
Insensé....(see 14)
La Diligence....27 B3
La Girafe....28 A3
Le Ban des Gourmands....29 D6
Le Petit Jardin....30 A3
Les Bains de Montpellier....31 B5
Tamarillos....32 B3
Tripti Kulai....33 C4
DRINKING
L'Heure Bleue....34 B3
ENTERTAINMENT
Café de la Mer....35 B3
Le Corum....36 C3
Le Heaven....(see 35)
Le Village....37 B3
Opéra-Comédie....38 C4
Rockstore....39 C5
TRANSPORT
Bus Station....40 B6
Eurolines....41 C5
TaM Office....42 C5
Vélostation Centrale TaM....43 C5
Av Bertrand Boulsson
Av St-Charles
Av Faubourg Boutonnet
R Achille-Bégé
R Auguste Broussonnet
Pl Albert Ier
Q des Tanneurs
Bd Pasteur
Bd Louis Blanc
To La Serre Amazonienne (3.25km); Agropolis (4km)
To Odysseum & Aquarium Mare Nostrum (3.5km)
To Nîmes (52km); Alès (81km)
Jardin des Plantes
Bd Henri IV
R du Cardinal de Cabrières
Cathéerale St-Pierre
R de l'Université
R des Écoles Laïques
Pl de la Chapelle Neuve
R de l'École de Médecine
Pl Candolle
R Candolle
R Jean-Jacques Rousseau
R Ste-Croix
R de la Vielle Intendance
R Fournarié
R de Girone
R de la Carbonnerie
Bd Bonne Nouvelle
Esplanade Charles de Gaulle
Pl Royale du Peyrou
R du Palais des Guilhem
Préfecture
Cambacérès
Pl du Marché aux Fleurs
R Delpech
Pl Pétrarque
R Foch
To Château d'Eau (250m); Aqueduct de St-Clément (250m)
Pl des Martyrs de la Résistance
R de l'Aiguillerie
R de la Petite Loge
R des Augustins
Pl Giral
Pl Castellane
Pl Jean Jaurès
R Collot
Bd Sarrail
R du Bras de Fer
R des Trésoriers de la Bourse
R Jacques Cœur
Passage Bruyas
Bd Ledru-Rollin
R Guisthem
R de l'Ancien Courrier
Pl St-Ravy
R Cauzit
R de la Loge
Pl de la Comédie
To Airport (8km); La Grande Motte (20km); Grau du Roi (26km); Aigues Mortes (31km)
Le Polygone Shopping Complex
R des Balances
R du Petit St-Jean
R Four des Flammes
Grand Rue Jean Moulin
R Vanneau
R Baudin
Bd du Jeu de Paume
R des Étuves
R de Verdun
R Flaugergues
R Boussairolles
To Gignac (30km); Lodève (56km); Millau (115km)
R En-Gondeau
R Loys
R Diderot
Richelieu
R Maguelone
R Aristide Olivier
To Antigone (100m)
R Joffre
Bd Victor Hugo
R Séran
Cours Gambetta
R Anatole France
R de le République
R Jules Ferry
R du Grand St-Jean
Pl Auguste Gibert
Train Station
R Rondelet
Pl Rondelet
R St-Denis
Av Georges Clemenceau
Pl Carnot
To A9 (4km); L'Oasis Palavasienne (4km); Espace Latipolia (10km); Palavas-les-Flots (12km); Carnon (19km); La Grande Motte (27km)
To Sète (29km); Agde (52km); Béziers (65km); Narbonne (94km); Perpignan (140km); Carcassonne (148km); Barcelona (345km)
To Lattes (4km)
LANGUEDOC-ROUSSILLON

population swelled dramatically in the 1960s when many French settlers left independent Algeria and settled here.

Orientation

Montpellier's mostly pedestrianised historic centre, girdled by wide boulevards, has at its heart place de la Comédie, known to locals as *l'œuf* (the egg), because of its ovoid shape. To its east is Le Polygone, a vast shopping complex, and Antigone, a mammoth 1980s neoclassical housing project.

Westwards, between rue de la Loge and Grand Rue Jean Moulin, sprawls the city's oldest quarter, a web of narrow alleys and fine *hôtels particuliers* (private mansions).

Information

BOOKSHOPS

Book in Bar (☎ 04 67 66 22 90; 8 rue du Bras de Fer) Large stock of new and second-hand books in English. Runs conversation exchanges and cultural events. Browse the British press for free.

Les Cinq Continents (☎ 04 67 66 46 70; 20 rue Jacques Cœur) Specialist travel bookshop with an excellent selection of maps and travel literature.

INTERNET ACCESS

Dimension 4 Cybercafé (11 rue des Balances; per hr €3; 10am-midnight)

Point Internet (54 rue de l'Aiguillerie; per hr €1.40; 9.30am-midnight Mon-Sat, 10.30am-midnight Sun)

LAUNDRY

Lavosud (19 rue de l'Université; 7am-9pm)

POST

Main Post Office (13 place Rondelet)

TOURIST INFORMATION

Main Tourist Office (☎ 04 67 60 60 60; www.ot-montpellier.fr; esplanade Charles de Gaulle; 9am-7.30pm Mon-Fri, 9.30am-1pm & 2.30-6pm Sat & Sun Jul-Sep; 9am-6.30pm Mon-Fri, 10am-6pm Sat, 10am-1pm & 2-5pm Sun Oct-Jun).

Sights

MUSEUMS

Musée Fabre (☎ 04 67 14 83 00; 39 bd Bonne Nouvelle; adult/child €6/4; core hr 10am-6pm Tue & Thu-Sun, 1-9pm Wed) is a delightfully spacious, superbly lit venue, with one of France's richest collections of European works from the 16th century onwards and seven galleries of bright, dynamic 20th-century art.

CITY CARD

The **Montpellier City Card** (per 1/2/3 days €14/20/26, children half-price), sold at the tourist office, allows free or reduced admission to several sites and spectacles, plus unlimited bus and tram travel and a place on a guided walking tour (ask at the tourist office for the current timetable).

Musée Languedocien (☎ 04 67 52 93 03; 7 rue Jacques Cœur; adult/student €6/3; 3-6pm Mon-Sat mid-Jun–mid-Sep, 2.30-5.30pm Mon-Sat rest of year) displays the area's rich archeological finds as well as objets d'art from the 16th to 19th centuries.

Musée du Vieux Montpellier (☎ 04 67 66 02 94; 2 place Pétrarque; admission free; 9.30am-noon & 1.30-5pm Tue-Sat) is a storehouse of the city's memorabilia from the Middle Ages to the Revolution.

Musée de l'Histoire de Montpellier (☎ 04 67 54 33 16; place Jean Jaurès; admission €1.50; 10.30-11.45am & 1.30-5.15pm Mon-Sat) in the crypt of the church of Notre Dame des Tables presents the city's history in high-tech mode.

Musée Atger (☎ 04 67 41 76 30; 2 rue de l'École de Médecine; admission free; 1.30-5.45pm Mon, Wed & Fri Sep-Jul), housed within the medical faculty, displays a striking collection of French, Italian and Flemish drawings.

HÔTELS PARTICULIERS

During the 17th and 18th centuries, Montpellier's wealthier merchants built grand private mansions, often externally quite sober but with resplendent inner courtyards (mostly, alas, closed to the public). Fine examples are **Hôtel de Varennes** (2 place Pétrarque), a harmonious blend of Romanesque and Gothic style, and **Hôtel St-Côme** (Grand Rue Jean Moulin), nowadays the city's Chamber of Commerce. The 17th-century **Hôtel des Trésoriers de France** (7 rue Jacques Cœur) today houses the Musée Languedocien (above). Within the old quarter are several other such mansions, each marked by a descriptive plaque in French.

AROUND PLACE ROYALE DU PEYROU

At the eastern end of this wide, tree-lined esplanade is the **Arc de Triomphe** (1692). From the **Château d'Eau**, an elaborate hexagonal water tower at its western limit, stretches the **Aqueduc de St-Clément**, spectacularly illuminated at night. North of the esplanade is the **Jardin des Plantes** (entry on bd Henri IV), France's oldest botanical garden, laid out in 1593 and still used as a research resource by the University of Montpellier.

OTHER SIGHTS

Agropolis (☎ 04 67 04 75 00; www.museum.agropolis.fr, in French; 951 av Agropolis; adult/11-18yr/child €5/2.50/free; 10am-12.30pm & 2-6pm Mon-Fri) Agropolis is all about food and how people around the world grow it. Historically, it follows our progression from hunter-gatherer to supermarket shopper. Fascinating stuff, it's at once didactic, enjoyable and pitched at both children and adults. The museum is located 4km north of the centre.

La Serre Amazonienne (☎ 04 67 54 45 23; 50 av Agropolis; adult/student/child €5/3/2.50, audioguide €2; 9am-5pm or 6pm), a 10-minute walk from Agropolis, is a spectacular recent addition to Montpellier's zoo. This humid hothouse replicates the Amazonian rainforest. Piranha and alligators swim in the first two tanks but it gets friendlier as you progress. Stars include a pair of bright-eyed young leopards, a family of Bolivian squirrel monkeys and flitting bats. Afterwards, you can explore the rest of the zoo, France's second-largest, for free.

For both venues, take tram 1 to the St-Eloi stop, from where a regular shuttle bus does a circular route.

Aquarium Mare Nostrum (☎ 04 67 13 05 50; adult/student/child €12.50/10/8.50; 10am-10pm Jul & Aug, 10am-7pm, 8pm or 10pm Tue-Sun Sep-Jun) takes you through 15 different aquatic environments, from polar waters to tropical forests. Montpellier's most recent attraction, it's part of **Odysseum**. At the end of tram line 1, 3.5km east of the centre, this expanding leisure complex also has an ice rink, planetarium and multiscreen cinema.

On esplanade Charles de Gaulle, children can enjoy a **pony ride** (per 1/5/10 circuits €4/15/20; 2-6pm or 8pm daily school holidays, Wed, Sat & Sun rest of year) on mounts ranging in size from little mannequin Shetlands to sturdy mules.

Festivals & Events

In June, Montpellier hosts **Printemps des Comédiens** (☎ 04 67 63 66 67; www.printempsdescomediens.com, in French), a popular theatre festival. **Montpellier Danse** (☎ 08 00 60 07 40; www.montpellierdanse.com, in French) is a two-week international dance festival held in June or July. The **Festival de Radio France et Montpellier** (☎ 04 67 02 02 01; www.festivalradiofrancemontpellier.com, in French) in the second half of July brings in top-notch classical music and jazz.

Sleeping

The closest campsites are around the suburb of Lattes, around 4km south of the city centre.

Auberge de Jeunesse (☎ 04 67 60 32 22; montpellier@fuaj.org; 2 impasse de la Petite Corraterie; B&B €15.20; mid-Jan–mid-Dec) Montpellier's HI-affiliated youth hostel is just off rue des Écoles Laïques. Rooms sleep two to 10 and there's a small, shaded garden. Take the tram to the Louis Blanc stop.

L'Oasis Palavasienne (☎ 04 67 15 11 61; www.oasis-palavasienne.com; rte de Palavas; site according to season €16-29; Apr–mid-Oct;) This shady campsite has a large heated pool and sauna. Take bus 17 from the bus station.

Hôtel des Étuves (☎ 04 67 60 78 19; www.hoteldesetuves.fr; 24 rue des Étuves; s €33-45, d €39-45;) This welcoming, 13-room family hotel, creeping around a spiral staircase like a vine, offers exceptional value. Room two, one of six overlooking the quiet pedestrian street, has a bath while the rest are equipped with showers. Does not take credit cards.

Hôtel le Mistral (☎ 04 67 58 45 25; www.hotel-le-mistral.com, in French; 25 rue Boussairolles; s €42-44, d €43-51) Behind its 19th-century facade, this spruce 20-room place is conveniently central. Spacious triples occupy the angle of the street. Other rooms are of ample size though bathrooms are cramped. Parking costs €10.

Hôtel de la Comédie (☎ 04 67 58 43 64; hoteldelacomedie@cegetel.net; 1bis rue Baudin; s €42-47, d €52-69;) This friendly, family-run place, just off place de la Comédie, is a favourite with visiting musicians and theatre troupes. All 20 rooms have air-con and heating and are double-glazed.

Hôtel du Parc (☎ 04 67 41 16 49; www.hotelduparc-montpellier.com; 8 rue Achille-Bégé; s €63-72, d €72-83, s/d with shower €45/50;) At this 18th-century former *hôtel particulier* with its grand curling wrought-iron staircase, bibelots and knick-knacks add an at-home touch to each of the 19 individually decorated rooms (ask for room seven, bedchamber of the previous owner, Comte Vivier de Châtelard). Those on the ground floor have a small balcony. Wi-fi and parking available.

Hôtel du Palais (☎ 04 67 60 47 38; www.hoteldupalais-montpellier.fr; 3 rue du Palais des Guilhem; s €62, d €67-79;) All 26 rooms of this delightful hotel overlooking a quiet square are decorated by a local artist and tastefully and individually furnished.

our pick **Hôtel Le Guilhem** (☎ 04 67 52 90 90; www.hotel-le-guilhem.com; 18 rue Jean-Jacques Rousseau; s €81-93, d €91-172;) Occupying a couple of interconnecting 16th-century buildings, Hôtel Le Guilhem's 35 rooms are exquisitely and individually furnished. Nearly all overlook the tranquil garden of nearby Restaurant Le Petit Jardin. Room 100 (€158) has its own little terrace and garden. It's wise to reserve at any time of year; Le Guilhem has its faithful clientele who return again and again. Free wi-fi.

Eating

You'll find plenty of cheap and cheerful eateries on rue de l'Université, rue des Écoles Laïques and the streets interlinking them.

Tripti Kulai (☎ 04 67 66 30 51; 20 rue Jacques Cœur; salads €9.50, menus €12-16.50; noon-9.30pm Mon-Sat) Barrel-vaulted and cosy, this popular vegetarian place stands out for the originality of many of its dishes.

Caves Jean Jaurès (☎ 04 67 60 27 33; 3 rue Collot; menu €18, mains €12-16; Tue-Sat, dinner Sun & Mon) Scan the range of tasty dishes on the chalkboard at this attractive restaurant with its mosaic-topped tables and polished wooden floor. A glass of wine? Select from the bottles of the day on the bar counter. Rather more? Pick from the shelves; every bottle has its price marked and the range is superlative.

Le Petit Jardin (☎ 04 67 60 78 78; 20 rue Jean-Jacques Rousseau; lunch menu €14, dinner menus €22-48, mains €22-28; Tue-Sun Feb-Dec) The Little Garden is just that: a restaurant offering imaginative cuisine, its big bay windows overlooking a shady, fairy-tale greenness at the rear, where you could be miles from Montpellier's bustle. The lunch *menu* (€14) is excellent value.

La Girafe (☎ 04 67 54 48 89; 14 rue du Palais des Guilhem; mains around €15; Tue-Sat) You're indeed greeted by a tall model giraffe as you enter. Dine in the intimate downstairs area with its ox-blood-red decor and original artwork or upstairs, beneath the cross arches of this former chapel. Chef Pascale Schmitt gets his ingredients fresh from the market and nothing's from the freezer, except the frogs' legs, which come simmered with snails and baby mushrooms in a creamy, peppery sauce. Other dishes are similarly creative.

Insensé (☎ 04 67 58 97 78; Musée Fabre; 2-/3-course lunch €19/26, mains around €15; lunch Tue-Sun, dinner Wed, Fri & Sat) Restaurant of Musée Fabre (p771), Insensé is just as contemporary and tasteful as you'd expect from such a venue. The dominant shade is black: tables, chairs, floor tiles – even the pepper pots. The innovative cuisine is altogether more colourful.

Le Ban des Gourmands (☎ 04 67 65 00 85; 5 place Carnot; menu €28, mains €16-25; Tue-Sat) South of the train station and a favourite of locals in the know, this appealing restaurant, run by a young family team, serves delicious local cuisine.

Les Bains de Montpellier (☎ 04 67 60 70 87; 6 rue Richelieu; 3-course menu €22, mains €17-21; Tue-Fri, lunch Sat & Mon) This former public bath is now a highly recommended restaurant. Tables are set around the old perimeter bathrooms where you can almost hear the gurgle and slurp of long-emptied tubs. For something light, try the *assiette des Bains*, a platter with salads, pasta, garnishes, vegetables and a hint of meat. If you're hungrier, enjoy a substantial hunk of *rôti de porc* (roast pork), succulent and still on the bone.

La Diligence (☎ 04 67 66 12 21; 2 place Pétrarque; lunch menu €20, dinner menus €26-66; Tue-Fri, dinner Sat & Mon) Dine beneath attractive vaults and arches at this former cloth warehouse. Savour the creative cuisine, impressive wine cellar and elegant rear patio overlooked by a gallery of the Hôtel de Varennes.

our pick **Tamarillos** (☎ 04 67 60 06 00; www.tamarillos.biz; 2 place du Marché aux Fleurs; lunch menus €25-38, menus €55-90; Tue-Sat & dinner Mon) 'A cuisine of fruit and flowers' is Tamarillos' motto, and indeed all dishes, sweet or savoury, have fruit as an ingredient or main element. Pace yourself; chef Philippe Chapon is *double champion de France de dessert* and taught a young Gordon Ramsay his pastry cooking.

SELF-CATERING

The city's food markets include **Halles Castellane** (rue de la Loge), the biggest, and **Halles Laissac** (rue Anatole France). There's a Saturday organic food market under the arches of Aqueduc de St-Clément (p771), and a farmers market every Sunday morning on av Samuel de Champlain in the Antigone complex.

Drinking

Place de la Comédie is alive with cafés where you can drink, grab a quick bite and watch street entertainers strut their stuff. Other popular venues are place Jean Jaurès and smaller, more intimate place St-Ravy.

L'Heure Bleue (1 rue de la Carbonnerie; ⌚ Tue-Sun) At this tea salon, you can sip Earl Grey to a background of classical music. It also does light lunches (around €12) with plenty of choice for vegetarians.

With nearly 80,000 students, Montpellier has a multitude of places to drink and dance. You'll find dense concentrations around rue En-Gondeau, off Grand Rue Jean Moulin, around place Jean Jaurès, and around the intersection of rue de l'Université and rue Candolle.

Entertainment

To find out what's on where, pick up the free weekly *Sortir à Montpellier*, available around town and at the tourist office.

Tickets for Montpellier's numerous theatres are sold at the box office of the **Opéra-Comédie** (☎ 04 67 60 19 80; place de la Comédie). **Le Corum** (☎ 04 67 61 67 61; esplanade Charles de Gaulle) is the city's prime concert venue.

Rockstore (☎ 04 67 06 80 00; www.rockstore.fr, in French; 20 rue de Verdun) In the heart of town, you'll recognise this long-standing discotheque and club by the rear of a classic American '70s car jutting out above the entrance. Opening days and times vary.

There's a critical mass of discos outside town in Espace Latipolia, about 10km from Montpellier on route de Palavas heading towards the coast. Major players include:

La Nitro (☎ 04 67 22 45 82) Thumps out techno and house.

Le Matchico (☎ 04 67 64 19 20) For retro music.

L'Amigo (€2.40), a night bus, does a circuit of Espace Latipolia and other dance venues on the periphery of town, leaving the train station at midnight and 1am, returning at 2.30am, 3.30am and (yawn!) 5am, Thursday to Saturday.

To tune into the active gay scene, call by:

Café de la Mer (5 place du Marché aux Fleurs) The friendly staff will arm you with a map of gay venues.

Le Heaven (1 rue Delpech; www.leheaven.fr, in French) Just around the corner from Café de la Mer, this bar for gay guys and gals gets busy from 8pm.

Le Village (3 rue Fournarié) A shop specialising in queer gear.

Getting There & Away

AIR

Montpellier's **airport** (☎ 04 67 20 85 00; www.montpellier.aeroport.fr) is 8km southeast of town. EasyJet flies to/from London (Gatwick) and Ryanair to/from London (Stansted).

BUS

The **bus station** (☎ 04 67 92 01 43; rue du Grand St-Jean) is an easy walk from the train station. **Hérault Transport** (☎ 08 25 34 01 34) runs buses approximately hourly to La Grande Motte (bus 106, €3.90, 35 minutes) via Carnon from Odysseum at the end of the tram line. Up to four daily services continue to Aigues Mortes (€5.90, 1¼ hours).

Eurolines (☎ 04 67 58 57 59; 8 rue de Verdun) has buses to Barcelona (€18, five hours) and most European destinations. **Linebus** (☎ 04 67 58 95 00) mainly operates services to destinations in Spain.

TRAIN

Major destinations from Montpellier's two-storey train station include Paris' Gare de Lyon (€96.50 to €112, 3½ hours, up to 10 daily), Carcassonne (€21.20, 1½ hours, nine daily), Millau (€24.30, 1¾ hours, one daily) and Perpignan (€21.60, 1¾ hours, frequent).

More than 20 trains daily go northwards to Nîmes (€8.20, 30 minutes) and southwards to Narbonne (€14, one hour).

Getting Around

TO/FROM THE AIRPORT

A frequent **shuttle bus** (☎ 08 25 34 01 34; tickets €4.90; ⌚ every 15 min) runs between the airport and the Place de l'Europe tram station.

BICYCLE

Montpellier is hugely bicycle-friendly. **Vélo-Magg**, an admirable urban initiative, has more than 1000 rental bikes, parked at 50 *vélostations* around town. To pick up a pass (€5 for 20 one-hour units), call by **Vélostation Centrale TaM** (☎ 04 67 22 87 82; 27 rue Maguelone; ⌚ 8am-8pm) with your passport or identity card.

CAR & MOTORCYCLE

The best and most eco-friendly option is to leave your vehicle in one of the vast car parks beside major tram stops. Just €4 gets you all-day parking and return tram tickets to the heart of town for up to five people.

PUBLIC TRANSPORT

Savour Montpellier's high-tech, high-speed, leave-your-car-at-home trams. Like city buses, they're run by **TaM** (☎ 04 67 22 87 87; www.tam-way.com, in French; 6 rue Jules Ferry).

Single-journey bus and tram tickets cost €1.30. A one-day pass/10-ticket carnet cost €3.20/10.80. Pick them up from newsagents or any tram station.

TAXI

Ring **Taxis Bleu** (☎ 04 67 03 20 00) or **Taxis Tram** (☎ 04 67 58 10 10).

AROUND MONTPELLIER

The closest beaches are at **Palavas-les-Flots**, 12km south of the city, and Montpellier-on-Sea in summer. Take TaM bus 131 from the Port Marianne tram stop. Heading north on the coastal road towards Carnon, you stand a chance of seeing flamingos hoovering the shallows of the lagoons either side of the D21.

Carnon itself comes out fairly low in the charm stakes despite its huge marina. Better to continue hugging the coast along the D59 (Le Petit Travers) alongside several kilometres of white sand beach, uncrowded and without a kiosk or café in sight.

Further northwards and 25km from Montpellier is **La Grande Motte**, purpose-built on the grand scale back in the 1960s to plug the tourist drain southwards into Spain. Its architecture, considered revolutionary at the time, now comes over as fairly heavy and leaden, contrasting with the more organic growth of adjacent **Grau du Roi**, deeper rooted and a still active fishing port.

Aigues Mortes, on the western edge of the Camargue, is another 11km eastwards.

SÈTE

pop 48,300

Sète is France's largest Mediterranean fishing port and biggest commercial entrepôt after Marseille. Established by Louis XIV in the 17th century, it prospered as the harbours of Aigues Mortes and Narbonne, to north and south respectively, were cut off from the sea by silt deposits.

Huddled beneath Mont St-Clair, Sète has lots in its favour: waterways and canals, beaches and shoals of fish and seafood restaurants.

The **tourist office** (☎ 04 67 74 71 71; www.ot-sete.fr; 60 Grand' Rue Mario Roustan; ⌚ 9.30am-7.30pm Jul & Aug, 9.30am-6pm Mon-Fri, 9.30am-5.30pm Sat & Sun Apr-Jun, 9.30am-6pm Mon-Fri, 9.30am-12.30pm & 2-5.30pm Sat & Sun Sep-Mar) rents out **audioguides** (per route €5) covering six walks (two with English commentary) in and around town.

Sète was the birthplace of the symbolist poet Paul Valéry (1871–1945), whose remains lie in the **Cimetière Marin** (Marine Cemetery), the inspiration for his most famous poem. The town was also the childhood home of singer and infinitely more accessible poet Georges Brassens (1921–81), whose mellow voice still speaks at multimedia **Espace Georges Brassens** (☎ 04 67 53 32 77; 67 bd Camille Blanc; adult/student/child €5/2/free; ⌚ 10am-noon & 2-6pm or 7pm Jun-Sep, Tue-Sun Oct-May).

From mid-February to mid-October, **Azur Croisières** (☎ 06 10 65 40 22) does a one-hour **harbour tour** (adult/child €10/5), leaving from Pont de la Savonnerie. In July and August, **Sète Croisières** (☎ 04 67 46 00 46; quai Général Durand) does a similar tour. Both also do fishing trips.

Over a long weekend in the first half of July, Sète celebrates **La Fête de la St-Pierre**, or Fête des Pêcheurs (Fisherfolk's Festival). The **Fête de la St-Louis** fills six frantic days around 25 August with *joutes nautiques*, where participants in competing boats try to knock each other into the water.

Sleeping & Eating

Auberge de Jeunesse (☎ 04 67 53 46 68; sete@fuaj.org; rue Général Revest; B&B €15.50; ⌚ mid-Jan–mid-Dec) Scarcely a kilometre northwest of the tourist office, it enjoys a lovely wooded site with great views over town and harbour.

L'Orque Bleue (☎ 04 67 74 72 13; www.hotel-orquebleue-sete.com; 10 quai Aspirant Herber; interior r €72-82, canalside r €105-110; ⌚ Feb-Dec; ❄ ⊠) Right on the quayside and prominent among its dowdier neighbours, this hotel occupies a former shipping magnate's mansion, clad everywhere in marble. To truly sense Sète as a living port, go for one of the more expensive nine rooms overlooking the canal, unless you're a light sleeper. Parking is available.

Tempting fish restaurants line quai Durand and quai Maximin Licciardi all the way from Pont de la Savonnerie to the wholesale fish market.

La Péniche (☎ 04 67 48 64 13; 1 quai des Moulins; menus €15-19.50, mains €11-13; ⌚ Mon-Fri, dinner Sat & lunch Sun) The service is brisk and friendly and the clientele a mix of local workers, suits and sweaters on this converted barge. For the *menu du matelot* (sailor's menu; €15), two pots of pâté, into which you dig at will, are slapped before you, followed by a significant dollop of Russian salad and half a lettuce. For the main course, it has to be the house speciality, *rouille sétoise* –

whole baby octopuses smothered in a peppery rouille sauce. Then comes dessert…

Au Bord du Canal (☎ 04 67 51 98 39; 9 quai Maximin Licciardi; menu €32; ⏰ Tue-Sat & lunch Sun) The fish could almost flop from the wholesale market opposite straight into this pleasantly furnished restaurant where not even the smallest sardine is frozen. It does a splendid midday grill (€15) of anything with fins that takes the chef's fancy that day.

AGDE

pop 20,000

There are three Agdes these days: the original settlement beside the River Hérault; Grau d'Agde, a small, modern fishing port; and Le Cap d'Agde, a vast summertime playground.

Of these, old Agde was originally a Phoenician then a Greek settlement, named after Agatha Tyche, the Greek goddess (its inhabitants are still called Agathois).

The **tourist office** (☎ 04 67 94 29 68; www.agde-herault.com, in French; ⏰ 9am-7pm Mon-Sat, 10am-1pm & 3-6pm Sun Jul & Aug, 9am-noon & 2-6pm Mon-Sat Sep-Jun) is at 1 place Molière. Ask for the English version of its walking-tour leaflet. It sells tickets for three companies that run short boat trips along the Canal du Midi, which joins the River Hérault just upstream from old Agde.

The dark grey basalt of the imposing *hotels particuliers* (private mansions) and the fortress-like, mainly 12th-century **Cathédrale St-Étienne** motivated Marco Polo to describe the town as the 'black pearl of the Mediterranean'.

The 26 well-displayed rooms of the **Musée Agathois** (☎ 04 67 94 82 51; 5 rue de la Fraternité; adult/child €4.50/1.80; ⏰ 9am-7pm Mon-Fri, noon-7pm Sat & Sun Jul & Aug, 9am-noon & 2-5pm Mon-Sat, 2-5pm Sun Sep-Jun), within an attractive 17th-century mansion, take you through Agde's long maritime and wine-producing history.

Hôtel le Donjon (☎ 04 67 94 12 32; www.hotelledonjon.com; place Jean Jaurès; r €42-79; ⊠) Once a convent then a coaching inn, this hotel is full of character. Each of its 20 rooms is large and attractively decorated in typical Midi blues and yellows. Parking is free.

A battery of restaurants with terraces splay along the quayside.

Lou Pescadou (☎ 04 67 21 17 10; 18 rue Chassefière; menu €15) has been serving the same take-it-or-leave-it five-course *menu* since 1965. First, a rich, fishy broth. After a steaming plate of mussels, piled high, comes a big bowl of pâté to dig into. Then it's a giant grilled fish or slab of steak followed by an equally gut-busting dessert. Come back tomorrow, next week, next year and repeat the experience; Lou Pescadou is one of life's few constants.

Buses (€2; at least hourly) ply the 6km route to the modern tourist resort of **Le Cap d'Agde**, famed for its long beaches and large nudist colony.

BÉZIERS

pop 71,600

Béziers, first settled by the Phoenicians, became an important military post in Roman times. It was almost completely destroyed in 1209 during the Albigensian Crusade, when some 20,000 'heretics', many seeking refuge in the cathedral, were slaughtered. In happier times, the local tax collector Paul Riquet (1604–80) moved heaven and earth to build the Unesco World Heritage–listed **Canal du Midi**, a 240km-long marvel of engineering with its aqueducts and more than 100 locks, enabling cargo vessels to sail from the Atlantic to the Mediterranean without having to circumnavigate Spain. There's a fine statue to Béziers' most famous son on allée Paul Riquet, a wide, leafy esplanade at the heart of the town.

The **tourist office** (☎ 04 67 76 84 00; www.beziers-tourisme.fr; 29 av St-Saens; ⏰ 9am-6.30pm Mon-Sat, 10am-1pm & 3-6pm Sun Jul & Aug, 9am-noon & 2-5pm or 6pm Mon-Sat Sep-Jun) is in the Palais des Congrès.

Fortified **Cathédrale St-Nazaire** (⏰ 9.30am-noon & 2.30-5.30pm), surrounded by narrow alleys, is typical of the area, with massive towers, an imposing facade and a huge 14th-century rose window.

Musée du Biterrois (☎ 04 67 36 81 61; place des Casernes; adult/child €2.60/1.80; ⏰ 10am-6pm Tue-Sun Jul & Aug, 9am-noon & 2-5pm or 6pm Tue-Sun Sep-Jun) is a well-displayed museum of the town's history, its largest sections devoted to Roman artefacts and winemaking.

Popular annual events include the week-long **Festa d'Oc**, a celebration of Mediterranean music and dance, in late July, and the **féria**, a five-day celebration with bullfights when the town's more Spanish than Languedocien, held around 15 August.

NARBONNE

pop 51,300

Once a coastal port but now a whole 13km inland because of silting up, Narbonne in its time was capital of Gallia Narbonensis and one of the principal Roman cities in Gaul.

The **tourist office** (04 68 65 15 60; www.narbonne-tourisme.com; 31 rue Jean Jaurès; 9am-7pm Apr–mid-Sep, 9am-12.30pm & 1.30-6pm Mon-Sat, 10am-5pm Sun mid-Sep–Mar) occupies smart new premises beside Canal de la Robine.

The splendid **Cathédrale St-Just** (entry on rue Armand Gauthier; 10am-7pm Jul-Sep, 9am-noon & 2-6pm Oct-Jun) is, in fact, no more than its towers and a soaring choir, construction having stopped in the early 14th century. The ambulatory chapel directly behind the main altar has a haunting alabaster *Virgin and Child* and fine, much knocked-about polychrome stone carving. The **treasury** (admission €2.20; 11am-6pm Jul-Sep, 2-5pm or 6pm Oct-Jun) has a beautiful Flemish tapestry of the Creation, while grotesque gargoyles peer down upon the 16th-century **cloister**.

Adjoining the cathedral to the south and facing place de l'Hôtel de Ville, the fortified **Palais des Archevêques** (Archbishops' Palace; 9.30am-12.15pm & 2-6pm Jul-Sep, 10am-noon & 2-5pm Mon-Sat Oct-Jun) houses Narbonne's **Musée d'Art et d'Histoire** and **Musée Archéologique**, the latter with an impressive collection of Roman mosaics and paintings on stucco. Nearby is the **Horreum** (same as Palais des Archevêques), an underground gallery of Gallo-Roman shops. A combined ticket (adult/child €5.20/3.70), valid for three days, gives access to all three sites.

The elaborate mock-Renaissance 19th-century facade of the **Hôtel de Ville** was designed by Viollet-le-Duc. Go inside for access to the **Donjon Gilles Aycelin** (adult/child €2.20/free; 10am-6pm Jul-Sep, 10am-noon & 2-5pm or 6pm Oct-Jun), a large, square 13th-century keep.

Take in also **Les Halles**, Narbonne's imposing art nouveau covered market, a colourful place to stock up on food and itself an architectural jewel.

Just off the A9, 15km south of Narbonne, is the **Réserve Africaine de Sigean** (04 68 48 20 20; www.reserveafricainesigean.fr; adult/child €24/19; 9am-4pm or 6.30pm), where lions, tigers and other 'safari' animals live in semiliberty. If you arrive by bike or on foot, there's free transport around the reserve.

CARCASSONNE

pop 45,500

From afar, Carcassonne looks like some fairy-tale medieval city. Bathed in late-afternoon sunshine and highlighted by dark clouds, La Cité, as the old walled city is known, is truly breathtaking. But once you're inside, La Cité loses its magic and mystery. Luring an estimated four million visitors annually, it can be a tourist hell in high summer. This said, you'll have to be fairly stone-hearted not to be moved.

But Carcassonne is more than La Cité. The Ville Basse (Lower Town), altogether more tranquil and established in the 13th century, is a more modest stepsister to camp Cinderella up the hill and also merits more than a browse.

History

The hill on which La Cité stands has been fortified across the centuries – by Gauls, Romans, Visigoths, Moors and Franks. In the 13th century, the walls protected one of the major Cathar strongholds (see boxed text, p799). Once Roussillon was annexed to France in 1659, Carcassonne, no longer a frontier town, sank into slow decline. By the 19th century La Cité was simply crumbling away. It was rescued by the elaborate intervention of Viollet-le-Duc, who also set his controversial stamp upon, for example, the cathedrals of Notre Dame in Paris and Vézelay in Burgundy.

Orientation

The River Aude separates the Ville Basse from La Cité, up on a hill 500m to the southeast. Pedestrianised rue Georges Clemenceau leads from the train station and Canal du Midi southwards through the heart of the lower town.

Information

INTERNET ACCESS

Alerte Rouge (73 rue de Verdun; per hr €3; 10am-10pm Mon-Thu, 10am-11pm Fri & Sat) Buy a drink and you can wi-fi for free for an hour. And here's a rare internet café that actually does great coffee.

LAUNDRY

La Lavandière (31 rue Aimé Ramond; 8am-7pm Mon-Sat)

TOURIST INFORMATION

Main Tourist Office (04 68 10 24 30; www.carcassonne-tourisme.com; 28 rue de Verdun; 9am-7pm Jul & Aug, 9am-6pm Mon-Sat, 9am-1pm Sun Sep-Jun) Borrow an audioguide to the Ville Basse (€3 for two hours).

Tourist Office Annexes La Cité (Porte Narbonnaise; year-round); Ville Basse (av Joffre; mid-Apr–Oct)

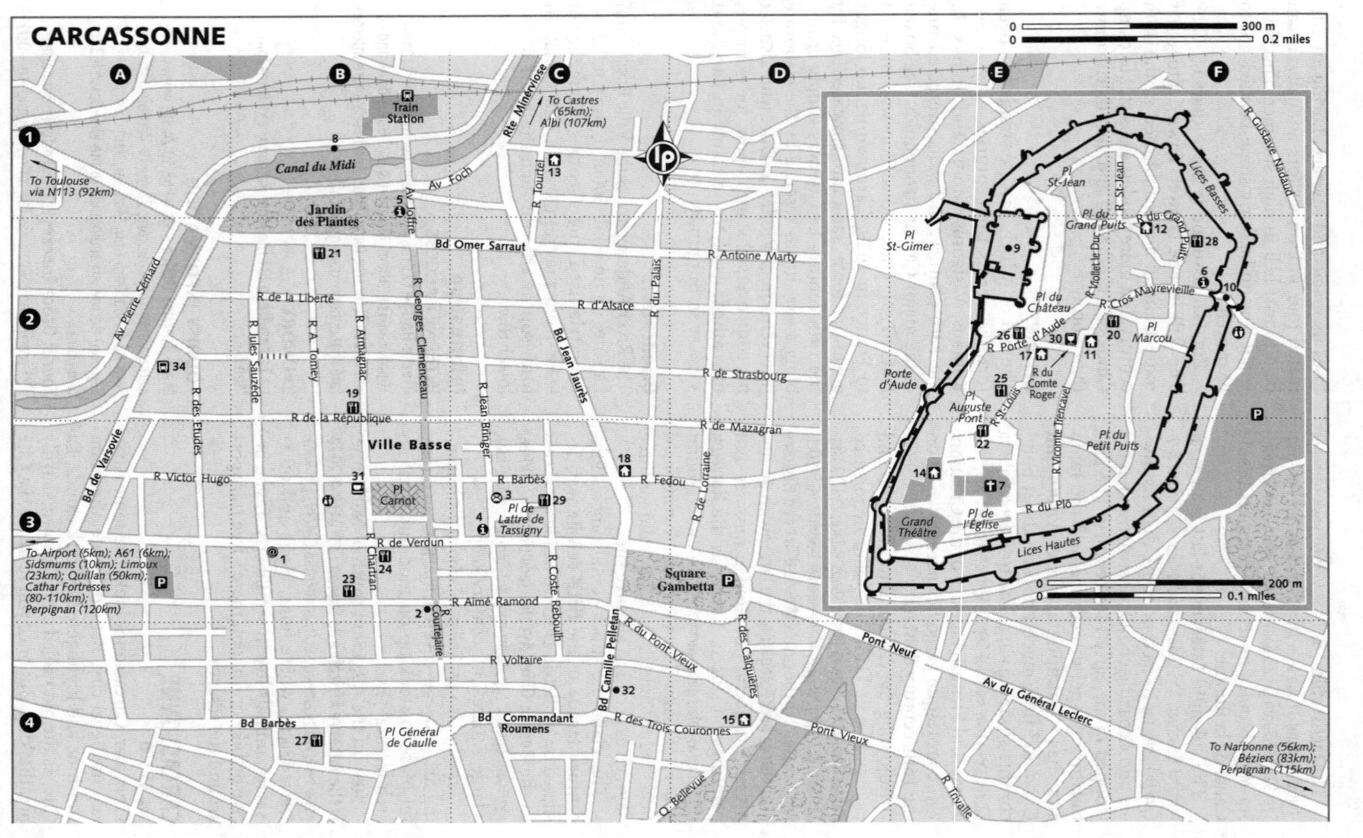
CARCASSONNE
0 300 m
0 0.2 miles
0 200 m
0 0.1 miles
To Toulouse via N113 (92km)
To Castres (65km); Albi (107km)
To Airport (5km); A61 (6km); Sidsmums (10km); Limoux (23km); Quillan (50km); Cathar Fortresses (80-110km); Perpignan (120km)
To Narbonne (56km); Béziers (83km); Perpignan (115km)
Canal du Midi
Train Station
Jardin des Plantes
Ville Basse
Pl Carnot
Pl de Lattre de Tassigny
Square Gambetta
Pl Général de Gaulle
Rte Minervoise
Av Foch
Av Joffre
Av Pierre Sémard
Bd de Varsovie
Bd Omer Sarraut
Bd Jean Jaurès
Bd Camille Pelletan
Bd Commandant Roumens
Bd Barbès
R Tourtel
R du Palais
R Antoine Marty
R d'Alsace
R de la Liberté
R de Strasbourg
R de Mazagran
R de la République
R de Lorraine
R Fedou
R Georges Clemenceau
R Armagnac
R A. Tomey
R Jules Sauzède
R des Etudes
R Victor Hugo
R Jean Bringer
R Barbès
R Coste Reboulh
R Aimé Ramond
R Courtejaire
R de Verdun
R Chartran
R Voltaire
R du Pont Vieux
R des Trois Couronnes
R des Calquières
Pont Neuf
Pont Vieux
Av du Général Leclerc
R Trivalle
Q Bellevue
R Gustave Nadaud
Lices Basses
Lices Hautes
R du Grand Puits
Pl du Grand Puits
R St-Jean
Pl St-Jean
R Viollet le Duc
R Cros Mayrevieille
Pl Marcou
Pl du Château
R Porte d'Aude
R du Comte Roger
R Vicomte Trencavel
Pl du Petit Puits
R St-Louis
Pl Auguste Pont
R du Plô
Pl de l'Église
Grand Théâtre
Porte d'Aude
Pl St-Gimer

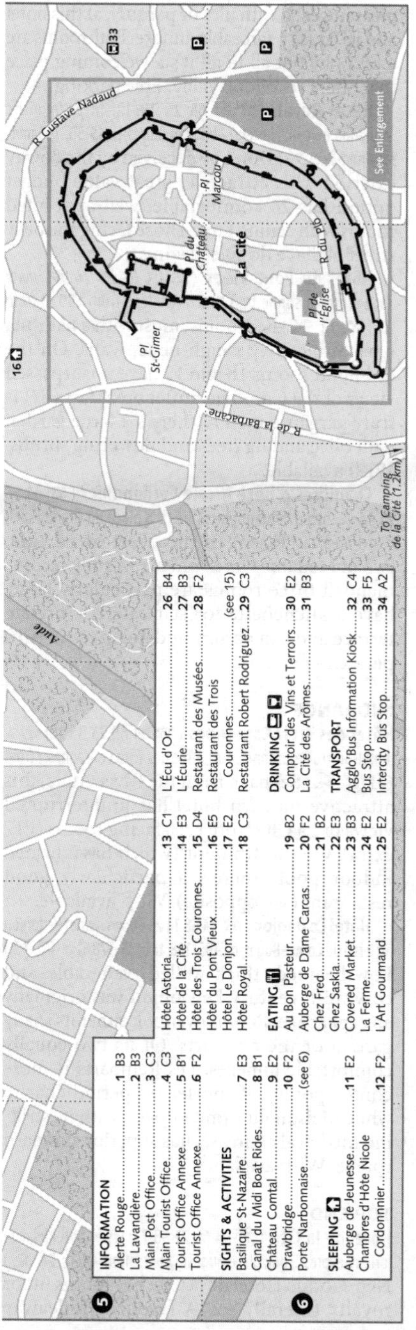

Sights & Activities

LA CITÉ

La Cité, dramatically illuminated at night and enclosed by two rampart walls punctuated by 52 stone towers, is one of Europe's largest city fortifications. But only the lower sections of the walls are original; the rest, including the anachronistic witches'-hat roofs (the originals were altogether flatter and weren't covered with slate), were stuck on by Viollet-le-Duc in the 19th century.

From square Gambetta, it's an attractive walk to La Cité across Pont Vieux, along rue de la Barbacane, then up and in through Porte d'Aude. Catching a bus to the main entrance is also an option.

If you pass over the **drawbridge** to enter via the main entrance, you're faced with a massive bastion, the **Porte Narbonnaise** and, just inside, the tourist office annexe. Rue Cros Mayrevieille, suffocating in kitschy souvenir shops, leads up to place du Château, heart of La Cité.

Through another archway and across a second dry moat is the 12th-century **Château Comtal** (adult/18-25yr/under 18yr €7.50/4.80/free; 10am-6.30pm Apr-Sep, 9.30am-5pm Oct-Mar). The entrance fee lets you look around the castle itself, enjoy an 11-minute film and join an optional 30- to 40-minute guided tour of the ramparts (tours in English, July and August). Descriptive panels around the castle, in both French and English, are explicit. For more detail, invest in an **audioguide** (1/2 persons €4/6).

South of place du Château is **Basilique St-Nazaire** (9am-11.45am & 1.45-5.30pm Mon-Sat, 9-10.45am & 2-6pm Sun). Highlights are the graceful Gothic transept arms with a pair of superb 13th- and 14th-century rose windows at each end.

The **Petit Train de la Cité** (20 min for adult/student/3-11yr/under 3yr €7/6/3/free; 10am-noon & 2-6pm May-Sep) with multilingual commentary beats the bounds of the ramparts. Alternatively, a horse-drawn **carriage** (adult/child €7/4; 10am-6pm Apr–mid-Nov), hauled by a pair of magnificent dray horses, does a shorter 20-minute trip.

If possible, linger after the crowds have left, when La Cité belongs only to its 100 or so inhabitants and the few visitors staying at the hotels within its ramparts.

BOAT RIDES

Lou Gabaret (04 68 71 61 26) and **Solal** (06 07 74 04 57) both chug along the Canal du Midi, departing from the bridge just south of the train station. **Sailings** (adult €8-10, child €6.50-7.50; 4 daily Jul & Aug, 1 or 2 daily Tue-Sun Apr-Jun, Sep & Oct) with commentary last around 1¾ or 2½ hours and prices vary accordingly.

SIMPLY STROLLING

Leave the crowds up high, cut loose and walk the landscaped banks of the River Aude.

Festivals & Events

Carcassonne knows how to party. On 14 July at 10.30pm, **L'Embrasement de la Cité** (Setting La Cité Ablaze) celebrates Bastille Day with a fireworks display rivalled only by Paris' pyrotechnics.

The **Festival de la Cité** (04 68 11 59 15; www.festivaldecarcassonne.com) brings music, dance and theatre to town for three weeks in July. During the same period, the **Festival de la Bastide** serves up around 70 free spectacles in the squares and public spaces.

Sleeping

BUDGET

Camping de la Cité (04 68 25 11 77; www.campeole.com; site €16-22.80, for hikers €9-12; mid-Mar–mid-Oct;) A walking and cycling trail leads from the site to both La Cité and the Ville Basse. From mid-June to mid-September, a shuttle bus connects the campsite with La Cité and the train station every 20 minutes.

Auberge de Jeunesse (04 68 25 23 16; carcassonne@fuaj.org; rue Vicomte Trencavel; B&B €16.90; Feb–mid-Dec) Carcassonne's cheery, welcoming, HI-affiliated youth hostel, in the heart of La Cité, has rooms sleeping four to six. It has a members' kitchen, a summertime snack bar, great outside terrace and one internet station. It rents out bikes (€8 per day) to hostellers. Although it has 120 beds, it's smart to reserve year-round.

Sidsmums (04 68 26 94 49; www.sidsmums.com; 11 chemin de la Croix d'Achille; dm €21, d with corridor bathroom €42-47.50) In Preixan, 10km south of Carcassonne, this is a splendid budget option. You can hire a bike, take a guided walk with George the dog, and cook for yourself in the self-contained kitchen. In the garden are four chalets (€46 to €51.50), each sleeping up to three. Lifts are possible by prior arrangement from Carcassonne town or airport. Otherwise, take the Quillan bus (four daily).

Hôtel Astoria (04 68 25 31 38; www.astoriacarcassonne.com, in French; 18 rue Tourtel; d/tr/q €49/59/72, r with shared bathroom €32; Mar-Jan) Rooms are fresh and pleasant, each with tiles or parquet, at this hotel and its equally agreeable annexe. Bathrooms are a bit poky but all in all it's a welcoming place that offers very good value. Free parking.

Hôtel Royal (04 68 25 19 12; http://monsite.wanadoo.fr/royal_hotel; 22 bd Jean Jaurès; r €45-50; mid-Jan–mid-Dec;) Don't be deceived by the dowdy exterior. This attractive, great-value budget option has 24 comfortable, well-appointed rooms with ceiling fans. Those facing the busy street all have double glazing.

Hôtel du Pont Vieux (04 68 25 24 99; www.lacitedecarcassonne.fr; 32 rue Trivalle; s from €50, d from €60;) Bedrooms, most with a bathtub, have attractively rough-hewn walls. On the 3rd floor, rooms 18 and 19 have unsurpassed views of the Cité. The buffet breakfast (€7) is truly gargantuan, and there's a large garden with olive and fig trees and flowering shrubs. Wi-fi available.

Chambres d'Hôte Nicole Cordonnier (04 68 25 16 67; http://legrandpuits.free.fr; 8 place du Grand Puits; d incl breakfast €52-65) In the heart of La Cité, two of Madame Cordonnier's warmly recommended three rooms are particularly large, have a kitchenette for self-caterers, private terrace and can accommodate up to six (€10 per extra person).

MIDRANGE

Hôtel des Trois Couronnes (04 68 25 36 10; www.hotel-destroiscouronnes.com; 2 rue des Trois Couronnes; r from €83;) Set back from the River Aude, this attractive modern hotel has uninterrupted views of La Cité from east-facing rooms (€17 extra). On the 4th floor (which has a heated indoor pool) there's a particularly good restaurant (see opposite). Wi-fi available.

Hôtel Le Donjon (04 68 11 23 00; www.hotel-donjon.fr; 2 rue du Comte Roger; d €105-158, tr €135-178;) Low-beamed, thick-walled, venerable and cosy, 15th-century Le Donjon was originally an orphanage. Rooms overlook either its shady garden or the ramparts. Of its two equally comfortable annexes, Les Remparts is more contemporary, if shorter on period charm, while Maison du Comte Roger, with its striking medieval staircase, has superior standard rooms. Wi-fi available.

TOP END

Hôtel de la Cité (04 68 71 98 71; www.hoteldelacite.orient-express.com; place Auguste Pont; r from €400;) Neo-Gothic Hôtel de la Cité has rooms fit for royalty (literally so: 'A favourite hideaway for Europe's crowned heads, film stars, writers and intellectuals,' proclaims its glossy brochure), should you fancy a retreat in such august company. Parking is €16.

Eating

Even if it's a boiling summer's day, don't leave town without trying the cassoulet, a piping-hot dish blending white beans, juicy pork cubes, even bigger cylinders of meaty sausage and, in the most popular local variant, a hunk of duck.

VILLE BASSE

Restaurant des Trois Couronnes (☎ 04 68 25 36 10; menus €21-29.50, mains €14-17) A particular bargain of this fine restaurant, on the 4th floor of Hôtel des Trois Couronnes (opposite) is its *le tout compris* ('everything included'; €21): three courses, a couple of glasses of wine, coffee and a magnificent panorama of La Cité thrown in.

Au Bon Pasteur (☎ 04 68 25 49 63; 29 rue Armagnac; menus €15-28; closed Sun & Mon Jul & Aug, Sun & Wed Sep-Jun) At this welcoming, intimate family restaurant, the simple wooden furniture belies the sophistication of the cooking. Warm yourself in winter with the yummy cassoulet or *choucroute* (sauerkraut), 100% authentic since the chef hails from the Vosges. Year-round, its *formule touristique* (a three-course special; €16.50), and *formules de midi* (lunch specials; €12.50 to €15.50) both represent excellent value.

L'Écurie (☎ 04 68 72 04 04; www.restaurant-lecurie.fr; 43 bd Barbès; menus €23.50-30; Mon-Sat & lunch Sun) Enjoy fine fare either within this attractively renovated 18th-century stable, all polished woodwork, brass and leather, or in the large, shaded garden. Pick from its long and choice selection of local wines.

Chez Fred (☎ 04 68 72 02 23; www.chez-fred.fr; 31 bd Omer Sarraut; menus €24-28; daily Jul-Sep, Mon-Fri & dinner Sat Oct-Jun) With a large window pierced in one of the walls of the ox-blood-red interior, you can peek at what Fred's chefs are rustling up; it's sure to be something creative. Alternatively, dine on its shaded tunnel of a terrace. The weekday *menu bistro* (lunch €16.50, dinner €20) is superb value.

LA CITÉ

Place Marcou is hemmed in on three sides by eateries and throughout La Cité every second building seems to be a café or restaurant. For those recommended here, it's wise to reserve, particularly for lunch.

Restaurant des Musées (☎ 06 17 05 24 90; 17 rue du Grand Puits; menus €9.50-18) This unpretentious place has three rear terraces with views of the ramparts. It bakes its own organic bread and offers excellent-value meals, including a vegetarian *menu* (€10.50). It doesn't take credit cards.

Auberge de Dame Carcas (☎ 04 68 71 23 23; 3 place du Château; menus €14.50-20.50; Thu-Tue) This casual restaurant specialises in suckling pig (model piggies displayed around the restaurant, give you a clue) and carries a fine selection of well-priced local wines. The ground floor is cosy and agreeably rustic, and you can see the chefs at work. The larger upstairs room offers more light, and there's a summer terrace too.

L'Écu d'Or (☎ 04 68 25 49 03; www.restaurant-ecudor.fr, in French; 7-9 rue Porte d'Aude; lunch menu €18, menus €25-33, mains €18-20) Step down to semi-basement level to dine in style within the thick stone walls of this friendly spot. It serves, among many other delightful dishes, five varieties of cassoulet and a delicious range of creative desserts.

Chez Saskia (☎ 04 68 71 98 71; place Auguste Pont; menus €26-45, mains around €25; Mar-Jan) This brasserie, where chef Jérome Ryon creates tasty, great-value dishes and a particularly rich range of desserts, belongs to Hótel de la Cité. All around its walls are photos of the great and good who have stayed at the hotel: Jacques Chirac, Winston Churchill, Yves Montand and many more, recognisable and less so.

RESTAURANT ROBERT RODRIGUEZ

Behind his bushy, curling Hercule Poirot moustache, Robert Rodriguez is as much culinary philosopher as chef. Indeed, describing himself as an artisan who works with raw, exclusively organic materials, he'd probably baulk at the very word 'chef'. Beaming with bonhomie, he calls his intimate **restaurant** (☎ 04 68 47 37 80; www.restaurantrobertrodriguez.com; 39 rue Coste Reboulh; 3-course lunch menu €20; menus €40-63, mains €28-38; Mon, Tue & Thu-Sat) his *atelier du goût* (a workshop creating tastes). *Fraicheur, saison, tradition, créativité* (fresh, seasonal, traditional, creative) is the leitmotif at this original and warmly recommended spot with its hugely innovative take on traditional Languedoc cuisine.

SELF-CATERING

La Ferme (☎ 04 68 25 02 15; 26 rue Chartran) A particularly well-stocked delicatessen, piled high with vintage cheeses, wines, sausages and lots of other *gourmandises,* including homemade crème Chantilly.

L'Art Gourmand (13 rue St-Louis) Chocolate fiends should descend upon this place, which sells a huge range of goodies. The ice cream is pretty great too – all 33 varieties of it.

Markets:

Covered market (rue Aimé Ramond; 🕑 Mon-Sat)

Open-air market (place Carnot; 🕑 Tue, Thu & Sat)

Drinking

Cafés overlooking place Carnot in the Ville Basse spill onto the square in summer. In La Cité, place Marcou is one big outside café.

La Cité des Arômes (14 place Carnot) In the north-western corner of place Carnot, this café wafts out scents of rich arabica and carries a huge selection of coffees.

Comptoir des Vins et Terroirs (☎ 04 68 26 44 76; 3 rue du Comte Roger; mains €11-13) This recently opened place in La Cité, affiliated to Hôtel le Donjon does tasty snacks and has plenty of wines by the glass on offer.

Getting There & Away

AIR

Ryanair is the only airline to fly in and out of Carcassonne's **airport** (☎ 04 68 71 96 46), 5.5km from town. It flies to/from London (Stansted), Liverpool and East Midlands in the UK, and Cork, Dublin and Shannon in Ireland.

BUS

We can only reiterate the advice of the tourist office: take the train. Eurolines and intercity buses stop on bd de Varsovie, 500m southwest of the train station.

TRAIN

Carcassonne is on the main line linking Toulouse (€13.30, 50 minutes, frequent) with Narbonne (€9.40, 30 minutes) and Montpellier (€21.20, 1½ hours). For Perpignan (€17.20, 1½ hours), change in Narbonne.

Getting Around

TO/FROM THE AIRPORT

Agglo'Bus's Navette Aéroport runs to and from the airport (€5, 25 minutes), leaving the train station approximately two hours before each Ryanair departure. By car, take the Carcassonne Ouest A61 motorway exit.

CAR & MOTORCYCLE

Several operators including **Europcar** (☎ 04 68 72 23 69), **Ada** (☎ 04 68 11 71 92) and **Hertz** (☎ 04 68 25 41 26) have booths at the airport.

For La Cité, leave your vehicle in the huge car park (€4.50 for three to six hours) just east of the main entrance.

PUBLIC TRANSPORT

At the time of writing, **Agglo'Bus** (☎ 04 68 47 82 22), the city bus company, had a temporary information kiosk beside a large tiled concrete dome on bd Camille Pelletan.

Buses run until about 7pm, Monday to Saturday. A single ticket/10-ticket carnet costs €1.10/7.80.

Bus 2 runs roughly hourly from the Ville Basse to La Cité's main entrance. From mid-June to mid-September, a **navette** (shuttle service; 🕑 10am-12.45pm & 2.15-7.30pm Mon-Sat) links La Cité, the town centre and the train station every 20 minutes.

TAXI

Ring ☎ 04 68 71 50 50 for a taxi.

HAUT-LANGUEDOC

Haut-Languedoc is a world away from the towns, vineyards and beaches of the broad coastal plain. More sparsely populated, it's a land of deeply incised gorges, high windswept plateaux and dense forest, ideal for those who love the open air.

MENDE

pop 12,600

Mende, a quiet little place straddling the River Lot, is the capital of Lozère, France's least populous *département.* Its oval-shaped centre is ringed by a one-way road that acts as something of a *cordon sanitaire,* leaving the old quarter almost traffic-free.

Information

Salle Antirouille (place du Foirail; per hr €1.60; 🕑 2pm or 3-8pm Tue-Fri, 9am-noon & 2-5pm Sat) Internet access; free wi-fi.

Tourist Office (☎ 04 66 94 00 23; www.ot-mende.fr; place du Foirail; 🕑 9am-12.30pm & 2-7pm Mon-Sat,

LANGUEDOC-ROUSSILLON

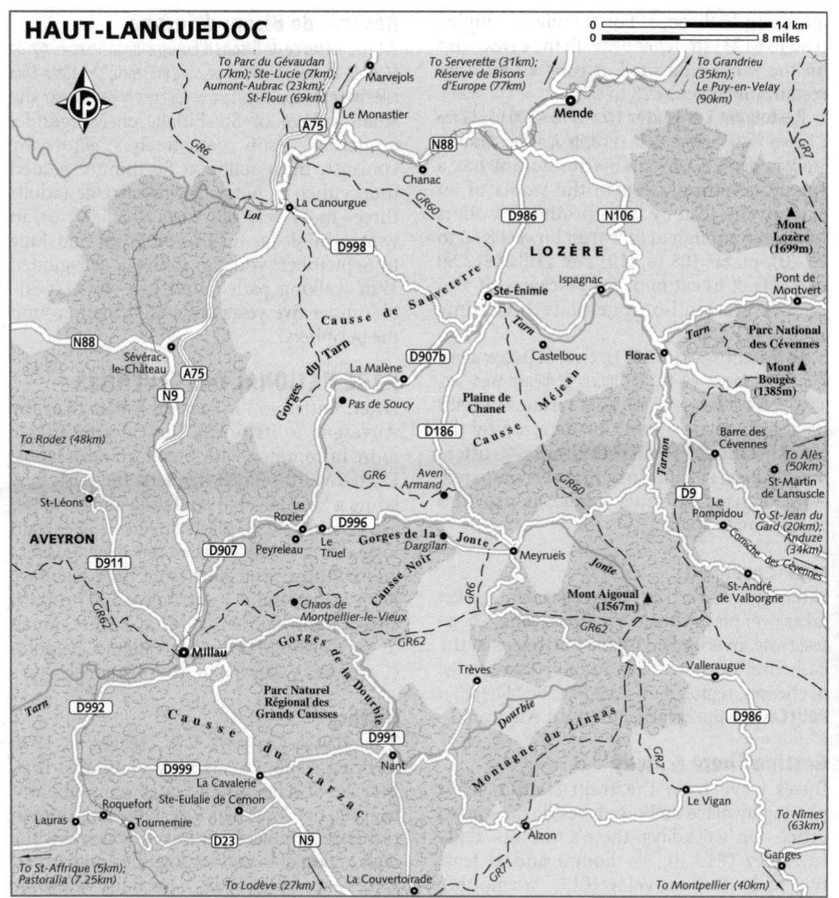

10am-noon & 2-4pm Sun Jul & Aug, 9am-noon & 2-6pm Mon-Fri, 9am-noon Sat Sep-Jun) Free wi-fi, which extends to the café terrace nearby.

Sights

The tourist office's brochure, *Discover Mende's Heritage*, highlights the town's main historical features. The dark interior of the 14th-century, twin-towered **Cathédrale Notre Dame** (place Urbain V) makes the pincushion panes of the 17th-century rose window at the west end positively glow, but you'll have to peer hard to make out detail on the eight 18th-century Aubusson tapestries, hung high above the nave, illustrating the life of the Virgin.

Sleeping & Eating

Hôtel le Commerce (☎ 04 66 65 13 73; www.lecommerce-mende.com, in French; 2 bd Henri Bourrillon; s/d/tr €41/51/55; closed 2 weeks in Apr & 2 in Oct; ☒) Opposite place du Foirail on the busy ring road, this agreeably labyrinthine hotel, run by the same family for three generations, has 10 impeccable rooms. The owner is an ale fanatic and his popular bar carries a great range of beers.

Hôtel de France (☎ 04 66 65 00 04; www.hoteldefrance-mende.com, in French; 9 bd Lucien Arnault; d €58-75; mid-Jan–Dec; 💻) Most rooms at this one-time coaching inn (whose owner speaks excellent English) have sweeping views over the valley and gardens below. Rooms one to three, eight and 10 are large, with separate toilet and gleaming bathroom. For families, a duplex (€93 to €123) stretches beneath the eaves. Also on the inner ring road, it runs a first-class restaurant (*menus* €28 to €31).

Restaurant Les Voûtes (☎ 04 66 49 00 05; 13 rue d'Aigues-Passes; menu €21; daily Jun-Aug, Mon-Sat Sep-May, closed 15-30 Sep) This restaurant has a splendid setting, deep in the vaults of an ex-convent. Run by three brothers, it offers salads big enough to fill a fruit bowl (€8.60 to €9.70), pizzas (€8 to €10) and grills (€12.50 to €14), all to eat in or for takeaway. It also does a great all-on-one-plate lunchtime special (€12.50).

Le Mazel (☎ 04 66 65 05 33; 25 rue du Collège; menus €15.50-28, mains €9-17; lunch & dinner Wed-Sun, lunch Mon mid-Mar–mid-Nov) This restaurant with its stylish decor – don't be deterred by the bleakly modern surroundings – offers mainly local cuisine, imaginatively prepared. A recognised gourmet venue, it provides exceptional value.

SELF-CATERING

Saturday is market day, when a farmers market takes over place Urbain V. **La Fromagerie** (30bis rue Soubeyran), overlooked by the buttresses of the cathedral's east end, has an impressive range of cheeses, regional meats and pâtés. There's a **Petit Casino** supermarket on rue d'Angiran.

Getting There & Away

Buses leave from the train station, most passing by place du Foirail, beside the tourist office. On weekdays, there's one bus daily to Rodez (€13.20, 3½ hours) and at least two to Le Puy-en-Velay (€17, two hours). Northbound, two SNCF buses run daily to/from Clermont-Ferrand in the Massif Central (€28.80, three hours).

The train station is 1km north of town across the River Lot. There are three trains daily to Alès (€16.20, 2½ hours).

AROUND MENDE

Wolves once prowled freely through the Lozère forests but today you'll see them only in the **Parc du Gévaudan** (☎ 04 66 32 09 22; www.loupsdugevaudan.com, in French; adult/child €6.50/3.50; 10am-7pm Jun-Aug, 10am-5pm or 6pm Feb-May & Sep-Dec) in Ste-Lucie, 7km north of Marvejols. The park sustains around 100 Mongolian, Canadian, Siberian and Polish wolves living in semifreedom.

Réserve de Bisons d'Europe

At the **Réserve de Bisons d'Europe** (Bison Reserve; ☎ 04 66 31 40 40; www.bisoneurope.com, in French; 10am-6pm mid-Jun–mid-Sep, 10am-5pm or 6pm rest of year) near the small village of Ste-Eulalie-en-Margeride, around 40 bison roam freely. Visitors, by contrast, must follow a 50-minute guided tour, either by horse-drawn carriage (adult/three- to 11-year-old costs €12/6.50) or, in winter, by sledge (€14.50/8). From mid-June to September, you can follow a self-guided 1km walking path (adult/five- to 11-year-old/under five years costs €6/4/free) around the periphery.

PARC NATIONAL DES CÉVENNES

Drier, hotter and in general leafier than the Auvergne to its north, the Cévennes have more in common with Mediterranean lands. Dotted with isolated hamlets, the park harbours a huge diversity of fauna and flora (an astounding 2250 plant species have been logged). Animals such as red deer, beavers and vultures, long gone from the park, have been successfully reintroduced. The park covers four main areas: Mont Lozère, much of the Causse Méjean, the Vallées Cévenoles (Cévennes Valleys) and Mont Aigoual.

History

The 910-sq-km park was created in 1970 to bring ecological stability to an area that, because of religious and later economic upheavals, has long had a destabilising human presence. Population influxes, which saw the destruction of forests for logging and pasture, were followed by mass desertions as people gave up the fight against the inhospitable climate and terrain. Emigration led to the abandonment of hamlets and farms, many of which have been snapped up by wealthy Parisians and foreigners.

Maps

The best map of the park is the IGN's *Parc National des Cévennes* (€6.20) at 1:100,000.

Mont Lozère

This 1699m-high lump of granite in the north of the park is shrouded in cloud and ice in winter and covered with heather and blueberries, peat bogs and flowing streams in summer. The **Musée du Mont Lozère** (☎ 04 66 45 80 73; adult/6-18yr/under 6yr incl audioguide €3.50/2.50/free;

CHESTNUT: THE ALL-PURPOSE TREE

In the Cévennes, the chestnut tree (known as *l'arbre à pain,* or bread tree) was the staple food of many Auvergnat families. The nuts were eaten raw, roasted and dried, or ground into flour. Blended with milk or wine, chestnuts were the essence of *bajanat,* a nourishing soup. Part of the harvest would feed the pigs while the leaves of pruned twigs and branches provided fodder for sheep and goats.

Harvested at ground level with small forks – of chestnut wood, of course – the prickly husks (called *hèrissons,* or hedgehogs) were removed by being trampled upon in spiky boots. Nowadays, they're the favourite food of the Cévennes' wild boars and still feature in a number of local sauces and desserts.

Nothing was wasted. Sections of hollowed-out trunk would serve as beehives, smaller branches would be woven into baskets while larger ones were whittled into stakes for fencing or used to build trellises. The wood, hard and resistant to parasites, was used for rafters, rakes and household furniture – everything from, quite literally, the cradle to the coffin.

10.30am-12.30pm & 2.30-6.30pm Easter-Sep), within a hideous concrete hulk at Pont de Montvert, 20km northeast of Florac, is a fascinating introduction to the region and its traditional rural crafts. Unfortunately, the English audio commentary is a disaster; you're better off reading the French text.

Vallées Cévenoles

First planted back in the Middle Ages, *châtaigniers* (sweet-chestnut trees) carpet the Vallées Cévenoles, the park's central area of plunging ravines and jagged ridges, along one of which runs the breathtaking Corniche des Cévennes.

Mont Aigoual

Mont Aigoual (1567m) and neighbouring Montagne du Lingas are renowned for their searing winds and heavy snowfall. The area is dense with beech trees, thanks to a reforestation program that counteracts years of uncontrolled logging. The observatory atop the summit has an **exhibition** (☎ 04 67 82 60 01; www.aigoual.asso.fr; admission free; 10am-7pm Jul & Aug, 10am-1pm & 2-6pm May, Jun & Sep) where you can learn about cloud formation, weather prediction, and much more. Captions are in French but much of the exhibition is highly visual.

Activities

In winter there's **cross-country skiing** (more than 100km of marked trails) on Mont Aigoual and Mont Lozère, while **donkey treks** are popular in the park in warmer months. There are 600km of donkey- and horse-riding trails and 200km marked out for mountain-bike enthusiasts.

An equally well-developed network of trails makes the park a **walking** paradise year-round. It's criss-crossed by a dozen GR *(grande randonnée)* trails and there are over 20 shorter signposted walks lasting between two and seven hours.

Florac's Maison du Parc (p786) has more than 11 excellent information kits (€5 each) describing circular walks from various starting points within the park. Ask about the **Festival Nature**, a summertime mix of outdoor activities, lectures and field trips.

Getting There & Away

By car, the most spectacular route is the Corniche des Cévennes, a ridge road that winds along the mountain crests of the Cévennes for 56km from St-Jean du Gard to Florac.

FLORAC

pop 2000

Florac, 79km northwest of Alès and 38km southeast of Mende, makes a great base for exploring the Parc National des Cévennes and the upper reaches of the Gorges du Tarn. Lively in summer and moribund for most of the rest of the year, it's draped along the west bank of River Tarnon, one of the tributaries of the Tarn, while the sheer cliffs of the Causse Méjean loom 1000m overhead.

Information

Florac Cyber Café (12 rue Armand Jullié; per 30min/1hr €3/4; 10am-8.30pm Jul & Aug, 2.30-8.30pm Sun & Mon, 10am-noon & 2.30-8.30pm Tue-Sat Sep-Jun) Internet access.

Laundrette (11 rue du Pêcher; 8.30am-7.30pm)

TRAVELS WITH A DONKEY

The Cévennes were even wilder and more untamed back in October 1878, when Scottish writer Robert Louis Stevenson crossed them with only a donkey, Modestine, for company.

'I was looked upon with contempt, like a man who should project a journey to the moon, but yet with a respectful interest, like one setting forth for the inclement Pole,' Stevenson wrote in his *Travels with a Donkey in the Cévennes*.

Accompanied by the wayward Modestine, bought for 65 francs and a glass of brandy, Stevenson took a respectable 12 days to travel the 232km on foot (Modestine carried his gear) from Le Monastier-sur-Gazelle, southeast of Le Puy-en-Velay, to St-Jean du Gard, west of Alès. Afterwards, he sold his ass – and wept.

The Stevenson trail, first retraced and marked with the cross of St Andrew by a Scottish woman in 1978, is nowadays designated the GR70 and extends from Le Puy to Alès.

Whether you're swaying on a donkey or simply walking, you'll find *The Robert Louis Stevenson Trail* by Alan Castle an excellent, practical, well-informed companion. Consult also www.chemin-stevenson.org and www.gr70-stevenson.com, and pick up the free pamphlet *Sur Le Chemin de Robert Louis Stevenson* (On The Robert Louis Stevenson Trail), stocked by tourist offices, which has a comprehensive list of accommodation en route.

Tourist Office (☎ 04 66 45 01 14; www.mescevennes.com; 33 av Jean Monestier; 🕑 9am-12.30pm & 1.30-7pm Jul & Aug, 9am-noon & 2-6pm Mon-Sat Sep-Jun)

Activities

The tourist office has details of a whole summer's worth of outdoor activities. For information on the park's rich walking potential, contact **Maison du Parc National des Cévennes** (☎ 04 66 49 53 01; www.cevennes-parcnational.fr; 🕑 9am-6.30pm Jul & Aug, 9.30am-12.15pm & 1.30-5.30pm Easter-Jun, Sep & Oct, 9.30am-12.15pm & 1.30-5.30pm Mon-Fri Nov-Easter). It occupies the handsome, restored 17th-century Château de Florac, stocks an English version of the guidebook *Parc National des Cévennes* (€15) and has a splendidly informative **interactive exhibition** (admission free), *Passagers du Paysage*, with captions, a recorded commentary in English (delivered, alas, by a couple of glum, monotone native speakers) and a 15-minute slide show.

DONKEY TREKS

Why not follow the lead of Robert Louis Stevenson and hire a pack animal? Several companies are in the donkey business. They include **Gentiâne** (☎ 04 66 41 04 16; anegenti@free.fr) in Castagnols and **Tramontane** (☎ 04 66 45 92 44; chantal.tramontane@nomade.fr) in St-Martin de Lansuscle. Typical prices are €45 per day and €210 to €275 per week, and both outfits can reserve accommodation along the route. Though each is outside Florac, they'll transport the donkeys to town or a place of your choosing for a fee (around €1 per kilometre).

OTHER ACTIVITIES

Cévennes Évasion (☎ 04 66 45 18 31; www.cevennes-evasion.com, in French; 5 place Boyer) rents out mountain bikes for €13/19 per half-/full day and furnishes riders with handy colour route maps. In summer Cévennes Évasion will take you for free (minimum five persons) up to the Causse Méjean, from where you can whiz effortlessly back down. It also arranges caving, rock-climbing and canyon-clambering expeditions (trust these guys; they hung the fireworks up high for the spectacular opening and closing ceremony pyrotechnics at the Athens Olympics). It also runs guided and independent walking holidays, where your accommodation is booked ahead and your luggage transported onwards daily.

Sleeping

Camping Le Pont du Tarn (☎ 04 66 45 18 26; www.campingpontdutarn.com; site & 2 persons €14; 🕑 Apr–mid-Oct; 🏊) At this large, attractive, shaded campsite, 2km from Florac beside the D998, you can swim either in the pool or river Tarn, which runs right by.

our pick La Ferme de la Borie (☎ 04 66 45 10 90; www.encevennes.com, in French; s incl breakfast €22-29, d €35-44; 🕑 Mar-Nov) You'll be bowled over by the sheer enthusiasm and joie de vivre of host Jean-Christophe Barthes. And you'll groan contentedly as you head to bed after a blow-out dinner of produce from this organic farm, accompanied by as much wine as you wish. Be sure to reserve – by phone since there's no email link from the website.

Hôtel Les Gorges du Tarn (☎ 04 66 45 00 63; www.hotel-gorgesdutarn.com; 48 rue du Pêcher; d €45-60; tr/q €70/80; Easter-Oct) Most rooms in both the main building and annexe of this 26-room Logis de France have been recently renovated and are bright as a new pin. Studios sleep up to four and have cooking facilities. Free parking and wi-fi.

Grand Hôtel du Parc (☎ 04 66 45 03 05; www.grandhotelduparc.fr; 47 av Jean Monestier; r €50-70; mid-Mar–mid-Nov;) This venerable building has 55 spacious rooms. It sits on its own extensive grounds with a pool, terrace and delightful, well-tended gardens shaded by mature cedars.

Eating

In summer L'Esplanade, a shady, pedestrianised avenue, becomes one long dining area where you can eat both well and economically.

Chez les Paysans (☎ 04 66 31 22 07; square Maury; menus €12-16, mains around €10) At this restaurant you can sample fresh, very reasonably priced local fare either inside or on its vine-shaded terrace. Its shop has a great selection of produce from small farmers in the area.

La Source du Pêcher (☎ 04 66 45 03 01; 1 rue de Remuret; menus €18-38; Apr-Oct) With a wonderful open-air terrace, perched above the little River Pêcher, it's very good and oh, they know it and show it (just look at the ostentatious display of medallions and shields from gastronomic bodies – most of them none too fresh, it must be said – that fringe the door). This said, you'll eat very well indeed, if you can stomach the prickly owner. They don't take reservations, so arrive early.

Maison du Pays Cévenol (3 rue du Pêcher) This gastronomic treasure trove sells local specialities – liqueurs, jams, Pélardon cheese and chestnuts in all their guises.

Florac has, in addition, two impressive hotel restaurants:

Grand Hôtel du Parc restaurant (☎ 04 66 45 03 05; 47 av Jean Monestier; menus €19-28, mains €9-14.50)

Adonis (☎ 04 66 45 00 63; 48 rue du Pêcher; menus €17-44, mains €17-20; Thu-Tue & lunch Wed) At Hôtel Les Gorges du Tarn.

Getting There & Away

It's a pain without your own vehicle. One **Transports Reilhes** (☎ 04 66 45 00 18, 06 60 58 58 10) minibus runs to/from Alès (€13.50, 1¼ hours), Monday to Saturday, leaving from the old railway station at 9am.

GORGES DU TARN

From the village of Ispagnac, 9km northwest of Florac, the deep, spectacular Gorges du Tarn wind southwest for about 50km, mark-

BIOMAN

In the 1990s, Jean-Christophe Barthes left his native Montpellier and bought himself 70 hectares of hillside and a seriously ruined farm whose buildings had languished unused since WWII.

After 10 years' hard labour, he now runs a successful organic farm that's all but self-sufficient. He gestures to the dinner table, groaning with sausages, fat and thin, cylindrical Tomme cheeses, tiny Pélardons and stout nameless ones furry with mould, pâtés, honey, jams and a wonderful concoction of beans, chestnuts and yet more sausages. 'Only the wine isn't mine,' he grins.

He shrugs off all the reconstruction. 'Yes, there are the buildings', he says. 'But what makes me even prouder is the way I've given new life to the land' – it had deteriorated into scrub and wilderness without the presence of animals and regular cropping for hay. 'And the return of the swallows too', he muses. 'At first just one or two and now a colony of annual nesters.' No animals means no flies and no dinner for the swallows. 'The more the flies, the more these graceful swallows', he grins.

His goats give the milk that makes the cheese. He feeds the litres of whey run-off from the cheese-making to his pigs, who finish up as truncheons of sausage hanging like stalactites in his cavernous storeroom. The cows? 'I have the space so why not?', he shrugs. And his bees busy themselves all alone and independently.

Nowadays it's not enough to be simply a farmer. With his boundless energy and infectious ready smile, Jean-Christophe runs a splendid *chambre d'hôte* (opposite) together with a *gîte d'étape* (walkers' guesthouse) for hikers walking the GR70 trail that passes nearby. He sells his produce in nearby markets, is a leading light in the local farmers' association and, in summer, arranges group visits to watch the milking of the goats, then follow them to pasture. On summer evenings, he puts on dinners of goat kid, roasted on a spit in the huge hearth of his equally grandly proportioned dining room. And somehow, some time, he manages to sleep, though you wonder how…

ing the boundary between the Causse Méjean to its south and the Causse de Sauveterre to the north. Until the construction of the riverside road in 1905, the only way to move through the gorges was by boat. Nowadays, this road (the D907bis) is often jammed with traffic: every summer's day, well over 2500 vehicles grind through Ste-Énimie.

Activities

CANOEING

Riding the River Tarn is at its best in high summer, when the river is usually low and the descent a lazy trip over mostly calm water. You can get as far as the impassable Pas de Soucy, a barrier of boulders about 9km downriver from La Malène. Downstream from here, there are further canoeing possibilities.

The Ste-Énimie tourist office carries information on the veritable flotilla of companies offering canoe and kayak descents. These include:

ADN La Cazelle (☎ 04 66 48 46 05; www.lacazelle.com, in French) In Ste-Énimie. Also rents out mountain bikes (per half-/full day €20/30).

Au Moulin de la Malène (☎ 04 66 48 51 14; www.canoeblanc.com) In La Malène.

Canoë 2000 (☎ 04 66 48 57 71; www.canoe2000.fr) In Ste-Énimie and La Malène.

Locanoë (☎ 04 66 48 55 57; www.gorges-du-tarn.fr, in French) In Castelbouc and Ste-Énimie.

Typical trips and tariffs for canoe and kayak descents are:

Trip	Cost (€)	Distance (km)	Duration
Castelbouc-Ste-Énimie	14	7	2hr
Ste-Énimie-La Malène	19	13	3½hr
Castelbouc-La Malène	22	20	1 day
Ste-Énimie-Les Baumes Basses	23	22	1 day

If you'd rather someone else did the hard work, spend a lazy, effortless hour with **Les Bateliers de la Malène** (☎ 04 66 48 51 10; ⌚ Apr-Oct), who, for €19.50/9.75 per adult/child under 10, will punt you down an 8km stretch of the gorge, leaving from La Malène, then drive you back.

Sleeping & Eating

Camping Les Gorges du Tarn (☎ 04 66 48 59 38; fax 04 66 48 59 37; 2 people tent & car €8.20; ⌚ Easter–mid-Nov; 🅿) About 800m upstream from Ste-Énimie, this is the cheapest of the several riverside campsites, and it also hires out canoes and kayaks.

Two splendid *chambres d'hôtes* lie at each end of the Gorges du Tarn.

La Pause (☎ 05 65 62 63 06; www.hebergement-gorgesdutarn.com; rte de Caplac; d/tr/ste incl breakfast €46/63/90; 🅿) At the southern end, in the village of Le Rozier, La Pause has three tastefully furnished rooms decorated in attractive colours, plus a couple of suites. At breakfast, jams – fig, quince, cherry and more – are all made by your hostess, Pierrette Espinasse. To get there, turn left (signed Capluc), after the village church.

La Maison de Marius (☎ 04 66 44 25 05; www.maisondemarius.info; 8 rue Pontet, Quézac; r incl breakfast €50-80; ⌚ Mar-Oct) At the gorges' northern limit, near Ispagnac, each of Dany Méjean's delightful rooms has its own character, and you've never tasted sweeter water, drawn from the nearby mineral springs. To get there, skirt the village (its main street is unidirectional against you) and follow signs from the church.

Ste-Énimie

pop 500

Ste-Énimie, 27km from Florac and 56km from Millau, tumbles like an avalanche of grey-brown stone, blending into the steep, once terraced slope behind it. Long isolated, it's now a popular destination for day visitors from Millau, Mende and Florac and a popular starting or finishing point for canoe or kayak descents of the Tarn.

Its **tourist office** (☎ 04 66 48 53 44; www.gorgesdutarn.net, in French; ⌚ 9am-1pm & 2-7pm Mon-Sat, 9.30am-12.30pm Sun Jul & Aug, 9.30am-12.30pm & 2-5.30pm or 6pm Mon-Fri Oct-Easter, also Sat Easter-Jun & Sep) stocks maps and walking guides, including IGN Top 25 map No 2640OT *Gorges du Tarn*. There's also a small seasonal **annexe** in La Malène.

Highlights of the small, cobbled old quarter, where most houses have been repainted and restored, are the 12th-century Romanesque **Église de Ste-Énimie**, and the **Halle aux Blés**, where cereal crops from the high Causses were bartered for wine, fresh fruit and walnut oil.

PARC NATUREL RÉGIONAL DES GRANDS CAUSSES

The Grands Causses, the Massif Central's most southerly expression, are mainly harsh limestone plateau. Scorched in summer and windswept in winter, the stony surface holds little moisture as water filters through the limestone to form an underground world, ideal for cavers.

The Rivers Tarn, Jonte and Dourbie have sliced deep gorges through the 5000-sq-km plateau, creating four *causses* ('plateaux' in the local patois): Sauveterre, Méjean, Noir and Larzac, each different in its delicate geological forms. One resembles a dark lunar surface, another's like a Scottish moor covered with the thinnest layer of grass, while the next is gentler and more fertile. But all are eerie and empty except for the occasional shepherd and his flock – and all offer magnificent walking and mountain biking.

Millau, at the heart of the park, is a good base for venturing into this wild area. The Gorges de la Jonte, where birds of prey wheel and swoop, skim the park's eastern boundary, rivalling in beauty the neighbouring, more famous Gorges du Tarn.

Information

Parc Naturel Régional des Grands Causses office (☎ 05 65 61 35 50; www.parc-grands-causses.fr, in French; 71 bd de l'Ayrolle, Millau; ⌚ 9am-noon or 12.30pm & 2-5pm or 6pm Mon-Fri)

Causse de Sauveterre

The northernmost of the *causses* is a gentle, hilly plateau dotted with a few compact and isolated farms resembling fortified villages. Every possible patch of fertile earth is cultivated, creating irregular, intricately patterned wheat fields.

Causse Méjean

Causse Méjean, the highest, is also the most barren and isolated. Defined to the north by the Gorges du Tarn and, southwards, by the Gorges de la Jonte, it looms over Florac on its eastern flank. It's a land of poor pasture enriched by occasional fertile depressions, where streams gurgle down into the limestone through sinkholes, funnels and fissures.

This combination of water and limestone has created some spectacular underground scenery. Within the cavern of **Aven Armand** (☎ 04 66 45 61 31; www.aven-armand.com; adult/16-20yr/5-15yr/under 5yr €8.50/7/5.80/free; ⌚ 9.30am-6pm Jul & Aug, 9.30am or 10am-noon & 1.30-5pm or 6pm Mar-Jun & Sep–mid-Nov), reached by a funicular railway that drops 60 vertical metres, bristles the world's greatest concentration of stalagmites. Guided visits, lasting about 45 minutes (there's an accompanying information sheet in English) head underground about every 20 minutes. A **combination ticket** (adult/16-20yr/5-15yr/under 5yr €11.80/9.30/7.80/free) also includes admission to the Chaos de Montpellier-le-Vieux.

Causse Noir

Rising immediately east of Millau, the 'Black Causse' is best known for the **Chaos de Montpellier-le-Vieux** (☎ 05 65 60 66 30; adult/5-15yr/under 5yr €5.30/3.80/free; ⌚ 9.30am-6pm or 7pm Apr–mid-Nov), 18km northeast of Millau overlooking the Gorges de la Dourbie. Water erosion has created more than 120 hectares of tortured limestone formations with fanciful names such as the Sphinx and the Elephant. Three trails, lasting one to three hours, cover the site, as does a **tourist train** (adult/5-15yr/under 5yr €3.40/2.40/free).

If you're here outside official opening times, there's nothing to stop you wandering around freely.

Causse du Larzac

The Causse du Larzac (800m to 1000m) is the largest of the four *causses*. An endless sweep of distant horizons and rocky steppes broken by medieval villages, it's known as the 'French Desert'.

You'll stumble across old, fortified villages such as **Ste-Eulalie de Cernon**, long the capital of the Larzac region, and **La Cavalerie**, both built by the Knights Templar, a religious military order that distinguished itself during the Crusades.

Gorges de la Jonte

The Gorges de la Jonte, 15km long, cleave east–west from Meyrueis to Le Rozier, separating in dramatic fashion the Causse Noir from Causse Méjean.

Just south of the gorge, **Dargilan** (☎ 04 66 45 60 20; www.grotte-dargilan.com; adult/6-18yr/under 6yr €8.50/5.80/free; ⌚ 10am-6.30pm Jul & Aug, 10am-noon & 2-4.30pm or 5.30pm Easter-Jun, Sep & Oct) is known as La Grotte Rose (the pink cave) for its dominant natural colouring. The culminating point of the one-hour, 1km tour through this vast chasm is a sudden, dazzling exit onto a ledge with a dizzying view of the Gorges de la Jonte way below.

Belvédère des Vautours (Vulture Viewing Point; ☎ 05 65 62 69 69; www.vautours-lozere.com, in French;

adult/5-12yr/under 5yr €6.50/3/free; 10am-7pm Jul & Aug, 10am-6pm Tue-Sun Apr-Jun, Sep & Oct) is just west of Le Truel on the D996. Reintroduced after having all but disappeared locally, the vultures now freely wheel and plane in the Causses skies and nest high in the sheer cliffs on the opposite side of the valley.

The viewing point has an impressive multimedia exhibition, including live video transmission from the nesting sites. It also organises half-day **birding walks** (adult/5-12yr/under 5yr €7/3.50/free; reservation essential) to the surrounding gorges.

MILLAU

pop 21,900

Millau (pronounced mee·yo) squeezes between the Causse Noir and Causse du Larzac at the confluence of the Rivers Tarn and Dourbie. Though falling just over the border into the Midi-Pyrénées *département* of Aveyron, it's tied to Languedoc historically and culturally. Famous within France for glove-making, it's also the main centre for the Parc Naturel Régional des Grands Causses, a take-off point for hiking and other outdoor activities – particularly hang-gliding and paragliding, exploiting the uplifting thermals.

Information

ABCD PC (cnr rue Droite & rue Solignac; per hr €3; 10am-7pm Mon-Sat Jul & Aug, 10am-12.15pm & 2-7pm Mon-Fri, 1-7pm Sat Sep-Jun) Internet access.
Laundrette (14 av Gambetta; 7am-9pm)
Main Post Office (12 av Alfred Merle)
Tourist Office (05 65 60 02 42; www.ot-millau.fr; 1 place du Beffroi; 9am-7pm Jul & Aug, 9am-12.30pm & 2-6.30pm Easter-Jun & Sep; closed Sun Oct-Easter)

Sights

The 42m-tall **beffroi** (belfry; rue Droite; adult/under 16yr €3/free; 10am-noon & 2-6pm mid-Jun–Sep) has a square base dating from the 12th century and tapers into a 17th-century octagonal tower, from where there's a great overview of town.

Musée de Millau (05 65 59 01 08; place Maréchal Foch; adult/19-25yr/under 19yr €5/3.70/free; 10am-6pm Jul & Aug, 10am-noon & 2-6pm Sep-Jun, closed Sat Oct-Apr) has a rich collection of fossils, including a 4m-long, almost intact skeleton of a prehistoric marine reptile from the Causse du Larzac. In the basement is a huge array of plates and vases from **La Graufesenque**, in its time the largest pottery workshop in the western Roman Empire. The 1st-floor leather and glove section illustrates Millau's tanneries and their products through the ages. A combined ticket, which costs €7, includes admission to La Graufesenque archeological site, at the confluence of the Rivers Tarn and Dourbie.

Causse Gantier (05 65 60 03 05; bd des Gantières; admission free; 9.30am-12.30pm & 2-7pm Mon-Sat) Causse Gantier is one of only two companies that still make gloves in Millau (all the rest import their leather goods and trade on their past reputations). Within this architecturally pleasing new building, both workshop and display, you can watch craftspeople at work. Buy here and you can be certain your gloves were made on the spot.

Activities

HANG-GLIDING & PARAGLIDING

Several outfits run introductory courses (around €325 for five days) and beginner flights with an instructor (€55 to €70). Two long-established players are:

Horizon (05 65 59 78 60; www.horizon-millau.com, in French; 6 place Lucien Grégoire) Also offers caving, canyon descents, rock climbing and Naturaventure, a multiadventure trail.
Roc et Canyon (05 65 61 17 77; www.roc-et-canyon.com, in French; 55 av Jean Jaurès) In summer it's based beside Pont de Cureplat. Also offers caving, rock climbing, canyon descents, rafting and bungee jumping.

ROCK CLIMBING

The high cliffs of the Gorges de la Jonte are an internationally renowned venue for climbers. Both Horizon and Roc et Canyon offer monitored climbs and can put you in touch with local climbers.

WALKING & CYCLING

Pick up a copy of *Les Belles Balades de l'Aveyron* (€8), on sale at the tourist office. You can navigate by the explicit maps even if you don't read French. It describes 22 walks in the area and also details 10 mountain-bike and 10 tourer routes.

Festivals & Events

During mid-August, the four-day **pétanque world series** is held in Millau. Its 16 competitions (including just two for women in this male-dominated sport) attract more than 10,000 players and over twice as many spectators.

Millau hosts a week-long **jazz festival** in mid-July.

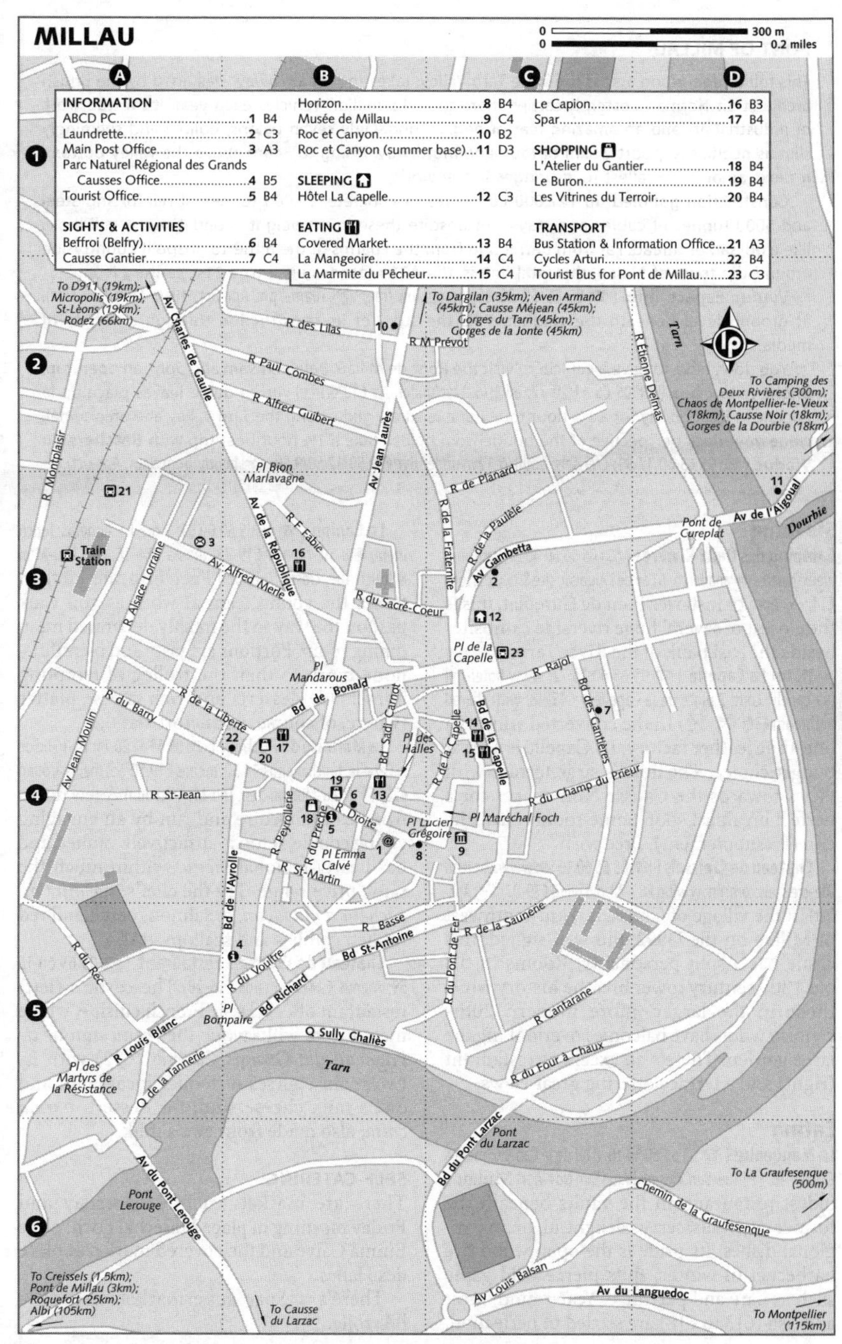
MILLAU
0 300 m
0 0.2 miles
A
B
C
D
1
2
3
4
5
6
INFORMATION
ABCD PC.....1 B4
Laundrette.....2 C3
Main Post Office.....3 A3
Parc Naturel Régional des Grands Causses Office.....4 B5
Tourist Office.....5 B4
SIGHTS & ACTIVITIES
Beffroi (Belfry).....6 B4
Causse Gantier.....7 C4
Horizon.....8 B4
Musée de Millau.....9 C4
Roc et Canyon.....10 B2
Roc et Canyon (summer base).....11 D3
SLEEPING
Hôtel La Capelle.....12 C3
EATING
Covered Market.....13 B4
La Mangeoire.....14 C4
La Marmite du Pêcheur.....15 C4
Le Capion.....16 B3
Spar.....17 B4
SHOPPING
L'Atelier du Gantier.....18 B4
Le Buron.....19 B4
Les Vitrines du Terroir.....20 B4
TRANSPORT
Bus Station & Information Office.....21 A3
Cycles Arturi.....22 B4
Tourist Bus for Pont de Millau.....23 C3
To D911 (19km); Micropolis (19km); St-Léons (19km); Rodez (66km)
To Dargilan (35km); Aven Armand (45km); Causse Méjean (45km); Gorges du Tarn (45km); Gorges de la Jonte (45km)
To Camping des Deux Rivières (300m); Chaos de Montpellier-le-Vieux (18km); Causse Noir (18km); Gorges de la Dourbie (18km)
Tarn
Dourbie
Av Charles de Gaulle
R des Lilas
R M Prévot
R Paul Combes
R Alfred Guibert
Av Jean Jaurès
R Étienne Delmas
R Montplaisir
Pl Bion Marlavagne
Av de la République
R F Fabié
R de Planard
R de la Fraternité
R de la Paulèle
Pont de Cureplat
Av de l'Aigoual
Train Station
R Alsace Lorraine
Av Alfred Merle
Av Gambetta
R du Sacré-Coeur
Pl de la Capelle
R Rajol
Pl Mandarous
Bd de Bonald
R du Barry
R de la Liberté
Bd Sadi Carnot
Pl des Halles
R de la Capelle
Bd de la Capelle
Bd des Gantières
Av Jean Moulin
R St-Jean
R du Champ du Prieur
R Peyrollerie
R Droite
Pl Maréchal Foch
Pl Lucien Grégoire
R du Pesche
Pl Emma Calvé
R St-Martin
Bd de l'Ayrolle
R Basse
R de la Saunerie
R du Pont de Fer
Bd St-Antoine
R du Voultre
R du Rec
Bd Richard
Pl Bompaire
R Cantarane
R Louis Blanc
Q Sully Chaliès
Pl des Martyrs de la Résistance
Q de la Tannerie
R du Four à Chaux
Bd du Pont Larzac
Pont du Larzac
Av du Pont Lerouge
Pont Lerouge
To La Graufesenque (500m)
Chemin de la Graufesenque
Av Louis Balsan
Av du Languedoc
To Creissels (1.5km); Pont de Millau (3km); Roquefort (25km); Albi (105km)
To Causse du Larzac
To Montpellier (115km)

PONT DE MILLAU

This toll bridge, slung across the wide Tarn Valley, takes the breath away. Designed by the British architect Sir Norman Foster, it carries more than 4.5 million vehicles each year. It's a true work of industrial art and an amazing feat of engineering. Only seven pylons, hollow and seemingly slim as needles, support 2.5km of four-lane motorway. Rising to 343m above the valley bottom, it ranks among the tallest road bridges in the world.

Construction gobbled up 127,000 cu metres of concrete, 19,000 tonnes of reinforcing steel and 5000 tonnes of cables and stays. Yet despite these heavyweight superlatives, it still looks like a gossamer thread. Far from detracting from the charms of the hitherto unspoilt countryside around the town of Millau, this vital link in the A75 motorway is a true 21st-century icon.

Viaduc Espace Info (☎ 05 65 58 80 65; admission free; ⏰ 10am-7pm Apr-Oct, 10am-5pm Nov-Mar), at ground level beneath the viaduct, tells the story of its construction through a variety of media.

You don't have to have a vehicle to visit the Pont de Millau. Between 9am and 5pm, an open-top, bright yellow **bus** (☎ 05 65 61 20 77; adult/6-12yr/under 6yr €10/6/free) with a guide leaves place de la Capelle at least hourly for a 1¾ hour tour. For a leisurely glide along the Tarn Valley and an original, crane-your-neck perspective of the bridge from below, take a 1½ hour boat trip with **Bateliers du Viaduc** (☎ 05 65 60 17 91; Creissels; adult/6-12yr/under 6yr €19.50/12.50/9.50; ⏰ hourly from 9am, Apr-Oct).

Sleeping

Camping des Deux Rivières (☎ 05 65 60 00 27; camping.deux-rivieres@wanadoo.fr; 61 av de l'Aigoual; site & two persons €14; ⏰ Apr-Oct) Just over Pont de Cureplat, this is the closest of several huge riverside campsites beside the east bank of the River Tarn.

Hôtel La Capelle (☎ 05 65 60 14 72; www.hotel-millau-capelle.com; 7 place de la Capelle; r €45-48, with shared bathroom €30; ❄ ⊠) In the converted wing of a one-time leather factory, La Capelle is a great budget choice. The hotel's large terrace with views towards the Causse Noir makes for a perfect breakfast spot. Some rooms have air-con (€5 supplement). Free wi-fi.

Château de Creissels (☎ 05 65 60 16 59; www.chateau-de-creissels.com; r new wing €63-72, old wing €79-97; ⏰ Apr-Oct) In the village of Creissels, 2km southwest of Millau on the D992 and well signed, this castle has a split personality. Rooms in the old 12th-century tower breathe history while those in the larger, more modern 20th-century wings have balconies overlooking the large garden. There's an excellent restaurant (right) and a terrace offering great views.

Eating

La Mangeoire (☎ 05 65 60 13 16; 8 bd de la Capelle; menus €19.50-46; ⏰ Tue-Sun, closed dinner Sun Nov-Apr) Millau's oldest restaurant, in the vaults beneath the former city walls, serves delightful, mainly regional dishes. Its pride is the open wood-fire barbecue. In winter, spits pierce wild game such as hare and partridge. Year-round, meat and fish (€13 to €18) are sizzled to perfection.

Le Capion (☎ 05 65 60 00 91; 3 rue J-F Alméras; lunch menu €13.50, menus €19-38, mains €14-18; ⏰ Thu-Mon & lunch Tue, closed 1-21 Jul) Peer into the kitchen to see the young team at work as you walk past on the way to the freshly decorated main dining room. Portions are tasty and plentiful – none more so than the trolley of tempting homemade desserts and rich cheese platter (where, of course, Roquefort stars).

La Marmite du Pêcheur (☎ 05 65 61 20 44; 14-16 bd de la Capelle; lunch menu €14.50, menus €19.50-55, mains around €20; ⏰ Wed-Mon Jul-Sep, Thu-Mon Oct-Jun) A few doors from La Mangeoire and run by an engaging young couple, it too is attractively vaulted and has hearty regional *menus* within much the same price range. Try the chef's *marmite du pêcheur à ma façon,* of salmon, perch and red mullet, gambas and scallops gratin.

Château de Creissels restaurant (☎ 05 65 60 16 59; menus €24-50, mains €16-20) The castle's (left) restaurant offers classic French cuisine, where meat lovers will savour the *menu autour de l'agneau des Grands Causses* (€32) with its two main courses of tender local lamb and ewe's-milk cheese, and, for dessert, *panna cotta,* also made from ewe's milk.

SELF-CATERING

There are markets each Wednesday and Friday morning in place Maréchal Foch, place Emma Calvé and the covered market at place des Halles.

There's a Spar supermarket on bd de l'Ayrolle.

Shopping

L'Atelier du Gantier (21 rue Droite) A wonderful little shop that sells gloves and only gloves of the softest leather. Hit the right moment and you can see staff sewing away at a trio of vintage Singer machines.

Les Vitrines du Terroir (17 bd de l'Ayrolle) and **Le Buron** (18 rue Droite) are delightfully rich and pungent cheese shops selling local specialities including Roquefort and Perail du Larzac cheeses.

Getting There & Away

The **bus station** (www.gareroutieredemillau.com, in French) is beside the train station; its **information office** (☎ 05 65 59 89 33) is inside. There are two buses daily to Albi (€17, 2¾ hours), one continuing to Toulouse (€26, four hours) and up to eight daily services to/from Montpellier (€17.70, 1¾ hours).

Train connections from Millau include Montpellier (€24.30, 1¾ hours, one daily) and Rodez (€11.30, 1½ hours, five daily).

Getting Around

Cycles Arturi (☎ 05 65 60 28 23; 2 rue du Barry; 🕑 Mon-Sat Jul & Aug, Tue-Sat Sep-Jun) rents out city bikes for €9/12 per half-/full day and mountain bikes for €11/15.

AROUND MILLAU

Roquefort

pop 700

In the heart of Parc Naturel Régional des Grands Causses and 25km southwest of Millau, the village of Roquefort (or, to give its full name, Roquefort-sur-Soulzon) turns ewe's milk into France's most famous blue cheese. Its steep, narrow streets lead to the cool natural caves, where seven producers ripen 22,000 tonnes of Roquefort cheese every year.

La Société (☎ 05 65 58 54 38; www.roquefort-societe.com) has one-hour **guided tours** (adult/under 16yr €3/free; 🕑 9.30am-6.30pm mid-Jul & Aug, core hr 9.30am-noon & 1.30-5pm rest of year) of the caves, which include a fairly feeble sound-and-light show and sampling of the three varieties the company makes. Established in 1842, it's the largest Roquefort producer, churning out 70% of the world's supply, over 30% of which is exported.

Tours of the equally pungent caves of **Le Papillon** (☎ 05 65 58 50 08; www.roquefort-papillon.com, in French; 8 rue de la Fontaine; 🕑 9am-6.30pm Jul & Aug, 9.30-11.30am & 1.30-4.30pm or 5.30pm Sep-Jun) are free, last 45 minutes to one hour and include a 15-minute film.

For a more rapid appreciation of the Roquefort making process, call by the showroom and sales outlet of **Gabriel Coulet** (☎ 05 65 59 90 21; www.gabriel-coulet.fr; admission free; 🕑 9.30am-6pm or 7pm Jun-Aug, 9.30am-noon & 1.30-5pm Sep-May) where you can descend into the vaulted, penicillin-streaked caves below the shop, wander at your own pace and take in the 10-minute video.

Roquefort's **tourist office** (☎ 05 65 58 56 00; www.roquefort.com; 🕑 9am-7pm Jul & Aug, 9am-6pm Mon-Sat Apr-Jun, Sep & Oct; 10am-5pm Mon-Sat Nov-Mar) is at the western entry to the village.

Micropolis

'La Cité des Insectes' (Insect City), **Micropolis** (☎ 05 65 58 50 50; www.micropolis.biz; adult/5-14yr/under 5yr €11.10/7.45/free; 🕑 10am-6pm Jul & Aug, 10am-4pm or 5pm daily Apr-Jun, Tue-Sun Sep–mid-Nov, Wed-Sun mid-Feb–Mar) is outside the village of St-Léons, off the D911 19km northwest of Millau.

Ever felt small? This mind-boggling high-tech experience happens in a building where grass grows 6m high. The swarms of facts about insect life, all compellingly presented, seem equally tall but all are true. Broadening its remit, Micropolis' newest gallery illustrates the theme of biodiversity. Captions are in French and English. Allow a good 1½ hours, perhaps rounding off with a meal at its pleasant, reasonably priced restaurant.

THE KING OF CHEESES

The mouldy blue-green veins that run through Roquefort are, in fact, the spores of microscopic mushrooms, cultivated on leavened bread.

As the cheeses are ripened in natural caves, enlarged and gouged from the mountainside, draughts of air called *fleurines* flow through, encouraging the blue *Penicillium roqueforti* to eat its way through the white cheese curds.

Roquefort is one of France's priciest and most noble cheeses. In 1407 Charles VI granted exclusive Roquefort cheese-making rights to the villagers, while in the 17th century the Sovereign Court of the Parliament of Toulouse imposed severe penalties against fraudulent cheesemakers trading under the Roquefort name.

Pastoralia

Pastoralia (☎ 05 65 98 10 23; www.pastoralia.com, in French; adult/6-12yr/under 6yr €4.50/3.20/free, 2 adults & 2 children €15; ⌚ 10am-6pm Jul & Aug, 10am-noon & 2-6pm daily Jun, Mon-Fri Sep & Oct), 3km west of St-Affrique, tells the story of the 800,000 ewes who graze the high plateaux, producing nearly 200 million litres of milk annually, over half of which is turned into Roquefort and other regional cheeses. There are interactive panels with English translation, a 10-minute film, and in summer you can feed the sheep.

ROUSSILLON

Roussillon, sometimes known as French Catalonia, sits on Spain's doorstep at the eastern end of the Pyrenees. It's the land of the Tramontane, a violent wind that howls down from the mountains, chilling to the bone in winter and in summer strong enough to overturn a caravan. Its only city is Perpignan, capital of the Pyrénées-Orientales *département*.

Long part of Catalonia (the name which nowadays officially designates only the semi-autonomous region over the border in north-east Spain), Roussillon retains many symbols of Catalan identity. The *sardane* folk dance is still performed, and the Catalan language, closely related to Provençal, is fairly widely spoken.

LANGUEDOC-ROUSSILLON

History

People have lived here since prehistoric times, and one of Europe's oldest skulls was found in a cave near Tautavel (p799).

Roussillon's relatively modern history was for a long time closely bound with events over the Pyrenees in present-day Spain. In 1172 it came under the control of Catalonia-Aragon. After flourishing for a time in its own right as the capital of the kingdom of Mallorca, it again fell under Aragonese rule for much of the late Middle Ages.

In 1640 the Catalans on both sides of the Pyrenees revolted against the Castilian kings in distant Madrid, who had engulfed Aragon. Perpignan endured a two-year siege, only relieved with the support of the French to the north. Peace came in 1659 with the Treaty of the Pyrenees, defining the border between Spain and France once and for all and ceding Roussillon (until then the northern section of Catalonia) to the French, much to the indignation of the locals.

PERPIGNAN

pop 115,000

As much Catalan as French, Perpignan (Perpinyà in Catalan) is far from the 'villainous ugly town', as sourly summarised by traveller Henry Swinburne in 1775. Its modern population is a mixed one. Iberian blood flows in the veins of the descendants of the thousands of refugees who fled over the mountains at the end of the Spanish Civil War. Many other families, Arab and displaced French settlers alike, have their recent origins in Algeria.

At the foothills of the Pyrenees and with the Côte Vermeille to its southeast, Perpignan is a good base for day trips along the coast or to the mountains and Cathar castles of the interior. It's commendably well documented; outside every major historical building is a free-standing sign with information in French, Catalan and English.

History

From 1278 to 1344 Perpignan was the capital of the kingdom of Mallorca, a Mediterranean force that stretched northwards as far as Montpellier and included the Balearic Islands. The town later became an important commercial centre and remains the third-largest Catalan city, after Barcelona and Lleida (Lérida) in Spain.

Orientation

Two rivers flow through the city: the Têt and its trickle of a tributary, the Basse, banked with trim gardens. Place de la Loge and place de la République are at the heart of the mostly pedestrianised old town.

Information

INTERNET ACCESS

Net & Games (45bis av Général Leclerc; per hr €3; ⌚ 8am-1am Mon-Sat, 1-8pm Sun)

LAUNDRY

Laverie Foch (23 rue du Maréchal Foch; ⌚ 7am-8.30pm)

POST

Main Post Office (quai de Barcelone)

TOURIST INFORMATION

Tourist Office (☎ 04 68 66 30 30; www.perpignantourisme.com; ⌚ 9am-7pm Mon-Sat, 10am-4pm Sun mid-Jun–mid-Sep; 9am-6pm Mon-Sat, 10am-1pm Sun mid-Sep–mid-Jun) In the Palais des Congrès, off promenade des Platanes.

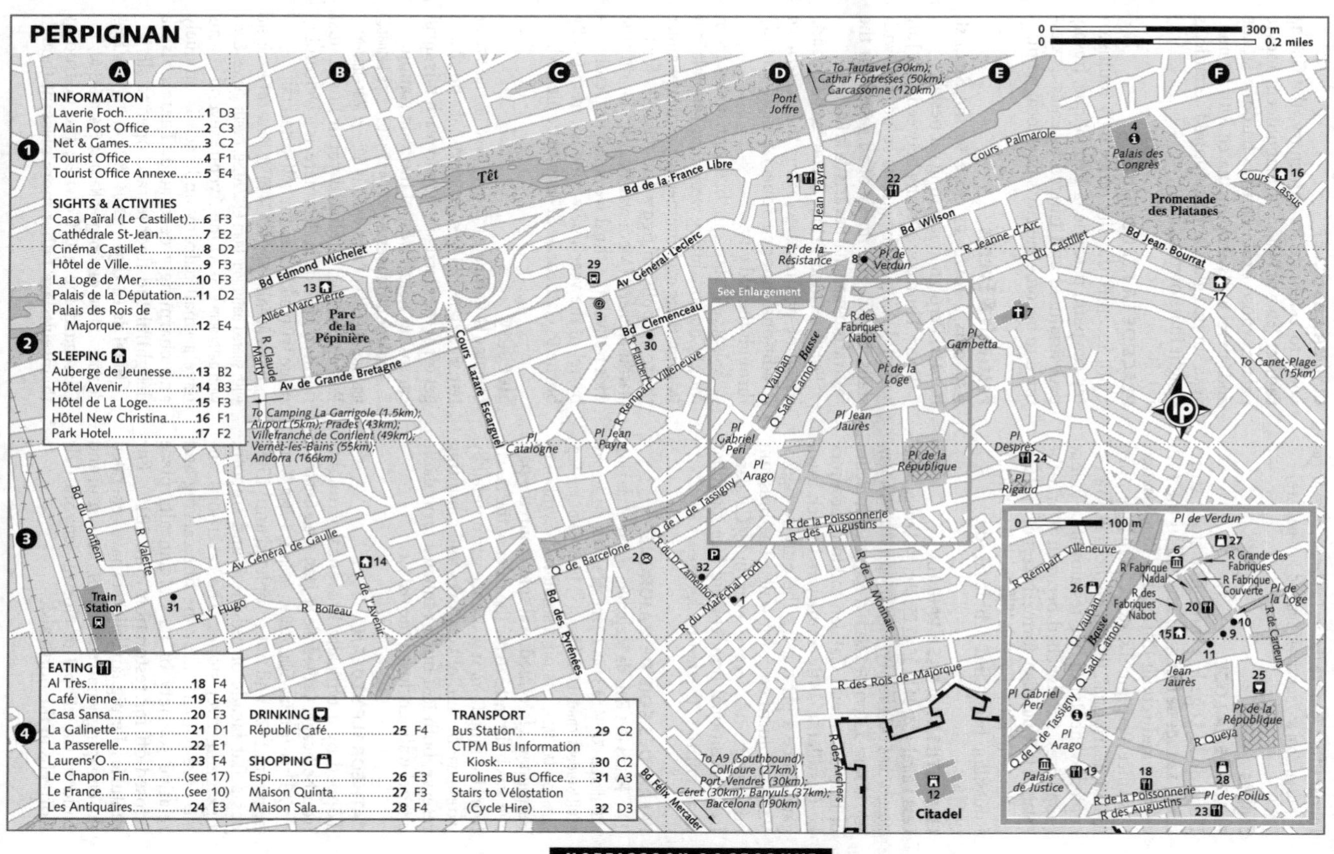
PERPIGNAN
0 300 m
0 0.2 miles
INFORMATION
Laverie Foch 1 D3
Main Post Office 2 C3
Net & Games 3 C2
Tourist Office 4 F1
Tourist Office Annexe 5 E4
SIGHTS & ACTIVITIES
Casa Païral (Le Castillet) 6 F3
Cathédrale St-Jean 7 E2
Cinéma Castillet 8 D2
Hôtel de Ville 9 F3
La Loge de Mer 10 F3
Palais de la Députation 11 D2
Palais des Rois de Majorque 12 E4
SLEEPING
Auberge de Jeunesse 13 B2
Hôtel Avenir 14 B3
Hôtel de La Loge 15 F3
Hôtel New Christina 16 F1
Park Hotel 17 F2
EATING
Al Très 18 F4
Café Vienne 19 E4
Casa Sansa 20 F3
La Galinette 21 D1
La Passerelle 22 E1
Laurens'O 23 F4
Le Chapon Fin (see 17)
Le France (see 10)
Les Antiquaires 24 E3
DRINKING
Républic Café 25 F4
SHOPPING
Espi 26 E3
Maison Quinta 27 F3
Maison Sala 28 F4
TRANSPORT
Bus Station 29 C2
CTPM Bus Information Kiosk 30 C2
Eurolines Bus Office 31 A3
Stairs to Vélostation (Cycle Hire) 32 D3
To Tautavel (30km); Cathar Fortresses (50km); Carcassonne (120km)
To Camping La Garrigole (1.5km); Airport (5km); Prades (43km); Villefranche de Conflent (49km); Vernet-les-Bains (55km); Andorra (166km)
To Canet-Plage (15km)
To A9 (Southbound); Collioure (27km); Port-Vendres (30km); Céret (30km); Banyuls (37km); Barcelona (190km)
Têt
Pont Joffre
Bd de la France Libre
Bd Wilson
Cours Palmarole
Palais des Congrès
Promenade des Platanes
Bd Jean Bourrat
Bd Edmond Michelet
Av Général Leclerc
Bd Clemenceau
Parc de la Pépinière
Cours Lazare Escarguel
Av de Grande Bretagne
Av Général de Gaulle
Bd des Pyrénées
Q de Barcelone
Train Station
Citadel
See Enlargement
Pl de la Résistance
Pl de Verdun
Pl Gambetta
Pl de la Loge
Pl Jean Jaurès
Pl de la République
Pl Gabriel Peri
Pl Arago
Pl Catalogne
Pl Jean Payra
Pl Desprès
Pl Rigaud
R de la Monnaie
R des Rois de Majorque
R des Archers
Bd Félix Mercader
0 100 m
Palais de Justice
Pl des Poilus

Tourist Office Annexe (Espace Palmarium, place Arago; 🕑 10am-6pm or 7pm; closed Sun mid-Jun–mid-Sep)

Sights

PLACE DE LA LOGE

Place de la Loge has three fine stone structures. **La Loge de Mer**, constructed in the 14th century and rebuilt during the Renaissance, was once Perpignan's stock exchange, then maritime tribunal. Its ground floor is now occupied by the stylish café-restaurant Le France (opposite). Sandwiched between it and the **Palais de la Députation**, formerly seat of the local parliament, is the **Hôtel de Ville** with its typically Roussillon brick-and-pebble facade.

LE CASTILLET & CASA PAÏRAL

Casa Païral (☎ 04 68 35 42 05; place de Verdun; adult/student/child €4/2/free; 🕑 11am-6.30pm Wed-Mon May-Sep, 10.30am-5.30pm Wed-Mon Oct-Apr), the museum of Roussillon and Catalan folklore, occupies Le Castillet, a 14th-century red-brick town gate. Once a prison, it's the only vestige of Vauban's fortified town walls. The museum houses bits and pieces of everything Catalan – from traditional bonnets and lace mantillas to an entire 17th-century kitchen.

PALAIS DES ROIS DE MAJORQUE

The **Palais des Rois de Majorque** (Palace of the Kings of Mallorca; ☎ 04 68 34 48 29; entrance on rue des Archers; adult/student/child €4/2/free; 🕑 10am-6pm Jun-Sep, 9am-5pm Oct-May) sits on a small hill. Symbol of Perpignan's late-medieval splendour, the palace was built in 1276 for the ruler of the newly founded kingdom. It was once surrounded by extensive fig and olive groves and a hunting reserve, both lost once Vauban's formidable citadel walls enclosed the palace.

CATHÉDRALE ST-JEAN

Topped by a typically Provençal wrought-iron bell cage, **Cathédrale St-Jean** (place Gambetta; 🕑 7.30am-7pm Tue-Sun, 7.30am-noon & 3-7pm Mon), begun in 1324 and not completed until 1509, has a flat facade of red brick and smooth, zigzagging river stones. The cavernous single nave is marked by the fine carving and relative sobriety of its Catalan altarpiece (closed off for restoration until 2010). For centuries, Perpignan believers have venerated the engagingly naive statue of the Virgin and child in the chapel of Nostra Senyora dels Correchs in the north aisle.

CINÉMA CASTILLET

Soon to celebrate its centenary, the **Cinéma Castillet** (place de Verdun), a magnificent movie palace whose exuberant neobaroque facade and lateral walls are punctuated with art nouveau stained glass and sculptured ceramic, is a sight in its own right.

PLACE DE LA RÉPUBLIQUE

Until recently the site of an ugly multistorey car park, place de la République, freshly pedestrianised and fringed by cafés, is destined to become the city's new focal point.

Festivals & Events

As befits a town so close to the Spanish border, Perpignan is strong on fiestas.

Every Thursday evening between mid-July and mid-August, the streets come alive with stalls, theatre and music of all genres for the **Festival International des Arts de la Rue**.

For the Good Friday **Procession de la Sanch**, barefoot penitents wearing the *caperutxa* (traditional hooded robes) parade silently through the old city.

A 'sacred' flame is brought down from Mont Canigou during week-long **Fête de la Sant Joan**, marking midsummer, while in September the town pulls on tights and wimples for the **Marché Médiéval** (Medieval Market). During the **wine festival**, the third weekend in October, a barrel of the year's new wine is ceremonially borne to Cathédrale St-Jean to be blessed.

Sleeping

Camping La Garrigole (☎ 04 68 54 66 10; 2 rue Maurice Lévy; site & 2 persons €13; 🕑 year-round) Take bus 2 and get off at the Garrigole stop to reach this small campsite, 1.5km west of the train station.

Auberge de Jeunesse (☎ 04 68 34 63 32; perpignan@fuaj.org; allée Marc Pierre; B&B €14.50; 🕑 Mar–mid-Nov) Perpignan's HI-affiliated youth hostel, just north of Parc de la Pépinière, is a welcoming place with a kitchen for self-caterers.

Hôtel Avenir (☎ 04 68 34 20 30; 11 rue de l'Avenir; s/d with shared bathroom from €18/20.50, r with shower €30, r with bathroom €35) At the Avenir, several rooms have a small balcony and each is uniquely and charmingly decorated. There's also a delightful 2nd-floor terrace, open to all.

Hôtel de La Loge (☎ 04 68 34 41 02; www.hoteldelaloge.fr; 1 rue des Fabriques Nabot; s €44, d €48-62; ❄) Disregard the gruff owner; the bedrooms themselves are rather more pleasant though their furniture varies from attractive and antique to flea market. Of the more expensive rooms, which have air-con, 106 and 206 overlook place de la Loge.

Park Hotel (☎ 04 68 35 14 14; www.parkhotel-fr.com; 18 bd Jean Bourrat; r from €80;) Each of this pleasant hotel's soundproofed rooms is individually and engagingly furnished and decorated. The *supérieure* rooms (from €110), with separate bathroom, shower cubicle and toilet, are a cut above the already attractive rest. The largest (ending in 04 and 05) overlook the park. Reputed chef Alexander Klimenko runs the hotel's impressive Le Chapon Fin restaurant. Wi-fi is available; parking costs €11.

Hôtel New Christina (☎ 04 68 35 12 21; www.hotel-newchristina.com; 51 cours Lassus; r €103;) Rooms are attractively decorated in blue and beige and bathrooms, all with bathtubs, are separate from toilets. Those at the front overlook a public park. The open-air pool, up on the roof, has Perpignan's only jacuzzi. Outside high season, rates (single/double €67/73) are a particular bargain. Wi-fi available.

Eating

Le France (☎ 04 68 51 61 71; place de la Loge; pizzas €10-15, mains €16-28; noon-10pm) Le France manages to insert harmoniously the ultramodern – right down to the all-glass handbasins in the toilets – within the historical setting of what was once Perpignan's stock exchange. Mains are smallish but attractively presented and there's a good selection of tapas and pizzas.

Al Trés (☎ 04 68 34 88 39; 3 rue de la Poissonnerie; 2-course lunch menu €13, mains €20-26; Tue-Sun) At this stylish place with its roughly plastered ox-blood-coloured walls and vast, carved wooden bar that could double up as an altar, you'll appreciate the freshness of the ingredients and innovative cuisine.

Café Vienne (☎ 04 68 34 80 00; 3 place Arago; 2-course lunch menu €17.50, mains €15-22; 10am-11pm) You're here for the ambience as much as the food. Dine on the terrace overlooking busy place Arago or inside in a recreation of a pre-WWII brasserie.

Laurens'O (☎ 04 68 34 66 66; 5 place des Poilus; mains €16-20; Tue-Sat) This cheerful modern locale with its striped tablecloths and orange and black decor offers innovative Mediterranean cooking. Its distinctly Italian flavour is garnished with a creative French twist and a little Thai touch here and there.

Casa Sansa (☎ 04 68 34 21 84; entrances 2 rue Fabrique Nadal & rue Fabrique Couverte; menus €19-29, mains €16-23) Here's another highly popular spot – or rather two adjacent places. Choose the older, more southerly one, its walls scarcely visible beneath photos of the famous and less famous who have enjoyed its fine Catalan cuisine.

Les Antiquaires (☎ 04 68 34 06 58; place Després; menus €24-43, mains €16-25; Tue-Sat & lunch Sun) The cuisine is as traditional, reliable and mature as both the clientele and the splendid line of vintage bottles displayed above the fireplace. Portions, from the 50g pack of butter discreetly placed before you to the three huge dollops of chocolate mousse for dessert, are mightily generous.

La Galinette (☎ 04 68 35 00 90; 23 rue Jean Payra; lunch menu €17, mains €28-30; Tue-Sat) In an elegant setting, La Galinette offers refined cuisine, delicately confectioned desserts and an ample selection of regional wines. For a frisson of the unexpected, go for the *menu confiance* fish menu (€50) and let the chef select the best that the sea can offer that day.

La Passerelle (☎ 04 68 51 30 65; 1 cours Palmarole; menus €30-60, mains €19-24; Tue-Sat & dinner Mon) The attractive marine decor hints at the riches within the kitchen. La Passerelle is *the* restaurant in Perpignan for Mediterranean fish, guaranteed fresh and without a hint of freezer or fish farm.

SELF-CATERING

There's a morning fresh fruit and vegetable market on place de la République daily except Monday. Saturday is organic day.

See also Espi and Maison Sala (p798).

Drinking

Républic Café (2 place de la République) Down your first coffee of the day on its busy terrace and return later to sip an aperitif and linger in its Gaudí-inspired interior, all sinuous shapes and white ceramic fragments.

Entertainment

The tourist office publishes **L'Agenda**, a comprehensive, free monthly guide to exhibitions and cultural events. **So Aware**, published monthly, and **Le Bizz**, out every two months, are what's-on tap-ins to the club scene and nightlife.

LANGUEDOC-ROUSSILLON

Shopping

Maison Quinta (3 rue Grande des Fabriques; ⌚ Tue-Sat) Take time to browse this Aladdin's cave of wares, tasteful, kitsch, utilitarian or unashamedly frivolous. They're piled high and higgledy-piggledy on three floors of this former noble mansion.

Espi (43bis quai Vauban) Gorge yourself on Espi's homemade chocolates, multicoloured macaroons and tempting ice creams. They'll even, given notice, knock you up a multistoreyed birthday cake.

Along short, scented rue Paratilla, known popularly to locals as rue des Épices (Spice St), shops sell dried fruits, herbs, jams, hams, cheeses and more. Most famous is **Maison Sala** (⌚ Tue-Sat & Sun morning) at No 1, run by the same family for nearly a century.

Getting There & Away

AIR

Perpignan's **airport** (☎ 04 68 52 60 70) is 5km northwest of the town centre. Flybe serves Southampton, BMI Baby flies to/from Manchester, and Ryanair runs flights to/from London (Stansted) and Birmingham.

The Navette Aéroport bus runs from the train station via place de Catalogne and the bus station.

BUS

From the **bus station** (☎ 04 68 35 29 02; av Général Leclerc), **Courriers Catalans** (☎ 04 68 55 68 00) services coastal resorts, with seven buses daily to/from Collioure and Port-Vendres, most continuing to Banyuls (1¼ hours from Perpignan).

Of the eight buses daily that travel along the Têt Valley to Prades (one hour) and Villefranche de Conflent (1¼ hours), four continue to Vernet-les-Bains (1½ hours from Perpignan).

Frequent buses run up the Tech Valley to Céret (50 minutes).

The **Eurolines office** (☎ 04 68 34 11 46; 10 av Général de Gaulle) is just east of the train station.

CAR

Rental companies include **Avis** (☎ airport 04 68 61 58 97) and **Budget** (☎ airport 04 68 56 95 95).

TRAIN

The train station is served by buses 1 and 2.

Trains cross the Pyrenees to Barcelona (€34 direct, twice daily; €18 changing at Cerbère/Portbou, at least three daily). There are frequent services to Montpellier (€21.60, 1¾ hours) via Narbonne (€9.90, 45 minutes) and Béziers (€13.10, one hour). For Carcassonne (€17.20, 1½ hours), change in Narbonne. Up to nine TGVs daily run to Paris' Gare de Lyon (€105, five hours).

Closer to home is Cerbère/Portbou on the Spanish border (€7.20, 40 minutes, around 15 daily) via Collioure (€5), Port-Vendres (€5.50) and Banyuls (€6.30).

Getting Around

The local bus company, CTPM, has an **information kiosk** (☎ 04 68 61 01 13; 27 bd Clemenceau). A ticket costs €1.10, a one-day pass is €4.10 and a 10-ticket carnet, €7.80. Spattered in cheerful polka dots, **Le P'tit Bus** is a free hop-on, hop-off minibus that plies a circular route around the town centre.

At **Vélostation** (☎ 04 68 35 45 82), on the 1st floor beneath street level of Parking Arago, you can hire a bike at the rock-bottom rate of €1.50/3 per half-/full day.

For a taxi, call **Accueil Perpignan Taxis** (☎ 04 68 35 15 15).

AROUND PERPIGNAN

Céret

pop 7600

It's mainly the **Musée d'Art Moderne** (☎ 04 68 87 27 76; www.musee-ceret.com, in French; 8 bd Maréchal Joffre; adult/student/child €8/6/free; ⌚ 10am-6pm daily May-Sep, Wed-Mon Oct-Apr) that draws visitors to Céret, settled snugly in the Pyrenean foothills just off the Tech Valley. Superbly endowed, the gallery's collection owes much to an earlier generation of visitors and residents, including Picasso, Braque, Chagall, Matisse, Miró and Dalí, all of whom donated their works (53 from Picasso alone).

Céret's **tourist office** (☎ 04 68 87 00 53; www.ot-ceret.fr, in French; 1 av Clemenceau; ⌚ 9am-1pm & 2-5pm Mon-Sat, 10am-1pm Sun Jul & Aug, core hr 10am-noon & 2-5pm Mon-Fri, 9.30am-12.30pm Sat rest of year) is just around the corner from the gallery.

Firmly Catalan and famous for its juicy cherries (the first pickings of the season are packed off to the French president), Céret is also a party town. First comes the **Fête de la Cerise** (Cherry Festival) in late May. Summer sees the **féria** with bullfights and general fun and **La Fête de la Sardane**, celebrating the *sardane,* Catalan folk dance par excellence. More sedately, **Les Méennes** is primarily a festival of classical music.

THE CATHARS

The term *le Pays Cathare* (Cathar Land) recalls the cruel Albigensian Crusade – the hounding and extermination of a religious sect called the Cathars.

The Cathars were the fundamentalists of their day: people of extreme beliefs, warily regarded by the mainstream yet convinced that they alone knew the one true way to salvation. Cathars (from the Greek word *katharos* meaning 'pure') believed that God's kingdom was locked in battle with Satan's evil world and that humans were base at heart. But, they reckoned, a pure life followed by several reincarnations could free the spirit. Reacting against worldly Rome and preaching in *langue d'oc,* the local tongue, the sect gained many followers. Their most extreme followers were the ascetic *parfaits* (perfects), who followed strict vegetarian diets and abstained from sex.

In 1208 Pope Innocent III preached a crusade against the Cathars. The Albigensian Crusade had a political as much as spiritual dimension, giving northern rulers the chance to expand their domains by ingesting Languedoc.

After long sieges, the major Cathar centres in Béziers, Carcassonne, Minerve and the dramatically sited fortresses of Montségur, Quéribus and Peyrepertuse were taken and hundreds of 'perfects' were burned as heretics. In Béziers as many as 20,000 faithful were slaughtered. Montségur witnessed another cruel massacre in 1244, when 200 Cathars, refusing to renounce their faith, were burned alive in a mass funerary pyre. In 1321 the burning of the last 'perfect', Guillaume Bélibaste, marked the end of Catharism in Languedoc.

our pick **Hôtel des Arcades** (☎ 04 68 87 12 30; www.hotel-arcades-ceret.com; r €42-57;) This friendly hotel overlooks place Picasso with its monumental plane trees and a sizeable hunk of the old town ramparts. Run with panache by a dynamic brother and sister duo, it's a gallery in its own right, where just about every square centimetre of wall space has its poster, photo or print. Parking is available.

Up to 12 daily buses run to/from Perpignan (50 minutes). If you're driving, head for the well-signed Musée d'Art Moderne car park.

Tautavel

The Arago Cave, on the slopes above the village of Tautavel, 27km northwest of Perpignan along the D117, has yielded a human skull, estimated to be 450,000 years old, along with a host of other prehistoric finds. The **Musée de Préhistoire** (Prehistory Museum; ☎ 04 68 29 07 76; www.tautavel.com; av Jean Jaurès; adult/child incl audioguide €7/3.50; 10am-7pm Jul & Aug, 10am-12.30pm & 2-5pm or 6pm Sep-Jun) has a full-size reproduction of the cave (in season, cameras show in real time archeologists excavating the real cave), together with holograms, dioramas, TVs dispensing knowledge from every corner and lots of fossilised bones and stone tools. The ticket includes entry to a secondary exhibition, at **Musée des Premiers Habitants d'Europe** (rue Anatole France; 11.30am-7.30pm Jul & Aug, 11.30am-1.30pm & 2.30pm-5.30pm or 6.30pm Sep-Jun), 300m away in the Palais des Congrès. Ask for its English-language sheet 'The First Inhabitants of Europe' and allow a good 1½ hours to take in both venues.

Cathar Fortresses

When the Albigensian Crusade forced the Cathars into the mountains that once marked the frontier between France and Aragon, they sought refuge in these inaccessible fortresses that had long protected the border. In a long but fulfilling 195km day of driving between Carcassonne and Perpignan you can take in the four major sites of **Puilaurens** (☎ 04 68 20 65 26; adult/child €3.50/1.50; 9am-8pm Jul & Aug, 10am-5pm or 6pm Sep–mid-Nov & Feb-Jun), which later functioned as a prison; **Peyrepertuse** (☎ 04 68 45 40 55; adult/child €5/3, audioguide €4; 9am-8.30pm Jun-Aug, 10am-5pm or 7pm Sep-May), the largest with a drop of several hundred metres on all sides; **Quéribus** (☎ 04 68 45 03 69; adult/child €5/3, audioguide €2; 9am-8pm Jul & Aug, 9.30am-7pm Apr-Jun & Sep, 10am-5pm or 6.30pm Oct-Mar), which marked the Cathars' last stand in 1255; and **Aguilar** (☎ 04 68 45 51 00; adult/child €3.50/1.50; 10am-7pm mid-Jun–Sep, 10.30am-5.30pm Apr–mid-Jun, 11am-5pm Oct–mid-Nov), the smallest and sadly in need of care and attention. Each clings to a clifftop, offers a dramatic wraparound panorama and requires a short, stiff climb from its car park. This is wild country, hot as hell in summer, so be sure to pack extra water.

Those deeply into Catharism might want to invest €3 in a *Passeport des Sites du Pays*

Cathare, which gives reductions to 20 sites, major and minor.

TÊT VALLEY

Fruit orchards carpet the lower reaches of the Têt Valley. Beyond the strategic fortress town of Villefranche de Conflent, the scenery becomes wilder, more open and undulating as the valley climbs towards Spanish Catalonia and Andorra.

Le Train Jaune

Carrying nearly half a million passengers during the three peak months of high summer, **Le Train Jaune** (Yellow Train; ☎ 04 68 96 63 62; 4 daily Jun-Sep, 2 daily Oct-May), also affectionately known as The Canary, runs from Villefranche to Latour de Carol (return €35.40) through spectacular Pyrenean scenery. You can't make reservations, and it's wise to arrive a good hour before departure in high summer.

Prades

pop 5600

Prades, at the heart of the Têt Valley and 44km from Perpignan, is internationally famed for its annual classical music festival. It's an attractive town with houses of river stone and brick, liberally adorned with pink marble from nearby quarries.

The **tourist office** (☎ 04 68 05 41 02; www.prades-tourisme.com; 4 rue des Marchands; 🕑 9am-12.30pm & 2.30-7pm Mon-Sat, 10am-noon Sun Jul & Aug, 9am-noon & 2-6pm Mon-Fri Sep-Jun) is just off place de la République, the main square.

The bell tower of **Église St-Pierre** (🕑 9am-noon & 2-6.30pm) is all that remains of the original Romanesque church, rebuilt in the 17th century. The wonderfully expressive, ill-lit 17th-century *Entombment of Christ* at its western end is by the Catalan sculptor Josep Sunyer, who also carved the exuberant main altarpiece, a chef-d'oeuvre of Catalan baroque.

The **Musée Pablo Casals** (☎ 04 68 96 28 55; 33 rue de L'Hospice; admission free; 🕑 9am-noon & 2-5pm Tue-Fri, 9am-1pm Sat Jul & Aug, 10am-1pm & 4-7pm Tue & Wed, 3-7pm Fri, 10am-1pm Sat Sep-Jun) commemorates the world-renowned Spanish cellist, who settled in Prades after fleeing Franco's Spain.

Hiking & Walking Around Prades details 20 easy-to-moderate walks lasting from 1¼ to 3½ hours. *Six Grandes Randonnées en Conflent* (in French) describes six more challenging day walks, including the classic ascent of Mont Canigou (2786m), an emotive symbol for Catalans on both sides of the border. The tourist office sells both (€3 each).

VTT en Conflent, also in French, details nine mountain-bike routes varying from easy to seriously tough. **Cycles Flament** (☎ 04 68 96 07 62; 8 rue Arago; 🕑 Tue-Sat), off the main square, rents out bikes (half-/full day €10/13).

The **Festival Pablo Casals** (☎ 04 68 96 33 07; www.prades-festival-casals.com, in French), held over two weeks in late July or early August, brings top-flight classical musicians to this small town.

There's a robust general market on place de la République every Tuesday and a farmers market each Saturday.

Villefranche de Conflent

pop 225

Villefranche, hemmed in by tall cliffs, sits at the strategic confluence of the valley of the Rivers Têt and Cady (hence the 'de Conflent' in its name). It's encircled by thick fortifications built by Vauban in the 17th century to

BEST OF LANGUEDOC FOOD MARKETS *Miles Roddis*

Narbonne Jostle and pick within Narbonne's art nouveau covered market, an architectural jewel in its own right.

Nîmes It's so vast, it could be a cathedral, and the restaurants that hang around its skirts wouldn't buy their produce anywhere else.

Mende Beneath the benign gaze of a statue of Pope Urbain V, the stalls of a farmers market take over Mende's cathedral square each Saturday.

Montpellier Locals who like their food fresh and real, pick and choose beneath the giant arches of Aqueduc de St-Clément at the city's Saturday organic food market.

Sète Watch and wonder at the riches from the deep, sold by the crate at the wholesale fish market of France's largest Mediterranean fishing port.

Uzès Farmers bring their fresh produce not once but twice a week, each Wednesday and Saturday, to colonnaded and cobbled place aux Herbes, one of the prettiest marketplaces in all France.

What's your recommendation?
www.lonelyplanet.com/france

augment the original 11th-century defences, which have survived intact.

Villefranche's **tourist information point** (☎ 04 68 96 22 96; www.villefranchedeconflent.fr; 32bis rue St-Jacques; ⏲ core hr 9am-noon & 2-5pm or 6pm Apr-Sep, 9am-noon Mon-Sat Sep-Mar) abuts the entrance to the spectacular **ramparts** (adult/child €4/1.50, audioguide €3; ⏲ 10am-7pm or 8pm Jun-Sep, hr vary Oct-Dec & Feb-May) is beside the western Porte d'Espagne.

The stronghold high above town, built by Vauban and strengthened under Napoléon III, is the heavily promoted **Château-Fort Liberia** (☎ 04 68 96 34 01; admission €5.50; ⏲ 9am-8pm Jun-Sep, 10am-6pm Oct-May), offering spectacular views.

Leave your vehicle in one of the car parks outside each of the two town gates.

Vernet-les-Bains

pop 1450

Busy in summer and a ghost town for the rest of the year, this charming little spa was much frequented by the British aristocracy in the late 19th century. Vernet has the status of *village arboretum* in recognition of more than 300 varieties of trees that flourish on its slopes, many brought in as seeds by overseas visitors.

The **tourist office** (☎ 04 68 05 55 35; www.ot-vernet-les-bains.fr; ⏲ 9am-noon & 2-6pm Mon-Sat May-Sep, closed Sat & Sun Oct-Apr) is on place de la République, the main square. Upstairs, there's a well-mounted free exhibition recounting Vernet's past.

Vernet is a great base for mountain biking and hiking – particularly for attacking **Mont Canigou**. Two tracks wind up from the village. To bag the summit an easier way, bounce up in a 4WD (€25 per person return) with **Garage Villacèque** (☎ 04 68 05 51 14; rue du Conflent) or **Jeeps de Canigou** (☎ 04 68 05 99 89; 17 bd des Pyrénées) as far as Les Cortalets (2175m), from where the summit is a three-hour return hike.

Randonnées dans la Vallée de Cady et le Massif du Canigou (€5), in French and with detailed maps, describes a holiday's worth of less demanding treks. A free tourist office pamphlet describes 12 signed mountain-bike trails that snake out from the village.

CÔTE VERMEILLE

The Côte Vermeille (Vermilion Coast) runs south from Collioure to Cerbère on the Spanish border, where the Pyrenees foothills dip to the sea. Against a backdrop of vineyards and pinched between the Mediterranean and the mountains, it's riddled with small, rocky bays and little ports.

If you're driving from Perpignan, leave the N114 at exit 13 and follow the lovely coastal corniche all the way to Banyuls.

Collioure

pop 2750

Collioure, where boats bob against a backdrop of houses washed in soft pastel colours, is the smallest and most picturesque of the Côte Vermeille resorts. Once Perpignan's port, it found fame in the early 20th century when it inspired the fauvist artists Henri Matisse and André Derain (see boxed text, below) and later both Picasso and Braque.

In summer Collioure is almost overwhelmed by visitors, drawn by its artistic reputation (there are over 30 galleries and workshops), its wine and the chance to buy the famed Collioure anchovies at source.

The **tourist office** (☎ 04 68 82 15 47; www.collioure.com; ⏲ 9am-8pm Mon-Sat, 10am-6pm Sun Jul & Aug, 9am-noon & 2-6pm or 7pm Mon-Sat Sep-Jun) is on place 18 Juin.

Across the creek is the **Château Royal** (☎ 04 68 82 06 43; adult/child €4/2; ⏲ 10am-5.30pm or 6.30pm Jun-Sep, 9am-4.30pm Oct-May), which enjoyed its greatest splendour as the summer residence of the kings of Mallorca. Vauban added its towering defensive walls in the 17th century.

The medieval church tower of **Notre Dame des Anges** at the northern end of the harbour once doubled as a lighthouse (the pink dome resembling a rampant penis was added in

THE FAUVISTES & COLLIOURE

'No sky in all France is more blue than that of Collioure. I only have to close the shutters of my room and there before me are all the colours of the Mediterranean.' So effused Henri Matisse (1869–1954), doyen of *les Fauves* (the Wild Animals), who worked with pure colour, filling their canvases with firm lines and stripes, rectangles and splashes of bright colour.

The **Chemin du Fauvisme** (Fauvism Trail) is a walking route around Collioure that takes you by 20 reproductions of works that Matisse and his younger colleague André Derain painted while living here. The tourist office carries a French-language guide booklet (€5.50).

1810). Inside is a superb altarpiece, crafted by the Catalan master Josep Sunyer.

The **Musée d'Art Moderne** (☎ 04 68 82 10 19; Villa Pams, rte de Port-Vendres; adult/child €2/1.50; ⌚ 10am-noon & 2-6pm or 7pm Jun-Sep, closed Tue Oct-May) has a good collection of 20th-century and contemporary canvases.

Just beside the museum's entrance gate, the **Cellier des Dominicains** (☎ 04 68 82 05 63; ⌚ 9am-noon & 2-6pm Mon-Fri, 10am-noon & 3-7pm Sat & Sun) is the place to sample and pick up some of the best local wine.

Le Trémail (☎ 04 68 82 16 10; 1 rue Arago; menus €23-35, mains €14.50-28; ⌚ daily Mar-Nov, Tue-Sat & lunch Sun Dec-Feb) It's primarily fresh fish at this engaging little restaurant that cures and cans its own anchovies. For local cuisine from starter to dessert, go for the *menu catalan* (€23).

Between May and September, leave your car in Parking Cap Dourats, at the top of the hill that plunges down to the village, and take the shuttle bus that runs to the village every 10 minutes. Year-round, there's a large car park behind the castle.

Port-Vendres

pop 5900

Three kilometres south of Collioure, Port-Vendres, Roussillon's only natural harbour and deep-water port, has been exploited ever since Greek mariners roamed the rocky coastline. Until the independence of France's North African territories in the 1960s, it was an important port linking them with the mainland. It's still a significant cargo and fishing harbour with everything from small coastal chuggers to giant deep-sea vessels bristling with radar. There's also a large leisure marina.

The **tourist office** (☎ 04 68 82 07 54; www.port-vendres.com; 1 quai François Joly; ⌚ 9am-7.30pm Jul & Aug, 9am-12.30pm & 2-5.30pm or 6.30pm Mon-Sat Sep-Jun) is in the port's northwest corner.

Banyuls

pop 4500

Banyuls, 7km south of Port-Vendres, has a pebbly beach, overlooked by the **tourist office** (☎ 04 68 88 31 58; www.banyuls-sur-mer.com; av de la République; ⌚ 8.30am-8pm Jul & Aug, 9am-noon & 2-6pm or 7pm Mon-Sat Sep-Jun).

At the promenade's southern limit is the **Aquarium du Laboratoire Arago** (☎ 04 68 88 73 39; adult/child €4.60/2.30; ⌚ 9am-1pm & 2-9pm Jul & Aug, 10am-noon & 2-6.30pm Sep-Jun). More than yet another commercial enterprise with smiling dolphins, this aquarium, which displays local Mediterranean marine life (and a collection of more than 250 stuffed sea and mountain birds), is also the oceanographic research station of Paris' Université Pierre et Marie Curie. It has recently acquired its first baby shark and constructed a small simulated rock pool, where children can dabble their fingers (the shark's elsewhere).

THE HIGH ROAD

The 15km alternative drive between Port-Vendres and Banyuls is a wonderful way to escape the summer coastal crawl and get the wind whistling through your hair. On the D914 near Port-Vendres, turn right at a sharp bend, just beyond the Cave Tambour wine producer's booth (don't call by; you'll need to keep your faculties sharp!). Signed Medaloc, the D86 winds inland, tight and single lane for most of its length. Views are breathtaking as, scarcely more than a track, it climbs above vineyards, almond and fig groves, through scrub and past bare schist outcrops.

More strenuously aquatic but well worth the effort is snorkelling for free around a 500m **underwater trail**. Just off Plage de Peyrefite, midway between Banyuls and Cerbère and within a protected marine area, it has five underwater information points. You can hire fins and masks (€7; from noon to 6pm in July and August). If you have your own gear, you can swim the trail at any time.

To taste the robust red and rosé wines of Banyuls and Collioure, visit the **Cellier des Templiers** (☎ 04 68 98 36 92; www.banyuls.com; rte du Mas Reig; admission free; ⌚ 10am-7.30pm Apr-Oct, 10am-1pm & 2.30pm-6.30pm Mon-Sat Nov-Mar), 1.75km inland. Tours are preceded by a 15-minute video (you'll probably loathe its posturing chef), subtitled in English, and followed by a tasting.

Restaurant Al Fanal (☎ 04 68 88 03 12; av Fontaulé; menu €28; ⌚ daily Easter–mid-Oct, Fri-Tue rest of year) with its appropriately nautical ambience overlooks the port. There's no à la carte selection, but there's an ample range of dishes, many with a regional flavour, within the three-course *menu*. Al Fanal also keeps an impressive cellar of local wines and has a few rooms (overlooking the garden, €60; with harbour views, €70).

Provence

Provence conjures up images of rolling lavender fields, blue skies, gorgeous villages, wonderful food and superb wine – most people's idea of a perfect holiday. It certainly delivers on all those fronts, but what many visitors don't expect is Provence's incredible diversity.

The Vaucluse and Luberon regions epitomise the Provençal cliché, but head south to the Alpilles with its craggy villages and olive groves and the light begins to change, a prelude to Camargue's bleached landscapes. It is this slanting, luminous air of southern Provence that has captivated so many illustrious painters, the likes of van Gogh, Cézanne and Gauguin. It's likely you will be smitten, too.

Further east, the spectacular Gorges du Verdon – with their 800m sheer-drop cliffs – set the scene for northeastern Provence's unspoilt wilderness, a divine mix of Alpine peaks, exceptional sunshine (in excess of 300 days a year) and Provençal flavours. The undisputed king of this little-explored wonderland is the majestic Parc National du Mercantour, with 3000m-plus summits, rare fauna and flora and thousands of unique prehistoric stone carvings.

It's amazing to think that this outstanding natural setting is headed by one of France's most explosive cities, sultry and intoxicating Marseille. In fact, you can rave just as much about Provence's cities – be it Avignon, Marseille, Aix-en-Provence or Arles – as you can about its countryside. In fact, the latter three won the French nominations to be European Capital of Culture in 2013, proof if it ever were needed that Provence is much more than lavender fields and eternal sunshine.

HIGHLIGHTS

- Soak up seething, heady **Marseille** (p805)
- Trail **van Gogh** (p829) around Arles, visiting spots where he painted some of his best-known canvases
- Canoe, canyon, raft or float down the vertigo-inducing **Gorges du Verdon** (p854)
- Take a walk on the wild side in the stunning, remote valleys of the **Parc National du Mercantour** (p858)
- Watch an opera at Orange's exceptional **Roman Theatre** (p845) on a balmy summer night
- Retrace the dinosaur's steps, literally, as you admire ammonites and prehistoric bird footprints at Digne-les-Bains' **Réserve Géologique** (p856)

Digne-les-Bains · Parc National du Mercantour · Orange · Gorges du Verdon · Arles · Marseille

POPULATION: 2,603,500	AREA: 25,851 SQ KM

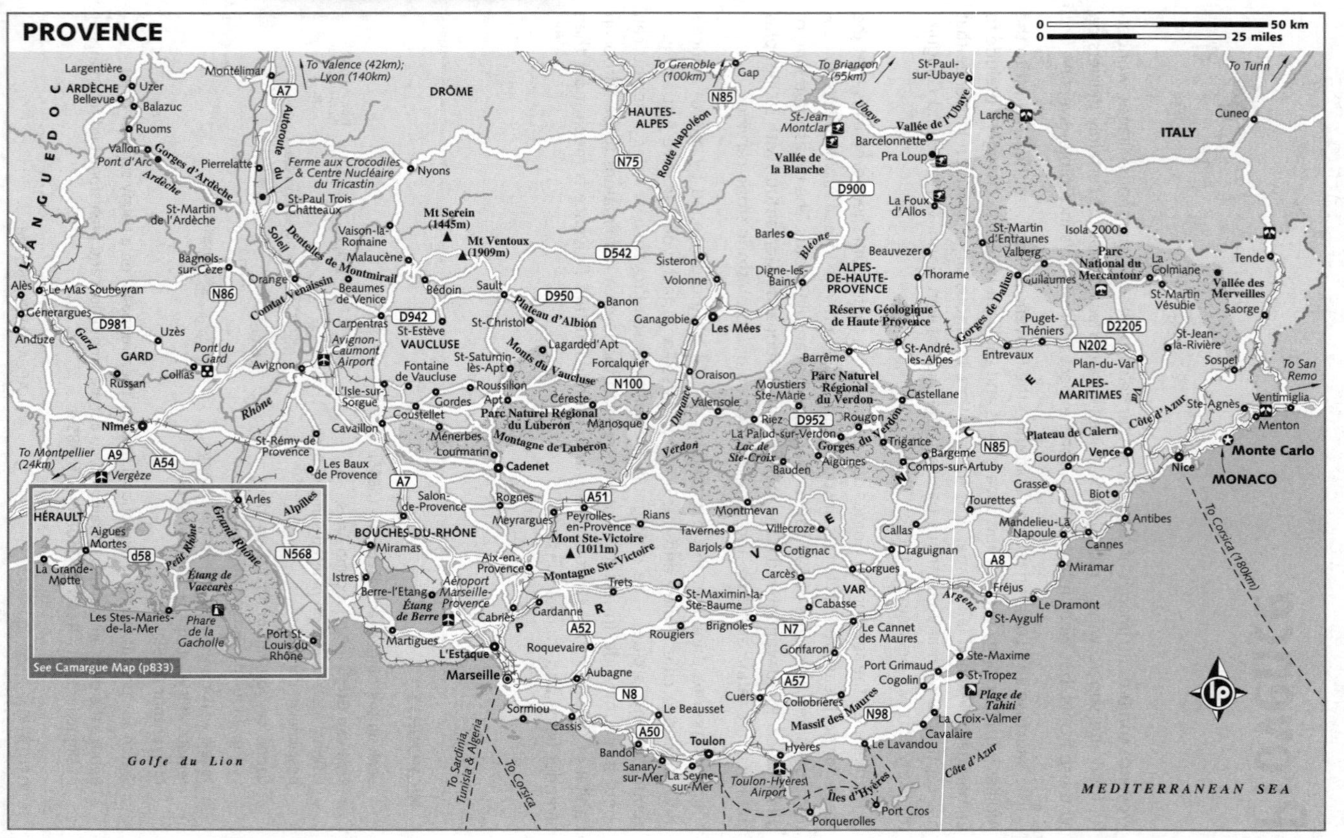
PROVENCE
0 50 km
0 25 miles
ITALY
MONACO
Monte Carlo
MEDITERRANEAN SEA
Golfe du Lion
To Turin
To San Remo
To Corsica (180km)
To Corsica
To Sardinia, Tunisia & Algeria
To Briançon (55km)
To Grenoble (100km)
To Valence (42km); Lyon (140km)
To Montpellier (24km)
Cuneo
Tende
Vallée des Merveilles
Saorge
Ventimiglia
Menton
Sospel
Ste-Agnès
Nice
Antibes
La Colmiane
St-Martin Vésubie
St-Jean-la-Rivière
Isola 2000
Parc National du Mercantour
D2205
N202
Plan-du-Var
Var
Côte d'Azur
ALPES-MARITIMES
Plateau de Calern
Vence
Biot
Cannes
Gourdon
Grasse
Mandelieu-La Napoule
Miramar
Le Dramont
St-Aygulf
Fréjus
A8
Argens
Tourettes
Ste-Maxime
St-Tropez
Plage de Tahiti
La Croix-Valmer
Cavalaire
Le Lavandou
Port Cros
Îles d'Hyères
Porquerolles
Hyères
Toulon-Hyères Airport
Toulon
La Seyne-sur-Mer
Sanary-sur-Mer
Bandol
Le Beausset
A50
Cassis
Sormiou
Marseille
L'Estaque
Cabriès
Gardanne
Roquevaire
Aubagne
N8
A52
Trets
Montagne Ste-Victoire
Mont Ste-Victoire (1011m)
Rians
Peyrolles-en-Provence
A51
Meyrargues
Rognes
Aix-en-Provence
Aéroport Marseille-Provence
Étang de Berre
Martigues
Berre-l'Étang
Miramas
Istres
Salon-de-Provence
A7
BOUCHES-DU-RHÔNE
Larche
St-Paul-sur-Ubaye
Vallée de l'Ubaye
Barcelonnette
Pra Loup
La Foux d'Allos
Ubaye
St-Jean Montclar
Vallée de la Blanche
D900
St-Martin d'Entraunes
Valberg
Guillaumes
Gorges de Dalius
Puget-Théniers
Entrevaux
N85
Beauvezer
Thorame
St-André-les-Alpes
Réserve Géologique de Haute Provence
ALPES-DE-HAUTE-PROVENCE
Castellane
Bargème
Comps-sur-Artuby
Trigance
Gorges du Verdon
Rougon
Aiguines
Parc Naturel Régional du Verdon
Moustiers Ste-Marie
D952
Riez
La Palud-sur-Verdon
Lac de Ste-Croix
Bauduen
Barrême
Digne-les-Bains
Bléone
Barles
Gap
Les Mées
Sisteron
Volonne
Route Napoléon
HAUTES-ALPES
N75
D542
Ganagobie
Oraison
Durance
Valensole
Verdon
Montmeyan
Villecroze
Cotignac
Callas
Draguignan
Lorgues
VAR
Le Cannet des Maures
Cabasse
Carcès
N7
Barjols
Tavernes
St-Maximin-la-Ste-Baume
Brignoles
Rougiers
Gonfaron
A57
Collobrières
Massif des Maures
N98
Cogolin
Port Grimaud
Cuers
Banon
Forcalquier
N100
Manosque
Céreste
Lagarde d'Apt
D950
Plateau d'Albion
St-Christol
Sault
Monts du Vaucluse
Parc Naturel Régional du Luberon
Montagne de Luberon
Cadenet
Lourmarin
Apt
Roussillon
St-Saturnin-lès-Apt
Gordes
Ménerbes
Coustellet
Fontaine de Vaucluse
L'Isle-sur-Sorgue
Cavaillon
Mt Ventoux (1909m)
Mt Serein (1445m)
Bédoin
St-Estève
D942
VAUCLUSE
Malaucène
Dentelles de Montmirail
Beaumes de Venice
Carpentras
Vaison-la-Romaine
Nyons
DRÔME
Comtat Venaissin
Avignon-Caumont Airport
Avignon
Les Baux de Provence
St-Rémy de Provence
Rhône
Orange
Autoroute du Soleil
Ferme aux Crocodiles & Centre Nucléaire du Tricastin
St-Paul Trois Châteaux
Montélimar
A7
Pierrelatte
N86
Bagnols-sur-Cèze
Pont du Gard
Collias
Uzès
St-Martin de l'Ardèche
Gorges d'Ardèche
Ardèche
Vallon Pont d'Arc
Ruoms
Balazuc
Uzer
Largentière
ARDÈCHE
Bellevue
LANGUEDOC
Alès
Le Mas Soubeyran
Générargues
Anduze
Gard
D981
GARD
Russan
Nîmes
A54
A9
Vergèze
Arles
Alpilles
N568
Grand Rhône
Petit Rhône
Étang de Vaccarès
Phare de la Gacholle
Port St-Louis du Rhône
Les Stes-Maries-de-la-Mer
d58
Aigues Mortes
La Grande-Motte
HÉRAULT
See Camargue Map (p833)

PROVENCE

History

Settled over the centuries variously by the Ligurians, the Celts and the Greeks, the area between the Alps, the sea and the Rhône River flourished following Julius Caesar's conquest in the mid-1st century BC. The Romans called the area *Provincia Romana,* which evolved into the name Provence. After the collapse of the Roman Empire in the late 5th century, Provence was invaded several times, by the Visigoths, Burgundians and Ostrogoths. The Arabs – who held the Iberian Peninsula and parts of France – were defeated in the 8th century.

During the 14th century, the Catholic Church – under a series of French-born popes – moved its headquarters from feud-riven Rome to Avignon, thus beginning the most resplendent period in the city's (and region's) history. Provence became part of France in 1481, but Avignon and Carpentras remained under papal control until the Revolution.

From the 12th to the 14th centuries, Provençal was the literary language of France, northern Spain and Italy, and the language of the medieval troubadours who romanticised courtly love in poems and melodies.

A movement for the revival of Provençal literature, culture and identity began in the mid-19th century, spearheaded by the poet Frédéric Mistral (1830–1914), recipient of the Nobel Prize for literature in 1904 (the region's furious 100km/h winds are named after him). In recent years the language has undergone a further revival, and in some areas signs are written in Provençal and French.

Getting There & Away

Thanks to the TGV, you can travel from Paris to Aix-en-Provence (three hours), Arles (four hours), Avignon (2¾ hours) and Marseille (three hours). On Saturdays in July and August, there's a direct Eurostar service from London to Avignon (p843). Aéroport Marseille-Provence (p818) is served by a smorgasbord of carriers. Ferries sail from Marseille to Sardinia, Tunisia and Corsica (p818).

MARSEILLE REGION

MARSEILLE

pop 826,700

There was a time when Marseille was the butt of French jokes and on the receiving end of some pretty bad press. No longer. The *cité phocéenne* has made an unprecedented comeback, undergoing a vast makeover. The results of her new self look rather fabulous: witness the Panier quarter, the new République neighbourhood with its swanky boutiques and Haussmannian buildings, the city's shiny new tram line, and, by 2010, the brand new docks and marina around the famous stripy Cathédrale de la Major.

Marseillais will tell you that the city's rough-and-tumble edginess is part of its charm and that, for all its flaws, it is a very endearing place. They're absolutely right: Marseille grows on you with its unique history, fusion of cultures, souklike markets, millennia-old port and corniches (coastal roads) chicaning around rocky inlets, coves and sun-baked beaches.

And then, of course, there are the Marseillais themselves, far too modest to ever admit that they are part of what makes Marseille so endearing: the accent, the warmth, the honesty, the Mediterranean flair. Marcel Pagnol really had it down to a *t.* And the ultimate vindication that Marseille no longer plays second fiddle to any other French city came in the form of its selection as European Capital of Culture in 2013.

History

Around 600 BC, Greek mariners founded Massilia, a trading post, at what is now Marseille's Vieux Port (Old Port). In the 1st century BC, the city lost out by backing Pompey the Great rather than Julius Caesar – Caesar's forces captured Massilia in 49 BC and directed Roman trade elsewhere. Massilia stayed a free port, remaining the last Western centre of Greek learning before falling into ruin. The city was revived in the early 10th century by the counts of Provence.

Marseille became part of France in the 1480s, but retained its rebellious streak. Its citizens embraced the Revolution, sending 500 volunteers to defend Paris in 1792. Heading north, they sang a rousing march, ever after dubbed 'La Marseillaise' – now the national anthem. Trade with North Africa escalated after France occupied Algeria in 1830, and the 1869 opening of the Suez Canal. During WWII Marseille was bombed by the Germans and Italians (in 1940), and the Allies (in 1943–44).

Postwar years brought with them a steady flow of migration from North Africa and the rapid expansion of Marseille's periphery. Today, Marseille is an important Mediterranean port at the centre of the new

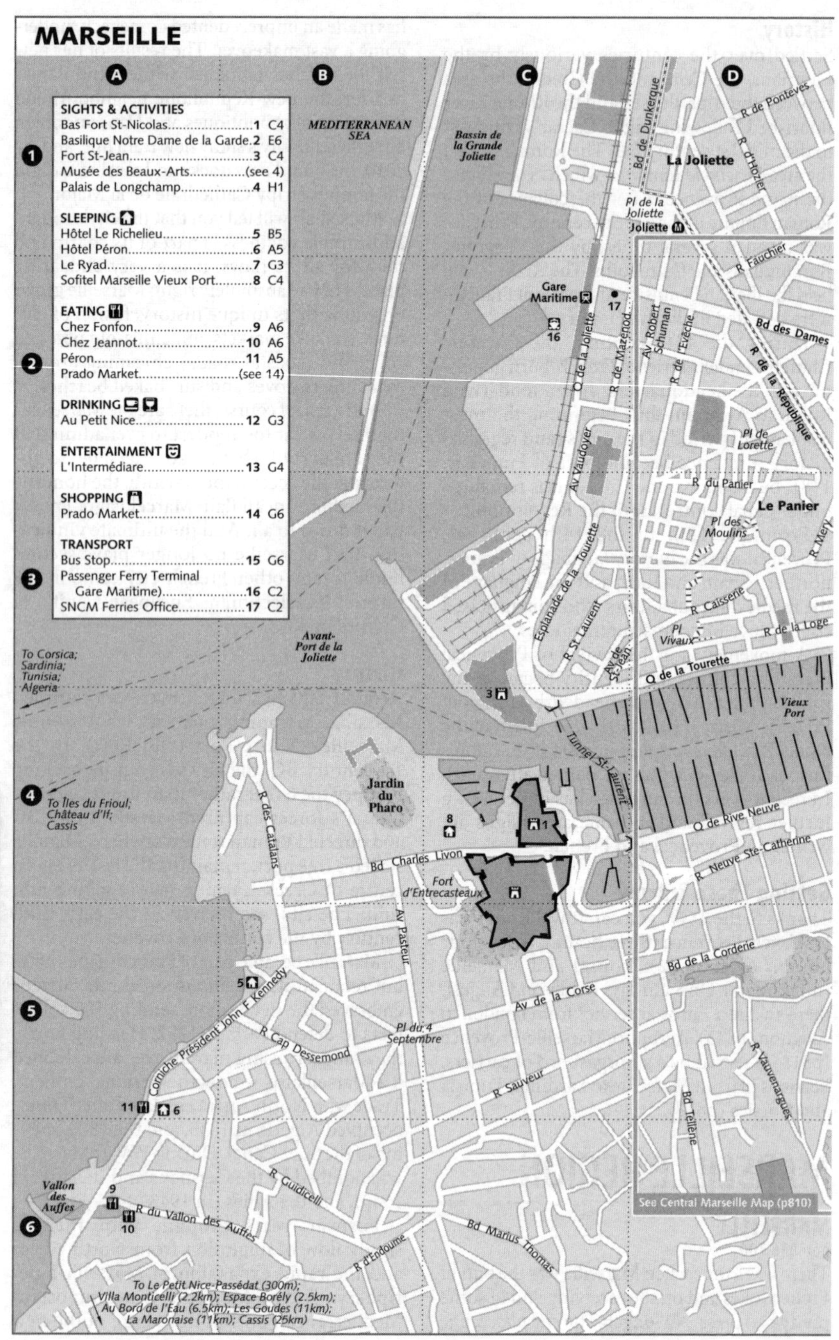
MARSEILLE
SIGHTS & ACTIVITIES
Bas Fort St-Nicolas....1 C4
Basilique Notre Dame de la Garde.2 E6
Fort St-Jean....3 C4
Musée des Beaux-Arts....(see 4)
Palais de Longchamp....4 H1
SLEEPING
Hôtel Le Richelieu....5 B5
Hôtel Péron....6 A5
Le Ryad....7 G3
Sofitel Marseille Vieux Port....8 C4
EATING
Chez Fonfon....9 A6
Chez Jeannot....10 A6
Péron....11 A5
Prado Market....(see 14)
DRINKING
Au Petit Nice....12 G3
ENTERTAINMENT
L'Intermédiare....13 G4
SHOPPING
Prado Market....14 G6
TRANSPORT
Bus Stop....15 G6
Passenger Ferry Terminal (Gare Maritime)....16 C2
SNCM Ferries Office....17 C2
MEDITERRANEAN SEA
Bassin de la Grande Joliette
La Joliette
Pl de la Joliette
Joliette
Gare Maritime
Avant-Port de la Joliette
To Corsica; Sardinia; Tunisia; Algeria
To Îles du Frioul; Château d'If; Cassis
Jardin du Pharo
Fort d'Entrecasteaux
Le Panier
Vieux Port
Tunnel St-Laurent
Vallon des Auffes
Pl du 4 Septembre
See Central Marseille Map (p810)
To Le Petit Nice-Passédat (300m); Villa Monticelli (2.2km); Espace Borély (2.5km); Au Bord de l'Eau (6.5km); Les Goudes (11km); La Maronaise (11km); Cassis (25km)

0 400 m
0 0.2 miles
E
F
G
H
To Aéroport Marseille-Provence (28km)
Autoroute Nord
Av du Général Leclerc
R de Crimée
Bd National
R Honnorat
Bd Camille Flammarion
R Jean de Bernardy
St-Charles
Pl Victor Hugo
Gare St-Charles
Bd Maurice Bourdet
Bd Charles Nédélec
R de la Joliette
Pl Jules Guesde
Jules Guesde
R Bernard du Bois
St-Charles
Pl des Marseillaises
Bd Voltaire
R Flégier
R des Petites Maries
R des Dominicaines
Bd d'Athènes
R Lafayette
R Ste-Barbe
R d'Aix
Colbert
Réformés Canebière
R Longue des Capucins
R Nationale
R Colbert
Square Léon Blum
Pl Sadi Carnot
Pl de l'Hôtel des Postes
Belsunce
Allées Léon Gambetta
Cours F Roosevelt
R Tapis Vert
Bd Dugommier
La Pleine
R Henri Barbusse
R Curiol
Grand Rue
Noailles
R Sénac de Meilhan
R St Savournin
La Canebière
Bd Garibaldi
R Coutelleine
R de Bir Hakeim
R Terrusse
Q du Port
Cours Belsunce
Vieux Port
Q des Belges
Pl du Général de Gaulle
R St-Ferréol
R d'Aubagne
Cours Lieutaud
Cours Julien
Pl Jean Jaurès
R des Trois Mages
R des Trois Rois
R Ferrari
R Francis Davso
R Estelle
Pl Thiars
Cours Honoré d'Estienne d'Orves
R Fort Notre Dame
Notre Dame du Mont-Cours Julien
R Auguste Blanqui
R Sainte
R Grignan
Pl N-D du Mont
R de la Loubière
To Hôpital de la Timone (700m)
R Montgrand
R de Lodi
Pl de la Préfecture
Estrangin Préfecture
R d'Italie
Cours Pierre Puget
Bd L Salvator
R Roux de Brignoles
R de Rome
R de Marengo
Bd Notre Dame
Bd André Aune
R Sylvabelle
R Breteuil
R du Dragon
R de Village
R Jules Moulet
R St-Suffren
R Paradis
Bd Baille
Pl Castellane
Castellane
R du Fort
Av du Prado
R de Rouet
Bd Vauban
To Le Bazar (1.7km); Stade Vélodrome (2.8km); Le Corbusier's Unité d'Habitation/Hôtel Le Corbusier (3km); Le Ventre de l'Architecte (3km); Auberge de Jeunesse de Bonneveine (4.5km); Le Millenium (6km)
2
4
7
12
13
14
15
PROVENCE

Euromed project (which seeks to gentrify the entire dockland area). The city has also produced one of France's most popular football players – the now-retired Zinedine Zidane (see p53) – as well as rising star Samir Nasri (who played for Olympique de Marseille and transferred to Arsenal in 2008).

Orientation

Stretching northeastwards from the Vieux Port (Old Port) is the city's main thoroughfare, the wide bd La Canebière (from the Provençal word *canebe*, meaning 'hemp', after Marseille's ship-rigging manufacturing industry).

The Gare St-Charles train station is north of La Canebière at the northern end of bd d'Athènes. Just a few blocks south of La Canebière, near the Notre Dame du Mont-Cours Julien metro station, is cours Julien, popular with young Marseillais for its hip cafés, restaurants and a Berlin vibe. To the north of the Vieux Port is Le Panier, Marseille's oldest quarter. The city's commercial heart around rue Paradis (southeast of Vieux Port) becomes more fashionable as you head south. The new ferry terminal is west of place de la Joliette.

Greater Marseille is divided into 16 arrondissements (suburbs); addresses in this book indicate arrondissements (1er, 2e etc).

Information

BOOKSHOPS

Fnac (Map p810; ☎ 08 25 02 00 20; Centre Bourse shopping centre; Ⓜ Vieux Port) On the top floor of the centre, off cours Belsunce (1er).

Librairie de la Bourse (Map p810; ☎ 04 91 33 63 06; 8 rue Paradis, 1er; Ⓜ Vieux Port) The best range of maps, travel books and Lonely Planet guides in Provence.

EMERGENCY

Préfecture de Police (Map p810; ☎ 04 91 39 80 00; place de la Préfecture, 1er; Ⓜ Estrangin Préfecture; 24hr)

INTERNET ACCESS

Info Café (Map p810; ☎ 04 91 33 74 98; 1 quai de Rive Neuve, 1er; Ⓜ Vieux Port; per hr adult/student €3.80/3; 9am-9pm Mon-Sat, 2.30-7.30pm Sun)

INTERNET RESOURCES

Découverte PACA (www.decouverte-paca.fr) Comprehensive information on the region (PACA stands for Provence-Alpes-Côte d'Azur), including eco-travel.

Visit Provence (www.visitprovence.com)

LAUNDRY

Laverie des Allées (Map p810; 15 allées Léon Gambetta, 1er; Ⓜ Réformés Canebière; 8am-8pm)

Laverie Self-Service (Map p810; 5 rue Breteuil, 1er; Ⓜ Vieux Port; 6.30am-8pm)

MEDICAL SERVICES

Hôpital de la Timone (☎ 04 91 38 60 00; 264 rue St-Pierre, 5e; Ⓜ La Timone) East of the city centre.

MONEY

There are a number of banks and exchange bureaux on La Canebière near the Vieux Port.

Canebière Change (Map p810; 39 La Canebière, 1er; Ⓜ Vieux Port; 8am-6pm Mon-Fri, 8.30am-noon & 2-4.30pm Sat)

POST

Main Post Office (Map p810; 1 place de l'Hôtel des Postes, 1er; Ⓜ Colbert) Offers currency exchange.

TOURIST INFORMATION

Tourist Office (Map p810; ☎ 04 91 13 89 00; www.marseille-tourisme.com; 4 La Canebière, 1er; Ⓜ Vieux Port; 9am-7pm Mon-Sat, 10am-5pm Sun)

Dangers & Annoyances

Marseille isn't a hotbed of crime, but petty crimes and muggings are commonplace. There is no need to fall into paranoia but you should avoid the Belsunce area (southwest of the train station, bounded by La Canebière, cours Belsunce and rue d'Aix, rue Bernard du Bois and bd d'Athènes).

Women *will* get unsolicited attention, anything from wolf-whistling to people walking up the street alongside them, trying to chat them up. It is generally harmless, so ignore the attention and press on.

Sights

MUSEUMS

Unless otherwise noted, museums listed here are open 10am to 5pm Tuesday to Sunday from October to May, and 11am to 6pm from June to September. Admission to permanent exhibitions costs €2/1 for adults/children. Temporary exhibitions usually cost €3/1.50. Entry is free for those under 12 or over 60.

Centre de la Vieille Charité

Initially built as a charity shelter for the town's poor, the stunning arched pink-stone courtyard of the **Centre de la Vieille Charité** (Old Charity Cultural Centre; Map p810; ☎ 04 91 14 58 80; 2 rue

PROVENCE

de la Charité, 2e; Ⓜ Joliette) now houses Marseille's beautiful **Musée d'Archéologie Méditerranéenne** (Museum of Mediterranean Archeology; ☎ 04 91 14 58 59) and **Musée d'Arts Africains, Océaniens & Amérindiens** (Museum of African, Oceanic & American Indian Art; ☎ 04 91 14 58 38). The latter houses a diverse and often striking collection, including masks from the Americas, Africa and the Pacific.

An all-inclusive ticket costs €5/2.50 per adult/student.

Musée d'Histoire de Marseille

A fascinating insight into Marseille's cultural heritage, the **Musée d'Histoire de Marseille** (Map p810; ☎ 04 91 90 42 22; ground fl, Centre Bourse shopping centre, 1er; Ⓜ Vieux Port; noon-7pm Mon-Sat) has some extraordinary exhibits, such as the remains of a merchant vessel discovered in the Vieux Port in 1974. The vessel plied the surrounding waters back in the early 3rd century AD. To preserve the soaked and decaying wood, it was freeze-dried right where it now sits behind glass. However, most of the explanatory notes are in French only.

Musée de la Mode

Contemplate contemporary fashion trends at the **Musée de la Mode** (Fashion Museum; Map p810; ☎ 04 96 17 06 00; 11 La Canebière, 1er; Ⓜ Vieux Port; adult/child €3/1.50). This stylish space has over 2000 garments and accessories in its permanent collection. Unfortunately, it regularly closes for two or three months at a time to switch exhibitions.

Musée du Santon

One of Provence's most enduring – and endearing – Christmas traditions are *santons* (from *santoùn* in Provençal, meaning 'little saint'). These plaster-moulded, kiln-fired nativity figures between 2.5cm and 15cm high were first created by Marseillais artisan Jean-Louis Lagnel (1764–1822). A private collection of 18th- and 19th-century *santons* is displayed at the **Musée du Santon** (Map p810; ☎ 04 91 54 26 58; 49 rue Neuve Ste-Catherine, 7e; Ⓜ Vieux Port; admission free; 10am-12.30pm & 2-6.30pm Tue-Sat). Entrance to the adjoining **ateliers** (workshops; 8am-1pm & 2-5pm Mon-Thu), where you can watch the figures being crafted, is also free.

Palais de Longchamp

The colonnaded **Palais de Longchamp** (Longchamp Palace; Map pp806-7; bd Philippon, 4e; Longchamp, Ⓜ Cinq Avenues Longchamp), constructed in the 1860s, was designed in part to disguise a *château d'eau* (water tower) at the terminus of an aqueduct from the River Durance. Its northern wing houses Marseille's oldest museum, the **Musée des Beaux-Arts** (☎ 04 91 14 59 30), under-

MARSEILLE IN...

Two Days

Breakfast or brunch at **Pain & Cie** (p816) before catching a boat to the **Château d'If** (p811). Revel in Monte-Cristo intrigues as you visit its cells and discover Marseille from out at sea. Back on the **Vieux Port** (p812), stroll along the quays and head up to the city's historical **Le Panier** (see boxed text, p818) area. Dine on **Chez Madie Les Galinettes'** (p815) *bouillabaisse* (fish chowder) or signature fish, and finish the evening with a mellow drink and a spot of jazz at **La Caravelle** (p817).

On the second day, get on yer bikes for a **cycling tour** (p813) to **Espace Borély**; energetic types can head all the way to Les Goudes while beach bums can chill on the beach. Catch **Le Grand Tour** (p813) to continue your visit and stop at **Basilique Notre Dame de la Garde** (p811) for sweeping views of the bay. Head to **Au Petit Nice** (p817) in artsy Cours Julien for a cheap *apéritif* and make a beeline for **Le Femina** (p815) and its barley semolina for a gigantic couscous. To finish off in style, try one of the city's clubs (p817).

Four Days

Follow the two-day itinerary. On the third day, head out to the magnificent turquoise waters of the Calanques, by boat in the summer, or by hiking in winter (p813). On the fourth day, check out the great **Musée d'Histoire de Marseille** (above) or the funky **Musée de la Mode** (above). Mooch around the many **markets** (p816) for picnic supplies and climb up to the sculpted stone benches at the **Jardin du Pharo** (p812). Hop on a bus to the beautiful **Vallon des Auffes** (p813) and finish your trip in style with a rooftop pizza at **Chez Jeannot** (p815).

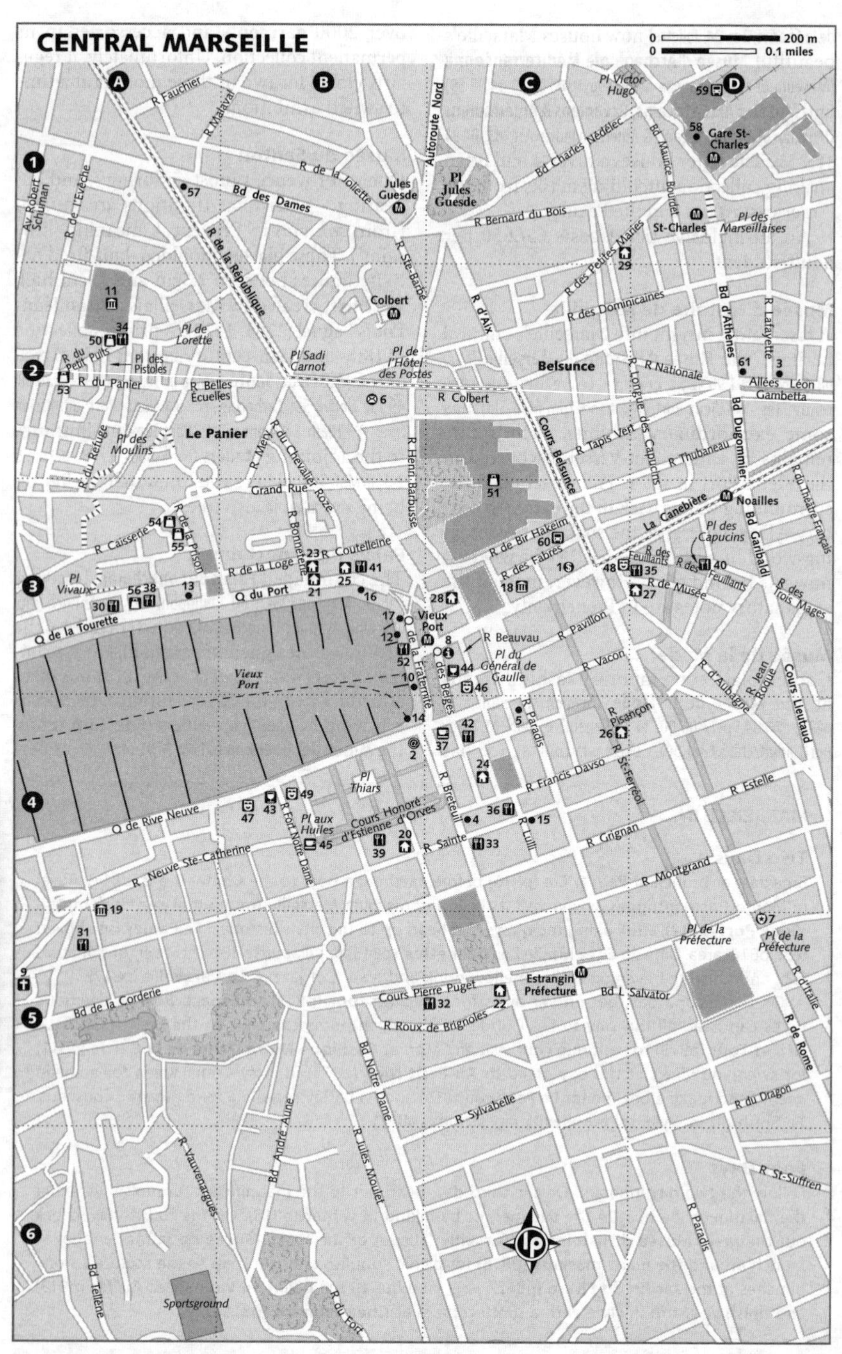
CENTRAL MARSEILLE
0 200 m
0 0.1 miles
R Fauchier
R Malaval
Autoroute Nord
Pl Victor Hugo
Gare St-Charles
Bd Charles Nédélec
Bd Maurice Bourdet
R de la Joliette
Jules Guesde
Pl Jules Guesde
Bd des Dames
Av Robert Schuman
R de l'Evêché
R de la République
R Bernard du Bois
St-Charles
Pl des Marseillaises
R des Petites Maries
R Ste-Barbe
Colbert
R d'Aix
R des Dominicaines
Bd d'Athènes
R Lafayette
Pl de Lorette
R du Petit Puits
Pl des Pistoles
R du Panier
Pl Sadi Carnot
Pl de l'Hôtel des Postes
Belsunce
R Nationale
Allées Léon Gambetta
R Belles Écuelles
R Colbert
R Longue des Capucins
Bd Dugommier
Le Panier
Pl des Moulins
R du Refuge
R Mery
R du Chevalier Roze
R Henri Barbusse
Cours Belsunce
R Tapis Vert
R Thubaneau
R du Théâtre Français
Grand Rue
R Bonneterie
La Canebière
Noailles
Bd Garibaldi
Pl des Capucins
R de la Prison
R Caisserie
R de Bir Hakeim
R des Fabres
R Coutellerie
R de la Loge
R des Feuillants
Pl Vivaux
Q du Port
R de Musée
R des Trois Mages
Q de la Tourette
Vieux Port
R de la Fraternité
R Beauvau
R Pavillon
Pl du Général de Gaulle
R Vacon
R des Belges
R d'Aubagne
R Jean Roque
Cours Lieutaud
R Paradis
R Pisançon
R St-Ferréol
Pl Thiars
R Breteuil
R Francis Davso
R Estelle
Q de Rive Neuve
R Fort Notre Dame
Pl aux Huiles
Cours Honoré d'Estienne d'Orves
R Sainte
R Lulli
R Grignan
R Neuve Ste-Catherine
R Montgrand
Pl de la Préfecture
Pl de la Préfecture
R d'Italie
Cours Pierre Puget
Estrangin Préfecture
Bd L Salvator
Bd de la Corderie
R Roux de Brignoles
R de Rome
Bd Notre Dame
R du Dragon
R Sylvabelle
R Vauvenargues
Bd André Aune
R Jules Moulet
R St-Suffren
R Paradis
Bd Tellène
Sportsground
R du Fort

PROVENCE

INFORMATION
Canebière Change ... 1 C3
Fnac ... (see 51)
Info Café ... 2 B4
Laverie des Allées ... 3 D2
Laverie Self-Service ... 4 C4
Librairie de la Bourse ... 5 C4
Main Post Office ... 6 B2
Préfecture de Police ... 7 D5
Tourist Office ... 8 C3

SIGHTS & ACTIVITIES
Abbaye St Victor ... 9 A5
Bus to Basilica ... 10 B3
Centre de la Vieille Charité ... 11 A2
Croisières Marseille Calanques Departure Point ... 12 B3
Croisières Marseille Calanques Office ... 13 A3
Frioul If Express ... 14 B4
La Bastide des Bains ... 15 C4
Le Grand Tour Departure Point ... 16 B3
Little Trains' Departure Point ... 17 B3
Musée d'Archéologie Méditerranéenne ... (see 11)
Musée d'Arts Africains, Océaniens & Amérindiens ... (see 11)
Musée de la Mode ... 18 C3
Musée d'Histoire de Marseille ... (see 51)
Musée du Santon ... 19 A4

SLEEPING
Etap Hotel ... 20 B4
Hôtel Belle-Vue ... 21 B3
Hôtel du Palais ... 22 C5
Hôtel Hermès ... 23 B3
Hôtel Relax ... 24 C4
Hôtel Résidence du Vieux Port ... 25 B3
Hôtel Saint-Ferréol ... 26 C4
Hôtel St-Louis ... 27 C3
New Hôtel Vieux Port ... 28 C3
Vertigo ... 29 C1

EATING
Chez Madie Les Galinettes ... 30 A3
Four des Navettes ... 31 A5
Fruit & Vegetable Market ... 32 C5
La Part des Anges ... 33 C4
Le Clan des Cigales ... 34 A2
Le Femina ... 35 D3
Le Mas ... 36 C4
Le Méditerranée ... 37 C4
Le Souk ... 38 A3
Les Arcenaulx ... 39 B4
Marché des Capucins ... 40 D3
Miramar ... 41 B3
O'Stop ... 42 C4

DRINKING
Le Bar de la Marine ... 43 B4
L'OM Café ... 44 C3
Pain & Cie ... 45 B4

ENTERTAINMENT
Kiut Bar ... 46 C3
La Caravelle ... (see 21)
Le Trolleybus ... 47 B4
OM's Boutique Officielle ... 48 C3
Pelle Mêle ... 49 B4

SHOPPING
72% Pétanque ... 50 A2
Centre Bourse Shopping Centre ... 51 C3
Ceramic Ateliers ... (see 50)
Fish Market ... 52 B3
La Chocolatière du Panier ... 53 A2
La Cie de Provence ... 54 A3
La Comptoir du Panier ... 55 A3
La Maison du Pastis ... 56 A3

TRANSPORT
Algérie Ferries ... 57 A1
Avis ... 58 D1
Bus Station ... 59 D1
Espace Infos RTM ... 60 C3
Eurolines ... 61 D2
Europcar ... (see 58)
SNCF Boutique ... (see 51)

going extensive renovations at press time and slated to reopen in 2012. The shaded park is one of the few green spaces in the centre.

BASILIQUE NOTRE DAME DE LA GARDE

Be blown away by the celestial bay and city views and knockout 19th-century architecture at the hilltop **Basilique Notre Dame de la Garde** (Map pp806-7; ☎ 04 91 13 40 80; montée de la Bonne Mère; admission free; basilica & crypt 7am-7pm, longer hr in summer), the opulent Romano-Byzantine basilica that dominates Marseille's skyline.

Found 1km south of the Vieux Port, the domed basilica was built between 1853 and 1864 and is ornamented with coloured marble, intricate gold-laid mosaics that were superbly restored in 2006, and murals. Its bell tower is crowned by a 9.7m-tall gilded statue of the Virgin Mary on a 12m-high pedestal. Bullet marks and vivid shrapnel scars on the cathedral's northern facade mark the fierce fighting that took place here during Marseille's Battle of Liberation (15–25 August 1944).

Bus 60 links the Vieux Port with the basilica. Otherwise, there's a **little train** (Map p810; per person €5; contact the tourist office for seasonal schedules), which departs from the port for the 20-minute trip up the steep hill. It gives you 20 minutes to look around before taking the trip back down. By foot, count on it taking about 30 minutes each way from the Vieux Port.

CHÂTEAU D'IF

Immortalised in Alexandre Dumas' classic 1840s novel *Le Comte de Monte Cristo* (The Count of Monte Cristo), the 16th-century fortress-turned-prison **Château d'If** (off Map pp806-7; ☎ 04 91 59 02 30; adult/student €5/3.50; 9.30am-6.30pm May-Aug, 9.30am-5.30pm Tue-Sun Sep-Mar, 9.30am-5.30pm daily Apr) sits on a 3-hectare island 3.5km west of the Vieux Port. Political prisoners of all persuasions were incarcerated here, along with hundreds of Protestants (many of whom perished in the dungeons), the Revolutionary hero Mirabeau (who didn't have such a bad time once he'd seduced the cook) and the Communards of 1871.

Boats run by **Frioul If Express** (Map p810; ☎ 04 91 46 54 65; www.frioul-if-express.com; 1 quai des Belges, 1er) leave for the Château d'If from the Vieux Port at the corner of quai de la Fraternité and quai de Rive Neuve. There are more than 15 boats a day in summer, with fewer in winter (€10 return, 20 minutes).

ÎLES DU FRIOUL

A few hundred metres west of the Château d'If are the islands of **Ratonneau** and **Pomègues**. The tiny islands (each about 2.5km long, and totalling 200 hectares) were linked by a dyke in the 1820s. From the 17th to 19th centuries they were used as a place of quarantine for people suspected of carrying the plague or cholera. Marseille's population was ravaged by the plague in 1720 when a merchant vessel carrying the disease broke the quarantine so as not to lose its shipment. The epidemics killed around 50,000 of the city's 90,000 inhabitants.

Sea birds and rare plants thrive on the islands today. The island of Ratonneau is still sprinkled with the ruins of the old yellow-fever quarantine hospital, Hôpital Caroline, and Fort Ratonneau (used by German troops during WWII). There is also a 700-boat marina on Pomègues.

Boats to the Château d'If also serve the Îles du Frioul (€10 return; €15 for a combined ticket; 35 minutes).

VIEUX PORT AREA

Ships have docked for more than 26 centuries at Marseille's colourful Vieux Port. Although the main commercial docks were transferred to the Joliette area on the coast north of here in the 1840s, it still overflows with fishing craft, yachts and local ferries.

Guarding the harbour are **Bas Fort St-Nicolas** (Map pp806–7) on the southern side and, across the water, **Fort St-Jean** (Map pp806–7), founded in the 13th century by the Knights Hospitaller of St John of Jerusalem.

In 1943 the neighbourhood on the northern side of the quai du Port, historic Le Panier quarter (Map p810; see p818), was dynamited, and much of it was rebuilt afterwards. Today its winding, narrow streets are a jumble of artisan's shops, and washing lines strung outside terraced houses.

MAX OUT MARSEILLE

To max out your time in Marseille, the **Marseille City Pass** (1-/2-day pass €20/27) gives you access to the city's museums; guided tours of the town; and unlimited travel on all public transport (as well as the little train). It also includes the boat trip and entrance to the Château d'If, and offers various discounts, such as for the Le Grand Tour tourist bus. For adults, the pass quickly pays for itself – however, it's not necessary for children under 12, as many attractions are greatly reduced or free.

Standing guard between the old and the 'new' port, is the striking Byzantine-style **Cathédrale de la Major**. Its 'stripy' facade is made of Cassis stone (local white stone) and green marble from Florence. Amazingly, this unique monument has stood in a bit of a wasteland for many years but it is set to become one of the centrepieces of the dockland redevelopment, so watch this space, literally!

On the Vieux Port's southern side, late-night restaurants and cafés pack the **place Thiars** and **cours Honoré d'Estienne d'Orves** pedestrian zone.

Northeast of La Canebière and cours Belsunce, the run-down **Belsunce** (Map p810) area is slowly being rehabilitated.

For chic, street-smart shopping, stroll west to the fashionable **6th arrondissement**, especially pedestrianised **Rue St-Ferréol**. The newly rehabilitated **rue de la République** is also fast becoming an alternative shop-till-you-drop main street.

Heading west of the Vieux Port brings you to the **Abbaye St-Victor** (Map p810), birthplace of Christianity in Marseille, built on a 3rd century BC necropolis. Perched at the edge of the peninsula is the **Jardin du Pharo** (Map pp806–7), a perfect picnic spot.

LE CORBUSIER'S UNITÉ D'HABITATION

Visionary architect Le Corbusier redefined urban living in 1952 with the completion of his vertical, 337-apartment 'garden city', **Unité d'Habitation** (off Map pp806-7; ☎ 04 91 16 78 00; www.hotellecorbusier.com; 280 bd Michelet, 8e; Ⓜ Le Corbusier; 🕑 by appointment), also known as Cité Radieuse (Radiant City). Along its darkened hallways, primary-coloured downlights create eerie tunnels leading to a minisupermarket, architectural bookshop and panoramic rooftop 'desert garden'.

Even if you're not staying at its hotel (p814), you can arrange to visit this tour de force or dine at its restaurant, **Le Ventre de l'Architecte** (☎ 04 91 16 78 00; mains €8 to €12; 🕑 lunch Mon-Fri, dinner Mon-Sat) – a gourmet bistro specialising in pâté de foie gras (duck or goose liver pâté), with shimmering views of the Mediterranean. Or you could look out for the proliferation of high-rises that Le Corbusier inspired. Catch bus 83 or 21 to Le Corbusier stop.

Acivities

From the Vieux Port, the **little train** (p811) tootles around Le Panier's hilly streets, but to

THE CALANQUES, SOON A NATIONAL PARK?

Just a few miles east of Marseille lies the **Calanques**, a small piece of perfectly unspoilt Mediterranean landscape: turquoise, translucent water lapping the sheer cliffs of the indented coast, interrupted every now and then by a small idyllic beach.

The area is cherished by Marseillais who love to come here to soak up some rays or go for a long Sunday walk. The site has always been protected but a project is now underway to turn the Calanques into a national park by 2010.

Whether or not the project goes ahead, you will still be able to go hiking along the many maquis-lined trails from October to June, and when the fire risks are too high over the summer months, you can take a boat trip. From Marseille, heading to the nearby village of Cassis makes for a great day trip – after a glorious morning travelling along the Calanques' coves, lunch and a bottle of crisp Cassis white at one of the port-side restaurants is just the ticket. If you're interested in wines of the area, **Cassis' tourist office** (☎ 04 42 01 71 17; quai des Moulins; 🕑 9am-12.30pm & 2-6pm Tue-Sat) supplies a free list and map of all the cellars you can visit for tastings.

see more of the city under your own steam – and for a wicked **cycling tour** – hop on one of Marseille's **le vélo** (see p819). Pedal up towards the Pharo area and then south along the corniche to take in the seascape. Stop at the cute **Vallon des Auffes** before pressing on towards the beaches and leisure areas of **Espace Borély**, where cycle lanes start. The trip is about 6km. For those feeling more energetic, it's a 10km return trip from Borély to the charming hamlet of **Les Goudes**, where it used to be all the rage to own a fishing cabin.

For a DIY walking tour, the free city map handed out by the tourist office outlines three **walking circuits**.

If you're in need of a little TLC after stomping around Marseille, **La Bastide des Bains** (☎ 04 91 33 39 13; www.bastide-des-bains.com, in French; 19 rue Sainte; 🕑 10am-8pm Mon-Sat, to 6pm Sun) runs a beautiful hammam with mixed and women-only opening hours. Entrance is €30; treatments are available.

Tours

Le Grand Tour (☎ 04 91 91 05 82; adult/student/child €16/13/8; 🕑 10am-4pm) is handy for getting around as well as for seeing the city. This hop-on, hop-off, open-topped double-decker bus travels between the main sights and museums, taking in the Vieux Port, the corniche and Basilique Notre Dame de la Garde, accompanied by a five-language audio guide. Buy tickets from the tourist office or on the bus. The best place to join the tour is at the Vieux Port.

The tourist office offers various guided tours, including an English-language **walking tour** (per person €6.50; 🕑 10am Sat Jul & Aug, 2pm every other Sat Sep-Jun) of Le Panier quarter.

Croisières Marseille Calanques (☎ 08 25 13 68 00; www.croisieres-marseille-calanques.com, in French; 74 quai du Port, 2e) runs boat trips (with French commentary only) from the Vieux Port to Cassis and back (€25). Trips pass by the coves and clear turquoise waters of the **Calanques** (see boxed text, above).

Sleeping

Marseille's hotel scene has come a long way in the last two or three years. There are now genuinely charming or funky addresses, although the hostel scene is still underdeveloped for a city of this size.

BUDGET

Auberge de Jeunesse de Bonneveine (off Map pp806-7; ☎ 04 91 17 63 30; www.fuaj.org; impasse du Docteur Bonfils, 8e; dm €17.10, d incl sheets & breakfast €40.60; 🕑 Feb-Dec; 💻 ⊠) The building looks like a primary school, the rooms are spartan and it is a fair way out of town, *but* it is close to the beach, and it organises loads of subsidised (ie cheap) activities such as kayaking, hiking and kitesurfing. It also has a bar with a pool table, a terrace and a small restaurant. Bus 44 (stop Bonnefon) is just 200m away.

our pick **Vertigo** (Map p810; ☎ 04 91 91 07 11; www.hotelvertigo.fr; 42 rue des Petites Maries, 1er; Ⓜ Gare St-Charles SNCF; dm €23.90, d €55-65; 💻) This new boutique hostel has kissed goodbye to dodgy bunk beds, itchy blankets and hospital-like decor. Here it's 'hello' to vintage posters, a designer chrome kitchen, groovy communal spaces and trendy multilingual staff. Obviously, there's no curfew. The double rooms are particularly funky, either in the two *cabanons* (traditional fishing cabins) at the back of the courtyard or in the main building, some with their own private terrace or balcony.

Hôtel Le Richelieu (Map pp806-7; ☎ 04 91 31 01 92; www.lerichelieu-marseille.com; 52 corniche Président John F Kennedy, 7e; d €46-110) This beach-house-type hotel has gone a little over-the-top on the old bright-coloured walls during its recent refurbishment, but the balconies, sea views, idyllic breakfast terrace and adjacent beach (June to September only) are still there, so no complaints.

Etap Hotel (Map p810; ☎ 08 92 68 05 82; fax 04 91 54 95 67; 46 rue Sainte, 1er; Ⓜ Vieux Port; s/d/tr €49/58/67;) Try for one of the large, wood-beamed rooms in the old building (a former sea captain's house), which add a smidgen of charm to this otherwise somewhat soulless chain establishment. English-speaking staff are super helpful, and there's a good buffet breakfast for only €5. There are also 13 prized covered parking spaces (€8).

Hôtel Relax (Map p810; ☎ 04 91 33 15 87; http://relaxhotel.free.fr, in French; 4 rue Corneille, 1er; Ⓜ Vieux Port; s €40, d €55-60;) In a dress-circle location overlooking Marseille's art deco Opera House, this 20-room hotel is run by a lovely family. Noise insulation between rooms is not great –you're likely to wake up at the same time as your neighbours. Rooms are, however, comfortable and clean, and a bargain for the location.

MIDRANGE

Hôtel Hermès (Map p810; ☎ 04 96 11 63 63; www.hotelmarseille.com; 2 rue Bonneterie, 2e; Ⓜ Vieux Port; s €50, d €68-85, nuptial ste €97;) The rooms are a little small and in need of a lick of paint, but they're otherwise clean and bright. There's a fabulous roof terrace on which to have breakfast or an evening drink. The elevated, rooftop nuptial suite, with its own private terrace and designer bathroom, will make you feel like you're on top of the world.

Hôtel Le Corbusier (off Map pp806-7; ☎ 04 91 16 78 00; www.hotellecorbusier.com; 280 bd Michelet, 8e; cabin with shared toilet €59, d €94-120;) It's not for everyone, but staying at the 20-room hotel within this iconic concrete monolith is certainly an architectural experience, and a chance to absorb Le Corbusier's legacy. The cabins can be quite unsettling but the recently spruced-up double rooms look very sharp indeed, particularly those with sublime sea views and Le Corbusier chairs. The owner is hugely knowledgeable. Catch bus 83 or 21 to Le Corbusier stop.

Hôtel Péron (Map pp806-7; ☎ 04 91 31 01 41; www.hotel-peron.com; 119 corniche Président John F Kennedy, 7e; d €60-85;) This unusual 1920s period piece houses museum-like rooms with preserved original art deco turquoise-and-black ceramic bathrooms and parquet floors inlaid with geometric motifs. Many rooms have balconies to enjoy the sea views, although you'll hear noise from the road below.

Hôtel St-Louis (Map p810; ☎ 04 91 54 02 74; www.hotel-st-louis.com; 2 rue des Récollettes, 1er; Canebière Garibaldi, Ⓜ Noailles; d €65-90;) Behind the beautiful red 1800s facade, with its wrought-iron balconies and pale green shutters, lies this gorgeous boutique place with character-filled rooms – round windows, high or sloping ceilings, four-poster beds, expensive mattresses and discreet vintage furniture. You'll get the idea as soon as you walk up to the reception area with its pretty breakfast room, glass-case bookshelves and reading corner.

Hôtel Belle-Vue (Map p810; ☎ 04 96 17 05 40; www.hotel-bellevue-marseille.fr; 34 quai du Port, 2e; Ⓜ Vieux Port; d €68-122, tr €137;) Don't be put off by the rambling facade of this seminal hotel: inside, the highly individual rooms all offer the same comfort, splendid views of the basilica and tasteful surroundings. And you only have to walk down a couple of floors to find one of Marseille's coolest bars (see La Caravelle, p817).

Le Ryad (Map pp806-7; ☎ 04 91 47 74 54; www.leryad.fr; 16 rue Sénac de Meilhan, 1er; Canebière Garibaldi, Ⓜ Noailles; s €75-120, d €95-140) With wrought-iron four-poster beds, arched alcoves, warm colours and minimalist decor, this latest addition to Marseille's hotel scene mixes Moroccan influences with modern tendencies. It is a tad over-priced so make the most of your Moroccan pancakes for breakfast.

Villa Monticelli (off Map pp806-7; ☎ 04 91 22 15 20; www.villamonticelli.com; 96 rue du Commandant Rolland, 8e; d €85-110) Colette and Jean are passionate about their city and will share with you all their secrets and best addresses. The five exquisite *chambre d'hôte* (B&B) rooms in their stunning villa are absolutely worth the slightly outer-city location. The amazing breakfast of homemade everything (jams, yoghurts, crêpes etc) will get you started in the morning, with panoramic views from the terrace to boot. It's probably the best value for money for this type of accommodation.

Hôtel Résidence du Vieux Port (Map p810; ☎ 04 91 91 91 22; www.hotelmarseille.com; 18 quai du Port, 2e;

PROVENCE

(M) Vieux Port; d €93-137, apt €165;) The views from here of the old port and Notre Dame de la Garde are the best in town, and the balconies on which to enjoy them are a godsend. However, the print wallpaper in the Provençal rooms is overwhelming, to say the least, so try for one of the 'traditional' rooms instead. The two-room apartments are great for families.

Hôtel Saint-Ferréol (Map p810; ☎ 04 91 33 12 21; www.hotelsaintferreol.com; 19 rue Pisançon, 1er; (M) Vieux Port; d €95-99;) On the corner of the city's most beautiful lamp-lit pedestrian shopping street, you'll find this very plush hotel with its individually and richly decorated rooms (many inspired by famous artists such as Van Gogh or Cézanne). There is wi-fi throughout, and very friendly staff.

Hôtel du Palais (Map pp806-7; ☎ 04 91 37 78 86; www.hotelmarseille.com; 26 rue Breteuil, 6e; (M) Estrangin Préfecture; d €95-109;) Ten of the 22 rooms at this stylish hotel have heavenly king-sized beds. As for colours, you'll have a choice of raspberry pink, pale lavender blues or serene beige. There is also a business corner and wi-fi.

TOP END

New Hôtel Vieux Port (Map p810; ☎ 04 91 99 23 23; www.new-hotel.com; 3bis rue Reine Elisabeth, 1er; (M) Vieux Port; s €140-220, d €160-240;) Sophisticated, central and decorated with an eye for detail, the rooms in this hotel are themed according to exotic locales such as Mexico, India, Morocco, Japan and Africa. The dining room with its high ceilings and seven French windows promises a grand start to the day.

Le Petit Nice-Passédat (off Map pp806-7; ☎ 04 91 59 25 92; www.passedat.fr; Anse de Maldormé, 7e; d low/high season from €230/370;) Nestled into the rocks above a petite cove, this is an idyllic hideaway of just 16 individually and exquisitely appointed rooms overlooking the mosaic-tiled saltwater pool and cacti garden. It's also home to Gerald Passédat's virtuoso restaurant (mains €51 to €95, open for lunch and dinner Tuesday to Saturday), which reached gastronomic consecration in 2008 by receiving its third Michelin star.

Sofitel Marseille Vieux Port (Map pp806-7; ☎ 04 91 15 59 55; www.sofitel-marseille-vieuxport.com; 36 bd Charles Livon, 7e; d from €195; (P)) Gaze at the beautiful old port while having a bath in the oversized square tub of the most recently renovated rooms; fall asleep the minute your head hits your 100% feather bed; and enjoy the enchanting views of the city and the port anywhere from the lobby, bar or restaurant. Excellent wheelchair access.

Eating

Marseille's signature dish *bouillabaisse* is a fish soup made from five different fish, along with tomatoes, white wine, fennel and saffron, and served with *rouille* (garlic mayonnaise) and croutons. It is therefore an expensive dish. Any less than €35 and it won't be the genuine article.

RESTAURANTS

The Vieux Port overflows with restaurants. For fare as diverse as Marseille itself, cours Julien and its surrounding streets are jammed with French, Indian, Antillean, Pakistani, Thai, Armenian, Lebanese, Tunisian and Italian restaurants.

Le Femina (Map p810; ☎ 04 91 54 03 56; 1 rue de Musée, 1er; Canebière Garibaldi, (M) Noailles; menus €15; closed Sun & Mon) Heading east from the Vieux Port towards cours Julien, Le Femina is a great – and affordable – traditional Algerian place for succulent couscous (you should definitely try the barley semolina).

our pick **Chez Madie Les Galinettes** (Map p810; ☎ 04 91 90 40 87; 138 quai du Port, 2e; mains €25-50, menus €15/22/27; lunch & dinner Mon-Sat, closed Sat lunch in summer) They're so friendly at Madie's that you'll leave feeling as though you've just had dinner with friends. The port-side terrace is perfect for those long summer evenings, and if the weather is not on your side, the great modern art collection on the walls inside will bring consolation. There's lots of fish on the menu, including the house speciality *Les Galinettes*, as well as a great *bouillabaisse* that you'll need to order in advance.

La Part des Anges (Map p810; ☎ 04 91 33 55 70; 33 rue Sainte; mains €15, lunch & dinner Mon-Sat, dinner Sun) The name *la part des anges* (angels' share) refers to the amount of alcohol that evaporates through a barrel during wine (or whisky) fermentation. But at this gem of a wine bistro in Marseille's centre, you'd be best not to lose an ounce or a drop of whatever you eat or drink: the French fare is cooked to perfection and the wine list is an oenologist's dream.

Chez Jeannot (Map pp806-7; ☎ 04 91 52 11 28; 129 rue du Vallon des Auffes; mains €15-22; lunch & dinner Tue-Sat, lunch Sun, closed Mon) An institution among Marseillais, the rooftop terrace overlooking the stunning Vallon des Auffes is booked out days in advance. The atmosphere is jovial and uncomplicated, just like the thin-crust pizzas, *grillades* (grilled meats) and seafood that land on your plate. One of the most authentic addresses in town.

Le Souk (Map p810; ☎ 04 91 91 29 29; 100 quai du Port, 2e; Ⓜ Vieux Port; menus €20-30; ⏰ lunch & dinner Tue-Sat, lunch Sun) Thanks to Marseille's heritage, you'll eat some of the best North African food this side of the Med. Le Souk is one such place, with great *tajines* (slow-cooked meat and vegetable stews) and wonderful almond and pistachio pastries saturated in honey.

Au Bord de l'Eau (off Map pp806-7; ☎ 04 91 72 68 04; 15 rue des Arapèdes, port de la Madrague Montredon, 8e; menus €25-30; ⏰ lunch & dinner Mon & Thu-Sun, lunch Tue Sep–mid-Jun, lunch & dinner Thu-Sun, dinner Mon-Wed mid-Jun–Aug)'At the water's edge' is the kind of place Marseillais cherish: easy on the frills, heavy on outdoor space, steady on the price and artistic on the plate. The *menus* (fixed-price menus) have the usual pizza, pasta and fresh fish. Catch bus 83 along the coast to av du Prado (by the statue of David), then take bus 19 further south along the coast.

Miramar (Map p810; ☎ 04 91 90 10 40; 12 quai du Port, 2e; Ⓜ Vieux Port; mains €25-50; ⏰ lunch & dinner Tue-Sat) Dine on expensive seafood or *bouillabaisse*, beneath glowing burgundy wall-mounted lamps in the dining rooms, or on a burgundy velveteen settee at the white-clothed tables on the *quai*-side (quay-side) terrace. The chef runs cooking classes (€120) where he reveals his seafood secrets; see the tourist office for information and bookings.

Le Mas (Map p810; ☎ 04 91 33 25 90; 4 rue Lulli; Ⓜ Estrangin Préfecture; menu €25; ⏰ lunch & dinner, open till 6am, closed Sun Oct-Apr) The walls of Le Mas are lined with photographs of stars, showbiz types, celebs and other insomniac artists who dine at this little late-night place that has become a Marseille institution. The food is rich, perfect for famished night-owls.

Les Arcenaulx (Map p810; ☎ 04 91 59 80 30; 27 cours Honoré d'Estienne d'Orves, 1er; Ⓜ Vieux Port; menus €30-50; ⏰ lunch & dinner Mon-Sat) Born out of the tumultuous arsenal's history, this cavernous complex contains an antiquarian and contemporary bookshop with a specialist interest in gastronomy, as well as a bookshelves-lined restaurant and *salon de thé* (tearoom) serving ice creams named after literary classics.

Chez Fonfon (Map pp806-7; ☎ 04 91 52 14 38; 140 rue du Vallon des Auffes, 7e; mains around €40; ⏰ lunch & dinner Tue-Sat, dinner Mon) Overlooking the enchanting little harbour Vallon des Auffes, Chez Fonfon is famed for its *bouillabaisse*. The place is quite formal, although the wonderful views brighten things up, as does the lush list of local rosés and crisp Cassis white wines. Book ahead.

Péron (Map pp806-7; ☎ 04 91 52 15 22; 56 corniche Président John F Kennedy, 7e; menus €56-68; ⏰ lunch & dinner Tue-Sat, lunch Sun) If you're going to throw budgetary caution to the wind, do it at this designer, sun-decked place perched on the edge of the corniche, opposite the Château d'If. The food (marinated tuna, scallops with lemon polenta) is phenomenal, and the views of the Med, particularly at sunset, are mesmerising.

CAFÉS

Cafés crowd quai de Rive Neuve and cours Honoré Estienne d'Orves (6e), a large, long, open square two blocks south of the quay. Another cluster overlooks place de la Préfecture, at the southern end of rue St-Ferréol (1er).

Le Méditerranée (Map p810; ☎ 04 91 55 58 32; 51 quai des Belges, 2e; Ⓜ Vieux Port; juice €4, snacks €3-6.50; ⏰ 9am-7pm winter, 9am-9pm summer) Get a vitamin fix with a freshly squeezed fruit juice or bite into tasty crêpes or panini as you wait for your boat to the Château d'If.

O'Stop (Map p810; ☎ 04 91 33 85 34; 15 rue St-Saëns, 1er; Ⓜ Vieux Port; menu €10; ⏰ 24hr) Ideal for late-night munchies, O'Stop is the only place in town to serve hot and cold sustenance around the clock.

Pain & Cie (Map p810; ☎ 04 91 33 55 00; 18 place aux Huiles, 1er; Ⓜ Vieux Port; brunch €19; ⏰ Tue-Sat 8am-10.30pm, 8am-6pm Sun & Mon) Trendy locals brunch here at the weekend or come for a quick *tartine* (posh French for 'sandwich') at lunchtime, or cake and coffee in the afternoon.

SELF-CATERING

Stock up on fruit and vegetables at **Marché des Capucins** (Map p810; place des Capucins, 1er; 🚊 Canebière Garibaldi, Ⓜ Noailles; ⏰ 8am-7pm Mon-Sat), one block south of La Canebière; and at the **fruit and vegetable market** (Map pp806-7; cours Pierre Puget, 6e; Ⓜ Estrangin Préfecture; ⏰ 8am-1pm Mon-Fri).

See opposite for more market listings.

For picnic treats, the **Four des Navettes** (Map pp806-7; ☎ 04 91 33 32 12; 136 rue Sainte) sells the iconic boat-shaped, orange-flower Navette biscuits by the half-dozen as well as other southern delicacies and bread.

There are a couple of supermarkets in the monstrous concrete bunker that is the Centre Bourse shopping centre (Map p810).

PROVENCE

Drinking

Options for a coffee or something stronger abound on and around the Vieux Port. Students and artists congregate at the alternative cafés and bars of cours Julien and its surrounding streets.

Au Petit Nice (Map pp806-7; ☎ 04 91 48 43 04; 28 place Jean Jaurès, 6e; Ⓜ Notre Dame du Mont-Cours Julien; 🕑 6.30am-2am) A living illustration of what cheap and cheerful means: €2 a drink, whatever it is – how could you not be happy?

Le Bar de la Marine (Map p810; ☎ 04 91 54 95 42; 15 quai de Rive Neuve, 7e; Ⓜ Vieux Port; 🕑 7am-1am) Marcel Pagnol filmed the card party scenes in *Marius* at this Marseille institution, which draws folks from every walk of life.

L'OM Café (Map p810; ☎ 04 91 33 80 33; 3 quai des Belges, 1er; Ⓜ Vieux Port; menus €15-25; 🕑 7am-1am) If you haven't managed to bag tickets to watch the city's football team play, this is the place to come and watch the game (unless you want to support the rival team, in which case you should leave Marseille).

Entertainment

Cultural events are covered in *L'Hebdo* (in French; €1.20), available around town. The website www.marseillebynight.com (in French) also has listings.

Tickets for most events are sold at *billetteries* (ticket counters) including Fnac (p808) as well as the tourist office.

To get a feel for Marseille's heart and soul, go and watch the city's cherished football team, Olympique de Marseille (OM), play at its home ground **Stade Vélodrome** (off Map pp806-7; 3 bd Michelet, 8e; Ⓜ rond point du Prado). It's almost more about supporters and atmosphere than about players and game. Tickets are sold in town at **OM's Boutique Officielle** (Map p810; ☎ 04 91 33 52 28; 44 La Canebière, 1er; 🚊 Canebière Garibaldi, Ⓜ Noailles; 🕑 10am-7pm Mon-Sat) and cost as little as €20.

LIVE MUSIC

La Caravelle (Map p810; ☎ 04 96 17 05 40; 34 quai du Port, 2e; Ⓜ Vieux Port; 🕑 7am-2am) Live jazz and chilled vibes are what's waiting for you at Hôtel Belle-Vue's (p814) 1st-floor bar. On balmy nights, a mojito on the small balcony overlooking the port is just the ticket, and in winter, the timber-lined walls, wooden tables and red vinyl upholstered chairs are wonderfully atmospheric.

Pelle Mêle (Map p810; ☎ 04 91 54 85 26; 8 place aux Huiles, 1er; Ⓜ Vieux Port; 🕑 5pm-1am) Jive to more good jazz at this lively bistro near the port. Bands start at around 10pm.

L'Intermédiaire (Map pp806-7; ☎ 04 91 47 01 25; 63 place Jean Jaurès, 6e; Ⓜ Notre Dame du Mont-Cours Julien; 🕑 7pm-2am Mon-Sat) This grungy venue with its graffitied walls is one of the best venues in town for live music, bands or DJs; and if you're game, the stage is yours every Tuesday night.

NIGHTCLUBS

La Maronaise (off Map pp806-7; ☎ 04 91 72 79 39; rte de la Maronaise, 8e; admission €20; 🕑 9am-5am Wed-Sat early May-early Sep) At this uberhip hang-out at Les Goudes on Cap Croisette, slide into a sun lounge and enjoy the private little sand beach before dancing under the stars till dawn. Take bus 19.

Other happenin' haunts:

Le Bazar (off Map pp806-7; ☎ 06 23 40 42 59; 90 bd Rabatau, 8e; admission €10-20, ladies free Fri; 🕑 midnight-6am Thu-Sun) Vast Moroccan-style space with bungalows and palms.

Le Millenium (off Map pp806-7; ☎ 06 15 62 54 97; rte de Cassis, 9e; admission €20; 🕑 11pm-6am Thu-Sat) Particularly popular with students living on the nearby campus, this is the place to listen to techno house beats. About 6km from the city.

Le Trolleybus (Map p810; ☎ 04 91 54 30 45; 24 quai de Rive Neuve, 7e; Ⓜ Vieux Port; 🕑 11pm-dawn Wed-Sat) Shake your booty to techno, funk, indie and more inside this tunnel-like harbourside club.

GAY & LESBIAN VENUES

The website www.gaymapmarseille.com has good coverage of Marseille's and Aix-en-Provence's gay scene, with everything from bars to bookshops. **Kiut Bar** (Map p810; ☎ 04 91 33 04 26; 10 rue Beauvau, 1e; Ⓜ Vieux Port; 🕑 6pm-late) is the most happening gay venue in town. It even has a see-through shower (yes) where you can err, wash (open *douche* on Tuesdays).

Shopping

You'll find artisan specialities in the streets spiralling out from the Vieux Port, especially in **Le Panier** (see boxed text, p818).

MARKETS

The small but enthralling **fish market** (Map p810; quai des Belges; Ⓜ Vieux Port; 🕑 8am-1pm) is a daily fixture at the Vieux Port docks. Cours Julien hosts a Wednesday-morning organic fruit and vegetable market and an Aladdin's cave bric-a-brac market every second Sunday of

MARSEILLE'S BASKET

North of the Vieux Port, Marseille's old city, Le Panier quarter (2e) translates as 'the basket', and was the site of the Greek *agora* (marketplace). In its history-woven streets you can get your fill of its past, as well as fill your shopping basket with products handmade by artisans in Marseille.

Sniff scented soaps at **La Cie de Provence** (Map p810; ☎ 04 91 56 20 94; 1 rue Caisserie), and pick up bathroom accoutrements like colourful towels at the neighbouring **La Comptoir du Panier** (Map p810; ☎ 04 91 91 29 65; 5 rue de la Prison). Olive soaps, olive oils and brilliantly named preserves (Gratte-Cul meaning 'Scratchy Ass' being just one of them; for the record, it's dog-rose jam) fill **72% Pétanque** (Map p810; ☎ 04 91 91 14 57; 10 rue du Petit Puits). Nearby are a clutch of ceramic ateliers with shops attached to their workshops, which you can just pop into. For sustenance, **Le Clan des Cigales** (Map p810; ☎ 06 63 78 07 83; 8 rue du Petit Puits) serves homemade aïoli (a traditional Provençal garlic mayonnaise served with cod, winkles, poached vegetables and hard-boiled eggs) on Fridays, savoury tarts and good vegetarian options.

For food shopping, try **La Chocolatière du Panier** (Map p810; ☎ 04 91 91 67 66; 49 rue du Petit Puits), with original flavours of handmade chocolates such as fig and *calisson* (marzipan). For drinks, head to **La Maison du Pastis** (Map p810; ☎ 04 91 90 86 77; 108 quai du Port), where you can sample more than 90 varieties of pastis (an aniseed-flavoured *apéritif*) or splash out on absinthe.

the month (running from 8am to 7pm; metro Notre Dame du Mont-Cours Julien).

Marseille's biggest market, the daily **Prado Market** (Map pp806-7; Ⓜ Castellane or Périer; ⌚ 8am-1pm) stretches from the Castellane metro station along av du Prado to the Périer metro station, with a staggering array of clothes, fruit, vegetables and speciality items – and a flower market on Friday morning.

Getting There & Away

AIR

Aéroport Marseille-Provence (☎ 04 42 14 14 14; www.marseille.aeroport.fr), also known as Aéroport Marseille-Marignane, is 25km northwest of town in Marignane. It has numerous flights to Europe and North Africa, including flights with low-cost airlines.

BOAT

Marseille's **passenger ferry terminal** (Map pp806-7; ☎ 04 91 39 40 00; www.marseille-port.fr; Ⓜ Joliette) is 250m south of place de la Joliette (1er).

The **Société Nationale Maritime Corse-Méditerranée** (SNCM; Map pp806-7; ☎ 08 25 88 80 88; www.sncm.fr; 61 bd des Dames, 2e; Ⓜ Joliette; ⌚ 8am-6pm Mon-Fri, 8.30am-noon & 2-5.30pm Sat) links Marseille with Corsica (see p907), Sardinia and Tunisia. It also serves Algeria, although services are prone to disruption/cancellation because of the political troubles there.

See the Transport chapter for more information on ferry services to/from North Africa (p967) and Sardinia (p967).

There is an office for **Algérie Ferries** (Map p810; ☎ 04 91 90 89 28; 58 bd des Dames, 2e; Ⓜ Colbert; ⌚ 9am-noon & 1-5pm Mon-Fri).

BUS

The **bus station** (Map p810; ☎ 08 91 02 40 25; 3 rue Honnorat, 3e; Ⓜ Gare St-Charles SNCF) is at the back of the train station. Tickets can be purchased from the information desk inside the train station or from the driver.

Buses travel to Aix-en-Provence (€4.60, 35 minutes via the autoroute or one hour via the N8, every five to 10 minutes), Avignon (€18.50, two hours, one daily), Cannes (€25, two hours, up to three daily), Carpentras (€14, two hours, three daily), Nice (€26.50, three hours, up to three daily), Nice airport, Orange and other destinations.

Services to some destinations, including Cassis, use the stop on **place Castellane** (Map pp806-7; 6e; Ⓜ Castellane), south of the centre. Bus drivers sell tickets.

Eurolines (☎ 08 92 89 90 91; www.eurolines.com; 3 allées Léon Gambetta; ⌚ 10am-6pm Mon-Fri, 10am-2pm Sat) has international coach services; see p964.

CAR

Rental agencies offering decent rates include **Avis** (Map p810; ☎ 08 20 61 16 36) and **Europcar** (Map p810; ☎ 08 25 82 56 80), both at the train station.

TRAIN

Marseille's passenger train station, **Gare St-Charles** (Map p810) is served by both metro

PROVENCE

lines. There's an **information and ticket reservation office** (⌚ 9am-8pm Mon-Sat, 5.15am-10pm for ticket purchases), as well as a **left-luggage office** (from €3.50; ⌚ 7.30am-10pm) next to platform A.

In town, tickets can be bought at the SNCF Boutique inside the Centre Bourse shopping centre (Map p810).

From Marseille there are trains to pretty much anywhere in France and beyond. Sample destinations and starting fares include Paris' Gare de Lyon (€80.20, three hours, 21 daily), Nice (€27.80, 2½ hours, 21 daily), Avignon (€23.10, 35 minutes, 27 daily) and Lyon (€57.60, 1¾ hours, 16 daily).

Getting Around

TO/FROM THE AIRPORT

Navette (Marseille ☎ 04 91 50 59 34; airport ☎ 04 42 14 31 27) shuttle buses link Aéroport Marseille-Provence (€8, 25 minutes) with Marseille's train station. There are buses every 20 minutes between 5.30am and 10.50pm.

BICYCLE

Pick up a bike from more than 100 bike stations across the city, and drop it off at one of those same stations. The system is called **le vélo** (www.levelo-mpm.fr); it's free for the first 30 minutes, costs €1 for the next 30, and is then €1 per hour thereafter. You'll need a credit card to register, and instructions are in French. There are stations all the way along the corniche to Anse de la Pointe Rouge (8km south of the Vieux Port) and throughout the centre.

BUS, METRO & TRAM

Marseille has two metro lines (Métro 1 and Métro 2), two tram lines (yellow and green) and an extensive bus network, all run by the Régie des Transports Marseillais (RTM).

The metro runs between 5am and 10.30pm Monday to Thursday and until 12.30am Friday to Sunday; the tram runs between 5am and 1am daily, year-round. Bus services generally stop around 9.30pm, when night buses take over until 12.30am – most start their run in front of the **Espace Infos RTM** (Map p810; ☎ 04 91 91 92 10; 6 rue des Fabres, 1er; Ⓜ Vieux Port; ⌚ 8.30am-6pm Mon-Fri, 9am-12.30pm & 2-5.30pm Sat), where you can obtain information and tickets for public transport.

Bus, metro or tram tickets (€1.70) can be used on any combination of metros and buses for one hour after they've been time-stamped. A pass for one/three days costs €4.50/10.

TAXI

It won't look anything like Luc Besson's celebrated vehicle, but there's a taxi stand to the right as you exit the train station through the main entrance. **Taxi Radio Marseille** (☎ 04 91 02 20 20) run taxis 24 hours a day.

AIX-EN-PROVENCE

pop 141,200

Aix-en-Provence is to Provence what the Left Bank is to Paris: a pocket of Bohemian chic with an edgy student crowd. It's hard to believe Aix (pronounced ex) is just 25km from chaotic, exotic Marseille. With some 30,000 students from the Université de Provence

CHRISTMAS IN PROVENCE *Emilie Filou*

If you thought Provence was only a summertime destination, think again. It has some of the quirkiest Christmas traditions.

Get your santons These traditional plaster-moulded figurines are used to depict nativity scenes. There 55 different kinds of characters, from Mary, Joseph and baby Jesus to shepherds and animals in the stable. Find out more at the Musée du Santon in Marseille (p809).

Eat 13 desserts You must sample all 13 desserts but it doesn't matter how much you eat of each (could be just one almond and one raisin for instance), otherwise it's bad luck for the following year: *Fougasse* or *pompe à l'huile* (traditional Provençal pastries – buy them at **Four des Navettes**; see p816); *nougat blanc* (white nougat); *nougat noir* (black nougat); dried figs; almonds; walnuts; raisins; pear; apple; orange or mandarin; dates; *calisson d'Aix* (see boxed text, p825); and quince jam or paste.

Shop at the Christmas markets Your 13 desserts, presents and *santons* can be bought at the amazing Christmas fairs in Marseille, Arles and Aix-en-Provence.

Ski or go to the beach If the weather's nice, people regularly go to the beach for Christmas. Alternatively, head to Provence's mountains and ski in **Pra Loup** (p858) or down **Mont Ventoux** (p848).

What's your recommendation?
www.lonelyplanet.com/france

PROVENCE

Aix-Marseille, including many foreign students, Aix is packed with bars, cafés, affordable restaurants and a wicked nightlife. The city itself is rich in culture, and elegant, with its plane-tree-shaded boulevards and chic boutiques. Were it not for its merry student population, it could be considered snobbish.

Aix marks the spot where, under the proconsul Sextius Calvinus, Roman forces enslaved the inhabitants of the Ligurian Celtic stronghold of Entremont. In 123 BC the military camp was named Aquae Sextiae (Waters of Sextius) for the thermal springs, which still flow today. In the 12th century the counts of Provence proclaimed Aix their capital, which it remained until the Revolution, when it was supplanted by Marseille. The city became a centre of culture under King René (1409–80); two of Aix' most famous sons are painter Paul Cézanne and novelist Émile Zola.

Testament to this rich heritage is Aix' nomination as European Capital of Culture for 2013 along with Marseille and Arles: expect even more to happen in this all-happening city.

Orientation

Cours Mirabeau extends eastwards to place Forbin from place du Général de Gaulle, a roundabout with a huge fountain (commonly referred to as just La Rotonde). The city's mostly pedestrianised old town, Vieil Aix, is north of cours Mirabeau. Radiating from La Rotonde, av des Belges leads southwest to the bus station, while av Victor Hugo brings you southeast to the train station – the tourist office is on the southern edge of La Rotonde. The TGV station is 8km from the city centre, linked by shuttle buses.

South of cours Mirabeau is the Quartier Mazarin, with a street grid that was laid out in the 17th century. The entire city centre is ringed by a series of maddening one-way boulevards.

PROVENCE

Information

BOOKSHOPS

Book in Bar (☎ 04 42 26 60 07; 4 rue Cabassol) The best selection of English-language books in town, with a great café offering homemade muffins.

Librairie Goulard (☎ 04 42 27 66 47; 37 cours Mirabeau) Aix' best selection of English-language Lonely Planet guides.

Paradox Librairie Internationale (☎ 04 42 26 47 99; 15 rue du 4 Septembre) A reasonable selection of fiction in English; the place also doubles up as a British grocery shop (Heinz tomato soup, Quavers and digestive biscuits – it's all here).

INTERNET ACCESS

Netgames (☎ 04 42 26 60 41; 52 rue Aumône Vieille; per hr €3; 🕒 10am-midnight) Central and state of the art.

LAUNDRY

Laundrettes (open from 7am or 8am to 8pm) can be found at 5 rue de la Fontaine, 36 cours Sextius and 60 rue Boulegon.

MONEY

Commercial banks mass along cours Mirabeau and cours Sextius, the latter running north–south to the west of La Rotonde.

Change Nazareth (7 rue Nazareth; 🕒 9am-7am Jul & Aug, 9am-6.30pm Mon-Sat Sep-Jun) Inside a jewellery shop.

POST

Post Office (place de l'Hôtel de Ville)

TOURIST INFORMATION

Tourist Office (☎ 04 42 16 11 61; www.aixenprovencetourism.com; 2 place du Général de Gaulle; 🕒 8.30am-7pm Mon-Sat, 10am-1pm & 2-6pm Sun) Longer hours in summer; very pro-active and helpful.

Sights & Activities

Art, culture and architecture abound in Aix. The tourist office has some great DIY walking tour maps. Otherwise, just follow your nose: Aix is a stroller's heaven.

The graceful **cours Mirabeau** is the literal and spiritual heart of Aix. Cafés spill out onto the footpaths on the sunny northern side. The southern side shelters a string of elegant Renaissance *hôtels particuliers* (private mansions). The mossy **fontaine d'Eau Thermale**, at the intersection of cours Mirabeau and rue du 4 Septembre, spouts 34°C water, a pleasant hint of what's awaiting you at the **Thermes Sextius** (thermal spa; ☎ 04 42 23 81 82; www.thermes-sextius.com; 55 av des Thermes; day pass incl 4 treatments from €84).

Quartier Mazarin, south of cours Mirabeau, is home to some of Aix' finest buildings. Further south still is the peaceful **parc Jourdan**, dominated by Aix' largest fountain and home to the town's **Boulodrome Municipal** – locals gather here to play *pétanque* (a game similar to lawn bowls, played with heavy metal balls on a sandy pitch) under the plane trees.

For more greenery (dry maquis, actually), the nearby **Montagne Ste-Victoire** offers dozens of walking and cycling tracks. The tourist

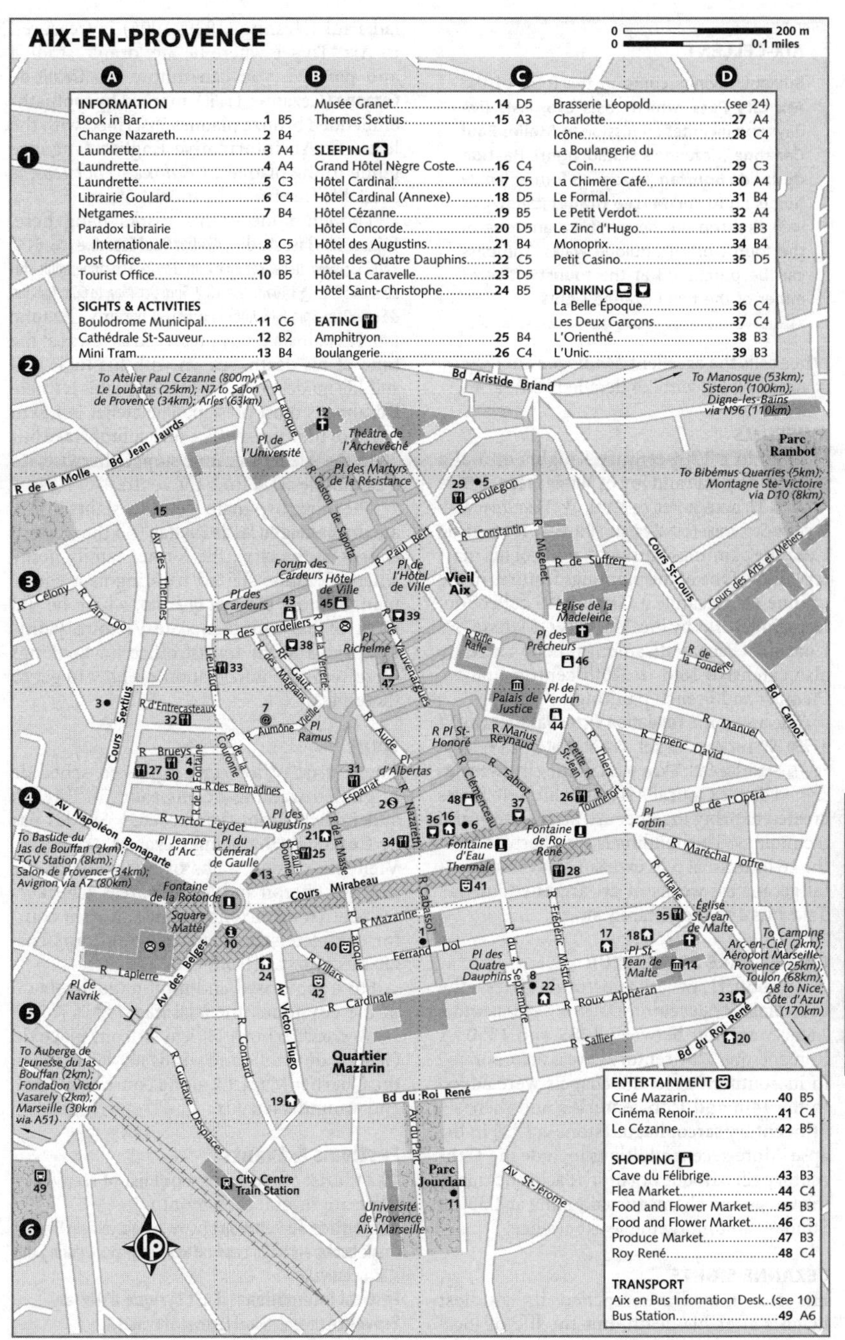
AIX-EN-PROVENCE
0 200 m
0 0.1 miles
A
B
C
D
1
2
3
4
5
6
INFORMATION
Book in Bar 1 B5
Change Nazareth 2 B4
Laundrette 3 A4
Laundrette 4 A4
Laundrette 5 C3
Librairie Goulard 6 C4
Netgames 7 B4
Paradox Librairie Internationale 8 C5
Post Office 9 B3
Tourist Office 10 B5
SIGHTS & ACTIVITIES
Boulodrome Municipal 11 C6
Cathédrale St-Sauveur 12 B2
Mini Tram 13 B4
Musée Granet 14 D5
Thermes Sextius 15 A3
SLEEPING
Grand Hôtel Nègre Coste 16 C4
Hôtel Cardinal 17 C5
Hôtel Cardinal (Annexe) 18 D5
Hôtel Cézanne 19 B5
Hôtel Concorde 20 D5
Hôtel des Augustins 21 B4
Hôtel des Quatre Dauphins 22 C5
Hôtel La Caravelle 23 D5
Hôtel Saint-Christophe 24 B5
EATING
Amphitryon 25 B4
Boulangerie 26 C4
Brasserie Léopold (see 24)
Charlotte 27 A4
Icône 28 C4
La Boulangerie du Coin 29 C3
La Chimère Café 30 A4
Le Formal 31 B4
Le Petit Verdot 32 A4
Le Zinc d'Hugo 33 B3
Monoprix 34 B4
Petit Casino 35 D5
DRINKING
La Belle Époque 36 C4
Les Deux Garçons 37 C4
L'Orienthé 38 B3
L'Unic 39 B3
ENTERTAINMENT
Ciné Mazarin 40 B5
Cinéma Renoir 41 C4
Le Cézanne 42 B5
SHOPPING
Cave du Félibrige 43 B3
Flea Market 44 C4
Food and Flower Market 45 B3
Food and Flower Market 46 C3
Produce Market 47 B3
Roy René 48 C4
TRANSPORT
Aix en Bus Infomation Desk (see 10)
Bus Station 49 A6
To Atelier Paul Cézanne (800m); Le Loubatas (25km); N7 to Salon de Provence (34km); Arles (63km)
To Manosque (53km); Sisteron (100km); Digne-les-Bains via N96 (110km)
Parc Rambot
To Bibémus Quarries (5km); Montagne Ste-Victoire via D10 (8km)
To Bastide du Jas de Bouffan (2km); TGV Station (8km); Salon de Provence (34km); Avignon via A7 (80km)
To Camping Arc-en-Ciel (2km); Aéroport Marseille-Provence (25km); Toulon (68km); A8 to Nice; Côte d'Azur (170km)
To Auberge de Jeunesse du Jas Bouffan (2km); Fondation Victor Vasarely (2km); Marseille (30km via A51)
Bd Aristide Briand
Bd Jean Jaurès
R de la Molle
R Laroque
Pl de l'Université
Théâtre de l'Archevêché
Pl des Martyrs de la Résistance
R Gaston de Saporta
R Boulegon
R Constantin
R Mignet
R de Suffren
Cours St-Louis
Cours des Arts et Métiers
Av des Thermes
R Célony
R Van Loo
Forum des Cardeurs
Pl des Cardeurs
Hôtel de Ville
Pl de l'Hôtel de Ville
R Paul Bert
Vieil Aix
Église de la Madeleine
Pl des Prêcheurs
R de la Fonderie
Bd Carnot
R des Cordeliers
R Lieutaud
R de la Verrerie
R des Magnans
RF Gaut
Pl Richelme
R de Vauvenargues
R Rifle Rafle
Palais de Justice
Pl de Verdun
R Manuel
R Emeric David
Cours Sextius
R d'Entrecasteaux
R Aumône Vieille
Pl Ramus
R Aude
R Pl St-Honoré
R Marius Reynaud
Petite R St-Jean
R Thiers
R Brueys
R de la Fontaine
R de la Couronne
R des Bernadines
Pl d'Albertas
R Espariat
R Clémenceau
R Fabrot
R Tournefort
Pl Forbin
R de l'Opéra
Av Napoléon Bonaparte
R Victor Leydet
Pl des Augustins
Pl Jeanne d'Arc
Pl du Général de Gaulle
R Paul Doumer
R de la Masse
R Nazareth
Fontaine d'Eau Thermale
Fontaine de Roi René
R Maréchal Joffre
R d'Italie
Fontaine de la Rotonde
Cours Mirabeau
Square Mattéi
R Cabassol
R Mazarine
R Laroque
R Frédéric Mistral
R du 4 Septembre
Église St-Jean de Malte
Pl St-Jean de Malte
Ferrand
Dol
Pl des Quatre Dauphins
R Lapierre
Pl de Navrik
Av des Belges
R Villars
R Cardinale
R Roux Alphéran
R Sallier
Bd du Roi René
R Gontard
Av Victor Hugo
Quartier Mazarin
R Gustave Desplaces
City Centre Train Station
Av du Parc
Parc Jourdan
Av St-Jérome
Université de Provence Aix-Marseille
PROVENCE

AIX-CELLENT

Brilliant savings come in the form of the **Aix City Pass**, which costs €15, lasts five days and includes admission to **Atelier Paul Cézanne** (Cézanne's studio; right), **Bastide du Jas de Bouffan** (Cézanne's former family home; right) and **Musée Granet** (below), as well as a trip on the minitram and one of the tourist office's guided walks. The pass can be purchased at the tourist office or either of the two Cézanne sights.

office sells the excellent *Montagne Ste-Victoire* map for €4.50, with 24 detailed itineraries.

MUSEUMS

Housed in a 17th-century Knights of Malta priory, the pride and joy of **Musée Granet** (☎ 04 42 52 88 32; place St-Jean de Malte; 🕑 11am-7pm Wed-Mon Jun-Sep, noon-6pm Wed-Mon Oct-May) is its nine Cézanne paintings (although none of his masterworks). One of the paintings features in the unique De Cézanne à Giacometti collection, featuring works by Picasso, Léger, Matisse, Tal Coat and Giacometti, among others. There are also extensive 16th- to 20th-century Italian, Flemish and French paintings.

The awesome **Fondation Victor Vasarely** (☎ 04 42 200 109; 1 av Marcel Pagnol; adult/student €7/4; 🕑 10am-1pm & 2-6pm Tue-Sat), 4km west of the city, was designed by the Optical Art leader himself. It was created to bring together art, architecture and technology. The building is a masterpiece, but the 16 hexagonal cells exposing his monumental geometric works of art are phenomenal. Take bus 4 to the Vasarely stop.

CATHÉDRALE ST-SAUVEUR

A potpourri of architectural styles, the **Cathédrale St-Sauveur** (rue Laroque; 🕑 8am-noon & 2-6pm) was built between 1285 and 1350. A Romanesque 12th-century nave is incorporated in its southern aisle; the chapels were added in the 14th and 15th centuries; and there's a 5th-century sarcophagus (stone coffin) in the apse. More-recent additions include the 18th-century gilt baroque organ. The acoustics make the Gregorian chants (usually sung at 4.30pm Sunday) an unforgettable experience.

CÉZANNE SIGHTS

His star may have reached its giddiest heights after his death, but the life of local lad Paul Cézanne (1839–1906) is treasured in Aix. To see where he ate, drank, studied and painted, you can follow the **Circuit de Cézanne** (Cézanne Trail), marked by footpath-embedded bronze plaques inscribed with the letter C. An informative English-language guide to the plaques, *Cézanne's Footsteps*, is available free from the tourist office.

Though none of his works hang here, Cézanne's last studio, **Atelier Paul Cézanne** (☎ 04 42 21 06 53; www.atelier-cezanne.com; 9 av Paul Cézanne; adult/student €5.50/2; 🕑 10am-noon & 2-5pm Oct-Mar, to 6pm Apr-Jun & Sep, 10am-6pm Jul & Aug) is a must for any Cézanne fan. It's painstakingly preserved as it was at the time of his death, strewn with his tools and still-life models; his admirers claim this is where Cézanne is most present. The atelier is 1.5km north of the tourist office on a hilltop; take bus 20 to the Atelier Cézanne stop. Otherwise, it's a 20 minute-walk from the centre.

The other two main Cézanne sights in Aix are the **Bastide du Jas de Bouffan** (on the western fringes of the city), the former family home where Cézanne started painting as a young man, and the **Bibémus quarries**, where he did most of his Montagne Ste-Victoire paintings. Head to the tourist office for bookings (required) and information on how to get to these sites.

Tours

The tourist office runs a packed schedule of guided walking or bus tours in English and French, from the expected 'Sur les pas de Cézanne' (Retracing Cézanne's steps), to Vieil Aix guided walks or bus tours of the nearby Luberon and Alpilles areas. Check its website (www.aixenprovencetourism.com) for complete schedules. Walking tours cost €8; bus tours are from €28.

For a motorised and multilingual version of the city tours, the **Mini Tram** (☎ 06 11 54 27 73; www.cpts.fr, in French; €6) leaves from place du Général de Gaulle and winds its way through the Quartier Mazarin, along cours Mirabeau, and around Vieil Aix.

Festivals & Events

The tourist office keeps a full list of festivities: there are several each month.

Rencontres du 9ème Art (www.bd-aix.com, in French) Comic books, animation and cartoon art feature during this March festival.

Festival International d'Art Lyrique d'Aix-en-Provence (International Festival of Lyrical Art;

www.festival-aix.com) The highlight of Aix' sumptuous cultural calendar is this month-long festival in July, which brings classical music, opera and ballet to city venues such as the Théâtre de l'Archevêché, and outside the Cathédrale St-Sauveur (see opposite), while buskers keep cours Mirabeau's festive spirits high.

Festival de le Roche d'Anthéron (www.festival-piano.com) Held in July, this is another biggie, dedicated to piano music and taking place across venues from Aix to the Luberon.

Sleeping

The tourist office has lists of *chambres d'hôtes* and *gîtes ruraux* (self-contained holiday cottages) in and around Aix. Accommodation bookings are coordinated through the **Centrale de Réservation** (☎ 04 42 16 11 84; resaix@aixenprovencetourism.com).

BUDGET

Auberge de Jeunesse du Jas de Bouffan (☎ 04 42 20 15 99; www.fuaj.org; 3 av Marcel Pagnol; dm incl breakfast & sheets €17.50-29.50; reception 7am-1pm & 5pm-midnight, closed mid-Dec–Jan) Shiny new with a bar, tennis courts, secure bike shed and massive barbecues in summer, this HI hostel is 2km west of the centre. It's such a shame that the motorway is just down below… Take bus 4 from La Rotonde to the Vasarely stop.

Camping Arc-en-Ciel (☎ 04 42 26 14 28; rte de Nice; camping site for 2 people plus car €18.50; Apr-Sep;) There are tranquil wooded hills out the back of this four-star place, but there's a busy motorway in front. It's 2km southeast of town, at Pont des Trois Sautets. Take bus 3 to Les Trois Sautets stop.

Hôtel La Caravelle (☎ 04 42 21 53 05; www.lacaravelle-hotel.com; 29 bd du Roi René; s €45, d €65-70) Central, serviceable and friendly, the 30 rooms here range from air-conditioned doubles overlooking a pretty (and sadly, neighbouring) garden to singles with toilets situated just outside the rooms. The hotel is on the southeastern ring; if you're driving you can pull up to drop off your luggage right out front. Wi-fi's free and wheelchair access is good.

Hôtel Concorde (☎ 04 42 26 03 95; 68 bd du Roi René; d €48-88;) Definitely ask for a room at the back if you don't want to be sung to sleep by the incessant traffic noise of the circular boulevard. The 50 rooms are functional, with good wheelchair access; 10 have small balconies, and higher-priced rooms come with air-con. Handy on-site parking is available for €7.50.

MIDRANGE

Hôtel des Quatre Dauphins (☎ 04 42 38 16 39; www.lesquatredauphins.fr; 54 rue Roux Alphéran; s €55-65, d €65-100;) Close to cours Mirabeau, this sweet 13-room hotel is a symphony of Wedgwood-blue, pale-pink and beige. The tall terracotta-tiled staircase leads to four charming attic rooms with sloped beamed ceilings (although maybe not ideal if you're pushing 6ft tall).

Hôtel Cardinal (☎ 04 42 38 32 30; www.hotel-cardinal-aix.com; 24 rue Cardinale; d €70, self-catering ste €110) Beneath stratospheric ceilings, Hôtel Cardinal's 29 romantic rooms are beautifully furnished with antiques, tasselled curtains, and newly tiled bathrooms. The choice picks are the six gigantic suites located in the annexe (about 100m further up the street), each with a kitchenette and dining room, ideal for longer stays.

Hôtel Saint-Christophe (☎ 04 42 26 01 24; www.hotel-saintchristophe.com; 2 av Victor Hugo; s €78.20-84.50, d €84.50-113;) Discreetly art deco and resolutely central (it's right behind the tourist office), the Saint-Christophe has very helpful staff, good wheelchair access, free wi-fi and a few rooms with private terraces. Brasserie Léopold (mains €15 to €20, open for lunch and dinner Tuesday to Sunday) downstairs is a sure bet for *steak-frites* (steak and fries).

Grand Hôtel Nègre Coste (☎ 04 42 27 74 22; www.hotelnegrecoste.com; 33 cours Mirabeau; d €90-145;) The only hotel right on cours Mirabeau isn't as grand as when Louis XIV stayed here in 1660. The place is a bit musty and the service blasé, but rooms still have a grand air about them, and it doesn't get more central than this. Garage parking is €10.

TOP END

Hôtel des Augustins (☎ 04 42 27 28 59; www.hotel-augustins.com; 3 rue de la Masse; standard/superior d €97-240;) Aix' oldest signature establishment has been resting, somewhat, on its laurels: the welcome is lukewarm, and the rooms, – in contrast with the grand lobby – are a little underwhelming (save for the most luxurious ones with Jacuzzi and private terrace). It's a shame, because this former 15th-century convent has volumes of history.

Hôtel Cézanne (☎ 04 42 91 11 11; www.hotelaix.com; 40 av Victor Hugo; d €170-195;) Apart from the beautifully crafted designer rooms and artistic surroundings, perhaps the best thing about Aix' hippest pad is the breakfast: smoked salmon and Champagne (bring on the Buck's Fizz!),

PROVENCE

as well as other more traditional treats such as delicate preserves, fresh bread and pastries.

Eating

You will be spoilt for choice in Aix: the centre runneth over with eateries, bistros, restaurants and gourmet haunts.

Le Formal (☎ 04 42 27 08 31; 32 rue Espariat; mains from €14; lunch & dinner Tue-Fri, dinner Sat;) The street entrance is rather discreet, but chef Jean-Luc Le Formal has received much attention since he opened his restaurant. The food is fantastic and elegantly presented but the portions err on the stingy side and the decibel level can get in the way of conversation.

Charlotte (☎ 04 42 26 77 56; 32 rue des Bernardines; 2-/3-course menu €14/17.50; lunch & dinner Tue-Sat) Townspeople congregate like a big extended family at this bustling place. It turns out delicious, simple home cooking, including terrines, homemade soups, grilled meat and savoury tarts, from its open kitchen. In summer, feasting takes place outdoors in the garden.

Le Zinc d'Hugo (☎ 04 42 27 69 69; 22 rue Lieutaud; mains €14-18; lunch & dinner Tue-Sat;) This rustic bistro of stone walls, wooden tables and a blackboard menu chalked with daily specials gets a little overwhelmed on market days when shoppers come up for the €14 lunchtime *menu*. You'll leave smelling as though you've been cooking all day, but that's the price to pay for authenticity!

Icône (☎ 04 42 27 59 82; 3 rue Frédéric Mistral; 2-/3-course menu €15/25; lunch & dinner Mon-Sat;) The designer Italian/Mediterranean fare matches the sleek, muted grey and glass setting at this glam place just off cours Mirabeau. There's a stainless steel bar and DJ spinning electro lounge beats if you'd rather sip a cocktail than devour lobster raviolis.

Le Petit Verdot (☎ 04 42 27 30 12; 7 rue Entrecasteaux; menu €17; dinner Mon-Sat;) At this cosy, wine-case-decorated establishment you'll choose food to accompany your wine (not the other way around). The wine list includes 100-odd choices, through which the staff will expertly guide you. And rest assured, the elegant French fare on your plate (mostly succulent meats, from duck breast to lamb shanks, including pig trotters!) will be just as divine as your tipple of choice.

La Chimère Café (☎ 04 42 38 30 00; 15 rue Brueys; 3-course menu €29.50; dinner Mon-Sat) Aix' yuppies lap up the cabaret atmosphere of this former nightclub: starry-night vaulted ceiling in the underground room; grand chandeliers with crimson, velvety furnishings above. As for the plate, it's a festival of decadent treats: crunchy *Pont l'Évêque* (a pale yellow, cow's-milk cheese) in cider caramel; cocoa-saturated fondant; scallops; lamb or whole sea bream.

Amphitryon (☎ 04 42 26 54 10; 2-4 rue Paul Doumer; 3-course menu €37; lunch & dinner Tue-Sat) Run by fiery duo maître d' Patrice Lesné and chef Bruno Ungaro, Amphitryon enjoys a solid reputation among Aix' bourgeoisie, particularly in summer for alfresco dining in the cloister-garden. The attached Comptoir de l'Amphi (mains €12 to €14) is a less-expensive alternative.

SELF-CATERING

Fresh, often still-warm loaves cram the shelves of **La Boulangerie du Coin** (4 rue Boulegon; Tue-Sun). It's also one of the few *boulangeries* (bakeries) to bake on Sunday, along with the **boulangerie** (5 rue Tournefort; 24hr) that never closes.

Aix is blessed with bountiful markets – see opposite.

Pick up groceries at **Monoprix** (cours Mirabeau; 8.30am-9pm Mon-Sat) and **Petit Casino** (rue d'Italie; 9am-7pm Mon-Sat).

Drinking

Open-air cafés saturate the city's squares, especially place des Cardeurs, place de Verdun and place de l'Hôtel de Ville.

Les Deux Garçons (☎ 04 42 26 00 51; 53 cours Mirabeau; 7am-2am) This is where Cézanne and Zola used to hang out, but this claim to fame no longer draws crowds like it used to. It's still a pleasant spot for a drink or a quiet bite, given its prime cours Mirabeau location.

L'Orienthé (5 rue de Félibre Gaut; 1pm-1am) A *1001 Nights'* soft-lit den ideal for lounge music, *sheeshas* (water pipes), dozens of different teas and a Zen atmosphere.

Entertainment

Flip through a copy of the monthly *In Aix* (free from the tourist office) to find out what's on, where.

CINEMAS

Aix' arty-intellectual student population ensures great cinema offerings, from Oscar contenders to cult flicks, often in English. Programs for the following cinemas can be found at www.lescinemasaixois.com (in French):

Ciné Mazarin (☎ 04 42 26 61 51; 6 rue Laroque; adult/student €8.10/7.10)

PROVENCE

Cinéma Renoir (☎ 04 42 26 61 51; 24 cours Mirabeau; adult/student €8.10/7.10)

Le Cézanne (☎ 04 42 26 61 51; 1 rue Marcel Guillaume; adult/student €8.90/7.30)

BARS & NIGHTCLUBS

Like all good student cities, the scene here is fun, but fickle. The areas on and around rue de la Verrerie and place Richelme (both about 300m north of cours Mirabeau) are prime for nightlife. Listings on the website www.marseille bynight.com (in French) also cover Aix.

La Belle Époque (☎ 04 42 27 65 66; 29 cours Mirabeau; 🕑 11am-midnight) The swanky, purple and fluoro-lit Belle Époque decor is a favourite of happening DJs and students alike. And don't be surprised if you receive two drinks when you've ordered just one; it's 'appy 'our between 7pm and 9pm every night.

L'Unic (☎ 04 42 96 38 28; 40 rue de Vauvenargues; 🕑 6am-2am) On one of the town's most charming squares, place Richelme, l'Unic is a timeless, reliable address serving anything from breakfast to *apéritifs,* cocktails and beers. Pensioners love it for the postmarket prelunch slot, while students crowd it to kick-start or simply while away their evening.

Shopping

Aix' chic-est shops are clustered along pedestrian rue Marius Reynaud, which winds behind the Palais de Justice on place de Verdun. Elegant boutiques also grace cours Mirabeau.

Local wine vendors include **Cave du Félibrige** (18 rue des Cordeliers), which has a splendid array – some *very* expensive.

MARKETS

Trestle tables set up each morning for a **produce market** (place Richelme), displaying olives, goats' cheese, garlic, lavender, honey, peaches, melons and other sun-kissed products. Another **food market** (place des Prêcheurs) takes place on Tuesday, Thursday and Saturday mornings.

Rainbows of flowers fill place des Prêcheurs during the Sunday-morning flower market, and place de l'Hôtel de Ville on Tuesday, Thursday and Saturday mornings. Quirky vintage items can also be found at the flea market (Tuesday, Thursday and Saturday mornings) on place de Verdun.

Getting There & Away

AIR

Aéroport Marseille-Provence (☎ 04 42 14 14 14; www.marseille.aeroport.fr), aka Aéroport Marseille-Marignane, is 25km from Aix-en-Provence and is served by regular shuttle buses.

BUS

Aix' **bus station** (☎ 08 91 02 40 25; av de l'Europe) is a 10-minute walk southwest from La Rotonde. Services include buses to Marseille (€4.60, 30 to 50 minutes depending on the traffic, every 10 minutes, every 20 minutes on Sunday), Arles (€10.40, 1½ hours, six daily Monday to Saturday), Avignon (€14, 1¼ hours, six daily Monday to Saturday) and Toulon (€10, one hour, five daily Monday to Saturday).

CAR & MOTORCYCLE

Circumnavigating the one-way, three-lane orbital system circling the old town is a nightmare. Street parking spaces are like hen's teeth, but secure, pricier covered parking is plentiful.

TRAIN

Aix' tiny **city centre train station** (🕑 7am-7pm) is at the southern end of av Victor Hugo. The only services there are those to Briançon (€32.90, four hours), Gap (€25, 2½ hours) and Marseille (€6.50, 50 minutes).

Aix' **TGV station**, 8km from the city centre and accessible by shuttle bus, has many more services. From there it's only 12 minutes to Marseille (€8), with about 20 services a day.

Getting Around

TO/FROM THE AIRPORT & TGV STATION

Aix' bus station is linked to both the TGV station (€3.70) and the airport (€7.90) from

SWEET TREAT

Aix' sweetest treat since King René's wedding banquet in 1473 is the marzipanlike local speciality, *calisson d'Aix,* a small, diamond-shaped, chewy delicacy made with ground almonds and fruit syrup, wrapped in a communion-wafer base and glazed with white icing sugar. Traditional *calissonniers* still make the sweets, including **Roy René** (☎ 04 42 26 67 86; www.calisson.com; 10 rue Clémenceau), which also runs guided **tours** (€1; 🕑 10am Tue & Thu) at its out-of-town factory-museum.

A GREEN GIANT

If you've been thinking about organising a big family reunion, or there's a group of you looking to rent somewhere a little unusual for a holiday in Provence, look no further: **Le Loubatas** (☎ 04 42 67 06 70; http://educ-envir.org/loubatas; Peyrolles-en-Provence; 6 nights incl sheets €650) might be just what you need.

Nestled in a beautiful Mediterranean forest 25km from Aix-en-Provence, at the crossroads of the Montagne Ste-Victoire, the Luberon and the Gorges du Verdon, Le Loubatas is a unique *eco-gîte* (eco-B&B). Designed using eco-friendly methods and materials, solar panels provide hot water, heating and electricity, while water comes from rainwater tanks and a local spring (the pump is solar powered).

Inside are dozens of interactive and highly informative gadgets to calculate and reduce electricity and water usage, including funky looking meters, cartoon reminders, timers etc.

The *gîte* has a capacity of 35 but it can be rented for smaller groups, starting at 12 people. Rooms are basic colourful dorms with bunk beds and communal showers. In the kitchen, recycling and composting are de rigueur. Dinner is served in the dining room, where an energy-efficient wood-stove keeps the place warm as toast in winter, or on the lovely terrace overlooking the forest in summer.

4.40am to 10.30pm by the half-hourly **Navette** (☎ 04 42 93 59 13) shuttle-bus services.

BUS

The city's 14 bus and three minibus lines are operated by **Aix en Bus** (☎ 04 42 26 37 28; 8.30am-7pm Mon-Sat). The information desk is inside the tourist office.

La Rotonde is the main bus hub. Most services run until 8pm. A single/*carnet* (book) of 10 tickets costs €1.10/7.70; a day pass costs €3.50. Minibus 2 links the train station with La Rotonde and cours Mirabeau. The Diabline electric shuttles go round Vieil Aix; flag them down for €0.50.

TAXI

You can find taxis outside the bus station. To order one, call **Taxi Radio Aixois** (☎ 04 42 27 71 11) or **Taxi Mirabeau** (☎ 04 42 21 61 61).

ARLES & THE CAMARGUE

ARLES

pop 52,400

Arles' poster boy is the celebrated impressionist painter Vincent van Gogh. If you're familiar with his work, you'll be familiar with Arles: the light, the colours, the landmarks, the atmosphere – all faithfully captured.

But long before Van Gogh captured this Grand Rhône River spot on canvas, the Romans had already been turned on to its charms. In 49 BC, Arles' prosperity and political standing rose meteorically when it backed a winner in Julius Caesar (who would never meet defeat in his entire career). After Caesar seized and plundered Marseille, which had supported his rival Pompey the Great, Arles eclipsed Marseille as the region's major port. Within a century and a half, it boasted a 12,000-seat theatre and a 20,000-seat amphitheatre to entertain its citizens with gruesome gladiatorial spectacles and chariot races.

Still impressively intact, the two structures now stage events including Arles' famous *ferias* (bull-running festivals), with their controversial bullfights and three-day street parties.

Arles' cultural significance was confirmed by its nomination as European Capital of Culture for 2013 along with Marseille and Aix-en-Provence.

Orientation

Arles is shoehorned between the Grand Rhône River to the northwest, bd Émile Combes to the east and, to the south, bd des Lices and bd Georges Clemenceau. The city centre is shaped like a foot, with the train station, place de la Libération and place Lamartine (where Van Gogh once lived) at the top, les Arènes at the anklebone and the tourist office under the arch. And – fittingly enough – its compact size means it's easily walkable.

Information

INTERNET ACCESS

Cyber Saladelle (☎ 04 90 93 13 56; 17 rue de la République; per hr €3.50; 10am-7pm Tue-Sat)

LAUNDRY

Laverie Mièle (12bis rue Portagnel; 8am-7pm)

MONEY

There are several banks along rue de la République.

POST

Post Office (5 bd des Lices)

TOURIST INFORMATION

Tourist Office main office (04 90 18 41 20; www.tourisme.ville-arles.fr; esplanade Charles de Gaulle; 9am-6.45pm Apr-Sep, 9am-4.45pm Mon-Sat, 10am-12.45pm Sun Oct-Mar); train station (04 90 43 33 57; 9am-1.30pm & 2.30-4.45pm Mon-Fri Apr-Sep) The main office is adjacent to the busy bd des Lices.

Sights & Activities

Unless otherwise noted, the last entry to all sights listed in this section is 30 minutes prior to closing.

ROMAN MONUMENTS

If you're keen to dig into Arles' Roman past, the 'Circuit Romain' combined ticket costing €9/7 for adults/children gives you access to the four following sites. The Pass Monument (€13.50/12) gives you access to all the museums and sites in Arles. You can buy the ticket at the tourist office or at any of the sites.

Les Arènes

Arles' remarkable Roman amphitheatre, **Les Arènes** (04 90 49 59 05; adult/student €5.50/4; 9am-6.30pm May-Sep, 9am-6pm Mar, Apr & Oct, 10am-5pm Nov-Feb), was built around the late 1st or early 2nd century. It was the venue for chariot races, and gladiatorial displays where slaves and criminals met their demise before jubilant crowds.

During the Arab invasions of early medieval times, the amphitheatre became a fortress. When it was decided in the 1820s to finally return it to its original state, there were still 212 houses and two churches on site. The amphitheatre is now undergoing restoration, but the polished finish of the renovated walls isn't popular with everyone. Debate is ongoing about what should be done to the metallic structure inside that seats 12,000 during Arles' bullfighting season (see boxed text, p829).

The *bureau de location* (ticket office) is on the northern side of the amphitheatre on rond point des Arènes.

Thermes de Constantin

Admission to the amphitheatre is also good for the **Thermes de Constantin** (rue du Grand Prieuré; adult/student €3/2.20; 9am-noon & 2-6.30pm May-Sep, 9am-noon & 2-6pm Mar, Apr & Oct, 10am-noon & 2-5pm Feb & Nov), partly preserved Roman baths near the river, built for Emperor Constantin's private use in the 4th century.

Théâtre Antique

Still regularly used for projections and plays, the **Théâtre Antique** (Roman Theatre; 04 90 49 59 05; entrance is on rue de la Calade; adult/student €3/2.20; 9am-6.30pm May-Sep, 9am-noon & 2-6pm Mar, Apr & Oct, 10am-noon & 2-5pm Nov-Feb) dates from the end of the 1st century BC. For hundreds of years it was used as a convenient source of construction materials, with workers chipping away at the 102m-diameter structure (the remaining column on the right-hand side near the entrance indicates the height of the original arcade).

Les Alyscamps

Works of Van Gogh and Gauguin feature this large **necropolis** (adult/student €3.50/2.60; 9am-6.30pm May-Sep, 9am-noon & 2-6pm Mar, Apr & Oct, 10am-noon & 2-5pm Nov-Feb). Situated 1km southeast of Les Arènes, it was founded by the Romans and taken over by Christians in the 4th century. It became a coveted resting place because of the tombs of martyr St Genest and Arles' first bishops.

Other Roman Sites

Under your feet as you stand on the place du Forum are the **Cryptoporticus du Forum** (entrance via Hôtel de Ville, place de la République; adult/student €5.50/4, incl entrance to amphitheatre; 9am-noon & 2-6.30pm May-Sep, 9am-noon & 2-6pm Oct, 9am-12.30pm & 2-6pm Mar & Apr, 10am-noon & 2-5pm Nov-Feb), underground storerooms carved out in the 1st century BC.

ÉGLISE ST-TROPHIME

Arles was an archbishopric from the 4th century until 1790, and this Romanesque-style **church** was once a cathedral. Built in the late 11th and 12th centuries on the site of several earlier churches, it's named after St Trophime, a late-2nd- or early-3rd-century bishop of Arles. If you look on the far right of the left-hand side of the western portal, you'll see an intricately sculpted facade of biblical scenes (more spectacular than the interior), with St Trophime holding a spiral staff in his right hand. Inside the austere church,

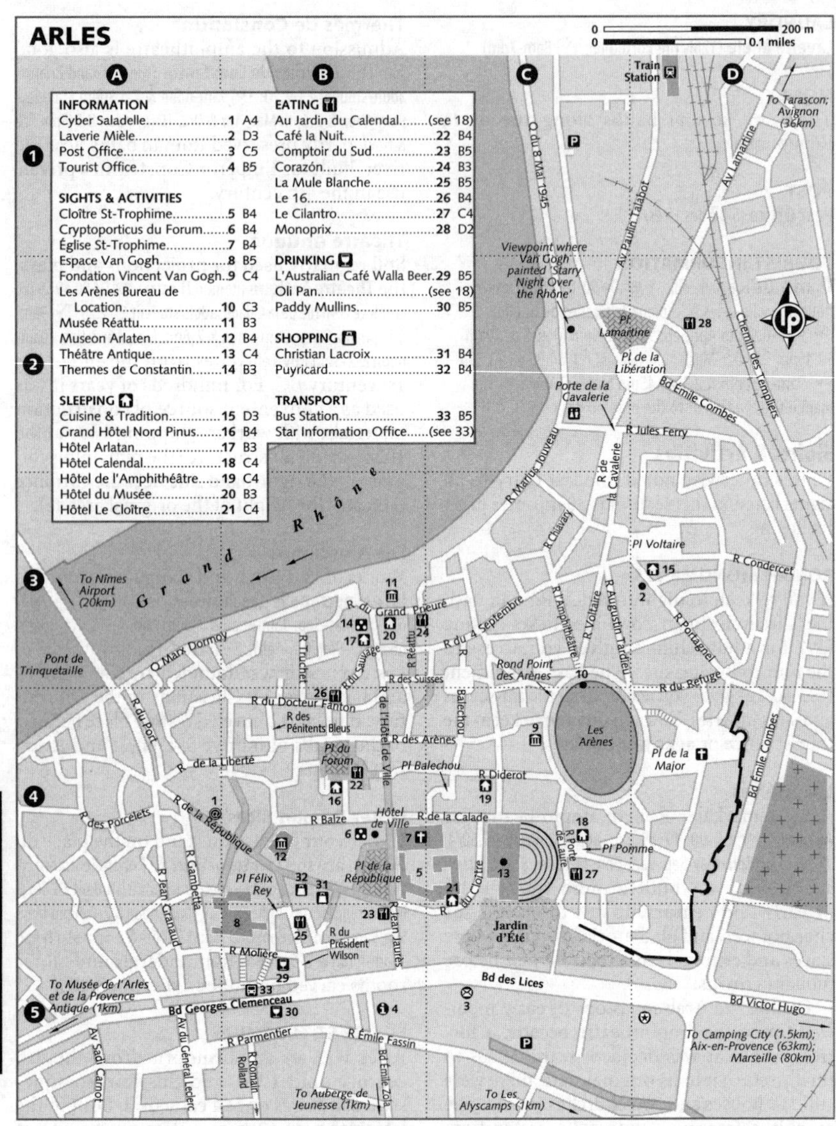

the most fascinating feature is the 'treasury', containing pieces of bone of Arles' bishops who were later canonised. Many of the broken statues inside were decapitated during the French Revolution.

Across the courtyard, the 12th- and 14th-century **Cloître St-Trophime** (St-Trophime Cloister; ☎ 04 90 49 36 36; adult/student €3.50/2.60; ⏰ 9am-6.30pm May-Sep, 9am-6pm Mar, Apr & Oct, 10am-5pm Nov-Feb) was built to accommodate the monks' daily lives. It comprises a reading room, dormitory and dining room.

MUSEUMS

Within a striking, state-of-the-art cobalt-blue building, the **Musée de l'Arles et de la Provence**

OF BULLS AND MEN

Animal lovers, fear not: some *corridas* (bullfights) do not end in a bloodbath. Usually, bulls are killed in a colourful and bloody spectacle involving *picadors* (horseback-riding bullfighters who use a lance), *banderilleros* (bullfighters who run close the bull, and use the *banderilla* – a type of dart), matadors and horses. When performed correctly – which is rarely the case – the matador and bull execute a kind of dance. After the event, the bull is carved up and sold for meat. The meat has a different taste from that of ordinary steers, as bulls bred for fighting graze free range, on grass.

However, in the local Camargue variation, the *course Camarguaise,* amateur *razeteurs* (from the word *razer,* 'shave') get as close as they dare to the bulls to remove rosettes and ribbons tied to the bull's horns. They do this using hooks held between their fingers. The bulls are local *camarguais* bulls, smaller and faster than their Spanish counterparts used in *corridas.*

Arles' bullfighting season begins around Easter with a festival known as the Feria (or Féria) Pascale, and charges through until the September rice harvest festival.

Antiques (☎ 04 90 18 88 88; av de la 1ère Division Française; adult/student/under 18yr €5.50/4/free; ⌚ 9am-7pm May-Oct, 10am-5pm Nov-Apr) is perched on the edge of what used to be the Roman chariot racing track (circus), 1.5km southwest of the tourist office. It has amassed a rich collection of pagan and Christian art, including stunning mosaics. The museum is also a leading mosaic restoration centre; you can watch the work in progress.

Museon Arlaten (☎ 04 90 93 58 11; 29 rue de la République; adult/student €4/3; ⌚ 9.30am-12.30pm & 2-6pm Jun-Aug, 9.30am-noon & 2-5.30pm Apr, May & Sep, 9.30am-noon & 2-4.30pm Oct-Mar) was founded by Nobel Prize–winning poet and dedicated Provençal preservationist Frédéric Mistral as a 'poem' for people who couldn't read. It occupies a 16th-century townhouse, with displays of traditional Provençal furniture, crafts, costumes, ceramics and wigs. It looks a bit dated now, but has retained a certain quaint charm. The last entry is one hour prior to closing.

Housed in a former 15th-century priory, the splendid **Musée Réattu** (☎ 04 90 96 37 68; 10 rue du Grand Prieuré; adult/student €4/3, temporary exhibitions €6/4.50; ⌚ 10am-12.30pm & 2-6.30pm Mar-Jun & mid-Sep–Oct, 10am-7pm Jul–mid-Sep, 1-5pm Nov-Feb) has two Picasso paintings, and 57 of his sketches from the early 1970s. It also has works by 18th- and 19th-century Provençal artists, but it's best known for its cutting-edge photographic displays.

VAN GOGH SIGHTS

Although Van Gogh painted around 200 canvases in Arles, not a single one remains here today. There's a certain poetic justice, considering that following his altercation with housemate Paul Gauguin in place Victor Hugo (see boxed text, p830), a petition was raised by fearful neighbours, and Van Gogh was committed for one month on the mayor's orders.

But Arles has admirably made up for it. Fitting tributes to Van Gogh's art include **Fondation Vincent Van Gogh** (☎ 04 90 49 94 04; 24bis Rond Point des Arènes; adult/student €7/5; ⌚ 10am-6pm Apr-Jun, 10am-7pm Jul-Sep, 11am-5pm Tue-Sun Oct-Mar), where important modern-day artists, including David Hockney, Francis Bacon and Fernando Botero, pay homage to the artist's distinctive style. The collection and its diversity show just how widely Van Gogh's influence has been felt in the artistic world.

Temporary art exhibitions regularly take place at **Espace Van Gogh** (☎ 04 90 49 37 40; place Félix Rey), housed in the former hospital where Van Gogh had his ear stitched and was later locked up.

The best way to get a sense of Van Gogh's time in Arles is to take the excellent **Van Gogh Trail**, a walking circuit of the city marked by footpath-embedded plaques. Accompanied by a brochure (in English) handed out by the tourist office, the trail takes in spots where Van Gogh set up his easel to paint canvases such as *Starry Night over the Rhône* (1888) and *The Amphitheatre* (1888). At each stop along the circuit, a lectern-style signboard with a reproduction of the painting has interpretative information (also in English).

Tours

In addition to the Van Gogh Trail, several other self-guided walking tours (Roman, medieval, Renaissance and classical) are marked along Arles' footpaths, in conjunction with an explanatory brochure.

VINCENT

It's easy to forget that Vincent van Gogh was only 37 when he died, as he appears much older in his self-portraits. His aged appearance may have been partly due to the effects of poverty – he sold only one painting in his lifetime.

Born in 1853, the Dutch painter arrived in Arles in 1888 after living in Paris with his younger brother Theo, an art dealer who financially supported Vincent from his own modest income. In Paris he became acquainted with seminal artists Edgar Degas, Camille Pissarro, Henri de Toulouse-Lautrec and Paul Gauguin. Revelling in Arles' intense light and bright colours, Van Gogh painted with a burning fervour, unfazed by howling mistrals. During a mistral he would kneel on his canvases and paint horizontally, or lash his easel to iron stakes driven deep into the ground. He sent paintings to Theo for him to try to sell, and dreamed of founding an artists' colony here, but only Gauguin followed up his invitation. Their differing artistic approaches – Gauguin believed in painting from imagination, Van Gogh painting what he saw – and their artistic temperaments, fuelled by absinthe, came to a head with the argument that led to Van Gogh lopping his ear, and his subsequent committal.

In May 1889 Van Gogh voluntarily entered an asylum in St-Rémy de Provence, 25km northeast of Arles over the Alpilles. It was here that he painted another 150-odd canvases during his one year, one week, and one day's confinement, including masterpieces like *Starry Night* (not to be confused with *Starry Night over the Rhône,* painted in Arles). In February 1890 his 1888 Arles-painted work *The Red Vines* was bought by Anne Boch, sister of his friend Eugene Boch, for 400 francs (around €50 today). It also now hangs in the Pushkin State Museum of Fine Arts.

On 16 May 1890 Van Gogh moved to Auvers-sur-Oise, just outside Paris, to be closer to Theo. However, on 27 July that year he shot and killed himself, possibly to avoid further financial burden for his brother, whose wife had just had a baby son (named Vincent). Theo was also supporting their ailing mother. He subsequently had a breakdown and was also committed, prior to succumbing to physical illness. He died, aged 33, just six months after Van Gogh. It would be less than a decade before Van Gogh's talent would start to achieve wide recognition, with major museums acquiring his works.

From July to September the tourist office runs thematic guided tours for around €6 for two hours, with the Vieil Arles tour in English on Saturdays at 5pm, and the Van Gogh tour on Tuesdays at 5pm.

Festivals & Events

Feria Pascale Around Easter, Arles heralds the beginning of the bullfighting season with this festival.

Fête des Gardians Held in May, this festival sees the crowning of the Queen of Arles, Camargue cowboys parading through the streets of town, and Camargue games in the amphitheatre.

Fêtes d'Arles From around the end of June, dance, theatre, music and poetry readings feature during this two-week festival.

Fête des Prémices du Riz This 10-day-long festival, held in September, marks the start of the rice harvest. The tourist office has detailed information.

Les Rencontres Internationales de la Photographie (International Photography Festival; www.rencontres-arles.com) In early July, this festival attracts photographers from around the world, with works displayed until September.

Sleeping

Except during festivals, bullfights and July and August, Arles has plenty of reasonably priced accommodation, including very good-value triple and quadruple rooms. Most hotels shut during January, if not during the entire low season – check ahead. There are lots of **gîtes ruraux** (☎ reservations 04 90 59 49 40) in the surrounding countryside, especially in the Camargue. Ask the tourist office for a list.

BUDGET

Auberge de Jeunesse (☎ 04 90 96 18 25; www.fuaj.org; 20 av Maréchal Foch; dm incl breakfast & sheets €15.20; Feb–mid-Dec) This sunlit, 100-bed place, made up of eight-bed dorms, is just 10 minutes' walk from the centre. There is a bar but it closes at 11pm, just like the hostel's gates (except during *ferias*).

Camping City (☎ 04 90 93 08 86; www.camping-city.com; 67 rte de Crau; camping per site €16; Apr-Sep;) This slightly out-of-centre campsite is the closest to town, 1.5km southeast on the road to Marseille. There are a couple of very

PROVENCE

big supermarkets nearby, and there's a pool on-site. Take bus 2 to the Hermite stop.

MIDRANGE

Hôtel du Musée (☎ 04 90 93 88 88; www.hoteldumusee.com; 11 rue du Grand Prieuré; d €48-68, tr & q €65-85; closed mid-Jan–mid-Feb;) The 28 rooms in this gorgeous 12th- to 13th-century building are all individually decorated and have been fitted with brand-new bathrooms. The €7 buffet breakfast is a steal, particularly in summer when you can savour it on the sun-filled flower-decked patios.

our pick **Hôtel Le Cloître** (☎ 04 90 96 29 50; www.hotelcloitre.com; 16 rue du Cloître; d €50-70, tr/q €70/80; mid-Mar–Oct) It has taken 18 years of painstaking renovation to get this old convent to be in its current stunning state. The wonderful Jean-François and Agnès (both sources of local information) will happily show you the 'before-and-after' photo album as well as some of the treasures they've unearthed (17th-century murals, traces of 12th-century paint, old doors etc). The rooms all feel like a little piece of history, from the grand dining room to rooms 18 and 20 with their prized views of the stone and marble St-Trophime cloister.

Hôtel de l'Amphithéâtre (☎ 04 90 96 10 30; www.hotelamphitheatre.fr; 5-7 rue Diderot; d €55-95;) Right near the hotel's namesake Roman amphitheatre, deep crimson decor dresses the steadfast, solid bones of this 1600s-built hotel. The building has kept many of its grand 17th century features such as a monumental fireplace and imposing stone staircases. Wheelchair access is good and there is free wi-fi.

Hôtel Calendal (☎ 04 90 96 11 89; www.lecalendal.com; 5 rue Porte de Laure; d €69-149; closed Jan;) Next to the amphitheatre and overlooking the Théâtre Antique, this picture of a place has good wheelchair access, and sports 38 rooms with beamed ceilings and bright Provençal fabrics. There's a peaceful garden terrace at the back with a giant chessboard, and a brand new spa.

Cuisine & Tradition (☎ 04 90 49 69 20; www.cuisineprovencale.com; 11 rue Portagnel; d incl breakfast €70) Initially set up to house chef Érick Vedel's cooking students, the five colour-themed rooms have a quaint romantic feel with their grand beds, draped curtains and open bathrooms. The top-floor room has great views of the Arènes. Breakfast is a delicious home-made affair. Érick runs weekend or week-long courses, and can customise half-day courses for as little as two people (€250 for a half day; €100 per person for three or more people).

Hôtel Arlatan (☎ 04 90 93 56 66; www.hotel-arlatan.fr; 26 rue du Sauvage; d €85-155; closed mid-Jan–mid-Feb;) The heated swimming pool, pretty garden and plush rooms decorated with antique furniture are just some of the things going for this hotel. Add to that a setting steeped in history, with Roman foundations visible through a glass floor in the lobby and 15th century paintings on one of the lounges' ceilings; this is a very classy choice. Good wheelchair access.

TOP END

Grand Hôtel Nord Pinus (☎ 04 90 93 44 44; www.nord-pinus.com; place du Forum; d €160-295;) Drawing on the town's Roma and Spanish heritage, this intimate hotel is lined with vintage *feria* posters and paraphernalia. The musical ambience is flamenco. The stunning room 10, nicknamed 'room of the matadors' is where many famous matadors have stayed (and still stay). The bar downstairs has been decorated with amazing B&W Peter Beard photographs of African wildlife.

Eating

Arles' restaurant terraces give even the most upmarket eating establishments a relaxed café atmosphere. The Roman place du Forum, shaded by outstretched plane trees, turns into a giant dining table at lunch and dinner during summer. It's also where you'll find **Café la Nuit**, thought to be the café captured on canvas by Van Gogh in his Café Terrace at Night (1888), now mostly a tourist trap.

Comptoir du Sud (☎ 04 90 96 22 17; 2 rue Jean Jaurès) Overlooking place de la République, this place is good for a quick bite. It sells wonderful gourmet sandwiches (tasty chutneys, succulent meat, foie gras) and divine little salads, all at rock-bottom prices.

Au Jardin du Calendal (☎ 04 90 96 11 89; 22 place Pomme; mains €11-19; lunch Tue-Sun May-Oct) Gaspacho, hummus, marinated red mullet fillets, salmon and dill terrine, organic red Camargue rice and a good cheese and dessert selection – Hôtel Calendal's restaurant is summer bliss for its wholesome fresh food as much as for its lush garden setting. It also serves afternoon tea, with scrumptious cakes.

La Mule Blanche (☎ 04 90 93 98 54; 8 rue du Président Wilson; mains €12.20-20; lunch Tue-Sun, dinner Wed-Sun summer, lunch Tue-Sat, dinner Wed-Sat winter) Jazz is often performed at the piano in the White Mule's domed interior, but the hottest tables are on the pavement terrace, the prettiest in town, perfect to savour a king-size salad or simple Mediterranean fare.

Le 16 (☎ 04 90 93 77 36; 16 rue du Docteur Fanton; mains €15; ⌚ lunch & dinner Mon-Fri, lunch Sat) Stripy tablecloths and candle-lit tables create a wonderfully warm atmosphere in which to savour the southwestern cuisine on your plate. Service is charming, and on most evenings a Jacques Brel–inspired singer comes in to scratch a tune or two on his guitar.

Corazón (☎ 04 90 96 32 53; 1bis rue Réattu; mains €18-25; ⌚ lunch & dinner Tue-Sat) This funky, crimson space in a recessed arcade combines a contemporary art gallery with a modern European restaurant. The restaurant serves fare as imaginative as the interior (the furniture is for sale, by the way): seafood sauerkraut, rabbit ravioli with pumpkin sauce or liquorice and rum lamb shoulder. Blimey.

Le Cilantro (☎ 04 90 18 25 05; 31 rue Porte de Laure; mains €32; ⌚ lunch Tue-Fri & Sun, dinner Tue-Sat) Arles' most buzzing tables are a result of the homecoming of Arlésian chef Jérôme Laurent, cooking accomplished dishes that change seasonally – ginger or cocoa pigeon, lard-roasted potatoes (yum!) and excellent veggie courses, too.

SELF-CATERING

Amble around the Saturday morning **market** (bd Georges Clemenceau & bd des Lices) that stretches the length of the main boulevard selling strong cheese, Camargue salt, olive oil and bull sausages. On Wednesday, market stalls set up along bd Émile Combes (east of Les Arènes).

Pick up groceries at **Monoprix** (place Lamartine; ⌚ 8.30am-7.30pm Mon-Sat).

Drinking

Oli Pan (☎ 04 90 96 11 89; 5 rue Porte de Laure; dishes €3-10; ⌚ 9am-7pm) The latest addition to the café scene, Le Calendal's new crowd-pleaser has organic sandwiches, Mövenpick ice creams, bottled beers and free wi-fi, all served on the great sunset-facing terrace or inside in a fresh candy-coloured room.

L'Australian Café Walla Beer (☎ 04 90 97 22 17; 7 rue Molière) Arles is pretty quiet at night outside of *ferias,* but this place is popular for an evening drink on the terrace that overlooks bd Clemenceau.

Paddy Mullins (☎ 04 90 49 67 25; 5 bd George Clemenceau; ⌚ 10am-2am) An Irish-style pub featuring regular live music. It's not the most genuine of pubs, but it brings some welcome oomph to an otherwise staid Arles.

Shopping

Next door to the first-ever boutique of home-grown fashion designer **Christian Lacroix** (52 rue de la République) is **Puyricard** (54 rue de la République), purveying exquisite Provençal chocolates.

Getting There & Away

AIR

Nîmes airport (p765) is 20km northwest of the city on the A54. There is no public transport between the airport and Arles.

BUS

The **bus station** (☎ 08 10 00 08 16; 24 bd Georges Clemenceau; ⌚ 8.30am-noon & 2-5.30pm Mon-Fri) is served by companies including **Telleschi** (☎ 04 42 28 40 22), which runs services to/from Aix-en-Provence (€10.40, 1½ hours). Buses to Nîmes take one hour (€6.60).

Buses also link Arles with various parts of the Camargue, including Les Stes-Maries-de-la-Mer (€5.20, one hour).

TRAIN

Some major rail destinations from Arles' **train station** (⌚ information office 9am-12.30pm & 2-6pm) include Nîmes (€7.20, 30 minutes), Marseille (€12.70, 55 minutes) and Avignon (€6.30, 20 minutes).

Getting Around

BUS

Local buses are operated by **Star** (☎ 08 10 00 08 16; information office 24 bd Georges Clemenceau; ⌚ 8.30am-noon & 2-5.30pm Mon-Fri). Star's office, situated west of the tourist office, is the main bus hub, although most buses also stop at place Lamartine, a short walk south of the train station. Star buses run from 6.30am to 7.30pm Monday to Saturday, and 9.30am to 5pm on Sunday. A single ticket costs €0.80. In addition to its 11 bus lines, Star runs free minibuses called Starlets, which make a circle around most of the old city every 30 minutes from 7.10am to 7.10pm Monday to Saturday.

TAXI

For a taxi call ☎ 04 90 96 90 03.

THE CAMARGUE

Just half an hour from Arles, Provence's rolling and brightly coloured landscapes morph into the flat, bleached, desolate wilderness of the Camargue. The light is harsher, the wind is stronger, but, thankfully, its people have retained some southern warmth.

The area is particularly famous for its teeming birdlife. King of all is the pink flamingo, who likes to winter in the Camargue's expansive wetlands. But there are at least another 500 species of birds regularly visiting the area, so birdwatchers should pack their binoculars and camera – and plenty of mosquito repellent. Other nature-lovers will revel in horse-riding trips across the patchwork of pink and purple salt-pans, meadows with grazing bulls and rice fields.

Enclosed by the Petit Rhône and Grand Rhône Rivers, most of the Camargue wetlands are within the 850-sq-km Parc Naturel Régional de Camargue. The park was established in 1970 to preserve the area's fragile ecosystems while sustaining local agriculture. On the periphery, the Étang de Vaccarès and nearby peninsulas and islands form the Réserve Nationale de Camargue, a 135-sq-km nature reserve.

The Camargue's two largest towns are the seaside pilgrim's outpost, Les Stes-Maries-de-la-Mer, and to the northwest, the walled town of Aigues Mortes.

INFORMATION

Réserve Nationale de Camargue Office (☎ 04 90 97 00 97; La Capelière; 🕑 9am-1pm & 2-6pm Apr-Sep, 9am-1pm & 2-5pm Wed-Mon Oct-Mar) Along the D36B, on the eastern side of Étang de Vaccarès, with exhibits on the Camargue's ecosystems, flora and fauna. Many trails and paths fan out from here.

SIGHTS & ACTIVITIES

Musée Camarguais

Inside an 1812-built sheep shed, the **Camargue Museum** (☎ 04 90 97 10 82; Mas du Pont de Rousty; adult/student €5/2.50; 🕑 9am-6pm Apr-Sep, 10am-5pm Wed-Mon Oct-Mar) is a fantastic introduction to this unique area. It covers the area's history and ecosystems, as well as traditional lifestyle in the new *gardian* (the Camargue version of cowboy!) room. From here, a 3.5km nature trail leads to an observation

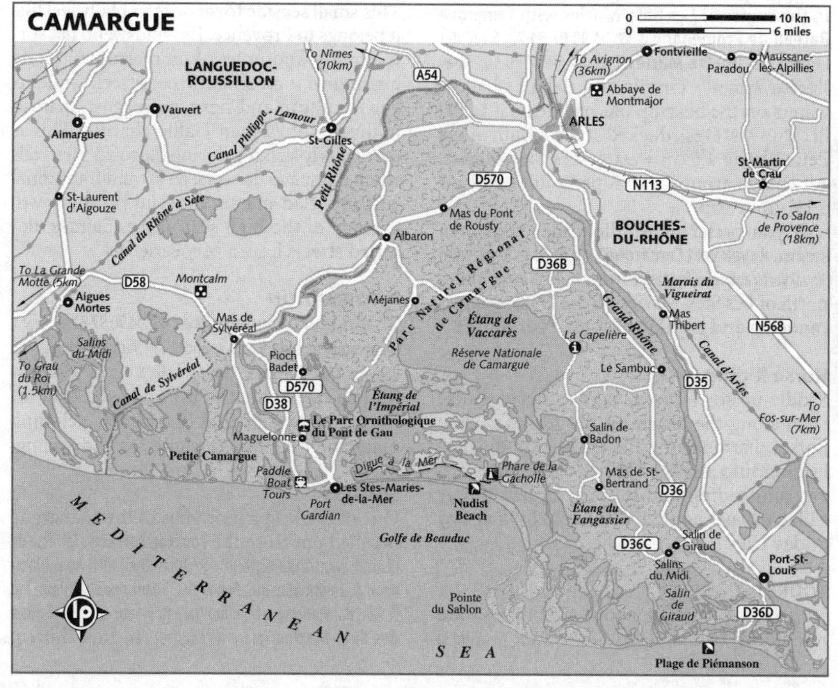

tower with bird's-eye views. The museum is 10km southwest of Arles on the D570 to Les Stes-Maries-de-la-Mer.

Le Parc Ornithologique du Pont de Gau

Get up close and personal with some 2000 pink flamingos at the wonderful **Parc Ornithologique du Pont de Gau** (☎ 04 90 97 82 62; adult/child €7/4; 🕑 9am-sunset Apr-Sep, 10am-sunset Oct-Mar), a semi-wild natural reserve 4km north of Les Stes-Maries on the D570. There are dozens more bird species living on the reserve, which you can watch from 7km of beautiful trails meandering through the site.

Walking

Walking paths and trails wend through the Parc Naturel Régional and the Réserve Nationale, on the embankments and along the coast. Bookshops sell detailed walking maps, including the 1:25,000 IGN Série Bleue maps 2943ET and 2944OT. Tourist offices also have plenty of good free maps.

Boating & Watersports

Experience the waterlogged Camargue by a boat excursion departing from Port Gardian in the centre of Les Stes-Maries with **Camargue Bateau de Promenade** (☎ 04 90 97 84 72; 5 rue des Launes) or **Quatre Maries** (☎ 04 90 97 70 10; 36 av Théodore Aubanel). Or ply the delta's shallow waters on the beat-up old paddle boat **Le Tiki III** (☎ 04 90 97 81 68), docked at the mouth of the Petit Rhône 1.5km west of Les Stes-Maries. All charge around €10/5 per adult/child for a 1½-hour trip.

If you prefer to paddle under your own steam, **Kayak Vert Camargue** (☎ 04 66 73 57 17; www.kayakvert-camargue.fr; Mas de Sylvéréal; prices vary), 14km north of Les Stes-Maries off the D38, arranges canoeing and kayaking on the Petit Rhône.

PROVENCE

Horse Riding

Saddle up for a *promenade à cheval* (horse ride) along the beach on the region's white horses. Farms along the D570 (Rte d'Arles) leading into Les Stes-Maries have signs advertising riding and lessons. Expect to pay €14 to €20 per hour, or €55 to €80 for half-day or day trips.

TOURS

Jeep safaris costing about €20 to €45 are offered by **Le Gitan** (☎ 04 66 70 09 65; 17 av de la République) on Les Stes-Maries' seafront, and by L'Auberge Cavalière (opposite).

GETTING THERE & AWAY

For details about bus connections to/from Arles, see p832. There are also two buses a day in July and August from Les Stes-Maries to Montpellier (€10.60, two hours) via Aigues Mortes.

GETTING AROUND

Bicycles are perfect for traversing the Camargue's flat (if windy) terrain. East of Les Stes-Maries, areas along the seafront and further inland are reserved for walkers and cyclists.

For an English-language list of cycling routes go to **Le Vélo Saintois** (☎ 04 90 97 74 56; 19 rue de la République, Les Stes-Maries), which hires out mountain bikes for €15/34 per day/three days. **Le Vélociste** (☎ 04 90 97 83 26; place Mireille, Les Stes-Maries) also rents out bikes, and organises cycling and horse-riding (€36) or cycling and canoeing (€30) packages.

Les Stes-Maries-de-la-Mer

pop 2500

This small seaside town doesn't really feel like it belongs to Provence. Its windswept, flat surroundings and miles of uninterrupted sandy beach give it an Atlantic coast feel, while its gypsy culture and heritage suggest Spanish inklings rather than Gallic charms. This is particularly striking during the town's festivals when flamenco dancers, *ferias* and traditional costume-clad masses descend on the town. Outside of the high season, Les Saintes' deserted streets have a very eerie feel.

INFORMATION

The modern **tourist office** (☎ 04 90 97 82 55; www.saintesmaries.com; 5 av Van Gogh; 🕑 9am-8pm Jul & Aug, 9am-7pm Apr-Jun & Sep, 9am-6pm Mar & Oct, 9am-5pm Nov-Feb) has an excellent website and stacks of information on activities in the area, including maps and itineraries for walking and cycling.

SIGHTS

One of the best panoramas of the Camargue is rolled out from the **rooftop terrace** (Terrasse de l'Église; adult/child €2/1.30; 🕑 10am-8pm Jul & Aug, 10am-noon & 2-6pm Mar-Jun, Sep & Oct, 10am-noon & 2-5pm Sat & Sun, daily during school holidays Nov-Feb) of the **Église des Stes-Maries** (place de l'Église). In this church,

A WASHED-UP LEGEND?

Catholicism first reached European shores in what's now the little township of Les Stes-Maries. So the stories go, Stes Marie-Salomé and Marie-Jacobé fled the Holy Land in a tiny boat and were caught in a storm, drifting at sea until washing ashore here.

Provençal and Catholic lore diverge at this point: Catholicism believes Sara, patron saint of the *gitans* (Roma Gitano people, also known as gypsies), travelled with the two Marys on the boat; Provençal legend says Sara was already here and was the first person to recognise their holiness. In 1448 skeletal remains said to belong to Sara and the Marys were found in a crypt in Les Stes-Maries.

Finer historical points aside, it's by no means a washed-up legend. *Gitans* continue to make the pilgrimage here on 24 and 25 May (often staying for up to three weeks), dancing and playing music in the streets, and parading a statue of Sara through town. The Sunday in October closest to the 22nd sees a second pilgrimage dedicated to the two Stes Maries, and *courses Camarguaises* (nonlethal bullfights) are also held at this time.

dating from the 12th to the 15th century, the relics of St Sara – the highly revered patron saint of the Roma – were found in the crypt by King René in 1448. These are enshrined in a wooden chest, stashed in the stone wall above the choir.

Tickets for **bullfights** at Les Stes-Maries' Arènes are sold at the arena – check with the tourist office for schedules.

Les Stes-Maries is fringed by around 30km of uninterrupted fine-sand **beaches**. For an all-over tan, the area around **Phare de la Gacholle**, the lighthouse 11km east of town, is the place for bathing *sans* (without) suit.

FESTIVALS & EVENTS

Les Stes-Maries spills over with colour and life during the animated **gitan pilgrimages** (see boxed text, above).

SLEEPING & EATING

Low-rise 'ranch-style' hotels line the D570 heading into Les Stes-Maries. A number of old *mas* (tradition Provençal stone houses) also surround the town, and often let out rooms. Accommodation is more limited in winter.

Camping La Brise (☎ 04 90 97 84 67; fax 04 90 97 72 01; av Marcel Carrière; per site winter €12, summer €18.90-20.50; ⏰ closed mid-Nov–mid-Dec; 🏊) Right on the beach, with not one but two swimming pools, this campsite is a good option for families. The site can be very windy, so pick somewhere sheltered.

Auberge de Jeunesse (☎ 04 90 97 51 72; www.auberge-de-jeunesse.fr, in French; Pioch Badet; dm incl breakfast, dinner & sheets €28.70; ⏰ reception 7.30-10.30am & 5-11pm Sep-Jun, to midnight Jul & Aug) Half-board is part of the package at this rural hostel, 8km north of Les Stes-Maries on the D570 to Arles. Buses from Arles' bus station drop you at the door.

Hôtel Méditerranée (☎ 04 90 97 82 09; www.mediterraneehotel.com, in French; 4 av Frédéric Mistral; d €40-55; ❄) Handily located in the centre of town (so a good bet if you don't have your own wheels), this place is one of the cheapest and most charming options in Les Stes. Rooms have all been renovated and some have air-con. Breakfast is taken on a patio overrun with flowers.

Mas de la Grenouillère (☎ 04 90 97 90 22; fax 04 90 97 70 94; d/tr incl breakfast from €67/95; ❄ 🏊) Horses, fields and silence is what's waiting for you at the 'frog farm'. The owners are horse breeders and organise horse-riding trips. The *mas* is 1.5km down a dirt track signposted 1km north of Les Stes-Maries off the D570.

L'Auberge Cavalière (☎ 04 90 97 88 88; www.aubergecavaliere.com; D570; s €130-160, d €140-170, half-board available; ❄ 💻 🏊) Approximately 1.5km north of Les Stes-Maries, this stunning yet salt-of-the-earth hotel spreads out over a typical Camargue landscape of wetlands and meadows. Rooms 340 to 345 look over a pond teeming with birdlife while the thatched *cabanes de gardian* (cabins) offer cosy independent quarters. The hotel runs horse-riding trips, including sunset and sunrise expeditions. The on-site restaurant (*menus* €28 to €38, open for lunch and dinner every day) serves great local fare, from bull-meat stews to Camargue rice.

Le Delta (☎ 04 90 97 81 12; 1 place Mireille; mains €11-15; ⏰ lunch & dinner Tue-Sat, lunch Sun) A local favourite, Le Delta is a great place to try Camargue specialities like *gardianne de taureau* (bull stew) and the area's thumbnail-sized clams called *tellines*.

Aigues-Mortes

pop 6800

Actually located over the border from Provence in the Gard *département* (administrative division of France), the town of Aigues-Mortes – meaning, somewhat eerily, 'dead waters' – is 28km northwest of Les Stes-Maries at the western extremity of the Camargue. Aigues-Mortes is set in flat marshland and encircled by walls. The town was established in the mid-13th century by Louis IX to give the French crown a Mediterranean port under its direct control, and in 1248 Louis IX's flotilla of 1500 ships massed here before setting sail to the Holy Land for the Seventh Crusade.

The cobbled streets inside the city walls are lined with restaurants, cafés and bars, giving it a festive atmosphere. It's definitely a charming option from which to explore the area.

INFORMATION

Tourist Office (☎ 04 66 53 73 00; www.ot-aiguesmortes.fr; place St-Louis; 🕑 9am-noon & 1-6pm Mon-Fri, 10am-noon & 2-6pm Sat & Sun Sep-Jun, 9am-8pm Jul & Aug) Inside the walled city.

SIGHTS & ACTIVITIES

Scaling the ramparts rewards you with a sweeping overview of the town's history, and of surrounding marshes. Head to the top of the tower, **Tour de Constance** (☎ 04 66 53 61 55; adult/student/under 17yr €6.50/4.50/free; 🕑 10am-5.30pm Sep-Apr, 10am-7pm May-Aug). The 1.6km wall-top walk takes about one hour.

The southern ramparts afford views of the stretching salt-pans (the Salins du Midi), which you can travel through aboard the **salt train** (☎ 04 66 73 40 24; www.salins.fr; adult/child €8.20/6; 🕑 Mar-Oct), accompanied by commentary in English. Book your tickets at the ticket office Porte de la Gardette, from where you will catch a bus to the salt-pan site.

SLEEPING & EATING

Parking within the town walls is practically impossible but there are plenty of car parks outside.

L'Escale (☎ 04 66 53 71 14; fax 04 66 53 76 74; http://hotel.escale.free.fr; 3 av Tour de Constance; d €26-48, 4-5-person r €55-65; 🅿) It should be compulsory for every town to have somewhere like L'Escale, which caters so well for budget travellers. The basic rooms are immaculate, as are the shared bathrooms and toilets of the cheaper rooms. Rooms in the annexe are bigger and good value for friends or families. The restaurant (mains €7 to €10), with red tablecloths and a flower-lined terrace, is one of the last bastions still churning out homemade *frites* to go with your steak.

L'Hermitage de St-Antoine (☎ 06 03 04 34 05; www.hermitagesa.com; 9 bd Intérieur Nord; d incl breakfast €74-79; ❄ ⊠) Inside the walled town, this pocket-sized *chambre d'hôte* has three exquisitely appointed rooms, one with a small private terrace, another under the sloped ceiling, and all with fresh, crisp decor. The continental breakfast takes on new dimensions in the sun-filled patio. Note: L'Hermitage de St-Antoine only caters to children aged over 12.

Le Café de Bouzigues (☎ 04 66 53 93 95; 7 rue Pasteur; menu €29.50; 🕑 lunch & dinner) This is an unexpected find in rather staid Camargue: Bouzigues is trendy, fun, unconventional – and loving it. Both the food and the interior have slightly wacky tendencies (hot and cold oysters with figs and an onion and ginger puree; duck leg with wheat, lard and hazelnut risotto), but either way it is a resounding success. The menu changes regularly, guaranteeing optimal novelty value.

THE VAUCLUSE

The Vaucluse is like every Provençal cliché rolled into one: lavender fields, scenic hills, rows upon rows of vineyards, enchanting villages and picturesque markets, traditional stone houses, beating summer sun and howling winter mistral. At the heart of Vaucluse – which means closed valley – is the exquisite town of Avignon, of historical nursery rhyme fame (see Pont St-Bénezet, opposite).

A car is the ideal way to cover the Vaucluse, but it's possible (if not expedient) to get from town to town by local bus.

AVIGNON

pop 90,800

Hooped by 4.3km of superbly preserved stone ramparts, this graceful city is the belle of Provence's ball. Its turn as the papal seat of power has bestowed Avignon with a treasury of magnificent art and architecture, none grander than the massive medieval fortress and papal palace, the Palais des Papes.

Famed for its annual performing arts festival, these days Avignon is also an animated student city and an ideal spot from which to step out into the surrounding region. In France and beyond, Avignon is perhaps best known for its fabled bridge, the Pont St-Bénezet, aka the Pont d'Avignon.

History

Avignon first gained its ramparts and its reputation as a city of art and culture during the 14th century, when Pope Clement V and his court fled political turmoil in Rome for Avignon. From 1309 to 1377, the seven French-born popes invested huge sums of money in building and decorating the papal palace. Under the popes' rule, Jews and political dissidents took shelter here. Pope Gregory XI left Avignon in 1376, but his death two years later led to the Great Schism (1378–1417), during which rival popes – up to three at one time – resided at Rome and Avignon, denouncing and excommunicating one another. Even after the schism was settled and an impartial pope – Martin V – established himself in Rome, Avignon remained under papal rule. The city and Comtat Venaissin (now the Vaucluse *département*) were ruled by papal legates until 1791, when they were annexed to France.

Orientation

The main avenue within the *intra-muros* (walled city) runs northwards from the train station to place de l'Horloge. South of the tourist office it's called cours Jean Jaurès, while north of the office it's rue de la République.

The café-clad central square place de l'Horloge is located 300m south of place du Palais, which abuts the Palais des Papes. The city gate nearest the train station is Porte de la République, while the city gate next to Pont Édouard Daladier, which leads to Villeneuve-lès-Avignon, is Porte de l'Oulle. The Quartier des Teinturiers (Dyers' Quarter), centred on rue des Teinturiers, southeast of place Pie, is the hang-out of Avignon's population of bohemian artists.

Information

BOOKSHOPS

Shakespeare (☎ 04 90 27 38 50; 155 rue de la Carreterie; 🕑 9.30am-noon & 2-6pm Tue-Sat) Enjoy homemade scones with your tomes at this English bookshop and *salon de thé*.

INTERNET ACCESS

Lots of internet cafés are around place Pie.

Chez W@m (☎ 04 90 86 19 03; 34 rue Bonneterie; per hr €3; 🕑 10am-8pm Mon-Thu & 10am-10pm Fri & Sat)

INTERNET RESOURCES

Provence Guide (www.provenceguide.com) Covers the Vaucluse region and includes B&Bs.

Visit Provence (www.visitprovence.com)

LAUNDRY

Lavmatic (9 rue du Chapeau Rouge; 🕑 7am-8.30pm) 21st-century laundrette with wi-fi.

MONEY

CIC (13 rue de la République) Has an ATM.

POST

Main Post Office (cours Président Kennedy) Offers currency exchange.

TOURIST INFORMATION

Tourist Office (☎ 04 32 74 32 74; www.avignon-tourisme.com; 41 cours Jean Jaurès; 🕑 9am-5pm Mon-Sat, 9.45am-5pm Sun Apr-Oct, 9am-7pm Mon-Sat, 9.45am-5pm Sun Jul, 9am-6pm Mon-Fri, 9am-5pm Sat & 10am-noon Sun Nov-Mar) Around 300m north of the train station.

Sights & Activities

Ticket offices for most sights close up to one hour before overall closing times. Admission to most sights is cheapter with the Avignon Passion pass (see the boxed text, p840).

PONT ST-BÉNEZET (PONT D'AVIGNON)

The fabled **Pont St-Bénezet** (St Bénezet's Bridge; ☎ 04 90 27 51 16; adult/student, 8-18yr/under 8yr €4.50/3.50/free; 🕑 9am-9pm Aug, 9am-8pm Jul & early–mid-Sep, 9am-7pm Apr-Jun & mid-Sep–Oct, 9.30am-5.45pm Nov-Mar), immortalised in the nursery rhyme *Sur le Pont d'Avignon*, was completed in 1185. It links Avignon with the settlement across the Rhône that later became Villeneuve-lès-Avignon. The 900m-long wooden structure was repaired and rebuilt several times before all but four of its 22 spans were washed away in the mid-1600s.

Entry is via cours Châtelet. If you don't feel like paying to visit the bridge, you can see it for free from the Rocher des Doms park, Pont Édouard Daladier or from across the river on the Île de la Barthelasse's chemin des Berges.

WALLED CITY

Wrapping around the city, Avignon's ramparts were built between 1359 and 1370.

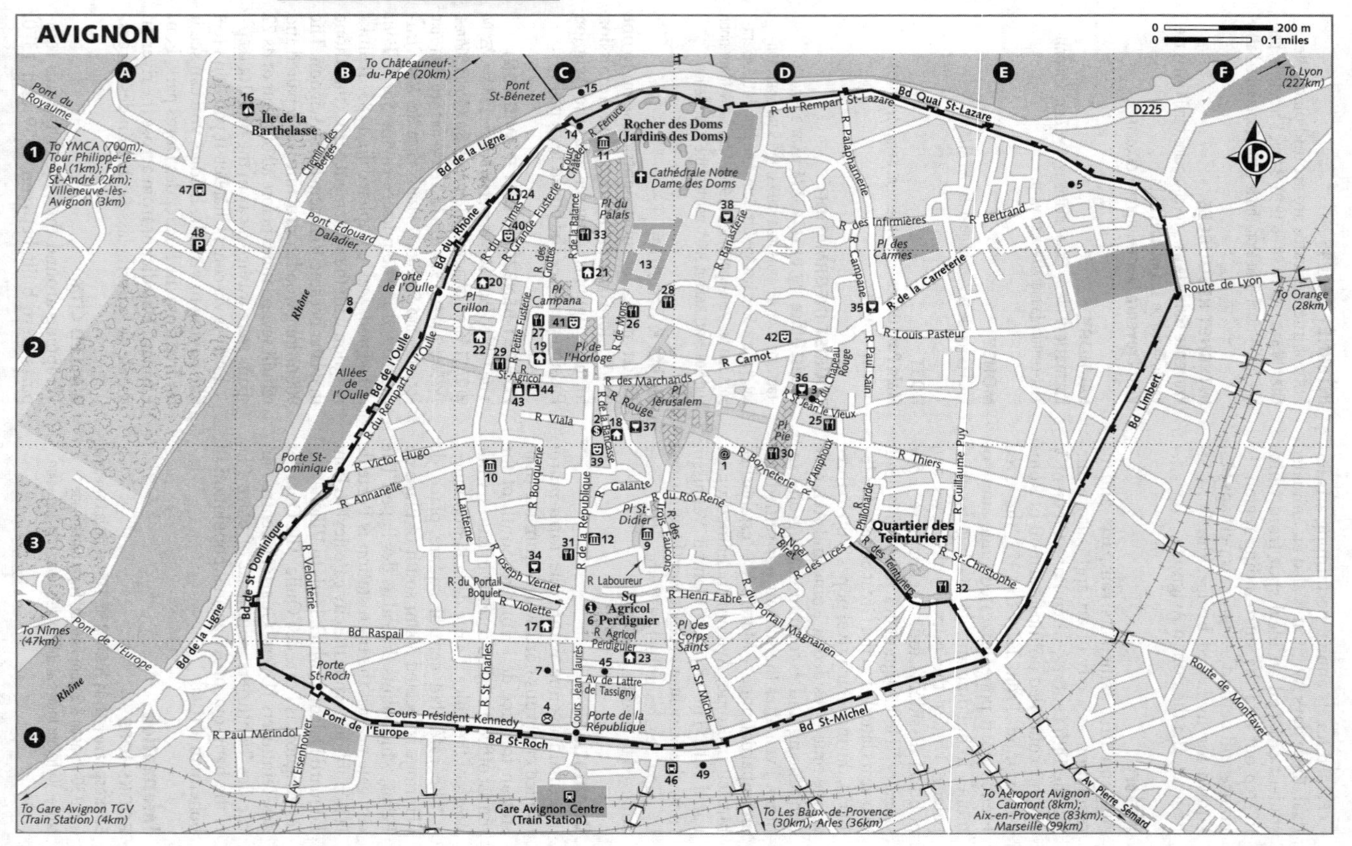
AVIGNON
0 200 m
0 0.1 miles
A
B
C
D
E
F
1
2
3
4
To Châteauneuf-du-Pape (20km)
Pont St-Bénezet
To Lyon (227km)
D225
Pont du Royaume
Île de la Barthelasse
Chemin des Berges
To YMCA (700m); Tour Philippe-le-Bel (1km); Fort St-André (2km); Villeneuve-lès-Avignon (3km)
Pont Édouard Daladier
Rhône
Bd de la Ligne
Bd du Rhône
R du Limas
R Grande Fusterie
Cours Châtelet
R Ferruce
Rocher des Doms (Jardins des Doms)
Cathédrale Notre Dame des Doms
Pl du Palais
R de la Balance
R des Grottes
Pl Campana
R Petite Fusterie
R St-Agricol
Pl de l'Horloge
R de Mons
R du Rempart St-Lazare
Bd Quai St-Lazare
R Palapharnerie
R Banasterie
R des Infirmières
R Bertrand
Pl des Carmes
R Campane
R de la Carreterie
Route de Lyon
To Orange (28km)
R Louis Pasteur
R Paul Saïn
R du Chapeau Rouge
R St Jean le Vieux
R Carnot
R des Marchands
Pl Jérusalem
R Rouge
R de la Bancasse
R Viala
Pl Pie
R Bonneterie
R d'Amphoux
R Thiers
R Guillaume Puy
Bd Limbert
Porte de l'Oulle
Pl Crillon
Allées de l'Oulle
Bd de l'Oulle
R du Rempart de l'Oulle
Porte St-Dominique
R Victor Hugo
R Annanelle
R Lanterne
R Bouquerie
R de la République
R Galante
R du Roi René
Pl St-Didier
R des Trois Faucons
R Philonarde
Quartier des Teinturiers
R Noël Biret
R des Lices
R des Teinturiers
R St-Christophe
R Joseph Vernet
R du Portail Boquier
R Violette
R Laboureur
Sq Agricol Perdiguier
R Henri Fabre
R du Portail Magnanen
Pl des Corps Saints
R Agricol Perdiguier
Bd de St Dominique
R Velouterie
Bd Raspail
R St Charles
Cours Jean Jaurès
Av de Lattre de Tassigny
R St Michel
Route de Montfavet
To Nîmes (47km)
Pont de l'Europe
Porte St-Roch
Cours Président Kennedy
Porte de la République
Bd St-Michel
R Paul Mérindol
Pont de l'Europe
Bd St-Roch
Av Eisenhower
Av Pierre Sémard
To Gare Avignon TGV (Train Station) (4km)
Gare Avignon Centre (Train Station)
To Les Baux-de-Provence (30km); Arles (36km)
To Aéroport Avignon-Caumont (8km); Aix-en-Provence (83km); Marseille (99km)

INFORMATION
Chez W@m....1 D3
CIC....2 C2
Lavmatic....3 D2
Main Post Office....4 C4
Shakespeare....5 E1
Tourist Office....6 C3

SIGHTS & ACTIVITIES
Autocars Lieutaud....(see 46)
Bureau du Festival....7 C4
Les Grands Bateaux de Provence..8 B2
Musée Angladon....9 C3
Musée Calvet....10 C3
Musée du Petit Palais....11 C1
Musée Lapidaire....12 C3
Palais des Papes....13 C2
Pont St-Bénezet Entrance....14 C1
Shuttleboat Embarkment Point..15 C1

SLEEPING
Auberge Bagatelle....(see 16)
Camping Bagatelle....16 B1
Hôtel Boquier....17 C3
Hôtel de Garlande....18 C2
Hôtel de l'Horloge....19 C2
Hôtel d'Europe....20 C2
Hôtel du Palais des Papes....21 C2
Hôtel Mignon....22 C2
Hôtel Splendid....23 C4
Le Limas....24 C1

EATING
Au Tout Petit....25 D2
Christian Etienne....26 C2
La Fourchette....27 C2
La Marmiton....28 C2
La Tropézienne....29 C2
Les Halles' Food Market....30 D3
Monoprix....31 C3
Numéro 75....32 E3
Restaurant Brunel....33 C1

DRINKING
La Compagnie des Comptoirs...34 C3
Le Cid Café....(see 20)
Mon Bar....35 D2
Red Sky....36 D2
Tapalocas....37 C2
Utopia Bar....38 D1

ENTERTAINMENT
Cinéma Utopia....(see 38)
Fnac....39 C3
L'Esclave....40 C1
Opéra d'Avignon....41 C2
Red Zone....42 D2

SHOPPING
Comtesse du Barry....43 C2
Oliviers & Co....44 C2

TRANSPORT
Agence Commerciale TCRA......45 C4
Bus 11 Stop....(see 4)
Bus Station....46 C4
Eurolines....(see 46)
La Barthelasse Bus Stop....47 A1
Linebús....(see 46)
Parking de L'Ile Piot....48 A1
Provence Bike....49 D4
TGV Shuttle Bus Stop....(see 4)

They were restored during the 19th century, minus their original moats – though even in the 14th century this defence system was hardly state-of-the-art, lacking machicolations (openings in the parapets for niceties such as pouring boiling oil on attackers, or for shooting out arrows).

Within the walls is a wealth of fine museums – the *Avignon Passion* booklet (see boxed text, p840) lists the whole gamut. The tourist office also has a French and English map with four suggested itineraries across the old town.

Palais des Papes

Flanked by the sprawling courtyard cours d'Honneur, the cavernous stone halls and extensive grounds of the **Palais des Papes** (Palace of the Popes; ☎ 04 90 27 50 00; place du Palais; adult/Avignon Passion pass, student & 12-18yr/under 12yr €6/3/free; 9am-9pm Aug, 9am-8pm Jul & early–mid-Sep, 9am-7pm Apr-Jun & mid-Sep–Oct, 9.30am-5.45pm Nov-Mar) testify to the fortune amassed by the papacy during the 'Babylonian Captivity'. Built during the 14th century and intended as a fortified palace for the pontifical court, it's the largest Gothic palace in Europe. Many of the 25 rooms are rather bare, save for the Pope's apartments and the odd stunning fresco or mosaic floor. To avoid the Babylonian cacophony of guides shouting their explanations to gaggles of organised tours, come at lunchtime when the groups have retreated to nearby restaurants.

The admission price includes a multilanguage audio guide.

Musée du Petit Palais

During the 14th and 15th centuries, **Musée du Petit Palais** (☎ 04 90 86 44 58; place du Palais; adult/Avignon Passion pass €6/3; 10am-6pm Wed-Mon Jun-Sep, 10am-1pm & 2-6pm Wed-Mon Oct-May) served as a bishops' and archbishops' palace. These days it's home to an outstanding collection of lavishly coloured 13th- to 16th-century Italian religious paintings created by artists including Botticelli, Carpaccio and Giovanni di Paolo. English-language interpretive information is available.

Musée Calvet

Impressive architecture and art intertwine at the elegant Hôtel de Villeneuve-Martignan (built 1741–54), where you'll find **Musée Calvet** (☎ 04 90 86 33 84; 65 rue Joseph Vernet; adult/student & 12-18yr/under 12yr €6/3/free; 10am-6pm Wed-Mon Jun-Sep, 10am-1pm & 2-6pm Wed-Mon Oct-May) Among its collections are 15th-century wrought-iron works and paintings from the 16th to 20th centuries.

Musée Lapidaire

Small and fairly random, the **Musée Lapidaire** (☎ 04 90 86 33 84; 27 rue de la République; adult/Avignon Passion pass/under 12yr €2/1/free; 10am-6pm Wed-Mon Jun-Sep, 10am-1pm & 2-6pm Wed-Mon Oct-May) houses a collection of Egyptian, Roman, Etruscan and early Christian pieces.

Musée Angladon

Born out of the private collection of couturier Jacques Doucet (1853–1929) and visionary

AVIGNON PASSION

Anyone passionate about Avignon's rich cultural heritage will want to pick up a free Avignon Passion pass from the tourist office. This nifty pass entitles you to 20% to 50% discounted entry on second and subsequent visits to museums and monuments (the equivalent of student prices), as well as reduced prices on the tourist office walking tours. It's valid for 15 days in all the museums of Avignon, as well as Villeneuve-lès-Avignon, and covers a family of five.

thinking of his heirs Jean and Paulette Angladon-Dubrujeaud, the charming **Musée Angladon** (☎ 04 90 82 29 03; www.angladon.com; 5 rue Laboureur; adult/students, 7-18yr/under 7yr €6/4/free; 🕑 1-6pm Tue-Sun mid-Mar–mid-Nov, 1-6pm Wed-Sun mid-Nov–mid-Mar) harbours Impressionist treasures. These include the only Van Gogh painting in Provence *(Railway Wagons)*, as well as works by Cézanne, Manet, Degas and other illustrious artists such as Picasso, Modigliani and Fujita. Upstairs is a collection of antique furniture and 16th and 17th-century paintings, many of which belonged to the Dubrujeauds, who were artists themselves.

BOATING

Les Grands Bateaux de Provence (☎ 04 90 85 62 25; www.mireio.net, in French; allées de l'Oulle) runs year-round excursions down the Rhône to Arles or the vineyard area of Châteauneuf-du-Pape on two restaurant boats (adult/Avignon Passion pass €46.50/41.85, including a meal). Less-ambitious destinations include Villeneuve-lès-Avignon and Île de la Barthelasse from two to five times daily from April to September.

A free **shuttle boat** (🕑 10am-12.30pm & 2-6.30pm Apr-Jun & Sep, 11am-9pm Jul & Aug, 2-5.30pm Wed, 10am-noon & 2-5.30pm Sat & Sun Oct-Dec & mid-Feb-Mar) adjacent to Pont St-Bénezet connects the walled city with the Île de la Barthelasse.

PROVENCE

Tours

Two-hour **guided tours** (adult/Avignon Passion pass, student, 8-18yr/under 8yr €11/8/free) of Avignon in English and French depart daily from the tourist office at 10am between April and October (Saturday only between November and March).

Autocars Lieutaud (☎ 04 90 86 36 75; www.cars-lieutaud.fr) runs half- and full-day bus tours throughout the year to nearby vineyards, the Pont du Gars or the Luberon (full price/Avignon Passion pass €45/40). For a more-authentic (and slower!) experience, do it in the archetypal French car: a Citroën 2CV (€145 for a three-hour chauffeured trip in the Alpilles).

Festivals & Events

Festival d'Avignon (www.festival-avignon.com) Hundreds of artists take to the stage and streets during this world-famous festival, founded in 1946 and held every year from early July to early August. Tickets for official festival performances in the Palais des Papes' cours d'Honneur cost around €25; reservations can be made from mid-June. Information can be obtained from the **Bureau du Festival** (☎ 04 90 27 66 50; Espace St-Louis, 20 rue du Portail Boquier).

Festival Off (☎ 04 90 85 13 08; www.avignonleoff.com, in French) Paralleling the official Avignon festival, this fringe event has an eclectic, cheaper program of experimental performances. A Carte Public Adhérent (€14) gives you a 30% discount on all Festival Off performances (each costing about €15 before the discount).

Sleeping

Avignon is one of the few places in Provence that caters well for budget-conscious travellers. You'll need to book many months ahead for a room during the festival, when prices soar.

BUDGET

Camping Bagatelle (☎ 04 90 86 30 39; camping.bagatelle@wanadoo.fr; Île de la Barthelasse; tent only per person €4.66-6.16, per 2 people with car €11.32-19.32; 🕑 reception 8am-9pm) Multilingual, shaded and only 20 minutes' walk from the centre on Île de la Barthelasse, this campsite offers great discounts to campers who come without a car.

Auberge Bagatelle (☎ 04 90 85 78 45; auberge.bagatelle@wanadoo.fr; Île de la Barthelasse; dm €15.90, s €35, d €40) Adjoining the campsite, the two- to eight-bed dorms are basic but serviceable. All rates include breakfast; sheets are €2.50. There are plenty of parties going on in the next-door bar-restaurant. Take bus 10 from the main post office to La Barthelasse stop, then follow the river to the campsite.

Hôtel Splendid (☎ 04 90 86 14 46; www.avignon-splendid-hotel.com; 17 rue Agricol Perdiguier; s €32-46, d €48-70, apt €70-90) This cyclist-friendly place has charming rooms, half of them overlooking the pretty neighbouring park, all with brand new bathrooms. The hotel also has three studio-flats equipped with kitchenette, ideal for longer stays in the heart of Provence; the ground-floor flat even has its own patio. The owners are also environmentally minded and use only natural cleaning products.

Hôtel Mignon (☎ 04 90 82 17 30; www.hotel-mignon.com; 12 rue Joseph Vernet; s €42-62, d €59-72;) Cute and comfy, this 16-room place within the walled city is a favourite for its small rooms in pretty shades (and small bathrooms – you'll see what we mean), its friendly, helpful staff, wi-fi, and a decent breakfast of croissants and rolls (€5).

YMCA-UCJG (☎ 04 90 25 46 20; www.ymca-avignon.com; 7bis chemin de la Justice; with/without bathroom d €45/30, tr €54/36, q €54/48; reception 8.30am-6pm, closed Dec-early Jan;) If you're after your own space on a shoestring budget, head to this spotless hostel across the river, just outside Villeneuve-lès-Avignon. There's a massive swimming pool and matching terrace with panoramic views of the city. Sheets are included, breakfast costs €5, and wheelchair access is good. Take bus 10 to the Monteau stop or take the 30-minute stroll across the bridge.

Hôtel Boquier (☎ 04 90 82 34 43; www.hotel-boquier.com, in French; 6 rue du Portail Boquier; d €45-66;) A wind of change is blowing through Hôtel Boquier: Sylvie and Pascal Sendra, the new owners, have been bowled over by their new city, and their infectious enthusiasm has swept through this central little place. It's bright, airy and spacious, and the themed rooms are particularly attractive (try for Morocco or Lavender).

MIDRANGE

Hôtel du Palais des Papes (☎ 04 90 86 04 13; www.hotel-avignon.com; 3 place du Palais des Papes; d €65-98) Strategically located at the crossroads between the Palais des Papes and the Place de l'Horloge, street-side rooms offer stunning views of both locations, while rooms overlooking the courtyard are whisper-quiet. Inside, the hotel has kept many of its original medieval features, the grandest being in the breakfast room and the excellent cavelike restaurant Le Lutrin (mains €24 to €28, open for lunch and dinner daily).

Hôtel de Garlande (☎ 04 90 80 08 85; www.hotelgarlande.com; 20 rue Galante; d €75-115;) Central for just about everything, Hôtel de Garlande is a sweet, familial little 12-room place housed in a historic *hôtel particulier* overlooking a narrow street. Rooms are elegantly decorated, with red clearly being the owner's colour of predilection. In the low season, ring ahead to check that there will be someone at reception when you arrive.

Hôtel de l'Horloge (☎ 04 90 16 42 00; www.hotels-ocre-azur.com; place de l'Horloge; d €85-170;) Most of rooms at this super central hotel, just off Avignon's main square, are pretty standard (comfortable, all mod cons – what you'd expect of a three-star place), but the five terrace rooms really have the edge with their sophisticated furnishings, linens and vantage point. *The* room to ask for is 505 with its incredible view of the Palais des Papes. Good wheelchair access.

our pick **Le Limas** (☎ 04 90 14 67 19; www.le-limas-avignon.com; 51 rue du Limas; d incl breakfast €100-160, tr incl breakfast €150-180;) Behind its discreet (easily missed) lavender door, this chic B&B in an 18th-century town house is like something out of *Vogue Living*. It is everything interior designers like to achieve when mixing old and new, from the state-of-the-art kitchen and minimalist white decor to antique fireplaces and 18th-century spiral staircase. Breakfast by the dining room's fireplace or on the sun-drenched terrace is a treat, as is the presence of the bubbly Marion.

TOP END

Hôtel d'Europe (☎ 04 90 14 76 76; www.heurope.com; 12 place Crillon; d €169-475;) You're in good company at this antique-laden hotel, established in 1799: guests have included illustrious leaders and dignitaries from Napoleon to Jacques Chirac, Charles Dickens, Jacqueline Kennedy-Onassis and Salvador Dali. The 44 rooms are befittingly sumptuous, subtly blending mod cons such as wi-fi and air-con with period tapestries and marble bathrooms.

Eating

Place de l'Horloge is a riot of cafés. They're popular with tourists, but the food is nothing to write home about. Restaurants are open seven days a week during the festival.

Numéro 75 (☎ 04 90 27 16 00; 75 rue Guillaume Puy; mains from €10; lunch & dinner Mon-Sat) Whether in the lush garden or inside the stunning dining room of absinthe inventor Jules Pernod's former *hôtel particulier*, the food at Numéro 75 is everything you'd want Mediterranean cuisine to be: super-fresh, packed with flavours, and ever so cheap.

Au Tout Petit (☎ 04 90 82 38 86; 4 rue d'Amphoux; lunch menu €10, dinner menu €18-24; lunch & dinner Mon-Sat, closed Wed night) If you're a foodie, the menu of 'The Teeny Tiny' is going to be music to your ears: so much imagination packed in such a small place! Asparagus ravioli and tandoori sauce, salmon lasagne and cardamom snails, apricot *tarte Tatin* with rosemary-and-madeleine ice cream – doesn't that just sound like food poetry to you?

Restaurant Brunel (☎ 04 90 85 24 83; 46 rue de la Balance; mains €11-16, menus €27.50-32.50; 🕑 lunch & dinner Tue-Sat) The elegant mirror-lined, muted red and grey dining room reflects the modern touch this restaurant adds to its Provençal fare. Lunchtime deals are a steal, as are the few outdoor tables in sunny weather. No wonder the locals like it here.

La Fourchette (☎ 04 90 85 20 93; 17 rue Racine; menus from €25; 🕑 lunch & dinner Mon-Fri) This perennial Avignon establishment does so well during the week that it can afford to close on weekends. Lucky them, and poor you, because on weekends you'll be missing out on great, unpretentious French cuisine (lamb, sardines, duck, and tasty desserts such as the melt-in-your-mouth ice cream meringue with praline) in a decor cluttered with old tools and frames.

Christian Etienne (☎ 04 90 86 16 50; 10 rue de Mons; mains €28-45; 🕑 lunch & dinner Tue-Sat Aug-Jun, lunch & dinner Jul) This is Avignon's top table. The restaurant's elevated dining room and leafy outdoor terrace are found in a 12th-century palace near the Palais des Papes. The refined Provençal cuisine (including an amazing and highly unusual starter-to-dessert tomato menu) is prepared by its eponymous master chef.

Le Marmiton (☎ 04 90 14 20 20; www.la-mirande.fr; 4 place de l'Amirande; lunch/dinner menus €38/49, table d'hôte €92; 🕑 restaurant lunch & dinner Thu-Mon, table d'hôte dinner Tue-Sat) Dine in one of France's famous gastronomic restaurants, or watch the preparation of classic Provençal food and then dine on the four-course feast – the meal that is created in front of you is cooked in the intimate kitchen of this 14th-century cardinals'-palace-turned-hotel (the exclusive Hôtel de la Mirande). Even better, try your hand in the exquisite 19th-century kitchen – Le Marmiton puts on a roll-call of visiting chefs who run phenomenal cooking courses year-round, from traditional half-day, three-course meal preparation (€110 to €135) to shorter dedicated chocolate or pastry courses (€80), or a decadent truffle weekend (€645, including accommodation).

PROVENCE

SELF-CATERING

Over 40 outlets fill **Les Halles' food market** (place Pie; 🕑 7am-1pm Tue-Sun), or pick up groceries at **Monoprix** (24 rue de la République; 🕑 8am-9pm Mon-Sat) and St-Tropez's famous cream-and-cake concoction, *tarte tropézienne*, and other Avignon treats at **La Tropézienne** (☎ 04 90 86 24 72; 22 rue St-Agricol; 🕑 8.30am-7.30pm Mon-Sat). Then make your way to Avignon's most picturesque picnic spot, **Rocher des Doms**, a bluff-top park with views spanning the Rhône, Pont St-Bénezet, Villeneuve-lès-Avignon and Mont Ventoux. Finish off with a *papaline d'Avignon* – a pink, chocolate ball filled with a potent Mont Ventoux herbal liqueur that packs a punch; available from speciality shops around town.

Drinking

Mon Bar (17 rue Portail-Matheron; 🕑 8am-8pm) This Parisian-looking bistro has been going for 70 years and looks set to go for another 70. It's an institution in the neighbourhood, so don't expect more than a scowl if you try to order your coffee in English. You have been warned.

La Compagnie des Comptoirs (☎ 04 90 85 99 04; 83 rue Joseph Vernet; lunch menu €9, mains €25-29; 🕑 noon-1am) Wrapped around a renovated cloister, La Compagnie has reached new heights in aesthetics: dine under the white-on-white arched alleyways, sip a cocktail by the palm-lined courtyard basin or simply nibble fusion snacks at the bar counter in the ground-floor rooms where DJs mix it up on weekends. The food still has some way to go to match the surroundings but it's definitely on the right track.

Tapalocas (☎ 04 90 82 56 84; 15 rue Galante; dishes from €3; 🕑 noon-1am) In the pedestrian area, tuck into a seemingly endless array of traditional Spanish tapas over a sangria or two.

Utopia Bar (☎ 04 90 27 04 96; 4 rue des escaliers Ste-Anne; 🕑 noon-midnight) At the foot of the imposing Palais des Papes walls, l'Utopia has something of a thespian bent with its red velvet benches, beautiful glass verandah and great mirrors throughout. It's the perfect place for a chilled glass of white; the *tartines* will fend off the hunger until you summon up the willpower to go elsewhere for a proper dinner.

Le Cid Café (☎ 04 90 82 30 28; 11 place de l'Horloge; 🕑 11am-late) DJs keep the beats coming at this fluoro-lit, all happening bar on Place de l'Horloge. Locals love it and so do visitors keen for a piece of the action.

Red Sky (☎ 04 90 85 93 23; rue St-Jean le Vieux; 🕑 10am-1am) Looking as though someone picked it up in central London and plonked it in Avignon, this cherry-red English pub has gigs, theme nights and plenty of live sport on TV.

Entertainment

The free *César* weekly magazine and the tourist office's fortnightly newsletter, *Rendez-vous d'Avignon* (both in French), carry events listings. Tickets for most events are sold at **Fnac** (☎ 08 25 02 00 20; 19 rue de la République; 10am-7pm Mon-Sat); the tourist office also sells tickets for many cultural fixtures.

Opéra d'Avignon (☎ 04 90 82 81 40; place de l'Horloge; box office 11am-6pm Tue-Sat) Housed in an imposing structure built in 1847, Opéra d'Avignon stages everything from operas to ballets.

Cinéma Utopia (☎ 04 90 82 65 36; 4 rue des escaliers Ste-Anne; adult/concession €5.50/3.50) In the cultural centre tucked behind the Palais des Papes, this cinema screens subtitled films.

NIGHTCLUBS

Red Zone (☎ 04 90 27 02 44; 25 rue Carnot; 9pm-3am) A studenty crowd gathers here for its regular gigs, boogying and always-buzzing bar.

L'Esclave (☎ 04 90 85 14 91; www.esclavebar.com, in French; 12 rue du Limas; hr vary) Avignon's inner-city gay hotspot has something on every night of the week. Check its website for tasters and details.

Shopping

Comtesse du Barry (☎ 04 90 82 62 92; 25 rue St-Agricol) Stock up on gourmet goodies like fine wine and foie gras.

Oliviers & Co (☎ 04 90 86 18 41; 19 rue St-Agricol) Fine olive oil and olive oil–based products such as soap, hand cream and biscuits.

Getting There & Away

AIR

The **Aéroport Avignon-Caumont** (☎ 04 90 81 51 51; www.avignon.aeroport.fr) is 8km southeast of Avignon. There are flights from Britain and Ireland from April to October.

BUS

The **bus station** (☎ 04 90 82 07 35; bd St-Roch; information window 8am-7pm Mon-Fri, 8am-1pm Sat) is in the basement of the building that's down the ramp to the right as you exit the train station. Tickets are sold on the buses.

Bus services include Aix-en-Provence (€14, one hour), Arles (€7.10, 1½ hours), Carpentras (€4.40, 35 minutes), Marseille (€18.50, two hours), Nîmes (€8.10, 1¼ hours) and Orange (€5.90, 45 minutes). Most lines operate on Sunday, with reduced frequency.

Long-haul bus companies **Linebús** (☎ 04 90 85 30 48) and **Eurolines** (☎ 04 90 85 27 60; www.eurolines.com) have offices at the far end of the bus platforms.

CAR & MOTORCYCLE

Most car-rental agencies are either inside the main train station complex or nearby (and they're well signed).

To reduce traffic within the walls, the city has over 900 free, monitored parking spaces at Parking de L'Ile Piot, which is served by a free shuttle bus.

TRAIN

Avignon has two train stations: Gare Avignon TGV, which is 4km southwest in the suburb of Courtine, and central **Gare Avignon Centre** (42 bd St-Roch), where local trains to/from Orange (€5.20, 20 minutes), Arles (€6.30, 20 minutes) and Nîmes (€8.10, 30 minutes) arrive and depart.

Some TGVs to/from Paris stop at Gare Avignon Centre, but TGV services such as to/from Marseille (€23.10, 35 minutes) and Nice (€51.80, three hours) only use Gare Avignon TGV.

In July and August there's a direct **Eurostar** (www.eurostar.com) service on Saturdays from London (from €125 return, six hours) to Gare Avignon Centre. See p965 for more details.

There is a **left luggage** (per bag from €4; 7am-7pm winter, 7am-10pm summer) facility inside the station.

Getting Around

TO/FROM THE AIRPORT

There is no public transport to the airport. A taxi will cost around €20.

BICYCLE

Bike-hire places in town include **Provence Bike** (☎ 04 90 27 92 61; www.provence-bike.com, in French; 52 bd St-Roch), which also rents out scooters and motorbikes.

BUS

Local **TCRA** (Transports en Commun de la Région d'Avignon; www.tcra.fr, in French) bus tickets cost €1.10 each, purchased on board. Buses run from 7am to about 7.40pm (less frequently on Sunday, from 8am to 6pm). The two most important bus transfer points are the Poste stop at the main post office and place Pie.

Carnets of 10 tickets (€9.40) and free *plan du réseau* (bus maps) are available at the

Agence Commerciale TCRA (☎ 04 32 74 18 32; av de Lattre de Tassigny; 🕑 8.30am-12.30pm & 1.30-6pm Mon-Fri).

Villeneuve-lès-Avignon is linked with Avignon by bus 11, which stops in front of the main post office and on the western side of the walled city near Porte de l'Oulle.

Navette (shuttle) buses link Gare Avignon TGV with the centre (€1.10, 10 to 13 minutes, half-hourly between 6.15am and 11.30pm); buses use the bus stop in front of the post office on cours Président Kennedy.

TAXI

Pick up a taxi outside the train station or call ☎ 04 90 82 20 20 around the clock.

AROUND AVIGNON

Villeneuve-lès-Avignon

pop 12,098

Across the Rhône from Avignon, the 13th-century Villeneuve-lès-Avignon (sometimes written as Villeneuve-lez-Avignon, and almost always just called Villeneuve, meaning 'new city') became known as the City of Cardinals as many archbishops affiliated with the papal court built large residences in the town, despite the fact that it was situated in territory ruled by the French crown, which in turn established a garrison here to keep an eye on events in the papal-controlled city across the river.

Just 3km from Avignon, Villeneuve is easily reached by foot (around 30 minutes) or bus 11 from Avignon's main post office. Sights are included in the *Avignon Passion* pass (see boxed text, p840).

Chartreuse du Val de Bénédiction (☎ 04 90 15 24 24; 58 rue de la République; full price/Avignon Passion pass €6.50/5.30; 🕑 9.30am-6pm Apr-Sep, 9.30am-5pm Mon-Fri, 10am-5pm Sat & Sun Oct-Mar) was once the largest and most important Carthusian monastery in France, and it still looks it today. The reconstructed cells give a good idea of what the austere life of the monks was like.

If you're remotely interested in religious art, check out Enguerrand Quarton's lavish and dramatic 1453 painting *The Crowning of the Virgin* and the rare 14th-century *Ivory Virgin* at **Musée Pierre de Luxembourg** (☎ 04 90 27 49 66; 3 rue de la République; full price/Avignon Passion pass €3/2; 🕑 10am-12.30pm & 2-6.30pm Tue-Sun Apr-Sep, 10am-noon & 2-5pm Tue-Sun Oct-Jan & Mar). Ask for the accompanying notes for an insight into its commissioning and its underpinning religious dogma.

If you're up for it, take the spiral steps to the top of **Tour Philippe-le-Bel** (☎ 04 32 70 08 57; adult/Avignon Passion pass €2/1.50; 🕑 10am-12.30pm & 2-6.30pm Tue-Sun Apr-Sep, 10am-noon & 2-5pm Tue-Sun Oct, Nov & Mar). This 14th-century defensive tower, built at what was the northwestern end of Pont St-Bénezet, has awesome views of the walled city.

Provençal panoramas are also plentiful from the majestic 14th-century **Fort St-André** (☎ 04 90 25 45 35; adult/Avignon Passion pass €5/4.20; 🕑 10am-1pm & 2-6pm mid-May–mid-Sep, to 5.30pm Apr–mid-May & mid-end Sep, to 5pm Oct-Mar).

Les Baux-de-Provence

pop 457

At the heart of the Alpilles and spectacularly perched above picture-perfect rolling hills of vineyards, olive groves and orchards is the intricate Provençal village of Les Baux-de-Provence, 30km south of Avignon towards Arles. Les Baux was vividly immortalised on canvas by Van Gogh during his time in nearby St-Rémy de Provence (see boxed text, p830).

Clawing precariously onto a 245m-high grey limestone *baou* (Provençal for rocky spur) is the rambling **Château des Baux** (☎ 04 90 54 55 56; adult/child €7.60/5.70; 🕑 9am-8.30pm summer, 9.30am-6pm autumn, 9.30am-5pm winter, 9am-6.30pm spring) at the top of the village. Thought to date back to the 10th century, it was largely destroyed during the reign of Louis XIII in 1633. Its remains are pitched on the edge of a sheer cliff, offering breathtaking panoramas of the valley below. Audioguides in several languages detail the history of the castle, village and region, and demonstrations of medieval warfare frequently feature in summer.

Les Baux-de-Provence is one of the most visited villages in France – aim for early evening after the caterpillar of tourist coaches has crawled back downhill. The **tourist office** (☎ 04 90 54 34 39; www.lesbauxdeprovence.com; 🕑 9.30am-1pm & 2-5.30pm Mon-Fri, 10am-noon & 2-5pm Sat & Sun) can give visitors information on Les Baux' handful of accommodation options. Parking within 800m of the village costs a flat €3 to €5 but you can park for free at **Cathédrale d'Images** (www.cathedrale-images.com; adult/child €7.50/3.50), which screens large-scale sound-and-light projections that flicker against the backdrop of a former quarry cave, just a few minutes' stroll north of the village.

ORANGE

pop 29,000

Considering how exceptional Orange's Roman theatre is (if you're only going to see one Roman site in France, make sure it's this one), the town itself is surprisingly untouristy, and really dead in the winter. It does mean accommodation is good value compared with that of neighbouring towns, but you'll struggle to find an open restaurant on a Sunday or Monday night.

The House of Orange – the princely dynasty that had ruled Orange since the 12th century – made its mark on the history of the Netherlands through a 16th-century marriage with the German House of Nassau. It later made its mark on English history through William III (William of Orange). Known as Arenja in Provençal, it had earlier been a stronghold of the Reformation, and was ceded to France in 1713 by the Treaty of Utrecht. To this day, many members of the royal house of the Netherlands are known as the princes and princesses of Orange-Nassau.

Orientation

Orange's train station is about 1.5km east of the city centre's place de la République, along av Frédéric Mistral, then rue de la République. Rue St-Martin links place de la République and nearby place Clemenceau with the tourist office, which is 250m to the west. Théâtre Antique is two blocks south of place de la République. The tiny River Meyne lies north of the centre. From the train station, bus 1 from the École Mistral school goes to the centre of town; get off at Pourtoules for the Théâtre Antique.

Information

Crédit Lyonnais (7 place de la République)

La Bugado (5 av Général Leclerc; ⌚ 7am-9pm) Laundrette.

Post Office (679 bd Édouard Daladier) The only place in Orange that changes money.

Tourist Office (☎ 04 90 34 70 88; www.otorange.fr; 5 cours Aristide Briand; ⌚ 9am-7.30pm Mon-Sat & 10am-1pm & 2-7pm Sun Jul & Aug, 9am-6.30pm Mon-Sat & 2-6.30pm Apr-Jun & Sep, 10am-1pm & 2-5pm Mon-Sat Oct-Mar)

Sights

THÉÂTRE ANTIQUE

Orange's **Roman theatre** (☎ 04 90 51 17 60; adult/student €7.70/5.90; ⌚ 9am-7pm Jun-Aug, 9am-6pm Apr, May & Sep, 9.30am-5.30pm Mar & Oct, 9.30am-4.30pm Nov-Feb) is by far the most impressive Roman sight in France. Its sheer size and age are awe-inspiring: designed to seat 10,000 spectators, it's thought to have been built during Augustus Caesar's rule (27 BC–AD 14). The 103m-wide, 37m-high stage wall is one of only three in the world still standing in its entirety – the other two are in Syria and Turkey – minus a few mosaics and the roof (its replacement is a modern addition). Admission includes a seven-language audioguide.

The theatre still regularly stages theatrical and musical performances (see below). Do catch a performance, if you can; balmy summer nights in this millennia-old venue are truly magical.

The admission price for the theatre is also good for entry to the **museum** (museum only adult/child €4.50/3.50; ⌚ opens/closes 15min after/before the theatre) across the road, which has some unassuming treasures of its own. These include segments of the Roman survey registers (a precursor to the tax department) and the friezes that formed part of the theatre's scenery.

Follow montée Philbert de Chalons or montée Lambert to the top of **Colline St-Eutrope** (St Eutrope Hill; elevation 97m) for a bird's-eye view of the theatre, and for phenomenal views of the Mont Ventoux and the Dentelles de Montmirail. En route you pass the ruins of a 12th-century **château**, the former residence of the princes of Orange.

ARC DE TRIOMPHE

Orange's 1st-century AD **triumphal arch** stands a proud 19m high and wide, and 8m thick, at the northern end of plane tree–lined av de l'Arc de Triomphe, about 450m northwest of the town centre. On its facade, ornate sculptures commemorate the Romans' victories over the Gauls in 49 BC.

Festivals & Events

In July and August Théâtre Antique comes alive with all-night concerts during **Les Chorégies d'Orange** (www.choregies.asso.fr), a series of weekend operas, classical concerts and choral performances. Festival tickets (€14 to €220, with good concession rates) must be reserved months beforehand. A week-long **jazz festival** swings into town in the last week of June.

Sleeping

Camping Le Jonquier (☎ 04 90 34 49 48; www.campinglejonquier.com, in French; 1321 rue Alexis Carrel; camping per 2 people €18.50-24; ⌚ Easter-Sep; 🏊) Perfect for activity junkies, at Le Jonquier you can splash in the pool, play minigolf, tennis or table tennis, or chill in the spa after a session at the gym. From the Arc de Triomphe walk 100m north, turn left onto rue du Bourbonnais and right again at the second roundabout onto rue Alexis Carrel. The campsite is 300m on your left.

Hôtel l'Herbier d'Orange (☎ 04 90 34 09 23; www.lherbierdorange.com, in French; 8 place aux Herbes; s €32-37, d €37-50, tr €50-55; reception 8am-noon & 3-5pm winter, 7am-11pm summer) The old adage of 'you get what you pay for' holds true at this 20-room hotel: cleanliness is patchy, some rooms *reek* of cigarettes, and noise insulation is minimal. It's a shame because the place has plenty going for it: nice building, bright rooms, tip-top location, wi-fi, private parking and helpful staff.

Hôtel St-Florent (☎ 04 90 34 18 53; www.hotelsaintflorent.com; 4 rue du Mazeau; d €35-77;) A skip and a hop from the Théâtre Antique, the St-Florent has 17 colourful, chintzy rooms with antique wooden beds and bathrooms in dire need of gutting, plus a breakfast room filled with a riot of fake flowers, iridescent orange tablecloths and Christmas lights. Private parking is €6 and wi-fi is free.

Le Glacier (☎ 04 90 34 02 01; www.le-glacier.com; 46 cours Aristide Briand; d €49-100;) Probably the best option in town, with individually decorated cosy, bright rooms, tip-top bathrooms and charming owners. The hotel also rents out bikes (per half-/full day €12/16), has wi-fi and is equidistant from the theatre, tourist office and town centre.

Hôtel Arène (☎ 04 90 11 40 40; www.bestwestern.fr; place de Langes; d €65-120;) With a whole floor dedicated to hypoallergenic, ecological rooms, the Italian-run Arène has managed to retain some individuality despite being integrated into a chain. The 'Italian' rooms, with their portrait-decorated doors, have stupendous bathrooms – some with panoramic bath tubs. The 'Provençal' rooms are a tad more subdued, but very cushy all the same. Wheelchair access is good and there is free wi-fi.

PROVENCE

Eating

Le Forum (☎ 04 90 34 01 09; 3 rue Mazeau; mains €15; lunch & dinner Tue-Fri & Sun, dinner Sat) You can either pick and choose on the *carte* or go for the whole hog with the restaurant's themed menus (duck, scallops or foie gras). Locals love both and regularly come back; just follow their lead.

Le Parvis (☎ 04 90 34 82 00; 55 cours Pourtoules; 2-course menu €20.50-22.50; lunch & dinner Tue-Sat, lunch Sun) The only noise you'll hear at Orange's gastronomic restaurant is the clinking of cutlery against plates and the hushed tones of its gourmet guests. It's all a little formal but the food is good (marinated lamb, grilled trout, and herbs and spices throughout the menu) – and very good-value, at that.

Classic fare stars at the terrace-only **Festival Café** (☎ 04 90 34 65 58; 5 place de la République; mains around €10; lunch & dinner), which sets up a marquee in inclement weather, and its indoor neighbour **Brasserie Le Palace** (☎ 04 90 34 13 51; 7 rue de la République; mains €9; 8am-7.30pm Mon-Sat summer, shorter hr winter), where you can squeeze into the red vinyl booths for a coffee or a *plat du jour* (daily special).

The town's central streets are lined with stalls each Thursday for its weekly market (if you need to move your car before the market wraps up, park at the edges of the city). Self-caterers can also pick up supplies at **Petit Casino** (35 rue St-Martin).

Getting There & Away

BUS

There's no longer a bus station, so buses stop on bd Édouard Daladier instead, southwest of the post office. Destinations include Avignon (€5.90, 40 minutes), Vaison-la-Romaine (€5.10, 45 minutes) and Carpentras (€4.80, 45 minutes).

TRAIN

Orange's **train station** (☎ 04 90 11 88 03; av Frédéric Mistral) has services south to Avignon (€5.20, 15 minutes), Marseille (€20.30, 1½ hours) and beyond, and north including Lyon (€25.60, two hours).

VAISON-LA-ROMAINE

pop 7060

Nestled in a valley at the crossroads of seven hills, Vaison-la-Romaine has long been a traditional exchange place. The tradition endures at the thriving Tuesday market, while the town's rich Roman legacy – the largest archaeological site in France – reveals its ancient roots.

Nowadays Vaison is a quintessential Provençal village, split by the temperamental waters of River l'Ouvèze into a delightful pedestrianised centre, with dappled plane trees, and the walled, cobbled street Cité Médiévale (Medieval City) on the hilltop. Nearby Mont Ventoux provides endless outdoor excursions for those tired of old stones.

Orientation

The ever-flooding River l'Ouvèze bisects Vaison. The modern centre is on the river's north bank; the Cité Médiévale is on its south side.

Pedestrianised Grand-rue heads northwest from the Pont Romain, changing its name near the Roman ruins to become av du Général de Gaulle.

To get from the bus station to the tourist office, turn left as you leave the station and then left again into rue Colonel Parazols, which leads past the Fouilles de Puymin excavations along rue Burrhus.

Information

Vaison's **tourist office** (☎ 04 90 36 02 11; www.vaison-la-romaine.com; place du Chanoine Sautel; 🕑 9am-12.30pm & 2-6.45pm Jul & Aug, 9am-noon & 2-5.45pm Mon-Sat, 9am-noon Sun Apr-Jun & Sep–mid-Oct, 9am-noon & 2-5.45pm Mon-Sat mid-Oct–Mar) is inside the Maison du Tourisme et des Vins, just off av du Général de Gaulle.

The post office, opposite place du 11 Novembre, has an exchange service.

Sights

GALLO-ROMAN RUINS

The ruined remains of Vasio Vocontiorum, the Roman city that flourished here from the 6th to 2nd centuries BC, are unearthed at two sites. The **Pass** (adult/child €8/3.50) ticket, valid for two days, includes admission to all Roman sites as well to the cathedral and cloister, and also includes a multilanguage audioguide.

At **Puymin** (av du Général de Gaulle; 🕑 9.30am-6.30pm Jun-Sep, 9am-6pm Apr & May, 10am-12.30pm & 2-5.30pm Mar & Oct, 10am-noon & 2-5pm Nov, Dec & Feb) you can see houses, mosaics, the still-functioning Théâtre Antique (built around AD 20 for an audience of 6000) and an **archaeological museum** (🕑 9.30am-6.30pm Jun-Sep, 9am-6pm Apr & May, 10am-12.30pm & 2-5.30pm Mar & Oct, 10am-noon & 2-5pm Nov, Dec & Feb) with a swag of statues – including likenesses of Hadrian and his wife Sabina.

Colonnaded shops, public baths' foundations and a limestone-paved street with an underground sewer are visible at **La Villasse** (🕑 10am-noon & 2.30-6.30pm Jun-Sep, 10am-noon & 2.30-6pm Apr & May, 10am-12.30pm & 2-5.30pm Mar & Oct, 10am-noon & 2-5pm Nov, Dec & Feb), to the west of the same road.

The 12th-century Romanesque **cloister** (🕑 10am-12.30pm & 2-6.30pm Jun-Sep, 10.30am-12.30pm & 2-6pm Apr & May, 10am-noon & 2-5pm Mar & Oct, closed Nov-Feb except school holidays) of the **Cathédrale Notre Dame de Nazareth** is five minutes' walk west across rue du Bon Ange from Fouilles de la Villasse.

From April to September there are regular **guided tours** (French only; free for Pass ticket holders) of the sites, as well as thematic tours such as Roman gastronomy or daily life in Roman times. Check the schedule at the tourist office.

CITÉ MÉDIÉVALE

Across the pretty **Pont Romain** (Roman Bridge), cobblestone alleyways carve through the stone walls up to the Cité Médiévale. The highest point is home to an imposing 12th-century **château** built by the counts of Toulouse, which was modernised in the 15th century only to be later abandoned. Entry to the château is available by guided tours (in French, €2) only – check with the tourist office for schedules.

Sleeping

The tourist office has comprehensive accommodation lists, including details on *chambres d'hôtes* and self-catering places in the surrounding region. Hotels are few and far between.

Camping du Théâtre Romain (☎ 04 90 28 78 66; www.camping-theatre.com; chemin de Brusquet; camping per 2 people €15-20; 🕑 15 Mar-15 Nov; 🏊) Opposite Théâtre Antique in the northern section of the Fouilles de Puymin, the site is a little exposed to the Provençal sun but there is a pool in which to cool off.

Le Moulin de César (☎ 04 90 36 00 78; www.escapade-vacances.com/vaison; av César Geoffray; d half-board €41-45; 🕑 Mar-Nov) Around 500m southeast of town along the river, this modern family resort is set over peaceful, sprawling grounds on the edge of the river, with views of Mont Ventoux. This being France, half-board (obligatory) includes wine.

Hôtel Le Burrhus (☎ 04 90 36 00 11; www.burrhus.com; 1 place de Montfort; d €46-82) Right on Vaison's vibrant central square, this might look like a quaint old place from the outside, but inside, its 38 rooms have ultramodern decors with cutting-edge designer fittings, artists' works on the walls and lush mosaic bathrooms.

Hostellerie Le Beffroi (☎ 04 90 36 04 71; www.le-beffroi.com; rue de l'Évêché; d €75-140; 🕑 Apr-Jan; 🏊) Within the medieval city's walls, this 1554-built *hostellerie* is housed over two buildings (the 'newer' one was built in 1690). A fairy-tale hideaway, its 22 rough-hewn stone-and-wood-beamed rooms are romantically furnished, and its restaurant (*menus* €28 to

€45) is one of Vaison's good addresses. It's been in the same family since 1904.

L'Évêché (☎ 04 90 36 13 46; http://eveche.free.fr; rue de l'Évêché, Cité Médiévale; d €78-130) With its groaning bookshelves, vaulted ceilings, higgledy-piggledy staircase, intimate lounges and exquisite art gracing the walls, this five-room *chambre d'hôte* is absolutely divine. Owners Jean-Loup and Aude can recommend all manner of excursions and good addresses. They can also lend you bikes to explore the area.

Eating

Moulin à Huile (☎ 04 90 36 20 67; www.moulin-huile.com; quai Maréchal Foch; mains €22-65; lunch & dinner Tue-Sat, lunch Sun) Enjoy chef Robert Bardot's gastronomic prowess in the draped, stone-wall dining room of this old oil mill or on the delightful summer terrace by the river. Try a cross-section of his creations with the €75 tasting menu or pick and choose from the old-school handwritten *carte* (which is actually quite difficult to read!).

Bistro Du'O (☎ 04 90 41 72 90; rue du Château; menus around €25; lunch & dinner Tue-Sat, lunch Sun) Housed in an old stable, this classy establishment serves knock-out dishes in any combination of starters, mains and desserts. The menu is short and changes every day to keep everything super fresh. Presentation is a work of art and every mouthful is a riot of taste. The same goes for the wine list: the bistro works with a vineyard from the very fine Gigondas area, so you'll be spoilt for choice.

SELF-CATERING

Wines (available from the tourist office's on-site boutique), as well as honey and nougat, are local specialities, but nothing compares with the area's delectable black truffles from the surrounding hillsides. They don't come cheap – €500 to €1000 per kg depending on the season and rainfall – but a few shavings are enough to transform any dish.

A magnificent market, which has become an attraction in its own right, snakes through the central streets every Tuesday from 6.30am to 1pm.

Getting There & Away

The bus station, where **Autocars Lieutaud** (Vaison ☎ 04 90 36 05 22; av des Choralies; Avignon bus station ☎ 04 90 86 36 75) has an office, is 400m east of the town centre. There are limited services from Vaison to Orange (€5.10, 45 minutes), Avignon (€7.70, 1½ hours) and Carpentras (€4.50, 45 minutes).

MONT VENTOUX

Visible from miles around, Mont Ventoux (1909m), nicknamed *le géant de Provence* (Provence's giant), stands like a sentinel over northern Provence. From its summit, accessible by road between May and October, vistas extend to the Alps and – on a clear day – as far as the Camargue.

Because of the mountain's dimensions, every European climate type is present on its slopes, from Mediterranean on its lower southern banks to Arctic on its exposed northern ridge. As you ascend the relentless gradients (which regularly feature in the Tour de France), temperatures can plummet by 20°C, and there's twice as much precipitation as on the plains below. The relentless mistral wind blows 130 days a year, sometimes at a speed of 250km/h. So bring warm clothes and rain gear, even in summer.

This unique and unusual climatic patchwork is reflected in the mountain's hugely diverse fauna and flora, which is now actively protected by Unesco Biosphere Reserve status.

In winter, visitors can take in the joys of snow at the **Mont Serein** (1445m) ski resort (www.stationdumontserein.com), 5km from Mont Ventoux' summit on the D974. The snow has generally all but melted by April, so the white glimmering stuff you can see in summer is not snow but are *lauzes* – broken white stones covering the top.

Piercing the sky to the west of Mont Ventoux are the spectacular limestone pinnacles of another walker's paradise, **Dentelles de Montmirail**. On the other side of the Dentelles sits the snug village of **Beaumes de Venise**, home to Frances's finest muscat.

The most common starting point for forays into the Ventoux area is the town of **Malaucène**, a former summer residence of the Avignon popes. It's about 10km south of Vaison-la-Romaine.

Information

Beaumes de Venise Tourist Office (☎ 04 90 62 94 39; www.ot-beaumesdevenise.com; place du marché; 9am-noon & 2-5pm Oct-Mar, to 6.30pm Apr-Jun, to 7pm Jul & Aug) Has plenty of info on the nearby Dentelles as well as a list and map of all the cellars and vineyards selling the famous muscat.

Destination Ventoux (www.destination-ventoux.com, in French)
Malaucène Tourist Office (☎ 04 90 65 22 59; ot-malaucene@wanadoo.fr; place de la Mairie; 🕑 10am-noon & 3-5pm Mon-Fri & 10am-noon Sat) A mine of info for those keen to explore under their own steam, be it walking or cycling.
Provence des Papes (www.hautvaucluse.com)

Activities

WALKING

Running from the River Ardèche east, the GR4 crosses the Dentelles de Montmirail before scaling the northern face of Mont Ventoux, where it meets the GR9. Both trails traverse the ridge before the GR4 branches eastwards to the Gorges du Verdon (p854).

Continuing on the GR9 takes you across the Monts du Vaucluse and the Luberon Range. Lonely Planet's *Walking in France* has information on walking in the latter.

Maps

Didier-Richard's 1:50,000 map *Massif du Ventoux* includes Mont Ventoux, the Monts du Vaucluse and the Dentelles de Montmirail. It's available at some of the area's larger tourist offices, bookshops and newsagents. More detailed are IGN's Série Bleue 1:25,000 *Mont Ventoux* (ref 3140ET) and *Carpentras/Vaison-la-Romaine/Dentelles de Montmirail* (ref 3040ET).

All tourist offices in the area also provide dozens of walking itineraries, including the excellent *Randonnées dans les Dentelles* (15 detailed, detachable itineraries in French, English and German; €5) at Beaumes' office.

CYCLING

The Mont Ventoux is on par with Alpe d'Huez (p566) when it comes to epic, legendary, leg-breaking cycling ascents. So before you gingerly hop on your bicycle to tackle the beast, you should know that pros polish off the climb in about an hour (depending on wind, weather etc). A 1½ to two-hour trip makes you Tour de France potential, and even 2½ hours requires serious pedal power. So if you're just top of your spinning class back home, you're in for a slog.

Ventoux aside, there are plenty more less-demanding cycling options in the area. The tourist office can provide maps and itineraries such as *Massif du Mont Ventoux, 9 itinéraires VTT* (free, but in French only).

Getting There & Around

Mont Ventoux can be reached by car from Sault via the D164 or – in summer – from Malaucène or St-Estève via the switchback D974, often snow-blocked until April. For information on bus services in the area, see p851.

Mag 2 Roues (☎ 04 90 37 18 67; cours des Isnards), next to the tourist office in Malaucène, rents out bikes.

CARPENTRAS

pop 27,000

If you can, try to come to Carpentras on a Friday morning, when the streets spill over with more than 350 stalls laden with breads, honeys, cheeses, olives, nuts, fruit, nougat and a rainbow of *berlingots* – Carpentras' striped, pillow-shaped hard-boiled sweets. During winter there's also a truffle market, with its pungent smell and hushed-tones transactions.

Markets aside, Carpentras wasn't always as quiet as it is today. It became the capital of the papal territory of the Comtat Venaissin in 1320. Pope Clement V was a frequent visitor in the 14th century, during which time Jews expelled from French crown territory took refuge in the Comtat Venaissin under papal protection. The 14th-century synagogue is the oldest in use in France.

Orientation

A heart-shaped ring of boulevards replaced the city's fortifications in the 19th century; the largely pedestrianised old city sits inside.

If you're arriving by bus, walk northeastwards to place Aristide Briand, a major intersection at the boulevards' southernmost point. The tourist office is across the crossroads on the small place 25 Août 1944. From here, the pedestrian-only rue de la République, which heads north, takes you to the 17th-century Palais de Justice and the cathedral.

Information

There are commercial banks on central place Aristide Briand and bd Albin Durand.
Blanc Ventoux Lavomatique (118 rue Porte de Monteux; 🕑 7am-8pm) Laundrette.
Post Office (65 rue d'Inguimbert)
Tourist Office (☎ 04 90 63 00 78; www.carpentras-ventoux.com; 97 place du 25 Août 1944; 🕑 9am-1pm & 2-7pm Mon-Sat, 9.30am-1pm Sun Jul & Aug, 9.30am-12.30pm & 2-6pm Mon-Sat Sep-Jun) Has an excellent website and organises guided city tours (adult/child

€4/2.50) in various languages from April to September. Also hands out a free English-language *Discovery Circuit* brochure, corresponding with a walking circuit of signposts marked with *berlingots*.

Sights

SYNAGOGUE

The centre of Jewish life for centuries and still a place of worship today, Carpentras' moving **synagogue** (☎ 04 90 63 39 97; place Juiverie; admission free; 🕑 10am-noon & 3-5pm Mon-Thu, 10am-noon & 3-4pm Fri) bears witness to the centuries of persecution that Jewish people have endured. Founded in 1367, it was rebuilt between 1741 and 1743 and restored in 1929 and 1954. In the 1st-floor wood-panelled sanctuary you can see 18th-century liturgical objects, while the ground floor houses older features such as the ablution basin and bakeries.

CATHEDRAL

Église St-Siffrein, once Carpentras' **cathedral** (🕑 7.30am-noon & 2-6.30pm, no visits during services), was built in the Méridional (southern French) Gothic style between 1405 and 1519 and is topped by a distinctive contemporary bell tower. Sadly, due to theft, its **Trésor d'Art Sacré** (Treasury of Religious Art) that holds precious 14th- to 19th-century religious relics is now not available for public viewing, except during the Fête de St-Siffrein (right).

MUSEUMS

Carpentras' museums are only open from April to September, from 10am to noon and 2pm to 6pm Wednesday to Monday. Admission is €2.

Musée Comtadin (243 bd Albin Durand), which displays artefacts relating to local history and folklore, and **Musée Duplessis** (243 bd Albin Durand), with paintings spanning nine centuries, are on the western side of the old city.

Musée Sobirats (112 rue du Collège), one block west of the cathedral, is an ornate 18th-century private residence filled with furniture, *faïence* and objets d'art in the Louis XV and Louis XVI styles.

The former 18th-century hospital in **Hôtel Dieu** (place Aristide Briand; 🕑 by arrangement with tourist office) has an incredibly preserved old-fashioned **pharmacy** and a **chapel**. However, the museum closed for renovation in 2008, and at the time of writing it was not clear when it would reopen. Check with the tourist office for details.

Sleeping & Eating

Hôtel La Lavande (☎ 04 90 63 13 49; 282 bd Alfred Rogier; r €32-70) Well, you sure won't miss the nearly luminescent purple cladding of Hôtel La Lavande. Thankfully, the interior is not as brash, with basic, clean rooms. The place generally lacks charm but the restaurant downstairs (mains €7 to €15, open for lunch and dinner daily) serves genuine North African fare as well as traditional, quick lunchtime fixes.

Hôtel du Fiacre (☎ 04 90 63 03 15; www.hotel-du-fiacre.com; 153 rue Vigne; d €62-90; ☒) This endearing 18th-century mansion grows on you the minute you walk in: everything from the beautiful patio to the canopied beds, grand interior and genuine warmth of its owners will want to make you stay a little bit longer. There is a private car park for €5, and wi-fi throughout.

Les Palmiers (☎ 04 90 63 12 31; 77 place du Général de Gaulle; mains from €9; 🕑 7am-10pm) This cheap and cheerful brasserie is packed to the rafters at lunchtime with colleagues and friends tucking into the €9 *plat du jour* and greedily lapping their *café gourmand* (an espresso served with miniature desserts; in this case, a chocolate fondant and crème anglaise – a rich custard) before heading back to work.

Chez Serge (☎ 04 90 63 21 24; 90 rue Cottier; lunch/dinner menus €17/35, mains €20-35; 🕑 lunch Sun-Fri, dinner Mon-Sat) Paris meets Provence by way of Armenia at this bistro where Serge serves up his culinary creations in a charming setting (love the old stone-wash basin in the patio). This being Carpentras, there is, of course, a good selection of truffle-flavoured dishes.

Shopping

Rue d'Inguimbert and most of av Jean Jaurès (and often the streets spilling off) are the site of Carpentras' fantastic Friday morning market. The town gets *very* quiet in the long lunch hours following.

In winter, Carpentras' 'black diamonds' are traded at the **truffle market** (place Aristide Briand; 🕑 9-10am Fri late Nov-Mar), attended by brokers, merchants and wholesalers from all over France. Carpentras' biggest fair, held during the Fête de St-Siffrein (Feast of St Siffrein) on 27 November, marks the opening of the truffle season with more than 1000 stalls and sellers spilling across town.

A Hansel and Gretel fantasy, **Chocolats Clavel** (☎ 04 90 63 07 59; 30 Porte d'Orange; 🕑 Mon-Sat) has spectacularly sculptured – and delicious – sweets.

Getting There & Away

The train station is served by goods trains only, so buses provide Carpentras' only intercity public transport. The **bus station** (place Terradou) is 150m southwest of place Aristide Briand. Schedules are available from across the square at **Cars Comtadins** (☎ 04 90 67 20 25; 192 av Clemenceau) and from **Cars Arnaud** (☎ 04 90 63 01 82; 8 av Victor Hugo).

There are half-hourly services to Avignon (€4.40, 45 minutes) and about three services a day to Marseille (€14, two hours). There are also infrequent runs to Vaison-la-Romaine (€4.50, 45 minutes) via Malaucène and Bédoin (€4.20, 40 minutes) at the southwestern foot of Mont Ventoux; and to Cavaillon (€5.40, 45 minutes) and L'Isle-sur-Sorgue (€3.80, 25 minutes), 7km west of Fontaine de Vaucluse.

FONTAINE DE VAUCLUSE

pop 650

Aptly named, Fontaine (meaning fountain) is Provence's main tap: all the rain that falls within 1200 sq km gushes out here as the River Sorgue. It is the world's fifth most powerful spring – and France's most powerful – and has fascinated specialists for centuries. Jacques Cousteau was one of many who attempted, unsuccessfully, to plumb the spring's depths before an unmanned submarine touched base (at 315m) in 1985. It's at its most dazzling after heavy rain, but in drought times, the normally surging hole looks like something out of a Harry Potter book, with eerily calm emerald water.

Information

Tourist Office (☎ 04 90 20 32 22; www.oti-delasorgue.fr; chemin de la Fontaine; ⏰ 9.30am-12.30pm & 1.30-5.30pm) Southeast of central place de la Colonne on the way to the spring. Has itineraries of local walks in French.

Sights

Most visitors come to see the spring, but this tiny village also has an eclectic collection of museums.

Musée d'Histoire 1939–1945 (☎ 04 90 20 24 00; chemin de la Fontaine; adult/student/under 12yr €3.50/1.50/free, combined ticket with Musée Pétrarque €4.60; ⏰ 10am-6pm Wed-Mon Jun-Sep, 10am-noon & 2-6pm Wed-Mon Apr & May, 10am-noon & 2-6pm Sat & Sun Mar, Nov & Dec, 10am-noon & 2-5pm Oct) showcases the resistance movement during WWII.

Musée Pétrarque (☎ 04 90 20 37 20; rive Gauche de la Sorgue; adult/student/under 12yr €3.50/1.50/free; ⏰ 10am-12.30pm & 1.30-6pm Wed-Mon Jun-Sep, 10am-noon & 2-6pm Wed-Mon Apr & May, 10am-noon & 2-5pm Oct) is devoted to the Italian Renaissance poet Francesco Petrarch, who lived in Fontaine de Vaucluse from 1337 to 1353. He expressed in heartbreaking verse his futile love for Laura, wife of Hugues de Sade.

At **Ecomusée du Gouffre** (☎ 04 90 20 34 13; chemin de la Fontaine; adult/child €5.50/4; ⏰ 9.30am-7.30pm Jul & Aug, 10am-noon & 2-6pm Feb-Jun & Sep–mid-Nov), follow a caving expert along underground tunnels to learn more about Fontaine's mysterious spring, the history of caving and how humans have used caves since the beginning of time. The tour finishes with an incredible collection of crystals of all shapes and forms.

Sleeping & Eating

Ask the tourist office for a regularly updated list of *chambres d'hôtes*.

Auberge de Jeunesse (☎ 04 90 20 31 65; www.fuaj.org; chemin de la Vignasse; dm incl breakfast & sheets €16.20; ⏰ reception 7.30-10am & 5.30-9pm, closed mid-Nov–Jan) In a lovely old farmhouse, about 800m south of Fontaine de Vaucluse in the direction of Lagnes, this peaceful hostel is popular with families and hikers (it's on the GR6 trail). In summer you can also pitch your tent in the garden. There's a good self-catering kitchen.

Hôtel du Poète (☎ 04 90 20 34 05; www.hoteldupoete.com; r €90-310; ⏰ closed late Dec–mid-Feb; ❄ 🏊) Fall asleep to the relaxing sound of rushing water in lyrically named rooms, stretch out by the pool and ponds, or chill in a Jacuzzi that straddles a stream. Find this stunning water wonderland by the river bank as you enter the village.

La Figuière (☎ 04 90 20 37 41; www.la-figuiere.com; chemin de la Grangette; menus €20 & €28) Just off the main village square, La Figuière has set up shop in a beautiful stone house. In summer, you can savour the Provençal dishes (rabbit, aïoli, sea bass etc) in the lovely front garden, or if you're staying in one of the three lovely *chambres d'hôtes*, wake up to the trickle of the fountain and a riot of cicadas.

Getting There & Away

Fontaine de Vaucluse is 21km southeast of Carpentras, 30km west of Apt, and 7km east of L'Isle-sur-Sorgue, a popular antiques centre. From Avignon, **Cars Arnaud** (☎ 04 90 82 07 35) has a bus (€4.80, one hour, two or three daily) with a stop at Fontaine de Vaucluse.

Fontaine is most easily reached by car, but you'll have to fork out for the privilege of parking (generally a €3 flat fee).

THE LUBERON

The Luberon's lush hills shot to fame following Peter Mayle's 1989 bestseller *A Year in Provence,* a light-hearted account of how he renovated a crumbling old farmhouse in deep rural Provence (just outside the village of Ménerbes), a story that highlighted classic English–French culture clash.

Until then the Luberon enjoyed a steady flow of dedicated Provence fans who came here for the area's rugged beauty, its relentless hills and cliffs, riot of purple, ochre, red and green, inhospitable forests and gastronomic treats (lavender honey, candied fruit, succulent fresh fruit, wines and much more).

Mayle's book, and subsequent works, triggered a huge interest in the Luberon, boosted by the existence of the 1200 sq km Parc Naturel Régional (the grade below a national park; see Maison du Parc, right) and a very fine cultural heritage that includes the Abbaye de Sénanque and the ancient, igloolike stone *bories* (dry-walled huts; see the boxed text, opposite).

The region's capital, Apt, is a good base from which to explore the area. The Luberon stretches from Cavaillon in the west to Manosque in the east, and from St-Saturnin-lès-Apt southwards to the River Durance. You'll undoubtedly come across many charming *chambres d'hôtes* and restaurants as you go: stumbling across them is what Provence is all about.

There are plenty of buses that can take you in and out of the Luberon, but you'll really need your own wheels (motorised or leg-powered) to explore. **Le Luberon en Vélo** (www.veloloisirluberon.com) network has signposted a 236km cycling itinerary with suggested stops in towns and villages across the park.

Apt

pop 11,300

Sleepy little Apt comes alive with its Saturday morning market, brimming with local specialities. The town's festive spirit peaks during its wine and cheese festival, held on the Ascension (May or June), when up to 30 châteaux show off their wares. In summer, the town overflows with contentedly strolling visitors living the Provence dream.

ORIENTATION

Maps

For hard-core exploring, the tourist office sells regional maps such as the 1:25,000 IGN map (3242OT) *Apt/Parc Naturel Régional du Luberon* (€9.70), or the *Cavaillon* map (3142OT), for €9.70.

The Maison du Parc sells an extensive range of guides and maps, including for hiking and cycling – such as the recommended topoguide *Le Parc Naturel Régional du Luberon à Pied* (€13.20), which details 24 walks including the GR9, GR92 and GR97 trails (in French only).

INFORMATION

Maison du Parc (☎ 04 90 04 42 00; www.parcduluberon.fr, in French; 60 place Jean Jaurès; 🕑 8.30am-noon & 1-6pm Mon-Fri, 8.30am-noon Sat Apr-Sep, closed Sat & Sun Oct-Mar) Has information on the Parc Naturel Régional du Luberon and the history of the area.

Tourist Office (☎ 04 90 74 03 18; www.ot-apt.fr; 20 av Philippe de Girard; 🕑 9am-7pm Mon-Sat Jul & Aug, 9am-noon & 2-6pm Mon-Sat Sep-Jun, 9.30am-12.30pm Sun May-Sep) Has enough suggestions for visits, excursions, activities and walks to last you an entire summer.

SIGHTS & ACTIVITIES

Retrace the steps of the industries that made Apt's fortunes at the **Musée de l'Aventure Industrielle du Pays d'Apt** (Industrial History Museum; ☎ 04 90 74 95 30; 14 place du Postel; adult/under 12yr €4/free; 🕑 10am-noon & 3-6.30pm Mon & Wed-Sat & 3-7pm Jun-Sun, 10am-noon & 2-5.30pm Mon & Wed-Sat Oct-May). In an old candied-fruit factory, it explains the area's candied-fruit trade, ochre mining and earthenware production from the 18th century.

SLEEPING & EATING

Camping Municipal Les Cèdres (☎/fax 04 90 74 14 61; www.camping-les-cedres.fr, in French; rte de Rustrel; campsite €8.80; 🕑 mid-Feb–mid-Nov) This back-to-basics riverside campsite is just out of town, with an Olympic-sized pool nearby.

Hôtel L'Aptois (☎ 04 90 74 02 02; www.aptois.fr, in French; 289 cours Lauze de Perret; d with bathroom €52-60, without bathroom €38-40) Found above an inexpensive café, this is a surprisingly stylish, cyclist-friendly hotel with good wheelchair access. It rents out bikes, which can be dropped off at points along the Le Luberon en Vélo bike routes. The rooms have colourful bedspreads and wallpapers.

Le Couvent (☎ 04 90 04 55 36; www.loucouvent.com, in French; 36 rue Louis Rousset; d incl breakfast €90-

WORTH A TRIP

You'll see beehive-shaped *bories* while you're buzzing around Provence, but the **Village des Bories** (☎ 04 90 72 03 48; adult/child €5.50/3; ⌚ 9am-sunset) has some of the finest models.

Reminiscent of Ireland's *clochàn,* these one- or two-storey dry-walled huts constructed from slivers of limestone were first built in the area in the Bronze Age. Their original purpose isn't known (shelter would seem most likely), but over time they've also been used as workshops, wine cellars and storage sheds. This 'village' contains about 20, dating back to the 18th century. Getting here requires your own wheels. You'll find the village 4km southwest of **Gordes** (population 2100), just off the D2. Gordes' **tourist office** (☎ 04 90 72 02 75; www.gordes-village.com; place du Château; ⌚ 9am-noon & 2-6pm Mon-Sat, 10am-noon & 2-6pm Sun) has information.

About 5km north of Gordes (turn left on the D177 in direction of Venasque as you enter Gordes) is the stunning **Abbaye de Sénanque** (☎ 04 90 72 02 05; www.senanque.fr, in French; adult/student/under 18yr €7/5/3). Fronted by a huge lavender field at the bottom of an isolated valley, it features on every postcard rack in Provence – but seeing it with your own eyes is a different thing altogether. You can only visit through guided tours, which are in French only, although multilingual leaflets are available; see the website or ask local tourist offices for tour times.

For another Provençal colour to add to your palette, head to ochre-rich **Roussillon** (population 1200), between the Vaucluse plateau and the Luberon Range. Two millennia ago the Romans used this distinctive earth to produce pottery glazes. These days the whole village – even the cemetery's gravestones – is built of the reddish stone.

From Roussillon, take a 45-minute walk along the fiery-coloured **Sentier des Ocres** (Ochre Trail; admission €2.50; ⌚ 9am-5pm Mar-11 Nov). The trail leads you through nature's powdery sunset-coloured palette of ochre formations that were created over centuries by erosion and winds. Don't wear white!

120; 💻 ⊠ 🅿) What you see today in this former 17th-century convent is the result of a painstaking labour of love: it was in ruins before Marie and Laurent worked to turn it into this exquisite B&B. At the time of our visit, plans were under way to increase the number of rooms from five to 12, turning it into a bona fide hotel. But, fear not – breakfast will still be served in the grand dining room, and there will still be classical music playing in the bathrooms.

Thym te voilà (☎ 04 90 74 28 25; 59 rue St-Martin; mains €10; ⌚ lunch Tue-Sat, dinner Fri & Sat, closed Christmas–mid-Apr) Head to this sweet little place for a taste of faraway climes combined with local staples. Lunch will be either in the sweet dining room or on the divine terrace on the square. Sadly, this is a short-lived treat, with the restaurant closing between Christmas and Easter.

Auberge du Luberon (☎ 04 90 74 12 50; www.auberge-luberon-peuzin.com; 8 place Faubourg du Ballet; lunch menu €29, dinner menus €35-57; ⌚ lunch & dinner Wed-Sat & dinner Tue, also open dinner Sun & Mon for hotel guests) Don't be fooled by the underwhelming appearance of this establishment on the bank of the river: here you'll find Apt's finest restaurant, the magnum opus of chef Serge Peuzin. The *menus* make much of Apt's culinary treasures (truffles and candied fruit), as well seasonal highlights. The 14 guest rooms (doubles €58 to €98) here are a little tired-looking in their Provençal prints, but they're comfortable.

GETTING THERE & AWAY

Buses going to Aix-en-Provence (€2, two hours, two daily) leave from the **bus station** (☎ 04 90 74 20 21; 250 av de la Libération) east of the centre. There are services to/from Avignon (€8.20, 1½ hours, eight daily), Digne-les-Bains (€11.40, 2¼ hours, one or two daily) and Cavaillon (€5.40, 45 minutes, four daily).

NORTHEASTERN PROVENCE

Northeastern Provence crowns the top of the Côte d'Azur with snowy peaks and spectacular Alp-cradled valleys.

The Route Napoléon, now the N85, which Bonaparte followed in 1815 en route to Paris after escaping from Elba, passes through Castellane. It continues north to Digne-les-Bains, a thermal spa retreat surrounded by serried lavender fields. Further north again are the winter ski slopes and summer mountain retreats of the Ubaye and Blanche Valleys.

GORGES DU VERDON

Europe's largest canyon, the plunging Gorges du Verdon (also known as the Grand Canyon du Verdon) slices a 25km swath through Provence's limestone plateau.

The gorges begin at Rougon near the confluence of the Verdon and the Jabron Rivers, and wind westwards until the Verdon's green waters flow into Lac de Ste-Croix. A dizzying 250m to 700m deep, the gorges' floor is just 8m to 90m wide, with its overhanging rims 200m to 1500m apart.

The two main jumping-off points for exploring the gorges are the villages of Castellane (population 1592) and the magical Moustiers Ste-Marie (population 705), which has a centuries-old gold star on a 227m-long chain strung between its cliffs.

Information

Castellane Tourist Office (☎ 04 92 83 61 14; www.castellane.org; rue Nationale; ⏲ 9am-1pm & 2-7pm Jul & Aug, 9.15am-noon & 2-6pm Mon-Fri Sep-Jun)

Moustiers Ste-Marie Tourist Office (☎ 04 92 74 67 84; www.moustiers.fr; ⏲ daily, hr vary monthly) This tip-top tourist office has resourceful staff and excellent documentation for exploring the area.

Sights & Activities

The gorges' depths are only accessible by foot or raft. Motorists and cyclists can take in staggering panoramas from two vertigo-inducing cliff-side roads.

CYCLING & DRIVING

The D952 corkscrews along the northern rim, past **Point Sublime**, which offers a fisheye-lens view of serrated rock formations falling away to the river below. The best view from the northern side is from **Belvédère de l'Escalès**, along rte de Crêtes (D23). Drive to the third bend and steel your nerves for the stunning drop-off into the gorge.

Also heart-palpitating, **La Corniche Sublime** (the D19 to the D71) twists along the southern rim, taking in landmarks such as the **Balcons de la Mescla** (Mescla Terraces) and **Pont de l'Artuby** (Artuby Bridge), the highest bridge in Europe.

A complete circuit of the Gorges du Verdon via Moustiers Ste-Marie involves about 140km of relentless hairpin-bend driving. Castellane's and Moustiers' tourist offices have multilanguage driving itineraries. The only village en route is **La Palud-sur-Verdon** (930m), 2km northeast of the northern bank of the gorges. In winter, roads can be icy or snowy, and heaven forbid that you get stuck behind a caravan in summer: opportunities to overtake on those single-lane roads are rare.

WALKING

From Point Sublime, the GR4 descends to the bottom of the canyon. Walkers and white-water rafters can experience an overwhelming series of cliffs and narrows. The GR4 is detailed by Didier-Richard's 1:50,000 map *Haute Provence-Verdon*. It's also included in the excellent English-language book *Canyon du Verdon – The Most Beautiful Hikes* (€4.60), available at the tourist offices, which lists 28 walks in the gorges. The multilingual *Canyon du Verdon* map also lists five walks with illustrated practical info. Bring a torch (flashlight) and drinking water. Short descents into the canyon are possible from a number of points. Camping on gravel beaches is illegal and dangerous because of sudden water level changes, which are due to the dam upstream.

OUTDOOR SPORTS

Castellane's and Moustiers' tourist offices have complete lists of companies offering rafting, canyoning, horse-riding, mountaineering, biking and more. Families should bear in mind that many activities are unsuitable for children under the age of eight.

Aboard Rafting (☎/fax 04 92 83 76 11; www.aboard-rafting.com; place de l'Eglise, Castellane; ⏲ Apr-Sep) runs white-water rafting (€33 to €75) as well as canyoning trips (€33 to €65).

Adrenaline-seekers can throw themselves off the 182m Artuby Bridge for a heart-popping *saut à l'élastique* (bungee jump). Contact Marseille-based **Latitude Challenge** (☎ 04 91 09 04 10; www.latitude-challenge.fr, in French) for prices and schedules.

The newest thrill-seeking pursuit is 'floating' (€50/90 per half-/full day) – it's like white-water rafting minus the raft, with a buoyancy bag strapped to your back. Contact **Guides Aventure** (www.guidesaventure.com) for details.

Sleeping & Eating

Both tourist offices have lists of numerous campsites and accommodation options, as well as restaurants and food shops.

CASTELLANE & AROUND

The nearby river is lined with seasonal camping areas. Hotels and restaurants cluster around the central square, place Marcel Sauvaire and place de l'Église.

Domaine de Chasteuil Provence (☎ 04 92 83 61 21; www.chasteuil-provence.com; camping per site €11.90-22.80; May–mid-Sep;) Just south of Castellane, this campsite has lovely, leafy grounds, optional powered sites, and timber chalets (from €335 for a week for four people).

Ma Petite Auberge (☎ 04 92 83 62 06; fax 04 92 83 68 49; 8 bd République; d €45-65; closed early Dec-early Mar) The key word in this establishment is 'simplicity'. The rooms are clean, basic and bright, with handy triples and quadruples for families or groups. The restaurant (*menus* from €15, open for lunch and dinner Friday to Tuesday) serves no-frills traditional French food at bargain prices.

MOUSTIERS & AROUND

Le Petit Lac (☎ 04 92 74 67 11; www.lepetitlac.com; rte du lac de Ste-Croix; tent per 2 people €13.90-19.90, 6-person eco-cabins per week from €359; camping mid-Jun–Sep, cabins Apr–mid-Oct;) In a peaceful lakeside spot, this activity-oriented campsite has great eco-cabins (two-night minimum) with hemp walls, solar hot water and low-output electricity.

Le Clos des Iris (☎ 04 92 74 63 46; www.closdesiris.fr; chemin de Quinson; d €63-120) The ode to Provence that is Le Clos des Iris comprises nine beautifully decorated rooms, with colourful tiled bathrooms and individual access to either the garden or a balcony. In summer, the garden loungers are perfect for topping up your tan or for finishing a novel.

La Ferme Rose (☎ 04 92 74 69 47; www.lafermerose.com; chemin de Quinson; d €78-148,) This fabulous converted farmhouse contains wonderfully quirky collections including antique toys, a Wurlitzer jukebox with 45rpm records, a display case of coffee grinders, and old telephones, telex machines, theatre lighting, projectors and a puppet theatre. Its dozen boutique rooms with their Provençal-colonial styles all have spectacular bathrooms. It's off the D952, 1km from Moustiers.

La Bastide de Moustiers (☎ 04 92 70 47 47; www.bastide-moustiers.com; d €160/335; menus €42-57;) This exquisite Provençal nest belonging to legendary chef Alain Ducasse is known up and down the country for its very fine cuisine – hence the helicopter pad in the garden. Rooms are equally sophisticated and breakfast is served on a terrace shaded by an old plane tree. The tree was saved in 1974 from the now-flooded village of Les Salles-sur-Verdon, following the completion of the Ste-Croix dam.

For local fare, dine under the oak trees at **Côté Jardin** (☎ 04 92 74 68 91; rue de Lérins; mains €19-27; closed Wed, dinner Tue low season, closed Nov & Dec), or try the fabulous **La Treille Muscate** (☎ 04 92 74 64 31; place de l'Église; menus €20-34; closed Thu & dinner Wed low season, closed Wed high season, closed mid-Nov–Jan).

Getting There & Away

Public transport to, from and around the Gorges du Verdon is limited. **Autocars Sumian** (☎ 04 42 54 72 82) runs buses from Marseille to Castellane (€19.90, 3½ hours) via Aix-en-Provence and Moustiers (€14.40, 2¼ hours).

Getting Around

Daily in July and August, and at weekends from April to September, the Navettes des Gorges (the gorges' shuttle) links Castellane with Point Sublime, La Palud, La Maline and Moustiers. Ask at the tourist offices for schedules; tickets cost €6. Both tourist offices (opposite) have bike rental information.

DIGNE-LES-BAINS

pop 17,600

The latter part of the name Digne-les-Bains refers to its thermal activity: the town's spring spurts out 49°C water, rich in minerals long known to help alleviate rheumatism and respiratory conditions such as asthma. It was the Romans who first spotted the spring, but 2000 years later, the French health system still sends some of its patients to Digne for treatment.

However, thermal activity aside, Digne is still a sleepy provincial town, nestled at the foot of the Alps. The town feels very isolated, almost other-worldly, which is perhaps why famous French adventurer Alexandra David-Néel decided to settle here for want of Tibetan wilderness. The geological sites in the surrounding area are world class, and so are the intensely purple summer lavender fields that flourish in Digne's dry climate.

Orientation

Digne hugs the eastern bank of the shallow River Bléone. The major roads into town converge at the Rond Point (roundabout) du 11 Novembre, 400m northeast of the train station. The main street, bd Gassendi, heads northeastwards from the roundabout and passes the large place du Général de Gaulle, the town's main square.

Information

Cybercafé (☎ 04 92 32 00 19; 48 rue de l'Hubac; internet access 1st 10min €1.50, per min thereafter €0.06; 10am-noon & 2-7pm Tue-Sat) In the centre of the town.

Laverie (☎ 04 92 31 11 75; 99 bd Gassendi; 9am-7pm)

Relais Départemental des Gîtes de France (☎ 04 92 31 30 40; www.gites-de-france.com; 8.30am-noon & 2-5pm Mon-Fri, 9am-noon Sat) Adjacent to the tourist office. It can book *gîtes* in the area.

Tourist Office (☎ 04 92 36 62 62; www.ot-digneles bains.fr; place du Tampinet; 10am-7pm Mon-Sat Jul & Aug, 10am-noon & 3-6pm Sun mid-Jun–Sep, 9am-noon & 2-6pm Mon-Fri Sep-Jun, 9am-noon Sat Sep-Mar, 9am-noon & 2-6pm Sat Apr-Jun) Has comprehensive regional info including walking and cycling maps.

Sights & Activities

FONDATION ALEXANDRA DAVID-NÉEL

Tibetan culture is celebrated at the **Fondation Alexandra David-Néel** (☎ 04 92 31 32 38; www.alexandra-david-neel.org; 27 av Maréchal Juin; admission free; 2hr tours 10am, 2pm & 3.30pm), in memory of Paris-born writer and philosopher Alexandra David-Néel, who made two incognito voyages to Tibet in the 1900s before settling in Digne. Her adventures, recounted in several books, inspired generations of travellers. The collection of B&W pictures David-Néel took during her trips is outstanding, and the Tibetan art room is an unusual jewel in the predominantly Roman heritage of this part of the world. Drive 1km along the Nice road or take bus 3 to the Stade Rolland stop.

MUSÉE GASSENDI

Everything from modern art to still lifes and exhibits on the 16th-century philosopher/scientist/painter Pierre Gassendi are displayed at the **Musée Gassendi** (☎ 04 92 31 45 29; 64 bd Gassendi; adult/child €4/2; 11am-7pm Wed-Mon Apr-Sep, 1.30-5.30pm Wed-Mon Oct-Mar) in the town centre.

RÉSERVE NATURELLE GÉOLOGIQUE DE HAUTE PROVENCE

Prehistoric birds' footprints, outsized ammonites and ram's horn spiral shells are some of the amazing fossil deposits in the **Réserve Naturelle Géologique**, which surrounds Digne. Getting to the 18 sites requires your own wheels; ask the tourist office for a detailed regional map.

The **Musée Promenade** (☎ 04 92 36 70 70; www.resgeol04.org; adult/child €4.60/2.75; 9am-1pm & 2-7pm Mon-Fri & 10.30am-12.30pm & 2-7pm Sat & Sun Jul & Aug, 9am-noon & 2-5.30pm Sat-Thu & to 4.30pm Fri Apr-Jun, Sep & Oct, 9am-noon & 2-5.30pm Mon-Thu, to 4.30pm Fri Nov-Mar), 2km north of town off the road to Barles, contains aquarium tanks, insect displays, and artistically presented fossils and plants put into evolutionary context. Take TUD bus 2 to the Champourcin stop; then take the road to the left.

THERMAL SPA

Ahhhh… Float in the thermal pool, slather yourself in mud and seaweed, or luxuriate in a lavender bath at the **Établissement Thermal** (☎ 04 92 32 58 46; www.eurothermes.com, in French; Mar-early Dec), 2km east of Digne's centre. A 50-minute essential oil massage costs €50.

Sleeping & Eating

France's first *gîte* was founded here in 1951; the headquarters of the Relais Départemental des Gîtes de France (left) has a list of locations.

Hôtel Central (☎ 04 92 31 31 91; www.lhotel-central.com; 26 bd Gassendi; s €31-49, d €39-53) With its traditional dark-wood furniture, beamed ceiling and brightly coloured quilts, the impeccable rooms of this (indeed) very central hotel are an unexpected bargain. There is also free wi-fi and the staff can recommend places to eat or visit.

Hôtel de Provence (☎ 04 92 31 32 19; 17 bd Thiers; s €40, d €50-58; P) This family-run hotel offers plenty in the way of comfort (it was entirely renovated in 2008) but not a huge amount in the way of charm. The 'family' welcome can also be a tad chaotic. However, it does have a few parking spaces, and wi-fi, so it is a practical option.

our pick **Hôtel Villa Gaia** (☎ 04 92 31 21 60; www.hotelvillagaia.fr; 24 rte de Nice; d €65-102, with half-board €148-170; Apr-Oct) Set in Italianate fountained gardens, the 1730 Villa Gaia is a timeless, utterly charming place. Anne-Françoise and Georges-Eric have opted for a beautiful wood-fired hammam rather than a swimming pool, and they serve simple, homemade food made with organic produce from their garden. Rooms have retained their period charm; children are well catered for with great family rooms. Dinner in the grand dining room or the terrace overlooking the valley is heavenly. Find the villa 2km southwest of town in the direction of Nice.

Le Grand Paris (☎ 04 92 31 11 15; www.hotel-grand-paris.com; 19 bd Thiers; d €88-137) Carpeted walls, heavy period furniture, chandeliers – you get the picture. This is Digne's elegant address, a vestige of the town's heyday as a thermal destination. But just like a good vintage, Le Grand Paris is going through old age gracefully, thanks in particular to the care of three generations of Ricaud. The restaurant (mains €23 to €37) has a lovely garden for alfresco dining.

Le Chaudron (☎ 04 92 31 24 87; 40 rue Hubac; mains €14-17; lunch & dinner Tue-Sat) Digne's unsung gastronomic treasure serves wonderful traditional cuisine at unbeatable prices: try the house speciality, the chef's great-grandmother's recipe of *pieds paquets* (pork-stuffed lamb), or the *filet mignon de porc à la crème aux morilles* (tenderloin pork in morel and crème-fraîche sauce).

SELF-CATERING

Wednesday and Saturday mornings are market days, with markets held on place du Général de Gaulle.

Stock up on groceries at the **8 à Huit** (33 bd Gassendi; 8.30am-12.30pm & 3.30-7.30pm).

Getting There & Away

The **bus station** (☎ 04 92 31 50 00; place du Tampinet; 6.30am-7.30pm Mon-Sat) is behind the tourist office. Destinations include Nice (€15.60, 2¼ hours) via Castellane (€5.60, 1¼ hours), Marseille (€15.10, 2½ hours) and Gap (€9.50, 1½ hours).

A shuttle bus links Digne with Aix-en-Provence's TGV station (€12.20, 1¾ hours), timed to coincide with the TGV to and from Paris, and with Marseille's airport (€14.50, 2¼ hours).

Even though Digne has a train station, there are no SNCF services running from the station. The only service that comes into Digne is the privately operated Train des Pignes from Nice (see boxed text, right).

Gallardo (☎ 04 92 31 05 29; 8 cours des Arès; 8am-noon & 2-7pm Tue-Fri, to 6pm Sat) rents out bikes (€14 per day).

THE PROVENCE ALPS

The terrain is mountainous but the sunshine (in excess of 300 days a year) is definitely Provençal. This combination hasn't escaped the attention of utility company Suez, who is building Europe's biggest solar power station in the village of Curbans near the Vallée de la Blanche.

> **THE PINE CONE TRAIN**
>
> Chug along a picturesque, narrow-gauge railway on **le Train des Pignes** (the Pine Cone Train). Operated by **Chemins de Fer de Provence** (www.trainprovence.com; Digne ☎ 04 92 31 01 58; Nice ☎ 04 97 03 80 80), the entire trip from Digne to Nice's Chemins de fer de Provence station (4bis rue Alfred Binet) takes about 3¼ hours (€17.65, four daily each direction).

Vallée de la Blanche

Remote and sparsely populated, the beautiful Vallée de la Blanche (www.valleedelablanche.com) is an unspoilt nature haven. The main 'resort' (although, it's so tiny that it seems funny to call it a resort), is the 1350m **St-Jean Montclar**. Set up in the 1970s by a farmers' cooperative desperate to stem the demographic decline of the area, it turned unfarmable land into a rather successful holiday destination. It's particularly great for families, with skiing in winter and trekking galore in summer. The **tourist office** (☎ 04 92 30 92 01; www.montclar.com) has plenty of info. The area is also the home of Montclar spring water, but you won't need to buy it while you're here – just turn on the tap.

One of the sweetest *chambres d'hôtes* is **Les Alisiers** (☎ 04 92 35 30 88; fax 04 92 35 02 72; d incl breakfast €52-56, 4-person self-catering apt per week €200-500; closed mid-Nov–mid-Dec), 800m past the ski station on your left as you head south. The chalet faces breathtaking 180-degree views of the surrounding peaks and valleys. For dinner, try the scrumptious *picatons* (tiny raviolis baked in a creamy, cheesy sauce with mushrooms) at the next door restaurant (☎ 04 92 35 34 90; mains €15; open for lunch and dinner Thursday to Tuesday).

St-Jean Montclar is 50km north of Dignes-les-Bains. Between late December and March, there's a bus service from Gap (€12, 45 minutes).

Vallée de l'Ubaye

At the edge of the wild, isolated **Parc National du Mercantour** (see boxed text, p858), the Vallée de l'Ubaye is ringed by a rollercoaster

WONDERFUL MERCANTOUR

Deeply isolated and breathtakingly beautiful, the **Parc National du Mercantour** (www.mercantour.eu) is one of the last bastions of true wilderness in France. Spread across six valleys (Roya-Bévéra, Vésubie, Tinée, Haut Var, Haut Verdon and Ubaye) and 685 sq km along the Italian border, it mixes Alpine snowy peaks with Mediterranean warmth.

The park was set up in 1979 and twinned with the Italian Alpi Marittime national park. Together, they form the first and only cross-border national park in Europe. Proof of this success was the controversial return of the wolf to France in 1992 from Italy, via the national park, after more than 70 years of absence. There are only about 50 wolves roaming the French side (in comparison with 1800 in Italy), but their presence has been highly unpopular with sheep farmers, because of attacks on flocks.

In a bid to show both sides of the debate, the mayor of the little town of St-Martin-Vésubie (pop 1146) decided in 2005 to open **Alpha** (☎ 04 93 02 33 69; www.alpha-loup.com; Le Boréon; adult/child €10/8; 🕑 10am-6.30pm Jun-Aug, to 6pm mid-Apr–May, 10am-6.30pm Tue, Sat & Sun Sep, 10am-5pm Sat-Wed Oct–mid-Nov, check with park directly for rest of year), a themed park exploring the pros and cons of the wolf's presence. Set high in the mountains of Le Boréon, three informative animated projections shown in renovated mountain stables present the arguments of scientists, sheep farmers and forest rangers. Further up in the park, visitors can also watch wolves in semiwild enclosures: the enclosures are big so that you may not see the wolves but you'll most certainly hear them. Their howling is absolutely enthralling.

In St-Martin-Vésubie, **La Bonne Auberge** (☎ 04 93 03 20 49; www.labonneauberge06.fr, in French; 98 allée de Verdun; d €50) is a wonderful stopover, with its huge fireplace and divine mountain fare (*menus* €20 to €27). The **tourist office** (☎ 04 93 03 21 28; place Félix Faure; 🕑 9am-noon & 2-6pm Mon-Sat, 9am-noon Sun Sep-Jun, longer hr summer) has plenty of information on walks and activities in this part of the park, including how to see some of the 36,000 outstanding Bronze Age **stone carvings** (visible only in summer) in the **Vallée des Merveilles** (Valley of Wonders), part of the Roya Valley. Public transport is minimal in the area but **TRAM** (☎ 04 93 85 92 60) operates two daily buses between Nice and St Martin.

of rugged mountains. The area's main town, **Barcelonnette** (population 2766), experienced strong emigration to Mexico in the 19th century. A few decades and many fortunes later, migrants returned to Barcelonnette and built bourgeois mansions with their Mexican monies, resulting in some very un-Alpine architecture. Rising 8.5km southwest are the twin ski resorts of **Pra Loup 1500** (sometimes called Les Molanes) and **Pra Loup 1600** (which has more infrastructure and nightlife). Both are connected by a lift system with the ski resort of La Foux d'Allos. Pra Loup's 50 lifts are between 1600m and 2600m, with 180km of runs and a vertical drop of almost 1000m. In summer, it's a hiker's and mountain biker's heaven (Pra Loup has been hosting the Mountain Bike Masters World Championship since 2007, and will host it for the last time in 2009).

Pra Loup's dynamic **tourist office** (☎ 04 92 84 10 04; www.praloup.com; 🕑 9am-noon & 2-6pm Jul & Aug, 9am-noon & 2-5pm Mon-Fri May, Jun & Sep-Nov, 9am-7pm Dec-Apr) and **École de Ski Français** (ESF; ☎ 04 92 84 11 05), the main ski school in France, are in Pra Loup 1600. Ski passes cost €27.50 per day.

Studios and apartments start from around €200 per week, climbing to around €800 in the peak ski season – the tourist office has lists. There's also a handful of hotels, like the wonderful storybook chalet **Hôtel Le Prieuré** (☎ 04 92 84 11 43; www.prieure.eu, in French; Pra Loup 1500; d €55-90, half-board per person €57-68; ⊠ 🅿), just across the road from the ski lift, with a restaurant (mains €13 to €26.55) serving heart-warming fondue.

The nearest train station to Pra Loup is at Gap, from where buses (usually a couple a day) travel to Barcelonnette (€7, 1½ hours). There is also one bus a day between Barcelonnette and Digne (€8.90, 1½ hours). Free shuttles operate between Barcelonnette and Pra Loup.

Côte d'Azur & Monaco

The Côte d'Azur (Azure Coast), with its glistening seas, idyllic beaches and lush hills, is a gift from the heavens. Nothing less. Greeks and Ligurians were quick to spot this, and were early settlers. Queens, tsars and assorted crowns followed a few centuries later, coming for mild winters and hedonistic lifestyles on what became known as the French Riviera.

The monarchs gone, celebrated artists and writers (Matisse, Chagall, Picasso, F Scott Fitzgerald, Cocteau) took over, propelling sleepy villages to fame and immortalising in a brush stroke or a verse what so many before them had quietly contemplated. You can admire or read their legacy the world over but the Riviera villages they inhabited have what no other museum on earth will ever have: their souls.

These days the Riviera is the destination de rigueur for the celebrity set. They like to hang out in glitzy St-Tropez, glamorous Cannes and sovereign Monaco. But the coast also beckons millions more for the simple pleasures of swimming in turquoise waters, walking along paradisaical shores, taking in the incessant song of millions of cicadas and buying shiny fruit and veg from groaning market stalls.

In summer, crowds are the price to pay for these pleasures. Spring and autumn are definitely best, but at any time of year, drive 15 minutes inland and the infinitely less-touristed hinterland offers rows of perfume-producing flower fields, acres of rosé-yielding vineyards, the rugged red Massif de l'Estérel, the forested slopes of Massif des Maures mountains, and the myriad hilltop villages proffering breathtaking Mediterranean views.

HIGHLIGHTS

- Retrace **Matisse's steps** (see boxed text, p867) in and around Nice
- Experience your own epiphany on the **Chemin de Nietzsche** (p898) between Èze and Èze-sur-Mer villages
- Party under the stars at Antibes' legendary beachside **La Siesta-Le Pearl** (p876) nightclub
- Head to Hyères' beaches for prime **kitesurfing** (p892)
- Catch a ferry to **Île de Port-Cros** (p890), France's only marine national park, for pristine Mediterranean land- and seascapes
- Wind your way through Bandol's **vineyards** (p897) and try some of the area's famed wines at **Maison des Vins** (p896)

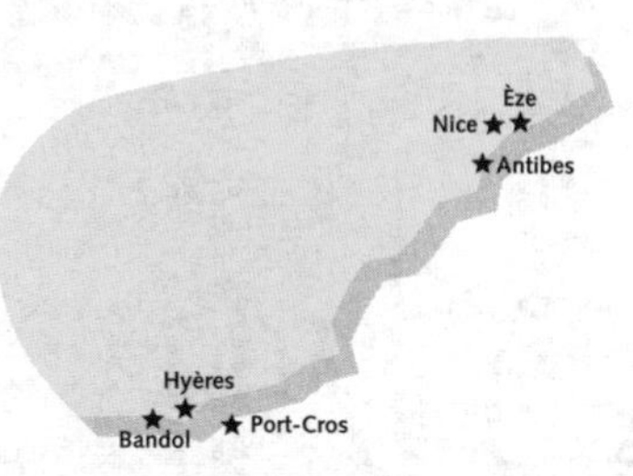

- POPULATION: 2,044,000
- AREA: 4300 SQ KM

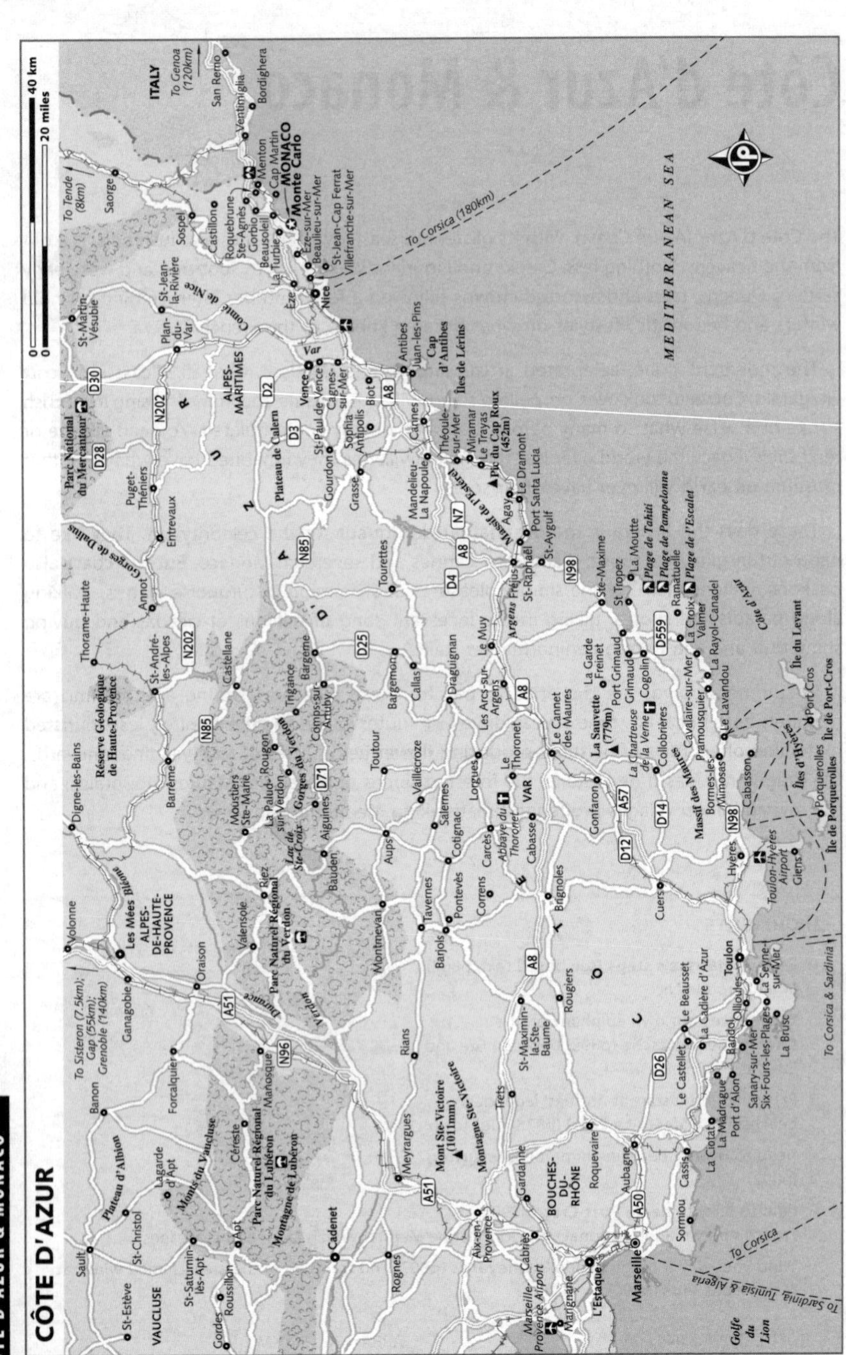
CÔTE D'AZUR
0 40 km
0 20 miles
ITALY
To Genoa (120km)
San Remo
Bordighera
Ventimiglia
MONACO
Monte Carlo
Cap Martin
Menton
Roquebrune
Ste-Agnès
Gorbio
Beausoleil
La Turbie
Èze-sur-Mer
Beaulieu-sur-Mer
St-Jean-Cap Ferrat
Villefranche-sur-Mer
Èze
Nice
To Tende (8km)
Saorge
Sospel
Castillon
St-Jean-la-Rivière
Comté de Nice
St-Martin-Vésubie
Plan-du-Var
Var
To Corsica (180km)
MEDITERRANEAN SEA
Antibes
Juan-les-Pins
Cap d'Antibes
Îles de Lérins
Cannes
Théoule-sur-Mer
Miramar
Le Trayas
Pic du Cap Roux (452m)
Le Dramont
Port Santa Lucia
Agay
Massif de l'Estérel
Mandelieu-La Napoule
Biot
Cagnes-sur-Mer
St-Paul de Vence
Vence
Sophia Antipolis
Grasse
Gourdon
Plateau de Calern
ALPES-MARITIMES
Parc National du Mercantour
Puget-Théniers
Entrevaux
Gorges de Daluis
Annot
Thorame-Haute
Réserve Géologique de Haute-Provence
St-André-les-Alpes
Castellane
Digne-les-Bains
Barrême
Moustiers Ste-Marie
La Palud-sur-Verdon
Rougon
Gorges du Verdon
Trigance
Bargème
Comps-sur-Artuby
Aiguines
Lac de Ste-Croix
Bauduen
Tourettes
Bargemon
Callas
Draguignan
Le Muy
Les Arcs-sur-Argens
Argens
Fréjus
St-Raphaël
St-Aygulf
Ste-Maxime
St Tropez
La Moutte
Plage de Tahiti
Plage de Pampelonne
Plage de l'Escalet
Ramatuelle
La Croix-Valmer
Côte d'Azur
Île du Levant
Port Cros
Île de Port-Cros
Porquerolles
Île de Porquerolles
Îles d'Hyères
Giens
Toulon-Hyères Airport
Hyères
Cabasson
Bormes-les-Mimosas
Le Lavandou
Pramousquier
Cavalaire-sur-Mer
La Rayol-Canadel
Massif des Maures
Collobrières
La Chartreuse de la Verne
Cogolin
Grimaud
Port Grimaud
La Garde Freinet
La Sauvette (779m)
Le Cannet des Maures
Le Thoronet
Abbaye du Thoronet
VAR
Lorgues
Salernes
Toutour
Vallécroze
Aups
Cotignac
Carcès
Cabasse
Gonfaron
Brignoles
Correns
Pontevès
Barjols
Tavernes
Montmeyan
Valensole
Riez
Parc Naturel Régional du Verdon
Verdon
Durance
Oraison
Les Mées
ALPES-DE-HAUTE-PROVENCE
Bléone
Volonne
Ganagobie
To Sisteron (7.5km); Gap (55km); Grenoble (140km)
Forcalquier
Manosque
Banon
Plateau d'Albion
St-Christol
Sault
Lagarde d'Apt
Monts du Vaucluse
Céreste
Parc Naturel Régional du Lubéron
Montagne du Lubéron
Apt
St-Saturnin-lès-Apt
VAUCLUSE
St-Estève
Roussillon
Gordes
Cadenet
Rognes
Meyrargues
Rians
Mont Ste-Victoire (1011mm)
Montagne Ste-Victoire
Trets
St-Maximin-la-Ste-Baume
Rougiers
Aix-en-Provence
Gardanne
Cabriès
BOUCHES-DU-RHÔNE
Roquevaire
Aubagne
Marseille-Provence Airport
Marignane
L'Estaque
Marseille
Sormiou
Cassis
La Ciotat
La Madrague
Port d'Alon
Le Castellet
Le Beausset
La Cadière d'Azur
Bandol
Sanary-sur-Mer
Six-Fours-les-Plages
Ollioules
La Seyne-sur-Mer
La Brusc
Toulon
Cuers
Golfe du Lion
To Corsica
To Sardinia, Tunisia & Algeria
To Corsica & Sardinia
A8
A50
A51
A57
D2
D3
D4
D12
D14
D25
D26
D28
D30
D71
D559
N7
N85
N96
N98
N202
C
O
T
E
D'
A
Z
U
R

History

The eastern part of France's Mediterranean coast, including the area now known as the Côte d'Azur, was occupied by the Ligurians from the 1st millennium BC. It was colonised around 600 BC by Greeks from Asia Minor, who settled along the coast in the areas of present-day Marseille, Hyères, St-Tropez, Antibes and Nice. Called in to help Massalia against the threat of invasion by Celto-Ligurians from Entremont, the Romans triumphed in 125 BC. They created Provincia Romana – the area between the Alps, the sea and the River Rhône – which ultimately became Provence.

In 1388 Nice, along with the Haute-Provence mountain towns Barcelonette and Puget-Théniers, was incorporated into the House of Savoy, while the rest of the surrounding Provençal region became part of the French kingdom in 1482. After Austrians were driven from northern Italy due to an agreement between Napoléon III and the House of Savoy in 1860, France took possession of Savoy.

Within the Provence-Alpes-Côte d'Azur *région* (administrative division of France – usually contains several *départements*), the Côte d'Azur encompasses most of the *départements* of the Alpes-Maritimes and the Var. In the 19th century, wealthy tourists and artists and writers added to the area's cachet. Little fishing ports morphed into exclusive resorts. Paid holidays for all French workers from 1936 and improved transportation saw visitors arrive in summer, making it a year-round holiday playground. But it's not all play, no work: since the late 20th century, the area inland of Antibes has been home to France's 'Silicon Valley', Sophia Antipolis, the country's largest industrial/technological hub.

Dangers & Annoyances

The Côte d'Azur isn't a dangerous area, but theft – from backpacks, pockets, bags, cars and even laundrettes – is rife. Watch your belongings, especially at train and bus stations, on overnight trains, and on the beach. Keep your passport, credit cards and cash on your person, not in your bags. Always drive with the doors locked and windows up as thieves often pounce at red lights. If you're travelling by bicycle, store it off-street overnight.

Getting There & Away

The efficient SNCF train network and regular bus connections link the Côte d'Azur with Provence and the rest of France. Excellent road networks make the region easy to access by car. There are international airports at Nice (the country's second busiest after Paris) and outside Toulon.

For information on ferry services from Nice and Toulon to Corsica, see p907.

Getting Around

SNCF trains shuttle along the coast between St-Raphaël and the Italian border, and north to Grasse. The coastal area between St-Raphaël and Toulon (where the train line veers inland) is served by regular buses. Boat services operate to St-Tropez in summer.

Except for the traffic-plagued high-summer season, the Côte d'Azur is easily accessible by car (and to get off the main tourist routes, you'll need one). The fastest thoroughfare is the uninspiring, speed-camera- and road-toll-ridden A8 motorway which, travelling west to east, starts near Aix-en-Provence, approaches the coast at Fréjus, skirts the Estérel range and runs more or less parallel to the coast from Cannes to the Italian border at Ventimiglia (Vintimille in French).

NICE TO TOULON

NICE

pop 346,900

> Most people come here for the light. Me, I'm from the north. What moved me are January's radiant colours and luminosity of daylight.
>
> *Henri Matisse*

The words are Matisse's but they could be those of any painter, or in fact, of any visitor who comes to Nice, for it's true: the light here is magical. The city also offers exceptional quality of life: shimmering Mediterranean shores, the very best of Mediterranean food, a unique historical heritage and Alpine wilderness within an hour's drive. No wonder that so many young French people have it high on their wishlist of places to live, and that tourists keep flooding in.

Thanks to its busy international airport, Nice has a very cosmopolitan and diverse crowd. Bars reverberate with a Babylonian hubbub of merry punters, the seafront is lined with strollers, in-line skaters, beach-goers,

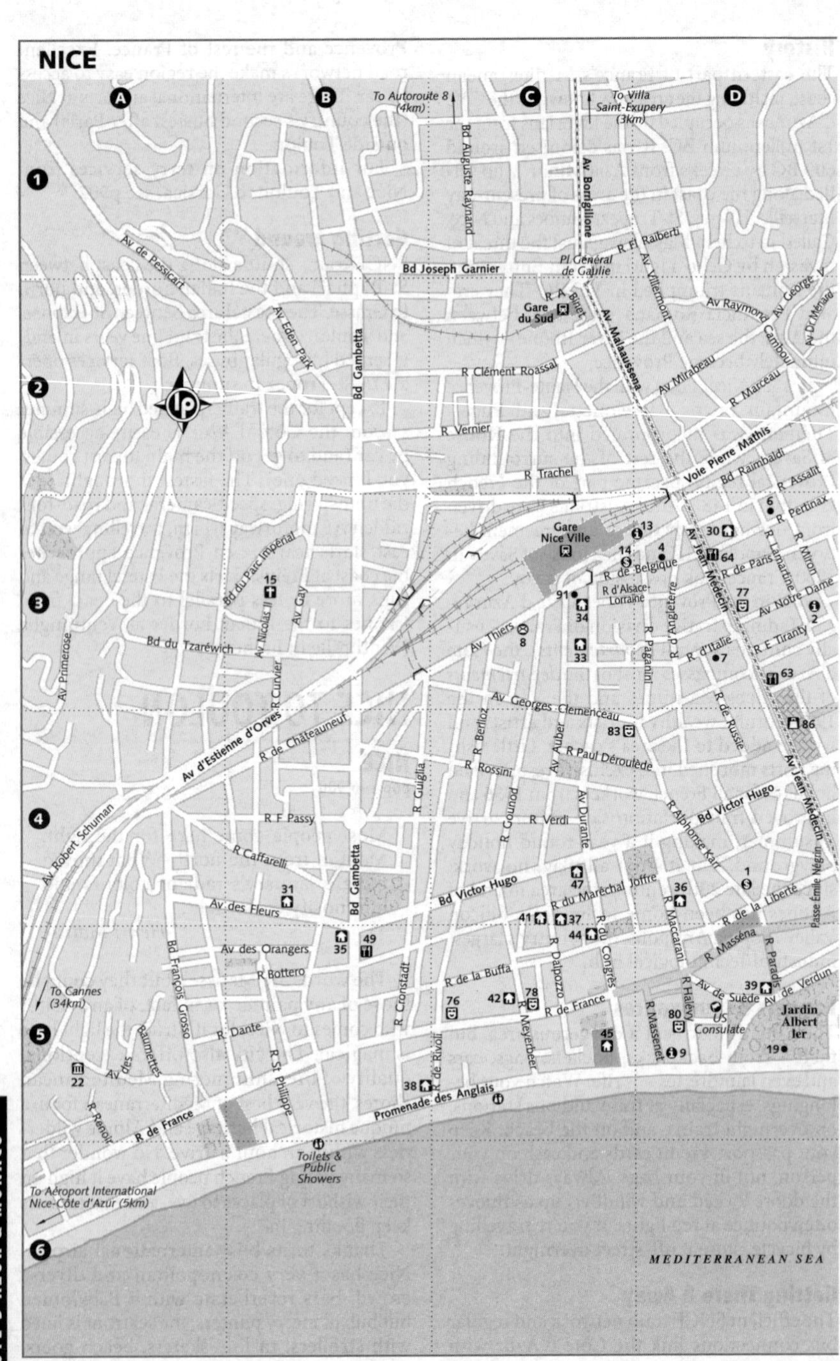
NICE
To Autoroute 8 (4km)
To Villa Saint-Exupery (3km)
Av Borriglione
Bd Auguste Raynaud
Av de Pessicart
Bd Joseph Garnier
Pl Général de Gaulle
R Fl Raiberti
Av Villermont
Gare du Sud
R A Binet
Av Malausséna
Av Raymond Comboul
Av George V
Av Dr Ménard
Av Eden Park
Bd Gambetta
R Clément Roassal
Av Mirabeau
R Marceau
R Vernier
Voie Pierre Mathis
R Trachel
Bd Raimbaldi
R Assalit
R Pertinax
Gare Nice Ville
Av Jean Médecin
R de Belgique
R de Paris
R Lamartine
R Miron
Bd du Parc Impérial
Av Nicolas II
Av Gay
R d'Alsace-Lorraine
R d'Angleterre
Av Notre Dame
Av Thiers
R Paganini
R d'Italie
R E Tiranty
Bd du Tzaréwich
Av Primerose
R Curvier
Av Georges Clemenceau
R de Russie
R de Châteauneuf
R Berlioz
Av Auber
R Paul Déroulède
Av d'Estienne d'Orves
R Rossini
R Guiglia
Av Robert Schuman
R F Passy
R Gounod
R Verdi
Av Durante
R Alphonse Karr
Bd Victor Hugo
R Caffarelli
Passe Émile Négrin
Av des Fleurs
R du Maréchal Joffre
R de la Liberté
Av des Orangers
R Maccarani
R du Congrès
Bd François Grosso
R Bottero
R Cronstadt
R de la Buffa
R Dalpozzo
R Masséna
R Paradis
Av de Suède
Av de Verdun
To Cannes (34km)
R de France
R Halévy
US Consulate
Jardin Albert Ier
R Dante
R Meyerbeer
R Massenet
Av des Baumettes
R St Philippe
R de Rivoli
Promenade des Anglais
R Renoir
Toilets & Public Showers
To Aéroport International Nice-Côte d'Azur (5km)
MEDITERRANEAN SEA

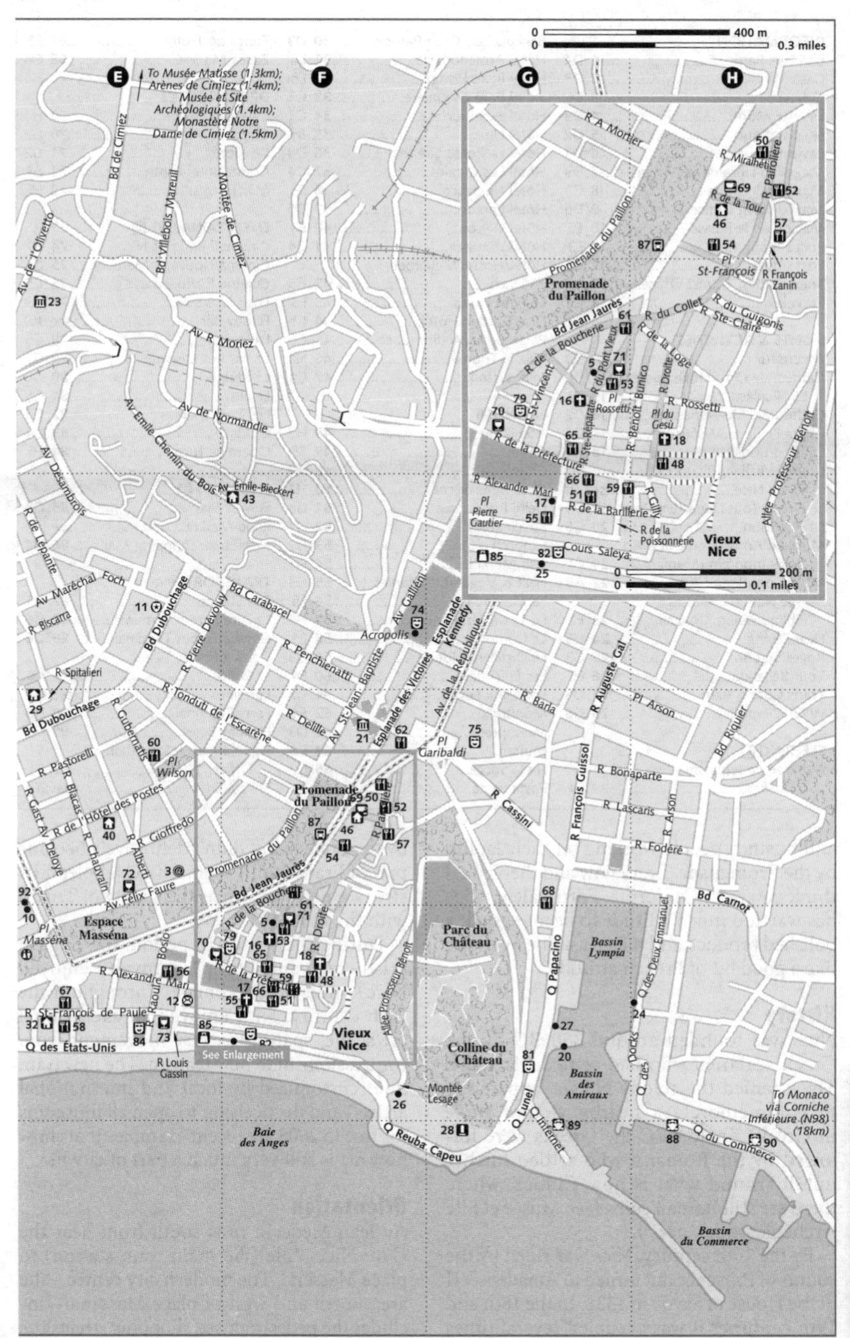

To Musée Matisse (1.3km); Arènes de Cimiez (1.4km); Musée et Site Archéologiques (1.4km); Monastère Notre Dame de Cimiez (1.5km)
Promenade du Paillon
Espace Masséna
Parc du Château
Colline du Château
Vieux Nice
Bassin Lympia
Bassin des Amiraux
Bassin du Commerce
Baie des Anges
To Monaco via Corniche Inférieure (N98) (18km)
See Enlargement

INFORMATION

Barclays Bank	1 D4
Cat's Whiskers	2 D3
Cyberpoint	3 E4
Laverie Mono	4 D3
Lavomatique	5 G2
Lavomatique	6 D3
Magellan Librairie de Voyages	7 D3
Main Post Office	8 C3
Main Tourist Office	9 D5
Maison de la Presse	10 E5
Police Station	11 E3
Post Office	12 E5
Train Station Tourist Office	13 D3
Travelex	14 C3

SIGHTS & ACTIVITIES

Ascenseur	(see 26)
Cathédrale Orthodoxe Russe St-Nicolas	15 B3
Cathédrale Ste-Réparate	16 G2
Chapelle de la Miséricorde	17 G3
Église du Gesù	18 H2
Guided Walking Tours of Vieux Nice	(see 9)
Le Grand Tour Departure Point	19 D5
Le Poséidon	20 G5
Musée d'Art Moderne et d'Art Contemporain (Mamac)	21 F4
Musée des Beaux-Arts	22 A5
Musée National Message Biblique Marc Chagall	23 E2
Nice Diving	24 H5
Roller Station	25 G3
Tour Bellanda	26 F5
Trans Côte d'Azur	27 G5
WWI Memorial	28 G6

SLEEPING

Auberge de Jeunesse - Les Camélias	29 E4
Backpackers Chez Patrick	30 D3
Hôtel Armenonville	31 B4
Hôtel Beau Rivage	32 E5
Hôtel Belle Meunière	33 C3
Hôtel Excelsior	34 C3
Hôtel Hi	35 B5
Hôtel La Petite Sirène	36 D4
Hôtel Les Cigales	37 C4
Hôtel Negresco	38 B5
Hôtel Paradis	39 D5
Hôtel Wilson	40 E4
Hôtel Windsor	41 C4
Hôtel/Hostel Meyerbeer Beach	42 C5
Le Petit Palais	43 F3
Nice Garden Hôtel	44 C5
Palais de la Méditerranée	45 C5
Villa la Tour	46 H1
Villa Victoria	47 C4

EATING

Acchiardo	48 H2
Casino	49 B5
Chantecler	(see 38)
Chez René Socca	50 H1
Delhi Belhi	51 G3
Escalinada	52 H1
Fenocchio	53 G2
Fish Market	54 H1
Fruit & Vegetable Market	55 G3
La Merenda	56 E5
La Table Alziari	57 H1
Le Comptoir	58 E5
Le Distilleries Idéales	59 G3
Les Épicuriens	60 E4
Lou Pilha Leva	61 G2
Monoprix	62 F4
Monoprix	63 D3
Multari	64 D3
Nissa Socca	65 G2
Pasta Basta	66 G3
Terres de Truffes	67 E5
Zucca Magica	68 G4

DRINKING

Cave de la Tour	69 H1
Chez Wayne's	70 G2
De Klomp	71 G2
Grand Hotel Aston	72 E4
Ma Nolan's	73 E5

ENTERTAINMENT

Cinemathèque de Nice	74 F3
Cinéma Nouveau Mercury	75 G4
Cinéma Rialto	76 C5
Fnac	77 D3
Happy Bar	(see 35)
La Havane	78 C5
Le Bar des Oiseaux	79 G2
Le Klub	80 D5
Le Nova	81 G5
Les Trois Diables	82 G3
L'Ôdace	83 C4
Opéra de Nice	84 E5

SHOPPING

Flower Market	85 G3
Food Market	(see 55)
Nice Étoile Shopping Mall	86 D4

TRANSPORT

Bus Station	87 H1
Corsica Ferries Terminal	88 H6
Corsica Ferries Terminal	89 G6
Corsica Ferries Ticket Office	(see 90)
Eurolines	(see 87)
Ferry Terminal	90 H6
Holiday Bikes	91 C3
Ligne d'Azur Information Office	92 E4
SNCM Office	(see 90)

and businesspeople working on their laptop by the Promenade. Every now and then you'd think you're in California. Fortunately, Nice has way too much attitude to become such a polished product, and that's just fine by us: we like a good bit of French attitude.

History

Nice was founded around 350 BC by the Greek seafarers who had settled Marseille. They named the colony Nikaia, apparently to commemorate a nearby victory (*nike* in Greek). In 154 BC the Greeks were followed by the Romans, who settled further uphill around what is now Cimiez, where there are still Roman ruins (see Musée et Site Archéologiques, p867).

By the 10th century, Nice was ruled by the counts of Provence but turned to Amadeus VII of the House of Savoy in 1388. In the 18th and 19th centuries it was occupied several times by the French, but didn't definitively become part of France until 1860, when Napoléon III struck a deal (known as the Treaty of Turin) with the House of Savoy.

During the Victorian period, the English aristocracy and European royalty enjoyed Nice's mild winter climate. Throughout the 20th century, Nice enjoyed an exceptional art scene, spanning every movement from Impressionism to new realism. The new tram line (customised by local and international artists) and the decision to open all museums for free in 2008 are recent examples that show how art is still very much a part of city life.

Orientation

Av Jean Médecin runs south from near the Gare Nice Ville (the main train station) to place Masséna. The modern city centre – the area north and west of place Masséna – includes the pedestrianised shopping streets rue de France and rue Masséna. The bus station is located three blocks east of place Masséna.

Promenade des Anglais follows the gently arced beachfront from the city centre to the airport, 6km west. Vieux Nice (Old Nice) is delineated by bd Jean Jaurès, quai des États-Unis and, east, the hill known as Colline du Château. The port is further east, on the other side of the Colline du Château.

The wealthy residential neighbourhood of Cimiez, home to outstanding museums, is just north of the city centre.

Information

BOOKSHOPS

Cat's Whiskers (☎ 04 93 80 02 66; 30 rue Lamartine; closed Mon morning & all Sun) Linda and her four-legged assistant Vodka will help you pick new and second-hand English-language books.
Magellan Librairie de Voyages (☎ 04 93 82 31 81; 3 rue d'Italie) Stellar selection of maps and travel guides, including Lonely Planet titles in English.
Maison de la Presse (1 place Masséna; to 7.30pm Oct-Jun, to midnight Jul-Sep) Maps and guides, plus books and magazines in English.

EMERGENCY

Police Station (☎ 04 92 17 22 22, Foreign Tourist Department 04 92 17 20 31; 1 av Maréchal Foch)

INTERNET ACCESS

New internet cafés abound (there are around 10 on rue Pertinax alone); you'll have no problems staying connected.
Cyberpoint (☎ 04 93 92 70 63; 10 av Félix Faure; per hr €4; 10am-9pm Mon-Sat, later in summer, 3-9pm Sun) An organised internet café with English keyboards.

INTERNET RESOURCES

Nice Tourism (www.nicetourisme.com) The tourist office's website.
PACA (www.crt-paca.fr) Umbrella site for all of Provence and the Côte d'Azur.
Riviera Guide (www.guideriviera.com) Covers the eastern Côte d'Azur.
Var Destination (www.vardestination.com) Info on the Côte d'Azur's western Var region.

LAUNDRY

Self-service laundrettes are plentiful, especially around Gare Nice Ville. Expect to pay about €3 for a small load of around 5kg.
Laverie Mono (8 rue Belgique; 7am-9pm)
Lavomatique rue Pertinax (22 rue Pertinax; 7am-8pm); rue du Pont Vieux (11 rue du Pont Vieux; 7am-8pm)

MONEY

Barclays Bank (2 rue Alphonse Karr) Has a change counter.
Travelex (☎ 04 93 88 59 99; 13 av Thiers; 8am-8pm Mon-Fri, 9am-5.30pm Sat & Sun) Opposite the station.

POST

Main Post Office (23 av Thiers)
Post Office (2 rue Louis Gassin) In Vieux Nice.

TOURIST INFORMATION

Airport Tourist Information Desk (☎ 08 92 70 74 07; 8am-9pm Jun-Sep, closed Sun Oct-May) In Terminal 1.
Main Tourist Office (☎ 08 92 70 74 07; 5 promenade des Anglais; 8am-8pm Mon-Sat, 9am-7pm Sun Jun-Sep, 9am-6pm Mon-Sat Oct-May) Right by the beach.
Train Station Tourist Office (☎ 08 92 35 35 35; av Thiers; 8am-8pm Mon-Sat, 9am-7pm Sun Jun-Sep, 8am-7pm Mon-Sat, 10am-5pm Sun Oct-May) Next to the Gare Nice Ville.

Sights

Nice has some great museums, most of which are free since the election of a new mayor in 2008. Only the Chagall Museum, which is a national museum, has retained a fee.

VIEUX NICE

Forget about maps and books for a moment, and embrace Nice's labyrinthine baroque old town. There is something really unique about this tangle of alleyways and backstreets bursting with local life and history. The northern end of this historical centre, running against bd Jean Jaurès, is packed with shops and holes in the wall, all claiming to sell *specialités niçoises* more genuine than their neighbours'. Further south, atmospheric squares fill with cafés, street artists and delighted *flâneurs* (strollers). Cours Saleya, running parallel to the seafront at the southern end of Vieux Nice, is the venue for one of the most vibrant, vividly hued local markets (p873) in the south of France.

Jutting above the rooflines are the spires of some historic churches including the baroque **Cathédrale Ste-Réparate** (place Rossetti) and its stunning glazed terracotta dome, built around 1650; the blue-grey and yellow **Église du Gesù** (place du Gesù), close to rue Rossetti, whose baroque ornamentation also dates from the mid-17th century; and the mid-18th-century **Chapelle de la Miséricorde**, next to place Pierre Gautier.

Perpendicular to rue Rossetti is the notorious **Rue Benoît Bunico**, Nice's old Jewish ghetto,

NICE IN…

Two Days

Kick-start the day with an espresso and pastry from **Multari** (p872) before an invigorating run or in-line skate along **promenade des Anglais** (p868). Browse the fragrant flower and produce **markets** (p873) for picnic supplies to take up to the **Parc du Château** (below). Amble the little alleys of **Vieux Nice** (p865), then laze away the afternoon on the beach, or sail the Baie des Anges on a **catamaran** (p868). Settle down for dinner at the fabulous **Les Épicuriens** (p872) and round off the night in your favourite **bar** or **pub** (p872). The following day, trace Matisse's artistic evolution at the **Musée Matisse** (below) and stroll along **Cimiez'** bourgeois avenues (p868). Grab some Nice-style tapas at **Chez René Socca** (p871) for lunch before getting a dose of pop culture at **Mamac** (below). Finish your day with a long *apéritif* at **Les Distilleries Idéales** (p872) and head to **La Havane** (p873) for a night of Latin flavour.

Four Days

Traverse the twisting cliff-side **corniches** (coast roads; p897) to the medieval village of **Èze** (p898), walk down along **Nietzsche's path** (p898) to Èze-sur-Mer and catch the train to **Monaco** (p900) for a punt at the **Casino de Monte Carlo** (p905), a tour of the aquarium at the **Musée Océanographique de Monaco** (p903) and a taste of the principality's culinary delights at **Castelroc** (p904). On the fourth day, go inland to **Grasse** (p883) to tour its **perfumeries** (p884) and, in season, its **flower-filled fields** (p884), or venture west to tackle one of the 100-odd hiking trails criss-crossing the jagged red crags of the **Massif de l'Estérel** (p885).

where a 1430 law ordered Jews to be locked in by gates at each end of the street from sunset to dawn.

PARC DU CHÂTEAU

From this 92m hilltop park the glittering views of Vieux Nice spires and the Baie des Anges are mesmerising.

The shaded hill and park, at the eastern end of quai des États-Unis, are named after a 12th-century château that was razed by Louis XIV in a fit of pique in 1706 and never rebuilt. To reach the park you can walk up montée Lesage or climb the steps at the eastern end of rue Rossetti, or take the **ascenseur** (lift; per person €1; 🕒 9am-8pm Jun-Aug, 9am-7pm Apr, May & Sep, 10am-6pm Oct-Mar) under Tour Bellanda.

MUSÉE D'ART MODERNE ET D'ART CONTEMPORAIN (MAMAC)

Designed by Yves Bayard and Henri Vidal, **Mamac** (Museum of Modern & Contemporary Art; ☎ 04 97 13 42 01; www.mamac-nice.org; Promenade des Arts; admission free; 🕒 10am-6pm Tue-Sun) is worth a visit for its stunning architecture alone, but it also houses some fantastic avant-garde art from the 1960s to the present. These include iconic pop art from Roy Lichtenstein, and Andy Warhol's 1965 *Campbell's Soup Can*. The marbled towers' glass walkways lead to highlights like Niki de St-Phalle's papier-mâché sculptures and a shopping trolley wrapped by Christo. An awesome panorama of Vieux Nice unfolds from the rooftop garden/gallery, which features works by Nice-born Yves Klein (1928–62).

MUSÉE NATIONAL MESSAGE BIBLIQUE MARC CHAGALL

This small **museum** (Marc Chagall Biblical Message Museum; ☎ 04 93 53 87 20; www.musee-chagall.fr, in French; 4 av Dr Ménard; permanent collection adult/student €6.50/4.50, temporary exhibitions additional €1.20; 🕒 10am-5pm Wed-Mon Oct-Jun, to 6pm Jul-Sep) houses the largest public collection of the Russian-born artist's seminal paintings of *Old Testament* scenes. Be sure to peek through a plate-glass window across a reflecting pond to view a mosaic of the rose window at Metz Cathedral. Take bus 22 from place Masséna (Masséna/Guitry stop) to the front of the museum or walk. The same bus goes to the Musée Matisse. Chagall (1887–1985) is buried in St-Paul de Vence (p877).

MUSÉE MATISSE

Heading northeast from the Chagall museum (about 2.5km from the city centre) brings you to the **Musée Matisse** (☎ 04 93 81 08 08; www.musee-matisse-nice.org; 164 av des Arènes de Cimiez; admission free; 🕒 10am-6pm Wed-Mon). Housed in a 17th-century Genoese mansion, this small museum reveals Matisse's evolution as an artist rather than wowing the crowds with masterpieces. There are some well-known works such as the blue paper cut-outs *Blue Nude IV* and *Woman with Amphora*, but you'll also see a number of less-well-known sculptures and experimental pieces using cloth, paper, oils, ink etc.

Take bus 17 from the bus station or bus 22 from Place Masséna to the Arènes stop. For other Matisse highlights in the Côte d'Azur, see boxed text, below.

MUSÉE ET SITE ARCHÉOLOGIQUES

Nice's little-spoken but lingering language, Nissart, derives most of its vocabulary from the Roman city of Cemenelum, founded by Augustus in 14 BC. Its ruins lie behind the Musée Matisse, on the eastern side of the Parc des Arènes, and are the focus of the **Musée et Site Archéologiques** (Archeology Museum & Site; ☎ 04 93 81 59 57; 160 av des Arènes de Cimiez; admission free; 🕑 10am-6pm Wed-Mon). You'll need a little imagination to picture the public baths, amphitheatre and original paved streets signposted across the site, but the relics inside the museum such as ceramics, glass, coins and tools bring it to life.

CATHÉDRALE ORTHODOXE RUSSE ST-NICOLAS

Crowned by six multicoloured onion domes, the **Cathédrale Orthodoxe Russe St-Nicolas** (Russian Orthodox Cathedral of St-Nicolas; ☎ 04 93 96 88 02; av Nicolas II; admission €3; 🕑 9am-noon & 2.30-5pm Mon-Sat, 2.30-5pm Sun) is an unexpected find on Nice's landscape. It was built between 1902 and 1912 in early-17th-century style, and is the largest cathedral outside Russia. Shorts, miniskirts and sleeveless shirts are forbidden.

MUSÉE DES BEAUX-ARTS

In a resplendent 1878 belle époque villa, the **Musée des Beaux-Arts** (Fine Arts Museum; ☎ 04 92 15 28 28; 33 av des Baumettes; admission free; 🕑 10am-6pm Tue-Sun) displays works by Fragonard, Monet, Sisley and Rodin, as well as an excellent collection of Dufy works.

Activities

For a breath of fresh air, head out to the stunning **Parc National du Mercantour** (see boxed text, p858), where walking and mountain-biking trails abound.

MAGICAL MATISSE TOUR

If you're mad about Matisse, you can cherry-pick a Côte d'Azur itinerary that takes in some of the major sites of his life in the area.

Born on New Year's Eve in 1869, Henri Matisse arrived in Nice from Paris in 1917 to recover from bronchitis. He remained here until his death in 1954 at his home and studio in the mansion-lined suburb, Cimiez.

Checking into the **Hôtel Beau Rivage** (p870), he went on to rent a flat on quai des États-Unis, then moved to what is now the **Palais de la Mediterranée** (p870), where he also exhibited. Many of the works he painted in Nice are housed in the city's **Musée Matisse** (opposite).

Matisse's visits to **Renoir's villa** (see boxed text, p878) in Cagnes-sur-Mer provided further inspiration for paintings, including the 1917 *Oliviers, Jardin de Renoir à Cagnes* (Olive Trees, Renoir's Garden in Cagnes).

During WWII, Matisse rented **Villa Le Rêve** in Vence, where he was visited by Picasso and Aragon, among others. To unleash your own creative streak, you can take a **painting course** (☎ 04 93 58 82 68, www.mclean.dk; 🕑 Mar-Nov) at the villa, with seven nights' accommodation, from around €650. While living here, Matisse's friendship with his former model-turned–Dominican Sister Jacques-Marie inspired him to design his masterwork, the nearby **Chapelle du Rosaire** (Rosary Chapel; ☎ 04 93 58 03 26; www.vence.fr/the-rosaire-chapel.html; 466 av Henri Matisse, Vence; admission €3; 🕑 2-5.30pm Mon, Wed & Sat, 10-11.30am & 2-5.30pm Tue & Thu, closed mid-Nov–mid-Dec), completed in 1951. Midmorning is the prime time to see sunlight streaming through the vast stained-glass windows. Matisse's artistic blueprints for the chapel, including 42 drawings, 21 paper cuttings, two stained-glass windows, two ceramic pieces and a sculpture, are on display in the Musée Matisse.

Matisse is buried at the **Monastère Notre Dame de Cimiez** (Cimiez Notre Dame Monastery; ☎ 04 93 81 00 04; 🕑 8.30am-12.30pm & 2.30-6.30pm), near the Musée Matisse; signs lead to his grave.

Tourist offices throughout the Côte d'Azur have an info-packed brochure (available in English) about tracing Matisse's footsteps.

CULTURE CARTE

If you're planning on making many visits and taking many tours in and around Nice, the **Nice Riviera Pass** is a good option for saving a few bob. Available for one, two or three days, it costs €24/36/54 and gives you free entry to Nice's paying sites – the Marc Chagall (p866) and the Cathédrale Orthodoxe Russe St-Nicolas (p867) – access to Le Grand Tour open-top bus (below), guided tours organised by Nice's tourist office and the Centre du Patrimoine (below), the Jardin Exotique in Monaco (p903), and the Musée Renoir (p878) and the Musée Picasso (p875) in Cagnes-sur-Mer. The pass also offers reductions in a number of shops and restaurants. See the tourist office for more details.

CITY WALKING

Established by English expats in 1822, wide, palm-lined **promenade des Anglais** (English promenade) is a timelessly elegant place for a beachfront stroll.

Continuing east along **quai des États-Unis** (named after the 1917 decision by President Wilson for the USA to enter WWI) to the end brings you to a colossal **WWI memorial** carved in the rock. It commemorates the 4000 people from Nice who died during the war.

Behind the quay is strolling heaven – Vieux Nice (p865).

Other pleasant spots include **Jardin Albert 1er** (west of Vieux Nice), which was laid out in the late 19th century; **Espace Masséna** (northeast of Jardin Albert 1er), a public square enlivened by fountains; the nearby atmospheric **place Masséna**, with its early-19th-century, neoclassical arcaded buildings in shades of ochre and red; and **Cimiez**, the most exclusive (and steep) quarter in Nice, just north of the city, with its turn-of-the-century villas, tree-lined avenues and vistas of the city.

IN-LINE SKATING

Smooth and flat, with great views to boot, the promenade des Anglais provides 7km of perfect skating ground between the port and the airport. **Roller Station** (☎ 04 93 62 99 05; 49 quai des États-Unis) rents out skates and kneepads for €8 a day and bikes for €15 a day. Some ID is required as a deposit.

BEACHES & WATER SPORTS

Made up of round pebbles, you'll need at least a beach mat to cushion your tush from Nice's **beaches**. Free sections of beach alternate with 15 sun lounge–lined **plages concédées** (private beaches; 🕒 late Apr or early May-15 Sep), for which you have to pay by renting a chair (around €15 a day) or mattress (around €10).

On the beach, operators hire out catamarans, paddleboats and jet skis; you can also parascend, waterski or paraglide. There are showers on every beach, and indoor toilets and showers opposite 50 promenade des Anglais.

Dive companies **Le Poséidon** (☎ 04 92 00 43 86; www.poseidon-nice.com; quai Lunel) and **Nice Diving** (☎ 04 93 89 42 44; www.nicediving.com; 14 quai des Docks) offer PADI courses and run diving expeditions in English. An introductory dive costs around €40, with equipment.

Tours

The tourist office–run **guided walking tours** (per 2½hr tour €12; 🕒 9.30am Sat) of Vieux Nice, in English, depart from the main office on the promenade des Anglais. The **Centre du Patrimoine** (☎ 04 92 00 41 90; www.nice.fr, in French) also runs 11 thematic 1½-hour walking tours in French and English, each costing €3. The tourist office has a full listing; tours must be booked 24 hours ahead.

With headphone commentary in several languages, the open-topped **Le Grand Tour** (☎ 04 92 29 17 00; adult/student/child €20/18/10) buses give you a good overview of Nice. Tours (1½ hours) depart from the Jardin Albert 1er on the promenade des Anglais.

Trans Côte d'Azur (☎ 04 92 00 42 30; www.trans-cote-azur.com; quai Lunel; 🕒 Apr-Oct) runs scenic one-hour coastal cruises (adult/child under 10 years €14/8.50) as well as day trips to the Îles de Lérins (adult/child €32/23; p880), St-Tropez (adult/child €52/39) and Monaco (adult/child €29/21).

To tour the coast in style, take a DIY day trip in a classic convertible. **Le Road-Show** (☎ 04 92 04 01 05; www.azur-roadshow.com, in French) offers packages for two people including car rental, lunch at a gourmet restaurant en route and a detailed driving itinerary (guaranteed getting lost–proof) plus fuel and insurance for €390.

Festivals & Events

Carnaval de Nice (www.nicecarnaval.com) This two-week carnival, held in February, is particularly famous for its battles of the flowers, where thousands of blooms are tossed into the crowds from passing floats, as well as its fantastic fireworks display.

Nice Jazz Festival (www.nicejazzfestival.fr) In July, Nice swings to the week-long jazz festival at the Arènes de Cimiez, amid the Roman ruins.

Les Nuits Musicales de Nice Moonlit classical-music concerts are held over three weeks in late July/early August at the Cloître du Monastère de Cimiez.

Sleeping

Nice has a suite of places to sleep, from stellar independent backpacker hostels to international art-filled icons. However, parking in the centre can be a nightmare. Prices jump during summer and also for regional festivals such as Monaco's Grand Prix or the Cannes Film Festival.

BUDGET

Hostels

Villa Saint-Exupéry (☎ 04 93 84 42 83; www.vsaint.com; 22 av Gravier; dm incl breakfast €18-25, s €35, d €55-80; 💻 ⊠) Why can't all hostels be like this? Set in a lovely converted monastery in the north of the city, this is a great place to put down your bags for a few days. Chill out in the 24-hour common room housed in the old stained-glass chapel, sip a €1 beer on the barbecue terrace, cook in the state-of-the-art self-catering kitchen, agonise over your choice of 12 different breakfast cereals, and stock up on travel tips. The villa staff will come and pick you up from the nearby Comte de Falicon tram stop or St Maurice stop for bus 23 (direct from the airport) when you first arrive.

Auberge de Jeunesse – Les Camélias (☎ 04 93 62 15 54; www.fuaj.org, in French; 3 rue Spitalieri; dm incl breakfast & sheets €20.70; 💻 ⊠) This squeaky-clean 136-bed hostel is a signature Fédération Unie des Auberges de Jeunesse (FUAJ) establishment: brightly coloured and spacious; equipped with bar, self-catering kitchen and laundry; and faithful to the dreaded midday lockout (11am to 3pm; no night curfew, though). The bright dorms sleep four to eight people and have in-room showers. There is good wheelchair access.

Backpackers Chez Patrick (☎ 04 93 80 30 72; www.chezpatrick.com; 32 rue Pertinax; dm/d €22/50; ❄ ⊠) Ultrahandy for the station, you'll find this 24-bed independent hostel inconspicuously situated on the 1st floor, above a restaurant (look for Chez Patrick's doorbell on the street below). Chill out in the air-conditioned, French-washed tiled common room, or in the high-ceilinged rooms. A word of warning however: check ahead that it will be open at the time of your visit.

Budget hotels that also have dorm beds available:

Hôtel/Hostel Meyerbeer Beach (☎ 04 93 88 95 65; www.come.to/meyerbeer; 15 rue Meyerbeer; dm from €16, d €54; 💻) Cramped, kitchenette-equipped rooms near the sea with free internet, soft drinks and beach mats.

Hôtel Belle Meunière (☎ 04 93 88 66 15; www.bellemeuniere.com; 21 av Durante; dm €17-22, d €45-60) Run by a lady who has travelled a lot herself, this beautiful 1870s mansion has huge, airy rooms. Numbers 8 and 9 sport an iron-lace balcony that overlooks the courtyard where breakfast is served until noon.

Hotels

our pick **Hôtel Wilson** (☎ 04 93 85 47 79; www.hotel-wilson-nice.com; 39 rue de l'Hôtel des Postes; s €29-50, d €34-65) Many years of travelling, an experimental nature and exquisite taste have turned Jean-Marie's rambling flat into a compelling place to stay. The 16 rooms have individual, carefully crafted decor, and share the eclectic dining room where photo albums, African statues and paintings offered by previous guests ornate the walls. Mind the two resident tortoises as you sit down for a breakfast of fresh bread and croissants (served until a very civilised noon). There's no lift, and the cheapest rooms do not come with attached bathrooms, but this place is absolutely worth it.

Hôtel Paradis (☎ 04 93 87 71 23; www.paradishotel.com; 1 rue Paradis; d €55-110; ⊠) This sun-filled, spotless budget hotel is a stone's throw from the promenade. Top-floor and courtyard rooms have air-con and all rooms are equipped with fridges, handy to keep those picnic supplies and beers chilled. Try to get your hands on one of the three rooms with balcony.

MIDRANGE

Villa la Tour (☎ 04 93 80 08 15; www.villa-la-tour.com; 4 rue de la Tour; s €45-129, d €48-139; ❄) Small but perfectly formed, the Villa la Tour is delightful, with warm, romantic Provençal rooms, a location at the heart of the Vieux Nice, and a diminutive, flower-decked roof-terrace with views of the Colline du Château and surrounding roofs.

Nice Garden Hôtel (☎ 04 93 87 35 63; www.nicegardenhotel.com; 11 rue du Congrès; d €60-98; ❄ ☒) Behind heavy iron gates hides this little gem of a hotel: nine beautifully appointed rooms displaying a subtle blend of old and new, overlooking an equally exquisite garden with a glorious orange tree (the fruit ends up on the breakfast table, in season). Amazingly, all this charm and peacefulness is just two blocks from the promenade.

Hôtel Armenonville (☎ 04 93 96 86 00; www.hotel-armenonville.com; 20 av des Fleurs; d €62-98, tr €79-112; 💻 P) Tucked away at the back of an alleyway and shielded by its large garden, this grand early-20th-century mansion has sober rooms, three of them (12, 13 and 14) with a huge terrace overlooking the garden. There is a free car park and wi-fi.

Hôtel La Petite Sirène (☎ 04 97 03 03 40; www.sirene-fr.com; 8 rue Maccarani; s €72-90, d €107-149, apt €147-318; ❄) Fresh and frescoed, rooms at the 'Little Mermaid' have good wheelchair access and a sun lounge–lined terrace (albeit with rather unfortunate fake grass) where you can sip cocktails from the in-house bar. Rooms 15 and 16 have their own private terrace (and no fake grass).

Hôtel Les Cigales (☎ 04 97 03 10 70; www.hotel-lescigales.com; 16 rue Dalpozzo; s €75-160, d €79-160, ❄) The Cicadas' brightly coloured rooms may be spacious and well located, but the hotel's real asset is its roof terrace. Think chilled rosé wine on long summer evenings or lazy breakfasts in the morning sun – now *that's* what we're talking about.

Villa Victoria (☎ 04 93 88 39 60; www.villa-victoria.com; 33 bd Victor Hugo; s €75-160, d €90-210; ❄ 💻) Its plastic furniture and heavily patterned materials do not make for the subtlest of decors, but this hotel does have its own botanic garden, complete with a fairy-lit gazebo. There's also a lovely breakfast room flanked by five sets of French doors. You can also rent bikes here.

Le Petit Palais (☎ 04 93 62 19 11; www.petitpalaisnice.fr, in French; 17 av Émile-Bieckert; s €80-140, d €90-170; ❄) In Cimiez' breezy heights, this yellow, neoclassical mansion offers breathtaking views of Nice – the views get better with every floor you climb (three in total). Ground-floor rooms are deprived of vistas but make up for it with private gardens. Decor is elegant throughout. The only downside is the *steep* 10 minutes' walk from bd Carabacel.

Hôtel Windsor (☎ 04 93 88 59 35; www.hotelwindsornice.com; 11 rue Dalpozzo; d €90-175; ❄ 💻 🏊) This original boutique hotel has let rip artists' imaginations – be it with the graffiti mural by the pool; the weird and wonderful artists' rooms customised from bathroom to bedspread; the more 'traditional' rooms (although there's no such thing as traditional at the Windsor) with their large frescoes; or the luxurious garden with its unconventional exotic plants.

Hôtel Excelsior (☎ 04 93 88 18 05; www.excelsiornice.com; 19 av Durante; d €120-195, 3–4-person apt €175-275; ❄) This 1892 building would not look out of place on a Parisian boulevard, but its handsome exterior hides big variations in the quality of rooms inside. Ask to change rooms if you're not satisfied. Apartments have kitchenettes. Good wheelchair access.

TOP END

Palais de la Méditerranée (☎ 04 92 14 77 00; www.lepalaisdelamediterranee.com; 13 promenade des Anglais; d €180-850; ❄ 💻 🏊) This opulent edifice is spectacularly recessed behind the massive pillars of its majestic 1929 art deco facade. Rooms are comfortable and well-appointed if a tad chain-like at times, but the staff are genuinely warm and helpful. There's a mosaic indoor/outdoor swimming pool, good wheelchair access and a private beach.

Hôtel Hi (☎ 04 97 07 26 26; www.hi-hotel.net; 3 av des Fleurs; s from €195, d €210-395; ❄ 💻 🏊) Think of what the most techno-funk, whacky, futuristic designer place would look like in your wildest dreams – now quadruple that, and you have Hôtel Hi. The downstairs lounge doubles as an übertrendy bar open to all, but you'll have to be a client to attend the rooftop, poolside cocktail parties with panoramic views of the Med and the Alps. Oh, and you can also ask for a goldfish in your room, if you're feeling lonely.

Hôtel Beau Rivage (☎ 04 92 47 82 82; www.nicebeaurivage.com; 24 rue St-François de Paule; d €210-700; ❄ 💻) This designer pad is one of Nice's oldest hotels, though with its modern, Asian Zen decor you'd never guess that Matisse and Chekhov used to be regulars. Its private beach is the biggest on the promenade but winter guests won't feel deprived thanks to the pebblelike armchairs in the bar.

Hôtel Negresco (☎ 04 93 16 64 00; www.hotel-negresco-nice.com; 37 promenade des Anglais; r €285-570; ❄ 💻) The pink-domed Negresco features some highly original rooms mixing kitsch, modern and period decors. It also houses priceless art and architecture, such as one of only three Hyacinthe Rigaud Louis XIV portraits – the others are in the Louvre and Versailles – and the Gustave Eiffel–designed stained-glass Salon Royal, bearing a one-tonne Baccarat crystal chandelier. Two hundred and fifty staff await, and so does the private beach.

Eating

Niçois nibbles include *socca* (a thin layer of chickpea flour and olive oil batter fried on a large griddle, served with pepper), *salade niçoise*, ratatouille and *farcis* (stuffed vegetables, each with a unique filling).

Restaurants in Vieux Nice are a mixed bag of what the French call *attrape touriste* (tourist trap) and genuine good finds. Follow your instincts, or our recommendations.

RESTAURANTS

Budget

Chez René Socca (☎ 04 93 92 05 73; 2 rue Miralhéti; dishes from €2; ⏰ 9am-9pm Tue-Sun, to 10.30pm Jul & Aug, closed Nov) Forget about presentation and manners; here, it's all about taste. Grab a portion of *socca* or a plate of *petits farçis* and head across the street to the bar for a *grand pointu* (glass) of red, white or rosé.

Lou Pilha Leva (10-13 rue du Collet; dishes from €3; ⏰ 10am-10pm) With its outdoor wooden tables crammed under a tight awning, this is Nice's version of a fast-food joint: courgette fritters, sugar-beet pie, or a bowl of *soupe au pistou* (soup of vegetables, noodles, beans, basil and garlic) – chop-chop!

Nissa Socca (☎ 04 93 80 18 35; 7 rue Ste-Réparate; mains from €8; ⏰ lunch & dinner Tue-Sat) This inexpensive joint in Nice's ambient old town is a good bet for authentic *niçoise* cuisine, from the eponymous *socca* to a slice of *pissaladière* (a thick crust covered with puréed onions and garlic, topped with anchovies and olives) or its Italian ancestor, the pizza.

La Table Alziari (☎ 04 93 80 34 03, 4 rue François Zanin; mains €8-14, ⏰ noon-2pm & 7.30-10pm Tue-Sat) Run by the grandson of the famous Alziari olive oil family, this citrus-coloured restaurant off the busy rue Pairolière is not here to brag about anything, though. The day's menu is chalked on a blackboard, with local specialities such as *morue à la niçoise* (cod served with potatoes, olives and a tomato sauce), *daube* (stew) or grilled goats' cheese washed down with regional wines.

La Merenda (4 rue Raoul Bosio; starters from €9, mains €12-15; ⏰ lunch & dinner Mon-Fri) You'd think that being closed at weekends, and not having a phone number or a credit card machine would be a recipe for disaster, but La Merenda is doing just fine, thank you very much. In fact, you'll have to be pretty determined to bag one of the house's 26 seats (queuing is what it comes down to) and feast on the unusual fare scribbled on a blackboard. Try tripe, stockfish (a local speciality soaked for days in running water, then simmered with onions, tomatoes, garlic, olives, peppers and potatoes), polenta with gorgonzola or *andouillettes* (mini sausages made from pork tripe).

Pasta Basta (☎ 04 93 80 03 57; 18 rue de la Préfecture; mains €13; ⏰ noon-2pm & 7-11pm) Choose a pasta, pick a sauce and – hey presto! – a plate of amazing pasta made on the premises. Enjoy it or a *supremo* pizza on the street-side terrace, and finish off with any of the Italian goodies on offer.

Midrange

Escalinada (☎ 04 93 62 11 71; 22 rue Pairolière; mains €12-20; ⏰ lunch & dinner) Lunch under a stripy awning or dine on the candle-lit terrace with a decent bottle of wine and good, unpretentious local fare such as *daube*, delicious homemade gnocchi, or, if you're game, the house speciality – *testicules de mouton panés* (sheep's testicles in batter).

Delhi Belhi (☎ 04 93 92 51 87; 22 rue de la Barillerie; mains €13, menus from €23; ⏰ dinner) For a change from Mediterranean flavours, Delhi Belhi is an absolute godsend: this is Indian food at its best. Biryanis, thalis, tandoori specialities and a raft of vegetarian options are served in a couple of dark-lit, wonderfully scented rooms just off cours Saleya. Locals have taken a shine to the place, so book.

Acchiardo (☎ 04 93 85 51 16; 38 rue Droite; mains €14-20; ⏰ lunch & dinner Mon-Fri) Going strong since 1927, locals flock to Acchiardo for the *plat du jour* (daily special), a glass of wine and a load of gossip served straight up on the counter. The food is simple and tasty – think lamb chops with a pile of green beans or a fine piece of steak with homemade French fries.

Zucca Magica (☎ 04 93 56 25 27; 4bis quai Papacino; lunch/dinner menus €17/27; ⏰ lunch & dinner Tue-Sat) The 'Magic Pumpkin' is a rare thing in France: a vegetarian restaurant that nonvegetarians actually like to visit. Bring an appetite: *menus* (fixed-price meals) comprise four set dishes plus dessert (five for dinner), depending on what green giant and chef Marco Folicaldi finds at the markets. Children under 13 eat for free.

Les Épicuriens (☎ 04 93 80 85 00; 6 place Wilson; mains €18-45.50; lunch & dinner Mon-Fri, dinner Sat) This aptly named elegant establishment is Nice's rising star. Famous for its *cocottes* (casseroles cooked in cast-iron dishes), it also excels in pretty much everything else: from the *pâté de foie gras* (duck or goose liver pâté) with grape compote to *brandade de cabillaud* (cod cooked in the oven with crème fraîche, olive oil, garlic, lemon juice and herbs), and whatever daily special takes the chef's fancy.

Le Comptoir (☎ 04 93 92 08 80; 20 rue St-François de Paule; mains €20-30; lunch & dinner Mon-Fri, dinner Sat) The bottle-lined wall at the end of the room is ominous: eating and drinking are serious business in this art deco–meets–ancient Greece establishment. Its proximity to the opera means it's especially popular for pre- and post-theatre sustenance.

Terres de Truffes (☎ 04 93 62 07 68; 11 rue St-François de Paule; mains €30; lunch & dinner Tue-Sat) At this small, exquisite place, head chef Arnaud Leclercq uses Provençal truffles to create seasonal sensations ranging from pastry-wrapped pigeon stuffed with *foie gras* and truffles to brie layered with truffles, to caramel of truffles. Obviously not the place to go if you're not a fan of the *Tuber melanosporum*…

Top End

Chantecler (☎ 04 93 16 64 00; 37 promenade des Anglais; menus €45-130; lunch & dinner Wed-Sun Feb-Dec) In a sumptuous Regency dining room, the Negresco's Michelin-starred restaurant, run by locally trained Jean-Denis Rieubland, is no ordinary restaurant. Make sure you're in a grand mood if you're going to splash out: the menu features treats such as sea bass in an almond crust with artichoke mousse or double-roasted veal cutlets served with a potato and black-pudding millefeuille.

CAFÉS

Fenocchio (☎ 04 93 80 72 52; 2 place Rossetti; ice cream from €2; 9am-midnight Feb-Oct) The best place to beat Nice's heat is this *glacier*, serving 50 flavours of ice cream – including beer and tomato-and-basil (both as scary as they sound).

Multari (☎ 04 93 92 01 99; 58bis av Jean Médecin; dishes from €3; 6.30am-7.30pm Mon-Sat) Now a small bakery empire, this Corsican family-run business has opened a couple of cafés where you can sit down and enjoy its scrumptious pastries with an espresso or a cup of tea. Its crêpes, sandwiches and salads also get the thumbs up.

Les Distilleries Idéales (☎ 04 93 62 10 66; 24 rue de la Préfecture; platters €2.90-4.40; 9am-12.30am) Whether you're after an espresso on your way to cours Saleya or a sundowner accompanied by a plate (chopping board, actually) of cheese or charcuterie, the atmosphere in this brilliant bistro is infectious: you're bound to leave with a skip in your step.

Cave de la Tour (☎ 04 93 80 03 31; 3 rue de la Tour; mains €8-12; 7am-8pm Tue-Sat) An old-town institution that combines a wonderful wine shop and a café/bar serving a couple of dishes a day, prepared from ingredients sourced at the nearby markets.

SELF-CATERING

Pack the ultimate picnic hamper from cours Saleya's fruit and vegetable market (part of the food market; see Shopping, opposite), and pick up freshly caught fish from the **fish market** (place St-François; 6am-1pm Tue-Sun).

Supermarkets and minimarkets abound:

Casino (20 bd Gambetta; 8.30am-8pm Mon-Sat) On the western side of the city.

Monoprix av Jean Médecin (42 av Jean Médecin; 8.30am-9pm Mon-Sat); place Garibaldi (place Garibaldi; 8.30am-8.45pm Mon-Sat)

Drinking

Vieux Nice's little streets runneth over with local bars and cafés: from a morning espresso to a lunchtime pastis (the tipple of choice in the south of France), a chilled evening beer or a midnight cocktail, the choice is yours.

Irish pub **Ma Nolans** (☎ 04 93 80 23 87; 2 rue St François de Paule; noon-2am Mon-Fri, 11pm-2am Sat & Sun) is a backpacker favourite with its Monday night pub quiz, televised sport, nightly live music, and full-English brekkie. Raucous watering hole **Chez Wayne's** (☎ 04 93 13 46 99; 15 rue de la Préfecture; 2.30pm-12.30am every day) also has live bands every night. A tad less rowdy is the beer-tastic **De Klomp** (☎ 04 93 92 42 85; 8 rue Mascoïnat; 5.30pm-2.30am Mon-Sat) with its 18 draught and 50 bottled beers. All three close around midnight on weekdays and around 3am on Friday and Saturday night.

If you're above those sorts of shenanigans, head for the rarefied rooftop bar at the **Grand Hotel Aston** (☎ 04 92 17 53 00; 12 av Félix Faure; 8am-11pm, closed Sun & Mon in winter), which has champagne views over Nice and the Med. Cocktail connoisseurs quaff at Hôtel La Petite Sirène (p870) with half-price cocktails from 5pm to 7pm Tuesday to Sunday, or at Hôtel Beau Rivage (p870), where the house special is sex-on-the-beach, as indicated by the pebble-themed bar.

Entertainment

The tourist office has info on Nice's cultural activities, which are listed in its free publications – *Nice Rendez-vous* (monthly) and *Côte d'Azur en Fêtes* (quarterly) – or consult the weekly *Semaine des Spectacles* (€1), available from newsstands on Wednesday. All are in French. Event tickets can be purchased at **fnac** (☎ 08 25 02 00 20; 44 av Jean Médecin).

CINEMAS

Catch nondubbed flicks at **Cinéma Nouveau Mercury** (☎ 08 36 68 81 06; 16 place Garibaldi) and **Cinéma Rialto** (☎ 08 36 68 00 41; 4 rue de Rivoli). Art films (usually in the original version with French subtitles) are screened at **Cinemathèque de Nice** (☎ 04 92 04 06 66; 3 esplanade Kennedy; 🕑 Tue-Sun), which is at the Acropolis conference centre and concert hall.

LIVE MUSIC

Opéra de Nice (☎ 04 92 17 40 00; 4-6 rue St-François de Paule; 🕑 box office 9am-5.45pm Tue-Sat, to 7.45pm Fri, closed mid-Jun–Sep) Built in 1885 and recently renovated, this grande dame hosts operas, ballets and orchestral concerts. Tickets cost €7 to €85.

Le Bar des Oiseaux (☎ 04 93 80 27 33; www.bardesoiseaux.com, in French; 5 rue St- Vincent; 🕑 lunch Mon-Fri, dinner Thu-Sat) Artistic types flock to this bohemian bar (and adjoining theatre) for live jazz, *chanson française* (French songs) and cabaret nights. There's a cover charge of about €5 when entertainment's on the bill; you can also dine here (*menus* around €20).

La Havane (☎ 04 93 16 36 16; 32 rue de France; mains €15-20; 🕑 2pm-2.30am) For sultry Latin vibes, this exotic bar-restaurant alternates live salsa and Latino jazz nights with *merengue* and *bachata* (two types of Latin American music) from Tuesday to Saturday. Musicians play three sets of 45 minutes, starting at 9.30pm.

NIGHTCLUBS

Happy Bar (☎ 04 97 07 26 26; www.hi-hotel.net; 3 av des Fleurs; 🕑 10pm with DJs to 2am Fri & Sat) The heart and soul of the hip Hôtel Hi hosts the gurus of the DJ world.

Les Trois Diables (☎ 04 93 62 47 00; 2 cours Saleya; 🕑 5pm-2.15am) 'The Three Devils' tempts a mainly local crowd with trip-hop, house and electro beats. Thursday is student night – don't forget your student ID to get in.

L'Ôdace (☎ 04 93 82 37 66; 29 rue Alphonse Karr; 🕑 midnight till late Thu-Sat Jul & Aug, Fri & Sat Sep-Jun) The vast industrial-style party temple has struggled to find its mojo, but it is the only place in town to party until dawn.

Other party options:

Le Klub (☎ 06 60 55 26 61; 6 rue Halevy; 🕑 11pm-5am) A thriving gay nightclub with a busy party schedule.

Le Nova (☎ 04 93 26 54 79; 26 quai Lunel; 🕑 6.30pm-2.30am) Party on at the port.

Shopping

Cours Saleya is split between its famous **flower market** (🕑 6am-5.30pm Tue-Sat, to 1.30pm Sun) selling bucketfuls of blooms in the western half, and a magnificent **food market** (🕑 6am-1.30pm Tue-Sun) at the eastern end, with long trestle tables displaying exotic spices, shiny fruit and veg, pastries, *fruits glacés* (glazed or candied fruits such as figs, ginger, tangerine and pears) and more. On Mondays from 6am to 6pm, cours Saleya also hosts an antiques market.

The best-value place for tasting and buying wine is a traditional wine cellar; try Cave de la Tour (opposite).

Designer names abound above the beautiful fashion boutiques along rue Paradis, av de Suède, rue Alphonse Karr and rue du Maréchal Joffre (all east of av Jean Médecin).

The massive **Nice Étoile shopping mall** (av Jean Médecin) spans a city block.

Getting There & Away

AIR

Nice's international airport, **Aéroport International Nice-Côte d'Azur** (☎ 08 20 42 33 33; www.nice.aeroport.fr), is about 6km west of the city centre. Its two terminals are connected by a free **shuttle bus** (🕑 every 10min 4.30am-midnight). The airport's served by numerous carriers, including the low-cost **BMIBaby** (www.bmibaby.com) and **easyJet** (www.easyjet.com).

For the shortest and most stylish transport to Monaco, board a **helicopter** (☎ 04 93 21 34 95; www.heliairmonaco.com). Seven-minute flights departing from Nice airport start at €99 per person, one way.

BOAT

The fastest and least expensive ferries from mainland France to Corsica depart from Nice (see p907). The **SNCM office** (☎ 08 25 88 80 88;

www.sncm.fr; ferry terminal, quai du Commerce) issues tickets – otherwise, try a travel agency in town. Italian-run **Corsica Ferries** (☎ 08 25 09 50 95; www.corsicaferries.com; quai Lunel) also sells tickets at the port. Take buses 9 or 10 off av Jean Médecin (stop Médecin/Pastorelli) to the Port stop.

BUS

Buses stop at the **bus station** (gare routière; ☎ 08 92 70 12 06; 5 bd Jean Jaurès).

A single €1 fare can take you anywhere in the Alpes-Maritimes *département* (with a few exceptions, such as the airport) and includes one connection, provided it is made within 74 minutes. There are services until about 7.30pm daily to Antibes (one hour), Cannes (1½ hours), Grasse (1½ hours), Menton (1½ hours) and Monaco (45 minutes). Buses also run to Vence (one hour) and St-Paul de Vence (55 minutes).

For long-haul travel, **Eurolines** (☎ 04 93 80 08 70), at the bus station, serves various European destinations.

TRAIN

Nice's main train station, **Gare Nice Ville** (av Thiers) is 1.2km north of the beach.

There are fast and frequent services (up to 40 trains a day in each direction) to coastal towns including Antibes (€3.80, 30 minutes), Cannes (€5.70, 30 to 40 minutes), Menton (€4.30, 35 minutes), Monaco (€3.20, 20 minutes) and St-Raphaël (€10, 50 minutes). Direct TGV trains link Nice with Paris' Gare de Lyon (€110, 5½ hours), with additional connecting services.

From July to September, the SNCF's Carte Isabelle (€12, available from train stations) lets you make unlimited trips in a single day (except TGV trains) from Fréjus to Ventimiglia in Italy, and from Nice to Tende.

Lost luggage and other problems are handled by **SOS Voyageurs** (☎ 04 93 16 02 61; 🕑 9am-noon & 3-6pm Mon-Fri).

For an enchanting train trip through the scarcely populated back country, **Chemins de fer de Provence** (www.trainprovence.com; ☎ 04 97 03 80 80) chugs four times daily from Nice's **Gare du Sud** (4bis rue Alfred Binet) to Digne-les-Bains (p857).

Getting Around

Travelling on the regional **Ligne d'Azur** (☎ 08 10 06 10 07; www.lignedazur.com; 3 place Masséna; 🕑 7.45am-6.30pm Mon-Fri & 8.30am-6pm Sat) transport network (including all local and intercity buses and the tram) costs just €1 per trip (except to the airport); the fare includes one connection. Tickets can be purchased from the driver or from ticket machines located at tram stops. An unlimited-travel day pass costs €4.

TO/FROM THE AIRPORT

Ligne d'Azur runs two airport bus services (€4). Route 99 shuttles approximately every half-hour direct between Gare Nice Ville and both airport terminals daily from around 8am to 9pm. Route 98 takes the slow route and departs from the bus station every 20 minutes (every 30 minutes on Sunday) from around 6am to around 9pm.

A taxi from the airport to the centre of Nice will cost €25 to €30, depending on the time of day and the terminal.

BUS

Walking or taking the tram (below) is the best way to get around the centre. But for anywhere beyond the station-Masséna-Garibaldi triangle, buses are the way to go. Four night buses (N1, N2, N3 and N4) run north, east and west from place Masséna every half-hour from 9.10pm until 2am.

CAR & MOTORCYCLE

All major car rental companies (Avis, Budget, Europcar, Hertz etc) have offices at the train station. The best deals are generally booked via their websites, and the earlier you do so, the better.

If you want to go native, go for two wheels. **Holiday Bikes** (☎ 04 93 16 01 62; 23 rue de Belgique; 🕑 closed 12.30-2.30pm & Sun Oct-May) rents out bicycles/50cc scooters/125cc motorcycles for €14/26/57. There's a hefty security deposit.

TAXI

To avoid getting taken for a ride (as it were), make sure the driver is using the meter and applying the right rate, which is clearly outlined in a laminated card that drivers are required to display. There are taxi stands outside the Gare Nice Ville and on av Félix Faure close to place Masséna; otherwise, you can order a taxi on ☎ 04 93 13 78 78.

TRAM

Nice's much awaited (and delayed) tram finally launched in November 2007. Line 1 runs a V-shape northwest-south-northeast itinerary from 4.30am to 1.30am, taking in useful areas such as the train station, the old town, and the Acropolis in the centre.

Fifteen international artists contributed to customising the trams' funky look, from original soundbites at each stop, to local artist Ben's stop-name calligraphy and futuristic art installations along the tram's itinerary.

ANTIBES-JUAN-LES-PINS

pop 75,000

Antibes is a concentrate of Mediterranean history. The town's sea walls bear witness to a defensive past (neighbouring Nice had switched allegiance to rival Savoy). Golfe Juan staged Napoléon Bonaparte's triumphant return from exile in Elba. Picasso painted in the Château Grimaldi and F Scott Fitzgerald wrote his seminal novel *Tender is the Night* based on life in Antibes.

Today, the town hasn't finished making its mark on history: its marina is the second biggest in Europe, attracting throngs of 'yachties' in search of seafaring adventures. Juan-les-Pins, Antibes' neighbouring town, with which it has more or less merged into one Riviera entity, holds an internationally-acclaimed jazz festival, and in the last decades, Antibes has enjoyed the presence of an affluent crowd of yuppies working in the nearby Sophia-Antipolis high-tech hub, keeping its population surprisingly young for this bit of the coast.

For visitors, Antibes provides a year-round buzz within its old walls. The cape is a perennial walking heaven and in summer, Juan's seamless 2km of sandy beach is a godsend for tender bottoms that have received the pebble treatment in Nice.

Orientation

Across the Baie des Anges from Nice, Antibes centres on place du Général de Gaulle, linked to Juan-les-Pins by bd du Président Wilson (1.5km) and to Cap d'Antibes by bd Albert 1er (700m). Av Robert Soleau links Antibes' train station (300m) with place du Général de Gaulle. The bus station is just a few steps away, linked by rue de la République, which continues east to the old town.

Information

Antibes Books-Heidi's English Bookshop (☎ 04 93 34 74 11; 24 rue Aubernon, Antibes; 🕑 10am-7pm) One of the best on the Côte.

Antibes Tourist Office (☎ 04 92 90 53 00; www.antibesjuanlespins.com; 11 place de Gaulle, Antibes; 🕑 9am-7pm Jul & Aug, 9am-12.30pm & 1.30-6pm Mon-Fri, 9am-noon & 2-6pm Sat Sep-Jun) In the town centre.

Eurochange (4 rue Georges Clémenceau, Antibes; 🕑 9am-6pm Mon-Sat)

Juan-les-Pins Tourist Office (☎ 04 92 90 53 05; 55 bd Charles Guillaumont, Juan-les-Pins) Keep similar hours to those of the Antibes Tourist Office.

Post Office (2 av Paul Doumer, Antibes)

Worstation Cyber Café (☎ 04 92 90 49 39; 1 av St Roch, Antibes; per hr €4.80; 🕑 9am-7.30pm Mon-Fri & 10am-6pm Sat & Sun)

Sights & Activities

Picasso used the 12th-century Château Grimaldi as a studio in 1946. It's now home to the **Musée Picasso** (☎ 04 92 90 54 28; Château Grimaldi, Antibes; adult/concession/under 18yr €6/3/free; 🕑 10am-noon & 2-6pm Tue-Sun mid-Sep–mid-Jun, 10am-6pm Tue-Sun mid-Jun–mid-Sep), which, following an extensive three-year refurbishment program, finally reopened at the time of going to press.

The light-hearted **Musée Peynet** (☎ 04 92 90 54 30; place Nationale, Antibes; adult/concession/under 18yr €3/1.50/free; 🕑 10am-noon & 2-6pm Tue-Sun Sep-Jun, 10am-noon & 2-6pm Tue, Thu, Sat & Sun, to 8pm Wed & Fri Jul & Aug) displays more than 300 humorous pictures, cartoons and costumes by Antibes-born cartoonist Raymond Peynet, as well as brilliant temporary exhibitions.

Antibes' small, sandy beach, **Plage de la Gravette**, gets packed; you'll find the best beaches in Juan-les-Pins, including some free beaches on bd Littoral and bd Charles Guillaumont.

Cap d'Antibes' 4.8km of wooded shores are the perfect setting for a walk-swim-walk-swim afternoon.

Festivals & Events

Next to the casino, Antibes' La Pinède park swings during mid-July's Jazz à Juan (also known as the Festival de Jazz d'Antibes-Juan-les-Pins). Book tickets at the tourist office or online from the tourist office's website, or try at the gate an hour before show time.

Sleeping & Eating

Relais International de la Jeunesse (☎ 04 93 61 34 40; www.clajsud.fr; 272 bd de la Garoupe, Cap d'Antibes; dm incl breakfast €17, sheets €3.10) In the most perfect of Mediterranean locations, with sea views the envy of neighbouring millionaires, this friendly hostel is particularly popular with 'yachties' looking for their next job in Antibes' port.

Le Relais du Postillon (☎ 04 93 34 20 77; www.relaisdupostillon.com; 8 rue Championnet, Antibes; d €46-89) Housed in a 17th-century coach house at the heart of the old town, Postillon's 16 rooms all have easy-on-the-eye decors; try for the Capri room and its sunny private patio. The buffet breakfast (€7), by the fire in winter or on the small terrace in summer, is good value.

Hôtel La Jabotte (☎ 04 93 61 45 89; www.jabotte.com; 13 av Max Maurey, Cap d'Antibes; d incl breakfast from €81) A hotel with *chambre d'hôte* (B&B) feel, La Jabotte is Antibes' hidden gem. A mere 50m from the beautiful Plage de la Salis, its 10 Provençal rooms all look out onto an exquisite patio where breakfast is served from spring to autumn. As for your hosts, you'll get a singing welcome from the reception's parakeets and Tommy the dog, while Yves and Claude will make you feel like long-lost friends.

Auberge Provençale (☎ 04 93 34 13 24; www.aubergeprovencale.com; 61 place Nationale, Antibes; d €120-200) Famed for its fabulous Provençal cuisine – seafood in particular (mains €26 to €60; open for lunch and dinner) – this *auberge* (inn) also features six grand, antique-filled romantic rooms, some of them the size of palatial suites. Rooms Céline and Emmanuelle will comfortably sleep four.

Hôtel Belles Rives (☎ 04 93 61 02 79; www.bellesrives.com; 33 bd Edouard Baudoin, Juan-les-Pins; d €255-740; ❄) In the mid-1920s, F Scott and Zelda Fitzgerald rented this entire villa (then the St-Louis). Since the early 1930s it's housed this classic Riviera establishment with its private beach and pier, top-notch restaurants and sought-after jazz bar.

Dining recommendations:

Le Broc en Bouche (☎ 04 93 34 75 60; 8 rue des Palmiers, Antibes; mains €15-30; ⏰ lunch & dinner, closed Tue night & Wed) You'll melt for Flo and Fred's gourmet bistro, their *foie gras*, their *magret de canard* (duck breast) and whatever daily special they'll come up with. And if you like what you see in the fantastic bric-a-brac decor, you could be going home with it: it's all for sale.

La Cafetière Fêlée (The Cracked Cafetière; ☎ 04 93 34 51 86; 18 rue du Marc, Antibes; mains €20-25; ⏰ lunch & dinner, closed Sun night & Mon) You'll eat things you've never even heard of at this Alice in Wonderland–like restaurant. But the presentation is a work of art and the fusion-style food is a knock-out.

Les Vieux Murs (The Old Walls; ☎ 04 93 34 06 73; 25 promenade Amiral de Grasse, Antibes; mains €30-40; ⏰ lunch & dinner, closed Mon & Tue lunch in winter) With its crystal chandeliers, silk curtains, panoramic views, sea-wall location and fresh Mediterranean food, this place is a complete and utter indulgence.

SELF-CATERING

Marché Provençal (cours Masséna, Antibes; ⏰ mornings daily Jun-Aug, Tue-Sun Sep-May) Antibes' heady Provençal marketplace is perfect for picking up picnic supplies.

Entertainment

La Siesta-Le Pearl (☎ 04 93 33 31 31; rte du Bord de Mer, Antibes; cover €15-20; ⏰ 11pm-5am) This legendary establishment is famous up and down the coast for its beachside nightclub (Le Pearl) and all-night dancing under the stars. Open from early June to mid-September only, you can still party at the indoor bar-lounge (Le Flamingo) during the rest of the year.

Getting There & Away

Antibes is an easy day trip by train from Nice (€3.80, 30 minutes) or Cannes (€2.40, 15 minutes).

The **bus station** (⏰ 04 93 34 37 60) has buses to surrounding towns such as Biot; buses also depart from adjacent to the tourist office.

BIOT

pop 9000

From the 16th to 18th century, the little hillside village of Biot was famous across the Med for the exceptional quality of its olive oil jars. But very little remains of that pottery hegemony. Biot is now famous for another much prettier, but far less pragmatic, art form: bubbled glass.

Biot's famous bubbles are produced by rolling molten glass in baking soda to create a chemical reaction, then trapping the bubbles with a second layer of glass; the latest frosted look uses acid dips.

You can watch work underway at the factory **La Verrerie de Biot** (The Glassworks of Biot; ☎ 04 93 65 03 00; www.verreriebiot.com; Chemin des Combes; admission free, 45min guided tour in English €6; ⏰ 9.30am-8pm Mon-Sat, 10.30am-1.30pm & 2.30-7.30pm Sun summer, 9.30am-6pm Mon-Sat, 10.30am-1.30pm & 2.30-6.30pm Sun winter), at the foot of the village.

Biot's **tourist office** (☎ 04 93 65 78 00; www.biot.fr, in French; 46 rue St-Sébastien; ⏰ 10am-7pm Mon-Fri, 2.30-7pm Sat & Sun Jul & Aug, 9am-noon & 2-6pm Mon-Fri, 2-6pm Sat & Sun Sep-Jun) has info and maps, as well as a list of *chambres d'hôtes*.

The enchanting hotel-restaurant **Galerie des Arcades** (☎ 04 93 65 01 04; www.hotel-restaurant-les-arcades.com; 16 place des Arcades; d €50-90, mains €15-22; ⏰ lunch & dinner, closed Mon & dinner Sun) has become an institution in Biot: the 15th-century building is now home to a prestigious modern art collection, the result of 50 years of friendship between André and Mimi Brothier (the owners) and the many artists living in Biot in postwar years such as César, Novaro, Vasarely and Léger. The more-expensive rooms, with their unique works of art, heavy oak furniture, monumental fireplaces and palatial bathrooms, are worth every penny.

Bus 10 (€1, 10 minutes) links the village and the Biot train station half-hourly. In summer, a free shuttle takes in the train station, the *verrerie* and the village.

ST-PAUL DE VENCE & AROUND

pop 3300

What's distinguished the medieval hilltop village of St-Paul de Vence from every other medieval hilltop village around is its phenomenal art legacy. St-Paul attracted many seminal 20th-century artists who lived, worked and sometimes even died in the village, many of them leaving significant legacies behind, such as Matisse's masterpiece the Chapelle du Rosaire (Rosary Chapel). Russian painter Marc Chagall, who lived in the village for 25 years, is now buried in St-Paul's interdenominational cemetery. The nearby Fondation Maeght, considered by many as one of the world's best modern art galleries, showcases an exceptional collection of 20th-century works.

St-Paul de Vence's cobblestone streets and 16th-century fortifications, dramatically floodlit at night, are an attraction in their own right, one that draws 2.5 million visitors a year.

Orientation & Information

Inside the fortifications, St-Paul de Vence is delineated by its main pedestrian thoroughfare, rue Grande. To take the road less travelled, turn right just by the **tourist office** (☎ 04 93 32 86 95; www.saint-pauldevence.com; 2 rue Grande; ⌚ 10am-7pm Jun-Sep, 10am-6pm Oct-May), follow the ramparts around to the far end, then turn left into rue Grande against the tide.

Matisse's stunning Chapelle du Rosaire and his former home Villa Le Rêve (see p867) are 4.8km north of St-Paul de Vence (800m north of the attractive medieval town of Vence; population 18,200), on rte de St-Jeannet (the D2210).

Sights

Browsing the gallery-lined village streets (64 galleries in total!) is a fine entrée for art lovers, but the main course is the **Fondation Maeght** (☎ 04 93 32 81 63; adult/student €11/9; ⌚ 10am-7pm Jul-Sep, 10am-6pm Oct-Jun), about 500m from the bus stop outside the old village. It was designed by architect Josep Luis Sert in conjunction with contemporary artists such as Chagall, who created an exterior mosaic. With an outdoor sculpture 'labyrinth' by Spanish surrealist Joan Miró, interspersed with reflecting pools and mosaics, it was inaugurated in 1964. Its extraordinary permanent collection of 40,000 works is exhibited on a rotating basis.

Sleeping & Eating

Chez Andréas (☎ 04 93 32 54 50; Rempart Ouest; tapas €5, mains €10; ⌚ noon-midnight) Perched on the ramparts, this popular bar teems with locals who come to feast on chilled beer, tasty tapas and panoramic views.

La Colombe d'Or (The Golden Dove; ☎ 04 93 32 80 02; www.la-colombe-dor.com, in French; lunch mains €20-60, dinner mains €60-70; ⌚ lunch & dinner) This world-famous inn could double up as the Fondation Maeght's annexe: La Colombe d'Or (located outside the walls, at the entrance of the village) was the party HQ of many 20th-century artists (Chagall, Braque, Matisse, Picasso etc) who often paid for their meals in kind, resulting in an incredible private art collection. Don't expect to get a table (or room, €280 to €350) unless you book weeks in advance. And lucky you if you manage it: every room houses unique art and vintage furniture, the chance to see what an art collector's house would be like.

There's a seven-day grocery store immediately to your right after entering the village, and there are plenty of benches for picnicking along the ramparts.

Getting There & Away

From Nice, the frequent bus 400 stops in St-Paul de Vence (€1, 55 minutes) and Vence (€1, one hour).

CANNES

pop 70,400

Most people have heard of Cannes and its eponymous film festival. The latter only lasts for two weeks in May, but the buzz and glitz are there year round, mostly thanks to regular visits from celebrities enjoying the creature comforts of bd de la Croisette's palaces.

However, what people may not know is that, for all its glamour, Cannes retains a genuine small-town feel: just like anywhere in the south, you'll witness pensioners hotly debating who won the last round of *pétanque* (a game not unlike lawn bowls) under the main square's plane trees (in this case, at Sq Lord Brougham). You'll also get a chance to escape to the miraculously unspoilt Îles de Lérins, and to become familiar with more than 2000 years of history – from Ligurian fishing communities in 200 BC to one of Europe's oldest religious communities (5th century AD), to the enigmatic Man in the Iron Mask and a stardom born out of antifascist efforts. Beat that!

Orientation

Cannes' glitter starts to appear along its main shopping street, rue d'Antibes, a couple of blocks south of the train and bus stations (rue Jean Jaurès). Several blocks further south, east of the Vieux Port (Old Port), is the huge Palais des Festivals et des Congrès, home to both the film festival and the tourist office.

The palm tree–lined waterfront promenade of bd de la Croisette begins at the Palais des Festivals and goes east along the Baie de Cannes to Pointe de la Croisette. Place Bernard Cornut Gentille, with the bus station that includes services to Nice, is on the northwestern corner of Vieux Port. The old town, Le Suquet quarter, is to the west of the Vieux Port.

Information

BOOKSHOPS

Cannes English Bookshop (☎ 04 93 99 40 08; 11 rue Bivouac Napoléon) Get your (English-language) summer reading from the lovely Christel and Wally.

INTERNET ACCESS

Cap Cyber (12 rue 24 Août; per hr €3; 🕑 10am-9pm Mon-Sat) Very central, with several QWERTY keyboards and Asian language software.

LAUNDRY

Laverie du Port (☎ 04 93 38 06 68; 36 rue Georges Clemenceau; per 7kg load €5.50, drying per 10min €1.50; 🕑 closed Sun & from noon Sat) Multilingual staff on-site.

MONEY

Scads of banks line rue d'Antibes and rue Buttura.

Crédit Lyonnais (13 rue d'Antibes) Has an ATM.

POST

Post Office (22 rue Bivouac Napoléon; 🕑 9am-7pm Mon-Fri, 9am-noon Sat) Has an ATM.

TOURIST INFORMATION

Tourist Office (☎ 04 92 99 84 22; www.cannes.travel; bd de la Croisette; 🕑 9am-8pm Jul & Aug, 9am-7pm Mon-Sat Sep-Jun) On the ground floor of the Palais des Festivals.

Tourist Office Annexe (☎ 04 93 99 19 77; 🕑 9am-7pm Mon-Sat) Next to the train station.

Sights & Activities

CANNES

Perched at the top of the Suquet old town, you could spend as long studying the beautifully presented ethnographic collections of the **Musée de la Castre** (☎ 04 93 38 55 26; place de la Castre, Le Suquet; adult/concession/student & under 18yr €3.20/2/free; 🕑 10am-7pm Jul & Aug, 10am-1pm & 2-6pm Tue-Sun Apr-Jun & Sep, 10am-1pm & 2-5pm Tue-Sun Oct-Mar) as you would admiring the view of the Baie de Cannes from the museum's grounds.

The central, sandy **beaches** along bd de la Croisette are sectioned off for hotel patrons (some accept day guests for prohibitive sums). A microscopic strip of sand near the Palais des Festivals is free, but you'll find better free sand on **Plages du Midi** and **Plages de la Bocca**, west from the Vieux Port along bd Jean Hibert and bd du Midi.

WORTH A TRIP

The conglomerated city of Cagnes-sur-Mer (population 45,000) comprises Le Haut de Cagnes, a medieval hill town; Le Cros de Cagnes, a former fishing village by the beach; and Cagnes Ville, euphemistically referred to as a 'modern town'. Amid the urban and semi-industrial sprawl are two pilgrimages for art devotees.

On the Haut de Cagnes hilltop, 14th-century **Château Grimaldi** (☎ 04 92 02 47 30; place Grimaldi; adult/child €3/1.50, combined ticket with Musée Renoir €4.50; 🕑 10am-noon & 2-5pm Wed-Mon Oct & Dec-Apr, to 6pm May-Sep) houses a museum showcasing contemporary Mediterranean art.

Near Cagnes Ville is Renoir's home and studio from 1907 to 1919, now **Musée Renoir** (☎ 04 93 20 61 07; chemin des Collettes; adult/concession/under 18yr €3/1.50/free; 🕑 10am-noon & 2-5pm Wed-Mon Oct & Dec-Apr, to 6pm May-Sep), set in dappled olive groves with original decor and several of Renoir's works on display.

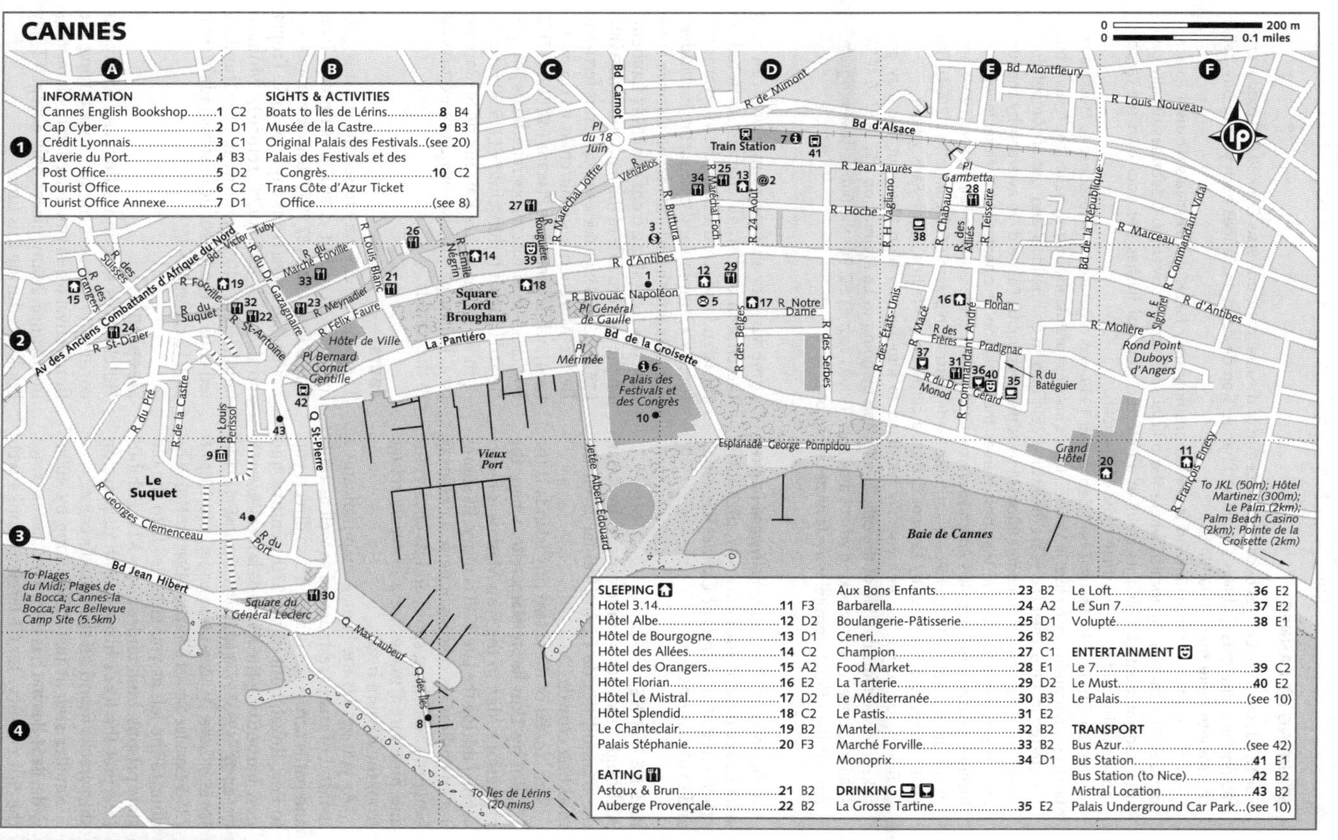

CÔTE D'AZUR & MONACO

STARRING AT CANNES

For 12 days in May, Cannes becomes the centre of the cinematic universe. Over 30,000 producers, distributors, directors, publicists, stars and hangers-on descend on Cannes each year to buy, sell or promote more than 2000 films.

At the centre of the whirlwind is the surprisingly ugly Palais des Festivals (Festival Palace; dubbed 'the bunker' by locals), where the official selection is screened. Celebrities usually get their big moment climbing its stairs in an electric storm of flashes (for your own red-carpet moment, the said carpet is there most of the year).

The first Cannes Film Festival, on 1 September 1939, was organised as a response to Mussolini's fascist propaganda film festival in Venice. Hitler's invasion of Poland abruptly halted the festival but it restarted in 1946. Over the years the festival split into 'in competition' and 'out of competition' selections. The goal of 'in competition' films is the prestigious Palme d'Or, awarded by the jury and its president to the film that best 'serves the evolution of cinematic art'. Notable winners include Francis Ford Coppola's *Apocalypse Now* (1979), Quentin Tarantino's *Pulp Fiction* (1994), and documentary maker Michael Moore's anti-Bush-administration polemic *Fahrenheit 9/11* (2004). The 2008 winner was *The Class* by Laurent Cantet, a chronicle of life in a tough Paris school.

Tickets to the festival are generally restricted to film-industry high fliers, but you may get tickets to see films outside of the official selection by going to **La Malmaison** (☎ 04 97 06 44 90; 47 bd de la Croisette) and checking what's available. Tickets cost €1.50. For the film-festival program, consult the official website: www.festival-cannes.org.

If the town's 12 massive **Hollywood-inspired murals** have piqued your curiosity, the tourist office's free *Murs Peints de Cannes* has a map and explanations.

ÎLES DE LÉRINS

Although just 20 minutes away by boat, the tranquil Îles de Lérins feel far from the madding crowd.

The closest of these two tiny islands is the 3.25km by 1km **Île Ste-Marguerite**, where the mysterious Man in the Iron Mask was incarcerated during the late 17th century. Its shores are an endless succession of perfect castaway beaches and fishing spots, and its eucalyptus and pine forest makes for a heavenly refuge from the Riviera heat.

As you get off the boat, a map indicates a handful of rustic restaurants as well as trails and paths across the island. It also directs you to Fort Royal, built in the 17th century, and now harbouring the **Musée de la Mer** (Museum of the Sea; ☎ 04 93 38 55 26; adult/concession/student & under 18yr €3.20/2/free; ⏲ 10am-5.45pm Jun-Sep, 10am-1.15pm & 2.15-5.45pm Tue-Sun Apr & May, to 4.45pm Oct-Mar). The door to the left as you enter leads to the old state prisons, built under Louis XIV. Exhibits interpret the fort's history, with displays on shipwrecks found off the island's coast.

Smaller still, at just 1.5km long by 400m wide, **Île St-Honorat** has been a monastery since the 5th century. Its Cistercian monks welcome visitors all year round: you can visit the church and small chapels scattered on the island and stroll among the vineyards and forests. Camping and cycling are forbidden.

Boats for the islands leave Cannes from quai des Îles (along from quai Max Laubeuf) on the western side of the harbour. **Riviera Lines** (☎ 04 92 98 71 31; ww.riviera-lines.com) runs ferries to Île Ste-Marguerite (adult/child €11/5.50 return), while **Compagnie Planaria** (☎ 04 92 98 71 38; www.cannes-ilesdelerins.com) operates boats going to Île St-Honorat (adult/child €11/5.50 return).

In St-Raphaël, Les Bateaux de St-Raphaël (see Tours, p886) also has daily excursions to the islands.

Tours

The most serene way to see the coast is gazing back from out at sea. In summer, **Trans Côte d'Azur** (☎ 04 92 98 71 30; www.trans-cote-azur.com; quai Max Laubeuf) runs day trips to St-Tropez (adult/child €37.50/24 return), Monaco (adult/child €40/24 return) and the stunning red cliffs of the Massif de l'Estérel (adult/child €20/12 return).

Sleeping

Hotel prices in Cannes fluctuate wildly according to the season, and soar during the film festival when you'll need to book months in advance. Many places only accept 12-day bookings during this time.

BUDGET

Parc Bellevue (04 93 47 28 97; www.parcbellevue.com; 67 av Maurice Chevalier, Cannes-la-Bocca; powered site per 2 adults, tent & car €26; Apr-Sep) About 5.5km west of the city, this is the closest campsite to Cannes, with a near-Olympic-sized pool and facilities galore. The 9 bus from the bus station on place Bernard Cornut Gentille stops 400m away.

Hôtel Albe (04 97 06 21 21; www.albe-hotel.fr; 31 rue Bivouac Napoléon; s/d from €35/45;) The rooms are nothing to write home about, but this hotel is right in the heart of the action: the street is about to become pedestrianised, which should bring some fancy neighbours and guarantee a good night's sleep. Wi-fi and friendly service are on the house.

Le Chanteclair (/fax 04 93 39 68 88; 12 rue Forville; d from €48; closed mid-Nov–mid-Jan) Right in the heart of Le Suquet and just moments from the Forville Provençal market, this sweet, simple 15-room place has an enchanting courtyard garden, and is handy for the harbourside restaurants.

Hôtel de Bourgogne (04 93 38 36 73; 11 rue du 24 Août; d from €50) Well placed for easy access to both the train station and the centre of town, this tired-looking hotel was planning some much-needed refurbishment at the time of research. Prices are likely to increase, but the same kind lady will be running it.

Hôtel Le Florian (04 93 39 24 82; www.hotel-leflorian.com; 31 rue Commandant André; s/d from €48/53;) It's simple, but Le Florian is sensationally located smack bang between rue d'Antibes and the beachfront bd de la Croisette. Its 20 rooms and 11 apartments are impeccable, and the super-kind owners will bend over backwards to help you out during your stay.

Hôtel des Allées (04 93 39 53 90; www.hotel-des-allees.com; 6 rue Émile Négrin; s/d €49/68;) You can be welcomed in four languages at this Swiss family-run hotel located on a vibrant pedestrian street. But you won't be lost in translation with the rooms: the spotless and brightly furnished courtyard rooms are blissfully quiet, while street-side rooms and their balconies make perfect vantage points from which to watch the world go by.

MIDRANGE

Hôtel Le Mistral (04 93 39 91 46; www.mistral-hotel.com; 13 rue des Belges; d from €77;) Wanna feel like a VIP without breaking the bank? Head straight to this small boutique hotel – 10 rooms with designer bathrooms, flattering plum and red tones, LCD TV screens, wi-fi, ace location, helpful staff and sea views for a couple of rooms on the top floor. Bring it on!

Hôtel des Orangers (04 93 39 99 92; www.hotel-orangers.com; 1 rue des Orangers; s/d from €74/81;) Perched at the edge of the old town, the water views from the bright west-facing rooms on the 2nd and 3rd floors are an unexpected treat. You'll also be able to work up an appetite in the pool before lazily ambling southeast down to rue du Suquet (5 minutes) for restaurants galore.

Hôtel Splendid (04 97 06 22 22; www.splendid-hotel-cannes.com; 4-6 rue Félix Faure; s/d from €115/128;) This elaborate 1871 building has everything it takes to rival the nearby palaces: beautifully decorated rooms, fabulous location, stunning views. But what the owners have also added is a touch of pragmatism: 15 of the 62 rooms are equipped with kitchenettes, your chance to make the very best of those balconies and sea views!

TOP END

Hôtel 3.14 (04 92 99 72 00; www.3-14hotel.com; 5 rue François Einesy; d from €155;) *Trois-quatorze* (three-fourteen) takes its status as Cannes' hottest design option *très* (very) seriously: themed 'world' decoration, a profusion of velvet and low lighting, Zen spa, trendy organic restaurant, weeknight DJ parties and a vertigo-inducing rooftop jacuzzi – make sure you hold on tight to that sparkling wine flute.

In a stratosphere of their own, there are the amazing beachfront palaces garlanding bd de la Croisette:

Palais Stéphanie (04 92 99 70 00; www.sofitel.com; 50 bd de la Croisette; d from €170;) On the historic site of the original Palais des Festivals. The views from the rooftop panoramic terrace (and pool) will take your breath away. Rooms are what you would expect from a four-star hotel: plush, with no comfort spared.

Hôtel Martinez (04 92 98 73 00; www.hotel-martinez.com; 73 bd de la Croisette; d from €260;) The *crème de la crème*, with an on-site Givenchy spa and two-starred Michelin restaurant (two-/three-course *menus* €79/104, open 12.30pm to 2pm and 8pm to 10pm Tuesday to Saturday).

Eating

RESTAURANTS

Generally, you'll find the least expensive restaurants on and around rue du Marché Forville, northeast of Vieux Port. Hipper and slightly pricier establishments line the buzzing rues St-Antoine and du Suquet.

Aux Bons Enfants (80 rue Meynadier; menu €23; lunch & dinner Tue-Sat) This familial little place doesn't have a phone, and there are no plans to get one any time soon: it's always full. The lucky ones who get a table (get there early or late) can feast on regional dishes made from ingredients picked up at the adjacent market.

Auberge Provençale (04 92 99 27 17; 10 rue St-Antoine; mains €24-55; lunch & dinner) Pesto-butter *gambas* (king prawns), roasted sea bass in fennel, beef medallion in foie gras sauce and a distinguished wine list – Cannes' oldest restaurant punches very high with its sun-drenched cuisine. Its rustic decor hasn't changed much in a century, to the delight of the locals who just keep coming back for more.

Le Pastis (04 92 98 95 40; 28 rue Commandant André; mains €25-30; 7.30am-11.30pm) With a name like this, it would be a crime if you didn't have an *apéritif* or two at this establishment. But you'd miss out if you stopped there – Le Pastis serves fabulous brasserie food (creamy risottos, tender steaks, delicious fish) in a setting of stone walls and vintage posters.

our pick **Mantel** (04 93 39 13 10; 22 rue St-Antoine; lunch menus €25, dinner menus €36-58; lunch & dinner, closed Wed & lunch Tue & Thu) The Italian maître d' will make you feel like a million dollars and you'll melt for Noël Mantel's divine cuisine and great value prices. Best of all, you get not one but two desserts with your menu (oh, the pannacotta…). Never mind the Croisette's palaces, you'll definitely have a regal night at Mantel.

Barbarella (04 92 99 17 33; 16 rue St-Dizier; mains €25-35; 7-11.30pm Tue-Sun) You've seen the film, now go to the err…restaurant. It is definitely as surreal as the movie (trompe l'œil–painted building, see-through chairs, psychedelic lighting, groovy atmosphere) and its fusion food is top notch.

Astoux & Brun (04 93 39 21 87; 27 rue Félix Faure; menus from €28; 12pm-1am) Seafood connoisseurs seldom need an introduction to this world-renowned place. And for those less familiar with bivalve mollusc consumption (read: shells), this is *the* place to try a fabulous seafood platter (oysters in particular).

Le Méditerranée (04 92 99 73 02; 2 bd Jean Hibert; lunch menu €42, dinner menus €52-72; lunch & dinner) On top of the port-side Sofitel hotel, adjoining the rooftop pool, it's hard to say which makes more of an impression – this contemporary French restaurant's cuisine or its 360-degree views across the Med to the red Massif de l'Estérel mountains.

CAFÉS

Cannes has copious numbers of coffee houses, cafés and *salons de thé* (tearooms).

La Tarterie (04 93 39 67 43; 33 rue Bivouac Napoléon; dishes €6-13; 8.30am-6pm Mon-Sat) Mega salads and fancy tarts, this place has gone one better than all the bakeries in town: think sit-down-meal at a fast-food price. We like it.

Volupté (04 93 39 60 32; 32 rue Hoche; snacks €4.50, mains €13-15; 9am-8pm Mon-Sat) This is *the* place to be seen in town. With its 140 types of teas, all neatly stocked in red and white tins spanning an entire wall, this elegant tearoom draws an all-happening crowd of young and beautiful things. Fashionistas aside, if you like what you're drinking, you can take some home from its retail outlet across the street, at 41 rue Hoche.

SELF-CATERING

The **Marché Forville** (rue du Marché Forville; mornings Tue-Sun) is where many of the city's restaurants shop and where you should get your picnic supplies. The **food market** (place Gambetta; morning) is another good address for fruit and veg.

Square Lord Brougham, next to the Vieux Port, is a great place for a picnic – watch the locals play *pétanque* while you bite into goodies bought at **Boulangerie-Pâtisserie** (12 rue Maréchal Foch). Locals go to **Ceneri** (22 rue Meynadier) for its wondrous cheeses.

Large supermarkets:

Champion (6 rue Meynadier; 8.30am-7.30pm Mon-Sat)

Monoprix (9 rue Maréchal Foch; 8.30am-8pm Mon-Sat)

Drinking

The party bloc in town is located between rue Macé and the Grand Hôtel, just north of La Croisette. But remember that popularity is a fickle thing, particularly in a town of stars: today's hot venue could be tomorrow's complete has-been.

To mingle with the rich and famous, Cannes' hotel palaces (p881) all have drop-dead-posh bars.

Mere mortals head to the following places.

Le Sun 7 (04 93 39 38 70; 5 rue du Dr Gérard Monod; 9pm-2.30am) The cocktail list is an arm long (literally), and it doesn't even include the 350 whiskies and many draught beers also served at this happening bar. The crowd is young on weekend nights when DJs spin their stuff, but it's much more eclectic during the week.

Also recommended:

La Grosse Tartine (☎ 04 93 68 59 28; 9 rue Batéguier; ⌚ hr vary) Fun local bistro that's not taking its Cannes location too seriously (any place that calls itself 'the big tart' wouldn't).

Le Loft (☎ 04 93 39 20 63; 13 rue du Dr Gérard Monod; ⌚ 7pm-2.30am Tue-Sat) A very beautiful place for very beautiful people. Schmooze the night away with designer cocktails and get those stilettos going with the DJ's chosen vibes.

Entertainment

Ask the tourist office for a copy of the free monthly *Le Mois à Cannes*, which lists what's on, where.

Dress up or you won't get in, and warm up your credit card: Cannes' nightlife ain't cheap.

Le Palais (www.palais-club.com; Palais des Festivals, bd de la Croisette; ⌚ midnight-dawn) Where else but in Cannes would you dance on 2000 sq metres of suspended gardens overlooking the sea? Going strong since 2006, this ephemeral nightclub (it's open only for 50 nights each year, in July and August) has become the hottest ticket in DJ land, a combination of the most happening names in music and its spectacular setting at the heart of the Palais des Festivals.

Le Must (14 rue du Batéguier; ⌚ 6pm-2.30am Tue-Sat) Ladies, if you're wearing a skirt, you're advised not to dance on the tables at this fun, super-friendly bar: Le Must's favourite gadget is an air pressure hose that will blow anything out of its way.

Le Palm (www.lepalmbeach.com, in French; place Franklin Roosevelt; ⌚ midnight-4am Fri & Sat, more often in summer) Located within the beautiful art deco Palm Beach Casino, anyone who's anyone will have partied at one of Le Palm's raucous nights. Its resident DJ also runs the coveted lounge nights at Hôtel 3.14 (see Sleeping, p881).

Le 7 (☎ 04 93 39 10 36; 7 rue Rouguière; ⌚ hr vary) Don't sit in the front row of the drag shows at this disco-and-house gay club unless you're up for being part of the spectacle.

Getting There & Away

BUS

Regular bus services to Nice (bus 200, €1, 1½ hours), Nice airport (bus 210, €14.20, 50 minutes, half-hourly from 8am to 6pm) and other destinations leave from the bus station on place Bernard Cornut Gentille.

TRAIN

There's an information desk and left-luggage facility at the train station.

Destinations within easy reach include Nice (€5.70, 30 to 40 minutes), Grasse (€3.60, 25 minutes) and Marseille (€24.80, two hours), as well as St-Raphaël (€6, 25 minutes), from where you can get buses to St-Tropez and Toulon.

Getting Around

BUS

Serving Cannes and destinations up to 7km away is **Bus Azur** (www.busazur.com; ☎ 08 25 82 55 99; place Bernard Cornut Gentille; tickets €1). Bus 8 runs along the coast to the port and Palm Beach Casino on Pointe de la Croisette.

For €0.60 per day you can hop on the electric Élo Bus. It has no set stops, so just flag it down as it passes. Its itinerary is marked by a blue line on the road and includes useful locations such as the bus hub at Hôtel de Ville, the Croisette, rue d'Antibes and the train station.

CAR & MOTORCYCLE

Car-rental agency **JKL** (☎ 04 97 06 37 77; www.jkl-forrent.com; 59 angle de la Croisette) offers cars fit for a star. There are plenty of paying car parks, including the Palais underground car park (€2.60 per hour) right next to the tourist office, which lends out free bicycles if you park here. Parking is free on Pointe de la Croisette.

Mistral Location (☎ 04 93 39 33 60; www.mistral-location.com; 4 rue Georges Clemenceau) rents out scooters from €26 a day.

TAXI

Taxis (☎ 08 90 71 22 27) can be ordered by phone. There are various taxi stands across towns, including outside the train station and the Palais des Festivals.

GRASSE

pop 49,100

Surrounded by fields of lavender, jasmine, centifolia roses, mimosa, orange blossom and violets, Grasse is one of France's leading perfume producers. Oddly, this international clout hardly comes across as you walk about the tightly wound streets of its ill-loved (read: neglected) centre. There is still plenty to see, and the tourist office has put together a trail of highlights, identified across town by interpretive golden-plate signs. But to really understand what makes this city tick, you'll have

CORINNE MARIE-TOSELLO, PERFUMER IN GRASSE

Corinne Marie-Tosello has two routes to work: one through olive groves, the other through fields overlooking the sea. Most people would revel in the view, but Corinne revels in their smells. Corinne is chief training officer at the prestigious Grasse perfumery Fragonard (see below). She is in charge of the 'olfactory education' of the perfumery's staff (scent identification, production process, types of perfumes etc) and she runs sought-after perfume workshops where perfume fanatics get a shot at producing their own scents. Life, therefore, revolves around her nose. She also works as an olfactory consultant (yes, they do exist), advising on scents destined to be used as incense, candles, air fresheners and so on.

So what's the best thing about living in Grasse? Grasse is very authentic – the perfumery industry is world famous but it remains very understated and hidden from the public. Many people don't believe us when we tell them it's so prominent. I also love Grasse's theatre; it puts on very original plays and films, although my teenage daughters prefer going out in glitzy Cannes! On the downside, driving is a nightmare because of the one-way system, and since the city is built on a hill, everything goes up and down; it's exhausting.

What do you like doing in the area? I love walking through flower fields (do the same at Domaine de Manon; see below): May roses and violets in the spring, lavender in early summer, and jasmine between August and October. I've taken Fragonard's staff on a couple of occasions so that they could see where the essences we work with come from. I also love going to Île St-Honorat (see p880): it's an olfactory paradise with eucalyptus, pine trees, dry wood and vine.

Favourite smells? Vetiver and galbanum (a resin produced from a Persian plant).

Least favourite smells? Anything that has been smoked, and artificial marine smells.

to visit one of its perfumeries and venture further out to its famous flower fields.

Orientation & Information

While the town of Grasse and its suburbs sprawl over a wide area of hill and valley, the old city is packed into the compact area formerly ringed by ramparts. The N85, better known as rte Napoléon (www.route-napoleon.com), runs right through Grasse, where it becomes the town's main thoroughfare, bd du Jeu de Ballon.

The town's **tourist office** (☎ 04 93 36 03 56; www.grasse.fr, in 7 languages; 22 cours Honoré Cresp; ⏲ 9am-7pm Mon-Sat, 9am-1pm & 2-6pm Sun Jul-Sep, 9am-12.30pm & 2-6pm Mon-Sat Oct-Jun) is inside the Palais de Congrès, and has information on accommodation in the town and surrounding area.

Banks abound on bd du Jeu de Ballon, but there are no change facilities in Grasse.

Place aux Aires is the heart of the old town, and it hosts a flower-filled morning market from Tuesday to Sunday. You'll find plenty of good eateries in nearby streets.

Sights & Activities

Grasse has more than 30 **perfumeries**, creating essences sold primarily to factories (for aromatically enhanced foodstuffs and soaps) as well as to prestigious couture houses. Several perfumeries offer free tours, taking you stage by stage through the perfume production process, from extraction and distillation to the work of the 'noses' (perfume creators who, after 10 years' training, are able to identify up to 3000 scents with one whiff). The perfumeries' showrooms sell fragrances for much less than traditional retailers, where you're mainly paying for the bottle.

Situated at the foot of the old town, **Fragonard** (☎ 04 93 36 44 65; 20 bd Fragonard; ⏲ 9am-6pm Feb-Oct, 9am-12.30pm & 2-6pm Nov-Jan) is the easiest perfumery to reach by foot; the tourist office provides information about other perfumeries that can be visited further afield.

For the ultimate field trip, it's possible to visit the **flower-growing fields** to learn about the blooms' cultivation and harvest. The family-run **Domaine de Manon** (☎ 04 93 60 12 76; www.domaine-manon.com; admission €6) runs tours of its rose fields from mid-May to mid-June, and its jasmine fields from July to late October.

Getting There & Away

From the **bus station** (☎ 04 93 36 37 37; place de la Buanderie) you can get regular buses to Nice (€1, 1½ hours) and Cannes (€1, 50 minutes).

About 2km south of the centre, Grasse's train station is linked to the old town and bus station by the free Farandole shuttle buses from 6.40am to 8pm. Regular trains leave for Cannes (€3.60, 25 minutes) and Nice (€8.20, one hour).

MASSIF DE L'ESTÉREL

Punctuated by pine, oak and eucalyptus trees, the rugged red mountain range Massif de l'Estérel contrasts dramatically with the brilliant blue sea.

Extending east from St-Raphaël to Mandelieu-La Napoule (near Cannes), a curling coastal road, the famous corniche de l'Estérel (also known as the corniche d'Or and the N98), passes through summer villages and inlets that are ideal for swimming. These include **Le Dramont**, where the 36th US Division landed on 15 August 1944; **Agay**, a sheltered bay with an excellent beach; and **Mandelieu-La Napoule**, a large pleasure-boat harbour near a fabulously restored 14th-century castle.

More than 100 hiking trails criss-cross the Massif de l'Estérel's interior, but for the more challenging trails you'll need a good map, such as IGN's *Série Bleue* (1:25,000) 3544ET. Many of the walks, such as those up to Pic de l'Ours (496m) and Pic du Cap Roux (452m), are signposted. Trails are open from 9am to 7pm – therefore, camping is not possible – and they're often closed in summer when fire danger's high.

FRÉJUS & ST-RAPHAËL

The twin towns of Fréjus (population 48,800) and St-Raphaël (population 32,700) bear the hallmarks of the area's history over the millennia.

The site of some exceptional Roman ruins, Fréjus was settled by Massiliots (the Greeks who founded Marseille) and colonised by Julius Caesar around 49 BC as Forum Julii. It was settled thanks to the extension of the Roman road Via Aurelia, which linked Italy with Arles. The town's commercial activity largely ceased after its harbour silted up in the 16th century. The Roman ruins are scattered in and around the lively pedestrianised town centre.

St-Raphaël is better known for its natural wonders. Sitting snug at the foot of the Massif de l'Estérel, it became a fashionable hang-out in the 1920s, when F Scott Fitzgerald wrote *Tender is the Night* here. With the development of diving activities, St-Raphaël sealed its fate as an adventure-prone destination.

Orientation

St-Raphaël is 2km southeast of Fréjus, but the towns' suburbs have become so intertwined that, essentially, they now form a single town. Fréjus comprises the hillside Fréjus Ville, about 3km from the seafront, and Fréjus Plage, on the Golfe de Fréjus. Most of the Roman remains are in Fréjus Ville.

Information

MONEY

Banque National de Paris (BNP; 232 rue Jean Jaurès, Fréjus) Just west of the tourist office; there's an ATM.

POST

Fréjus Post Office (av Aristide Briand)
St-Raphaël Post Office (av Victor Hugo)

TOURIST INFORMATION

Fréjus Tourist Office (☎ 04 94 51 83 83; www.frejus.fr; 249 rue Jean Jaurès; 9.30am-6pm Mon-Sat Sep-May, Sun 9.30am-6pm school holidays, 9am-7pm Jul & Aug)
St-Raphaël Tourist Office (☎ 04 94 19 52 52; www.saint-raphael.com; 99 quai Albert 1er; 9am-7pm Jul & Aug, 9am-12.30pm & 2-6.30pm Mon-Sat Sep-Jun) On the port, inside the futuristic-looking Palais des Congrès.
Tourist Office Kiosk (☎ 04 94 51 48 42; 9.30am-noon & 3-6pm Jul & Aug) By the beach opposite 11 bd de la Libération in Fréjus.

Sights

The most economical way to see Fréjus' Roman sights is to purchase the seven-day **Fréjus Pass Intégral** (€6.60), available from the tourist office, which includes entry to all the main sites.

ROMAN RUINS

Fréjus' Roman-times population is calculated at 10,000, based on the capacity of its 1st- and 2nd-century **arènes** (amphitheatres; ☎ 04 94 51 34 31; rue Henri Vadon; admission €2; 9.30am-12.30pm & 2-6pm Mon-Sat May-Oct, 9.30am-12.30pm & 2-5pm Mon-Sat Nov-Apr). It's hoped that current restoration projects and further archeological work will restore one of France's oldest entertainment venues to its previous glory, allowing it to house shows and concerts. The **Roman theatre** (rue du Théâtre Romain; admission €2; as for amphitheatre), north of the old town, houses theatre and music festivals in summer.

LE GROUPE ÉPISCOPAL

The jewel in the crown of the dramatic **Episcopal ensemble** (☎ 04 94 51 26 30; 58 rue de Fleury,

Fréjus; adult/18-25yr/under 17yr €5/3.50/free; 🕑 9am-6.30pm Jun-Sep, 9am-noon & 2-5pm Tue-Sun Oct-May) is the series of rare, intricate 14th-century painted cornices of the **cloister** ceiling, depicting fabled as well as real animals and characters.

Built on the site of a Roman temple, the ensemble includes the 11th- and 12th-century **cathedral** and a unique 5th-century octagonal **baptistry**. The 12th- and 13th-century cloister acted as the antichamber of the cathedral. Some of its columns come from the podium of the Roman theatre. Admission includes a 10-minute film in multiple languages.

Adjoining the cloister is the small but fascinating **Musée Archéologique** (Archeological Museum; ☎ 04 94 52 15 78; place Calvini; admission €2; 🕑 9.30am-12.30pm & 2-6pm Tue-Sun mid-Apr–mid-Oct, 9.30am-12.30pm & 2-5pm Tue-Sun mid-Oct–mid-Apr), whose unearthed treasures include a double-faced marble statue of Hermes, a head of Jupiter and a stunning 3rd-century mosaic depicting a leopard.

Activities

With its 36 kilometres of coastline, St-Raphaël claims no less than 30 **beaches** running the gamut of beach possibilities: sandy, pebbly, rocky, long, covelike, nudist…you name it, St Raph' has it.

Taking in 11km of this coastal wonder is the clearly marked **sentier du littoral** (coastal trail), with yellow markers. Starting at Port Santa Lucia, southeast of the city centre, and finishing at the Beaumette lighthouse, you can cut short at any stage by heading back up to the coastal road and catching bus 8 home (bus stops every 500m). The whole path takes about 4½ hours to complete.

St-Raphaël is also a leading **dive** centre, with numerous **WWII shipwrecks** off the coast. **Aventure Sous-Marine** (☎ 06 09 58 43 52; 165 quai Albert 1er, Galerie du Parvis, St-Raphaël) and **CIP** (☎ 04 94 52 34 99; www.cip-frejus.com; east port, Fréjus) organise night and day dives and courses for beginners.

Tours

A guided tour, run by the Fréjus tourist office (€5, two hours), available in English on request, is the best way to get the most out of Fréjus' rich heritage.

Les Bateaux de St-Raphaël (☎ 04 94 95 17 46; www.tmr-saintraphael.com; Gare Maritime, St-Raphaël) organises boat excursions from St-Raphaël to Île Ste-Marguerite (return adult €18 to €24, child €10 to €13) and the nearby Estérel mountains (return adult €14, child €8). It also runs daily boats to St-Tropez (single/return adult €13/22, child €8/12); check for seasonal schedules.

Sleeping & Eating

Auberge de Jeunesse Fréjus-St-Raphaël (☎ 04 94 53 18 75; www.fuaj.org; chemin du Counillier, Fréjus; dm incl breakfast & sheets €15.70; 🕑 reception 8am-noon & 5.30-11.30pm, closed mid-Nov–Feb) A rambling Hostelling International–affiliated hostel set in 10 hectares of pine trees where you can also pitch your tent in the summer. From St-Raphaël's train station, take bus 7. From the Fréjus train station, take bus 7, 10 or 13 to Les Chênes, cross the roundabout and take chemin de Counillier on your left (there's a supermarket on your right); the hostel's 600m ahead.

Holiday Green (☎ 04 94 19 88 30; www.holidaygreen.com; rte de Bagnols, Fréjus; camping €27-37; 🕑 Apr-end Sep; 🏊) The extra-large swimming pool and lovely pine forest grounds more than make up for the 7km trip to the beach. Buses 1 and 11 stop right opposite.

Hôtel Cyrnos (☎ 04 94 95 17 13; www.hotel-cyrnos.com; 840 bd Alphonse Juin, St Raphaël; d €40-95) You'll never want to leave once you arrive: the beautiful 1883 mansion has kept so much of its early-20th-century Riviera charm, with its grand staircase, terracotta-tiled floors, understated decor, spacious balconies and wonderfully cool garden. A mere 300m from the beach, it's also ideally located for the *sentier du littoral* walks.

Hôtel Provençal (☎ 04 98 11 80 00; www.hotel-provencal.com; 195 rue de la Garonne, St-Raphaël; d €55-80; ❄) Centrally located near St Raphaël's pretty port, the plain but clean and friendly Hôtel Provençal is good value, particularly if you bag a room with sea views. The breakfast buffet will keep you going all day, and you also get wi-fi thrown in for good measure.

L'Aréna (☎ 04 94 17 09 40; www.arena-hotel.com; 145 rue du Général de Gaulle, Fréjus; s €70-90, d €85-155; ❄ 💻 🏊) This elegant hotel with its sienna-coloured walls and lush garden would not have looked out of place as a luxurious Roman villa a couple of millennia back. Nowadays, it's the perfect location from which to explore the neighbouring sites; the restaurant (mains €20 to €25; closed Monday and Saturday lunch) is also a favourite for alfresco Mediterranean dinners.

Les Potiers (The Potters; ☎ 04 94 51 33 74; 135 rue des Potiers, Fréjus; mains €20; 🕑 lunch & dinner, closed Tue & lunch Wed) Not a potter in sight at this tiny restaurant, but some very tasty regional food instead. You'll also get a peek at local artists' work on the walls.

L'Arbousier (☎ 04 94 95 25 00; 6 av de Valescure; lunch menus €28, dinner menus €36-59; 🕑 lunch & dinner, closed Mon & Tue in winter) One of St-Raphaël's best restaurants, the cuisine is a subtle blend of French *gastronomie* and world influences best enjoyed under the shade of the *arbousiers* (strawberry trees).

Getting There & Away

Bus 5, part of the **AggloBus** (☎ in St-Raphaël 04 94 83 87 63) network, links Fréjus train station and place Paul Vernet (also in Fréjus) with St-Raphaël.

Fréjus and St-Raphaël are on the train line from Nice to Marseille. There's a frequent service (€10, 50 minutes) from Nice to St-Raphaël Valescure train station, with breathtaking views of the Med and red slopes of the Estérel.

ST-TROPEZ

pop 5635

In the soft autumn or winter light, it's hard to believe that the pretty terracotta fishing village of St-Tropez is yet another stop on the Riviera celebrity circuit. It seems far removed from its glitzy siblings further up the coast, but come spring or summer, it's a different world: the town's population increases tenfold, prices triple, and celebrities (particularly French, including crooner Johnny Hallyday) and their party apparatchiks monopolise town.

To get a glimpse of what attracted so many artists to these beautiful shores, avoid visiting in July and August. And take heart if you're only around in the summer: it's always fun to play 'I spy…' (a celebrity).

History

St-Tropez acquired its name in AD 68 when a Roman officer named Torpes was beheaded on Nero's orders in Pisa, and packed into a boat with a dog and a rooster to devour his remains. His headless corpse washed up here intact, leading the villagers to adopt him as their patron saint.

For centuries St-Tropez remained a peaceful little fishing village, attracting painters like pointillist Paul Signac, but few tourists. That changed dramatically in 1956 when *Et Dieu Créa la Femme* (And God Created Woman) was shot here starring Brigitte Bardot (aka BB), catapulting the village into the international limelight.

Orientation

The beaches where A+-listers sunbathe, in the Baie de Pampelonne, lie 4km southeast of town. The village itself is at the tip of a petite peninsula on the southern side of the Baie de St-Tropez, across from the Massif des Maures. The old town sits snugly between quai Jean Jaurès (the main quay of the luxury yacht-packed Vieux Port), place des Lices (an elongated square a few blocks back from the port) and a lofty 16th-century citadel overlooking the town from the northeastern edge.

Information

INTERNET ACCESS

Kreatik Café (☎ 04 94 97 40 61; 19 av Gal Lerclerc; per hr €7; 🕑 9.30am-9pm Mon-Sat, 2-8pm Sun) Even the internet café looks fit for celebrities.

INTERNET RESOURCES

Bay of St-Tropez (www.bay-of-saint-tropez.com) A good information source for the surrounding towns and beaches.

LAUNDRY

Laverie du Pin (☎ 04 94 43 09 09; 13 quai de l'Épi; 🕑 8am-7pm, to 9pm in summer)

MONEY

Crédit Lyonnais (21 quai Suffren) At the port.

Master Change (18 rue du Général Allard) A *bureau de change* (exchange bureau).

POST

Post Office (place Celli) One block from the port.

TOURIST INFORMATION

The English-language brochure *Out and About* is available in tourist offices in the area.

Tourist Office (☎ 04 94 97 45 21; www.ot-saint-tropez.com; quai Jean Jaurès; 🕑 9.30am-8pm Jul & Aug, 9.30am-12.30pm & 2-7pm Apr-Jun & Sep–mid-Oct, 9.30am-12.30pm & 2-6pm mid-Oct–Mar) Keeps a useful list of hotels and restaurants that are open out of season.

Sights

Any amount of wandering about the historical quarter should dismiss any preconceived belief that St-Tropez is all glitz, no substance. For the sceptics (or the culture vultures), the tourist office organises 1½-hour **guided walking tours** (tours €6; 🕑 10am Wed Apr-Oct) in French; call to see if an English-speaking guide is available.

Dramatically displayed in a disused chapel, the **Musée de l'Annonciade** (☎ 04 94 17 84 10; place Grammont, Vieux Port; adult/student €5/3, exhibitions €6/4; 🕑 10am-noon & 3-7pm Wed-Mon Jun-Sep, 10am-noon & 2-6pm Wed-Mon Oct & Dec-May) displays an impressive collection of works by Matisse, Bonnard, Dufy and especially Signac, who set up his home and studio in St-Tropez.

The panoramas of St-Tropez' bay from the elevated 17th-century **Citadelle de St-Tropez** (☎ 04 94 97 59 43; admission €2.50; 🕑 10am-6.30pm Apr-Sep, 10am-12.30pm & 1.30-5.30pm Oct-Mar) are definitely worth the climb. The citadel also houses regular exhibitions (€5.50).

Activities

BEACHES

The glistening sandy beach **Plage de Tahiti**, 4km southeast of town, morphs into the 5km-long **Plage de Pampelonne**, which in summer incorporates a sequence of exclusive restaurant/clubs. To get here, head out of town along av de la Résistance (south of place des Lices) to rte de la Belle Isnarde and then rte de Tahiti. Otherwise, the bus to Ramatuelle, south of St-Tropez, stops at various points along a road that runs about 1km inland from the beach. Beach mats can be rented for around €15 per day.

WALKING

Marked by yellow ('easy') blazes, a 35km **sentier du littoral** (coastal trail) starts from St-Tropez' sandy fishing cove to the east of the 15th-century Tour du Portalet, in the old fishing quarter La Ponche, and arcs around to Cavalaire-sur-Mer along a spectacular series of rocky outcrops and hidden bays. If you're short on time or energy, you can walk as far as Ramatuelle and return by bus. The tourist office has a free, easy-to-follow map showing distances and average walking times.

Sleeping

BUDGET & MIDRANGE

St-Tropez is no shoestring destination, but there are plenty of multistar camping grounds to the southeast along Plage de Pampelonne. Alternatively, during summer St-Tropez makes a scenic day trip by boat from St-Raphaël or Nice, which have hostels. Most hotels close at some stage in winter; the tourist office keeps a list.

Hôtel La Méditerranée (☎ 04 94 97 00 44; www.hotelmediterranee.org; 21 bd Louis Blanc; d low season €50-100, d high season €85-250; ❄) It is remarkable that such authentic places still exist in St-Tropez. Solveig has beautifully renovated each of her 16 rooms with a simple but romantic decor. You may even be asked your opinion on her latest DIY during your visit! The garden of the bar-restaurant (mains €15) is pure summer evening bliss.

Les Palmiers (☎ 04 94 97 01 61; www.hotel-les-palmiers.com; 26 bd Vasserot; d low season €68-139, d high season €109-215; ❄) Opposite the place des Lices, at the back of a lovely shaded courtyard, this friendly and comfortable hotel also has a handful of parking spaces (ie every inch of its front street space). Rooms in the annexe are noisy – choose those in the main building.

Hôtel Sube (☎ 04 94 97 30 04; www.hotel-sube.com; 15 quai Suffren; d low season €115-190, d high season €140-290; ❄) This marine-style hotel has the most coveted location in town, right on the waterfront. Port-side rooms and their fabulous views provide the perfect excuse to stare unashamedly at the yachts moored below. The 1st-floor wood-panelled bar has a diminutive but popular balcony and an imposing stone fireplace for cosy winter evenings.

AU NATUREL

Not a fan of tan lines? The coastline from Le Lavandou to the St-Tropez peninsula is well endowed with *naturiste* (nudist) beaches. Naturism is also legal in some other spots in the area, like the secluded beach, **Plage de l'Escalet**, on the southern side of Cap Camarat. There's a bus to Ramatuelle from St-Tropez, but you'll have to walk the 4km southeast to the beach. Closer to St-Tropez is **La Moutte**, 4.5km east of town – take rte des Salins.

Most isolated is the oldest and largest *naturiste* colony in the region, which occupies half of the 8km-long island **Île du Levant** (p891).

The coast's laid-back, let-it-all-hang-out attitude was the premise of Jean Girault's cult 1964 farce film *Le Gendarme de St-Tropez*, in which Louis de Funès starred as the policeman of the title, who attempted to crack down on local nudists.

TOP END

La Maison Blanche (☎ 04 94 97 52 66; www.hotellamaisonblanche.com; place des Lices; d low season €180-290, d high season €240-390; closed Feb;) Don't forget your sunglasses at the ode to minimalist design that is the Maison Blanche, and see how many shades of white you've counted by the end of your stay.

La Mistralée (☎ 04 98 12 91 12; www.hotel-mistralee.com; 1 av du Général Leclerc; d low season €190-390, d high season €460-790;) The flamboyant former home of hairdresser to the stars, Alexandre (famously *sans* surname), this totally over-the-top 1960s-decorated hotel includes, for example, fabric presented to Alexandre by the king of Morocco. The restaurant (*menus* €50 to €60), tucked at the back of the luxurious garden by the mosaic-lined pool, feels like a *1001 Nights'* palace at night.

Pastis (☎ 04 98 12 56 50; www.pastis-st-tropez.com; 61 av du Général Leclerc; d low season €200-350, d high season €350-600;) This stunning hotel is the brainchild of an English couple besotted with Provence and passionate about modern art. If it doesn't sound like an obvious combination, one look at Pastis will dispel any doubt: you'll die for the pop-art-inspired interior and long for a swim in the emerald green pool and a snooze under the centenary palm trees.

Eating

Quai Jean Jaurès on the old port is littered with restaurants and cafés – they have mediocre menus, but strategic views of the opulent wealth of nearby yachts. More-appealing places can be found on Port des Pêcheurs at the northern end of rue des Remparts, and wedged in the pedestrian alleys running south of rue Allard.

Ö Vents d'Anges (☎ 04 94 43 31 33; 7 quai de l'Epi; mains €12-25; lunch & dinner) Right by the port, in one of the town's party corners, this cheap and cheerful place serves up grilled fish and meat, a good option for a lighter meal on a scorching summer day.

La Table du Marché (☎ 04 94 97 85 20; 38 rue Georges Clémenceau; mains €24-36; lunch & dinner) Chef Christophe Leroy's St-Tropez pad is a must, be it for scrumptious tea-time *pâtisseries* (pastries and cakes) or heavenly cuisine come dinner time. The lobster gratin is unforgettable, and, for once, vegetarians are properly catered for. Take a leaf of out Leroy's recipe book at one of his cooking lessons (5-person minimum, €100 per person).

La Nouvelle Bohême (☎ 04 94 95 12 63; 3 rue Charrons; menus €25; dinner Tue-Sun) With its corset-shaped fluffy cushions, candle-lit atmosphere, low-beamed ceiling and whitewashed walls, this irreverent, superfriendly restaurant serves the best seafood tagliatelle in town. Its chocolate cake is a chocoholic's dream come true.

Auberge de l'Oumède (☎ 04 94 44 11 11; Chemin de l'Oumède, Ramatuelle; menu €75; dinner Apr-Oct, closed Mon Apr–mid-Jun, Sep & Oct) Epicureans come from far and wide to savour Jean-Pierre Frezia's divine Provençal cuisine in the idyllic setting of his hilltop *mas* (traditional Provençal stone building). Red mullet and spinach cannelloni, grilled catch of the day and sensational desserts, all accompanied by some *very* fine wines; dining at l'Oumède is a once in a lifetime treat.

CAFÉS

Sénéquier (☎ 04 94 97 00 90; cnr quai Jean Jaurès & place aux Herbes; dishes €5-12.50; 8am-2am Apr-Oct, 8am-7pm Nov-Mar) This quintessential St-Tropez quay-side café opened in 1887, and Sartre worked on *Les Chemins de la Liberté* (Roads to Freedom) here. Its fire-engine-red terrace is a prized drinking spot, and our extensive field research has also concluded that its nougat is the best under the sun.

Le Café (☎ 04 94 97 44 69; place des Lices; mains €20, menu €30; lunch & dinner) If you've been itching to have a go at *pétanque,* Le Café will lend you a set of bowls to play out front while you sip a glass of rosé or an evening kir. And you could do worse than staying for dinner: the Provençal fare at this institution is of the finest variety.

SELF-CATERING

The **place des Lices market** (mornings Tue & Sat) is a highlight of local life: people come for the gossip as much as the colourful stalls groaning under the weight of plump fruit and veg, mounds of olives, local cheeses, tasty chestnut purée and fragrant herbs. The **fish market** (Tue-Sun, daily in summer) on place aux Herbes is joined by a fruit and veg market in summer.

A must-try is the local speciality, *tarte Tropézienne,* an orange blossom–flavoured double sponge cake filled with a thick cream, created nearby by a Polish baker and christened by BB in the '50s. **La Tarte Tropézienne** (☎ 04 94 97 71 42; 36 rue Georges Clémenceau; 7am-7.30pm) turns them out along with freshly filled sandwiches on home-baked bread.

For groceries, try **Monoprix** (9 av du Général Leclerc; 8am-8pm Mon-Sat).

Entertainment

The good news: most bars open from around 11pm to dawn. The bad? Drinks start at €15 and door policies are formidable. Try to look as famous as possible.

In winter, most bars only open on weekends; in summer, it's party central seven days a week.

Chez Maggy (04 94 97 16 12; 5 rue Sibille) Gay-friendly disco.

Le Pigeonnier (04 94 97 84 26; 13 rue de la Ponche) Small in size, big in reputation; run by the pioneer of *Tropézienne* nights.

Les Caves du Roy (04 94 97 16 02; Hôtel Byblos, av Paul Signac) Star-studded.

L'Esquinade (04 94 97 87 45; 2 rue du Four) *The* gay bar in town.

Papagayo (04 94 54 82 89; Résidence du Nouveau Port; summer & Christmas-time) Your best bet for gaining entry, and usually the most fun.

Shopping

The old-town streets and arcades are dripping with designer boutiques. For your chance to own a Prada or Gucci number, try the brilliant vintage **De L'une à L'autre** (04 98 12 66 14; 6 rue Joseph Quaranta; 10am-1pm & 3-8pm Jul & Aug, 10am-12.30pm & 2.30-6.30pm Tue-Sat Sep-Jun), St-Tropez's answer to charity shops. The lovely Anne will help you unearth hardly worn and infinitely cheaper (we didn't say cheap) couture treasures from her stocks.

Getting There & Away

BOAT

Les Bateaux Verts (04 94 49 29 39; www.bateauxverts.com; Ste-Maxime) operates a shuttle-boat service from St-Tropez to Ste-Maxime (one way adult/child €6.60/3.50, 20 minutes) and Port Grimaud (one way adult/child €6.50/3.50, 15 minutes), with reduced schedules outside peak season. In summer and autumn, Les Bateaux de St-Raphaël (see p886) runs boats from St-Tropez to St-Raphaël.

Trans Côte d'Azur runs day trips from Nice (see p868) and Cannes (see p880) between Easter and September.

BUS

St-Tropez' **bus station** (av Général de Gaulle) is on the southwestern edge of town on the main road. There's an **information office** (04 94 54 62 36; 8.30am-noon & 2-4.30pm Mon-Fri, 8.30am-noon Sat) at the station. **Sodetrav** (08 25 00 06 50) runs eight buses daily (15 in summer) from St-Raphaël Valescure train station to St-Tropez bus station (€10.30, 1¼ hours), via Fréjus. The eight daily buses from St-Tropez to Toulon (€19.70, 2¼ hours) also stop at Le Lavandou and Hyères. Bus 111 serves Toulon-Hyères' airport (€20.90, one hour) from Friday to Sunday, April to October only.

CAR & MOTORCYCLE

To avoid the worst of the high season traffic, approach from the Provençale Autoroute (the A8) and exit at Le Muy (exit 35). Take the D558 road across the Massif des Maures and via La Garde Freinet to Port Grimaud, then park here and take the shuttle boat that runs to St-Tropez from Easter to October.

Getting Around

If you'd like to retain some sort of inner peace while in St-Tropez, you're strongly advised to opt for two wheels rather than four: parking is the bane of Riviera life. **MAS** (04 94 97 00 60; 3-5 rue Joseph Quaranta) rents out mountain bikes and scooters. And if you must drive, there are several car-hire places lining av du Général Leclerc.

To order a taxi, ring 04 94 97 05 27. For a taxi boat call **Marine Service** (06 09 57 31 22; Le Pilon).

ST-TROPEZ TO TOULON

Massif des Maures

Shrouded by a forest of pine, chestnut and cork oak trees, the Massif des Maures arcs inland between Hyères and Fréjus. Roamed by wild boars, its near-black vegetation gives rise to its name, derived from the Provençal word *mauro* (dark-pine wood).

Within the forest, the village of **Collobrières** concocts wonderful chestnut purée and *marrons glacé* (candied chestnuts).

Hiking and cycling opportunities abound, especially around La Sauvette (779m), the massif's highest peak. St-Tropez' tourist office distributes an English-language map/guide called *Tours in the Gulf of St-Tropez – Pays des Maures*, detailing driving, cycling and walking itineraries.

Îles d'Hyères

For some inexplicable reason, these paradisaical islands (also known as Îles d'Or –

Golden Islands – for their shimmering mica rock) have remained mostly unknown to foreign crowds.

The easternmost and largest of this trio of islands is the discreet **Île du Levant**, split into an odd combination of army land and nudist colony. **Île de Port-Cros**, the middle and smallest island, is the jewel in the islands' crown. France's only marine **parc national** (national park; ☎ 04 94 12 82 30; www.portcrosparcnational.fr, in French; 50 rue St Claire, Hyères), it boasts exceptional marine fauna and flora, which makes it a **snorkelling** paradise. The island is also covered with 30km of marked trails through thick forest, ragged clifftops and deserted beaches.

The largest and westernmost island is **Île de Porquerolles** (www.porquerolles.com). Run as a hacienda in the early 20th century, it has kept many of its sprawling plantation features. There are plenty of walking trails, but the best way to get around is by cycling. There are several bicycle-rental places, as well as a few restaurants and hotels.

For more information, contact Hyères' tourist office (see p892) or check www.provence-azur.com.

Boats to the Îles d'Hyères leave from various towns along the coast. **Vedettes Îles d'Or** (☎ 04 94 71 01 02; www.vedettesilesdor.fr) in Le Lavandou operates boats to all three islands (Porquerolles return adult/child €30.60/23.90, 40 minutes each way; Port-Cros and Île du Levant return adult/child €23.50/19.60, 35 and 60 minutes respectively). In summer, there are boats between Port-Cros and Porquerolles.

TLV-TVM (☎ for Porquerolles 04 94 58 21 81, ☎ for Port-Cros & Levant 04 94 57 44 07; www.tlv-tvm.com) runs services from Hyères' two ports: La Tour Fondue, at the bottom of the Giens Peninsula, is only 10 minutes from Porquerolles (return adult/child €16/14), while Hyères's port at the top of the peninsula has services to

HIDDEN VAR TREASURES

The Var *département*, which stretches from the Estérel mountains to Marseille, is packed with coastal gems. At the edge of the Massif des Maures, the 26km-long coastal road (part of the D559), also known as **Corniche des Maures**, snakes from La Croix-Valmer to Le Lavandou. In addition to stunning views, there are some superb spots for swimming, sunbathing, windsurfing and walking.

La Croix-Valmer's **Gigaro** beach is one not to miss, as is the walking path towards Cap Lardier, which is one of the most magnificent, least-trodden bits of the entire southern coast.

Le Lavandou (population 5825; www.ot-lelavandou.fr) is also famous for its 12km of fine beaches and 12 types of sand. The town has also retained a beautiful historical centre, and its 1000-boat marina is a prime evening-stroll venue. **Hotel Le Rabelais** (☎ 04 94 71 00 56; www.le-rabelais.fr; 2 rue Rabelais; d €45-105) is one of the best options in the area. Smack bang in front of the marina, the simply decorated rooms have prized views of the port and nearby islands, or of surrounding hills at the back. And what better place to discuss what beach or village to visit each day than on the sun-drenched breakfast terrace?

Up in the hills, you'll find the quintessential Provençal village of **Bormes-les-Mimosas**. The *vieux* (old) village is spectacularly flowered year round, with the eponymous mimosas in winter, and deep-fuchsia bougainvilleas in summer. Old cobbled streets are lined with artists' galleries, and with boutiques filled with traditional Provençal products, natural soap and essential oils.

For breathtaking views of the islands, the **rte des Crêtes** winds its way through maquis-covered hills some 400m above the sea. Take the D41 as you head out of Bormes-les-Mimosas past the Chapelle St-François; 500m up the hill on your right is Chemin du Landon, which then turns into the rte des Crêtes. Eight kilometres and many bends and picture stops later, you'll get to the sensational **our pick** **Relais du Vieux Sauvaire** (☎ 04 94 05 84 22; rte des Crêtes; mains €18-30; lunch & dinner May-Sep;), with 180-degree views you could only dream of. Owner Roland Gallo has been here since 1960 and clearly has no intention of ever going anywhere else (you'll understand why when you get there). The food is as sunny as the views: pizzas, melon and Parma ham, whole sea bass in salt crust – and there's even a swimming-pool in which to cool off. The rte des Crêtes goes back down towards Le Rayol-Canadel on the coastal D559 after the restaurant.

You'll need a car to travel along the rte des Crêtes, but the coastal road is on the itinerary of the Toulon to St-Tropez bus (see opposite), which stops in most towns, including Le Lavandou.

Port-Cros (40 to 60 minutes, summer only) and Le Levant (50 to 90 minutes; adult/child return trip €23.50/20.50).

Hyères

pop 53,700

The reason you come to Hyères seldom has to do with its small, neglected medieval town centre or profusion of palm trees. The city's real assets are the **Giens Peninsula** to the south and the three **Îles d'Hyères** stretching east along the coast.

A protected wetland area, the peninsula harbours amazing birdlife including pink flamingos, herons, terns, egrets, sandpipers, teals and cormorants. The **tourist office** (☎ 04 94 01 84 50; 3 av Ambroise Thomas; 8.30am-7.30pm Jul & Aug, 9am-6pm Mon-Fri, 10am-4pm Sat Sep-Jun) runs 1½-hour tours for €7.

On the peninsula's northwestern edge, the beaches of Almanarre are internationally famed for windsurfing and kitesurfing. For windsurfing lessons, contact **Funboard Center** (☎ 04 94 57 95 33; www.funboardcenter.com; rte l'Almanarre) or for kitesurfing lessons, contact **École Kite** (☎ 06 60 79 37 69; www.ecolekite.fr; Mahalo Surf Shop, rte l'Almanarre). Toulon-Hyères' international airport (p895) is on the other side of the peninsula.

TOULON

pop 167,400

Toulon still has a long way to go before it's a prime travellers' destination. The town has remained hermetically sealed against the Côte d'Azur's charms, mostly because of its naval activities and half a century of neglect.

To give the town its due, much has happened since mayor Hubert Falco was elected in 2002 (and re-elected in 2008). The opera house has been renovated, and there is a brand new bus station and the most energetic and proactive tourist office you'll find anywhere on the coast. The town has also made much of its 500-year-old arsenal and rich military history.

As the western gateway of the Côte d'Azur, Toulon has excellent train connections as well as ferry services and, at neighbouring Hyères, an expanding international airport.

History

Initially a Roman colony, Toulon became part of France in 1481 – the city grew in importance after Henri IV founded an arsenal here. In the 17th century the port was enlarged by Vauban. The young Napoléon Bonaparte made a name for himself in 1793 during a siege in which the English, who had taken over Toulon, were expelled. In 1942 almost the entire fleet scuttled in the *rade* (sheltered bay lined with quays) to escape German forces, and the city was practically razed following the 1944 Allied landing. Following the war, Toulon languished for much of the second half of the 20th century.

Orientation

Toulon wraps itself around a bay. To the west is the naval base and to the east the ferry terminal, where boats sail for Corsica. The city is at its liveliest along quai de la Sinse and quai Stalingrad (the departure point for Îles d'Hyères ferries) and in the old city. The train station is northwest of the old city.

Women travelling solo should take care at night in some of the old city streets, such as rue Chevalier Paul and the western end of rue Pierre Sémard.

Information

Many commercial banks flourish along bd de Strasbourg.

Arobase (18 rue Paul Landrin; internet access per hr €2.50; 9.30am-10.30pm)

Change du Port (☎ 04 94 92 60 40; 15 quai Cronstadt; 8.30am-noon & 1.30-4.45pm Mon-Fri) A bureau de change.

Laverie (10 rue Zola; 7am-9pm) One of several laundrettes in the old city.

Post Office (rue Dr Jean Bertholet) There's a second entrance on rue Ferrero.

Tourist Office (☎ 04 94 18 53 00; www.toulontourisme.com; 334 av de la République; 9am-6pm Mon-Sat, 10am-noon Sun Sep-Jun, 9am-8pm Mon-Sat, 10am-noon Sun Jul & Aug) Distributes a useful monthly agenda summarising museum opening hours and events in town.

Sights & Activities

Housed in an imperial arsenal building, the **Musée de la Marine** (Naval Museum; ☎ 04 94 02 02 01; place Monsenergue; adult/child €5/free; 10am-6pm Wed-Mon) has some intricate scale models of old ships and historic paintings of Toulon.

The compact but high-calibre photographic museum, **Maison de la Photographie** (☎ 04 94 93 07 59; rue Nicolas Laugier, place du Globe; admission free; noon-6pm Tue-Sat), exhibits contemporary works in a two-tiered, light-filled space.

Towering over the old city to the north is **Mont Faron** (580m), offering a fantastic

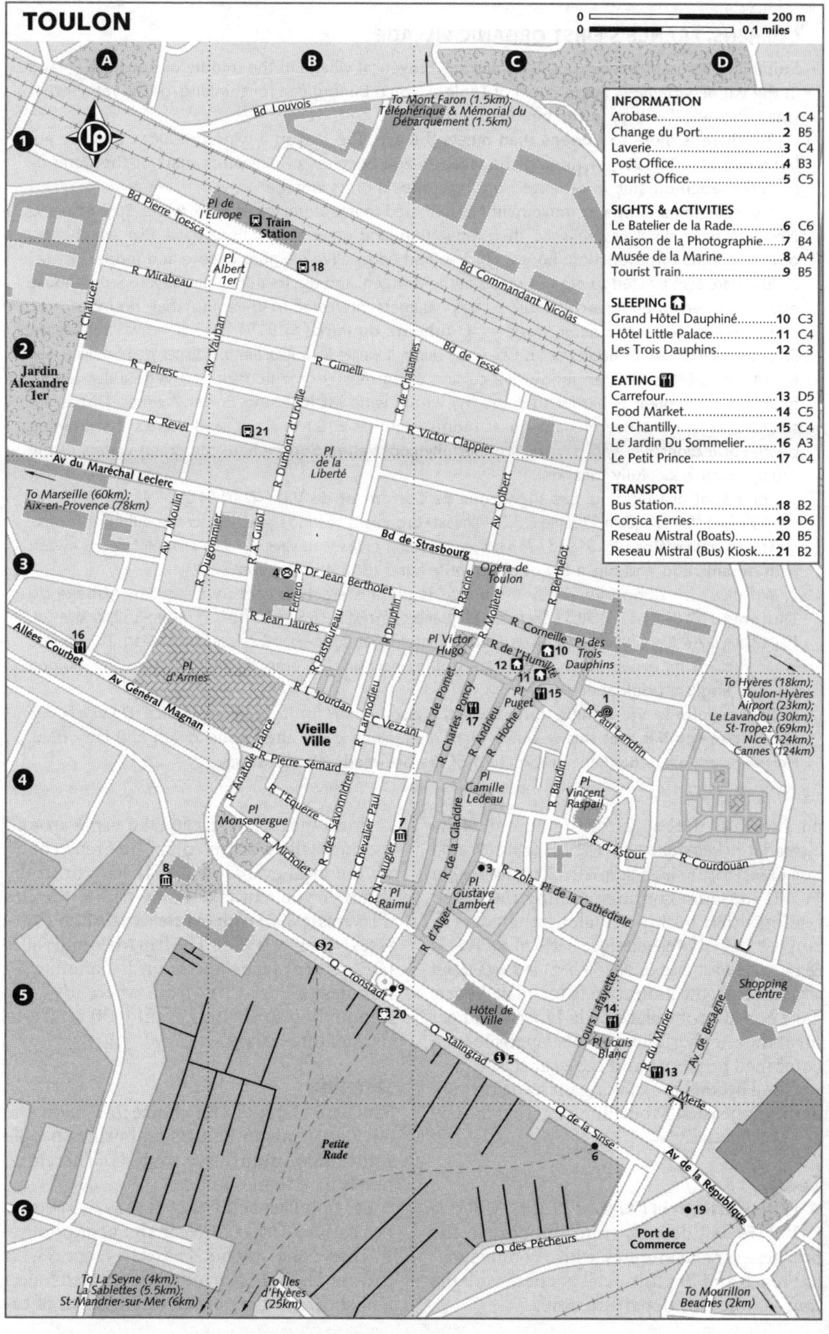
TOULON
0 200 m
0 0.1 miles
INFORMATION
Arobase 1 C4
Change du Port 2 B5
Laverie 3 C4
Post Office 4 B3
Tourist Office 5 C5
SIGHTS & ACTIVITIES
Le Batelier de la Rade 6 C6
Maison de la Photographie 7 B4
Musée de la Marine 8 A4
Tourist Train 9 B5
SLEEPING
Grand Hôtel Dauphiné 10 C3
Hôtel Little Palace 11 C4
Les Trois Dauphins 12 C3
EATING
Carrefour 13 D5
Food Market 14 C5
Le Chantilly 15 C4
Le Jardin Du Sommelier 16 A3
Le Petit Prince 17 C4
TRANSPORT
Bus Station 18 B2
Corsica Ferries 19 D6
Reseau Mistral (Boats) 20 B5
Reseau Mistral (Bus) Kiosk 21 B2
To Mont Faron (1.5km); Téléphérique & Mémorial du Débarquement (1.5km)
Bd Louvois
Bd Pierre Toesca
Pl de l'Europe
Train Station
Pl Albert 1er
R Mirabeau
Bd Commandant Nicolas
R Chalucet
Jardin Alexandre 1er
R Peiresc
Av Vauban
R Gimelli
R de Chabannes
Bd de Tessé
R Revel
R Dumont d'Urville
R Victor Clappier
Pl de la Liberté
Av du Maréchal Leclerc
To Marseille (60km); Aix-en-Provence (78km)
Av J Moulin
R Dugommier
R A Guiol
Av Colbert
Bd de Strasbourg
R Berthelot
Opéra de Toulon
R Dr Jean Bertholet
R Ferrero
R Racine
R Jean Jaurès
R Dauphin
R Molière
R Corneille
Pl des Trois Dauphins
Pl Victor Hugo
R de l'Humilité
Allées Courbet
Pl d'Armes
R Pastoureau
Av Général Magnan
R L Jourdan
Pl Puget
To Hyères (18km); Toulon-Hyères Airport (23km); Le Lavandou (30km); St-Tropez (69km); Nice (124km); Cannes (124km)
R Paul Landrin
C Vezzani
R Larmodieu
R de Pomet
R Charles Poncy
R Andrieu
R Hoche
Vieille Ville
R Anatole France
R Pierre Sémard
Pl Camille Ledeau
R Baudin
Pl Vincent Raspail
R l'Equerre
Pl Monsenergue
R des Savonnières
R Chevalier Paul
R de la Glacière
R d'Astour
R Courdouan
R Micholet
R N Laugier
R Zola
Pl de la Cathédrale
Pl Raimu
Pl Gustave Lambert
R d'Alger
Q Cronstadt
Shopping Centre
Hôtel de Ville
Cours Lafayette
Av de Besagne
Q Stalingrad
Pl Louis Blanc
R du Murier
R Merle
Q de la Sinse
Petite Rade
Av de la République
Port de Commerce
Q des Pêcheurs
To La Seyne (4km); La Sablettes (5.5km); St-Mandrier-sur-Mer (6km)
To Îles d'Hyères (25km)
To Mourillon Beaches (2km)

CORRENS, FRANCE'S FIRST ORGANIC VILLAGE

Stumbling across **Correns** (pop 800), a small Provençal village in the middle of nowhere (inland in the Var *département*, 50km north of Toulon), you'd be forgiven for thinking 'great, yet another small, Provençal village in the middle of nowhere'.

But there is more to Correns than meets the eye. The mayor, a wine producer, had the enlightened idea in 1997 of turning the village's 200 hectares of vineyards (part of the *Côtes de Provence* label) organic in order to boost the appeal of its vintage.

A decade on, the organic movement has gathered momentum: wines (30% white, 50% rosé and 20% red) have slowly established their reputation, and other productions have also switched to organic means of production: honey, chicken and eggs, olive oil, goat cheese and fodder. School children are also treated to organic meals at the canteen, and the town hall has developed in-house expertise in eco-friendly architecture to help villagers interested in 'greening' their houses.

To sample Correns' organic wonders, **L'Auberge du Parc** (☎ 04 94 59 53 52; www.aubergeduparc.fr; 34 place du Général de Gaulle; menus €25-35; ⏲ lunch & dinner Jul & Aug, lunch & dinner Wed-Sat, lunch Sun Apr-Jun, Sep & Oct) serves an innovative cuisine using mostly organic fruit and vegetables (good-quality organic meat is harder to come by) with a wine list featuring Correns' wines. Dishes are sizeable, as are the five elegant guest rooms (doubles €100 to €130, and there's a swimming pool). For a digestive walk, try the wonderfully cool **Vallon Soun** where the green waters of the Argens River peacefully meander.

For a spot of shopping, **Les Vignerons de Correns et du Val** (☎ 04 94 59 59 46; rue de l'Eglise; ⏲ 3.30-7pm Mon-Fri, 10am-12.30pm & 3.30-7pm Sat) organises tastings and stocks the village's wines.

The **tourist office** (☎ 04 94 37 21 31; www.correns.fr; 2 rue Cabassonne; ⏲ 9am-noon Mon-Sat) is awash with organic info and has a list of *chambres d'hôtes* (B&BS) in the area.

Worth a visit during your stay in Correns is the austere 12th-century Cistercian **Abbaye du Thoronet** (☎ 04 94 60 43 90; Le Thoronet; adult/under 25yr/child €6.50/4.50/free; ⏲ 10am-6.30pm Mon-Sat, 10am-noon & 2-6.30pm Sun Apr-Sep, 10am-1pm & 2-5pm Mon-Sat, 10am-noon & 2-5pm Sun Oct-Mar). The church is famous for its exceptional acoustics – guides occasionally sing, to demonstrate. For guided tours in English, book ahead.

St-Maximim-la-Ste-Baume, further west, is also famous for its religious edifice. *Da Vinci Code* fans will remember that this is where Mary Magdalene came after Jesus' death and later died. Her relics are allegedly kept in the crypt of the **Ste-Madeleine Basilica**.

panorama of the bay. Near the summit is the **Mémorial du Débarquement** (☎ 04 94 88 08 09; adult/child €3.80/1.55; ⏲ 10am-noon & 2-5.30pm Tue-Sun), a WWII museum commemorating the Allied landings that took place along the coast in August 1944. A **téléphérique** (cablecar; ☎ 04 94 92 68 25; return adult/child €6.30/4.50; ⏲ check with tourist office) ascends the mountain from bd de Vence. Take bus 40 from place de la Liberté and get off at the téléphérique stop. See opposite for a combined bus, boat and cablecar ticket.

Good **beaches** for soaking up some rays are 2km southeast at Mourillon or across the bay at Les Sablettes.

Tours

A little **tourist train** (☎ 06 94 36 01 32; adult/child €5/3; ⏲ Feb-Oct) departs from the port to the beaches every 30 minutes, with a commentary in French and English – call or check with the tourist office for departure times.

From the port, you can take a spin around the *rade*, with a commentary (in French only) on the local events of WWII (€9), or in the summer you can take a day trip to the Îles d'Hyères (p890) with **Le Batelier de la Rade** (☎ 04 94 46 24 65; quai de la Sinse). The trip to Porquerolles (€22 return) takes one hour. It's another 40 minutes to Port-Cros, from where it's a 20-minute hop to Île du Levant (€30 return to tour all three islands).

Sleeping

You won't be spoilt for choice in Toulon: the clientele tends to be passing businesspeople rather than inquisitive tourists. Therefore, hotels tend to be soulless.

Les Trois Dauphins (☎ 04 94 92 65 79; 9 place des Trois Dauphins; d from €32) Near the opera house, this basic one-star hotel has a few rooms with bathrooms and a few more with shared toilets and shower. Many of the rooms smell of tobacco so ask to see rooms before you settle. It's run by the same family as at Little Palace.

Hôtel Little Palace (☎ 04 94 92 26 62; www.hotel-littlepalace.com; 6-8 rue Berthelot; s/d €45-54) The slightly over-the-top Italian-inspired decor lacks a little authenticity but its owners definitely don't. The energetic Madame Masson has become the neighbourhood's matriarch and the cute breakfast corner quickly fills with people on errands stopping by for coffee and gossip.

Grand Hôtel Dauphiné (☎ 04 94 92 20 28; www.grandhoteldauphine.com; 10 rue Berthelot; s/d €54/60; ❄) 'Life is like a box of chocolates. You never know what you're gonna get.' Forrest Gump's famous line could have been written for this hotel: rooms vary wildly in quality so ask to see one first (and ask for nonsmoking if you're not keen on the smell of stale tobacco). Thankfully, the staff is accommodating and the €8 buffet breakfast is superb.

Eating

Le Chantilly (☎ 04 94 92 24 37; place Puget; mains €10-25; 🕑 6.30am-11pm) Whether you're here for an early morning breakfast, a mound of *moules-frites* (mussels and chips) at lunchtime or an evening drink to wind down, you're certain to find this stalwart of local life packed with Toulonnais. Going strong since 1907, Le Chantilly's popularity shows no sign of receding any time soon.

Le Petit Prince (☎ 04 94 93 03 45; 16 rue Charles Poncy; mains from €15; 🕑 lunch & dinner Mon-Fri, dinner Sat) A few doors down from the opera house, the sweet 'Little Prince' dishes up good ol' French staples such as *entrecôte* (rib steak), *souris d'agneau* (top of a leg of lamb) or *tagliatelles aux ceps et au foie gras* (tagliatelle with mushroom and foie gras) in a cosy atmosphere.

Le Jardin Du Sommelier (☎ 04 94 62 03 27; 20 allées Courbet; mains €25, menu €38; 🕑 lunch & dinner Mon-Fri, dinner Sat) The less-than-inspiring location is saved by an impressive wine list (including a tasting formula of three different glasses of wine for €15), seasonally changing Provençal cuisine and elaborate desserts.

SELF-CATERING

Under the plane trees of cours Lafayette you'll find the elongated, open-air **food market** (🕑 7.30am-12.30pm Tue-Sun). Once the picnic-perfect food stalls have packed up for the day, bric-a-brac and clothes traders take over. Two blocks east, there's a **Carrefour** (rue du Mûrier; 🕑 8.30am-9pm Mon-Sat) supermarket inside the Centre Commercial Mayol (mall).

Getting There & Away

The small international **Toulon-Hyères Airport** (☎ 08 25 01 83 87; www.toulon-hyeres.aeroport.fr) is located 23km east of Toulon, on the edge of the Giens Peninsula (5km south of Hyères). There are regular flights to/from Amsterdam, Brussels, London and Rome.

Ferries to Corsica and Sardinia are run by **Corsica Ferries** (☎ 08 25 09 50 95; Port de Commerce). See p907 for details.

From Toulon's **bus station** (☎ 04 94 24 60 00; bd de Tessé), next to the train station, bus 103 to St-Tropez (eight buses daily) runs east along the coast via Hyères (€1.40, 35 minutes) and Le Lavandou (€12.60, one hour).

There are frequent train connections to coastal cities including Marseille (€10.40, 40 minutes), St-Raphaël (€13.70, 50 minutes), Cannes (€17.80, 1¼ hours), Monaco (€22.90, 2¼ hours) and Nice (€21.40, 1¾ hours).

Getting Around

Bus 102 (five daily) links the airport with Toulon's bus and train station (€1.40, 40 minutes) and Hyères' town centre (€1.40, 10 minutes).

Local buses are run by **Réseau Mistral** (☎ 04 94 03 87 03; rue Revel; 🕑 7.30am-7pm Mon-Fri, 8.30am-12.30pm & 2-6pm Sat). Tickets cost €1.40 each, or €10 for a book of 10. Buses generally run until around 7.30pm or 8.30pm. Sunday service is limited. Bus 7 links the train station with quai Stalingrad.

Réseau Mistral also runs boats that link quai Stalingrad with the towns on the peninsula across the harbour, including La Seyne (line 8M), St-Mandrier-sur-Mer (line 28M) and Sablettes (line 18M). The 20-minute ride costs €2 (€3.90 for an all-day bus and boat ticket, or €6 including a cablecar return trip). Boats run from around 6am to 8pm; line 28M also has a couple of night boats at around 11pm.

WEST OF TOULON

Bandol

pop 8645

To many, the name Bandol conjures up images of rosés chilled to perfection and noble reds elevating meat dishes to new heights. The seaside resort town of Bandol itself is lesser known, but with its 1600-boat marina, pretty beaches and steep hills proffering uninterrupted sea views, it's a long-standing favourite of French holiday-home owners.

ORIENTATION & INFORMATION

Bandol's centre is located on an anchor-shaped peninsula: the port, marina and historical centre run along an elongated eastern edge while the western side is carved by the picture-perfect Anse de Renécros. From the tip of the peninsula it's only a few breaststrokes to the tiny Île de Bendor. Bandol's train station is 10 minutes' walk north of the marina.

The energetic **tourist office** (☎ 04 94 29 41 35; www.bandol.fr; Allées Vivien; 9am-noon & 2-6pm Mon-Fri & Sat 9am-noon Sep-Jun, 9.30am-6.30pm Jul-Aug) hands out a comprehensive practical guide in French and English.

Banque Populaire (☎ 04 94 29 32 90; 31 quai de Gaulle), on the marina, has a *bureau de change*.

SIGHTS & ACTIVITIES

Bandol wines have enjoyed surprising popularity throughout their 2000-year history. In Roman times, the then Massilia wines were famous across Gaul; their ability to mature at sea meant they travelled far beyond their home shores in the 16th and 17th centuries (Louis XV was rumoured to be an insatiable fan). Nowadays, Bandol's 49 vineyards carefully manage their prized production (collectively held under the *Appellation d'Origine Contrôlée Vins de Bandol* label) of red, rosé and white. You can drive around the scenic **vineyards** (see opposite) or go to the **Maison des Vins** (☎ 04 94 29 45 03; Place Artaud; 10am-12.30pm & 3-6.30pm Tue-Sat), where Pascal Perier – aka living Bandol encyclopedia – organises tastings and keeps a well-supplied shop.

The tiny **Île de Bendor**, belonging to the Ricard family (of international pastis fame; pastis is an aniseed-flavoured *apéritif*), is an easy trip from the mainland. It takes just seven minutes by **boat** (☎ 04 94 10 75 93; return €8; 7.45am-5pm low season; 7am-7pm mid-season; 7am-2am high season) from Bandol, but in summer that's the difference between 'can't-even-see-the-sand-it's-so-overcrowded' beach and 'wow-space-to-breathe' (the beaches are artificial). On the downside, the buildings on the island look like a tacky movie set.

Much more authentic is the yellow-marked **sentier du littoral**, which runs 12km (allow 3½ to four hours) from Bandol's port to La Madrague in St-Cyr-Les-Lecques, with the stunning **Calanque de Port d'Alon** roughly halfway. The easiest way of doing it is to take the bus from Bandol to Les-Lecques (the tourist office has timetables) and walk back to Bandol at your own pace.

Wednesday's colourful **grand marché** (mornings) in Sanary-sur-Mer is the area's main market, drawing crowds from miles around.

SLEEPING & EATING

Camping Les Girelles (☎ 04 94 74 13 18; www.lesgirelles.com; 1003 Chemin de Beaucours; tent per 2 people low/high season €15.90/25; Easter-Sep) On the Baie de Bandol, in the direction of Sanary, this campsite has bagged the best location on the coast, a mere 30m from the water's edge. There's plenty of shade for pitching your tent, and there's a pizzeria-bar on site.

Key Largo (☎ 04 94 29 46 93; www.hotel-key-largo.com; 19 corniche Bonaparte; d €49-99) Strategically located halfway between the port and the pretty beach of Renécros, the eight rooms with sea views (and private terrace for three of them) are an absolute steal. The remaining 10 still enjoy the same simple but stylish decor and look out on neighbouring gardens. And there are homemade cakes for breakfast no matter where you sleep.

L'Assiette des Saveurs (☎ 04 94 29 80 08; 1 rue Louis Marçon; mains €10; lunch & dinner) One street back from the busy marina, with its pretty street-side terrace, L'Assiette prepares classic recipes with a cheeky fusion twist – such as monkfish in orange sauce or satay lamb chops. It gets our vote for best value in town.

La Chipote (☎ 04 94 29 41 62; 12 corniche Bonaparte; menus €28; lunch daily, dinner Fri & Sat) Not content with its stunning location (right on the Renécros beach, with a terrace, panoramic dining room and massive sliding windows letting in the sea breeze), La Chipote also delivers on the plate: fresh fish, tip-top presentation and ace desserts.

GETTING THERE & AWAY

Bandol is on the train line between Toulon (€3.20, 15 minutes) and Marseille (€8.30, 45 minutes), with regular services year round.

Littoral Cars (☎ 04 94 74 01 35) operates a regular bus service between Bandol and Toulon (€4.30,

50 minutes) via Sanary (€1.80, 10 minutes) from around 6am to 7.30pm.

Around Bandol

Bandol's 1500 hectares of **vineyards** spread inland across scenic rolling landscapes and stunning villages (you'll need wheels to get around). The most famous village of all is the hilltop **Le Castellet**, a medieval wonder culminating in a 12th-century castle. Its steep, boutique-lined pedestrian streets are chock-a-block in summer, when the pace often slows to a crawl.

A few hairpin bends down from the village is the fabulous our pick **Les Quatre Saisons** (☎ 04 94 25 24 90; www.lesquatresaisons.org; 370 montée des Oliviers, rte du Brûlat, Le Castellet; d incl breakfast €90-140;). In their *mas* (traditional Provençal stone house), Patrice and Didier have decorated five exquisite rooms in the purest Provençal style. All rooms open on to a central swimming pool; some also offer breathtaking views of the area. Patrice's *table d'hôtes* (set menu; €40, including drinks) is worth every penny. Make sure you try his divine *vin d'orange amère* (bitter orange liquor). For a share of Patrice's culinary secrets, try his half-day cooking course (€40 per person).

Back on the coast, the pretty-as-a-picture seaside town of **Sanary-sur-Mer** is a stroller's dream. Watch the fishermen unload their catch on the quay, or admire the traditional fishing boats from one of the seafront's cafés. For a chance to eat your own catch, get on board the *Mistigri-Albacore* at the crack of dawn for a day of **deep-sea fishing** (pêche au gros; ☎ 06 07 39 05 48; port de Sanary-sur-Mer; per day €170; Jul-Oct), for usually tuna and swordfish. The port is opposite the town hall.

Sanary's charismatic portside **Hôtel de la Tour** (☎ 04 94 74 10 10; www.sanary-hoteldelatour.com; 24 quai du Général de Gaulle; d incl breakfast €76-103;) has cheerful rooms, all with brilliant views, to boot. On the downside, such central location comes with a fair amount of background noise.

For a divine meal amid the vines, the recently opened **La Parenthèse de Terrebrune** (☎ 04 94 88 36 19; Domaine de Terrebrune, 724 chemin de la Tourelle, Ollioules; lunch menu €32, dinner menu €55; lunch & dinner) serves gourmet seasonal cuisine. Hurry, before Michelin stars start raining on young chef Jérôme Laffont and his wonderful cuisine becomes out of your reach.

NICE TO MENTON

THE CORNICHES

Some of the Côte d'Azur's most spectacular scenery stretches between Nice and Menton. A trio of corniches (coastal roads) hugs the cliffs between Nice and Monaco, each higher up the hill than the last. The middle corniche ends in Monaco; the upper and lower continue to Menton. (If you're in a hurry, you can take the uninspiring A8, a bit further inland.)

Corniche Inférieure

Skimming the villa-lined waterfront, the Corniche Inférieure (also known as the Basse Corniche, the Lower Corniche or the N98) sticks pretty close to the train line, passing (west to east) through Villefranche-sur-Mer, St-Jean-Cap Ferrat, Beaulieu-sur-Mer, Èze-sur-Mer and Cap d'Ail.

VILLEFRANCHE-SUR-MER

pop 6650

This picturesque pastel-coloured, terracotta-rooved fishing port overlooking the Cap Ferrat peninsula was a favourite with Jean Cocteau, who painted the frescoes in the 17th-century **Chapelle St-Pierre**. Steps split the steep cobblestone streets that weave through the old town, including the oldest, rue Obscure, an eerie vaulted passageway built in 1295. Looking down on the township is the 16th-century citadel. Beyond the port is a sandy **beach** offering picture-perfect views of the town.

ST-JEAN-CAP FERRAT

pop 2100

On the Cap Ferrat peninsula, the fishing-village-turned-playground-for-the-wealthy, St-Jean-Cap Ferrat, conceals an enclave of millionaires' villas, with illustrious residents both present and past. On the narrow isthmus of the town, the extravagant **Musée de Béatrice Ephrussi de Rothschild** (☎ 04 93 01 33 09; www.villa-ephrussi.com; adult/student €10/7.30; 10am-7pm Jul & Aug, to 6pm mid-Feb–Jun, Sep & Oct, 2-6pm Mon-Fri & 10am-6pm Sat & Sun Nov–mid-Feb) gives you an appreciation of the area's wealth. Housed in a 1912 Tuscan-style villa built for the Baroness de Rothschild, it's full of 18th-century furniture, paintings, tapestries and porcelain. A combined ticket with the Villa Grecque Kérylos in Beaulieu costs €15/10.40 for adults/students. The peninsula also has three **walking trails** with glimmering seascapes, and secluded coves for swimming.

BEAULIEU-SUR-MER

pop 3720, boats 800

Some of the best-preserved belle époque architecture along the coast is in the seaside holiday town of Beaulieu-sur-Mer, including its elaborate 1904 **rotunda** with Corinthian columns capped by a cupola. Another belle époque beauty is the **Villa Grecque Kérylos** (☎ 04 93 01 47 29; www.villa-kerylos.com; av Gustave Eiffel; adult/student €8.50/6.20; 🕑 10am-7pm Jul & Aug, to 6pm mid-Feb–Jun, Sep & Oct, 2-6pm Mon-Fri & 10am-6pm Sat & Sun Nov–mid-Feb), a reproduction of an Athenian villa built by archeologist Théodore Reinach in 1902.

Moyenne Corniche

The Moyenne Corniche – the middle coastal road (the N7) – clings to the hillside. It was here that Alfred Hitchcock filmed *To Catch a Thief*, which starred Grace Kelly. The actress met Prince Rainier of Monaco at that time, and it was here that she later lost her life in a car crash. If you want to enjoy the views, the bus to Monaco takes this road, so bag a seat on the right from Nice to Monaco (on the left in the opposite direction). From Nice, the Moyenne Corniche travels past Col de Villefranche, through Èze and to Beausoleil, the French town bordering Monte Carlo.

ÈZE

pop 2930

At the pinnacle of a 427m peak is the medieval stone village of Èze. Once occupied by Ligurians and Phoenicians, today it's home to one-off galleries and artisan boutiques within its enclosed walls (there's only one doorway in or out of the village). The high point is the **Jardin Èze** (admission €5; 🕑 9am-sunset), a slanting cliff-side garden of exotic cacti with views of the Med all the way to Corsica (on a good day).

To explore the village's nooks and crannies after the tour buses have left, donkeys can cart your luggage uphill from the car park to **Château Eza** (☎ 04 93 41 12 24; www.chateaueza.com; rue de la Pise; d from €180; ❄ ⊠), which also has a lofty gastronomic restaurant and terrace (lunch *menus* €45 to €55, dinner mains €45), with views of the Med on a plate.

On the seaside below is the village's coastal and very belle époque counterpart, Èze-sur-Mer (where U2's Bono has a villa). Èze-sur-Mer and Èze village are connected by a spectacular (and steep!) walking path, where German philosopher Friedrich Nietzsche (1844–1900) mused about the theories that formed the basis of his work *Thus Spoke Zarathustra*. Now labelled **Chemin de Nietzsche**, the rocky path takes about an hour, and in winter it's the only link without your own wheels. In summer a shuttle bus meets every train (Èze-sur-Mer is on the train line between Nice and Ventimiglia, which also stops at Monaco and Menton). Year-round, buses 82 and 112 run direct to Èze village from Nice (€1, 20 minutes). There's a helpful **tourist office** (☎ 04 93 41 26 00; www.eze-riviera.com; place du Général de Gaulle) at the base of the village.

Grande Corniche

The Grande Corniche, whose panoramas are the most dramatic of all, leaves Nice as the D2564. It passes **La Turbie** (population 3150), which sits on a promontory directly above Monaco and offers vertigo-inducing views of the principality. The best views are from the town's **Trophée des Alps** (☎ 04 93 41 20 84; cours Albert 1; adult/child €5/3.50; 🕑 10am-1.30pm & 2.30-5pm Tue-Sun Sep-May, longer in summer), one of only two Roman trophy monuments in the world (the other's in Romania), built by Augustus in 6 BC. The corniche continues to **Roquebrune** (population 12,800), a hilltop village where architect Le Corbusier is buried.

MENTON

pop 27,300

To the east of Monaco, the pastel-shaded, palm-lined seaside town of Menton is within walking distance of the Italian border.

Protected by the surrounding mountains, Menton enjoys a warm, near-subtropical climate that has made its good fortune: 19th-century European royals moved their winter residences to its shores, and Menton was Europe's biggest lemon producer until the 1930s. Production is much smaller these days but the sun-coloured fruit is celebrated every year during the February Fête de Citrons.

The town's annual 316 days of sunshine have also made it a popular retirement destination, an image that Menton's authorities have tried to shake up in the last few years. But as a visitor, Menton's staid character might actually come as a welcome break from the hustle and bustle of the rest of the coast.

FRUITY FÊTE

Since the 1930s, Menton's lemon cultivation has been embraced during its **Fête du Citron** (Lemon Festival; www.feteducitron.com). Every February, kitsch lemon-adorned floats weave processions along the seafront, accompanied by marching bands, and giant wire-framed sculptures bearing thousands of lemons fill the Jardins Biovès.

Five metric tonnes of the total 150 are used to replace fruit that rots during the course of the festival. Undamaged fruit is sold off at bargain prices out the front of the Palais de l'Europe at the end of the festival, once sculptures have been dismantled. Ironically, the lemons used for the festival come from Spain because Menton's lemons are too irregularly shaped to fit neatly on the floats.

Year-round, you can view Europe's largest variety of citrus in the gardens of the **Palais Carnolès** (☎ 04 93 35 49 71; 3 av de la Madone; admission free; 🕑 10am-noon & 2-6pm Wed-Mon). The tourist office has bucketloads of info about the town's favourite fruit.

Orientation

Promenade du Soleil runs southwest to northeast along the beach. Av Édouard VII links the train station with the beach. Av Boyer, home to the tourist office, is 350m to the east. From the station, turn left and walk along av de la Gare, then take the second right; the tourist office is about halfway down av Boyer. The bus station is approximately 500m north along av Boyer from the tourist office.

Av Boyer and its parallel to the west, av Verdun, are divided by the Jardins Biovès, an elongated sequence of parks where the annual Lemon Festival displays are held.

On and around the hill at the northeastern end of promenade du Soleil is the old town; the Vieux Port lies just beyond it.

Information

BOOKSHOPS

Librairie de la Presse (25 av Félix Faure) Stocks a fine range of guides, travel books and foreign-language newspapers.

INTERNET ACCESS

Café des Arts (☎ 04 93 35 78 67; 16 rue de la République; per hr €6; 🕑 internet access 7.30-11am & 2-8pm Mon-Sat, restaurant 7.30am-10pm Mon-Sat) Also a funky café with mains from €9 to €14.

MONEY

There are plenty of banks with exchange facilities along rue Partouneaux.

Banque Populaire Côte d'Azur (☎ 04 92 10 43 80; 31 av Félix Faure) Has an automatic exchange machine outside.

Crédit Lyonnais (☎ 04 92 41 81 11; 4 av Boyer) Two doors down from the tourist office. Has a 24-hour currency machine.

POST

Post Office (cours George V)

TOURIST INFORMATION

Service du Patrimoine (Heritage Office; ☎ 04 92 10 97 10; 24 rue St-Michel; 🕑 10am-12.30pm & 1.30-6pm Tue-Sat) Runs thematic organised tours (Jean Cocteau and Menton, artists, gardens etc) for €5 to €8 per person.

Tourist Office (☎ 04 92 41 76 76; www.menton.fr; 8 av Boyer; 🕑 9am-7pm mid-Jun–mid-Sep, 8.30am-12.30pm & 2-6pm Mon-Sat, 9am-12.30pm Sun mid-Sep–mid-Jun) In the Palais de l'Europe.

Sights & Activities

Step back in time in the peaceful **old town**, dominated by the **Basilique St-Michel** (🕑 10am-noon & 3-5.15pm Mon-Fri, 3-5.15pm Sat & Sun). The ornate, Italian-inspired early-17th-century basilica is accessed by a labyrinth of little staircases from the old town's narrow lanes.

In a seafront bastion dating from 1636, the **Musée Jean Cocteau** (☎ 04 93 57 72 30; quai Napoléon III; admission €3; 🕑 10am-noon & 2-6pm Wed-Mon) displays drawings, tapestries and mosaics by the multitalented poet, dramatist, artist and film director. You can view Cocteau's frescoes in the **Salle des Mariages** (Marriage Hall; place Ardoïno; admission €1.50; 🕑 8.30am-12.30pm & 2-5pm Mon-Fri) in the Hôtel de Ville.

Yes, Menton has a **beach**, along promenade du Soleil, and yes, it's free, but no, there's no sand, only pebbles. You'll find sandy private beaches directly north of the Vieux Port, and east of Port de Garavan, the main pleasure-boat harbour.

Sleeping

Camping Saint Michel (☎ 04 93 35 81 23; rte des Ciappes de Castellar; per 2 adults & tent €15; 🕑 Apr–mid-Oct) This two-star ground has dreamy views of town. Get here on bus 6.

Auberge de Jeunesse (☎ 04 93 35 93 14; www.fuaj.org; Plateau St-Michel; dm incl breakfast & sheets €16.20; reception 7-10am & 5-10pm, closed Nov–mid-March) Menton's HI hostel is a 1.5km hike uphill from the train station. Take the (infrequent) bus 6 to the campsite, situated 500m from the hostel.

Hôtel Richelieu (☎ 04 93 35 74 71; www.richelieu-menton.com; 26 rue Partouneaux; s €45-52, d €52-92) Many of the rooms in this central bourgeois hotel have kept beautiful period features such as grand fireplaces. The owner is a well of knowledge on the area, particularly inland and on the Mercantour national park (p858).

Hôtel Claridges (☎ 04 93 35 72 53; www.claridges-menton.com; 39 av de Verdun; s €47-52, d €56-71) This is the cheapest hotel in town, but sensitive design souls should abstain, or brace themselves for the festival of clashing patterned materials in the rooms. On the bright side, it's clean, there's free internet access and the train and bus stations are nearby.

Le Royal Westminster (☎ 04 93 28 69 69; www.vacancesbleues.com; 1510 promenade du Soleil; s €65-109, d €80-134;) This shiny 1870 building right on the promenade is part of a chain, but you wouldn't know it. Rooms are fairly bog-standard but those with sea views definitely have some 'wow' factor. It has good wheelchair access.

Eating

Menton is very popular with groups (pensioners in particular), so it's well endowed with cheerful, inexpensive restaurants. Anywhere in the old town and the centre's pedestrian streets is a good bet.

Al Vicoletto (☎ 04 93 28 18 40; Impasse Bellecour, 40 rue Partouneaux; mains €9-14; lunch & dinner) With Italy being just a hop and a skip from Menton, the Italian food in town is guaranteed to be the genuine article. This is just one example, with lots of veal on the menu and great fresh pasta.

L'Occitan (☎ 04 93 41 67 76; 7 & 11 rue des marins; 3-course lunch menu €16, mains €15; lunch & dinner Tue-Sat, lunch Sun) The southern flavours in this popular brasserie's cuisine come from the southwest (foie gras, *magret* etc), but that doesn't seem to faze southeastern residents, who love coming here on market days.

A Braijade Méridiounale (☎ 04 93 35 65 65; 66 rue longue; mains €17-25; lunch & dinner Thu-Tue Sep-Jun, dinner Jul & Aug) Unsurprisingly, lemons feature prominently on the menu of this rustic, stone-walled restaurant, found in one the old town's tiny lanes: stuffed lemons, red mullet fillet in parsley-and-lemon sauce, lemon-marinaded chicken…even the menus are yellow!

If you're planning a beach picnic, fill your basket at the old town's covered market, **Marché Municipal** (Les Halles; quai de Monléon; 5am-1pm Tue-Sun), or pop into the supermarket **8 à Huit** (7 rue Amiral Courbet; 9am-7.45pm Mon-Sat, 12.30-7.45pm Sun).

Getting There & Away

The **bus station** (☎ 04 93 28 43 27, information office 04 93 35 93 60) is next to 12 promenade Maréchal Leclerc, the northern continuation of av Boyer. Services are run by **Bus RCA** (☎ 04 93 85 64 44), and all fares cost €1 (except to Nice airport, a trip that costs €18 and takes 1½ hours): Monaco (30 minutes), Nice (1¼ hours), Ste-Agnès (45 minutes) and Sospel (45 minutes).

Trains going to Ventimiglia cost €2.30 and take around 15 minutes. For more information on train services along the Côte d'Azur, see p874.

TUM (Transports Urbains de Menton; ☎ 04 93 35 93 60) runs nine bus lines in the area. Lines 1 and 2 link the train station with the old town. Tickets cost €1.

MONACO (PRINCIPAUTÉ DE MONACO)

pop 32,000 / ☎ 377

Your first glimpse of this pocket-sized principality will probably make your heart sink: after all the gorgeous medieval hilltop villages, glittering beaches and secluded peninsulas of the surrounding area, Monaco's concrete high-rises, reclaimed land and astronomic prices might come as a shock.

But Monaco has a surprising amount to offer, much more, in fact, than the customary spin at its casino's roulette table. In its 1.95 sq km, the world's second-smallest state (a smidgen bigger than the Vatican) has managed to squeeze in a thriving performing art and sport scene (Formula One, but also a world-famous circus festival and a tennis open), a world-class aquarium, a beautiful old town, stunning gardens, interesting architecture throughout and a royal family on a par with British royals for best gossip fodder.

In terms of practicalities, Monaco is a sovereign state but there is no border control. It has its own flag (red and white), national holiday (19 November), postal system (good for the card home to grandma) and telephone country code (377), but the official language is French and the country uses the euro even though it is not part of the European Union.

History

Originally from the nearby Genoa region of Italy (hence the Monégasque language's similarity with the Genoese dialect), the Grimaldi family has ruled Monaco for most of the period since 1297, except for its occupation during the French Revolution, and its loss of territories in 1848. Its independence was again recognised by France in 1860. Five years later, a monetary agreement with France and the opening of the Monte Carlo casino revived the country's fortunes. Today there are just 7800 Monégasque citizens, by either parentage or marriage, out of a total population of 32,000 (and 107 nationalities); they live an idyllic tax-free life of cradle-to-grave security. Alas, all other residents and businesses pay tax.

Ever since the marriage of Prince Rainier III of Monaco (who ruled between 1949 and 2005) to Hollywood actress Grace Kelly, Monaco's ruling family has regularly featured in gossip magazines. Albert II, prince since his father's death in 2005, hasn't escaped media scrutiny (he has no legitimate heirs but two illegitimate children), but his achievements as an athlete (he played for the Monaco football team and is a black belt in judo), his charity work and promotion of the arts have earned him favourable press.

Orientation

Monaco is made up of six main areas: Monaco Ville (also known as the old city or Rocher de Monaco), with its narrow, medieval streets leading to the Palais du Prince (Prince's Palace) on a 60m-high outcrop of rock on the southern side of the port; the capital, Monte Carlo, which is north of the port; La Condamine, the predominantly flat area immediately to the southwest of the port; Fontvieille, the industrial area southwest of Monaco Ville; Moneghetti, the hillside suburb west of La Condamine; and Larvotto, the beach area north of Monte Carlo, from where the French town of Beausoleil is just three streets uphill.

Information

BOOKSHOPS

Scruples (☎ 93 50 43 52; 9 rue Princesse Caroline) Well-stocked English-language bookshop.

INTERNET ACCESS

Stars 'n' Bars (☎ 97 97 95 95; www.starsnbars.com; 6 quai Antoine 1er; per 15min €2.50; ⏰ 11am-midnight) There's a cybercorner and wi-fi inside this rockin' restaurant/bar (see Drinking, p904).

LAUNDRY

Laverie (1 Escalier de la Riviera, Beausoleil; ⏰ 7am-7pm)

MEDICAL SERVICES

Centre Hospitalier Princesse Grace (☎ emergency 97 98 97 69, switchboard 97 98 99 00; av Pasteur)

MONEY

Monaco-imprinted euro coins are rarely spotted in circulation, and are quickly pocketed by collectors.

There are (of course!) numerous banks near the casino. In La Condamine, you'll find banks on bd Albert 1er.

Change Bureau (Jardins du Casino; ⏰ 9am-7.30pm)

POST

Monégasque stamps must be used to post mail within Monaco and to countries beyond; rates are the same as for France. There are post office branches in each of Monaco's districts.

Post Office (1 av Henri Dunant) In Monte Carlo.

TELEPHONE

Calls between Monaco and France are international calls. Dial 00 followed by Monaco's country code (377) when calling Monaco from France or elsewhere abroad. To phone France from Monaco, dial 00 and France's country code (33), even if you're only calling from the eastern side of bd de France (in Monaco) to its western side (in France)!

TOURIST INFORMATION

Tourist Office (☎ 92 16 61 16; www.visitmonaco.com; 2a bd des Moulins; ⏰ 9am-7pm Mon-Sat, 10am-1pm Sun) Across the public gardens from the casino. From mid-June to late-September additional tourist information kiosks open around the harbour and the train station.

Sights & Activities

PALAIS DU PRINCE

At 11.55am every day, guards are changed at Monaco's **Palais du Prince** (Prince's Palace;

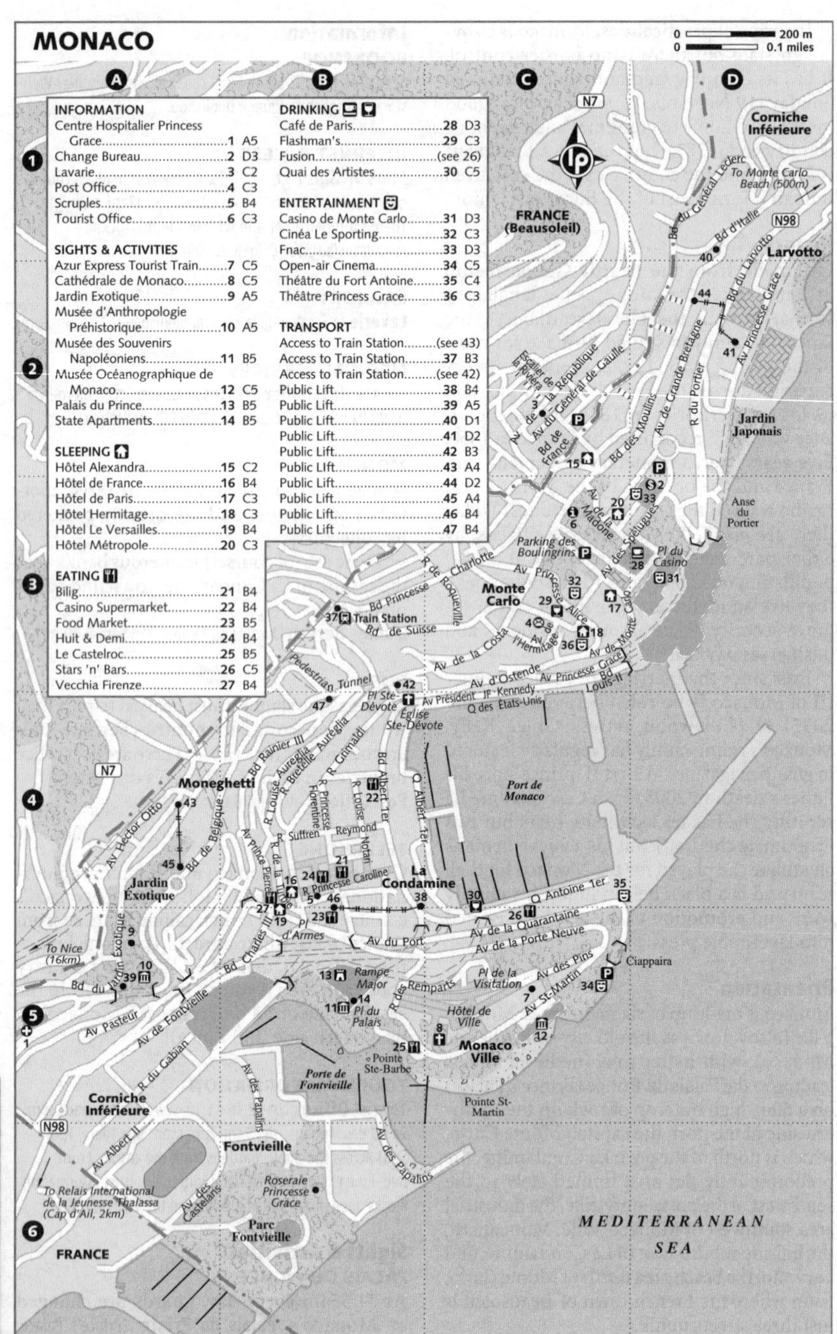
MONACO
INFORMATION
Centre Hospitalier Princess Grace....1 A5
Change Bureau....2 D3
Lavarie....3 C2
Post Office....4 C3
Scruples....5 B4
Tourist Office....6 C3
SIGHTS & ACTIVITIES
Azur Express Tourist Train....7 C5
Cathédrale de Monaco....8 C5
Jardin Exotique....9 A5
Musée d'Anthropologie Préhistorique....10 A5
Musée des Souvenirs Napoléoniens....11 B5
Musée Océanographique de Monaco....12 C5
Palais du Prince....13 B5
State Apartments....14 B5
SLEEPING
Hôtel Alexandra....15 C2
Hôtel de France....16 B4
Hôtel de Paris....17 C3
Hôtel Hermitage....18 C3
Hôtel Le Versailles....19 B4
Hôtel Métropole....20 C3
EATING
Bilig....21 B4
Casino Supermarket....22 B4
Food Market....23 B5
Huit & Demi....24 B4
Le Castelroc....25 B5
Stars 'n' Bars....26 C5
Vecchia Firenze....27 B4
DRINKING
Café de Paris....28 D3
Flashman's....29 C3
Fusion....(see 26)
Quai des Artistes....30 C5
ENTERTAINMENT
Casino de Monte Carlo....31 D3
Cinéa Le Sporting....32 C3
Fnac....33 D3
Open-air Cinema....34 C5
Théâtre du Fort Antoine....35 C4
Théâtre Princess Grace....36 C3
TRANSPORT
Access to Train Station....(see 43)
Access to Train Station....37 B3
Access to Train Station....(see 42)
Public Lift....38 B4
Public Lift....39 A5
Public Lift....40 D1
Public Lift....41 D2
Public Lift....42 B3
Public Lift....43 A4
Public Lift....44 D2
Public Lift....45 A4
Public Lift....46 B4
Public Lift....47 B4
Corniche Inférieure
To Monte Carlo Beach (500m)
FRANCE (Beausoleil)
Larvotto
Jardin Japonais
Anse du Portier
Monte Carlo
Train Station
Pedestrian Tunnel
Église Ste-Dévote
Port de Monaco
Moneghetti
Jardin Exotique
La Condamine
To Nice (16km)
Rampe Major
Pl du Palais
Hôtel de Ville
Monaco Ville
Pointe Ste-Barbe
Porte de Fontvieille
Pointe St-Martin
Ciappaira
Fontvieille
Roseraie Princesse Grace
Parc Fontvieille
To Relais International de la Jeunesse Thalassa (Cap d'Ail, 2km)
FRANCE
MEDITERRANEAN SEA

(☎ 93 25 18 31), at the southern end of rue des Remparts in Monaco Ville. For a half-hour inside glimpse into royal life, you can tour the **state apartments** (adult/child €7/3.50; ⏰ 9.30am-6.30pm May-Sep, 10.30am-6pm Apr, 10am-5.30pm Oct) with an 11-language audioguide.

A combined ticket, which also lets you view a display of Napoléon's personal effects in the southern wing of the palace at the **Musée des Souvenirs Napoléoniens** (⏰ 10.30am-5pm Dec-Mar, to 5.30pm Oct & Apr, 9.30am-6.30pm May-Sep), costs €9 (children €4.50).

MUSÉE OCÉANOGRAPHIQUE DE MONACO

Propped on a sheer cliff-face, the graceful **Musée Océanographique de Monaco** (☎ 93 15 36 00; av St-Martin; adult/student €12.50/6; ⏰ 9.30am-7pm Jul & Aug, to 6.30pm Apr-Jun & Sep, to 6pm Oct-Mar), built in 1910, houses a fantastic aquarium. There are eerie sharks and bemusing tropical fish, a tactile basin where you can touch a variety of sea creatures, and daily sessions with the aquarium's technicians to find out more about the ins and outs of running an aquarium. All signs are translated into English, Italian and German. One vast, columned floor explores the evolution of oceanography with amazing fossils and ship replicas. Even if you're not dining at the rooftop restaurant (mains €11 to €21, with lunch served from noon to 3.30pm, and a snack bar open from 9.30am to 6pm), come up for a squiz at the spectacular views.

CATHÉDRALE DE MONACO

An adoring crowd continually shuffles past Prince Rainier's and Princess Grace's graves, located on the western side of the cathedral choir of the 1875 Romanesque-Byzantine **Cathédrale de Monaco** (4 rue Colonel). Monaco's boys' choir, Les Petits Chanteurs de Monaco, sings Sunday Mass at 10am between September and June.

JARDIN EXOTIQUE

Flowering year-round, over 1000 species of cacti and succulents tumble down the slopes of the **Jardin Exotique** (☎ 93 15 29 80; 62 bd du Jardin Exotique; adult/student €6.90/3.60; ⏰ 9am-7pm mid-May–mid-Sep, 9am-6pm mid-Sep–mid-May). For non-gardeners, the main draw is undoubtedly the spectacular vistas over the principality and endless Med. Admission also includes a half-hour guided visit of the stalactites and stalagmites in the **Observatory Caves**. From the tourist office, take bus 2 to the Jardin Exotique terminus.

BEACHES

A few kilometres east of Monte Carlo, Monaco's nearest beaches are the free **Plages du Larvotto** and the €50-a-day **Monte Carlo Beach** the latter including a sun lounge, security for your accoutrements while you bathe, and parking.

Tours

A saviour from all those hills is the **Azur Express tourist train** (☎ 92 05 64 38; tour €6). Starting opposite the Musée Océanographique, multi-language, 30-minute city tours run every day from 10am to 5pm.

Festivals & Events

Brazilian triple-world champion Nelson Piquet famously likened driving Monaco's **Formula One Grand Prix** with 'riding a bicycle around your living room'. Monaco's cachet nonetheless means it's the most coveted trophy, and the narrow lanes, tortuous road layout and hairpin bends means spectators can get closer to the action than at most circuits. Trackside tickets (from about €70 standing, €270 seated) for the May event can be purchased from the Automobile Club de Monaco (www.formula1monaco.com), but get in early as demand is steeper than the near-vertical streets. If you're dead keen, you can walk the 3.2km circuit; the tourist office has maps.

Also death-defying, the **International Circus Festival of Monaco** (www.montecarlofestivals.com), held each year in late January, showcases heart-stopping acts from around the globe.

Sleeping

BUDGET

If your shoestring budget's fraying, consider basing yourself at one of Nice's hostels or budget hotels and taking the quick 20-minute train trip to Monaco. The neighbouring French town of Beausoleil is also a good hunting ground for lower-priced accommodation.

Relais International de la Jeunesse Thalassa (☎ 04 93 78 18 58; 2 av Gramaglia, Cap d'Ail; dm incl sheets €17; ⏰ closed Nov-Mar) If you're not up for the Nice–Monaco train trip, try staying at the closest hostel to Monaco, in a beautiful spot right by the sea on Cap d'Ail.

MIDRANGE

Hôtel Le Versailles (☎ 93 50 79 34; 4-6 av Prince Pierre; s €70-90, d €100-160;) Run by a gregarious family, this sun-filled hotel is good value for Monaco: refurbishment was coming to an end at the time of research and all rooms have wooden floors, simple but tasteful decor, flat screen TVs, wi-fi, and best of all, fridges to keep your grub budget.

Hôtel de France (☎ 93 30 24 64; fax 92 16 13 34; 6 rue de la Turbie; s/d/tr €80/90/108) This is the cheapest place is town, which unfortunately comes at the expense of friendly service. Centrally located in the Condamine district, you can also find nearby 24-hour parking for €7.50.

Hôtel Alexandra (☎ 93 50 63 13; fax 92 16 06 48; 35 bd Princesse Charlotte; s €100-125, d €120-160, tr €170-190;) This turn-of-the-20th-century hotel is conveniently located in Monte Carlo, close to the train stations, but its 56 spacious rooms are in need of a revamp. Breakfast is a hefty €15.

TOP END

Here are some world-famous places at which to blow your winnings.

Hôtel Hermitage (☎ 98 06 40 00; www.montecarloresort.com; sq Beaumarchais; d low season from €370, high season €460, grand prix and first two weeks of August €510;) This opulent fresco-cloistered Italianate landmark hotel with good wheelchair access features a stained-glass winter garden built by Gustave Eiffel, a sea-water swimming pool, and a gastronomic restaurant with arresting Med views serving wondrous seafood.

Hôtel Métropole (☎ 93 15 15 15; www.metropole.com; 4 av de la Madone; d low season from €400, high season €500, grand prix and first two weeks of August €590;) A sumptuously renovated 1889 palace in the heart of Monte Carlo, with black and white diamond-laid marble floors, huge walk-in showers and carpet so deep that your feet sink in. The restaurant downstairs is the playground of internationally famous Joël Rebuchon (*menus* €70 and €170, open for lunch and dinner daily).

Eating

Decently priced restaurants congregate in La Condamine along place d'Armes and rue Princesse Caroline, and there's a raft of sandwich bars and cheap eateries along quai Albert 1er. In Monte Carlo, there are a few snack stops inside the Métropole shopping centre. However, if you're living it *way* up, head to the dining rooms of the sumptuous hotels.

Bilig (☎ 97 98 20 43; 11bis rue Princesse Caroline; mains €6-12; 11am-6pm Mon-Sat winter, to 10pm summer) A small café serving big portions of wonderful salads, tasty crêpes and the odd meat dish or two on a pretty sundeck.

Vecchia Firenze (☎ 93 30 27 70; 4-6 av Prince Pierre; mains €12-27; lunch & dinner Tue-Fri, dinner Sat) This Italian brasserie is run by the same family as at Hôtel Le Versailles. The pasta and pizza could not be more authentic and there is seldom French spoken inside the art deco glasshouse.

Huit & Demi (☎ 93 50 97 02; cnr rue Langlé & rue Princesse Caroline; mains €13-27; noon-3pm & 7-11pm Mon-Fri, 7-11pm Sat) Very chic and very popular. You can savour your Italian fare indoors amid crimson-coloured walls lined with celebrity B&W portraits, or on the street-side terrace from February to December, when the sun is shining.

Le Castelroc (☎ 93 30 36 68; place du Palais; mains €22-27; 9am-3pm daily, dinner Tue-Sat May-Sep) Right across from the palace, and behind the souvenir stalls, hides the authentic Le Castelroc. Its alfresco terrace is the perfect place to try genuine Monégasque specialities like *barbajuan* (a beignet filled with spinach and cheese) and *cundyun* (Monaco's version of *salade niçoise*).

SELF-CATERING

Pit stops for self-catering include a **food market** (place d'Armes; 7am-2pm) and a **Casino Supermarket** (bd Albert 1er), both in La Condamine. The principality's parks have plenty of benches for picnicking.

Drinking

Café de Paris (☎ 98 06 76 23; place du Casino; mains €17-53; 7am-2am) Adjacent to the opulent Monte Carlo Casino, this is a fabulous spot for a classy lunch or a decadent coffee with liqueur and pastry whilst limo-spotting from the sprawling 300-seat terrace.

Stars 'n' Bars (☎ 97 97 95 95; 6 quai Antoine 1er; mains €14.50-22; noon-2.30am Tue-Sun) Any star worth his or her reputation has partied at this American western saloon: check out the gazillion pictures of in-situ celebrities and admire the Grand Prix paraphernalia while you tuck into humongous burgers and wash the lot down with bottled beers or heavy-duty cocktails.

Fusion (☎ 97 97 95 95; 6 quai Antoine 1er; mains €15-25; 7pm-2.30am Mon-Sat) A self-proclaimed specialist in 'mixology', Fusion's cocktails are priced on a par with its Asian food, ie expensive. However, it gets points for removing the endangered red tuna off its menu and for the slightly surreal cruise liner–like interior.

Quai des Artistes (☎ 97 97 97 77; 4 quai Antoine 1er; mains €15-35; ⏰ noon-1am) Another themed portside restaurant/cocktail bar, this time devoted to acting's noble form – theatre. Fancy seafood platters and drinks are served under massive chandeliers, pictures of actors on stage and puppets in stage costumes.

Entertainment

Pack your evening wear for concerts, opera and ballet, which are held at various venues. The tourist office has a schedule of local events. Tickets for most cultural events are sold at **fnac** (☎ 93 10 81 81; Centre Commercial le Métropole, 17 av des Spélugues).

Flashman's (☎ 93 30 09 03; 7 av Princesse Alice; ⏰ 8am-5am Mon & Wed-Fri, 7pm-5am Sat & Sun) The retro American diner–style decor with fluoro lights and chrome counter is rather funky at night. If you're not up for a boogie, there's a small outdoor booth in which to chill out.

CASINOS

Living out your James Bond fantasies just doesn't get any better than at Monte Carlo's monumental, richly decorated showpiece, the 1910-built **Casino de Monte Carlo** (☎ 98 06 21 21; www.casinomontecarlo.com; place du Casino; ⏰ European Rooms from noon Sat & Sun, from 2pm Mon-Fri). You have to pay even before you play: admission is €10 for the European Rooms, with poker/slot machines, French roulette and *trente et quarante* (a card game), and €20 for the Private Rooms, which offer baccarat, blackjack, craps and American roulette. The jacket-and-tie dress code kicks in after 10pm.

Minimum entry age for both types of rooms is 18; bring photo ID.

CINEMAS

Cinéma Le Sporting (☎ 08 36 68 00 72; place du Casino; adult/student €9/6.50) often has movies in their original language. An **open-air cinema** (parking des Pêcheurs; adult/student €10/7) has nightly shows from June to September, specialising in crowd-pleasing blockbusters, mostly in English.

THEATRE

The 18th-century fortress-turned–outdoor theatre, **Théâtre du Fort Antoine** (☎ 93 50 80 00; av de la Quarantaine; ⏰ plays 9pm Mon Jul & Aug), is a great spot to while away a summer evening.

In winter, Monte Carlo's **Théâtre Princesse Grace** (☎ 93 25 32 27; www.tpgmonaco.com; 12 av d'Ostende; tickets €27-42), designed by the late princess, stages anything from magic shows to gospel music and comedy.

Getting There & Away

BUS

Buses to France leave from various stops around the city; the tourist office has schedules and maps.

CAR & MOTORCYCLE

Some 25 official paying car parks are scattered around the principality. One of the most convenient is the Parking des Boulingrins under the casino, from where you exit next to the tourist office. The first hour is free; the next six hours costs €2.40 per hour, and it's €0.80 per hour beyond that.

If you're driving (not really necessary in this compact little country), note that you can't take your car into Monaco Ville unless you have either a Monaco or a 06 (Alpes-Maritimes) licence plate.

TRAIN

Trains to and from Monaco's **train station** (av Prince Pierre) are run by the French SNCF.

A train trip along the coast offers mesmerising views of the Mediterranean Sea and the mountains. There are frequent trains to Nice (€3.20, 20 minutes), and east to Menton (€1.80, 10 minutes), and to the first town across the border in Italy, Ventimiglia (€3.20, 20 minutes).

Getting Around

BUS

Several urban bus lines traverse Monaco; bus 4 links the train station with the tourist office and also with the casino. Tickets cost €1.

LIFTS

About 15 *ascenseurs publics* (public lifts) whisk you up and down the hillsides. Most operate 24 hours; others run between 6am and midnight or 1am.

TAXI

Expect to pay around €14 for a 10-minute taxi ride. To order one, call ☎ 04 93 15 01 01.

Corsica

Kallisté to the Greeks, Corse to the French, and 'La Montagne en Mer' (mountain in the sea) to the island's more poetically minded inhabitants, the mysterious island of Corsica goes under many sobriquets. But there's one that sums up the island in a nutshell – the *île de beauté* (beautiful island). Crowned by sawtooth peaks, mantled in forest cloaks of green oak, chestnut and pine, and shot through with rushing rivers and tumbling cascades, it's one of the most dramatic, diverse and downright gorgeous islands in the Mediterranean.

Officially a part of France, and yet fiercely proud of its own culture, history and language, Corsica has long had a love-hate relationship with the mainland: you'll see plenty of anti-French slogans on the walls, and French-language road signs are an enduring target for nationalist spray-cans. Despite the political posturing and its reputation for aloofness, Corsica has long hosted a hotchpotch of cultures: everyone from ancient Greeks to Genoese settlers has helped shape the island's history, and you can still feel the cultural melting pot at work today.

While most people make a beeline for the glittering bays, glitzy ports and bone-white beaches around the 1000km coastline, Corsica's mountainous interior is where you'll find the island's rugged heart and soul. Shrouded in dense shrubs, gnarled trees and unruly scrubland known as the maquis (whose wild herbs flavour the island's cheeses and charcuterie), Corsica's mountains and pastures were traditionally the preserve of bandits and *bergers* (shepherds). But today, the high-altitude trails are more often frequented by trekkers: the GR20 hike cuts down the island's spine through an otherworldly landscape of peaks, forests, waterfalls and shimmering mountain lakes. Prepare to be dazzled by France's diamond in the rough.

HIGHLIGHTS

- Discover your own pocket-sized island paradise for a day on the **Îles Lavezzi** (p934)
- Ponder the architectural ambitions of ancestors at **Filitosa** (p932) and **Alignement de Paddaghiu** (p932)
- Explore the remote peninsula of **Cap Corse** (p914) by way of winding coastal roads
- Cruise the sapphire waters of the **Réserve Naturelle de Scandola** (Scandola Nature Reserve; p922)
- Wander the backstreets and bask on the beaches around **Bonifacio** (p932)
- Bone up on your Bonaparte around Napoléon's hometown, **Ajaccio** (p926)

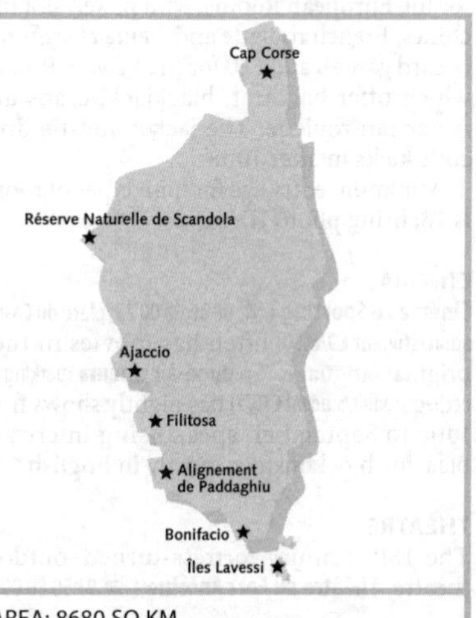

- POPULATION: 260,150
- AREA: 8680 SQ KM

History

From the 11th to 13th centuries Corsica was ruled by the Italian city-state of Pisa, superseded in 1284 by its arch-rival, Genoa. To prevent seaborne raids, a massive system of coastal citadels and watchtowers was constructed, many of which still ring the coastline.

In 1755, after 25 years of sporadic warfare against the Genoese, Corsicans declared their independence, led by Pascal Paoli (1725–1807). Under Paoli's rule they established a National Assembly and founded the most democratic constitution in Europe. They also adopted *La Tête de Maure* (the Moor's Head) – a profile of a black head wearing a white bandanna and a hooped earring, which first appeared in Corsica in 1297 – as a national emblem. According to legend, the bandanna originally covered the Moor's eyes, and was raised to the forehead to symbolise the island's liberation.

Corsicans made the inland town of Corte their capital, outlawed vendettas and established a university, but the island's independence was short-lived. In 1768 the Genoese ceded Corsica to Louis XV, whose troops crushed Paoli's army in 1769. The island has since been part of France, except for 1794–96, when it was briefly under English domination, and during the Axis occupation of 1940–43.

Corsicans have long cared for their island's ecology. In 1972 the formation of the Parc Naturel Régional de Corse (PNRC) protected more than a third (3505 sq km) of the island.

The 1998 assassination of Corsica's *préfet* (prefect; the State's representative), Claude Erignac, in Ajaccio, rocked Corsica. In 2001, the French parliament granted Corsica limited autonomy in exchange for an end to separatist violence. The bill was later overturned by the French high court because it threatened the principal of national unity.

Despite ongoing media coverage, relatively few Corsicans support the separatist Front de Libération Nationale de la Corse (FLNC). In 2003 a long-awaited referendum, which would have united the island's two *départements* (administrative divisions of France) of Haute-Corse and Corse-du-Sud, and granted the island greater autonomy, was rejected despite a nail-biting electoral race. Nevertheless, the nationalist issue remains a burning topic: several FLNC bombs exploded across the island in 2005, and in December of 2007 the militant nationalist Yvan Colonna was sentenced to life imprisonment for the assassination of Claude Erignac nine years earlier. Typically for a Corsican, after five years on the run he was discovered hiding out in a shepherd's hut.

Internet Resources

Corse Matin (www.corsematin.com) The island's daily newspaper.

Gites de France Corse (www.gites-corsica.com) Rural *gîtes* (cottages for rent) and *chambres d'hôtes* (B&Bs) on the island.

Parc Naturel Régional de Corse (www.parc-naturel-corse.com, in French) Official site for the natural park.

Visit Corsica (www.visit-corsica.com) Main tourism portal, with practical info and accommodation details.

Getting There & Away

AIR

Corsica's main airports are at Ajaccio, Bastia, Figari (near Bonifacio) and Calvi.

Air France (☎ 08 20 82 08 20; www.airfrance.com) and **Compagnie Corse Méditerranée** (CCM; ☎ 08 20 82 08 20; www.aircorsica.com) collectively provide year-round flights from Paris, Marseille, Lyon and Nice to all of Corsica's airports, with seasonal flights from Bordeaux, Lille, Nantes, Mulhouse, Strasbourg, Clermont-Ferrand and Brest to Bastia, Ajaccio and occasionally Figari.

British Airways (☎ in France 08 25 82 54 00, ☎ in UK 0844 493 0 787; www.ba.com) has seasonal flights from London to Ajaccio, Bastia and Figari; there are also summer charter flights from other regional airports in the UK.

BOAT

Mainland France

Several companies run between the French mainland and Corsica's main ferry ports (Ajaccio, Bastia, Calvi, Île Rousse, Porto-Vecchio and Propriano):

Corsica Ferries (☎ France 08 25 09 50 95; www.corsicaferries.com) Year-round from Nice to Ajaccio, Bastia, Calvi and Île Rousse, and from Toulon to Ajaccio, Bastia and Île Rousse.

La Méridionale/CMN (☎ France 08 10 20 13 20; www.cmn.fr) This Société Nationale Maritime Corse-Méditerranée subsidiary has year-round sailings between Marseille and Ajaccio, Bastia and Propriano.

Société Nationale Maritime Corse-Méditerranée (SNCM; ☎ 08 91 70 18 01; www.sncm.fr) Year-round ferries from Nice and Marseille to all of Corsica's ports, plus high-speed *navettes à grandes vitesses* (NGVs) from Nice to Ajaccio and Île Rousse in summer.

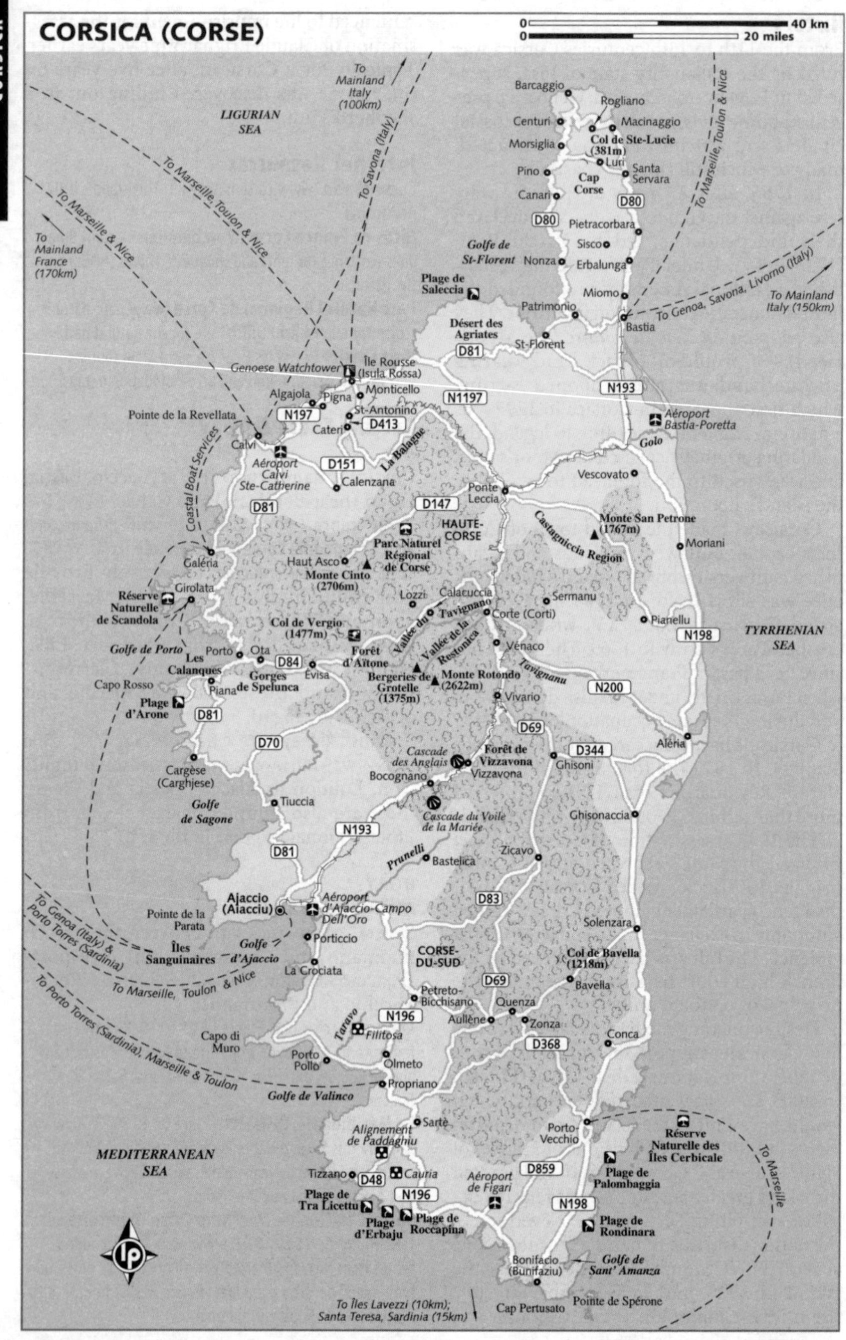
CORSICA (CORSE)
0 40 km
0 20 miles
LIGURIAN SEA
TYRRHENIAN SEA
MEDITERRANEAN SEA
To Mainland Italy (100km)
To Mainland France (170km)
To Mainland Italy (150km)
To Marseille, Toulon & Nice
To Marseille & Nice
To Savona (Italy)
To Genoa, Savona, Livorno (Italy)
To Genoa (Italy) & Porto Torres (Sardinia)
To Marseille, Toulon & Nice
To Porto Torres (Sardinia), Marseille & Toulon
To Marseille
To Îles Lavezzi (10km); Santa Teresa, Sardinia (15km)
Coastal Boat Services
Barcaggio
Rogliano
Centuri
Macinaggio
Morsiglia
Col de Ste-Lucie (381m)
Luri
Pino
Santa Servara
Cap Corse
Canari
Pietracorbara
Sisco
Golfe de St-Florent
Nonza
Erbalunga
Miomo
Plage de Saleccia
Patrimonio
Bastia
Désert des Agriates
St-Florent
Genoese Watchtower
Île Rousse (Isula Rossa)
Algajola
Pigna
Monticello
St-Antonino
Cateri
Pointe de la Revellata
Calvi
Aéroport Calvi Ste-Catherine
Calenzana
La Balagne
Aéroport Bastia-Poretta
Golo
Vescovato
Ponte Leccia
HAUTE-CORSE
Parc Naturel Régional de Corse
Castagniccia Region
Monte San Petrone (1767m)
Moriani
Galéria
Haut Asco
Monte Cinto (2706m)
Girolata
Réserve Naturelle de Scandola
Lozzi
Calacuccia
Sermanu
Corte (Corti)
Pianellu
Col de Vergio (1477m)
Vallée du Tavignano
Vallée de la Restonica
Golfe de Porto
Les Calanques
Porto
Ota
Forêt d'Aïtone
Vénaco
Gorges de Spelunca
Évisa
Bergeries de Grotelle (1375m)
Monte Rotondo (2622m)
Tavignanu
Capo Rosso
Piana
Plage d'Arone
Vivario
Aléria
Cascade des Anglais
Forêt de Vizzavona
Vizzavona
Ghisoni
Cargèse (Carghjese)
Bocognano
Tiuccia
Cascade du Voile de la Mariée
Golfe de Sagone
Ghisonaccia
Prunelli
Bastelica
Zicavo
Ajaccio (Aiacciu)
Aéroport d'Ajaccio-Campo Dell'Oro
Pointe de la Parata
Solenzara
Îles Sanguinaires
Golfe d'Ajaccio
Porticcio
CORSE-DU-SUD
Col de Bavella (1218m)
La Crociata
Bavella
Petreto-Bicchisano
Quenza
Aullène
Zonza
Taravo
Filitosa
Capo di Muro
Conca
Porto Pollo
Olmeto
Propriano
Golfe de Valinco
Sartè
Porto Vecchio
Alignement de Paddaghiu
Réserve Naturelle des Îles Cerbicale
Tizzano
Cauria
Aéroport de Figari
Plage de Palombaggia
Plage de Tra Licettu
Plage d'Erbaju
Plage de Roccapina
Plage de Rondinara
Bonifacio (Bunifaziu)
Golfe de Sant' Amanza
Cap Pertusato
Pointe de Spérone
D80
D81
N1197
N193
N197
D413
D151
D147
D84
N198
N200
D69
D344
D70
D83
N196
D368
D859
D48

TAMING THE TREMBLER

Famous among trainspotters and railway fanatics, Corsica's venerable single-track railway, the **Chemins de Fer de Corse (CFC)**, has been clattering its way around the island for over a century, traversing a network of 32 tunnels and 76 bridges and viaducts (including one designed by a certain Gustave Eiffel). The first CFC line opened for business in 1888, an engineering marvel on an island still largely reliant on mules for transport – although even in its heyday it was never renowned for its reliability, smoothness or punctuality (the train was affectionately dubbed *'U Trinighellu'* – 'The Trembler' – and impromptu stops for sheep, goats and cows were a regular occurrence). But change is afoot even for this most hallowed Corsican institution: the old TGV (*train à grand vibration*) and its vintage *micheline* carriages are being phased out in favour of smoother, more efficient and altogether less characterful trains – good for journey times, not so good for trainspotters. But CFC bosses insist that some of the old cars will be retained for posterity, and for the moment, the **Tramway de la Balagne** (see p921) has resisted the relentless urge for modernisation…

The quickest NGVs from Nice take about three hours, with normal ferries taking between four and five hours; ferries from Marseille and Toulon take between eight and 10 hours depending on your destination port. There can be as many as 10 boats a day in the high season, dropping to a single daily sailing in winter: reservations are essential in summer. In bad weather, boats can be cancelled at very short notice (often on the day of departure).

The fare structure varies depending on your route. Fares are broadly similar for all three main companies, starting at around €20 and rising to around €70 per person, with various discounts offered throughout the year. Private cabins will set you back €54 to €159, or you'll pay €17 to €23 for a shared-berth cabin. Vehicles cost between €44 and €156; bikes costs a flat €3. Remember to factor in taxes of €7 to €12 per person, plus €5 to €10 per vehicle.

Italy

Between April and October, ferries link Corsica with the Italian ports of Genoa, Livorno and Savona, and Porto Torres on Sardinia. Fares vary depending on the crossing time and route, with one-way trips starting as low as €10 per adult. It costs around €35 to transport a small car (add €18 to €25 for taxes).

Operators on the island include the following:

Corsica Ferries (☎ Livorno 0586 88 13 80, Savona 019 215 62 47) Livorno to Bastia (April to early November) and from Savona to Bastia, Calvi and Île Rousse (April to September).

La Méridionale/CMN (☎ France 08 10 20 13 20; www.cmn.fr) Ferries (April to October) between Porto Torres (Sardinia) and Propriano and Ajaccio.

Moby Lines (☎ Corsica 04 95 34 84 94, Genoa 010 254 15 13, Livorno 0565 93 61; www.mobylines.it) Ferries (May to September) from Genoa and Livorno to Bastia, plus small ferries from Santa Teresa di Gallura (Sardinia) to Bonifacio from April to September.

Getting Around

BUS

Travelling around Corsica by bus can be hard work, as there are a multitude of companies and (except in summer) buses rarely run on Sundays. **Eurocorse** (☎ Ajaccio 04 95 21 06 30, Bastia 04 95 31 73 76) handles the main intercity routes.

There's a useful online resource for bus timetables at www.corsicabus.org – although as it's run by a private enthusiast, updates can be a little erratic.

CAR & MOTORCYCLE

Driving is the most convenient way to explore Corsica, but navigating its narrow, twisting roads is not easy (take particular care on the treacherous coast road between Calvi, Porto and Les Calanques). A good road map is indispensable – Michelin's 1:150,000 *Corsica* (Map No #345) or IGN's 1:250,000 *Regional Touring Map to Corsica* (Map #R19) are both excellent, or there are a number of alternatives available on the island.

TRAIN

Corsica's railway system is operated by **Chemins de Fer de Corse** (CFC; ☎ Bastia 04 95 32 80 61; www.ter-sncf.com/corse, in French) The two lines meet at Ponte Leccia: the Bastia–Corte–Ajaccio line is served by four daily trains, with two connections from Ponte Leccia to Calvi via Île Rousse. Services are greatly reduced in winter and on public holidays.

Under 12s travel half-price; under fours (and, bizarrely, dogs in a basket) travel free. Return journeys of more than 200km qualify for a 25% discount (known as the *billet touristique*), or 10% for journeys of more than 75km in summer. There are also discounts for Société Nationale des Chemins de Fer Français (SNCF) family ticket-holders (between 30% and 70%) and InterRail travellers (50%). The CFC sells its own rail pass – the Carte Zoom – which costs €48 for seven days' unlimited train travel.

BASTIA AREA

BASTIA

pop 37,800

Tucked into the island's northeastern corner, the bustling old port of Bastia is many people's first glimpse of Corsica. However, surprisingly few visitors take the time to explore this dynamic little city, put off by its hectic traffic, peeling paintwork and ramshackle tenement blocks. And that's a shame: while Bastia might not measure up to the sexy style of Ajaccio or the architectural appeal of Bonifacio, in many ways it's a more authentic snapshot of modern-day Corsica, a lived-in, well-loved city that's resisted the urge to polish up its image just to please the tourists. Narrow alleyways climb from the old harbour to the 16th-century citadel, which was the former seat of the town's Genoese governors, and is presently the site of one of the largest (and costliest) renovation projects in the island's history.

Orientation

Place St-Nicolas is the central hub. The train station is northwest along av Maréchal Sébastiani; west are the city's main shopping streets, bd Paoli and rue César Campinchi. The city's three older neighbourhoods are south of place St-Nicolas: Terra Vecchia (centred on place de l'Hôtel de Ville), the Vieux Port (Old Port) and the citadel.

Information

BOOKSHOPS

Librairie Album (☎ 04 95 31 08 59; 19 bd Paoli; ⏰ 8am-noon & 1.30-7.30pm Mon-Sat, 9am-12.30pm Sun) Big bookshop with an excellent travel section.

Librairie-Papeterie Papi (☎ 04 95 31 00 96; 5 rue César Campinchi; ⏰ 7.30am-noon & 1.30-7pm Mon-Sat) Sells walking maps, topoguides and travel books.

EMERGENCY

Centre Hospitalier Général Paese Nuovo (☎ 04 95 59 11 11; Rue Impériale) Located south of town.

Police Nationale (☎ 04 95 54 50 22; av Paul Giacobbi) Near the northern ferry terminal.

INTERNET ACCESS

Oxy Cyber Café (☎ 06 84 76 11 65; 1 rue Salvatore Viale; per hr €3.10; ⏰ 10am-2am Mon-Sat, 1pm-2am Sun)

LAUNDRY

Le Lavoir du Port (⏰ 7am-9pm) In the car park near the end of rue du Commandant Luce de Casabianca.

MONEY

Most of the big French banks are dotted along place St-Nicolas, rue César Campinchi and rue du Conventionnel Salicetti. Most have ATMs.

POST

Post Office (av Maréchal Sébastiani; ⏰ 8am-7pm Mon-Fri, 8am-noon Sat)

TOURIST INFORMATION

Tourist Office (☎ 04 95 54 20 40; www.bastia-tourisme.com; place St-Nicolas; ⏰ 8am-8pm Mon-Sat, 9am-noon & 4-7pm Sun Jul & Aug, 8.30am-noon & 2-6pm Mon-Sat, 9.30am-1pm Sun Apr-Jun, Sep & Oct, 8.30am-noon & 2-6pm Mon-Fri, 8.30am-noon Sun Nov-Mar) Multilingual tourist office in a hut on place St-Nicholas.

Sights

Even by Corsican standards, Bastia is a pocket-sized city, and you can tick off the main sights in an afternoon. The 19th-century square of **place St-Nicholas** sprawls along the seafront between the ferry port and the harbour. Named after the patron saint of sailors – a nod to Corsica's seagoing heritage – the square is lined with plane trees and busy cafés, as well as a **statue of Napoléon Bonaparte** depicted as a cross between a Grecian warrior-hero and a pumped-up bodybuilder.

A network of narrow lanes leads south towards the old port and the neighbourhood of **Terra Vecchia**, a muddle of crumbling apartments and balconied blocks. The shady **place de l'Hôtel de Ville** hosts Bastia's lively morning market from Tuesday to Saturday.

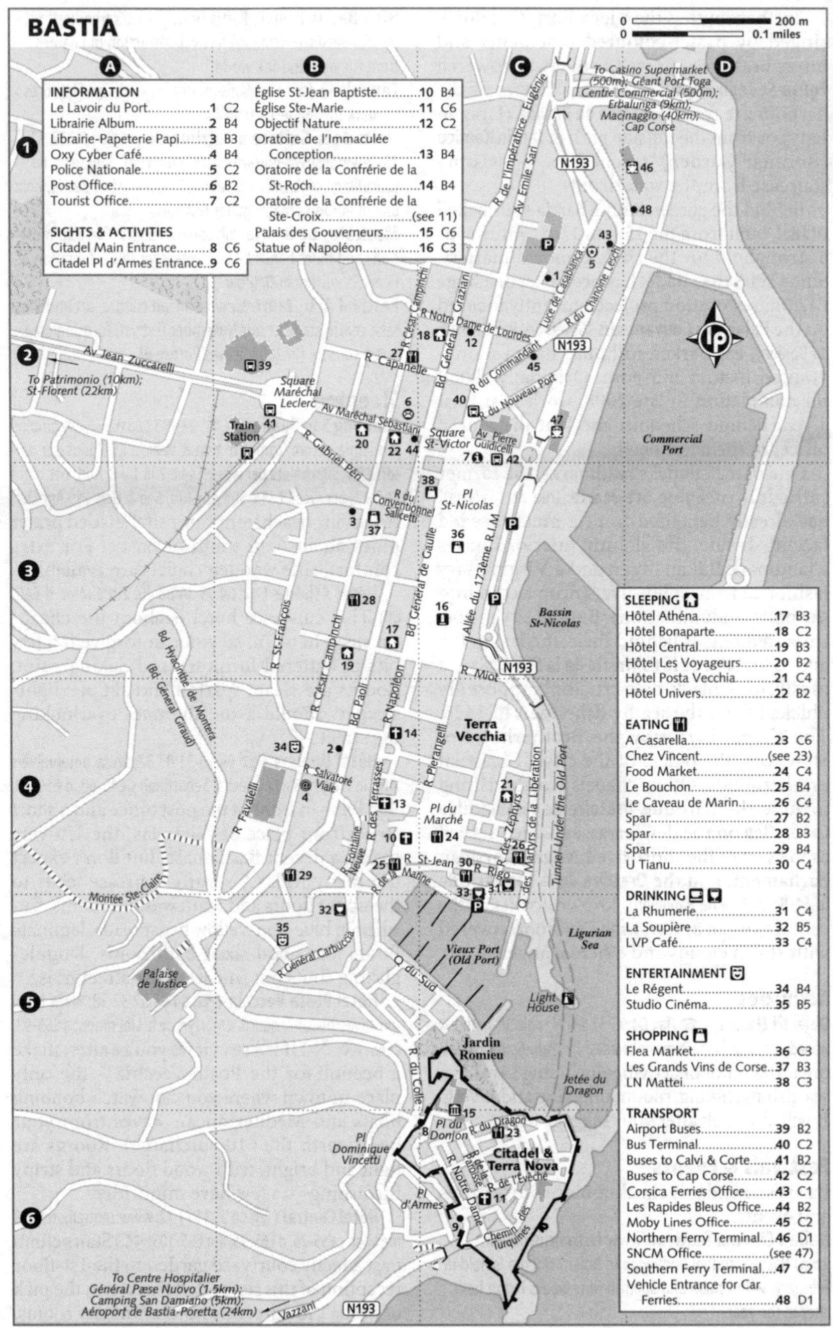
BASTIA
0 200 m
0 0.1 miles
INFORMATION
Le Lavoir du Port 1 C2
Librairie Album 2 B4
Librairie-Papeterie Papi 3 B3
Oxy Cyber Café 4 B4
Police Nationale 5 C2
Post Office 6 B2
Tourist Office 7 C2
SIGHTS & ACTIVITIES
Citadel Main Entrance 8 C6
Citadel Pl d'Armes Entrance 9 C6
Église St-Jean Baptiste 10 B4
Église Ste-Marie 11 C6
Objectif Nature 12 C2
Oratoire de l'Immaculée Conception 13 B4
Oratoire de la Confrérie de la St-Roch 14 B4
Oratoire de la Confrérie de la Ste-Croix (see 11)
Palais des Gouverneurs 15 C6
Statue of Napoléon 16 C3
SLEEPING
Hôtel Athéna 17 B3
Hôtel Bonaparte 18 C2
Hôtel Central 19 B3
Hôtel Les Voyageurs 20 B2
Hôtel Posta Vecchia 21 C4
Hôtel Univers 22 B2
EATING
A Casarella 23 C6
Chez Vincent (see 23)
Food Market 24 C4
Le Bouchon 25 B4
Le Caveau de Marin 26 C4
Spar 27 B2
Spar 28 B3
Spar 29 B4
U Tianu 30 C4
DRINKING
La Rhumerie 31 C4
La Soupière 32 B5
LVP Café 33 C4
ENTERTAINMENT
Le Régent 34 B4
Studio Cinéma 35 B5
SHOPPING
Flea Market 36 C3
Les Grands Vins de Corse 37 B3
LN Mattei 38 C3
TRANSPORT
Airport Buses 39 B2
Bus Terminal 40 C2
Buses to Calvi & Corte 41 B2
Buses to Cap Corse 42 C2
Corsica Ferries Office 43 C1
Les Rapides Bleus Office 44 B2
Moby Lines Office 45 C2
Northern Ferry Terminal 46 D1
SNCM Office (see 47)
Southern Ferry Terminal 47 C2
Vehicle Entrance for Car Ferries 48 D1
To Casino Supermarket (500m); Géant Port Toga Centre Commercial (500m); Erbalunga (9km); Macinaggio (40km); Cap Corse
To Patrimonio (10km); St-Florent (22km)
To Centre Hospitalier Général Pæse Nuovo (1.5km); Camping San Damiano (5km); Aéroport de Bastia-Poretta (24km)
Av Jean Zuccarelli
Square Maréchal Leclerc
Train Station
Av Maréchal Sébastiani
R Gabriel Péri
Square St-Victor
Av Pierre Guidicelli
Pl St-Nicolas
R du Conventionnel Salicetti
R César Campinchi
Bd Général Graziani
R Notre Dame de Lourdes
R Capanelle
R du Commandant
R du Nouveau Port
R de l'Impératrice Eugénie
Av Emile Sari
Luce de Casabianca
R du Chanoine Leschi
Commercial Port
Bassin St-Nicolas
Allée du 173ème R.I.M
Bd Général de Gaulle
R Miot
Terra Vecchia
R St-François
Bd Hyacinthe de Montera (Bd Général Giraud)
Bd Paoli
R Napoléon
R Pierangeli
R Salvatore Viale
R Favatelli
R des Terrasses
R Fontaine Neuve
Pl du Marché
R St-Jean
R de la Marine
R Rigo
R des Zéphyrs
Q des Martyrs de la Libération
Tunnel Under the Old Port
Montée Ste-Claire
R Général Carbuccia
Q du Sud
Vieux Port (Old Port)
Ligurian Sea
Light House
Palais de Justice
Jardin Romieu
R du Colle
Jetée du Dragon
Pl du Donjon
R du Dragon
Pl Dominique Vincetti
Citadel & Terra Nova
R de la Paroisse
R Notre Dame
R de l'Évêché
Pl d'Armes
Chemin des Turquines
Vazzani
N193

Further south is the Vieux Port (Old Port), ringed by pastel-coloured tenements and buzzy brasseries, as well as the twin-towered **Église St-Jean Baptiste**. The best views of the harbour are from the **Jetée du Dragon** (Dragon Jetty) or from the hillside park of **Jardin Romieu** (Romieu Garden) reached via a twisting staircase from the waterfront.

Behind the garden looms Bastia's sunbaked **citadel**, built from the 15th to 17th centuries as a stronghold for the city's Genoese masters. Since 2005 the citadel has been part of a huge €12.5m restoration project, currently focused on the **Palais des Gouverneurs** (Governors' Palace; place du Donjon), earmarked to house Bastia's long-awaited history museum. Originally slated for completion in late 2008, work is at least a year behind schedule; check at the tourist office for the latest news.

One of the citadel's landmarks, the former cathedral of **Église Ste-Marie** (rue de l'Évêché), has already benefited from a much-needed facelift. Inside, the gloomy interior houses a landmark Italian organ and a Virgin Mary fashioned from solid silver (drop a coin into the box for illumination). But the city's most treasured relic is behind the cathedral in the gilded **Oratoire de la Confrérie de la Ste-Croix** – a mysterious black-oak crucifix supposedly plucked from the sea by fishermen in 1428. The chapel is run by the Brotherhood of Ste-Croix, the oldest of the city's Christian brotherhoods. Other chapels worth visiting include the baroque **Oratoire de l'Immaculée Conception** on rue des Terrasses, which served as the seat of the short-lived Anglo-Corsican parliament, and the **Oratoire de la Confrérie de la St-Roch** (rue de Napoléon), known for its 18th-century organ and *trompe l'œil* roof, covered with storm clouds and ethereal angels.

Activities

Objectif Nature (☎/fax 04 95 32 54 34; objectif-nature@wanadoo.fr; 3 rue Notre Dame de Lourdes; 🕑 9am-6pm Mon-Sat) organises outdoor activities including kayaking, sea-fishing, hiking, mountaineering and diving. It will also look after your luggage for €3.

Festivals & Events

Bastia's calendar is chock-a-bloc with festivals and events.

Italian Cinema Festival (www.festivalcineitalien.com) Bastia's annual *hommage* to Italian cinema is held in February, with British and Spanish film-weeks being held later in the year.

BD à Bastia In April, Bastia hosts France's trendiest *bandes dessinées* (comics) festival, attracting big names from the pen-and-ink world.

Feux de la St-Jean Midsummer fireworks and bonfires to mark the longest day in June.

Nuits de la Guitare à Patrimonio (☎ 04 95 37 12 15; www.festival-guitare-patrimonio.com) July sees the tiny village of Patrimonio, about 10km west of Bastia, host one of Europe's major guitar festivals.

Musicales de Bastia Polyphonic singers, Corsican musicians and blues bands fill the streets for this celebration of Corsican culture in October.

Festival Arte-Maré Mediterranean culture, art and films take centre stage at this November festival, focusing on a guest country (in 2008, it was Portugal).

Sleeping

Camping San Damiano (☎ 04 95 33 68 02; www.campingsandamiano.com; campsite tent & vehicle €5-7 plus per person €5-7.50, chalets per week €441-798 Jul & Aug, per night €45-72, per week €315-504 Apr-Jun, Sep & Oct; 🕑 Apr-Oct) An idyllic beachfront campsite, shaded under pines about 6km south of Bastia. For extra comfort, cute wooden chalets are available.

Hôtel Athéna (☎ 04 95 34 88 40; 2 rue Miot; d €40-60) This cut-price hotel is about the cheapest sleep in town, so you can forgive it a few bits of battered furniture and flaking paint. Rooms are clean, spartan and simple: light-sleepers should avoid the ones overlooking the street.

Hôtel Univers (☎ 04 95 31 03 38; www.hotelunivers.org, in French; 3 av Maréchal Sébastiani; s €45-60, d €50-70; ❄) Bang in front of the post office and a short stroll from place St-Nicholas, the Univers makes a decent Bastia base, but don't expect too many frills. A scruffy staircase leads to the upper floors and whitewashed rooms, finished in blue-and-yellow bedspreads, laminate floors and good-sized bathrooms. Double-glazing shuts out (most) of the street noise.

Hôtel Posta Vecchia (☎ 04 95 32 32 38; www.hotel-postavecchia.com; quai des Martyrs de la Libération; d €55-92, f €65-100; ❄) If it's sea views you're after, make a beeline for the Posta Vecchia – the only place in town where you can watch bobbing boats and Mediterranean waves from your bed (worth the €10 surcharge). Rooms are light and bright, with wood floors and stripy furnishings – a few have minifridges.

Hôtel Central (☎ 04 95 31 71 12; www.centralhotel.fr; 3 rue Miot; s €55-75, d €65-95, apt €85-105; ❄) Stairs climb past a teeny courtyard garden to the 1st-floor reception of this renovated tenement, the pick of Bastia's town-centre hotels. Unfussy rooms, most with timber floors, checks and nautical pictures, are dotted around the corridors: a €10 supplement buys a titchy balcony above the garden, or you could splash out on an 'apartment' with self-contained kitchenette.

Hôtel Les Voyageurs (☎ 04 95 34 90 80; www.hotel-lesvoyageurs.com; 9 av Maréchal Sébastiani; s €70-75, d €80-95, tr €90-110; ❄ P) Swish furnishings and efficient service make this fancy hotel popular with business travellers and well-heeled tourists. Buttermilk walls, modern-art prints and blindingly white en suites fill the rooms; you'll secure more space, plush sofas and a minifridge if you splash more cash. There's covered parking (€6) and free wi-fi.

Hôtel Bonaparte (☎ 04 95 34 07 10; www.hotel-bonaparte-bastia.com; 45 bd Général Graziani; s €70-80, d €75-160; ❄ P) A cute little three-star place with a cluster of eclectic rooms: some small, snug and carpeted in mix-and-match fabrics, others larger with white-tiled floors, Mediterranean colours and street-front balconies, plus a couple of suites with separate sitting areas. Parking costs €8.

Eating

You'll find endless restaurants around the old port and quai des Martyrs, but quality can suffer in the high season.

Chez Vincent (☎ 04 95 31 62 50; 12 rue St-Michel; mains €8-18; ⏰ lunch & dinner Mon-Fri, dinner Sat) Not up to the gastronomic heights of A Casarella (see below), but this next-door neighbour still offers Corsican staples and wood-fired pizzas. The *Assiette du Bandit Corse* (€18) features a smorgasbord of local nosh, including Corsican meats, chestnuts, cheese and boar.

our pick A Casarella (☎ 04 95 32 02 32; rue du Dragon; mains €9-28; ⏰ lunch Mon-Fri, dinner Mon-Sat) Poised above the old port in the heart of the citadel, this well-hidden restaurant boasts the loveliest patio in Bastia. Tuck into inventive variations on traditional Corsican cuisine – tuna with caramelised figs, or Brocciu (ewe's- or goat's-milk cheese)-stuffed sardines – with the twinkling lights of the harbour below, or on colder nights duck into the dining room, filled with bric-a-brac and black-and-white prints.

Le Bouchon (☎ 04 95 58 14 22; 4bis rue St-Jean; mains €15-21, no credit cards; ⏰ closed Sun) Dinky, down-to-earth bistro from the Lyonnaise school, with a blackboard of specials running the gamut from Corsican sausages to pork steaks. The food's filling, the welcome's warm, and the tables are packed in tight – go for the terrace in warm weather, illuminated by candles stuffed into old bottles.

U Tianu (☎ 04 95 31 36 67; 4 rue Rigo; menus €19; ⏰ dinner Mon-Sat, closed Aug) A favourite Bastiais hideaway for aeons, this is as close as you'll come to a traditional Corsican kitchen. Hunting rifles, country knick-knacks and dog-eared posters cover the walls, and you'll tuck into five-course platters of Corsican food including cheese, aperitif and coffee, whipped up by the venerable mamas in charge of the kitchen.

Le Caveau de Marin (☎ 04 95 31 62 31; quai des Martyrs de la Libération; ⏰ closed lunch Sat-Mon) Maritime paraphernalia and a shipshape atmosphere defines this longstanding seafood restaurant, especially strong on sea-fresh fish – oysters, grilled sea bass, giant-sized mussel platters and sea urchins, with a choice of tables in the vaulted dining room or on the portside patio.

SELF-CATERING

Cheese, fish, fruit, veg and Corsican charcuterie fills the morning **food market** (place de l'Hôtel de Ville; ⏰ Tue-Sun), or you can pick up supplies at Spar supermarkets on rue César Campinchi and bd Paoli. For big shops, head out of town for the Casino supermarket at the Géant Port Toga Centre Commercial.

Drinking

Cafés line the edges of place St-Nicolas and the backstreets around the Vieux Port.

La Rhumerie (☎ 06 86 37 09 32; place Galetta; ⏰ 8pm-2am Mon-Sat Jun-Aug, Wed-Sat Sep-May) If you can look beyond the dodgy fibreglass pirates guarding the doorway, you'll find a treasure chest of rums behind the bar of this popular drinking hole, not to mention beers and cocktails.

LVP Café (quai du 1er Bataillon de Choc, Vieux Port; ⏰ 10am-2am) Currently the hot-tip of Bastia's port-side bars, crammed to bursting with bright young things sipping pastis and Pietras.

La Soupière (☎ 06 42 85 44 11; ⏰ 6.30pm-2am) Hidden behind the old port on a cobbled ramp next to rue Général Carbuccia, this *café litteraire* (literary café) hosts regular poetry readings and open-mike nights.

Entertainment

Le Régent (☎ 04 95 31 30 31; www.leregent.fr; rue César Campinchi) A multiscreen cinema screening the latest releases (nearly always in French).

Studio Cinéma (☎ 04 95 31 12 94; www.studio-cinema.com; rue Miséricorde) A small arts cinema where you can catch French and international flicks, often in *version originale* (the original language version).

Shopping

LN Mattei (15 bd Général de Gaulle) An institution in Basti – founded by local man Louis Napoléon Mattei (who also cooked up the local liqueur, Cap Corse). It's *the* place for local delicacies, including liqueurs, jams, honeys and olive oils.

For Corsican wines, drop by **Les Grands Vins de Corse** (☎ 04 95 31 24 94; www.lesvinscorse.com, in French; 24 rue César Campinchi).

A Sunday flea market takes place on place St-Nicholas, but the bargains go early, so pitch up before 9am.

Getting There & Around

AIR

Aéroport Bastia-Poretta (☎ 04 95 54 54 54; www.bastia.aeroport.fr) is 24km south of the city. Buses (€8.50, eight daily) depart from outside the Préfecture building. The first bus from town is around 6am and the last bus from the airport is around 9pm; schedules are posted at the bus stop. A taxi will set you back €37/50 during the day/night with **Taxis Bleus** (☎ 04 95 32 70 70).

BOAT

Bastia has two ferry terminals connected by a free shuttle bus. All the ferry companies have information offices in the southern terminal, which usually opens for same-day ticket sales a couple of hours before each sailing. If the kiosks for Corsica Ferries or Moby Lines are closed, try stopping by the main offices nearby.

Corsica Ferries (☎ 04 95 32 95 95; www.corsicaferries.com; 15bis rue Chanoine Leschi; 🕒 8.30am-noon & 2-6pm Mon-Fri, 9am-noon Sat) Opposite the northern terminal.

Moby Lines (☎ 04 95 34 84 94; www.mobylines.it; 4 rue du Commandant Luce de Casabianca; 🕒 8am-noon & 2-6pm Mon-Fri, 8am-noon Sat)

SNCM (☎ 04 95 54 66 81; www.sncm.com; inside Southern Terminal; 🕒 8-11.45am & 2-5.45pm Mon-Fri, 8am-noon Sat)

BUS

There are three bus stops in Bastia: outside the tourist office, at the train station, and at the 'bus terminal' (actually a car park) north of Square St-Victor.

Autocars Cortenais (☎ 04 95 46 02 12) Travels to Corte (€10, two hours) once daily on Monday, Wednesday and Friday. Buses leave from the train station.

Beaux Voyages (☎ 04 95 65 11 35) Travels to Île Rousse (€10, 90 minutes) and Calvi (€16, two hours) daily except Sunday. Buses leave from the train station.

Eurocorse (☎ 04 95 31 73 76) travels to Ajaccio (€22, three hours) via Corte (€11, two hours) twice daily except on Sundays from Bastia's 'bus station'.

Les Rapides Bleus (☎ 04 95 31 03 79; 1 av Maréchal Sébastiani) Runs buses to Porto-Vecchio (€20, per baggage item €1, bikes €8, three hours) every day except Sundays and holidays.

For buses to Cap Corse, see p916.

TRAIN

The **train station** (☎ 04 95 32 80 61; av Maréchal Sébastiani; 🕒 6am-8.30pm Mon-Sat, 8.30am-8.30pm Sun) is beside the large roundabout on Square Maréchal Leclerc. Main destinations include Ajaccio (€23.90, four daily) via Corte (€11.20), and Calvi (€18.10. three hours, three or four daily) via Île Rousse (€15).

CAP CORSE

Poking an accusatory finger towards mainland France, Corsica's northerly peninsula feels one step removed from the rest of the island – hardly surprising, since before the road arrived the only way to reach the peninsula was by mule track or boat. Genoese watchtowers and hidden coves line the coastline, while maquis-covered slopes flank the peninsula's hilly spine. The twisting coastal roads make for adventurous driving; factor in plenty of time to account for caravans and roadside goats in summer.

From Bastia, the coast unfolds through seaside resorts and small beaches towards the quaint harbour of **Erbalunga**, 9km north, famous for its August music festival (☎ 04 95 33 20 84), and **Pietracorbara**, the sexiest stretch of sand on the east coast.

At Santa Servara, the road splits: the west fork climbs to the Col de Ste-Lucie and its hilltop tower (supposedly where the Roman poet-philosopher Seneca was exiled in the 1st century). The second fork continues north to the little port of **Macinaggio**, where you'll find a smattering of hotels and bistros and the cape's sole **tourist office** (☎ 04 95 35 40 34; www.ot-rogliano-macinaggio.com; Port de Plaisance de Macinaggio; 🕒 9am-noon & 2-7pm Mon-Sat, 9am-noon Sun Jul & Aug, 9am-noon & 2-5pm Mon-Fri, 9am-noon Sat Sep-Jun). Boat trips putter along the coastline from the

CORSICA'S GRANDES RANDONNÉES

The holy grail for many a hardy hiker, the **GR20** (aka the Frá Li Monti, 'between the mountains'), cuts through the middle of the island for a distance of 168km, from Calenzana (10km southeast of Calvi) to Conca (20km north of Porto-Vecchio) in the southwest. It's a stunning traverse through high mountain scenery, but it's not for novices – the terrain is tough, the route is long, steep and often dizzyingly lofty, and creature comforts (hotels, ATMs, supply shops and food stores) are nonexistent. Much of the route is above the snowline at 2000m and passable only from mid-June to October: you'll need camping equipment, ample food supplies, drinking water and a stove, and at least 15 days to complete it. Parc Naturel Régional de Corse (PNRC) *refuges* (mountain huts) are dotted along the trail, but they don't accept reservations. Wild camping and the lighting of fires are strictly forbidden.

Lonely Planet's *Corsica* and *Walking in France* guides have extensive sections on hiking the GR20, with full day-by-day route guides, accommodation listings and practical advice. Despite the challenges, the 10,000 walkers who tackle the trail every year receive a justifiable sense of achievement upon completing the route – you can rightly count yourself a *grand randonneur* if you reach the end in one piece.

If you don't feel like taking on the full-blown route, it's possible to divide the GR20 into smaller sections: Vizzavona makes a convenient halfway stage. Alternatively you could take on one of Corsica's other *grandes randonnées;* the **Maison d'Information Randonnées du Parc Naturel Régional de Corse** (☎ 04 95 51 79 10; www.parc-naturel-corse.com) provides information.

Trails within Corsica:

Mare a Mare Centre A seven-day trail linking Porticcio (south of Ajaccio) with Ghisonaccia. Open May to November.

Mare a Mare Nord Cargèse (north of Ajaccio) to Moriani (40km south of Bastia), one route (of two alternatives) passing through the forest of Vizzavona and the village of Vénaco. Allow seven to 12 days. Open May to November.

Mare a Mare Sud Five days from Propriano (south of Ajaccio) to Porto-Vecchio, passing Zonza en route. Open year-round.

Mare e Monti Nord Cargèse to Calenzana (via Évisa, Ota, Girolata and Galéria) in around 10 days. Open all year, but best in spring and autumn.

Mare e Monti Sud Porticcio to Propriano via Porto Pollo and Olmeto; open year-round.

harbour, and a coastal trail – the Sentier des Douaniers – leads north to the remote village of **Barcaggio**.

Round the peninsula's tip, the road sweeps along the western side, wilder and grander than the east, with clifftop villages, jagged coves and houses hidden deep in the maquis. A restored windmill overlooks the village of **Centuri**, but the highlight of the west coast is **Nonza**, perched above a black-sand beach with an 11th-century chapel dedicated to St Julia (Corsica's patron saint, martyred here in the 5th century). The final stretch sweeps past sandy bays to the touristy harbour of **St-Florent**.

Sleeping & Eating

CAMPING

Cap Corse has several lovely campsites.

Camping La Pietra (☎ 04 95 35 27 49; www.la-pietra.com; Pietracorbara; campsites per adult €7.70-9.80, tent €3.30-4.70; Apr–mid-Oct;) Regally equipped campsite with lots of tree-shaded pitches (some wheelchair accessible), tennis courts, a buffet-bar and a fantastic swimming pool.

Camping U Stazzu (☎ 04 95 35 43 76; campsites €15; May-Sep) Pleasant campground handy for Tamarone beach, just north of Macinaggio.

HOTELS

Relais du Cap (☎ 04 95 37 86 53; www.relaisducap.com; d €45-70; Apr-Oct) For the ultimate seaside escape, bag one of the four doubles or the roomy apartment at this tiny little B&B perched on the sands of a pocket-sized pebble beach, 5km south of Nonza. Beachside barbecues, a private boat and fabulous watery views make for a gold-dust getaway.

Casa Maria (☎ 04 95 37 80 95; www.casamaria-corse.com, in French; d €70-90, ste €120-160;) What a find – a bewitching little hideaway in Nonza, coolly refurbished with whitewashed walls, wrought-iron staircases and reclaimed beams, and an endearingly pastoral ambience that makes for a great refuge from the outside world.

Le Vieux Moulin (☎ 04 95 35 60 15; www.le-vieux-moulin.net, in French; d incl half-board €100-280) Split over two buildings (a lovely colonial-style holiday house and a more modern annexe) in Centuri, this is one of the poshest places to stay on the peninsula. It's a real pamper-pad crammed with rugs, antique pots and chaise longues. The annexe rooms are disappointingly bland, but the restaurant's top-notch (mains €15 to €25).

Hôtel Castel Brando (☎ 04 95 30 10 30; www.castelbrando.com; Erbalunga; d €105-210;) Smart, swish, sophisticated hotel in Erbalunga, with four grades of rooms ranging from 'Charming' to 'Suite ', and a choice of buildings (19th-century mansion or modern annexe). Peaches and yellows dominate the decor; some rooms have private patios, others flat-screen TVs and sea views. Wi-fi is standard throughout, and the beach couldn't be much closer.

Osteria di U Portu (☎ 04 95 35 40 49; Macinaggio; mains €15-25; lunch & dinner) Fab seafood straight off the quayside of Macinaggio, supplemented by a quartet of simple *chambres d'hôtes* (d €40 to €60) in summer.

Getting There & Away

The main road around Cap Corse is the D80. **Société des Transports Interurbains Bastiais** (☎ 04 95 31 06 65) runs several buses to Cap Corse from Bastia, with destinations including Erbalunga (€2), Sisco (€2) and Pietracorbara (€2.60). **Transport Micheli** (☎ 04 95 35 14 64) runs to Macinaggio (€6.40, two daily Sunday to Friday, one on Saturday). Buses leave from outside the Bastia tourist office.

THE NORTH COAST

ÎLE ROUSSE (ISULA ROSSA)

pop 2300

Sun-worshippers, celebrities and holidaying yachties all buzz around the busy beach town of Île Rousse, straddling a long, sandy curve of land backed by maquis-cloaked mountains and a sparkling beach. Originally founded by Pascal Paoli in 1758 as a rival port to pro-Genoese Calvi, 24km to the southwest, the town was later renamed after the russet-coloured rock of Île de la Pietra offshore (now home to the town's ferry-port and lighthouse).

Orientation

The **tourist office** (☎ 04 95 60 04 35; www.balagne-corsica.com; place Paoli; 9am-7pm mid-Jun–mid-Sep, 9am-12.30pm & 2-6pm May, early Jun & late Sep, 9am-noon & 2-6pm Mon-Fri Oct-Apr) is on the southern side of place Paoli. The station is north along the Rte du Port, which joins the mainland to the Île de la Pietra and the ferry port.

Sights

The modern-day town is short on sights, but the backstreets around the grand marketplace (complete with 21 neo-Grecian columns) are worth a stroll. All roads in Île Rousse lead to the tree-shaded place Paoli, where you can watch nightly boules contests courtesy of the local gents while you sip *eau de vie* (clear fruit or nut brandy) at one of the square-side cafés.

Île Rousse's beaches stretch along the seafront, known as **Promenade a Marinella**, for 3km east of town, but things get very crowded in the summer months – you can usually find more room at **Algajola**, 7km to the west, accessible via the clanking **Tramway de la Balagne** (p921). Ask at the tourist office or the train station for timetables.

The ferry-port is north of town on the **Île de la Pietra**, where you'll also find an old Genovese **watchtower** and a **lighthouse**. You can rent out jet skis, dinghies and sailing boats from **Club Nautique** (☎ 04 95 60 22 55), based on the beach running alongside the Rte du Port.

Four kilometres inland from Île Rousse in the village of Monticello is the **Parc de Saleccia** (☎ 04 95 36 88 83; adult/child €7/5; 10am-8pm Jul & Aug, 9.30am-7pm Mon-Sat, 10am-8pm Sun, occasionally closed Mon & Sat mornings mid-Mar–Jun & early Sep–mid-Sep), a 7-hectare park reclaimed from fire-ravaged land and now brimming with native Corsican plants, including cypresses, olive trees, myrtles and wildflowers.

Sleeping & Eating

Splendid Hotel (☎ 04 95 60 00 24; www.le-splendid-hotel.com; s €53-85, d €58-100, tr €79-138; late Mar-Oct; P) This coral-pink tower has been sheltering seaside travellers in Île Rousse for decades (it even served as a field hospital during WWII), but despite the name, rooms are satisfactory rather than splendid. The decor's dated, but the facilities are decent – palm-shaded pool, wi-fi and a swish cocktail bar, to boot; the sea-view rooms are well worth the €5 supplement.

L'Amiral (☎ 04 95 60 28 05; www.hotel-amiral.com; 163 bd Charles Marie Savelli; d €65-100; Apr-Oct;) This neo-Cubist lump would be more at home on the Costa del Sol than the Corsican coastline, but for beach babies it's ideal – seafront bars and soft white sand nearby, and most of the boxy modern rooms have bay-view balconies. Just don't expect much character.

L'Escale (☎ 04 95 60 10 53; rue Notre-Dame; mains €11-25) For sea-view dining, head for the wood-decked terrace at L'Escale, where you can tuck into huge seafood platters, mussels, pastas and fresh lobster plucked (literally) straight from the tank, all with unparalleled vistas of the blue, blue sea.

Restaurant L'Île d'Or (☎ 04 95 60 12 05; place Paoli; menus €12.50-35) There's something to suit all budgets at this venerable bistro, which offers front-row seats for the town's nightly boules contests. The *menu* (fixed-price meal) takes in everything from wood-fired pizzas to gourmet salads and *fruits de mer* (seafood).

U Lubecciu (☎ 04 95 60 13 82; 3 rue Paoli; mains €15-22; lunch & dinner) A short hop from the market and decked out with slatted chairs and black umbrellas, this restaurant serves up the town's best seafood – swordfish kebabs, scorpionfish fillet and lots and lots of mussels (try them with chorizo, pancetta, Roquefort or the house Cap Corse sauce).

Stop by the buzzy **covered market** (place Paoli; 8am-1pm) for fish, vegetables, fruit and Corsican delicacies.

Getting There & Away

Les Beaux Voyages (☎ 04 95 65 11 35) runs a morning bus from Calvi (€4, 15 minutes) to Bastia (€10, two hours), which stops at Île Rousse. There's also an afternoon bus in the opposite direction. The service runs from Monday to Saturday year-round.

In summer, **Transports Santini** (☎ 04 95 37 02 98) runs two daily buses to St-Florent (€10, one hour, two daily Monday to Saturday from July to August).

The **train station** (☎ 04 95 60 00 50) has two daily trains to Bastia (€15, 2½ hours) and Ajaccio (€24.60, four hours) via Corte (€12, 2¼ hours) year-round.

For ferries to Île Rousse, see p907. **Corse Voyages** (☎ 04 95 60 11 19; place Paoli) and **Tramar** (☎ 04 95 60 09 56; av Joseph Calizi; 8.30am-noon & 2-5.30pm Mon-Fri, 8.30am-noon Sat) both sell tickets.

LA BALAGNE

Stretching inland from the barren 5000-hectare **Désert des Agriates** east of Île Rousse to the snowy crest of Monte Cinto, the Balagne is a remote and traditional area, dotted with scrubby knolls, maquis-covered hills and tiny backcountry villages. A century ago this was one of the island's richest agricultural regions, colloquially known as the Garden of Corsica – a fertile landscape covered with olive farms, orange plantations and fig orchards. But economic decline and steady depopulation during the early 20th century emptied many of the orchards and farming communities, and it's only in recent years that the area has rediscovered its soul as a centre for local craftwork and small-scale cultivation.

A signposted route, the **Strada di L'Artiagni** (Route des Artisans, in French), links up the region's most attractive villages, and details local workshops belonging to potters, beekeepers and luthiers. You can pick up a route map from the tourist offices in Calvi and Île Rousse.

Of particular interest is the craft centre of **Pigna**, 7km from Île Rousse, where dotted around the cobbled streets you'll find makers of everything from candles to lutes and music boxes, and **Calenzana**, the northern terminus of the GR20 and Mare e Monti trails (see p915).

Casa Musicale (☎ 04 95 61 76 57; www.casa-musicale.org; Pigna; d €50-94; P) Riding Pigna's Bohemian vibe, this charming hotel has quirky rooms finished with painted frescoes and fabulous valley views, and it hosts regular concerts of local music. The patio restaurant brims with Balagne ingredients.

our pick U Palazzu (☎ 04 95 47 32 78; www.hotel-palazzu.com; Pigna; d €130-210, ste €210-260; P) A palace indeed! This wonderfully luxurious place occupies a Pignan 18th-century mansion, with three super-plush doubles (shared patio) and two regal suites (private terrace). All boast rich fabrics, antique furniture, original carpentry and period features; some have jaw-dropping views of the Bay of Algajola. Not convinced? Stop by the rustic restaurant, which serves Corsican dishes inside a refurbished olive mill. Trust us – you'll never want to leave.

CALVI

pop 5600

Basking between the fiery orange bastions of its 15th-century citadel and the glittering waters of a moon-shaped bay, Calvi feels closer to the chi-chi sophistication of a Côte d'Azur resort than a historic Corsican port. Palatial yachts and private cruisers jostle for space along its harbourside, lined with up-market brasseries and cafés, while high above the quay the watchtowers and battlements of the town's Genoese stronghold stand guard, proffering sweeping views inland to Monte Cinto (2706m). Unsurprisingly, Calvi is one of Corsica's most popular tourist spots and in summer it's crammed to bursting (and chronically overpriced) – pitch up in the shoulder seasons, when you'll be able to stroll the citadel's cobbled alleys in relative peace and quiet.

Orientation

The citadel – also known as the Haute Ville (Upper City) – sits on a rocky promontory northeast of the Basse Ville (Lower Town). Bd Wilson, the major thoroughfare through town, is uphill from the marina.

Information

Banks, including Crédit Lyonnais, can be found along bd Wilson.

Antenne Médicale du SAMU (☎ 04 95 65 11 22; rue de Santore)
Café de l'Orient (☎ 04 95 65 00 16; quai Landry; internet access connection €1 plus per min €0.10; 🕑 9am-late)
Citadel Tourist Office (citadel gate; 🕑 9am-noon Mon-Sat Jun-Sep)
Hall de la Presse (☎ 04 95 65 05 14; 13 bd Wilson; 🕑 9am-noon & 2-6pm Mon-Sat) Sells topoguides and walking maps.
Main Tourist Office (☎ 04 95 65 16 67; www.balagne-corsica.com; Port de Plaisance; 🕑 9am-noon & 3-6.30pm Jul & Aug, 9am-noon & 2-6pm Mon-Sat May, Jun, Sep & Oct, 9am-noon & 2-6pm Mon-Fri Nov-Apr)
Post Office (bd Wilson)

Sights & Activities

CITADEL

Set atop a lofty promontory, Calvi's massive fortified citadel completely dominates the harbour skyline. Built by the town's Genoese governors, Calvi's citadel has seen off several major assaults down the centuries, fending off everyone from Franco-Turkish raiders to Anglo-Corsican armies, notably during the siege of 1794 when the citadel was attacked by the forces of the revolutionary leader Pascal Paoli. During the ensuing battle, a young British captain by the name of Horatio Nelson lost his right eye.

Inside the battlements, the **Palais des Gouverneurs** (Governors' Palace; place d'Armes) was the seat of power for the Genoese administration and now serves (under the name Caserne Sampiero) as a base for the French Foreign Legion. Look out for soldiers wearing the regiment's distinctive white *kepis* (military caps) around town. The citadel's enduring loyalty to Genoa is recalled by the motto *Civitas Calvi Semper Fidelis* (The City of Calvi, Forever Faithful) carved over the citadel gateway.

Uphill from Caserne Sampiero is the 13th-century **Église St-Jean Baptiste**, rebuilt in 1570 following an explosion at a nearby gunpowder store. The church's most celebrated relic is the ebony *Christ des Miracles*, credited with saving the town from Saracen invasion in 1553; legend has it that the besieging Turkish fleet fell back after the statue was paraded around Calvi's streets.

In the northern part of the citadel, a **plaque** marks the house where navigator Christopher Columbus was supposedly born. However, despite the assertions of many Corsican historians, it's generally accepted that the globetrotting explorer was actually born in Genoa.

BEACHES

Sunworshippers don't have far to stroll – Calvi's stellar 4km beach begins at the marina and runs east around the Golfe de Calvi. You can rent out kayaks and windsurfers from the **Calvi Nautique Club** (☎ 04 95 65 10 65; www.calvinc.org; Base Nautique, Port de Plaisance; 🕑 May-Oct).

Tours

Croisières Colombo Line (☎ 04 95 65 32 10; www.colombo-line.com; marina; 🕑 Apr-Oct) runs glass-bottomed boat excursions to the Réserve Naturelle de Scandola (Scandola Natural Reserve), starting from around €35.

Festivals & Events

La Semaine Sainte Easter festival, culminating in street processions on Good Friday.
Calvi Jazz festival Corsica's biggest jazz festival, in June.
Rencontres Polyphoniques Traditional Corsican chants – traditionally sung *a cappella* (without instrumental accompaniment) – can be heard at this five-day music festival in September. The stirring *paghjellas* feature three male voices – a tenor, baritone and bass – and mark the passage of life.
Le Festival du Vent (☎ 04 95 65 16 67; www.le-festival-du-vent.com) In autumn, this festival celebrates wind in all its forms, with musical instrument and theatre

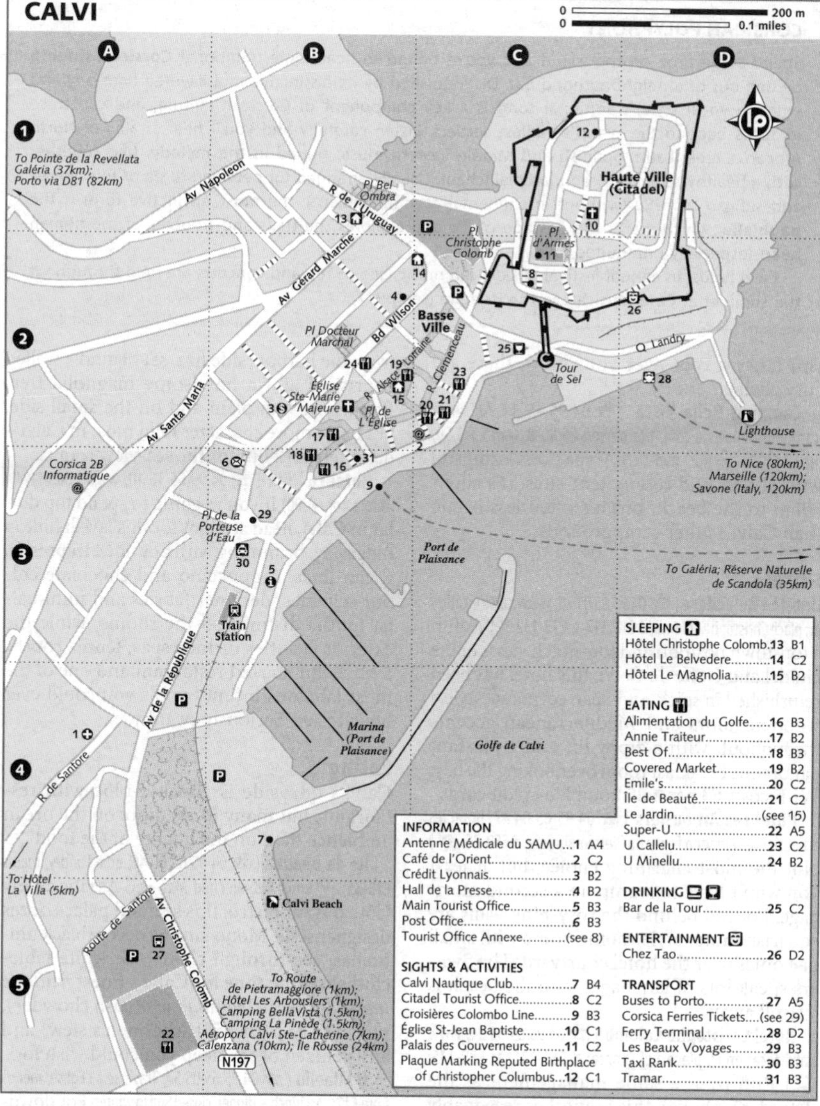

performances, art exhibitions, sailing and windsurfing, and paragliding and air displays.

Sleeping

Despite the eye-watering prices, Calvi's hotels are packed out in summer, so book well ahead unless you fancy kipping on the beach.

CAMPING

Calvi has plenty of campsites.

Camping La Pinède (☎ 04 95 65 17 80; www.camping-calvi.com; rte de la Pinède; adult €6.50-9, tent €2.50-3.50, car €2.50-3.50; mid-May–mid-Oct; P) Handy for Calvi town and the beach, this shady spot has sites sheltered under tall pines, and, if

CORSICAN POLYPHONY

Spend some time on the island and you're bound to hear some traditional **Corsican singing** belting out of a neighbourhood bar. Distinguished by its distinctive multilayered harmony and emotive vocal style, traditional song is a key component of Corsican culture, and can trace its roots back to the island's earliest settlers. Listen carefully and you'll hear strains of North African, Greek, Latin, Spanish and Middle Eastern music buried in the melody, tied together with a healthy strain of Gregorian plainchant. Usually arranged for between three or four voices and sung *a cappella* (without instrumental accompaniment), the most distinctive form is the **paghjella**, which marks the passage of life and explores the trials and troubles of the human heart (especially unrequited love).

Calvi holds an annual festival of Corsican music (see p918), and concerts are held throughout the summer at Casa Musicale in the Balagne (see p917).

you fancy a roof over your head, there are cosy chalets.

Camping Bella Vista (☎ 04 95 65 11 76; www.camping-bellavista.com; per person €5.50-8, tent €3-3.50, car €2.50-3; ⌚ Apr–mid-Oct) A spacious campsite with chalets and roomy tent-sites. It's about 500m to the beach, but it's often less hectic than Calvi's other campgrounds.

HOTELS

Hôtel Le Belvedere (☎ 04 95 65 01 25; www.calvi-location.fr; place Christophe Colomb; d €47-117, tr €72-132; ❄) With a top-town position and top-notch views of the citadel and Golfe de Calvi, this hotel has been refurbished in spick-and-span corporate style – wooden floors and Mediterranean accents throughout, with a zippy lift and a pleasant panoramic breakfast room overlooking the bay. Wi-fi costs €3 per half-hour. No credit cards.

Hôtel Les Arbousiers (☎ 04 95 65 04 47; hotel.lesarbousiers@wanadoo.fr; rte du Pietramaggiore; d €50-76; Ⓟ) Not the most charming choice, but at least you won't have to stump up a second mortgage. Lodged behind the rosy-pink walls are squarish motel-style rooms, some with small balconies over the hotel courtyard. The owners speak lots of languages, and the beach is a stroll away.

Hôtel Christophe Colomb (☎ 04 95 65 06 04; www.calvi-location.fr; place Bel Ombra; d €55-115, tr €85-135; 💻) Run by the same management as the Belvedere (above), this is another reasonably priced option within striking distance of the citadel. Rooms are comfortable if unremarkable: Mediterranean colourwashes and cheery fabrics keep things jolly, and there's a pleasant ground-floor lounge where you can hook up to the hotel's wi-fi.

Hôtel Le Magnolia (☎ 04 95 65 19 16; www.hotel-le-magnolia.com; rue Alsace Lorraine; r €60-140) An oasis from the harbourside fizz, set behind a walled courtyard and a handsome magnolia tree. Rooms are old, plain and on the small side, but boast more character than most in Calvi – definitely fork out for the sea-view rooms.

Hôtel La Villa (☎ 04 95 65 10 10; www.hotel-lavilla.com; r from €200) If you're going to spend top dollar in Calvi, head straight for this lavish hilltop hideaway, brimming with boutique trappings. Clean lines, cappuccino-and-chocolate colour schemes, designer fabrics and minimalist motifs distinguish the rooms, while the exterior facilities include spas, tennis courts, a Michelin-starred restaurant and one of the most fabulous infinity pools you could ever hope to see. Seriously swanky.

Eating

Calvi's quayside is chock-a-bloc with restaurants, but many focus more on the ocean ambience than on the quality of the food.

Île de Beauté (☎ 04 95 65 00 46; quai Landry; mains €15-35; ⌚ lunch & dinner mid-Mar–Dec) As chic as any Côte d'Azur bistro, this seafood palace oozes designer style. Monochrome decor (black umbrellas, see-through chairs, ice-white tablecloths) set the tone for Calvi's finest *fruits de mer* – authentic *bouillabaisse* (fish chowder), *marmite de pêcheurs* (fishermen's stew) and any denizen of the deep you could wish for.

U Minellu (☎ 04 95 65 05 52; Traverse à l'Église; menus from €17; ⌚ lunch & dinner, closed Sun in winter) For down-to-earth cooking, you can't top this family-run operation opposite Église Ste-Marie Majeure. Duck under the ramshackle awning and prepare for hearty portions of wild boar stew, Brocciu cannelloni and chestnut cake.

Le Jardin (☎ 04 95 65 19 16; rue Alsace Lorraine; mains €18-28, menus €21/27) You couldn't ask for a more romantic setting than the Magnolia Hotel's (opposite) courtyard restaurant, sheltering beneath the boughs of the eponymous tree. Corsican produce and seafood take centre stage, with a *menu* including crayfish stew, stir-fried scallops and lobster in 'hell-fire' sauce.

U Callelu (☎ 04 95 65 22 18; quai Landry; menu €23, mains €12-28) The *menu* chases the changing seasons at this homespun eatery, run with passion and flair by a born-and-bred islander who tracks down the best local ingredients for his dishes: meat and veg from the market, wine direct from the vineyards, fish straight off the boats. Who needs sexy decor when the food's this good?

Emile's (☎ 04 95 65 09 60; quai Landry; menus €23-120, mains €24-60; lunch & dinner Apr, dinner May-Oct) If you want to blow the budget, climb the stairs from the quayside to this gastronomic sanctuary. Roast pigeon, caviar and langoustines grace the super-chic *carte* (menu), or you can let the chef choose the dishes with the multicourse 'signature' *menu* (€120).

QUICK EATS & SELF-CATERING

Piping-hot panini, flatbreads and stuffed pittas are available from the *sandwicherie* **Best Of** (1 rue Clemenceau; sandwiches €4-7; 11.30am-10pm). You can pick up fresh fruit and veg from the **Alimentation du Golfe** (rue Clemenceau; Apr-Oct) across the street or the **covered market** (marché couvert; 8am-noon Mon-Sat) near Église Ste-Marie Majeure. If you're doing a big shop, you'll be better off at the **Super U** (av Christophe Colomb) near the bus station.

For souvenirs and Corsican goodies, seek out **Annie Traiteur** (rue Clemenceau; Apr-Oct), where the shelves are creaking with *artisanal* jams, honeys, Corsican charcuterie and umpteen varieties of *canistrelli* (sweet Corsican biscuits).

Drinking & Entertainment

There are plenty of places around town at which to whet your whistle: the best views are from the laid-back **Bar de la Tour** (☎ 04 95 46 39 74) at the end of the quay, which serves cocktails, cold beers and chilled wine till late, but for historical provenance swing by **Chez Tao** (☎ 04 95 65 00 73; May-Oct), inside the citadel. It's a super-smooth piano bar that was founded in 1935 by Tao Kanbey de Kerekoff, an escaping member of the Russian White Cavalry, and it still attracts hedonistic hipsters seven decades later.

Getting There & Away

AIR

Seven kilometres southeast of town is **Aéroport Calvi Ste-Catherine** (☎ 04 95 65 88 88; www.calvi.aeroport.fr), with regular Air France (CCM) flights to Nice, Marseille and Paris Orly, plus selected seasonal flights. There's no airport bus: taxis with **Radio Taxis Calvis** (☎ 04 95 65 30 36) or **Association Abeille Taxis** (☎ 04 95 65 03 10) cost about €25.

BOAT

Calvi's ferry terminal is at the northeastern end of quai Landry, with regular ferries to Nice offered by SNCM and Corsica Ferries.

Ferry tickets can be bought at the port two hours before departure. At other times, SNCM tickets are handled by **Tramar** (☎ 04 95 65 01 38; quai Landry; 9am-noon & 2-5pm Mon-Fri, 9am-noon Sat). Tickets for Corsica Ferries are handled by **Les Beaux Voyages** (☎ 04 95 65 15 02; place de la Porteuse d'Eau).

BUS

Les Beaux Voyages (☎ 04 95 65 15 02; place de la Porteuse d'Eau) runs daily buses to Bastia (€16, two hours) via Algajola and Île Rousse (€4, 15 minutes).

Autocars Ceccaldi (SAIB Autocars; ☎ 04 95 22 41 99; www.autocarsiledebeaute.com) runs a daily bus to Porto (€17, 2¾ hours) leaving from opposite the Super U supermarket in Calvi and the main road opposite the pharmacy in Porto. There's one bus daily from July to mid-September. From mid-May to June, and late September, there's no bus on Sundays. There's no service at all from October to mid-May.

TRAIN

Calvi's **train station** (☎ 04 95 65 00 61; to 7.30pm) has connections to Ajaccio (€27.80, five hours, two daily) via Corte (€15.10, four hours two daily). You'll need to change trains at Ponte-Lecchia. There are also two daily trains to Bastia (€18.10, three hours).

From April to October, the CFC's **Tramway de la Balagne** clatters along the coast between Calvi and Île Rousse (45 minutes). The line has three sectors – you need one ticket for each sector. *Carnets* (books) of six tickets (€8) are sold at stations.

PORTO TO AJACCIO

PORTO (PORTU)

pop 250

Lodged at the base of a thickly forested valley trammelled on either side by crimson peaks, Porto has one of the most dramatic locations of any of Corsica's westerly ports. Buzzing in season and practically deserted in winter, it's a fantastic spot for exploring the shimmering seas around the Réserve Naturelle de Scandola, a Unesco-protected marine reservation (the only one in Corsica), or venturing inland to the plunging canyons around the Gorges de Spelunca and the valley villages of Ota and Évisa (p924).

Orientation

Porto is split into three sections: the seaside marina; the Vaita quarter (Guaïta in Corsican), 800m further uphill; and the main road from Calvi, 1.3km from the sea. There are shops, hotels and restaurants in all three districts.

Information

Le Moulin (internet access per 1/2hr €5/8; 2pm-2am Apr-Oct, 2-10pm Oct-Mar) Pricey cybercafé downhill from Camping Les Oliviers.

Post Office Next to Hôtel Lonza in Vaita.

Tourist Office (04 95 26 10 55; www.porto-tourisme.com, in French; 9am-7pm Mon-Sat Jun-Sep, 9am-6pm Mon-Sat Apr & May, 9am-5pm Mon-Fri Oct-Mar) Just behind the marina's upper car park.

Sights & Activities

Porto's main sights are all dotted around the harbour. Once you've climbed the russet-coloured rocks up to the **Genoese tower** (adult/under 12yr €2.50/free; 9am-9pm Jul & Aug, 11am-7pm Sep-Jun), you can stroll round to the bustling marina, from where an arched footbridge crosses the estuary to a **eucalyptus grove** and Porto's pebbly patch of beach. Fish-fanatics can drop by the **Aquarium de la Poudrière** (04 95 26 19 24; adult/7-12yr €5.50/3, joint ticket with Tour Génoise €6.50/3), which houses fishy specimens from around the Golfe de Porto.

The best way to appreciate Porto's beautiful location is (ironically) by leaving it: the view of Porto's natural harbour and the surrounding coastline from way out to sea is utterly unforgettable, and if you have the time it's well worth exploring further afield to the **Réserve Naturelle de Scandola** and the tiny seaside village of **Girolata**, accessible only on foot or by boat.

BOAT TRIPS

Lots of operators based around Porto's marina offer boat trips from April to October. Expect to pay €20 to €25 for trips to the Calanques, or €35 to €45 for trips including Réserve Naturelle de Scandola (Scandola Nature Reserve) and Girolata. Most offer informative commentaries (usually in French) – a few of the captains speak passable English, so ask at the quay before booking your boat. Some operators located near the quayside:

Nave Va (04 95 26 15 16; www.naveva.com) The slickest operator with one of the poshest (and biggest) boats. Info from Restaurant Les Flots Bleus.

Pass'Partout (06 75 99 13 15; www.lepasspartout.com) Smaller firm with a more personal feel. Info from Restaurant Le Cyrnée.

Porto Linea (04 95 21 52 22; www.portolinea.com) Trips to the Calanches, plus Scandola and Girolata aboard the twin Mare Nostrum vessels. Info from Hôtel Monte Rosso.

Via Mare (06 07 28 72 72) Experienced operator with a selection of trips and good commentaries. Info from Hôtel Le Golfe.

BOAT HIRE

Hiring your own vessel can be a good way to escape the crowds, but you'll obviously miss out on the local knowledge. Smaller vessels don't require a licence – most places charge the same fees, at around €75/115 per half/full day.

Patrick & Toussaint (06 81 41 70 03; wwwpatrickettoussaint.com)

Porto Bateaux Locations (06 88 84 49 87; www.portobateaulocation.com)

DIVING

Porto is one of the island's best-known diving spots. If you're a qualified submariner you'll be in seventh heaven, especially around the Capo Rasso area and the edges of the Scandola reserve – although diving within the protected zone itself is strictly forbidden. Porto is well stocked with accredited outfits, all offering single- and multi-trip dives (from around €35, including equipment) as well as courses and *baptême* (introductory) sessions.

Centre de Plongée du Golfe de Porto (04 95 26 10 29; www.plongeeporto.com; Porto Marina; Easter-Nov)

École de Plongée Génération Bleue (04 95 26 24 88; www.generation-bleue.com; Porto Marina; May-Oct)

Méditerranée Porto Sub (MPS; 04 95 26 19 47; www.plongeecose.fr; Porto Marina; mid-Apr–Sep)

HIKING

There are many stunning hikes around Porto, Ota and Évisa, 28 of which are detailed in *Hikes & Walks in the Area of Porto* (€2.50), available from the tourist office.

CORSICAN ESSENTIALS

If there's one thing that gets the Corsicans fired up, it's their food. We've listed a few delicacies to look out for on your travels, but this is really just a start – you'll find lots of other variations on traditional dishes scattered across the island, so it's well worth asking for local recommendations.

Cheese

King of the island's cheeses is Brocciu, a crumbly white ewes'- or goats'-milk cheese protected by its own *Appellation d'Origine Contrôlée* (AOC), and used in lots of Corsican dishes. The classics to try are *omelette au brocciu* and *cannelloni au brocciu.*

Chestnuts

Since the 16th century, Corsicans have been lovingly tending their *chataigniers* (chestnut trees), sometimes affectionately dubbed *l'arbre à pain* (the bread tree). Look out for chestnut fritters, chestnut flour, chestnut mousse, chestnut jam, chestnut biscuits – and even chestnut beer (Pietra).

Sausages

Lonzu, figatellu, coppu, salsiccia – Corsica has more varieties of sausage than you could count on one trotter, but make sure you're getting the real McCoy. To avoid knock-offs, buy only from good delis, local market stalls or high-quality restaurants.

Wild boar

Sanglier (wild boar) is traditionally eaten in the rich meaty stew known as *civet de sanglier,* and is a must-try for committed carnivores.

Wine

Corsica's wines are rapidly growing in reputation, with nine AOC-labelled areas and over 7000 hectares of vines on the islands: areas to watch out for are Patrimonio, Cap Corse, Ajaccio and Sartène.

Corsica Cola

Corsica's own answer to 'the real thing', produced by the makers of Pietra beer and dubbed 'the cola for hotheads' by the adverts. Can you taste the difference? Well yes, frankly.

Oursin

Corsica is renowned for its fantastic shellfish, but gastronomic adventurers should try the local speciality, *oursin* (sea urchin). These spiny critters definitely look as though they don't want to be eaten, but the local fishermen swear by 'em.

Sleeping

Even by Corsican standards, Porto's hotel prices are truly out of this world in July and August, and many places shut up shop between November and March.

Camping Sol e Vista (☎ 04 95 26 15 71; www.camping-sol-e-vista.com; per person €5.50-5.70, tent €2.20-2.50, car €2.20-2.50, 4-bed chalet per week €400-550) Climbing the hillside beside the Spar supermarket, this terraced campground is basic but still very attractive, with spacious sites, laundry facilities and a small café.

Camping Les Oliviers (☎ 04 95 26 14 49; www.campinglesoliviers.com; per person €6.80-9.10, tent €3-6.50, car €2.50-3.50, 5-bed chalet per week €429-826; late Mar-early Nov;) Idyllically set among overhanging olive trees, this campsite's deluxe facilities include a gym, pizzeria and rock-surround swimming pool, plus wooden chalets straight out of *Little House on the Prairie*. Expect company in the high season.

Bon Accueil (☎ 04 95 26 19 50; BA20150@aol.com; Vaita; d €41-51;) About the cheapest option in town, removed from the harbour hustle above a café-cum-souvenir shop in Vaita. For this kind of cash you can expect clean, spartan rooms with minimal frills: bag a balcony room and you won't even notice the lack of furniture.

Le Belvedere (☎ 04 95 26 12 01; www.hotel-le-belvedere.com; d €45-110; ❄) Our pick of the seemingly endless hotels around Porto's marina (as long as you're not staying in high summer, when prices skyrocket). It's modern and functional, and has top-drawer bay-view balconies, shiny bathroom suites, ice-cold air-con and a sunset aspect worth triple the price.

M'Hôtel Corsica (☎ 04 95 26 10 89; www.hotel-corsica-porto.com; d €55-85; ❄) Get past the livid-pink facade and you'll be hard-pushed to find a better-value spot in Porto. It's a reliable hotel occupying a valley spot framed by eucalyptus, riotous plants and a top-drawer pool (squint a bit and it's Caribbeanesque). Admittedly, the decor's dated, but the valley views are super; kitchenettes and air-con are optional extras.

Le Colombo (☎ 04 95 26 10 14; www.hotellecolombo.com, in French; rte de Calvi; d incl breakfast €62-127; 🕑 Apr-Oct; ❄) A cut above Porto's cookie-cutter condo-hotels, this quirky little place has an eclectic jumble of rooms. Most are a soothing sky-blue with views of garden, sea and mountain, supplemented by offbeat touches such as tree-branch table lamps and a Corsican brekkie served up by the *patronne* (owner).

Eating

Le Sud (☎ 04 95 26 14 11; mains €24-28; 🕑 Apr-Oct) An excellent fish and seafood restaurant with Mediterranean overtones and a lovely verandah overlooking the port and watchtower. Try the *lotte au chorizo* (monkfish with chorizo) or plump for the fish of the day (decent value at €7 per 100g).

Self-caterers have two side-by-side supermarkets: **Spar** (🕑 8.30am-12.30pm & 3-7.30pm Mon-Sat, 8.30am-12.15pm Sun) and **Banco** (🕑 8.30am-12.30pm & 3-7.30pm Mon-Sat, 8.30am-12.30pm Sun) on the main Calvi road, plus an excellent bakery in Vaita.

Getting There & Around

Autocars Ceccaldi (☎ 04 95 22 41 99) operates buses from Porto to Ajaccio (€11, 2½ hours, two daily, no Sunday buses except from July to mid-September), stopping at Piana and Cargèse en route. For buses from Porto to Calvi, see p921).

Transports Mordiconi (☎ 04 95 48 00 44) links Porto with Ota (€4) and Évisa (€8), the Col de Vergio (€14, 2¼ hours) and Corte (€20, 2¾ hours) once daily except on Sundays from July to mid-September. Buses leave from behind the beach near the Restaurant Mini-Golf.

Opposite the supermarkets, **Porto Locations** (☎ /fax 04 95 26 10 13) hires out bikes (€15/58 per day/week), scooters (€46/198) and cars (€58/298).

For a taxi contact **Chez Félix** (☎ 04 95 26 12 92).

OTA & ÉVISA

pop 300

Hidden in the hills inland from Porto, the twin villages of Ota and Évisa dangle defiantly above a plunging canyon blanketed with thick woods of pine, oak and chestnut, hemmed in by sky-reaching peaks and plunging defiles. Quintessentially Corsican, these magical mountain villages are a haven for hikers, positioned halfway along the Mare e Monti trail and within striking distance of the Foret d'Aïtone and Corsica's answer to the Grand Canyon – the Gorges de Spelunca.

The Porto tourist office (see p922) provides information on Évisa, Ota and the surrounding areas, including tips on hiking trails.

Sights & Activities

Carpeting the slopes east of Évisa is the **Forêt d'Aïtone**, home of Corsica's most impressive stands of Laricio pines. These arrow-straight, 60m-high trees once provided beams and masts for Genoese ships. The Évisa area is also famous for its chestnuts (which have been granted their very own AOC label), and every year the village celebrates its nutty produce at the **Fête du Marron** in November.

Between Ota and Évisa plunges the unforgettable **Gorges de Spelunca**, one of the deepest natural canyons in Corsica. Until the D84 was carved out from the mountainside, the only link between the villages was a tiny mule track via two Genoese bridges, the Ponte Vecchju and Ponte Zaghlia. The track is now part of the Mare e Monti hiking trail. The stretch between Ota and Évisa makes a fantastic day-hike, winding along the valley floor past the rushing River Porto and soaring orange cliffs, some more than a kilometre high. The whole Ota–Évisa route takes about five hours return, or you can follow the two-hour section between the bridges: pick the trail up at the arched road-bridge 2km east of Ota.

There are lots of other wonderful hikes in the area, including the **Sentier de Chataignes** (2½ hours, 7km return from Évisa), which winds through chestnut forest and mountain pools to the crashing Cascades d'Aïtone (Aïtone Falls, 7km return). There are also several trails venturing off from the 1477m-high **Col de Vergio**.

Sleeping & Eating

Hôtel L'Aïtone (☎ 04 95 26 20 04; www.hotel-aitone.com, in French; d €35-110; 🕑 Feb-Nov; 🏊 🅿) Plonked at the top of Évisa, the endearingly old-world Aïtone feels like it's dropped out of a wormhole to the 19th century. The rooms are plainly furnished and pretty basic (cheaper rooms have a shared loo), and the rustic restaurant – complete with roaring fire and sweeping valley view – is hardly haute cuisine (mains €12 to €20), but somehow it's still delightful. Make sure you get a valley outlook and leave time to lounge in the lovely panoramic pool.

La Châtaigneraie (☎ 04 95 26 24 47; www.hotel-la-chataigneraie.com, in French; d €40-53, tr €59-67) In the lower part of the village, on the left-hand side as you drive up from Ota, this sweet little stone house is run by an engaging American-Corsican couple (and their energetic kids): expect apple-green shutters, chintzy, comfy rooms and home-cooked food prepared by *la patronne*.

If you're tramping on the trail, you'll find cut-price *gîte* beds and solid food at **Chez Félix** (☎ 04 95 26 12 92; place de la Fontaine; dm €13) and **Chez Marie** (☎ 04 95 26 11 37; dm €16), both in Ota.

Getting There & Away

There's a daily bus from Monday to Saturday from Évisa to Porto (€8, 40 minutes) and Corte (€17, two hours).

PIANA

pop 500

Teetering above the Golfe de Porto and surrounded by the scarlet pillars of Les Calanques, Piana makes for a less frenzied base than nearby Porto in the high season, and is a useful launching pad for exploring the idyllic beaches of **Ficajola** (4km from Piana) and **Arone** (11km southwest on the D824). The town's main landmark is the Église Ste-Marie, the focus for the annual Good Friday procession of La Granitola.

The **Tourist Office** (Syndicat d'Initiative ☎ 04 95 27 84 42; www.sipiana.com; place Mairie; 🕑 9am-6pm Mon-Fri) is next to the post office.

Piana has a limited supply of hotels.

Le Scandola (☎ 04 95 27 80 07; www.hotelscandola.com; d €50-100), uphill from the village on the left-hand side of the D81 as you drive towards Cargèse, near the turn-off to Ficajola, might resemble a Costa del Sol reject, but give it a chance; the rooms are bright and breezy, bathrooms are spotless, and the balconies have some of the best views in town.

The best budget option is **Hôtel Continental** (☎ 04 95 27 83 12; www.continentalpiana.com; d €54-80, tr €64-67; 🕑 Apr-Sep), in the middle of Piana on the main road near the petrol station, which has two buildings separated by a grassy garden. The blue-shuttered 19th-century townhouse has the older rooms; more modern, beach-style rooms (with town-view balconies) are found in the annexe.

Corsica's original luxury hotel, **Hôtel des Roches Rouges** (☎ 04 95 27 81 81; www.lesrochesrouges.com; D81; d €90-105, tr €135, q €129-160; 🕑 mid-Mar–mid-Nov), built in 1912, is still one of the most idyllic places to stay on the island. It's on the right-hand side of the D81 as you drive from Porto, just before Piana. The rambling corridors and musty rooms are full of early-20th-century ambience, despite modern en suites, wi-fi and phone lines – you half expect Hercule Poirot to wander round the corner twiddling his moustache. Don't even consider cutting costs by not taking a sea-view room – you'll regret it.

Buses between Porto and Ajaccio stop near the church and the post office.

LES CALANQUES

Flaming fiery red in the sunlight, the crimson cliffs and weird rock pillars of Les Calanques de Piana (E Calanche in Corsican) are one of Corsica's most photogenic sights, carved out by centuries of sun, wind and rain. Several trails wind their way around these dramatic rock formations, many of which start near the Pont de Mezzanu, a road bridge near the Chalet des Roches Bleues souvenir shop, about 3km from Piana along the D81. The Piana tourist office has a free leaflet detailing more walks.

Four trails begin nearby:

Chemin des Muletiers The old 'Mule-Drivers' Trail' that once linked Piana and Ota is a classic, with some of the best Calanche views; look out for the signed trailhead 50m from the Pont de Mezzanu.

Chemin du Château Fort A one-hour trail to a fortress-shaped rock with stunning views of the Golfe de Porto. The trailhead is on the D81 beside the distinctive Tête de Chien (Dog's Head) rock, 3.5km east of Piana.

La Forêt de Piana Three possible routes through pine and chestnut woods, starting about 1.5km from Porto near the Pont de Mezzanu.

La Tour de Capo Rosso A stiff three-hour walk to the Tour de Turghiu (331m) and the Capo Rosso, Corsica's most westerly point. The trail starts about 6km from Piana on the D824 towards Arone.

CARGÈSE (CARGHJESE)

pop 900

With its whitewashed houses and sunbaked streets, Cargèse feels more like a Grecian hilltop village than a Corsican harbour – this is hardly surprising, since the village was founded by refugee Greeks fleeing their Ottoman-controlled homeland in the 19th century. The town is known for its **twin churches** – one Eastern (Orthodox), the other Western (Catholic) – that eye each other across vegetable plots, like boxers squaring up for a bout. The interior of the 19th-century Greek church contains original relics carried across by settlers from their Peloponnese homeland.

The **tourist office** (☎ 04 95 26 41 31; www.cargese.net; rue du Docteur Dragacci; 🕑 9am-7pm Jun-Sep, 9am-12.30pm & 2.30-6pm Mon-Sat Oct-May) is a little way north of the churches, while the town's harbour is downhill to the south. Boat trips with **Nave Va** (☎ 04 95 28 02 66; www.naveva.com) and **Crosières Grand Bleu** (☎ 04 95 26 40 24) sail to Scandola, Girolata and Les Calanques in summer.

One kilometre north of Cargèse is the small strip of Plage de Pero, overlooked by a couple of Genoese watchtowers, but for more space you'll need to push on south towards the popular bay of Sagone, about 10km further along the coastal D81.

Hôtel Cyrnos (☎ 04 95 26 49 47; www.torraccia.com, in French; rue de la République; d €35-60), a lemon-yellow townhouse in the heart of Cargèse, has freshly decorated, good-value rooms. The pick of these have dinky balconies teetering over the town's rooftops.

Tumble straight from your room onto the soft sands of Pero beach at lovely little **Hôtel Thalassa** (☎ 04 95 26 40 08; www.thalassalura.com; d €70-80; 🕑 May-Sep; Ⓟ), which is simply but sweetly furnished with views of garden and ocean. There are great weekly and half-board deals if you fancy sticking around to soak up the sunshine.

Two daily buses from Ota (1½ hours) via Porto (one hour) to Ajaccio (one hour) stop in front of the post office. There are no buses on Sunday except in July and August.

AJACCIO (AJACCIU)

pop 52,880

The spectre of Corsica's great (little) general looms over the elegant port city of Ajaccio (pronounced a·zhaks·jo). Napoléon Bonaparte was born here in 1769, and the city is dotted with relics relating to the diminutive dictator, from his childhood home to seafront statues, historic museums and countless street-names. Often dubbed *La Cité Imperiale* in recognition of its historic importance, Ajaccio is the capital of the Corse-du-Sud *département* and is the island's main metropolis.

Orientation

Ajaccio's main street, cours Napoléon, stretches from place de Gaulle northwards to the train station and beyond. The old city is south of place Foch. The port is on the eastern side of town, from where a promenade leads west along plage St-François.

Information

BOOKSHOPS

Album (☎ 04 95 21 81 18; 2 place Foch; 🕑 8.30am-noon & 2.30-7pm Mon-Sat, 8.30am-noon Sun Oct-May)

EMERGENCY

Centre Hospitalier Notre-Dame de la Miséricorde (☎ 04 95 29 90 90; 27 av de l'Impératrice Eugénie; 🕑 24hr)

Police Station (☎ 04 95 11 17 17; rue Général Fiorella)

INTERNET ACCESS

Cyber Espace (rue Docteur Versini; per 30min/1hr €2/3; 🕑 10am-12.30am Mon-Sat)

LAUNDRY

Lavomatique (rue du Maréchal Ornano; 🕑 8am-10pm)

MONEY

Banks with ATMs are found along place de Gaulle, place Foch and cours Napoléon.

POST

Post Office (13 cours Napoléon)

TOURIST INFORMATION

Tourist Office (☎ 04 95 51 53 03; www.ajaccio-tourisme.com; 3 bd du Roi Jérôme; 🕑 9am-6pm Mon-Sat, 9am-1pm Sun Jun-Sep, 8.30-11.30am & 1.30-4pm Mon-Fri Oct-May) Free internet kiosk.

Maison d'Information Randonnées du Parc Naturel Régional de Corse (☎ 04 95 51 79 10; www.parc-naturel-corse.com; 2 rue Sergent Casalonga; 🕑 8am-noon & 2-6pm Mon-Fri Jun-Sep, 8am-noon &

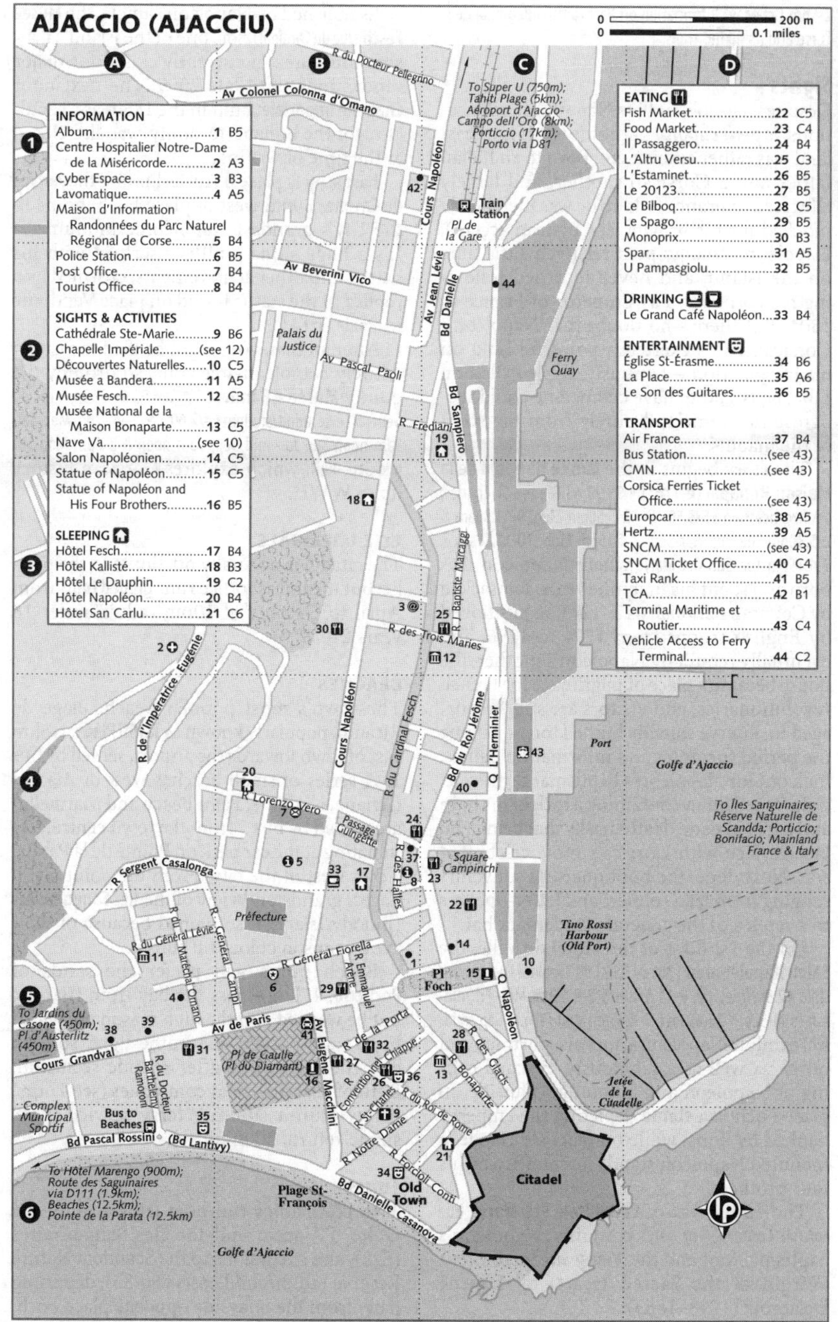
AJACCIO (AJACCIU)
0 200 m
0 0.1 miles
A B C D
1 2 3 4 5 6
INFORMATION
Album.....1 B5
Centre Hospitalier Notre-Dame de la Miséricorde.....2 A3
Cyber Espace.....3 B3
Lavomatique.....4 A5
Maison d'Information Randonnées du Parc Naturel Régional de Corse.....5 B4
Police Station.....6 B5
Post Office.....7 B4
Tourist Office.....8 B4
SIGHTS & ACTIVITIES
Cathédrale Ste-Marie.....9 B6
Chapelle Impériale.....(see 12)
Découvertes Naturelles.....10 C5
Musée a Bandera.....11 A5
Musée Fesch.....12 C3
Musée National de la Maison Bonaparte.....13 C5
Nave Va.....(see 10)
Salon Napoléonien.....14 C5
Statue of Napoléon.....15 C5
Statue of Napoléon and His Four Brothers.....16 B5
SLEEPING
Hôtel Fesch.....17 B4
Hôtel Kallisté.....18 B3
Hôtel Le Dauphin.....19 C2
Hôtel Napoléon.....20 B4
Hôtel San Carlu.....21 C6
EATING
Fish Market.....22 C5
Food Market.....23 C4
Il Passaggero.....24 B4
L'Altru Versu.....25 C3
L'Estaminet.....26 B5
Le 20123.....27 B5
Le Bilboq.....28 C5
Le Spago.....29 B5
Monoprix.....30 B3
Spar.....31 A5
U Pampasgiolu.....32 B5
DRINKING
Le Grand Café Napoléon.....33 B4
ENTERTAINMENT
Église St-Érasme.....34 B6
La Place.....35 A6
Le Son des Guitares.....36 B5
TRANSPORT
Air France.....37 B4
Bus Station.....(see 43)
CMN.....(see 43)
Corsica Ferries Ticket Office.....(see 43)
Europcar.....38 A5
Hertz.....39 A5
SNCM.....(see 43)
SNCM Ticket Office.....40 C4
Taxi Rank.....41 B5
TCA.....42 B1
Terminal Maritime et Routier.....43 C4
Vehicle Access to Ferry Terminal.....44 C2
R du Docteur Pellegrino
Av Colonel Colonna d'Omano
To Super U (750m); Tahiti Plage (5km); Aéroport d'Ajaccio-Campo dell'Oro (8km); Porticcio (17km); Porto via D81
Cours Napoléon
Train Station
Pl de la Gare
Av Beverini Vico
Av Jean Lévie
Bd Danielle
Palais du Justice
Av Pascal Paoli
Ferry Quay
Bd Sampiero
R Frediani
R J Baptiste Marcaggi
R des Trois Maries
R de l'Impératrice Eugénie
R du Cardinal Fesch
Bd du Roi Jérôme
Q L'Herminier
Port
Golfe d'Ajaccio
To Îles Sanguinaires; Réserve Naturelle de Scandda; Porticcio; Bonifacio; Mainland France & Italy
R Lorenzo Vero
Passage Guingette
R des Halles
Square Campinchi
R Sergent Casalonga
Préfecture
R du Général Lévie
R du Maréchal Ornano
R Général Campi
R Général Fiorella
R Emmanuel Arène
Pl Foch
Q Napoléon
Tino Rossi Harbour (Old Port)
To Jardins du Casone (450m); Pl d'Austerlitz (450m)
Av de Paris
Cours Grandval
R du Docteur Barthélemy Ramorol
Pl de Gaulle (Pl du Diamant)
Av Eugène Macchini
R de la Porta
R Conventionnel Chappe
R St-Charles
R du Roi de Rome
R Bonaparte
R des Glacis
R Notre Dame
R Forcioli Conti
Jetée de la Citadelle
Complex Municipal Sportif
Bus to Beaches
Bd Pascal Rossini
(Bd Lantivy)
Citadel
To Hôtel Marengo (900m); Route des Saguinaires via D111 (1.9km); Beaches (12.5km); Pointe de la Parata (12.5km)
Plage St-François
Old Town
Bd Danielle Casanova
Golfe d'Ajaccio

2-5pm Oct-May) Information on Parc Naturel Régional de Corse and its hiking trails.

Sights

Despite Ajaccio's endless Napoléonic connections, *le petit caporal's* attitude to his home island was rather ambivalent. Born to an Italian father and a Corsican mother, and largely educated in France (where he was mercilessly mocked for his provincial Corsican accent), Napoléon actually spent relatively little time on the island, and never returned following his coronation as Emperor of France in 1804. But there's no doubt that Napoléon's Corsican roots exerted a powerful hold on his imagination – famously, while exiled on Elba, he is said to have claimed he could recognise his homeland purely from the scent of the maquis.

The story begins at the **Musée National de la Maison Bonaparte** (☎ 04 95 21 43 89; rue St-Charles; adult/concession €5/3.50; ⏰ 2-5.50pm Mon, 9-11.30am & 2-5.30pm Tue-Sun Apr-Sep, 2-4.15pm Mon, 10-11.30am & 2-4.15pm Tue-Sun Oct-Mar), where Napoléon was born and spent his first nine years. Ransacked by Corsican nationalists in 1793, requisitioned by English troops from 1794 to 1796, and eventually rebuilt by Napoléon's mother, the house became a place of pilgrimage for French revolutionaries, and visitors are still encouraged to observe suitably hushed tones. Among the period furniture and information panels, look out for Napoléon's baptismal certificate; a glass medallion containing a lock of his hair; and a trio of eerie death masks that bring you face-to-face with Corsica's most celebrated son. Next door, the boutique sells souvenirs ranging from lead soldiers and letter-openers to a replica of the general's trademark hat.

On the 1st floor of the Hôtel de Ville, the **Salon Napoléonien** (☎ 04 95 21 90 15; place Foch; adult/child €2.30/free; ⏰ 9-11.45am & 2-5.45pm Mon-Fri mid-Jun–mid-Sep, 9-11.45am & 2-4.45pm Mon-Fri mid-Sep–mid-Jun) exhibits Napoléonic medals, portraits and busts, as well as a fabulously frescoed ceiling of Napoléon and entourage. Outside on place Foch is a **statue** depicting the emperor flanked by lions, while on place de Gaulle, a mounted Napoléon stands surrounded by his four brothers.

The 16th-century **Cathédrale Ste-Marie** (rue Forcioli Conti; ⏰ hr vary) contains Napoléon's baptismal font and the *Vierge au Sacré-Cœur* (Virgin of the Sacred Heart) by Eugène Delacroix (1798–1863).

Established by Napoléon's uncle, the **Musée Fesch** (rue du Cardinal Fesch), one of the island's flagship museums, is currently closed for major renovations until late 2009. The next-door **Chapelle Impériale**, built in the 1850s as a sepulchre for the Bonaparte family, was also closed at the time of writing.

Last stop is place d'Austerlitz and the **Jardins du Casone**, 800m west of place Foch, home to the city's grandest Napoléonic monument. It's a huge stone plinth, inscribed with his battles and other achievements, crowned by a replica of the statue found on place Vendôme in Paris (p141).

After all that, you might be glad to visit an entirely Napoléon-free zone, so drop by the quirky **Musée a Bandera** (☎ 04 95 51 07 34; 1 rue du Général Lévie; adult/student €4/2.60; ⏰ 9am-7pm Mon-Sat, 9am-noon Sun Jul–mid-Sep, 9am-noon & 2-6pm Mon-Sat mid-Sep–Jun), which explores Corsican history up to WWII.

CITÉ IMPÉRIALE

The citadel is normally off-limits to the public, but the tourist office runs **guided tours** from April to October at 10pm (adult/under 18 years €10/8).

BEACHES

The town's most popular beach, Plage de Ricanto, popularly known as **Tahiti Plage**, is 5km east of town towards the airport, served by bus 1. A series of small beaches west of Ajaccio (Ariane, Neptune, Palm Beach and Marinella) are served by bus 5 from the town centre, terminating at the car park on Pointe de la Parata, 12km west of the city. From the point you'll have a grandstand view of the **Îles Sanguinaires** (Bloody Islands), so named because of their vivid crimson colours at sunset.

Beach bums will prefer the sands of **Porticcio**, 17km across the bay from Ajaccio, but be warned – in the high season the windbreaks are packed in sardine-tight, so look elsewhere if you're after seaside seclusion. Both of Ajaccio's boat companies (see Tours, below) run a summer ferry service (€5/8 single/return, 30 minutes).

Tours

Two companies run boat trips around the Golfe d'Ajaccio and the Îles Sanguinaires (€25), and excursions to the Scandola Nature Reserve (adult/child costs €50/35), departing daily from the quayside opposite place Foch.

Découvertes Naturelles (☎ 06 24 69 48 80; www.promenades-en-mer.org; ⏲ May-Sep) Also offers a sunset cruise to the Îles Sanguinaires (€25), returning around 10pm.
Nave Va (☎ 04 95 51 31 31; www.naveva.com; ⏲ May-Sep) Also offers a cultural tour (adult/child costs €28/20) and a voyage down to Bonifacio (€57/40), including a four-hour stop on shore.

Festivals & Events

Like many of Corsica's towns, Ajaccio has a line-up of annual festivities that adds some extra spice to the town's streets.

Chants Polyphoniques Corsican concerts are held every Wednesday at 7pm in Église St-Érasme.
Festival de la St-Érasme Fishy festival in honour of the patron saint of pêcheurs, held around 2 June.
Fêtes Napoléoniennes Ajaccio's biggest bash celebrates Napoléon's birthday on 15 August, with military-themed parades, street spectacles and a huge fireworks display.
La relève de la Garde Impériale Every Thursday at 7pm in summer, you can watch the pomp and ceremony of the changing of the guard on place Foch in front of the town hall.

Sleeping

Ajaccio's hotels are steeply priced, especially in the high season – book well ahead for big events such as the WRC Car Rally and the Fêtes Napoléoniennes.

our pick Hôtel Kallisté (☎ 04 95 51 34 45; www.hotel-kalliste-ajaccio.com, in French; 51 cours Napoléon; s €56-69, d €64-79, tr €79-99; ❄ 💻 ⊠) Exposed brick, neutral tones, terracotta tiles and a funky glass lift conjure a neo-boutique feel at the Kallisté. Double-glazing and electric shutters keep out the traffic hum from nearby cours Napoléon, and the facilities are fab – wi-fi, satellite TV, an on-site laundry and a stonking buffet brekkie. Unfortunately, the secret's out, so book ahead.

Hôtel Marengo (☎ 04 95 21 43 66; www.hotel-marengo.com; 2 rue Marengo; d €61-79, tr €75-95; ❄) For something more personal, try this jolly, hospitably run little bolthole. Country prints and vintage furniture throughout, plus pastel rooms (all with balconies) and a quiet flower-filled courtyard, all just a stroll from the beach.

Hôtel Fesch (☎ 04 95 51 62 62; www.hotel-fesch.com; 7 rue du Cardinal Fesch; s €61-86, d €66-97, tr €87-122; ⏲ closed mid-Dec–mid-Jan; ❄) A grand old dame that's starting to show her years, but if it's old-fashioned service and traditional rooms you're after, the Fesch fits the bill. Free wi-fi (ask for the code) and flat-screen TVs meet old-fashioned furniture in the 77 rooms, but the cheaper rooms are poky (wheelchair users and baggage-luggers won't appreciate the weird 1st-floor lift).

Hôtel San Carlu (☎ 04 95 21 13 84; www.hotel-sancarlu.com; 8 bd Danielle Casanova; s €76-86, d €85-99; ❄) About the only place to stay in the old city, the San Carlu occupies a fine position opposite the citadel – but don't even think about getting a room without a view, as the motel-style decor is hardly cutting edge.

Other options:

Hôtel Le Dauphin (☎ 04 95 21 12 94; www.ledauphinhotel.com; 11 bd Sampiero; s €52-59, d €60-79, tr €79-96; ❄) Ajaccio's idea of a budget hotel, with cheap(ish), functional rooms, some with port-view balconies overlooking the hectic road and ground-floor café-bar.
Hôtel Napoléon (☎ 04 95 51 54 00; www.hotel-napoleon-ajaccio.fr; 4 rue Lorenzo Vero; s €65-92, d €77-109; ❄ P) Modernish rooms in a quiet spot, all with complimentary wi-fi, LCD TVs and safes.

Eating

Tiny street-side restaurants cram the old quarter, and eating out there on a sultry summer night is an experience not to be missed.

Il Passaggero (☎ 04 95 21 30 52; 3 bd du Roi Jérôme; mains €12-18; ⏲ daily) Hip new Italian-cum-Mediterranean restaurant by the harbour, specialising in authentic pastas, fresh fish and inventive risottos – try the one made with *oursin* (sea urchin).

Le Spago (☎ 04 95 21 15 71; rue Emmanuel Arène; mains €14-22; ⏲ lunch & dinner Mon-Fri, dinner Sat) Sleekly styled bistro with a metropolitan edge, from the space-age lime-green chairs to the customised oil dispensers and retro lighting. Fusion food fills the *carte* – chicken kebabs, pesto gnocchi, Moroccan *tajines* (slow-cooked meat and vegetable stews) – and the clientele is cool and classy.

U Pampasgiolu (☎ 06 09 39 26 92; 15 rue de la Porta; mains €14-24, platters €26-27; ⏲ dinner) The rustic arch-vaulted dining room of this Ajaccio institution is packed with punters nearly every night of the week. They come for the first-rate Corsican food – from pork fillets in chestnut-honey to veal cutlets and farm-fresh *fromage de brebis* (sheep's cheese). If you're a novice, the *planches* (platters) offer bite-sized dishes – the *planche spuntinu* concentrates on country tucker while the *planche de la mer* offers fruits of the sea.

L'Altru Versu (☎ 04 95 50 05 22; 16 rue J Baptiste Marcaggi; mains €22-28; ⏲ lunch Tue-Sat, dinner Tue-Sun) One of the top tables for Corsican cuisine: dishes at 'The Other Side' include prawn and Brocciu tart, pork with Cotticcio almonds, and even sorbet tinged with Pietra beer. It's cosy and convivial: pans clatter, waiters hustle and Corsican *sons et guitares* (guitar players) serenade the terrace on Friday and Saturday nights.

Le 20123 (☎ 04 95 21 50 05; 2 rue du Roi de Rome; menus €32; ⏰ dinner Tue-Sun) This one-of-a-kind place started life in the village of Pila Canale (postcode 20123 – get it?), and when the owner upped sticks to Ajaccio he decided to take the old village with him – water pump, washing line, central square et al. It sounds completely daft, and it is – but you won't find many more characterful places in Corsica. Needless to say, the food is 100% authentic, too.

Also recommended:

Le Bilboq (☎ 04 95 51 35 40; 2 rue des Glacis) An unpretentious diner with lots of Corsican staples and a sweet vine-covered patio.

L'Estaminet (☎ 04 95 50 10 42; 5 rue du Roi de Rome; mains €15.50-24.50, menus €18.50 & €25) An old-style brasserie decked out with shiny wood and polished brass, plus plenty of heart-and-soul country classics.

SELF-CATERING

The open-air **food market** (square Campinchi; ⏰ to noon, closed Mon) is stacked with cheese, sausages, jams, fruit and veg, while piscatorial treats are available at the nearby fish market.

Self-caterers have a **Spar** (cours Grandval; ⏰ 8.30am-12.30pm & 3-7.30pm Mon-Sat) and **Monoprix** (cours Napoléon; ⏰ 8.30am-7.15pm Mon-Sat) in the city centre, or a huge **Super U** (19 cours Prince Impérial; ⏰ 9am-8.30pm Mon-Sat) on the outskirts.

For Corsican goodies, there's only one address that matters: **U Stazzu** (☎ 04 95 51 10 80; 1 rue Bonaparte; ⏰ 9am-12.30pm & 2.30-7pm), famous for its handmade charcuterie.

Drinking & Entertainment

Le Grand Café Napoléon (10 cours Napoléon; ⏰ 8am-midnight daily) Ajaccio's jet-set dines in expensive style inside the chandelier-strewn dining room of this historic brasserie, but mere mortals can soak up the ritzy ambience with coffee on the streetside terrace.

Le Son des Guitares (☎ 04 95 51 15 47; 7 rue du Roi de Rome) Local guitarists serenade the punters at this cosy bar from around 10pm.

La Place (☎ 04 95 51 09 10; bd Lantivy; ⏰ 11pm-3am Fri-Sat) Ajaccio's only club is hardly cutting-edge, but local DJs host house and techno nights at weekends.

Getting There & Away

AIR

Aéroport d'Ajaccio-Campo dell'Oro (☎ 04 95 23 56 56) is 8km east of the city centre. Charter airlines have kiosks at the airport, but **Air France** (☎ 08 20 82 08 20; 3 bd du Roi Jérôme) also has an office in town.

BOAT

Boats depart from **Terminal Maritime et Routier** (quai l'Herminier), the combined bus/ferry terminal.

CMN (☎ 08 10 20 13 20; www.cmn.fr; bd Sampiero; ⏰ 8.15am-6pm Mon-Fri, 8.15am-noon Sat, open to 7pm Mon-Fri & from 4.30-7pm Sat on departure days) Located inside the terminal.

Corsica Ferries (☎ 08 25 09 50 95; www.corsicaferries.fr) Inside the terminal.

SNCM (☎ 04 95 29 66 99; www.sncm.fr; ⏰ 8am-8pm Tue-Fri, 8am-1pm Sat) The main office is on quai L'Herminier, and there's a ticket and information kiosk inside the terminal, which opens before most sailings.

BUS

Lots of local bus companies have kiosks inside the terminal building. As always in Corsica, expect reduced services on Sunday and during the winter months. The bus station information desk (☎ 04 95 51 42 56) can supply timetables.

Ceccaldi/SAIB (☎ 04 95 22 41 99) Travels to Porto (€11, two hours, two daily) via Tiuccia (30 minutes), Cargèse (55 minutes), and Piana (one hour and 25 minutes).

Eurocorse (☎ 04 95 21 06 30) Travels to Bastia (€22, three hours, two daily) via Vizzavona (one hour), Corte (1¾ hours) and Ponte Lecchia (two hours). Connecting buses travel from Ponte Lecchia to Calvi. There's also a route to Bonifacio (€22, four hours, two daily) via Propriano (1½ hours) and Sartène (€13.60, two hours).

CAR

The main car-rental companies also have airport bureaux.

Europcar (☎ 04 95 21 05 49; 16 cours Grandval)

Hertz (☎ 04 95 21 70 94; 8 cours Grandval)

Hôtel Kallisté (p929) rents out cars and mopeds cheaply.

TRAIN

The **train station** (☎ 04 95 23 11 03; place de la Gare) is staffed until 6.30pm (to 8pm May to September). Services include Bastia (€23.90, four hours, three to four daily), Corte (€12.70, two hours, three to four daily) and Calvi (€27.80, five hours, two daily; change at Ponte Leccia).

Getting Around

TO/FROM THE AIRPORT

Transports Corse d'Ajaccio (TCA) bus 8 links the airport with Ajaccio's train and bus stations (€4.50). Hourly buses run from around 6am to 7pm from the bus station, and from 9am to 11pm from the airport. A taxi costs €30 to €35.

BUS

TCA (☎ 04 95 23 29 41; 75 cours Napoléon) operates Ajaccio's municipal bus network. A single ticket/*carnet* of 10 costs €1.20/9. Most buses operate from place de Gaulle and cours Napoléon; useful lines include number 5 to Pointe de la Parata and number 8 to the airport.

TAXI

There's a **taxi rank** (☎ 04 95 21 00 87) on place de Gaulle.

SOUTH OF AJACCIO

SARTÈNE (SARTÈ)

pop 3500

With its grey granite houses, secretive culs-de-sac and slightly sombre, introspective air, Sartène has long been said to encapsulate Corsica's rugged spirit (French novelist Prosper Mérimée dubbed it the 'most Corsican of Corsican towns'). There's no doubt that Sartène feels a long way from the glitter of the Corsican coast; the hillside houses are endearingly ramshackle, the streets are shady and scruffy, and life still crawls along at a traditional tilt. But it offers a much more convincing glimpse of how life was once lived in rural Corsica than do any of the island's more well-heeled towns. Notorious for its banditry and bloody vendettas in the 19th century, Sartène has more recently found fame thanks to the annual Procession du Catenacciu, a re-enactment of the Passion that takes place in the town every Good Friday.

Orientation & Information

Sartène's main square is place Porta (sometimes called place de la Libération), connecting the main streets of cours Sœur Amélie and cours Général de Gaulle. The Santa Anna quarter is north of place de la Libération.

Crédit Lyonnais (14 cours Général de Gaulle) Has an ATM.

Post Office (rue du Marché) Has an ATM.

Tourist Office (☎ 04 95 77 15 40; ot-sartene@wanadoo.fr; cours Sœur Amélie; 9am-12.30pm & 2-6.30pm Mon-Fri, plus 9am-12.30pm & 2.30-6.30pm Sat in high season)

Sights & Activities

The only way to explore Sartène is on foot, and the town's corkscrew alleyways and shady staircases make an agreeable stroll on a blazing summer's afternoon. An archway through the **town hall** (formerly the Governors' Palace) leads to the residential **Santa Anna quarter**, where you'll find the town's most atmospheric streets.

Near the **WWI memorial** on place Porta is the granite **Église Ste-Marie**, which houses the 35kg cross and 17kg chain used in the annual **Procession du Catenacciu**. Since the Middle Ages, every Good Friday the Catenacciu ('chained one') has lugged this massive hunk of wood through town in a re-enactment of Christ's journey to Calvary. Barefoot, red-robed and cowled (to preserve his anonymity), the penitent is chosen by the parish priest to atone for a grave sin – in times gone by, legend has it that notorious bandits descended from the maquis to expiate their crimes.

South of Sartène are several lovely beaches, including windswept **Roccapina**, the remote beaches of **Erbaju** and **Tra Licettu**, and the heart-meltingly pretty little port of **Tizzano**, at the end of the D48.

Sleeping & Eating

Hôtel La Villa Piana (☎ 04 95 77 07 04; www.lavillapiana.com; d €50-115; Apr–mid-Oct;) This attractive villa-style hotel mixes up-to-date-comfort and good old-fashioned service. Run with trademark efficiency by the bustling madame, you'll find spacious rooms decked out in solemn beiges and dark wood. Outside, drink in views of Sartène from the hilltop pool and breakfast patio. The excellent restaurant across the street, L'Instant (mains €16 to €28), serves some of Sartène's most contemporary food.

Hôtel des Roches (☎ 04 95 77 07 61; www.sartenehotel.fr; s €54-90, d €64-100; Apr-Oct) It won't win any beauty contests, but Sartène's only central hotel still packs in the coach parties thanks to its central location and (at least in some rooms) plunging valley views. Boxy, modern rooms are plainly furnished and a bit threadbare in places; management can be a little offish, too.

Self-caterers can stock up at **Spar** (14 cours Général de Gaulle) or **Atac** (cours Sœur Amélie) supermarkets, or pick up Corsican delicacies

STONES OF THE SARTÈNAIS

Dotted around the granite hilltops of the Sartènais are Corsica's most astonishing prehistoric sites. Some time around 4000–3000 BC, Corsica developed its own megalithic faith (possibly imported by seafaring settlers from mainland Europe); most of the island's standing stones and menhirs date from this period. The most important site is **Filitosa** (☎ 04 95 74 00 91; admission €5; 🕑 8am-8pm Apr-Oct), northwest of Sartène, where a collection of extraordinary carved menhirs were discovered in 1946 by the land's owner, Charles-Antoine Césari (an episode memorably recounted in Dorothy Carrington's classic book on Corsica, *Granite Island*). The Filitosa menhirs are highly unusual: several have detailed faces, anatomical features (such as ribcages) and even swords and armour, suggesting that they may commemorate specific warriors or chieftains. A small **museum** displays arrowheads, pottery and other archaeological artefacts.

Southwest of Sartène are the **Cauria** alignments – the **Alignement de Stantari** and the **Alignement de Renaju** – several of which show similar anatomical details and weaponry to those of Filitosa. Nearby is one of Corsica's few burial chambers, the **Fontanaccia** dolmen, with its supporting pillars and capstones. Look out for the turn-off about 8km along the D48 towards Tizzano.

Four kilometres further on from the turn-off is the Mediterranean's largest alignment of standing stones, the **Alignement de Paddaghiu**, with four distinct rows of huge menhirs perfectly aligned to face the rising sun. The site is reached via a rough track from the car park near the Mosconi vineyard.

What did these strange sites signify for their megalithic architects? Were they ritual temples? Sacred graveyards? Mythical armies? Or even celestial timepieces? Despite countless theories, PhD papers and academic postulations, no one has the foggiest idea.

at **U Maggiu** (☎ 04 95 77 21 36; 🕑 Apr-Oct), near pl Porta, just along from the town hall.

Getting There & Away

Sartène is on the twice-daily **Eurocorse** (☎ 04 95 21 06 30) bus line linking Ajaccio with Bonifacio.

BONIFACIO (BUNIFAZIU)

pop 2700

With its glittering harbour, creamy white cliffs and stout citadel teetering above the cornflower-blue waters of the Bouches de Bonifacio, this dazzling port is an essential stop on everyone's Corsican itinerary. Just a short hop from Sardinia, Bonifacio has a distinctly Italianate feel: sun-bleached townhouses, dangling washing lines and murky chapels cram the web of alleyways of the old citadel, while down below on the harbourside, brasseries and boat-kiosks tout their wares to the droves of day-trippers. Perfectly positioned for exploring the island's southerly beaches and the Îles Lavezzi, Bonifacio is the minxish little sister to Corsica's more grown-up towns.

Orientation

Bonifacio is split in two: the hilltop citadel (often referred to as the Haute Ville), reached via av Charles de Gaulle or on foot by two sets of steps, and the harbour, which sits beneath the citadel at the southeastern corner of Goulet de Bonifacio. The ferry terminal is northwest of the citadel.

Information

Boniboom (☎ 04 95 73 55 45; quai Jérôme Comparetti; internet access per 30min/1hr €3/5; 🕑 7am-midnight) Internet café.

Lavoir de la Marine (1 quai Jérôme Comparetti; 🕑 7am-10pm) Wash your beach togs here.

Post Office (place Carrega; 🕑 8.30am-12.30pm & 2-4pm Mon-Fri, 8.30am-noon Sat) Has an ATM.

Société Générale (38 rue St-Érasme; 🕑 Mon-Fri) ATM and currency exchange.

Tourist Office (☎ 04 95 73 11 88; www.bonifacio.fr; 2 rue Fred Scamaroni; 🕑 9am-8pm Jul & Aug, 9am-7pm May, Jun & Sep, 9am-noon & 2-6pm Mon-Fri Oct-Apr)

Tourist Office Annexe (Le Port; 🕑 9am-7pm Jun-Sep) Seasonal office by the harbour.

Sights & Activities

CITADEL (HAUTE VILLE)

A long slog from the harbour via the double staircases of Montée Rastello and Montée St-Roch brings you to the citadel's old gateway, the **Porte de Gênes**, complete with its original 16th-century drawbridge. Inside the gateway is the 13th-century **Bastion l'Étendard**, which

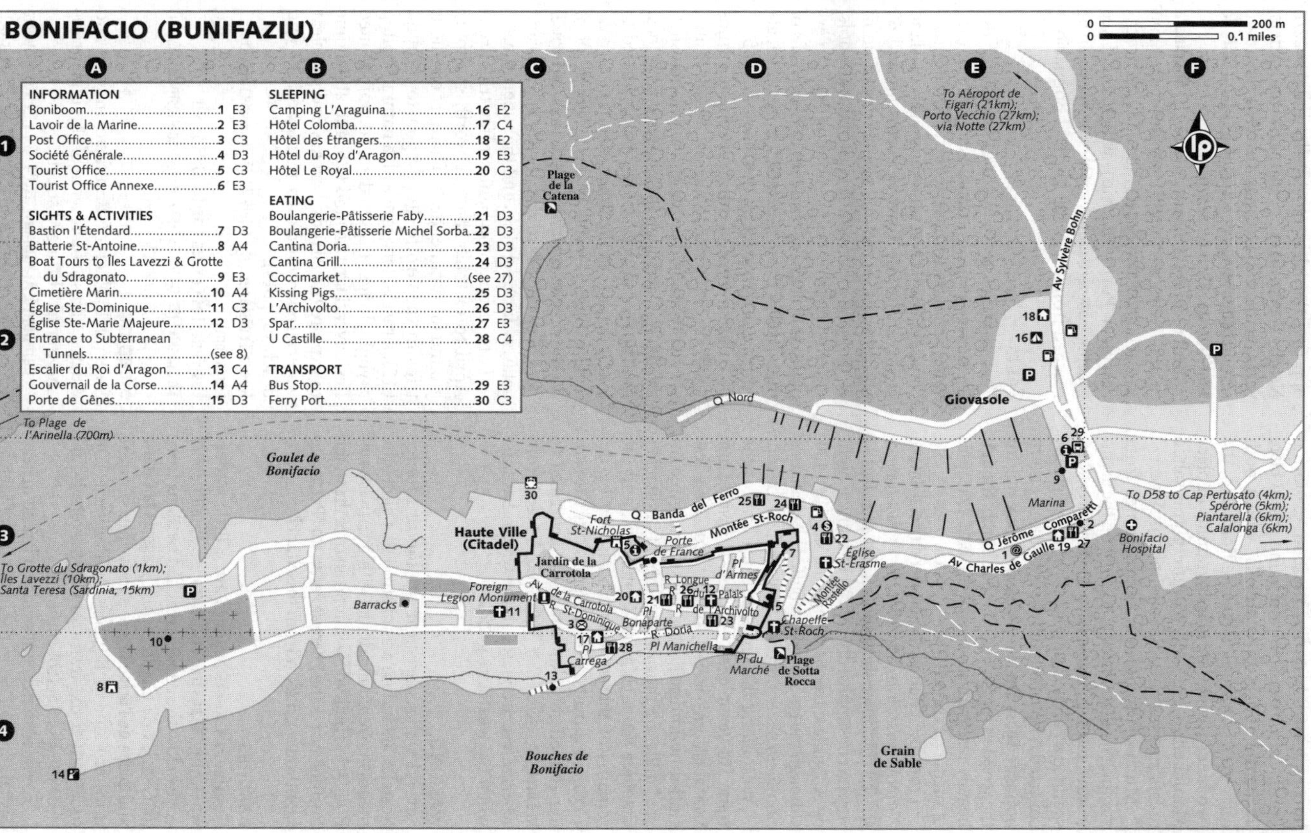
BONIFACIO (BUNIFAZIU)
INFORMATION
Boniboom 1 E3
Lavoir de la Marine 2 E3
Post Office 3 C3
Société Générale 4 D3
Tourist Office 5 C3
Tourist Office Annexe 6 E3
SIGHTS & ACTIVITIES
Bastion l'Étendard 7 D3
Batterie St-Antoine 8 A4
Boat Tours to Îles Lavezzi & Grotte du Sdragonato 9 E3
Cimetière Marin 10 A4
Église Ste-Dominique 11 C3
Église Ste-Marie Majeure 12 D3
Entrance to Subterranean Tunnels (see 8)
Escalier du Roi d'Aragon 13 C4
Gouvernail de la Corse 14 A4
Porte de Gênes 15 D3
SLEEPING
Camping L'Araguina 16 E2
Hôtel Colomba 17 C4
Hôtel des Étrangers 18 E2
Hôtel du Roy d'Aragon 19 E3
Hôtel Le Royal 20 C3
EATING
Boulangerie-Pâtisserie Faby 21 D3
Boulangerie-Pâtisserie Michel Sorba 22 D3
Cantina Doria 23 D3
Cantina Grill 24 D3
Coccimarket (see 27)
Kissing Pigs 25 D3
L'Archivolto 26 D3
Spar 27 E3
U Castille 28 C4
TRANSPORT
Bus Stop 29 E3
Ferry Port 30 C3
200 m
0.1 miles
To Aéroport de Figari (21km); Porto Vecchio (27km) via Notte (27km)
To D58 to Cap Pertusato (4km); Spérone (5km); Piantarella (6km); Calalonga (6km)
To Plage de l'Arinella (700m)
To Grotte du Sdragonato (1km); Îles Lavezzi (10km); Santa Teresa (Sardinia, 15km)
Av Sylvère Bohn
Bonifacio Hospital
Giovasole
Marina
Q Jérôme Comparetti
Av Charles de Gaulle
Q Nord
Q Banda del Ferro
Montée St-Roch
Plage de la Catena
Goulet de Bonifacio
Haute Ville (Citadel)
Jardin de la Carrotola
Fort St-Nicholas
Porte de France
Église St-Erasme
Montée Rastello
Chapelle St-Roch
Plage de Sotta Rocca
Pl du Marché
Pl Manichella
Pl d'Armes
Foreign Legion Monument
Barracks
Bouches de Bonifacio
Grain de Sable

houses a small historical museum exploring Bonifacio's past. Stroll the ramparts to **place du Marché** and **place Manichella**, which both offer views of the Bouches de Bonifacio; the two holes covered by glass pyramids in place Manichella were used to store grain, salted meats and supplies during times of siege.

Much of Bonifacio's charm comes from strolling its shady streets, soaking up the architecture and the atmosphere. Several streets are spanned by arched aqueducts, which originally collected rainwater to fill the communal cistern opposite **Église Ste-Marie Majeure**. Look out for the wooden loggia outside the church: though heavily restored, it's one of the best examples of medieval carpentry in Corsica.

From the citadel, the **Escalier du Roi d'Aragon** (King of Aragon's stairway; admission €2.50; 9am-7pm mid-Apr–Sep) cuts down the southern cliff-face. Its 187 steps were supposedly carved in a single night by Aragonese troops during the siege of 1420, although the troops were rebuffed by retaliating Bonifacio residents once they reached the top.

West along the limestone headland is the **Église Ste-Dominique** (9.30am-12.30pm & 3-6pm Mon-Sat mid-Jun–mid-Sep), one of Corsica's few Gothic buildings. Further west, near three ruined mills, are the ornate tombs of Bonifacio's **Cimetière Marin** (Marine Cemetery), and the remains of **subterranean tunnels** dug by the Germans during WWII, overlooking the rudder-shaped rock known as the **Gouvernail de la Corse** (admission €2.50; 9am-noon & 2-6pm) from where there are views all the way to Sardinia when the weather's good.

WALKING

Several walks start near the top of Montée Rastello, including a 2km stroll east along the maquis-covered headland with great views of Bonifacio's buildings arching out over the water. Further east is the **Phare de Pertusato** (Pertusato Lighthouse), 5.6km from the citadel.

BEACHES

Bonifacio's town beaches are a little underwhelming. **Plage de Sotta Rocca** is a small pebbly cove below the citadel, reached by steps from av Charles de Gaulle, while **plage de la Catena** and **plage de l'Arinella** are sandy inlets on the northern side of Bouches de Bonifacio. On foot, follow the trail from av Sylvère Bohn, near the Esso petrol station.

For finer stretches of sand you'll need to head east along the D58 to the little cove of **Spérone**, opposite the islets of Cavallo and Lavezzi. Nearby **Piantarella** is popular with windsurfers, while further east is shingly **Calalonga**. There are several other lovely beaches around the **Golfe de Sant'Amanza**, 8km east of Bonifacio.

Best of all is the horseshoe bay of **Rondinara** (about 18km northeast from Bonifacio) and tree-fringed **Palombaggia** (about 30km northeast near Porto-Vecchio), which you'll see gracing postcards all over Corsica. Both can be reached from the N198 north of Bonifacio.

Tours

You couldn't leave without exploring the idyllic waters around Bonifacio – thought by some scholars to have featured in Homer's *Odyssey*. The largest (and most visited) island of the group, Île Lavezzi, covers around 65 hectares and marks the southernmost point of Corsica; there are lots of natural pools, deserted beaches and swimming holes to explore, as well as a monument to the victims of the wreck of the Sémillante, a military frigate which came to grief on the island in 1855.

To reach some of the more remote islands you'll probably need your own yacht (you'll see plenty moored up around the islands' sheltered bays), although the skippers of the local tour boats can occasionally be persuaded to take a detour via the other islands.

The superexclusive Île de Cavallo is one of the only regularly inhabited islands, but you'll need deep pockets to visit; it's a favourite island getaway for celebrities and the super-rich.

Lots of boat companies offer trips from April to October, but it's worth shopping around for summer deals. There are one-hour trips to the Grotte du Sdragonato (around €15), a vast watery cave with a natural rooftop skylight; longer trips to the wild, uninhabited Îles Lavezzi cost around €25, and allow time to explore the islands' beaches and gin-clear waters (take your own picnic, drinks and beach supplies).

Rocca Croisières (04 95 73 13 96; www.rocca-croisieres.com)

Les Vedettes Corsica (06 03 48 58 59)

Thalassa (04 95 73 10 17; www.vedettesthalassa.com)

Sleeping

Steer well clear of Bonifacio in July and August unless you're a fan of sky-high prices and tourist-thronged streets.

Camping L'Araguina (04 95 73 02 96; av Sylvère Bohn; per person/tent/car €5.85/2.40/2.40; Mar-Oct)

Bonifacio's main campsite is near the Hôtel des Étrangers, with plenty of tent sites and rental chalets, but the roadside location can be less than soothing.

Hôtel des Étrangers (☎ 04 95 73 01 09; hoteldesetrangers.ifrance.com; av Sylvère Bohn; d €35-70; 🕑 Apr-Oct; ❄ P) Bunking down in Bonifacio doesn't have to shatter your budget, thanks to the Foreigners' Hotel. It's a solid, unfussy place offering spick-and-span rooms, all with tiled floors, clean bathrooms and simple colour schemes (more-expensive ones have air-con). Yes, it's basic, and the main road outside's a bother, but for this price it's a steal.

Hôtel Le Royal (☎ 04 95 73 00 51; fax 04 95 73 04 68; 8 rue Fred Scamaroni; s €40-95, d €45-105; ❄) This bare-bones hotel above a popular brasserie-bar is the cheapest option inside the citadel. In exchange for the top-drawer location you'll have to make some sacrifices: street noise, dullish decor and faded furnishings – but score a sea-view room and you won't give a fig.

Hotel du Roy d'Aragon (☎ 04 95 73 03 99; www.royaragon.com; 13 quai Jérôme Comparetti; d €50-150, ste from €130; ❄ ⊠) In summer it's as overpriced as anywhere on Bonifacio's quayside, but pitch up out of season and you'll bag a top-drawer sea view for a knock-down price. Despite the upmarket location, the room décor is surprisingly generic (creams, peaches, watercolour prints); don't let yourself be fobbed off with a rear or side-view room – you're paying seaside prices, remember.

Hôtel Colomba (☎ 04 95 73 73 44; www.hotel-bonifacio.fr; rue Simon Varsi; d €78-155; ❄) A newish addition to Bonifacio's hotel scene, and a welcome one – a not-quite-boutique hotel in a picturesque side street, bang in the heart of the old town. The rooms are all pleasantly individual – wrought-iron bedsteads and country fabrics in some, carved bedheads and chequerboard tiles in others – and while they're all on the small side, they have a whole lot more character than at many places in Bonifacio.

Eating

Swish terrace restaurants pack the quayside, but the food isn't always as fancy as the ambience suggests.

Kissing Pigs (☎ 04 95 73 56 09; quai Banda del Ferro; mains €8-15; 🕑 lunch & dinner daily) Sporting quite possibly the oddest name of any restaurant in Corsica, Kissing Pigs is a cosy wine bar and temple to cheese and charcuterie. Diners pack in among swinging sausages for platters of Corsican meats and cheeses – committed carnivores go for *l'incontournable* (all meat; €18), while undecideds plump for the *moitié-moitié* (half cheese, half meat; €15).

Cantina Doria (☎ 04 95 73 50 49; 27 rue Doria; mains €10-14; 🕑 Apr-Oct) The Doria is *the* place in Bonifacio for Corsican country food. Squeeze onto wooden benches amid copper pots, rustic tools and dented signs, and tuck into *soupe Corse, aubergines à la Bonifacienne* (aubergines stuffed with breadcrumbs and cheese) and slabs of beef, veal and pork. It's so popular, it's opened a sister place with a fishier focus on the quay – Cantina Grill (☎ 04 95 70 49 86). You'll find the Grill at 3 quai Banda del Ferro (open April to October), with mains costing €9 to €15.

our pick **L'Archivolto** (☎ 04 95 73 17 58; rue de l'Archivolto; mains €10-16; 🕑 dinner Mon-Sat mid-Mar–Oct) Steps from the Église Ste-Marie Majeure, this gloriously offbeat bistro is part jumble sale, part hippie-chic antique shop and part fine-dining restaurant. Bric-a-brac, rustic curios, dangling guitars and mix-and-match furniture fill the salon from floor to ceiling, and the chalked-up menu is just as eclectic, swinging from seared tuna to chicken in Pietra beer. Choose a seat among the clutter or on the alleyway patio – either way, you'll be charmed.

U Castille (☎ 04 95 73 04 99; rue Simon Varsi; menus €14-22; 🕑 lunch & dinner in summer, closed Mon & Sun in winter) Tucked away up a gut-squeezing alleyway off place Bonaparte, this cosy little alcove restaurant offers Corsican meats, cheeses and salads, as well as pasta and pizza from next door.

SELF-CATERING

Bonifacio has two wonderful bakeries where you can buy local specialities such as *pain des morts* (a nut-and-raisin brioche traditionally eaten for the Fête des Morts – Festival of the Dead – on 2 November), *fugazzi* (aniseed and orange cakes) and *tarte brocciu* (Brocciu tart). Pick them up at **Boulangerie-Pâtisserie Faby** (4 rue St-Jean Baptiste; 🕑 8am-8pm Jul & Aug, 8am-12.30pm & 4-7pm Sep-Jun) in the citadel or **Boulangerie-Pâtisserie Michel Sorba** (1-3 rue St-Érasme; 🕑 6am-8pm Jul & Aug, 8am-12.30pm & 4.30-7pm Tue-Sat, 8am-12.30pm Sun Sep-Jun) by the quay.

There are side-by-side supermarkets on quai Jérôme Comparetti: **Spar** (🕑 8am-12.30pm & 3.30-7.30pm Mon-Sat, 8am-12.30pm Sun) and Coccimarket (with the same opening hours as at Spar).

Getting There & Away

AIR

Bonifacio's airport, **Aéroport de Figari** (☎ 04 95 71 10 10), is 21km north of town. A shuttle bus runs from the town centre in July and August (€9, 30 to 40 minutes) five times daily.

BOAT

Sardinia's main ferry operators, **Saremar** (☎ 04 95 73 00 96; www.saremar.it, in Italian) and **Moby Lines** (☎ 04 95 73 00 29; www.mobylines.it), offer services between Bonifacio and Santa Teresa in summer. Costs vary according to the time and day of sailing, but range from around €9 to €18 one-way plus taxes; the crossing lasts about an hour.

BUS

From Monday to Saturday, **Eurocorse** (☎ 04 95 21 06 30) has a twice-daily service to Porto-Vecchio (€7.50, 30 minutes), with onward connections to Ajaccio (€22, four hours) via Sartène and Propriano. Buses leave from behind the tourist office annexe, with greatly reduced numbers of services outside summer.

CORTE AREA

CORTE (CORTI)

pop 5700 / elevation 400m

The mountain town of Corte (pronounced cor·tay) is the heart and soul of Corsica, both geographically and politically. Hemmed in by high mountains, and frequently blanketed in cloud, Corte has been at the centre of the island's fortunes since Pascal Paoli made it the capital of his short-lived Corsican republic in 1755. With its high-rise apartment blocks, tatty tenements and rough-and-ready streets – not to mention a liberal smattering of nationalist graffiti – it's certainly not the island's smartest town, but if you're after Corsican culture in the raw, then this is definitely the place. Around the town's cobbled streets you'll find the national history museum, a historic inland citadel and Corsica's university, Università di Corsica Pasquale Paoli. Founded by Paoli in 1765, the university closed four years later following the fall of the republic, reopened to great fanfare in 1981, and is now playing a vital role in the ongoing renaissance of the Corsican language.

Orientation

Corte's main thoroughfare is cours Paoli. At its southern end is place Paoli, from where the narrow streets of the Haute Ville (Upper Town) continue uphill to the citadel. The train station is 500m downhill from cours Paoli.

Information

Banks with ATMs are found along cours Paoli.

Grand Café (22 cours Paoli; internet access per 15min/1hr €1/3.50; ⏰ 7am-2am) Late-night café with internet terminals.

Maison de la Presse (cours Paoli; ⏰ 8am-6pm) Maps, walking guides and lots of Corsican books.

Post Office (av du Baron Mariani)

Tourist Office (☎ 04 95 46 26 70; www.corte-tourisme.com; citadelle; ⏰ 9am-12.30pm & 2-5.30pm Mon-Thu, 9am-noon & 2-5pm Fri, longer hr summer)

Video Games (av du Président Pierucci; internet access per hr €4; ⏰ 10am-midnight) Online gamers' hang-out with net access.

Sights

Of Corsica's six citadels, Corte's is the only one not on the coast. Jutting out above the Rivers Tavignanu and Restonica and the cobbled alleyways of the Haute Ville, the citadel's highest point is the **château** (known as the Nid d'Aigle – the Eagle's Nest), built in 1419 by Vincentello d'Istria, a Corsican nobleman rebelling against Genoese occupation.

The town's finest views are from the **belvédère** (viewing platform), reached via a steep staircase just outside the citadel's ramparts. Inside the walls are the former barracks and administrative buildings, which previously served as a WWII prison and a French Foreign Legion base. They now house the tourist office and the **Museu di a Corsica** (Museum of Corsica; ☎ 04 95 45 25 45; adult/student €5.30/3.80; ⏰ 10am-8pm mid-Jun–mid-Sep, 10am-6pm Tue-Sun Apr–mid-Jun & mid-Sep-Oct, 10am-5pm Tue-Sat Nov-Mar), Corsica's main national museum. Dramatically designed by Italian architect Andrea Bruno, the museum is split into two sections. The Galerie Doazan houses over 3000 artefacts exploring traditional crafts such as shepherding, weaving, agriculture and rustic life in Corsica, while the Museum in Motion explores Corsican history and industry through an eclectic collection ranging from vintage tourist posters to a reconstructed asbestos factory. English audioguides cost €1.50.

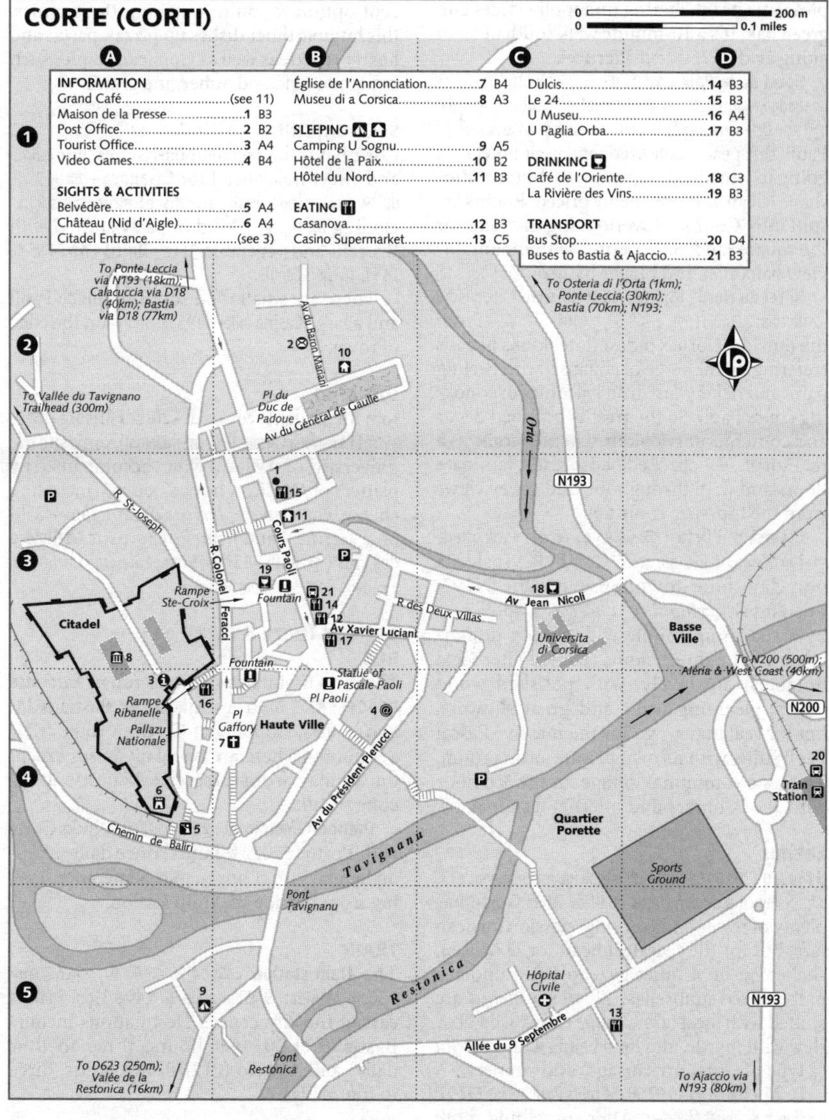

Further downhill is the 15th-century **Église de l'Annonciation** (place Gaffory). The walls of nearby houses are pock-marked with bullet holes, reputedly from Corsica's war of independence.

Situated halfway along the Mare a Mare Nord, and surrounded by mountain trails, Corte is also rapidly becoming one of Corsica's main hiking centres (see p938).

Sleeping

Camping U Sognu (☎ 04 95 46 09 07; per tent/person/car €6.50/2.50/2.50) The pick of Corte's campsites, with lovely views of the city, and lots of pleasant sites sheltering under olive trees and green oak. It's a 10-minute walk south of town along av du Président Pierucci.

Hôtel de la Paix (☎ 04 95 46 06 72; http://monsite.wanadoo.fr/socoget/; av du Général de Gaulle; d €35-62; ⏲ Apr-Oct) On a quiet cul-de-sac just off cours Paoli, this peach-coloured tenement hotel isn't going to win any design awards, but it's shipshape, clean and reasonably priced. Rooms are split into 'Confort' (overlooking the valley or the square) and 'Superieure', with mountain-view balconies and bigger bathrooms.

Hôtel du Nord (☎ 04 95 46 00 68; www.hoteldunord-corte.com; 22 cours Paoli; d €68-83, tr €105-134; 💻) From the outside, Corte's oldest hotel looks like it's teetering on the verge of collapse, with peeling paint and rickety cast-iron balconies overlooking cours Paoli. So the freshly polished decor and contemporary colour schemes come as a real surprise – checked bedspreads, laminate floors and wi-fi throughout, and valley views from the top-spec rooms.

Osteria di l'Orta (☎ 04 95 61 06 41; www.osteria-di-l-orta.com; d €70-80, ste €110; 💻 P) Inside a porcelain-blue townhouse on the N193, this fantastic *chambre d'hôte* is a spoil, run by a charming couple with a keen designer's eye. The three rooms (named after local notables) are lovely, with polished wood floors, gleaming walls and great showers, but for real luxury, go for the massive Pascal Paoli suite, with its own private sitting room. There's a communal lounge on the 3rd floor with DVD, library and internet terminal.

Eating

U Museu (☎ 04 95 61 08 36; rampe Ribanelle; menus €13-17; ⏲ lunch & dinner, closed mid-Nov–Mar) Corte has plenty of restaurants serving 'classic' Corsican fare, but for the real deal head for U Museu, sheltering on a quiet gazebo patio under a brace of red umbrellas. Three set *menus* are stuffed with local fare – *soupe Corse,* wild boar stew with myrtle, and lima beans with *figatellu* (a type of Corsican sausage) and peppers.

Le 24 (☎ 04 95 46 02 90; 24 cours Paoli; mains €13-22; ⏲ lunch & dinner Mon-Sat) After something more upmarket? Then swing by Corte's foodie spot, Le Vingt-Quatre, where top-quality local ingredients take precedence on the seasonal menu, and traditional dishes are given a contemporary twist. Rustic stone and just-so reclaimed wooden furniture continue the up-to-date vibe.

U Paglia Orba (☎ 04 95 61 07 89; 5 av Xavier Luciani; menu €15, mains €7-18; ⏲ lunch & dinner Mon-Sat) A decent option if you're watching the pennies, this humble diner dishes up pizzas, pastas and hearty steaks, as well as Corsican staples such as pigeon pâté and aubergine gratin.

SELF-CATERING

Corte has some excellent patisseries. For cakes and sweet treats head for **Casanova** (☎ 04 95 46 00 79; 6 cours Paoli), and for local savouries (including *bastelle,* a kind of pasty stuffed with Brocciu and vegetables), try **Dulcis** (☎ 04 95 46 24 91; 10 cours Paoli).

There are small food shops on place Paoli and a large **Casino** (allée du 9 Septembre) on the edge of town.

Drinking

Join the student crowds at **Café de l'Oriente** (☎ 04 95 61 11 17; av Jean Nicoli; ⏲ 9am-midnight), opposite the university, or try local wines accompanied by platters of Corsican hors d'oeuvre (including cheese, charcuterie, *terrine de sanglier* – wild boar terrine – and *figatellu*) at rustic **La Rivière des Vins** (☎ 04 95 46 37 04; 5 rampe Ste-Croix; menu €16; ⏲ noon-3pm & 6-11pm Mon-Sat).

Getting There & Away

BUS

The most useful bus service is run by **Eurocorse** (☎ 04 95 31 73 76) from Ajaccio to Bastia (€11, two hours), stopping at Corte en route (€11, 2¾ hours). There are two daily buses except on Sunday from Brasserie Majestic at 19 cours Paoli.

Transports Mordiconi (☎ 04 95 48 00 44) links Corte with Porto (€20, 2¾ hours) once daily except on Sundays from July to mid-September, leaving from outside the train station.

TRAIN

The **train station** (☎ 04 95 46 00 97; ⏲ 6.30am-8.30pm Mon-Sat, 9.45am-noon & 4.45-8.35pm Sun) is east of the city centre. Destinations include Bastia (€11.20, two hours, three to four daily) and Ajaccio (€12.70, two hours, three to four daily).

AROUND CORTE

If you're a trail junkie, the area around Corte offers some of the finest hiking on the island. Key spots include the **Vallée de la Restonica**, accessed via the D623 and choked with traffic in July and August. From the car park at **Bergeries de Grotelle** (1375m), 16km from Corte, an hour-long walk leads up the dramatic valley to the high-mountain tarns of **Lac de Mello** (Melu; 1711m) and **Lac de Capitello** (Capitellu; 1930m), 45 minutes' walk further on.

West of Corte, and usually much quieter than Restonica, is the remote trail through the **Vallée du Tavignano** all the way up to **Lac Nino** (Ninu; 1743m) on the GR20, a tough 9½-hour slog from Corte. If you're really up for a challenge, the six-hour ascent to the crest of **Monte Cinto** (2706m), Corsica's highest mountain, starts at the tiny village of Lozzi – don't even think about attempting the mountain without hiking supplies, trail maps and a favourable weather forecast.

South of Corte, there are less-challenging trails through the pine and oak woods of the **Forêt de Vizzavona**. Two waterfalls, the **Cascade des Anglais**, accessible from Vizzavona, and the **Cascade du Voile de la Mariée**, near Bocognano, are both worth the walk.

Directory

CONTENTS

ACCOMMODATION

Be it a fairy-tale château, an urban boutique hideaway or a mountain refuge, France has accommodation to suit every taste and pocket.

In this guide, accommodation options listed as 'budget' have doubles with private bathroom costing up to €60 (€70 in Paris); 'midrange' hotels charge €61 to €140 (to €160 in Paris); and top-end rooms cost anything upwards of €141 (€161 in Paris). Some hotels offer rooms with a *lavabo* (washbasin), ie with a hall shower (free unless otherwise noted) and/or a hall toilet.

During periods of heavy tourism, popular destinations are packed out and prices soar. Ski resorts charge their highest rates over Christmas and New Year and the February–March school holidays, while beach resorts are priciest in summer, especially July and August, and particularly from 14 July to 15 August. On the other hand, hotels in inland cities charge low-season rates while everyone is on the coast. In cities whose hotels get mainly business clients, rooms are most expensive from Monday to Thursday and cheaper over the weekend. Rates listed in this guide are generally high-season rates.

Some tourist offices make room reservations, often for a fee of €5, but many only do so if you stop by in person. In the Alps, tourist offices for ski resorts run a central reservation service for booking accommodation.

B&Bs

Some of France's most charming accommodation comes in the form of *chambres d'hôtes* (B&Bs) – up to five bed-and-breakfast rooms attached to a private home. Many hosts cook up a homemade evening meal *(table d'hôte)* for an extra charge (usually €20 to €25). Tourist offices have lists of local *chambres d'hôtes* – urban rarities but plentiful in rural areas.

Gîtes de France acts as an umbrella organisation for B&B properties. Ask at local tourist offices about Gîtes de France brochures and offices, or contact the **Fédération Nationale des Gîtes de France** (Map pp120-1; ☎ 01 49 70 75 75; www.gites-de-france.fr; 59 rue St-Lazare, 9e, Paris; Ⓜ Trinité). Check out their annual catalogue *Gîtes de Charme* (€20) (online at www.gites-de-france-charme.com).

Bienvenue à la Ferme (Map pp118-19; ☎ 01 53 57 11 44; www.bienvenue-a-la-ferme.com; 9 av George V, 8e, Paris; Ⓜ Alma-Marceau, George V) has *chambres d'hôte* on farms. Search online or order a catalogue.

Other useful websites: **Fleurs de Soleil** (http://fleursdesoleil.fr, in French), **Samedi Midi Éditions** (www.samedimidi.com) and **...en France** (www.bbfrance.com).

> **BOOK YOUR STAY ONLINE**
>
> For more accommodation reviews and recommendations by Lonely Planet authors, check out lonelyplanet.com/hotels. You'll find the true, insider lowdown on the best places to stay. Reviews are thorough and independent. Best of all, you can book online.

PRACTICALITIES

- France uses the metric system for weights and measures.
- Plugs have two round pins, so visitors from the English-speaking lands will need an adaptor; the electric current is 220V at 50Hz AC (you may need a transformer for 110V electrical appliances).
- Videos in France work on the PAL system; TV is Secam.
- Locals read their news in centre-left, highly intellectual *Le Monde* (www.lemonde.fr), right-leaning *Le Figaro* (www.lefigaro.fr) or left-leaning *Libération* (www.liberation.fr).
- For radio news, tune in to the French-language Radio France Info (105.5MHz or thereabouts in most areas), the multilanguage RFI (738kHz or 89MHz in Paris) or, in northwestern France, the BBC World Service (648kHz) and BBC Radio 4 (198kHz).
- In many areas, Autoroute Info (107.7MHz) has round-the-clock information on autoroute travel conditions.
- Popular national FM music stations include NRJ (pronounced 'energy'; www.nrj.fr, in French), Skyrock (www.skyrock.fm, in French) and Nostalgie (www.nostalgie.fr, in French).
- Pick up the free *FUSAC* (France USA Contacts; www.fusac.fr) in Anglophone haunts in Paris for classified ads about housing, babysitting, jobs and language exchanges.

Camping

France has thousands of campsites, most near rivers, lakes or the sea. Most are open from March or April to October. A few hostels let travellers pitch tents in their grounds.

In this book, 'camping' refers to fixed-price deals for two or three people including a tent and a car. Otherwise the price is broken down per person/tent/car. Camping-ground offices are often closed for most of the day. Getting to/from many sites without your own transport can be slow and costly.

Camping in nondesignated spots *(camping sauvage)* is illegal in France. Except in Corsica, you probably won't have problems if you're at least 1500m from a camping area (or, in national parks, at least an hour's walk from the road). Camping on the beach is not a good idea in areas with high tidal variations. Always ask permission before camping on private land.

Gîtes de France and Bienvenue à la Ferme (opposite and opposite) coordinate camping on farms.

In recent years, creative camping options for couples and families – some *écolo chic* (eco-chic), others adventurous – have sprung up. A *cabane dans les arbres* (also known as a *cabane perchée*) is a sort of Robinson Crusoe–style tree house built high off the ground in a lime, oak or sequoia tree. If you prefer keeping your feet on the ground, you might keep your eyes open for a place that rents a *tipi* (tepee), or lets you snooze in a giant hammock.

Homestays

Under an arrangement known as *hôtes payants* or *hébergement chez l'habitant*, students, young people and tourists stay with French families. In general you rent a room and have access to the bathroom and the kitchen (sometimes limited); meals may also be available. If you're sensitive to smoke or pets make sure you mention this. Language schools often arrange this type of accommodation for their students, as do the following organisations:

Accueil Familial des Jeunes Étrangers (Map pp124-5; ☎ 01 42 22 50 34; www.afje-paris.org; 23 rue du Cherche Midi, 6e, Paris; Ⓜ Sèvres Babylone) Homestays in or near Paris from €555 a month with breakfast.

France Lodge (Map pp118-19; ☎ 01 56 33 85 85; www.apartments-in-paris.com; 2 rue Meissonier, 17e, Paris; Ⓜ Wagram) Accommodation in private Parisian homes; €25 to €60 a night for one person, €40 to €75 for two.

Hostels

A dormitory bed in an *auberge de jeunesse* (youth hostel) costs about €25 in Paris, and anything from €10.30 to €28 in the provinces, depending on location, amenities and facilities; sheets are included and breakfast often is, too (or is available for about €3.50). To prevent outbreaks of bed bugs, sleeping bags are no longer permitted. Hostels on the seashore or in the mountains sometimes offer seasonal outdoor activities. All hostels are totally nonsmoking.

Some hostels are little more than a few spartan rooms set aside in a hostel for young workers *(foyer de jeunes travailleurs/travailleuses)*. In university towns, *foyers d'étudiant* (student dormitories) are sometimes converted for use by travellers during summer.

Guests need to purchase an annual Hostelling International card (€11/16 for under/over 26s) or a nightly Welcome Stamp (€1.80 to €2.90, up to a maximum of six) to stay at hostels run by the two French hostelling associations:

Fédération Unie des Auberges de Jeunesse (FUAJ; Map pp120-1; ☎ 01 44 89 87 27; www.fuaj.org; 27 rue Pajol, 18e, Paris; Ⓜ Marx Dormoy).

Ligue Française pour les Auberges de la Jeunesse (LFAJ; Map pp114-15; ☎ 01 44 16 78 78; www.auberges-de-jeunesse.com; 7 rue Vergniaud, 13e, Paris; Ⓜ Glacière)

Hotels

In this book we have tried to feature well-situated, independent (ie nonchain) hotels that offer good value, a warm welcome, at least a bit of charm and a palpable sense of place.

Hotels in France are rated with one to four stars, although the ratings are based on objective criteria (eg the size of the entry hall), not the quality of the service, the decor or cleanliness. Prices often reflect these intangibles far more than they do the number of stars.

French hotels almost never include breakfast in their advertised nightly rates. Unless specified otherwise, prices quoted in this guide don't include breakfast, which costs around €6.50/8/18 in a budget/midrange/top-end hotel. When you book, hotels usually ask for a credit-card number and, occasionally, written (faxed) confirmation; some require a deposit.

A double room generally has one double bed (often two pushed-together singles!); a room with twin beds *(deux lits)* is usually more expensive, as is a room with a bathtub instead of a shower. Triples and quads usually have two or three beds.

The small, often family-run hotels rated by **Logis de France** (☎ 01 45 84 83 84; www.logis-de-france.fr) with one to three chimneys are known for their charm and warm welcome. It publishes an annual guide with maps.

Independent hotels, each with its own unique local character, are grouped by **Arcantis** (www.arcantis-hotels.com), which brings together two- and three-star places; **Best Western** (www.bestwestern.com), whose hotels are generally on the upper end of midrange; **Citôtel** (www.citotel.com); **Contact Hôtel** (www.contact-hotel.com); and **Inter-Hotel** (www.inter-hotel.fr). Superluxury establishments can be found through **Relaix & Châteaux** (www.relaischateaux.com) and **Grandes Étapes Françaises** (www.grandesetapes.fr).

> **SMOKE-FREE HOTEL ROOMS**
>
> Almost all French hotels, except a few budget ones, now have at least some nonsmoking rooms. The nonsmoking icon (⊠) appears only when an establishment is 100% nonsmoking.

More French hotel rooms than ever are controlled by a few huge chains offering predictable, cookie-cutter establishments, often along main access roads, that place predictability and convenience over atmosphere.

From cheapest to poshest, the brands belonging to the **Accor group** (www.accor.com) include **Formule 1** (www.hotelformule1.com), **Etap** (www.etaphotel.com), **Ibis** (www.ibishotel.com), **Mercure** (www.mercure.com), **Novotel** (www.novotel.com) and **Sofitel** (www.sofitel.com).

The **Louvre Hotels group** (www.louvrehotels.com) has four brands (from cheapest to most expensive): **Première Classe** (www.premiereclasse.com), **Campanile** (www.campanile.com), **Kyriad** (www.kyriad.com) and **Kyriad Prestige** (www.kyriadprestige.com).

Choice Hotels (www.choicehotels.com) brands in France include **Comfort Inn** (www.comfortinn.com), **Quality Inn** (www.qualityinn.com), **Clarion** (www.clarionhotel.com) and **Sleep Inn** (www.sleepinn.com).

Other inexpensive chain options include **Balladins** (☎ 08 25 08 84 53; www.balladins.com), **B&B Hôtels** (www.hotel-bb.com), **Bonsaï Hôtels** (☎ 08 10 63 72 71; www.bonsai-hotels.fr) and **Hôtel Stars** (www.starshotels.com).

Refuges & Gîtes d'Étape

A *refuge* (mountain hut or shelter) is a bog-basic cabin established along trails in uninhabited mountainous areas and operated by national-park authorities, the **Club Alpin Français** (CAF; www.ffcam.fr, in French) or other private organisations. *Refuges* are marked on hiking and climbing maps. A bunk in the dorm generally costs €10 to €20. Hot meals are sometimes available and, in a few cases, mandatory, pushing the price of a bed up to €30 or beyond. Advance reservations and a weather check are essential before setting out.

Gîtes d'étape, better equipped and more comfortable than *refuges* (some even have showers), are situated along walking trails in less remote areas, often villages. Gîtes de France (p940) publishes an annual guide, *Gîtes d'Étapes et de Séjour* (€10).

Rental Accommodation

Renting a furnished studio, apartment or villa can be an economical alternative for stays of a few days or more, plus it gives you the chance to live a little bit like a local, with trips to the farmers market and the *boulangerie*. Cleaning, linen rental and electricity fees usually cost extra.

In rural areas, Gîtes de France (p940) handles some of the most charming *gîtes ruraux* (self-contained holiday cottages).

Finding an apartment for long-term rental can be gruelling. Landlords, many of whom prefer locals to foreigners, usually require substantial proof of financial responsibility and sufficient funds in France; many ask for a *caution* (guarantee) and a hefty deposit.

Classified ads appear in **De Particulier à Particulier** (www.pap.fr), published Thursday and sold at newsstands. **FUSAC** (p941) also has short- and long-term apartment ads.

For apartments outside Paris it's best to be on-site. Check places like bars and *tabacs* (tobacconists) for free local newspapers (often named after the number of the *département*) with classifieds listings.

ACTIVITIES

From the peaks, rivers and canyons of the Alps to the mountains and volcanic peaks of the Massif Central – not to mention 3200km of coastline stretching from Italy to Spain and from the Basque country to the Straits of Dover – France offers a cornucopia of exhilarating outdoor adventures.

See this book's destination listings for details and check with local and regional tourist offices (or consult their websites) for information on local activities, clubs and companies.

Some youth hostels (p941) offer week-long sports *stages* (courses).

Adventure Sports

Be it canyoning, diving, ice-driving or kitesurfing (on snow or water!), France sets the pulse racing. In larger cities and picturesque regions like the Côte d'Azur and the Alps, local companies offer all kinds of high-adrenaline pursuits; see regional chapters for details.

Adventures in *alpinisme* (mountaineering), *escalade* (rock climbing), *escalade de glace* (ice climbing) and other highland activities with a professional guide can be arranged through the **Club Alpin Français** (www.ffcam.fr, in French).

Deltaplane (hang-gliding) and *parapente* (paragliding) are all the rage in the Pyrenees, Brittany, Massif Central and Languedoc-Roussillon regions; see those chapters for details. The Nice-based **Fédération Française de Vol Libre** (☎ 04 97 03 82 82; http://federation.ffvl.fr, in French) groups regional clubs specialising in these pursuits as well as *le kite-surf* (kitesurfing), popular at spots all along France's Atlantic and Mediterranean coasts.

Vol à voile (gliding) is popular in southern France, where temperatures are warmer and thermals better. The Causse Méjean (p789) in Languedoc is a popular spot. The **Fédération Française de Vol à Voile** (FFVV; ☎ 01 45 44 04 78; www.ffvv.org, in French; 29 rue de Sèvres, 6e, Paris) provides details of gliding clubs countrywide.

Speleology was pioneered in France and there are still some great spots for cave exploration; the **CAF** (www.ffcam.fr, in French) has information.

Cycling

The French take cycling very seriously. Whole parts of the country – except, it's rumoured, for some pharmacies – grind to a halt during the famous annual Tour de France (p54).

A *vélo tout-terrain* (VTT, or mountain bike) is a fantastic tool for exploring the countryside. Some GR *(grandes randonnées)* and GRP *(grandes randonnées de pays)* trails (see p944) are open to mountain bikers. A *piste cyclable* or a *voie cyclable* is a cycling path or lane.

Some of the best areas for mountain biking (with varying gradients and grades of difficulty) are around Annecy and Chambéry in the Alps and throughout the Pyrenees. In southwestern France, the Dordogne and Quercy offer a vast network of scenic, tranquil roads for pedal-powered tourists. The Loire Valley, Alsace, Burgundy, the Lubéron in Provence and coastal regions like Brittany, Normandy and the Atlantic coast offer a wealth of easier (flatter) options.

For details on companies that offer cycling tours of France, see p975.

For maps, see p953. Lonely Planet's *Cycling France* includes essential maps, advice, directions and technical tips. For information on transporting your bicycle by train and bike rental, see p969. Details on places that rent out bikes – though not always helmets – appear in each city or town listing under Getting Around.

The **Fête du Vélo** (www.feteduvelo.fr, in French), a national cycling festival, takes place all over the country on the first weekend in June.

Cycling organisations:

Association Française de Développement des Véloroutes et Voies Vertes (www.af3v.org) Has a database of 250 signposted *véloroutes* (bike paths) and *voies vertes* (greenways) for cycling and in-line skating.

Cartovélo (www.cartovelo.fr) Sells cycling guides.

Fédération Française de Cyclisme (www.ffc.fr, in French) Founded 1881, the French Cycling Federation organises competitive cycling in France, including (as of 2008) the Tour de France.

Fédération Française de Cyclotourisme (www.ffct.org, in French) Founded in 1923, this organisation promotes bicycle touring and mountain biking.

Union Touristique Les Amis de la Nature (http://troisv.amis-nature.org, in French) Has details on local, regional and long-distance *véloroutes* (cycling routes) around France.

In-Line Skating

Over 10,000 in-line skaters – accompanied by skating police – race through the streets of Paris from 10pm to 1am every Friday night. The free, 30km ride, whose purpose – in addition to fun – is to promote in-line skating as a mode of urban transport, is the largest such event in the world. For details see the website of **Pari Roller** (www.pari-roller.com).

The **Fédération Française de Roller Skating** (http://parcours.ffrs.asso.fr, in French) can provide details on routes suitable for in-line skating.

Skiing & Snowboarding

France sports more than 400 ski resorts in the Alps, the Jura, the Pyrenees, the Vosges and Massif Central – and even the mountains of Corsica. The season generally lasts from mid-December to late March or April. January and February tend to have the best overall conditions but the slopes get very crowded during the February–March school holidays.

The high Alps have some of the world's priciest and most fashionable resorts (see p524 for the full scoop on winter and summer Alpine skiing), although smaller, low-altitude stations in the Alps, the Pyrenees and the Massif Central are cheaper. Cross-country skiing is possible at Alpine resorts but best done in the valleys; the Jura (p570) has some lovely trails. Some lower-altitude stations are examining their options should global warming make the ski season too short and/or unpredictable.

One of the cheapest ways to ski or snowboard is with a package deal, though thanks to budget airlines flying to/from Lyon, Grenoble, Chambéry and Geneva (Switzerland), arranging Alpine breaks independently is equally viable.

Paris-based **Ski France** (www.skifrance.fr) has information and an annual brochure covering more than 90 ski resorts. **CAF** (www.ffcam.fr, in French) can also provide information on mountain activities.

SKIING SUPERLATIVES

France can claim a fair few superlatives in the world of skiing:

- The world's largest ski area is Les Portes du Soleil (p539), northwest of Chamonix.
- Europe's highest station is Val Thorens (2300m; p551), west of Méribel.
- Europe's largest skiable glacier, which has 120 hectares of marked slopes, is at Les Deux Alpes (p565), in the spectacular Parc National des Écrins.
- One of France's longest off-piste trails (20km) is the legendary Vallée Blanche (p532) at Chamonix; the longest official (groomed) one – some 16km – is black-marked La Sarenne (p566) at Alpe d'Huez.

Walking

The French countryside is criss-crossed by a staggering 120,000km of *sentiers balisés* (marked walking paths), which pass through every imaginable terrain in every region of the country. No permit is needed to hike. For details on *topoguides* (walking guides), see p953.

Probably the best-known trails are the *sentiers de grande randonnée* (GR), long-distance paths marked by red-and-white-striped track indicators. Some – like the GR5, which goes from the Netherlands through the French Alps to Nice – are hundreds of kilometres long.

The *grandes randonnées de pays* (GRP) trails, whose markings are yellow, are designed for intense exploration of one particular area. Other types of trails include *sentiers de promenade randonnée* (PR), walking paths marked in yellow; *drailles,* paths used by cattle to get to high-altitude summer pastures; and *chemins de halage,* canal towpaths. Shorter day-hike trails are often known as *sentiers de petites randonnées* or *sentiers de pays.*

The **Fédération Française de la Randonnée Pédestre** (FFRP; French Ramblers' Association; www.ffrp.asso.fr, in French) has an **information centre** (Map pp114-15; ☎ 01 44 89 93 93; 64 rue du Dessous des Berges, 13e, Paris; Ⓜ Bibliothèque François Mitterrand) in Paris. Another good resource is the **Club Alpin Français** (www.ffcam.fr, in French), which groups 240 local mountain sports clubs.

Lonely Planet's *Walking in France* is full of lively detail and essential information. For information on *refuges* and other overnight accommodation for walkers, such as *gîtes d'étape*, see p942. For information on maps, see p953.

Water Sports

France has fine beaches along all its coasts – the English Channel, the Atlantic and the Mediterranean. The beautifully sandy beaches stretching along the family-oriented Atlantic Coast (eg near La Rochelle) are less crowded than their rather pebbly counterparts on the Côte d'Azur. Corsica has some truly magnificent spots. Brittany, Normandy and the Channel coast are also popular, albeit cooler, beach destinations. The general public is free to use any beach not marked as private.

The best surfing is on the Atlantic Coast around Biarritz (p685), where waves reach heights of 4m. Windsurfing is popular wherever there's water and a breeze, and equipment is often rented out near beaches and lakes.

White-water rafting, canoeing and kayaking are practised on many French rivers, especially in the Massif Central and the Alps, but also in Burgundy's Parc Naturel Régional du Morvan and along the Gorges de l'Allier, Gorges de l'Ardèche, Gorges du Tarn and Gorges du Verdon.

For kitesurfing see p943.

All French cities and towns have public swimming pools. Some may require that swimming suits be made of Lycra.

BUSINESS HOURS

French business hours are regulated by a maze of government regulations, including the 35-hour working week. Shop hours are usually 9am or 9.30am to 7pm or 8pm, often with a break from noon or 1pm to 2pm or 3pm. The midday break is uncommon in Paris but, in general, gets longer the further south you go. French law requires that most businesses close on Sunday; exceptions include grocery stores, *boulangeries*, cake shops, florists and businesses catering exclusively to the tourist trade. In some places shops close on Monday.

Restaurants generally serve lunch from noon or 12.30pm to 2pm or 2.30pm and dinner from 7pm or 7.30pm until 9.30pm or 10pm; they are often closed one or two days of the week, chosen according to the owner's whim. Cafés are usually open all day long, from early morning until around midnight. Many bars open in the early evening and close at 1am or 2am.

Most (but not all) national museums are closed on Tuesday, while most local museums are closed on Monday, though in summer some open daily. Many museums close at lunchtime.

Banks are usually open from 8am or 9am to some time between 11.30am or 1pm and then from 1.30pm or 2pm to 4.30pm or 5pm, Monday to Friday or Tuesday to Saturday. Exchange services may end half an hour before closing time.

Post offices generally open from 8.30am or 9am to 5pm or 6pm on weekdays (7pm in Paris), perhaps with a midday break, and on Saturday from 8am to noon.

Supermarkets usually open Monday to Saturday from about 9am to 7pm or 8pm, with a midday break in some smaller towns; some open on Sunday morning. Small food shops (except for *boulangeries*) often shut on Monday also, so Saturday may be your last chance to stock up on provisions until Tuesday. Most open-air markets start at between 6am to 8am and finish at 12.30pm or 1pm. Many service stations have groceries open 24 hours a day.

CHILDREN

Rural France can be a great place for travel with children and, while big cities can present a variety of difficulties, lots of activities are on offer for *les enfants*, especially in Paris.

Practicalities

France is reasonably child-friendly, although French parents don't usually take their children to a restaurant any more sophisticated than a corner café. Chain restaurants like Hippopotamus and Bistro Romain are casual and serve food that most kids like, and many nicer restaurants have a reasonably priced children's menu. Take drinks and snacks with you on sightseeing days if you want to avoid costly stops in cafés. Picnics are a great way to feed the troops and enjoy local produce.

In Paris, weekly magazine *L'Officiel des Spectacles* (p190) advertises babysitting services *(gardes d'enfants, baby-sitting)*. Elsewhere, tourist offices often have lists of babysitters, or try www.bebe-annonce.com (in French).

RAIN, HAIL, SNOW OR SHINE

Check out the French weather forecasts at www.meteofrance.com (in French) or call one of the following for €0.34 per minute:

National, city, marine and mountain forecasts

☎ 3250 Local & *département* forecasts

☎ 08 92 68 02 + two-digit *département* number

Car-rental firms have children's safety seats for hire at a nominal cost; book them in advance. High chairs and cots (cribs) are standard in midrange restaurants and hotels. The choice of baby food, infant formula, soy and cow's milk, nappies (diapers) and the like in French supermarkets is similar to that in any developed country, but remember that opening hours may be more limited – run out of nappies on Saturday evening and you could be facing a long and messy weekend. (Should disaster strike, pharmacies – of which there is always one open for at least a few hours on a Sunday – also sell baby paraphernalia, and in Paris a number of pharmacies are open 24/7.)

Staying in a *chambre d'hôte* (B&B; p940) that also does a *table d'hôte* is fab for families; little kids can sweetly slumber upstairs while weary parents wine and dine in peace downstairs (don't forget your baby monitor!) Fancier camping grounds have pools and facilities for kids.

Sights & Activities

Include the kids in the trip planning: Lonely Planet's *Travel with Children* is a useful info source.

Paris' narrow streets and metro stairways can be a trial, but the capital has wonderful parks with amusements and activities like pony rides and puppet shows. For more information about Paris for children, see p162. Beaches are great kid-pleasers, the Atlantic coast being especially popular with families (note: some beaches have strong undertows). The French Alps also have lots of outdoor activities year-round, like horse riding, snowshoeing, light hiking and biking (most bike rental places carry children's bicycles).

CLIMATE CHARTS

France has a temperate climate with generally mild winters, except in mountainous areas and the far northeast (Lorraine and Alsace). For climatic considerations, see p18.

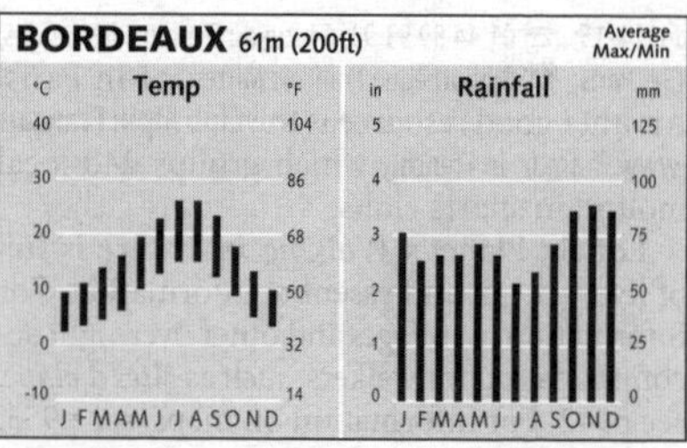

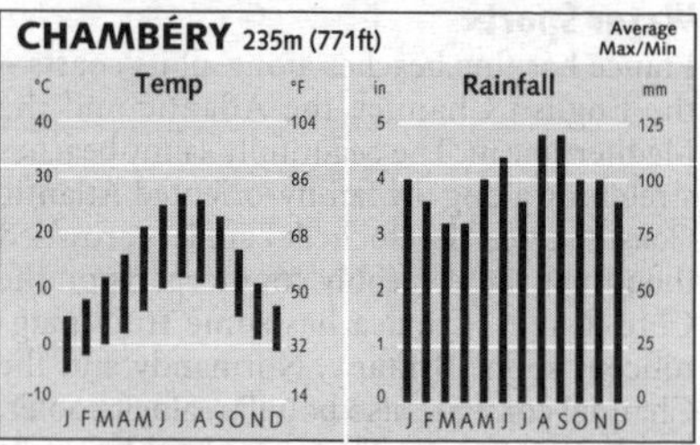

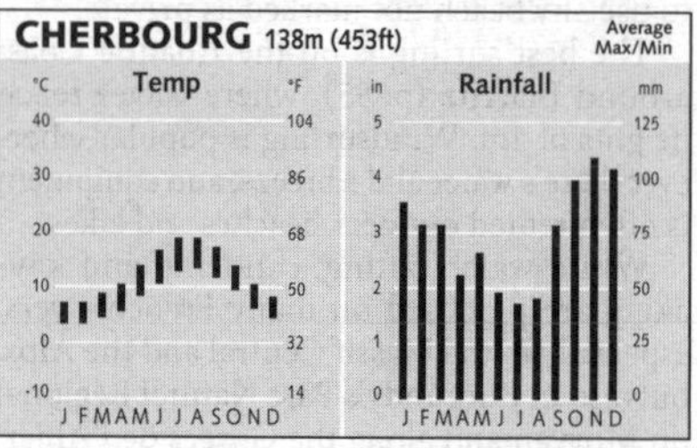

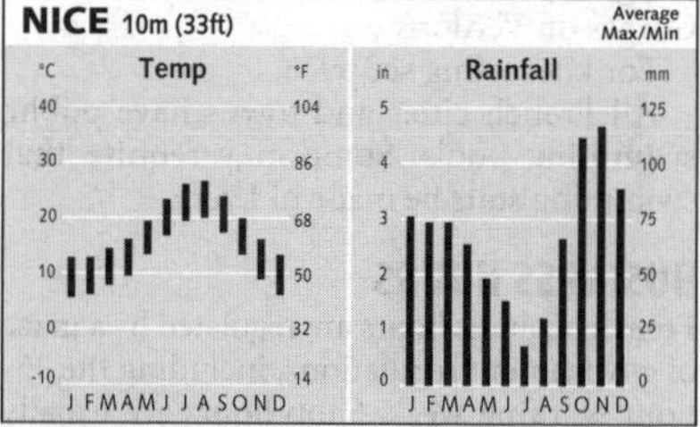

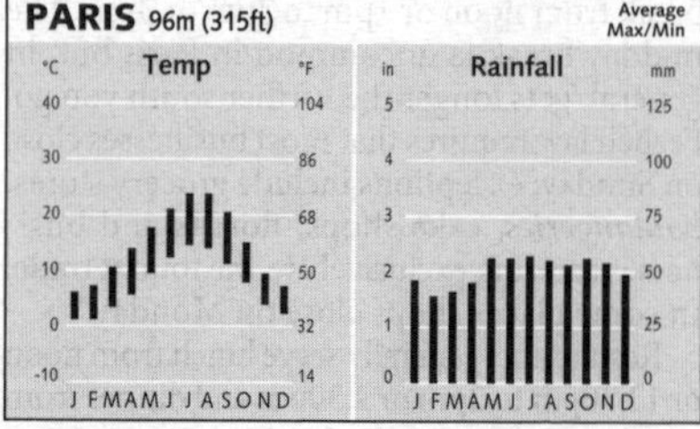

COURSES

Art, cooking, wine, language, film – the best of France is there for the learning. The website www.studyabroadlinks.com can help you find specific courses and summer programs, while www.edufrance.fr/en has information about university study.

Cooking

For short cooking courses and specialised sessions such as pastry making, see p86.

Language

All manner of French language courses are available in Paris and provincial towns and cities; many also arrange accommodation. Prices and courses vary greatly and the content can often be tailored to your specific needs (for a fee). The government site www.diplomatie.gouv.fr (under 'Francophony') and www.europa-pages.com/france list language schools in France. Some schools you might consider:

Alliance Française (Map pp124-5; ☎ 01 42 84 90 00; www.alliancefr.org; 101 bd Raspail, 6e, Paris; Ⓜ St-Placide) Venerable institution for the worldwide promotion of French language and civilisation, with intensive and extensive classes, including literature and business French.

Centre de Linguistique Appliquée de Besançon (☎ 03 81 66 52 00; http://cla.univ-fcomte.fr; 6 rue Gabriel Plançon, Besançon) One of France's largest language schools, in a beautiful city, with a variety of language and culture classes.

Centre Méditerranéen d'Études Françaises (☎ 04 93 78 21 59; www.monte-carlo.mc/centremed; chemin des Oliviers, Cap d'Ail) Côte d'Azur school dating to 1952, with an open-air amphitheatre designed by Jean Cocteau overlooking the sparkling blue Med.

Eurocentre d'Amboise (☎ 02 47 23 10 60; www.eurocentres.com; 9 mail St-Thomas, Amboise) Small, well-organised school in the charming Loire Valley. Eurocentre has branches in La Rochelle and Paris.

Université de Provence (☎ 04 42 95 32 17; http://sites.univ-provence.fr/wscefee; 29 av Robert Schumann, Aix-en-Provence) A hot choice in lovely Aix: semester-long language courses as well as shorter summer classes.

CUSTOMS

Goods brought in and out of countries within the EU incur no additional taxes provided duty has been paid somewhere within the EU and the goods are for personal consumption. Duty-free shopping is available only if you're leaving the EU.

Coming from non-EU countries (including the Channel Islands), duty-free allowances (for adults) are: 200 cigarettes, 50 cigars, 1L of spirits, 2L of wine, 50ml of perfume, 250ml *eau de toilette* and other goods up to the value of €175 (€90 for under 15s). Higher limits apply if you're coming from Andorra. Anything over these limits must be declared. For details, see www.douane.gouv.fr (partly in English).

DANGERS & ANNOYANCES

France is generally a safe place in which to live and travel but crime has risen dramatically in the last few years. Although property crime is a major problem, it's extremely unlikely that you will be physically assaulted while walking down the street. Always check your government's travel advisory warnings. Safety advice for women travellers is on p959.

Hunters

The hunting season runs from September to February. If you see signs reading *'chasseurs'* or *'chasse gardée'* strung up or tacked to trees, think twice about wandering into the area. As well as millions of wild animals, 25 French hunters die each year after being shot by other hunters.

Hunting is traditional and commonplace in all rural areas in France, especially the Vosges, the Sologne, the southwest and the Baie de Somme.

Natural Dangers

There are powerful tides and strong undertows at many places along the Atlantic Coast, from the Spanish border north to Brittany and Normandy.

Only swim in *zones de baignade surveillée* (beaches monitored by life guards). Be aware of tide times and, if sleeping on a beach, always make sure you are above the high-tide mark.

Thunderstorms in the mountains and the hot southern plains can be extremely sudden and violent. Check the weather report before setting out on a long walk and be prepared for sudden storms and temperature drops if you're heading into the high country of the Alps or Pyrenees.

Avalanches pose an enormous danger in the French Alps (see p525).

Smoking

As of 2007, smoking is illegal in all public spaces, including restaurants and pubs – and, to the surprise of some, the law is actually obeyed!

Strikes

France is the only European country in which public workers enjoy an unlimited right to strike, and they avail themselves of it with carefree abandon. Aggrieved truck drivers often block motorways and farmers agitating for more government support sometimes dump tonnes of produce on major arteries.

Getting caught in one of the 'social dialogues' that characterise labour relations in France can put a serious crimp in your travel plans. It's best to leave some wriggle room in your schedule, particularly around the departure times.

Riots

Attacks on the police and public buildings, such as those that swept French cities and their poor suburbs in November 2005 (p56), are very much the exception.

Theft

The security problem you're most likely to encounter is theft, including pick-pocketing and bag snatching (eg in dense crowds and public places). A common ploy is for one person to distract you while another steals your wallet, camera or bag. Tired tourists on the train from the airport are a frequent target for thieves. Big cities – notably Paris, Marseille and Nice – have the highest crime levels. Particularly in Paris, museums are beset by organised gangs of seemingly innocuous children who are actually trained pickpockets.

There's no need whatsoever to travel in fear. Taking a few simple precautions will minimise your chances of being ripped off.

- A hidden money belt is the safest way to carry money, credit cards and important documents.
- Take only what you need on busy sightseeing days; use the hotel/hostel safe for the rest.
- On trains, keep bags as close to you as possible: the luggage racks (if in use) at the ends of the carriage are an easy target for thieves; in sleeping compartments, lock the door carefully at night.
- Be especially vigilant for bag-snatchers at train stations, airports, fast-food outlets, cinemas, outdoor cafés and beaches and on public transport.
- Photocopy your passport, credit cards, plane tickets, driver's licence and other important documents – leave one copy at home and keep another one with you, separate from the originals.

TRAVELLING BY CAR

Break-ins to parked cars are a widespread problem. Gangs cruise seemingly tranquil tourist areas for unattended vehicles – out-of-town or foreign plates and rental stickers are a dead giveaway. *Never, ever* leave anything valuable – or anything not valuable – inside your car. Hiding your bags in the trunk is risky; in hatchbacks it's practically an open invitation to theft.

Aggressive theft from cars stopped at red lights, eg by motorcycle-borne thieves, is occasionally a problem, especially in the south (specifically in and around Marseille and sometimes Nice). As a precaution, lock your car doors and roll up the windows.

DISCOUNT CARDS

Camping Card International

The Camping Card International (www.campingcardinternational.com) is a form of ID that can be used instead of a passport when checking into a camping ground and includes third-party liability insurance. As a result, many camping grounds offer a 5% to 20% discount if you sign in with one. CCIs are issued by automobile associations, camping federations and, sometimes, on the spot at camping grounds.

Seniors Cards

People over 60 or 65 are entitled to discounts on things like public transport, museum admission fees and theatres. For details on the SNCF's Carte Sénior, see p976.

Student, Youth & Teachers' Cards

These cards, available from student unions and travel agencies, often yield fantastic discounts. An **International Student Identity Card** (ISIC; €12) can easily pay for itself through half-price admissions and cheap meals in student cafeterias. Many places stipulate a maximum age, usually 24 or 25 (ie 'under 25' or 'under 26'). For more details, check the website of the **International Student Travel Confederation** (ISTC; www.istc.org or www.isic.fr, in French).

If you're under 26 but not a student, you can apply for an **International Youth Travel Card** (IYTC or Go25, €12), also issued by ISTC, which entitles you to many of the same discounts as an ISIC. The **European Youth Card** (Euro<26 card) offers similar discounts across 41 European countries to anyone under 26; see www.euro26.org.

Teachers, professional artists, museum conservators and certain categories of students are admitted to some museums free. Bring along proof of affiliation – for example, an **International Teacher Identity Card** (ITIC).

EMBASSIES & CONSULATES

French Embassies & Consulates

France's diplomatic and consular representatives abroad are listed on the website www.diplomatie.gouv.fr/en.

Australia Canberra (☎ 02-6216 0100; www.ambafrance-au.org; 6 Perth Ave, Yarralumla, ACT 2600); Sydney Consulate (☎ 02-9268 2400; Level 26, St Martin's Tower, 31 Market St, Sydney, NSW 2000) There are also seven consular agencies.

Belgium Brussels (☎ 02 548 8711; www.ambafrance-be.org; 65 rue Ducale, Brussels 1000); Brussels Consulate (☎ 02-548 8811; www.consulfrance-bruxelles.org; 42 bd du Régent, Brussels 1000)

Canada Ottawa (☎ 613-789-1795; www.ambafrance-ca.org; 42 Sussex Drive, Ottawa, Ontario K1M 2C9); Toronto Consulate (☎ 416-847-1900; www.consulfrance-toronto.org; 2 Bloor St East, Ste 2200, Toronto M4W 1A8)

Germany Berlin (☎ 030-590 039 000; www.botschaft-frankreich.de; Pariser Platz 5, Berlin 10117, public entry at Wilhelmstrasse 69); Munich Consulate (☎ 089-419 4110; 3rd fl, Heimeranstrasse 31, Munich 80339)

Ireland Dublin (☎ 01-277 5000; www.ambafrance-ie.org; 36 Ailesbury Rd, Ballsbridge, Dublin 4)

Italy Rome (☎ 06 68 60 11; www.ambafrance-it.org; Piazza Farnese 67, 00186 Rome)

Netherlands The Hague (☎ 070-312 58 00; www.ambafrance-nl.org; Smidsplein 1, 2514 BT Den Haag); Amsterdam Consulate (☎ 020-530 6969; www.consulfrance-amsterdam.org; Vijzelgracht 2, 1017 HR Amsterdam)

New Zealand Wellington (☎ 04-384 2555; www.ambafrance-nz.org; 13th fl, Rural Bank Bldg, 34-42 Manners St, PO Box 11-343, Wellington)

South Africa Pretoria (☎ 012-425 1600; www.ambafrance-rsa.org; 250 Melk St, New Muckleneuk, 0181 Pretoria)

Spain Madrid (☎ 91 423 89 00; www.ambafrance-es.org; Calle de Salustiano Olozaga 9, 28001 Madrid); Barcelona Consulate (☎ 93 270 30 00; www.consulfrance-barcelone.org; Ronda Universitat 22, 08007 Barcelona)

Switzerland Bern (☎ 031 359 21 11; www.ambafrance-ch.org; Schosshaldenstrasse 46, 3006 Berne)

UK London Embassy (☎ 020-7073 1000; www.ambafrance-uk.org; 58 Knightsbridge, London SW1X 7JT); London Consulate (☎ 020-7073 1200; www.consulfrance-londres.org; 21 Cromwell Rd, London SW7 2EN); London Visa Section (☎ 020-7073 1250; 6A Cromwell Pl, London SW7 2EW)

USA Washington (☎ 202-944-6000; www.ambafrance-us.org; 4101 Reservoir Rd NW, Washington, DC 20007); New York Consulate (☎ 212-606-3600; www.consulfrance-newyork.org; 934 Fifth Ave, New York, NY 10021)

Embassies & Consulates in France

All foreign embassies are in Paris. Many countries – including the Canada, Japan, the UK, USA and most European countries – also have consulates in other major cities such as Bordeaux, Lyon, Nice, Marseille and Strasbourg. To find an embassy not listed here, look up *'ambassade'* under Paris in the super user-friendly **Pages Jaunes** (Yellow Pages; www.pagesjaunes.fr).

Australia Paris (Map pp124-5; ☎ 01 40 59 33 00; www.france.embassy.gov.au; 4 rue Jean Rey, 15e; Ⓜ Bir Hakeim)

Belgium Paris (Map pp118-19; ☎ 01 44 09 39 39; www.diplomatie.be/paris; 9 rue de Tilsitt, 17e; Ⓜ Charles de Gaulle-Étoile)

Canada Paris (Map pp118-19; ☎ 01 44 43 29 00; www.amb-canada.fr; 35 av Montaigne, 8e; Ⓜ Franklin D Roosevelt); Nice consulate (☎ 04 93 92 93 22; 10 rue Lamartine)

Germany Paris Embassy & Consulate (Map pp118-19; ☎ 01 53 83 45 00; www.paris.diplo.de, in French & German; 13 av Franklin D Roosevelt, 8e; Ⓜ Franklin D Roosevelt)

Ireland Paris (Map pp118-19; ☎ 01 44 17 67 00; www.embassyofirelandparis.com; 12 av Foch, 16e; Ⓜ Argentine)

Italy Paris Embassy (Map pp124-5; ☎ 01 49 54 03 00; www.amb-italie.fr; 51 rue de Varenne, 7e; Ⓜ Rue du Bac); Paris Consulate (Map pp114-15; ☎ 01 44 30 47 00; 5 bd Émile Augier, 16e; Ⓜ La Muette)

Japan Paris (Map pp118-19; ☎ 01 48 88 62 00; www.amb-japon.fr; 7 av Hoche, 8e; Ⓜ Courcelles)

Netherlands Paris (Map pp124-5; ☎ 01 40 62 33 00; www.amb-pays-bas.fr; 7 rue Eblé, 7e; Ⓜ St-François Xavier)

New Zealand Paris (Map pp118-19; ☎ 01 45 01 43 43; www.nzembassy.com; 7ter rue Léonard de Vinci, 16e; Ⓜ Victor Hugo)

South Africa Paris (Map pp124-5; ☎ 01 53 59 23 23; www.afriquesud.net; 59 quai d'Orsay, 7e; Ⓜ Invalides)

Spain Paris (Map pp118-19; ☎ 01 44 43 18 00; www.amb-espagne.fr; 22 av Marceau, 8e; Ⓜ Alma-Marceau)

Switzerland Paris Embassy (Map pp124-5; ☎ 01 49 55 67 00; www.amb-suisse.fr; 142 rue de Grenelle, 7e; Ⓜ Varenne);

UK Paris Embassy (Map pp118-19; ☎ 01 44 51 31 00;

www.amb-grandebretagne.fr; 35 rue du Faubourg St-Honoré, 8e; Ⓜ Concorde); Paris Consulate (Map pp118-19; ☎ 01 44 51 31 00; 18bis rue d'Anjou, 8e; Ⓜ Madeleine); Marseille Consulate (☎ 04 91 54 92 00; place Varian Fry, 6e)
USA Paris Embassy (Map pp118-19; ☎ 01 43 12 22 22; http://france.usembassy.gov; 2 av Gabriel, 8e; Ⓜ Concorde); US citizen services (☎ 01 43 12 26 71; 4 av Gabriel, 8e; Ⓜ Concorde; 9am-noon Mon-Fri except US & French holidays); Nice Consular Agency (Map pp862-3; ☎ 04 93 88 89 55; 3rd fl, 7 av Gustave V); Marseille Consulate (☎ 04 91 54 92 00; place Varian Fry, 6e)

FESTIVALS & EVENTS

Most French cities and towns have at least one major music, dance, theatre, cinema or art festival each year and many have several. Villages hold *foires* (fairs) and *fêtes* (festivals) to honour anything from a local saint to the year's garlic crop. We list many of these important annual events in city and town sections; more details are available from tourist-office websites. During big events towns get extremely busy and accommodation can get booked out in advance.

Tickets for many events can be purchased at tourist offices and *billetteries* (ticket agencies) run by **Fnac** (☎ 08 92 68 36 22 for €0.34 a min; www.fnacspectacles.com, in French) and **Virgin** (☎ 08 25 12 91 39 for €0.15 a min; www.virginmega.fr, in French); both charge a commission of €1 to €6.

FEBRUARY

Carnaval de Nice (p869; www.nicecarnaval.com) Merrymaking in Nice, on the Riviera, during France's largest street carnival (last half of February)

MARCH & APRIL

Feria Pascale (p830; www.feriaarles.com, in French) In the ancient *arène* (arena) of Arles, the Feria kicks off the bullfight season with much cavorting and merriment (Easter).

MAY & JUNE

May Day Across France, workers' day is celebrated with trade-union parades and diverse protests. People give each other *muguets* (lilies of the valley) for good luck. No one works – except waiters and *muguet* sellers (1 May).
International Film Festival (p880; www.festival-cannes.com) The stars walk the red carpet at Cannes, the biggest of Europe's see-and-be-seen cinema extravaganzas (mid-May).
Pélerinage des Gitans (p835; www.gitans.fr, in French) Twice a year *gitans* (Roma Gitano people) from all over Europe make their way to the Camargue for a flamboyant street fiesta of music, dancing and dipping their toes in the sea (24-25 May and Sunday nearest 22 October).
Fête de la Musique (www.fetedelamusique.culture.fr, in French) Bands, orchestras, crooners, buskers and spectators take to the streets for this nationwide celebration of music (21 June).
Gay Pride (www.gaypride.fr, in French) Sizzling street parades, performances and parties throughout Paris and other major cities (late June in Paris, mid-May to early July in other cities).

JULY

Festival d'Aix-en-Provence (p822; www.festival-aix.com) Attracts some of the world's best classical music, opera, ballet and buskers (late June to mid-July).
Bastille Day Fireworks, balls, processions – including a military parade down Paris' Champs-Élysées – and all-round hoo-ha mark France's National Day, on the anniversary of the storming of the Bastille in 1789 (14 July).
Festival d'Avignon (p840; www.festival-avignon.com) Actors, dancers and musicians flock to Avignon to perform in the official and fringe art festivals (mid-July).
Nice Jazz Festival (p869; www.nicejazzfest.fr) See jazz cats and other pop, rock and world artists take over public spaces and the Roman ruins of Nice (mid-July).
Paris Plages (p164; www.paris.fr, search for 'Paris plages') Tan on a sandy Seine-side beach in the capital (mid-July–mid-August).
Fêtes de Bayonne (p691; www.fetes-de-bayonne.com) Bullfighting, cow-chasing and Basque music are the order of the day at Bayonne's biggest event (late July-early August).

AUGUST & SEPTEMBER

Festival Interceltique de Lorient (p339; www.festival-interceltique.com) Hundreds of thousands of Celts from Brittany and abroad flock to Lorient to celebrate Celtic culture (early August).
Fêtes d'Arvor (p346; www.fetes-arvor.org, in French) A passionate celebration of local Breton culture in Vannes, with street parades, concerts and numerous *festoù-noz* (night festivals; mid-August).
Braderie de Lille (p231) Three days of mussel-munching as this colossal flea market engulfs the city with antiques, handicrafts and bric-a-brac (first weekend in September).
Festival du Cinema Américain (p294; www.festival-deauville.com) The silver screen flickers next to the sea at this celebration of American cinema in Deauville (early September).
Journées du Patrimoine Countrywide festivals that see some of France's most important public buildings open to the public (third weekend in September).

DECEMBER

Christmas Markets in Alsace (p381) Colourful, traditional pre-Christmas markets and celebrations (last weekend in November through Christmas or New Year).

Fête des Lumières (p506; www.lumieres.lyon.fr) France's biggest and best light show transforms Lyon (8 December).

FOOD

The food and drink chapter (p77 and p69) bursts with succulent information about French gastronomy.

In this book's restaurant listings, we almost always indicate the price of *menus* (two- or three-course set menus), the quickie lunchtime version of which is also known as a *formule* (literally 'formula'). Ordering à la carte (choosing individual items from the menu) generally works out to be rather more expensive.

At eateries listed under 'budget', *menus* cost up to €15. At midrange places, with more atmosphere and seasonal specialities, *menus* go for €15 to €50. Top-end restaurants – some with one to three Michelin stars – have impeccable service, outstanding cuisine and *menus* costing anything upwards of €50.

GAY & LESBIAN TRAVELLERS

France is one of Europe's most liberal countries when it comes to homosexuality, in part because of a long tradition of public tolerance towards people who choose not to live by conventional social codes. Paris has been a thriving gay and lesbian centre since the late 1970s. Bordeaux, Lille, Lyon, Montpellier, Toulouse and many other towns also have significant active communities. Attitudes towards homosexuality tend to be more conservative in the countryside and villages. France's lesbian scene is less public than its gay male counterpart and is centred mainly on women's cafés and bars, also the best places to find information.

Gay Pride marches (opposite) are held in major French cities in mid-May to early July.

Internet Resources

CitéGAY (www.citegay.fr, in French) Low-down on gay and lesbian events.

France Queer Resources Directory (www.france.qrd.org, in French) Directory for gays and lesbians, including matters of interest to travellers.

French Government Tourist Office (http://us.franceguide.com/Special-Interests/Gay-friendly) Information about 'the gay-friendly destination par excellence'.

Gayscape (www.gayscape.com) Hundreds of links to gay- and lesbian-related sites.

Tasse de Thé (www.tassedethe.com, in French) A *webzine lesbien* with lots of useful links.

Organisations

Most major gay and lesbian organisations are based in Paris:

Act Up-Paris (Map pp132-3; ☎ 01 48 06 13 89; www.actupparis.org, in French; 45 rue Sedaine, 11e; Ⓜ Voltaire) An activist group focusing on the battle against HIV/AIDS and the rights of people who are *séropositif* (have tested positive for HIV).

AIDES (Map pp114-15; ☎ 08 20 16 00 11, 01 53 27 63 00; www.aides.org; 119 rue des Pyrénées, 20e; Ⓜ Jourdain) France-wide activist organisation bringing together people directly and indirectly affected by AIDS.

Association des Médecins Gais (☎ 01 48 05 81 71; www.medecins-gays.org, in French; 63 rue Beaubourg, 3e; Ⓜ Rambuteau) Association of Gay Doctors, based in the Centre Lesbien Gai Bi & Trans; deals with gay-related health issues.

Centre Lesbien Gai Bi & Trans (LGBT; Map pp126-7; ☎ 01 43 57 21 47; www.cglparis.org, in French; 63 rue Beaubourg, 3e; Ⓜ Rambuteau; ⏲ 6-8pm Mon, 4-8pm Tue, 12.30-8pm Wed, Fri & Sat, 3-8pm Thu, 4-7pm Sun, women-only 8-10pm 1st & 3rd Fri of month) A welcome and support centre.

SIDA Info service (☎ 08 00 84 08 00; www.sida-info-service.org, in French) HIV/AIDS information service that helps with anonymous HIV testing and treatment; advice available in foreign languages.

Publications

Damron (www.damron.com) Publishes English-language international travel guides, including the *Damron Women's Traveller* for lesbians and the *Damron Men's Travel Guide* for gays.

Gayvox (www.gayvox.com/guide3, in French) Online travel guide to France, with listings by region.

Lesbia French-language lesbian monthly with articles and useful listings.

Spartacus International Gay Guide (www.spartacusworld.com) Annual English-language travel guide for men.

Têtu (www.tetu.com, in French) A glossy monthly that bills itself as *le magazine des gais et des lesbiennes*. Has a France-wide directory of bars, clubs and hotels.

HOLIDAYS

The following *jours fériés* (public holidays) are observed in France:

New Year's Day (Jour de l'An) 1 January – parties in larger cities; fireworks are subdued by international standards.

Easter Sunday & Monday (Pâques & lundi de Pâques) Late March/April.

May Day (Fête du Travail) 1 May – traditional parades.

Victoire 1945 8 May – commemorates the Allied victory in Europe that ended WWII.

Ascension Thursday (Ascension) May – celebrated on the 40th day after Easter.

Pentecost/Whit Sunday & Whit Monday (Pentecôte & lundi de Pentecôte) Mid-May to mid-June – celebrated on the seventh Sunday after Easter.
Bastille Day/National Day (Fête Nationale) 14 July – *the* national holiday.
Assumption Day (Assomption) 15 August.
All Saints' Day (Toussaint) 1 November.
Remembrance Day (L'onze novembre) 11 November – marks the WWI armistice.
Christmas (Noël) 25 December.

The following are *not* public holidays in France: Shrove Tuesday (Mardi Gras; the first day of Lent); Maundy (or Holy) Thursday and Good Friday, just before Easter; and Boxing Day (26 December).

Note: Good Friday and Boxing Day *are* public holidays in Alsace.

INSURANCE

See p978 for health insurance and p973 for car insurance.

Travel Insurance

Getting travel insurance to cover theft, loss and medical problems is highly recommended. Some policies specifically exclude dangerous activities such as scuba diving, motorcycling, skiing and even trekking so read the fine print. Check that the policy covers ambulances or an emergency flight home.

You may prefer a policy that pays doctors or hospitals directly rather than reimbursing you for expenditures after the fact. If you have to claim later, make sure you keep all documentation.

Paying for your airline ticket with a credit card often provides limited travel accident insurance – ask your credit-card company what it's prepared to cover.

INTERNET ACCESS

Wireless access points can now be found at major airports, in many (if not most) hotels and at lots of cafés. Many tourist offices tout wi-fi hot spots that let laptop owners hook up for free.

Internet cafés can be found in towns and cities countrywide; they are listed under Information in the regional chapters. Prices range from €2 to €6 per hour. Public libraries *(bibliothèques or médiathèques)* often have free or inexpensive internet access, though hours are limited and you may have to fill in some forms.

If you'll be accessing dial-up ISPs with your laptop, you'll need a telephone-plug adaptor, available at large supermarkets.

For useful national French websites, see p20.

WHAT THE COMPUTER ICON MEANS

Throughout this guide, only accommodation providers that have an actual computer that guests can use to access the internet are flagged with a computer icon (💻); those that offer wi-fi access, but have no computer, are not. Paris is the exception: places offering wi-fi only as well as places offering the use of a computer receive the 💻 icon in the Paris chapter.

LAUNDRY

Virtually all French cities and towns have at least one *laverie libre-service* (self-service laundrette), mentioned in town listings under Information. In most, *machines à laver* (washing machines), *séchoirs* (dryers) and the *lessive* (washing powder) dispenser are operated by a *centrale de paiement* (central payment gadget) that runs on coins – bring plenty in various denominations in case the change-maker is on the fritz. In general, you punch in the number of the machine you'd like to operate and insert coins in the sum indicated; the machine will then launch automatically so make sure you've already chosen your temperature and cycle.

Useful vocabulary includes *blanc* (whites), *couleur* (colours), *synthetique* (synthetics), *laine* (wool), *prélavage* (prewash cycle), *lavage* (wash cycle), *rinçage* (rinse cycle) and *essorage* (spin-dry cycle).

LEGAL MATTERS

Drugs & Alcohol

Contrary to popular belief, French law does not distinguish between 'hard' and 'soft' drugs. The penalty for any personal use of *stupéfiants* (including cannabis, amphetamines, ecstasy and heroin) can be a one-year jail sentence and a €3750 fine, but depending on the circumstances it might be anything from a stern word to a compulsory rehab program.

Importing, possessing, selling or buying drugs can get you up to 10 years' prison and a fine of up to €500,000. Police have been known to search chartered coaches, cars and train passengers for drugs just because they're coming from Amsterdam.

Ivresse (drunkeness) in public is punishable by a €150 fine.

Police

French police have wide powers of search and seizure and can ask you to prove your identity at any time – whether or not there is 'probable cause'. Foreigners must be able to prove their legal status in France (eg passport, visa, residency permit) without delay.

If the police stop you for any reason, be polite and remain calm. Verbally (and of course physically) abusing a police officer can lead to a hefty fine, and even imprisonment. You may refuse to sign a police statement, and have the right to ask for a copy. People who are arrested are considered innocent until proven guilty, but can be held in custody until trial.

Because of the threat of terrorism, French police are very strict about security. Do not leave baggage unattended, especially at airports or train stations: suspicious objects may be summarily blown up.

LOCAL GOVERNMENT

Metropolitan France (the mainland and Corsica) is made up of 22 *régions* (regions), which group the country's 96 *départements* (departments), each ruled by a Paris-appointed *préfet* (prefect) who rules from the departmental capital, the *préfecture*. *Départements* are subdivided into 324 arrondissements, which are in turn subdivided into *cantons*, which are split into 36,400 *communes*.

Almost always named after a geographic feature, *départements* have two-digit codes (see the map, p954) that do extra duty as the first two digits of all postcodes.

LEGAL AGE

- Driving: 18
- Buying alcohol: 16
- Age of majority: 18
- Age of sexual consent for everyone: 15
- Age considered minor under anti-child-pornography and child-prostitution laws: 18
- Voting: 18

MAPS

France's two major map publishers are **Michelin** (http://boutiquecartesetguides.michelin.fr, in French, www.viamichelin.com for online maps) and the **Institut Géographique National** (IGN; www.ign.fr), which also publishes themed maps showing wine regions, museums and so on. Countrywide, road and city maps are available at Maisons de la Presse (large newsagencies), bookshops, tourist offices and newspaper kiosks. In Paris, the full range of IGN maps is on offer at **Espace IGN** (Map pp118-19; ☎ 01 43 98 80 00; 107 rue la Boétie, Paris 8e; Ⓜ Franklin D Roosevelt).

The book in your hand contains around 140 city and town maps; Lonely Planet also publishes a laminated *Paris City Map*. Plans-Guides Blay (www.blayfoldex.com, in French) produces over 180 orange-jacketed street maps of French cities and towns. Michelin has excellent city maps of Paris and Lyon.

Michelin's green-jacketed *Environs de Paris* and *Banlieue de Paris* maps (€4.30), both available from airport newsagents, will help you with the very confusing drive into and out of Paris. Michelin's yellow-orange 1:200,000 scale (1cm = 2km) regional maps (€6.50) are perfect for cross-country driving; if you'll be covering more than a few regions the national *Atlas Routier France* (€15.90) is better value.

The IGN also has regional fold-out maps as well as an all-France volume, *France – Routes, Autoroutes*.

Walking & Cycling

The **FFRP** (www.ffrp.asso.fr, in French) publishes around 120 *topoguides* – map-equipped booklets about major trails (eg GRs) – in French. Local organisations also produce topoguides that supply details on trail conditions, flora, fauna, mountain shelters and so on; ask for these at tourist offices and local bookshops.

IGN has a variety of great topoguides and 1:50,000-scale maps that are ideal for hiking, biking or walking. Its specialised *cyclocartes* (cycle maps) show dozens of suggested bicycle tours around France.

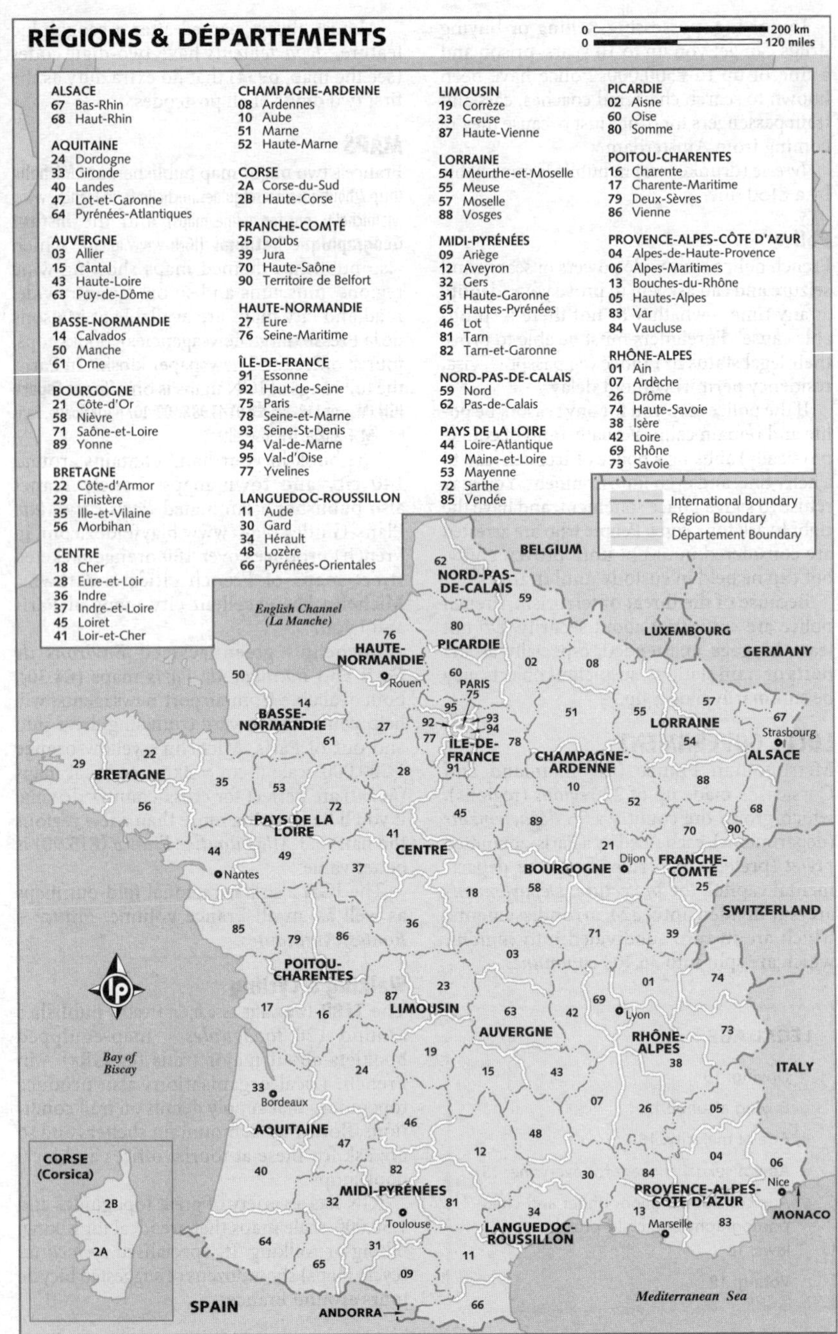
RÉGIONS & DÉPARTEMENTS
0 200 km
0 120 miles
ALSACE
67 Bas-Rhin
68 Haut-Rhin
AQUITAINE
24 Dordogne
33 Gironde
40 Landes
47 Lot-et-Garonne
64 Pyrénées-Atlantiques
AUVERGNE
03 Allier
15 Cantal
43 Haute-Loire
63 Puy-de-Dôme
BASSE-NORMANDIE
14 Calvados
50 Manche
61 Orne
BOURGOGNE
21 Côte-d'Or
58 Nièvre
71 Saône-et-Loire
89 Yonne
BRETAGNE
22 Côte-d'Armor
29 Finistère
35 Ille-et-Vilaine
56 Morbihan
CENTRE
18 Cher
28 Eure-et-Loir
36 Indre
37 Indre-et-Loire
45 Loiret
41 Loir-et-Cher
CHAMPAGNE-ARDENNE
08 Ardennes
10 Aube
51 Marne
52 Haute-Marne
CORSE
2A Corse-du-Sud
2B Haute-Corse
FRANCHE-COMTÉ
25 Doubs
39 Jura
70 Haute-Saône
90 Territoire de Belfort
HAUTE-NORMANDIE
27 Eure
76 Seine-Maritime
ÎLE-DE-FRANCE
91 Essonne
92 Haut-de-Seine
75 Paris
78 Seine-et-Marne
93 Seine-St-Denis
94 Val-de-Marne
95 Val-d'Oise
77 Yvelines
LANGUEDOC-ROUSSILLON
11 Aude
30 Gard
34 Hérault
48 Lozère
66 Pyrénées-Orientales
LIMOUSIN
19 Corrèze
23 Creuse
87 Haute-Vienne
LORRAINE
54 Meurthe-et-Moselle
55 Meuse
57 Moselle
88 Vosges
MIDI-PYRÉNÉES
09 Ariège
12 Aveyron
32 Gers
31 Haute-Garonne
65 Hautes-Pyrénées
46 Lot
81 Tarn
82 Tarn-et-Garonne
NORD-PAS-DE-CALAIS
59 Nord
62 Pas-de-Calais
PAYS DE LA LOIRE
44 Loire-Atlantique
49 Maine-et-Loire
53 Mayenne
72 Sarthe
85 Vendée
PICARDIE
02 Aisne
60 Oise
80 Somme
POITOU-CHARENTES
16 Charente
17 Charente-Maritime
79 Deux-Sèvres
86 Vienne
PROVENCE-ALPES-CÔTE D'AZUR
04 Alpes-de-Haute-Provence
06 Alpes-Maritimes
13 Bouches-du-Rhône
05 Hautes-Alpes
83 Var
84 Vaucluse
RHÔNE-ALPES
01 Ain
07 Ardèche
26 Drôme
74 Haute-Savoie
38 Isère
42 Loire
69 Rhône
73 Savoie
International Boundary
Région Boundary
Département Boundary
BELGIUM
LUXEMBOURG
GERMANY
SWITZERLAND
ITALY
SPAIN
ANDORRA
MONACO
English Channel (La Manche)
Bay of Biscay
Mediterranean Sea
NORD-PAS-DE-CALAIS
PICARDIE
HAUTE-NORMANDIE
BASSE-NORMANDIE
BRETAGNE
PAYS DE LA LOIRE
CENTRE
ÎLE-DE-FRANCE
CHAMPAGNE-ARDENNE
LORRAINE
ALSACE
BOURGOGNE
FRANCHE-COMTÉ
POITOU-CHARENTES
LIMOUSIN
AUVERGNE
RHÔNE-ALPES
AQUITAINE
MIDI-PYRÉNÉES
LANGUEDOC-ROUSSILLON
PROVENCE-ALPES-CÔTE D'AZUR
CORSE (Corsica)
Rouen
PARIS
Strasbourg
Nantes
Dijon
Lyon
Bordeaux
Toulouse
Marseille
Nice

MONEY

ATMs

Automated Teller Machines (ATMs) – known as *distributeurs automatiques de billets* (DAB) or *points d'argent* in French – are the cheapest and most convenient way to get money. ATMs connected to international networks are situated in all cities and towns and usually offer an excellent exchange rate.

Cash

You always get a better exchange rate in-country but it's a good idea to arrive in France with enough euros to take a taxi to a hotel if you have to.

Credit & Debit Cards

Credit and debit cards are convenient, relatively secure and usually offer a better exchange rate than travellers cheques or cash exchanges. Credit cards issued in France have embedded chips – you have to type in a PIN code to make a purchase.

Credit cards are accepted almost everywhere in France. Visa, MasterCard and Amex can be used in shops and supermarkets and for train travel, car rentals and motorway tolls, though some places (eg 24-hour petrol stations, some autoroute toll machines) only take French-style credit cards with chips and PINs (for security reasons, these are now being issued by more and more banks worldwide). Don't assume that you can pay for a meal or a budget hotel with a credit card – inquire first.

Cash advances are a supremely convenient way to stay stocked up with euros. However, getting cash with a credit card involves both fees (sometimes US$10 or more) and interest – ask your credit-card issuer for details. Debit-card fees are usually much less.

For lost cards, these numbers operate 24 hours:

Amex (☎ 01 47 77 72 00)
Diners Club (☎ 08 10 31 41 59)
MasterCard (☎ 08 00 90 13 87)
Visa (Carte Bleue; ☎ 08 00 90 11 79)

Currency

The euro has been the official currency of France since 2002. One euro is divided into 100 cents or centimes, with one-, two-, five-, 10-, 20- and 50-centime coins. Notes come in denominations of five, 10, 20, 50, 100, 200 and 500 euros. Euro notes and coins issued in France are valid throughout the other 14 countries in the euro zone: Austria, Belgium, Cyprus, Finland, Germany, Greece, Ireland, Italy, Luxembourg, Malta, the Netherlands, Portugal, Slovenia and Spain.

Exchange rates at publication time are given on the inside front cover of this book and a guide to costs can be found on p18.

Moneychangers

Commercial banks usually charge a stiff €3 to €5 fee per foreign-currency transaction – if they even bother to offer exchange services any more. In Paris and major cities, *bureaux de change* (exchange bureaux) are faster and easier, open longer hours and often give better rates than banks. Some post-office branches exchange travellers cheques and banknotes in a variety of currencies but charge a €5 commission for cash; most won't take US$100 bills.

Tipping

By law, restaurant and bar prices are *service compris* (include a 15% service charge) so there's no expectation of a *pourboire* (tip), though if you're satisfied you might leave a few coins (for a cup of coffee) or round up to the nearest euro or two. Except in very upscale establishments, that is, where 5% is the norm. Taxi drivers are usually tipped 10%. If you stay in a hotel for several days, it's good form to leave €1 or €2 for the people who clean your room (more in top-end places, where the porter, the bellboy and other staff should be tipped if you've asked them to carry out extra services).

Travellers Cheques

Travellers cheques, a relic of the 19th and 20th centuries, cannot be used to pay most French merchants directly and so have to be changed into euro banknotes at banks, exchange bureaux or post offices.

POST

French post offices are flagged with a yellow or brown sign reading 'La Poste'. Since La Poste also has banking, finance and bill-paying functions, queues can be long but automatic machines dispense postage stamps.

Postal Rates

Domestic letters (including to French overseas territories) weighing up to 20g cost €0.55.

For international post, a letter/package under 20g/2kg costs €0.65/12.30 to Zone 1 (EU and Switzerland) and €0.85/14 to Zone 2 (the rest of the world). Worldwide express-mail delivery, called **Chronopost** (☎ 08 10 82 18 21; www.fr.chronopost.com), costs a fortune and may not be as rapid as advertised.

All mail to France *must* include the five-digit *code postal* (postcode/ZIP code), which begins with the two-digit number of the *département*. For French postcodes, see www.france-codepostal.fr/en or www.codeposte.com (in French). The notation 'CEDEX' after a town name simply means that mail sent to that address is collected at the post office, rather than delivered to the door.

SHOPPING

France is renowned for its luxury goods, particularly haute couture, high-quality clothing accessories (eg Hermès scarves), lingerie, perfume and cosmetics. However, such goods may not be any cheaper in France than at home.

Soldes (sales) – held, by law, for three weeks in January and July – offer significant discounts and can be a gold mine for fashionistas. The budget-conscious should also look out for the words *degriffés* (name-brand products with the labels cut out) or *dépôt-vente* (ex-showroom garments sold at steep mark-downs). Factory-outlet shops can be found in Troyes (p369) and Calais (p238).

For local arts and crafts go directly to the source. In Brittany, look for colourful Quimper *faïence* (earthenware), and in Normandy you can pick up Rouen *faïence* or intricate lace from Alençon. Other possibilities include deluxe crystal and glassware from Baccarat in southern Lorraine or enamel and porcelain from Limoges in Limousin.

Wines from Bordeaux, Burgundy, Alsace and Champagne are available all around France but you'll find a better selection at local wine shops. Buying direct from wineries – after a *dégustation* (tasting session), of course – is an even more enjoyable option! Local brandies make good souvenirs since they may not be available in your home country; look out for cognacs (from Cognac!), Calvados (apple brandy), *pommeau* (a mixture of unfermented apple juice and Calvados) or Fécamp Bénédictine (from Normandy). Corsicans sell unusual liqueurs in local markets, and Charentes is the place to pick up Pineau de Charentes.

Goodies that travel well include macaroons from St-Émilion and Alsace, *calissons* (a chewy, marzipan-like sweet) from Aix-en-Provence and candied fruit from Nice. For information on local shopping options, see the individual towns and cities.

In some shops and department stores, non-EU residents can arrange a rebate of some of the 19.6% value-added tax (VAT) if they spend enough. There are forms to fill out in-store, which must be shown, with the purchases, as you leave the country (eg at an airport).

SOLO TRAVELLERS

Travelling solo in France is easy and rewarding. One economic drawback, though, is that single rooms tend to cost almost as much as doubles. It is quite common for people to eat in restaurants alone in France, particularly at lunch. Women travelling alone are unlikely to encounter any particular problems beyond some minor hassles (for more information, see p959).

TELEPHONE

Four decades ago France had one of the worst telephone systems in Western Europe but thanks to massive investment, the country now has one of the most modern – and overpriced – telecommunications systems in the world.

Domestic Dialling

French telephone numbers have 10 digits, except for a few commercial access numbers that have four digits and some emergency numbers that have just two or three. Emergency numbers (see inside the front cover) can be dialled from public phones without a phonecard.

Numbers beginning with ☎ 08 00 or ☎ 08 05 are free but other ☎ 08 numbers are not – per-minute tariffs include €0.12 for ☎ 08 20 and ☎ 08 21, €0.15 for ☎ 08 25 and ☎ 08 26, and €0.34 for ☎ 08 92; a ☎ 08 10 number costs the same as a local call. French law requires that prices be marked wherever such numbers are publicised.

Dialling a mobile phone (ie a number that begins with ☎ 06) from a fixed-line phone or another mobile can be very expensive.

For France Telecom's *service des renseignements* (directory inquiries) dial ☎ 11 87 12 (€1.18 per call from a fixed-line phone). Not all operators speak English. For help in English with all France Telecom's services, see www.francetelecom.com or call ☎ 08 00 36 47 75.

Hotels, *gîtes,* hostels and pensions are free to meter their calls as they like. The surcharge is usually around €0.30 per minute but can be higher.

Public Phones & Telephone Cards

To get explanations in English and other languages on how to use a public telephone, push the button engraved with a two-flags icon.

For both international and domestic calling, most public phones operate using either a credit card or two kinds of *télécartes* (phonecards): *cartes à puce* (cards with a magnetic chip) issued by France Télécom and sold at post offices for €8 or €15; and *cartes à code* (cards that you can use from public or private phones by dialling a free access number and then the card's scratch-off code), marketed by an array of companies and sold at *tabacs,* newsagents and post offices.

Phonecards with codes offer *much* better international rates than do France Télécom chip cards or Country Direct services (for which you're billed at home by your long-distance carrier). The shop you buy a phonecard from should be able to tell you which type is best for the country you'd like to call. Using phonecards from a home phone is much cheaper that using them from public phones or mobile phones.

International Dialling

To call France from another country, dial your country's international access code, then ☎ 33 (France's country code), then the 10-digit local number *without* the initial ☎ 0.

To call internationally from France, dial ☎ 00 (the international access code), the *indicatif* (country code), the area code (without the initial zero if there is one) and the local number. Some country codes are posted in public telephones.

For directory inquiries for numbers outside France, dial ☎ 11 87 00 (€2 or €3).

To make a reverse-charges (collect) call *(en PCV)* or a person-to-person call *(avec préavis)* from France, dial ☎ 31 23. For the USA and Canada you can dial ☎ 08 00 99 00 11, and for Australia (Telstra) ☎ 08 00 99 00 61.

Mobile Phones

French mobile phones have numbers that begin with ☎ 06.

France uses GSM 900/1800, which is compatible with the rest of Europe and Australia but not with the North American GSM 1900 or the totally different system in Japan (though some North Americans have tri-band phones that work here). Check with your service provider about roaming charges – using a mobile phone outside your home country can be hideously expensive!

It may be cheaper to buy your own French SIM card – and locals you meet are much more likely to ring you if your number is French. If you already have a compatible phone, you can slip in a SIM card (€20 to €30) and rev it up with prepaid credit, though this is likely to run out fast as domestic prepaid calls cost about €0.50 a minute. Recharge cards are sold at most *tabacs* and newsagents. In general, SIMs that lie dormant for six months are deactivated.

SIMs are available at the ubiquitous outlets run by France's three mobile phone companies, **Bouygues** (☎ 08 10 63 01 00; www.bouyguestelecom.fr), France Telecom's **Orange** (www.orange.fr, in French) and **SFR** (☎ 08 11 70 70 73; www.sfr.com).

TIME

France uses the 24-hour clock and is on Central European Time, which is one hour ahead of GMT/UTC. During daylight-saving time, which runs from the last Sunday in March to the last Sunday in October, France is two hours ahead of GMT/UTC.

Without taking daylight-saving time into account, when it's noon in Paris it's 3am in San Francisco, 6am in New York, 11am in London, 8pm in Tokyo, 9pm in Sydney and 11pm in Auckland. Australia's east coast is between eight and 10 hours ahead of France. Refer to the time-zone world map on pp1018–19 for additional data.

TOURIST INFORMATION

Local Tourist Offices

Almost every city, town, village and hamlet has an *office de tourisme* (a tourist office run by some unit of local government) or *syndicat d'initiative* (a tourist office run by an organisation of local merchants). Both are excellent resources and can supply you with local maps as well as details on accommodation, restaurants and activities. If you have a special interest such as walking, cycling, architecture or wine sampling, ask about it. Many tourist offices make local hotel and B&B reservations, sometimes for a small fee. Some have limited currency-exchange services. Details on tourist offices appear under Information at the beginning of each city, town or area listing.

Comités régionaux de tourisme (CRTs; regional tourist boards), their *départemental* analogues (CDTs), and their websites are a superb source of information and hyperlinks. CRT websites can be found at www.fncrt.com (in French).

Tourist Offices Abroad

French government tourist offices (usually called Maisons de la France) provide every imaginable sort of tourist information on France. See www.franceguide.com for links to country-specific websites.

Australia (☎ 02-9231 5244; Level 13, 25 Bligh St, Sydney, NSW 2000)
Canada (☎ 514-288 2026; Ste 1010, 1800 McGill College Ave, Montreal, Quebec H3A 3J6)
UK (☎ 09068-244 123; Lincoln House, 300 High Holborn, London WC1V 7JH)
USA New York (☎ 514-288-1904; 29th fl, 825 Third Ave, entrance on 50th St, New York, NY 10022); Los Angeles (☎ 310-271-6665; 9454 Wilshire Bd, Ste 210, Beverly Hills, CA 90212-2967)

TRAVELLERS WITH DISABILITIES

France is not well equipped for *handicapés* (people with disabilities): cobblestone streets are a nightmare to navigate in a wheelchair; kerb ramps are often lacking; older public facilities and budget hotels frequently lack lifts; and the Paris metro, most of it built decades ago, is hopeless. But travellers with disabilities who would like to visit France can overcome these difficulties.

Tourisme et Handicaps (☎ 01 44 11 10 41; www.tourisme-handicaps.org, in French; 43 rue Marx Dormoy, 18e, Paris) issues the 'Tourisme et Handicap' label to tourist sites, restaurants and hotels that comply with strict accessibility and usability standards. Different symbols indicate the sort of access afforded to people with physical, mental, hearing and/or visual disabilities.

Details on rail access for people with disabilities appear in the SNCF's French-language booklet *Guide des Voyageurs Handicapés et à Mobilité Réduite,* available at train stations. You can also contact the **Centre du Service Accès Plus** (☎ 08 90 64 06 50; www.accessibilite.sncf.fr, in French), to check station accessibility or to arrange for a *fauteuil roulant* (wheelchair) or to receive help getting on or off a train. For the Paris region, contact **Accès Plus Transilien** (☎ 08 10 76 74 33; www.infomobi.com).

Access Project (www.accessproject-phsp.org; 39 Bradley Gardens, West Ealing, London W13 8HE) publishes a useful guide, *Access in Paris,* which was recently updated and can be downloaded as PDF files. The **Paris Convention & Visitors Bureau** (p137) also has information and brochures.

If you speak French, Petit Futé (www.petitfute.fr, in French) publishes a national guide, *Handitourisme* (€16), and the portal www.jaccede.com (in French) has loads of information and reviews. **Mobile en Ville** (www.mobile-en-ville.asso.fr) works to make Paris wheelchair accessible and publishes *Paris Comme sur les Roulettes,* which showcases 20 tours of the city.

Michelin's *Guide Rouge* uses icons to indicate hotels with lifts and with facilities that make them at least partly accessible to people with disabilities, while Gîtes de France (see p940) can provide details on *gîtes ruraux* and *chambres d'hôtes* with 'disabled access' (this is one of their website's search criteria).

Specialised travel agencies abroad include UK-based **Access Travel** (☎ in UK 01942-888 844; www.access-travel.co.uk).

Tourism for All (☎ in UK 0845-124 9971; www.tourismforall.info) is a UK-based group that provides tips and information for travellers with disabilities.

VISAS

For up-to-date details on visa requirements, see the **French Foreign Affairs Ministry site** (www.diplomatie.gouv.fr) and click 'Going to France'.

EU nationals and citizens of Iceland, Norway and Switzerland need only a passport or a national identity card in order to enter France and stay in the country. However, nationals of the 12 countries that joined the EU in 2004 and 2007 are subject to various limitations on living and working in France.

Citizens of Australia, Canada, Israel, Hong Kong, Japan, Malaysia, New Zealand, Singapore, the USA and many Latin American countries do not need visas to visit France as tourists for up to 90 days.

Other people wishing to come to France as tourists have to apply for a **Schengen Visa**, named after the agreements that abolished passport controls between 15 European countries: Austria, Belgium, Denmark, Finland, France, Germany, Greece, Iceland, Italy, Luxembourg, the Netherlands, Norway, Portugal, Spain and Sweden. It allows unlimited travel throughout the entire zone for a 90-day period. Application should be made to the consulate of the country you are entering first, or that will be your main destination. Among other things, you will need travel and repatriation insurance and be able to show that you have sufficient funds to support yourself.

Tourist visas *cannot* be extended except in emergencies (such as medical problems). When your visa expires you'll need to leave and reapply from outside France.

Carte de Séjour

EU passport-holders and citizens of Switzerland, Iceland and Norway do not need a *carte de séjour* (residence permit) to reside or work in France.

Nationals of other countries with long-stay visas must contact the local *mairie* (city hall) or *préfecture* (prefecture) to apply for a *carte de séjour*. Usually, you are required to do so within eight days of arrival in France. Make sure you have all the necessary documents before you arrive.

Students of all nationalities studying in Paris must apply for a *carte de séjour* either through their university (if the option exists) or at the **Centre des Étudiants Étrangers** (Map pp124-5; 13 rue Miollis, 15e, Paris; Ⓜ Cambronne or Ségur) in Paris. For more information see the website of Paris' **Préfecture de Police** (www.prefecture-police-paris.interieur.gouv.fr, in French).

Long-Stay & Student Visas

EU nationals and citizens of Iceland, Norway and Switzerland do not require visas for stays of over 90 days in France but everybody else does. Contact the French embassy or consulate nearest your residence and begin your application well in advance as it can take months. Tourist visas cannot be changed into student visas after arrival. However, short-term visas are available for students sitting university-entrance exams in France.

Working Holiday Visa

Citizens of Australia, Canada, Japan and New Zealand aged between 18 and 30 are eligible for a 12-month, multiple-entry Working Holiday Visa, allowing combined tourism and employment in France. You have to apply to the embassy or consulate in your home country and must prove you have a return ticket, insurance and sufficient funding to get you through the start of your stay. Apply early as there are annual quotas.

Once you have arrived in France and have found a job, you must apply for an *autorisation provisoire de travail* (temporary work permit), which will only be valid for the duration of the employment offered. The permit can be renewed under the same conditions up to the limit of the authorised length of stay. You can also study or do training programs but the visa cannot be extended, nor can it turned into a student visa. After one year you *must* go home.

Once in France, the Centre d'Information et Documentation Jeunesse (CIDJ; p960) can help with information.

VOLUNTEERING

Websites like www.volunteerabroad.com and www.transitionsabroad.com throw up a colourful selection of volunteering opportunities in France: helping out on a family farm in the Alps, restoring an historic monument in Provence or participating in a summertime archaeological excavation are but some of the golden opportunities awaiting those keen to volunteer their skills and services.

Interesting volunteer organisations include the following:

Rempart (Map pp126-7; ☎ 01 42 71 96 55; www.rempart.com; 1 rue des Guillemites, 4e, Paris) Brings together 170 organisations countrywide committed to preserving France's religious, military, civil, industrial and natural heritage.

Volunteers for Peace (☎ 802-259-2759; www.vfp.org; 1034 Tiffany Rd, Belmont, Vermont 05730 USA) Can link you up with a voluntary service project dealing with social work, the environment, education or the arts.

World Wide Opportunities on Organic Farms (WWOOF; www.wwoof.org & www.wwoof.fr) Work on a small farm or other organic venture (harvesting chestnuts, renovating an abandoned olive farm near Nice etc).

WOMEN TRAVELLERS

For information about health issues while travelling, see p980.

Safety Precautions

Women tend to attract more unwanted attention than men but need not walk around in fear; people are rarely assaulted on the street. Be aware of your surroundings and of situations that could be dangerous: empty streets, lonely beaches, dark corners of large train stations. Using metros late at night is generally OK, as stations are rarely deserted, but there are a few in Paris that it's best to avoid (see p137).

In some places women may have to deal with what might be called low-intensity sexual harassment: 'playful' comments and invitations that can become overbearing or aggressive, and which some women find threatening or offensive. Remain polite and keep your distance. Hearing a foreign accent may provoke further unwanted attention.

Be alert to vibes in cheap hotels, sometimes staffed by apparently unattached men who may pay far more attention to your comings and goings than you would like. Change hotels if you feel uncomfortable, or allude to the imminent arrival of your husband (whether you have one or not).

On overnight trains, you may prefer to ask (when reserving) if there's a women's compartment available. If your compartment companions are overly attentive, don't hesitate to ask the conductor for a change of compartment. Sleeping cars, which have their own bathrooms, offer greater security than a couchette.

In an emergency, contact the **police** (☎ 17), who will take you to the hospital if you have been attacked or injured. You can reach France's national **rape crisis hotline** (☎ 08 00 05 95 95; 10am-7pm Mon-Fri) toll-free from any telephone without using a phonecard.

Organisations

The women-only **Maison des Femmes de Paris** (Map pp134-5; ☎ 01 43 43 41 13; http://maisondesfemmes.free.fr, in French; 163 rue de Charenton, 12e, Paris; Ⓜ Reuilly Diderot; 9am-7pm Mon-Fri) is a meeting place for women of all ages and nationalities.

WORK

EU nationals, except those from the 12 countries that joined the EU in 2004 and 2007, have an automatic right to work in France. Pretty much anyone else who'd like a French job will need a hard-to-get work permit, issued at the request of your employer, who will have to show that no one in France – or the entire European Economic Area – can do your job. Exceptions may be made for artists, computer engineers and translation specialists.

Working 'in the black' (that is, without documents) is difficult and risky for non-EU nationals. The only instance in which the government turns a blind eye to workers without documents is during fruit harvests (mid-May to November) and the *vendange* (grape harvest; mid-September to mid- or late October).

Au-pair work is also very popular and can be done legally even by non-EU citizens. To apply, contact a placement agency from your home country at least three months in advance.

For details on a Working Holiday Visa, see p959.

EU Nationals

EU nationals with the right to work in France can find summer and casual work in restaurants, bars and hotels (particularly in the Alps during the winter skiing season; for bar work check out www.mountainpub.com). Teaching English is another option, either for a company or through private lessons. Paris-based mag **FUSAC** (France USA Contacts; www.fusac.fr) advertises jobs for English speakers, including au-pair work, babysitting and language teaching.

France's national employment service, the **Agence National pour l'Emploi** (ANPE; www.anpe.fr, in French), has offices throughout France; the website has job listings.

The **Centre d'Information et de Documentation Jeunesse** (CIDJ; www.cidj.com, in French) provides young people with information on jobs (including seasonal summer jobs), housing, education and more. It has offices all over France, including **Paris** (Map pp124-5; ☎ 01 44 49 12 00; 101 quai Branly, 15e; Ⓜ Champ de Mars).

Transport

CONTENTS

GETTING THERE & AWAY

ENTERING THE COUNTRY

Entering France from other parts of the EU is usually a breeze – no border checkpoints and no customs – thanks to the Schengen Agreements, signed and fully implemented by all of France's neighbours except the UK, the Channel Islands and Switzerland. For these three entities, old-fashioned document and customs checks are still the norm, at least when exiting France.

If you're arriving from a non-EU country, you will have to show your passport (and your visa if you need one – see p958) or EU identity card, and clear customs.

AIR

Budget carriers account for an increasing share of intra-European flights.

Airports

France's two major international airports, both just outside Paris, are **Roissy Charles de Gaulle** (☎ 01 48 62 22 80; www.aeroportsdeparis.fr; airport code CDG) and **Orly** (☎ 01 49 75 15 15; www.aeroportsdeparis.fr; airport code ORY). For details, see p198.

THINGS CHANGE...

The information in this chapter is particularly vulnerable to change, especially as the price of oil skyrockets. Check directly with the transport provider or a travel agent to make sure you understand how a fare (and the ticket you may buy) works, and be aware of the security requirements for international travel. The details given in this chapter should be regarded as pointers and are not a substitute for your own careful, up-to-date research.

French airports with significant international services, mainly within Europe and to North Africa include the following:

Bordeaux (☎ 05 56 34 50 50; www.bordeaux.aeroport.fr; airport code BOD)
Lille (☎ 03 20 49 67 47, 08 91 67 32 10; www.lille.aeroport.fr; airport code LIL)
Lyon (☎ 08 26 80 08 26; www.lyon.aeroport.fr; airport code LYS)
Marseille (☎ 04 42 14 14 14; www.mrsairport.com; airport code MRS)
Mulhouse-Basel-Freiburg (EuroAirport; ☎ 03 89 90 31 11; www.euroairport.com; airport codes MLH, BSL, EAP)
Nantes (☎ 02 40 84 80 00; www.nantes.aeroport.fr; airport code NTE)
Nice (☎ 08 20 42 33 33; www.nice.aeroport.fr; airport code NCE)
Strasbourg (☎ 03 88 64 67 67; www.strasbourg.aeroport.fr; airport code SXB)
Toulouse (☎ 08 25 38 00 00; www.toulouse.aeroport.fr; airport code TLS)

Smaller provincial airports with international flights, mainly to/from the UK, continental Europe and North Africa, include Angoulême, Beauvais-Tillé (Paris-Beauvais), Bergerac, Béziers, Biarritz, Brest, Caen, Carcassonne, Deauville, Dinard, Grenoble, La Rochelle, Le Touquet, Limoges, Montpellier, Nîmes, Pau, Perpignan, Poitiers, Rennes, Rodez, St-Étienne, Toulon and Tours. Relevant local airports, including those on Corsica, are listed in destination chapters.

Airlines

The new Open Skies Agreement between the EU and the United States lets any European airline fly to any US destination and any US airline fly anywhere in the EU. As a result, unprecedented trans-Atlantic flight options are likely to start appearing.

Major airlines serving France include:

Aer Lingus (☎ 08 21 23 02 67; www.aerlingus.com; airline code EI; hub Dublin)

Air Canada (☎ 08 25 88 29 00; www.aircanada.ca; airline code AC; hub Toronto)

Air France (☎ 36 54; www.airfrance.com; airline code AF; hub Paris) France's flag carrier, now joined with KLM. Subsidiaries include Brit Air (www.britair.fr) and Régional (www.regional.com).

Alitalia (☎ 08 20 31 53 15; www.alitalia.com; airline code AZ; hub Rome)

American Airlines (☎ 01 55 17 43 41; www.americanairlines.com; airline code AA; hub Dallas)

Austrian Airlines (☎ 08 20 81 68 16; www.austrianairlines.com; airline code OS; hub Vienna)

BMI British Midland (☎ in UK 0870-6070 555 or 01332-64 8181; www.flybmi.com; airline code BD; hub London)

British Airways (☎ 08 25 82 54 00; www.britishairways.com; airline code BA; hub London)

Cathay Pacific (☎ 01 41 43 75 75; www.cathaypacific.com; airline code CX; hub Hong Kong)

Continental Airlines (☎ 01 71 23 03 35; www.continental.com; airline code CO; hub Houston)

Iberia (☎ 08 25 80 09 65; www.iberia.com; airline code IB; hub Madrid)

KLM (☎ 32 72; www.klm.com; airline code KL; hub Amsterdam) Now joined with Air France.

Lufthansa (☎ 08 26 10 33 34; www.lufthansa.com; airline code LH; hub Frankfurt)

Northwest Airlines (☎ 08 90 71 07 10; NWA; www.nwa.com) Works closely with KLM.

Olympic Airlines (☎ 01 44 94 58 58; www.olympicairlines.com; airline code OA; hub Athens)

Qantas Airways (☎ 08 11 98 00 02; www.qantas.com; airline code QF; hub Sydney)

Singapore Airlines (☎ 08 21 23 03 80; www.singaporeair.com; airline code SQ; hub Singapore)

South African Airways (☎ 08 25 80 09 69; www.flysaa.com; airline code SA; hub Johannesburg)

Thai Airways International (☎ 01 55 68 80 70; www.thaiair.com; airline code TG; hub Bangkok)

Turkish Airlines (☎ 08 25 80 09 02; www.thy.com; airline code TK; hub Istanbul)

An ever-morphing panoply of low-budget, no-frills carriers, many with strict baggage weight limits, serve Paris and/or provincial French cities:

Aer Arann (www.aerarann.com) Links Ireland to cities on France's west coast.

Air Berlin (www.airberlin.com) Links EuroAirport (Mulhouse) and Nice with destinations around Western Europe.

Air Transat (www.airtransat.com) Flights from Canada.

Atlas Blue (www.atlas-blue.com) Moroccan budget airline.

BMI Baby (www.bmibaby.com) Budget subsidiary of BMI British Midland; generally offers good ticket flexibility.

Corsairfly (www.corsairfly.com) Links Paris with Quebec, the Caribbean, Morocco and the Indian Ocean.

easyJet (www.easyjet.com) UK budget carrier; also has domestic flights within France.

Flybe (www.flybe.com) Links a dozen French cities with the UK.

Flyglobespan (www.flyglobespan.com) Scottish budget carrier.

Germanwings (www.germanwings.com) Cologne-based German budget carrier.

Jet2.com (www.jet2.com) Links French cities with the UK.

Jet4you (www.jet4you.com) Flights to Morocco.

Myair (www.myair.com) Flights to Italy.

New Axis Airways (www.axis-airways.com) Marseille-based carrier serving Europe, North Africa and the Middle East.

Ryanair (www.ryanair.com) Services from Ireland and the UK to destinations throughout France.

Transavia.com (www.transavia.com) Budget subsidiary of the Air France–KLM Group.

TUIfly (www.tuifly.com) German budget carrier.

Wizz Air (http://wizzair.com) Links Hungary and Poland with Beauvais-Tillé near Paris.

Tickets

Checking internet sites and scouring major newspapers' travel sections can result in significant savings on your air ticket. Start early: some of the cheapest tickets have to be bought well in advance.

AUSTRALIA & NEW ZEALAND

Both **Flight Centre** (Australia ☎ 133 133; www.flightcentre.com.au; New Zealand ☎ 0800 24 35 44; www.flightcentre.co.nz) and **STA Travel** (Australia ☎ 1300 733 035; www.statravel.com.au; New Zealand ☎ 0508 782 872; www.statravel.co.nz) have branches throughout Australia and New Zealand. For online bookings, try www.travel.com.au.

CLIMATE CHANGE & TRAVEL

Climate change is a serious threat to the ecosystems that humans rely upon, and air travel is the fastest-growing contributor to the problem. Lonely Planet regards travel, overall, as a global benefit, but believes we all have a responsibility to limit our personal impact on global warming.

Flying and Climate Change

Pretty much every form of motorised travel generates CO2 (the main cause of human-induced climate change) but planes are far and away the worst offenders, not just because of the sheer distances they allow us to travel, but because they release greenhouse gases high into the atmosphere. The statistics are frightening: two people taking a return flight between Europe and the US will contribute as much to climate change as an average household's gas and electricity consumption over a whole year.

Carbon Offset Schemes

Climatecare.org and other websites use 'carbon calculators' that allow travellers to offset the level of greenhouse gases they are responsible for with financial contributions to sustainable travel schemes that reduce global warming – including projects in India, Honduras, Kazakhstan and Uganda.

Lonely Planet, together with Rough Guides and other concerned partners in the travel industry, support the carbon offset scheme run by climatecare.org. Lonely Planet offsets all of its staff and author travel.

For more information check out our website, lonelyplanet.com.

CANADA

Travel Cuts (☎ 800-667-2887; www.travelcuts.com) is Canada's national student travel agency. For online bookings try www.expedia.ca and www.travelocity.ca.

UK & IRELAND

Advertisements for travel agencies appear in the travel pages of the weekend broadsheet newspapers, *Time Out* and the *Evening Standard,* as well as in the free online magazine *TNT* (www.tntmagazine.com), but some of the best deals are available direct from budget airlines.

Recommended travel agencies and online ticket sales:

ebookers.com (www.ebookers.com)
Flight Centre (www.flightcentre.co.uk)
Trailfinders (www.trailfinders.com)
USIT (www.usit.ie)

USA

San Francisco is the ticket consolidator capital of America, although some good deals can be found in Los Angeles, New York and other big cities.

The following agencies are recommended for online bookings:

CheapTickets (www.cheaptickets.com)
Expedia (www.expedia.com)
lowestfare.com (www.lowestfare.com)
Orbitz (www.orbitz.com)
STA Travel (www.statravel.com)
Travelocity (www.travelocity.com)

Other rock-bottom options for discounted trans-Atlantic air travel include stand-by and courier flights. For details:

Airhitch (www.airhitch.org)
Courier Travel (www.couriertravel.org)
International Association of Air Travel Couriers (www.courier.org)

LAND

Bus and train passes can often be effectively combined with discount airfares to keep travel costs down.

Bus

Europe's international buses are slower and less comfortable than trains but are considerably cheaper, especially if you are under 26 or over 60, or get a promotional fare.

BUSABOUT

Buses run by London-based **Busabout** (☎ in UK 0207-950 1661; www.busabout.com; 1/2/3 loops

US$639/1069/1319) link 29 continental European cities in nine countries every other day from early May to October.

You can travel at your own pace and hop on or off as you like. In many places, the pick-up/drop-off point is a central hostel. In France, which is on the Western Loop (one of three), stops are in Bordeaux, Tours, Paris, Avignon and Nice.

EUROLINES

Eurolines (☎ 08 92 89 90 91; www.eurolines.eu) is a grouping of 32 long-haul coach operators that link cities all across Europe and in Morocco and Russia. Return fares are about 20% cheaper than two one-ways. In summer it's best to make reservations at least two working days in advance.

From London, the standard one-way fare to Paris is UK£39 but Funfares, available online, can work out much cheaper. From Paris, a one-way ticket to London costs €32; supplements of €4 to €11 sometimes apply. Channel crossings are by ferry.

The Eurolines Travel Pass (www.eurolines-pass.eu) allows unlimited international travel for 15 or 30 days between 40 European cities, including eight in France – but you cannot use the pass to get from one French city to another.

Car & Motorcycle

Arriving in France by car is easy. At some border points you may be asked for a passport or EU national identity card (your driver's licence will not be sufficient ID). Police searches are not uncommon for vehicles entering France, particularly from Spain and Belgium (via which drugs from Morocco or the Netherlands can enter France). See p971 for details about driving in France.

EUROTUNNEL

The Channel Tunnel, inaugurated in 1994, is the first dry-land link between England and France since the last ice age.

High-speed **Eurotunnel shuttle trains** (☎ in UK 08705-35 35 35, in France 08 10 63 03 04; www.eurotunnel.com) whisk bicycles, motorcycles, cars and coaches from Folkestone through the Channel Tunnel to Coquelles, 5km southwest of Calais, in air-conditioned and soundproofed comfort in just 35 minutes. Shuttles run 24 hours a day, every day of the year, with up to three departures an hour during peak periods. LPG and CNG tanks are not permitted, which eliminates gas-powered cars and many campers and caravans.

Eurotunnel sets its fares the way budget airlines do: the longer in advance you book and the lower the demand for a particular crossing, the less you pay; same-day fares can cost a fortune.

Depending on the date and, especially, the time of day, one-way car fares range from UK£49 to UK£145 (€69 to €217), including all passengers, unlimited luggage and taxes. The fee for a bicycle, including its rider, is UK£16 one-way; cyclists must make advance reservations (☎ in UK 01303-28 22 01).

Train

Rail services link France with virtually every country in Europe. For details on train travel within France, see p975.

You can book tickets and get information from **Rail Europe** (www.raileurope.com). In France ticketing is handled by **SNCF** (☎ in France 36 35, from abroad 08 92 35 35 35; www.sncf.com); telephone and internet bookings are possible but they won't post tickets outside France.

For details on Europe's 200,000km rail network, see www.railpassenger.info, set up by a grouping of European rail companies. Information on 'seamless high-speed rail travel' between France, Belgium, the Netherlands, Germany and Austria, and under the English Channel to London, is available from www.railteam.co.uk and www.tgv-europe.com.

Certain rail services between France and its continental neighbours are marketed under a number of peculiar brand names: **Alleo** heads to Germany; **Artésia** (www.artesia.eu) takes you to Italian cities such as Milan, Venice, Florence and Rome; **Elipsos** (www.elipsos.com) has luxurious 'train-hotel' services to Spain; and **TGV Lyria** (www.tgv-lyria.fr) takes passengers to Switzerland. **Thalys** (www.thalys.com) links Paris' Gare du Nord with destinations including Brussels-Midi (from €82, 82 minutes, up to 25 per day), Amsterdam CS (from €105, 4¼ hours, seven per day) and Cologne's Hauptbahnhof (€91, 3¾ hours, six per day).

A very useful resource is the information-packed website **The Man in Seat 61** (www.seat61.com).

The following are some sample train routes linking France with various cities in Europe.

Route	Full Fare (€)	Duration (hr)
Geneva–Lyon	22.90	2
Geneva–Marseille	50.20–76.40	4½-8
Vienna–Strasbourg	133.40	10
Brussels–Paris	82	1½
Rome–Nice	51.50	8½-10
Berlin–Paris	179.50	9
Frankfurt–Paris	99	4
Amsterdam–Paris	105	4½
Barcelona–Montpellier	53	4½

EUROPEAN RAIL PASSES

Eurail Passes (www.eurail.com), available to non-European residents, are valid in up to 20 countries, including France. Benefits include a 'Pass-holder' discount on the London-to-Paris Eurostar (one-way/return UK£50/100); foot passenger discounts on Dover-Calais ferries (50% on SeaFrance and 25% on P&O); 30% off the adult pedestrian fare for Irish Ferries crossings between Ireland and France (make sure you book ahead); and 50% off trains in Corsica.

Residents of Europe can get an **InterRail Global Pass** (www.interrailnet.com) for travel in 30 countries except the one they live in.

These passes, worthwhile only if you plan to really clock up the kilometres, must be validated at a train-station ticket window before you begin your first journey. The best deals are available to people under 26.

EUROSTAR

Thanks to the long-awaited high-speed track recently put into operation in England, the highly civilised **Eurostar** (☎ in UK 08705-186 186, in France 08 92 35 35 39; www.eurostar.com) now whisks you between London and Paris in just 2¼ hours. Except late at night, trains link London (St Pancras International) with Paris (Gare du Nord; hourly), Calais (Calais-Fréthun; one hour, two or three daily), Lille (Gare Lille-Europe; 1½ hours, 10 daily) and Disneyland Resort Paris (2½ hours, one or two daily), with less frequent services departing from Ebbsfleet and Ashford, both in Kent. Ski trains – which, unlike airplanes, don't hasten the greenhouse processes that threaten the very existence of Alpine skiing – connect London and Ashford with the French Alps on weekends from late December to mid-April.

Eurostar offers a bewildering array of fares. A standard 2nd-class one-way/return ticket from London to Paris costs a whopping UK£154.50/309 (€232.50/435), but super-discount returns go for as little as UK£59.

You'll get the best deals if you buy a return ticket, stay over a Saturday night, book well in advance (the cheapest fares sell out early) and don't mind nonexchangeability and nonrefundability. Special fares are also available if you're under 26 or over 60 on your departure date. Booking by phone incurs a UK£5 surcharge. Student travel agencies may have youth fares not available directly from Eurostar.

SEA

Tickets for car- and passenger-ferry travel to/from France are available from most travel agencies in France and the countries served, though it's generally cheapest to book online.

Except where noted, the prices given below are for standard one-way tickets; in some cases, return fares cost less than two one-way tickets. Prices vary tremendously according to the season (July and August are priciest) and demand. People under 25 and over 60 may qualify for discounts. Many companies charge a supplement if you book by phone.

If you're travelling with a vehicle, for safety reasons you are usually denied access to it during the voyage.

International ferry companies serving France:

Brittany Ferries (☎ in UK 0871-244 0744, in Ireland 021 4277 801, in France 08 25 82 88 28; www.brittany-ferries.co.uk, www.brittanyferries.ie)

Celtic Link Ferries (☎ in UK 0844-576 8834; www.celticlinkferries.com)

Comanav (☎ in Morocco, Casablanca office 22 30 24 12; www.comanav.ma, in French)

Comarit (☎ in Morocco, Tangier office 39 32 00 32; www.comarit.com, in French)

Condor Ferries (☎ in UK 0845-609 1024, in France 08 25 13 51 35; www.condorferries.com)

CTN (Compagnie Tunisienne de Navigation; ☎ Marseille office 04 91 91 55 71; www.ctn.com.tn)

HD Ferries (☎ in UK 0844-576 8831, in France 08 25 04 17 03; www.hdferries.com)

Irish Ferries (☎ in Ireland 0818 300 400, in France 08 10 00 13 57; in Cherbourg 02 33 23 44 44, in Roscoff 02 98 61 17 17; www.irishferries.ie, www.shamrock-irlande.com, in French)

LD Lines (☎ in UK 0844-576 8836, in France 08 25 30 43 04; www.ldlines.co.uk)

Manche Îles Express (☎ on Jersey 01534-880 756, on Guernsey 01481-701 316, in France 08 25 13 30 50; www.manche-iles-express.com)

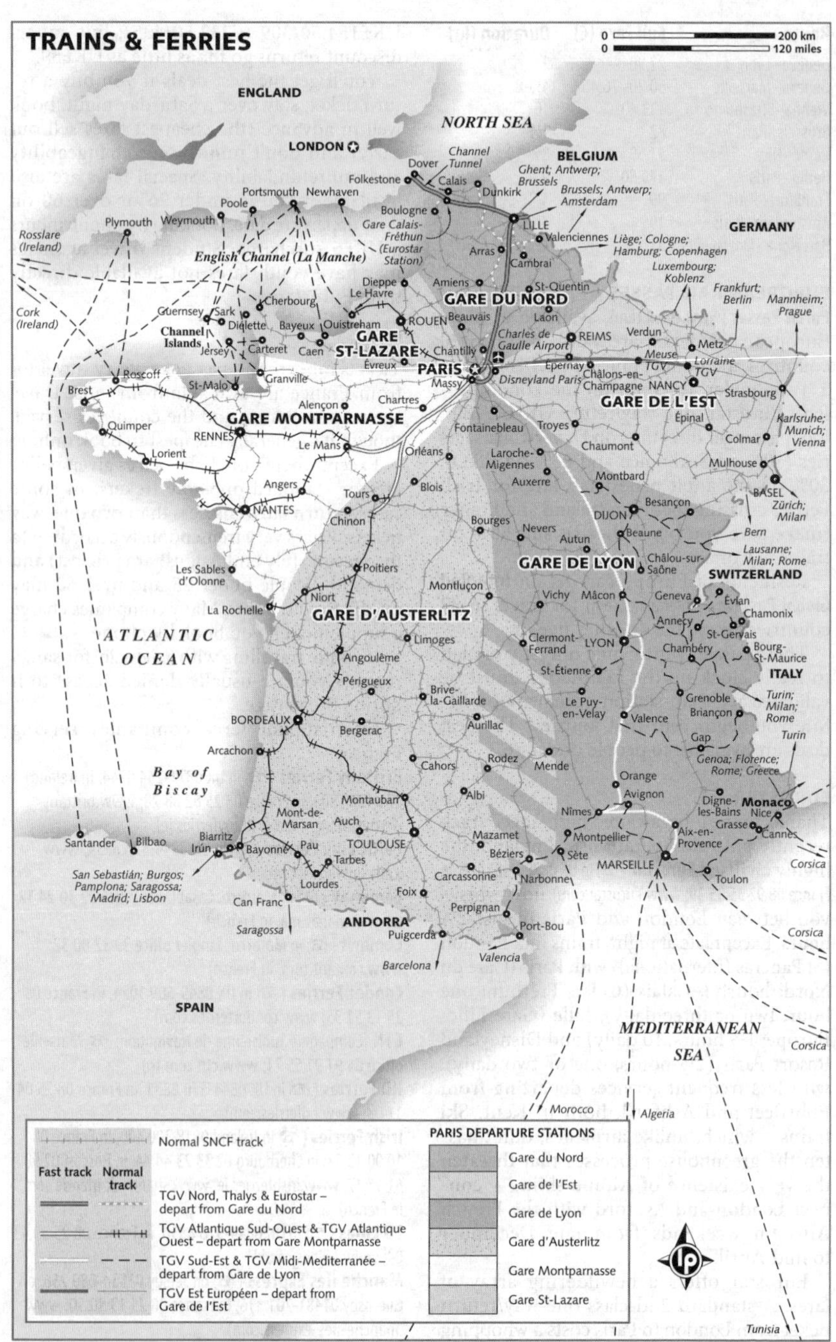

TRAINS & FERRIES
0 200 km
0 120 miles
ENGLAND
NORTH SEA
LONDON
BELGIUM
GERMANY
SWITZERLAND
ITALY
ANDORRA
SPAIN
ATLANTIC OCEAN
Bay of Biscay
MEDITERRANEAN SEA
English Channel (La Manche)
GARE DU NORD
GARE ST-LAZARE
GARE MONTPARNASSE
GARE DE L'EST
GARE DE LYON
GARE D'AUSTERLITZ
PARIS
Normal SNCF track
Fast track
Normal track
TGV Nord, Thalys & Eurostar – depart from Gare du Nord
TGV Atlantique Sud-Ouest & TGV Atlantique Ouest – depart from Gare Montparnasse
TGV Sud-Est & TGV Midi-Mediterranée – depart from Gare de Lyon
TGV Est Européen – depart from Gare de l'Est
PARIS DEPARTURE STATIONS
Gare du Nord
Gare de l'Est
Gare de Lyon
Gare d'Austerlitz
Gare Montparnasse
Gare St-Lazare

Norfolk Line (☎ in UK 0870 8701 020, in France 03 28 59 01 01; www.norfolkline.com)
P&O Ferries (☎ in UK 08716 645 645, in France 08 25 12 01 56; www.poferries.com)
SeaFrance (☎ in UK 0870 5711 711, in France 08 25 82 60 00; www.seafrance.com)
SNCM (Société Nationale Maritime Corse-Méditerranée; ☎ in France 08 25 88 80 88; www.sncm.fr)
Speed Ferries (☎ in UK 0871-222 7456, in France 03 21 10 50 00; www.speedferries.com)
Transmanche Ferries (☎ in UK 0800-917 1201, in France 08 00 65 01 00; www.transmancheferries.com)

The Channel Islands

Passenger ferries run by **Manche Îles Express** link Normandy's west coast with Jersey, Guernsey (Guernesey) and Sark (Sercq); passage takes 45 to 70 minutes. The Granville-Jersey line runs at least three times a week (daily from May to September); lines from Carteret and/or Diélette operate almost daily from April to September. Same-day return fares cost €39 to €50 (€23.50 to €30.50 for a child).

Year-round, fast car ferries run by **HD Ferries** and **Condor Ferries** link the Breton port of St-Malo with Jersey (one to 1¼ hours) and Guernsey (1½ to 2½ hours). On HD Ferries, whose services run daily in summer and four times a week in winter, one-way passage for two adults with a small car costs €58 to €75 to Jersey and €60 to €91 to Guernsey.

Ireland

Irish Ferries has overnight services from Rosslare to either Cherbourg (17½ hours) or Roscoff (17½ hours; mid-May to mid-September only) every other day (three times a week from October to May, except late December and January). One-way, foot passengers pay €56 to €69, while a car with a driver costs from €99 to €230, not including a reserved seat (€15) or a cabin (from €80 to €95 for a two-berth cabin). Bicycles cost €10.

A mainly freight ship run by **Celtic Link Ferries** links Rosslare with Cherbourg (18½ hours, two or three weekly except mid-December to mid-January). A car with a driver costs €119 to €269, not including a mandatory sleeping berth. Foot passengers are not allowed.

From about March to early November, **Brittany Ferries** runs a car ferry at 4pm on Saturday from Cork (Ringaskiddy) to Roscoff (14 hours) and at 9.30pm on Friday in the other direction. One-way, a car with two passengers costs €140 to €290 and carless foot passengers pay €75 to €110, not including mandatory on-board accommodation (€95 to €125 for a two-bunk inside cabin).

Italy

Every two or three days during the warm half of the year, **SNCM** runs an overnight car ferry from Marseille to Porto Torres on the Italian island of Sardinia (Sardaigne). The crossing takes 14½ to 17½ hours.

Several ferry companies ply the waters between Corsica and Italy. For details, see p909.

North Africa

SNCM and **CTN** link Marseille (and sometimes Toulon) with the Tunisian capital, Tunis (21 hours, three or four a week) and, occasionally, Bizerte, Sfax and Sousse.

Every day or two, **SNCM** car ferries – or ferries bookable via SNCM – link Marseille (and sometimes Sète and Toulon) with five ports in Algeria: Algiers (Alger; 21 hours), Annaba, Béjaia, Oran and Skikda.

Two Moroccan companies, **Comanav** and **Comarit**, link Sète – 26km (20 minutes by train) southwest of Montpellier – with the Moroccan port of Tangier (Tanger; 22 hours, three or four times weekly). In France ticketing is handled by **SNCM** (☎ Sète office 04 67 46 68 00).

The UK

Like Eurotunnel, trans-Channel ferry companies have started setting fares the way budget airlines do: the longer in advance you book and the lower the demand for a particular sailing, the less you pay, with the cheapest tickets costing just a third of the priciest ones. Seasonal demand is a crucial factor (July and August are especially busy), as is the time of day (an early evening ferry can cost much more than one at 4am). On some routes, three- or five-day excursion (return) fares often cost about the same as regular one-way tickets, and same-day returns can be even cheaper (though conditions apply). Deals available in the UK may not be on offer in France, and vice versa.

To get the best fare by comparing prices on various trans-Channel options, check out the booking service offered by **Ferry Savers** (☎ in UK 0844-576 8835; www.ferrysavers.com). Booking by phone incurs a UK£25 fee.

If you pay the foot-passenger fare, transporting a bicycle is often (but not always) free.

Foot passengers are not allowed on Dover–Boulogne and Dover–Dunkirk crossings and at night on Dover–Calais sailings.

TO BRITTANY

Condor Ferries runs car ferries from Poole to St-Malo (from 4½ hours) almost daily from late May to September; and from Weymouth to St-Malo (5¼ hours) daily from late March to October and at least once a week in winter, with a change of boat in Jersey or Guernsey from late May to September.

Brittany Ferries links Plymouth with Roscoff (6½ hours by day, nine hours overnight, one to three daily from mid-March to early November, almost daily in winter); and Portsmouth with St-Malo (8¾ hours by day, 10¾ hours overnight, one daily from March to October, almost daily in winter).

TO FAR NORTHERN FRANCE

The extremely popular Dover–Calais crossing is handled by **SeaFrance** (80 to 90 minutes, 15 daily) and **P&O Ferries** (75 to 90 minutes, 35 daily). Foot passengers, who are not allowed on night sailings (ie sailings departing after sometime between 7pm and 9.30pm and before 7am or 8am), pay about UK£14 one-way on SeaFrance and UK£20 one-way on P&O (less if you reserve ahead). Car fares vary greatly – for a vehicle and up to nine passengers they can be as low as UK£25 or as high as UK£70. Promotional fares you can book on the internet may not be available at company offices.

Car ferries run by **Norfolk Line** link Loon Plage, about 25km west of Dunkirk (Dunkerque), with Dover (1¾ hours) for UK£19 to UK£93 one-way for a vehicle and up to four passengers. Cheap tickets are first come, first served. Foot passengers are not allowed.

Ultramodern, ultrafast, low-cost car catamarans run by **Speed Ferries** link Dover with Boulogne-sur-Mer (50 minutes, three to five daily). The one-way fare for a car with up to five passengers ranges from UK£18 to UK£67. Foot passengers and camping trailers cannot be accommodated but cyclists can. Has a straightforward, easy-to-use website.

TO NORMANDY

Transmanche Ferries operates year-round car ferries from Newhaven to Dieppe (up to three daily, four hours). A one-way foot-passenger fare starts at €19; the one-way fare for a car and two adults usually ranges from UK£37.50 to UK£90.

Year-round, **LD Lines** offers a 5pm car ferry service (foot passengers welcome) from Portsmouth to Le Havre (5½ hours) and an overnight crossing (eight hours) in the opposite direction. One-way passage for a car and two adults generally costs UK£32.50 to UK£89.50. From May to mid-September, the company's ferries also link Newhaven with Le Havre (five hours).

Brittany Ferries links Cherbourg with both Poole (high-speed ferry 2¼ hours, regular ferry 4½ to 6½ hours, two or three daily) and Portsmouth (three hours, one or two sailings daily). The company also has car-ferry services from Portsmouth to Ouistreham (5¾ to seven hours, two to four daily), 14km northeast of Caen; high-speed ferries (3¾ hours) ply this route from mid-March to late October.

Condor Ferries links Portsmouth with Cherbourg (5½ hours) each Sunday from late May to early September.

The USA, Canada & Elsewhere

The days when you could earn your passage to Europe on a freighter are long gone, but it's still possible to travel as a passenger on a cargo ship from North America and East Asia to France's Atlantic Coast (eg Le Havre). Expect to pay from around US$90 to US$135 per day. Such vessels typically carry five to 12 passengers (more than 12 would require a doctor on board). Useful websites:

Freighter World Cruises (www.freighterworld.com) Based in California.

The Cruise People (www.cruisepeople.co.uk) Based in London.

GETTING AROUND

This section provides details on travelling both by car – the simplest way to get around except in traffic-plagued, parking-starved city centres – and on the excellent public transport network, which covers every corner of the land except some rural areas. In addition to its environmental benefits, travelling by train, metro, tram and bus lets you experience France the way many ordinary French people do, taking in the sights, encountering the unexpected and meeting locals at a pace set by the leisurely rhythm of day-to-day life.

The state-owned Société Nationale des Chemins de Fer Français (SNCF) takes care of almost all land transport between *départements*. Transport within *départements* is handled by a combination of short-haul trains, SNCF buses and local bus companies that are either government-owned or government-contracted. All cities and towns have public transport systems.

Domestic air travel has been partly deregulated but smaller carriers still struggle.

AIR

All of France's major cities – as well as many minor ones – have airports, which we mention in the destination chapters.

Air France (☎ 36 54; www.airfrance.com) and its subsidiaries **Brit Air** (www.britair.fr) and **Régional** (☎ 36 54; www.regional.com) continue to control the lion's share of France's long-protected domestic airline industry. Significant discounts are available to people aged 12 to 24 (26 or under in the case of students) or over 60, and couples who are married or can prove they live together. You can save up to 84% if you buy your ticket well in advance (at least 42 days ahead for the best deals); stay over a Saturday night; and/or don't mind tickets that can't be changed or reimbursed. Special last-minute offers are posted on the Air France website every Wednesday.

Budget carriers offering flights within France include **easyJet** (www.easyjet.com), **Airlinair** (www.airlinair.com) and **Twin Jet** (www.twinjet.net).

Any French travel agency can make air bookings and supply details on fare options.

France's vaunted TGV (*Train à Grande Vitesse*, ie High-Speed Train) network, which has a minimal carbon footprint because it's powered by nuclear-generated electricity, has made rail travel between some cities (eg from Paris to Lyon and Marseille) faster and easier than flying.

BICYCLE

France is generally a great place to cycle. Not only is much of the countryside drop-dead gorgeous but it has a growing number of urban and rural *pistes cyclables* (bike paths and lanes), some linking one town to the next, and an extensive network of secondary and tertiary roads with relatively light traffic. One pitfall: back roads rarely have proper shoulders so wearing a fluorescent reflective vest is highly recommended.

French law dictates that bicycles must have two functioning brakes, a bell, a red reflector on the back, and yellow reflectors on the pedals. After sunset and when visibility is poor, cyclists must turn on a white light at the front and a red one at the rear. When being overtaken by a vehicle, cyclists are required to ride in single file. Towing children in a bike trailer is permitted.

Never leave your bicycle locked up outside overnight if you want to see it or most of its parts again. Some hotels can provide enclosed bicycle parking.

The **Fédération Française des Usagers de la Bicyclette** (French Bicycle Users Federation; www.fubicy.org, in French) promotes cycling for transport.

More information of interest to cyclists can be found on p943.

Transportation

The SNCF does its best to make travelling with a bicycle easy and even has a special website dealing with bikes and trains, www.velo.sncf.com (in French).

Bicycles, in their natural, rideable state (ie not disassembled), can be taken along as carry-on luggage on most long-distance intercity trains, subject to space availability – look for a bicycle pictogram on train schedules. There's no charge on Corail Intercité trains but TGV, Téoz and Lunéa trains (see p975) require a €10 reservation that needs to be made when you purchase your passenger ticket (at the time of research, it was not possible to make bike reservations via the internet).

Bicycles that have been partly disassembled and put in a box *(housse)*, with maximum dimensions of 1.20m by 90cm, can be taken along for no charge in the baggage compartments of TGV, Téoz, Lunéa and Corail Intercité trains.

Bicycles can be brought along for no charge on all intraregional TER trains in Alsace, Aquitaine, Auvergne, Languedoc-Roussillon, Limousin, Provence-Côte d'Azur and Rhône-Alpes, subject to space availability. In other regions, check TER regional train schedules for a bicycle pictogram.

In the Paris area, bicycles are allowed aboard Transilien and RER trains except during rush hour periods from Monday to Friday (6.30am to 9am for trains heading into and around Paris, 4.30pm to 7pm for trains travelling around and out of the city).

With precious few exceptions, bicycles are not allowed on metros, trams and local, intra-*département* and SNCF buses (the latter replace trains on some runs).

On trans-Channel ferries, foot passengers can usually (but not always) bring along a bicycle for no charge. On Eurotunnel shuttle trains through the Channel Tunnel, the fee for a bicycle, including its rider, is UK£16 one-way. For details on taking your bike on an international train to France, see www.railpassenger.info.

European Bike Express (☎ in UK 01430-422 111; www.bike-express.co.uk) transports cyclists and their bikes from the UK to places around France.

Bike Rental

Most French cities and towns have at least one bike shop that rents out *vélos tout terrains* (mountain bikes; generally €10 to €20 a day), popularly known as VTTs; more road-oriented *vélos tout chemin* (VTCs); or cheaper city bikes. You usually have to leave ID and/or a deposit (often a credit-card slip) that you forfeit if the bike is damaged or stolen. Some cities, such as Strasbourg and La Rochelle, have inexpensive rental agencies run by the municipality, and in some places (eg Dijon) tourist offices rent out bicycles. For details on rental options, see Getting Around under city and town listings throughout this book.

A growing number of cities – most famously, Paris and Lyon, but also Rennes, La Rochelle, Orléans, Montpellier, Aix-en-Provence, Mulhouse, Besançon, Marseille, Nancy, Toulouse, Rouen, Amiens, Perpignan, Dijon, Caen, and Nantes – have automatic bike rental systems, intended to encourage cycling as a form of urban transport, with computerised pick-up and drop-off sites all over town. In general, you have to sign up either short-term or long-term, providing credit-card details, and can then use the bikes for no charge for the first half hour. For details on Paris' Vélib' system, see p201.

If you'll be doing lots of cycling but don't want to bring your bike from home, it may be worthwhile to buy a VTT (prices start at around €250) and resell it at the end of your trip for around two-thirds of its purchase price, something that's possible at certain bike shops. The website www.velo101.com (in French) has classified ads and advice.

BOAT

For information on ferry services that operate along France's coasts and to offshore islands, see individual town and city sections. For information on ferry services from other countries, see p965.

Canal Boating

Transportation and tranquillity are usually mutually exclusive – but not if you rent a houseboat and cruise along France's canals and navigable rivers, stopping at whim to pick up supplies, dine at a village restaurant or check out a local château by bicycle. Changes in altitude are taken care of by a system of *écluses* (locks).

Boats generally accommodate from two to 12 passengers and are fully outfitted with bedding and cooking facilities. Anyone over 18 can pilot a riverboat but first-time skippers are given a short instruction session so they qualify for a *carte de plaisance* (a temporary cruising permit). The speed limit is 6km/h on canals and 8km/h on rivers.

Prices start at around €450 a week for a small boat and can top €3000 for a large, luxurious craft. Except in July and August, you can often rent over a weekend (Friday to Monday; from €280) or from Monday to Friday.

Advance reservations are essential for holiday periods, over long weekends and in July and August, especially for larger boats.

Online rental agencies include **Canal Boat Holidays** (www.canalboatholidays.com), **H2olidays** (Barging in France; www.barginginfrance.com) and **Worldwide River Cruise** (www.worldwide-river-cruise.com). For more rental companies, see the Burgundy chapter (p456) and the Limousin, the Dordogne & Quercy chapter (p607).

BUS

Buses are widely used for short-distance travel within *départements*, especially in rural areas with relatively few train lines (eg Brittany and Normandy). Unfortunately, services in some regions are infrequent and slow, in part because they were designed to get children to their schools in the towns rather than transport visitors around the countryside.

Over the years, certain uneconomical train lines have been replaced by SNCF buses, which – unlike regional buses – are free if you've got a rail pass.

ROAD DISTANCES (KM)

	Bayonne	Bordeaux	Brest	Caen	Cahors	Calais	Chambéry	Cherbourg	Clermont-Ferrand	Dijon	Grenoble	Lille	Lyon	Marseille	Nantes	Nice	Paris	Perpignan	Strasbourg	Toulouse
Bordeaux	184																			
Brest	811	623																		
Caen	764	568	376																	
Cahors	307	218	788	661																
Calais	164	876	710	339	875															
Chambéry	860	651	120	800	523	834														
Cherbourg	835	647	399	124	743	461	923													
Clermont-Ferrand	564	358	805	566	269	717	295	689												
Dijon	807	619	867	548	378	572	273	671	279											
Grenoble	827	657	1126	806	501	863	56	929	300	302										
Lille	997	809	725	353	808	112	767	476	650	505	798									
Lyon	831	528	1018	698	439	755	103	820	171	194	110	687								
Marseille	700	651	1271	1010	521	1067	344	1132	477	506	273	999	314							
Nantes	513	326	298	292	491	593	780	317	462	656	787	609	618	975						
Nice	858	810	1429	1168	679	1225	410	1291	636	664	337	1157	473	190	1131					
Paris	771	583	596	232	582	289	565	355	424	313	571	222	462	775	384	932				
Perpignan	499	451	1070	998	320	1149	478	1094	441	640	445	1081	448	319	773	476	857			
Strasbourg	1254	1066	1079	730	847	621	496	853	584	335	551	522	488	803	867	804	490	935		
Toulouse	300	247	866	865	116	991	565	890	890	727	533	923	536	407	568	564	699	205	1022	
Tours	536	348	490	246	413	531	611	369	369	418	618	463	449	795	197	952	238	795	721	593

CAR & MOTORCYCLE

Having your own wheels gives you exceptional freedom and makes it easy to visit more remote parts of France. Unfortunately driving can be expensive, and in the cities traffic and finding a place to park are frequently a major headache. Motorcyclists will find France great for touring, with winding roads of good quality and lots of stunning scenery. Just make sure your wet-weather gear is up to scratch.

France (along with Belgium) has the densest highway network in Europe. There are four types of intercity roads, which have alphanumeric designations:

Autoroutes (highway names beginning with A) Multilane divided highways, usually with tolls *(péages)*, that are generously outfitted with rest stops.

Routes Nationales (N, RN) National highways, often with sections with a divider strip.

Routes Départementales (D) Local roads.

Routes Communales (C, V) Minor rural roads.

Information on tolls, rest areas, traffic and weather is available from www.autoroutes.fr. The websites www.viamichelin.com and www.mappy.fr plot itineraries between your departure and arrival points.

Theft from cars is a major problem in France, especially in the south – see p948.

Make sure your car is fitted with winter or all-season tyres if there's a chance you'll be driving through snow. During holiday periods and over long weekends, roads throughout France get backed up with *bouchons* (traffic jams).

By autoroute, the drive from Paris to Nice (about 950km; eight hours of driving) in a small car costs at least €150 in petrol and autoroute tolls. By comparison, a regular one-way, 2nd-class TGV ticket for the 5½-hour Paris–Nice run costs around €80 to €110 per person (and often much less – see p976).

Bringing Your Own Vehicle

A right-hand-drive vehicle brought to France from the UK or Ireland must have deflectors affixed to the headlights to avoid dazzling oncoming traffic.

A foreign motor vehicle entering France must display a sticker or licence plate identifying its country of registration. In the UK, information on driving in France is available from the **RAC** (☎ in UK 0870-0106 382; www.rac.co.uk, click 'Driving Abroad') and the **AA** (☎ in UK 0870-6000 371; www.theaa.com, click 'European Driving').

TRANSPORT

Car Hire

To hire a car in France, you'll generally need to be over 21 years old, have had a driver's licence for at least a year, and have an international credit card. Drivers under 25 usually have to pay a surcharge *(frais jeune conducteur)* of €25 to €35 per day.

Car-rental companies provide mandatory third-party liability insurance but things such as collision-damage waivers (CDW, or *assurance tous risques*) vary greatly from company to company. When comparing rates and conditions (ie the fine print), the most important thing to check is the *franchise* (excess), which for a small car is usually around €600 for damage and €800 for theft. With many companies, you can reduce the excess to zero (or at least to half) by paying a daily insurance supplement of €10 to €16. Your credit card may cover CDW if you use it to pay for the car rental but the rental company won't know anything about this – verify conditions and details with your credit-card issuer to be sure.

Arranging your car rental or fly/drive package before you leave home is usually considerably cheaper than a walk-in rental but beware of website offers that don't include a CDW or you may be liable for up to 100% of the car's value.

Major rental companies include the following:

ADA (☎ 08 25 16 91 69; www.ada.fr, in French)
Avis (☎ 08 20 05 05 05; www.avis.com)
Budget (☎ 08 25 00 35 64; www.budget.com or www.budget.fr, in French)
Easycar (☎ in UK 0906-333 333 3; www.easycar.com)
Europcar (☎ 08 25 35 83 58; www.europcar.com)
Hertz (☎ 01 39 38 38 38; www.hertz.com)
National-Citer (www.nationalcar.com or www.citer.fr)
Renault Rent (☎ 08 10 40 50 60; www.renault-rent.com, in French) Renault's new car-rental arm.
Sixt (☎ 08 20 00 74 98; www.sixt.fr, in French)

Deals can be found on the internet, with travel agencies and through companies like **Auto Europe** (☎ in USA 1-888-223-5555; www.autoeurope.com) in the US, **DriveAway Holidays** (☎ in Australia 1300 723 972; www.driveaway.com.au) in Australia and **Holiday Autos** (☎ in UK 0871-472 5229; www.holidayautos.co.uk) in the UK. In this book, car-rental addresses are listed under large cities and towns.

Note that rental cars with automatic transmission are very much the exception in France. You will usually need to order one well in advance, with a much smaller (and invariably costlier) range of models to choose from.

Hybrid-car hire is in its infancy but Hertz now has a few Toyota Priuses available in France and, despite the higher rental rates, more companies are sure to follow suit. For more information, see www.greencarsite.co.uk/green-car-hire.htm.

For insurance reasons, you are usually not allowed to take rental cars on ferries, eg to Corsica.

All rental cars registered in France have a distinctive number on the licence plate, making them easily identifiable – including to thieves, so *never* leave anything of value in a parked car, even in the boot.

Driving Licence & Documents

All drivers must carry at all times: an EU national ID card or passport; a valid driver's licence (*permis de conduire;* most foreign licences can be used in France for up to a year); car-ownership papers, known as a *carte grise* (grey card); and proof of third-party liability *assurance* (insurance).

An International Driving Permit (IDP), valid only if accompanied by your original licence (an IDP is basically just a translation), is good for a year and can be issued by your local automobile association before you leave home.

Fuel & Spare Parts

Essence (petrol), also known as *carburant* (fuel), costs around €1.40/L for 95 unleaded (Sans Plomb 95 or SP95, usually available from a green pump) and €1.30 for diesel (*diesel, gazole* or *gasoil,* usually available from a yellow pump). Filling up *(faire le plein)* is most expensive at the rest stops along the autoroutes and often cheapest at hypermarkets.

Many small petrol stations close on Sunday afternoons, and, even in cities, it can be hard to find a staffed station open late at night. In general, after-hours purchases (eg at hypermarkets' 24-hour stations) can only be made with a credit card that has an embedded PIN chip, so if all you've got is cash or a magnetic-strip credit card, you could be stuck.

If your car is *en panne* (breaks down), you'll have to find a garage that handles your *marque* (make of car). Peugeot, Renault and Citroën garages are common, but if you have a non-French car, you may have trouble finding someone to service it in more remote areas.

Insurance

Third-party liability insurance *(assurance au tiers)* is compulsory for all vehicles in France, including cars brought in from abroad. Normally, cars registered and insured in other European countries can circulate freely in France, but it's a good idea to contact your insurance company before you leave home to make sure you've got coverage – and to check who to contact in case of a breakdown or accident.

If you get into a minor accident with no injuries, the easiest way for drivers to sort things out with their insurance companies is to fill out a **Constat Aimable d'Accident Automobile** (European Accident Statement), a standardised way of recording important details about what happened. In rental cars it's usually in the packet of documents in the glove compartment. Make sure the report includes any information that will help you prove that the accident was not your fault. Remember, if it was your fault you may be liable for a hefty insurance excess. Don't sign anything you don't fully understand. If problems crop up, call the **police** (☎ 17).

French-registered cars have details on their insurance company printed on a little green square affixed to their windscreens (from inside the car, in the lower-right-hand corner).

Motorbike Hire

Motorcycle and moped rental is popular in southern France, especially in the beach resorts, but accidents are all too common. Where relevant, details on rental options appear at the end of city and town listings.

To rent a moped, scooter or motorcycle, you usually have to leave a large *caution* (deposit), which you then forfeit – up to the value of the damage – if you cause an accident or if the bike is damaged or stolen.

Parking

In city centres, most on-the-street parking places are *payant* (metered) from about 9am to 7pm (sometimes with a break from noon to 2pm) from Monday to Saturday, except bank holidays. Details on places near city centres where parking is free, and without the usual two-hour time limits, appear in the Getting Around section of many city listings.

Purchase-Repurchase Plans

If you'll be needing a car in France (or Europe) for one to six months (up to one year if you'll be studying or teaching in France), by far the cheapest option is to 'purchase' a brand-new one from **Citroën** (Eurocar TT, DriveEurope or Citroën TT; www.eurocartt.com, www.citroendriveeurope.com.au or www.citroentt.com), **Peugeot** (Open Europe or Sodexa; www.peugeot-openeurope.com) or **Renault** (Eurodrive; www.eurodrive.renault.com) and then 'sell' it back to them at the end of your trip. In reality, you pay only for the number of days you have the vehicle but the paperwork means that the car is registered under your name – and that the whole deal is exempt from all sorts of taxes. Eligibility is restricted to people who are not residents of the EU (citizens of EU countries are eligible if they live outside the EU). Pricing and special offers depend on your home country.

Prices include unlimited kilometres, 24-hour towing and breakdown service, and comprehensive insurance with – incredibly – no excess, so returning the car is totally hassle-free, even if it's damaged. Extending your contract is possible (using a credit card) but you'll end up paying about double the prepaid per-day rate.

Cars – which have special red licence plates – can be picked up at about three-dozen cities and airports all over France and dropped off at any other purchase-repurchase centre. You can also pick up or return your car in some cities outside France for a fee.

Road Rules

Enforcement of traffic laws has been stepped up in France in recent years and speed cameras are becoming ever more common.

French law requires that all passengers, including those in the back seat, wear seat belts. Babies weighing less than 13kg must travel in the rear in backward-facing child seats; children up to 18kg must ride in child seats. Children under 10 must sit in the back unless it's already occupied by other children under 10. North American drivers should remember that turning right on a red light is illegal in France.

Speed limits outside built-up areas:

- 90km/h (80km/h if it's raining) on undivided N and D highways
- 110km/h (100km/h if it's raining) on nonautoroute divided highways
- 130km/h (110km/h in the rain, 60km/h in icy conditions) on autoroutes

There is talk of reducing the autoroute speed limit in some areas, eg Alsace, to 110km/h to reduce fuel consumption, in light of climate change.

Unless otherwise posted, a limit of 50km/h applies in *all* areas designated as built up, no matter how rural they may appear. You must slow to 50km/h the moment you come to a white sign with a red border and a place name written on it; you can resume your previous speed when you pass an identical sign with a horizontal bar through it. You can be fined for going 10km over the speed limit.

Under the *priorité à droite* rule, any car entering an intersection (including a T-junction and a roundabout) from a road on your right has the right of way, unless the intersection is marked *vous n'avez pas la priorité* (you do not have right of way) or *cédez le passage* (give way). *Priorité à droite* is also suspended on priority roads, which are marked by an upended yellow square with a black square in the middle.

It is illegal to drive with a blood-alcohol concentration over 0.05% (0.5g per litre of blood) – the equivalent of two glasses of wine for a 75kg adult. Police often conduct breathalyser tests at random and penalties can be severe, including imprisonment. Mobile phones may only be used when accompanied by a hands-free kit or speakerphone.

Since July 2008, all French vehicles must now carry a reflective safety jacket and a reflective triangle; the fine for not carrying one/both is €90/135. Radar detectors are illegal.

Riders of any type of two-wheeled vehicle with a motor (except motor-assisted bicycles) must wear a helmet. No special licence is required to ride a motorbike whose engine is smaller than 50cc, which is why you often find places renting scooters rated at 49.9cc.

HITCHING

Hitching is never entirely safe in any country in the world, and we don't recommend it. Travellers who decide to hitch should understand that they are taking a small but potentially serious risk. Remember that it's safer to travel in pairs and be sure to inform someone of your intended destination. Hitching is not really part of French culture and is not recommended for women in France, even in pairs.

Hitching from city centres is pretty much hopeless, so your best bet is to take public transport to the outskirts. It is illegal to hitch on autoroutes but you can stand near an entrance ramp as long as you don't block traffic. Remote rural areas are a better bet, but once you get off the *routes nationales* traffic can be light and local. If your itinerary includes a ferry crossing, it's worth trying to score a ride before the ferry since vehicle tickets sometimes include a number of passengers free of charge. At dusk, give up and think about finding somewhere to stay.

Ride Share

A number of organisations around France arrange *covoiturage* (car sharing), ie putting people looking for rides in touch with drivers going to the same destination. You generally pay a per-kilometre fee to the driver as well as a flat administration fee. The best known is Paris-based **Allostop** (☎ 01 53 20 42 42; www.allostop.net, in French; 30 rue Pierre Sémard, 9e, Paris), though you might also try www.123envoiture.com, www.covoiturage.com, www.carecole.com, www.carjob.org and www.carvoyage.com.

LOCAL TRANSPORT

France's cities and larger towns have excellent public-transport systems. There are *métros* (underground subway systems) in Paris, Lyon, Marseille, Lille and Toulouse and ultramodern light-rail lines *(tramways)* in cities such as Bordeaux, Grenoble, Lille, Lyon, Nancy, Nantes, Nice, Rouen and Strasbourg, as well as parts of Paris. Details on routes and fares are available at tourist offices and from local transport companies – see Getting Around under city and town listings.

See p943 and p969 for information on bicycles and bike hire.

Taxi

All medium and large train stations – and many small ones – have a taxi stand out front. For details on the tariffs and regulations applicable in major cities, see p204. In small cities and towns, where taxi drivers are unlikely to find another fare anywhere near where they let you off, one-way and return trips often cost the same. Tariffs are about 30% higher at night and on Sundays and holidays. Having a cab wait for you while you visit something costs about €18 an hour. There may be a surcharge to get picked up at a train station or airport and a small additional fee for a fourth passenger and/or for suitcases.

TOURS

Local tourist offices, museums, wineries, châteaux and private companies all over France offer a wide variety of guided walking, cycling and minibus tours with expert commentary. In chapter subsections and city listings, details appear either under Tours or under Activities.

The **Association of British Travel Organisers to France** (www.holidayfrance.org.uk) has an online list of UK-based companies offering trips to France – click 'ABTOF Members' under 'Directory'.

A multitude of companies run activities-based tours, usually including accommodation, meals and transport.

ATG Oxford (www.atg-oxford.co.uk) Cycling and rambling holidays for independent travellers.
Butterfield & Robinson (www.butterfield.com) Canada-based upmarket walking and biking holidays.
CBT Tours (www.biketrip.net) Cycling tours are the speciality of this US-based outfit.
Classic Bike Provence (www.classicbikeprovence.com) Motorcycling tours in Provence and beyond astride classic bikes from the '50s to the '80s.
Cycling for Softies (www.cycling-for-softies.co.uk) Unescorted cycling trips through rural France.
French Wine Explorers (www.wine-tours-france.com) US-based outfit offering small-group wine tours.
Olde Ipswich Tours (www.ipswichtours.com) Specialist 'gourmet' tours (based in the USA).
Ramblers Worldwide Holidays (www.ramblersholidays.co.uk) Tours based around walking, trekking and cross-country skiing.

TRAIN

Travelling by train is a comfortable, classy, urbane and environmentally sustainable way to see France. Since many train stations have car-rental agencies, it's easy to combine rail travel with rural exploration by motorcar.

The jewel in the crown of France's public transport system – alongside the Paris *métro* – is its extensive rail network, almost all run by the state-owned **SNCF** (☎ 36 35; www.sncf.com). Although it employs the most advanced rail technology, the network's layout reflects the country's centuries-old Paris-centric nature: most of the principal rail lines radiate out from Paris like the spokes of a wheel, the result being that services between provincial towns situated on different spurs can be infrequent and slow. For details, see the map on p966. Up-to-the-minute information on *perturbations* (service disruptions), eg because of strikes, can be found on www.infolignes.com (in French).

Since its inauguration in the 1980s, the pride and joy of SNCF – and the French – is the world-renowned **TGV** (Train à Grande Vitesse, ie 'high-speed train'; www.tgv.com), pronounced teh zheh veh, which zips passengers along at speeds of up to 320km/h (198mph). In 2008, the French company Alstom unveiled the next generation TGV, known as the AGV (Automotrice Grande Vitesse), which will be able to travel up to 360km/h. Instead of having locomotives at each end, motors will be situated under each carriage. In 2007, a specially modified TGV achieved a new speed record for non-maglev (magnetic levitation) trains: 574.8km/h.

The four main TGV lines head due north, due east, southeast and southwest from Paris:

TGV Nord, Thalys & Eurostar These link Paris' Gare du Nord with Arras, Lille, Calais, Brussels, Amsterdam, Cologne and, via the Channel Tunnel, Ashford, Ebbsfleet and London St Pancras.
TGV Est Européen Inaugurated in 2007, this new line connects Paris' Gare de l'Est with Reims, Nancy, Metz, Strasbourg, Zurich and Germany, including Frankfurt and Stuttgart. At the time of research, super-high-speed track stretched only as far east as Lorraine but it's supposed to reach Strasbourg in 2012.
TGV Sud-Est & TGV Midi-Méditerranée These lines link Paris' Gare de Lyon with the southeast, including Dijon, Lyon, Geneva, the Alps, Avignon, Marseille, Nice and Montpellier.
TGV Atlantique Sud-Ouest & TGV Atlantique Ouest These link Paris' Gare Montparnasse with western and southwestern France, including Brittany (Rennes, Brest, Quimper), Nantes, Tours, Poitiers, La Rochelle, Bordeaux, Biarritz and Toulouse.

TGV lines are interconnected, making it possible to go directly from, say, Lyon to Nantes or Bordeaux to Lille without switching trains in Paris – or, even worse, having to transfer from one of Paris' six main train stations to another. Stops on the link-up, which runs east and south of Paris, include Roissy Charles de Gaulle airport and Disneyland Resort Paris. For details on international rail travel, see p964.

In an effort to make train travel both affordable and hip for the iPod generation, the SNCF has recently launched a new website, www.idtgv.com, which sells tickets for as little as €19 for TGV travel on 20 routes to/from Paris.

A train that is not a TGV is often referred to as a *corail*, a *classique* or a **TER** (Train Express

Régional; www.ter-sncf.com, in French). Certain non-TGV services have been given funny names:

Corail Intercités Medium-haul routes.

Lunéa (www.coraillunea.fr, in French) Overnight trains for cross-country travel, eg from Paris' Gare d'Austerlitz to Biarritz, Quimper to Lyon, or Strasbourg to Nice. Goes to the Alps in winter.

Téoz (www.corailteoz.com, in French) Especially comfortable trains that run southward from Paris' Gare d'Austerlitz to Clermont-Ferrand, Limoges, Cahors, Toulouse, Montpellier, Perpignan, Marseille and Nice.

Transilien (www.transilien.com) SNCF services in the Île de France (the Paris region).

For details on especially scenic train routes all around France, see www.trainstouristiques-ter.com.

Long-distance trains sometimes split at a station – that is, each half of the train heads off for a different destination. Check the destination panel on your car as you board or you could wind up very, very far from wherever it was you intended to go.

Classes & Sleeping Cars

Most French trains have both 1st- and 2nd-class sections. Full-fare tickets for the former cost 50% more than the latter.

On overnight trains, the 2nd-class couchette compartments have six berths while those in 1st class have four. Certain overnight trains have 1st-class *voitures-lits* (sleeping cars), which provide private facilities for one or two people and a continental breakfast. Some couchette compartments are reserved for women travelling alone or with children.

Costs

Full-fare tickets can be quite expensive – for instance, a one-way low-/peak-period trip by TGV from Paris to Lyon will drain your wallet of €61/79.50. Full-fare return passage costs twice as much as one-way fares. Children aged under four travel for free; those aged four to 11 pay half price. For details on discounts, see below.

SNCF DISCOUNTS

The SNCF's most heavily discounted tickets are, oddly, known as **Prem's**. They can be booked on the internet, by phone, at ticket windows and from ticket machines a maximum of 90 days and a minimum of four days before your travel date, though the very cheapest seats (eg Paris to Colmar for €22) often sell out early on. Once you buy a Prem's ticket, it's use it or lose it – getting your money back or changing the time is not allowed.

Corail fares that require neither a discount card nor advance purchase but get you 25% off include **Loisir Week-End** rates, good for return travel that includes a Saturday night at your destination or involves travel on a Saturday or Sunday; and **Découverte** fares, available for low-demand 'blue-period' trains to young people aged 12 to 25, seniors and the adult travel companions of children under 12. **Mini-Groupe** tickets can save lots for three to six people travelling together, provided you spend a Saturday night at your destination.

Reductions of at least 25% (for last-minute bookings), and up to 40%, 50% or even 60% (if you reserve ahead or travel during low-volume 'blue' periods), are available with several discount cards, valid for a year:

Carte 12-25 (www.12-25-sncf.com in, French; €49) Available to travellers aged 12 to 25.

Carte Enfant Plus (www.enfantplus-sncf.com, in French; €65) For one to four adults travelling with a child aged four to 11.

Carte Sénior (www.senior-sncf.com, in French; €55) For travellers over 60.

Carte Escapades (www.escapades-sncf.com, in French; €85) For people aged 26 to 59. Gets you discounts on return journeys of at least 200km that either include a Saturday night away or only involve travel on a Saturday or Sunday.

The new **Bons Plans** fares, a grab bag of really cheap options on a changing array of routes and dates, are advertised on www.voyages-sncf.com.

Certain French *régions* (eg Basse Normandie and Alsace) offer great deals on intraregional TER transport for day trips or weekend travel.

An **InterRail One Country Pass** (www.interrailnet.com) valid in France entitles nonresidents of France to unlimited travel on SNCF trains for three to eight days over the course of a month. For three/four/six/eight days, the cost is €189/209/269/299 for adults and €125/139/175/194 for young people aged 12 to 25.

LEFT-LUGGAGE FACILITIES

Because of security concerns, French train stations no longer have left-luggage lockers, but in some larger stations you can leave your bags in a *consigne manuelle* (staffed left-luggage facility), where items are handed over in person and x-rayed before being stowed. To find out which stations let you leave your bags and when their *consignes* are open, go to www.gares-en-mouvement.com (in French), choose a city, click 'Infos Pratiques' and then 'Services'.

Ticket prices for some trains, including most TGVs, reflect supply and demand and so are pricier during peak periods, eg during workday rush hours, on Friday evening and at the beginning and end of holiday periods.

Pooches (and other pets) under 6kg travel for free as long as they're in a pouch. Dogs that weigh more than that – except guide dogs – need a ticket, available for 50% of a standard fare.

Tickets & Reservations

Large stations often have separate ticket windows for *international, grandes lignes* (long-haul) and *banlieue* (suburban) lines, and for people whose train is about to leave (*départ immédiat* or *départ dans l'heure*). Nearly every SNCF station has at least one *borne libre-service* (self-service terminal) or *billeterie automatique* (automatic ticket machine) that accepts both cash and computer-chip credit cards. Push on the Union Jack for instructions in English.

Using a credit card, you can buy a ticket by phone or via the SNCF's internet booking site (www.voyages-sncf.com, in French) and either have it sent to you by post (if you have an address in France) or collect it from any SNCF ticket office or from train-station ticket machines.

Before boarding the train, you must validate *(composter)* your ticket by time-stamping it in a *composteur,* one of those yellow posts located on the way to the platform. If you forget (or don't have a ticket for some other reason), find a conductor on the train before they find you – otherwise you can be fined.

In general, reserving a place on a specific train – something you can do by phone, on the internet or at stations – is optional, although there are exceptions:

- travel by TGV, Eurostar, Thalys, Lunéa or Téoz
- couchettes (sleeping berths; €18 for 2nd class)
- travelling during peak holiday periods

For trains that do not require reservations (eg Corail Intercités and TER trains), full-fare tickets are useable whenever you like for 61 days from the date they were purchased. Like all SNCF tickets, they cannot be replaced if lost or stolen.

If you've got a full-fare Loisir Week-End ticket, you can change your reservation by phone, internet or at train stations for no charge until the day before your departure; changes made on the day of your reserved trip incur a charge of €10 (€3 for tickets bought with a discount card). Pro tickets (eg TGV Pro, Téoz Pro) cost extra and allow full reimbursement up to the time of departure and, if you're running a bit late, let you board the next train to the same destination up to an hour after your scheduled departure. Very cheap promotional tickets (eg Prem's) cannot be modified and are nonreimbursable.

Health

CONTENTS

France is a healthy place so your main risks are likely to be sunburn, foot blisters, insect bites and mild stomach problems from eating and drinking with too much gusto.

BEFORE YOU GO

Prevention is the key to staying healthy while abroad. A little planning before departure, particularly for pre-existing illnesses, will save trouble later. See your dentist before a long trip, carry a spare pair of contact lenses and glasses, and take your optical prescription with you. Bring medications in their original, clearly labelled, containers. A signed and dated letter from your physician describing your medical conditions and medications, including generic names (French medicine names are often completely different than those in other countries), is also a good idea. If carrying syringes or needles, be sure to have a physician's letter documenting their medical necessity.

INSURANCE

Citizens of the EU, Switzerland, Iceland, Norway or Liechtenstein receive free or reduced-cost state-provided health-care cover with the European Health Insurance Card (EHIC) for medical treatment that becomes necessary while in France. (The EHIC replaced the E111 in 2006.) Each family member will need a separate card. In the UK, get application forms from post offices, or download them from the Department of Health website (www.dh.gov.uk), which has comprehensive information about the card's coverage.

Citizens from other countries will need to check if there is a reciprocal arrangement for free medical care between their country and France. If you need health insurance, strongly consider a policy covering the worst possible scenario, such as an accident requiring an emergency flight home. Find out in advance if your insurance plan will make payments directly to providers or reimburse you later for overseas health expenditures.

RECOMMENDED VACCINATIONS

No vaccinations are required to travel to France. However, the World Health Organization (WHO) recommends that all travellers be covered for diphtheria, tetanus, measles, mumps, rubella and polio, regardless of their destination.

IN TRANSIT

DEEP VEIN THROMBOSIS (DVT)

Blood clots may form in the legs during plane flights, chiefly because of prolonged immobility. The main symptom of DVT is swelling or pain of the foot, ankle or calf, usually but not always on just one side. When a blood clot travels to the lungs it may cause chest pain and breathing difficulties. Travellers with any of these symptoms should immediately seek medical attention.

To prevent the development of DVT on long flights, walk about the cabin, contract the leg muscles while sitting, drink plenty of fluids and avoid alcohol and tobacco.

JET LAG

To avoid jet lag (common when crossing more than five time zones), drink plenty of non-alcoholic fluids and eat light meals. Upon arrival, get exposure to natural sunlight and readjust your schedule (for meals, sleep and so on) as soon as possible.

IN FRANCE

AVAILABILITY & COST OF HEALTH CARE

Visitors to France can get excellent health care from the emergency room/casualty ward *(salle des urgences)* of a hospital *(hôpital)* and at a doctors' office *(cabinet médical)*, and for minor illnesses trained staff in pharmacies – flagged in every village and town with a green-cross sign outside that flashes when open – give valuable advice and sell medications.

They can also tell you when more specialised help is needed and point you in the right direction. Dental care is usually good; however, it is sensible to have a dental check-up before a long trip.

DIARRHOEA

If you develop diarrhoea, drink plenty of fluids, preferably an oral rehydration solution (eg Dioralyte). If diarrhoea is bloody, persists for more than 72 hours, or is accompanied by fever, shaking, chills or severe abdominal pain, seek immediate medical attention.

ENVIRONMENTAL HAZARDS

Altitude Sickness

Lack of oxygen at high altitudes (over 2500m) affects most people to some extent. Symptoms of Acute Mountain Sickness (AMS) usually develop in the first 24 hours at altitude but may be delayed up to three weeks. Mild symptoms are headache, lethargy, dizziness, difficulty sleeping and loss of appetite. Severe symptoms are breathlessness, a dry, irritative cough (followed by the production of pink, frothy sputum), severe headache, lack of coordination and balance, confusion, vomiting, irrational behaviour, drowsiness and unconsciousness. There's no rule as to what is too high: AMS can be fatal at 3000m, but 3500m to 4500m is the usual range.

Treat mild symptoms by resting at the same altitude until you recover, which usually takes a day or two. Paracetamol (acetaminophen) or aspirin can be taken for headaches. If symptoms persist or grow worse, however, *immediate descent is necessary;* even 500m can help. Drug treatments should never be used to avoid descent or to enable further ascent. Diamox (acetazolamide) reduces the headache of AMS and helps the body acclimatise to the lack of oxygen. It is only available on prescription.

To prevent AMS:

- Ascend slowly – have frequent rest days, spending two to three nights at each rise of 1000m. Acclimatisation takes place gradually.
- Sleep at a lower altitude than the greatest height reached during the day, if possible. Also, once above 3000m, care should be taken not to increase the sleeping altitude by more than 300m per day.
- Drink extra fluids. Monitor hydration by ensuring that urine is clear and plentiful.
- Eat light, high-carbohydrate meals for more energy.
- Avoid alcohol, sedatives and tobacco.

Heat Exhaustion

Heat exhaustion follows excessive fluid loss with inadequate replacement of fluids and salt. Symptoms include headache, dizziness and tiredness. Dehydration is already happening by the time you feel thirsty – aim to drink enough water to produce pale, diluted urine. To treat heat exhaustion, replace lost fluids by drinking water and/or fruit juice, and cool the body with cold water and fans.

Hypothermia

Even on a hot day France's mountain weather can change rapidly so always carry waterproof garments and warm layers, and inform others of your route. Acute hypothermia follows a sudden drop of body temperature over a short time, while chronic hypothermia is caused by a gradual loss of body temperature over hours.

Hypothermia starts with shivering, loss of judgment and clumsiness. Unless rewarming occurs, the sufferer deteriorates into apathy, confusion and coma. Prevent further heat loss by seeking shelter, warm dry clothing, hot sweet drinks and shared bodily warmth.

SEXUAL HEALTH

Emergency contraception is available with a doctor's prescription in France. Condoms *(les préservatifs)* are readily available. Be sure to keep them in a cool dry place or they may crack.

It is estimated that 0.4% of France's adult population (aged 15 to 49) is living with HIV/AIDS (in French: *VIH/SIDA*).

TRAVELLING WITH CHILDREN

All travellers with children should know how to treat minor ailments and when to seek medical advice. Be sure children are up to date with routine vaccinations, and discuss possible travel vaccines well before departure, as some vaccines are not suitable for children under a year.

If your child has vomiting or diarrhoea, lost fluids and salts must be replaced. It may be helpful to take along rehydration powders for reconstituting with boiled water.

WOMEN'S HEALTH

Emotional stress, exhaustion and travelling across time zones can all contribute to an upset in the menstrual pattern. If using oral contraceptives, remember some antibiotics, diarrhoea and vomiting can stop the pill from working and lead to the risk of pregnancy – remember to take condoms with you just in case. Time zones, gastrointestinal upsets and antibiotics do not affect injectable contraception.

Travelling during pregnancy is usually possible but you should always consult your doctor before planning your trip. The most risky times for travel are during the first 12 weeks of pregnancy and after 30 weeks.

Language

CONTENTS

Modern French developed from the *langue d'oïl*, a group of dialects spoken north of the Loire River that grew out of the vernacular Latin used during the late Gallo-Roman period. The *langue d'oïl* – particularly the Francien dialect spoken in the Île de France – eventually displaced the *langue d'oc*, the dialect spoken in the south of the country and from which the Mediterranean region of Languedoc got its name.

Standard French is taught and spoken throughout France, but its various accents and dialects are an important source of identity in certain regions. In addition, some of the peoples subjected to French rule many centuries ago have preserved their traditional languages. These include Dutch (known locally as Flemish) in the far north; Alsatian (a German dialect) in Alsace; Breton (a Celtic tongue akin to Welsh) in Brittany; Basque (a language unrelated to any other) in the Basque Country; Catalan in Roussillon (Catalan is the official language of nearby Andorra as well as the first language of many in the Spanish province of Catalonia); Provençal (an Occitan dialect) in Provence; and Corsican (linked to archaic Latin-Italian forms) on Corsica.

For more language about food and dining in France, see p87. If you'd like a more comprehensive guide to the French language, Lonely Planet's *French Phrasebook* will cover most of your travel needs.

PRONUNCIATION

The pronunciation guides included with each French phrase should help in getting your message across. Here are a few letters of written French that may cause confusion:

c before **e** and **i**, as the 's' in 'sit'; before **a**, **o** and **u** it's pronounced as English 'k'. When carrying a 'cedilla' (**ç**), it's always pronounced as the 's' in 'sit'.

j **zh** in the pronunciation guides; as the 's' in 'leisure', eg *jour*, zhoor (day)

n, m where a syllable ends in a single **n** or **m**, these letters are not pronounced, but the preceding vowel is given a nasal pronunciation

r pronounced from the back of the throat while constricting the muscles to restrict the flow of air

BE POLITE!

You'll find any attempt to communicate in French will be much appreciated. What is often perceived as arrogance can be just a subtle objection to the assumption by many travellers that they should be able to speak English anywhere, in any situation, and be understood. You can easily avoid the problem by approaching people and addressing them in French. Even if the only sentence you can put together is *Pardon, madame/monsieur, parlez-vous anglais?* (Excuse me, madam/sir, do you speak English?), you're sure to be more warmly received than if you stick to English.

An important distinction is made in French between *tu* and *vous*, which both mean 'you'. *Tu* is only used when addressing people you know well, children or animals. If you're addressing an adult who isn't a personal friend, *vous* should be used unless the person invites you to use *tu*. In general, younger people insist less on this distinction between polite and informal, and you will find that in many cases they use *tu* from the beginning of an acquaintance.

GENDER

All nouns in French are either masculine or feminine and adjectives reflect the gender of the noun they modify. The feminine form of many nouns and adjectives is indicated by a silent **e** added to the masculine form, as in *ami* and *amie* (the masculine and feminine for 'friend').

In the following phrases, both masculine and feminine forms have been indicated where necessary. The masculine form comes first and is separated from the feminine by a slash. The gender of a noun is often indicated by a preceding article: 'the/a/some', *le/un/du* (m), *la/une/de la* (f); or one of the possessive adjectives, 'my/your/his, her', *mon/ton/son* (m), *ma/ta/sa* (f). In French, unlike English, the possessive adjective agrees in number and gender with the thing in question – eg 'his/her mother', *sa mère.*

ACCOMMODATION

I'm looking for a ...	*Je cherche ...*	zher shersh ...
campsite	*un camping*	un kom·peeng
guest house	*une pension (de famille)*	ewn pon·syon (der fa·mee·yer)
hotel	*un hôtel*	un o·tel
youth hostel	*une auberge de jeunesse*	ewn o·berzh der zher·nes

Where can I find a cheap hotel?
Où est-ce qu'on peut trouver un hôtel pas cher?
oo es·kon per troo·vay un o·tel pa shair

What is the address?
Quelle est l'adresse?
kel ay la·dres

Could you write the address, please?
Est-ce que vous pourriez écrire l'adresse, s'il vous plaît?
es·ker voo poo·ryay ay·kreer la·dres seel voo play

Do you have any rooms available?
Est-ce que vous avez des chambres libres?
es·ker voo·za·vay day shom·brer lee·brer

I'd like (a) ...	*Je voudrais ...*	zher voo·dray ...
single room	*une chambre à un lit*	ewn shom·brer a un lee
double-bed room	*une chambre avec un grand lit*	ewn shom·brer a·vek un gron lee
twin room (with two beds)	*une chambre avec des lits jumeaux*	ewn shom·brer a·vek day lee zhew·mo
room with a bathroom	*une chambre avec une salle de bains*	ewn shom·brer a·vek ewn sal der bun
to share a dorm	*coucher dans un dortoir*	koo·shay don zun dor·twa

How much is it ...?	*Quel est le prix ...?*	kel ay ler pree ...
per night	*par nuit*	par nwee
per person	*par personne*	par per·son

May I see it?
Est-ce que je peux voir la chambre? es·ker zher per vwa la shom·brer

Where is the bathroom?
Où est la salle de bains? oo ay la sal der bun

Where is the toilet?
Où sont les toilettes? oo·son lay twa·let

I'm leaving today.
Je pars aujourd'hui. zher par o·zhoor·dwee

We're leaving today.
Nous partons aujourd'hui. noo par·ton o·zhoor·dwee

MAKING A RESERVATION

(for phone or written requests)

To ...	*À l'attention de ...*
From ...	*De la part de ...*
Date	*Date*
I'd like to book ...	*Je voudrais réserver ...*
in the name of ...	*au nom de ...*
from ... to ... (date)	*du ... au ...*
credit card	*carte de crédit*
number	*numéro*
expiry date	*date d'expiration*
Please confirm availability and price.	*Veuillez confirmer la disponibilité et le prix.*

CONVERSATION & ESSENTIALS

Hello.	*Bonjour.*	bon·zhoor
Goodbye.	*Au revoir.*	o·rer·vwa
Yes.	*Oui.*	wee
No.	*Non.*	non
Please.	*S'il vous plaît.*	seel voo play
Thank you.	*Merci.*	mair·see

You're welcome.
Je vous en prie. (pol) zher voo·zon pree
De rien. (inf) der ree·en

Excuse me.
Excusez-moi. ek·skew·zay·mwa
Sorry. (forgive me)
Pardon. par·don
What's your name?
Comment vous appelez-vous? (pol) ko·mon voo·za·play voo
Comment tu t'appelles? (inf) ko·mon tew ta·pel
My name is ...
Je m'appelle ... zher ma·pel ...
Where are you from?
De quel pays êtes-vous? (pol) der kel pay·ee et·voo
De quel pays es-tu? (inf) der kel pay·ee ay·tew

I'm from ...	*Je viens de ...*	zher vyen der ...
I like ...	*J'aime ...*	zhem ...
I don't like ...	*Je n'aime pas ...*	zher nem pa ...
Just a minute.	*Une minute.*	ewn mee·newt

SIGNS

Entrée	Entrance
Sortie	Exit
Renseignements	Information
Ouvert	Open
Fermé	Closed
Interdit	Prohibited
Chambres Libres	Rooms Available
Complet	Full/No Vacancies
Commissariat de Police	Police Station
Toilettes/WC	Toilets
Hommes	Men
Femmes	Women

DIRECTIONS

Where is ...?
Où est ...? oo ay ...
Go straight ahead.
Continuez tout droit. kon·teen·way too drwa
Turn left.
Tournez à gauche. toor·nay a gosh
Turn right.
Tournez à droite. toor·nay a drwat
at the corner/at the traffic lights
au coin/aux feux o kwun/o fer

behind	*derrière*	dair·ryair
in front of	*devant*	der·von
far (from)	*loin (de)*	lwun (der)
near (to)	*près (de)*	pray (der)
opposite	*en face de*	on fas der

EMERGENCIES

Help!
Au secours! o skoor
There's been an accident!
Il y a eu un accident! eel ya ew un ak·see·don
I'm lost.
Je me suis égaré/e. (m/f) zhe me swee·zay·ga·ray
Leave me alone!
Fichez-moi la paix! fee·shay·mwa la pay

Call ...!	*Appelez ...!*	a·play ...
a doctor	*un médecin*	un mayd·sun
the police	*la police*	la po·lees

beach	*la plage*	la plazh
bridge	*le pont*	ler pon
castle	*le château*	ler sha·to
cathedral	*la cathédrale*	la ka·tay·dral
church	*l'église*	lay·gleez
island	*l'île*	leel
lake	*le lac*	ler lak
main square	*la place centrale*	la plas son·tral
museum	*le musée*	ler mew·zay
old city (town)	*la vieille ville*	la vyay veel
palace	*le palais*	ler pa·lay
quay	*le quai*	ler kay
river bank	*la rive*	la reev
ruins	*les ruines*	lay rween
sea	*la mer*	la mair
square	*la place*	la plas
tourist office	*l'office de tourisme*	lo·fees der too·rees·mer
tower	*la tour*	la toor

HEALTH

I'm ill.	*Je suis malade.*	zher swee ma·lad
It hurts here.	*J'ai une douleur ici.*	zhay ewn doo·ler ee·see

I'm ...	*Je suis ...*	zher swee(z) ...
asthmatic	*asthmatique*	as·ma·teek
diabetic	*diabétique*	dee·a·bay·teek
epileptic	*épileptique*	ay·pee·lep·teek

I'm allergic to ...	*Je suis allergique ...*	zher swee za·lair·zheek ...
antibiotics	*aux antibiotiques*	o zon·tee·byo·teek
bees	*aux abeilles*	o za·bay·yer
walnuts	*aux noix*	o nwa
peanuts	*aux cacahuètes*	o ka·ka·wet
penicillin	*à la pénicilline*	a la pay·nee·see·leen

antiseptic	*l'antiseptique*	lon·tee·sep·teek
aspirin	*l'aspirine*	las·pee·reen
condoms	*des préservatifs*	day pray·zair·va·teef
contraceptive	*le contraceptif*	ler kon·tra·sep·teef
diarrhoea	*la diarrhée*	la dya·ray
medicine	*le médicament*	ler may·dee·ka·mon
nausea	*la nausée*	la no·zay
sunblock cream	*la crème solaire*	la krem so·lair
tampons	*des tampons hygiéniques*	day tom·pon ee·zhen·eek

LANGUAGE DIFFICULTIES

Do you speak English?
Parlez-vous anglais? par·lay·voo ong·glay
Does anyone here speak English?
Y a-t-il quelqu'un qui parle anglais? ya·teel kel·kung kee parl ong·glay
How do you say ... in French?
Comment est-ce qu'on dit ... en français? ko·mon es·kon dee ... on fron·say
What does ... mean?
Que veut dire ...? ker ver deer ...
I don't understand.
Je ne comprends pas. zher ner kom·pron pa
Could you write it down, please?
Est-ce que vous pourriez l'écrire, s'il vous plaît? es·ker voo poo·ryay lay·kreer seel voo play
Can you show me (on the map)?
Pouvez-vous m'indiquer (sur la carte)? poo·vay·voo mun·dee·kay (sewr la kart)

NUMBERS

0	*zéro*	zay·ro
1	*un*	un
2	*deux*	der
3	*trois*	trwa
4	*quatre*	ka·trer
5	*cinq*	sungk
6	*six*	sees
7	*sept*	set
8	*huit*	weet
9	*neuf*	nerf
10	*dix*	dees
11	*onze*	onz
12	*douze*	dooz
13	*treize*	trez
14	*quatorze*	ka·torz
15	*quinze*	kunz
16	*seize*	sez
17	*dix-sept*	dee·set
18	*dix-huit*	dee·zweet
19	*dix-neuf*	deez·nerf
20	*vingt*	vung
21	*vingt et un*	vung tay un
22	*vingt-deux*	vung·der
30	*trente*	tront
40	*quarante*	ka·ront
50	*cinquante*	sung·kont
60	*soixante*	swa·sont
70	*soixante-dix*	swa·son·dees
80	*quatre-vingts*	ka·trer·vung
90	*quatre-vingt-dix*	ka·trer·vung·dees
100	*cent*	son
1000	*mille*	meel

PAPERWORK

name	*nom*	nom
nationality	*nationalité*	na·syo·na·lee·tay
date/place of birth	*date/place de naissance*	dat/plas der nay·sons
sex/gender	*sexe*	seks
passport	*passeport*	pas·por
visa	*visa*	vee·za

QUESTION WORDS

Who?	*Qui?*	kee
What?	*Quoi?*	kwa
What is it?	*Qu'est-ce que c'est?*	kes·ker say
When?	*Quand?*	kon
Where?	*Où?*	oo
Which?	*Quel/Quelle?* (m/f)	kel
Why?	*Pourquoi?*	poor·kwa
How?	*Comment?*	ko·mon

SHOPPING & SERVICES

I'd like to buy ...
Je voudrais acheter ... zher voo·dray ash·tay ...
How much is it?
C'est combien? say kom·byun
I don't like it.
Cela ne me plaît pas. ser·la ner mer play pa
May I look at it?
Est-ce que je peux le voir? es·ker zher per ler vwar
I'm just looking.
Je regarde. zher rer·gard
It's cheap.
Ce n'est pas cher. ser nay pa shair
It's too expensive.
C'est trop cher. say tro shair
I'll take it.
Je le prends. zher ler pron

Can I pay by ...?	*Est-ce que je peux payer avec ...?*	es·ker zher per pay·yay a·vek ...
credit card	*ma carte de crédit*	ma kart der kray·dee
travellers cheques	*des chèques de voyage*	day shek der vwa·yazh

more	*plus*	plew
less	*moins*	mwun
smaller	*plus petit*	plew per·tee
bigger	*plus grand*	plew gron

I'm looking for ...	*Je cherche ...*	zhe shersh ...
a bank	*une banque*	ewn bonk
the ... embassy	*l'ambassade de ...*	lam·ba·sahd der ...
the hospital	*l'hôpital*	lo·pee·tal
an internet café	*un cybercafé*	un see·bair·ka·fay
the market	*le marché*	ler mar·shay
the police	*la police*	la po·lees
the post office	*le bureau de poste*	ler bew·ro der post
a public phone	*une cabine téléphonique*	ewn ka·been tay·lay·fo·neek
a public toilet	*les toilettes*	lay twa·let

TIME & DATES

What time is it?	*Quelle heure est-il?*	kel er ay til
It's (8) o'clock.	*Il est (huit) heures.*	il ay (weet) er
It's half past ...	*Il est (...) heures et demie.*	il ay (...) er ay day·mee

in the morning	*du matin*	dew ma·tun
in the afternoon	*de l'après-midi*	der la·pray·mee·dee
in the evening	*du soir*	dew swar
today	*aujourd'hui*	o·zhoor·dwee
tomorrow	*demain*	der·mun
yesterday	*hier*	yair

Monday	*lundi*	lun·dee
Tuesday	*mardi*	mar·dee
Wednesday	*mercredi*	mair·krer·dee
Thursday	*jeudi*	zher·dee
Friday	*vendredi*	von·drer·dee
Saturday	*samedi*	sam·dee
Sunday	*dimanche*	dee·monsh

January	*janvier*	zhon·vyay
February	*février*	fayv·ryay
March	*mars*	mars
April	*avril*	a·vreel
May	*mai*	may
June	*juin*	zhwun
July	*juillet*	zhwee·yay
August	*août*	oot
September	*septembre*	sep·tom·brer
October	*octobre*	ok·to·brer
November	*novembre*	no·vom·brer
December	*décembre*	day·som·brer

TRANSPORT

Public Transport

What time does ... leave/arrive?	*À quelle heure part/arrive ...?*	a kel er par/a·reev ...
boat	*le bateau*	ler ba·to
bus	*le bus*	ler bews
plane	*l'avion*	la·vyon
train	*le train*	ler trun

I'd like a ... ticket.	*Je voudrais un billet ...*	zher voo·dray un bee·yay ...
one-way	*simple*	sum·pler
return	*aller et retour*	a·lay ay rer·toor
1st-class	*de première classe*	der prem·yair klas
2nd-class	*de deuxième classe*	der der·zyem klas

I want to go to ...
Je voudrais aller à ... zher voo·dray a·lay a ...
The train has been delayed.
Le train est en retard. ler trun ay ton rer·tar
The train has been cancelled.
Le train a été annulé. ler trun a ay·tay a·new·lay

the first	*le premier* (m) *la première* (f)	ler prer·myay la prer·myair
the last	*le dernier* (m) *la dernière* (f)	ler dair·nyay la dair·nyair
platform number	*le numéro de quai*	ler new·may·ro der kay
ticket office	*le guichet*	ler gee·shay
timetable	*l'horaire*	lo·rair
train station	*la gare*	la gar

Private Transport

I'd like to hire a/an...	*Je voudrais louer ...*	zher voo·dray loo·way ...
car	*une voiture*	ewn vwa·tewr
4WD	*un quatre-quatre*	un kat·kat
motorbike	*une moto*	ewn mo·to
bicycle	*un vélo*	un vay·lo

Is this the road to ...?
C'est la route pour ...? say la root poor ...
Where's a service station?
Où est-ce qu'il y a une station-service? oo es·keel ya ewn sta·syon·ser·vees
Please fill it up.
Le plein, s'il vous plaît. ler plun seel voo play
I'd like ... litres.
Je voudrais ... litres. zher voo·dray ... lee·trer

petrol/gas	*essence*	ay·sons
diesel	*diesel*	dyay·zel

ROAD SIGNS

Cédez la Priorité	Give Way
Danger	Danger
Défense de Stationner	No Parking
Entrée	Entrance
Interdiction de Doubler	No Overtaking
Péage	Toll
Ralentissez	Slow Down
Sens Interdit	No Entry
Sens Unique	One Way
Sortie	Exit

(How long) Can I park here?
(Combien de temps) Est-ce que je peux stationner ici?
(kom·byun der tom) es·ker zher per sta·syo·nay ee·see?

Where do I pay?
Où est-ce que je paie?
oo es·ker zher pay?

I need a mechanic.
J'ai besoin d'un mécanicien.
zhay ber·zwun dun may·ka·nee·syun

The car/motorbike has broken down (at ...).
La voiture/moto est tombée en panne (à ...).
la vwa·tewr/mo·to ay tom·bay on pan (a ...).

The car/motorbike won't start.
La voiture/moto ne veut pas démarrer.
la vwa·tewr/mo·to ner ver pa day·ma·ray

I have a flat tyre.
Mon pneu est à plat.
mom pner ay ta pla

I've run out of petrol.
Je suis en panne d'essence.
zher swee zon pan day·sons

I've had an accident.
J'ai eu un accident.
zhay ew un ak·see·don

TRAVEL WITH CHILDREN

Is there a/an ...?	*Y a-t-il ...?*	ya teel ...
I need a/an ...	*J'ai besoin ...*	zhay ber·zwun ...
baby change room	*d'un endroit pour changer le bébé*	dun on·drwa poor shon·zhay ler bay·bay
car baby seat	*d'un siège-enfant*	dun syezh·on·fon
children's menu	*d'un menu pour enfants*	dun mer·new poor on·fon
disposable nappies/diapers	*de couches-culottes*	der koosh·kew·lot
formula (milk)	*de lait maternisé*	de lay ma·ter·nee·zay
(English-speaking) babysitter	*d'une baby-sitter (qui parle anglais)*	dewn ba·bee·see·ter (kee parl ong·glay)
highchair	*d'une chaise haute*	dewn shay zot
potty	*d'un pot de bébé*	dun po der bay·bay

Do you mind if I breastfeed here?
Cela vous dérange si j'allaite mon bébé ici? ser·la voo day·ron·zhe see zha·layt mon bay·bay ee·see

Are children allowed?
Les enfants sont permis? lay zon·fon son pair·mee

LANGUAGE

Glossary

For a glossary of food and drink terms, see the Food & Drink chapter (p77).

(m) indicates masculine gender, (f) feminine gender and (pl) plural

accès – (track) access
accueil (m) – reception
alignements (m pl) – a series of standing stones, or menhirs, in straight lines
alimentation (f) – grocery store
AOC – Appellation d'Origine Contrôlée; system of French wine classification
arrondissement (m) – administrative division within a large city; abbreviated on signs as 1er (1st arrondissement), 2e (2nd), 3e (3rd) etc
atelier (m) – workshop or studio
auberge (m) – inn
auberge de jeunesse (f) – youth hostel

baie (f) – bay
bassin (m) – bay or basin
bastide (f) – medieval settlement in southwestern France, usually built on a grid plan and surrounding an arcaded square; also a country house in Provence
belle époque (f) – literally 'beautiful age'; era of elegance and gaiety characterising fashionable Parisian life in the period preceding WWI
billet (m) – ticket
billet jumelé (m) – combination ticket, good for more than one site, museum etc
billetterie (f) – ticket office or counter
bouchon – Lyonnais bistro
boulangerie (f) – bakery or bread shop
boules (f pl) – a game not unlike lawn bowls played with heavy metal balls on a sandy pitch; also called *pétanque*
BP – *boîte postale;* post office box
brasserie (f) – restaurant usually serving food all day (original meaning: brewery)
bureau de change (m) – exchange bureau
bureau de poste (m) or **poste** (f) – post office

CAF – Club Alpin Français
carnet (m) – a book of five or 10 bus, tram or metro tickets sold at a reduced rate
carrefour (m) – crossroad
carte (f) – card; menu; map
caserne (f) – military barracks
cave (f) – wine cellar
chambre (f) – room
chambre d'hôte (f) – B&B
charcuterie (f) – pork butcher's shop and delicatessen; the prepared meats it sells
cimetière (m) – cemetery
col (m) – mountain pass
consigne or **consigne manuelle** (f) – left-luggage office
consigne automatique (f) – left-luggage locker
correspondance (f) – linking tunnel or walkway, eg in the metro; rail or bus connection
couchette (f) – sleeping berth on a train or ferry
cour (f) – courtyard
crémerie (f) – dairy or cheese shop
cyclisme (m) – cycling

dégustation (f) – tasting
demi (m) – 330mL glass of beer
demi-pension (f) – half board (B&B with either lunch or dinner)
département (m) – administrative division of France
donjon (m) – castle keep
douane (f) – customs

église (f) – church
embarcadère (m) – pier or jetty
épicerie (f) – small grocery store
ESF – École de Ski Français; France's leading ski school

fauteuil (m) – seat on trains, ferries or at the theatre
fest-noz or **festoù-noz** (pl) – night festival
fête (f) – festival
FN – Front National; National Front
forêt (f) – forest
formule or **formule rapide** (f) – similar to a *menu* but allows choice of whichever two of three courses you want (eg starter and main course or main course and dessert)
fouilles (f pl) – excavations at an archaeological site
foyer (m) – workers or students hostel
fromagerie (f) – cheese shop
FUAJ – Fédération Unie des Auberges de Jeunesse; France's major hostel association
funiculaire (m) – funicular railway

galerie (f) – covered shopping centre or arcade
gare or **gare SNCF** (f) – railway station
gare maritime (f) – ferry terminal
gare routière (f) – bus station
gendarmerie (f) – police station; police force
gîte d'étape (m) – hikers accommodation, usually in a village
gîte rural (m) – country cottage

golfe (m) – gulf
GR – Grande Randonnée; long-distance hiking trail
grand cru (m) – wine of exceptional quality

halles (f pl) – covered market; central food market
halte routière (f) – bus stop
horaire (m) – timetable or schedule
hostellerie – hostelry
hôte payant (m) – paying guest
hôtel de ville (m) – city or town hall
hôtel particulier (m) – private mansion

intra-muros – old city (literally 'within the walls')

jardin (m) – garden
jardin botanique (m) – botanic garden
jours fériés (m pl) – public holidays

laverie (f) or **lavomatique** (m) – launderette

mairie (f) – city or town hall
maison de la presse (f) – newsagent
maison du parc (f) – a national park's headquarters and/or visitors centre
marché (m) – market
marché aux puces (m) – flea market
marché couvert (m) – covered market
mas (m) – farmhouse in southern France
menu (m) – fixed-price meal with two or more courses
mistral (m) – incessant north wind in southern France said to drive people crazy
musée (m) – museum

navette (f) – shuttle bus, train or boat

palais de justice (m) – law courts
parapente – paragliding
pardon (m) – religious pilgrimage
parlement (m) – parliament
parvis (m) – square
pâtisserie (f) – cake and pastry shop
patron(ne) (m/f) – boss
péage (m) – toll
pensions de famille (f pl) – similar to B&Bs
pétanque (f) – a game not unlike lawn bowls played with heavy metal balls on a sandy pitch; also called *boules*
piste cyclable (f) – bicycle path
place (f) – square or plaza
plage (f) – beach
plan (m) – city map
plan du quartier (m) – map of nearby streets (hung on the wall near metro exits)
plat du jour (m) – daily special in a restaurant
pont (m) – bridge
port (m) – harbour or port
port de plaisance (m) – marina or pleasure-boat harbour
porte (f) – gate in a city wall
poste (f) or **bureau de poste** (m) – post office
préfecture (f) – prefecture (capital of a *département*)
presqu'île (f) – peninsula
pression (f) – draught beer
puy (m) – volcanic cone or peak

quai (m) – quay; railway platform
quartier (m) – quarter or district

refuge (m) – mountain hut, basic shelter for hikers
région (f) – administrative division of France
rez-de-chausée (m) – ground floor
rive (f) – bank of a river
rond point (m) – roundabout
routier (m) – trucker; truckers restaurant

sentier (m) – trail
service des urgences (f) – casualty ward
ski de fond – cross-country skiing
SNCF – Société Nationale des Chemins de Fer; state-owned railway company
SNCM – Société Nationale Maritime Corse-Méditerranée; state-owned ferry company linking Corsica and mainland France
sortie (f) – exit
spectacle (m) – performance, play or theatrical show
square (m) – public garden
supplément (m) – supplement or additional cost
syndicat d'initiative (m) – tourist office

tabac (m) – tobacconist (also selling bus tickets, phonecards etc)
table d'orientation (f) – viewpoint indicator
taxe de séjour (f) – municipal tourist tax
télécarte (f) – phonecard
téléphérique (m) – cableway or cable car
télésiège (m) – chairlift
téléski (m) – ski lift or tow
TGV – Train à Grande Vitesse; high-speed train or bullet train
tour (f) – tower
tour d'horloge (f) – clock tower

vallée (f) – valley
vf (f) – *version française*; a film dubbed in French
vieille ville (f) – old town or old city
ville neuve (f) – new town or new city
vo (f) – *version originale*; a nondubbed film with French subtitles
voie (f) – train platform
VTT – *vélo tout terrain;* mountain bike

winstub – traditional Alsatian eateries

The Authors

NICOLA WILLIAMS

A British writer living on the southern (French) side of Lake Geneva in a house with lake and Jura mountain views, Nicola is well and truly spoilt…so much so that she only eats in places that cook up real-McCoy lake fish (most comes from Eastern Europe) and, if the sky is not blue, she refuses to ski. A journalist by trade, she worked in the Baltic region as a newspaper features editor and later as an In Your Pocket city-guide editor for several years before trading in Lithuanian *cepelinai* for Lyonnais *andouillette* in 1997. She has authored numerous titles for Lonely Planet, including first editions of *The Loire, Provence & the Côte d'Azur* and *Languedoc-Roussillon*.

OLIVER BERRY

Oliver has been travelling to France since the tender age of two, and over the last decade his writing has carried him from the rural corners of the Lot Valley to the snowy hump of Mont Blanc and the chestnut forests of Corsica. Having worked on several previous editions of the *France* guide, for this edition he plumbed the depths of prehistoric caves in the Vézère Valley, wandered the hallways of obscure Loire châteaux, clambered to the top of dormant volcanoes in the Massif Central and conquered the old mule track in the spectacular Gorges de Spelunca. When he's not out on the road, Oliver lives and works in Cornwall as a writer and photographer.

STEVE FALLON

Steve, who has worked on every edition of France except the first, visited the City of Light for the first time at age 16 with his half-French best friend, where they spent a week drinking vin ordinaire from plastic bottles, keeping several paces ahead of irate café waiters demanding to be paid, and learning French swear words that shocked even them. Despite this inexcusable behaviour, the PAF (border police) let him back in five years later to complete a degree in French at the Sorbonne. Now based in East London, Steve will be just one Underground stop away from Paris when Eurostar trains begin departing from Stratford in 2010. *C'est si bon…*

LONELY PLANET AUTHORS

Why is our travel information the best in the world? It's simple: our authors are passionate, dedicated travellers. They don't take freebies in exchange for positive coverage so you can be sure the advice you're given is impartial. They travel widely to all the popular spots, and off the beaten track. They don't research using just the internet or phone. They discover new places not included in any other guidebook. They personally visit thousands of hotels, restaurants, palaces, trails, galleries, temples and more. They speak with dozens of locals every day to make sure you get the kind of insider knowledge only a local could tell you. They take pride in getting all the details right, and in telling it how it is. Think you can do it? Find out how at **lonelyplanet.com**.

EMILIE FILOU

Emilie was born in Paris but spent most of her childhood holidays roaming the south of France and the Alps. Bigger summits beckoned when she turned 18 and spent a year in Nepal before going to university. She read geography at Oxford, where she had to endure colouring-in jokes for three years but managed to bag a field trip to Niger for her dissertation on nomadic tribes. More travel in French-speaking Africa, southeast Asia, Australia and New Zealand ensued. She now works as a business and travel journalist in London.

CATHERINE LE NEVEZ

Catherine's wanderlust kicked in when she lived in and road-tripped throughout France aged four and she's been road-tripping here at every opportunity since, completing her Doctorate of Creative Arts in Writing, Masters in Professional Writing, and postgrad qualifications in Editing and Publishing along the way.

Catherine's writing on France includes the previous editions of this book as well as Lonely Planet's *Paris Encounter* and *Provence & the Côte d'Azur* guidebooks, newspaper and radio reportage covering Paris' literary scene, and several hundred Lonely Planet online accommodation reviews nationwide. When not scouting out hidden corners of France, Catherine has followed Lonely Planet travel writing assignments to neighbouring Italy, Germany, Belgium and (across the pond) Ireland, among others.

DANIEL ROBINSON

Over the past two decades, Daniel's articles and guidebooks – published in nine languages – have covered every region of France, but he has a particular fondness for those bits of the Hexagon in which Celtic, Romance and Germanic cultures have mingled for over two millennia. Seeking out enchanting corners of rust-belt France is a long-time hobby, and he takes particular interest in the creativity and panache – and foresighted public-transport initiatives – of dynamic northern cities such as Lille, Nancy and Strasbourg.

Daniel grew up in the United States and Israel and holds degrees from Princeton University and Tel Aviv University. He is based in Tel Aviv and Los Angeles.

MILES RODDIS

Miles studied French at university and spent an idyllic sandwich year in Neuville-sur-Saône, a place quite rightly overlooked by the best guidebooks, including the one in your hand. Living over the Pyrenees in Valencia, Spain, he and his wife, Ingrid, cross the mountains to France for work or fun at least once a year. He has travelled the length of Languedoc, and usually Roussillon too, on seven occasions for Lonely Planet guidebooks, each time returning home several kilos and a case of fine red wine heavier.

Miles has written or contributed to more than 30 Lonely Planet titles including *France, Brittany & Normandy* and – most satisfyingly of all – *Walking in France*.

Behind the Scenes

THIS BOOK

For this 8th edition of France, Nicola Williams coordinated a skilled team of authors composed of Oliver Berry, Steve Fallon, Emilie Filou, Catherine Le Nevez, Daniel Robinson and Miles Roddis. Nicola, Oliver, Steve, Catherine, Daniel and Miles also made major contributions to previous editions, as did Teresa Fisher, Jeremy Gray, Annabel Hart, Paul Hellander, Jonathan Knight, Leanne Logan, Oda O'Carroll, Jeanne Oliver and Andrew Stone.

This guidebook was commissioned in Lonely Planet's London office, and produced by the following:

Commissioning Editor Caroline Sieg
Coordinating Editor Robyn Loughnane
Coordinating Cartographer Anita Banh
Coordinating Layout Designer Pablo Gastar
Managing Editor Bruce Evans
Managing Cartographer Mark Griffiths
Managing Layout Designer Laura Jane
Assisting Editors Barbara Delissen, Penelope Goodes, Kim Hutchins, Amy Karafin, Helen Koehne, Joanne Newell, Branislava Vladisavljevic, Helen Yeates
Assisting Cartographers Fatima Basic, Barbara Benson, Tony Fankhauser, Valentina Kremenchutskaya, Jolyon Philcox, Malisa Plesa
Assisting Layout Designers Carol Jackson
Cover Designer Pepi Bluck
Project Manager Glenn van der Knijff, Fabrice Rocher
Language Content Coordinator Quentin Frayne
Thanks to Yvonne Bischofberger, Helen Christinis, Ryan Evans, Jennifer Garrett, Rachel Imeson, Lisa Knights, Katie Lynch, Anna Metcalfe, Wayne Murphy, Katie O'Connell, Trent Paton, Lyahna Spencer, Simon Tillema, Clifton Wilkinson

THANKS

NICOLA WILLIAMS

The enormous graciousness, professionalism and good humour of the contributing authors of this book and commissioning editor Caroline Sieg cannot be stressed enough: Thank you. In that vibrant, fantastic, happening, nearly southern French city I called home for so long, *un grand merci* to chefs Nicolas Le Bec and Josiane Chanaux; and to old friends for keeping me in the Lyonnais loop, Chiara Buttiglione, David Reid, Lise Pedersen, Jo Kelly, Stéphane Lange and Jean-Phi included. Thanks to Thomas Salacroup in Toulouse and, on the lakefront I now call home, oodles of lollipop- and chocolate-flavoured *bisous* to Matthias, Niko and Mischa for tolerating the long hours and absences with a smile.

OLIVER BERRY

Back home a huge thanks as always to Susie Berry for keeping me fed and watered during long nights of typing, Jenks and the o-region boys for keeping

THE LONELY PLANET STORY

Fresh from an epic journey across Europe, Asia and Australia in 1972, Tony and Maureen Wheeler sat at their kitchen table stapling together notes. The first Lonely Planet guidebook, *Across Asia on the Cheap,* was born.

Travellers snapped up the guides. Inspired by their success, the Wheelers began publishing books to Southeast Asia, India and beyond. Demand was prodigious, and the Wheelers expanded the business rapidly to keep up. Over the years, Lonely Planet extended its coverage to every country and into the virtual world via lonelyplanet.com and the Thorn Tree message board.

As Lonely Planet became a globally loved brand, Tony and Maureen received several offers for the company. But it wasn't until 2007 that they found a partner whom they trusted to remain true to the company's principles of travelling widely, treading lightly and giving sustainably. In October of that year, BBC Worldwide acquired a 75% share in the company, pledging to uphold Lonely Planet's commitment to independent travel, trustworthy advice and editorial independence.

Today, Lonely Planet has offices in Melbourne, London and Oakland, with over 500 staff members and 300 authors. Tony and Maureen are still actively involved with Lonely Planet. They're travelling more often than ever, and they're devoting their spare time to charitable projects. And the company is still driven by the philosophy of *Across Asia on the Cheap*: 'All you've got to do is decide to go and the hardest part is over. So go!'

things ticking over Kernowside while I was on the road, TSP for serial long distance Skype-ing, and the Hobo for constantly keeping my shadow company. Special thanks across the Channel go to Philippe Camba and all the excellent tour guides around the Vézère Valley (especially the staff of Rouffignac), Stéphane Michon and the Mushroom Museum, the Hotel Aïtone in Évisa (always a pleasure!), Thierry Dupont and the team, and the countless people who helped me out and gave their time along the way.

STEVE FALLON

A number of people helped in the updating of my portion of *France,* in particular resident Brenda Turnnidge, who provided invaluable support and insider's information with her usual efficiency and enthusiasm. Thanks too to Zahia Hafs, Caroline Guilleminot, Olivier Cirendini, Bryan Manning, Dominique and Martine Bodez and Nick Franklin for assistance, ideas and/or a few laughs along the way. Daniel Meyers and Patricia Ribault were overwhelmingly hospitable to a stranger and I (no longer same) am very grateful. A very special *merci* to co-ordinating author Nicola Williams, a true professional. As always, I'd like to dedicate my share of *France* to my partner Michael Rothschild, a veritable walking *Larousse Gastronomique*.

EMILIE FILOU

Thanks first and foremost to my family, and in particular my Mum and Patrick for the stays at La Cadière, the loan of the car and my amazing *bottes des sept lieux;* my Dad and Laurence for the surprise birthday visit and one hell of a walk down memory lane; Pierre-Yves for that meticulous review of Marseille; and Loïc for the hot Grenoble tips. Thanks also to coordinating author extraordinaire Nicola Williams for her help all along and to commissioning editor Caroline Sieg for giving me the chance to do this. And last but not least, thanks to my wonderful boyfriend Adolfo for letting me go just two weeks after we'd moved in together, for his silly jokes on the road, his patience and quiet-but-unwavering support; thank you.

CATHERINE LE NEVEZ

To thank all of the locals, tourism professionals and fellow travellers who helped on my journey throughout the Atlantic Coast, French Basque Country, Pyrenees and Brittany individually would unfortunately (or rather, fortunately!) take up several pages. So instead, a heartfelt *merci* to you all – your insights and assistance were invaluable. Special thanks in particular to Christiane, Laurence, Perrine, Sandrine and Stéphanie. At Lonely Planet, cheers to Caroline Sieg for giving me the gig, Mark Griffiths, Nicola Williams and the *France* team, and the editors and cartos who helped me juggle simultaneous *Encounter* AQs. As ever, *merci surtout* to my family.

DANIEL ROBINSON

Countless people went out of their way to help me with my research, including many incredibly patient tourist-office staffers – alas, I can thank by name only a handful.

In Normandy, Isabelle Robert-Attard; *cidre* and Calvados producer Gerard Desvoye; Jane Fitte; and Samuel and Galit Vacrate were incredibly generous with their time. My work in Far Northern France was enriched by Laurent Courouble and Anny Monet, whom I met through Adrienne Costanzo, editor of this book's 1st edition.

MILES RODDIS

Huge thanks, as every time, everywhere, on every book to Ingrid. John and Buffy Rodenbeck were generous with hospitality and shared their knowledge of and enthusiasm for the Montagne Noire. Tourist-office staff were unfailingly keen to promote their towns and regions. Thanks once again to Nicolas (Perpignan), Amélie (Vernet-les-Bains), Aude (Prades), Lucie (Narbonne), Amy (Béziers), Adrien (Sète), Yannick (Ax-les-Thermes), Sylvette and Séverine (Foix), Sarah Seguy (Carcassonne), Dominique (Nîmes), Myriam (Millau), Delphine Atché (Roquefort), Monique Rocher (Florac), Juliette and Ricardo (Mende) and Mme Argilier (Parc National des Cévennes, Florac).

OUR READERS

Many thanks to the travellers who used the last edition and wrote to us with helpful hints, useful advice and interesting anecdotes:

A Jon Alford, Stephen Allen, Bill Atwood **B** Laura Barnhouse, Cendrine Barral, Theresa Boteilho, Miriam Brauch, Matthieu Bugeon, Paige Burgess **C** Ed Casilino, Helen Cavill, Justine and Ian Charman, Helen Christian, Laura Cochrane, Elisabeth Cox, John Cox, Kylie Crawley **D** Wouter De Sutter **E** Kevin Eddy, Robin Edwards, G C Elliott, Michael Ellis, Sarah Evans **F** John Fenn, David Feterston, Jill Fraser, Jon Furholt **G** Ethna Gallacher, Marie-Laure Genin, Noel Gibney, Charlotte Girardot, George Goudriaan, Louise Grainger, Warwick Grainger **H** Andrew Hackett, Paul Harris, Harrison Heyl, Calvin Hilton, Douglas Holder, Ralph Hounslow, Winona Hubbard, Lucy Hunt, Kasrynne Huolohan, Sunkee Hwang **J** Andy Johnston, Norma Johnston, Caroline Jongma, Basia Jóźwiak, Helen Jury, Laurie Jury **K** Zvi Kam, Margriet Katoen, Susannah Kingston **L** Priscille Lacoste, Lisa Lamb, Donna Leone **M** Lara Mantovani, Thomas Mayes, Blair McNamara, Lisa Melessaccio, Eddie Moore, Amanda Morrow, Laurence Mory, Claude Mourier, Gunter Muehl, Anky Mulder **N** Marie Navillod, Pascale Navillod, Brett Nietschke, Martin Nolan **O** Martina O'Doherty, Beverley Orgill **P** Alexandra Pasquer, Gordon Payne, Jim Personett, Maxine

SEND US YOUR FEEDBACK

We love to hear from travellers – your comments keep us on our toes and help make our books better. Our well-travelled team reads every word on what you loved or loathed about this book. Although we cannot reply individually to postal submissions, we always guarantee that your feedback goes straight to the appropriate authors, in time for the next edition. Each person who sends us information is thanked in the next edition – and the most useful submissions are rewarded with a free book.

To send us your updates – and find out about Lonely Planet events, newsletters and travel news – visit our award-winning website: **lonelyplanet.com/contact.**

Note: we may edit, reproduce and incorporate your comments in Lonely Planet products such as guidebooks, websites and digital products, so let us know if you don't want your comments reproduced or your name acknowledged. For a copy of our privacy policy visit lonelyplanet.com /privacy.

Persson, John Peterson, David Pollard, Kitty Price, Elizabeth Pringault **Q** Graham Quintal **R** Mark Reason, Lynette Rieper, Michael Rodin, Nell Roversi-Deal **S** Richard Sanderson, Karin Schaedler, Heinrich Schlasche-Töpel, Yoash Shapira, Melissa Shearer, Natashya Sherbot, Jacqueline Shervington, Mark Shervington, Bo Sjoholm, Kate Smith **T** Lisa Tam, Rob Tolchard, Andrea Turrell **V** David Vacelet, Emilie Velut **W** Jessica and Henry Wadsworth, Tony Wheeler, Rebekah Wike, Emyr Williams, Marilyn Williams **Y** Wei Yan

ACKNOWLEDGMENTS

Many thanks to the following for the use of their content:

Globe on title page ©Mountain High Maps 1993 Digital Wisdom, Inc

RATP for the use of its transit map © RATP – CML Agence Cartographique

Internal photographs p100 (#1) Owen Franken/ Corbis. All other photographs by Lonely Planet Images, and by Alice Grulich-Jones p93; John Banagan p94 (#1); Will Salter p94 (#2); Glenn Beanland p95 (#3); Izzet Keribar p95 (#4); Jean-Bernard Carillet p96; Grant Dixon p97 (#2); Sally Dillon p97 (#3); Christopher Groenhout p98; Bill Wassman p99 (#2); Barbara van Zanten p99 (#3); Juliet Coombe p99 (#4); David Tomlinson p100 (#2).

Index

000 Map pages
000 Photograph pages

INDEX

D

INDEX

000 Map pages
000 Photograph pages

000 Map pages
000 Photograph pages

INDEX

000 Map pages
000 Photograph pages

T

INDEX

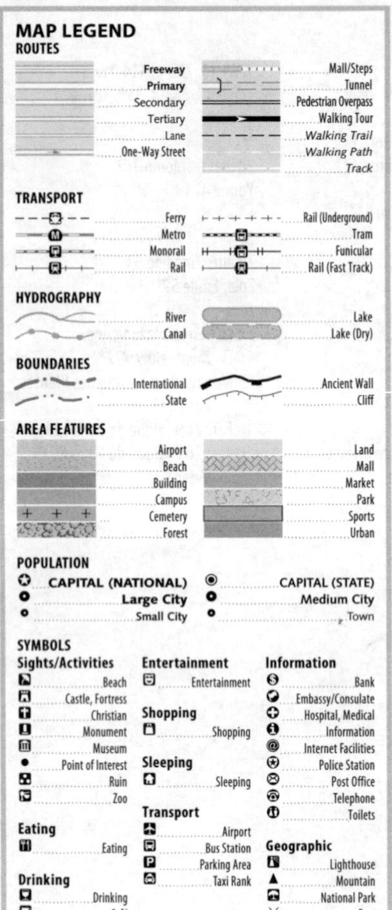

LONELY PLANET OFFICES

Australia
Head Office
Locked Bag 1, Footscray, Victoria 3011
☎ 03 8379 8000, fax 03 8379 8111
talk2us@lonelyplanet.com.au

USA
150 Linden St, Oakland, CA 94607
☎ 510 250 6400, toll free 800 275 8555
fax 510 893 8572
info@lonelyplanet.com

UK
2nd fl, 186 City Rd,
London EC1V 2NT
☎ 020 7106 2100, fax 020 7106 2101
go@lonelyplanet.co.uk

Published by Lonely Planet Publications Pty Ltd
ABN 36 005 607 983

Cover photograph: Route de Vin, Rhin (Haut), Hunawihr, C Bowman/Age Fotostock. Many of the images in this guide are available for licensing from Lonely Planet Images: www.lonelyplanetimages.com.

Printed by SNP Security Printing Pte Ltd, Singapore.